THE WORLD FACTBOOK

2002
(CIA's 2001 Edition)

Prepared by the Central Intelligence Agency

Brassey's
Washington, D.C.

Brassey's Edition 2002 (CIA's 2001 Edition)

In general, information available as of 1 January 2001 was used in the preparation of this edition.

The World Factbook is prepared by the Central Intelligence Agency for the use of US Government officials, and the style, format, coverage, and content are designed to meet their specific requirements. Information is provided by Antarctic Information Program (National Science Foundation), Bureau of the Census (Department of Commerce), Bureau of Labor Statistics (Department of Labor, Central Intelligence Agency, Council of Managers of National Antarctic Programs, Defense Intelligence Agency (Department of Defense), Department of State, Fish and Wildlife Service (Department of the Interior), Maritime Administration (Department of Transportation), National Imagery and Mapping Agency (Department of Defense), Naval Facilities Engineering Command (Department of Defense), Office of Insular Affairs (Department of Interior), US Transportation Command (Department of Defense), and other public and private sources.

Brassey's has published a commercial version of *The World Factbook* for ten years in order to extend the limited audience reached by the CIA's publication. This annual is a valuable primary source of information, and Brassey's seeks to make it more readily available to bookstores and libraries so that the taxpayers who fund the US government can directly benefit from this excellent effort. Brassey's makes no claim to copyright to this publication. Brassey's editions differ in two minor aspects from the CIA publications. This current Brassey's edition is identified by the year 2002, following the pattern Brassey's uses in other annual publications. The CIA completes its volume late each year, and Brassey's republishes it the following year. Also, as a commercial publisher, Brassey's does not include the very simple but expensive four-color maps contained in the CIA publication. The cost to the consumer would be prohibitive, and these maps are not unique and are readily available elsewhere.

ISBN 1-57488-475-1 (alk. paper)

Printed in the United States of America on acid-free paper that meets the American National Standards Institute Z39-48 Standard.

Brassey's, Inc.
22841 Quicksilver Drive
Dulles, Virginia 20166

First Edition

10 9 8 7 6 5 4 3 2 1

Contents

		Page
	Notes and Definitions	vii
	Guide to Country Profiles	xxix
A	Afghanistan	1
	Albania	3
	Algeria	5
	American Samoa	8
	Andorra	10
	Angola	12
	Anguilla	14
	Antarctica	16
	Antigua and Barbuda	18
	Arctic Ocean	20
	Argentina	21
	Armenia	24
	Aruba	26
	Ashmore and Cartier Islands	28
	Atlantic Ocean	28
	Australia	29
	Austria	32
	Azerbaijan	34
B	Bahamas, The	37
	Bahrain	39
	Baker Island	41
	Bangladesh	41
	Barbados	44
	Bassas da India	46
	Belarus	46
	Belgium	49
	Belize	51
	Benin	53
	Bermuda	56
	Bhutan	58
	Bolivia	60
	Bosnia and Herzegovina	62
	Botswana	65
	Bouvet Island	67
	Brazil	68
	British Indian Ocean Territory	70
	British Virgin Islands	71
	Brunei	73
	Bulgaria	75
	Burkina Faso	78
	Burma	80
	Burundi	83
C	Cambodia	85
	Cameroon	88
	Canada	90
	Cape Verde	93
	Cayman Islands	95

		Page
	Central African Republic	96
	Chad	99
	Chile	101
	China (also see separate Hong Kong, Macau, and Taiwan entries)	104
	Christmas Island	107
	Clipperton Island	108
	Cocos (Keeling) Islands	109
	Colombia	110
	Comoros	113
	Congo, Democratic Republic of the	115
	Congo, Republic of the	117
	Cook Islands	120
	Coral Sea Islands	121
	Costa Rica	122
	Cote d'Ivoire	124
	Croatia	127
	Cuba	130
	Cyprus	133
	Czech Republic	136
D	Denmark	138
	Djibouti	141
	Dominica	143
	Dominican Republic	145
E	Ecuador	147
	Egypt	149
	El Salvador	152
	Equatorial Guinea	154
	Eritrea	156
	Estonia	159
	Ethiopia	161
	Europa Island	164
F	Falkland Islands (Islas Malvinas)	164
	Faroe Islands	166
	Fiji	168
	Finland	170
	France	173
	French Guiana	176
	French Polynesia	178
	French Southern and Antarctic Lands	180
G	Gabon	181
	Gambia, The	183
	Gaza Strip	185
	Georgia	187
	Germany	189
	Ghana	192
	Gibraltar	194
	Glorioso Islands	196
	Greece	197

		Page
	Greenland	199
	Grenada	201
	Guadeloupe	203
	Guam	205
	Guatemala	207
	Guernsey	209
	Guinea	211
	Guinea-Bissau	213
	Guyana	216
H	Haiti	218
	Heard Island and McDonald Islands	220
	Holy See (Vatican City)	221
	Honduras	222
	Hong Kong	225
	Howland Island	227
	Hungary	228
I	Iceland	231
	India	233
	Indian Ocean	236
	Indonesia	237
	Iran	239
	Iraq	242
	Ireland	245
	Israel (also see separate Gaza Strip and West Bank entries)	247
	Italy	250
J	Jamaica	253
	Jan Mayen	255
	Japan	256
	Jarvis Island	258
	Jersey	259
	Johnston Atoll	261
	Jordan	262
	Juan de Nova Island	264
K	Kazakhstan	265
	Kenya	268
	Kingman Reef	270
	Kiribati	271
	Korea, North	273
	Korea, South	275
	Kuwait	278
	Kyrgyzstan	280
L	Laos	282
	Latvia	285
	Lebanon	287
	Lesotho	290
	Liberia	292
	Libya	294
	Liechtenstein	297

		Page
	Lithuania	299
	Luxembourg	301
M	Macau	303
	Macedonia, The Former Yugoslav Republic of	305
	Madagascar	308
	Malawi	310
	Malaysia	312
	Maldives	315
	Mali	317
	Malta	319
	Man, Isle of	321
	Marshall Islands	323
	Martinique	325
	Mauritania	327
	Mauritius	329
	Mayotte	331
	Mexico	333
	Micronesia, Federated States of	336
	Midway Islands	338
	Moldova	339
	Monaco	341
	Mongolia	343
	Montserrat	345
	Morocco	347
	Mozambique	350
N	Namibia	352
	Nauru	354
	Navassa Island	356
	Nepal	357
	Netherlands	360
	Netherlands Antilles	362
	New Caledonia	364
	New Zealand	366
	Nicaragua	369
	Niger	371
	Nigeria	374
	Niue	376
	Norfolk Island	378
	Northern Mariana Islands	379
	Norway	381
O	Oman	384
P	Pacific Ocean	386
	Pakistan	387
	Palau	389
	Palmyra Atoll	391
	Panama	392
	Papua New Guinea	395
	Paracel Islands	397
	Paraguay	398

		Page
	Peru	400
	Philippines	403
	Pitcairn Islands	405
	Poland	407
	Portugal	410
	Puerto Rico	412
Q	Qatar	414
R	Reunion	417
	Romania	419
	Russia	421
	Rwanda	425
S	Saint Helena	427
	Saint Kitts and Nevis	429
	Saint Lucia	431
	Saint Pierre and Miquelon	433
	Saint Vincent and the Grenadines	435
	Samoa	437
	San Marino	439
	Sao Tome and Principe	441
	Saudi Arabia	443
	Senegal	445
	Seychelles	447
	Sierra Leone	449
	Singapore	452
	Slovakia	454
	Slovenia	457
	Solomon Islands	459
	Somalia	461
	South Africa	464
	South Georgia and the South Sandwich Islands	466
	Southern Ocean	467
	Spain	468
	Spratly Islands	471
	Sri Lanka	472
	Sudan	474
	Suriname	477
	Svalbard	479
	Swaziland	481
	Sweden	483
	Switzerland	486
	Syria	488
T	Taiwan entry follows Zimbabwe	
	Tajikistan	491
	Tanzania	493
	Thailand	496
	Togo	499
	Tokelau	501
	Tonga	503
	Trinidad and Tobago	505

		Page
	Tromelin Island	507
	Tunisia	507
	Turkey	510
	Turkmenistan	513
	Turks and Caicos Islands	515
	Tuvalu	517
U	Uganda	519
	Ukraine	521
	United Arab Emirates	524
	United Kingdom	527
	United States	530
	Uruguay	533
	Uzbekistan	536
V	Vanuatu	538
	Venezuela	540
	Vietnam	543
	Virgin Islands	545
W	Wake Island	547
	Wallis and Futuna	548
	West Bank	550
	Western Sahara	552
	World	553
Y	Yemen	555
	Yugoslavia	557
Z	Zambia	560
	Zimbabwe	563
	Taiwan	565

		Page
Appendixes	A: Abbreviations	568
	B: International Organizations and Groups	575
	C: Selected International Environmental Agreements	610
	D: Cross-Reference List of Country Data Codes	618
	E: Cross-Reference List of Hydrographic Data Codes	626
	F: Cross-Reference List of Geographic Names	627

Notes and Definitions

In addition to the updating of information, the following changes have been made in this edition of *The World Factbook*. The entity of Serbia and Montenegro is now officially known as Yugoslavia. There are new entries on: **Currency code, HIV/AIDS – adult prevalence rate, HIV/AIDS – people living with HIV/AIDS, HIV/AIDS – deaths, Internet users**, and **Internet country code**. The **Background** entry, which was introduced in the 1999 edition, has now been completed for all 267 entities in the *Factbook*. The individual country maps are being revised. Some new maps with elevation extremes and a partial geographic grid are included in this edition.

Abbreviations: This information is included in **Appendix A: Abbreviations**, which includes all abbreviations and acronyms used in the *Factbook*, with their expansions.

Acronyms: An acronym is an abbreviation coined from the initial letter of each successive word in a term or phrase. In general, an acronym made up solely from the first letter of the major words in the expanded form is rendered in all capital letters (NATO from North Atlantic Treaty Organization; an exception would be ASEAN for Association of Southeast Asian Nations). In general, an acronym made up of more than the first letter of the major words in the expanded form is rendered with only an initial capital letter (Comsat from Communications Satellite Corporation; an exception would be NAM from Nonaligned Movement). Hybrid forms are sometimes used to distinguish between initially identical terms (WTO: WTrO for World Trade Organization and WToO for World Tourism Organization.)

Administrative divisions: This entry generally gives the numbers, designatory terms, and first-order administrative divisions as approved by the US Board on Geographic Names (BGN). Changes that have been reported but not yet acted on by BGN are noted.

Age structure: This entry provides the distribution of the population according to age. Information is included by sex and age group (0-14 years, 15-64 years, 65 years and over). The age structure of a population affects a nation's key socioeconomic issues. Countries with young populations (high percentage under age 15) need to invest more in schools, while countries with older populations (high percentage ages 65 and over) need to invest more in the health sector. The age structure can also be used to help predict potential political issues. For example, the rapid growth of a young adult population unable to find employment can lead to unrest.

Agriculture - products: This entry is a rank ordering of major crops and products starting with the most important.

Airports: This entry gives the total number of airports. The runway(s) may be paved (concrete or asphalt surfaces) or unpaved (grass, dirt, sand, or gravel surfaces), but must be usable. Not all airports have facilities for refueling, maintenance, or air traffic control.

Airports - with paved runways: This entry gives the total number of airports with paved runways (concrete or asphalt surfaces). For airports with more than one runway, only the longest runway is included according to the following five groups - (1) over 3,047 m, (2) 2,438 to 3,047 m, (3) 1,524 to 2,437 m, (4) 914 to 1,523 m, and (5) under 914 m. Only airports with usable runways are included in this listing. Not all airports have facilities for refueling, maintenance, or air traffic control.

Notes and Definitions *(continued)*

Airports - with unpaved runways: This entry gives the total number of airports with unpaved runways (grass, dirt, sand, or gravel surfaces). For airports with more than one runway, only the longest runway is included according to the following five groups - (1) over 3,047 m, (2) 2,438 to 3,047 m, (3) 1,524 to 2,437 m, (4) 914 to 1,523 m, and (5) under 914 m. Only airports with usable runways are included in this listing. Not all airports have facilities for refueling, maintenance, or air traffic control

Appendixes: This section includes *Factbook*-related material by topic.

Area: This entry includes three subfields. *Total area* is the sum of all land and water areas delimited by international boundaries and/or coastlines. *Land area* is the aggregate of all surfaces delimited by international boundaries and/or coastlines, excluding inland water bodies (lakes, reservoirs, rivers). *Water area* is the sum of all water surfaces delimited by international boundaries and/or coastlines, including inland water bodies (lakes, reservoirs, rivers).

Area - comparative: This entry provides an area comparison based on total area equivalents. Most entities are compared with the entire US or one of the 50 states based on area measurements (1990 revised) provided by the US Bureau of the Census. The smaller entities are compared with Washington, DC (178 sq km, 69 sq mi) or The Mall in Washington, DC (0.59 sq km, 0.23 sq mi, 146 acres).

Background: This entry usually highlights major historic events and current issues and may include a statement about one or two key future trends.

Birth rate: This entry gives the average annual number of births during a year per 1,000 persons in the population at midyear; also known as crude birth rate. The birth rate is usually the dominant factor in determining the rate of population growth. It depends on both the level of fertility and the age structure of the population.

Budget: This entry includes revenues, total expenditures, and capital expenditures. These figures are calculated on an exchange rate basis, i.e., not in purchasing power parity (PPP) terms

Capital: This entry gives the location of the seat of government.

Climate: This entry includes a brief description of typical weather regimes throughout the year.

Coastline: This entry gives the total length of the boundary between the land area (including islands) and the sea.

Communications: This category deals with the means of exchanging information and includes the telephone, radio, television, and Internet service provider entries.

Communications - note: This entry includes miscellaneous communications information of significance not included elsewhere.

Constitution: This entry includes the dates of adoption, revisions, and major amendments.

Country data codes: see **Data codes**

Country map: Most versions of the *Factbook* provide a country map in color. The maps were produced from the best information available at the time of preparation. Names and/or boundaries may have changed subsequently.

Notes and Definitions (continued)

Country name: This entry includes all forms of the country's name approved by the US Board on Geographic Names (Italy is used as an example): *conventional long form* (Italian Republic), *conventional short form* (Italy), *local long form* (Repubblica Italiana), *local short form* (Italia), *former* (Kingdom of Italy), as well as the *abbreviation*. Also see the **Terminology** note.

Currency: This entry identifies the national medium of exchange and its basic subunit.

Currency code: This entry gives the ISO 4217 alphabetic currency code for each country.

Data codes: This information is presented in **Appendix D: Cross-Reference List of Country Data Codes** and **Appendix E: Cross-Reference List of Hydrographic Data Codes**. This appendix includes the US Government approved Federal Information Processing Standards (FIPS) codes, the International Organization for Standardization (ISO) codes, and Internet codes for land entities. The appendix also includes the International Hydrographic Organization (IHO) codes, Aeronautical Chart and Information Center (ACIC; now a part of the National Imagery and Mapping Agency or NIMA) codes, and Defense Intelligence Agency (DIA) codes for hydrographic entities. The US Government has not yet approved a standard for hydrographic data codes similar to the FIPS 10-4 standard for country data codes.

Date of information: In general, information available as of 1 January 2001, was used in the preparation of this edition.

Death rate: This entry gives the average annual number of deaths during a year per 1,000 population at midyear; also known as crude death rate. The death rate, while only a rough indicator of the mortality situation in a country, accurately indicates the current mortality impact on population growth. This indicator is significantly affected by age distribution, and most countries will eventually show a rise in the overall death rate, in spite of continued decline in mortality at all ages, as declining fertility results in an aging population.

Debt - external: This entry gives the total amount of public foreign financial obligations.

Dependency status: This entry describes the formal relationship between a particular nonindependent entity and an independent state.

Dependent areas: This entry contains an alphabetical listing of all nonindependent entities associated in some way with a particular independent state.

Diplomatic representation: The US Government has diplomatic relations with 185 independent states, including 183 of the 189 UN members (excluded UN members are Bhutan, Cuba, Iran, Iraq, North Korea, and the US itself). In addition, the US has diplomatic relations with 2 independent states that are not in the UN - Holy See and Switzerland.

Diplomatic representation from the US: This entry includes the *chief of mission*, *embassy* address, *mailing address*, telephone number, *FAX* number, *branch office* locations, *consulate general* locations, and *consulate* locations.

Notes and Definitions *(continued)*

Disputes - international: This entry includes a wide variety of situations that range from traditional bilateral boundary disputes to unilateral claims of one sort or another. Information regarding disputes over international terrestrial and maritime boundaries has been reviewed by the US Department of State. References to other situations involving borders or frontiers may also be included, such as resource disputes, geopolitical questions, or irredentist issues; however, inclusion does not necessarily constitute official acceptance or recognition by the US Government.

Economic aid - donor: This entry refers to net official development assistance (ODA) from OECD nations to developing countries and multilateral organizations. ODA is defined as financial assistance that is concessional in character, has the main objective to promote economic development and welfare of the less developed countries (LDCs), and contains a grant element of at least 25%. The entry does not cover other official flows (OOF) or private flows.

Economic aid - recipient: This entry, which is subject to major problems of definition and statistical coverage, refers to the net inflow of Official Development Finance (ODF) to recipient countries. The figure includes assistance from the World Bank, the IMF, and other international organizations and from individual nation donors. Formal commitments of aid are included in the data. Omitted from the data are grants by private organizations. Aid comes in various forms including outright grants and loans. The entry thus is the difference between new inflows and repayments.

Economy: This category includes the entries dealing with the size, development, and management of productive resources, i.e., land, labor, and capital.

Economy - overview: This entry briefly describes the type of economy, including the degree of market orientation, the level of economic development, the most important natural resources, and the unique areas of specialization. It also characterizes major economic events and policy changes in the most recent 12 months and may include a statement about one or two key future macroeconomic trends.

Electricity - consumption: This entry consists of total electricity generated annually plus imports and minus exports, expressed in kilowatt-hours. The discrepancy between the amount of electricity generated and/or imported and the amount consumed and/or exported is accounted for as loss in transmission and distribution.

Electricity - exports: This entry is the total exported electricity in kilowatt-hours.

Electricity - imports: This entry is the total imported electricity in kilowatt-hours.

Electricity - production: This entry is the annual electricity generated expressed in kilowatt-hours. The discrepancy between the amount of electricity generated and/or imported and the amount consumed and/or exported is accounted for as loss in transmission and distribution.

Electricity - production by source: This entry indicates the percentage share of annual electricity production of each energy source. These are fossil fuel, hydro, nuclear, and other (solar, geothermal, and wind).

Elevation extremes: This entry includes both the *highest point* and the *lowest point*.

Notes and Definitions *(continued)*

Entities: Some of the independent states, dependencies, areas of special sovereignty, and governments included in this publication are not independent, and others are not officially recognized by the US Government. "Independent state" refers to a people politically organized into a sovereign state with a definite territory. "Dependencies" and "areas of special sovereignty" refer to a broad category of political entities that are associated in some way with an independent state. "Country" names used in the table of contents or for page headings are usually the short-form names as approved by the US Board on Geographic Names and may include independent states, dependencies, and areas of special sovereignty, or other geographic entities. There are a total of 267 separate geographic entities in *The World Factbook* that may be categorized as follows:

INDEPENDENT STATES
191 Afghanistan, Albania, Algeria, Andorra, Angola, Antigua and Barbuda, Argentina, Armenia, Australia, Austria, Azerbaijan, The Bahamas, Bahrain, Bangladesh, Barbados, Belarus, Belgium, Belize, Benin, Bhutan, Bolivia, Bosnia and Herzegovina, Botswana, Brazil, Brunei, Bulgaria, Burkina Faso, Burma, Burundi, Cambodia, Cameroon, Canada, Cape Verde, Central African Republic, Chad, Chile, China, Colombia, Comoros, Democratic Republic of the Congo, Republic of the Congo, Costa Rica, Cote d'Ivoire, Croatia, Cuba, Cyprus, Czech Republic, Denmark, Djibouti, Dominica, Dominican Republic, Ecuador, Egypt, El Salvador, Equatorial Guinea, Eritrea, Estonia, Ethiopia, Fiji, Finland, France, Gabon, The Gambia, Georgia, Germany, Ghana, Greece, Grenada, Guatemala, Guinea, Guinea-Bissau, Guyana, Haiti, Holy See, Honduras, Hungary, Iceland, India, Indonesia, Iran, Iraq, Ireland, Israel, Italy, Jamaica, Japan, Jordan, Kazakhstan, Kenya, Kiribati, North Korea, South Korea, Kuwait, Kyrgyzstan, Laos, Latvia, Lebanon, Lesotho, Liberia, Libya, Liechtenstein, Lithuania, Luxembourg, The Former Yugoslav Republic of Macedonia, Madagascar, Malawi, Malaysia, Maldives, Mali, Malta, Marshall Islands, Mauritania, Mauritius, Mexico, Federated States of Micronesia, Moldova, Monaco, Mongolia, Morocco, Mozambique, Namibia, Nauru, Nepal, Netherlands, NZ, Nicaragua, Niger, Nigeria, Norway, Oman, Pakistan, Palau, Panama, Papua New Guinea, Paraguay, Peru, Philippines, Poland, Portugal, Qatar, Romania, Russia, Rwanda, Saint Kitts and Nevis, Saint Lucia, Saint Vincent and the Grenadines, Samoa, San Marino, Sao Tome and Principe, Saudi Arabia, Senegal, Seychelles, Sierra Leone, Singapore, Slovakia, Slovenia, Solomon Islands, Somalia, South Africa, Spain, Sri Lanka, Sudan, Suriname, Swaziland, Sweden, Switzerland, Syria, Tajikistan, Tanzania, Thailand, Togo, Tonga, Trinidad and Tobago, Tunisia, Turkey, Turkmenistan, Tuvalu, Uganda, Ukraine, UAE, UK, US, Uruguay, Uzbekistan, Vanuatu, Venezuela, Vietnam, Yemen, Yugoslavia, Zambia, Zimbabwe

OTHER
1 Taiwan

DEPENDENCIES AND AREAS OF SPECIAL SOVEREIGNTY
6 Australia - Ashmore and Cartier Islands, Christmas Island, Cocos (Keeling) Islands, Coral Sea Islands, Heard Island and McDonald Islands, Norfolk Island
2 China - Hong Kong, Macau
2 Denmark - Faroe Islands, Greenland
16 France - Bassas da India, Clipperton Island, Europa Island, French Guiana, French Polynesia, French Southern and Antarctic Lands, Glorioso Islands, Guadeloupe, Juan de Nova Island, Martinique, Mayotte, New Caledonia, Reunion, Saint Pierre and Miquelon, Tromelin Island, Wallis and Futuna

Notes and Definitions (continued)

    2   Netherlands - Aruba, Netherlands Antilles
    3   New Zealand - Cook Islands, Niue, Tokelau
    3   Norway - Bouvet Island, Jan Mayen, Svalbard
  15   UK - Anguilla, Bermuda, British Indian Ocean Territory, British Virgin Islands, Cayman Islands, Falkland Islands, Gibraltar, Guernsey, Jersey, Isle of Man, Montserrat, Pitcairn Islands, Saint Helena, South Georgia and the South Sandwich Islands, Turks and Caicos Islands
  14   US - American Samoa, Baker Island, Guam, Howland Island, Jarvis Island, Johnston Atoll, Kingman Reef, Midway Islands, Navassa Island, Northern Mariana Islands, Palmyra Atoll, Puerto Rico, Virgin Islands, Wake Island

MISCELLANEOUS
    6   Antarctica, Gaza Strip, Paracel Islands, Spratly Islands, West Bank, Western Sahara

OTHER ENTITIES
    5   oceans - Arctic Ocean, Atlantic Ocean, Indian Ocean, Pacific Ocean, Southern Ocean
    <u>1   World</u>
267   total

Environment - current issues: This entry lists the most pressing and important environmental problems. The following terms and abbreviations are used throughout the entry:

    acidification - the lowering of soil and water pH due to acid precipitation and deposition usually through precipitation; this process disrupts ecosystem nutrient flows and may kill freshwater fish and plants dependent on more neutral or alkaline conditions (see acid rain).

    acid rain - characterized as containing harmful levels of sulfur dioxide or nitrogen oxide; acid rain is damaging and potentially deadly to the earth's fragile ecosystems; acidity is measured using the pH scale where 7 is neutral, values greater that 7 are considered alkaline, and anything measured below 5.6 is considered acid precipitation; note - a pH of 2.4 (the acidity of vinegar) has been measured in rainfall in New England.

    aerosol - a collection of airborne particles dispersed in a gas, smoke, or fog.

    afforestation - converting a bare or agricultural space by planting trees and plants; reforestation involves replanting trees on areas that have been cut or destroyed by fire.

    asbestos - a naturally occurring soft fibrous mineral commonly used in fireproofing materials and considered to be highly carcinogenic in particulate form.

    biodiversity - also biological diversity; the relative number of species, diverse in form and function, at the genetic, organism, community, and ecosystem level; loss of biodiversity reduces an ecosystem's ability to recover from natural or man-induced disruption.

    bio-indicators - a plant or animal species whose presence, abundance, and health reveal the general condition of its habitat.

    biomass - the total weight or volume of living matter in a given area or volume.

    carbon cycle - the term used to describe the exchange of carbon (in various forms, e.g., as carbon dioxide) between the atmosphere, ocean, terrestrial biosphere, and geological deposits.

    catchments - assemblages used to capture and retain rainwater and runoff; an important water management technique in areas with limited freshwater resources, such as Gibraltar.

    DDT (dichloro-diphenyl-trichloro-ethane) - a colorless, odorless insecticide that has toxic effects on most animals; the use of DDT was banned in the US in 1972.

Notes and Definitions (continued)

defoliants - chemicals which cause plants to lose their leaves artificially; often used in agricultural practices for weed control, and may have detrimental impacts on human and ecosystem health.

deforestation - the destruction of vast areas of forest (e.g., unsustainable forestry practices, agricultural and range land clearing, and the over exploitation of wood products for use as fuel) without planting new growth.

desertification - the spread of desert-like conditions in arid or semi-arid areas, due to overgrazing, loss of agriculturally productive soils, or climate change.

dredging - the practice of deepening an existing waterway; also, a technique used for collecting bottom-dwelling marine organisms (e.g., shellfish) or harvesting coral, often causing significant destruction of reef and ocean-floor ecosystems.

drift-net fishing - done with a net, miles in extent, that is generally anchored to a boat and left to float with the tide; often results in an over harvesting and waste of large populations of non-commercial marine species (by-catch) by its effect of "sweeping the ocean clean".

ecosystems - ecological units comprised of complex communities of organisms and their specific environments.

effluents - waste materials, such as smoke, sewage, or industrial waste which are released into the environment, subsequently polluting it.

endangered species - a species that is threatened with extinction either by direct hunting or habitat destruction.

freshwater - water with very low soluble mineral content; sources include lakes, streams, rivers, glaciers, and underground aquifers.

greenhouse gas - a gas that "traps" infrared radiation in the lower atmosphere causing surface warming; water vapor, carbon dioxide, nitrous oxide, methane, hydrofluorocarbons, and ozone are the primary greenhouse gases in the Earth's atmosphere.

groundwater - water sources found below the surface of the earth often in naturally occurring reservoirs in permeable rock strata; the source for wells and natural springs.

Highlands Water Project - a series of dams constructed jointly by Lesotho and South Africa to redirect Lesotho's abundant water supply into a rapidly growing area in South Africa; while it is the largest infrastructure project in southern Africa, it is also the most costly and controversial; objections to the project include claims that it forces people from their homes, submerges farmlands, and squanders economic resources.

Inuit Circumpolar Conference (ICC) - represents the 125,000 Inuits of Russia, Alaska, Canada, and Greenland in international environmental issues; a panel convenes every three years to determine the focus of the ICC; the most current concerns are long-range transport of pollutants, sustainable development, and climate change.

metallurgical plants - industries which specialize in the science, technology, and processing of metals; these plants produce highly concentrated and toxic wastes which can contribute to pollution of ground water and air when not properly disposed.

noxious substances - injurious, very harmful to living beings.

overgrazing - the grazing of animals on plant material faster than it can naturally regrow leading to the permanent loss of plant cover, a common effect of too many animals grazing limited range land.

ozone shield - a layer of the atmosphere composed of ozone gas (O_3) that resides approximately 25 miles above the Earth's surface and absorbs solar ultraviolet radiation that can be harmful to living organisms.

poaching - the illegal killing of animals or fish, a great concern with respect to endangered or threatened species.

Notes and Definitions (continued)

pollution - the contamination of a healthy environment by man-made waste.

potable water - water that is drinkable, safe to be consumed.

salination - the process through which fresh (drinkable) water becomes salt (undrinkable) water; hence, desalination is the reverse process; also involves the accumulation of salts in topsoil caused by evaporation of excessive irrigation water, a process that can eventually render soil incapable of supporting crops.

siltation - occurs when water channels and reservoirs become clotted with silt and mud, a side effect of deforestation and soil erosion.

slash-and-burn agriculture - a rotating cultivation technique in which trees are cut down and burned in order to clear land for temporary agriculture; the land is used until its productivity declines at which point a new plot is selected and the process repeats; this practice is sustainable while population levels are low and time is permitted for regrowth of natural vegetation; conversely, where these conditions do not exist, the practice can have disastrous consequences for the environment.

soil degradation - damage to the land's productive capacity because of poor agricultural practices such as the excessive use of pesticides or fertilizers, soil compaction from heavy equipment, or erosion of topsoil, eventually resulting in reduced ability to produce agricultural products.

soil erosion - the removal of soil by the action of water or wind, compounded by poor agricultural practices, deforestation, overgrazing, and desertification.

ultraviolet (UV) radiation - a portion of the electromagnetic energy emitted by the sun and naturally filtered in the upper atmosphere by the ozone layer; UV radiation can be harmful to living organisms and has been linked to increasing rates of skin cancer in humans.

water-born diseases - those in which the bacteria survive in, and is transmitted through, water; always a serious threat in areas with an untreated water supply.

Environment - international agreements: This entry separates country participation in international environmental agreements into two levels - *party to* and *signed but not ratified*. Agreements are listed in alphabetical order by the abbreviated form of the full name.

Environmental agreements: This information is presented in **Appendix C: Selected International Environmental Agreements**, which includes the name, abbreviation, date opened for signature, date entered into force, objective, and parties by category.

Ethnic groups: This entry provides a rank ordering of ethnic groups starting with the largest and normally includes the percent of total population.

Exchange rates: This entry provides the official value of a country's monetary unit at a given date or over a given period of time, as expressed in units of local currency per US dollar and as determined by international market forces or official fiat.

Executive branch: This entry includes several subfields. *Chief of state* includes the name and title of the titular leader of the country who represents the state at official and ceremonial functions but may not be involved with the day-to-day activities of the government. *Head of government* includes the name and title of the top administrative leader who is designated to manage the day-to-day activities of the government. For example, in the UK, the monarch is the chief of state, and the prime minister is the head of government. In the US, the president is both the chief of state and the head of government. *Cabinet* includes the official name for this body of high-ranking advisers and the method for selection of members. *Elections* includes the nature of election process or accession to power, date of the last election, and date of the next election. *Election results* includes the percent of vote for each candidate in the last election.

Notes and Definitions (continued)

Exports: This entry provides the total US dollar amount of exports on an f.o.b. (free on board) basis.

Exports - commodities: This entry provides a rank ordering of exported products starting with the most important; it sometimes includes the percent of total dollar value.

Exports - partners: This entry provides a rank ordering of trading partners starting with the most important; it sometimes includes the percent of total dollar value.

Fiscal year: This entry identifies the beginning and ending months for a country's accounting period of 12 months, which often is the calendar year but which may begin in any month. All yearly references are for the calendar year (CY) unless indicated as a noncalendar fiscal year (FY).

Flag description: This entry provides a written flag description produced from actual flags or the best information available at the time the entry was written. The flags of independent states are used by their dependencies unless there is an officially recognized local flag. Some disputed and other areas do not have flags.

Flag graphic: Most versions of the *Factbook* include a color flag at the beginning of the country profile. The flag graphics were produced from actual flags or the best information available at the time of preparation. The flags of independent states are used by their dependencies unless there is an officially recognized local flag. Some disputed and other areas do not have flags.

GDP: This entry gives the gross domestic product (GDP) or value of all final goods and services produced within a nation in a given year. GDP dollar estimates in the Factbook are derived from purchasing power parity (PPP) calculations. See the note on **GDP methodology** for more information.

GDP methodology: In the **Economy** section, GDP dollar estimates for all countries are derived from purchasing power parity (PPP) calculations rather than from conversions at official currency exchange rates. The PPP method involves the use of standardized international dollar price weights, which are applied to the quantities of final goods and services produced in a given economy. The data derived from the PPP method provide the best available starting point for comparisons of economic strength and well-being between countries. The division of a GDP estimate in domestic currency by the corresponding PPP estimate in dollars gives the PPP conversion rate. Whereas PPP estimates for OECD countries are quite reliable, PPP estimates for developing countries are often rough approximations. Most of the GDP estimates are based on extrapolation of PPP numbers published by the UN International Comparison Program (UNICP) and by Professors Robert Summers and Alan Heston of the University of Pennsylvania and their colleagues. In contrast, the currency exchange rate method involves a variety of international and domestic financial forces that often have little relation to domestic output. In developing countries with weak currencies the exchange rate estimate of GDP in dollars is typically one-fourth to one-half the PPP estimate. Furthermore, exchange rates may suddenly go up or down by 10% or more because of market forces or official fiat whereas real output has remained unchanged. On 12 January 1994, for example, the 14 countries of the African Financial Community (whose currencies are tied to the French franc) devalued their currencies by 50%. This move, of course, did not cut the real output of these countries by half. One important caution: the proportion of, say, defense

Notes and Definitions (continued)

expenditures as a percentage of GDP in local currency accounts may differ substantially from the proportion when GDP accounts are expressed in PPP terms, as, for example, when an observer tries to estimate the dollar level of Russian or Japanese military expenditures. Note: the numbers for GDP and other economic data can not be chained together from successive volumes of the *Factbook* because of changes in the US dollar measuring rod, revisions of data by statistical agencies, use of new or different sources of information, and changes in national statistical methods and practices.

GDP - composition by sector: This entry gives the percentage contribution of *agriculture, industry,* and *services* to total GDP.

GDP - per capita: This entry shows GDP on a purchasing power parity basis divided by population as of 1 July for the same year.

GDP - real growth rate: This entry gives GDP growth on an annual basis adjusted for inflation and expressed as a percent.

Geographic coordinates: This entry includes rounded latitude and longitude figures for the purpose of finding the approximate geographic center of an entity and is based on the *Gazetteer of Conventional Names*, Third Edition, August 1988, US Board on Geographic Names and on other sources.

Geographic names: This information is presented in **Appendix F: Cross-Reference List of Geographic Names**. It includes a listing of various alternate names, former names, local names, and regional names referenced to one or more related Factbook entries. Spellings are normally, but not always, those approved by the US Board on Geographic Names (BGN). Alternate names and additional information are included in parentheses.

Geography: This category includes the entries dealing with the natural environment and the effects of human activity.

Geography - note: This entry includes miscellaneous geographic information of significance not included elsewhere.

GNP: Gross national product (GNP) is the value of all final goods and services produced within a nation in a given year, plus income earned by its citizens abroad, minus income earned by foreigners from domestic production. *The Factbook*, following current practice, uses GDP rather than GNP to measure national production. However, the user must realize that in certain countries net remittances from citizens working abroad may be important to national well-being.

Government: This category includes the entries dealing with the system for the adoption and administration of public policy.

Government type: This entry gives the basic form of government (e.g., republic, constitutional monarchy, federal republic, parliamentary democracy, military dictatorship).

Government - note: This entry includes miscellaneous government information of significance not included elsewhere.

Gross domestic product: see **GDP**

Gross national product: see **GNP**

Notes and Definitions (continued)

Gross world product: see **GWP**

GWP: This entry gives the gross world product (GWP) or aggregate value of all final goods and services produced worldwide in a given year.

Heliports: This entry gives the total number of established helicopter takeoff and landing sites (which may or may not have fuel or other services).

Highways: This entry includes the *total* length of the highway system as well as the length of the *paved* and *unpaved* components.

HIV/AIDS – adult prevalence rate: This entry gives an estimate of the percentage of adults (aged 15-49) living with HIV/AIDS. The adult prevalence rate is calculated by dividing the estimated number of adults living with HIV/AIDS at yearend by the total adult population at yearend.

HIV/AIDS – deaths: This entry gives an estimate of the number of adults and children who died of AIDS during a given calendar year.

HIV/AIDS – people living with HIV/AIDS: This entry gives an estimate of all people (adults and children) alive at yearend with HIV infection, whether or not they have developed symptoms of AIDS.

Household income or consumption by percentage share: Data on household income or consumption come from household surveys, the results adjusted for household size. Nations use different standards and procedures in collecting and adjusting the data. Surveys based on income will normally show a more unequal distribution than surveys based on consumption. The quality of surveys is improving with time, yet caution is still necessary in making inter-country comparisons.

Hydrographic data codes: see **Data codes**

Illicit drugs: This entry gives information on the five categories of illicit drugs - narcotics, stimulants, depressants (sedatives), hallucinogens, and cannabis. These categories include many drugs legally produced and prescribed by doctors as well as those illegally produced and sold outside of medical channels.

Cannabis (Cannabis sativa) is the common hemp plant, which provides hallucinogens with some sedative properties, and includes marijuana (pot, Acapulco gold, grass, reefer), tetrahydrocannabinol (THC, Marinol), hashish (hash), and hashish oil (hash oil).

Coca (mostly Erythroxylum coca) is a bush with leaves that contain the stimulant used to make cocaine. Coca is not to be confused with cocoa, which comes from cacao seeds and is used in making chocolate, cocoa, and cocoa butter.

Cocaine is a stimulant derived from the leaves of the coca bush.

Depressants (sedatives) are drugs that reduce tension and anxiety and include chloral hydrate, barbiturates (Amytal, Nembutal, Seconal, phenobarbital), benzodiazepines (Librium, Valium), methaqualone (Quaalude), glutethimide (Doriden), and others (Equanil, Placidyl, Valmid).

Drugs are any chemical substances that effect a physical, mental, emotional, or behavioral change in an individual.

Drug abuse is the use of any licit or illicit chemical substance that results in physical, mental, emotional, or behavioral impairment in an individual.

Notes and Definitions (continued)

Hallucinogens are drugs that affect sensation, thinking, self-awareness, and emotion. Hallucinogens include LSD (acid, microdot), mescaline and peyote (mexc, buttons, cactus), amphetamine variants (PMA, STP, DOB), phencyclidine (PCP, angel dust, hog), phencyclidine analogues (PCE, PCPy, TCP), and others (psilocybin, psilocyn).

Hashish is the resinous exudate of the cannabis or hemp plant (Cannabis sativa).

Heroin is a semisynthetic derivative of morphine.

Mandrax is a trade name for methaqualone, a pharmaceutical depressant.

Marijuana is the dried leaf of the cannabis or hemp plant (Cannabis sativa).

Methaqualone is a pharmaceutical depressant, referred to as mandrax in Southwest Asia and Africa.

Narcotics are drugs that relieve pain, often induce sleep, and refer to opium, opium derivatives, and synthetic substitutes. Natural narcotics include opium (paregoric, parepectolin), morphine (MS-Contin, Roxanol), codeine (Tylenol with codeine, Empirin with codeine, Robitussan AC), and thebaine. Semisynthetic narcotics include heroin (horse, smack), and hydromorphone (Dilaudid). Synthetic narcotics include meperidine or Pethidine (Demerol, Mepergan), methadone (Dolophine, Methadose), and others (Darvon, Lomotil).

Opium is the brown, gummy exudate of the incised, unripe seedpod of the opium poppy.

Opium poppy (Papaver somniferum) is the source for the natural and semisynthetic narcotics.

Poppy straw concentrate is the alkaloid derived from the mature, dried opium poppy.

Qat (kat, khat) is a stimulant from the buds or leaves of Catha edulis that is chewed or drunk as tea.

Quaaludes is the North American slang term for methaqualone, a pharmaceutical depressant.

Stimulants are drugs that relieve mild depression, increase energy and activity, and include cocaine (coke, snow, crack), amphetamines (Desoxyn, Dexedrine), ephedrine, ecstasy (clarity, essence, doctor, Adam), phenmetrazine (Preludin), methylphenidate (Ritalin), and others (Cylert, Sanorex, Tenuate).

Imports: This entry provides the total US dollar amount of imports on a c.i.f. (cost, insurance, and freight) or f.o.b. (free on board) basis.

Imports - commodities: This entry provides a rank ordering of imported products starting with the most important; it sometimes includes the percent of total dollar value.

Imports - partners: This entry provides a rank ordering of trading partners starting with the most important; it sometimes includes the percent of total dollar value.

Independence: For most countries, this entry gives the date that sovereignty was achieved and from which nation, empire, or trusteeship. For the other countries, the date given may not represent "independence" in the strict sense, but rather some significant nationhood event such as the traditional founding date or the date of unification, federation, confederation, establishment, fundamental change in the form of government, or state succession. Dependent areas include the notation "none" followed by the nature of their dependency status. Also see the **Terminology** note.

Notes and Definitions (continued)

Industrial production growth rate: This entry gives the annual percentage increase in industrial production (includes manufacturing, mining, and construction).

Industries: This entry provides a rank ordering of industries starting with the largest by value of annual output.

Infant mortality rate: This entry gives the number of deaths of infants under one year old in a given year per 1,000 live births in the same year. This rate is often used as an indicator of the level of health in a country.

Inflation rate (consumer prices): This entry furnishes the annual percent change in consumer prices compared with the previous year's consumer prices.

Internet country code: This entry includes the two-letter codes maintained by the International Organization for Standardization (ISO) in the ISO 3166 Alpha-2 list and used by the Internet Assigned Numbers Authority (IANA) to establish country-coded top-level domains (ccTLDs).

Internet Service Providers (ISPs): This entry supplies the number of Internet Service Providers within a country. An ISP is defined as a company that provides access to the Internet.

Internet users: This entry gives the number of users within a country that access the Internet. Statistics vary from country to country and may include users who access the Internet at least several times a week to those who access it only once within a period of several months.

International disputes: see **Disputes - international**

International organization participation: This entry lists in alphabetical order by abbreviation those international organizations in which the subject country is a member or participates in some other way.

International organizations: This information is presented in **Appendix B: International Organizations and Groups** which includes the name, abbreviation, date established, aim, and members by category.

Introduction: This category includes one entry, **Background**.

Irrigated land: This entry gives the number of square kilometers of land area that is artificially supplied with water.

Judicial branch: This entry contains the name(s) of the highest court(s) and a brief description of the selection process for members.

Labor force: This entry contains the total labor force figure.

Labor force - by occupation: This entry contains a rank ordering of component parts of the labor force by occupation.

Land boundaries: This entry contains the total length of all land boundaries and the individual lengths for each of the contiguous border countries.

Land use: This entry contains the percentage shares of total land area for five different types of land use: *arable land* - land cultivated for crops that are replanted after each harvest like wheat, maize, and rice; *permanent crops* - land cultivated

Notes and Definitions (continued)

for crops that are not replanted after each harvest like citrus, coffee, and rubber; *permanent pastures* - land permanently used for herbaceous forage crops; *forests and woodland* - land under dense or open stands of trees; *other* - any land type not specifically mentioned above, such as urban areas, roads, desert, etc.

Languages: This entry provides a rank ordering of languages starting with the largest and sometimes includes the percent of total population speaking that language.

Legal system: This entry contains a brief description of the legal system's historical roots, role in government, and acceptance of International Court of Justice (ICJ) jurisdiction.

Legislative branch: This entry contains information on the structure (unicameral, bicameral, tricameral), formal name, number of seats, and term of office. *Elections* includes the nature of election process or accession to power, date of the last election, and date of the next election. *Election results* includes the percent of vote and/or number of seats held by each party in the last election.

Life expectancy at birth: This entry contains the average number of years to be lived by a group of people born in the same year, if mortality at each age remains constant in the future. The entry includes total population as well as the male and female components. Life expectancy at birth is also a measure of overall quality of life in a country and summarizes the mortality at all ages. It can also be thought of as indicating the potential return on investment in human capital and is necessary for the calculation of various actuarial measures.

Literacy: This entry includes a definition of literacy and Census Bureau percentages for the total population, males, and females. There are no universal definitions and standards of literacy. Unless otherwise specified, all rates are based on the most common definition - the ability to read and write at a specified age. Detailing the standards that individual countries use to assess the ability to read and write is beyond the scope of the *Factbook*. Information on literacy, while not a perfect measure of educational results, is probably the most easily available and valid for international comparisons. Low levels of literacy, and education in general, can impede the economic development of a country in the current rapidly changing, technology-driven world.

Location: This entry identifies the country's regional location, neighboring countries, and adjacent bodies of water.

Map references: This entry includes the name of the *Factbook* reference map on which a country may be found. The entry on **Geographic coordinates** may be helpful in finding some smaller countries.

Maritime claims: This entry includes the following claims: contiguous zone, continental shelf, exclusive economic zone, exclusive fishing zone, extended fishing zone, none (usually for a landlocked country), other (unique maritime claims like Libya's Gulf of Sidra Closing Line or North Korea's Military Boundary Line), and territorial sea. The proximity of neighboring states may prevent some national claims from being extended the full distance.

Merchant marine: Merchant marine may be defined as all ships engaged in the carriage of goods; or all commercial vessels (as opposed to all nonmilitary ships), which excludes tugs, fishing vessels, offshore oil rigs, etc.; or a grouping of

Notes and Definitions *(continued)*

merchant ships by nationality or register. This entry contains information in two subfields - *total and ships by type. Total* includes the total number of ships (1,000 GRT or over), total DWT for those ships, and total GRT for those ships. DWT or dead weight tonnage is the total weight of cargo, plus bunkers, stores, etc. that a ship can carry when immersed to the appropriate load line. GRT or gross register tonnage is a figure obtained by measuring the entire sheltered volume of the ship available for cargo and passengers and converting it to tons on the basis of 100 cubic feet per ton; there is no stable relationship between GRT and DWT. *Ships by type* includes a listing of barge carriers, bulk cargo ships, cargo ships, chemical tankers, combination bulk carriers, combination ore/oil carriers, container ships, liquefied gas tankers, livestock carriers, multifunctional large-load carriers, petroleum tankers, passenger ships, passenger/cargo ships, railcar carriers, refrigerated cargo ships, roll-on/roll-off cargo ships, short-sea passenger ships, specialized tankers, and vehicle carriers.

A captive register is a register of ships maintained by a territory, possession, or colony primarily or exclusively for the use of ships owned in the parent country; it is also referred to as an offshore register, the offshore equivalent of an internal register. Ships on a captive register will fly the same flag as the parent country, or a local variant of it, but will be subject to the maritime laws and taxation rules of the offshore territory. Although the nature of a captive register makes it especially desirable for ships owned in the parent country, just as in the internal register, the ships may also be owned abroad. The captive register then acts as a flag of convenience register, except that it is not the register of an independent state.

A flag of convenience register is a national register offering registration to a merchant ship not owned in the flag state. The major flags of convenience (FOC) attract ships to their registers by virtue of low fees, low or nonexistent taxation of profits, and liberal manning requirements. True FOC registers are characterized by having relatively few of the registered ships actually owned in the flag state. Thus, while virtually any flag can be used for ships under a given set of circumstances, an FOC register is one where the majority of the merchant fleet is owned abroad. It is also referred to as an open register.

A flag state is the nation in which a ship is registered and which holds legal jurisdiction over operation of the ship, whether at home or abroad. Maritime legislation of the flag state determines how a ship is crewed and taxed and whether a foreign-owned ship may be placed on the register.

An internal register is a register of ships maintained as a subset of a national register. Ships on the internal register fly the national flag and have that nationality but are subject to a separate set of maritime rules from those on the main national register. These differences usually include lower taxation of profits, use of foreign nationals as crewmembers, and, usually, ownership outside the flag state (when it functions as an FOC register). The Norwegian International Ship Register and Danish International Ship Register are the most notable examples of an internal register. Both have been instrumental in stemming flight from the national flag to flags of convenience and in attracting foreign-owned ships to the Norwegian and Danish flags.

A merchant ship is a vessel that carries goods against payment of freight; it is commonly used to denote any nonmilitary ship but accurately restricted to commercial vessels only.

A register is the record of a ship's ownership and nationality as listed with the maritime authorities of a country; also, it is the compendium of such individual ships' registrations. Registration of a ship provides it with a nationality and makes it subject to the laws of the country in which registered (the flag state) regardless of the nationality of the ship's ultimate owner.

Notes and Definitions (continued)

Military: This category includes the entries dealing with a country's military structure, manpower, and expenditures.

Military branches: This entry lists the names of the ground, naval, air, marine, and other defense or security forces.

Military expenditures - dollar figure: This entry gives current military expenditures in US dollars; the figure is calculated by multiplying the estimated defense spending in percentage terms by the gross domestic product (GDP) calculated on an exchange rate basis *not* purchasing power parity (PPP) terms. However, in the case of Russia, estimates of military expenditures have been made using PPP. Dollar figures for military expenditures should be treated with caution because of different price patterns and accounting methods among nations, as well as wide variations in the strength of their currencies.

Military expenditures - percent of GDP: This entry gives current military expenditures as an estimated percent of gross domestic product (GDP).

Military manpower - availability: This entry gives the total numbers of males and females age 15-49 and assumes that every individual is fit to serve.

Military manpower - fit for military service: This entry gives the number of males and females age 15-49 fit for military service. This is a more refined measure of potential military manpower availability which tries to correct for the health situation in the country and reduces the maximum potential number to a more realistic estimate of the actual number fit to serve.

Military manpower - military age: This entry gives the minimum age at which an individual may volunteer for military service or be subject to conscription.

Military manpower - reaching military age annually: This entry gives the number of draft-age males and females entering the military manpower pool in any given year and is a measure of the availability of draft-age young adults.

Military - note: This entry includes miscellaneous military information of significance not included elsewhere.

Money figures: All money figures are expressed in contemporaneous US dollars unless otherwise indicated.

National holiday: This entry gives the primary national day of celebration - usually independence day.

Nationality: This entry provides the identifying terms for citizens - *noun* and *adjective*.

Natural hazards: This entry lists potential natural disasters.

Natural resources: This entry lists a country's mineral, petroleum, hydropower, and other resources of commercial importance.

Net migration rate: This entry includes the figure for the difference between the number of persons entering and leaving a country during the year per 1,000 persons (based on midyear population). An excess of persons entering the country is referred to as net immigration (e.g., 3.56 migrants/1,000 population); an

Notes and Definitions (continued)

excess of persons leaving the country as net emigration (e.g., -9.26 migrants/ 1,000 population). The net migration rate indicates the contribution of migration to the overall level of population change. High levels of migration can cause problems such as increasing unemployment and potential ethnic strife (if people are coming in) or a reduction in the labor force, perhaps in certain key sectors (if people are leaving).

People: This category includes the entries dealing with the characteristics of the people and their society.

People - note: This entry includes miscellaneous demographic information of significance not included elsewhere.

Personal Names - Capitalization: The *Factbook* capitalizes the surname or family name of individuals for the convenience of our users who are faced with a world of different cultures and naming conventions. An example would be President SADDAM Husayn of Iraq. Saddam is his name and Husayn is his father's name. He may be referred to as President SADDAM Husayn or President SADDAM, but **not** President Husayn. The need for capitalization, bold type, underlining, italics, or some other indicator of the individual's surname is apparent in the following examples: MAO Zedong, Fidel CASTRO Ruz, George W. BUSH, and TUNKU SALAHUDDIN Abdul Aziz Shah ibni Al-Marhum Sultan Hisammuddin Alam Shah. By knowing the surname, a short form without all capital letters can be used with confidence as in President Saddam, President Castro, Chairman Mao, President Bush, or Sultan Tunku Salahuddin. The same system of capitalization is extended to the names of leaders with surnames that are not commonly used such as Queen ELIZABETH II.

Personal Names - Spelling: The romanization of personal names in the *Factbook* normally follows the same transliteration system used by the US Board on Geographic Names for spelling place names. At times, however, a foreign leader expressly indicates a preference for, or the media or official documents regularly use, a romanized spelling that differs from the transliteration derived from the US Government standard. In such cases, the *Factbook* uses the alternative spelling.

Personal Names - Titles: The *Factbook* capitalizes any valid title (or short form of it) immediately preceding a person's name. A title standing alone is lowercased. Examples: President PUTIN and President BUSH are chiefs of state. In Russia, the president is chief of state and the premier is the head of the government, while in the US, the president is both chief of state and head of government.

Pipelines: This entry gives the lengths and types of pipelines for transporting products like natural gas, crude oil, or petroleum products.

Political parties and leaders: This entry includes a listing of significant political organizations and their leaders.

Political pressure groups and leaders: This entry includes a listing of organizations with leaders involved in politics, but not standing for legislative election.

Population: This entry gives an estimate from the US Bureau of the Census based on statistics from population censuses, vital statistics registration systems, or sample surveys pertaining to the recent past and on assumptions about future trends. The total population presents one overall measure of the potential impact

Notes and Definitions *(continued)*

of the country on the world and within its region. Note: starting with the 1993 *Factbook*, demographic estimates for some countries (mostly African) have explicitly taken into account the effects of the growing impact of the HIV/AIDS epidemic. These countries are currently: The Bahamas, Benin, Botswana, Brazil, Burkina Faso, Burma, Burundi, Cambodia, Cameroon, Central African Republic, Democratic Republic of the Congo, Republic of the Congo, Cote d'Ivoire, Ethiopia, Gabon, Ghana, Guyana, Haiti, Honduras, Kenya, Lesotho, Malawi, Mozambique, Namibia, Nigeria, Rwanda, South Africa, Swaziland, Tanzania, Thailand, Togo, Uganda, Zambia, and Zimbabwe.

Population below poverty line: National estimates of the percentage of the population lying below the poverty line are based on surveys of sub-groups, with the results weighted by the number of people in each group. Definitions of poverty vary considerably among nations. For example, rich nations generally employ more generous standards of poverty than poor nations.

Population growth rate: The average annual percent change in the population, resulting from a surplus (or deficit) of births over deaths and the balance of migrants entering and leaving a country. The rate may be positive or negative. The growth rate is a factor in determining how great a burden would be imposed on a country by the changing needs of its people for infrastructure (e.g., schools, hospitals, housing, roads), resources (e.g., food, water, electricity), and jobs. Rapid population growth can be seen as threatening by neighboring countries.

Ports and harbors: This entry lists the major ports and harbors selected on the basis of overall importance to each country. This is determined by evaluating a number of factors (e.g., dollar value of goods handled, gross tonnage, facilities, military significance).

Radio broadcast stations: This entry includes the total number of AM, FM, and shortwave broadcast stations.

Radios: This entry gives the total number of radio receivers.

Railways: This entry includes the *total* route length of the railway network and of its component parts by gauge: *broad, dual, narrow, standard,* and *other.*

Reference maps: This section includes world, regional, and special or current interest maps.

Religions: This entry includes a rank ordering of religions by adherents starting with the largest group and sometimes includes the percent of total population.

Sex ratio: This entry includes the number of males for each female in five age groups - *at birth, under 15 years, 15-64 years, 65 years and over,* and for the *total population*. Sex ratio at birth has recently emerged as an indicator of certain kinds of sex discrimination in some countries. For instance, high sex ratios at birth in some Asian countries are now attributed to sex-selective abortion and infanticide due to a strong preference for sons. This will affect future marriage patterns and fertility patterns. Eventually it could cause unrest among young adult males who are unable to find partners.

Suffrage: This entry gives the age at enfranchisement and whether the right to vote is universal or restricted.

Notes and Definitions (continued)

Telephone numbers: All telephone numbers in the *Factbook* consist of the country code in brackets, the city or area code (where required) in parentheses, and the local number. The one component that is not presented is the international access code, which varies from country to country. For example, an international direct dial telephone call placed from the US to Madrid, Spain, would be as follows:

011 [34] (1) 577-xxxx, where
011 is the international access code for station-to-station calls
(01 is for calls other than station-to-station calls),
[34] is the country code for Spain,
(1) is the city code for Madrid,
577 is the local exchange, and
xxxx is the local telephone number.

An international direct dial telephone call placed from another country to the US would be as follows:

international access code + [1] (202) 939-xxxx, where
[1] is the country code for the US,
(202) is the area code for Washington, DC,
939 is the local exchange, and
xxxx is the local telephone number.

Telephone system: This entry includes a brief characterization of the system with details on the *domestic* and *international* components. The following terms and abbreviations are used throughout the entry:

Africa ONE - a fiber-optic submarine cable link encircling the continent of Africa.

Arabsat - Arab Satellite Communications Organization (Riyadh, Saudi Arabia).

Autodin - Automatic Digital Network (US Department of Defense).

CB - citizen's band mobile radio communications.

cellular telephone system - the telephones in this system are radio transceivers, with each instrument having its own private radio frequency and sufficient radiated power to reach the booster station in its area (cell), from which the telephone signal is fed to a regular telephone exchange.

Central American Microwave System - a trunk microwave radio relay system that links the countries of Central America and Mexico with each other.

coaxial cable - a multichannel communication cable consisting of a central conducting wire, surrounded by and insulated from a cylindrical conducting shell; a large number of telephone channels can be made available within the insulated space by the use of a large number of carrier frequencies.

Comsat - Communications Satellite Corporation (US).

DSN - Defense Switched Network (formerly Automatic Voice Network or Autovon); basic general-purpose, switched voice network of the Defense Communications System (US Department of Defense).

Eutelsat - European Telecommunications Satellite Organization (Paris).

fiber-optic cable - a multichannel communications cable using a thread of optical glass fibers as a transmission medium in which the signal (voice, video, etc.) is in the form of a coded pulse of light.

GSM - a global system for mobile (cellular) communications devised by the Groupe Special Mobile of the pan-European standardization organization, Conference Europeanne des Posts et Telecommunications (CEPT) in 1982.

HF – high frequency; any radio frequency in the 3,000- to 30,000-kHz range.

Inmarsat - International Mobile Satellite Organization (London); provider of global mobile satellite communications for commercial, distress, and safety applications at sea, in the air, and on land.

Notes and Definitions *(continued)*

Intelsat - International Telecommunications Satellite Organization (Washington, DC).

Intersputnik - International Organization of Space Communications (Moscow); first established in the former Soviet Union and the East European countries, it is now marketing its services worldwide with earth stations in North America, Africa, and East Asia.

landline - communication wire or cable of any sort that is installed on poles or buried in the ground.

Marecs - Maritime European Communications Satellite used in the Inmarsat system on lease from the European Space Agency.

Marisat - satellites of the Comsat Corporation that participate in the Inmarsat system.

Medarabtel - the Middle East Telecommunications Project of the International Telecommunications Union (ITU) providing a modern telecommunications network, primarily by microwave radio relay, linking Algeria, Djibouti, Egypt, Jordan, Libya, Morocco, Saudi Arabia, Somalia, Sudan, Syria, Tunisia, and Yemen; it was initially started in Morocco in 1970 by the Arab Telecommunications Union (ATU) and was known at that time as the Middle East Mediterranean Telecommunications Network.

microwave radio relay - transmission of long distance telephone calls and television programs by highly directional radio microwaves that are received and sent on from one booster station to another on an optical path.

NMT - Nordic Mobile Telephone; an analog cellular telephone system that was developed jointly by the national telecommunications authorities of the Nordic countries (Denmark, Finland, Iceland, Norway, and Sweden).

Orbita - a Russian television service; also the trade name of a packet-switched digital telephone network.

radiotelephone communications - the two-way transmission and reception of sounds by broadcast radio on authorized frequencies using telephone handsets.

PanAmSat - PanAmSat Corporation (Greenwich, CT).

satellite communication system - a communication system consisting of two or more earth stations and at least one satellite that provide long distance transmission of voice, data, and television; the system usually serves as a trunk connection between telephone exchanges; if the earth stations are in the same country, it is a domestic system.

satellite earth station - a communications facility with a microwave radio transmitting and receiving antenna and required receiving and transmitting equipment for communicating with satellites.

satellite link - a radio connection between a satellite and an earth station permitting communication between them, either one-way (down link from satellite to earth station - television receive-only transmission) or two-way (telephone channels).

SHF – super high frequency; any radio frequency in the 3,000- to 30,000-MHz range.

shortwave - radio frequencies (from 1.605 to 30 MHz) that fall above the commercial broadcast band and are used for communication over long distances.

Solidaridad - geosynchronous satellites in Mexico's system of international telecommunications in the Western Hemisphere.

Statsionar - Russia's geostationary system for satellite telecommunications.

submarine cable - a cable designed for service under water.

TAT - Trans-Atlantic Telephone; any of a number of high-capacity submarine coaxial telephone cables linking Europe with North America.

telefax - facsimile service between subscriber stations via the public switched telephone network or the international Datel network.

Notes and Definitions (continued)

    telegraph - a telecommunications system designed for unmodulated electric impulse transmission.
    telex - a communication service involving teletypewriters connected by wire through automatic exchanges.
    tropospheric scatter - a form of microwave radio transmission in which the troposphere is used to scatter and reflect a fraction of the incident radio waves back to earth; powerful, highly directional antennas are used to transmit and receive the microwave signals; reliable over-the-horizon communications are realized for distances up to 600 miles in a single hop; additional hops can extend the range of this system for very long distances.
    trunk network - a network of switching centers, connected by multichannel trunk lines.
    UHF – ultra high frequency; any radio frequency in the 300- to 3,000-MHz range.
    VHF – very high frequency; any radio frequency in the 30- to 300-MHz range.

Telephones - main lines in use: This entry gives the total number of main telephone lines in use.

Telephones - mobile cellular: This entry gives the total number of mobile cellular telephones in use.

Television - broadcast stations: This entry gives the total number of separate broadcast stations plus any repeater stations.

Televisions: This entry gives the total number of television sets.

Terminology: Due to the highly structured nature of the *Factbook* database, some collective generic terms have to be used. For example, the word **Country** in the **Country name** entry refers to a wide variety of dependencies, areas of special sovereignty, uninhabited islands, and other entities in addition to the traditional countries or independent states. **Military** is also used as an umbrella term for various civil defense, security, and defense activities in many entries. The **Independence** entry includes the usual colonial independence dates and former ruling states as well as other significant nationhood dates such as the traditional founding date or the date of unification, federation, confederation, establishment, or state succession that are not strictly independence dates. Dependent areas have the nature of their dependency status noted in this same entry.

Terrain: This entry contains a brief description of the topography.

Total fertility rate: This entry gives a figure for the average number of children that would be born per woman if all women lived to the end of their childbearing years and bore children according to a given fertility rate at each age. The total fertility rate is a more direct measure of the level of fertility than the crude birth rate, since it refers to births per woman. This indicator shows the potential for population growth in the country. High rates will also place some limits on the labor force participation rates for women. Large numbers of children born to women indicate large family sizes that might limit the ability of the families to feed and educate their children.

Transnational Issues: This category includes only two entries at the present time - **Disputes - international** and **Illicit drugs** - that deal with current issues going beyond national boundaries.

Notes and Definitions *(continued)*

Transportation: This category includes the entries dealing with the means for movement of people and goods.

Transportation - note: This entry includes miscellaneous transportation information of significance not included elsewhere.

Unemployment rate: This entry contains the percent of the labor force that is without jobs. Substantial underemployment might be noted.

Waterways: This entry gives the total length and individual names of navigable rivers, canals, and other inland bodies of water.

Years: All year references are for the calendar year (CY) unless indicated as fiscal year (FY). The calendar year is an accounting period of 12 months from 1 January to 31 December. The fiscal year is an accounting period of 12 months other than 1 January to 31 December.

Guide to Country Profiles (Categories, Fields, and *subfields*)

Introduction
Background

Geography
Location
Geographic coordinates
Map references
Area
 total
 land
 water
Area - comparative
Land boundaries
 total
 border countries
Coastline
Maritime claims
 contiguous zone
 exclusive fishing zone
 continental shelf
 exclusive economic zone
 territorial sea
 extended fishing zone
Climate
Terrain
Elevation extremes
 lowest point
 highest point
Natural resources
Land use
 arable land
 permanent crops
 permanent pastures
 forests and woodland
 other
Irrigated land
Natural hazards
Environment - current issues
Environment - international agreements
 party to
 signed, but not ratified
Geography - note

People
Population
Age structure
 0-14 years
 15-64 years
 65 years and over
Population growth rate
Birth rate
Death rate
Net migration rate
Sex ratio
 at birth
 under 15 years
 15-64 years
 65 years and over
 total population
 Infant mortality rate
Life expectancy at birth
 total population
 male
 female
Total fertility rate
HIV/AIDS - adult prevalence rate
HIV/AIDS - people living with HIV/AIDS
HIV/AIDS - deaths
Nationality
 noun
 adjective
Ethnic groups
Religions
Languages
Literacy
 definition
 total population
 male
 female
People - note

Government
Country name
 conventional long form
 conventional short form
 local long form
 local short form
 former
 abbreviation
Dependency status
Government type
Capital
Administrative divisions
Dependent areas
Independence
National holiday
Constitution
Legal system
Suffrage
Executive branch
 chief of state
 head of government
 cabinet
 elections
 election results
Legislative branch
 elections
 election results
Judicial branch
Political parties and leaders
Political pressure groups and leaders
International organization participation
Diplomatic representation in the US
 chief of mission
 chancery
 telephone
 FAX
 consulate(s) general
 consulate(s)
 honorary consulate(s) general
 honorary consulate(s)
Diplomatic representation from the US
 chief of mission
 embassy
 mailing address
 telephone
 FAX
 consulate(s) general
 consulate(s)
 branch office(s)
Flag description
Government - note

Economy
Economy - overview
GDP
GDP - real growth rate
GDP - per capita
GDP - composition by sector
 agriculture
 industry
 services
Population below poverty line
Household income or consumption by percentage share
 lowest 10%
 highest 10%
Inflation rate (consumer prices)
Labor force
Labor force - by occupation
Unemployment rate
Budget
 revenues
 expenditures
Industries
Industrial production growth rate
Electricity - production
Electricity - production by source
 fossil fuel
 hydro
 nuclear
 other
Electricity - consumption
Electricity - exports
Electricity - imports
Agriculture - products
Exports
Exports - commodities
Exports - partners
Imports
Imports - commodities
Imports - partners
Debt - external
Economic aid - donor
Economic aid - recipient
Currency
Currency code
Exchange rates
Fiscal year

Communications
Telephones - main lines in use
Telephones - mobile cellular
Telephone system
 general assessment
 domestic
 international
Radio broadcast stations
Radios
Television broadcast stations
Televisions
Internet country code
Internet Service Providers (ISPs)
Internet users
Communications - note

Transportation
Railways
 total
 broad gauge
 standard gauge
 narrow gauge
 dual gauge
Highways
 total
 paved
 unpaved
Waterways
Pipelines
Ports and harbors
Merchant marine
 total
 ships by type
Airports
Airports - with paved runways
 total
 over 3,047 m
 2,438 to 3,047 m
 1,524 to 2,437 m
 914 to 1,523 m
 under 914 m
Airports - with unpaved runways
 total
 over 3,047 m
 2,438 to 3,047 m
 1,524 to 2,437 m
 1,524 to2,437 m
 914 to 1,523 m
 under 914 m
Heliports
Transportation - note

Military
Military branches
Military manpower - military age
Military manpower - availability
 males age 15-49
 females age 15-49
Military manpower - fit for military service
 males age 15-49
 females age 15-49
Military manpower - reaching military age annually
 males
 females
Military expenditures - dollar figure
Military expenditures - percent of GDP
Military - note

Transnational Issues
Disputes - international
Illicit drugs

Afghanistan

Introduction

Background: Afghanistan was invaded and occupied by the Soviet Union in 1979. The USSR was forced to withdraw 10 years later by anti-communist mujahidin forces supplied and trained by the US, Saudi Arabia, Pakistan, and others. Fighting subsequently continued among the various mujahidin factions, but the fundamentalist Islamic Taliban movement has been able to seize most of the country. In addition to the continuing civil strife, the country suffers from enormous poverty, a crumbling infrastructure, and widespread land mines.

Geography

Location: Southern Asia, north and west of Pakistan, east of Iran
Geographic coordinates: 33 00 N, 65 00 E
Map references: Asia
Area:
total: 647,500 sq km
land: 647,500 sq km
water: 0 sq km
Area - comparative: slightly smaller than Texas
Land boundaries:
total: 5,529 km
border countries: China 76 km, Iran 936 km, Pakistan 2,430 km, Tajikistan 1,206 km, Turkmenistan 744 km, Uzbekistan 137 km
Coastline: 0 km (landlocked)
Maritime claims: none (landlocked)
Climate: arid to semiarid; cold winters and hot summers
Terrain: mostly rugged mountains; plains in north and southwest
Elevation extremes:
lowest point: Amu Darya 258 m
highest point: Nowshak 7,485 m
Natural resources: natural gas, petroleum, coal, copper, chromite, talc, barites, sulfur, lead, zinc, iron ore, salt, precious and semiprecious stones
Land use:
arable land: 12%
permanent crops: 0%
permanent pastures: 46%
forests and woodland: 3%
other: 39% (1993 est.)
Irrigated land: 30,000 sq km (1993 est.)
Natural hazards: damaging earthquakes occur in Hindu Kush mountains; flooding; droughts
Environment - current issues: soil degradation; overgrazing; deforestation (much of the remaining forests are being cut down for fuel and building materials); desertification
Environment - international agreements:
party to: Desertification, Endangered Species, Environmental Modification, Marine Dumping, Nuclear Test Ban, Ship Pollution
signed, but not ratified: Biodiversity, Climate Change, Hazardous Wastes, Law of the Sea, Marine Life Conservation
Geography - note: landlocked

People

Population: 26,813,057 (July 2001 est.)
Age structure:
0-14 years: 42.2% (male 5,775,921; female 5,538,836)
15-64 years: 55.01% (male 7,644,242; female 7,106,568)
65 years and over: 2.79% (male 394,444; female 353,046) (2001 est.)
Population growth rate: 3.48% (2001 est.)
note: this rate reflects the continued return of refugees from Iran
Birth rate: 41.42 births/1,000 population (2001 est.)
Death rate: 17.72 deaths/1,000 population (2001 est.)
Net migration rate: 11.11 migrant(s)/1,000 population (2001 est.)
Sex ratio:
at birth: 1.05 male(s)/female
under 15 years: 1.04 male(s)/female
15-64 years: 1.08 male(s)/female
65 years and over: 1.12 male(s)/female
total population: 1.06 male(s)/female (2001 est.)
Infant mortality rate: 147.02 deaths/1,000 live births (2001 est.)
Life expectancy at birth:
total population: 46.24 years
male: 46.97 years
female: 45.47 years (2001 est.)
Total fertility rate: 5.79 children born/woman (2001 est.)
HIV/AIDS - adult prevalence rate: less than 0.01% (1999 est.)
HIV/AIDS - people living with HIV/AIDS: NA
HIV/AIDS - deaths: NA
Nationality:
noun: Afghan(s)
adjective: Afghan
Ethnic groups: Pashtun 38%, Tajik 25%, Hazara 19%, minor ethnic groups (Aimaks, Turkmen, Baloch, and others) 12%, Uzbek 6%
Religions: Sunni Muslim 84%, Shi'a Muslim 15%, other 1%
Languages: Pashtu 35%, Afghan Persian (Dari) 50%, Turkic languages (primarily Uzbek and Turkmen) 11%, 30 minor languages (primarily Balochi and Pashai) 4%, much bilingualism
Literacy:
definition: age 15 and over can read and write
total population: 31.5%
male: 47.2%
female: 15% (1999 est.)

Government

Country name:
conventional long form: Islamic State of Afghanistan; note - the self-proclaimed Taliban government refers to the country as Islamic Emirate of Afghanistan
conventional short form: Afghanistan
local long form: Dowlat-e Eslami-ye Afghanestan
local short form: Afghanestan
former: Republic of Afghanistan
Government type: no functioning central government, administered by factions
Capital: Kabul
Administrative divisions: 30 provinces (velayat, singular - velayat); Badakhshan, Badghis, Baghlan, Balkh, Bamian, Farah, Faryab, Ghazni, Ghowr, Helmand, Herat, Jowzjan, Kabol, Kandahar, Kapisa, Konar, Kondoz, Laghman, Lowgar, Nangarhar, Nimruz, Oruzgan, Paktia, Paktika, Parvan, Samangan, Sar-e Pol, Takhar, Vardak, Zabol; note - there may be two new provinces of Nurestan (Nuristan) and Khowst
Independence: 19 August 1919 (from UK control over Afghan foreign affairs)
National holiday: Independence Day, 19 August (1919)
Constitution: none
Legal system: a new legal system has not been adopted but all factions tacitly agree they will follow Shari'a (Islamic law)
Suffrage: NA; previously males 15-50 years of age
Executive branch: on 27 September 1996, the ruling members of the Afghan Government were displaced by members of the Islamic Taliban movement; the Islamic State of Afghanistan has no functioning government at this time, and the country remains divided among fighting factions
note: the Taliban have declared themselves the legitimate government of Afghanistan; however, the UN still recognizes the government of Burhanuddin RABBANI; the Organization of the Islamic Conference has left the Afghan seat vacant until the question of legitimacy can be resolved through negotiations among the warring factions; the country is essentially divided along ethnic lines; the Taliban controls the capital of Kabul and approximately two-thirds of the country including the predominately ethnic Pashtun

Afghanistan (continued)

areas in southern Afghanistan; opposing factions have their stronghold in the ethnically diverse north
Legislative branch: non-functioning as of June 1993
Judicial branch: upper courts were non-functioning as of March 1995 (local Shari'a or Islamic law courts are functioning throughout the country)
Political parties and leaders: Taliban (Religious Students Movement) [Mullah Mohammad OMAR]; United National Islamic Front for the Salvation of Afghanistan or UNIFSA [Burhanuddin RABBANI, chairman; Gen. Abdul Rashid DOSTAM, vice chairman; Ahmad Shah MASOOD, military commander; Mohammed Yunis QANUNI, spokesman]; note - made up of 13 parties opposed to the Taliban including Harakat-i-Islami Afghanistan (Islamic Movement of Afghanistan), Hizb-i-Islami (Islamic Party), Hizb-i-Wahdat-i-Islami (Islamic Unity Party), Jumaat-i-Islami Afghanistan (Islamic Afghan Society), Jumbish-i-Milli (National Front), Mahaz-i-Milli-i-Islami (National Islamic Front)
Political pressure groups and leaders: Afghan refugees in Pakistan, Australia, US, and elsewhere have organized politically; Mellat (Social Democratic Party) [leader NA]; Peshawar, Pakistan-based groups such as the Coordination Council for National Unity and Understanding in Afghanistan or CUNUA [Ishaq GAILANI]; tribal elders represent traditional Pashtun leadership; Writers Union of Free Afghanistan or WUFA [A. Rasul AMIN]
International organization participation: AsDB, CP, ECO, ESCAP, FAO, G-77, IAEA, IBRD, ICAO, ICRM, IDA, IDB, IFAD, IFC, IFRCS, ILO, IMF, Intelsat, IOC, IOM (observer), ITU, NAM, OIC, OPCW, UN, UNCTAD, UNESCO, UNIDO, UPU, WFTU, WHO, WMO, WToO
Diplomatic representation in the US: none; note - embassy operations suspended 21 August 1997
consulate(s) general: New York
Diplomatic representation from the US: the US embassy in Kabul has been closed since January 1989 due to security concerns
Flag description: three equal horizontal bands of green (top), white, and black with a gold emblem centered on the three bands; the emblem features a temple-like structure with Islamic inscriptions above and below, encircled by a wreath on the left and right and by a bolder Islamic inscription above, all of which are encircled by two crossed scimitars
note: the Taliban uses a plain white flag

Economy

Economy - overview: Afghanistan is an extremely poor, landlocked country, highly dependent on farming and livestock raising (sheep and goats). Economic considerations have played second fiddle to political and military upheavals during two decades of war, including the nearly 10-year Soviet military occupation (which ended 15 February 1989). During that conflict one-third of the population fled the country, with Pakistan and Iran sheltering a combined peak of more than 6 million refugees. In early 2000, 2 million Afghan refugees remained in Pakistan and about 1.4 million in Iran. Gross domestic product has fallen substantially over the past 20 years because of the loss of labor and capital and the disruption of trade and transport; severe drought added to the nation's difficulties in 1998-2000. The majority of the population continues to suffer from insufficient food, clothing, housing, and medical care. Inflation remains a serious problem throughout the country. International aid can deal with only a fraction of the humanitarian problem, let alone promote economic development. In 1999-2000, internal civil strife continued, hampering both domestic economic policies and international aid efforts. Numerical data are likely to be either unavailable or unreliable. Afghanistan was by far the largest producer of opium poppies in 2000, and narcotics trafficking is a major source of revenue.
GDP: purchasing power parity - $21 billion (2000 est.)
GDP - real growth rate: NA%
GDP - per capita: purchasing power parity - $800 (2000 est.)
GDP - composition by sector:
agriculture: 53%
industry: 28.5%
services: 18.5% (1990)
Population below poverty line: NA%
Household income or consumption by percentage share:
lowest 10%: NA%
highest 10%: NA%
Inflation rate (consumer prices): NA%
Labor force: 10 million (2000 est.)
Labor force - by occupation: agriculture 70%, industry 15%, services 15% (1990 est.)
Unemployment rate: NA%
Budget:
revenues: $NA
expenditures: $NA, including capital expenditures of $NA
Industries: small-scale production of textiles, soap, furniture, shoes, fertilizer, and cement; handwoven carpets; natural gas, oil, coal, copper
Electricity - production: 420 million kWh (1999)
Electricity - production by source:
fossil fuel: 35.71%
hydro: 64.29%
nuclear: 0%
other: 0% (1999)
Electricity - consumption: 480.6 million kWh (1999)
Electricity - exports: 0 kWh (1999)
Electricity - imports: 90 million kWh (1999)
Agriculture - products: opium poppies, wheat, fruits, nuts; wool, mutton, karakul pelts
Exports: $80 million (does not include opium) (1996 est.)
Exports - commodities: opium, fruits and nuts, handwoven carpets, wool, cotton, hides and pelts, precious and semi-precious gems
Exports - partners: FSU, Pakistan, Iran, Germany, India, UK, Belgium, Luxembourg, Czech Republic
Imports: $150 million (1996 est.)
Imports - commodities: capital goods, food and petroleum products; most consumer goods
Imports - partners: FSU, Pakistan, Iran, Japan, Singapore, India, South Korea, Germany
Debt - external: $5.5 billion (1996 est.)
Economic aid - recipient: US provided about $70 million in humanitarian assistance in 1997; US continues to contribute to multilateral assistance through the UN programs of food aid, immunization, land mine removal, and a wide range of aid to refugees and displaced persons
Currency: afghani (AFA)
Currency code: AFA
Exchange rates: afghanis per US dollar - 4,700 (January 2000), 4,750 (February 1999), 17,000 (December 1996), 7,000 (January 1995), 1,900 (January 1994), 1,019 (March 1993), 850 (1991); note - these rates reflect the free market exchange rates rather than the official exchange rate, which was fixed at 50.600 afghanis to the dollar until 1996, when it rose to 2,262.65 per dollar, and finally became fixed again at 3,000.00 per dollar in April 1996
Fiscal year: 21 March - 20 March

Communications

Telephones - main lines in use: 29,000 (1996)
note: there were 21,000 main lines in service in Kabul in 1998
Telephones - mobile cellular: NA
Telephone system:
general assessment: very limited telephone and telegraph service
domestic: in 1997, telecommunications links were established between Mazar-e Sharif, Herat, Kandahar, Jalalabad, and Kabul through satellite and microwave systems
international: satellite earth stations - 1 Intelsat (Indian Ocean) linked only to Iran and 1 Intersputnik (Atlantic Ocean region); commercial satellite telephone center in Ghazni
Radio broadcast stations: AM 7 (6 are inactive; the active station is in Kabul), FM 1, shortwave 1 (broadcasts in Pushtu, Dari, Urdu, and English) (1999)
Radios: 167,000 (1999)
Television broadcast stations: at least 10 (one government run central television station in Kabul and regional stations in nine of the 30 provinces; the regional stations operate on a reduced schedule; also, in 1997, there was a station in Mazar-e Sharif reaching four northern Afghanistan provinces) (1998)
Televisions: 100,000 (1999)
Internet country code: .af
Internet Service Providers (ISPs): 1 (2000)
Internet users: NA

Afghanistan (continued)

Transportation

Railways:
total: 24.6 km
broad gauge: 9.6 km 1.524-m gauge from Gushgy (Turkmenistan) to Towraghondi; 15 km 1.524-m gauge from Termiz (Uzbekistan) to Kheyrabad transshipment point on south bank of Amu Darya
Highways:
total: 21,000 km
paved: 2,793 km
unpaved: 18,207 km (1998 est.)
Waterways: 1,200 km
note: chiefly Amu Darya, which handles vessels with DWT up to about 500 (2001)
Pipelines: petroleum products - Uzbekistan to Bagram and Turkmenistan to Shindand; natural gas 180 km
Ports and harbors: Kheyrabad, Shir Khan
Airports: 45 (2000 est.)
Airports - with paved runways:
total: 10
over 3,047 m: 3
2,438 to 3,047 m: 4
1,524 to 2,437 m: 2
under 914 m: 1 (2000 est.)
Airports - with unpaved runways:
total: 35
2,438 to 3,047 m: 4
1,524 to 2,437 m: 15
914 to 1,523 m: 4
under 914 m: 12 (2000 est.)
Heliports: 3 (2000 est.)

Military

Military branches: NA; note - the military does not exist on a national basis; some elements of the former Army, Air and Air Defense Forces, National Guard, Border Guard Forces, National Police Force (Sarandoi), and tribal militias still exist but are factionalized among the various groups
Military manpower - military age: 22 years of age
Military manpower - availability:
males age 15-49: 6,645,023 (2001 est.)
Military manpower - fit for military service:
males age 15-49: 3,561,957 (2001 est.)
Military manpower - reaching military age annually:
males: 252,869 (2001 est.)
Military expenditures - dollar figure: $NA
Military expenditures - percent of GDP: NA%

Transnational Issues

Disputes - international: support to Islamic militants worldwide by some factions; question over which group should hold Afghanistan's seat at the UN
Illicit drugs: world's largest illicit opium producer, surpassing Burma (potential production in 1999 - 1,670 metric tons; cultivation in 1999 - 51,500 hectares, a 23% increase over 1998); a major source of hashish; increasing number of heroin-processing laboratories being set up in the country; major political factions in the country profit from drug trade

Albania

Introduction

Background: In 1990 Albania ended 44 years of xenophobic communist rule and established a multiparty democracy. The transition has proven difficult as corrupt governments have tried to deal with high unemployment, a dilapidated infrastructure, widespread gangsterism, and disruptive political opponents. International observers judged local elections in 2000 to be acceptable and a step toward democratic development, but serious deficiencies remain to be corrected before the the 2001 parliamentary elections.

Geography

Location: Southeastern Europe, bordering the Adriatic Sea and Ionian Sea, between Greece and the Federal Republic of Yugoslavia
Geographic coordinates: 41 00 N, 20 00 E
Map references: Europe
Area:
total: 28,748 sq km
land: 27,398 sq km
water: 1,350 sq km
Area - comparative: slightly smaller than Maryland
Land boundaries:
total: 720 km
border countries: Greece 282 km, The Former Yugoslav Republic of Macedonia 151 km, Yugoslavia 287 km
Coastline: 362 km
Maritime claims:
continental shelf: 200-m depth or to the depth of exploitation
territorial sea: 12 NM
Climate: mild temperate; cool, cloudy, wet winters; hot, clear, dry summers; interior is cooler and wetter
Terrain: mostly mountains and hills; small plains along coast
Elevation extremes:
lowest point: Adriatic Sea 0 m
highest point: Maja e Korabit (Golem Korab) 2,753 m
Natural resources: petroleum, natural gas, coal, chromium, copper, timber, nickel, hydropower
Land use:
arable land: 21%
permanent crops: 5%
permanent pastures: 15%
forests and woodland: 38%
other: 21% (1993 est.)
Irrigated land: 3,410 sq km (1993 est.)
Natural hazards: destructive earthquakes; tsunamis occur along southwestern coast; drought
Environment - current issues: deforestation; soil erosion; water pollution from industrial and domestic effluents
Environment - international agreements:
party to: Biodiversity, Climate Change, Desertification, Hazardous Wastes, Marine Dumping, Ozone Layer Protection, Ship Pollution, Wetlands
signed, but not ratified: none of the selected agreements
Geography - note: strategic location along Strait of Otranto (links Adriatic Sea to Ionian Sea and Mediterranean Sea)

People

Population: 3,510,484 (July 2001 est.)
Age structure:
0-14 years: 29.53% (male 536,495; female 500,026)
15-64 years: 63.48% (male 1,073,351; female 1,155,115)
65 years and over: 6.99% (male 107,476; female 138,021) (2001 est.)
Population growth rate: 0.88% (2001 est.)
Birth rate: 19.01 births/1,000 population (2001 est.)
Death rate: 6.5 deaths/1,000 population (2001 est.)
Net migration rate: -3.69 migrant(s)/1,000 population (2001 est.)
Sex ratio:
at birth: 1.08 male(s)/female
under 15 years: 1.07 male(s)/female
15-64 years: 0.93 male(s)/female
65 years and over: 0.78 male(s)/female
total population: 0.96 male(s)/female (2001 est.)
Infant mortality rate: 39.99 deaths/1,000 live births (2001 est.)
Life expectancy at birth:
total population: 71.83 years
male: 69.01 years
female: 74.87 years (2001 est.)
Total fertility rate: 2.32 children born/woman (2001 est.)
HIV/AIDS - adult prevalence rate: less than 0.01% (1999 est.)
HIV/AIDS - people living with HIV/AIDS: less than 100 (2000 est.)
HIV/AIDS - deaths: less than 100 (1999 est.)
Nationality:
noun: Albanian(s)
adjective: Albanian
Ethnic groups: Albanian 95%, Greeks 3%, other 2% (Vlachs, Gypsies, Serbs, and Bulgarians) (1989 est.)

Albania (continued)

note: in 1989, other estimates of the Greek population ranged from 1% (official Albanian statistics) to 12% (from a Greek organization)
Religions: Muslim 70%, Albanian Orthodox 20%, Roman Catholic 10%
note: all mosques and churches were closed in 1967 and religious observances prohibited; in November 1990, Albania began allowing private religious practice
Languages: Albanian (Tosk is the official dialect), Greek
Literacy:
definition: age 9 and over can read and write
total population: 93% (1997 est.)
male: NA%
female: NA%

Government

Country name:
conventional long form: Republic of Albania
conventional short form: Albania
local long form: Republika e Shqiperise
local short form: Shqiperia
former: People's Socialist Republic of Albania
Government type: emerging democracy
Capital: Tirana
Administrative divisions: 36 districts (rrethe, singular - rreth) and 1 municipality* (bashki); Berat, Bulqize, Delvine, Devoll (Bilisht), Diber (Peshkopi), Durres, Elbasan, Fier, Gjirokaster, Gramsh, Has (Krume), Kavaje, Kolonje (Erseke), Korce, Kruje, Kucove, Kukes, Kurbin, Lezhe, Librazhd, Lushnje, Malesi e Madhe (Koplik), Mallakaster (Ballsh), Mat (Burrel), Mirdite (Rreshen), Peqin, Permet, Pogradec, Puke, Sarande, Shkoder, Skrapar (Corovode), Tepelene, Tirane (Tirana), Tirane* (Tirana), Tropoje (Bajram Curri), Vlore
note: administrative divisions have the same names as their administrative centers (exceptions have the administrative center name following in parentheses)
Independence: 28 November 1912 (from Ottoman Empire)
National holiday: Independence Day, 28 November (1912)
Constitution: a new constitution was adopted by popular referendum on 28 November 1998; note - the opposition Democratic Party boycotted the vote
Legal system: has not accepted compulsory ICJ jurisdiction
Suffrage: 18 years of age; universal and compulsory
Executive branch:
chief of state: President of the Republic Rexhep MEIDANI (since 24 July 1997)
head of government: Prime Minister Ilir META (since 29 October 1999)
cabinet: Council of Ministers nominated by the prime minister and approved by the president
elections: president elected by the People's Assembly for a five-year term; election last held 24 July 1997 (next to be held NA 2002); prime minister appointed by the president
election results: Rexhep MEIDANI elected president; People's Assembly vote by number - total votes 122, for 110, against 3, abstained 2, invalid 7
Legislative branch: unicameral People's Assembly or Kuvendi Popullor (155 seats; most members are elected by direct popular vote and some by proportional vote for four-year terms)
elections: last held 29 June 1997 (next held 24 June 2001, 2nd round 8 July 2001)
election results: percent of vote by party - PS 53.36%, PD 25.33%, PSD 2.5%, PBDNJ 2.78%, PBK 2.36%, PAD 2.85%, PR 2.25%, PLL 3.09%, PDK 1.00%, PBSD 0.84%; seats by party - PS 101, PD 27, PSD 8, PBDNJ 4, PBK 3, PAD 2, PR 2, PLL 2, PDK 1, PBSD 1, PUK 1, independents 3
Judicial branch: Supreme Court (chairman is elected by the People's Assembly for a four-year term)
Political parties and leaders: Albanian National Front (Balli Kombetar) or PBK [Abaz ERMENJI]; Albanian Republican Party or PR [Fatmir MEDIU]; Albanian Socialist Party or PS (formerly the Albania Workers Party) [Fatos NANO, chairman]; Christian Democratic Party or PDK [Zef BUSHATI]; Democratic Alliance or PAD [Neritan CEKA]; Democratic Party or PD [Sali BERISHA]; Group of Reformist Democrats [Leonard NDOKA]; Liberal Union Party [Teodor LACO]; note - Teodor LACO of the Liberal Union Party was leader of the Social Democratic Union of Albania or PBSD; Movement of Legality Party or PLL [Nderim KUPI]; OMONIA [Vagjelis DULES]; Party of National Unity or PUK [Idajet BEQUIRI]; Social Democratic Party or PSD [Skender GJINUSHI]; Unity for Human Rights Party or PBDNJ [Vasil MELO, chairman]
Political pressure groups and leaders: NA
International organization participation: ACCT (associate), BSEC, CCC, CE, CEI, EAPC, EBRD, ECE, FAO, IAEA, IBRD, ICAO, ICRM, IDA, IDB, IFAD, IFC, IFRCS, ILO, IMF, IMO, Intelsat (nonsignatory user), Interpol, IOC, IOM, ISO (correspondent), ITU, OIC, OPCW, OSCE, PFP, UN, UNCTAD, UNESCO, UNIDO, UNOMIG, UPU, WFTU, WHO, WIPO, WMO, WToO, WTrO
Diplomatic representation in the US:
chief of mission: Ambassador Petrit BUSHATI
chancery: 2100 S Street NW, Washington, DC 20008
telephone: [1] (202) 223-4942
FAX: [1] (202) 628-7342
Diplomatic representation from the US:
chief of mission: Ambassador Joseph LIMPRECHT
embassy: Rruga Elbasanit Labinoti 103, Tirana
mailing address: PSC 59, Box 100(A), APO AE 09624
telephone: [355] (42) 32875, 33520
FAX: [355] (42) 32222
Flag description: red with a black two-headed eagle in the center

Economy

Economy - overview: Poor by European standards, Albania is making the difficult transition to a more open-market economy. The economy rebounded in 1993-95 after a severe depression accompanying the end of the previous centrally planned system in 1990 and 1991. However, a weakening of government resolve to maintain stabilization policies in the election year of 1996 contributed to renewal of inflationary pressures, spurred by the budget deficit which exceeded 12% of GDP. The collapse of financial pyramid schemes in early 1997 - which had attracted deposits from a substantial portion of Albania's population - triggered severe social unrest which led to more than 1,500 deaths, widespread destruction of property, and a 7% drop in GDP. The government has taken measures to curb violent crime and to revive economic activity and trade. The economy is bolstered by remittances from some 20% of the labor force that works abroad, mostly in Greece and Italy. These remittances supplement GDP and help offset the large foreign trade deficit. Most agricultural land was privatized in 1992, substantially improving peasant incomes. In 1998, Albania recovered the 7% drop in GDP of 1997 and pushed ahead by 8% in 1999 and by 7.5% in 2000. International aid helped defray the high costs of receiving and returning refugees from the Kosovo conflict. Privatization scored some successes in 2000, but other reforms lagged.
GDP: purchasing power parity - $10.5 billion (2000 est.)
GDP - real growth rate: 7.5% (2000 est.)
GDP - per capita: purchasing power parity - $3,000 (2000 est.)
GDP - composition by sector:
agriculture: 55%
industry: 24%
services: 21% (2000)
Population below poverty line: 19.6% (1996 est.)
Household income or consumption by percentage share:
lowest 10%: NA%
highest 10%: NA%
Inflation rate (consumer prices): 1% (2000 est.)
Labor force: 1.692 million (including 352,000 emigrant workers and 261,000 domestically unemployed) (1994 est.)
Labor force - by occupation: agriculture 50%, industry and services 50%
Unemployment rate: 16% (2000 est.) officially; may be as high as 25%
Budget:
revenues: $393 million
expenditures: $676 million, including capital expenditures of $NA (1997 est.)
Industries: food processing, textiles and clothing; lumber, oil, cement, chemicals, mining, basic metals, hydropower
Industrial production growth rate: 9% (2000 est.)
Electricity - production: 5.332 billion kWh (1999)
Electricity - production by source:
fossil fuel: 3.81%
hydro: 96.19%
nuclear: 0%
other: 0% (1999)
Electricity - consumption: 5.379 billion kWh (1999)
Electricity - exports: 100 million kWh (1999)
Electricity - imports: 600 million kWh (2000)

Albania (continued)

Agriculture - products: wheat, corn, potatoes, vegetables, fruits, sugar beets, grapes; meat, dairy products
Exports: $310 million (f.o.b., 2000 est.)
Exports - commodities: textiles and footwear; asphalt, metals and metallic ores, crude oil; vegetables, fruits, tobacco
Exports - partners: Italy 67%, Greece 15%, Germany 5%, Austria 2%, The Former Yugoslav Republic of Macedonia 2% (2000)
Imports: $1 billion (f.o.b., 2000 est.)
Imports - commodities: machinery and equipment, foodstuffs, textiles, chemicals
Imports - partners: Italy 37%, Greece 28%, Turkey 6%, Germany 6%, Bulgaria 3% (2000)
Debt - external: $1 billion (2000)
Economic aid - recipient: $NA; aid for energy from China, Germany, Norway (2000)
Currency: lek (ALL)
Currency code: ALL
Exchange rates: leke per US dollar - 146.08 (December 2000),143.71 (2000) 137.69 (1999), 150.63 (1998), 148.93 (1997), 104.50 (1996); note - leke is the plural of lek
Fiscal year: calendar year

Communications

Telephones - main lines in use: 87,000 (1997)
Telephones - mobile cellular: 3,100 (1999)
Telephone system:
general assessment: Albania has the poorest telephone service in Europe with fewer than two telephones per 100 inhabitants; it is doubtful that every village has telephone service
domestic: obsolete wire system; no longer provides a telephone for every village; in 1992, following the fall of the communist government, peasants cut the wire to about 1,000 villages and used it to build fences
international: inadequate; international traffic carried by microwave radio relay from the Tirana exchange to Italy and Greece
Radio broadcast stations: AM 16, FM 3, shortwave 2 (1999)
Radios: 810,000 (1997)
Television broadcast stations: 9 (plus 264 repeaters) (1995)
Televisions: 405,000 (1997)
Internet country code: .al
Internet Service Providers (ISPs): 7 (2000)
Internet users: 2,500 (2000)

Transportation

Railways:
total: 447 km
standard gauge: 447 km 1.435-m gauge (2001)
Highways:
total: 18,000 km
paved: 5,400 km
unpaved: 12,600 km (1998 est.)
Waterways: 43 km
note: includes Albanian sections of Lake Scutari, Lake Ohrid, and Lake Prespa (1990)

Pipelines: crude oil 145 km; petroleum products 55 km; natural gas 64 km (1991)
Ports and harbors: Durres, Sarande, Shengjin, Vlore
Merchant marine:
total: 9 ships (1,000 GRT or over) totaling 17,797 GRT/26,324 DWT
ships by type: cargo 9 (2000 est.)
Airports: 11 (2000 est.)
Airports - with paved runways:
total: 3
2,438 to 3,047 m: 3 (2000 est.)
Airports - with unpaved runways:
total: 8
over 3,047 m: 1
1,524 to 2,437 m: 1
914 to 1,523 m: 2
under 914 m: 4 (2000 est.)
Heliports: 1 (2000 est.)

Military

Military branches: Army, Navy, Air and Air Defense Forces, Interior Ministry Troops, Border Guards
Military manpower - military age: 19 years of age
Military manpower - availability:
males age 15-49: 870,768 (2001 est.)
Military manpower - fit for military service:
males age 15-49: 712,763 (2001 est.)
Military manpower - reaching military age annually:
males: 35,792 (2001 est.)
Military expenditures - dollar figure: $42 million (FY99)
Military expenditures - percent of GDP: 1.5% (FY99)

Transnational Issues

Disputes - international: the Albanian Government supports protection of the rights of ethnic Albanians outside of its borders but has downplayed them to further its primary foreign policy goal of regional cooperation; Albanian majority in Kosovo seeks independence from Yugoslavia; Albanians in The Former Yugoslav Republic of Macedonia claim discrimination in education, access to public-sector jobs, and representation in government
Illicit drugs: increasingly active transshipment point for Southwest Asian opiates, hashish, and cannabis transiting the Balkan route and - to a far lesser extent - cocaine from South America destined for Western Europe; limited opium and cannabis production; ethnic Albanian narcotrafficking organizations active and rapidly expanding in Europe

Algeria

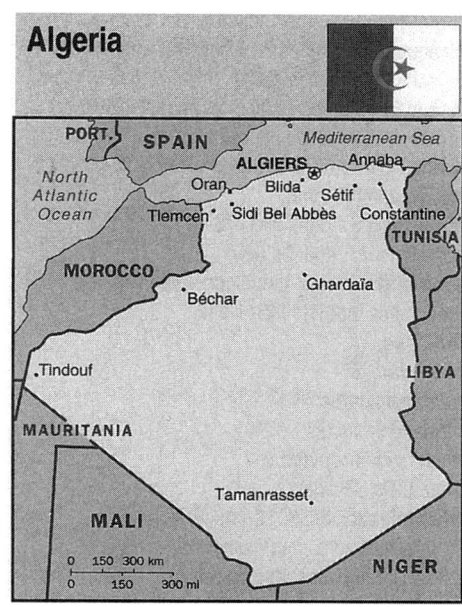

Introduction

Background: After a century of rule by France, Algeria became independent in 1962. The surprising first round success of the fundamentalist FIS (Islamic Salvation Front) party in December 1991 balloting caused the army to intervene, crack down on the FIS, and postpone the subsequent elections. The FIS response has resulted in a continuous low-grade civil conflict with the secular state apparatus, which nonetheless has allowed elections featuring pro-government and moderate religious-based parties. FIS's armed wing, the Islamic Salvation Army, disbanded itself in January 2000 and many armed militants surrendered under an amnesty program designed to promote national reconciliation. Nevertheless, residual fighting continues. Other concerns include large-scale unemployment and the need to diversify the petroleum-based economy.

Geography

Location: Northern Africa, bordering the Mediterranean Sea, between Morocco and Tunisia
Geographic coordinates: 28 00 N, 3 00 E
Map references: Africa
Area:
total: 2,381,740 sq km
land: 2,381,740 sq km
water: 0 sq km
Area - comparative: slightly less than 3.5 times the size of Texas
Land boundaries:
total: 6,343 km
border countries: Libya 982 km, Mali 1,376 km, Mauritania 463 km, Morocco 1,559 km, Niger 956 km, Tunisia 965 km, Western Sahara 42 km
Coastline: 998 km
Maritime claims:
exclusive fishing zone: 32-52 NM
territorial sea: 12 NM

Algeria (continued)

Climate: arid to semiarid; mild, wet winters with hot, dry summers along coast; drier with cold winters and hot summers on high plateau; sirocco is a hot, dust/sand-laden wind especially common in summer
Terrain: mostly high plateau and desert; some mountains; narrow, discontinuous coastal plain
Elevation extremes:
lowest point: Chott Melrhir -40 m
highest point: Tahat 3,003 m
Natural resources: petroleum, natural gas, iron ore, phosphates, uranium, lead, zinc
Land use:
arable land: 3%
permanent crops: 0%
permanent pastures: 13%
forests and woodland: 2%
other: 82% (1993 est.)
Irrigated land: 5,550 sq km (1993 est.)
Natural hazards: mountainous areas subject to severe earthquakes; mud slides
Environment - current issues: soil erosion from overgrazing and other poor farming practices; desertification; dumping of raw sewage, petroleum refining wastes, and other industrial effluents is leading to the pollution of rivers and coastal waters; Mediterranean Sea, in particular, becoming polluted from oil wastes, soil erosion, and fertilizer runoff; inadequate supplies of potable water
Environment - international agreements:
party to: Biodiversity, Climate Change, Desertification, Endangered Species, Environmental Modification, Hazardous Wastes, Law of the Sea, Marine Dumping, Ozone Layer Protection, Ship Pollution, Wetlands
signed, but not ratified: Nuclear Test Ban
Geography - note: second-largest country in Africa (after Sudan)

People

Population: 31,736,053 (July 2001 est.)
Age structure:
0-14 years: 34.21% (male 5,528,755; female 5,328,083)
15-64 years: 61.72% (male 9,901,319; female 9,687,449)
65 years and over: 4.07% (male 594,973; female 695,474) (2001 est.)
Population growth rate: 1.71% (2001 est.)
Birth rate: 22.76 births/1,000 population (2001 est.)
Death rate: 5.22 deaths/1,000 population (2001 est.)
Net migration rate: -0.45 migrant(s)/1,000 population (2001 est.)
Sex ratio:
at birth: 1.04 male(s)/female
under 15 years: 1.04 male(s)/female
15-64 years: 1.02 male(s)/female
65 years and over: 0.86 male(s)/female
total population: 1.02 male(s)/female (2001 est.)
Infant mortality rate: 40.56 deaths/1,000 live births (2001 est.)
Life expectancy at birth:
total population: 69.95 years
male: 68.6 years
female: 71.34 years (2001 est.)
Total fertility rate: 2.72 children born/woman (2001 est.)
HIV/AIDS - adult prevalence rate: 0.07% (1999 est.)
HIV/AIDS - people living with HIV/AIDS: NA
HIV/AIDS - deaths: NA
Nationality:
noun: Algerian(s)
adjective: Algerian
Ethnic groups: Arab-Berber 99%, European less than 1%
Religions: Sunni Muslim (state religion) 99%, Christian and Jewish 1%
Languages: Arabic (official), French, Berber dialects
Literacy:
definition: age 15 and over can read and write
total population: 61.6%
male: 73.9%
female: 49% (1995 est.)

Government

Country name:
conventional long form: People's Democratic Republic of Algeria
conventional short form: Algeria
local long form: Al Jumhuriyah al Jaza'iriyah ad Dimuqratiyah ash Sha'biyah
local short form: Al Jaza'ir
Government type: republic
Capital: Algiers
Administrative divisions: 48 provinces (wilayas, singular - wilaya); Adrar, Ain Defla, Ain Temouchent, Alger, Annaba, Batna, Bechar, Bejaia, Biskra, Blida, Bordj Bou Arreridj, Bouira, Boumerdes, Chlef, Constantine, Djelfa, El Bayadh, El Oued, El Tarf, Ghardaia, Guelma, Illizi, Jijel, Khenchela, Laghouat, Mascara, Medea, Mila, Mostaganem, M'Sila, Naama, Oran, Ouargla, Oum el Bouaghi, Relizane, Saida, Setif, Sidi Bel Abbes, Skikda, Souk Ahras, Tamanghasset, Tebessa, Tiaret, Tindouf, Tipaza, Tissemsilt, Tizi Ouzou, Tlemcen
Independence: 5 July 1962 (from France)
National holiday: Revolution Day, 1 November (1954)
Constitution: 19 November 1976, effective 22 November 1976; revised 3 November 1988, 23 February 1989, and 28 November 1996; note - referendum approving the revisions of 28 November 1996 was signed into law 7 December 1996
Legal system: socialist, based on French and Islamic law; judicial review of legislative acts in ad hoc Constitutional Council composed of various public officials, including several Supreme Court justices; has not accepted compulsory ICJ jurisdiction
Suffrage: 18 years of age; universal
Executive branch:
chief of state: President Abdelaziz BOUTEFLIKA (since 28 April 1999)
head of government: Prime Minister Ali BENFLIS (since 26 August 2000)
cabinet: Cabinet of Ministers appointed by the president
elections: president elected by popular vote for a five-year term; election last held 15 April 1999 (next to be held NA April 2004); prime minister appointed by the president
election results: Abdelaziz BOUTEFLIKA elected president; percent of vote - Abdelaziz BOUTEFLIKA over 70%; note - his six opposing candidates withdrew on the eve of the election citing electoral fraud
Legislative branch: bicameral Parliament consists of the National People's Assembly or Al-Majlis Ech-Chaabi Al-Watani (380 seats; members elected by popular vote to serve five-year terms) and the Council of Nations (144 seats; one-third of the members appointed by the president, two-thirds elected by indirect vote; members serve six-year terms; the constitution requires half the council to be renewed every three years)
elections: National People's Assembly - last held 5 June 1997 (next to be held NA 2002); Council of Nations - last held 30 December 2000 (next to be held NA 2003)
election results: National People's Assembly - percent of vote by party - RND 40.8%, MSP 18.2%, FLN 16.8%, Nahda Movement 8.9%, FFS 5%, RCD 5%, PT 1.1%, Progressive Republican Party 0.8%, Union for Democracy and Liberty 0.3%, Social Liberal Party 0.3%, independents 2.8%; seats by party - RND 155, MSP 69, FLN 64, Nahda Movement 34, FFS 19, RCD 19, PT 4, Progressive Republican Party 3, Union for Democracy and Liberty 1, Social Liberal Party 1, independents 11; Council of Nations - percent of vote by party - NA%; seats by party - RND 79, FLN 12, FFS 4, MSP 1 (remaining 48 seats appointed by the president, party breakdown NA)
Judicial branch: Supreme Court or Cour Supreme
Political parties and leaders: Democratic National Rally or RND [Ahmed OUYAHIA, chairman]; Islamic Salvation Front or FIS (outlawed April 1992) [Ali BELHADJ and Dr. Abassi MADANI (imprisoned), Rabeh KEBIR (self-exile in Germany)]; Movement of a Peaceful Society or MSP [Mahfoud NAHNAH, chairman]; National Liberation Front or FLN [Boualem BENHAMOUDA, secretary general]; Progressive Republican Party [Khadir DRISS]; Rally for Culture and Democracy or RCD [Said SAADI, secretary general]; Renaissance Movement or EnNahda Movement [Lahbib ADAMI]; Social Liberal Party or PSL [Ahmed KHELIL]; Socialist Forces Front or FFS [Hocine Ait AHMED, secretary general (self-exile in Switzerland)]; Union for Democracy and Liberty [Mouley BOUKHALAFA]; Workers Party or PT [Louisa HANOUN]
note: a party law banning political parties based on religion was enacted in March 1997
Political pressure groups and leaders: NA

Algeria (continued)

International organization participation: ABEDA, AfDB, AFESD, AL, AMF, AMU, CCC, ECA, FAO, G-15, G-19, G-24, G-77, IAEA, IBRD, ICAO, ICC, ICFTU, ICRM, IDA, IDB, IFAD, IFC, IFRCS, IHO, ILO, IMF, IMO, Inmarsat, Intelsat, Interpol, IOC, IOM, ISO, ITU, MONUC, NAM, OAPEC, OAS (observer), OAU, OIC, OPCW, OPEC, OSCE (partner), UN, UNCTAD, UNESCO, UNHCR, UNIDO, UNMEE, UPU, WHO, WIPO, WMO, WToO, WTrO (observer)
Diplomatic representation in the US:
chief of mission: Ambassador Idriss JAZAIRY
chancery: 2118 Kalorama Road NW, Washington, DC 20008
telephone: [1] (202) 265-2800
FAX: [1] (202) 667-2174
Diplomatic representation from the US:
chief of mission: Ambassador Janet A. SANDERSON
embassy: 4 Chemin Cheikh Bachir El-Ibrahimi, Algiers
mailing address: B. P. Box 549, Alger-Gare, 16000 Algiers
telephone: [213] (21) 69-11-86, 69-12-55, 69-18-54, 69-38-75
FAX: [213] (21) 69-39-79
Flag description: two equal vertical bands of green (hoist side) and white; a red, five-pointed star within a red crescent centered over the two-color boundary; the crescent, star, and color green are traditional symbols of Islam (the state religion)

Economy

Economy - overview: The hydrocarbons sector is the backbone of the economy, accounting for roughly 60% of budget revenues, 30% of GDP, and over 95% of export earnings. Algeria has the fifth-largest reserves of natural gas in the world and is the second largest gas exporter; it ranks fourteenth for oil reserves. Algiers' efforts to reform one of the most centrally planned economies in the Arab world stalled in 1992 as the country became embroiled in political turmoil. Algeria's financial and economic indicators improved during the mid-1990s, in part because of policy reforms supported by the IMF and debt rescheduling from the Paris Club. Algeria's finances in 2000 benefited from the spike in oil prices and the government's tight fiscal policy, leading to a large increase in the trade surplus, the near tripling of foreign exchange reserves, and reduction in foreign debt. The government continues efforts to diversify the economy by attracting foreign and domestic investment outside the energy sector, but has had little success in reducing high unemployment and improving living standards.
GDP: purchasing power parity - $171 billion (2000 est.)
GDP - real growth rate: 5% (2000 est.)
GDP - per capita: purchasing power parity - $5,500 (2000 est.)
GDP - composition by sector:
agriculture: 11%
industry: 37%
services: 52% (1999 est.)
Population below poverty line: 23% (1999 est.)
Household income or consumption by percentage share:
lowest 10%: 2.8%
highest 10%: 26.8% (1995)
Inflation rate (consumer prices): 2% (2000 est.)
Labor force: 9.1 million (2000 est.)
Labor force - by occupation: government 29%, agriculture 25%, construction and public works 15%, industry 11%, other 20% (1996 est.)
Unemployment rate: 30% (1999 est.)
Budget:
revenues: $15.8 billion
expenditures: $16 billion, including capital expenditures of $5.3 billion (2001 est.)
Industries: petroleum, natural gas, light industries, mining, electrical, petrochemical, food processing
Industrial production growth rate: 7% (1999 est.)
Electricity - production: 23.215 billion kWh (1999)
Electricity - production by source:
fossil fuel: 99.14%
hydro: 0.86%
nuclear: 0%
other: 0% (1999)
Electricity - consumption: 21.613 billion kWh (1999)
Electricity - exports: 307 million kWh (1999)
Electricity - imports: 330 million kWh (1999)
Agriculture - products: wheat, barley, oats, grapes, olives, citrus, fruits; sheep, cattle
Exports: $19.6 billion (f.o.b., 2000 est.)
Exports - commodities: petroleum, natural gas, and petroleum products 97%
Exports - partners: Italy 22%, US 15%, France 12%, Spain 11%, Brazil 8%, Netherlands 5% (1999)
Imports: $9.2 billion (f.o.b., 2000 est.)
Imports - commodities: capital goods, food and beverages, consumer goods
Imports - partners: France 30%, Italy 9%, Germany 7%, Spain 6%, US 5%, Turkey 5% (1999)
Debt - external: $25 billion (2000 est.)
Economic aid - recipient: $100 million (1999 est.)
Currency: Algerian dinar (DZD)
Currency code: DZD
Exchange rates: Algerian dinars per US dollar - 74.813 (January 2001), 75.260 (2000), 66.574 (1999), 58.739 (1998), 57.707 (1997), 54.749 (1996)
Fiscal year: calendar year

Communications

Telephones - main lines in use: 2.3 million (1998)
Telephones - mobile cellular: 33,500 (1999)
Telephone system:
general assessment: telephone density in Algeria is very low, not exceeding five telephones per 100 persons; the number of fixed main lines has been increased in the last few years to a little more than 2,000,000, but only about two-thirds of these have subscribers; much of the infrastructure is outdated and inefficient
domestic: good service in north but sparse in south; domestic satellite system with 12 earth stations (20 additional domestic earth stations are planned)
international: 5 submarine cables; microwave radio relay to Italy, France, Spain, Morocco, and Tunisia; coaxial cable to Morocco and Tunisia; participant in Medarabtel; satellite earth stations - 2 Intelsat (1 Atlantic Ocean and 1 Indian Ocean), 1 Intersputnik, and 1 Arabsat (1998)
Radio broadcast stations: AM 25, FM 1, shortwave 8 (1999)
Radios: 7.1 million (1997)
Television broadcast stations: 46 (plus 216 repeaters) (1995)
Televisions: 3.1 million (1997)
Internet country code: .dz
Internet Service Providers (ISPs): 2 (2000)
Internet users: 20,000 (2000)

Transportation

Railways:
total: 4,820 km
standard gauge: 3,664 km 1.435-m gauge (301 km electrified; 215 km double track)
narrow gauge: 1,156 km 1.055-m gauge (1996)
Highways:
total: 104,000 km
paved: 71,656 km (including 640 km of expressways)
unpaved: 32,344 km (1996 est.)
Waterways: none
Pipelines: crude oil 6,612 km; petroleum products 298 km; natural gas 2,948 km
Ports and harbors: Algiers, Annaba, Arzew, Bejaia, Beni Saf, Dellys, Djendjene, Ghazaouet, Jijel, Mostaganem, Oran, Skikda, Tenes
Merchant marine:
total: 73 ships (1,000 GRT or over) totaling 896,911 GRT/1,047,991 DWT
ships by type: bulk 9, cargo 25, chemical tanker 7, liquefied gas 10, petroleum tanker 4, roll on/roll off 13, short-sea passenger 4, specialized tanker 1 (2000 est.)
Airports: 135 (2000 est.)
Airports - with paved runways:
total: 51
over 3,047 m: 9
2,438 to 3,047 m: 24
1,524 to 2,437 m: 12
914 to 1,523 m: 5
under 914 m: 1 (2000 est.)
Airports - with unpaved runways:
total: 84
2,438 to 3,047 m: 3
1,524 to 2,437 m: 23
914 to 1,523 m: 40
under 914 m: 18 (2000 est.)
Heliports: 1 (2000 est.)

Algeria (continued)

Military

Military branches: National Popular Army, Navy, Air Force, Territorial Air Defense, National Gendarmerie
Military manpower - military age: 19 years of age
Military manpower - availability:
males age 15-49: 8,794,622 (2001 est.)
Military manpower - fit for military service:
males age 15-49: 5,383,770 (2001 est.)
Military manpower - reaching military age annually:
males: 388,939 (2001 est.)
Military expenditures - dollar figure: $1.87 billion (FY99)
Military expenditures - percent of GDP: 4.1% (FY99)

Transnational Issues

Disputes - international: part of southeastern region claimed by Libya; Algeria supports exiled West Saharan Polisario Front and rejects Moroccan administration of Western Sahara

American Samoa
(territory of the US)

Introduction

Background: Settled as early as 1000 B.C., Samoa was "discovered" by European explorers in the 18th century. International rivalries in the latter half of the 19th century were settled by an 1899 treaty in which Germany and the US divided the Samoan archipelago. The US formally occupied its portion - a smaller group of eastern islands with the excellent harbor of Pago Pago - the following year.

Geography

Location: Oceania, group of islands in the South Pacific Ocean, about one-half of the way from Hawaii to New Zealand
Geographic coordinates: 14 20 S, 170 00 W
Map references: Oceania
Area:
total: 199 sq km
land: 199 sq km
water: 0 sq km
note: includes Rose Island and Swains Island
Area - comparative: slightly larger than Washington, DC
Land boundaries: 0 km
Coastline: 116 km
Maritime claims:
exclusive economic zone: 200 NM
territorial sea: 12 NM
Climate: tropical marine, moderated by southeast trade winds; annual rainfall averages about 3 m; rainy season from November to April, dry season from May to October; little seasonal temperature variation
Terrain: five volcanic islands with rugged peaks and limited coastal plains, two coral atolls (Rose Island, Swains Island)
Elevation extremes:
lowest point: Pacific Ocean 0 m
highest point: Lata 966 m
Natural resources: pumice, pumicite
Land use:
arable land: 5%
permanent crops: 10%
permanent pastures: 0%
forests and woodland: 70%
other: 15% (1993 est.)
Irrigated land: NA sq km
Natural hazards: typhoons common from December to March
Environment - current issues: limited natural fresh water resources; the water division of the government has spent substantial funds in the past few years to improve water catchments and pipelines
Geography - note: Pago Pago has one of the best natural deepwater harbors in the South Pacific Ocean, sheltered by shape from rough seas and protected by peripheral mountains from high winds; strategic location in the South Pacific Ocean

People

Population: 67,084 (July 2001 est.)
Age structure:
0-14 years: 38.44% (male 13,278; female 12,512)
15-64 years: 56.57% (male 18,784; female 19,163)
65 years and over: 4.99% (male 1,779; female 1,568) (2001 est.)
Population growth rate: 2.42% (2001 est.)
Birth rate: 24.88 births/1,000 population (2001 est.)
Death rate: 4.31 deaths/1,000 population (2001 est.)
Net migration rate: 3.58 migrant(s)/1,000 population (2001 est.)
Sex ratio:
at birth: 1.06 male(s)/female
under 15 years: 1.06 male(s)/female
15-64 years: 0.98 male(s)/female
65 years and over: 1.13 male(s)/female
total population: 1.02 male(s)/female (2001 est.)
Infant mortality rate: 10.36 deaths/1,000 live births (2001 est.)
Life expectancy at birth:
total population: 75.32 years
male: 70.89 years
female: 80.02 years (2001 est.)
Total fertility rate: 3.5 children born/woman (2001 est.)
HIV/AIDS - adult prevalence rate: NA%
HIV/AIDS - people living with HIV/AIDS: NA
HIV/AIDS - deaths: NA
Nationality:
noun: American Samoan(s)
adjective: American Samoan
Ethnic groups: Samoan (Polynesian) 89%, Caucasian 2%, Tongan 4%, other 5%
Religions: Christian Congregationalist 50%, Roman Catholic 20%, Protestant and other 30%
Languages: Samoan (closely related to Hawaiian and other Polynesian languages), English
note: most people are bilingual

American Samoa (continued)

Literacy:
definition: age 15 and over can read and write
total population: 97%
male: 98%
female: 97% (1980 est.)

Government

Country name:
conventional long form: Territory of American Samoa
conventional short form: American Samoa
abbreviation: AS
Dependency status: unincorporated and unorganized territory of the US; administered by the Office of Insular Affairs, US Department of the Interior
Government type: NA
Capital: Pago Pago
Administrative divisions: none (territory of the US); there are no first-order administrative divisions as defined by the US Government, but there are three districts and two islands* at the second order; Eastern, Manu'a, Rose Island*, Swains Island*, Western
Independence: none (territory of the US)
National holiday: Flag Day, 17 April (1900)
Constitution: ratified 1966, in effect 1967
Legal system: NA
Suffrage: 18 years of age; universal
Executive branch:
chief of state: President George W. BUSH of the US (since 20 January 2001) and Vice President Richard B. CHENEY (since 20 January 2001)
head of government: Governor Tauese P. SUNIA (since 3 January 1997) and Lieutenant Governor Togiola TULAFONO (since 3 January 1997)
cabinet: NA
elections: US president and vice president elected on the same ticket for four-year terms; governor and lieutenant governor elected on the same ticket by popular vote for four-year terms; election last held 7 November 2000 (next to be held NA November 2004)
election results: Tauese P. SUNIA reelected governor; percent of vote - Tauese P. SUNIA (Democrat) 50.7%, Lealaifuaneva Peter REID (independent) 47.8%
Legislative branch: bicameral Fono or Legislative Assembly consists of the House of Representatives (21 seats - 20 of which are elected by popular vote and 1 is an appointed, nonvoting delegate from Swains Island; members serve two-year terms) and the Senate (18 seats; members are elected from local chiefs and serve four-year terms)
elections: House of Representatives - last held 7 November 2000 (next to be held NA November 2002); Senate - last held 7 November 2000 (next to be held NA November 2004)
election results: House of Representatives - percent of vote by party - NA%; seats by party - NA; Senate - percent of vote by party - NA%; seats by party - NA; note - only independents elected
note: American Samoa elects one delegate to the US House of Representatives; election last held 7 November 2000 (next to be held NA November 2002); results - Eni F. H. FALEOMAVAEGA (Democrat) reelected as delegate for a sixth term
Judicial branch: High Court (chief justice and associate justices are appointed by the US Secretary of the Interior
Political parties and leaders: Democratic Party [leader NA]; Republican Party [leader NA]
Political pressure groups and leaders: NA
International organization participation: ESCAP (associate), Interpol (subbureau), IOC, SPC
Diplomatic representation in the US: none (territory of the US)
Diplomatic representation from the US: none (territory of the US)
Flag description: blue, with a white triangle edged in red that is based on the outer side and extends to the hoist side; a brown and white American bald eagle flying toward the hoist side is carrying two traditional Samoan symbols of authority, a staff and a war club

Economy

Economy - overview: This is a traditional Polynesian economy in which more than 90% of the land is communally owned. Economic activity is strongly linked to the US, with which American Samoa conducts the great bulk of its foreign trade. Tuna fishing and tuna processing plants are the backbone of the private sector, with canned tuna the primary export. Transfers from the US Government add substantially to American Samoa's economic well-being. Attempts by the government to develop a larger and broader economy are restrained by Samoa's remote location, its limited transportation, and its devastating hurricanes. Tourism, a developing sector, has been held back by the recurring financial difficulties in East Asia.
GDP: purchasing power parity - $500 million (2000 est.)
GDP - real growth rate: NA%
GDP - per capita: purchasing power parity - $8,000 (2000 est.)
GDP - composition by sector:
agriculture: NA%
industry: NA%
services: NA%
Population below poverty line: NA%
Household income or consumption by percentage share:
lowest 10%: NA%
highest 10%: NA%
Inflation rate (consumer prices): NA%
Labor force: 14,000 (1996)
Labor force - by occupation: government 33%, tuna canneries 34%, other 33% (1990)
Unemployment rate: 16% (1993)
Budget:
revenues: $121 million (37% in local revenue and 63% in US grants)
expenditures: $127 million, including capital expenditures of $NA (FY96/97)
Industries: tuna canneries (largely dependent on foreign fishing vessels), handicrafts
Industrial production growth rate: NA%
Electricity - production: 130 million kWh (1999)
Electricity - production by source:
fossil fuel: 100%
hydro: 0%
nuclear: 0%
other: 0% (1999)
Electricity - consumption: 120.9 million kWh (1999)
Electricity - exports: 0 kWh (1999)
Electricity - imports: 0 kWh (1999)
Agriculture - products: bananas, coconuts, vegetables, taro, breadfruit, yams, copra, pineapples, papayas; dairy products, livestock
Exports: $500 million (1998)
Exports - commodities: canned tuna 93%
Exports - partners: US 99.6%
Imports: $471 million (1996)
Imports - commodities: materials for canneries 56%, food 8%, petroleum products 7%, machinery and parts 6%
Imports - partners: US 62%, Japan 9%, NZ 7%, Australia 11%, Fiji 4%, other 7%
Debt - external: $NA
Economic aid - recipient: important financial support from the US, more than $40 million in 1994
Currency: US dollar (USD)
Currency code: USD
Exchange rates: the US dollar is used
Fiscal year: 1 October - 30 September

Communications

Telephones - main lines in use: 13,000 (1997)
Telephones - mobile cellular: 2,550 (1997)
Telephone system:
general assessment: NA
domestic: good telex, telegraph, facsimile and cellular telephone services; domestic satellite system with 1 Comsat earth station
international: satellite earth station - 1 Intelsat (Pacific Ocean)
Radio broadcast stations: AM 1, FM 1, shortwave 0 (1998)
Radios: 57,000 (1997)
Television broadcast stations: 1 (1997)
Televisions: 14,000 (1997)
Internet country code: .as
Internet Service Providers (ISPs): 1 (2000)
Internet users: NA

Transportation

Railways: 0 km
Highways:
total: 350 km
paved: 150 km
unpaved: 200 km
Waterways: none
Ports and harbors: Aunu'u (new construction), Auasi, Faleosao, Ofu, Pago Pago, Ta'u
Merchant marine: none (2000 est.)
Airports: 4 (2000 est.)

American Samoa *(continued)*

Airports - with paved runways:
total: 2
2,438 to 3,047 m: 1
under 914 m: 1 (2000 est.)
Airports - with unpaved runways:
total: 2
under 914 m: 2 (2000 est.)

Military

Military - note: defense is the responsibility of the US

Transnational Issues

Disputes - international: none

Andorra

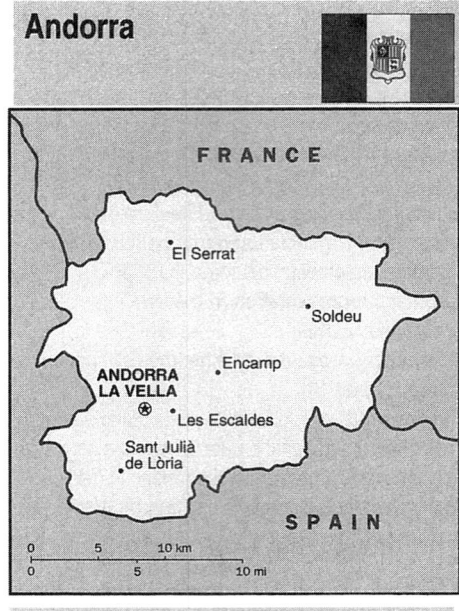

Introduction

Background: Long isolated and impoverished, mountainous Andorra has achieved considerable prosperity since World War II through its tourist industry. Many immigrants (legal and illegal) are attracted to the thriving economy with its lack of income taxes.

Geography

Location: Southwestern Europe, between France and Spain
Geographic coordinates: 42 30 N, 1 30 E
Map references: Europe
Area:
total: 468 sq km
land: 468 sq km
water: 0 sq km
Area - comparative: 2.5 times the size of Washington, DC
Land boundaries:
total: 120.3 km
border countries: France 56.6 km, Spain 63.7 km
Coastline: 0 km (landlocked)
Maritime claims: none (landlocked)
Climate: temperate; snowy, cold winters and warm, dry summers
Terrain: rugged mountains dissected by narrow valleys
Elevation extremes:
lowest point: Riu Runer 840 m
highest point: Coma Pedrosa 2,946 m
Natural resources: hydropower, mineral water, timber, iron ore, lead
Land use:
arable land: 4%
permanent crops: 0%
permanent pastures: 45%
forests and woodland: 35%
other: 16% (1998 est.)
Irrigated land: NA sq km
Natural hazards: snowslides, avalanches
Environment - current issues: deforestation; overgrazing of mountain meadows contributes to soil erosion; air pollution; wastewater treatment and solid waste disposal
Environment - international agreements:
party to: Hazardous Wastes, Marine Dumping, Ship Pollution
signed, but not ratified: none of the selected agreements
Geography - note: landlocked

People

Population: 67,627 (July 2001 est.)
Age structure:
0-14 years: 15.29% (male 5,425; female 4,917)
15-64 years: 72.06% (male 25,654; female 23,078)
65 years and over: 12.65% (male 4,299; female 4,254) (2001 est.)
Population growth rate: 1.17% (2001 est.)
Birth rate: 10.29 births/1,000 population (2001 est.)
Death rate: 5.41 deaths/1,000 population (2001 est.)
Net migration rate: 6.82 migrant(s)/1,000 population (2001 est.)
Sex ratio:
at birth: 1.07 male(s)/female
under 15 years: 1.1 male(s)/female
15-64 years: 1.11 male(s)/female
65 years and over: 1.01 male(s)/female
total population: 1.1 male(s)/female (2001 est.)
Infant mortality rate: 4.08 deaths/1,000 live births (2001 est.)
Life expectancy at birth:
total population: 83.47 years
male: 80.57 years
female: 86.57 years (2001 est.)
Total fertility rate: 1.25 children born/woman (2001 est.)
HIV/AIDS - adult prevalence rate: NA%
HIV/AIDS - people living with HIV/AIDS: NA
HIV/AIDS - deaths: NA
Nationality:
noun: Andorran(s)
adjective: Andorran
Ethnic groups: Spanish 43%, Andorran 33%, Portuguese 11%, French 7%, other 6% (1998)
Religions: Roman Catholic (predominant)
Languages: Catalan (official), French, Castilian
Literacy:
definition: NA
total population: 100%
male: NA%
female: NA%

Government

Country name:
conventional long form: Principality of Andorra
conventional short form: Andorra
local long form: Principat d'Andorra
local short form: Andorra

Andorra (continued)

Government type: parliamentary democracy (since March 1993) that retains as its heads of state a coprincipality; the two princes are the president of France and bishop of Seo de Urgel, Spain, who are represented locally by coprinces' representatives
Capital: Andorra la Vella
Administrative divisions: 7 parishes (parroquies, singular - parroquia); Andorra la Vella, Canillo, Encamp, La Massana, Escaldes-Engordany, Ordino, Sant Julia de Loria
Independence: 1278 (was formed under the joint suzerainty of France and Spain)
National holiday: Our Lady of Meritxell Day, 8 September (1278)
Constitution: Andorra's first written constitution was drafted in 1991; approved by referendum 14 March 1993; came into force 4 May 1993
Legal system: based on French and Spanish civil codes; no judicial review of legislative acts; has not accepted compulsory ICJ jurisdiction
Suffrage: 18 years of age; universal
Executive branch:
chief of state: French Coprince Jacques CHIRAC (since 17 May 1995), represented by Frederic de SAINT-SERNIN (since NA); Spanish Coprince Episcopal Monseigneur Joan MARTI Alanis (since 31 January 1971), represented by Nemesi MARQUES OSTE (since NA)
head of government: Executive Council President Marc FORNE Molne (since 21 December 1994)
cabinet: Executive Council or Govern designated by the Executive Council president
elections: Executive Council president elected by the General Council and formally appointed by the coprinces for a four-year term; election last held 16 February 1997 (next to be held NA 2001)
election results: Marc FORNE Molne elected executive council president; percent of General Council vote - 64%
Legislative branch: unicameral General Council of the Valleys or Consell General de las Valls (28 seats; members are elected by direct popular vote, 14 from a single national constituency and 14 to represent each of the 7 parishes; members serve four-year terms)
elections: last held 16 February 1997 (next to be held NA February 2001)
election results: percent of vote by party - UL 57%, AND 21%, IDN 7%, ND 7%, other 8%; seats by party - UL 16, AND 6, ND 2, IDN 2, UPO 2
Judicial branch: Tribunal of Judges or Tribunal de Batlles; Tribunal of the Courts or Tribunal de Corts; Supreme Court of Justice of Andorra or Tribunal Superior de Justicia d'Andorra; Supreme Council of Justice or Consell Superior de la Justicia; Fiscal Ministry or Ministeri Fiscal; Constitutional Tribunal or Tribunal Constitucional
Political parties and leaders: Liberal Union or UL [Marc Forne MOLNE] (renamed Liberal Party of Andorra or PLA); National Democratic Group or AND [Ladislau BARO SOLA]; National Democratic Initiative or IDN [Vincenc MATEU Zamora]; New Democracy or ND [Jaume BARTOMEU Cassany]; Union of the People of Ordino (Unio Parroquial d'Ordino) or UPO [Simo DURO Coma]
note: there are two other small parties
Political pressure groups and leaders: NA
International organization participation: CCC, CE, ECE, ICAO, ICRM, IFRCS, Interpol, IOC, ITU, OSCE, UN, UNESCO, WHO, WIPO, WToO, WTrO (observer)
Diplomatic representation in the US:
chief of mission: Ambassador Juli MINOVES-TRIQUELL (also Permanent Representative to the UN)
chancery: 2 United Nations Plaza, 25th Floor, New York, NY 10017
telephone: [1] (212) 750-8064
FAX: [1] (212) 750-6630
Diplomatic representation from the US: the US does not have an embassy in Andorra; the US Ambassador to Spain is accredited to Andorra; US interests in Andorra are represented by the Consulate General's office in Barcelona (Spain); mailing address: Paseo Reina Elisenda, 23, 08034 Barcelona, Spain; telephone: (3493) 280-2227; FAX: (3493) 205-7705
Flag description: three equal vertical bands of blue (hoist side), yellow, and red with the national coat of arms centered in the yellow band; the coat of arms features a quartered shield; similar to the flags of Chad and Romania, which do not have a national coat of arms in the center, and the flag of Moldova, which does bear a national emblem

Economy

Economy - overview: Tourism, the mainstay of Andorra's tiny, well-to-do economy, accounts for roughly 80% of GDP. An estimated 9 million tourists visit annually, attracted by Andorra's duty-free status and by its summer and winter resorts. Andorra's comparative advantage has recently eroded as the economies of neighboring France and Spain have been opened up, providing broader availability of goods and lower tariffs. The banking sector, with its "tax haven" status, also contributes substantially to the economy. Agricultural production is limited by a scarcity of arable land, and most food has to be imported. The principal livestock activity is sheep raising. Manufacturing output consists mainly of cigarettes, cigars, and furniture. Andorra is a member of the EU Customs Union and is treated as an EU member for trade in manufactured goods (no tariffs) and as a non-EU member for agricultural products.
GDP: purchasing power parity - $1.2 billion (1996 est.)
GDP - real growth rate: NA%
GDP - per capita: purchasing power parity - $18,000 (1996 est.)
GDP - composition by sector:
agriculture: NA%
industry: NA%
services: NA%
Population below poverty line: NA%
Household income or consumption by percentage share:
lowest 10%: NA%
highest 10%: NA%
Inflation rate (consumer prices): 1.62% (1998)
Labor force: 30,787 salaried employees (1998)
Labor force - by occupation: agriculture 1%, industry 21%, services 78% (1998)
Unemployment rate: 0%
Budget:
revenues: $385 million
expenditures: $342 million, including capital expenditures of $NA (1997)
Industries: tourism (particularly skiing), cattle raising, timber, tobacco, banking
Industrial production growth rate: NA%
Electricity - production by source:
fossil fuel: NA%
hydro: NA%
nuclear: NA%
other: NA%
Electricity - consumption: NA kWh
Electricity - exports: NA kWh
Electricity - imports: NA kWh
note: most electricity supplied by Spain and France; Andorra generates a small amount of hydropower
Agriculture - products: small quantities of tobacco, rye, wheat, barley, oats, vegetables; sheep
Exports: $58 million (f.o.b., 1998)
Exports - commodities: tobacco products, furniture
Exports - partners: France 34%, Spain 58% (1998)
Imports: $1.077 billion (c.i.f., 1998)
Imports - commodities: consumer goods, food, electricity
Imports - partners: Spain 48%, France 35%, US 2.3% (1998)
Debt - external: $NA
Economic aid - recipient: none
Currency: French franc (FRF); Spanish peseta (ESP); euro (EUR)
Currency code: FRF; ESP; EUR
Exchange rates: euros per US dollar - 1.0659 (January 2001), 1.0854 (2000), 0.9386 (1999); French francs per US dollar - 5.8995 (1998), 5.8367 (1997), 5.1155 (1996); Spanish pesetas per US dollar - 149.40 (1998), 146.41 (1997), 126.66 (1996)
Fiscal year: calendar year

Communications

Telephones - main lines in use: 32,946 (December 1998)
Telephones - mobile cellular: 14,117 (December 1998)
Telephone system:
general assessment: NA
domestic: modern system with microwave radio relay connections between exchanges
international: landline circuits to France and Spain
Radio broadcast stations: AM 0, FM 15, shortwave 0 (1998)
Radios: 16,000 (1997)
Television broadcast stations: 0 (1997)

Andorra (continued)

Televisions: 27,000 (1997)
Internet country code: .ad
Internet Service Providers (ISPs): 1 (2000)
Internet users: 5,000 (2000)

Transportation

Railways: 0 km
Highways:
total: 269 km
paved: 198 km
unpaved: 71 km (1994 est.)
Waterways: none
Ports and harbors: none
Airports: none (2000 est.)

Military

Military - note: defense is the responsibility of France and Spain

Transnational Issues

Disputes - international: none

Angola

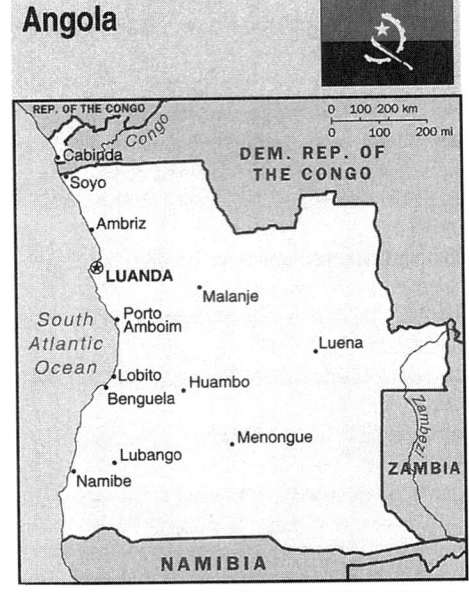

Introduction

Background: Civil war has been the norm in Angola since independence from Portugal in 1975. A 1994 peace accord between the government and the National Union for the Total Independence of Angola (UNITA) provided for the integration of former UNITA insurgents into the government and armed forces. A national unity government was installed in April of 1997, but serious fighting resumed in late 1998, rendering hundreds of thousands of people homeless. Up to 1.5 million lives may have been lost in fighting over the past quarter century.

Geography

Location: Southern Africa, bordering the South Atlantic Ocean, between Namibia and Democratic Republic of the Congo
Geographic coordinates: 12 30 S, 18 30 E
Map references: Africa
Area:
total: 1,246,700 sq km
land: 1,246,700 sq km
water: 0 sq km
Area - comparative: slightly less than twice the size of Texas
Land boundaries:
total: 5,198 km
border countries: Democratic Republic of the Congo 2,511 km (of which 220 km is the boundary of discontiguous Cabinda Province), Republic of the Congo 201 km, Namibia 1,376 km, Zambia 1,110 km
Coastline: 1,600 km
Maritime claims:
contiguous zone: 24 NM
exclusive economic zone: 200 NM
territorial sea: 12 NM
Climate: semiarid in south and along coast to Luanda; north has cool, dry season (May to October) and hot, rainy season (November to April)
Terrain: narrow coastal plain rises abruptly to vast interior plateau
Elevation extremes:
lowest point: Atlantic Ocean 0 m
highest point: Morro de Moco 2,620 m
Natural resources: petroleum, diamonds, iron ore, phosphates, copper, feldspar, gold, bauxite, uranium
Land use:
arable land: 2%
permanent crops: 0%
permanent pastures: 23%
forests and woodland: 43%
other: 32% (1993 est.)
Irrigated land: 750 sq km (1993 est.)
Natural hazards: locally heavy rainfall causes periodic flooding on the plateau
Environment - current issues: overuse of pastures and subsequent soil erosion attributable to population pressures; desertification; deforestation of tropical rain forest, in response to both international demand for tropical timber and to domestic use as fuel, resulting in loss of biodiversity; soil erosion contributing to water pollution and siltation of rivers and dams; inadequate supplies of potable water
Environment - international agreements:
party to: Biodiversity, Climate Change, Desertification, Law of the Sea, Marine Dumping, Ozone Layer Protection, Ship Pollution
signed, but not ratified: none of the selected agreements
Geography - note: Cabinda is separated from rest of country by the Democratic Republic of the Congo

People

Population: 10,366,031 (July 2001 est.)
Age structure:
0-14 years: 43.31% (male 2,266,870; female 2,222,262)
15-64 years: 53.98% (male 2,847,089; female 2,748,091)
65 years and over: 2.71% (male 127,798; female 153,921) (2001 est.)
Population growth rate: 2.15% (2001 est.)
Birth rate: 46.54 births/1,000 population (2001 est.)
Death rate: 24.68 deaths/1,000 population (2001 est.)
Net migration rate: -0.34 migrant(s)/1,000 population (2001 est.)
Sex ratio:
at birth: 1.05 male(s)/female
under 15 years: 1.02 male(s)/female
15-64 years: 1.04 male(s)/female
65 years and over: 0.83 male(s)/female
total population: 1.02 male(s)/female (2001 est.)
Infant mortality rate: 193.72 deaths/1,000 live births (2001 est.)
Life expectancy at birth:
total population: 38.59 years
male: 37.36 years
female: 39.87 years (2001 est.)
Total fertility rate: 6.48 children born/woman (2001 est.)

Angola (continued)

HIV/AIDS - adult prevalence rate: 2.78% (1999 est.)
HIV/AIDS - people living with HIV/AIDS: 160,000 (1999 est.)
HIV/AIDS - deaths: 15,000 (1999 est.)
Nationality:
noun: Angolan(s)
adjective: Angolan
Ethnic groups: Ovimbundu 37%, Kimbundu 25%, Bakongo 13%, mestico (mixed European and Native African) 2%, European 1%, other 22%
Religions: indigenous beliefs 47%, Roman Catholic 38%, Protestant 15% (1998 est.)
Languages: Portuguese (official), Bantu and other African languages
Literacy:
definition: age 15 and over can read and write
total population: 42%
male: 56%
female: 28% (1998 est.)

Government

Country name:
conventional long form: Republic of Angola
conventional short form: Angola
local long form: Republica de Angola
local short form: Angola
former: People's Republic of Angola
Government type: transitional government, nominally a multiparty democracy with a strong presidential system
Capital: Luanda
Administrative divisions: 18 provinces (provincias, singular - provincia); Bengo, Benguela, Bie, Cabinda, Cuando Cubango, Cuanza Norte, Cuanza Sul, Cunene, Huambo, Huila, Luanda, Lunda Norte, Lunda Sul, Malanje, Moxico, Namibe, Uige, Zaire
Independence: 11 November 1975 (from Portugal)
National holiday: Independence Day, 11 November (1975)
Constitution: 11 November 1975; revised 7 January 1978, 11 August 1980, 6 March 1991, and 26 August 1992
Legal system: based on Portuguese civil law system and customary law; recently modified to accommodate political pluralism and increased use of free markets
Suffrage: 18 years of age; universal
Executive branch:
chief of state: President Jose Eduardo DOS SANTOS (since 21 September 1979); note - the president is both chief of state and head of government
head of government: President Jose Eduardo DOS SANTOS (since 21 September 1979); note - the president is both chief of state and head of government
cabinet: Council of Ministers appointed by the president
elections: President DOS SANTOS originally elected (in 1979) without opposition under a one-party system and stood for reelection in Angola's first multiparty elections 29-30 September 1992 (next to be held NA)
election results: DOS SANTOS 49.6%, Jonas SAVIMBI 40.1%, making a run-off election necessary; the run-off was not held and SAVIMBI's National Union for the Total Independence of Angola (UNITA) repudiated the results of the first election; the civil war resumed
Legislative branch: unicameral National Assembly or Assembleia Nacional (220 seats; members elected by proportional vote to serve four-year terms)
elections: last held 29-30 September 1992 (next to be held NA)
election results: percent of vote by party - MPLA 54%, UNITA 34%, others 12%; seats by party - MPLA 129, UNITA 70, PRS 6, FNLA 5, PLD 3, others 7
Judicial branch: Supreme Court or Tribunal da Relacao (judges are appointed by the president)
Political parties and leaders: Liberal Democratic Party or PLD [Analia de Victoria PEREIRA]; National Front for the Liberation of Angola or FNLA [disputed leadership: Lucas NGONDA, Holden ROBERTO]; National Union for the Total Independence of Angola or UNITA [Jonas SAVIMBI], largest opposition party has engaged in years of armed resistance; Popular Movement for the Liberation of Angola or MPLA [Jose Eduardo DOS SANTOS] ruling party in power since 1975; Social Renewal Party or PRS [disputed leadership: Eduardo KUANGANA, Antonio MUACHICUNGO]; UNITA-Renovada [Eugenio NGOLO "Manuvakola", leader]
note: about a dozen minor parties participated in the 1992 elections but won few seats and have little influence in the National Assembly
Political pressure groups and leaders: Front for the Liberation of the Enclave of Cabinda or FLEC [N'zita Henriques TIAGO; Antonio Bento BEMBE]
note: FLEC is waging a small-scale, highly factionalized, armed struggle for the independence of Cabinda Province
International organization participation: ACP, AfDB, CCC, CEEAC, ECA, FAO, G-77, IAEA, IBRD, ICAO, ICFTU, ICRM, IDA, IFAD, IFC, IFRCS, ILO, IMF, IMO, Intelsat, Interpol, IOC, IOM, ITU, NAM, OAS (observer), OAU, SADC, UN, UNCTAD, UNESCO, UNIDO, UPU, WFTU, WHO, WIPO, WMO, WToO, WTrO
Diplomatic representation in the US:
chief of mission: Ambassador Josefina Perpetua Pitra DIAKIDI
chancery: 1615 M Street, NW, Suite 900, Washington, DC 20036
telephone: [1] (202) 785-1156
FAX: [1] (202) 785-1258
consulate(s) general: New York
Diplomatic representation from the US:
chief of mission: Ambassador Joseph G. SULLIVAN
embassy: number 32 Rua Houari Boumeddienne, Luanda
mailing address: international mail: Caixa Postal 6484, Luanda; pouch: American Embassy Luanda, Department of State, Washington, DC 20521-2550
telephone: [244] (2) 345-481, 346-418
FAX: [244] (2) 346-924
Flag description: two equal horizontal bands of red (top) and black with a centered yellow emblem consisting of a five-pointed star within half a cogwheel crossed by a machete (in the style of a hammer and sickle)

Economy

Economy - overview: Angola is an economy in disarray because of a quarter century of nearly continuous warfare. Despite its abundant natural resources, output per capita is among the world's lowest. Subsistence agriculture provides the main livelihood for 85% of the population. Oil production and the supporting activities are vital to the economy, contributing about 45% to GDP and 90% of exports. Violence continues, millions of land mines remain, and many farmers are reluctant to return to their fields. As a result, much of the country's food must still be imported. To fully take advantage of its rich resources - gold, diamonds, extensive forests, Atlantic fisheries, and large oil deposits - Angola will need to end its conflict and continue reforming government policies. Despite the increase in the pace of civil warfare in late 1998, the economy grew by an estimated 5% in 2000. The government introduced new currency denominations in 1999, including 1 and 5 kwanza notes. Internal strife discourages investment outside of the petroleum sector, which is producing roughly 800,000 barrels of oil per day. Angola has entered into a Staff Monitored Program (SMP) with the IMF. Continued growth depends on sharp cuts in inflation, further economic reform, and a lessening of fighting.
GDP: purchasing power parity - $10.1 billion (2000 est.)
GDP - real growth rate: 4.9% (2000 est.)
GDP - per capita: purchasing power parity - $1,000 (2000 est.)
GDP - composition by sector:
agriculture: 7%
industry: 60%
services: 33% (1999 est.)
Population below poverty line: NA%
Household income or consumption by percentage share:
lowest 10%: NA%
highest 10%: NA%
Inflation rate (consumer prices): 325% (2000 est.)
Labor force: 5 million (1997 est.)
Labor force - by occupation: agriculture 85%, industry and services 15% (1997 est.)
Unemployment rate: extensive unemployment and underemployment affecting more than half the population (2000 est.)
Budget:
revenues: $928 million
expenditures: $2.5 billion, including capital expenditures of $963 million (1992 est.)
Industries: petroleum; diamonds, iron ore, phosphates, feldspar, bauxite, uranium, and gold; cement; basic metal products; fish processing; food processing; brewing; tobacco products; sugar; textiles

Angola (continued)

Industrial production growth rate: NA%
Electricity - production: 1.475 billion kWh (1999)
Electricity - production by source:
fossil fuel: 32.2%
hydro: 67.8%
nuclear: 0%
other: 0% (1999)
Electricity - consumption: 1.372 billion kWh (1999)
Electricity - exports: 0 kWh (1999)
Electricity - imports: 0 kWh (1999)
Agriculture - products: bananas, sugarcane, coffee, sisal, corn, cotton, manioc (tapioca), tobacco, vegetables, plantains; livestock; forest products; fish
Exports: $7.8 billion (f.o.b., 2000 est.)
Exports - commodities: crude oil 90%, diamonds, refined petroleum products, gas, coffee, sisal, fish and fish products, timber, cotton
Exports - partners: US 54%, South Korea 14%, Benelux 11%, China 7%, Taiwan 6% (1999)
Imports: $2.5 billion (f.o.b., 2000 est.)
Imports - commodities: machinery and electrical equipment, vehicles and spare parts; medicines, food, textiles, military goods
Imports - partners: South Korea 16%, Portugal 15%, US 13%, South Africa 10%, France 8% (1999)
Debt - external: $10.8 billion (2000 est.)
Economic aid - recipient: $493.1 million (1995)
Currency: kwanza (AOA)
Currency code: AOA
Exchange rates: kwanza per US dollar - 17,910,800 (January 2001), 10,041,000 (2000), 2,790,706 (1999), 392,824 (1998), 229,040 (1997), 128,029 (1996); note - in December 1999 the kwanza was revalued with six zeroes dropped off the old value
Fiscal year: calendar year

Communications

Telephones - main lines in use: 62,000 (1997)
Telephones - mobile cellular: 7,052 (1997)
Telephone system:
general assessment: telephone service limited mostly to government and business use; HF radiotelephone used extensively for military links
domestic: limited system of wire, microwave radio relay, and tropospheric scatter
international: satellite earth stations - 2 Intelsat (Atlantic Ocean)
Radio broadcast stations: AM 34, FM 7, shortwave 9 (1999)
Radios: 630,000 (1997)
Television broadcast stations: 7 (1999)
Televisions: 150,000 (1997)
Internet country code: .ao
Internet Service Providers (ISPs): 1 (2000)
Internet users: 12,000 (1999)

Transportation

Railways:
total: 2,952 km (inland, much of the track is unusable because of land mines still in place from the civil war)
narrow gauge: 2,798 km 1.067-m gauge; 154 km 0.600-m gauge (1997)

Highways:
total: 76,626 km
paved: 19,156 km
unpaved: 57,470 km (1997)
Waterways: 1,295 km
Pipelines: crude oil 179 km
Ports and harbors: Ambriz, Cabinda, Lobito, Luanda, Malongo, Mocamedes, Namibe, Porto Amboim, Soyo
Merchant marine:
total: 9 ships (1,000 GRT or over) totaling 39,305 GRT/63,067 DWT
ships by type: cargo 8, petroleum tanker 1 (2000 est.)
Airports: 247 (2000 est.)
Airports - with paved runways:
total: 31
over 3,047 m: 4
2,438 to 3,047 m: 8
1,524 to 2,437 m: 12
914 to 1,523 m: 6
under 914 m: 1 (2000 est.)
Airports - with unpaved runways:
total: 216
over 3,047 m: 2
2,438 to 3,047 m: 5
1,524 to 2,437 m: 30
914 to 1,523 m: 96
under 914 m: 83 (2000 est.)

Military

Military branches: Army, Navy, Air and Air Defense Forces, National Police Force
Military manpower - military age: 18 years of age
Military manpower - availability:
males age 15-49: 2,480,016 (2001 est.)
Military manpower - fit for military service:
males age 15-49: 1,246,224 (2001 est.)
Military manpower - reaching military age annually:
males: 103,807 (2001 est.)
Military expenditures - dollar figure: $1.2 billion (FY97)
Military expenditures - percent of GDP: 22% (1999)

Transnational Issues

Disputes - international: none
Illicit drugs: increasingly used as a transshipment point for cocaine and heroin destined for Western Europe and other African states

Anguilla
(overseas territory of the UK)

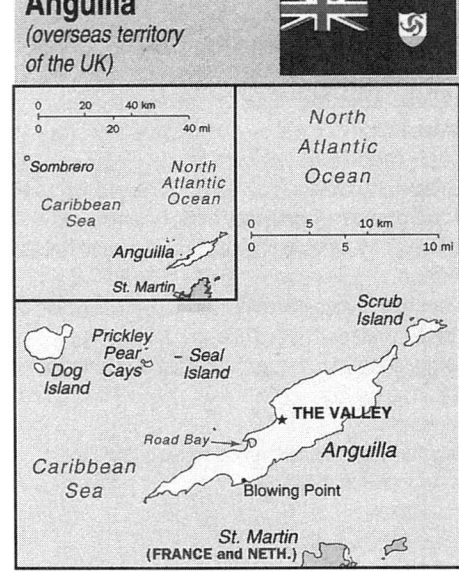

Introduction

Background: Colonized by English settlers from Saint Kitts in 1650, Anguilla was administered by Great Britain until the early 19th century, when the island - against the wishes of the inhabitants - was incorporated into a single British dependency along with Saint Kitts and Nevis. Several attempts at separation failed. In 1971, two years after a revolt, Anguilla was finally allowed to secede; this arrangement was formally recognized in 1980 with Anguilla becoming a separate British dependency.

Geography

Location: Caribbean, island in the Caribbean Sea, east of Puerto Rico
Geographic coordinates: 18 15 N, 63 10 W
Map references: Central America and the Caribbean
Area:
total: 91 sq km
land: 91 sq km
water: 0 sq km
Area - comparative: about half the size of Washington, DC
Land boundaries: 0 km
Coastline: 61 km
Maritime claims:
exclusive fishing zone: 200 NM
territorial sea: 3 NM
Climate: tropical; moderated by northeast trade winds
Terrain: flat and low-lying island of coral and limestone
Elevation extremes:
lowest point: Caribbean Sea 0 m
highest point: Crocus Hill 65 m
Natural resources: salt, fish, lobster
Land use:
arable land: 0%
permanent crops: 0%

Anguilla (continued)

permanent pastures: 0%
forests and woodland: 0%
other: 100% (mostly rock with sparse scrub oak, few trees, some commercial salt ponds)
Irrigated land: NA sq km
Natural hazards: frequent hurricanes and other tropical storms (July to October)
Environment - current issues: supplies of potable water sometimes cannot meet increasing demand largely because of poor distribution system

People

Population: 12,132 (July 2001 est.)
Age structure:
0-14 years: 25.55% (male 1,574; female 1,526)
15-64 years: 67.47% (male 4,200; female 3,985)
65 years and over: 6.98% (male 376; female 471) (2001 est.)
Population growth rate: 2.68% (2001 est.)
Birth rate: 15.17 births/1,000 population (2001 est.)
Death rate: 5.61 deaths/1,000 population (2001 est.)
Net migration rate: 17.23 migrant(s)/1,000 population (2001 est.)
Sex ratio:
at birth: 1.03 male(s)/female
under 15 years: 1.03 male(s)/female
15-64 years: 1.05 male(s)/female
65 years and over: 0.8 male(s)/female
total population: 1.03 male(s)/female (2001 est.)
Infant mortality rate: 24.56 deaths/1,000 live births (2001 est.)
Life expectancy at birth:
total population: 76.31 years
male: 73.41 years
female: 79.29 years (2001 est.)
Total fertility rate: 1.79 children born/woman (2001 est.)
HIV/AIDS - adult prevalence rate: NA%
HIV/AIDS - people living with HIV/AIDS: NA
HIV/AIDS - deaths: NA
Nationality:
noun: Anguillan(s)
adjective: Anguillan
Ethnic groups: black
Religions: Anglican 40%, Methodist 33%, Seventh-Day Adventist 7%, Baptist 5%, Roman Catholic 3%, other 12%
Languages: English (official)
Literacy:
definition: age 12 and over can read and write
total population: 95%
male: 95%
female: 95% (1984 est.)

Government

Country name:
conventional long form: none
conventional short form: Anguilla
Dependency status: overseas territory of the UK
Government type: NA
Capital: The Valley
Administrative divisions: none (overseas territory of the UK)
Independence: none (overseas territory of the UK)
National holiday: Anguilla Day, 30 May
Constitution: Anguilla Constitutional Order 1 April 1982; amended 1990
Legal system: based on English common law
Suffrage: 18 years of age; universal
Executive branch:
chief of state: Queen ELIZABETH II (since 6 February 1952); represented by Governor Peter JOHNSTON (since NA February 2000)
head of government: Chief Minister Osbourne FLEMING (since 3 March 2000)
cabinet: Executive Council appointed by the governor from among the elected members of the House of Assembly
elections: none; the monarch is hereditary; governor appointed by the monarch; chief minister appointed by the governor from among the members of the House of Assembly
Legislative branch: unicameral House of Assembly (11 seats total, 7 elected by direct popular vote, 2 ex officio members and 2 appointed; members serve five-year terms)
elections: last held 3 March 2000 (next to be held NA March 2005)
election results: percent of vote by party - NA%; seats by party - UF 4, AUM 2, independent 1
Judicial branch: High Court (judge provided by Eastern Caribbean Supreme Court)
Political parties and leaders: Anguilla United Movement or AUM [Hubert HUGHES]; The United Front or UF [Osbourne FLEMMING, Victor BANKS], a coalition of the Anguilla Democratic Party or ADP and the Anguilla National Alliance or ANA
Political pressure groups and leaders: NA
International organization participation: Caricom (associate), CDB, Interpol (subbureau), OECS (associate), ECLAC (associate)
Diplomatic representation in the US: none (overseas territory of the UK)
Diplomatic representation from the US: none (overseas territory of the UK)
Flag description: blue, with the flag of the UK in the upper hoist-side quadrant and the Anguillan coat of arms centered in the outer half of the flag; the coat of arms depicts three orange dolphins in an interlocking circular design on a white background with blue wavy water below

Economy

Economy - overview: Anguilla has few natural resources, and the economy depends heavily on luxury tourism, offshore banking, lobster fishing, and remittances from emigrants. The economy, and especially the tourism sector, suffered a setback in late 1995 due to the effects of Hurricane Luis in September but recovered in 1996. Increased activity in the tourism industry, which has spurred the growth of the construction sector, has contributed to economic growth. Anguillan officials have put substantial effort into developing the offshore financial sector. A comprehensive package of financial services legislation was enacted in late 1994. In the medium term, prospects for the economy will depend on the tourism sector and, therefore, on continuing income growth in the industrialized nations as well as favorable weather conditions.
GDP: purchasing power parity - $96 million (1999 est.)
GDP - real growth rate: 7% (1999 est.)
GDP - per capita: purchasing power parity - $8,200 (1999 est.)
GDP - composition by sector:
agriculture: 4%
industry: 18%
services: 78% (1997 est.)
Population below poverty line: NA%
Household income or consumption by percentage share:
lowest 10%: NA%
highest 10%: NA%
Inflation rate (consumer prices): 2.5% (1998 est.)
Labor force: 4,400 (1992)
Labor force - by occupation: commerce 36%, services 29%, construction 18%, transportation and utilities 10%, manufacturing 3%, agriculture/fishing/forestry/mining 4%
Unemployment rate: 7% (1992 est.)
Budget:
revenues: $20.4 million
expenditures: $23.3 million, including capital expenditures of $3.8 million (1997 est.)
Industries: tourism, boat building, offshore financial services
Industrial production growth rate: 3.1% (1997 est.)
Electricity - production: NA kWh
Electricity - production by source:
fossil fuel: NA%
hydro: NA%
nuclear: NA%
other: NA%
Electricity - consumption: NA kWh
Agriculture - products: small quantities of tobacco, vegetables; cattle raising
Exports: $4.5 million (1998)
Exports - commodities: lobster, fish, livestock, salt
Exports - partners: NA
Imports: $57.6 million (1998)
Imports - commodities: NA
Imports - partners: NA
Debt - external: $8.8 million (1998)
Economic aid - recipient: $3.5 million (1995)
Currency: East Caribbean dollar (XCD)
Currency code: XCD
Exchange rates: East Caribbean dollars per US dollar - 2.7000 (fixed rate since 1976)
Fiscal year: 1 April - 31 March

Anguilla (continued)

Communications

Telephones - main lines in use: 5,000 (1997)
Telephones - mobile cellular: NA
Telephone system:
general assessment: NA
domestic: modern internal telephone system
international: microwave radio relay to island of Saint Martin (Guadeloupe and Netherlands Antilles)
Radio broadcast stations: AM 5, FM 6, shortwave 1 (1998)
Radios: 3,000 (1997)
Television broadcast stations: 1 (1997)
Televisions: 1,000 (1997)
Internet country code: .ai
Internet Service Providers (ISPs): 16 (2000)
Internet users: NA

Transportation

Railways: 0 km
Highways:
total: 279 km
paved: 253 km
unpaved: 26 km (1998 est.)
Waterways: none
Ports and harbors: Blowing Point, Road Bay
Merchant marine: none (2000 est.)
Airports: 3 (2000 est.)
Airports - with paved runways:
total: 1
914 to 1,523 m: 1 (2000 est.)
Airports - with unpaved runways:
total: 2
under 914 m: 2 (2000 est.)

Military

Military - note: defense is the responsibility of the UK

Transnational Issues

Disputes - international: none
Illicit drugs: transshipment point for South American narcotics destined for the US and Europe

Antarctica

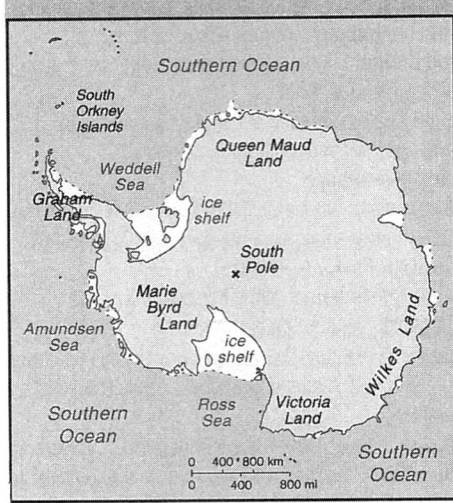

Introduction

Background: Speculation over the existence of a "southern land" was not confirmed until the early 1820s when British and American commercial operators and British and Russian national expeditions began exploring the Peninsula region and areas south of the Antarctic Circle. Not until 1838 was it established that Antarctica was indeed a continent and not just a group of islands. Various "firsts" were achieved in the early 20th century, including: 1902, first balloon flight (by British explorer Robert Falcon SCOTT); 1912, first to the South Pole (five Norwegian explorers under Roald AMUNDSEN); 1928, first fixed-wing aircraft flight (by Australian adventurer/explorer Sir Hubert WILKINS); 1929, first flight over the South Pole (by Americans Richard BYRD and Bernt BALCHEN); and 1935, first transantarctic flight (American Lincoln ELLSWORTH). Following World War II, there was an upsurge in scientific research on the continent. A number of countries have set up year-round research stations on Antarctica. Seven have made territorial claims, but no other country recognizes these claims. In order to form a legal framework for the activities of nations on the continent, an Antarctic Treaty was negotiated that neither denies nor gives recognition to existing territorial claims; signed in 1959, it entered into force in 1961.

Geography

Location: continent mostly south of the Antarctic Circle
Geographic coordinates: 90 00 S, 0 00 E
Map references: Antarctic Region
Area:
total: 14 million sq km
land: 14 million sq km (280,000 sq km ice-free, 13.72 million sq km ice-covered) (est.)
note: fifth-largest continent, following Asia, Africa, North America, and South America, but larger than Australia and the subcontinent of Europe
Area - comparative: slightly less than 1.5 times the size of the US
Land boundaries: 0 km
note: see entry on International disputes
Coastline: 17,968 km
Maritime claims: none; nineteen of 26 Antarctic consultative nations have made no claims to Antarctic territory (although Russia and the US have reserved the right to do so) and do not recognize the claims of the other nations; also see the Disputes - international entry
Climate: severe low temperatures vary with latitude, elevation, and distance from the ocean; East Antarctica is colder than West Antarctica because of its higher elevation; Antarctic Peninsula has the most moderate climate; higher temperatures occur in January along the coast and average slightly below freezing
Terrain: about 98% thick continental ice sheet and 2% barren rock, with average elevations between 2,000 and 4,000 meters; mountain ranges up to 5,140 meters; ice-free coastal areas include parts of southern Victoria Land, Wilkes Land, the Antarctic Peninsula area, and parts of Ross Island on McMurdo Sound; glaciers form ice shelves along about half of the coastline, and floating ice shelves constitute 11% of the area of the continent
Elevation extremes:
lowest point: Bentley Subglacial Trench -2,540 m
highest point: Vinson Massif 5,140 m
note: the lowest known land point in Antarctica is hidden in the Bentley Subglacial Trench; at its surface is the deepest ice yet discovered and the world's lowest elevation not under sea water
Natural resources: iron ore, chromium, copper, gold, nickel, platinum and other minerals, and coal and hydrocarbons have been found in small uncommercial quantities; none presently exploited; krill, finfish, and crab have been taken by commercial fisheries
Land use:
arable land: 0%
permanent crops: 0%
permanent pastures: 0%
forests and woodland: 0%
other: 100% (ice 98%, barren rock 2%)
Irrigated land: 0 sq km (1993)
Natural hazards: katabatic (gravity-driven) winds blow coastward from the high interior; frequent blizzards form near the foot of the plateau; cyclonic storms form over the ocean and move clockwise along the coast; volcanism on Deception Island and isolated areas of West Antarctica; other seismic activity rare and weak; large icebergs may calve from ice shelf
Environment - current issues: in 1998, NASA satellite data showed that the antarctic ozone hole was the largest on record, covering 27 million square kilometers; researchers in 1997 found that increased ultraviolet light coming through the hole damages the DNA of icefish, an antarctic fish lacking hemoglobin; ozone depletion earlier was shown to harm one-celled antarctic marine plants

Antarctica (continued)

Geography - note: the coldest, windiest, highest (on average), and driest continent; during summer, more solar radiation reaches the surface at the South Pole than is received at the Equator in an equivalent period; mostly uninhabitable

People

Population: no indigenous inhabitants, but there are seasonally staffed research stations
note: approximately 29 nations, all signatory to the Antarctic Treaty, send personnel to perform seasonal (summer) and year-round research on the continent and in its surrounding oceans; the population of persons doing and supporting science on the continent and its nearby islands south of 60 degrees south latitude (the region covered by the Antarctic Treaty) varies from approximately 4,000 in summer to 1,000 in winter; in addition, approximately 1,000 personnel including ship's crew and scientists doing onboard research are present in the waters of the treaty region; Summer (January) population - 3,687 total; Argentina 302, Australia 201, Belgium 13, Brazil 80, Bulgaria 16, Chile 352, China 70, Finland 11, France 100, Germany 51, India 60, Italy 106, Japan 136, South Korea 14, Netherlands 10, NZ 60, Norway 40, Peru 28, Poland 70, Russia 254, South Africa 80, Spain 43, Sweden 20, UK 192, US 1,378 (1998-99); Winter (July) population - 964 total; Argentina 165, Australia 75, Brazil 12, Chile 129, China 33, France 33, Germany 9, India 25, Japan 40, South Korea 14, NZ 10, Poland 20, Russia 102, South Africa 10, UK 39, US 248 (1998-99); year-round stations - 42 total; Argentina 6, Australia 4, Brazil 1, Chile 4, China 2, Finland 1, France 1, Germany 1, India 1, Italy 1, Japan 1, South Korea 1, NZ 1, Norway 1, Poland 1, Russia 6, South Africa 1, Spain 1, Ukraine 1, UK 2, US 3, Uruguay 1 (1998-99); Summer-only stations - 32 total; Argentina 3, Australia 4, Bulgaria 1, Chile 7, Germany 1, India 1, Japan 3, NZ 1, Peru 1, Russia 3, Sweden 2, UK 5 (1998-99); in addition, during the austral summer some nations have numerous occupied locations such as tent camps, summer-long temporary facilities, and mobile traverses in support of research (July 2001 est.)

Government

Country name:
conventional long form: none
conventional short form: Antarctica
Government type: Antarctic Treaty Summary - the Antarctic Treaty, signed on 1 December 1959 and entered into force on 23 June 1961, establishes the legal framework for the management of Antarctica. The 23rd Antarctic Treaty Consultative Meeting was held in Peru in May 1999. At the end of 2000, there were 44 treaty member nations: 27 consultative and 17 non-consultative. Consultative (voting) members include the seven nations that claim portions of Antarctica as national territory (some claims overlap) and 20 nonclaimant nations. The US and Russia have reserved the right to make claims. The US does not recognize the claims of others. Antarctica is administered through meetings of the consultative member nations. Decisions from these meetings are carried out by these member nations (within their areas) in accordance with their own national laws. The year in parentheses indicates when an acceding nation was voted to full consultative (voting) status, while no date indicates the country was an original 1959 treaty signatory. Claimant nations are - Argentina, Australia, Chile, France, New Zealand, Norway, and the UK. Nonclaimant consultative nations are - Belgium, Brazil (1983), Bulgaria (1998) China (1985), Ecuador (1990), Finland (1989), Germany (1981), India (1983), Italy (1987), Japan, South Korea (1989), Netherlands (1990), Peru (1989), Poland (1977), Russia, South Africa, Spain (1988), Sweden (1988), Uruguay (1985), and the US. Non-consultative (nonvoting) members, with year of accession in parentheses, are - Austria (1987), Canada (1988), Colombia (1989), Cuba (1984), Czech Republic (1993), Denmark (1965), Greece (1987), Guatemala (1991), Hungary (1984), North Korea (1987), Papua New Guinea (1981), Romania (1971), Slovakia (1993), Switzerland (1990), Turkey (1995), Ukraine (1992), and Venezuela (1999). Article 1 - area to be used for peaceful purposes only; military activity, such as weapons testing, is prohibited, but military personnel and equipment may be used for scientific research or any other peaceful purpose; Article 2 - freedom of scientific investigation and cooperation shall continue; Article 3 - free exchange of information and personnel, cooperation with the UN and other international agencies; Article 4 - does not recognize, dispute, or establish territorial claims and no new claims shall be asserted while the treaty is in force; Article 5 - prohibits nuclear explosions or disposal of radioactive wastes; Article 6 - includes under the treaty all land and ice shelves south of 60 degrees 00 minutes south and reserves high seas rights; Article 7 - treaty-state observers have free access, including aerial observation, to any area and may inspect all stations, installations, and equipment; advance notice of all expeditions and of the introduction of military personnel must be given; Article 8 - allows for jurisdiction over observers and scientists by their own states; Article 9 - frequent consultative meetings take place among member nations; Article 10 - treaty states will discourage activities by any country in Antarctica that are contrary to the treaty; Article 11 - disputes to be settled peacefully by the parties concerned or, ultimately, by the ICJ; Articles 12, 13, 14 - deal with upholding, interpreting, and amending the treaty among involved nations. Other agreements - some 200 recommendations adopted at treaty consultative meetings and ratified by governments include - Agreed Measures for Fauna and Flora (1964) which were later incorporated into the Environmental Protocol; Convention for the Conservation of Antarctic Seals (1972); Convention on the Conservation of Antarctic Marine Living Resources (1980); a mineral resources agreement was signed in 1988 but remains unratified; the Protocol on Environmental Protection to the Antarctic Treaty was signed 4 October 1991 and entered into force 14 January 1998; this agreement provides for the protection of the Antarctic environment through five specific annexes: 1) marine pollution, 2) fauna and flora, 3) environmental impact assessments, 4) waste management, and 5) protected area management; it prohibits all activities relating to mineral resources except scientific research.
Legal system: Antarctica is administered through meetings of the consultative member nations. Decisions from these meetings are carried out by these member nations (within their areas) in accordance with their own national laws. US law, including certain criminal offenses by or against US nationals, such as murder, may apply extra-territorially. Some US laws directly apply to Antarctica. For example, the Antarctic Conservation Act, 16 U.S.C. section 2401 et seq., provides civil and criminal penalties for the following activities, unless authorized by regulation of statute: the taking of native mammals or birds; the introduction of nonindigenous plants and animals; entry into specially protected areas; the discharge or disposal of pollutants; and the importation into the US of certain items from Antarctica. Violation of the Antarctic Conservation Act carries penalties of up to $10,000 in fines and one year in prison. The National Science Foundation and Department of Justice share enforcement responsibilities. Public Law 95-541, the US Antarctic Conservation Act of 1978, as amended in 1996, requires expeditions from the US to Antarctica to notify, in advance, the Office of Oceans and Polar Affairs, Room 5801, Department of State, Washington, DC 20520, which reports such plans to other nations as required by the Antarctic Treaty. For more information, contact Permit Office, Office of Polar Programs, National Science Foundation, Arlington, Virginia 22230; telephone: (703) 292-8030, or see their website at www.nsf.gov.

Economy

Economy - overview: Fishing off the coast and tourism, both based abroad, account for the limited economic activity. Antarctic fisheries in 1998-99 (1 July-30 June) reported landing 119,898 metric tons. Unregulated fishing landed five to six times more than the regulated fishery, and allegedly illegal fishing in antarctic waters in 1998 resulted in the seizure (by France and Australia) of at least eight fishing ships. Companies interested in commercial fishing activities in Antarctica have put forward proposals. The Convention on the Conservation of Antarctic Marine Living Resources determines the recommended catch limits for marine species. A total of 13,193 tourists visited in the 1999-2000 summer, up from the 10,013 who visited the previous year. Nearly all of them were passengers on 24 commercial (nongovernmental) ships and several yachts that made 143 trips during the summer. Most tourist trips lasted approximately two weeks.

Antarctica (continued)

Communications

Telephones - main lines in use: 0
note: information for US bases only (2001)
Telephones - mobile cellular: NA
Telephone system:
general assessment: NA
domestic: NA
international: NA
Radio broadcast stations: AM NA, FM 2, shortwave 1
note: information for US bases only (1998)
Radios: NA
Television broadcast stations: 1 (the US Navy Antarctic Support Group operates a cable system with six channels for the American Forces Antarctic Network-McMurdo)
note: information for US bases only (2000)
Televisions: several hundred at McMurdo Sound
note: information for US bases only (2001)
Internet country code: .aq
Internet Service Providers (ISPs): NA

Transportation

Ports and harbors: there are no developed ports and harbors in Antarctica; most coastal stations have offshore anchorages, and supplies are transferred from ship to shore by small boats, barges, and helicopters; a few stations have a basic wharf facility US coastal stations include McMurdo (77 51 S, 166 40 E), Palmer (64 43 S, 64 03 W); government use only except by permit (see Permit Office under "Legal System"); offshore anchorage is sparse and intermittent
Airports: 19
note: 27 stations, operated by 16 national governments party to the Antarctic Treaty, have aircraft landing facilities for either helicopters and/or fixed-wing aircraft; commercial enterprises operate two additional aircraft landing facilities; helicopter pads are available at 27 stations; runways at 15 locations are gravel, sea-ice, blue-ice, or compacted snow suitable for landing wheeled, fixed-wing aircraft; of these, 1 is greater than 3 km in length, 6 are between 2 km and 3 km in length, 3 are between 1 km and 2 km in length, 3 are less than 1 km in length, and 2 are of unknown length; snow surface skiways, limited to use by ski-equipped, fixed-wing aircraft, are available at another 15 locations; of these, 4 are greater than 3 km in length, 3 are between 2 km and 3 km in length, 2 are between 1 km and 2 km in length, 2 are less than 1 km in length, and 4 are of unknown length; aircraft landing facilities generally subject to severe restrictions and limitations resulting from extreme seasonal and geographic conditions; aircraft landing facilities do not meet ICAO standards; advance approval from the respective governmental or nongovernmental operating organization required for landing (2001 est.)
Airports - with unpaved runways:
total: 19
over 3,047 m: 6
2,438 to 3,047 m: 3
1,524 to 2,437 m: 1
914 to 1,523 m: 4
under 914 m: 5 (2000 est.)
Heliports: 27 stations have helicopter landing facilities (helipads) (2001 est.)

Military

Military - note: the Antarctic Treaty prohibits any measures of a military nature, such as the establishment of military bases and fortifications, the carrying out of military maneuvers, or the testing of any type of weapon; it permits the use of military personnel or equipment for scientific research or for any other peaceful purposes

Transnational Issues

Disputes - international: Antarctic Treaty freezes claims (see Antarctic Treaty Summary in Government type entry); sections (some overlapping) claimed by Argentina, Australia, Chile, France, New Zealand, Norway, and UK; the US and most other nations do not recognize the territorial claims of other nations and have made no claims themselves (the US and Russia reserve the right to do so); no claims have been made in the sector between 90 degrees west and 150 degrees west

Antigua and Barbuda

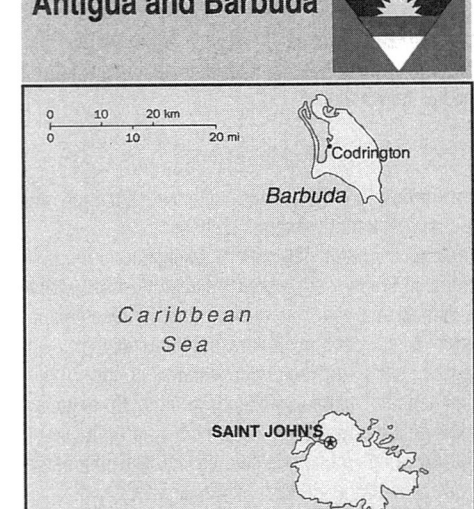

Introduction

Background: The islands of Antigua and Barbuda became an independent state within the British Commonwealth of Nations in 1981. Some 3,000 refugees fleeing a volcanic eruption on nearby Montserrat have settled in Antigua and Barbuda since 1995.

Geography

Location: Caribbean, islands between the Caribbean Sea and the North Atlantic Ocean, east-southeast of Puerto Rico
Geographic coordinates: 17 03 N, 61 48 W
Map references: Central America and the Caribbean
Area:
total: 442 sq km (Antigua 281 sq km; Barbuda 161 sq km)
land: 442 sq km
water: 0 sq km
note: includes Redonda
Area - comparative: 2.5 times the size of Washington, DC
Land boundaries: 0 km
Coastline: 153 km
Maritime claims:
contiguous zone: 24 NM
continental shelf: 200 NM or to the edge of the continental margin
exclusive economic zone: 200 NM
territorial sea: 12 NM
Climate: tropical marine; little seasonal temperature variation
Terrain: mostly low-lying limestone and coral islands, with some higher volcanic areas
Elevation extremes:
lowest point: Caribbean Sea 0 m
highest point: Boggy Peak 402 m
Natural resources: NEGL; pleasant climate fosters tourism

Antigua and Barbuda (continued)

Land use:
arable land: 18%
permanent crops: 0%
permanent pastures: 9%
forests and woodland: 11%
other: 62% (1993 est.)
Irrigated land: NA sq km
Natural hazards: hurricanes and tropical storms (July to October); periodic droughts
Environment - current issues: water management - a major concern because of limited natural fresh water resources - is further hampered by the clearing of trees to increase crop production, causing rainfall to run off quickly
Environment - international agreements:
party to: Biodiversity, Climate Change, Climate Change-Kyoto Protocol, Desertification, Endangered Species, Environmental Modification, Hazardous Wastes, Law of the Sea, Marine Dumping, Nuclear Test Ban, Ozone Layer Protection, Ship Pollution, Whaling
signed, but not ratified: none of the selected agreements

People

Population: 66,970 (July 2001 est.)
Age structure:
0-14 years: 27.97% (male 9,527; female 9,203)
15-64 years: 67.15% (male 22,450; female 22,519)
65 years and over: 4.88% (male 1,360; female 1,911) (2001 est.)
Population growth rate: 0.74% (2001 est.)
Birth rate: 19.5 births/1,000 population (2001 est.)
Death rate: 5.87 deaths/1,000 population (2001 est.)
Net migration rate: -6.27 migrant(s)/1,000 population (2001 est.)
Sex ratio:
at birth: 1.05 male(s)/female
under 15 years: 1.04 male(s)/female
15-64 years: 1 male(s)/female
65 years and over: 0.71 male(s)/female
total population: 0.99 male(s)/female (2001 est.)
Infant mortality rate: 22.33 deaths/1,000 live births (2001 est.)
Life expectancy at birth:
total population: 70.74 years
male: 68.45 years
female: 73.14 years (2001 est.)
Total fertility rate: 2.31 children born/woman (2001 est.)
HIV/AIDS - adult prevalence rate: NA%
HIV/AIDS - people living with HIV/AIDS: NA
HIV/AIDS - deaths: NA
Nationality:
noun: Antiguan(s), Barbudan(s)
adjective: Antiguan, Barbudan
Ethnic groups: black, British, Portuguese, Lebanese, Syrian
Religions: Anglican (predominant), other Protestant, some Roman Catholic
Languages: English (official), local dialects

Literacy:
definition: age 15 and over has completed five or more years of schooling
total population: 89%
male: 90%
female: 88% (1960 est.)

Government

Country name:
conventional long form: none
conventional short form: Antigua and Barbuda
Government type: constitutional monarchy with UK-style parliament
Capital: Saint John's
Administrative divisions: 6 parishes and 2 dependencies*; Barbuda*, Redonda*, Saint George, Saint John, Saint Mary, Saint Paul, Saint Peter, Saint Philip
Independence: 1 November 1981 (from UK)
National holiday: Independence Day, 1 November (1981)
Constitution: 1 November 1981
Legal system: based on English common law
Suffrage: 18 years of age; universal
Executive branch:
chief of state: Queen ELIZABETH II (since 6 February 1952), represented by Governor General James B. CARLISLE (since NA 1993)
head of government: Prime Minister Lester Bryant BIRD (since 8 March 1994)
cabinet: Council of Ministers appointed by the governor general on the advice of the prime minister
elections: none; the monarch is hereditary; governor general chosen by the monarch on the advice of the prime minister; prime minister appointed by the governor general
Legislative branch: bicameral Parliament consists of the Senate (17-member body appointed by the governor general) and the House of Representatives (17 seats; members are elected by proportional representation to serve five-year terms)
elections: House of Representatives - last held 9 March 1999 (next to be held NA March 2004)
election results: percent of vote by party - NA%; seats by party - ALP 12, UPP 4, independent 1
Judicial branch: Eastern Caribbean Supreme Court (based in Saint Lucia; one judge of the Supreme Court is a resident of the islands and presides over the Court of Summary Jurisdiction)
Political parties and leaders: Antigua Labor Party or ALP [Lester Bryant BIRD]; Barbuda People's Movement or BPM [Thomas H. FRANK]; United Progressive Party or UPP [Baldwin SPENCER] (a coalition of three opposition parties - United National Democratic Party or UNDP, Antigua Caribbean Liberation Movement or ACLM, and Progressive Labor Movement or PLM)
Political pressure groups and leaders: Antigua Trades and Labor Union or ATLU [William ROBINSON]; People's Democratic Movement or PDM [Hugh MARSHALL]

International organization participation: ACP, C, Caricom, CDB, ECLAC, FAO, G-77, IBRD, ICAO, ICFTU, ICRM, IFAD, IFC, IFRCS, ILO, IMF, IMO, Intelsat (nonsignatory user), Interpol, IOC, ITU, NAM (observer), OAS, OECS, OPANAL, UN, UNCTAD, UNESCO, UPU, WCL, WFTU, WHO, WIPO, WMO, WTrO
Diplomatic representation in the US:
chief of mission: Ambassador Lionel Alexander HURST
chancery: 3216 New Mexico Avenue NW, Washington, DC 20016
telephone: [1] (202) 362-5211
FAX: [1] (202) 362-5225
consulate(s) general: Miami
Diplomatic representation from the US: the US does not have an embassy in Antigua and Barbuda (embassy closed 30 June 1994); the US Ambassador to Barbados is accredited to Antigua and Barbuda
Flag description: red, with an inverted isosceles triangle based on the top edge of the flag; the triangle contains three horizontal bands of black (top), light blue, and white, with a yellow rising sun in the black band

Economy

Economy - overview: Tourism continues to be the dominant activity in the economy accounting directly or indirectly for more than half of GDP. The budding offshore financial sector has been seriously hurt by financial sanctions imposed by the US and UK as a result of the loosening of its money-laundering controls. The government has made efforts to comply with international demands in order to get the sanctions lifted. Antigua and Barbuda was listed as a tax haven by the OECD in 2000. The dual island nation's agricultural production is mainly directed to the domestic market; the sector is constrained by the limited water supply and labor shortages that reflect the pull of higher wages in tourism and construction. Manufacturing comprises enclave-type assembly for export with major products being bedding, handicrafts, and electronic components. Prospects for economic growth in the medium term will continue to depend on income growth in the industrialized world, especially in the US, which accounts for about one-third of all tourist arrivals.
GDP: purchasing power parity - $533 million (1999 est.)
GDP - real growth rate: 4.6% (1999 est.)
GDP - per capita: purchasing power parity - $8,200 (1999 est.)
GDP - composition by sector:
agriculture: 4%
industry: 12.5%
services: 83.5% (1996 est.)
Population below poverty line: NA%
Household income or consumption by percentage share:
lowest 10%: NA%
highest 10%: NA%
Inflation rate (consumer prices): 1.6% (1999 est.)

Antigua and Barbuda (continued)

Labor force: 30,000
Labor force - by occupation: commerce and services 82%, agriculture 11%, industry 7% (1983)
Unemployment rate: 7% (1999 est.)
Budget:
revenues: $122.6 million
expenditures: $141.2 million, including capital expenditures of $17.3 million (1997 est.)
Industries: tourism, construction, light manufacturing (clothing, alcohol, household appliances)
Industrial production growth rate: 6% (1997 est.)
Electricity - production: 95 million kWh (1999)
Electricity - production by source:
fossil fuel: 100%
hydro: 0%
nuclear: 0%
other: 0% (1999)
Electricity - consumption: 88.4 million kWh (1999)
Electricity - exports: 0 kWh (1999)
Electricity - imports: 0 kWh (1999)
Agriculture - products: cotton, fruits, vegetables, bananas, coconuts, cucumbers, mangoes, sugarcane; livestock
Exports: $38 million (1998)
Exports - commodities: petroleum products 48%, manufactures 23%, machinery and transport equipment 17%, food and live animals 4%, other 8%
Exports - partners: OECS 26%, Barbados 15%, Guyana 4%, Trinidad and Tobago 2%, US 0.3%
Imports: $330 million (1998)
Imports - commodities: food and live animals, machinery and transport equipment, manufactures, chemicals, oil
Imports - partners: US 27%, UK 16%, Canada 4%, OECS 3%
Debt - external: $357 million (1998)
Economic aid - recipient: $2.3 million (1995)
Currency: East Caribbean dollar (XCD)
Currency code: XCD
Exchange rates: East Caribbean dollars per US dollar - 2.7000 (fixed rate since 1976)
Fiscal year: 1 April - 31 March

Communications

Telephones - main lines in use: 28,000 (1996)
Telephones - mobile cellular: 1,300 (1996)
Telephone system:
general assessment: NA
domestic: good automatic telephone system
international: 1 coaxial submarine cable; satellite earth station - 1 Intelsat (Atlantic Ocean); tropospheric scatter to Saba (Netherlands Antilles) and Guadeloupe
Radio broadcast stations: AM 4, FM 2, shortwave 0 (1998)
Radios: 36,000 (1997)
Television broadcast stations: 2 (1997)
Televisions: 31,000 (1997)
Internet country code: .ag
Internet Service Providers (ISPs): 16 (2000)
Internet users: 8,000 (2000)

Transportation

Railways:
total: 77 km
narrow gauge: 64 km 0.760-m gauge; 13 km 0.610-m gauge (used almost exclusively for handling sugarcane)
Highways:
total: 1,165 km
paved: 384 km
unpaved: 781 km (1999 est.)
Waterways: none
Ports and harbors: Saint John's
Merchant marine:
total: 681 ships (1,000 GRT or over) totaling 4,070,390 GRT/5,289,904 DWT
ships by type: bulk 15, cargo 424, chemical tanker 10, combination bulk 4, container 176, liquefied gas 4, multi-functional large-load carrier 6, petroleum tanker 2, refrigerated cargo 11, roll on/roll off 29
note: includes some foreign-owned ships registered here as a flag of convenience: Cyprus 2, Germany 4, Slovenia 2 (2000 est.)
Airports: 3 (2000 est.)
Airports - with paved runways:
total: 2
2,438 to 3,047 m: 1
under 914 m: 1 (2000 est.)
Airports - with unpaved runways:
total: 1
under 914 m: 1 (2000 est.)

Military

Military branches: Royal Antigua and Barbuda Defense Force, Royal Antigua and Barbuda Police Force (includes Coast Guard)
Military expenditures - dollar figure: $NA
Military expenditures - percent of GDP: NA%

Transnational Issues

Disputes - international: none
Illicit drugs: considered a minor transshipment point for narcotics bound for the US and Europe; more significant as a drug-money-laundering center

Arctic Ocean

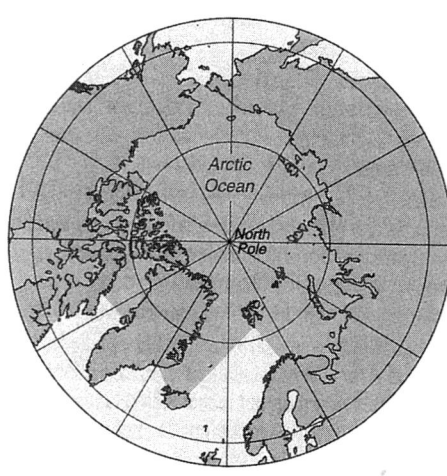

Introduction

Background: The Arctic Ocean is the smallest of the world's five oceans (after the Pacific Ocean, Atlantic Ocean, Indian Ocean, and the recently delimited Southern Ocean). The Northwest Passage (US and Canada) and Northern Sea Route (Norway and Russia) are two important seasonal waterways. A sparse network of air, ocean, river, and land routes circumscribes the Arctic Ocean.

Geography

Location: body of water between Europe, Asia, and North America, mostly north of the Arctic Circle
Geographic coordinates: 90 00 N, 0 00 E
Map references: Arctic Region
Area:
total: 14.056 million sq km
note: includes Baffin Bay, Barents Sea, Beaufort Sea, Chukchi Sea, East Siberian Sea, Greenland Sea, Hudson Bay, Hudson Strait, Kara Sea, Laptev Sea, Northwest Passage, and other tributary water bodies
Area - comparative: slightly less than 1.5 times the size of the US
Coastline: 45,389 km
Climate: polar climate characterized by persistent cold and relatively narrow annual temperature ranges; winters characterized by continuous darkness, cold and stable weather conditions, and clear skies; summers characterized by continuous daylight, damp and foggy weather, and weak cyclones with rain or snow
Terrain: central surface covered by a perennial drifting polar icepack that averages about 3 meters in thickness, although pressure ridges may be three times that size; clockwise drift pattern in the Beaufort Gyral Stream, but nearly straight-line movement from the New Siberian Islands (Russia) to Denmark Strait (between Greenland and Iceland); the icepack is surrounded by open seas during the summer, but more than doubles in size during the winter and

Arctic Ocean (continued)

extends to the encircling landmasses; the ocean floor is about 50% continental shelf (highest percentage of any ocean) with the remainder a central basin interrupted by three submarine ridges (Alpha Cordillera, Nansen Cordillera, and Lomonosov Ridge)
Elevation extremes:
lowest point: Fram Basin -4,665 m
highest point: sea level 0 m
Natural resources: sand and gravel aggregates, placer deposits, polymetallic nodules, oil and gas fields, fish, marine mammals (seals and whales)
Natural hazards: ice islands occasionally break away from northern Ellesmere Island; icebergs calved from glaciers in western Greenland and extreme northeastern Canada; permafrost in islands; virtually ice locked from October to June; ships subject to superstructure icing from October to May
Environment - current issues: endangered marine species include walruses and whales; fragile ecosystem slow to change and slow to recover from disruptions or damage; thinning polar icepack
Geography - note: major chokepoint is the southern Chukchi Sea (northern access to the Pacific Ocean via the Bering Strait); strategic location between North America and Russia; shortest marine link between the extremes of eastern and western Russia; floating research stations operated by the US and Russia; maximum snow cover in March or April about 20 to 50 centimeters over the frozen ocean; snow cover lasts about 10 months

Economy

Economy - overview: Economic activity is limited to the exploitation of natural resources, including petroleum, natural gas, fish, and seals.

Transportation

Ports and harbors: Churchill (Canada), Murmansk (Russia), Prudhoe Bay (US)
Transportation - note: sparse network of air, ocean, river, and land routes; the Northwest Passage (North America) and Northern Sea Route (Eurasia) are important seasonal waterways

Transnational Issues

Disputes - international: some maritime disputes (see littoral states)

Argentina

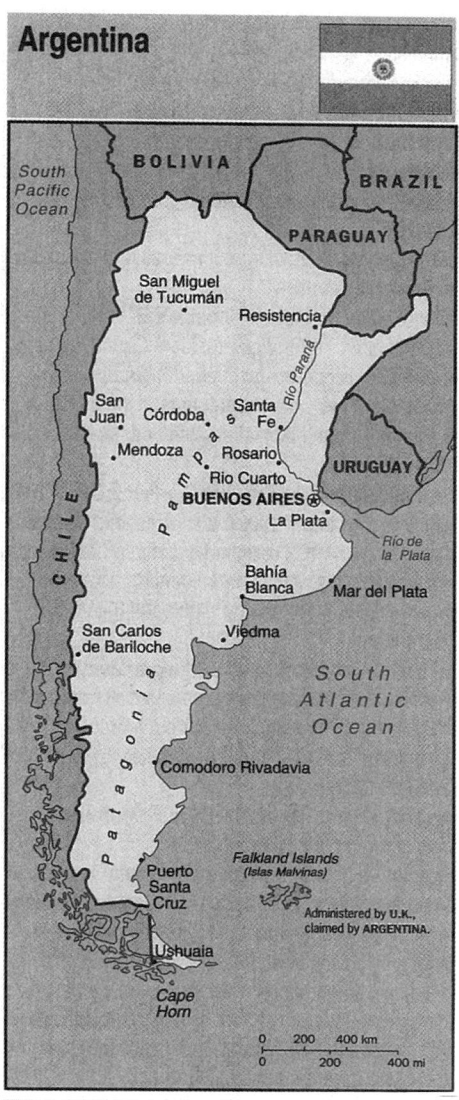

Introduction

Background: Following independence from Spain in 1816, Argentina experienced periods of internal political conflict between conservatives and liberals and between civilian and military factions. After World War II, a long period of Peronist dictatorship was followed by a military junta that took power in 1976. Democracy returned in 1983, and numerous elections since then have underscored Argentina's progress in democratic consolidation.

Geography

Location: Southern South America, bordering the South Atlantic Ocean, between Chile and Uruguay
Geographic coordinates: 34 00 S, 64 00 W
Map references: South America
Area:
total: 2,766,890 sq km
land: 2,736,690 sq km
water: 30,200 sq km
Area - comparative: slightly less than three-tenths the size of the US
Land boundaries:
total: 9,665 km
border countries: Bolivia 832 km, Brazil 1,224 km, Chile 5,150 km, Paraguay 1,880 km, Uruguay 579 km
Coastline: 4,989 km
Maritime claims:
contiguous zone: 24 NM
continental shelf: 200 NM or to the edge of the continental margin
exclusive economic zone: 200 NM
territorial sea: 12 NM
Climate: mostly temperate; arid in southeast; subantarctic in southwest
Terrain: rich plains of the Pampas in northern half, flat to rolling plateau of Patagonia in south, rugged Andes along western border
Elevation extremes:
lowest point: Salinas Chicas -40 m (located on Peninsula Valdes)
highest point: Cerro Aconcagua 6,960 m
Natural resources: fertile plains of the Pampas, lead, zinc, tin, copper, iron ore, manganese, petroleum, uranium
Land use:
arable land: 9%
permanent crops: 1%
permanent pastures: 52%
forests and woodland: 19%
other: 19% (1993 est.)
Irrigated land: 17,000 sq km (1993 est.)
Natural hazards: San Miguel de Tucuman and Mendoza areas in the Andes subject to earthquakes; pamperos are violent windstorms that can strike the Pampas and northeast; heavy flooding
Environment - current issues: environmental problems (urban and rural) typical of an industrializing economy such as soil degradation, desertification, air pollution, and water pollution
note: Argentina is a world leader in setting voluntary greenhouse gas targets
Environment - international agreements:
party to: Antarctic-Environmental Protocol, Antarctic-Marine Living Resources, Antarctic Seals, Antarctic Treaty, Biodiversity, Climate Change, Desertification, Endangered Species, Environmental Modification, Hazardous Wastes, Law of the Sea, Marine Dumping, Nuclear Test Ban, Ozone Layer Protection, Ship Pollution, Wetlands, Whaling
signed, but not ratified: Climate Change-Kyoto Protocol, Marine Life Conservation
Geography - note: second-largest country in South America (after Brazil); strategic location relative to sea lanes between South Atlantic and South Pacific Oceans (Strait of Magellan, Beagle Channel, Drake Passage)

People

Population: 37,384,816 (July 2001 est.)
Age structure:
0-14 years: 26.54% (male 5,077,593; female 4,842,811)
15-64 years: 63.04% (male 11,795,282; female 11,773,855)

Argentina (continued)

65 years and over: 10.42% (male 1,609,672; female 2,285,603) (2001 est.)
Population growth rate: 1.15% (2001 est.)
Birth rate: 18.41 births/1,000 population (2001 est.)
Death rate: 7.58 deaths/1,000 population (2001 est.)
Net migration rate: 0.64 migrant(s)/1,000 population (2001 est.)
Sex ratio:
at birth: 1.05 male(s)/female
under 15 years: 1.05 male(s)/female
15-64 years: 1 male(s)/female
65 years and over: 0.7 male(s)/female
total population: 0.98 male(s)/female (2001 est.)
Infant mortality rate: 17.75 deaths/1,000 live births (2001 est.)
Life expectancy at birth:
total population: 75.26 years
male: 71.88 years
female: 78.82 years (2001 est.)
Total fertility rate: 2.44 children born/woman (2001 est.)
HIV/AIDS - adult prevalence rate: 0.69% (1999 est.)
HIV/AIDS - people living with HIV/AIDS: 130,000 (1999 est.)
HIV/AIDS - deaths: 1,800 (1999 est.)
Nationality:
noun: Argentine(s)
adjective: Argentine
Ethnic groups: white (mostly Spanish and Italian) 97%, mestizo, Amerindian, or other nonwhite groups 3%
Religions: nominally Roman Catholic 92% (less than 20% practicing), Protestant 2%, Jewish 2%, other 4%
Languages: Spanish (official), English, Italian, German, French
Literacy:
definition: age 15 and over can read and write
total population: 96.2%
male: 96.2%
female: 96.2% (1995 est.)

Government

Country name:
conventional long form: Argentine Republic
conventional short form: Argentina
local long form: Republica Argentina
local short form: Argentina
Government type: republic
Capital: Buenos Aires
Administrative divisions: 23 provinces (provincias, singular - provincia), and 1 autonomous city* (distrito federal); Buenos Aires; Buenos Aires Capital Federal*; Catamarca; Chaco; Chubut; Cordoba; Corrientes; Entre Rios; Formosa; Jujuy; La Pampa; La Rioja; Mendoza; Misiones; Neuquen; Rio Negro; Salta; San Juan; San Luis; Santa Cruz; Santa Fe; Santiago del Estero; Tierra del Fuego, Antartica e Islas del Atlantico Sur; Tucuman
note: the US does not recognize any claims to Antarctica
Independence: 9 July 1816 (from Spain)
National holiday: Revolution Day, 25 May (1810)
Constitution: 1 May 1853; revised August 1994
Legal system: mixture of US and West European legal systems; has not accepted compulsory ICJ jurisdiction
Suffrage: 18 years of age; universal and mandatory
Executive branch:
chief of state: President Fernando DE LA RUA (since 10 December 1999); Vice President Carlos "Chacho" ALVAREZ resigned 6 October 2000 and a replacement has not yet been named; note - the president is both the chief of state and head of government
head of government: President Fernando DE LA RUA (since 10 December 1999); Vice President Carlos "Chacho" ALVAREZ resigned 6 October 2000 and a replacement has not yet been named; note - the president is both the chief of state and head of government
cabinet: Cabinet appointed by the president
elections: president and vice president elected on the same ticket by popular vote for four-year terms; election last held 24 October 1999 (next to be held NA October 2003)
election results: Fernando DE LA RUA elected president; percent of vote - 48.5%
Legislative branch: bicameral National Congress or Congreso Nacional consists of the Senate (72 seats; formerly, three members appointed by each of the provincial legislatures; presently transitioning to one-third of the members being elected every two years to six-year terms) and the Chamber of Deputies (257 seats; one-half of the members elected every two years to four-year terms)
elections: Senate - transition phase will begin in the 2001 elections when all seats will be fully contested; winners will randomly draw to determine whether they will serve a two-year, four-year, or full six-year term, beginning a rotating cycle renovating one-third of the body every two years; Chamber of Deputies - last held 24 October 1999 (next to be held NA October 2001)
election results: Senate - percent of vote by bloc or party - NA%; seats by bloc or party - Peronist 40, UCR 20, Frepaso 1, other 11; Chamber of Deputies - percent of vote by bloc or party - NA%; seats by bloc or party - Alliance 124 (UCR 85, Frepaso 36, others 3), Peronist 101, AR 12, other 20
Judicial branch: Supreme Court or Corte Suprema (the nine Supreme Court judges are appointed by the president with approval by the Senate)
Political parties and leaders: Action for the Republic or AR [Domingo CAVALLO]; Front for a Country in Solidarity or Frepaso (a four-party coalition) [Carlos ALVAREZ]; Justicialist Party or PJ [Carlos Saul MENEM] (Peronist umbrella political organization); Radical Civic Union or UCR [Raul ALFONSIN]; several provincial parties
Political pressure groups and leaders: Argentine Association of Pharmaceutical Labs (CILFA); Argentine Industrial Union (manufacturers' association); Argentine Rural Society (large landowners' association); business organizations; General Confederation of Labor or CGT (Peronist-leaning umbrella labor organization); Peronist-dominated labor movement; Roman Catholic Church; students
International organization participation: AfDB, Australia Group, BCIE, BIS, CCC, ECLAC, FAO, G-6, G-11, G-15, G-19, G-24, G-77, IADB, IAEA, IBRD, ICAO, ICC, ICFTU, ICRM, IDA, IFAD, IFC, IFRCS, IHO, ILO, IMF, IMO, Inmarsat, Intelsat, Interpol, IOC, IOM, ISO, ITU, LAES, LAIA, Mercosur, MINURSO, MIPONUH, MTCR, NSG, OAS, OPANAL, OPCW, PCA, RG, UN, UNCTAD, UNESCO, UNFICYP, UNHCR, UNIDO, UNIKOM, UNMEE, UNMIBH, UNMIK, UNMOP, UNTSO, UNU, UPU, WCL, WFTU, WHO, WIPO, WMO, WToO, WTrO, ZC
Diplomatic representation in the US:
chief of mission: Ambassador Guillermo Enrique GONZALEZ
chancery: 1600 New Hampshire Avenue NW, Washington, DC 20009
telephone: [1] (202) 238-6400
FAX: [1] (202) 332-3171
consulate(s) general: Atlanta, Chicago, Houston, Los Angeles, Miami, New York
Diplomatic representation from the US:
chief of mission: Ambassador James D. WALSH
embassy: Avenida Colombia 4300, 1425 Buenos Aires
mailing address: international mail: use street address; APO address: Unit 4334, APO AA 34034
telephone: [54] (11) 4777-4533/4534
FAX: [54] (11) 4511-4997
Flag description: three equal horizontal bands of light blue (top), white, and light blue; centered in the white band is a radiant yellow sun with a human face known as the Sun of May

Economy

Economy - overview: Argentina benefits from rich natural resources, a highly literate population, an export-oriented agricultural sector, and a diversified industrial base. However, when President Carlos MENEM took office in 1989, the country had piled up huge external debts, inflation had reached 200% per month, and output was plummeting. To combat the economic crisis, the government embarked on a path of trade liberalization, deregulation, and privatization. In 1991, it implemented radical monetary reforms which pegged the peso to the US dollar and limited the growth in the monetary base by law to the growth in reserves. Inflation fell sharply in subsequent years. In 1995, the Mexican peso crisis produced capital flight, the loss of banking system deposits, and a severe, but short-lived, recession; a series of reforms to bolster the domestic banking system followed. Real GDP growth recovered strongly, reaching 8% in 1997. In

Argentina (continued)

1998, international financial turmoil caused by Russia's problems and increasing investor anxiety over Brazil produced the highest domestic interest rates in more than three years, halving the growth rate of the economy. Conditions worsened in 1999 with GDP falling by 3%. President Fernando DE LA RUA, who took office in December 1999, sponsored tax increases and spending cuts to reduce the deficit, which had ballooned to 2.5% of GDP in 1999. Growth in 2000 was a disappointing 0.8%, as both domestic and foreign investors remained skeptical of the government's ability to pay debts and maintain its fixed exchange rate with the US dollar. One bright spot at the start of 2001 was the IMF's offer of $13.7 billion in support.

GDP: purchasing power parity - $476 billion (2000 est.)
GDP - real growth rate: 0.8% (2000 est.)
GDP - per capita: purchasing power parity - $12,900 (2000 est.)
GDP - composition by sector:
agriculture: 6%
industry: 32%
services: 62% (2000 est.)
Population below poverty line: 37% (1999 est.)
Household income or consumption by percentage share:
lowest 10%: NA%
highest 10%: NA%
Inflation rate (consumer prices): -0.9% (2000 est.)
Labor force: 15 million (1999)
Labor force - by occupation: agriculture NA%, industry NA%, services NA%
Unemployment rate: 15% (December 2000)
Budget:
revenues: $44 billion
expenditures: $48 billion, including capital expenditures of $NA billion (2000 est.)
Industries: food processing, motor vehicles, consumer durables, textiles, chemicals and petrochemicals, printing, metallurgy, steel
Industrial production growth rate: 1% (2000 est.)
Electricity - production: 77.087 billion kWh (1999)
Electricity - production by source:
fossil fuel: 60.3%
hydro: 30.7%
nuclear: 8.75%
other: 0.25% (1999)
Electricity - consumption: 77.111 billion kWh (1999)
Electricity - exports: 1.08 billion kWh (1999)
Electricity - imports: 6.5 billion kWh (1999)
Agriculture - products: sunflower seeds, lemons, soybeans, grapes, corn, tobacco, peanuts, tea, wheat; livestock
Exports: $26.5 billion (f.o.b., 2000 est.)
Exports - commodities: edible oils, fuels and energy, cereals, feed, motor vehicles
Exports - partners: Brazil 24%, EU 21%, US 11% (1999 est.)
Imports: $25.2 billion (f.o.b., 2000 est.)
Imports - commodities: machinery and equipment, motor vehicles, chemicals, metal manufactures, plastics
Imports - partners: EU 28%, US 22%, Brazil 21% (1999 est.)
Debt - external: $154 billion (2000 est.)
Economic aid - recipient: IMF offer of $13.7 billion (January 2001)
Currency: Argentine peso (ARS)
Currency code: ARS
Exchange rates: Argentine pesos per US dollar - 1.000 (fixed rate pegged to the US dollar)
Fiscal year: calendar year

Communications

Telephones - main lines in use: 7.5 million (1998)
Telephones - mobile cellular: 3 million (December 1999)
Telephone system:
general assessment: by opening the telecommunications market to competition and foreign investment with the "Telecommunications Liberalization Plan of 1998", Argentina encouraged the growth of modern telecommunication technology; fiber-optic cable trunk lines are being installed between all major cities; the major networks are entirely digital and the availability of telephone service is being improved; however, telephone density is presently minimal, and making telephone service universally available will take some time
domestic: microwave radio relay, fiber-optic cable, and a domestic satellite system with 40 earth stations serve the trunk network; more than 110,000 pay telephones are installed and mobile telephone use is rapidly expanding
international: satellite earth stations - 8 Intelsat (Atlantic Ocean); Atlantis II and Unisur submarine cables; two international gateways near Buenos Aires (1999)
Radio broadcast stations: AM 260 (including 10 inactive stations), FM NA (probably more than 1,000, mostly unlicensed), shortwave 6 (1998)
Radios: 24.3 million (1997)
Television broadcast stations: 42 (plus 444 repeaters) (1997)
Televisions: 7.95 million (1997)
Internet country code: .ar
Internet Service Providers (ISPs): 33 (2000)
Internet users: 900,000 (2000)

Transportation

Railways:
total: 38,326 km (160 km electrified)
broad gauge: 24,481 km 1.676-m gauge (134 km electrified)
standard gauge: 2,765 km 1.435-m gauge (26 km electrified)
narrow gauge: 11,080 km 1.000-m gauge (1999)
Highways:
total: 215,434 km
paved: 63,553 km (including 734 km of expressways)
unpaved: 151,881 km (1998 est.)
Waterways: 10,950 km
Pipelines: crude oil 4,090 km; petroleum products 2,900 km; natural gas 9,918 km
Ports and harbors: Bahia Blanca, Buenos Aires, Comodoro Rivadavia, Concepcion del Uruguay, La Plata, Mar del Plata, Necochea, Rio Gallegos, Rosario, Santa Fe, Ushuaia
Merchant marine:
total: 26 ships (1,000 GRT or over) totaling 185,355 GRT/281,475 DWT
ships by type: cargo 9, petroleum tanker 11, railcar carrier 1, refrigerated cargo 2, roll on/roll off 1, short-sea passenger 2 (2000 est.)
Airports: 1,359 (2000 est.)
Airports - with paved runways:
total: 143
over 3,047 m: 4
2,438 to 3,047 m: 25
1,524 to 2,437 m: 57
914 to 1,523 m: 48
under 914 m: 9 (2000 est.)
Airports - with unpaved runways:
total: 1,216
over 3,047 m: 2
2,438 to 3,047 m: 2
1,524 to 2,437 m: 56
914 to 1,523 m: 601
under 914 m: 555 (2000 est.)

Military

Military branches: Argentine Army, Navy of the Argentine Republic (includes Naval Aviation, Marines, and Coast Guard), Argentine Air Force, National Gendarmerie, National Aeronautical Police Force
Military manpower - military age: 20 years of age
Military manpower - availability:
males age 15-49: 9,404,434 (2001 est.)
Military manpower - fit for military service:
males age 15-49: 7,625,425 (2001 est.)
Military manpower - reaching military age annually:
males: 335,085 (2001 est.)
Military expenditures - dollar figure: $4.3 billion (FY99)
Military expenditures - percent of GDP: 1.3% (FY99)

Transnational Issues

Disputes - international: claims UK-administered Falkland Islands (Islas Malvinas); claims UK-administered South Georgia and the South Sandwich Islands; territorial claim in Antarctica partially overlaps British and Chilean claims
Illicit drugs: use as a transshipment country for cocaine headed for Europe and the US; increasing use as a money-laundering center; domestic consumption of drugs in urban centers is increasing

Armenia

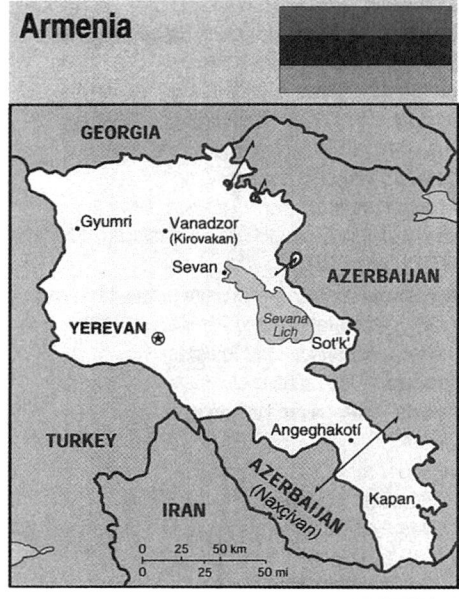

Introduction

Background: An Orthodox Christian country, Armenia was incorporated into Russia in 1828 and the USSR in 1920. Armenian leaders remain preoccupied by the long conflict with Azerbaijan over Nagorno-Karabakh, a primarily Armenian-populated exclave, assigned to Soviet Azerbaijan in the 1920s by Moscow. Armenia and Azerbaijan began fighting over the exclave in 1988; the struggle escalated after both countries attained independence from the Soviet Union in 1991. By May 1994, when a cease-fire took hold, Armenian forces held not only Nagorno-Karabakh but also a significant portion of Azerbaijan proper. The economies of both sides have been hurt by their inability to make substantial progress toward a peaceful resolution.

Geography

Location: Southwestern Asia, east of Turkey
Geographic coordinates: 40 00 N, 45 00 E
Map references: Commonwealth of Independent States
Area:
total: 29,800 sq km
land: 28,400 sq km
water: 1,400 sq km
Area - comparative: slightly smaller than Maryland
Land boundaries:
total: 1,254 km
border countries: Azerbaijan-proper 566 km, Azerbaijan-Naxcivan exclave 221 km, Georgia 164 km, Iran 35 km, Turkey 268 km
Coastline: 0 km (landlocked)
Maritime claims: none (landlocked)
Climate: highland continental, hot summers, cold winters
Terrain: Armenian Highland with mountains; little forest land; fast flowing rivers; good soil in Aras River valley
Elevation extremes:
lowest point: Debed River 400 m
highest point: Aragats Lerr 4,095 m
Natural resources: small deposits of gold, copper, molybdenum, zinc, alumina
Land use:
arable land: 17%
permanent crops: 3%
permanent pastures: 24%
forests and woodland: 15%
other: 41% (1993 est.)
Irrigated land: 2,870 sq km (1993 est.)
Natural hazards: occasionally severe earthquakes; droughts
Environment - current issues: soil pollution from toxic chemicals such as DDT; energy blockade, the result of conflict with Azerbaijan, has led to deforestation when citizens scavenged for firewood; pollution of Hrazdan (Razdan) and Aras Rivers; the draining of Sevana Lich (Lake Sevan), a result of its use as a source for hydropower, threatens drinking water supplies; restart of Metsamor nuclear power plant without adequate (IAEA-recommended) safety and backup systems
Environment - international agreements:
party to: Air Pollution, Biodiversity, Climate Change, Desertification, Hazardous Wastes, Marine Dumping, Nuclear Test Ban, Ozone Layer Protection, Ship Pollution, Wetlands
signed, but not ratified: Air Pollution-Persistent Organic Pollutants
Geography - note: landlocked

People

Population: 3,336,100 (July 2001 est.)
Age structure:
0-14 years: 23.23% (male 394,194; female 380,911)
15-64 years: 67.04% (male 1,094,646; female 1,141,760)
65 years and over: 9.73% (male 135,477; female 189,112) (2001 est.)
Population growth rate: -0.21% (2001 est.)
Birth rate: 11.47 births/1,000 population (2001 est.)
Death rate: 9.74 deaths/1,000 population (2001 est.)
Net migration rate: -3.87 migrant(s)/1,000 population (2001 est.)
Sex ratio:
at birth: 1.05 male(s)/female
under 15 years: 1.03 male(s)/female
15-64 years: 0.96 male(s)/female
65 years and over: 0.72 male(s)/female
total population: 0.95 male(s)/female (2001 est.)
Infant mortality rate: 41.27 deaths/1,000 live births (2001 est.)
Life expectancy at birth:
total population: 66.49 years
male: 62.12 years
female: 71.08 years (2001 est.)
Total fertility rate: 1.5 children born/woman (2001 est.)
HIV/AIDS - adult prevalence rate: 0.01% (1999 est.)
HIV/AIDS - people living with HIV/AIDS: less than 500 (1999 est.)
HIV/AIDS - deaths: less than 100 (1999 est.)
Nationality:
noun: Armenian(s)
adjective: Armenian
Ethnic groups: Armenian 93%, Azeri 3%, Russian 2%, other (mostly Yezidi Kurds) 2% (1989)
note: as of the end of 1993, virtually all Azeris had emigrated from Armenia
Religions: Armenian Orthodox 94%
Languages: Armenian 96%, Russian 2%, other 2%
Literacy:
definition: age 15 and over can read and write
total population: 99%
male: 99%
female: 98% (1989 est.)

Government

Country name:
conventional long form: Republic of Armenia
conventional short form: Armenia
local long form: Hayastani Hanrapetut'yun
local short form: Hayastan
former: Armenian Soviet Socialist Republic; Armenian Republic
Government type: republic
Capital: Yerevan
Administrative divisions: 10 provinces (marzer, singular - marz) and 1 city* (k'aghak'ner, singular - k'aghak'); Aragatsotn, Ararat, Armavir, Geghark'unik', Kotayk', Lorri, Shirak, Syunik', Tavush, Vayots' Dzor, Yerevan*
Independence: 21 September 1991 (from Soviet Union)
National holiday: Independence Day, 21 September (1991)
Constitution: adopted by nationwide referendum 5 July 1995
Legal system: based on civil law system
Suffrage: 18 years of age; universal
Executive branch:
chief of state: President Robert KOCHARIAN (since 30 March 1998)
head of government: Prime Minister Andranik MARKARYAN (since 12 May 2000)
cabinet: Council of Ministers appointed by the prime minister
elections: president elected by popular vote for a five-year term; special election last held 30 March 1998 (next to be held NA March 2003); prime minister appointed by the president
election results: Robert KOCHARIAN elected president; percent of vote - Robert KOCHARIAN 59.5%, Karen DEMIRCHYAN 40.5%

Armenia (continued)

Legislative branch: unicameral National Assembly (Parliament) or Azgayin Zhoghov (131 seats; members serve four-year terms)
elections: last held 30 May 1999 (next to be held in the spring of 2003)
election results: percent of vote by party - NA%; seats by party - unity bloc 61 (Republican Party 41, People's Party of Armenia 20), Stability Group (independent Armenian deputies who have formed a bloc) 21, ACP 10, ARF (Dashnak) 8, Law and Unity Party 7, NDU 6, Law-Governed Party 6, independents 10, unfilled 2; note - seats by party change frequently
Judicial branch: Supreme Court; Constitutional Court
Political parties and leaders: Armenia Party [Myasnik ALKHASYAN]; Armenian Communist Party or ACP [Vladimir DARBINYAN]; Armenian Revolutionary Federation ("Dashnak" Party) or ARF [Hrant MARKARYAN]; Christian Democratic Union or CDU [Azat ARSHAKYN, chairman]; Democratic Liberal Party [Ramkavar AZATAKAN, chairman]; Free Armenian's Mission [Ruben MNATSANIAN, chairman]; Law and Unity Party [Artashes GEGAMIAN, chairman]; Law-Governed Party [Artur BAGDASARIAN, chairman]; Mission Party [Artush PAPOIAN, chairman]; National Democratic Union or NDU [Vazgen MANUKIAN]; National State Party [Samvel SHAGINIAN]; Pan-Armenian National Movement or PANM [Vano SIRADEGHYAN]; People's Party of Armenia [Stepan DEMIRCHYAN]; Republican Party or RPA [Andranik MARKARYAN]; Shamiram Women's Movement or SWM [Gayane SARUKHYAN]; Social Democratic (Hnchakian) Party [Ernst SOGOMONYAN]; Stability Group [Vartan AYVAZIAN, chairman]; Union of National Self-Determination or NSDU [Paruir HAIRIKIAN, chairman]; Unity Bloc [Stepan DEMIRCHIAN and Andranik MARKARYAN] (a coalition of the Republican Party and People's Party of Armenia)
Political pressure groups and leaders: NA
International organization participation: BSEC, CCC, CE, CIS, EAPC, EBRD, ECE, ESCAP, FAO, IAEA, IBRD, ICAO, ICRM, IDA, IFAD, IFC, IFRCS, ILO, IMF, Intelsat, Interpol, IOC, IOM, ISO, ITU, NAM (observer), OPCW, OSCE, PFP, UN, UNCTAD, UNESCO, UNIDO, UPU, WFTU, WHO, WIPO, WMO, WToO, WTrO (observer)
Diplomatic representation in the US:
chief of mission: Ambassador Arman KIRAKOSIAN
chancery: 2225 R Street NW, Washington, DC 20008
telephone: [1] (202) 319-1976
FAX: [1] (202) 319-2982
consulate(s) general: Los Angeles
Diplomatic representation from the US:
chief of mission: Ambassador Michael C. LEMMON
embassy: 18 Marshal Bagramian Avenue, Yerevan
mailing address: American Embassy Yerevan, Department of State, Washington, DC 20521-7020
telephone: [374] (2) 52-16-11
FAX: [374] (2) 151-550
Flag description: three equal horizontal bands of red (top), blue, and orange

Economy

Economy - overview: Under the old Soviet central planning system, Armenia had developed a modern industrial sector, supplying machine tools, textiles, and other manufactured goods to sister republics in exchange for raw materials and energy. Since the implosion of the USSR in December 1991, Armenia has switched to small-scale agriculture away from the large agroindustrial complexes of the Soviet era. The agricultural sector has long-term needs for more investment and updated technology. The privatization of industry has been at a slower pace, but has been given renewed emphasis by the current administration. Armenia is a food importer, and its mineral deposits (gold, bauxite) are small. The ongoing conflict with Azerbaijan over the ethnic Armenian-dominated region of Nagorno-Karabakh and the breakup of the centrally directed economic system of the former Soviet Union contributed to a severe economic decline in the early 1990s. By 1994, however, the Armenian Government had launched an ambitious IMF-sponsored economic program that has resulted in positive growth rates in 1995-2000. Armenia also managed to slash inflation and to privatize most small- and medium-sized enterprises. The chronic energy shortages Armenia suffered in recent years have been largely offset by the energy supplied by one of its nuclear power plants at Metsamor. Armenia's severe trade imbalance, importing three times its exports, has been offset somewhat by international aid, domestic restructuring of the economy, and foreign direct investment.
GDP: purchasing power parity - $10 billion (2000 est.)
GDP - real growth rate: 5% (2000 est.)
GDP - per capita: purchasing power parity - $3,000 (2000 est.)
GDP - composition by sector:
agriculture: 40%
industry: 25%
services: 35% (1999 est.)
Population below poverty line: 45% (1999 est.)
Household income or consumption by percentage share:
lowest 10%: NA%
highest 10%: NA%
Inflation rate (consumer prices): 1% (1999 est.)
Labor force: 1.5 million (1999)
Labor force - by occupation: agriculture 55%, services 25%, industry 20% (1999 est.)
Unemployment rate: 20% (1998 est.)
note: official rate is 9.3% for 1998
Budget:
revenues: $360 million
expenditures: $566 million, including capital expenditures of $NA (1999 est.)
Industries: metal-cutting machine tools, forging-pressing machines, electric motors, tires, knitted wear, hosiery, shoes, silk fabric, chemicals, trucks, instruments, microelectronics, gem cutting, jewelry manufacturing, software development, brandy
Industrial production growth rate: 5% (2000 est.)
Electricity - production: 6.668 billion kWh (1999)
Electricity - production by source:
fossil fuel: 45.56%
hydro: 23.25%
nuclear: 31.19%
other: 0% (1999)
Electricity - consumption: 6.201 billion kWh (1999)
Electricity - exports: 0 kWh (1999)
Electricity - imports: 0 kWh (1999)
Agriculture - products: fruit (especially grapes), vegetables; livestock
Exports: $284 million (f.o.b., 2000 est.)
Exports - commodities: diamonds, scrap metal, machinery and equipment, brandy, copper ore
Exports - partners: Belgium 36%, Iran 15%, Russia 14%, US 7%, Turkmenistan, Georgia (1999)
Imports: $913 million (f.o.b., 2000 est.)
Imports - commodities: natural gas, petroleum, tobacco products, foodstuffs, diamonds
Imports - partners: Russia 17%, US 11%, Belgium 11%, Iran 10%, UK, Turkey (1999)
Debt - external: $836 million (January 2001)
Economic aid - recipient: $245.5 million (1995)
Currency: dram (AMD)
Currency code: AMD
Exchange rates: drams per US dollar - 554.29 (1 February 2001), 539.53 (2000), 535.06 (1999), 504.92 (1998), 490.85 (1997), 414.04 (1996)
Fiscal year: calendar year

Communications

Telephones - main lines in use: 568,000 (1997)
Telephones - mobile cellular: 6,220 (1997)
Telephone system:
general assessment: system inadequate; now 90% privately owned and undergoing modernization and expansion
domestic: the majority of subscribers and the most modern equipment are in Yerevan (this includes paging and mobile cellular service)
international: Yerevan is connected to the Trans-Asia-Europe fiber-optic cable through Iran; additional international service is available by microwave radio relay and landline connections to the other countries of the Commonwealth of Independent States and through the Moscow international switch and by satellite to the rest of the world; satellite earth stations - 1 Intelsat
Radio broadcast stations: AM 9, FM 6, shortwave 1 (1998)
Radios: 850,000 (1997)
Television broadcast stations: 4 (1998)
Televisions: 825,000 (1997)
Internet country code: .am
Internet Service Providers (ISPs): 1 (1999)
Internet users: 30,000 (2000)

Armenia (continued)

Transportation

Railways:
total: 852 km in common carrier service; does not include industrial lines
broad gauge: 852 km 1.520-m gauge (779 km electrified) (2001)
Highways:
total: 8,431 km ()
paved: NA
unpaved: NA (1997)
Waterways: NA km
Pipelines: natural gas 900 km (1991)
Ports and harbors: none
Airports: 7 (2000 est.)
Airports - with unpaved runways:
total: 7
over 3,047 m: 1
1,524 to 2,437 m: 2
914 to 1,523 m: 3
under 914 m: 1 (2000 est.)

Military

Military branches: Army, Air Force and Air Defense Aviation, Air Defense Force, Security Forces (internal and border troops)
Military manpower - military age: 18 years of age
Military manpower - availability:
males age 15-49: 905,154 (2001 est.)
Military manpower - fit for military service:
males age 15-49: 715,734 (2001 est.)
Military manpower - reaching military age annually:
males: 34,998 (2001 est.)
Military expenditures - dollar figure: $75 million (FY99)
Military expenditures - percent of GDP: 4% (FY99)

Transnational Issues

Disputes - international: Armenia supports ethnic Armenians in the Nagorno-Karabakh region of Azerbaijan in the longstanding, separatist conflict against the Azerbaijani Government; traditional demands regarding former Armenian lands in Turkey have subsided
Illicit drugs: illicit cultivator of cannabis mostly for domestic consumption; increasingly used as a transshipment point for illicit drugs - mostly opium and hashish - to Western Europe and the US via Iran, Central Asia, and Russia

Aruba
(part of the Kingdom of the Netherlands)

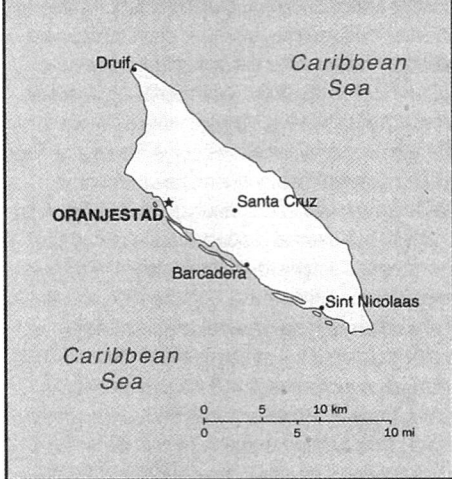

Introduction

Background: Discovered and claimed for Spain in 1499, Aruba was acquired by the Dutch in 1636. The island's economy has been dominated by three main industries. A 19th century gold rush was followed by prosperity brought on by the opening in 1924 of an oil refinery. The last decades of the 20th century saw a boom in the tourism industry. Aruba seceded from the Netherlands Antilles in 1986 and became a separate, autonomous member of the Kingdom of the Netherlands. Movement toward full independence was halted at Aruba's request in 1990.

Geography

Location: Caribbean, island in the Caribbean Sea, north of Venezuela
Geographic coordinates: 12 30 N, 69 58 W
Map references: Central America and the Caribbean
Area:
total: 193 sq km
land: 193 sq km
water: 0 sq km
Area - comparative: slightly larger than Washington, DC
Land boundaries: 0 km
Coastline: 68.5 km
Maritime claims:
territorial sea: 12 NM
Climate: tropical marine; little seasonal temperature variation
Terrain: flat with a few hills; scant vegetation
Elevation extremes:
lowest point: Caribbean Sea 0 m
highest point: Mount Jamanota 188 m
Natural resources: NEGL; white sandy beaches
Land use:
arable land: 7% (including aloe 0.01%)
permanent crops: 0%
permanent pastures: 0%
forests and woodland: 0%
other: 93% (1993 est.)
Irrigated land: 0.01 sq km
Natural hazards: lies outside the Caribbean hurricane belt
Environment - current issues: NA

People

Population: 70,007 (July 2001 est.)
Age structure:
0-14 years: 21.29% (male 7,709; female 7,193)
15-64 years: 68.52% (male 23,111; female 24,859)
65 years and over: 10.19% (male 2,954; female 4,181) (2001 est.)
Population growth rate: 0.64% (2001 est.)
Birth rate: 12.64 births/1,000 population (2001 est.)
Death rate: 6.21 deaths/1,000 population (2001 est.)
Net migration rate: NEGL
Sex ratio:
at birth: 1.05 male(s)/female
under 15 years: 1.07 male(s)/female
15-64 years: 0.93 male(s)/female
65 years and over: 0.71 male(s)/female
total population: 0.93 male(s)/female (2001 est.)
Infant mortality rate: 6.39 deaths/1,000 live births (2001 est.)
Life expectancy at birth:
total population: 78.52 years
male: 75.16 years
female: 82.04 years (2001 est.)
Total fertility rate: 1.8 children born/woman (2001 est.)
HIV/AIDS - adult prevalence rate: NA%
HIV/AIDS - people living with HIV/AIDS: NA
HIV/AIDS - deaths: NA
Nationality:
noun: Aruban(s)
adjective: Aruban; Dutch
Ethnic groups: mixed white/Caribbean Amerindian 80%
Religions: Roman Catholic 82%, Protestant 8%, Hindu, Muslim, Confucian, Jewish
Languages: Dutch (official), Papiamento (a Spanish, Portuguese, Dutch, English dialect), English (widely spoken), Spanish
Literacy:
definition: NA
total population: 97%
male: NA%
female: NA%

Government

Country name:
conventional long form: none
conventional short form: Aruba
Dependency status: part of the Kingdom of the Netherlands; full autonomy in internal affairs obtained in 1986 upon separation from the Netherlands Antilles; Dutch Government responsible for defense and foreign affairs
Government type: parliamentary democracy
Capital: Oranjestad

Aruba (continued)

Administrative divisions: none (part of the Kingdom of the Netherlands)
Independence: none (part of the Kingdom of the Netherlands)
National holiday: Flag Day, 18 March
Constitution: 1 January 1986
Legal system: based on Dutch civil law system, with some English common law influence
Suffrage: 18 years of age; universal
Executive branch:
chief of state: Queen BEATRIX Wilhelmina Armgard of the Netherlands (since 30 April 1980), represented by Governor General Olindo KOOLMAN (since 1 January 1992)
head of government: Prime Minister Jan (Henny) H. EMAN (since 29 July 1994) and Deputy Prime Minister Lili BEKE-MARTINEZ
cabinet: Council of Ministers (elected by the Staten)
elections: the monarch is hereditary; governor general appointed for a six-year term by the monarch; prime minister and deputy prime minister elected by the Staten for four-year terms; election last held 12 July 1997 (next to be held by December 2001)
election results: Jan (Henny) H. EMAN elected prime minister; percent of legislative vote - NA%; Lili BEKE-MARTINEZ elected deputy prime minister; percent of legislative vote - NA%
Legislative branch: unicameral Legislature or Staten (21 seats; members elected by direct, popular vote to serve four-year terms)
elections: last held 12 December 1997 (next to be held by NA December 2001)
election results: percent of vote by party - AVP 43%, MEP 39%, OLA 9% PPA 4%, ADN 2%, PARA 1%, MAS 0.5%; seats by party - AVP 10, MEP 9, OLA 2
Judicial branch: Joint High Court of Justice (judges are appointed by the monarch)
Political parties and leaders: Aruba Solidarity Movement or MAS [leader NA]; Aruban Democratic Party or PDA [Leo BERLINSKI]; Aruban Liberal Party or OLA [Glenbert CROES]; Aruban Patriotic Party or PPA [Benny NISBET]; Aruban People's Party or AVP [Tico CROES]; Electoral Movement Party or MEP [Nelson ODUBER]; For a Restructured Aruba Now or PARA [leader NA]; National Democratic Action or ADN [Pedro Charro KELLY]
Political pressure groups and leaders: NA
International organization participation: Caricom (observer), ECLAC (associate), Interpol, IOC, UNESCO (associate), WCL, WToO (associate)
Diplomatic representation in the US: none (represented by the Kingdom of the Netherlands)
Diplomatic representation from the US:
chief of mission: Consul General Barbara J. STEPHENSON
embassy: J. B. Gorsiraweg #1, Curacao
mailing address: P. O. Box 158, Willemstad, Curacao
telephone: [599] (9) 461-3066
FAX: [599] (9) 461-6489
Flag description: blue, with two narrow, horizontal, yellow stripes across the lower portion and a red, four-pointed star outlined in white in the upper hoist-side corner

Economy

Economy - overview: Tourism is the mainstay of the Aruban economy, although offshore banking and oil refining and storage are also important. The rapid growth of the tourism sector over the last decade has resulted in a substantial expansion of other activities. Construction has boomed, with hotel capacity five times the 1985 level. In addition, the reopening of the country's oil refinery in 1993, a major source of employment and foreign exchange earnings, has further spurred growth. Aruba's small labor force and less than 1% unemployment rate have led to a large number of unfilled job vacancies, despite sharp rises in wage rates in recent years.
GDP: purchasing power parity - $2 billion (2000 est.)
GDP - real growth rate: 3.5% (2000 est.)
GDP - per capita: purchasing power parity - $28,000 (2000 est.)
GDP - composition by sector:
agriculture: NA%
industry: NA%
services: NA%
Population below poverty line: NA%
Household income or consumption by percentage share:
lowest 10%: NA%
highest 10%: NA%
Inflation rate (consumer prices): 4.2% (2000 est.)
Labor force: 41,501 (1997 est.)
Labor force - by occupation: most employment is in wholesale and retail trade and repair, followed by hotels and restaurants; oil refining
Unemployment rate: 0.6% (1999 est.)
Budget:
revenues: $NA
expenditures: $541 million, including capital expenditures of $NA (2000 est.)
Industries: tourism, transshipment facilities, oil refining
Industrial production growth rate: NA%
Electricity - production: 450 million kWh (1999)
Electricity - production by source:
fossil fuel: 100%
hydro: 0%
nuclear: 0%
other: 0% (1999)
Electricity - consumption: 418.5 million kWh (1999)
Electricity - exports: 0 kWh (1999)
Electricity - imports: 0 kWh (1999)
Agriculture - products: aloes; livestock; fish
Exports: $2.2 billion (including oil reexports) (2000 est.)
Exports - commodities: live animals and animal products, art and collectibles, machinery and electrical equipment, transport equipment
Exports - partners: US 42%, Colombia 20%, Netherlands 12% (1999)
Imports: $2.5 billion (2000 est.)
Imports - commodities: machinery and electrical equipment, crude oil for refining and reexport, chemicals; foodstuffs
Imports - partners: US 63%, Netherlands 11%, Netherlands Antilles 3%, Japan (1999)
Debt - external: $285 million (1996)
Economic aid - recipient: $26 million (1995); note - the Netherlands provided a $127 million aid package to Aruba and Suriname in 1996
Currency: Aruban guilder/florin (AWG)
Currency code: AWG
Exchange rates: Aruban guilders/florins per US dollar - 1.7900 (fixed rate since 1986)
Fiscal year: calendar year

Communications

Telephones - main lines in use: 33,000 (1997)
Telephones - mobile cellular: 3,402 (1997)
Telephone system:
general assessment: NA
domestic: more than adequate
international: 1 submarine cable to Sint Maarten (Netherlands Antilles); extensive interisland microwave radio relay links
Radio broadcast stations: AM 4, FM 6, shortwave 0 (1998)
Radios: 50,000 (1997)
Television broadcast stations: 1 (1997)
Televisions: 20,000 (1997)
Internet country code: .aw
Internet Service Providers (ISPs): NA
Internet users: 4,000 (2000)

Transportation

Railways: 0 km
Highways:
total: 800 km
paved: 513 km
unpaved: 287 km
note: most coastal roads are paved, while unpaved roads serve large tracts of the interior (1995)
Waterways: none
Ports and harbors: Barcadera, Oranjestad, Sint Nicolaas
Merchant marine:
total: 1 ship (1,000 GRT or over) totaling 3,120 GRT/ 3,635 DWT
ships by type: cargo 1 (2000 est.)
Airports: 1 (2000 est.)
Airports - with paved runways:
total: 1
2,438 to 3,047 m: 1 (2000 est.)

Military

Military branches: Royal Dutch Navy and Marines, Coast Guard
Military - note: defense is the responsibility of the Kingdom of the Netherlands

Transnational Issues

Disputes - international: none
Illicit drugs: drug-money-laundering center and transit point for narcotics bound for the US and Europe

Ashmore and Cartier Islands
(territory of Australia)

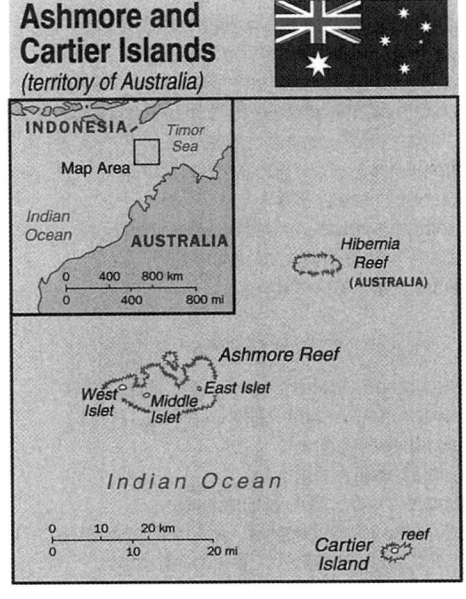

Introduction

Background: These uninhabited islands came under Australian authority in 1931; formal administration began two years later. Ashmore Reef supports a rich and diverse avian and marine habitat; in 1983 it became a National Nature Reserve. Recent geological explorations have indicated promising petroleum formations.

Geography

Location: Southeastern Asia, islands in the Indian Ocean, northwest of Australia
Geographic coordinates: 12 14 S, 123 05 E
Map references: Southeast Asia
Area:
total: 5 sq km
land: 5 sq km
water: 0 sq km
note: includes Ashmore Reef (West, Middle, and East Islets) and Cartier Island
Area - comparative: about eight times the size of The Mall in Washington, DC
Land boundaries: 0 km
Coastline: 74.1 km
Maritime claims:
contiguous zone: 12 NM
continental shelf: 200-m depth or to the depth of exploitation
exclusive fishing zone: 200 NM
territorial sea: 3 NM
Climate: tropical
Terrain: low with sand and coral
Elevation extremes:
lowest point: Indian Ocean 0 m
highest point: unnamed location 3 m
Natural resources: fish
Land use:
arable land: 0%
permanent crops: 0%
permanent pastures: 0%
forests and woodland: 0%
other: 100% (all grass and sand)
Irrigated land: 0 sq km (1993)
Natural hazards: surrounded by shoals and reefs that can pose maritime hazards
Environment - current issues: NA
Geography - note: Ashmore Reef National Nature Reserve established in August 1983

People

Population: no indigenous inhabitants
note: there are only seasonal caretakers (July 2001 est.)

Government

Country name:
conventional long form: Territory of Ashmore and Cartier Islands
conventional short form: Ashmore and Cartier Islands
Dependency status: territory of Australia; administered from Canberra by the Australian Department of the Environment, Sport, and Territories
Legal system: the laws of the Northern Territory of Australia, where applicable, apply
Diplomatic representation in the US: none (territory of Australia)
Diplomatic representation from the US: none (territory of Australia)
Flag description: the flag of Australia is used

Economy

Economy - overview: no economic activity

Transportation

Waterways: none
Ports and harbors: none; offshore anchorage only

Military

Military - note: defense is the responsibility of Australia; periodic visits by the Royal Australian Navy and Royal Australian Air Force

Transnational Issues

Disputes - international: none

Atlantic Ocean

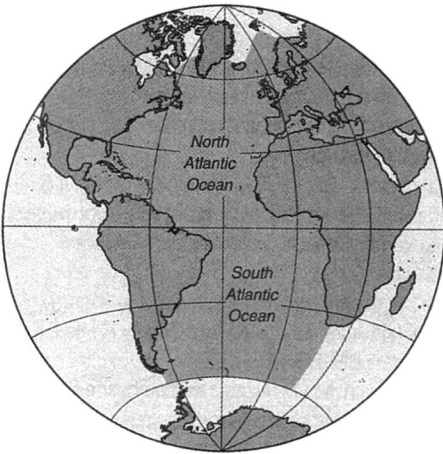

Introduction

Background: The Atlantic Ocean is the second-largest of the world's five oceans (after the Pacific Ocean, but larger than the Indian Ocean, Southern Ocean, and Arctic Ocean). The Kiel Canal (Germany), Oresund (Denmark-Sweden), Bosporus (Turkey), Strait of Gibraltar (Morocco-Spain), and the St. Lawrence Seaway (Canada-US) are important strategic access waterways. The decision by the International Hydrographic Organization in the spring of 2000 to delimit a fifth world ocean, the Southern Ocean, removed the portion of the Atlantic Ocean south of 60 degrees south.

Geography

Location: body of water between Africa, Europe, the Southern Ocean, and the Western Hemisphere
Geographic coordinates: 0 00 N, 25 00 W
Map references: World
Area:
total: 76.762 million sq km
note: includes Baltic Sea, Black Sea, Caribbean Sea, Davis Strait, Denmark Strait, part of the Drake Passage, Gulf of Mexico, Mediterranean Sea, North Sea, Norwegian Sea, almost all of the Scotia Sea, and other tributary water bodies
Area - comparative: slightly less than 6.5 times the size of the US
Coastline: 111,866 km
Climate: tropical cyclones (hurricanes) develop off the coast of Africa near Cape Verde and move westward into the Caribbean Sea; hurricanes can occur from May to December, but are most frequent from August to November
Terrain: surface usually covered with sea ice in Labrador Sea, Denmark Strait, and Baltic Sea from October to June; clockwise warm-water gyre (broad, circular system of currents) in the northern Atlantic, counterclockwise warm-water gyre in the southern Atlantic; the ocean floor is dominated by the

Atlantic Ocean (continued)

Mid-Atlantic Ridge, a rugged north-south centerline for the entire Atlantic basin
Elevation extremes:
lowest point: Milwaukee Deep in the Puerto Rico Trench -8,605 m
highest point: sea level 0 m
Natural resources: oil and gas fields, fish, marine mammals (seals and whales), sand and gravel aggregates, placer deposits, polymetallic nodules, precious stones
Natural hazards: icebergs common in Davis Strait, Denmark Strait, and the northwestern Atlantic Ocean from February to August and have been spotted as far south as Bermuda and the Madeira Islands; ships subject to superstructure icing in extreme northern Atlantic from October to May; persistent fog can be a maritime hazard from May to September; hurricanes (May to December)
Environment - current issues: endangered marine species include the manatee, seals, sea lions, turtles, and whales; drift net fishing is hastening the decline of fish stocks and contributing to international disputes; municipal sludge pollution off eastern US, southern Brazil, and eastern Argentina; oil pollution in Caribbean Sea, Gulf of Mexico, Lake Maracaibo, Mediterranean Sea, and North Sea; industrial waste and municipal sewage pollution in Baltic Sea, North Sea, and Mediterranean Sea
Geography - note: major chokepoints include the Dardanelles, Strait of Gibraltar, access to the Panama and Suez Canals; strategic straits include the Strait of Dover, Straits of Florida, Mona Passage, The Sound (Oresund), and Windward Passage; the Equator divides the Atlantic Ocean into the North Atlantic Ocean and South Atlantic Ocean

Economy

Economy - overview: The Atlantic Ocean provides some of the world's most heavily trafficked sea routes, between and within the Eastern and Western Hemispheres. Other economic activity includes the exploitation of natural resources, e.g., fishing, the dredging of aragonite sands (The Bahamas), and production of crude oil and natural gas (Caribbean Sea, Gulf of Mexico, and North Sea).

Transportation

Ports and harbors: Alexandria (Egypt), Algiers (Algeria), Antwerp (Belgium), Barcelona (Spain), Buenos Aires (Argentina), Casablanca (Morocco), Colon (Panama), Copenhagen (Denmark), Dakar (Senegal), Gdansk (Poland), Hamburg (Germany), Helsinki (Finland), Las Palmas (Canary Islands, Spain), Le Havre (France), Lisbon (Portugal), London (UK), Marseille (France), Montevideo (Uruguay), Montreal (Canada), Naples (Italy), New Orleans (US), New York (US), Oran (Algeria), Oslo (Norway), Peiraiefs or Piraeus (Greece), Rio de Janeiro (Brazil), Rotterdam (Netherlands), Saint Petersburg (Russia), Stockholm (Sweden)

Transportation - note: Kiel Canal and Saint Lawrence Seaway are two important waterways; significant domestic commercial and recreational use of Intracoastal Waterway on central and south Atlantic seaboard and Gulf of Mexico coast of US

Transnational Issues

Disputes - international: some maritime disputes (see littoral states)

Australia

Introduction

Background: Australia became a commonwealth of the British Empire in 1901. It was able to take advantage of its natural resources to rapidly develop its agricultural and manufacturing industries and to make a major contribution to the British effort in World Wars I and II. Long-term concerns include pollution, particularly depletion of the ozone layer, and management and conservation of coastal areas, especially the Great Barrier Reef. A referendum to change Australia's status, from a commonwealth headed by the British monarch to an independent republic, was defeated in 1999.

Geography

Location: Oceania, continent between the Indian Ocean and the South Pacific Ocean
Geographic coordinates: 27 00 S, 133 00 E
Map references: Oceania
Area:
total: 7,686,850 sq km
land: 7,617,930 sq km
water: 68,920 sq km
note: includes Lord Howe Island and Macquarie Island
Area - comparative: slightly smaller than the US
Land boundaries: 0 km
Coastline: 25,760 km
Maritime claims:
contiguous zone: 24 NM
continental shelf: 200 NM or to the edge of the continental margin
exclusive economic zone: 200 NM
territorial sea: 12 NM
Climate: generally arid to semiarid; temperate in south and east; tropical in north
Terrain: mostly low plateau with deserts; fertile plain in southeast
Elevation extremes:
lowest point: Lake Eyre -15 m

Australia (continued)

highest point: Mount Kosciuszko 2,229 m
Natural resources: bauxite, coal, iron ore, copper, tin, silver, uranium, nickel, tungsten, mineral sands, lead, zinc, diamonds, natural gas, petroleum
Land use:
arable land: 6%
permanent crops: 0%
permanent pastures: 54%
forests and woodland: 19%
other: 21% (1993 est.)
Irrigated land: 21,070 sq km (1993 est.)
Natural hazards: cyclones along the coast; severe droughts
Environment - current issues: soil erosion from overgrazing, industrial development, urbanization, and poor farming practices; soil salinity rising due to the use of poor quality water; desertification; clearing for agricultural purposes threatens the natural habitat of many unique animal and plant species; the Great Barrier Reef off the northeast coast, the largest coral reef in the world, is threatened by increased shipping and its popularity as a tourist site; limited natural fresh water resources
Environment - international agreements:
party to: Antarctic-Environmental Protocol, Antarctic-Marine Living Resources, Antarctic Seals, Antarctic Treaty, Biodiversity, Climate Change, Desertification, Endangered Species, Environmental Modification, Hazardous Wastes, Law of the Sea, Marine Dumping, Marine Life Conservation, Nuclear Test Ban, Ozone Layer Protection, Ship Pollution, Tropical Timber 83, Tropical Timber 94, Wetlands, Whaling
signed, but not ratified: Climate Change-Kyoto Protocol
Geography - note: world's smallest continent but sixth-largest country; population concentrated along the eastern and southeastern coasts; regular, tropical, invigorating, sea breeze known as "the Doctor" occurs along the west coast in the summer

People

Population: 19,357,594 (July 2001 est.)
Age structure:
0-14 years: 20.64% (male 2,045,892; female 1,948,949)
15-64 years: 66.86% (male 6,538,096; female 6,405,014)
65 years and over: 12.5% (male 1,059,107; female 1,360,536) (2001 est.)
Population growth rate: 0.99% (2001 est.)
Birth rate: 12.86 births/1,000 population (2001 est.)
Death rate: 7.18 deaths/1,000 population (2001 est.)
Net migration rate: 4.19 migrant(s)/1,000 population (2001 est.)
Sex ratio:
at birth: 1.05 male(s)/female
under 15 years: 1.05 male(s)/female
15-64 years: 1.02 male(s)/female
65 years and over: 0.78 male(s)/female
total population: 0.99 male(s)/female (2001 est.)

Infant mortality rate: 4.97 deaths/1,000 live births (2001 est.)
Life expectancy at birth:
total population: 79.87 years
male: 77.02 years
female: 82.87 years (2001 est.)
Total fertility rate: 1.77 children born/woman (2001 est.)
HIV/AIDS - adult prevalence rate: 0.15% (1999 est.)
HIV/AIDS - people living with HIV/AIDS: 14,000 (1999 est.)
HIV/AIDS - deaths: 100 (1999 est.)
Nationality:
noun: Australian(s)
adjective: Australian
Ethnic groups: Caucasian 92%, Asian 7%, aboriginal and other 1%
Religions: Anglican 26.1%, Roman Catholic 26%, other Christian 24.3%, non-Christian 11%
Languages: English, native languages
Literacy:
definition: age 15 and over can read and write
total population: 100%
male: 100%
female: 100% (1980 est.)

Government

Country name:
conventional long form: Commonwealth of Australia
conventional short form: Australia
Government type: democratic, federal-state system recognizing the British monarch as sovereign
Capital: Canberra
Administrative divisions: 6 states and 2 territories*; Australian Capital Territory*, New South Wales, Northern Territory*, Queensland, South Australia, Tasmania, Victoria, Western Australia
Dependent areas: Ashmore and Cartier Islands, Christmas Island, Cocos (Keeling) Islands, Coral Sea Islands, Heard Island and McDonald Islands, Norfolk Island
Independence: 1 January 1901 (federation of UK colonies)
National holiday: Australia Day, 26 January (1788)
Constitution: 9 July 1900, effective 1 January 1901
Legal system: based on English common law; accepts compulsory ICJ jurisdiction, with reservations
Suffrage: 18 years of age; universal and compulsory
Executive branch:
chief of state: Queen ELIZABETH II (since 6 February 1952), represented by Governor General Rev. Peter HOLLINGSWORTH (since 29 June 2001)
head of government: Prime Minister John Winston HOWARD (since 11 March 1996); Deputy Prime Minister John ANDERSON (since NA)
cabinet: Cabinet selected from among the members of Federal Parliament by the governor general on the advice of the prime minister
elections: none; the monarch is hereditary; governor general appointed by the monarch; following legislative elections, the leader of the majority party or leader of a majority coalition is usually appointed prime minister by the governor general for a three-year term
note: government coalition - Liberal Party and National Party
Legislative branch: bicameral Federal Parliament consists of the Senate (76 seats - 12 from each of the six states and two from each of the two territories; one-half of the members elected every three years by popular vote to serve six-year terms) and the House of Representatives (148 seats; members elected by popular vote on the basis of proportional representation to serve three-year terms; no state can have fewer than five representatives)
elections: Senate - last held 3 October 1998 (next to be held by October 2001); House of Representatives - last held 3 October 1998 (next to be held by October 2001)
election results: Senate - percent of vote by party - NA%; seats by party - Liberal Party-National Party coalition 35, Australian Labor Party 29, Australian Democratic Party 9, Green Party 1, One Nation Party 1, independent 1; House of Representatives - percent of vote by party - NA%; seats by party - Liberal Party-National Party coalition 80, Australian Labor Party 67, independent 1
Judicial branch: High Court (the chief justice and six other justices are appointed by the governor general)
Political parties and leaders: Australian Democratic Party [Meg LEES]; Australian Labor Party [Kim BEAZLEY]; Green Party [Bob BROWN]; Liberal Party [John Winston HOWARD]; National Party [John ANDERSON]; One Nation Party [Pauline HANSON]
Political pressure groups and leaders: Australian Democratic Labor Party (anti-Communist Labor Party splinter group); Peace and Nuclear Disarmament Action (Nuclear Disarmament Party splinter group)
International organization participation: ANZUS, APEC, ARF (dialogue partner), AsDB, ASEAN (dialogue partner), Australia Group, BIS, C, CCC, CP, EBRD, ESCAP, FAO, IAEA, IBRD, ICAO, ICC, ICFTU, ICRM, IDA, IEA, IFAD, IFC, IFRCS, IHO, ILO, IMF, IMO, Inmarsat, Intelsat, Interpol, IOC, IOM, ISO, ITU, NAM (guest), NEA, NSG, OECD, OPCW, PCA, Sparteca, SPC, SPF, UN, UNCTAD, UNESCO, UNHCR, UNMEE, UNTAET, UNTSO, UNU, UPU, WFTU, WHO, WIPO, WMO, WTrO, ZC
Diplomatic representation in the US:
chief of mission: Ambassador Michael THAWLEY
chancery: 1601 Massachusetts Avenue NW, Washington, DC 20036
telephone: [1] (202) 797-3000
FAX: [1] (202) 797-3168
consulate(s) general: Atlanta, Honolulu, Los Angeles, New York, and San Francisco
Diplomatic representation from the US:
chief of mission: Ambassador Edward W. GNEHM, Jr.
embassy: Moonah Place, Yarralumla, Canberra, Australian Capital Territory 2600
mailing address: APO AP 96549

Australia (continued)

telephone: [61] (02) 6214-5600
FAX: [61] (02) 6214-5970
consulate(s) general: Sydney
consulate(s): Melbourne and Perth
Flag description: blue with the flag of the UK in the upper hoist-side quadrant and a large seven-pointed star in the lower hoist-side quadrant; the remaining half is a representation of the Southern Cross constellation in white with one small five-pointed star and four, larger, seven-pointed stars

Economy

Economy - overview: Australia has a prosperous Western-style capitalist economy, with a per capita GDP at the level of the four dominant West European economies. Rich in natural resources, Australia is a major exporter of agricultural products, minerals, metals, and fossil fuels. Commodities account for 57% of the value of total exports, so that a downturn in world commodity prices can have a big impact on the economy. The government is pushing for increased exports of manufactured goods, but competition in international markets continues to be severe. While Australia has suffered from the low growth and high unemployment characterizing the OECD countries in the early 1990s and during the recent financial problems in East Asia, the economy has expanded at a solid 4% annual growth pace in the last five years. Canberra's emphasis on reforms is a key factor behind the economy's resilience to the regional crisis and its stronger than expected growth rate. Growth in 2001 will depend on key international commodity prices, the extent of recovery in nearby Asian economies, and the strength of US and European markets.
GDP: purchasing power parity - $445.8 billion (2000 est.)
GDP - real growth rate: 4.7% (2000 est.)
GDP - per capita: purchasing power parity - $23,200 (2000 est.)
GDP - composition by sector:
agriculture: 3%
industry: 26%
services: 71% (1999 est.)
Population below poverty line: NA%
Household income or consumption by percentage share:
lowest 10%: 2%
highest 10%: 25.4% (1994)
Inflation rate (consumer prices): 1.4% (2000 est.)
Labor force: 9.5 million (December 1999)
Labor force - by occupation: services 73%, industry 22%, agriculture 5% (1997 est.)
Unemployment rate: 6.4% (2000)
Budget:
revenues: $94 billion
expenditures: $103 billion, including capital expenditures of $NA (1999 est.)
Industries: mining, industrial and transportation equipment, food processing, chemicals, steel
Industrial production growth rate: 1.5% (1999 est.)
Electricity - production: 191.727 billion kWh (1999)
Electricity - production by source:
fossil fuel: 89.93%
hydro: 8.36%
nuclear: 0%
other: 1.71% (1999)
Electricity - consumption: 178.306 billion kWh (1999)
Electricity - exports: 0 kWh (1999)
Electricity - imports: 0 kWh (1999)
Agriculture - products: wheat, barley, sugarcane, fruits; cattle, sheep, poultry
Exports: $69 billion (f.o.b., 2000 est.)
Exports - commodities: coal, gold, meat, wool, alumina, iron ore, wheat, machinery and transport equipment
Exports - partners: Japan 19%, EU 14%, ASEAN 12%, US 9%, South Korea, NZ, Taiwan, Hong Kong, China (1999)
Imports: $77 billion (f.o.b., 2000 est.)
Imports - commodities: machinery and transport equipment, computers and office machines, telecommunication equipment and parts; crude oil and petroleum products
Imports - partners: EU 24%, US 22%, Japan 14%, ASEAN 13% (1999)
Debt - external: $220.6 billion (2000)
Economic aid - donor: ODA, $1.43 billion (FY97/98)
Currency: Australian dollar (AUD)
Currency code: AUD
Exchange rates: Australian dollars per US dollar - 1.7995 (January 2001), 1.7173 (2000), 1.5497 (1999), 1.5888 (1998), 1.3439 (1997), 1.2773 (1996)
Fiscal year: 1 July - 30 June

Communications

Telephones - main lines in use: 9.58 million (1998)
Telephones - mobile cellular: 6.4 million (1998)
Telephone system:
general assessment: excellent domestic and international service
domestic: domestic satellite system; much use of radiotelephone in areas of low population density; rapid growth of mobile cellular telephones
international: submarine cables to New Zealand, Papua New Guinea, and Indonesia; satellite earth stations - 10 Intelsat (4 Indian Ocean and 6 Pacific Ocean), 2 Inmarsat (Indian and Pacific Ocean regions) (1998)
Radio broadcast stations: AM 262, FM 345, shortwave 1 (1998)
Radios: 25.5 million (1997)
Television broadcast stations: 104 (1997)
Televisions: 10.15 million (1997)
Internet country code: .au
Internet Service Providers (ISPs): 264 (2000)
Internet users: 7.77 million (2000)

Transportation

Railways:
total: 33,819 km (2,540 km electrified)
broad gauge: 3,719 km 1.600-m gauge
standard gauge: 15,422 km 1.435-m gauge
narrow gauge: 14,506 km 1.067-m gauge
dual gauge: 172 km NA gauges (1999)
Highways:
total: 913,000 km
paved: 353,331 km (including 1,363 km of expressways)
unpaved: 559,669 km (1996)
Waterways: 8,368 km (mainly used by small, shallow-draft craft)
Pipelines: crude oil 2,500 km; petroleum products 500 km; natural gas 5,600 km
Ports and harbors: Adelaide, Brisbane, Cairns, Darwin, Devonport (Tasmania), Fremantle, Geelong, Hobart (Tasmania), Launceston (Tasmania), Mackay, Melbourne, Sydney, Townsville
Merchant marine:
total: 54 ships (1,000 GRT or over) totaling 1,558,371 GRT/2,038,776 DWT
ships by type: bulk 26, cargo 3, chemical tanker 5, container 1, liquefied gas 4, passenger 2, petroleum tanker 7, roll on/roll off 6 (2000 est.)
Airports: 411 (2000 est.)
Airports - with paved runways:
total: 271
over 3,047 m: 10
2,438 to 3,047 m: 12
1,524 to 2,437 m: 118
914 to 1,523 m: 122
under 914 m: 9 (2000 est.)
Airports - with unpaved runways:
total: 140
1,524 to 2,437 m: 17
914 to 1,523 m: 112
under 914 m: 11 (2000 est.)

Military

Military branches: Australian Army, Royal Australian Navy, Royal Australian Air Force
Military manpower - military age: 17 years of age
Military manpower - availability:
males age 15-49: 4,990,107 (2001 est.)
Military manpower - fit for military service:
males age 15-49: 4,303,966 (2001 est.)
Military manpower - reaching military age annually:
males: 138,971 (2001 est.)
Military expenditures - dollar figure: $6.9 billion (FY98/99)
Military expenditures - percent of GDP: 1.9% (FY98/99)

Transnational Issues

Disputes - international: territorial claim in Antarctica (Australian Antarctic Territory)
Illicit drugs: Tasmania is one of the world's major suppliers of licit opiate products; government maintains strict controls over areas of opium poppy cultivation and output of poppy straw concentrate

Austria

Introduction

Background: Once the center of power for the large Austro-Hungarian Empire, Austria was reduced to a small republic after its defeat in World War I. Following annexation by Nazi Germany in 1938 and subsequent occupation by the victorious Allies, Austria's 1955 State Treaty declared the country "permanently neutral" as a condition of Soviet military withdrawal. Neutrality, once ingrained as part of the Austrian cultural identity, has been called into question since the Soviet collapse of 1991 and Austria's increasingly prominent role in European affairs. A prosperous country, Austria joined the European Union in 1995 and the euro monetary system in 1999.

Geography

Location: Central Europe, north of Italy and Slovenia
Geographic coordinates: 47 20 N, 13 20 E
Map references: Europe
Area:
total: 83,858 sq km
land: 82,738 sq km
water: 1,120 sq km
Area - comparative: slightly smaller than Maine
Land boundaries:
total: 2,562 km
border countries: Czech Republic 362 km, Germany 784 km, Hungary 366 km, Italy 430 km, Liechtenstein 35 km, Slovakia 91 km, Slovenia 330 km, Switzerland 164 km
Coastline: 0 km (landlocked)
Maritime claims: none (landlocked)
Climate: temperate; continental, cloudy; cold winters with frequent rain in lowlands and snow in mountains; cool summers with occasional showers
Terrain: in the west and south mostly mountains (Alps); along the eastern and northern margins mostly flat or gently sloping
Elevation extremes:
lowest point: Neusiedler See 115 m
highest point: Grossglockner 3,798 m
Natural resources: iron ore, oil, timber, magnesite, lead, coal, lignite, copper, hydropower
Land use:
arable land: 17%
permanent crops: 1%
permanent pastures: 23%
forests and woodland: 39%
other: 20% (1996 est.)
Irrigated land: 457 sq km (1995 est.)
Natural hazards: NA
Environment - current issues: some forest degradation caused by air and soil pollution; soil pollution results from the use of agricultural chemicals; air pollution results from emissions by coal- and oil-fired power stations and industrial plants and from trucks transiting Austria between northern and southern Europe
Environment - international agreements:
party to: Air Pollution, Air Pollution-Nitrogen Oxides, Air Pollution-Sulphur 85, Air Pollution-Sulphur 94, Air Pollution-Volatile Organic Compounds, Antarctic Treaty, Biodiversity, Climate Change, Desertification, Endangered Species, Environmental Modification, Hazardous Wastes, Law of the Sea, Marine Dumping, Nuclear Test Ban, Ozone Layer Protection, Ship Pollution, Tropical Timber 83, Tropical Timber 94, Wetlands, Whaling
signed, but not ratified: Air Pollution-Persistent Organic Pollutants, Antarctic-Environmental Protocol, Climate Change-Kyoto Protocol
Geography - note: landlocked; strategic location at the crossroads of central Europe with many easily traversable Alpine passes and valleys; major river is the Danube; population is concentrated on eastern lowlands because of steep slopes, poor soils, and low temperatures elsewhere

People

Population: 8,150,835 (July 2001 est.)
Age structure:
0-14 years: 16.57% (male 691,925; female 658,375)
15-64 years: 68.05% (male 2,802,019; female 2,744,536)
65 years and over: 15.38% (male 478,498; female 775,482) (2001 est.)
Population growth rate: 0.24% (2001 est.)
Birth rate: 9.74 births/1,000 population (2001 est.)
Death rate: 9.8 deaths/1,000 population (2001 est.)
Net migration rate: 2.45 migrant(s)/1,000 population (2001 est.)
Sex ratio:
at birth: 1.05 male(s)/female
under 15 years: 1.05 male(s)/female
15-64 years: 1.02 male(s)/female
65 years and over: 0.62 male(s)/female
total population: 0.95 male(s)/female (2001 est.)
Infant mortality rate: 4.44 deaths/1,000 live births (2001 est.)
Life expectancy at birth:
total population: 77.84 years
male: 74.68 years
female: 81.15 years (2001 est.)
Total fertility rate: 1.39 children born/woman (2001 est.)
HIV/AIDS - adult prevalence rate: 0.23% (1999 est.)
HIV/AIDS - people living with HIV/AIDS: 9,000 (1999 est.)
HIV/AIDS - deaths: less than 100 (1999 est.)
Nationality:
noun: Austrian(s)
adjective: Austrian
Ethnic groups: German 98%, Croatian, Slovene, other (includes Hungarians, Czechs, Slovaks, Roma)
Religions: Roman Catholic 78%, Protestant 5%, Muslim and other 17%
Languages: German
Literacy:
definition: age 15 and over can read and write
total population: 98%
male: NA%
female: NA%

Government

Country name:
conventional long form: Republic of Austria
conventional short form: Austria
local long form: Republik Oesterreich
local short form: Oesterreich
Government type: federal republic
Capital: Vienna
Administrative divisions: 9 states (bundeslaender, singular - bundesland); Burgenland, Kaernten, Niederoesterreich, Oberoesterreich, Salzburg, Steiermark, Tirol, Vorarlberg, Wien
Independence: 1156 (from Bavaria)
National holiday: National Day, 26 October (1955); note - commemorates the passage of the law on permanent neutrality
Constitution: 1920; revised 1929 (reinstated 1 May 1945)
Legal system: civil law system with Roman law origin; judicial review of legislative acts by the Constitutional Court; separate administrative and civil/penal supreme courts; has not accepted compulsory ICJ jurisdiction
Suffrage: 19 years of age; universal; compulsory for presidential elections
Executive branch:
chief of state: President Thomas KLESTIL (since 8 July 1992)
head of government: Chancellor Wolfgang SCHUESSEL (OeVP)(since 4 February 2000); Vice Chancellor Susanne RIESS-PASSER (FPOe) (since 4 February 2000)
cabinet: Council of Ministers chosen by the president on the advice of the chancellor
elections: president elected by direct popular vote for a six-year term; presidential election last held

Austria (continued)

19 April 1998 (next to be held in the spring of 2004); chancellor traditionally chosen by the president from the plurality party in the National Council; in the case of the current coalition, the chancellor was chosen from another party after the plurality party failed to form a government; vice chancellor chosen by the president on the advice of the chancellor
election results: Thomas KLESTIL reelected president; percent of vote - Thomas KLESTIL 63%, Gertraud KNOLL 14%, Heide SCHMIDT 11%, Richard LUGNER 10%, Karl NOWAK 2%
note: government coalition - OeVP and FPOe
Legislative branch: bicameral Federal Assembly or Bundesversammlung consists of Federal Council or Bundesrat (64 members; members represent each of the states on the basis of population, but with each state having at least three representatives; members serve a four- or six-year term) and the National Council or Nationalrat (183 seats; members elected by direct popular vote to serve four-year terms)
elections: National Council - last held 3 October 1999 (next to be held in the fall of 2003)
election results: National Council - percent of vote by party - SPOe 33.2%, OeVP 26.9%, FPOe 26.9%, Greens 7.4%; seats by party - SPOe 65, OeVP 52, FPOe 52, Greens 14
Judicial branch: Supreme Judicial Court or Oberster Gerichtshof; Administrative Court or Verwaltungsgerichtshof; Constitutional Court or Verfassungsgerichtshof
Political parties and leaders: Austrian People's Party or OeVP [Wolfgang SCHUESSEL]; Freedom Party of Austria or FPOe [Susanne RIESS-PASSER]; Social Democratic Party of Austria or SPOe [Alfred GUSENBAUER]; The Greens Alternative or GA [Alexander VAN DER BELLEN]
Political pressure groups and leaders: Austrian Trade Union Federation (primarily Socialist) or OeGB; Federal Economic Chamber; OeVP-oriented League of Austrian Industrialists or VOel; Roman Catholic Church, including its chief lay organization, Catholic Action; three composite leagues of the Austrian People's Party or OeVP representing business, labor, and farmers
International organization participation: AfDB, AsDB, Australia Group, BIS, BSEC (observer), CCC, CE, CEI, CERN, EAPC, EBRD, ECE, EIB, EMU, ESA, EU, FAO, G- 9, IADB, IAEA, IBRD, ICAO, ICC, ICFTU, ICRM, IDA, IEA, IFAD, IFC, IFRCS, ILO, IMF, IMO, Intelsat, Interpol, IOC, IOM, ISO, ITU, MINURSO, NAM (guest), NEA, NSG, OAS (observer), OECD, OPCW, OSCE, PCA, PFP, UN, UNCTAD, UNDOF, UNESCO, UNFICYP, UNHCR, UNIDO, UNIKOM, UNITAR, UNMEE, UNMIBH, UNMIK, UNMOT, UNOMIG, UNTAET, UNTSO, UPU, WCL, WEU (observer), WFTU, WHO, WIPO, WMO, WToO, WTrO, ZC
Diplomatic representation in the US:
chief of mission: Ambassador Peter MOSER
chancery: 3524 International Court NW, Washington, DC 20008-3035
telephone: [1] (202) 895-6700
FAX: [1] (202) 895-6750
consulate(s) general: Chicago, Los Angeles, and New York
Diplomatic representation from the US:
chief of mission: Ambassador Kathryn Walt HALL
embassy: Boltzmanngasse 16, A-1091, Vienna
mailing address: use embassy street address
telephone: [43] (1) 313-39-2060
FAX: [43] (1) 313-39-2057
Flag description: three equal horizontal bands of red (top), white, and red

Economy

Economy - overview: Austria with its well-developed market economy and high standard of living is closely tied to other EU economies, especially Germany's. Membership in the EU has drawn an influx of foreign investors attracted by Austria's access to the single European market and proximity to EU aspirant economies. In 2000, Austria moved to further cut government spending and raise taxes to meet EMU deficit targets after facing unexpected difficulties in reducing the public deficit. To meet increased competition from both EU and Central European countries, Austria will need to emphasize knowledge-based sectors of the economy and continue to deregulate the service sector. Growth is expected to remain at about 3% in 2001.
GDP: purchasing power parity - $203 billion (2000 est.)
GDP - real growth rate: 3.1% (2000 est.)
GDP - per capita: purchasing power parity - $25,000 (2000 est.)
GDP - composition by sector:
agriculture: 2.2%
industry: 30.4%
services: 67.4% (1999 est.)
Population below poverty line: NA%
Inflation rate (consumer prices): 2% (2000 est.)
Labor force: 3.7 million (1999)
Labor force - by occupation: services 68%, industry and crafts 29%, agriculture and forestry 3% (1999 est.)
Unemployment rate: 5.4% (2000 est.)
Budget:
revenues: $56.3 billion
expenditures: $60.5 billion, including capital expenditures of $NA (2000 est.)
Industries: construction, machinery, vehicles and parts, food, chemicals, lumber and wood processing, paper and paperboard, communications equipment, tourism
Industrial production growth rate: 4.2% (2000)
Electricity - production: 59.283 billion kWh (1999)
Electricity - production by source:
fossil fuel: 29.53%
hydro: 67.65%
nuclear: 0%
other: 2.82% (1999)
Electricity - consumption: 53.231 billion kWh (1999)
Electricity - exports: 13.507 billion kWh (1999)
Electricity - imports: 11.605 billion kWh (1999)
Agriculture - products: grains, potatoes, sugar beets, wine, fruit; dairy products, cattle, pigs, poultry; lumber
Exports: $63.2 billion (2000 est.)
Exports - commodities: machinery and equipment, paper and paperboard, metal goods, chemicals, iron and steel; textiles, foodstuffs
Exports - partners: EU 64.2% (Germany 35.7%, Italy 8.7%, France 4.5%), Switzerland 5.9%, US 4.5%, Hungary 3.9% (1999)
Imports: $65.6 billion (2000 est.)
Imports - commodities: machinery and equipment, chemicals, metal goods, oil and oil products; foodstuffs
Imports - partners: EU 70.3% (Germany 42.5%, Italy 7.9%, France 5.3%), US 5.4%, Switzerland 3.0%, Hungary 2.8% (1999)
Debt - external: $16 billion (1999)
Economic aid - donor: ODA, $472 million (1999)
Currency: Austrian schilling (ATS); euro (EUR)
note: on 1 January 1999, the EU introduced the euro as a common currency that is now being used by financial institutions in Austria at a fixed rate of 13.7603 Austrian shillings per euro and will replace the local currency for all transactions in 2002
Currency code: ATS; EUR
Exchange rates: euros per US dollar - 1.0659 (January 2001), 1.0854 (2000), 0.9386 (1999); Austrian schillings per US dollar - 11.86 (January 1999), 12.91 (1999), 12.379 (1998), 12.204 (1997), 10.587 (1996)
Fiscal year: calendar year

Communications

Telephones - main lines in use: 4 million (3,600,000 analog main lines plus 400,000 ISDN or Integrated Services Digital Network connections) (1999)
Telephones - mobile cellular: 4.5 million (2000)
Telephone system:
general assessment: highly developed and efficient
domestic: there are 48 main lines for every 100 persons and the system is nearly 100% digital; the fiber optic net is very extensive; all telephone applications and Internet services are available
international: satellite earth stations - 2 Intelsat (1 Atlantic Ocean and 1 Indian Ocean) and 2 Eutelsat (1999)
Radio broadcast stations: AM 1, FM 61 (plus several hundred repeaters), shortwave 1 (1998)
Radios: 6.08 million (1997)
Television broadcast stations: 45 (plus 960 repeaters) (1995)
Televisions: 4.25 million (1997)
Internet country code: .at
Internet Service Providers (ISPs): 37 (2000)
Internet users: 2.6 million (2000)

Austria (continued)

Transportation

Railways:
total: 6,095.2 km (3,643.3 km electrified)
standard gauge: 5,564.2 km 1.435-m gauge (3,521.2 km electrified)
narrow gauge: 497.1 km (33.9 km 1.000-m gauge - 28.1 km electrified, 497.1 km 0.760-m gauge - 94 km electrified) (2001)
Highways:
total: 133,361 km
paved: 133,361 km (including 1,613 km of expressways)
unpaved: 0 km (1998)
Waterways: 358 km (1999)
Pipelines: crude oil 777 km; natural gas 840 km (1999)
Ports and harbors: Linz, Vienna, Enns, Krems
Merchant marine:
total: 23 ships (1,000 GRT or over) totaling 86,905 GRT/117,417 DWT
ships by type: bulk 1, cargo 18, combination bulk 2, container 2 (2000 est.)
Airports: 55 (2000 est.)
Airports - with paved runways:
total: 24
over 3,047 m: 1
2,438 to 3,047 m: 5
1,524 to 2,437 m: 1
914 to 1,523 m: 3
under 914 m: 14 (2000 est.)
Airports - with unpaved runways:
total: 31
1,524 to 2,437 m: 1
914 to 1,523 m: 3
under 914 m: 27 (2000 est.)
Heliports: 1 (2000 est.)

Military

Military branches: Army (includes Flying Division)
Military manpower - military age: 19 years of age
Military manpower - availability:
males age 15-49: 2,091,263 (2001 est.)
Military manpower - fit for military service:
males age 15-49: 1,731,383 (2001 est.)
Military manpower - reaching military age annually:
males: 50,580 (2001 est.)
Military expenditures - dollar figure: $1.7 billion (FY98)
Military expenditures - percent of GDP: 1.2% (FY98)

Transnational Issues

Disputes - international: minor disputes with Czech Republic and Slovenia over nuclear power plants and post-World War II treatment of German-speaking minorities
Illicit drugs: transshipment point for Southwest Asian heroin and South American cocaine destined for Western Europe

Azerbaijan

Introduction

Background: Azerbaijan - a nation of Turkic Muslims - has been an independent republic since the collapse of the Soviet Union in 1991. Despite a cease-fire, in place since 1994, Azerbaijan has yet to resolve its conflict with Armenia over the Azerbaijani Nagorno-Karabakh enclave (largely Armenian populated). Azerbaijan has lost almost 20% of its territory and must support some 750,000 refugees and internally displaced persons (IDPs) as a result of the conflict. Corruption is ubiquitous and the promise of widespread wealth from Azerbaijan's undeveloped petroleum resources remains largely unfulfilled.

Geography

Location: Southwestern Asia, bordering the Caspian Sea, between Iran and Russia
Geographic coordinates: 40 30 N, 47 30 E
Map references: Commonwealth of Independent States
Area:
total: 86,600 sq km
land: 86,100 sq km
water: 500 sq km
note: includes the exclave of Naxcivan Autonomous Republic and the Nagorno-Karabakh region; the region's autonomy was abolished by Azerbaijani Supreme Soviet on 26 November 1991
Area - comparative: slightly smaller than Maine
Land boundaries:
total: 2,013 km
border countries: Armenia (with Azerbaijan-proper) 566 km, Armenia (with Azerbaijan-Naxcivan exclave) 221 km, Georgia 322 km, Iran (with Azerbaijan-proper) 432 km, Iran (with Azerbaijan-Naxcivan exclave) 179 km, Russia 284 km, Turkey 9 km
Coastline: 0 km (landlocked); note - Azerbaijan borders the Caspian Sea (800 km, est.)
Maritime claims: none (landlocked)
Climate: dry, semiarid steppe
Terrain: large, flat Kur-Araz Ovaligi (Kura-Araks Lowland) (much of it below sea level) with Great Caucasus Mountains to the north, Qarabag Yaylasi (Karabakh Upland) in west; Baku lies on Abseron Yasaqligi (Apsheron Peninsula) that juts into Caspian Sea
Elevation extremes:
lowest point: Caspian Sea -28 m
highest point: Bazarduzu Dagi 4,485 m
Natural resources: petroleum, natural gas, iron ore, nonferrous metals, alumina
Land use:
arable land: 18%
permanent crops: 5%
permanent pastures: 25%
forests and woodland: 11%
other: 41% (1993 est.)
Irrigated land: 10,000 sq km (1993 est.)
Natural hazards: droughts; some lowland areas threatened by rising levels of the Caspian Sea
Environment - current issues: local scientists consider the Abseron Yasaqligi (Apsheron Peninsula) (including Baku and Sumqayit) and the Caspian Sea to be the ecologically most devastated area in the world because of severe air, water, and soil pollution; soil pollution results from the use of DDT as a pesticide and also from toxic defoliants used in the production of cotton
Environment - international agreements:
party to: Biodiversity, Climate Change, Climate Change-Kyoto Protocol, Desertification, Endangered Species, Marine Dumping, Ozone Layer Protection, Ship Pollution
signed, but not ratified: none of the selected agreements
Geography - note: landlocked

People

Population: 7,771,092 (July 2001 est.)
Age structure:
0-14 years: 28.95% (male 1,146,315; female 1,103,393)
15-64 years: 63.93% (male 2,415,678; female 2,552,759)
65 years and over: 7.12% (male 219,549; female 333,398) (2001 est.)
Population growth rate: 0.32% (2001 est.)
Birth rate: 18.44 births/1,000 population (2001 est.)
Death rate: 9.55 deaths/1,000 population (2001 est.)
Net migration rate: -5.67 migrant(s)/1,000 population (2001 est.)
Sex ratio:
at birth: 1.05 male(s)/female
under 15 years: 1.04 male(s)/female
15-64 years: 0.95 male(s)/female
65 years and over: 0.66 male(s)/female
total population: 0.95 male(s)/female (2001 est.)
Infant mortality rate: 83.08 deaths/1,000 live births (2001 est.)

Azerbaijan (continued)

Life expectancy at birth:
total population: 62.96 years
male: 58.65 years
female: 67.49 years (2001 est.)
Total fertility rate: 2.24 children born/woman (2001 est.)
HIV/AIDS - adult prevalence rate: less than 0.01% (1999 est.)
HIV/AIDS - people living with HIV/AIDS: less than 500 (1999 est.)
HIV/AIDS - deaths: less than 100 (1999 est.)
Nationality:
noun: Azerbaijani(s)
adjective: Azerbaijani
Ethnic groups: Azeri 90%, Dagestani 3.2%, Russian 2.5%, Armenian 2%, other 2.3% (1998 est.)
note: almost all Armenians live in the separatist Nagorno-Karabakh region
Religions: Muslim 93.4%, Russian Orthodox 2.5%, Armenian Orthodox 2.3%, other 1.8% (1995 est.)
note: religious affiliation is still nominal in Azerbaijan; percentages for actual practicing adherents are much lower
Languages: Azerbaijani (Azeri) 89%, Russian 3%, Armenian 2%, other 6% (1995 est.)
Literacy:
definition: age 15 and over can read and write
total population: 97%
male: 99%
female: 96% (1989 est.)

Government

Country name:
conventional long form: Republic of Azerbaijan
conventional short form: Azerbaijan
local long form: Azarbaycan Respublikasi
local short form: none
former: Azerbaijan Soviet Socialist Republic
Government type: republic
Capital: Baku (Baki)
Administrative divisions: 59 rayons (rayonlar; rayon - singular), 11 cities* (saharlar; sahar - singular), 1 autonomous republic** (muxtar respublika); Abseron Rayonu, Agcabadi Rayonu, Agdam Rayonu, Agdas Rayonu, Agstafa Rayonu, Agsu Rayonu, Ali Bayramli Sahari*, Astara Rayonu, Baki Sahari*, Balakan Rayonu, Barda Rayonu, Beylaqan Rayonu, Bilasuvar Rayonu, Cabrayil Rayonu, Calilabad Rayonu, Daskasan Rayonu, Davaci Rayonu, Fuzuli Rayonu, Gadabay Rayonu, Ganca Sahari*, Goranboy Rayonu, Goycay Rayonu, Haciqabul Rayonu, Imisli Rayonu, Ismayilli Rayonu, Kalbacar Rayonu, Kurdamir Rayonu, Lacin Rayonu, Lankaran Rayonu, Lankaran Sahari*, Lerik Rayonu, Masalli Rayonu, Mingacevir Sahari*, Naftalan Sahari*, Naxcivan Muxtar Respublikasi**, Neftcala Rayonu, Oguz Rayonu, Qabala Rayonu, Qax Rayonu, Qazax Rayonu, Qobustan Rayonu, Quba Rayonu, Qubadli Rayonu, Qusar Rayonu, Saatli Rayonu, Sabirabad Rayonu, Saki Rayonu, Saki Sahari*, Salyan Rayonu, Samaxi Rayonu, Samkir Rayonu, Samux Rayonu, Siyazan Rayonu, Sumqayit Sahari*, Susa Rayonu, Susa Sahari*, Tartar Rayonu, Tovuz Rayonu, Ucar Rayonu, Xacmaz Rayonu, Xankandi Sahari*, Xanlar Rayonu, Xizi Rayonu, Xocali Rayonu, Xocavand Rayonu, Yardimli Rayonu, Yevlax Rayonu, Yevlax Sahari*, Zangilan Rayonu, Zaqatala Rayonu, Zardab Rayonu
Independence: 30 August 1991 (from Soviet Union)
National holiday: Founding of the Democratic Republic of Azerbaidzhan, 28 May (1918)
Constitution: adopted 12 November 1995
Legal system: based on civil law system
Suffrage: 18 years of age; universal
Executive branch:
chief of state: President Heydar ALIYEV (since 18 June 1993)
head of government: Prime Minister Artur RASIZADE (since 26 November 1996)
cabinet: Council of Ministers appointed by the president and confirmed by the National Assembly
elections: president elected by popular vote to a five-year term; election last held 11 October 1998 (next to be held NA October 2003); prime minister and first deputy prime ministers appointed by the president and confirmed by the National Assembly
election results: Heydar ALIYEV reelected president; percent of vote - Heydar ALIYEV 77.6%, Etibar MAMEDOV 11.8%, Nizami SULEYMANOV 8.2%
Legislative branch: unicameral National Assembly or Milli Mejlis (125 seats; members elected by popular vote to serve five-year terms)
elections: last held 4 November 2000 (next to be held NA November 2005)
election results: percent of vote by party - NA%; seats by party - NAP and allies 108, APF 6, CSP 3, PNIA 2, Musavat Party 2, CPA 2, APF "traditionalist" 1, Compatriot Party 1
Judicial branch: Supreme Court
Political parties and leaders: Alliance for Azerbaijan Party [Abutalyb SAMADOV]; Azerbaijani Democratic Party or ADP [Sardar JALAL]; Azerbaijani Independent Democratic Party or AMDP [Leyla YUNUSOVA]; Azerbaijan Popular Front or APF [Ali KERIMOV, leader of "reform faction"; Mirmahmud FATTAYEV, leader of "traditionalist" faction]; Civic Solidarity Party or CSP [Sabir RUSTAMKHANLY]; Civic Union Party [Ayaz MUTALIBOV]; Communist Party of Azerbaijan or CPA [Ramiz AHMADOV]; Communist Party of Azerbaijan or CPA-2 [Firudin HASANOV]; Compatriot Party [Mais SAFARLI]; Democratic Enlightenment Party [Mammadhanifu MUSAYEV]; Democratic Party for Azerbaijan or DPA [Ilyus ISMAILOV and Rasul QULIYEV, co-chairman]; Democratic World Party of Azerbaijan [Mamnad ALIZADE]; Liberal Party of Azerbaijan [Lala Shvkat HAJIYEVA]; Motherland Party [Fazail AGAMALI]; National Congress Party of Azerbaijan [Ihtiyar SHIRIN]; National Movement Party [Samir JAFAROV]; National Statehood Party [Sabir TARIVERDIYEV]; Musavat [Isa GAMBAR, chairman]; New Azerbaijan Party or NAP [Heydar ALIYEV, chairman]; Party for National Independence of Azerbaijan or PNIA [Etibar MAMMADOV, chairman]; People's Democratic Party of Azerbaijan or PDPA [Rafig TURABKHANOGLU]; Social Democratic Party of Azerbaijan or SDP [Zardusht ALIZADE, chairman]
note: opposition parties regularly factionalize and form new parties
Political pressure groups and leaders: Sadval, Lezgin movement; self-proclaimed Armenian Nagorno-Karabakh Republic; Talysh independence movement
International organization participation: AsDB, BSEC, CCC, CE, CIS, EAPC, EBRD, ECE, ECO, ESCAP, FAO, IBRD, ICAO, ICFTU, ICRM, IDA, IDB, IFAD, IFC, IFRCS, ILO, IMF, IMO, Intelsat, Interpol, IOC, ISO (correspondent), ITU, NAM (observer), OAS (observer), OIC, OPCW, OSCE, PFP, UN, UNCTAD, UNESCO, UNIDO, UPU, WFTU, WHO, WIPO, WMO, WTrO (observer)
Diplomatic representation in the US:
chief of mission: Ambassador Hafiz Mir Jalal PASHAYEV
chancery: (temporary) Suite 700, 927 15th Street NW, Washington, DC 20005 or P. O. Box 28790, Washington, DC 20038-8790
telephone: [1] (202) 842-0001
FAX: [1] (202) 842-0004
Diplomatic representation from the US:
chief of mission: Ambassador Ross WILSON
embassy: Azadliq Prospekt 83, Baku 370007
mailing address: American Embassy Baku, Department of State, Washington, DC 20521-7050
telephone: [9] (9412) 98-03-35, 36, 37
FAX: [9] (9412) 90-66-71
Flag description: three equal horizontal bands of blue (top), red, and green; a crescent and eight-pointed star in white are centered in red band

Economy

Economy - overview: Azerbaijan's most prominent products are oil, cotton, and natural gas. Azerbaijan's oil production declined through 1997 but has registered an increase every year since. Negotiation of 19 production-sharing arrangements (PSAs) with foreign firms, which have thus far committed $60 billion to oil field development, should generate the funds needed to spur future industrial development. Oil production under the first of these PSAs, with the Azerbaijan International Operating Company, began in November 1997. Azerbaijan shares all the formidable problems of the former Soviet republics in making the transition from a command to a market economy, but its considerable energy resources brighten its long-term prospects. Baku has only recently begun making progress on economic reform, and old economic ties and structures are slowly being replaced. An obstacle to economic progress, including stepped up foreign investment, is the continuing conflict with Armenia over the Nagorno-Karabakh region. Trade with Russia and the other former Soviet republics is declining in importance while trade is building up with Turkey, Iran, UAE, and the nations of Europe. Long-term prospects will depend on world oil prices, the location of new pipelines in the region, and Azerbaijan's ability to manage its oil wealth.

Azerbaijan *(continued)*

GDP: purchasing power parity - $23.5 billion (2000 est.)
GDP - real growth rate: 11.4% (2000 est.)
GDP - per capita: purchasing power parity - $3,000 (2000 est.)
GDP - composition by sector:
agriculture: 22%
industry: 33%
services: 45% (1999 est.)
Population below poverty line: 60% (2000 est.)
Household income or consumption by percentage share:
lowest 10%: NA%
highest 10%: NA%
Inflation rate (consumer prices): 1.8% (2000 est.)
Labor force: 2.9 million (1997)
Labor force - by occupation: agriculture and forestry 32%, industry 15%, services 53% (1997)
Unemployment rate: 20% (1999 est.)
Budget:
revenues: $777 million
expenditures: $995 million, including capital expenditures of $NA (1999 est.)
Industries: petroleum and natural gas, petroleum products, oilfield equipment; steel, iron ore, cement; chemicals and petrochemicals; textiles
Industrial production growth rate: 6.9% (2000 est.)
Electricity - production: 16.378 billion kWh (1999)
Electricity - production by source:
fossil fuel: 86.46%
hydro: 13.54%
nuclear: 0%
other: 0% (1999)
Electricity - consumption: 15.432 billion kWh (1999)
Electricity - exports: 600 million kWh (1999)
Electricity - imports: 800 million kWh (1999)
Agriculture - products: cotton, grain, rice, grapes, fruit, vegetables, tea, tobacco; cattle, pigs, sheep, goats
Exports: $1.9 billion (f.o.b., 2000 est.)
Exports - commodities: oil and gas 75%, machinery, cotton, foodstuffs
Exports - partners: Italy, Turkey, Russia, Georgia, Iran
Imports: $1.4 billion (f.o.b., 2000 est.)
Imports - commodities: machinery and equipment, foodstuffs, metals, chemicals
Imports - partners: Russia, Turkey, Ukraine, UAE, Iran
Debt - external: $1 billion (2000)
Economic aid - recipient: ODA, $113 million (1996)
Currency: Azerbaijani manat (AZM)
Currency code: AZM
Exchange rates: Azerbaijani manats per US dollar - 4,579 (1 February 2001), 4,342 (October 1999), 4,373 (1999), 3,869 (1998), 3,985.38 (1997), 4,301.26 (1996)
Fiscal year: calendar year

Communications

Telephones - main lines in use: 663,000 (1997)
Telephones - mobile cellular: 40,000 (1997)
Telephone system:
general assessment: inadequate; requires considerable expansion and modernization; teledensity of 8.6 main lines per 100 persons is very low
domestic: the majority of telephones are in Baku and other industrial centers - about 700 villages still do not have public telephone service; satellite service connects Baku to a modern switch in its exclave of Naxcivan
international: the old Soviet system of cable and microwave is still serviceable; a satellite connection to Turkey enables Baku to reach about 200 additional countries, some of which are directly connected to Baku by satellite providers other than Turkey (1997)
Radio broadcast stations: AM 10, FM 17, shortwave 1 (1998)
Radios: 175,000 (1997)
Television broadcast stations: 2 (1997)
Televisions: 170,000 (1997)
Internet country code: .az
Internet Service Providers (ISPs): 2 (2000)
Internet users: 8,000 (2000)

Transportation

Railways:
total: 2,125 km in common carrier service; does not include industrial lines
broad gauge: 2,125 km 1.520-m gauge (1,278 km electrified) (1993)
Highways:
total: 24,981 km
paved: 23,057 km (these roads are said to be hard-surfaced, and include, in addition to conventionally paved roads, some that are surfaced with gravel or other coarse aggregate, making them trafficable in all weather)
unpaved: 1,924 km (these roads are made of unstabilized earth and are difficult to negotiate in wet weather) (1998)
Waterways: none
Pipelines: crude oil 1,130 km; petroleum products 630 km; natural gas 1,240 km
Ports and harbors: Baku (Baki)
Merchant marine:
total: 56 ships (1,000 GRT or over) totaling 253,882 GRT/313,252 DWT
ships by type: bulk 1, cargo 12, petroleum tanker 40, roll on/roll off 2, short-sea passenger 1 (2000 est.)
Airports: 52 (2000 est.)
Airports - with paved runways:
total: 9
2,438 to 3,047 m: 5
1,524 to 2,437 m: 4 (2000 est.)
Airports - with unpaved runways:
total: 43
1,524 to 2,437 m: 7
914 to 1,523 m: 8
under 914 m: 28 (2000 est.)

Military

Military branches: Army, Navy, Air and Air Defense Forces, Border Guards
Military manpower - military age: 18 years of age
Military manpower - availability:
males age 15-49: 2,102,780 (2001 est.)
Military manpower - fit for military service:
males age 15-49: 1,684,673 (2001 est.)
Military manpower - reaching military age annually:
males: 77,099 (2001 est.)
Military expenditures - dollar figure: $121 million (FY99)
Military expenditures - percent of GDP: 2.6% (FY99)

Transnational Issues

Disputes - international: Armenia supports ethnic Armenians in the Nagorno-Karabakh region of Azerbaijan in the longstanding, separatist conflict against the Azerbaijani Government; Caspian Sea boundaries are not yet determined among Azerbaijan, Iran, Kazakhstan, Russia, and Turkmenistan
Illicit drugs: limited illicit cultivation of cannabis and opium poppy, mostly for CIS consumption; limited government eradication program; transshipment point for opiates via Iran, Central Asia, and Russia to Western Europe

Bahamas, The

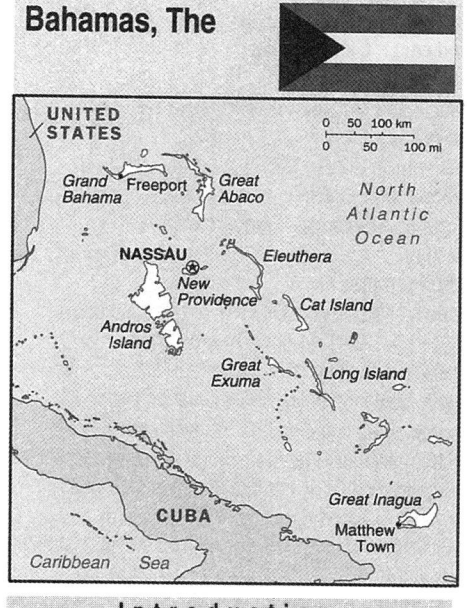

Introduction

Background: Since attaining independence from the UK in 1973, The Bahamas have prospered through tourism and international banking and investment management. Because of its geography, the country is a major transshipment point for illegal drugs, particularly shipments to the US, and its territory is used for smuggling illegal migrants into the US.

Geography

Location: Caribbean, chain of islands in the North Atlantic Ocean, southeast of Florida
Geographic coordinates: 24 15 N, 76 00 W
Map references: Central America and the Caribbean
Area:
total: 13,940 sq km
land: 10,070 sq km
water: 3,870 sq km
Area - comparative: slightly smaller than Connecticut
Land boundaries: 0 km
Coastline: 3,542 km
Maritime claims:
continental shelf: 200-m depth or to the depth of exploitation
exclusive economic zone: 200 NM
territorial sea: 12 NM
Climate: tropical marine; moderated by warm waters of Gulf Stream
Terrain: long, flat coral formations with some low rounded hills
Elevation extremes:
lowest point: Atlantic Ocean 0 m
highest point: Mount Alvernia, on Cat Island 63 m
Natural resources: salt, aragonite, timber, arable land
Land use:
arable land: 1%
permanent crops: 0%
permanent pastures: 0%
forests and woodland: 32%
other: 67% (1993 est.)
Irrigated land: NA sq km
Natural hazards: hurricanes and other tropical storms that cause extensive flood and wind damage
Environment - current issues: coral reef decay; solid waste disposal
Environment - international agreements:
party to: Biodiversity, Climate Change, Climate Change-Kyoto Protocol, Desertification, Endangered Species, Hazardous Wastes, Law of the Sea, Marine Dumping, Nuclear Test Ban, Ozone Layer Protection, Ship Pollution, Wetlands
signed, but not ratified: none of the selected agreements
Geography - note: strategic location adjacent to US and Cuba; extensive island chain

People

Population: 297,852
note: estimates for this country explicitly take into account the effects of excess mortality due to AIDS; this can result in lower life expectancy, higher infant mortality and death rates, lower population and growth rates, and changes in the distribution of population by age and sex than would otherwise be expected (July 2001 est.)
Age structure:
0-14 years: 29.43% (male 44,179; female 43,486)
15-64 years: 64.46% (male 94,329; female 97,674)
65 years and over: 6.11% (male 7,618; female 10,566) (2001 est.)
Population growth rate: 0.93% (2001 est.)
Birth rate: 19.1 births/1,000 population (2001 est.)
Death rate: 7.14 deaths/1,000 population (2001 est.)
Net migration rate: -2.65 migrant(s)/1,000 population (2001 est.)
Sex ratio:
at birth: 1.02 male(s)/female
under 15 years: 1.02 male(s)/female
15-64 years: 0.97 male(s)/female
65 years and over: 0.72 male(s)/female
total population: 0.96 male(s)/female (2001 est.)
Infant mortality rate: 17.03 deaths/1,000 live births (2001 est.)
Life expectancy at birth:
total population: 70.46 years
male: 67.27 years
female: 73.71 years (2001 est.)
Total fertility rate: 2.3 children born/woman (2001 est.)
HIV/AIDS - adult prevalence rate: 4.13% (1999 est.)
HIV/AIDS - people living with HIV/AIDS: 6,900 (1999 est.)
HIV/AIDS - deaths: 500 (1999 est.)
Nationality:
noun: Bahamian(s)
adjective: Bahamian
Ethnic groups: black 85%, white 12%, Asian and Hispanic 3%
Religions: Baptist 32%, Anglican 20%, Roman Catholic 19%, Methodist 6%, Church of God 6%, other Protestant 12%, none or unknown 3%, other 2%
Languages: English, Creole (among Haitian immigrants)
Literacy:
definition: age 15 and over can read and write
total population: 98.2%
male: 98.5%
female: 98% (1995 est.)

Government

Country name:
conventional long form: Commonwealth of The Bahamas
conventional short form: The Bahamas
Government type: constitutional parliamentary democracy
Capital: Nassau
Administrative divisions: 21 districts; Acklins and Crooked Islands, Bimini, Cat Island, Exuma, Freeport, Fresh Creek, Governor's Harbour, Green Turtle Cay, Harbour Island, High Rock, Inagua, Kemps Bay, Long Island, Marsh Harbour, Mayaguana, New Providence, Nicholls Town and Berry Islands, Ragged Island, Rock Sound, Sandy Point, San Salvador and Rum Cay
Independence: 10 July 1973 (from UK)
National holiday: Independence Day, 10 July (1973)
Constitution: 10 July 1973
Legal system: based on English common law
Suffrage: 18 years of age; universal
Executive branch:
chief of state: Queen ELIZABETH II (since 6 February 1952), represented by Governor General Sir Orville TURNQUEST (since 2 January 1995)
head of government: Prime Minister Hubert Alexander INGRAHAM (since 19 August 1992) and Deputy Prime Minister Frank WATSON (since December 1994)
cabinet: Cabinet appointed by the governor general on the prime minister's recommendation
elections: none; the monarch is hereditary; governor general appointed by the monarch; prime minister and deputy prime minister appointed by the governor general
Legislative branch: bicameral Parliament consists of the Senate (16-member body appointed by the governor general upon the advice of the prime minister and the opposition leader for five-year terms) and the House of Assembly (40 seats; members elected by direct popular vote to serve five-year terms)
elections: last held 14 March 1997 (next to be held by March 2002)
election results: percent of vote by party - NA%; seats by party - FNM 35, PLP 5
Judicial branch: Supreme Court; Court of Appeal; magistrates courts

Bahamas, The (continued)

Political parties and leaders: Free National Movement or FNM [Hubert Alexander INGRAHAM]; Progressive Liberal Party or PLP [Perry CHRISTIE]
Political pressure groups and leaders: NA
International organization participation: ACP, C, Caricom, CCC, CDB, ECLAC, FAO, G-77, IADB, IBRD, ICAO, ICFTU, ICRM, IFC, IFRCS, ILO, IMF, IMO, Inmarsat, Intelsat, Interpol, IOC, ITU, LAES, NAM, OAS, OPANAL, OPCW, UN, UNCTAD, UNESCO, UNIDO, UPU, WHO, WIPO, WMO, WTrO (observer)
Diplomatic representation in the US:
chief of mission: Ambassador Joshua SEARS
chancery: 2220 Massachusetts Avenue NW, Washington, DC 20008
telephone: [1] (202) 319-2660
FAX: [1] (202) 319-2668
consulate(s) general: Miami and New York
Diplomatic representation from the US:
chief of mission: Ambassador-designate J. Richard BLANKENSHIP
embassy: Queen Street, Nassau
mailing address: local or express mail address: P. O. Box N-8197, Nassau; stateside address: American Embassy Nassau, P. O. Box 599009, Miami, FL 33159-9009; pouch address: Nassau, Department of State, Washington, DC 20521-3370
telephone: [1] (242) 322-1181, 328-2206
FAX: [1] (242) 356-0222
Flag description: three equal horizontal bands of aquamarine (top), gold, and aquamarine, with a black equilateral triangle based on the hoist side

Economy

Economy - overview: The Bahamas is a stable, developing nation with an economy heavily dependent on tourism and offshore banking. Tourism alone accounts for more than 60% of GDP and directly or indirectly employs 40% of the archipelago's labor force. Moderate growth in tourism receipts and a boom in construction of new hotels, resorts, and residences led to an increase of the country's GDP by an estimated 3% in 1998, 6% in 1999, and 4.5% in 2000. Manufacturing and agriculture together contribute only 10% of GDP and show little growth, despite government incentives aimed at those sectors. Overall growth prospects in the short run will depend heavily on the fortunes of the tourism sector and continued sturdy growth in the US, which accounts for the majority of tourist visitors.
GDP: purchasing power parity - $4.5 billion (2000 est.)
GDP - real growth rate: 4.5% (2000 est.)
GDP - per capita: purchasing power parity - $15,000 (2000 est.)
GDP - composition by sector:
agriculture: 3%
industry: 7%
services: 90% (1999 est.)
Population below poverty line: NA%
Household income or consumption by percentage share:
lowest 10%: NA%
highest 10%: NA%
Inflation rate (consumer prices): 1.9% (2000 est.)
Labor force: 156,000 (1999)
Labor force - by occupation: tourism 40%, other services 50%, industry 5%, agriculture 5% (1995 est.)
Unemployment rate: 9% (1998 est.)
Budget:
revenues: $766 million
expenditures: $845 million, including capital expenditures of $97 million (FY97/98)
Industries: tourism, banking, cement, oil refining and transshipment, salt, rum, aragonite, pharmaceuticals, spiral-welded steel pipe
Industrial production growth rate: NA%
Electricity - production: 1.465 billion kWh (1999)
Electricity - production by source:
fossil fuel: 100%
hydro: 0%
nuclear: 0%
other: 0% (1999)
Electricity - consumption: 1.362 billion kWh (1999)
Electricity - exports: 0 kWh (1999)
Electricity - imports: 0 kWh (1999)
Agriculture - products: citrus, vegetables; poultry
Exports: $376.8 million (2000 est.)
Exports - commodities: pharmaceuticals, cement, rum, crawfish, refined petroleum products
Exports - partners: US 22.3%, Switzerland 15.6%, UK 15%, Denmark 7.4% (1998)
Imports: $1.73 billion (2000 est.)
Imports - commodities: foodstuffs, manufactured goods, crude oil, vehicles, electronics
Imports - partners: US 27.3%, Italy 26.5%, Japan 10%, Denmark 4.2% (1998)
Debt - external: $385.8 million (2000 est.)
Economic aid - recipient: $9.8 million (1995)
Currency: Bahamian dollar (BSD)
Currency code: BSD
Exchange rates: Bahamian dollars per US dollar - 1.000 (fixed rate pegged to the dollar)
Fiscal year: 1 July - 30 June

Communications

Telephones - main lines in use: 96,000 (1997)
Telephones - mobile cellular: 6,152 (1997)
Telephone system:
general assessment: modern facilities
domestic: totally automatic system; highly developed
international: tropospheric scatter and submarine cable to Florida; 3 coaxial submarine cables; satellite earth station - 1 Intelsat (Atlantic Ocean) (1997)
Radio broadcast stations: AM 3, FM 4, shortwave 0 (1998)
Radios: 215,000 (1997)
Television broadcast stations: 1 (1997)
Televisions: 67,000 (1997)
Internet country code: .bs
Internet Service Providers (ISPs): 19 (2000)
Internet users: 15,000 (2000)

Transportation

Railways: 0 km
Highways:
total: 2,693 km
paved: 1,546 km
unpaved: 1,147 km (1997)
Waterways: none
Ports and harbors: Freeport, Matthew Town, Nassau
Merchant marine:
total: 1,049 ships (1,000 GRT or over) totaling 30,000,221 GRT/44,601,471 DWT
ships by type: bulk 185, cargo 214, chemical tanker 36, combination bulk 15, combination ore/oil 22, container 66, liquefied gas 33, livestock carrier 1, multi-functional large-load carrier 4, passenger 79, passenger/cargo 1, petroleum tanker 182, railcar carrier 1, refrigerated cargo 118, roll on/roll off 50, short-sea passenger 15, specialized tanker 3, vehicle carrier 24
note: includes some foreign-owned ships registered here as a flag of convenience: Algeria 2, Australia 1, Austria 1, Bermuda 6, Belgium 14, Canada 1, Cuba 1, Cyprus 2, Denmark 17, Finland 7, France 9, Germany 9, Greece 89, Hong Kong 7, Indonesia 2, India 1, Israel 4, Italy 8, Japan 23, Jamaica 1, Kenya 1, Lebanon 2, Luxembourg 2, Monaco 15, Malaysia 1, Netherlands 16, Norway 139, Poland 3, Portugal 2, Russia 2, Saudi Arabia 5, Singapore 12, Spain 7, Sweden 14, Syria 1, Switzerland 7, UAE 1, Trinidad and Tobago 2, UK 67, Ukraine 3, US 50, British Virgin Islands 1, British Virgin Islands 1 (2000 est.)
Airports: 65 (2000 est.)
Airports - with paved runways:
total: 36
over 3,047 m: 2
2,438 to 3,047 m: 2
1,524 to 2,437 m: 16
914 to 1,523 m: 13
under 914 m: 3 (2000 est.)
Airports - with unpaved runways:
total: 29
914 to 1,523 m: 6
under 914 m: 23 (2000 est.)
Heliports: 1 (2000 est.)

Military

Military branches: Royal Bahamas Defense Force (Coast Guard only), Royal Bahamas Police Force
Military expenditures - dollar figure: $20 million (FY95/96)
Military expenditures - percent of GDP: NA%

Transnational Issues

Disputes - international: none
Illicit drugs: transshipment point for cocaine and marijuana bound for US and Europe; banking industry vulnerable to money laundering

Bahrain

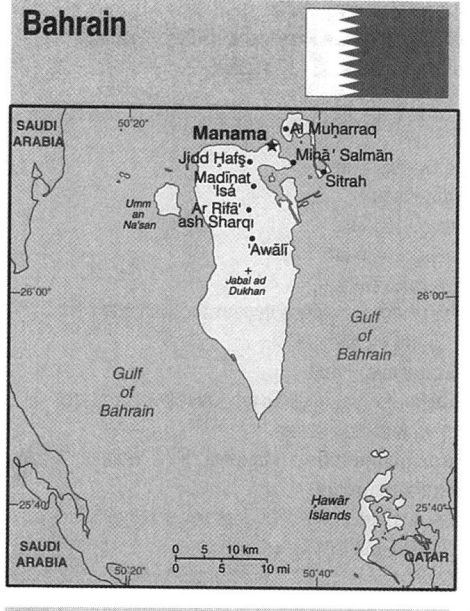

Introduction

Background: Bahrain's small size and central location among Persian Gulf countries require it to play a delicate balancing act in foreign affairs among its larger neighbors. Possessing minimal oil reserves, Bahrain has turned to petroleum processing and refining, and has transformed itself into an international banking center. The new amir is pushing economic and political reforms, and has worked to improve relations with the Shi'a community. In 2001, the International Court of Justice awarded the Hawar Islands, long disputed with Qatar, to Bahrain.

Geography

Location: Middle East, archipelago in the Persian Gulf, east of Saudi Arabia
Geographic coordinates: 26 00 N, 50 33 E
Map references: Middle East
Area:
total: 620 sq km
land: 620 sq km
water: 0 sq km
Area - comparative: 3.5 times the size of Washington, DC
Land boundaries: 0 km
Coastline: 161 km
Maritime claims:
contiguous zone: 24 NM
continental shelf: extending to boundaries to be determined
territorial sea: 12 NM
Climate: arid; mild, pleasant winters; very hot, humid summers
Terrain: mostly low desert plain rising gently to low central escarpment
Elevation extremes:
lowest point: Persian Gulf 0 m
highest point: Jabal ad Dukhan 122 m
Natural resources: oil, associated and nonassociated natural gas, fish, pearls
Land use:
arable land: 1%
permanent crops: 1%
permanent pastures: 6%
forests and woodland: 0%
other: 92% (1993 est.)
Irrigated land: 10 sq km (1993 est.)
Natural hazards: periodic droughts; dust storms
Environment - current issues: desertification resulting from the degradation of limited arable land, periods of drought, and dust storms; coastal degradation (damage to coastlines, coral reefs, and sea vegetation) resulting from oil spills and other discharges from large tankers, oil refineries, and distribution stations; no natural fresh water resources so that groundwater and sea water are the only sources for all water needs
Environment - international agreements:
party to: Biodiversity, Climate Change, Desertification, Hazardous Wastes, Law of the Sea, Marine Dumping, Ozone Layer Protection, Ship Pollution, Wetlands
signed, but not ratified: none of the selected agreements
Geography - note: close to primary Middle Eastern petroleum sources; strategic location in Persian Gulf which much of Western world's petroleum must transit to reach open ocean

People

Population: 645,361
note: includes 228,424 non-nationals (July 2001 est.)
Age structure:
0-14 years: 29.6% (male 96,697; female 94,330)
15-64 years: 67.43% (male 257,360; female 177,839)
65 years and over: 2.97% (male 9,721; female 9,414) (2001 est.)
Population growth rate: 1.73% (2001 est.)
Birth rate: 20.07 births/1,000 population (2001 est.)
Death rate: 3.92 deaths/1,000 population (2001 est.)
Net migration rate: 1.1 migrant(s)/1,000 population (2001 est.)
Sex ratio:
at birth: 1.03 male(s)/female
under 15 years: 1.03 male(s)/female
15-64 years: 1.45 male(s)/female
65 years and over: 1.03 male(s)/female
total population: 1.29 male(s)/female (2001 est.)
Infant mortality rate: 19.77 deaths/1,000 live births (2001 est.)
Life expectancy at birth:
total population: 73.2 years
male: 70.81 years
female: 75.67 years (2001 est.)
Total fertility rate: 2.79 children born/woman (2001 est.)
HIV/AIDS - adult prevalence rate: 0.15% (1999 est.)
HIV/AIDS - people living with HIV/AIDS: NA
HIV/AIDS - deaths: NA
Nationality:
noun: Bahraini(s)
adjective: Bahraini
Ethnic groups: Bahraini 63%, Asian 19%, other Arab 10%, Iranian 8%
Religions: Shi'a Muslim 70%, Sunni Muslim 30%
Languages: Arabic, English, Farsi, Urdu
Literacy:
definition: age 15 and over can read and write
total population: 85.2%
male: 89.1%
female: 79.4% (1995 est.)

Government

Country name:
conventional long form: State of Bahrain
conventional short form: Bahrain
local long form: Dawlat al Bahrayn
local short form: Al Bahrayn
former: Dilmun
Government type: constitutional monarchy
Capital: Manama
Administrative divisions: 12 municipalities (manatiq, singular - mintaqah); Al Hadd, Al Manamah, Al Mintaqah al Gharbiyah, Al Mintaqah al Wusta, Al Mintaqah ash Shamaliyah, Al Muharraq, Ar Rifa' wa al Mintaqah al Janubiyah, Jidd Hafs, Madinat Hamad, Madinat 'Isa, Juzur Hawar, Sitrah
note: all municipalities administered from Manama
Independence: 15 August 1971 (from UK)
National holiday: National Day, 16 December (1971); note - 15 August 1971 is the date of independence from the UK, 16 December 1971 is the date of independence from British protection
Constitution: adopted late December 2000 (new constitution calls for a partially elected legislature, a constitutional monarchy, and an independent judiciary)
Legal system: based on Islamic law and English common law
Suffrage: none
Executive branch:
chief of state: Amir HAMAD bin Isa Al Khalifa (since 6 March 1999); Heir Apparent Crown Prince SALMAN bin Hamad (son of the monarch, born 21 October 1969)
head of government: Prime Minister KHALIFA bin Salman Al Khalifa (since NA 1971)
cabinet: Cabinet appointed by the monarch
elections: none; the monarch is hereditary; prime minister appointed by the monarch
Legislative branch: unicameral National Assembly was dissolved 26 August 1975 and legislative powers were assumed by the Cabinet; appointed Advisory Council established 16 December 1992; the National Action Charter created a bicameral legislature on 23 December 2000; approved by referendum of 14 February 2001
Judicial branch: High Civil Appeals Court
Political parties and leaders: political parties prohibited

Bahrain (continued)

Political pressure groups and leaders: Shi'a activists fomented unrest sporadically 1994-97, demanding the return of an elected National Assembly and an end to unemployment; several small, clandestine leftist and Islamic fundamentalist groups are active
International organization participation: ABEDA, AFESD, AL, AMF, ESCWA, FAO, G-77, GCC, IBRD, ICAO, ICC, ICRM, IDB, IFC, IFRCS, IHO, ILO, IMF, IMO, Inmarsat, Intelsat, Interpol, IOC, ISO (correspondent), ITU, NAM, OAPEC, OIC, OPCW, UN, UNCTAD, UNESCO, UNIDO, UPU, WFTU, WHO, WIPO, WMO, WTrO
Diplomatic representation in the US:
chief of mission: Ambassador (vacant)
chancery: 3502 International Drive NW, Washington, DC 20008
telephone: [1] (202) 342-0741
FAX: [1] (202) 362-2192
consulate(s) general: New York
Diplomatic representation from the US:
chief of mission: Ambassador Johnny YOUNG
embassy: #979, Road 3119 (next to Al-Ahli Sports Club), Block 321, Zinj District, Manama
mailing address: American Embassy Manama, PSC 451, FPO AE 09834-5100; international mail: American Embassy, Box 26431, Manama
telephone: [973] 273-300
FAX: [973] 272-594
Flag description: red with a white serrated band (eight white points) on the hoist side

Economy

Economy - overview: In Bahrain, petroleum production and refining account for about 60% of export receipts, 60% of government revenues, and 30% of GDP. With its highly developed communication and transport facilities, Bahrain is home to numerous multinational firms with business in the Gulf. Bahrain is dependent on Saudi Arabia for oil revenue granted as aid. A large share of exports consists of petroleum products made from imported crude. Construction proceeds on several major industrial projects. Unemployment, especially among the young, and the depletion of both oil and underground water resources are major long-term economic problems.
GDP: purchasing power parity - $10.1 billion (2000 est.)
GDP - real growth rate: 5% (2000 est.)
GDP - per capita: purchasing power parity - $15,900 (2000 est.)
GDP - composition by sector:
agriculture: 1%
industry: 46%
services: 53% (1996 est.)
Population below poverty line: NA%
Household income or consumption by percentage share:
lowest 10%: NA%
highest 10%: NA%
Inflation rate (consumer prices): 2% (2000 est.)
Labor force: 295,000 (1998 est.)
note: 44% of the population in the 15-64 age group is non-national (July 1998 est.)
Labor force - by occupation: industry, commerce, and service 79%, government 20%, agriculture 1% (1997 est.)
Unemployment rate: 15% (1998 est.)
Budget:
revenues: $1.8 billion
expenditures: $2.2 billion, including capital expenditures of $NA (2001 est.)
Industries: petroleum processing and refining, aluminum smelting, offshore banking, ship repairing; tourism
Industrial production growth rate: 2% (2000 est.)
Electricity - production: 6.185 billion kWh (1999)
Electricity - production by source:
fossil fuel: 100%
hydro: 0%
nuclear: 0%
other: 0% (1999)
Electricity - consumption: 5.752 billion kWh (1999)
Electricity - exports: 0 kWh (1999)
Electricity - imports: 0 kWh (1999)
Agriculture - products: fruit, vegetables; poultry, dairy products; shrimp, fish
Exports: $5.8 billion (f.o.b., 2000)
Exports - commodities: petroleum and petroleum products 61%, aluminum 7%
Exports - partners: India 14%, Saudi Arabia 5%, US 5%, UAE 5%, Japan 4%, South Korea 4% (1999)
Imports: $4.2 billion (f.o.b., 2000)
Imports - commodities: nonoil 59%, crude oil 41%
Imports - partners: France 20%, US 14%, UK 8%, Saudi Arabia 7%, Japan 5% (1999)
Debt - external: $2.7 billion (2000)
Economic aid - recipient: $48.4 million (1995)
Currency: Bahraini dinar (BHD)
Currency code: BHD
Exchange rates: Bahraini dinars per US dollar - 0.3760 (fixed rate pegged to the US dollar)
Fiscal year: calendar year

Communications

Telephones - main lines in use: 152,000 (1997)
Telephones - mobile cellular: 58,543 (1997)
Telephone system:
general assessment: modern system
domestic: modern fiber-optic integrated services; digital network with rapidly growing use of mobile cellular telephones
international: tropospheric scatter to Qatar and UAE; microwave radio relay to Saudi Arabia; submarine cable to Qatar, UAE, and Saudi Arabia; satellite earth stations - 2 Intelsat (1 Atlantic Ocean and 1 Indian Ocean) and 1 Arabsat (1997)
Radio broadcast stations: AM 2, FM 3, shortwave 0 (1998)
Radios: 338,000 (1997)
Television broadcast stations: 4 (1997)
Televisions: 275,000 (1997)
Internet country code: .bh
Internet Service Providers (ISPs): 1 (2000)
Internet users: 37,500 (2000)

Transportation

Railways: 0 km
Highways:
total: 3,164 km
paved: 2,433 km
unpaved: 731 km
note: there is a paved causeway connecting Bahrain to Saudi Arabia (1997)
Waterways: none
Pipelines: crude oil 56 km; petroleum products 16 km; natural gas 32 km
Ports and harbors: Manama, Mina' Salman, Sitrah
Merchant marine:
total: 7 ships (1,000 GRT or over) totaling 175,609 GRT/207,652 DWT
ships by type: bulk 2, cargo 3, container 2 (2000 est.)
Airports: 3 (2000 est.)
Airports - with paved runways:
total: 2
over 3,047 m: 2 (2000 est.)
Airports - with unpaved runways:
total: 1
1,524 to 2,437 m: 1 (2000 est.)
Heliports: 1 (2000 est.)

Military

Military branches: Ground Force, Navy, Air Force, Coast Guard, Police Force
Military manpower - military age: 15 years of age
Military manpower - availability:
males age 15-49: 222,141 (2001 est.)
Military manpower - fit for military service:
males age 15-49: 121,833 (2001 est.)
Military manpower - reaching military age annually:
males: 5,926 (2001 est.)
Military expenditures - dollar figure: $318 million (FY99)
Military expenditures - percent of GDP: 5.2% (FY99)

Transnational Issues

Disputes - international: in March of 2001, the International Court of Justice (ICJ) awarded the Hawar Islands to Bahrain and also adjusted Bahrain's maritime boundary with Qatar

Baker Island
(territory of the US)

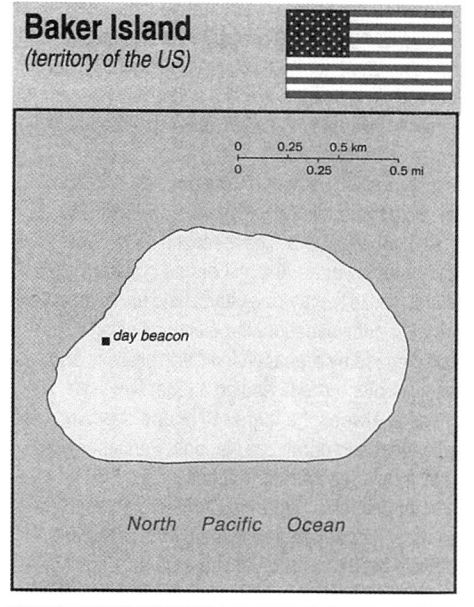

Introduction
Background: The US took possession of the island in 1857, and its guano deposits were mined by US and British companies during the second half of the 19th century. In 1935, a short-lived attempt at colonization was begun on this island - as well as on nearby Howland Island - but was disrupted by World War II and thereafter abandoned. Presently the island is a National Wildlife Refuge run by the US Department of the Interior; a day beacon is situated near the middle of the west coast.

Geography
Location: Oceania, atoll in the North Pacific Ocean, about one-half of the way from Hawaii to Australia
Geographic coordinates: 0 13 N, 176 31 W
Map references: Oceania
Area:
total: 1.4 sq km
land: 1.4 sq km
water: 0 sq km
Area - comparative: about 2.5 times the size of The Mall in Washington, DC
Land boundaries: 0 km
Coastline: 4.8 km
Maritime claims:
exclusive economic zone: 200 NM
territorial sea: 12 NM
Climate: equatorial; scant rainfall, constant wind, burning sun
Terrain: low, nearly level coral island surrounded by a narrow fringing reef
Elevation extremes:
lowest point: Pacific Ocean 0 m
highest point: unnamed location 8 m
Natural resources: guano (deposits worked until 1891), terrestrial and aquatic wildlife
Land use:
arable land: 0%
permanent crops: 0%
permanent pastures: 0%
forests and woodland: 0%
other: 100%
Irrigated land: 0 sq km (1993)
Natural hazards: the narrow fringing reef surrounding the island can be a maritime hazard
Environment - current issues: no natural fresh water resources
Geography - note: treeless, sparse, and scattered vegetation consisting of grasses, prostrate vines, and low growing shrubs; primarily a nesting, roosting, and foraging habitat for seabirds, shorebirds, and marine wildlife

People
Population: uninhabited
note: American civilians evacuated in 1942 after Japanese air and naval attacks during World War II; occupied by US military during World War II, but abandoned after the war; public entry is by special-use permit from US Fish and Wildlife Service only and generally restricted to scientists and educators; a cemetery and remnants of structures from early settlement are located near the middle of the west coast; visited annually by US Fish and Wildlife Service (July 2001 est.)

Government
Country name:
conventional long form: none
conventional short form: Baker Island
Dependency status: unincorporated territory of the US; administered from Washington, DC, by the Fish and Wildlife Service of the US Department of the Interior as part of the National Wildlife Refuge system
Legal system: the laws of the US, where applicable, apply
Flag description: the flag of the US is used

Economy
Economy - overview: no economic activity

Transportation
Waterways: none
Ports and harbors: none; offshore anchorage only; note - there is one small boat landing area along the middle of the west coast
Airports: 1 abandoned World War II runway of 1,665 m, completely covered with vegetation and unusable (2000 est.)
Transportation - note: there is a day beacon near the middle of the west coast

Military
Military - note: defense is the responsibility of the US; visited annually by the US Coast Guard

Transnational Issues
Disputes - international: none

Bangladesh

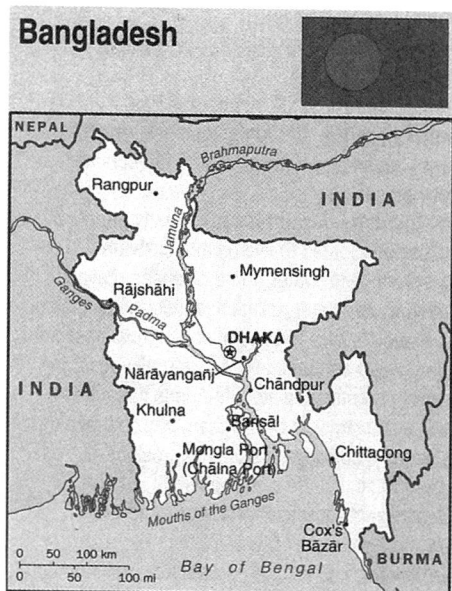

Introduction
Background: Bangladesh came into existence in 1971 when Bengali East Pakistan seceded from its union with West Pakistan. About a third of this extremely poor country annually floods during the monsoon rainy season, hampering economic development.

Geography
Location: Southern Asia, bordering the Bay of Bengal, between Burma and India
Geographic coordinates: 24 00 N, 90 00 E
Map references: Asia
Area:
total: 144,000 sq km
land: 133,910 sq km
water: 10,090 sq km
Area - comparative: slightly smaller than Wisconsin
Land boundaries:
total: 4,246 km
border countries: Burma 193 km, India 4,053 km
Coastline: 580 km
Maritime claims:
contiguous zone: 18 NM
continental shelf: up to the outer limits of the continental margin
exclusive economic zone: 200 NM
territorial sea: 12 NM
Climate: tropical; mild winter (October to March); hot, humid summer (March to June); humid, warm rainy monsoon (June to October)
Terrain: mostly flat alluvial plain; hilly in southeast
Elevation extremes:
lowest point: Indian Ocean 0 m
highest point: Keokradong 1,230 m
Natural resources: natural gas, arable land, timber, coal
Land use:
arable land: 73%
permanent crops: 2%

Bangladesh (continued)

permanent pastures: 5%
forests and woodland: 15%
other: 5% (1993 est.)
Irrigated land: 31,000 sq km (1993 est.)
Natural hazards: droughts, cyclones; much of the country routinely inundated during the summer monsoon season
Environment - current issues: many people are landless and forced to live on and cultivate flood-prone land; water-borne diseases prevalent in surface water; water pollution, especially of fishing areas, results from the use of commercial pesticides; ground water contaminated by naturally-occurring arsenic; intermittent water shortages because of falling water tables in the northern and central parts of the country; soil degradation and erosion; deforestation; severe overpopulation
Environment - international agreements:
party to: Biodiversity, Climate Change, Desertification, Endangered Species, Environmental Modification, Hazardous Wastes, Marine Dumping, Nuclear Test Ban, Ozone Layer Protection, Ship Pollution, Wetlands
signed, but not ratified: Law of the Sea

People

Population: 131,269,860 (July 2001 est.)
Age structure:
0-14 years: 35.04% (male 23,550,607; female 22,451,006)
15-64 years: 61.6% (male 41,432,123; female 39,434,633)
65 years and over: 3.36% (male 2,389,639; female 2,011,852) (2001 est.)
Population growth rate: 1.59% (2001 est.)
Birth rate: 25.3 births/1,000 population (2001 est.)
Death rate: 8.6 deaths/1,000 population (2001 est.)
Net migration rate: -0.76 migrant(s)/1,000 population (2001 est.)
Sex ratio:
at birth: 1.06 male(s)/female
under 15 years: 1.05 male(s)/female
15-64 years: 1.05 male(s)/female
65 years and over: 1.19 male(s)/female
total population: 1.05 male(s)/female (2001 est.)
Infant mortality rate: 69.85 deaths/1,000 live births (2001 est.)
Life expectancy at birth:
total population: 60.54 years
male: 60.74 years
female: 60.33 years (2001 est.)
Total fertility rate: 2.78 children born/woman (2001 est.)
HIV/AIDS - adult prevalence rate: 0.02% (1999 est.)
HIV/AIDS - people living with HIV/AIDS: 13,000 (1999 est.)
HIV/AIDS - deaths: 1,000 (1999 est.)
Nationality:
noun: Bangladeshi(s)
adjective: Bangladeshi

Ethnic groups: Bengali 98%, tribal groups, non-Bengali Muslims (1998)
Religions: Muslim 83%, Hindu 16%, other 1% (1998)
Languages: Bangla (official, also known as Bengali), English
Literacy:
definition: age 15 and over can read and write
total population: 56%
male: 63%
female: 49% (2000 est.)

Government

Country name:
conventional long form: People's Republic of Bangladesh
conventional short form: Bangladesh
former: East Pakistan
Government type: parliamentary democracy
Capital: Dhaka
Administrative divisions: 5 divisions; Barisal, Chittagong, Dhaka, Khulna, Rajshahi; note - there may be one additional division named Sylhet
Independence: 16 December 1971 (from West Pakistan); note - 26 March 1971 is the date of independence from West Pakistan, 16 December 1971 is known as Victory Day and commemorates the official creation of the state of Bangladesh
National holiday: Independence Day, 26 March (1971); note - 26 March 1971 is the date of independence from West Pakistan, 16 December 1971 is Victory Day and commemorates the official creation of the state of Bangladesh
Constitution: 4 November 1972, effective 16 December 1972, suspended following coup of 24 March 1982, restored 10 November 1986, amended many times
Legal system: based on English common law
Suffrage: 18 years of age; universal
Executive branch:
chief of state: President Shahabuddin AHMED (since 9 October 1996); note - the president's duties are normally ceremonial, but with the 13th amendment to the constitution ("Caretaker Government Amendment"), the president's role becomes significant at times when Parliament is dissolved and a caretaker government is installed - at presidential direction - to supervise the elections
head of government: Prime Minister Sheikh HASINA (since 13 July 1996)
cabinet: Cabinet selected by the prime minister and appointed by the president
elections: president elected by National Parliament for a five-year term; election last held 24 July 1996 (next to be held by NA October 2001); following legislative elections, the leader of the party that wins the most seats is usually appointed prime minister by the president
election results: Shahabuddin AHMED elected president without opposition; percent of National Parliament vote - NA%

Legislative branch: unicameral National Parliament or Jatiya Sangsad (330 seats; 300 elected by popular vote from single territorial constituencies, 30 seats reserved for women; members serve five-year terms)
elections: last held 12 June 1996 (next to be held before 13 October 2001)
election results: percent of vote by party - AL 33.87%, BNP 30.87%; seats by party - AL 178, BNP 113, JP 33, JI 3, other 3; note - the elections of 12 June 1996 brought to power an Awami League government for the first time in twenty-one years; held under a neutral, caretaker administration, the elections were characterized by a peaceful, orderly process and massive voter turnout, ending a bitter two-year impasse between the former BNP and opposition parties that had paralyzed National Parliament and led to widespread street violence
Judicial branch: Supreme Court (the chief justices and other judges are appointed by the president)
Political parties and leaders: Awami League or AL [Sheikh HASINA]; Bangladesh Communist Party or BCP [Saifuddin Ahmed MANIK]; Bangladesh Nationalist Party or BNP [Khaleda ZIAur Rahman]; Islami Oikya Jote or IOJ [Azizol HAQ]; Jamaat-E-Islami or JI [Motiur Rahman NIZAMI]; Jatiya Party or JP [Hussain Mohammad ERSHAD]
Political pressure groups and leaders: NA
International organization participation: AsDB, C, CCC, CP, ESCAP, FAO, G-77, IAEA, IBRD, ICAO, ICC, ICFTU, ICRM, IDA, IDB, IFAD, IFC, IFRCS, IHO (pending member), ILO, IMF, IMO, Inmarsat, Intelsat, Interpol, IOC, IOM, ISO, ITU, MINURSO, MONUC, NAM, OIC, OPCW, SAARC, UN, UN Security Council (temporary), UNCTAD, UNESCO, UNHCR, UNIDO, UNIKOM, UNMEE, UNMIBH, UNMIK, UNMOP, UNMOT, UNOMIG, UNTAET, UNU, UPU, WCL, WFTU, WHO, WIPO, WMO, WToO, WTrO
Diplomatic representation in the US:
chief of mission: Ambassador-designate A. Tariq KARIM
chancery: 3510 International Drive NW, Washington, DC 20008
telephone: [1] (202) 244-0183
consulate(s) general: Los Angeles and New York
Diplomatic representation from the US:
chief of mission: Ambassador Mary Ann PETERS
embassy: Road 27, House 110, Banani, Dhaka
mailing address: G. P. O. Box 323, Dhaka 1000
telephone: [880] (2) 8824700 through 8824722
FAX: [880] (2) 8823744
Flag description: green with a large red disk slightly to the hoist side of center; the red sun of freedom represents the blood shed to achieve independence; the green field symbolizes the lush countryside, and secondarily, the traditional color of Islam

Bangladesh (continued)

Economy

Economy - overview: Despite sustained domestic and international efforts to improve economic and demographic prospects, Bangladesh remains one of the world's poorest, most densely populated, and least developed nations. Although more than half of GDP is generated through the service sector, nearly two-thirds of Bangladeshis are employed in the agriculture sector, with rice as the single most important product. Major impediments to growth include frequent cyclones and floods, inefficient state-owned enterprises, inadequate port facilities, a rapidly growing labor force that cannot be absorbed by agriculture, delays in exploiting energy resources (natural gas), insufficient power supplies, and slow implementation of economic reforms. Reform is stalled in many instances by political infighting and corruption at all levels of government. Even so, Prime Minister Sheikh HASINA's Awami League government has made some headway improving the climate for foreign investors and liberalizing the capital markets. Progress on other economic reforms has been halting because of opposition from the bureaucracy, public sector unions, and other vested interest groups.
GDP: purchasing power parity - $203 billion (2000 est.)
GDP - real growth rate: 5.3% (2000 est.)
GDP - per capita: purchasing power parity - $1,570 (2000 est.)
GDP - composition by sector:
agriculture: 30%
industry: 18%
services: 52% (2000 est.)
Population below poverty line: 35.6% (FY95/96 est.)
Household income or consumption by percentage share:
lowest 10%: 3.9%
highest 10%: 28.6% (1995-96 est.)
Inflation rate (consumer prices): 5.8% (2000 est.)
Labor force: 64.1 million (1998)
note: extensive export of labor to Saudi Arabia, Kuwait, UAE, Oman, Qatar, and Malaysia; workers' remittances estimated at $1.71 billion in 1998-99
Labor force - by occupation: agriculture 63%, services 26%, industry 11% (FY95/96)
Unemployment rate: 35.2% (1996)
Budget:
revenues: $4.9 billion
expenditures: $6.8 billion, including capital expenditures of $NA (FY99/00 est.)
Industries: cotton textiles, jute, garments, tea processing, paper newsprint, cement, chemical fertilizer, light engineering, sugar
Industrial production growth rate: 6.1% (2000 est.)
Electricity - production: 12.06 billion kWh (1999)
Electricity - production by source:
fossil fuel: 93.7%
hydro: 6.3%
nuclear: 0%
other: 0% (1999)
Electricity - consumption: 11.216 billion kWh (1999)
Electricity - exports: 0 kWh (1999)
Electricity - imports: 0 kWh (1999)
Agriculture - products: rice, jute, tea, wheat, sugarcane, potatoes, tobacco, pulses, oilseeds, spices, fruit; beef, milk, poultry
Exports: $5.9 billion (2000)
Exports - commodities: garments, jute and jute goods, leather, frozen fish and seafood
Exports - partners: US 31.2%, Germany 9.95%, UK 8.06%, France 5.82%, Italy 4.42% (1999)
Imports: $8.1 billion (2000)
Imports - commodities: machinery and equipment, chemicals, iron and steel, textiles, raw cotton, food, crude oil and petroleum products, cement
Imports - partners: India 12.2%, Singapore 7.8%, Japan 6.7%, China 6.4%, US 5.3% (1999)
Debt - external: $17 billion (2000)
Economic aid - recipient: $1.575 billion (2000 est.)
Currency: taka (BDT)
Currency code: BDT
Exchange rates: taka per US dollar - 54.000 (January 2001), 52.142 (2000), 49.085 (1999), 46.906 (1998), 43.892 (1997), 41.794 (1996)
Fiscal year: 1 July - 30 June

Communications

Telephones - main lines in use: 500,000 (2000)
Telephones - mobile cellular: 283,000 (2000)
Telephone system:
general assessment: totally inadequate for a modern country
domestic: modernizing; introducing digital systems; trunk systems include VHF and UHF microwave radio relay links, and some fiber-optic cable in cities
international: satellite earth stations - 2 Intelsat (Indian Ocean); international radiotelephone communications and landline service to neighboring countries (2000)
Radio broadcast stations: AM 12, FM 12, shortwave 2 (1999)
Radios: 6.15 million (1997)
Television broadcast stations: 15 (1999)
Televisions: 770,000 (1997)
Internet country code: .bd
Internet Service Providers (ISPs): 10 (2000)
Internet users: 30,000 (2000)

Transportation

Railways:
total: 2,745 km
broad gauge: 923 km 1.676-m gauge
narrow gauge: 1,822 km 1.000-m gauge (2000)
Highways:
total: 201,182 km
paved: 19,112 km
unpaved: 182,070 km (1997)
Waterways: up to 8,046 km depending on season
note: includes 3,058 km main cargo routes
Pipelines: natural gas 1,250 km
Ports and harbors: Chittagong, Dhaka, Mongla Port, Narayanganj (2001)
Merchant marine:
total: 35 ships (1,000 GRT or over) totaling 268,566 GRT/375,110 DWT
ships by type: bulk 2, cargo 25, container 3, petroleum tanker 2, refrigerated cargo 1, roll on/roll off 2 (2000 est.)
Airports: 18 (2000 est.)
Airports - with paved runways:
total: 15
over 3,047 m: 2
2,438 to 3,047 m: 3
1,524 to 2,437 m: 4
914 to 1,523 m: 1
under 914 m: 5 (2000 est.)
Airports - with unpaved runways:
total: 3
1,524 to 2,437 m: 1
under 914 m: 2 (2000 est.)

Military

Military branches: Army, Navy, Coast Guard, Air Force, paramilitary forces (includes Bangladesh Rifles, Bangladesh Ansars, Village Defense Parties, National Cadet Corps), Armed Police battalions
Military manpower - availability:
males age 15-49: 36,005,553 (2001 est.)
Military manpower - fit for military service:
males age 15-49: 21,362,279 (2001 est.)
Military expenditures - dollar figure: $559 million (FY96/97)
Military expenditures - percent of GDP: 1.8% (FY96/97)

Transnational Issues

Disputes - international: a portion of the boundary with India is indefinite; exchange of 151 enclaves along border with India subject to ratification by Indian parliament; dispute with India over South Talpatty/New Moore Island
Illicit drugs: transit country for illegal drugs produced in neighboring countries

Barbados

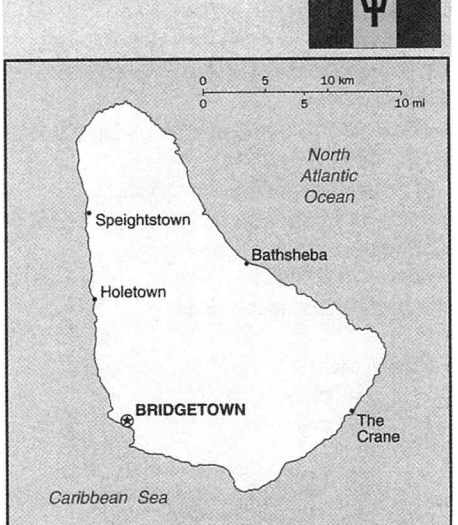

Introduction

Background: The island was uninhabited when first settled by the British in 1627. Its economy remained heavily dependent on sugar, rum, and molasses production through most of the 20th century. In the 1990s, tourism and manufacturing surpassed the sugar industry in economic importance.

Geography

Location: Caribbean, island between the Caribbean Sea and the North Atlantic Ocean, northeast of Venezuela
Geographic coordinates: 13 10 N, 59 32 W
Map references: Central America and the Caribbean
Area:
total: 430 sq km
land: 430 sq km
water: 0 sq km
Area - comparative: 2.5 times the size of Washington, DC
Land boundaries: 0 km
Coastline: 97 km
Maritime claims:
exclusive economic zone: 200 NM
territorial sea: 12 NM
Climate: tropical; rainy season (June to October)
Terrain: relatively flat; rises gently to central highland region
Elevation extremes:
lowest point: Atlantic Ocean 0 m
highest point: Mount Hillaby 336 m
Natural resources: petroleum, fish, natural gas
Land use:
arable land: 37%
permanent crops: 0%
permanent pastures: 5%
forests and woodland: 12%
other: 46% (1993 est.)
Irrigated land: NA sq km
Natural hazards: infrequent hurricanes; periodic landslides
Environment - current issues: pollution of coastal waters from waste disposal by ships; soil erosion; illegal solid waste disposal threatens contamination of aquifers
Environment - international agreements:
party to: Climate Change, Climate Change-Kyoto Protocol, Desertification, Endangered Species, Hazardous Wastes, Law of the Sea, Marine Dumping, Ozone Layer Protection, Ship Pollution
signed, but not ratified: Biodiversity
Geography - note: easternmost Caribbean island

People

Population: 275,330 (July 2001 est.)
Age structure:
0-14 years: 21.68% (male 30,122; female 29,572)
15-64 years: 69.44% (male 93,283; female 97,915)
65 years and over: 8.88% (male 9,432; female 15,006) (2001 est.)
Population growth rate: 0.46% (2001 est.)
Birth rate: 13.47 births/1,000 population (2001 est.)
Death rate: 8.53 deaths/1,000 population (2001 est.)
Net migration rate: -0.32 migrant(s)/1,000 population (2001 est.)
Sex ratio:
at birth: 1.01 male(s)/female
under 15 years: 1.02 male(s)/female
15-64 years: 0.95 male(s)/female
65 years and over: 0.63 male(s)/female
total population: 0.93 male(s)/female (2001 est.)
Infant mortality rate: 12.04 deaths/1,000 live births (2001 est.)
Life expectancy at birth:
total population: 73.25 years
male: 70.66 years
female: 75.86 years (2001 est.)
Total fertility rate: 1.64 children born/woman (2001 est.)
HIV/AIDS - adult prevalence rate: 1.17% (1999 est.)
HIV/AIDS - people living with HIV/AIDS: 1,800 (1999 est.)
HIV/AIDS - deaths: 130 (1999 est.)
Nationality:
noun: Barbadian(s) or Bajan (colloquial)
adjective: Barbadian or Bajan (colloquial)
Ethnic groups: black 80%, white 4%, other 16%
Religions: Protestant 67% (Anglican 40%, Pentecostal 8%, Methodist 7%, other 12%), Roman Catholic 4%, none 17%, other 12%
Languages: English
Literacy:
definition: age 15 and over has ever attended school
total population: 97.4%
male: 98%
female: 96.8% (1995 est.)

Government

Country name:
conventional long form: none
conventional short form: Barbados
Government type: parliamentary democracy; independent sovereign state within the Commonwealth
Capital: Bridgetown
Administrative divisions: 11 parishes; Christ Church, Saint Andrew, Saint George, Saint James, Saint John, Saint Joseph, Saint Lucy, Saint Michael, Saint Peter, Saint Philip, Saint Thomas; note - the city of Bridgetown may be given parish status
Independence: 30 November 1966 (from UK)
National holiday: Independence Day, 30 November (1966)
Constitution: 30 November 1966
Legal system: English common law; no judicial review of legislative acts
Suffrage: 18 years of age; universal
Executive branch:
chief of state: Queen ELIZABETH II (since 6 February 1952), represented by Governor General Sir Clifford Straughn HUSBANDS (since 1 June 1996)
head of government: Prime Minister Owen Seymour ARTHUR (since 6 September 1994); Deputy Prime Minister Billie MILLER (since 6 September 1994)
cabinet: Cabinet appointed by the governor general on the advice of the prime minister
elections: none; the monarch is hereditary; governor general appointed by the monarch; prime minister appointed by the governor general
Legislative branch: bicameral Parliament consists of the Senate (21-member body appointed by the governor general) and the House of Assembly (28 seats; members are elected by direct popular vote to serve five-year terms)
elections: House of Assembly - last held 20 January 1999 (next to be held by January 2004)
election results: House of Assembly - percent of vote by party - NA%; seats by party - BLP 26, DLP 2
Judicial branch: Supreme Court of Judicature (judges are appointed by the Service Commissions for the Judicial and Legal Services)
Political parties and leaders: Barbados Labor Party or BLP [Owen ARTHUR]; Democratic Labor Party or DLP [David THOMPSON]; National Democratic Party or NDP [Richard HAYNES]
Political pressure groups and leaders: Barbados Workers Union [Leroy TROTMAN]; Clement Payne Labor Union [David COMMISSIONG]; People's Progressive Movement [Eric SEALY]; Worker's Party of Barbados [Dr. George BELLE]
International organization participation: ACP, C, Caricom, CCC, CDB, ECLAC, FAO, G-77, IADB, IBRD, ICAO, ICFTU, ICRM, IFAD, IFC, IFRCS, ILO, IMF, IMO, Intelsat, Interpol, IOC, ISO, ITU, LAES, NAM, OAS, OPANAL, UN, UNCTAD, UNESCO, UNIDO, UPU, WFTU, WHO, WIPO, WMO, WTrO

Barbados (continued)

Diplomatic representation in the US:
chief of mission: Ambassador Michael KING
chancery: 2144 Wyoming Avenue NW, Washington, DC 20008
telephone: [1] (202) 939-9200
FAX: [1] (202) 332-7467
consulate(s) general: Miami and New York
consulate(s): Los Angeles

Diplomatic representation from the US:
chief of mission: Ambassador James A. DALEY
embassy: Canadian Imperial Bank of Commerce Building, Broad Street, Bridgetown
mailing address: P. O. Box 302, Bridgetown; FPO AA 34055
telephone: [1] (246) 436-4950
FAX: [1] (246) 429-5246

Flag description: three equal vertical bands of blue (hoist side), gold, and blue with the head of a black trident centered on the gold band; the trident head represents independence and a break with the past (the colonial coat of arms contained a complete trident)

Economy

Economy - overview: Historically, the Barbadian economy had been dependent on sugarcane cultivation and related activities, but production in recent years has diversified into manufacturing and tourism. The start of the Port Charles Marina project in Speightstown helped the tourism industry continue to expand in 1996-2000. Offshore finance and information services are important foreign exchange earners, and there is also a light manufacturing sector. The government continues its efforts to reduce unemployment, encourage direct foreign investment, and privatize remaining state-owned enterprises. Growth should remain steady in 2001, with new tourist facilities a plus factor.

GDP: purchasing power parity - $4 billion (2000 est.)
GDP - real growth rate: 2.8% (2000 est.)
GDP - per capita: purchasing power parity - $14,500 (2000 est.)
GDP - composition by sector:
agriculture: 4%
industry: 16%
services: 80% (1998)
Population below poverty line: NA%
Household income or consumption by percentage share:
lowest 10%: NA%
highest 10%: NA%
Inflation rate (consumer prices): 2% (2000 est.)
Labor force: 136,000 (1998 est.)
Labor force - by occupation: services 75%, industry 15%, agriculture 10% (1996 est.)
Unemployment rate: 11% (1999 est.)
Budget:
revenues: $725.5 million
expenditures: $750.6 million, including capital expenditures of $126.3 million (FY97/98 est.)
Industries: tourism, sugar, light manufacturing, component assembly for export
Industrial production growth rate: 0.8% (1996)
Electricity - production: 718 million kWh (1999)
Electricity - production by source:
fossil fuel: 100%
hydro: 0%
nuclear: 0%
other: 0% (1999)
Electricity - consumption: 667.7 million kWh (1999)
Electricity - exports: 0 kWh (1999)
Electricity - imports: 0 kWh (1999)
Agriculture - products: sugarcane, vegetables, cotton
Exports: $260 million (2000 est.)
Exports - commodities: sugar and molasses, rum, other foods and beverages, chemicals, electrical components, clothing
Exports - partners: UK 14.8%, US 11.6%, Trinidad and Tobago 7.6%, Venezuela 6.1%, Jamaica 5.8% (1998)
Imports: $800.3 million (2000 est.)
Imports - commodities: consumer goods, machinery, foodstuffs, construction materials, chemicals, fuel, electrical components
Imports - partners: US 30.7%, Trinidad and Tobago 10.2%, Japan 8.3%, UK 7.7%, Canada 2.2% (1998)
Debt - external: $425 million (2000 est.)
Economic aid - recipient: $9.1 million (1995)
Currency: Barbadian dollar (BBD)
Currency code: BBD
Exchange rates: Barbadian dollars per US dollar - 2.0000 (fixed rate pegged to the US dollar)
Fiscal year: 1 April - 31 March

Communications

Telephones - main lines in use: 108,000 (1997)
Telephones - mobile cellular: 8,013 (1997)
Telephone system:
general assessment: NA
domestic: island-wide automatic telephone system
international: satellite earth stations - 4 Intelsat (Atlantic Ocean); tropospheric scatter to Trinidad and Saint Lucia
Radio broadcast stations: AM 2, FM 3, shortwave 0 (1998)
Radios: 237,000 (1997)
Television broadcast stations: 1 (plus two cable channels) (1997)
Televisions: 76,000 (1997)
Internet country code: .bb
Internet Service Providers (ISPs): 19 (2000)
Internet users: 6,000 (2000)

Transportation

Railways: 0 km
Highways:
total: 1,600 km
paved: 1,578 km
unpaved: 22 km (1998)
Waterways: none
Ports and harbors: Bridgetown, Speightstown (Port Charles Marina)
Merchant marine:
total: 47 ships (1,000 GRT or over) totaling 671,545 GRT/1,125,635 DWT
ships by type: bulk 10, cargo 28, combination bulk 1, container 2, petroleum tanker 4, refrigerated cargo 1, roll on/roll off 1
note: includes some foreign-owned ships registered here as a flag of convenience: Canada 2, Hong Kong 1 (2000 est.)
Airports: 1 (2000 est.)
Airports - with paved runways:
total: 1
over 3,047 m: 1 (2000 est.)

Military

Military branches: Royal Barbados Defense Force (includes Ground Forces and Coast Guard), Royal Barbados Police Force
Military manpower - availability:
males age 15-49: 78,069 (2001 est.)
Military manpower - fit for military service:
males age 15-49: 53,576 (2001 est.)
Military expenditures - dollar figure: $NA
Military expenditures - percent of GDP: NA%

Transnational Issues

Disputes - international: none
Illicit drugs: one of many Caribbean transshipment points for narcotics bound for Europe and the US

Bassas da India
(possession of France)

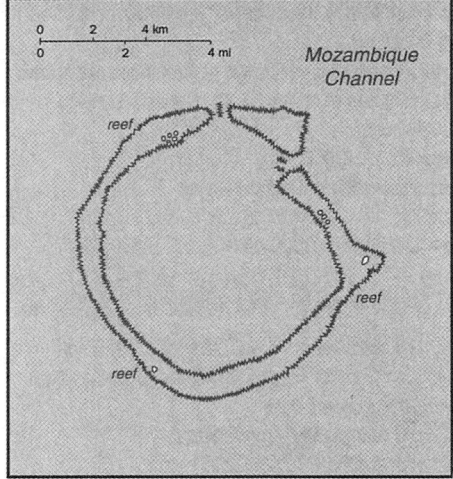

Introduction
Background: This atoll is a volcanic rock surrounded by reefs and is awash at high tide. A French possession since 1897, it was placed under the administration of a commissioner residing in Reunion in 1968.

Geography
Location: Southern Africa, islands in the southern Mozambique Channel, about one-half of the way from Madagascar to Mozambique
Geographic coordinates: 21 30 S, 39 50 E
Map references: Africa
Area:
total: 0.2 sq km
land: 0.2 sq km
water: 0 sq km
Area - comparative: about one-third the size of The Mall in Washington, DC
Land boundaries: 0 km
Coastline: 35.2 km
Maritime claims:
exclusive economic zone: 200 NM
territorial sea: 12 NM
Climate: tropical
Terrain: volcanic rock
Elevation extremes:
lowest point: Indian Ocean 0 m
highest point: unnamed location 2.4 m
Natural resources: none
Land use:
arable land: 0%
permanent crops: 0%
permanent pastures: 0%
forests and woodland: 0%
other: 100% (all rock)
Irrigated land: 0 sq km (1993)
Natural hazards: maritime hazard since it is usually under water during high tide and surrounded by reefs; subject to periodic cyclones
Environment - current issues: NA

People
Population: uninhabited (July 2001 est.)

Government
Country name:
conventional long form: none
conventional short form: Bassas da India
Dependency status: possession of France; administered by a high commissioner of the Republic, resident in Reunion
Legal system: the laws of France, where applicable, apply
Flag description: the flag of France is used

Economy
Economy - overview: no economic activity

Transportation
Waterways: none
Ports and harbors: none; offshore anchorage only

Military
Military - note: defense is the responsibility of France

Transnational Issues
Disputes - international: claimed by Madagascar

Belarus

Introduction
Background: After seven decades as a constituent republic of the USSR, Belarus attained its independence in 1991. It has retained closer political and economic ties to Russia than any of the other former Soviet republics. Belarus and Russia signed a treaty on a two-state union on 8 December 1999 envisioning greater political and economic integration but, to date, neither side has actively sought to implement the accord.

Geography
Location: Eastern Europe, east of Poland
Geographic coordinates: 53 00 N, 28 00 E
Map references: Commonwealth of Independent States
Area:
total: 207,600 sq km
land: 207,600 sq km
water: 0 sq km
Area - comparative: slightly smaller than Kansas
Land boundaries:
total: 3,098 km
border countries: Latvia 141 km, Lithuania 502 km, Poland 605 km, Russia 959 km, Ukraine 891 km
Coastline: 0 km (landlocked)
Maritime claims: none (landlocked)
Climate: cold winters, cool and moist summers; transitional between continental and maritime
Terrain: generally flat and contains much marshland
Elevation extremes:
lowest point: Nyoman River 90 m
highest point: Dzyarzhynskaya Hara 346 m
Natural resources: forests, peat deposits, small quantities of oil and natural gas
Land use:
arable land: 29%
permanent crops: 1%
permanent pastures: 15%
forests and woodland: 34%
other: 21% (1993 est.)

Belarus (continued)

Irrigated land: 1,000 sq km (1993 est.)
Natural hazards: NA
Environment - current issues: soil pollution from pesticide use; southern part of the country contaminated with fallout from 1986 nuclear reactor accident at Chornobyl' in northern Ukraine
Environment - international agreements:
party to: Air Pollution, Air Pollution-Nitrogen Oxides, Air Pollution-Sulphur 85, Biodiversity, Climate Change, Endangered Species, Environmental Modification, Hazardous Wastes, Marine Dumping, Ozone Layer Protection, Ship Pollution, Wetlands
signed, but not ratified: Law of the Sea
Geography - note: landlocked

People

Population: 10,350,194 (July 2001 est.)
Age structure:
0-14 years: 17.93% (male 947,820; female 908,210)
15-64 years: 68.21% (male 3,428,920; female 3,631,290)
65 years and over: 13.86% (male 473,992; female 959,962) (2001 est.)
Population growth rate: -0.15% (2001 est.)
Birth rate: 9.57 births/1,000 population (2001 est.)
Death rate: 13.97 deaths/1,000 population (2001 est.)
Net migration rate: 2.89 migrant(s)/1,000 population (2001 est.)
Sex ratio:
at birth: 1.05 male(s)/female
under 15 years: 1.04 male(s)/female
15-64 years: 0.94 male(s)/female
65 years and over: 0.49 male(s)/female
total population: 0.88 male(s)/female (2001 est.)
Infant mortality rate: 14.38 deaths/1,000 live births (2001 est.)
Life expectancy at birth:
total population: 68.14 years
male: 62.06 years
female: 74.52 years (2001 est.)
Total fertility rate: 1.28 children born/woman (2001 est.)
HIV/AIDS - adult prevalence rate: 0.28% (1999 est.)
HIV/AIDS - people living with HIV/AIDS: 14,000 (1999 est.)
HIV/AIDS - deaths: 400 (1999 est.)
Nationality:
noun: Belarusian(s)
adjective: Belarusian
Ethnic groups: Byelorussian 81.2%, Russian 11.4%, Polish, Ukrainian, and other 7.4%
Religions: Eastern Orthodox 80%, other (including Roman Catholic, Protestant, Jewish, and Muslim) 20% (1997 est.)
Languages: Byelorussian, Russian, other
Literacy:
definition: age 15 and over can read and write
total population: 98%
male: 99%
female: 97% (1989 est.)

Government

Country name:
conventional long form: Republic of Belarus
conventional short form: Belarus
local long form: Respublika Byelarus'
local short form: none
former: Belorussian (Byelorussian) Soviet Socialist Republic
Government type: republic
Capital: Minsk
Administrative divisions: 6 voblastsi (singular - voblasts') and one municipality* (harady, singular - horad); Brestskaya (Brest), Homyel'skaya (Homyel'), Horad Minsk*, Hrodzyenskaya (Hrodna), Mahilyowskaya (Mahilyow), Minskaya, Vitsyebskaya (Vitsyebsk); note - when using a place name with the adjectival ending 'skaya' the word voblasts' should be added to the place name
note: voblasti have the administrative center name following in parentheses
Independence: 25 August 1991 (from Soviet Union)
National holiday: Independence Day, 3 July (1944); note - 3 July 1944 was the date Minsk was liberated from German troops, 25 August 1991 was the date of independence from the Soviet Union
Constitution: 30 March 1994; revised by national referendum of 24 November 1996 giving the presidency greatly expanded powers and became effective 27 November 1996
Legal system: based on civil law system
Suffrage: 18 years of age; universal
Executive branch:
chief of state: President Aleksandr LUKASHENKO (since 20 July 1994)
head of government: Prime Minister Vladimir YERMOSHIN (since 18 February 2000); First Deputy Prime Minister Andrey KOBYAKOV (since 13 March 2000); Deputy Prime Ministers Mikhail DEMCHUK (since 14 July 2000), Mikhail KHORSTOV (since 27 November 2000), Valeriy KOKOREV (since 23 August 1994), Leonid KOZIK (since 4 February 1997), Gennadiy NOVITSKIY (since 11 February 1997), Aleksandr POPKOV (since 10 November 1998)
cabinet: Council of Ministers
elections: president elected by popular vote for a five-year term; first election took place 23 June and 10 July 1994 (next to be held NA; according to the 1994 constitution, the next election should have been held in 1999, however LUKASHENKO extended his term to 2001 via the November 1996 referendum); prime minister and deputy prime ministers appointed by the president
election results: Aleksandr LUKASHENKO elected president; percent of vote - Aleksandr LUKASHENKO 85%, Vyacheslav KEBICH 15%
Legislative branch: bicameral Parliament or Natsionalnoye Sobranie consists of the Council of the Republic or Soviet Respubliki (64 seats) and the Chamber of Representatives or Palata Pretsaviteley (110 seats)
elections: last held October 2000 (next to be held NA)
election results: party affiliation data unavailable; under present political conditions party designations are meaningless
Judicial branch: Supreme Court (judges are appointed by the president); Constitutional Court (half of the judges appointed by the president and half appointed by the Chamber of Representatives)
Political parties and leaders: Agrarian Party or AP [Semyon SHARETSKY, chairman]; Belarusian Communist Party or KPB [Viktor CHIKIN, chairman]; Belarusian Ecological Green Party (merger of Belarusian Ecological Party and Green Party of Belarus) [leader NA]; Belarusian Patriotic Movement (Belarusian Patriotic Party) or BPR [Anatoliy BARANKEVICH, chairman]; Belarusian Popular Front or BNF [Vintsuk VYACHORKA]; Belarusian Social-Democrat or SDBP [Nikolay STATKEVICH, chairman]; Belarusian Social-Democratic Party Hromada [Stanislav SHUSHKEVICH, chairman]; Belarusian Socialist Party [Vyacheslav KUZNETSOV]; Civic Accord Bloc (United Civic Party) or CAB [Stanislav BOGDANKEVICH, chairman]; Liberal Democratic Party or LDPB [Sergei GAYDUKEVICH, chairman]; Party of Communists Belarusian or PKB [Sergei KALYAKIN, chairman]; Republican Party of Labor and Justice or RPPS [Anatoliy NETYLKIN, chairman]; Social-Democrat Party of Popular Accord or PPA [Leanid SECHKA]; Women's Party Nadezhda [Valentina POLEVIKOVA, chairperson]
Political pressure groups and leaders: NA
International organization participation: CCC, CEI, CIS, EAPC, EBRD, ECE, IAEA, IBRD, ICAO, ICRM, IFC, IFRCS, ILO, IMF, Inmarsat, Intelsat (nonsignatory user), Interpol, IOC, IOM (observer), ISO, ITU, NAM, NSG, OPCW, OSCE, PCA, PFP, UN, UNCTAD, UNESCO, UNIDO, UPU, WFTU, WHO, WIPO, WMO, WTrO (observer)
Diplomatic representation in the US:
chief of mission: Ambassador Valeriy TSEPAKLO
chancery: 1619 New Hampshire Avenue NW, Washington, DC 20009
telephone: [1] (202) 986-1604
FAX: [1] (202) 986-1805
consulate(s) general: New York
Diplomatic representation from the US:
chief of mission: Ambassador Michael KOZAK
embassy: 46 Starovilenskaya St., Minsk 220002
mailing address: use embassy street address
telephone: [375] (17) 210-12-83
FAX: [375] (17) 234-7853
Flag description: red horizontal band (top) and green horizontal band one-half the width of the red band; a white vertical stripe on the hoist side bears the Belarusian national ornament in red

Belarus (continued)

Economy

Economy - overview: Belarus has seen little structural reform since 1995, when President LUKASHENKO launched the country on the path of "market socialism." In keeping with this policy, LUKASHENKO reimposed administrative controls over prices and currency exchange rates and expanded the state's right to intervene in the management of private enterprise. In addition to the burdens imposed by extremely high inflation, businesses have been subject to pressure on the part of central and local governments, e.g., arbitrary changes in regulations, numerous rigorous inspections, and retroactive application of new business regulations prohibiting practices that had been legal. Further economic problems are two consecutive bad harvests, 1998-99, and persistent trade deficits. Close relations with Russia, possibly leading to reunion, color the pattern of economic developments. For the time being, Belarus remains self-isolated from the West and its open-market economies.
GDP: purchasing power parity - $78.8 billion (2000 est.)
GDP - real growth rate: 4% (2000 est.)
GDP - per capita: purchasing power parity - $7,500 (2000 est.)
GDP - composition by sector:
agriculture: 13%
industry: 46%
services: 41% (1999 est.)
Population below poverty line: 22% (1995 est.)
Household income or consumption by percentage share:
lowest 10%: 4.9%
highest 10%: 19.4% (1993)
Inflation rate (consumer prices): 200% (2000 est.)
Labor force: 4.8 million (2000)
Labor force - by occupation: industry and construction NA%, agriculture and forestry NA%, services NA%
Unemployment rate: 2.1% officially registered unemployed (December 2000); large number of underemployed workers
Budget:
revenues: $4 billion
expenditures: $4.1 billion, including capital expenditures of $180 million (1997 est.)
Industries: metal-cutting machine tools, tractors, trucks, earth movers, motorcycles, television sets, chemical fibers, fertilizer, textiles, radios, refrigerators
Industrial production growth rate: 5% (2000 est.)
Electricity - production: 24.911 billion kWh (1999)
Electricity - production by source:
fossil fuel: 99.9%
hydro: 0.1%
nuclear: 0%
other: 0% (1999)
Electricity - consumption: 27.647 billion kWh (1999)
Electricity - exports: 2.62 billion kWh (1999)
Electricity - imports: 7.1 billion kWh (1999)
Agriculture - products: grain, potatoes, vegetables, sugar beets, flax; beef, milk
Exports: $7.4 billion (f.o.b., 2000)
Exports - commodities: machinery and equipment, chemicals, metals, textiles, foodstuffs
Exports - partners: Russia 66%, Ukraine, Poland, Germany, Lithuania (1998)
Imports: $8.3 billion (f.o.b., 2000)
Imports - commodities: mineral products, machinery and equipment, metals, chemicals, foodstuffs
Imports - partners: Russia 54%, Ukraine, Germany, Poland, Lithuania (1998)
Debt - external: $1 billion (2000 est.)
Economic aid - recipient: $194.3 million (1995)
Currency: Belarusian ruble (BYB/BYR)
Currency code: BYB/BYR
Exchange rates: Belarusian rubles per US dollar - 1,180 (yearend 2000), 730,000 (15 December 1999), 139,000 (25 January 1999), 46,080 (second quarter 1998), 25,964 (1997), 15,500 (yearend 1996); note - on 1 January 2000, the national currency was redenominated at one new ruble to 2,000 old rubles
Fiscal year: calendar year

Communications

Telephones - main lines in use: 2.313 million (1997)
Telephones - mobile cellular: 8,167 (1997)
Telephone system:
general assessment: the Ministry of Telecommunications controls all telecommunications through its carrier (a joint stock company) Beltelcom which is a monopoly
domestic: local - Minsk has a digital metropolitan network and a cellular NMT-450 network; waiting lists for telephones are long; local service outside Minsk is neglected and poor; intercity - Belarus has a partly developed fiber-optic backbone system presently serving at least 13 major cities (1998); Belarus's fiber optics form synchronous digital hierarchy rings through other countries' systems; an inadequate analog system remains operational
international: Belarus is a member of the Trans-European Line (TEL), Trans-Asia-Europe (TAE) fiber-optic line, and has access to the Trans-Siberia Line (TSL); three fiber-optic segments provide connectivity to Latvia, Poland, Russia, and Ukraine; worldwide service is available to Belarus through this infrastructure; additional analog lines to Russia; Intelsat, Eutelsat, and Intersputnik earth stations
Radio broadcast stations: AM 28, FM 37, shortwave 11 (1998)
Radios: 3.02 million (1997)
Television broadcast stations: 47 (plus 27 repeaters) (1995)
Televisions: 2.52 million (1997)
Internet country code: .by
Internet Service Providers (ISPs): 4 (2000)
Internet users: 10,000 (2000)

Transportation

Railways:
total: 5,563 km
broad gauge: 5,563 km 1.520-m gauge (894 km electrified)
Highways:
total: 63,355 km
paved: 60,567 km (these roads are said to be hard-surfaced, and include, in addition to conventionally paved roads, some that are surfaced with gravel or other coarse aggregate, making them trafficable in all weather)
unpaved: 2,788 km (these roads are made of unstabilized earth and are difficult to negotiate in wet weather) (1998)
Waterways: NA km; note - Belarus has extensive and widely used canal and river systems
Pipelines: crude oil 1,470 km; refined products 1,100 km; natural gas 1,980 km (1992)
Ports and harbors: Mazyr
Airports: 136 (2000 est.)
Airports - with paved runways:
total: 33
over 3,047 m: 2
2,438 to 3,047 m: 19
1,524 to 2,437 m: 1
under 914 m: 11 (2000 est.)
Airports - with unpaved runways:
total: 103
over 3,047 m: 3
2,438 to 3,047 m: 10
1,524 to 2,437 m: 11
914 to 1,523 m: 14
under 914 m: 65 (2000 est.)

Military

Military branches: Army, Air Force, Air Defense Force, Interior Ministry Troops, Border Guards
Military manpower - military age: 18 years of age
Military manpower - availability:
males age 15-49: 2,729,956 (2001 est.)
Military manpower - fit for military service:
males age 15-49: 2,138,743 (2001 est.)
Military manpower - reaching military age annually:
males: 86,396 (2001 est.)
Military expenditures - dollar figure: $156 million (FY98)
Military expenditures - percent of GDP: 1.2% (FY98)

Transnational Issues

Disputes - international: none
Illicit drugs: limited cultivation of opium poppy and cannabis, mostly for the domestic market; transshipment point for illicit drugs to and via Russia, and to the Baltics and Western Europe

Belgium

Introduction

Background: Belgium became independent from the Netherlands in 1830 and was occupied by Germany during World Wars I and II. It has prospered in the past half century as a modern, technologically advanced European state and member of NATO and the EU. Tensions between the Dutch-speaking Flemings of the north and the French-speaking Walloons of the south have led in recent years to constitutional amendments granting these regions formal recognition and autonomy.

Geography

Location: Western Europe, bordering the North Sea, between France and the Netherlands
Geographic coordinates: 50 50 N, 4 00 E
Map references: Europe
Area:
total: 30,510 sq km
land: 30,230 sq km
water: 280 sq km
Area - comparative: about the size of Maryland
Land boundaries:
total: 1,385 km
border countries: France 620 km, Germany 167 km, Luxembourg 148 km, Netherlands 450 km
Coastline: 66 km
Maritime claims:
continental shelf: median line with neighbors
exclusive fishing zone: median line with neighbors (extends about 68 km from coast)
territorial sea: 12 NM
Climate: temperate; mild winters, cool summers; rainy, humid, cloudy
Terrain: flat coastal plains in northwest, central rolling hills, rugged mountains of Ardennes Forest in southeast
Elevation extremes:
lowest point: North Sea 0 m
highest point: Signal de Botrange 694 m
Natural resources: coal, natural gas
Land use:
arable land: 24%
permanent crops: 1%
permanent pastures: 20%
forests and woodland: 21%
other: 34%
Irrigated land: NA sq km
Natural hazards: flooding is a threat in areas of reclaimed coastal land, protected from the sea by concrete dikes
Environment - current issues: the environment is exposed to intense pressures from human activities: urbanization, dense transportation network, industry, intense animal breeding and crop cultivation; air and water pollution also have repercussions for neighboring countries; uncertainties regarding federal and regional responsibilities (now resolved) have impeded progress in tackling environmental challenges
Environment - international agreements:
party to: Air Pollution, Air Pollution-Nitrogen Oxides, Air Pollution-Sulphur 94, Air Pollution-Volatile Organic Compounds, Air Pollution-Sulphur 85, Antarctic-Environmental Protocol, Antarctic-Marine Living Resources, Antarctic Seals, Antarctic Treaty, Biodiversity, Climate Change, Desertification, Endangered Species, Environmental Modification, Hazardous Wastes, Law of the Sea, Marine Dumping, Marine Life Conservation, Nuclear Test Ban, Ozone Layer Protection, Ship Pollution, Tropical Timber 83, Tropical Timber 94, Wetlands
signed, but not ratified: Air Pollution-Persistent Organic Pollutants, Climate Change-Kyoto Protocol
Geography - note: crossroads of Western Europe; majority of West European capitals within 1,000 km of Brussels which is the seat of both the EU and NATO

People

Population: 10,258,762 (July 2001 est.)
Age structure:
0-14 years: 17.48% (male 916,957; female 876,029)
15-64 years: 65.57% (male 3,390,145; female 3,336,908)
65 years and over: 16.95% (male 709,212; female 1,029,511) (2001 est.)
Population growth rate: 0.16% (2001 est.)
Birth rate: 10.74 births/1,000 population (2001 est.)
Death rate: 10.1 deaths/1,000 population (2001 est.)
Net migration rate: 0.97 migrant(s)/1,000 population (2001 est.)
Sex ratio:
at birth: 1.05 male(s)/female
under 15 years: 1.05 male(s)/female
15-64 years: 1.02 male(s)/female
65 years and over: 0.69 male(s)/female
total population: 0.96 male(s)/female (2001 est.)
Infant mortality rate: 4.7 deaths/1,000 live births (2001 est.)
Life expectancy at birth:
total population: 77.96 years
male: 74.63 years
female: 81.46 years (2001 est.)
Total fertility rate: 1.61 children born/woman (2001 est.)
HIV/AIDS - adult prevalence rate: 0.15% (1999 est.)
HIV/AIDS - people living with HIV/AIDS: 7,700 (1999 est.)
HIV/AIDS - deaths: less than 100 (1999 est.)
Nationality:
noun: Belgian(s)
adjective: Belgian
Ethnic groups: Fleming 58%, Walloon 31%, mixed or other 11%
Religions: Roman Catholic 75%, Protestant or other 25%
Languages: Dutch 58%, French 32%, German 10%, legally bilingual (Dutch and French)
Literacy:
definition: age 15 and over can read and write
total population: 98%
male: NA%
female: NA%

Government

Country name:
conventional long form: Kingdom of Belgium
conventional short form: Belgium
local long form: Royaume de Belgique/Koninkrijk Belgie
local short form: Belgique/Belgie
Government type: federal parliamentary democracy under a constitutional monarch
Capital: Brussels
Administrative divisions: 10 provinces (French: provinces, singular - province; Flemish: provincien, singular - provincie); Antwerpen, Brabant Wallon, Hainaut, Liege, Limburg, Luxembourg, Namur, Oost-Vlaanderen, Vlaams Brabant, West-Vlaanderen; note - the Brussels Capitol Region is not included within the 10 provinces
Independence: 21 July 1831 (from the Netherlands)
National holiday: Independence Day, 21 July (1831)
Constitution: 7 February 1831, last revised 14 July 1993; parliament approved a constitutional package creating a federal state
Legal system: civil law system influenced by English constitutional theory; judicial review of legislative acts; accepts compulsory ICJ jurisdiction, with reservations
Suffrage: 18 years of age; universal and compulsory
Executive branch:
chief of state: King ALBERT II (since 9 August 1993); Heir Apparent Prince PHILIPPE, son of the monarch
head of government: Prime Minister Guy VERHOFSTADT (since 13 July 1999)
cabinet: Council of Ministers appointed by the monarch and approved by Parliament

Belgium (continued)

elections: none; the monarch is hereditary; prime minister appointed by the monarch and then approved by Parliament
note: government coalition - VLD, PRL, PS, SP, AGALEV, and ECOLO
Legislative branch: bicameral Parliament consists of a Senate or Senaat in Dutch, Senat in French (71 seats; 40 members are directly elected by popular vote, 31 are indirectly elected; members serve four-year terms) and a Chamber of Deputies or Kamer van Volksvertegenwoordigers in Dutch, Chambre des Representants in French (150 seats; members are directly elected by popular vote on the basis of proportional representation to serve four-year terms)
elections: Senate and Chamber of Deputies - last held 13 June 1999 (next to be held in NA 2003)
election results: Senate - percent of vote by party - VLD 15.4%, CVP 14.7%, PRL 10.6%, PS 9.7%, VB 9.4%, SP 8.9%, ECOLO 7.4%, AGALEV 7.1%, PSC 6.0%, VU 5.1%; seats by party - VLD 11, CVP 10, PS 10, PRL 9, VB 6, SP 6, ECOLO 6, AGALEV 5, PSC 5, VU 3; Chamber of Deputies - percent of vote by party - VLD 14.3%, CVP 14.1%, PS 10.2%, PRL 10.1%, VB 9.9%, SP 9.5%, ECOLO 7.4%, AGALEV 7.0%, PSC 5.9%, VU 5.6%; seats by party - VLD 23, CVP 22, PS 19, PRL 18, VB 15, SP 14, ECOLO 11, PSC 10, AGALEV 9, VU 8, FN 1
note: as a result of the 1993 constitutional revision that furthered devolution into a federal state, there are now three levels of government (federal, regional, and linguistic community) with a complex division of responsibilities; this reality leaves six governments each with its own legislative assembly; for other acronyms of the listed parties see Political parties and leaders
Judicial branch: Supreme Court of Justice or Hof van Cassatie (in Dutch) or Cour de Cassation (in French) (judges are appointed for life by the monarch)
Political parties and leaders: AGALEV (Flemish Greens) [Dos GEYSELS]; ECOLO (Francophone Greens) [no president]; Flemish Christian Democrats or CVP (Christian People's Party) [Stefaan DE CLERCK, president]; Flemish Liberal Democrats or VLD [Karel DE GUCHT, president]; Flemish Socialist Party or SP [Patrick JANSSENS, president]; Francophone Christian Democrats or PSC (Social Christian Party) [Joelle MILQUET, president]; Francophone Liberal Reformation Party or PRL [Daniel DUCARME, president]; Francophone Socialist Party or PS [Elio DI RUPO, president]; National Front or FN [Daniel FERET]; Vlaams Blok or VB [Frank VANHECKE]; Volksunie or VU [leader vacant]; other minor parties
Political pressure groups and leaders: Christian and Socialist Trade Unions; Federation of Belgian Industries; numerous other associations representing bankers, manufacturers, middle-class artisans, and the legal and medical professions; various organizations represent the cultural interests of Flanders and Wallonia; various peace groups such as Pax Christi and groups representing immigrants

International organization participation: ACCT, AfDB, AsDB, Australia Group, Benelux, BIS, CCC, CE, CERN, EAPC, EBRD, ECE, EIB, EMU, ESA, EU, FAO, G- 9, G-10, IADB, IAEA, IBRD, ICAO, ICC, ICFTU, ICRM, IDA, IEA, IFAD, IFC, IFRCS, IHO, ILO, IMF, IMO, Inmarsat, Intelsat, Interpol, IOC, IOM, ISO, ITU, MINURSO, MONUC, NATO, NEA, NSG, OAS (observer), OECD, OPCW, OSCE, PCA, UN, UNCTAD, UNESCO, UNHCR, UNIDO, UNMIK, UNMOGIP, UNMOP, UNRWA, UNTSO, UPU, WADB (nonregional), WCL, WEU, WHO, WIPO, WMO, WTrO, ZC
Diplomatic representation in the US:
chief of mission: Ambassador Alexis REYN
chancery: 3330 Garfield Street NW, Washington, DC 20008
telephone: [1] (202) 333-6900
FAX: [1] (202) 333-3079
consulate(s) general: Atlanta, Chicago, Los Angeles, and New York
Diplomatic representation from the US:
chief of mission: Ambassador (vacant)
embassy: 27 Boulevard du Regent, B-1000 Brussels
mailing address: PSC 82, Box 002, APO AE 09710
telephone: [32] (2) 508-2111
FAX: [32] (2) 511-2725
Flag description: three equal vertical bands of black (hoist side), yellow, and red; the design was based on the flag of France

Economy

Economy - overview: This modern private enterprise economy has capitalized on its central geographic location, highly developed transport network, and diversified industrial and commercial base. Industry is concentrated mainly in the populous Flemish area in the north, although the government is encouraging investment in the southern region of Wallonia. With few natural resources, Belgium must import substantial quantities of raw materials and export a large volume of manufactures, making its economy unusually dependent on the state of world markets. About three-quarters of its trade is with other EU countries. Belgium's public debt is expected to fall below 100% of GDP in 2002, and the government has succeeded in balancing is budget. Belgium became a charter member of the European Monetary Union (EMU) in January 1999. Economic growth in 2000 was broad based, putting the government in a good position to pursue its energy market liberalization policies and planned tax cuts.
GDP: purchasing power parity - $259.2 billion (2000 est.)
GDP - real growth rate: 4.1% (2000 est.)
GDP - per capita: purchasing power parity - $25,300 (2000 est.)
GDP - composition by sector:
agriculture: 1.4%
industry: 26%
services: 72.6% (2000 est.)
Population below poverty line: 4%

Household income or consumption by percentage share:
lowest 10%: 3.7%
highest 10%: 20.2% (1992)
Inflation rate (consumer prices): 2.2% (2000 est.)
Labor force: 4.34 million (1999)
Labor force - by occupation: services 73%, industry 25%, agriculture 2% (1999 est.)
Unemployment rate: 8.4% (2000 est.)
Budget:
revenues: $114.8 billion
expenditures: $117 billion, including capital expenditures of $7.6 billion (1999)
Industries: engineering and metal products, motor vehicle assembly, processed food and beverages, chemicals, basic metals, textiles, glass, petroleum, coal
Industrial production growth rate: 5.5% (2000 est.)
Electricity - production: 79.829 billion kWh (1999)
Electricity - production by source:
fossil fuel: 40.01%
hydro: 0.42%
nuclear: 58.33%
other: 1.24% (1999)
Electricity - consumption: 75.089 billion kWh (1999)
Electricity - exports: 8.207 billion kWh (1999)
Electricity - imports: 9.055 billion kWh (1999)
Agriculture - products: sugar beets, fresh vegetables, fruits, grain, tobacco; beef, veal, pork, milk
Exports: $181.4 billion (f.o.b., 2000)
Exports - commodities: machinery and equipment, chemicals, diamonds, metals and metal products
Exports - partners: EU 76% (Germany 18%, France 18%, Netherlands 12%, UK 10%) (1999)
Imports: $166 billion (c.i.f., 2000)
Imports - commodities: machinery and equipment, chemicals, metals and metal products
Imports - partners: EU 71% (Germany 18%, Netherlands 17%, France 14%, UK 9%) (1999)
Debt - external: $28.3 billion (1999 est.)
Economic aid - donor: ODA, $764 million (1997)
Currency: Belgian franc (BEF); euro (EUR)
note: on 1 January 1999, the EU introduced the euro as a common currency that is now being used by financial institutions in Belgium at a fixed rate of 40.3399 Belgian francs per euro and will replace the local currency for all transactions in 2002
Currency code: BEF; EUR
Exchange rates: euros per US dollar - 1.0659 (January 2001), 1.0854 (2000), 0.9386 (1999); Belgian francs per US dollar - 34.77 (January 1999), 36.229 (1998), 35.774 (1997), 30.962 (1996)
Fiscal year: calendar year

Belgium (continued)

Communications

Telephones - main lines in use: 4.769 million (1997)
Telephones - mobile cellular: 974,494 (1997)
Telephone system:
general assessment: highly developed, technologically advanced, and completely automated domestic and international telephone and telegraph facilities
domestic: nationwide cellular telephone system; extensive cable network; limited microwave radio relay network
international: 5 submarine cables; satellite earth stations - 2 Intelsat (Atlantic Ocean) and 1 Eutelsat
Radio broadcast stations: FM 79, AM 7, shortwave 1 (1998)
Radios: 8.075 million (1997)
Television broadcast stations: 25 (plus 10 repeaters) (1997)
Televisions: 4.72 million (1997)
Internet country code: .be
Internet Service Providers (ISPs): 61 (2000)
Internet users: 2.7 million (2000)

Transportation

Railways:
total: 3,437 km (2,446 km electrified; 2,563 km double track)
standard gauge: 3,437 km 1.435-m gauge (1998)
Highways:
total: 145,774 km
paved: 116,182 km (including 1,674 km of expressways)
unpaved: 29,592 km (1999)
Waterways: 2,043 km (1,528 km in regular commercial use)
Pipelines: crude oil 161 km; petroleum products 1,167 km; natural gas 3,300 km
Ports and harbors: Antwerp (one of the world's busiest ports), Brugge, Gent, Hasselt, Liege, Mons, Namur, Oostende, Zeebrugge
Merchant marine:
total: 21 ships (1,000 GRT or over) totaling 32,912 GRT/53,161 DWT
ships by type: cargo 6, chemical tanker 9, petroleum tanker 6 (2000 est.)
Airports: 42 (2000 est.)
Airports - with paved runways:
total: 24
over 3,047 m: 6
2,438 to 3,047 m: 8
1,524 to 2,437 m: 3
914 to 1,523 m: 1
under 914 m: 6 (2000 est.)
Airports - with unpaved runways:
total: 18
914 to 1,523 m: 2
under 914 m: 16 (2000 est.)
Heliports: 1 (2000 est.)

Military

Military branches: Army, Navy, Air Force, National Gendarmerie, Medical Service
Military manpower - military age: 19 years of age
Military manpower - availability:
males age 15-49: 2,517,596 (2001 est.)
Military manpower - fit for military service:
males age 15-49: 2,079,624 (2001 est.)
Military manpower - reaching military age annually:
males: 63,247 (2001 est.)
Military expenditures - dollar figure: $2.5 billion (FY01)
Military expenditures - percent of GDP: 1.2% (FY99)

Transnational Issues

Disputes - international: none
Illicit drugs: growing producer of synthetic drugs; transit point for US-bound ecstasy; source of precursor chemicals for South American cocaine processors; transshipment point for cocaine, heroin, hashish, and marijuana entering Western Europe

Belize

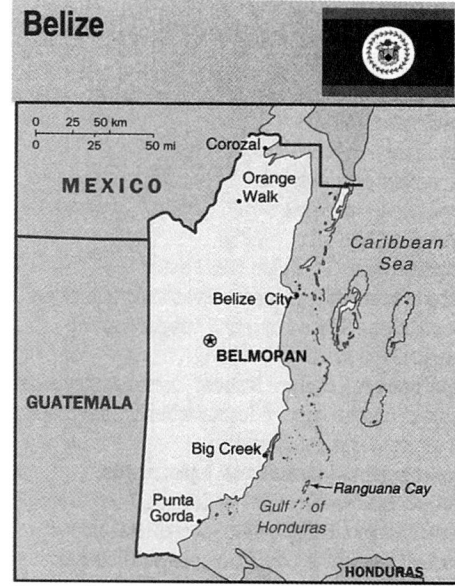

Introduction

Background: Territorial disputes between the UK and Guatemala delayed the independence of Belize (formerly British Honduras) until 1981. Guatemala refused to recognize the new nation until 1992. Tourism has become the mainstay of the economy. The country remains plagued by high unemployment, growing involvement in the South American drug trade, and increased urban crime.

Geography

Location: Middle America, bordering the Caribbean Sea, between Guatemala and Mexico
Geographic coordinates: 17 15 N, 88 45 W
Map references: Central America and the Caribbean
Area:
total: 22,966 sq km
land: 22,806 sq km
water: 160 sq km
Area - comparative: slightly smaller than Massachusetts
Land boundaries:
total: 516 km
border countries: Guatemala 266 km, Mexico 250 km
Coastline: 386 km
Maritime claims:
exclusive economic zone: 200 NM
territorial sea: 12 NM in the north, 3 NM in the south; note - from the mouth of the Sarstoon River to Ranguana Cay, Belize's territorial sea is 3 NM; according to Belize's Maritime Areas Act, 1992, the purpose of this limitation is to provide a framework for the negotiation of a definitive agreement on territorial differences with Guatemala
Climate: tropical; very hot and humid; rainy season (May to November); dry season (February to May)
Terrain: flat, swampy coastal plain; low mountains in south
Elevation extremes:
lowest point: Caribbean Sea 0 m

Belize (continued)

highest point: Victoria Peak 1,160 m
Natural resources: arable land potential, timber, fish, hydropower
Land use:
arable land: 10%
permanent crops: 1%
permanent pastures: 2%
forests and woodland: 84%
other: 3% (2000 est.)
Irrigated land: 20 sq km (1993 est.)
Natural hazards: frequent, devastating hurricanes (September to December) and coastal flooding (especially in south)
Environment - current issues: deforestation; water pollution from sewage, industrial effluents, agricultural runoff; solid waste disposal
Environment - international agreements:
party to: Biodiversity, Climate Change, Desertification, Endangered Species, Hazardous Wastes, Law of the Sea, Ozone Layer Protection, Marine Dumping, Ship Pollution, Wetlands
signed, but not ratified: none of the selected agreements
Geography - note: only country in Central America without a coastline on the North Pacific Ocean

People

Population: 256,062 (July 2001 est.)
Age structure:
0-14 years: 42.04% (male 54,876; female 52,780)
15-64 years: 54.43% (male 70,534; female 68,837)
65 years and over: 3.53% (male 4,403; female 4,632) (2001 est.)
Population growth rate: 2.7% (2001 est.)
Birth rate: 31.69 births/1,000 population (2001 est.)
Death rate: 4.7 deaths/1,000 population (2001 est.)
Net migration rate: 0 migrant(s)/1,000 population (2001 est.)
Sex ratio:
at birth: 1.05 male(s)/female
under 15 years: 1.04 male(s)/female
15-64 years: 1.02 male(s)/female
65 years and over: 0.95 male(s)/female
total population: 1.03 male(s)/female (2001 est.)
Infant mortality rate: 25.14 deaths/1,000 live births (2001 est.)
Life expectancy at birth:
total population: 71.19 years
male: 68.91 years
female: 73.57 years (2001 est.)
Total fertility rate: 4.05 children born/woman (2001 est.)
HIV/AIDS - adult prevalence rate: 2.01% (1999 est.)
HIV/AIDS - people living with HIV/AIDS: 2,400 (1999 est.)
HIV/AIDS - deaths: 170 (1999 est.)
Nationality:
noun: Belizean(s)
adjective: Belizean
Ethnic groups: mestizo 43.7%, Creole 29.8%, Maya 10%, Garifuna 6.2%, other 10.3%
Religions: Roman Catholic 62%, Protestant 30% (Anglican 12%, Methodist 6%, Mennonite 4%, Seventh-Day Adventist 3%, Pentecostal 2%, Jehovah's Witnesses 1%, other 2%), none 2%, other 6% (1980)
Languages: English (official), Spanish, Mayan, Garifuna (Carib), Creole
Literacy:
definition: age 15 and over can read and write
total population: 70.3%
male: 70.3%
female: 70.3% (1991 est.)
note: other sources list the literacy rate as high as 75%

Government

Country name:
conventional long form: none
conventional short form: Belize
former: British Honduras
Government type: parliamentary democracy
Capital: Belmopan
Administrative divisions: 6 districts; Belize, Cayo, Corozal, Orange Walk, Stann Creek, Toledo
Independence: 21 September 1981 (from UK)
National holiday: Independence Day, 21 September (1981)
Constitution: 21 September 1981
Legal system: English law
Suffrage: 18 years of age; universal
Executive branch:
chief of state: Queen ELIZABETH II (since 6 February 1952), represented by Governor General Sir Colville YOUNG (since 17 November 1993)
head of government: Prime Minister Said MUSA (since 27 August 1998); Deputy Prime Minister John BRICENO (since 1 September 1998)
cabinet: Cabinet appointed by the governor general on the advice of the prime minister
elections: none; the monarch is hereditary; governor general appointed by the monarch; governor general appoints the member of the House of Representatives who is leader of the majority party to be prime minister
Legislative branch: bicameral National Assembly consists of the Senate (eight members, five appointed on the advice of the prime minister, two on the advice of the leader of the opposition, and one by the governor general; members are appointed for five-year terms); and the House of Representatives (29 seats; members are elected by direct popular vote to serve five-year terms)
elections: House of Representatives - last held 27 August 1998 (next to be held by NA August 2003)
election results: percent of vote by party - PUP 59.2%, UDP 40.8%; seats by party - PUP 26, UDP 3
Judicial branch: Supreme Court (the chief justice is appointed by the governor general on the advice of the prime minister)
Political parties and leaders: People's United Party or PUP [Said MUSA]; United Democratic Party or UDP [Manuel ESQUIVEL, Dean BARROW, Doug SINGH]
Political pressure groups and leaders: Society for the Promotion of Education and Research or SPEAR [Diane HAYLOCK]; United Worker's Front

International organization participation: ACP, C, Caricom, CDB, ECLAC, FAO, G-77, IADB, IBRD, ICAO, ICFTU, ICRM, IDA, IFAD, IFC, IFRCS, ILO, IMF, IMO, Intelsat (nonsignatory user), Interpol, IOC, IOM, ITU, LAES, NAM, OAS, OPANAL, UN, UNCTAD, UNESCO, UNIDO, UPU, WCL, WHO, WIPO, WMO, WTrO
Diplomatic representation in the US:
chief of mission: Ambassador Lisa M. SHOMAN
chancery: 2535 Massachusetts Avenue NW, Washington, DC 20008
telephone: [1] (202) 332-9636
FAX: [1] (202) 332-6888
consulate(s) general: Los Angeles
Diplomatic representation from the US:
chief of mission: Ambassador Carolyn CURIEL
embassy: 29 Gabourel Lane and Hutson Street, Belize City
mailing address: P. O. Box 286, Unit 7401, APO AA 34025
telephone: [501] (2) 77161
FAX: [501] (2) 30802
Flag description: blue with a narrow red stripe along the top and the bottom edges; centered is a large white disk bearing the coat of arms; the coat of arms features a shield flanked by two workers in front of a mahogany tree with the related motto SUB UMBRA FLOREO (I Flourish in the Shade) on a scroll at the bottom, all encircled by a green garland

Economy

Economy - overview: The small, essentially private enterprise economy is based primarily on agriculture, agro-based industry, and merchandising, with tourism and construction assuming greater importance. Sugar, the chief crop, accounts for nearly half of exports, while the banana industry is the country's largest employer. The government's tough austerity program in 1997 resulted in an economic slowdown that continued in 1998. The trade deficit has been growing, mostly as a result of low export prices for sugar and bananas. The tourist and construction sectors strengthened in early 1999, supporting growth of 6% in 1999 and 4% in 2000. Aided by international donors, the government's key short-term objective remains the reduction of poverty.
GDP: purchasing power parity - $790 million (2000 est.)
GDP - real growth rate: 4% (2000 est.)
GDP - per capita: purchasing power parity - $3,200 (2000 est.)
GDP - composition by sector:
agriculture: 18%
industry: 24%
services: 58% (2000 est.)
Population below poverty line: 33% (1999 est.)
Household income or consumption by percentage share:
lowest 10%: NA%
highest 10%: NA%
Inflation rate (consumer prices): 2% (2000 est.)

Belize (continued)

Labor force: 71,000
note: shortage of skilled labor and all types of technical personnel (1997 est.)
Labor force - by occupation: agriculture 38%, industry 32%, services 30% (1994)
Unemployment rate: 12.8% (1999)
Budget:
revenues: $157 million
expenditures: $279 million, including capital expenditures of $NA (1999 est.)
Industries: garment production, food processing, tourism, construction
Industrial production growth rate: 4.6% (1999)
Electricity - production: 185 million kWh (1999)
Electricity - production by source:
fossil fuel: 56.76%
hydro: 43.24%
nuclear: 0%
other: 0% (1999)
Electricity - consumption: 172.1 million kWh (1999)
Electricity - exports: 0 kWh (1999)
Electricity - imports: 0 kWh (1999)
Agriculture - products: bananas, coca, citrus, sugarcane; lumber; fish, cultured shrimp
Exports: $235.7 million (f.o.b., 2000 est.)
Exports - commodities: sugar, bananas, citrus, clothing, fish products, molasses, wood
Exports - partners: US 42%, UK 33%, EU 12%, Caricom 4.8%, Canada 2%, Mexico 1% (1999)
Imports: $413 million (c.i.f., 2000 est.)
Imports - commodities: machinery and transportation equipment, manufactured goods; food, beverages, tobacco; fuels, chemicals, pharmaceuticals
Imports - partners: US 58%, Mexico 12%, UK 5%, EU 5%, Central America 5%, Caricom 4% (1998)
Debt - external: $338 million (1998)
Economic aid - recipient: $NA
Currency: Belizean dollar (BZD)
Currency code: BZD
Exchange rates: Belizean dollars per US dollar - 2.0000 (fixed rate pegged to the US dollar)
Fiscal year: 1 April - 31 March

Communications

Telephones - main lines in use: 31,000 (1997)
Telephones - mobile cellular: 3,023 (1997)
Telephone system:
general assessment: above-average system
domestic: trunk network depends primarily on microwave radio relay
international: satellite earth station - 1 Intelsat (Atlantic Ocean)
Radio broadcast stations: AM 1, FM 12, shortwave 0 (1998)
Radios: 133,000 (1997)
Television broadcast stations: 2 (1997)
Televisions: 41,000 (1997)
Internet country code: .bz
Internet Service Providers (ISPs): 2 (2000)
Internet users: 12,000 (2000)

Transportation

Railways: 0 km
Highways:
total: 2,872 km
paved: 488 km
unpaved: 2,384 km (1998 est.)
Waterways: 825 km (river network used by shallow-draft craft; seasonally navigable)
Ports and harbors: Belize City, Big Creek, Corozol, Punta Gorda
Merchant marine:
total: 402 ships (1,000 GRT or over) totaling 1,575,851 GRT/2,241,731 DWT
ships by type: bulk 27, cargo 265, chemical tanker 6, combination ore/oil 1, container 14, passenger 1, passenger/cargo 2, petroleum tanker 56, refrigerated cargo 18, roll on/roll off 7, short-sea passenger 1, specialized tanker 1, vehicle carrier 3
note: includes some foreign-owned ships registered here as a flag of convenience: Cuba 1, Singapore 1, US 1 (2000 est.)
Airports: 44 (2000 est.)
Airports - with paved runways:
total: 4
1,524 to 2,437 m: 1
914 to 1,523 m: 1
under 914 m: 2 (2000 est.)
Airports - with unpaved runways:
total: 40
2,438 to 3,047 m: 1
914 to 1,523 m: 10
under 914 m: 29 (2000 est.)

Military

Military branches: Belize Defense Force (includes Army, Maritime Wing, Air Wing, and Volunteer Guard)
Military manpower - military age: 18 years of age
Military manpower - availability:
males age 15-49: 62,698 (2001 est.)
Military manpower - fit for military service:
males age 15-49: 37,174 (2001 est.)
Military manpower - reaching military age annually:
males: 2,847 (2001 est.)
Military expenditures - dollar figure: $17 million (FY98/99)
Military expenditures - percent of GDP: 2.4% (FY98/99)

Transnational Issues

Disputes - international: Guatemala periodically asserts claims to territory in southern Belize; to deter cross-border squatting, both states in 2000 agreed to a "line of adjacency" based on the de facto boundary, which is not recognized by Guatemala
Illicit drugs: minor transshipment point for cocaine; small-scale illicit producer of cannabis for the international drug trade; minor money-laundering center

Benin

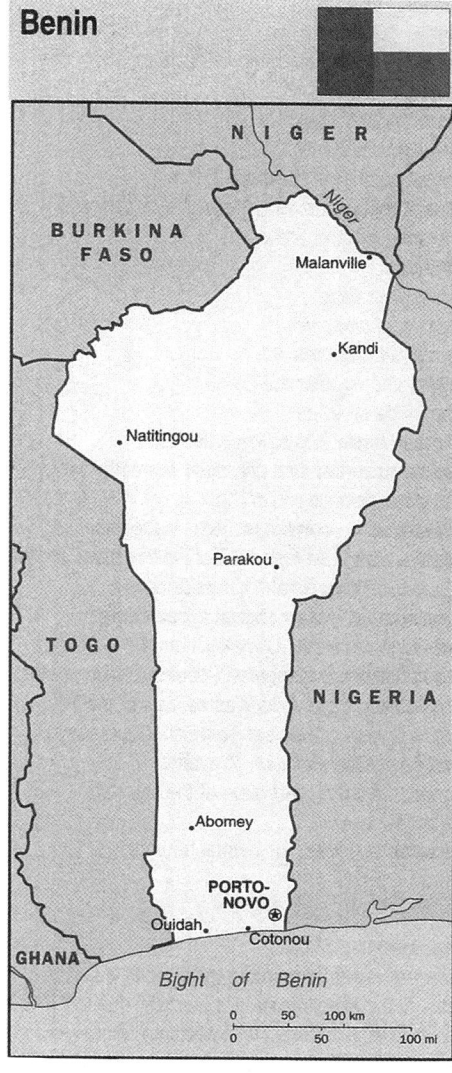

Introduction

Background: Dahomey gained its independence from France in 1960; the name was changed to Benin in 1975. From 1974 to 1989 the country was a socialist state; free elections were reestablished in 1991.

Geography

Location: Western Africa, bordering the North Atlantic Ocean, between Nigeria and Togo
Geographic coordinates: 9 30 N, 2 15 E
Map references: Africa
Area:
total: 112,620 sq km
land: 110,620 sq km
water: 2,000 sq km
Area - comparative: slightly smaller than Pennsylvania
Land boundaries:
total: 1,989 km
border countries: Burkina Faso 306 km, Niger 266 km, Nigeria 773 km, Togo 644 km
Coastline: 121 km
Maritime claims:
territorial sea: 200 NM

Benin (continued)

Climate: tropical; hot, humid in south; semiarid in north
Terrain: mostly flat to undulating plain; some hills and low mountains
Elevation extremes:
lowest point: Atlantic Ocean 0 m
highest point: Mont Sokbaro 658 m
Natural resources: small offshore oil deposits, limestone, marble, timber
Land use:
arable land: 13%
permanent crops: 4%
permanent pastures: 4%
forests and woodland: 31%
other: 48% (1993 est.)
Irrigated land: 100 sq km (1993 est.)
Natural hazards: hot, dry, dusty harmattan wind may affect north in winter
Environment - current issues: inadequate supplies of potable water; poaching threatens wildlife populations; deforestation; desertification
Environment - international agreements:
party to: Biodiversity, Climate Change, Desertification, Endangered Species, Environmental Modification, Hazardous Wastes, Law of the Sea, Marine Dumping, Nuclear Test Ban, Ozone Layer Protection, Ship Pollution, Wetlands
signed, but not ratified: none of the selected agreements
Geography - note: no natural harbors

People

Population: 6,590,782
note: estimates for this country explicitly take into account the effects of excess mortality due to AIDS; this can result in lower life expectancy, higher infant mortality and death rates, lower population and growth rates, and changes in the distribution of population by age and sex than would otherwise be expected (July 2001 est.)
Age structure:
0-14 years: 47.32% (male 1,574,124; female 1,544,741)
15-64 years: 50.38% (male 1,607,900; female 1,712,360)
65 years and over: 2.3% (male 64,756; female 86,901) (2001 est.)
Population growth rate: 2.97% (2001 est.)
Birth rate: 44.23 births/1,000 population (2001 est.)
Death rate: 14.51 deaths/1,000 population (2001 est.)
Net migration rate: 0 migrant(s)/1,000 population (2001 est.)
Sex ratio:
at birth: 1.03 male(s)/female
under 15 years: 1.02 male(s)/female
15-64 years: 0.94 male(s)/female
65 years and over: 0.75 male(s)/female
total population: 0.97 male(s)/female (2001 est.)
Infant mortality rate: 89.68 deaths/1,000 live births (2001 est.)
Life expectancy at birth:
total population: 49.94 years
male: 49.02 years
female: 50.88 years (2001 est.)
Total fertility rate: 6.23 children born/woman (2001 est.)
HIV/AIDS - adult prevalence rate: 2.45% (1999 est.)
HIV/AIDS - people living with HIV/AIDS: 70,000 (1999 est.)
HIV/AIDS - deaths: 5,600 (1999 est.)
Nationality:
noun: Beninese (singular and plural)
adjective: Beninese
Ethnic groups: African 99% (42 ethnic groups, most important being Fon, Adja, Yoruba, Bariba), Europeans 5,500
Religions: indigenous beliefs 50%, Christian 30%, Muslim 20%
Languages: French (official), Fon and Yoruba (most common vernaculars in south), tribal languages (at least six major ones in north)
Literacy:
definition: age 15 and over can read and write
total population: 37.5%
male: 52.2%
female: 23.6% (2000)

Government

Country name:
conventional long form: Republic of Benin
conventional short form: Benin
local long form: Republique du Benin
local short form: Benin
former: Dahomey
Government type: republic under multiparty democratic rule; dropped Marxism-Leninism December 1989; democratic reforms adopted February 1990; transition to multiparty system completed 4 April 1991
Capital: Porto-Novo is the official capital; Cotonou is the seat of government
Administrative divisions: 6 provinces; Atakora, Atlantique, Borgou, Mono, Oueme, Zou; note - six additional provinces have been reported but not confirmed; they are Alibori, Collines, Couffo, Donga, Littoral, and Plateau; moreover, the term "province" may have been changed to "department"
Independence: 1 August 1960 (from France)
National holiday: National Day, 1 August (1960)
Constitution: December 1990
Legal system: based on French civil law and customary law; has not accepted compulsory ICJ jurisdiction
Suffrage: 18 years of age; universal
Executive branch:
chief of state: President Mathieu KEREKOU (since 4 April 1996); note - the president is both the chief of state and head of government
head of government: President Mathieu KEREKOU (since 4 April 1996); note - the president is both the chief of state and head of government
cabinet: Council of Ministers appointed by the president
elections: president reelected by popular vote for a five-year term; runoff election held 22 March 2001 (next to be held NA March 2006)
election results: Mathieu KEREKOU reelected president; percent of vote - Mathieu KEREKOU 84.1%, Bruno AMOUSSOU 15.9%
note: the four top-ranking contenders following the first round presidential elections were: Mathieu KEREKOU (incumbent) 45.4%, Nicephore SOGOLO (former president) 27.1%, Adrien HOUNGBEDJI (National Assembly Speaker) 12.6%, and Bruno AMOUSSOU (Minister of State) 8.6%; the second round balloting, originally scheduled for 18 March, was postponed four days because both SOGOLO and HOUNGBEDJI withdrew alleging electoral fraud; this left KEREKOU to run against his own Minister of State, AMOUSSOU, in what was termed a "friendly match"
Legislative branch: unicameral National Assembly or Assemblee Nationale (83 seats; members are elected by direct popular vote to serve four-year terms)
elections: last held 30 March 1999 (next to be held NA March 2003)
election results: percent of vote by party - NA%; seats by party - RB 27, PRD 11, FARD-ALAFIA 10, PSD 9, MADEP 6, E'toile 4, Alliance IPD 4, Car-DUNYA 3, MERCI 2, other 7
Judicial branch: Constitutional Court or Cour Constitutionnelle; Supreme Court or Cour Supreme; High Court of Justice
Political parties and leaders: African Movement for Democracy and Progress or MADEP [Sefou FAGBOHOUN]; Alliance for Democracy and Progress or ADP [Sylvain Adekpedjou AKINDES]; Alliance of the Social Democratic Party or PSD and the National Union for Solidarity and Progress or UNSP [Bruno AMOUSSOU]; Cameleon Alliance or AC [leader NA]; Car-DUNYA [Saka SALEY]; Communist Party of Benin or PCB [Pascal FANTONDJI, first secretary]; Democratic Renewal Party or PRD [Adrien HOUNGBEDJI]; Front for Renewal and Development or FARD-ALAFIA [Jerome Sakia KINA]; Impulse for Progress and Democracy or IPD [Bertin BORNA]; Liberal Democrats' Rally for National Reconstruction-Vivoten or RDL-Vivoten [Severin ADJOVI]; Movement for Citizens' Commitment and Awakening or MERCI [Severin ADJOVI]; New Generation for the Republic or NGR [Paul DOSSOU]; Our Common Cause or NCC [Francois Odjo TANKPINON]; Party Democratique du Benin or PDB [Col. Soule DANKORO]; Rally for Democracy and Pan-Africanism or RDP [Dominique HOYMINOU, Dr. Giles Auguste MINONTIN]; Renaissance Party du Benin or RB [Nicephore SOGLO]; The Star Alliance (Alliance E'toile) [Sacca LAFIA]; Union for National Democracy and Solidarity or UDS [Adamou N'Diaye MAMA]
note: the Coalition of Democratic Forces is an alliance of parties and organizations supporting President KEREKOU [Gatien HOUNGBEDJI]

Benin (continued)

Political pressure groups and leaders: NA
International organization participation: ACCT, ACP, AfDB, CCC, ECA, ECOWAS, Entente, FAO, FZ, G-77, IAEA, IBRD, ICAO, ICFTU, ICRM, IDA, IDB, IFAD, IFC, IFRCS, ILO, IMF, IMO, Intelsat, Interpol, IOC, IOM, ISO (subscriber), ITU, MIPONUH, MONUC, NAM, OAU, OIC, OPCW, UN, UNCTAD, UNESCO, UNIDO, UNMEE, UNTAET, UPU, WADB, WADB (regional), WAEMU, WCL, WFTU, WHO, WIPO, WMO, WToO, WTrO
Diplomatic representation in the US:
chief of mission: Ambassador Lucien Edgar TONOUKOUIN
chancery: 2737 Cathedral Avenue NW, Washington, DC 20008
telephone: [1] (202) 232-6656
FAX: [1] (202) 265-1996
Diplomatic representation from the US:
chief of mission: Ambassador Pamela E. BRIDGEWATER
embassy: Rue Caporal Bernard Anani, Cotonou
mailing address: B. P. 2012, Cotonou
telephone: [229] 30-06-50, 30-05-13, 30-17-92
FAX: [229] 30-14-39, 30-19-74
Flag description: two equal horizontal bands of yellow (top) and red with a vertical green band on the hoist side

Economy

Economy - overview: The economy of Benin remains underdeveloped and dependent on subsistence agriculture, cotton production, and regional trade. Growth in real output averaged a sound 5% in 1996-99, but a rapid population rise offset much of this growth. Inflation has subsided over the past several years. Commercial and transport activities, which make up a large part of GDP, are vulnerable to developments in Nigeria, particularly fuel shortages. The Paris Club and bilateral creditors have eased the external debt situation in recent years. While high fuel prices constrained growth in 2000, increased cotton production - enabled by a major restructuring program - and an expansion of the Cotonou port, may lead to increased growth in 2001.
GDP: purchasing power parity - $6.6 billion (2000 est.)
GDP - real growth rate: 5% (2000 est.)
GDP - per capita: purchasing power parity - $1,030 (2000 est.)
GDP - composition by sector:
agriculture: 37.9%
industry: 13.5%
services: 48.6% (1999)
Population below poverty line: 37.2% (1999 est.)
Household income or consumption by percentage share:
lowest 10%: NA%
highest 10%: NA%
Inflation rate (consumer prices): 3% (2000 est.)
Labor force: NA
Unemployment rate: NA%
Budget:
revenues: $299 million
expenditures: $445 million, including capital expenditures of $14 million (1995 est.)
Industries: textiles, cigarettes; beverages, food; construction materials, petroleum
Industrial production growth rate: 6.9% (2000 est.)
Electricity - production: 226 million kWh (1999)
Electricity - production by source:
fossil fuel: 24.78%
hydro: 75.22%
nuclear: 0%
other: 0% (1999)
Electricity - consumption: 510.2 million kWh (1999)
Electricity - exports: 0 kWh (1999)
Electricity - imports: 300 million kWh (1999)
Agriculture - products: corn, sorghum, cassava (tapioca), yams, beans, rice, cotton, palm oil, peanuts; poultry, livestock
Exports: $396 million (f.o.b., 1999)
Exports - commodities: cotton, crude oil, palm products, cocoa
Exports - partners: Brazil 14%, Libya 5%, Indonesia 4%, Italy 4% (1999)
Imports: $566 million (c.i.f., 1999)
Imports - commodities: foodstuffs, tobacco, petroleum products, capital goods
Imports - partners: France 38%, China 16%, UK 9%, Cote d'Ivoire 5% (1999)
Debt - external: $1.6 billion (1998 est.)
Economic aid - recipient: $274.6 million (1997)
Currency: Communaute Financiere Africaine franc (XOF); note - responsible authority is the Central Bank of the West African States
Currency code: XOF
Exchange rates: Communaute Financiere Africaine francs (XOF) per US dollar - 699.21 (January 2001), 711.98 (2000), 615.70 (1999), 589.95 (1998), 583.67 (1997), 511.55 (1996); note - from 1 January 1999, the XOF is pegged to the euro at a rate of 655.957 XOF per euro
Fiscal year: calendar year

Communications

Telephones - main lines in use: 36,000 (1997)
Telephones - mobile cellular: 4,295 (1997)
Telephone system:
general assessment: NA
domestic: fair system of open wire, microwave radio relay, and cellular connections
international: satellite earth station - 1 Intelsat (Atlantic Ocean); submarine cable
Radio broadcast stations: AM 2, FM 9, shortwave 4 (1998)
Radios: 620,000 (1997)
Television broadcast stations: 2 (one privately-owned) (1997)
Televisions: 60,000 (1997)
Internet country code: .bj
Internet Service Providers (ISPs): 1 (2000)
Internet users: 10,000 (2000)

Transportation

Railways:
total: 578 km (single track)
narrow gauge: 578 km 1.000-m gauge (1995 est.)
Highways:
total: 6,787 km
paved: 1,357 km (including 10 km of expressways)
unpaved: 5,430 km (1997 est.)
Waterways: streams navigable along small sections, important only locally
Ports and harbors: Cotonou, Porto-Novo
Merchant marine: none (2000 est.)
Airports: 5 (2000 est.)
Airports - with paved runways:
total: 1
1,524 to 2,437 m: 1 (2000 est.)
Airports - with unpaved runways:
total: 4
2,438 to 3,047 m: 1
1,524 to 2,437 m: 1
914 to 1,523 m: 2 (2000 est.)

Military

Military branches: Armed Forces (includes Army, Navy, Air Force), National Gendarmerie
Military manpower - military age: 18 years of age
Military manpower - availability:
males age 15-49: 1,455,433
females age 15-49: 1,489,947
note: both sexes are liable for military service (2001 est.)
Military manpower - fit for military service:
males age 15-49: 743,980
females age 15-49: 755,149 (2001 est.)
Military manpower - reaching military age annually:
males: 70,088
females: 73,618 (2001 est.)
Military expenditures - dollar figure: $27 million (FY96)
Military expenditures - percent of GDP: 1.2% (FY96)

Transnational Issues

Disputes - international: none
Illicit drugs: transshipment point for narcotics associated with Nigerian trafficking organizations and most commonly destined for Western Europe and the US

Bermuda
(overseas territory of the UK)

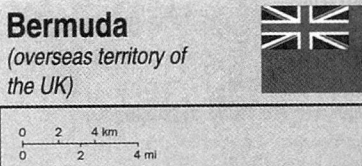

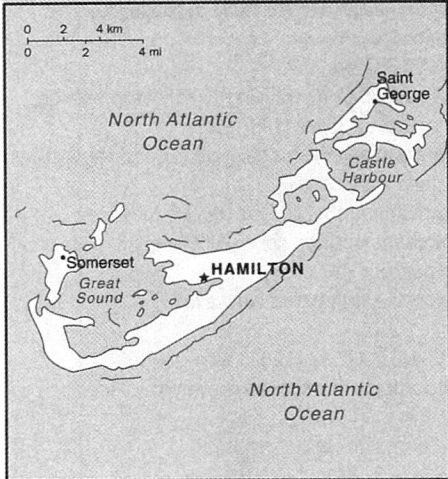

Introduction

Background: Bermuda was first settled in 1609 by shipwrecked English colonists headed for Virginia. Tourism to the island to escape North American winters first developed in Victorian times. Bermuda has developed into a highly successful offshore financial center. A referendum on independence was soundly defeated in 1995.

Geography

Location: North America, group of islands in the North Atlantic Ocean, east of North Carolina (US)
Geographic coordinates: 32 20 N, 64 45 W
Map references: North America
Area:
total: 58.8 sq km
land: 58.8 sq km
water: 0 sq km
Area - comparative: about 0.3 times the size of Washington, DC
Land boundaries: 0 km
Coastline: 103 km
Maritime claims:
exclusive fishing zone: 200 NM
territorial sea: 12 NM
Climate: subtropical; mild, humid; gales, strong winds common in winter
Terrain: low hills separated by fertile depressions
Elevation extremes:
lowest point: Atlantic Ocean 0 m
highest point: Town Hill 76 m
Natural resources: limestone, pleasant climate fostering tourism
Land use:
arable land: 6%
permanent crops: 0%
permanent pastures: 0%
forests and woodland: 0%
other: 94% (55% developed, 39% rural/open space) (1997 est.)
Irrigated land: NA sq km
Natural hazards: hurricanes (June to November)
Environment - current issues: asbestos disposal; water pollution; preservation of open space
Geography - note: consists of about 360 small coral islands with ample rainfall, but no rivers or freshwater lakes; some land, reclaimed and otherwise, was leased by US Government from 1941 to 1995

People

Population: 63,503 (July 2001 est.)
Age structure:
0-14 years: 19.4% (male 6,091; female 6,230)
15-64 years: 69.43% (male 21,783; female 22,309)
65 years and over: 11.17% (male 3,073; female 4,017) (2001 est.)
Population growth rate: 0.74% (2001 est.)
Birth rate: 12.16 births/1,000 population (2001 est.)
Death rate: 7.42 deaths/1,000 population (2001 est.)
Net migration rate: 2.66 migrant(s)/1,000 population (2001 est.)
Sex ratio:
at birth: 0.94 male(s)/female
under 15 years: 0.98 male(s)/female
15-64 years: 0.98 male(s)/female
65 years and over: 0.76 male(s)/female
total population: 0.95 male(s)/female (2001 est.)
Infant mortality rate: 9.55 deaths/1,000 live births (2001 est.)
Life expectancy at birth:
total population: 77.12 years
male: 75.04 years
female: 79.06 years (2001 est.)
Total fertility rate: 1.81 children born/woman (2001 est.)
HIV/AIDS - adult prevalence rate: NA%
HIV/AIDS - people living with HIV/AIDS: NA
HIV/AIDS - deaths: NA
Nationality:
noun: Bermudian(s)
adjective: Bermudian
Ethnic groups: black 58%, white 36%, other 6%
Religions: non-Anglican Protestant 39%, Anglican 27%, Roman Catholic 15%, other 19%
Languages: English (official), Portuguese
Literacy:
definition: age 15 and over can read and write
total population: 98%
male: 98%
female: 99% (1970 est.)

Government

Country name:
conventional long form: none
conventional short form: Bermuda
former: Somers Islands
Dependency status: overseas territory of the UK
Government type: parliamentary British overseas territory with internal self-government
Capital: Hamilton
Administrative divisions: 9 parishes and 2 municipalities*; Devonshire, Hamilton, Hamilton*, Paget, Pembroke, Saint George*, Saint Georges, Sandys, Smiths, Southampton, Warwick
Independence: none (overseas territory of the UK)
National holiday: Bermuda Day, 24 May
Constitution: 8 June 1968, amended 1989
Legal system: English law
Suffrage: 18 years of age; universal
Executive branch:
chief of state: Queen ELIZABETH II (since 6 February 1952), represented by Governor Thorold MASEFIELD (since NA June 1997)
head of government: Premier Jennifer SMITH (since 10 November 1998)
cabinet: Cabinet nominated by the premier, appointed by the governor
elections: none; the monarch is hereditary; governor appointed by the monarch; governor invites leader of largest party in Parliament to form a government as premier
Legislative branch: bicameral Parliament consists of the Senate (an 11-member body appointed by the governor) and the House of Assembly (40 seats; members are elected by popular vote to serve five-year terms)
elections: last held 9 November 1998 (next to be held NA November 2003)
election results: percent of vote by party - PLP 54%, UBP 44%, NLP 1%, independents 1%; seats by party - PLP 26, UBP 14
Judicial branch: Supreme Court; Court of Appeal; Magistrate Courts
Political parties and leaders: National Liberal Party or NLP [Dessaline WALDRON]; Progressive Labor Party or PLP [Jennifer SMITH]; United Bermuda Party or UBP [Pamela GORDON]
Political pressure groups and leaders: Bermuda Industrial Union or BIU [Derrick BURGESS]; Bermuda Public Services Association or BPSA [Betty CHRISTOPHER]
International organization participation: Caricom (observer), CCC, ICFTU, Interpol (subbureau), IOC
Diplomatic representation in the US: none (overseas territory of the UK)
Diplomatic representation from the US:
chief of mission: Consul General Lawrence D. OWEN
consulate(s) general: Crown Hill, 16 Middle Road, Devonshire, Hamilton
mailing address: P. O. Box HM325, Hamilton HMBX; American Consulate General Hamilton, Department of State, Washington, DC 20520-5300
telephone: [1] (441) 295-1342
FAX: [1] (441) 295-1592
Flag description: red, with the flag of the UK in the upper hoist-side quadrant and the Bermudian coat of arms (white and green shield with a red lion holding a scrolled shield showing the sinking of the ship Sea Venture off Bermuda in 1609) centered on the outer half of the flag

Bermuda *(continued)*

Economy

Economy - overview: Bermuda enjoys one of the highest per capita incomes in the world, having successfully exploited its location by providing financial services for international firms and luxury tourist facilities for 360,000 visitors annually. The tourist industry, which accounts for an estimated 28% of GDP, attracts 84% of its business from North America. The industrial sector is small, and agriculture is severely limited by a lack of suitable land. About 80% of food needs are imported. International business contributes over 60% of Bermuda's economic output; a failed independence vote in late 1995 can be partially attributed to Bermudian fears of scaring away foreign firms. Government economic priorities are the further strengthening of the tourist and international financial sectors.
GDP: purchasing power parity - $2.1 billion (2000 est.)
GDP - real growth rate: 1.5% (2000 est.)
GDP - per capita: purchasing power parity - $33,000 (2000 est.)
GDP - composition by sector:
agriculture: 1%
industry: 10%
services: 89% (1995 est.)
Population below poverty line: NA%
Household income or consumption by percentage share:
lowest 10%: NA%
highest 10%: NA%
Inflation rate (consumer prices): 2.7% (2000 est.)
Labor force: 35,296 (1997)
Labor force - by occupation: clerical 23%, services 22%, laborers 17%, professional and technical 17%, administrative and managerial 12%, sales 7%, agriculture and fishing 2% (1996)
Unemployment rate: NEGL% (1995)
Budget:
revenues: $504.6 million
expenditures: $537 million, including capital expenditures of $75 million (FY97/98)
Industries: tourism, finance, insurance, structural concrete products, paints, perfumes, pharmaceuticals, ship repairing
Industrial production growth rate: NA%
Electricity - production: 550 million kWh (1999)
Electricity - production by source:
fossil fuel: 100%
hydro: 0%
nuclear: 0%
other: 0% (1999)
Electricity - consumption: 511.5 million kWh (1999)
Electricity - exports: 0 kWh (1999)
Electricity - imports: 0 kWh (1999)
Agriculture - products: bananas, vegetables, citrus, flowers; dairy products
Exports: $56 million (2000 est.)
Exports - commodities: reexports of pharmaceuticals
Exports - partners: UK 29.5%, US 9.8% (1997)
Imports: $739 million (2000 est.)
Imports - commodities: machinery and transport equipment, construction materials, chemicals, food and live animals
Imports - partners: US 34%, UK 9%, Mexico 8% (1997)
Debt - external: $NA
Economic aid - recipient: $27.9 million (1995)
Currency: Bermudian dollar (BMD)
Currency code: BMD
Exchange rates: Bermudian dollar per US dollar - 1.0000 (fixed rate pegged to the US dollar)
Fiscal year: 1 April - 31 March

Communications

Telephones - main lines in use: 52,000 (1997)
Telephones - mobile cellular: 7,980 (1996)
Telephone system:
general assessment: NA
domestic: modern, fully automatic telephone system
international: 3 submarine cables; satellite earth stations - 3 Intelsat (Atlantic Ocean)
Radio broadcast stations: AM 5, FM 3, shortwave 0 (1998)
Radios: 82,000 (1997)
Television broadcast stations: 3 (1997)
Televisions: 66,000 (1997)
Internet country code: .bm
Internet Service Providers (ISPs): 20 (2000)
Internet users: 25,000 (2000)

Transportation

Railways: 0 km
Highways:
total: 225 km
paved: 225 km
unpaved: 0 km
note: in addition, there are 232 km of paved and unpaved roads that are privately owned (1997)
Waterways: none
Ports and harbors: Hamilton, Saint George
Merchant marine:
total: 105 ships (1,000 GRT or over) totaling 5,836,538 GRT/9,728,045 DWT
ships by type: bulk 27, cargo 4, container 15, liquefied gas 7, passenger 2, petroleum tanker 23, refrigerated cargo 16, roll on/roll off 8, short-sea passenger 3
note: includes some foreign-owned ships registered here as a flag of convenience: Canada 10, Hong Kong 10, Japan 1, Nigeria 4, Saudi Arabia 1, Sweden 3, Switzerland 2, UK 10, US 7 (2000 est.)
Airports: 1 (2000 est.)
Airports - with paved runways:
total: 1
2,438 to 3,047 m: 1 (2000 est.)

Military

Military branches: Bermuda Regiment, Bermuda Police Force, Bermuda Reserve Constabulary
Military expenditures - dollar figure: $NA
Military expenditures - percent of GDP: NA%
Military - note: defense is the responsibility of the UK

Transnational Issues

Disputes - international: none

Bhutan

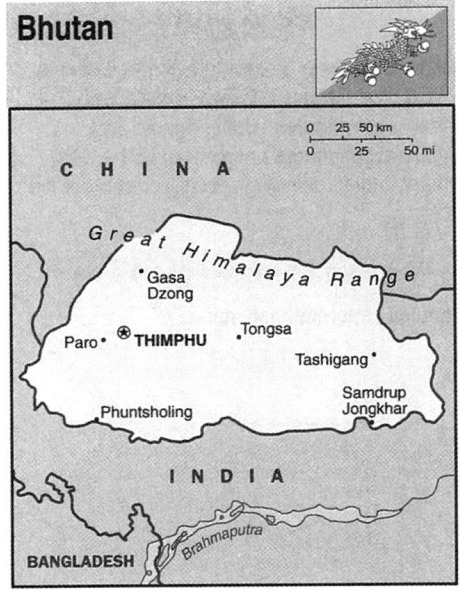

Introduction

Background: Under British influence a monarchy was set up in 1907; three years later a treaty was signed whereby the country became a British protectorate. Independence was attained in 1949, with India subsequently guiding foreign relations and supplying aid. A refugee issue of some 100,000 Bhutanese in Nepal remains unresolved; 90% of these displaced persons are housed in seven United Nations Office of the High Commissioner for Refugees (UNHCR) camps. Maoist Assamese separatists from India, who have established themselves in the southeast portion of Bhutan, have drawn Indian cross-border incursions.

Geography

Location: Southern Asia, between China and India
Geographic coordinates: 27 30 N, 90 30 E
Map references: Asia
Area:
total: 47,000 sq km
land: 47,000 sq km
water: 0 sq km
Area - comparative: about half the size of Indiana
Land boundaries:
total: 1,075 km
border countries: China 470 km, India 605 km
Coastline: 0 km (landlocked)
Maritime claims: none (landlocked)
Climate: varies; tropical in southern plains; cool winters and hot summers in central valleys; severe winters and cool summers in Himalayas
Terrain: mostly mountainous with some fertile valleys and savanna
Elevation extremes:
lowest point: Drangme Chhu 97 m
highest point: Kula Kangri 7,553 m
Natural resources: timber, hydropower, gypsum, calcium carbide
Land use:
arable land: 2%
permanent crops: 0%
permanent pastures: 6%
forests and woodland: 66%
other: 26% (1993 est.)
Irrigated land: 340 sq km (1993 est.)
Natural hazards: violent storms coming down from the Himalayas are the source of the country's name which translates as Land of the Thunder Dragon; frequent landslides during the rainy season
Environment - current issues: soil erosion; limited access to potable water
Environment - international agreements:
party to: Biodiversity, Climate Change, Marine Dumping, Nuclear Test Ban, Ship Pollution
signed, but not ratified: Law of the Sea
Geography - note: landlocked; strategic location between China and India; controls several key Himalayan mountain passes

People

Population: 2,049,412 (July 2001 est.)
note: other estimates range as low as 800,000
Age structure:
0-14 years: 39.99% (male 424,832; female 394,725)
15-64 years: 56.05% (male 591,152; female 557,498)
65 years and over: 3.96% (male 41,125; female 40,080) (2001 est.)
Population growth rate: 2.17% (2001 est.)
Birth rate: 35.73 births/1,000 population (2001 est.)
Death rate: 14.03 deaths/1,000 population (2001 est.)
Net migration rate: 0 migrant(s)/1,000 population (2001 est.)
Sex ratio:
at birth: 1.05 male(s)/female
under 15 years: 1.08 male(s)/female
15-64 years: 1.06 male(s)/female
65 years and over: 1.03 male(s)/female
total population: 1.07 male(s)/female (2001 est.)
Infant mortality rate: 108.89 deaths/1,000 live births (2001 est.)
Life expectancy at birth:
total population: 52.79 years
male: 53.16 years
female: 52.41 years (2001 est.)
Total fertility rate: 5.07 children born/woman (2001 est.)
HIV/AIDS - adult prevalence rate: less than 0.01% (1999 est.)
HIV/AIDS - people living with HIV/AIDS: less than 100 (1999 est.)
HIV/AIDS - deaths: NA
Nationality:
noun: Bhutanese (singular and plural)
adjective: Bhutanese
Ethnic groups: Bhote 50%, ethnic Nepalese 35%, indigenous or migrant tribes 15%
Religions: Lamaistic Buddhist 75%, Indian- and Nepalese-influenced Hinduism 25%
Languages: Dzongkha (official), Bhotes speak various Tibetan dialects, Nepalese speak various Nepalese dialects
Literacy:
definition: age 15 and over can read and write
total population: 42.2%
male: 56.2%
female: 28.1% (1995 est.)
People - note: refugee issue over the presence in Nepal of approximately 98,700 Bhutanese refugees, 90% of whom are in seven United Nations Office of the High Commissioner for Refugees (UNHCR) camps

Government

Country name:
conventional long form: Kingdom of Bhutan
conventional short form: Bhutan
Government type: monarchy; special treaty relationship with India
Capital: Thimphu
Administrative divisions: 18 districts (dzongkhag, singular and plural); Bumthang, Chhukha, Chirang, Daga, Geylegphug, Ha, Lhuntshi, Mongar, Paro, Pemagatsel, Punakha, Samchi, Samdrup Jongkhar, Shemgang, Tashigang, Thimphu, Tongsa, Wangdi Phodrang
note: there may be two new districts named Gasa and Yangtse
Independence: 8 August 1949 (from India)
National holiday: National Day (Ugyen WANGCHUCK became first hereditary king), 17 December (1907)
Constitution: no written constitution or bill of rights; note - Bhutan uses 1953 Royal decree for the Constitution of the National Assembly; on 7 July 1998, a Royal edict was ratified giving the National Assembly additional powers
Legal system: based on Indian law and English common law; has not accepted compulsory ICJ jurisdiction
Suffrage: each family has one vote in village-level elections
Executive branch:
chief of state: King Jigme Singye WANGCHUCK (since 24 July 1972)
head of government: Chairman of the Council of Ministers Sangay NGEDUP (since NA 1999)
cabinet: Council of Ministers (Lhengye Shungtsog) nominated by the monarch, approved by the National Assembly; members serve fixed, five-year terms; note - there is also a Royal Advisory Council (Lodoi Tsokde), members nominated by the monarch
elections: none; the monarch is hereditary, but democratic reforms in July 1998 give the National Assembly authority to remove the monarch with two-thirds vote
Legislative branch: unicameral National Assembly or Tshogdu (150 seats; 105 elected from village constituencies, 10 represent religious bodies, and 35 are designated by the monarch to represent government and other secular interests; members serve three-year terms)

Bhutan (continued)

elections: last held NA (next to be held NA)
election results: NA
Judicial branch: Supreme Court of Appeal (the monarch); High Court (judges appointed by the monarch)
Political parties and leaders: no legal parties
Political pressure groups and leaders: Buddhist clergy; ethnic Nepalese organizations leading militant antigovernment campaign; Indian merchant community; United Front for Democracy (exiled)
International organization participation: AsDB, CP, ESCAP, FAO, G-77, IBRD, ICAO, IDA, IFAD, IMF, Intelsat, IOC, IOM (observer), ITU, NAM, OPCW, SAARC, UN, UNCTAD, UNESCO, UNIDO, UPU, WHO, WIPO, WTrO (observer)
Diplomatic representation in the US: none; note - Bhutan has a Permanent Mission to the UN; address: 2 United Nations Plaza, 27th Floor, New York, NY 10017; telephone [1] (212) 826-1919; the Bhutanese mission to the UN has consular jurisdiction in the US
consulate(s) general: New York
Diplomatic representation from the US: the US and Bhutan have no formal diplomatic relations, although informal contact is maintained between the Bhutanese and US Embassy in New Delhi (India)
Flag description: divided diagonally from the lower hoist side corner; the upper triangle is yellow and the lower triangle is orange; centered along the dividing line is a large black and white dragon facing away from the hoist side

Economy

Economy - overview: The economy, one of the world's smallest and least developed, is based on agriculture and forestry, which provide the main livelihood for more than 90% of the population. Agriculture consists largely of subsistence farming and animal husbandry. Rugged mountains dominate the terrain and make the building of roads and other infrastructure difficult and expensive. The economy is closely aligned with India's through strong trade and monetary links. The industrial sector is technologically backward, with most production of the cottage industry type. Most development projects, such as road construction, rely on Indian migrant labor. Bhutan's hydropower potential and its attraction for tourists are key resources. The Bhutanese Government has made some progress in expanding the nation's productive base and improving social welfare. Model education, social, and environment programs in Bhutan are underway with support from multilateral development organizations. Each economic program takes into account the government's desire to protect the country's environment and cultural traditions. Detailed controls and uncertain policies in areas like industrial licensing, trade, labor, and finance continue to hamper foreign investment.
GDP: purchasing power parity - $2.3 billion (2000 est.)
GDP - real growth rate: 6% (2000 est.)
GDP - per capita: purchasing power parity - $1,100 (2000 est.)
GDP - composition by sector:
agriculture: 38%
industry: 37%
services: 25% (2000 est.)
Population below poverty line: NA%
Household income or consumption by percentage share:
lowest 10%: NA%
highest 10%: NA%
Inflation rate (consumer prices): 7% (2000 est.)
Labor force: NA
note: massive lack of skilled labor
Labor force - by occupation: agriculture 93%, services 5%, industry and commerce 2%
Unemployment rate: NA%
Budget:
revenues: $146 million
expenditures: $152 million, including capital expenditures of $NA (FY95/96 est.)
note: the government of India finances nearly three-fifths of Bhutan's budget expenditures
Industries: cement, wood products, processed fruits, alcoholic beverages, calcium carbide
Industrial production growth rate: 9.3% (1996 est.)
Electricity - production: 1.856 billion kWh (1999)
Electricity - production by source:
fossil fuel: 0.05%
hydro: 99.95%
nuclear: 0%
other: 0% (1999)
Electricity - consumption: 191.1 million kWh (1999)
Electricity - exports: 1.55 billion kWh (1999)
Electricity - imports: 15 million kWh (1999)
Agriculture - products: rice, corn, root crops, citrus, foodgrains; dairy products, eggs
Exports: $154 million (f.o.b., 2000 est.)
Exports - commodities: cardamom, gypsum, timber, handicrafts, cement, fruit, electricity (to India), precious stones, spices
Exports - partners: India 94%, Bangladesh
Imports: $269 million (c.i.f., 2000 est.)
Imports - commodities: fuel and lubricants, grain, machinery and parts, vehicles, fabrics, rice
Imports - partners: India 77%, Japan, UK, Germany, US
Debt - external: $120 million (1998)
Economic aid - recipient: $73.8 million (1995)
Currency: ngultrum (BTN); Indian rupee (INR)
Currency code: BTN; INR
Exchange rates: ngultrum per US dollar - 46.540 (January 2001), 44.942 (2000), 43.055 (1999), 41.259 (1998), 36.313 (1997), 35.433 (1996); note - the Bhutanese ngultrum is at par with the Indian rupee which is also legal tender
Fiscal year: 1 July - 30 June

Communications

Telephones - main lines in use: 6,000 (1997)
Telephones - mobile cellular: NA
Telephone system:
general assessment: NA
domestic: domestic telephone service is very poor with few telephones in use
international: international telephone and telegraph service is by landline through India; a satellite earth station was planned (1990)
Radio broadcast stations: AM 0, FM 1, shortwave 1 (1998)
Radios: 37,000 (1997)
Television broadcast stations: 0 (1997)
Televisions: 11,000 (1997)
Internet country code: .bt
Internet Service Providers (ISPs): NA
Internet users: 500 (2000)

Transportation

Railways: 0 km
Highways:
total: 3,285 km
paved: 1,994 km
unpaved: 1,291 km (1996)
Waterways: none
Ports and harbors: none
Airports: 2 (2000 est.)
Airports - with paved runways:
total: 1
1,524 to 2,437 m: 1 (2000 est.)
Airports - with unpaved runways:
total: 1
914 to 1,523 m: 1 (2000 est.)

Military

Military branches: Royal Bhutan Army, National Militia, Royal Bhutan Police, Royal Body Guards, Forest Guards (paramilitary)
Military manpower - military age: 18 years of age
Military manpower - availability:
males age 15-49: 504,342 (2001 est.)
Military manpower - fit for military service:
males age 15-49: 269,251 (2001 est.)
Military manpower - reaching military age annually:
males: 21,167 (2001 est.)
Military expenditures - dollar figure: $NA
Military expenditures - percent of GDP: NA%

Transnational Issues

Disputes - international: approximately 98,700 Bhutanese refugees in Nepal

Bolivia

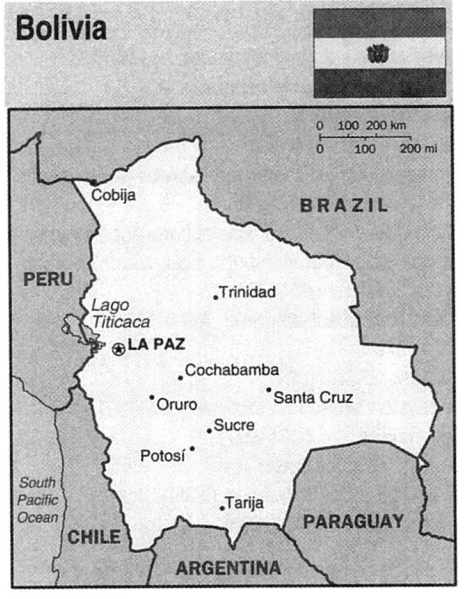

Introduction

Background: Bolivia, named after independence fighter Simon BOLIVAR, broke away from Spanish rule in 1825; much of its subsequent history has consisted of a series of nearly 200 coups and counter-coups. Comparatively democratic civilian rule was established in the 1980s, but leaders have faced difficult problems of deep-seated poverty, social unrest, and drug production. Current goals include attracting foreign investment, strengthening the educational system, continuing the privatization program, and waging an anti-corruption campaign.

Geography

Location: Central South America, southwest of Brazil
Geographic coordinates: 17 00 S, 65 00 W
Map references: South America
Area:
total: 1,098,580 sq km
land: 1,084,390 sq km
water: 14,190 sq km
Area - comparative: slightly less than three times the size of Montana
Land boundaries:
total: 6,743 km
border countries: Argentina 832 km, Brazil 3,400 km, Chile 861 km, Paraguay 750 km, Peru 900 km
Coastline: 0 km (landlocked)
Maritime claims: none (landlocked)
Climate: varies with altitude; humid and tropical to cold and semiarid
Terrain: rugged Andes Mountains with a highland plateau (Altiplano), hills, lowland plains of the Amazon Basin
Elevation extremes:
lowest point: Rio Paraguay 90 m
highest point: Nevado Sajama 6,542 m
Natural resources: tin, natural gas, petroleum, zinc, tungsten, antimony, silver, iron, lead, gold, timber, hydropower
Land use:
arable land: 2%
permanent crops: 0%
permanent pastures: 24%
forests and woodland: 53%
other: 21% (1993 est.)
Irrigated land: 1,750 sq km (1993 est.)
Natural hazards: flooding in the northeast (March-April)
Environment - current issues: the clearing of land for agricultural purposes and the international demand for tropical timber are contributing to deforestation; soil erosion from overgrazing and poor cultivation methods (including slash-and-burn agriculture); desertification; loss of biodiversity; industrial pollution of water supplies used for drinking and irrigation
Environment - international agreements:
party to: Biodiversity, Climate Change, Climate Change-Kyoto Protocol, Desertification, Endangered Species, Hazardous Wastes, Law of the Sea, Marine Dumping, Nuclear Test Ban, Ship Pollution, Tropical Timber 83, Tropical Timber 94, Wetlands
signed, but not ratified: Environmental Modification, Marine Dumping, Marine Life Conservation, Ozone Layer Protection
Geography - note: landlocked; shares control of Lago Titicaca, world's highest navigable lake (elevation 3,805 m), with Peru

People

Population: 8,300,463 (July 2001 est.)
Age structure:
0-14 years: 38.46% (male 1,626,698; female 1,565,748)
15-64 years: 57.07% (male 2,315,098; female 2,421,987)
65 years and over: 4.47% (male 166,986; female 203,946) (2001 est.)
Population growth rate: 1.76% (2001 est.)
Birth rate: 27.27 births/1,000 population (2001 est.)
Death rate: 8.2 deaths/1,000 population (2001 est.)
Net migration rate: -1.45 migrant(s)/1,000 population (2001 est.)
Sex ratio:
at birth: 1.05 male(s)/female
under 15 years: 1.04 male(s)/female
15-64 years: 0.96 male(s)/female
65 years and over: 0.82 male(s)/female
total population: 0.98 male(s)/female (2001 est.)
Infant mortality rate: 58.98 deaths/1,000 live births (2001 est.)
Life expectancy at birth:
total population: 64.06 years
male: 61.53 years
female: 66.72 years (2001 est.)
Total fertility rate: 3.51 children born/woman (2001 est.)
HIV/AIDS - adult prevalence rate: 0.1% (1999 est.)
HIV/AIDS - people living with HIV/AIDS: 4,200 (1999 est.)
HIV/AIDS - deaths: 380 (1999 est.)
Nationality:
noun: Bolivian(s)
adjective: Bolivian
Ethnic groups: Quechua 30%, Aymara 25%, mestizo (mixed white and Amerindian ancestry) 30%, white 15%
Religions: Roman Catholic 95%, Protestant (Evangelical Methodist)
Languages: Spanish (official), Quechua (official), Aymara (official)
Literacy:
definition: age 15 and over can read and write
total population: 83.1%
male: 90.5%
female: 76% (1995 est.)

Government

Country name:
conventional long form: Republic of Bolivia
conventional short form: Bolivia
local long form: Republica de Bolivia
local short form: Bolivia
Government type: republic
Capital: La Paz (seat of government); Sucre (legal capital and seat of judiciary)
Administrative divisions: 9 departments (departamentos, singular - departamento); Chuquisaca, Cochabamba, Beni, La Paz, Oruro, Pando, Potosi, Santa Cruz, Tarija
Independence: 6 August 1825 (from Spain)
National holiday: Independence Day, 6 August (1825)
Constitution: 2 February 1967; revised in August 1994
Legal system: based on Spanish law and Napoleonic Code; has not accepted compulsory ICJ jurisdiction
Suffrage: 18 years of age, universal and compulsory (married); 21 years of age, universal and compulsory (single)
Executive branch:
chief of state: President Hugo BANZER Suarez (since 6 August 1997); Vice President Jorge Fernando QUIROGA Ramirez (since 6 August 1997); note - the president is both the chief of state and head of government
head of government: President Hugo BANZER Suarez (since 6 August 1997); Vice President Jorge Fernando QUIROGA Ramirez (since 6 August 1997); note - the president is both the chief of state and head of government
cabinet: Cabinet appointed by the president
elections: president and vice president elected on the same ticket by popular vote for five-year terms; election last held 1 June 1997 (next to be held May or June 2002)
election results: Hugo BANZER Suarez elected president; percent of vote - Hugo BANZER Suarez (ADN) 22%; Jaime PAZ Zamora (MIR) 17%, Juan Carlos DURAN (MNR) 18%, Ivo KULJIS (UCS) 16%, Remedios LOZA (CONDEPA) 17%; no candidate received a majority of the popular vote; Hugo

Bolivia (continued)

BANZER Suarez won a congressional runoff election on 5 August 1997 after forming a "megacoalition" with MIR, UCS, CONDEPA, NFR, and PDC
Legislative branch: bicameral National Congress or Congreso Nacional consists of Chamber of Senators or Camara de Senadores (27 seats; members are directly elected by popular vote to serve five-year terms) and Chamber of Deputies or Camara de Diputados (130 seats; members are directly elected by popular vote to serve five-year terms; note - some members are drawn from party lists, thus not directly elected)
elections: Chamber of Senators and Chamber of Deputies - last held 1 June 1997 (next to be held NA June 2002)
election results: Chamber of Senators - percent of vote by party - NA%; seats by party - ADN 11, MIR 7, MNR 4, CONDEPA 3, UCS 2; Chamber of Deputies - percent of vote by party - NA%; seats by party - ADN 32, MNR 26, MIR 23, UCS 21, CONDEPA 19, MBL 5, IU 4
Judicial branch: Supreme Court or Corte Suprema (judges appointed for 10-year terms by National Congress); District Courts (one in each department); provincial and local courts (to try minor cases)
Political parties and leaders: Christian Democratic Party or PDC [leader NA]; Civic Solidarity Union or UCS [Johnny FERNANDEZ]; Conscience of the Fatherland or CONDEPA [Remedios LOZA Alvarado]; Free Bolivia Movement or MBL [Antonio ARANIBAR]; Movement of the Revolutionary Left or MIR [Jaime PAZ Zamora]; Nationalist Democratic Action or ADN [Hugo BANZER Suarez]; Nationalist Revolutionary Movement or MNR [Gonzalo SANCHEZ DE LOZADA]; New Republican Force or NFR [leader NA]; Pachacuti Indigenous Movement [Filipe QUISPE]; United Left or IU [Marcos DOMIC]
note: the ADN, MIR, and UCS comprise the ruling coalition
Political pressure groups and leaders: Cocalero Groups; indigenous organizations; labor unions
International organization participation: CAN, CCC, ECLAC, FAO, G-11, G-77, IADB, IAEA, IBRD, ICAO, ICRM, IDA, IFAD, IFC, IFRCS, ILO, IMF, IMO, Intelsat, Interpol, IOC, IOM, ITU, LAES, LAIA, Mercosur (associate), MONUC, NAM, OAS, OPANAL, OPCW, PCA, RG, UN, UNCTAD, UNESCO, UNIDO, UNMIK, UNTAET, UPU, WCL, WFTU, WHO, WIPO, WMO, WToO, WTrO
Diplomatic representation in the US:
chief of mission: Ambassador Marlene FERNANDEZ del Granado
chancery: 3014 Massachusetts Avenue NW, Washington, DC 20008
telephone: [1] (202) 483-4410
FAX: [1] (202) 328-3712
consulate(s) general: Los Angeles, Miami, New York, and San Francisco
Diplomatic representation from the US:
chief of mission: Ambassador V. Manuel ROCHA
embassy: Avenida Arce 2780, San Jorge, La Paz
mailing address: P. O. Box 425, La Paz; APO AA 34032
telephone: [591] (2) 432254
FAX: [591] (2) 433854
Flag description: three equal horizontal bands of red (top), yellow, and green with the coat of arms centered on the yellow band; similar to the flag of Ghana, which has a large black five-pointed star centered in the yellow band

Economy

Economy - overview: Bolivia, long one of the poorest and least developed Latin American countries, has made considerable progress toward the development of a market-oriented economy. Successes under President SANCHEZ DE LOZADA (1993-97) included the signing of a free trade agreement with Mexico and joining the Southern Cone Common Market (Mercosur), as well as the privatization of the state airline, telephone company, railroad, electric power company, and oil company. His successor, Hugo BANZER Suarez has tried to further improve the country's investment climate with an anticorruption campaign. Growth slowed in 1999, in part due to tight government budget policies, which limited needed appropriations for anti-poverty programs, and the fallout from the Asian financial crisis. In 2000, major civil disturbances in April, and again in September and October, held down overall growth to 2.5%.
GDP: purchasing power parity - $20.9 billion (2000 est.)
GDP - real growth rate: 2.5% (2000 est.)
GDP - per capita: purchasing power parity - $2,600 (2000 est.)
GDP - composition by sector:
agriculture: 16%
industry: 31%
services: 53% (1999 est.)
Population below poverty line: 70% (1999 est.)
Household income or consumption by percentage share:
lowest 10%: 2.3%
highest 10%: 31.7% (1990)
Inflation rate (consumer prices): 4.4% (2000 est.)
Labor force: 2.5 million
Labor force - by occupation: agriculture NA%, industry NA%, services NA%
Unemployment rate: 11.4% (1997)
note: widespread underemployment
Budget:
revenues: $2.7 billion
expenditures: $2.7 billion, including capital expenditures of $NA (1998)
Industries: mining, smelting, petroleum, food and beverages, tobacco, handicrafts, clothing
Industrial production growth rate: 4% (1995 est.)
Electricity - production: 3.625 billion kWh (1999)
Electricity - production by source:
fossil fuel: 56.61%
hydro: 41.6%
nuclear: 0%
other: 1.79% (1999)
Electricity - consumption: 3.377 billion kWh (1999)
Electricity - exports: 4 million kWh (1999)
Electricity - imports: 10 million kWh (1999)
Agriculture - products: soybeans, coffee, coca, cotton, corn, sugarcane, rice, potatoes; timber
Exports: $1.26 billion (f.o.b., 2000 est.)
Exports - commodities: soybeans, natural gas, zinc, gold, wood
Exports - partners: UK 16%, US 12%, Peru 11%, Argentina 10%, Colombia 7% (1998)
Imports: $1.86 billion (f.o.b., 2000 est.)
Imports - commodities: capital goods, raw materials and semi-manufactures, chemicals, petroleum, food
Imports - partners: US 32%, Japan 24%, Brazil 12%, Argentina 12%, Chile 7%, Peru 4%, Germany 3%, other 6% (1998)
Debt - external: $6.6 billion (2000)
Economic aid - recipient: $588 million (1997)
Currency: boliviano (BOB)
Currency code: BOB
Exchange rates: bolivianos per US dollar - 6.4071 (January 2001), 6.1835 (2000), 5.8124 (1999), 5.5101 (1998), 5.2543 (1997), 5.0746 (1996)
Fiscal year: calendar year

Communications

Telephones - main lines in use: 327,600 (1996)
Telephones - mobile cellular: 116,000 (1997)
Telephone system:
general assessment: new subscribers face bureaucratic difficulties; most telephones are concentrated in La Paz and other cities; mobile cellular telephone use expanding rapidly
domestic: primary trunk system, which is being expanded, employs digital microwave radio relay; some areas are served by fiber-optic cable; mobile cellular systems are being expanded
international: satellite earth station - 1 Intelsat (Atlantic Ocean)
Radio broadcast stations: AM 171, FM 73, shortwave 77 (1999)
Radios: 5.25 million (1997)
Television broadcast stations: 48 (1997)
Televisions: 900,000 (1997)
Internet country code: .bo
Internet Service Providers (ISPs): 9 (2000)
Internet users: 35,000 (2000)

Transportation

Railways:
total: 3,691 km (single track)
narrow gauge: 3,652 km 1.000-m gauge; 39 km 0.760-m gauge (13 km electrified) (1995)
Highways:
total: 49,400 km
paved: 2,500 km (including 30 km of expressways)
unpaved: 46,900 km (1996)
Waterways: 10,000 km (commercially navigable)
Pipelines: crude oil 1,800 km; petroleum products 580 km; natural gas 1,495 km

Bolivia (continued)

Ports and harbors: none; however, Bolivia has free port privileges in maritime ports in Argentina, Brazil, Chile, and Paraguay
Merchant marine:
total: 42 ships (1,000 GRT or over) totaling 141,017 GRT/211,058 DWT
ships by type: bulk 5, cargo 20, chemical tanker 3, container 1, petroleum tanker 10, roll on/roll off 3 (2000 est.)
Airports: 1,093 (2000 est.)
Airports - with paved runways:
total: 13
over 3,047 m: 4
2,438 to 3,047 m: 3
1,524 to 2,437 m: 4
914 to 1,523 m: 2 (2000 est.)
Airports - with unpaved runways:
total: 1,080
2,438 to 3,047 m: 3
1,524 to 2,437 m: 65
914 to 1,523 m: 212
under 914 m: 800 (2000 est.)

Military

Military branches: Army (Ejercito Boliviano), Navy (Fuerza Naval Boliviana, includes Marines), Air Force (Fuerza Aerea Boliviana), National Police Force (Policia Nacional de Bolivia)
Military manpower - military age: 19 years of age
Military manpower - availability:
males age 15-49: 2,005,660 (2001 est.)
Military manpower - fit for military service:
males age 15-49: 1,306,452 (2001 est.)
Military manpower - reaching military age annually:
males: 90,120 (2001 est.)
Military expenditures - dollar figure: $147 million (FY99)
Military expenditures - percent of GDP: 1.8% (FY99)

Transnational Issues

Disputes - international: has wanted a sovereign corridor to the South Pacific Ocean since the Atacama area was lost to Chile in 1884; dispute with Chile over Rio Lauca water rights
Illicit drugs: world's third-largest cultivator of coca (after Colombia and Peru, a distant second) with an estimated 14,600 hectares under cultivation in 2000, a 33% decrease in overall cultivation of coca from 1999 levels; intermediate coca products and cocaine exported to or through Colombia, Brazil, Argentina, and Chile to the US and other international drug markets; eradication and alternative crop programs have slashed illicit coca cultivation during the BANZER administration beginning in 1997

Bosnia and Herzegovina

Introduction

Background: Bosnia and Herzegovina's declaration of sovereignty in October 1991, was followed by a referendum for independence from the former Yugoslavia in February 1992. The Bosnian Serbs - supported by neighboring Serbia - responded with armed resistance aimed at partitioning the republic along ethnic lines and joining Serb-held areas to form a "greater Serbia." In March 1994, Bosniaks and Croats reduced the number of warring factions from three to two by signing an agreement creating a joint Bosniak/Croat Federation of Bosnia and Herzegovina. On 21 November 1995, in Dayton, Ohio, the warring parties signed a peace agreement that brought to a halt the three years of interethnic civil strife (the final agreement was signed in Paris on 14 December 1995). The Dayton Agreement retained Bosnia and Herzegovina's international boundaries and created a joint multi-ethnic and democratic government. This national government is charged with conducting foreign, economic, and fiscal policy. Also recognized was a second tier of government comprised of two entities roughly equal in size: the Bosniak/Croat Federation of Bosnia and Herzegovina and the Bosnian Serb-led Republika Srpska (RS). The Federation and RS governments are charged with overseeing internal functions. In 1995-96, a NATO-led international peacekeeping force (IFOR) of 60,000 troops served in Bosnia to implement and monitor the military aspects of the agreement. IFOR was succeeded by a smaller, NATO-led Stabilization Force (SFOR) whose mission is to deter renewed hostilities. SFOR remains in place at a level of approximately 21,000 troops.

Geography

Location: Southeastern Europe, bordering the Adriatic Sea and Croatia
Geographic coordinates: 44 00 N, 18 00 E
Map references: Bosnia and Herzegovina, Europe
Area:
total: 51,129 sq km
land: 51,129 sq km
water: 0 sq km
Area - comparative: slightly smaller than West Virginia
Land boundaries:
total: 1,459 km
border countries: Croatia 932 km, Yugoslavia 527 km
Coastline: 20 km
Maritime claims: NA
Climate: hot summers and cold winters; areas of high elevation have short, cool summers and long, severe winters; mild, rainy winters along coast
Terrain: mountains and valleys
Elevation extremes:
lowest point: Adriatic Sea 0 m
highest point: Maglic 2,386 m
Natural resources: coal, iron, bauxite, manganese, forests, copper, chromium, lead, zinc, hydropower
Land use:
arable land: 14%
permanent crops: 5%
permanent pastures: 20%
forests and woodland: 39%
other: 22% (1993 est.)
Irrigated land: 20 sq km (1993 est.)
Natural hazards: destructive earthquakes
Environment - current issues: air pollution from metallurgical plants; sites for disposing of urban waste are limited; water shortages and destruction of infrastructure because of the 1992-95 civil strife
Environment - international agreements:
party to: Air Pollution, Climate Change, Law of the Sea, Marine Dumping, Marine Life Conservation, Nuclear Test Ban, Ozone Layer Protection, Ship Pollution
signed, but not ratified: none of the selected agreements
Geography - note: within Bosnia and Herzegovina's recognized borders, the country is divided into a joint Bosniak/Croat Federation (about 51% of the territory) and the Bosnian Serb-led Republika Srpska or RS (about 49% of the territory); the region called Herzegovina is contiguous to Croatia and traditionally has been settled by an ethnic Croat majority

People

Population: 3,922,205
note: all data dealing with population are subject to considerable error because of the dislocations caused by military action and ethnic cleansing (July 2001 est.)
Age structure:
0-14 years: 20.13% (male 405,713; female 383,850)
15-64 years: 70.78% (male 1,422,796; female 1,353,410)
65 years and over: 9.09% (male 150,802; female 205,634) (2001 est.)
Population growth rate: 1.38% (2001 est.)
Birth rate: 12.86 births/1,000 population (2001 est.)
Death rate: 7.99 deaths/1,000 population (2001 est.)

Bosnia and Herzegovina (continued)

Net migration rate: 8.91 migrant(s)/1,000 population (2001 est.)
Sex ratio:
at birth: 1.07 male(s)/female
under 15 years: 1.06 male(s)/female
15-64 years: 1.05 male(s)/female
65 years and over: 0.73 male(s)/female
total population: 1.02 male(s)/female (2001 est.)
Infant mortality rate: 24.35 deaths/1,000 live births (2001 est.)
Life expectancy at birth:
total population: 71.75 years
male: 69.04 years
female: 74.65 years (2001 est.)
Total fertility rate: 1.71 children born/woman (2001 est.)
HIV/AIDS - adult prevalence rate: 0.04% (1999 est.)
HIV/AIDS - people living with HIV/AIDS: NA
HIV/AIDS - deaths: less than 100 (1999 est.)
Nationality:
noun: Bosnian(s), Herzegovinian(s)
adjective: Bosnian, Herzegovinian
Ethnic groups: Serb 31%, Bosniak 44%, Croat 17%, Yugoslav 5.5%, other 2.5% (1991)
note: Bosniak has replaced muslim as an ethnic term in part to avoid confusion with the religious term Muslim - an adherent of Islam
Religions: Muslim 40%, Orthodox 31%, Roman Catholic 15%, Protestant 4%, other 10%
Languages: Croatian, Serbian, Bosnian
Literacy:
definition: NA
total population: NA%
male: NA%
female: NA%

Government

Country name:
conventional long form: none
conventional short form: Bosnia and Herzegovina
local long form: none
local short form: Bosna i Hercegovina
Government type: emerging democracy
Capital: Sarajevo
Administrative divisions: there are two first-order administrative divisions - the Bosniak/Croat Federation of Bosnia and Herzegovina (Federacija Bosna i Hercegovina) and the Bosnian Serb-led Republika Srpska; note - Brcko in northeastern Bosnia is a self-governing administrative unit under the sovereignty of Bosnia and Herzegovina; it is not part of either the Federation or Republika Srpska
Independence: 1 March 1992 (from Yugoslavia)
National holiday: National Day, 25 November (1943)
Constitution: the Dayton Agreement, signed 14 December 1995, included a new constitution now in force
Legal system: based on civil law system
Suffrage: 16 years of age, if employed; 18 years of age, universal

Executive branch:
chief of state: Chairman of the Presidency Jozo KRIZANOVI (chairman since 14 June 2001, presidency member since NA March 2001 - Croat); other members of the three-member rotating (every 8 months) presidency: Zivko RADISIC (since 13 October 1998 - Serb) and Beriz BELKIC (since NA March 2001 - Bosniak); note - Ante JELAVIC was dismissed from his post by the UN High Representative in March 2001
head of government: Chairman of the Council of Ministers Bozidar MATIC (since 22 February 2001)
cabinet: Council of Ministers nominated by the council chairman; approved by the National House of Representatives
elections: the three members of the presidency (one Bosniak, one Croat, one Serb) are elected by popular vote for a four-year term; the member with the most votes becomes the chairman unless he or she was the incumbent chairman at the time of the election; election last held 12-13 September 1998 (next to be held NA September 2002); the chairman of the Council of Ministers is appointed by the presidency and confirmed by the National House of Representatives
election results: percent of vote - Zivko RADISIC with 52% of the Serb vote was elected chairman of the collective presidency for the first 8 months; Ante JELAVIC with 52% of the Croat vote followed RADISIC in the rotation; Alija IZETBEGOVIC with 87% of the Bosniak vote won the highest number of votes in the election but was ineligible to serve a second term until RADISIC and JELAVIC had each served a first term as Chairman of the Presidency; IZETBEGOVIC retired from the presidency 14 October 2000 and was temporarily replaced by Halid GENJAC; Ante JELAVIC was replaced by Jozo KRIZANOVIC in March 2001
note: President of the Federation of Bosnia and Herzegovina: Karlo FILIPOVIC (since 27 February 2001); Vice President Safet HALILOVIC (since 27 February 2001); note - president and vice president rotate every year; President of the Republika Srpska: Mirko SAROVIC (since 11 November 2000)
Legislative branch: bicameral Parliamentary Assembly or Skupstina consists of the National House of Representatives or Predstavnicki Dom (42 seats - 14 Serb, 14 Croat, and 14 Bosniak; members elected by popular vote to serve two-year terms) and the House of Peoples or Dom Naroda (15 seats - 5 Bosniak, 5 Croat, 5 Serb; members elected by the Bosniak/Croat Federation's House of Representatives and the Republika Srpska's National Assembly to serve two-year terms); note - as of 1 January 2001, Bosnia and Herzegovina does not have a permanent election law; a draft law specifies four-year terms for the state and first-order administrative division entity legislatures; officials elected in 2000 were elected to two-year terms on the presumption that a permanent law would be in place before 2002

elections: National House of Representatives - elections last held 11 November 2000 (next to be held in the fall of 2002); House of Peoples - last constituted after the 11 November 2000 elections (next to be constituted in the fall of 2002)
election results: National House of Representatives - percent of vote by party/coalition - NA%; seats by party/coalition - SDP 9, SDA 8, SDS 6, HDZ-BiH 5, SBH 5, PDP 2, NHI 1, BPS 1, DPS 1, SNS 1, SNSD-DSP 1, DNZ 1, SPRS 1; House of Peoples - percent of vote by party/coalition - NA%; seats by party/coalition - NA
note: the Bosniak/Croat Federation has a bicameral legislature that consists of a House of Representatives (140 seats; members elected by popular vote to serve four-year terms); elections last held 11 November 2000 (next to be held NA 2002); percent of vote by party - NA%; seats by party/coalition - SDA 38, SDP 37, HDZ-BiH 25, SBH 21, DNZ 3, NHI 2, BPS 2, DPS 2, BOSS 2, GDS 1, RP 1, HSS 1, LDS 1, Pensioners' Party of FBiH 1, SNSD-DSP 1, HKDU 1, HSP 1; and a House of Peoples (74 seats - 30 Bosniak, 30 Croat, and 14 others); last constituted November 2000; the Republika Srpska has a National Assembly (83 seats; members elected by popular vote to serve four-year terms); elections last held 11 November 2000 (next to be held NA 2002); percent of vote by party - NA%; seats by party/coalition - SDS 31, PDP 11, SNSD 11, SDA 6, DSP 4, SDP 4, SPRS 4, SBH 4, DNS 3, SNS 2, NHI 1, DSRS 1, Pensioners' Party 1; as of 1 January 2001, Bosnia and Herzegovina does not have a permanent election law; a draft law specifies four-year terms for the state and first-order administrative division entity legislatures; officials elected in 2000 were elected to two-year terms on the presumption that a permanent law would be in place before 2002
Judicial branch: BiH Constitutional Court (consists of nine members: four members are selected by the Bosniak/Croat Federation's House of Representatives, two members by the Republika Srpska's National Assembly, and three non-Bosnian members by the president of the European Court of Human Rights)
note: a new state court, established in November 1999, has jurisdiction over cases related to state-level law and appellate jurisdiction over cases initiated in the entities; the entities each have a Supreme Court; each entity also has a number of lower courts; there are ten cantonal courts in the Federation, plus a number of municipal courts; the Republika Srpska has five municipal courts
Political parties and leaders: Bosnian Party or BOSS [Mirnes AJANOVIC]; Bosnian Patriotic Party or BPS [Sefer HALILOVIC]; Civic Democratic Party of BiH or GDS [Ibrahim SPAHIC]; Croat Christian Democratic Union or HKDU BiH [Ante PASALIC]; Croatian Democratic Union of BiH or HDZ-BiH [leader vacant]; Croatian Party of Rights or HSP [Zdravko HRSTIC]; Croatian Peasants Party of BiH or HSS-BiH [Ilija SIMIC]; Democratic Action Party or SDA [Alija

Bosnia and Herzegovina (continued)

IZETBEGOVIC]; Democratic National Alliance or DNS [Dragan KOSTIC]; Democratic Party of Pensioners or DPS [Alojz KNEZOVIC]; Democratic Party of RS or DSRS [Dragomir DUMIC]; Democratic Peoples Union or DNZ [Fikret ABDIC]; Democratic Socialist Party or DSP [Nebojsa RADMANOVIC]; Liberal Democratic Party or LDS [Rasim KADIC]; New Croatian Initiative or NHI [Kresimir ZUBAK]; Party for Bosnia and Herzegovina or SBH [Haris SILAJDZIC]; Party of Democratic Progress or PDP [Mladen IVANIC]; Party of Independent Social Democrats or SNSD [Milorad DODIK]; Pensioners' Party of FBiH [Husein VOJNIKOVIC]; Pensioners' Party of SR [Stojan BOGOSAVAC]; Republican Party of BiH or RP [Stjepan KLJUIC]; Serb Democratic Party or Serb Lands or SDS [Dragan KALINIC]; Serb National Alliance (Serb People's Alliance) or SNS [Biljana PLAVSIC]; Social Democratic Party BIH or SDP-BiH [Zlatko LAGUMDZIJA]; Socialist Party of Republika Srpska or SPRS [Zivko RADISIC]
Political pressure groups and leaders: NA
International organization participation: BIS, CE (guest), CEI, EBRD, ECE, FAO, G-77, IAEA, IBRD, ICAO, IDA, IFAD, IFC, ILO, IMF, IMO, Inmarsat, Intelsat, Interpol, IOC, IOM (observer), ISO, ITU, NAM (guest), OAS (observer), OIC (observer), OPCW, OSCE, UN, UNCTAD, UNESCO, UNIDO, UNMEE, UNTAET, UPU, WHO, WIPO, WMO, WToO, WTrO (observer)
Diplomatic representation in the US:
chief of mission: Ambassador Igor DAVIDOVIC
chancery: 2109 E Street NW, Washington, DC 20037
telephone: [1] (202) 337-1500
FAX: [1] (202) 337-1502
consulate(s) general: New York
Diplomatic representation from the US:
chief of mission: Ambassador Thomas J. MILLER
embassy: Alipasina 43, 71000 Sarajevo
mailing address: use street address
telephone: [387] (33) 445-700
FAX: [387] (33) 659-722
Branch Office(s): Banja Luka, Mostar
Flag description: a wide medium blue vertical band on the fly side with a yellow isosceles triangle abutting the band and the top of the flag; the remainder of the flag is medium blue with seven full five-pointed white stars and two half stars top and bottom along the hypotenuse of the triangle
Government - note: The Dayton Agreement, signed in Paris on 14 December 1995, retained Bosnia and Herzegovina's exterior border and created a joint multi-ethnic and democratic government. This national government - based on proportional representation similar to that which existed in the former socialist regime - is charged with conducting foreign, economic, and fiscal policy. The Dayton Agreement also recognized a second tier of government, comprised of two entities - a joint Bosniak/Croat Federation of Bosnia and Herzegovina and the Bosnian Serb Republika Srpska (RS) - each presiding over roughly one-half the territory. The Federation and RS governments are charged with overseeing internal functions. The Dayton Agreement established the Office of the High Representative (OHR) to oversee the implementation of the civilian aspects of the agreement. About 250 international and 450 local staff members are employed by the OHR.

Economy

Economy - overview: Bosnia and Herzegovina ranked next to The Former Yugoslav Republic of Macedonia as the poorest republic in the old Yugoslav federation. Although agriculture is almost all in private hands, farms are small and inefficient, and the republic traditionally is a net importer of food. Industry has been greatly overstaffed, one reflection of the socialist economic structure of Yugoslavia. TITO had pushed the development of military industries in the republic with the result that Bosnia hosted a large share of Yugoslavia's defense plants. The bitter interethnic warfare in Bosnia caused production to plummet by 80% from 1990 to 1995, unemployment to soar, and human misery to multiply. With an uneasy peace in place, output recovered in 1996-98 at high percentage rates from a low base; but output growth slowed appreciably in 1999 and 2000, and GDP remains far below the 1990 level. Economic data are of limited use because, although both entities issue figures, national-level statistics are not available. Moreover, official data do not capture the large share of activity that occurs on the black market. The marka - the national currency introduced in 1998 - has gained wide acceptance, and the Central Bank of Bosnia and Herzegovina has dramatically increased its reserve holdings. Implementation of privatization, however, has been slower than anticipated. Banking reform accelerated in early 2001 as all the communist-era payments bureaus were shut down. The country receives substantial amounts of reconstruction assistance and humanitarian aid from the international community but will have to prepare for an era of declining assistance.
GDP: purchasing power parity - $6.5 billion (2000 est.)
GDP - real growth rate: 8% (2000 est.)
GDP - per capita: purchasing power parity - $1,700 (2000 est.)
GDP - composition by sector:
agriculture: 19%
industry: 23%
services: 58% (1996 est.)
Population below poverty line: NA%
Household income or consumption by percentage share:
lowest 10%: NA%
highest 10%: NA%
Inflation rate (consumer prices): 8% (2000 est.)
Labor force: 1.026 million
Labor force - by occupation: agriculture NA%, industry NA%, services NA%
Unemployment rate: 35%-40% (1999 est.)
Budget:
revenues: $1.9 billion
expenditures: $2.2 billion, including capital expenditures of $NA (1999 est.)
Industries: steel, coal, iron ore, lead, zinc, manganese, bauxite, vehicle assembly, textiles, tobacco products, wooden furniture, tank and aircraft assembly, domestic appliances, oil refining
Industrial production growth rate: 10% (2000 est.)
Electricity - production: 2.585 billion kWh (1999)
Electricity - production by source:
fossil fuel: 38.68%
hydro: 61.32%
nuclear: 0%
other: 0% (1999)
Electricity - consumption: 2.684 billion kWh (1999)
Electricity - exports: 150 million kWh (1999)
Electricity - imports: 430 million kWh (1999)
Agriculture - products: wheat, corn, fruits, vegetables; livestock
Exports: $950 million (f.o.b., 2000 est.)
Exports - commodities: NA
Exports - partners: Croatia, Switzerland, Italy, Germany
Imports: $2.45 billion (f.o.b., 2000 est.)
Imports - commodities: NA
Imports - partners: Croatia, Slovenia, Germany, Italy
Debt - external: $3.4 billion (2000 est.)
Economic aid - recipient: $1 billion (1999 est.)
Currency: marka (BAM)
Currency code: BAM
Exchange rates: marka per US dollar - 2.10 (2000), 1.83 (1999), 1.76 (1998)
Fiscal year: calendar year

Communications

Telephones - main lines in use: 303,000 (1997)
Telephones - mobile cellular: 9,000 (1997)
Telephone system:
general assessment: telephone and telegraph network is in need of modernization and expansion; many urban areas are below average when compared with services in other former Yugoslav republics
domestic: NA
international: no satellite earth stations
Radio broadcast stations: AM 8, FM 16, shortwave 1 (1998)
Radios: 940,000 (1997)
Television broadcast stations: 33 (plus 277 repeaters) (September 1995)
Televisions: NA
Internet country code: .ba
Internet Service Providers (ISPs): 3 (2000)
Internet users: 3,500 (2000)

Transportation

Railways:
total: 1,021 km (electrified 795 km; operating as diesel or steam until grids are repaired)
standard gauge: 1,021 km 1.435-m gauge (1995); note - many segments still need repair and/or reconstruction

Bosnia and Herzegovina (continued)

Highways:
total: 21,846 km
paved: 14,020 km
unpaved: 7,826 km
note: road system is in need of maintenance and repair (2001)
Waterways: NA km; large sections of the Sava blocked by downed bridges, silt, and debris
Pipelines: crude oil 174 km; natural gas 90 km (1992)
Ports and harbors: Bosanska Gradiska, Bosanski Brod, Bosanski Samac, and Brcko (all inland waterway ports on the Sava), Orasje
Merchant marine: none (2000 est.)
Airports: 28 (2000 est.)
Airports - with paved runways:
total: 9
2,438 to 3,047 m: 4
1,524 to 2,437 m: 2
under 914 m: 3 (2000 est.)
Airports - with unpaved runways:
total: 19
1,524 to 2,437 m: 1
914 to 1,523 m: 7
under 914 m: 11 (2000 est.)
Heliports: 4 (2000 est.)

Military

Military branches: Federation Army or VF (composed of both Croatian and Bosniak elements), Republika Srpska Army or VRS (composed of Bosnian Serb elements); note - within both of these forces air and air defense are subordinate commands
Military manpower - military age: 19 years of age
Military manpower - availability:
males age 15-49: 1,127,146 (2001 est.)
Military manpower - fit for military service:
males age 15-49: 895,780 (2001 est.)
Military manpower - reaching military age annually:
males: 29,757 (2001 est.)
Military expenditures - dollar figure: $NA
Military expenditures - percent of GDP: NA%

Transnational Issues

Disputes - international: none
Illicit drugs: minor transit point for marijuana and opiate trafficking routes to Western Europe

Botswana

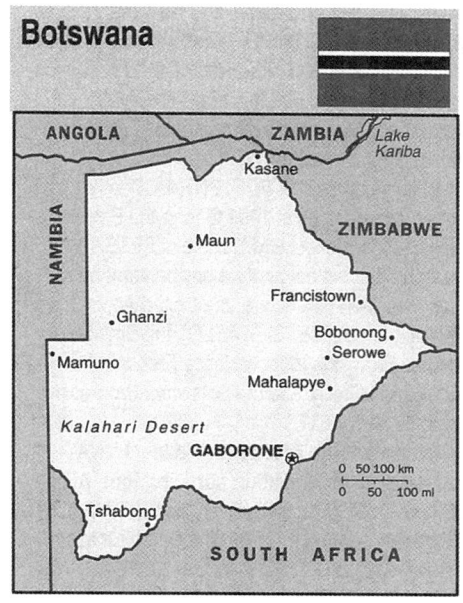

Introduction

Background: Formerly the British protectorate of Bechuanaland, Botswana adopted its new name upon independence in 1966. The economy, one of the most robust on the continent, is dominated by diamond mining.

Geography

Location: Southern Africa, north of South Africa
Geographic coordinates: 22 00 S, 24 00 E
Map references: Africa
Area:
total: 600,370 sq km
land: 585,370 sq km
water: 15,000 sq km
Area - comparative: slightly smaller than Texas
Land boundaries:
total: 4,013 km
border countries: Namibia 1,360 km, South Africa 1,840 km, Zimbabwe 813 km
Coastline: 0 km (landlocked)
Maritime claims: none (landlocked)
Climate: semiarid; warm winters and hot summers
Terrain: predominantly flat to gently rolling tableland; Kalahari Desert in southwest
Elevation extremes:
lowest point: junction of the Limpopo and Shashe Rivers 513 m
highest point: Tsodilo Hills 1,489 m
Natural resources: diamonds, copper, nickel, salt, soda ash, potash, coal, iron ore, silver
Land use:
arable land: 1%
permanent crops: 0%
permanent pastures: 46%
forests and woodland: 47%
other: 6% (1993 est.)
Irrigated land: 20 sq km (1993 est.)
Natural hazards: periodic droughts; seasonal August winds blow from the west, carrying sand and dust across the country, which can obscure visibility
Environment - current issues: overgrazing; desertification; limited fresh water resources
Environment - international agreements:
party to: Biodiversity, Climate Change, Desertification, Endangered Species, Hazardous Wastes, Law of the Sea, Marine Dumping, Nuclear Test Ban, Ozone Layer Protection, Ship Pollution, Wetlands
signed, but not ratified: none of the selected agreements
Geography - note: landlocked; population concentrated in eastern part of the country

People

Population: 1,586,119
note: estimates for this country explicitly take into account the effects of excess mortality due to AIDS; this can result in lower life expectancy, higher infant mortality and death rates, lower population and growth rates, and changes in the distribution of population by age and sex than would otherwise be expected (July 2001 est.)
Age structure:
0-14 years: 40.3% (male 321,164; female 318,007)
15-64 years: 55.56% (male 423,954; female 457,227)
65 years and over: 4.14% (male 26,691; female 39,076) (2001 est.)
Population growth rate: 0.47% (2001 est.)
Birth rate: 28.85 births/1,000 population (2001 est.)
Death rate: 24.18 deaths/1,000 population (2001 est.)
Net migration rate: 0 migrant(s)/1,000 population (2001 est.)
Sex ratio:
at birth: 1.03 male(s)/female
under 15 years: 1.01 male(s)/female
15-64 years: 0.93 male(s)/female
65 years and over: 0.68 male(s)/female
total population: 0.95 male(s)/female (2001 est.)
Infant mortality rate: 63.2 deaths/1,000 live births (2001 est.)
Life expectancy at birth:
total population: 37.13 years
male: 36.77 years
female: 37.51 years (2001 est.)
Total fertility rate: 3.7 children born/woman (2001 est.)
HIV/AIDS - adult prevalence rate: 35.8% (1999 est.)
HIV/AIDS - people living with HIV/AIDS: 290,000 (1999 est.)
HIV/AIDS - deaths: 24,000 (1999 est.)
Nationality:
noun: Motswana (singular), Batswana (plural)
adjective: Motswana (singular), Batswana (plural)
Ethnic groups: Tswana (or Setswana) 79%, Kalanga 11%, Basarwa 3%, other, including Kgalagadi and white 7%

Botswana (continued)

Religions: indigenous beliefs 50%, Christian 50%
Languages: English (official), Setswana
Literacy:
definition: age 15 and over can read and write
total population: 69.8%
male: 80.5%
female: 59.9% (1995 est.)

Government

Country name:
conventional long form: Republic of Botswana
conventional short form: Botswana
former: Bechuanaland
Government type: parliamentary republic
Capital: Gaborone
Administrative divisions: 10 districts and four town councils*; Central, Chobe, Francistown*, Gaborone*, Ghanzi, Kgalagadi, Kgatleng, Kweneng, Lobatse*, Ngamiland, North-East, Selebi-Pikwe*, South-East, Southern
Independence: 30 September 1966 (from UK)
National holiday: Independence Day, 30 September (1966)
Constitution: March 1965, effective 30 September 1966
Legal system: based on Roman-Dutch law and local customary law; judicial review limited to matters of interpretation; has not accepted compulsory ICJ jurisdiction
Suffrage: 18 years of age; universal
Executive branch:
chief of state: President Festus MOGAE (since 1 April 1998) and Vice President Seretse Ian KHAMA (since 13 July 1998); note - the president is both the chief of state and head of government
head of government: President Festus MOGAE (since 1 April 1998) and Vice President Seretse Ian KHAMA (since 13 July 1998); note - the president is both the chief of state and head of government
cabinet: Cabinet appointed by the president
elections: president elected by the National Assembly for a five-year term; election last held 16 October 1999 (next to be held NA October 2004); vice president appointed by the president
election results: Festus MOGAE elected president; percent of National Assembly vote - 54.3%
Legislative branch: bicameral Parliament consists of the House of Chiefs (a largely advisory 15-member body consisting of the chiefs of the eight principal tribes, four elected subchiefs, and three members selected by the other 12) and the National Assembly (44 seats, 40 members are directly elected by popular vote and 4 appointed by the majority party; members serve five-year terms)
elections: National Assembly elections last held 16 October 1999 (next to be held NA October 2004)
election results: percent of vote by party - BDP 57.2%, BNF 26%, other 16.8%; seats by party - BDP 33, BNF 6, other 1
Judicial branch: High Court; Court of Appeal; Magistrates' Courts (one in each district)

Political parties and leaders: Botswana Democratic Party or BDP [Festus MOGAE]; Botswana National Front or BNF [Kenneth KOMA]; Botswana Congress Party or BCP [Michael DINGAKE]; Botswana Alliance Movement or BAM [Ephraim Lepetu SETSHWAELO]
note: main parties are: BDP, BNF, BCP; other minor parties joined forces in 1999 to form the Botswana Alliance Movement or BAM [Ephraim SETSHWAELO, chairman] but did not capture any parliamentary seats; the BAM parties are: the United Action Party [Ephraim Lepetu SETSHWAELO], the Botswana Peoples Party, the Independence Freedom Party [Motsamai MPHO], and the Botswana Progressive Union [D. K. KWELE]
Political pressure groups and leaders: NA
International organization participation: ACP, AfDB, C, CCC, ECA, FAO, G-77, IBRD, ICAO, ICFTU, ICRM, IDA, IFAD, IFC, IFRCS, ILO, IMF, Intelsat, Interpol, IOC, ISO, ITU, NAM, OAU, OPCW, SACU, SADC, UN, UNCTAD, UNESCO, UNIDO, UPU, WFTU, WHO, WIPO, WMO, WToO, WTrO
Diplomatic representation in the US:
chief of mission: Ambassador Kgosi SEEPAPITSO IV
chancery: 1531-1533 New Hampshire Avenue NW, Washington, DC 20036
telephone: [1] (202) 244-4990
FAX: [1] (202) 244-4164
Diplomatic representation from the US:
chief of mission: Ambassador John E. LANGE
embassy: address NA, Gaborone
mailing address: P. O. Box 90, Gaborone
telephone: [267] 353982
FAX: [267] 356947
Flag description: light blue with a horizontal white-edged black stripe in the center

Economy

Economy - overview: Botswana has maintained one of the world's highest growth rates since independence in 1966. Through fiscal discipline and sound management, Botswana has transformed itself from one of the poorest countries in the world to a middle-income country with a per capita GDP of $6,600 in 2000. Diamond mining has fueled much of Botswana's economic expansion and currently accounts for more than one-third of GDP and for three-fourths of export earnings. Tourism, subsistence farming, and cattle raising are other key sectors. The government must deal with high rates of unemployment and poverty. Unemployment officially is 19%, but unofficial estimates place it closer to 40%. HIV/AIDS infection rates are the highest in the world and threaten Botswana's impressive economic gains.
GDP: purchasing power parity - $10.4 billion (2000 est.)
GDP - real growth rate: 6% (2000 est.)
GDP - per capita: purchasing power parity - $6,600 (2000 est.)
GDP - composition by sector:
agriculture: 4%
industry: 46% (including 36% mining)
services: 50% (1998 est.)
Population below poverty line: 47% (2000 est.)
Household income or consumption by percentage share:
lowest 10%: NA%
highest 10%: NA%
Inflation rate (consumer prices): 8.6% (2000 est.)
Labor force: 235,000 formal sector employees (1995)
Labor force - by occupation: 100,000 public sector; 135,000 private sector, including 14,300 who are employed in various mines in South Africa; most others engaged in cattle raising and subsistence agriculture (1995 est.)
Unemployment rate: 40% (2000 est.)
Budget:
revenues: $1.6 billion
expenditures: $1.8 billion, including capital expenditures of $560 million (FY96)
Industries: diamonds, copper, nickel, coal, salt, soda ash, potash; livestock processing
Industrial production growth rate: 6.2% (2000 est.)
Electricity - production: 610 million kWh (1999)
Electricity - production by source:
fossil fuel: 100%
hydro: 0%
nuclear: 0%
other: 0% (1999)
Electricity - consumption: 1.517 billion kWh (1999)
Electricity - exports: 0 kWh (1999)
Electricity - imports: 950 million kWh (1999)
Agriculture - products: sorghum, corn, millet, pulses, groundnuts (peanuts), beans, cowpeas, sunflower seed; livestock
Exports: $2.6 billion (f.o.b., 2000 est.)
Exports - commodities: diamonds 72%, vehicles, copper, nickel, meat (1998)
Exports - partners: EU 77%, Southern African Customs Union (SACU) 18%, Zimbabwe 3% (1998)
Imports: $2.2 billion (f.o.b., 2000 est.)
Imports - commodities: foodstuffs, machinery and transport equipment, textiles, petroleum products
Imports - partners: Southern African Customs Union (SACU) 76%, Europe 10%, South Korea 5% (1998)
Debt - external: $455 million (2000)
Economic aid - recipient: $73 million (1995)
Currency: pula (BWP)
Currency code: BWP
Exchange rates: pulas per US dollar - 5.4585 (January 2001), 5.1018 (2000), 4.6244 (1999), 4.2259 (1998), 3.6508 (1997), 3.3242 (1996)
Fiscal year: 1 April - 31 March

Communications

Telephones - main lines in use: 86,000 (1997)
Telephones - mobile cellular: NA
Telephone system:
general assessment: sparse system
domestic: small system of open-wire lines, microwave radio relay links, and a few radiotelephone communication stations

Botswana (continued)

international: two international exchanges; digital microwave radio relay links to Zambia, Zimbabwe, and South Africa; satellite earth station - 1 Intelsat (Indian Ocean)
Radio broadcast stations: AM 7, FM 15, shortwave 5 (1998)
Radios: 237,000 (1997)
Television broadcast stations: 0 (1997)
Televisions: 31,000 (1997)
Internet country code: .bw
Internet Service Providers (ISPs): 3 (2000)
Internet users: 12,000 (2000)

Transportation

Railways:
total: 971 km
narrow gauge: 971 km 1.067-m gauge (1995)
Highways:
total: 18,482 km
paved: 4,343 km
unpaved: 14,139 km (1996)
Waterways: none
Ports and harbors: none
Airports: 92 (2000 est.)
Airports - with paved runways:
total: 11
2,438 to 3,047 m: 2
1,524 to 2,437 m: 8
914 to 1,523 m: 1 (2000 est.)
Airports - with unpaved runways:
total: 81
1,524 to 2,437 m: 3
914 to 1,523 m: 56
under 914 m: 22 (2000 est.)

Military

Military branches: Botswana Defense Force (includes Army and Air Wing), Botswana National Police
Military manpower - military age: 18 years of age
Military manpower - availability:
males age 15-49: 380,152 (2001 est.)
Military manpower - fit for military service:
males age 15-49: 199,995 (2001 est.)
Military manpower - reaching military age annually:
males: 19,479 (2001 est.)
Military expenditures - dollar figure: $61 million (FY99)
Military expenditures - percent of GDP: 1.2% (FY99)

Transnational Issues

Disputes - international: none

Bouvet Island
(territory of Norway)

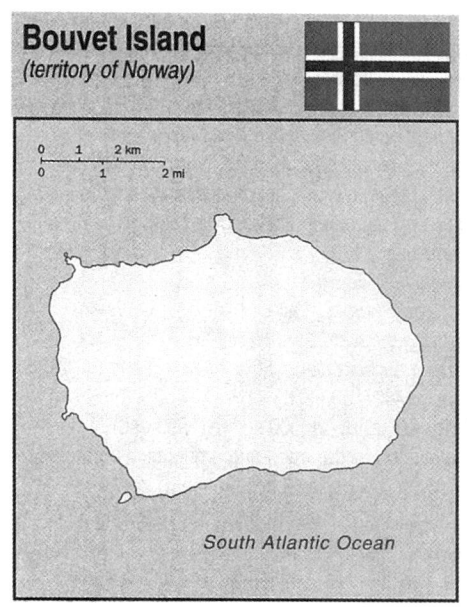

Introduction

Background: This uninhabited volcanic island is almost entirely covered by glaciers and is difficult to approach. It was discovered in 1739 by a French naval officer after whom the island was named. No claim was made until 1825 when the British flag was raised. In 1928, the UK waived its claim in favor of Norway, which had occupied the island the previous year. In 1971, Bouvet Island and the adjacent territorial waters were designated a nature reserve. Since 1977, Norway has run an automated meteorological station on the island.

Geography

Location: Southern Africa, island in the South Atlantic Ocean, south-southwest of the Cape of Good Hope (South Africa)
Geographic coordinates: 54 26 S, 3 24 E
Map references: Antarctic Region
Area:
total: 58.5 sq km
land: 58.5 sq km
water: 0 sq km
Area - comparative: about 0.3 times the size of Washington, DC
Land boundaries: 0 km
Coastline: 29.6 km
Maritime claims:
territorial sea: 4 NM
Climate: antarctic
Terrain: volcanic; maximum elevation about 800 m; coast is mostly inaccessible
Elevation extremes:
lowest point: South Atlantic Ocean 0 m
highest point: Olav Peak 935 m
Natural resources: none
Land use:
arable land: 0%
permanent crops: 0%
permanent pastures: 0%
forests and woodland: 0%
other: 100% (93% ice)
Irrigated land: 0 sq km (1993)
Natural hazards: NA
Environment - current issues: NA
Geography - note: covered by glacial ice; declared a nature reserve

People

Population: uninhabited (July 2001 est.)

Government

Country name:
conventional long form: none
conventional short form: Bouvet Island
Dependency status: territory of Norway; administered by the Polar Department of the Ministry of Justice and Police from Oslo
Legal system: the laws of Norway, where applicable, apply
Flag description: the flag of Norway is used

Economy

Economy - overview: no economic activity; declared a nature reserve

Communications

Internet country code: .bv
Communications - note: automatic meteorological station

Transportation

Waterways: none
Ports and harbors: none; offshore anchorage only

Military

Military - note: defense is the responsibility of Norway

Transnational Issues

Disputes - international: none

Brazil

Introduction

Background: Following three centuries under the rule of Portugal, Brazil became an independent nation in 1822. By far the largest and most populous country in South America, Brazil has overcome more than half a century of military intervention in the governance of the country to pursue industrial and agricultural growth and development of the interior. Exploiting vast natural resources and a large labor pool, Brazil became Latin America's leading economic power by the 1970s. Highly unequal income distribution remains a pressing problem.

Geography

Location: Eastern South America, bordering the Atlantic Ocean
Geographic coordinates: 10 00 S, 55 00 W
Map references: South America
Area:
total: 8,511,965 sq km
land: 8,456,510 sq km
water: 55,455 sq km
note: includes Arquipelago de Fernando de Noronha, Atol das Rocas, Ilha da Trindade, Ilhas Martin Vaz, and Penedos de Sao Pedro e Sao Paulo
Area - comparative: slightly smaller than the US
Land boundaries:
total: 14,691 km
border countries: Argentina 1,224 km, Bolivia 3,400 km, Colombia 1,643 km, French Guiana 673 km, Guyana 1,119 km, Paraguay 1,290 km, Peru 1,560 km, Suriname 597 km, Uruguay 985 km, Venezuela 2,200 km
Coastline: 7,491 km
Maritime claims:
contiguous zone: 24 NM
continental shelf: 200 NM
exclusive economic zone: 200 NM
territorial sea: 12 NM
Climate: mostly tropical, but temperate in south
Terrain: mostly flat to rolling lowlands in north; some plains, hills, mountains, and narrow coastal belt
Elevation extremes:
lowest point: Atlantic Ocean 0 m
highest point: Pico da Neblina 3,014 m
Natural resources: bauxite, gold, iron ore, manganese, nickel, phosphates, platinum, tin, uranium, petroleum, hydropower, timber
Land use:
arable land: 5%
permanent crops: 1%
permanent pastures: 22%
forests and woodland: 58%
other: 14% (1993 est.)
Irrigated land: 28,000 sq km (1993 est.)
Natural hazards: recurring droughts in northeast; floods and occasional frost in south
Environment - current issues: deforestation in Amazon Basin destroys the habitat and endangers the existence of a multitude of plant and animal species indigenous to the area; air and water pollution in Rio de Janeiro, Sao Paulo, and several other large cities; land degradation and water pollution caused by improper mining activities
note: President CARDOSO in September 1999 signed into force an environmental crime bill which for the first time defines pollution and deforestation as crimes punishable by stiff fines and jail sentences
Environment - international agreements:
party to: Antarctic-Environmental Protocol, Antarctic-Marine Living Resources, Antarctic Seals, Antarctic Treaty, Biodiversity, Climate Change, Desertification, Endangered Species, Environmental Modification, Hazardous Wastes, Law of the Sea, Marine Dumping, Nuclear Test Ban, Ozone Layer Protection, Ship Pollution, Tropical Timber 83, Tropical Timber 94, Wetlands, Whaling
signed, but not ratified: Climate Change-Kyoto Protocol
Geography - note: largest country in South America; shares common boundaries with every South American country except Chile and Ecuador

People

Population: 174,468,575
note: Brazil took an intercensal count in August 1996 which reported a population of 157,079,573; that figure was about 5% lower than projections by the US Census Bureau, which is close to the implied underenumeration of 4.6% for the 1991 census; estimates for this country explicitly take into account the effects of excess mortality due to AIDS; this can result in lower life expectancy, higher infant mortality and death rates, lower population and growth rates, and changes in the distribution of population by age and sex than would otherwise be expected (July 2001 est.)
Age structure:
0-14 years: 28.57% (male 25,390,039; female 24,449,902)
15-64 years: 65.98% (male 56,603,895; female 58,507,289)
65 years and over: 5.45% (male 3,857,564; female 5,659,886) (2001 est.)
Population growth rate: 0.91% (2001 est.)
Birth rate: 18.45 births/1,000 population (2001 est.)
Death rate: 9.34 deaths/1,000 population (2001 est.)
Net migration rate: -0.03 migrant(s)/1,000 population (2001 est.)
Sex ratio:
at birth: 1.05 male(s)/female
under 15 years: 1.04 male(s)/female
15-64 years: 0.97 male(s)/female
65 years and over: 0.68 male(s)/female
total population: 0.97 male(s)/female (2001 est.)
Infant mortality rate: 36.96 deaths/1,000 live births (2001 est.)
Life expectancy at birth:
total population: 63.24 years
male: 58.96 years
female: 67.73 years (2001 est.)
Total fertility rate: 2.09 children born/woman (2001 est.)
HIV/AIDS - adult prevalence rate: 0.57% (1999 est.)
HIV/AIDS - people living with HIV/AIDS: 540,000 (1999 est.)
HIV/AIDS - deaths: 18,000 (1999 est.)
Nationality:
noun: Brazilian(s)
adjective: Brazilian
Ethnic groups: white (includes Portuguese, German, Italian, Spanish, Polish) 55%, mixed white and black 38%, black 6%, other (includes Japanese, Arab, Amerindian) 1%
Religions: Roman Catholic (nominal) 80%
Languages: Portuguese (official), Spanish, English, French
Literacy:
definition: age 15 and over can read and write
total population: 83.3%
male: 83.3%
female: 83.2% (1995 est.)

Government

Country name:
conventional long form: Federative Republic of Brazil
conventional short form: Brazil
local long form: Republica Federativa do Brasil
local short form: Brasil
Government type: federative republic
Capital: Brasilia
Administrative divisions: 26 states (estados, singular - estado) and 1 federal district* (distrito federal); Acre, Alagoas, Amapa, Amazonas, Bahia, Ceara, Distrito Federal*, Espirito Santo, Goias, Maranhao, Mato Grosso, Mato Grosso do Sul, Minas Gerais, Para, Paraiba, Parana, Pernambuco, Piaui, Rio de Janeiro, Rio Grande do Norte, Rio Grande do Sul, Rondonia, Roraima, Santa Catarina, Sao Paulo, Sergipe, Tocantins
Independence: 7 September 1822 (from Portugal)

Brazil (continued)

National holiday: Independence Day, 7 September (1822)
Constitution: 5 October 1988
Legal system: based on Roman codes; has not accepted compulsory ICJ jurisdiction
Suffrage: voluntary between 16 and 18 years of age and over 70; compulsory over 18 and under 70 years of age
Executive branch:
chief of state: President Fernando Henrique CARDOSO (since 1 January 1995); Vice President Marco MACIEL (since 1 January 1995); note - the president is both the chief of state and head of government
head of government: President Fernando Henrique CARDOSO (since 1 January 1995); Vice President Marco MACIEL (since 1 January 1995); note - the president is both the chief of state and head of government
cabinet: Cabinet appointed by the president
elections: president and vice president elected on the same ticket by popular vote for four-year terms; election last held 4 October 1998 (next to be held NA October 2002)
election results: Fernando Henrique CARDOSO reelected president; percent of vote - 53%
Legislative branch: bicameral National Congress or Congresso Nacional consists of the Federal Senate or Senado Federal (81 seats; three members from each state or federal district elected according to the principle of majority to serve eight-year terms; one-third elected after a four year period, two-thirds elected after the next four-year period) and the Chamber of Deputies or Camara dos Deputados (513 seats; members are elected by proportional representation to serve four-year terms)
elections: Federal Senate - last held 4 October 1998 for one-third of Senate (next to be held NA October 2002 for two-thirds of the Senate); Chamber of Deputies - last held 4 October 1998 (next to be held NA October 2002)
election results: Federal Senate - percent of vote by party - NA%; seats by party - PMDB 27, PFL 20, PSDB 16, PT 7, PPB 5, PSB 3, PDT 2, PPS 1; Chamber of Deputies - percent of vote by party - NA%; seats by party - PFL 106, PSDB 99, PMDB 82, PPB 60, PT 58, PTB 31, PDT 25, PSB 19, PL 12, PCdoB 7, other 14
Judicial branch: Supreme Federal Tribunal (11 ministers are appointed by the president and confirmed by the Senate); Higher Tribunal of Justice; Regional Federal Tribunals (judges are appointed for life)
Political parties and leaders: Brazilian Democratic Movement Party or PMDB [Jader BARBALHO, president]; Brazilian Labor Party or PTB [Roberto JEFFERSON]; Brazilian Social Democracy Party or PSDB [Teotonio VILELA Filno]; Brazilian Socialist Party or PSB [Miguel ARRAES, president]; Brazilian Progressive Party or PPB [Paulo Salim MALUF]; Communist Party of Brazil or PCdoB [Sergio Roberto Gomes SOUZA, chairman]; Democratic Labor Party or PDT [Leonel BRIZOLA, president]; Liberal Front Party or PFL [Jorge BORNHAUSEN, president]; Liberal Party or PL [Francisco Teixeira de OLIVEIRA]; Popular Socialist Party or PPS [Ciro GOMEZ, president]; Worker's Party or PT [Jose DIRCEU, president]
Political pressure groups and leaders: left wing of the Catholic Church, Landless Worker's Movement, and labor unions allied to leftist Worker's Party are critical of government's social and economic policies
International organization participation: AfDB, BIS, CCC, ECLAC, FAO, G-11, G-15, G-19, G-24, G-77, IADB, IAEA, IBRD, ICAO, ICC, ICFTU, ICRM, IDA, IFAD, IFC, IFRCS, IHO, ILO, IMF, IMO, Inmarsat, Intelsat, Interpol, IOC, IOM (observer), ISO, ITU, LAES, LAIA, Mercosur, NAM (observer), NSG, OAS, OPANAL, OPCW, PCA, RG, UN, UNCTAD, UNESCO, UNHCR, UNIDO, UNITAR, UNMOP, UNTAET, UNU, UPU, WCL, WFTU, WHO, WIPO, WMO, WToO, WTrO
Diplomatic representation in the US:
chief of mission: Ambassador Rubens Antonio BARBOSA
chancery: 3006 Massachusetts Avenue NW, Washington, DC 20008
telephone: [1] (202) 238-2700
FAX: [1] (202) 238-2827
consulate(s) general: Boston, Chicago, Houston, Los Angeles, Miami, New York, and San Francisco
Diplomatic representation from the US:
chief of mission: Ambassador Anthony S. HARRINGTON
embassy: Avenida das Nacoes, Quadra 801, Lote 3, Distrito Federal Cep 70403-900, Brasilia
mailing address: Unit 3500, APO AA 34030
telephone: [55] (061) 321-7272
FAX: [55] (061) 225-9136
consulate(s) general: Rio de Janeiro, Sao Paulo
consulate(s): Recife
Flag description: green with a large yellow diamond in the center bearing a blue celestial globe with 27 white five-pointed stars (one for each state and the Federal District) arranged in the same pattern as the night sky over Brazil; the globe has a white equatorial band with the motto ORDEM E PROGRESSO (Order and Progress)

Economy

Economy - overview: Possessing large and well-developed agricultural, mining, manufacturing, and service sectors, Brazil's economy outweighs that of all other South American countries and is expanding its presence in world markets. In the late eighties and early nineties, high inflation hindered economic activity and investment. "The Real Plan", instituted in the spring of 1994, sought to break inflationary expectations by pegging the real to the US dollar. Inflation was brought down to single digit annual figures, but not fast enough to avoid substantial real exchange rate appreciation during the transition phase of the "Real Plan". This appreciation meant that Brazilian goods were now more expensive relative to goods from other countries, which contributed to large current account deficits. However, no shortage of foreign currency ensued because of the financial community's renewed interest in Brazilian markets as inflation rates stabilized and the debt crisis of the eighties faded from memory. The maintenance of large current account deficits via capital account surpluses became problematic as investors became more risk averse to emerging market exposure as a consequence of the Asian financial crisis in 1997 and the Russian bond default in August 1998. After crafting a fiscal adjustment program and pledging progress on structural reform, Brazil received a $41.5 billion IMF-led international support program in November 1998. In January 1999, the Brazilian Central Bank announced that the real would no longer be pegged to the US dollar. This devaluation helped moderate the downturn in economic growth in 1999 that investors had expressed concerns about over the summer of 1998. Brazil's debt to GDP ratio for 1999 beat the IMF target and helped reassure investors that Brazil will maintain tight fiscal and monetary policy even with a floating currency. The economy continued to recover in 2000, with inflation remaining in the single digits and expected growth for 2001 of 4.5%. Foreign direct investment set a record of more than $30 billion in 2000.
GDP: purchasing power parity - $1.13 trillion (2000 est.)
GDP - real growth rate: 4.2% (2000 est.)
GDP - per capita: purchasing power parity - $6,500 (2000 est.)
GDP - composition by sector:
agriculture: 9%
industry: 29%
services: 62% (1999 est.)
Population below poverty line: 17.4% (1990 est.)
Household income or consumption by percentage share:
lowest 10%: 1%
highest 10%: 47.6% (1996)
Inflation rate (consumer prices): 6% (2000)
Labor force: 79 million (1999 est.)
Labor force - by occupation: services 53.2%, agriculture 23.1%, industry 23.7%
Unemployment rate: 7.1% (2000 est.)
Budget:
revenues: $151 billion
expenditures: $149 billion, including capital expenditures of $36 billion (1998)
Industries: textiles, shoes, chemicals, cement, lumber, iron ore, tin, steel, aircraft, motor vehicles and parts, other machinery and equipment
Industrial production growth rate: 6.9% (2000 est.)
Electricity - production: 337.44 billion kWh (1999)
Electricity - production by source:
fossil fuel: 5.28%
hydro: 90.66%
nuclear: 1.12%
other: 2.94% (1999)
Electricity - consumption: 353.674 billion kWh

Brazil (continued)

(1999)
Electricity - exports: 5 million kWh (1999)
Electricity - imports: 39.86 billion kWh
note: supplied by Paraguay (1999)
Agriculture - products: coffee, soybeans, wheat, rice, corn, sugarcane, cocoa, citrus; beef
Exports: $55.1 billion (f.o.b., 2000)
Exports - commodities: manufactures, iron ore, soybeans, footwear, coffee
Exports - partners: US 23%, Argentina 11%, Germany 5%, Netherlands 5%, Japan 5% (1999)
Imports: $55.8 billion (f.o.b., 2000)
Imports - commodities: machinery and equipment, chemical products, oil, electricity
Imports - partners: US 24%, Argentina 12%, Germany 10%, Japan 5%, Italy 5% (1999)
Debt - external: $232 billion (2000)
Economic aid - recipient: NA
Currency: real (BRL)
Currency code: BRL
Exchange rates: reals per US dollar - 1.954 (January 2001), 1.830 (2000), 1.815 (1999), 1.161 (1998), 1.078 (1997), 1.005 (1996)
note: from October 1994 through 14 January 1999, the official rate was determined by a managed float; since 15 January 1999, the official rate floats independently with respect to the US dollar
Fiscal year: calendar year

Communications

Telephones - main lines in use: 17.039 million (1997)
Telephones - mobile cellular: 4.4 million (1997)
Telephone system:
general assessment: good working system
domestic: extensive microwave radio relay system and a domestic satellite system with 64 earth stations
international: 3 coaxial submarine cables; satellite earth stations - 3 Intelsat (Atlantic Ocean), 1 Inmarsat (Atlantic Ocean region east), connected by microwave relay system to MERCOSUR Brazilsat B3 satellite earth station
Radio broadcast stations: AM 1,365, FM 296, shortwave 161 (of which 91 are collocated with AM stations) (1999)
Radios: 71 million (1997)
Television broadcast stations: 138 (1997)
Televisions: 36.5 million (1997)
Internet country code: .br
Internet Service Providers (ISPs): 50 (2000)
Internet users: 8.65 million (2000)

Transportation

Railways:
total: 27,882 km (1,122 km electrified); note - excludes urban rail
broad gauge: 4,057 km 1.600-m gauge
narrow gauge: 23,489 km 1.000-m gauge
dual gauge: 336 km 1.000-m and 1.600-m gauges (three rails) (1999 est.)
Highways:
total: 1.98 million km
paved: 184,140 km
unpaved: 1,795,860 km (1996)
Waterways: 50,000 km
Pipelines: crude oil 2,980 km; petroleum products 4,762 km; natural gas 4,246 km (1998)
Ports and harbors: Belem, Fortaleza, Ilheus, Imbituba, Manaus, Paranagua, Porto Alegre, Recife, Rio de Janeiro, Rio Grande, Salvador, Santos, Vitoria
Merchant marine:
total: 171 ships (1,000 GRT or over) totaling 3,788,999 GRT/6,067,314 DWT
ships by type: bulk 33, cargo 26, chemical tanker 5, combination ore/oil 9, container 12, liquefied gas 11, multi-functional large-load carrier 1, passenger/cargo 5, petroleum tanker 56, roll on/roll off 12, short-sea passenger 1 (2000 est.)
Airports: 3,264 (2000 est.)
Airports - with paved runways:
total: 570
over 3,047 m: 5
2,438 to 3,047 m: 21
1,524 to 2,437 m: 141
914 to 1,523 m: 370
under 914 m: 33 (2000 est.)
Airports - with unpaved runways:
total: 2,694
1,524 to 2,437 m: 68
914 to 1,523 m: 1,279
under 914 m: 1,347 (2000 est.)

Military

Military branches: Brazilian Army, Brazilian Navy (includes naval air and marines), Brazilian Air Force, Federal Police (paramilitary)
Military manpower - military age: 18 years of age
Military manpower - availability:
males age 15-49: 48,298,486 (2001 est.)
Military manpower - fit for military service:
males age 15-49: 32,388,786 (2001 est.)
Military manpower - reaching military age annually:
males: 1,762,740 (2001 est.)
Military expenditures - dollar figure: $13.408 billion (FY99)
Military expenditures - percent of GDP: 1.9% (FY99)

Transnational Issues

Disputes - international: none
Illicit drugs: limited illicit producer of cannabis, minor coca cultivation in the Amazon region, mostly used for domestic consumption; government has a large-scale eradication program to control cannabis; important transshipment country for Bolivian, Colombian, and Peruvian cocaine headed for the US and Europe; also used by traffickers as a way station for narcotics air transshipments between Peru and Colombia; upsurge in drug-related violence and weapons smuggling; important market for Bolivian, Peruvian, and Colombian cocaine

British Indian Ocean Territory
(overseas territory of the UK)

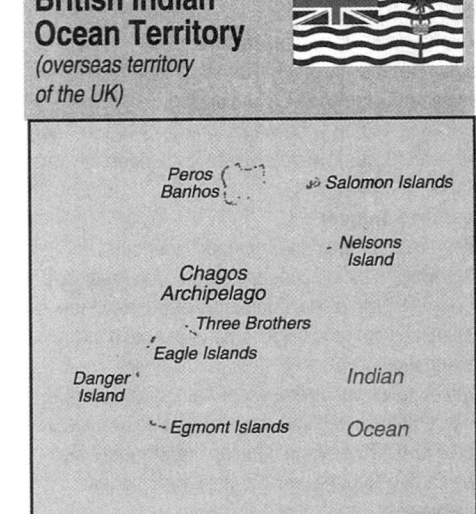

Introduction

Background: Established as a territory of the UK in 1965, a number of the British Indian Ocean Territory (BIOT) islands were transferred to the Seychelles when it attained independence in 1976. Subsequently, BIOT has consisted only of the six main island groups comprising the Chagos Archipelago. The largest and most southerly of the islands, Diego Garcia, contains a joint UK-US naval support facility. All of the remaining islands are uninhabited. Former agricultural workers, earlier resident in the islands, were relocated primarily to Mauritius but also to the Seychelles, between 1967 and 1973. In 2000, a British High Court ruling invalidated the local immigration order which had excluded them from the archipelago, but upheld the special military status of Diego Garcia.

Geography

Location: Southern Asia, archipelago in the Indian Ocean, about one-half the way from Africa to Indonesia
Geographic coordinates: 6 00 S, 71 30 E
Map references: World
Area:
total: 60 sq km
land: 60 sq km
water: 0 sq km
note: includes the entire Chagos Archipelago
Area - comparative: about 0.3 times the size of Washington, DC
Land boundaries: 0 km
Coastline: 698 km
Maritime claims:
exclusive fishing zone: 200 NM
territorial sea: 3 NM
Climate: tropical marine; hot, humid, moderated by trade winds

British Indian Ocean Territory (continued)

Terrain: flat and low (most areas do not exceed four meters in elevation)
Elevation extremes:
lowest point: Indian Ocean 0 m
highest point: unnamed location on Diego Garcia 15 m
Natural resources: coconuts, fish, sugarcane
Land use:
arable land: 0%
permanent crops: 0%
permanent pastures: 0%
forests and woodland: NA%
other: NA%
Irrigated land: 0 sq km (1993)
Natural hazards: NA
Environment - current issues: NA
Geography - note: archipelago of 2,300 islands; Diego Garcia, largest and southernmost island, occupies strategic location in central Indian Ocean; island is site of joint US-UK military facility

People

Population: no indigenous inhabitants
note: approximately 1,200 former agricultural workers resident in the Chagos Archipelago, often referred to as Chagossians or Ilois, were relocated to Mauritius and the Seychelles around the time of the construction of UK-US military facilities; in 1995, there were approximately 1,700 UK and US military personnel and 1,500 civilian contractors living on the island of Diego Garcia

Government

Country name:
conventional long form: British Indian Ocean Territory
conventional short form: none
abbreviation: BIOT
Dependency status: overseas territory of the UK; administered by a commissioner, resident in the Foreign and Commonwealth Office in London
Legal system: the laws of the UK, where applicable, apply
Executive branch:
chief of state: Queen ELIZABETH II (since 6 February 1952)
head of government: Commissioner John WHITE (since NA); Administrator Louise SAVILL (since NA); note - both reside in the UK
cabinet: NA
elections: none; the monarch is hereditary; commissioner and administrator appointed by the monarch
Diplomatic representation in the US: none (overseas territory of the UK)
Diplomatic representation from the US: none (overseas territory of the UK)
Flag description: white with six blue wavy horizontal stripes; the flag of the UK is in the upper hoist-side quadrant; the striped section bears a palm tree and yellow crown centered on the outer half of the flag

Economy

Economy - overview: All economic activity is concentrated on the largest island of Diego Garcia, where joint UK-US defense facilities are located. Construction projects and various services needed to support the military installations are done by military and contract employees from the UK, Mauritius, the Philippines, and the US. There are no industrial or agricultural activities on the islands. When the Ilois return, they plan to reestablish sugarcane production and fishing.
Electricity - production: NA kWh; note - electricity supplied by the US military
Electricity - consumption: NA kWh

Communications

Telephones - main lines in use: NA
Telephone system:
general assessment: separate facilities for military and public needs are available
domestic: all commercial telephone services are available, including connection to the Internet
international: international telephone service is carried by satellite (2000)
Radio broadcast stations: AM 1, FM 2, shortwave 0 (1998)
Radios: NA
Television broadcast stations: 1 (1997)
Televisions: NA
Internet country code: .io
Internet Service Providers (ISPs): 1 (2000)

Transportation

Highways:
total: NA km
paved: short stretch of paved road of NA km between port and airfield on Diego Garcia
unpaved: NA km
Waterways: none
Ports and harbors: Diego Garcia
Airports: 1 (2000 est.)
Airports - with paved runways:
total: 1
over 3,047 m: 1 (2000 est.)

Military

Military - note: defense is the responsibility of the UK; the US lease on Diego Garcia expires in 2016

Transnational Issues

Disputes - international: the Chagos Archipelago is claimed by Mauritius and Seychelles

British Virgin Islands
(overseas territory of the UK)

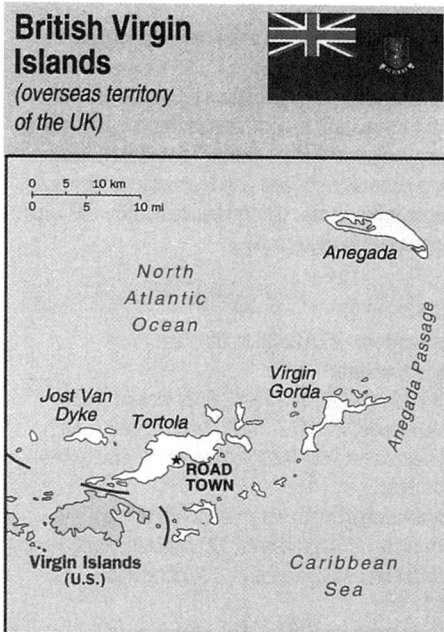

Introduction

Background: First settled by the Dutch in 1648, the islands were soon after (1672) annexed by the English. The economy is closely tied to the larger and more populous US Virgin Islands to the west; the US dollar is the legal currency.

Geography

Location: Caribbean, between the Caribbean Sea and the North Atlantic Ocean, east of Puerto Rico
Geographic coordinates: 18 30 N, 64 30 W
Map references: Central America and the Caribbean
Area:
total: 150 sq km
land: 150 sq km
water: 0 sq km
note: includes the island of Anegada
Area - comparative: about 0.9 times the size of Washington, DC
Land boundaries: 0 km
Coastline: 80 km
Maritime claims:
exclusive fishing zone: 200 NM
territorial sea: 3 NM
Climate: subtropical; humid; temperatures moderated by trade winds
Terrain: coral islands relatively flat; volcanic islands steep, hilly
Elevation extremes:
lowest point: Caribbean Sea 0 m
highest point: Mount Sage 521 m
Natural resources: NEGL
Land use:
arable land: 20%
permanent crops: 7%
permanent pastures: 33%
forests and woodland: 7%
other: 33% (1993 est.)

British Virgin Islands (continued)

Irrigated land: NA sq km
Natural hazards: hurricanes and tropical storms (July to October)
Environment - current issues: limited natural fresh water resources (except for a few seasonal streams and springs on Tortola, most of the islands' water supply comes from wells and rainwater catchment)
Geography - note: strong ties to nearby US Virgin Islands and Puerto Rico

People

Population: 20,812 (July 2001 est.)
Age structure:
0-14 years: 22.77% (male 2,399; female 2,339)
15-64 years: 72.31% (male 7,741; female 7,309)
65 years and over: 4.92% (male 555; female 469) (2001 est.)
Population growth rate: 2.22% (2001 est.)
Birth rate: 15.18 births/1,000 population (2001 est.)
Death rate: 4.42 deaths/1,000 population (2001 est.)
Net migration rate: 11.39 migrant(s)/1,000 population (2001 est.)
Sex ratio:
at birth: 1.05 male(s)/female
under 15 years: 1.03 male(s)/female
15-64 years: 1.06 male(s)/female
65 years and over: 1.18 male(s)/female
total population: 1.06 male(s)/female (2001 est.)
Infant mortality rate: 20.3 deaths/1,000 live births (2001 est.)
Life expectancy at birth:
total population: 75.64 years
male: 74.74 years
female: 76.59 years (2001 est.)
Total fertility rate: 1.72 children born/woman (2001 est.)
HIV/AIDS - adult prevalence rate: NA%
HIV/AIDS - people living with HIV/AIDS: NA
HIV/AIDS - deaths: NA
Nationality:
noun: British Virgin Islander(s)
adjective: British Virgin Islander
Ethnic groups: black 90%, white, Asian
Religions: Protestant 86% (Methodist 45%, Anglican 21%, Church of God 7%, Seventh-Day Adventist 5%, Baptist 4%, Jehovah's Witnesses 2%, other 2%), Roman Catholic 6%, none 2%, other 6% (1981)
Languages: English (official)
Literacy:
definition: age 15 and over can read and write
total population: 97.8% (1991 est.)
male: NA%
female: NA%

Government

Country name:
conventional long form: none
conventional short form: British Virgin Islands
abbreviation: BVI
Dependency status: overseas territory of the UK
Government type: NA
Capital: Road Town
Administrative divisions: none (overseas territory of the UK)
Independence: none (overseas territory of the UK)
National holiday: Territory Day, 1 July
Constitution: 1 June 1977
Legal system: English law
Suffrage: 18 years of age; universal
Executive branch:
chief of state: Queen ELIZABETH II (since 6 February 1952), represented by Governor Francis J. SAVAGE (since NA)
head of government: Chief Minister Ralph T. O'NEAL (since 15 May 1995)
cabinet: Executive Council appointed by the governor from members of the Legislative Council
elections: none; the monarch is hereditary; governor appointed by the monarch; chief minister appointed by the governor from among the members of the Legislative Council
Legislative branch: unicameral Legislative Council (13 seats; members are elected by direct popular vote, one member from each of 9 electoral districts, four at-large members; members serve five-year terms)
elections: last held 17 May 1999 (next to be held NA 2004)
election results: percent of vote by party - NA%; seats by party - VIP 7, CCM 1, NDP 5
Judicial branch: Eastern Caribbean Supreme Court, consisting of the High Court of Justice and the Court of Appeal (one judge of the Supreme Court is a resident of the islands and presides over the High Court); Magistrate's Court; Juvenile Court; Court of Summary Jurisdiction
Political parties and leaders: Concerned Citizens Movement or CCM [Ethlyn SMITH]; National Democratic Party or NDP [Orlando SMITH]; United Party or UP [Gregory MADURO]; Virgin Islands Party or VIP [Ralph T. O'NEAL]
Political pressure groups and leaders: NA
International organization participation: Caricom (associate), CDB, ECLAC (associate), Interpol (subbureau), IOC, OECS (associate), UNESCO (associate)
Diplomatic representation in the US: none (overseas territory of the UK)
Diplomatic representation from the US: none (overseas territory of the UK)
Flag description: blue, with the flag of the UK in the upper hoist-side quadrant and the Virgin Islander coat of arms centered in the outer half of the flag; the coat of arms depicts a woman flanked on either side by a vertical column of six oil lamps above a scroll bearing the Latin word VIGILATE (Be Watchful)

Economy

Economy - overview: The economy, one of the most stable and prosperous in the Caribbean, is highly dependent on tourism, which generates an estimated 45% of the national income. An estimated 350,000 tourists, mainly from the US, visited the islands in 1997. In the mid-1980s, the government began offering offshore registration to companies wishing to incorporate in the islands, and incorporation fees now generate substantial revenues. An estimated 250,000 companies were on the offshore registry by yearend 1997. The adoption of a comprehensive insurance law in late 1994, which provides a blanket of confidentiality with regulated statutory gateways for investigation of criminal offenses, is expected to make the British Virgin Islands even more attractive to international business. Livestock raising is the most important agricultural activity; poor soils limit the islands' ability to meet domestic food requirements. Because of traditionally close links with the US Virgin Islands, the British Virgin Islands has used the dollar as its currency since 1959.
GDP: purchasing power parity - $311 million (2000 est.)
GDP - real growth rate: 6% (2000 est.)
GDP - per capita: purchasing power parity - $16,000 (2000 est.)
GDP - composition by sector:
agriculture: 1.8%
industry: 6.2%
services: 92% (1996 est.)
Population below poverty line: NA%
Household income or consumption by percentage share:
lowest 10%: NA%
highest 10%: NA%
Inflation rate (consumer prices): 2% (2000)
Labor force: 4,911 (1980)
Labor force - by occupation: agriculture NA%, industry NA%, services NA%
Unemployment rate: 3% (1995)
Budget:
revenues: $121.5 million
expenditures: $115.5 million, including capital expenditures of $NA (1997)
Industries: tourism, light industry, construction, rum, concrete block, offshore financial center
Industrial production growth rate: 4% (1985)
Electricity - production: 42 million kWh (1999)
Electricity - production by source:
fossil fuel: 100%
hydro: 0%
nuclear: 0%
other: 0% (1999)
Electricity - consumption: 39.1 million kWh (1999)
Electricity - exports: 0 kWh (1999)
Electricity - imports: 0 kWh (1999)
Agriculture - products: fruits, vegetables; livestock, poultry; fish
Exports: $6.2 million (2000 est.)
Exports - commodities: rum, fresh fish, fruits, animals; gravel, sand
Exports - partners: Virgin Islands (US), Puerto Rico, US
Imports: $220 million (2000 est.)
Imports - commodities: building materials, automobiles, foodstuffs, machinery

British Virgin Islands (continued)

Imports - partners: Virgin Islands (US), Puerto Rico, US
Debt - external: $36.1 million (1997)
Economic aid - recipient: $2.6 million (1995)
Currency: US dollar (USD)
Currency code: USD
Exchange rates: the US dollar is used
Fiscal year: 1 April - 31 March

Communications

Telephones - main lines in use: 10,000 (1996)
Telephones - mobile cellular: NA
Telephone system:
general assessment: worldwide telephone service
domestic: NA
international: submarine cable to Bermuda
Radio broadcast stations: AM 1, FM 4, shortwave 0 (1998)
Radios: 9,000 (1997)
Television broadcast stations: 1 (plus one cable company) (1997)
Televisions: 4,000 (1997)
Internet country code: .vg
Internet Service Providers (ISPs): 16 (2000)
Internet users: NA

Transportation

Railways: 0 km
Highways:
total: 132 km
paved: 132 km
unpaved: 0 km (1997)
Waterways: none
Ports and harbors: Road Town
Merchant marine:
total: 1 ship (1,000 GRT or over) totaling 70,285 GRT/ 6,946 DWT
ships by type: passenger 1 (2000 est.)
Airports: 3 (2000 est.)
Airports - with paved runways:
total: 2
914 to 1,523 m: 1
under 914 m: 1 (2000 est.)
Airports - with unpaved runways:
total: 1
914 to 1,523 m: 1 (2000 est.)

Military

Military - note: defense is the responsibility of the UK

Transnational Issues

Disputes - international: none
Illicit drugs: transshipment point for South American narcotics destined for the US and Europe

Brunei

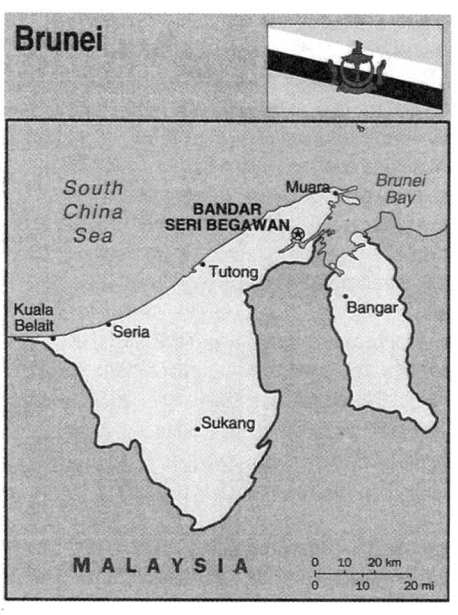

Introduction

Background: The Sultanate of Brunei's heyday occurred between the 15th and 17th centuries, when its control extended over coastal areas of northwest Borneo and the southern Philippines. Brunei subsequently entered a period of decline brought on by internal strife over royal succession, colonial expansion of European powers, and piracy. In 1888, Brunei became a British protectorate; independence was achieved in 1984. Brunei benefits from extensive petroleum and natural gas fields, the source of one of the highest per capita GDPs in the less developed countries. The same family has now ruled in Brunei for over six centuries.

Geography

Location: Southeastern Asia, bordering the South China Sea and Malaysia
Geographic coordinates: 4 30 N, 114 40 E
Map references: Southeast Asia
Area:
total: 5,770 sq km
land: 5,270 sq km
water: 500 sq km
Area - comparative: slightly smaller than Delaware
Land boundaries:
total: 381 km
border countries: Malaysia 381 km
Coastline: 161 km
Maritime claims:
exclusive economic zone: 200 NM or to median line
territorial sea: 12 NM
Climate: tropical; hot, humid, rainy
Terrain: flat coastal plain rises to mountains in east; hilly lowland in west
Elevation extremes:
lowest point: South China Sea 0 m
highest point: Bukit Pagon 1,850 m
Natural resources: petroleum, natural gas, timber
Land use:
arable land: 1%
permanent crops: 1%
permanent pastures: 1%
forests and woodland: 85%
other: 12% (1993 est.)
Irrigated land: 10 sq km (1993 est.)
Natural hazards: typhoons, earthquakes, and severe flooding are very rare
Environment - current issues: seasonal smoke/haze resulting from forest fires in Indonesia
Environment - international agreements:
party to: Endangered Species, Law of the Sea, Marine Dumping, Ozone Layer Protection, Ship Pollution
signed, but not ratified: none of the selected agreements
Geography - note: close to vital sea lanes through South China Sea linking Indian and Pacific Oceans; two parts physically separated by Malaysia; almost an enclave of Malaysia

People

Population: 343,653 (July 2001 est.)
Age structure:
0-14 years: 30.77% (male 53,977; female 51,772)
15-64 years: 66.52% (male 121,601; female 107,007)
65 years and over: 2.71% (male 4,449; female 4,847) (2001 est.)
Population growth rate: 2.11% (2001 est.)
Birth rate: 20.45 births/1,000 population (2001 est.)
Death rate: 3.38 deaths/1,000 population (2001 est.)
Net migration rate: 4.07 migrant(s)/1,000 population (2001 est.)
Sex ratio:
at birth: 1.06 male(s)/female
under 15 years: 1.04 male(s)/female
15-64 years: 1.14 male(s)/female
65 years and over: 0.92 male(s)/female
total population: 1.1 male(s)/female (2001 est.)
Infant mortality rate: 14.4 deaths/1,000 live births (2001 est.)
Life expectancy at birth:
total population: 73.82 years
male: 71.45 years
female: 76.31 years (2001 est.)
Total fertility rate: 2.44 children born/woman (2001 est.)
HIV/AIDS - adult prevalence rate: 0.2% (1999 est.)
HIV/AIDS - people living with HIV/AIDS: less than 100 (1999 est.)
HIV/AIDS - deaths: NA
Nationality:
noun: Bruneian(s)
adjective: Bruneian
Ethnic groups: Malay 67%, Chinese 15%, indigenous 6%, other 12%
Religions: Muslim (official) 67%, Buddhist 13%, Christian 10%, indigenous beliefs and other 10%
Languages: Malay (official), English, Chinese

Brunei (continued)

Literacy:
definition: age 15 and over can read and write
total population: 88.2%
male: 92.6%
female: 83.4% (1995 est.)

Government

Country name:
conventional long form: Negara Brunei Darussalam
conventional short form: Brunei
Government type: constitutional sultanate
Capital: Bandar Seri Begawan
Administrative divisions: 4 districts (daerah-daerah, singular - daerah); Belait, Brunei and Muara, Temburong, Tutong
Independence: 1 January 1984 (from UK)
National holiday: National Day, 23 February (1984); note - 1 January 1984 was the date of independence from the UK, 23 February 1984 was the date of independence from British protection
Constitution: 29 September 1959 (some provisions suspended under a State of Emergency since December 1962, others since independence on 1 January 1984)
Legal system: based on English common law; for Muslims, Islamic Shari'a law supersedes civil law in a number of areas
Suffrage: none
Executive branch:
chief of state: Sultan and Prime Minister Sir HASSANAL Bolkiah (since 5 October 1967); note - the monarch is both the chief of state and head of government
head of government: Sultan and Prime Minister Sir HASSANAL Bolkiah (since 5 October 1967); note - the monarch is both the chief of state and head of government
cabinet: Council of Cabinet Ministers appointed and presided over by the monarch; deals with executive matters; note - there is also a Religious Council (members appointed by the monarch) that advises on religious matters, a Privy Council (members appointed by the monarch) that deals with constitutional matters, and the Council of Succession (members appointed by the monarch) that determines the succession to the throne if the need arises
elections: none; the monarch is hereditary
Legislative branch: unicameral Legislative Council or Majlis Masyuarat Megeri (a privy council that serves only in a consultative capacity; NA seats; members appointed by the monarch)
elections: last held in March 1962
note: in 1970 the Council was changed to an appointive body by decree of the monarch; an elected Legislative Council is being considered as part of constitutional reform, but elections are unlikely for several years
Judicial branch: Supreme Court (chief justice and judges are sworn in by the monarch for three-year terms)

Political parties and leaders: Brunei Solidarity National Party or PPKB in Malay [Haji Mohd HATTA bin Haji Zainal Abidin, president]; the PPKB is the only legal political party in Brunei; it was registered in 1985, but became largely inactive after 1988, it was revived in 1995 and again in 1998; it has less than 200 registered party members; other parties include Brunei People's Party or PRB (banned in 1962) and Brunei National Democratic Party (registered in May 1965, deregistered by the Brunei Government in 1988)
Political pressure groups and leaders: NA
International organization participation: APEC, ARF, ASEAN, C, CCC, ESCAP, G-77, IBRD, ICAO, ICRM, IDB, IFRCS, IMF, IMO, Inmarsat, Intelsat, Interpol, IOC, ISO (correspondent), ITU, NAM, OIC, OPCW, UN, UNCTAD, UPU, WHO, WIPO, WMO, WTrO
Diplomatic representation in the US:
chief of mission: Ambassador Pengiran Anak Dato Haji PUTEH Ibni Mohammad Alam
chancery: 3520 International Court NW, Washington, DC 20008
telephone: [1] (202) 342-0159
FAX: [1] (202) 342-0158
Diplomatic representation from the US:
chief of mission: Ambassador Sylvia Gaye STANFIELD
embassy: Third Floor, Teck Guan Plaza, Jalan Sultan, Bandar Seri Begawan
mailing address: PSC 470 (BSB), FPO AP 96507
telephone: [673] (2) 229670
FAX: [673] (2) 225293
Flag description: yellow with two diagonal bands of white (top, almost double width) and black starting from the upper hoist side; the national emblem in red is superimposed at the center; the emblem includes a swallow-tailed flag on top of a winged column within an upturned crescent above a scroll and flanked by two upraised hands

Economy

Economy - overview: This small, wealthy economy is a mixture of foreign and domestic entrepreneurship, government regulation and welfare measures, and village tradition. Exports of crude oil and natural gas account for over half of GDP. Per capita GDP is far above most other Third World countries, and substantial income from overseas investment supplements income from domestic production. The government provides for all medical services and subsidizes rice and housing. Brunei's leaders are concerned that steadily increased integration in the world economy will undermine internal social cohesion although it became a more prominent player by serving as chairman for the 2000 APEC (Asian Pacific Economic Cooperation) forum. Plans for the future include upgrading the labor force, reducing unemployment, strengthening the banking and tourist sectors, and, in general, a further widening of the economic base beyond oil and gas.

GDP: purchasing power parity - $5.9 billion (2000 est.)
GDP - real growth rate: 3% (2000 est.)
GDP - per capita: purchasing power parity - $17,600 (2000 est.)
GDP - composition by sector:
agriculture: 5%
industry: 46%
services: 49% (1996 est.)
Population below poverty line: NA%
Household income or consumption by percentage share:
lowest 10%: NA%
highest 10%: NA%
Inflation rate (consumer prices): 1% (1999 est.)
Labor force: 144,000 (1995 est.); note - includes foreign workers and military personnel
note: temporary residents make up 41% of labor force (1991)
Labor force - by occupation: government 48%, production of oil, natural gas, services, and construction 42%, agriculture, forestry, and fishing 10% (1999 est.)
Unemployment rate: 4.9% (1995 est.)
Budget:
revenues: $2.5 billion
expenditures: $2.6 billion, including capital expenditures of $1.35 billion (1997 est.)
Industries: petroleum, petroleum refining, liquefied natural gas, construction
Industrial production growth rate: 4% (1997 est.)
Electricity - production: 2.445 billion kWh (1999)
Electricity - production by source:
fossil fuel: 100%
hydro: 0%
nuclear: 0%
other: 0% (1999)
Electricity - consumption: 2.274 billion kWh (1999)
Electricity - exports: 0 kWh (1999)
Electricity - imports: 0 kWh (1999)
Agriculture - products: rice, vegetables, fruits, chickens, water buffalo
Exports: $2.55 billion (f.o.b., 1999 est.)
Exports - commodities: crude oil, natural gas, refined products
Exports - partners: Japan 42%, US 17%, South Korea 14%, Thailand 3% (1999)
Imports: $1.3 billion (c.i.f., 1999 est.)
Imports - commodities: machinery and transport equipment, manufactured goods, food, chemicals
Imports - partners: Singapore 34%, UK 15%, Malaysia 15%, US 5% (1999)
Debt - external: $0
Economic aid - recipient: $4.3 million (1995)
Currency: Bruneian dollar (BND)
Currency code: BND
Exchange rates: Bruneian dollars per US dollar - 1.7365 (January 2001), 1.7240 (2000), 1.6950 (1999), 1.6736 (1998), 1.4848 (1997), 1.4100 (1996); note - the Bruneian dollar is at par with the Singapore dollar
Fiscal year: calendar year

Brunei (continued)

Communications

Telephones - main lines in use: 79,000 (1996)
Telephones - mobile cellular: 43,524 (1996)
Telephone system:
general assessment: service throughout country is excellent; international service good to Europe, US, and East Asia
domestic: every service available
international: satellite earth stations - 2 Intelsat (1 Indian Ocean and 1 Pacific Ocean); digital submarine cable links to Malaysia, Singapore, and Philippines (2001)
Radio broadcast stations: AM 3, FM 10, shortwave 0 (1998)
Radios: 329,000 (1998)
Television broadcast stations: 2 (1997)
Televisions: 201,900 (1998)
Internet country code: .bn
Internet Service Providers (ISPs): 2 (2000)
Internet users: 28,000 (2001)

Transportation

Railways:
total: 13 km (private line)
narrow gauge: 13 km 0.610-m gauge
Highways:
total: 1,712 km
paved: 1,284 km
unpaved: 428 km (1996)
Waterways: 209 km; navigable by craft drawing less than 1.2 m
Pipelines: crude oil 135 km; petroleum products 418 km; natural gas 920 km
Ports and harbors: Bandar Seri Begawan, Kuala Belait, Muara, Seria, Tutong
Merchant marine:
total: 7 ships (1,000 GRT or over) totaling 348,476 GRT/340,635 DWT
ships by type: liquefied gas 7 (2000 est.)
Airports: 2 (2000 est.)
Airports - with paved runways:
total: 1
over 3,047 m: 1 (2000 est.)
Airports - with unpaved runways:
total: 1
914 to 1,523 m: 1 (2000 est.)
Heliports: 3 (2000 est.)

Military

Military branches: Land Forces, Navy, Air Force, Royal Brunei Police
Military manpower - military age: 18 years of age
Military manpower - availability:
males age 15-49: 106,725 (2001 est.)
Military manpower - fit for military service:
males age 15-49: 61,640 (2001 est.)
Military manpower - reaching military age annually:
males: 3,005 (2001 est.)
Military expenditures - dollar figure: $343 million (FY98)
Military expenditures - percent of GDP: 5.1% (FY98)

Transnational Issues

Disputes - international: possibly involved in a complex dispute over the Spratly Islands with China, Malaysia, Philippines, Taiwan, and Vietnam; in 1984, Brunei established an exclusive fishing zone that encompasses Louisa Reef in the southern Spratly Islands, but has not publicly claimed the island
Illicit drugs: drug trafficking and illegally importing controlled substances are serious offenses in Brunei and carry a mandatory death penalty

Bulgaria

Introduction

Background: Bulgaria earned its independence from the Ottoman Empire in 1878, but having fought on the losing side in both World Wars, it fell within the Soviet sphere of influence and became a People's Republic in 1946. Communist domination ended in 1990, when Bulgaria held its first multi-party election since World War II and began the contentious process of moving toward political democracy and a market economy while combating inflation, unemployment, corruption, and crime. Today, reforms and democratization keep Bulgaria on a path toward eventual integration into NATO and the EU - with which it began accession negotiations in 2000.

Geography

Location: Southeastern Europe, bordering the Black Sea, between Romania and Turkey
Geographic coordinates: 43 00 N, 25 00 E
Map references: Europe
Area:
total: 110,910 sq km
land: 110,550 sq km
water: 360 sq km
Area - comparative: slightly larger than Tennessee
Land boundaries:
total: 1,808 km
border countries: Greece 494 km, The Former Yugoslav Republic of Macedonia 148 km, Romania 608 km, Yugoslavia 318 km, Turkey 240 km
Coastline: 354 km
Maritime claims:
contiguous zone: 24 NM
exclusive economic zone: 200 NM
territorial sea: 12 NM
Climate: temperate; cold, damp winters; hot, dry summers
Terrain: mostly mountains with lowlands in north and southeast

Bulgaria (continued)

Elevation extremes:
lowest point: Black Sea 0 m
highest point: Musala 2,925 m
Natural resources: bauxite, copper, lead, zinc, coal, timber, arable land
Land use:
arable land: 43%
permanent crops: 2%
permanent pastures: 14%
forests and woodland: 38%
other: 3% (1999 est.)
Irrigated land: 12,370 sq km (1993 est.)
Natural hazards: earthquakes, landslides
Environment - current issues: air pollution from industrial emissions; rivers polluted from raw sewage, heavy metals, detergents; deforestation; forest damage from air pollution and resulting acid rain; soil contamination from heavy metals from metallurgical plants and industrial wastes
Environment - international agreements:
party to: Air Pollution, Air Pollution-Nitrogen Oxides, Air Pollution-Sulphur 85, Air Pollution-Volatile Organic Compounds, Antarctic-Environmental Protocol, Antarctic-Marine Living Resources, Antarctic Treaty, Biodiversity, Climate Change, Endangered Species, Environmental Modification, Hazardous Wastes, Law of the Sea, Marine Dumping, Nuclear Test Ban, Ozone Layer Protection, Ship Pollution, Wetlands
signed, but not ratified: Air Pollution-Persistent Organic Pollutants, Air Pollution-Sulphur 94, Climate Change-Kyoto Protocol
Geography - note: strategic location near Turkish Straits; controls key land routes from Europe to Middle East and Asia

People

Population: 7,707,495 (July 2001 est.)
Age structure:
0-14 years: 15.11% (male 597,765; female 567,030)
15-64 years: 68.17% (male 2,588,805; female 2,665,736)
65 years and over: 16.72% (male 543,665; female 744,494) (2001 est.)
Population growth rate: -1.14% (2001 est.)
Birth rate: 8.06 births/1,000 population (2001 est.)
Death rate: 14.53 deaths/1,000 population (2001 est.)
Net migration rate: -4.9 migrant(s)/1,000 population (2001 est.)
Sex ratio:
at birth: 1.06 male(s)/female
under 15 years: 1.05 male(s)/female
15-64 years: 0.97 male(s)/female
65 years and over: 0.73 male(s)/female
total population: 0.94 male(s)/female (2001 est.)
Infant mortality rate: 14.65 deaths/1,000 live births (2001 est.)
Life expectancy at birth:
total population: 71.2 years
male: 67.72 years
female: 74.89 years (2001 est.)

Total fertility rate: 1.13 children born/woman (2001 est.)
HIV/AIDS - adult prevalence rate: 0.01% (1999 est.)
HIV/AIDS - people living with HIV/AIDS: NA
HIV/AIDS - deaths: less than 100 (1999 est.)
Nationality:
noun: Bulgarian(s)
adjective: Bulgarian
Ethnic groups: Bulgarian 83%, Turk 8.5%, Roma 2.6%, Macedonian, Armenian, Tatar, Gagauz, Circassian, others (1998)
Religions: Bulgarian Orthodox 83.5%, Muslim 13%, Roman Catholic 1.5%, Uniate Catholic 0.2%, Jewish 0.8%, Protestant, Gregorian-Armenian, and other 1% (1998)
Languages: Bulgarian, secondary languages closely correspond to ethnic breakdown
Literacy:
definition: age 15 and over can read and write
total population: 98%
male: 99%
female: 98% (1999)

Government

Country name:
conventional long form: Republic of Bulgaria
conventional short form: Bulgaria
Government type: parliamentary democracy
Capital: Sofia
Administrative divisions: 28 provinces (oblasti, singular - oblast); Blagoevgrad, Burgas, Dobrich, Gabrovo, Khaskovo, Kurdzhali, Kyustendil, Lovech, Montana, Pazardzhik, Pernik, Pleven, Plovdiv, Razgrad, Ruse, Shumen, Silistra, Sliven, Smolyan, Sofiya, Sofiya-Grad, Stara Zagora, Turgovishte, Varna, Veliko Turnovo, Vidin, Vratsa, Yambol
Independence: 3 March 1878 (from Ottoman Empire)
National holiday: Liberation Day, 3 March (1878)
Constitution: adopted 12 July 1991
Legal system: civil law and criminal law based on Roman law; accepts compulsory ICJ jurisdiction
Suffrage: 18 years of age; universal
Executive branch:
chief of state: President Petar STOYANOV (since 22 January 1997); Vice President Todor KAVALDZHIEV (since 22 January 1997)
head of government: Chairman of the Council of Ministers (Prime Minister) Ivan KOSTOV (since 19 May 1997); Deputy Prime Minister Petur ZHOTEV (since 21 December 1999)
cabinet: Council of Ministers elected by the National Assembly
elections: president and vice president elected on the same ticket by popular vote for five-year terms; election last held 27 October and 3 November 1996 (next to be held NA 2001); chairman of the Council of Ministers (prime minister) nominated by the president; deputy prime ministers nominated by the prime minister
election results: Petar STOYANOV elected president; percent of vote - Petar STOYANOV 59.73%

Legislative branch: unicameral National Assembly or Narodno Sobranie (240 seats; members elected by popular vote to serve four-year terms)
elections: last held 17 June 2001 (next to be held NA June 2005)
election results: percent of vote by party - NA%; seats by party - National Movement for Simeon II 120, UDF 51, BSP 48, DPS 21
Judicial branch: Supreme Administrative Court; Supreme Court of Cassation; Constitutional Court (12 justices appointed or elected for nine-year terms); Supreme Judicial Council (consists of the chairmen of the two Supreme Courts, the Chief Prosecutor, and 22 other members; responsible for appointing the justices, prosecutors, and investigating magistrates in the justice system; members of the Supreme Judicial Council elected for five-year terms, 11 elected by the National Assembly and 11 by bodies of the judiciary)
Political parties and leaders: Alliance for National Salvation or ANS (coalition led mainly by Movement for Rights and Freedoms or MRF) [Ahmed DOGAN]; Bulgarian Business Bloc or BBB [Georgi GANCHEV]; Bulgarian Socialist Party or BSP [Georgi PURVANOV, chairman]; Democratic Left or DL (bloc led by BSP, includes Ecoglasnost Political Club and Bulgarian Agrarian National Union) [leader NA]; Euro-left [Aleksandur TOMOV]; Internal Macedonian Revolutionary Organization or UMRO [Aleksander KARAKACHNOV]; Kingdom of Bulgaria Federation [leader NA]; Movement for Rights and Freedom or DPS [Ahmed DOGAN]; National Movement for Simeon II [Simeon II, former king]; New Civic Party for Bulgaria [Bogomil BONEV]; People's Union or PU (includes Bulgarian Agrarian People's Union and Democratic Party) [Anastasiya MOZER]; St. George's Day [Lyuben DILOV]; Union of Democratic Forces or UDF (an alliance of pro-democratic parties) [Ivan KOSTOV]
Political pressure groups and leaders: agrarian movement; Bulgarian Democratic Center; Confederation of Independent Trade Unions of Bulgaria or CITUB; Democratic Alliance for the Republic or DAR; New Union for Democracy or NUD; Podkrepa Labor Confederation; numerous regional, ethnic, and national interest groups with various agendas
International organization participation: ACCT, BIS, BSEC, CCC, CE, CEI, CERN, EAPC, EBRD, ECE, EU (applicant), FAO, G- 9, IAEA, IBRD, ICAO, ICFTU, ICRM, IFC, IFRCS, IHO (pending member), ILO, IMF, IMO, Inmarsat, Intelsat, Interpol, IOC, IOM, ISO, ITU, NAM (guest), NSG, OAS (observer), OPCW, OSCE, PCA, PFP, UN, UNCTAD, UNESCO, UNIDO, UNMEE, UNMIBH, UNMIK, UNMOP, UPU, WCL, WEU (associate partner), WFTU, WHO, WIPO, WMO, WTOO, WTrO, ZC
Diplomatic representation in the US:
chief of mission: Ambassador Philip DIMITROV
chancery: 1621 22nd Street NW, Washington, DC 20008
telephone: [1] (202) 387-7969
FAX: [1] (202) 234-7973

Bulgaria (continued)

consulate(s): New York

Diplomatic representation from the US:
chief of mission: Ambassador Richard M. MILES
embassy: 1 Suborna Street, Sofia
mailing address: American Embassy Sofia, Department of State, Washington, DC 20521-5740
telephone: [359] (2) 980-52-41
FAX: [359] (2) 981-89-77

Flag description: three equal horizontal bands of white (top), green, and red; the national emblem formerly on the hoist side of the white stripe has been removed - it contained a rampant lion within a wreath of wheat ears below a red five-pointed star and above a ribbon bearing the dates 681 (first Bulgarian state established) and 1944 (liberation from Nazi control)

Economy

Economy - overview: Bulgaria, a former communist country struggling to enter the European market economy, suffered a major economic downturn in 1996 and 1997, with triple digit inflation and GDP contraction of 10.6% and 6.9%. The current government - which took office in May 1997 after pre-term parliamentary elections - stabilized the economy and promoted growth by implementing a currency board, practicing sound financial policies, invigorating privatization, and pursuing structural reforms. Additionally, strong assistance from international financial institutions - most notably the IMF which approved a three-year Extended Fund Facility worth approximately $900 million in September 1998 - played a critical role in turning the economy around. After several years of tumult, Bulgaria's economy has stabilized. Its better-than-expected economic performance in 1999 - despite the impact of the Kosovo conflict, the 1998 Russian financial crisis, and structural reforms - and strong growth in 2000 portends solid growth over the next few years; this assumes continued fiscal restraint, additional structural reforms, aid from abroad, and prosperous times in the EU economy.

GDP: purchasing power parity - $48 billion (2000 est.)

GDP - real growth rate: 5% (2000 est.)

GDP - per capita: purchasing power parity - $6,200 (2000 est.)

GDP - composition by sector:
agriculture: 15%
industry: 29%
services: 56% (2000 est.)

Population below poverty line: 35% (2000 est.)

Household income or consumption by percentage share:
lowest 10%: 3.4%
highest 10%: 22.5% (1995)

Inflation rate (consumer prices): 10.4% (2000 est.)

Labor force: 3.83 million (2000 est.)

Labor force - by occupation: agriculture 26%, industry 31%, services 43% (1998 est.)

Unemployment rate: 17.7% (2000 est.)

Budget:
revenues: $4.85 billion
expenditures: $4.92 billion, including capital expenditures of $NA (2000 est.)

Industries: electricity, gas and water; food, beverages and tobacco; machinery and equipment, base metals, chemical products, coke, refined petroleum, nuclear fuel

Industrial production growth rate: 10.8% (2000 est.)

Electricity - production: 36.217 billion kWh (1999)

Electricity - production by source:
fossil fuel: 51.52%
hydro: 8.35%
nuclear: 40.12%
other: 0.01% (1999)

Electricity - consumption: 33.182 billion kWh (1999)

Electricity - exports: 2.2 billion kWh (1999)

Electricity - imports: 1.7 billion kWh (1999)

Agriculture - products: vegetables, fruits, tobacco, livestock, wine, wheat, barley, sunflowers, sugar beets

Exports: $4.8 billion (f.o.b., 2000 est.)

Exports - commodities: clothing, footwear, iron and steel, machinery and equipment, fuels

Exports - partners: Italy 14%, Turkey 10%, Germany 9%, Greece 8%, Yugoslavia 8%, Belgium 6%, France 5%, US 4% (2000)

Imports: $5.9 billion (f.o.b., 2000 est.)

Imports - commodities: fuels, minerals, and raw materials; machinery and equipment; metals and ores; chemicals and plastics; food, textiles

Imports - partners: Russia 24%, Germany 14%, Italy 8%, Greece 5%, France 5%, Romania 4%, Turkey 3%, US 3% (2000)

Debt - external: $10.4 billion (2000 est.)

Economic aid - recipient: $1 billion (1999 est.)

Currency: lev (BGL)

Currency code: BGL

Exchange rates: leva per US dollar - 2.0848 (January 2001), 2.1233 (2000), 1.8364 (1999), 1,760.36 (1998), 1,681.88 (1997), 177.89 (1996)
note: on 5 July 1999, the lev was redenominated; the post-5 July 1999 lev is equal to 1,000 of the pre-5 July 1999 lev

Fiscal year: calendar year

Communications

Telephones - main lines in use: 3.255 million (2000)

Telephones - mobile cellular: 596,000 (2000)

Telephone system:
general assessment: extensive but antiquated
domestic: more than two-thirds of the lines are residential; telephone service is available in most villages; a fairly modern digital cable trunk line now connects switching centers in most of the regions, the others are connected by digital microwave radio relay
international: direct dialing to 58 countries; satellite earth stations - 1 Intersputnik (Atlantic Ocean region); 2 Intelsat (Atlantic and Indian Ocean regions)

Radio broadcast stations: AM 24, FM 93, shortwave 2 (1998)

Radios: 4.51 million (1997)

Television broadcast stations: 96 (plus 1,030 repeaters) (1995)

Televisions: 3.31 million (1997)

Internet country code: .bg

Internet Service Providers (ISPs): 26 (2000)

Internet users: 200,000 (2000)

Transportation

Railways:
total: 4,294 km
standard gauge: 4,049 km 1.435-m gauge (2,710 km electrified; 917 km double track)
narrow gauge: 245 km 0.760-m gauge (1998)

Highways:
total: 36,724 km
paved: 33,786 km (including 314 km of expressways)
unpaved: 2,938 km (1999)

Waterways: 470 km (1987)

Pipelines: petroleum products 525 km; natural gas 1,500 km (1999)

Ports and harbors: Burgas, Lom, Nesebur, Ruse, Varna, Vidin

Merchant marine:
total: 81 ships (1,000 GRT or over) totaling 938,706 GRT/1,440,374 DWT
ships by type: bulk 44, cargo 16, chemical tanker 4, container 2, passenger/cargo 1, petroleum tanker 6, railcar carrier 2, refrigerated cargo 1, roll on/roll off 3, short-sea passenger 1, specialized tanker 1 (2000 est.)

Airports: 215 (2000 est.)

Airports - with paved runways:
total: 128
over 3,047 m: 1
2,438 to 3,047 m: 19
1,524 to 2,437 m: 15
914 to 1,523 m: 1
under 914 m: 92 (2000 est.)

Airports - with unpaved runways:
total: 87
1,524 to 2,437 m: 2
914 to 1,523 m: 10
under 914 m: 75 (2000 est.)

Heliports: 1 (2000 est.)

Military

Military branches: Army, Navy, Air and Air Defense Forces, Civil Defense Forces, Internal Troops

Military manpower - military age: 19 years of age

Military manpower - availability:
males age 15-49: 1,891,498 (2001 est.)

Military manpower - fit for military service:
males age 15-49: 1,581,697 (2001 est.)

Military manpower - reaching military age annually:
males: 56,104 (2001 est.)

Military expenditures - dollar figure: $344 million (FY00)

Bulgaria (continued)

Military expenditures - percent of GDP: 2.4% (FY00)

Transnational Issues

Illicit drugs: major European transshipment point for Southwest Asian heroin and, to a lesser degree, South American cocaine for the European market; limited producer of precursor chemicals

Burkina Faso

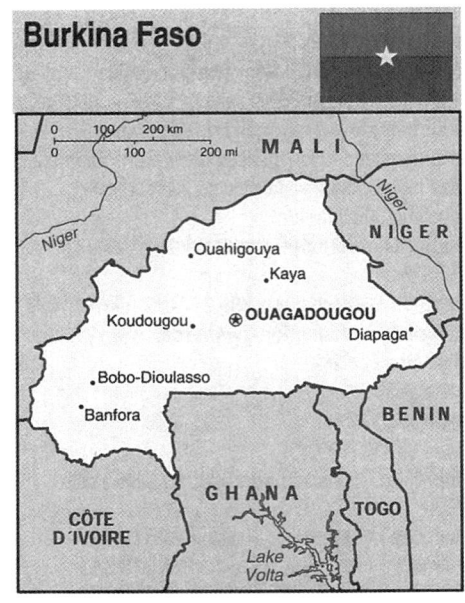

Introduction

Background: Independence from France came to Burkina Faso (formerly Upper Volta) in 1960. Governmental instability during the 1970s and 1980s was followed by multiparty elections in the early 1990s. Several hundred thousand farm workers migrate south every year to Cote d'Ivoire and Ghana.

Geography

Location: Western Africa, north of Ghana
Geographic coordinates: 13 00 N, 2 00 W
Map references: Africa
Area:
total: 274,200 sq km
land: 273,800 sq km
water: 400 sq km
Area - comparative: slightly larger than Colorado
Land boundaries:
total: 3,192 km
border countries: Benin 306 km, Cote d'Ivoire 584 km, Ghana 548 km, Mali 1,000 km, Niger 628 km, Togo 126 km
Coastline: 0 km (landlocked)
Maritime claims: none (landlocked)
Climate: tropical; warm, dry winters; hot, wet summers
Terrain: mostly flat to dissected, undulating plains; hills in west and southeast
Elevation extremes:
lowest point: Mouhoun (Black Volta) River 200 m
highest point: Tena Kourou 749 m
Natural resources: manganese, limestone, marble; small deposits of gold, antimony, copper, nickel, bauxite, lead, phosphates, zinc, silver
Land use:
arable land: 13%
permanent crops: 0%
permanent pastures: 22%
forests and woodland: 50%
other: 15% (1993 est.)
Irrigated land: 200 sq km (1993 est.)
Natural hazards: recurring droughts
Environment - current issues: recent droughts and desertification severely affecting agricultural activities, population distribution, and the economy; overgrazing; soil degradation; deforestation
Environment - international agreements:
party to: Biodiversity, Climate Change, Desertification, Endangered Species, Hazardous Wastes, Marine Dumping, Marine Life Conservation, Ozone Layer Protection, Ship Pollution, Wetlands
signed, but not ratified: Law of the Sea, Nuclear Test Ban
Geography - note: landlocked

People

Population: 12,272,289
note: estimates for this country explicitly take into account the effects of excess mortality due to AIDS; this can result in lower life expectancy, higher infant mortality and death rates, lower population and growth rates, and changes in the distribution of population by age and sex than would otherwise be expected (July 2001 est.)
Age structure:
0-14 years: 47.5% (male 2,937,285; female 2,892,107)
15-64 years: 49.59% (male 2,903,153; female 3,183,121)
65 years and over: 2.91% (male 150,688; female 205,935) (2001 est.)
Population growth rate: 2.68% (2001 est.)
Birth rate: 44.79 births/1,000 population (2001 est.)
Death rate: 17.05 deaths/1,000 population (2001 est.)
Net migration rate: -0.97 migrant(s)/1,000 population (2001 est.)
Sex ratio:
at birth: 1.03 male(s)/female
under 15 years: 1.02 male(s)/female
15-64 years: 0.91 male(s)/female
65 years and over: 0.73 male(s)/female
total population: 0.95 male(s)/female (2001 est.)
Infant mortality rate: 106.92 deaths/1,000 live births (2001 est.)
Life expectancy at birth:
total population: 46.41 years
male: 45.86 years
female: 46.98 years (2001 est.)
Total fertility rate: 6.35 children born/woman (2001 est.)
HIV/AIDS - adult prevalence rate: 6.44% (1999 est.)
HIV/AIDS - people living with HIV/AIDS: 350,000 (1999 est.)
HIV/AIDS - deaths: 43,000 (1999 est.)
Nationality:
noun: Burkinabe (singular and plural)
adjective: Burkinabe
Ethnic groups: Mossi over 40%, Gurunsi, Senufo, Lobi, Bobo, Mande, Fulani

Burkina Faso (continued)

Religions: indigenous beliefs 40%, Muslim 50%, Christian (mainly Roman Catholic) 10%
Languages: French (official), native African languages belonging to Sudanic family spoken by 90% of the population
Literacy:
definition: age 15 and over can read and write
total population: 19.2%
male: 29.5%
female: 9.2% (1995 est.)

Government

Country name:
conventional long form: none
conventional short form: Burkina Faso
former: Upper Volta, Republic of Upper Volta
Government type: parliamentary
Capital: Ouagadougou
Administrative divisions: 30 provinces; Bam, Bazega, Bougouriba, Boulgou, Boulkiemde, Ganzourgou, Gnagna, Gourma, Houe, Kadiogo, Kenedougou, Komoe, Kossi, Kouritenga, Mouhoun, Namentenga, Naouri, Oubritenga, Oudalan, Passore, Poni, Sanguie, Sanmatenga, Seno, Sissili, Soum, Sourou, Tapoa, Yatenga, Zoundweogo
note: a new electoral code was approved by the National Assembly in January 1997; the number of administrative provinces was increased from 30 to 45 (Bale, Bam, Banwa, Bazega, Bougouriba, Boulgou, Boulkiemde, Comoe, Ganzourgou, Gnagna, Gourma, Houet, Ioba, Kadiogo, Kenedougou, Komandjari, Kompienga, Kossi, Koupelogo, Kouritenga, Kourweogo, Leraba, Loroum, Mouhoun, Nahouri, Namentenga, Nayala, Naumbiel, Oubritenga, Oudalan, Passore, Poni, Samentenga, Sanguie, Seno, Sissili, Soum, Sourou, Tapoa, Tuy, Yagha, Yatenga, Ziro, Zondomo, Zoundweogo), however, this change has not yet been confirmed by the US Board on Geographic Names
Independence: 5 August 1960 (from France)
National holiday: Republic Day, 11 December (1958)
Constitution: 2 June 1991 approved by referendum; 11 June 1991 formally adopted
Legal system: based on French civil law system and customary law
Suffrage: universal
Executive branch:
chief of state: President Blaise COMPAORE (since 15 October 1987)
head of government: Prime Minister Ernest Paramanga YONLI (since 6 November 2000)
cabinet: Council of Ministers appointed by the president on the recommendation of the prime minister
elections: president elected by popular vote for a seven-year term; the president may serve unlimited terms; election last held 15 November 1998 (next to be held NA 2005); prime minister appointed by the president with the consent of the legislature
election results: Blaise COMPAORE reelected president with 87.5% percent of the vote, 56% of voter turnout
note: President COMPAORE faces an increasingly well-coordinated opposition; recent charges against a former member of his Presidential Guard in the 1998 assassination of a newspaper editor signify an attempt to defuse chronic areas of dissatisfaction
Legislative branch: bicameral; consists of a National Assembly or Assemblee des Deputes Populaires (111 seats; members are elected by popular vote to serve five-year terms) and the purely consultative Chamber of Representatives or Chambre des Representants (178 seats; members are appointed to serve three-year terms)
elections: National Assembly election last held 11 May 1997 (next to be held NA 2002)
election results: percent of vote by party - NA%; seats by party - CDP 101, PDP 6, RDA 2, ADF 2
Judicial branch: Supreme Court; Appeals Court
Political parties and leaders: African Democratic Rally-Alliance for Democracy and Federation or RDA-ADF [Herman YAMEOGO]; Congress for Democracy and Progress or CDP [Roch Marc-Christian KABORE]; Movement for Tolerance and Progress or MTP [Noyabtigungu Congo KABORE]; Party for African Independence or PAI [Philippe OUEDRAOGO]; Party for Democracy and Progress or PDP [Joseph KI-ZERBO]; Union of Greens for the Development of Burkina Faso or UVDB [Ram OVEDRAGO]
Political pressure groups and leaders: Burkinabe General Confederation of Labor or CGTB; Burkinabe Movement for Human Rights or HBDHP; Group of 14 February; National Confederation of Burkinabe Workers or CNTB; National Organization of Free Unions or ONSL; watchdog/political action groups throughout the country in both organizations and communities
International organization participation: ACCT, ACP, AfDB, CCC, ECA, ECOWAS, Entente, FAO, FZ, G-77, IAEA, IBRD, ICAO, ICC, ICFTU, ICRM, IDA, IDB, IFAD, IFC, IFRCS, ILO, IMF, Intelsat, Interpol, IOC, IOM, ISO (subscriber), ITU, MONUC, NAM, OAU, OIC, OPCW, UN, UNCTAD, UNESCO, UNIDO, UPU, WADB, WAEMU, WCL, WFTU, WHO, WIPO, WMO, WToO, WTrO
Diplomatic representation in the US:
chief of mission: Ambassador Bruno ZIDOUEMBA
chancery: 2340 Massachusetts Avenue NW, Washington, DC 20008
telephone: [1] (202) 332-5577
FAX: [1] (202) 667-1882
Diplomatic representation from the US:
chief of mission: Ambassador Jimmy J. KOLKER
embassy: 602 Avenue Raoul Follerau, Koulouba, Secteur 4, Ouagadougou
mailing address: B. P. 35, Ouagadougou 01
telephone: [226] 306723
FAX: [226] 303890
Flag description: two equal horizontal bands of red (top) and green with a yellow five-pointed star in the center; uses the popular pan-African colors of Ethiopia

Economy

Economy - overview: One of the poorest countries in the world, landlocked Burkina Faso has a high population density, few natural resources, and a fragile soil. About 90% of the population is engaged in (mainly subsistence) agriculture which is highly vulnerable to variations in rainfall. Industry remains dominated by unprofitable government-controlled corporations. Following the African franc currency devaluation in January 1994 the government updated its development program in conjunction with international agencies, and exports and economic growth have increased. Maintenance of its macroeconomic progress in 2001-02 depends on continued low inflation, reduction in the trade deficit, and reforms designed to encourage private investment.
GDP: purchasing power parity - $12 billion (2000 est.)
GDP - real growth rate: 5% (2000 est.)
GDP - per capita: purchasing power parity - $1,000 (2000 est.)
GDP - composition by sector:
agriculture: 26%
industry: 27%
services: 47% (1998)
Population below poverty line: NA%
Household income or consumption by percentage share:
lowest 10%: 2.2%
highest 10%: 39.5% (1994)
Inflation rate (consumer prices): 1.5% (2000 est.)
Labor force: 5 million (1999)
note: a large part of the male labor force migrates annually to neighboring countries for seasonal employment
Labor force - by occupation: agriculture 90% (2000 est.)
Unemployment rate: NA%
Budget:
revenues: $277 million
expenditures: $492 million, including capital expenditures of $233 million (1995 est.)
Industries: cotton lint, beverages, agricultural processing, soap, cigarettes, textiles, gold
Industrial production growth rate: 4.2% (1995)
Electricity - production: 285 million kWh (1999)
Electricity - production by source:
fossil fuel: 71.93%
hydro: 28.07%
nuclear: 0%
other: 0% (1999)
Electricity - consumption: 265.1 million kWh (1999)
Electricity - exports: 0 kWh (1999)
Electricity - imports: 0 kWh (1999)
Agriculture - products: peanuts, shea nuts, sesame, cotton, sorghum, millet, corn, rice; livestock
Exports: $220 million (f.o.b, 2000 est.)
Exports - commodities: cotton, animal products, gold

Burkina Faso (continued)

Exports - partners: Italy 13%, France 10%, Indonesia 8%, Thailand 7% (1999)
Imports: $610 million (f.o.b., 2000 est.)
Imports - commodities: machinery, food products, petroleum
Imports - partners: Cote d'Ivoire 30%, France 28%, Spain 3%, Benelux 3% (1999)
Debt - external: $1.3 billion (1997)
Economic aid - recipient: $484.1 million (1995)
Currency: Communaute Financiere Africaine franc (XOF); note - responsible authority is the Central Bank of the West African States
Currency code: XOF
Exchange rates: Communaute Financiere Africaine francs (XOF) per US dollar - 699.21 (January 2001), 711.98 (2000), 615.70 (1999), 589.95 (1998), 583.67 (1997), 511.55 (1996); note - from 1 January 1999, the XOF is pegged to the euro at a rate of 655.957 XOF per euro
Fiscal year: calendar year

Communications

Telephones - main lines in use: 36,000 (1997)
Telephones - mobile cellular: 1,503 (1997)
Telephone system:
general assessment: all services only fair
domestic: microwave radio relay, open wire, and radiotelephone communication stations
international: satellite earth station - 1 Intelsat (Atlantic Ocean)
Radio broadcast stations: AM 2, FM 17, shortwave 1 (1998)
Radios: 370,000 (1997)
Television broadcast stations: 1 (1997)
Televisions: 100,000 (1997)
Internet country code: .bf
Internet Service Providers (ISPs): 1 (2000)
Internet users: 4,000 (2000)

Transportation

Railways:
total: 622 km (517 km from Ouagadougou to the Cote d'Ivoire border and 105 km from Ouagadougou to Kaya)
narrow gauge: 622 km 1.000-m gauge (1995 est.)
Highways:
total: 12,506 km
paved: 2,001 km
unpaved: 10,505 km (1996)
Waterways: none
Ports and harbors: none
Airports: 33 (2000 est.)
Airports - with paved runways:
total: 2
over 3,047 m: 1
2,438 to 3,047 m: 1 (2000 est.)
Airports - with unpaved runways:
total: 31
1,524 to 2,437 m: 3
914 to 1,523 m: 12
under 914 m: 16 (2000 est.)

Military

Military branches: Army, Air Force, National Gendarmerie, National Police, People's Militia
Military manpower - availability:
males age 15-49: 2,592,974 (2001 est.)
Military manpower - fit for military service:
males age 15-49: 1,329,995 (2001 est.)
Military expenditures - dollar figure: $66 million (FY96)
Military expenditures - percent of GDP: 2% (FY96)

Transnational Issues

Disputes - international: none

Burma

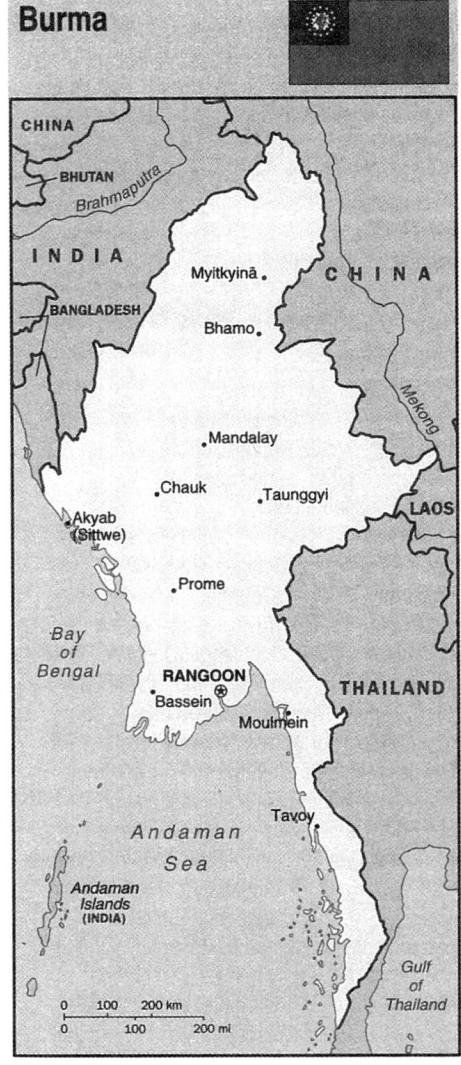

Introduction

Background: Despite multiparty elections in 1990 that resulted in the main opposition party winning a decisive victory, the military junta ruling the country refused to hand over power. Key opposition leader and Nobel Peace Prize recipient AUNG San Suu Kyi, under house arrest from 1989 to 1995, was again placed under house detention in September 2000; her supporters are routinely harassed or jailed.

Geography

Location: Southeastern Asia, bordering the Andaman Sea and the Bay of Bengal, between Bangladesh and Thailand
Geographic coordinates: 22 00 N, 98 00 E
Map references: Southeast Asia
Area:
total: 678,500 sq km
land: 657,740 sq km
water: 20,760 sq km
Area - comparative: slightly smaller than Texas
Land boundaries:
total: 5,876 km

Burma (continued)

border countries: Bangladesh 193 km, China 2,185 km, India 1,463 km, Laos 235 km, Thailand 1,800 km
Coastline: 1,930 km
Maritime claims:
contiguous zone: 24 NM
continental shelf: 200 NM or to the edge of the continental margin
exclusive economic zone: 200 NM
territorial sea: 12 NM
Climate: tropical monsoon; cloudy, rainy, hot, humid summers (southwest monsoon, June to September); less cloudy, scant rainfall, mild temperatures, lower humidity during winter (northeast monsoon, December to April)
Terrain: central lowlands ringed by steep, rugged highlands
Elevation extremes:
lowest point: Andaman Sea 0 m
highest point: Hkakabo Razi 5,881 m
Natural resources: petroleum, timber, tin, antimony, zinc, copper, tungsten, lead, coal, some marble, limestone, precious stones, natural gas, hydropower
Land use:
arable land: 15%
permanent crops: 1%
permanent pastures: 1%
forests and woodland: 49%
other: 34% (1993 est.)
Irrigated land: 10,680 sq km (1993 est.)
Natural hazards: destructive earthquakes and cyclones; flooding and landslides common during rainy season (June to September); periodic droughts
Environment - current issues: deforestation; industrial pollution of air, soil, and water; inadequate sanitation and water treatment contribute to disease
Environment - international agreements:
party to: Biodiversity, Climate Change, Desertification, Endangered Species, Law of the Sea, Marine Dumping, Nuclear Test Ban, Ozone Layer Protection, Ship Pollution, Tropical Timber 83, Tropical Timber 94
signed, but not ratified: none of the selected agreements
Geography - note: strategic location near major Indian Ocean shipping lanes

People

Population: 41,994,678
note: estimates for this country explicitly take into account the effects of excess mortality due to AIDS; this can result in lower life expectancy, higher infant mortality and death rates, lower population and growth rates, and changes in the distribution of population by age and sex than would otherwise be expected (July 2001 est.)
Age structure:
0-14 years: 29.14% (male 6,245,798; female 5,992,074)
15-64 years: 66.08% (male 13,779,571; female 13,970,707)
65 years and over: 4.78% (male 895,554; female 1,110,974) (2001 est.)
Population growth rate: 0.6% (2001 est.)
Birth rate: 20.13 births/1,000 population (2001 est.)
Death rate: 12.3 deaths/1,000 population (2001 est.)
Net migration rate: -1.84 migrant(s)/1,000 population (2001 est.)
Sex ratio:
at birth: 1.06 male(s)/female
under 15 years: 1.04 male(s)/female
15-64 years: 0.99 male(s)/female
65 years and over: 0.81 male(s)/female
total population: 0.99 male(s)/female (2001 est.)
Infant mortality rate: 73.71 deaths/1,000 live births (2001 est.)
Life expectancy at birth:
total population: 55.16 years
male: 53.73 years
female: 56.68 years (2001 est.)
Total fertility rate: 2.3 children born/woman (2001 est.)
HIV/AIDS - adult prevalence rate: 1.99% (1999 est.)
HIV/AIDS - people living with HIV/AIDS: 530,000 (1999 est.)
HIV/AIDS - deaths: 48,000 (1999 est.)
Nationality:
noun: Burmese (singular and plural)
adjective: Burmese
Ethnic groups: Burman 68%, Shan 9%, Karen 7%, Rakhine 4%, Chinese 3%, Mon 2%, Indian 2%, other 5%
Religions: Buddhist 89%, Christian 4% (Baptist 3%, Roman Catholic 1%), Muslim 4%, animist 1%, other 2%
Languages: Burmese, minority ethnic groups have their own languages
Literacy:
definition: age 15 and over can read and write
total population: 83.1%
male: 88.7%
female: 77.7% (1995 est.)
note: these are official statistics; estimates of functional literacy are likely closer to 30% (1999 est.)

Government

Country name:
conventional long form: Union of Burma
conventional short form: Burma
local long form: Pyidaungzu Myanma Naingngandaw (translated by the US Government as Union of Myanma and by the Burmese as Union of Myanmar)
local short form: Myanma Naingngandaw
former: Socialist Republic of the Union of Burma
Government type: military regime
Capital: Rangoon (regime refers to the capital as Yangon)
Administrative divisions: 7 divisions* (yin-mya, singular - yin) and 7 states (pyine-mya, singular - pyine); Chin State, Ayeyarwady*, Bago*, Kachin State, Kayin State, Kayah State, Magway*, Mandalay*, Mon State, Rakhine State, Sagaing*, Shan State, Tanintharyi*, Yangon*
Independence: 4 January 1948 (from UK)
National holiday: Independence Day, 4 January (1948)
Constitution: 3 January 1974 (suspended since 18 September 1988); national convention started on 9 January 1993 to draft a new constitution; progress has since been stalled
Legal system: has not accepted compulsory ICJ jurisdiction
Suffrage: 18 years of age; universal
Executive branch:
chief of state: Prime Minister and Chairman of the State Peace and Development Council Gen. THAN SHWE (since 23 April 1992); note - the prime minister is both the chief of state and head of government
head of government: Prime Minister and Chairman of the State Peace and Development Council Gen. THAN SHWE (since 23 April 1992); note - the prime minister is both the chief of state and head of government
cabinet: State Peace and Development Council (SPDC); military junta, so named 15 November 1997, which initially assumed power 18 September 1988 under the name State Law and Order Restoration Council; the SPDC oversees the cabinet
elections: none; the prime minister assumed power upon resignation of the former prime minister
Legislative branch: unicameral People's Assembly or Pyithu Hluttaw (485 seats; members elected by popular vote to serve four-year terms)
elections: last held 27 May 1990, but Assembly never convened
election results: percent of vote by party - NA%; seats by party - NLD 392, SNLD 23, NUP 10, other 60
Judicial branch: remnants of the British-era legal system are in place, but there is no guarantee of a fair public trial; the judiciary is not independent of the executive
Political parties and leaders: National League for Democracy or NLD [AUNG SHWE, chairman, AUNG SAN SUU KYI, general secretary]; National Unity Party or NUP (proregime) [THA KYAW]; Shan Nationalities League for Democracy or SNLD [U KHUN TUN OO]; Union Solidarity and Development Association or USDA (proregime, a social and political organization) [THAN AUNG, general secretary]; and other smaller parties
Political pressure groups and leaders: All Burma Student Democratic Front or ABSDF; Kachin Independence Army or KIA; Karen National Union or KNU; National Coalition Government of the Union of Burma or NCGUB [Dr. SEIN WIN] consists of individuals legitimately elected to the People's Assembly but not recognized by the military regime; the group fled to a border area and joined with insurgents in December 1990 to form a parallel government; several Shan factions; United Wa State Army or UWSA
International organization participation: ARF, AsDB, ASEAN, CCC, CP, ESCAP, FAO, G-77, IAEA, IBRD, ICAO, ICRM, IDA, IFAD, IFC, IFRCS, ILO, IMF, IMO, Intelsat (nonsignatory user), Interpol, IOC, ITU,

Burma (continued)

NAM, OPCW, UN, UNCTAD, UNESCO, UNIDO, UPU, WHO, WIPO, WMO, WToO, WTrO

Diplomatic representation in the US:
chief of mission: Ambassador-designate U LINN MYAING
chancery: 2300 S Street NW, Washington, DC 20008
telephone: [1] (202) 332-9044
FAX: [1] (202) 332-9046
consulate(s) general: New York

Diplomatic representation from the US:
chief of mission: Permanent Charge d'Affaires Priscilla A. CLAPP
embassy: 581 Merchant Street, Rangoon (GPO 521)
mailing address: Box B, APO AP 96546
telephone: [95] (1) 282055, 282182
FAX: [95] (1) 280409

Flag description: red with a blue rectangle in the upper hoist-side corner bearing, all in white, 14 five-pointed stars encircling a cogwheel containing a stalk of rice; the 14 stars represent the 14 administrative divisions

Economy

Economy - overview: Burma has a mixed economy with private activity dominant in agriculture, light industry, and transport, and with substantial state-controlled activity, mainly in energy, heavy industry, and the rice trade. Government policy in the 1990s has aimed at revitalizing the economy after three decades of tight central planning. Private activity markedly increased in the early to mid-1990s, but began to decline in the past several years due to frustrations with the unfriendly business environment and political pressure from western nations. Published estimates of Burma's foreign trade are greatly understated because of the volume of black-market, illicit, and border trade. A major ongoing problem is the failure to achieve monetary and fiscal stability. Burma remains a poor Asian country and living standards for the majority have not improved over the past decade. Short-term growth will continue to be restrained because of poor government planning and minimal foreign investment.

GDP: purchasing power parity - $63.7 billion (2000 est.)
GDP - real growth rate: 4.9% (2000 est.)
GDP - per capita: purchasing power parity - $1,500 (2000 est.)
GDP - composition by sector:
agriculture: 42%
industry: 17%
services: 41% (2000 est.)
Population below poverty line: 23% (1997 est.)
Household income or consumption by percentage share:
lowest 10%: 2.8%
highest 10%: 32.4% (1998)
Inflation rate (consumer prices): 18% (1999)
Labor force: 19.7 million (FY98/99 est.)
Labor force - by occupation: agriculture 65%, industry 10%, services 25% (1999 est.)
Unemployment rate: 7.1% (official FY97/98 est.)

Budget:
revenues: $7.9 billion
expenditures: $12.2 billion, including capital expenditures of $5.7 billion (FY96/97)
Industries: agricultural processing; textiles and footwear; wood and wood products; copper, tin, tungsten, iron; construction materials; pharmaceuticals; fertilizer
Industrial production growth rate: NA%
Electricity - production: 4.813 billion kWh (1999)
Electricity - production by source:
fossil fuel: 68.56%
hydro: 31.44%
nuclear: 0%
other: 0% (1999)
Electricity - consumption: 4.476 billion kWh (1999)
Electricity - exports: 0 kWh (1999)
Electricity - imports: 0 kWh (1999)
Agriculture - products: paddy rice, corn, oilseed, sugarcane, pulses; hardwood
Exports: $1.3 billion (f.o.b., 1999)
Exports - commodities: apparel 36%, foodstuffs 22%, wood products 21%, precious stones 5% (1999)
Exports - partners: India 13%, Singapore 11%, China 11%, US 8% (1999 est.)
note: official trade statistics do not include trade in illicit goods - such as narcotics, teak, and gems - or the largely unrecorded border trade with China and Thailand
Imports: $2.5 billion (f.o.b., 1999)
Imports - commodities: machinery, transport equipment, construction materials, food products
Imports - partners: Singapore 28%, Thailand 12%, China 10%, Japan 10%, South Korea 9% (1999 est.)
Debt - external: $6 billion (FY99/00 est.)
Economic aid - recipient: $99 million (FY98/99)
Currency: kyat (MMK)
Currency code: MMK
Exchange rates: kyats per US dollar - official rate - 6.5972 (January 2001), 6.5167 (2000), 6.2858 (1999), 6.3432 (1998), 6.2418 (1997), 5.9176 (1996); kyats per US dollar - black market exchange rate - 435 (yearend 2000)
Fiscal year: 1 April - 31 March

Communications

Telephones - main lines in use: 250,000 (2000)
Telephones - mobile cellular: 8,492 (1997)
Telephone system:
general assessment: meets minimum requirements for local and intercity service for business and government; international service is good
domestic: NA
international: satellite earth station - 1 Intelsat (Indian Ocean)
Radio broadcast stations: AM 2, FM 3, shortwave 3 (1998)
Radios: 4.2 million (1997)
Television broadcast stations: 2 (1998)
Televisions: 320,000 (2000)
Internet country code: .mm

Internet Service Providers (ISPs): 1
note: as of September 2000, Internet connections were legal only for the government, tourist offices, and a few large businesses (2000)
Internet users: 500 (2000)

Transportation

Railways:
total: 3,991 km
narrow gauge: 3,991 km 1.000-m gauge
Highways:
total: 28,200 km
paved: 3,440 km
unpaved: 24,760 km (1996)
Waterways: 12,800 km
note: 3,200 km navigable by large commercial vessels
Pipelines: crude oil 1,343 km; natural gas 330 km
Ports and harbors: Bassein, Bhamo, Chauk, Mandalay, Moulmein, Myitkyina, Rangoon, Akyab (Sittwe), Tavoy
Merchant marine:
total: 37 ships (1,000 GRT or over) totaling 411,181 GRT/632,769 DWT
ships by type: bulk 11, cargo 20, container 1, passenger/cargo 3, petroleum tanker 2
note: includes some foreign-owned ships registered here as a flag of convenience: Japan 2 (2000 est.)
Airports: 80 (2000 est.)
Airports - with paved runways:
total: 9
over 3,047 m: 3
2,438 to 3,047 m: 1
1,524 to 2,437 m: 4
914 to 1,523 m: 1 (2000 est.)
Airports - with unpaved runways:
total: 71
over 3,047 m: 2
1,524 to 2,437 m: 15
914 to 1,523 m: 22
under 914 m: 32 (2000 est.)
Heliports: 1 (2000 est.)

Military

Military branches: Army, Navy, Air Force
Military manpower - military age: 18 years of age
Military manpower - availability:
males age 15-49: 12,050,964
females age 15-49: 12,070,017
note: both sexes liable for military service (2001 est.)
Military manpower - fit for military service:
males age 15-49: 6,425,514
females age 15-49: 6,419,677 (2001 est.)
Military manpower - reaching military age annually:
males: 470,667
females: 479,691 (2001 est.)
Military expenditures - dollar figure: $39 million (FY97/98)
Military expenditures - percent of GDP: 2.1% (FY97/98)

Burma (continued)

Transnational Issues

Disputes - international: sporadic border hostilities with Thailand over border alignment and ethnic Shan rebels operating in cross-border region

Illicit drugs: world's second largest producer of illicit opium, after Afghanistan (potential production in 1999 - 1,090 metric tons, down 38% due to drought; cultivation in 1999 - 89,500 hectares, a 31% decline from 1998); surrender of drug warlord KHUN SA's Mong Tai Army in January 1996 was hailed by Rangoon as a major counternarcotics success, but lack of government will and ability to take on major narcotrafficking groups and lack of serious commitment against money laundering continues to hinder the overall antidrug effort; becoming a major source of methamphetamine for regional consumption

Burundi

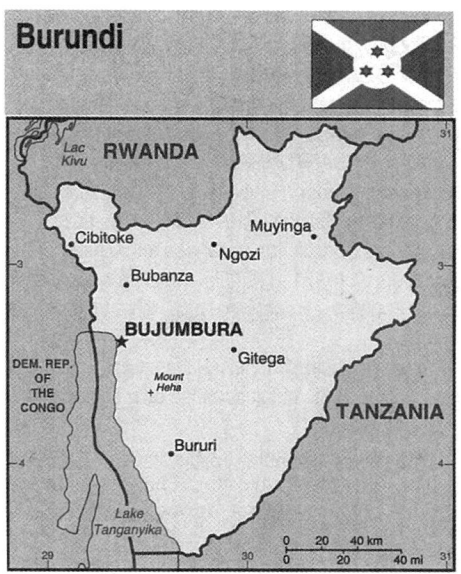

Introduction

Background: Between 1993 and 2000, wide-spread, often intense ethnic violence between Hutu and Tutsi factions in Burundi created hundreds of thousands of refugees and left tens of thousands dead. Although some refugees have returned from neighboring countries, continued ethnic strife has forced many others to flee. Burundian troops, seeking to secure their borders, have intervened in the conflict in the Democratic Republic of the Congo.

Geography

Location: Central Africa, east of Democratic Republic of the Congo
Geographic coordinates: 3 30 S, 30 00 E
Map references: Africa
Area:
total: 27,830 sq km
land: 25,650 sq km
water: 2,180 sq km
Area - comparative: slightly smaller than Maryland
Land boundaries:
total: 974 km
border countries: Democratic Republic of the Congo 233 km, Rwanda 290 km, Tanzania 451 km
Coastline: 0 km (landlocked)
Maritime claims: none (landlocked)
Climate: equatorial; high plateau with considerable altitude variation (772 m to 2,670 m above sea level); average annual temperature varies with altitude from 23 to 17 degrees centigrade but is generally moderate as the average altitude is about 1,700 m; average annual rainfall is about 150 cm; wet seasons from February to May and September to November, and dry seasons from June to August and December to January
Terrain: hilly and mountainous, dropping to a plateau in east, some plains
Elevation extremes:
lowest point: Lake Tanganyika 772 m
highest point: Mount Heha 2,670 m
Natural resources: nickel, uranium, rare earth oxides, peat, cobalt, copper, platinum (not yet exploited), vanadium, arable land, hydropower
Land use:
arable land: 44%
permanent crops: 9%
permanent pastures: 36%
forests and woodland: 3%
other: 8% (1993 est.)
Irrigated land: 140 sq km (1993 est.)
Natural hazards: flooding, landslides, drought
Environment - current issues: soil erosion as a result of overgrazing and the expansion of agriculture into marginal lands; deforestation (little forested land remains because of uncontrolled cutting of trees for fuel); habitat loss threatens wildlife populations
Environment - international agreements:
party to: Biodiversity, Climate Change, Desertification, Endangered Species, Hazardous Wastes, Marine Dumping, Ozone Layer Protection, Ship Pollution
signed, but not ratified: Law of the Sea, Nuclear Test Ban
Geography - note: landlocked; straddles crest of the Nile-Congo watershed

People

Population: 6,223,897
note: estimates for this country explicitly take into account the effects of excess mortality due to AIDS; this can result in lower life expectancy, higher infant mortality and death rates, lower population and growth rates, and changes in the distribution of population by age and sex than would otherwise be expected (July 2001 est.)
Age structure:
0-14 years: 46.82% (male 1,472,618; female 1,441,548)
15-64 years: 50.37% (male 1,541,131; female 1,593,743)
65 years and over: 2.81% (male 71,984; female 102,873) (2001 est.)
Population growth rate: 2.38% (2001 est.)
Birth rate: 40.13 births/1,000 population (2001 est.)
Death rate: 16.36 deaths/1,000 population (2001 est.)
Net migration rate: 0 migrant(s)/1,000 population (2001 est.)
Sex ratio:
at birth: 1.03 male(s)/female
under 15 years: 1.02 male(s)/female
15-64 years: 0.97 male(s)/female
65 years and over: 0.7 male(s)/female
total population: 0.98 male(s)/female (2001 est.)
Infant mortality rate: 70.74 deaths/1,000 live births (2001 est.)
Life expectancy at birth:
total population: 46.06 years
male: 45.15 years
female: 46.99 years (2001 est.)

Burundi (continued)

Total fertility rate: 6.16 children born/woman (2001 est.)
HIV/AIDS - adult prevalence rate: 11.32% (1999 est.)
HIV/AIDS - people living with HIV/AIDS: 360,000 (1999 est.)
HIV/AIDS - deaths: 39,000 (1999 est.)
Nationality:
noun: Burundian(s)
adjective: Burundi
Ethnic groups: Hutu (Bantu) 85%, Tutsi (Hamitic) 14%, Twa (Pygmy) 1%, Europeans 3,000, South Asians 2,000
Religions: Christian 67% (Roman Catholic 62%, Protestant 5%), indigenous beliefs 23%, Muslim 10%
Languages: Kirundi (official), French (official), Swahili (along Lake Tanganyika and in the Bujumbura area)
Literacy:
definition: age 15 and over can read and write
total population: 35.3%
male: 49.3%
female: 22.5% (1995 est.)

Government

Country name:
conventional long form: Republic of Burundi
conventional short form: Burundi
local long form: Republika y'u Burundi
local short form: Burundi
former: Urundi
Government type: republic
Capital: Bujumbura
Administrative divisions: 16 provinces; Bubanza, Bujumbura, Bururi, Cankuzo, Cibitoke, Gitega, Karuzi, Kayanza, Kirundo, Makamba, Muramvya, Muyinga, Mwaro, Ngozi, Rutana, Ruyigi
Independence: 1 July 1962 (from UN trusteeship under Belgian administration)
National holiday: Independence Day, 1 July (1962)
Constitution: 13 March 1992; provided for establishment of a plural political system; supplanted on 6 June 1998 by a Transitional Constitution which enlarged the National Assembly and created two vice presidents
Legal system: based on German and Belgian civil codes and customary law; has not accepted compulsory ICJ jurisdiction
Suffrage: NA years of age; universal adult
Executive branch:
chief of state: President Pierre BUYOYA (interim president since 27 September 1996, officially sworn in 11 June 1998), First Vice President Frederic BAMVUGINYUMVIRA (since NA June 1998), Second Vice President Mathias SINAMENYE (since NA June 1998); note - the president is both chief of state and head of government
head of government: President Pierre BUYOYA (interim president since 27 September 1996, officially sworn in 11 June 1998), First Vice President Frederic BAMVUGINYUMVIRA (since NA June 1998), Second Vice President Mathias SINAMENYE (since NA June 1998); note - the president is both chief of state and head of government
cabinet: Council of Ministers appointed by president
elections: NA; current president assumed power following a coup on 25 July 1996 in which former President NTIBANTUNGANYA was overthrown
Legislative branch: unicameral National Assembly or Assemblee Nationale (121 seats; note - new Transitional Constitution expanded the number of seats from 81 to 121 in 1998; members are elected by popular vote on a proportional basis to serve five-year terms)
elections: last held 29 June 1993 (next was scheduled to be held in 1998, but suspended by presidential decree in 1996)
election results: percent of vote by party - FRODEBU 71.04%, UPRONA 21.4%, other 7.56%; seats by party - FRODEBU 65, UPRONA 16, various other parties 40
Judicial branch: Supreme Court or Cour Supreme; Constitutional Court; Courts of Appeal (there are three in separate locations); Tribunals of First Instance (17 at the province level and 123 small local tribunals)
Political parties and leaders: Two national, mainstream governing parties are: Unity for National Progress or UPRONA [Luc RUKINGAMA, president]; Burundi Democratic Front or FRODEBU [Jean MINANI, president]
note: A multiparty system was introduced after 1998, included are: Burundi African Alliance for the Salvation or ABASA [Terrence NSANZE]; Rally for Democracy and Economic and Social Development or RADDES [Joseph NZENZIMANA]; Party for National Redress or PARENA [Jean-Baptiste BAGAZA]; People's Reconciliation Party or PRP [Mathias HITIMANA]
Political pressure groups and leaders: Loosely organized Tutsi militias, often affiliated with Tutsi extremist parties
International organization participation: ACCT, ACP, AfDB, CCC, CEEAC, CEPGL, ECA, FAO, G-77, IBRD, ICAO, ICRM, IDA, IFAD, IFC, IFRCS, ILO, IMF, Intelsat (nonsignatory user), Interpol, IOC, ITU, NAM, OAU, OPCW, UN, UNCTAD, UNESCO, UNIDO, UPU, WHO, WIPO, WMO, WToO, WTrO
Diplomatic representation in the US:
chief of mission: Ambassador Thomas NDIKUMANA
chancery: Suite 212, 2233 Wisconsin Avenue NW, Washington, DC 20007
telephone: [1] (202) 342-2574
FAX: [1] (202) 342-2578
Diplomatic representation from the US:
chief of mission: Ambassador Mary Carlin YATES
embassy: Avenue des Etats-Unis, Bujumbura
mailing address: B. P. 1720, Bujumbura
telephone: [257] 223454
FAX: [257] 222926
Flag description: divided by a white diagonal cross into red panels (top and bottom) and green panels (hoist side and outer side) with a white disk superimposed at the center bearing three red six-pointed stars outlined in green arranged in a triangular design (one star above, two stars below)

Economy

Economy - overview: Burundi is a landlocked, resource-poor country with an underdeveloped manufacturing sector. The economy is predominantly agricultural with roughly 90% of the population dependent on subsistence agriculture. Its economic health depends on the coffee crop, which accounts for 80% of foreign exchange earnings. The ability to pay for imports therefore rests largely on the vagaries of the climate and the international coffee market. Since October 1993 the nation has suffered from massive ethnic-based violence which has resulted in the death of perhaps 250,000 persons and the displacement of about 800,000 others. Only one in four children go to school, and one in nine adults has HIV/AIDS. Foods, medicines, and electricity remain in short supply.
GDP: purchasing power parity - $4.4 billion (2000 est.)
GDP - real growth rate: 1.8% (2000 est.)
GDP - per capita: purchasing power parity - $720 (2000 est.)
GDP - composition by sector:
agriculture: 50%
industry: 18%
services: 32% (1999 est.)
Population below poverty line: 36.2% (1990 est.)
Household income or consumption by percentage share:
lowest 10%: 3.4%
highest 10%: 26.6% (1992)
Inflation rate (consumer prices): 22% (2000 est.)
Labor force: 1.9 million
Labor force - by occupation: NA
Unemployment rate: NA%
Budget:
revenues: $125 million
expenditures: $176 million, including capital expenditures of $NA (2000 est.)
Industries: light consumer goods such as blankets, shoes, soap; assembly of imported components; public works construction; food processing
Industrial production growth rate: 6.3% (1999 est.)
Electricity - production: 141 million kWh (1999)
Electricity - production by source:
fossil fuel: 0.71%
hydro: 99.29%
nuclear: 0%
other: 0% (1999)
Electricity - consumption: 160.1 million kWh (1999)
Electricity - exports: 0 kWh (1999)
Electricity - imports: 29 million kWh
note: supplied by the Democratic Republic of the Congo (1999)
Agriculture - products: coffee, cotton, tea, corn, sorghum, sweet potatoes, bananas, manioc (tapioca); beef, milk, hides
Exports: $32 million (f.o.b., 2000)
Exports - commodities: coffee, tea, sugar, cotton, hides

Burundi (continued)

Exports - partners: Germany 17%, Belgium 14%, US 8%, France 6%, Switzerland 4% (1999)
Imports: $110 million (f.o.b., 2000)
Imports - commodities: capital goods, petroleum products, foodstuffs
Imports - partners: Belgium 20%, Zambia 11%, Kenya 8%, South Africa 5%, France 4% (1999)
Debt - external: $1.12 billion (1999 est.)
Economic aid - recipient: $1.344 billion (1999 est.)
Currency: Burundi franc (BIF)
Currency code: BIF
Exchange rates: Burundi francs per US dollar - 782.36 (January 2001), 720.67 (2000), 563.56 (1999), 477.77 (1998), 352.35 (1997), 302.75 (1996)
Fiscal year: calendar year

Communications

Telephones - main lines in use: 16,000 (1997)
Telephones - mobile cellular: 619 (1997)
Telephone system:
general assessment: primitive system
domestic: sparse system of open wire, radiotelephone communications, and low-capacity microwave radio relay
international: satellite earth station - 1 Intelsat (Indian Ocean)
Radio broadcast stations: AM 2, FM 2, shortwave 0 (1998)
Radios: 440,000 (1997)
Television broadcast stations: 1 (1999)
Televisions: 25,000 (1997)
Internet country code: .bi
Internet Service Providers (ISPs): 1 (2000)
Internet users: 2,000 (2000)

Transportation

Railways: 0 km
Highways:
total: 14,480 km
paved: 1,028 km
unpaved: 13,452 km (1996)
Waterways: Lake Tanganyika
Ports and harbors: Bujumbura
Airports: 4 (2000 est.)
Airports - with paved runways:
total: 1
over 3,047 m: 1 (2000 est.)
Airports - with unpaved runways:
total: 3
914 to 1,523 m: 3 (2000 est.)

Military

Military branches: Army (includes naval and air units), paramilitary Gendarmerie
Military manpower - military age: 16 years of age
Military manpower - availability:
males age 15-49: 1,394,273 (2001 est.)
Military manpower - fit for military service:
males age 15-49: 728,326 (2001 est.)
Military manpower - reaching military age annually:
males: 79,360 (2001 est.)
Military expenditures - dollar figure: $57 million (FY97)
Military expenditures - percent of GDP: 6.1% (FY97)

Transnational Issues

Disputes - international: none

Cambodia

Introduction

Background: Following a five-year struggle, communist Khmer Rouge forces captured Phnom Penh in 1975 and ordered the evacuation of all cities and towns; over 1 million displaced people died from execution or enforced hardships. A 1978 Vietnamese invasion drove the Khmer Rouge into the countryside and touched off 13 years of fighting. UN-sponsored elections in 1993 helped restore some semblance of normalcy, as did the rapid diminishment of the Khmer Rouge in the mid-1990s. A coalition government, formed after national elections in 1998, brought renewed political stability and the surrender of remaining Khmer Rouge forces.

Geography

Location: Southeastern Asia, bordering the Gulf of Thailand, between Thailand, Vietnam, and Laos
Geographic coordinates: 13 00 N, 105 00 E
Map references: Southeast Asia
Area:
total: 181,040 sq km
land: 176,520 sq km
water: 4,520 sq km
Area - comparative: slightly smaller than Oklahoma
Land boundaries:
total: 2,572 km
border countries: Laos 541 km, Thailand 803 km, Vietnam 1,228 km
Coastline: 443 km
Maritime claims:
contiguous zone: 24 NM
continental shelf: 200 NM
exclusive economic zone: 200 NM
territorial sea: 12 NM
Climate: tropical; rainy, monsoon season (May to November); dry season (December to April); little seasonal temperature variation
Terrain: mostly low, flat plains; mountains in southwest and north

Cambodia (continued)

Elevation extremes:
lowest point: Gulf of Thailand 0 m
highest point: Phnum Aoral 1,810 m
Natural resources: timber, gemstones, some iron ore, manganese, phosphates, hydropower potential
Land use:
arable land: 13%
permanent crops: 0%
permanent pastures: 11%
forests and woodland: 66%
other: 10% (1993 est.)
Irrigated land: 920 sq km (1993 est.)
Natural hazards: monsoonal rains (June to November); flooding; occasional droughts
Environment - current issues: illegal logging activities throughout the country and strip mining for gems in the western region along the border with Thailand have resulted in habitat loss and declining biodiversity (in particular, destruction of mangrove swamps threatens natural fisheries); soil erosion; in rural areas, a majority of the population does not have access to potable water; toxic waste delivery from Taiwan sparked unrest in Kampong Saom (Sihanoukville) in December 1998
Environment - international agreements:
party to: Biodiversity, Climate Change, Desertification, Endangered Species, Marine Dumping, Marine Life Conservation, Ship Pollution, Tropical Timber 94, Wetlands
signed, but not ratified: Law of the Sea, Marine Dumping
Geography - note: a land of paddies and forests dominated by the Mekong River and Tonle Sap

People

Population: 12,491,501
note: estimates for this country explicitly take into account the effects of excess mortality due to AIDS; this can result in lower life expectancy, higher infant mortality and death rates, lower population and growth rates, and changes in the distribution of population by age and sex than would otherwise be expected (July 2001 est.)
Age structure:
0-14 years: 41.25% (male 2,626,821; female 2,526,510)
15-64 years: 55.28% (male 3,253,611; female 3,651,129)
65 years and over: 3.47% (male 177,577; female 255,853) (2001 est.)
Population growth rate: 2.25% (2001 est.)
Birth rate: 33.16 births/1,000 population (2001 est.)
Death rate: 10.65 deaths/1,000 population (2001 est.)
Net migration rate: 0 migrant(s)/1,000 population (2001 est.)
Sex ratio:
at birth: 1.05 male(s)/female
under 15 years: 1.04 male(s)/female
15-64 years: 0.89 male(s)/female
65 years and over: 0.69 male(s)/female
total population: 0.94 male(s)/female (2001 est.)
Infant mortality rate: 65.41 deaths/1,000 live births (2001 est.)
Life expectancy at birth:
total population: 56.82 years
male: 54.62 years
female: 59.12 years (2001 est.)
Total fertility rate: 4.74 children born/woman (2001 est.)
HIV/AIDS - adult prevalence rate: 4.04% (1999 est.)
HIV/AIDS - people living with HIV/AIDS: 220,000 (1999 est.)
HIV/AIDS - deaths: 14,000 (1999 est.)
Nationality:
noun: Cambodian(s)
adjective: Cambodian
Ethnic groups: Khmer 90%, Vietnamese 5%, Chinese 1%, other 4%
Religions: Theravada Buddhist 95%, other 5%
Languages: Khmer (official) 95%, French, English
Literacy:
definition: age 15 and over can read and write
total population: 35%
male: 48%
female: 22% (1990 est.)

Government

Country name:
conventional long form: Kingdom of Cambodia
conventional short form: Cambodia
local long form: Preahreacheanachakr Kampuchea
local short form: Kampuchea
former: Khmer Republic, Kampuchea Republic
Government type: multiparty liberal democracy under a constitutional monarchy established in September 1993
Capital: Phnom Penh
Administrative divisions: 20 provinces (khett, singular and plural) and 4 municipalities* (krong, singular and plural); Banteay Mean Cheay, Batdambang, Kampong Cham, Kampong Chhnang, Kampong Spoe, Kampong Thum, Kampot, Kandal, Kaoh Kong, Keb*, Kracheh, Mondol Kiri, Otdar Mean Cheay, Pailin*, Phnum Penh*, Pouthisat, Preah Seihanu* (Sihanoukville), Preah Vihear, Prey Veng, Rotanah Kiri, Siem Reab, Stoeng Treng, Svay Rieng, Takev
Independence: 9 November 1953 (from France)
National holiday: Independence Day, 9 November (1953)
Constitution: promulgated 21 September 1993
Legal system: primarily a civil law mixture of French-influenced codes from the United Nations Transitional Authority in Cambodia (UNTAC) period, royal decrees, and acts of the legislature, with influences of customary law and remnants of communist legal theory; increasing influence of common law in recent years
Suffrage: 18 years of age; universal
Executive branch:
chief of state: King Norodom SIHANOUK (reinstated 24 September 1993)
head of government: Prime Minister HUN SEN (since 30 November 1998)
cabinet: Council of Ministers appointed by the monarch
elections: none; the monarch is chosen by a Royal Throne Council; prime minister appointed by the monarch after a vote of confidence by the National Assembly
Legislative branch: bicameral consists of the National Assembly (122 seats; members elected by popular vote to serve five-year terms) and the Senate (61 seats; two members appointed by the monarch, two elected by the National Assembly, and 57 elected by "functional constituencies"; members serve five-year terms
elections: National Assembly - last held 26 July 1998 (next to be held NA 2003); Senate - last held 2 March 1999 (next to be held NA 2004)
election results: National Assembly - percent of vote by party - CPP 41%, FUNCINPEC 32%, SRP 14%, other 13%; seats by party - CPP 64, FUNCINPEC 43, SRP 15; Senate - seats by party - CPP 31, FUNCINPEC 21, SRP 7
Judicial branch: Supreme Council of the Magistracy (provided for in the constitution and formed in December 1997); Supreme Court (and lower courts) exercises judicial authority
Political parties and leaders: Buddhist Liberal Party or BLP [IENG MOULY]; Cambodian Pracheachon Party or Cambodian People's Party or CPP [CHEA SIM]; Khmer Citizen Party or KCP [NGUON SOEUR]; National United Front for an Independent, Neutral, Peaceful, and Cooperative Cambodia or FUNCINPEC [Prince NORODOM RANARIDDH]; Sam Rangsi Party or SRP (formerly Khmer Nation Party or KNP) [SAM RANGSI]
Political pressure groups and leaders: NA
International organization participation: ACCT, ARF, AsDB, ASEAN, CP, ESCAP, FAO, G-77, IAEA, IBRD, ICAO, ICRM, IDA, IFAD, IFC, IFRCS, ILO, IMF, IMO, Intelsat (nonsignatory user), Interpol, IOC, IOM (observer), ISO (subscriber), ITU, NAM, OPCW, UN, UNCTAD, UNESCO, UNIDO, UPU, WFTU, WHO, WIPO, WMO, WToO, WTrO (observer)
Diplomatic representation in the US:
chief of mission: Ambassador Roland ENG
chancery: 4500 16th Street NW, Washington, DC 20011
telephone: [1] (202) 726-7742
FAX: [1] (202) 726-8381
Diplomatic representation from the US:
chief of mission: Ambassador Kent M. WIEDEMANN
embassy: 16-18 Mongkol lem St. 228, Phnom Penh
mailing address: Box P, APO AP 96546
telephone: [855] (23) 216-436
FAX: [855] (23) 216-437
Flag description: three horizontal bands of blue (top), red (double width), and blue with a white three-towered temple representing Angkor Wat outlined in black in the center of the red band

Cambodia (continued)

Economy

Economy - overview: Cambodia's economy slowed dramatically in 1997-98 due to the regional economic crisis, civil violence, and political infighting. Foreign investment and tourism fell off. In 1999, the first full year of peace in 30 years, progress was made on economic reforms and growth resumed at 4%. GDP growth for 2000 had been projected to reach 5.5%, but the worst flooding in 70 years severely damaged agricultural crops, and high oil prices hurt industrial production, and growth for the year is estimated at only 4%. Tourism is Cambodia's fastest growing industry, with arrivals up 34% in 2000. The long-term development of the economy after decades of war remains a daunting challenge. The population lacks education and productive skills, particularly in the poverty-ridden countryside, which suffers from an almost total lack of basic infrastructure. Fear of renewed political instability and corruption within the government discourage foreign investment and delay foreign aid. On the brighter side, the government is addressing these issues with assistance from bilateral and multilateral donors.
GDP: purchasing power parity - $16.1 billion (2000 est.)
GDP - real growth rate: 4% (2000 est.)
GDP - per capita: purchasing power parity - $1,300 (2000 est.)
GDP - composition by sector:
agriculture: 43%
industry: 20%
services: 37% (1998 est.)
Population below poverty line: 36% (1997 est.)
Household income or consumption by percentage share:
lowest 10%: 2.9%
highest 10%: 33.8% (1997)
Inflation rate (consumer prices): 1.6% (2000 est.)
Labor force: 6 million (1998 est.)
Labor force - by occupation: agriculture 80% (1999 est.)
Unemployment rate: 2.8% (1999 est.)
Budget:
revenues: $363 million
expenditures: $532 million, including capital expenditures of $225 million (2000 est.)
Industries: garments, tourism, rice milling, fishing, wood and wood products, rubber, cement, gem mining, textiles
Industrial production growth rate: NA%
Electricity - production: 147 million kWh (1999)
Electricity - production by source:
fossil fuel: 59.18%
hydro: 40.82%
nuclear: 0%
other: 0% (1999)
Electricity - consumption: 136.7 million kWh (1999)
Electricity - exports: 0 kWh (1999)
Electricity - imports: 0 kWh (1999)
Agriculture - products: rice, rubber, corn, vegetables
Exports: $942 million (f.o.b., 2000 est.)
Exports - commodities: timber, garments, rubber, rice, fish
Exports - partners: Vietnam 18%, Thailand 15%, US 10%, Singapore 8%, China 5% (1997)
Imports: $1.3 billion (f.o.b., 2000 est.)
Imports - commodities: cigarettes, gold, construction materials, petroleum products, machinery, motor vehicles
Imports - partners: Thailand 16%, Vietnam 9%, Japan 7%, Hong Kong 5%, China 5% (1997)
Debt - external: $829 million (1999 est.)
Economic aid - recipient: $548 million pledged in grants and concessional loans for 2001 by international donors
Currency: riel (KHR)
Currency code: KHR
Exchange rates: riels per US dollar - 3,909.0 (January 2001), 3,840.8 (2000), 3,807.8 (1999), 3,744.4 (1998), 2,946.3 (1997), 2,624.1 (1996)
Fiscal year: calendar year

Communications

Telephones - main lines in use: 21,800 (mid-1998)
Telephones - mobile cellular: 80,000 (2000)
Telephone system:
general assessment: adequate landline and/or cellular service in Phnom Penh and other provincial cities; rural areas have little telephone service
domestic: NA
international: adequate but expensive landline and cellular service available to all countries from Phnom Penh and major provincial cities; satellite earth station - 1 Intersputnik (Indian Ocean region)
Radio broadcast stations: AM 7, FM 3, shortwave 3 (1999)
Radios: 1.34 million (1997)
Television broadcast stations: 5 (1999)
Televisions: 94,000 (1997)
Internet country code: .kh
Internet Service Providers (ISPs): 2 (2000)
Internet users: NA

Transportation

Railways:
total: 603 km
narrow gauge: 603 km 1.000-m gauge
Highways:
total: 35,769 km
paved: 4,165 km
unpaved: 31,604 km (1997)
Waterways: 3,700 km
note: navigable all year to craft drawing 0.6 m or less; 282 km navigable to craft drawing as much as 1.8 m
Ports and harbors: Kampong Saom (Sihanoukville), Kampot, Krong Kaoh Kong, Phnom Penh
Merchant marine:
total: 295 ships (1,000 GRT or over) totaling 1,305,932 GRT/1,853,487 DWT
ships by type: bulk 22, cargo 237, chemical tanker 1, combination bulk 3, container 8, liquefied gas 1, livestock carrier 2, multi-functional large-load carrier 1, passenger/cargo 1, petroleum tanker 7, refrigerated cargo 6, roll on/roll off 5, short-sea passenger 1
note: includes some foreign-owned ships registered here as a flag of convenience: Cyprus 3, South Korea 1, Malta 1, Panama 1, Russia 1, Singapore 1 (2000 est.)
Airports: 19 (2000 est.)
Airports - with paved runways:
total: 6
2,438 to 3,047 m: 2
1,524 to 2,437 m: 2
914 to 1,523 m: 2 (2000 est.)
Airports - with unpaved runways:
total: 13
1,524 to 2,437 m: 2
914 to 1,523 m: 11 (2000 est.)
Heliports: 3 (2000 est.)

Military

Military branches: Royal Cambodian Armed Forces (RCAF), including Army, Navy, and Air Force - created in 1993 by the merger of the Cambodian People's Armed Forces and the two noncommunist resistance armies
note: Khmer Rouge and royalist insurgent forces were integrated into the RCAF in 1999
Military manpower - military age: 18 years of age
Military manpower - availability:
males age 15-49: 2,877,137 (2001 est.)
Military manpower - fit for military service:
males age 15-49: 1,610,761 (2001 est.)
Military manpower - reaching military age annually:
males: 162,643 (2001 est.)
Military expenditures - dollar figure: $112 million (FY01 est.)
Military expenditures - percent of GDP: 3% (FY01 est.)

Transnational Issues

Disputes - international: portions of boundary with Vietnam are disputed; parts of border with Thailand are indefinite
Illicit drugs: possible money laundering; narcotics-related corruption reportedly involving some in the government, military, and police; possible small-scale opium, heroin, and amphetamine production; large producer of cannabis for the international market

Cameroon

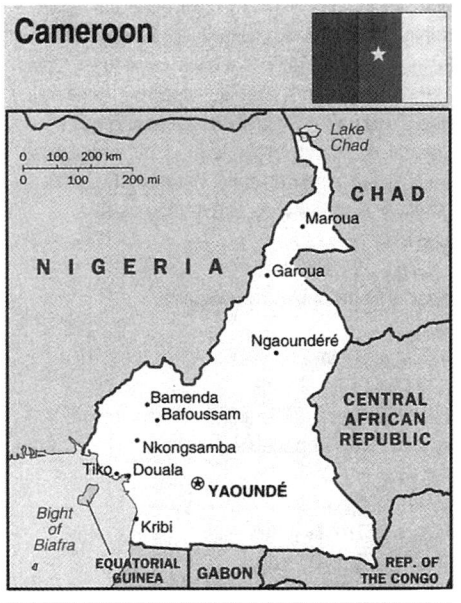

Introduction

Background: The former French Cameroon and part of British Cameroon merged in 1961 to form the present country. Cameroon has generally enjoyed stability, which has permitted the development of agriculture, roads, and railways, as well as a petroleum industry. Despite movement toward democratic reform, political power remains firmly in the hands of an ethnic oligarchy.

Geography

Location: Western Africa, bordering the Bight of Biafra, between Equatorial Guinea and Nigeria
Geographic coordinates: 6 00 N, 12 00 E
Map references: Africa
Area:
total: 475,440 sq km
land: 469,440 sq km
water: 6,000 sq km
Area - comparative: slightly larger than California
Land boundaries:
total: 4,591 km
border countries: Central African Republic 797 km, Chad 1,094 km, Republic of the Congo 523 km, Equatorial Guinea 189 km, Gabon 298 km, Nigeria 1,690 km
Coastline: 402 km
Maritime claims:
territorial sea: 50 NM
Climate: varies with terrain, from tropical along coast to semiarid and hot in north
Terrain: diverse, with coastal plain in southwest, dissected plateau in center, mountains in west, plains in north
Elevation extremes:
lowest point: Atlantic Ocean 0 m
highest point: Fako 4,095 m
Natural resources: petroleum, bauxite, iron ore, timber, hydropower
Land use:
arable land: 13%
permanent crops: 2%
permanent pastures: 4%
forests and woodland: 78%
other: 3% (1993 est.)
Irrigated land: 210 sq km (1993 est.)
Natural hazards: recent volcanic activity with release of poisonous gases
Environment - current issues: water-borne diseases are prevalent; deforestation; overgrazing; desertification; poaching; overfishing
Environment - international agreements:
party to: Biodiversity, Climate Change, Desertification, Endangered Species, Hazardous Wastes, Law of the Sea, Marine Dumping, Ozone Layer Protection, Ship Pollution, Tropical Timber 83, Tropical Timber 94
signed, but not ratified: Nuclear Test Ban
Geography - note: sometimes referred to as the hinge of Africa

People

Population: 15,803,220
note: estimates for this country explicitly take into account the effects of excess mortality due to AIDS; this can result in lower life expectancy, higher infant mortality and death rates, lower population and growth rates, and changes in the distribution of population by age and sex than would otherwise be expected (July 2001 est.)
Age structure:
0-14 years: 42.37% (male 3,385,898; female 3,310,504)
15-64 years: 54.28% (male 4,305,354; female 4,271,958)
65 years and over: 3.35% (male 244,419; female 285,087) (2001 est.)
Population growth rate: 2.41% (2001 est.)
Birth rate: 36.12 births/1,000 population (2001 est.)
Death rate: 11.99 deaths/1,000 population (2001 est.)
Net migration rate: 0 migrant(s)/1,000 population (2001 est.) NA migrant(s)/1,000 population
Sex ratio:
at birth: 1.03 male(s)/female
under 15 years: 1.02 male(s)/female
15-64 years: 1.01 male(s)/female
65 years and over: 0.86 male(s)/female
total population: 1.01 male(s)/female (2001 est.)
Infant mortality rate: 69.83 deaths/1,000 live births (2001 est.)
Life expectancy at birth:
total population: 54.59 years
male: 53.76 years
female: 55.44 years (2001 est.)
Total fertility rate: 4.8 children born/woman (2001 est.)
HIV/AIDS - adult prevalence rate: 7.73% (1999 est.)
HIV/AIDS - people living with HIV/AIDS: 540,000 (1999 est.)
HIV/AIDS - deaths: 52,000 (1999 est.)
Nationality:
noun: Cameroonian(s)
adjective: Cameroonian
Ethnic groups: Cameroon Highlanders 31%, Equatorial Bantu 19%, Kirdi 11%, Fulani 10%, Northwestern Bantu 8%, Eastern Nigritic 7%, other African 13%, non-African less than 1%
Religions: indigenous beliefs 40%, Christian 40%, Muslim 20%
Languages: 24 major African language groups, English (official), French (official)
Literacy:
definition: age 15 and over can read and write
total population: 63.4%
male: 75%
female: 52.1% (1995 est.)

Government

Country name:
conventional long form: Republic of Cameroon
conventional short form: Cameroon
former: French Cameroon
Government type: unitary republic; multiparty presidential regime (opposition parties legalized in 1990)
note: preponderance of power remains with the president
Capital: Yaounde
Administrative divisions: 10 provinces; Adamaoua, Centre, Est, Extreme-Nord, Littoral, Nord, Nord-Ouest, Ouest, Sud, Sud-Ouest
Independence: 1 January 1960 (from French-administered UN trusteeship)
National holiday: Republic Day, 20 May (1972)
Constitution: 20 May 1972 approved by referendum; 2 June 1972 formally adopted; revised January 1996
Legal system: based on French civil law system, with common law influence; has not accepted compulsory ICJ jurisdiction
Suffrage: 20 years of age; universal
Executive branch:
chief of state: President Paul BIYA (since 6 November 1982)
head of government: Prime Minister Peter Mafany MUSONGE (since 19 September 1996)
cabinet: Cabinet appointed by the president from proposals submitted by the Prime Minister
elections: president elected by popular vote for a seven-year term; election last held 12 October 1997 (next to be held NA October 2004); prime minister appointed by the president
election results: President Paul BIYA reelected; percent of vote - Paul BIYA 92.6%; note - supporters of the opposition candidates boycotted the elections, making a comparison of vote shares relatively meaningless
Legislative branch: unicameral National Assembly or Assemblee Nationale (180 seats; members are elected by direct popular vote to serve five-year terms;

Cameroon (continued)

note - the president can either lengthen or shorten the term of the legislature)
elections: last held 17 May 1997 (next to be held NA 2002)
election results: percent of vote by party - NA%; seats by party - RDCP 109, SDF 43, UNDP 13, UDC 5, UPC-K 1, MDR 1, MLJC 1; note - results from 7 contested seats were cancelled by the Supreme Court, further elections on 3 August 1997 gave these seats to the RDCP
note: the constitution calls for an upper chamber for the legislature, to be called a Senate, but it has yet to be established
Judicial branch: Supreme Court (judges are appointed by the president); High Court of Justice (consists of nine judges and 6 substitute judges, elected by the National Assembly)
Political parties and leaders: Cameroonian Democratic Union or UDC [Adamou NDAM NJOYA]; Democratic Rally of the Cameroon People or RDCP [Paul BIYA]; Movement for the Defense of the Republic or MDR [Dakole DAISSALA]; Movement for the Liberation and Development of Cameroon or MLDC [leader NA]; Movement for the Youth of Cameroon or MLJC [Marcel YONDO]; National Union for Democracy and Progress or UNDP [Maigari BELLO BOUBA, chairman]; Social Democratic Front or SDF [John FRU NDI]; Union of Cameroonian Populations has two sections UPC-N [Ndeh NTUMAZAH] and UPC-K [Augustin Frederic KODOCK]
Political pressure groups and leaders: Cameroon Anglophone Movement or CAM [Vishe FAI, secretary general]; Southern Cameroon National Council [Nfor Ngala NFOR, acting]
International organization participation: ACCT, ACP, AfDB, BDEAC, C, CCC, CEEAC, CEMAC, ECA, FAO, FZ, G-19, G-77, IAEA, IBRD, ICAO, ICC, ICFTU, ICRM, IDA, IDB, IFAD, IFC, IFRCS, ILO, IMF, IMO, Inmarsat, Intelsat, Interpol, IOC, ISO (correspondent), ITU, NAM, OAU, OIC, OPCW, UN, UNCTAD, UNESCO, UNIDO, UNITAR, UPU, WCL, WFTU, WHO, WIPO, WMO, WToO, WTrO
Diplomatic representation in the US:
chief of mission: Ambassador Jerome MENDOUGA
chancery: 2349 Massachusetts Avenue NW, Washington, DC 20008
telephone: [1] (202) 265-8790
FAX: [1] (202) 387-3826
Diplomatic representation from the US:
chief of mission: Ambassador John M. YATES
embassy: Rue Nachtigal, Yaounde
mailing address: P. O. Box 817, Yaounde; pouch: American Embassy, Department of State, Washington, DC 20521-2520
telephone: [237] 23-40-14, 22-25-89, 23-05-12, 22-17-94
FAX: [237] 23-07-53
Branch Office(s): Douala
Flag description: three equal vertical bands of green (hoist side), red, and yellow with a yellow five-pointed star centered in the red band; uses the popular pan-African colors of Ethiopia

Economy

Economy - overview: Because of its oil resources and favorable agricultural conditions, Cameroon has one of the best-endowed primary commodity economies in sub-Saharan Africa. Still, it faces many of the serious problems facing other underdeveloped countries, such as a top-heavy civil service and a generally unfavorable climate for business enterprise. Since 1990, the government has embarked on various IMF and World Bank programs designed to spur business investment, increase efficiency in agriculture, improve trade, and recapitalize the nation's banks. In June 2000, the government completed an IMF-sponsored, three-year structural adjustment program; however, the IMF is pressing for more reforms, including increased budget transparency and privatization. Higher oil prices in 2000 helped to offset the country's lower cocoa export revenues. A rebound in the cocoa market should increase growth to over 5% in 2001.
GDP: purchasing power parity - $26 billion (2000 est.)
GDP - real growth rate: 4.4% (2000 est.)
GDP - per capita: purchasing power parity - $1,700 (2000 est.)
GDP - composition by sector:
agriculture: 43.4%
industry: 20.1%
services: 36.5% (1999 est.)
Population below poverty line: 48% (2000 est.)
Household income or consumption by percentage share:
lowest 10%: NA%
highest 10%: NA%
Inflation rate (consumer prices): 2% (2000 est.)
Labor force: NA
Labor force - by occupation: agriculture 70%, industry and commerce 13%, other 17%
Unemployment rate: 30% (1998 est.)
Budget:
revenues: $2.1 billion
expenditures: $2.1 billion, including capital expenditures of $NA (FY00/01 est.)
Industries: petroleum production and refining, food processing, light consumer goods, textiles, lumber
Industrial production growth rate: 4.2% (1999 est.)
Electricity - production: 3.47 billion kWh (1999)
Electricity - production by source:
fossil fuel: 2.59%
hydro: 97.41%
nuclear: 0%
other: 0% (1999)
Electricity - consumption: 3.227 billion kWh (1999)
Electricity - exports: 0 kWh (1999)
Electricity - imports: 0 kWh (1999)
Agriculture - products: coffee, cocoa, cotton, rubber, bananas, oilseed, grains, root starches; livestock; timber
Exports: $2.1 billion (f.o.b., 2000 est.)
Exports - commodities: crude oil and petroleum products, lumber, cocoa beans, aluminum, coffee, cotton
Exports - partners: Italy 24%, France 18%, Netherlands 10% (2000 est.)
Imports: $1.6 billion (f.o.b., 2000 est.)
Imports - commodities: machines and electrical equipment, transport equipment, fuel, food
Imports - partners: France 29%, Germany 7%, US 6%, Japan 6% (2000 est.)
Debt - external: $10.9 billion (2000 est.)
Economic aid - recipient: on 23 January 2001, the Paris Club agreed to reduce Cameroon's debt of $1.3 billion by $900 million; total debt relief now amounts to $1.26 billion
Currency: Communaute Financiere Africaine franc (XAF); note - responsible authority is the Bank of the Central African States
Currency code: XAF
Exchange rates: Communaute Financiere Africaine francs (XAF) per US dollar - 699.21 (January 2001), 711.98 (2000), 615.70 (1999), 589.95 (1998), 583.67 (1997), 511.55 (1996); note - from 1 January 1999, the XAF is pegged to the euro at a rate of 655.957 XAF per euro
Fiscal year: 1 July - 30 June

Communications

Telephones - main lines in use: 75,000 (1997)
Telephones - mobile cellular: 4,200 (1997)
Telephone system:
general assessment: available only to business and government
domestic: cable, microwave radio relay, and tropospheric scatter
international: satellite earth stations - 2 Intelsat (Atlantic Ocean)
Radio broadcast stations: AM 11, FM 8, shortwave 3 (1998)
Radios: 2.27 million (1997)
Television broadcast stations: 1 (1998)
Televisions: 450,000 (1997)
Internet country code: .cm
Internet Service Providers (ISPs): 1 (2000)
Internet users: 20,000 (2000)

Transportation

Railways:
total: 1,104 km
narrow gauge: 1,104 km 1.000-m gauge (1995 est.)
Highways:
total: 34,300 km
paved: 4,288 km
unpaved: 30,012 km (1995)
Waterways: 2,090 km (of decreasing importance)
Ports and harbors: Bonaberi, Douala, Garoua, Kribi, Tiko
Airports: 49 (2000 est.)
Airports - with paved runways:
total: 11
over 3,047 m: 2

Cameroon (continued)

2,438 to 3,047 m: 4
1,524 to 2,437 m: 3
914 to 1,523 m: 1
under 914 m: 1 (2000 est.)
Airports - with unpaved runways:
total: 38
1,524 to 2,437 m: 7
914 to 1,523 m: 21
under 914 m: 10 (2000 est.)

Military

Military branches: Army, Navy (includes Naval Infantry), Air Force, National Gendarmerie, Presidential Guard
Military manpower - military age: 18 years of age
Military manpower - availability:
males age 15-49: 3,762,369 (2001 est.)
Military manpower - fit for military service:
males age 15-49: 1,903,149 (2001 est.)
Military manpower - reaching military age annually:
males: 174,308 (2001 est.)
Military expenditures - dollar figure: $118.6 million (FY00/01)
Military expenditures - percent of GDP: 1.4% (FY98/99)

Transnational Issues

Disputes - international: delimitation of international boundaries in the vicinity of Lake Chad, the lack of which led to border incidents in the past, is complete and awaits ratification by Cameroon, Chad, Niger, and Nigeria; tripartite maritime boundary and economic zone dispute with Equatorial Guinea and Nigeria is currently before the ICJ

Canada

Introduction

Background: A land of vast distances and rich natural resources, Canada became a self-governing dominion in 1867 while retaining ties to the British crown. Economically and technologically the nation has developed in parallel with the US, its neighbor to the south across an unfortified border. Its paramount political problem continues to be the relationship of the province of Quebec, with its French-speaking residents and unique culture, to the remainder of the country.

Geography

Location: Northern North America, bordering the North Atlantic Ocean and North Pacific Ocean, north of the conterminous US
Geographic coordinates: 60 00 N, 95 00 W
Map references: North America
Area:
total: 9,976,140 sq km
land: 9,220,970 sq km
water: 755,170 sq km
Area - comparative: slightly larger than the US
Land boundaries:
total: 8,893 km
border countries: US 8,893 km (includes 2,477 km with Alaska)
Coastline: 243,791 km
Maritime claims:
contiguous zone: 24 NM
continental shelf: 200 NM or to the edge of the continental margin
exclusive economic zone: 200 NM
territorial sea: 12 NM
Climate: varies from temperate in south to subarctic and arctic in north
Terrain: mostly plains with mountains in west and lowlands in southeast
Elevation extremes:
lowest point: Atlantic Ocean 0 m
highest point: Mount Logan 5,959 m
Natural resources: iron ore, nickel, zinc, copper, gold, lead, molybdenum, potash, silver, fish, timber, wildlife, coal, petroleum, natural gas, hydropower
Land use:
arable land: 5%
permanent crops: 0%
permanent pastures: 3%
forests and woodland: 54%
other: 38% (1993 est.)
Irrigated land: 7,100 sq km (1993 est.)
Natural hazards: continuous permafrost in north is a serious obstacle to development; cyclonic storms form east of the Rocky Mountains, a result of the mixing of air masses from the Arctic, Pacific, and North American interior, and produce most of the country's rain and snow
Environment - current issues: air pollution and resulting acid rain severely affecting lakes and damaging forests; metal smelting, coal-burning utilities, and vehicle emissions impacting on agricultural and forest productivity; ocean waters becoming contaminated due to agricultural, industrial, mining, and forestry activities
Environment - international agreements:
party to: Air Pollution, Air Pollution-Nitrogen Oxides, Air Pollution-Persistent Organic Pollutants, Air Pollution-Sulphur 85, Air Pollution-Sulphur 94, Antarctic-Marine Living Resources, Antarctic Seals, Antarctic Treaty, Biodiversity, Climate Change, Desertification, Endangered Species, Environmental Modification, Hazardous Wastes, Marine Dumping, Nuclear Test Ban, Ozone Layer Protection, Ship Pollution, Tropical Timber 83, Tropical Timber 94, Wetlands
signed, but not ratified: Air Pollution-Volatile Organic Compounds, Antarctic-Environmental Protocol, Climate Change-Kyoto Protocol, Law of the Sea, Marine Life Conservation
Geography - note: second-largest country in world (after Russia); strategic location between Russia and

Canada (continued)

US via north polar route; approximately 85% of the population is concentrated within 300 km of the US/Canada border

People

Population: 31,592,805 (July 2001 est.)
Age structure:
0-14 years: 18.95% (male 3,067,102; female 2,918,839)
15-64 years: 68.28% (male 10,846,151; female 10,725,800)
65 years and over: 12.77% (male 1,715,071; female 2,319,842) (2001 est.)
Population growth rate: 0.99% (2001 est.)
Birth rate: 11.21 births/1,000 population (2001 est.)
Death rate: 7.47 deaths/1,000 population (2001 est.)
Net migration rate: 6.13 migrant(s)/1,000 population (2001 est.)
Sex ratio:
at birth: 1.05 male(s)/female
under 15 years: 1.05 male(s)/female
15-64 years: 1.01 male(s)/female
65 years and over: 0.74 male(s)/female
total population: 0.98 male(s)/female (2001 est.)
Infant mortality rate: 5.02 deaths/1,000 live births (2001 est.)
Life expectancy at birth:
total population: 79.56 years
male: 76.16 years
female: 83.13 years (2001 est.)
Total fertility rate: 1.6 children born/woman (2001 est.)
HIV/AIDS - adult prevalence rate: 0.3% (1999 est.)
HIV/AIDS - people living with HIV/AIDS: 49,000 (1999 est.)
HIV/AIDS - deaths: 400 (1999 est.)
Nationality:
noun: Canadian(s)
adjective: Canadian
Ethnic groups: British Isles origin 28%, French origin 23%, other European 15%, Amerindian 2%, other, mostly Asian, African, Arab 6%, mixed background 26%
Religions: Roman Catholic 42%, Protestant 40%, other 18%
Languages: English 59.3% (official), French 23.2% (official), other 17.5%
Literacy:
definition: age 15 and over can read and write
total population: 97% (1986 est.)
male: NA%
female: NA%

Government

Country name:
conventional long form: none
conventional short form: Canada
Government type: confederation with parliamentary democracy
Capital: Ottawa
Administrative divisions: 10 provinces and 3 territories*; Alberta, British Columbia, Manitoba, New Brunswick, Newfoundland, Northwest Territories*, Nova Scotia, Nunavut*, Ontario, Prince Edward Island, Quebec, Saskatchewan, Yukon Territory*
Independence: 1 July 1867 (from UK)
National holiday: Independence Day/Canada Day, 1 July (1867)
Constitution: 17 April 1982 (Constitution Act); originally, the machinery of the government was set up in the British North America Act of 1867; charter of rights and unwritten customs
Legal system: based on English common law, except in Quebec, where civil law system based on French law prevails; accepts compulsory ICJ jurisdiction, with reservations
Suffrage: 18 years of age; universal
Executive branch:
chief of state: Queen ELIZABETH II (since 6 February 1952), represented by Governor General Adrienne CLARKSON (since 7 October 1999)
head of government: Prime Minister Jean CHRETIEN (since 4 November 1993)
cabinet: Federal Ministry chosen by the prime minister from among the members of his own party sitting in Parliament
elections: none; the monarch is hereditary; governor general appointed by the monarch on the advice of the prime minister for a five-year term; following legislative elections, the leader of the majority party in the House of Commons is automatically designated by the governor general to become prime minister
Legislative branch: bicameral Parliament or Parlement consists of the Senate or Senat (a body whose members are appointed to serve until reaching 75 years of age by the governor general and selected on the advice of the prime minister; its normal limit is 104 senators) and the House of Commons or Chambre des Communes (301 seats; members elected by direct popular vote to serve five-year terms)
elections: House of Commons - last held 27 November 2000 (next to be held 2005)
election results: percent of vote by party as of January 2001 - Liberal Party 42%, Canadian Alliance 22%, Bloc Quebecois 13%, New Democratic Party 4%, Progressive Conservative Party 4%; seats by party as of January 2001 - Liberal Party 172, Canadian Alliance 66, Bloc Quebecois 38, New Democratic Party 13, Progressive Conservative Party 12
Judicial branch: Supreme Court of Canada (judges are appointed by the prime minister through the governor general); Federal Court of Canada; Federal Court of Appeal; Provincial Courts (these are named variously Court of Appeal, Court of Queens Bench, Superior Court, Supreme Court, and Court of Justice)
Political parties and leaders: Bloc Quebecois [Gilles DUCEPPE]; Canadian Alliance [Stockwell DAY]; Liberal Party [Jean CHRETIEN]; New Democratic Party [Alexa MCDONOUGH]; Progressive Conservative Party [Joe CLARK]
Political pressure groups and leaders: NA
International organization participation: ABEDA, ACCT, AfDB, APEC, ARF (dialogue partner), AsDB, ASEAN (dialogue partner), Australia Group, BIS, C, CCC, CDB (non-regional), CE (observer), EAPC, EBRD, ECE, ECLAC, ESA (cooperating state), FAO, G-7, G-10, IADB, IAEA, IBRD, ICAO, ICC, ICFTU, ICRM, IDA, IEA, IFAD, IFC, IFRCS, IHO, ILO, IMF, IMO, Inmarsat, Intelsat, Interpol, IOC, IOM, ISO, ITU, MINURCA, MIPONUH, MONUC, NAM (guest), NATO, NEA, NSG, OAS, OECD, OPCW, OSCE, PCA, UN, UNCTAD, UNDOF, UNESCO, UNFICYP, UNHCR, UNIKOM, UNMEE, UNMIBH, UNMIK, UNMOP, UNTAET, UNTSO, UNU, UPU, WCL, WFTU, WHO, WIPO, WMO, WToO, WTrO, ZC
Diplomatic representation in the US:
chief of mission: Ambassador Michael KERGIN
chancery: 501 Pennsylvania Avenue NW, Washington, DC 20001
telephone: [1] (202) 682-1740
FAX: [1] (202) 682-7726
consulate(s) general: Atlanta, Boston, Buffalo, Chicago, Dallas, Detroit, Los Angeles, Minneapolis, New York, and Seattle
consulate(s): Miami, Princeton, San Francisco, and San Jose
Diplomatic representation from the US:
chief of mission: Ambassador Gordon D. GIFFIN
embassy: 490 Sussex Drive, Ottawa, Ontario K1N 1G8
mailing address: P. O. Box 5000, Ogdensburg, NY 13669-0430
telephone: [1] (613) 238-5335, 4470
FAX: [1] (613) 238-5720
consulate(s) general: Calgary, Halifax, Montreal, Quebec, Toronto, and Vancouver
Flag description: three vertical bands of red (hoist side), white (double width, square), and red with a red maple leaf centered in the white band

Economy

Economy - overview: As an affluent, high-tech industrial society, Canada today closely resembles the US in its market-oriented economic system, pattern of production, and high living standards. Since World War II, the impressive growth of the manufacturing, mining, and service sectors has transformed the nation from a largely rural economy into one primarily industrial and urban. Real rates of growth have averaged nearly 3.0% since 1993. Unemployment is falling and government budget surpluses are being partially devoted to reducing the large public sector debt. The 1989 US-Canada Free Trade Agreement (FTA) and 1994 North American Free Trade Agreement (NAFTA) (which included Mexico) have touched off a dramatic increase in trade and economic integration with the US. With its great natural resources, skilled labor force, and modern capital plant Canada enjoys solid economic prospects. Two shadows loom, the first being the continuing constitutional impasse between English- and French-speaking areas, which has been raising the possibility of a split in the federation. Another

Canada (continued)

long-term concern is the flow south to the US of professional persons lured by higher pay, lower taxes, and the immense high-tech infrastructure.
GDP: purchasing power parity - $774.7 billion (2000 est.)
GDP - real growth rate: 4.3% (2000 est.)
GDP - per capita: purchasing power parity - $24,800 (2000 est.)
GDP - composition by sector:
agriculture: 3%
industry: 31%
services: 66% (2000 est.)
Population below poverty line: NA%
Household income or consumption by percentage share:
lowest 10%: 2.8%
highest 10%: 23.8% (1994)
Inflation rate (consumer prices): 2.6% (2000)
Labor force: 16.1 million (2000)
Labor force - by occupation: services 74%, manufacturing 15%, construction 5%, agriculture 3%, other 3% (2000)
Unemployment rate: 6.8% (2000 est.)
Budget:
revenues: $126.1 billion
expenditures: $125.3 billion, including capital expenditures of $14.8 billion (2000)
Industries: processed and unprocessed minerals, food products, wood and paper products, transportation equipment, chemicals, fish products, petroleum and natural gas
Industrial production growth rate: 4.5% (2000 est.)
Electricity - production: 567.193 billion kWh (1999)
Electricity - production by source:
fossil fuel: 26.38%
hydro: 60%
nuclear: 12.31%
other: 1.31% (1999)
Electricity - consumption: 497.532 billion kWh (1999)
Electricity - exports: 42.911 billion kWh (1999)
Electricity - imports: 12.953 billion kWh (1999)
Agriculture - products: wheat, barley, oilseed, tobacco, fruits, vegetables; dairy products; forest products; fish
Exports: $272.3 billion (f.o.b., 2000 est.)
Exports - commodities: motor vehicles and parts, newsprint, wood pulp, timber, crude petroleum, machinery, natural gas, aluminum, telecommunications equipment, electricity
Exports - partners: US 86%, Japan 3%, UK, Germany, South Korea, Netherlands, China (1999)
Imports: $238.2 billion (f.o.b., 2000 est.)
Imports - commodities: machinery and equipment, crude oil, chemicals, motor vehicles and parts, durable consumer goods, electricity
Imports - partners: US 76%, Japan 3%, UK, Germany, France, Mexico, Taiwan, South Korea (1999)
Debt - external: $1.9 billion (2000)
Economic aid - donor: ODA, $1.3 billion (1999)

Currency: Canadian dollar (CAD)
Currency code: CAD
Exchange rates: Canadian dollars per US dollar - 1.5032 (January 2001), 1.4851 (2000), 1.4857 (1999), 1.4835 (1998), 1.3846 (1997), 1.3635 (1996)
Fiscal year: 1 April - 31 March

Communications

Telephones - main lines in use: 18.5 million (1999)
Telephones - mobile cellular: 4.207 million (1997)
Telephone system:
general assessment: excellent service provided by modern technology
domestic: domestic satellite system with about 300 earth stations
international: 5 coaxial submarine cables; satellite earth stations - 5 Intelsat (4 Atlantic Ocean and 1 Pacific Ocean) and 2 Intersputnik (Atlantic Ocean region)
Radio broadcast stations: AM 535, FM 53, shortwave 6 (1998)
Radios: 32.3 million (1997)
Television broadcast stations: 80 (plus many repeaters) (1997)
Televisions: 21.5 million (1997)
Internet country code: .ca
Internet Service Providers (ISPs): 760 (2000 est.)
Internet users: 13.28 million (1999)

Transportation

Railways:
total: 36,114 km; note - there are two major transcontinental freight railway systems: Canadian National (privatized November 1995) and Canadian Pacific Railway; passenger service provided by government-operated firm VIA, which has no trackage of its own
standard gauge: 36,114 km 1.435-m gauge (156 km electrified) (1998)
Highways:
total: 901,902 km
paved: 318,371 km (including 16,571 km of expressways)
unpaved: 583,531 km (1999)
Waterways: 3,000 km (including Saint Lawrence Seaway)
Pipelines: crude and refined oil 23,564 km; natural gas 74,980 km
Ports and harbors: Becancour (Quebec), Churchill, Halifax, Hamilton, Montreal, New Westminster, Prince Rupert, Quebec, Saint John (New Brunswick), St. John's (Newfoundland), Sept Isles, Sydney, Trois-Rivieres, Thunder Bay, Toronto, Vancouver, Windsor
Merchant marine:
total: 121 ships (1,000 GRT or over) totaling 1,767,259 GRT/2,633,290 DWT
ships by type: barge carrier 1, bulk 67, cargo 13, chemical tanker 5, combination bulk 1, passenger 3, passenger/cargo 1, petroleum tanker 17, railcar carrier 2, roll on/roll off 7, short-sea passenger 3, specialized tanker 1 (2000 est.)

Airports: 1,417 (2000 est.)
Airports - with paved runways:
total: 517
over 3,047 m: 18
2,438 to 3,047 m: 15
1,524 to 2,437 m: 151
914 to 1,523 m: 244
under 914 m: 89 (2000 est.)
Airports - with unpaved runways:
total: 900
1,524 to 2,437 m: 74
914 to 1,523 m: 362
under 914 m: 464 (2000 est.)
Heliports: 18 (2000 est.)

Military

Military branches: Canadian Forces (includes Land Forces Command or LC, Maritime Command or MC, Air Command or AC, Communications Command or CC, Training Command or TC), Royal Canadian Mounted Police (RCMP)
Military manpower - military age: 17 years of age
Military manpower - availability:
males age 15-49: 8,325,084 (2001 est.)
Military manpower - fit for military service:
males age 15-49: 7,114,851 (2001 est.)
Military manpower - reaching military age annually:
males: 215,627 (2001 est.)
Military expenditures - dollar figure: $7.5 billion (FY00/01)
Military expenditures - percent of GDP: 1.3% (FY00/01)

Transnational Issues

Disputes - international: maritime boundary disputes with the US (Dixon Entrance, Beaufort Sea, Strait of Juan de Fuca, Machias Seal Island)
Illicit drugs: illicit producer of cannabis for the domestic drug market; use of hydroponics technology permits growers to plant large quantities of high-quality marijuana indoors; transit point for heroin and cocaine entering the US market

Cape Verde

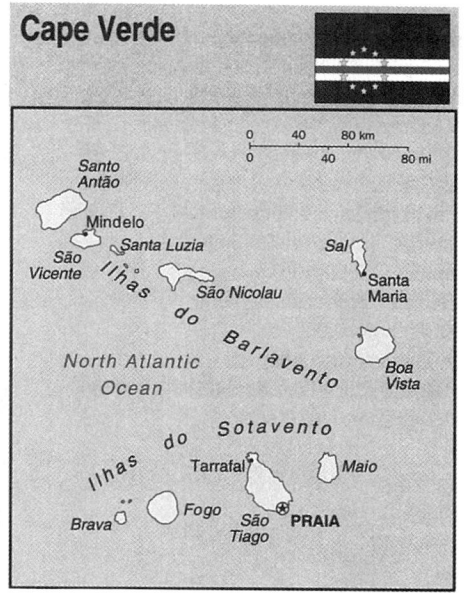

Introduction

Background: The uninhabited islands were discovered and colonized by the Portuguese in the 15th century; they subsequently became a trading center for African slaves. Most Cape Verdeans descend from both groups. Independence was achieved in 1975.

Geography

Location: Western Africa, group of islands in the North Atlantic Ocean, west of Senegal
Geographic coordinates: 16 00 N, 24 00 W
Map references: World
Area:
total: 4,033 sq km
land: 4,033 sq km
water: 0 sq km
Area - comparative: slightly larger than Rhode Island
Land boundaries: 0 km
Coastline: 965 km
Maritime claims: measured from claimed archipelagic baselines
contiguous zone: 24 NM
exclusive economic zone: 200 NM
territorial sea: 12 NM
Climate: temperate; warm, dry summer; precipitation meager and very erratic
Terrain: steep, rugged, rocky, volcanic
Elevation extremes:
lowest point: Atlantic Ocean 0 m
highest point: Mt. Fogo 2,829 m (a volcano on Fogo Island)
Natural resources: salt, basalt rock, pozzuolana (a siliceous volcanic ash used to produce hydraulic cement), limestone, kaolin, fish
Land use:
arable land: 11%
permanent crops: 0%
permanent pastures: 6%
forests and woodland: 0%
other: 83% (1993 est.)
Irrigated land: 1,500 to 2,000 hectares (1999)
Natural hazards: prolonged droughts; harmattan wind can obscure visibility; volcanically and seismically active
Environment - current issues: overgrazing of livestock and improper land use such as the cultivation of crops on steep slopes has led to soil erosion; demand for wood used as fuel has resulted in deforestation; desertification; environmental damage has threatened several species of birds and reptiles; overfishing
Environment - international agreements:
party to: Biodiversity, Climate Change, Desertification, Environmental Modification, Hazardous Wastes, Law of the Sea, Marine Dumping, Ship Pollution
signed, but not ratified: none of the selected agreements
Geography - note: strategic location 500 km from west coast of Africa near major north-south sea routes; important communications station; important sea and air refueling site

People

Population: 405,163 (July 2001 est.)
Age structure:
0-14 years: 42.79% (male 87,458; female 85,895)
15-64 years: 50.76% (male 97,812; female 107,834)
65 years and over: 6.45% (male 10,204; female 15,960) (2001 est.)
Population growth rate: 0.92% (2001 est.)
Birth rate: 28.71 births/1,000 population (2001 est.)
Death rate: 7.19 deaths/1,000 population (2001 est.)
Net migration rate: -12.37 migrant(s)/1,000 population (2001 est.)
Sex ratio:
at birth: 1.03 male(s)/female
under 15 years: 1.02 male(s)/female
15-64 years: 0.91 male(s)/female
65 years and over: 0.64 male(s)/female
total population: 0.93 male(s)/female (2001 est.)
Infant mortality rate: 53.22 deaths/1,000 live births (2001 est.)
Life expectancy at birth:
total population: 69.21 years
male: 65.93 years
female: 72.6 years (2001 est.)
Total fertility rate: 4.05 children born/woman (2001 est.)
HIV/AIDS - adult prevalence rate: NA%
HIV/AIDS - people living with HIV/AIDS: NA
HIV/AIDS - deaths: NA
Nationality:
noun: Cape Verdean(s)
adjective: Cape Verdean
Ethnic groups: Creole (mulatto) 71%, African 28%, European 1%
Religions: Roman Catholic (infused with indigenous beliefs); Protestant (mostly Church of the Nazarene)
Languages: Portuguese, Crioulo (a blend of Portuguese and West African words)
Literacy:
definition: age 15 and over can read and write
total population: 71.6%
male: 81.4%
female: 63.8% (1995 est.)

Government

Country name:
conventional long form: Republic of Cape Verde
conventional short form: Cape Verde
local long form: Republica de Cabo Verde
local short form: Cabo Verde
Government type: republic
Capital: Praia
Administrative divisions: 14 districts (concelhos, singular - concelho); Boa Vista, Brava, Fogo, Maio, Paul, Praia, Porto Novo, Ribeira Grande, Sal, Santa Catarina, Santa Cruz, Sao Nicolau, Sao Vicente, Tarrafal; note - there may be a new administrative structure of 16 districts (Boa Vista, Brava, Maio, Mosteiros, Paul, Praia, Porto Novo, Ribeira Grande, Sal, Santa Catarina, Santa Cruz, Sao Domingos, Sao Nicolau, Sao Filipe, Sao Vicente, Tarrafal)
Independence: 5 July 1975 (from Portugal)
National holiday: Independence Day, 5 July (1975)
Constitution: new constitution came into force 25 September 1992; underwent a major revision on 23 November 1995, substantially increasing the powers of the president
Legal system: derived from the legal system of Portugal
Suffrage: 18 years of age; universal
Executive branch:
chief of state: President Pedro PIRES (since 22 March 2001)
head of government: Prime Minister Jose Maria Pereira NEVES (since 1 February 1991)
cabinet: Council of Ministers appointed by the president on the recommendation of the prime minister from among the members of the National Assembly
elections: president elected by popular vote for a five-year term; election last held 11 and 25 February 2001 (next to be held NA February 2006); prime minister nominated by the National Assembly and appointed by the president
election results: Pedro PIRES elected president; percent of vote - Pedro PIRES (PAICV) 49.43%, Carlos VIEGA (MPD) 49.42%; note: the election was won by only twelve votes
Legislative branch: unicameral National Assembly or Assembleia Nacional (72 seats; members are elected by popular vote to serve five-year terms)
elections: last held 14 January 2001 (next to be held NA December 2005)
election results: percent of vote by party - PAICV 47.3%, MPD 39.8%, ADM 6%, other 6.9%; seats by party - PAICV 40, MPD 30, ADM 2
Judicial branch: Supreme Tribunal of Justice or Supremo Tribunal de Justia

Cape Verde (continued)

Political parties and leaders: African Party for Independence of Cape Verde or PAICV [Jose Maria NEVES, chairman]; Democratic Alliance for Change or ADM [Dr. Eurico MONTEIRO] (a coalition of PCD, PTS, and UCID); Democratic Renovation Party or PRD [Jacinto SANTOS, president]; Movement for Democracy or MPD [Antonio Gualberto do ROSARIO, president]; Party for Democratic Convergence or PCD [Dr. Eurico MONTEIRO, president]; Party of Work and Solidarity or PTS [Dr. Oresimo SILVEIRA, president]; Social Democratic Party or PSD [Joao ALEM, president]; Union for an Independent Democratic Cape Verde or UCID [Antonio MONTEIRO, president]
Political pressure groups and leaders: NA
International organization participation: ACCT, ACP, AfDB, CCC, ECA, ECOWAS, FAO, G-77, IBRD, ICAO, ICFTU, ICRM, IDA, IFAD, IFC, IFRCS, ILO, IMF, IMO, Intelsat, Interpol, IOC, IOM (observer), ITU, NAM, OAU, OPCW, UN, UNCTAD, UNESCO, UNIDO, UNTAET, UPU, WHO, WIPO, WMO, WTrO (observer)
Diplomatic representation in the US:
chief of mission: Ambassador Ferdinand Amilcar Spencer LOPES
chancery: 3415 Massachusetts Avenue NW, Washington, DC 20007
telephone: [1] (202) 965-6820
FAX: [1] (202) 965-1207
consulate(s) general: Boston
Diplomatic representation from the US:
chief of mission: Ambassador Michael D. METELITS
embassy: Rua Abilio Macedo 81, Praia
mailing address: C. P. 201, Praia
telephone: [238] 61 56 16
FAX: [238] 61 13 55
Flag description: three horizontal bands of light blue (top, double width), white (with a horizontal red stripe in the middle third), and light blue; a circle of 10 yellow five-pointed stars is centered on the hoist end of the red stripe and extends into the upper and lower blue bands

Economy

Economy - overview: Cape Verde's low per capita GDP reflects a poor natural resource base, including serious water shortages exacerbated by cycles of long-term drought. The economy is service-oriented, with commerce, transport, and public services accounting for almost 70% of GDP. Although nearly 70% of the population lives in rural areas, the share of agriculture in GDP in 1998 was only 13%, of which fishing accounts for 1.5%. About 90% of food must be imported. The fishing potential, mostly lobster and tuna, is not fully exploited. Cape Verde annually runs a high trade deficit, financed by foreign aid and remittances from emigrants; remittances constitute a supplement to GDP of more than 20%. Economic reforms, launched by the new democratic government in 1991, are aimed at developing the private sector and attracting foreign investment to diversify the economy. Prospects for 2001 depend heavily on the maintenance of aid flows, remittances, and the momentum of the government's development program.
GDP: purchasing power parity - $670 million (2000 est.)
GDP - real growth rate: 6% (2000 est.)
GDP - per capita: purchasing power parity - $1,700 (2000 est.)
GDP - composition by sector:
agriculture: 13%
industry: 19%
services: 68% (1998)
Population below poverty line: NA%
Household income or consumption by percentage share:
lowest 10%: NA%
highest 10%: NA%
Inflation rate (consumer prices): 4% (2000)
Labor force: NA
Unemployment rate: 24% (1999 est.)
Budget:
revenues: $188 million
expenditures: $228 million, including capital expenditures of $116 million (1996)
Industries: food and beverages, fish processing, shoes and garments, salt mining, ship repair
Industrial production growth rate: NA%
Electricity - production: 40 million kWh (1999)
Electricity - production by source:
fossil fuel: 100%
hydro: 0%
nuclear: 0%
other: 0% (1999)
Electricity - consumption: 37.2 million kWh (1999)
Electricity - exports: 0 kWh (1999)
Electricity - imports: 0 kWh (1999)
Agriculture - products: bananas, corn, beans, sweet potatoes, sugarcane, coffee, peanuts; fish
Exports: $40 million (f.o.b., 2000 est.)
Exports - commodities: fuel, shoes, garments, fish, bananas, hides
Exports - partners: Portugal, UK, Germany, Spain, France, Malaysia
Imports: $250 million (f.o.b., 2000 est.)
Imports - commodities: foodstuffs, industrial products, transport equipment, fuels
Imports - partners: Portugal, Netherlands, France, UK, Spain, US
Debt - external: $260 million (2000)
Economic aid - recipient: $111.3 million (1995)
Currency: Cape Verdean escudo (CVE)
Currency code: CVE
Exchange rates: Cape Verdean escudos per US dollar - 123.080 (December 2000), 115.877 (2000), 102.700 (1999), 98.158 (1998), 93.177 (1997), 82.591 (1996)
Fiscal year: calendar year

Communications

Telephones - main lines in use: 45,644 (2000)
Telephones - mobile cellular: 19,729 (1997)
Telephone system:
general assessment: effective system, being improved
domestic: interisland microwave radio relay system with both analog and digital exchanges; work is in progress on a submarine fiber-optic cable system which was scheduled for completion in 1998
international: 2 coaxial submarine cables; HF radiotelephone to Senegal and Guinea-Bissau; satellite earth station - 1 Intelsat (Atlantic Ocean)
Radio broadcast stations: AM 0, FM 11 (and 14 repeaters), shortwave 0 (1998)
Radios: 73,000 (1997)
Television broadcast stations: 1 (1997)
Televisions: 2,000 (1997)
Internet country code: .cv
Internet Service Providers (ISPs): 1 (2000)
Internet users: 5,000 (2000)

Transportation

Railways: 0 km
Highways:
total: 1,100 km
paved: 858 km
unpaved: 242 km (1996)
Waterways: none
Ports and harbors: Mindelo, Praia, Tarrafal
Merchant marine:
total: 5 ships (1,000 GRT or over) totaling 9,523 GRT/ 11,798 DWT
ships by type: cargo 4, chemical tanker 1 (2000 est.)
Airports: 8 (2000)
Airports - with paved runways:
total: 8
over 3,047 m: 1
914 to 1,523 m: 7 (2000)

Military

Military branches: Army, Coast Guard/Marines
Military manpower - availability:
males age 15-49: 89,543 (2001 est.)
Military manpower - fit for military service:
males age 15-49: 50,615 (2001 est.)
Military expenditures - dollar figure: $4 million (FY96)
Military expenditures - percent of GDP: 1.8% (FY96)

Transnational Issues

Disputes - international: none
Illicit drugs: used as a transshipment point for illicit drugs moving from Latin America and Africa destined for Western Europe

Cayman Islands
(overseas territory of the UK)

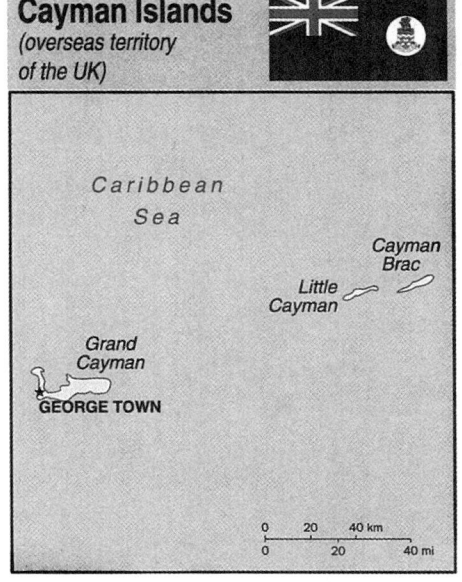

Introduction

Background: The Cayman Islands were colonized from Jamaica by the British during the 18th and 19th centuries. Administered by Jamaica from 1863, they remained a British dependency after 1962 when the former became independent.

Geography

Location: Caribbean, island group in Caribbean Sea, nearly one-half of the way from Cuba to Honduras
Geographic coordinates: 19 30 N, 80 30 W
Map references: Central America and the Caribbean
Area:
total: 259 sq km
land: 259 sq km
water: 0 sq km
Area - comparative: 1.5 times the size of Washington, DC
Land boundaries: 0 km
Coastline: 160 km
Maritime claims:
exclusive fishing zone: 200 NM
territorial sea: 12 NM
Climate: tropical marine; warm, rainy summers (May to October) and cool, relatively dry winters (November to April)
Terrain: low-lying limestone base surrounded by coral reefs
Elevation extremes:
lowest point: Caribbean Sea 0 m
highest point: The Bluff 43 m
Natural resources: fish, climate and beaches that foster tourism
Land use:
arable land: 0%
permanent crops: 0%
permanent pastures: 8%
forests and woodland: 23%
other: 69% (1993 est.)
Irrigated land: NA sq km
Natural hazards: hurricanes (July to November)
Environment - current issues: no natural fresh water resources; drinking water supplies must be met by rainwater catchment
Geography - note: important location between Cuba and Central America

People

Population: 35,527 (July 2001 est.)
Age structure:
0-14 years: 22.21% (male 3,807; female 4,084)
15-64 years: 69.74% (male 12,102; female 12,676)
65 years and over: 8.05% (male 1,318; female 1,540) (2001 est.)
Population growth rate: 2.12% (2001 est.)
Birth rate: 13.79 births/1,000 population (2001 est.)
Death rate: 5.15 deaths/1,000 population (2001 est.)
Net migration rate: 12.58 migrant(s)/1,000 population (2001 est.)
note: major destination for Cubans trying to migrate to the US
Sex ratio:
at birth: 0.86 male(s)/female
under 15 years: 0.93 male(s)/female
15-64 years: 0.95 male(s)/female
65 years and over: 0.86 male(s)/female
total population: 0.94 male(s)/female (2001 est.)
Infant mortality rate: 10.16 deaths/1,000 live births (2001 est.)
Life expectancy at birth:
total population: 79.03 years
male: 76.24 years
female: 81.43 years (2001 est.)
Total fertility rate: 2.04 children born/woman (2001 est.)
HIV/AIDS - adult prevalence rate: NA%
HIV/AIDS - people living with HIV/AIDS: NA
HIV/AIDS - deaths: NA
Nationality:
noun: Caymanian(s)
adjective: Caymanian
Ethnic groups: mixed 40%, white 20%, black 20%, expatriates of various ethnic groups 20%
Religions: United Church (Presbyterian and Congregational), Anglican, Baptist, Roman Catholic, Church of God, other Protestant
Languages: English
Literacy:
definition: age 15 and over has ever attended school
total population: 98%
male: 98%
female: 98% (1970 est.)

Government

Country name:
conventional long form: none
conventional short form: Cayman Islands
Dependency status: overseas territory of the UK
Government type: British crown colony
Capital: George Town
Administrative divisions: 8 districts; Creek, Eastern, Midland, South Town, Spot Bay, Stake Bay, West End, Western
Independence: none (overseas territory of the UK)
National holiday: Constitution Day, first Monday in July
Constitution: 1959, revised 1972 and 1992
Legal system: British common law and local statutes
Suffrage: 18 years of age; universal
Executive branch:
chief of state: Queen ELIZABETH II (since 6 February 1952); Governor and President of the Executive Council Peter SMITH (since 5 May 1999)
head of government: Kurt TIBBETTS (since November 2000)
cabinet: Executive Council (three members appointed by the governor, four members elected by the Legislative Assembly)
elections: none; the monarch is hereditary; the governor is appointed by the monarch
Legislative branch: unicameral Legislative Assembly (18 seats, three appointed members and 15 elected by popular vote; members serve four-year terms)
elections: last held 8 November 2000 (next to be held NA November 2004)
election results: percent of vote - NA%; seats - NA
Judicial branch: Summary Court; Grand Court; Cayman Islands Court of Appeal
Political parties and leaders: there are no formal political parties but the following loose groupings act as political organizations; National Team; Democratic Alliance; Team Cayman
Political pressure groups and leaders: NA
International organization participation: Caricom (observer), CDB, Interpol (subbureau), IOC, UNESCO (associate)
Diplomatic representation in the US: none (overseas territory of the UK)
Diplomatic representation from the US: none (overseas territory of the UK)
Flag description: blue, with the flag of the UK in the upper hoist-side quadrant and the Caymanian coat of arms on a white disk centered on the outer half of the flag; the coat of arms includes a pineapple and turtle above a shield with three stars (representing the three islands) and a scroll at the bottom bearing the motto HE HATH FOUNDED IT UPON THE SEAS

Economy

Economy - overview: With no direct taxation, the islands are a thriving offshore financial center. More than 40,000 companies were registered in the Cayman Islands as of 1997, including almost 600 banks and trust companies; banking assets exceed $500 billion. A stock exchange was opened in 1997. Tourism is also a mainstay, accounting for about 70% of GDP and 75% of foreign currency earnings. The tourist industry is aimed at the luxury market and caters mainly to visitors from North America. Total

Cayman Islands (continued)

tourist arrivals exceeded 1.2 million visitors in 1997. About 90% of the islands' food and consumer goods must be imported. The Caymanians enjoy one of the highest outputs per capita and one of the highest standards of living in the world.
GDP: purchasing power parity - $930 million (1997 est.)
GDP - real growth rate: 4.9% (1999 est.)
GDP - per capita: purchasing power parity - $24,500 (1997 est.)
GDP - composition by sector:
agriculture: 1.4%
industry: 3.2%
services: 95.4% (1994 est.)
Population below poverty line: NA%
Household income or consumption by percentage share:
lowest 10%: NA%
highest 10%: NA%
Inflation rate (consumer prices): 3% (1998)
Labor force: 19,820 (1995)
Labor force - by occupation: agriculture 1.4%, industry 12.6%, services 86% (1995)
Unemployment rate: 4.1% (1997)
Budget:
revenues: $265.2 million
expenditures: $248.9 million, including capital expenditures of $NA (1997)
Industries: tourism, banking, insurance and finance, construction, construction materials, furniture
Industrial production growth rate: NA%
Electricity - production: 330 million kWh (1999)
Electricity - production by source:
fossil fuel: 100%
hydro: 0%
nuclear: 0%
other: 0% (1999)
Electricity - consumption: 306.9 million kWh (1999)
Electricity - exports: 0 kWh (1999)
Electricity - imports: 0 kWh (1999)
Agriculture - products: vegetables, fruit; livestock, turtle farming
Exports: $1.5 million (1998)
Exports - commodities: turtle products, manufactured consumer goods
Exports - partners: mostly US
Imports: $507.6 million (1998)
Imports - commodities: foodstuffs, manufactured goods
Imports - partners: US, Trinidad and Tobago, UK, Netherlands Antilles, Japan
Debt - external: $70 million (1996)
Economic aid - recipient: $NA
Currency: Caymanian dollar (KYD)
Currency code: KYD
Exchange rates: Caymanian dollars per US dollar - 0.83 (3 November 1995), 0.85 (22 November 1993)
Fiscal year: 1 April - 31 March

Communications

Telephones - main lines in use: 19,000 (1995)
Telephones - mobile cellular: 2,534 (1995)
Telephone system:
general assessment: NA
domestic: NA
international: 1 submarine coaxial cable; satellite earth station - 1 Intelsat (Atlantic Ocean)
Radio broadcast stations: AM 1, FM 5, shortwave 0 (1998)
Radios: 36,000 (1997)
Television broadcast stations: NA
Televisions: 7,000 (1997)
Internet country code: .ky
Internet Service Providers (ISPs): 16 (2000)
Internet users: NA

Transportation

Railways: 0 km
Highways:
total: 406 km
paved: 304 km
unpaved: 102 km
Waterways: none
Ports and harbors: Cayman Brac, George Town
Merchant marine:
total: 106 ships (1,000 GRT or over) totaling 1,656,452 GRT/2,643,036 DWT
ships by type: bulk 21, cargo 5, chemical tanker 27, container 4, liquefied gas 1, petroleum tanker 13, refrigerated cargo 30, roll on/roll off 4, specialized tanker 1
note: includes some foreign-owned ships registered here as a flag of convenience: Cyprus 2, Denmark 2, Finland 1, Greece 11, Norway 3, UK 3, US 3 (2000 est.)
Airports: 3 (2000 est.)
Airports - with paved runways:
total: 2
1,524 to 2,437 m: 2 (2000 est.)
Airports - with unpaved runways:
total: 1
914 to 1,523 m: 1 (2000 est.)

Military

Military branches: Royal Cayman Islands Police Force (RCIPF)
Military - note: defense is the responsibility of the UK

Transnational Issues

Disputes - international: none
Illicit drugs: vulnerable to drug money laundering and drug transshipment to the US and Europe

Central African Republic

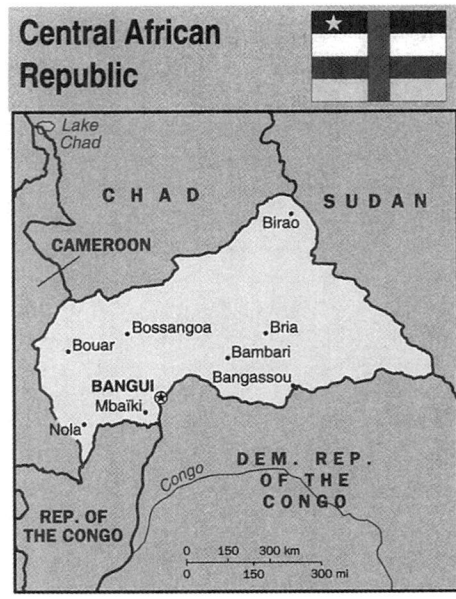

Introduction

Background: The former French colony of Ubangi-Shari became the Central African Republic upon independence in 1960. After three tumultuous decades of misrule - mostly by military governments - a civilian government was installed in 1993.

Geography

Location: Central Africa, north of Democratic Republic of the Congo
Geographic coordinates: 7 00 N, 21 00 E
Map references: Africa
Area:
total: 622,984 sq km
land: 622,984 sq km
water: 0 sq km
Area - comparative: slightly smaller than Texas
Land boundaries:
total: 5,203 km
border countries: Cameroon 797 km, Chad 1,197 km, Democratic Republic of the Congo 1,577 km, Republic of the Congo 467 km, Sudan 1,165 km
Coastline: 0 km (landlocked)
Maritime claims: none (landlocked)
Climate: tropical; hot, dry winters; mild to hot, wet summers
Terrain: vast, flat to rolling, monotonous plateau; scattered hills in northeast and southwest
Elevation extremes:
lowest point: Oubangui River 335 m
highest point: Mont Ngaoui 1,420 m
Natural resources: diamonds, uranium, timber, gold, oil, hydropower
Land use:
arable land: 3%
permanent crops: 0%
permanent pastures: 5%
forests and woodland: 75%
other: 17% (1993 est.)
Irrigated land: NA sq km

Central African Republic (continued)

Natural hazards: hot, dry, dusty harmattan winds affect northern areas; floods are common
Environment - current issues: tap water is not potable; poaching has diminished its reputation as one of the last great wildlife refuges; desertification; deforestation
Environment - international agreements:
party to: Biodiversity, Climate Change, Desertification, Endangered Species, Marine Dumping, Nuclear Test Ban, Ozone Layer Protection, Ship Pollution, Tropical Timber 94
signed, but not ratified: Law of the Sea
Geography - note: landlocked; almost the precise center of Africa

People

Population: 3,576,884
note: estimates for this country explicitly take into account the effects of excess mortality due to AIDS; this can result in lower life expectancy, higher infant mortality and death rates, lower population and growth rates, and changes in the distribution of population by age and sex than would otherwise be expected (July 2001 est.)
Age structure:
0-14 years: 43.23% (male 778,885; female 767,414)
15-64 years: 53% (male 929,717; female 965,947)
65 years and over: 3.77% (male 59,364; female 75,557) (2001 est.)
Population growth rate: 1.85% (2001 est.)
Birth rate: 37.05 births/1,000 population (2001 est.)
Death rate: 18.53 deaths/1,000 population (2001 est.)
Net migration rate: 0 migrant(s)/1,000 population (2001 est.)
Sex ratio:
at birth: 1.03 male(s)/female
under 15 years: 1.01 male(s)/female
15-64 years: 0.96 male(s)/female
65 years and over: 0.79 male(s)/female
total population: 0.98 male(s)/female (2001 est.)
Infant mortality rate: 105.25 deaths/1,000 live births (2001 est.)
Life expectancy at birth:
total population: 43.8 years
male: 42.17 years
female: 45.48 years (2001 est.)
Total fertility rate: 4.86 children born/woman (2001 est.)
HIV/AIDS - adult prevalence rate: 13.84% (1999 est.)
HIV/AIDS - people living with HIV/AIDS: 240,000 (1999 est.)
HIV/AIDS - deaths: 23,000 (1999 est.)
Nationality:
noun: Central African(s)
adjective: Central African
Ethnic groups: Baya 34%, Banda 27%, Sara 10%, Mandjia 21%, Mboum 4%, M'Baka 4%, Europeans 6,500 (including 1,500 French)
Religions: indigenous beliefs 24%, Protestant 25%, Roman Catholic 25%, Muslim 15%, other 11%
note: animistic beliefs and practices strongly influence the Christian majority
Languages: French (official), Sangho (lingua franca and national language), Arabic, Hunsa, Swahili
Literacy:
definition: age 15 and over can read and write
total population: 60%
male: 68.5%
female: 52.4% (1995 est.)

Government

Country name:
conventional long form: Central African Republic
conventional short form: none
local long form: Republique Centrafricaine
local short form: none
former: Ubangi-Shari, Central African Empire
abbreviation: CAR
Government type: republic
Capital: Bangui
Administrative divisions: 14 prefectures (prefectures, singular - prefecture), 2 economic prefectures* (prefectures economiques, singular - prefecture economique), and 1 commune**; Bamingui-Bangoran, Bangui**, Basse-Kotto, Gribingui*, Haute-Kotto, Haute-Sangha, Haut-Mbomou, Kemo-Gribingui, Lobaye, Mbomou, Nana-Mambere, Ombella-Mpoko, Ouaka, Ouham, Ouham-Pende, Sangha*, Vakaga
Independence: 13 August 1960 (from France)
National holiday: Republic Day, 1 December (1958)
Constitution: passed by referendum 29 December 1994; adopted 7 January 1995
Legal system: based on French law
Suffrage: 21 years of age; universal
Executive branch:
chief of state: President Ange-Felix PATASSE (since 22 October 1993)
head of government: Prime Minister Martin ZIGUELE (since 1 April 2001)
cabinet: Council of Ministers
elections: president elected by popular vote for a six-year term; election last held 19 September 1999 (next to be held NA 2005); prime minister appointed by the president
election results: Ange-Felix PATASSE reelected president; percent of vote - Ange-Felix PATASSE 51.63%, Andre KOLINGBA 19.38%, David DACKO 11.15%
Legislative branch: unicameral National Assembly or Assemblee Nationale (109 seats; members are elected by popular vote to serve five-year terms; note - there were 85 seats in the National Assembly before the 1998 election)
elections: last held 22-23 November and 13 December 1998 (next to be held NA 2003)
election results: percent of vote by party - MLPC 43%, RDC 18%, MDD 9%, FPP 6%, PSD 5%, ADP 4%, PUN 3%, FODEM 2%, PLD 2%, UPR 1%, FC 1%, independents 6%; seats by party - MLPC 47, RDC 20, MDD 8, FPP 7, PSD 6, ADP 5, PUN 3, FODEM 2, PLD 2, UPR 1, FC 1, independents 7
note: the National Assembly is advised by the Economic and Regional Council or Conseil Economique et Regional; when they sit together they are called the Congress or Congres
Judicial branch: Supreme Court or Cour Supreme; Constitutional Court (all judges appointed by the president); Court of Appeal; Criminal Courts
Political parties and leaders: Alliance for Democracy and Progress or ADP [Francois PEHOUA]; Central African Democratic Assembly or RDC [Andre KOLINGBA]; Civic Forum or FC [Gen. Timothee MALENDOMA]; Democratic Forum or FODEM [Charles MASSI]; Liberal Democratic Party or PLD [Nestor KOMBO-NAGUEMON]; Movement for Democracy and Development or MDD [David DACKO]; Movement for the Liberation of the Central African People or MLPC [the party of the president, Ange-Felix PATASSE]; Patriotic Front for Progress or FPP [Abel GOUMBA]; People's Union for the Republic or UPR [leader NA]; National Unity Party or PUN [Jean-Paul NGOUPANDE]; Social Democratic Party or PSD [Enoch LAKOUE]
Political pressure groups and leaders: NA
International organization participation: ACCT, ACP, AfDB, BDEAC, CCC, CEEAC, CEMAC, ECA, FAO, FZ, G-77, IBRD, ICAO, ICFTU, ICRM, IDA, IFAD, IFC, IFRCS, ILO, IMF, Intelsat, Interpol, IOC, ITU, NAM, OAU, OIC (observer), OPCW, UN, UNCTAD, UNESCO, UNIDO, UPU, WCL, WHO, WIPO, WMO, WToO, WTrO
Diplomatic representation in the US:
chief of mission: Ambassador Emmanuel TOUABOY
chancery: 1618 22nd Street NW, Washington, DC 20008
telephone: [1] (202) 483-7800
FAX: [1] (202) 332-9893
Diplomatic representation from the US:
chief of mission: Ambassador Robert C. PERRY
embassy: Avenue David Dacko, Bangui
mailing address: B. P. 924, Bangui
telephone: [236] 61 02 00
FAX: [236] 61 44 94
Flag description: four equal horizontal bands of blue (top), white, green, and yellow with a vertical red band in center; there is a yellow five-pointed star on the hoist side of the blue band

Economy

Economy - overview: Subsistence agriculture, together with forestry, remains the backbone of the economy of the Central African Republic (CAR), with more than 70% of the population living in outlying areas. The agricultural sector generates half of GDP. Timber has accounted for about 16% of export earnings and the diamond industry for nearly 54%. Important constraints to economic development include the CAR's landlocked position, a poor transportation system, a largely unskilled work force, and a legacy of misdirected macroeconomic policies. The 50% devaluation of the currencies of 14 Francophone African nations on 12 January 1994 had mixed effects on the CAR's economy. Diamond,

Central African Republic (continued)

timber, coffee, and cotton exports increased, leading an estimated rise of GDP of 7% in 1994 and nearly 5% in 1995. Military rebellions and social unrest in 1996 were accompanied by widespread destruction of property and a drop in GDP of 2%. The IMF approved an Extended Structure Adjustment Facility in 1998 and the World Bank extended further credits in 1999 and approved a $10 million loan in early 2001. The government has set targets of 3.5% GDP growth in 2001 and 2002. As of January 2001, many civil servants were owed as much as 30 months pay, leading them to go on strike and further damaging the economy.

GDP: purchasing power parity - $6.1 billion (2000 est.)
GDP - real growth rate: 3.5% (2000 est.)
GDP - per capita: purchasing power parity - $1,700 (2000 est.)
GDP - composition by sector:
agriculture: 53%
industry: 20%
services: 27% (1999 est.)
Population below poverty line: NA%
Household income or consumption by percentage share:
lowest 10%: 0.7%
highest 10%: 47.7% (1993)
Inflation rate (consumer prices): 3% (2000 est.)
Labor force: NA
Unemployment rate: 6% (1993)
Budget:
revenues: $638 million
expenditures: $1.9 billion, including capital expenditures of $888 million (1994 est.)
Industries: diamond mining, sawmills, breweries, textiles, footwear, assembly of bicycles and motorcycles
Industrial production growth rate: NA%
Electricity - production: 102 million kWh (1999)
Electricity - production by source:
fossil fuel: 20.59%
hydro: 79.41%
nuclear: 0%
other: 0% (1999)
Electricity - consumption: 94.9 million kWh (1999)
Electricity - exports: 0 kWh (1999)
Electricity - imports: 0 kWh (1999)
Agriculture - products: cotton, coffee, tobacco, manioc (tapioca), yams, millet, corn, bananas; timber
Exports: $166 million (f.o.b., 2000)
Exports - commodities: diamonds, timber, cotton, coffee, tobacco
Exports - partners: Benelux 64%, Cote d'Ivoire, Spain, China, Egypt, France (1999)
Imports: $154 million (f.o.b., 2000)
Imports - commodities: food, textiles, petroleum products, machinery, electrical equipment, motor vehicles, chemicals, pharmaceuticals, consumer goods, industrial products
Imports - partners: France 35%, Cameroon 13%, Benelux, Cote d'Ivoire, Germany, Japan (1999)
Debt - external: $790 million (1999 est.)
Economic aid - recipient: $172.2 million (1995); note - traditional budget subsidies from France
Currency: Communaute Financiere Africaine franc (XAF); note - responsible authority is the Bank of the Central African States
Currency code: XAF
Exchange rates: Communaute Financiere Africaine francs (XAF) per US dollar - 699.21 (January 2001), 711.98 (2000), 615.70 (1999), 589.95 (1998), 583.67 (1997), 511.55 (1996); note - from 1 January 1999, the XAF is pegged to the euro at a rate of 655.957 XAF per euro
Fiscal year: calendar year

Communications

Telephones - main lines in use: 10,000 (1997)
Telephones - mobile cellular: 570 (1997)
Telephone system:
general assessment: fair system
domestic: network consists principally of microwave radio relay and low-capacity, low-powered radiotelephone communication
international: satellite earth station - 1 Intelsat (Atlantic Ocean)
Radio broadcast stations: AM 1, FM 3, shortwave 1 (1998)
Radios: 283,000 (1997)
Television broadcast stations: NA
Televisions: 18,000 (1997)
Internet country code: .cf
Internet Service Providers (ISPs): 1 (2000)
Internet users: 1,000 (2000)

Transportation

Railways: 0 km
Highways:
total: 23,810 km
paved: 429 km
unpaved: 23,381 km (1998 est.)
Waterways: 900 km
note: traditional trade carried on by means of shallow-draft dugouts; Oubangui is the most important river, navigable all year to craft drawing 0.6 m or less; 282 km navigable to craft drawing as much as 1.8 m
Ports and harbors: Bangui, Nola
Airports: 52 (2000 est.)
Airports - with paved runways:
total: 3
2,438 to 3,047 m: 1
1,524 to 2,437 m: 2 (2000 est.)
Airports - with unpaved runways:
total: 49
2,438 to 3,047 m: 1
1,524 to 2,437 m: 10
914 to 1,523 m: 23
under 914 m: 15 (2000 est.)

Military

Military branches: Central African Armed Forces (includes Army, Air Force, Presidential Guard, National Gendarmerie, Police Force)
Military manpower - availability:
males age 15-49: 824,139 (2001 est.)
Military manpower - fit for military service:
males age 15-49: 430,922 (2001 est.)
Military expenditures - dollar figure: $29 million (FY96)
Military expenditures - percent of GDP: 2.2% (FY96)

Transnational Issues

Disputes - international: none

Chad

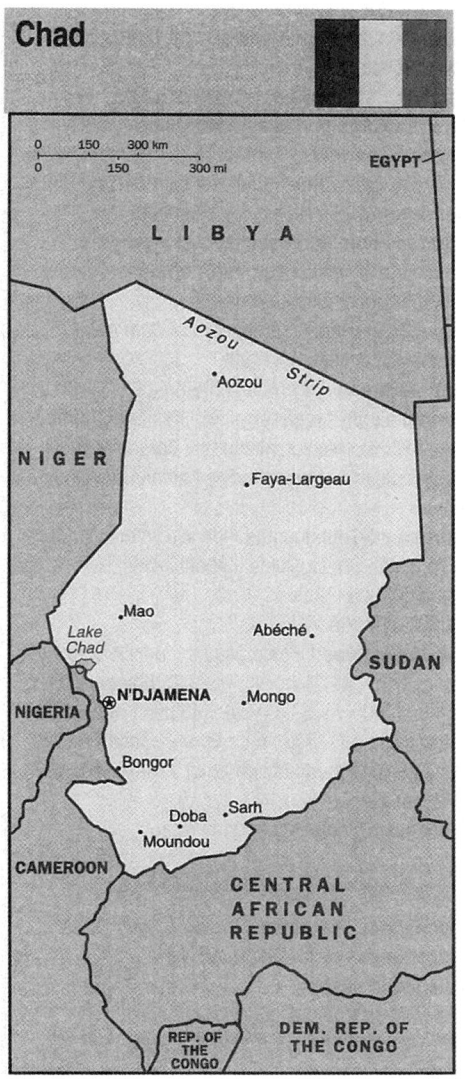

Introduction

Background: Chad, part of France's African holdings until 1960, endured three decades of ethnic warfare as well as invasions by Libya before a semblance of peace was finally restored in 1990. The government eventually suppressed or came to terms with most political-military groups, settled a territorial dispute with Libya on terms favorable to Chad, drafted a democratic constitution, and held multiparty presidential and National Assembly elections in 1996 and 1997 respectively. In 1998 a new rebellion broke out in northern Chad, which continued to escalate throughout 2000. Despite movement toward democratic reform, power remains in the hands of a northern ethnic oligarchy.

Geography

Location: Central Africa, south of Libya
Geographic coordinates: 15 00 N, 19 00 E
Map references: Africa
Area:
total: 1.284 million sq km
land: 1,259,200 sq km
water: 24,800 sq km
Area - comparative: slightly more than three times the size of California
Land boundaries:
total: 5,968 km
border countries: Cameroon 1,094 km, Central African Republic 1,197 km, Libya 1,055 km, Niger 1,175 km, Nigeria 87 km, Sudan 1,360 km
Coastline: 0 km (landlocked)
Maritime claims: none (landlocked)
Climate: tropical in south, desert in north
Terrain: broad, arid plains in center, desert in north, mountains in northwest, lowlands in south
Elevation extremes:
lowest point: Djourab Depression 160 m
highest point: Emi Koussi 3,415 m
Natural resources: petroleum (unexploited but exploration under way), uranium, natron, kaolin, fish (Lake Chad)
Land use:
arable land: 3%
permanent crops: 0%
permanent pastures: 36%
forests and woodland: 26%
other: 35% (1993 est.)
Irrigated land: 140 sq km (1993 est.)
Natural hazards: hot, dry, dusty harmattan winds occur in north; periodic droughts; locust plagues
Environment - current issues: inadequate supplies of potable water; improper waste disposal in rural areas contributes to soil and water pollution; desertification
Environment - international agreements:
party to: Biodiversity, Climate Change, Desertification, Endangered Species, Marine Dumping, Nuclear Test Ban, Ozone Layer Protection, Ship Pollution, Wetlands
signed, but not ratified: Law of the Sea, Marine Dumping
Geography - note: landlocked; Lake Chad is the most significant water body in the Sahel

People

Population: 8,707,078 (July 2001 est.)
Age structure:
0-14 years: 47.73% (male 2,091,724; female 2,064,514)
15-64 years: 49.46% (male 2,035,099; female 2,271,389)
65 years and over: 2.81% (male 101,579; female 142,773) (2001 est.)
Population growth rate: 3.29% (2001 est.)
Birth rate: 48.28 births/1,000 population (2001 est.)
Death rate: 15.4 deaths/1,000 population (2001 est.)
Net migration rate: 0 migrant(s)/1,000 population (2001 est.)
Sex ratio:
at birth: 1.04 male(s)/female
under 15 years: 1.01 male(s)/female
15-64 years: 0.9 male(s)/female
65 years and over: 0.71 male(s)/female
total population: 0.94 male(s)/female (2001 est.)
Infant mortality rate: 95.06 deaths/1,000 live births (2001 est.)
Life expectancy at birth:
total population: 50.88 years
male: 48.86 years
female: 52.98 years (2001 est.)
Total fertility rate: 6.56 children born/woman (2001 est.)
HIV/AIDS - adult prevalence rate: 2.69% (1999 est.)
HIV/AIDS - people living with HIV/AIDS: 92,000 (1999 est.)
HIV/AIDS - deaths: 10,000 (1999 est.)
Nationality:
noun: Chadian(s)
adjective: Chadian
Ethnic groups: Muslims, commonly referred to as "northerners" or "gorane" (Arabs, Toubou, Hadjerai, Fulbe, Kotoko, Kanembou, Baguirmi, Boulala, Zaghawa, and Maba); non-Muslims, commonly referred to as "southerners" (Sara, Ngambaye, Mbaye, Goulaye, Moundang, Moussei, Massa) including nonindigenous 150,000 (of whom 1,000 are French)
note: ethnicity and regional background more commonly used to identify Chadians than religious affiliation
Religions: Muslim 50%, Christian 25%, indigenous beliefs (mostly animism) 25%
Languages: French (official), Arabic (official), Sara and Sango (in south), more than 100 different languages and dialects
Literacy:
definition: age 15 and over can read and write French or Arabic
total population: 48.1%
male: 62.1%
female: 34.7% (1995 est.)

Government

Country name:
conventional long form: Republic of Chad
conventional short form: Chad
local long form: Republique du Tchad
local short form: Tchad
Government type: republic
Capital: N'Djamena
Administrative divisions: 14 prefectures (prefectures, singular - prefecture); Batha, Biltine, Borkou-Ennedi-Tibesti, Chari-Baguirmi, Guera, Kanem, Lac, Logone Occidental, Logone Oriental, Mayo-Kebbi, Moyen-Chari, Ouaddai, Salamat, Tandjile
Independence: 11 August 1960 (from France)
National holiday: Independence Day, 11 August (1960)
Constitution: passed by referendum 31 March 1995
Legal system: based on French civil law system and Chadian customary law; has not accepted compulsory ICJ jurisdiction
Suffrage: 18 years of age; universal

Chad (continued)

Executive branch:
chief of state: President Lt. Gen. Idriss DEBY (since 4 December 1990)
head of government: Prime Minister Nagoum YAMASSOUM (since 13 December 1999)
cabinet: Council of State, members appointed by the president on the recommendation of the prime minister
elections: president elected by popular vote to serve five-year term; if no candidate receives at least 50% of the total vote, the two candidates receiving the most votes must stand for a second round of voting; last held 20 May 2001 (next to be held NA 2006); prime minister appointed by the president
election results: Lt. Gen. Idriss DEBY elected president; percent of vote - Lt. Gen. Idriss DEBY 63%, Ngarlegy YORONGAR 16%, Saleh KEBZABO 7%
note: government coalition - MPS, UNDR, and URD
Legislative branch: unicameral National Assembly (125 seats; members elected by popular vote to serve four-year terms); replaces the Higher Transitional Council or the Conseil Superieur de Transition
elections: National Assembly - last held in two rounds on 5 January and 23 February 1997 (next to be held in late 2001); in the first round of voting some candidates won clear victories by receiving 50% or more of the vote; where that did not happen, the two highest scoring candidates stood for a second round of voting
election results: percent of vote by party - NA%; seats by party - MPS 65, URD 29, UNDR 15, RDP 3, others 13
Judicial branch: Supreme Court; Court of Appeal; Criminal Courts; Magistrate Courts
Political parties and leaders: National Union for Development and Renewal or UNDR [Saleh KEBZABO]; Patriotic Salvation Movement or MPS [Mahamat Saleh AHMAT, chairman] (originally in opposition but now the party in power and the party of the president); Rally for Democracy and Progress or RDP [Lal Mahamat CHOUA]; Union for Renewal and Democracy or URD [Gen. Wadal Abdelkader KAMOUGUE]
Political pressure groups and leaders: NA
International organization participation: ACCT, ACP, AfDB, BDEAC, CEEAC, CEMAC, ECA, FAO, FZ, G-77, IBRD, ICAO, ICFTU, ICRM, IDA, IDB, IFAD, IFC, IFRCS, ILO, IMF, Intelsat, Interpol, IOC, ITU, NAM, OAU, OIC, OPCW, UN, UNCTAD, UNESCO, UNIDO, UPU, WCL, WHO, WIPO, WMO, WToO, WTrO
Diplomatic representation in the US:
chief of mission: Ambassador Hassaballah Abdelhadi Ahmat SOUBIANE
chancery: 2002 R Street NW, Washington, DC 20009
telephone: [1] (202) 462-4009
FAX: [1] (202) 265-1937
Diplomatic representation from the US:
chief of mission: Ambassador Christopher E. GOLDTHWAIT
embassy: Avenue Felix Eboue, N'Djamena
mailing address: B. P. 413, N'Djamena
telephone: [235] (51) 70-09, (51) 90-52, (51) 92-33
FAX: [235] (51) 56-54
Flag description: three equal vertical bands of blue (hoist side), yellow, and red; similar to the flag of Romania; also similar to the flags of Andorra and Moldova, both of which have a national coat of arms centered in the yellow band; design was based on the flag of France

Economy

Economy - overview: Landlocked Chad's economic development suffers from its geographic remoteness, drought, lack of infrastructure, and political turmoil. About 85% of the population depends on agriculture, including the herding of livestock. Of Africa's Francophone countries, Chad benefited least from the 50% devaluation of their currencies in January 1994. Financial aid from the World Bank, the African Development Fund, and other sources is directed largely at the improvement of agriculture, especially livestock production. The World Bank's decision to back the Doba oil field development and the Chad-Cameroon pipeline will add Chad to the group of already booming West African oil exporters. However, the rank and file may not benefit much from the oil development projects.
GDP: purchasing power parity - $8.1 billion (2000 est.)
GDP - real growth rate: 4% (2000 est.)
GDP - per capita: purchasing power parity - $1,000 (2000 est.)
GDP - composition by sector:
agriculture: 40%
industry: 14%
services: 46% (1998)
Population below poverty line: 64% (1995 est.)
Household income or consumption by percentage share:
lowest 10%: NA%
highest 10%: NA%
Inflation rate (consumer prices): 3% (2000 est.)
Labor force: NA
Labor force - by occupation: agriculture 85% (subsistence farming, herding, and fishing)
Unemployment rate: NA%
Budget:
revenues: $198 million
expenditures: $218 million, including capital expenditures of $146 million (1998 est.)
Industries: cotton textiles, meatpacking, beer brewing, natron (sodium carbonate), soap, cigarettes, construction materials
Industrial production growth rate: 5% (1995)
Electricity - production: 90 million kWh (1999)
Electricity - production by source:
fossil fuel: 100%
hydro: 0%
nuclear: 0%
other: 0% (1999)
Electricity - consumption: 83.7 million kWh (1999)
Electricity - exports: 0 kWh (1999)
Electricity - imports: 0 kWh (1999)
Agriculture - products: cotton, sorghum, millet, peanuts, rice, potatoes, manioc (tapioca); cattle, sheep, goats, camels
Exports: $172 million (f.o.b., 2000 est.)
Exports - commodities: cotton, cattle, textiles
Exports - partners: Portugal 38%, Germany 12%, Thailand, Costa Rica, South Africa, France (1999)
Imports: $223 million (f.o.b., 2000 est.)
Imports - commodities: machinery and transportation equipment, industrial goods, petroleum products, foodstuffs, textiles
Imports - partners: France 40%, Cameroon 13%, Nigeria 12%, India 5% (1999)
Debt - external: $1 billion (1999 est.)
Economic aid - recipient: $238.3 million (1995); note - $125 million committed by Taiwan (August 1997); $30 million committed by African Development Bank
Currency: Communaute Financiere Africaine franc (XAF); note - responsible authority is the Bank of the Central African States
Currency code: XAF
Exchange rates: Communaute Financiere Africaine francs (XAF) per US dollar - 699.21 (January 2001), 711.98 (2000), 615.70 (1999), 589.95 (1998), 583.67 (1997), 511.55 (1996); note - from 1 January 1999, the XAF is pegged to the euro at a rate of 655.957 XAF per euro
Fiscal year: calendar year

Communications

Telephones - main lines in use: 7,000 (1997)
Telephones - mobile cellular: NA
Telephone system:
general assessment: primitive system
domestic: fair system of radiotelephone communication stations
international: satellite earth station - 1 Intelsat (Atlantic Ocean)
Radio broadcast stations: AM 2, FM 3, shortwave 5 (1998)
Radios: 1.67 million (1997)
Television broadcast stations: 1 (1997)
Televisions: 10,000 (1997)
Internet country code: .td
Internet Service Providers (ISPs): 1 (2000)
Internet users: 1,000 (2000)

Transportation

Railways: 0 km
Highways:
total: 33,400 km
paved: 267 km
unpaved: 33,133 km (1996)
Waterways: 2,000 km
Ports and harbors: none
Airports: 50 (2000 est.)
Airports - with paved runways:
total: 7
over 3,047 m: 2
2,438 to 3,047 m: 3

Chad (continued)

1,524 to 2,437 m: 1
under 914 m: 1 (2000 est.)
Airports - with unpaved runways:
total: 43
1,524 to 2,437 m: 12
914 to 1,523 m: 20
under 914 m: 11 (2000 est.)

Military

Military branches: Armed Forces (includes Ground Force, Air Force, and Gendarmerie), Republican Guard, Rapid Intervention Force, Police, Rural and Nomadic Guard (GNNT)
Military manpower - military age: 20 years of age
Military manpower - availability:
males age 15-49: 1,814,578 (2001 est.)
Military manpower - fit for military service:
males age 15-49: 949,997 (2001 est.)
Military manpower - reaching military age annually:
males: 82,003 (2001 est.)
Military expenditures - dollar figure: $39 million (FY96)
Military expenditures - percent of GDP: 3.5% (FY96)

Transnational Issues

Disputes - international: delimitation of international boundaries in the vicinity of Lake Chad, the lack of which led to border incidents in the past, has been completed and awaits ratification by Cameroon, Chad, Niger, and Nigeria

Chile

Introduction

Background: A three-year-old Marxist government was overthrown in 1973 by a dictatorial military regime led by Augusto PINOCHET, which ruled until a freely elected president was installed in 1990. Sound economic policies, first implemented by the PINOCHET dictatorship, led to unprecedented growth in 1991-97 and have helped secure the country's commitment to democratic and representative government. Growth slowed in 1998-99, but recovered strongly in 2000.

Geography

Location: Southern South America, bordering the South Atlantic Ocean and South Pacific Ocean, between Argentina and Peru
Geographic coordinates: 30 00 S, 71 00 W
Map references: South America
Area:
total: 756,950 sq km
land: 748,800 sq km
water: 8,150 sq km
note: includes Easter Island (Isla de Pascua) and Isla Sala y Gomez
Area - comparative: slightly smaller than twice the size of Montana
Land boundaries:
total: 6,171 km
border countries: Argentina 5,150 km, Bolivia 861 km, Peru 160 km
Coastline: 6,435 km
Maritime claims:
contiguous zone: 24 NM
continental shelf: 200/350 NM
exclusive economic zone: 200 NM
territorial sea: 12 NM
Climate: temperate; desert in north; Mediterranean in central region; cool and damp in south
Terrain: low coastal mountains; fertile central valley; rugged Andes in east
Elevation extremes:
lowest point: Pacific Ocean 0 m
highest point: Nevado Ojos del Salado 6,880 m
Natural resources: copper, timber, iron ore, nitrates, precious metals, molybdenum, hydropower
Land use:
arable land: 5%
permanent crops: 0%
permanent pastures: 18%
forests and woodland: 22%
other: 55% (1993 est.)
Irrigated land: 12,650 sq km (1993 est.)
Natural hazards: severe earthquakes; active volcanism; tsunamis
Environment - current issues: air pollution from industrial and vehicle emissions; water pollution from raw sewage
Environment - international agreements:
party to: Antarctic-Environmental Protocol, Antarctic-Marine Living Resources, Antarctic Seals, Antarctic Treaty, Biodiversity, Climate Change, Desertification, Endangered Species, Environmental Modification, Hazardous Wastes, Law of the Sea, Marine Dumping, Ozone Layer Protection, Ship Pollution, Wetlands, Whaling
signed, but not ratified: Climate Change-Kyoto Protocol, Nuclear Test Ban
Geography - note: strategic location relative to sea lanes between Atlantic and Pacific Oceans (Strait of Magellan, Beagle Channel, Drake Passage); Atacama Desert is one of world's driest regions

People

Population: 15,328,467 (July 2001 est.)
Age structure:
0-14 years: 27.25% (male 2,135,755; female 2,041,552)
15-64 years: 65.39% (male 4,993,416; female 5,029,739)
65 years and over: 7.36% (male 467,477; female 660,528) (2001 est.)
Population growth rate: 1.13% (2001 est.)
Birth rate: 16.8 births/1,000 population (2001 est.)
Death rate: 5.55 deaths/1,000 population (2001 est.)

Chile (continued)

Net migration rate: 0 migrant(s)/1,000 population (2001 est.)
Sex ratio:
at birth: 1.05 male(s)/female
under 15 years: 1.05 male(s)/female
15-64 years: 0.99 male(s)/female
65 years and over: 0.71 male(s)/female
total population: 0.98 male(s)/female (2001 est.)
Infant mortality rate: 9.36 deaths/1,000 live births (2001 est.)
Life expectancy at birth:
total population: 75.94 years
male: 72.63 years
female: 79.42 years (2001 est.)
Total fertility rate: 2.16 children born/woman (2001 est.)
HIV/AIDS - adult prevalence rate: 0.19% (1999 est.)
HIV/AIDS - people living with HIV/AIDS: 15,000 (1999 est.)
HIV/AIDS - deaths: 1,000 (1999 est.)
Nationality:
noun: Chilean(s)
adjective: Chilean
Ethnic groups: white and white-Amerindian 95%, Amerindian 3%, other 2%
Religions: Roman Catholic 89%, Protestant 11%, Jewish NEGL%
Languages: Spanish
Literacy:
definition: age 15 and over can read and write
total population: 95.2%
male: 95.4%
female: 95% (1995 est.)

Government

Country name:
conventional long form: Republic of Chile
conventional short form: Chile
local long form: Republica de Chile
local short form: Chile
Government type: republic
Capital: Santiago
Administrative divisions: 13 regions (regiones, singular - region); Aisen del General Carlos Ibanez del Campo, Antofagasta, Araucania, Atacama, Bio-Bio, Coquimbo, Libertador General Bernardo O'Higgins, Los Lagos, Magallanes y de la Antartica Chilena, Maule, Region Metropolitana (Santiago), Tarapaca, Valparaiso
note: the US does not recognize claims to Antarctica
Independence: 18 September 1810 (from Spain)
National holiday: Independence Day, 18 September (1810)
Constitution: 11 September 1980, effective 11 March 1981, amended 30 July 1989, 1993, and 1997
Legal system: based on Code of 1857 derived from Spanish law and subsequent codes influenced by French and Austrian law; judicial review of legislative acts in the Supreme Court; has not accepted compulsory ICJ jurisdiction
Suffrage: 18 years of age; universal and compulsory
Executive branch:
chief of state: President Ricardo LAGOS Escobar (since 11 March 2000); note - the president is both the chief of state and head of government
head of government: President Ricardo LAGOS Escobar (since 11 March 2000); note - the president is both the chief of state and head of government
cabinet: Cabinet appointed by the president
elections: president elected by popular vote for a six-year term; election last held 12 December 1999, with runoff election held 16 January 2000 (next to be held NA December 2005)
election results: Ricardo LAGOS Escobar elected president; percent of vote - Ricardo LAGOS Escobar 51.32%, Joaquin LAVIN 48.68%
Legislative branch: bicameral National Congress or Congreso Nacional consists of the Senate or Senado (48 seats, 38 elected by popular vote and 10 appointed (all former presidents who served 6 years are senators for life); members serve eight-year terms - one-half elected every four years) and the Chamber of Deputies or Camara de Diputados (120 seats; members are elected by popular vote to serve four-year terms)
elections: Senate - last held 11 December 1997 (next to be held NA December 2001); Chamber of Deputies - last held 11 December 1997 (next to be held NA December 2001)
election results: Senate - percent of vote by party - NA%; seats by party - CPD (PDC 14, PS 4, PPD 2), RN 7, UDI 10, UCCP 1, independents 10; Chamber of Deputies - percent of vote by party - CPD 50.55% (PDC 22.98%, PS 11.10%, PPD 12.55%, PRSD 3.13%), RN 16.78%, UDI 14.43%; seats by party - CPD 70 (PDC 39, PPD 16, PRSD 4, PS 11), RN 24, UDI 21, Socialist Party 1, right-wing independents 4
Judicial branch: Supreme Court or Corte Suprema (judges are appointed by the president and ratified by the Senate from lists of candidates provided by the court itself; the president of the Supreme Court is elected by the 21-member court); Constitutional Tribunal
Political parties and leaders: Center-Center Union Party or UCCP [Francisco Javier ERRAZURIZ]; Christian Democratic Party or PDC [Ricardo HORMAZABAL]; Coalition of Parties for Democracy ("Concertacion") or CPD - including PDC, PS, PPD, PRSD; Independent Democratic Union or UDI [Pablo LONGUEIRA]; National Renewal or RN [Alberto CARDEMIL]; Party for Democracy or PPD [Guido GIRARDI]; Radical Social Democratic Party or PRSD [Anselmo SULE]; Socialist Party or PS [Ricardo NUNEZ]
Political pressure groups and leaders: revitalized university student federations at all major universities; Roman Catholic Church; United Labor Central or CUT includes trade unionists from the country's five largest labor confederations
International organization participation: APEC, CCC, ECLAC, FAO, G-11, G-77, IADB, IAEA, IBRD, ICAO, ICC, ICFTU, ICRM, IDA, IFAD, IFC, IFRCS, IHO, ILO, IMF, IMO, Inmarsat, Intelsat, Interpol, IOC, IOM, ISO, ITU, LAES, LAIA, Mercosur (associate), NAM, OAS, OPANAL, OPCW, PCA, RG, UN, UNCTAD, UNESCO, UNHCR, UNIDO, UNITAR, UNMIBH, UNMOGIP, UNTAET, UNTSO, UNU, UPU, WCL, WFTU, WHO, WIPO, WMO, WToO, WTrO
Diplomatic representation in the US:
chief of mission: Ambassador Andres BIANCHI
chancery: 1140 Connecticut Avenue NW, Washington, DC 20036
telephone: [1] (202) 785-1746
FAX: [1] (202) 887-5579
consulate(s) general: Chicago, Houston, Los Angeles, Miami, New York, Philadelphia, San Francisco, and San Juan (Puerto Rico)
Diplomatic representation from the US:
chief of mission: Ambassador John O'LEARY
embassy: Avenida Andres Bello 2800, Las Condes, Santiago
mailing address: APO AA 34033
telephone: [56] (2) 232-2600
FAX: [56] (2) 339-3710
Flag description: two equal horizontal bands of white (top) and red; there is a blue square the same height as the white band at the hoist-side end of the white band; the square bears a white five-pointed star in the center; design was based on the US flag

Economy

Economy - overview: Chile has a market-oriented economy characterized by a high level of foreign trade. During the early 1990s, Chile's reputation as a role model for economic reform was strengthened when the democratic government of Patricio AYLWIN - which took over from the military in 1990 - deepened the economic reform initiated by the military government. Growth in real GDP averaged 8% during 1991-97, but fell to half that level in 1998 because of tight monetary policies implemented to keep the current account deficit in check and lower export earnings - the latter a product of the global financial crisis. A severe drought exacerbated the recession in 1999, reducing crop yields and causing hydroelectric shortfalls and electricity rationing, and Chile experienced negative economic growth for the first time in more than 15 years. Despite the effects of the recession, Chile maintained its reputation for strong financial institutions and sound policy that have given it the strongest sovereign bond rating in South America. By the end of 1999, exports and economic activity had begun to recover, and growth rebounded to 5.5% in 2000. Unemployment remains stubbornly high, however, putting pressure on President LAGOS to improve living standards. Meanwhile, Chile has launched free trade negotiations with the US.
GDP: purchasing power parity - $153.1 billion (2000 est.)
GDP - real growth rate: 5.5% (2000 est.)
GDP - per capita: purchasing power parity - $10,100 (2000 est.)
GDP - composition by sector:
agriculture: 8%

Chile (continued)

industry: 38%
services: 54% (2000)
Population below poverty line: 22% (1998 est.)
Household income or consumption by percentage share:
lowest 10%: 1.2%
highest 10%: 41.3% (1998)
Inflation rate (consumer prices): 4.5% (2000 est.)
Labor force: 5.8 million (1999 est.)
Labor force - by occupation: agriculture 14%, industry 27%, services 59% (1997 est.)
Unemployment rate: 9% (December 2000)
Budget:
revenues: $16 billion
expenditures: $17 billion, including capital expenditures of $NA (2000 est.)
Industries: copper, other minerals, foodstuffs, fish processing, iron and steel, wood and wood products, transport equipment, cement, textiles
Industrial production growth rate: 6% (2000 est.)
Electricity - production: 38.092 billion kWh (1999)
Electricity - production by source:
fossil fuel: 61%
hydro: 35%
nuclear: 0%
other: 4% (1999)
Electricity - consumption: 35.426 billion kWh (1999)
Electricity - exports: 0 kWh (1999)
Electricity - imports: 0 kWh (1999)
Agriculture - products: wheat, corn, grapes, beans, sugar beets, potatoes, fruit; beef, poultry, wool; fish; timber
Exports: $18 billion (f.o.b., 2000)
Exports - commodities: copper, fish, fruits, paper and pulp, chemicals
Exports - partners: EU 27%, US 16%, Japan 14%, Brazil 6%, Argentina 5% (1998)
Imports: $17 billion (f.o.b., 2000)
Imports - commodities: consumer goods, chemicals, motor vehicles, fuels, electrical machinery, heavy industrial machinery, food
Imports - partners: US 24%, EU 23%, Argentina 11%, Brazil 6%, Japan 6%, Mexico 5% (1998)
Debt - external: $39 billion (2000)
Economic aid - recipient: ODA, $40 million (2001 est.)
Currency: Chilean peso (CLP)
Currency code: CLP
Exchange rates: Chilean pesos per US dollar - 571.12 (January 2001), 535.47 (2000), 508.78 (1999), 460.29 (1998), 419.30 (1997), 412.27 (1996)
Fiscal year: calendar year

Communications

Telephones - main lines in use: 2.603 million (1998)
Telephones - mobile cellular: 944,225 (1998)
Telephone system:
general assessment: modern system based on extensive microwave radio relay facilities
domestic: extensive microwave radio relay links; domestic satellite system with 3 earth stations
international: satellite earth stations - 2 Intelsat (Atlantic Ocean)
Radio broadcast stations: AM 180 (eight inactive), FM 64, shortwave 17 (one inactive) (1998)
Radios: 5.18 million (1997)
Television broadcast stations: 63 (plus 121 repeaters) (1997)
Televisions: 3.15 million (1997)
Internet country code: .cl
Internet Service Providers (ISPs): 7 (2000)
Internet users: 625,000 (2000)

Transportation

Railways:
total: 6,782 km
broad gauge: 3,743 km 1.676-m gauge (1,653 km electrified)
narrow gauge: 116 km 1.067-m gauge; 2,923 km 1.000-m gauge (40 km electrified) (1995)
Highways:
total: 79,800 km
paved: 11,012 km
unpaved: 68,788 km (1996)
Waterways: 725 km
Pipelines: crude oil 755 km; petroleum products 785 km; natural gas 320 km
Ports and harbors: Antofagasta, Arica, Chanaral, Coquimbo, Iquique, Puerto Montt, Punta Arenas, San Antonio, San Vicente, Talcahuano, Valparaiso
Merchant marine:
total: 44 ships (1,000 GRT or over) totaling 606,506 GRT/884,023 DWT
ships by type: bulk 11, cargo 7, chemical tanker 8, container 4, liquefied gas 2, passenger 3, petroleum tanker 4, roll on/roll off 3, vehicle carrier 2 (2000 est.)
Airports: 366 (2000 est.)
Airports - with paved runways:
total: 69
over 3,047 m: 6
2,438 to 3,047 m: 6
1,524 to 2,437 m: 22
914 to 1,523 m: 21
under 914 m: 14 (2000 est.)
Airports - with unpaved runways:
total: 297
over 3,047 m: 1
2,438 to 3,047 m: 4
1,524 to 2,437 m: 11
914 to 1,523 m: 62
under 914 m: 219 (2000 est.)

Military

Military branches: Army, Navy (includes Naval Air, Coast Guard, and Marines), Air Force, Carabineros of Chile (National Police), Investigations Police
note: Carabineros and Investigations Police are normally administered by the Ministry of Interior, but in times of national emergency, they are considered part of the military
Military manpower - military age: 19 years of age
Military manpower - availability:
males age 15-49: 4,057,466 (2001 est.)
Military manpower - fit for military service:
males age 15-49: 3,003,134 (2001 est.)
Military manpower - reaching military age annually:
males: 136,830 (2001 est.)
Military expenditures - dollar figure: $2.5 billion (FY99)
Military expenditures - percent of GDP: 3.1% (FY99)

Transnational Issues

Disputes - international: Bolivia has wanted a sovereign corridor to the South Pacific Ocean since the Atacama area was lost to Chile in 1884; dispute with Bolivia over Rio Lauca water rights; territorial claim in Antarctica (Chilean Antarctic Territory) partially overlaps Argentine and British claims
Illicit drugs: a growing transshipment country for cocaine destined for the US and Europe; economic prosperity has made Chile more attractive to traffickers seeking to launder drug profits; imported precursors passed on to Bolivia; domestic cocaine consumption is rising

China
(also see separate Hong Kong, Macau, and Taiwan entries)

Introduction

Background: For centuries China has stood as a leading civilization, outpacing the rest of the world in the arts and sciences. But in the first half of the 20th century, China was beset by major famines, civil unrest, military defeats, and foreign occupation. After World War II, the Communists under MAO Zedong established a dictatorship that, while ensuring China's sovereignty, imposed strict controls over everyday life and cost the lives of tens of millions of people. After 1978, his successor DENG Xiaoping gradually introduced market-oriented reforms and decentralized economic decision making. Output quadrupled in the next 20 years and China now has the world's second largest GDP. Political controls remain tight even while economic controls continue to weaken.

Geography

Location: Eastern Asia, bordering the East China Sea, Korea Bay, Yellow Sea, and South China Sea, between North Korea and Vietnam
Geographic coordinates: 35 00 N, 105 00 E
Map references: Asia
Area:
total: 9,596,960 sq km
land: 9,326,410 sq km
water: 270,550 sq km
Area - comparative: slightly smaller than the US
Land boundaries:
total: 22,147.24 km
border countries: Afghanistan 76 km, Bhutan 470 km, Burma 2,185 km, Hong Kong 30 km, India 3,380 km, Kazakhstan 1,533 km, North Korea 1,416 km, Kyrgyzstan 858 km, Laos 423 km, Macau 0.34 km, Mongolia 4,676.9 km, Nepal 1,236 km, Pakistan 523 km, Russia (northeast) 3,605 km, Russia (northwest) 40 km, Tajikistan 414 km, Vietnam 1,281 km
Coastline: 14,500 km
Maritime claims:
contiguous zone: 24 NM
continental shelf: 200 NM or to the edge of the continental margin
territorial sea: 12 NM
Climate: extremely diverse; tropical in south to subarctic in north
Terrain: mostly mountains, high plateaus, deserts in west; plains, deltas, and hills in east
Elevation extremes:
lowest point: Turpan Pendi -154 m
highest point: Mount Everest 8,850 m (1999 est.)
Natural resources: coal, iron ore, petroleum, natural gas, mercury, tin, tungsten, antimony, manganese, molybdenum, vanadium, magnetite, aluminum, lead, zinc, uranium, hydropower potential (world's largest)
Land use:
arable land: 10%
permanent crops: 0%
permanent pastures: 43%
forests and woodland: 14%
other: 33% (1993 est.)
Irrigated land: 498,720 sq km (1993 est.)
Natural hazards: frequent typhoons (about five per year along southern and eastern coasts); damaging floods; tsunamis; earthquakes; droughts
Environment - current issues: air pollution (greenhouse gases, sulfur dioxide particulates) from reliance on coal, produces acid rain; water shortages, particularly in the north; water pollution from untreated wastes; deforestation; estimated loss of one-fifth of agricultural land since 1949 to soil erosion and economic development; desertification; trade in endangered species
Environment - international agreements:
party to: Antarctic-Environmental Protocol, Antarctic Treaty, Biodiversity, Climate Change, Desertification, Endangered Species, Hazardous Wastes, Law of the Sea, Marine Dumping, Nuclear Test Ban, Ozone Layer Protection, Ship Pollution, Tropical Timber 83, Tropical Timber 94, Wetlands, Whaling
signed, but not ratified: Climate Change-Kyoto Protocol, Marine Life Conservation
Geography - note: world's fourth-largest country (after Russia, Canada, and US)

People

Population: 1,273,111,290 (July 2001 est.)
Age structure:
0-14 years: 25.01% (male 166,754,893; female 151,598,117)
15-64 years: 67.88% (male 445,222,858; female 418,959,646)
65 years and over: 7.11% (male 42,547,296; female 48,028,480) (2001 est.)
Population growth rate: 0.88% (2001 est.)
Birth rate: 15.95 births/1,000 population (2001 est.)
Death rate: 6.74 deaths/1,000 population (2001 est.)
Net migration rate: -0.39 migrant(s)/1,000 population (2001 est.)
Sex ratio:
at birth: 1.09 male(s)/female
under 15 years: 1.1 male(s)/female
15-64 years: 1.06 male(s)/female
65 years and over: 0.89 male(s)/female
total population: 1.06 male(s)/female (2001 est.)
Infant mortality rate: 28.08 deaths/1,000 live births (2001 est.)
Life expectancy at birth:
total population: 71.62 years
male: 69.81 years
female: 73.59 years (2001 est.)
Total fertility rate: 1.82 children born/woman (2001 est.)
HIV/AIDS - adult prevalence rate: 0.07% (1999 est.)
HIV/AIDS - people living with HIV/AIDS: 500,000 (1999 est.)
HIV/AIDS - deaths: 17,000 (1999 est.)
Nationality:
noun: Chinese (singular and plural)
adjective: Chinese
Ethnic groups: Han Chinese 91.9%, Zhuang, Uygur, Hui, Yi, Tibetan, Miao, Manchu, Mongol, Buyi, Korean, and other nationalities 8.1%
Religions: Daoist (Taoist), Buddhist, Muslim 2%-3%, Christian 1% (est.)
note: officially atheist
Languages: Standard Chinese or Mandarin (Putonghua, based on the Beijing dialect), Yue (Cantonese), Wu (Shanghaiese), Minbei (Fuzhou), Minnan (Hokkien-Taiwanese), Xiang, Gan, Hakka dialects, minority languages (see Ethnic groups entry)
Literacy:
definition: age 15 and over can read and write
total population: 81.5%
male: 89.9%
female: 72.7% (1995 est.)

China (continued)

Government

Country name:
conventional long form: People's Republic of China
conventional short form: China
local long form: Zhonghua Renmin Gongheguo
local short form: Zhong Guo
abbreviation: PRC
Government type: Communist state
Capital: Beijing
Administrative divisions: 23 provinces (sheng, singular and plural), 5 autonomous regions* (zizhiqu, singular and plural), and 4 municipalities** (shi, singular and plural); Anhui, Beijing**, Chongqing**, Fujian, Gansu, Guangdong, Guangxi*, Guizhou, Hainan, Hebei, Heilongjiang, Henan, Hubei, Hunan, Jiangsu, Jiangxi, Jilin, Liaoning, Nei Mongol*, Ningxia*, Qinghai, Shaanxi, Shandong, Shanghai**, Shanxi, Sichuan, Tianjin**, Xinjiang*, Xizang* (Tibet), Yunnan, Zhejiang; note - China considers Taiwan its 23rd province; see separate entries for the special administrative regions of Hong Kong and Macau
Independence: 221 BC (unification under the Qin or Ch'in Dynasty 221 BC; Qing or Ch'ing Dynasty replaced by the Republic on 12 February 1912; People's Republic established 1 October 1949)
National holiday: Founding of the People's Republic of China, 1 October (1949)
Constitution: most recent promulgation 4 December 1982
Legal system: a complex amalgam of custom and statute, largely criminal law; rudimentary civil code in effect since 1 January 1987; new legal codes in effect since 1 January 1980; continuing efforts are being made to improve civil, administrative, criminal, and commercial law
Suffrage: 18 years of age; universal
Executive branch:
chief of state: President JIANG Zemin (since 27 March 1993) and Vice President HU Jintao (since 16 March 1998)
head of government: Premier ZHU Rongji (since 18 March 1998); Vice Premiers QIAN Qichen (since 29 March 1993), LI Lanqing (29 March 1993), WU Banggou (since 17 March 1995), and WEN Jiabao (since 18 March 1998)
cabinet: State Council appointed by the National People's Congress (NPC)
elections: president and vice president elected by the National People's Congress for five-year terms; elections last held 16-18 March 1998 (next to be held NA March 2003); premier nominated by the president, confirmed by the National People's Congress
election results: JIANG Zemin reelected president by the Ninth National People's Congress with a total of 2,882 votes (36 delegates voted against him, 29 abstained, and 32 did not vote); HU Jintao elected vice president by the Ninth National People's Congress with a total of 2,841 votes (67 delegates voted against him, 39 abstained, and 32 did not vote)
Legislative branch: unicameral National People's Congress or Quanguo Renmin Daibiao Dahui (2,979 seats; members elected by municipal, regional, and provincial people's congresses to serve five-year terms)
elections: last held NA December 1997-NA February 1998 (next to be held late 2002-NA March 2003)
election results: percent of vote - NA%; seats - NA
Judicial branch: Supreme People's Court (judges appointed by the National People's Congress); Local Peoples Courts (comprise higher, intermediate and local courts); Special Peoples Courts (primarily military, maritime, and railway transport courts)
Political parties and leaders: Chinese Communist Party or CCP [JIANG Zemin, General Secretary of the Central Committee]; eight registered small parties controlled by CCP
Political pressure groups and leaders: no substantial political opposition groups exist, although the government has identified the Falungong sect and the China Democracy Party as potential rivals
International organization participation: AfDB, APEC, ARF (dialogue partner), AsDB, ASEAN (dialogue partner), BIS, CCC, CDB (non-regional), ESCAP, FAO, G-77, IAEA, IBRD, ICAO, ICC, ICFTU, ICRM, IDA, IFAD, IFC, IFRCS, IHO, ILO, IMF, IMO, Inmarsat, Intelsat, Interpol, IOC, ISO, ITU, LAIA (observer), MINURSO, NAM (observer), OPCW, PCA, UN, UN Security Council, UNAMSIL, UNCTAD, UNESCO, UNHCR, UNIDO, UNIKOM, UNITAR, UNMEE, UNTAET, UNTSO, UNU, UPU, WHO, WIPO, WMO, WToO, WTrO (observer), ZC
Diplomatic representation in the US:
chief of mission: Ambassador-designate YANG Jiechi
chancery: 2300 Connecticut Avenue NW, Washington, DC 20008
telephone: [1] (202) 328-2500
consulate(s) general: Chicago, Houston, Los Angeles, New York, and San Francisco
Diplomatic representation from the US:
chief of mission: Ambassador Joseph W. PRUEHER
embassy: Xiu Shui Bei Jie 3, 100600 Beijing
mailing address: PSC 461, Box 50, FPO AP 96521-0002
telephone: [86] (10) 6532-3431
FAX: [86] (10) 6532-6422
consulate(s) general: Chengdu, Guangzhou, Shanghai, Shenyang
Flag description: red with a large yellow five-pointed star and four smaller yellow five-pointed stars (arranged in a vertical arc toward the middle of the flag) in the upper hoist-side corner

Economy

Economy - overview: In late 1978 the Chinese leadership began moving the economy from a sluggish Soviet-style centrally planned economy to a more market-oriented system. Whereas the system operates within a political framework of strict Communist control, the economic influence of non-state managers and enterprises has been steadily increasing. The authorities have switched to a system of household responsibility in agriculture in place of the old collectivization, increased the authority of local officials and plant managers in industry, permitted a wide variety of small-scale enterprise in services and light manufacturing, and opened the economy to increased foreign trade and investment. The result has been a quadrupling of GDP since 1978. In 2000, with its 1.26 billion people but a GDP of just $3,600 per capita, China stood as the second largest economy in the world after the US (measured on a purchasing power parity basis). Agricultural output doubled in the 1980s, and industry also posted major gains, especially in coastal areas near Hong Kong and opposite Taiwan, where foreign investment helped spur output of both domestic and export goods. On the darker side, the leadership has often experienced in its hybrid system the worst results of socialism (bureaucracy and lassitude) and of capitalism (windfall gains and stepped-up inflation). Beijing thus has periodically backtracked, retightening central controls at intervals. The government has struggled to (a) collect revenues due from provinces, businesses, and individuals; (b) reduce corruption and other economic crimes; and (c) keep afloat the large state-owned enterprises many of which had been shielded from competition by subsides and had been losing the ability to pay full wages and pensions. From 80 to 120 million surplus rural workers are adrift between the villages and the cities, many subsisting through part-time low-paying jobs. Popular resistance, changes in central policy, and loss of authority by rural cadres have weakened China's population control program, which is essential to maintaining growth in living standards. Another long-term threat to continued rapid economic growth is the deterioration in the environment, notably air pollution, soil erosion, and the steady fall of the water table especially in the north. China continues to lose arable land because of erosion and economic development. Weakness in the global economy in 2001 could hamper growth in exports. Beijing will intensify efforts to stimulate growth through spending on infrastructure--such as water control and power grids--and poverty relief and through rural tax reform aimed at eliminating arbitrary local levies on farmers.
GDP: purchasing power parity - $4.5 trillion (2000 est.)
GDP - real growth rate: 8% (2000 est.)
GDP - per capita: purchasing power parity - $3,600 (2000 est.)
GDP - composition by sector:
agriculture: 15%
industry: 50%
services: 35% (2000 est.)
Population below poverty line: 10% (1999 est.)
Household income or consumption by percentage share:
lowest 10%: 2.4%
highest 10%: 30.4% (1998)
Inflation rate (consumer prices): 0.4% (2000 est.)
Labor force: 700 million (1998 est.)
Labor force - by occupation: agriculture 50%, industry 24%, services 26% (1998)

China (continued)

Unemployment rate: urban unemployment roughly 10%; substantial unemployment and underemployment in rural areas (2000 est.)
Budget:
revenues: $NA
expenditures: $NA, including capital expenditures of $NA
Industries: iron and steel, coal, machine building, armaments, textiles and apparel, petroleum, cement, chemical fertilizers, footwear, toys, food processing, automobiles, consumer electronics, telecommunications
Industrial production growth rate: 10% (2000 est.)
Electricity - production: 1.173 trillion kWh (1999)
Electricity - production by source:
fossil fuel: 79.82%
hydro: 18.98%
nuclear: 1.2%
other: 0.01% (1999)
Electricity - consumption: 1.084 trillion kWh (1999)
Electricity - exports: 7.2 billion kWh (1999)
Electricity - imports: 90 million kWh (1999)
Agriculture - products: rice, wheat, potatoes, sorghum, peanuts, tea, millet, barley, cotton, oilseed; pork; fish
Exports: $232 billion (f.o.b., 2000)
Exports - commodities: machinery and equipment; textiles and clothing, footwear, toys and sporting goods; mineral fuels
Exports - partners: US 21%, Hong Kong 18%, Japan 17%, South Korea, Germany, Netherlands, UK, Singapore, Taiwan (2000)
Imports: $197 billion (f.o.b., 2000)
Imports - commodities: machinery and equipment, mineral fuels, plastics, iron and steel, chemicals
Imports - partners: Japan 18%, Taiwan 11%, US 10%, South Korea 10%, Germany, Hong Kong, Russia, Malaysia (2000)
Debt - external: $162 billion (2000 est.)
Economic aid - recipient: $NA
Currency: yuan (CNY)
Currency code: CNY
Exchange rates: yuan per US dollar - 8.2776 (January 2001), 8.2785 (2000), 8.2783 (1999), 8.2790 (1998), 8.2898 (1997), 8.3142 (1996)
note: beginning 1 January 1994, the People's Bank of China quotes the midpoint rate against the US dollar based on the previous day's prevailing rate in the interbank foreign exchange market
Fiscal year: calendar year

Communications

Telephones - main lines in use: 135 million (2000)
Telephones - mobile cellular: 65 million (January 2001)
Telephone system:
general assessment: domestic and international services are increasingly available for private use; unevenly distributed domestic system serves principal cities, industrial centers, and many towns
domestic: interprovincial fiber-optic trunk lines and cellular telephone systems have been installed; a domestic satellite system with 55 earth stations is in place
international: satellite earth stations - 5 Intelsat (4 Pacific Ocean and 1 Indian Ocean), 1 Intersputnik (Indian Ocean region) and 1 Inmarsat (Pacific and Indian Ocean regions); several international fiber-optic links to Japan, South Korea, Hong Kong, Russia, and Germany (2000)
Radio broadcast stations: AM 369, FM 259, shortwave 45 (1998)
Radios: 417 million (1997)
Television broadcast stations: 3,240 (of which 209 are operated by China Central Television, 31 are provincial TV stations and nearly 3,000 are local city stations) (1997)
Televisions: 400 million (1997)
Internet country code: .cn
Internet Service Providers (ISPs): 3 (2000)
Internet users: 22 million (January 2001)

Transportation

Railways:
total: 67,524 km (including 5,400 km of provincial "local" rails)
standard gauge: 63,924 km 1.435-m gauge (13,362 km electrified; 20,250 km double track)
narrow gauge: 3,600 km 0.750-m and 1.000-m gauge local industrial lines (1998 est.)
note: a new total of 68,000 km was estimated for early 1999 to take new construction programs into account (1999)
Highways:
total: 1.4 million km
paved: 271,300 km (with at least 16,000 km of expressways)
unpaved: 1,128,700 km (1999)
Waterways: 110,000 km (1999)
Pipelines: crude oil 9,070 km; petroleum products 560 km; natural gas 9,383 km (1998)
Ports and harbors: Dalian, Fuzhou, Guangzhou, Haikou, Huangpu, Lianyungang, Nanjing, Nantong, Ningbo, Qingdao, Qinhuangdao, Shanghai, Shantou, Tianjin, Xiamen, Xingang, Yantai, Zhanjiang
Merchant marine:
total: 1,745 ships (1,000 GRT or over) totaling 16,533,521 GRT/24,746,859 DWT
ships by type: barge carrier 2, bulk 324, cargo 825, chemical tanker 21, combination bulk 11, combination ore/oil 1, container 132, liquefied gas 24, multi-functional large-load carrier 5, passenger 7, passenger/cargo 45, petroleum tanker 258, refrigerated cargo 22, roll on/roll off 23, short-sea passenger 41, specialized tanker 3, vehicle carrier 1 (2000 est.)
Airports: 489 (2000 est.)
Airports - with paved runways:
total: 324
over 3,047 m: 27
2,438 to 3,047 m: 88
1,524 to 2,437 m: 147
914 to 1,523 m: 30
under 914 m: 32 (2000 est.)
Airports - with unpaved runways:
total: 165
over 3,047 m: 1
2,438 to 3,047 m: 1
1,524 to 2,437 m: 29
914 to 1,523 m: 56
under 914 m: 78 (2000 est.)

Military

Military branches: People's Liberation Army (PLA) - which includes Ground Forces, Navy (includes Marines and Naval Aviation), Air Force, Second Artillery Corps (the strategic missile force), People's Armed Police (internal security troops, nominally subordinate to Ministry of Public Security, but included by the Chinese as part of the "armed forces" and considered to be an adjunct to the PLA in wartime)
Military manpower - military age: 18 years of age
Military manpower - availability:
males age 15-49: 366,306,353 (2001 est.)
Military manpower - fit for military service:
males age 15-49: 200,886,946 (2001 est.)
Military manpower - reaching military age annually:
males: 10,089,458 (2001 est.)
Military expenditures - dollar figure: $12.608 billion (FY99); note - China's real defense spending may be several times higher than the official figure because a number of significant items are funded elsewhere
Military expenditures - percent of GDP: 1.2% (FY99)

Transnational Issues

Disputes - international: most of boundary with India in dispute; dispute over at least two small sections of the boundary with Russia remains to be settled, despite 1997 boundary agreement; portions of the boundary with Tajikistan are indefinite; 33-km section of boundary with North Korea in the Paektu-san (mountain) area is indefinite; involved in a complex dispute over the Spratly Islands with Malaysia, Philippines, Taiwan, Vietnam, and possibly Brunei; maritime boundary agreement with Vietnam in the Gulf of Tonkin awaits ratification; Paracel Islands occupied by China, but claimed by Vietnam and Taiwan; claims Japanese-administered Senkaku-shoto (Senkaku Islands/Diaoyu Tai), as does Taiwan
Illicit drugs: major transshipment point for heroin produced in the Golden Triangle; growing domestic drug abuse problem; source country for chemical precursors and methamphetamine

Christmas Island
(territory of Australia)

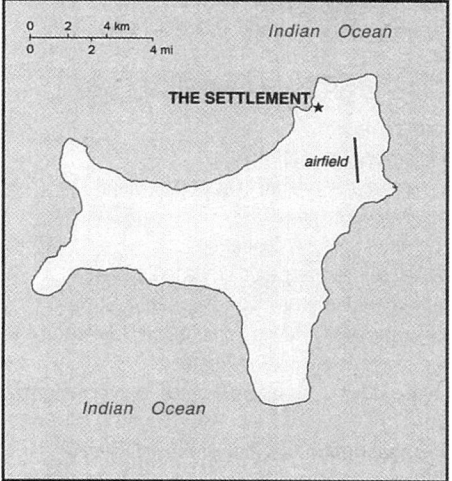

Introduction

Background: Named in 1643 for the day of its discovery, the island was annexed and settlement was begun by the UK in 1888. Phosphate mining began in the 1890s. The UK transferred sovereignty to Australia in 1958. The phosphate mine, closed in 1987, was reopened four years later, but the need for an alternative industry has spurred investment in tourism. Old mining areas are being restored, and almost two-thirds of the island has been declared a national park.

Geography

Location: Southeastern Asia, island in the Indian Ocean, south of Indonesia
Geographic coordinates: 10 30 S, 105 40 E
Map references: Southeast Asia
Area:
total: 135 sq km
land: 135 sq km
water: 0 sq km
Area - comparative: about 0.7 times the size of Washington, DC
Land boundaries: 0 km
Coastline: 138.9 km
Maritime claims:
contiguous zone: 12 NM
exclusive fishing zone: 200 NM
territorial sea: 3 NM
Climate: tropical; heat and humidity moderated by trade winds
Terrain: steep cliffs along coast rise abruptly to central plateau
Elevation extremes:
lowest point: Indian Ocean 0 m
highest point: Murray Hill 361 m
Natural resources: phosphate
Land use:
arable land: NA%
permanent crops: NA%
permanent pastures: NA%
forests and woodland: NA%
other: NA%
note: mainly tropical rainforest of which 60%-70% is in a national park
Irrigated land: NA sq km
Natural hazards: the narrow fringing reef surrounding the island can be a maritime hazard
Environment - current issues: NA
Geography - note: located along major sea lanes of Indian Ocean

People

Population: 2,771 (July 2001 est.)
Age structure:
0-14 years: NA%
15-64 years: NA%
65 years and over: NA%
Population growth rate: 7.77% (2001 est.)
Birth rate: NA births/1,000 population
Death rate: NA deaths/1,000 population
Net migration rate: NA migrant(s)/1,000 population
Infant mortality rate: NA deaths/1,000 live births
Life expectancy at birth:
total population: NA years
male: NA years
female: NA years
Total fertility rate: NA children born/woman
HIV/AIDS - adult prevalence rate: NA%
HIV/AIDS - people living with HIV/AIDS: NA
HIV/AIDS - deaths: NA
Nationality:
noun: Christmas Islander(s)
adjective: Christmas Island
Ethnic groups: Chinese 61%, Malay 25%, European 11%, other 3%, no indigenous population
Religions: Buddhist 55%, Christian 15%, Muslim 10%, other 20% (1991)
Languages: English, Chinese, Malay

Government

Country name:
conventional long form: Territory of Christmas Island
conventional short form: Christmas Island
Dependency status: territory of Australia; administered from Canberra by the Australian Department of the Environment, Sport, and Territories
Government type: NA
Capital: The Settlement
Administrative divisions: none (territory of Australia)
Independence: none (territory of Australia)
National holiday: NA
Constitution: Christmas Island Act of 1958
Legal system: under the authority of the governor general of Australia and Australian law
Executive branch:
chief of state: Queen ELIZABETH II (since 6 February 1952), represented by the Australian governor general
head of government: Administrator William Leonard TAYLOR (since 4 February 1999)
elections: none; the monarch is hereditary; administrator appointed by the governor general of Australia and represents the monarch and Australia
Legislative branch: unicameral Christmas Island Shire Council (9 seats; members elected by popular vote to serve one-year terms)
elections: last held NA December 2000 (next to be held NA December 2001)
election results: percent of vote - NA%; seats - independents 9
Judicial branch: Supreme Court; District Court; Magistrate's Court
Political parties and leaders: none
Political pressure groups and leaders: none
International organization participation: none
Diplomatic representation in the US: none (territory of Australia)
Diplomatic representation from the US: none (territory of Australia)
Flag description: the flag of Australia is used

Economy

Economy - overview: Phosphate mining had been the only significant economic activity, but in December 1987 the Australian Government closed the mine. In 1991, the mine was reopened by union workers. With the support of the government, Australian-based Casinos Austria International Ltd. built a $34 million casino on Christmas Island, which opened in 1993. As of yearend 1999, gaming facilities at the casino were temporarily closed but were expected to reopen in early 2000. Another economic prospect is the possible location of a space-launching site on the island.
GDP: purchasing power parity - $NA
GDP - real growth rate: NA%
GDP - per capita: purchasing power parity - $NA
GDP - composition by sector:
agriculture: NA%
industry: NA%
services: NA%
Population below poverty line: NA%
Household income or consumption by percentage share:
lowest 10%: NA%
highest 10%: NA%
Inflation rate (consumer prices): NA%
Labor force: NA
Labor force - by occupation: tourism 400 people, mining 100 people (1995)
Unemployment rate: NA%
Budget:
revenues: $NA
expenditures: $NA, including capital expenditures of $NA
Industries: tourism, phosphate extraction (near depletion)
Industrial production growth rate: NA%
Electricity - production: NA kWh

Christmas Island (continued)

Electricity - production by source:
fossil fuel: NA%
hydro: NA%
nuclear: NA%
other: NA%
Electricity - consumption: NA kWh
Agriculture - products: NA
Exports: $NA
Exports - commodities: phosphate
Exports - partners: Australia, NZ
Imports: $NA
Imports - commodities: consumer goods
Imports - partners: principally Australia
Debt - external: $NA
Economic aid - recipient: $NA
Currency: Australian dollar (AUD)
Currency code: AUD
Exchange rates: Australian dollars per US dollar - 1.7995 (January 2001), 1.7173 (2000), 1.5497 (1999), 1.5888 (1998), 1.3439 (1997), 1.2773 (1996)
Fiscal year: 1 July - 30 June

Communications

Telephones - main lines in use: NA
Telephones - mobile cellular: 0 (1999)
Telephone system:
general assessment: NA
domestic: NA
international: satellite earth stations - one Intelsat earth station provides telephone and telex service
Radio broadcast stations: AM 1, FM 1, shortwave 0 (1998)
Radios: 1,000 (1997)
Television broadcast stations: NA
Televisions: 600 (1997)
Internet country code: .cx
Internet Service Providers (ISPs): 2 (2000)
Internet users: NA

Transportation

Railways: 24 km to serve phosphate mines
Highways:
total: 140 km (not including 100 km that is maintained by private industry)
paved: 30 km
unpaved: 110 km (1999)
Waterways: none
Ports and harbors: Flying Fish Cove
Merchant marine: none (2000 est.)
Airports: 1 (2000 est.)
Airports - with paved runways:
total: 1
1,524 to 2,437 m: 1 (2000 est.)

Military

Military - note: defense is the responsibility of Australia

Transnational Issues

Disputes - international: none

Clipperton Island
(possession of France)

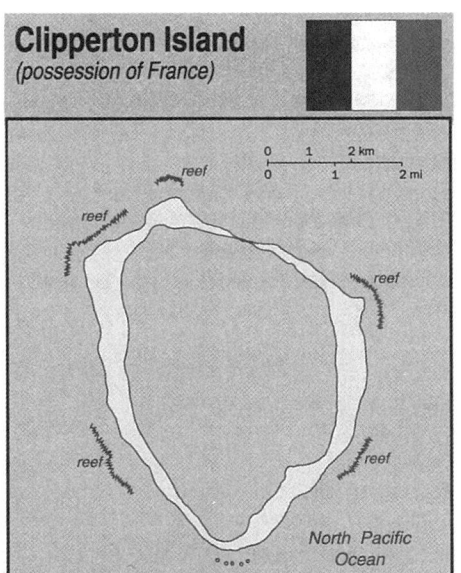

Introduction

Background: This isolated island was named for John CLIPPERTON, a pirate who made it his hideout early in the 18th century. Annexed by France in 1855, it was seized by Mexico in 1897. Arbitration eventually awarded the island to France, which took possession in 1935.

Geography

Location: Middle America, atoll in the North Pacific Ocean, 1,120 km southwest of Mexico
Geographic coordinates: 10 17 N, 109 13 W
Map references: World
Area:
total: 7 sq km
land: 7 sq km
water: 0 sq km
Area - comparative: about 12 times the size of The Mall in Washington, DC
Land boundaries: 0 km
Coastline: 11.1 km
Maritime claims:
exclusive economic zone: 200 NM
territorial sea: 12 NM
Climate: tropical, humid, average temperature 20-32 degrees C, rains May-October
Terrain: coral atoll
Elevation extremes:
lowest point: Pacific Ocean 0 m
highest point: Rocher Clipperton 29 m
Natural resources: fish
Land use:
arable land: 0%
permanent crops: 0%
permanent pastures: 0%
forests and woodland: 0%
other: 100% (all coral)
Irrigated land: 0 sq km (1993)
Natural hazards: NA
Environment - current issues: NA
Geography - note: reef about 8 km in circumference

People

Population: uninhabited (July 2001 est.)

Government

Country name:
conventional long form: none
conventional short form: Clipperton Island
local long form: none
local short form: Ile Clipperton
former: sometimes called Ile de la Passion
Dependency status: possession of France; administered by France from French Polynesia by a high commissioner of the Republic
Legal system: the laws of France, where applicable, apply
Flag description: the flag of France is used

Economy

Economy - overview: Although 115 species of fish have been identified in the territorial waters of Clipperton Island, the only economic activity is tuna fishing.

Transportation

Waterways: none
Ports and harbors: none; offshore anchorage only

Military

Military - note: defense is the responsibility of France

Transnational Issues

Disputes - international: none

Cocos (Keeling) Islands
(territory of Australia)

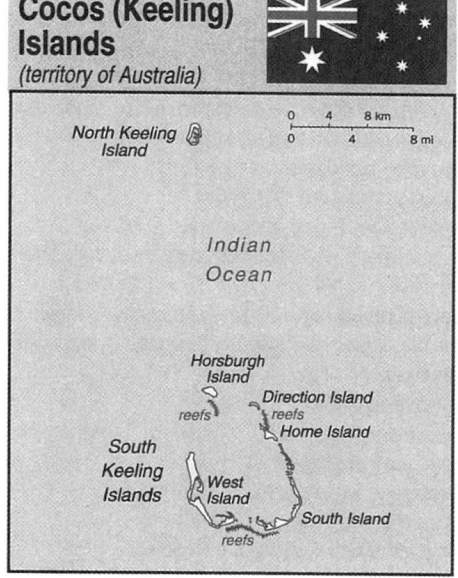

Introduction

Background: The islands were discovered in 1609, but remained uninhabited until the 19th century. Annexed by the UK in 1857, they were transferred to the Australian Government in 1955. The population on the two inhabited islands is split between the mostly Europeans on West Island and the Malays on Home Island.

Geography

Location: Southeastern Asia, group of islands in the Indian Ocean, south of Indonesia, about one-half of the way from Australia to Sri Lanka
Geographic coordinates: 12 30 S, 96 50 E
Map references: Southeast Asia
Area:
total: 14 sq km
land: 14 sq km
water: 0 sq km
note: includes the two main islands of West Island and Home Island
Area - comparative: about 24 times the size of The Mall in Washington, DC
Land boundaries: 0 km
Coastline: 2.6 km
Maritime claims:
exclusive fishing zone: 200 NM
territorial sea: 3 NM
Climate: pleasant, modified by the southeast trade winds for about nine months of the year; moderate rainfall
Terrain: flat, low-lying coral atolls
Elevation extremes:
lowest point: Indian Ocean 0 m
highest point: unnamed location 5 m
Natural resources: fish
Land use:
arable land: 0%
permanent crops: 0%
permanent pastures: 0%
forests and woodland: 0%
other: 100% (1993 est.)
Irrigated land: NA sq km
Natural hazards: cyclones may occur in the early months of the year
Environment - current issues: fresh water resources are limited to rainwater accumulations in natural underground reservoirs
Geography - note: two coral atolls thickly covered with coconut palms and other vegetation

People

Population: 633 (July 2001 est.)
Age structure:
0-14 years: NA%
15-64 years: NA%
65 years and over: NA%
Population growth rate: -0.21% (2001 est.)
Birth rate: NA births/1,000 population
Death rate: NA deaths/1,000 population
Net migration rate: NA migrant(s)/1,000 population
Infant mortality rate: NA deaths/1,000 live births
Life expectancy at birth:
total population: NA years
male: NA years
female: NA years
Total fertility rate: NA children born/woman
HIV/AIDS - adult prevalence rate: NA%
HIV/AIDS - people living with HIV/AIDS: NA
HIV/AIDS - deaths: NA
Nationality:
noun: Cocos Islander(s)
adjective: Cocos Islander
Ethnic groups: Europeans, Cocos Malays
Religions: Sunni Muslim 57%, Christian 22%, other 21% (1981 est.)
Languages: English, Malay

Government

Country name:
conventional long form: Territory of Cocos (Keeling) Islands
conventional short form: Cocos (Keeling) Islands
Dependency status: territory of Australia; administered from Canberra by the Australian Department of the Environment, Sport, and Territories
Government type: NA
Capital: West Island
Administrative divisions: none (territory of Australia)
Independence: none (territory of Australia)
National holiday: NA
Constitution: Cocos (Keeling) Islands Act of 1955
Legal system: based upon the laws of Australia and local laws
Suffrage: NA
Executive branch:
chief of state: Queen ELIZABETH II (since 6 February 1952), represented by the Australian governor general
head of government: Administrator (non-resident) William Leonard TAYLOR (since 4 February 1999)
cabinet: NA
elections: none; the monarch is hereditary; administrator appointed by the governor general of Australia and represents the monarch and Australia
Legislative branch: unicameral Cocos (Keeling) Islands Shire Council (NA seats)
Judicial branch: Supreme Court; Magistrate's Court
Political parties and leaders: none
Political pressure groups and leaders: none
International organization participation: none
Diplomatic representation in the US: none (territory of Australia)
Diplomatic representation from the US: none (territory of Australia)
Flag description: the flag of Australia is used

Economy

Economy - overview: Grown throughout the islands, coconuts are the sole cash crop. Copra and fresh coconuts are the major export earners. Small local gardens and fishing contribute to the food supply, but additional food and most other necessities must be imported from Australia.
GDP: purchasing power parity - $NA
GDP - real growth rate: NA%
GDP - per capita: purchasing power parity - $NA
GDP - composition by sector:
agriculture: NA%
industry: NA%
services: NA%
Population below poverty line: NA%
Household income or consumption by percentage share:
lowest 10%: NA%
highest 10%: NA%
Inflation rate (consumer prices): NA%
Labor force: NA
Labor force - by occupation: the Cocos Islands Cooperative Society Ltd. employs construction workers, stevedores, and lighterage workers; tourism employs others
Budget:
revenues: $NA
expenditures: $NA, including capital expenditures of $NA
Industries: copra products and tourism
Industrial production growth rate: NA%
Electricity - production: NA kWh
Electricity - production by source:
fossil fuel: NA%
hydro: NA%
nuclear: NA%
other: NA%
Electricity - consumption: NA kWh
Agriculture - products: vegetables, bananas, pawpaws, coconuts
Exports: $NA
Exports - commodities: copra
Exports - partners: Australia
Imports: $NA
Imports - commodities: foodstuffs
Imports - partners: Australia

Cocos (Keeling) Islands (continued)

Debt - external: $NA
Economic aid - recipient: $NA
Currency: Australian dollar (AUD)
Currency code: AUD
Exchange rates: Australian dollars per US dollar - 1.7995 (January 2001), 1.7173 (2000), 1.5497 (1999), 1.5888 (1998), 1.3439 (1997), 1.2773 (1996)
Fiscal year: 1 July - 30 June

Communications

Telephones - main lines in use: NA (1999)
Telephones - mobile cellular: 0 (1999)
Telephone system:
general assessment: NA
domestic: NA
international: telephone, telex, and facsimile communications with Australia and elsewhere via satellite; 1 satellite earth station of NA type
Radio broadcast stations: AM 1, FM 0, shortwave 0 (1998)
Radios: 300 (1992)
Television broadcast stations: 0 (1997)
Televisions: NA
Internet country code: .cc
Internet Service Providers (ISPs): 2 (2000)
Internet users: NA

Transportation

Railways: 0 km
Highways:
total: 15 km
paved: NA km
unpaved: NA km (2001)
Waterways: none
Ports and harbors: none; lagoon anchorage only
Merchant marine: none (2000 est.)
Airports: 1 (2000 est.)
Airports - with paved runways:
total: 1
1,524 to 2,437 m: 1 (2000 est.)

Military

Military - note: defense is the responsibility of Australia

Transnational Issues

Disputes - international: none

Colombia

Introduction

Background: Colombia was one of the three countries that emerged from the collapse of Gran Colombia in 1830 (the others being Ecuador and Venezuela). A 40-year insurgent campaign to overthrow the Colombian Government escalated during the 1990s, undergirded in part by funds from the drug trade. Although the violence is deadly and large swaths of the countryside are under guerrilla influence, the movement lacks the military strength or popular support necessary to overthrow the government. While Bogota continues to try to negotiate a settlement, neighboring countries worry about the violence spilling over their borders.

Geography

Location: Northern South America, bordering the Caribbean Sea, between Panama and Venezuela, and bordering the North Pacific Ocean, between Ecuador and Panama
Geographic coordinates: 4 00 N, 72 00 W
Map references: South America, Central America and the Caribbean
Area:
total: 1,138,910 sq km
land: 1,038,700 sq km
water: 100,210 sq km
note: includes Isla de Malpelo, Roncador Cay, Serrana Bank, and Serranilla Bank
Area - comparative: slightly less than three times the size of Montana
Land boundaries:
total: 6,004 km
border countries: Brazil 1,643 km, Ecuador 590 km, Panama 225 km, Peru 1,496 km (est.), Venezuela 2,050 km
Coastline: 3,208 km (Caribbean Sea 1,760 km, North Pacific Ocean 1,448 km)
Maritime claims:
continental shelf: 200-m depth or to the depth of exploitation
exclusive economic zone: 200 NM
territorial sea: 12 NM
Climate: tropical along coast and eastern plains; cooler in highlands
Terrain: flat coastal lowlands, central highlands, high Andes Mountains, eastern lowland plains
Elevation extremes:
lowest point: Pacific Ocean 0 m
highest point: Pico Cristobal Colon 5,775 m
note: nearby Pico Simon Bolivar also has the same elevation
Natural resources: petroleum, natural gas, coal, iron ore, nickel, gold, copper, emeralds, hydropower
Land use:
arable land: 4%
permanent crops: 1%
permanent pastures: 39%
forests and woodland: 48%
other: 8% (1993 est.)
Irrigated land: 5,300 sq km (1993 est.)
Natural hazards: highlands subject to volcanic eruptions; occasional earthquakes; periodic droughts
Environment - current issues: deforestation; soil damage from overuse of pesticides; air pollution, especially in Bogota, from vehicle emissions
Environment - international agreements:
party to: Antarctic Treaty, Biodiversity, Climate Change, Desertification, Endangered Species, Hazardous Wastes, Marine Dumping, Marine Life Conservation, Nuclear Test Ban, Ozone Layer Protection, Ship Pollution, Tropical Timber 83, Tropical Timber 94, Wetlands
signed, but not ratified: Antarctic-Environmental Protocol, Law of the Sea, Marine Dumping
Geography - note: only South American country with coastlines on both North Pacific Ocean and Caribbean Sea

People

Population: 40,349,388 (July 2001 est.)
Age structure:
0-14 years: 31.88% (male 6,507,282; female 6,354,454)
15-64 years: 63.37% (male 12,452,182; female 13,117,707)
65 years and over: 4.75% (male 859,967; female 1,057,796) (2001 est.)
Population growth rate: 1.64% (2001 est.)
Birth rate: 22.41 births/1,000 population (2001 est.)
Death rate: 5.69 deaths/1,000 population (2001 est.)
Net migration rate: -0.33 migrant(s)/1,000 population (2001 est.)
Sex ratio:
at birth: 1.03 male(s)/female
under 15 years: 1.02 male(s)/female
15-64 years: 0.95 male(s)/female
65 years and over: 0.81 male(s)/female
total population: 0.97 male(s)/female (2001 est.)
Infant mortality rate: 23.96 deaths/1,000 live births (2001 est.)

Colombia (continued)

Life expectancy at birth:
total population: 70.57 years
male: 66.71 years
female: 74.55 years (2001 est.)
Total fertility rate: 2.66 children born/woman (2001 est.)
HIV/AIDS - adult prevalence rate: 0.31% (1999 est.)
HIV/AIDS - people living with HIV/AIDS: 71,000 (1999 est.)
HIV/AIDS - deaths: 1,700 (1999 est.)
Nationality:
noun: Colombian(s)
adjective: Colombian
Ethnic groups: mestizo 58%, white 20%, mulatto 14%, black 4%, mixed black-Amerindian 3%, Amerindian 1%
Religions: Roman Catholic 90%
Languages: Spanish
Literacy:
definition: age 15 and over can read and write
total population: 91.3%
male: 91.2%
female: 91.4% (1995 est.)

Government

Country name:
conventional long form: Republic of Colombia
conventional short form: Colombia
local long form: Republica de Colombia
local short form: Colombia
Government type: republic; executive branch dominates government structure
Capital: Bogota
Administrative divisions: 32 departments (departamentos, singular - departamento) and 1 capital district* (distrito capital); Amazonas, Antioquia, Arauca, Atlantico, Bolivar, Boyaca, Caldas, Caqueta, Casanare, Cauca, Cesar, Choco, Cordoba, Cundinamarca, Guainia, Guaviare, Huila, La Guajira, Magdalena, Meta, Narino, Norte de Santander, Putumayo, Quindio, Risaralda, San Andres y Providencia, Distrito Capital de Santa Fe de Bogota*, Santander, Sucre, Tolima, Valle del Cauca, Vaupes, Vichada
Independence: 20 July 1810 (from Spain)
National holiday: Independence Day, 20 July (1810)
Constitution: 5 July 1991
Legal system: based on Spanish law; a new criminal code modeled after US procedures was enacted in 1992-93; judicial review of executive and legislative acts; accepts compulsory ICJ jurisdiction, with reservations
Suffrage: 18 years of age; universal
Executive branch:
chief of state: President Andres PASTRANA (since 7 August 1998); Vice President Gustavo BELL Lemus (since 7 August 1998); note - the president is both the chief of state and head of government
head of government: President Andres PASTRANA (since 7 August 1998); Vice President Gustavo BELL Lemus (since 7 August 1998); note - the president is both the chief of state and head of government
cabinet: Cabinet Cabinet consists of a coalition of the two dominant parties - the PL and PSC - and independents
elections: president elected by popular vote for a four-year term; election last held 31 May 1998 (next to be held NA May 2002); vice president elected by popular vote for a four-year term in a new procedure that replaces the traditional designation of vice presidents by newly elected presidents; election last held 31 May 1998 (next to be held NA May 2002)
election results: no candidate received more than 50% of the total vote, therefore, a run-off election to select a president from the two leading candidates was held 21 June 1998; Andres PASTRANA elected president; percent of vote - 50.3%; Gustavo BELL elected vice president; percent of vote - 50.3%
Legislative branch: bicameral Congress or Congreso consists of the Senate or Senado (102 seats; members are elected by popular vote to serve four-year terms) and the House of Representatives or Camara de Representantes (163 seats; members are elected by popular vote to serve four-year terms)
elections: Senate - last held 8 March 1998 (next to be held NA March 2002); House of Representatives - last held 8 March 1998 (next to be held NA March 2002)
election results: Senate - percent of vote by party - PL 50%, PSC 24%, smaller parties (many aligned with conservatives) 26%; seats by party - PL 58, PSC 28, smaller parties 16; House of Representatives - percent of vote by party - PL 52%, PSC 17%, other 31%; seats by party - PL 98, PSC 52, indigenous parties 2, others 11
Judicial branch: four, coequal, supreme judicial organs; Supreme Court of Justice or Corte Suprema de Justical (highest court of criminal law; judges are selected from the nominees of the Higher Council of Justice for eight-year terms); Council of State (highest court of administrative law, judges are selected from the nominees of the Higher Council of Justice for eight-year terms); Constitutional Court (guards integrity and supremacy of the constitution, rules on constitutionality of laws, amendments to the constitution, and international treaties); Higher Council of Justice (administers and disciplines the civilian judiciary; members of the disciplinary chamber resolve jurisdictional conflicts arising between other courts; members are elected by three sister courts and Congress for eight-year terms)
Political parties and leaders: Conservative Party or PSC [Ciro RAMIREZ Anzon]; Liberal Party or PL [Luis Guillermo VELEZ]; Patriotic Union or UP is a legal political party formed by Revolutionary Armed Forces of Colombia or FARC and Colombian Communist Party or PCC [Jaime CAICEDO]; 19 of April Movement or M-19 [Antonio NAVARRO Wolff]
Political pressure groups and leaders: two largest insurgent groups active in Colombia - National Liberation Army or ELN and Revolutionary Armed Forces of Colombia or FARC; largest paramilitary group is United Self-Defense Groups of Colombia or AUC
International organization participation: BCIE, CAN, Caricom (observer), CCC, CDB, ECLAC, FAO, G- 3, G-11, G-24, G-77, IADB, IAEA, IBRD, ICAO, ICC, ICFTU, ICRM, IDA, IFAD, IFC, IFRCS, IHO, ILO, IMF, IMO, Inmarsat, Intelsat, Interpol, IOC, IOM, ISO, ITU, LAES, LAIA, NAM, OAS, OPANAL, OPCW, PCA, RG, UN, UN Security Council (temporary), UNCTAD, UNESCO, UNHCR, UNIDO, UNU, UPU, WCL, WFTU, WHO, WIPO, WMO, WToO, WTrO
Diplomatic representation in the US:
chief of mission: Ambassador Luis Alberto MORENO Mejia
chancery: 2118 Leroy Place NW, Washington, DC 20008
telephone: [1] (202) 387-8338
FAX: [1] (202) 232-8643
consulate(s) general: Boston, Chicago, Houston, Los Angeles, Miami, New Orleans, New York, San Francisco, San Juan (Puerto Rico), and Washington, DC
consulate(s): Atlanta
Diplomatic representation from the US:
chief of mission: Ambassador Anne W. PATTERSON
embassy: Calle 22D-BIS, numbers 47-51, Apartado Aereo 3831
mailing address: Carrera 45 #22D-45, Bogota, D.C., APO AA 34038
telephone: [57] (1) 315-0811
FAX: [57] (1) 315-2197
Flag description: three horizontal bands of yellow (top, double-width), blue, and red; similar to the flag of Ecuador, which is longer and bears the Ecuadorian coat of arms superimposed in the center

Economy

Economy - overview: Colombia is poised for muted growth in the next several years, marking continued recovery from the severe 1999 recession when GDP fell by about 4%. President PASTRANA's well-respected economic team is working to keep the economy on track, maintaining low interest rates, for example. In accordance with its IMF loan agreement, the administration also is taking steps to improve the public sector's fiscal health. However, many challenges to improved prosperity remain. Unemployment was stuck at a record 20% in 2000, contributing to the extreme inequality in income distribution. Two of Colombia's leading exports, oil and coffee, face an uncertain future; new exploration is needed to offset declining oil production, while coffee harvests and prices are depressed. The lack of public security is a key concern for investors, making progress in the government's peace negotiations with insurgent groups an important driver of economic performance. Colombia is looking for continued support from the international community to boost economic and peace prospects.
GDP: purchasing power parity - $250 billion (2000 est.)
GDP - real growth rate: 3% (2000 est.)
GDP - per capita: purchasing power parity - $6,200 (2000 est.)

Colombia (continued)

GDP - composition by sector:
agriculture: 19%
industry: 26%
services: 55% (1999 est.)
Population below poverty line: 55% (1999)
Household income or consumption by percentage share:
lowest 10%: 1%
highest 10%: 44% (1999)
Inflation rate (consumer prices): 9% (2000)
Labor force: 18.3 million (1999 est.)
Labor force - by occupation: services 46%, agriculture 30%, industry 24% (1990)
Unemployment rate: 20% (2000 est.)
Budget:
revenues: $22 billion
expenditures: $24 billion, including capital expenditures of $NA (2000 est.)
Industries: textiles, food processing, oil, clothing and footwear, beverages, chemicals, cement; gold, coal, emeralds
Industrial production growth rate: 11% (2000 est.)
Electricity - production: 43.574 billion kWh (1999)
Electricity - production by source:
fossil fuel: 22.27%
hydro: 76.19%
nuclear: 0%
other: 1.54% (1999)
Electricity - consumption: 40.532 billion kWh (1999)
Electricity - exports: 27 million kWh (1999)
Electricity - imports: 35 million kWh (1999)
Agriculture - products: coffee, cut flowers, bananas, rice, tobacco, corn, sugarcane, cocoa beans, oilseed, vegetables; forest products; shrimp
Exports: $14.5 billion (f.o.b., 2000 est.)
Exports - commodities: petroleum, coffee, coal, apparel, bananas, cut flowers
Exports - partners: US 50%, EU 14%, Andean Community of Nations 16%, Japan 2% (2000 est.)
Imports: $12.4 billion (f.o.b., 2000 est.)
Imports - commodities: industrial equipment, transportation equipment, consumer goods, chemicals, paper products, fuels, electricity
Imports - partners: US 35%, EU 16%, Andean Community of Nations 15%, Japan 5% (2000 est.)
Debt - external: $34 billion (2000 est.)
Economic aid - recipient: $40.7 million (1995)
Currency: Colombian peso (COP)
Currency code: COP
Exchange rates: Colombian pesos per US dollar - 2,241.43 (January 2001), 2087.90 (2000), 1,756.23 (1999), 1,426.04 (1998), 1,140.96 (1997), 1,036.69 (1996)
Fiscal year: calendar year

Communications

Telephones - main lines in use: 5,433,565 (December 1997)
Telephones - mobile cellular: 1,800,229 (December 1998)
Telephone system:
general assessment: modern system in many respects
domestic: nationwide microwave radio relay system; domestic satellite system with 41 earth stations; fiber-optic network linking 50 cities
international: satellite earth stations - 6 Intelsat, 1 Inmarsat; 3 fully digitalized international switching centers; 8 submarine cables
Radio broadcast stations: AM 454, FM 34, shortwave 27 (1999)
Radios: 21 million (1997)
Television broadcast stations: 60 (includes seven low-power stations) (1997)
Televisions: 4.59 million (1997)
Internet country code: .co
Internet Service Providers (ISPs): 18 (2000)
Internet users: 600,000 (2000)

Transportation

Railways:
total: 3,380 km
standard gauge: 150 km 1.435-m gauge (connects Cerrejon coal mines to maritime port at Bahia de Portete)
narrow gauge: 3,230 km 0.914-m gauge (1,830 km in use) (1995)
Highways:
total: 110,000 km
paved: 26,000 km
unpaved: 84,000 km (2000)
Waterways: 18,140 km (navigable by river boats) (April 1996)
Pipelines: crude oil 3,585 km; petroleum products 1,350 km; natural gas 830 km; natural gas liquids 125 km
Ports and harbors: Bahia de Portete, Barranquilla, Buenaventura, Cartagena, Leticia, Puerto Bolivar, San Andres, Santa Marta, Tumaco, Turbo
Merchant marine:
total: 13 ships (1,000 GRT or over) totaling 53,322 GRT/69,444 DWT
ships by type: bulk 5, cargo 4, container 1, multi-functional large-load carrier 1, petroleum tanker 2 (2000 est.)
Airports: 1,091 (2000 est.)
Airports - with paved runways:
total: 92
over 3,047 m: 2
2,438 to 3,047 m: 8
1,524 to 2,437 m: 38
914 to 1,523 m: 36
under 914 m: 8 (2000 est.)
Airports - with unpaved runways:
total: 999
2,438 to 3,047 m: 1
1,524 to 2,437 m: 64
914 to 1,523 m: 321
under 914 m: 613 (2000 est.)

Military

Military branches: Army (Ejercito Nacional), Navy (Armada Nacional, includes Marines and Coast Guard), Air Force (Fuerza Aerea Colombiana), National Police (Policia Nacional)
Military manpower - military age: 18 years of age
Military manpower - availability:
males age 15-49: 10,779,148 (2001 est.)
Military manpower - fit for military service:
males age 15-49: 7,205,211 (2001 est.)
Military manpower - reaching military age annually:
males: 379,295 (2001 est.)
Military expenditures - dollar figure: $3 billion (FY00)
Military expenditures - percent of GDP: 3.4% (FY00)

Transnational Issues

Disputes - international: maritime boundary dispute with Venezuela in the Gulf of Venezuela; territorial disputes with Nicaragua over Archipelago de San Andres y Providencia and Quita Sueno Bank
Illicit drugs: illicit producer of coca, opium poppies, and cannabis; world's leading coca cultivator (cultivation of coca in 1999 - 122,500 hectares, a 20.3% increase over 1998); cultivation of opium in 1999 increased to 7,500 hectares from 6,100 hectares in 1998; potential production of opium in 1999 - 75 metric tons, a 25% increase over 1998; potential production of heroin in 1999 - nearly 8 metric tons, as compared with 6 tons in 1998; the world's largest processor of coca derivatives into cocaine; supplier of about 90% of the cocaine to the US and the great majority of cocaine to other international drug markets, and an important supplier of heroin to the US market; active aerial eradication program

Comoros

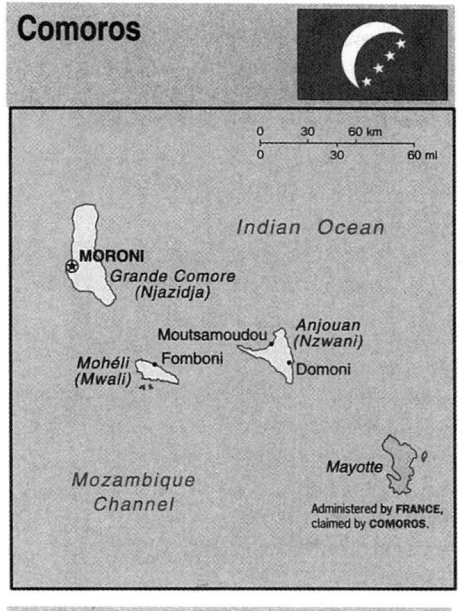

Introduction

Background: Unstable Comoros has endured 19 coups or attempted coups since gaining independence from France in 1975. In 1997, the islands of Anjouan and Moheli declared their independence from Comoros. In 1999, military chief Col. AZALI seized power. He has pledged to resolve the secessionist crisis through the 2000 Fomboni Accord, a confederal arrangement that the Organization of African Unity has yet to recognize.

Geography

Location: Southern Africa, group of islands in the Mozambique Channel, about two-thirds of the way between northern Madagascar and northern Mozambique
Geographic coordinates: 12 10 S, 44 15 E
Map references: Africa
Area:
total: 2,170 sq km
land: 2,170 sq km
water: 0 sq km
Area - comparative: slightly more than 12 times the size of Washington, DC
Land boundaries: 0 km
Coastline: 340 km
Maritime claims:
exclusive economic zone: 200 NM
territorial sea: 12 NM
Climate: tropical marine; rainy season (November to May)
Terrain: volcanic islands, interiors vary from steep mountains to low hills
Elevation extremes:
lowest point: Indian Ocean 0 m
highest point: Le Kartala 2,360 m
Natural resources: NEGL
Land use:
arable land: 35%
permanent crops: 10%
permanent pastures: 7%
forests and woodland: 18%
other: 30% (1993 est.)
Irrigated land: NA sq km
Natural hazards: cyclones possible during rainy season (December to April); Le Kartala on Grand Comore is an active volcano
Environment - current issues: soil degradation and erosion results from crop cultivation on slopes without proper terracing; deforestation
Environment - international agreements:
party to: Biodiversity, Climate Change, Desertification, Endangered Species, Hazardous Wastes, Law of the Sea, Marine Dumping, Ozone Layer Protection, Ship Pollution, Wetlands
signed, but not ratified: none of the selected agreements
Geography - note: important location at northern end of Mozambique Channel

People

Population: 596,202 (July 2001 est.)
Age structure:
0-14 years: 42.81% (male 127,955; female 127,267)
15-64 years: 54.26% (male 159,560; female 163,949)
65 years and over: 2.93% (male 8,326; female 9,145) (2001 est.)
Population growth rate: 3.02% (2001 est.)
Birth rate: 39.52 births/1,000 population (2001 est.)
Death rate: 9.35 deaths/1,000 population (2001 est.)
Net migration rate: NEGL migrant(s)/1,000 population (2001 est.)
Sex ratio:
at birth: 1.03 male(s)/female
under 15 years: 1.01 male(s)/female
15-64 years: 0.97 male(s)/female
65 years and over: 0.91 male(s)/female
total population: 0.98 male(s)/female (2001 est.)
Infant mortality rate: 84.07 deaths/1,000 live births (2001 est.)
Life expectancy at birth:
total population: 60.41 years
male: 58.2 years
female: 62.68 years (2001 est.)
Total fertility rate: 5.32 children born/woman (2001 est.)
HIV/AIDS - adult prevalence rate: 0.12% (1999 est.)
HIV/AIDS - people living with HIV/AIDS: NA
HIV/AIDS - deaths: NA
Nationality:
noun: Comoran(s)
adjective: Comoran
Ethnic groups: Antalote, Cafre, Makoa, Oimatsaha, Sakalava
Religions: Sunni Muslim 98%, Roman Catholic 2%
Languages: Arabic (official), French (official), Comoran (a blend of Swahili and Arabic)
Literacy:
definition: age 15 and over can read and write
total population: 57.3%
male: 64.2%
female: 50.4% (1995 est.)

Government

Country name:
conventional long form: Federal Islamic Republic of the Comoros
conventional short form: Comoros
local long form: Republique Federale Islamique des Comores
local short form: Comores
Government type: independent republic
Capital: Moroni
Administrative divisions: 3 islands; Grande Comore (Njazidja), Anjouan (Nzwani), and Moheli (Mwali); note - there are also four municipalities named Domoni, Fomboni, Moroni, and Moutsamoudou
Independence: 6 July 1975 (from France)
National holiday: Independence Day, 6 July (1975)
Constitution: 20 October 1996
Legal system: French and Muslim law in a new consolidated code
Suffrage: 18 years of age; universal
Executive branch:
chief of state: President AZALI Assoumani (since 6 May 1999); note - the interim government of President Tajiddine Ben Said MASSOUNDE, which had assumed power on 6 November 1998 upon the death of President Mohamed TAKI Abdulkarim, was overthrown in a bloodless coup on 30 April 1999
head of government: Prime Minister Hamada MADI (since late November 2000)
cabinet: Council of Ministers appointed by the president
elections: president elected by popular vote for a five-year term; election last held 6 and 16 March 1996 (next to be held NA); prime minister appointed by the president
note: President AZALI claimed a one-year term at the time of the coup; but elections, promised for spring 2000, were not held
election results: results of the last presidential election before the coup were: Mohamed TAKI Abdulkarim elected president; percent of vote - 64.3%
Legislative branch: bicameral legislature consists of the Senate (15 seats: five from each island); members selected by regional councils for six-year terms) and a Federal Assembly or Assemblee Federale (43 seats; members elected by popular vote to serve five-year terms); note - the Federal Assembly was dissolved following the coup of 30 April 1999
elections: Federal Assembly - last held 1 and 8 December 1996 (next to be held NA)
election results: Federal Assembly - percent of vote by party - NA%; seats by party - RND 39, FNJ 3, independent 1
note: the constitution stipulates that only parties that win six seats in the Federal Assembly (two from each island) are permitted to be in opposition, but if no party accomplishes that, the second most successful party will be in opposition; in the elections of December 1996 the FNJ appeared to qualify as opposition

Comoros (continued)

Judicial branch: Supreme Court or Cour Supremes (two members appointed by the president, two members elected by the Federal Assembly, one elected by the Council of each island, and others are former presidents of the republic)

Political parties and leaders: Front National pour la Justice or FNJ (Islamic party in opposition) [Ahmed Abdallah MOHAMED, Ahmed ABOUBACAR, Soidiki M'BAPANOZA]; Rassemblement National pour le Development or RND (party of the government) [Ali Bazi SELIM]

Political pressure groups and leaders: NA

International organization participation: ACCT, ACP, AfDB, AFESD, AL, CCC, ECA, FAO, FZ, G-77, IBRD, ICAO, ICRM, IDA, IDB, IFAD, IFC, IFRCS (associate), ILO, IMF, InOC, Intelsat, Interpol, IOC, ISO (subscriber), ITU, NAM, OAU, OIC, OPCW, UN, UNCTAD, UNESCO, UNIDO, UPU, WHO, WMO, WTrO (applicant)

Diplomatic representation in the US:
chief of mission: Deputy Permanent Representative Mahmoud Mohamed ABOUD (acting)
chancery: (temporary) care of the Permanent Mission of the Federal and Islamic Republic of the Comoros to the United Nations, 420 East 50th Street, New York, NY 10022
telephone: [1] (212) 972-8010
FAX: [1] (212) 983-4712

Diplomatic representation from the US: the US does not have an embassy in Comoros; the ambassador to Mauritius is accredited to Comoros

Flag description: green with a white crescent in the center of the field, its points facing downward; there are four white five-pointed stars placed in a line between the points of the crescent; the crescent, stars, and color green are traditional symbols of Islam; the four stars represent the four main islands of the archipelago - Mwali, Njazidja, Nzwani, and Mayotte (a territorial collectivity of France, but claimed by Comoros); the design, the most recent of several, is described in the constitution approved by referendum on 7 June 1992

Economy

Economy - overview: One of the world's poorest countries, Comoros is made up of three islands that have inadequate transportation links, a young and rapidly increasing population, and few natural resources. The low educational level of the labor force contributes to a subsistence level of economic activity, high unemployment, and a heavy dependence on foreign grants and technical assistance. Agriculture, including fishing, hunting, and forestry, is the leading sector of the economy. It contributes 40% to GDP, employs 80% of the labor force, and provides most of the exports. The country is not self-sufficient in food production; rice, the main staple, accounts for the bulk of imports. The government is struggling to upgrade education and technical training, to privatize commercial and industrial enterprises, to improve health services, to diversify exports, to promote tourism, and to reduce the high population growth rate. Continued foreign support is essential if the goal of 4% annual GDP growth is to be met. Remittances from 150,000 Comorans abroad help supplement GDP.

GDP: purchasing power parity - $419 million (2000 est.)

GDP - real growth rate: 0.5% (2000 est.)

GDP - per capita: purchasing power parity - $720 (2000 est.)

GDP - composition by sector:
agriculture: 40%
industry: 4%
services: 56% (2000 est.)

Population below poverty line: NA%

Household income or consumption by percentage share:
lowest 10%: NA%
highest 10%: NA%

Inflation rate (consumer prices): 3.5% (1999)

Labor force: 144,500 (1996 est.)

Labor force - by occupation: agriculture 80%

Unemployment rate: 20% (1996 est.)

Budget:
revenues: $48 million
expenditures: $53 million, including capital expenditures of $NA (1997)

Industries: tourism, perfume distillation, textiles, furniture, jewelry, construction materials, soft drinks

Industrial production growth rate: -2% (1999 est.)

Electricity - production: 17 million kWh (1999)

Electricity - production by source:
fossil fuel: 88.24%
hydro: 11.76%
nuclear: 0%
other: 0% (1999)

Electricity - consumption: 15.8 million kWh (1999)

Electricity - exports: 0 kWh (1999)

Electricity - imports: 0 kWh (1999)

Agriculture - products: vanilla, cloves, perfume essences, copra, coconuts, bananas, cassava (tapioca)

Exports: $7.9 million (f.o.b., 1999 est.)

Exports - commodities: vanilla, ylang-ylang, cloves, perfume oil, copra

Exports - partners: France 50%, Germany 25% (1998)

Imports: $55.1 million (f.o.b., 1999 est.)

Imports - commodities: rice and other foodstuffs, consumer goods; petroleum products, cement, transport equipment

Imports - partners: France 38%, Pakistan 13%, South Africa 8%, Kenya 8% (1998)

Debt - external: $197 million (1997 est.)

Economic aid - recipient: $28.1 million (1997)

Currency: Comoran franc (KMF)

Currency code: KMF

Exchange rates: Comoran francs per US dollar - 524.41 (January 2001), 533.98 (2000), 461.77 (1999), 442.46 (1998), 437.75 (1997), 383.66 (1996)
note: prior to January 1999, the official rate was pegged to the French franc at 75 Comoran francs per French franc; since 1 January 1999, the Comoran franc is pegged to the euro at a rate of 491.9677 Comoran francs per euro

Fiscal year: calendar year

Communications

Telephones - main lines in use: 6,000 (1997)

Telephones - mobile cellular: NA

Telephone system:
general assessment: sparse system of microwave radio relay and HF radiotelephone communication stations
domestic: HF radiotelephone communications and microwave radio relay
international: HF radiotelephone communications to Madagascar and Reunion

Radio broadcast stations: AM 1, FM 2, shortwave 1 (1998)

Radios: 90,000 (1997)

Television broadcast stations: 0 (1998)

Televisions: 1,000 (1997)

Internet country code: .km

Internet Service Providers (ISPs): 1 (2000)

Internet users: 800 (2000)

Transportation

Railways: 0 km

Highways:
total: 880 km
paved: 673 km
unpaved: 207 km (1996)

Waterways: none

Ports and harbors: Fomboni, Moroni, Moutsamoudou

Merchant marine:
total: 2 ships (1,000 GRT or over) totaling 19,122 GRT/29,817 DWT
ships by type: cargo 2 (2000 est.)

Airports: 4 (2000 est.)

Airports - with paved runways:
total: 4
2,438 to 3,047 m: 1
914 to 1,523 m: 3 (2000 est.)

Military

Military branches: Comoran Security Force

Military manpower - availability:
males age 15-49: 141,120 (2001 est.)

Military manpower - fit for military service:
males age 15-49: 83,920 (2001 est.)

Military expenditures - dollar figure: $NA

Military expenditures - percent of GDP: NA%

Transnational Issues

Disputes - international: claims French-administered Mayotte; the island of Anjouan (Nzwani) has moved to secede from Comoros

Congo, Democratic Republic of the

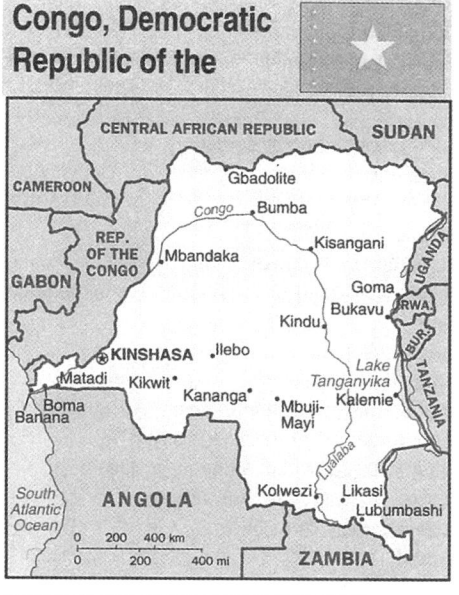

Introduction

Background: Since 1994 the Democratic Republic of the Congo (DROC; formerly called Zaire) has been rent by ethnic strife and civil war, touched off by a massive inflow of refugees from the fighting in Rwanda and Burundi. The government of former president MOBUTU Sese Seko was toppled by a rebellion led by Laurent KABILA in May 1997; his regime was subsequently challenged by a Rwanda- and Uganda-backed rebellion in August 1998. Troops from Zimbabwe, Angola, Namibia, Chad, and Sudan intervened to support the Kinshasa regime. A cease-fire was signed on 10 July 1999, but sporadic fighting continued. KABILA was assassinated in January 2001 and his son Joseph KABILA was named head of state. The new president quickly began overtures to end the war.

Geography

Location: Central Africa, northeast of Angola
Geographic coordinates: 0 00 N, 25 00 E
Map references: Africa
Area:
total: 2,345,410 sq km
land: 2,267,600 sq km
water: 77,810 sq km
Area - comparative: slightly less than one-fourth the size of the US
Land boundaries:
total: 10,744 km
border countries: Angola 2,511 km, Burundi 233 km, Central African Republic 1,577 km, Republic of the Congo 2,410 km, Rwanda 217 km, Sudan 628 km, Tanzania 473 km, Uganda 765 km, Zambia 1,930 km
Coastline: 37 km
Maritime claims:
exclusive economic zone: boundaries with neighbors
territorial sea: 12 NM
Climate: tropical; hot and humid in equatorial river basin; cooler and drier in southern highlands; cooler and wetter in eastern highlands; north of Equator - wet season April to October, dry season December to February; south of Equator - wet season November to March, dry season April to October
Terrain: vast central basin is a low-lying plateau; mountains in east
Elevation extremes:
lowest point: Atlantic Ocean 0 m
highest point: Pic Marguerite on Mont Ngaliema (Mount Stanley) 5,110 m
Natural resources: cobalt, copper, cadmium, petroleum, industrial and gem diamonds, gold, silver, zinc, manganese, tin, germanium, uranium, radium, bauxite, iron ore, coal, hydropower, timber
Land use:
arable land: 3%
permanent crops: 0%
permanent pastures: 7%
forests and woodland: 77%
other: 13% (1993 est.)
Irrigated land: 100 sq km (1993 est.)
Natural hazards: periodic droughts in south; volcanic activity
Environment - current issues: poaching threatens wildlife populations; water pollution; deforestation; refugees who arrived in mid-1994 were responsible for significant deforestation, soil erosion, and wildlife poaching in the eastern part of the country (most of those refugees were repatriated in November and December 1996)
Environment - international agreements:
party to: Biodiversity, Climate Change, Desertification, Endangered Species, Hazardous Wastes, Law of the Sea, Marine Dumping, Nuclear Test Ban, Ozone Layer Protection, Ship Pollution, Tropical Timber 83, Tropical Timber 94, Wetlands
signed, but not ratified: Environmental Modification
Geography - note: straddles Equator; very narrow strip of land that controls the lower Congo river and is only outlet to South Atlantic Ocean; dense tropical rain forest in central river basin and eastern highlands

People

Population: 53,624,718
note: estimates for this country explicitly take into account the effects of excess mortality due to AIDS; this can result in lower life expectancy, higher infant mortality and death rates, lower population and growth rates, and changes in the distribution of population by age and sex than would otherwise be expected (July 2001 est.)
Age structure:
0-14 years: 48.24% (male 12,988,488; female 12,878,232)
15-64 years: 49.21% (male 12,931,886; female 13,459,109)
65 years and over: 2.55% (male 575,113; female 791,890) (2001 est.)
Population growth rate: 3.1% (2001 est.)
Birth rate: 46.02 births/1,000 population (2001 est.)
Death rate: 15.15 deaths/1,000 population (2001 est.)
Net migration rate: 0.14 migrant(s)/1,000 population (2001 est.)
note: one million refugees fled into Zaire (now called the Democratic Republic of the Congo or DROC) in 1994 to escape the fighting between the Hutus and the Tutsis; fighting in the DROC between rebels and government forces in October 1996 caused 875,000 refugees to return to Rwanda in late 1996 and early 1997; an additional 173,000 Rwandan refugees disappeared in early 1997 and are assumed to have been killed by Zairian forces; fighting between the Congolese government and Uganda- and Rwanda-backed Congolese rebels spawned a regional war in DROC in August 1998, which left 1.8 million Congolese displaced in DROC and caused 300,000 Congolese refugees to flee to surrounding countries
Sex ratio:
at birth: 1.03 male(s)/female
under 15 years: 1.01 male(s)/female
15-64 years: 0.96 male(s)/female
65 years and over: 0.73 male(s)/female
total population: 0.98 male(s)/female (2001 est.)
Infant mortality rate: 99.88 deaths/1,000 live births (2001 est.)
Life expectancy at birth:
total population: 48.94 years
male: 46.96 years
female: 50.98 years (2001 est.)
Total fertility rate: 6.84 children born/woman (2001 est.)
HIV/AIDS - adult prevalence rate: 5.07% (1999 est.)
HIV/AIDS - people living with HIV/AIDS: 1.1 million (1999 est.)
HIV/AIDS - deaths: 95,000 (1999 est.)
Nationality:
noun: Congolese (singular and plural)
adjective: Congolese or Congo
Ethnic groups: over 200 African ethnic groups of which the majority are Bantu; the four largest tribes - Mongo, Luba, Kongo (all Bantu), and the Mangbetu-Azande (Hamitic) make up about 45% of the population
Religions: Roman Catholic 50%, Protestant 20%, Kimbanguist 10%, Muslim 10%, other syncretic sects and indigenous beliefs 10%
Languages: French (official), Lingala (a lingua franca trade language), Kingwana (a dialect of Kiswahili or Swahili), Kikongo, Tshiluba
Literacy:
definition: age 15 and over can read and write French, Lingala, Kingwana, or Tshiluba
total population: 77.3%
male: 86.6%
female: 67.7% (1995 est.)

Government

Country name:
conventional long form: Democratic Republic of the Congo
conventional short form: none

Congo, Democratic Republic of the (continued)

local long form: Republique Democratique du Congo
local short form: none
former: Congo Free State, Belgian Congo, Congo/Leopoldville, Congo/Kinshasa, Zaire
abbreviation: DROC
Government type: dictatorship; presumably undergoing a transition to representative government
Capital: Kinshasa
Administrative divisions: 10 provinces (provinces, singular - province) and one city* (ville); Bandundu, Bas-Congo, Equateur, Kasai-Occidental, Kasai-Oriental, Katanga, Kinshasa*, Maniema, Nord-Kivu, Orientale, Sud-Kivu
Independence: 30 June 1960 (from Belgium)
National holiday: Independence Day, 30 June (1960)
Constitution: 24 June 1967, amended August 1974, revised 15 February 1978, amended April 1990; transitional constitution promulgated in April 1994; in November 1998, a draft constitution was approved by former President Laurent KABILA but it has not been ratified by a national referendum
Legal system: based on Belgian civil law system and tribal law; has not accepted compulsory ICJ jurisdiction
Suffrage: 18 years of age; universal and compulsory
Executive branch:
chief of state: Joseph KABILA (since 26 January 2001); note - the president succeeded his father Laurent Desire KABILA after his assassination on 16 January 2001; as president he is both chief of state and head of government
head of government: Joseph KABILA (since 26 January 2001); note - the president succeeded his father Laurent Desire KABILA after his assassination on 16 January 2001; as president he is both chief of state and head of government
cabinet: National Executive Council, appointed by the president
elections: before Laurent Desire KABILA seized power, the president was elected by popular vote for a seven-year term; election last held 29 July 1984 (next was scheduled to be held in May 1997); formerly, the prime minister was elected by the High Council of the Republic; note - elections were not held in 1991 as called for by the constitution
election results: results of the last election were: MOBUTU Sese Seko Kuku Ngbendu wa Za Banga reelected president in 1984 without opposition
note: Marshal MOBUTU Sese Seko Kuku Ngbendu wa Za Banga was president from 24 November 1965 until forced into exile on 16 May 1997 when his government was overthrown militarily by Laurent Desire KABILA, who immediately assumed governing authority; KABILA pledged to hold elections by April 1999, but in December 1998 announced that elections would be postponed until all foreign military forces attempting to topple the government had withdrawn from the country; KABILA was assassinated in January 2001 and was succeeded by his son Joseph KABILA

Legislative branch: a 300-member Transitional Constituent Assembly established in August 2000
elections: NA; members of the Transitional Constituent Assembly were appointed by former President KABILA
Judicial branch: Supreme Court or Cour Supreme
Political parties and leaders: Democratic Social Christian Party or PDSC [Andre BO-BOLIKO]; Popular Movement of the Revolution or MPR [leader NA]; Unified Lumumbast Party or PALU [Antoine GIZENGA]; Union for Democracy and Social Progress or UDPS [Etienne TSHISEKEDI wa Mulumba]; Union of Federalists and Independent Republicans or UFERI [Kouyoumba MUCHULI Mulembe]
Political pressure groups and leaders: NA
International organization participation: ACCT, ACP, AfDB, CCC, CEEAC, CEPGL, ECA, FAO, G-19, G-24, G-77, IAEA, IBRD, ICAO, ICFTU, ICRM, IDA, IFAD, IFC, IFRCS, IHO, ILO, IMF, IMO, Intelsat, Interpol, IOC, IOM (observer), ISO (correspondent), ITU, NAM, OAU, OPCW, PCA, SADC, UN, UNCTAD, UNESCO, UNHCR, UNIDO, UPU, WCL, WFTU, WHO, WIPO, WMO, WToO, WTrO
Diplomatic representation in the US:
chief of mission: Ambassador Faida MITIFU
chancery: 1800 New Hampshire Avenue NW, Washington, DC 20009
telephone: [1] (202) 234-7690, 7691
FAX: [1] (202) 234-2609
Diplomatic representation from the US:
chief of mission: Ambassador William Lacy SWING
embassy: 310 Avenue des Aviateurs, Kinshasa
mailing address: Unit 31550, APO AE 09828
telephone: [243] (12) 21804, 21807
FAX: [243] (88) 43805
Flag description: light blue with a large yellow five-pointed star in the center and a columnar arrangement of six small yellow five-pointed stars along the hoist side

Economy

Economy - overview: The economy of the Democratic Republic of the Congo - a nation endowed with vast potential wealth - has declined drastically since the mid-1980s. The new government instituted a tight fiscal policy that initially curbed inflation and currency depreciation, but these small gains were quickly reversed when the foreign-backed rebellion in the eastern part of the country began in August 1998. The war has dramatically reduced national output and government revenue and has increased external debt. Foreign businesses have curtailed operations due to uncertainty about the outcome of the conflict and because of increased government harassment and restrictions. The war has intensified the impact of such basic problems as an uncertain legal framework, corruption, raging inflation, and lack of openness in government economic policy and financial operations. A number of IMF and World Bank missions have met with the government to help it develop a coherent economic plan but associated reforms are on hold.

GDP: purchasing power parity - $31 billion (2000 est.)
GDP - real growth rate: -15% (2000 est.)
GDP - per capita: purchasing power parity - $600 (2000 est.)
GDP - composition by sector:
agriculture: 58%
industry: 17%
services: 25% (1997 est.)
Population below poverty line: NA%
Household income or consumption by percentage share:
lowest 10%: NA%
highest 10%: NA%
Inflation rate (consumer prices): 540% (2000 est.)
Labor force: 14.51 million (1993 est.)
Labor force - by occupation: agriculture 65%, industry 16%, services 19% (1991 est.)
Unemployment rate: NA%
Budget:
revenues: $269 million
expenditures: $244 million, including capital expenditures of $24 million (1996 est.)
Industries: mining (diamonds, copper, zinc), mineral processing, consumer products (including textiles, footwear, cigarettes, processed foods and beverages), cement
Industrial production growth rate: NA%
Electricity - production: 5.268 billion kWh (1999)
Electricity - production by source:
fossil fuel: 2.05%
hydro: 97.95%
nuclear: 0%
other: 0% (1999)
Electricity - consumption: 4.55 billion kWh (1999)
Electricity - exports: 404 million kWh (1999)
Electricity - imports: 55 million kWh (1999)
Agriculture - products: coffee, sugar, palm oil, rubber, tea, quinine, cassava (tapioca), palm oil, bananas, root crops, corn, fruits; wood products
Exports: $960 million (f.o.b., 2000 est.)
Exports - commodities: diamonds, copper, coffee, cobalt, crude oil
Exports - partners: Benelux 62%, US 18%, South Africa, Finland, Italy (1999)
Imports: $660 million (c.i.f., 2000 est.)
Imports - commodities: foodstuffs, mining and other machinery, transport equipment, fuels
Imports - partners: South Africa 28%, Benelux 14%, Nigeria 9%, Kenya 7%, China (1999)
Debt - external: $13 billion (1998 est.)
Economic aid - recipient: $195.3 million (1995)
Currency: Congolese franc (CDF)
Currency code: CDF
Exchange rates: Congolese francs per US dollar - 50 (January 2001), 4.5 (January 2000), 4.02 (1999), 1.61 (1998), 1.31 (1997), 0.50 (1996)
note: on 30 June 1998 the Congolese franc was introduced, replacing the new zaire
Fiscal year: calendar year

Congo, Democratic Republic of the (continued)

Communications

Telephones - main lines in use: 21,000 (1997)
Telephones - mobile cellular: 8,900 (1997)
Telephone system:
general assessment: NA
domestic: barely adequate wire and microwave radio relay service in and between urban areas; domestic satellite system with 14 earth stations
international: satellite earth station - 1 Intelsat (Atlantic Ocean)
Radio broadcast stations: AM 3, FM 12, shortwave 1 (1999)
Radios: 18.03 million (1997)
Television broadcast stations: 20 (1999)
Televisions: 6.478 million (1997)
Internet country code: .cd
Internet Service Providers (ISPs): 2 (2000)
Internet users: 1,500 (1999)

Transportation

Railways:
total: 5,138 km (1995); note - severely reduced route-distance in use because of damage to facilities by civil strife
narrow gauge: 3,987 km 1.067-m gauge (858 km electrified); 125 km 1.000-m gauge; 1,026 km 0.600-m gauge
Highways:
total: 157,000 km (including 30 km of expressways)(1996)
paved: NA km
unpaved: NA km
Waterways: 15,000 km (including the Congo and its tributaries, and unconnected lakes)
Pipelines: petroleum products 390 km
Ports and harbors: Banana, Boma, Bukavu, Bumba, Goma, Kalemie, Kindu, Kinshasa, Kisangani, Matadi, Mbandaka
Merchant marine: none (2000 est.)
Airports: 232 (2000 est.)
Airports - with paved runways:
total: 24
over 3,047 m: 4
2,438 to 3,047 m: 3
1,524 to 2,437 m: 15
914 to 1,523 m: 2 (2000 est.)
Airports - with unpaved runways:
total: 208
1,524 to 2,437 m: 20
914 to 1,523 m: 96
under 914 m: 92 (2000 est.)

Military

Military branches: Army, Navy, Air Force, Special Presidential Security Group
Military manpower - availability:
males age 15-49: 11,615,554 (2001 est.)
Military manpower - fit for military service:
males age 15-49: 5,915,251 (2001 est.)
Military expenditures - dollar figure: $250 million (FY97)
Military expenditures - percent of GDP: 4.6% (FY97)

Transnational Issues

Disputes - international: the Democratic Republic of the Congo is in the grip of a civil war that has drawn in military forces from neighboring states, with Uganda and Rwanda supporting the rebel movements that occupy much of the eastern portion of the state; most of the Congo river boundary with the Republic of the Congo is indefinite (no agreement has been reached on the division of the river or its islands, except in the Pool Malebo/Stanley Pool area)
Illicit drugs: illicit producer of cannabis, mostly for domestic consumption

Congo, Republic of the

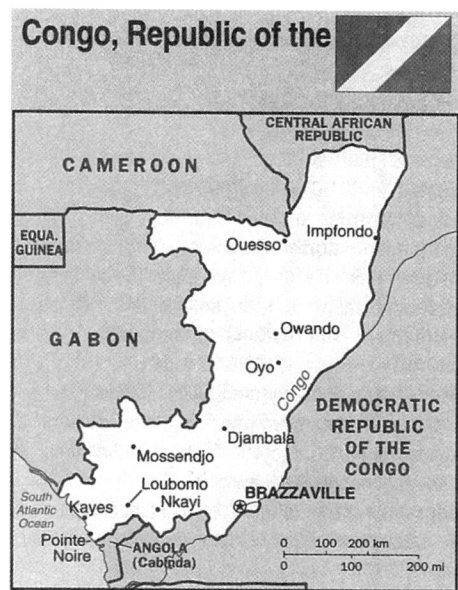

Introduction

Background: Upon independence in 1960, the former French region of Middle Congo became the Republic of the Congo. A quarter century of experimentation with Marxism was abandoned in 1990 and a democratically elected government installed in 1992. A brief civil war in 1997 restored former Marxist President SASSOU-NGUESSO.

Geography

Location: Western Africa, bordering the South Atlantic Ocean, between Angola and Gabon
Geographic coordinates: 1 00 S, 15 00 E
Map references: Africa
Area:
total: 342,000 sq km
land: 341,500 sq km
water: 500 sq km
Area - comparative: slightly smaller than Montana
Land boundaries:
total: 5,504 km
border countries: Angola 201 km, Cameroon 523 km, Central African Republic 467 km, Democratic Republic of the Congo 2,410 km, Gabon 1,903 km
Coastline: 169 km
Maritime claims:
territorial sea: 200 NM
Climate: tropical; rainy season (March to June); dry season (June to October); constantly high temperatures and humidity; particularly enervating climate astride the Equator
Terrain: coastal plain, southern basin, central plateau, northern basin
Elevation extremes:
lowest point: Atlantic Ocean 0 m
highest point: Mount Berongou 903 m
Natural resources: petroleum, timber, potash, lead, zinc, uranium, copper, phosphates, natural gas, hydropower

Congo, Republic of the (continued)

Land use:
arable land: 0%
permanent crops: 0%
permanent pastures: 29%
forests and woodland: 62%
other: 9% (1993 est.)
Irrigated land: 10 sq km (1993 est.)
Natural hazards: seasonal flooding
Environment - current issues: air pollution from vehicle emissions; water pollution from the dumping of raw sewage; tap water is not potable; deforestation
Environment - international agreements:
party to: Biodiversity, Climate Change, Desertification, Endangered Species, Marine Dumping, Ozone Layer Protection, Ship Pollution, Tropical Timber 83, Tropical Timber 94, Wetlands
signed, but not ratified: Law of the Sea
Geography - note: about 70% of the population lives in Brazzaville, Pointe-Noire, or along the railroad between them

People

Population: 2,894,336
note: estimates for this country explicitly take into account the effects of excess mortality due to AIDS; this can result in lower life expectancy, higher infant mortality and death rates, lower population and growth rates, and changes in the distribution of population by age and sex than would otherwise be expected (July 2001 est.)
Age structure:
0-14 years: 42.43% (male 618,411; female 609,633)
15-64 years: 54.23% (male 765,501; female 804,125)
65 years and over: 3.34% (male 38,772; female 57,894) (2001 est.)
Population growth rate: 2.2% (2001 est.)
Birth rate: 38.24 births/1,000 population (2001 est.)
Death rate: 16.22 deaths/1,000 population (2001 est.)
Net migration rate: 0 migrant(s)/1,000 population (2001 est.)
Sex ratio:
at birth: 1.03 male(s)/female
under 15 years: 1.01 male(s)/female
15-64 years: 0.95 male(s)/female
65 years and over: 0.67 male(s)/female
total population: 0.97 male(s)/female (2001 est.)
Infant mortality rate: 99.73 deaths/1,000 live births (2001 est.)
Life expectancy at birth:
total population: 47.57 years
male: 44.38 years
female: 50.85 years (2001 est.)
Total fertility rate: 5 children born/woman (2001 est.)
HIV/AIDS - adult prevalence rate: 6.43% (1999 est.)
HIV/AIDS - people living with HIV/AIDS: 86,000 (1999 est.)
HIV/AIDS - deaths: 8,600 (1999 est.)
Nationality:
noun: Congolese (singular and plural)
adjective: Congolese or Congo
Ethnic groups: Kongo 48%, Sangha 20%, M'Bochi 12%, Teke 17%, Europeans NA%; note - Europeans estimated at 8,500, mostly French, before the 1997 civil war; may be half that of 1998, following the widespread destruction of foreign businesses in 1997
Religions: Christian 50%, animist 48%, Muslim 2%
Languages: French (official), Lingala and Monokutuba (lingua franca trade languages), many local languages and dialects (of which Kikongo has the most users)
Literacy:
definition: age 15 and over can read and write
total population: 74.9%
male: 83.1%
female: 67.2% (1995 est.)

Government

Country name:
conventional long form: Republic of the Congo
conventional short form: none
local long form: Republique du Congo
local short form: none
former: Middle Congo, Congo/Brazzaville, Congo
Government type: republic
Capital: Brazzaville
Administrative divisions: 9 regions (regions, singular - region) and 1 commune*; Bouenza, Brazzaville*, Cuvette, Kouilou, Lekoumou, Likouala, Niari, Plateaux, Pool, Sangha
Independence: 15 August 1960 (from France)
National holiday: Independence Day, 15 August (1960)
Constitution: Draft constitution approved by transitional parliament in September 2000
Legal system: based on French civil law system and customary law
Suffrage: 18 years of age; universal
Executive branch:
chief of state: President Denis SASSOU-NGUESSO (since 25 October 1997, following the civil war in which he toppled elected president Pascal LISSOUBA); note - the president is both the chief of state and head of government
head of government: President Denis SASSOU-NGUESSO (since 25 October 1997, following the civil war in which he toppled elected president Pascal LISSOUBA); note - the president is both the chief of state and head of government
cabinet: Council of Ministers appointed by the president
elections: president elected by popular vote for a five-year term; election last held 16 August 1992 (next was to be held 27 July 1997 but will be delayed for several years pending the drafting of a new constitution)
election results: Pascal LISSOUBA elected president in 1992; percent of vote - Pascal LISSOUBA 61.3%, Bernard KOLELAS 38.7%; note - LISSOUBA was deposed in 1997, replaced by Denis SASSOU-NGUESSO
Legislative branch: unicameral National Transitional Council (75 seats, members elected by reconciliation forum of 1,420 delegates on NA January 1998); note - the National Transitional Council replaced the bicameral Parliament
elections: National Transitional Council - last held NA January 1998 (next to be held NA 2001); note - at that election the National Transitional Council is to be replaced by a bicameral assembly
election results: National Transitional Council - percent of vote by party - NA%; seats by party - NA
Judicial branch: Supreme Court or Cour Supreme
Political parties and leaders: the most important of the many parties are the Democratic and Patriotic Forces or FDP (an alliance of Convention for Alternative Democracy, Congolese Labor Party or PCT, Liberal Republican Party, National Union for Democracy and Progress, Patriotic Union for the National Reconstruction, and Union for the National Renewal) [Denis SASSOU-NGUESSO, president]; Association for Democracy and Social Progress or RDPS [Jean-Pierre Thystere TCHICAYA, president]; Congolese Movement for Democracy and Integral Development or MCDDI [Michel MAMPOUYA]; Pan-African Union for Social Development or UPADS [Martin MBERI]; Union of Democratic Forces or UFD [Sebastian EBAO]
Political pressure groups and leaders: Congolese Trade Union Congress or CSC; General Union of Congolese Pupils and Students or UGEEC; Revolutionary Union of Congolese Women or URFC; Union of Congolese Socialist Youth or UJSC
International organization participation: ACCT, ACP, AfDB, BDEAC, CCC, CEEAC, CEMAC, ECA, FAO, FZ, G-77, IBRD, ICAO, ICFTU, ICRM, IDA, IFAD, IFC, IFRCS, ILO, IMF, IMO, Intelsat, Interpol, IOC, IOM (observer), ITU, NAM, OAU, OPCW, UN, UNCTAD, UNESCO, UNIDO, UPU, WCL, WFTU, WHO, WIPO, WMO, WToO, WTrO
Diplomatic representation in the US:
chief of mission: (vacant); Charge d'Affaires ad interim Serge MOMBOULI
chancery: 4891 Colorado Avenue NW, Washington, DC 20011
telephone: [1] (202) 726-5500
FAX: [1] (202) 726-1860
Diplomatic representation from the US:
chief of mission: Ambassador David H. KAEUPER
embassy: NA
mailing address: NA
telephone: [243] (88) 43608
FAX: [243] (88) 41036
note: the embassy is temporarily collocated with the US Embassy in the Democratic Republic of the Congo (US Embassy Kinshasa, 310 Avenue des Aviateurs, Kinshasa)
Flag description: divided diagonally from the lower hoist side by a yellow band; the upper triangle (hoist side) is green and the lower triangle is red; uses the popular pan-African colors of Ethiopia

Congo, Republic of the *(continued)*

Economy

Economy - overview: The economy is a mixture of village agriculture and handicrafts, an industrial sector based largely on oil, support services, and a government characterized by budget problems and overstaffing. Oil has supplanted forestry as the mainstay of the economy, providing a major share of government revenues and exports. In the early 1980s, rapidly rising oil revenues enabled the government to finance large-scale development projects with GDP growth averaging 5% annually, one of the highest rates in Africa. Moreover, the government has mortgaged a substantial portion of its oil earnings, contributing to the government's shortage of revenues. The 12 January 1994 devaluation of Franc Zone currencies by 50% resulted in inflation of 61% in 1994, but inflation has subsided since. Economic reform efforts continued with the support of international organizations, notably the World Bank and the IMF. The reform program came to a halt in June 1997 when civil war erupted. Denis SASSOU-NGUESSO, who returned to power when the war ended in October 1997, publicly expressed interest in moving forward on economic reforms and privatization and in renewing cooperation with international financial institutions. However, economic progress was badly hurt by slumping oil prices and the resumption of armed conflict in December 1998, which worsened the Republic of the Congo's budget deficit. Even with the IMF's renewed confidence and high world oil prices, Congo is unlikely to realize growth of more than 5% in 2001-02. With the return to fragile peace, the IMF approved a $14 million credit in November 2000 to aid post-conflict reconstruction.
GDP: purchasing power parity - $3.1 billion (2000 est.)
GDP - real growth rate: 3.8% (2000 est.)
GDP - per capita: purchasing power parity - $1,100 (2000 est.)
GDP - composition by sector:
agriculture: 10%
industry: 48%
services: 42% (1999 est.)
Population below poverty line: NA%
Household income or consumption by percentage share:
lowest 10%: NA%
highest 10%: NA%
Inflation rate (consumer prices): 3.5% (2000 est.)
Labor force: NA
Unemployment rate: NA%
Budget:
revenues: $870 million
expenditures: $970 million, including capital expenditures of $NA (1997 est.)
Industries: petroleum extraction, cement kilning, lumbering, brewing, sugar milling, palm oil, soap, flour, cigarette making
Industrial production growth rate: NA%
Electricity - production: 302 million kWh (1999)
Electricity - production by source:
fossil fuel: 0.66%
hydro: 99.34%
nuclear: 0%
other: 0% (1999)
Electricity - consumption: 406.9 million kWh (1999)
Electricity - exports: 0 kWh (1999)
Electricity - imports: 126 million kWh (1999)
Agriculture - products: cassava (tapioca), sugar, rice, corn, peanuts, vegetables, coffee, cocoa; forest products
Exports: $2.6 billion (f.o.b., 2000)
Exports - commodities: petroleum 50%, lumber, plywood, sugar, cocoa, coffee, diamonds
Exports - partners: US 23%, Benelux 14%, Germany, Italy, Taiwan, China (1998)
Imports: $870 million (f.o.b., 2000)
Imports - commodities: petroleum products, capital equipment, construction materials, foodstuffs
Imports - partners: France 23%, US 9%, Belgium 8%, UK 7%, Italy (1997 est.)
Debt - external: $5 billion (1999 est.)
Economic aid - recipient: $159.1 million (1995)
Currency: Communaute Financiere Africaine franc (XAF); note - responsible authority is the Bank of the Central African States
Currency code: XAF
Exchange rates: Communaute Financiere Africaine francs (XAF) per US dollar - 699.21 (January 2001), 711.98 (2000), 615.70 (1999), 589.95 (1998), 583.67 (1997), 511.55 (1996); note - from 1 January 1999, the XAF is pegged to the euro at a rate of 655.957 XAF per euro
Fiscal year: calendar year

Communications

Telephones - main lines in use: 22,000 (1997)
Telephones - mobile cellular: 1,000 (1996)
Telephone system:
general assessment: services barely adequate for government use; key exchanges are in Brazzaville, Pointe-Noire, and Loubomo; intercity lines frequently out-of-order
domestic: primary network consists of microwave radio relay and coaxial cable
international: satellite earth station - 1 Intelsat (Atlantic Ocean)
Radio broadcast stations: AM 1, FM 5, shortwave 1 (1999)
Radios: 341,000 (1997)
Television broadcast stations: 1 (1999)
Televisions: 33,000 (1997)
Internet country code: .cg
Internet Service Providers (ISPs): 1 (2000)
Internet users: 500 (2000)

Transportation

Railways:
total: 795 km (includes 285 km private track)
narrow gauge: 795 km 1.067-m gauge (1995 est.)
Highways:
total: 12,800 km
paved: 1,242 km
unpaved: 11,558 km (1996)
Waterways: 1,120 km
note: the Congo and Ubangi (Oubangui) rivers provide 1,120 km of commercially navigable water transport; other rivers are used for local traffic only
Pipelines: crude oil 25 km
Ports and harbors: Brazzaville, Impfondo, Ouesso, Oyo, Pointe-Noire
Airports: 33 (2000 est.)
Airports - with paved runways:
total: 4
over 3,047 m: 1
1,524 to 2,437 m: 3 (2000 est.)
Airports - with unpaved runways:
total: 29
1,524 to 2,437 m: 7
914 to 1,523 m: 12
under 914 m: 10 (2000 est.)

Military

Military branches: Army, Air Force, Navy, Gendarmerie
Military manpower - military age: 20 years of age
Military manpower - availability:
males age 15-49: 684,922 (2001 est.)
Military manpower - fit for military service:
males age 15-49: 347,946 (2001 est.)
Military manpower - reaching military age annually:
males: 32,350 (2001 est.)
Military expenditures - dollar figure: $110 million (FY93)
Military expenditures - percent of GDP: 3.8% (FY93)

Transnational Issues

Disputes - international: most of the Congo river boundary with the Democratic Republic of the Congo is indefinite (no agreement has been reached on the division of the river or its islands, except in the Stanley Pool/Pool Malebo area)

Cook Islands
(self-governing in free association with New Zealand)

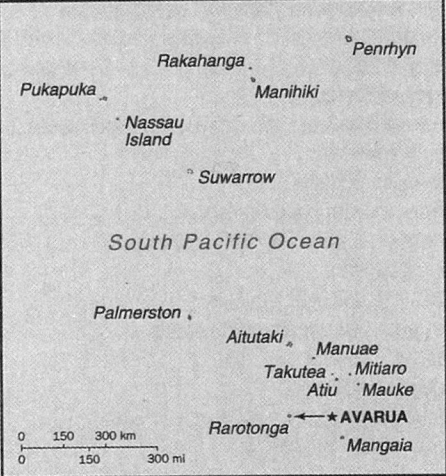

Introduction

Background: Named after Captain Cook, who sighted them in 1770, the islands became a British protectorate in 1888. By 1900, administrative control was transferred to New Zealand; in 1965 residents chose self-government in free association with New Zealand. The emigration of skilled workers to New Zealand and government deficits are continuing problems.

Geography

Location: Oceania, group of islands in the South Pacific Ocean, about one-half of the way from Hawaii to New Zealand
Geographic coordinates: 21 14 S, 159 46 W
Map references: Oceania
Area:
total: 240 sq km
land: 240 sq km
water: 0 sq km
Area - comparative: 1.3 times the size of Washington, DC
Land boundaries: 0 km
Coastline: 120 km
Maritime claims:
continental shelf: 200 NM or to the edge of the continental margin
exclusive economic zone: 200 NM
territorial sea: 12 NM
Climate: tropical; moderated by trade winds
Terrain: low coral atolls in north; volcanic, hilly islands in south
Elevation extremes:
lowest point: Pacific Ocean 0 m
highest point: Te Manga 652 m
Natural resources: NEGL
Land use:
arable land: 9%
permanent crops: 13%
permanent pastures: 0%
forests and woodland: 0%
other: 78% (1993 est.)
Irrigated land: NA sq km
Natural hazards: typhoons (November to March)
Environment - current issues: NA
Environment - international agreements:
party to: Biodiversity, Climate Change, Desertification, Law of the Sea
signed, but not ratified: Climate Change-Kyoto Protocol

People

Population: 20,611 (July 2001 est.)
Age structure:
0-14 years: NA%
15-64 years: NA%
65 years and over: NA%
HIV/AIDS - adult prevalence rate: NA%
HIV/AIDS - people living with HIV/AIDS: NA
HIV/AIDS - deaths: NA
Nationality:
noun: Cook Islander(s)
adjective: Cook Islander
Ethnic groups: Polynesian (full blood) 81.3%, Polynesian and European 7.7%, Polynesian and non-European 7.7%, European 2.4%, other 0.9%
Religions: Christian (majority of populace are members of the Cook Islands Christian Church)
Languages: English (official), Maori
Literacy:
definition: NA
total population: 95%
male: NA%
female: NA%

Government

Country name:
conventional long form: none
conventional short form: Cook Islands
former: Harvey Islands
Dependency status: self-governing in free association with New Zealand; Cook Islands is fully responsible for internal affairs; New Zealand retains responsibility for external affairs, in consultation with the Cook Islands
Government type: self-governing parliamentary democracy
Capital: Avarua
Administrative divisions: none
Independence: none (became self-governing in free association with New Zealand on 4 August 1965 and has the right at any time to move to full independence by unilateral action)
National holiday: Constitution Day, first Monday in August (1965)
Constitution: 4 August 1965
Legal system: based on New Zealand law and English common law
Suffrage: NA years of age; universal adult
Executive branch:
chief of state: Queen ELIZABETH II (since 6 February 1952), represented by Apenera SHORT (since NA); New Zealand High Commissioner Jon JONESSEN (since NA January 1998), representative of New Zealand
head of government: Prime Minister Dr. Terepai MAOATE (since 18 November 1999); Deputy Prime Minister Norman GEORGE (since NA)
cabinet: Cabinet chosen by the prime minister; collectively responsible to Parliament
elections: none; the monarch is hereditary; the UK representative is appointed by the monarch; the New Zealand high commissioner is appointed by the New Zealand Government; following legislative elections, the leader of the party that wins the most seats usually becomes prime minister
note: ten years of rule by the Cook Islands Party (CIP) came to an end 18 November 1999 with the resignation of Prime Minister Joe WILLIAMS; WILLIAMS had led a minority government since October 1999 when the New Alliance Party (NAP) left the government coalition and joined the main opposition Democratic Alliance Party (DAP); on 18 November 1999, DAP leader Dr. Terepai MAOATE was sworn in as prime minister
Legislative branch: unicameral Parliament (25 seats; members elected by popular vote to serve five-year terms)
elections: last held NA June 1999 (next to be held by NA 2004)
election results: percent of vote by party - NA%; seats by party - CIP 12, DAP 12, NAP 1
note: the House of Ariki (chiefs) advises on traditional matters, but has no legislative powers
Judicial branch: High Court
Political parties and leaders: Cook Islands People's Party or CIP [Tai CARPENTER]; Democratic Alliance Party or DAP [Terepai MAOATE]; New Alliance Party or NAP [Norman GEORGE]
Political pressure groups and leaders: NA
International organization participation: ACP, AsDB, ESCAP (associate), FAO, ICAO, ICFTU, IFAD, Intelsat (nonsignatory user), IOC, OPCW, Sparteca, SPC, SPF, UNESCO, WHO, WMO
Diplomatic representation in the US: none (self-governing in free association with New Zealand)
Diplomatic representation from the US: none (self-governing in free association with New Zealand)
Flag description: blue, with the flag of the UK in the upper hoist-side quadrant and a large circle of 15 white five-pointed stars (one for every island) centered in the outer half of the flag

Economy

Economy - overview: Like many other South Pacific island nations, the Cook Islands' economic development is hindered by the isolation of the country from foreign markets, the limited size of domestic markets, lack of natural resources, periodic devastation from natural disasters, and inadequate infrastructure. Agriculture provides the economic base

Cook Islands (continued)

with major exports made up of copra and citrus fruit. Manufacturing activities are limited to fruit processing, clothing, and handicrafts. Trade deficits are made up for by remittances from emigrants and by foreign aid, overwhelmingly from New Zealand. In the 1980s and 1990s, the country lived beyond its means, maintaining a bloated public service and accumulating a large foreign debt. Subsequent reforms, including the sale of state assets, the strengthening of economic management, the encouragement of tourism, and a debt restructuring agreement, have rekindled investment and growth.

GDP: purchasing power parity - $100 million (1999 est.)
GDP - real growth rate: 2.9% (1999 est.)
GDP - per capita: purchasing power parity - $5,000 (1999 est.)
GDP - composition by sector:
agriculture: 18%
industry: 9%
services: 73% (1995)
Population below poverty line: NA%
Household income or consumption by percentage share:
lowest 10%: NA%
highest 10%: NA%
Inflation rate (consumer prices): 1.6% (1999 est.)
Labor force: 6,601 (1993)
Labor force - by occupation: agriculture 29%, industry 15%, services 56% (1995) note - shortage of skilled labor
Unemployment rate: NA%
Budget:
revenues: $25 million
expenditures: $23 million, including capital expenditures of $NA (FY 99/00)
Industries: fruit processing, tourism, fishing
Industrial production growth rate: NA%
Electricity - production: 21 million kWh (1999)
Electricity - production by source:
fossil fuel: 100%
hydro: 0%
nuclear: 0%
other: 0% (1999)
Electricity - consumption: 19.5 million kWh (1999)
Electricity - exports: 0 kWh (1999)
Electricity - imports: 0 kWh (1999)
Agriculture - products: copra, citrus, pineapples, tomatoes, beans, pawpaws, bananas, yams, taro, coffee; pigs, poultry
Exports: $3 million (f.o.b., 1999 est.)
Exports - commodities: copra, papayas, fresh and canned citrus fruit, coffee; fish; pearls and pearl shells; clothing
Exports - partners: Japan 42%, New Zealand 25%, US 9%, Australia 9% (1999)
Imports: $85 million (c.i.f., 1994)
Imports - commodities: foodstuffs, textiles, fuels, timber, capital goods
Imports - partners: NZ 70%, Australia 8% (1999)
Debt - external: $141 million (1996 est.)
Economic aid - recipient: $13.1 million (1995); note - New Zealand continues to furnish the greater part
Currency: New Zealand dollar (NZD)
Currency code: NZD
Exchange rates: New Zealand dollars per US dollar - 2.2502 (January 2001), 2.1863 (2000), 1.8886 (1999), 1.8632 (1998), 1.5083 (1997), 1.4543 (1996)
Fiscal year: 1 April - 31 March

Communications

Telephones - main lines in use: 5,000 (1997)
Telephones - mobile cellular: 0 (1994)
Telephone system:
general assessment: NA
domestic: the individual islands are connected by a combination of satellite earth stations, microwave systems, and VHF and HF radiotelephone; within the islands, service is provided by small exchanges connected to subscribers by open wire, cable, and fiber-optic cable
international: satellite earth station - 1 Intelsat (Pacific Ocean)
Radio broadcast stations: AM 1, FM 2, shortwave 0 (1998)
Radios: 14,000 (1997)
Television broadcast stations: 2 (plus eight low-power repeaters) (1997)
Televisions: 4,000 (1997)
Internet country code: .ck
Internet Service Providers (ISPs): 3 (2000)
Internet users: NA

Transportation

Railways: 0 km
Highways:
total: 320 km (1992)
paved: NA
unpaved: NA
Waterways: none
Ports and harbors: Avarua, Avatiu
Merchant marine:
total: 1 ship (1,000 GRT or over) totaling 2,310 GRT/ 2,181 DWT
ships by type: cargo 1 (2000 est.)
Airports: 7 (2000 est.)
Airports - with paved runways:
total: 1
1,524 to 2,437 m: 1 (2000 est.)
Airports - with unpaved runways:
total: 6
1,524 to 2,437 m: 3
914 to 1,523 m: 3 (2000 est.)

Military

Military - note: defense is the responsibility of New Zealand, in consultation with the Cook Islands and at its request

Transnational Issues

Disputes - international: none

Coral Sea Islands (territory of Australia)

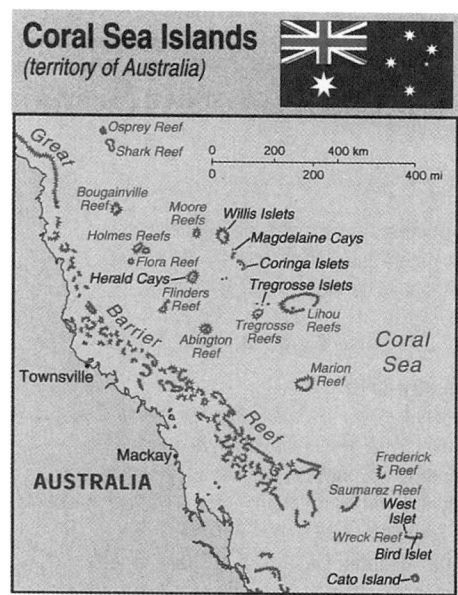

Introduction

Background: Scattered over some 1 million square kilometers of ocean, the Coral Sea Islands were declared a territory of Australia in 1969. They are uninhabited except for a small meteorological staff on Willis Island. Automated weather stations, beacons, and a lighthouse occupy many other islands and reefs.

Geography

Location: Oceania, islands in the Coral Sea, northeast of Australia
Geographic coordinates: 18 00 S, 152 00 E
Map references: Oceania
Area:
total: less than 3 sq km
land: less than 3 sq km
water: 0 sq km
note: includes numerous small islands and reefs scattered over a sea area of about 1 million sq km, with the Willis Islets the most important
Area - comparative: NA
Land boundaries: 0 km
Coastline: 3,095 km
Maritime claims:
exclusive fishing zone: 200 NM
territorial sea: 3 NM
Climate: tropical
Terrain: sand and coral reefs and islands (or cays)
Elevation extremes:
lowest point: Pacific Ocean 0 m
highest point: unnamed location on Cato Island 6 m
Natural resources: NEGL
Land use:
arable land: 0%
permanent crops: 0%
permanent pastures: 0%
forests and woodland: 0%
other: 100% (mostly grass or scrub cover)
Irrigated land: 0 sq km (1993)

Coral Sea Islands (continued)

Natural hazards: occasional tropical cyclones
Environment - current issues: no permanent fresh water resources
Geography - note: important nesting area for birds and turtles

People

Population: no indigenous inhabitants
note: there is a staff of three to four at the meteorological station (July 2001 est.)

Government

Country name:
conventional long form: Coral Sea Islands Territory
conventional short form: Coral Sea Islands
Dependency status: territory of Australia; administered from Canberra by the Department of the Environment, Sport, and Territories
Legal system: the laws of Australia, where applicable, apply
Executive branch: administered from Canberra by the Department of the Environment, Sport, and Territories
Diplomatic representation in the US: none (territory of Australia)
Diplomatic representation from the US: none (territory of Australia)
Flag description: the flag of Australia is used

Economy

Economy - overview: no economic activity

Communications

Communications - note: there are automatic weather stations on many of the isles and reefs relaying data to the mainland

Transportation

Waterways: none
Ports and harbors: none; offshore anchorage only

Military

Military - note: defense is the responsibility of Australia; visited regularly by the Royal Australian Navy; Australia has control over the activities of visitors

Transnational Issues

Disputes - international: none

Costa Rica

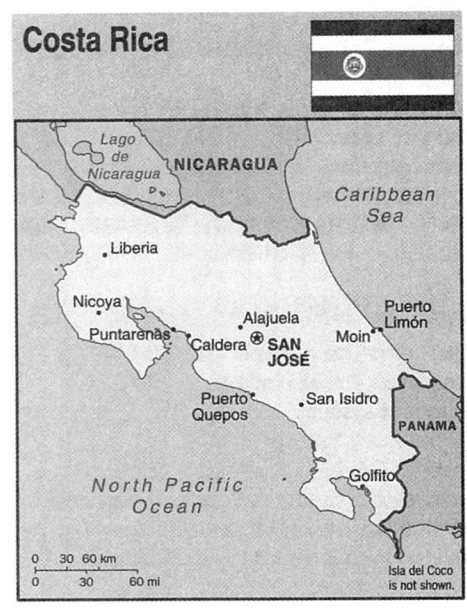

Introduction

Background: Costa Rica is a Central American success story: since the late 19th century, only two brief periods of violence have marred its democratic development. Although still a largely agricultural country, it has achieved a relatively high standard of living. Land ownership is widespread. Tourism is a rapidly expanding industry.

Geography

Location: Middle America, bordering both the Caribbean Sea and the North Pacific Ocean, between Nicaragua and Panama
Geographic coordinates: 10 00 N, 84 00 W
Map references: Central America and the Caribbean
Area:
total: 51,100 sq km
land: 50,660 sq km
water: 440 sq km
note: includes Isla del Coco
Area - comparative: slightly smaller than West Virginia
Land boundaries:
total: 639 km
border countries: Nicaragua 309 km, Panama 330 km
Coastline: 1,290 km
Maritime claims:
exclusive economic zone: 200 NM
territorial sea: 12 NM
Climate: tropical and subtropical; dry season (December to April); rainy season (May to November); cooler in highlands
Terrain: coastal plains separated by rugged mountains
Elevation extremes:
lowest point: Pacific Ocean 0 m
highest point: Cerro Chirripo 3,810 m
Natural resources: hydropower
Land use:
arable land: 6%
permanent crops: 5%
permanent pastures: 46%
forests and woodland: 31%
other: 12% (1993 est.)
Irrigated land: 1,200 sq km (1993 est.)
Natural hazards: occasional earthquakes, hurricanes along Atlantic coast; frequent flooding of lowlands at onset of rainy season and landslides; active volcanoes
Environment - current issues: deforestation and land use change, largely a result of the clearing of land for cattle ranching and agriculture; soil erosion; water pollution (rivers); coastal marine pollution; wetlands degradation; fisheries protection; solid waste management; air pollution
Environment - international agreements:
party to: Biodiversity, Climate Change, Desertification, Endangered Species, Environmental Modification, Hazardous Wastes, Law of the Sea, Marine Dumping, Nuclear Test Ban, Ozone Layer Protection, Ship Pollution, Wetlands, Whaling
signed, but not ratified: Climate Change-Kyoto Protocol, Marine Life Conservation

People

Population: 3,773,057 (July 2001 est.)
Age structure:
0-14 years: 31.38% (male 605,728; female 578,128)
15-64 years: 63.37% (male 1,209,084; female 1,181,754)
65 years and over: 5.25% (male 92,314; female 106,049) (2001 est.)
Population growth rate: 1.65% (2001 est.)
Birth rate: 20.27 births/1,000 population (2001 est.)
Death rate: 4.3 deaths/1,000 population (2001 est.)
Net migration rate: 0.53 migrant(s)/1,000 population (2001 est.)
Sex ratio:
at birth: 1.05 male(s)/female
under 15 years: 1.05 male(s)/female
15-64 years: 1.02 male(s)/female
65 years and over: 0.87 male(s)/female
total population: 1.02 male(s)/female (2001 est.)
Infant mortality rate: 11.18 deaths/1,000 live births (2001 est.)
Life expectancy at birth:
total population: 76.02 years
male: 73.49 years
female: 78.68 years (2001 est.)
Total fertility rate: 2.47 children born/woman (2001 est.)
HIV/AIDS - adult prevalence rate: 0.54% (1999 est.)
HIV/AIDS - people living with HIV/AIDS: 12,000 (1999 est.)
HIV/AIDS - deaths: 750 (1999 est.)
Nationality:
noun: Costa Rican(s)
adjective: Costa Rican

Costa Rica (continued)

Ethnic groups: white (including mestizo) 94%, black 3%, Amerindian 1%, Chinese 1%, other 1%
Religions: Roman Catholic 76.3%, Evangelical 13.7%, other Protestant 0.7%, Jehovah's Witnesses 1.3%, other 4.8%, none 3.2%
Languages: Spanish (official), English spoken around Puerto Limon
Literacy:
definition: age 15 and over can read and write
total population: 94.8%
male: 94.7%
female: 95% (1995 est.)

Government

Country name:
conventional long form: Republic of Costa Rica
conventional short form: Costa Rica
local long form: Republica de Costa Rica
local short form: Costa Rica
Government type: democratic republic
Capital: San Jose
Administrative divisions: 7 provinces (provincias, singular - provincia); Alajuela, Cartago, Guanacaste, Heredia, Limon, Puntarenas, San Jose
Independence: 15 September 1821 (from Spain)
National holiday: Independence Day, 15 September (1821)
Constitution: 7 November 1949
Legal system: based on Spanish civil law system; judicial review of legislative acts in the Supreme Court; has accepted compulsory ICJ jurisdiction
Suffrage: 18 years of age; universal and compulsory
Executive branch:
chief of state: President Miguel Angel RODRIGUEZ (since 8 May 1998); First Vice President Astrid FISCHEL Volio (since 8 May 1998), Second Vice President Elizabeth ODIO Benito (since 8 May 1998); note - president is both the chief of state and head of government
head of government: President Miguel Angel RODRIGUEZ (since 8 May 1998); First Vice President Astrid FISCHEL Volio (since 8 May 1998), Second Vice President Elizabeth ODIO Benito (since 8 May 1998); note - president is both the chief of state and head of government
cabinet: Cabinet selected by the president
elections: president and vice presidents elected on the same ticket by popular vote for four-year terms; election last held 1 February 1998 (next to be held 3 February 2002)
election results: Miguel Angel RODRIGUEZ elected president; percent of vote - Miguel Angel RODRIGUEZ (PUSC) 46.6%, Jose Miguel CORRALES (PLN) 44.6%
Legislative branch: unicameral Legislative Assembly or Asamblea Legislativa (57 seats; members are elected by direct, popular vote to serve four-year terms)
elections: last held 1 February 1998 (next to be held 3 February 2002)
election results: percent of vote by party - PUSC 41%, PLN 35%, minority parties 24%; seats by party - PUSC 27, PLN 23, minority parties 7
Judicial branch: Supreme Court or Corte Suprema (22 justices are elected for eight-year terms by the Legislative Assembly)
Political parties and leaders: Agricultural Labor Action or PALA [Carlos Alberto SOLIS Blanco]; Costa Rican Renovation Party or PRC [Justo OROZCO]; Democratic Force Party or PFD [Jose M. NUNEZ]; Libertarian Movement Party or PML [Otto GUEVARA Guth]; National Christian Alliance Party or ANC [Alejandro MADRIGAL]; National Independent Party or PNI [Jorge GONZALEZ Marten]; National Integration Party or PIN [Walter MUNOZ Cespedes]; National Liberation Party or PLN [Sonia PICADO]; Social Christian Unity Party or PUSC [Luis Manuel CHACON]
note: mainly a two-party system - PUSC and PLN; numerous small parties share less than 25% of population's support
Political pressure groups and leaders: Authentic Confederation of Democratic Workers or CATD (Communist Party affiliate); Chamber of Coffee Growers; Confederated Union of Workers or CUT (Communist Party affiliate); Costa Rican Confederation of Democratic Workers or CCTD (Liberation Party affiliate); Federation of Public Service Workers or FTSP; National Association for Economic Development or ANFE; National Association of Educators or ANDE; Rerum Novarum or CTRN (PLN affiliate) [Gilbert Brown]
International organization participation: BCIE, CACM, ECLAC, FAO, G-77, IADB, IAEA, IBRD, ICAO, ICFTU, ICRM, IDA, IFAD, IFC, IFRCS, ILO, IMF, IMO, Inmarsat, Intelsat, Interpol, IOC, IOM, ISO, ITU, LAES, LAIA (observer), NAM (observer), OAS, OPANAL, OPCW, PCA, UN, UNCTAD, UNESCO, UNIDO, UNU, UPU, WCL, WFTU, WHO, WIPO, WMO, WToO, WTrO
Diplomatic representation in the US:
chief of mission: Ambassador Jaime DAREMBLUM Rosenstein
chancery: 2114 S Street NW, Washington, DC 20008
telephone: [1] (202) 234-2945
FAX: [1] (202) 265-4795
consulate(s) general: Atlanta, Boston, Chicago, Denver, Houston, Los Angeles, Miami, New Orleans, New York, Phoenix, San Antonio, San Francisco, St. Paul, and Tampa
consulate(s): Austin
Diplomatic representation from the US:
chief of mission: Ambassador Thomas J. DODD
embassy: Calle 120 Avenida O, Pavas, San Jose
mailing address: APO AA 34020
telephone: [506] 220-3939
FAX: [506] 220-2305
Flag description: five horizontal bands of blue (top), white, red (double width), white, and blue, with the coat of arms in a white disk on the hoist side of the red band

Economy

Economy - overview: Costa Rica's basically stable economy depends on tourism, agriculture, and electronics exports. Poverty has been substantially reduced over the past 15 years, and a strong social safety net has been put into place. Foreign investors remain attracted by the country's political stability and high education levels, and tourism continues to bring in foreign exchange. However, traditional export sectors have not kept pace. Low coffee prices and an overabundance of bananas have hurt the agricultural sector. The government continues to grapple with its large deficit and massive internal debt and with the need to modernize the state-owned electricity and telecommunications sector.
GDP: purchasing power parity - $25 billion (2000 est.)
GDP - real growth rate: 3% (2000 est.)
GDP - per capita: purchasing power parity - $6,700 (2000 est.)
GDP - composition by sector:
agriculture: 12.5%
industry: 30.7%
services: 56.8% (1999)
Population below poverty line: 20.6% (1999 est.)
Household income or consumption by percentage share:
lowest 10%: 1.3%
highest 10%: 34.7% (1996)
Inflation rate (consumer prices): 11% (2000 est.)
Labor force: 1.9 million (1999)
Labor force - by occupation: agriculture 20%, industry 22%, services 58% (1999 est.)
Unemployment rate: 5.2% (2000 est.)
Budget:
revenues: $1.95 billion
expenditures: $2.4 billion, including capital expenditures of $NA (2000 est.)
Industries: microprocessors, food processing, textiles and clothing, construction materials, fertilizer, plastic products
Industrial production growth rate: 4.3% (2000)
Electricity - production: 5.805 billion kWh (1999)
Electricity - production by source:
fossil fuel: 2.41%
hydro: 83.32%
nuclear: 0%
other: 14.27% (1999)
Electricity - consumption: 5.303 billion kWh (1999)
Electricity - exports: 165 million kWh (1999)
Electricity - imports: 69 million kWh (1999)
Agriculture - products: coffee, pineapples, bananas, sugar, corn, rice, beans, potatoes; beef; timber
Exports: $6.1 billion (f.o.b., 2000 est.)
Exports - commodities: coffee, bananas, sugar; pineapples; textiles, electronic components, medical equipment
Exports - partners: US 54.1%, EU 21.3%, Central America 8.6% (1999)
Imports: $5.9 billion (f.o.b., 2000 est.)

Costa Rica (continued)

Imports - commodities: raw materials, consumer goods, capital equipment, petroleum
Imports - partners: US 56.4%, EU 9%, Mexico 5.4%, Japan 4.7%, (1999)
Debt - external: $4.2 billion (2000 est.)
Currency: Costa Rican colon (CRC)
Currency code: CRC
Exchange rates: Costa Rican colones per US dollar - 318.95 (2001), 308.19 (2000), 285.68 (1999), 257.23 (1998), 232.60 (1997), 207.69 (1996)
Fiscal year: calendar year

Communications

Telephones - main lines in use: 450,000 (1998)
note: 584,000 installed in 1997, but only about 450,000 were in use 1998
Telephones - mobile cellular: 143,000 (2000)
Telephone system:
general assessment: very good domestic telephone service
domestic: point-to-point and point-to-multi-point microwave, fiber-optic, and coaxial cable link rural areas; Internet service is available
international: connected to Central American Microwave System; satellite earth stations - 2 Intelsat (Atlantic Ocean); two submarine cables (1999)
Radio broadcast stations: AM 50, FM 43, shortwave 19 (1998)
Radios: 980,000 (1997)
Television broadcast stations: 6 (plus 11 repeaters) (1997)
Televisions: 525,000 (1997)
Internet country code: .cr
Internet Service Providers (ISPs): 3 (of which only one is legal) (2000)
Internet users: 150,000 (2000)

Transportation

Railways:
total: 950 km
narrow gauge: 950 km 1.067-m gauge (260 km electrified)
Highways:
total: 37,273 km
paved: 7,827 km
unpaved: 29,446 km (1998 est.)
Waterways: 730 km (seasonally navigable)
Pipelines: petroleum products 176 km
Ports and harbors: Caldera, Golfito, Moin, Puerto Limon, Puerto Quepos, Puntarenas
Merchant marine:
total: 1 ship (1,000 GRT or over) totaling 1,716 GRT/NA DWT
ships by type: passenger 1 (2000 est.)
Airports: 152 (2000 est.)
Airports - with paved runways:
total: 29
2,438 to 3,047 m: 2
1,524 to 2,437 m: 1
914 to 1,523 m: 19
under 914 m: 7 (2000 est.)
Airports - with unpaved runways:
total: 123
914 to 1,523 m: 28
under 914 m: 95 (2000 est.)

Military

Military branches: Coast Guard, Air Section, Ministry of Public Security Force (Fuerza Publica)
note: Costa Rica has no military, only domestic police forces, including the Coast Guard and Air Section
Military manpower - military age: 18 years of age
Military manpower - availability:
males age 15-49: 1,035,090 (2001 est.)
Military manpower - fit for military service:
males age 15-49: 692,973 (2001 est.)
Military manpower - reaching military age annually:
males: 39,411 (2001 est.)
Military expenditures - dollar figure: $69 million (FY99)
Military expenditures - percent of GDP: 1.6% (FY99)

Transnational Issues

Disputes - international: legal dispute over navigational rights of Rio San Juan on border with Nicaragua
Illicit drugs: transshipment country for cocaine and heroin from South America; illicit production of cannabis on small, scattered plots; domestic cocaine consumption is rising, particularly crack cocaine; those who previously only trafficked are now becoming users

Cote d'Ivoire

Introduction

Background: Close ties to France since independence in 1960, the development of cocoa production for export, and foreign investment made Cote d'Ivoire one of the most prosperous of the tropical African states. Falling cocoa prices and political turmoil, however, sparked an economic downturn in 1999 and 2000. On 25 December 1999, a military coup - the first ever in Cote d'Ivoire's history - overthrew the government led by President Henri Konan BEDIE. Presidential and legislative elections held in October and December 2000 provoked violence due to the exclusion of opposition leader Alassane OUATTARA. In October 2000, Laurent GBAGBO replaced junta leader Robert GUEI as president, ending 10 months of military rule.

Geography

Location: Western Africa, bordering the North Atlantic Ocean, between Ghana and Liberia
Geographic coordinates: 8 00 N, 5 00 W
Map references: Africa
Area:
total: 322,460 sq km
land: 318,000 sq km
water: 4,460 sq km
Area - comparative: slightly larger than New Mexico
Land boundaries:
total: 3,110 km
border countries: Burkina Faso 584 km, Ghana 668 km, Guinea 610 km, Liberia 716 km, Mali 532 km
Coastline: 515 km
Maritime claims:
continental shelf: 200 NM
exclusive economic zone: 200 NM
territorial sea: 12 NM
Climate: tropical along coast, semiarid in far north; three seasons - warm and dry (November to March), hot and dry (March to May), hot and wet (June to October)

Cote d'Ivoire *(continued)*

Terrain: mostly flat to undulating plains; mountains in northwest
Elevation extremes:
lowest point: Gulf of Guinea 0 m
highest point: Mont Nimba 1,752 m
Natural resources: petroleum, natural gas, diamonds, manganese, iron ore, cobalt, bauxite, copper, hydropower
Land use:
arable land: 8%
permanent crops: 4%
permanent pastures: 41%
forests and woodland: 22%
other: 25% (1993 est.)
Irrigated land: 680 sq km (1993 est.)
Natural hazards: coast has heavy surf and no natural harbors; during the rainy season torrential flooding is possible
Environment - current issues: deforestation (most of the country's forests - once the largest in West Africa - have been heavily logged); water pollution from sewage and industrial and agricultural effluents
Environment - international agreements:
party to: Biodiversity, Climate Change, Desertification, Endangered Species, Hazardous Wastes, Law of the Sea, Marine Dumping, Nuclear Test Ban, Ozone Layer Protection, Ship Pollution, Tropical Timber 83, Tropical Timber 94, Wetlands
signed, but not ratified: none of the selected agreements

People

Population: 16,393,221
note: estimates for this country explicitly take into account the effects of excess mortality due to AIDS; this can result in lower life expectancy, higher infant mortality and death rates, lower population and growth rates, and changes in the distribution of population by age and sex than would otherwise be expected (July 2001 est.)
Age structure:
0-14 years: 46.21% (male 3,802,397; female 3,773,455)
15-64 years: 51.57% (male 4,343,518; female 4,110,805)
65 years and over: 2.22% (male 180,463; female 182,583) (2001 est.)
Population growth rate: 2.51% (2001 est.)
Birth rate: 40.38 births/1,000 population (2001 est.)
Death rate: 16.65 deaths/1,000 population (2001 est.)
Net migration rate: 1.4 migrant(s)/1,000 population (2001 est.)
note: after Liberia's civil war started in 1990, more than 350,000 refugees fled to Cote d'Ivoire; by the end of 1999 most Liberian refugees were assumed to have returned
Sex ratio:
at birth: 1.03 male(s)/female
under 15 years: 1.01 male(s)/female
15-64 years: 1.06 male(s)/female
65 years and over: 0.99 male(s)/female
total population: 1.03 male(s)/female (2001 est.)
Infant mortality rate: 93.65 deaths/1,000 live births (2001 est.)
Life expectancy at birth:
total population: 44.93 years
male: 43.58 years
female: 46.33 years (2001 est.)
Total fertility rate: 5.7 children born/woman (2001 est.)
HIV/AIDS - adult prevalence rate: 10.76% (1999 est.)
HIV/AIDS - people living with HIV/AIDS: 760,000 (1999 est.)
HIV/AIDS - deaths: 72,000 (1999 est.)
Nationality:
noun: Ivorian(s)
adjective: Ivorian
Ethnic groups: Akan 42.1%, Voltaiques or Gur 17.6%, Northern Mandes 16.5%, Krous 11%, Southern Mandes 10%, other 2.8% (1998)
Religions: Christian 34%, Muslim 27%, no religion 21%, animist 15%, other 3% (1998)
note: the majority of foreigners (migratory workers) are Muslim (70%) and Christian (20%)
Languages: French (official), 60 native dialects with Dioula the most widely spoken
Literacy:
definition: age 15 and over can read and write
total population: 48.5%
male: 57%
female: 40%

Government

Country name:
conventional long form: Republic of Cote d'Ivoire
conventional short form: Cote d'Ivoire
local long form: Republique de Cote d'Ivoire
local short form: Cote d'Ivoire
former: Ivory Coast
Government type: republic; multiparty presidential regime established 1960
Capital: Yamoussoukro; note - although Yamoussoukro has been the official capital since 1983, Abidjan remains the administrative center; the US, like other countries, maintains its Embassy in Abidjan
Administrative divisions: 50 departments (departements, singular - departement); Abengourou, Abidjan, Aboisso, Adzope, Agboville, Agnibilekrou, Bangolo, Beoumi, Biankouma, Bondoukou, Bongouanou, Bouafle, Bouake, Bouna, Boundiali, Dabakala, Daloa, Danane, Daoukro, Dimbokro, Divo, Duekoue, Ferkessedougou, Gagnoa, Grand-Lahou, Guiglo, Issia, Katiola, Korhogo, Lakota, Man, Mankono, Mbahiakro, Odienne, Oume, Sakassou, San-Pedro, Sassandra, Seguela, Sinfra, Soubre, Tabou, Tanda, Tingrela, Tiassale, Touba, Toumodi, Vavoua, Yamoussoukro, Zuenoula
note: Cote d'Ivoire may have a new administrative structure consisting of 58 departments; the following additional departments have been reported but not yet confirmed by the US Board on Geographic Names (BGN); Adiake', Ale'pe', Dabon, Grand Bassam, Jacqueville, Tiebissou, Toulepleu, Bocanda
Independence: 7 August (1960) (from France)
National holiday: Independence Day, 7 August (1960)
Constitution: 3 November 1960; has been amended numerous times, last time 27 July 1998
Legal system: based on French civil law system and customary law; judicial review in the Constitutional Chamber of the Supreme Court; has not accepted compulsory ICJ jurisdiction
Suffrage: 18 years of age; universal
Executive branch:
chief of state: President Laurent GBAGBO (since 26 October 2000); note - took power following a popular overthrow of the interim leader Gen. Robert GUEI who had claimed a dubious victory in presidential elections; Gen. GUEI himself had assumed power on 25 December 1999, following a military coup against the government of former President Henri Konan BEDIE
head of government: Prime Minister and Minister of Planning and Development Affi N'GUESSAN (since 27 October 2000) appointed by the president
cabinet: Council of Ministers appointed by the president
elections: president elected by popular vote for a five-year term; election last held 26 October 2000 (next is scheduled to be held NA 2005); prime minister appointed by the president
election results: Laurent GBAGBO elected president; percent of vote - Laurent GBAGBO 59.4%, Robert GUEI 32.7%, Francis WODIE 5.7%, other 2.2%
Legislative branch: unicameral National Assembly or Assemblee Nationale (225 seats; members are elected in single- and multi-district elections by direct popular vote to serve five-year terms)
elections: elections last held 10 December 2000 with by-elections on 14 January 2001 (next to be held NA 2005)
election results: percent of vote by party - NA%; seats by party - FPI 96, PDCI-RDA 94, RDR 5, PIT 4, other 2, independents 22, vacant 2
note: a Senate is scheduled to be created in the next full election in 2005
Judicial branch: Supreme Court or Cour Supreme consists of four chambers: Judicial Chamber for criminal cases, Audit Chamber for financial cases, Constitutional Chamber for judicial review cases, and Administrative Chamber for civil cases; there is no legal limit to the number of members
Political parties and leaders: Democratic Party of Cote d'Ivoire-African Democratic Rally or PDCI-RDA [Aime Henri Konan BEDIE]; Ivorian Popular Front or FPI [Laurent GBAGBO]; Ivorian Worker's Party or PIT [Francis WODIE]; Rally of the Republicans or RDR [Henriette DAGRI-DIABATE]; Union for Democracy and Peace [Gen. Robert GUEI]; over 20 smaller parties
Political pressure groups and leaders: NA

Cote d'Ivoire (continued)

International organization participation: ACP, AfDB, CCC, ECA, ECOWAS, Entente, FAO, FZ, G-24, G-77, IAEA, IBRD, ICAO, ICC, ICFTU, ICRM, IDA, IFAD, IFC, IFRCS, ILO, IMF, IMO, Intelsat, Interpol, IOC, IOM, ISO (correspondent), ITU, NAM, OAU, OIC (observer), OPCW, UN, UNCTAD, UNESCO, UNHCR, UNIDO, UPU, WADB, WADB (regional), WAEMU, WCL, WFTU, WHO, WIPO, WMO, WToO, WTrO
Diplomatic representation in the US:
chief of mission: Ambassador Youssouf BAMBA
chancery: 3421 Massachusetts Avenue NW, Washington, DC 20007
telephone: [1] (202) 797-0300
Diplomatic representation from the US:
chief of mission: Ambassador George MU
embassy: 5 Rue Jesse Owens, Abidjan
mailing address: B. P. 1712, Abidjan 01
telephone: [225] 20 21 09 79
FAX: [225] 20 22 32 59
Flag description: three equal vertical bands of orange (hoist side), white, and green; similar to the flag of Ireland, which is longer and has the colors reversed - green (hoist side), white, and orange; also similar to the flag of Italy, which is green (hoist side), white, and red; design was based on the flag of France

Economy

Economy - overview: Cote d'Ivoire is among the world's largest producers and exporters of coffee, cocoa beans, and palm oil. Consequently, the economy is highly sensitive to fluctuations in international prices for these products and to weather conditions. Despite government attempts to diversify the economy, it is still largely dependent on agriculture and related activities, which engage roughly 68% of the population. After several years of lagging performance, the Ivorian economy began a comeback in 1994, due to the 50% devaluation of the CFA franc and improved prices for cocoa and coffee, growth in nontraditional primary exports such as pineapples and rubber, limited trade and banking liberalization, offshore oil and gas discoveries, and generous external financing and debt rescheduling by multilateral lenders and France. Moreover, government adherence to donor-mandated reforms led to a jump in growth to 5% annually in 1996-99. Growth was negative in 2000 because of the difficulty of meeting the conditions of international donors, continued low prices of key exports, and post-coup instability. In 2001-02, a moderate rebound in the cocoa market could boost growth back above 3%; however, political instability could impede growth again.
GDP: purchasing power parity - $26.2 billion (2000 est.)
GDP - real growth rate: -0.3% (2000 est.)
GDP - per capita: purchasing power parity - $1,600 (2000 est.)
GDP - composition by sector:
agriculture: 32%
industry: 18%
services: 50% (1998)
Population below poverty line: NA%
Household income or consumption by percentage share:
lowest 10%: 3.1%
highest 10%: 28.8% (1995)
Inflation rate (consumer prices): 2.5% (2000 est.)
Labor force: 68% agricultural (2000 est.)
Unemployment rate: 13% in urban areas (1998 est.)
Budget:
revenues: $1.5 billion
expenditures: $2.1 billion, including capital expenditures of $420 million (2000 est.)
Industries: foodstuffs, beverages; wood products, oil refining, truck and bus assembly, textiles, fertilizer, building materials, electricity
Industrial production growth rate: 15% (1998 est.)
Electricity - production: 4.06 billion kWh (1999)
Electricity - production by source:
fossil fuel: 75.37%
hydro: 24.63%
nuclear: 0%
other: 0% (1999)
Electricity - consumption: 3.183 billion kWh (1999)
Electricity - exports: 593 million kWh (1999)
Electricity - imports: 0 kWh (1999)
Agriculture - products: coffee, cocoa beans, bananas, palm kernels, corn, rice, manioc (tapioca), sweet potatoes, sugar, cotton, rubber; timber
Exports: $3.8 billion (f.o.b., 2000 est.)
Exports - commodities: cocoa 33%, coffee, tropical woods, petroleum, cotton, bananas, pineapples, palm oil, cotton, fish (1999)
Exports - partners: France 15%, US 8%, Netherlands 7%, Germany 6%, Italy 6% (1999)
Imports: $2.5 billion (f.o.b., 2000 est.)
Imports - commodities: food, consumer goods; capital goods, fuel, transport equipment
Imports - partners: France 26%, Nigeria 10%, China 7%, Italy 5%, Germany 4% (1999)
Debt - external: $13.9 billion (2000 est.)
Economic aid - recipient: ODA, $1 billion (1996 est.)
Currency: Communaute Financiere Africaine franc (XOF); note - responsible authority is the Central Bank of the West African States
Currency code: XOF
Exchange rates: Communaute Financiere Africaine francs (XOF) per US dollar - 699.21 (January 2001), 711.98 (2000), 615.70 (1999), 589.95 (1998), 583.67 (1997), 511.55 (1996); note - from 1 January 1999, the XOF is pegged to the euro at a rate of 655.957 XOF per euro
Fiscal year: calendar year

Communications

Telephones - main lines in use: 219,283 (31 December 1999)
Telephones - mobile cellular: 322,500 (May 2000)
Telephone system:
general assessment: well developed by African standards but operating well below capacity
domestic: open-wire lines and microwave radio relay; 90% digitalized
international: satellite earth stations - 2 Intelsat (1 Atlantic Ocean and 1 Indian Ocean); 2 coaxial submarine cables (June 1999)
Radio broadcast stations: AM 2, FM 8, shortwave 3 (1998)
Radios: 2.26 million (1997)
Television broadcast stations: 14 (1999)
Televisions: 900,000 (1997)
Internet country code: .ci
Internet Service Providers (ISPs): 5 (2001)
Internet users: 20,000 (2000)

Transportation

Railways:
total: 660 km
narrow gauge: 660 km 1.000-meter gauge; 25 km double track (1995 est.)
Highways:
total: 50,400 km
paved: 4,889 km
unpaved: 45,511 km (1996)
Waterways: 980 km (navigable rivers, canals, and numerous coastal lagoons)
Ports and harbors: Abidjan, Aboisso, Dabou, San-Pedro
Merchant marine:
total: 1 ship (1,000 GRT or over) totaling 1,200 GRT/ 1,500 DWT
ships by type: petroleum tanker 1 (2000 est.)
Airports: 36 (2000 est.)
Airports - with paved runways:
total: 7
over 3,047 m: 1
2,438 to 3,047 m: 2
1,524 to 2,437 m: 4 (2000 est.)
Airports - with unpaved runways:
total: 29
1,524 to 2,437 m: 8
914 to 1,523 m: 12
under 914 m: 9 (2000 est.)

Military

Military branches: Army, Navy, Air Force, paramilitary Gendarmerie, Republican Guard (includes Presidential Guard), Sapeur-Pompier (Military Fire Group)
Military manpower - military age: 18 years of age
Military manpower - availability:
males age 15-49: 3,851,432 (2001 est.)
Military manpower - fit for military service:
males age 15-49: 2,010,862 (2001 est.)
Military manpower - reaching military age annually:
males: 188,411 (2001 est.)
Military expenditures - dollar figure: $94 million (FY96)

Cote d'Ivoire (continued)

Military expenditures - percent of GDP: 1% (FY96)

Transnational Issues

Disputes - international: none
Illicit drugs: illicit producer of cannabis, mostly for local consumption; transshipment point for Southwest and Southeast Asian heroin to Europe and occasionally to the US, and for Latin American cocaine destined for Europe

Croatia

Introduction

Background: In 1918, the Croats, Serbs, and Slovenes formed a kingdom known after 1929 as Yugoslavia. Following World War II, Yugoslavia became an independent communist state under the strong hand of Marshal TITO. Although Croatia declared its independence from Yugoslavia in 1991, it took four years of sporadic, but often bitter, fighting before occupying Serb armies were mostly cleared from Croatian lands. Under UN supervision the last Serb-held enclave in eastern Slavonia was returned to Croatia in 1998.

Geography

Location: Southeastern Europe, bordering the Adriatic Sea, between Bosnia and Herzegovina and Slovenia
Geographic coordinates: 45 10 N, 15 30 E
Map references: Europe
Area:
total: 56,542 sq km
land: 56,414 sq km
water: 128 sq km
Area - comparative: slightly smaller than West Virginia
Land boundaries:
total: 2,028 km
border countries: Bosnia and Herzegovina 932 km, Hungary 329 km, Yugoslavia 266 km, Slovenia 501 km
Coastline: 5,835 km (mainland 1,777 km, islands 4,058 km)
Maritime claims:
continental shelf: 200-m depth or to the depth of exploitation
territorial sea: 12 NM
Climate: Mediterranean and continental; continental climate predominant with hot summers and cold winters; mild winters, dry summers along coast
Terrain: geographically diverse; flat plains along Hungarian border, low mountains and highlands near Adriatic coastline and islands
Elevation extremes:
lowest point: Adriatic Sea 0 m
highest point: Dinara 1,830 m
Natural resources: oil, some coal, bauxite, low-grade iron ore, calcium, natural asphalt, silica, mica, clays, salt, hydropower
Land use:
arable land: 21%
permanent crops: 2%
permanent pastures: 20%
forests and woodland: 38%
other: 19% (1993 est.)
Irrigated land: 30 sq km (1993 est.)
Natural hazards: destructive earthquakes
Environment - current issues: air pollution (from metallurgical plants) and resulting acid rain is damaging the forests; coastal pollution from industrial and domestic waste; landmine removal and reconstruction of infrastructure consequent to 1992-95 civil strife
Environment - international agreements:
party to: Air Pollution, Air Pollution-Sulphur 94, Biodiversity, Climate Change, Desertification, Endangered Species, Hazardous Wastes, Law of the Sea, Marine Dumping, Nuclear Test Ban, Ozone Layer Protection, Ship Pollution, Wetlands
signed, but not ratified: Air Pollution-Persistent Organic Pollutants, Climate Change-Kyoto Protocol
Geography - note: controls most land routes from Western Europe to Aegean Sea and Turkish Straits

People

Population: 4,334,142 (July 2001 est.)
Age structure:
0-14 years: 18.16% (male 403,722; female 383,151)
15-64 years: 66.61% (male 1,452,872; female 1,434,086)
65 years and over: 15.23% (male 245,727; female 414,584) (2001 est.)
Population growth rate: 1.48% (2001 est.)
Birth rate: 12.82 births/1,000 population (2001 est.)
Death rate: 11.41 deaths/1,000 population (2001 est.)
Net migration rate: 13.37 migrant(s)/1,000 population (2001 est.)
Sex ratio:
at birth: 1.06 male(s)/female
under 15 years: 1.05 male(s)/female
15-64 years: 1.01 male(s)/female
65 years and over: 0.59 male(s)/female
total population: 0.94 male(s)/female (2001 est.)
Infant mortality rate: 7.21 deaths/1,000 live births (2001 est.)
Life expectancy at birth:
total population: 73.9 years
male: 70.28 years
female: 77.73 years (2001 est.)
Total fertility rate: 1.94 children born/woman (2001 est.)

Croatia (continued)

HIV/AIDS - adult prevalence rate: 0.02% (1999 est.)
HIV/AIDS - people living with HIV/AIDS: 350 (1999 est.)
HIV/AIDS - deaths: less than 100 (1999 est.)
Nationality:
noun: Croat(s)
adjective: Croatian
Ethnic groups: Croat 78.1%, Serb 12.2%, Bosniak 0.9%, Hungarian 0.5%, Slovenian 0.5%, Czech 0.4%, Albanian 0.3%, Montenegrin 0.3%, Roma 0.2%, others 6.6% (1991)
Religions: Roman Catholic 76.5%, Orthodox 11.1%, Muslim 1.2%, Protestant 0.4%, others and unknown 10.8% (1991)
Languages: Croatian 96%, other 4% (including Italian, Hungarian, Czech, Slovak, and German)
Literacy:
definition: age 15 and over can read and write
total population: 97%
male: 99%
female: 95% (1991 est.)

Government

Country name:
conventional long form: Republic of Croatia
conventional short form: Croatia
local long form: Republika Hrvatska
local short form: Hrvatska
Government type: presidential/parliamentary democracy
Capital: Zagreb
Administrative divisions: 20 counties (zupanije, zupanija - singular), 1 city (grad -singular)*: Bjelovarsko-Bilogorska Zupanija, Brodsko-Posavska Zupanija, Dubrovacko-Neretvanska Zupanija, Istarska Zupanija, Karlovacka Zupanija, Koprivnicko-Krizevacka Zupanija, Krapinsko-Zagorska Zupanija, Licko-Senjska Zupanija, Medimurska Zupanija, Osjecko-Baranjska Zupanija, Pozesko-Slavonska Zupanija, Primorsko-Goranska Zupanija, Sibensko-Kninska Zupanija, Sisacko-Moslavacka Zupanija, Splitsko-Dalmatinska Zupanija, Varazdinska Zupanija, Viroviticko-Podravska Zupanija, Vukovarsko-Srijemska Zupanija, Zadarska Zupanija, Zagreb*, Zagrebacka Zupanija
Independence: 25 June 1991 (from Yugoslavia)
National holiday: Republic Day/Statehood Day, 30 May (1990)
Constitution: adopted on 22 December 1990
Legal system: based on civil law system
Suffrage: 18 years of age; universal (16 years of age, if employed)
Executive branch:
chief of state: President Stjepan (Stipe) MESIC (since 18 February 2000)
head of government: Prime Minister Ivica RACAN (since 27 January 2000); Deputy Prime Ministers Goran GRANIC (since 27 January 2000), Zeljka ANTUNOVIC (since 27 January 2000), Slavko LINIC (since 27 January 2000)
cabinet: Council of Ministers named by the prime minister and approved by the House of Representatives
elections: president elected by popular vote for a five-year term; election last held 7 February 2000 (next to be held NA 2005); prime minister nominated by the president in line with the balance of power in the Assembly
election results: Stjepan MESIC elected president; percent of vote - Stjepan MESIC (HNS) 56%, Drazen BUDISA (HSLS) 44%
note: government coalition - SDP, HSLS, HSS, LP, HNS, IDS
Legislative branch: bicameral Assembly or Sabor consists of the House of Counties or Zupanijski Dom (68 seats, 63 directly elected by popular vote, 5 appointed by the president; members serve four-year terms; note - House of Counties to be abolished in 2001) and House of Representatives or the Zastupnicki Dom (151 seats; members elected by popular vote to serve four-year terms)
elections: House of Counties - last held 13 April 1997; House of Representatives - last held 2-3 January 2000 (next to be held NA 2004)
election results: House of Counties - percent of vote by party - NA%; seats by party - HDZ 42, HSLS/HSS 11, HSS 2, IDS 2, SDP/PGS/HNS 2, SDP/HNS 2, HSLS/HSS/HNS 1, HSLS 1; note - in some districts certain parties ran as coalitions, while in others they ran alone; House of Representatives - percent of vote by party - NA%; seats by party - HDZ 46, SDP 44, HSLS 24, HSS 17, HSP/HKDU 5, IDS 4, HNS 2, independents 4, minority representatives 5
Judicial branch: Supreme Court; Constitutional Court; judges for both courts appointed for eight-year terms by the Judicial Council of the Republic, which is elected by the House of Representatives
Political parties and leaders: Alliance of Croatian Coast and Mountains Department or PGS [Luciano SUSANJ]; Croatian Christian Democratic Union or HKDU [Marko VESELICA]; Croatian Democratic Union or HDZ [Ivo SANADER]; Croatian Party of Rights or HSP [Dobroslav PARAGA]; Croatian Peasant Party or HSS [Zlatko TOMCIC]; Croatian People's Party or HNS [Vesna PUSIC]; Croatian Social Liberal Party or HSLS [Drazen BUDISA]; Independent Democratic Serb Party or SDSS [Vojislav STANIMIROVIC]; Istrian Democratic Assembly or IDS [Ivan JAKOVCIC]; Liberal Party or LP [leader NA]; Social Democratic Party of Croatia or SDP [Ivica RACAN]
note: the Social Democratic Party or SDP and the Croatian Social Liberal Party or HSLS formed a coalition as did the HSS, HNS, LP, and IDS, which together defeated the Croatian Democratic Union or HDZ in the 2000 lower house parliamentary election
Political pressure groups and leaders: NA
International organization participation: BIS, CCC, CE, CEI, EAPC, EBRD, ECE, FAO, IADB, IAEA, IBRD, ICAO, ICFTU, ICRM, IDA, IFAD, IFC, IFRCS, IHO, ILO, IMF, IMO, Inmarsat, Intelsat, Interpol, IOC, IOM, ISO, ITU, NAM (observer), OAS (observer), OPCW, OSCE, PCA, PFP, UN, UNCTAD, UNESCO, UNIDO, UPU, WHO, WIPO, WMO, WToO, WTrO
Diplomatic representation in the US:
chief of mission: Ambassador Ivan GRDESIC
chancery: 2343 Massachusetts Avenue NW, Washington, DC 20008
telephone: [1] (202) 588-5899
FAX: [1] (202) 588-8936
consulate(s) general: Chicago, Cleveland, Los Angeles, New York
Diplomatic representation from the US:
chief of mission: Ambassador Lawrence G. ROSSIN
embassy: Andrije Hebranga 2, 100000 Zagreb
mailing address: use street address
telephone: [385] (1) 455-55-00
FAX: [385] (1) 455-85-85
Flag description: red, white, and blue horizontal bands with Croatian coat of arms (red and white checkered)

Economy

Economy - overview: Before the dissolution of Yugoslavia, the Republic of Croatia, after Slovenia, was the most prosperous and industrialized area, with a per capita output perhaps one-third above the Yugoslav average. Croatia faces considerable economic problems stemming from: the legacy of longtime communist mismanagement of the economy; damage during the internecine fighting to bridges, factories, power lines, buildings, and houses; the large refugee and displaced population, both Croatian and Bosnian; and the disruption of economic ties. Stepped-up Western aid and investment, especially in the tourist and oil industries, would help bolster the economy. The economy emerged from its mild recession in 2000 with tourism the main factor. Massive unemployment remains a key negative element. The government's failure to press the economic reforms needed to spur growth is largely the result of coalition politics and public resistance, particularly from the trade unions, to measures that would cut jobs, wages, or social benefits.
GDP: purchasing power parity - $24.9 billion (2000 est.)
GDP - real growth rate: 3.2% (2000 est.)
GDP - per capita: purchasing power parity - $5,800 (2000 est.)
GDP - composition by sector:
agriculture: 10%
industry: 19%
services: 71% (1999 est.)
Population below poverty line: 4% (1999 est.)
Household income or consumption by percentage share:
lowest 10%: NA%
highest 10%: NA%
Inflation rate (consumer prices): 6% (2000 est.)
Labor force: 1.68 million (October 2000)
Labor force - by occupation: agriculture NA%, industry NA%, services NA%

Croatia (continued)

Unemployment rate: 22% (October 2000)
Budget:
revenues: $6 billion
expenditures: $4.7 billion, including capital expenditures of $NA (1999 est.)
Industries: chemicals and plastics, machine tools, fabricated metal, electronics, pig iron and rolled steel products, aluminum, paper, wood products, construction materials, textiles, shipbuilding, petroleum and petroleum refining, food and beverages; tourism
Industrial production growth rate: 1.7% (2000)
Electricity - production: 10.96 billion kWh (1999)
Electricity - production by source:
fossil fuel: 40.89%
hydro: 59%
nuclear: 0%
other: 0.11% (1999)
Electricity - consumption: 13.643 billion kWh (1999)
Electricity - exports: 1 billion kWh (1999)
Electricity - imports: 4.45 billion kWh (1999)
Agriculture - products: wheat, corn, sugar beets, sunflower seed, alfalfa, clover, olives, citrus, grapes, soy beans, potatoes; livestock, dairy products
Exports: $4.3 billion (f.o.b., 1999)
Exports - commodities: transport equipment, textiles, chemicals, foodstuffs, fuels
Exports - partners: Italy 18%, Germany 15.7%, Bosnia and Herzegovina 12.8%, Slovenia 10.6%, Austria 6.2% (1999)
Imports: $7.8 billion (c.i.f., 1999)
Imports - commodities: machinery, transport and electrical equipment, chemicals, fuels and lubricants, foodstuffs
Imports - partners: Germany 18.5%, Italy 15.9%, Russia 8.6%, Slovenia 7.9%, Austria 7.1% (1999)
Debt - external: $9.9 billion (December 1999)
Economic aid - recipient: $NA
Currency: kuna (HRK)
Currency code: HRK
Exchange rates: kuna per US dollar - 8.089 (January 2001), 8.277 (2000), 7.112 (1999), 6.362 (1998), 6.101 (1997), 5.434 (1996)
Fiscal year: calendar year

Communications

Telephones - main lines in use: 1.488 million (1997)
Telephones - mobile cellular: 187,000 (yearend 1998)
Telephone system:
general assessment: NA
domestic: reconstruction plan calls for replacement of all analog circuits with digital and enlarging the network; a backup will be included in the plan for the main trunk
international: digital international service is provided through the main switch in Zagreb; Croatia participates in the Trans-Asia-Europe (TEL) fiber-optic project which consists of two fiber-optic trunk connections with Slovenia and a fiber-optic trunk line from Rijeka to Split and Dubrovnik; Croatia is also investing in ADRIA 1, a joint fiber-optic project with Germany, Albania, and Greece (2000)
Radio broadcast stations: AM 16, FM 98, shortwave 5 (1999)
Radios: 1.51 million (1997)
Television broadcast stations: 36 (plus 321 repeaters) (September 1995)
Televisions: 1.22 million (1997)
Internet country code: .hr
Internet Service Providers (ISPs): 9 (2000)
Internet users: 100,000 (1999)

Transportation

Railways:
total: 2,296 km
standard gauge: 2,296 km 1.435-m gauge (983 km electrified) (1997)
Highways:
total: 27,840 km
paved: 23,497 km (including 330 km of expressways)
unpaved: 4,343 km (1998)
Waterways: 785 km
note: (perennially navigable; large sections of Sava blocked by downed bridges, silt, and debris)
Pipelines: crude oil 670 km; petroleum products 20 km; natural gas 310 km (1992)
Ports and harbors: Dubrovnik, Dugi Rat, Omisalj, Ploce, Pula, Rijeka, Sibenik, Split, Vukovar (inland waterway port on Danube), Zadar
Merchant marine:
total: 53 ships (1,000 GRT or over) totaling 631,853 GRT/969,739 DWT
ships by type: bulk 11, cargo 18, chemical tanker 1, combination bulk 5, container 3, multi-functional large-load carrier 3, passenger 1, petroleum tanker 2, refrigerated cargo 2, roll on/roll off 4, short-sea passenger 3 (2000 est.)
Airports: 67 (2000 est.)
Airports - with paved runways:
total: 22
over 3,047 m: 2
2,438 to 3,047 m: 6
1,524 to 2,437 m: 2
914 to 1,523 m: 4
under 914 m: 8 (2000 est.)
Airports - with unpaved runways:
total: 45
1,524 to 2,437 m: 1
914 to 1,523 m: 8
under 914 m: 36 (2000 est.)
Heliports: 1 (2000 est.)

Military

Military branches: Ground Forces, Naval Forces, Air and Air Defense Forces
Military manpower - military age: 19 years of age
Military manpower - availability:
males age 15-49: 1,085,877 (2001 est.)
Military manpower - fit for military service:
males age 15-49: 859,621 (2001 est.)
Military manpower - reaching military age annually:
males: 30,037 (2001 est.)
Military expenditures - dollar figure: $575 million (2000)
Military expenditures - percent of GDP: 3.8% (2000)

Transnational Issues

Disputes - international: Croatia and Italy made progress toward resolving a bilateral issue dating from World War II over property and ethnic minority rights; progress with Slovenia on discussions of adjustments to land boundary, but problems remain in defining maritime boundary in Gulf of Piran; Croatia and Yugoslavia are negotiating the status of the strategically important Prevlaka Peninsula, which is currently under a UN military observer mission (UNMOP)
Illicit drugs: transit point along the Balkan route for Southwest Asian heroin to Western Europe; a minor transit point for maritime shipments of South American cocaine bound for Western Europe

Cuba

Introduction

Background: Fidel CASTRO led a rebel army to victory in 1959; his iron rule has held the country together since. Cuba's communist revolution, with Soviet support, was exported throughout Latin America and Africa during the 1960s, 70s, and 80s. The country is now slowly recovering from a severe economic recession in 1990, following the withdrawal of former Soviet subsidies, worth $4 billion to $6 billion annually. Havana portrays its difficulties as the result of the US embargo in place since 1961. Illicit migration to the US - using homemade rafts, alien smugglers, or falsified visas - is a continuing problem. Some 3,000 Cubans took to the Straits of Florida in 2000; the US Coast Guard interdicted only about 35% of these.

Geography

Location: Caribbean, island between the Caribbean Sea and the North Atlantic Ocean, south of Florida
Geographic coordinates: 21 30 N, 80 00 W
Map references: Central America and the Caribbean
Area:
total: 110,860 sq km
land: 110,860 sq km
water: 0 sq km
Area - comparative: slightly smaller than Pennsylvania
Land boundaries:
total: 29 km
border countries: US Naval Base at Guantanamo Bay 29 km
note: Guantanamo Naval Base is leased by the US and thus remains part of Cuba
Coastline: 3,735 km
Maritime claims:
exclusive economic zone: 200 NM
territorial sea: 12 NM
Climate: tropical; moderated by trade winds; dry season (November to April); rainy season (May to October)
Terrain: mostly flat to rolling plains, with rugged hills and mountains in the southeast
Elevation extremes:
lowest point: Caribbean Sea 0 m
highest point: Pico Turquino 2,005 m
Natural resources: cobalt, nickel, iron ore, copper, manganese, salt, timber, silica, petroleum, arable land
Land use:
arable land: 24%
permanent crops: 7%
permanent pastures: 27%
forests and woodland: 24%
other: 18% (1993 est.)
Irrigated land: 9,100 sq km (1993 est.)
Natural hazards: the east coast is subject to hurricanes from August to October (in general, the country averages about one hurricane every other year); droughts are common
Environment - current issues: pollution of Havana Bay; overhunting threatens wildlife populations; deforestation
Environment - international agreements:
party to: Antarctic Treaty, Biodiversity, Climate Change, Desertification, Endangered Species, Environmental Modification, Hazardous Wastes, Law of the Sea, Marine Dumping, Ozone Layer Protection, Ship Pollution
signed, but not ratified: Antarctic-Environmental Protocol, Climate Change-Kyoto Protocol, Marine Life Conservation
Geography - note: largest country in Caribbean

People

Population: 11,184,023 (July 2001 est.)
Age structure:
0-14 years: 20.99% (male 1,205,159; female 1,142,070)
15-64 years: 69.14% (male 3,876,432; female 3,855,878)
65 years and over: 9.87% (male 511,589; female 592,895) (2001 est.)
Population growth rate: 0.37% (2001 est.)
Birth rate: 12.36 births/1,000 population (2001 est.)
Death rate: 7.33 deaths/1,000 population (2001 est.)
Net migration rate: -1.36 migrant(s)/1,000 population (2001 est.)
Sex ratio:
at birth: 1.06 male(s)/female
under 15 years: 1.06 male(s)/female
15-64 years: 1.01 male(s)/female
65 years and over: 0.86 male(s)/female
total population: 1 male(s)/female (2001 est.)
Infant mortality rate: 7.39 deaths/1,000 live births (2001 est.)
Life expectancy at birth:
total population: 76.41 years
male: 74.02 years
female: 78.94 years (2001 est.)
Total fertility rate: 1.6 children born/woman (2001 est.)
HIV/AIDS - adult prevalence rate: 0.03% (1999 est.)
HIV/AIDS - people living with HIV/AIDS: 1,950 (1999 est.)
HIV/AIDS - deaths: 120 (1999 est.)
Nationality:
noun: Cuban(s)
adjective: Cuban
Ethnic groups: mulatto 51%, white 37%, black 11%, Chinese 1%
Religions: nominally 85% Roman Catholic prior to CASTRO assuming power; Protestants, Jehovah's Witnesses, Jews, and Santeria are also represented
Languages: Spanish
Literacy:
definition: age 15 and over can read and write
total population: 95.7%
male: 96.2%
female: 95.3% (1995 est.)
People - note: illicit migration is a continuing problem; Cubans attempt to depart the island and enter the US using homemade rafts, alien smugglers, direct flights, or falsified visas; some 3,000 Cubans took to the Straits of Florida in 2000; the US Coast Guard interdicted about 35% of these migrants; Cubans also use non-maritime routes to enter the US; some 2,400 Cubans arrived overland via the southwest border and direct flights to Miami

Government

Country name:
conventional long form: Republic of Cuba
conventional short form: Cuba
local long form: Republica de Cuba
local short form: Cuba
Government type: Communist state
Capital: Havana
Administrative divisions: 14 provinces (provincias, singular - provincia) and 1 special municipality* (municipio especial); Camaguey, Ciego de Avila, Cienfuegos, Ciudad de La Habana, Granma, Guantanamo, Holguin, Isla de la Juventud*, La

Cuba (continued)

Habana, Las Tunas, Matanzas, Pinar del Rio, Sancti Spiritus, Santiago de Cuba, Villa Clara
Independence: 20 May 1902 (from US)
National holiday: Independence Day, 10 October (1868); note - 10 October 1868 is the date of independence from Spain, 20 May 1902 is the date of independence from US administration
Constitution: 24 February 1976, amended July 1992
Legal system: based on Spanish and American law, with large elements of Communist legal theory; has not accepted compulsory ICJ jurisdiction
Suffrage: 16 years of age; universal
Executive branch:
chief of state: President of the Council of State and President of the Council of Ministers Fidel CASTRO Ruz (prime minister from February 1959 until 24 February 1976 when office was abolished; president since 2 December 1976); First Vice President of the Council of State and First Vice President of the Council of Ministers Gen. Raul CASTRO Ruz (since 2 December 1976); note - the president is both the chief of state and head of government
head of government: President of the Council of State and President of the Council of Ministers Fidel CASTRO Ruz (prime minister from February 1959 until 24 February 1976 when office was abolished; president since 2 December 1976); First Vice President of the Council of State and First Vice President of the Council of Ministers Gen. Raul CASTRO Ruz (since 2 December 1976); note - the president is both the chief of state and head of government
cabinet: Council of Ministers proposed by the president of the Council of State, appointed by the National Assembly; note - there is also a Council of State whose members are elected by the National Assembly
elections: president and vice president elected by the National Assembly; election last held 24 February 1998 (next election unscheduled)
election results: Fidel CASTRO Ruz elected president; percent of legislative vote - 100%; Raul CASTRO Ruz elected vice president; percent of legislative vote - 100%
Legislative branch: unicameral National Assembly of People's Power or Asemblea Nacional del Poder Popular (601 seats, elected directly from slates approved by special candidacy commissions; members serve five-year terms)
elections: last held 11 January 1998 (next to be held in 2003)
election results: percent of vote - PCC 94.39%; seats - PCC 601
Judicial branch: People's Supreme Court or Tribunal Supremo Popular (president, vice president, and other judges are elected by the National Assembly)
Political parties and leaders: only party - Cuban Communist Party or PCC [Fidel CASTRO Ruz, first secretary]
Political pressure groups and leaders: NA
International organization participation: CCC, ECLAC, FAO, G-77, IAEA, ICAO, ICC, ICRM, IFAD, IFRCS, IHO, ILO, IMO, Inmarsat, Intelsat (nonsignatory user), Interpol, IOC, IOM (observer), ISO, ITU, LAES, LAIA, NAM, OAS (excluded from formal participation since 1962), OPCW, PCA, UN, UNCTAD, UNESCO, UNIDO, UPU, WCL, WFTU, WHO, WIPO, WMO, WToO, WTrO
Diplomatic representation in the US: none; note - Cuba has an Interests Section in the Swiss Embassy, headed by Principal Officer Fernando REMIREZ DE ESTENOZ; address: Cuban Interests Section, Swiss Embassy, 2630 16th Street NW, Washington, DC 20009; telephone: [1] (202) 797-8518
Diplomatic representation from the US: none; note - the US has an Interests Section in the Swiss Embassy, headed by Principal Officer Vicki HUDDLESTON; address: USINT, Swiss Embassy, Calzada between L and M Streets, Vedado Seccion, Havana; telephone: 33-3551 through 3559 (operator assistance required); FAX: 33-3700; protecting power in Cuba is Switzerland
Flag description: five equal horizontal bands of blue (top and bottom) alternating with white; a red equilateral triangle based on the hoist side bears a white, five-pointed star in the center

Economy

Economy - overview: The government, the primary player in the economy, has undertaken limited reforms in recent years to stem excess liquidity, increase enterprise efficiency, and alleviate serious shortages of food, consumer goods, and services, but prioritizing of political control makes extensive reforms unlikely. Living standards for the average Cuban, without access to dollars, remain at a depressed level compared with 1990. The liberalized farmers' markets introduced in 1994, sell above-quota production at market prices, expand legal consumption alternatives, and reduce black market prices. Income taxes and increased regulations introduced since 1996 have sharply reduced the number of legally self-employed from a high of 208,000 in January 1996. Havana announced in 1995 that GDP declined by 35% during 1989-93 as a result of lost Soviet aid and domestic inefficiencies. The slide in GDP came to a halt in 1994 when Cuba reported growth in GDP of 0.7%. Cuba reported that GDP increased by 2.5% in 1995 and 7.8% in 1996, before slowing down in 1997 and 1998 to 2.5% and 1.2% respectively. Growth recovered with a 6.2% increase in GDP in 1999 and a 5.6% increase in 2000. Much of Cuba's recovery can be attributed to tourism revenues and foreign investment. Growth in 2001 should continue at the same level as the government balances the need for economic loosening against its concern for firm political control.
GDP: purchasing power parity - $19.2 billion (2000 est.)
GDP - real growth rate: 5.6% (2000 est.)
GDP - per capita: purchasing power parity - $1,700 (2000 est.)
GDP - composition by sector:
agriculture: 7%
industry: 37%
services: 56% (1998 est.)
Population below poverty line: NA%
Household income or consumption by percentage share:
lowest 10%: NA%
highest 10%: NA%
Inflation rate (consumer prices): 0.3% (1999 est.)
Labor force: 4.3 million (2000 est.)
note: state sector 75%, non-state sector 25% (1998)
Labor force - by occupation: agriculture 25%, industry 24%, services 51% (1998)
Unemployment rate: 5.5% (2000 est.)
Budget:
revenues: $13.5 billion
expenditures: $14.3 billion, including capital expenditures of $NA (2000 est.)
Industries: sugar, petroleum, tobacco, chemicals, construction, services, nickel, steel, cement, agricultural machinery
Industrial production growth rate: 5% (2000 est.)
Electricity - production: 14.358 billion kWh (1999)
Electricity - production by source:
fossil fuel: 94.2%
hydro: 0.7%
nuclear: 0%
other: 5.1% (1999)
Electricity - consumption: 13.353 billion kWh (1999)
Electricity - exports: 0 kWh (1999)
Electricity - imports: 0 kWh (1999)
Agriculture - products: sugar, tobacco, citrus, coffee, rice, potatoes, beans; livestock
Exports: $1.8 billion (f.o.b., 2000 est.)
Exports - commodities: sugar, nickel, tobacco, fish, medical products, citrus, coffee
Exports - partners: Russia 23%, Netherlands 23%, Canada 13% (1999)
Imports: $3.4 billion (f.o.b., 2000 est.)
Imports - commodities: petroleum, food, machinery, chemicals, semifinished goods, transport equipment, consumer goods
Imports - partners: Spain 18%, Venezuela 13%, Canada 8% (1999)
Debt - external: $11.1 billion (convertible currency, 1999); another $15 billion -$20 billion owed to Russia (2000)
Economic aid - recipient: $68.2 million (1997 est.)
Currency: Cuban peso (CUP)
Currency code: CUP
Exchange rates: Cuban pesos per US dollar - 1.0000 (nonconvertible, official rate, for international transactions, pegged to the US dollar); convertible peso sold for domestic use at a rate of 1.00 US dollar per 22 pesos by the Government of Cuba (January 2001)
Fiscal year: calendar year

Cuba (continued)

Communications

Telephones - main lines in use: 473,031 (2000)
Telephones - mobile cellular: 2,994 (1997)
Telephone system:
general assessment: NA
domestic: principal trunk system, end to end of country, is coaxial cable; fiber-optic distribution in Havana and on Isla de la Juventud; 2 microwave radio relay installations (one is old, US-built; the other newer, Soviet-built); both analog and digital mobile cellular service established
international: satellite earth station - 1 Intersputnik (Atlantic Ocean region)
Radio broadcast stations: AM 169, FM 55, shortwave 1 (1998)
Radios: 3.9 million (1997)
Television broadcast stations: 58 (1997)
Televisions: 2.64 million (1997)
Internet country code: .cu
Internet Service Providers (ISPs): 4 (2001)
Internet users: 60,000 (2000)

Transportation

Railways:
total: 11,969 km
standard gauge: 4,807 km 1.435-m gauge (147 km electrified)
note: in addition to the 4,807 km of standard gauge track in public use, 7,162 km of track is in private use by sugar plantations; about 90% of the private use track is standard gauge and the rest is narrow gauge
Highways:
total: 60,858 km
paved: 29,820 km (including 638 km of expressway)
unpaved: 31,038 km (1997)
Waterways: 240 km
Ports and harbors: Cienfuegos, Havana, Manzanillo, Mariel, Matanzas, Nuevitas, Santiago de Cuba
Merchant marine:
total: 15 ships (1,000 GRT or over) totaling 54,821 GRT/78,062 DWT
ships by type: bulk 1, cargo 7, liquefied gas 1, petroleum tanker 1, refrigerated cargo 5 (2000 est.)
Airports: 171 (2000 est.)
Airports - with paved runways:
total: 77
over 3,047 m: 7
2,438 to 3,047 m: 9
1,524 to 2,437 m: 16
914 to 1,523 m: 10
under 914 m: 35 (2000 est.)
Airports - with unpaved runways:
total: 94
914 to 1,523 m: 31
under 914 m: 63 (2000 est.)

Military

Military branches: Revolutionary Armed Forces (FAR) includes ground forces, Revolutionary Navy (MGR), Air and Air Defense Force (DAAFAR), Territorial Troops Militia (MTT), and Youth Labor Army (EJT); the Border Guard (TGF) is controlled by the Interior Ministry
Military manpower - military age: 17 years of age
Military manpower - availability:
males age 15-49: 3,090,633
females age 15-49: 3,029,274 (2001 est.)
Military manpower - fit for military service:
males age 15-49: 1,911,160
females age 15-49: 1,867,958 (2001 est.)
Military manpower - reaching military age annually:
males: 79,562
females: 85,650 (2001 est.)
Military expenditures - dollar figure: $NA
Military expenditures - percent of GDP: roughly 4% (FY95 est.)
Military - note: Moscow, for decades the key military supporter and supplier of Cuba, cut off almost all military aid by 1993

Transnational Issues

Disputes - international: US Naval Base at Guantanamo Bay is leased to US and only mutual agreement or US abandonment of the area can terminate the lease
Illicit drugs: territorial waters and air space serve as transshipment zone for cocaine bound for the US and Europe; established the death penalty for certain drug-related crimes in 1999

Cyprus

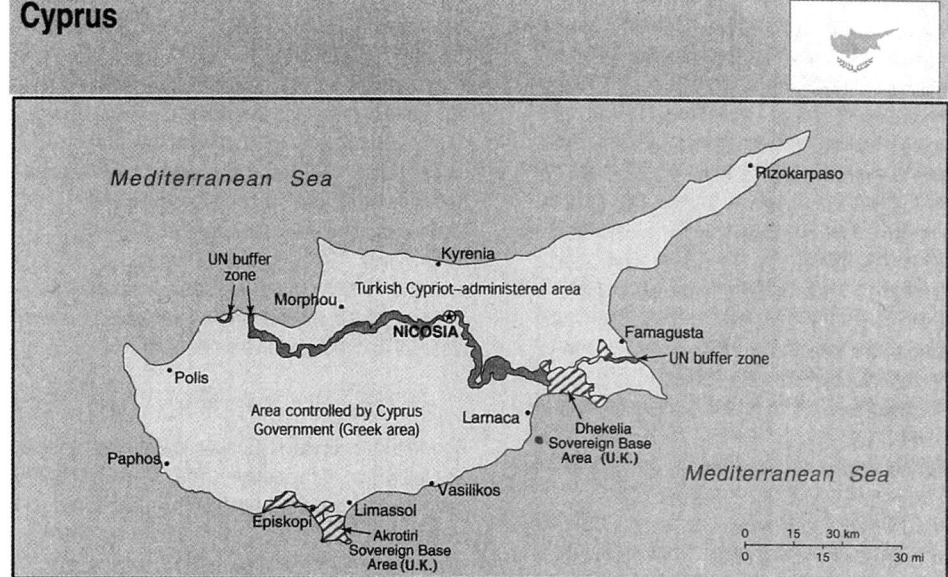

Introduction

Background: Independence from the UK was approved in 1960 with constitutional guarantees by the Greek Cypriot majority to the Turkish Cypriot minority. In 1974, a Greek-sponsored attempt to seize the government was met by military intervention from Turkey, which soon controlled almost 40% of the island. In 1983, the Turkish-held area declared itself the "Turkish Republic of Northern Cyprus", but it is recognized only by Turkey. UN-led talks on the status of Cyprus resumed in December 1999 to prepare the ground for meaningful negotiations leading to a comprehensive settlement.

Geography

Location: Middle East, island in the Mediterranean Sea, south of Turkey
Geographic coordinates: 35 00 N, 33 00 E
Map references: Middle East
Area:
total: 9,250 sq km (of which 3,355 sq km are in the Turkish Cypriot area)
land: 9,240 sq km
water: 10 sq km
Area - comparative: about 0.6 times the size of Connecticut
Land boundaries: 0 km
Coastline: 648 km
Maritime claims:
continental shelf: 200-m depth or to the depth of exploitation
territorial sea: 12 NM
Climate: temperate, Mediterranean with hot, dry summers and cool, winters
Terrain: central plain with mountains to north and south; scattered but significant plains along southern coast
Elevation extremes:
lowest point: Mediterranean Sea 0 m
highest point: Olympus 1,951 m

Natural resources: copper, pyrites, asbestos, gypsum, timber, salt, marble, clay earth pigment
Land use:
arable land: 12%
permanent crops: 5%
permanent pastures: 0%
forests and woodland: 13%
other: 70% (1993 est.)
Irrigated land: 390 sq km (1993 est.)
Natural hazards: moderate earthquake activity; droughts
Environment - current issues: water resource problems (no natural reservoir catchments, seasonal disparity in rainfall, sea water intrusion to island's largest aquifer, increased salination in the north); water pollution from sewage and industrial wastes; coastal degradation; loss of wildlife habitats from urbanization
Environment - international agreements:
party to: Air Pollution, Biodiversity, Climate Change, Climate Change-Kyoto Protocol, Desertification, Endangered Species, Environmental Modification, Hazardous Wastes, Law of the Sea, Marine Dumping, Nuclear Test Ban, Ozone Layer Protection, Ship Pollution
signed, but not ratified: Air Pollution-Persistent Organic Pollutants

People

Population: 762,887 (July 2001 est.)
Age structure:
0-14 years: 22.95% (male 89,532; female 85,518)
15-64 years: 66.26% (male 255,368; female 250,140)
65 years and over: 10.79% (male 35,864; female 46,465) (2001 est.)
Population growth rate: 0.59% (2001 est.)
Birth rate: 13.08 births/1,000 population (2001 est.)
Death rate: 7.65 deaths/1,000 population (2001 est.)
Net migration rate: 0.44 migrant(s)/1,000 population (2001 est.)

Sex ratio:
at birth: 1.05 male(s)/female
under 15 years: 1.05 male(s)/female
15-64 years: 1.02 male(s)/female
65 years and over: 0.77 male(s)/female
total population: 1 male(s)/female (2001 est.)
Infant mortality rate: 7.89 deaths/1,000 live births (2001 est.)
Life expectancy at birth:
total population: 76.89 years
male: 74.6 years
female: 79.3 years (2001 est.)
Total fertility rate: 1.93 children born/woman (2001 est.)
HIV/AIDS - adult prevalence rate: 0.1% (1999 est.)
HIV/AIDS - people living with HIV/AIDS: 400 (1999 est.)
HIV/AIDS - deaths: NA
Nationality:
noun: Cypriot(s)
adjective: Cypriot
Ethnic groups: Greek 78% (99.5% of the Greeks live in the Greek Cypriot area; 0.5% of the Greeks live in the Turkish Cypriot area), Turkish 18% (1.3% of the Turks live in the Greek Cypriot area; 98.7% of the Turks live in the Turkish Cypriot area), other 4% (99.2% of the other ethnic groups live in the Greek Cypriot area; 0.8% of the other ethnic groups live in the Turkish Cypriot area)
Religions: Greek Orthodox 78%, Muslim 18%, Maronite, Armenian Apostolic, and other 4%
Languages: Greek, Turkish, English
Literacy:
definition: age 15 and over can read and write
total population: 94%
male: 98%
female: 91% (1987 est.)

Government

Country name:
conventional long form: Republic of Cyprus
conventional short form: Cyprus
note: the Turkish Cypriot area refers to itself as the "Turkish Republic of Northern Cyprus" (TRNC)
Government type: republic
note: a disaggregation of the two ethnic communities inhabiting the island began following the outbreak of communal strife in 1963; this separation was further solidified after the Turkish intervention in July 1974 after a Greek junta-based coup attempt gave the Turkish Cypriots de facto control in the north; Greek Cypriots control the only internationally recognized government; on 15 November 1983 Turkish Cypriot "President" Rauf DENKTASH declared independence and the formation of a "Turkish Republic of Northern Cyprus" (TRNC), recognized only by Turkey; both sides publicly support a settlement based on a federation (Greek Cypriot position) or confederation (Turkish Cypriot position)
Capital: Nicosia

Cyprus (continued)

Administrative divisions: 6 districts; Famagusta, Kyrenia, Larnaca, Limassol, Nicosia, Paphos; note - Turkish Cypriot area's administrative divisions include Kyrenia, all but a small part of Famagusta, and small parts of Lefkosa (Nicosia) and Larnaca

Independence: 16 August 1960 (from UK); note - Turkish Cypriot area proclaimed self-rule on 13 February 1975

National holiday: Independence Day, 1 October (1960); note - Turkish Cypriot area celebrates 15 November (1983) as Independence Day

Constitution: 16 August 1960; negotiations to create the basis for a new or revised constitution to govern the island and to better relations between Greek and Turkish Cypriots have been held intermittently; in 1975 Turkish Cypriots created their own constitution and governing bodies within the "Turkish Federated State of Cyprus," which was renamed the "Turkish Republic of Northern Cyprus" in 1983; a new constitution for the Turkish Cypriot area passed by referendum on 5 May 1985

Legal system: based on common law, with civil law modifications

Suffrage: 18 years of age; universal

Executive branch:
chief of state: President Glafcos CLERIDES (since 28 February 1993); note - the president is both the chief of state and head of government; post of vice president is currently vacant; under the 1960 constitution, the post is reserved for a Turkish Cypriot
head of government: President Glafcos CLERIDES (since 28 February 1993); note - the president is both the chief of state and head of government; post of vice president is currently vacant; under the 1960 constitution, the post is reserved for a Turkish Cypriot
cabinet: Council of Ministers appointed jointly by the president and vice president
elections: president elected by popular vote for a five-year term; election last held 15 February 1998 (next to be held NA February 2003)
election results: Glafcos CLERIDES reelected president; percent of vote - Glafcos CLERIDES 50.8%, George IAKOVOU 49.2%
note: Rauf R. DENKTASH has been "president" of the Turkish Cypriot area since 13 February 1975 ("president" elected by popular vote for a five-year term); elections last held 15 April 2000 (next to be held NA April 2005); results - Rauf R. DENKTASH reelected president after the other contender withdrew; Dervis EROGLU has been "prime minister" of the Turkish Cypriot area since 16 August 1996; there is a Council of Ministers (cabinet) in the Turkish Cypriot area

Legislative branch: unicameral - Greek Cypriot area: House of Representatives or Vouli Antiprosopon (80 seats; 56 assigned to the Greek Cypriots, 24 to Turkish Cypriots; note - only those assigned to Greek Cypriots are filled; members are elected by popular vote to serve five-year terms); Turkish Cypriot area: Assembly of the Republic or Cumhuriyet Meclisi (50 seats; members are elected by popular vote to serve five-year terms)
elections: Greek Cypriot area: last held 27 May 2001 (next to be held NA May 2006); Turkish Cypriot area: last held 6 December 1998 (next to be held NA December 2003)
election results: Greek Cypriot area: House of Representatives - percent of vote by party - NA%; seats by party - AKEL (Communist) 20, DISY 19, DIKO 9, KISOS 4, others 4; Turkish Cypriot area: Assembly of the Republic - percent of vote by party - UBP 40.3%, DP 22.6%, TKP 15.4%, CTP 13.4%, UDP 4.6%, YBH 2.5%, BP 1.2%; seats by party - UBP 24, DP 13, TKP 7, CTP 6

Judicial branch: Supreme Court (judges are appointed by the Supreme Council of Judicature)
note: there is also a Supreme Court in the Turkish Cypriot area

Political parties and leaders: Greek Cypriot area: Democratic Party or DIKO [Tassos PAPADOPOULOS]; Democratic Rally or DISY [Nikos ANASTASIADHIS]; Restorative Party of the Working People or AKEL (Communist Party) [Dimitrios CHRISTOFIAS]; Social Democrats Movement or KISOS (formerly United Democratic Union of Cyprus or EDEK) [Vassos LYSSARIDIS]; United Democrats Movement or EDE (formerly Free Democrats Movement or KED) [George VASSILIOU]; Turkish Cypriot area: Communal Liberation Party or TKP [Mustafa AKINCI]; Democratic Party or DP [Salih COSAR]; National Birth Party or UDP [Enver EMIN]; National Unity Party or UBP [Dervis EROGLU]; Our Party or BP [Okyay SADIKOGLU]; Patriotic Unity Movement or YBH [Izzet IZCAN]; Republican Turkish Party or CTP [Mehmet ALI TALAT]

Political pressure groups and leaders: Confederation of Cypriot Workers or SEK (pro-West); Confederation of Revolutionary Labor Unions or Dev-Is; Federation of Turkish Cypriot Labor Unions or Turk-Sen; Pan-Cyprian Labor Federation or PEO (Communist controlled)

International organization participation: Australia Group, C, CCC, CE, EBRD, ECE, EU (applicant), FAO, G-77, IAEA, IBRD, ICAO, ICC, ICFTU, IDA, IFAD, IFC, IFRCS (associate), IHO, ILO, IMF, IMO, Inmarsat, Intelsat, Interpol, IOC, IOM, ISO, ITU, NAM, NSG, OAS (observer), OPCW, OSCE, PCA, UN, UNCTAD, UNESCO, UNIDO, UPU, WCL, WFTU, WHO, WIPO, WMO, WToO, WTrO

Diplomatic representation in the US:
chief of mission: Ambassador Erato KOZAKOU-MARCOULLIS
chancery: 2211 R Street NW, Washington, DC 20008
telephone: [1] (202) 462-5772
FAX: [1] (202) 483-6710
consulate(s) general: New York
note: representative of the Turkish Cypriot area in the US is Ahmet ERDENGIZ; office at 1667 K Street NW, Washington, DC; telephone [1] (202) 887-6198

Diplomatic representation from the US:
chief of mission: Ambassador Donald K. BANDLER
embassy: corner of Metochiou and Ploutarchou Streets, Engomi, 2407 Nicosia
mailing address: P. O. Box 4536, FPO AE 09836
telephone: [357] (2) 776400
FAX: [357] (2) 780944

Flag description: white with a copper-colored silhouette of the island (the name Cyprus is derived from the Greek word for copper) above two green crossed olive branches in the center of the flag; the branches symbolize the hope for peace and reconciliation between the Greek and Turkish communities
note: the Turkish Cypriot flag has a horizontal red stripe at the top and bottom between which is a red crescent and red star on a white field

Economy

Economy - overview: Economic affairs are affected by the division of the country. The Greek Cypriot economy is prosperous but highly susceptible to external shocks. Erratic growth rates in the 1990s reflect the economy's vulnerability to swings in tourist arrivals, caused by political instability on the island and fluctuations in economic conditions in Western Europe. Economic policy is focused on meeting the criteria for admission to the EU. As in the Turkish sector, water shortage is a growing problem, and several desalination plants are planned. The Turkish Cypriot economy has about one-fifth the population and one-third the per capita GDP of the south. Because it is recognized only by Turkey, it has had much difficulty arranging foreign financing, and foreign firms have hesitated to invest there. It remains heavily dependent on agriculture and government service, which together employ about half of the work force. Moreover, the small, vulnerable economy has suffered because the Turkish lira is legal tender. To compensate for the economy's weakness, Turkey provides direct and indirect aid to tourism, education, industry, etc.

GDP: Greek Cypriot area: purchasing power parity - $9.7 billion (2000 est.); Turkish Cypriot area: purchasing power parity - $830 million (1999 est.)

GDP - real growth rate: Greek Cypriot area: 4.2% (2000 est.); Turkish Cypriot area: 4.9% (1999 est.)

GDP - per capita: Greek Cypriot area: purchasing power parity - $16,000 (2000 est.); Turkish Cypriot area: purchasing power parity - $5,300 (1999 est.)

GDP - composition by sector: Greek Cypriot area: agriculture 6.3%, industry 22.4%, services 71.3% (1998); Turkish Cypriot area: agriculture 11.8%, industry 20.5%, services 67.7% (1998)

Population below poverty line: NA%

Household income or consumption by percentage share:
lowest 10%: NA%
highest 10%: NA%

Inflation rate (consumer prices): Greek Cypriot area: 4.2% (2000 est.); Turkish Cypriot area: 58% (1999 est.)

Labor force: Greek Cypriot area: 291,000; Turkish Cypriot area: 86,300 (2000)

Cyprus (continued)

Labor force - by occupation: Greek Cypriot area: services 73%, industry 22%, agriculture 5% (2000); Turkish Cypriot area: services 56.4%, industry 22.8%, agriculture 20.8% (1998)
Unemployment rate: Greek Cypriot area: 3.6% (2000 est.); Turkish Cypriot area: 6% (1998 est.)
Budget:
revenues: Greek Cypriot area - $2.9 billion (2000 est.); Turkish Cypriot area - $294 million (2000 est.)
expenditures: Greek Cypriot area - $3.2 billion, including capital expenditures of $324 million (2000 est.); Turkish Cypriot $495 million, including capital expenditures of $60 million (2000 est.)
Industries: food, beverages, textiles, chemicals, metal products, tourism, wood products
Industrial production growth rate: Greek Cypriot area: 2.2% (1999); Turkish Cypriot area: -0.3% (1999)
Electricity - production: 2.951 billion kWh (1999); Turkish Cypriot area: NA kWh
Electricity - production by source:
fossil fuel: 100%
hydro: 0%
nuclear: 0%
other: 0% (1999)
Electricity - consumption: 2.744 billion kWh (1999); Turkish Cypriot area: NA kWh
Electricity - exports: 0 kWh (1999)
Electricity - imports: 0 kWh (1999)
Agriculture - products: potatoes, citrus, vegetables, barley, grapes, olives, vegetables
Exports: Greek Cypriot area: $1 billion (f.o.b., 1999 est.); Turkish Cypriot area: $51.1 million (f.o.b., 1999)
Exports - commodities: Greek Cypriot area: citrus, potatoes, grapes, wine, cement, clothing and shoes; Turkish Cypriot area: citrus, potatoes, textiles
Exports - partners: Greek Cypriot area: UK 17.3%, Greece 9.7%, Russia 7.0%, Lebanon 5.2% (1999); Turkish Cypriot area: Turkey 51%, UK 31%, other EU 16.5% (1999)
Imports: Greek Cypriot area: $3.6 billion (f.o.b., 1999 est.); Turkish Cypriot area: $402 million (f.o.b., 1999)
Imports - commodities: Greek Cypriot area: consumer goods, petroleum and lubricants, food and feed grains, machinery; Turkish Cypriot area: food, minerals, chemicals, machinery
Imports - partners: Greek Cypriot area: UK 11.2%, US 10.6%, Italy 8.8%, Greece 8.2%, Germany 6.7% (1999); Turkish Cypriot area: Turkey 58.6%, UK 12.5%, other EU 13% (1999)
Debt - external: Greek Cypriot area: $NA; Turkish Cypriot area: $NA
Economic aid - recipient: Greek Cypriot area - $17 million (1998); Turkish Cypriot area - $700 million from Turkey in grants and loans (1990-97) that are usually forgiven
Currency: Greek Cypriot area: Cypriot pound (CYP); Turkish Cypriot area: Turkish lira (TRL)
Currency code: CYP; TRL

Exchange rates: Cypriot pounds per US dollar - 0.6146 (January 2001), 0.6208 (2000), 0.5423 (1999), 0.5170 (1998), 0.5135 (1997), 0.4663 (1996); Turkish liras per US dollar - 677,621 (December 2000), 625,219 (2000), 418,783 (1999), 260,724 (1998), 151,865 (1997), 81,405 (1996)
Fiscal year: calendar year

Communications

Telephones - main lines in use: Greek Cypriot area: 405,000 (1998); Turkish Cypriot area: 83,162 (1998)
Telephones - mobile cellular: Greek Cypriot area: 68,000 (1998); Turkish Cypriot area: 70,000 (1999)
Telephone system:
general assessment: excellent in both the Greek Cypriot and Turkish Cypriot areas
domestic: open wire, fiber-optic cable, and microwave radio relay
international: tropospheric scatter; 3 coaxial and 5 fiber-optic submarine cables; satellite earth stations - 3 Intelsat (1 Atlantic Ocean and 2 Indian Ocean), 2 Eutelsat, 2 Intersputnik, and 1 Arabsat
Radio broadcast stations: Greek Cypriot area: AM 7, FM 60, shortwave 1 (1998); Turkish Cypriot area: AM 3, FM 11, shortwave 1 (1998)
Radios: Greek Cypriot area: 310,000 (1997); Turkish Cypriot area: 56,450 (1994)
Television broadcast stations: Greek Cypriot area: 4 (plus 225 low-power repeaters) (September 1995); Turkish Cypriot area: 4 (plus 5 repeaters) (September 1995)
Televisions: Greek Cypriot area: 248,000 (1997); Turkish Cypriot area: 52,300 (1994)
Internet country code: .cy
Internet Service Providers (ISPs): 6 (2000)
Internet users: 80,000 (2000)

Transportation

Railways: 0 km
Highways:
total: Greek Cypriot area: 10,663 km (1998 est.); Turkish Cypriot area: 2,350 km (1996 est.)
paved: Greek Cypriot area: 6,249 km (1998 est.); Turkish Cypriot area: 1,370 km (1996 est.)
unpaved: Greek Cypriot area: 4,414 km (1998 est.); Turkish Cypriot area: 980 km (1996 est.)
Waterways: none
Ports and harbors: Famagusta, Kyrenia, Larnaca, Limassol, Paphos, Vasilikos
Merchant marine:
total: 1,328 ships (1,000 GRT or over) totaling 22,905,542 GRT/36,312,219 DWT
ships by type: barge carrier 2, bulk 431, cargo 438, chemical tanker 23, combination bulk 36, combination ore/oil 4, container 140, liquefied gas 6, passenger 8, passenger/cargo 1, petroleum tanker 143, refrigerated cargo 40, roll on/roll off 42, short-sea passenger 9, specialized tanker 2, vehicle carrier 3

note: includes some foreign-owned ships registered here as a flag of convenience: Austria 8, Belgium 7, China 10, Cuba 10, Denmark 2, Germany 79, Greece 385, Hong Kong 9, Croatia 2, India 5, Iran 1, Israel 4, Italy 2, Japan 19, South Korea 3, Latvia 10, Lithuania 1, Monaco 1, Netherlands 13, Norway 11, Poland 9, Portugal 3, Russia 42, Singapore 1, Spain 5, Sudan 2, Sweden 3, Switzerland 2, UAE 6, UK 8, Ukraine 2, US 9, Venezuela 2 (2000 est.)
Airports: 15 (2000 est.)
Airports - with paved runways:
total: 12
2,438 to 3,047 m: 7
1,524 to 2,437 m: 1
914 to 1,523 m: 3
under 914 m: 1 (2000 est.)
Airports - with unpaved runways:
total: 3
914 to 1,523 m: 1
under 914 m: 2 (2000 est.)
Heliports: 7 (2000 est.)

Military

Military branches: Greek Cypriot area: Greek Cypriot National Guard (GCNG; includes air and naval elements), Hellenic Forces Contingent on Cyprus (ELDYK), Greek Cypriot Police; Turkish Cypriot area: Turkish Cypriot Security Force (TCSF), Turkish mainland army units
Military manpower - military age: 18 years of age
Military manpower - availability:
males age 15-49: 198,275 (2001 est.)
Military manpower - fit for military service:
males age 15-49: 136,147 (2001 est.)
Military manpower - reaching military age annually:
males: 6,616 (2001 est.)
Military expenditures - dollar figure: $370 million (FY00)
Military expenditures - percent of GDP: 4.2% (FY00)

Transnational Issues

Disputes - international: 1974 hostilities divided the island into two de facto autonomous areas, a Greek Cypriot area controlled by the internationally recognized Cypriot Government (59% of the island's land area) and a Turkish-Cypriot area (37% of the island), that are separated by a UN buffer zone (4% of the island); there are two UK sovereign base areas mostly within the Greek Cypriot portion of the island
Illicit drugs: minor transit point for heroin and hashish via air routes and container traffic to Europe, especially from Lebanon and Turkey; some cocaine transits as well

Czech Republic

Introduction

Background: After World War II, Czechoslovakia fell within the Soviet sphere of influence. In 1968, an invasion by Warsaw Pact troops ended the efforts of the country's leaders to liberalize party rule and create "socialism with a human face." Anti-Soviet demonstrations the following year ushered in a period of harsh repression. With the collapse of Soviet authority in 1989, Czechoslovakia regained its freedom through a peaceful "Velvet Revolution." On 1 January 1993, the country underwent a "velvet divorce" into its two national components, the Czech Republic and Slovakia. Now a member of NATO, the Czech Republic has moved toward integration in world markets, a development that poses both opportunities and risks.

Geography

Location: Central Europe, southeast of Germany
Geographic coordinates: 49 45 N, 15 30 E
Map references: Europe
Area:
total: 78,866 sq km
land: 77,276 sq km
water: 1,590 sq km
Area - comparative: slightly smaller than South Carolina
Land boundaries:
total: 1,881 km
border countries: Austria 362 km, Germany 646 km, Poland 658 km, Slovakia 215 km
Coastline: 0 km (landlocked)
Maritime claims: none (landlocked)
Climate: temperate; cool summers; cold, cloudy, humid winters
Terrain: Bohemia in the west consists of rolling plains, hills, and plateaus surrounded by low mountains; Moravia in the east consists of very hilly country
Elevation extremes:
lowest point: Elbe River 115 m
highest point: Snezka 1,602 m
Natural resources: hard coal, soft coal, kaolin, clay, graphite, timber
Land use:
arable land: 41%
permanent crops: 2%
permanent pastures: 11%
forests and woodland: 34%
other: 12% (1993 est.)
Irrigated land: 240 sq km (1993 est.)
Natural hazards: flooding
Environment - current issues: air and water pollution in areas of northwest Bohemia and in northern Moravia around Ostrava present health risks; acid rain damaging forests
Environment - international agreements:
party to: Air Pollution, Air Pollution-Nitrogen Oxides, Air Pollution-Sulphur 85, Air Pollution-Sulphur 94, Air Pollution-Volatile Organic Compounds, Antarctic Treaty, Biodiversity, Climate Change, Desertification, Endangered Species, Environmental Modification, Hazardous Wastes, Law of the Sea, Marine Dumping, Nuclear Test Ban, Ozone Layer Protection, Ship Pollution, Wetlands
signed, but not ratified: Air Pollution-Persistent Organic Pollutants, Antarctic-Environmental Protocol, Climate Change-Kyoto Protocol
Geography - note: landlocked; strategically located astride some of oldest and most significant land routes in Europe; Moravian Gate is a traditional military corridor between the North European Plain and the Danube in central Europe

People

Population: 10,264,212 (July 2001 est.)
Age structure:
0-14 years: 16.09% (male 847,219; female 804,731)
15-64 years: 69.99% (male 3,592,984; female 3,590,802)
65 years and over: 13.92% (male 549,538; female 878,938) (2001 est.)
Population growth rate: -0.07% (2001 est.)
Birth rate: 9.11 births/1,000 population (2001 est.)
Death rate: 10.81 deaths/1,000 population (2001 est.)
Net migration rate: 0.96 migrant(s)/1,000 population (2001 est.)
Sex ratio:
at birth: 1.06 male(s)/female
under 15 years: 1.05 male(s)/female
15-64 years: 1 male(s)/female
65 years and over: 0.63 male(s)/female
total population: 0.95 male(s)/female (2001 est.)
Infant mortality rate: 5.55 deaths/1,000 live births (2001 est.)
Life expectancy at birth:
total population: 74.73 years
male: 71.23 years
female: 78.43 years (2001 est.)
Total fertility rate: 1.18 children born/woman (2001 est.)
HIV/AIDS - adult prevalence rate: 0.04% (1999 est.)
HIV/AIDS - people living with HIV/AIDS: 2,200 (1999 est.)
HIV/AIDS - deaths: less than 100 (1999 est.)
Nationality:
noun: Czech(s)
adjective: Czech
Ethnic groups: Czech 81.2%, Moravian 13.2%, Slovak 3.1%, Polish 0.6%, German 0.5%, Silesian 0.4%, Roma 0.3%, Hungarian 0.2%, other 0.5% (1991)
Religions: atheist 39.8%, Roman Catholic 39.2%, Protestant 4.6%, Orthodox 3%, other 13.4%
Languages: Czech
Literacy:
definition: NA
total population: 99.9% (1999 est.)
male: NA%
female: NA%

Government

Country name:
conventional long form: Czech Republic
conventional short form: Czech Republic
local long form: Ceska Republika
local short form: Ceska Republika
Government type: parliamentary democracy
Capital: Prague
Administrative divisions: 13 regions (kraje, singular - kraj) and 1 capital city* (hlavni mesto); Brnensky, Budejovicky, Jihlavsky, Karlovarsky, Kralovehradecky, Liberecky, Olomoucky, Ostravsky, Pardubicky, Plzensky, Praha*, Stredocesky, Ustecky, Zlinsky
Independence: 1 January 1993 (Czechoslovakia split into the Czech Republic and Slovakia)
National holiday: Czech Founding Day, 28 October (1918)
Constitution: ratified 16 December 1992; effective 1 January 1993
Legal system: civil law system based on Austro-Hungarian codes; has not accepted compulsory ICJ jurisdiction; legal code modified to bring it in line with Organization on Security and Cooperation in Europe (OSCE) obligations and to expunge Marxist-Leninist legal theory
Suffrage: 18 years of age; universal
Executive branch:
chief of state: President Vaclav HAVEL (since 2 February 1993)
head of government: Prime Minister Milos ZEMAN (since 17 July 1998); Deputy Prime Ministers Vladimir SPIDLA (since 22 July 1998), Pavel RYCHETSKY (since 22 July 1998), Jan KAVAN (since 8 December 1999)
cabinet: Cabinet appointed by the president on the recommendation of the prime minister

Czech Republic (continued)

elections: president elected by Parliament for a five-year term; election last held 20 January 1998 (next to be held NA January 2003); prime minister appointed by the president
election results: Vaclav HAVEL reelected president; Vaclav HAVEL received 47 of 81 votes in the Senate and 99 out of 200 votes in the Chamber of Deputies (second round of voting)
Legislative branch: bicameral Parliament or Parliament consists of the Senate or Senat (81 seats; members are elected by popular vote to serve six-year terms; one-third elected every two years) and the Chamber of Deputies or Poslanecka snemovna (200 seats; members are elected by popular vote to serve four-year terms)
elections: Senate - last held 12 and 19 November 2000 (next to be held NA November 2002); Chamber of Deputies - last held 19-20 June 1998 (next to be held by NA June 2002)
election results: Senate - percent of vote by party - NA%; seats by party - KDU-CSL 28, ODS 22, CSSD 15, ODA 7, US 4, KSCM 3, independents 2; Chamber of Deputies - percent of vote by party - CSSD 32.3%, ODS 27.7%, KSCM 11%, KDU-CSL 9.0%, US 8.6%; seats by party - CSSD 74, ODS 63, KSCM 24, KDU-CSL 20, US 18, CSNS 1
Judicial branch: Supreme Court; Constitutional Court; chairman and deputy chairmen are appointed by the president for a 10-year term
Political parties and leaders: Christian and Democratic Union-Czechoslovak People's Party or KDU-CSL [Jan KASAL, chairman]; Civic Democratic Alliance or ODA [Daniel KROUPA, chairman]; Civic Democratic Party or ODS [Vaclav KLAUS, chairman]; Communist Party of Bohemia and Moravia or KSCM [Miroslav GREBENICEK, chairman]; Communist Party of Czechoslovakia or KSC [Miroslav STEPAN, chairman]; Czech National Social Party of CSNS [Jan SULA, chairman]; Czech Social Democratic Party or CSSD [Milos ZEMAN, chairman]; Democratic Union or DEU [Ratibor MAJZLIK, chairman]; Freedom Union or US [Karel KUEHNL, chairman]; Quad Coalition [Cyril SVOBODA, chairman] (includes KDU-CSL, US, ODA, DEU); Republicans of Miroslav SLADEK or RMS [Miroslav SLADEK, chairman]
Political pressure groups and leaders: Czech-Moravian Confederation of Trade Unions [Richard FALBR]
International organization participation: ACCT (observer), Australia Group, BIS, CCC, CE, CEI, CERN, EAPC, EBRD, ECE, EU (applicant), FAO, IAEA, IBRD, ICAO, ICC, ICFTU, ICRM, IDA, IEA, IFC, IFRCS, ILO, IMF, IMO, Inmarsat, Intelsat, Interpol, IOC, IOM, ISO, ITU, MONUC, NATO, NEA, NSG, OAS (observer), OECD, OPCW, OSCE, PCA, PFP, UN, UNCTAD, UNESCO, UNIDO, UNMEE, UNMIBH, UNMIK, UNMOP, UNMOT, UNOMIG, UPU, WCL, WEU (associate), WFTU, WHO, WIPO, WMO, WToO, WTrO, ZC
Diplomatic representation in the US:
chief of mission: Ambassador Alexsandr VONDRA
chancery: 3900 Spring of Freedom Street NW, Washington, DC 20008
telephone: [1] (202) 274-9100
FAX: [1] (202) 966-8540
consulate(s) general: Los Angeles and New York
Diplomatic representation from the US:
chief of mission: Ambassador (vacant); Charge d'Affaires Steven J. COFFEY
embassy: Trziste 15, 11801 Prague 1
mailing address: use embassy street address
telephone: [420] (2) 5753-0663
FAX: [420] (2) 5753-0583
Flag description: two equal horizontal bands of white (top) and red with a blue isosceles triangle based on the hoist side (identical to the flag of the former Czechoslovakia)

Economy

Economy - overview: Basically one of the most stable and prosperous of the post-Communist states, the Czech Republic has been recovering from recession since mid-1999. The economy grew about 2.5% in 2000 and should achieve somewhat higher growth in 2001. Growth is led by exports to the EU, especially Germany, and foreign investment, while domestic demand is reviving. Uncomfortably high fiscal and current account deficits could be future problems. Unemployment is down to 8.7% as job creation continues in the rebounding economy; inflation is up to 3.8% but still moderate. The EU put the Czech Republic just behind Poland and Hungary in preparations for accession, which will give further impetus and direction to structural reform. Moves to complete banking, telecommunications and energy privatization will add to foreign investment, while intensified restructuring among large enterprises and banks and improvements in the financial sector should strengthen output growth.
GDP: purchasing power parity - $132.4 billion (2000 est.)
GDP - real growth rate: 2.5% (2000 est.)
GDP - per capita: purchasing power parity - $12,900 (2000 est.)
GDP - composition by sector:
agriculture: 3.7%
industry: 41.8%
services: 54.5% (1999)
Population below poverty line: NA%
Household income or consumption by percentage share:
lowest 10%: 4.3%
highest 10%: 22.4% (1996)
Inflation rate (consumer prices): 3.8% (2000 est.)
Labor force: 5.203 million (1999 est.)
Labor force - by occupation: agriculture 5%, industry 40%, services 55% (2000 est.)
Unemployment rate: 8.7% (2000 est.)
Budget:
revenues: $16.7 billion
expenditures: $18 billion, including capital expenditures of $NA (2001 est.)
Industries: metallurgy, machinery and equipment, motor vehicles, glass, armaments
Industrial production growth rate: 7.6% (2000)
Electricity - production: 67.642 billion kWh (2000)
Electricity - production by source:
fossil fuel: 77.8%
hydro: 3.43%
nuclear: 18.77%
other: 0% (2000)
Electricity - consumption: 52.898 billion kWh (2000)
Electricity - exports: 18.744 billion kWh (2000)
Electricity - imports: 8.735 billion kWh (2000)
Agriculture - products: wheat, potatoes, sugar beets, hops, fruit; pigs, poultry
Exports: $28.3 billion (f.o.b., 2000)
Exports - commodities: machinery and transport equipment 44%, other manufactured goods 40%, chemicals 7%, raw materials and fuel 7% (1999)
Exports - partners: Germany 43%, Slovakia 8.4%, Austria 6.6%, Poland 5.6%, France 4% (1999)
Imports: $31.4 billion (f.o.b., 2000)
Imports - commodities: machinery and transport equipment 42%, other manufactured goods 33%, chemicals 12%, raw materials and fuels 10% (1999)
Imports - partners: Germany 37.5%, Slovakia 6.7%, Austria 6.2%, Italy 5.9%, France 5.4% (1999)
Debt - external: $21.3 billion (2000)
Economic aid - recipient: $NA
Currency: Czech koruna (CZK)
Currency code: CZK
Exchange rates: koruny per US dollar - 37.425 (January 2001), 38.598 (2000), 34.569 (1999), 32.281 (1998), 31.698 (1997), 27.145 (1996)
Fiscal year: calendar year

Communications

Telephones - main lines in use: 3.869 million (2000)
Telephones - mobile cellular: 4.346 million (2000)
Telephone system:
general assessment: privatization and modernization of the Czech telecommunication system got a late start but is advancing steadily; growth in the use of mobile cellular telephones is particularly vigorous
domestic: 86% of exchanges now digital; existing copper subscriber systems now being enhanced with Asymmetric Digital Subscriber Line (ADSL) equipment to accommodate Internet and other digital signals; trunk systems include fiber-optic cable and microwave radio relay
international: satellite earth stations - 2 Intersputnik (Atlantic and Indian Ocean regions), 1 Intelsat, 1 Eutelsat, 1 Inmarsat, 1 Globalstar
Radio broadcast stations: AM 31, FM 304, shortwave 17 (2000)
Radios: 3,159,134 (December 2000)
Television broadcast stations: 150 (plus 1,434 repeaters) (2000)
Televisions: 3,405,834 (December 2000)
Internet country code: .cz
Internet Service Providers (ISPs): more than 300 (2000)
Internet users: 900,000 (2000)

Czech Republic (continued)

Transportation

Railways:
total: 9,444 km
standard gauge: 9,350 km 1.435-m standard gauge (2,843 km electrified at three voltages; 1,929 km double track)
narrow gauge: 94 km 0.760-m narrow gauge (2000)
Highways:
total: 55,432 km
paved: 55,432 km (including 499 km of expressways)
unpaved: 0 km (2000)
Waterways: 303 km
note: (the Labe (Elbe) is the principal river) (2000)
Pipelines: natural gas 3,550 km (2000)
Ports and harbors: Decin, Prague, Usti nad Labem
Airports: 114 (2000 est.)
Airports - with paved runways:
total: 43
over 3,047 m: 2
2,438 to 3,047 m: 10
1,524 to 2,437 m: 14
914 to 1,523 m: 1
under 914 m: 16 (2000 est.)
Airports - with unpaved runways:
total: 71
1,524 to 2,437 m: 1
914 to 1,523 m: 28
under 914 m: 42 (2000 est.)
Heliports: 1 (2000 est.)

Military

Military branches: Army, Air and Air Defense Forces, Territorial Defense, Railroad Units
Military manpower - military age: 18 years of age
Military manpower - availability:
males age 15-49: 2,653,456 (2001 est.)
Military manpower - fit for military service:
males age 15-49: 2,024,070 (2001 est.)
Military manpower - reaching military age annually:
males: 69,393 (2001 est.)
Military expenditures - dollar figure: $1.2 billion (FY01)
Military expenditures - percent of GDP: 2.2% (FY01)

Transnational Issues

Disputes - international: Liechtenstein's royal family claims restitution for 1,600 sq km of land in the Czech Republic confiscated in 1918; individual Sudeten German claims for restitution of property confiscated in connection with their expulsion after World War II; Austria has minor dispute with Czech Republic over nuclear power plants and post-World War II treatment of German-speaking minorities
Illicit drugs: major transshipment point for Southwest Asian heroin and minor transit point for Latin American cocaine to Western Europe; domestic consumption - especially of locally produced synthetic drugs - on the rise

Denmark

Introduction

Background: Once the seat of Viking raiders and later a major north European power, Denmark has evolved into a modern, prosperous nation that is participating in the political and economic integration of Europe. So far, however, the country has opted out of some aspects of the European Union's Maastricht Treaty, including the economic and monetary system (EMU) and issues concerning certain internal affairs.

Geography

Location: Northern Europe, bordering the Baltic Sea and the North Sea, on a peninsula north of Germany
Geographic coordinates: 56 00 N, 10 00 E
Map references: Europe
Area:
total: 43,094 sq km
land: 42,394 sq km
water: 700 sq km
note: includes the island of Bornholm in the Baltic Sea and the rest of metropolitan Denmark (the Jutland Peninsula, and the major islands of Sjaeland and Fyn), but excludes the Faroe Islands and Greenland
Area - comparative: slightly less than twice the size of Massachusetts
Land boundaries:
total: 68 km
border countries: Germany 68 km
Coastline: 7,314 km
Maritime claims:
contiguous zone: 24 NM
continental shelf: 200-m depth or to the depth of exploitation
exclusive economic zone: 200 NM
territorial sea: 12 NM
Climate: temperate; humid and overcast; mild, windy winters and cool summers
Terrain: low and flat to gently rolling plains
Elevation extremes:
lowest point: Lammefjord -7 m
highest point: Yding Skovhoej 173 m
Natural resources: petroleum, natural gas, fish, salt, limestone, stone, gravel and sand
Land use:
arable land: 60%
permanent crops: 0%
permanent pastures: 5%
forests and woodland: 10%
other: 25% (1993 est.)
Irrigated land: 4,350 sq km (1993 est.)
Natural hazards: flooding is a threat in some areas of the country (e.g., parts of Jutland, along the southern coast of the island of Lolland) that are protected from the sea by a system of dikes
Environment - current issues: air pollution, principally from vehicle and power plant emissions; nitrogen and phosphorus pollution of the North Sea; drinking and surface water becoming polluted from animal wastes and pesticides
Environment - international agreements:
party to: Air Pollution, Air Pollution-Nitrogen Oxides, Air Pollution-Sulphur 85, Air Pollution-Sulphur 94, Air Pollution-Volatile Organic Compounds, Antarctic Treaty, Biodiversity, Climate Change, Desertification, Endangered Species, Environmental Modification, Hazardous Wastes, Marine Dumping, Marine Life Conservation, Nuclear Test Ban, Ozone Layer Protection, Ship Pollution, Tropical Timber 83, Tropical Timber 94, Wetlands, Whaling
signed, but not ratified: Air Pollution-Persistent Organic Pollutants, Antarctic-Environmental Protocol, Climate Change-Kyoto Protocol, Law of the Sea
Geography - note: controls Danish Straits (Skagerrak and Kattegat) linking Baltic and North Seas; about one-quarter of the population lives in greater Copenhagen

People

Population: 5,352,815 (July 2001 est.)
Age structure:
0-14 years: 18.59% (male 510,826; female 484,385)
15-64 years: 66.56% (male 1,804,617; female 1,758,019)
65 years and over: 14.85% (male 331,906; female 463,062) (2001 est.)
Population growth rate: 0.3% (2001 est.)
Birth rate: 11.96 births/1,000 population (2001 est.)
Death rate: 10.9 deaths/1,000 population (2001 est.)
Net migration rate: 1.98 migrant(s)/1,000 population (2001 est.)
Sex ratio:
at birth: 1.06 male(s)/female
under 15 years: 1.05 male(s)/female
15-64 years: 1.03 male(s)/female
65 years and over: 0.72 male(s)/female
total population: 0.98 male(s)/female (2001 est.)
Infant mortality rate: 5.04 deaths/1,000 live births (2001 est.)
Life expectancy at birth:
total population: 76.72 years
male: 74.12 years

Denmark (continued)

female: 79.47 years (2001 est.)
Total fertility rate: 1.73 children born/woman (2001 est.)
HIV/AIDS - adult prevalence rate: 0.17% (1999 est.)
HIV/AIDS - people living with HIV/AIDS: 4,300 (1999 est.)
HIV/AIDS - deaths: less than 100 (1999 est.)
Nationality:
noun: Dane(s)
adjective: Danish
Ethnic groups: Scandinavian, Inuit, Faroese, German, Turkish, Iranian, Somali
Religions: Evangelical Lutheran 95%, other Protestant and Roman Catholic 3%, Muslims 2%
Languages: Danish, Faroese, Greenlandic (an Inuit dialect), German (small minority)
note: English is the predominant second language
Literacy:
definition: age 15 and over can read and write
total population: 100%
male: NA%
female: NA%

Government

Country name:
conventional long form: Kingdom of Denmark
conventional short form: Denmark
local long form: Kongeriget Danmark
local short form: Danmark
Government type: constitutional monarchy
Capital: Copenhagen
Administrative divisions: metropolitan Denmark - 14 counties (amter, singular - amt) and 2 kommunes*; Arhus, Bornholm, Fredericksberg*, Frederiksborg, Fyn, Kobenhavn, Kobenhavns*, Nordjylland, Ribe, Ringkobing, Roskilde, Sonderjylland, Storstrom, Vejle, Vestsjalland, Viborg
note: see separate entries for the Faroe Islands and Greenland, which are part of the Kingdom of Denmark and are self-governing administrative divisions
Independence: first organized as a unified state in 10th century; in 1849 became a constitutional monarchy
National holiday: Constitution Day, 5 June
Constitution: 1849 was the original constitution; there was a major overhaul 5 June 1953, allowing for a unicameral legislature and a female chief of state
Legal system: civil law system; judicial review of legislative acts; accepts compulsory ICJ jurisdiction, with reservations
Suffrage: 18 years of age; universal
Executive branch:
chief of state: Queen MARGRETHE II (since 14 January 1972); Heir Apparent Crown Prince FREDERIK, elder son of the monarch (born 26 May 1968)
head of government: Prime Minister Poul Nyrup RASMUSSEN (since 25 January 1993)
cabinet: Cabinet appointed by the prime minister and approved by Parliament
elections: none; the monarch is hereditary; prime minister appointed by the monarch
Legislative branch: unicameral Parliament or Folketing (179 seats, including 2 from Greenland and 2 from the Faroe Islands; members are elected by popular vote on the basis of proportional representation to serve four-year terms)
elections: last held 11 March 1998 (next to be held by March 2002)
election results: percent of vote by party - NA%; seats by party - progovernment parties: Social Democratic Party 65, Socialist People's Party 13, Social Liberal Party 7, Red-Green Unity List 5; opposition: Liberal Party 43, Conservative Party 17, Danish People's Party 13, Center Democratic Party 8, Christian People's Party 4, Progress Party 4; seats by party as of 1 January 2001: government coalition parties - Social Democrats 63, Social Liberals 7; pro-government parties - Socialist People's Party 13, Unity List 5; opposition - Liberals 42, Conservatives 16, Danish People's Party 13, Center Democrats 8, Christian People's Party 4, Progress Party 4 (now named Freedom 2000); does not include the 4 overseas seats
Judicial branch: Supreme Court (judges are appointed by the monarch for life)
Political parties and leaders: Center Democratic Party [Mimi JAKOBSEN]; Christian People's Party [Jann SJURSEN]; Conservative Party (sometimes known as Conservative People's Party) [Bendt BENDTSEN]; Danish People's Party [Pia KJAERSGAARD]; Liberal Party [Anders Fogh RASMUSSEN]; Progress Party (now named Freedom 2000) [Kim BEHNKE]; Social Democratic Party [Poul Nyrup RASMUSSEN]; Social Liberal Party (sometimes called the Radical Left) [Marianne JELVED, leader; Johannes LEBECH, chairman]; Socialist People's Party [Holger K. NIELSEN]; Red-Green Unity List (bloc includes Left Socialist Party, Communist Party of Denmark, Socialist Workers' Party) [collective leadership]
Political pressure groups and leaders: NA
International organization participation: AfDB, AsDB, Australia Group, BIS, CBSS, CCC, CE, CERN, EAPC, EBRD, ECE, EIB, ESA, EU, FAO, G- 9, IADB, IAEA, IBRD, ICAO, ICC, ICFTU, ICRM, IDA, IEA, IFAD, IFC, IFRCS, IHO, ILO, IMF, IMO, Inmarsat, Intelsat, Interpol, IOC, IOM, ISO, ITU, MONUC, NATO, NC, NEA, NIB, NSG, OAS (observer), OECD, OPCW, OSCE, PCA, UN, UNCTAD, UNESCO, UNHCR, UNIDO, UNIKOM, UNMEE, UNMIBH, UNMIK, UNMOGIP, UNMOP, UNMOT, UNOMIG, UNTAET, UNTSO, UPU, WEU (observer), WHO, WIPO, WMO, WTrO, ZC
Diplomatic representation in the US:
chief of mission: Ambassador Ulrik Andreas FEDERSPIEL
chancery: 3200 Whitehaven Street NW, Washington, DC 20008
telephone: [1] (202) 234-4300
FAX: [1] (202) 328-1470
consulate(s) general: Chicago, Los Angeles, and New York
Diplomatic representation from the US:
chief of mission: Ambassador Richard N. SWETT (scheduled to depart 6 July 2001); Ambassador-designate Stuart BERNSTEIN
embassy: Dag Hammarskjolds Alle 24, 2100 Copenhagen
mailing address: PSC 73, APO AE 09716
telephone: [45] 35 55 31 44
FAX: [45] 35 38 96 16
Flag description: red with a white cross that extends to the edges of the flag; the vertical part of the cross is shifted to the hoist side, and that design element of the Dannebrog (Danish flag) was subsequently adopted by the other Nordic countries of Finland, Iceland, Norway, and Sweden

Economy

Economy - overview: This thoroughly modern market economy features high-tech agriculture, up-to-date small-scale and corporate industry, extensive government welfare measures, comfortable living standards, and high dependence on foreign trade. Denmark is a net exporter of food and energy and has a comfortable balance of payments surplus. The center-left coalition government has reduced the formerly high unemployment rate and attained a budget surplus as well as followed the previous government's policies of maintaining low inflation and a stable currency. The coalition has lowered marginal income tax rates and raised environmental taxes thus maintaining overall tax revenues. Problems of bottlenecks, and longer term demographic changes reducing the labor force, are being addressed through labor market reforms. The government has been successful in meeting, and even exceeding, the economic convergence criteria for participating in the third phase (a common European currency) of the European Monetary Union (EMU), but Denmark, in a September 2000 referendum, reconfirmed its decision not to join the 11 other EU members in the euro. Even so, the Danish currency remains pegged to the euro.
GDP: purchasing power parity - $136.2 billion (2000 est.)
GDP - real growth rate: 2.8% (2000 est.)
GDP - per capita: purchasing power parity - $25,500 (2000 est.)
GDP - composition by sector:
agriculture: 3%
industry: 25%
services: 72% (2000 est.)
Population below poverty line: NA%
Household income or consumption by percentage share:
lowest 10%: 2%
highest 10%: 24% (2000 est.)
Inflation rate (consumer prices): 2.9% (2000 est.)
Labor force: 2.856 million (2000 est.)
Labor force - by occupation: services 79%, industry 17%, agriculture 4% (2000 est.)
Unemployment rate: 5.3% (2000)

Denmark (continued)

Budget:
revenues: $52.9 billion
expenditures: $51.3 billion, including capital expenditures of $500 million (2001 est.)
Industries: food processing, machinery and equipment, textiles and clothing, chemical products, electronics, construction, furniture, and other wood products, shipbuilding, windmills
Industrial production growth rate: 3% (2000 est.)
Electricity - production: 37.885 billion kWh (1999)
Electricity - production by source:
fossil fuel: 88.4%
hydro: 0.07%
nuclear: 0%
other: 11.53% (1999)
Electricity - consumption: 32.916 billion kWh (1999)
Electricity - exports: 7.28 billion kWh (1999)
Electricity - imports: 4.963 billion kWh (1999)
Agriculture - products: grain, potatoes, rape, sugar beets; pork and beef, dairy products; fish
Exports: $50.8 billion (f.o.b., 2000)
Exports - commodities: machinery and instruments, meat and meat products, dairy products, fish, chemicals, furniture, ships, windmills
Exports - partners: EU 66.5% (Germany 20.1%, Sweden 11.7%, UK 9.6%, France 5.3%, Netherlands 4.7%), Norway 5.8%, US 5.4% (1999)
Imports: $43.6 billion (f.o.b., 2000)
Imports - commodities: machinery and equipment, raw materials and semimanufactures for industry, chemicals, grain and foodstuffs, consumer goods
Imports - partners: EU 72.1% (Germany 21.6%, Sweden 12.4%, UK 8.0%, Netherlands 8.0%, France 5.8%), Norway 4.2%, US 4.5% (1999)
Debt - external: $21.7 billion (2000)
Economic aid - donor: ODA, $1.63 billion (1999)
Currency: Danish krone (DKK)
Currency code: DKK
Exchange rates: Danish kroner per US dollar - 7.951 (January 2001), 8.083 (2000), 6.976 (1999), 6.701 (1998), 6.604 (1997), 5.799 (1996); note - the Danes rejected the Euro in a 28 September 2000 referendum
Fiscal year: calendar year

Communications

Telephones - main lines in use: 4.785 million (1997)
Telephones - mobile cellular: 1,444,016 (1997)
Telephone system:
general assessment: excellent telephone and telegraph services
domestic: buried and submarine cables and microwave radio relay form trunk network, 4 cellular mobile communications systems
international: 18 submarine fiber-optic cables linking Denmark with Norway, Sweden, Russia, Poland, Germany, Netherlands, UK, Faroe Islands, Iceland, and Canada; satellite earth stations - 6 Intelsat, 10 Eutelsat, 1 Orion, 1 Inmarsat (Blaavand-Atlantic-East); note - the Nordic countries (Denmark, Finland, Iceland, Norway, and Sweden) share the Danish earth station and the Eik, Norway, station for worldwide Inmarsat access (1997)
Radio broadcast stations: AM 2, FM 355, shortwave 0 (1998)
Radios: 6.02 million (1997)
Television broadcast stations: 26 (plus 51 repeaters) (1998)
Televisions: 3.121 million (1997)
Internet country code: .dk
Internet Service Providers (ISPs): 13 (2000)
Internet users: 2.3 million (2000)

Transportation

Railways:
total: 2,859 km (508 km privately owned and operated)
standard gauge: 2,859 km 1.435-m gauge (600 km electrified; 760 km double track) (1998)
Highways:
total: 71,474 km
paved: 71,474 km (including 880 km of expressways)
unpaved: 0 km (1999)
Waterways: 417 km
Pipelines: crude oil 110 km; petroleum products 578 km; natural gas 700 km
Ports and harbors: Abenra, Alborg, Arhus, Copenhagen, Esbjerg, Fredericia, Kolding, Odense, Roenne (Bornholm), Vejle
Merchant marine:
total: 342 ships (1,000 GRT or over) totaling 6,073,489 GRT/8,027,002 DWT
ships by type: bulk 10, cargo 128, chemical tanker 27, container 76, liquefied gas 26, livestock carrier 6, petroleum tanker 22, railcar carrier 1, refrigerated cargo 13, roll on/roll off 23, short-sea passenger 7, specialized tanker 3
note: includes some foreign-owned ships registered here as a flag of convenience: Finland 1 (2000 est.)
Airports: 119 (2000 est.)
Airports - with paved runways:
total: 28
over 3,047 m: 2
2,438 to 3,047 m: 7
1,524 to 2,437 m: 4
914 to 1,523 m: 12
under 914 m: 3 (2000 est.)
Airports - with unpaved runways:
total: 91
1,524 to 2,437 m: 1
914 to 1,523 m: 7
under 914 m: 83 (2000 est.)

Military

Military branches: Royal Danish Army, Royal Danish Navy, Royal Danish Air Force, Home Guard
Military manpower - military age: 18 years of age
Military manpower - availability:
males age 15-49: 1,292,619 (2001 est.)
Military manpower - fit for military service:
males age 15-49: 1,106,094 (2001 est.)
Military manpower - reaching military age annually:
males: 29,212 (2001 est.)
Military expenditures - dollar figure: $2.47 billion (FY99)
Military expenditures - percent of GDP: 1.4% (FY99)

Transnational Issues

Disputes - international: Rockall continental shelf dispute involving Iceland and the UK (Ireland and the UK have signed a boundary agreement in the Rockall area); dispute with Iceland over the Faroe Islands fisheries median line boundary within 200 NM; disputes with Iceland, the UK, and Ireland over the Faroe Islands continental shelf boundary outside 200 NM

Djibouti

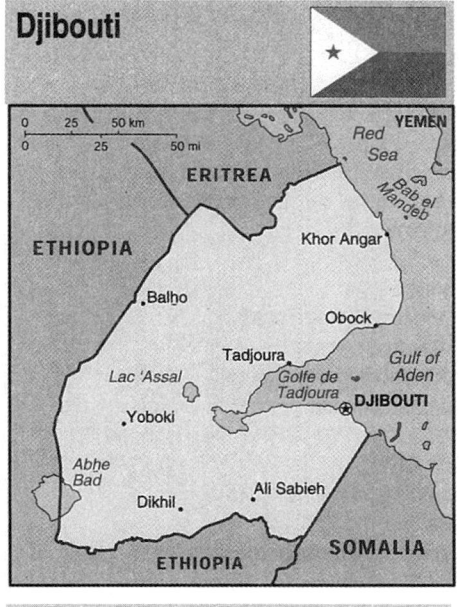

Introduction

Background: The French Territory of the Afars and the Issas became Djibouti in 1977. A peace accord in 1994 ended a three-year uprising by Afars rebels.

Geography

Location: Eastern Africa, bordering the Gulf of Aden and the Red Sea, between Eritrea and Somalia
Geographic coordinates: 11 30 N, 43 00 E
Map references: Africa
Area:
total: 22,000 sq km
land: 21,980 sq km
water: 20 sq km
Area - comparative: slightly smaller than Massachusetts
Land boundaries:
total: 508 km
border countries: Eritrea 113 km, Ethiopia 337 km, Somalia 58 km
Coastline: 314 km
Maritime claims:
contiguous zone: 24 NM
exclusive economic zone: 200 NM
territorial sea: 12 NM
Climate: desert; torrid, dry
Terrain: coastal plain and plateau separated by central mountains
Elevation extremes:
lowest point: Lac Assal -155 m
highest point: Moussa Ali 2,028 m
Natural resources: geothermal areas
Land use:
arable land: 0%
permanent crops: 0%
permanent pastures: 9%
forests and woodland: 0%
other: 91% (1993 est.)
Irrigated land: NA sq km
Natural hazards: earthquakes; droughts; occasional cyclonic disturbances from the Indian Ocean bring heavy rains and flash floods
Environment - current issues: inadequate supplies of potable water; desertification
Environment - international agreements:
party to: Biodiversity, Climate Change, Desertification, Endangered Species, Law of the Sea, Marine Dumping, Ozone Layer Protection, Ship Pollution
signed, but not ratified: none of the selected agreements
Geography - note: strategic location near world's busiest shipping lanes and close to Arabian oilfields; terminus of rail traffic into Ethiopia; mostly wasteland

People

Population: 460,700 (July 2001 est.)
Age structure:
0-14 years: 42.58% (male 98,314; female 97,859)
15-64 years: 54.58% (male 132,619; female 118,841)
65 years and over: 2.84% (male 6,787; female 6,280) (2001 est.)
Population growth rate: 2.6% (2001 est.)
Birth rate: 40.66 births/1,000 population (2001 est.)
Death rate: 14.66 deaths/1,000 population (2001 est.)
Net migration rate: 0 migrant(s)/1,000 population (2001 est.)
Sex ratio:
at birth: 1.03 male(s)/female
under 15 years: 1 male(s)/female
15-64 years: 1.12 male(s)/female
65 years and over: 1.08 male(s)/female
total population: 1.07 male(s)/female (2001 est.)
Infant mortality rate: 101.51 deaths/1,000 live births (2001 est.)
Life expectancy at birth:
total population: 51.21 years
male: 49.37 years
female: 53.1 years (2001 est.)
Total fertility rate: 5.72 children born/woman (2001 est.)
HIV/AIDS - adult prevalence rate: 11.75% (1999 est.)
HIV/AIDS - people living with HIV/AIDS: 37,000 (1999 est.)
HIV/AIDS - deaths: 3,100 (1999 est.)
Nationality:
noun: Djiboutian(s)
adjective: Djiboutian
Ethnic groups: Somali 60%, Afar 35%, French, Arab, Ethiopian, and Italian 5%
Religions: Muslim 94%, Christian 6%
Languages: French (official), Arabic (official), Somali, Afar
Literacy:
definition: age 15 and over can read and write
total population: 46.2%
male: 60.3%
female: 32.7% (1995 est.)

Government

Country name:
conventional long form: Republic of Djibouti
conventional short form: Djibouti
former: French Territory of the Afars and Issas, French Somaliland
Government type: republic
Capital: Djibouti
Administrative divisions: 5 districts (cercles, singular - cercle); 'Ali Sabih, Dikhil, Djibouti, Obock, Tadjoura
Independence: 27 June 1977 (from France)
National holiday: Independence Day, 27 June (1977)
Constitution: multiparty constitution approved by referendum 4 September 1992
Legal system: based on French civil law system, traditional practices, and Islamic law
Suffrage: NA years of age; universal adult
Executive branch:
chief of state: President GUELLEH Ismail Omar (since 8 May 1999);
head of government: Prime Minister DILLEITA Mohamed Dilleita (since 4 March 2001)
cabinet: Council of Ministers responsible to the president
elections: president elected by popular vote for a six-year term; election last held 9 April 1999 (next to be held NA 2005); prime minister appointed by the president
election results: GUELLEH Ismail Omar elected president; percent of vote - GUELLEH Ismail Omar 74.4%, IDRIS Moussa Ahmed 25.6%
Legislative branch: unicameral Chamber of Deputies or Chambre des Deputes (65 seats; members elected by popular vote for five-year terms)
elections: last held 19 December 1997 (next to be held NA 2002)
election results: percent of vote - NA%; seats - RPP 65; note - RPP (the ruling party) dominated the election
Judicial branch: Supreme Court or Cour Supreme
Political parties and leaders: Democratic National Party or PND [ADEN Robleh Awaleh]; Democratic Renewal Party or PRD [Abdillahi HAMARITEH]; People's Progress Assembly or RPP (governing party) [Ismail Omar GELLEH]
Political pressure groups and leaders: Front for the Restoration of Unity and Democracy or FRUD and affiliates; Movement for Unity and Democracy or MUD
International organization participation: ACCT, ACP, AfDB, AFESD, AL, AMF, ECA, FAO, G-77, IBRD, ICAO, ICFTU, ICRM, IDA, IDB, IFAD, IFC, IFRCS, IGAD, ILO, IMF, IMO, Intelsat (nonsignatory user), Interpol, IOC, ITU, NAM, OAU, OIC, OPCW, UN, UNCTAD, UNESCO, UNIDO, UPU, WFTU, WHO, WMO, WToO, WTrO
Diplomatic representation in the US:
chief of mission: Ambassador ROBLE Olhaye Oudine
chancery: Suite 515, 1156 15th Street NW, Washington, DC 20005

Djibouti (continued)

telephone: [1] (202) 331-0270
FAX: [1] (202) 331-0302
Diplomatic representation from the US:
chief of mission: Ambassador Donald YAMAMOTO
embassy: Plateau du Serpent, Boulevard Marechal Joffre, Djibouti
mailing address: B. P. 185, Djibouti
telephone: [253] 35 39 95
FAX: [253] 35 39 40
Flag description: two equal horizontal bands of light blue (top) and light green with a white isosceles triangle based on the hoist side bearing a red five-pointed star in the center

Economy

Economy - overview: The economy is based on service activities connected with the country's strategic location and status as a free trade zone in northeast Africa. Two-thirds of the inhabitants live in the capital city, the remainder being mostly nomadic herders. Scanty rainfall limits crop production to fruits and vegetables, and most food must be imported. Djibouti provides services as both a transit port for the region and an international transshipment and refueling center. It has few natural resources and little industry. The nation is, therefore, heavily dependent on foreign assistance to help support its balance of payments and to finance development projects. An unemployment rate of 40% to 50% continues to be a major problem. Inflation is not a concern, however, because of the fixed tie of the franc to the US dollar. Per capita consumption dropped an estimated 35% over the last seven years because of recession, civil war, and a high population growth rate (including immigrants and refugees). Faced with a multitude of economic difficulties, the government has fallen in arrears on long-term external debt and has been struggling to meet the stipulations of foreign aid donors. The year 2001 will see only small growth as port activity should decrease now that Ethiopia has more trade route options.
GDP: purchasing power parity - $574 million (2000 est.)
GDP - real growth rate: 2% (2000 est.)
GDP - per capita: purchasing power parity - $1,300 (2000 est.)
GDP - composition by sector:
agriculture: 3%
industry: 22%
services: 75% (1998 est.)
Population below poverty line: NA%
Household income or consumption by percentage share:
lowest 10%: NA%
highest 10%: NA%
Inflation rate (consumer prices): 2% (2000 est.)
Labor force: 282,000
Labor force - by occupation: agriculture 75%, industry 11%, services 14% (1991 est.)
Unemployment rate: 50% (2000 est.)
Budget:
revenues: $133 million
expenditures: $187 million, including capital expenditures of $NA (1999 est.)
Industries: limited to a few small-scale enterprises, such as dairy products and mineral-water bottling
Industrial production growth rate: 3% (1996 est.)
Electricity - production: 180 million kWh (1999)
Electricity - production by source:
fossil fuel: 100%
hydro: 0%
nuclear: 0%
other: 0% (1999)
Electricity - consumption: 167.4 million kWh (1999)
Electricity - exports: 0 kWh (1999)
Electricity - imports: 0 kWh (1999)
Agriculture - products: fruits, vegetables; goats, sheep, camels
Exports: $260 million (f.o.b., 1999 est.)
Exports - commodities: reexports, hides and skins, coffee (in transit)
Exports - partners: Somalia 53%, Yemen 23%, Ethiopia 5%, (1998)
Imports: $440 million (f.o.b., 1999 est.)
Imports - commodities: foods, beverages, transport equipment, chemicals, petroleum products
Imports - partners: France 13%, Ethiopia 12%, Italy 9%, Saudi Arabia 6%, UK 6% (1998)
Debt - external: $356 million (1999 est.)
Economic aid - recipient: $106.3 million (1995)
Currency: Djiboutian franc (DJF)
Currency code: DJF
Exchange rates: Djiboutian francs per US dollar - 177.721 (fixed rate since 1973)
Fiscal year: calendar year

Communications

Telephones - main lines in use: 8,000 (1997)
Telephones - mobile cellular: 203 (1997)
Telephone system:
general assessment: telephone facilities in the city of Djibouti are adequate as are the microwave radio relay connections to outlying areas of the country
domestic: microwave radio relay network
international: submarine cable to Jiddah, Suez, Sicily, Marseilles, Colombo, and Singapore; satellite earth stations - 1 Intelsat (Indian Ocean) and 1 Arabsat; Medarabtel regional microwave radio relay telephone network
Radio broadcast stations: AM 2, FM 2, shortwave 0 (1998)
Radios: 52,000 (1997)
Television broadcast stations: 1 (plus 5 low-power repeaters) (1998)
Televisions: 28,000 (1997)
Internet country code: .dj
Internet Service Providers (ISPs): 1 (2000)
Internet users: 1,000 (2000)

Transportation

Railways:
total: 100 km (Djibouti segment of the Addis Ababa-Djibouti railroad)
narrow gauge: 100 km 1.000-m gauge
note: Djibouti and Ethiopia plan to revitalize the century-old railroad that links their capitals by 2003
Highways:
total: 2,890 km
paved: 364 km
unpaved: 2,526 km (1996)
Waterways: none
Ports and harbors: Djibouti
Merchant marine:
total: 1 ship (1,000 GRT or over) totaling 1,369 GRT/ 3,030 DWT
ships by type: cargo 1 (2000 est.)
Airports: 12 (2000 est.)
Airports - with paved runways:
total: 2
over 3,047 m: 1
2,438 to 3,047 m: 1 (2000 est.)
Airports - with unpaved runways:
total: 10
1,524 to 2,437 m: 2
914 to 1,523 m: 5
under 914 m: 3 (2000 est.)

Military

Military branches: Djibouti National Army (includes Navy and Air Force)
Military manpower - availability:
males age 15-49: 108,038 (2001 est.)
Military manpower - fit for military service:
males age 15-49: 63,589 (2001 est.)
Military expenditures - dollar figure: $23 million (FY97)
Military expenditures - percent of GDP: 4.5% (FY97)

Transnational Issues

Disputes - international: none

Dominica

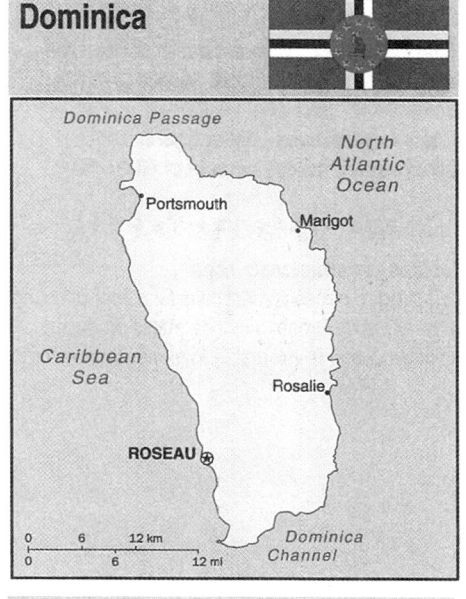

Introduction

Background: Dominica was the last of the Caribbean islands to be colonized by Europeans, due chiefly to the fierce resistance of the native Caribs. France ceded possession to Great Britain in 1763, which made the island a colony in 1805. In 1980, two years after independence, Dominica's fortunes improved when a corrupt and tyrannical administration was replaced by that of Mary Eugenia CHARLES, the first female prime minister in the Caribbean, who remained in office for 15 years.

Geography

Location: Caribbean, island between the Caribbean Sea and the North Atlantic Ocean, about one-half of the way from Puerto Rico to Trinidad and Tobago
Geographic coordinates: 15 25 N, 61 20 W
Map references: Central America and the Caribbean
Area:
total: 754 sq km
land: 754 sq km
water: 0 sq km
Area - comparative: slightly more than four times the size of Washington, DC
Land boundaries: 0 km
Coastline: 148 km
Maritime claims:
contiguous zone: 24 NM
exclusive economic zone: 200 NM
territorial sea: 12 NM
Climate: tropical; moderated by northeast trade winds; heavy rainfall
Terrain: rugged mountains of volcanic origin
Elevation extremes:
lowest point: Caribbean Sea 0 m
highest point: Morne Diablatins 1,447 m
Natural resources: timber, hydropower, arable land
Land use:
arable land: 9%
permanent crops: 13%
permanent pastures: 3%
forests and woodland: 67%
other: 8% (1993 est.)
Irrigated land: NA sq km
Natural hazards: flash floods are a constant threat; destructive hurricanes can be expected during the late summer months
Environment - current issues: NA
Environment - international agreements:
party to: Biodiversity, Climate Change, Desertification, Endangered Species, Environmental Modification, Hazardous Wastes, Law of the Sea, Marine Dumping, Ozone Layer Protection, Ship Pollution, Whaling
signed, but not ratified: none of the selected agreements

People

Population: 70,786 (July 2001 est.)
Age structure:
0-14 years: 28.72% (male 10,300; female 10,027)
15-64 years: 63.45% (male 23,056; female 21,855)
65 years and over: 7.83% (male 2,267; female 3,281) (2001 est.)
Population growth rate: -0.98% (2001 est.)
Birth rate: 17.81 births/1,000 population (2001 est.)
Death rate: 7.19 deaths/1,000 population (2001 est.)
Net migration rate: -20.37 migrant(s)/1,000 population (2001 est.)
Sex ratio:
at birth: 1.05 male(s)/female
under 15 years: 1.03 male(s)/female
15-64 years: 1.05 male(s)/female
65 years and over: 0.69 male(s)/female
total population: 1.01 male(s)/female (2001 est.)
Infant mortality rate: 16.54 deaths/1,000 live births (2001 est.)
Life expectancy at birth:
total population: 73.6 years
male: 70.74 years
female: 76.61 years (2001 est.)
Total fertility rate: 2.03 children born/woman (2001 est.)
HIV/AIDS - adult prevalence rate: NA%
HIV/AIDS - people living with HIV/AIDS: NA
HIV/AIDS - deaths: NA
Nationality:
noun: Dominican(s)
adjective: Dominican
Ethnic groups: black, Carib Amerindian
Religions: Roman Catholic 77%, Protestant 15% (Methodist 5%, Pentecostal 3%, Seventh-Day Adventist 3%, Baptist 2%, other 2%), none 2%, other 6%
Languages: English (official), French patois
Literacy:
definition: age 15 and over has ever attended school
total population: 94%
male: 94%
female: 94% (1970 est.)

Government

Country name:
conventional long form: Commonwealth of Dominica
conventional short form: Dominica
Government type: parliamentary democracy; republic within the Commonwealth
Capital: Roseau
Administrative divisions: 10 parishes; Saint Andrew, Saint David, Saint George, Saint John, Saint Joseph, Saint Luke, Saint Mark, Saint Patrick, Saint Paul, Saint Peter
Independence: 3 November 1978 (from UK)
National holiday: Independence Day, 3 November (1978)
Constitution: 3 November 1978
Legal system: based on English common law
Suffrage: 18 years of age; universal
Executive branch:
chief of state: President Vernon Lordon SHAW (since 6 October 1998)
head of government: Prime Minister Pierre CHARLES (since 1 October 2000); note - assumed post after death of Roosevelt DOUGLAS
cabinet: Cabinet appointed by the president on the advice of the prime minister
elections: president elected by the House of Assembly for a five-year term; election last held 6 October 1998 (next to be held NA October 2003); prime minister appointed by the president
election results: Vernon Lordon SHAW elected president; percent of legislative vote - NA%
Legislative branch: unicameral House of Assembly (30 seats, 9 appointed senators, 21 elected by popular vote; members serve five-year terms)
elections: last held 31 January 2000 (next to be held by NA 2005)
election results: percent of vote by party - NA%; seats by party -DLP 11, UWP 8, DFP 2
Judicial branch: Eastern Caribbean Supreme Court, consisting of the Court of Appeal and the High Court (located in Saint Lucia; one of the six judges must reside in Dominica and preside over the Court of Summary Jurisdiction)
Political parties and leaders: Dominica Freedom Party or DFP [Charles SAVARIN]; Dominica Labor Party or DLP [Pierre CHARLES]; United Workers Party or UWP [Edison JAMES]
Political pressure groups and leaders: Dominica Liberation Movement or DLM (a small leftist party)
International organization participation: ACCT, ACP, C, Caricom, CDB, ECLAC, FAO, G-77, IBRD, ICFTU, ICRM, IDA, IFAD, IFC, IFRCS, ILO, IMF, IMO, Interpol, IOC, ITU, NAM (observer), OAS, OECS, OPANAL, OPCW, UN, UNCTAD, UNESCO, UNIDO, UPU, WCL, WHO, WIPO, WMO, WTrO
Diplomatic representation in the US:
chief of mission: Ambassador Nicholas J. O. LIVERPOOL (resident in Dominica)
chancery: 3216 New Mexico Avenue NW, Washington, DC 20016
telephone: [1] (202) 364-6781

Dominica *(continued)*

FAX: [1] (202) 364-6791
consulate(s) general: New York
Diplomatic representation from the US: the US does not have an embassy in Dominica; US interests are served by the embassy in Bridgetown, Barbados
Flag description: green, with a centered cross of three equal bands - the vertical part is yellow (hoist side), black, and white and the horizontal part is yellow (top), black, and white; superimposed in the center of the cross is a red disk bearing a sisserou parrot encircled by 10 green, five-pointed stars edged in yellow; the 10 stars represent the 10 administrative divisions (parishes)

Economy

Economy - overview: The economy depends on agriculture and is highly vulnerable to climatic conditions, notably tropical storms. Agriculture, primarily bananas, accounts for 21% of GDP and employs 40% of the labor force. Development of the tourist industry remains difficult because of the rugged coastline, lack of beaches, and the lack of an international airport. Hurricane Luis devastated the country's banana crop in September 1995; tropical storms had wiped out one-quarter of the crop in 1994 as well. The subsequent recovery has been fueled by increases in construction, soap production, and tourist arrivals. The government is attempting to develop an offshore financial industry in order to diversify the island's production base.
GDP: purchasing power parity - $290 million (2000 est.)
GDP - real growth rate: 0.5% (2000 est.)
GDP - per capita: purchasing power parity - $4,000 (2000 est.)
GDP - composition by sector:
agriculture: 21%
industry: 16%
services: 63% (1999 est.)
Population below poverty line: NA%
Household income or consumption by percentage share:
lowest 10%: NA%
highest 10%: NA%
Inflation rate (consumer prices): 2.5% (2000 est.)
Labor force: 25,000
Labor force - by occupation: agriculture 40%, industry and commerce 32%, services 28%
Unemployment rate: 20% (1999 est.)
Budget:
revenues: $72 million
expenditures: $79.9 million, including capital expenditures of $11.5 million (FY97/98)
Industries: soap, coconut oil, tourism, copra, furniture, cement blocks, shoes
Industrial production growth rate: -10% (1997 est.)
Electricity - production: 62 million kWh (1999)
Electricity - production by source:
fossil fuel: 48.39%
hydro: 51.61%
nuclear: 0%
other: 0% (1999)
Electricity - consumption: 57.7 million kWh (1999)
Electricity - exports: 0 kWh (1999)
Electricity - imports: 0 kWh (1999)
Agriculture - products: bananas, citrus, mangoes, root crops, coconuts, cocoa; forest and fishery potential not exploited
Exports: $60.7 million (2000 est.)
Exports - commodities: bananas, soap, bay oil, vegetables, grapefruit, oranges
Exports - partners: Caricom countries 47%, UK 36%, US 7% (1996 est.)
Imports: $126 million (2000 est.)
Imports - commodities: manufactured goods, machinery and equipment, food, chemicals
Imports - partners: US 41%, Caricom countries 25%, UK 13%, Netherlands, Canada (1996 est.)
Debt - external: $108.9 million (1999)
Economic aid - recipient: $24.4 million (1995)
Currency: East Caribbean dollar (XCD)
Currency code: XCD
Exchange rates: East Caribbean dollars per US dollar - 2.7000 (fixed rate since 1976)
Fiscal year: 1 July - 30 June

Communications

Telephones - main lines in use: 19,000 (1996)
Telephones - mobile cellular: 461 (1996)
Telephone system:
general assessment: NA
domestic: fully automatic network
international: microwave radio relay and SHF radiotelephone links to Martinique and Guadeloupe; VHF and UHF radiotelephone links to Saint Lucia
Radio broadcast stations: AM 3, FM 10, shortwave 0 (1998)
Radios: 46,000 (1997)
Television broadcast stations: 0 (however, there is one cable television company) (1997)
Televisions: 6,000 (1997)
Internet country code: .dm
Internet Service Providers (ISPs): 16 (2000)
Internet users: 2,000 (2000)

Transportation

Railways: 0 km
Highways:
total: 750 km
paved: 375 km
unpaved: 375 km (2001)
Waterways: none
Ports and harbors: Portsmouth, Roseau
Merchant marine: none (2000 est.)
Airports: 2 (2000 est.)
Airports - with paved runways:
total: 2
914 to 1,523 m: 2 (2000 est.)

Military

Military branches: Commonwealth of Dominica Police Force (includes Special Service Unit, Coast Guard)
Military expenditures - dollar figure: $NA
Military expenditures - percent of GDP: NA%

Transnational Issues

Disputes - international: none
Illicit drugs: transshipment point for narcotics bound for the US and Europe; minor cannabis producer; banking industry is vulnerable to money laundering

Dominican Republic

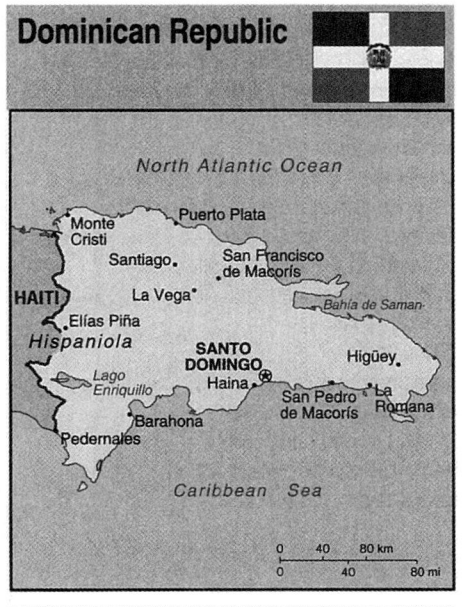

Introduction

Background: A legacy of unsettled, mostly non-representative, rule for much of the 20th century was brought to an end in 1996 when free and open elections ushered in a new government.

Geography

Location: Caribbean, eastern two-thirds of the island of Hispaniola, between the Caribbean Sea and the North Atlantic Ocean, east of Haiti
Geographic coordinates: 19 00 N, 70 40 W
Map references: Central America and the Caribbean
Area:
total: 48,730 sq km
land: 48,380 sq km
water: 350 sq km
Area - comparative: slightly more than twice the size of New Hampshire
Land boundaries:
total: 275 km
border countries: Haiti 275 km
Coastline: 1,288 km
Maritime claims:
contiguous zone: 24 NM
continental shelf: 200 NM or to the edge of the continental margin
exclusive economic zone: 200 NM
territorial sea: 6 NM
Climate: tropical maritime; little seasonal temperature variation; seasonal variation in rainfall
Terrain: rugged highlands and mountains with fertile valleys interspersed
Elevation extremes:
lowest point: Lago Enriquillo -46 m
highest point: Pico Duarte 3,175 m
Natural resources: nickel, bauxite, gold, silver
Land use:
arable land: 21%
permanent crops: 9%
permanent pastures: 43%
forests and woodland: 12%
other: 15% (1993 est.)
Irrigated land: 2,300 sq km (1993 est.)
Natural hazards: lies in the middle of the hurricane belt and subject to severe storms from June to October; occasional flooding; periodic droughts
Environment - current issues: water shortages; soil eroding into the sea damages coral reefs; deforestation; Hurricane Georges damage
Environment - international agreements:
party to: Biodiversity, Climate Change, Desertification, Endangered Species, Hazardous Wastes, Marine Dumping, Marine Life Conservation, Nuclear Test Ban, Ozone Layer Protection, Ship Pollution
signed, but not ratified: Law of the Sea
Geography - note: shares island of Hispaniola with Haiti (eastern two-thirds is the Dominican Republic, western one-third is Haiti)

People

Population: 8,581,477 (July 2001 est.)
Age structure:
0-14 years: 34.11% (male 1,495,477; female 1,431,406)
15-64 years: 60.99% (male 2,664,679; female 2,569,398)
65 years and over: 4.9% (male 199,240; female 221,277) (2001 est.)
Population growth rate: 1.63% (2001 est.)
Birth rate: 24.77 births/1,000 population (2001 est.)
Death rate: 4.7 deaths/1,000 population (2001 est.)
Net migration rate: -3.81 migrant(s)/1,000 population (2001 est.)
Sex ratio:
at birth: 1.05 male(s)/female
under 15 years: 1.04 male(s)/female
15-64 years: 1.04 male(s)/female
65 years and over: 0.9 male(s)/female
total population: 1.03 male(s)/female (2001 est.)
Infant mortality rate: 34.67 deaths/1,000 live births (2001 est.)
Life expectancy at birth:
total population: 73.44 years
male: 71.34 years
female: 75.64 years (2001 est.)
Total fertility rate: 2.97 children born/woman (2001 est.)
HIV/AIDS - adult prevalence rate: 2.8% (1999 est.)
HIV/AIDS - people living with HIV/AIDS: 130,000 (1999 est.)
HIV/AIDS - deaths: 4,900 (1999 est.)
Nationality:
noun: Dominican(s)
adjective: Dominican
Ethnic groups: white 16%, black 11%, mixed 73%
Religions: Roman Catholic 95%
Languages: Spanish
Literacy:
definition: age 15 and over can read and write
total population: 82.1%
male: 82%
female: 82.2% (1995 est.)

Government

Country name:
conventional long form: Dominican Republic
conventional short form: none
local long form: Republica Dominicana
local short form: none
Government type: representative democracy
Capital: Santo Domingo
Administrative divisions: 29 provinces (provincias, singular - provincia) and 1 district* (distrito); Azua, Baoruco, Barahona, Dajabon, Distrito Nacional*, Duarte, Elias Pina, El Seibo, Espaillat, Hato Mayor, Independencia, La Altagracia, La Romana, La Vega, Maria Trinidad Sanchez, Monsenor Nouel, Monte Cristi, Monte Plata, Pedernales, Peravia, Puerto Plata, Salcedo, Samana, Sanchez Ramirez, San Cristobal, San Juan, San Pedro de Macoris, Santiago, Santiago Rodriguez, Valverde
Independence: 27 February 1844 (from Haiti)
National holiday: Independence Day, 27 February (1844)
Constitution: 28 November 1966
Legal system: based on French civil codes
Suffrage: 18 years of age, universal and compulsory; married persons regardless of age
note: members of the armed forces and police cannot vote
Executive branch:
chief of state: President Rafael Hipolito MEJIA Dominguez (since 16 August 2000); Vice President Milagros ORTIZ-BOSCH (since 16 August 2000); note - the president is both the chief of state and head of government
head of government: President Rafael Hipolito MEJIA Dominguez (since 16 August 2000); Vice President Milagros ORTIZ-BOSCH (since 16 August 2000); note - the president is both the chief of state and head of government
cabinet: Cabinet nominated by the president
elections: president and vice president elected on the same ticket by popular vote for four-year term; election last held 16 May 2000 (next to be held NA May 2004)
election results: Raphael Hipolito MEJIA Dominguez elected president; percent of vote - Rafael Hipolito MEJIA Dominguez (PRD) 49.87%, Danilo MEDINA (PLD) 24.95%, Joaquin BALAGUER (PRSC) 24.6%
Legislative branch: bicameral National Congress or Congreso Nacional consists of the Senate or Senado (30 seats; members are elected by popular vote to serve four-year terms) and the Chamber of Deputies or Camara de Diputados (149 seats; members are elected by popular vote to serve four-year terms)
elections: Senate - last held 16 May 1998 (next to be held NA May 2002); Chamber of Deputies - last held 16 May 1998 (next to be held NA May 2002)
election results: Senate - percent of vote by party - NA%; seats by party - PRD 24, PLD 3, PRSC 3; Chamber of Deputies - percent of vote by party - NA%; seats by party - PRD 83, PLD 49, PRSC 17

Dominican Republic (continued)

Judicial branch: Supreme Court or Corte Suprema (judges are elected by a Council made up of members of the legislative and executive branches with the president presiding)
Political parties and leaders: Dominican Liberation Party or PLD [Leonel FERNANDEZ Reyna]; Dominican Revolutionary Party or PRD [Hatuey DE CAMPS]; Social Christian Reformist Party or PRSC [Joaquin BALAGUER Ricardo]
Political pressure groups and leaders: Collective of Popular Organizations or COP
International organization participation: ACP, Caricom (observer), ECLAC, FAO, G-11, G-77, IADB, IAEA, IBRD, ICAO, ICFTU, ICRM, IDA, IFAD, IFC, IFRCS, IHO, ILO, IMF, IMO, Intelsat, Interpol, IOC, IOM, ISO (subscriber), ITU, LAES, LAIA (observer), NAM (observer), OAS, OPANAL, OPCW, PCA, UN, UNCTAD, UNESCO, UNIDO, UPU, WCL, WFTU, WHO, WIPO, WMO, WToO, WTrO
Diplomatic representation in the US:
chief of mission: Ambassador Roberto Bienvenido SALADIN-SELIN
chancery: 1715 22nd Street NW, Washington, DC 20008
telephone: [1] (202) 332-6280
FAX: [1] (202) 265-8057
consulate(s) general: Boston, Chicago, Mayaguez (Puerto Rico), Miami, New Orleans, New York, Philadelphia, San Francisco, and San Juan (Puerto Rico)
consulate(s): Houston, Jacksonville, Mobile, and Ponce (Puerto Rico)
Diplomatic representation from the US:
chief of mission: Ambassador Charles T. MANATT
embassy: corner of Calle Cesar Nicolas Penson and Calle Leopoldo Navarro, Santo Domingo
mailing address: Unit 5500, APO AA 34041-5500
telephone: [1] (809) 221-2171
FAX: [1] (809) 686-7437
Flag description: a centered white cross that extends to the edges divides the flag into four rectangles - the top ones are blue (hoist side) and red, and the bottom ones are red (hoist side) and blue; a small coat of arms is at the center of the cross

Economy

Economy - overview: The Dominican economy experienced dramatic growth over the last decade, even though the economy was hit hard by Hurricane Georges in 1998. Although the country has long been viewed primarily as an exporter of sugar, coffee, and tobacco, in recent years the service sector has overtaken agriculture as the economy's largest employer, due to growth in tourism and free trade zones. The country suffers from marked income inequality; the poorest half of the population receives less than one-fifth of GNP, while the richest ten percent enjoy 40% of national income. In December 2000, the new MEJIA administration passed broad new tax legislation which it hopes will provide enough revenue to offset rising oil prices and to service foreign debt.
GDP: purchasing power parity - $48.3 billion (2000 est.)
GDP - real growth rate: 8% (2000 est.)
GDP - per capita: purchasing power parity - $5,700 (2000 est.)
GDP - composition by sector:
agriculture: 11.3%
industry: 32.2%
services: 56.5% (1999 est.)
Population below poverty line: 25% (1999 est.)
Household income or consumption by percentage share:
lowest 10%: 1.6%
highest 10%: 39.6% (1989)
Inflation rate (consumer prices): 7.9% (2000 est.)
Labor force: 2.3 million - 2.6 million
Labor force - by occupation: services and government 58.7%, industry 24.3%, agriculture 17% (1998 est.)
Unemployment rate: 13.8% (1999 est.)
Budget:
revenues: $2.3 billion
expenditures: $2.9 billion, including capital expenditures of $867 million (1999 est.)
Industries: tourism, sugar processing, ferronickel and gold mining, textiles, cement, tobacco
Industrial production growth rate: 8% (2000 est.)
Electricity - production: 7.29 billion kWh (1999)
Electricity - production by source:
fossil fuel: 87.19%
hydro: 12.4%
nuclear: 0%
other: 0.41% (1999)
Electricity - consumption: 6.78 billion kWh (1999)
Electricity - exports: 0 kWh (1999)
Electricity - imports: 0 kWh (1999)
Agriculture - products: sugarcane, coffee, cotton, cocoa, tobacco, rice, beans, potatoes, corn, bananas; cattle, pigs, dairy products, beef, eggs
Exports: $5.8 billion (f.o.b., 2000)
Exports - commodities: ferronickel, sugar, gold, silver, coffee, cocoa, tobacco, meats
Exports - partners: US 66.1%, Netherlands 7.8%, Canada 7.6%, Russia 7.4%, UK 4.5% (1999 est.)
Imports: $9.6 billion (f.o.b., 2000 est.)
Imports - commodities: foodstuffs, petroleum, cotton and fabrics, chemicals and pharmaceuticals
Imports - partners: US 25.7%, Venezuela 9.2%, Mexico 4%, Japan 3%, Panama 2.6% (1999 est.)
Debt - external: $4.7 billion (2000 est.)
Economic aid - recipient: $239.6 million (1995)
Currency: Dominican peso (DOP)
Currency code: DOP
Exchange rates: Dominican pesos per US dollar - 16.888 (January 2001), 16.415 (2000), 16.033 (1999), 15.267 (1998), 14.265 (1997), 13.775 (1996)
Fiscal year: calendar year

Communications

Telephones - main lines in use: 709,000 (1997)
Telephones - mobile cellular: 130,149 (1997)
Telephone system:
general assessment: NA
domestic: relatively efficient system based on islandwide microwave radio relay network
international: 1 coaxial submarine cable; satellite earth station - 1 Intelsat (Atlantic Ocean)
Radio broadcast stations: AM 120, FM 56, shortwave 4 (1998)
Radios: 1.44 million (1997)
Television broadcast stations: 25 (1997)
Televisions: 770,000 (1997)
Internet country code: .do
Internet Service Providers (ISPs): 24 (2000)
Internet users: 25,000 (1999)

Transportation

Railways:
total: 757 km
standard gauge: 375 km 1.435-m gauge (Central Romana Railroad)
narrow gauge: 142 km 0.762-m gauge (Dominican Republic Government Railway); 240 km operated by sugar companies in various gauges (0.558-m, 0.762-m, 1.067-m gauges) (1995)
Highways:
total: 12,600 km
paved: 6,224 km
unpaved: 6,376 km (1996)
Waterways: none
Pipelines: crude oil 96 km; petroleum products 8 km
Ports and harbors: Barahona, La Romana, Puerto Plata, San Pedro de Macoris, Santo Domingo
Merchant marine:
total: 1 ship (1,000 GRT or over) totaling 1,587 GRT/ 1,165 DWT
ships by type: cargo 1 (2000 est.)
Airports: 29 (2000 est.)
Airports - with paved runways:
total: 13
over 3,047 m: 3
2,438 to 3,047 m: 2
1,524 to 2,437 m: 4
914 to 1,523 m: 3
under 914 m: 1 (2000 est.)
Airports - with unpaved runways:
total: 16
1,524 to 2,437 m: 2
914 to 1,523 m: 4
under 914 m: 10 (2000 est.)

Military

Military branches: Army, Navy, Air Force, National Police
Military manpower - military age: 18 years of age
Military manpower - availability:
males age 15-49: 2,281,035 (2001 est.)
Military manpower - fit for military service:
males age 15-49: 1,430,776 (2001 est.)

Dominican Republic (continued)

Military manpower - reaching military age annually:
males: 87,404 (2001 est.)
Military expenditures - dollar figure: $180 million (FY98)
Military expenditures - percent of GDP: 1.1% (FY98)

Transnational Issues

Disputes - international: none
Illicit drugs: transshipment point for South American drugs destined for the US and Europe; has become a transshipment point for ecstasy from the Netherlands and Belgium destined for US and Canada

Ecuador

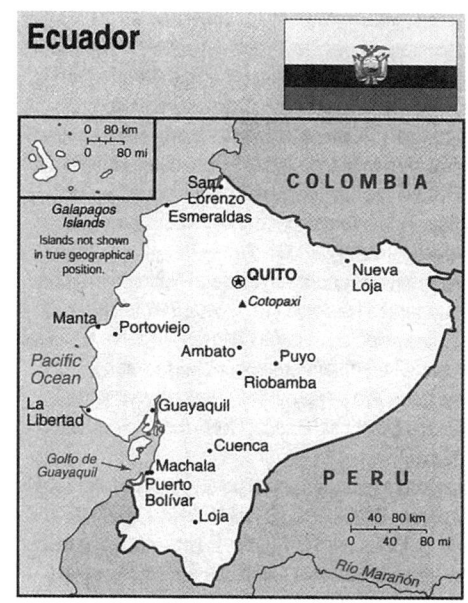

Introduction

Background: The "Republic of the Equator" was one of three countries that emerged from the collapse of Gran Colombia in 1830 (the others being Colombia and Venezuela). Between 1904 and 1942, Ecuador lost territories in a series of conflicts with its neighbors. A border war with Peru that flared in 1995 was resolved in 1999.

Geography

Location: Western South America, bordering the Pacific Ocean at the Equator, between Colombia and Peru
Geographic coordinates: 2 00 S, 77 30 W
Map references: South America
Area:
total: 283,560 sq km
land: 276,840 sq km
water: 6,720 sq km
note: includes Galapagos Islands
Area - comparative: slightly smaller than Nevada
Land boundaries:
total: 2,010 km
border countries: Colombia 590 km, Peru 1,420 km
Coastline: 2,237 km
Maritime claims:
continental shelf: claims continental shelf between mainland and Galapagos Islands
territorial sea: 200 NM
Climate: tropical along coast, becoming cooler inland at higher elevations; tropical in Amazonian jungle lowlands
Terrain: coastal plain (costa), inter-Andean central highlands (sierra), and flat to rolling eastern jungle (oriente)
Elevation extremes:
lowest point: Pacific Ocean 0 m
highest point: Chimborazo 6,267 m
Natural resources: petroleum, fish, timber, hydropower
Land use:
arable land: 6%
permanent crops: 5%
permanent pastures: 18%
forests and woodland: 56%
other: 15% (1993 est.)
Irrigated land: 5,560 sq km (1993 est.)
Natural hazards: frequent earthquakes, landslides, volcanic activity; periodic droughts
Environment - current issues: deforestation; soil erosion; desertification; water pollution; pollution from oil production wastes
Environment - international agreements:
party to: Antarctic-Environmental Protocol, Antarctic Treaty, Biodiversity, Climate Change, Climate Change-Kyoto Protocol, Desertification, Endangered Species, Hazardous Wastes, Marine Dumping, Nuclear Test Ban, Ozone Layer Protection, Ship Pollution, Tropical Timber 83, Tropical Timber 94, Wetlands
signed, but not ratified: none of the selected agreements
Geography - note: Cotopaxi in Andes is highest active volcano in world

People

Population: 13,183,978 (July 2001 est.)
Age structure:
0-14 years: 35.8% (male 2,398,801; female 2,320,537)
15-64 years: 59.81% (male 3,900,193; female 3,984,797)
65 years and over: 4.39% (male 269,372; female 310,278) (2001 est.)
Population growth rate: 2% (2001 est.)
Birth rate: 25.99 births/1,000 population (2001 est.)
Death rate: 5.44 deaths/1,000 population (2001 est.)
Net migration rate: -0.55 migrant(s)/1,000 population (2001 est.)
Sex ratio:
at birth: 1.05 male(s)/female
under 15 years: 1.03 male(s)/female
15-64 years: 0.98 male(s)/female
65 years and over: 0.87 male(s)/female
total population: 0.99 male(s)/female (2001 est.)
Infant mortality rate: 34.08 deaths/1,000 live births (2001 est.)
Life expectancy at birth:
total population: 71.33 years
male: 68.52 years
female: 74.28 years (2001 est.)
Total fertility rate: 3.12 children born/woman (2001 est.)
HIV/AIDS - adult prevalence rate: 0.29% (1999 est.)
HIV/AIDS - people living with HIV/AIDS: 19,000 (1999 est.)
HIV/AIDS - deaths: 1,400 (1999 est.)
Nationality:
noun: Ecuadorian(s)
adjective: Ecuadorian

Ecuador (continued)

Ethnic groups: mestizo (mixed Amerindian and white) 65%, Amerindian 25%, Spanish and others 7%, black 3%
Religions: Roman Catholic 95%
Languages: Spanish (official), Amerindian languages (especially Quechua)
Literacy:
definition: age 15 and over can read and write
total population: 90.1%
male: 92%
female: 88.2% (1995 est.)

Government

Country name:
conventional long form: Republic of Ecuador
conventional short form: Ecuador
local long form: Republica del Ecuador
local short form: Ecuador
Government type: republic
Capital: Quito
Administrative divisions: 22 provinces (provincias, singular - provincia); Azuay, Bolivar, Canar, Carchi, Chimborazo, Cotopaxi, El Oro, Esmeraldas, Galapagos, Guayas, Imbabura, Loja, Los Rios, Manabi, Morona-Santiago, Napo, Orellana, Pastaza, Pichincha, Sucumbios, Tungurahua, Zamora-Chinchipe
Independence: 24 May 1822 (from Spain)
National holiday: Independence Day (independence of Quito), 10 August (1809)
Constitution: 10 August 1998
Legal system: based on civil law system; has not accepted compulsory ICJ jurisdiction
Suffrage: 18 years of age; universal, compulsory for literate persons ages 18-65, optional for other eligible voters
Executive branch:
chief of state: President Gustavo NOBOA Bejarano (since 22 January 2000) selected president following coup that deposed President MAHUAD; Vice President Pedro PINTO Rubianes (since 28 January 2000) elected by National Congress from a slate of candidates submitted by President NABOA; note - the president is both the chief of state and head of government
head of government: President Gustavo NOBOA Bejarano (since 22 January 2000) selected president following coup that deposed President MAHUAD; Vice President Pedro PINTO Rubianes (since 28 January 2000) elected by National Congress from a slate of candidates submitted by President NABOA; note - the president is both the chief of state and head of government
cabinet: Cabinet appointed by the president
elections: president and vice president elected on the same ticket by popular vote for four-year term (no reelection); election last held 31 May 1998; runoff election held 12 July 1998 (next to be held NA 2002)
election results: results of the last election prior to the coup were: Jamil MAHUAD elected president; percent of vote - 51%
note: a military-indigenous coup toppled democratically elected President Jamil MAHAUD on 21 January 2000; the military quickly handed power over to Vice President Gustavo NOBOA on 22 January; National Congress then elected a new vice president from a slate of candidates submitted by NOBOA; the new administration is scheduled to complete the remainder of MAHAUD's term, due to expire in January 2003
Legislative branch: unicameral National Congress or Congreso Nacional (121 seats; 79 members are popularly elected at-large nationally to serve four-year terms; 42 members are popularly elected by province - two per province - for four-year terms)
elections: last held 31 May 1998 (next to be held NA 2002)
election results: percent of vote by party - NA%; seats by party - DP 32, PSC 27, PRE 24, ID 18, P-NP 9, FRA 5, PCE 3, MPD 2, CFP 1; note - defections by members of National Congress are commonplace, resulting in frequent changes in the numbers of seats held by the various parties
Judicial branch: Supreme Court or Corte Suprema (new justices are elected by the full Supreme Court)
Political parties and leaders: Concentration of Popular Forces or CFP [Averroes BUCARAM]; Democratic Left or ID [Rodrigo BORJA Cevallos]; Ecuadorian Conservative Party or PCE [Sixto DURAN Ballen]; Independent National Movement or MIN [leader NA]; Pachakutik-New Country or P-NP [Rafael PANDAM]; Popular Democracy or DP [Ramiro RIVERA]; Popular Democratic Movement or MPD [leader NA]; Radical Alfarista Front or FRA [Fabian ALARCON, director]; Roldosist Party or PRE [Abdala BUCARAM Ortiz, director]; Social Christian Party or PSC [Jaime NEBOT Saadi, president]
Political pressure groups and leaders: Confederation of Indigenous Nationalities of Ecuador or CONAIE [Antonio VARGAS]; Coordinator of Social Movements or CMS [F. Napoleon SANTOS]; Popular Front or FP [Luis VILLACIS]
International organization participation: CAN, CCC, ECLAC, FAO, G-11, G-77, IADB, IAEA, IBRD, ICAO, ICC, ICFTU, ICRM, IDA, IFAD, IFC, IFRCS, IHO, ILO, IMF, IMO, Intelsat, Interpol, IOC, IOM, ISO, ITU, LAES, LAIA, NAM, OAS, OPANAL, OPCW, PCA, RG, UN, UNCTAD, UNESCO, UNIDO, UPU, WCL, WFTU, WHO, WIPO, WMO, WToO, WTrO
Diplomatic representation in the US:
chief of mission: Ambassador Ivonne A-BAKI
chancery: 2535 15th Street NW, Washington, DC 20009
telephone: [1] (202) 234-7200
FAX: [1] (202) 667-3482
consulate(s) general: Chicago, Houston, Los Angeles, Miami, New Orleans, New York, Newark, Philadelphia, and San Francisco
Diplomatic representation from the US:
chief of mission: Ambassador Gwen C. CLARE
embassy: Avenida 12 de Octubre y Avenida Patria, Quito
mailing address: APO AA 34039
telephone: [593] (2) 562-890
FAX: [593] (2) 502-052
consulate(s) general: Guayaquil
Flag description: three horizontal bands of yellow (top, double width), blue, and red with the coat of arms superimposed at the center of the flag; similar to the flag of Colombia which is shorter and does not bear a coat of arms

Economy

Economy - overview: Ecuador has substantial oil resources and rich agricultural areas. Because the country exports primary products such as oil, bananas, and shrimp, fluctuations in world market prices can have a substantial domestic impact. Ecuador joined the World Trade Organization in 1996, but has failed to comply with many of its accession commitments. In recent years, growth has been uneven due to ill-conceived fiscal stabilization measures. The aftermath of El Nino and depressed oil market of 1997-98 drove Ecuador's economy into a free-fall in 1999. The beginning of 1999 saw the banking sector collapse, which helped precipitate an unprecedented default on external loans later that year. Continued economic instability drove a 70% depreciation of the currency throughout 1999, which eventually forced a desperate government to "dollarize" the currency regime in 2000. The move stabilized the currency, but did not stave off the ouster of the government. The new president, Gustavo NOBOA has yet to complete negotiations for a long sought IMF accord. He will find it difficult to push through the reforms necessary to make "dollarization" work in the long run.
GDP: purchasing power parity - $37.2 billion (2000 est.)
GDP - real growth rate: 0.8% (2000 est.)
GDP - per capita: purchasing power parity - $2,900 (2000 est.)
GDP - composition by sector:
agriculture: 14%
industry: 36%
services: 50% (1999 est.)
Population below poverty line: 50% (1999 est.)
Household income or consumption by percentage share:
lowest 10%: 2.2%
highest 10%: 33.8% (1995)
Inflation rate (consumer prices): 96% (2000 est.)
Labor force: 4.2 million
Labor force - by occupation: agriculture 30%, industry 25%, services 45% (1999 est.)
Unemployment rate: 13%; note - widespread underemployment (2000 est.)
Budget:
revenues: planned $5.1 billion (not including revenue from potential privatizations)
expenditures: $5.1 billion, including capital expenditures of $NA (1999)
Industries: petroleum, food processing, textiles, metal work, paper products, wood products, chemicals, plastics, fishing, lumber

Ecuador (continued)

Industrial production growth rate: 2.4% (1997 est.)
Electricity - production: 10.065 billion kWh (1999)
Electricity - production by source:
fossil fuel: 29.51%
hydro: 70.49%
nuclear: 0%
other: 0% (1999)
Electricity - consumption: 9.386 billion kWh (1999)
Electricity - exports: 0 kWh (1999)
Electricity - imports: 25 million kWh (1999)
Agriculture - products: bananas, coffee, cocoa, rice, potatoes, manioc (tapioca), plantains, sugarcane; cattle, sheep, pigs, beef, pork, dairy products; balsa wood; fish, shrimp
Exports: $5.6 billion (f.o.b., 2000 est.)
Exports - commodities: petroleum, bananas, shrimp, coffee, cocoa, cut flowers, fish
Exports - partners: US 37%, Colombia 5%, Italy 5%, Chile 5%, Peru 4% (1999)
Imports: $3.4 billion (f.o.b., 2000 est.)
Imports - commodities: machinery and equipment, raw materials, fuels; consumer goods
Imports - partners: US 30%, Colombia 13%, Venezuela 6%, Japan 5%, Venezuela 6%, Mexico 3% (1998)
Debt - external: $15 billion (1999)
Economic aid - recipient: $695.7 million (1995)
Currency: US dollar (USD)
Currency code: USD
Exchange rates: sucres per US dollar - 25,000 (January 2001), 24,988.4 (2000), 11,786.8 (1999), 5,446.6 (1998), 3,988.3 (1997), 3,189.5 (1996)
note: on 7 January 2000, the government passed a decree "dollarizing" the economy; on 13 March 2000, the National Congress approved a new exchange system whereby the US dollar is adopted as the main legal tender in Ecuador for all purposes; on 20 March 2000, the Central Bank of Ecuador started to exchange sucres for US dollars at a fixed rate of 25,000 sucres per US dollar; since 30 April 2000, all transactions are denominated in US dollars
Fiscal year: calendar year

Communications

Telephones - main lines in use: 899,000 (1997)
Telephones - mobile cellular: 160,061 (1997)
Telephone system:
general assessment: NA
domestic: facilities generally inadequate and unreliable
international: satellite earth station - 1 Intelsat (Atlantic Ocean)
Radio broadcast stations: AM 392, FM 27, shortwave 29 (1998)
Radios: 4.15 million (1997)
Television broadcast stations: 15 (including one station on the Galapagos Islands) (1997)
Televisions: 1.55 million (1997)
Internet country code: .ec
Internet Service Providers (ISPs): 13 (2000)
Internet users: 20,000 (2000)

Transportation

Railways:
total: 812 km (single track)
narrow gauge: 812 km 1.067-m gauge
Highways:
total: 43,197 km
paved: 8,165 km
unpaved: 35,032 km (1999 est.)
Waterways: 1,500 km
Pipelines: crude oil 800 km; petroleum products 1,358 km
Ports and harbors: Esmeraldas, Guayaquil, La Libertad, Manta, Puerto Bolivar, San Lorenzo
Merchant marine:
total: 30 ships (1,000 GRT or over) totaling 233,312 GRT/385,784 DWT
ships by type: cargo 2, chemical tanker 1, liquefied gas 1, passenger 3, petroleum tanker 22, specialized tanker 1 (2000 est.)
Airports: 180 (2000 est.)
Airports - with paved runways:
total: 59
over 3,047 m: 2
2,438 to 3,047 m: 5
1,524 to 2,437 m: 18
914 to 1,523 m: 15
under 914 m: 19 (2000 est.)
Airports - with unpaved runways:
total: 121
914 to 1,523 m: 32
under 914 m: 89 (2000 est.)
Heliports: 1 (2000 est.)

Military

Military branches: Army (Ejercito Ecuatoriano), Navy (Armada Ecuatoriana, includes Marines), Air Force (Fuerza Aerea Ecuatoriana), National Police (Policia Nacional)
Military manpower - military age: 20 years of age
Military manpower - availability:
males age 15-49: 3,382,567 (2001 est.)
Military manpower - fit for military service:
males age 15-49: 2,280,899 (2001 est.)
Military manpower - reaching military age annually:
males: 132,978 (2001 est.)
Military expenditures - dollar figure: $720 million (FY98)
Military expenditures - percent of GDP: 3.4% (FY98)

Transnational Issues

Disputes - international: none
Illicit drugs: significant transit country for cocaine and derivatives of coca originating in Colombia and Peru; importer of precursor chemicals used in production of illicit narcotics; important money-laundering hub; increased activity on the northern frontier by trafficking groups and Colombian insurgents

Egypt

Introduction

Background: Nominally independent from the UK in 1922, Egypt acquired full sovereignty following World War II. The completion of the Aswan High Dam in 1971 and the resultant Lake Nasser have altered the time-honored place of the Nile river in the agriculture and ecology of Egypt. A rapidly growing population (the largest in the Arab world), limited arable land, and dependence on the Nile all continue to overtax resources and stress society. The government has struggled to ready the economy for the new millennium through economic reform and massive investment in communications and physical infrastructure.

Geography

Location: Northern Africa, bordering the Mediterranean Sea, between Libya and the Gaza Strip
Geographic coordinates: 27 00 N, 30 00 E
Map references: Africa
Area:
total: 1,001,450 sq km
land: 995,450 sq km
water: 6,000 sq km
Area - comparative: slightly more than three times the size of New Mexico
Land boundaries:
total: 2,689 km
border countries: Gaza Strip 11 km, Israel 255 km, Libya 1,150 km, Sudan 1,273 km
Coastline: 2,450 km
Maritime claims:
contiguous zone: 24 NM
continental shelf: 200-m depth or to the depth of exploitation
exclusive economic zone: 200 NM
territorial sea: 12 NM
Climate: desert; hot, dry summers with moderate winters

Egypt (continued)

Terrain: vast desert plateau interrupted by Nile valley and delta
Elevation extremes:
lowest point: Qattara Depression -133 m
highest point: Mount Catherine 2,629 m
Natural resources: petroleum, natural gas, iron ore, phosphates, manganese, limestone, gypsum, talc, asbestos, lead, zinc
Land use:
arable land: 2%
permanent crops: 0%
permanent pastures: 0%
forests and woodland: 0%
other: 98% (1993 est.)
Irrigated land: 32,460 sq km (1993 est.)
Natural hazards: periodic droughts; frequent earthquakes, flash floods, landslides, volcanic activity; hot, driving windstorm called khamsin occurs in spring; dust storms, sandstorms
Environment - current issues: agricultural land being lost to urbanization and windblown sands; increasing soil salination below Aswan High Dam; desertification; oil pollution threatening coral reefs, beaches, and marine habitats; other water pollution from agricultural pesticides, raw sewage, and industrial effluents; very limited natural fresh water resources away from the Nile which is the only perennial water source; rapid growth in population overstraining natural resources
Environment - international agreements:
party to: Biodiversity, Climate Change, Desertification, Endangered Species, Environmental Modification, Hazardous Wastes, Law of the Sea, Marine Dumping, Nuclear Test Ban, Ozone Layer Protection, Ship Pollution, Tropical Timber 83, Tropical Timber 94, Wetlands
signed, but not ratified: Climate Change-Kyoto Protocol
Geography - note: controls Sinai Peninsula, only land bridge between Africa and remainder of Eastern Hemisphere; controls Suez Canal, shortest sea link between Indian Ocean and Mediterranean Sea; size, and juxtaposition to Israel, establish its major role in Middle Eastern geopolitics; dependence on upstream neighbors; dominance of Nile basin issues; prone to influxes of refugees

People

Population: 69,536,644 (July 2001 est.)
Age structure:
0-14 years: 34.59% (male 12,313,585; female 11,739,072)
15-64 years: 61.6% (male 21,614,284; female 21,217,978)
65 years and over: 3.81% (male 1,160,967; female 1,490,758) (2001 est.)
Population growth rate: 1.69% (2001 est.)
Birth rate: 24.89 births/1,000 population (2001 est.)
Death rate: 7.7 deaths/1,000 population (2001 est.)
Net migration rate: -0.24 migrant(s)/1,000 population (2001 est.)

Sex ratio:
at birth: 1.05 male(s)/female
under 15 years: 1.05 male(s)/female
15-64 years: 1.02 male(s)/female
65 years and over: 0.78 male(s)/female
total population: 1.02 male(s)/female (2001 est.)
Infant mortality rate: 60.46 deaths/1,000 live births (2001 est.)
Life expectancy at birth:
total population: 63.69 years
male: 61.62 years
female: 65.85 years (2001 est.)
Total fertility rate: 3.07 children born/woman (2001 est.)
HIV/AIDS - adult prevalence rate: 0.02% (1999 est.)
HIV/AIDS - people living with HIV/AIDS: NA
HIV/AIDS - deaths: NA
Nationality:
noun: Egyptian(s)
adjective: Egyptian
Ethnic groups: Eastern Hamitic stock (Egyptians, Bedouins, and Berbers) 99%, Greek, Nubian, Armenian, other European (primarily Italian and French) 1%
Religions: Muslim (mostly Sunni) 94%, Coptic Christian and other 6%
Languages: Arabic (official), English and French widely understood by educated classes
Literacy:
definition: age 15 and over can read and write
total population: 51.4%
male: 63.6%
female: 38.8% (1995 est.)

Government

Country name:
conventional long form: Arab Republic of Egypt
conventional short form: Egypt
local long form: Jumhuriyat Misr al-Arabiyah
local short form: Misr
former: United Arab Republic (with Syria)
Government type: republic
Capital: Cairo
Administrative divisions: 26 governorates (muhafazat, singular - muhafazah); Ad Daqahliyah, Al Bahr al Ahmar, Al Buhayrah, Al Fayyum, Al Gharbiyah, Al Iskandariyah, Al Isma'iliyah, Al Jizah, Al Minufiyah, Al Minya, Al Qahirah, Al Qalyubiyah, Al Wadi al Jadid, Ash Sharqiyah, As Suways, Aswan, Asyut, Bani Suwayf, Bur Sa'id, Dumyat, Janub Sina', Kafr ash Shaykh, Matruh, Qina, Shamal Sina', Suhaj
Independence: 28 February 1922 (from UK)
National holiday: Revolution Day, 23 July (1952)
Constitution: 11 September 1971
Legal system: based on English common law, Islamic law, and Napoleonic codes; judicial review by Supreme Court and Council of State (oversees validity of administrative decisions); accepts compulsory ICJ jurisdiction, with reservations
Suffrage: 18 years of age; universal and compulsory

Executive branch:
chief of state: President Mohammed Hosni MUBARAK (since 14 October 1981)
head of government: Prime Minister Atef OBEID (since 5 October 1999)
cabinet: Cabinet appointed by the president
elections: president nominated by the People's Assembly for a six-year term, the nomination must then be validated by a national, popular referendum; national referendum last held 26 September 1999 (next to be held NA October 2005); prime minister appointed by the president
election results: national referendum validated President MUBARAK's nomination by the People's Assembly to a fourth term
Legislative branch: bicameral system consists of the People's Assembly or Majlis al-Sha'b (454 seats; 444 elected by popular vote, 10 appointed by the president; members serve five-year terms) and the Advisory Council or Majlis al-Shura - which functions only in a consultative role (264 seats; 176 elected by popular vote, 88 appointed by the president; members serve NA-year terms)
elections: People's Assembly - three-phase voting - last held 19 October, 29 October, 8 November 2000 (next to be held NA November 2005); Advisory Council - last held 7 June 1995 (next to be held NA)
election results: People's Assembly - percent of vote by party - NDP 88%, independents 8%, opposition 4%; seats by party - NDP 398, NWP 7, Tagammu 6, Nasserists 2, LSP 1, independents 38, undecided 2; Advisory Council - percent of vote by party - NDP 99%, independents 1%; seats by party - NA
Judicial branch: Supreme Constitutional Court
Political parties and leaders: Nasserist Arab Democratic Party or Nasserists [Dia' al-din DAWUD]; National Democratic Party or NDP [President Mohammed Hosni MUBARAK, leader] - governing party; National Progressive Unionist Grouping or Tagammu [Khalid MUHI AL-DIN]; New Wafd Party or NWP [No'man GOMA]; Socialist Liberal Party or LSP [leader NA]
note: formation of political parties must be approved by government
Political pressure groups and leaders: despite a constitutional ban against religious-based parties, the technically illegal Muslim Brotherhood constitutes MUBARAK's potentially most significant political opposition; MUBARAK tolerated limited political activity by the Brotherhood for his first two terms, but moved more aggressively since then to block its influence; civic society groups are sanctioned, but constrained in practical terms; trade unions and professional associations are officially sanctioned
International organization participation: ABEDA, ACC, ACCT (associate), AfDB, AFESD, AL, AMF, BSEC (observer), CAEU, CCC, EBRD, ECA, ESCWA, FAO, G-15, G-19, G-24, G-77, IAEA, IBRD, ICAO, ICC, ICRM, IDA, IDB, IFAD, IFC, IFRCS, IHO, ILO, IMF, IMO, Inmarsat, Intelsat, Interpol, IOC, IOM, ISO, ITU, MINURSO, MONUC, NAM, OAPEC, OAS (observer), OAU, OIC, OSCE (partner), PCA, UN,

Egypt (continued)

UNAMSIL, UNCTAD, UNESCO, UNIDO, UNITAR, UNMIBH, UNMIK, UNMOP, UNOMIG, UNRWA, UNTAET, UPU, WFTU, WHO, WIPO, WMO, WToO, WTrO

Diplomatic representation in the US:
chief of mission: Ambassador Nabil FAHMY
chancery: 3521 International Court NW, Washington, DC 20008
telephone: [1] (202) 895-5400
FAX: [1] (202) 244-4319, 5131
consulate(s) general: Chicago, Houston, New York, and San Francisco

Diplomatic representation from the US:
chief of mission: Ambassador Daniel C. KURTZER
embassy: 5 Latin America St., Garden City, Cairo
mailing address: Unit 64900, APO AE 09839-4900
telephone: [20] (2) 795-7371
FAX: [20] (2) 797-2000

Flag description: three equal horizontal bands of red (top), white, and black with the national emblem (a shield superimposed on a golden eagle facing the hoist side above a scroll bearing the name of the country in Arabic) centered in the white band; similar to the flag of Yemen, which has a plain white band; also similar to the flag of Syria, which has two green stars, and to the flag of Iraq, which has three green stars (plus an Arabic inscription) in a horizontal line centered in the white band

Economy

Economy - overview: A series of IMF arrangements - along with massive external debt relief resulting from Egypt's participation in the Gulf war coalition - helped Egypt improve its macroeconomic performance during the 1990s. Sound fiscal and monetary policies through the mid-1990s helped to tame inflation, slash budget deficits, and build up foreign reserves, while structural reforms such as privatization and new business legislation prompted increased foreign investment. By mid-1998, however, the pace of structural reform slackened, and lower combined hard currency earnings resulted in pressure on the Egyptian pound and sporadic US dollar shortages. External payments were not in crisis, but Cairo's attempts to curb demand for foreign exchange convinced some investors and currency traders that government financial operations lacked transparency and coordination. Monetary pressures have since eased, however, with the 1999-2000 higher oil prices, a rebound in tourism, and a series of mini-devaluations of the pound. The development of a gas export market is a major plus factor in future growth.

GDP: purchasing power parity - $247 billion (2000 est.)
GDP - real growth rate: 5% (2000 est.)
GDP - per capita: purchasing power parity - $3,600 (2000 est.)
GDP - composition by sector:
agriculture: 17%
industry: 32%
services: 51% (1999)

Population below poverty line: 22.9% (FY95/96 est.)
Household income or consumption by percentage share:
lowest 10%: 4.4%
highest 10%: 25% (1995)
Inflation rate (consumer prices): 3% (2000)
Labor force: 19.9 million (2000 est.)
Labor force - by occupation: agriculture 29%, services 49%, industry 22% (FY99)
Unemployment rate: 11.5% (2000 est.)
Budget:
revenues: $22.6 billion
expenditures: $26.2 billion, including capital expenditures of $NA (FY99)
Industries: textiles, food processing, tourism, chemicals, hydrocarbons, construction, cement, metals
Industrial production growth rate: 2.1% (2000 est.)
Electricity - production: 64.685 billion kWh (1999)
Electricity - production by source:
fossil fuel: 76.59%
hydro: 23.41%
nuclear: 0%
other: 0% (1999)
Electricity - consumption: 60.157 billion kWh (1999)
Electricity - exports: 0 kWh (1999)
Electricity - imports: 0 kWh (1999)
Agriculture - products: cotton, rice, corn, wheat, beans, fruits, vegetables; cattle, water buffalo, sheep, goats
Exports: $7.3 billion (f.o.b., 2000 est.)
Exports - commodities: crude oil and petroleum products, cotton, textiles, metal products, chemicals
Exports - partners: EU 35%, Middle East 17%, Afro-Asian countries 14%, US 12% (1999)
Imports: $17 billion (f.o.b., 2000 est.)
Imports - commodities: machinery and equipment, foodstuffs, chemicals, wood products, fuels
Imports - partners: EU 36%, US 14%, Afro-Asian countries 14%, Middle East 6% (1999)
Debt - external: $31 billion (2000 est.)
Economic aid - recipient: ODA, $2.25 billion (1999)
Currency: Egyptian pound (EGP)
Currency code: EGP
Exchange rates: Egyptian pounds per US dollar - market rate - 3.8400 (January 2001), 3.6900 (2000), 3.4050 (1999), 3.3880 (1998), 3.3880 (1997), 3.3880 (1996)
Fiscal year: 1 July - 30 June

Communications

Telephones - main lines in use: 3,971,500 (December 1998)
Telephones - mobile cellular: 380,000 (1999)
Telephone system:
general assessment: large system; underwent extensive upgrading during 1990s and is reasonably modern; Internet access and cellular service are available
domestic: principal centers at Alexandria, Cairo, Al Mansurah, Ismailia, Suez, and Tanta are connected by coaxial cable and microwave radio relay
international: satellite earth stations - 2 Intelsat (Atlantic Ocean and Indian Ocean), 1 Arabsat, and 1 Inmarsat; 5 coaxial submarine cables; tropospheric scatter to Sudan; microwave radio relay to Israel; a participant in Medarabtel and a signatory to Project Oxygen (a global submarine fiber-optic cable system)
Radio broadcast stations: AM 42 (plus 15 repeaters), FM 14, shortwave 3 (1999)
Radios: 20.5 million (1997)
Television broadcast stations: 98 (September 1995)
Televisions: 7.7 million (1997)
Internet country code: .eg
Internet Service Providers (ISPs): 50 (2000)
Internet users: 300,000 (2000)

Transportation

Railways:
total: 4,955 km
standard gauge: 4,955 km 1,435-m gauge (42 km electrified; 1,560 km double track)
Highways:
total: 64,000 km
paved: 50,000 km
unpaved: 14,000 km (1996)
Waterways: 3,500 km
note: including the Nile, Lake Nasser, Alexandria-Cairo Waterway, and numerous smaller canals in the delta; Suez Canal (193.5 km including approaches), used by oceangoing vessels drawing up to 16.1 m of water
Pipelines: crude oil 1,171 km; petroleum products 596 km; natural gas 460 km
Ports and harbors: Alexandria, Al Ghardaqah, Aswan, Asyut, Bur Safajah, Damietta, Marsa Matruh, Port Said, Suez
Merchant marine:
total: 181 ships (1,000 GRT or over) totaling 1,336,678 GRT/1,982,220 DWT
ships by type: bulk 23, cargo 61, container 2, liquefied gas 1, passenger 61, petroleum tanker 15, roll on/roll off 15, short-sea passenger 3 (2000 est.)
Airports: 90 (2000 est.)
Airports - with paved runways:
total: 69
over 3,047 m: 12
2,438 to 3,047 m: 35
1,524 to 2,437 m: 17
914 to 1,523 m: 2
under 914 m: 3 (2000 est.)
Airports - with unpaved runways:
total: 21
2,438 to 3,047 m: 2
1,524 to 2,437 m: 2
914 to 1,523 m: 7
under 914 m: 10 (2000 est.)
Heliports: 2 (2000 est.)

Egypt (continued)

Military

Military branches: Army, Navy, Air Force, Air Defense Command
Military manpower - military age: 20 years of age
Military manpower - availability:
males age 15-49: 18,562,994 (2001 est.)
Military manpower - fit for military service:
males age 15-49: 12,020,059 (2001 est.)
Military manpower - reaching military age annually:
males: 712,983 (2001 est.)
Military expenditures - dollar figure: $4.04 billion (FY99/00)
Military expenditures - percent of GDP: 4.1% (FY99/00)

Transnational Issues

Disputes - international: Egypt asserts its claim to the "Hala'ib Triangle," a barren area of 20,580 sq km under partial Sudanese administration that is defined by an administrative boundary which supersedes the treaty boundary of 1899
Illicit drugs: a transit point for Southwest Asian and Southeast Asian heroin and opium moving to Europe, Africa, and the US; popular transit stop for Nigerian couriers

El Salvador

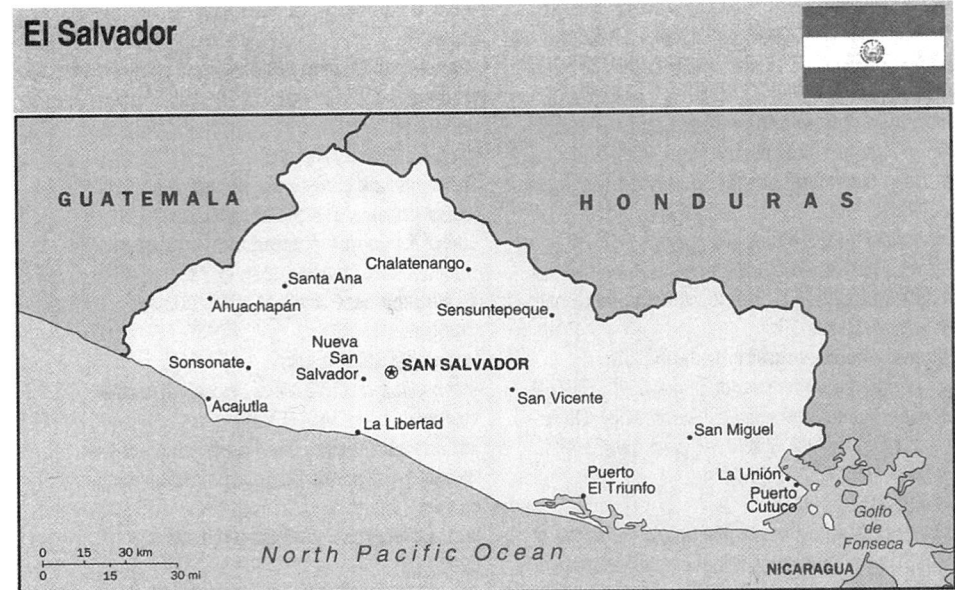

Introduction

Background: El Salvador achieved independence from Spain in 1821 and from the Central American Federation in 1839. A 12-year civil war, which cost the lives of some 75,000 people, was brought to a close in 1992 when the government and leftist rebels signed a treaty that provided for military and political reforms.

Geography

Location: Middle America, bordering the North Pacific Ocean, between Guatemala and Honduras
Geographic coordinates: 13 50 N, 88 55 W
Map references: Central America and the Caribbean
Area:
total: 21,040 sq km
land: 20,720 sq km
water: 320 sq km
Area - comparative: slightly smaller than Massachusetts
Land boundaries:
total: 545 km
border countries: Guatemala 203 km, Honduras 342 km
Coastline: 307 km
Maritime claims:
territorial sea: 200 NM
Climate: tropical; rainy season (May to October); dry season (November to April); tropical on coast; temperate in uplands
Terrain: mostly mountains with narrow coastal belt and central plateau
Elevation extremes:
lowest point: Pacific Ocean 0 m
highest point: Cerro El Pital 2,730 m
Natural resources: hydropower, geothermal power, petroleum, arable land
Land use:
arable land: 27%
permanent crops: 8%
permanent pastures: 29%
forests and woodland: 5%
other: 31% (1993 est.)
Irrigated land: 1,200 sq km (1993 est.)
Natural hazards: known as the Land of Volcanoes; frequent and sometimes very destructive earthquakes and volcanic activity
Environment - current issues: deforestation; soil erosion; water pollution; contamination of soils from disposal of toxic wastes; Hurricane Mitch damage
Environment - international agreements:
party to: Biodiversity, Climate Change, Climate Change-Kyoto Protocol, Desertification, Endangered Species, Hazardous Wastes, Marine Dumping, Nuclear Test Ban, Ozone Layer Protection, Ship Pollution, Wetlands
signed, but not ratified: Law of the Sea
Geography - note: smallest Central American country and only one without a coastline on Caribbean Sea

People

Population: 6,237,662 (July 2001 est.)
Age structure:
0-14 years: 37.68% (male 1,198,623; female 1,151,584)
15-64 years: 57.27% (male 1,693,865; female 1,878,254)
65 years and over: 5.05% (male 142,345; female 172,991) (2001 est.)
Population growth rate: 1.85% (2001 est.)
Birth rate: 28.67 births/1,000 population (2001 est.)
Death rate: 6.18 deaths/1,000 population (2001 est.)
Net migration rate: -3.95 migrant(s)/1,000 population (2001 est.)
Sex ratio:
at birth: 1.05 male(s)/female
under 15 years: 1.04 male(s)/female
15-64 years: 0.9 male(s)/female

El Salvador (continued)

65 years and over: 0.82 male(s)/female
total population: 0.95 male(s)/female (2001 est.)
Infant mortality rate: 28.4 deaths/1,000 live births (2001 est.)
Life expectancy at birth:
total population: 70.03 years
male: 66.43 years
female: 73.81 years (2001 est.)
Total fertility rate: 3.34 children born/woman (2001 est.)
HIV/AIDS - adult prevalence rate: 0.6% (1999 est.)
HIV/AIDS - people living with HIV/AIDS: 20,000 (1999 est.)
HIV/AIDS - deaths: 1,300 (1999 est.)
Nationality:
noun: Salvadoran(s)
adjective: Salvadoran
Ethnic groups: mestizo 90%, Amerindian 1%, white 9%
Religions: Roman Catholic 86%
note: there is extensive activity by Protestant groups throughout the country; by the end of 1992, there were an estimated 1 million Protestant evangelicals in El Salvador
Languages: Spanish, Nahua (among some Amerindians)
Literacy:
definition: age 10 and over can read and write
total population: 71.5%
male: 73.5%
female: 69.8% (1995 est.)

Government

Country name:
conventional long form: Republic of El Salvador
conventional short form: El Salvador
local long form: Republica de El Salvador
local short form: El Salvador
Government type: republic
Capital: San Salvador
Administrative divisions: 14 departments (departamentos, singular - departamento); Ahuachapan, Cabanas, Chalatenango, Cuscatlan, La Libertad, La Paz, La Union, Morazan, San Miguel, San Salvador, Santa Ana, San Vicente, Sonsonate, Usulutan
Independence: 15 September 1821 (from Spain)
National holiday: Independence Day, 15 September (1821)
Constitution: 23 December 1983
Legal system: based on civil and Roman law, with traces of common law; judicial review of legislative acts in the Supreme Court; accepts compulsory ICJ jurisdiction, with reservations
Suffrage: 18 years of age; universal
Executive branch:
chief of state: President Francisco FLORES Perez (since 1 June 1999); Vice President Carlos QUINTANILLA Schmidt (since 1 June 1999); note - the president is both the chief of state and head of government
head of government: President Francisco FLORES Perez (since 1 June 1999); Vice President Carlos QUINTANILLA Schmidt (since 1 June 1999); note - the president is both the chief of state and head of government
cabinet: cabinet selected by the president
elections: president and vice president elected on the same ticket by popular vote for five-year terms; election last held 7 March 1999 (next to be held NA March 2004)
election results: Francisco FLORES Perez elected president; percent of vote - Francisco FLORES (ARENA) 52%, Facundo GUARDADO (FMLN) 29%, Ruben ZAMORA (CDU) 7.5%, other (no individual above 3%) 11.5%
Legislative branch: unicameral Legislative Assembly or Asamblea Legislativa (84 seats; members are elected by direct popular vote to serve three-year terms)
elections: last held 12 March 2000 (next to be held NA March 2003)
election results: percent of vote by party - ARENA 36.1%, FMLN 35.14%, PCN 8.76%, PDC 7.08%, CD 5.32%, PAN 3.75%, USC 1.47%, PLD 1.29%; seats by party - ARENA 28, FMLN 31, PCN 14, PDC 5, CD 3, PAN 1, independent 2
Judicial branch: Supreme Court or Corte Suprema (judges are selected by the Legislative Assembly)
Political parties and leaders: Christian Democratic Party or PDC [Rene AGUILUZ]; Democratic Convergence or CD (includes PSD, MNR, MPSC) [Ruben ZAMORA, secretary general]; Democratic Party or PD [Jorge MELENDEZ]; Farabundo Marti National Liberation Front or FMLN [Fabio CASTILLO]; Liberal Democratic Party or PLD [Kirio Waldo SALGADO, president]; National Action Party or PAN [Gustavo Rogelio SALINAS, secretary general]; National Conciliation Party or PCN [Ciro CRUZ Zepeda, president]; National Republican Alliance or ARENA [Walter ARAUJO]; Social Christian Union or USC (formed by the merger of Christian Social Renewal Party or PRSC and Unity Movement or MU) [Abraham RODRIGUEZ, president]
Political pressure groups and leaders:
labor organizations: Electrical Industry Union of El Salvador or SIES; Federation of the Construction Industry, Similar Transport and other activities, or FESINCONTRANS; National Confederation of Salvadoran Workers or CNTS; National Union of Salvadoran Workers or UNTS; Port Industry Union of El Salvador or SIPES; Salvadoran Union of Ex-Petrolleros and Peasant Workers or USEPOC; Salvadoran Workers Central or CTS; Workers Union of Electrical Corporation or STCEL
business organizations: National Association of Small Enterprise or ANEP; Salvadoran Assembly Industry Association or ASIC; Salvadoran Industrial Association or ASI
International organization participation: BCIE, CACM, ECLAC, FAO, G-77, IADB, IAEA, IBRD, ICAO, ICFTU, ICRM, IDA, IFAD, IFC, IFRCS, ILO, IMF, IMO, Intelsat, Interpol, IOC, IOM, ISO (correspondent), ITU, LAES, LAIA (observer), MINURSO, NAM (observer), OAS, OPANAL, OPCW, PCA, UN, UNCTAD, UNESCO, UNIDO, UPU, WCL, WFTU, WHO, WIPO, WMO, WToO, WTrO
Diplomatic representation in the US:
chief of mission: Ambassador Rene Antonio LEON Rodriguez
chancery: 2308 California Street NW, Washington, DC 20008
telephone: [1] (202) 265-9671
consulate(s) general: Chicago, Dallas, Houston, Los Angeles, Miami, New Orleans, New York, and San Francisco
consulate(s): Boston
Diplomatic representation from the US:
chief of mission: Ambassador Rose M. LIKINS
embassy: Boulevard Santa Elena Final, Antiguo Cuscatlan, La Libertad, San Salvador
mailing address: Unit 3116, APO AA 34023
telephone: [503] 278-4444
FAX: [503] 278-6011
Flag description: three equal horizontal bands of blue (top), white, and blue with the national coat of arms centered in the white band; the coat of arms features a round emblem encircled by the words REPUBLICA DE EL SALVADOR EN LA AMERICA CENTRAL; similar to the flag of Nicaragua, which has a different coat of arms centered in the white band - it features a triangle encircled by the words REPUBLICA DE NICARAGUA on top and AMERICA CENTRAL on the bottom; also similar to the flag of Honduras, which has five blue stars arranged in an X pattern centered in the white band

Economy

Economy - overview: El Salvador is a struggling Central American economy which has been suffering from a weak tax collection system, factory closings, the aftermaths of Hurricane Mitch of 1998 and the devastating earthquakes of early 2001, and weak world coffee prices. On the bright side, in recent years inflation has fallen to single digit levels, and total exports have grown substantially. The trade deficit has been offset by remittances (an estimated $1.6 billion in 2000) from Salvadorans living abroad and by external aid. As of 1 January 2001, the US dollar was made legal tender alongside the colon.
GDP: purchasing power parity - $24 billion (2000 est.)
GDP - real growth rate: 2.5% (2000 est.)
GDP - per capita: purchasing power parity - $4,000 (2000 est.)
GDP - composition by sector:
agriculture: 12%
industry: 28%
services: 60% (1999 est.)
Population below poverty line: 48% (1999 est.)
Household income or consumption by percentage share:
lowest 10%: 1.2%
highest 10%: 38.3% (1995)

El Salvador (continued)

Inflation rate (consumer prices): 2.5% (2000 est.)
Labor force: 2.35 million (1999)
Labor force - by occupation: agriculture 30%, industry 15%, services 55% (1999 est.)
Unemployment rate: 10% (2000 est.)
Budget:
revenues: $1.8 billion
expenditures: $2.2 billion, including capital expenditures of $NA (1999 est.)
Industries: food processing, beverages, petroleum, chemicals, fertilizer, textiles, furniture, light metals
Industrial production growth rate: 5% (2000 est.)
Electricity - production: 3.641 billion kWh (1999)
Electricity - production by source:
fossil fuel: 45.65%
hydro: 41.01%
nuclear: 0%
other: 13.34% (1999)
Electricity - consumption: 3.638 billion kWh (1999)
Electricity - exports: 208 million kWh (1999)
Electricity - imports: 460 million kWh (1999)
Agriculture - products: coffee, sugar, corn, rice, beans, oilseed, cotton, sorghum; shrimp; beef, dairy products
Exports: $2.8 billion (f.o.b., 2000)
Exports - commodities: offshore assembly exports, coffee, sugar, shrimp, textiles, chemicals, electricity
Exports - partners: US 63%, Guatemala 11%, Honduras 7%, Costa Rica 4% (1999)
Imports: $4.6 billion (f.o.b., 2000)
Imports - commodities: raw materials, consumer goods, capital goods, fuels, foodstuffs, petroleum, electricity
Imports - partners: US 52%, Guatemala 9%, Mexico 6%, Costa Rica 3% (1999)
Debt - external: $4.1 billion (2000 est.)
Economic aid - recipient: total $252 million; $57 million from US (1999 est.)
Currency: Salvadoran colon (SVC); US dollar (USD)
Currency code: SVC; USD
Exchange rates: Salvadoran colones per US dollar - 8.755 (fixed rate since 1993)
Fiscal year: calendar year

Communications

Telephones - main lines in use: 380,000 (1998)
Telephones - mobile cellular: 40,163 (1997)
Telephone system:
general assessment: NA
domestic: nationwide microwave radio relay system
international: satellite earth station - 1 Intelsat (Atlantic Ocean); connected to Central American Microwave System
Radio broadcast stations: AM 61 (plus 24 repeaters), FM 30, shortwave 0 (1998)
Radios: 2.75 million (1997)
Television broadcast stations: 5 (1997)
Televisions: 600,000 (1990)
Internet country code: .sv
Internet Service Providers (ISPs): 4 (2000)
Internet users: 40,000 (2000)

Transportation

Railways:
total: 602 km (single track; note - some sections abandoned, unusable, or operating at reduced capacity)
narrow gauge: 602 km 0.914-m gauge
Highways:
total: 10,029 km
paved: 1,986 km (including 327 km of expressways)
unpaved: 8,043 km (1997)
Waterways: Rio Lempa partially navigable
Ports and harbors: Acajutla, Puerto Cutuco, La Libertad, La Union, Puerto El Triunfo
Merchant marine: none (2000 est.)
Airports: 83 (2000 est.)
Airports - with paved runways:
total: 4
over 3,047 m: 1
1,524 to 2,437 m: 1
914 to 1,523 m: 2 (2000 est.)
Airports - with unpaved runways:
total: 79
914 to 1,523 m: 17
under 914 m: 62 (2000 est.)
Heliports: 1 (2000 est.)

Military

Military branches: Army, Navy, Air Force
Military manpower - military age: 18 years of age
Military manpower - availability:
males age 15-49: 1,464,898 (2001 est.)
Military manpower - fit for military service:
males age 15-49: 929,263 (2001 est.)
Military manpower - reaching military age annually:
males: 68,103 (2001 est.)
Military expenditures - dollar figure: $112 million (FY99)
Military expenditures - percent of GDP: 0.7% (FY99)

Transnational Issues

Disputes - international: with respect to the maritime boundary in the Golfo de Fonseca, the ICJ referred to the line determined by the 1900 Honduras-Nicaragua Mixed Boundary Commission and advised that some tripartite resolution among El Salvador, Honduras and Nicaragua likely would be required
Illicit drugs: transshipment point for cocaine; marijuana produced for local consumption; domestic drug abuse on the rise

Equatorial Guinea

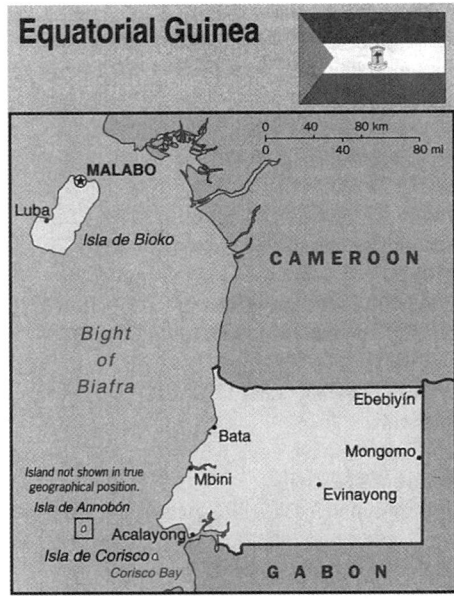

Introduction

Background: Composed of a mainland portion and five inhabited islands, Equatorial Guinea has been ruled by ruthless leaders who have badly mismanaged the economy since independence from 190 years of Spanish rule in 1968. Although nominally a constitutional democracy since 1991, the 1996 presidential and 1999 legislative elections were widely seen as being flawed.

Geography

Location: Western Africa, bordering the Bight of Biafra, between Cameroon and Gabon
Geographic coordinates: 2 00 N, 10 00 E
Map references: Africa
Area:
total: 28,051 sq km
land: 28,051 sq km
water: 0 sq km
Area - comparative: slightly smaller than Maryland
Land boundaries:
total: 539 km
border countries: Cameroon 189 km, Gabon 350 km
Coastline: 296 km
Maritime claims:
exclusive economic zone: 200 NM
territorial sea: 12 NM
Climate: tropical; always hot, humid
Terrain: coastal plains rise to interior hills; islands are volcanic
Elevation extremes:
lowest point: Atlantic Ocean 0 m
highest point: Pico Basile 3,008 m
Natural resources: oil, petroleum, timber, small unexploited deposits of gold, manganese, uranium
Land use:
arable land: 5%
permanent crops: 4%
permanent pastures: 4%
forests and woodland: 46%
other: 41% (1993 est.)

Equatorial Guinea (continued)

Irrigated land: NA sq km
Natural hazards: violent windstorms, flash floods
Environment - current issues: tap water is not potable; desertification
Environment - international agreements:
party to: Biodiversity, Climate Change, Climate Change-Kyoto Protocol, Desertification, Endangered Species, Law of the Sea, Marine Dumping, Ship Pollution
signed, but not ratified: none of the selected agreements
Geography - note: insular and continental regions rather widely separated

People

Population: 486,060 (July 2001 est.)
Age structure:
0-14 years: 42.56% (male 103,909; female 102,946)
15-64 years: 53.68% (male 124,808; female 136,088)
65 years and over: 3.76% (male 8,178; female 10,131) (2001 est.)
Population growth rate: 2.46% (2001 est.)
Birth rate: 37.72 births/1,000 population (2001 est.)
Death rate: 13.11 deaths/1,000 population (2001 est.)
Net migration rate: NEGL migrant(s)/1,000 population (2001 est.)
Sex ratio:
at birth: 1.03 male(s)/female
under 15 years: 1.01 male(s)/female
15-64 years: 0.92 male(s)/female
65 years and over: 0.81 male(s)/female
total population: 0.95 male(s)/female (2001 est.)
Infant mortality rate: 92.9 deaths/1,000 live births (2001 est.)
Life expectancy at birth:
total population: 53.95 years
male: 51.89 years
female: 56.07 years (2001 est.)
Total fertility rate: 4.88 children born/woman (2001 est.)
HIV/AIDS - adult prevalence rate: 0.51% (1999 est.)
HIV/AIDS - people living with HIV/AIDS: 1,100 (1999 est.)
HIV/AIDS - deaths: 120 (1999 est.)
Nationality:
noun: Equatorial Guinean(s) or Equatoguinean(s)
adjective: Equatorial Guinean or Equatoguinean
Ethnic groups: Bioko (primarily Bubi, some Fernandinos), Rio Muni (primarily Fang), Europeans less than 1,000, mostly Spanish
Religions: nominally Christian and predominantly Roman Catholic, pagan practices
Languages: Spanish (official), French (official), pidgin English, Fang, Bubi, Ibo
Literacy:
definition: age 15 and over can read and write
total population: 78.5%
male: 89.6%
female: 68.1% (1995 est.)

Government

Country name:
conventional long form: Republic of Equatorial Guinea
conventional short form: Equatorial Guinea
local long form: Republica de Guinea Ecuatorial
local short form: Guinea Ecuatorial
former: Spanish Guinea
Government type: republic
Capital: Malabo
Administrative divisions: 7 provinces (provincias, singular - provincia); Annobon, Bioko Norte, Bioko Sur, Centro Sur, Kie-Ntem, Litoral, Wele-Nzas
Independence: 12 October 1968 (from Spain)
National holiday: Independence Day, 12 October (1968)
Constitution: approved by national referendum 17 November 1991; amended January 1995
Legal system: partly based on Spanish civil law and tribal custom
Suffrage: 18 years of age; universal adult
Executive branch:
chief of state: President Brig. Gen. (Ret.) Teodoro OBIANG NGUEMA MBASOGO (since 3 August 1979 when he seized power in a military coup)
head of government: Prime Minister Candido Muatetema RIVAS (since 26 February 2001); First Deputy Prime Minister Miguel OYONO NDONG (since NA January 1998); Deputy Prime Minister Demetrio Elo NDONG NZE FUMU (since NA January 1998)
cabinet: Council of Ministers appointed by the president
elections: president elected by popular vote to a seven-year term; election last held 25 February 1996 (next to be held NA February 2003); prime minister and vice prime ministers appointed by the president
election results: President Teodoro OBIANG NGUEMA MBASOGO reelected with 98% of popular vote in elections marred by widespread fraud
Legislative branch: unicameral House of People's Representatives or Camara de Representantes del Pueblo (80 seats; members directly elected by popular vote to serve five-year terms)
elections: last held 7 March 1999 (next to be held NA 2004)
election results: percent of vote by party - PDGE 80%, UP 6%, CPDS 5%; seats by party - PDGE 75, UP 4 and CPDS 1
note: opposition parties have refused to take up their seats in the House to protest widespread irregularities in the 1999 legislative elections
Judicial branch: Supreme Tribunal
Political parties and leaders: Convergence Party for Social Democracy or CPDS [Placido Miko ABOGO]; Democratic Party for Equatorial Guinea or PDGE (ruling party) [Teodoro OBIANG NGUEMA MBASOGO]; Party for Progress of Equatorial Guinea or PPGE [Severo MOTO]; Popular Action of Equatorial Guinea or APGE [Miguel Esono EMAN]; Popular Union or UP [Andres Moises Bda ADA]; Progressive Democratic Alliance or ADP [Victorino Bolekia BONAY, mayor of Malabo]; Union of Independent Democrats of UDI [Daniel OYONO]
Political pressure groups and leaders: NA
International organization participation: ACCT, ACP, AfDB, BDEAC, CEEAC, CEMAC, ECA, FAO, FZ, G-77, IBRD, ICAO, ICRM, IDA, IFAD, IFC, IFRCS, ILO, IMF, IMO, Intelsat, Interpol, IOC, ITU, NAM, OAS (observer), OAU, OPCW, UN, UNCTAD, UNESCO, UNIDO, UPU, WHO, WIPO, WToO, WTrO (applicant)
Diplomatic representation in the US:
chief of mission: Ambassador Teodoro BIYOGO NSUEA
chancery: 2020 16th Street NW, Washington, DC 20009
telephone: [1] (202) 518-5700
FAX: [1] (202) 528-5252
Diplomatic representation from the US:
chief of mission: Ambassador John M. YATES; note - the US does not have an embassy in Equatorial Guinea (embassy closed September 1995); US relations with Equatorial Guinea are handled through the US Embassy in Yaounde, Cameroon; the US State Department is considering opening a Consulate Agency in Malabo
Flag description: three equal horizontal bands of green (top), white, and red with a blue isosceles triangle based on the hoist side and the coat of arms centered in the white band; the coat of arms has six yellow six-pointed stars (representing the mainland and five offshore islands) above a gray shield bearing a silk-cotton tree and below which is a scroll with the motto UNIDAD, PAZ, JUSTICIA (Unity, Peace, Justice)

Economy

Economy - overview: The discovery and exploitation of large oil reserves have contributed to dramatic economic growth in recent years. Forestry, farming, and fishing are also major components of GDP. Subsistence farming predominates. Although pre-independence Equatorial Guinea counted on cocoa production for hard currency earnings, the deterioration of the rural economy under successive brutal regimes has diminished potential for agriculture-led growth. A number of aid programs sponsored by the World Bank and the IMF have been cut off since 1993 because of the government's gross corruption and mismanagement. Businesses, for the most part, are owned by government officials and their family members. Undeveloped natural resources include titanium, iron ore, manganese, uranium, and alluvial gold. The country responded favorably to the devaluation of the CFA franc in January 1994. Boosts in production and high world oil prices stimulated growth in 2000, with oil accounting for 90% of greatly increased exports.
GDP: purchasing power parity - $960 million (2000 est.)
GDP - real growth rate: 12% (2000 est.)
GDP - per capita: purchasing power parity - $2,000 (2000 est.)

Equatorial Guinea (continued)

GDP - composition by sector:
agriculture: 20%
industry: 60%
services: 20% (1999 est.)
Population below poverty line: NA%
Household income or consumption by percentage share:
lowest 10%: NA%
highest 10%: NA%
Inflation rate (consumer prices): 6% (1999 est.)
Labor force: NA
Unemployment rate: 30% (1998 est.)
Budget:
revenues: $47 million
expenditures: $43 million, including capital expenditures of $7 million (1996 est.)
Industries: petroleum, fishing, sawmilling, natural gas
Industrial production growth rate: 7.4% (1994 est.)
Electricity - production: 21 million kWh (1999)
Electricity - production by source:
fossil fuel: 85.71%
hydro: 14.29%
nuclear: 0%
other: 0% (1999)
Electricity - consumption: 19.5 million kWh (1999)
Electricity - exports: 0 kWh (1999)
Electricity - imports: 0 kWh (1999)
Agriculture - products: coffee, cocoa, rice, yams, cassava (tapioca), bananas, palm oil nuts; livestock; timber
Exports: $860 million (f.o.b., 2000 est.)
Exports - commodities: petroleum, timber, cocoa
Exports - partners: US 62%, Spain 17%, China 9%, France 3%, Japan 3%, (1997)
Imports: $300 million (f.o.b., 1999)
Imports - commodities: manufactured goods and equipment
Imports - partners: US 35%, France 15%, Spain 10%, Cameroon 10%, UK 6% (1997)
Debt - external: $290 million (1999 est.)
Economic aid - recipient: $33.8 million (1995)
Currency: Communaute Financiere Africaine franc (XAF); note - responsible authority is the Bank of the Central African States
Currency code: XAF
Exchange rates: Communaute Financiere Africaine francs (XAF) per US dollar - 699.21 (January 2001), 711.98 (2000), 615.70 (1999), 589.95 (1998), 583.67 (1997), 511.55 (1996); note - from 1 January 1999, the XAF is pegged to the euro at a rate of 655.957 XAF per euro
Fiscal year: 1 April - 31 March

Communications

Telephones - main lines in use: 4,000 (1996)
Telephones - mobile cellular: NA
Telephone system:
general assessment: poor system with adequate government services
domestic: NA
international: international communications from Bata and Malabo to African and European countries; satellite earth station - 1 Intelsat (Indian Ocean)
Radio broadcast stations: AM 0, FM 2, shortwave 4 (1998)
Radios: 180,000 (1997)
Television broadcast stations: 1 (1997)
Televisions: 4,000 (1997)
Internet country code: .gq
Internet Service Providers (ISPs): 1 (2000)
Internet users: 500 (2000)

Transportation

Railways:
total: 0 km
Highways:
total: 2,880 km
paved: 0 km
unpaved: 2,880 km (1996)
Waterways: none
Ports and harbors: Bata, Luba, Malabo
Merchant marine:
total: 12 ships (1,000 GRT or over) totaling 26,035 GRT/27,927 DWT
ships by type: bulk 1, cargo 7, combination bulk 1, passenger 2, passenger/cargo 1 (2000 est.)
Airports: 3 (2000 est.)
Airports - with paved runways:
total: 2
2,438 to 3,047 m: 1
1,524 to 2,437 m: 1 (2000 est.)
Airports - with unpaved runways:
total: 1
under 914 m: 1 (2000 est.)

Military

Military branches: Army, Navy, Air Force, Rapid Intervention Force, National Police
Military manpower - availability:
males age 15-49: 108,973 (2001 est.)
Military manpower - fit for military service:
males age 15-49: 55,347 (2001 est.)
Military expenditures - dollar figure: $3 million (FY97/98)
Military expenditures - percent of GDP: 0.6% (FY97/98)

Transnational Issues

Disputes - international: tripartite maritime boundary and economic zone dispute with Cameroon and Nigeria is currently before the ICJ; maritime boundary dispute with Gabon because of disputed sovereignty over islands in Corisco Bay

Eritrea

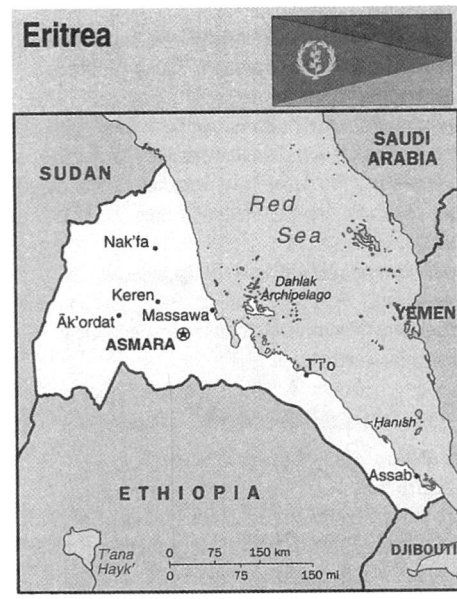

Introduction

Background: Eritrea was awarded to Ethiopia in 1952 as part of a federation. Ethiopia's annexation of Eritrea as a province 10 years later sparked a 30-year struggle for independence that ended in 1991 with Eritrean rebels defeating governmental forces; independence was overwhelmingly approved in a 1993 referendum. A two and a half year border war with Ethiopia that erupted in 1998 ended under UN auspices on 12 December 2000.

Geography

Location: Eastern Africa, bordering the Red Sea, between Djibouti and Sudan
Geographic coordinates: 15 00 N, 39 00 E
Map references: Africa
Area:
total: 121,320 sq km
land: 121,320 sq km
water: 0 sq km
Area - comparative: slightly larger than Pennsylvania
Land boundaries:
total: 1,630 km
border countries: Djibouti 113 km, Ethiopia 912 km, Sudan 605 km
Coastline: 2,234 km total; mainland on Red Sea 1,151 km, islands in Red Sea 1,083 km
Maritime claims:
territorial sea: 12 NM
Climate: hot, dry desert strip along Red Sea coast; cooler and wetter in the central highlands (up to 61 cm of rainfall annually); semiarid in western hills and lowlands; rainfall heaviest during June-September except in coastal desert
Terrain: dominated by extension of Ethiopian north-south trending highlands, descending on the east to a coastal desert plain, on the northwest to hilly terrain and on the southwest to flat-to-rolling plains

Eritrea (continued)

Elevation extremes:
lowest point: near Kulul within the Denakil depression -75 m
highest point: Soira 3,018 m
Natural resources: gold, potash, zinc, copper, salt, possibly oil and natural gas, fish
Land use:
arable land: 12%
permanent crops: 1%
permanent pastures: 49%
forests and woodland: 6%
other: 32% (1998 est.)
Irrigated land: 280 sq km (1993 est.)
Natural hazards: frequent droughts; locust swarms
Environment - current issues: deforestation; desertification; soil erosion; overgrazing; loss of infrastructure from civil warfare
Environment - international agreements:
party to: Biodiversity, Climate Change, Desertification, Endangered Species, Marine Dumping, Ship Pollution
signed, but not ratified: none of the selected agreements
Geography - note: strategic geopolitical position along world's busiest shipping lanes; Eritrea retained the entire coastline of Ethiopia along the Red Sea upon de jure independence from Ethiopia on 24 May 1993

People

Population: 4,298,269 (July 2001 est.)
Age structure:
0-14 years: 42.85% (male 922,691; female 918,916)
15-64 years: 53.87% (male 1,147,927; female 1,167,705)
65 years and over: 3.28% (male 71,232; female 69,798) (2001 est.)
Population growth rate: 3.84% (2001 est.)
Birth rate: 42.52 births/1,000 population (2001 est.)
Death rate: 12.07 deaths/1,000 population (2001 est.)
Net migration rate: 7.91 migrant(s)/1,000 population (2001 est.)
note: according to the UNHCR, about 150,000 Eritrean refugees in Sudan have registered for voluntary repatriation, following the restoration of diplomatic relations between Eritrea and Sudan in January 2000
Sex ratio:
at birth: 1.03 male(s)/female
under 15 years: 1 male(s)/female
15-64 years: 0.98 male(s)/female
65 years and over: 1.02 male(s)/female
total population: 0.99 male(s)/female (2001 est.)
Infant mortality rate: 75.14 deaths/1,000 live births (2001 est.)
Life expectancy at birth:
total population: 56.18 years
male: 53.73 years
female: 58.71 years (2001 est.)
Total fertility rate: 5.87 children born/woman (2001 est.)
HIV/AIDS - adult prevalence rate: 2.87% (1999 est.)
HIV/AIDS - people living with HIV/AIDS: NA
HIV/AIDS - deaths: NA
Nationality:
noun: Eritrean(s)
adjective: Eritrean
Ethnic groups: ethnic Tigrinya 50%, Tigre and Kunama 40%, Afar 4%, Saho (Red Sea coast dwellers) 3%
Religions: Muslim, Coptic Christian, Roman Catholic, Protestant
Languages: Afar, Amharic, Arabic, Tigre and Kunama, Tigrinya, other Cushitic languages
Literacy:
definition: NA
total population: 25%
male: NA%
female: NA%

Government

Country name:
conventional long form: State of Eritrea
conventional short form: Eritrea
local long form: Hagere Ertra
local short form: Ertra
former: Eritrea Autonomous Region in Ethiopia
Government type: transitional government
note: following a successful referendum on independence for the Autonomous Region of Eritrea on 23-25 April 1993, a National Assembly, composed entirely of the People's Front for Democracy and Justice or PFDJ, was established as a transitional legislature; a Constitutional Commission was also established to draft a constitution; ISAIAS Afworki was elected president by the transitional legislature; the constitution, ratified in May 1997, did not enter into effect, pending parliamentary and presidential elections; parliamentary elections have now been scheduled to take place in December 2001
Capital: Asmara (formerly Asmera)
Administrative divisions: 8 provinces (singular - awraja); Akale Guzay, Barka, Denkel, Hamasen, Sahil, Semhar, Senhit, Seraye
note: in May 1995 the National Assembly adopted a resolution stating that the administrative structure of Eritrea, which had been established by former colonial powers, would consist of only six provinces when the new constitution, then being drafted, became effective in 1997; the new provinces, the names of which had not been recommended by the US Board on Geographic Names for recognition by the US Government, pending acceptable definition of the boundaries, were: Anseba, Debub, Debubawi Keyih Bahri, Gash-Barka, Maakel, and Semanawi Keyih Bahri; more recently, it has been reported that these provinces have been redesignated regions and renamed Southern Red Sea, Northern Red Sea, Anseba, Gash-Barka, Southern, and Central
Independence: 24 May 1993 (from Ethiopia)
National holiday: Independence Day, 24 May (1993)
Constitution: the transitional constitution, decreed on 19 May 1993, was replaced by a new constitution adopted on 23 May 1997, but not yet implemented
Legal system: operates on the basis of transitional laws that incorporate pre-independence statutes of the Eritrean People's Liberation Front, revised Ethiopian laws, customary laws, and post independence enacted laws
Suffrage: 18 years of age; universal
Executive branch:
chief of state: President ISAIAS Afworki (since 8 June 1993); note - the president is both the chief of state and head of government and is head of the State Council and National Assembly
head of government: President ISAIAS Afworki (since 8 June 1993); note - the president is both the chief of state and head of government and is head of the State Council and National Assembly
cabinet: State Council is the collective executive authority
elections: president elected by the National Assembly; election last held 8 June 1993 (next tentatively scheduled for December 2001)
election results: ISAIAS Afworki elected president; percent of National Assembly vote - ISAIAS Afworki 95%
Legislative branch: unicameral National Assembly (150 seats; term limits not established)
elections: in May 1997, following the adoption of the new constitution, 75 members of the PFDJ Central Committee (the old Central Committee of the EPLF), 60 members of the 527-member Constituent Assembly which had been established in 1997 to discuss and ratify the new constitution, and 15 representatives of Eritreans living abroad were formed into a Transitional National Assembly to serve as the country's legislative body until country-wide elections to a National Assembly are held; only 75 members will be elected to the National Assembly - the other 75 will be members of the Central Committee of the PFDJ; parliamentary elections are now scheduled for NA December 2001
Judicial branch: Supreme Court; 10 provincial courts; 29 district courts
Political parties and leaders: People's Front for Democracy and Justice or PFDJ, the only party recognized by the government [ISAIAS Afworki, PETROS Solomon]; note - the National Assembly has appointed a committee to draft a law on political parties
Political pressure groups and leaders: Eritrean Islamic Jihad or EIJ; Eritrean Liberation Front or ELF [ABDULLAH Muhammed]; Eritrean Liberation Front-Revolutionary Council or ELF-RC [Ahmed NASSER]; Eritrean Liberation Front-United Organization or ELF-UO [Mohammed Said NAWD]
International organization participation: ACP, AfDB, CCC, ECA, FAO, IBRD, ICAO, ICFTU, IDA, IFAD, IFC, IGAD, ILO, IMF, IMO, Intelsat (nonsignatory user), Interpol, IOC, ITU, NAM, OAU, OPCW, UN, UNCTAD, UNESCO, UNIDO, UPU, WFTU, WHO, WIPO, WMO, WToO

Eritrea (continued)

Diplomatic representation in the US:
chief of mission: Ambassador GIRMA Asmerom
chancery: 1708 New Hampshire Avenue NW, Washington, DC 20009
telephone: [1] (202) 319-1991
FAX: [1] (202) 319-1304

Diplomatic representation from the US:
chief of mission: Ambassador William D. CLARKE
embassy: Franklin D. Roosevelt Street, Asmara
mailing address: P. O. Box 211, Asmara
telephone: [291] (1) 120004
FAX: [291] (1) 127584

Flag description: red isosceles triangle (based on the hoist side) dividing the flag into two right triangles; the upper triangle is green, the lower one is blue; a gold wreath encircling a gold olive branch is centered on the hoist side of the red triangle

Economy

Economy - overview: With independence from Ethiopia on 24 May 1993, Eritrea faced the economic problems of a small, desperately poor country. The economy is largely based on subsistence agriculture, with 80% of the population involved in farming and herding. The small industrial sector consists mainly of light industries with outmoded technologies. Domestic output (GDP) is substantially augmented by worker remittances from abroad. Government revenues come from custom duties and taxes on income and sales. Road construction is a top domestic priority. In the long term, Eritrea may benefit from the development of offshore oil, offshore fishing, and tourism. Eritrea's economic future depends on its ability to master fundamental social and economic problems, e.g., by reducing illiteracy, promoting job creation, expanding technical training, attracting foreign investment, and streamlining the bureaucracy. Eritrea's agriculture over the last two years was severely weakened by war and drought, and many farmlands must wait to be demined. Another major difficulty is the ports, which prior to the war were Ethiopia's preferred outlets but since have seen trade dry up.

GDP: purchasing power parity - $2.9 billion (2000 est.)
GDP - real growth rate: -1% (2000 est.)
GDP - per capita: purchasing power parity - $710 (2000 est.)
GDP - composition by sector:
agriculture: 16%
industry: 27%
services: 57% (2000 est.)
Population below poverty line: NA%
Household income or consumption by percentage share:
lowest 10%: NA%
highest 10%: NA%
Inflation rate (consumer prices): 14% (2000 est.)
Labor force: NA
Labor force - by occupation: agriculture 80%, industry and services 20%
Unemployment rate: NA%
Budget:
revenues: $283.9 million
expenditures: $351.6 million, including capital expenditures of $NA (1997 est.)
Industries: food processing, beverages, clothing and textiles
Industrial production growth rate: NA%
Electricity - production: 165 million kWh (1999)
Electricity - production by source:
fossil fuel: 100%
hydro: 0%
nuclear: 0%
other: 0% (1999)
Electricity - consumption: 153.5 million kWh (1999)
Electricity - exports: 0 kWh NA kWh (1999)
Electricity - imports: 0 kWh NA kWh (1999)
Agriculture - products: sorghum, lentils, vegetables, corn, cotton, tobacco, coffee, sisal; livestock, goats; fish
Exports: $26 million (f.o.b., 1999)
Exports - commodities: livestock, sorghum, textiles, food, small manufactures
Exports - partners: Sudan 27.2%, Ethiopia 26.5%, Japan 13.2%, UAE 7.3%, Italy 5.3% (1998)
Imports: $560 million (c.i.f., 1999)
Imports - commodities: machinery, petroleum products, food, manufactured goods
Imports - partners: Italy 17.4%, UAE 16.2%, Germany 5.7%, UK 4.5%, Korea 4.4% (1998)
Debt - external: $281 million (2000 est.)
Economic aid - recipient: $77 million (1999)
Currency: nakfa (ERN)
Currency code: ERN
Exchange rates: nakfa per US dollar = 9.5 (January 2000), 7.6 (January 1999), 7.2 (March 1998 est.)
Fiscal year: calendar year

Communications

Telephones - main lines in use: 23,578 (2000)
Telephones - mobile cellular: NA
Telephone system:
general assessment: NA
domestic: very inadequate; most telephones are in Asmara; government is seeking international tenders to improve the system
international: NA
Radio broadcast stations: AM 2, FM 1, shortwave 2 (2000)
Radios: 345,000 (1997)
Television broadcast stations: 1 (2000)
Televisions: 1,000 (1997)
Internet country code: .er
Internet Service Providers (ISPs): 4 (2000)
Internet users: 500 (2000)

Transportation

Railways:
total: 317 km
narrow gauge: 317 km 0.950-m gauge (1999)
note: links Ak'ordat and Asmara with the port of Massawa; nonoperational since 1978 except for about a 5 km stretch that was reopened in Massawa in 1994; rehabilitation of the remainder and of the rolling stock is under way
Highways:
total: 3,850 km
paved: 810 km
unpaved: 3,040 km (2000)
Waterways: none
Ports and harbors: Assab (Aseb), Massawa (Mits'iwa)
Merchant marine:
total: 5 ships (1,000 GRT or over) totaling 16,069 GRT/19,549 DWT
ships by type: bulk 1, cargo 1, liquefied gas 1, petroleum tanker 1, roll on/roll off 1 (2000 est.)
Airports: 20 (2000 est.)
Airports - with paved runways:
total: 2
over 3,047 m: 1
2,438 to 3,047 m: 1 (2000 est.)
Airports - with unpaved runways:
total: 18
over 3,047 m: 2
2,438 to 3,047 m: 2
1,524 to 2,437 m: 5
914 to 1,523 m: 7
under 914 m: 2 (2000 est.)

Military

Military branches: Army, Navy, Air Force
Military expenditures - dollar figure: $160 million (2000 est.)
Military expenditures - percent of GDP: 29.4% (2000 est.)

Transnational Issues

Disputes - international: as a result of the 12 December 2000 peace agreement ending a two-year war with Ethiopia, the UN will administer a 25-km wide temporary security zone within Eritrea until a joint boundary commission delimits and demarcates a final boundary

Estonia

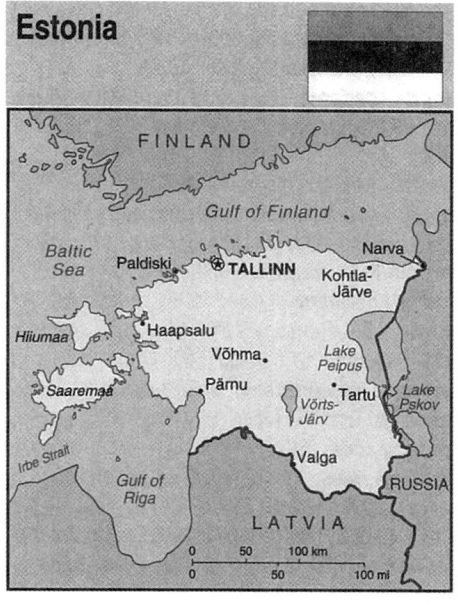

Introduction

Background: After centuries of Swedish and Russian rule, Estonia attained independence in 1918. Forcibly incorporated into the USSR in 1940, it regained its freedom in 1991 with the collapse of the Soviet Union. Since the last Russian troops left in 1994, Estonia has been free to promote economic and political ties with Western Europe.

Geography

Location: Eastern Europe, bordering the Baltic Sea and Gulf of Finland, between Latvia and Russia
Geographic coordinates: 59 00 N, 26 00 E
Map references: Europe
Area:
total: 45,226 sq km
land: 43,211 sq km
water: 2,015 sq km
note: includes 1,520 islands in the Baltic Sea
Area - comparative: slightly smaller than New Hampshire and Vermont combined
Land boundaries:
total: 633 km
border countries: Latvia 339 km, Russia 294 km
Coastline: 3,794 km
Maritime claims:
exclusive economic zone: limits fixed in coordination with neighboring states
territorial sea: 12 NM
Climate: maritime, wet, moderate winters, cool summers
Terrain: marshy, lowlands
Elevation extremes:
lowest point: Baltic Sea 0 m
highest point: Suur Munamagi 318 m
Natural resources: shale oil (kukersite), peat, phosphorite, amber, cambrian blue clay, limestone, dolomite, arable land
Land use:
arable land: 25%
permanent crops: 0%
permanent pastures: 11%
forests and woodland: 44%
other: 20% (1996 est.)
Irrigated land: 110 sq km (1996 est.)
Natural hazards: flooding occurs frequently in the spring
Environment - current issues: air heavily polluted with sulfur dioxide from oil-shale burning power plants in northeast; contamination of soil and groundwater with petroleum products, chemicals at former Soviet military bases; Estonia has more than 1,400 natural and manmade lakes, the smaller of which in agricultural areas are heavily affected by organic waste; coastal sea water is polluted in many locations
Environment - international agreements:
party to: Air Pollution, Air Pollution-Nitrogen Oxides, Air Pollution-Sulphur 85, Air Pollution-Volatile Organic Compounds, Biodiversity, Climate Change, Endangered Species, Hazardous Wastes, Marine Dumping, Ship Pollution, Ozone Layer Protection, Wetlands
signed, but not ratified: Climate Change-Kyoto Protocol

People

Population: 1,423,316 (July 2001 est.)
Age structure:
0-14 years: 17.08% (male 123,997; female 119,166)
15-64 years: 68.14% (male 466,823; female 503,032)
65 years and over: 14.78% (male 68,802; female 141,496) (2001 est.)
Population growth rate: -0.55% (2001 est.)
Birth rate: 8.7 births/1,000 population (2001 est.)
Death rate: 13.48 deaths/1,000 population (2001 est.)
Net migration rate: -0.76 migrant(s)/1,000 population (2001 est.)
Sex ratio:
at birth: 1.05 male(s)/female
under 15 years: 1.04 male(s)/female
15-64 years: 0.93 male(s)/female
65 years and over: 0.49 male(s)/female
total population: 0.86 male(s)/female (2001 est.)
Infant mortality rate: 12.62 deaths/1,000 live births (2001 est.)
Life expectancy at birth:
total population: 69.73 years
male: 63.72 years
female: 76.05 years (2001 est.)
Total fertility rate: 1.21 children born/woman (2001 est.)
HIV/AIDS - adult prevalence rate: 0.04% (1999 est.)
HIV/AIDS - people living with HIV/AIDS: less than 500 (1999 est.)
HIV/AIDS - deaths: less than 100 (1999 est.)
Nationality:
noun: Estonian(s)
adjective: Estonian
Ethnic groups: Estonian 65.1%, Russian 28.1%, Ukrainian 2.5%, Byelorussian 1.5%, Finn 1%, other 1.8% (1998)
Religions: Evangelical Lutheran, Russian Orthodox, Estonian Orthodox, Baptist, Methodist, Seventh-Day Adventist, Roman Catholic, Pentecostal, Word of Life, Jewish
Languages: Estonian (official), Russian, Ukrainian, English, Finnish, other
Literacy:
definition: age 15 and over can read and write
total population: 100%
male: 100%
female: 100% (1998 est.)

Government

Country name:
conventional long form: Republic of Estonia
conventional short form: Estonia
local long form: Eesti Vabariik
local short form: Eesti
former: Estonian Soviet Socialist Republic
Government type: parliamentary democracy
Capital: Tallinn
Administrative divisions: 15 counties (maakonnad, singular - maakond): Harjumaa (Tallinn), Hiiumaa (Kardla), Ida-Virumaa (Johvi), Jarvamaa (Paide), Jogevamaa (Jogeva), Laanemaa (Haapsalu), Laane-Virumaa (Rakvere), Parnumaa (Parnu), Polvamaa (Polva), Raplamaa (Rapla), Saaremaa (Kuessaare), Tartumaa (Tartu), Valgamaa (Valga), Viljandimaa (Viljandi), Vorumaa (Voru)
note: counties have the administrative center name following in parentheses
Independence: 6 September 1991 (from Soviet Union)
National holiday: Independence Day, 24 February (1918); note - 24 February 1918 was the date of independence from Soviet Russia, 6 September 1991 was the date of independence from the Soviet Union
Constitution: adopted 28 June 1992
Legal system: based on civil law system; no judicial review of legislative acts
Suffrage: 18 years of age; universal for all Estonian citizens
Executive branch:
chief of state: President Lennart MERI (since 5 October 1992)
head of government: Prime Minister Mart LAAR (since 29 March 1999)
cabinet: Council of Ministers appointed by the prime minister, approved by Parliament
elections: president elected by Parliament for a five-year term; if he or she does not secure two-thirds of the votes after three rounds of balloting, then an electoral assembly (made up of Parliament plus members of local governments) elects the president, choosing between the two candidates with the largest percentage of votes; election last held August-September 1996 (next to be held in the fall of 2001); prime minister nominated by the president and approved by Parliament

Estonia (continued)

election results: Lennart MERI reelected president by an electoral assembly after Parliament was unable to break a deadlock between MERI and RUUTEL; percent of electoral assembly vote - Lennart MERI 61%, Arnold RUUTEL 39%

Legislative branch: unicameral Parliament or Riigikogu (101 seats; members are elected by popular vote to serve four-year terms)

elections: last held 7 March 1999 (next to be held NA March 2003)

election results: percent of vote by party - NA%; seats by party - Center Party 28, Union of Pro Patria (Fatherland League) 18, Reform Party 18, Moderates 17, Country People's Party (Agrarians) 7, Coalition Party 7, UPPE 6

Judicial branch: National Court (chairman appointed by Parliament for life)

Political parties and leaders: Center Party or K [Edgar SAVISAAR, chairman]; Christian People's Party [Aldo VINKEL]; Coalition Party and Rural Union or KMU [Andrus OOBEL, chairman]; Estonian Democratic Party (formerly Estonian Blue Party) [Jaan LAAS]; Estonian Independence Party [leader NA]; Estonian National Democratic Party or ENDP [leader NA]; Estonian Pensioners and Families Party [Mai TREIAL]; Estonian Progressive Party [Andra VEIDEMANN]; Estonian Republican Party [leader NA]; Estonian Social-Democratic Labor Party [Tiit TOOMSALU]; Estonian Rural People's Union (1999 merger of Estonian Country People's Party and the Estonian Rural Union) [Arvo SIRENDI]; Party of Consolidation Today [leader NA]; People's Party Moderates (1999 merger of People's Party and Moderates) [Andres TARAND]; Reform Party or RE [Siim KALLAS, chairman]; Russian Party in Estonia [Nikolai MASPANOV]; Russian Unity Party [Igor SEDASHEV]; Union of Pro Patria or Fatherland League (Isamaaliit) [Mart LAAR, chairman]; United People's Party or UPPE [Viktor ANDREJEV, chairman]

Political pressure groups and leaders: NA

International organization participation: BIS, CBSS, CCC, CE, EAPC, EBRD, ECE, EU (applicant), FAO, IAEA, IBRD, ICAO, ICFTU, ICRM, IFC, IFRCS, IHO, ILO, IMF, IMO, Interpol, IOC, IOM (observer), ISO (correspondent), ITU, OPCW, OSCE, PFP, UN, UNCTAD, UNESCO, UNMIBH, UNMIK, UNTSO, UPU, WEU (associate partner), WHO, WIPO, WMO, WTrO

Diplomatic representation in the US:
chief of mission: Ambassador Sven JURGENSON
chancery: 2131 Massachusetts Avenue NW, Washington, DC 20008
telephone: [1] (202) 588-0101
FAX: [1] (202) 588-0108
consulate(s) general: New York

Diplomatic representation from the US:
chief of mission: Ambassador Melissa WELLS
embassy: Kentmanni 20, 15099 Tallinn
mailing address: use embassy street address
telephone: [372] 668-8100
FAX: [372] 668-8134

Flag description: pre-1940 flag restored by Supreme Soviet in May 1990 - three equal horizontal bands of blue (top), black, and white

Economy

Economy - overview: In 2000, Estonia rebounded from the Russian financial crisis by scaling back its budget and reorienting trade away from Russian markets into EU member states. After GDP shrank 1.1% in 1999, the economy made a strong recovery in 2000, with growth estimated at 6.4% - the highest in Central and Eastern Europe. Estonia joined the World Trade Organization in November 1999 - the second Baltic state to join - and continues its EU accession talks. For 2001, Estonians predict GDP to grow around 6%, inflation of between 4.2%-5.3%, and a balanced budget. Substantial gains were made in completing privatization of Estonia's few remaining large, state-owned companies in 2000, and this momentum is expected to continue in 2001. Estonia hopes to join the EU during the next round of enlargement tentatively set for 2004.

GDP: purchasing power parity - $14.7 billion (2000 est.)

GDP - real growth rate: 6.4% (2000 est.)

GDP - per capita: purchasing power parity - $10,000 (2000 est.)

GDP - composition by sector:
agriculture: 3.6%
industry: 30.7%
services: 65.7% (1999)

Population below poverty line: 8.9% (1995 est.)

Household income or consumption by percentage share:
lowest 10%: 3.2%
highest 10%: 28.5% (1996)

Inflation rate (consumer prices): 4.1% (1999 est.)

Labor force: 785,500 (1999 est.)

Labor force - by occupation: industry 20%, agriculture 11%, services 69% (1999 est.)

Unemployment rate: 11.7% (1999 est.)

Budget:
revenues: $1.37 billion
expenditures: $1.37 billion, including capital expenditures of $NA (1997 est.)

Industries: oil shale, shipbuilding, phosphates, electric motors, excavators, cement, furniture, clothing, textiles, paper, shoes, apparel

Industrial production growth rate: 5% (2000 est.)

Electricity - production: 7.782 billion kWh (1999)

Electricity - production by source:
fossil fuel: 99.72%
hydro: 0.09%
nuclear: 0%
other: 0.19% (1999)

Electricity - consumption: 6.807 billion kWh (1999)

Electricity - exports: 530 million kWh (1999)

Electricity - imports: 100 million kWh (1999)

Agriculture - products: potatoes, fruits, vegetables; livestock and dairy products; fish

Exports: $3.1 billion (f.o.b., 2000)

Exports - commodities: machinery and equipment 24%, wood products 20%, textiles 17%, food products 9%, metals, chemical products (1999)

Exports - partners: Finland 19.4%, Sweden 18.8%, Russia 9.2%, Latvia 8.7%, Germany 7.5%, US 2.5% (1999)

Imports: $4 billion (f.o.b., 2000)

Imports - commodities: machinery and equipment 31%, chemical products 13%, foodstuffs 11%, metal products 8%, textiles 8% (1999)

Imports - partners: Finland 22.8%, Russia 13.5%, Sweden 9.3%, Germany 9.3%, Japan 4.7% (1999)

Debt - external: $1.6 billion (2000 est.)

Economic aid - recipient: $137.3 million (1995)

Currency: Estonian kroon (EEK)

Currency code: EEK

Exchange rates: krooni per US dollar - 16.663 (January 2001), 16.969 (2000), 14.678 (1999), 14.075 (1998), 13.882 (1997), 12.034 (1996); note - krooni are tied to the German deutsche mark at a fixed rate of 8 to 1

Fiscal year: calendar year

Communications

Telephones - main lines in use: 476,078 (yearend 1998)

Telephones - mobile cellular: 475,000 (yearend 2000)

Telephone system:
general assessment: foreign investment in the form of joint business ventures greatly improved telephone service; Internet services available throughout most of the country; about 150,000 unfilled subscriber requests
domestic: local - the Ministry of Transport and Communications is expanding cellular telephone services to form rural networks; intercity - highly developed fiber-optic backbone (double loop) system presently serving at least 16 major cities (1998)
international: fiber-optic cables to Finland, Sweden, Latvia, and Russia provide worldwide packet-switched service; two international switches are located in Tallinn

Radio broadcast stations: AM 3 (all AM stations inactive since July 1998), FM 82, shortwave 1 (1998)

Radios: 1.01 million (1997)

Television broadcast stations: 31 (plus five repeaters) (September 1995)

Televisions: 605,000 (1997)

Internet country code: .ee

Internet Service Providers (ISPs): 28 (2000)

Internet users: 309,000 (2000)

Transportation

Railways:
total: 1,018 km common carrier lines only; does not include dedicated industrial lines
broad gauge: 1,018 km 1.520-m gauge (132 km electrified) (1995)

Highways:
total: 30,300 km

Estonia (continued)

paved: 29,200 km (including 75 km of expressways); note - these roads are said to be hard-surfaced, and include, in addition to conventionally paved roads, some that are surfaced with gravel or other coarse aggregate, making them trafficable in all weather
unpaved: 1,100 km (2000)
Waterways: 320 km (perennially navigable)
Pipelines: natural gas 420 km (1992)
Ports and harbors: Haapsalu, Kunda, Muuga, Paldiski, Parnu, Tallinn
Merchant marine:
total: 44 ships (1,000 GRT or over) totaling 253,460 GRT/219,727 DWT
ships by type: bulk 2, cargo 19, combination bulk 1, container 5, petroleum tanker 1, roll on/roll off 10, short-sea passenger 6 (2000 est.)
Airports: 32 (2000 est.)
Airports - with paved runways:
total: 8
2,438 to 3,047 m: 7
under 914 m: 1 (2000 est.)
Airports - with unpaved runways:
total: 24
over 3,047 m: 1
2,438 to 3,047 m: 5
1,524 to 2,437 m: 7
914 to 1,523 m: 5
under 914 m: 6 (2000 est.)

Military

Military branches: Ground Forces, Navy/Coast Guard, Air and Air Defense Force (not officially sanctioned), Maritime Border Guard, Volunteer Defense League (Kaitseliit), Security Forces (internal and border troops)
Military manpower - military age: 18 years of age
Military manpower - availability:
males age 15-49: 359,677 (2001 est.)
Military manpower - fit for military service:
males age 15-49: 282,418 (2001 est.)
Military manpower - reaching military age annually:
males: 11,164 (2001 est.)
Military expenditures - dollar figure: $70 million (FY99)
Military expenditures - percent of GDP: 1.2% (FY99)

Transnational Issues

Disputes - international: Estonian and Russian negotiators reached a technical border agreement in December 1996 which has not been signed nor ratified by Russia as of February 2001
Illicit drugs: transshipment point for opiates and cannabis from Southwest Asia and the Caucasus via Russia, cocaine from Latin America to Western Europe and Scandinavia, and synthetic drugs from Western Europe to Scandinavia; possible precursor manufacturing and/or trafficking; synthetic drug production growing, trafficked to Russia, Baltics, Finland

Ethiopia

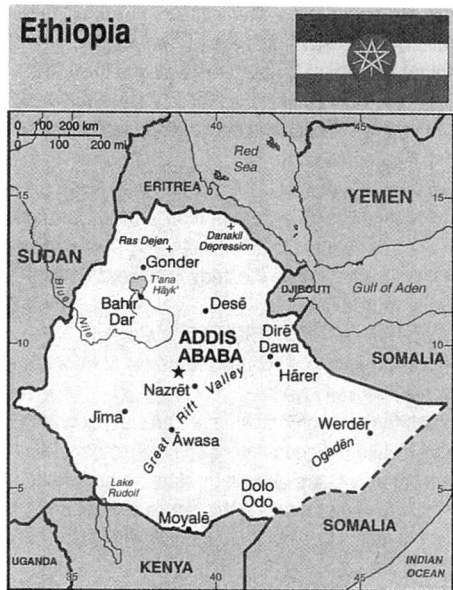

Introduction

Background: Unique among African countries, the ancient Ethiopian monarchy maintained its freedom from colonial rule, one exception being the Italian occupation of 1936-41. In 1974 a military junta, the Derg, deposed Emperor Haile SELASSIE (who had ruled since 1930) and established a socialist state. Torn by bloody coups, uprisings, wide-scale drought, and massive refugee problems, the regime was finally toppled by a coalition of rebel forces, the Ethiopian People's Revolutionary Democratic Front (EPRDF), in 1991. A constitution was adopted in 1994 and Ethiopia's first multiparty elections were held in 1995. A two and a half year border war with Eritrea that ended with a peace treaty on 12 December 2000 has strengthened the ruling coalition, but has hurt the nation's economy.

Geography

Location: Eastern Africa, west of Somalia
Geographic coordinates: 8 00 N, 38 00 E
Map references: Africa
Area:
total: 1,127,127 sq km
land: 1,119,683 sq km
water: 7,444 sq km
Area - comparative: slightly less than twice the size of Texas
Land boundaries:
total: 5,311 km
border countries: Djibouti 337 km, Eritrea 912 km, Kenya 830 km, Somalia 1,626 km, Sudan 1,606 km
Coastline: 0 km (landlocked)
Maritime claims: none (landlocked)
Climate: tropical monsoon with wide topographic-induced variation
Terrain: high plateau with central mountain range divided by Great Rift Valley
Elevation extremes:
lowest point: Denakil Depression -125 m
highest point: Ras Dejen 4,620 m
Natural resources: small reserves of gold, platinum, copper, potash, natural gas, hydropower
Land use:
arable land: 12%
permanent crops: 1%
permanent pastures: 40%
forests and woodland: 25%
other: 22% (1993 est.)
Irrigated land: 1,900 sq km (1993 est.)
Natural hazards: geologically active Great Rift Valley susceptible to earthquakes, volcanic eruptions; frequent droughts
Environment - current issues: deforestation; overgrazing; soil erosion; desertification
Environment - international agreements:
party to: Biodiversity, Climate Change, Desertification, Endangered Species, Hazardous Wastes, Marine Dumping, Ozone Layer Protection, Ship Pollution
signed, but not ratified: Environmental Modification, Law of the Sea, Nuclear Test Ban
Geography - note: landlocked - entire coastline along the Red Sea was lost with the de jure independence of Eritrea on 24 May 1993

People

Population: 65,891,874
note: estimates for this country explicitly take into account the effects of excess mortality due to AIDS; this can result in lower life expectancy, higher infant mortality and death rates, lower population and growth rates, and changes in the distribution of population by age and sex than would otherwise be expected (July 2001 est.)
Age structure:
0-14 years: 47.18% (male 15,647,675; female 15,442,348)
15-64 years: 50.03% (male 16,584,765; female 16,378,060)
65 years and over: 2.79% (male 834,825; female 1,004,201) (2001 est.)
Population growth rate: 2.7% (2001 est.)
Birth rate: 44.68 births/1,000 population (2001 est.)
Death rate: 17.84 deaths/1,000 population (2001 est.)
Net migration rate: 0.13 migrant(s)/1,000 population (2001 est.)
note: repatriation of Ethiopians who fled to Sudan for refuge from war and famine in earlier years is expected to continue for several years; small numbers of Sudanese and Somali refugees, who fled to Ethiopia from the fighting or famine in their own countries, continue to return to their homes
Sex ratio:
at birth: 1.03 male(s)/female
under 15 years: 1.01 male(s)/female
15-64 years: 1.01 male(s)/female
65 years and over: 0.83 male(s)/female
total population: 1.01 male(s)/female (2001 est.)
Infant mortality rate: 99.96 deaths/1,000 live births (2001 est.)

Ethiopia (continued)

Life expectancy at birth:
total population: 44.68 years
male: 43.88 years
female: 45.51 years (2001 est.)
Total fertility rate: 7 children born/woman (2001 est.)
HIV/AIDS - adult prevalence rate: 10.63% (1999 est.)
HIV/AIDS - people living with HIV/AIDS: 3 million (1999 est.)
HIV/AIDS - deaths: 280,000 (1999 est.)
Nationality:
noun: Ethiopian(s)
adjective: Ethiopian
Ethnic groups: Oromo 40%, Amhara and Tigre 32%, Sidamo 9%, Shankella 6%, Somali 6%, Afar 4%, Gurage 2%, other 1%
Religions: Muslim 45%-50%, Ethiopian Orthodox 35%-40%, animist 12%, other 3%-8%
Languages: Amharic, Tigrinya, Oromigna, Guaragigna, Somali, Arabic, other local languages, English (major foreign language taught in schools)
Literacy:
definition: age 15 and over can read and write
total population: 35.5%
male: 45.5%
female: 25.3% (1995 est.)

Government

Country name:
conventional long form: Federal Democratic Republic of Ethiopia
conventional short form: Ethiopia
local long form: Ityop'iya Federalawi Demokrasiyawi Ripeblik
local short form: Ityop'iya
former: Abyssinia, Italian East Africa
abbreviation: FDRE
Government type: federal republic
Capital: Addis Ababa
Administrative divisions: 9 ethnically-based states (kililoch, singular - kilil) and 2 self-governing administrations* (astedaderoch, singular - astedader): Adis Abeba* (Addis Ababa); Afar; Amara, Binshangul Gumuz; Dire Dawa*; Gambela Hizboch; Hareri Hizb; Oromiya; Sumale; Tigray; YeDebub Biheroch Biheresboch na Hizboch (Southern Nations, Nationalities, and Peoples Region)
Independence: oldest independent country in Africa and one of the oldest in the world - at least 2,000 years
National holiday: National Day (defeat of MENGISTU regime), 28 May (1991)
Constitution: ratified December 1994; effective 22 August 1995
Legal system: currently transitional mix of national and regional courts
Suffrage: 18 years of age; universal
Executive branch:
chief of state: President NEGASSO Gidada (since 22 August 1995)
head of government: Prime Minister MELES Zenawi (since NA August 1995)
cabinet: Council of Ministers as provided for in the December 1994 constitution; ministers are selected by the prime minister and approved by the House of People's Representatives
elections: president elected by the House of People's Representatives for a six-year term; election last held NA June 1995 (next to be held NA May 2001); prime minister designated by the party in power following legislative elections
election results: NEGASSO Gidada elected president; percent of vote by the House of People's Representatives - NA%
Legislative branch: bicameral Parliament consists of the House of Federation or upper chamber (108 seats; members are chosen by state assemblies to serve five-year terms) and the House of People's Representatives or lower chamber (548 seats; members are directly elected by popular vote from single-member districts to serve five-year terms)
elections: last held 14 May 2000 (next to be held NA May 2005)
election results: percent of vote - NA%; seats - OPDO 177, ANDM 134, TPLF 38, WGGPDO 27, EPRDF 19, SPDO 18, GNDM 15, KSPDO 10, ANDP 8, GPRDF 7, SOPDM 7, BGPDUF 6, BMPDO 5, KAT 4, other regional political groupings 22, independents 8; note - 43 seats unconfirmed
note: irregularities and violence at a number of polling stations necessitated the rescheduling of voting in certain constituencies; voting postponed in Somali regional state because of severe drought
Judicial branch: Federal Supreme Court (the president and vice president of the Federal Supreme Court are recommended by the prime minister and appointed by the House of People's Representatives; for other federal judges, the prime minister submits to the House of People's Representatives for appointment candidates selected by the Federal Judicial Administrative Council)
Political parties and leaders: Afar National Democratic Party or ANDP [leader NA]; All-Amhara People's Organization or AAPO [KEGNAZ MATCH Neguea Tibeb]; Amhara National Democratic Movement or ANDM [TEFERA Walwa]; Bench Madji People's Democratic Organization or BMPDO [leader NA]; Benishangul Gumuz People's Democratic Unity Front or BGPDUF [leader NA]; Coalition of Alternative Forces for Peace and Democracy or CAFPD [Kifle TIGNEH Abate and BEYENE Petros]; Ethiopian Democratic Unity Party or EDUP [Lt. Gen. TESFAYE Gebre Kidan]; Ethiopian National Democratic Party or ENDP [FEKADU Gedamu]; Ethiopian People's Revolutionary Democratic Front or EPRDF [MELES Zenawi] (an alliance of the ANDM, OPDO, and TPLF); Gedeyo People's Revolutionary Democratic Movement or GPRDF [leader NA]; Gurange Nationalities Democratic Movement or GNDM [leader NA]; Kafa Shaka People's Democratic Organization or KSPDO [leader NA]; Kembata, Alabaa, and Tembaro or KAT [leader NA]; Oromo Liberation Front or OLF [DAOUD Ibsa Gudina]; Oromo People's Democratic Organization or OPDO [KUMA Demeksa]; Sidama People's Democratic Organization or SPDO [leader NA]; South Omo People's Democratic Movement or SOPDM [leader NA]; Tigrai People's Liberation Front or TPLF [MELES Zenawi]; Walayta, Gamo, Gofa, Dawro, Konta People's Democratic Organization or WGGPDO [leader NA]; dozens of small parties
Political pressure groups and leaders: Southern Ethiopia People's Democratic Coalition; numerous small, ethnically based groups have formed since the defeat of the former MENGISTU regime in 1991, including several Islamic militant groups
International organization participation: ACP, AfDB, CCC, ECA, FAO, G-24, G-77, IAEA, IBRD, ICAO, ICRM, IDA, IFAD, IFC, IFRCS, IGAD, ILO, IMF, IMO, Intelsat, Interpol, IOC, IOM (observer), ISO, ITU, NAM, OAU, OPCW, UN, UNCTAD, UNESCO, UNHCR, UNIDO, UNU, UPU, WFTU, WHO, WIPO, WMO, WToO
Diplomatic representation in the US:
chief of mission: Ambassador (vacant)
chancery: 3506 International Drive NW, Washington, DC 20008
telephone: [1] (202) 364-1200
FAX: [1] (202) 686-9857
Diplomatic representation from the US:
chief of mission: Ambassador Tibor P. NAGY, Jr.
embassy: Entoto Street, Addis Ababa
mailing address: P. O. Box 1014, Addis Ababa
telephone: [251] (1) 550666
FAX: [251] (1) 551328
Flag description: three equal horizontal bands of green (top), yellow, and red with a yellow pentagram and single yellow rays emanating from the angles between the points on a light blue disk centered on the three bands; Ethiopia is the oldest independent country in Africa, and the colors of her flag were so often adopted by other African countries upon independence that they became known as the pan-African colors

Economy

Economy - overview: Ethiopia's economy is based on agriculture, which accounts for half of GDP, 90% of exports, and 80% of total employment. The agricultural sector suffers from frequent periods of drought and poor cultivation practices, and as many as 4.6 million people need food assistance annually. Coffee is critical to the Ethiopian economy, and Ethiopia earned $267 million in 1999 by exporting 105,000 metric tons. According to current estimates, coffee contributes 10% of Ethiopia's GDP. More than 15 million people (25% of the population) derive their livelihood from the coffee sector. Other exports include live animals, hides, gold, and qat. In December 1999, Ethiopia signed a $1.4 billion joint venture deal to develop a huge natural gas field in the Somali Regional State. The war with Eritrea forced the government to spend scarce resources on the military and to scale back ambitious development plans. Foreign investment has declined significantly.

Ethiopia (continued)

Government taxes imposed in late 1999 to raise money for the war depressed an already weak economy. The war forced the government to improve roads and other parts of the previously neglected infrastructure, but only certain regions of the nation benefited. Recovery from the war is mostly contingent on natural factors. A drought has continued into the end of 2000 and food relief is expected to be needed through mid-2001 at least. Ethiopia may receive Highly Indebted Poor Countries (HIPC) debt relief by the end of the year.

GDP: purchasing power parity - $39.2 billion (2000 est.)
GDP - real growth rate: 2% (2000 est.)
GDP - per capita: purchasing power parity - $600 (2000 est.)
GDP - composition by sector:
agriculture: 45%
industry: 12%
services: 43% (1999 est.)
Population below poverty line: NA%
Household income or consumption by percentage share:
lowest 10%: 3%
highest 10%: 33.7% (1995)
Inflation rate (consumer prices): 5% (2000 est.)
Labor force: NA
Labor force - by occupation: agriculture and animal husbandry 80%, government and services 12%, industry and construction 8% (1985)
Unemployment rate: NA%
Budget:
revenues: $1 billion
expenditures: $1.48 billion, including capital expenditures of $415 million (FY96/97)
Industries: food processing, beverages, textiles, chemicals, metals processing, cement
Industrial production growth rate: NA%
Electricity - production: 1.625 billion kWh (1999)
Electricity - production by source:
fossil fuel: 3.08%
hydro: 96.92%
nuclear: 0%
other: 0% (1999)
Electricity - consumption: 1.511 billion kWh (1999)
Electricity - exports: 0 kWh (1999)
Electricity - imports: 0 kWh (1999)
Agriculture - products: cereals, pulses, coffee, oilseed, sugarcane, potatoes, qat; hides, cattle, sheep, goats
Exports: $460 million (f.o.b., 1999)
Exports - commodities: coffee, gold, leather products, oilseeds, qat
Exports - partners: Germany 16%, Japan 13%, Djibouti 10%, Saudi Arabia 7% (1999 est.)
Imports: $1.25 billion (f.o.b., 1999)
Imports - commodities: food and live animals, petroleum and petroleum products, chemicals, machinery, motor vehicles
Imports - partners: Saudi Arabia 28%, Italy 10%, Russia 7%, US 6% (1999 est.)
Debt - external: $10 billion (1999 est.)
Economic aid - recipient: $367 million (FY95/96)
Currency: birr (ETB)
Currency code: ETB
Exchange rates: birr per US dollar (end of period) - 8.3140 (December 2000), 8.3140 (2000), 8.1340 (1999), 7.5030 (1998), 6.8640 (1997), 6.4260 (1996)
note: since May 1993, the birr market rate has been determined in an interbank market supported by weekly wholesale auction
Fiscal year: 8 July - 7 July

Communications

Telephones - main lines in use: 157,000 (1997)
Telephones - mobile cellular: 4,000 (1999)
Telephone system:
general assessment: open wire and microwave radio relay system adequate for government use
domestic: open wire; microwave radio relay; radio communication in the HF, VHF, and UHF frequencies; two domestic satellites provide the national trunk service
international: open wire to Sudan and Djibouti; microwave radio relay to Kenya and Djibouti; satellite earth stations - 3 Intelsat (1 Atlantic Ocean and 2 Pacific Ocean)
Radio broadcast stations: AM 5, FM 0, shortwave 2 (1999)
Radios: 11.75 million (1997)
Television broadcast stations: 25 (1999)
Televisions: 320,000 (1997)
Internet country code: .et
Internet Service Providers (ISPs): 1 (2000)
Internet users: 7,200 (1999)

Transportation

Railways:
total: 681 km (Ethiopian segment of the Addis Ababa-Djibouti railroad)
narrow gauge: 681 km 1.000-m gauge
note: in April 1998, Djibouti and Ethiopia announced plans to revitalize the century-old railroad that links their capitals; since May 1998 Ethiopia has expended considerable effort to repair and maintain the lines
Highways:
total: 24,145 km
paved: 3,290 km
unpaved: 20,855 km (1998)
Waterways: none
Ports and harbors: none; Ethiopia is landlocked and was by agreement with Eritrea using the ports of Assab and Massawa; since the border dispute with Eritrea flared, Ethiopia has used the port of Djibouti for nearly all of its imports
Merchant marine:
total: 11 ships (1,000 GRT or over) totaling 85,382 GRT/108,526 DWT
ships by type: cargo 6, container 1, petroleum tanker 1, roll on/roll off 3 (2000 est.)
Airports: 86 (2000 est.)
Airports - with paved runways:
total: 12
over 3,047 m: 3
2,438 to 3,047 m: 5
1,524 to 2,437 m: 3
914 to 1,523 m: 1 (2000 est.)
Airports - with unpaved runways:
total: 74
over 3,047 m: 2
2,438 to 3,047 m: 7
1,524 to 2,437 m: 10
914 to 1,523 m: 35
under 914 m: 20 (2000 est.)

Military

Military branches: Ground Forces, Air Force, Police, Militia
note: Ethiopia is landlocked and has no navy; following the independence of Eritrea, Ethiopian naval facilities remained in Eritrean possession and ships which belonged to the former Ethiopian Navy and based at Djibouti have been sold
Military manpower - military age: 18 years of age
Military manpower - availability:
males age 15-49: 14,537,884 (2001 est.)
Military manpower - fit for military service:
males age 15-49: 7,581,815 (2001 est.)
Military manpower - reaching military age annually:
males: 703,625 (2001 est.)
Military expenditures - dollar figure: $138 million (FY98/99)
Military expenditures - percent of GDP: 2.5% (FY98/99)

Transnational Issues

Disputes - international: most of the southern half of the boundary with Somalia is a Provisional Administrative Line; as a result of the 12 December 2000 peace agreement ending a two year war with Eritrea, the UN will administer a 25-km wide temporary security zone within Eritrea until a joint boundary commission delimits and demarcates a final boundary; dispute over alignment of boundary with Eritrea led to armed conflict in 1998; a peace accord signed in December 2000 provides for UN-assisted arbitration and demarcation of the border
Illicit drugs: transit hub for heroin originating in Southwest and Southeast Asia and destined for Europe and North America as well as cocaine destined for markets in southern Africa; cultivates qat (khat) for local use and regional export, principally to Djibouti and Somalia

Europa Island
(possession of France)

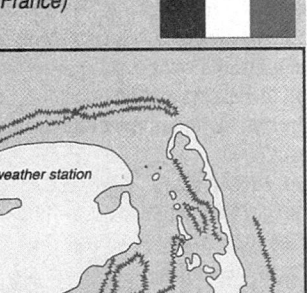

Introduction

Background: A French possession since 1897, the island is heavily wooded; it is the site of a small military garrison that staffs a weather station.

Geography

Location: Southern Africa, island in the Mozambique Channel, about one-half of the way from southern Madagascar to southern Mozambique
Geographic coordinates: 22 20 S, 40 22 E
Map references: Africa
Area:
total: 28 sq km
land: 28 sq km
water: 0 sq km
Area - comparative: about 0.16 times the size of Washington, DC
Land boundaries: 0 km
Coastline: 22.2 km
Maritime claims:
exclusive economic zone: 200 NM
territorial sea: 12 NM
Climate: tropical
Terrain: low and flat
Elevation extremes:
lowest point: Indian Ocean 0 m
highest point: unnamed location 24 m
Natural resources: NEGL
Land use:
arable land: 0%
permanent crops: 0%
permanent pastures: 0%
forests and woodland: 100%
other: 0%
Irrigated land: 0 sq km (1993)
Natural hazards: NA
Environment - current issues: NA
Geography - note: wildlife sanctuary

People

Population: no indigenous inhabitants
note: there is a small French military garrison (July 2001 est.)

Government

Country name:
conventional long form: none
conventional short form: Europa Island
local long form: none
local short form: Ile Europa
Dependency status: possession of France; administered by a high commissioner of the Republic, resident in Reunion
Legal system: the laws of France, where applicable, apply
Flag description: the flag of France is used

Economy

Economy - overview: no economic activity

Communications

Communications - note: 1 meteorological station

Transportation

Waterways: none
Ports and harbors: none; offshore anchorage only
Airports: 1 (2000 est.)
Airports - with unpaved runways:
total: 1
914 to 1,523 m: 1 (2000 est.)

Military

Military - note: defense is the responsibility of France

Transnational Issues

Disputes - international: claimed by Madagascar

Falkland Islands
(Islas Malvinas)
(overseas territory of the UK; also claimed by Argentina)

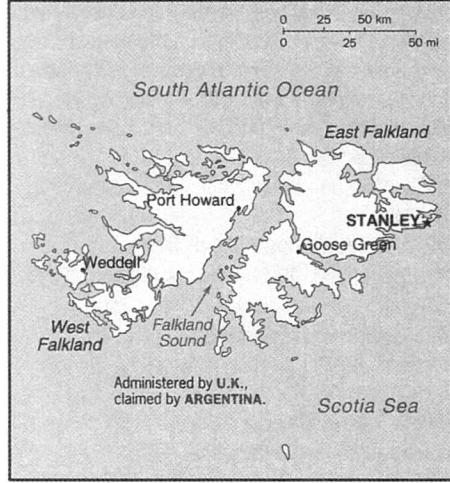

Introduction

Background: Although first sighted by an English navigator in 1592, the first landing (English) did not occur until almost a century later in 1690, and the first settlement (French) was not established until 1764. The colony was turned over to Spain two years later and the islands have since been the subject of a territorial dispute, first between Britain and Spain, then between Britain and Argentina. The UK asserted its claim to the islands by establishing a naval garrison there in 1833. Argentina invaded the islands on 2 April 1982. The British responded with an expeditionary force that landed seven weeks later and after fierce fighting forced Argentine surrender on 14 June 1982.

Geography

Location: Southern South America, islands in the South Atlantic Ocean, east of southern Argentina
Geographic coordinates: 51 45 S, 59 00 W
Map references: South America
Area:
total: 12,173 sq km
land: 12,173 sq km
water: 0 sq km
note: includes the two main islands of East and West Falkland and about 200 small islands
Area - comparative: slightly smaller than Connecticut
Land boundaries: 0 km
Coastline: 1,288 km
Maritime claims:
continental shelf: 200 NM
exclusive fishing zone: 200 NM
territorial sea: 12 NM
Climate: cold marine; strong westerly winds, cloudy, humid; rain occurs on more than half of days in year; occasional snow all year, except in January and February, but does not accumulate

Falkland Islands (Islas Malvinas)
(continued)

Terrain: rocky, hilly, mountainous with some boggy, undulating plains
Elevation extremes:
lowest point: Atlantic Ocean 0 m
highest point: Mount Usborne 705 m
Natural resources: fish, wildlife
Land use:
arable land: 0%
permanent crops: 0%
permanent pastures: 99%
forests and woodland: 0%
other: 1% (1993 est.)
Irrigated land: NA sq km
Natural hazards: strong winds persist throughout the year
Environment - current issues: NA
Geography - note: deeply indented coast provides good natural harbors; short growing season

People

Population: 2,895 (July 2001 est.)
Age structure:
0-14 years: NA%
15-64 years: NA%
65 years and over: NA%
Population growth rate: 2.43% (2001 est.)
Birth rate: NA births/1,000 population
Death rate: NA deaths/1,000 population
Net migration rate: NA migrant(s)/1,000 population
Infant mortality rate: NA deaths/1,000 live births
Life expectancy at birth:
total population: NA years
male: NA years
female: NA years
Total fertility rate: NA children born/woman
HIV/AIDS - adult prevalence rate: NA%
HIV/AIDS - people living with HIV/AIDS: NA
HIV/AIDS - deaths: NA
Nationality:
noun: Falkland Islander(s)
adjective: Falkland Island
Ethnic groups: British
Religions: primarily Anglican, Roman Catholic, United Free Church, Evangelist Church, Jehovah's Witnesses, Lutheran, Seventh-Day Adventist
Languages: English

Government

Country name:
conventional long form: none
conventional short form: Falkland Islands (Islas Malvinas)
Dependency status: overseas territory of the UK, also claimed by Argentina
Government type: NA
Capital: Stanley
Administrative divisions: none (overseas territory of the UK; also claimed by Argentina)
Independence: none (overseas territory of the UK; also claimed by Argentina)
National holiday: Liberation Day, 14 June (1982)
Constitution: 3 October 1985; amended 1997 and 1998
Legal system: English common law
Suffrage: 18 years of age; universal
Executive branch:
chief of state: Queen ELIZABETH II (since 6 February 1952)
head of government: Governor Donald LAMONT (since NA May 1999); Chief Executive A. M. GURR (since NA); Financial Secretary D. F. HOWATT (since NA)
cabinet: Executive Council; three members elected by the Legislative Council, two ex officio members (chief executive and the financial secretary), and the governor
elections: none; the monarch is hereditary; governor appointed by the monarch
Legislative branch: unicameral Legislative Council (10 seats - 2 ex officio, 8 elected by popular vote, members serve four-year terms) presided over by the governor
elections: last held 9 October 1997 (next to be held NA October 2001)
election results: percent of vote - NA%; seats - independents 8
Judicial branch: Supreme Court (chief justice is a nonresident); Magistrates Court (senior magistrate presides over civil and criminal divisions)
Political parties and leaders: none; all independents
Political pressure groups and leaders: none
International organization participation: ICFTU
Diplomatic representation in the US: none (overseas territory of the UK; also claimed by Argentina)
Diplomatic representation from the US: none (overseas territory of the UK; also claimed by Argentina)
Flag description: blue with the flag of the UK in the upper hoist-side quadrant and the Falkland Island coat of arms in a white disk centered on the outer half of the flag; the coat of arms contains a white ram (sheep raising is the major economic activity) above the sailing ship Desire (whose crew discovered the islands) with a scroll at the bottom bearing the motto DESIRE THE RIGHT

Economy

Economy - overview: The economy was formerly based on agriculture, mainly sheep farming, but today fishing contributes the bulk of economic activity. In 1987 the government began selling fishing licenses to foreign trawlers operating within the Falklands exclusive fishing zone. These license fees total more than $40 million per year, which goes to support the island's health, education, and welfare system. Squid accounts for 75% of the fish taken. Dairy farming supports domestic consumption; crops furnish winter fodder. Exports feature shipments of high-grade wool to the UK and the sale of postage stamps and coins. To encourage tourism, the Falkland Islands Development Corporation has built three lodges for visitors attracted by the abundant wildlife and trout fishing. The islands are now self-financing except for defense. The British Geological Survey announced a 200-mile oil exploration zone around the islands in 1993, and early seismic surveys suggest substantial reserves capable of producing 500,000 barrels per day; to date no exploitable site has been identified. An agreement between Argentina and the UK in 1995 seeks to defuse licensing and sovereignty conflicts that would dampen foreign interest in exploiting potential oil reserves.
GDP: purchasing power parity - $52 million (FY95/96 est.)
GDP - real growth rate: 1% (FY95/96 est.)
GDP - per capita: purchasing power parity - $19,000 (FY95/96 est.)
GDP - composition by sector:
agriculture: NA%
industry: NA%
services: NA%
Population below poverty line: NA%
Household income or consumption by percentage share:
lowest 10%: NA%
highest 10%: NA%
Inflation rate (consumer prices): 3.6% (1998)
Labor force: 1,100 (est.)
Labor force - by occupation: agriculture 95% (mostly sheepherding and fishing)
Unemployment rate: full employment; labor shortage
Budget:
revenues: $66.2 million
expenditures: $67.9 million, including capital expenditures of $23.2 million (FY98/99 est.)
Industries: wool and fish processing; sale of stamps and coins
Industrial production growth rate: NA%
Electricity - production: 12 million kWh (1999)
Electricity - production by source:
fossil fuel: 100%
hydro: 0%
nuclear: 0%
other: 0% (1999)
Electricity - consumption: 11.2 million kWh (1999)
Electricity - exports: 0 kWh (1999)
Electricity - imports: 0 kWh (1999)
Agriculture - products: fodder and vegetable crops; sheep, dairy products
Exports: $7.6 million (1995)
Exports - commodities: wool, hides, meat
Exports - partners: UK, Japan, Chile, NZ
Imports: $24.7 million (1995)
Imports - commodities: fuel, food and drink, building materials, clothing
Imports - partners: UK, Japan, Chile, NZ
Debt - external: $NA
Economic aid - recipient: $1.7 million (1995)
Currency: Falkland pound (FKP)
Currency code: FKP

Falkland Islands (Islas Malvinas)
(continued)

Exchange rates: Falkland pounds per US dollar - 0.6764 (January 2001), 0.6596 (2000), 0.6180 (1999), 0.6037 (1998), 0.6106 (1997), 0.6403 (1996); note - the Falkland pound is at par with the British pound
Fiscal year: 1 April - 31 March

Communications

Telephones - main lines in use: NA
Telephones - mobile cellular: NA
Telephone system:
general assessment: NA
domestic: government-operated radiotelephone and private VHF/CB radiotelephone networks provide effective service to almost all points on both islands
international: satellite earth station - 1 Intelsat (Atlantic Ocean) with links through London to other countries
Radio broadcast stations: AM 1, FM 7, shortwave 0 (1998)
Radios: 1,000 (1997)
Television broadcast stations: 2 (operated by the British Forces Broadcasting Service) (1997)
Televisions: 1,000 (1997)
Internet country code: .fk
Internet Service Providers (ISPs): 2 (2000)
Internet users: NA

Transportation

Railways: 0 km
Highways:
total: 440 km
paved: 50 km
unpaved: 390 km
Waterways: none
Ports and harbors: Stanley
Merchant marine: none (2000 est.)
Airports: 5 (2000 est.)
Airports - with paved runways:
total: 2
2,438 to 3,047 m: 1
under 914 m: 1 (2000 est.)
Airports - with unpaved runways:
total: 3
under 914 m: 3 (2000 est.)

Military

Military branches: British Forces Falkland Islands (includes Army, Royal Air Force, Royal Navy, and Royal Marines), Police Force
Military expenditures - dollar figure: $NA
Military expenditures - percent of GDP: NA%
Military - note: defense is the responsibility of the UK

Transnational Issues

Disputes - international: claimed by Argentina

Faroe Islands
(part of the Kingdom of Denmark)

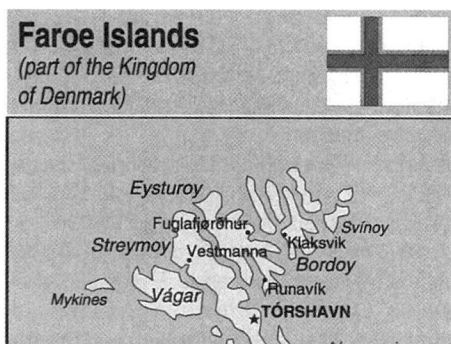

Introduction

Background: The population of the Faroe Islands is largely descended from Viking settlers who arrived in the 9th century. The islands have been connected politically to Denmark since the 14th century. A high degree of self-government was attained in 1948.

Geography

Location: Northern Europe, island group between the Norwegian Sea and the North Atlantic Ocean, about one-half of the way from Iceland to Norway
Geographic coordinates: 62 00 N, 7 00 W
Map references: Europe
Area:
total: 1,399 sq km
land: 1,399 sq km
water: 0 sq km (some lakes and streams)
Area - comparative: eight times the size of Washington, DC
Land boundaries: 0 km
Coastline: 1,117 km
Maritime claims:
exclusive fishing zone: 200 NM
territorial sea: 3 NM
Climate: mild winters, cool summers; usually overcast; foggy, windy
Terrain: rugged, rocky, some low peaks; cliffs along most of coast
Elevation extremes:
lowest point: Atlantic Ocean 0 m
highest point: Slaettaratindur 882 m
Natural resources: fish, whales, hydropower
Land use:
arable land: 6%
permanent crops: 0%
permanent pastures: 0%
forests and woodland: 0%
other: 94% (1996)
Irrigated land: 0 sq km
Natural hazards: NA
Environment - current issues: NA
Geography - note: archipelago of 17 inhabited islands and one uninhabited island, and a few uninhabited islets; strategically located along important sea lanes in northeastern Atlantic; precipitous terrain limits habitation to small coastal lowlands

People

Population: 45,661 (July 2001 est.)
Age structure:
0-14 years: 22.62% (male 5,193; female 5,136)
15-64 years: 63.64% (male 15,463; female 13,596)
65 years and over: 13.74% (male 2,802; female 3,471) (2001 est.)
Population growth rate: 0.78% (2001 est.)
Birth rate: 13.64 births/1,000 population (2001 est.)
Death rate: 8.69 deaths/1,000 population (2001 est.)
Net migration rate: 2.89 migrant(s)/1,000 population (2001 est.)
Sex ratio:
at birth: 1 male(s)/female
under 15 years: 1.01 male(s)/female
15-64 years: 1.14 male(s)/female
65 years and over: 0.81 male(s)/female
total population: 1.06 male(s)/female (2001 est.)
Infant mortality rate: 6.8 deaths/1,000 live births (2001 est.)
Life expectancy at birth:
total population: 78.59 years
male: 75.12 years
female: 82.06 years
Total fertility rate: 2.3 children born/woman (2001 est.)
HIV/AIDS - adult prevalence rate: NA%
HIV/AIDS - people living with HIV/AIDS: NA
HIV/AIDS - deaths: NA
Nationality:
noun: Faroese (singular and plural)
adjective: Faroese
Ethnic groups: Scandinavian
Religions: Evangelical Lutheran
Languages: Faroese (derived from Old Norse), Danish
Literacy:
definition: NA
total population: NA%
male: NA%
female: NA%
note: similar to Denmark proper

Government

Country name:
conventional long form: none
conventional short form: Faroe Islands
local long form: none
local short form: Foroyar
Dependency status: part of the Kingdom of Denmark; self-governing overseas administrative division of Denmark since 1948

Faroe Islands (continued)

Government type: NA
Capital: Torshavn
Administrative divisions: none (part of the Kingdom of Denmark; self-governing overseas administrative division of Denmark); there are no first-order administrative divisions as defined by the US Government, but there are 49 municipalities
Independence: none (part of the Kingdom of Denmark; self-governing overseas administrative division of Denmark)
National holiday: Olaifest, 29 July
Constitution: 5 June 1953 (Danish constitution)
Legal system: Danish
Suffrage: 18 years of age; universal
Executive branch:
chief of state: Queen MARGRETHE II of Denmark (since 14 January 1972), represented by High Commissioner Ms. Vibeke LARSEN, chief administrative officer (since NA)
head of government: Prime Minister Anfinn KALLSBERG (since 15 May 1998)
cabinet: Landsstyri appointed by the prime minister
elections: the monarch is hereditary; high commissioner appointed by the monarch; following legislative elections, the leader of the party that wins the most seats is usually elected prime minister by the Faroese Parliament; election last held 30 April 1998 (next to be held no later than April 2002)
election results: Anfinn KALLSBERG elected prime minister; percent of parliamentary vote - NA%
note: coalition of People's Party, Republican Party and Home Rule Party
Legislative branch: unicameral Faroese Parliament or Logting (32 seats; members are elected by popular vote on a proportional basis from the seven constituencies to serve four-year terms)
elections: last held 30 April 1998 (next to be held not later than April 2002)
election results: percent of vote by party - Republican Party 23.8%, People's Party 21.3%, Social Democratic Party 21.9%, Union Party 18%, Home Rue Party 7.7%, Center Party 4.1%; seats by party - Republican Party 8, People's Party 8, Social Democratic Party 7, Union Party 6, Home Rule Party 2, Center Party 1
note: election of 2 seats to the Danish Parliament was last held on 11 March 1998 (next to be held not later than March 2002); results - percent of vote by party - NA; seats by party - Social Democratic Party 1, People's Party 1
Judicial branch: none
Political parties and leaders: Center Party [Jenis A. RANA]; Home Rule Party [Helena Dam a NEYSTABO]; People's Party [Oli BRECKMANN]; Republican Party [Hogni HOYDAL]; Social Democratic Party [Joannes EIDESGAARD]; Union Party [Edmund JOENSEN]
Political pressure groups and leaders: NA
International organization participation: NC, NIB
Diplomatic representation in the US: none (self-governing overseas administrative division of Denmark)
Diplomatic representation from the US: none (self-governing overseas administrative division of Denmark)
Flag description: white with a red cross outlined in blue that extends to the edges of the flag; the vertical part of the cross is shifted to the hoist side in the style of the Dannebrog (Danish flag)

Economy

Economy - overview: The Faroese economy has had a strong performance since 1994, mostly as a result of increasing fish landings and high and stable export prices. Unemployment is falling and there are signs of labor shortages in several sectors. The positive economic development has helped the Faroese Home Rule Government produce increasing budget surpluses which in turn help to reduce the large public debt, most of it owed to Denmark. However, the total dependence on fishing makes the Faroese economy extremely vulnerable, and the present fishing efforts appear in excess of what is required to ensure a sustainable level of fishing in the long term. Oil finds close to the Faroese area give hope for deposits in the immediate Faroese area, which may eventually lay the basis for a more diversified economy and thus less dependence on Denmark and Danish economic assistance. Aided by a substantial annual subsidy (15% of GDP) from Denmark, the Faroese have a standard of living not far below the Danes and other Scandinavians.
GDP: purchasing power parity - $910 million (2000 est.)
GDP - real growth rate: 5% (2000 est.)
GDP - per capita: purchasing power parity - $20,000 (2000 est.)
GDP - composition by sector:
agriculture: 27%
industry: 11%
services: 62% (1999)
Population below poverty line: NA%
Household income or consumption by percentage share:
lowest 10%: NA%
highest 10%: NA%
Inflation rate (consumer prices): 5.1% (1999)
Labor force: 24,250 (October 2000)
Labor force - by occupation: fishing, fish processing, and manufacturing, construction and private services, public services
Unemployment rate: 1% (October 2000)
Budget:
revenues: $488 million
expenditures: $484 million, including capital expenditures of $21 million (1999)
Industries: fishing, fish processing, shipbuilding, construction, handicrafts
Industrial production growth rate: 8% (1999 est.)
Electricity - production: 170 million kWh (1999)
Electricity - production by source:
fossil fuel: 58.82%
hydro: 41.18%
nuclear: 0%
other: 0% (1999)
Electricity - consumption: 158.1 million kWh (1999)
Electricity - exports: 0 kWh (1999)
Electricity - imports: 0 kWh (1999)
Agriculture - products: milk, potatoes, vegetables; sheep; salmon, other fish
Exports: $471 million (f.o.b., 1999)
Exports - commodities: fish and fish products 94%, stamps, ships (1999)
Exports - partners: Denmark 32%, UK 21%, France 9%, Germany 7%, Iceland 5%, US 5% (1996)
Imports: $469 million (c.i.f., 1999)
Imports - commodities: machinery and transport equipment 29%, consumer goods 36%, raw materials and semi-manufactures 32%, fuels, fish and salt (1999)
Imports - partners: Denmark 28%, Norway 26%, Germany 7%, UK 6% Sweden 5%, Iceland 4%, US (1999)
Debt - external: $64 million (1999)
Economic aid - recipient: $135 million (annual subsidy from Denmark) (1999)
Currency: Danish krone (DKK)
Currency code: DKK
Exchange rates: Danish kroner per US dollar - 7.951 (January 2001), 8.093 (2000), 6.976 (1999), 6.701 (1998), 6.604 (1997), 5.799 (1966)
Fiscal year: calendar year

Communications

Telephones - main lines in use: 24,851 (1999)
Telephones - mobile cellular: 10,761 (1999)
Telephone system:
general assessment: good international communications; good domestic facilities
domestic: digitalization was to have been completed in 1998; both NMT (analog) and GSM (digital) mobile telephone systems are installed
international: satellite earth stations - 1 Orion; 1 fiber-optic submarine cable to the Shetland Islands, linking the Faroe Islands with Denmark and Iceland; fiber-optic submarine cable connection to Canada-Europe cable
Radio broadcast stations: AM 1, FM 13, shortwave 0 (1998)
Radios: 26,000 (1997)
Television broadcast stations: 3 (plus 43 low-power repeaters) (September 1995)
Televisions: 15,000 (1997)
Internet country code: .fo
Internet Service Providers (ISPs): 2 (2000)
Internet users: 3,000 (2000)

Transportation

Railways: 0 km
Highways:
total: 463 km
paved: 454 km
unpaved: 9 km (1999)
Waterways: none

Faroe Islands (continued)

Ports and harbors: Torshavn, Klaksvik, Tvoroyri, Runavik, Fuglafjorour
Merchant marine:
total: 6 ships (1,000 GRT or over) totaling 23,247 GRT/11,736 DWT
ships by type: cargo 2, petroleum tanker 1, refrigerated cargo 1, roll on/roll off 1, short-sea passenger 1 (2000 est.)
Airports: 1 (2000 est.)
Airports - with paved runways:
total: 1
914 to 1,523 m: 1 (2000 est.)

Military

Military branches: defense is the responsibility of Denmark; no organized native military forces; only a small Police Force and Coast Guard are maintained
Military expenditures - dollar figure: $NA
Military expenditures - percent of GDP: NA%
Military - note: defense is the responsibility of Denmark

Transnational Issues

Disputes - international: Faroese are considering proposals for full independence

Fiji

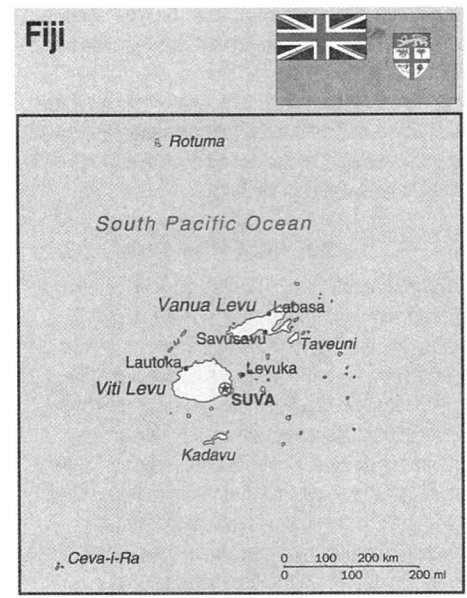

Introduction

Background: Fiji became independent in 1970, after nearly a century as a British colony. Democratic rule was interrupted by two military coups in 1987, caused by concern over a government perceived as dominated by the Indian community (descendants of contract laborers brought to the islands by the British in the 19th century). A 1990 constitution favored native Melanesian control of Fiji, but led to heavy Indian emigration; the population loss resulted in economic difficulties, but ensured that Melanesians became the majority. Amendments enacted in 1997 made the constitution more equitable. Free and peaceful elections in 1999 resulted in a government led by an Indo-Fijian, but a coup in May of 2000 ushered in a prolonged period of political turmoil. New elections are scheduled for August 2001.

Geography

Location: Oceania, island group in the South Pacific Ocean, about two-thirds of the way from Hawaii to New Zealand
Geographic coordinates: 18 00 S, 175 00 E
Map references: Oceania
Area:
total: 18,270 sq km
land: 18,270 sq km
water: 0 sq km
Area - comparative: slightly smaller than New Jersey
Land boundaries: 0 km
Coastline: 1,129 km
Maritime claims: measured from claimed archipelagic baselines
continental shelf: 200-m depth or to the depth of exploitation; rectilinear shelf claim added
exclusive economic zone: 200 NM
territorial sea: 12 NM
Climate: tropical marine; only slight seasonal temperature variation
Terrain: mostly mountains of volcanic origin
Elevation extremes:
lowest point: Pacific Ocean 0 m
highest point: Tomanivi 1,324 m
Natural resources: timber, fish, gold, copper, offshore oil potential, hydropower
Land use:
arable land: 10%
permanent crops: 4%
permanent pastures: 10%
forests and woodland: 65%
other: 11% (1993 est.)
Irrigated land: 10 sq km (1993 est.)
Natural hazards: cyclonic storms can occur from November to January
Environment - current issues: deforestation; soil erosion
Environment - international agreements:
party to: Biodiversity, Climate Change, Climate Change-Kyoto Protocol, Desertification, Endangered Species, Law of the Sea, Marine Dumping, Marine Life Conservation, Nuclear Test Ban, Ozone Layer Protection, Ship Pollution, Tropical Timber 83, Tropical Timber 94
signed, but not ratified: none of the selected agreements
Geography - note: includes 332 islands of which approximately 110 are inhabited

People

Population: 844,330 (July 2001 est.)
Age structure:
0-14 years: 32.92% (male 141,724; female 136,216)
15-64 years: 63.52% (male 268,411; female 267,871)
65 years and over: 3.56% (male 14,007; female 16,101) (2001 est.)
Population growth rate: 1.41% (2001 est.)
Birth rate: 23.33 births/1,000 population (2001 est.)
Death rate: 5.75 deaths/1,000 population (2001 est.)
Net migration rate: -3.45 migrant(s)/1,000 population (2001 est.)
Sex ratio:
at birth: 1.05 male(s)/female
under 15 years: 1.04 male(s)/female
15-64 years: 1 male(s)/female
65 years and over: 0.87 male(s)/female
total population: 1.01 male(s)/female (2001 est.)
Infant mortality rate: 14.08 deaths/1,000 live births (2001 est.)
Life expectancy at birth:
total population: 68.25 years
male: 65.83 years
female: 70.78 years (2001 est.)
Total fertility rate: 2.86 children born/woman (2001 est.)
HIV/AIDS - adult prevalence rate: 0.07% (1999 est.)
HIV/AIDS - people living with HIV/AIDS: NA
HIV/AIDS - deaths: NA
Nationality:
noun: Fijian(s)
adjective: Fijian

Fiji (continued)

Ethnic groups: Fijian 51% (predominantly Melanesian with a Polynesian admixture), Indian 44%, European, other Pacific Islanders, overseas Chinese, and other 5% (1998 est.)
Religions: Christian 52% (Methodist 37%, Roman Catholic 9%), Hindu 38%, Muslim 8%, other 2%
note: Fijians are mainly Christian, Indians are Hindu, and there is a Muslim minority (1986)
Languages: English (official), Fijian, Hindustani
Literacy:
definition: age 15 and over can read and write
total population: 91.6%
male: 93.8%
female: 89.3% (1995 est.)

Government

Country name:
conventional long form: Republic of the Fiji Islands
conventional short form: Fiji
Government type: republic
note: military coup leader Maj. Gen. Sitiveni RABUKA formally declared Fiji a republic on 6 October 1987
Capital: Suva
Administrative divisions: 4 divisions and 1 dependency*; Central, Eastern, Northern, Rotuma*, Western
Independence: 10 October 1970 (from UK)
National holiday: Independence Day, second Monday of October (1970)
Constitution: 10 October 1970 (suspended 1 October 1987); a new constitution was proposed on 23 September 1988 and promulgated on 25 July 1990; amended 25 July 1997 to allow nonethnic Fijians greater say in government and to make multiparty government mandatory; entered into force 28 July 1998; note - the May 1999 election was the first test of the amended constitution and introduced open voting - not racially prescribed - for the first time at the national level
Legal system: based on British system
Suffrage: 21 years of age; universal
Executive branch:
note: armed ethnic Fijian terrorists, led by George SPEIGHT stormed the Parliament building on 19 May 2000; ethnic Indo-Fijian Prime Minister Mahendra CHAUDHRY and his government were held hostage for 56 days; following the attempted coup, the Commander of the Fiji Military Forces, naval Commodore Frank BAINIMARAMA declared martial law and dissolved the government on 29 May 2000; an interim government, headed by interim Prime Minister Laisenia QARASE, was appointed to serve until a new constitution was initiated and subsequent elections held; in November 2000, Fiji's High Court upheld the 1997 constitution and ruled that Ratu Sir Kamisese MARA remained the president; Justice Anthony GATES concluded that MARA should recall the pre-May 19th Parliament and appoint a prime minister to form a new government; the Fiji Court of Appeals upheld GATES' decision on 1 March 2001; it ruled that the 1997 constitution had not been abrogated, Parliament had not been dissolved, only prorogued for six months, and that the presidency remained vacant since MARA's resignation took effect 15 December 2000; President Ratu Josefa ILOILO reinstated QARASE's interim government as the caretaker government and elections were scheduled for August 2001; approximately 23 fluid political parties are currently jockeying for power
chief of state: President Ratu Josefa ILOILO (since NA 2000); Vice President Jope SENILOLI (since NA 2000)
head of government: Prime Minister Laisenia QARASE (since NA 2000); Deputy Prime Minister Epeli NAILATIKAU (since NA 2000)
cabinet: Cabinet appointed by the prime minister from among the members of Parliament and is responsible to Parliament; note -there is also a Presidential Council that advises the president on matters of national importance and a Great Council of Chiefs which consists of the highest ranking members of the traditional chiefly system
elections: president elected by the Great Council of Chiefs for a five-year term; prime minister appointed by the president
election results: Ratu Josefa ILOILO elected president by the Great Council of Chiefs; percent of vote - NA%
Legislative branch: bicameral Parliament consists of the Senate (32 seats; 14 appointed by the Great Council of Chiefs, nine appointed by the prime minister, eight appointed by the leader of the opposition, and one appointed by the council of Rotuma) and the House of Representatives (71 seats; 23 reserved for ethnic Fijians, 19 reserved for ethnic Indians, three reserved for other ethnic groups, one reserved for the council of Rotuma constituency encompassing the whole of Fiji, and 25 open; members serve five-year terms)
elections: House of Representatives - last held 11 May 1999 (next to be held NA May 2004)
election results: House of Representatives - percent of vote by party - NA%; seats by party - Fiji Labor Party 37, others 34
Judicial branch: Supreme Court (judges are appointed by the president)
Political parties and leaders: Fiji Labor Party or FLP [Mahendra CHAUDHRY]; Fijian Nationalist Federation Party or NFP [Singh RAKKA]; Fijian Political Party or SVT (primarily Fijian) [Maj. Gen. Sitiveni RABUKA]; National Federation Party or NFP (primarily Indian) [Jai Ram REDDY]; United General Party or UGP [David PICKERING]
Political pressure groups and leaders: NA
International organization participation: ACP, AsDB, C, CCC, CP, ESCAP, FAO, G-77, IBRD, ICAO, ICFTU, ICRM, IDA, IFAD, IFC, IFRCS, IHO, ILO, IMF, IMO, Intelsat, Interpol, IOC, ISO (subscriber), ITU, OPCW, Sparteca, SPC, SPF, UN, UNCTAD, UNESCO, UNIDO, UNIFIL, UNIKOM, UNMIBH, UNMIK, UNTAET, UPU, WFTU, WHO, WIPO, WMO, WToO, WTrO
Diplomatic representation in the US:
chief of mission: Ambassador (vacant); Charge d'Affaires ad interim Salaseini Lelelvawalu VOSAILAGI
chancery: Suite 240, 2233 Wisconsin Avenue NW, Washington, DC 20007
telephone: [1] (202) 337-8320
FAX: [1] (202) 337-1996
Diplomatic representation from the US:
chief of mission: Ambassador Osman M. SIDDIQUE
embassy: 31 Loftus Street, Suva
mailing address: P. O. Box 218, Suva
telephone: [679] 314466
FAX: [679] 300081
Flag description: light blue with the flag of the UK in the upper hoist-side quadrant and the Fijian shield centered on the outer half of the flag; the shield depicts a yellow lion above a white field quartered by the cross of Saint George featuring stalks of sugarcane, a palm tree, bananas, and a white dove

Economy

Economy - overview: Fiji, endowed with forest, mineral, and fish resources, is one of the most developed of the Pacific island economies, though still with a large subsistence sector. Sugar exports and a growing tourist industry are the major sources of foreign exchange. Sugar processing makes up one-third of industrial activity. Roughly 300,000 tourists visit each year, including thousands of Americans following the start of regularly scheduled non-stop air service from Los Angeles. Fiji's growth slowed in 1997 because the sugar industry suffered from low world prices and rent disputes between farmers and landowners. Drought in 1998 further damaged the sugar industry, but its recovery in 1999 contributed to robust GDP growth. Long-term problems include low investment and uncertain property rights. The political turmoil in Fiji has had a severe impact with the economy shrinking by 8% in 1999 and over 7,000 people losing their jobs. The interim government's 2001 budget is an attempt to attract foreign investment and restart economic activity. The government's ability to manage the budget and fulfill predictions of 4% growth for 2001 will depend on a return to stability, a regaining of investor confidence, and the absence of international sanctions (which could cripple Fiji's sugar and textile industry).
GDP: purchasing power parity - $5.9 billion (1999 est.)
GDP - real growth rate: -8% (1999 est.)
GDP - per capita: purchasing power parity - $7,300 (1999 est.)
GDP - composition by sector:
agriculture: 16%
industry: 30%
services: 54% (1999 est.)
Population below poverty line: NA%
Household income or consumption by percentage share:
lowest 10%: NA%
highest 10%: NA%
Inflation rate (consumer prices): 0% (1999 est.)
Labor force: 235,000

Fiji (continued)

Labor force - by occupation: subsistence agriculture 67%, wage earners 18%, salary earners 15% (1987)
Unemployment rate: 6% (1997 est.)
Budget:
revenues: $610 million
expenditures: $501 million, including capital expenditures of $NA (1999 est.)
Industries: tourism, sugar, clothing, copra, gold, silver, lumber, small cottage industries
Industrial production growth rate: 2.9% (1995)
Electricity - production: 510 million kWh (1999)
Electricity - production by source:
fossil fuel: 17.65%
hydro: 82.35%
nuclear: 0%
other: 0% (1999)
Electricity - consumption: 474.3 million kWh (1999)
Electricity - exports: 0 kWh (1999)
Electricity - imports: 0 kWh (1999)
Agriculture - products: sugarcane, coconuts, cassava (tapioca), rice, sweet potatoes, bananas; cattle, pigs, horses, goats; fish
Exports: $537 million (f.o.b., 1999)
Exports - commodities: sugar, garments, gold, timber, fish
Exports - partners: Australia 33.1%, US 14.8%, UK 13.8%, other Pacific island countries 8.8%, NZ 4.5%, Japan 4.5% (1999)
Imports: $653 million (f.o.b., 1999)
Imports - commodities: manufactured goods, machinery and transport equipment, petroleum products, food, chemicals
Imports - partners: Australia 41.9%, US 14%, NZ 13.3%, Japan 4.8%, Taiwan 1.9% (1999)
Debt - external: $193 million (1998)
Economic aid - recipient: $40.3 million (1995)
Currency: Fijian dollar (FJD)
Currency code: FJD
Exchange rates: Fijian dollars per US dollar - 2.1814 (January 2001), 2.1286 (2000), 1.9696 (1999), 1.9868 (1998), 1.4437 (1997), 1.4033 (1996)
Fiscal year: calendar year

Communications

Telephones - main lines in use: 72,000 (1997)
Telephones - mobile cellular: 5,200 (1997)
Telephone system:
general assessment: modern local, interisland, and international (wire/radio integrated) public and special-purpose telephone, telegraph, and teleprinter facilities; regional radio communications center
domestic: NA
international: access to important cable links between US and Canada as well as between NZ and Australia; satellite earth station - 1 Intelsat (Pacific Ocean)
Radio broadcast stations: AM 13, FM 40, shortwave 0 (1998)
Radios: 500,000 (1997)
Television broadcast stations: NA
Televisions: 21,000 (1997)
Internet country code: .fj
Internet Service Providers (ISPs): 2 (2000)
Internet users: 7,500 (2000)

Transportation

Railways:
total: 597 km; note - belongs to the government-owned Fiji Sugar Corporation
narrow gauge: 597 km 0.610-m gauge (1995)
Highways:
total: 3,440 km
paved: 1,692 km
unpaved: 1,748 km (1996)
Waterways: 203 km
note: 122 km navigable by motorized craft and 200-metric-ton barges
Ports and harbors: Lambasa, Lautoka, Levuka, Savusavu, Suva
Merchant marine:
total: 6 ships (1,000 GRT or over) totaling 11,870 GRT/14,787 DWT
ships by type: chemical tanker 2, passenger 1, petroleum tanker 1, roll on/roll off 1, specialized tanker 1 (2000 est.)
Airports: 27 (2000 est.)
Airports - with paved runways:
total: 3
over 3,047 m: 1
1,524 to 2,437 m: 1
914 to 1,523 m: 1 (2000 est.)
Airports - with unpaved runways:
total: 24
1,524 to 2,437 m: 1
914 to 1,523 m: 4
under 914 m: 19 (2000 est.)

Military

Military branches: Republic of Fiji Military Forces (RFMF; includes ground and naval forces)
Military manpower - military age: 18 years of age
Military manpower - availability:
males age 15-49: 227,599 (2001 est.)
Military manpower - fit for military service:
males age 15-49: 125,238 (2001 est.)
Military manpower - reaching military age annually:
males: 9,471 (2001 est.)
Military expenditures - dollar figure: $24 million (FY98)
Military expenditures - percent of GDP: 1.1% (FY98)

Transnational Issues

Disputes - international: none

Finland

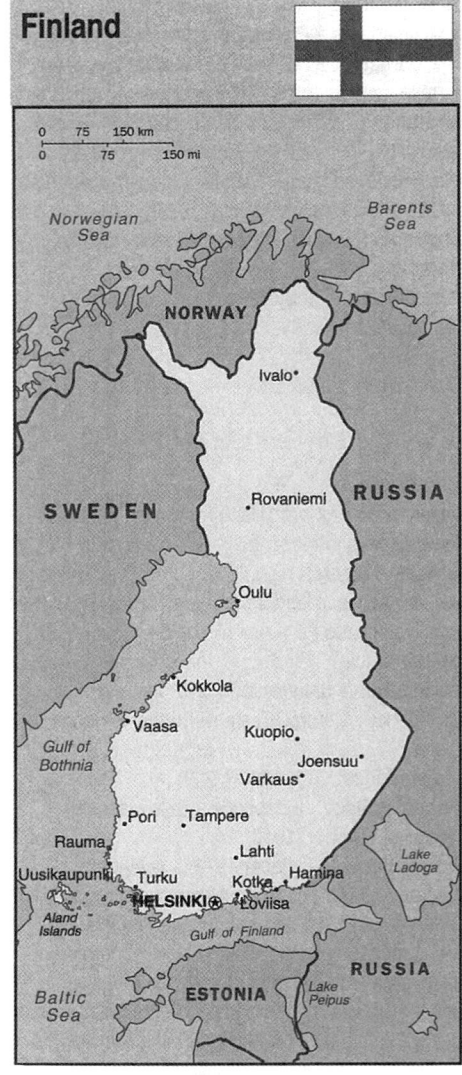

Introduction

Background: Ruled by Sweden from the 12th to the 19th centuries and by Russia from 1809, Finland finally won its independence in 1917. During World War II, it was able to successfully defend its freedom and fend off invasions by the Soviet Union and Germany. In the subsequent half century, the Finns have made a remarkable transformation from a farm/forest economy to a diversified modern industrial economy; per capita income is now on par with Western Europe. As a member of the European Union, Finland was the only Nordic state to join the euro system at its initiation in January 1999.

Geography

Location: Northern Europe, bordering the Baltic Sea, Gulf of Bothnia, and Gulf of Finland, between Sweden and Russia
Geographic coordinates: 64 00 N, 26 00 E
Map references: Europe
Area:
total: 337,030 sq km
land: 305,470 sq km
water: 31,560 sq km

Finland (continued)

Area - comparative: slightly smaller than Montana
Land boundaries:
total: 2,628 km
border countries: Norway 729 km, Sweden 586 km, Russia 1,313 km
Coastline: 1,126 km (excludes islands and coastal indentations)
Maritime claims:
continental shelf: 200-m depth or to the depth of exploitation
exclusive fishing zone: 12 NM
territorial sea: 12 NM (in the Gulf of Finland - 3 NM)
Climate: cold temperate; potentially subarctic, but comparatively mild because of moderating influence of the North Atlantic Current, Baltic Sea, and more than 60,000 lakes
Terrain: mostly low, flat to rolling plains interspersed with lakes and low hills
Elevation extremes:
lowest point: Baltic Sea 0 m
highest point: Haltiatunturi 1,328 m
Natural resources: timber, copper, zinc, iron ore, silver
Land use:
arable land: 8%
permanent crops: 0%
permanent pastures: 0%
forests and woodland: 76%
other: 16% (1993 est.)
Irrigated land: 640 sq km (1993 est.)
Natural hazards: NA
Environment - current issues: air pollution from manufacturing and power plants contributing to acid rain; water pollution from industrial wastes, agricultural chemicals; habitat loss threatens wildlife populations
Environment - international agreements:
party to: Air Pollution, Air Pollution-Nitrogen Oxides, Air Pollution-Sulphur 85, Air Pollution-Sulphur 94, Air Pollution-Volatile Organic Compounds, Antarctic-Environmental Protocol, Antarctic-Marine Living Resources, Antarctic Treaty, Biodiversity, Climate Change, Desertification, Endangered Species, Environmental Modification, Hazardous Wastes, Law of the Sea, Marine Dumping, Marine Life Conservation, Nuclear Test Ban, Ozone Layer Protection, Ship Pollution, Tropical Timber 83, Tropical Timber 94, Wetlands, Whaling
signed, but not ratified: Air Pollution-Persistent Organic Pollutants, Climate Change-Kyoto Protocol
Geography - note: long boundary with Russia; Helsinki is northernmost national capital on European continent; population concentrated on small southwestern coastal plain

People

Population: 5,175,783 (July 2001 est.)
Age structure:
0-14 years: 18% (male 474,967; female 456,584)
15-64 years: 66.97% (male 1,750,660; female 1,715,358)
65 years and over: 15.03% (male 300,569; female 477,645) (2001 est.)
Population growth rate: 0.16% (2001 est.)
Birth rate: 10.69 births/1,000 population (2001 est.)
Death rate: 9.75 deaths/1,000 population (2001 est.)
Net migration rate: 0.61 migrant(s)/1,000 population (2001 est.)
Sex ratio:
at birth: 1.03 male(s)/female
under 15 years: 1.04 male(s)/female
15-64 years: 1.02 male(s)/female
65 years and over: 0.63 male(s)/female
total population: 0.95 male(s)/female (2001 est.)
Infant mortality rate: 3.79 deaths/1,000 live births (2001 est.)
Life expectancy at birth:
total population: 77.58 years
male: 73.92 years
female: 81.36 years (2001 est.)
Total fertility rate: 1.7 children born/woman (2001 est.)
HIV/AIDS - adult prevalence rate: 0.05% (1999 est.)
HIV/AIDS - people living with HIV/AIDS: 1,100 (1999 est.)
HIV/AIDS - deaths: less than 100 (1999 est.)
Nationality:
noun: Finn(s)
adjective: Finnish
Ethnic groups: Finn 93%, Swede 6%, Sami 0.11%, Roma 0.12%, Tatar 0.02%
Religions: Evangelical Lutheran 89%, Greek Orthodox 1%, none 9%, other 1%
Languages: Finnish 93.4% (official), Swedish 5.9% (official), small Lapp- and Russian-speaking minorities
Literacy:
definition: age 15 and over can read and write
total population: 100% (1980 est.)
male: NA%
female: NA%

Government

Country name:
conventional long form: Republic of Finland
conventional short form: Finland
local long form: Suomen Tasavalta
local short form: Suomi
Government type: republic
Capital: Helsinki
Administrative divisions: 6 provinces (laanit, singular - laani); Aland, Etela-Suomen Laani, Ita-Suomen Laani, Lansi-Suomen Laani, Lappi, Oulun Laani
Independence: 6 December 1917 (from Russia)
National holiday: Independence Day, 6 December (1917)
Constitution: 17 July 1919
Legal system: civil law system based on Swedish law; Supreme Court may request legislation interpreting or modifying laws; accepts compulsory ICJ jurisdiction, with reservations
Suffrage: 18 years of age; universal
Executive branch:
chief of state: President Tarja HALONEN (since 1 March 2000)
head of government: Prime Minister Paavo LIPPONEN (since 13 April 1995) and Deputy Prime Minister Sauli NIINISTO (since 13 April 1995)
cabinet: Council of State or Valtioneuvosto appointed by the president, responsible to Parliament
elections: president elected by popular vote for a six-year term; election last held 6 February 2000 (next to be held NA February 2006); prime minister and deputy prime minister appointed from the majority party by the president after parliamentary elections
election results: Tarja HALONEN elected president; percent of vote - Tarja HALONEN (SDP) 51.6%, Esco AHO (Kesk) 48.4%
note: government coalition - SDP, Kok, Leftist Alliance (People's Democratic Union and Democratic Alternative), SFP, and Green Union
Legislative branch: unicameral Parliament or Eduskunta (200 seats; members are elected by popular vote on a proportional basis to serve four-year terms)
elections: last held 21 March 1999 (next to be held NA March 2003)
election results: percent of vote by party - SDP 22.9%, Kesk 22.5%, Kok 21.0%, Leftist Alliance (Communist) 10.9%, SFP 5.1%, Green Union 7.2%, SKL 4.2%; seats by party - SDP 51, Kesk 48, Kok 46, Leftist Alliance (Communist) 20, SFP 11, Green Union 11, SKL 10, other 3
Judicial branch: Supreme Court or Korkein Oikeus (judges appointed by the president)
Political parties and leaders: Center Party or Kesk [Esko AHO]; Finnish Christian Union or SKL [C. P. Bjarne KALLIS]; Green Union [Satu HASSI]; Leftist Alliance (Communist) composed of People's Democratic League and Democratic Alternative [Suvi-Anne SIIMES]; National Coalition (conservative) Party or Kok [Sauli NIINISTO]; Reform Group [Risto KUISMA]; Social Democratic Party or SDP [Paavo LIPPONEN]; Swedish People's Party or SFP [Jan-Erik ENESTAM]; True Finns [Timo SOINI]
Political pressure groups and leaders: Communist Workers Party [Timo LAHDENMAKI]; Constitutional Rightist Party; Finnish Communist Party-Unity [Yrjo HAKANEN]; Finnish Pensioners Party
International organization participation: AfDB, AsDB, Australia Group, BIS, CBSS, CCC, CE, CERN, EAPC, EBRD, ECE, EIB, EMU, ESA, EU, FAO, G- 9, IADB, IAEA, IBRD, ICAO, ICC, ICFTU, ICRM, IDA, IEA, IFAD, IFC, IFRCS, IHO, ILO, IMF, IMO, Inmarsat, Intelsat, Interpol, IOC, IOM, ISO, ITU, NAM (guest), NC, NEA, NIB, NSG, OAS (observer), OECD, OPCW, OSCE, PCA, PFP, UN, UNCTAD, UNESCO, UNFICYP, UNHCR, UNIDO, UNIFIL, UNIKOM, UNMEE, UNMIBH, UNMIK, UNMOGIP, UNMOP, UNTSO, UPU, WEU (observer), WFTU, WHO, WIPO, WMO, WToO, WTrO, ZC
Diplomatic representation in the US:
chief of mission: Ambassador Jaakko Tapani LAAJAVA

Finland (continued)

chancery: 3301 Massachusetts Avenue NW, Washington, DC 20008
telephone: [1] (202) 298-5800
FAX: [1] (202) 298-6030
consulate(s) general: Los Angeles and New York
Diplomatic representation from the US:
chief of mission: Ambassador (vacant); Charge d'Affaires Carol VAN VOORST
embassy: Itainen Puistotie 14B, FIN-00140, Helsinki
mailing address: APO AE 09723
telephone: [358] (9) 171931
FAX: [358] (9) 174681
Flag description: white with a blue cross that extends to the edges of the flag; the vertical part of the cross is shifted to the hoist side in the style of the Dannebrog (Danish flag)

Economy

Economy - overview: Finland has a highly industrialized, largely free-market economy, with per capita output roughly that of the UK, France, Germany, and Italy. Its key economic sector is manufacturing - principally the wood, metals, engineering, telecommunications, and electronics industries. Trade is important, with exports equaling more than one-third of GDP. Except for timber and several minerals, Finland depends on imports of raw materials, energy, and some components for manufactured goods. Because of the climate, agricultural development is limited to maintaining self-sufficiency in basic products. Forestry, an important export earner, provides a secondary occupation for the rural population. Rapidly increasing integration with Western Europe - Finland was one of the 11 countries joining the euro monetary system (EMU) on 1 January 1999 - will dominate the economic picture over the next several years. Growth in 2001 will be bolstered by strong private consumption, yet may be 1 or 2 points lower than in 2000, largely because of a weakening in export demand.
GDP: purchasing power parity - $118.3 billion (2000 est.)
GDP - real growth rate: 5.6% (2000 est.)
GDP - per capita: purchasing power parity - $22,900 (2000 est.)
GDP - composition by sector:
agriculture: 3.5%
industry: 29%
services: 67.5% (1999)
Population below poverty line: NA%
Household income or consumption by percentage share:
lowest 10%: 4.2%
highest 10%: 21.6% (1991)
Inflation rate (consumer prices): 3.4% (2000 est.)
Labor force: 2.6 million (2000 est.)
Labor force - by occupation: public services 32%, industry 22%, commerce 14%, finance, insurance, and business services 10%, agriculture and forestry 8%, transport and communications 8%, construction 6%
Unemployment rate: 9.8% (2000 est.)

Budget:
revenues: $36.1 billion
expenditures: $31 billion, including capital expenditures of $NA (2000 est.)
Industries: metal products, shipbuilding, pulp and paper, copper refining, foodstuffs, chemicals, textiles, clothing
Industrial production growth rate: 7.5% (2000)
Electricity - production: 75.792 billion kWh (1999)
Electricity - production by source:
fossil fuel: 41.88%
hydro: 16.77%
nuclear: 28.82%
other: 12.53% (1999)
Electricity - consumption: 81.611 billion kWh (1999)
Electricity - exports: 232 million kWh (1999)
Electricity - imports: 11.356 billion kWh (1999)
Agriculture - products: cereals, sugar beets, potatoes; dairy cattle; fish
Exports: $44.4 billion (f.o.b., 2000)
Exports - commodities: machinery and equipment, chemicals, metals; timber, paper, pulp
Exports - partners: EU 58% (Germany 13%, Sweden 10%, UK 9%, France 5%, Netherlands 4%), US 8%, Russia, Japan (1999)
Imports: $32.7 billion (f.o.b., 2000)
Imports - commodities: foodstuffs, petroleum and petroleum products, chemicals, transport equipment, iron and steel, machinery, textile yarn and fabrics, grains
Imports - partners: EU 60% (Germany 15%, Sweden 11%, UK 7%), US 8%, Russia 7%, Japan 6% (1999)
Debt - external: $30 billion (December 1993)
Economic aid - donor: ODA, $379 million (1997)
Currency: markka (FIM); euro (EUR)
note: on 1 January 1999, the EU introduced the euro as a common currency that is now being used by financial institutions in Finland at a fixed rate of 5.94573 markkaa per euro and will replace the local currency for all transactions in 2002
Currency code: FIM; EUR
Exchange rates: euros per US dollar - 1.0659 (January 2001), 1.0854 (2000), 0.9386 (1999); markkaa per US dollar - 5.3441 (1998), 5.1914 (1997), 4.5936 (1996)
Fiscal year: calendar year

Communications

Telephones - main lines in use: 2.861 million (1997)
Telephones - mobile cellular: 2,162,574 (1997)
Telephone system:
general assessment: modern system with excellent service
domestic: cable, microwave radio relay, and an extensive cellular net provide domestic needs
international: 1 submarine cable; satellite earth stations - access to Intelsat transmission service via a Swedish satellite earth station, 1 Inmarsat (Atlantic and Indian Ocean regions); note - Finland shares the Inmarsat earth station with the other Nordic countries (Denmark, Iceland, Norway, and Sweden)

Radio broadcast stations: AM 2, FM 186, shortwave 1 (1998)
Radios: 7.7 million (1997)
Television broadcast stations: 130 (plus 385 repeaters) (1995)
Televisions: 3.2 million (1997)
Internet country code: .fi
Internet Service Providers (ISPs): 23 (2000)
Internet users: 2.27 million (2000)

Transportation

Railways:
total: 5,865 km
broad gauge: 5,865 km 1.524-m gauge (2,192 km electrified; 480 km double or multiple track) (1998)
Highways:
total: 77,796 km
paved: 49,789 km (including 444 km of expressways)
unpaved: 28,042 km (1999)
Waterways: 6,675 km
note: includes Saimaa Canal; 3,700 km suitable for large ships
Pipelines: natural gas 580 km
Ports and harbors: Hamina, Helsinki, Kokkola, Kotka, Loviisa, Oulu, Pori, Rauma, Turku, Uusikaupunki, Varkaus
Merchant marine:
total: 98 ships (1,000 GRT or over) totaling 1,172,808 GRT/1,138,175 DWT
ships by type: bulk 9, cargo 23, chemical tanker 5, passenger 1, petroleum tanker 11, railcar carrier 1, roll on/roll off 37, short-sea passenger 11 (2000 est.)
Airports: 159 (2000 est.)
Airports - with paved runways:
total: 69
over 3,047 m: 3
2,438 to 3,047 m: 26
1,524 to 2,437 m: 10
914 to 1,523 m: 20
under 914 m: 10 (2000 est.)
Airports - with unpaved runways:
total: 90
914 to 1,523 m: 6
under 914 m: 84 (2000 est.)

Military

Military branches: Army, Navy, Air Force, Frontier Guard (includes Sea Guard)
Military manpower - military age: 17 years of age
Military manpower - availability:
males age 15-49: 1,251,700 (2001 est.)
Military manpower - fit for military service:
males age 15-49: 1,033,188 (2001 est.)
Military manpower - reaching military age annually:
males: 33,883 (2001 est.)
Military expenditures - dollar figure: $1.8 billion (FY98)
Military expenditures - percent of GDP: 2% (FY98)

Transnational Issues

Disputes - international: none

France

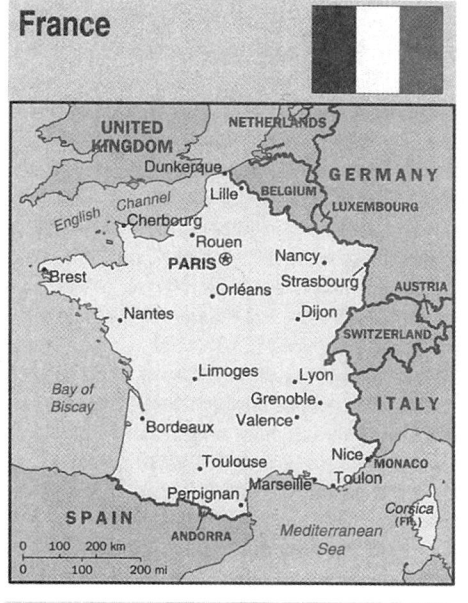

Introduction

Background: Although ultimately a victor in World Wars I and II, France suffered extensive losses in its empire, wealth, manpower, and rank as a dominant nation-state. Nevertheless, France today is one of the most modern countries in the world and is a leader among European nations. Since 1958, it has constructed a presidential democracy resistant to the instabilities experienced in earlier parliamentary democracies. In recent years, its reconciliation and cooperation with Germany have proved central to the economic integration of Europe, including the advent of the euro in January 1999. Presently, France is at the forefront of European states seeking to exploit the momentum of monetary union to advance the creation of a more unified and capable European defense and security apparatus.

Geography

Location: Western Europe, bordering the Bay of Biscay and English Channel, between Belgium and Spain, southeast of the UK; bordering the Mediterranean Sea, between Italy and Spain
Geographic coordinates: 46 00 N, 2 00 E
Map references: Europe
Area:
total: 547,030 sq km
land: 545,630 sq km
water: 1,400 sq km
note: includes only metropolitan France, but excludes the overseas administrative divisions
Area - comparative: slightly less than twice the size of Colorado
Land boundaries:
total: 2,889 km
border countries: Andorra 56.6 km, Belgium 620 km, Germany 451 km, Italy 488 km, Luxembourg 73 km, Monaco 4.4 km, Spain 623 km, Switzerland 573 km
Coastline: 3,427 km
Maritime claims:
contiguous zone: 24 NM
continental shelf: 200-m depth or to the depth of exploitation
exclusive economic zone: 200 NM (does not apply to the Mediterranean)
territorial sea: 12 NM
Climate: generally cool winters and mild summers, but mild winters and hot summers along the Mediterranean; occasional strong, cold, dry, north-to-northwesterly wind known as mistral
Terrain: mostly flat plains or gently rolling hills in north and west; remainder is mountainous, especially Pyrenees in south, Alps in east
Elevation extremes:
lowest point: Rhone River delta -2 m
highest point: Mont Blanc 4,807 m
Natural resources: coal, iron ore, bauxite, zinc, potash, timber, fish
Land use:
arable land: 33%
permanent crops: 2%
permanent pastures: 20%
forests and woodland: 27%
other: 18% (1993 est.)
Irrigated land: 16,300 sq km (1995 est.)
Natural hazards: flooding; avalanches
Environment - current issues: some forest damage from acid rain (major forest damage occurred as a result of severe December 1999 windstorm); air pollution from industrial and vehicle emissions; water pollution from urban wastes, agricultural runoff
Environment - international agreements:
party to: Air Pollution, Air Pollution-Nitrogen Oxides, Air Pollution-Sulphur 85, Air Pollution-Sulphur 94, Air Pollution-Volatile Organic Compounds, Antarctic-Environmental Protocol, Antarctic-Marine Living Resources, Antarctic Seals, Antarctic Treaty, Biodiversity, Climate Change, Desertification, Endangered Species, Hazardous Wastes, Law of the Sea, Marine Dumping, Marine Life Conservation, Ozone Layer Protection, Ship Pollution, Tropical Timber 83, Tropical Timber 94, Wetlands, Whaling
signed, but not ratified: Air Pollution-Persistent Organic Pollutants, Climate Change-Kyoto Protocol
Geography - note: largest West European nation

People

Population: 59,551,227 (July 2001 est.)
Age structure:
0-14 years: 18.68% (male 5,698,604; female 5,426,838)
15-64 years: 65.19% (male 19,424,018; female 19,399,588)
65 years and over: 16.13% (male 3,900,579; female 5,701,600) (2001 est.)
Population growth rate: 0.37% (2001 est.)
Birth rate: 12.1 births/1,000 population (2001 est.)
Death rate: 9.09 deaths/1,000 population (2001 est.)
Net migration rate: 0.64 migrant(s)/1,000 population (2001 est.)
Sex ratio:
at birth: 1.06 male(s)/female
under 15 years: 1.05 male(s)/female
15-64 years: 1 male(s)/female
65 years and over: 0.68 male(s)/female
total population: 0.95 male(s)/female (2001 est.)
Infant mortality rate: 4.46 deaths/1,000 live births (2001 est.)
Life expectancy at birth:
total population: 78.9 years
male: 75.01 years
female: 83.01 years (2001 est.)
Total fertility rate: 1.75 children born/woman (2001 est.)
HIV/AIDS - adult prevalence rate: 0.44% (1999 est.)
HIV/AIDS - people living with HIV/AIDS: 130,000 (1999 est.)
HIV/AIDS - deaths: 2,000 (1999 est.)
Nationality:
noun: Frenchman(men), Frenchwoman(women)
adjective: French
Ethnic groups: Celtic and Latin with Teutonic, Slavic, North African, Indochinese, Basque minorities
Religions: Roman Catholic 90%, Protestant 2%, Jewish 1%, Muslim (North African workers) 3%, unaffiliated 4%
Languages: French 100%, rapidly declining regional dialects and languages (Provencal, Breton, Alsatian, Corsican, Catalan, Basque, Flemish)
Literacy:
definition: age 15 and over can read and write
total population: 99%
male: 99%
female: 99% (1980 est.)

Government

Country name:
conventional long form: French Republic
conventional short form: France
local long form: Republique Francaise
local short form: France
Government type: republic
Capital: Paris
Administrative divisions: 22 regions (regions, singular - region); Alsace, Aquitaine, Auvergne, Basse-Normandie, Bourgogne, Bretagne, Centre, Champagne-Ardenne, Corse, Franche-Comte, Haute-Normandie, Ile-de-France, Languedoc-Roussillon, Limousin, Lorraine, Midi-Pyrenees, Nord-Pas-de-Calais, Pays de la Loire, Picardie, Poitou-Charentes, Provence-Alpes-Cote d'Azur, Rhone-Alpes
note: metropolitan France is divided into 22 regions (including the "territorial collectivity" of Corse or Corsica) and is subdivided into 96 departments; see separate entries for the overseas departments (French Guiana, Guadeloupe, Martinique, Reunion) and the overseas territorial collectivities (Mayotte, Saint Pierre and Miquelon)
Dependent areas: Bassas da India, Clipperton Island, Europa Island, French Polynesia, French Southern and Antarctic Lands, Glorioso Islands, Juan de Nova Island, New Caledonia, Tromelin Island, Wallis and Futuna

France (continued)

note: the US does not recognize claims to Antarctica
Independence: 486 (unified by Clovis)
National holiday: Bastille Day, 14 July (1789)
Constitution: 28 September 1958, amended concerning election of president in 1962, amended to comply with provisions of EC Maastricht Treaty in 1992; amended to tighten immigration laws 1993
Legal system: civil law system with indigenous concepts; review of administrative but not legislative acts
Suffrage: 18 years of age; universal
Executive branch:
chief of state: President Jacques CHIRAC (since 17 May 1995)
head of government: Prime Minister Lionel JOSPIN (since 3 June 1997)
cabinet: Council of Ministers appointed by the president on the suggestion of the prime minister
elections: president elected by popular vote for a seven-year term; election last held 23 April and 7 May 1995 (next to be held by May 2002); prime minister nominated by the National Assembly majority and appointed by the president
election results: Jacques CHIRAC elected president; percent of vote, second ballot - Jacques CHIRAC (RPR) 52.64%, Lionel JOSPIN (PS) 47.36%
Legislative branch: bicameral Parliament or Parlement consists of the Senate or Senat (321 seats - 296 for metropolitan France, 13 for overseas departments and territories, and 12 for French nationals abroad; members are indirectly elected by an electoral college to serve nine-year terms; elected by thirds every three years) and the National Assembly or Assemblee Nationale (577 seats; members are elected by popular vote under a single-member majoritarian system to serve five-year terms)
elections: Senate - last held 27 September 1998 (next to be held September 2001); National Assembly - last held 25 May-1 June 1997 (next to be held NA May 2002)
election results: Senate - percent of vote by party - NA%; seats by party - RPR 99, UDC 52, DL 47, PS 78, PCF 16, other 29; National Assembly - percent of vote by party - NA%; seats by party - PS 245, RPR 140, UDF 109, PCF 37, PRS 13, MEI 8, MDC 7, LDI-MPF 1, FN 1, various left 9, various right 7
Judicial branch: Supreme Court of Appeals or Cour de Cassation (judges are appointed by the president from nominations of the High Council of the Judiciary); Constitutional Council or Conseil Constitutionnel (three members appointed by the president, three appointed by the president of the National Assembly, and three appointed by the president of the Senate); Council of State or Conseil d'Etat
Political parties and leaders: Citizens Movement or MdC [Jean Pierre CHEVENEMENT]; French Communist Party or PCF [Robert HUE]; Independent Ecological Movement or MEI [Antoine WAECHTER]; Left Radical Party or PRG (previously Radical Socialist Party or PRS and the Left Radical Movement or MRG) [Jean-Michel BAYLET]; Liberal Democracy or DL (originally Republican Party or PR) [Alain MADELIN]; Movement for France or MPF [Philippe DEVILLIERS]; National Front or FN [Jean-Marie LE PEN]; Rally for the Republic or RPR [Michelle ALLIOT-MARIE]; Socialist Party or PS [Francois HOLLANDE]; Union for French Democracy or UDF (coalition of UDC, FD, RRRS, PPDF) [Francois BAYROU]; Union of the Center or UDC [leader NA]
Political pressure groups and leaders: Communist-controlled labor union (Confederation Generale du Travail) or CGT, nearly 2.4 million members (claimed); independent labor union or Force Ouvriere, 1 million members (est.); independent white-collar union or Confederation Generale des Cadres, 340,000 members (claimed); National Council of French Employers (Conseil National du Patronat Francais) or CNPF or Patronat; Socialist-leaning labor union (Confederation Francaise Democratique du Travail) or CFDT, about 800,000 members (est.)
International organization participation: ACCT, AfDB, AsDB, Australia Group, BDEAC, BIS, CCC, CDB (non-regional), CE, CERN, EAPC, EBRD, ECA (associate), ECE, ECLAC, EIB, EMU, ESA, ESCAP, EU, FAO, FZ, G-5, G-7, G-10, IADB, IAEA, IBRD, ICAO, ICC, ICFTU, ICRM, IDA, IEA, IFAD, IFC, IFRCS, IHO, ILO, IMF, IMO, Inmarsat, InOC, Intelsat, Interpol, IOC, IOM, ISO, ITU, MINURSO, MIPONUH, MONUC, NAM (guest), NATO, NEA, NSG, OAS (observer), OECD, OPCW, OSCE, PCA, SPC, UN, UN Security Council, UNCTAD, UNESCO, UNHCR, UNIDO, UNIFIL, UNIKOM, UNITAR, UNMEE, UNMIBH, UNMIK, UNOMIG, UNRWA, UNTAET, UNTSO, UNU, UPU, WADB (nonregional), WCL, WEU, WFTU, WHO, WIPO, WMO, WToO, WTrO, ZC
Diplomatic representation in the US:
chief of mission: Ambassador Francois V. BUJON DE L'ESTANG
chancery: 4101 Reservoir Road NW, Washington, DC 20007
telephone: [1] (202) 944-6000
FAX: [1] (202) 944-6166
consulate(s) general: Atlanta, Boston, Chicago, Houston, Los Angeles, Miami, New Orleans, New York, and San Francisco
Diplomatic representation from the US:
chief of mission: Ambassador-designate Howard H. LEACH; Charge d'Affaires Douglas L. McELHANEY
embassy: 2 Avenue Gabriel, 75382 Paris Cedex 08
mailing address: PSC 116, APO AE 09777
telephone: [33] (1) 43-12-22-22
FAX: [33] (1) 42 66 97 83
consulate(s) general: Marseille, Strasbourg
Flag description: three equal vertical bands of blue (hoist side), white, and red; known as the French Tricouleur (Tricolor); the design and/or colors are similar to a number of other flags, including those of Belgium, Chad, Ireland, Cote d'Ivoire, Luxembourg, and Netherlands; the official flag for all French dependent areas

Economy

Economy - overview: France is in the midst of transition, from an economy that featured extensive government ownership and intervention to one that relies more on market mechanisms. The government remains dominant in some sectors, particularly power, public transport, and defense industries, but it has been relaxing its control since the mid-1980s. The Socialist-led government has sold off part of its holdings in France Telecom, Air France, Thales, Thomson Multimedia, and the European Aerospace and Defense Company (EADS). The telecommunications sector is gradually being opened to competition. France's leaders remain committed to a capitalism in which they maintain social equity by means of laws, tax policies, and social spending that reduce income disparity and the impact of free markets on public health and welfare. The government has done little to cut generous unemployment and retirement benefits which impose a heavy tax burden and discourage hiring. It has also shied from measures that would dramatically increase the use of stock options and retirement investment plans; such measures would boost the stock market and fast-growing IT firms as well as ease the burden on the pension system, but would disproportionately benefit the rich. In addition to the tax burden, the reduction of the work week to 35-hours has drawn criticism for lowering the competitiveness of French companies.
GDP: purchasing power parity - $1.448 trillion (2000 est.)
GDP - real growth rate: 3.1% (2000 est.)
GDP - per capita: purchasing power parity - $24,400 (2000 est.)
GDP - composition by sector:
agriculture: 3.3%
industry: 26.1%
services: 70.6% (1999)
Population below poverty line: NA%
Household income or consumption by percentage share:
lowest 10%: 2.8%
highest 10%: 25.1% (1995)
Inflation rate (consumer prices): 1.7% (2000 est.)
Labor force: 25 million (2000)
Labor force - by occupation: services 71%, industry 25%, agriculture 4% (1997)
Unemployment rate: 9.7% (2000 est.)
Budget:
revenues: $210 billion
expenditures: $240 billion, including capital expenditures of $NA (2000 est.)
Industries: machinery, chemicals, automobiles, metallurgy, aircraft, electronics; textiles, food processing; tourism
Industrial production growth rate: 3.5% (2000 est.)
Electricity - production: 497.26 billion kWh (1999)
Electricity - production by source:
fossil fuel: 9.69%
hydro: 14.39%

France (continued)

nuclear: 75.43%
other: 0.49% (1999)
Electricity - consumption: 398.752 billion kWh (1999)
Electricity - exports: 68.7 billion kWh (1999)
Electricity - imports: 5 billion kWh (1999)
Agriculture - products: wheat, cereals, sugar beets, potatoes, wine grapes; beef, dairy products; fish
Exports: $325 billion (f.o.b., 2000 est.)
Exports - commodities: machinery and transportation equipment, aircraft, plastics, chemicals, pharmaceutical products, iron and steel, beverages
Exports - partners: EU 63% (Germany 16%, UK 10%, Spain 9%, Italy 9%, Belgium-Luxembourg 8%), US 8% (1999)
Imports: $320 billion (f.o.b., 2000 est.)
Imports - commodities: machinery and equipment, vehicles, crude oil, aircraft, plastics, chemicals
Imports - partners: EU 62% (Germany 16%, Belgium-Luxembourg 11%, Italy 9%, UK 8%), US 7% (2000 est.)
Debt - external: $106 billion (1998)
Economic aid - donor: ODA, $6.3 billion (1997)
Currency: French franc (FRF); euro (EUR)
note: on 1 January 1999, the EU introduced the euro as a common currency that is now being used by financial institutions in France at a fixed rate of 6.55957 French francs per euro and will replace the local currency for all transactions in 2002
Currency code: FRF; EUR
Exchange rates: euros per US dollar - 1.0659 (January 2001), 1.0854 (2000), 0.9386 (1999); French francs per US dollar - 5.65 (January 1999), 5.8995 (1998), 5.8367 (1997), 5.1155 (1996)
Fiscal year: calendar year

Communications

Telephones - main lines in use: 34.86 million (yearend 1998)
Telephones - mobile cellular: 11.078 million (yearend 1998)
Telephone system:
general assessment: highly developed
domestic: extensive cable and microwave radio relay; extensive introduction of fiber-optic cable; domestic satellite system
international: satellite earth stations - 2 Intelsat (with total of 5 antennas - 2 for Indian Ocean and 3 for Atlantic Ocean), NA Eutelsat, 1 Inmarsat (Atlantic Ocean region); HF radiotelephone communications with more than 20 countries
Radio broadcast stations: AM 41, FM about 3,500 (this figure is an approximation and includes many repeaters), shortwave 2 (1998)
Radios: 55.3 million (1997)
Television broadcast stations: 584 (plus 9,676 repeaters) (1995)
Televisions: 34.8 million (1997)
Internet country code: .fr
Internet Service Providers (ISPs): 62 (2000)
Internet users: 9 million (2000)

Transportation

Railways:
total: 31,939 km (31,939 km are operated by French National Railways (SNCF); 14,176 km of SNCF routes are electrified and 12,132 km are double- or multiple-tracked)
standard gauge: 31,840 km 1.435-m gauge
narrow gauge: 99 km 1.000-m gauge (1998)
Highways:
total: 892,900 km
paved: 892,900 km (including 9,900 km of expressways)
unpaved: 0 km (1999)
Waterways: 14,932 km (6,969 km heavily traveled)
Pipelines: crude oil 3,059 km; petroleum products 4,487 km; natural gas 24,746 km
Ports and harbors: Bordeaux, Boulogne, Cherbourg, Dijon, Dunkerque, La Pallice, Le Havre, Lyon, Marseille, Mullhouse, Nantes, Paris, Rouen, Saint Nazaire, Saint Malo, Strasbourg
Merchant marine:
total: 46 ships (1,000 GRT or over) totaling 942,333 GRT/1,304,754 DWT
ships by type: bulk 3, cargo 4, chemical tanker 6, combination bulk 1, container 1, liquefied gas 3, multi-functional large-load carrier 1, passenger 3, petroleum tanker 17, roll on/roll off 4, short-sea passenger 3
note: includes some foreign-owned ships registered here as a flag of convenience: Germany 1 (2000 est.)
Airports: 475 (2000 est.)
Airports - with paved runways:
total: 268
over 3,047 m: 14
2,438 to 3,047 m: 30
1,524 to 2,437 m: 94
914 to 1,523 m: 72
under 914 m: 58 (2000 est.)
Airports - with unpaved runways:
total: 207
1,524 to 2,437 m: 4
914 to 1,523 m: 73
under 914 m: 130 (2000 est.)
Heliports: 3 (2000 est.)

Military

Military branches: Army (includes Marines), Navy (includes Naval Air), Air Force (includes Air Defense), National Gendarmerie
Military manpower - military age: 18 years of age
Military manpower - availability:
males age 15-49: 14,573,199 (2001 est.)
Military manpower - fit for military service:
males age 15-49: 12,127,793 (2001 est.)
Military manpower - reaching military age annually:
males: 390,064 (2001 est.)
Military expenditures - dollar figure: $39.831 billion (FY97)
Military expenditures - percent of GDP: 2.5% (FY97)

Transnational Issues

Disputes - international: Madagascar claims Bassas da India, Europa Island, Glorioso Islands, Juan de Nova Island, and Tromelin Island; Comoros claims Mayotte; Mauritius claims Tromelin Island; territorial dispute between Suriname and French Guiana; territorial claim in Antarctica (Adelie Land); Matthew and Hunter Islands east of New Caledonia claimed by France and Vanuatu
Illicit drugs: transshipment point for and consumer of South American cocaine, Southwest Asian heroin, and European synthetics

French Guiana
(overseas department of France)

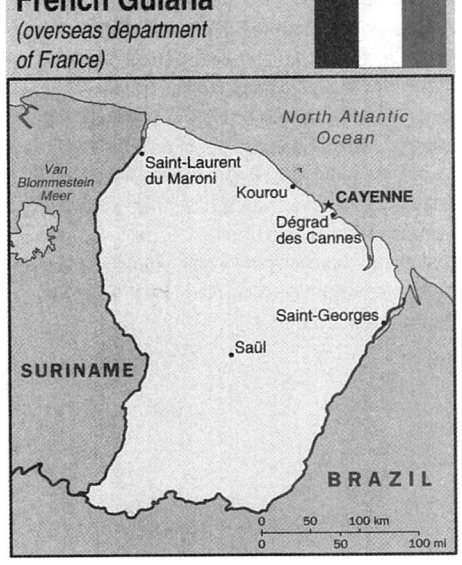

Introduction

Background: First settled by the French in 1604, French Guiana was the site of notorious penal settlements until 1951. The European Space Agency launches its communication satellites from Kourou.

Geography

Location: Northern South America, bordering the North Atlantic Ocean, between Brazil and Suriname
Geographic coordinates: 4 00 N, 53 00 W
Map references: South America
Area:
total: 91,000 sq km
land: 89,150 sq km
water: 1,850 sq km
Area - comparative: slightly smaller than Indiana
Land boundaries:
total: 1,183 km
border countries: Brazil 673 km, Suriname 510 km
Coastline: 378 km
Maritime claims:
exclusive economic zone: 200 NM
territorial sea: 12 NM
Climate: tropical; hot, humid; little seasonal temperature variation
Terrain: low-lying coastal plains rising to hills and small mountains
Elevation extremes:
lowest point: Atlantic Ocean 0 m
highest point: Bellevue de l'Inini 851 m
Natural resources: bauxite, timber, gold (widely scattered), cinnabar, kaolin, fish
Land use:
arable land: 0%
permanent crops: 0%
permanent pastures: 0%
forests and woodland: 90%
other: 10% (1996 est.)
Irrigated land: 20 sq km (1993 est.)
Natural hazards: high frequency of heavy showers and severe thunderstorms; flooding
Environment - current issues: NA
Geography - note: mostly an unsettled wilderness

People

Population: 177,562 (July 2001 est.)
Age structure:
0-14 years: 30.47% (male 27,669; female 26,428)
15-64 years: 64.05% (male 61,457; female 52,266)
65 years and over: 5.48% (male 4,937; female 4,805) (2001 est.)
Population growth rate: 2.74% (2001 est.)
Birth rate: 22.02 births/1,000 population (2001 est.)
Death rate: 4.77 deaths/1,000 population (2001 est.)
Net migration rate: 10.14 migrant(s)/1,000 population (2001 est.)
Sex ratio:
at birth: 1.05 male(s)/female
under 15 years: 1.05 male(s)/female
15-64 years: 1.18 male(s)/female
65 years and over: 1.03 male(s)/female
total population: 1.13 male(s)/female (2001 est.)
Infant mortality rate: 13.61 deaths/1,000 live births (2001 est.)
Life expectancy at birth:
total population: 76.3 years
male: 72.97 years
female: 79.79 years (2001 est.)
Total fertility rate: 3.17 children born/woman (2001 est.)
HIV/AIDS - adult prevalence rate: NA%
HIV/AIDS - people living with HIV/AIDS: NA
HIV/AIDS - deaths: NA
Nationality:
noun: French Guianese (singular and plural)
adjective: French Guianese
Ethnic groups: black or mulatto 66%, white 12%, East Indian, Chinese, Amerindian 12%, other 10%
Religions: Roman Catholic
Languages: French
Literacy:
definition: age 15 and over can read and write
total population: 83%
male: 84%
female: 82% (1982 est.)

Government

Country name:
conventional long form: Department of Guiana
conventional short form: French Guiana
local long form: none
local short form: Guyane
Dependency status: overseas department of France
Government type: NA
Capital: Cayenne
Administrative divisions: none (overseas department of France)
Independence: none (overseas department of France)
National holiday: Bastille Day, 14 July (1789)
Constitution: 28 September 1958 (French Constitution)
Legal system: French legal system
Suffrage: 18 years of age; universal
Executive branch:
chief of state: President Jacques CHIRAC of France (since 17 May 1995), represented by Prefect Dominique VIAN (since NA January 1997)
head of government: President of the General Council Andre LECANTE (since NA March 1998); President of the Regional Council Antoine KARAM (since 22 March 1992)
cabinet: NA
elections: French president elected by popular vote for a seven-year term; prefect appointed by the French president on the advice of the French Ministry of Interior; presidents of the General and Regional Councils are appointed by the members of those councils
Legislative branch: unicameral General Council or Conseil General (19 seats; members are elected by popular vote to serve six-year terms) and a unicameral Regional Council or Conseil Regional (31 seats; members are elected by popular vote to serve six-year terms)
elections: General Council - last held NA March 2000 (next to be held NA 2006); Regional Council - last held 15 March 1998 (next to be held NA 2004)
election results: General Council - percent of vote by party - NA%; seats by party - NA; Regional Council - percent of vote by party - PS 28.28%, various left parties 22.56%, RPR 15.91%, independents 8.6%, Walwari Committee 6%; seats by party - PS 11, various left parties 9, RPR 6, independents 3, Walwari Committee 2
note: one seat was elected to the French Senate on 27 September 1998 (next to be held NA September 2007); results - percent of vote by party - NA; seats by party - NA; 2 seats were elected to the French National Assembly on 25 May - 1 June 1997 (next to be held NA 2002); results - percent of vote by party - NA; seats by party - RPR 1, PSG 1
Judicial branch: Court of Appeals or Cour d'Appel (highest local court based in Martinique with jurisdiction over Martinique, Guadeloupe, and French Guiana)
Political parties and leaders: Guianese Socialist Party or PSG [Antoine KARAM]; Guyana Democratic Forces or FDG [Georges OTHILY]; Rally for the Republic or RPR [Roland HO-WEN-SZE]; Socialist Party or PS [Pierre RIBARDIERE] (may be a subset of PSG); Walwari Committee [Christine TAUBIRA-DELANON]
Political pressure groups and leaders: NA
International organization participation: FZ, WCL, WFTU
Diplomatic representation in the US: none (overseas department of France)
Diplomatic representation from the US: none (overseas department of France)
Flag description: the flag of France is used

French Guiana (continued)

Economy

Economy - overview: The economy is tied closely to that of France through subsidies and imports. Besides the French space center at Kourou, fishing and forestry are the most important economic activities. The large reserves of tropical hardwoods, not fully exploited, support an expanding sawmill industry which provides sawn logs for export. Cultivation of crops is limited to the coastal area, where the population is largely concentrated; rice and manioc are the major crops. French Guiana is heavily dependent on imports of food and energy. Unemployment is a serious problem, particularly among younger workers.
GDP: purchasing power parity - $1 billion (1998 est.)
GDP - real growth rate: NA%
GDP - per capita: purchasing power parity - $6,000 (1998 est.)
GDP - composition by sector:
agriculture: NA%
industry: NA%
services: NA%
Population below poverty line: NA%
Household income or consumption by percentage share:
lowest 10%: NA%
highest 10%: NA%
Inflation rate (consumer prices): 2.5% (1992)
Labor force: 58,800 (1997)
Labor force - by occupation: services, government, and commerce 60.6%, industry 21.2%, agriculture 18.2% (1980)
Unemployment rate: 21.4% (1998)
Budget:
revenues: $225 million
expenditures: $390 million, including capital expenditures of $105 million (1996)
Industries: construction, shrimp processing, forestry products, rum, gold mining
Industrial production growth rate: NA%
Electricity - production: 440 million kWh (1999)
Electricity - production by source:
fossil fuel: 100%
hydro: 0%
nuclear: 0%
other: 0% (1999)
Electricity - consumption: 409.2 million kWh (1999)
Electricity - exports: 0 kWh (1999)
Electricity - imports: 0 kWh (1999)
Agriculture - products: rice, manioc (tapioca), sugar, cocoa, vegetables, bananas; cattle, pigs, poultry
Exports: $155 million (f.o.b., 1997)
Exports - commodities: shrimp, timber, gold, rum, rosewood essence, clothing
Exports - partners: France 62%, Switzerland 7%, US 2% (1997)
Imports: $625 million (c.i.f., 1997)
Imports - commodities: food (grains, processed meat), machinery and transport equipment, fuels and chemicals
Imports - partners: France 52%, US 14%, Trinidad and Tobago 6% (1997)
Debt - external: $1.2 billion (1988)
Economic aid - recipient: $NA
Currency: French franc (FRF); euro (EUR)
Currency code: FRF; EUR
Exchange rates: Euros per US dollar - 1.0659 (January 2001), 1.0854 (2000), 0.9386 (1999); French francs per US dollar - 5.8995 (1998), 5.8367 (1997), 5.1155 (1996)
Fiscal year: calendar year

Communications

Telephones - main lines in use: 47,000 (1997)
Telephones - mobile cellular: NA
Telephone system:
general assessment: NA
domestic: fair open wire and microwave radio relay system
international: satellite earth station - 1 Intelsat (Atlantic Ocean)
Radio broadcast stations: AM 2, FM 14 (including 6 repeaters), shortwave 6 (including 5 repeaters) (1998)
Radios: 104,000 (1997)
Television broadcast stations: 3 (plus eight low-power repeaters) (1997)
Televisions: 30,000 (1997)
Internet country code: .gf
Internet Service Providers (ISPs): 2 (2000)
Internet users: 2,000 (2000)

Transportation

Railways: 0 km (1995)
Highways:
total: 1,817 km
paved: 727 km
unpaved: 1,090 km (1995)
Waterways: 3,300 km navigable by native craft
note: 460 km navigable by small oceangoing vessels and coastal and river steamers
Ports and harbors: Cayenne, Degrad des Cannes, Saint-Laurent du Maroni
Merchant marine: none (2000 est.)
Airports: 11 (2000 est.)
Airports - with paved runways:
total: 4
over 3,047 m: 1
914 to 1,523 m: 2
under 914 m: 1 (2000 est.)
Airports - with unpaved runways:
total: 7
914 to 1,523 m: 2
under 914 m: 5 (2000 est.)

Military

Military branches: French Forces, Gendarmerie
Military manpower - availability:
males age 15-49: 49,495 (2001 est.)
Military manpower - fit for military service:
males age 15-49: 32,052 (2001 est.)
Military expenditures - dollar figure: $NA
Military expenditures - percent of GDP: NA%
Military - note: defense is the responsibility of France

Transnational Issues

Disputes - international: Suriname claims area between Riviere Litani and Riviere Marouini (both headwaters of the Lawa)
Illicit drugs: small amount of marijuana grown for local consumption; minor transshipment point to Europe

French Polynesia
(overseas territory of France)

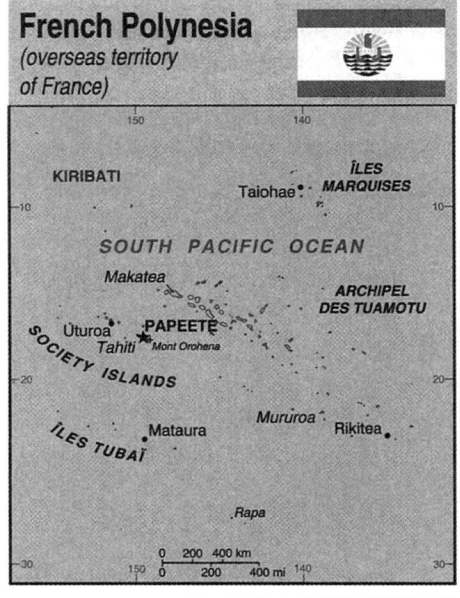

Introduction

Background: The French annexed various Polynesian island groups during the 19th century. In September 1995, France stirred up widespread protests by resuming nuclear testing on the Mururoa atoll after a three-year moratorium. The tests were suspended in January 1996.

Geography

Location: Oceania, archipelago in the South Pacific Ocean, about one-half of the way from South America to Australia
Geographic coordinates: 15 00 S, 140 00 W
Map references: Oceania
Area:
total: 4,167 sq km (118 islands and atolls)
land: 3,660 sq km
water: 507 sq km
Area - comparative: slightly less than one-third the size of Connecticut
Land boundaries: 0 km
Coastline: 2,525 km
Maritime claims:
exclusive economic zone: 200 NM
territorial sea: 12 NM
Climate: tropical, but moderate
Terrain: mixture of rugged high islands and low islands with reefs
Elevation extremes:
lowest point: Pacific Ocean 0 m
highest point: Mont Orohena 2,241 m
Natural resources: timber, fish, cobalt, hydropower
Land use:
arable land: 1%
permanent crops: 6%
permanent pastures: 5%
forests and woodland: 31%
other: 57% (1993 est.)
Irrigated land: NA sq km
Natural hazards: occasional cyclonic storms in January
Environment - current issues: NA
Geography - note: includes five archipelagoes; Makatea in French Polynesia is one of the three great phosphate rock islands in the Pacific Ocean - the others are Banaba (Ocean Island) in Kiribati and Nauru

People

Population: 253,506 (July 2001 est.)
Age structure:
0-14 years: 29.74% (male 38,473; female 36,925)
15-64 years: 65.17% (male 86,128; female 79,076)
65 years and over: 5.09% (male 6,481; female 6,423) (2001 est.)
Population growth rate: 1.72% (2001 est.)
Birth rate: 18.6 births/1,000 population (2001 est.)
Death rate: 4.45 deaths/1,000 population (2001 est.)
Net migration rate: 3.09 migrant(s)/1,000 population (2001 est.)
Sex ratio:
at birth: 1.05 male(s)/female
under 15 years: 1.04 male(s)/female
15-64 years: 1.09 male(s)/female
65 years and over: 1.01 male(s)/female
total population: 1.07 male(s)/female (2001 est.)
Infant mortality rate: 9.12 deaths/1,000 live births (2001 est.)
Life expectancy at birth:
total population: 75.01 years
male: 72.67 years
female: 77.46 years (2001 est.)
Total fertility rate: 2.23 children born/woman (2001 est.)
HIV/AIDS - adult prevalence rate: NA%
HIV/AIDS - people living with HIV/AIDS: NA
HIV/AIDS - deaths: NA
Nationality:
noun: French Polynesian(s)
adjective: French Polynesian
Ethnic groups: Polynesian 78%, Chinese 12%, local French 6%, metropolitan French 4%
Religions: Protestant 54%, Roman Catholic 30%, other 16%
Languages: French (official), Tahitian (official)
Literacy:
definition: age 14 and over can read and write
total population: 98%
male: 98%
female: 98% (1977 est.)

Government

Country name:
conventional long form: Territory of French Polynesia
conventional short form: French Polynesia
local long form: Territoire de la Polynesie Francaise
local short form: Polynesie Francaise
former: French Colony of Oceania
Dependency status: overseas territory of France since 1946
Government type: NA
Capital: Papeete
Administrative divisions: none (overseas territory of France); there are no first-order administrative divisions as defined by the US Government, but there are 5 archipelagic divisions named Archipel des Marquises, Archipel des Tuamotu, Archipel des Tubuai, Iles du Vent, and Iles Sous-le-Vent
note: Clipperton Island is administered by France from French Polynesia
Independence: none (overseas territory of France)
National holiday: Bastille Day, 14 July (1789)
Constitution: 28 September 1958 (French Constitution)
Legal system: based on French system
Suffrage: 18 years of age; universal
Executive branch:
chief of state: President Jacques CHIRAC of France (since 17 May 1995), represented by High Commissioner of the Republic Paul RONCIERE (since NA 1994)
head of government: President of the Territorial Government of French Polynesia Gaston FLOSSE (since 4 April 1991); President of the Territorial Assembly Justin ARAPARI (since 13 May 1996)
cabinet: Council of Ministers; president submits a list of members of the Territorial Assembly for approval by them to serve as ministers
elections: French president elected by popular vote for a seven-year term; high commissioner appointed by the French president on the advice of the French Ministry of Interior; president of the Territorial Government and the president of the Territorial Assembly are elected by the members of the assembly
Legislative branch: unicameral Territorial Assembly or Assemblee Territoriale (41 seats; members are elected by popular vote to serve five-year terms)
elections: last held 12 May 1996 (next to be held NA 2001)
election results: percent of vote by party - NA%; seats by party - People's Rally for the Republic (Gaullist) 22, Independent Front for the Liberation of Polynesia 10, New Fatherland Party 5, other 4
note: one seat was elected to the French Senate on 24 September 1989 (next to be held NA September 1998); results - percent of vote by party - NA; seats by party - UC 1; two seats were elected to the French National Assembly on 25 May - 1 June 1997 (next to be held NA 2002); results - percent of vote by party - NA; seats by party - People's Rally for the Republic (Gaullist) 2
Judicial branch: Court of Appeal or Cour d'Appel; Court of the First Instance or Tribunal de Premiere Instance; Court of Administrative Law or Tribunal Administratif
Political parties and leaders: Centrist Union or UC [leader NA]; Independent Front for the Liberation of Polynesia (Tavini Huiraatira) [Oscar TEMARU]; New Fatherland Party (Ai'a Api) [Emile VERNAUDON]; People's Rally for the Republic (Tahoeraa Huiraatira) [Gaston FLOSSE]
Political pressure groups and leaders: NA
International organization participation: ESCAP (associate), FZ, ICFTU, SPC, WMO

French Polynesia (continued)

Diplomatic representation in the US: none (overseas territory of France)
Diplomatic representation from the US: none (overseas territory of France)
Flag description: two narrow red horizontal bands encase a wide white band; centered on the white band is a disk with blue and white wave pattern on the lower half and gold and white ray pattern on the upper half; a stylized red, blue and white ship rides on the wave pattern; the French flag is used for official occasions

Economy

Economy - overview: Since 1962, when France stationed military personnel in the region, French Polynesia has changed from a subsistence economy to one in which a high proportion of the work force is either employed by the military or supports the tourist industry. Tourism accounts for about one-fourth of GDP and is a primary source of hard currency earnings. The small manufacturing sector primarily processes agricultural products. The territory benefited from a five-year (1994-98) development agreement with France aimed principally at creating new jobs.
GDP: purchasing power parity - $2.6 billion (1997 est.)
GDP - real growth rate: 2.5% (1997 est.)
GDP - per capita: purchasing power parity - $10,800 (1997 est.)
GDP - composition by sector:
agriculture: 4%
industry: 18%
services: 78% (1997)
Population below poverty line: NA%
Household income or consumption by percentage share:
lowest 10%: NA%
highest 10%: NA%
Inflation rate (consumer prices): 1.5% (1994)
Labor force: 70,000 (1996)
Labor force - by occupation: agriculture 13%, industry 19%, services 68% (1997)
Unemployment rate: 15% (1992 est.)
Budget:
revenues: $1 billion
expenditures: $900 million, including capital expenditures of $185 million (1996)
Industries: tourism, pearls, agricultural processing, handicrafts
Industrial production growth rate: NA%
Electricity - production: 430 million kWh (1999)
Electricity - production by source:
fossil fuel: 51.16%
hydro: 48.84%
nuclear: 0%
other: 0% (1999)
Electricity - consumption: 399.9 million kWh (1999)
Electricity - exports: 0 kWh (1999)
Electricity - imports: 0 kWh (1999)
Agriculture - products: coconuts, vanilla, vegetables, fruits; poultry, beef, dairy products

Exports: $205 million (f.o.b., 1999)
Exports - commodities: cultured pearls 50%, coconut products, mother-of-pearl, vanilla, shark meat (1997)
Exports - partners: Japan 62%, US 21% (1999)
Imports: $749 million (f.o.b., 1999)
Imports - commodities: fuels, foodstuffs, equipment
Imports - partners: France 53%, US 13%, Australia 10% (1999)
Debt - external: $NA
Economic aid - recipient: $367 million (1997)
Currency: Comptoirs Francais du Pacifique franc (XPF)
Currency code: XPF
Exchange rates: Comptoirs Francais du Pacifique francs (XPF) per US dollar - 127.11 (January 2001), 129.44 (2000), 111.93 (1999), 107.25 (1998), 106.11 (1997), 93.00 (1996); note - pegged at the rate of 119.25 XPF to the euro
Fiscal year: calendar year

Communications

Telephones - main lines in use: 52,000 (1997)
Telephones - mobile cellular: 5,427 (1997)
Telephone system:
general assessment: NA
domestic: NA
international: satellite earth station - 1 Intelsat (Pacific Ocean)
Radio broadcast stations: AM 2, FM 14, shortwave 2 (1998)
Radios: 128,000 (1997)
Television broadcast stations: 7 (plus 17 low-power repeaters) (1997)
Televisions: 40,000 (1997)
Internet country code: .pf
Internet Service Providers (ISPs): 2 (2000)
Internet users: 5,000 (2000)

Transportation

Railways: 0 km
Highways:
total: 792 km
paved: 264 km
unpaved: 528 km (2000)
Waterways: none
Ports and harbors: Mataura, Papeete, Rikitea, Uturoa
Merchant marine:
total: 4 ships (1,000 GRT or over) totaling 5,240 GRT/7,765 DWT
ships by type: cargo 1, passenger/cargo 2, refrigerated cargo 1 (2000 est.)
Airports: 45 (2000 est.)
Airports - with paved runways:
total: 32
over 3,047 m: 2
1,524 to 2,437 m: 5
914 to 1,523 m: 19
under 914 m: 6 (2000 est.)

Airports - with unpaved runways:
total: 13
914 to 1,523 m: 3
under 914 m: 10 (2000 est.)

Military

Military branches: French Forces (includes Army, Navy, Air Force), Gendarmerie
Military - note: defense is the responsibility of France

Transnational Issues

Disputes - international: none

French Southern and Antarctic Lands
(overseas territory of France)

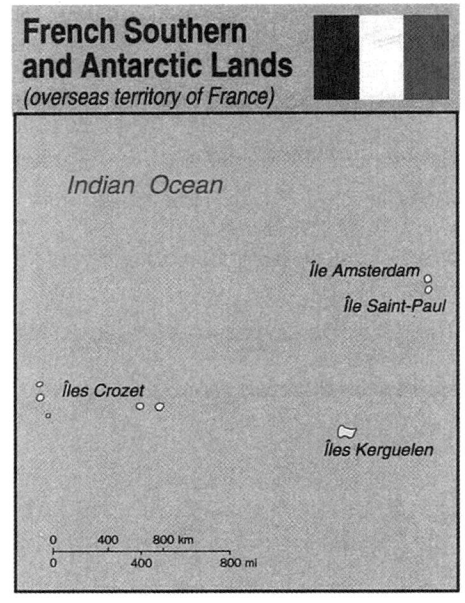

Introduction

Background: The Southern Lands consist of two archipelagos, Iles Crozet and Iles Kerguelen, and two volcanic islands, Ile Amsterdam and Ile Saint-Paul. They contain no permanent inhabitants and are visited only by researchers studying the native fauna. The Antarctic portion consists of "Adelie Land," a thin slice of the Antarctic continent discovered and claimed by the French in 1840.

Geography

Location: south of Africa, islands in the southern Indian Ocean, about equidistant between Africa, Antarctica, and Australia; note - French Southern and Antarctic Lands includes Ile Amsterdam, Ile Saint-Paul, Iles Crozet, and Iles Kerguelen in the southern Indian Ocean, along with the French-claimed sector of Antarctica, "Adelie Land"; the US does not recognize the French claim to "Adelie Land"
Geographic coordinates: 43 00 S, 67 00 E
Map references: Antarctic Region
Area:
total: 7,781 sq km
land: 7,781 sq km
water: 0 sq km
note: includes Ile Amsterdam, Ile Saint-Paul, Iles Crozet and Iles Kerguelen; excludes "Adelie Land" claim of about 500,000 sq km in Antarctica that is not recognized by the US
Area - comparative: slightly less than 1.3 times the size of Delaware
Land boundaries: 0 km
Coastline: 1,232 km
Maritime claims:
exclusive economic zone: 200 NM from Iles Kerguelen only
territorial sea: 12 NM
Climate: antarctic
Terrain: volcanic
Elevation extremes:
lowest point: Indian Ocean 0 m
highest point: Mont Ross on Iles Kerguelen 1,850 m
Natural resources: fish, crayfish
Land use:
arable land: 0%
permanent crops: 0%
permanent pastures: 0%
forests and woodland: 0%
other: 100%
Irrigated land: 0 sq km (1993)
Natural hazards: Ile Amsterdam and Ile Saint-Paul are extinct volcanoes
Environment - current issues: NA
Geography - note: islands component is widely scattered across remote locations in the southern Indian Ocean

People

Population: no indigenous inhabitants (July 2001 est.)
note: in 1997, there were about 100 researchers whose numbers vary from winter (July) to summer (January)

Government

Country name:
conventional long form: Territory of the French Southern and Antarctic Lands
conventional short form: French Southern and Antarctic Lands
local long form: Territoire des Terres Australes et Antarctiques Francaises
local short form: Terres Australes et Antarctiques Francaises
Dependency status: overseas territory of France since 1955; administered from Paris by High Commissioner of the Republic Brigitte GIRARDIN (since 25 March 1998), assisted by Secretary General Jean-Yves HERMOSO (since NA)
Administrative divisions: none (overseas territory of France); there are no first-order administrative divisions as defined by the US Government, but there are 3 districts named Ile Crozet, Iles Kerguelen, and Iles Saint-Paul et Amsterdam; excludes "Adelie Land" claim in Antarctica that is not recognized by the US
Legal system: the laws of France, where applicable, apply
Diplomatic representation in the US: none (overseas territory of France)
Diplomatic representation from the US: none (overseas territory of France)
Flag description: the flag of France is used

Economy

Economy - overview: Economic activity is limited to servicing meteorological and geophysical research stations and French and other fishing fleets. The fish catches landed on Iles Kerguelen by foreign ships are exported to France and Reunion.

Communications

Internet country code: .tf

Transportation

Waterways: none
Ports and harbors: none; offshore anchorage only
Merchant marine:
total: 74 ships (1,000 GRT or over) totaling 3,024,194 GRT/5,255,703 DWT
ships by type: bulk 7, cargo 5, chemical tanker 9, container 11, liquefied gas 7, petroleum tanker 23, roll on/roll off 12
note: includes some foreign-owned ships registered here as a flag of convenience: France 1 (2000 est.)
Airports: none

Military

Military - note: defense is the responsibility of France

Transnational Issues

Disputes - international: "Adelie Land" claim in Antarctica is not recognized by the US

Gabon

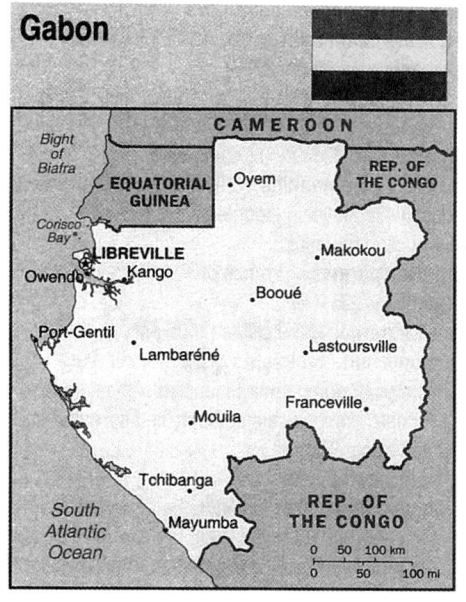

Introduction

Background: Ruled by autocratic presidents since independence from France in 1960, Gabon introduced a multiparty system and a new constitution in the early 1990s that allowed for a more transparent electoral process and for reforms of governmental institutions. A small population, abundant natural resources, and foreign private investment have helped make Gabon one of the more prosperous black African countries.

Geography

Location: Western Africa, bordering the Atlantic Ocean at the Equator, between Republic of the Congo and Equatorial Guinea
Geographic coordinates: 1 00 S, 11 45 E
Map references: Africa
Area:
total: 267,667 sq km
land: 257,667 sq km
water: 10,000 sq km
Area - comparative: slightly smaller than Colorado
Land boundaries:
total: 2,551 km
border countries: Cameroon 298 km, Republic of the Congo 1,903 km, Equatorial Guinea 350 km
Coastline: 885 km
Maritime claims:
contiguous zone: 24 NM
exclusive economic zone: 200 NM
territorial sea: 12 NM
Climate: tropical; always hot, humid
Terrain: narrow coastal plain; hilly interior; savanna in east and south
Elevation extremes:
lowest point: Atlantic Ocean 0 m
highest point: Mont Iboundji 1,575 m
Natural resources: petroleum, manganese, uranium, gold, timber, iron ore, hydropower
Land use:
arable land: 1%
permanent crops: 1%
permanent pastures: 18%
forests and woodland: 77%
other: 3% (1993 est.)
Irrigated land: 40 sq km (1993 est.)
Natural hazards: NA
Environment - current issues: deforestation; poaching
Environment - international agreements:
party to: Biodiversity, Climate Change, Desertification, Endangered Species, Law of the Sea, Marine Dumping, Nuclear Test Ban, Ozone Layer Protection, Ship Pollution, Tropical Timber 83, Tropical Timber 94, Wetlands
signed, but not ratified: none of the selected agreements

People

Population: 1,221,175
note: estimates for this country explicitly take into account the effects of excess mortality due to AIDS; this can result in lower life expectancy, higher infant mortality and death rates, lower population and growth rates, and changes in the distribution of population by age and sex than would otherwise be expected (July 2001 est.)
Age structure:
0-14 years: 33.29% (male 203,677; female 202,833)
15-64 years: 60.77% (male 373,828; female 368,282)
65 years and over: 5.94% (male 35,867; female 36,688) (2001 est.)
Population growth rate: 1.02% (2001 est.)
Birth rate: 27.42 births/1,000 population (2001 est.)
Death rate: 17.22 deaths/1,000 population (2001 est.)
Net migration rate: 0 migrant(s)/1,000 population (2001 est.)
Sex ratio:
at birth: 1.03 male(s)/female
under 15 years: 1 male(s)/female
15-64 years: 1.02 male(s)/female
65 years and over: 0.98 male(s)/female
total population: 1.01 male(s)/female (2001 est.)
Infant mortality rate: 94.91 deaths/1,000 live births (2001 est.)
Life expectancy at birth:
total population: 49.59 years
male: 48.47 years
female: 50.75 years (2001 est.)
Total fertility rate: 3.69 children born/woman (2001 est.)
HIV/AIDS - adult prevalence rate: 4.16% (1999 est.)
HIV/AIDS - people living with HIV/AIDS: 23,000 (1999 est.)
HIV/AIDS - deaths: 2,000 (1999 est.)
Nationality:
noun: Gabonese (singular and plural)
adjective: Gabonese
Ethnic groups: Bantu tribes including four major tribal groupings (Fang, Eshira, Bapounou, Bateke), other Africans and Europeans 154,000, including 10,700 French and 11,000 persons of dual nationality
Religions: Christian 55%-75%, animist, Muslim less than 1%
Languages: French (official), Fang, Myene, Bateke, Bapounou/Eschira, Bandjabi
Literacy:
definition: age 15 and over can read and write
total population: 63.2%
male: 73.7%
female: 53.3% (1995 est.)

Government

Country name:
conventional long form: Gabonese Republic
conventional short form: Gabon
local long form: Republique Gabonaise
local short form: Gabon
Government type: republic; multiparty presidential regime (opposition parties legalized in 1990)
Capital: Libreville
Administrative divisions: 9 provinces; Estuaire, Haut-Ogooue, Moyen-Ogooue, Ngounie, Nyanga, Ogooue-Ivindo, Ogooue-Lolo, Ogooue-Maritime, Woleu-Ntem
Independence: 17 August 1960 (from France)
National holiday: Founding of the Gabonese Democratic Party (PDG), 12 March (1968)
Constitution: adopted 14 March 1991
Legal system: based on French civil law system and customary law; judicial review of legislative acts in Constitutional Chamber of the Supreme Court; has not accepted compulsory ICJ jurisdiction
Suffrage: 21 years of age; universal
Executive branch:
chief of state: President El Hadj Omar BONGO (since 2 December 1967)
head of government: Prime Minister Jean-Francois NTOUTOUME-EMANE (since 23 January 1999)
cabinet: Council of Ministers appointed by the prime minister in consultation with the president
elections: president elected by popular vote for a seven-year term; election last held 6 December 1998 (next to be held NA 2005); prime minister appointed by the president
election results: President El Hadj Omar BONGO reelected; percent of vote - El Hadj Omar BONGO 66.6%, Pierre MAMBOUNDOU 16.5%, Fr. Paul M'BA-ABESSOLE 13.4%
Legislative branch: bicameral legislature consists of the Senate (91 seats) and the National Assembly or Assemblee Nationale (120 seats); members are elected by direct popular vote to serve five-year terms
elections: National Assembly - last held 15 and 29 December 1996 (next to be held NA December 2001); Senate - last held 26 January and 9 February 1997 (next to be held in January 2002)
election results: National Assembly - percent of vote by party - NA%; seats by party - PDG 89, PGP 9, RNB 6, CLR 3, UPG 2, USG 2, independents 4, others 5; Senate - percent of vote by party - NA%; seats by party - PDG 53, RNB 20, PGP 4, ADERE 3, RDP 1, CLR 1, independents 9

Gabon (continued)

Judicial branch: Supreme Court or Cour Supreme consisting of three chambers - Judicial, Administrative, and Accounts; Constitutional Court; Courts of Appeal; Court of State Security; County Courts

Political parties and leaders: African Forum for Reconstruction or FAR [Leon MBOU-YEMBI]; Circle of Liberal Reformers or CLR [General Jean Boniface ASSELE]; Democratic and Republican Alliance or ADERE [Divungui-di-Ndinge DIDJOB]; Gabonese Democratic Party or PDG, former sole party [Simplice Nguedet MANZELA, secretary general]; Gabonese Party for Progress or PGP [Pierre-Louis AGONDJO-OKAWE, president]; Gabonese People's Union or UPG [Pierre MAMBOUNDOU]; Gabonese Socialist Union or USG [Serge MBA BEKALE]; National Rally of Woodcutters (Bucherons) or RNB [Fr. Paul M'BA-ABESSOLE]; People's Unity Party or PUP [Louis Gaston MAYILA]; Rally for Democracy and Progress or RDP [Pierre EMBONI]; Social Democratic Party or PSD [Pierre Claver MAGANGA-MOUSSAVOU]

Political pressure groups and leaders: NA

International organization participation: ACCT, ACP, AfDB, BDEAC, CCC, CEEAC, CEMAC, ECA, FAO, FZ, G-24, G-77, IAEA, IBRD, ICAO, ICFTU, IDA, IDB, IFAD, IFC, IFRCS (associate), ILO, IMF, IMO, Inmarsat, Intelsat, Interpol, IOC, ITU, NAM, OAU, OIC, OPCW, UN, UNCTAD, UNESCO, UNIDO, UPU, WCL, WHO, WIPO, WMO, WToO, WTrO

Diplomatic representation in the US:
chief of mission: Ambassador Paul BOUNDOUKOU-LATHA
chancery: Suite 200, 2034 20th Street NW, Washington, DC 20009
telephone: [1] (202) 797-1000
FAX: [1] (202) 332-0668
consulate(s): New York

Diplomatic representation from the US:
chief of mission: Ambassador James V. LEDESMA
embassy: Boulevard de la Mer, Libreville
mailing address: B. P. 4000, Libreville
telephone: [241] 76 20 03 through 76 20 04, 74 34 92
FAX: [241] 74 55 07

Flag description: three equal horizontal bands of green (top), yellow, and blue

Economy

Economy - overview: Gabon enjoys a per capita income four times that of most nations of sub-Saharan Africa. This has supported a sharp decline in extreme poverty; yet because of high income inequality a large proportion of the population remains poor. Gabon depended on timber and manganese until oil was discovered offshore in the early 1970s. The oil sector now accounts for 50% of GDP. Gabon continues to face fluctuating prices for its oil, timber, manganese, and uranium exports. Despite the abundance of natural wealth, the economy is hobbled by poor fiscal management. In 1992, the fiscal deficit widened to 2.4% of GDP, and Gabon failed to settle arrears on its bilateral debt, leading to a cancellation of rescheduling agreements with official and private creditors. Devaluation of its Francophone currency by 50% on 12 January 1994 sparked a one-time inflationary surge, to 35%; the rate dropped to 6% in 1996. The IMF provided a one-year standby arrangement in 1994-95, a three-year Enhanced Financing Facility (EFF) at near commercial rates beginning in late 1995, and stand-by credit of $119 million in October 2000. Those agreements mandate progress in privatization and fiscal discipline. France provided additional financial support in January 1997 after Gabon had met IMF targets for mid-1996. In 1997, an IMF mission to Gabon criticized the government for overspending on off-budget items, overborrowing from the central bank, and slipping on its schedule for privatization and administrative reform. The rebound of oil prices in 1999-2000 helped growth, but drops in production hampered Gabon from fully realizing potential gains. An expected decline in oil output may lead to contraction in GDP in 2001-02.

GDP: purchasing power parity - $7.7 billion (2000 est.)

GDP - real growth rate: 1.2% (2000 est.)

GDP - per capita: purchasing power parity - $6,300 (2000 est.)

GDP - composition by sector:
agriculture: 10%
industry: 60%
services: 30% (1999 est.)

Population below poverty line: NA%

Household income or consumption by percentage share:
lowest 10%: NA%
highest 10%: NA%

Inflation rate (consumer prices): 1.5% (2000 est.)

Labor force: 600,000

Labor force - by occupation: agriculture 60%, services and government 25%, industry and commerce 15%

Unemployment rate: 21% (1997 est.)

Budget:
revenues: $1.5 billion
expenditures: $1.3 billion, including capital expenditures of $302 million (1996 est.)

Industries: food and beverage; textile; lumbering and plywood; cement; petroleum extraction and refining; manganese, uranium, and gold mining; chemicals; ship repair

Industrial production growth rate: 2.3% (1995)

Electricity - production: 1.02 billion kWh (1999)

Electricity - production by source:
fossil fuel: 29.9%
hydro: 70.1%
nuclear: 0%
other: 0% (1999)

Electricity - consumption: 948.6 million kWh (1999)

Electricity - exports: 0 kWh (1999)

Electricity - imports: 0 kWh (1999)

Agriculture - products: cocoa, coffee, sugar, palm oil, rubber; cattle; okoume (a tropical softwood); fish

Exports: $3.4 billion (f.o.b., 2000 est.)

Exports - commodities: crude oil 75%, timber, manganese, uranium (1998)

Exports - partners: US 47%, France 19%, China 8%, Japan 1.3% (1999)

Imports: $1 billion (f.o.b., 2000 est.)

Imports - commodities: machinery and equipment, foodstuffs, chemicals, petroleum products, construction materials

Imports - partners: France 64%, US 4%, UK 2%, Netherlands 2%, (1999)

Debt - external: $3.9 billion (2000 est.)

Economic aid - recipient: $331 million (1995)

Currency: Communaute Financiere Africaine franc (XAF); note - responsible authority is the Bank of the Central African States

Currency code: XAF

Exchange rates: Communaute Financiere Africaine francs (XAF) per US dollar - 699.21 (January 2001), 711.98 (2000), 615.70 (1999), 589.95 (1998), 583.67 (1997), 511.55 (1996); note - from 1 January 1999, the XAF is pegged to the euro at a rate of 655.957 XAF per euro

Fiscal year: calendar year

Communications

Telephones - main lines in use: 37,000 (1997)

Telephones - mobile cellular: 9,500 (1997)

Telephone system:
general assessment: NA
domestic: adequate system of cable, microwave radio relay, tropospheric scatter, radiotelephone communication stations, and a domestic satellite system with 12 earth stations
international: satellite earth stations - 3 Intelsat (Atlantic Ocean)

Radio broadcast stations: AM 6, FM 7, shortwave 6 (1998)

Radios: 208,000 (1997)

Television broadcast stations: 4 (plus five low-power repeaters) (1997)

Televisions: 63,000 (1997)

Internet country code: .ga

Internet Service Providers (ISPs): 1 (2000)

Internet users: 5,000 (2000)

Transportation

Railways:
total: 649 km (Gabon State Railways or OCTRA)
standard gauge: 649 km 1.435-m gauge; single track (1994)

Highways:
total: 7,670 km
paved: 629 km (including 30 km of expressways)
unpaved: 7,041 km (1996)

Waterways: 1,600 km (perennially navigable)

Pipelines: crude oil 270 km; petroleum products 14 km

Ports and harbors: Cap Lopez, Kango, Lambarene, Libreville, Mayumba, Owendo, Port-Gentil

Airports: 59 (2000 est.)

Gabon (continued)

Airports - with paved runways:
total: 10
over 3,047 m: 1
2,438 to 3,047 m: 1
1,524 to 2,437 m: 7
914 to 1,523 m: 1 (2000 est.)
Airports - with unpaved runways:
total: 49
1,524 to 2,437 m: 8
914 to 1,523 m: 17
under 914 m: 24 (2000 est.)

Military

Military branches: Army, Navy, Air Force, Republican Guard (charged with protecting the president and other senior officials), National Gendarmerie, National Police
Military manpower - military age: 20 years of age
Military manpower - availability:
males age 15-49: 281,218 (2001 est.)
Military manpower - fit for military service:
males age 15-49: 145,062 (2001 est.)
Military manpower - reaching military age annually:
males: 11,304 (2001 est.)
Military expenditures - dollar figure: $91 million (FY96)
Military expenditures - percent of GDP: 1.6% (FY96)

Transnational Issues

Disputes - international: maritime boundary dispute with Equatorial Guinea because of disputed sovereignty over islands in Corisco Bay

Gambia, The

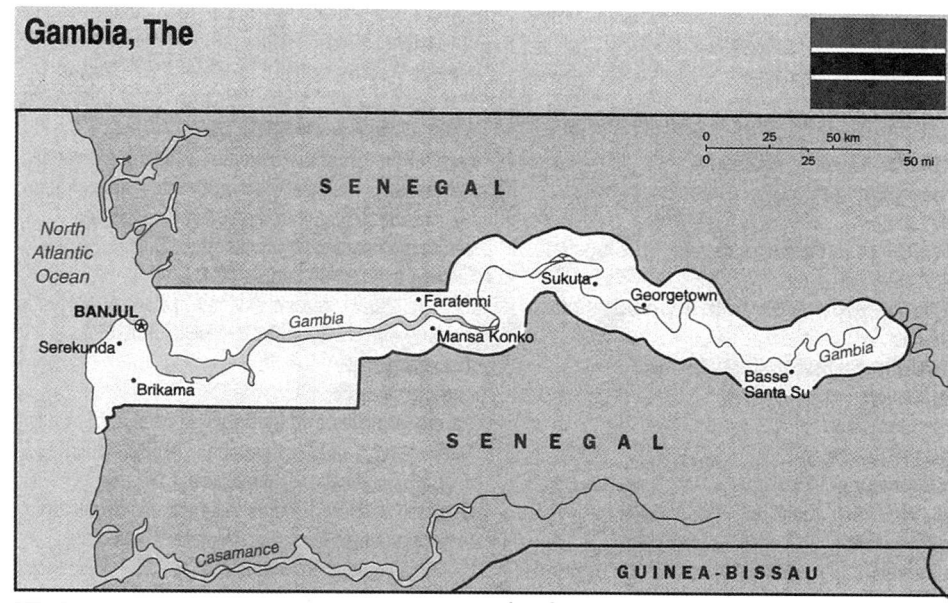

Introduction

Background: The Gambia gained its independence from the UK in 1965; it formed a short-lived federation of Senegambia with Senegal between 1982 and 1989. In 1991 the two nations signed a friendship and cooperation treaty. A military coup in 1994 overthrew the president and banned political activity, but a new 1996 constitution and presidential elections, followed by parliamentary balloting in 1997, have completed a nominal return to civilian rule.

Geography

Location: Western Africa, bordering the North Atlantic Ocean and Senegal
Geographic coordinates: 13 28 N, 16 34 W
Map references: Africa
Area:
total: 11,300 sq km
land: 10,000 sq km
water: 1,300 sq km
Area - comparative: slightly less than twice the size of Delaware
Land boundaries:
total: 740 km
border countries: Senegal 740 km
Coastline: 80 km
Maritime claims:
contiguous zone: 18 NM
continental shelf: not specified
exclusive fishing zone: 200 NM
territorial sea: 12 NM
Climate: tropical; hot, rainy season (June to November); cooler, dry season (November to May)
Terrain: flood plain of the Gambia river flanked by some low hills
Elevation extremes:
lowest point: Atlantic Ocean 0 m
highest point: unnamed location 53 m
Natural resources: fish
Land use:
arable land: 18%
permanent crops: 0%
permanent pastures: 9%
forests and woodland: 28%
other: 45% (1993 est.)
Irrigated land: 150 sq km (1993 est.)
Natural hazards: drought (rainfall has dropped by 30% in the last 30 years)
Environment - current issues: deforestation; desertification; water-borne diseases prevalent
Environment - international agreements:
party to: Biodiversity, Climate Change, Desertification, Endangered Species, Hazardous Wastes, Law of the Sea, Marine Dumping, Nuclear Test Ban, Ozone Layer Protection, Ship Pollution, Wetlands
signed, but not ratified: none of the selected agreements
Geography - note: almost an enclave of Senegal; smallest country on the continent of Africa

People

Population: 1,411,205 (July 2001 est.)
Age structure:
0-14 years: 45.22% (male 320,458; female 317,647)
15-64 years: 52.13% (male 364,900; female 370,717)
65 years and over: 2.65% (male 19,660; female 17,823) (2001 est.)
Population growth rate: 3.14% (2001 est.)
Birth rate: 41.76 births/1,000 population (2001 est.)
Death rate: 12.92 deaths/1,000 population (2001 est.)
Net migration rate: 2.59 migrant(s)/1,000 population (2001 est.)
Sex ratio:
at birth: 1.03 male(s)/female
under 15 years: 1.01 male(s)/female
15-64 years: 0.98 male(s)/female
65 years and over: 1.1 male(s)/female
total population: 1 male(s)/female (2001 est.)

Gambia, The (continued)

Infant mortality rate: 77.84 deaths/1,000 live births (2001 est.)
Life expectancy at birth:
total population: 53.59 years
male: 51.65 years
female: 55.58 years (2001 est.)
Total fertility rate: 5.68 children born/woman (2001 est.)
HIV/AIDS - adult prevalence rate: 1.95% (1999 est.)
HIV/AIDS - people living with HIV/AIDS: 13,000 (1999 est.)
HIV/AIDS - deaths: 1,400 (1999 est.)
Nationality:
noun: Gambian(s)
adjective: Gambian
Ethnic groups: African 99% (Mandinka 42%, Fula 18%, Wolof 16%, Jola 10%, Serahuli 9%, other 4%), non-African 1%
Religions: Muslim 90%, Christian 9%, indigenous beliefs 1%
Languages: English (official), Mandinka, Wolof, Fula, other indigenous vernaculars
Literacy:
definition: age 15 and over can read and write
total population: 47.5%
male: 58.4%
female: 37.1% (2001 est.)

Government

Country name:
conventional long form: Republic of The Gambia
conventional short form: The Gambia
Government type: republic under multiparty democratic rule
Capital: Banjul
Administrative divisions: 5 divisions and 1 city*; Banjul*, Lower River, Central River, North Bank, Upper River, Western
Independence: 18 February 1965 (from UK)
National holiday: Independence Day, 18 February (1965)
Constitution: 24 April 1970; suspended July 1994; rewritten and approved by national referendum 8 August 1996; reestablished in January 1997
Legal system: based on a composite of English common law, Koranic law, and customary law; accepts compulsory ICJ jurisdiction, with reservations
Suffrage: 18 years of age; universal
Executive branch:
chief of state: President Yahya A. J. J. JAMMEH (since 18 October 1996); Vice President Isatou Njie SAIDY (since 20 March 1997); note - the president is both the chief of state and head of government
head of government: President Yahya A. J. J. JAMMEH (since 18 October 1996); Vice President Isatou Njie SAIDY (since 20 March 1997); note - the president is both the chief of state and head of government
cabinet: Cabinet is appointed by the president
elections: the president is elected by popular vote for a five-year term; the number of terms is not restricted; election last held 26 September 1996 (next to be held NA October 2001)
election results: Yahya A. J. J. JAMMEH elected president; percent of vote - Yahya A. J. J. JAMMEH 55.8%, Ousainou DARBOE 35.8%
Legislative branch: unicameral National Assembly (49 seats; 45 elected by popular vote, 4 appointed by the president; members serve five-year terms)
elections: last popular election held 2 January 1997 (next to be held NA January 2002)
election results: percent of vote by party - NA%; seats by party - APRC 33, UDP 7, NRP 2, PDOIS 1, independents 2
Judicial branch: Supreme Court
Political parties and leaders: Alliance for Patriotic Reorientation and Construction or APRC [Yahya A. J. J. JAMMEH]; National Reconciliation Party or NRP [Hamat N. K. BAH]; People's Democratic Organization for Independence and Socialism or PDOIS [Sidia JATTA]; United Democratic Party or UDP [Ousainou DARBOE]
note: in August 1996 the government banned the following from participation in the elections of 1996: People's Progressive Party or PPP [former President Dawda K. JAWARA (in exile)], and two opposition parties - the National Convention Party or NCP [former Vice President Sheriff DIBBA] and the Gambian People's Party or GPP [Hassan Musa CAMARA]
Political pressure groups and leaders: NA
International organization participation: ACP, AfDB, C, CCC, ECA, ECOWAS, FAO, G-77, IBRD, ICAO, ICFTU, ICRM, IDA, IDB, IFAD, IFC, IFRCS, ILO, IMF, IMO, Intelsat (nonsignatory user), Interpol, IOC, ITU, NAM, OAU, OIC, OPCW, UN, UNCTAD, UNESCO, UNIDO, UNMEE, UPU, WCL, WFTU, WHO, WIPO, WMO, WToO, WTrO
Diplomatic representation in the US:
chief of mission: Ambassador John P. BOJANG
chancery: Suite 1000, 1155 15th Street NW, Washington, DC 20005
telephone: [1] (202) 785-1399
FAX: [1] (202) 785-1430
Diplomatic representation from the US:
chief of mission: Ambassador George W. B. HALEY
embassy: Fajara, Kairaba Avenue, Banjul
mailing address: P. M. B. No. 19, Banjul
telephone: [220] 392856, 392858, 391970, 391971
FAX: [220] 392475
Flag description: three equal horizontal bands of red (top), blue with white edges, and green

Economy

Economy - overview: The Gambia has no important mineral or other natural resources and has a limited agricultural base. About 75% of the population depends on crops and livestock for its livelihood. Small-scale manufacturing activity features the processing of peanuts, fish, and hides. Reexport trade normally constitutes a major segment of economic activity, but a 1999 government-imposed preshipment inspection plan, instability of the Gambian dalasi, and the stable political situation in Senegal have drawn some of the reexport trade away from Banjul. The government's 1998 seizure of the private peanut firm Alimenta eliminated the largest purchaser of Gambian groundnuts; the following two marketing seasons have seen significantly lower prices and sales. A decline in tourism from 1999 to 2000 has also held back growth. Unemployment and underemployment rates are extremely high. Shortrun economic progress remains highly dependent on sustained bilateral and multilateral aid, on responsible government economic management as forwarded by IMF technical help and advice, and on expected growth in the construction sector.
GDP: purchasing power parity - $1.5 billion (2000 est.)
GDP - real growth rate: 4.9% (2000 est.)
GDP - per capita: purchasing power parity - $1,100 (2000 est.)
GDP - composition by sector:
agriculture: 21%
industry: 12%
services: 67% (1998 est.)
Population below poverty line: NA%
Household income or consumption by percentage share:
lowest 10%: NA%
highest 10%: NA%
Inflation rate (consumer prices): 3.4% (2000 est.)
Labor force: 400,000
Labor force - by occupation: agriculture 75%, industry, commerce, and services 19%, government 6%
Unemployment rate: NA%
Budget:
revenues: $90.5 million
expenditures: $80.9 million, including capital expenditures of $4.1 million (2001 est.)
Industries: processing peanuts, fish, and hides; tourism; beverages; agricultural machinery assembly, woodworking, metalworking; clothing
Industrial production growth rate: NA%
Electricity - production: 75 million kWh (1999)
Electricity - production by source:
fossil fuel: 100%
hydro: 0%
nuclear: 0%
other: 0% (1999)
Electricity - consumption: 69.8 million kWh (1999)
Electricity - exports: 0 kWh (1999)
Electricity - imports: 0 kWh (1999)
Agriculture - products: peanuts, millet, sorghum, rice, corn, sesame, cassava (tapioca), palm kernels; cattle, sheep, goats; forest and fishery resources not fully exploited
Exports: $125.8 million (f.o.b., 1999)
Exports - commodities: peanuts and peanut products, fish, cotton lint, palm kernels
Exports - partners: Benelux 59%, Japan 20%, UK 7%, Spain 2% (1999)
Imports: $202.5 million (f.o.b., 1999)
Imports - commodities: foodstuffs, manufactures, fuel, machinery and transport equipment

Gambia, The (continued)

Imports - partners: China (including Hong Kong) 49%, UK 15%, Netherlands 11.6%, Brazil 10%, Senegal 10% (1997)
Debt - external: $440 million (2001 est.)
Economic aid - recipient: $45.4 million (1995)
Currency: dalasi (GMD)
Currency code: GMD
Exchange rates: dalasi per US dollar - 15.000 (January 2001), 12.729 (3d quarter 1999), 11.395 (1999), 10.643 (1998), 10.200 (1997), 9.789 (1996)
Fiscal year: calendar year

Communications

Telephones - main lines in use: 31,900 (2000)
Telephones - mobile cellular: 5,624 (2000)
Telephone system:
general assessment: adequate; a packet switched data network is available
domestic: adequate network of microwave radio relay and open wire
international: microwave radio relay links to Senegal and Guinea-Bissau; satellite earth station - 1 Intelsat (Atlantic Ocean)
Radio broadcast stations: AM 3, FM 5, shortwave 0 (2000)
Radios: 196,000 (1997)
Television broadcast stations: 1 (government-owned) (1997)
Televisions: 5,000 (2000)
Internet country code: .gm
Internet Service Providers (ISPs): 2 (2001)
Internet users: 5,000 (2001)

Transportation

Railways: 0 km
Highways:
total: 2,700 km
paved: 956 km
unpaved: 1,744 km (1996)
Waterways: 400 km
Ports and harbors: Banjul
Merchant marine: none (2000 est.)
Airports: 1 (2000 est.)
Airports - with paved runways:
total: 1
over 3,047 m: 1 (2000 est.)

Military

Military branches: Army (includes marine unit), National Police, Presidential Guard
Military manpower - availability:
males age 15-49: 316,873 (2001 est.)
Military manpower - fit for military service:
males age 15-49: 159,764 (2001 est.)
Military expenditures - dollar figure: $2.6 million (2001 est.)
Military expenditures - percent of GDP: 2% (FY96/97)

Transnational Issues

Disputes - international: none

Gaza Strip

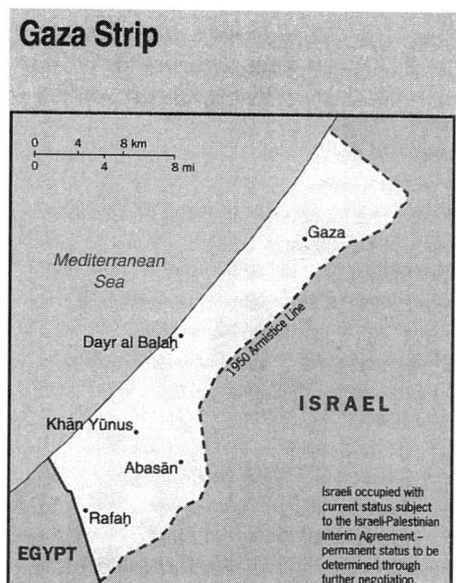

Introduction

Background: The Israel-PLO Declaration of Principles on Interim Self-Government Arrangements (the DOP), signed in Washington on 13 September 1993, provided for a transitional period not exceeding five years of Palestinian interim self-government in the Gaza Strip and the West Bank. Under the DOP, Israel agreed to transfer certain powers and responsibilities to the Palestinian Authority, which includes the Palestinian Legislative Council elected in January 1996, as part of the interim self-governing arrangements in the West Bank and Gaza Strip. A transfer of powers and responsibilities for the Gaza Strip and Jericho took place pursuant to the Israel-PLO 4 May 1994 Cairo Agreement on the Gaza Strip and the Jericho Area and in additional areas of the West Bank pursuant to the Israel-PLO 28 September 1995 Interim Agreement, the Israel-PLO 15 January 1997 Protocol Concerning Redeployment in Hebron, the Israel-PLO 23 October 1998 Wye River Memorandum, and the 4 September 1999 Sharm el-Sheikh Agreement. The DOP provides that Israel will retain responsibility during the transitional period for external security and for internal security and public order of settlements and Israeli citizens. Permanent status is to be determined through direct negotiations, which resumed in September 1999 after a three-year hiatus. An intifadah broke out in September 2000; the resulting widespread violence in the West Bank and Gaza Strip, Israel's military response, and instability in the Palestinian Authority are undermining progress toward a permanent settlement.

Geography

Location: Middle East, bordering the Mediterranean Sea, between Egypt and Israel
Geographic coordinates: 31 25 N, 34 20 E
Map references: Middle East
Area:
total: 360 sq km
land: 360 sq km
water: 0 sq km
Area - comparative: slightly more than twice the size of Washington, DC
Land boundaries:
total: 62 km
border countries: Egypt 11 km, Israel 51 km
Coastline: 40 km
Maritime claims: Israeli-occupied with current status subject to the Israeli-Palestinian Interim Agreement - permanent status to be determined through further negotiation
Climate: temperate, mild winters, dry and warm to hot summers
Terrain: flat to rolling, sand- and dune-covered coastal plain
Elevation extremes:
lowest point: Mediterranean Sea 0 m
highest point: Abu 'Awdah (Joz Abu 'Auda) 105 m
Natural resources: arable land, natural gas
Land use:
arable land: 24%
permanent crops: 39%
permanent pastures: 0%
forests and woodland: 11%
other: 26% (1993 est.)
Irrigated land: 120 sq km (1993 est.)
Natural hazards: droughts
Environment - current issues: desertification; salination of fresh water; sewage treatment; water-borne disease; soil degradation
Geography - note: there are 25 Israeli settlements and civilian land use sites in the Gaza Strip (August 2000 est.)

People

Population: 1,178,119 (July 2001 est.)
note: in addition, there are some 6,900 Israeli settlers in the Gaza Strip (August 2000 est.)
Age structure:
0-14 years: 49.89% (male 301,288; female 286,481)
15-64 years: 47.32% (male 283,274; female 274,189)
65 years and over: 2.79% (male 14,121; female 18,766) (2001 est.)
Population growth rate: 4.01% (2001 est.)
Birth rate: 42.48 births/1,000 population (2001 est.)
Death rate: 4.21 deaths/1,000 population (2001 est.)
Net migration rate: 1.8 migrant(s)/1,000 population (2001 est.)
Sex ratio:
at birth: 1.05 male(s)/female
under 15 years: 1.05 male(s)/female
15-64 years: 1.03 male(s)/female
65 years and over: 0.75 male(s)/female
total population: 1.03 male(s)/female (2001 est.)
Infant mortality rate: 25.37 deaths/1,000 live births (2001 est.)
Life expectancy at birth:
total population: 71.01 years
male: 69.76 years
female: 72.32 years (2001 est.)

Gaza Strip (continued)

Total fertility rate: 6.42 children born/woman (2001 est.)
HIV/AIDS - adult prevalence rate: NA%
HIV/AIDS - people living with HIV/AIDS: NA
HIV/AIDS - deaths: NA
Nationality:
noun: NA
adjective: NA
Ethnic groups: Palestinian Arab and other 99.4%, Jewish 0.6%
Religions: Muslim (predominantly Sunni) 98.7%, Christian 0.7%, Jewish 0.6%
Languages: Arabic, Hebrew (spoken by Israeli settlers and many Palestinians), English (widely understood)
Literacy:
definition: NA
total population: NA%
male: NA%
female: NA%

Government

Country name:
conventional long form: none
conventional short form: Gaza Strip
local long form: none
local short form: Qita Ghazzah

Economy

Economy - overview: Economic output in the Gaza Strip - which comes under the responsibility of the Palestinian Authority since the Cairo Agreement of May 1994 - declined perhaps one-third between 1992 and 1996. The downturn was largely the result of Israeli closure policies - the imposition of generalized border closures in response to security incidents in Israel - which disrupted previously established labor and commodity market relationships between Israel and the WBGS (West Bank and Gaza Strip). The most serious negative social effect of this downturn was the emergence of high unemployment; unemployment in the WBGS during the 1980s was generally under 5%; by 1995 it had risen to over 20%. Since 1997 Israel's use of comprehensive closures has decreased and, in 1998, Israel implemented new policies to reduce the impact of closures and other security procedures on the movement of Palestinian goods and labor. These changes fueled an almost three-year long economic recovery in the West Bank and Gaza Strip; real GDP grew by 5% in 1998 and 6% in 1999. Recovery was upended in the last quarter of 2000 with the outbreak of Palestinian violence, which triggered tight Israeli closures of Palestinian self-rule areas and a severe disruption of trade and labor movements.
GDP: purchasing power parity - $1.11 billion (2000 est.)
GDP - real growth rate: -7.5% (2000 est.)
GDP - per capita: purchasing power parity - $1,000 (2000 est.)
GDP - composition by sector:
agriculture: 9%
industry: 28%
services: 63% (1999 est., includes West Bank)
Population below poverty line: NA%
Household income or consumption by percentage share:
lowest 10%: NA%
highest 10%: NA%
Inflation rate (consumer prices): 3% (includes West Bank) (2000 est.)
Labor force: NA
Labor force - by occupation: services 66%, industry 21%, agriculture 13% (1996)
Unemployment rate: 40% (includes West Bank) (yearend 2000)
Budget:
revenues: $1.6 billion
expenditures: $1.73 billion, including capital expenditures of $NA
note: includes West Bank (1999 est.)
Industries: generally small family businesses that produce textiles, soap, olive-wood carvings, and mother-of-pearl souvenirs; the Israelis have established some small-scale modern industries in an industrial center
Industrial production growth rate: NA%
Electricity - production: NA kWh; note - electricity supplied by Israel
Electricity - consumption: NA kWh
Electricity - exports: 0 kWh (1999)
Electricity - imports: NA kWh; note - electricity supplied by Israel
Agriculture - products: olives, citrus, vegetables; beef, dairy products
Exports: $682 million (f.o.b., 1998 est.) (includes West Bank)
Exports - commodities: citrus, flowers
Exports - partners: Israel, Egypt, West Bank
Imports: $2.5 billion (c.i.f., 1998 est.) (includes West Bank)
Imports - commodities: food, consumer goods, construction materials
Imports - partners: Israel, Egypt, West Bank
Debt - external: $108 million (1997 est.) (includes West Bank)
Economic aid - recipient: $121 million disbursed (2000) (includes West Bank)
Currency: new Israeli shekel (ILS)
Currency code: ILS
Exchange rates: new Israeli shekels per US dollar - 4.0810 (December 2000), 4.0773 (2000), 4.1397 (1999), 3.8001 (1998), 3.4494 (1997), 3.1917 (1996)
Fiscal year: calendar year

Communications

Telephones - main lines in use: 95,729 (total for Gaza Strip and West Bank) (1997)
Telephones - mobile cellular: NA
Telephone system:
general assessment: NA
domestic: rudimentary telephone services provided by an open wire system
international: NA
Radio broadcast stations: AM 0, FM 0, shortwave 0 (1998)
Radios: NA; note - most Palestinian households have radios (1999)
Television broadcast stations: 2 (operated by the Palestinian Broadcasting Corporation) (1997)
Televisions: NA; note - most Palestinian households have televisions (1997)
Internet Service Providers (ISPs): 3 (1999)
Internet users: 23,520 (1999) (includes West Bank)

Transportation

Railways:
total: NA km; note - one line, abandoned and in disrepair, little trackage remains
Highways:
total: NA km
paved: NA km
unpaved: NA km
note: small, poorly developed road network
Waterways: none
Ports and harbors: Gaza
Airports: 2
note: includes Gaza International Airport that opened on 24 November 1998 as part of agreements stipulated in the September 1995 Oslo II Accord and the 23 October 1998 Wye River Memorandum (2000 est.)
Airports - with paved runways:
total: 1
over 3,047 m: 1 (2000 est.)
Airports - with unpaved runways:
total: 1
under 914 m: 1 (2000 est.)

Military

Military branches: NA
Military expenditures - dollar figure: $NA
Military expenditures - percent of GDP: NA%

Transnational Issues

Disputes - international: West Bank and Gaza Strip are Israeli-occupied with current status subject to the Israeli-Palestinian Interim Agreement - permanent status to be determined through further negotiation

Georgia

Introduction

Background: Georgia was absorbed into the Russian Empire in the 19th century. Independent for three years (1918-1921) following the Russian revolution, it was forcibly incorporated into the USSR until the Soviet Union dissolved in 1991. Russian troops remain garrisoned at four military bases and as peacekeepers in the separatist regions of Abkhazia and South Ossetia (but are scheduled to withdraw from two of the bases by July 2001). Despite a badly degraded transportation network - brought on by ethnic conflict, criminal activities, and fuel shortages - the country continues to move toward a market economy and greater integration with Western institutions.

Geography

Location: Southwestern Asia, bordering the Black Sea, between Turkey and Russia
Geographic coordinates: 42 00 N, 43 30 E
Map references: Commonwealth of Independent States
Area:
total: 69,700 sq km
land: 69,700 sq km
water: 0 sq km
Area - comparative: slightly smaller than South Carolina
Land boundaries:
total: 1,461 km
border countries: Armenia 164 km, Azerbaijan 322 km, Russia 723 km, Turkey 252 km
Coastline: 310 km
Maritime claims: NA
Climate: warm and pleasant; Mediterranean-like on Black Sea coast
Terrain: largely mountainous with Great Caucasus Mountains in the north and Lesser Caucasus Mountains in the south; Kolkhet'is Dablobi (Kolkhida Lowland) opens to the Black Sea in the west; Mtkvari River Basin in the east; good soils in river valley flood plains, foothills of Kolkhida Lowland
Elevation extremes:
lowest point: Black Sea 0 m
highest point: Mt'a Mqinvartsveri (Gora Kazbek) 5,048 m
Natural resources: forests, hydropower, manganese deposits, iron ore, copper, minor coal and oil deposits; coastal climate and soils allow for important tea and citrus growth
Land use:
arable land: 9%
permanent crops: 4%
permanent pastures: 25%
forests and woodland: 34%
other: 28% (1993 est.)
Irrigated land: 4,000 sq km (1993 est.)
Natural hazards: earthquakes
Environment - current issues: air pollution, particularly in Rust'avi; heavy pollution of Mtkvari River and the Black Sea; inadequate supplies of potable water; soil pollution from toxic chemicals
Environment - international agreements:
party to: Air Pollution, Biodiversity, Climate Change, Climate Change-Kyoto Protocol, Desertification, Endangered Species, Hazardous Wastes, Law of the Sea, Marine Dumping, Ozone Layer Protection, Ship Pollution, Wetlands
signed, but not ratified: none of the selected agreements

People

Population: 4,989,285 (July 2001 est.)
Age structure:
0-14 years: 19.59% (male 498,575; female 478,663)
15-64 years: 67.91% (male 1,632,338; female 1,755,910)
65 years and over: 12.5% (male 241,824; female 381,975) (2001 est.)
Population growth rate: -0.59% (2001 est.)
Birth rate: 11.18 births/1,000 population (2001 est.)
Death rate: 14.58 deaths/1,000 population (2001 est.)
Net migration rate: -2.48 migrant(s)/1,000 population (2001 est.)
Sex ratio:
at birth: 1.05 male(s)/female
under 15 years: 1.04 male(s)/female
15-64 years: 0.93 male(s)/female
65 years and over: 0.63 male(s)/female
total population: 0.91 male(s)/female (2001 est.)
Infant mortality rate: 52.37 deaths/1,000 live births (2001 est.)
Life expectancy at birth:
total population: 64.57 years
male: 61.04 years
female: 68.28 years (2001 est.)
Total fertility rate: 1.45 children born/woman (2001 est.)
HIV/AIDS - adult prevalence rate: less than 0.01% (1999 est.)
HIV/AIDS - people living with HIV/AIDS: less than 500 (1999 est.)
HIV/AIDS - deaths: less than 100 (1999 est.)
Nationality:
noun: Georgian(s)
adjective: Georgian
Ethnic groups: Georgian 70.1%, Armenian 8.1%, Russian 6.3%, Azeri 5.7%, Ossetian 3%, Abkhaz 1.8%, other 5%
Religions: Georgian Orthodox 65%, Muslim 11%, Russian Orthodox 10%, Armenian Apostolic 8%, unknown 6%
Languages: Georgian 71% (official), Russian 9%, Armenian 7%, Azeri 6%, other 7%
note: Abkhaz is the official language in Abkhazia
Literacy:
definition: age 15 and over can read and write
total population: 99%
male: 100%
female: 98% (1989 est.)

Government

Country name:
conventional long form: none
conventional short form: Georgia
local long form: none
local short form: Sak'art'velo
former: Georgian Soviet Socialist Republic
Government type: republic
Capital: T'bilisi
Administrative divisions: 53 rayons (raionebi, singular - raioni), 9 cities* (k'alak'ebi, singular - k'alak'i), and 2 autonomous republics** (avtomnoy respubliki, singular - avtom respublika); Abashis, Abkhazia or Ap'khazet'is Avtonomiuri Respublika** (Sokhumi), Adigenis, Ajaria or Acharis Avtonomiuri Respublika** (Bat'umi), Akhalgoris, Akhalk'alak'is, Akhalts'ikhis, Akhmetis, Ambrolauris, Aspindzis, Baghdat'is, Bolnisis, Borjomis, Chiat'ura*, Ch'khorotsqus, Ch'okhatauris, Dedop'listsqaros, Dmanisis, Dushet'is, Gardabanis, Gori*, Goris, Gurjaanis, Javis, K'arelis, Kaspis, Kharagaulis, Khashuris, Khobis, Khonis, K'ut'aisi*, Lagodekhis, Lanch'khut'is, Lentekhis, Marneulis, Martvilis, Mestiis,

Georgia (continued)

Mts'khet'is, Ninotsmindis, Onis, Ozurget'is, P'ot'i*, Qazbegis, Qvarlis, Rust'avi*, Sach'kheris, Sagarejos, Samtrediis, Senakis, Sighnaghis, T'bilisi*, T'elavis, T'erjolis, T'et'ritsqaros, T'ianet'is, Tqibuli*, Ts'ageris, Tsalenjikhis, Tsalkis, Tsqaltubo*, Vanis, Zestap'onis, Zugdidi*, Zugdidis
note: administrative divisions have the same names as their administrative centers (exceptions have the administrative center name following in parentheses)
Independence: 9 April 1991 (from Soviet Union)
National holiday: Independence Day, 26 May (1918); note - 26 May 1918 is the date of independence from Soviet Russia, 9 April 1991 is the date of independence from the Soviet Union
Constitution: adopted 17 October 1995
Legal system: based on civil law system
Suffrage: 18 years of age; universal
Executive branch:
chief of state: President Eduard Amvrosiyevich SHEVARDNADZE (previously elected chairman of the Government Council 10 March 1992; Council has since been disbanded; previously elected chairman of Parliament 11 October 1992; president since 26 November 1995); note - the president is both the chief of state and head of government
head of government: President Eduard Amvrosiyevich SHEVARDNADZE (previously elected chairman of the Government Council 10 March 1992; Council has since been disbanded; previously elected chairman of Parliament 11 October 1992; president since 26 November 1995); note - the president is both the chief of state and head of government
cabinet: Cabinet of Ministers
elections: president elected by popular vote for a five-year term; election last held 9 April 2000 (next to be held NA 2005)
election results: Eduard SHEVARDNADZE reelected president; percent of vote - Eduard SHEVARDNADZE 80%
Legislative branch: unicameral Supreme Council (commonly referred to as Parliament) or Umaghiesi Sabcho (235 seats; members are elected by popular vote to serve four-year terms)
elections: last held 31 October and 14 November 1999 (next to be held NA 2003)
election results: percent of vote by party - CUG 41.85%, AGUR 25.65%, IWSG 7.8%, all other parties received less than 7% each; seats by party - CUG 130, AGUR 58, IWSG 15, Abkhaz deputies 12, independents 17, other 3
Judicial branch: Supreme Court (judges elected by the Supreme Council on the president's recommendation); Constitutional Court
Political parties and leaders: Citizen's Union of Georgia or CUG [Eduard SHEVARDNADZE]; Georgian United Communist Party or UCPG [Panteleimon GIORGADZE, chairman]; Industry Will Save Georgia or IWSG [Georgi TOPADZE]; National Democratic Party or NDP [Irina SARISHVILI-CHANTURIA]; Socialist Party or SPG [Temur GAMTSEMLIDZE]; Union for "Revival" Party or AGUR [Alsan ABASHIDZE]; United Republican Party or URP [Nodar NATADZE, chairman]

Political pressure groups and leaders: Georgian refugees from Abkhazia (Abkhaz faction in Georgian Parliament); separatist elements in the breakaway region of Abkhazia; supporters of the late ousted President Zviad GAMSAKHURDYA remain a source of opposition
International organization participation: BSEC, CCC, CE, CIS, EAPC, EBRD, ECE, FAO, IAEA, IBRD, ICAO, ICFTU, IDA, IFAD, IFC, IFRCS, ILO, IMF, IMO, Inmarsat, Interpol, IOC, IOM (observer), ITU, OPCW, OSCE, PFP, UN, UNCTAD, UNESCO, UNIDO, UPU, WHO, WIPO, WMO, WToO, WTrO
Diplomatic representation in the US:
chief of mission: Ambassador Tedo JAPARIDZE
chancery: Suite 300, 1615 New Hampshire Avenue NW, Washington, DC 20009
telephone: [1] (202) 387-2390
FAX: [1] (202) 393-4537
Diplomatic representation from the US:
chief of mission: Ambassador Kenneth S. YALOWITZ
embassy: #25 Antoneli Street, T'bilisi 380026
mailing address: use embassy street address
telephone: [995] (32) 989-967/68
FAX: [995] (32) 933-759
Flag description: maroon field with small rectangle in upper hoist side corner; rectangle divided horizontally with black on top, white below

Economy

Economy - overview: Georgia's economy has traditionally revolved around Black Sea tourism; cultivation of citrus fruits, tea, and grapes; mining of manganese and copper; and output of a small industrial sector producing wine, metals, machinery, chemicals, and textiles. The country imports the bulk of its energy needs, including natural gas and oil products. Its only sizable internal energy resource is hydropower. Despite the severe damage the economy has suffered due to civil strife, Georgia, with the help of the IMF and World Bank, has made substantial economic gains since 1995, increasing GDP growth and slashing inflation. The Georgian economy continues to experience large budget deficits due to a failure to collect tax revenues. Georgia also still suffers from energy shortages; it privatized the distribution network in 1998, and deliveries are steadily improving. The country is pinning its hopes for long-term recovery on the development of an international transportation corridor through the key Black Sea ports of P'ot'i and Bat'umi. The growing trade deficit, continuing problems with tax evasion and corruption, and political uncertainties cloud the short-term economic picture.
GDP: purchasing power parity - $22.8 billion (2000 est.)
GDP - real growth rate: 1.9% (2000 est.)
GDP - per capita: purchasing power parity - $4,600 (2000 est.)
GDP - composition by sector:
agriculture: 32%
industry: 23%
services: 45% (1999 est.)

Population below poverty line: 60% (1999 est.)
Household income or consumption by percentage share:
lowest 10%: NA%
highest 10%: NA%
Inflation rate (consumer prices): 4.1% (2000 est.)
Labor force: 3.08 million (1997)
Labor force - by occupation: industry 20%, agriculture 40%, services 40% (1999 est.)
Unemployment rate: 14.9% (1999 est.)
Budget:
revenues: $437 million
expenditures: $626 million, including capital expenditures of $60 million (1999)
Industries: steel, aircraft, machine tools, electric locomotives, trucks, tractors, textiles, shoes, chemicals, wood products, wine
Industrial production growth rate: -0.3% (1998 est.)
Electricity - production: 7.975 billion kWh (1999)
Electricity - production by source:
fossil fuel: 20.38%
hydro: 79.62%
nuclear: 0%
other: 0% (1999)
Electricity - consumption: 7.117 billion kWh (1999)
Electricity - exports: 850 million kWh (1999)
Electricity - imports: 550 million kWh (1999)
Agriculture - products: citrus, grapes, tea, vegetables, potatoes; livestock
Exports: $372 million (2000 est.)
Exports - commodities: citrus fruits, tea, wine, other agricultural products; diverse types of machinery and metals; chemicals; fuel reexports; textiles
Exports - partners: Russia 19%, Turkey 16%, Azerbaijan 8%, Armenia 6% (1999)
Imports: $898 million (2000 est.)
Imports - commodities: fuel, grain and other foods, machinery and parts, transport equipment
Imports - partners: EU 22%, Russia 19%, Turkey 12%, US 12% (1999)
Debt - external: $1.9 billion (2000)
Economic aid - recipient: $212.7 million (1995)
Currency: lari (GEL)
Currency code: GEL
Exchange rates: lari per US dollar - 1.9798 (December 2000), 1.9762 (2000), 2.0245 (1999), 1.3898 (1998), 1.2975 (1997), 1.2628 (1996)
Fiscal year: calendar year

Communications

Telephones - main lines in use: 620,000 (1997)
Telephones - mobile cellular: 30,000 (1997)
Telephone system:
general assessment: NA
domestic: local - T'bilisi and K'ut'aisi have cellular telephone networks; urban telephone density is about 20 per 100 people; rural telephone density is about 4 per 100 people; intercity facilities include a fiber-optic line between T'bilisi and K'ut'aisi; nationwide pager service is available

Georgia (continued)

international: Georgia and Russia are working on a fiber-optic line between P'ot'i and Sochi (Russia); present international service is available by microwave, landline, and satellite through the Moscow switch; international electronic mail and telex service are available
Radio broadcast stations: AM 7, FM 12, shortwave 4 (1998)
Radios: 3.02 million (1997)
Television broadcast stations: 12 (plus repeaters) (1998)
Televisions: 2.57 million (1997)
Internet country code: .ge
Internet Service Providers (ISPs): 6 (2000)
Internet users: 20,000 (2000)

Transportation

Railways:
total: 1,583 km in common carrier service; does not include industrial lines
broad gauge: 1,583 km 1.520-m gauge (1993)
Highways:
total: 33,900 km
paved: 29,500 km (these roads are said to be hard-surfaced, and include, in addition to conventionally paved roads, some that are surfaced with gravel or other coarse aggregate, making them trafficable in all weather)
unpaved: 4,400 km (these roads are made of unstabilized earth and are difficult to negotiate in wet weather) (1990)
Waterways: none
Pipelines: crude oil 370 km; refined products 300 km; natural gas 440 km (1992)
Ports and harbors: Bat'umi, P'ot'i, Sokhumi
Merchant marine:
total: 37 ships (1,000 GRT or over) totaling 131,316 GRT/190,289 DWT
ships by type: bulk 3, cargo 25, chemical tanker 2, container 2, petroleum tanker 4, roll on/roll off 1 (2000 est.)
Airports: 31 (2000 est.)
Airports - with paved runways:
total: 16
over 3,047 m: 1
2,438 to 3,047 m: 8
1,524 to 2,437 m: 2
914 to 1,523 m: 2
under 914 m: 3 (2000 est.)
Airports - with unpaved runways:
total: 15
2,438 to 3,047 m: 1
1,524 to 2,437 m: 4
914 to 1,523 m: 4
under 914 m: 6 (2000 est.)
Transportation - note: transportation network is in poor condition resulting from ethnic conflict, criminal activities, and fuel shortages; network lacks maintenance and repair

Military

Military branches: Ground Forces, Navy, Air Force and Air Defense Forces, National Guard, Security Forces (internal and border troops)
Military manpower - military age: 18 years of age
Military manpower - availability:
males age 15-49: 1,296,199 (2001 est.)
Military manpower - fit for military service:
males age 15-49: 1,024,574 (2001 est.)
Military manpower - reaching military age annually:
males: 41,561 (2001 est.)
Military expenditures - dollar figure: $23 million (FY00)
Military expenditures - percent of GDP: 0.59% (FY00)
Military - note: a CIS peacekeeping force consisting of Russian troops is deployed in the Abkhazia region of Georgia together with a UN military observer group; a Russian peacekeeping battalion is deployed in South Ossetia

Transnational Issues

Disputes - international: none
Illicit drugs: limited cultivation of cannabis and opium poppy, mostly for domestic consumption; used as transshipment point for opiates via Central Asia to Western Europe and Russia

Germany

Introduction

Background: As Western Europe's richest and most populous nation, Germany remains a key member of the continent's economic, political, and defense organizations. European power struggles immersed the country in two devastating World Wars in the first half of the 20th century and left the country occupied by the victorious Allied powers of the US, UK, France, and the Soviet Union in 1945. With the advent of the Cold War, two German states were formed in 1949: the western Federal Republic of Germany (FRG) and the eastern German Democratic Republic (GDR). The democratic FRG embedded itself in key Western economic and security organizations, the EC and NATO, while the communist GDR was on the front line of the Soviet-led Warsaw Pact. The decline of the USSR and the end of the Cold War allowed for German unification in 1990. Since then Germany has expended considerable funds to bring eastern productivity and wages up to western standards. In January 1999, Germany and 10 other EU countries formed a common European currency, the euro.

Geography

Location: Central Europe, bordering the Baltic Sea and the North Sea, between the Netherlands and Poland, south of Denmark
Geographic coordinates: 51 00 N, 9 00 E
Map references: Europe
Area:
total: 357,021 sq km
land: 349,223 sq km
water: 7,798 sq km
Area - comparative: slightly smaller than Montana
Land boundaries:
total: 3,618 km
border countries: Austria 784 km, Belgium 167 km, Czech Republic 646 km, Denmark 68 km, France 451 km, Luxembourg 135 km, Netherlands 577 km, Poland 456 km, Switzerland 334 km

Germany (continued)

Coastline: 2,389 km
Maritime claims:
continental shelf: 200-m depth or to the depth of exploitation
exclusive economic zone: 200 NM
territorial sea: 12 NM
Climate: temperate and marine; cool, cloudy, wet winters and summers; occasional warm foehn wind
Terrain: lowlands in north, uplands in center, Bavarian Alps in south
Elevation extremes:
lowest point: Freepsum Lake -2 m
highest point: Zugspitze 2,963 m
Natural resources: iron ore, coal, potash, timber, lignite, uranium, copper, natural gas, salt, nickel, arable land
Land use:
arable land: 33%
permanent crops: 1%
permanent pastures: 15%
forests and woodland: 31%
other: 20% (1993 est.)
Irrigated land: 4,750 sq km (1993 est.)
Natural hazards: flooding
Environment - current issues: emissions from coal-burning utilities and industries contribute to air pollution; acid rain, resulting from sulfur dioxide emissions, is damaging forests; pollution in the Baltic Sea from raw sewage and industrial effluents from rivers in eastern Germany; hazardous waste disposal; government currently attempting to define mechanism for ending the use of nuclear power; government working to meet EU commitment to identify nature preservation areas in line with the EU's Flora, Fauna, and Habitat directive
Environment - international agreements:
party to: Air Pollution, Air Pollution-Nitrogen Oxides, Air Pollution-Sulphur 85, Air Pollution-Sulphur 94, Air Pollution-Volatile Organic Compounds, Antarctic-Environmental Protocol, Antarctic-Marine Living Resources, Antarctic Seals, Antarctic Treaty, Biodiversity, Climate Change, Desertification, Endangered Species, Environmental Modification, Hazardous Wastes, Law of the Sea, Marine Dumping, Nuclear Test Ban, Ozone Layer Protection, Ship Pollution, Tropical Timber 83, Tropical Timber 94, Wetlands, Whaling
signed, but not ratified: Air Pollution-Persistent Organic Pollutants, Climate Change-Kyoto Protocol
Geography - note: strategic location on North European Plain and along the entrance to the Baltic Sea

People

Population: 83,029,536 (July 2001 est.)
Age structure:
0-14 years: 15.57% (male 6,635,328; female 6,289,994)
15-64 years: 67.82% (male 28,619,237; female 27,691,698)
65 years and over: 16.61% (male 5,336,664; female 8,456,615) (2001 est.)
Population growth rate: 0.27% (2001 est.)
Birth rate: 9.16 births/1,000 population (2001 est.)
Death rate: 10.42 deaths/1,000 population (2001 est.)
Net migration rate: 4 migrant(s)/1,000 population (2001 est.)
Sex ratio:
at birth: 1.06 male(s)/female
under 15 years: 1.05 male(s)/female
15-64 years: 1.03 male(s)/female
65 years and over: 0.63 male(s)/female
total population: 0.96 male(s)/female (2001 est.)
Infant mortality rate: 4.71 deaths/1,000 live births (2001 est.)
Life expectancy at birth:
total population: 77.61 years
male: 74.47 years
female: 80.92 years (2001 est.)
Total fertility rate: 1.38 children born/woman (2001 est.)
HIV/AIDS - adult prevalence rate: 0.1% (1999 est.)
HIV/AIDS - people living with HIV/AIDS: 37,000 (1999 est.)
HIV/AIDS - deaths: 600 (1999 est.)
Nationality:
noun: German(s)
adjective: German
Ethnic groups: German 91.5%, Turkish 2.4%, other 6.1% (made up largely of Serbo-Croatian, Italian, Russian, Greek, Polish, Spanish)
Religions: Protestant 38%, Roman Catholic 34%, Muslim 1.7%, unaffiliated or other 26.3%
Languages: German
Literacy:
definition: age 15 and over can read and write
total population: 99% (1977 est.)
male: NA%
female: NA%

Government

Country name:
conventional long form: Federal Republic of Germany
conventional short form: Germany
local long form: Bundesrepublik Deutschland
local short form: Deutschland
former: German Empire, German Republic, German Reich
Government type: federal republic
Capital: Berlin
Administrative divisions: 16 states (Laender, singular - Land); Baden-Wuerttemberg, Bayern, Berlin, Brandenburg, Bremen, Hamburg, Hessen, Mecklenburg-Vorpommern, Niedersachsen, Nordrhein-Westfalen, Rheinland-Pfalz, Saarland, Sachsen, Sachsen-Anhalt, Schleswig-Holstein, Thueringen
Independence: 18 January 1871 (German Empire unification); divided into four zones of occupation (UK, US, USSR, and later, France) in 1945 following World War II; Federal Republic of Germany (FRG or West Germany) proclaimed 23 May 1949 and included the former UK, US, and French zones; German Democratic Republic (GDR or East Germany) proclaimed 7 October 1949 and included the former USSR zone; unification of West Germany and East Germany took place 3 October 1990; all four powers formally relinquished rights 15 March 1991
National holiday: Unity Day, 3 October (1990)
Constitution: 23 May 1949, known as Basic Law; became constitution of the united German people 3 October 1990
Legal system: civil law system with indigenous concepts; judicial review of legislative acts in the Federal Constitutional Court; has not accepted compulsory ICJ jurisdiction
Suffrage: 18 years of age; universal
Executive branch:
chief of state: President Johannes RAU (since 1 July 1999)
head of government: Chancellor Gerhard SCHROEDER (since 27 October 1998)
cabinet: Cabinet or Bundesminister (Federal Ministers) appointed by the president on the recommendation of the chancellor
elections: president elected for a five-year term by a Federal Convention including all members of the Federal Assembly and an equal number of delegates elected by the state parliaments; election last held 23 May 1999 (next to be held 23 May 2004); chancellor elected by an absolute majority of the Federal Assembly for a four-year term; election last held 27 September 1998 (next to be held in the fall of 2002)
election results: Johannes RAU elected president; percent of Federal Convention vote - 57.6%; Gerhard SCHROEDER elected chancellor; percent of Federal Assembly - 52.7%
Legislative branch: bicameral Parliament or Parliament consists of the Federal Assembly or Bundestag (656 seats usually, but 669 for the 1998 term; elected by popular vote under a system combining direct and proportional representation; a party must win 5% of the national vote or three direct mandates to gain representation; members serve four-year terms) and the Federal Council or Bundesrat (69 votes; state governments are directly represented by votes; each has 3 to 6 votes depending on population and are required to vote as a block)
elections: Federal Assembly - last held 27 September 1998 (next to be held by the fall of 2002); note - there are no elections for the Bundesrat; composition is determined by the composition of the state-level governments; the composition of the Bundesrat has the potential to change any time one of the 16 states holds an election
election results: Federal Assembly - percent of vote by party - SPD 40.9%, Alliance '90/Greens 6.7%, CDU/CSU 35.1%, FDP 6.2%, PDS 5.1%; seats by party - SPD 298, Alliance '90/Greens 47, CDU/CSU 245, FDP 43, PDS 36; Federal Council - current composition - votes by party - SPD-led states 26, CDU-led states 28, grand coalitions 15

Germany (continued)

Judicial branch: Federal Constitutional Court or Bundesverfassungsgericht (half the judges are elected by the Bundestag and half by the Bundesrat)
Political parties and leaders: Alliance '90/Greens [Renate KUENAST and Fritz KUHN]; Christian Democratic Union or CDU [Angela MERKEL]; Christian Social Union or CSU [Edmund STOIBER, chairman]; Free Democratic Party or FDP [Wolfgang GERHARDT, chairman]; note - Wolfgang GERHARDT will probably be replaced by Guido WESTERWELLE in May 2001; Party of Democratic Socialism or PDS [Gabi ZIMMER]; Social Democratic Party or SPD [Gerhard SCHROEDER, chairman]
Political pressure groups and leaders: employers' organizations; expellee, refugee, trade unions, and veterans groups
International organization participation: AfDB, AsDB, Australia Group, BDEAC, BIS, CBSS, CCC, CDB (non-regional), CE, CERN, EAPC, EBRD, ECE, EIB, EMU, ESA, EU, FAO, G- 5, G- 7, G-10, IADB, IAEA, IBRD, ICAO, ICC, ICFTU, ICRM, IDA, IEA, IFAD, IFC, IFRCS, IHO, ILO, IMF, IMO, Inmarsat, Intelsat, Interpol, IOC, IOM, ISO, ITU, MONUC, NAM (guest), NATO, NEA, NSG, OAS (observer), OECD, OPCW, OSCE, PCA, UN, UNCTAD, UNESCO, UNHCR, UNIDO, UNIKOM, UNMIBH, UNMIK, UNOMIG, UPU, WADB (nonregional), WEU, WHO, WIPO, WMO, WToO, WTrO, ZC
Diplomatic representation in the US:
chief of mission: Ambassador Juergen CHROBOG
chancery: 4645 Reservoir Road NW, Washington, DC 20007
telephone: [1] (202) 298-8141
FAX: [1] (202) 298-4249
consulate(s) general: Atlanta, Boston, Chicago, Detroit, Houston, Los Angeles, Miami, New York, San Francisco, Seattle
consulate(s): Wellington (America Samoa)
Diplomatic representation from the US:
chief of mission: Ambassador John C. KORNBLUM (was due to resign on 20 January 2001)
embassy: Neustaedtische Kirchstrasse 4-5, 10117 Berlin
mailing address: PSC 120, Box 1000, APO AE 09265
telephone: [49] (30) 238-5174
FAX: [49] (30) 238-6290
consulate(s) general: Duesseldorf, Frankfurt am Main, Hamburg, Leipzig, Munich
Flag description: three equal horizontal bands of black (top), red, and gold

Economy

Economy - overview: Germany possesses the world's third most technologically powerful economy after the US and Japan, but structural market rigidities - including the substantial non-wage costs of hiring new workers - have made unemployment a long-term, not just a cyclical, problem. Germany's aging population, combined with high unemployment, has pushed social security outlays to a level exceeding contributions from workers. The modernization and integration of the eastern German economy remains a costly long-term problem, with annual transfers from western Germany amounting to roughly $70 billion. Growth picked up to 3% in 2000, largely due to recovering global demand; newly passed business and income tax cuts are expected to keep growth strong in 2001. Corporate restructuring and growing capital markets are transforming the German economy to meet the challenges of European economic integration and globalization in general.
GDP: purchasing power parity - $1.936 trillion (2000 est.)
GDP - real growth rate: 3% (2000 est.)
GDP - per capita: purchasing power parity - $23,400 (2000 est.)
GDP - composition by sector:
agriculture: 1.2%
industry: 30.4%
services: 68.4% (1999)
Population below poverty line: NA%
Inflation rate (consumer prices): 2% (2000 est.)
Labor force: 40.5 million (1999 est.)
Labor force - by occupation: industry 33.4%, agriculture 2.8%, services 63.8% (1999)
Unemployment rate: 9.9% (2000 est.)
Budget:
revenues: $996 billion
expenditures: $1.036 trillion, including capital expenditures of $NA (1999 est.)
Industries: among the world's largest and most technologically advanced producers of iron, steel, coal, cement, chemicals, machinery, vehicles, machine tools, electronics, food and beverages; shipbuilding; textiles
Industrial production growth rate: 4.7% (2000)
Electricity - production: 531.377 billion kWh (1999)
Electricity - production by source:
fossil fuel: 63.29%
hydro: 3.59%
nuclear: 30.3%
other: 2.82% (1999)
Electricity - consumption: 495.181 billion kWh (1999)
Electricity - exports: 39.5 billion kWh (1999)
Electricity - imports: 40.5 billion kWh (1999)
Agriculture - products: potatoes, wheat, barley, sugar beets, fruit, cabbages; cattle, pigs, poultry
Exports: $578 billion (f.o.b., 2000 est.)
Exports - commodities: machinery, vehicles, chemicals, metals and manufactures, foodstuffs, textiles
Exports - partners: EU 55.3% (France 11.3%, UK 8.3%, Italy 7.3%, Netherlands 6.3%, Belgium/Luxembourg 5.1%), US 10.1%, Japan 2.0% (1999)
Imports: $505 billion (f.o.b., 2000 est.)
Imports - commodities: machinery, vehicles, chemicals, foodstuffs, textiles, metals
Imports - partners: EU 52.2% (France 10.5%, Netherlands 7.6%, Italy 7.4%, UK 6.9%, Belgium/Luxembourg 5.6%), US 8.1%, Japan 4.9% (1999)
Debt - external: $NA
Economic aid - donor: ODA, $5.6 billion (1998)
Currency: deutsche mark (DEM); euro (EUR)
note: on 1 January 1999, the EU introduced the euro as a common currency that is now being used by financial institutions in Germany at a fixed rate of 1.95583 deutsche marks per euro and will replace the local currency for all transactions in 2002
Currency code: DEM; EUR
Exchange rates: euros per US dollar - 1.0659 (January 2001), 1.0854 (2000), 0.9386 (1999); deutsche marks per US dollar - 1.69 (January 1999), 1.7597 (1998), 1.7341 (1997), 1.5048 (1996)
Fiscal year: calendar year

Communications

Telephones - main lines in use: 45.2 million (1997)
note: 46.5 million main lines were installed by yearend 1998
Telephones - mobile cellular: 15.318 million (April 1999)
Telephone system:
general assessment: Germany has one of the world's most technologically advanced telecommunications systems; as a result of intensive capital expenditures since reunification, the formerly backward system of the eastern part of the country has been modernized and integrated with that of the western part
domestic: Germany is served by an extensive system of automatic telephone exchanges connected by modern networks of fiber-optic cable, coaxial cable, microwave radio relay, and a domestic satellite system; cellular telephone service is widely available and includes roaming service to many foreign countries
international: satellite earth stations - 14 Intelsat (12 Atlantic Ocean and 2 Indian Ocean), 1 Eutelsat, 1 Inmarsat (Atlantic Ocean region), 2 Intersputnik (1 Atlantic Ocean region and 1 Indian Ocean region); 7 submarine cable connections; 2 HF radiotelephone communication centers; tropospheric scatter links
Radio broadcast stations: AM 51, FM 767, shortwave 4 (1998)
Radios: 77.8 million (1997)
Television broadcast stations: 373 (plus 8,042 repeaters) (1995)
Televisions: 51.4 million (1998)
Internet country code: .de
Internet Service Providers (ISPs): 123 (2000)
Internet users: 18 million (2000)

Transportation

Railways:
total: 40,826 km including at least 14,253 km electrified and 14,768 km double- or multiple-tracked (1998)
note: since privatization in 1994, Deutsche Bahn AG (DBAG) no longer publishes details of the tracks it owns; in addition to the DBAG system there are 102 privately owned railway companies which own an approximate 3,000 km to 4,000 km of the total tracks
Highways:
total: 656,140 km
paved: 650,891 km (including 11,400 km of expressways)

Germany (continued)

unpaved: 5,249 km (all-weather) (1998 est.)
Waterways: 7,500 km
note: major rivers include the Rhine and Elbe; Kiel Canal is an important connection between the Baltic Sea and North Sea (1999)
Pipelines: crude oil 2,500 km (1998)
Ports and harbors: Berlin, Bonn, Brake, Bremen, Bremerhaven, Cologne, Dresden, Duisburg, Emden, Hamburg, Karlsruhe, Kiel, Luebeck, Magdeburg, Mannheim, Rostock, Stuttgart
Merchant marine:
total: 457 ships (1,000 GRT or over) totaling 6,414,724 GRT/7,952,776 DWT
ships by type: cargo 169, chemical tanker 10, combination ore/oil 1, container 243, liquefied gas 2, passenger 3, petroleum tanker 7, railcar carrier 2, refrigerated cargo 1, roll on/roll off 12, short-sea passenger 7 (2000 est.)
Airports: 613 (2000 est.)
Airports - with paved runways:
total: 322
over 3,047 m: 13
2,438 to 3,047 m: 55
1,524 to 2,437 m: 67
914 to 1,523 m: 63
under 914 m: 124 (2000 est.)
Airports - with unpaved runways:
total: 291
over 3,047 m: 2
2,438 to 3,047 m: 6
1,524 to 2,437 m: 5
914 to 1,523 m: 53
under 914 m: 225 (2000 est.)
Heliports: 59 (2000 est.)

Military

Military branches: Army, Navy (includes Naval Air Arm), Air Force, Medical Corps, Border Police, Coast Guard
Military manpower - military age: 18 years of age
Military manpower - availability:
males age 15-49: 20,851,022 (2001 est.)
Military manpower - fit for military service:
males age 15-49: 17,760,412 (2001 est.)
Military manpower - reaching military age annually:
males: 482,318 (2001 est.)
Military expenditures - dollar figure: $32.8 billion (FY98)
Military expenditures - percent of GDP: 1.5% (FY98)

Transnational Issues

Disputes - international: none
Illicit drugs: source of precursor chemicals for South American cocaine processors; transshipment point for and consumer of Southwest Asian heroin, Latin American cocaine, and European-produced synthetic drugs

Ghana

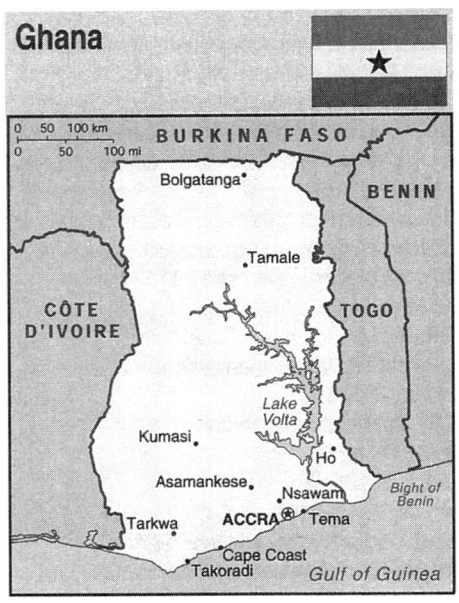

Introduction

Background: Formed from the merger of the British colony of the Gold Coast and the Togoland trust territory, Ghana in 1957 became the first country in colonial Africa to gain its independence. A long series of coups resulted in the suspension of the constitution in 1981 and the banning of political parties. A new constitution, restoring multiparty politics, was approved in 1992. Lt. Jerry RAWLINGS, head of state since 1981, won presidential elections in 1992 and 1996, but was constitutionally prevented from running for a third term in 2000. He was succeeded by John KUFUOR.

Geography

Location: Western Africa, bordering the Gulf of Guinea, between Cote d'Ivoire and Togo
Geographic coordinates: 8 00 N, 2 00 W
Map references: Africa
Area:
total: 238,540 sq km
land: 230,020 sq km
water: 8,520 sq km
Area - comparative: slightly smaller than Oregon
Land boundaries:
total: 2,093 km
border countries: Burkina Faso 548 km, Cote d'Ivoire 668 km, Togo 877 km
Coastline: 539 km
Maritime claims:
contiguous zone: 24 NM
continental shelf: 200 NM
exclusive economic zone: 200 NM
territorial sea: 12 NM
Climate: tropical; warm and comparatively dry along southeast coast; hot and humid in southwest; hot and dry in north
Terrain: mostly low plains with dissected plateau in south-central area
Elevation extremes:
lowest point: Atlantic Ocean 0 m
highest point: Mount Afadjato 880 m
Natural resources: gold, timber, industrial diamonds, bauxite, manganese, fish, rubber, hydropower
Land use:
arable land: 12%
permanent crops: 7%
permanent pastures: 22%
forests and woodland: 35%
other: 24% (1993 est.)
Irrigated land: 60 sq km (1993 est.)
Natural hazards: dry, dusty, harmattan winds occur from January to March; droughts
Environment - current issues: recent drought in north severely affecting agricultural activities; deforestation; overgrazing; soil erosion; poaching and habitat destruction threatens wildlife populations; water pollution; inadequate supplies of potable water
Environment - international agreements:
party to: Biodiversity, Climate Change, Desertification, Endangered Species, Environmental Modification, Law of the Sea, Marine Dumping, Nuclear Test Ban, Ozone Layer Protection, Ship Pollution, Tropical Timber 83, Tropical Timber 94, Wetlands
signed, but not ratified: Marine Life Conservation
Geography - note: Lake Volta is the world's largest artificial lake; northeasterly harmattan wind (January to March)

People

Population: 19,894,014
note: estimates for this country explicitly take into account the effects of excess mortality due to AIDS; this can result in lower life expectancy, higher infant mortality and death rates, lower population and growth rates, and changes in the distribution of population by age and sex than would otherwise be expected (July 2001 est.)
Age structure:
0-14 years: 41.18% (male 4,123,317; female 4,068,786)
15-64 years: 55.35% (male 5,455,577; female 5,555,278)
65 years and over: 3.47% (male 328,809; female 362,247) (2001 est.)
Population growth rate: 1.79% (2001 est.)
Birth rate: 28.95 births/1,000 population (2001 est.)
Death rate: 10.26 deaths/1,000 population (2001 est.)
Net migration rate: -0.83 migrant(s)/1,000 population (2001 est.)
Sex ratio:
at birth: 1.03 male(s)/female
under 15 years: 1.01 male(s)/female
15-64 years: 0.98 male(s)/female
65 years and over: 0.91 male(s)/female
total population: 0.99 male(s)/female (2001 est.)
Infant mortality rate: 56.54 deaths/1,000 live births (2001 est.)

Ghana (continued)

Life expectancy at birth:
total population: 57.24 years
male: 55.86 years
female: 58.66 years (2001 est.)
Total fertility rate: 3.82 children born/woman (2001 est.)
HIV/AIDS - adult prevalence rate: 3.6% (1999 est.)
HIV/AIDS - people living with HIV/AIDS: 340,000 (1999 est.)
HIV/AIDS - deaths: 33,000 (1999 est.)
Nationality:
noun: Ghanaian(s)
adjective: Ghanaian
Ethnic groups: black African 99.8% (major tribes - Akan 44%, Moshi-Dagomba 16%, Ewe 13%, Ga 8%), European and other 0.2%
Religions: indigenous beliefs 38%, Muslim 30%, Christian 24%, other 8%
Languages: English (official), African languages (including Akan, Moshi-Dagomba, Ewe, and Ga)
Literacy:
definition: age 15 and over can read and write
total population: 64.5%
male: 75.9%
female: 53.5% (1995 est.)

Government

Country name:
conventional long form: Republic of Ghana
conventional short form: Ghana
former: Gold Coast
Government type: constitutional democracy
Capital: Accra
Administrative divisions: 10 regions; Ashanti, Brong-Ahafo, Central, Eastern, Greater Accra, Northern, Upper East, Upper West, Volta, Western
Independence: 6 March 1957 (from UK)
National holiday: Independence Day, 6 March (1957)
Constitution: new constitution approved 28 April 1992
Legal system: based on English common law and customary law; has not accepted compulsory ICJ jurisdiction
Suffrage: 18 years of age; universal
Executive branch:
chief of state: President John Agyekum KUFUOR (since 7 January 2001); Vice President Alhaji Aliu MAHAMA (since 7 January 2001); note - the president is both the chief of state and head of government
head of government: President John Agyekum KUFUOR (since 7 January 2001); Vice President Alhaji Aliu MAHAMA (since 7 January 2001); note - the president is both the chief of state and head of government
cabinet: Council of Ministers; president nominates members subject to approval by Parliament
elections: president and vice president elected on the same ticket by popular vote for four-year terms; election last held 7 and 28 December 2000 (next to be held NA December 2004)
election results: John Agyekum KUFUOR elected president in runoff; percent of vote - John KUFUOR 56.4%, John Atta MILLS 43.6%
Legislative branch: unicameral Parliament (200 seats; members are elected by direct popular vote to serve four-year terms)
elections: last held 7 December 2000 (next to be held NA December 2004)
election results: percent of vote by party - NA%; seats by party - NPP 100, NDC 92, PNC 3, CPP 1, independents 4
Judicial branch: Supreme Court
Political parties and leaders: Every Ghanaian Living Everywhere or EGLE [Owuraku AMOFA, chairman]; National Convention Party or NCP [Sarpong KUMA-KUMA]; National Democratic Congress or NDC [Dr. Huudu YAHAYA, general secretary]; New Patriotic Party or NPP [Samuel Arthur ODOI-SYKES]; People's Convention Party or PCP [P. K. DONKOH-AYIFI, acting chairman]; People's Heritage Party or PHP [Emmanuel Alexander ERSKINE]; People's National Convention or PNC [Edward MAHAMA]
Political pressure groups and leaders: NA
International organization participation: ABEDA, ACP, AfDB, C, CCC, ECA, ECOWAS, FAO, G-24, G-77, IAEA, IBRD, ICAO, ICC, ICFTU, ICRM, IDA, IFAD, IFC, IFRCS, ILO, IMF, IMO, Inmarsat, Intelsat, Interpol, IOC, IOM (observer), ISO, ITU, MINURSO, NAM, OAS (observer), OAU, OPCW, UN, UNCTAD, UNESCO, UNIDO, UNIFIL, UNIKOM, UNITAR, UNMEE, UNMIBH, UNMIK, UNMOP, UNMOT, UNTAET, UNU, UPU, WCL, WFTU, WHO, WIPO, WMO, WToO, WTrO
Diplomatic representation in the US:
chief of mission: Ambassador Kobena KOOMSON
chancery: 3512 International Drive NW, Washington, DC 20008
telephone: [1] (202) 686-4520
FAX: [1] (202) 686-4527
consulate(s) general: New York
Diplomatic representation from the US:
chief of mission: Ambassador Kathryn D. ROBINSON
embassy: Ring Road East, East of Danquah Circle, Accra
mailing address: P. O. Box 194, Accra
telephone: [233] (21) 775348
FAX: [233] (21) 776008
Flag description: three equal horizontal bands of red (top), yellow, and green with a large black five-pointed star centered in the yellow band; uses the popular pan-African colors of Ethiopia; similar to the flag of Bolivia, which has a coat of arms centered in the yellow band

Economy

Economy - overview: Well endowed with natural resources, Ghana has twice the per capita output of the poorer countries in West Africa. Even so, Ghana remains heavily dependent on international financial and technical assistance. Gold, timber, and cocoa production are major sources of foreign exchange. The domestic economy continues to revolve around subsistence agriculture, which accounts for 36% of GDP and employs 60% of the work force, mainly small landholders. In 1995-97, Ghana made mixed progress under a three-year structural adjustment program in cooperation with the IMF. On the minus side, public sector wage increases and regional peacekeeping commitments have led to continued inflationary deficit financing, depreciation of the cedi, and rising public discontent with Ghana's austerity measures. Political uncertainty and a depressed cocoa market led to disappointing growth in 2000. A rebound in the cocoa market should push growth over 4% in 2001-02.
GDP: purchasing power parity - $37.4 billion (2000 est.)
GDP - real growth rate: 3% (2000 est.)
GDP - per capita: purchasing power parity - $1,900 (2000 est.)
GDP - composition by sector:
agriculture: 36%
industry: 25%
services: 39% (2000 est.)
Population below poverty line: 31.4% (1992 est.)
Household income or consumption by percentage share:
lowest 10%: 3.6%
highest 10%: 26.1% (1997)
Inflation rate (consumer prices): 22.8% (2000 est.)
Labor force: 9 million (2000 est.)
Labor force - by occupation: agriculture 60%, industry 15%, services 25% (1999 est.)
Unemployment rate: 20% (1997 est.)
Budget:
revenues: $1.39 billion
expenditures: $1.47 billion, including capital expenditures of $370 million (1996 est.)
Industries: mining, lumbering, light manufacturing, aluminum smelting, food processing
Industrial production growth rate: 4.2% (1996 est.)
Electricity - production: 5.466 billion kWh (1999)
Electricity - production by source:
fossil fuel: 26.82%
hydro: 73.18%
nuclear: 0%
other: 0% (1999)
Electricity - consumption: 5.573 billion kWh (1999)
Electricity - exports: 400 million kWh (1999)
Electricity - imports: 890 million kWh (1999)
Agriculture - products: cocoa, rice, coffee, cassava (tapioca), peanuts, corn, shea nuts, bananas; timber
Exports: $1.6 billion (f.o.b., 2000)
Exports - commodities: gold, cocoa, timber, tuna, bauxite, aluminum, manganese ore, diamonds
Exports - partners: Togo, UK, Italy, Netherlands, Germany, US, France (1998)
Imports: $2.2 billion (f.o.b., 2000)
Imports - commodities: capital equipment, petroleum, foodstuffs
Imports - partners: UK, Nigeria, US, Germany, Italy, Spain (1998)

Ghana (continued)

Debt - external: $7 billion (1999 est.)
Economic aid - recipient: $477.3 million (1995)
Currency: cedi (GHC)
Currency code: GHC
Exchange rates: cedis per US dollar - 6,895.77 (January 2001), 5,321.68 (2000), 2,647.32 (1999), 2,314.15 (1998), 2,050.17 (1997), 1,637.23 (1996)
Fiscal year: calendar year

Communications

Telephones - main lines in use: 200,000 (1998)
Telephones - mobile cellular: 30,000 (yearend 1998)
Telephone system:
general assessment: poor to fair system; Internet accessible; many rural communities not yet connected; expansion of services is underway
domestic: primarily microwave radio relay; wireless local loop has been installed
international: satellite earth stations - 4 Intelsat (Atlantic Ocean); microwave radio relay link to Panaftel system connects Ghana to its neighbors
Radio broadcast stations: AM 0, FM 18, shortwave 3 (1999)
Radios: 4.4 million (1997)
Television broadcast stations: 11 (1999)
Televisions: 1.73 million (1997)
Internet country code: .gh
Internet Service Providers (ISPs): 1 (2000)
Internet users: 20,000 (2000)

Transportation

Railways:
total: 953 km (undergoing major rehabilitation)
narrow gauge: 953 km 1.067-m gauge (32 km double track) (1997 est.)
Highways:
total: 39,409 km
paved: 11,653 km (including 30 km of expressways)
unpaved: 27,756 km (1997)
Waterways: 1,293 km
note: Volta, Ankobra, and Tano Rivers provide 168 km of perennial navigation for launches and lighters; Lake Volta provides 1,125 km of arterial and feeder waterways
Pipelines: 0 km
Ports and harbors: Takoradi, Tema
Merchant marine:
total: 6 ships (1,000 GRT or over) totaling 13,484 GRT/18,583 DWT
ships by type: petroleum tanker 2, refrigerated cargo 4 (2000 est.)
Airports: 12 (2000 est.)
Airports - with paved runways:
total: 6
2,438 to 3,047 m: 1
1,524 to 2,437 m: 3
914 to 1,523 m: 2 (2000 est.)
Airports - with unpaved runways:
total: 6
1,524 to 2,437 m: 1
914 to 1,523 m: 3
under 914 m: 2 (2000 est.)

Military

Military branches: Army, Navy, Air Force, National Police Force, Palace Guard, Civil Defense
Military manpower - military age: 18 years of age
Military manpower - availability:
males age 15-49: 4,890,483 (2001 est.)
Military manpower - fit for military service:
males age 15-49: 2,713,584 (2001 est.)
Military manpower - reaching military age annually:
males: 213,237 (2001 est.)
Military expenditures - dollar figure: $53 million (FY99)
Military expenditures - percent of GDP: 0.7% (FY99)

Transnational Issues

Disputes - international: none
Illicit drugs: illicit producer of cannabis for the international drug trade; transit hub for Southwest and Southeast Asian heroin and South American cocaine destined for Europe and the US

Gibraltar
(overseas territory of the UK)

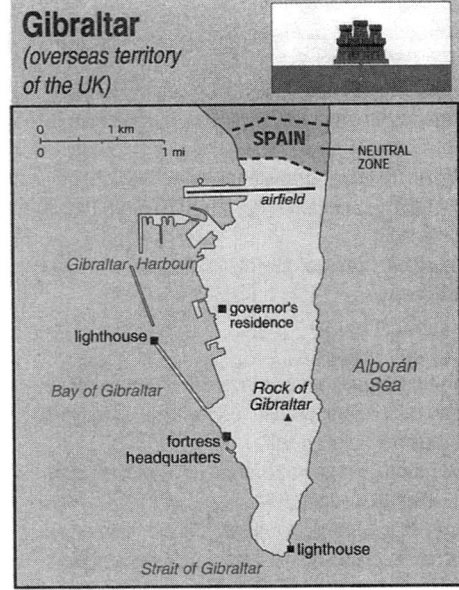

Introduction

Background: Strategically important, Gibraltar was ceded to Great Britain by Spain in the 1713 Treaty of Utrecht; the British garrison was formally declared a colony in 1830. In a 1967 referendum, Gibraltarians ignored Spanish pressure and voted overwhelmingly to remain a British dependency.

Geography

Location: Southwestern Europe, bordering the Strait of Gibraltar, which links the Mediterranean Sea and the North Atlantic Ocean, on the southern coast of Spain
Geographic coordinates: 36 11 N, 5 22 W
Map references: Europe
Area:
total: 6.5 sq km
land: 6.5 sq km
water: 0 sq km
Area - comparative: about 11 times the size of The Mall in Washington, DC
Land boundaries:
total: 1.2 km
border countries: Spain 1.2 km
Coastline: 12 km
Maritime claims:
territorial sea: 3 NM
Climate: Mediterranean with mild winters and warm summers
Terrain: a narrow coastal lowland borders the Rock of Gibraltar
Elevation extremes:
lowest point: Mediterranean Sea 0 m
highest point: Rock of Gibraltar 426 m
Natural resources: NEGL
Land use:
arable land: 0%
permanent crops: 0%
permanent pastures: 0%
forests and woodland: 0%
other: 100% (1993 est.)

Gibraltar (continued)

Irrigated land: NA sq km
Natural hazards: NA
Environment - current issues: limited natural freshwater resources; large concrete or natural rock water catchments collect rainwater
Geography - note: strategic location on Strait of Gibraltar that links the North Atlantic Ocean and Mediterranean Sea

People

Population: 27,649 (July 2001 est.)
Age structure:
0-14 years: 18.73% (male 2,652; female 2,528)
15-64 years: 66.33% (male 9,473; female 8,866)
65 years and over: 14.94% (male 1,733; female 2,397) (2001 est.)
Population growth rate: 0.24% (2001 est.)
Birth rate: 11.25 births/1,000 population (2001 est.)
Death rate: 8.82 deaths/1,000 population (2001 est.)
Net migration rate: NEGL migrant(s)/1,000 population (2001 est.)
Sex ratio:
at birth: 1.05 male(s)/female
under 15 years: 1.05 male(s)/female
15-64 years: 1.07 male(s)/female
65 years and over: 0.72 male(s)/female
total population: 1 male(s)/female (2001 est.)
Infant mortality rate: 5.49 deaths/1,000 live births (2001 est.)
Life expectancy at birth:
total population: 79.09 years
male: 76.23 years
female: 82.1 years (2001 est.)
Total fertility rate: 1.64 children born/woman (2001 est.)
HIV/AIDS - adult prevalence rate: NA%
HIV/AIDS - people living with HIV/AIDS: NA
HIV/AIDS - deaths: NA
Nationality:
noun: Gibraltarian(s)
adjective: Gibraltar
Ethnic groups: Spanish, Italian, English, Maltese, Portuguese
Religions: Roman Catholic 76.9%, Church of England 6.9%, Muslim 6.9%, Jewish 2.3%, none or other 7% (1991)
Languages: English (used in schools and for official purposes), Spanish, Italian, Portuguese, Russian
Literacy:
definition: NA
total population: above 80%
male: NA%
female: NA%

Government

Country name:
conventional long form: none
conventional short form: Gibraltar
Dependency status: overseas territory of the UK
Government type: NA
Capital: Gibraltar
Administrative divisions: none (overseas territory of the UK)
Independence: none (overseas territory of the UK)
National holiday: Commonwealth Day, second Monday of March
Constitution: 30 May 1969
Legal system: English law
Suffrage: 18 years of age; universal, plus other UK subjects who have been residents six months or more
Executive branch:
chief of state: Queen ELIZABETH II (since 6 February 1952), represented by Governor and Commander-in-Chief David DURIE (since 5 April 2000); note - DURIE was appointed in February 2000 but took office in April 2000
head of government: Chief Minister Peter CARUANA (since 17 May 1996)
cabinet: Council of Ministers appointed from among the 15 elected members of the House of Assembly by the governor in consultation with the chief minister; note - there is also a Gibraltar Council that advises the governor
elections: none; the monarch is hereditary; governor appointed by the monarch; chief minister appointed by the governor
Legislative branch: unicameral House of Assembly (18 seats - 15 elected by popular vote, one appointed for the Speaker, and two ex officio members; members serve four-year terms)
elections: last held 10 February 2000 (next to be held NA 2004)
election results: percent of vote by party - GSD 58%, GSLP 41%; seats by party - GSD 8, GSLP 7
Judicial branch: Supreme Court; Court of Appeal
Political parties and leaders: Gibraltar Social Democrats or GSD [Peter CARUANA]; Gibraltar Socialist Labor Party or GSLP [Joseph John BOSSANO]
Political pressure groups and leaders: Chamber of Commerce; Gibraltar Representatives Organization; Housewives Association
International organization participation: Interpol (subbureau)
Diplomatic representation in the US: none (overseas territory of the UK)
Diplomatic representation from the US: none (overseas territory of the UK)
Flag description: two horizontal bands of white (top, double width) and red with a three-towered red castle in the center of the white band; hanging from the castle gate is a gold key centered in the red band

Economy

Economy - overview: Gibraltar benefits from an extensive shipping trade, offshore banking, and its position as an international conference center. The British military presence has been sharply reduced and now contributes about 11% to the local economy. The financial sector accounts for 20% of GDP; tourism (almost 6 million visitors in 1998), shipping services fees, and duties on consumer goods also generate revenue. In recent years, Gibraltar has seen major structural change from a public to a private sector economy, but changes in government spending still have a major impact on the level of employment.
GDP: purchasing power parity - $500 million (1997 est.)
GDP - real growth rate: NA%
GDP - per capita: purchasing power parity - $17,500 (1997 est.)
GDP - composition by sector:
agriculture: NA%
industry: NA%
services: NA%
Population below poverty line: NA%
Household income or consumption by percentage share:
lowest 10%: NA%
highest 10%: NA%
Inflation rate (consumer prices): 1.5% (1998)
Labor force: 14,800 (including non-Gibraltar laborers)
Labor force - by occupation: services 60%, industry 40%, agriculture NEGL%
Unemployment rate: 13.5% (1996)
Budget:
revenues: $307 million
expenditures: $284 million, including capital expenditures of $NA (FY00/01 est.)
Industries: tourism, banking and finance, ship-building and repairing; support to large UK naval and air bases; tobacco, mineral water, beer, canned fish
Industrial production growth rate: NA%
Electricity - production: 95 million kWh (1999)
Electricity - production by source:
fossil fuel: 100%
hydro: 0%
nuclear: 0%
other: 0% (1999)
Electricity - consumption: 88.4 million kWh (1999)
Electricity - exports: 0 kWh (1999)
Electricity - imports: 0 kWh (1999)
Agriculture - products: none
Exports: $81.1 million (f.o.b., 1997)
Exports - commodities: (principally reexports) petroleum 51%, manufactured goods 41%, other 8%
Exports - partners: UK, Morocco, Portugal, Netherlands, Spain, US, Germany
Imports: $492 million (c.i.f., 1997)
Imports - commodities: fuels, manufactured goods, and foodstuffs
Imports - partners: UK, Spain, Japan, Netherlands
Debt - external: $NA
Economic aid - recipient: $NA
Currency: Gibraltar pound (GIP)
Currency code: GIP
Exchange rates: Gibraltar pounds per US dollar - 0.6764 (January 2001), 0.6596 (2000), 0.6180 (1999), 0.6037 (1998), 0.6106 (1997), 0.6403 (1996); note - the Gibraltar pound is at par with the British pound
Fiscal year: 1 July - 30 June

Gibraltar (continued)

Communications

Telephones - main lines in use: 19,000 (1997)
Telephones - mobile cellular: 1,620 (1997)
Telephone system:
general assessment: adequate, automatic domestic system and adequate international facilities
domestic: automatic exchange facilities
international: radiotelephone; microwave radio relay; satellite earth station - 1 Intelsat (Atlantic Ocean)
Radio broadcast stations: AM 1, FM 5, shortwave 0 (1998)
Radios: 37,000 (1997)
Television broadcast stations: 1 (plus three low-power repeaters) (1997)
Televisions: 10,000 (1997)
Internet country code: .gi
Internet Service Providers (ISPs): 2 (2000)
Internet users: NA

Transportation

Railways:
total: NA km; 1.000-m gauge system in dockyard area only
Highways:
total: 46.25 km
paved: 46.25 km
unpaved: 0 km (2001)
Waterways: none
Pipelines: 0 km
Ports and harbors: Gibraltar
Merchant marine:
total: 49 ships (1,000 GRT or over) totaling 669,056 GRT/1,003,809 DWT
ships by type: bulk 1, cargo 15, chemical tanker 6, container 7, multi-functional large-load carrier 3, passenger 2, petroleum tanker 14, roll on/roll off 1 (2000 est.)
Airports: 1 (2000 est.)
Airports - with paved runways:
total: 1
1,524 to 2,437 m: 1 (2000 est.)

Military

Military branches: British Army, Royal Navy, Royal Air Force
Military - note: defense is the responsibility of the UK

Transnational Issues

Disputes - international: source of friction between Spain and the UK

Glorioso Islands
(possession of France)

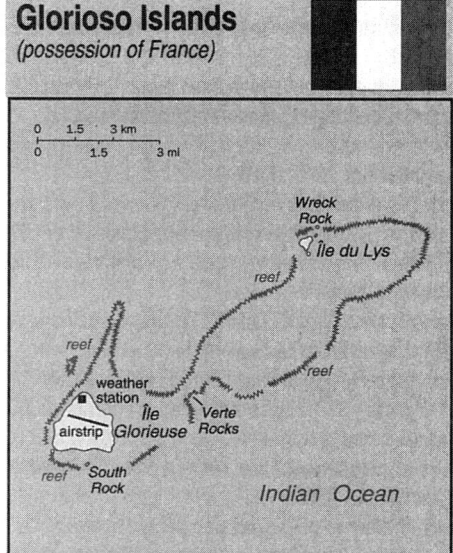

Introduction

Background: A French possession since 1892, the Glorioso Islands are composed of two lushly vegetated islands (Ile Glorieuse and Ile du Lys) and three rock islets. A military garrison operates a weather and radio station on Ile Glorieuse.

Geography

Location: Southern Africa, group of islands in the Indian Ocean, northwest of Madagascar
Geographic coordinates: 11 30 S, 47 20 E
Map references: Africa
Area:
total: 5 sq km
land: 5 sq km
water: 0 sq km
note: includes Ile Glorieuse, Ile du Lys, Verte Rocks, Wreck Rock, and South Rock
Area - comparative: about eight times the size of The Mall in Washington, DC
Land boundaries: 0 km
Coastline: 35.2 km
Maritime claims:
exclusive economic zone: 200 NM
territorial sea: 12 NM
Climate: tropical
Terrain: low and flat
Elevation extremes:
lowest point: Indian Ocean 0 m
highest point: unnamed location 12 m
Natural resources: guano, coconuts
Land use:
arable land: 0%
permanent crops: 0%
permanent pastures: 0%
forests and woodland: 0%
other: 100% (all lush vegetation and coconut palms)
Irrigated land: 0 sq km (1993)
Natural hazards: periodic cyclones
Environment - current issues: NA

People

Population: no indigenous inhabitants
note: there is a small French military garrison (July 2001 est.)

Government

Country name:
conventional long form: none
conventional short form: Glorioso Islands
local long form: none
local short form: Iles Glorieuses
Dependency status: possession of France; administered by a high commissioner of the Republic, resident in Reunion
Legal system: the laws of France, where applicable, apply
Diplomatic representation in the US: none (possession of France)
Diplomatic representation from the US: none (possession of France)
Flag description: the flag of France is used

Economy

Economy - overview: no economic activity

Communications

Communications - note: 1 meteorological station

Transportation

Waterways: none
Ports and harbors: none; offshore anchorage only
Airports: 1 (2000 est.)
Airports - with unpaved runways:
total: 1
914 to 1,523 m: 1 (2000 est.)

Military

Military - note: defense is the responsibility of France

Transnational Issues

Disputes - international: claimed by Madagascar

Greece

Introduction

Background: Greece achieved its independence from the Ottoman Empire in 1829. During the second half of the 19th century and the first half of the 20th century, it gradually added neighboring islands and territories with Greek-speaking populations. Following the defeat of communist rebels in 1949, Greece joined NATO in 1952. A military dictatorship, which in 1967 suspended many political liberties and forced the king to flee the country, lasted seven years. Democratic elections in 1974 and a referendum created a parliamentary republic and abolished the monarchy; Greece joined the European Community or EC in 1981 (which became the EU in 1992).

Geography

Location: Southern Europe, bordering the Aegean Sea, Ionian Sea, and the Mediterranean Sea, between Albania and Turkey
Geographic coordinates: 39 00 N, 22 00 E
Map references: Europe
Area:
total: 131,940 sq km
land: 130,800 sq km
water: 1,140 sq km
Area - comparative: slightly smaller than Alabama
Land boundaries:
total: 1,210 km
border countries: Albania 282 km, Bulgaria 494 km, Turkey 206 km, The Former Yugoslav Republic of Macedonia 228 km
Coastline: 13,676 km
Maritime claims:
continental shelf: 200-m depth or to the depth of exploitation
territorial sea: 6 NM
Climate: temperate; mild, wet winters; hot, dry summers
Terrain: mostly mountains with ranges extending into the sea as peninsulas or chains of islands
Elevation extremes:
lowest point: Mediterranean Sea 0 m
highest point: Mount Olympus 2,917 m
Natural resources: bauxite, lignite, magnesite, petroleum, marble, hydropower potential
Land use:
arable land: 19%
permanent crops: 8%
permanent pastures: 41%
forests and woodland: 20%
other: 12% (1993 est.)
Irrigated land: 13,140 sq km (1993 est.)
Natural hazards: severe earthquakes
Environment - current issues: air pollution; water pollution
Environment - international agreements:
party to: Air Pollution, Air Pollution-Nitrogen Oxides, Air Pollution-Sulphur 94, Antarctic-Environmental Protocol, Antarctic-Marine Living Resources, Biodiversity, Climate Change, Desertification, Endangered Species, Environmental Modification, Hazardous Wastes, Law of the Sea, Marine Dumping, Nuclear Test Ban, Ozone Layer Protection, Ship Pollution, Tropical Timber 83, Tropical Timber 94, Wetlands
signed, but not ratified: Air Pollution-Persistent Organic Pollutants, Air Pollution-Volatile Organic Compounds, Antarctic Treaty, Climate Change-Kyoto Protocol
Geography - note: strategic location dominating the Aegean Sea and southern approach to Turkish Straits; a peninsular country, possessing an archipelago of about 2,000 islands

People

Population: 10,623,835 (July 2001 est.)
Age structure:
0-14 years: 14.98% (male 820,219; female 771,466)
15-64 years: 67.3% (male 3,580,535; female 3,569,755)
65 years and over: 17.72% (male 834,234; female 1,047,626) (2001 est.)
Population growth rate: 0.21% (2001 est.)
Birth rate: 9.83 births/1,000 population (2001 est.)
Death rate: 9.73 deaths/1,000 population (2001 est.)
Net migration rate: 1.96 migrant(s)/1,000 population (2001 est.)
Sex ratio:
at birth: 1.07 male(s)/female
under 15 years: 1.06 male(s)/female
15-64 years: 1 male(s)/female
65 years and over: 0.8 male(s)/female
total population: 0.97 male(s)/female (2001 est.)
Infant mortality rate: 6.38 deaths/1,000 live births (2001 est.)
Life expectancy at birth:
total population: 78.59 years
male: 76.03 years
female: 81.32 years (2001 est.)
Total fertility rate: 1.33 children born/woman (2001 est.)
HIV/AIDS - adult prevalence rate: 0.16% (1999 est.)
HIV/AIDS - people living with HIV/AIDS: 8,000 (1999 est.)
HIV/AIDS - deaths: less than 100 (1999 est.)
Nationality:
noun: Greek(s)
adjective: Greek
Ethnic groups: Greek 98%, other 2%
note: the Greek Government states there are no ethnic divisions in Greece
Religions: Greek Orthodox 98%, Muslim 1.3%, other 0.7%
Languages: Greek 99% (official), English, French
Literacy:
definition: age 15 and over can read and write
total population: 95%
male: 98%
female: 93% (1991 est.)

Government

Country name:
conventional long form: Hellenic Republic
conventional short form: Greece
local long form: Elliniki Dhimokratia
local short form: Ellas or Ellada
former: Kingdom of Greece
Government type: parliamentary republic; monarchy rejected by referendum 8 December 1974
Capital: Athens
Administrative divisions: 51 prefectures (nomoi, singular - nomos)and 1 autonomous region*; Ayion Oros* (Mt. Athos), Aitolia kai Akarnania, Akhaia, Argolis, Arkadhia, Arta, Attiki, Dhodhekanisos, Drama, Evritania, Evros, Evvoia, Florina, Fokis, Fthiotis, Grevena, Ilia, Imathia, Ioannina, Irakleion, Kardhitsa, Kastoria, Kavala, Kefallinia, Kerkyra, Khalkidhiki, Khania, Khios, Kikladhes, Kilkis, Korinthia, Kozani, Lakonia, Larisa, Lasithi, Lesvos, Levkas, Magnisia, Messinia, Pella, Pieria, Preveza, Rethimni, Rodhopi, Samos, Serrai, Thesprotia, Thessaloniki, Trikala, Voiotia, Xanthi, Zakinthos
Independence: 1829 (from the Ottoman Empire)
National holiday: Independence Day, 25 March (1821)
Constitution: 11 June 1975; amended March 1986
Legal system: based on codified Roman law; judiciary divided into civil, criminal, and administrative courts
Suffrage: 18 years of age; universal and compulsory
Executive branch:
chief of state: President Konstandinos (Kostis) STEPHANOPOULOS (since 10 March 1995)
head of government: Prime Minister Konstandinos SIMITIS (since 19 January 1996)
cabinet: Cabinet appointed by the president on the recommendation of the prime minister
elections: president elected by Parliament for a five-year term; election last held 8 February 2000 (next to be held by NA March 2005); prime minister appointed by the president

Greece (continued)

election results: Konstandinos STEPHANOPOULOS reelected president; percent of Parliament vote - 90%
Legislative branch: unicameral Parliament or Vouli ton Ellinon (300 seats; members are elected by direct popular vote to serve four-year terms)
elections: elections last held 9 April 2000 (next to be held by NA April 2004)
election results: percent of vote by party - PASOK 43.8%, ND 42.7%, KKE 5.5%, Coalition of the Left and Progress 3.2%; seats by party - PASOK 158, ND 125, KKE 11, Coalition of the Left and Progress 6
Judicial branch: Supreme Judicial Court; Special Supreme Tribunal; all judges appointed for life by the president after consultation with a judicial council
Political parties and leaders: Coalition of the Left and Progress (Synaspismos) [Nikolaos KONSTANDOPOULOS]; Communist Party of Greece or KKE [Aleka PAPARIGA]; New Democracy or ND (conservative) [Konstandinos KARAMANLIS]; Panhellenic Socialist Movement or PASOK [Konstandinos SIMITIS]
Political pressure groups and leaders: NA
International organization participation: Australia Group, BIS, BSEC, CCC, CE, CERN, EAPC, EBRD, ECE, EIB, EMU, EU, FAO, G- 6, IAEA, IBRD, ICAO, ICC, ICFTU, ICRM, IDA, IEA, IFAD, IFC, IFRCS, IHO, ILO, IMF, IMO, Inmarsat, Intelsat, Interpol, IOC, IOM, ISO, ITU, MINURSO, NAM (guest), NATO, NEA, NSG, OAS (observer), OECD, OPCW, OSCE, PCA, UN, UNCTAD, UNESCO, UNHCR, UNIDO, UNIKOM, UNMIBH, UNOMIG, UPU, WEU, WFTU, WHO, WIPO, WMO, WToO, WTrO, ZC
Diplomatic representation in the US:
chief of mission: Ambassador Alexandros PHILON
chancery: 2221 Massachusetts Avenue NW, Washington, DC 20008
telephone: [1] (202) 939-5800
FAX: [1] (202) 939-5824
consulate(s) general: Boston, Chicago, Los Angeles, New York, and San Francisco
consulate(s): Atlanta, Houston, and New Orleans
Diplomatic representation from the US:
chief of mission: Ambassador R. Nicholas BURNS
embassy: 91 Vasilissis Sophias Boulevard, 10160 Athens
mailing address: PSC 108, APO AE 09842-0108
telephone: [30] (1) 721-2951
FAX: [30] (1) 645-6282
consulate(s) general: Thessaloniki
Flag description: nine equal horizontal stripes of blue alternating with white; there is a blue square in the upper hoist-side corner bearing a white cross; the cross symbolizes Greek Orthodoxy, the established religion of the country

Economy

Economy - overview: Greece has a mixed capitalist economy with the public sector accounting for about half of GDP. Tourism is a key industry, providing a large portion of GDP and foreign exchange earnings. Greece is a major beneficiary of EU aid, equal to about 4% of GDP. The economy has improved steadily over the last few years, as the government has tightened policy in the run-up to Greece's entry into the EU's Economic and Monetary Union (EMU) on 1 January 2001. In particular, Greece has cut its budget deficit to below 1% of GDP and tightened monetary policy, with the result that inflation fell from 20% in 1990 to 3.1% in 2000. Major challenges remaining include the reduction of unemployment and further restructuring of the economy, including the privatization of some leading state enterprises. Growth, 3.8% in 2000, may fall off to 3%-3.5% in 2001.
GDP: purchasing power parity - $181.9 billion (2000 est.)
GDP - real growth rate: 3.8% (2000 est.)
GDP - per capita: purchasing power parity - $17,200 (2000 est.)
GDP - composition by sector:
agriculture: 8.3%
industry: 27.3%
services: 64.4% (1998)
Population below poverty line: NA%
Household income or consumption by percentage share:
lowest 10%: 3%
highest 10%: 25.3% (1993 est.)
Inflation rate (consumer prices): 3.1% (2000 est.)
Labor force: 4.32 million (1999 est.)
Labor force - by occupation: industry 21%, agriculture 20%, services 59% (2000 est.)
Unemployment rate: 11.3% (2000 est.)
Budget:
revenues: $45 billion
expenditures: $47.6 billion, including capital expenditures of $NA (1998 est.)
Industries: tourism; food and tobacco processing, textiles; chemicals, metal products; mining, petroleum
Industrial production growth rate: 7% (2000 est.)
Electricity - production: 46.432 billion kWh (1999)
Electricity - production by source:
fossil fuel: 89.6%
hydro: 9.72%
nuclear: 0%
other: 0.68% (1999)
Electricity - consumption: 43.343 billion kWh (1999)
Electricity - exports: 1.65 billion kWh (1999)
Electricity - imports: 1.811 billion kWh (1999)
Agriculture - products: wheat, corn, barley, sugar beets, olives, tomatoes, wine, tobacco, potatoes; beef, dairy products
Exports: $15.8 billion (f.o.b., 2000)
Exports - commodities: manufactured goods, food and beverages, petroleum products
Exports - partners: EU 49% (Germany 15%, Italy 13%, UK 6%), US 6% (1999)
Imports: $33.9 billion (c.i.f., 2000)
Imports - commodities: manufactured goods, foodstuffs, fuels, chemicals
Imports - partners: EU 66% (Italy 15%, Germany 15%, France 9%, UK 6%) (1999)
Debt - external: $57 billion (2000 est.)
Economic aid - recipient: $5.4 billion from EU (1997 est.)
Currency: drachma (GRD); euro (EUR)
note: on 1 January 1999, the EU introduced the euro as a common currency that is now being used by financial institutions in Greece (which entered the European Monetary Union on 1 January 2001) at a fixed rate of 340.750 drachmae per euro and will replace the local currency for all transactions in 2002
Currency code: GRD; EUR
Exchange rates: drachmae per US dollar - 380.21 (December 2000), 365.40 (2000), 305.65 (1999), 295.53 (1998), 273.06 (1997), 240.71 (1996)
Fiscal year: calendar year

Communications

Telephones - main lines in use: 5.431 million (1997)
Telephones - mobile cellular: 937,700 (1997)
Telephone system:
general assessment: adequate, modern networks reach all areas; good mobile telephone and international service
domestic: microwave radio relay trunk system; extensive open wire connections; submarine cable to offshore islands
international: tropospheric scatter; 8 submarine cables; satellite earth stations - 2 Intelsat (1 Atlantic Ocean and 1 Indian Ocean), 1 Eutelsat, and 1 Inmarsat (Indian Ocean region)
Radio broadcast stations: AM 26, FM 88, shortwave 4 (1998)
Radios: 5.02 million (1997)
Television broadcast stations: 36 (plus 1,341 low-power repeaters); also two stations in the US Armed Forces Radio and Television Service (1995)
Televisions: 2.54 million (1997)
Internet country code: .gr
Internet Service Providers (ISPs): 27 (2000)
Internet users: 1.33 million (1999)

Transportation

Railways:
total: 2,548 km
standard gauge: 1,565 km 1.435-m gauge (36 km electrified; 23 km double track)
narrow gauge: 961 km 1.000-m gauge; 22 km 0.750-m gauge (a rack-type railway for steep grades)
Highways:
total: 117,000 km
paved: 107,406 km (including 470 km of expressways)
unpaved: 9,594 km (1996)
Waterways: 80 km
note: system consists of three coastal canals including the Corinth Canal (6 km) which crosses the Isthmus of Corinth connecting the Gulf of Corinth with the Saronic Gulf and shortens the sea voyage from the Adriatic to Peiraiefs (Piraeus) by 325 km; there are also three unconnected rivers

Greece (continued)

Pipelines: crude oil 26 km; petroleum products 547 km
Ports and harbors: Alexandroupolis, Elefsis, Irakleion (Crete), Kavala, Kerkyra, Chalkis, Igoumenitsa, Lavrion, Patrai, Peiraiefs (Piraeus), Thessaloniki, Volos
Merchant marine:
total: 780 ships (1,000 GRT or over) totaling 25,564,988 GRT/44,761,916 DWT
ships by type: bulk 272, cargo 55, chemical tanker 22, combination bulk 5, combination ore/oil 6, container 51, liquefied gas 5, multi-functional large-load carrier 1, passenger 14, passenger/cargo 2, petroleum tanker 255, refrigerated cargo 3, roll on/roll off 20, short-sea passenger 63, specialized tanker 5, vehicle carrier 1
note: includes some foreign-owned ships registered here as a flag of convenience: South Korea 1, UK 4 (2000 est.)
Airports: 81 (2000 est.)
Airports - with paved runways:
total: 65
over 3,047 m: 6
2,438 to 3,047 m: 15
1,524 to 2,437 m: 19
914 to 1,523 m: 16
under 914 m: 9 (2000 est.)
Airports - with unpaved runways:
total: 16
over 3,047 m: 1
1,524 to 2,437 m: 1
914 to 1,523 m: 4
under 914 m: 10 (2000 est.)
Heliports: 2 (2000 est.)

Military

Military branches: Hellenic Army, Hellenic Navy, Hellenic Air Force, National Guard, Police
Military manpower - military age: 21 years of age
Military manpower - availability:
males age 15-49: 2,673,539 (2001 est.)
Military manpower - fit for military service:
males age 15-49: 2,040,227 (2001 est.)
Military manpower - reaching military age annually:
males: 77,976 (2001 est.)
Military expenditures - dollar figure: $6.12 billion (FY99/00 est.)
Military expenditures - percent of GDP: 4.91% (FY99/00 est.)

Transnational Issues

Disputes - international: complex maritime, air, and territorial disputes with Turkey in Aegean Sea; Cyprus question with Turkey; dispute with The Former Yugoslav Republic of Macedonia over its name
Illicit drugs: a gateway to Europe for traffickers smuggling cannabis and heroin from the Middle East and Southwest Asia to the West and precursor chemicals to the East; some South American cocaine transits or is consumed in Greece

Greenland
(part of the Kingdom of Denmark)

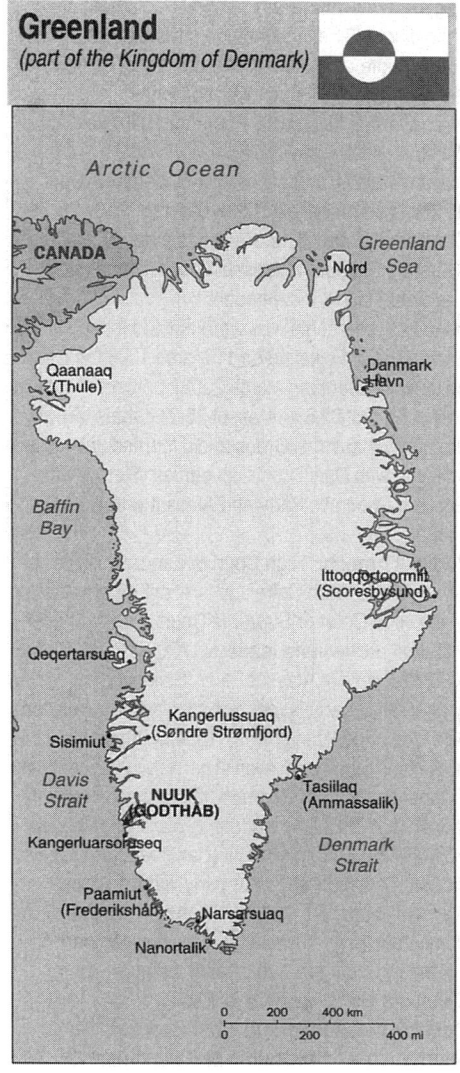

Introduction

Background: The world's largest island, about 84% ice-capped, Greenland was granted self-government in 1978 by the Danish parliament. The law went into effect the following year. Denmark continues to exercise control of Greenland's foreign affairs.

Geography

Location: Northern North America, island between the Arctic Ocean and the North Atlantic Ocean, northeast of Canada
Geographic coordinates: 72 00 N, 40 00 W
Map references: Arctic Region
Area:
total: 2,175,600 sq km
land: 2,175,600 sq km (341,700 sq km ice-free, 1,833,900 sq km ice-covered) (est.)
Area - comparative: slightly more than three times the size of Texas
Land boundaries: 0 km
Coastline: 44,087 km
Maritime claims:
continental shelf: 200 NM or agreed boundaries or median line
exclusive fishing zone: 200 NM or agreed boundaries or median line
territorial sea: 3 NM
Climate: arctic to subarctic; cool summers, cold winters
Terrain: flat to gradually sloping icecap covers all but a narrow, mountainous, barren, rocky coast
Elevation extremes:
lowest point: Atlantic Ocean 0 m
highest point: Gunnbjorn 3,700 m
Natural resources: zinc, lead, iron ore, coal, molybdenum, gold, platinum, uranium, fish, seals, whales, hydropower, possible oil and gas
Land use:
arable land: 0%
permanent crops: 0%
permanent pastures: 1%
forests and woodland: 0%
other: 99% (1998 est.)
Irrigated land: NA sq km
Natural hazards: continuous permafrost over northern two-thirds of the island
Environment - current issues: protection of the arctic environment; preservation of the Inuit traditional way of life, including whaling and seal hunting
Geography - note: dominates North Atlantic Ocean between North America and Europe; sparse population confined to small settlements along coast, but close to one-quarter of the population lives in the capital, Nuuk; world's second largest ice cap

People

Population: 56,352 (July 2001 est.)
Age structure:
0-14 years: 26.69% (male 7,649; female 7,392)
15-64 years: 67.87% (male 20,868; female 17,376)
65 years and over: 5.44% (male 1,385; female 1,682) (2001 est.)
Population growth rate: 0.06% (2001 est.)
Birth rate: 16.52 births/1,000 population (2001 est.)
Death rate: 7.58 deaths/1,000 population (2001 est.)
Net migration rate: -8.38 migrant(s)/1,000 population (2001 est.)
Sex ratio:
at birth: 1.02 male(s)/female
under 15 years: 1.03 male(s)/female
15-64 years: 1.2 male(s)/female
65 years and over: 0.82 male(s)/female
total population: 1.13 male(s)/female (2001 est.)
Infant mortality rate: 17.77 deaths/1,000 live births (2001 est.)
Life expectancy at birth:
total population: 68.37 years
male: 64.82 years
female: 72.01 years (2001 est.)
Total fertility rate: 2.44 children born/woman (2001 est.)
HIV/AIDS - adult prevalence rate: NA%
HIV/AIDS - people living with HIV/AIDS: 100 (1999)
HIV/AIDS - deaths: NA

Greenland (continued)

Nationality:
noun: Greenlander(s)
adjective: Greenlandic
Ethnic groups: Greenlander 88% (Inuit and Greenland-born whites), Danish and others 12% (January 2000)
Religions: Evangelical Lutheran
Languages: Greenlandic (East Inuit), Danish, English
Literacy:
definition: NA
total population: NA%
male: NA%
female: NA%
note: similar to Denmark proper

Government

Country name:
conventional long form: none
conventional short form: Greenland
local long form: none
local short form: Kalaallit Nunaat
Dependency status: part of the Kingdom of Denmark; self-governing overseas administrative division of Denmark since 1979
Government type: parliamentary democracy within a constitutional monarchy
Capital: Nuuk (Godthab)
Administrative divisions: 3 districts (landsdele); Avannaa (Nordgronland), Tunu (Ostgronland), Kitaa (Vestgronland)
note: there are 18 municipalities in Greenland
Independence: none (part of the Kingdom of Denmark; self-governing overseas administrative division of Denmark since 1979)
note: foreign affairs is the responsibility of Denmark, but Greenland actively participates in international agreements relating to Greenland
National holiday: June 21 (longest day)
Constitution: 5 June 1953 (Danish constitution)
Legal system: Danish
Suffrage: 18 years of age; universal
Executive branch:
chief of state: Queen MARGRETHE II of Denmark (since 14 January 1972), represented by High Commissioner Gunnar MARTENS (since NA 1995)
head of government: Prime Minister Jonathan MOTZFELDT (since 19 September 1997)
cabinet: Home Rule Government is elected by the Parliament (Landstinget) on the basis of the strength of parties
elections: the monarch is hereditary; high commissioner appointed by the monarch; prime minister is elected by Parliament (usually the leader of the majority party); election last held 16 February 1999 (next to be held NA February 2003)
election results: Jonathan MOTZFELDT reelected prime minister following the 16 February 1999 elections; percent of parliamentary vote - 57.3%
note: government coalition - Siumut and Inuit Ataqatigiit (IA)
Legislative branch: unicameral Parliament or Landstinget (31 seats; members are elected by popular vote on the basis of proportional representation to serve four-year terms)
elections: last held on 16 February 1999 (next to be held by NA February 2003)
election results: percent of vote by party - Siumut 35.2%, Inuit Ataqatigiit 22.1%, Atassut Party 25.2%, Candidate's League 12.3%, independent 5.2%; seats by party - Siumut 11, Atassut 8, Inuit Ataqatigiit 7, Candidate List 4, independent 1
note: two representatives were elected to the Danish Parliament or Folketing on 11 March 1998 (next to be held by not later than March 2002); percent of vote by party - Siumut 35.6%, Atassut 35.2%; seats by party - Siumut 1, Atassut 1; Greenlandic representatives are affiliated with Danish political parties (Siumut with Social Democratic Party and Atassut with Liberal Party)
Judicial branch: High Court or Landsret (appeals can be made to the Ostre Landsret or Eastern Division of the High Court or Supreme Court in Copenhagen)
Political parties and leaders: Akulliit Party [Bjarne KREUTZMANN]; Atassut Party (Solidarity, a conservative party favoring continuing close relations with Denmark) [Daniel SKIFTE]; Inuit Ataqatigiit or IA (Eskimo Brotherhood, a leftist party favoring complete independence from Denmark rather than home rule) [Josef MOTZFELDT]; Issituup (Polar Party) [Nicolai HEINRICH]; Kattusseqatigiit (Candidate List, an independent right-of-center party with no official platform [leader NA]; Siumut (Forward Party, a social democratic party advocating more distinct Greenlandic identity and greater autonomy from Denmark) [Jonathan MOTZFELDT]
Political pressure groups and leaders: NA
International organization participation: ICC, NC, NIB
Diplomatic representation in the US: none (self-governing overseas administrative division of Denmark)
Diplomatic representation from the US: none (self-governing overseas administrative division of Denmark)
Flag description: two equal horizontal bands of white (top) and red with a large disk slightly to the hoist side of center - the top half of the disk is red, the bottom half is white

Economy

Economy - overview: The economy remains critically dependent on exports of fish and substantial support from the Danish Government, which supplies about half of government revenues. The public sector, including publicly owned enterprises and the municipalities, plays the dominant role in the economy. Despite several interesting hydrocarbon and minerals exploration activities, it will take several years before production can materialize. Tourism is the only sector offering any near-term potential and even this is limited due to a short season and high costs.
GDP: purchasing power parity - $1.1 billion (2000 est.)
GDP - real growth rate: NA%
GDP - per capita: purchasing power parity - $20,000 (2000 est.)
GDP - composition by sector:
agriculture: NA%
industry: NA%
services: NA%
Population below poverty line: NA%
Household income or consumption by percentage share:
lowest 10%: NA%
highest 10%: NA%
Inflation rate (consumer prices): 1.6% (1999 est.)
Labor force: 24,500 (1999 est.)
Unemployment rate: 7% (1999 est.)
Budget:
revenues: $646 million
expenditures: $629 million, including capital expenditures of $85 million (1999)
Industries: fish processing (mainly shrimp and Greenland halibut), handicrafts, furs, small shipyards
Industrial production growth rate: NA%
Electricity - production: 250 million kWh (1999)
Electricity - production by source:
fossil fuel: 41%
hydro: 59%
nuclear: 0%
other: 0%
note: Greenland is shifting its electricity production from fossil fuel to hydroelectric power production (1999)
Electricity - consumption: 232.5 million kWh (1999)
Electricity - exports: 0 kWh (1999)
Electricity - imports: 0 kWh (1999)
Agriculture - products: forage crops, garden and greenhouse vegetables; sheep, reindeer; fish
Exports: $276 million (f.o.b., 1999)
Exports - commodities: fish and fish products 94%
Exports - partners: EU (mainly Denmark) 85%, Japan 8%, US 2% (1999)
Imports: $400 million (c.i.f., 1999)
Imports - commodities: machinery and transport equipment, manufactured goods, food, petroleum products
Imports - partners: EU (mostly Denmark), Norway, US, Canada
Debt - external: $25 million (1999)
Economic aid - recipient: $380 million subsidy from Denmark (1999)
Currency: Danish krone (DKK)
Currency code: DKK
Exchange rates: Danish kroner per US dollar - 7.951 (January 2001), 8.083 (2000), 6.976 (1999), 6.701 (1998), 6.604 (1997), 5.799 (1996)
Fiscal year: calendar year

Greenland (continued)

Communications

Telephones - main lines in use: 25,617 (end 1999)
Telephones - mobile cellular: 12,676 (end 1999)
Telephone system:
general assessment: adequate domestic and international service provided by satellite, cables and microwave radio relay; totally digitalized in 1995
domestic: microwave radio relay and satellite
international: satellite earth stations - 12 Intelsat, 1 Eutelsat, 2 Americom GE-2 (all Atlantic Ocean)
Radio broadcast stations: AM 5, FM 12, shortwave 0 (1998)
Radios: 30,000 (1998 est.)
Television broadcast stations: 1 publicly-owned station, some local low-power stations, and three AFRTS (US Air Force) stations (1997)
Televisions: 22,000 (1997)
Internet country code: .gl
Internet Service Providers (ISPs): 1 (2000)
Internet users: 4,008 (1999)

Transportation

Railways: 0 km
Highways:
total: 150 km
paved: 60 km
unpaved: 90 km
Waterways: none
Ports and harbors: Aasiaat (Egedesminde), Ilulissat (Jakobshavn), Kangerlussuaq, Nanortalik, Narsarsuaq, Nuuk (Godthab), Qaqortoq (Julianehab), Sisimiut (Holsteinsborg), Tasiilaq (March 2001)
Merchant marine:
total: 2 ships (1,000 GRT or over) totaling 3,289 GRT/ 1,500 DWT
ships by type: cargo 1, passenger 1 (2000 est.)
Airports: 13 (2000 est.)
Airports - with paved runways:
total: 8
over 3,047 m: 1
2,438 to 3,047 m: 1
1,524 to 2,437 m: 1
914 to 1,523 m: 1
under 914 m: 4 (2000 est.)
Airports - with unpaved runways:
total: 5
1,524 to 2,437 m: 1
914 to 1,523 m: 3
under 914 m: 1 (2000 est.)

Military

Military - note: defense is the responsibility of Denmark

Transnational Issues

Disputes - international: none

Grenada

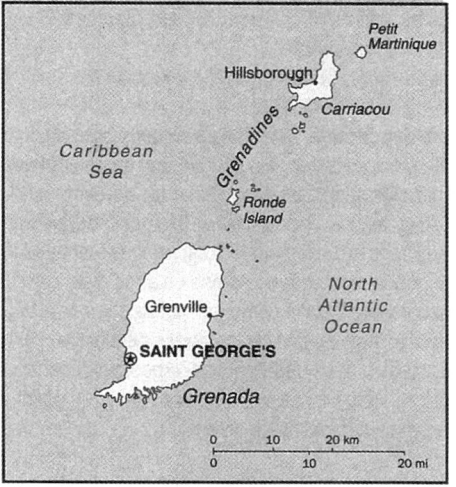

Introduction

Background: One of the smallest independent countries in the western hemisphere, Grenada was seized by a Marxist military council on 19 October 1983. Six days later the island was invaded by US forces and those of six other Caribbean nations, which quickly captured the ringleaders and their hundreds of Cuban advisers. Free elections were reinstituted the following year.

Geography

Location: Caribbean, island between the Caribbean Sea and Atlantic Ocean, north of Trinidad and Tobago
Geographic coordinates: 12 07 N, 61 40 W
Map references: Central America and the Caribbean
Area:
total: 340 sq km
land: 340 sq km
water: 0 sq km
Area - comparative: twice the size of Washington, DC
Land boundaries: 0 km
Coastline: 121 km
Maritime claims:
exclusive economic zone: 200 NM
territorial sea: 12 NM
Climate: tropical; tempered by northeast trade winds
Terrain: volcanic in origin with central mountains
Elevation extremes:
lowest point: Caribbean Sea 0 m
highest point: Mount Saint Catherine 840 m
Natural resources: timber, tropical fruit, deepwater harbors
Land use:
arable land: 15%
permanent crops: 18%
permanent pastures: 3%
forests and woodland: 9%
other: 55% (1993 est.)
Irrigated land: NA sq km
Natural hazards: lies on edge of hurricane belt; hurricane season lasts from June to November
Environment - current issues: NA
Environment - international agreements:
party to: Biodiversity, Climate Change, Desertification, Endangered Species, Law of the Sea, Marine Dumping, Ozone Layer Protection, Ship Pollution, Whaling
signed, but not ratified: none of the selected agreements
Geography - note: the administration of the islands of the Grenadines group is divided between Saint Vincent and the Grenadines and Grenada

People

Population: 89,227 (July 2001 est.)
Age structure:
0-14 years: 37.05% (male 16,739; female 16,318)
15-64 years: 59.03% (male 27,850; female 24,820)
65 years and over: 3.92% (male 1,592; female 1,908) (2001 est.)
Population growth rate: -0.06% (2001 est.)
Birth rate: 23.12 births/1,000 population (2001 est.)
Death rate: 7.82 deaths/1,000 population (2001 est.)
Net migration rate: -15.86 migrant(s)/1,000 population (2001 est.)
Sex ratio:
at birth: 1 male(s)/female
under 15 years: 1.03 male(s)/female
15-64 years: 1.12 male(s)/female
65 years and over: 0.83 male(s)/female
total population: 1.07 male(s)/female (2001 est.)
Infant mortality rate: 14.63 deaths/1,000 live births (2001 est.)
Life expectancy at birth:
total population: 64.52 years
male: 62.74 years
female: 66.31 years (2001 est.)
Total fertility rate: 2.54 children born/woman (2001 est.)
HIV/AIDS - adult prevalence rate: NA%
HIV/AIDS - people living with HIV/AIDS: NA
HIV/AIDS - deaths: NA
Nationality:
noun: Grenadian(s)
adjective: Grenadian
Ethnic groups: black 82% some South Asians (East Indians) and Europeans, trace Arawak/Carib Amerindian
Religions: Roman Catholic 53%, Anglican 13.8%, other Protestant 33.2%
Languages: English (official), French patois
Literacy:
definition: age 15 and over can read and write
total population: 98%
male: 98%
female: 98% (1970 est.)

Grenada (continued)

Government

Country name:
conventional long form: none
conventional short form: Grenada
Government type: constitutional monarchy with Westminster-style parliament
Capital: Saint George's
Administrative divisions: 6 parishes and 1 dependency*; Carriacou and Petit Martinique*, Saint Andrew, Saint David, Saint George, Saint John, Saint Mark, Saint Patrick
Independence: 7 February 1974 (from UK)
National holiday: Independence Day, 7 February (1974)
Constitution: 19 December 1973
Legal system: based on English common law
Suffrage: 18 years of age; universal
Executive branch:
chief of state: Queen ELIZABETH II (since 6 February 1952), represented by Governor General Daniel WILLIAMS (since 9 August 1996)
head of government: Prime Minister Keith MITCHELL (since 22 June 1995)
cabinet: Cabinet appointed by the governor general on the advice of the prime minister
elections: none; the monarch is hereditary; governor general appointed by the monarch; prime minister appointed by the governor general from among the members of the House of Assembly
Legislative branch: bicameral Parliament consists of the Senate (a 13-member body, 10 appointed by the government and three by the leader of the opposition) and the House of Representatives (15 seats; members are elected by popular vote to serve five-year terms)
elections: last held on 18 January 1999 (next to be held by NA October 2004)
election results: House of Representatives - percent of vote by party - NA%; seats by party - NNP 14, GULP 1
Judicial branch: West Indies Associate States Supreme Court (an associate judge resides in Grenada)
Political parties and leaders: Grenada United Labor Party or GULP [Herbert PREUDHOMME]; National Democratic Congress or NDC [leader vacant]; New National Party or NNP [George McGUIRE]
Political pressure groups and leaders: NA
International organization participation: ACP, C, Caricom, CDB, ECLAC, FAO, G-77, IBRD, ICAO, ICFTU, ICRM, IDA, IFAD, IFC, IFRCS, ILO, IMF, IMO, Interpol, IOC, ISO (subscriber), ITU, LAES, NAM, OAS, OECS, OPANAL, OPCW, UN, UNCTAD, UNESCO, UNIDO, UPU, WHO, WIPO, WTrO
Diplomatic representation in the US:
chief of mission: Ambassador Denis G. ANTOINE
chancery: 1701 New Hampshire Avenue NW, Washington, DC 20009
telephone: [1] (202) 265-2561
consulate(s) general: New York
Diplomatic representation from the US:
chief of mission: the ambassador to Barbados is accredited to Grenada
embassy: Point Salines, Saint George's
mailing address: P. O. Box 54, Saint George's, Grenada, West Indies
telephone: [1] (473) 444-1173 through 1176
FAX: [1] (473) 444-4820
Flag description: a rectangle divided diagonally into yellow triangles (top and bottom) and green triangles (hoist side and outer side), with a red border around the flag; there are seven yellow, five-pointed stars with three centered in the top red border, three centered in the bottom red border, and one on a red disk superimposed at the center of the flag; there is also a symbolic nutmeg pod on the hoist-side triangle (Grenada is the world's second-largest producer of nutmeg, after Indonesia); the seven stars represent the seven administrative divisions

Economy

Economy - overview: In this island economy progress in fiscal reforms and prudent macroeconomic management have kept annual growth steady since 1998. The increase in economic activity has been led by construction and trade. Tourist facilities are being expanded; tourism is the leading foreign exchange earner. Major short-term concerns are the rising fiscal deficit and the deterioration in the external account balance. Grenada shares a common central bank and a common currency with seven other members of the Organization of Eastern Caribbean States (OECS).
GDP: purchasing power parity - $394 million (2000 est.)
GDP - real growth rate: 7% (2000 est.)
GDP - per capita: purchasing power parity - $4,400 (2000 est.)
GDP - composition by sector:
agriculture: 9.7%
industry: 15%
services: 75.3% (1996 est.)
Population below poverty line: NA%
Household income or consumption by percentage share:
lowest 10%: NA%
highest 10%: NA%
Inflation rate (consumer prices): 2.5% (2000 est.)
Labor force: 42,300 (1996)
Labor force - by occupation: services 62%, agriculture 24%, industry 14% (1999 est.)
Unemployment rate: 15% (1997)
Budget:
revenues: $85.8 million
expenditures: $102.1 million, including capital expenditures of $28 million (1997)
Industries: food and beverages, textiles, light assembly operations, tourism, construction
Industrial production growth rate: 0.7% (1997 est.)
Electricity - production: 120 million kWh (1999)
Electricity - production by source:
fossil fuel: 100%
hydro: 0%
nuclear: 0%
other: 0% (1999)
Electricity - consumption: 111.6 million kWh (1999)
Electricity - exports: 0 kWh (1999)
Electricity - imports: 0 kWh (1999)
Agriculture - products: bananas, cocoa, nutmeg, mace, citrus, avocados, root crops, sugarcane, corn, vegetables
Exports: $62.3 million (2000 est.)
Exports - commodities: bananas, cocoa, nutmeg, fruit and vegetables, clothing, mace
Exports - partners: Caricom 32.3%, UK 20%, US 13%, Netherlands 8.8% (1991)
Imports: $217.5 million (2000 est.)
Imports - commodities: food, manufactured goods, machinery, chemicals, fuel (1989)
Imports - partners: US 31.2%, Caricom 23.6%, UK 13.8%, Japan 7.1% (1991)
Debt - external: $182.8 million (1998)
Economic aid - recipient: $8.3 million (1995)
Currency: East Caribbean dollar (XCD)
Currency code: XCD
Exchange rates: East Caribbean dollars per US dollar - 2.7000 (fixed rate since 1976)
Fiscal year: calendar year

Communications

Telephones - main lines in use: 27,000 (1997)
Telephones - mobile cellular: 976 (1997)
Telephone system:
general assessment: automatic, islandwide telephone system
domestic: interisland VHF and UHF radiotelephone links
international: new SHF radiotelephone links to Trinidad and Tobago and Saint Vincent; VHF and UHF radio links to Trinidad
Radio broadcast stations: AM 2, FM 1, shortwave 0 (1998)
Radios: 57,000 (1997)
Television broadcast stations: 2 (1997)
Televisions: 33,000 (1997)
Internet country code: .gd
Internet Service Providers (ISPs): 14 (2000)
Internet users: 2,000 (2000)

Transportation

Railways: 0 km
Highways:
total: 1,040 km
paved: 638 km
unpaved: 402 km (1996)
Waterways: none
Ports and harbors: Grenville, Saint George's
Merchant marine: none (2000 est.)
Airports: 3 (2000 est.)

Grenada (continued)

Airports - with paved runways:
total: 3
2,438 to 3,047 m: 1
1,524 to 2,437 m: 1
under 914 m: 1 (2000 est.)

Military

Military branches: Royal Grenada Police Force (includes Special Service Unit), Coast Guard
Military expenditures - dollar figure: $NA
Military expenditures - percent of GDP: NA%

Transnational Issues

Disputes - international: none
Illicit drugs: small-scale cannabis cultivation; lesser transshipment point for marijuana and cocaine to US

Guadeloupe
(overseas department of France)

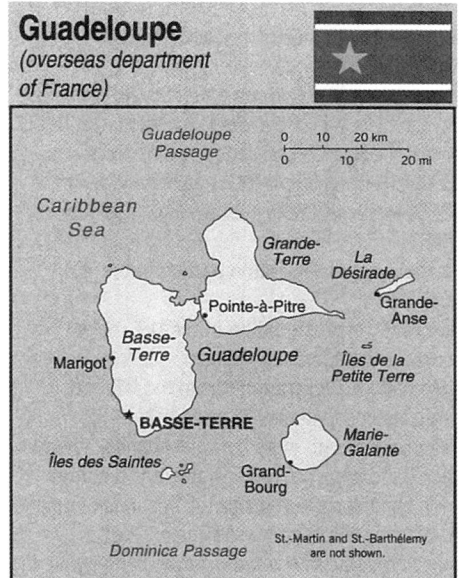

Introduction

Background: Guadeloupe has been a French possession since 1635. The island of Saint-Martin is divided with the Netherlands (whose southern portion is named Sint Maarten and is part of the Netherlands Antilles).

Geography

Location: Caribbean, islands in the eastern Caribbean Sea, southeast of Puerto Rico
Geographic coordinates: 16 15 N, 61 35 W
Map references: Central America and the Caribbean
Area:
total: 1,780 sq km
land: 1,706 sq km
water: 74 sq km
note: Guadeloupe is an archipelago of nine inhabited islands, including Basse-Terre, Grande-Terre, Marie-Galante, La Desirade, Iles des Saintes (2), Saint-Barthelemy, Iles de la Petite Terre, and Saint-Martin (French part of the island of Saint Martin
Area - comparative: 10 times the size of Washington, DC
Land boundaries:
total: 10.2 km
border countries: Netherlands Antilles (Sint Maarten) 10.2 km
Coastline: 306 km
Maritime claims:
exclusive economic zone: 200 NM
territorial sea: 12 NM
Climate: subtropical tempered by trade winds; moderately high humidity
Terrain: Basse-Terre is volcanic in origin with interior mountains; Grande-Terre is low limestone formation; most of the seven other islands are volcanic in origin
Elevation extremes:
lowest point: Caribbean Sea 0 m
highest point: Soufriere 1,467 m
Natural resources: cultivable land, beaches and climate that foster tourism
Land use:
arable land: 14%
permanent crops: 4%
permanent pastures: 14%
forests and woodland: 39%
other: 29% (1993 est.)
Irrigated land: 30 sq km (1993 est.)
Natural hazards: hurricanes (June to October); Soufriere is an active volcano
Environment - current issues: NA

People

Population: 431,170 (July 2001 est.)
Age structure:
0-14 years: 24.99% (male 55,030; female 52,722)
15-64 years: 66.22% (male 141,294; female 144,232)
65 years and over: 8.79% (male 15,901; female 21,991) (2001 est.)
Population growth rate: 1.07% (2001 est.)
Birth rate: 16.91 births/1,000 population (2001 est.)
Death rate: 6.02 deaths/1,000 population (2001 est.)
Net migration rate: -0.15 migrant(s)/1,000 population (2001 est.)
Sex ratio:
at birth: 1.05 male(s)/female
under 15 years: 1.04 male(s)/female
15-64 years: 0.98 male(s)/female
65 years and over: 0.72 male(s)/female
total population: 0.97 male(s)/female (2001 est.)
Infant mortality rate: 9.53 deaths/1,000 live births (2001 est.)
Life expectancy at birth:
total population: 77.16 years
male: 74.01 years
female: 80.48 years (2001 est.)
Total fertility rate: 1.93 children born/woman (2001 est.)
HIV/AIDS - adult prevalence rate: NA%
HIV/AIDS - people living with HIV/AIDS: NA
HIV/AIDS - deaths: NA
Nationality:
noun: Guadeloupian(s)
adjective: Guadeloupe
Ethnic groups: black or mulatto 90%, white 5%, East Indian, Lebanese, Chinese less than 5%
Religions: Roman Catholic 95%, Hindu and pagan African 4%, Protestant 1%
Languages: French (official) 99%, Creole patois
Literacy:
definition: age 15 and over can read and write
total population: 90%
male: 90%
female: 90% (1982 est.)

Government

Country name:
conventional long form: Department of Guadeloupe
conventional short form: Guadeloupe
local long form: Departement de la Guadeloupe
local short form: Guadeloupe

Guadeloupe (continued)

Dependency status: overseas department of France
Government type: NA
Capital: Basse-Terre
Administrative divisions: none (overseas department of France)
Independence: none (overseas department of France)
National holiday: Bastille Day, 14 July (1789)
Constitution: 28 September 1958 (French Constitution)
Legal system: French legal system
Suffrage: 18 years of age; universal
Executive branch:
chief of state: President Jacques CHIRAC of France (since 17 May 1995), represented by Prefect Jean FEDINI (since NA 1996)
head of government: President of the General Council Marcellin LUBETH (since NA March 1998); President of the Regional Council Lucette MICHAUX-CHEVRY (since 22 March 1992)
cabinet: NA
elections: French president elected by popular vote for a seven-year term; prefect appointed by the French president on the advice of the French Ministry of Interior; the presidents of the General and Regional Councils are elected by the members of those councils
election results: NA
Legislative branch: unicameral General Council or Conseil General (42 seats; members are elected by popular vote to serve six-year terms) and the unicameral Regional Council or Conseil Regional (41 seats; members are elected by popular vote to serve six-year terms)
elections: General Council - last held 22 March 1998 (next to be held by NA 2004); Regional Council - last held 15 March 1998 (next to be held NA 2004)
election results: General Council - percent of vote by party - NA%; seats by party - diverse left parties 11, PS 8, RPR 8, PPDG 6, diverse right parties 5, PCG 3, UDF 1; Regional Council - percent of vote by party - RPR 48.03%, PS/PPDG/diverse left parties 24.49%, PCG 5.29%, diverse right parties 5.73%; seats by party - RPR 25, PS/PPDG/diverse left parties 12, PCG 2, diverse right parties 2
note: Guadeloupe elects two representatives to the French Senate; elections last held NA September 1995 (next to be held NA September 2004); percent of vote by party - NA; seats by party - RPR 1, FGPS 1; Guadeloupe elects four representatives to the French National Assembly; elections last held 25 May - 1 June 1997 (next to be held NA 2002); percent of vote by party - NA; seats by party - FGPS 2, RPR 1, PPDG 1
Judicial branch: Court of Appeal or Cour d'Appel with jurisdiction over Guadeloupe, French Guiana, and Martinique
Political parties and leaders: Communist Party of Guadeloupe or PCG [Christian CELESTE]; Progressive Democratic Party or PPDG [Henri BANGOU]; Rally for the Republic or RPR [Aldo BLAISE]; Socialist Party or PS [Georges LOUISOR]; Union for French Democracy or UDF [Marcel ESDRAS]
Political pressure groups and leaders: Christian Movement for the Liberation of Guadeloupe or KLPG; General Federation of Guadeloupe Workers or CGT-G; General Union of Guadeloupe Workers or UGTG; Movement for Independent Guadeloupe or MPGI
International organization participation: FZ, WCL, WFTU
Diplomatic representation in the US: none (overseas department of France)
Diplomatic representation from the US: none (overseas department of France)
Flag description: three horizontal bands, a narrow green band (top), a wide red band, and a narrow green band; the green bands are separated from the red band by two narrow white stripes; a gold five-pointed star is centered in the red band toward the hoist side; the flag of France is used for official occasions

Economy

Economy - overview: The economy depends on agriculture, tourism, light industry, and services. It also depends on France for large subsidies and imports. Tourism is a key industry, with most tourists from the US; an increasingly large number of cruise ships visit the islands. The traditional sugarcane crop is slowly being replaced by other crops, such as bananas (which now supply about 50% of export earnings), eggplant, and flowers. Other vegetables and root crops are cultivated for local consumption, although Guadeloupe is still dependent on imported food, mainly from France. Light industry features sugar and rum production. Most manufactured goods and fuel are imported. Unemployment is especially high among the young. Hurricanes periodically devastate the economy.
GDP: purchasing power parity - $3.7 billion (1997 est.)
GDP - real growth rate: NA%
GDP - per capita: purchasing power parity - $9,000 (1997 est.)
GDP - composition by sector:
agriculture: 15%
industry: 17%
services: 68% (1997 est.)
Population below poverty line: NA%
Household income or consumption by percentage share:
lowest 10%: NA%
highest 10%: NA%
Inflation rate (consumer prices): NA
Labor force: 125,900 (1997)
Labor force - by occupation: NA
Unemployment rate: 27.8% (1998)
Budget:
revenues: $225 million
expenditures: $390 million, including capital expenditures of $105 million (1996)
Industries: construction, cement, rum, sugar, tourism
Industrial production growth rate: NA%
Electricity - production: 1.3 billion kWh (1999)
Electricity - production by source:
fossil fuel: 100%
hydro: 0%
nuclear: 0%
other: 0% (1999)
Electricity - consumption: 1.209 billion kWh (1999)
Electricity - exports: 0 kWh (1999)
Electricity - imports: 0 kWh (1999)
Agriculture - products: bananas, sugarcane, tropical fruits and vegetables; cattle, pigs, goats
Exports: $140 million (f.o.b., 1997)
Exports - commodities: bananas, sugar, rum
Exports - partners: France 60%, Martinique 18%, US 4% (1997)
Imports: $1.7 billion (c.i.f., 1997)
Imports - commodities: foodstuffs, fuels, vehicles, clothing and other consumer goods, construction materials
Imports - partners: France 63%, Germany 4%, US 3%, Japan 2%, Netherlands Antilles 2% (1997)
Debt - external: $NA
Economic aid - recipient: $NA; note - substantial annual French subsidies
Currency: French franc (FRF); euro (EUR)
Currency code: FRF; EUR
Exchange rates: Euros per US dollar - 1.0659 (January 2001), 1.0854 (2000), 0.9386 (1999); French francs per US dollar - 5.8995 (1998), 5.8367 (1997), 5.1155 (1996)
Fiscal year: calendar year

Communications

Telephones - main lines in use: 171,000 (1996)
Telephones - mobile cellular: NA
Telephone system:
general assessment: domestic facilities inadequate
domestic: NA
international: satellite earth station - 1 Intelsat (Atlantic Ocean); microwave radio relay to Antigua and Barbuda, Dominica, and Martinique
Radio broadcast stations: AM 1, FM 17, shortwave 0 (1998)
Radios: 113,000 (1997)
Television broadcast stations: 5 (plus several low-power repeaters) (1997)
Televisions: 118,000 (1997)
Internet country code: .gp
Internet Service Providers (ISPs): 3 (2000)
Internet users: 4,000 (2000)

Transportation

Railways:
total: NA km; privately owned, narrow-gauge plantation lines
Highways:
total: 2,560 km
paved: 965 km
unpaved: 1,595 km (1996)

Guadeloupe (continued)

Waterways: none
Ports and harbors: Basse-Terre, Gustavia (on Saint Barthelemy), Marigot, Pointe-a-Pitre
Merchant marine:
total: 1 ship (1,000 GRT or over) totaling 1,240 GRT/ 109 DWT
ships by type: passenger 1 (2000 est.)
Airports: 9 (2000 est.)
Airports - with paved runways:
total: 8
over 3,047 m: 1
914 to 1,523 m: 2
under 914 m: 5 (2000 est.)
Airports - with unpaved runways:
total: 1
under 914 m: 1 (2000 est.)

Military

Military branches: French Forces, Gendarmerie
Military - note: defense is the responsibility of France

Transnational Issues

Disputes - international: none

Guam
(territory of the US)

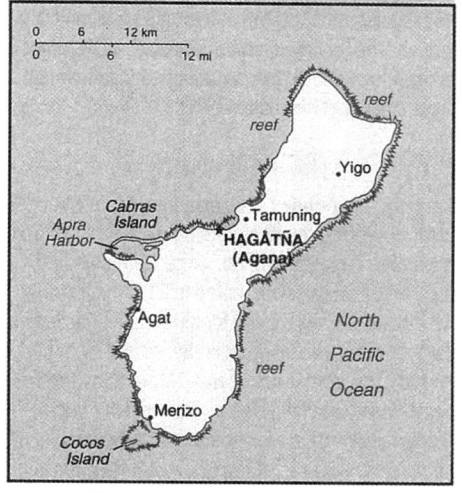

Introduction

Background: Guam was ceded to the US by Spain in 1898. Captured by the Japanese in 1941, it was retaken by the US three years later. The military installation on the island is one of the most strategically important US bases in the Pacific.

Geography

Location: Oceania, island in the North Pacific Ocean, about three-quarters of the way from Hawaii to the Philippines
Geographic coordinates: 13 28 N, 144 47 E
Map references: Oceania
Area:
total: 549 sq km
land: 549 sq km
water: 0 sq km
Area - comparative: three times the size of Washington, DC
Land boundaries: 0 km
Coastline: 125.5 km
Maritime claims:
exclusive economic zone: 200 NM
territorial sea: 12 NM
Climate: tropical marine; generally warm and humid, moderated by northeast trade winds; dry season from January to June, rainy season from July to December; little seasonal temperature variation
Terrain: volcanic origin, surrounded by coral reefs; relatively flat coralline limestone plateau (source of most fresh water), with steep coastal cliffs and narrow coastal plains in north, low-rising hills in center, mountains in south
Elevation extremes:
lowest point: Pacific Ocean 0 m
highest point: Mount Lamlam 406 m
Natural resources: fishing (largely undeveloped), tourism (especially from Japan)
Land use:
arable land: 11%
permanent crops: 11%
permanent pastures: 15%
forests and woodland: 18%
other: 45% (1993 est.)
Irrigated land: NA sq km
Natural hazards: frequent squalls during rainy season; relatively rare, but potentially very destructive typhoons (especially in August)
Environment - current issues: extirpation of native bird population by the rapid proliferation of the brown tree snake, an exotic species
Geography - note: largest and southernmost island in the Mariana Islands archipelago; strategic location in western North Pacific Ocean

People

Population: 157,557 (July 2001 est.)
Age structure:
0-14 years: 35.07% (male 28,978; female 26,270)
15-64 years: 58.78% (male 48,704; female 43,902)
65 years and over: 6.15% (male 4,871; female 4,832) (2001 est.)
Population growth rate: 2.09% (2001 est.)
Birth rate: 25.07 births/1,000 population (2001 est.)
Death rate: 4.2 deaths/1,000 population (2001 est.)
Net migration rate: 0 migrant(s)/1,000 population (2001 est.)
Sex ratio:
at birth: 1.14 male(s)/female
under 15 years: 1.1 male(s)/female
15-64 years: 1.11 male(s)/female
65 years and over: 1.01 male(s)/female
total population: 1.1 male(s)/female (2001 est.)
Infant mortality rate: 6.71 deaths/1,000 live births (2001 est.)
Life expectancy at birth:
total population: 77.94 years
male: 75.66 years
female: 80.55 years (2001 est.)
Total fertility rate: 3.85 children born/woman (2001 est.)
HIV/AIDS - adult prevalence rate: NA%
HIV/AIDS - people living with HIV/AIDS: NA
HIV/AIDS - deaths: NA
Nationality:
noun: Guamanian(s)
adjective: Guamanian
Ethnic groups: Chamorro 47%, Filipino 25%, white 10%, Chinese, Japanese, Korean, and other 18%
Religions: Roman Catholic 85%, other 15% (1999 est.)
Languages: English, Chamorro, Japanese
Literacy:
definition: age 15 and over can read and write
total population: 99%
male: 99%
female: 99% (1990 est.)

Guam (continued)

Government

Country name:
conventional long form: Territory of Guam
conventional short form: Guam
Dependency status: organized, unincorporated territory of the US with policy relations between Guam and the US under the jurisdiction of the Office of Insular Affairs, US Department of the Interior
Government type: NA
Capital: Hagatna (Agana)
Administrative divisions: none (territory of the US)
Independence: none (territory of the US)
National holiday: Discovery Day, first Monday in March (1521)
Constitution: Organic Act of 1 August 1950
Legal system: modeled on US; US federal laws apply
Suffrage: 18 years of age; universal; US citizens, but do not vote in US presidential elections
Executive branch:
chief of state: President George W. BUSH of the US (since 20 January 2001); Vice President Richard B. CHENEY (since 20 January 2001)
head of government: Governor Carl GUTIERREZ (since 8 November 1994) and Lieutenant Governor Madeleine BORDALLO (since 8 November 1994)
cabinet: executive departments; heads appointed by the governor with the consent of the Guam legislature
elections: US president and vice president elected on the same ticket for a four-year term; governor and lieutenant governor elected on the same ticket by popular vote for four-year terms; election last held 3 November 1998 (next to be held NA November 2002)
election results: Carl GUTIERREZ reelected governor; percent of vote - Carl GUTIERREZ (Democrat) 53.2%, Joseph ADA (Republican) 46.8%
Legislative branch: unicameral Legislature (15 seats; members are elected by popular vote to serve two-year terms)
elections: last held 7 November 2000 (next to be held NA November 2002)
election results: percent of vote by party - NA%; seats by party - Republican Party 8, Democratic Party 7
note: Guam elects one delegate to the US House of Representatives; election last held 7 November 2000 (next to be held NA November 2002); results - Robert UNDERWOOD was reelected as delegate; percent of vote by party - NA%; seats by party - Democratic Party 1
Judicial branch: Federal District Court (judge is appointed by the president); Territorial Superior Court (judges appointed for eight-year terms by the governor)
Political parties and leaders: Democratic Party (party of the Governor) [leader NA]; Republican Party (controls the legislature) [leader NA]
Political pressure groups and leaders: NA
International organization participation: ESCAP (associate), Interpol (subbureau), IOC, SPC
Diplomatic representation in the US: none (territory of the US)
Diplomatic representation from the US: none (territory of the US)
Flag description: territorial flag is dark blue with a narrow red border on all four sides; centered is a red-bordered, pointed, vertical ellipse containing a beach scene, outrigger canoe with sail, and a palm tree with the word GUAM superimposed in bold red letters; US flag is the national flag

Economy

Economy - overview: The economy depends on US military spending, tourism, and the export of fish and handicrafts. Total US grants, wage payments, and procurement outlays amounted to $1 billion in 1998. Over the past 20 years, the tourist industry has grown rapidly, creating a construction boom for new hotels and the expansion of older ones. More than 1 million tourists visit Guam each year. The industry has recently suffered setbacks because of the continuing Japanese slowdown; the Japanese normally make up almost 90% of the tourists. Most food and industrial goods are imported. Guam faces the problem of building up the civilian economic sector to offset the impact of military downsizing.
GDP: purchasing power parity - $3.2 billion (2000 est.)
GDP - real growth rate: NA%
GDP - per capita: purchasing power parity - $21,000 (2000 est.)
GDP - composition by sector:
agriculture: NA%
industry: 15% (1993)
services: NA%
Population below poverty line: NA%
Household income or consumption by percentage share:
lowest 10%: NA%
highest 10%: NA%
Inflation rate (consumer prices): 0% (1999 est.)
Labor force: 60,000 (2000 est.)
Labor force - by occupation: federal and territorial government 26%, private 74% (trade 24%, other services 40%, industry 10%) (2000 est.)
Unemployment rate: 15% (2000 est.)
Budget:
revenues: $605.3 million
expenditures: $654.2 million, including capital expenditures of $NA (2000)
Industries: US military, tourism, construction, transshipment services, concrete products, printing and publishing, food processing, textiles
Industrial production growth rate: NA%
Electricity - production: 800 million kWh (1999)
Electricity - production by source:
fossil fuel: 100%
hydro: 0%
nuclear: 0%
other: 0% (1999)
Electricity - consumption: 744 million kWh (1999)
Electricity - exports: 0 kWh (1999)
Electricity - imports: 0 kWh (1999)
Agriculture - products: fruits, copra, vegetables; eggs, pork, poultry, beef
Exports: $75.7 million (f.o.b., 1999)
Exports - commodities: mostly transshipments of refined petroleum products; construction materials, fish, food and beverage products
Exports - partners: US 25%
Imports: $203 million (f.o.b., 1999 est.)
Imports - commodities: petroleum and petroleum products, food, manufactured goods
Imports - partners: US 23%, Japan 19%
Debt - external: $NA
Economic aid - recipient: Guam receives large transfer payments from the US Federal Treasury ($143 million in 1997) into which Guamanians pay no income or excise taxes; under the provisions of a special law of Congress, the Guam Treasury, rather than the US Treasury, receives federal income taxes paid by military and civilian Federal employees stationed in Guam
Currency: US dollar (USD)
Currency code: USD
Exchange rates: the US dollar is used
Fiscal year: 1 October - 30 September

Communications

Telephones - main lines in use: 84,134 (1998)
Telephones - mobile cellular: 55,000 (1998)
Telephone system:
general assessment: modern system, integrated with US facilities for direct dialing, including free use of 800 numbers
domestic: modern digital system, including cellular mobile service and local access to the Internet
international: satellite earth stations - 2 Intelsat (Pacific Ocean); submarine cables to US and Japan (Guam is a trans-Pacific communications hub for MCI, Sprint, AT&T, IT&E, and GTE, linking the US and Asia)
Radio broadcast stations: AM 4, FM 7, shortwave 0 (1998)
Radios: 221,000 (1997)
Television broadcast stations: 5 (1997)
Televisions: 106,000 (1997)
Internet country code: .gu
Internet Service Providers (ISPs): 20 (2000)
Internet users: 5,000 (2000)

Transportation

Railways: 0 km
Highways:
total: 885 km
paved: 675 km
unpaved: 210 km
note: there are also 685 km of roads classified non-public, including roads located on federal government installations
Waterways: none
Ports and harbors: Apra Harbor
Merchant marine: none (2000 est.)
Airports: 5 (2000 est.)

Guam (continued)

Airports - with paved runways:
total: 4
over 3,047 m: 2
2,438 to 3,047 m: 1
914 to 1,523 m: 1 (2000 est.)
Airports - with unpaved runways:
total: 1
under 914 m: 1 (2000 est.)

Military

Military - note: defense is the responsibility of the US

Transnational Issues

Disputes - international: none

Guatemala

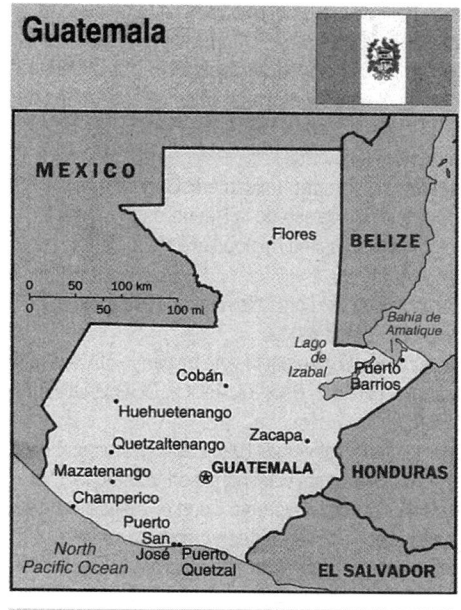

Introduction

Background: Guatemala was freed of Spanish colonial rule in 1821. During the second half of the 20th century, it experienced a variety of military and civilian governments as well as a 36-year guerrilla war. In 1996, the government signed a peace agreement formally ending the conflict, which had led to the death of more than 100,000 people and had created some 1 million refugees.

Geography

Location: Middle America, bordering the Caribbean Sea, between Honduras and Belize and bordering the North Pacific Ocean, between El Salvador and Mexico
Geographic coordinates: 15 30 N, 90 15 W
Map references: Central America and the Caribbean
Area:
total: 108,890 sq km
land: 108,430 sq km
water: 460 sq km
Area - comparative: slightly smaller than Tennessee
Land boundaries:
total: 1,687 km
border countries: Belize 266 km, El Salvador 203 km, Honduras 256 km, Mexico 962 km
Coastline: 400 km
Maritime claims:
continental shelf: 200-m depth or to the depth of exploitation
exclusive economic zone: 200 NM
territorial sea: 12 NM
Climate: tropical; hot, humid in lowlands; cooler in highlands
Terrain: mostly mountains with narrow coastal plains and rolling limestone plateau (Peten)
Elevation extremes:
lowest point: Pacific Ocean 0 m
highest point: Volcan Tajumulco 4,211 m
Natural resources: petroleum, nickel, rare woods, fish, chicle, hydropower
Land use:
arable land: 12%
permanent crops: 5%
permanent pastures: 24%
forests and woodland: 54%
other: 5% (1993 est.)
Irrigated land: 1,250 sq km (1993 est.)
Natural hazards: numerous volcanoes in mountains, with occasional violent earthquakes; Caribbean coast subject to hurricanes and other tropical storms
Environment - current issues: deforestation; soil erosion; water pollution; Hurricane Mitch damage
Environment - international agreements:
party to: Antarctic Treaty, Biodiversity, Climate Change, Climate Change-Kyoto Protocol, Desertification, Endangered Species, Environmental Modification, Hazardous Wastes, Law of the Sea, Marine Dumping, Nuclear Test Ban, Ozone Layer Protection, Ship Pollution, Wetlands
signed, but not ratified: Antarctic-Environmental Protocol
Geography - note: no natural harbors on west coast

People

Population: 12,974,361 (July 2001 est.)
Age structure:
0-14 years: 42.11% (male 2,789,189; female 2,674,747)
15-64 years: 54.25% (male 3,518,209; female 3,519,851)
65 years and over: 3.64% (male 220,640; female 251,725) (2001 est.)
Population growth rate: 2.6% (2001 est.)
Birth rate: 34.61 births/1,000 population (2001 est.)
Death rate: 6.79 deaths/1,000 population (2001 est.)
Net migration rate: -1.84 migrant(s)/1,000 population (2001 est.)
Sex ratio:
at birth: 1.05 male(s)/female
under 15 years: 1.04 male(s)/female
15-64 years: 1 male(s)/female
65 years and over: 0.88 male(s)/female
total population: 1.01 male(s)/female (2001 est.)
Infant mortality rate: 45.79 deaths/1,000 live births (2001 est.)
Life expectancy at birth:
total population: 66.51 years
male: 63.85 years
female: 69.31 years (2001 est.)
Total fertility rate: 4.58 children born/woman (2001 est.)
HIV/AIDS - adult prevalence rate: 1.38% (1999 est.)
HIV/AIDS - people living with HIV/AIDS: 73,000 (1999 est.)
HIV/AIDS - deaths: 3,600 (1999 est.)
Nationality:
noun: Guatemalan(s)

Guatemala (continued)

adjective: Guatemalan
Ethnic groups: Mestizo (mixed Amerindian-Spanish or assimilated Amerindian - in local Spanish called Ladino), approximately 55%, Amerindian or predominantly Amerindian, approximately 43%, whites and others 2%
Religions: Roman Catholic, Protestant, indigenous Mayan beliefs
Languages: Spanish 60%, Amerindian languages 40% (more than 20 Amerindian languages, including Quiche, Cakchiquel, Kekchi, Mam, Garifuna, and Xinca)
Literacy:
definition: age 15 and over can read and write
total population: 63.6%
male: 68.7%
female: 58.5% (2000 est.)

Government

Country name:
conventional long form: Republic of Guatemala
conventional short form: Guatemala
local long form: Republica de Guatemala
local short form: Guatemala
Government type: constitutional democratic republic
Capital: Guatemala
Administrative divisions: 22 departments (departamentos, singular - departamento); Alta Verapaz, Baja Verapaz, Chimaltenango, Chiquimula, El Progreso, Escuintla, Guatemala, Huehuetenango, Izabal, Jalapa, Jutiapa, Peten, Quetzaltenango, Quiche, Retalhuleu, Sacatepequez, San Marcos, Santa Rosa, Solola, Suchitepequez, Totonicapan, Zacapa
Independence: 15 September 1821 (from Spain)
National holiday: Independence Day, 15 September (1821)
Constitution: 31 May 1985, effective 14 January 1986; note - suspended 25 May 1993 by former President SERRANO; reinstated 5 June 1993 following ouster of president; amended November 1993
Legal system: civil law system; judicial review of legislative acts; has not accepted compulsory ICJ jurisdiction
Suffrage: 18 years of age; universal (active duty members of the armed forces may not vote)
Executive branch:
chief of state: President Alfonso Antonio PORTILLO Cabrera (since 14 January 2000); Vice President Juan Francisco REYES Lopez (since 14 January 2000); note - the president is both the chief of state and head of government
head of government: President Alfonso Antonio PORTILLO Cabrera (since 14 January 2000); Vice President Juan Francisco REYES Lopez (since 14 January 2000); note - the president is both the chief of state and head of government
cabinet: Council of Ministers named by the president
elections: president elected by popular vote for a four-year term; election last held 7 November 1999; runoff held 26 December 1999 (next to be held NA November 2003)
election results: Alfonso Antonio PORTILLO Cabrera elected president; percent of vote - Alfonso Antonio PORTILLO Cabrera (FRG) 68%, Oscar BERGER Perdomo (PAN) 32%
Legislative branch: unicameral Congress of the Republic or Congreso de la Republica (113 seats; members are elected by popular vote to serve four-year terms)
elections: last held on 7 November 1999 (next to be held in November 2003)
election results: percent of vote by party - NA%; seats by party - FRG 63, PAN 37, ANN 9, DCG 2, UD/LOV 1, PLP 1
note: for the 7 November 1999 election, the number of congressional seats was increased from 80 to 113
Judicial branch: Supreme Court of Justice or Corte Suprema de Justicia (thirteen members serve concurrent five-year terms and elect a president of the Court each year from among their number; the president of the Supreme Court of Justice also supervises trial judges around the country, who are named to five-year terms); Constitutional Court or Corte de Constitutcionalidad (five judges are elected for concurrent five-year terms by Congress, each serving one year as president of the Constitutional Court; one is elected by Congress, one elected by the Supreme Court of Justice, one appointed by the President, one elected by Superior Counsel of Universidad San Carlos de Guatemala, and one by Colegio de Abogados)
Political parties and leaders: Authentic Integral Development or DIA [Jorge Luis ORTEGA]; Democratic Union or UD [Jose Luis CHEA Urruela]; Green Party or LOV [Jose ASTURIAS Rudecke]; Guatemalan Christian Democracy or DCG [Vinicio CEREZO Arevalo]; Guatemalan National Revolutionary Unity or URNG [Pablo MONSANTO, also known as Jorge SOTO]; Guatemalan Republican Front or FRG [Efrain RIOS Montt]; New Nation Alliance or ANN [leader NA], which includes the URNG; National Advancement Party or PAN [Leonel LOPEZ Rodas]; Progressive Liberator Party or PLP [Acisclo VALLADARES Molina]
Political pressure groups and leaders: Agrarian Owners Group or UNAGRO; Alliance Against Impunity or AAI; Committee for Campesino Unity or CUC; Coordinating Committee of Agricultural, Commercial, Industrial, and Financial Associations or CACIF; Mutual Support Group or GAM
International organization participation: BCIE, CACM, CCC, ECLAC, FAO, G-24, G-77, IADB, IAEA, IBRD, ICAO, ICFTU, ICRM, IDA, IFAD, IFC, IFRCS, IHO, ILO, IMF, IMO, Intelsat, Interpol, IOC, IOM, ISO (correspondent), ITU, LAES, LAIA (observer), NAM, OAS, OPANAL, OPCW, PCA, UN, UNCTAD, UNESCO, UNIDO, UNU, UPU, WCL, WFTU, WHO, WIPO, WMO, WToO, WTrO
Diplomatic representation in the US:
chief of mission: Ambassador Ariel RIVERA Irias
chancery: 2220 R Street NW, Washington, DC 20008
telephone: [1] (202) 745-4952
FAX: [1] (202) 745-1908
consulate(s) general: Chicago, Houston, Los Angeles, Miami, New York, and San Francisco
Diplomatic representation from the US:
chief of mission: Ambassador Prudence BUSHNELL
embassy: 7-01 Avenida Reforma, Zone 10, Guatemala City
mailing address: APO AA 34024
telephone: [502] 331-1541/55
FAX: [502] 334-8477
Flag description: three equal vertical bands of light blue (hoist side), white, and light blue with the coat of arms centered in the white band; the coat of arms includes a green and red quetzal (the national bird) and a scroll bearing the inscription LIBERTAD 15 DE SEPTIEMBRE DE 1821 (the original date of independence from Spain) all superimposed on a pair of crossed rifles and a pair of crossed swords and framed by a wreath

Economy

Economy - overview: The agricultural sector accounts for about one-fourth of GDP, two-thirds of exports, and half of the labor force. Coffee, sugar, and bananas are the main products. Former President ARZU (1996-2000) worked to implement a program of economic liberalization and political modernization. The 1996 signing of the peace accords, which ended 36 years of civil war, removed a major obstacle to foreign investment. In 1998, Hurricane Mitch caused relatively little damage to Guatemala compared to its neighbors. Ongoing challenges include increasing government revenues, negotiating further assistance from international donors, and increasing the efficiency and openness of both government and private financial operations. Despite low international prices for Guatemala's main commodities, the economy grew by 3% in 2000 and is forecast to grow by 4% in 2001. Guatemala, along with Honduras and El Salvador, recently concluded a free trade agreement with Mexico and has moved to protect international property rights. However, the PORTILLO administration has undertaken a review of privatizations under the previous administration, thereby creating some uncertainty among investors.
GDP: purchasing power parity - $46.2 billion (2000 est.)
GDP - real growth rate: 3% (2000 est.)
GDP - per capita: purchasing power parity - $3,700 (2000 est.)
GDP - composition by sector:
agriculture: 23%
industry: 20%
services: 57% (2000 est.)
Population below poverty line: 60% (2000 est.)
Household income or consumption by percentage share:
lowest 10%: 0.6%
highest 10%: 46.6% (1989)
Inflation rate (consumer prices): 6% (2000 est.)
Labor force: 4.2 million (1999 est.)

Guatemala (continued)

Labor force - by occupation: agriculture 50%, industry 15%, services 35% (1999 est.)
Unemployment rate: 7.5% (1999 est.)
Budget:
revenues: $2.2 billion
expenditures: $1.8 billion, including capital expenditures of $NA (2001 est.)
Industries: sugar, textiles and clothing, furniture, chemicals, petroleum, metals, rubber, tourism
Industrial production growth rate: 4.1% (1999)
Electricity - production: 3.785 billion kWh (1999)
Electricity - production by source:
fossil fuel: 38.31%
hydro: 61.69%
nuclear: 0%
other: 0% (1999)
Electricity - consumption: 3.295 billion kWh (1999)
Electricity - exports: 435 million kWh (1999)
Electricity - imports: 210 million kWh (1999)
Agriculture - products: sugarcane, corn, bananas, coffee, beans, cardamom; cattle, sheep, pigs, chickens
Exports: $2.9 billion (f.o.b., 2000)
Exports - commodities: coffee, sugar, bananas, fruits and vegetables, cardamom, meat, apparel, petroleum, electricity
Exports - partners: US 51.4%, El Salvador 8.7%, Honduras 5%, Costa Rica 3.4%, Germany 2.7% (1998)
Imports: $4.4 billion (f.o.b., 2000)
Imports - commodities: fuels, machinery and transport equipment, construction materials, grain, fertilizers, electricity
Imports - partners: US 42.8%, Mexico 9.9%, Japan 4.8%, El Salvador 4.3%, Venezuela 3.8% (1998)
Debt - external: $4.7 billion (2000 est.)
Economic aid - recipient: $212 million (1995)
Currency: quetzal (GTQ), US dollar (USD), others allowed
Currency code: GTQ; USD
Exchange rates: quetzales per US dollar - 7.8020 (January 2001), 7.7632 (2000), 7.3856 (1999), 6.3947 (1998), 6.0653 (1997), 6.0495 (1996), 5.8103 (1995)
Fiscal year: calendar year

Communications

Telephones - main lines in use: 665,061 (June 2000)
Telephones - mobile cellular: 663,296 (September 2000)
Telephone system:
general assessment: fairly modern network centered in the city of Guatemala
domestic: NA
international: connected to Central American Microwave System; satellite earth station - 1 Intelsat (Atlantic Ocean)
Radio broadcast stations: AM 130, FM 487, shortwave 15 (2000)
Radios: 835,000 (1997)
Television broadcast stations: 26 (plus 27 repeaters) (1997)
Televisions: 1.323 million (1997)
Internet country code: .gt
Internet Service Providers (ISPs): 5 (2000)
Internet users: 65,000 (2000)

Transportation

Railways:
total: 884 km (102 km privately owned)
narrow gauge: 884 km 0.914-m gauge (single track)
Highways:
total: 13,856 km
paved: 4,370 km (including 140 km of expressways)
unpaved: 9,486 km (1998)
Waterways: 990 km
note: 260 km navigable year round; additional 730 km navigable during highwater season
Pipelines: crude oil 275 km
Ports and harbors: Champerico, Puerto Barrios, Puerto Quetzal, San Jose, Santo Tomas de Castilla
Merchant marine: none (2000 est.)
Airports: 477 (2000 est.)
Airports - with paved runways:
total: 11
2,438 to 3,047 m: 3
1,524 to 2,437 m: 1
914 to 1,523 m: 5
under 914 m: 2 (2000 est.)
Airports - with unpaved runways:
total: 466
2,438 to 3,047 m: 1
1,524 to 2,437 m: 9
914 to 1,523 m: 124
under 914 m: 332 (2000 est.)

Military

Military branches: Army, Navy, Air Force
Military manpower - military age: 18 years of age
Military manpower - availability:
males age 15-49: 3,092,050 (2001 est.)
Military manpower - fit for military service:
males age 15-49: 2,018,636 (2001 est.)
Military manpower - reaching military age annually:
males: 140,358 (2001 est.)
Military expenditures - dollar figure: $120 million (FY99)
Military expenditures - percent of GDP: 0.6% (FY99)

Transnational Issues

Disputes - international: Guatemala periodically asserts claims to territory in southern Belize; to deter cross-border squatting, both states in 2000 agreed to a "line of adjacency" based on the de facto boundary, which is not recognized by Guatemala
Illicit drugs: transit country for cocaine and heroin; minor producer of illicit opium poppy and cannabis for the international drug trade; proximity to Mexico makes Guatemala a major staging area for drugs (cocaine and heroin shipments); money laundering is probably increasing

Guernsey
(British crown dependency)

Introduction

Background: The island of Guernsey and the other Channel Islands represent the last remnants of the medieval Dukedom of Normandy, which held sway in both France and England. The islands were the only British soil occupied by German troops in World War II.

Geography

Location: Western Europe, islands in the English Channel, northwest of France
Geographic coordinates: 49 28 N, 2 35 W
Map references: Europe
Area:
total: 194 sq km
land: 194 sq km
water: 0 sq km
note: includes Alderney, Guernsey, Herm, Sark, and some other smaller islands
Area - comparative: slightly larger than Washington, DC
Land boundaries: 0 km
Coastline: 50 km
Maritime claims:
exclusive fishing zone: 12 NM
territorial sea: 3 NM
Climate: temperate with mild winters and cool summers; about 50% of days are overcast
Terrain: mostly level with low hills in southwest
Elevation extremes:
lowest point: Atlantic Ocean 0 m
highest point: unnamed location on Sark 114 m
Natural resources: cropland
Land use:
arable land: NA%
permanent crops: NA%
permanent pastures: NA%
forests and woodland: NA%
other: NA%
Irrigated land: NA sq km
Natural hazards: NA

Guernsey (continued)

Environment - current issues: NA
Geography - note: large, deepwater harbor at Saint Peter Port

People

Population: 64,342 (July 2001 est.)
Age structure:
0-14 years: 16.22% (male 5,285; female 5,151)
15-64 years: 66.67% (male 21,264; female 21,630)
65 years and over: 17.11% (male 4,546; female 6,466) (2001 est.)
Population growth rate: 0.39% (2001 est.)
Birth rate: 9.9 births/1,000 population (2001 est.)
Death rate: 9.87 deaths/1,000 population (2001 est.)
Net migration rate: 3.89 migrant(s)/1,000 population (2001 est.)
Sex ratio:
at birth: 1.04 male(s)/female
under 15 years: 1.03 male(s)/female
15-64 years: 0.98 male(s)/female
65 years and over: 0.7 male(s)/female
total population: 0.94 male(s)/female (2001 est.)
Infant mortality rate: 5 deaths/1,000 live births (2001 est.)
Life expectancy at birth:
total population: 79.78 years
male: 76.78 years
female: 82.88 years (2001 est.)
Total fertility rate: 1.36 children born/woman (2001 est.)
HIV/AIDS - adult prevalence rate: NA%
HIV/AIDS - people living with HIV/AIDS: NA
HIV/AIDS - deaths: NA
Nationality:
noun: Channel Islander(s)
adjective: Channel Islander
Ethnic groups: UK and Norman-French descent
Religions: Anglican, Roman Catholic, Presbyterian, Baptist, Congregational, Methodist
Languages: English, French, Norman-French dialect spoken in country districts
Literacy:
definition: NA
total population: NA%
male: NA%
female: NA%

Government

Country name:
conventional long form: Bailiwick of Guernsey
conventional short form: Guernsey
Dependency status: British crown dependency
Government type: NA
Capital: Saint Peter Port
Administrative divisions: none (British crown dependency); there are no first-order administrative divisions as defined by the US Government, but there are 10 parishes including St. Peter Port, St. Sampson, Vale, Castel, St. Saviour, St. Pierre du Bois, Torteval, Forest, St. Martin, St. Andrew
Independence: none (British crown dependency)
National holiday: Liberation Day, 9 May (1945)
Constitution: unwritten; partly statutes, partly common law and practice
Legal system: English law and local statute; justice is administered by the Royal Court
Suffrage: 18 years of age; universal
Executive branch:
chief of state: Queen ELIZABETH II (since 6 February 1952)
head of government: Lieutenant Governor and Commander-in-Chief Lt. Gen. Sir John FOLEY (since NA 2000) and Bailiff De Vic G. CAREY (since NA)
cabinet: Advisory and Finance Committee appointed by the Assembly of the States
elections: none; the monarch is hereditary; lieutenant governor appointed by the monarch; bailiff appointed by the monarch
Legislative branch: unicameral Assembly of the States; consists of the Bailiff, 10 Douzaine (parish council) representatives, 45 People's Deputies elected by popular franchise, 2 Alderney representatives, HM Procureur (Attorney General), HM Comptroller (Solicitor General) and HM Greffier (Court Recorder and Registrar General)
elections: last held 12 April 2000 (next to be held NA 2006)
election results: percent of vote - NA%; seats - all independents
Judicial branch: Royal Court
Political parties and leaders: none; all independents
Political pressure groups and leaders: none
International organization participation: none
Diplomatic representation in the US: none (British crown dependency)
Diplomatic representation from the US: none (British crown dependency)
Flag description: white with the red cross of Saint George (patron saint of England) extending to the edges of the flag and a yellow equal-armed cross of William the Conqueror superimposed on the Saint George cross

Economy

Economy - overview: Financial services - banking, fund management, insurance, etc. - account for about 55% of total income in this tiny Channel Island economy. Tourism, manufacturing, and horticulture, mainly tomatoes and cut flowers, have been declining. Light tax and death duties make Guernsey a popular tax haven. The evolving economic integration of the EU nations is changing the rules of the game under which Guernsey operates.
GDP: purchasing power parity - $1.3 billion (1999 est.)
GDP - real growth rate: 5.7% (1999 est.)
GDP - per capita: purchasing power parity - $20,000 (1999 est.)
GDP - composition by sector:
agriculture: 3%
industry: 10%
services: 87% (2000)
Population below poverty line: NA%
Household income or consumption by percentage share:
lowest 10%: NA%
highest 10%: NA%
Inflation rate (consumer prices): 3.99% (2000 est.)
Labor force: 31,322 (2000)
Unemployment rate: 0.5% (1999 est.)
Budget:
revenues: $381.3 million
expenditures: $368.8 million, including capital expenditures of $NA (2000 est.)
Industries: tourism, banking
Industrial production growth rate: NA%
Electricity - production: NA kWh
Electricity - production by source:
fossil fuel: NA%
hydro: NA%
nuclear: NA%
other: NA%
Electricity - consumption: NA kWh
Electricity - exports: NA kWh
Electricity - imports: NA kWh
Agriculture - products: tomatoes, greenhouse flowers, sweet peppers, eggplant, fruit; Guernsey cattle
Exports: $NA
Exports - commodities: tomatoes, flowers and ferns, sweet peppers, eggplant, other vegetables
Exports - partners: UK (regarded as internal trade)
Imports: $NA
Imports - commodities: coal, gasoline, oil, machinery and equipment
Imports - partners: UK (regarded as internal trade)
Debt - external: $NA
Economic aid - recipient: $NA
Currency: British pound (GBP); note - there is also a Guernsey pound
Currency code: GBP
Exchange rates: Guernsey pounds per US dollar - 0.6764 (January 2001), 0.6596 0.6180 (1999), 0.6037 (1998), 0.6106 (1997), 0.6403 (1996); note - the Guernsey pound is at par with the British pound
Fiscal year: calendar year

Communications

Telephones - main lines in use: 44,000 (1996)
Telephones - mobile cellular: 12,000 (1997)
Telephone system:
general assessment: NA
domestic: NA
international: 1 submarine cable
Radio broadcast stations: AM 1, FM 1, shortwave 0 (1998)
Radios: NA
Television broadcast stations: 1 (1997)
Televisions: NA
Internet country code: .gg
Internet Service Providers (ISPs): NA
Internet users: NA

Guernsey (continued)

Transportation

Railways: 0 km
Highways:
total: NA km
paved: NA km
unpaved: NA km
Waterways: none
Ports and harbors: Saint Peter Port, Saint Sampson
Merchant marine: none (2000 est.)
Airports: 2 (2000 est.)
Airports - with paved runways:
total: 2
914 to 1,523 m: 1
under 914 m: 1 (2000 est.)

Military

Military - note: defense is the responsibility of the UK

Transnational Issues

Disputes - international: none

Guinea

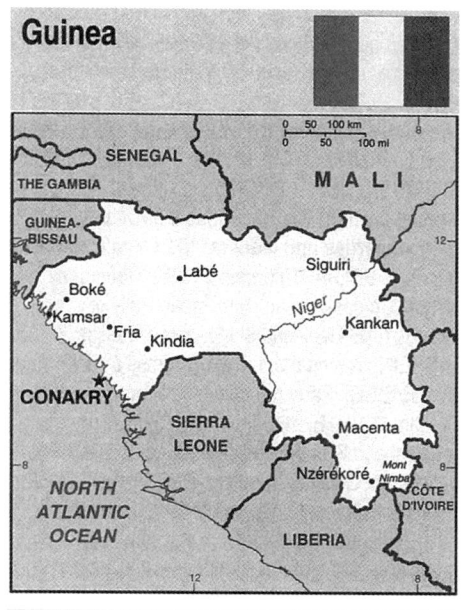

Introduction

Background: Independent from France since 1958, Guinea did not hold democratic elections until 1993 when Gen. Lansana CONTE (head of the military government) was elected president of the civilian government. He was reelected in 1998. Unrest in Sierra Leone has spilled over into Guinea, threatening stability and creating a humanitarian emergency.

Geography

Location: Western Africa, bordering the North Atlantic Ocean, between Guinea-Bissau and Sierra Leone
Geographic coordinates: 11 00 N, 10 00 W
Map references: Africa
Area:
total: 245,857 sq km
land: 245,857 sq km
water: 0 sq km
Area - comparative: slightly smaller than Oregon
Land boundaries:
total: 3,399 km
border countries: Cote d'Ivoire 610 km, Guinea-Bissau 386 km, Liberia 563 km, Mali 858 km, Senegal 330 km, Sierra Leone 652 km
Coastline: 320 km
Maritime claims:
exclusive economic zone: 200 NM
territorial sea: 12 NM
Climate: generally hot and humid; monsoonal-type rainy season (June to November) with southwesterly winds; dry season (December to May) with northeasterly harmattan winds
Terrain: generally flat coastal plain, hilly to mountainous interior
Elevation extremes:
lowest point: Atlantic Ocean 0 m
highest point: Mont Nimba 1,752 m
Natural resources: bauxite, iron ore, diamonds, gold, uranium, hydropower, fish
Land use:
arable land: 2%
permanent crops: 0%
permanent pastures: 22%
forests and woodland: 59%
other: 17% (1993 est.)
Irrigated land: 930 sq km (1993 est.)
Natural hazards: hot, dry, dusty harmattan haze may reduce visibility during dry season
Environment - current issues: deforestation; inadequate supplies of potable water; desertification; soil contamination and erosion; overfishing, overpopulation in forest region
Environment - international agreements:
party to: Biodiversity, Climate Change, Climate Change-Kyoto Protocol, Desertification, Endangered Species, Hazardous Wastes, Law of the Sea, Marine Dumping, Ozone Layer Protection, Ship Pollution, Wetlands, Whaling
signed, but not ratified: none of the selected agreements

People

Population: 7,613,870 (July 2001 est.)
Age structure:
0-14 years: 43.12% (male 1,637,000; female 1,645,786)
15-64 years: 54.19% (male 2,015,199; female 2,110,745)
65 years and over: 2.69% (male 84,586; female 120,554) (2001 est.)
Population growth rate: 1.96% (2001 est.)
Birth rate: 39.78 births/1,000 population (2001 est.)
Death rate: 17.53 deaths/1,000 population (2001 est.)
Net migration rate: -2.63 migrant(s)/1,000 population (2001 est.)
note: as a result of civil war in neighboring countries, Guinea is host to almost half a million Liberian and Sierra Leonean refugees
Sex ratio:
at birth: 1.03 male(s)/female
under 15 years: 0.99 male(s)/female
15-64 years: 0.95 male(s)/female
65 years and over: 0.7 male(s)/female
total population: 0.96 male(s)/female (2001 est.)
Infant mortality rate: 129.03 deaths/1,000 live births (2001 est.)
Life expectancy at birth:
total population: 45.91 years
male: 43.49 years
female: 48.42 years (2001 est.)
Total fertility rate: 5.39 children born/woman (2001 est.)
HIV/AIDS - adult prevalence rate: 1.54% (1999 est.)
HIV/AIDS - people living with HIV/AIDS: 55,000 (1999 est.)
HIV/AIDS - deaths: 5,600 (1999 est.)
Nationality:
noun: Guinean(s)
adjective: Guinean

Guinea (continued)

Ethnic groups: Peuhl 40%, Malinke 30%, Soussou 20%, smaller ethnic groups 10%
Religions: Muslim 85%, Christian 8%, indigenous beliefs 7%
Languages: French (official), each ethnic group has its own language
Literacy:
definition: age 15 and over can read and write
total population: 35.9%
male: 49.9%
female: 21.9% (1995 est.)

Government

Country name:
conventional long form: Republic of Guinea
conventional short form: Guinea
local long form: Republique de Guinee
local short form: Guinee
former: French Guinea
Government type: republic
Capital: Conakry
Administrative divisions: 33 prefectures and 1 special zone (zone special)*; Beyla, Boffa, Boke, Conakry*, Coyah, Dabola, Dalaba, Dinguiraye, Dubreka, Faranah, Forecariah, Fria, Gaoual, Gueckedou, Kankan, Kerouane, Kindia, Kissidougou, Koubia, Koundara, Kouroussa, Labe, Lelouma, Lola, Macenta, Mali, Mamou, Mandiana, Nzerekore, Pita, Siguiri, Telimele, Tougue, Yomou
Independence: 2 October 1958 (from France)
National holiday: Independence Day, 2 October (1958)
Constitution: 23 December 1990 (Loi Fundamentale)
Legal system: based on French civil law system, customary law, and decree; legal codes currently being revised; has not accepted compulsory ICJ jurisdiction
Suffrage: 18 years of age; universal
Executive branch:
chief of state: President Lansana CONTE (head of military government since 5 April 1984, elected president 19 December 1993)
head of government: Prime Minister Lamine SIDIME (since 8 March 1999)
cabinet: Council of Ministers appointed by the president
elections: president elected by popular vote for a five-year term; candidate must receive a majority of the votes cast to be elected president; election last held 14 December 1998 (next to be held NA December 2003); the prime minister is appointed by the president
election results: Lansana CONTE reelected president; percent of vote - Lansana CONTE (PUP) 56.1%, Mamadou Boye BA (UNR-PRP) 24.6%, Alpha CONDE (RPG) 16.6%,
Legislative branch: unicameral People's National Assembly or Assemblee Nationale Populaire (114 seats; members are elected by direct popular vote to serve five-year terms)
elections: last held 11 June 1995 (next scheduled for 26 November 2000 postponed indefinitely due to border fighting with rebels from Sierra Leone and Liberia)
election results: percent of vote by party - NA%; seats by party - PUP 71, RPG 19, PRP 9, UNR 9, UPG 2, PDG-AST 1, UNP 1, PDG-RDA 1, other 1
Judicial branch: Court of Appeal or Cour d'Appel
Political parties and leaders: Democratic Party of Guinea or PDG-AST [Marcel CROS]; Democratic Party of Guinea-African Democratic Rally or PDG-RDA [El Hadj Ismael Mohamed Gassim GUSHEIN]; National Union for Progress or UNP [Paul Louis FABER]; Party for Unity and Progress or PUP [Lansana CONTE] - the governing party; Party for Renewal and Progress or PRP [Siradiou DIALLO]; Rally for the Guinean People or RPG [Alpha CONDE]; Union for Progress of Guinea or UPG [Jean-Marie DORE, secretary-general]; Union for the New Republic or UNR [Mamadou Boye BA]; Union of Republican Forces or UFR [Sidya TOURE]
Political pressure groups and leaders: NA
International organization participation: ACCT, ACP, AfDB, CCC, ECA, ECOWAS, FAO, G-77, IBRD, ICAO, ICFTU, ICRM, IDA, IDB, IFAD, IFC, IFRCS, ILO, IMF, IMO, Intelsat, Interpol, IOC, IOM, ISO (correspondent), ITU, MINURSO, NAM, OAU, OIC, OPCW, UN, UNAMSIL, UNCTAD, UNESCO, UNIDO, UPU, WCL, WFTU, WHO, WIPO, WMO, WToO, WTrO
Diplomatic representation in the US:
chief of mission: Ambassador Mohamed Aly THIAM
chancery: 2112 Leroy Place NW, Washington, DC 20008
telephone: [1] (202) 483-9420
FAX: [1] (202) 483-8688
Diplomatic representation from the US:
chief of mission: Charge d'Affaires Timberlake FOSTER
embassy: Rue Ka 038, Conakry
mailing address: B. P. 603, Conakry
telephone: [224] 41 15 20, 41 15 21, 41 15 23
FAX: [224] 41 15 22
Flag description: three equal vertical bands of red (hoist side), yellow, and green; uses the popular pan-African colors of Ethiopia; similar to the flag of Rwanda, which has a large black letter R centered in the yellow band

Economy

Economy - overview: Guinea possesses major mineral, hydropower, and agricultural resources, yet remains a poor underdeveloped nation. The country possesses over 30% of the world's bauxite reserves and is the second largest bauxite producer. The mining sector accounted for about 75% of exports in 1999. Long-run improvements in government fiscal arrangements, literacy, and the legal framework are needed if the country is to move out of poverty. The government made encouraging progress in budget management in 1997-99, and reform progress was praised in the World Bank/IMF October 2000 assessment. However, escalating fighting along the Sierra Leonean and Liberian borders will cause major economic disruptions. In addition to direct defense costs, the violence has led to a sharp decline in investor confidence. Foreign mining companies have reduced expatriate staff, while panic buying has created food shortages and inflation in local markets. Real GDP growth is expected to fall to 2% in 2001.
GDP: purchasing power parity - $10 billion (2000 est.)
GDP - real growth rate: 5% (2000 est.)
GDP - per capita: purchasing power parity - $1,300 (2000 est.)
GDP - composition by sector:
agriculture: 22.3%
industry: 35.3%
services: 42.4% (1998 est.)
Population below poverty line: 40% (1994 est.)
Household income or consumption by percentage share:
lowest 10%: 2.6%
highest 10%: 32% (1994)
Inflation rate (consumer prices): 6% (2000 est.)
Labor force: 3 million (1999)
Labor force - by occupation: agriculture 80%, industry and services 20% (2000 est.)
Unemployment rate: NA%
Budget:
revenues: $NA
expenditures: $417.7 million, including capital expenditures of $NA million (2000 est.)
Industries: bauxite, gold, diamonds; alumina refining; light manufacturing and agricultural processing industries
Industrial production growth rate: 3.2% (1994)
Electricity - production: 750 million kWh (1999)
Electricity - production by source:
fossil fuel: 46.67%
hydro: 53.33%
nuclear: 0%
other: 0% (1999)
Electricity - consumption: 697.5 million kWh (1999)
Electricity - exports: 0 kWh (1999)
Electricity - imports: 0 kWh (1999)
Agriculture - products: rice, coffee, pineapples, palm kernels, cassava (tapioca), bananas, sweet potatoes; cattle, sheep, goats; timber
Exports: $820 million (f.o.b., 2000 est.)
Exports - commodities: bauxite, alumina, gold, diamonds, coffee, fish, agricultural products
Exports - partners: US, Benelux, Ukraine, Ireland (1999)
Imports: $634 million (f.o.b., 2000 est.)
Imports - commodities: petroleum products, metals, machinery, transport equipment, textiles, grain and other foodstuffs
Imports - partners: France, Belgium, US, Cote d'Ivoire (1999)
Debt - external: $3.6 billion (1999 est.)

Guinea (continued)

Economic aid - recipient: $359.2 million (1998)
Currency: Guinean franc (GNF)
Currency code: GNF
Exchange rates: Guinean francs per US dollar - 1,855.0 (October 2000), 1,572.0 (2000), 1,387.4 (1999), 1,236.8 (1998), 1,095.3 (1997), 1,004.0 (1996)
Fiscal year: calendar year

Communications

Telephones - main lines in use: 20,000 (1997)
Telephones - mobile cellular: 2,868 (1997)
Telephone system:
general assessment: poor to fair system of open-wire lines, small radiotelephone communication stations, and new microwave radio relay system
domestic: microwave radio relay and radiotelephone communication
international: satellite earth station - 1 Intelsat (Atlantic Ocean)
Radio broadcast stations: AM 4, FM 8, shortwave 3 (1998)
Radios: 357,000 (1997)
Television broadcast stations: 6 (1997)
Televisions: 85,000 (1997)
Internet country code: .gn
Internet Service Providers (ISPs): 1 (2000)
Internet users: 5,000 (2000)

Transportation

Railways:
total: 1,086 km
standard gauge: 279 km 1.435-m gauge
narrow gauge: 807 km 1.000-m gauge (includes 662 km in common carrier service from Kankan to Conakry)
Highways:
total: 30,500 km
paved: 5,033 km
unpaved: 25,467 km (1996)
Waterways: 1,295 km (navigable by shallow-draft native craft)
Ports and harbors: Boke, Conakry, Kamsar
Merchant marine: none (2000 est.)
Airports: 15 (2000 est.)
Airports - with paved runways:
total: 5
over 3,047 m: 1
2,438 to 3,047 m: 1
1,524 to 2,437 m: 3 (2000 est.)
Airports - with unpaved runways:
total: 10
1,524 to 2,437 m: 6
914 to 1,523 m: 3
under 914 m: 1 (2000 est.)

Military

Military branches: Army, Navy, Air Force, Republican Guard, Presidential Guard, paramilitary National Gendarmerie, National Police Force (Surete National)
Military manpower - availability:
males age 15-49: 1,764,912 (2001 est.)
Military manpower - fit for military service:
males age 15-49: 891,166 (2001 est.)
Military expenditures - dollar figure: $56 million (FY96)
Military expenditures - percent of GDP: 1.4% (FY96)

Transnational Issues

Disputes - international: border incursions by Revolutionary United Front combatants from Sierra Leone; civil war in that country has engendered a massive flow of refugees to southern Guinea and Liberia

Guinea-Bissau

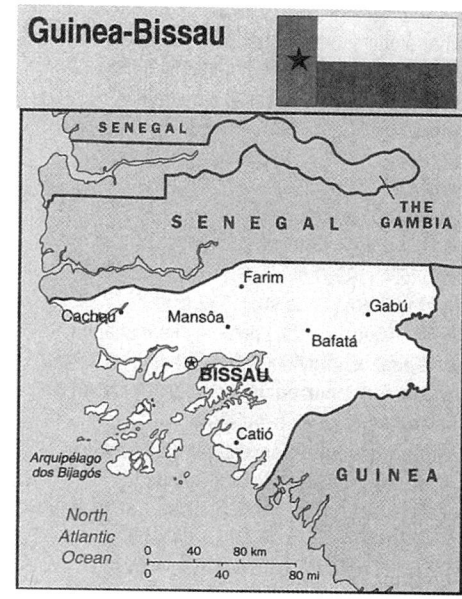

Introduction

Background: In 1994, 20 years after independence from Portugal, the country's first multiparty legislative and presidential elections were held. An army uprising that triggered a bloody civil war in 1998, created hundreds of thousands of displaced persons. The president was ousted by a military junta in May 1999. An interim government turned over power in February 2000 when opposition leader Koumba YALLA took office following two rounds of transparent presidential elections. Guinea-Bissau's transition back to democracy will be complicated by a crippled economy devastated by civil war and the military's predilection for governmental meddling.

Geography

Location: Western Africa, bordering the North Atlantic Ocean, between Guinea and Senegal
Geographic coordinates: 12 00 N, 15 00 W
Map references: Africa
Area:
total: 36,120 sq km
land: 28,000 sq km
water: 8,120 sq km
Area - comparative: slightly less than three times the size of Connecticut
Land boundaries:
total: 724 km
border countries: Guinea 386 km, Senegal 338 km
Coastline: 350 km
Maritime claims:
exclusive economic zone: 200 NM
territorial sea: 12 NM
Climate: tropical; generally hot and humid; monsoonal-type rainy season (June to November) with southwesterly winds; dry season (December to May) with northeasterly harmattan winds
Terrain: mostly low coastal plain rising to savanna in east
Elevation extremes:
lowest point: Atlantic Ocean 0 m

Guinea-Bissau (continued)

highest point: unnamed location in the northeast corner of the country 300 m
Natural resources: fish, timber, phosphates, bauxite, unexploited deposits of petroleum
Land use:
arable land: 11%
permanent crops: 1%
permanent pastures: 38%
forests and woodland: 38%
other: 12% (1993 est.)
Irrigated land: 17 sq km (1993 est.)
Natural hazards: hot, dry, dusty harmattan haze may reduce visibility during dry season; brush fires
Environment - current issues: deforestation; soil erosion; overgrazing; overfishing
Environment - international agreements:
party to: Biodiversity, Climate Change, Desertification, Endangered Species, Law of the Sea, Marine Dumping, Ship Pollution, Wetlands
signed, but not ratified: none of the selected agreements

People

Population: 1,315,822 (July 2001 est.)
Age structure:
0-14 years: 42.09% (male 276,312; female 277,536)
15-64 years: 55.05% (male 344,493; female 379,889)
65 years and over: 2.86% (male 16,850; female 20,742) (2001 est.)
Population growth rate: 2.23% (2001 est.)
Birth rate: 39.29 births/1,000 population (2001 est.)
Death rate: 15.33 deaths/1,000 population (2001 est.)
Net migration rate: -1.66 migrant(s)/1,000 population (2001 est.)
Sex ratio:
at birth: 1.03 male(s)/female
under 15 years: 1 male(s)/female
15-64 years: 0.91 male(s)/female
65 years and over: 0.81 male(s)/female
total population: 0.94 male(s)/female (2001 est.)
Infant mortality rate: 110.4 deaths/1,000 live births (2001 est.)
Life expectancy at birth:
total population: 49.42 years
male: 47.12 years
female: 51.78 years (2001 est.)
Total fertility rate: 5.2 children born/woman (2001 est.)
HIV/AIDS - adult prevalence rate: 2.5% (1999 est.)
HIV/AIDS - people living with HIV/AIDS: 14,000 (1999 est.)
HIV/AIDS - deaths: 1,300 (1999 est.)
Nationality:
noun: Guinean (s)
adjective: Guinean
Ethnic groups: African 99% (Balanta 30%, Fula 20%, Manjaca 14%, Mandinga 13%, Papel 7%), European and mulatto less than 1%
Religions: indigenous beliefs 50%, Muslim 45%, Christian 5%

Languages: Portuguese (official), Crioulo, African languages
Literacy:
definition: age 15 and over can read and write
total population: 53.9%
male: 67.1%
female: 40.7% (1997 est.)

Government

Country name:
conventional long form: Republic of Guinea-Bissau
conventional short form: Guinea-Bissau
local long form: Republica da Guine-Bissau
local short form: Guine-Bissau
former: Portuguese Guinea
Government type: republic, multiparty since mid-1991
Capital: Bissau
Administrative divisions: 9 regions (regioes, singular - regiao); Bafata, Biombo, Bissau, Bolama, Cacheu, Gabu, Oio, Quinara, Tombali; note - Bolama may have been renamed Bolama/Bijagos
Independence: 24 September 1973 (unilaterally declared by Guinea-Bissau); 10 September 1974 (recognized by Portugal)
National holiday: Independence Day, 24 September (1973)
Constitution: 16 May 1984, amended 4 May 1991, 4 December 1991, 26 February 1993, 9 June 1993, and 1996
Legal system: NA
Suffrage: 18 years of age; universal
Executive branch:
chief of state: President Koumba YALLA (since 18 February 2000)
head of government: Prime Minister Faustino IMBALI (since 20 March 2001)
cabinet: NA
elections: president elected by popular vote for a five-year term; election last held 28 November 1999 and 16 January 2000 (next to be held NA 2004); prime minister appointed by the president after consultation with party leaders in the legislature
election results: Koumba YALLA elected president; percent of vote, second ballot - Koumba YALLA (PRS) 72%, Malan Bacai SANHA (PAIGC) 28%
Legislative branch: unicameral National People's Assembly or Assembleia Nacional Popular (100 seats; members are elected by popular vote to serve a maximum of four years)
elections: last held 28 November 1999 (next to be held by NA 2003)
election results: percent of vote by party - NA%; seats by party - PRS 37, RGB 27, PAIGC 25, 11 remaining seats went to 5 of the remaining 10 parties that fielded candidates
Judicial branch: Supreme Court or Supremo Tribunal da Justica (consists of nine justices who are appointed by the president and serve at his pleasure; final court of appeals in criminal and civil cases); Regional Courts (one in each of nine regions; first court of appeals for Sectoral Court decisions; hear all felony cases and civil cases valued at over $1,000); 24 Sectoral Courts (judges are not necessarily trained lawyers; they hear civil cases under $1,000 and misdemeanor criminal cases)
Political parties and leaders: African Party for the Independence of Guinea-Bissau and Cape Verde or PAIGC [Francisco BENANTE]; Front for the Liberation and Independence of Guinea or FLING [Francois MENDY]; Guinea-Bissau Resistance-Ba Fata Movement or RGB-MB [Helder Vaz LOPES]; Guinean Civic Forum or FCG [Antonieta Rosa GOMES]; International League for Ecological Protection or LIPE [Alhaje Bubacar DJALO, president]; National Union for Democracy and Progress or UNDP [Abubacer BALDE, secretary general]; Party for Democratic Convergence or PCD [Victor MANDINGA]; Social Renovation Party or PRS [Koumba YALLA]; Union for Change or UM [Jorge MANDINGA, president, Dr. Anne SAAD, secretary general]; United Social Democratic Party or PUSD [Victor Sau'de MARIA]
Political pressure groups and leaders: NA
International organization participation: ACCT (associate), ACP, AfDB, ECA, ECOWAS, FAO, FZ, G-77, IBRD, ICAO, ICFTU, ICRM, IDA, IDB, IFAD, IFC, IFRCS, ILO, IMF, IMO, Intelsat (nonsignatory user), Interpol, IOC, IOM, ITU, NAM, OAU, OIC, OPCW, UN, UNCTAD, UNESCO, UNIDO, UPU, WADB (regional), WAEMU, WFTU, WHO, WIPO, WMO, WToO, WTrO
Diplomatic representation in the US:
chief of mission: Ambassador Mario LOPES DA ROSA
chancery: Suite 519, 1511 K Street, NW, Washington, DC 20005
telephone: [1] (202) 347-3950
FAX: [1] (202) 347-3954
Diplomatic representation from the US: the US Embassy suspended operations on 14 June 1998 in the midst of violent conflict between forces loyal to then President VIEIRA and military-led junta
Flag description: two equal horizontal bands of yellow (top) and green with a vertical red band on the hoist side; there is a black five-pointed star centered in the red band; uses the popular pan-African colors of Ethiopia

Economy

Economy - overview: One of the 20 poorest countries in the world, Guinea-Bissau depends mainly on farming and fishing. Cashew crops have increased remarkably in recent years, and the country now ranks sixth in cashew production. Guinea-Bissau exports fish and seafood along with small amounts of peanuts, palm kernels, and timber. Rice is the major crop and staple food. However, intermittent fighting between Senegalese-backed government troops and a military junta destroyed much of the country's infrastructure and caused widespread damage to the economy in 1998; the civil war led to a 28% drop in GDP that year, with partial recovery in 1999-2000. Before the war, trade reform and price liberalization were the most successful part of the country's structural adjustment

Guinea-Bissau (continued)

program under IMF sponsorship. The tightening of monetary policy and the development of the private sector had also begun to reinvigorate the economy. Because of high costs, the development of petroleum, phosphate, and other mineral resources is not a near-term prospect. However, unexploited offshore oil reserves could provide much-needed revenue in the long run.

GDP: purchasing power parity - $1.1 billion (2000 est.)
GDP - real growth rate: 7.6% (2000 est.)
GDP - per capita: purchasing power parity - $850 (2000 est.)
GDP - composition by sector:
agriculture: 54%
industry: 15%
services: 31% (1997 est.)
Population below poverty line: 50% (1991 est.)
Household income or consumption by percentage share:
lowest 10%: 0.5%
highest 10%: 42.4% (1991)
Inflation rate (consumer prices): 3% (2000 est.)
Labor force: 480,000
Labor force - by occupation: agriculture 78%
Unemployment rate: NA%
Budget:
revenues: $NA
expenditures: $NA, including capital expenditures of $NA
Industries: agricultural products processing, beer, soft drinks
Industrial production growth rate: 2.6% (1997 est.)
Electricity - production: 55 million kWh (1999)
Electricity - production by source:
fossil fuel: 100%
hydro: 0%
nuclear: 0%
other: 0% (1999)
Electricity - consumption: 51.2 million kWh (1999)
Electricity - exports: 0 kWh (1999)
Electricity - imports: 0 kWh (1999)
Agriculture - products: rice, corn, beans, cassava (tapioca), cashew nuts, peanuts, palm kernels, cotton; timber; fish
Exports: $80 million (f.o.b., 2000 est.)
Exports - commodities: cashew nuts 70%, shrimp, peanuts, palm kernels, sawn lumber (1996)
Exports - partners: India 59%, Singapore 12%, Italy 10% (1998)
Imports: $55.2 million (f.o.b., 2000 est.)
Imports - commodities: foodstuffs, machinery and transport equipment, petroleum products (1996)
Imports - partners: Portugal 26%, France 8%, Senegal 8%, Netherlands 7% (1998)
Debt - external: $964 million (1998 est.)
Economic aid - recipient: $115.4 million (1995)
Currency: Communaute Financiere Africaine franc (XOF); note - responsible authority is the Central Bank of the West African States; previously the Guinea-Bissau peso (GWP) was used
Currency code: XOF; GWP
Exchange rates: Communaute Financiere Africaine francs (XOF) per US dollar - 699.21 (January 2001), 711.98 (2000), 615.70 (1999), 589.95 (1998), 583.67 (1997); Guinea-Bissauan pesos per US dollar - 26,373 (1996)
note: as of 1 May 1997, Guinea-Bissau adopted the CFA franc as the national currency; since 1 January 1999, the CFA franc is pegged to the euro at a rate of 655.957 CFA francs per euro
Fiscal year: calendar year

Communications

Telephones - main lines in use: 8,000 (1997)
Telephones - mobile cellular: NA
Telephone system:
general assessment: small system
domestic: combination of microwave radio relay, open-wire lines, radiotelephone, and cellular communications
international: NA
Radio broadcast stations: AM 1, FM 2, shortwave 0 (1998)
Radios: 49,000 (1997)
Television broadcast stations: 2 (1997)
Televisions: NA
Internet country code: .gw
Internet Service Providers (ISPs): 1 (2000)
Internet users: 1,500 (2000)

Transportation

Railways: 0 km
Highways:
total: 4,400 km
paved: 453 km
unpaved: 3,947 km (1996)
Waterways: several rivers are accessible to coastal shipping
Ports and harbors: Bissau, Buba, Cacheu, Farim
Merchant marine: none (2000 est.)
Airports: 29 (2000 est.)
Airports - with paved runways:
total: 3
over 3,047 m: 1
1,524 to 2,437 m: 1
914 to 1,523 m: 1 (2000 est.)
Airports - with unpaved runways:
total: 26
1,524 to 2,437 m: 1
914 to 1,523 m: 4
under 914 m: 21 (2000 est.)

Military

Military branches: People's Revolutionary Armed Force (FARP; includes Army, Navy, and Air Force), paramilitary force
Military manpower - availability:
males age 15-49: 305,071 (2001 est.)
Military manpower - fit for military service:
males age 15-49: 173,703 (2001 est.)
Military expenditures - dollar figure: $8 million (FY96)
Military expenditures - percent of GDP: 2.8% (FY96)

Transnational Issues

Disputes - international: none

Guyana

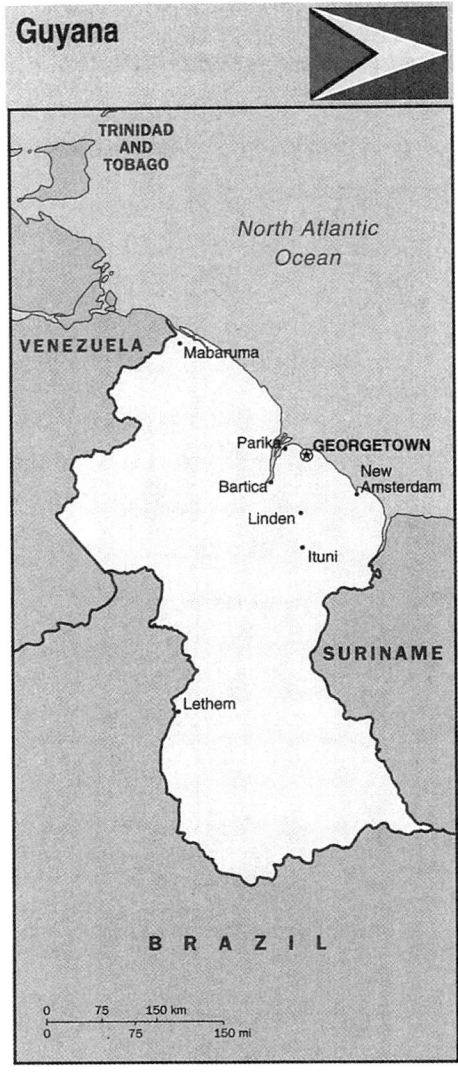

Introduction

Background: Guyana achieved independence from the UK in 1966 and became a republic in 1970. In 1989 Guyana launched an Economic Recovery Program, which marked a dramatic reversal from a state-controlled, socialist economy towards a more open, free market system. Results through the first decade have proven encouraging.

Geography

Location: Northern South America, bordering the North Atlantic Ocean, between Suriname and Venezuela
Geographic coordinates: 5 00 N, 59 00 W
Map references: South America
Area:
total: 214,970 sq km
land: 196,850 sq km
water: 18,120 sq km
Area - comparative: slightly smaller than Idaho
Land boundaries:
total: 2,462 km
border countries: Brazil 1,119 km, Suriname 600 km, Venezuela 743 km
Coastline: 459 km
Maritime claims:
continental shelf: 200 NM or to the outer edge of the continental margin
exclusive economic zone: 200 NM
territorial sea: 12 NM
Climate: tropical; hot, humid, moderated by northeast trade winds; two rainy seasons (May to mid-August, mid-November to mid-January)
Terrain: mostly rolling highlands; low coastal plain; savanna in south
Elevation extremes:
lowest point: Atlantic Ocean 0 m
highest point: Mount Roraima 2,835 m
Natural resources: bauxite, gold, diamonds, hardwood timber, shrimp, fish
Land use:
arable land: 2%
permanent crops: 0%
permanent pastures: 6%
forests and woodland: 84%
other: 8% (1993 est.)
Irrigated land: 1,300 sq km (1993 est.)
Natural hazards: flash floods are a constant threat during rainy seasons
Environment - current issues: water pollution from sewage and agricultural and industrial chemicals; deforestation
Environment - international agreements:
party to: Biodiversity, Climate Change, Desertification, Endangered Species, Law of the Sea, Marine Dumping, Ozone Layer Protection, Ship Pollution, Tropical Timber 83, Tropical Timber 94
signed, but not ratified: none of the selected agreements

People

Population: 697,181
note: estimates for this country explicitly take into account the effects of excess mortality due to AIDS; this can result in lower life expectancy, higher infant mortality and death rates, lower population and growth rates, and changes in the distribution of population by age and sex than would otherwise be expected (July 2001 est.)
Age structure:
0-14 years: 28.19% (male 100,194; female 96,309)
15-64 years: 66.89% (male 234,976; female 231,360)
65 years and over: 4.92% (male 15,324; female 19,018) (2001 est.)
Population growth rate: 0.07% (2001 est.)
Birth rate: 17.92 births/1,000 population (2001 est.)
Death rate: 8.87 deaths/1,000 population (2001 est.)
Net migration rate: -8.38 migrant(s)/1,000 population (2001 est.)
Sex ratio:
at birth: 1.05 male(s)/female
under 15 years: 1.04 male(s)/female
15-64 years: 1.02 male(s)/female
65 years and over: 0.81 male(s)/female
total population: 1.01 male(s)/female (2001 est.)
Infant mortality rate: 38.72 deaths/1,000 live births (2001 est.)
Life expectancy at birth:
total population: 63.31 years
male: 60.52 years
female: 66.24 years (2001 est.)
Total fertility rate: 2.1 children born/woman (2001 est.)
HIV/AIDS - adult prevalence rate: 3.01% (1999 est.)
HIV/AIDS - people living with HIV/AIDS: 15,000 (1999 est.)
HIV/AIDS - deaths: 900 (1999 est.)
Nationality:
noun: Guyanese (singular and plural)
adjective: Guyanese
Ethnic groups: East Indian 49%, black 32%, mixed 12%, Amerindian 6%, white and Chinese 1%
Religions: Christian 50%, Hindu 33%, Muslim 9%, other 8%
Languages: English, Amerindian dialects, Creole, Hindi, Urdu
Literacy:
definition: age 15 and over has ever attended school
total population: 98.1%
male: 98.6%
female: 97.5% (1995 est.)

Government

Country name:
conventional long form: Co-operative Republic of Guyana
conventional short form: Guyana
former: British Guiana
Government type: republic within the Commonwealth
Capital: Georgetown
Administrative divisions: 10 regions; Barima-Waini, Cuyuni-Mazaruni, Demerara-Mahaica, East Berbice-Corentyne, Essequibo Islands-West Demerara, Mahaica-Berbice, Pomeroon-Supenaam, Potaro-Siparuni, Upper Demerara-Berbice, Upper Takutu-Upper Essequibo
Independence: 26 May 1966 (from UK)
National holiday: Republic Day, 23 February (1970)
Constitution: 6 October 1980
Legal system: based on English common law with certain admixtures of Roman-Dutch law; has not accepted compulsory ICJ jurisdiction
Suffrage: 18 years of age; universal
Executive branch:
chief of state: President Bharrat JAGDEO (since 11 August 1999); note - assumed presidency after resignation of President JAGAN
head of government: Prime Minister Samuel HINDS (since NA December 1997)
cabinet: Cabinet of Ministers appointed by the president, responsible to the legislature
elections: president elected by the majority party in the National Assembly following legislative elections, which must be held at least every five years; elections

Guyana (continued)

last held 19 March 2001 (next to be held NA); prime minister appointed by the president
election results: President Bharrat JAGDEO reelected; percent of legislative vote - NA%
Legislative branch: unicameral National Assembly (65 seats, 53 elected by popular vote, 10 elected by the ten Regional Democratic Councils, and 2 elected by the National Congress of Local Democratic Organs; members serve five-year terms)
elections: last held 19 March 2001 (next to be held NA March 2006)
election results: percent of vote by party - NA%; seats by party - PPP/C 34, PNC 27, GAP and WPA 2, ROAR 1, TUF 1
Judicial branch: Supreme Court of Judicature; Judicial Court of Appeal; High Court
Political parties and leaders: Alliance for Guyana or AFG (includes Guyana Labor Party or GLP and Working People's Alliance or WPA [Rupert ROOPNARINE]; Guyana Action Party or GAP [leader NA]; Guyana Labor Party or GLP [leader NA]; People's National Congress or PNC [Hugh Desmond HOYTE]; People's Progressive Party or PPP [Janet JAGEN]; Rise, Organize and Rebuild or ROAR [Ravi DEV]; The United Force or TUF [Manzoor NADIR]; Working People's Alliance or WPA [Rupert ROOPARNINE]
Political pressure groups and leaders: Civil Liberties Action Committee or CLAC; Guyana Council of Indian Organizations or GCIO; Rise, Organize and Rebuild or ROAR [Ravi DEV]; Trades Union Congress or TUC
note: the GCIO and the CLAC are small and active but not well organized
International organization participation: ACP, C, Caricom, CCC, CDB, ECLAC, FAO, G-77, IADB, IBRD, ICAO, ICFTU, ICRM, IDA, IFAD, IFC, IFRCS, ILO, IMF, IMO, Intelsat (nonsignatory user), Interpol, IOC, ISO (subscriber), ITU, LAES, NAM, OAS, OIC, OPANAL, OPCW, PCA, UN, UNCTAD, UNESCO, UNIDO, UPU, WCL, WFTU, WHO, WIPO, WMO, WTrO
Diplomatic representation in the US:
chief of mission: Ambassador Dr. Ali Odeen ISHMAEL
chancery: 2490 Tracy Place NW, Washington, DC 20008
telephone: [1] (202) 265-6900
consulate(s) general: New York
Diplomatic representation from the US:
chief of mission: Ambassador Ronald D. GODARD
embassy: 100 Young and Duke Streets, Kingston, Georgetown
mailing address: P. O. Box 10507, Georgetown
telephone: [592] (2) 54900 through 54909, 57960 through 57969
FAX: [592] (2) 58497
Flag description: green, with a red isosceles triangle (based on the hoist side) superimposed on a long, yellow arrowhead; there is a narrow, black border between the red and yellow, and a narrow, white border between the yellow and the green

Economy

Economy - overview: Severe drought and political turmoil contributed to Guyana's negative growth of -1.8% for 1998 following six straight years of growth of 5% or better. Growth came back to a positive 1.8% in 1999 and 3% in 2000. Underlying growth factors have included expansion in the key agricultural and mining sectors, a more favorable atmosphere for business initiative, a more realistic exchange rate, a moderate inflation rate, and continued support by international organizations. President JAGDEO, the former finance minister, is taking steps to reform the economy, including drafting an investment code and restructuring the inefficient and unresponsive public sector. Problems include a shortage of skilled labor and a deficient infrastructure. The government must persist in efforts to manage its sizable external debt and attract new investment.
GDP: purchasing power parity - $3.4 billion (2000 est.)
GDP - real growth rate: 3% (2000 est.)
GDP - per capita: purchasing power parity - $4,800 (2000 est.)
GDP - composition by sector:
agriculture: 34.7%
industry: 32.5%
services: 32.8% (1998 est.)
Population below poverty line: NA%
Household income or consumption by percentage share:
lowest 10%: NA%
highest 10%: NA%
Inflation rate (consumer prices): 5.9% (2000 est.)
Labor force: 245,492 (1992)
Labor force - by occupation: agriculture NA%, industry NA%, services NA%
Unemployment rate: 12% (1992 est.)
Budget:
revenues: $220.1 million
expenditures: $286.4 million, including capital expenditures of $86.6 million (1998)
Industries: bauxite, sugar, rice milling, timber, fishing (shrimp), textiles, gold mining
Industrial production growth rate: 7.1% (1997 est.)
Electricity - production: 455 million kWh (1999)
Electricity - production by source:
fossil fuel: 98.9%
hydro: 1.1%
nuclear: 0%
other: 0% (1999)
Electricity - consumption: 423.2 million kWh (1999)
Electricity - exports: 0 kWh (1999)
Electricity - imports: 0 kWh (1999)
Agriculture - products: sugar, rice, wheat, vegetable oils; beef, pork, poultry, dairy products; forest and fishery potential not exploited
Exports: $570 million (f.o.b., 2000 est.)
Exports - commodities: sugar, gold, bauxite/alumina, rice, shrimp, molasses, rum, timber
Exports - partners: US 22%, Canada 22%, UK 18%, Netherlands Antilles 11%, Jamaica (1999)
Imports: $660 million (c.i.f., 2000 est.)
Imports - commodities: manufactures, machinery, petroleum, food
Imports - partners: US 29%, Trinidad and Tobago 18%, Netherlands Antilles 16%, UK 7%, Japan (1999)
Debt - external: $1.1 billion (2000)
Economic aid - recipient: $84 million (1995), Heavily Indebted Poor Country Initiative (HIPC) $253 million (1997)
Currency: Guyanese dollar (GYD)
Currency code: GYD
Exchange rates: Guyanese dollars per US dollar - 184.1 (November 2000), 182.2 (2000), 178.0 (1999), 150.5 (1998), 142.4 (1997), 140.4 (1996)
Fiscal year: calendar year

Communications

Telephones - main lines in use: 70,000 (2000)
Telephones - mobile cellular: 6,100 (2000)
Telephone system:
general assessment: fair system for long-distance calling
domestic: microwave radio relay network for trunk lines
international: tropospheric scatter to Trinidad; satellite earth station - 1 Intelsat (Atlantic Ocean)
Radio broadcast stations: AM 3, FM 3, shortwave 1 (1998)
Radios: 420,000 (1997)
Television broadcast stations: 3 (one public station; two private stations which relay US satellite services) (1997)
Televisions: 46,000 (1997)
Internet country code: .gy
Internet Service Providers (ISPs): 3 (2000)
Internet users: 3,000 (2000)

Transportation

Railways:
total: 187 km (all dedicated to ore transport)
standard gauge: 139 km 1.435-m gauge
narrow gauge: 48 km 0.914-m gauge
Highways:
total: 7,970 km
paved: 590 km
unpaved: 7,380 km (1996)
Waterways: 5,900 km (total length of navigable waterways)
note: Berbice, Demerara, and Essequibo rivers are navigable by oceangoing vessels for 150 km, 100 km, and 80 km, respectively
Ports and harbors: Bartica, Georgetown, Linden, New Amsterdam, Parika
Merchant marine:
total: 2 ships (1,000 GRT or over) totaling 2,929 GRT/4,507 DWT
ships by type: cargo 2 (2000 est.)
Airports: 51 (2000 est.)

Guyana (continued)

Airports - with paved runways:
total: 6
1,524 to 2,437 m: 3
914 to 1,523 m: 1
under 914 m: 2 (2000 est.)
Airports - with unpaved runways:
total: 45
1,524 to 2,437 m: 1
914 to 1,523 m: 8
under 914 m: 36 (2000 est.)

Military

Military branches: Guyana Defense Force (GDF; includes Ground Forces, Coast Guard, and Air Corps), Guyana People's Militia (GPM), Guyana National Service (GNS), Guyana Police Force
Military manpower - availability:
males age 15-49: 204,938 (2001 est.)
Military manpower - fit for military service:
males age 15-49: 154,259 (2001 est.)
Military expenditures - dollar figure: $7 million (FY94)
Military expenditures - percent of GDP: 1.7% (FY94)

Transnational Issues

Disputes - international: all of the area west of the Essequibo (river) claimed by Venezuela; Suriname claims area between New (Upper Courantyne) and Courantyne/Kutari [Koetari] rivers (all headwaters of the Courantyne)
Illicit drugs: transshipment point for narcotics from South America - primarily Venezuela - to Europe and the US; producer of cannabis

Haiti

Introduction

Background: One of the poorest countries in the Western Hemisphere, Haiti has been plagued by political violence for most of its history. Over three decades of dictatorship followed by military rule ended in 1990 when Jean-Bertrand ARISTIDE was elected president. Most of his term was usurped by a military takeover, but he was able to return to office in 1994 and oversee the installation of a close associate to the presidency in 1996. ARISTIDE won a second term as president in 2000, and took office early the following year.

Geography

Location: Caribbean, western one-third of the island of Hispaniola, between the Caribbean Sea and the North Atlantic Ocean, west of the Dominican Republic
Geographic coordinates: 19 00 N, 72 25 W
Map references: Central America and the Caribbean
Area:
total: 27,750 sq km
land: 27,560 sq km
water: 190 sq km
Area - comparative: slightly smaller than Maryland
Land boundaries:
total: 275 km
border countries: Dominican Republic 275 km
Coastline: 1,771 km
Maritime claims:
contiguous zone: 24 NM
continental shelf: to depth of exploitation
exclusive economic zone: 200 NM
territorial sea: 12 NM
Climate: tropical; semiarid where mountains in east cut off trade winds
Terrain: mostly rough and mountainous
Elevation extremes:
lowest point: Caribbean Sea 0 m
highest point: Chaine de la Selle 2,680 m
Natural resources: bauxite, copper, calcium carbonate, gold, marble, hydropower
Land use:
arable land: 20%
permanent crops: 13%
permanent pastures: 18%
forests and woodland: 5%
other: 44% (1993 est.)
Irrigated land: 750 sq km (1993 est.)
Natural hazards: lies in the middle of the hurricane belt and subject to severe storms from June to October; occasional flooding and earthquakes; periodic droughts
Environment - current issues: extensive deforestation (much of the remaining forested land is being cleared for agriculture and used as fuel); soil erosion; inadequate supplies of potable water
Environment - international agreements:
party to: Biodiversity, Climate Change, Desertification, Law of the Sea, Marine Dumping, Marine Life Conservation, Ozone Layer Protection, Ship Pollution
signed, but not ratified: Hazardous Wastes, Nuclear Test Ban
Geography - note: shares island of Hispaniola with Dominican Republic (western one-third is Haiti, eastern two-thirds is the Dominican Republic)

People

Population: 6,964,549
note: estimates for this country explicitly take into account the effects of excess mortality due to AIDS; this can result in lower life expectancy, higher infant mortality and death rates, lower population and growth rates, and changes in the distribution of population by age and sex than would otherwise be expected (July 2001 est.)
Age structure:
0-14 years: 40.31% (male 1,421,945; female 1,385,580)
15-64 years: 55.52% (male 1,869,323; female 1,997,246)
65 years and over: 4.17% (male 140,556; female 149,899) (2001 est.)
Population growth rate: 1.4% (2001 est.)
Birth rate: 31.68 births/1,000 population (2001 est.)
Death rate: 15 deaths/1,000 population (2001 est.)
Net migration rate: -2.64 migrant(s)/1,000 population (2001 est.)
Sex ratio:
at birth: 1.05 male(s)/female
under 15 years: 1.03 male(s)/female
15-64 years: 0.94 male(s)/female
65 years and over: 0.94 male(s)/female
total population: 0.97 male(s)/female (2001 est.)
Infant mortality rate: 95.23 deaths/1,000 live births (2001 est.)
Life expectancy at birth:
total population: 49.38 years
male: 47.67 years
female: 51.17 years (2001 est.)

Haiti (continued)

Total fertility rate: 4.4 children born/woman (2001 est.)
HIV/AIDS - adult prevalence rate: 5.17% (1999 est.)
HIV/AIDS - people living with HIV/AIDS: 210,000 (1999 est.)
HIV/AIDS - deaths: 23,000 (1999 est.)
Nationality:
noun: Haitian(s)
adjective: Haitian
Ethnic groups: black 95%, mulatto and white 5%
Religions: Roman Catholic 80%, Protestant 16% (Baptist 10%, Pentecostal 4%, Adventist 1%, other 1%), none 1%, other 3% (1982)
note: roughly one-half of the population also practices Voodoo
Languages: French (official), Creole (official)
Literacy:
definition: age 15 and over can read and write
total population: 45%
male: 48%
female: 42.2% (1995 est.)

Government

Country name:
conventional long form: Republic of Haiti
conventional short form: Haiti
local long form: Republique d'Haiti
local short form: Haiti
Government type: elected government
Capital: Port-au-Prince
Administrative divisions: 9 departments (departements, singular - departement); Artibonite, Centre, Grand'Anse, Nord, Nord-Est, Nord-Ouest, Ouest, Sud, Sud-Est
Independence: 1 January 1804 (from France)
National holiday: Independence Day, 1 January (1804)
Constitution: approved March 1987; suspended June 1988, with most articles reinstated March 1989; in October 1991, government claimed to be observing the constitution; return to constitutional rule, October 1994
Legal system: based on Roman civil law system; accepts compulsory ICJ jurisdiction
Suffrage: 18 years of age; universal
Executive branch:
chief of state: President Jean-Bertrand ARISTIDE (since 7 February 2001)
head of government: Prime Minister Jean-Marie CHERESTAL (since 9 February 2001)
cabinet: Cabinet chosen by the prime minister in consultation with the president
elections: president elected by popular vote for a five-year term; election last held 26 November 2000 (next to be held NA 2005); prime minister appointed by the president, ratified by the Congress
election results: Jean-Bertrand ARISTIDE elected president; percent of vote - Jean-Bertrand ARISTIDE 92%
Legislative branch: bicameral National Assembly or Assemblee Nationale consists of the Senate (27 seats; members serve six-year terms; one-third elected every two years) and the Chamber of Deputies (83 seats; members are elected by popular vote to serve four-year terms)
elections: Senate - last held for two-thirds of seats 21 May 2000, with runoffs on 9 July boycotted by the opposition; about eight seats still disputed; election for remaining one-third held on 26 November 2000 (next to be held NA 2002); Chamber of Deputies - last held 21 May 2000, with runoffs on 30 July boycotted by the opposition; one vacant seat rerun 26 November 2000 (next election NA 2004)
election results: Senate - percent of vote by party - NA%; seats by party - FL 26, independent 1; Chamber of Deputies - percent of vote by party - NA%; seats by party - FL 73, OPL 1, other minor parties and independents 9
Judicial branch: Supreme Court or Cour de Cassation
Political parties and leaders: Alliance for the Liberation and Advancement of Haiti or ALAH [Reynold GEORGES]; Assembly of Progressive National Democrats or RDNP [Leslie MANIGAT]; Convergence (opposition coalition composed of ESPACE, OPL, and MOCHRENA) [Gerard PIERRE-CHARLES, Evans PAUL, Luc MESADIEU, Victor BENOIT]; Democratic Consultation Group coalition or ESPACE [Evans PAUL, Victor Benoit] composed of the following parties: National Congress of Democratic Movements or KONAKOM, National Progressive Revolutionary Party or PANPRA, Generation 2004, and Haiti Can; Haitian Christian Democratic Party or PDCH [Marie-France CLAUDE]; Haitian Democratic Party or PADEM [Clark PARENT]; Lavalas Family or FL [Jean-Bertrand ARISTIDE]; Mobilization for National Development or MDN [Hubert DE RONCERAY]; Movement for National Reconstruction or MRN [Rene THEODORE]; Movement for the Installation of Democracy in Haiti or MIDH [Marc BAZIN]; Movement for the Organization of the Country or MOP [Gesner COMEAU and Jean MOLIERE]; National Front for Change and Democracy or FNCD [Evans PAUL and Turneb DELPE]; New Christian Movement for a New Haiti or MOCHRENA [Luc MESADIEU]; Struggling People's Organization or OPL [Gerard PIERRE-CHARLES]
Political pressure groups and leaders: Autonomous Haitian Workers or CATH; Confederation of Haitian Workers or CTH; Federation of Workers Trade Unions or FOS; National Popular Assembly or APN; Papaye Peasants Movement or MPP; Popular Organizations Gathering Power or PROP; Roman Catholic Church
International organization participation: ACCT, ACP, Caricom (observer), CCC, ECLAC, FAO, G-77, IADB, IAEA, IBRD, ICAO, ICRM, IDA, IFAD, IFC, IFRCS, ILO, IMF, IMO, Intelsat, Interpol, IOC, IOM, ITU, LAES, OAS, OPANAL, OPCW, PCA, UN, UNCTAD, UNESCO, UNIDO, UPU, WCL, WFTU, WHO, WIPO, WMO, WToO, WTrO
Diplomatic representation in the US:
chief of mission: Ambassador (vacant); Charge d'Affaires Louis Harold JOSEPH
chancery: 2311 Massachusetts Avenue NW, Washington, DC 20008
telephone: [1] (202) 332-4090
FAX: [1] (202) 745-7215
consulate(s) general: Boston, Chicago, Miami, New York, and San Juan (Puerto Rico)
Diplomatic representation from the US:
chief of mission: Ambassador Brian Dean CURRAN
embassy: 5 Harry Truman Boulevard, Port-au-Prince
mailing address: P. O. Box 1761, Port-au-Prince
telephone: [509] 222-0354, 222-0269, 222-0200, 223-4776
FAX: [509] 23-1641
Flag description: two equal horizontal bands of blue (top) and red with a centered white rectangle bearing the coat of arms, which contains a palm tree flanked by flags and two cannons above a scroll bearing the motto L'UNION FAIT LA FORCE (Union Makes Strength)

Economy

Economy - overview: About 80% of the population lives in abject poverty. Nearly 70% of all Haitians depend on the agriculture sector, which consists mainly of small-scale subsistence farming and employs about two-thirds of the economically active work force. The country has experienced little job creation since the former President PREVAL took office in February 1996, although the informal economy is growing. Following legislative elections in May 2000, fraught with irregularities, international donors - including the US and EU - suspended almost all aid to Haiti. This destabilized the Haitian currency, the gourde, and, combined with a 40% fuel price hike in September, caused widespread price increases. Prices appear to have leveled off in January 2001.
GDP: purchasing power parity - $12.7 billion (2000 est.)
GDP - real growth rate: 1.2% (2000 est.)
GDP - per capita: purchasing power parity - $1,800 (2000 est.)
GDP - composition by sector:
agriculture: 32%
industry: 20%
services: 48% (1999 est.)
Population below poverty line: 80% (1998 est.)
Household income or consumption by percentage share:
lowest 10%: NA%
highest 10%: NA%
Inflation rate (consumer prices): 19% (2000 est.)
Labor force: 3.6 million (1995)
note: shortage of skilled labor, unskilled labor abundant (1998)
Labor force - by occupation: agriculture 66%, services 25%, industry 9%
Unemployment rate: widespread unemployment and underemployment; more than two-thirds of the labor force do not have formal jobs (1999)
Budget:
revenues: $317 million
expenditures: $362 million, including capital expenditures of $84 million (FY99/00 est.)

Haiti (continued)

Industries: sugar refining, flour milling, textiles, cement, tourism, light assembly industries based on imported parts
Industrial production growth rate: 0.6% (1997 est.)
Electricity - production: 672 million kWh (1999)
Electricity - production by source:
fossil fuel: 52.83%
hydro: 47.17%
nuclear: 0%
other: 0% (1999)
Electricity - consumption: 625 million kWh (1999)
Electricity - exports: 0 kWh (1999)
Electricity - imports: 0 kWh (1999)
Agriculture - products: coffee, mangoes, sugarcane, rice, corn, sorghum; wood
Exports: $186 million (f.o.b., 1999)
Exports - commodities: manufactures, coffee, oils, mangoes
Exports - partners: US 89%, EU 8% (1999)
Imports: $1.2 billion (c.i.f., 1999)
Imports - commodities: food, machinery and transport equipment, fuels, raw materials
Imports - partners: US 60%, EU 13% (1999)
Debt - external: $1 billion (1998 est.)
Economic aid - recipient: $730.6 million (1995)
Currency: gourde (HTG)
Currency code: HTG
Exchange rates: gourdes per US dollar - 23.761 (January 2001), 22.524 (2000), 17.965 (1999), 16.505 (1998), 17.311 (1997), 15.093 (1996)
Fiscal year: 1 October - 30 September

Communications

Telephones - main lines in use: 60,000 (1997)
Telephones - mobile cellular: 0 (1995)
Telephone system:
general assessment: domestic facilities barely adequate; international facilities slightly better
domestic: coaxial cable and microwave radio relay trunk service
international: satellite earth station - 1 Intelsat (Atlantic Ocean)
Radio broadcast stations: AM 41, FM 26, shortwave 0 (1999)
Radios: 415,000 (1997)
Television broadcast stations: 2 (plus a cable TV service) (1997)
Televisions: 38,000 (1997)
Internet country code: .ht
Internet Service Providers (ISPs): 3 (2000)
Internet users: 6,000 (2000)

Transportation

Railways:
total: 40 km (single track; privately owned industrial line) - closed in early 1990s
narrow gauge: 40 km 0.760-m gauge
Highways:
total: 4,160 km
paved: 1,011 km
unpaved: 3,149 km (1996)
Waterways: NEGL; less than 100 km navigable
Ports and harbors: Cap-Haitien, Gonaives, Jacmel, Jeremie, Les Cayes, Miragoane, Port-au-Prince, Port-de-Paix, Saint-Marc
Merchant marine: none (2000 est.)
Airports: 13 (2000 est.)
Airports - with paved runways:
total: 3
2,438 to 3,047 m: 1
914 to 1,523 m: 2 (2000 est.)
Airports - with unpaved runways:
total: 10
914 to 1,523 m: 2
under 914 m: 8 (2000 est.)

Military

Military branches: Haitian National Police (HNP)
note: the regular Haitian Army, Navy, and Air Force have been demobilized but still exist on paper until constitutionally abolished
Military manpower - military age: 18 years of age
Military manpower - availability:
males age 15-49: 1,635,253 (2001 est.)
Military manpower - fit for military service:
males age 15-49: 888,305 (2001 est.)
Military manpower - reaching military age annually:
males: 87,049 (2001 est.)
Military expenditures - dollar figure: $NA; note - mainly for police and security activities
Military expenditures - percent of GDP: NA%

Transnational Issues

Disputes - international: claims US-administered Navassa Island
Illicit drugs: major Caribbean transshipment point for cocaine en route to the US and Europe; vulnerable to money laundering

Heard Island and McDonald Islands
(territory of Australia)

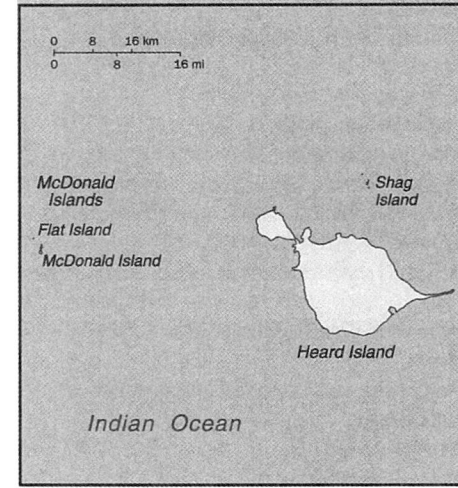

Introduction

Background: These uninhabited, barren islands were transferred from the UK to Australia in 1947. Populated by large numbers of seal and bird species, the islands have been designated a nature preserve.

Geography

Location: Southern Africa, islands in the Indian Ocean, about two-thirds of the way from Madagascar to Antarctica
Geographic coordinates: 53 06 S, 72 31 E
Map references: Antarctic Region
Area:
total: 412 sq km
land: 412 sq km
water: 0 sq km
Area - comparative: slightly more than two times the size of Washington, DC
Land boundaries: 0 km
Coastline: 101.9 km
Maritime claims:
exclusive fishing zone: 200 NM
territorial sea: 3 NM
Climate: antarctic
Terrain: Heard Island - bleak and mountainous, with a quiescent volcano; McDonald Islands - small and rocky
Elevation extremes:
lowest point: Southern Ocean 0 m
highest point: Big Ben 2,745 m
Natural resources: none
Land use:
arable land: 0%
permanent crops: 0%
permanent pastures: 0%
forests and woodland: 0%
other: 100%
Irrigated land: 0 sq km (1993)

Heard Island and McDonald Islands
(continued)

Natural hazards: Heard Island is dominated by a dormant volcano called Big Ben
Environment - current issues: NA
Geography - note: primarily used for research stations

People

Population: uninhabited (July 2001 est.)

Government

Country name:
conventional long form: Territory of Heard Island and McDonald Islands
conventional short form: Heard Island and McDonald Islands
Dependency status: territory of Australia; administered from Canberra by the Department of the Environment, Sport, and Territories
Legal system: the laws of Australia, where applicable, apply
Diplomatic representation in the US: none (territory of Australia)
Diplomatic representation from the US: none (territory of Australia)
Flag description: the flag of Australia is used

Economy

Economy - overview: no economic activity

Communications

Internet country code: .hm

Transportation

Waterways: none
Ports and harbors: none; offshore anchorage only

Military

Military - note: defense is the responsibility of Australia

Transnational Issues

Disputes - international: none

Holy See (Vatican City)

Introduction

Background: Popes in their secular role ruled much of the Italian peninsula for more than a thousand years until the mid 19th century, when many of the Papal States were seized by the newly united Kingdom of Italy. In 1870, the pope's holdings were further circumscribed when Rome itself was annexed. Disputes between a series of "prisoner" popes and Italy were resolved in 1929 by three Lateran Treaties, which established the independent state of Vatican City and granted Roman Catholicism special status in Italy. In 1984, a concordat between the Vatican and Italy modified certain of the earlier treaty provisions, including the primacy of Roman Catholicism as the Italian state religion. Present concerns of the Holy See include the failing health of Pope John Paul II, interreligious dialogue and reconciliation, and the adjustment of church doctrine in an era of rapid change and globalization. About 1 billion people worldwide profess the Catholic faith.

Geography

Location: Southern Europe, an enclave of Rome (Italy)
Geographic coordinates: 41 54 N, 12 27 E
Map references: Europe
Area:
total: 0.44 sq km
land: 0.44 sq km
water: 0 sq km
Area - comparative: about 0.7 times the size of The Mall in Washington, DC
Land boundaries:
total: 3.2 km
border countries: Italy 3.2 km
Coastline: 0 km (landlocked)
Maritime claims: none (landlocked)
Climate: temperate; mild, rainy winters (September to mid-May) with hot, dry summers (May to September)
Terrain: low hill
Elevation extremes:
lowest point: unnamed location 19 m
highest point: unnamed location 75 m
Natural resources: none
Land use:
arable land: 0%
permanent crops: 0%
permanent pastures: 0%
forests and woodland: 0%
other: 100% (urban area)
Irrigated land: 0 sq km (1993)
Natural hazards: NA
Environment - current issues: NA
Environment - international agreements:
party to: Marine Dumping, Ship Pollution
signed, but not ratified: Air Pollution, Environmental Modification
Geography - note: urban; landlocked; enclave of Rome, Italy; world's smallest state; outside the Vatican City, 13 buildings in Rome and Castel Gandolfo (the pope's summer residence) enjoy extraterritorial rights

People

Population: 890 (July 2001 est.)
Population growth rate: 1.15% (2001 est.)
HIV/AIDS - adult prevalence rate: NA%
HIV/AIDS - people living with HIV/AIDS: NA
HIV/AIDS - deaths: NA
Nationality:
noun: none
adjective: none
Ethnic groups: Italians, Swiss, other
Religions: Roman Catholic
Languages: Italian, Latin, French, various other languages
Literacy:
definition: NA
total population: 100%
male: NA%
female: NA%

Government

Country name:
conventional long form: The Holy See (State of the Vatican City)
conventional short form: Holy See (Vatican City)
local long form: Santa Sede (Stato della Citta del Vaticano)
local short form: Santa Sede (Citta del Vaticano)
Government type: ecclesiastical
Capital: Vatican City
Independence: 11 February 1929 (from Italy)
National holiday: Coronation Day of Pope JOHN PAUL II, 22 October (1978)
Constitution: Apostolic Constitution of 1967 (effective 1 March 1968)
Legal system: NA
Suffrage: limited to cardinals less than 80 years old

Holy See (Vatican City) (continued)

Executive branch:
chief of state: Pope JOHN PAUL II (since 16 October 1978)
head of government: Secretary of State Cardinal Angelo SODANO (since 2 December 1990)
cabinet: Pontifical Commission appointed by the pope
elections: pope elected for life by the College of Cardinals; election last held 16 October 1978 (next to be held after the death of the current pope); secretary of state appointed by the pope
election results: Karol WOJTYLA elected pope
Legislative branch: unicameral Pontifical Commission
Judicial branch: none; normally handled by Italy
Political parties and leaders: none
Political pressure groups and leaders: none (exclusive of influence exercised by church officers)
International organization participation: CE (observer), IAEA, ICFTU, Intelsat, IOM (observer), ITU, NAM (guest), OAS (observer), OPCW, OSCE, UN (observer), UNCTAD, UNHCR, UPU, WHO (observer), WIPO, WToO (observer), WTrO (observer)
Diplomatic representation in the US:
chief of mission: Apostolic Nuncio Archbishop Gabriele MONTALVO
chancery: 3339 Massachusetts Avenue NW, Washington, DC 20008
telephone: [1] (202) 333-7121
Diplomatic representation from the US:
chief of mission: Ambassador (vacant)
embassy: Villa Domiziana, Via delle Terme Deciane 26, 00162 Rome
mailing address: PSC 59, Box F, APO AE 09624
telephone: [39] (06) 4674-3428
FAX: [39] (06) 5758346
Flag description: two vertical bands of yellow (hoist side) and white with the crossed keys of Saint Peter and the papal miter centered in the white band

Economy

Economy - overview: This unique, noncommercial economy is supported financially by contributions (known as Peter's Pence) from Roman Catholics throughout the world, the sale of postage stamps and tourist mementos, fees for admission to museums, and the sale of publications. The incomes and living standards of lay workers are comparable to, or somewhat better than, those of counterparts who work in the city of Rome.
Population below poverty line: NA%
Household income or consumption by percentage share:
lowest 10%: NA%
highest 10%: NA%
Labor force: NA
Labor force - by occupation: agriculture NA%, industry NA%, services NA%; note - dignitaries, priests, nuns, guards, and 3,000 lay workers live outside the Vatican
Budget:
revenues: $209.6 million
expenditures: $198.5 million, including capital expenditures of $NA (1997)
Industries: printing and production of a small amount of mosaics and staff uniforms; worldwide banking and financial activities
Electricity - production by source:
fossil fuel: NA%
hydro: NA%
nuclear: NA%
other: NA%
Electricity - consumption: NA kWh
Electricity - imports: NA kWh; note - electricity supplied by Italy
Economic aid - recipient: none
Currency: Italian lira (ITL); euro (EUR)
Currency code: ITL; EUR
Exchange rates: euros per US dollar - 1.0659 (January 2001), 1.0854 (2000), 0.9386 (1999); Vatican lire per US dollar - 2,099 (2000), 1817.2 (1999), 1,736.2 (1998), 1,703.1 (1997), 1,542.9 (1996); note - the Vatican lira is at par with the Italian lira; the Vatican will start using euros in 2002 in conjunction with Italy at a fixed rate of 1,936.17 lire per euro
Fiscal year: calendar year

Communications

Telephones - main lines in use: NA
Telephones - mobile cellular: NA
Telephone system:
general assessment: automatic exchange
domestic: tied into Italian system
international: uses Italian system
Radio broadcast stations: AM 3, FM 4, shortwave 2 (1998)
Radios: NA
Television broadcast stations: 1 (1996)
Televisions: NA
Internet country code: .va
Internet Service Providers (ISPs): 93 (Holy See and Italy) (2000)
Internet users: NA

Transportation

Railways:
total: 862 m; note - a spur of the Italian Railways system, serving Rome's Saint Peter's station
standard gauge: 862 m 1.435-m gauge (1999)
Highways: none; all city streets
Waterways: none
Ports and harbors: none
Airports: none
Heliports: 1 (2000 est.)

Military

Military - note: defense is the responsibility of Italy; Swiss Papal Guards are posted at entrances to the Vatican City to provide security and protect the Pope

Transnational Issues

Disputes - international: none

Honduras

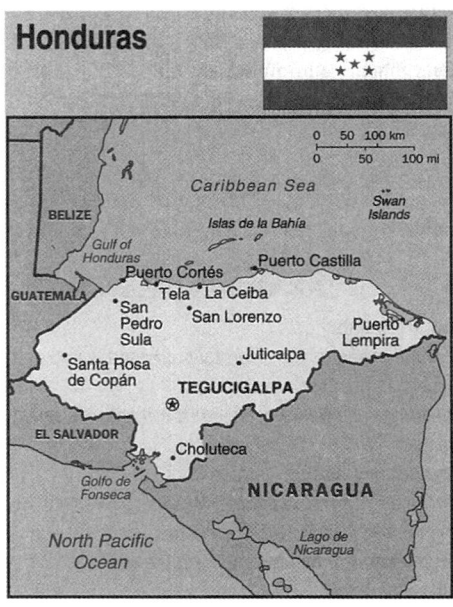

Introduction

Background: Part of Spain's vast empire in the New World, Honduras became an independent nation in 1821. After two and one-half decades of mostly military rule, a freely elected civilian government came to power in 1982. During the 1980s, Honduras proved a haven for anti-Sandinista contras fighting the Marxist Nicaraguan Government and an ally to Salvadoran Government forces fighting against leftist guerrillas.

Geography

Location: Middle America, bordering the Caribbean Sea, between Guatemala and Nicaragua and bordering the North Pacific Ocean, between El Salvador and Nicaragua
Geographic coordinates: 15 00 N, 86 30 W
Map references: Central America and the Caribbean
Area:
total: 112,090 sq km
land: 111,890 sq km
water: 200 sq km
Area - comparative: slightly larger than Tennessee
Land boundaries:
total: 1,520 km
border countries: Guatemala 256 km, El Salvador 342 km, Nicaragua 922 km
Coastline: 820 km
Maritime claims:
contiguous zone: 24 NM
continental shelf: natural extension of territory or to 200 NM
exclusive economic zone: 200 NM
territorial sea: 12 NM
Climate: subtropical in lowlands, temperate in mountains
Terrain: mostly mountains in interior, narrow coastal plains

Honduras (continued)

Elevation extremes:
lowest point: Caribbean Sea 0 m
highest point: Cerro Las Minas 2,870 m
Natural resources: timber, gold, silver, copper, lead, zinc, iron ore, antimony, coal, fish, hydropower
Land use:
arable land: 15%
permanent crops: 3%
permanent pastures: 14%
forests and woodland: 54%
other: 14% (1993 est.)
Irrigated land: 740 sq km (1993 est.)
Natural hazards: frequent, but generally mild, earthquakes; damaging hurricanes and floods along Caribbean coast
Environment - current issues: urban population expanding; deforestation results from logging and the clearing of land for agricultural purposes; further land degradation and soil erosion hastened by uncontrolled development and improper land use practices such as farming of marginal lands; mining activities polluting Lago de Yojoa (the country's largest source of fresh water) as well as several rivers and streams with heavy metals; severe Hurricane Mitch damage
Environment - international agreements:
party to: Biodiversity, Climate Change, Climate Change-Kyoto Protocol, Desertification, Endangered Species, Hazardous Wastes, Law of the Sea, Marine Dumping, Nuclear Test Ban, Ozone Layer Protection, Ship Pollution, Tropical Timber 83, Tropical Timber 94, Wetlands
signed, but not ratified: none of the selected agreements

People

Population: 6,406,052
note: estimates for this country explicitly take into account the effects of excess mortality due to AIDS; this can result in lower life expectancy, higher infant mortality and death rates, lower population and growth rates, and changes in the distribution of population by age and sex than would otherwise be expected (July 2001 est.)
Age structure:
0-14 years: 42.22% (male 1,381,823; female 1,322,684)
15-64 years: 54.21% (male 1,719,593; female 1,753,003)
65 years and over: 3.57% (male 108,271; female 120,678) (2001 est.)
Population growth rate: 2.43% (2001 est.)
Birth rate: 31.94 births/1,000 population (2001 est.)
Death rate: 5.52 deaths/1,000 population (2001 est.)
Net migration rate: -2.12 migrant(s)/1,000 population (2001 est.)
Sex ratio:
at birth: 1.05 male(s)/female
under 15 years: 1.04 male(s)/female
15-64 years: 0.98 male(s)/female
65 years and over: 0.9 male(s)/female
total population: 1 male(s)/female (2001 est.)
Infant mortality rate: 30.88 deaths/1,000 live births (2001 est.)
Life expectancy at birth:
total population: 69.35 years
male: 67.51 years
female: 71.28 years (2001 est.)
Total fertility rate: 4.15 children born/woman (2001 est.)
HIV/AIDS - adult prevalence rate: 1.92% (1999 est.)
HIV/AIDS - people living with HIV/AIDS: 63,000 (1999 est.)
HIV/AIDS - deaths: 4,200 (1999 est.)
Nationality:
noun: Honduran(s)
adjective: Honduran
Ethnic groups: mestizo (mixed Amerindian and European) 90%, Amerindian 7%, black 2%, white 1%
Religions: Roman Catholic 97%, Protestant minority
Languages: Spanish, Amerindian dialects
Literacy:
definition: age 15 and over can read and write
total population: 72.7%
male: 72.6%
female: 72.7% (1995 est.)

Government

Country name:
conventional long form: Republic of Honduras
conventional short form: Honduras
local long form: Republica de Honduras
local short form: Honduras
Government type: democratic constitutional republic
Capital: Tegucigalpa
Administrative divisions: 18 departments (departamentos, singular - departamento); Atlantida, Choluteca, Colon, Comayagua, Copan, Cortes, El Paraiso, Francisco Morazan, Gracias a Dios, Intibuca, Islas de la Bahia, La Paz, Lempira, Ocotepeque, Olancho, Santa Barbara, Valle, Yoro
Independence: 15 September 1821 (from Spain)
National holiday: Independence Day, 15 September (1821)
Constitution: 11 January 1982, effective 20 January 1982; amended 1995
Legal system: rooted in Roman and Spanish civil law with increasing influence of English common law; recent judicial reforms include abandoning Napoleonic legal codes in favor of the oral adversarial system; accepts ICJ jurisdiction, with reservations
Suffrage: 18 years of age; universal and compulsory
Executive branch:
chief of state: President Carlos Roberto FLORES Facusse (since 27 January 1998); note - the president is both the chief of state and head of government; First Vice President William HANDAL (since NA); Second Vice President Gladys CABALLERO de Arevalo (since NA); Third Vice President Hector Vidal CERRATO Hernandez (since NA)
head of government: President Carlos Roberto FLORES Facusse (since 27 January 1998); note - the president is both the chief of state and head of government; First Vice President William HANDAL (since NA); Second Vice President Gladys CABALLERO de Arevalo (since NA); Third Vice President Hector Vidal CERRATO Hernandez (since NA)
cabinet: Cabinet appointed by president
elections: president elected by popular vote for a four-year term; election last held 30 November 1997 (next to be held 25 November 2001)
election results: Carlos Roberto FLORES Facusse elected president; percent of vote - Carlos Roberto FLORES Facusse (PL) 50%, Nora de MELGAR (PN) 40%, other 10%
Legislative branch: unicameral National Congress or Congreso Nacional (128 seats; members are elected proportionally to the number of votes their party's presidential candidate receives to serve four-year terms)
elections: last held on 30 November 1997 (next to be held 25 November 2001)
election results: percent of vote by party - PL 46%, PN 38%, PINU-SD 4%, PDC 2%, PUD 2%; seats by party - PL 67, PN 55, PINU-SD 3, PDC 2, PUD 1
Judicial branch: Supreme Court of Justice or Corte Suprema de Justicia (judges are elected for four-year terms by the National Congress)
Political parties and leaders: Christian Democratic Party or PDC [Efrain DIAZ Arrivillaga, president]; Democratic Unification Party or PUD [Marias FUNES Valladares, president]; Liberal Party or PL [Carlos Roberto FLORES Facusse, president]; National Innovation and Unity Party-Social Democratic Party or PINU-SD [Olban VALLADARES, president]; National Party of Honduras or PN [Carlos URBIZO, president]
Political pressure groups and leaders: Committee for the Defense of Human Rights in Honduras or CODEH; Confederation of Honduran Workers or CTH; Coordinating Committee of Popular Organizations or CCOP; General Workers Confederation or CGT; Honduran Council of Private Enterprise or COHEP; National Association of Honduran Campesinos or ANACH; National Union of Campesinos or UNC; Popular Bloc or BP; United Federation of Honduran Workers or FUTH
International organization participation: BCIE, CACM, ECLAC, FAO, G-77, IADB, IBRD, ICAO, ICFTU, ICRM, IDA, IFAD, IFC, IFRCS, ILO, IMF, IMO, Intelsat, Interpol, IOC, IOM, ISO (correspondent), ITU, LAES, LAIA (observer), MINURSO, NAM, OAS, OPANAL, OPCW, PCA, UN, UNCTAD, UNESCO, UNIDO, UPU, WCL, WFTU, WHO, WIPO, WMO, WTrO
Diplomatic representation in the US:
chief of mission: Ambassador Hugo NOE PINO
chancery: Suite 4-M, 3007 Tilden Street NW, Washington, DC 20008
telephone: [1] (202) 966-7702
FAX: [1] (202) 966-9751
consulate(s) general: Chicago, Houston, Los Angeles, Miami, New Orleans, New York, San Francisco, San Juan (Puerto Rico)

Honduras (continued)

consulate(s), honorary: Boston, Detroit, and Jacksonville
Diplomatic representation from the US:
chief of mission: Ambassador Frank ALMAGUER
embassy: Avenida La Paz, Apartado Postal No. 3453, Tegucigalpa
mailing address: American Embassy, APO AA 34022, Tegucigalpa
telephone: [504] 238-5114, 236-9320
FAX: [504] 236-9037
Flag description: three equal horizontal bands of blue (top), white, and blue with five blue five-pointed stars arranged in an X pattern centered in the white band; the stars represent the members of the former Federal Republic of Central America - Costa Rica, El Salvador, Guatemala, Honduras, and Nicaragua; similar to the flag of El Salvador, which features a round emblem encircled by the words REPUBLICA DE EL SALVADOR EN LA AMERICA CENTRAL centered in the white band; also similar to the flag of Nicaragua, which features a triangle encircled by the word REPUBLICA DE NICARAGUA on top and AMERICA CENTRAL on the bottom, centered in the white band

Economy

Economy - overview: Honduras, one of the poorest countries in the Western Hemisphere, is banking on expanded trade privileges under the Enhanced Caribbean Basin Initiative and on debt relief under the Heavily Indebted Poor Countries (HIPC) initiative. While reconstruction from 1998's Hurricane Mitch is at an advanced stage, and the country has met most of its macroeconomic targets, it failed to meet the IMF's goals to liberalize its energy and telecommunications sectors. Economic growth has rebounded nicely since the hurricane and should continue in 2001.
GDP: purchasing power parity - $17 billion (2000 est.)
GDP - real growth rate: 5% (2000 est.)
GDP - per capita: purchasing power parity - $2,700 (2000 est.)
GDP - composition by sector:
agriculture: 16.2%
industry: 31.9%
services: 51.9% (1999 est.)
Population below poverty line: 53% (1993 est.)
Household income or consumption by percentage share:
lowest 10%: 1.2%
highest 10%: 42.1% (1996)
Inflation rate (consumer prices): 11% (2000 est.)
Labor force: 2.3 million (1997 est.)
Labor force - by occupation: agriculture 29%, industry 21%, services 50% (1998 est.)
Unemployment rate: 28% (2000 est.)
Budget:
revenues: $607 million
expenditures: $411.9 million, including capital expenditures of $106 million (1999 est.)
Industries: sugar, coffee, textiles, clothing, wood products
Industrial production growth rate: 4% (1999 est.)
Electricity - production: 3.319 billion kWh (1999)
Electricity - production by source:
fossil fuel: 44.71%
hydro: 55.29%
nuclear: 0%
other: 0% (1999)
Electricity - consumption: 3.232 billion kWh (1999)
Electricity - exports: 0 kWh (1999)
Electricity - imports: 145 million kWh (1999)
Agriculture - products: bananas, coffee, citrus; beef; timber; shrimp
Exports: $2 billion (f.o.b., 2000 est.)
Exports - commodities: coffee, bananas, shrimp, lobster, meat; zinc, lumber
Exports - partners: US 35.4%, Germany 7.5%, El Salvador 6.4%, Guatemala 5.8%, Nicaragua 4.8% (1999)
Imports: $2.8 billion (f.o.b., 2000 est.)
Imports - commodities: machinery and transport equipment, industrial raw materials, chemical products, fuels, foodstuffs
Imports - partners: US 47.1%, Guatemala 7.4%, El Salvador 5.9%, Mexico 4.8%, Japan 4.7% (1999)
Debt - external: $5.4 billion (2000)
Economic aid - recipient: $557.8 million (1999)
Currency: lempira (HNL)
Currency code: HNL
Exchange rates: lempiras per US dollar - 15.1407 (December 2000), 15.1407 (2000), 14.5039 (1999), 13.8076 (1998), 13.0942 (1997), 12.8694 (1996)
Fiscal year: calendar year

Communications

Telephones - main lines in use: 234,000 (1997)
Telephones - mobile cellular: 14,427 (1997)
Telephone system:
general assessment: inadequate system
domestic: NA
international: satellite earth stations - 2 Intelsat (Atlantic Ocean); connected to Central American Microwave System
Radio broadcast stations: AM 241, FM 53, shortwave 12 (1998)
Radios: 2.45 million (1997)
Television broadcast stations: 11 (plus 17 repeaters) (1997)
Televisions: 570,000 (1997)
Internet country code: .hn
Internet Service Providers (ISPs): 8 (2000)
Internet users: 20,000 (2000)

Transportation

Railways:
total: 595 km
narrow gauge: 349 km 1.067-m gauge; 246 km 0.914-m gauge (1999)
Highways:
total: 15,400 km
paved: 3,126 km
unpaved: 12,274 km (1999 est.)
Waterways: 465 km (navigable by small craft)
Ports and harbors: La Ceiba, Puerto Castilla, Puerto Cortes, San Lorenzo, Tela, Puerto Lempira
Merchant marine:
total: 313 ships (1,000 GRT or over) totaling 760,819 GRT/820,582 DWT
ships by type: bulk 21, cargo 187, chemical tanker 7, container 4, livestock carrier 2, passenger 2, passenger/cargo 4, petroleum tanker 52, refrigerated cargo 17, roll on/roll off 8, short-sea passenger 5, specialized tanker 2, vehicle carrier 2
note: includes some foreign-owned ships registered here as a flag of convenience: Russia 4, Singapore 2, Vietnam 1 (2000 est.)
Airports: 119 (2000 est.)
Airports - with paved runways:
total: 12
2,438 to 3,047 m: 3
1,524 to 2,437 m: 2
914 to 1,523 m: 4
under 914 m: 3 (2000 est.)
Airports - with unpaved runways:
total: 107
1,524 to 2,437 m: 2
914 to 1,523 m: 21
under 914 m: 84 (2000 est.)

Military

Military branches: Army, Navy (includes Marines), Air Force
Military manpower - military age: 18 years of age
Military manpower - availability:
males age 15-49: 1,515,101 (2001 est.)
Military manpower - fit for military service:
males age 15-49: 902,220 (2001 est.)
Military manpower - reaching military age annually:
males: 72,335 (2001 est.)
Military expenditures - dollar figure: $35 million (FY99)
Military expenditures - percent of GDP: 0.6% (FY99)

Transnational Issues

Disputes - international: with respect to the maritime boundary in the Golfo de Fonseca, the ICJ referred to the line determined by the 1900 Honduras-Nicaragua Mixed Boundary Commission and advised that some tripartite resolution among El Salvador, Honduras, and Nicaragua likely would be required; the maritime boundary dispute with Nicaragua in the Caribbean Sea is before the ICJ
Illicit drugs: transshipment point for drugs and narcotics; illicit producer of cannabis, cultivated on small plots and used principally for local consumption; corruption is a major problem; vulnerable to money laundering

Hong Kong
(special administrative region of China)

Introduction

Background: Occupied by the UK in 1841, Hong Kong was formally ceded by China the following year; various adjacent lands were added later in the 19th century. Pursuant to an agreement signed by China and the UK on 19 December 1984, Hong Kong became the Hong Kong Special Administrative Region (SAR) of China on 1 July 1997. In this agreement, China has promised that, under its "one country, two systems" formula, China's socialist economic system will not be practiced in Hong Kong and that Hong Kong will enjoy a high degree of autonomy in all matters except foreign and defense affairs for the next 50 years.

Geography

Location: Eastern Asia, bordering the South China Sea and China
Geographic coordinates: 22 15 N, 114 10 E
Map references: Southeast Asia
Area:
total: 1,092 sq km
land: 1,042 sq km
water: 50 sq km
Area - comparative: six times the size of Washington, DC
Land boundaries:
total: 30 km
border countries: China 30 km
Coastline: 733 km
Maritime claims:
territorial sea: 3 NM
Climate: tropical monsoon; cool and humid in winter, hot and rainy from spring through summer, warm and sunny in fall
Terrain: hilly to mountainous with steep slopes; lowlands in north
Elevation extremes:
lowest point: South China Sea 0 m
highest point: Tai Mo Shan 958 m

Natural resources: outstanding deepwater harbor, feldspar
Land use:
arable land: 6%
permanent crops: 1%
permanent pastures: 1%
forests and woodland: 20%
other: 72% (1997 est.)
Irrigated land: 20 sq km (1997 est.)
Natural hazards: occasional typhoons
Environment - current issues: air and water pollution from rapid urbanization
Geography - note: more than 200 islands

People

Population: 7,210,505 (July 2001 est.)
Age structure:
0-14 years: 17.73% (male 677,785; female 600,781)
15-64 years: 71.52% (male 2,554,329; female 2,602,662)
65 years and over: 10.75% (male 354,199; female 420,749) (2001 est.)
Population growth rate: 1.3% (2001 est.)
Birth rate: 11.13 births/1,000 population (2001 est.)
Death rate: 6.02 deaths/1,000 population (2001 est.)
Net migration rate: 7.9 migrant(s)/1,000 population (2001 est.)
Sex ratio:
at birth: 1.07 male(s)/female
under 15 years: 1.13 male(s)/female
15-64 years: 0.98 male(s)/female
65 years and over: 0.84 male(s)/female
total population: 0.99 male(s)/female (2001 est.)
Infant mortality rate: 5.83 deaths/1,000 live births (2001 est.)
Life expectancy at birth:
total population: 79.67 years
male: 76.97 years
female: 82.55 years (2001 est.)
Total fertility rate: 1.29 children born/woman (2001 est.)
HIV/AIDS - adult prevalence rate: 0.06% (1999 est.)
HIV/AIDS - people living with HIV/AIDS: 2,500 (1999 est.)
HIV/AIDS - deaths: less than 100 (1999 est.)
Nationality:
noun: Chinese
adjective: Chinese
Ethnic groups: Chinese 95%, other 5%
Religions: eclectic mixture of local religions 90%, Christian 10%
Languages: Chinese (Cantonese), English; both are official
Literacy:
definition: age 15 and over has ever attended school
total population: 92.2%
male: 96%
female: 88.2% (1996 est.)

Government

Country name:
conventional long form: Hong Kong Special Administrative Region
conventional short form: Hong Kong
local long form: Xianggang Tebie Xingzhengqu
local short form: Xianggang
abbreviation: HK
Dependency status: special administrative region of China
Government type: NA
Administrative divisions: none (special administrative region of China)
Independence: none (special administrative region of China)
National holiday: National Day (Anniversary of the Founding of the People's Republic of China), 1 October (1949); note - 1 July 1997 is celebrated as Hong Kong Special Administrative Region Establishment Day
Constitution: Basic Law approved in March 1990 by China's National People's Congress is Hong Kong's "mini-constitution"
Legal system: based on English common law
Suffrage: direct election 18 years of age; universal for permanent residents living in the territory of Hong Kong for the past seven years; indirect election limited to about 100,000 members of functional constituencies and an 800-member election committee drawn from broad regional groupings, municipal organizations, and central government bodies
Executive branch:
chief of state: President of China JIANG Zemin (since 27 March 1993)
head of government: Chief Executive TUNG Chee-hwa (since 1 July 1997)
cabinet: Executive Council consists of three ex-officio members and 10 appointed members; ex-officio members are: Chief Secretary Anson CHAN (since 29 November 1993), Financial Secretary Donald TSANG (since 7 March 1995), and Secretary of Justice Elsie LEUNG (since 1 July 1997)
elections: NA
Legislative branch: unicameral Legislative Council or LEGCO (60 seats; 30 indirectly elected by functional constituencies, 24 elected by popular vote, and 6 elected by an 800-member election committee; members serve four-year terms)
elections: last held 10 September 2000 (next to be held NA 2004)
election results: percent of vote by party - NA%; seats by party - Democratic Party 12, Democratic Alliance for the Betterment of Hong Kong 10, Liberal Party 7, Frontier Party 5, Hong Kong Progressive Alliance 4, New Century Forum 2, Hong Kong Association for Democracy and People's Livelihood 1, independents 19
Judicial branch: The Court of Final Appeal in the Hong Kong Special Administrative Region

Hong Kong (continued)

Political parties and leaders: Association for Democracy and People's Livelihood [Frederick FUNG Kin-kee, chairman]; Citizens Party [leader NA]; Democratic Alliance for the Betterment of Hong Kong [Jasper TSANG Yok-sing, chairman]; Democratic Party [Martin LEE Chu-ming, chairman]; Frontier Party [Emily LAU Wai-hing, chairwoman]; Hong Kong Association for Democracy and People's Livelihood [leader NA]; Hong Kong Progressive Alliance [Ambrose LAU Hon-chuen]; Liberal Party [James TIEN Pei-chun, chairman]; New Century Forum [NQ Ching-fai, chairman]

note: political blocs include: pro-democracy - Association for Democracy and People's Livelihood, Citizens Party, Democratic Party, Frontier Party; pro-Beijing - Democratic Alliance for the Betterment of Hong Kong, Hong Kong Progressive Alliance, Liberal Party, New Century Forum

Political pressure groups and leaders: Chinese General Chamber of Commerce (pro-China); Chinese Manufacturers' Association of Hong Kong; Confederation of Trade Unions (pro-democracy) [LAU Chin-shek, president; LEE Cheuk-yan, general secretary]; Federation of Hong Kong Industries; Federation of Trade Unions (pro-China) [LEE Chark-tim, president]; Hong Kong Alliance in Support of the Patriotic Democratic Movement in China [Szeto WAH, chairman]; Hong Kong and Kowloon Trade Union Council (pro-Taiwan); Hong Kong General Chamber of Commerce; Hong Kong Professional Teachers' Union [CHEUNG Man-kwong, president]; Liberal Democratic Federation [HU Fa-kuang, chairman]

International organization participation: APEC, AsDB, BIS, CCC, ESCAP (associate), ICC, ICFTU, IMO (associate), Interpol (subbureau), IOC, ISO (correspondent), WCL, WMO, WToO (associate), WTrO

Diplomatic representation in the US: none (special administrative region of China)

Diplomatic representation from the US:
chief of mission: Consul General Michael KLOSSON
consulate(s) general: 26 Garden Road, Hong Kong
mailing address: PSC 464, Box 30, FPO AP 96522-0002
telephone: [852] 2523-9011
FAX: [852] 2845-1598

Flag description: red with a stylized, white, five-petal bauhinia flower in the center

Economy

Economy - overview: Hong Kong has a bustling free market economy highly dependent on international trade. Natural resources are limited, and food and raw materials must be imported. Indeed, imports and exports, including reexports, each exceed GDP in dollar value. Even before Hong Kong reverted to Chinese administration on 1 July 1997 it had extensive trade and investment ties with China. Per capita GDP compares with the level in the four big countries of Western Europe. GDP growth averaged a strong 5% in 1989-97. The widespread Asian economic difficulties in 1998 hit this trade-dependent economy quite hard, with GDP down 5%. The economy is undergoing a rapid recovery, with growth of 10% in 2000 to be followed by projected growth of 5% in 2001.

GDP: purchasing power parity - $181 billion (2000 est.)
GDP - real growth rate: 10% (2000 est.)
GDP - per capita: purchasing power parity - $25,400 (2000 est.)
GDP - composition by sector:
agriculture: 0.1%
industry: 14.3%
services: 85.6% (1999 est.)
Population below poverty line: NA%
Household income or consumption by percentage share:
lowest 10%: NA%
highest 10%: NA%
Inflation rate (consumer prices): 3.7% (2000 est.)
Labor force: 3.39 million (2000 est.)
Labor force - by occupation: wholesale and retail trade, restaurants, and hotels 31.5%, community and social services 24%, financing, insurance, and real estate 14.5%, transport and communications 11.6%, manufacturing 7.7%, construction 2.6% (October 1999)
Unemployment rate: 4.5% (2000 est.)
Budget:
revenues: $20.8 billion
expenditures: $24.5 billion, including capital expenditures of $NA (FY99/00)
Industries: textiles, clothing, tourism, electronics, plastics, toys, watches, clocks
Industrial production growth rate: 2.1% (2000)
Electricity - production: 27.726 billion kWh (1999)
Electricity - production by source:
fossil fuel: 100%
hydro: 0%
nuclear: 0%
other: 0% (1999)
Electricity - consumption: 32.202 billion kWh (1999)
Electricity - exports: 633 million kWh (1999)
Electricity - imports: 7.05 billion kWh (1999)
Agriculture - products: fresh vegetables; poultry
Exports: $204 billion (including reexports; f.o.b., 2000 est.)
Exports - commodities: clothing, textiles, footwear, electrical appliances, watches and clocks, toys
Exports - partners: China 33%, US 24%, Japan 5%, UK 4%, Germany, Singapore (1999)
Imports: $215 billion (f.o.b., 2000)
Imports - commodities: foodstuffs, transport equipment, raw materials, semimanufactures, petroleum; a large share is reexported
Imports - partners: China 44%, Japan 12%, US 7%, Taiwan 7%, South Korea, Singapore (1999)
Debt - external: $48.1 billion (1999)
Currency: Hong Kong dollar (HKD)
Currency code: HKD
Exchange rates: Hong Kong dollars per US dollar - 7.7990 (January 2001), 7.7912 (2000), 7.7575 (1999), 7.7453 (1998), 7.7421 (1997), 7.7343 (1996); note - Hong Kong became a special administrative region of China on 1 July 1997; before then, the Hong Kong dollar was linked to the US dollar at the rate of about 7.8 Hong Kong dollars per US dollar
Fiscal year: 1 April - 31 March

Communications

Telephones - main lines in use: 3.839 million (1999)
Telephones - mobile cellular: 3.7 million (December 1999)
Telephone system:
general assessment: modern facilities provide excellent domestic and international services
domestic: microwave radio relay links and extensive fiber-optic network
international: satellite earth stations - 3 Intelsat (1 Pacific Ocean and 2 Indian Ocean); coaxial cable to Guangzhou, China; access to 5 international submarine cables providing connections to ASEAN member nations, Japan, Taiwan, Australia, Middle East, and Western Europe
Radio broadcast stations: AM 7, FM 13, shortwave 0 (1998)
Radios: 4.45 million (1997)
Television broadcast stations: 4 (plus two repeaters) (1997)
Televisions: 1.84 million (1997)
Internet country code: .hk
Internet Service Providers (ISPs): 17 (2000)
Internet users: 1.85 million (2000)

Transportation

Railways:
total: 34 km
standard gauge: 34 km 1.435-m gauge (all electrified) (1996 est.)
Highways:
total: 1,831 km
paved: 1,831 km
unpaved: 0 km (1997)
Waterways: none
Ports and harbors: Hong Kong
Merchant marine:
total: 354 ships (1,000 GRT or over) totaling 10,330,662 GRT/17,227,315 DWT
ships by type: barge carrier 1, bulk 208, cargo 36, chemical tanker 7, combination bulk 2, container 59, liquefied gas 6, multi-functional large-load carrier 2, petroleum tanker 26, refrigerated cargo 3, short-sea passenger 1, vehicle carrier 3
note: includes some foreign-owned ships registered here as a flag of convenience: Bermuda 2, Belgium 1, Canada 2, China 9, Japan 3, Mongolia 1, Norway 1, South Africa 1, UK 7 (2000 est.)
Airports: 3 (2000 est.)

Hong Kong (continued)

Airports - with paved runways:
total: 3
over 3,047 m: 2
1,524 to 2,437 m: 1 (2000 est.)
Heliports: 2 (2000 est.)

Military

Military branches: Hong Kong garrison of China's People's Liberation Army (PLA) including elements of the PLA Ground Forces, PLA Navy, and PLA Air Force; these forces are under the direct leadership of the Central Military Commission in Beijing and under administrative control of the adjacent Guangzhou Military Region
Military manpower - military age: 18 years of age
Military manpower - availability:
males age 15-49: 2,020,937 (2001 est.)
Military manpower - fit for military service:
males age 15-49: 1,520,531 (2001 est.)
Military manpower - reaching military age annually:
males: 47,139 (2001 est.)
Military expenditures - dollar figure: $NA; note - separate budget for Hong Kong not established by China
Military expenditures - percent of GDP: NA%
Military - note: defense is the responsibility of China

Transnational Issues

Disputes - international: none
Illicit drugs: a hub for Southeast Asian heroin and regional stimulants trade; transshipment and money-laundering center; increasing indigenous amphetamine abuse

Howland Island
(territory of the US)

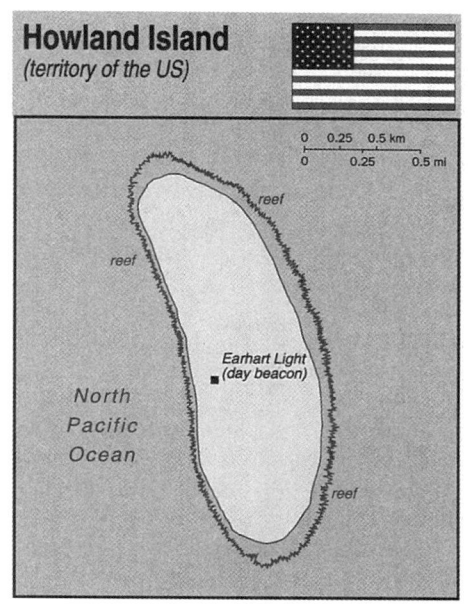

Introduction

Background: Discovered by the US early in the 19th century, the island was officially claimed by the US in 1857. Both US and British companies mined for guano until about 1890. Earhart Light is a day beacon near the middle of the west coast that was partially destroyed during World War II, but has since been rebuilt; it is named in memory of famed aviatrix Amelia EARHART. The island is administered by the US Department of the Interior as a National Wildlife Refuge.

Geography

Location: Oceania, island in the North Pacific Ocean, about one-half of the way from Hawaii to Australia
Geographic coordinates: 0 48 N, 176 38 W
Map references: Oceania
Area:
total: 1.6 sq km
land: 1.6 sq km
water: 0 sq km
Area - comparative: about three times the size of The Mall in Washington, DC
Land boundaries: 0 km
Coastline: 6.4 km
Maritime claims:
exclusive economic zone: 200 NM
territorial sea: 12 NM
Climate: equatorial; scant rainfall, constant wind, burning sun
Terrain: low-lying, nearly level, sandy, coral island surrounded by a narrow fringing reef; depressed central area
Elevation extremes:
lowest point: Pacific Ocean 0 m
highest point: unnamed location 3 m
Natural resources: guano (deposits worked until late 1800s), terrestrial and aquatic wildlife
Land use:
arable land: 0%
permanent crops: 0%
permanent pastures: 0%
forests and woodland: 5%
other: 95%
Irrigated land: 0 sq km (1998)
Natural hazards: the narrow fringing reef surrounding the island can be a maritime hazard
Environment - current issues: no natural fresh water resources
Geography - note: almost totally covered with grasses, prostrate vines, and low-growing shrubs; small area of trees in the center; primarily a nesting, roosting, and foraging habitat for seabirds, shorebirds, and marine wildlife

People

Population: uninhabited
note: American civilians evacuated in 1942 after Japanese air and naval attacks during World War II; occupied by US military during World War II, but abandoned after the war; public entry is by special-use permit from US Fish and Wildlife Service only and generally restricted to scientists and educators; visited annually by US Fish and Wildlife Service (July 2001 est.)

Government

Country name:
conventional long form: none
conventional short form: Howland Island
Dependency status: unincorporated territory of the US; administered from Washington, DC, by the Fish and Wildlife Service of the US Department of the Interior as part of the National Wildlife Refuge system
Legal system: the laws of the US, where applicable, apply
Flag description: the flag of the US is used

Economy

Economy - overview: no economic activity

Transportation

Waterways: none
Ports and harbors: none; offshore anchorage only; note - there is one small boat landing area along the middle of the west coast
Airports: airstrip constructed in 1937 for scheduled refueling stop on the round-the-world flight of Amelia EARHART and Fred NOONAN - they left Lae, New Guinea, for Howland Island, but were never seen again; the airstrip is no longer serviceable (2000 est.)
Transportation - note: Earhart Light is a day beacon near the middle of the west coast that was partially destroyed during World War II, but has since been rebuilt; named in memory of famed aviatrix Amelia EARHART

Howland Island (continued)

Military

Military - note: defense is the responsibility of the US; visited annually by the US Coast Guard

Transnational Issues

Disputes - international: none

Hungary

Introduction

Background: Hungary was part of the polyglot Austro-Hungarian Empire, which collapsed during World War I. The country fell under communist rule following World War II. In 1956, a revolt and announced withdrawal from the Warsaw Pact were met with a massive military intervention by Moscow. In the more open GORBACHEV years, Hungary led the movement to dissolve the Warsaw Pact and steadily shifted toward multiparty democracy and a market-oriented economy. Following the collapse of the USSR in 1991, Hungary developed close political and economic ties to Western Europe. It joined NATO in 1999 and is a frontrunner in a future expansion of the EU.

Geography

Location: Central Europe, northwest of Romania
Geographic coordinates: 47 00 N, 20 00 E
Map references: Europe
Area:
total: 93,030 sq km
land: 92,340 sq km
water: 690 sq km
Area - comparative: slightly smaller than Indiana
Land boundaries:
total: 2,009 km
border countries: Austria 366 km, Croatia 329 km, Romania 443 km, Yugoslavia 151 km, Slovakia 515 km, Slovenia 102 km, Ukraine 103 km
Coastline: 0 km (landlocked)
Maritime claims: none (landlocked)
Climate: temperate; cold, cloudy, humid winters; warm summers
Terrain: mostly flat to rolling plains; hills and low mountains on the Slovakian border
Elevation extremes:
lowest point: Tisza River 78 m
highest point: Kekes 1,014 m
Natural resources: bauxite, coal, natural gas, fertile soils, arable land
Land use:
arable land: 51%
permanent crops: 3.6%
permanent pastures: 12.4%
forests and woodland: 19%
other: 14% (1999)
Irrigated land: 2,060 sq km (1993 est.)
Environment - current issues: the approximation of Hungary's standards in waste management, energy efficiency, and air, soil, and water pollution with environmental requirements for EU accession will require large investments
Environment - international agreements:
party to: Air Pollution, Air Pollution-Nitrogen Oxides, Air Pollution-Sulphur 85, Air Pollution-Volatile Organic Compounds, Antarctic Treaty, Biodiversity, Climate Change, Desertification, Endangered Species, Environmental Modification, Hazardous Wastes, Marine Dumping, Nuclear Test Ban, Ozone Layer Protection, Ship Pollution, Wetlands
signed, but not ratified: Air Pollution-Persistent Organic Pollutants, Air Pollution-Sulphur 94, Antarctic-Environmental Protocol, Law of the Sea
Geography - note: landlocked; strategic location astride main land routes between Western Europe and Balkan Peninsula as well as between Ukraine and Mediterranean basin

People

Population: 10,106,017 (July 2001 est.)
Age structure:
0-14 years: 16.63% (male 862,468; female 818,052)
15-64 years: 68.66% (male 3,406,717; female 3,532,008)
65 years and over: 14.71% (male 546,992; female 939,780) (2001 est.)
Population growth rate: -0.32% (2001 est.)
Birth rate: 9.32 births/1,000 population (2001 est.)
Death rate: 13.21 deaths/1,000 population (2001 est.)

Hungary (continued)

Net migration rate: 0.74 migrant(s)/1,000 population (2001 est.)
Sex ratio:
at birth: 1.07 male(s)/female
under 15 years: 1.05 male(s)/female
15-64 years: 0.96 male(s)/female
65 years and over: 0.58 male(s)/female
total population: 0.91 male(s)/female (2001 est.)
Infant mortality rate: 8.96 deaths/1,000 live births (2001 est.)
Life expectancy at birth:
total population: 71.63 years
male: 67.28 years
female: 76.3 years (2001 est.)
Total fertility rate: 1.25 children born/woman (2001 est.)
HIV/AIDS - adult prevalence rate: 0.05% (1999 est.)
HIV/AIDS - people living with HIV/AIDS: 2,500 (1999 est.)
HIV/AIDS - deaths: less than 100 (1999 est.)
Nationality:
noun: Hungarian(s)
adjective: Hungarian
Ethnic groups: Hungarian 89.9%, Roma 4%, German 2.6%, Serb 2%, Slovak 0.8%, Romanian 0.7%
Religions: Roman Catholic 67.5%, Calvinist 20%, Lutheran 5%, atheist and other 7.5%
Languages: Hungarian 98.2%, other 1.8%
Literacy:
definition: age 15 and over can read and write
total population: 99%
male: 99%
female: 98% (1980 est.)

Government

Country name:
conventional long form: Republic of Hungary
conventional short form: Hungary
local long form: Magyar Koztarsasag
local short form: Magyarorszag
Government type: parliamentary democracy
Capital: Budapest
Administrative divisions: 19 counties (megyek, singular - megye), 20 urban counties* (singular - megyei varos), and 1 capital city** (fovaros); Bacs-Kiskun, Baranya, Bekes, Bekescsaba*, Borsod-Abauj-Zemplen, Budapest**, Csongrad, Debrecen*, Dunaujvaros*, Eger*, Fejer, Gyor*, Gyor-Moson-Sopron, Hajdu-Bihar, Heves, Hodmezovasarhely*, Jasz-Nagykun-Szolnok, Kaposvar*, Kecskemet*, Komarom-Esztergom, Miskolc*, Nagykanizsa*, Nograd, Nyiregyhaza*, Pecs*, Pest, Somogy, Sopron*, Szabolcs-Szatmar-Bereg, Szeged*, Szekesfehervar*, Szolnok*, Szombathely*, Tatabanya*, Tolna, Vas, Veszprem, Veszprem*, Zala, Zalaegerszeg*
Independence: 1001 (unification by King Stephen I)
National holiday: St. Stephen's Day, 20 August

Constitution: 18 August 1949, effective 20 August 1949, revised 19 April 1972; 18 October 1989 revision ensured legal rights for individuals and constitutional checks on the authority of the prime minister and also established the principle of parliamentary oversight; 1997 amendment streamlined the judicial system
Legal system: rule of law based on Western model
Suffrage: 18 years of age; universal
Executive branch:
chief of state: Ferenc MADL (since NA August 2000)
head of government: Prime Minister Viktor ORBAN (since 6 July 1998)
cabinet: Council of Ministers elected by the National Assembly on the recommendation of the president
elections: president elected by the National Assembly for a five-year term; election last held 6 June 2000 (next to be held by June 2005); prime minister elected by the National Assembly on the recommendation of the president
election results: Ferenc MADL elected president; percent of legislative vote - NA% (but by a simple majority in the third round of voting); Viktor ORBAN elected prime minister; percent of legislative vote - NA%
note: to be elected, the president must win two-thirds of legislative vote in the first two rounds or a simple majority in the third round
Legislative branch: unicameral National Assembly or Orszaggyules (386 seats; members are elected by popular vote under a system of proportional and direct representation to serve four-year terms)
elections: last held on 10 and 24 May 1998 (next to be held May/June 2002)
election results: percent of vote by party (5% or more of the vote required for parliamentary representation in the first round) - MSZP 32.0%, FIDESZ 28.2%, FKGP 13.8%, SZDSZ 7.9%, MIEP 5.5%, MMP 4.1%, MDF 2.8%, KDNP 2.3%, MDNP 1.5%; seats by party - MSZP 134, FIDESZ 148, FKGP 48, SZDSZ 24, MDF 17, MIEP 14, independent 1; note - seating as of 2000 by party - MSZP 136, FIDESZ 141, FKGP 48, SZDSZ 24, MDF 16, MIEP 12, independents 9
Judicial branch: Constitutional Court (judges are elected by the National Assembly for nine-year terms)
Political parties and leaders: Alliance of Free Democrats or SZDSZ [Gabor DEMSZKY]; Christian Democratic People's Party or KDNP [Gyorgy GICZY, president]; Federation of Young Democrats-Hungarian Civic Party or FYD-HCP [Laszlo KOVER]; note - used to be Hungarian Civic Party or FIDESZ; Hungarian Democratic Forum or MDF [Ibolya DAVID]; Hungarian Democratic People's Party or MDNP [Erzsebet PUSZTAI, chairman]; Hungarian Justice and Life Party or MIEP [Istvan CSURKA, chairman]; Hungarian Socialist Party or MSZP [Laszlo KOVACS, chairman]; Hungarian Workers' Party or MMP [Gyula THURMER, chairman]; Independent Smallholders or FKGP [Jozsef TORGYAN, president]
Political pressure groups and leaders: NA

International organization participation: ABEDA, Australia Group, BIS, CCC, CE, CEI, CERN, EAPC, EBRD, ECE, EU (applicant), FAO, G- 9, IAEA, IBRD, ICAO, ICC, ICFTU, ICRM, IDA, IEA, IFC, IFRCS, ILO, IMF, IMO, Inmarsat, Intelsat, Interpol, IOC, IOM, ISO, ITU, MINURSO, NAM (guest), NATO, NEA, NSG, OAS (observer), OECD, OPCW, OSCE, PCA, PFP, UN, UNCTAD, UNESCO, UNFICYP, UNHCR, UNIDO, UNIKOM, UNMIBH, UNMIK, UNMOGIP, UNOMIG, UNU, UPU, WCL, WEU (associate), WFTU, WHO, WIPO, WMO, WToO, WTrO, ZC
Diplomatic representation in the US:
chief of mission: Ambassador Geza JESZENSZKY
chancery: 3910 Shoemaker Street NW, Washington, DC 20008
telephone: [1] (202) 362-6730
FAX: [1] (202) 966-8135
consulate(s) general: Los Angeles and New York
Diplomatic representation from the US:
chief of mission: Ambassador Peter F. TUFO
embassy: Szabadsag Ter 12, H.-1054 Budapest
mailing address: pouch: American Embassy Budapest, 5270 Budapest Place, Department of State, Washington, DC 20521-5270
telephone: [36] (1) 475-4400, 475-4703 (after hours)
FAX: [36] (1) 475-4764
Flag description: three equal horizontal bands of red (top), white, and green

Economy

Economy - overview: Hungary continues to demonstrate strong economic growth and to work toward accession to the European Union. The private sector accounts for over 80% of GDP. Foreign ownership of and investment in Hungarian firms is widespread, with cumulative foreign direct investment totaling $23 billion by 2000. Hungarian sovereign debt was upgraded in 2000 to the second-highest rating among all the Central European transition economies. Inflation - a top economic concern in 2000 - is still high at almost 10%, pushed upward by higher world oil and gas and domestic food prices. Economic reform measures such as health care reform, tax reform, and local government financing have not yet been addressed by the ORBAN government.
GDP: purchasing power parity - $113.9 billion (2000 est.)
GDP - real growth rate: 5.5% (2000 est.)
GDP - per capita: purchasing power parity - $11,200 (2000 est.)
GDP - composition by sector:
agriculture: 5%
industry: 35%
services: 60% (2000 est.)
Population below poverty line: 8.6% (1993 est.)
Household income or consumption by percentage share:
lowest 10%: 3.9%
highest 10%: 24.8% (1996)
Inflation rate (consumer prices): 9.8% (1999 est.)
Labor force: 4.2 million (1997)

Hungary (continued)

Labor force - by occupation: services 65%, industry 27%, agriculture 8% (1996)
Unemployment rate: 9.4% (2000 est.)
Budget:
revenues: $13 billion
expenditures: $14.4 billion, including capital expenditures of $NA (2000 est.)
Industries: mining, metallurgy, construction materials, processed foods, textiles, chemicals (especially pharmaceuticals), motor vehicles
Industrial production growth rate: 18% (2000 est.)
Electricity - production: 36.75 billion kWh (1999)
Electricity - production by source:
fossil fuel: 61.09%
hydro: 0.51%
nuclear: 38.4%
other: 0% (1999)
Electricity - consumption: 35.234 billion kWh (1999)
Electricity - exports: 2.35 billion kWh (1999)
Electricity - imports: 3.406 billion kWh (1999)
Agriculture - products: wheat, corn, sunflower seed, potatoes, sugar beets; pigs, cattle, poultry, dairy products
Exports: $25.2 billion (f.o.b., 2000)
Exports - commodities: machinery and equipment 59.5%, other manufactures 29.4%, food products 6.9%, raw materials 2.4%, fuels and electricity 1.8% (2000)
Exports - partners: Germany 37%, Austria 9%, Italy 6%, Netherlands 5% (2000)
Imports: $27.6 billion (f.o.b., 2000)
Imports - commodities: machinery and equipment 51.1%, other manufactures 35.9%, fuels and electricity 8.1%, food products 2.8%, raw materials 2.1% (2000)
Imports - partners: Germany 25%, Russia 8%, Austria 7%, Italy 7% (2000)
Debt - external: $29.6 billion (2000)
Economic aid - recipient: $122.7 million (1995)
Currency: forint (HUF)
Currency code: HUF
Exchange rates: forints per US dollar - 282.240 (January 2001), 282.179 (2000), 237.146 (1999), 214.402 (1998), 186.789 (1997), 152.647 (1996)
Fiscal year: calendar year

Communications

Telephones - main lines in use: 3.095 million (1997)
Telephones - mobile cellular: 1.269 million (July 1999)
Telephone system:
general assessment: the telephone system has been modernized and is capable of satisfying all requests for telecommunication service
domestic: the system is digitalized and highly automated; trunk services are carried by fiber-optic cable and digital microwave radio relay; a program for fiber-optic subscriber connections was initiated in 1996; heavy use is made of mobile cellular telephones
international: Hungary has fiber-optic cable connections with all neighboring countries; the international switch is in Budapest; satellite earth stations - 2 Intelsat (Atlantic Ocean and Indian Ocean regions), 1 Inmarsat, 1 very small aperture terminal (VSAT) system of ground terminals
Radio broadcast stations: AM 17, FM 57, shortwave 3 (1998)
Radios: 7.01 million (1997)
Television broadcast stations: 35 (plus 161 low-power repeaters) (1995)
Televisions: 4.42 million (1997)
Internet country code: .hu
Internet Service Providers (ISPs): 16 (2000)
Internet users: 650,000 (2000)

Transportation

Railways:
total: 7,606 km
broad gauge: 36 km 1.524-m gauge
standard gauge: 7,394 km 1.435-m gauge (2,270 km electrified; 1,236 km double track)
narrow gauge: 176 km 0.760-m gauge (1998)
note: Hungary and Austria jointly manage the cross-border standard-gauge railway connecting Gyor, Sopron, and Ebenfurt (Gysev railroad) a distance of about 101 km in Hungary and 65 km in Austria
Highways:
total: 188,203 km
paved: 81,680 km (including 448 km of expressways)
unpaved: 106,523 km (1998 est.)
Waterways: 1,373 km (permanently navigable) (1997)
Pipelines: crude oil 1,204 km; natural gas 4,387 km (1991)
Ports and harbors: Budapest, Dunaujvaros
Merchant marine:
total: 1 ship (1,000 GRT or over) totaling 1,199 GRT/ 1,050 DWT
ships by type: cargo 1 (2000 est.)
Airports: 43 (2000 est.)
Airports - with paved runways:
total: 16
over 3,047 m: 2
2,438 to 3,047 m: 8
1,524 to 2,437 m: 4
914 to 1,523 m: 1
under 914 m: 1 (2000 est.)
Airports - with unpaved runways:
total: 27
2,438 to 3,047 m: 3
1,524 to 2,437 m: 4
914 to 1,523 m: 12
under 914 m: 8 (2000 est.)
Heliports: 5 (2000 est.)

Military

Military branches: Ground Forces, Air Force; note - there is a paramilitary Border Guard which is under the Ministry of Interior
Military manpower - military age: 18 years of age
Military manpower - availability:
males age 15-49: 2,573,119 (2001 est.)
Military manpower - fit for military service:
males age 15-49: 2,050,404 (2001 est.)
Military manpower - reaching military age annually:
males: 64,121 (2001 est.)
Military expenditures - dollar figure: $822 million (FY00)
Military expenditures - percent of GDP: 1.6% (FY00)

Transnational Issues

Disputes - international: Gabcikovo/Nagymaros Dam dispute with Slovakia is before the ICJ
Illicit drugs: major transshipment point for Southwest Asian heroin and cannabis and transit point for South American cocaine destined for Western Europe; limited producer of precursor chemicals, particularly for amphetamine and methamphetamine

Iceland

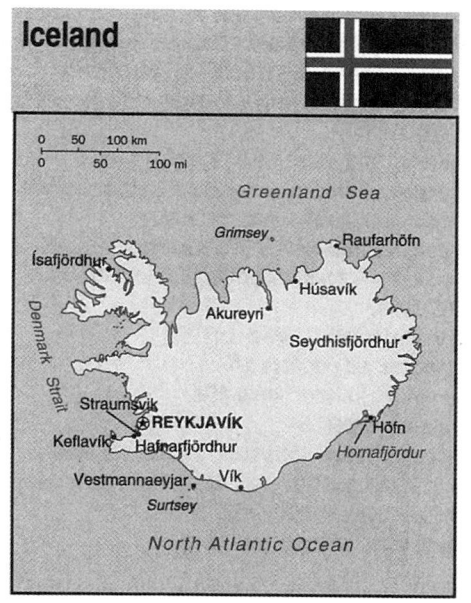

Introduction

Background: Settled by Norwegian and Celtic (Scottish and Irish) immigrants during the late 9th and 10th centuries A.D., Iceland boasts the world's oldest functioning legislative assembly, the Althing, established in 930. Independent for over 300 years, Iceland was subsequently ruled by Norway and Denmark. Fallout from the Askja volcano of 1875 devastated the Icelandic economy and caused widespread famine. Over the next quarter century, 20% of the island's population emigrated, mostly to Canada and the US. Limited home rule from Denmark was granted in 1874 and complete independence attained in 1944. Literacy, longevity, income, and social cohesion are first-rate by world standards.

Geography

Location: Northern Europe, island between the Greenland Sea and the North Atlantic Ocean, northwest of the UK
Geographic coordinates: 65 00 N, 18 00 W
Map references: Arctic Region
Area:
total: 103,000 sq km
land: 100,250 sq km
water: 2,750 sq km
Area - comparative: slightly smaller than Kentucky
Land boundaries: 0 km
Coastline: 4,988 km
Maritime claims:
continental shelf: 200 NM or to the edge of the continental margin
exclusive economic zone: 200 NM
territorial sea: 12 NM
Climate: temperate; moderated by North Atlantic Current; mild, windy winters; damp, cool summers
Terrain: mostly plateau interspersed with mountain peaks, icefields; coast deeply indented by bays and fiords
Elevation extremes:
lowest point: Atlantic Ocean 0 m
highest point: Hvannadalshnukur 2,119 m
Natural resources: fish, hydropower, geothermal power, diatomite
Land use:
arable land: 0%
permanent crops: 0%
permanent pastures: 23%
forests and woodland: 1%
other: 76% (1993 est.)
Irrigated land: NA sq km
Natural hazards: earthquakes and volcanic activity
Environment - current issues: water pollution from fertilizer runoff; inadequate wastewater treatment
Environment - international agreements:
party to: Air Pollution, Biodiversity, Climate Change, Desertification, Endangered Species, Environmental Modification, Hazardous Wastes, Law of the Sea, Marine Dumping, Nuclear Test Ban, Ozone Layer Protection, Ship Pollution, Wetlands
signed, but not ratified: Air Pollution-Persistent Organic Pollutants, Marine Life Conservation
Geography - note: strategic location between Greenland and Europe; westernmost European country; Reykjavik is the northernmost national capital in the world; more land covered by glaciers than in all of continental Europe

People

Population: 277,906 (July 2001 est.)
Age structure:
0-14 years: 23.18% (male 33,238; female 31,191)
15-64 years: 65.01% (male 91,095; female 89,583)
65 years and over: 11.81% (male 14,681; female 18,118) (2001 est.)
Population growth rate: 0.54% (2001 est.)
Birth rate: 14.62 births/1,000 population (2001 est.)
Death rate: 6.89 deaths/1,000 population (2001 est.)
Net migration rate: -2.28 migrant(s)/1,000 population (2001 est.)
Sex ratio:
at birth: 1.08 male(s)/female
under 15 years: 1.07 male(s)/female
15-64 years: 1.02 male(s)/female
65 years and over: 0.81 male(s)/female
total population: 1 male(s)/female (2001 est.)
Infant mortality rate: 3.56 deaths/1,000 live births (2001 est.)
Life expectancy at birth:
total population: 79.52 years
male: 77.31 years
female: 81.92 years (2001 est.)
Total fertility rate: 2.01 children born/woman (2001 est.)
HIV/AIDS - adult prevalence rate: 0.14% (1999 est.)
HIV/AIDS - people living with HIV/AIDS: 200 (1999 est.)
HIV/AIDS - deaths: less than 100 (1999 est.)
Nationality:
noun: Icelander(s)
adjective: Icelandic
Ethnic groups: homogeneous mixture of descendants of Norse and Celts
Religions: Evangelical Lutheran 93%, other Protestant and Roman Catholic, none (1997)
Languages: Icelandic
Literacy:
definition: age 15 and over can read and write
total population: 99.9% (1997 est.)
male: NA%
female: NA%

Government

Country name:
conventional long form: Republic of Iceland
conventional short form: Iceland
local long form: Lyoveldio Island
local short form: Island
Government type: constitutional republic
Capital: Reykjavik
Administrative divisions: 23 counties (syslar, singular - sysla) and 14 independent towns* (kaupstadhir, singular - kaupstadhur); Akranes*, Akureyri*, Arnessysla, Austur-Bardhastrandarsysla, Austur-Hunavatnssysla, Austur-Skaftafellssysla, Borgarfjardharsysla, Dalasysla, Eyjafjardharsysla, Gullbringusysla, Hafnarfjordhur*, Husavik*, Isafjordhur*, Keflavik*, Kjosarsysla, Kopavogur*, Myrasysla, Neskaupstadhur*, Nordhur-Isafjardharsysla, Nordhur-Mulasys-la, Nordhur-Thingeyjarsysla, Olafsfjordhur*, Rangarvallasysla, Reykjavik*, Saudharkrokur*, Seydhisfjordhur*, Siglufjordhur*, Skagafjardharsysla, Snaefellsnes-og Hnappadalssysla, Strandasysla, Sudhur-Mulasysla, Sudhur-Thingeyjarsysla, Vesttmannaeyjar*, Vestur-Bardhastrandarsysla, Vestur-Hunavatnssysla, Vestur-Isafjardharsysla, Vestur-Skaftafellssysla
note: there may be four other counties
Independence: 17 June 1944 (from Denmark)
National holiday: Independence Day, 17 June (1944)
Constitution: 16 June 1944, effective 17 June 1944
Legal system: civil law system based on Danish law; has not accepted compulsory ICJ jurisdiction
Suffrage: 18 years of age; universal
Executive branch:
chief of state: President Olafur Ragnar GRIMSSON (since 1 August 1996)
head of government: Prime Minister David ODDSSON (since 30 April 1991)
cabinet: Cabinet appointed by the prime minister and approved by Parliament
elections: president elected by popular vote for a four-year term; election last held 29 June 1996 (next to be held NA June 2004); President GRIMSSON ran unopposed in June 2000 so there were no elections; prime minister appointed by the president
election results: Olafur Ragnar GRIMSSON elected president; President GRIMSSON ran unopposed

Iceland (continued)

Legislative branch: unicameral Parliament or Althing (63 seats; members are elected by popular vote to serve four-year terms)
elections: last held on 8 May 1999 (next to be held by April 2003)
election results: percent of vote by party - Independence Party 40.7%, The Alliance (PA, People's Party, Women's List) 26.8%, Progressive Party 18.4%, Left-Green Alliance 9.1%, Liberal Party 4.2%; seats by party - Independence Party 26, The Alliance 17, Progressive Party 12, Left-Green Alliance 6, Liberal Party 2
Judicial branch: Supreme Court or Haestirettur (justices are appointed for life by the president)
Political parties and leaders: Independence Party (conservative) or IP [David ODDSSON]; Left-Green Alliance [Steinsvimur SIGFUSSON]; Liberal Party [Sverrir HERMANNSSON]; People's Party (Social Democratic Party) or SDP [Sighvatyr BJORGIVINSSON]; Progressive Party (liberal) or PP [Halldor ASGRIMSSON]; The Alliance (includes People's Alliance or PA, Social Democratic Party or SVP, People's Movement, Women's List) [Ossur SKARPHEDINSSON]; Women's List or WL [Kristin ASTGEIRSDOTTIR]
Political pressure groups and leaders: NA
International organization participation: Australia Group, BIS, CBSS, CCC, CE, EAPC, EBRD, ECE, EFTA, FAO, IAEA, IBRD, ICAO, ICC, ICFTU, ICRM, IDA, IEA (observer), IFC, IFRCS, IHO, ILO, IMF, IMO, Inmarsat, Intelsat, Interpol, IOC, ISO, ITU, NATO, NC, NEA, NIB, OECD, OPCW, OSCE, UN, UNCTAD, UNESCO, UNHCR, UNMIBH, UNMIK, UNU, UPU, WEU (associate), WHO, WIPO, WMO, WTrO
Diplomatic representation in the US:
chief of mission: Ambassador Jon-Baldvin HANNIBALSSON
chancery: Suite 1200, 1156 15th Street NW, Washington, DC 20005
telephone: [1] (202) 265-6653
FAX: [1] (202) 265-6656
consulate(s) general: New York
Diplomatic representation from the US:
chief of mission: Ambassador Barbara J. GRIFFITHS
embassy: Laufasvegur 21, Reykjavik
mailing address: US Embassy, PSC 1003, Box 40, FPO AE 09728-0340
telephone: [354] 5629100
FAX: [354] 5629118
Flag description: blue with a red cross outlined in white that extends to the edges of the flag; the vertical part of the cross is shifted to the hoist side in the style of the Dannebrog (Danish flag)

Economy

Economy - overview: Iceland's Scandinavian-type economy is basically capitalistic, yet with an extensive welfare system, low unemployment, and remarkably even distribution of income. In the absence of other natural resources (except for abundant hydrothermal and geothermal power), the economy depends heavily on the fishing industry, which provides 70% of export earnings and employs 12% of the work force. The economy remains sensitive to declining fish stocks as well as to drops in world prices for its main exports: fish and fish products, aluminum, and ferrosilicon. The center-right government plans to continue its policies of reducing the budget and current account deficits, limiting foreign borrowing, containing inflation, revising agricultural and fishing policies, diversifying the economy, and privatizing state-owned industries. The government remains opposed to EU membership, primarily because of Icelanders' concern about losing control over their fishing resources. Iceland's economy has been diversifying into manufacturing and service industries in the last decade, and new developments in software production, biotechnology, and financial services are taking place. The tourism sector is also expanding, with the recent trends in ecotourism and whale watching. Growth has been remarkably steady over the past five years at 4%-5%.
GDP: purchasing power parity - $6.85 billion (2000 est.)
GDP - real growth rate: 4.3% (2000 est.)
GDP - per capita: purchasing power parity - $24,800 (2000 est.)
GDP - composition by sector:
agriculture: 15% (includes fishing 13%)
industry: 21%
services: 64% (1999 est.)
Population below poverty line: NA%
Household income or consumption by percentage share:
lowest 10%: NA%
highest 10%: NA%
Inflation rate (consumer prices): 3.5% (2000 est.)
Labor force: 159,000 (2000)
Labor force - by occupation: agriculture 5.1%, fishing and fish processing 11.8%, manufacturing 12.9%, construction 10.7%, other services 59.5% (1999)
Unemployment rate: 2.7% (January 2001)
Budget:
revenues: $3.5 billion
expenditures: $3.3 billion, including capital expenditures of $467 million (1999)
Industries: fish processing; aluminum smelting, ferrosilicon production, geothermal power; tourism
Industrial production growth rate: 1.5% (2000 est.)
Electricity - production: 7.069 billion kWh (1999)
Electricity - production by source:
fossil fuel: 0.07%
hydro: 84.64%
nuclear: 0%
other: 15.29% (1999)
Electricity - consumption: 6.574 billion kWh (1999)
Electricity - exports: 0 kWh (1999)
Electricity - imports: 0 kWh (1999)
Agriculture - products: potatoes, turnips; cattle, sheep; fish
Exports: $2 billion (f.o.b., 2000)
Exports - commodities: fish and fish products 70%, animal products, aluminum, diatomite, ferrosilicon
Exports - partners: EU 64% (UK 20%, Germany 13%, France 5%, Denmark 5%), US 15%, Japan 5% (1999)
Imports: $2.2 billion (f.o.b., 2000)
Imports - commodities: machinery and equipment, petroleum products; foodstuffs, textiles
Imports - partners: EU 56% (Germany 12%, UK 9%, Denmark 8%, Sweden 6%), US 11%, Norway 10% (1999)
Debt - external: $2.6 billion (1999)
Economic aid - donor: $NA
Currency: Icelandic krona (ISK)
Currency code: ISK
Exchange rates: Icelandic kronur per US dollar - 84.810 (January 2001), 78.676 (2000), 72.335 (1999), 70.958 (1998), 70.904 (1997), 66.500 (1996)
Fiscal year: calendar year

Communications

Telephones - main lines in use: 168,000 (1997)
Telephones - mobile cellular: 65,746 (1997)
Telephone system:
general assessment: adequate domestic service
domestic: the trunk network consists of coaxial and fiber-optic cables and microwave radio relay links
international: satellite earth stations - 2 Intelsat (Atlantic Ocean), 1 Inmarsat (Atlantic and Indian Ocean regions); note - Iceland shares the Inmarsat earth station with the other Nordic countries (Denmark, Finland, Norway, and Sweden)
Radio broadcast stations: AM 3, FM about 70 (including repeaters), shortwave 1 (1998)
Radios: 260,000 (1997)
Television broadcast stations: 14 (plus 156 low-power repeaters) (1997)
Televisions: 98,000 (1997)
Internet country code: .is
Internet Service Providers (ISPs): 7 (2000)
Internet users: 144,000 (2000)

Transportation

Railways: 0 km
Highways:
total: 12,689 km
paved: 3,439 km
unpaved: 9,250 km (1998 est.)
Waterways: none
Ports and harbors: Akureyri, Hornafjordur, Isafjordhur, Keflavik, Raufarhofn, Reykjavik, Seydhisfjordhur, Straumsvik, Vestmannaeyjar
Merchant marine:
total: 2 ships (1,000 GRT or over) totaling 3,435 GRT/4,538 DWT
ships by type: chemical tanker 1, petroleum tanker 1 (2000 est.)
Airports: 87 (2000 est.)
Airports - with paved runways:
total: 12
over 3,047 m: 1

Iceland (continued)

1,524 to 2,437 m: 4
914 to 1,523 m: 7 (2000 est.)
Airports - with unpaved runways:
total: 75
1,524 to 2,437 m: 3
914 to 1,523 m: 20
under 914 m: 52 (2000 est.)

Military

Military branches: no regular armed forces; Police, Coast Guard; note - Iceland's defense is provided by the US-manned Icelandic Defense Force (IDF) headquartered at Keflavik
Military manpower - availability:
males age 15-49: 71,241 (2001 est.)
Military manpower - fit for military service:
males age 15-49: 62,704 (2001 est.)
Military expenditures - dollar figure: $0
Military - note: defense is provided by the US-manned Icelandic Defense Force (IDF) headquartered at Keflavik

Transnational Issues

Disputes - international: Rockall continental shelf dispute involving Denmark and the UK (Ireland and the UK have signed a boundary agreement in the Rockall area); dispute with Denmark over the Faroe Islands fisheries median line boundary within 200 NM; disputes with Denmark, the UK, and Ireland over the Faroe Islands continental shelf boundary outside 200 NM

India

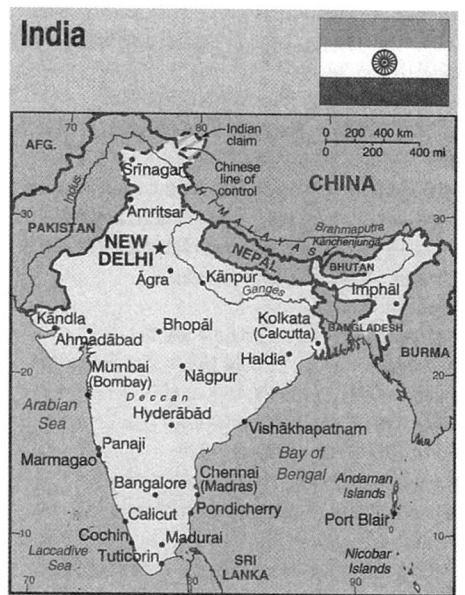

Introduction

Background: The Indus Valley civilization, one of the oldest in the world, goes back at least 5,000 years. Aryan tribes from the northwest invaded about 1500 B.C.; their merger with the earlier inhabitants created classical Indian culture. Arab incursions starting in the 8th century and Turkish in 12th were followed by European traders beginning in the late 15th century. By the 19th century, Britain had assumed political control of virtually all Indian lands. Nonviolent resistance to British colonialism under Mohandas GANDHI and Jawaharlal NEHRU led to independence in 1947. The subcontinent was divided into the secular state of India and the smaller Muslim state of Pakistan. A third war between the two countries in 1971 resulted in East Pakistan becoming the separate nation of Bangladesh. Fundamental concerns in India include the ongoing dispute with Pakistan over Kashmir, massive overpopulation, environmental degradation, extensive poverty, and ethnic strife, all this despite impressive gains in economic investment and output.

Geography

Location: Southern Asia, bordering the Arabian Sea and the Bay of Bengal, between Burma and Pakistan
Geographic coordinates: 20 00 N, 77 00 E
Map references: Asia
Area:
total: 3,287,590 sq km
land: 2,973,190 sq km
water: 314,400 sq km
Area - comparative: slightly more than one-third the size of the US
Land boundaries:
total: 14,103 km
border countries: Bangladesh 4,053 km, Bhutan 605 km, Burma 1,463 km, China 3,380 km, Nepal 1,690 km, Pakistan 2,912 km
Coastline: 7,000 km
Maritime claims:
contiguous zone: 24 NM
continental shelf: 200 NM or to the edge of the continental margin
exclusive economic zone: 200 NM
territorial sea: 12 NM
Climate: varies from tropical monsoon in south to temperate in north
Terrain: upland plain (Deccan Plateau) in south, flat to rolling plain along the Ganges, deserts in west, Himalayas in north
Elevation extremes:
lowest point: Indian Ocean 0 m
highest point: Kanchenjunga 8,598 m
Natural resources: coal (fourth-largest reserves in the world), iron ore, manganese, mica, bauxite, titanium ore, chromite, natural gas, diamonds, petroleum, limestone, arable land
Land use:
arable land: 56%
permanent crops: 1%
permanent pastures: 4%
forests and woodland: 23%
other: 16% (1993 est.)
Irrigated land: 535,100 sq km (1995/96 est.)
Natural hazards: droughts, flash floods, severe thunderstorms common; earthquakes
Environment - current issues: deforestation; soil erosion; overgrazing; desertification; air pollution from industrial effluents and vehicle emissions; water pollution from raw sewage and runoff of agricultural pesticides; tap water is not potable throughout the country; huge and growing population is overstraining natural resources
Environment - international agreements:
party to: Antarctic-Environmental Protocol, Antarctic-Marine Living Resources, Antarctic Treaty, Biodiversity, Climate Change, Desertification, Endangered Species, Environmental Modification, Hazardous Wastes, Law of the Sea, Marine Dumping, Nuclear Test Ban, Ozone Layer Protection, Ship Pollution, Tropical Timber 83, Tropical Timber 94, Wetlands, Whaling
signed, but not ratified: none of the selected agreements
Geography - note: dominates South Asian subcontinent; near important Indian Ocean trade routes

People

Population: 1,029,991,145 (July 2001 est.)
Age structure:
0-14 years: 33.12% (male 175,630,537; female 165,540,672)
15-64 years: 62.2% (male 331,790,850; female 308,902,864)
65 years and over: 4.68% (male 24,439,022; female 23,687,200) (2001 est.)
Population growth rate: 1.55% (2001 est.)
Birth rate: 24.28 births/1,000 population (2001 est.)
Death rate: 8.74 deaths/1,000 population (2001 est.)

India (continued)

Net migration rate: -0.08 migrant(s)/1,000 population (2001 est.)
Sex ratio:
at birth: 1.05 male(s)/female
under 15 years: 1.06 male(s)/female
15-64 years: 1.07 male(s)/female
65 years and over: 1.03 male(s)/female
total population: 1.07 male(s)/female (2001 est.)
Infant mortality rate: 63.19 deaths/1,000 live births (2001 est.)
Life expectancy at birth:
total population: 62.86 years
male: 62.22 years
female: 63.53 years (2001 est.)
Total fertility rate: 3.04 children born/woman (2001 est.)
HIV/AIDS - adult prevalence rate: 0.7% (1999 est.)
HIV/AIDS - people living with HIV/AIDS: 3.7 million (1999 est.)
HIV/AIDS - deaths: 310,000 (1999 est.)
Nationality:
noun: Indian(s)
adjective: Indian
Ethnic groups: Indo-Aryan 72%, Dravidian 25%, Mongoloid and other 3% (2000)
Religions: Hindu 81.3%, Muslim 12%, Christian 2.3%, Sikh 1.9%, other groups including Buddhist, Jain, Parsi 2.5% (2000)
Languages: English enjoys associate status but is the most important language for national, political, and commercial communication, Hindi the national language and primary tongue of 30% of the people, Bengali (official), Telugu (official), Marathi (official), Tamil (official), Urdu (official), Gujarati (official), Malayalam (official), Kannada (official), Oriya (official), Punjabi (official), Assamese (official), Kashmiri (official), Sindhi (official), Sanskrit (official), Hindustani (a popular variant of Hindi/Urdu spoken widely throughout northern India)
note: 24 languages each spoken by a million or more persons; numerous other languages and dialects, for the most part mutually unintelligible
Literacy:
definition: age 15 and over can read and write
total population: 52%
male: 65.5%
female: 37.7% (1995 est.)

Government

Country name:
conventional long form: Republic of India
conventional short form: India
Government type: federal republic
Capital: New Delhi
Administrative divisions: 28 states and 7 union territories*; Andaman and Nicobar Islands*, Andhra Pradesh, Arunachal Pradesh, Assam, Bihar, Chandigarh*, Chhattisgarh, Dadra and Nagar Haveli*, Daman and Diu*, Delhi*, Goa, Gujarat, Haryana, Himachal Pradesh, Jammu and Kashmir, Jharkhand, Karnataka, Kerala, Lakshadweep*, Madhya Pradesh, Maharashtra, Manipur, Meghalaya, Mizoram, Nagaland, Orissa, Pondicherry*, Punjab, Rajasthan, Sikkim, Tamil Nadu, Tripura, Uttaranchal, Uttar Pradesh, West Bengal
Independence: 15 August 1947 (from UK)
National holiday: Republic Day, 26 January (1950)
Constitution: 26 January 1950
Legal system: based on English common law; limited judicial review of legislative acts; accepts compulsory ICJ jurisdiction, with reservations
Suffrage: 18 years of age; universal
Executive branch:
chief of state: President Kicheril Raman NARAYANAN (since 25 July 1997); Vice President Krishnan KANT (since 21 August 1997)
head of government: Prime Minister Atal Behari VAJPAYEE (since 19 March 1998)
cabinet: Council of Ministers appointed by the president on the recommendation of the prime minister
elections: president elected by an electoral college consisting of elected members of both houses of Parliament and the legislatures of the states for a five-year term; election last held 14 July 1997 (next to be held NA July 2002); vice president elected by both houses of Parliament for a five-year term; election last held 16 August 1997 (next to be held NA August 2002); prime minister elected by parliamentary members of the majority party following legislative elections; election last held NA October 1999 (next to be held NA October 2004)
election results: Kicheril Raman NARAYANAN elected president; percent of electoral college vote - NA%; Krishnan KANT elected vice president; percent of Parliament vote - NA%; Atal Behari VAJPAYEE elected prime minister; percent of vote - NA%
Legislative branch: bicameral Parliament or Sansad consists of the Council of States or Rajya Sabha (a body consisting of not more than 250 members, up to 12 of which are appointed by the president, the remainder are chosen by the elected members of the state and territorial assemblies; members serve six-year terms) and the People's Assembly or Lok Sabha (545 seats; 543 elected by popular vote, 2 appointed by the president; members serve five-year terms)
elections: People's Assembly - last held 5 September through 3 October 1999 (next to be held NA 2004)
election results: People's Assembly - percent of vote by party - BJP alliance 40.8%, Congress alliance 33.8%, other 25.4%; seats by party - BJP alliance 304, Congress alliance 134, other 107
Judicial branch: Supreme Court (judges are appointed by the president and remain in office until they reach the age of 65)
Political parties and leaders: All India Anna Dravida Munnetra Kazhagam or AIADMK [C. Jayalalitha JAYARAM]; All India Forward Bloc or AIFB [Prem Dutta PALIWAL (chairman), Chitta BASU (general secretary)]; Asom Gana Parishad [Prafulla Kumar MAHANTA]; Bahujan Samaj Party or BSP [Kanshi RAM]; Bharatiya Janata Party or BJP [Bangaru LAXMAN, president]; Biju Janata Dal or BJD [Naveen PATNAIK]; Communist Party of India or CPI [Ardhendu Bhushan BARDHAN]; Communist Party of India/Marxist-Leninist or CPI/ML [Vinod MISHRA]; Congress (I) Party [Sonia GANDHI, president]; Dravida Munnetra Kazagham or DMK (a regional party in Tamil Nadu) [M. KARUNANIDHI]; Indian National League [Suliaman SAIT]; Janata Dal (Secular) [H. D. Deve GOWDA]; Janata Dal (United) or JDU [Sharad YADAV, president, I. K. GUJRAL]; Kerala Congress (Mani faction) [K. M. MANI]; Marumalarchi Dravida Munnetra Kazhagam or MDMK [VAIKO]; Muslim League [G. M. BANATWALA]; Nationalist Congress Party or NCP [Sharad PAWAR]; National Democratic Alliance, a 16-party alliance including BJP, DMK, Janata Dal (U), SHS, Shiromani Akali Dal, Telugu Desam, BJD, Rinamool Congress]; Rashtriya Janata Dal or RJD [Laloo Prasad YADAV]; Revolutionary Socialist Party or RSP [Tridip CHOWDHURY]; Samajwadi Party or SP [Mulayam Singh YADAV, president]; Shiromani Akali Dal [Prakash Singh BADAL]; Shiv Sena [Bal THACKERAY]; Tamil Maanila Congress [G. K. MOOPANAR]; Telugu Desam Party or TDP (a regional party in Andhra Pradesh) [Chandrababu NAIDU]; Trinamool Congress [Mamata BANERJEE]
Political pressure groups and leaders: numerous religious or militant/chauvinistic organizations, including Vishwa Hindu Parishad, Bajrang Dal, and Rashtriya Swayamsevak Sangh; various separatist groups seeking greater communal and/or regional autonomy, including the All Parties Hurriyat Conference
International organization participation: AfDB, ARF (dialogue partner), AsDB, ASEAN (dialogue partner), BIS, C, CCC, CP, ESCAP, FAO, G- 6, G-15, G-19, G-24, G-77, IAEA, IBRD, ICAO, ICC, ICFTU, ICRM, IDA, IEA (observer), IFAD, IFC, IFRCS, IHO, ILO, IMF, IMO, Inmarsat, Intelsat, Interpol, IOC, IOM (observer), ISO, ITU, MINURSO, MIPONUH, MONUC, NAM, OAS (observer), OPCW, PCA, SAARC, UN, UNCTAD, UNESCO, UNHCR, UNIDO, UNIFIL, UNIKOM, UNMEE, UNMIBH, UNMIK, UNU, UPU, WCL, WFTU, WHO, WIPO, WMO, WToO, WTrO
Diplomatic representation in the US:
chief of mission: Ambassador Naresh CHANDRA
chancery: 2107 Massachusetts Avenue NW, Washington, DC 20008; note - Embassy located at 2536 Massachusetts Avenue NW, Washington, DC 20008
telephone: [1] (202) 939-7000
FAX: [1] (202) 483-3972
consulate(s) general: Chicago, Houston, New York, and San Francisco
Diplomatic representation from the US:
chief of mission: Ambassador Richard F. CELESTE
embassy: Shantipath, Chanakyapuri, New Delhi 110021
mailing address: use embassy street address
telephone: [91] (11) 688-9033, 611-3033
FAX: [91] (11) 419-0025
consulate(s) general: Chennai (Madras), Kolkata (Calcutta), Mumbai (Bombay)

India (continued)

Flag description: three equal horizontal bands of orange (top), white, and green with a blue chakra (24-spoked wheel) centered in the white band; similar to the flag of Niger, which has a small orange disk centered in the white band

Economy

Economy - overview: India's economy encompasses traditional village farming, modern agriculture, handicrafts, a wide range of modern industries, and a multitude of support services. More than a third of the population is too poor to be able to afford an adequate diet. India's international payments position remained strong in 2000 with adequate foreign exchange reserves, moderately depreciating nominal exchange rates, and booming exports of software services. Growth in manufacturing output slowed, and electricity shortages continue in many regions.
GDP: purchasing power parity - $2.2 trillion (2000 est.)
GDP - real growth rate: 6% (2000 est.)
GDP - per capita: purchasing power parity - $2,200 (2000 est.)
GDP - composition by sector:
agriculture: 25%
industry: 24%
services: 51% (2000)
Population below poverty line: 35% (1994 est.)
Household income or consumption by percentage share:
lowest 10%: 3.5%
highest 10%: 33.5% (1997)
Inflation rate (consumer prices): 5.4% (2000 est.)
Labor force: NA
Labor force - by occupation: agriculture 67%, services 18%, industry 15% (1995 est.)
Unemployment rate: NA%
Budget:
revenues: $44.3 billion
expenditures: $73.6 billion, including capital expenditures of $NA (FY00/01 est.)
Industries: textiles, chemicals, food processing, steel, transportation equipment, cement, mining, petroleum, machinery, software
Industrial production growth rate: 7.5% (2000 est.)
Electricity - production: 454.561 billion kWh (1999)
Electricity - production by source:
fossil fuel: 79.41%
hydro: 17.77%
nuclear: 2.52%
other: 0.3% (1999)
Electricity - consumption: 424.032 billion kWh (1999)
Electricity - exports: 200 million kWh (1999)
Electricity - imports: 1.49 billion kWh (1999)
Agriculture - products: rice, wheat, oilseed, cotton, jute, tea, sugarcane, potatoes; cattle, water buffalo, sheep, goats, poultry; fish
Exports: $43.1 billion (f.o.b., 2000)
Exports - commodities: textile goods, gems and jewelry, engineering goods, chemicals, leather manufactures
Exports - partners: US 22%, UK 6%, Germany 5%, Japan 5%, Hong Kong 5%, UAE 4% (1999)
Imports: $60.8 billion (f.o.b., 2000)
Imports - commodities: crude oil, machinery, gems, fertilizer, chemicals
Imports - partners: US 9%, Benelux 8%, UK 6%, Saudi Arabia 6%, Japan 6%, Germany 5% (1999)
Debt - external: $99.6 billion (2000)
Economic aid - recipient: $2.9 billion (FY98/99)
Currency: Indian rupee (INR)
Currency code: INR
Exchange rates: Indian rupees per US dollar - 46.540 (January 2001), 44.942 (2000), 43.055 (1999), 41.259 (1998), 36.313 (1997), 35.433 (1996)
Fiscal year: 1 April - 31 March

Communications

Telephones - main lines in use: 27.7 million (October 2000)
Telephones - mobile cellular: 2.93 million (November 2000)
Telephone system:
general assessment: mediocre service; local and long distance service provided throughout all regions of the country, with services primarily concentrated in the urban areas; major objective is to continue to expand and modernize long-distance network in order to keep pace with rapidly growing number of local subscriber lines; steady improvement is taking place with the recent admission of private and private-public investors, but, with telephone density at about two for each 100 persons and a waiting list of over 2 million, demand for main line telephone service will not be satisfied for a very long time
domestic: local service is provided by microwave radio relay and coaxial cable, with open wire and obsolete electromechanical and manual switchboard systems still in use in rural areas; starting in the 1980s, a substantial amount of digital switch gear has been introduced for local and long-distance service; long-distance traffic is carried mostly by coaxial cable and low-capacity microwave radio relay; since 1985 significant trunk capacity has been added in the form of fiber-optic cable and a domestic satellite system with 254 earth stations; mobile cellular service is provided in four metropolitan cities
international: satellite earth stations - 8 Intelsat (Indian Ocean) and 1 Inmarsat (Indian Ocean region); nine gateway exchanges operating from Mumbai (Bombay), New Delhi, Kolkata (Calcutta), Chennai (Madras), Jalandhar, Kanpur, Gaidhinagar, Hyderabad, and Ernakulam; 4 submarine cables - LOCOM linking Chennai (Madras) to Penang; Indo-UAE-Gulf cable linking Mumbai (Bombay) to Al Fujayrah, UAE; India-SEA-ME-WE-3, SEA-ME-WE-2 with landing sites at Cochin and Mumbai (Bombay); Fiber-Optic Link Around the Globe (FLAG) with landing site at Mumbai (Bombay) (2000)
Radio broadcast stations: AM 153, FM 91, shortwave 68 (1998)
Radios: 116 million (1997)
Television broadcast stations: 562 (of which 82 stations have 1 kW or greater power and 480 stations have less than 1 kW of power) (1997)
Televisions: 63 million (1997)
Internet country code: .in
Internet Service Providers (ISPs): 43 (2000)
Internet users: 4.5 million (2000)

Transportation

Railways:
total: 62,915 km (12,307 km electrified; 12,617 km double track)
broad gauge: 40,620 km 1.676-m gauge
narrow gauge: 18,501 km 1.000-m gauge; 3,794 km 0.762-m and 0.610-m gauge (1998 est.)
Highways:
total: 3,319,644 km
paved: 1,517,077 km
unpaved: 1,802,567 km (1996)
Waterways: 16,180 km
note: 3,631 km navigable by large vessels
Pipelines: crude oil 3,005 km; petroleum products 2,687 km; natural gas 1,700 km (1995)
Ports and harbors: Chennai (Madras), Cochin, Jawaharal Nehru, Kandla, Kolkata (Calcutta), Mumbai (Bombay), Vishakhapatnam
Merchant marine:
total: 315 ships (1,000 GRT or over) totaling 6,433,831 GRT/10,691,973 DWT
ships by type: bulk 117, cargo 70, chemical tanker 15, combination bulk 1, combination ore/oil 3, container 15, liquefied gas 9, passenger/cargo 5, petroleum tanker 76, short-sea passenger 2, specialized tanker 2 (2000 est.)
Airports: 337 (2000 est.)
Airports - with paved runways:
total: 235
over 3,047 m: 13
2,438 to 3,047 m: 48
1,524 to 2,437 m: 81
914 to 1,523 m: 77
under 914 m: 16 (2000 est.)
Airports - with unpaved runways:
total: 102
2,438 to 3,047 m: 1
1,524 to 2,437 m: 6
914 to 1,523 m: 40
under 914 m: 55 (2000 est.)
Heliports: 16 (2000 est.)

Military

Military branches: Army, Navy (including naval air arm), Air Force, various security or paramilitary forces (includes Border Security Force, Assam Rifles, Rashtriya Rifles, and National Security Guards)
Military manpower - military age: 17 years of age
Military manpower - availability:
males age 15-49: 280,204,502 (2001 est.)

India (continued)

Military manpower - fit for military service:
males age 15-49: 164,410,461 (2001 est.)
Military manpower - reaching military age annually:
males: 10,879,384 (2001 est.)
Military expenditures - dollar figure: $13.02 billion (FY01)
Military expenditures - percent of GDP: 2.5% (FY00)

Transnational Issues

Disputes - international: boundary with China in dispute; status of Kashmir with Pakistan; water-sharing problems with Pakistan over the Indus River (Wular Barrage); a portion of the boundary with Bangladesh is indefinite; exchange of 151 enclaves along border with Bangladesh subject to ratification by Indian parliament; dispute with Bangladesh over New Moore/South Talpatty Island

Illicit drugs: world's largest producer of licit opium for the pharmaceutical trade, but an undetermined quantity of opium is diverted to illicit international drug markets; transit country for illicit narcotics produced in neighboring countries; illicit producer of hashish and methaqualone

Indian Ocean

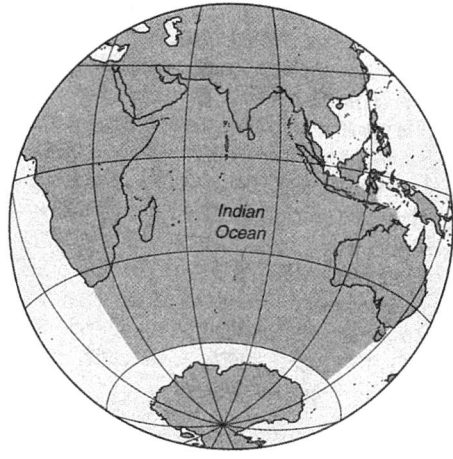

Introduction

Background: The Indian Ocean is the third-largest of the world's five oceans (after the Pacific Ocean and Atlantic Ocean, but larger than the Southern Ocean and Arctic Ocean). Four critically important access waterways are the Suez Canal (Egypt), Bab el Mandeb (Djibouti-Yemen), Strait of Hormuz (Iran-Oman), and Strait of Malacca (Indonesia-Malaysia). The decision by the International Hydrographic Organization in the spring of 2000 to delimit a fifth ocean, the Southern Ocean, removed the portion of the Indian Ocean south of 60 degrees south.

Geography

Location: body of water between Africa, the Southern Ocean, Asia, and Australia
Geographic coordinates: 20 00 S, 80 00 E
Map references: World
Area:
total: 68.556 million sq km
note: includes Andaman Sea, Arabian Sea, Bay of Bengal, Great Australian Bight, Gulf of Aden, Gulf of Oman, Mozambique Channel, Persian Gulf, Red Sea, Strait of Malacca, and other tributary water bodies
Area - comparative: about 5.5 times the size of the US
Coastline: 66,526 km
Climate: northeast monsoon (December to April), southwest monsoon (June to October); tropical cyclones occur during May/June and October/November in the northern Indian Ocean and January/February in the southern Indian Ocean
Terrain: surface dominated by counterclockwise gyre (broad, circular system of currents) in the southern Indian Ocean; unique reversal of surface currents in the northern Indian Ocean; low atmospheric pressure over southwest Asia from hot, rising, summer air results in the southwest monsoon and southwest-to-northeast winds and currents, while high pressure over northern Asia from cold, falling, winter air results in the northeast monsoon and northeast-to-southwest winds and currents; ocean floor is dominated by the Mid-Indian Ocean Ridge and subdivided by the Southeast Indian Ocean Ridge, Southwest Indian Ocean Ridge, and Ninetyeast Ridge
Elevation extremes:
lowest point: Java Trench -7,258 m
highest point: sea level 0 m
Natural resources: oil and gas fields, fish, shrimp, sand and gravel aggregates, placer deposits, polymetallic nodules
Natural hazards: occasional icebergs pose navigational hazard in southern reaches
Environment - current issues: endangered marine species include the dugong, seals, turtles, and whales; oil pollution in the Arabian Sea, Persian Gulf, and Red Sea
Geography - note: major chokepoints include Bab el Mandeb, Strait of Hormuz, Strait of Malacca, southern access to the Suez Canal, and the Lombok Strait

Economy

Economy - overview: The Indian Ocean provides major sea routes connecting the Middle East, Africa, and East Asia with Europe and the Americas. It carries a particularly heavy traffic of petroleum and petroleum products from the oilfields of the Persian Gulf and Indonesia. Its fish are of great and growing importance to the bordering countries for domestic consumption and export. Fishing fleets from Russia, Japan, South Korea, and Taiwan also exploit the Indian Ocean, mainly for shrimp and tuna. Large reserves of hydrocarbons are being tapped in the offshore areas of Saudi Arabia, Iran, India, and western Australia. An estimated 40% of the world's offshore oil production comes from the Indian Ocean. Beach sands rich in heavy minerals and offshore placer deposits are actively exploited by bordering countries, particularly India, South Africa, Indonesia, Sri Lanka, and Thailand.

Transportation

Ports and harbors: Chennai (Madras; India), Colombo (Sri Lanka), Durban (South Africa), Jakarta (Indonesia), Kolkata (Calcutta; India) Melbourne (Australia), Mumbai (Bombay; India), Richards Bay (South Africa)

Transnational Issues

Disputes - international: some maritime disputes (see littoral states)

Indonesia

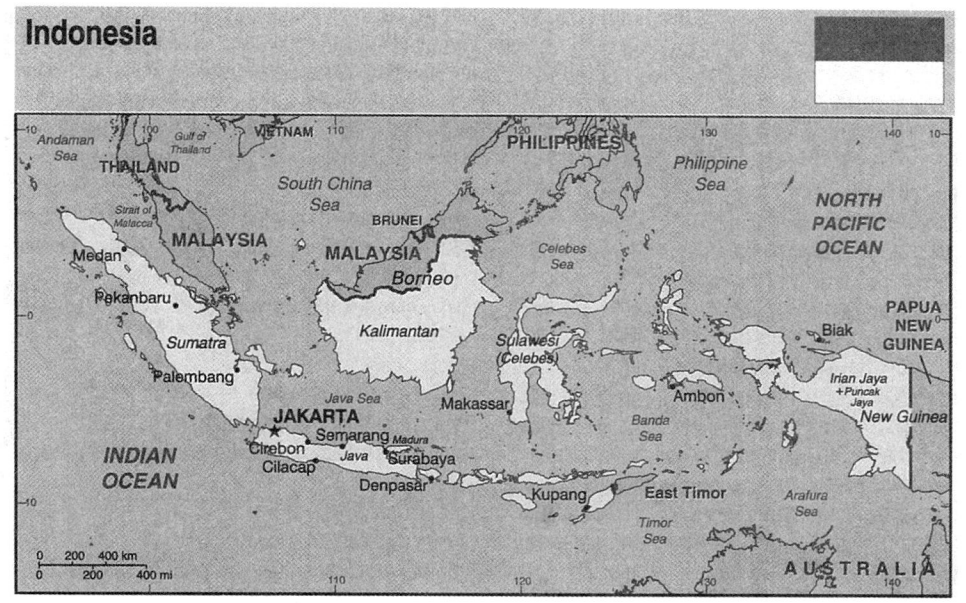

Introduction

Background: The world's largest archipelago, Indonesia achieved independence from the Netherlands in 1949. Current issues include: implementing IMF-mandated reforms of the banking sector, effecting a transition to a popularly elected government after four decades of authoritarianism, addressing charges of cronyism and corruption, holding the military accountable for human rights violations, and resolving growing separatist pressures in Aceh and Irian Jaya. On 30 August 1999 a provincial referendum for independence was overwhelmingly approved by the people of Timor Timur. Concurrence followed by Indonesia's national legislature, and the name East Timor was provisionally adopted. The independent status of East Timor - now under UN administration - has yet to be formally established.

Geography

Location: Southeastern Asia, archipelago between the Indian Ocean and the Pacific Ocean
Geographic coordinates: 5 00 S, 120 00 E
Map references: Southeast Asia
Area:
total: 1,919,440 sq km
land: 1,826,440 sq km
water: 93,000 sq km
Area - comparative: slightly less than three times the size of Texas
Land boundaries:
total: 2,602 km
border countries: Malaysia 1,782 km, Papua New Guinea 820 km
Coastline: 54,716 km
Maritime claims: measured from claimed archipelagic baselines
exclusive economic zone: 200 NM
territorial sea: 12 NM
Climate: tropical; hot, humid; more moderate in highlands
Terrain: mostly coastal lowlands; larger islands have interior mountains
Elevation extremes:
lowest point: Indian Ocean 0 m
highest point: Puncak Jaya 5,030 m
Natural resources: petroleum, tin, natural gas, nickel, timber, bauxite, copper, fertile soils, coal, gold, silver
Land use:
arable land: 10%
permanent crops: 7%
permanent pastures: 7%
forests and woodland: 62%
other: 14% (1993 est.)
Irrigated land: 45,970 sq km (1993 est.)
Natural hazards: occasional floods, severe droughts, tsunamis, earthquakes, volcanoes
Environment - current issues: deforestation; water pollution from industrial wastes, sewage; air pollution in urban areas; smoke and haze from forest fires
Environment - international agreements:
party to: Biodiversity, Climate Change, Desertification, Endangered Species, Hazardous Wastes, Law of the Sea, Marine Dumping, Nuclear Test Ban, Ozone Layer Protection, Ship Pollution, Tropical Timber 83, Tropical Timber 94, Wetlands
signed, but not ratified: Climate Change-Kyoto Protocol, Marine Life Conservation
Geography - note: archipelago of 17,000 islands (6,000 inhabited); straddles Equator; strategic location astride or along major sea lanes from Indian Ocean to Pacific Ocean

People

Population: 228,437,870 (July 2001 est.)
Age structure:
0-14 years: 30.26% (male 35,144,702; female 33,973,879)
15-64 years: 65.11% (male 74,273,519; female 74,458,291)
65 years and over: 4.63% (male 4,641,816; female 5,945,663) (2001 est.)
Population growth rate: 1.6% (2001 est.)
Birth rate: 22.26 births/1,000 population (2001 est.)
Death rate: 6.3 deaths/1,000 population (2001 est.)
Net migration rate: 0 migrant(s)/1,000 population (2001 est.)
Sex ratio:
at birth: 1.05 male(s)/female
under 15 years: 1.03 male(s)/female
15-64 years: 1 male(s)/female
65 years and over: 0.78 male(s)/female
total population: 1 male(s)/female (2001 est.)
Infant mortality rate: 40.91 deaths/1,000 live births (2001 est.)
Life expectancy at birth:
total population: 68.27 years
male: 65.9 years
female: 70.75 years (2001 est.)
Total fertility rate: 2.58 children born/woman (2001 est.)
HIV/AIDS - adult prevalence rate: 0.05% (1999 est.)
HIV/AIDS - people living with HIV/AIDS: 52,000 (1999 est.)
HIV/AIDS - deaths: 3,100 (1999 est.)
Nationality:
noun: Indonesian(s)
adjective: Indonesian
Ethnic groups: Javanese 45%, Sundanese 14%, Madurese 7.5%, coastal Malays 7.5%, other 26%
Religions: Muslim 88%, Protestant 5%, Roman Catholic 3%, Hindu 2%, Buddhist 1%, other 1% (1998)
Languages: Bahasa Indonesia (official, modified form of Malay), English, Dutch, local dialects, the most widely spoken of which is Javanese
Literacy:
definition: age 15 and over can read and write
total population: 83.8%
male: 89.6%
female: 78% (1995 est.)

Government

Country name:
conventional long form: Republic of Indonesia
conventional short form: Indonesia
local long form: Republik Indonesia
local short form: Indonesia
former: Netherlands East Indies; Dutch East Indies
Government type: republic
Capital: Jakarta
Administrative divisions: 27 provinces (propinsi-propinsi, singular - propinsi), 2 special regions* (daerah-daerah istimewa, singular - daerah istimewa), and 1 special capital city district** (daerah khusus ibukota); Aceh*, Bali, Banten, Bengkulu, Gorontalo, Irian Jaya, Jakarta Raya**, Jambi, Jawa Barat, Jawa Tengah, Jawa Timur, Kalimantan Barat, Kalimantan Selatan, Kalimantan Tengah, Kalimantan Timur, Kepulauan Bangka Belitung, Lampung, Maluku, Maluku Utara, Nusa Tenggara Barat, Nusa Tenggara Timur, Riau, Sulawesi Selatan, Sulawesi Tengah, Sulawesi Tenggara, Sulawesi Utara, Sumatera Barat, Sumatera Selatan, Sumatera Utara,

Indonesia (continued)

Yogyakarta*; note - the province of Irian Jaya may have been divided into two new provinces - Central Irian Jaya and West Irian Jaya; with the implementation of decentralization on 1 January 2001, the 357 districts (regencies) may become the key administrative units

note: following the 30 August 1999 provincial referendum for independence which was overwhelmingly approved by the people of Timor Timur and the October 1999 concurrence of Indonesia's national legislature, the name East Timor was adopted as a provisional name for the political entity formerly known as Propinsi Timor Timur; East Timor is under UN administration pending its formal independence

Independence: 17 August 1945 (proclaimed independence; on 27 December 1949, Indonesia became legally independent from the Netherlands)

National holiday: Independence Day, 17 August (1945)

Constitution: August 1945, abrogated by Federal Constitution of 1949 and Provisional Constitution of 1950, restored 5 July 1959

Legal system: based on Roman-Dutch law, substantially modified by indigenous concepts and by new criminal procedures code; has not accepted compulsory ICJ jurisdiction

Suffrage: 17 years of age; universal and married persons regardless of age

Executive branch:
chief of state: President Abdurrahman WAHID (since 20 October 1999) and Vice President MEGAWATI Sukarnoputri (since 21 October 1999); note - the president is both the chief of state and head of government
head of government: President Abdurrahman WAHID (since 20 October 1999) and Vice President MEGAWATI Sukarnoputri (since 21 October 1999); note - the president is both the chief of state and head of government
cabinet: Cabinet appointed by the president
elections: president and vice president elected separately by the 700-member People's Consultative Assembly or MPR for five-year terms; election last held 20 and 21 October 1999 (next to be held by NA 2004)
election results: Abdurrahman WAHID elected president, receiving 373 votes to 313 votes for MEGAWATI Sukarnoputri; MEGAWATI Sukarnoputri elected vice president, defeating Hamzah HAZ; vote totals NA
note: the People's Consultative Assembly (Majelis Permusyawaratan Rakyat or MPR) includes the House of Representatives (Dewan Perwakilan Rakyat or DPR) plus 200 indirectly selected members; it meets every five years to elect the president and vice president and to approve the broad outlines of national policy

Legislative branch: unicameral House of Representatives or Dewan Perwakilan Rakyat (DPR) (500 seats; 462 elected by popular vote, 38 are appointed military representatives; members serve five-year terms)
elections: last held 7 June 1999 (next to be held NA June 2004)
election results: percent of vote by party - PDI-P 37.4%, Golkar 20.9%, PKB 17.4%, PPP 10.7%, PAN 7.3%, PBB 1.8%, other 4.5%; seats by party - PDI-P 154, Golkar 120, PPP 58, PKB 51, PAN 35, PBB 14, other 30

Judicial branch: Supreme Court or Mahkamah Agung (justices appointed by the president from a list of candidates approved by the legislature)

Political parties and leaders: Crescent Moon and Star Party or PBB [Yusril Ihza MAHENDRA, chairman]; Development Unity Party or PPP (federation of former Islamic parties) [Hamzah HAZ, chairman]; Federation of Functional Groups or Golkar [Akbar TANJUNG, general chairman]; Indonesia Democracy Party or PDI (federation of former Nationalist and Christian Parties) [Budi HARDJONO, chairman]; Indonesia Democracy Party-Struggle or PDI-P [MEGAWATI Sukarnoputri, chairperson]; National Awakening Party or PKB [Matori Abdul DJALIL, chairman]; National Mandate Party or PAN [Amien RAIS, chairman]

Political pressure groups and leaders: NA

International organization participation: APEC, ARF, AsDB, ASEAN, CCC, CP, ESCAP, FAO, G-15, G-19, G-77, IAEA, IBRD, ICAO, ICC, ICFTU, ICRM, IDA, IDB, IFAD, IFC, IFRCS, IHO, ILO, IMF, IMO, Inmarsat, Intelsat, Interpol, IOC, IOM (observer), ISO, ITU, NAM, OIC, OPCW, OPEC, UN, UNCTAD, UNESCO, UNIDO, UNIKOM, UNMIBH, UNMOP, UNMOT, UNOMIG, UPU, WCL, WFTU, WHO, WIPO, WMO, WToO, WTrO

Diplomatic representation in the US:
chief of mission: Ambassador DORODJATUN Kuntjoro-Jakti
chancery: 2020 Massachusetts Avenue NW, Washington, DC 20036
telephone: [1] (202) 775-5200
FAX: [1] (202) 775-5365
consulate(s) general: Chicago, Houston, Los Angeles, New York, and San Francisco

Diplomatic representation from the US:
chief of mission: Ambassador Robert GELBARD
embassy: Jalan Merdeka Selatan 4-5, Jakarta 10110
mailing address: Unit 8129, Box 1, APO AP 96520
telephone: [62] (21) 3435-9000
FAX: [62] (21) 3435-9922
consulate(s) general: Surabaya

Flag description: two equal horizontal bands of red (top) and white; similar to the flag of Monaco, which is shorter; also similar to the flag of Poland, which is white (top) and red

Economy

Economy - overview: Indonesia, a vast polyglot nation, faces severe economic problems, stemming from secessionist movements and the low level of security in the regions, the lack of reliable legal recourse in contract disputes, corruption, weaknesses in the banking system, and strained relations with the IMF. Investor confidence will remain low and few new jobs will be created under these circumstances. Growth of 4.8% in 2000 is not sustainable, being attributable to favorable short-term factors, including high world oil prices, a surge in nonoil exports, and increased domestic demand for consumer durables.

GDP: purchasing power parity - $654 billion (2000 est.)

GDP - real growth rate: 4.8% (2000 est.)

GDP - per capita: purchasing power parity - $2,900 (2000 est.)

GDP - composition by sector:
agriculture: 21%
industry: 35%
services: 44% (1999 est.)

Population below poverty line: 20% (1998)

Household income or consumption by percentage share:
lowest 10%: 3.6%
highest 10%: 30.3% (1996)

Inflation rate (consumer prices): 9% (2000 est.)

Labor force: 99 million (1999)

Labor force - by occupation: agriculture 45%, industry 16%, services 39% (1999 est.)

Unemployment rate: 15%-20% (1998 est.)

Budget:
revenues: $26 billion
expenditures: $30 billion, including capital expenditures of $NA (2000 est.)

Industries: petroleum and natural gas; textiles, apparel, and footwear; mining, cement, chemical fertilizers, plywood; rubber; food; tourism

Industrial production growth rate: 7.5% (2000 est.)

Electricity - production: 78.674 billion kWh (1999)

Electricity - production by source:
fossil fuel: 80.36%
hydro: 14.63%
nuclear: 0%
other: 5.01% (1999)

Electricity - consumption: 73.167 billion kWh (1999)

Electricity - exports: 0 kWh (1999)

Electricity - imports: 0 kWh (1999)

Agriculture - products: rice, cassava (tapioca), peanuts, rubber, cocoa, coffee, palm oil, copra; poultry, beef, pork, eggs

Exports: $64.7 billion (f.o.b., 2000 est.)

Exports - commodities: oil and gas, plywood, textiles, rubber

Exports - partners: Japan 21%, US 14%, Singapore 10%, South Korea 7%, Netherlands 3%, Australia 3%, Hong Kong, China, Taiwan (1999 est.)

Imports: $40.4 billion (c.i.f., 2000 est.)

Imports - commodities: machinery and equipment; chemicals, fuels, foodstuffs

Imports - partners: Japan 12%, US 12%, Singapore 10%, Germany 6%, Australia 6%, South Korea 6%, Taiwan, China (1999 est.)

Debt - external: $144 billion (2000 est.)

Economic aid - recipient: $43 billion from IMF program and other official external financing (1997-2000)

Indonesia (continued)

Currency: Indonesian rupiah (IDR)
Currency code: IDR
Exchange rates: Indonesian rupiahs per US dollar - 10,000 (January 2001), 8,421.8 (2000), 7,855.2 (1999), 10,013.6 (1998), 2,909.4 (1997), 2,342.3 (1996)
Fiscal year: calendar year; note - previously was 1 April - 31 March, but starting with 2001, has been changed to calendar year

Communications

Telephones - main lines in use: 5,588,310 (1998)
Telephones - mobile cellular: 1.07 million (1998)
Telephone system:
general assessment: domestic service fair, international service good
domestic: interisland microwave system and HF radio police net; domestic satellite communications system
international: satellite earth stations - 2 Intelsat (1 Indian Ocean and 1 Pacific Ocean)
Radio broadcast stations: AM 678, FM 43, shortwave 82 (1998)
Radios: 31.5 million (1997)
Television broadcast stations: 41 (1999)
Televisions: 13.75 million (1997)
Internet country code: .id
Internet Service Providers (ISPs): 24 (2000)
Internet users: 400,000 (2000)

Transportation

Railways:
total: 6,458 km
narrow gauge: 5,961 km 1.067-m gauge (101 km electrified; 101 km double track); 497 km 0.750-m gauge (1995)
Highways:
total: 342,700 km
paved: 158,670 km
unpaved: 184,030 km (1997)
Waterways: 21,579 km total
note: Sumatra 5,471 km, Java and Madura 820 km, Kalimantan 10,460 km, Sulawesi (Celebes) 241 km, Irian Jaya 4,587 km
Pipelines: crude oil 2,505 km; petroleum products 456 km; natural gas 1,703 km (1989)
Ports and harbors: Cilacap, Cirebon, Jakarta, Kupang, Makassar, Palembang, Semarang, Surabaya
Merchant marine:
total: 609 ships (1,000 GRT or over) totaling 2,698,157 GRT/3,723,933 DWT
ships by type: bulk 36, cargo 357, chemical tanker 10, container 25, liquefied gas 3, livestock carrier 1, passenger 7, passenger/cargo 14, petroleum tanker 117, refrigerated cargo 1, roll on/roll off 15, short-sea passenger 8, specialized tanker 10, vehicle carrier 5 (2000 est.)
Airports: 453 (2000 est.)
Airports - with paved runways:
total: 136
over 3,047 m: 4
2,438 to 3,047 m: 12
1,524 to 2,437 m: 39
914 to 1,523 m: 44
under 914 m: 37 (2000 est.)
Airports - with unpaved runways:
total: 317
1,524 to 2,437 m: 6
914 to 1,523 m: 28
under 914 m: 283 (2000 est.)
Heliports: 4 (2000 est.)

Military

Military branches: Army, Navy, Air Force, Marines
note: as of 1 July 2000, the National Police became an independent organization that reports directly to the president
Military manpower - military age: 18 years of age
Military manpower - availability:
males age 15-49: 64,046,049 (2001 est.)
Military manpower - fit for military service:
males age 15-49: 37,418,755 (2001 est.)
Military manpower - reaching military age annually:
males: 2,263,706 (2001 est.)
Military expenditures - dollar figure: $1 billion (FY98/99)
Military expenditures - percent of GDP: 1.3% (FY98/99)

Transnational Issues

Disputes - international: Sipadan and Ligitan Islands in dispute with Malaysia
Illicit drugs: illicit producer of cannabis largely for domestic use; possible growing role as transshipment point for Golden Triangle heroin

Iran

Introduction

Background: Known as Persia until 1935, Iran became an Islamic republic in 1979 after the ruling shah was forced into exile. Conservative clerical forces subsequently crushed westernizing liberal elements. Militant Iranian students seized the US Embassy in Tehran on 4 November 1979 and held it until 20 January 1981. During 1980-88, Iran fought a bloody, indecisive war with Iraq over disputed territory. The key current issue is how rapidly the country should open up to the modernizing influences of the outside world.

Geography

Location: Middle East, bordering the Gulf of Oman, the Persian Gulf, and the Caspian Sea, between Iraq and Pakistan
Geographic coordinates: 32 00 N, 53 00 E
Map references: Middle East
Area:
total: 1.648 million sq km
land: 1.636 million sq km
water: 12,000 sq km
Area - comparative: slightly larger than Alaska
Land boundaries:
total: 5,440 km
border countries: Afghanistan 936 km, Armenia 35 km, Azerbaijan-proper 432 km, Azerbaijan-Naxcivan exclave 179 km, Iraq 1,458 km, Pakistan 909 km, Turkey 499 km, Turkmenistan 992 km
Coastline: 2,440 km; note - Iran also borders the Caspian Sea (740 km)
Maritime claims:
contiguous zone: 24 NM
continental shelf: natural prolongation
exclusive economic zone: bilateral agreements or median lines in the Persian Gulf
territorial sea: 12 NM
Climate: mostly arid or semiarid, subtropical along Caspian coast

Iran (continued)

Terrain: rugged, mountainous rim; high, central basin with deserts, mountains; small, discontinuous plains along both coasts
Elevation extremes:
lowest point: Caspian Sea -28 m
highest point: Qolleh-ye Damavand 5,671 m
Natural resources: petroleum, natural gas, coal, chromium, copper, iron ore, lead, manganese, zinc, sulfur
Land use:
arable land: 10%
permanent crops: 1%
permanent pastures: 27%
forests and woodland: 7%
other: 55% (1993 est.)
Irrigated land: 94,000 sq km (1993 est.)
Natural hazards: periodic droughts, floods; dust storms, sandstorms; earthquakes along western border and in the northeast
Environment - current issues: air pollution, especially in urban areas, from vehicle emissions, refinery operations, and industrial effluents; deforestation; overgrazing; desertification; oil pollution in the Persian Gulf; inadequate supplies of potable water
Environment - international agreements:
party to: Biodiversity, Climate Change, Desertification, Endangered Species, Hazardous Wastes, Marine Dumping, Nuclear Test Ban, Ozone Layer Protection, Ship Pollution, Wetlands
signed, but not ratified: Environmental Modification, Law of the Sea, Marine Life Conservation

People

Population: 66,128,965 (July 2001 est.)
Age structure:
0-14 years: 32.97% (male 11,150,053; female 10,654,884)
15-64 years: 62.38% (male 20,765,001; female 20,488,672)
65 years and over: 4.65% (male 1,617,045; female 1,453,310) (2001 est.)
Population growth rate: 0.72% (2001 est.)
Birth rate: 17.1 births/1,000 population (2001 est.)
Death rate: 5.41 deaths/1,000 population (2001 est.)
Net migration rate: -4.51 migrant(s)/1,000 population (2001 est.)
Sex ratio:
at birth: 1.05 male(s)/female
under 15 years: 1.05 male(s)/female
15-64 years: 1.01 male(s)/female
65 years and over: 1.11 male(s)/female
total population: 1.03 male(s)/female (2001 est.)
Infant mortality rate: 29.04 deaths/1,000 live births (2001 est.)
Life expectancy at birth:
total population: 69.95 years
male: 68.61 years
female: 71.37 years (2001 est.)
Total fertility rate: 2.02 children born/woman (2001 est.)
HIV/AIDS - adult prevalence rate: less than 0.01% (1999 est.)
HIV/AIDS - people living with HIV/AIDS: NA
HIV/AIDS - deaths: NA
Nationality:
noun: Iranian(s)
adjective: Iranian
Ethnic groups: Persian 51%, Azeri 24%, Gilaki and Mazandarani 8%, Kurd 7%, Arab 3%, Lur 2%, Baloch 2%, Turkmen 2%, other 1%
Religions: Shi'a Muslim 89%, Sunni Muslim 10%, Zoroastrian, Jewish, Christian, and Baha'i 1%
Languages: Persian and Persian dialects 58%, Turkic and Turkic dialects 26%, Kurdish 9%, Luri 2%, Balochi 1%, Arabic 1%, Turkish 1%, other 2%
Literacy:
definition: age 15 and over can read and write
total population: 72.1%
male: 78.4%
female: 65.8% (1994 est.)

Government

Country name:
conventional long form: Islamic Republic of Iran
conventional short form: Iran
local long form: Jomhuri-ye Eslami-ye Iran
local short form: Iran
former: Persia
Government type: theocratic republic
Capital: Tehran
Administrative divisions: 28 provinces (ostanha, singular - ostan); Ardabil, Azarbayjan-e Gharbi, Azarbayjan-e Sharqi, Bushehr, Chahar Mahall va Bakhtiari, Esfahan, Fars, Gilan, Golestan, Hamadan, Hormozgan, Ilam, Kerman, Kermanshah, Khorasan, Khuzestan, Kohgiluyeh va Buyer Ahmad, Kordestan, Lorestan, Markazi, Mazandaran, Qazvin, Qom, Semnan, Sistan va Baluchestan, Tehran, Yazd, Zanjan
Independence: 1 April 1979 (Islamic Republic of Iran proclaimed)
National holiday: Republic Day, 1 April (1979)
Constitution: 2-3 December 1979; revised 1989 to expand powers of the presidency and eliminate the prime ministership
Legal system: the Constitution codifies Islamic principles of government
Suffrage: 15 years of age; universal
Executive branch:
chief of state: Leader of the Islamic Revolution Ayatollah Ali Hoseini-KHAMENEI (since 4 June 1989)
head of government: President (Ali) Mohammad KHATAMI-Ardakani (since 3 August 1997); First Vice President Hasan Ebrahim HABIBI (since NA August 1989)
cabinet: Council of Ministers selected by the president with legislative approval
elections: leader of the Islamic Revolution appointed for life by the Assembly of Experts; president elected by popular vote for a four-year term; election last held 8 June 2001 (next to be held NA 2005)
election results: (Ali) Mohammad KHATAMI-Ardakani reelected president; percent of vote - (Ali) Mohammad KHATAMI-Ardakani 76%
Legislative branch: unicameral Islamic Consultative Assembly or Majles-e-Shura-ye Eslami (290 seats, note - changed from 270 seats with the 18 February 2000 election; members elected by popular vote to serve four-year terms)
elections: last held 18 February-NA April 2000 (next to be held NA 2004)
election results: percent of vote - NA%; seats by party - reformers 170, conservatives 45, and independents 10; 65 seats were up for runoff election on 5 May 2000 (reformers 52, conservatives 10, independents 3)
Judicial branch: Supreme Court
Political parties and leaders: the following organizations appeared to have achieved considerable success at elections to the sixth Majlis in early 2000: Assembly of the Followers of the Imam's Line, Freethinkers' Front, Islamic Iran Participation Front, Moderation and Development Party, Servants of Construction Party, Society of Self-sacrificing Devotees
Political pressure groups and leaders: active student groups include the pro-reform "Organization for Strengthening Unity" and "the Union of Islamic Student Societies'; groups that generally support the Islamic Republic include Ansar-e Hizballah, Mojahedin of the Islamic Revolution, Muslim Students Following the Line of the Imam, and the Islamic Coalition Association; opposition groups include the Liberation Movement of Iran and the Nation of Iran party; armed political groups that have been almost completely repressed by the government include Mojahedin-e Khalq Organization (MEK), People's Fedayeen, Democratic Party of Iranian Kurdistan; the Society for the Defense of Freedom
International organization participation: CCC, CP, ECO, ESCAP, FAO, G-19, G-24, G-77, IAEA, IBRD, ICAO, ICC, ICRM, IDA, IDB, IFAD, IFC, IFRCS, IHO, ILO, IMF, IMO, Inmarsat, Intelsat, Interpol, IOC, IOM (observer), ISO, ITU, NAM, OIC, OPCW, OPEC, PCA, UN, UNCTAD, UNESCO, UNHCR, UNIDO, UPU, WCL, WFTU, WHO, WMO, WToO
Diplomatic representation in the US: none; note - Iran has an Interests Section in the Pakistani Embassy; address: Iranian Interests Section, Pakistani Embassy, 2209 Wisconsin Avenue NW, Washington, DC 20007; telephone: [1] (202) 965-4990
Diplomatic representation from the US: none; note - protecting power in Iran is Switzerland
Flag description: three equal horizontal bands of green (top), white, and red; the national emblem (a stylized representation of the word Allah) in red is centered in the white band; ALLAH AKBAR (God is Great) in white Arabic script is repeated 11 times along the bottom edge of the green band and 11 times along the top edge of the red band

Iran (continued)

Economy

Economy - overview: Iran's economy is a mixture of central planning, state ownership of oil and other large enterprises, village agriculture, and small-scale private trading and service ventures. President KHATAMI has continued to follow the market reform plans of former President RAFSANJANI and has indicated that he will pursue diversification of Iran's oil-reliant economy although he has made little progress toward that goal. The strong oil market in 1996 helped ease financial pressures on Iran and allowed for Tehran's timely debt service payments. Iran's financial situation tightened in 1997 and deteriorated further in 1998 because of lower oil prices. The subsequent zoom in oil prices in 1999-2000 afforded Iran fiscal breathing room but does not solve Iran's structural economic problems, including the encouragement of foreign investment.
GDP: purchasing power parity - $413 billion (2000 est.)
GDP - real growth rate: 3% (2000 est.)
GDP - per capita: purchasing power parity - $6,300 (2000 est.)
GDP - composition by sector:
agriculture: 24%
industry: 28%
services: 48% (2000 est.)
Population below poverty line: 53% (1996 est.)
Household income or consumption by percentage share:
lowest 10%: NA%
highest 10%: NA%
Inflation rate (consumer prices): 16% (2000 est.)
Labor force: 17.3 million
note: shortage of skilled labor (1998)
Labor force - by occupation: agriculture 33%, industry 25%, services 42% (1999 est.)
Unemployment rate: 14% (1999 est.)
Budget:
revenues: $27 billion
expenditures: $27 billion, including capital expenditures of $NA (1999)
Industries: petroleum, petrochemicals, textiles, cement and other construction materials, food processing (particularly sugar refining and vegetable oil production), metal fabricating, armaments
Industrial production growth rate: 4.4% (nonoil) (1999)
Electricity - production: 103.054 billion kWh (1999)
Electricity - production by source:
fossil fuel: 93.16%
hydro: 6.84%
nuclear: 0%
other: 0% (1999)
Electricity - consumption: 95.84 billion kWh (1999)
Electricity - exports: 0 kWh (1999)
Electricity - imports: 0 kWh (1999)
Agriculture - products: wheat, rice, other grains, sugar beets, fruits, nuts, cotton; dairy products, wool; caviar
Exports: $25 billion (f.o.b., 2000 est.)
Exports - commodities: petroleum 85%, carpets, fruits and nuts, iron and steel, chemicals
Exports - partners: Japan, Italy, UAE, South Korea, France, China
Imports: $15 billion (f.o.b., 2000 est.)
Imports - commodities: industrial raw materials and intermediate goods, capital goods, foodstuffs and other consumer goods, technical services, military supplies
Imports - partners: Germany, South Korea, Italy, UAE, France, Japan
Debt - external: $7.5 billion (2000 est.)
Economic aid - recipient: $116.5 million (1995)
Currency: Iranian rial (IRR)
Currency code: IRR
Exchange rates: Iranian rials per US dollar - 1,754.71 (January 2001), 1,764.43 (2000), 1,725.93 (1999), 1,751.86 (1998), 1,752.92 (1997), 1,750.76 (1996)
note: Iran has three officially recognized exchange rates; the averages for 1999 are as follows: the official floating rate of 1,750 rials per US dollar, the "export" rate of 3,000 rials per US dollar, and the variable Tehran Stock Exchange rate, which averages 7,863 rials per US dollar; the market rate averages 8,615 rials per US dollar
Fiscal year: 21 March - 20 March

Communications

Telephones - main lines in use: 6.313 million (1997)
Telephones - mobile cellular: 265,000 (August 1998)
Telephone system:
general assessment: inadequate but currently being modernized and expanded with the goal of not only improving the efficiency and increasing the volume of the urban service but also bringing telephone service to several thousand villages, not presently connected
domestic: as a result of heavy investing in the telephone system since 1994, the number of long-distance channels in the microwave radio relay trunk has grown substantially; many villages have been brought into the net; the number of main lines in the urban systems has approximately doubled; and thousands of mobile cellular subscribers are being served; moreover, the technical level of the system has been raised by the installation of thousands of digital switches
international: HF radio and microwave radio relay to Turkey, Azerbaijan, Pakistan, Afghanistan, Turkmenistan, Syria, Kuwait, Tajikistan, and Uzbekistan; submarine fiber-optic cable to UAE with access to Fiber-Optic Link Around the Globe (FLAG); Trans-Asia-Europe (TAE) fiber-optic line runs from Azerbaijan through the northern portion of Iran to Turkmenistan with expansion to Georgia and Azerbaijan; satellite earth stations - 9 Intelsat and 4 Inmarsat; Internet service available but limited to electronic mail to promote Iranian culture
Radio broadcast stations: AM 72, FM 5, shortwave 5 (1998)
Radios: 17 million (1997)
Television broadcast stations: 28 (plus 450 low-power repeaters) (1997)
Televisions: 4.61 million (1997)
Internet country code: .ir
Internet Service Providers (ISPs): 8 (2000)
Internet users: 100,000 (2000)

Transportation

Railways:
total: 5,600 km
broad gauge: 94 km 1.676-m gauge
standard gauge: 5,506 km 1.435-m gauge (146 km electrified)
note: broad gauge track is employed at the borders with Azerbaijan and Turkmenistan which have broad-gauge rail systems (2001)
Highways:
total: 140,200 km
paved: 49,440 km (including 470 km of expressways)
unpaved: 90,760 km (1998 est.)
Waterways: 904 km
note: the Shatt al Arab is usually navigable by maritime traffic for about 130 km; channel has been dredged to 3 m and is in use
Pipelines: crude oil 5,900 km; petroleum products 3,900 km; natural gas 4,550 km
Ports and harbors: Abadan (largely destroyed in fighting during 1980-88 war), Ahvaz, Bandar 'Abbas, Bandar-e Anzali, Bushehr, Bandar-e Emam Khomeyni, Bandar-e Lengeh, Bandar-e Mahshahr, Bandar-e Torkaman, Chabahar (Bandar Beheshti), Jazireh-ye Khark, Jazireh-ye Lavan, Jazireh-ye Sirri, Khorramshahr (limited operation since November 1992), Now Shahr
Merchant marine:
total: 152 ships (1,000 GRT or over) totaling 4,097,977 GRT/7,131,688 DWT
ships by type: bulk 49, cargo 38, chemical tanker 4, combination bulk 1, container 10, liquefied gas 1, multi-functional large-load carrier 6, petroleum tanker 32, refrigerated cargo 1, roll on/roll off 9, short-sea passenger 1
note: includes some foreign-owned ships registered here as a flag of convenience: Singapore 1 (2000 est.)
Airports: 317 (2000 est.)
Airports - with paved runways:
total: 117
over 3,047 m: 38
2,438 to 3,047 m: 23
1,524 to 2,437 m: 25
914 to 1,523 m: 24
under 914 m: 7 (2000 est.)
Airports - with unpaved runways:
total: 200
over 3,047 m: 2
2,438 to 3,047 m: 3
1,524 to 2,437 m: 13
914 to 1,523 m: 122
under 914 m: 60 (2000 est.)
Heliports: 11 (2000 est.)

Iran (continued)

Military

Military branches: Islamic Republic of Iran regular forces (includes Ground Forces, Navy, Air and Air Defense Forces), Revolutionary Guards (includes Ground, Air, Navy, Qods, and Basij-mobilization-forces), Law Enforcement Forces
Military manpower - military age: 21 years of age
Military manpower - availability:
males age 15-49: 18,319,328 (2001 est.)
Military manpower - fit for military service:
males age 15-49: 10,872,407 (2001 est.)
Military manpower - reaching military age annually:
males: 823,040 (2001 est.)
Military expenditures - dollar figure: $5.787 billion (FY98/99)
Military expenditures - percent of GDP: 2.9% (FY98/99)

Transnational Issues

Disputes - international: Iran and Iraq restored diplomatic relations in 1990 but are still trying to work out written agreements settling outstanding disputes from their eight-year war concerning border demarcation, prisoners-of-war, and freedom of navigation and sovereignty over the Shatt al Arab waterway; Iran occupies two islands in the Persian Gulf claimed by the UAE: Lesser Tunb (called Tunb as Sughra in Arabic by UAE and Jazireh-ye Tonb-e Kuchek in Persian by Iran) and Greater Tunb (called Tunb al Kubra in Arabic by UAE and Jazireh-ye Tonb-e Bozorg in Persian by Iran); Iran jointly administers with the UAE an island in the Persian Gulf claimed by the UAE (called Abu Musa in Arabic by UAE and Jazireh-ye Abu Musa in Persian by Iran) - over which Iran has taken steps to exert unilateral control since 1992, including access restrictions and a military build-up on the island; the UAE has garnered significant diplomatic support in the region in protesting these Iranian actions; Caspian Sea boundaries are not yet determined among Azerbaijan, Iran, Kazakhstan, Russia, and Turkmenistan
Illicit drugs: despite substantial interdiction efforts, Iran remains a key transshipment point for Southwest Asian heroin to Europe; domestic consumption of narcotics remains a persistent problem and Iranian press reports estimate that there are at least 1.2 million drug users in the country

Iraq

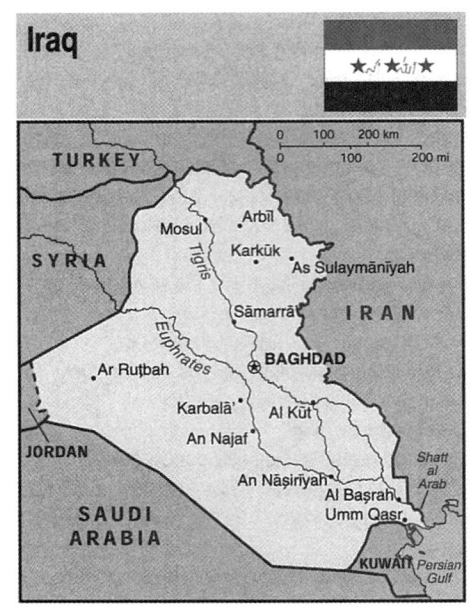

Introduction

Background: Formerly part of the Ottoman Empire, Iraq became an independent kingdom in 1932. A "republic" was proclaimed in 1958, but in actuality a series of military strongmen have ruled the country since then, the latest being SADDAM Husayn. Territorial disputes with Iran led to an inconclusive and costly eight-year war (1980-1988). In August 1990 Iraq seized Kuwait, but was expelled by US-led, UN coalition forces during January-February 1991. The victors did not occupy Iraq, however, thus allowing the regime to stay in control. Following Kuwait's liberation, the UN Security Council (UNSC) required Iraq to scrap all weapons of mass destruction and long-range missiles and to allow UN verification inspections. UN trade sanctions remain in effect due to incomplete Iraqi compliance with relevant UNSC resolutions.

Geography

Location: Middle East, bordering the Persian Gulf, between Iran and Kuwait
Geographic coordinates: 33 00 N, 44 00 E
Map references: Middle East
Area:
total: 437,072 sq km
land: 432,162 sq km
water: 4,910 sq km
Area - comparative: slightly more than twice the size of Idaho
Land boundaries:
total: 3,631 km
border countries: Iran 1,458 km, Jordan 181 km, Kuwait 242 km, Saudi Arabia 814 km, Syria 605 km, Turkey 331 km
Coastline: 58 km
Maritime claims:
continental shelf: not specified
territorial sea: 12 NM
Climate: mostly desert; mild to cool winters with dry, hot, cloudless summers; northern mountainous regions along Iranian and Turkish borders experience cold winters with occasionally heavy snows that melt in early spring, sometimes causing extensive flooding in central and southern Iraq
Terrain: mostly broad plains; reedy marshes along Iranian border in south with large flooded areas; mountains along borders with Iran and Turkey
Elevation extremes:
lowest point: Persian Gulf 0 m
highest point: Haji Ibrahim 3,600 m
Natural resources: petroleum, natural gas, phosphates, sulfur
Land use:
arable land: 12%
permanent crops: 0%
permanent pastures: 9%
forests and woodland: 0%
other: 79% (1993 est.)
Irrigated land: 25,500 sq km (1993 est.)
Natural hazards: dust storms, sandstorms, floods
Environment - current issues: government water control projects have drained most of the inhabited marsh areas east of An Nasiriyah by drying up or diverting the feeder streams and rivers; a once sizable population of Shi'a Muslims, who have inhabited these areas for thousands of years, has been displaced; furthermore, the destruction of the natural habitat poses serious threats to the area's wildlife populations; inadequate supplies of potable water; development of Tigris-Euphrates Rivers system contingent upon agreements with upstream riparian Turkey; air and water pollution; soil degradation (salination) and erosion; desertification
Environment - international agreements:
party to: Law of the Sea, Marine Dumping, Nuclear Test Ban, Ship Pollution
signed, but not ratified: Environmental Modification

People

Population: 23,331,985 (July 2001 est.)
Age structure:
0-14 years: 41.64% (male 4,934,340; female 4,781,206)
15-64 years: 55.28% (male 6,528,854; female 6,368,823)
65 years and over: 3.08% (male 335,953; female 382,809) (2001 est.)
Population growth rate: 2.84% (2001 est.)
Birth rate: 34.64 births/1,000 population (2001 est.)
Death rate: 6.21 deaths/1,000 population (2001 est.)
Net migration rate: 0 migrant(s)/1,000 population (2001 est.)
Sex ratio:
at birth: 1.05 male(s)/female
under 15 years: 1.03 male(s)/female
15-64 years: 1.03 male(s)/female
65 years and over: 0.88 male(s)/female
total population: 1.02 male(s)/female (2001 est.)

Iraq (continued)

Infant mortality rate: 60.05 deaths/1,000 live births (2001 est.)
Life expectancy at birth:
total population: 66.95 years
male: 65.92 years
female: 68.03 years (2001 est.)
Total fertility rate: 4.75 children born/woman (2001 est.)
HIV/AIDS - adult prevalence rate: less than 0.01% (1999 est.)
HIV/AIDS - people living with HIV/AIDS: NA
HIV/AIDS - deaths: NA
Nationality:
noun: Iraqi(s)
adjective: Iraqi
Ethnic groups: Arab 75%-80%, Kurdish 15%-20%, Turkoman, Assyrian or other 5%
Religions: Muslim 97% (Shi'a 60%-65%, Sunni 32%-37%), Christian or other 3%
Languages: Arabic, Kurdish (official in Kurdish regions), Assyrian, Armenian
Literacy:
definition: age 15 and over can read and write
total population: 58%
male: 70.7%
female: 45% (1995 est.)

Government

Country name:
conventional long form: Republic of Iraq
conventional short form: Iraq
local long form: Al Jumhuriyah al Iraqiyah
local short form: Al Iraq
Government type: republic
Capital: Baghdad
Administrative divisions: 18 provinces (muhafazat, singular - muhafazah); Al Anbar, Al Basrah, Al Muthanna, Al Qadisiyah, An Najaf, Arbil, As Sulaymaniyah, At Ta'mim, Babil, Baghdad, Dahuk, Dhi Qar, Diyala, Karbala', Maysan, Ninawa, Salah ad Din, Wasit
Independence: 3 October 1932 (from League of Nations mandate under British administration)
National holiday: Revolution Day, 17 July (1968)
Constitution: 22 September 1968, effective 16 July 1970 (provisional constitution); new constitution drafted in 1990 but not adopted
Legal system: based on Islamic law in special religious courts, civil law system elsewhere; has not accepted compulsory ICJ jurisdiction
Suffrage: 18 years of age; universal
Executive branch:
chief of state: President SADDAM Husayn (since 16 July 1979); Vice Presidents Taha Muhyi al-Din MARUF (since 21 April 1974) and Taha Yasin RAMADAN (since 23 March 1991)
head of government: Prime Minister SADDAM Husayn (since 29 May 1994); Deputy Prime Ministers Tariq Mikhail AZIZ (since NA 1979) and Hikmat Mizban Ibrahim al-AZZAWI (since 30 July 1999)
cabinet: Council of Ministers; note - there is also a Revolutionary Command Council or RCC (Chairman SADDAM Husayn, Vice Chairman Izzat IBRAHIM al-Duri) which controls the ruling Ba'th Party, and is the most powerful political entity in the country
elections: president and vice presidents elected by a two-thirds majority of the Revolutionary Command Council; election last held 17 October 1995 (next to be held NA 2002)
election results: SADDAM Husayn reelected president; percent of vote - 99%; Taha Muhyi al-Din MARUF and Taha Yasin RAMADAN elected vice presidents; percent of vote - NA%
Legislative branch: unicameral National Assembly or Majlis al-Watani (250 seats; 30 appointed by the president to represent the three northern provinces of Dahuk, Arbil, and As Sulaymaniyah; 220 elected by popular vote; members serve four-year terms)
elections: last held 27 March 2000 (next to be held NA March 2004)
election results: percent of vote by party - NA%; seats by party - NA
Judicial branch: Court of Cassation
Political parties and leaders: Ba'th Party [SADDAM Husayn, central party leader]
Political pressure groups and leaders: any formal political activity must be sanctioned by the government; opposition to regime from Kurdish groups and southern Shi'a dissidents
International organization participation: ABEDA, ACC, AFESD, AL, AMF, CAEU, CCC, EAPC, ESCWA, FAO, G-19, G-77, IAEA, IBRD, ICAO, ICRM, IDA, IDB, IFAD, IFC, IFRCS, ILO, IMF, IMO, Inmarsat, Intelsat, Interpol, IOC, ITU, NAM, OAPEC, OIC, OPEC, PCA, UN, UNCTAD, UNESCO, UNIDO, UPU, WFTU, WHO, WIPO, WMO, WToO
Diplomatic representation in the US: none; note - Iraq has an Interest Section in the Algerian Embassy headed by Akram AL DOURI; address: Iraqi Interests Section, Algerian Embassy, 1801 P Street NW, Washington, DC 20036; telephone: [1] (202) 483-7500; FAX: [1] (202) 462-5066
Diplomatic representation from the US: none; note - the US has an Interests Section in the Polish Embassy in Baghdad; address: P. O. Box 2051 Hay Babel, Baghdad; telephone: [964] (1) 718-9267; FAX: [964] (1) 718-9297
Flag description: three equal horizontal bands of red (top), white, and black with three green five-pointed stars in a horizontal line centered in the white band; the phrase ALLAHU AKBAR (God is Great) in green Arabic script - Allahu to the right of the middle star and Akbar to the left of the middle star - was added in January 1991 during the Persian Gulf crisis; similar to the flag of Syria which has two stars but no script and the flag of Yemen which has a plain white band; also similar to the flag of Egypt which has a symbolic eagle centered in the white band

Economy

Economy - overview: Iraq's economy is dominated by the oil sector, which has traditionally provided about 95% of foreign exchange earnings. In the 1980s, financial problems caused by massive expenditures in the eight-year war with Iran and damage to oil export facilities by Iran led the government to implement austerity measures, borrow heavily, and later reschedule foreign debt payments; Iraq suffered economic losses of at least $100 billion from the war. After the end of hostilities in 1988, oil exports gradually increased with the construction of new pipelines and restoration of damaged facilities. Iraq's seizure of Kuwait in August 1990, subsequent international economic sanctions, and damage from military action by an international coalition beginning in January 1991 drastically reduced economic activity. Although government policies supporting large military and internal security forces and allocating resources to key supporters of the regime have hurt the economy, implementation of the UN's oil-for-food program in December 1996 has helped improve conditions for the average Iraqi citizen. For the first six, six-month phases of the program, Iraq was allowed to export limited amounts of oil in exchange for food, medicine, and some infrastructure spare parts. In December 1999, the UN Security Council authorized Iraq to export under the program as much oil as required to meet humanitarian needs. Oil exports are now more than three-quarters their prewar level. Per capita food imports have increased significantly, while medical supplies and health care services are steadily improving. Per capita output and living standards are still well below the prewar level, but any estimates have a wide range of error.
GDP: purchasing power parity - $57 billion (2000 est.)
GDP - real growth rate: 15% (2000 est.)
GDP - per capita: purchasing power parity - $2,500 (2000 est.)
GDP - composition by sector:
agriculture: 6%
industry: 13%
services: 81% (1993 est.)
Population below poverty line: NA%
Household income or consumption by percentage share:
lowest 10%: NA%
highest 10%: NA%
Inflation rate (consumer prices): 100% (2000 est.)
Labor force: 4.4 million (1989)
Labor force - by occupation: agriculture NA%, industry NA%, services NA%
Unemployment rate: NA%
Budget:
revenues: $NA
expenditures: $NA, including capital expenditures of $NA
Industries: petroleum, chemicals, textiles, construction materials, food processing

Iraq (continued)

Industrial production growth rate: NA%
Electricity - production: 29.42 billion kWh (1999)
Electricity - production by source:
fossil fuel: 97.96%
hydro: 2.04%
nuclear: 0%
other: 0% (1999)
Electricity - consumption: 27.361 billion kWh (1999)
Electricity - exports: 0 kWh (1999)
Electricity - imports: 0 kWh (1999)
Agriculture - products: wheat, barley, rice, vegetables, dates, cotton; cattle, sheep
Exports: $21.8 billion (2000 est.)
Exports - commodities: crude oil
Exports - partners: Russia, France, Switzerland, China (2000)
Imports: $13.8 billion (2000 est.)
Imports - commodities: food, medicine, manufactures
Imports - partners: Egypt, Russia, France, Vietnam (2000)
Debt - external: $139 billion (2000 est.)
Economic aid - recipient: $327.5 million (1995)
Currency: Iraqi dinar (IQD)
Currency code: IQD
Exchange rates: Iraqi dinars per US dollar - 0.3109 (fixed official rate since 1982); black market rate - Iraqi dinars per US dollar - 1,910 (December 1999), 1,815 (December 1998), 1,530 (December 1997), 910 (December 1996), 3,000 (December 1995); note - subject to wide fluctuations
Fiscal year: calendar year

Communications

Telephones - main lines in use: 675,000 (1997)
Telephones - mobile cellular: NA; service available in northern Iraq (2001)
Telephone system:
general assessment: reconstitution of damaged telecommunication facilities began after the Gulf war; most damaged facilities have been rebuilt
domestic: the network consists of coaxial cables and microwave radio relay links
international: satellite earth stations - 2 Intelsat (1 Atlantic Ocean and 1 Indian Ocean), 1 Intersputnik (Atlantic Ocean region), and 1 Arabsat (inoperative); coaxial cable and microwave radio relay to Jordan, Kuwait, Syria, and Turkey; Kuwait line is probably nonoperational
Radio broadcast stations: AM 19 (5 are inactive), FM 51, shortwave 4 (1998)
Radios: 4.85 million (1997)
Television broadcast stations: 13 (1997)
Televisions: 1.75 million (1997)
Internet country code: .iq
Internet Service Providers (ISPs): 1 (2000)
Internet users: NA

Transportation

Railways:
total: 2,032 km
standard gauge: 2,032 km 1.435-m gauge
note: rail link between Iraq and Syria restored in 2000 after 19 years
Highways:
total: 45,550 km
paved: 38,400 km
unpaved: 7,150 km (1996 est.)
Waterways: 1,015 km
note: Shatt al Arab is usually navigable by maritime traffic for about 130 km; channel has been dredged to 3 m and is in use; Tigris and Euphrates Rivers have navigable sections for shallow-draft boats; Shatt al Basrah canal was navigable by shallow-draft craft before closing in 1991 because of the Gulf war
Pipelines: crude oil 4,350 km; petroleum products 725 km; natural gas 1,360 km
Ports and harbors: Umm Qasr, Khawr az Zubayr, and Al Basrah have limited functionality
Merchant marine:
total: 30 ships (1,000 GRT or over) totaling 453,273 GRT/779,662 DWT
ships by type: cargo 14, passenger 1, passenger/cargo 1, petroleum tanker 12, refrigerated cargo 1, roll on/roll off 1 (2000 est.)
Airports: 110 (2000 est.)
Airports - with paved runways:
total: 76
over 3,047 m: 20
2,438 to 3,047 m: 36
1,524 to 2,437 m: 6
914 to 1,523 m: 7
under 914 m: 7 (2000 est.)
Airports - with unpaved runways:
total: 34
over 3,047 m: 3
2,438 to 3,047 m: 5
1,524 to 2,437 m: 4
914 to 1,523 m: 10
under 914 m: 12 (2000 est.)
Heliports: 4 (2000 est.)

Military

Military branches: Army, Republican Guard, Navy, Air Force, Air Defense Force, Border Guard Force, Fedayeen Saddam
Military manpower - military age: 18 years of age
Military manpower - availability:
males age 15-49: 5,902,215 (2001 est.)
Military manpower - fit for military service:
males age 15-49: 3,301,880 (2001 est.)
Military manpower - reaching military age annually:
males: 274,035 (2001 est.)
Military expenditures - dollar figure: $NA
Military expenditures - percent of GDP: NA%

Transnational Issues

Disputes - international: Iran and Iraq restored diplomatic relations in 1990 but are still trying to work out written agreements settling outstanding disputes from their eight-year war concerning border demarcation, prisoners-of-war, and freedom of navigation and sovereignty over the Shatt al Arab waterway; in November 1994, Iraq formally accepted the UN-demarcated border with Kuwait which had been spelled out in Security Council Resolutions 687 (1991), 773 (1993), and 883 (1993); this formally ends earlier claims to Kuwait and to Bubiyan and Warbah islands although the government continues periodic rhetorical challenges; dispute over water development plans by Turkey for the Tigris and Euphrates rivers

Ireland

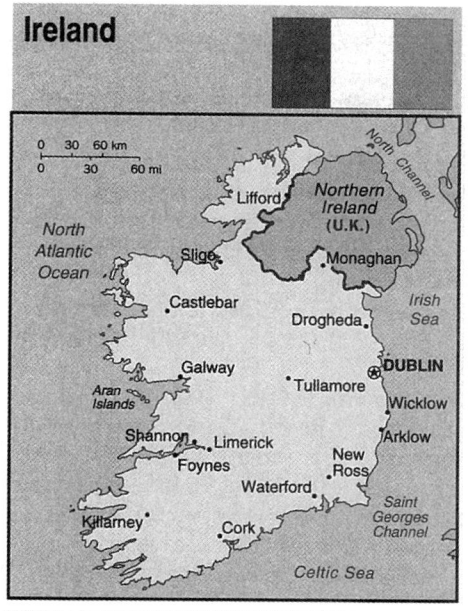

Introduction

Background: A failed 1916 Easter Monday Rebellion touched off several years of guerrilla warfare that in 1921 resulted in independence from the UK for the 26 southern counties; the six northern counties (Ulster) remained part of Great Britain. In 1948 Ireland withdrew from the British Commonwealth; it joined the European Community in 1973. Irish governments have sought the peaceful unification of Ireland and have cooperated with Britain against terrorist groups. A peace settlement for Northern Ireland, approved in 1998, was implemented the following year.

Geography

Location: Western Europe, occupying five-sixths of the island of Ireland in the North Atlantic Ocean, west of Great Britain
Geographic coordinates: 53 00 N, 8 00 W
Map references: Europe
Area:
total: 70,280 sq km
land: 68,890 sq km
water: 1,390 sq km
Area - comparative: slightly larger than West Virginia
Land boundaries:
total: 360 km
border countries: UK 360 km
Coastline: 1,448 km
Maritime claims:
continental shelf: not specified
exclusive fishing zone: 200 NM
territorial sea: 12 NM
Climate: temperate maritime; modified by North Atlantic Current; mild winters, cool summers; consistently humid; overcast about half the time
Terrain: mostly level to rolling interior plain surrounded by rugged hills and low mountains; sea cliffs on west coast
Elevation extremes:
lowest point: Atlantic Ocean 0 m
highest point: Carrauntoohil 1,041 m
Natural resources: zinc, lead, natural gas, barite, copper, gypsum, limestone, dolomite, peat, silver
Land use:
arable land: 13%
permanent crops: 0%
permanent pastures: 68%
forests and woodland: 5%
other: 14% (1993 est.)
Irrigated land: NA sq km
Natural hazards: NA
Environment - current issues: water pollution, especially of lakes, from agricultural runoff
Environment - international agreements:
party to: Air Pollution, Air Pollution-Nitrogen Oxides, Air Pollution-Sulphur 94, Biodiversity, Climate Change, Desertification, Environmental Modification, Hazardous Wastes, Law of the Sea, Marine Dumping, Nuclear Test Ban, Ozone Layer Protection, Ship Pollution, Tropical Timber 83, Tropical Timber 94, Wetlands, Whaling
signed, but not ratified: Air Pollution-Persistent Organic Pollutants, Climate Change-Kyoto Protocol, Endangered Species, Marine Life Conservation
Geography - note: strategic location on major air and sea routes between North America and northern Europe; over 40% of the population resides within 97 km of Dublin

People

Population: 3,840,838 (July 2001 est.)
Age structure:
0-14 years: 21.57% (male 425,328; female 403,204)
15-64 years: 67.08% (male 1,290,002; female 1,286,312)
65 years and over: 11.35% (male 188,868; female 247,124) (2001 est.)
Population growth rate: 1.12% (2001 est.)
Birth rate: 14.57 births/1,000 population (2001 est.)
Death rate: 8.07 deaths/1,000 population (2001 est.)
Net migration rate: 4.69 migrant(s)/1,000 population (2001 est.)
Sex ratio:
at birth: 1.07 male(s)/female
under 15 years: 1.05 male(s)/female
15-64 years: 1 male(s)/female
65 years and over: 0.76 male(s)/female
total population: 0.98 male(s)/female (2001 est.)
Infant mortality rate: 5.53 deaths/1,000 live births (2001 est.)
Life expectancy at birth:
total population: 76.99 years
male: 74.23 years
female: 79.93 years (2001 est.)
Total fertility rate: 1.9 children born/woman (2001 est.)
HIV/AIDS - adult prevalence rate: 0.1% (1999 est.)
HIV/AIDS - people living with HIV/AIDS: 2,200 (1999 est.)
HIV/AIDS - deaths: less than 100 (1999 est.)
Nationality:
noun: Irishman(men), Irishwoman(women), Irish (collective plural)
adjective: Irish
Ethnic groups: Celtic, English
Religions: Roman Catholic 91.6%, Church of Ireland 2.5%, other 5.9% (1998)
Languages: English is the language generally used, Irish (Gaelic) spoken mainly in areas located along the western seaboard
Literacy:
definition: age 15 and over can read and write
total population: 98% (1981 est.)
male: NA%
female: NA%

Government

Country name:
conventional long form: none
conventional short form: Ireland
Government type: republic
Capital: Dublin
Administrative divisions: 26 counties; Carlow, Cavan, Clare, Cork, Donegal, Dublin, Galway, Kerry, Kildare, Kilkenny, Laois, Leitrim, Limerick, Longford, Louth, Mayo, Meath, Monaghan, Offaly, Roscommon, Sligo, Tipperary, Waterford, Westmeath, Wexford, Wicklow
Independence: 6 December 1921 (from UK by treaty)
National holiday: Saint Patrick's Day, 17 March
Constitution: 29 December 1937; adopted 1 July 1937 by plebiscite
Legal system: based on English common law, substantially modified by indigenous concepts; judicial review of legislative acts in Supreme Court; has not accepted compulsory ICJ jurisdiction
Suffrage: 18 years of age; universal
Executive branch:
chief of state: President Mary MCALEESE (since 11 November 1997)
head of government: Prime Minister Bertie AHERN (since 26 June 1997)
cabinet: Cabinet appointed by the president with previous nomination by the prime minister and approval of the House of Representatives
elections: president elected by popular vote for a seven-year term; election last held 31 October 1997 (next to be held NA November 2004); prime minister nominated by the House of Representatives and appointed by the president
election results: Mary MCALEESE elected president; percent of vote - Mary MCALEESE 44.8%, Mary BANOTTI 29.6%
note: government coalition - Fianna Fail and the Progressive Democrats
Legislative branch: bicameral Parliament or Oireachtas consists of the Senate or Seanad Eireann (60 seats - 49 elected by the universities and from candidates put forward by five vocational panels, 11 are nominated by the prime minister; members serve

Ireland (continued)

five-year terms) and the House of Representatives or Dail Eireann (166 seats; members are elected by popular vote on the basis of proportional representation to serve five-year terms)
elections: Senate - last held NA August 1997 (next to be held NA 2002); House of Representatives - last held 6 June 1997 (next to be held NA 2002)
election results: Senate - percent of vote by party - NA%; seats by party - Fianna Fail 29, Fine Gael 16, Labor Party 4, Progressive Democrats 4, others 7; House of Representatives - percent of vote by party - NA%; seats by party - Fianna Fail 76, Fine Gael 53, Labor Party 19, Progressive Democrats 4, Democratic Left 4, Green Alliance 2, Sinn Fein 1, independents 7; note - seats by party in the House of Representatives as of 1 January 2001 were as follows: Fianna Fail 76, Fine Gael 54, Labor Party 21, Progressive Democrats 4, Green Alliance 2, Socialist Party 1, Sinn Fein 1, independents 7
Judicial branch: Supreme Court (judges appointed by the president on the advice of the prime minister and cabinet)
Political parties and leaders: Democratic Left [Proinsias DE ROSSA]; Fianna Fail [Bertie AHERN]; Fine Gael [Michael NOONAN]; Green Party [Mary BOWERS]; Labor Party [Ruairi QUINN]; Progressive Democrats [Mary HARNEY]; Sinn Fein [Gerry ADAMS]; Socialist Party [Joe HIGGINS]; The Workers' Party [Tom FRENCH]
Political pressure groups and leaders: NA
International organization participation: Australia Group, BIS, CCC, CE, EBRD, ECE, EIB, EMU, ESA, EU, FAO, IAEA, IBRD, ICAO, ICC, ICFTU, ICRM, IDA, IEA, IFAD, IFC, IFRCS, ILO, IMF, IMO, Intelsat, Interpol, IOC, IOM (observer), ISO, ITU, MINURSO, NAM (guest), NEA, NSG, OAS (observer), OECD, OPCW, OSCE, PFP, UN, UN Security Council (temporary), UNCTAD, UNESCO, UNFICYP, UNHCR, UNIDO, UNIFIL, UNIKOM, UNITAR, UNMIBH, UNMIK, UNMOP, UNTAET, UNTSO, UPU, WEU (observer), WHO, WIPO, WMO, WTrO, ZC
Diplomatic representation in the US:
chief of mission: Ambassador Sean O'HUIGINN
chancery: 2234 Massachusetts Avenue NW, Washington, DC 20008
telephone: [1] (202) 462-3939
FAX: [1] (202) 232-5993
consulate(s) general: Boston, Chicago, New York, and San Francisco
Diplomatic representation from the US:
chief of mission: Ambassador Michael J. SULLIVAN
embassy: 42 Elgin Road, Ballsbridge, Dublin 4
mailing address: use embassy street address
telephone: [353] (1) 668-7122/668-8777
FAX: [353] (1) 668-9946
Flag description: three equal vertical bands of green (hoist side), white, and orange; similar to the flag of Cote d'Ivoire, which is shorter and has the colors reversed - orange (hoist side), white, and green; also similar to the flag of Italy, which is shorter and has colors of green (hoist side), white, and red

Economy

Economy - overview: Ireland is a small, modern, trade-dependent economy with growth averaging a robust 9% in 1995-2000. Agriculture, once the most important sector, is now dwarfed by industry, which accounts for 38% of GDP and about 80% of exports and employs 28% of the labor force. Although exports remain the primary engine for Ireland's robust growth, the economy is also benefiting from a rise in consumer spending and recovery in both construction and business investment. Over the past decade, the Irish government has implemented a series of national economic programs designed to curb inflation, reduce government spending, increase labor force skills, and promote foreign investment. Ireland joined in launching the euro currency system in January 1999 along with 10 other EU nations. The Irish economy is in danger of overheating, with the tight labor market driving up wage demands and inflation.
GDP: purchasing power parity - $81.9 billion (2000 est.)
GDP - real growth rate: 9.9% (2000 est.)
GDP - per capita: purchasing power parity - $21,600 (2000 est.)
GDP - composition by sector:
agriculture: 4%
industry: 38%
services: 58% (1999)
Population below poverty line: 10% (1997 est.)
Household income or consumption by percentage share:
lowest 10%: 2%
highest 10%: 27.3% (1997)
Inflation rate (consumer prices): 5.6% (2000)
Labor force: 1.82 million (2000 est.)
Labor force - by occupation: services 64%, industry 28%, agriculture 8% (2000 est.)
Unemployment rate: 4.1% (2000)
Budget:
revenues: $25.7 billion
expenditures: $19.2 billion, including capital expenditures of $2 billion (2000)
Industries: food products, brewing, textiles, clothing; chemicals, pharmaceuticals, machinery, transportation equipment, glass and crystal; software
Industrial production growth rate: 14% (2000 est.)
Electricity - production: 19.542 billion kWh (1999)
Electricity - production by source:
fossil fuel: 94.42%
hydro: 4.23%
nuclear: 0%
other: 1.35% (1999)
Electricity - consumption: 18.414 billion kWh (1999)
Electricity - exports: 50 million kWh (1999)
Electricity - imports: 290 million kWh (1999)
Agriculture - products: turnips, barley, potatoes, sugar beets, wheat; beef, dairy products
Exports: $73.5 billion (f.o.b., 2000)
Exports - commodities: machinery and equipment, computers, chemicals, pharmaceuticals; live animals, animal products
Exports - partners: EU 59% (UK 19%, Germany 9%, France 7%), US 20% (2000)
Imports: $45.7 billion (f.o.b., 2000 est.)
Imports - commodities: data processing equipment, other machinery and equipment, chemicals; petroleum and petroleum products, textiles, clothing
Imports - partners: EU 54% (UK 29%, Germany 6%, France 5%), US 18%, Japan 5%, Singapore 4% (2000)
Debt - external: $11 billion (1998)
Economic aid - donor: ODA, $245 million (2000)
Currency: Irish pound (IEP); euro (EUR)
note: on 1 January 1999, the EU introduced the euro as a common currency that is now being used by financial institutions in Ireland at a fixed rate of 0.787564 Irish pounds per euro and will replace the local currency for all transactions in 2002
Currency code: IEP; EUR
Exchange rates: Irish pounds per US dollar - 1.0658 (January 2001), 1.0823 (2000), 0.9374 (1999), 0.7014 (1998), 0.6588 (1997), 0.6248 (1996)
Fiscal year: calendar year

Communications

Telephones - main lines in use: 1.59 million (2001)
Telephones - mobile cellular: 2 million (2001)
Telephone system:
general assessment: modern digital system using cable and microwave radio relay
domestic: microwave radio relay
international: satellite earth station - 1 Intelsat (Atlantic Ocean)
Radio broadcast stations: AM 9, FM 106, shortwave 0 (1998)
Radios: 2.55 million (1997)
Television broadcast stations: 4 (many low-power repeaters) (2001)
Televisions: 1.82 million (2001)
Internet country code: .ie
Internet Service Providers (ISPs): 22 (2000)
Internet users: 1 million (2001)

Transportation

Railways:
total: 1,947 km
broad gauge: 1,947 km 1.600-m gauge (38 km electrified; 485 km double track) (1998)
Highways:
total: 92,500 km
paved: 87,043 km (including 115 km of expressways)
unpaved: 5,457 km (1999 est.)
Waterways: 700 km (limited facilities for commercial traffic) (1998)
Pipelines: natural gas 7,592 km (transmission 1,158 km; distribution 6,434 km) (2000)
Ports and harbors: Arklow, Cork, Drogheda, Dublin, Foynes, Galway, Limerick, New Ross, Waterford

Ireland (continued)

Merchant marine:
total: 29 ships (1,000 GRT or over) totaling 115,554 GRT/135,391 DWT
ships by type: bulk 4, cargo 22, container 2, short-sea passenger 1 (2000 est.)
Airports: 44 (2000 est.)
Airports - with paved runways:
total: 17
over 3,047 m: 1
2,438 to 3,047 m: 1
1,524 to 2,437 m: 3
914 to 1,523 m: 5
under 914 m: 7 (2000 est.)
Airports - with unpaved runways:
total: 27
914 to 1,523 m: 2
under 914 m: 25 (2000 est.)

Military

Military branches: Army (includes Naval Service and Air Corps), National Police (Garda Siochana)
Military manpower - military age: 17 years of age
Military manpower - availability:
males age 15-49: 1,004,469 (2001 est.)
Military manpower - fit for military service:
males age 15-49: 809,808 (2001 est.)
Military manpower - reaching military age annually:
males: 32,287 (2001 est.)
Military expenditures - dollar figure: $738 million (2001 est.)
Military expenditures - percent of GDP: 0.75% (2001 est.)

Transnational Issues

Disputes - international: Northern Ireland issue with the UK (historic peace agreement signed 10 April 1998); disputes with Iceland, Denmark, and the UK over the Faroe Islands continental shelf boundary outside 200 NM
Illicit drugs: transshipment point for and consumer of hashish from North Africa to the UK and Netherlands and of European-produced synthetic drugs; minor transshipment point for heroin and cocaine destined for Western Europe

Israel
(also see separate Gaza Strip and West Bank entries)

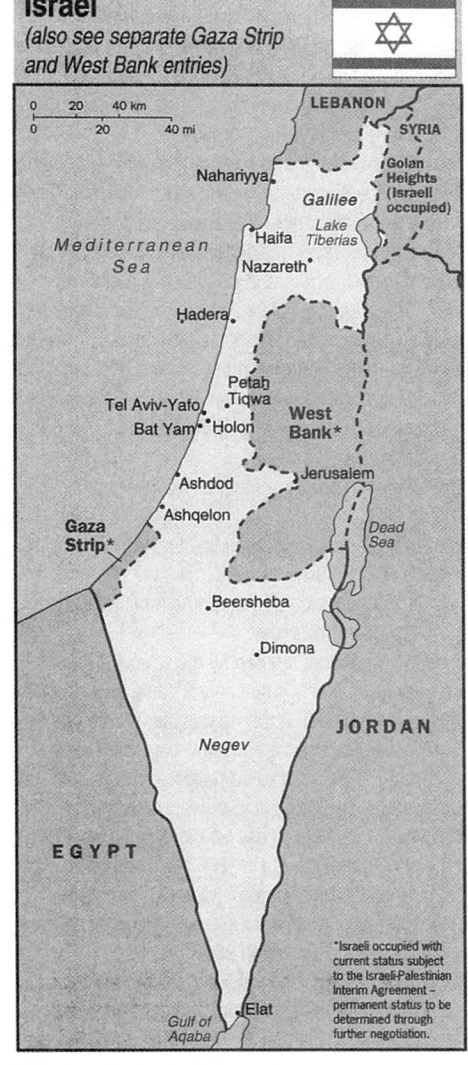

Introduction

Background: Following World War II, the British withdrew from their mandate of Palestine, and the UN partitioned the area into Arab and Jewish states, an arrangement rejected by the Arabs. Subsequently, the Israelis defeated the Arabs in a series of wars without ending the deep tensions between the two sides. The territories occupied by Israel since the 1967 war are not included in the Israel country profile, unless otherwise noted. In keeping with the framework established at the Madrid Conference in October 1991, bilateral negotiations are being conducted between Israel and Palestinian representatives (from the Israeli-occupied West Bank and Gaza Strip) and Israel and Syria, to achieve a permanent settlement. On 25 April 1982, Israel withdrew from the Sinai pursuant to the 1979 Israel-Egypt Peace Treaty. Outstanding territorial and other disputes with Jordan were resolved in the 26 October 1994 Israel-Jordan Treaty of Peace. On 25 May 2000, Israel withdrew unilaterally from southern Lebanon, which it had occupied since 1982.

Geography

Location: Middle East, bordering the Mediterranean Sea, between Egypt and Lebanon
Geographic coordinates: 31 30 N, 34 45 E
Map references: Middle East
Area:
total: 20,770 sq km
land: 20,330 sq km
water: 440 sq km
Area - comparative: slightly smaller than New Jersey
Land boundaries:
total: 1,006 km
border countries: Egypt 255 km, Gaza Strip 51 km, Jordan 238 km, Lebanon 79 km, Syria 76 km, West Bank 307 km
Coastline: 273 km
Maritime claims:
continental shelf: to depth of exploitation
territorial sea: 12 NM
Climate: temperate; hot and dry in southern and eastern desert areas
Terrain: Negev desert in the south; low coastal plain; central mountains; Jordan Rift Valley
Elevation extremes:
lowest point: Dead Sea -408 m
highest point: Har Meron 1,208 m
Natural resources: timber, potash, copper ore, natural gas, phosphate rock, magnesium bromide, clays, sand, oil
Land use:
arable land: 17%
permanent crops: 4%
permanent pastures: 7%
forests and woodland: 6%
other: 66% (1993 est.)
Irrigated land: 1,800 sq km (1993 est.)
Natural hazards: sandstorms may occur during spring and summer; droughts
Environment - current issues: limited arable land and natural fresh water resources pose serious constraints; desertification; air pollution from industrial and vehicle emissions; groundwater pollution from industrial and domestic waste, chemical fertilizers, and pesticides
Environment - international agreements:
party to: Biodiversity, Climate Change, Desertification, Endangered Species, Hazardous Wastes, Marine Dumping, Nuclear Test Ban, Ozone Layer Protection, Ship Pollution, Wetlands
signed, but not ratified: Climate Change-Kyoto Protocol, Marine Life Conservation
Geography - note: there are 231 Israeli settlements and civilian land use sites in the West Bank, 42 in the Israeli-occupied Golan Heights, 25 in the Gaza Strip, and 29 in East Jerusalem (August 2000 est.)

People

Population: 5,938,093 (July 2001 est.)
note: includes about 176,000 Israeli settlers in the West Bank, about 20,000 in the Israeli-occupied Golan Heights, about 6,900 in the Gaza Strip, and about 173,000 in East Jerusalem (August 2000 est.)

Israel (continued)

Age structure:
0-14 years: 27.36% (male 831,523; female 792,982)
15-64 years: 62.73% (male 1,869,114; female 1,855,707)
65 years and over: 9.91% (male 253,105; female 335,662) (2001 est.)
Population growth rate: 1.58% (2001 est.)
Birth rate: 19.12 births/1,000 population (2001 est.)
Death rate: 6.22 deaths/1,000 population (2001 est.)
Net migration rate: 2.85 migrant(s)/1,000 population (2001 est.)
Sex ratio:
at birth: 1.05 male(s)/female
under 15 years: 1.05 male(s)/female
15-64 years: 1.01 male(s)/female
65 years and over: 0.75 male(s)/female
total population: 0.99 male(s)/female (2001 est.)
Infant mortality rate: 7.72 deaths/1,000 live births (2001 est.)
Life expectancy at birth:
total population: 78.71 years
male: 76.69 years
female: 80.84 years (2001 est.)
Total fertility rate: 2.57 children born/woman (2001 est.)
HIV/AIDS - adult prevalence rate: 0.08% (1999 est.)
HIV/AIDS - people living with HIV/AIDS: 2,400 (1999 est.)
HIV/AIDS - deaths: less than 100 (1999 est.)
Nationality:
noun: Israeli(s)
adjective: Israeli
Ethnic groups: Jewish 80.1% (Europe/America-born 32.1%, Israel-born 20.8%, Africa-born 14.6%, Asia-born 12.6%), non-Jewish 19.9% (mostly Arab) (1996 est.)
Religions: Jewish 80.1%, Muslim 14.6% (mostly Sunni Muslim), Christian 2.1%, other 3.2% (1996 est.)
Languages: Hebrew (official), Arabic used officially for Arab minority, English most commonly used foreign language
Literacy:
definition: age 15 and over can read and write
total population: 95%
male: 97%
female: 93% (1992 est.)

Government

Country name:
conventional long form: State of Israel
conventional short form: Israel
local long form: Medinat Yisra'el
local short form: Yisra'el
Government type: parliamentary democracy
Capital: Jerusalem; note - Israel proclaimed Jerusalem as its capital in 1950, but the US, like nearly all other countries, maintains its Embassy in Tel Aviv
Administrative divisions: 6 districts (mehozot, singular - mehoz); Central, Haifa, Jerusalem, Northern, Southern, Tel Aviv
Independence: 14 May 1948 (from League of Nations mandate under British administration)
National holiday: Independence Day, 14 May (1948); note - Israel declared independence on 14 May 1948, but the Jewish calendar is lunar and the holiday may occur in April or May
Constitution: no formal constitution; some of the functions of a constitution are filled by the Declaration of Establishment (1948), the Basic Laws of the parliament (Knesset), and the Israeli citizenship law
Legal system: mixture of English common law, British Mandate regulations, and, in personal matters, Jewish, Christian, and Muslim legal systems; in December 1985, Israel informed the UN Secretariat that it would no longer accept compulsory ICJ jurisdiction
Suffrage: 18 years of age; universal
Executive branch:
chief of state: President Moshe KATSAV (since 31 July 2000)
head of government: Prime Minister Ariel SHARON (since 2 March 2001)
cabinet: Cabinet selected by prime minister and approved by the Knesset
elections: president elected by the Knesset for a five-year term; election last held 31 July 2000 (next to be held NA July 2005); prime minister elected by popular vote for a four-year term; election last held 6 February 2001 (next to be held NA 2005); note - in March 1992, the Knesset approved legislation, effective in 1996, which allowed for the direct election of the prime minister, but in 2001 the Knesset voted to restore the previous method under which the legislators will choose the next prime minister after the next legislative elections in 2003
election results: Moshe KATSAV elected president by the 120-member Knesset with a total of 60 votes, other candidate, Shimon PERES, received 57 votes (there were three abstentions); Ariel SHARON elected prime minister; percent of vote - Ariel SHARON 62.5%, Ehud BARAK 37.4%; note - after the next legislative elections scheduled for 2003, the prime minister will be elected by the Knesset
Legislative branch: unicameral Knesset or parliament (120 seats; members elected by popular vote to serve four-year terms)
elections: last held 17 May 1999 (next to be held NA November 2003)
election results: percent of vote by party - One Israel 20.2%, Likud Party 14.1%, Shas 13%, MERETZ 7.6%, Yisra'el Ba'Aliya 5.1%, Shinui 5%, Center Party 5%, National Religious Party 4.2%, United Torah Judaism 3.7%, United Arab List 3.4%, National Union 3%, Hadash 2.6%, Yisra'el Beiteinu 2.6%, Balad 1.9%, One Nation 1.9%, Democratic Movement NA (party formed after election, members elected under Yisra'el Ba'Aliya list); seats by party - One Israel 26, Likud Party 19, Shas 17, MERETZ 10, Yisra'el Ba'Aliya 4, Shinui 6, Center Party 6, National Religious Party 5, United Torah Judaism 5, United Arab List 5, National Union 4, Hadash 3, Yisra'el Beiteinu 4, Democratic Movement 2 (party formed after election, members elected under Yisra'el Ba'Aliya list), Balad 2, One Nation 2
Judicial branch: Supreme Court (justices appointed for life by the president)
Political parties and leaders: Balad or National Democratic Alliance [Amnon LIPKIN-SHAHAK]; Center Party [Yitzhak MORDECHAI]; Democratic Movement [Roman BRONFMAN]; Gesher [David LEVI]; Hadash [Muhammad BARAKA]; Labor Party [leader vacant]; Likud Party [Ariel SHARON]; MERETZ [Yossi SARID]; National Democratic Alliance (Balad) [leader NA]; National Religious Party [Yitzhak LEVY]; National Union [Rehavam ZEEVI] (includes Herut, Tekuma, and Moledet); One Israel [leader NA] (includes Labor, Gesher, and Meimad); One Nation [Amir PERETZ]; Shas [Eliyahu YISHAI]; Shinui [Tommy LAPID]; United Arab List [Abd al-Malik DAHAMSHAH]; United Torah Judaism [Rabbi Eliezer SHACK, spiritual leader]; Yisra'el Ba'Aliya [Natan SHARANSKY]; Yisra'el Beiteinu [Avigdor LIEBERMAN]
Political pressure groups and leaders: Gush Emunim, Israeli nationalists advocating Jewish settlement on the West Bank and Gaza Strip; Peace Now supports territorial concessions in the West Bank and is critical of government's Lebanon policy
International organization participation: BSEC (observer), CCC, CE (observer), CERN (observer), EBRD, ECE, FAO, IADB, IAEA, IBRD, ICAO, ICC, ICFTU, IDA, IFAD, IFC, ILO, IMF, IMO, Inmarsat, Intelsat, Interpol, IOC, IOM, ISO, ITU, OAS (observer), OPCW, OSCE (partner), PCA, UN, UNCTAD, UNESCO, UNHCR, UNIDO, UPU, WHO, WIPO, WMO, WToO, WTrO
Diplomatic representation in the US:
chief of mission: Ambassador David IVRY
chancery: 3514 International Drive NW, Washington, DC 20008
telephone: [1] (202) 364-5500
FAX: [1] (202) 364-5607
consulate(s) general: Atlanta, Boston, Chicago, Houston, Los Angeles, Miami, New York, Philadelphia, and San Francisco
Diplomatic representation from the US:
chief of mission: Ambassador Martin S. INDYK
embassy: 71 Hayarkon Street, Tel Aviv
mailing address: PSC 98, Unit 7228, APO AE 09830
telephone: [972] (3) 519-7575
FAX: [972] (3) 517-3227
consulate(s) general: Jerusalem; note - an independent US mission, established in 1928, whose members are not accredited to a foreign government
Flag description: white with a blue hexagram (six-pointed linear star) known as the Magen David (Shield of David) centered between two equal horizontal blue bands near the top and bottom edges of the flag

Economy

Economy - overview: Israel has a technologically advanced market economy with substantial government participation. It depends on imports of crude oil, grains, raw materials, and military equipment. Despite limited natural resources, Israel has intensively developed its agricultural and

Israel (continued)

industrial sectors over the past 20 years. Israel is largely self-sufficient in food production except for grains. Cuts diamonds, high-technology equipment, and agricultural products (fruits and vegetables) are the leading exports. Israel usually posts sizable current account deficits, which are covered by large transfer payments from abroad and by foreign loans. Roughly half of the government's external debt is owed to the US, which is its major source of economic and military aid. The influx of Jewish immigrants from the former USSR topped 750,000 during the period 1989-99, bringing the population of Israel from the former Soviet Union to 1 million, one-sixth of the total population, and adding scientific and professional expertise of substantial value for the economy's future. The influx, coupled with the opening of new markets at the end of the Cold War, energized Israel's economy, which grew rapidly in the early 1990s. But growth began moderating in 1996 when the government imposed tighter fiscal and monetary policies and the immigration bonus petered out. Growth was a strong 5.9% in 2000. But the outbreak of Palestinian unrest in late September and the collapse of the BARAK Government - coupled with a cooling off in the high-technology and tourist sectors - undercut the boom and foreshadows a slowdown to 2%-3% in 2001.

GDP: purchasing power parity - $110.2 billion (2000 est.)
GDP - real growth rate: 5.9% (2000 est.)
GDP - per capita: purchasing power parity - $18,900 (2000 est.)
GDP - composition by sector:
agriculture: 4%
industry: 37%
services: 59% (1999 est.)
Population below poverty line: NA%
Household income or consumption by percentage share:
lowest 10%: 2.8%
highest 10%: 26.9% (1992)
Inflation rate (consumer prices): 0.1% (2000 est.)
Labor force: 2.4 million (2000 est.)
Labor force - by occupation: public services 31.2%, manufacturing 20.2%, finance and business 13.1%, commerce 12.8%, construction 7.5%, personal and other services 6.4%, transport, storage, and communications 6.2%, agriculture, forestry, and fishing 2.6% (1996)
Unemployment rate: 9% (2000 est.)
Budget:
revenues: $40 billion
expenditures: $42.4 billion, including capital expenditures of $NA (2000 est.)
Industries: high-technology projects (including aviation, communications, computer-aided design and manufactures, medical electronics), wood and paper products, potash and phosphates, food, beverages, and tobacco, caustic soda, cement, diamond cutting
Industrial production growth rate: 7% (2000)
Electricity - production: 35.437 billion kWh (1999)

Electricity - production by source:
fossil fuel: 99.89%
hydro: 0.11%
nuclear: 0%
other: 0% (1999)
Electricity - consumption: 31.899 billion kWh (1999)
Electricity - exports: 1.061 billion kWh (1999)
Electricity - imports: 4 million kWh (1999)
Agriculture - products: citrus, vegetables, cotton; beef, poultry, dairy products
Exports: $31.5 billion (f.o.b., 2000)
Exports - commodities: machinery and equipment, software, cut diamonds, agricultural products, chemicals, textiles and apparel
Exports - partners: US 36%, UK 6%, Benelux 5%, Hong Kong 4%, Netherlands 4% (1999)
Imports: $35.1 billion (f.o.b., 2000)
Imports - commodities: raw materials, military equipment, investment goods, rough diamonds, fuels, consumer goods
Imports - partners: US 20%, Benelux 11%, Germany 8%, UK 8%, Switzerland 6%, Italy 5% (1999)
Debt - external: $38 billion (2000 est.)
Economic aid - recipient: $1.1 billion from the US (1999)
Currency: new Israeli shekel (ILS)
Currency code: ILS
Exchange rates: new Israeli shekels per US dollar - 4.0810 (December 2000), 4.0773 (2000), 4.1397 (1999), 3.8001 (1998), 3.4494 (1997), 3.1917 (1996)
Fiscal year: calendar year

Communications

Telephones - main lines in use: 2.8 million (1999)
Telephones - mobile cellular: 2.5 million (1999)
Telephone system:
general assessment: most highly developed system in the Middle East although not the largest
domestic: good system of coaxial cable and microwave radio relay; all systems are digital
international: 3 submarine cables; satellite earth stations - 3 Intelsat (2 Atlantic Ocean and 1 Indian Ocean)
Radio broadcast stations: AM 23, FM 15, shortwave 2 (1998)
Radios: 3.07 million (1997)
Television broadcast stations: 17 (plus 36 low-power repeaters) (1995)
Televisions: 1.69 million (1997)
Internet country code: .il
Internet Service Providers (ISPs): 21 (2000)
Internet users: 1 million (2000)

Transportation

Railways:
total: 610 km
standard gauge: 610 km 1.435-m gauge (1996)
Highways:
total: 15,965 km

paved: 15,965 km (including 56 km of expressways)
unpaved: 0 km (1998 est.)
Waterways: none
Pipelines: crude oil 708 km; petroleum products 290 km; natural gas 89 km
Ports and harbors: Ashdod, Ashqelon, Elat (Eilat), Hadera, Haifa, Tel Aviv-Yafo
Merchant marine:
total: 17 ships (1,000 GRT or over) totaling 631,582 GRT/745,011 DWT
ships by type: container 16, roll on/roll off 1 (2000 est.)
Airports: 55 (2000 est.)
Airports - with paved runways:
total: 30
over 3,047 m: 2
2,438 to 3,047 m: 4
1,524 to 2,437 m: 7
914 to 1,523 m: 10
under 914 m: 7 (2000 est.)
Airports - with unpaved runways:
total: 25
1,524 to 2,437 m: 1
914 to 1,523 m: 4
under 914 m: 20 (2000 est.)
Heliports: 2 (2000 est.)

Military

Military branches: Israel Defense Forces (includes ground, naval, and air components), Pioneer Fighting Youth (Nahal), Frontier Guard, Chen (women); note - historically there have been no separate Israeli military services
Military manpower - military age: 18 years of age
Military manpower - availability:
males age 15-49: 1,522,003
females age 15-49: 1,482,027 (2001 est.)
Military manpower - fit for military service:
males age 15-49: 1,245,757
females age 15-49: 1,208,973 (2001 est.)
Military manpower - reaching military age annually:
males: 49,206
females: 53,379 (2001 est.)
Military expenditures - dollar figure: $8.7 billion (FY99)
Military expenditures - percent of GDP: 9.4% (FY99)

Transnational Issues

Disputes - international: West Bank and Gaza Strip are Israeli-occupied with current status subject to the Israeli-Palestinian Interim Agreement - permanent status to be determined through further negotiation; Golan Heights is Israeli-occupied (Lebanon claims the Shab'a Farms area of Golan Heights)
Illicit drugs: increasingly concerned about cocaine and heroin abuse; drugs arrive in country from Lebanon and increasingly Jordan

Italy

Introduction

Background: Italy became a nation-state belatedly in 1861 when the city-states of the peninsula, along with Sardinia and Sicily, were united under King Victor EMMANUEL. An era of parliamentary government came to a close in the early 1920s when Benito MUSSOLINI established a Fascist dictatorship. His disastrous alliance with Nazi Germany led to Italy's defeat in World War II. A democratic republic replaced the monarchy in 1946 and economic revival followed. Italy was a charter member of NATO and the European Economic Community (EEC). It has been at the forefront of European economic and political unification, joining the European Monetary Union in 1999. Persistent problems include illegal immigration, the ravages of organized crime, corruption, high unemployment, and the low incomes and technical standards of southern Italy compared with the more prosperous north.

Geography

Location: Southern Europe, a peninsula extending into the central Mediterranean Sea, northeast of Tunisia
Geographic coordinates: 42 50 N, 12 50 E
Map references: Europe
Area:
total: 301,230 sq km
land: 294,020 sq km
water: 7,210 sq km
note: includes Sardinia and Sicily
Area - comparative: slightly larger than Arizona
Land boundaries:
total: 1,932.2 km
border countries: Austria 430 km, France 488 km, Holy See (Vatican City) 3.2 km, San Marino 39 km, Slovenia 232 km, Switzerland 740 km
Coastline: 7,600 km
Maritime claims:
continental shelf: 200-m depth or to the depth of exploitation
territorial sea: 12 NM
Climate: predominantly Mediterranean; Alpine in far north; hot, dry in south
Terrain: mostly rugged and mountainous; some plains, coastal lowlands
Elevation extremes:
lowest point: Mediterranean Sea 0 m
highest point: Mont Blanc (Monte Bianco) 4,807 m
Natural resources: mercury, potash, marble, sulfur, natural gas and crude oil reserves, fish, coal, arable land
Land use:
arable land: 31%
permanent crops: 10%
permanent pastures: 15%
forests and woodland: 23%
other: 21% (1993 est.)
Irrigated land: 27,100 sq km (1993 est.)
Natural hazards: regional risks include landslides, mudflows, avalanches, earthquakes, volcanic eruptions, flooding; land subsidence in Venice
Environment - current issues: air pollution from industrial emissions such as sulfur dioxide; coastal and inland rivers polluted from industrial and agricultural effluents; acid rain damaging lakes; inadequate industrial waste treatment and disposal facilities
Environment - international agreements:
party to: Air Pollution, Air Pollution-Nitrogen Oxides, Air Pollution-Sulphur 85, Air Pollution-Sulphur 94, Air Pollution-Volatile Organic Compounds, Antarctic-Environmental Protocol, Antarctic-Marine Living Resources, Antarctic Seals, Antarctic Treaty, Biodiversity, Climate Change, Desertification, Endangered Species, Environmental Modification, Hazardous Wastes, Law of the Sea, Marine Dumping, Nuclear Test Ban, Ozone Layer Protection, Ship Pollution, Tropical Timber 83, Tropical Timber 94, Wetlands, Whaling
signed, but not ratified: Air Pollution-Persistent Organic Pollutants, Climate Change-Kyoto Protocol
Geography - note: strategic location dominating central Mediterranean as well as southern sea and air approaches to Western Europe

People

Population: 57,679,825 (July 2001 est.)
Age structure:
0-14 years: 14.17% (male 4,209,102; female 3,964,765)
15-64 years: 67.48% (male 19,375,742; female 19,546,332)
65 years and over: 18.35% (male 4,368,264; female 6,215,620) (2001 est.)
Population growth rate: 0.07% (2001 est.)
Birth rate: 9.05 births/1,000 population (2001 est.)
Death rate: 10.07 deaths/1,000 population (2001 est.)
Net migration rate: 1.73 migrant(s)/1,000 population (2001 est.)
Sex ratio:
at birth: 1.07 male(s)/female
under 15 years: 1.06 male(s)/female
15-64 years: 0.99 male(s)/female
65 years and over: 0.7 male(s)/female
total population: 0.94 male(s)/female (2001 est.)
Infant mortality rate: 5.84 deaths/1,000 live births (2001 est.)
Life expectancy at birth:
total population: 79.14 years
male: 75.97 years
female: 82.52 years (2001 est.)
Total fertility rate: 1.18 children born/woman (2001 est.)
HIV/AIDS - adult prevalence rate: 0.35% (1999 est.)
HIV/AIDS - people living with HIV/AIDS: 95,000 (1999 est.)
HIV/AIDS - deaths: 1,000 (1999 est.)
Nationality:
noun: Italian(s)
adjective: Italian
Ethnic groups: Italian (includes small clusters of German-, French-, and Slovene-Italians in the north and Albanian-Italians and Greek-Italians in the south)
Religions: predominately Roman Catholic with mature Protestant and Jewish communities and a growing Muslim immigrant community
Languages: Italian (official), German (parts of Trentino-Alto Adige region are predominantly German speaking), French (small French-speaking minority in Valle d'Aosta region), Slovene (Slovene-speaking minority in the Trieste-Gorizia area)
Literacy:
definition: age 15 and over can read and write
total population: 98% (1998)
male: NA%
female: NA%

Government

Country name:
conventional long form: Italian Republic
conventional short form: Italy
local long form: Repubblica Italiana
local short form: Italia
former: Kingdom of Italy
Government type: republic
Capital: Rome
Administrative divisions: 20 regions (regioni, singular - regione); Abruzzi, Basilicata, Calabria, Campania, Emilia-Romagna, Friuli-Venezia Giulia, Lazio, Liguria, Lombardia, Marche, Molise, Piemonte, Puglia, Sardegna, Sicilia, Toscana, Trentino-Alto Adige, Umbria, Valle d'Aosta, Veneto
Independence: 17 March 1861 (Kingdom of Italy proclaimed; Italy was not finally unified until 1870)
National holiday: Republic Day, 2 June (1946)
Constitution: 1 January 1948
Legal system: based on civil law system; appeals treated as new trials; judicial review under certain conditions in Constitutional Court; has not accepted compulsory ICJ jurisdiction
Suffrage: 18 years of age; universal (except in senatorial elections, where minimum age is 25)

Italy (continued)

Executive branch:
chief of state: President Carlo Azeglio CIAMPI (since 13 May 1999)
head of government: Prime Minister (referred to in Italy as the president of the Council of Ministers) Silvio BERLUSCONI (since 10 June 2001)
cabinet: Council of Ministers nominated by the prime minister and approved by the president
elections: president elected by an electoral college consisting of both houses of Parliament and 58 regional representatives for a seven-year term; election last held 13 May 1999 (next to be held NA May 2006); prime minister appointed by the president and confirmed by parliament
election results: Carlo Azeglio CIAMPI elected president; percent of electoral college vote - 70%
note: a 12-party government coalition; note - BERLUSCONI's coalition includes Forza Italian, National Alliance, Christian Democratic Center, Christian Northern League
Legislative branch: bicameral Parliament or Parlamento consists of the Senate or Senato della Repubblica (315 seats elected by popular vote of which 232 are directly elected and 83 are elected by regional proportional representation plus, in addition, there are a small number of senators-for-life including former presidents of the republic; members serve five-year terms) and the Chamber of Deputies or Camera dei Deputati (630 seats; 475 are directly elected, 155 by regional proportional representation; members serve five-year terms)
elections: Senate - last held 13 May 2001 (next to be held NA 2006); Chamber of Deputies - last held 13 May 2001 (next to be held NA 2006)
election results: Senate - percent of vote by party - NA%; seats by party - House of Liberties 177 (Forza Italia 82, National Alliance 46, CCD-CDU 29, Northern League 17, others 3), Olive Tree 128 (Democrats of the Left 62, Daisy Alliance 42, Sunflower Alliance 16, Italian Communist Party 3, independents 5), non-affiliated with either coalition 10, senators for life 9; Chamber of Deputies - percent of vote by party - NA%; seats by party - House of Liberties 367 (Forza Italia 189, National Alliance 96, CCD-CDU 40, Northern League 30, others 12), Olive Tree 248 (Democrats of the Left 138, Daisy Alliance 76, Sunflower Alliance 18, Italian Communist Party 9, independents 7), non-affiliated with either coalition 15
Judicial branch: Constitutional Court or Corte Costituzionale (composed of 15 judges: one-third appointed by the president, one-third elected by Parliament, one-third elected by the ordinary and administrative Supreme Courts)
Political parties and leaders: Center-Left Olive Tree Coalition [Francesco RUTELLI] - Democrats of the Left, Daisy Alliance (including Italian Popular Party, Italian Renewal, Union of Democrats for Europe, The Democrats), Sunflower Alliance (including Green Federation, Italian Democratic Socialists), Italian Communist Party; Christian Democratic Center or CDC [Pier Ferdinando CASINI]; Christian Democratic Union or CDU [Rocco BUTTIGLIONE]; Communist Renewal or RC [Fausto BERTINOTTI]; Forza Italia or FI [Silvio BERLUSCONI]; Green Federation [Grazia FRANCESCATO]; House of Liberties (formerly Freedom Alliance, a center-right coalition) [leader Silvio BERLUSCONI] - Forza Italian, National Alliance, Christian Democratic Center, Christian Democratic Union, Northern League; Italian Communist Party or PdCI [Oliviero DILIBERTO]; Italian Democratic Socialists [Enrico BOSELLI]; Italian Popular Party [Pierluigi CASTAGNETTI]; Italian Renewal [Lamberto DINI]; Italian Social Movement-Tricolored Flame or MSI-FI [Pino RAUTI]; National Alliance or AN [Gianfranco FINI]; Northern League or NL [Umberto BOSSI]; Radical Party (formerly Panella Reformers and Autonomous List) [Marco PANNELLA]; Southern Tyrols People's Party or SVP (German speakers) [Siegfried BRUGGER]; Union of Democrats for Europe [Clemente MASTELLA]; The Democrats [Arturo PARISI]
Political pressure groups and leaders: Italian manufacturers and merchants associations (Confindustria, Confcommercio); organized farm groups (Confcoltivatori, Confagricoltura); Roman Catholic Church; three major trade union confederations (Confederazione Generale Italiana del Lavoro or CGIL [Sergio COFFERATI] which is left wing, Confederazione Italiana dei Sindacati Lavoratori or CISL [Sergio D'ANTONI] which is Catholic centrist, and Unione Italiana del Lavoro or UIL [Pietro LARIZZA] which is lay centrist)
International organization participation: AfDB, AsDB, Australia Group, BIS, BSEC (observer), CCC, CDB (non-regional), CE, CEI, CERN, EAPC, EBRD, ECE, ECLAC, EIB, EMU, ESA, EU, FAO, G-7, G-10, IADB, IAEA, IBRD, ICAO, ICC, ICFTU, ICRM, IDA, IEA, IFAD, IFC, IFRCS, IHO, ILO, IMF, IMO, Inmarsat, Intelsat, Interpol, IOC, IOM, ISO, ITU, LAIA (observer), MINURSO, NAM (guest), NATO, NEA, NSG, OAS (observer), OECD, OPCW, OSCE, PCA, UN, UNCTAD, UNESCO, UNHCR, UNIDO, UNIFIL, UNIKOM, UNMEE, UNMIBH, UNMIK, UNMOGIP, UNTSO, UPU, WCL, WEU, WHO, WIPO, WMO, WToO, WTrO, ZC
Diplomatic representation in the US:
chief of mission: Ambassador Ferdinando SALLEO
chancery: 3000 Whitehaven Street NW, Washington, DC 20008
telephone: [1] (202) 612-4400
FAX: [1] (202) 518-2154
consulate(s) general: Boston, Chicago, Houston, Miami, New York, Los Angeles, Philadelphia, and San Francisco
consulate(s): Detroit
Diplomatic representation from the US:
chief of mission: Ambassador (vacant)
embassy: Via Veneto 119/A, 00187-Rome
mailing address: PSC 59, Box 100, APO AE 09624
telephone: [39] (06) 46741
FAX: [39] (06) 488-2672
consulate(s) general: Florence, Milan, Naples
Flag description: three equal vertical bands of green (hoist side), white, and red; similar to the flag of Ireland, which is longer and is green (hoist side), white, and orange; also similar to the flag of the Cote d'Ivoire, which has the colors reversed - orange (hoist side), white, and green
note: inspired by the French flag brought to Italy by Napoleon in 1797

Economy

Economy - overview: Italy has a diversified industrial economy with roughly the same total and per capita output as France and the UK. This capitalistic economy remains divided into a developed industrial north, dominated by private companies, and a less developed agricultural south, with more than 20% unemployment. Most raw materials needed by industry and more than 75% of energy requirements are imported. Since 1992, Italy has adopted budgets compliant with the requirements of the European Monetary Union (EMU); wage moderation agreements by representatives of government, labor, and employers have helped to bring Italy's inflation into conformity with EMU requirements. Italy's economic performance, however, has lagged behind that of its EU partners and it must work to stimulate employment, promote labor flexibility, reform its expensive pension system, and tackle the informal economy.
GDP: purchasing power parity - $1.273 trillion (2000 est.)
GDP - real growth rate: 2.7% (2000 est.)
GDP - per capita: purchasing power parity - $22,100 (2000 est.)
GDP - composition by sector:
agriculture: 2.5%
industry: 30.4%
services: 67.1% (2000 est.)
Population below poverty line: NA%
Household income or consumption by percentage share:
lowest 10%: 3.5%
highest 10%: 21.8% (1995)
Inflation rate (consumer prices): 2.5% (2000)
Labor force: 23.4 million (2000)
Labor force - by occupation: services 61.9%, industry 32.6%, agriculture 5.5% (1999)
Unemployment rate: 10.4% (2000 est.)
Budget:
revenues: $488 billion
expenditures: $501 billion, including capital expenditures of $NA (2000 est.)
Industries: tourism, machinery, iron and steel, chemicals, food processing, textiles, motor vehicles, clothing, footwear, ceramics
Industrial production growth rate: 1.9% (2000)
Electricity - production: 247.679 billion kWh (1999)
Electricity - production by source:
fossil fuel: 79.09%
hydro: 18.08%
nuclear: 0%
other: 2.83% (1999)

Italy (continued)

Electricity - consumption: 272.35 billion kWh (1999)
Electricity - exports: 530 million kWh (1999)
Electricity - imports: 42.539 billion kWh (1999)
Agriculture - products: fruits, vegetables, grapes, potatoes, sugar beets, soybeans, grain, olives; beef, dairy products; fish
Exports: $241.1 billion (f.o.b., 2000)
Exports - commodities: engineering products, textiles and clothing, production machinery, motor vehicles, transport equipment, chemicals; food, beverages and tobacco; minerals and nonferrous metals
Exports - partners: EU 56.8% (Germany 16.4%, France 12.9%, Netherlands 7.1%, Spain 6.3%, Netherlands 2.9%), US 9.5% (1999)
Imports: $231.4 billion (f.o.b., 2000)
Imports - commodities: engineering products, chemicals, transport equipment, energy products, minerals and nonferrous metals, textiles and clothing; food, beverages and tobacco
Imports - partners: EU 61% (Germany 19.3%, France 12.6%, Netherlands 6.3%, Spain 4.4%), US 5.0% (1999)
Debt - external: $NA
Economic aid - donor: ODA, $1.3 billion (1997)
Currency: Italian lira (ITL); euro (EUR)
note: on 1 January 1999, the EU introduced the euro as a common currency that is now being used by financial institutions in Italy at a fixed rate of 1,936.27 Italian lire per euro and will replace the local currency for all transactions in 2002
Currency code: ITL; EUR
Exchange rates: euros per US dollar - 1.0659 (January 2001), 1.0854 (2000), 0.9386 (1999); Italian lire per US dollar - 1,688.7 (January 1999), 1,736.2 (1998), 1,703.1 (1997), 1,542.9 (1996)
Fiscal year: calendar year

Communications

Telephones - main lines in use: 25 million (1999)
Telephones - mobile cellular: 20.5 million (1999)
Telephone system:
general assessment: modern, well developed, fast; fully automated telephone, telex, and data services
domestic: high-capacity cable and microwave radio relay trunks
international: satellite earth stations - 3 Intelsat (with a total of 5 antennas - 3 for Atlantic Ocean and 2 for Indian Ocean), 1 Inmarsat (Atlantic Ocean region), and NA Eutelsat; 21 submarine cables
Radio broadcast stations: AM about 100, FM about 4,600, shortwave 9 (1998)
Radios: 50.5 million (1997)
Television broadcast stations: 358 (plus 4,728 repeaters) (1995)
Televisions: 30.3 million (1997)
Internet country code: .it
Internet Service Providers (ISPs): 93 (Italy and Holy See) (2000)
Internet users: 11.6 million (2000)

Transportation

Railways:
total: 19,394 km
standard gauge: 18,071 km 1.435-m gauge; Italian Railways (FS) operates 16,014 km of the total standard gauge routes (11,322 km electrified)
narrow gauge: 112 km 1.000-m gauge (112 km electrified); 1,211 km 0.950-m gauge (153 km electrified) (1998)
Highways:
total: 654,676 km
paved: 654,676 km (including 6460 km of expressways)
unpaved: 0 km (1997)
Waterways: 2,400 km
note: for various types of commercial traffic, although of limited overall value
Pipelines: crude oil 1,703 km; petroleum products 2,148 km; natural gas 19,400 km
Ports and harbors: Augusta (Sicily), Bagnoli, Bari, Brindisi, Gela, Genoa, La Spezia, Livorno, Milazzo, Naples, Porto Foxi, Porto Torres (Sardinia), Salerno, Savona, Taranto, Trieste, Venice (2001)
Merchant marine:
total: 445 ships (1,000 GRT or over) totaling 8,005,136 GRT/10,556,244 DWT
ships by type: bulk 44, cargo 41, chemical tanker 77, combination ore/oil 4, container 24, liquefied gas 38, multi-functional large-load carrier 1, passenger 11, petroleum tanker 85, refrigerated cargo 1, roll on/roll off 64, short-sea passenger 26, specialized tanker 14, vehicle carrier 15 (2000 est.)
Airports: 135 (2000 est.)
Airports - with paved runways:
total: 97
over 3,047 m: 5
2,438 to 3,047 m: 32
1,524 to 2,437 m: 17
914 to 1,523 m: 31
under 914 m: 12 (2000 est.)
Airports - with unpaved runways:
total: 38
1,524 to 2,437 m: 2
914 to 1,523 m: 18
under 914 m: 18 (2000 est.)
Heliports: 4 (2000 est.)

Military

Military branches: Army, Navy, Air Force, Carabinieri
Military manpower - military age: 18 years of age
Military manpower - availability:
males age 15-49: 14,248,674 (2001 est.)
Military manpower - fit for military service:
males age 15-49: 12,244,166 (2001 est.)
Military manpower - reaching military age annually:
males: 304,369 (2001 est.)
Military expenditures - dollar figure: $20.7 billion (FY00/01)
Military expenditures - percent of GDP: 1.7% (FY00/01)

Transnational Issues

Disputes - international: Croatia and Italy made progress toward resolving a bilateral issue dating from World War II over property and ethnic minority rights
Illicit drugs: important gateway for and consumer of Latin American cocaine and Southwest Asian heroin entering the European market

Jamaica

Introduction

Background: Jamaica gained full independence within the British Commonwealth in 1962. Deteriorating economic conditions during the 1970s led to recurrent violence and a dropoff in tourism. Elections in 1980 saw the democratic socialists voted out of office. Subsequent governments have been open market oriented. Political violence marred elections during the 1990s.

Geography

Location: Caribbean, island in the Caribbean Sea, south of Cuba
Geographic coordinates: 18 15 N, 77 30 W
Map references: Central America and the Caribbean
Area:
total: 10,990 sq km
land: 10,830 sq km
water: 160 sq km
Area - comparative: slightly smaller than Connecticut
Land boundaries: 0 km
Coastline: 1,022 km
Maritime claims: measured from claimed archipelagic baselines
contiguous zone: 24 NM
continental shelf: 200-m depth or to the depth of exploitation
exclusive economic zone: 200 NM
territorial sea: 12 NM
Climate: tropical; hot, humid; temperate interior
Terrain: mostly mountains, with narrow, discontinuous coastal plain
Elevation extremes:
lowest point: Caribbean Sea 0 m
highest point: Blue Mountain Peak 2,256 m
Natural resources: bauxite, gypsum, limestone
Land use:
arable land: 14%
permanent crops: 6%
permanent pastures: 24%
forests and woodland: 17%
other: 39% (1993 est.)
Irrigated land: 350 sq km (1993 est.)
Natural hazards: hurricanes (especially July to November)
Environment - current issues: heavy rates of deforestation; coastal waters polluted by industrial waste, sewage, and oil spills; damage to coral reefs; air pollution in Kingston results from vehicle emissions
Environment - international agreements:
party to: Biodiversity, Climate Change, Climate Change-Kyoto Protocol, Desertification, Endangered Species, Law of the Sea, Marine Dumping, Marine Life Conservation, Nuclear Test Ban, Ozone Layer Protection, Ship Pollution, Wetlands
signed, but not ratified: none of the selected agreements
Geography - note: strategic location between Cayman Trench and Jamaica Channel, the main sea lanes for Panama Canal

People

Population: 2,665,636 (July 2001 est.)
Age structure:
0-14 years: 29.7% (male 405,189; female 386,555)
15-64 years: 63.52% (male 845,226; female 847,944)
65 years and over: 6.78% (male 80,667; female 100,055) (2001 est.)
Population growth rate: 0.51% (2001 est.)
Birth rate: 18.12 births/1,000 population (2001 est.)
Death rate: 5.48 deaths/1,000 population (2001 est.)
Net migration rate: -7.52 migrant(s)/1,000 population (2001 est.)
Sex ratio:
at birth: 1.05 male(s)/female
under 15 years: 1.05 male(s)/female
15-64 years: 1 male(s)/female
65 years and over: 0.81 male(s)/female
total population: 1 male(s)/female (2001 est.)
Infant mortality rate: 14.16 deaths/1,000 live births (2001 est.)
Life expectancy at birth:
total population: 75.42 years
male: 73.45 years
female: 77.49 years (2001 est.)
Total fertility rate: 2.08 children born/woman (2001 est.)
HIV/AIDS - adult prevalence rate: 0.71% (1999 est.)
HIV/AIDS - people living with HIV/AIDS: 9,900 (1999 est.)
HIV/AIDS - deaths: 650 (1999 est.)
Nationality:
noun: Jamaican(s)
adjective: Jamaican
Ethnic groups: black 90.9%, East Indian 1.3%, white 0.2%, Chinese 0.2%, mixed 7.3%, other 0.1%
Religions: Protestant 61.3% (Church of God 21.2%, Baptist 8.8%, Anglican 5.5%, Seventh-Day Adventist 9%, Pentecostal 7.6%, Methodist 2.7%, United Church 2.7%, Brethren 1.1%, Jehovah's Witness 1.6%, Moravian 1.1%), Roman Catholic 4%, other, including some spiritual cults 34.7%
Languages: English, Creole
Literacy:
definition: age 15 and over has ever attended school
total population: 85%
male: 80.8%
female: 89.1% (1995 est.)

Government

Country name:
conventional long form: none
conventional short form: Jamaica
Government type: constitutional parliamentary democracy
Capital: Kingston
Administrative divisions: 14 parishes; Clarendon, Hanover, Kingston, Manchester, Portland, Saint Andrew, Saint Ann, Saint Catherine, Saint Elizabeth, Saint James, Saint Mary, Saint Thomas, Trelawny, Westmoreland
Independence: 6 August 1962 (from UK)
National holiday: Independence Day, first Monday in August (1962)
Constitution: 6 August 1962
Legal system: based on English common law; has not accepted compulsory ICJ jurisdiction
Suffrage: 18 years of age; universal
Executive branch:
chief of state: Queen ELIZABETH II (since 6 February 1952), represented by Governor General Sir Howard Felix COOKE (since 1 August 1991)
head of government: Prime Minister Percival James PATTERSON (since 30 March 1992) and Deputy Prime Minister Seymour MULLINGS (since NA 1993)
cabinet: Cabinet appointed by the governor general on the advice of the prime minister
elections: none; the monarch is hereditary; governor general appointed by the monarch on the recommendation of the prime minister; prime minister and deputy prime minister appointed by the governor general

Jamaica (continued)

Legislative branch: bicameral Parliament consists of the Senate (a 21-member body appointed by the governor general on the recommendations of the prime minister and the leader of the opposition; ruling party is allocated 13 seats, and the opposition is allocated eight seats) and the House of Representatives (60 seats; members are elected by popular vote to serve five-year terms)
elections: last held 18 December 1997 (next to be held by March 2002)
election results: percent of vote by party - NA%; seats by party - PNP 50, JLP 10
Judicial branch: Supreme Court (judges appointed by the governor general on the advice of the prime minister); Court of Appeal
Political parties and leaders: Jamaica Labor Party or JLP [Edward SEAGA]; National Democratic Movement or NDM [Bruce GOLDING]; People's National Party or PNP [Percival James PATTERSON]
Political pressure groups and leaders: New Beginnings Movement or NBM; Rastafarians (black religious/racial cultists, pan-Africanists)
International organization participation: ACP, C, Caricom, CCC, CDB, ECLAC, FAO, G-15, G-19, G-77, IADB, IAEA, IBRD, ICAO, ICFTU, ICRM, IFAD, IFC, IFRCS, IHO (pending member), ILO, IMF, IMO, Intelsat, Interpol, IOC, IOM (observer), ISO, ITU, LAES, NAM, OAS, OPANAL, OPCW, UN, UN Security Council (temporary), UNCTAD, UNESCO, UNIDO, UPU, WFTU, WHO, WIPO, WMO, WToO, WTrO
Diplomatic representation in the US:
chief of mission: Ambassador Richard Leighton BERNAL
chancery: 1520 New Hampshire Avenue NW, Washington, DC 20036
telephone: [1] (202) 452-0660
FAX: [1] (202) 452-0081
consulate(s) general: Miami and New York
Diplomatic representation from the US:
chief of mission: Ambassador Stanley Louis MCLELLAND
embassy: Jamaica Mutual Life Center, 2 Oxford Road, 3rd floor, Kingston 5
mailing address: use embassy street address
telephone: [1] (876) 929-4850 through 4859
FAX: [1] (876) 926-6743
Flag description: diagonal yellow cross divides the flag into four triangles - green (top and bottom) and black (hoist side and outer side)

Economy

Economy - overview: Key sectors in this island economy are bauxite (alumina and bauxite account for more than half of exports) and tourism. Since assuming office in 1992, Prime Minister PATTERSON has eliminated most price controls, streamlined tax schedules, and privatized government enterprises. Continued tight monetary and fiscal policies have helped slow inflation - although inflationary pressures are mounting - and stabilize the exchange rate, but have resulted in the slowdown of economic growth (moving from 1.5% in 1992 to 0.5% in 1995). In 1996, GDP showed negative growth (-1.4%) and remained negative through 1999. Serious problems include: high interest rates; increased foreign competition; the weak financial condition of business in general resulting in receiverships or closures and downsizings of companies; the shift in investment portfolios to non-productive, short-term high yield instruments; a pressured, sometimes sliding, exchange rate; a widening merchandise trade deficit; and a growing internal debt for government bailouts to various ailing sectors of the economy, particularly the financial sector. Depressed economic conditions in 1999-2000 led to increased civil unrest, including a mounting crime rate. Jamaica's medium-term prospects will depend upon encouraging investment in the productive sectors, maintaining a competitive exchange rate, stabilizing the labor environment, selling off reacquired firms, and implementing proper fiscal and monetary policies.
GDP: purchasing power parity - $9.7 billion (2000 est.)
GDP - real growth rate: 0.2% (2000 est.)
GDP - per capita: purchasing power parity - $3,700 (2000 est.)
GDP - composition by sector:
agriculture: 7.4%
industry: 35.2%
services: 57.4% (1999 est.)
Population below poverty line: 34.2% (1992 est.)
Household income or consumption by percentage share:
lowest 10%: 2.9%
highest 10%: 28.9% (1996)
Inflation rate (consumer prices): 8.8% (2000 est.)
Labor force: 1.13 million (1998)
Labor force - by occupation: services 60%, agriculture 21%, industry 19% (1998)
Unemployment rate: 16% (2000 est.)
Budget:
revenues: $2.23 billion
expenditures: $2.56 billion, including capital expenditures of $232.5 million (FY99/00 est.)
Industries: tourism, bauxite, textiles, food processing, light manufactures, rum, cement, metal, paper, chemical products
Industrial production growth rate: -2% (2000 est.)
Electricity - production: 6.53 billion kWh (1999)
Electricity - production by source:
fossil fuel: 92.28%
hydro: 1.36%
nuclear: 0%
other: 6.36% (1999)
Electricity - consumption: 6.073 billion kWh (1999)
Electricity - exports: 0 kWh (1999)
Electricity - imports: 0 kWh (1999)
Agriculture - products: sugarcane, bananas, coffee, citrus, potatoes, vegetables; poultry, goats, milk
Exports: $1.7 billion (f.o.b., 2000 est.)
Exports - commodities: alumina, bauxite; sugar, bananas, rum
Exports - partners: US 35.7%, EU (excluding UK) 15.8%, UK 13%, Canada 10.5% (1999)
Imports: $3 billion (f.o.b., 2000 est.)
Imports - commodities: machinery and transport equipment, construction materials, fuel, food, chemicals, fertilizers
Imports - partners: US 47.8%, Caricom countries 12.4%, Latin America 7.2%, EU (excluding UK) 4.7% (1999)
Debt - external: $4.7 billion (2000 est.)
Economic aid - recipient: $102.7 million (1995)
Currency: Jamaican dollar (JMD)
Currency code: JMD
Exchange rates: Jamaican dollars per US dollar - 45.557 (January 2001), 42.701 (2000), 39.044 (1999), 36.550 (1998), 35.404 (1997), 37.120 (1996)
Fiscal year: 1 April - 31 March

Communications

Telephones - main lines in use: 353,000 (1996)
Telephones - mobile cellular: 54,640 (1996)
Telephone system:
general assessment: fully automatic domestic telephone network
domestic: NA
international: satellite earth stations - 2 Intelsat (Atlantic Ocean); 3 coaxial submarine cables
Radio broadcast stations: AM 10, FM 13, shortwave 0 (1998)
Radios: 1.215 million (1997)
Television broadcast stations: 7 (1997)
Televisions: 460,000 (1997)
Internet country code: .jm
Internet Service Providers (ISPs): 21 (2000)
Internet users: 60,000 (2000)

Transportation

Railways:
total: 370 km
standard gauge: 370 km 1.435-m gauge; note - 207 km belong to the Jamaica Railway Corporation in common carrier service, but are no longer operational; the remaining track is privately owned and used to transport bauxite
Highways:
total: 18,700 km
paved: 13,100 km
unpaved: 5,600 km (1997 est.)
Waterways: none
Pipelines: petroleum products 10 km
Ports and harbors: Alligator Pond, Discovery Bay, Kingston, Montego Bay, Ocho Rios, Port Antonio, Rocky Point, Port Esquivel (Longswharf)
Merchant marine:
total: 1 ship (1,000 GRT or over) totaling 1,930 GRT/3,065 DWT
ships by type: petroleum tanker 1 (2000 est.)
Airports: 35 (2000 est.)
Airports - with paved runways:
total: 11
2,438 to 3,047 m: 2

Jamaica (continued)

1,524 to 2,437 m: 1
914 to 1,523 m: 3
under 914 m: 5 (2000 est.)
Airports - with unpaved runways:
total: 24
914 to 1,523 m: 2
under 914 m: 22 (2000 est.)

Military

Military branches: Jamaica Defense Force (includes Ground Forces, Coast Guard, and Air Wing), Jamaica Constabulary Force
Military manpower - military age: 18 years of age
Military manpower - availability:
males age 15-49: 736,627 (2001 est.)
Military manpower - fit for military service:
males age 15-49: 517,077 (2001 est.)
Military manpower - reaching military age annually:
males: 27,729 (2001 est.)
Military expenditures - dollar figure: $30 million (FY95/96 est.)
Military expenditures - percent of GDP: NA%

Transnational Issues

Disputes - international: none
Illicit drugs: major transshipment point for cocaine from South America to North America and Europe; illicit cultivation of cannabis; government has an active manual cannabis eradication program; corruption is a major concern

Jan Mayen (territory of Norway)

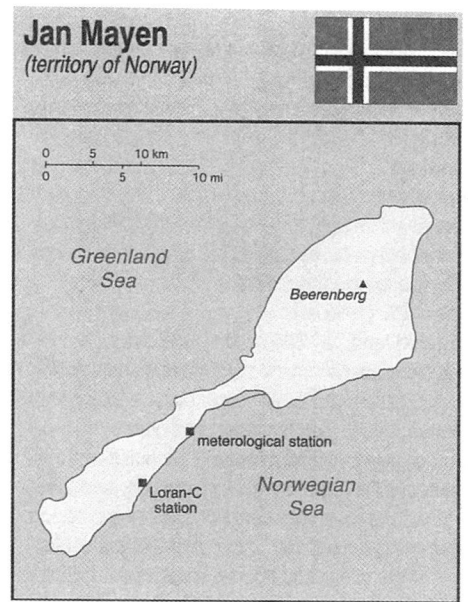

Introduction

Background: This desolate, mountainous island was named after a Dutch whaling captain who indisputably discovered it in 1614 (earlier claims are inconclusive). Visited only occasionally by seal hunters and trappers over the following centuries, the island came under Norwegian sovereignty in 1929. The long dormant Beerenberg volcano resumed activity in 1970; it is the northernmost active volcano on earth.

Geography

Location: Northern Europe, island between the Greenland Sea and the Norwegian Sea, northeast of Iceland
Geographic coordinates: 71 00 N, 8 00 W
Map references: Arctic Region
Area:
total: 373 sq km
land: 373 sq km
water: 0 sq km
Area - comparative: slightly more than twice the size of Washington, DC
Land boundaries: 0 km
Coastline: 124.1 km
Maritime claims:
contiguous zone: 10 NM
continental shelf: 200-m depth or to the depth of exploitation
exclusive economic zone: 200 NM
territorial sea: 4 NM
Climate: arctic maritime with frequent storms and persistent fog
Terrain: volcanic island, partly covered by glaciers
Elevation extremes:
lowest point: Norwegian Sea 0 m
highest point: Haakon VII Toppen/Beerenberg 2,277 m
Natural resources: none
Land use:
arable land: 0%
permanent crops: 0%
permanent pastures: 0%
forests and woodland: 0%
other: 100%
Irrigated land: 0 sq km (1993)
Natural hazards: dominated by the volcano Haakon VII Toppen/Beerenberg; volcanic activity resumed in 1970
Environment - current issues: NA
Geography - note: barren volcanic island with some moss and grass

People

Population: no indigenous inhabitants
note: there are personnel who operate the Long Range Navigation (Loran-C) base and the weather and coastal services radio station (July 2001 est.)

Government

Country name:
conventional long form: none
conventional short form: Jan Mayen
Dependency status: territory of Norway; administered from Oslo through a governor (sysselmann) resident in Longyearbyen (Svalbard); however, authority has been delegated to a station commander of the Norwegian Defense Communication Service
Legal system: the laws of Norway, where applicable, apply
Flag description: the flag of Norway is used

Economy

Economy - overview: Jan Mayen is a volcanic island with no exploitable natural resources. Economic activity is limited to providing services for employees of Norway's radio and meteorological stations located on the island.

Communications

Radio broadcast stations: AM NA, FM NA, shortwave NA
note: there is one radio and meteorological station (1998)
Internet Service Providers (ISPs): 13 (Jan Mayen and Svalbard) (2000)

Transportation

Waterways: none
Ports and harbors: none; offshore anchorage only
Airports: 1 (2000 est.)
Airports - with unpaved runways:
total: 1
1,524 to 2,437 m: 1 (2000 est.)

Military

Military - note: defense is the responsibility of Norway

Transnational Issues

Disputes - international: none

Japan

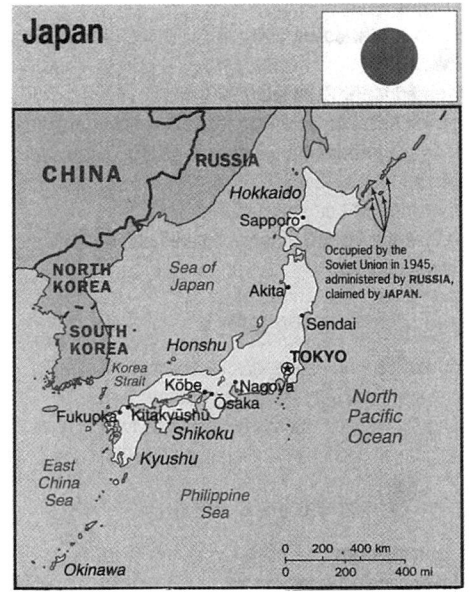

Introduction

Background: While retaining its time-honored culture, Japan rapidly absorbed Western technology during the late 19th and early 20th centuries. After its devastating defeat in World War II, Japan recovered to become the second most powerful economy in the world and a staunch ally of the US. While the emperor retains his throne as a symbol of national unity, actual power rests in networks of powerful politicians, bureaucrats, and business executives. The economy experienced a major slowdown in the 1990s following three decades of unprecedented growth.

Geography

Location: Eastern Asia, island chain between the North Pacific Ocean and the Sea of Japan, east of the Korean Peninsula
Geographic coordinates: 36 00 N, 138 00 E
Map references: Asia
Area:
total: 377,835 sq km
land: 374,744 sq km
water: 3,091 sq km
note: includes Bonin Islands (Ogasawara-gunto), Daito-shoto, Minami-jima, Okino-tori-shima, Ryukyu Islands (Nansei-shoto), and Volcano Islands (Kazan-retto)
Area - comparative: slightly smaller than California
Land boundaries: 0 km
Coastline: 29,751 km
Maritime claims:
contiguous zone: 24 NM
exclusive economic zone: 200 NM
territorial sea: 12 NM; between 3 NM and 12 NM in the international straits - La Perouse or Soya, Tsugaru, Osumi, and Eastern and Western Channels of the Korea or Tsushima Strait
Climate: varies from tropical in south to cool temperate in north
Terrain: mostly rugged and mountainous
Elevation extremes:
lowest point: Hachiro-gata -4 m
highest point: Fujiyama 3,776 m
Natural resources: negligible mineral resources, fish
Land use:
arable land: 11%
permanent crops: 1%
permanent pastures: 2%
forests and woodland: 67%
other: 19% (1993 est.)
Irrigated land: 27,820 sq km (1993 est.)
Natural hazards: many dormant and some active volcanoes; about 1,500 seismic occurrences (mostly tremors) every year; tsunamis; typhoons
Environment - current issues: air pollution from power plant emissions results in acid rain; acidification of lakes and reservoirs degrading water quality and threatening aquatic life; Japan is one of the largest consumers of fish and tropical timber, contributing to the depletion of these resources in Asia and elsewhere
Environment - international agreements:
party to: Antarctic-Environmental Protocol, Antarctic-Marine Living Resources, Antarctic Seals, Antarctic Treaty, Biodiversity, Climate Change, Desertification, Endangered Species, Environmental Modification, Hazardous Wastes, Law of the Sea, Marine Dumping, Nuclear Test Ban, Ozone Layer Protection, Ship Pollution, Tropical Timber 83, Tropical Timber 94, Wetlands, Whaling
signed, but not ratified: Climate Change-Kyoto Protocol
Geography - note: strategic location in northeast Asia

People

Population: 126,771,662 (July 2001 est.)
Age structure:
0-14 years: 14.64% (male 9,510,296; female 9,043,074)
15-64 years: 67.83% (male 43,202,513; female 42,790,187)
65 years and over: 17.53% (male 9,351,340; female 12,874,252) (2001 est.)
Population growth rate: 0.17% (2001 est.)
Birth rate: 10.04 births/1,000 population (2001 est.)
Death rate: 8.34 deaths/1,000 population (2001 est.)
Net migration rate: 0 migrant(s)/1,000 population (2001 est.)
Sex ratio:
at birth: 1.05 male(s)/female
under 15 years: 1.05 male(s)/female
15-64 years: 1.01 male(s)/female
65 years and over: 0.73 male(s)/female
total population: 0.96 male(s)/female (2001 est.)
Infant mortality rate: 3.88 deaths/1,000 live births (2001 est.)
Life expectancy at birth:
total population: 80.8 years
male: 77.62 years
female: 84.15 years (2001 est.)
Total fertility rate: 1.41 children born/woman (2001 est.)
HIV/AIDS - adult prevalence rate: 0.02% (1999 est.)
HIV/AIDS - people living with HIV/AIDS: 10,000 (1999 est.)
HIV/AIDS - deaths: 150 (1999 est.)
Nationality:
noun: Japanese (singular and plural)
adjective: Japanese
Ethnic groups: Japanese 99.4%, Korean 0.6% (1999)
Religions: observe both Shinto and Buddhist 84%, other 16% (including Christian 0.7%)
Languages: Japanese
Literacy:
definition: age 15 and over can read and write
total population: 99% (1970 est.)
male: NA%
female: NA%

Government

Country name:
conventional long form: none
conventional short form: Japan
Government type: constitutional monarchy with a parliamentary government
Capital: Tokyo
Administrative divisions: 47 prefectures; Aichi, Akita, Aomori, Chiba, Ehime, Fukui, Fukuoka, Fukushima, Gifu, Gumma, Hiroshima, Hokkaido, Hyogo, Ibaraki, Ishikawa, Iwate, Kagawa, Kagoshima, Kanagawa, Kochi, Kumamoto, Kyoto, Mie, Miyagi, Miyazaki, Nagano, Nagasaki, Nara, Niigata, Oita, Okayama, Okinawa, Osaka, Saga, Saitama, Shiga, Shimane, Shizuoka, Tochigi, Tokushima, Tokyo, Tottori, Toyama, Wakayama, Yamagata, Yamaguchi, Yamanashi
Independence: 660 BC (traditional founding by Emperor Jimmu)
National holiday: Birthday of Emperor AKIHITO, 23 December (1933)
Constitution: 3 May 1947
Legal system: modeled after European civil law system with English-American influence; judicial review of legislative acts in the Supreme Court; accepts compulsory ICJ jurisdiction, with reservations
Suffrage: 20 years of age; universal
Executive branch:
chief of state: Emperor AKIHITO (since 7 January 1989)
head of government: Prime Minister Junichiro KOIZUMI (since 24 April 2001)
cabinet: Cabinet appointed by the prime minister
elections: none; the monarch is hereditary; the Diet designates the prime minister; the constitution requires that the prime minister must command a parliamentary majority, therefore, following legislative elections, the leader of the majority party or leader of a majority coalition in the House of Representatives usually becomes prime minister

Japan (continued)

note: following the resignation of Prime Minister Yoshiro MORI, Junichiro KOIZUMI was elected as the new president of the majority Liberal Democratic Party, and soon thereafter designated by the Diet to become the next prime minister

Legislative branch: bicameral Diet or Kokkai consists of the House of Councillors or Sangi-in (252 seats; one-half of the members elected every three years - 76 seats of which are elected from the 47 multi-seat prefectural districts and 50 of which are elected from a single nationwide list; members elected by popular vote to serve six-year terms) and the House of Representatives or Shugi-in (480 seats - 180 of which are elected from 11 regional blocks on a proportional representation basis and 300 of which are elected from 300 single-seat districts; members elected by popular vote to serve four-year terms)
elections: House of Councillors - last held 12 July 1998 (next to be held NA July 2001); House of Representatives - last held 25 June 2000 (next to be held by June 2004)
election results: House of Councillors - percent of vote by party - NA%; seats by party - LDP 102, DPJ 47, JCP 23, Komeito 22, SDP 13, Liberal Party 12, independents 26, others 7; note - the distribution of seats as of February 2001 is as follows - LDP 112, DPJ 58, Komeito 24, JCP 23, SDP 13, Liberal Party 5, independents 7, others 10; House of Representatives - percent of vote by party - NA%; seats by party - LDP 233, DPJ 127, Komeito 31, Liberal Party 22, JCP 20, SDP 19, other 28; note - the distribution of seats as of February 2001 is as follows - LDP 239, DPJ 129, Komeito 31, Liberal Party 22, JCP 20, SDP 19, other 20

Judicial branch: Supreme Court (chief justice is appointed by the monarch after designation by the cabinet; all other justices are appointed by the cabinet)

Political parties and leaders: Democratic Party of Japan or DPJ [Yukio HATOYAMA, leader, Naoto KAN, secretary general]; Japan Communist Party or JCP [Kazuo SHII, chairman, Tadaaki ICHIDA, secretary general]; Komeito [Takenori KANZAKI, president, Tetsuzo FUYUSHIBA, secretary general]; Liberal Democratic Party or LDP [Junichiro KOIZUMI, president, Taku YAMASAKI, secretary general]; Liberal Party [Ichiro OZAWA, president, Hirohisa FUJII, secretary general]; New Conservative Party [Chikage OGI, president, Takeshi NODA, secretary general]; Social Democratic Party or SDP [Takako DOI, chairperson, Sadao FUCHIGAMI, secretary general]

Political pressure groups and leaders: NA

International organization participation: AfDB, APEC, ARF (dialogue partner), AsDB, ASEAN (dialogue partner), Australia Group, BIS, CCC, CE (observer), CERN (observer), CP, EBRD, ESCAP, FAO, G-5, G-7, G-10, IADB, IAEA, IBRD, ICAO, ICC, ICFTU, ICRM, IDA, IEA, IFAD, IFC, IFRCS, IHO, ILO, IMF, IMO, Inmarsat, Intelsat, Interpol, IOC, IOM, ISO, ITU, NAM (guest), NEA, NSG, OAS (observer), OECD, OPCW, OSCE (partner), PCA, UN, UNCTAD, UNDOF, UNESCO, UNHCR, UNIDO, UNITAR, UNRWA, UNU, UPU, WFTU, WHO, WIPO, WMO, WToO, WTrO, ZC

Diplomatic representation in the US:
chief of mission: Ambassador Shunji YANAI
chancery: 2520 Massachusetts Avenue NW, Washington, DC 20008
telephone: [1] (202) 238-6700
FAX: [1] (202) 328-2187
consulate(s) general: Anchorage, Atlanta, Boston, Chicago, Denver, Detroit, Hagatna (Guam), Honolulu, Houston, Kansas City (Missouri), Los Angeles, Miami, New Orleans, New York, Portland (Oregon), San Francisco, and Seattle
consulate(s): Saipan (Northern Mariana Islands)

Diplomatic representation from the US:
chief of mission: Ambassador-designate Howard H. BAKER, Jr.
embassy: 10-5 Akasaka 1-chome, Minato-ku, Tokyo 107-8420
mailing address: Unit 45004, Box 205, APO AP 96337-5004
telephone: [81] (03) 3224-5000
FAX: [81] (03) 3224-5856
consulate(s) general: Naha (Okinawa), Osaka-Kobe, Sapporo
consulate(s): Fukuoka, Nagoya

Flag description: white with a large red disk (representing the sun without rays) in the center

Economy

Economy - overview: Government-industry cooperation, a strong work ethic, mastery of high technology, and a comparatively small defense allocation (1% of GDP) have helped Japan advance with extraordinary rapidity to the rank of second most technologically powerful economy in the world after the US and third largest economy in the world after the US and China. One notable characteristic of the economy is the working together of manufacturers, suppliers, and distributors in closely-knit groups called keiretsu. A second basic feature has been the guarantee of lifetime employment for a substantial portion of the urban labor force. Both features are now eroding. Industry, the most important sector of the economy, is heavily dependent on imported raw materials and fuels. The much smaller agricultural sector is highly subsidized and protected, with crop yields among the highest in the world. Usually self-sufficient in rice, Japan must import about 50% of its requirements of other grain and fodder crops. Japan maintains one of the world's largest fishing fleets and accounts for nearly 15% of the global catch. For three decades overall real economic growth had been spectacular: a 10% average in the 1960s, a 5% average in the 1970s, and a 4% average in the 1980s. Growth slowed markedly in the 1990s largely because of the aftereffects of overinvestment during the late 1980s and contractionary domestic policies intended to wring speculative excesses from the stock and real estate markets. Government efforts to revive economic growth have met little success and were further hampered in late 2000 by the slowing of the US and Asian economies. The crowding of habitable land area and the aging of the population are two major long-run problems. Robotics constitutes a key long-term economic strength, with Japan possessing 410,000 of the world's 720,000 "working robots".

GDP: purchasing power parity - $3.15 trillion (2000 est.)

GDP - real growth rate: 1.3% (2000 est.)

GDP - per capita: purchasing power parity - $24,900 (2000 est.)

GDP - composition by sector:
agriculture: 2%
industry: 35%
services: 63% (1999 est.)

Population below poverty line: NA%

Household income or consumption by percentage share:
lowest 10%: 4.8%
highest 10%: 21.7% (1993)

Inflation rate (consumer prices): -0.7% (2000 est.)

Labor force: 67.7 million (December 2000)

Labor force - by occupation: services 65%, industry 30%, agriculture 5%

Unemployment rate: 4.7% (2000)

Budget:
revenues: $441 billion
expenditures: $718 billion, including capital expenditures (public works only) of about $84 billion (FY01/02 est.)

Industries: among world's largest and technologically advanced producers of motor vehicles, electronic equipment, machine tools, steel and nonferrous metals, ships, chemicals; textiles, processed foods

Industrial production growth rate: 5.3% (2000 est.)

Electricity - production: 1.018 trillion kWh (1999)

Electricity - production by source:
fossil fuel: 58.91%
hydro: 8.35%
nuclear: 30.31%
other: 2.43% (1999)

Electricity - consumption: 947.038 billion kWh (1999)

Electricity - exports: 0 kWh (1999)

Electricity - imports: 0 kWh (1999)

Agriculture - products: rice, sugar beets, vegetables, fruit; pork, poultry, dairy products, eggs; fish

Exports: $450 billion (f.o.b., 2000)

Exports - commodities: motor vehicles, semiconductors, office machinery, chemicals

Exports - partners: US 30%, Taiwan 7%, South Korea 6.4%, China 6.2%, Hong Kong 5.6% (2000 est.)

Imports: $355 billion (c.i.f., 2000)

Imports - commodities: fuels, foodstuffs, chemicals, textiles, office machinery

Imports - partners: US 19%, China 14.5%, South Korea 5.4%, Taiwan 4.8%, Indonesia 4.3%, Australia 3.9% (2000 est.)

Japan (continued)

Debt - external: $NA
Economic aid - donor: ODA, $9.1 billion (1999)
Currency: yen (JPY)
Currency code: JPY
Exchange rates: yen per US dollar - 117.10 (January 2001), 107.77 (2000), 113.91 (1999), 130.91 (1998), 120.99 (1997), 108.78 (1996)
Fiscal year: 1 April - 31 March

Communications

Telephones - main lines in use: 60.381 million (1997)
Telephones - mobile cellular: 63.88 million (2000)
Telephone system:
general assessment: excellent domestic and international service
domestic: high level of modern technology and excellent service of every kind
international: satellite earth stations - 5 Intelsat (4 Pacific Ocean and 1 Indian Ocean), 1 Intersputnik (Indian Ocean region), and 1 Inmarsat (Pacific and Indian Ocean regions); submarine cables to China, Philippines, Russia, and US (via Guam) (1999)
Radio broadcast stations: AM 190, FM 88, shortwave 24 (1999)
Radios: 120.5 million (1997)
Television broadcast stations: 7,108 (plus 441 repeaters; note - in addition, US Forces are served by 3 TV stations and 2 TV cable services) (1999)
Televisions: 86.5 million (1997)
Internet country code: .jp
Internet Service Providers (ISPs): 73 (2000)
Internet users: 27.06 million (2000)

Transportation

Railways:
total: 23,670.7 km
standard gauge: 2,893.1 km 1.435-m gauge (entirely electrified)
narrow gauge: 89.8 km 1.372-m gauge (89.8 km electrified); 20,656.8 km 1.067-m gauge (10,383.6 km electrified); 31 km 0.762-m gauge (3.6 km electrified) (1994)
Highways:
total: 1,152,207 km
paved: 863,003 km (including 6,114 km of expressways)
unpaved: 289,204 km (1997 est.)
Waterways: 1,770 km approximately
note: seagoing craft ply all coastal inland seas
Pipelines: crude oil 84 km; petroleum products 322 km; natural gas 1,800 km
Ports and harbors: Akita, Amagasaki, Chiba, Hachinohe, Hakodate, Higashi-Harima, Himeji, Hiroshima, Kawasaki, Kinuura, Kobe, Kushiro, Mizushima, Moji, Nagoya, Osaka, Sakai, Sakaide, Shimizu, Tokyo, Tomakomai
Merchant marine:
total: 630 ships (1,000 GRT or over) totaling 11,691,174 GRT/15,484,848 DWT
ships by type: bulk 137, cargo 51, chemical tanker 15, combination bulk 22, combination ore/oil 3, container 22, liquefied gas 49, passenger 9, passenger/cargo 2, petroleum tanker 194, refrigerated cargo 15, roll on/roll off 49, short-sea passenger 6, vehicle carrier 56 (2000 est.)
Airports: 173 (2000 est.)
Airports - with paved runways:
total: 142
over 3,047 m: 8
2,438 to 3,047 m: 36
1,524 to 2,437 m: 38
914 to 1,523 m: 30
under 914 m: 30 (2000 est.)
Airports - with unpaved runways:
total: 31
914 to 1,523 m: 4
under 914 m: 27 (2000 est.)
Heliports: 16 (2000 est.)

Military

Military branches: Japan Ground Self-Defense Force (Army), Japan Maritime Self-Defense Force (Navy), Japan Air Self-Defense Force (Air Force)
Military manpower - military age: 18 years of age
Military manpower - availability:
males age 15-49: 29,926,614 (2001 est.)
Military manpower - fit for military service:
males age 15-49: 25,876,484 (2001 est.)
Military manpower - reaching military age annually:
males: 765,817 (2001 est.)
Military expenditures - dollar figure: $43 billion (FY01)
Military expenditures - percent of GDP: 0.96% (FY01)

Transnational Issues

Disputes - international: islands of Etorofu, Kunashiri, and Shikotan, and the Habomai group occupied by the Soviet Union in 1945, now administered by Russia, claimed by Japan; Liancourt Rocks (Takeshima/Tokdo) disputed with South Korea; Senkaku-shoto (Senkaku Islands) claimed by China and Taiwan

Jarvis Island
(territory of the US)

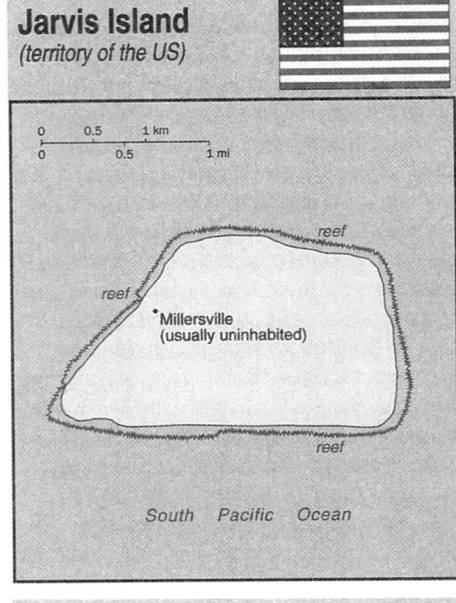

Introduction

Background: First discovered by the British in 1821, the uninhabited island was annexed by the US in 1858, but abandoned in 1879 after tons of guano had been removed. The UK annexed the island in 1889, but never carried out plans for further exploitation. The US occupied and reclaimed the island in 1935. Abandoned after World War II, the island is currently a National Wildlife Refuge administered by the US Department of the Interior; a day beacon is situated near the middle of the west coast.

Geography

Location: Oceania, island in the South Pacific Ocean, about one-half of the way from Hawaii to the Cook Islands
Geographic coordinates: 0 22 S, 160 03 W
Map references: Oceania
Area:
total: 4.5 sq km
land: 4.5 sq km
water: 0 sq km
Area - comparative: about eight times the size of The Mall in Washington, DC
Land boundaries: 0 km
Coastline: 8 km
Maritime claims:
exclusive economic zone: 200 NM
territorial sea: 12 NM
Climate: tropical; scant rainfall, constant wind, burning sun
Terrain: sandy, coral island surrounded by a narrow fringing reef
Elevation extremes:
lowest point: Pacific Ocean 0 m
highest point: unnamed location 7 m
Natural resources: guano (deposits worked until late 1800s), terrestrial and aquatic wildlife

Jarvis Island (continued)

Land use:
arable land: 0%
permanent crops: 0%
permanent pastures: 0%
forests and woodland: 0%
other: 100%
Irrigated land: 0 sq km (1998)
Natural hazards: the narrow fringing reef surrounding the island can be a maritime hazard
Environment - current issues: no natural fresh water resources
Geography - note: sparse bunch grass, prostrate vines, and low-growing shrubs; primarily a nesting, roosting, and foraging habitat for seabirds, shorebirds, and marine wildlife

People

Population: uninhabited
note: Millersville settlement on western side of island occasionally used as a weather station from 1935 until World War II, when it was abandoned; reoccupied in 1957 during the International Geophysical Year by scientists who left in 1958; public entry is by special-use permit from US Fish and Wildlife Service only and generally restricted to scientists and educators; visited annually by US Fish and Wildlife Service (July 2001 est.)

Government

Country name:
conventional long form: none
conventional short form: Jarvis Island
Dependency status: unincorporated territory of the US; administered from Washington, DC, by the Fish and Wildlife Service of the US Department of the Interior as part of the National Wildlife Refuge system
Legal system: the laws of the US, where applicable, apply
Flag description: the flag of the US is used

Economy

Economy - overview: no economic activity

Transportation

Waterways: none
Ports and harbors: none; offshore anchorage only; note - there is one small boat landing area in the middle of the west coast and another near the southwest corner of the island
Transportation - note: there is a day beacon near the middle of the west coast

Military

Military - note: defense is the responsibility of the US; visited annually by the US Coast Guard

Transnational Issues

Disputes - international: none

Jersey
(British crown dependency)

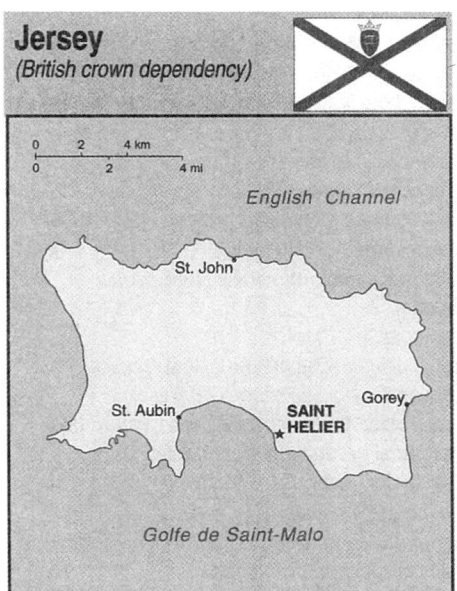

Introduction

Background: The island of Jersey and the other Channel Islands represent the last remnants of the medieval Dukedom of Normandy that held sway in both France and England. These islands were the only British soil occupied by German troops in World War II.

Geography

Location: Western Europe, island in the English Channel, northwest of France
Geographic coordinates: 49 15 N, 2 10 W
Map references: Europe
Area:
total: 116 sq km
land: 116 sq km
water: 0 sq km
Area - comparative: about 0.7 times the size of Washington, DC
Land boundaries: 0 km
Coastline: 70 km
Maritime claims:
exclusive fishing zone: 12 NM
territorial sea: 3 NM
Climate: temperate; mild winters and cool summers
Terrain: gently rolling plain with low, rugged hills along north coast
Elevation extremes:
lowest point: Atlantic Ocean 0 m
highest point: unnamed location 143 m
Natural resources: arable land
Land use:
arable land: 66%
permanent crops: 0%
permanent pastures: 0%
forests and woodland: 0%
other: 34%
Irrigated land: NA sq km
Natural hazards: NA
Environment - current issues: NA
Geography - note: largest and southernmost of Channel Islands; about 30% of population concentrated in Saint Helier

People

Population: 89,361 (July 2001 est.)
Age structure:
0-14 years: 17.77% (male 8,214; female 7,667)
15-64 years: 67.59% (male 30,065; female 30,331)
65 years and over: 14.64% (male 5,603; female 7,481) (2001 est.)
Population growth rate: 0.48% (2001 est.)
Birth rate: 11.28 births/1,000 population (2001 est.)
Death rate: 9.27 deaths/1,000 population (2001 est.)
Net migration rate: 2.8 migrant(s)/1,000 population (2001 est.)
Sex ratio:
at birth: 1.08 male(s)/female
under 15 years: 1.07 male(s)/female
15-64 years: 0.99 male(s)/female
65 years and over: 0.75 male(s)/female
total population: 0.96 male(s)/female (2001 est.)
Infant mortality rate: 5.62 deaths/1,000 live births (2001 est.)
Life expectancy at birth:
total population: 78.63 years
male: 76.21 years
female: 81.23 years (2001 est.)
Total fertility rate: 1.56 children born/woman (2001 est.)
HIV/AIDS - adult prevalence rate: NA%
HIV/AIDS - people living with HIV/AIDS: NA
HIV/AIDS - deaths: NA
Nationality:
noun: Channel Islander(s)
adjective: Channel Islander
Ethnic groups: UK and Norman-French descent
Religions: Anglican, Roman Catholic, Baptist, Congregational New Church, Methodist, Presbyterian
Languages: English (official), French (official), Norman-French dialect spoken in country districts
Literacy:
definition: NA
total population: NA
male: NA
female: NA

Government

Country name:
conventional long form: Bailiwick of Jersey
conventional short form: Jersey
Dependency status: British crown dependency
Government type: NA
Capital: Saint Helier
Administrative divisions: none (British crown dependency)
Independence: none (British crown dependency)
National holiday: Liberation Day, 9 May (1945)
Constitution: unwritten; partly statutes, partly common law and practice

Jersey (continued)

Legal system: English law and local statute
Suffrage: NA years of age; universal adult
Executive branch:
chief of state: Queen ELIZABETH II (since 6 February 1952)
head of government: Lieutenant Governor and Commander in Chief Air Chief Marshall Sir John CHESHIRE (since 24 January 2001) and Bailiff Philip Martin BAILHACHE (since NA February 1995)
cabinet: committees appointed by the Assembly of the States
elections: none; the monarch is hereditary; lieutenant governor and bailiff appointed by the monarch
Legislative branch: unicameral Assembly of the States (55 voting members - 12 senators, 12 constables or heads of parishes, 29 deputies; all elected for six-year terms, half elected every third year; the bailiff and the deputy bailiff; and 3 non-voting members - the Dean of Jersey, the Attorney General and the Solicitor General all appointed by the monarch
elections: last held NA (next to be held NA)
election results: percent of vote - NA%; seats - independents 52
Judicial branch: Royal Court (judges elected by an electoral college and the bailiff)
Political parties and leaders: none; all independents
Political pressure groups and leaders: none
Diplomatic representation in the US: none (British crown dependency)
Diplomatic representation from the US: none (British crown dependency)
Flag description: white with a diagonal red cross extending to the corners of the flag and in the upper quadrant, surmounted by a yellow crown, a red shield holding the three lions of England in yellow

Economy

Economy - overview: The economy is based largely on international financial services, agriculture, and tourism. Potatoes, cauliflower, tomatoes, and especially flowers are important export crops, shipped mostly to the UK. The Jersey breed of dairy cattle is known worldwide and represents an important export income earner. Milk products go to the UK and other EU countries. In 1996 the finance sector accounted for about 60% of the island's output. Tourism, another mainstay of the economy, accounts for 24% of GDP. In recent years, the government has encouraged light industry to locate in Jersey, with the result that an electronics industry has developed alongside the traditional manufacturing of knitwear. All raw material and energy requirements are imported, as well as a large share of Jersey's food needs. Light taxes and death duties make the island a popular tax haven.
GDP: purchasing power parity - $2.2 billion (1999 est.)
GDP - real growth rate: NA%
GDP - per capita: purchasing power parity - $24,800 (1999 est.)
GDP - composition by sector:
agriculture: 5%
industry: 2%
services: 93% (1996)
Population below poverty line: NA%
Household income or consumption by percentage share:
lowest 10%: NA%
highest 10%: NA%
Inflation rate (consumer prices): 4.7% (1998)
Labor force: 57,050 (1996)
Unemployment rate: 0.7% (1998 est.)
Budget:
revenues: $601 million
expenditures: $588 million, including capital expenditures of $98 million (2000 est.)
Industries: tourism, banking and finance, dairy
Industrial production growth rate: NA%
Electricity - imports: NA kWh
note: electricity supplied by France
Agriculture - products: potatoes, cauliflower, tomatoes; beef, dairy products
Exports: $NA
Exports - commodities: light industrial and electrical goods, foodstuffs, textiles
Exports - partners: UK
Imports: $NA
Imports - commodities: machinery and transport equipment, manufactured goods, foodstuffs, mineral fuels, chemicals
Imports - partners: UK
Debt - external: none
Economic aid - recipient: none
Currency: British pound (GBP); note - there is also a Jersey pound
Currency code: GBP
Exchange rates: Jersey pounds per US dollar - 0.6764 (January 2001), 0.6596 (2000), 0.6180 (1999), 0.6037 (1998), 0.6106 (1997), 0.6403 (1996); the Jersey pound is at par with the British pound
Fiscal year: 1 April - 31 March

Communications

Telephones - main lines in use: 65,500 (1997)
Telephones - mobile cellular: 4,400 (1997)
Telephone system:
general assessment: NA
domestic: NA
international: 3 submarine cables
Radio broadcast stations: AM NA, FM 1, shortwave 0 (1998)
Radios: NA
Television broadcast stations: 1 (1997)
Televisions: NA
Internet country code: .je
Internet Service Providers (ISPs): NA
Internet users: NA

Transportation

Railways: 0 km
Highways:
total: 577 km
paved: NA km
unpaved: NA km (1995)
Waterways: none
Ports and harbors: Gorey, Saint Aubin, Saint Helier
Merchant marine: none (2000 est.)
Airports: 1 (2000 est.)
Airports - with paved runways:
total: 1
1,524 to 2,437 m: 1 (2000 est.)

Military

Military - note: defense is the responsibility of the UK

Transnational Issues

Disputes - international: none

Johnston Atoll
(territory of the US)

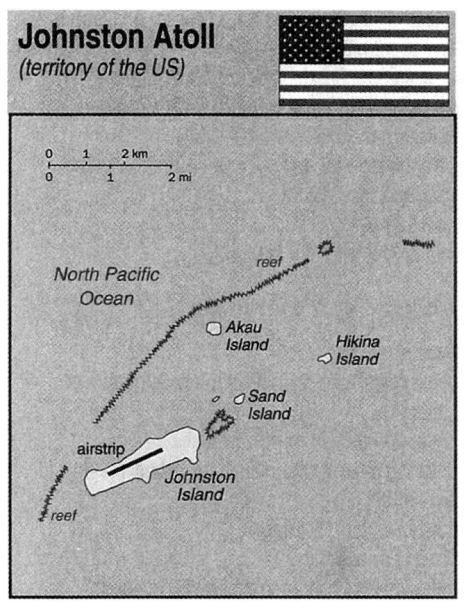

Introduction

Background: Both the US and the Kingdom of Hawaii annexed Johnston Atoll in 1858, but it was the US that mined the guano deposits until the late 1880s. The US Navy took over the atoll in 1934, and subsequently the US Air Force assumed control in 1948. The site was used for high altitude nuclear tests in the 1950s and 1960s, and until late in 2000 the atoll was maintained as a storage and disposal site for chemical weapons. Munitions destruction is now complete, and cleanup and closure of the facility is progressing.

Geography

Location: Oceania, atoll in the North Pacific Ocean 717 NM (1328 km) southwest of Honolulu, Hawaii, about one-third of the way from Hawaii to the Marshall Islands
Geographic coordinates: 16 45 N, 169 31 W
Map references: Oceania
Area:
total: 2.8 sq km
land: 2.8 sq km
water: 0 sq km
Area - comparative: about 4.7 times the size of The Mall in Washington, DC
Land boundaries: 0 km
Coastline: 10 km
Maritime claims:
exclusive economic zone: 200 NM
territorial sea: 12 NM
Climate: tropical, but generally dry; consistent northeast trade winds with little seasonal temperature variation
Terrain: mostly flat
Elevation extremes:
lowest point: Pacific Ocean 0 m
highest point: Summit Peak 5 m
Natural resources: guano deposits worked until depletion about 1890, terrestrial and aquatic wildlife
Land use:
arable land: 0%
permanent crops: 0%
permanent pastures: 0%
forests and woodland: 0%
other: 100%
Irrigated land: 0 sq km (1998)
Natural hazards: NA
Environment - current issues: no natural fresh water resources
Geography - note: strategic location in the North Pacific Ocean; Johnston Island and Sand Island are natural islands, which have been expanded by coral dredging; North Island (Akau) and East Island (Hikina) are manmade islands formed from coral dredging; egg-shaped reef is 34 km in circumference; closed to the public; former US nuclear weapons test site; site of Johnston Atoll Chemical Agent Disposal System (JACADS); some low-growing vegetation

People

Population: no indigenous inhabitants
note: in previous years, there was an average of 1,100 US military and civilian contractor personnel present; as of 1 October 2000, population decreased to approximately 970 when US Army Chemical Activity Pacific (USACAP) departed (January 2001 est.)
Population growth rate: -5.94% (2001 est.)

Government

Country name:
conventional long form: none
conventional short form: Johnston Atoll
Dependency status: unincorporated territory of the US; administered from Washington, DC, by Pacific Air Forces, Hickam AFB, and the Fish and Wildlife Service of the US Department of the Interior as part of the National Wildlife Refuge system
Legal system: the laws of the US, where applicable, apply
Flag description: the flag of the US is used

Economy

Economy - overview: Economic activity is limited to providing services to US military personnel and contractors located on the island. All food and manufactured goods must be imported.
Electricity - production: approximately 1,000,000 kWh weekly; note - there are six 25,000 kWh generators supplied by the base operating support contractor (1999)
Electricity - consumption: NA kWh

Communications

Telephone system:
general assessment: 13 outgoing and 10 incoming commercial lines; adequate telecommunications
domestic: 60-channel submarine cable, 22 DSN circuits by satellite, Autodin with standard remote terminal, digital telephone switch, Military Affiliated Radio System (MARS station), UHF/VHF air-ground radio, a link to the Pacific Consolidated Telecommunications Network (PCTN) satellite
international: NA
Radio broadcast stations: AM NA, FM NA, shortwave NA
Television broadcast stations: commercial satellite television system, with 16 channels (1997)
Internet Service Providers (ISPs): NA

Transportation

Waterways: none
Ports and harbors: Johnston Island
Airports: 1; note - six flights per week; three commercial, three military (2001 est.)
Airports - with paved runways:
total: 1
2,438 to 3,047 m: 1 (2000 est.)

Military

Military - note: defense is the responsibility of the US

Transnational Issues

Disputes - international: none

Jordan

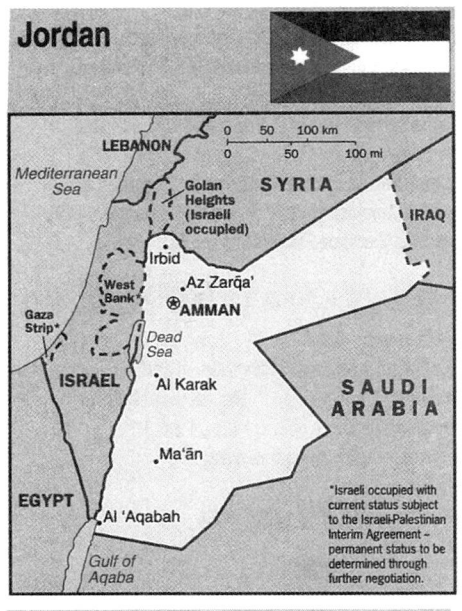

Introduction

Background: For most of its history since independence from British administration in 1946, Jordan was ruled by King HUSSEIN (1953-1999). A pragmatic ruler, he successfully navigated competing pressures from the major powers (US, USSR, and UK), various Arab states, Israel, and a large internal Palestinian population, through several wars and coup attempts. In 1989 he resumed parliamentary elections and gradually permitted political liberalization; in 1994 a formal peace treaty was signed with Israel. King ABDALLAH II - the eldest son of King HUSSEIN and Princess MUNA - assumed the throne following his father's death in February 1999. Since then, he has consolidated his power and established his domestic priorities.

Geography

Location: Middle East, northwest of Saudi Arabia
Geographic coordinates: 31 00 N, 36 00 E
Map references: Middle East
Area:
total: 92,300 sq km
land: 91,971 sq km
water: 329 sq km
Area - comparative: slightly smaller than Indiana
Land boundaries:
total: 1,619 km
border countries: Iraq 181 km, Israel 238 km, Saudi Arabia 728 km, Syria 375 km, West Bank 97 km
Coastline: 26 km
Maritime claims:
territorial sea: 3 NM
Climate: mostly arid desert; rainy season in west (November to April)
Terrain: mostly desert plateau in east, highland area in west; Great Rift Valley separates East and West Banks of the Jordan River
Elevation extremes:
lowest point: Dead Sea -408 m
highest point: Jabal Ram 1,734 m

Natural resources: phosphates, potash, shale oil
Land use:
arable land: 4%
permanent crops: 1%
permanent pastures: 9%
forests and woodland: 1%
other: 85% (1993 est.)
Irrigated land: 630 sq km (1993 est.)
Natural hazards: droughts
Environment - current issues: limited natural fresh water resources; deforestation; overgrazing; soil erosion; desertification
Environment - international agreements:
party to: Biodiversity, Climate Change, Desertification, Endangered Species, Hazardous Wastes, Law of the Sea, Marine Dumping, Nuclear Test Ban, Ozone Layer Protection, Ship Pollution, Wetlands
signed, but not ratified: none of the selected agreements

People

Population: 5,153,378 (July 2001 est.)
Age structure:
0-14 years: 37.23% (male 980,345; female 938,081)
15-64 years: 59.44% (male 1,633,579; female 1,429,631)
65 years and over: 3.33% (male 84,815; female 86,927) (2001 est.)
Population growth rate: 3% (2001 est.)
Birth rate: 25.44 births/1,000 population (2001 est.)
Death rate: 2.62 deaths/1,000 population (2001 est.)
Net migration rate: 7.18 migrant(s)/1,000 population (2001 est.)
Sex ratio:
at birth: 1.06 male(s)/female
under 15 years: 1.05 male(s)/female
15-64 years: 1.14 male(s)/female
65 years and over: 0.98 male(s)/female
total population: 1.1 male(s)/female (2001 est.)
Infant mortality rate: 20.36 deaths/1,000 live births (2001 est.)
Life expectancy at birth:
total population: 77.53 years
male: 75.1 years
female: 80.12 years (2001 est.)
Total fertility rate: 3.29 children born/woman (2001 est.)
HIV/AIDS - adult prevalence rate: 0.02% (1999 est.)
HIV/AIDS - people living with HIV/AIDS: NA
HIV/AIDS - deaths: NA
Nationality:
noun: Jordanian(s)
adjective: Jordanian
Ethnic groups: Arab 98%, Circassian 1%, Armenian 1%
Religions: Sunni Muslim 92%, Christian 6% (majority Greek Orthodox, but some Greek Catholics, Roman Catholics, Syrian Orthodox, Coptic Orthodox, Armenian Orthodox, and Protestant denominations), other 2% (several small Shi'a Muslim and Druze populations) (2000 est.)
Languages: Arabic (official), English widely understood among upper and middle classes
Literacy:
definition: age 15 and over can read and write
total population: 86.6%
male: 93.4%
female: 79.4% (1995 est.)

Government

Country name:
conventional long form: Hashemite Kingdom of Jordan
conventional short form: Jordan
local long form: Al Mamlakah al Urduniyah al Hashimiyah
local short form: Al Urdun
former: Transjordan
Government type: constitutional monarchy
Capital: Amman
Administrative divisions: 12 governorates (muhafazat, singular - muhafazah); Ajlun, Al 'Aqabah, Al Balqa', Al Karak, Al Mafraq, 'Amman, At Tafilah, Az Zarqa', Irbid, Jarash, Ma'an, Madaba
Independence: 25 May 1946 (from League of Nations mandate under British administration)
National holiday: Independence Day, 25 May (1946)
Constitution: 8 January 1952
Legal system: based on Islamic law and French codes; judicial review of legislative acts in a specially provided High Tribunal; has not accepted compulsory ICJ jurisdiction
Suffrage: 20 years of age; universal
Executive branch:
chief of state: King ABDALLAH II (since 7 February 1999); Crown Prince HAMZAH (half brother of the monarch, born 29 March 1980)
head of government: Prime Minister Ali Abul RAGHEB (since 19 June 2000)
cabinet: Cabinet appointed by the prime minister in consultation with the monarch
elections: none; the monarch is hereditary; prime minister appointed by the monarch
Legislative branch: bicameral National Assembly or Majlis al-'Umma consists of the Senate (a 40-member body appointed by the monarch from designated categories of public figures; members serve four-year terms) and the House of Representatives (80 seats; members elected by popular vote on the basis of proportional representation to serve four-year terms)
elections: House of Representatives - last held 4 November 1997 (next to be held NA November 2001)
election results: House of Representatives - percent of vote by party - NA%; seats by party - National Constitutional Party 2, Arab Land Party 1, independents 75, other 2
note: the House of Representatives has been convened and dissolved by the monarch several times since 1974; in November 1989 the first parliamentary elections in 22 years were held

Jordan (continued)

Judicial branch: Court of Cassation; Supreme Court (court of final appeal)
Political parties and leaders: Al-Umma (Nation) Party [Ahmad al-HANANDEH, secretary general]; Arab Land Party [Dr. Muhammad al-'ORAN, secretary general]; Jordanian Democratic Popular Unity Party [Sa'eed THIYAB, secretary general]; National Constitutional Party [Abdul Hadi MAJALI, secretary general]
Political pressure groups and leaders: Council of Professional Association Presidents [Ahmad al-QADIRI, chairman]; Jordanian Press Association [Sayf al-SHARIF, president]; Muslim Brotherhood [Abd-al-Majid DHUNAYBAT, secretary general]
International organization participation: ABEDA, ACC, AFESD, AL, AMF, CAEU, CCC, ESCWA, FAO, G-77, IAEA, IBRD, ICAO, ICC, ICFTU, ICRM, IDA, IDB, IFAD, IFC, IFRCS, ILO, IMF, IMO, Intelsat, Interpol, IOC, IOM, ISO (correspondent), ITU, MINURSO, MONUC, NAM, OIC, OPCW, OSCE (partner), PCA, UN, UNAMSIL, UNCTAD, UNESCO, UNIDO, UNMEE, UNMIBH, UNMIK, UNMOP, UNMOT, UNOMIG, UNRWA, UNTAET, UPU, WFTU, WHO, WIPO, WMO, WToO, WTrO
Diplomatic representation in the US:
chief of mission: Ambassador Marwan Jamil MUASHER
chancery: 3504 International Drive NW, Washington, DC 20008
telephone: [1] (202) 966-2664
FAX: [1] (202) 966-3110
Diplomatic representation from the US:
chief of mission: Ambassador William J. BURNS
embassy: Abdoum, Amman
mailing address: P. O. Box 354, Amman 11118 Jordan; APO AE 09892-0200
telephone: [962] (6) 5920101
FAX: [962] (6) 5920121
Flag description: three equal horizontal bands of black (top, the Abbassid Caliphate of Islam), white (the Ummayyad Caliphate of Islam), and green (the Fatimid Caliphate of Islam) with a red isosceles triangle (representing the Great Arab Revolt of 1916) based on the hoist side bearing a small white seven-pointed star symbolizing the seven verses of the opening Sura (Al-Fatiha) of the Holy Koran; the seven points on the star represent faith in One God, humanity, national spirit, humility, social justice, virtue, and aspirations

Economy

Economy - overview: Jordan is a small Arab country with inadequate supplies of water and other natural resources such as oil. The Persian Gulf crisis, which began in August 1990, aggravated Jordan's already serious economic problems, forcing the government to stop most debt payments and suspend rescheduling negotiations. Aid from Gulf Arab states, worker remittances, and trade revenues contracted. Refugees flooded the country, producing serious balance-of-payments problems, stunting GDP growth, and straining government resources. The economy rebounded in 1992, largely due to the influx of capital repatriated by workers returning from the Gulf. After averaging 9% in 1992-95, GDP growth averaged only 1.5% during 1996-99. In an attempt to spur growth, King ABDALLAH has undertaken limited economic reform, including partial privatization of some state-owned enterprises and Jordan's entry in January 2000 into the World Trade Organization (WTrO). Debt, poverty, and unemployment are fundamental ongoing economic problems.
GDP: purchasing power parity - $17.3 billion (2000 est.)
GDP - real growth rate: 2% (2000 est.)
GDP - per capita: purchasing power parity - $3,500 (2000 est.)
GDP - composition by sector:
agriculture: 3%
industry: 25%
services: 72% (1998 est.)
Population below poverty line: 30% (1998 est.)
Household income or consumption by percentage share:
lowest 10%: 2.4%
highest 10%: 34.7% (1991)
Inflation rate (consumer prices): 0.7% (2000 est.)
Labor force: 1.15 million
note: in addition, at least 300,000 workers are employed abroad (1997 est.)
Labor force - by occupation: industry 11.4%, commerce, restaurants, and hotels 10.5%, construction 10%, transport and communications 8.7%, agriculture 7.4%, other services 52% (1992)
Unemployment rate: 15% official rate; actual rate is 25%-30% (1999 est.)
Budget:
revenues: $2.8 billion
expenditures: $3.1 billion, including capital expenditures of $NA (2000 est.)
Industries: phosphate mining, petroleum refining, cement, potash, light manufacturing, tourism
Industrial production growth rate: 3.8% (2000 est.)
Electricity - production: 6.657 billion kWh (1999)
Electricity - production by source:
fossil fuel: 99.79%
hydro: 0.21%
nuclear: 0%
other: 0% (1999)
Electricity - consumption: 6.594 billion kWh (1999)
Electricity - exports: 4 million kWh (1999)
Electricity - imports: 407 million kWh (1999)
Agriculture - products: wheat, barley, citrus, tomatoes, melons, olives; sheep, goats, poultry
Exports: $2 billion (f.o.b., 2000 est.)
Exports - commodities: phosphates, fertilizers, potash, agricultural products, manufactures
Exports - partners: India, Iraq, Saudi Arabia, EU, Indonesia, UAE, Lebanon, Kuwait, Syria, Ethiopia
Imports: $4 billion (f.o.b., 2000 est.)
Imports - commodities: crude oil, machinery, transport equipment, food, live animals, manufactured goods
Imports - partners: Iraq, Germany, US, Japan, UK, Italy, Turkey, Malaysia, Syria, China
Debt - external: $8 billion (2000 est.)
Economic aid - recipient: ODA, $850 million (1996 est.)
Currency: Jordanian dinar (JOD)
Currency code: JOD
Exchange rates: Jordanian dinars per US dollar - 0.7090 (1996-present)
note: since May 1989, the Jordanian dinar has been pegged to a group of currencies
Fiscal year: calendar year

Communications

Telephones - main lines in use: 403,000 (1997)
Telephones - mobile cellular: 11,500 (1995)
Telephone system:
general assessment: service has improved recently with the increased use of digital switching equipment, but better access to the telephone system is needed in the rural areas and easier access to pay telephones is needed by the urban public
domestic: microwave radio relay transmission and coaxial and fiber-optic cable are employed on trunk lines; considerable use is made of mobile cellular systems; Internet service is available
international: satellite earth stations - 3 Intelsat, 1 Arabsat, and 29 land and maritime Inmarsat terminals; fiber-optic cable to Saudi Arabia and microwave radio relay link with Egypt and Syria; connection to international submarine cable FLAG (Fiber-Optic Link Around the Globe); participant in MEDARABTEL; international links total about 4,000
Radio broadcast stations: AM 6, FM 5, shortwave 1 (1999)
Radios: 1.66 million (1997)
Television broadcast stations: 20 (plus 96 repeaters) (1995)
Televisions: 500,000 (1997)
Internet country code: .jo
Internet Service Providers (ISPs): 5 (2000)
Internet users: 87,500 (2000)

Transportation

Railways:
total: 677 km
narrow gauge: 677 km 1.050-m gauge (2000)
Highways:
total: 8,000 km
paved: 8,000 km
unpaved: 0 km (2000 est.)
Waterways: none
Pipelines: crude oil 209 km; note - may not be in use
Ports and harbors: Al 'Aqabah
Merchant marine:
total: 6 ships (1,000 GRT or over) totaling 40,919 GRT/57,777 DWT
ships by type: bulk 1, cargo 3, container 1, roll on/roll off 1 (2000 est.)
Airports: 18 (2000 est.)

Jordan (continued)

Airports - with paved runways:
total: 15
over 3,047 m: 7
2,438 to 3,047 m: 6
914 to 1,523 m: 1
under 914 m: 1 (2000 est.)
Airports - with unpaved runways:
total: 3
under 914 m: 3 (2000 est.)
Heliports: 1 (2000 est.)

Military

Military branches: Jordanian Armed Forces (JAF; includes Royal Jordanian Land Force, Royal Naval Force, and Royal Jordanian Air Force); Ministry of the Interior's Public Security Force (falls under JAF only in wartime or crisis situations)
Military manpower - military age: 18 years of age
Military manpower - availability:
males age 15-49: 1,458,571 (2001 est.)
Military manpower - fit for military service:
males age 15-49: 1,034,109 (2001 est.)
Military manpower - reaching military age annually:
males: 57,131 (2001 est.)
Military expenditures - dollar figure: $608.9 million (FY98/99)
Military expenditures - percent of GDP: 7.8% (FY98/99)

Transnational Issues

Disputes - international: none

Juan de Nova Island
(possession of France)

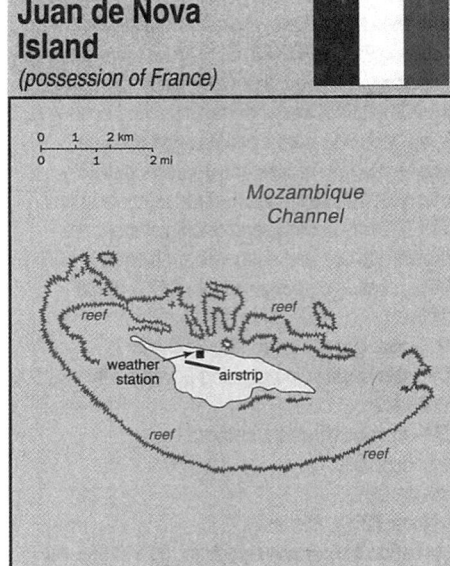

Introduction

Background: Named after a famous 15th century Spanish navigator and explorer, the island has been a French possession since 1897. It has been exploited for its guano and phosphate. Presently a small military garrison oversees a meteorological station.

Geography

Location: Southern Africa, island in the Mozambique Channel, about one-third of the way between Madagascar and Mozambique
Geographic coordinates: 17 03 S, 42 45 E
Map references: Africa
Area:
total: 4.4 sq km
land: 4.4 sq km
water: 0 sq km
Area - comparative: about seven times the size of The Mall in Washington, DC
Land boundaries: 0 km
Coastline: 24.1 km
Maritime claims:
continental shelf: 200-m depth or to the depth of exploitation
exclusive economic zone: 200 NM
territorial sea: 12 NM
Climate: tropical
Terrain: low and flat
Elevation extremes:
lowest point: Indian Ocean 0 m
highest point: unnamed location 10 m
Natural resources: guano deposits and other fertilizers
Land use:
arable land: 0%
permanent crops: 0%
permanent pastures: 0%
forests and woodland: 90%
other: 10%
Irrigated land: 0 sq km (1993)
Natural hazards: periodic cyclones
Environment - current issues: NA
Geography - note: wildlife sanctuary

People

Population: no indigenous inhabitants
note: there is a small French military garrison (July 2001 est.)

Government

Country name:
conventional long form: none
conventional short form: Juan de Nova Island
local long form: none
local short form: Ile Juan de Nova
Dependency status: possession of France; administered by a high commissioner of the Republic, resident in Reunion
Legal system: the laws of France, where applicable, apply
Diplomatic representation in the US: none (possession of France)
Diplomatic representation from the US: none (possession of France)
Flag description: the flag of France is used

Economy

Economy - overview: Up to 12,000 tons of guano are mined per year.

Communications

Communications - note: 1 meteorological station

Transportation

Railways:
total: NA km; short line going to a jetty
Waterways: none
Ports and harbors: none; offshore anchorage only
Airports: 1 (2000 est.)
Airports - with unpaved runways:
total: 1
914 to 1,523 m: 1 (2000 est.)

Military

Military - note: defense is the responsibility of France

Transnational Issues

Disputes - international: claimed by Madagascar

Kazakhstan

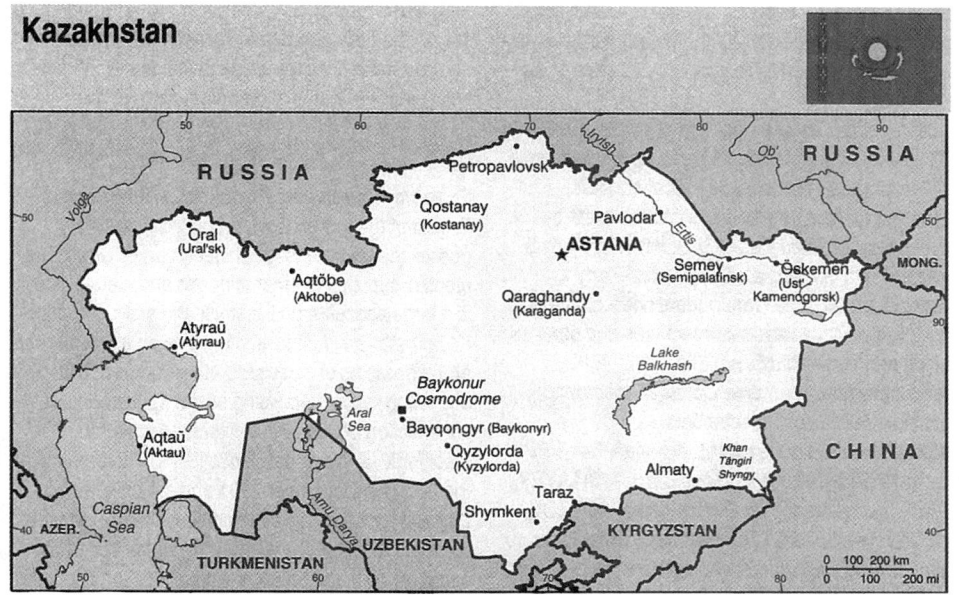

Introduction

Background: Native Kazakhs, a mix of Turkic and Mongol nomadic tribes who migrated into the region in the 13th century, were rarely united as a single nation. The area was conquered by Russia in the 18th century and Kazakhstan became a Soviet Republic in 1936. During the 1950s and 1960s agricultural "Virgin Lands" program, Soviet citizens were encouraged to help cultivate Kazakhstan's northern pastures. This influx of immigrants (mostly Russians, but also some other deported nationalities) skewed the ethnic mixture and enabled non-Kazakhs to outnumber natives. Independence has caused many of these newcomers to emigrate. Current issues include: developing a cohesive national identity; expanding the development of the country's vast energy resources and exporting them to world markets; and continuing to strengthen relations with neighboring states and other foreign powers.

Geography

Location: Central Asia, northwest of China
Geographic coordinates: 48 00 N, 68 00 E
Map references: Commonwealth of Independent States
Area:
total: 2,717,300 sq km
land: 2,669,800 sq km
water: 47,500 sq km
Area - comparative: slightly less than four times the size of Texas
Land boundaries:
total: 12,012 km
border countries: China 1,533 km, Kyrgyzstan 1,051 km, Russia 6,846 km, Turkmenistan 379 km, Uzbekistan 2,203 km
Coastline: 0 km (landlocked); note - Kazakhstan borders the Aral Sea, now split into two bodies of water (1,070 km), and the Caspian Sea (1,894 km)
Maritime claims: none (landlocked)
Climate: continental, cold winters and hot summers, arid and semiarid
Terrain: extends from the Volga to the Altai Mountains and from the plains in western Siberia to oases and desert in Central Asia
Elevation extremes:
lowest point: Vpadina Kaundy -132 m
highest point: Khan Tangiri Shyngy (Pik Khan-Tengri) 6,995 m
Natural resources: major deposits of petroleum, natural gas, coal, iron ore, manganese, chrome ore, nickel, cobalt, copper, molybdenum, lead, zinc, bauxite, gold, uranium
Land use:
arable land: 12%
permanent crops: 11%
permanent pastures: 57%
forests and woodland: 4%
other: 16% (1996 est.)
Irrigated land: 22,000 sq km (1996 est.)
Natural hazards: earthquakes in the south, mudslides around Almaty
Environment - current issues: radioactive or toxic chemical sites associated with its former defense industries and test ranges are found throughout the country and pose health risks for humans and animals; industrial pollution is severe in some cities; because the two main rivers which flowed into the Aral Sea have been diverted for irrigation, it is drying up and leaving behind a harmful layer of chemical pesticides and natural salts; these substances are then picked up by the wind and blown into noxious dust storms; pollution in the Caspian Sea; soil pollution from overuse of agricultural chemicals and salination from poor infrastructure and wasteful irrigation practices
Environment - international agreements:
party to: Air Pollution, Biodiversity, Climate Change, Desertification, Endangered Species, Marine Dumping, Ozone Layer Protection, Ship Pollution
signed, but not ratified: Climate Change-Kyoto Protocol
Geography - note: landlocked; Russia leases approximately 6,000 sq km of territory enclosing the Baykonur Cosmodrome

People

Population: 16,731,303 (July 2001 est.)
Age structure:
0-14 years: 26.73% (male 2,271,866; female 2,200,078)
15-64 years: 66.03% (male 5,358,535; female 5,688,550)
65 years and over: 7.24% (male 412,761; female 799,513) (2001 est.)
Population growth rate: 0.03% (2001 est.)
Birth rate: 17.3 births/1,000 population (2001 est.)
Death rate: 10.61 deaths/1,000 population (2001 est.)
Net migration rate: -6.43 migrant(s)/1,000 population (2001 est.)
Sex ratio:
at birth: 1.05 male(s)/female
under 15 years: 1.03 male(s)/female
15-64 years: 0.94 male(s)/female
65 years and over: 0.52 male(s)/female
total population: 0.93 male(s)/female (2001 est.)
Infant mortality rate: 59.17 deaths/1,000 live births (2001 est.)
Life expectancy at birth:
total population: 63.29 years
male: 57.87 years
female: 68.97 years (2001 est.)
Total fertility rate: 2.07 children born/woman (2001 est.)
HIV/AIDS - adult prevalence rate: 0.04% (1999 est.)
HIV/AIDS - people living with HIV/AIDS: 3,500 (1999 est.)
HIV/AIDS - deaths: less than 100 (1999 est.)
Nationality:
noun: Kazakhstani(s)
adjective: Kazakhstani
Ethnic groups: Kazakh (Qazaq) 53.4%, Russian 30%, Ukrainian 3.7%, Uzbek 2.5%, German 2.4%, Uighur 1.4%, other 6.6% (1999 census)
Religions: Muslim 47%, Russian Orthodox 44%, Protestant 2%, other 7%
Languages: Kazakh (Qazaq, state language) 40%, Russian (official, used in everyday business) 66%
Literacy:
definition: age 15 and over can read and write
total population: 98%
male: 99%
female: 96% (1989 est.)

Government

Country name:
conventional long form: Republic of Kazakhstan
conventional short form: Kazakhstan
local long form: Qazaqstan Respublikasy
local short form: none
former: Kazakh Soviet Socialist Republic
Government type: republic

Kazakhstan (continued)

Capital: Astana; note - the government moved from Almaty to Astana in December 1998
Administrative divisions: 14 oblystar (singular - oblysy) and 3 cities (qala, singular - qalasy)*; Almaty, Almaty*, Aqmola (Astana), Aqtobe, Astana*, Atyrau, Batys Qazaqstan (Oral), Bayqongyr*, Mangghystau (Aqtau; formerly Shevchenko), Ongtustik Qazaqstan (Shymkent), Pavlodar, Qaraghandy, Qostanay, Qyzylorda, Shyghys Qazaqstan (Oskemen; formerly Ust'-Kamenogorsk), Soltustik Qazaqstan (Petropavl), Zhambyl (Taraz; formerly Dzhambul)
note: administrative divisions have the same names as their administrative centers (exceptions have the administrative center name following in parentheses); in 1995 the Governments of Kazakhstan and Russia entered into an agreement whereby Russia would lease for a period of 20 years an area of 6,000 sq km enclosing the Baykonur space launch facilities and the city of Bayqongyr (Baykonyr, formerly Leninsk)
Independence: 16 December 1991 (from the Soviet Union)
National holiday: Republic Day, 25 October (1990)
Constitution: adopted by national referendum 30 August 1995; first post-independence constitution was adopted 28 January 1993
Legal system: based on civil law system
Suffrage: 18 years of age; universal
Executive branch:
chief of state: President Nursultan A. NAZARBAYEV (chairman of the Supreme Soviet from 22 February 1990, elected president 1 December 1991)
head of government: Prime Minister Kazymzhomart TOKAYEV (since 2 October 1999)
cabinet: Council of Ministers appointed by the president
elections: president elected by popular vote for a seven-year term; election last held 10 January 1999, a year before it was previously scheduled (next to be held NA 2006); note - President NAZARBAYEV's previous term had been extended to 2000 by a nationwide referendum held 30 April 1995; prime minister and first deputy prime minister appointed by the president
election results: Nursultan A. NAZARBAYEV reelected president; percent of vote - Nursultan A. NAZARBAYEV 81.7%, Serikbolsyn ABDILDIN 12.1%, Gani KASYMOV 4.7%, other 1.5%
note: President NAZARBAYEV expanded his presidential powers by decree: only he can initiate constitutional amendments, appoint and dismiss the government, dissolve Parliament, call referenda at his discretion, and appoint administrative heads of regions and cities
Legislative branch: bicameral Parliament consists of the Senate (47 seats; 7 senators are appointed by the president; other members are popularly elected, two from each of the former oblasts and the former capital of Almaty, to serve six-year terms) and the Majilis (67 seats; the addition of 10 "Party List" seats brings the total to 77; members are popularly elected to serve five-year terms; note - with the oblasts being reduced to 14, the Senate will eventually be reduced to 37; a number of Senate seats come up for reelection every two years

elections: Senate - (indirect) last held 17 September 1999 (next to be held NA 2001); Majilis - last held 10 and 24 October and 26 December 1999 (next to be held NA 2004)
election results: Senate - percent of vote by party - NA%; seats by party - NA; 16 seats up for election in 1999, candidates nominated by local councils; Majilis - percent of vote by party - NA%; seats by party - Otan 23, Civic Party 13, Communist Party 3, Agrarian Party 3, People's Cooperative Party 1, independents 34; note - most independent candidates are affiliated with parastatal enterprises and other pro-government institutions
Judicial branch: Supreme Court (44 members); Constitutional Council (7 members)
Political parties and leaders: Agrarian Party [Romin MADENOV]; Alash [Soverkazhy AKATAYEV]; AZAMAT Movement [Petr SVOIK, Murat AUEZOV, and Galym ABILSIITOV, cochairmen]; Civic Party [Azat PERUASHEV, first secretary]; Communist Party or KPK [Serikbolsyn ABDILDIN, first secretary]; Forum of Democratic Forces [Nurbulat MASANOV, Deputy Chairman of the Republican People's Party of Kazakhstan (RNPK); Amirzhan KOSANOV, RNPK activist; Seidakhmet KUTTYKADAM, Orleu Movement; cochairmen]; Labor and Worker's Movement [Madel ISMAILOV, chairman]; Orleu Movement [Seidakhmet KUTTYKADAM]; Otan [Sergei TERESCHENKO, chairman]; Pensioners Movement or Pokoleniye [Irina SAVOSTINA, chairwoman]; People's Congress of Kazakhstan of NKK [Olzhas SULEIMENOV, chairman]; People's Cooperative Party [Umirzak SARSENOV]; People's Unity Party or PUP [Nursultan A. NAZARBAYEV]; Republican People's Party of Kazakhstan or RNPK [Akezhan KAZHEGELDIN]
Political pressure groups and leaders: Kazakhstan International Bureau on Human Rights [Yevgeniy ZHOVTIS, executive director]
International organization participation: AsDB, CCC, CIS, EAPC, EBRD, ECE, ECO, ESCAP, FAO, IAEA, IBRD, ICAO, IDA, IDB, IFAD, IFC, ILO, IMF, IMO, Intelsat, Interpol, IOC, IOM (observer), ISO, ITU, NAM (observer), OAS (observer), OIC, OPCW, OSCE, PFP, UN, UNCTAD, UNESCO, UNIDO, UPU, WFTU, WHO, WIPO, WMO, WToO, WTrO (observer)
Diplomatic representation in the US:
chief of mission: Ambassador Kanat SAUDABAYEV
chancery: 1401 16th Street, NW, Washington, DC 20036
telephone: [1] (202) 232-5488
FAX: [1] (202) 232-5845
consulate(s): New York
Diplomatic representation from the US:
chief of mission: Ambassador Richard H. JONES
embassy: 99/97A Furmanova Street, Almaty, Republic of Kazakhstan 480091
mailing address: American Embassy Almaty, Department of State, Washington, DC 20521-7030
telephone: [7] (3272) 63-39-21, 50-76-23, 50-76-27 (emergency number)
FAX: [7] (3272) 63-38-83, 50-76-24

Flag description: sky blue background representing the endless sky and a gold sun with 32 rays soaring above a golden steppe eagle in the center; on the hoist side is a "national ornamentation" in gold

Economy

Economy - overview: Kazakhstan, the second largest of the former Soviet republics in territory, possesses enormous fossil fuel reserves as well as plentiful supplies of other minerals and metals. It also is a large agricultural - livestock and grain - producer. Kazakhstan's industrial sector rests on the extraction and processing of these natural resources and also on a growing machine-building sector specializing in construction equipment, tractors, agricultural machinery, and some defense items. The breakup of the USSR in December 1991 and the collapse of demand for Kazakhstan's traditional heavy industry products resulted in a short-term contraction of the economy, with the steepest annual decline occurring in 1994. In 1995-97, the pace of the government program of economic reform and privatization quickened, resulting in a substantial shifting of assets into the private sector. The Caspian Pipeline Consortium agreement to build a new pipeline from western Kazakhstan's Tengiz oil field to the Black Sea increases prospects for substantially larger oil exports in several years. Kazakhstan's economy again turned downward in 1998 with a 2% decline in GDP due to slumping oil prices and the August financial crisis in Russia. The recovery of international oil prices in 1999, combined with a well-timed tenge devaluation and a bumper grain harvest, pulled the economy out of recession in 2000. Astana has embarked upon an industrial policy designed to diversify the economy away from overdependence on the oil sector by developing light industry.
GDP: purchasing power parity - $85.6 billion (2000 est.)
GDP - real growth rate: 10.5% (2000 est.)
GDP - per capita: purchasing power parity - $5,000 (2000 est.)
GDP - composition by sector:
agriculture: 10%
industry: 30%
services: 60% (1999 est.)
Population below poverty line: 35% (1999 est.)
Household income or consumption by percentage share:
lowest 10%: 2.7%
highest 10%: 26.3% (1996)
Inflation rate (consumer prices): 13.4% (2000 est.)
Labor force: 8.8 million (1997)
Labor force - by occupation: industry 27%, agriculture 23%, services 50% (1996)
Unemployment rate: 13.7% (1998 est.)
Budget:
revenues: $3.1 billion
expenditures: $3.6 billion, including capital expenditures of $NA (1999 est.)

Kazakhstan (continued)

Industries: oil, coal, iron ore, manganese, chromite, lead, zinc, copper, titanium, bauxite, gold, silver, phosphates, sulfur, iron and steel, nonferrous metal, tractors and other agricultural machinery, electric motors, construction materials
Industrial production growth rate: 14.9% (2000 est.)
Electricity - production: 44.36 billion kWh (1999)
Electricity - production by source:
fossil fuel: 87.12%
hydro: 12.65%
nuclear: 0.23%
other: 0% (1999)
Electricity - consumption: 44.132 billion kWh (1999)
Electricity - exports: 200 million kWh (1999)
Electricity - imports: 3.077 billion kWh (1999)
Agriculture - products: grain (mostly spring wheat), cotton; wool, livestock
Exports: $8.8 billion (f.o.b., 2000 est.)
Exports - commodities: oil 40%, ferrous and nonferrous metals, machinery, chemicals, grain, wool, meat, coal
Exports - partners: EU 23%, Russia 20%, China 8% (1999)
Imports: $6.9 billion (f.o.b., 2000 est.)
Imports - commodities: machinery and parts, industrial materials, oil and gas, vehicles
Imports - partners: Russia 37%, US, Uzbekistan, Turkey, UK, Germany, Ukraine, South Korea (1999)
Debt - external: $12.5 billion (2000 est.)
Economic aid - recipient: $409.6 million (1995)
Currency: tenge (KZT)
Currency code: KZT
Exchange rates: tenge per US dollar - 145.09 (January 2001), 142.13 (2000), 119.52 (1999), 78.30 (1998), 75.44 (1997), 67.30 (1996)
Fiscal year: calendar year

Communications

Telephones - main lines in use: 1.818 million (1997)
Telephones - mobile cellular: 11,202 (1997)
Telephone system:
general assessment: service is poor; equipment antiquated
domestic: intercity by landline and microwave radio relay; mobile cellular systems are available in most of Kazakhstan
international: international traffic with other former Soviet republics and China carried by landline and microwave radio relay; with other countries by satellite and by the Trans-Asia-Europe (TAE) fiber-optic cable; satellite earth stations - 2 Intelsat
Radio broadcast stations: AM 60, FM 17, shortwave 9 (1998)
Radios: 6.47 million (1997)
Television broadcast stations: 12 (plus nine repeaters) (1998)
Televisions: 3.88 million (1997)
Internet country code: .kz
Internet Service Providers (ISPs): NA
Internet users: 70,000 (2000)

Transportation

Railways:
total: 14,400 km in common carrier service; does not include industrial lines
broad gauge: 14,400 km 1.520-m gauge (3,299 km electrified) (1997)
Highways:
total: NA km
paved: 150,000 km (these roads are said to be hard-surfaced, and include, in addition to conventionally paved roads, some that are surfaced with gravel or other coarse aggregate, making them trafficable in all weather)
unpaved: NA km (these roads are made of unstabilized earth and are difficult to negotiate in wet weather) (2000 est.)
Waterways: 3,900 km
note: on the Syrdariya (Syr Darya) and Ertis (Irtysh) rivers
Pipelines: crude oil 2,850 km; refined products 1,500 km; natural gas 3,480 km (1992)
Ports and harbors: Aqtau (Shevchenko), Atyrau (Gur'yev), Oskemen (Ust-Kamenogorsk), Pavlodar, Semey (Semipalatinsk)
Airports: 449 (2000 est.)
Airports - with paved runways:
total: 28
over 3,047 m: 6
2,438 to 3,047 m: 14
1,524 to 2,437 m: 5
under 914 m: 3 (2000 est.)
Airports - with unpaved runways:
total: 421
over 3,047 m: 11
2,438 to 3,047 m: 18
1,524 to 2,437 m: 45
914 to 1,523 m: 101
under 914 m: 246 (2000 est.)

Military

Military branches: General Purpose Forces (Army), Air Force, Border Guards, Navy, Republican Guard
Military manpower - military age: 18 years of age
Military manpower - availability:
males age 15-49: 4,509,179 (2001 est.)
Military manpower - fit for military service:
males age 15-49: 3,598,859 (2001 est.)
Military manpower - reaching military age annually:
males: 163,628 (2001 est.)
Military expenditures - dollar figure: $322 million (FY99)
Military expenditures - percent of GDP: 1.5% (FY99)

Transnational Issues

Disputes - international: Caspian Sea boundaries are not yet determined among Azerbaijan, Iran, Kazakhstan, Russia, and Turkmenistan
Illicit drugs: significant illicit cultivation of cannabis and limited cultivation of opium poppy and ephedra (for the drug ephedrone); limited government eradication program; cannabis consumed largely in the CIS; used as transshipment point for illicit drugs to Russia, North America, and Western Europe from Southwest Asia; developing heroin addiction problem

Kenya

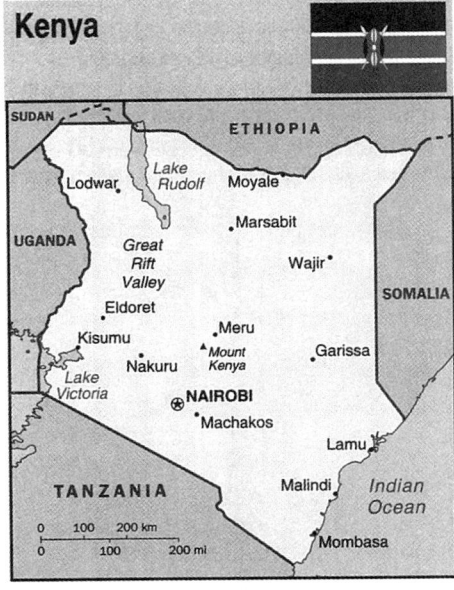

Introduction

Background: Revered president and liberation struggle icon Jomo KENYATTA led Kenya from independence until his death in 1978, when current President Daniel Toroitich arap MOI took power in a constitutional succession. The country was a de facto one-party state from 1969 until 1982 when the ruling Kenya African National Union (KANU) made itself the sole legal party in Kenya. MOI acceded to internal and external pressure for political liberalization in late 1991. The ethnically fractured opposition failed to dislodge KANU from power in elections in 1992 and 1997, which were marred by violence and fraud, but are viewed as having generally reflected the will of the Kenyan people. The country faces a period of political uncertainty because MOI is constitutionally required to step down at the next elections that have to be held by early 2003.

Geography

Location: Eastern Africa, bordering the Indian Ocean, between Somalia and Tanzania
Geographic coordinates: 1 00 N, 38 00 E
Map references: Africa
Area:
total: 582,650 sq km
land: 569,250 sq km
water: 13,400 sq km
Area - comparative: slightly more than twice the size of Nevada
Land boundaries:
total: 3,446 km
border countries: Ethiopia 830 km, Somalia 682 km, Sudan 232 km, Tanzania 769 km, Uganda 933 km
Coastline: 536 km
Maritime claims:
continental shelf: 200-m depth or to the depth of exploitation
exclusive economic zone: 200 NM
territorial sea: 12 NM
Climate: varies from tropical along coast to arid in interior
Terrain: low plains rise to central highlands bisected by Great Rift Valley; fertile plateau in west
Elevation extremes:
lowest point: Indian Ocean 0 m
highest point: Mount Kenya 5,199 m
Natural resources: gold, limestone, soda ash, salt barites, rubies, fluorspar, garnets, wildlife, hydropower
Land use:
arable land: 7%
permanent crops: 1%
permanent pastures: 37%
forests and woodland: 30%
other: 25% (1993 est.)
Irrigated land: 660 sq km (1993 est.)
Natural hazards: recurring drought in northern and eastern regions; flooding during rainy seasons
Environment - current issues: water pollution from urban and industrial wastes; degradation of water quality from increased use of pesticides and fertilizers; water hyacinth infestation in Lake Victoria; deforestation; soil erosion; desertification; poaching
Environment - international agreements:
party to: Biodiversity, Climate Change, Desertification, Endangered Species, Hazardous Wastes, Law of the Sea, Marine Dumping, Marine Life Conservation, Nuclear Test Ban, Ozone Layer Protection, Ship Pollution, Wetlands, Whaling
signed, but not ratified: none of the selected agreements
Geography - note: the Kenyan Highlands comprise one of the most successful agricultural production regions in Africa; glaciers on Mt. Kenya; unique physiography supports abundant and varied wildlife of scientific and economic value

People

Population: 30,765,916
note: estimates for this country explicitly take into account the effects of excess mortality due to AIDS; this can result in lower life expectancy, higher infant mortality and death rates, lower population and growth rates, and changes in the distribution of population by age and sex than would otherwise be expected (July 2001 est.)
Age structure:
0-14 years: 41.95% (male 6,524,776; female 6,381,192)
15-64 years: 55.26% (male 8,529,842; female 8,471,609)
65 years and over: 2.79% (male 376,151; female 482,346) (2001 est.)
Population growth rate: 1.27% (2001 est.)
Birth rate: 28.5 births/1,000 population (2001 est.)
Death rate: 14.35 deaths/1,000 population (2001 est.)
Net migration rate: -1.5 migrant(s)/1,000 population (2001 est.)
note: according to UNHCR, by the end of 1999 Kenya was host to 223,700 refugees from neighboring countries, including: Somalia 141,000 and Sudan 64,250
Sex ratio:
at birth: 1.03 male(s)/female
under 15 years: 1.02 male(s)/female
15-64 years: 1.01 male(s)/female
65 years and over: 0.78 male(s)/female
total population: 1.01 male(s)/female (2001 est.)
Infant mortality rate: 67.99 deaths/1,000 live births (2001 est.)
Life expectancy at birth:
total population: 47.49 years
male: 46.57 years
female: 48.44 years (2001 est.)
Total fertility rate: 3.5 children born/woman (2001 est.)
HIV/AIDS - adult prevalence rate: 13.95% (1999 est.)
HIV/AIDS - people living with HIV/AIDS: 2.1 million (1999 est.)
HIV/AIDS - deaths: 180,000 (1999 est.)
Nationality:
noun: Kenyan(s)
adjective: Kenyan
Ethnic groups: Kikuyu 22%, Luhya 14%, Luo 13%, Kalenjin 12%, Kamba 11%, Kisii 6%, Meru 6%, other African 15%, non-African (Asian, European, and Arab) 1%
Religions: Protestant 38%, Roman Catholic 28%, indigenous beliefs 26%, Muslim 7%, other 1%
note: a large majority of Kenyans are Christian, but estimates for the percentage of the population that adheres to Islam or indigenous beliefs vary widely
Languages: English (official), Kiswahili (official), numerous indigenous languages
Literacy:
definition: age 15 and over can read and write
total population: 78.1%
male: 86.3%
female: 70% (1995 est.)

Government

Country name:
conventional long form: Republic of Kenya
conventional short form: Kenya
former: British East Africa
Government type: republic
Capital: Nairobi
Administrative divisions: 7 provinces and 1 area*; Central, Coast, Eastern, Nairobi Area*, North Eastern, Nyanza, Rift Valley, Western
Independence: 12 December 1963 (from UK)
National holiday: Independence Day, 12 December (1963)
Constitution: 12 December 1963, amended as a republic 1964; reissued with amendments 1979, 1983, 1986, 1988, 1991, 1992, and 1997
Legal system: based on English common law, tribal law, and Islamic law; judicial review in High Court; accepts compulsory ICJ jurisdiction, with reservations; constitutional amendment of 1982 making Kenya a de jure one-party state repealed in 1991
Suffrage: 18 years of age; universal

Kenya (continued)

Executive branch:
chief of state: President Daniel Toroitich arap MOI (since 14 October 1978); note - the president is both the chief of state and head of government
head of government: President Daniel Toroitich arap MOI (since 14 October 1978); note - the president is both the chief of state and head of government
cabinet: Cabinet appointed by the president
elections: president elected by popular vote from among the members of the National Assembly for a five-year term; in addition to receiving the largest number of votes in absolute terms, the presidential candidate must also win 25% or more of the vote in at least five of Kenya's seven provinces and one area to avoid a runoff; election last held 29 December 1997 (next to be held by early 2003); vice president appointed by the president
election results: President Daniel Toroitich arap MOI reelected; percent of vote - Daniel T. arap MOI (KANU) 40.6%, Mwai KIBAKI (DP) 31.5%, Raila ODINGA (NDP) 11.1%, Michael WAMALWA (FORD-K) 8.4%, Charity NGILU (SDP) 7.8%
Legislative branch: unicameral National Assembly or Bunge (222 seats; 210 members elected by popular vote to serve five-year terms, 12 so-called "nominated" members who are appointed by the president, but selected by the parties in proportion to their parliamentary vote totals)
elections: last held 29 December 1997 (next to be held by early 2003)
election results: percent of vote by party - NA%; seats by party - KANU 107, FORD-A 1, FORD-K 17, FORD-People 3, DP 39, NDP 21, SDP 15, SAFINA 5, smaller parties 2; seats appointed by the president - KANU 6, FORD-K 1, DP 2, SDP 1, NDP 1, SAFINA 1
Judicial branch: Court of Appeal (chief justice is appointed by the president); High Court
Political parties and leaders: Democratic Party of Kenya or DP [Mwai KIBAKI]; Forum for the Restoration of Democracy-Asili or FORD-A [Martin SHIKUKU, secretary general]; Forum for the Restoration of Democracy-Kenya or FORD-K [Michael Kijana WAMALWA]; Forum for the Restoration of Democracy-People or FORD-People [Kimaniwa NYOIKE, chairman]; Kenya African National Union or KANU [President Daniel Toroitich arap MOI] - the governing party; National Development Party or NDP [Raila ODINGA, president]; SAFINA [Farah MAALIM, chairman]; Social Democratic Party or SDP [Dr. Apollo NJONJO, secretary general and Justus NYANG'AYA, chairman]
Political pressure groups and leaders: human rights groups; labor unions; Muslim organizations; National Convention Executive Council or NCEC, a proreform coalition of political parties and nongovernment organizations [Kivutha KIBWANA]; Protestant National Council of Churches of Kenya or NCCK [Mutava MUSYIMI]; Roman Catholic and other Christian churches; Supreme Council of Kenya Muslims or SUPKEM [Shaykh Abdul Gafur al-BUSAIDY, chairman]

International organization participation: ACP, AfDB, C, CCC, EADB, ECA, FAO, G-77, IAEA, IBRD, ICAO, ICFTU, ICRM, IDA, IFAD, IFC, IFRCS, IGAD, ILO, IMF, IMO, Inmarsat, Intelsat, Interpol, IOC, IOM, ISO, ITU, MINURSO, MONUC, NAM, OAU, OPCW, UN, UNAMSIL, UNCTAD, UNESCO, UNIDO, UNIKOM, UNMEE, UNMIBH, UNMIK, UNMOP, UNTAET, UNU, UPU, WHO, WIPO, WMO, WToO, WTrO
Diplomatic representation in the US:
chief of mission: Ambassador Yusuf Abdulraham NZIBO
chancery: 2249 R Street NW, Washington, DC 20008
telephone: [1] (202) 387-6101
FAX: [1] (202) 462-3829
consulate(s) general: offices in Los Angeles and New York are closed; mission to the UN remains open
Diplomatic representation from the US:
chief of mission: Ambassador Johnnie CARSON
embassy: US Embassy, Mombasa Road, Nairobi
mailing address: P. O. Box 30137, Box 21A, Unit 64100, APO AE 09831
telephone: [254] (2) 537-800
FAX: [254] (2) 537-810
Flag description: three equal horizontal bands of black (top), red, and green; the red band is edged in white; a large warrior's shield covering crossed spears is superimposed at the center

Economy

Economy - overview: Kenya is well placed to serve as an engine of growth in East Africa, but its economy has been stagnating because of poor management and uneven commitment to reform. In 1993, the government of Kenya implemented a program of economic liberalization and reform that included the removal of import licensing, price controls, and foreign exchange controls. With the support of the World Bank, IMF, and other donors, the reforms led to a brief turnaround in economic performance following a period of negative growth in the early 1990s. Kenya's real GDP grew 5% in 1995 and 4% in 1996, and inflation remained under control. Growth slowed after 1997, averaging only 1.5% in 1997-2000. In 1997, political violence damaged the tourist industry, and Kenya's Enhanced Structural Adjustment Program lapsed due to the government's failure to maintain reform or address public sector corruption. Severe drought in 1999 and 2000 caused water and energy rationing and reduced agricultural sector productivity. A new economic team was put in place in 1999 to revitalize the reform effort, strengthen the civil service, and curb corruption. The IMF and World Bank renewed their support to Kenya in mid-2000, but a number of setbacks to the economic reform program in late 2000 have renewed donor and private sector concern about the government's commitment to sound governance. Long-term barriers to development include electricity shortages, inefficient government dominance of key sectors, endemic corruption, and high population growth.

GDP: purchasing power parity - $45.6 billion (2000 est.)
GDP - real growth rate: 0.4% (2000 est.)
GDP - per capita: purchasing power parity - $1,500 (2000 est.)
GDP - composition by sector:
agriculture: 25%
industry: 13%
services: 62% (1999 est.)
Population below poverty line: 42% (1992 est.)
Household income or consumption by percentage share:
lowest 10%: 1.8%
highest 10%: 34.9% (1994)
Inflation rate (consumer prices): 7% (2000 est.)
Labor force: 9.2 million (1998 est.)
Labor force - by occupation: agriculture 75%-80%
Unemployment rate: 50% (1998 est.)
Budget:
revenues: $2.91 billion
expenditures: $2.97 billion, including capital expenditures of $NA (2000 est.)
Industries: small-scale consumer goods (plastic, furniture, batteries, textiles, soap, cigarettes, flour), agricultural products processing; oil refining, cement; tourism
Industrial production growth rate: 0.5% (2000 est.)
Electricity - production: 4.225 billion kWh (1999)
Electricity - production by source:
fossil fuel: 31%
hydro: 67%
nuclear: 0%
other: 2% (1999 est.)
Electricity - consumption: 4.075 billion kWh (1999)
Electricity - exports: 0 kWh (1999)
Electricity - imports: 146 million kWh (1999)
Agriculture - products: coffee, tea, corn, wheat, sugarcane, fruit, vegetables; dairy products, beef, pork, poultry, eggs
Exports: $1.7 billion (f.o.b., 2000 est.)
Exports - commodities: tea, coffee, horticultural products, petroleum products, fish, cement
Exports - partners: Uganda 18%, UK 15%, Tanzania 12%, Pakistan 8% (1999)
Imports: $3 billion (f.o.b., 2000 est.)
Imports - commodities: machinery and transportation equipment, petroleum products, iron and steel
Imports - partners: UK 12%, UAE 8%, Japan 8%, US 7% (1999)
Debt - external: $6.2 billion (2000)
Economic aid - recipient: $457 million (1997)
Currency: Kenyan shilling (KES)
Currency code: KES
Exchange rates: Kenyan shillings per US dollar - 78.733 (December 2000), 76.176 (2000), 70.326 (1999), 60.367 (1998), 58.732 (1997), 57.115 (1996)
Fiscal year: 1 July - 30 June

Kenya (continued)

Communications

Telephones - main lines in use: 290,000 (1998)
Telephones - mobile cellular: 5,345 (1997)
Telephone system:
general assessment: unreliable; little attempt to modernize except for service to business
domestic: trunks are primarily microwave radio relay; business data commonly transferred by a very small aperture terminal (VSAT) system
international: satellite earth stations - 4 Intelsat
Radio broadcast stations: AM 24, FM 8, shortwave 6 (1999)
Radios: 3.07 million (1997)
Television broadcast stations: 8 (1997)
Televisions: 730,000 (1997)
Internet country code: .ke
Internet Service Providers (ISPs): 5 (2000)
Internet users: 45,000 (1999)

Transportation

Railways:
total: 2,778 km
narrow gauge: 2,778 km 1.000-m gauge
note: the line connecting Nairobi with the port of Mombasa is the most important in the country
Highways:
total: 63,800 km
paved: 8,868 km
unpaved: 54,932 km (1996)
Waterways: NA
note: part of the Lake Victoria system is within the boundaries of Kenya
Pipelines: petroleum products 483 km
Ports and harbors: Kisumu, Lamu, Mombasa
Merchant marine:
total: 2 ships (1,000 GRT or over) totaling 4,893 GRT/ 6,255 DWT
ships by type: petroleum tanker 1, roll on/roll off 1 (2000 est.)
Airports: 230 (2000 est.)
Airports - with paved runways:
total: 22
over 3,047 m: 4
2,438 to 3,047 m: 1
1,524 to 2,437 m: 3
914 to 1,523 m: 13
under 914 m: 1 (2000 est.)
Airports - with unpaved runways:
total: 208
2,438 to 3,047 m: 1
1,524 to 2,437 m: 14
914 to 1,523 m: 109
under 914 m: 84 (2000 est.)

Military

Military branches: Army, Navy, Air Force, paramilitary General Service Unit of the Police
Military manpower - availability:
males age 15-49: 7,712,402 (2001 est.)
Military manpower - fit for military service:
males age 15-49: 4,774,889 (2001 est.)
Military expenditures - dollar figure: $197 million (FY98/99)
Military expenditures - percent of GDP: 1.9% (FY98/99)

Transnational Issues

Disputes - international: administrative boundary with Sudan does not coincide with international boundary
Illicit drugs: widespread harvesting of small plots of marijuana; transit country for South Asian heroin destined for Europe and North America; Indian methaqualone also transits on way to South Africa

Kingman Reef
(territory of the US)

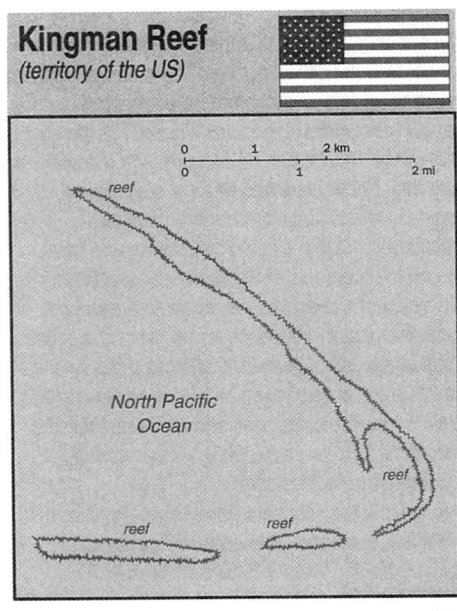

Introduction

Background: The US annexed the reef in 1922. Its sheltered lagoon served as a way station for flying boats on Hawaii-to-American Samoa flights during the late 1930s. There is no flora on the reef, which is frequently awash, but it does support an abundant and diverse marine fauna. In 2001, the waters surrounding the reef were designated a National Wildlife Refuge.

Geography

Location: Oceania, reef in the North Pacific Ocean, about one-half of the way from Hawaii to American Samoa
Geographic coordinates: 6 24 N, 162 24 W
Map references: Oceania
Area:
total: 1 sq km
land: 1 sq km
water: 0 sq km
Area - comparative: about 1.7 times the size of The Mall in Washington, DC
Land boundaries: 0 km
Coastline: 3 km
Maritime claims:
exclusive economic zone: 200 NM
territorial sea: 12 NM
Climate: tropical, but moderated by prevailing winds
Terrain: low and nearly level
Elevation extremes:
lowest point: Pacific Ocean 0 m
highest point: unnamed location 1 m
Natural resources: terrestrial and aquatic wildlife
Land use:
arable land: 0%
permanent crops: 0%
permanent pastures: 0%
forests and woodland: 0%
other: 100%
Irrigated land: 0 sq km (1996)

Kingman Reef (continued)

Natural hazards: wet or awash most of the time, maximum elevation of about 1 meter makes Kingman Reef a maritime hazard
Environment - current issues: none
Geography - note: barren coral atoll with deep interior lagoon; closed to the public

People

Population: uninhabited (July 2001 est.)

Government

Country name:
conventional long form: none
conventional short form: Kingman Reef
Dependency status: unincorporated territory of the US; administered from Washington, DC, by the US Fish and Wildlife Service of the Department of the Interior
note: on 1 September 2000, the Department of the Interior accepted restoration of its administrative jurisdiction over Kingman Reef from the Department of the Navy; Executive Order 3223 signed 18 January 2001 established Kingman Reef National Wildlife Refuge to be administered by the Director, US Fish and Wildlife Service; this refuge is managed to protect the terrestrial and aquatic wildlife of Kingman Reef out to the twelve nautical mile territorial sea limit
Legal system: the laws of the US, where applicable, apply
Flag description: the flag of the US is used

Economy

Economy - overview: no economic activity

Transportation

Waterways: none
Ports and harbors: none; offshore anchorage only
Airports: lagoon was used as a halfway station between Hawaii and American Samoa by Pan American Airways for flying boats in 1937 and 1938 (2000 est.)

Military

Military - note: defense is the responsibility of the US

Transnational Issues

Disputes - international: none

Kiribati

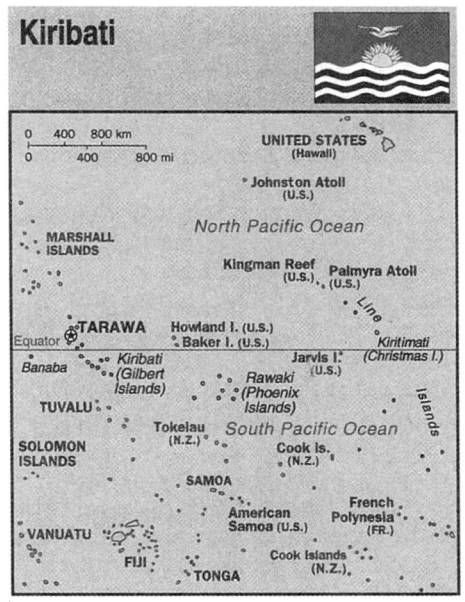

Introduction

Background: The Gilbert Islands were granted self-rule by the UK in 1971 and complete independence in 1979 under the new name of Kiribati. The US relinquished all claims to the sparsely inhabited Phoenix and Line Island groups in a 1979 treaty of friendship with Kiribati.

Geography

Location: Oceania, group of islands in the Pacific Ocean, straddling the equator, about one-half of the way from Hawaii to Australia; note - on 1 January 1995, Kiribati proclaimed that all of its territory lies in the same time zone as its Gilbert Islands group (GMT +12) even though the Phoenix Islands and the Line Islands under its jurisdiction lie on the other side of the International Date Line
Geographic coordinates: 1 25 N, 173 00 E
Map references: Oceania
Area:
total: 717 sq km
land: 717 sq km
water: 0 sq km
note: includes three island groups - Gilbert Islands, Line Islands, Phoenix Islands
Area - comparative: four times the size of Washington, DC
Land boundaries: 0 km
Coastline: 1,143 km
Maritime claims:
exclusive economic zone: 200 NM
territorial sea: 12 NM
Climate: tropical; marine, hot and humid, moderated by trade winds
Terrain: mostly low-lying coral atolls surrounded by extensive reefs
Elevation extremes:
lowest point: Pacific Ocean 0 m
highest point: unnamed location on Banaba 81 m
Natural resources: phosphate (production discontinued in 1979)
Land use:
arable land: 0%
permanent crops: 51%
permanent pastures: 0%
forests and woodland: 3%
other: 46% (1993 est.)
Irrigated land: NA sq km
Natural hazards: typhoons can occur any time, but usually November to March; occasional tornadoes; low level of some of the islands make them very sensitive to changes in sea level
Environment - current issues: heavy pollution in lagoon of south Tarawa atoll due to heavy migration mixed with traditional practices such as lagoon latrines and open-pit dumping; ground water at risk
Environment - international agreements:
party to: Biodiversity, Climate Change, Climate Change-Kyoto Protocol, Desertification, Hazardous Wastes, Marine Dumping, Ozone Layer Protection, Ship Pollution
signed, but not ratified: none of the selected agreements
Geography - note: 20 of the 33 islands are inhabited; Banaba (Ocean Island) in Kiribati is one of the three great phosphate rock islands in the Pacific Ocean - the others are Makatea in French Polynesia, and Nauru

People

Population: 94,149 (July 2001 est.)
Age structure:
0-14 years: 40.53% (male 19,322; female 18,833)
15-64 years: 56.27% (male 26,136; female 26,841)
65 years and over: 3.2% (male 1,291; female 1,726) (2001 est.)
Population growth rate: 2.31% (2001 est.)
Birth rate: 31.98 births/1,000 population (2001 est.)
Death rate: 8.88 deaths/1,000 population (2001 est.)
Net migration rate: 0 migrant(s)/1,000 population (2001 est.)
Sex ratio:
at birth: 1.05 male(s)/female
under 15 years: 1.03 male(s)/female
15-64 years: 0.97 male(s)/female
65 years and over: 0.75 male(s)/female
total population: 0.99 male(s)/female (2001 est.)
Infant mortality rate: 54 deaths/1,000 live births (2001 est.)
Life expectancy at birth:
total population: 60.16 years
male: 57.25 years
female: 63.22 years (2001 est.)
Total fertility rate: 4.36 children born/woman (2001 est.)
HIV/AIDS - adult prevalence rate: NA%
HIV/AIDS - people living with HIV/AIDS: NA
HIV/AIDS - deaths: NA

Kiribati (continued)

Nationality:
noun: I-Kiribati (singular and plural)
adjective: I-Kiribati
Ethnic groups: predominantly Micronesian with some Polynesian
Religions: Roman Catholic 54%, Protestant (Congregational) 30%, some Seventh-Day Adventist, Baha'i, Latter-day Saints, and Church of God (1996)
Languages: English (official), I-Kiribati
Literacy:
definition: NA
total population: NA%
male: NA%
female: NA%

Government

Country name:
conventional long form: Republic of Kiribati
conventional short form: Kiribati
note: pronounced kir-ih-bahss
former: Gilbert Islands
Government type: republic
Capital: Tarawa
Administrative divisions: 3 units; Gilbert Islands, Line Islands, Phoenix Islands; note - in addition, there are 6 districts (Banaba, Central Gilberts, Line Islands, Northern Gilberts, Southern Gilberts, Tarawa) and 21 island councils - one for each of the inhabited islands (Abaiang, Abemama, Aranuka, Arorae, Banaba, Beru, Butaritari, Kanton, Kiritimati, Kuria, Maiana, Makin, Marakei, Nikunau, Nonouti, Onotoa, Tabiteuea, Tabuaeran, Tamana, Tarawa, Teraina)
Independence: 12 July 1979 (from UK)
National holiday: Independence Day, 12 July (1979)
Constitution: 12 July 1979
Legal system: NA
Suffrage: 18 years of age; universal
Executive branch:
chief of state: President Teburoro TITO (since 1 October 1994); Vice President Tewareka TENTOA (since 12 October 1994); note - the president is both the chief of state and head of government
head of government: President Teburoro TITO (since 1 October 1994); Vice President Tewareka TENTOA (since 12 October 1994); note - the president is both the chief of state and head of government
cabinet: Cabinet appointed by the president from among the members of the House of Assembly, includes the president, vice president, attorney general, and up to eight other ministers
elections: the House of Assembly chooses the presidential candidates from among their members and then those candidates compete in a general election; president is elected by popular vote for a four-year term; election last held 27 November 1998 (next to be held by NA November 2002); vice president appointed by the president
election results: Teburoro TITO reelected president; percent of vote - Teburoro TITO 52.3%, Dr. Harry TONG 45.8%, Amberoti NIKORA 1.9%, Taberannang TIMEON 0%

Legislative branch: unicameral House of Assembly or Maneaba Ni Maungatabu (41 seats; 39 elected by popular vote, one ex officio member, and one nominated to represent Banaba; members serve four-year terms)
elections: last held 23 September 1998 (next to be held by NA September 2002)
election results: percent of vote by party - NA%; seats by party - Maneaban Te Mauri Party 14, National Progressive Party 11, independents 14
Judicial branch: Court of Appeal; High Court; 26 Magistrates' courts; judges at all levels are appointed by the president
Political parties and leaders: Maneaban Te Mauri Party [Teburoro TITO]; National Progressive Party [Teatao TEANNAKI]
note: there is no tradition of formally organized political parties in Kiribati; they more closely resemble factions or interest groups because they have no party headquarters, formal platforms, or party structures
Political pressure groups and leaders: NA
International organization participation: ACP, AsDB, C, ESCAP, FAO, IBRD, ICAO, ICFTU, ICRM, IDA, IFC, IFRCS, ILO, IMF, Intelsat (nonsignatory user), ITU, OPCW, Sparteca, SPC, SPF, UN, UNESCO, UPU, WHO, WTrO (applicant)
Diplomatic representation in the US: Kiribati does not have an embassy in the US; there is an honorary consulate in Honolulu
Diplomatic representation from the US: the US does not have an embassy in Kiribati; the ambassador to the Marshall Islands is accredited to Kiribati
Flag description: the upper half is red with a yellow frigate bird flying over a yellow rising sun, and the lower half is blue with three horizontal wavy white stripes to represent the ocean

Economy

Economy - overview: A remote country of 33 scattered coral atolls, Kiribati has few national resources. Commercially viable phosphate deposits were exhausted at the time of independence from the UK in 1979. Copra and fish now represent the bulk of production and exports. The economy has fluctuated widely in recent years. Economic development is constrained by a shortage of skilled workers, weak infrastructure, and remoteness from international markets. Tourism provides more than one-fifth of GDP. The financial sector is at an early stage of development as is the expansion of private sector initiatives. Foreign financial aid, largely from the UK and Japan, is a critical supplement to GDP, equal to 25%-50% of GDP in recent years. Remittances from workers abroad account for more than $5 million each year. Performance in 2000 fell short of the 2.5% growth in 1999, which benefited from increased copra production and exceptionally large revenues from fishing licenses.
GDP: purchasing power parity - $76 million (2000 est.), supplemented by a nearly equal amount from external sources
GDP - real growth rate: 1% (2000 est.)
GDP - per capita: purchasing power parity - $850 (2000 est.)
GDP - composition by sector:
agriculture: 14%
industry: 7%
services: 79% (1996 est.)
Population below poverty line: NA%
Household income or consumption by percentage share:
lowest 10%: NA%
highest 10%: NA%
Inflation rate (consumer prices): 2% (1999 est.)
Labor force: 7,870 economically active, not including subsistence farmers (1985 est.)
Unemployment rate: 2%; underemployment 70% (1992 est.)
Budget:
revenues: $33.3 million
expenditures: $47.7 million, including capital expenditures of $NA million (1996 est.)
Industries: fishing, handicrafts
Industrial production growth rate: 0.7% (1992 est.)
Electricity - production: 7 million kWh (1999)
Electricity - production by source:
fossil fuel: 100%
hydro: 0%
nuclear: 0%
other: 0% (1999)
Electricity - consumption: 6.5 million kWh (1999)
Electricity - exports: 0 kWh (1999)
Electricity - imports: 0 kWh (1999)
Agriculture - products: copra, taro, breadfruit, sweet potatoes, vegetables; fish
Exports: $6 million (f.o.b., 1998)
Exports - commodities: copra 62%, coconuts, seaweed, fish
Exports - partners: Bangladesh, Australia, US, Hong Kong (1999)
Imports: $44 million (c.i.f., 1999)
Imports - commodities: foodstuffs, machinery and equipment, miscellaneous manufactured goods, fuel
Imports - partners: Australia, Fiji, Japan, NZ, China (1999)
Debt - external: $10 million (1999 est.)
Economic aid - recipient: $15.5 million (1995), largely from UK and Japan
Currency: Australian dollar (AUD)
Currency code: AUD
Exchange rates: Australian dollars per US dollar - 1.7995 (January 2001), 1.7173 (2000), 1.5497 (1999), 1.5888 (1998), 1.3439 (1997), 1.2773 (1996)
Fiscal year: NA

Communications

Telephones - main lines in use: 2,000 (1997)
Telephones - mobile cellular: NA
Telephone system:
general assessment: NA
domestic: NA
international: satellite earth station - 1 Intelsat (Pacific Ocean)

Kiribati (continued)

note: Kiribati is being linked to the Pacific Ocean Cooperative Telecommunications Network, which should improve telephone service
Radio broadcast stations: AM 1, FM 1, shortwave 1 (1998)
Radios: 17,000 (1997)
Television broadcast stations: 1 (1997)
Televisions: 1,000 (1997)
Internet country code: .ki
Internet Service Providers (ISPs): 1 (2000)
Internet users: 1,000 (2000)

Transportation

Railways: 0 km
Highways:
total: 670 km
paved: NA km
unpaved: NA km (1996)
Waterways: 5 km (small network of canals in Line Islands)
Ports and harbors: Banaba, Betio, English Harbor, Kanton
Merchant marine:
total: 1 ship (1,000 GRT or over) totaling 1,291 GRT/1,295 DWT
ships by type: passenger/cargo 1 (2000 est.)
Airports: 21 (2000 est.)
Airports - with paved runways:
total: 4
1,524 to 2,437 m: 4 (2000 est.)
Airports - with unpaved runways:
total: 17
914 to 1,523 m: 12
under 914 m: 5 (2000 est.)

Military

Military branches: no regular military forces; Police Force (carries out law enforcement functions and paramilitary duties; small police posts are on all islands)
Military expenditures - dollar figure: $NA
Military expenditures - percent of GDP: NA%
Military - note: Kiribati does not have military forces; defense assistance is provided by Australia and NZ

Transnational Issues

Disputes - international: none

Korea, North

Introduction

Background: Following World War II, Korea was split into a northern, communist half and a southern, Western-oriented half. KIM Chong-il has ruled North Korea since his father and the country's founder, president KIM Il-song, died in 1994. After decades of mismanagement, the North relies heavily on international food aid to feed its population, while continuing to expend resources to maintain an army of about 1 million. North Korea's long-range missile development and research into nuclear and chemical weapons are of major concern to the international community.

Geography

Location: Eastern Asia, northern half of the Korean Peninsula bordering the Korea Bay and the Sea of Japan, between China and South Korea
Geographic coordinates: 40 00 N, 127 00 E
Map references: Asia
Area:
total: 120,540 sq km
land: 120,410 sq km
water: 130 sq km
Area - comparative: slightly smaller than Mississippi
Land boundaries:
total: 1,673 km
border countries: China 1,416 km, South Korea 238 km, Russia 19 km
Coastline: 2,495 km
Maritime claims:
territorial sea: 12 NM
exclusive economic zone: 200 NM
note: military boundary line 50 NM in the Sea of Japan and the exclusive economic zone limit in the Yellow Sea where all foreign vessels and aircraft without permission are banned
Climate: temperate with rainfall concentrated in summer
Terrain: mostly hills and mountains separated by deep, narrow valleys; coastal plains wide in west, discontinuous in east
Elevation extremes:
lowest point: Sea of Japan 0 m
highest point: Paektu-san 2,744 m
Natural resources: coal, lead, tungsten, zinc, graphite, magnesite, iron ore, copper, gold, pyrites, salt, fluorspar, hydropower
Land use:
arable land: 14%
permanent crops: 2%
permanent pastures: 0%
forests and woodland: 61%
other: 23% (1993 est.)
Irrigated land: 14,600 sq km (1993 est.)
Natural hazards: late spring droughts often followed by severe flooding; occasional typhoons during the early fall
Environment - current issues: water pollution; inadequate supplies of potable water; water-borne disease; deforestation; soil erosion and degradation
Environment - international agreements:
party to: Antarctic Treaty, Biodiversity, Climate Change, Environmental Modification, Marine Dumping, Ozone Layer Protection, Ship Pollution
signed, but not ratified: Antarctic-Environmental Protocol, Law of the Sea
Geography - note: strategic location bordering China, South Korea, and Russia; mountainous interior is isolated and sparsely populated

People

Population: 21,968,228 (July 2001 est.)
Age structure:
0-14 years: 25.52% (male 2,873,390; female 2,733,163)
15-64 years: 67.63% (male 7,301,531; female 7,556,554)
65 years and over: 6.85% (male 486,805; female 1,016,785) (2001 est.)
Population growth rate: 1.22% (2001 est.)
Birth rate: 19.1 births/1,000 population (2001 est.)
Death rate: 6.92 deaths/1,000 population (2001 est.)
Net migration rate: 0 migrant(s)/1,000 population (2001 est.)
Sex ratio:
at birth: 1.05 male(s)/female
under 15 years: 1.05 male(s)/female
15-64 years: 0.97 male(s)/female
65 years and over: 0.48 male(s)/female
total population: 0.94 male(s)/female (2001 est.)
Infant mortality rate: 23.55 deaths/1,000 live births (2001 est.)
Life expectancy at birth:
total population: 71.02 years
male: 68.04 years
female: 74.15 years (2001 est.)
Total fertility rate: 2.26 children born/woman (2001 est.)
HIV/AIDS - adult prevalence rate: NA%

Korea, North (continued)

HIV/AIDS - people living with HIV/AIDS: NA
HIV/AIDS - deaths: NA
Nationality:
noun: Korean(s)
adjective: Korean
Ethnic groups: racially homogeneous; there is a small Chinese community and a few ethnic Japanese
Religions: traditionally Buddhist and Confucianist, some Christian and syncretic Chondogyo (Religion of the Heavenly Way)
note: autonomous religious activities now almost nonexistent; government-sponsored religious groups exist to provide illusion of religious freedom
Languages: Korean
Literacy:
definition: age 15 and over can read and write Korean
total population: 99%
male: 99%
female: 99% (1990 est.)

Government

Country name:
conventional long form: Democratic People's Republic of Korea
conventional short form: North Korea
local long form: Choson-minjujuui-inmin-konghwaguk
local short form: none
note: the North Koreans generally use the term "Choson" to refer to their country
abbreviation: DPRK
Government type: authoritarian socialist; one-man dictatorship
Capital: P'yongyang
Administrative divisions: 9 provinces (do, singular and plural) and 3 special cities* (si, singular and plural); Chagang-do (Chagang Province), Hamgyong-bukto (North Hamgyong Province), Hamgyong-namdo (South Hamgyong Province), Hwanghae-bukto (North Hwanghae Province), Hwanghae-namdo (South Hwanghae Province), Kaesong-si* (Kaesong City), Kangwon-do (Kangwon Province), Namp'o-si* (Namp'o City), P'yongan-bukto (North P'yongan Province), P'yongan-namdo (South P'yongan Province), P'yongyang-si* (P'yongyang City), Yanggang-do (Yanggang Province)
Independence: 15 August 1945 (from Japan)
National holiday: Founding of the Democratic People's Republic of Korea (DPRK), 9 September (1948)
Constitution: adopted 1948, completely revised 27 December 1972, revised again in April 1992 and September 1998
Legal system: based on German civil law system with Japanese influences and Communist legal theory; no judicial review of legislative acts; has not accepted compulsory ICJ jurisdiction
Suffrage: 17 years of age; universal
Executive branch:
chief of state: KIM Chong-il (since NA July 1994); note - in September 1998, KIM Chong-il was reelected Chairman of the National Defense Commission, a position accorded the nation's "highest administrative authority"; KIM Yong-nam was named President of the Supreme People's Assembly Presidium and given the responsibility of representing the state and receiving diplomatic credentials
head of government: Premier HONG Song-nam (since 5 September 1998)
cabinet: Cabinet (Naegak), members, except for the Minister of People's Armed Forces, are appointed by the Supreme People's Assembly
elections: premier elected by the Supreme People's Assembly; election last held NA September 1998 (next to be held NA)
election results: HONG Song-nam elected premier; percent of Supreme People's Assembly vote - NA%
Legislative branch: unicameral Supreme People's Assembly or Ch'oego Inmin Hoeui (687 seats; members elected by popular vote to serve five-year terms)
elections: last held 26 July 1998 (next to be held NA 2003)
election results: percent of vote by party - NA%; seats by party - the KWP approves a single list of candidates who are elected without opposition; minor parties hold a few seats
Judicial branch: Central Court (judges are elected by the Supreme People's Assembly)
Political parties and leaders: Chondoist Chongu Party [YU Mi-yong, chairwoman]; Korean Social Democratic Party [KIM Pyong-sik, chairman]; major party - Korean Workers' Party or KWP [KIM Chong-il, General Secretary]
Political pressure groups and leaders: NA
International organization participation: ARF (dialogue partner), ESCAP, FAO, G-77, ICAO, ICRM, IFAD, IFRCS, IHO, IMO, Intelsat (nonsignatory user), IOC, ISO, ITU, NAM, UN, UNCTAD, UNESCO, UNIDO, UPU, WFTU, WHO, WIPO, WMO, WToO
Diplomatic representation in the US: none; note - North Korea has a Permanent Mission to the UN in New York, headed by YI Hyong-chol
Diplomatic representation from the US: none (Swedish Embassy in P'yongyang represents the US as consular protecting power)
Flag description: three horizontal bands of blue (top), red (triple width), and blue; the red band is edged in white; on the hoist side of the red band is a white disk with a red five-pointed star

Economy

Economy - overview: North Korea, one of the world's most centrally planned and isolated economies, faces desperate economic conditions. Industrial capital stock is nearly beyond repair as a result of years of underinvestment and spare parts shortages. The nation faces its seventh year of food shortages because of weather-related problems, including major drought in 2000, and chronic shortages of fertilizer and fuel. Massive international food aid deliveries have allowed the regime to escape the major consequence of spreading economic failure, such as mass starvation, but the population remains vulnerable to prolonged malnutrition and deteriorating living conditions. Large-scale military spending eats up resources needed for expanding investment and consumption goods. In 2000, the regime placed emphasis on expanding foreign trade links, embracing modern technology, and attracting foreign investment, but in no way at the expense of relinquishing central control over key national assets or undergoing market-oriented reforms.
GDP: purchasing power parity - $22 billion (2000 est.)
GDP - real growth rate: -3% (2000 est.)
GDP - per capita: purchasing power parity - $1,000 (2000 est.)
GDP - composition by sector:
agriculture: 30%
industry: 42%
services: 28% (1999 est.)
Population below poverty line: NA%
Household income or consumption by percentage share:
lowest 10%: NA%
highest 10%: NA%
Inflation rate (consumer prices): NA%
Labor force: 9.6 million
Labor force - by occupation: agricultural 36%, nonagricultural 64%
Unemployment rate: NA%
Budget:
revenues: $NA
expenditures: $NA, including capital expenditures of $NA
Industries: military products; machine building, electric power, chemicals; mining (coal, iron ore, magnesite, graphite, copper, zinc, lead, and precious metals), metallurgy; textiles, food processing; tourism
Industrial production growth rate: NA%
Electricity - production: 28.6 billion kWh (1999)
Electricity - production by source:
fossil fuel: 34.62%
hydro: 65.38%
nuclear: 0%
other: 0% (1999)
Electricity - consumption: 26.598 billion kWh (1999)
Electricity - exports: 0 kWh (1999)
Electricity - imports: 0 kWh (1999)
Agriculture - products: rice, corn, potatoes, soybeans, pulses; cattle, pigs, pork, eggs
Exports: $520 million (f.o.b., 1999 est.)
Exports - commodities: minerals, metallurgical products, manufactures (including armaments); agricultural and fishery products
Exports - partners: Japan 28%, South Korea 21%, China 5%, Germany 4%, Russia 1% (1995)
Imports: $960 million (c.i.f., 1999 est.)
Imports - commodities: petroleum, coking coal, machinery and equipment; consumer goods, grain
Imports - partners: China 33%, Japan 17%, Russia 5%, South Korea 4%, Germany 3% (1995)

Korea, North (continued)

Debt - external: $12 billion (1996 est.)
Economic aid - recipient: $NA; note - an estimated $200 million to $300 million in humanitarian aid from US, South Korea, Japan, and EU in 1997 plus much additional aid from the UN and non-governmental organizations; substantial continuing humanitarian aid, 1998-2000
Currency: North Korean won (KPW)
Currency code: KPW
Exchange rates: official: North Korean won per US dollar - 2.15 (May 1994), 2.13 (May 1992), 2.14 (September 1991), 2.1 (January 1990), 2.3 (December 1989); market: North Korean won per US dollar - 200
Fiscal year: calendar year

Communications

Telephones - main lines in use: 1.1 million (1997)
Telephones - mobile cellular: NA
Telephone system:
general assessment: NA
domestic: NA
international: satellite earth stations - 1 Intelsat (Indian Ocean) and 1 Russian (Indian Ocean region); other international connections through Moscow and Beijing
Radio broadcast stations: AM 16, FM 14, shortwave 12 (1999)
Radios: 3.36 million (1997)
Television broadcast stations: 38 (1999)
Televisions: 1.2 million (1997)
Internet country code: .kp
Internet Service Providers (ISPs): 1 (2000)
Internet users: NA

Transportation

Railways:
total: 5,000 km
standard gauge: 4,095 km 1.435-m gauge (3,500 km electrified; 159 km double track)
narrow gauge: 665 km 0.762-m gauge
dual gauge: 240 km 1.435-m and 1.600-m gauges (four rails interlaced) (1996 est.)
Highways:
total: 31,200 km
paved: 1,997 km
unpaved: 29,203 km (1996)
Waterways: 2,253 km
note: mostly navigable by small craft only
Pipelines: crude oil 37 km; petroleum product 180 km
Ports and harbors: Ch'ongjin, Haeju, Hungnam (Hamhung), Kimch'aek, Kosong, Najin, Namp'o, Sinuiju, Songnim, Sonbong (formerly Unggi), Ungsang, Wonsan
Merchant marine:
total: 110 ships (1,000 GRT or over) totaling 661,792 GRT/903,367 DWT
ships by type: bulk 4, cargo 94, combination bulk 1, multi-functional large-load carrier 1, passenger 2, passenger/cargo 1, petroleum tanker 4, refrigerated cargo 1, short-sea passenger 2 (2000 est.)

Airports: 87 (2000 est.)
Airports - with paved runways:
total: 39
over 3,047 m: 3
2,438 to 3,047 m: 26
1,524 to 2,437 m: 8
914 to 1,523 m: 1
under 914 m: 1 (2000 est.)
Airports - with unpaved runways:
total: 48
2,438 to 3,047 m: 3
1,524 to 2,437 m: 24
914 to 1,523 m: 13
under 914 m: 8 (2000 est.)

Military

Military branches: Korean People's Army (includes Army, Navy, Air Force), Civil Security Forces
Military manpower - military age: 18 years of age
Military manpower - availability:
males age 15-49: 5,943,735 (2001 est.)
Military manpower - fit for military service:
males age 15-49: 3,574,050 (2001 est.)
Military manpower - reaching military age annually:
males: 179,136 (2001 est.)
Military expenditures - dollar figure: $3.7 billion to $4.9 billion (FY98 est.)
Military expenditures - percent of GDP: 25% to 33% (FY98 est.)

Transnational Issues

Disputes - international: 33-km section of boundary with China in the Paektu-san (mountain) area is indefinite; Demarcation Line with South Korea

Korea, South

Introduction

Background: After World War II, a republic was set up in the southern half of the Korean Peninsula while a communist-style government was installed in the north. The Korean War (1950-53) had US and other UN forces intervene to defend South Korea from North Korean attacks supported by the Chinese. An armistice was signed in 1953 splitting the peninsula at the 38th parallel known as the DMZ. Thereafter, South Korea achieved rapid economic growth, with per capita income rising to 13 times the level of North Korea. In 1997, the nation suffered a severe financial crisis from which it continues to make a solid recovery. South Korea has also maintained its commitment to democratize its political processes. In June 2000, a historic first south-north summit took place between the south's President KIM Dae-jung and the north's leader KIM Chong-il. In December 2000, President KIM Dae-jung won the Noble Peace Prize for his lifeling committment to democracy and human rights in Asia. He is the first Korean to win a Nobel Prize.

Geography

Location: Eastern Asia, southern half of the Korean Peninsula bordering the Sea of Japan and the Yellow Sea
Geographic coordinates: 37 00 N, 127 30 E
Map references: Asia
Area:
total: 98,480 sq km
land: 98,190 sq km
water: 290 sq km
Area - comparative: slightly larger than Indiana
Land boundaries:
total: 238 km
border countries: North Korea 238 km
Coastline: 2,413 km
Maritime claims:
contiguous zone: 24 NM
continental shelf: not specified

Korea, South (continued)

exclusive economic zone: 200 NM
territorial sea: 12 NM; between 3 NM and 12 NM in the Korea Strait
Climate: temperate, with rainfall heavier in summer than winter
Terrain: mostly hills and mountains; wide coastal plains in west and south
Elevation extremes:
lowest point: Sea of Japan 0 m
highest point: Halla-san 1,950 m
Natural resources: coal, tungsten, graphite, molybdenum, lead, hydropower potential
Land use:
arable land: 19%
permanent crops: 2%
permanent pastures: 1%
forests and woodland: 65%
other: 13% (1993 est.)
Irrigated land: 13,350 sq km (1993 est.)
Natural hazards: occasional typhoons bring high winds and floods; low-level seismic activity common in southwest
Environment - current issues: air pollution in large cities; acid rain; water pollution from the discharge of sewage and industrial effluents; drift net fishing
Environment - international agreements:
party to: Antarctic-Environmental Protocol, Antarctic-Marine Living Resources, Antarctic Treaty, Biodiversity, Climate Change, Desertification, Endangered Species, Environmental Modification, Hazardous Wastes, Law of the Sea, Marine Dumping, Nuclear Test Ban, Ozone Layer Protection, Ship Pollution, Tropical Timber 83, Tropical Timber 94, Wetlands, Whaling
signed, but not ratified: Climate Change-Kyoto Protocol

People

Population: 47,904,370 (July 2001 est.)
Age structure:
0-14 years: 21.59% (male 5,475,453; female 4,864,918)
15-64 years: 71.14% (male 17,291,202; female 16,789,380)
65 years and over: 7.27% (male 1,352,312; female 2,131,105) (2001 est.)
Population growth rate: 0.89% (2001 est.)
Birth rate: 14.85 births/1,000 population (2001 est.)
Death rate: 5.93 deaths/1,000 population (2001 est.)
Net migration rate: 0 migrant(s)/1,000 population (2001 est.)
Sex ratio:
at birth: 1.11 male(s)/female
under 15 years: 1.13 male(s)/female
15-64 years: 1.03 male(s)/female
65 years and over: 0.63 male(s)/female
total population: 1.01 male(s)/female (2001 est.)
Infant mortality rate: 7.71 deaths/1,000 live births (2001 est.)

Life expectancy at birth:
total population: 74.65 years
male: 70.97 years
female: 78.74 years (2001 est.)
Total fertility rate: 1.72 children born/woman (2001 est.)
HIV/AIDS - adult prevalence rate: 0.01% (1999 est.)
HIV/AIDS - people living with HIV/AIDS: 3,800 (1999 est.)
HIV/AIDS - deaths: 180 (1999 est.)
Nationality:
noun: Korean(s)
adjective: Korean
Ethnic groups: homogeneous (except for about 20,000 Chinese)
Religions: Christian 49%, Buddhist 47%, Confucianist 3%, Shamanist, Chondogyo (Religion of the Heavenly Way), and other 1%
Languages: Korean, English widely taught in junior high and high school
Literacy:
definition: age 15 and over can read and write
total population: 98%
male: 99.3%
female: 96.7% (1995 est.)

Government

Country name:
conventional long form: Republic of Korea
conventional short form: South Korea
local long form: Taehan-min'guk
local short form: none
note: the South Koreans generally use the term "Han-guk" to refer to their country
abbreviation: ROK
Government type: republic
Capital: Seoul
Administrative divisions: 9 provinces (do, singular and plural) and 7 metropolitan cities* (gwangyoksi, singular and plural); Cheju-do, Cholla-bukto, Cholla-namdo, Ch'ungch'ong-bukto, Ch'ungch'ong-namdo, Inch'on-gwangyoksi*, Kangwon-do, Kwangju-gwangyoksi*, Kyonggi-do, Kyongsang-bukto, Kyongsang-namdo, Pusan-gwangyoksi*, Soul-t'ukpyolsi*, Taegu-gwangyoksi*, Taejon-gwangyoksi*, Ulsan-gwangyoksi*
Independence: 15 August 1945 (from Japan)
National holiday: Liberation Day, 15 August (1945)
Constitution: 25 February 1988
Legal system: combines elements of continental European civil law systems, Anglo-American law, and Chinese classical thought
Suffrage: 20 years of age; universal
Executive branch:
chief of state: President KIM Dae-jung (since 25 February 1998)
head of government: Prime Minister YI Han-tong (since 23 May 2000)
cabinet: State Council appointed by the president on the prime minister's recommendation
elections: president elected by popular vote for a single five-year term; election last held 18 December 1997 (next to be held by 18 December 2002); prime minister appointed by the president; deputy prime ministers appointed by the president on the prime minister's recommendation
election results: KIM Dae-jung elected president; percent of vote - KIM Dae-jung (NCNP) 40.3% (with ULD partnership), YI Hoe-chang (GNP) 38.7%, YI In-che (NPP) 19.2%
Legislative branch: unicameral National Assembly or Kukhoe (273 seats total - 227 elected by direct, popular vote; members serve four-year terms)
elections: last held 13 April 2000 (next to be held NA April 2004)
election results: percent of vote by party - NA%; seats by party - GNP 133, MDP 115, ULD 17, other 8
Judicial branch: Supreme Court (justices are appointed by the president with the consent of the National Assembly)
Political parties and leaders: Grand National Party or GNP [YI Hoe-chang, president]; Millennium Democratic Party or MDP [KIM Dae-jung, president]; United Liberal Democrats or ULD [KIM Chong-p'il, honorary chairman, KIM Chong-ho, acting president]
note: on 20 January 2000, the National Congress for New Politics or NCNP was renamed the Millennium Democratic Party or MDP
Political pressure groups and leaders: Federation of Korean Industries; Federation of Korean Trade Unions; Korean Confederation of Trade Unions; Korean National Council of Churches; Korean Traders Association; Korean Veterans' Association; National Council of Labor Unions; National Democratic Alliance of Korea; National Federation of Farmers' Associations; National Federation of Student Associations
International organization participation: AfDB, APEC, ARF (dialogue partner), AsDB, ASEAN (dialogue partner), Australia Group, BIS, CCC, CP, EBRD, ESCAP, FAO, G-77, IAEA, IBRD, ICAO, ICC, ICFTU, ICRM, IDA, IEA (observer), IFAD, IFC, IFRCS, IHO, ILO, IMF, IMO, Inmarsat, Intelsat, Interpol, IOC, IOM, ISO, ITU, MINURSO, NAM (guest), NEA, NSG, OAS (observer), OECD, OPCW, OSCE (partner), PCA, UN, UNCTAD, UNESCO, UNHCR, UNIDO, UNMOGIP, UNOMIG, UNTAET, UNU, UPU, WHO, WIPO, WMO, WToO, WTrO, ZC
Diplomatic representation in the US:
chief of mission: Ambassador YANG Song-chol
chancery: 2450 Massachusetts Avenue NW, Washington, DC 20008
telephone: [1] (202) 939-5600
FAX: [1] (202) 387-0205
consulate(s) general: Anchorage, Atlanta, Boston, Chicago, Honolulu, Houston, Los Angeles, Miami, New York, San Francisco, and Seattle
consulate(s): Hagatna (Guam)

Korea, South (continued)

Diplomatic representation from the US:
chief of mission: Ambassador (vacant)
embassy: 82 Sejong-ro, Chongro-ku, Seoul 110-710
mailing address: American Embassy, Unit 15550, APO AP 96205-0001
telephone: [82] (2) 397-4114
FAX: [82] (2) 738-8845
Flag description: white with a red (top) and blue yin-yang symbol in the center; there is a different black trigram from the ancient I Ching (Book of Changes) in each corner of the white field

Economy

Economy - overview: As one of the Four Dragons of East Asia, South Korea has achieved an incredible record of growth. Three decades ago GDP per capita was comparable with levels in the poorer countries of Africa and Asia. Today its GDP per capita is seven times India's, 16 times North Korea's, and comparable to the lesser economies of the European Union. This success through the late 1980s was achieved by a system of close government/business ties, including directed credit, import restrictions, sponsorship of specific industries, and a strong labor effort. The government promoted the import of raw materials and technology at the expense of consumer goods and encouraged savings and investment over consumption. The Asian financial crisis of 1997-99 exposed certain longstanding weaknesses in South Korea's development model, including high debt/equity ratios, massive foreign borrowing, and an undisciplined financial sector. By 1999 GDP growth had recovered, reversing the substantial decline of 1998. Seoul has pressed the country's largest business groups to restructure and to strengthen their financial base. Growth in 2001 likely will be a more sustainable rate of 5%.
GDP: purchasing power parity - $764.6 billion (2000 est.)
GDP - real growth rate: 9% (2000 est.)
GDP - per capita: purchasing power parity - $16,100 (2000 est.)
GDP - composition by sector:
agriculture: 5.6%
industry: 41.4%
services: 53% (1999 est.)
Population below poverty line: NA%
Household income or consumption by percentage share:
lowest 10%: 2.9%
highest 10%: 24.3% (1993)
Inflation rate (consumer prices): 2.3% (2000)
Labor force: 22 million (2000)
Labor force - by occupation: services 68%, industry 20%, agriculture 12% (1999)
Unemployment rate: 4.1% (2000 est.)
Budget:
revenues: $81.8 billion
expenditures: $94.9 billion, including capital expenditures of $6.1 billion (1999)
Industries: electronics, automobile production, chemicals, shipbuilding, steel, textiles, clothing, footwear, food processing
Industrial production growth rate: 17% (2000)
Electricity - production: 250.287 billion kWh (1999)
Electricity - production by source:
fossil fuel: 59.22%
hydro: 1.64%
nuclear: 39.12%
other: 0.02% (1999)
Electricity - consumption: 232.767 billion kWh (1999)
Electricity - exports: 0 kWh (1999)
Electricity - imports: 0 kWh (1999)
Agriculture - products: rice, root crops, barley, vegetables, fruit; cattle, pigs, chickens, milk, eggs; fish
Exports: $172.6 billion (f.o.b., 2000)
Exports - commodities: electronic products, machinery and equipment, motor vehicles, steel, ships; textiles, clothing, footwear; fish
Exports - partners: US 20.5%, Japan 11%, China 9.5%, Hong Kong 6.3%, Taiwan 4.4% (1999)
Imports: $160.5 billion (f.o.b., 2000)
Imports - commodities: machinery, electronics and electronic equipment, oil, steel, transport equipment, textiles, organic chemicals, grains
Imports - partners: US 20.8%, Japan 20.2%, China 7.4%, Saudi Arabia 4.7%, Australia 3.9% (1999)
Debt - external: $137 billion (November 2000)
Economic aid - recipient: $NA
Currency: South Korean won (KRW)
Currency code: KRW
Exchange rates: South Korean won per US dollar - 1,271.89 (January 2001), 1,130.96 (2000), 1,188.82 (1999), 1,401.44 (1998), 951.29 (1997), 804.45 (1996)
Fiscal year: calendar year

Communications

Telephones - main lines in use: 24 million (1999)
Telephones - mobile cellular: 27 million (June 2000)
Telephone system:
general assessment: excellent domestic and international services
domestic: NA
international: fiber-optic submarine cable to China; the Russia-Korea-Japan submarine cable; satellite earth stations - 3 Intelsat (2 Pacific Ocean and 1 Indian Ocean) and 1 Inmarsat (Pacific Ocean region)
Radio broadcast stations: AM 106, FM 97, shortwave 6 (1999)
Radios: 47.5 million (1997)
Television broadcast stations: 121 (plus 850 repeater stations and the eight-channel American Forces Korea Network) (1999)
Televisions: 15.9 million (1997)
Internet country code: .kr
Internet Service Providers (ISPs): 11 (2000)
Internet users: 15.3 million (2000)

Transportation

Railways:
total: 6,240 km
standard gauge: 6,240 km 1.435-m gauge (525 km electrified) (1998 est.)
Highways:
total: 87,534 km
paved: 65,388 km (including 1,996 km of expressways)
unpaved: 22,146 km (1999)
Waterways: 1,609 km
note: restricted to small native craft
Pipelines: petroleum products 455 km; note - additionally, there is a parallel petroleum, oils, and lubricants (POL) pipeline being completed
Ports and harbors: Chinhae, Inch'on, Kunsan, Masan, Mokp'o, P'ohang, Pusan, Tonghae-hang, Ulsan, Yosu
Merchant marine:
total: 496 ships (1,000 GRT or over) totaling 5,421,993 GRT/8,757,034 DWT
ships by type: bulk 105, cargo 168, chemical tanker 38, combination bulk 5, container 49, liquefied gas 16, multi-functional large-load carrier 1, passenger 3, petroleum tanker 70, refrigerated cargo 27, roll on/roll off 4, short-sea passenger 1, specialized tanker 4, vehicle carrier 5 (2000 est.)
Airports: 102 (2000 est.)
Airports - with paved runways:
total: 68
over 3,047 m: 2
2,438 to 3,047 m: 18
1,524 to 2,437 m: 16
914 to 1,523 m: 11
under 914 m: 21 (2000 est.)
Airports - with unpaved runways:
total: 34
914 to 1,523 m: 2
under 914 m: 32 (2000 est.)
Heliports: 203 (2000 est.)

Military

Military branches: Army, Navy, Air Force, Marine Corps, National Maritime Police (Coast Guard)
Military manpower - military age: 18 years of age
Military manpower - availability:
males age 15-49: 14,148,552 (2001 est.)
Military manpower - fit for military service:
males age 15-49: 8,979,778 (2001 est.)
Military manpower - reaching military age annually:
males: 394,397 (2001 est.)
Military expenditures - dollar figure: $12 billion (2000)
Military expenditures - percent of GDP: 3.2% (FY98/99)

Transnational Issues

Disputes - international: Demarcation Line with North Korea; Liancourt Rocks (Takeshima/Tokdo) disputed with Japan

Kuwait

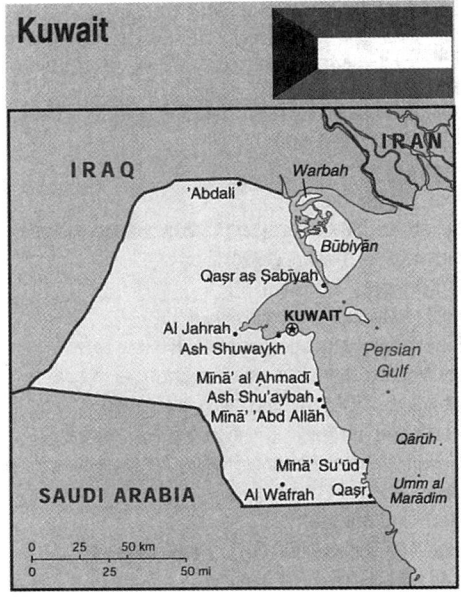

Introduction

Background: Kuwait was attacked and overrun by Iraq on 2 August 1990. Following several weeks of aerial bombardment, a US-led UN coalition began a ground assault on 23 February 1991 that completely liberated Kuwait in four days. Kuwait has spent more than $5 billion to repair oil infrastructure damaged during 1990-91.

Geography

Location: Middle East, bordering the Persian Gulf, between Iraq and Saudi Arabia
Geographic coordinates: 29 30 N, 45 45 E
Map references: Middle East
Area:
total: 17,820 sq km
land: 17,820 sq km
water: 0 sq km
Area - comparative: slightly smaller than New Jersey
Land boundaries:
total: 464 km
border countries: Iraq 242 km, Saudi Arabia 222 km
Coastline: 499 km
Maritime claims:
territorial sea: 12 NM
Climate: dry desert; intensely hot summers; short, cool winters
Terrain: flat to slightly undulating desert plain
Elevation extremes:
lowest point: Persian Gulf 0 m
highest point: unnamed location 306 m
Natural resources: petroleum, fish, shrimp, natural gas
Land use:
arable land: 0%
permanent crops: 0%
permanent pastures: 8%
forests and woodland: 0%
other: 92% (1993 est.)
Irrigated land: 20 sq km (1993 est.)
Natural hazards: sudden cloudbursts are common from October to April; they bring inordinate amounts of rain which can damage roads and houses; sandstorms and dust storms occur throughout the year, but are most common between March and August
Environment - current issues: limited natural fresh water resources; some of world's largest and most sophisticated desalination facilities provide much of the water; air and water pollution; desertification
Environment - international agreements:
party to: Climate Change, Desertification, Environmental Modification, Hazardous Wastes, Law of the Sea, Marine Dumping, Nuclear Test Ban, Ozone Layer Protection, Ship Pollution
signed, but not ratified: Biodiversity, Endangered Species, Marine Dumping
Geography - note: strategic location at head of Persian Gulf

People

Population: 2,041,961
note: includes 1,159,913 non-nationals (July 2001 est.)
Age structure:
0-14 years: 28.76% (male 299,080; female 288,125)
15-64 years: 68.82% (male 897,839; female 507,527)
65 years and over: 2.42% (male 31,843; female 17,547) (2001 est.)
Population growth rate: 3.38% (2001 est.)
note: this rate reflects a return to pre-Gulf crisis immigration of expatriates
Birth rate: 21.91 births/1,000 population (2001 est.)
Death rate: 2.45 deaths/1,000 population (2001 est.)
Net migration rate: 14.31 migrant(s)/1,000 population (2001 est.)
Sex ratio:
at birth: 1.04 male(s)/female
under 15 years: 1.04 male(s)/female
15-64 years: 1.77 male(s)/female
65 years and over: 1.81 male(s)/female
total population: 1.51 male(s)/female (2001 est.)
Infant mortality rate: 11.18 deaths/1,000 live births (2001 est.)
Life expectancy at birth:
total population: 76.27 years
male: 75.42 years
female: 77.15 years (2001 est.)
Total fertility rate: 3.2 children born/woman (2001 est.)
HIV/AIDS - adult prevalence rate: 0.12% (1999 est.)
HIV/AIDS - people living with HIV/AIDS: NA
HIV/AIDS - deaths: NA
Nationality:
noun: Kuwaiti(s)
adjective: Kuwaiti
Ethnic groups: Kuwaiti 45%, other Arab 35%, South Asian 9%, Iranian 4%, other 7%
Religions: Muslim 85% (Sunni 45%, Shi'a 40%), Christian, Hindu, Parsi, and other 15%
Languages: Arabic (official), English widely spoken
Literacy:
definition: age 15 and over can read and write
total population: 78.6%
male: 82.2%
female: 74.9% (1995 est.)

Government

Country name:
conventional long form: State of Kuwait
conventional short form: Kuwait
local long form: Dawlat al Kuwayt
local short form: Al Kuwayt
Government type: nominal constitutional monarchy
Capital: Kuwait
Administrative divisions: 5 governorates (muhafazat, singular - muhafazah); Al Ahmadi, Al Farwaniyah, Al 'Asimah, Al Jahra', Hawalli
Independence: 19 June 1961 (from UK)
National holiday: National Day, 25 February (1950)
Constitution: approved and promulgated 11 November 1962
Legal system: civil law system with Islamic law significant in personal matters; has not accepted compulsory ICJ jurisdiction
Suffrage: adult males who have been naturalized for 30 years or more or have resided in Kuwait since before 1920 and their male descendants at age 21
note: only 10% of all citizens are eligible to vote; in 1996, naturalized citizens who do not meet the pre-1920 qualification but have been naturalized for 30 years were eligible to vote for the first time
Executive branch:
chief of state: Amir JABIR al-Ahmad al-Jabir Al Sabah (since 31 December 1977)
head of government: Prime Minister and Crown Prince SAAD al-Abdallah al-Salim Al Sabah (since 8 February 1978); First Deputy Prime Minister SABAH al-Ahmad al-Jabir Al Sabah (since 17 October 1992); Deputy Prime Ministers JABIR MUBARAK al-Hamud Al Sabah (since NA) and MUHAMMAD KHALID al-Hamed Al Sabah (since NA)
cabinet: Council of Ministers appointed by the prime minister and approved by the monarch
elections: none; the monarch is hereditary; prime minister and deputy prime ministers appointed by the monarch
Legislative branch: unicameral National Assembly or Majlis al-Umma (50 seats; members elected by popular vote to serve four-year terms)
elections: last held 3 July 1999 (next to be held NA 2003)
election results: percent of vote - NA%; seats - independents 50; note - all cabinet ministers are also ex officio members of the National Assembly
Judicial branch: High Court of Appeal
Political parties and leaders: none; formation of political parties is illegal
Political pressure groups and leaders: several political groups act as de facto parties: Bedouins, merchants, Sunni and Shi'a activists, and secular leftists and nationalists

Kuwait (continued)

International organization participation: ABEDA, AfDB, AFESD, AL, AMF, BDEAC, CAEU, CCC, ESCWA, FAO, G-77, GCC, IAEA, IBRD, ICAO, ICC, ICRM, IDA, IDB, IFAD, IFC, IFRCS, ILO, IMF, IMO, Inmarsat, Intelsat, Interpol, IOC, ISO, ITU, NAM, OAPEC, OIC, OPCW, OPEC, UN, UNCTAD, UNESCO, UNIDO, UNITAR, UPU, WFTU, WHO, WIPO, WMO, WToO, WTrO

Diplomatic representation in the US:
chief of mission: Ambassador (vacant)
chancery: 2940 Tilden Street NW, Washington, DC 20008
telephone: [1] (202) 966-0702
FAX: [1] (202) 966-0517

Diplomatic representation from the US:
chief of mission: Ambassador James A. LAROCCO
embassy: Bayan, near the Bayan palace, Kuwait City
mailing address: P. O. Box 77 Safat, 13001 Safat, Kuwait Unit 69000, APO AE 09880-9000
telephone: [965] 539-5307
FAX: [965] 538-0282

Flag description: three equal horizontal bands of green (top), white, and red with a black trapezoid based on the hoist side

Economy

Economy - overview: Kuwait is a small, relatively open economy with proved crude oil reserves of about 94 billion barrels - 10% of world reserves. Petroleum accounts for nearly half of GDP, 90% of export revenues, and 75% of government income. Kuwait's climate limits agricultural development. Consequently, with the exception of fish, it depends almost wholly on food imports. About 75% of potable water must be distilled or imported. Higher oil prices put the FY99/00 budget into a $2 billion surplus. The FY00/01 budget covers only nine months because of a change in the fiscal year. The budget for FY01/02, which begins 1 April, contains higher expenditures for salaries, construction, and other general categories. Kuwait continues its discussions with foreign oil companies to develop fields in the northern part of the country.

GDP: purchasing power parity - $29.3 billion (2000 est.)
GDP - real growth rate: 6% (2000 est.)
GDP - per capita: purchasing power parity - $15,000 (2000 est.)
GDP - composition by sector:
agriculture: 0%
industry: 55%
services: 45% (1996)
Population below poverty line: NA%
Household income or consumption by percentage share:
lowest 10%: NA%
highest 10%: NA%
Inflation rate (consumer prices): 3% (2000)
Labor force: 1.3 million (1998 est.)
note: 68% of the population in the 15-64 age group is non-national (July 1998 est.)

Labor force - by occupation: agriculture NA%, industry NA%, services NA%
Unemployment rate: 1.8% (official 1996 est.)
Budget:
revenues: $11.5 billion
expenditures: $17.2 billion, including capital expenditures of $NA (FY01/02)
Industries: petroleum, petrochemicals, desalination, food processing, construction materials
Industrial production growth rate: 1% (1997 est.)
Electricity - production: 31.567 billion kWh (1999)
Electricity - production by source:
fossil fuel: 100%
hydro: 0%
nuclear: 0%
other: 0% (1999)
Electricity - consumption: 29.357 billion kWh (1999)
Electricity - exports: 0 kWh (1999)
Electricity - imports: 0 kWh (1999)
Agriculture - products: practically no crops; fish
Exports: $23.2 billion (f.o.b., 2000 est.)
Exports - commodities: oil and refined products, fertilizers
Exports - partners: Japan 23%, US 12%, Singapore 8%, Netherlands 7% (1999)
Imports: $7.6 billion (f.o.b., 2000 est.)
Imports - commodities: food, construction materials, vehicles and parts, clothing
Imports - partners: US 15%, Japan 10%, UK 7%, Germany 7% (1999)
Debt - external: $6.9 billion (2000 est.)
Economic aid - recipient: $27.6 million (1995)
Currency: Kuwaiti dinar (KWD)
Currency code: KWD
Exchange rates: Kuwaiti dinars per US dollar - 0.3057 (January 2001), 0.3067 (2000), 0.3044 (1999), 0.3047 (1998), 0.3033 (1997), 0.2994 (1996)
Fiscal year: 1 April - 31 March

Communications

Telephones - main lines in use: 412,000 (1997)
Telephones - mobile cellular: 210,000 (1997)
Telephone system:
general assessment: the quality of service is excellent
domestic: new telephone exchanges provide a large capacity for new subscribers; trunk traffic is carried by microwave radio relay, coaxial cable, open wire, and fiber-optic cable; a cellular telephone system operates throughout Kuwait, and the country is well supplied with pay telephones
international: coaxial cable and microwave radio relay to Saudi Arabia; linked to Bahrain, Qatar, UAE via the Fiber-Optic Gulf (FOG) cable; satellite earth stations - 3 Intelsat (1 Atlantic Ocean, 2 Indian Ocean), 1 Inmarsat (Atlantic Ocean), and 2 Arabsat
Radio broadcast stations: AM 6, FM 11, shortwave 1 (1998)
Radios: 1.175 million (1997)
Television broadcast stations: 13 (plus several satellite channels) (1997)

Televisions: 875,000 (1997)
Internet country code: .kw
Internet Service Providers (ISPs): 3 (2000)
Internet users: 100,000 (2000)

Transportation

Railways: 0 km
Highways:
total: 4,450 km
paved: 3,590 km
unpaved: 860 km (1999 est.)
Pipelines: crude oil 877 km; petroleum products 40 km; natural gas 165 km
Ports and harbors: Ash Shu'aybah, Ash Shuwaykh, Kuwait, Mina' 'Abd Allah, Mina' al Ahmadi, Mina' Su'ud
Merchant marine:
total: 45 ships (1,000 GRT or over) totaling 2,461,072 GRT/3,966,645 DWT
ships by type: bulk 1, cargo 6, container 6, liquefied gas 7, livestock carrier 5, petroleum tanker 20 (2000 est.)
Airports: 8 (2000 est.)
Airports - with paved runways:
total: 4
over 3,047 m: 2
2,438 to 3,047 m: 2 (2000 est.)
Airports - with unpaved runways:
total: 4
1,524 to 2,437 m: 1
under 914 m: 3 (2000 est.)
Heliports: 3 (2000 est.)

Military

Military branches: Army, Navy, Air Force, National Police Force, National Guard, Coast Guard
Military manpower - military age: 18 years of age
Military manpower - availability:
males age 15-49: 780,559 (2001 est.)
Military manpower - fit for military service:
males age 15-49: 466,521 (2001 est.)
Military manpower - reaching military age annually:
males: 18,309 (2001 est.)
Military expenditures - dollar figure: $1.9 billion (FY00/01)
Military expenditures - percent of GDP: 8.7% (FY00/01)

Transnational Issues

Disputes - international: in November 1994, Iraq formally accepted the UN-demarcated border with Kuwait which had been spelled out in Security Council Resolutions 687 (1991), 773 (1993), and 883 (1993); this formally ends earlier claims to Kuwait and to Bubiyan and Warbah islands

Kyrgyzstan

Introduction

Background: A Central Asian country of incredible natural beauty and proud nomadic traditions, Kyrgyzstan was annexed by Russia in 1864; it achieved independence from the Soviet Union in 1991. Current concerns include: privatization of state-owned enterprises, expansion of democracy and political freedoms, inter-ethnic relations, and terrorism.

Geography

Location: Central Asia, west of China
Geographic coordinates: 41 00 N, 75 00 E
Map references: Commonwealth of Independent States
Area:
total: 198,500 sq km
land: 191,300 sq km
water: 7,200 sq km
Area - comparative: slightly smaller than South Dakota
Land boundaries:
total: 3,878 km
border countries: China 858 km, Kazakhstan 1,051 km, Tajikistan 870 km, Uzbekistan 1,099 km
Coastline: 0 km (landlocked)
Maritime claims: none (landlocked)
Climate: dry continental to polar in high Tien Shan; subtropical in southwest (Fergana Valley); temperate in northern foothill zone
Terrain: peaks of Tien Shan and associated valleys and basins encompass entire nation
Elevation extremes:
lowest point: Kara-Darya 132 m
highest point: Jengish Chokusu (Pik Pobedy) 7,439 m
Natural resources: abundant hydropower; significant deposits of gold and rare earth metals; locally exploitable coal, oil, and natural gas; other deposits of nepheline, mercury, bismuth, lead, and zinc
Land use:
arable land: 7%
permanent crops: 0%
permanent pastures: 44%
forests and woodland: 4%
other: 45% (1993 est.)
note: Kyrgyzstan has the world's largest natural growth walnut forest
Irrigated land: 9,000 sq km (1993 est.)
Natural hazards: NA
Environment - current issues: water pollution; many people get their water directly from contaminated streams and wells; as a result, water-borne diseases are prevalent; increasing soil salinity from faulty irrigation practices
Environment - international agreements:
party to: Air Pollution, Biodiversity, Climate Change, Desertification, Hazardous Wastes, Marine Dumping, Ozone Layer Protection, Ship Pollution
signed, but not ratified: none of the selected agreements
Geography - note: landlocked

People

Population: 4,753,003 (July 2001 est.)
Age structure:
0-14 years: 35.03% (male 841,029; female 823,723)
15-64 years: 58.83% (male 1,369,842; female 1,426,522)
65 years and over: 6.14% (male 110,340; female 181,547) (2001 est.)
Population growth rate: 1.44% (2001 est.)
Birth rate: 26.18 births/1,000 population (2001 est.)
Death rate: 9.13 deaths/1,000 population (2001 est.)
Net migration rate: -2.66 migrant(s)/1,000 population (2001 est.)
Sex ratio:
at birth: 1.05 male(s)/female
under 15 years: 1.02 male(s)/female
15-64 years: 0.96 male(s)/female
65 years and over: 0.61 male(s)/female
total population: 0.95 male(s)/female (2001 est.)
Infant mortality rate: 76.5 deaths/1,000 live births (2001 est.)
Life expectancy at birth:
total population: 63.46 years
male: 59.2 years
female: 67.94 years (2001 est.)
Total fertility rate: 3.19 children born/woman (2001 est.)
HIV/AIDS - adult prevalence rate: less than 0.01% (1999 est.)
HIV/AIDS - people living with HIV/AIDS: less than 100 (1999 est.)
HIV/AIDS - deaths: less than 100 (1999 est.)
Nationality:
noun: Kyrgyzstani(s)
adjective: Kyrgyzstani
Ethnic groups: Kirghiz 52.4%, Russian 18%, Uzbek 12.9%, Ukrainian 2.5%, German 2.4%, other 11.8%
Religions: Muslim 75%, Russian Orthodox 20%, other 5%
Languages: Kirghiz (Kyrgyz) - official language, Russian - official language
note: in May 2000, the Kyrgyzstani legislature made Russian an official language, equal in status to Kirghiz
Literacy:
definition: age 15 and over can read and write
total population: 97%
male: 99%
female: 96% (1989 est.)

Government

Country name:
conventional long form: Kyrgyz Republic
conventional short form: Kyrgyzstan
local long form: Kyrgyz Respublikasy
local short form: none
former: Kirghiz Soviet Socialist Republic
Government type: republic
Capital: Bishkek
Administrative divisions: 7 oblastlar (singular - oblast) and 1 city* (singular - shaar); Batken Oblasty, Bishkek Shaary*, Chuy Oblasty (Bishkek), Jalal-Abad Oblasty, Naryn Oblasty, Osh Oblasty, Talas Oblasty, Ysyk-Kol Oblasty (Karakol)
note: administrative divisions have the same names as their administrative centers (exceptions have the administrative center name following in parentheses)
Independence: 31 August 1991 (from Soviet Union)
National holiday: Independence Day, 31 August (1991)
Constitution: adopted 5 May 1993; note - amendment proposed by President AKAYEV and passed in a national referendum on 10 February 1996 significantly expands the powers of the president at the expense of the legislature
Legal system: based on civil law system
Suffrage: 18 years of age; universal
Executive branch:
chief of state: President Askar AKAYEV (since 28 October 1990)

Kyrgyzstan (continued)

head of government: Prime Minister Kurmanbek BAKIYEV (since 22 December 2000)
cabinet: Cabinet of Ministers appointed by the president on the recommendation of the prime minister
elections: president reelected by popular vote for a five-year term; elections last held 29 October 2000 (next to be held November or December 2005); prime minister appointed by the president
election results: Askar AKAYEV reelected president; percent of vote - Askar AKAYEV 74%, Omurbek TEKEBAYEV 14%, other candidates 12%; note - election marred by serious irregularities
Legislative branch: bicameral Supreme Council or Zhogorku Kenesh consists of the Assembly of People's Representatives (70 seats; members are elected by popular vote to serve five-year terms) and the Legislative Assembly (35 seats; members are elected by popular vote to serve five-year terms)
elections: Assembly of People's Representatives - last held 20 February and 12 March 2000 (next to be held NA February 2005); Legislative Assembly - last held 20 February and 12 March 2000 (next to be held NA February 2005)
election results: Assembly of People's Representatives - percent of vote by party - NA%; percent of vote by party - NA; and Legislative Assembly - percent of vote by party - NA%; seats by party - NA; note - total seats by party in the Supreme Council were as follows: Union of Democratic Forces 12, Communists 6, My Country Party of Action 4, independents 73, other 10
note: the legislature became bicameral for the 5 February 1995 elections; the 2000 election results include both the Assembly of People's Representatives and the Legislative Assembly
Judicial branch: Supreme Court (judges are appointed for 10-year terms by the Supreme Council on the recommendation of the president); Constitutional Court; Higher Court of Arbitration
Political parties and leaders: Agrarian Labor Party of Kyrgyzstan [Uson S. SYDYKOV]; Agrarian Party of Kyrgyzstan [Arkin ALIYEV]; Ata-Meken Socialist Party or Fatherland [Onurbek TEKEBAYEV]; Banner National Revival Party or ASABA [Chaprashty BAZARBAY]; Democratic Movement of Kyrgyzstan or DDK [Jypar JEKSHEYEV]; Democratic Women's Party of Kyrgyzstan [T. A. SHAILIYEVA]; Dignity Party [Feliks KULOV]; Erkin Kyrgyzstan Progressive and Democratic Party [Tursunbay Bakir UULU]; Justice Party [Chingiz AYTMATOV]; Movement for the People's Salvation [Jumgalbek AMAMBAYEV]; Mutual Help Movement or Ashar [Jumagazy USUPOV]; My Country of Action [Almazbek ISMANKULOV]; National Unity Democratic Movement or DDNE [Yury RAZGULYAYEV]; Party of Communists of Kyrgyzstan or KCP [Absamat M. MASALIYEV]; Party of the Veterans of the War in Afghanistan [leader NA]; Peasant Party [leader NA]; People's Party [Melis ESHIMKANOV]; Poor and Unprotected People's Party [Daniyar USENOV]; Republican Popular Party of Kyrgyzstan [J. SHARSHENALIYEV]; Social Democratic Party or PSD [J. IBRAMOV]; Union of Democratic Forces (composed of Social Democratic Party of Kyrgyzstan or PSD [J. IBRAMOV], Economic Revival Party, and Birimdik Party
Political pressure groups and leaders: Council of Free Trade Unions; Kyrgyz Committee on Human Rights [Ramazan DYRYIDAYEV]; National Unity Democratic Movement; Union of Entrepreneurs
International organization participation: AsDB, CCC, CIS, EAPC, EBRD, ECE, ECO, ESCAP, FAO, IBRD, ICAO, ICRM, IDA, IDB, IFAD, IFC, IFRCS, ILO, IMF, Intelsat, Interpol, IOC, IOM, ISO (correspondent), ITU, NAM (observer), OIC, OPCW, OSCE, PFP, UN, UNAMSIL, UNCTAD, UNESCO, UNIDO, UNMIK, UPU, WFTU, WHO, WIPO, WMO, WToO, WTrO
Diplomatic representation in the US:
chief of mission: Ambassador Bakyt ABDRISAYEV
chancery: 1732 Wisconsin Avenue NW, Washington, DC 20007
telephone: [1] (202) 338-5141
FAX: [1] (202) 338-5139
Diplomatic representation from the US:
chief of mission: Ambassador John M. O'KEEFE
embassy: 171 Prospect Mira, 720016 Bishkek
mailing address: use embassy street address
telephone: [996] (312) 551-241, (517) 777-217
FAX: [996] (312) 551-264
Flag description: red field with a yellow sun in the center having 40 rays representing the 40 Kirghiz tribes; on the obverse side the rays run counterclockwise, on the reverse, clockwise; in the center of the sun is a red ring crossed by two sets of three lines, a stylized representation of the roof of the traditional Kirghiz yurt

Economy

Economy - overview: Kyrgyzstan is a small, poor, mountainous country with a predominantly agricultural economy. Cotton, wool, and meat are the main agricultural products and exports. Industrial exports include gold, mercury, uranium, and electricity. Kyrgyzstan has been one of the most progressive countries of the former Soviet Union in carrying out market reforms. Following a successful stabilization program, which lowered inflation from 88% in 1994 to 15% for 1997, attention is turning toward stimulating growth. Much of the government's stock in enterprises has been sold. Drops in production had been severe since the breakup of the Soviet Union in December 1991, but by mid-1995 production began to recover and exports began to increase. Pensioners, unemployed workers, and government workers with salary arrears continue to suffer. Foreign assistance played a substantial role in the country's economic turnaround in 1996-97. Growth was held down to 2.1% in 1998 largely because of the spillover from Russia's economic difficulties, but moved ahead to 3.6% in 1999 and an estimated 5.7% in 2000. The government has adopted a series of measures to combat such persistent problems as excessive external debt, inflation, and inadequate revenue collection.
GDP: purchasing power parity - $12.6 billion (2000 est.)
GDP - real growth rate: 5.7% (2000 est.)
GDP - per capita: purchasing power parity - $2,700 (2000 est.)
GDP - composition by sector:
agriculture: 39%
industry: 22%
services: 39% (1999 est.)
Population below poverty line: 51% (1997 est.)
Household income or consumption by percentage share:
lowest 10%: 2.7%
highest 10%: 31.7% (1997)
Inflation rate (consumer prices): 18.7% (2000 est.)
Labor force: 1.7 million
Labor force - by occupation: agriculture 55%, industry 15%, services 30% (1999 est.)
Unemployment rate: 6% (1998 est.)
Budget:
revenues: $207.4 million
expenditures: $238.7 million, including capital expenditures of $NA (1999 est.)
Industries: small machinery, textiles, food processing, cement, shoes, sawn logs, refrigerators, furniture, electric motors, gold, rare earth metals
Industrial production growth rate: 7% (2000 est.)
Electricity - production: 12.981 billion kWh (1999)
Electricity - production by source:
fossil fuel: 6.67%
hydro: 93.33%
nuclear: 0%
other: 0% (1999)
Electricity - consumption: 10.236 billion kWh (1999)
Electricity - exports: 2.02 billion kWh (1999)
Electricity - imports: 184 million kWh (1999)
Agriculture - products: tobacco, cotton, potatoes, vegetables, grapes, fruits and berries; sheep, goats, cattle, wool
Exports: $482 million (f.o.b., 2000 est.)
Exports - commodities: cotton, wool, meat, tobacco; gold, mercury, uranium, hydropower; machinery; shoes
Exports - partners: Germany 33%, Russia 16%, Kazakhstan 10%, Uzbekistan 10%, China 6% (1999)
Imports: $579 million (f.o.b., 2000 est.)
Imports - commodities: oil and gas, machinery and equipment, foodstuffs
Imports - partners: Russia 18%, Kazakhstan 12%, US 9%, Germany 8%, Uzbekistan 8%, China (1999)
Debt - external: $1.4 billion (2000 est.)
Economic aid - recipient: $329.4 million (1995)
Currency: Kyrgyzstani som (KGS)
Currency code: KGS
Exchange rates: soms per US dollar - 48.701 (January 2001), 47.704 (2000), 39.008 (1999), 20.838 (1998), 17.362 (1997), 12.810 (1996)
Fiscal year: calendar year

Kyrgyzstan (continued)

Communications

Telephones - main lines in use: 351,000 (1997)
Telephones - mobile cellular: NA
Telephone system:
general assessment: poorly developed; about 100,000 unsatisfied applications for household telephones
domestic: principally microwave radio relay; one cellular provider, probably limited to Bishkek region
international: connections with other CIS countries by landline or microwave radio relay and with other countries by leased connections with Moscow international gateway switch and by satellite; satellite earth stations - 1 Intersputnik and 1 Intelsat; connected internationally by the Trans-Asia-Europe (TAE) fiber-optic line
Radio broadcast stations: AM 12 (plus 10 repeater stations), FM 14, shortwave 2 (1998)
Radios: 520,000 (1997)
Television broadcast stations: NA (repeater stations throughout the country relay programs from Russia, Uzbekistan, Kazakhstan, and Turkey) (1997)
Televisions: 210,000 (1997)
Internet country code: .kg
Internet Service Providers (ISPs): NA
Internet users: 10,000 (2000)

Transportation

Railways:
total: 370 km in common carrier service; does not include industrial lines
broad gauge: 370 km 1.520-m gauge (1990)
Highways:
total: 18,500 km (including 140 km of expressways)
paved: 16,854 km (these roads are said to be hard-surfaced, and include, in addition to conventionally paved roads, some that are surfaced with gravel or other coarse aggregate, making them trafficable in all weather)
unpaved: 1,646 km (these roads are made of unstabilized earth and are difficult to negotiate in wet weather) (1996)
Waterways: 600 km (1990)
Pipelines: natural gas 200 km
Ports and harbors: Balykchy (Ysyk-Kol or Rybach'ye)
Airports: 50 (2000 est.)
Airports - with paved runways:
total: 4
over 3,047 m: 1
2,438 to 3,047 m: 1
1,524 to 2,437 m: 1
914 to 1,523 m: 1 (2000 est.)
Airports - with unpaved runways:
total: 46
2,438 to 3,047 m: 3
1,524 to 2,437 m: 5
914 to 1,523 m: 6
under 914 m: 32 (2000 est.)

Military

Military branches: Army, Air and Air Defense, Security Forces, Border Troops
Military manpower - military age: 18 years of age
Military manpower - availability:
males age 15-49: 1,203,001 (2001 est.)
Military manpower - fit for military service:
males age 15-49: 975,744 (2001 est.)
Military manpower - reaching military age annually:
males: 50,590 (2001 est.)
Military expenditures - dollar figure: $12 million (FY99)
Military expenditures - percent of GDP: 1% (FY99)

Transnational Issues

Disputes - international: territorial dispute with Tajikistan on southwestern boundary in Isfara Valley area; periodic target of Islamic insurgents from Uzbekistan, Tajikistan, and Afghanistan
Illicit drugs: limited illicit cultivator of cannabis and opium poppy, mostly for CIS consumption; limited government eradication program; increasingly used as transshipment point for illicit drugs to Russia and Western Europe from Southwest Asia

Laos

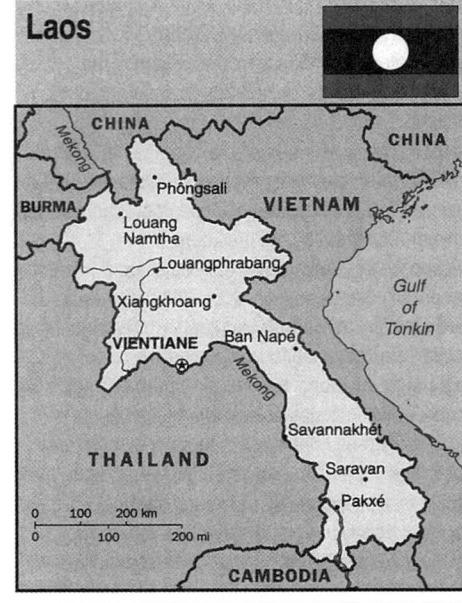

Introduction

Background: In 1975 the communist Pathet Lao took control of the government, ending a six-century-old monarchy. Initial closer ties to Vietnam and socialization were replaced with a gradual return to private enterprise, an easing of foreign investment laws, and the admission into ASEAN in 1997.

Geography

Location: Southeastern Asia, northeast of Thailand, west of Vietnam
Geographic coordinates: 18 00 N, 105 00 E
Map references: Southeast Asia
Area:
total: 236,800 sq km
land: 230,800 sq km
water: 6,000 sq km
Area - comparative: slightly larger than Utah
Land boundaries:
total: 5,083 km
border countries: Burma 235 km, Cambodia 541 km, China 423 km, Thailand 1,754 km, Vietnam 2,130 km
Coastline: 0 km (landlocked)
Maritime claims: none (landlocked)
Climate: tropical monsoon; rainy season (May to November); dry season (December to April)
Terrain: mostly rugged mountains; some plains and plateaus
Elevation extremes:
lowest point: Mekong River 70 m
highest point: Phou Bia 2,817 m
Natural resources: timber, hydropower, gypsum, tin, gold, gemstones
Land use:
arable land: 3%
permanent crops: 0%
permanent pastures: 3%
forests and woodland: 54%
other: 40% (1993 est.)

Laos (continued)

Irrigated land: 1,250 sq km (1993 est.)
note: rainy season irrigation - 2,169 sq km; dry season irrigation - 750 sq km (1998 est.)
Natural hazards: floods, droughts, and blight
Environment - current issues: unexploded ordnance; deforestation; soil erosion; a majority of the population does not have access to potable water
Environment - international agreements:
party to: Biodiversity, Climate Change, Desertification, Environmental Modification, Law of the Sea, Marine Dumping, Nuclear Test Ban, Ozone Layer Protection, Ship Pollution
signed, but not ratified: none of the selected agreements
Geography - note: landlocked

People

Population: 5,635,967 (July 2001 est.)
Age structure:
0-14 years: 42.75% (male 1,212,577; female 1,196,795)
15-64 years: 53.94% (male 1,494,927; female 1,544,851)
65 years and over: 3.31% (male 85,632; female 101,185) (2001 est.)
Population growth rate: 2.48% (2001 est.)
Birth rate: 37.84 births/1,000 population (2001 est.)
Death rate: 13.02 deaths/1,000 population (2001 est.)
Net migration rate: 0 migrant(s)/1,000 population (2001 est.)
Sex ratio:
at birth: 1.03 male(s)/female
under 15 years: 1.01 male(s)/female
15-64 years: 0.97 male(s)/female
65 years and over: 0.85 male(s)/female
total population: 0.98 male(s)/female (2001 est.)
Infant mortality rate: 92.89 deaths/1,000 live births (2001 est.)
Life expectancy at birth:
total population: 53.48 years
male: 51.58 years
female: 55.44 years (2001 est.)
Total fertility rate: 5.12 children born/woman (2001 est.)
HIV/AIDS - adult prevalence rate: 0.05% (1999 est.)
HIV/AIDS - people living with HIV/AIDS: 1,400 (1999 est.)
HIV/AIDS - deaths: 130 (1999 est.)
Nationality:
noun: Lao(s) or Laotian(s)
adjective: Lao or Laotian
Ethnic groups: Lao Loum (lowland) 68%, Lao Theung (upland) 22%, Lao Soung (highland) including the Hmong ("Meo") and the Yao (Mien) 9%, ethnic Vietnamese/Chinese 1%
Religions: Buddhist 60%, animist and other 40%
Languages: Lao (official), French, English, and various ethnic languages

Literacy:
definition: age 15 and over can read and write
total population: 57%
male: 70%
female: 44% (1999 est.)

Government

Country name:
conventional long form: Lao People's Democratic Republic
conventional short form: Laos
local long form: Sathalanalat Paxathipatai Paxaxon Lao
local short form: none
Government type: Communist state
Capital: Vientiane
Administrative divisions: 16 provinces (khoueng, singular and plural), 1 municipality* (kampheng nakhon, singular and plural), and 1 special zone** (khetphiset, singular and plural); Attapu, Bokeo, Bolikhamxai, Champasak, Houaphan, Khammouan, Louangnamtha, Louangphabang, Oudomxai, Phongsali, Salavan, Savannakhet, Viangchan*, Viangchan, Xaignabouli, Xaisomboun**, Xekong, Xiangkhoang
Independence: 19 July 1949 (from France)
National holiday: Republic Day, 2 December (1975)
Constitution: promulgated 14 August 1991
Legal system: based on traditional customs, French legal norms and procedures, and Socialist practice
Suffrage: 18 years of age; universal
Executive branch:
chief of state: President Gen. KHAMTAI Siphandon (since 26 February 1998) and Vice President Lt. Gen. CHOUMMALI Saignason (since NA March 2001)
head of government: Prime Minister BOUNGNANG Volachit (since NA March 2001); Deputy Prime Ministers THONGLOUN Sisolit (since NA March 2001), SOMSAVAT Lengsavat (since 26 February 1998)
cabinet: Council of Ministers appointed by the president, approved by the National Assembly
elections: president elected by the National Assembly for a five-year term; election last held 21 December 1997 (next to be held NA 2002); prime minister appointed by the president with the approval of the National Assembly for a five-year term
election results: KHAMTAI Siphandon elected president; percent of National Assembly vote - NA%
Legislative branch: unicameral National Assembly (99 seats; members elected by popular vote to serve five-year terms; note - by presidential decree, on 27 October 1997, the number of seats increased from 85 to 99)
elections: last held 21 December 1997 (next to be held NA 2002)
election results: percent of vote by party - NA%; seats by party - LPRP or LPRP-approved (independent, non-party members) 99
Judicial branch: People's Supreme Court (the president of the People's Supreme Court is elected by the National Assembly on the recommendation of the National Assembly Standing Committee; the vice president of the People's Supreme Court and the judges are appointed by the National Assembly Standing Committee)
Political parties and leaders: Lao People's Revolutionary Party or LPRP [KHAMTAI Siphandon, party president]; other parties proscribed
Political pressure groups and leaders: noncommunist political groups proscribed; most opposition leaders fled the country in 1975
International organization participation: ACCT, ARF, AsDB, ASEAN, CP, ESCAP, FAO, G-77, IBRD, ICAO, ICRM, IDA, IFAD, IFC, IFRCS, ILO, IMF, Intelsat (nonsignatory user), Interpol, IOC, ITU, NAM, OPCW, PCA, UN, UNCTAD, UNESCO, UNIDO, UPU, WFTU, WHO, WIPO, WMO, WToO, WTrO (observer)
Diplomatic representation in the US:
chief of mission: Ambassador VANG Rattanavong
chancery: 2222 S Street NW, Washington, DC 20008
telephone: [1] (202) 332-6416
FAX: [1] (202) 332-4923
Diplomatic representation from the US:
chief of mission: Ambassador (vacant); Charge d'Affairs Karen Brevard STEWART
embassy: 19 Rue Bartholonie, B. P. 114, Vientiane
mailing address: American Embassy, Box V, APO AP 96546
telephone: [856] (21) 212581, 212582, 212585
FAX: [856] (21) 212584
Flag description: three horizontal bands of red (top), blue (double width), and red with a large white disk centered in the blue band

Economy

Economy - overview: The government of Laos - one of the few remaining official communist states - began decentralizing control and encouraging private enterprise in 1986. The results, starting from an extremely low base, were striking - growth averaged 7% during 1988-97. Reform efforts subsequently slowed, and GDP growth dropped an average of 3 percentage points. Because Laos depends heavily on its trade with Thailand, it was damaged by the regional financial crisis beginning in 1997. Government mismanagement deepened the crisis, and from June 1997 to June 1999 the Lao kip lost 87% of its value. Laos' foreign exchange problems peaked in September 1999 when the kip fell from 3,500 kip to the dollar to 9,000 kip to the dollar in a matter of weeks. Now that the currency has stabilized, however, the government seems content to let the current situation persist, despite limited government revenue and foreign exchange reserves. A landlocked country with a primitive infrastructure, Laos has no railroads, a rudimentary road system, and limited external and internal telecommunications. Electricity is available in only a few urban areas. Subsistence agriculture accounts for half of GDP and provides 80% of total employment. For the foreseeable future the economy will continue to depend on aid from the IMF and other international

Laos (continued)

sources; Japan is currently the largest bilateral aid donor; aid from the former USSR/Eastern Europe has been cut sharply.
GDP: purchasing power parity - $9 billion (2000 est.)
GDP - real growth rate: 4% (2000 est.)
GDP - per capita: purchasing power parity - $1,700 (2000 est.)
GDP - composition by sector:
agriculture: 51%
industry: 22%
services: 27% (1999 est.)
Population below poverty line: 46.1% (1993 est.)
Household income or consumption by percentage share:
lowest 10%: 4.2%
highest 10%: 26.4% (1992)
Inflation rate (consumer prices): 33% (2000 est.)
Labor force: 1 million - 1.5 million
Labor force - by occupation: agriculture 80% (1997 est.)
Unemployment rate: 5.7% (1997 est.)
Budget:
revenues: $211 million
expenditures: $462 million, including capital expenditures of $NA (FY98/99 est.)
Industries: tin and gypsum mining, timber, electric power, agricultural processing, construction, garments, tourism
Industrial production growth rate: 7.5% (1999 est.)
Electricity - production: 792 million kWh (1999)
Electricity - production by source:
fossil fuel: 2.78%
hydro: 97.22%
nuclear: 0%
other: 0% (1999)
Electricity - consumption: 173.6 million kWh (1999)
Electricity - exports: 705 million kWh (1999)
Electricity - imports: 142 million kWh (1999)
Agriculture - products: sweet potatoes, vegetables, corn, coffee, sugarcane, tobacco, cotton; tea, peanuts, rice; water buffalo, pigs, cattle, poultry
Exports: $323 million (f.o.b., 2000 est.)
Exports - commodities: wood products, garments, electricity, coffee, tin
Exports - partners: Vietnam, Thailand, Germany, France, Belgium
Imports: $540 million (f.o.b., 2000 est.)
Imports - commodities: machinery and equipment, vehicles, fuel
Imports - partners: Thailand, Japan, Vietnam, China, Singapore, Hong Kong
Debt - external: $2.46 billion (1998 est.)
Economic aid - recipient: $345 million (1999 est.)
Currency: kip (LAK)
Currency code: LAK
Exchange rates: kips per US dollar - 7,578.00 (December 2000), 7,102.03 (1999), 3,298.33 (1998), 1,259.98 (1997), 921.02 (1996)
Fiscal year: 1 October - 30 September

Communications

Telephones - main lines in use: 25,000 (1997)
Telephones - mobile cellular: 4,915 (1997)
Telephone system:
general assessment: service to general public is poor but improving, with over 20,000 telephones currently in service and an additional 48,000 expected by 2001; the government relies on a radiotelephone network to communicate with remote areas
domestic: radiotelephone communications
international: satellite earth station - 1 Intersputnik (Indian Ocean region)
Radio broadcast stations: AM 12, FM 1, shortwave 4 (1998)
Radios: 730,000 (1997)
Television broadcast stations: 4 (1999)
Televisions: 52,000 (1997)
Internet country code: .la
Internet Service Providers (ISPs): 1 (2000)
Internet users: 2,000 (2000)

Transportation

Railways: 0 km
Highways:
total: 14,000 km
paved: 3,360 km
unpaved: 10,640 km (1991)
Waterways: 4,587 km approximately
note: primarily Mekong and tributaries; 2,897 additional km are intermittently navigable by craft drawing less than 0.5 m
Pipelines: petroleum products 136 km
Ports and harbors: none
Merchant marine:
total: 1 ship (1,000 GRT or over) totaling 2,370 GRT/ 3,000 DWT
ships by type: cargo 1 (2000 est.)
Airports: 51 (2000 est.)
Airports - with paved runways:
total: 8
2,438 to 3,047 m: 1
1,524 to 2,437 m: 5
914 to 1,523 m: 2 (2000 est.)
Airports - with unpaved runways:
total: 43
1,524 to 2,437 m: 1
914 to 1,523 m: 17
under 914 m: 25 (2000 est.)

Military

Military branches: Lao People's Army (LPA; includes riverine element), Air Force, National Police Department
Military manpower - military age: 18 years of age
Military manpower - availability:
males age 15-49: 1,319,537 (2001 est.)
Military manpower - fit for military service:
males age 15-49: 710,627 (2001 est.)
Military manpower - reaching military age annually:
males: 64,437 (2001 est.)
Military expenditures - dollar figure: $55 million (FY98)
Military expenditures - percent of GDP: 4.2% (FY96/97)

Transnational Issues

Disputes - international: parts of the border with Thailand are indefinite
Illicit drugs: world's third-largest illicit opium producer (estimated cultivation in 1999 - 21,800 hectares, a 16% decrease over 1998; estimated potential production in 1999 - 140 metric tons, about the same as in 1998); potential heroin producer; transshipment point for heroin and methamphetamine produced in Burma; illicit producer of cannabis

Latvia

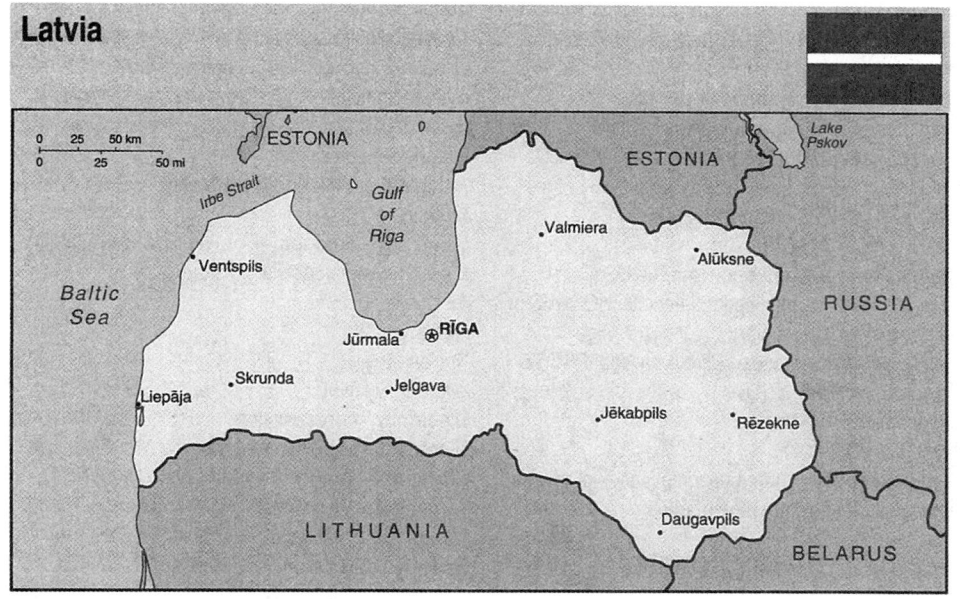

Introduction

Background: After a brief period of independence between the two World Wars, Latvia was annexed by the USSR in 1940. It reestablished its independence in 1991 following the breakup of the Soviet Union. Although the last Russian troops left in 1994, the status of the Russian minority (some 30% of the population) remains of concern to Moscow. Latvia continues to revamp its economy for eventual integration into various Western European political and economic institutions.

Geography

Location: Eastern Europe, bordering the Baltic Sea, between Estonia and Lithuania
Geographic coordinates: 57 00 N, 25 00 E
Map references: Europe
Area:
total: 64,589 sq km
land: 64,589 sq km
water: 0 sq km
Area - comparative: slightly larger than West Virginia
Land boundaries:
total: 1,150 km
border countries: Belarus 141 km, Estonia 339 km, Lithuania 453 km, Russia 217 km
Coastline: 531 km
Maritime claims:
continental shelf: 200-m depth or to the depth of exploitation
exclusive economic zone: 200 NM
territorial sea: 12 NM
Climate: maritime; wet, moderate winters
Terrain: low plain
Elevation extremes:
lowest point: Baltic Sea 0 m
highest point: Gaizinkalns 312 m
Natural resources: minimal; amber, peat, limestone, dolomite, hydropower, arable land
Land use:
arable land: 27%
permanent crops: 0%
permanent pastures: 13%
forests and woodland: 46%
other: 14% (1993 est.)
Irrigated land: 160 sq km (1993 est.)
Natural hazards: NA
Environment - current issues: air and water pollution because of a lack of waste conversion equipment; Gulf of Riga and Daugava River heavily polluted; contamination of soil and groundwater with chemicals and petroleum products at military bases
Environment - international agreements:
party to: Air Pollution, Biodiversity, Climate Change, Endangered Species, Hazardous Wastes, Marine Dumping, Ozone Layer Protection, Ship Pollution, Wetlands
signed, but not ratified: Air Pollution-Persistent Organic Pollutants, Climate Change-Kyoto Protocol

People

Population: 2,385,231 (July 2001 est.)
Age structure:
0-14 years: 16.55% (male 201,746; female 193,036)
15-64 years: 68.15% (male 776,509; female 848,908)
65 years and over: 15.3% (male 118,110; female 246,922) (2001 est.)
Population growth rate: -0.81% (2001 est.)
Birth rate: 8.03 births/1,000 population (2001 est.)
Death rate: 14.8 deaths/1,000 population (2001 est.)
Net migration rate: -1.27 migrant(s)/1,000 population (2001 est.)
Sex ratio:
at birth: 1.05 male(s)/female
under 15 years: 1.05 male(s)/female
15-64 years: 0.91 male(s)/female
65 years and over: 0.48 male(s)/female
total population: 0.85 male(s)/female (2001 est.)
Infant mortality rate: 15.34 deaths/1,000 live births (2001 est.)
Life expectancy at birth:
total population: 68.7 years
male: 62.8 years
female: 74.9 years (2001 est.)
Total fertility rate: 1.15 children born/woman (2001 est.)
HIV/AIDS - adult prevalence rate: 0.11% (1999 est.)
HIV/AIDS - people living with HIV/AIDS: 1,250 (1999 est.)
HIV/AIDS - deaths: less than 100 (1999 est.)
Nationality:
noun: Latvian(s)
adjective: Latvian
Ethnic groups: Latvian 56.5%, Russian 30.4%, Byelorussian 4.3%, Ukrainian 2.8%, Polish 2.6%, other 3.4%
Religions: Lutheran, Roman Catholic, Russian Orthodox
Languages: Latvian or Lettish (official), Lithuanian, Russian, other
Literacy:
definition: age 15 and over can read and write
total population: 100%
male: 100%
female: 99% (1989 est.)

Government

Country name:
conventional long form: Republic of Latvia
conventional short form: Latvia
local long form: Latvijas Republika
local short form: Latvija
former: Latvian Soviet Socialist Republic
Government type: parliamentary democracy
Capital: Riga
Administrative divisions: 26 counties (singular - rajons) and 7 municipalities*: Aizkraukles Rajons, Aluksnes Rajons, Balvu Rajons, Bauskas Rajons, Cesu Rajons, Daugavpils*, Daugavpils Rajons, Dobeles Rajons, Gulbenes Rajons, Jekabpils Rajons, Jelgava*, Jelgavas Rajons, Jurmala*, Kraslavas Rajons, Kuldigas Rajons, Leipaja*, Liepajas Rajons, Limbazu Rajons, Ludzas Rajons, Madonas Rajons, Ogres Rajons, Preilu Rajons, Rezekne*, Rezeknes Rajons, Riga*, Rigas Rajons, Saldus Rajons, Talsu Rajons, Tukuma Rajons, Valkas Rajons, Valmieras Rajons, Ventspils*, Ventspils Rajons
Independence: 18 November 1991 (from Soviet Union)
National holiday: Independence Day, 18 November (1918); note - 18 November 1918 is the date of independence from Soviet Russia, 18 November 1991 is the date of independence from the Soviet Union
Constitution: the 1991 Constitutional Law which supplements the 1922 constitution, provides for basic rights and freedoms

Latvia (continued)

Legal system: based on civil law system
Suffrage: 18 years of age; universal for Latvian citizens
Executive branch:
chief of state: President Vaira VIKE-FREIBERGA (since 8 July 1999)
head of government: Prime Minister Andris BERZINS (since 5 May 2000)
cabinet: Council of Ministers nominated by the prime minister and appointed by the Parliament
elections: president elected by Parliament for a four-year term; election last held 17 June 1999 (next to be held by NA June 2003); prime minister appointed by the president
election results: Vaira VIKE-FREIBERGA elected as a compromise candidate in second phase of balloting, second round (after five rounds in first phase failed); percent of parliamentary vote - Vaira VIKE-FREIBERGA 53%, Valdis BIRKAVS 20%, Ingrida UDRE 9%
Legislative branch: unicameral Parliament or Saeima (100 seats; members are elected by direct popular vote to serve four-year terms)
elections: last held 3 October 1998 (next to be held NA October 2002)
election results: percent of vote by party - People's Party 21%, LC 18%, TSP 14%, TB/LNNK 14%, Social Democrats 13%, New Party 7%; seats by party - People's Party 24, LC 21, TB/LNNK 17, TSP 16, Social Democrats 14, New Party 8
Judicial branch: Supreme Court (judges' appointments are confirmed by Parliament)
Political parties and leaders: Anticommunist Union or PA [P. MUCENIEKS]; Christian Democrat Union or LKDS [Talavs JUNDZIS]; Christian People's Party or KTP [Uldis AUGSTKALNS]; Democratic Party "Saimnieks" or DPS [Ziedonis CEVERS, chairman]; For Fatherland and Freedom or TB [Maris GRINBLATS], merged with LNNK; For Human Rights in a United Latvia [Janis JURKANS], a coalition of the People's Harmony Party or TSP, the Latvian Socialist Party or LSP, and the Equal Rights Movement; Green Party or LZP [Olegs BATAREVSKI]; Latvian Liberal Party or LLP [J. DANOSS]; Latvian National Conservative Party or LNNK [Andrejs KRASTINS]; Latvian National Democratic Party or LNDP [A. MALINS]; Latvian Social-Democratic Workers Party (Social Democrats) or LSDWU [Juris BOJARS and Janis ADAMSONS, leaders]; Latvian Unity Party or LVP [Alberis KAULS]; Latvia's Way or LC [Andrei PANTELEJEVS]; New Christian Party [Ainars SLESERS]; New Faction [Ingrida UDRE]; "Our Land" or MZ [M. DAMBEKALNE]; Party of Russian Citizens or LKPP [V. SOROCHIN, V. IVANOV]; People's Party [Andris SKELE]; Political Union of Economists or TPA [Edvins KIDE]
Political pressure groups and leaders: NA
International organization participation: BIS, CBSS, CCC, CE, EAPC, EBRD, ECE, EU (applicant), FAO, IAEA, IBRD, ICAO, ICFTU, ICRM, IDA, IFC, IFRCS, ILO, IMF, IMO, Intelsat (nonsignatory user), Interpol, IOC, IOM, ISO (correspondent), ITU, NSG, OAS (observer), OPCW, OSCE, PFP, UN, UNCTAD, UNESCO, UPU, WEU (associate partner), WHO, WIPO, WMO, WTrO
Diplomatic representation in the US:
chief of mission: Ambassador Aivis RONIS
chancery: 4325 17th Street NW, Washington, DC 20011
telephone: [1] (202) 726-8213, 8214
FAX: [1] (202) 726-6785
Diplomatic representation from the US:
chief of mission: Ambassador James H. HOLMES
embassy: Raina Boulevard 7, LV-1510, Riga
mailing address: American Embassy Riga, PSC 78, Box Riga, APO AE 09723
telephone: [371] 721-0005
FAX: [371] 782-0047
Flag description: three horizontal bands of maroon (top), white (half-width), and maroon

Economy

Economy - overview: In 2000, Latvia's transitional economy recovered from the 1998 Russian financial crisis, largely due to the SKELE government's budget stringency and a gradual reorientation of exports toward EU countries, lessening Latvia's trade dependency on Russia. Latvia officially joined the World Trade Organization in February 1999 - the first Baltic state to join - and was invited at the Helsinki EU Summit in December 1999 to begin accession talks in early 2000. Unemployment fell to 7.8% in 2000, down from 9.6% in 1999, and 9.2% in 1998. Privatization of large state-owned utilities and the shipping industry faced more delays in 2000, and political instability will continue to delay completion of the privatization process over the next year. Latvia projects 6% GDP growth, 2.5%-3.0% inflation, and a 1.7% fiscal deficit in 2001. Preparing for EU membership over the next few years remains a top foreign policy goal.
GDP: purchasing power parity - $17.3 billion (2000 est.)
GDP - real growth rate: 5.5% (2000 est.)
GDP - per capita: purchasing power parity - $7,200 (2000 est.)
GDP - composition by sector:
agriculture: 5%
industry: 33%
services: 62% (1999)
Population below poverty line: NA%
Household income or consumption by percentage share:
lowest 10%: 2.9%
highest 10%: 25.9% (1998)
Inflation rate (consumer prices): 2.7% (2000)
Labor force: 1.4 million (2000 est.)
Labor force - by occupation: agriculture 10%, industry 25%, services 65% (2000 est.)
Unemployment rate: 7.8% (2000 est.)
Budget:
revenues: $1.33 billion
expenditures: $1.27 billion, including capital expenditures of $NA (1998 est.)
Industries: buses, vans, street and railroad cars, synthetic fibers, agricultural machinery, fertilizers, washing machines, radios, electronics, pharmaceuticals, processed foods, textiles; note - dependent on imports for energy, raw materials, and intermediate products
Industrial production growth rate: 6.3% (2000 est.)
Electricity - production: 3.996 billion kWh (1999)
Electricity - production by source:
fossil fuel: 31.78%
hydro: 68.22%
nuclear: 0%
other: 0% (1999)
Electricity - consumption: 4.316 billion kWh (1999)
Electricity - exports: 400 million kWh (1999)
Electricity - imports: 1 billion kWh (1999)
Agriculture - products: grain, sugar beets, potatoes, vegetables; beef, milk, eggs; fish
Exports: $2.1 billion (f.o.b., 2000)
Exports - commodities: wood and wood products, machinery and equipment, metals, textiles, foodstuffs
Exports - partners: Germany 16%, UK 11%, Sweden 11%, Russia 7% (1999)
Imports: $3.2 billion (f.o.b., 2000)
Imports - commodities: machinery and equipment, chemicals, fuels
Imports - partners: Russia 15%, Germany 10%, Finland 9%, Sweden 7% (1999)
Debt - external: $800 million (2000 est.)
Economic aid - recipient: $96.2 million (1995)
Currency: Latvian lat (LVL)
Currency code: LVL
Exchange rates: lati per US dollar - 0.614 (January 2001), 0.607 (2000), 0.585 (1999), 0.590 (1998), 0.581 (1997), 0.551 (1996)
Fiscal year: calendar year

Communications

Telephones - main lines in use: 748,000 (1997)
Telephones - mobile cellular: 77,100 (1997)
Telephone system:
general assessment: inadequate, but is being modernized to provide an international capability independent of the Moscow international switch; more facilities are being installed for individual use
domestic: expansion underway in intercity trunk line connections, rural exchanges, and mobile systems; still many unsatisfied subscriber applications
international: international connections are now available via cable and a satellite earth station at Riga, enabling direct connections for most calls (1998)
Radio broadcast stations: AM 8, FM 56, shortwave 1 (1998)
Radios: 1.76 million (1997)
Television broadcast stations: 44 (plus 31 repeaters) (1995)
Televisions: 1.22 million (1997)
Internet country code: .lv
Internet Service Providers (ISPs): 42 (2000)
Internet users: 234,000 (2000)

Latvia (continued)

Transportation

Railways:
total: 2,412 km
broad gauge: 2,379 km 1.520-m gauge (271 km electrified) (1992)
narrow gauge: 33 km 0.750-m gauge (1994)
Highways:
total: 59,178 km
paved: 22,843 km
unpaved: 36,335 km (1998 est.)
Waterways: 300 km (perennially navigable)
Pipelines: crude oil 750 km; refined products 780 km; natural gas 560 km (1992)
Ports and harbors: Daugavpils, Liepaja, Riga, Ventspils
Merchant marine:
total: 8 ships (1,000 GRT or over) totaling 27,984 GRT/29,978 DWT
ships by type: cargo 2, petroleum tanker 3, refrigerated cargo 3 (2000 est.)
Airports: 25 (2000 est.)
Airports - with paved runways:
total: 13
2,438 to 3,047 m: 7
1,524 to 2,437 m: 1
914 to 1,523 m: 1
under 914 m: 4 (2000 est.)
Airports - with unpaved runways:
total: 12
2,438 to 3,047 m: 1
1,524 to 2,437 m: 2
914 to 1,523 m: 2
under 914 m: 7 (2000 est.)

Military

Military branches: Ground Forces, Navy, Air and Air Defense Forces, Security Forces, Border Guard, Home Guard (Zemessardze)
Military manpower - military age: 18 years of age
Military manpower - availability:
males age 15-49: 590,784 (2001 est.)
Military manpower - fit for military service:
males age 15-49: 463,944 (2001 est.)
Military manpower - reaching military age annually:
males: 19,114 (2001 est.)
Military expenditures - dollar figure: $60 million (FY99)
Military expenditures - percent of GDP: 0.9% (FY99)

Transnational Issues

Disputes - international: draft treaty delimiting the boundary with Russia has not been signed; has not ratified 1998 maritime boundary agreement with Lithuania (primary concern is oil exploration rights)
Illicit drugs: transshipment point for opiates and cannabis from Central and Southwest Asia to Western Europe and Scandinavia and Latin American cocaine and some synthetics from Western Europe to CIS; limited production of illicit amphetamine, ephedrine, and ecstasy for export

Lebanon

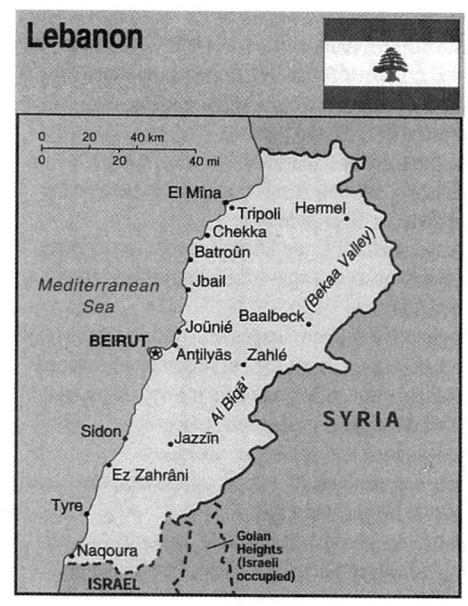

Introduction

Background: Lebanon has made progress toward rebuilding its political institutions and regaining its national sovereignty since 1991 and the end of the devastating 16-year civil war. Under the Ta'if Accord - the blueprint for national reconciliation - the Lebanese have established a more equitable political system, particularly by giving Muslims a greater say in the political process while institutionalizing sectarian divisions in the government. Since the end of the war, the Lebanese have conducted several successful elections, most of the militias have been weakened or disbanded, and the Lebanese Armed Forces (LAF) have extended central government authority over about two-thirds of the country. Hizballah, the radical Shi'a party, retains its weapons. Syria maintains about 25,000 troops in Lebanon based mainly in Beirut, North Lebanon, and the Bekaa Valley. Syria's troop deployment was legitimized by the Arab League during Lebanon's civil war and in the Ta'if Accord. Damascus justifies its continued military presence in Lebanon by citing the continued weakness of the LAF, Beirut's requests, and the failure of the Lebanese Government to implement all of the constitutional reforms in the Ta'if Accord. Israel's withdrawal from its security zone in southern Lebanon in May of 2000, however, has emboldened some Lebanese Christians and Druze to demand that Syria withdraw its forces as well.

Geography

Location: Middle East, bordering the Mediterranean Sea, between Israel and Syria
Geographic coordinates: 33 50 N, 35 50 E
Map references: Middle East
Area:
total: 10,400 sq km
land: 10,230 sq km
water: 170 sq km
Area - comparative: about 0.7 times the size of Connecticut
Land boundaries:
total: 454 km
border countries: Israel 79 km, Syria 375 km
Coastline: 225 km
Maritime claims:
territorial sea: 12 NM
Climate: Mediterranean; mild to cool, wet winters with hot, dry summers; Lebanon mountains experience heavy winter snows
Terrain: narrow coastal plain; Al Biqa' (Bekaa Valley) separates Lebanon and Anti-Lebanon Mountains
Elevation extremes:
lowest point: Mediterranean Sea 0 m
highest point: Qurnat as Sawda' 3,088 m
Natural resources: limestone, iron ore, salt, water-surplus state in a water-deficit region, arable land
Land use:
arable land: 18%
permanent crops: 9%
permanent pastures: 1%
forests and woodland: 8%
other: 64% (1996 est.)
Irrigated land: 860 sq km (1993 est.)
Natural hazards: dust storms, sandstorms
Environment - current issues: deforestation; soil erosion; desertification; air pollution in Beirut from vehicular traffic and the burning of industrial wastes; pollution of coastal waters from raw sewage and oil spills
Environment - international agreements:
party to: Biodiversity, Climate Change, Desertification, Hazardous Wastes, Law of the Sea, Marine Dumping, Nuclear Test Ban, Ozone Layer Protection, Ship Pollution, Wetlands
signed, but not ratified: Environmental Modification, Marine Dumping, Marine Life Conservation
Geography - note: Nahr al Litani only major river in Near East not crossing an international boundary; rugged terrain historically helped isolate, protect, and develop numerous factional groups based on religion, clan, and ethnicity

People

Population: 3,627,774 (July 2001 est.)
Age structure:
0-14 years: 27.57% (male 509,975; female 490,031)
15-64 years: 65.72% (male 1,136,995; female 1,247,184)
65 years and over: 6.71% (male 110,964; female 132,625) (2001 est.)
Population growth rate: 1.38% (2001 est.)
Birth rate: 20.16 births/1,000 population (2001 est.)
Death rate: 6.39 deaths/1,000 population (2001 est.)
Net migration rate: 0 migrant(s)/1,000 population (2001 est.)
Sex ratio:
at birth: 1.05 male(s)/female
under 15 years: 1.04 male(s)/female
15-64 years: 0.91 male(s)/female
65 years and over: 0.84 male(s)/female
total population: 0.94 male(s)/female (2001 est.)

Lebanon (continued)

Infant mortality rate: 28.35 deaths/1,000 live births (2001 est.)
Life expectancy at birth:
total population: 71.52 years
male: 69.13 years
female: 74.03 years (2001 est.)
Total fertility rate: 2.05 children born/woman (2001 est.)
HIV/AIDS - adult prevalence rate: 0.09% (1999 est.)
HIV/AIDS - people living with HIV/AIDS: NA
HIV/AIDS - deaths: NA
Nationality:
noun: Lebanese (singular and plural)
adjective: Lebanese
Ethnic groups: Arab 95%, Armenian 4%, other 1%
Religions: Muslim 70% (including Shi'a, Sunni, Druze, Isma'ilite, Alawite or Nusayri), Christian 30% (including Orthodox Christian, Catholic, Protestant), Jewish NEGL%
Languages: Arabic (official), French, English, Armenian
Literacy:
definition: age 15 and over can read and write
total population: 86.4%
male: 90.8%
female: 82.2% (1997 est.)

Government

Country name:
conventional long form: Lebanese Republic
conventional short form: Lebanon
local long form: Al Jumhuriyah al Lubnaniyah
local short form: Lubnan
Government type: republic
Capital: Beirut
Administrative divisions: 5 governorates (mohafazat, singular - mohafazah); Beyrouth, Ech Chimal, Ej Jnoub, El Bekaa, Jabal Loubnane
Independence: 22 November 1943 (from League of Nations mandate under French administration)
National holiday: Independence Day, 22 November (1943)
Constitution: 23 May 1926, amended a number of times, most recently Charter of Lebanese National Reconciliation (Taif Accord) of October 1989
Legal system: mixture of Ottoman law, canon law, Napoleonic code, and civil law; no judicial review of legislative acts; has not accepted compulsory ICJ jurisdiction
Suffrage: 21 years of age; compulsory for all males; authorized for women at age 21 with elementary education
Executive branch:
chief of state: President Emile LAHUD (since 24 November 1998)
head of government: Prime Minister Rafiq HARIRI (since 23 October 2000); Deputy Prime Minister Issam FARES (since 23 October 2000)
cabinet: Cabinet chosen by the prime minister in consultation with the president and members of the National Assembly; the current Cabinet was formed in 1998
elections: president elected by the National Assembly for a six-year term; election last held 15 October 1998 (next to be held NA 2004); prime minister and deputy prime minister appointed by the president in consultation with the National Assembly; by custom, the president is a Maronite Christian, the prime minister is a Sunni Muslim, and the speaker of the legislature is a Shi'a Muslim
election results: Emile LAHUD elected president; National Assembly vote - 118 votes in favor, 0 against, 10 abstentions
Legislative branch: unicameral National Assembly or Majlis Alnuwab (Arabic) or Assemblee Nationale (French) (128 seats; members elected by popular vote on the basis of sectarian proportional representation to serve four-year terms)
elections: last held 27 August and 3 September 2000 (next to be held NA 2004)
election results: percent of vote by party - Muslim 57% (of which Sunni 25%, Sh'ite 25%, Druze 6%, Alawite less than 1%), Christian 43% (of which Maronite 23%); seats by party - Muslim 64 (of which Sunni 27, Sh'ite 27, Druze 8, Alawite 2), Christian 64 (of which Maronite 34)
Judicial branch: four Courts of Cassation (three courts for civil and commercial cases and one court for criminal cases); Constitutional Council (called for in Ta'if Accord - rules on constitutionality of laws); Supreme Council (hears charges against the president and prime minister as needed)
Political parties and leaders: political party activity is organized along largely sectarian lines; numerous political groupings exist, consisting of individual political figures and followers motivated by religious, clan, and economic considerations
Political pressure groups and leaders: NA
International organization participation: ABEDA, ACCT, AFESD, AL, AMF, CCC, ESCWA, FAO, G-24, G-77, IAEA, IBRD, ICAO, ICC, ICFTU, ICRM, IDA, IDB, IFAD, IFC, IFRCS, ILO, IMF, IMO, Inmarsat, Intelsat, Interpol, IOC, ISO (correspondent), ITU, NAM, OAS (observer), OIC, PCA, UN, UNCTAD, UNESCO, UNHCR, UNIDO, UNRWA, UPU, WFTU, WHO, WIPO, WMO, WToO, WTrO (observer)
Diplomatic representation in the US:
chief of mission: Ambassador Dr. Farid ABBOUD
chancery: 2560 28th Street NW, Washington, DC 20008
telephone: [1] (202) 939-6300
FAX: [1] (202) 939-6324
consulate(s) general: Detroit, New York, and Los Angeles
Diplomatic representation from the US:
chief of mission: Ambassador David M. SATTERFIELD
embassy: Antelias, Beirut
mailing address: P. O. Box 70-840, Antelias, Beirut; PSC 815, Box 2, FPO AE 09836-0002
telephone: [961] (4) 543600, 543600
FAX: [961] (4) 544136
Flag description: three horizontal bands of red (top), white (double width), and red with a green and brown cedar tree centered in the white band

Economy

Economy - overview: The 1975-91 civil war seriously damaged Lebanon's economic infrastructure, cut national output by half, and all but ended Lebanon's position as a Middle Eastern entrepot and banking hub. Peace enabled the central government to restore control in Beirut, begin collecting taxes, and regain access to key port and government facilities. Economic recovery was helped by a financially sound banking system and resilient small- and medium-scale manufacturers. Family remittances, banking services, manufactured and farm exports, and international aid provided the main sources of foreign exchange. Lebanon's economy has made impressive gains since the launch in 1993 of "Horizon 2000," the government's $20 billion reconstruction program. Real GDP grew 8% in 1994, 7% in 1995, 4% per year in 1996 and 1997 but slowed to 2% in 1998, -1% in 1999, and 1% in 2000. Annual inflation fell during the course of the 1990s from more than 100% to 0%, and foreign exchange reserves jumped from $1.4 billion to more than $6 billion. Burgeoning capital inflows have generated foreign payments surpluses, and the Lebanese pound has remained very stable for the past two years. Lebanon has rebuilt much of its war-torn physical and financial infrastructure. Solidere, a $2-billion firm, has managed the reconstruction of Beirut's central business district; the stock market reopened in January 1996; and international banks and insurance companies are returning. The government nonetheless faces serious challenges in the economic arena. It has funded reconstruction by tapping foreign exchange reserves and by borrowing heavily - mostly from domestic banks. The newly re-installed HARIRI government's announced policies fail to address the ever-increasing budgetary deficits and national debt burden. The gap between rich and poor has widened in the 1990s, resulting in grassroots dissatisfaction over the skewed distribution of the reconstruction's benefits.
GDP: purchasing power parity - $18.2 billion (2000 est.)
GDP - real growth rate: 1% (2000 est.)
GDP - per capita: purchasing power parity - $5,000 (2000 est.)
GDP - composition by sector:
agriculture: 12%
industry: 27%
services: 61% (1999 est.)
Population below poverty line: 28% (1999 est.)
Household income or consumption by percentage share:
lowest 10%: NA%
highest 10%: NA%
Inflation rate (consumer prices): 0% (2000 est.)
Labor force: 1.3 million (1999 est.)
note: in addition, there are as many as 1 million foreign workers (1997 est.)
Labor force - by occupation: services NA%, industry NA%, agriculture NA%

Lebanon *(continued)*

Unemployment rate: 18% (1997 est.)
Budget:
revenues: $3.31 billion
expenditures: $5.55 billion, including capital expenditures of $NA (2000 est.)
Industries: banking; food processing; jewelry; cement; textiles; mineral and chemical products; wood and furniture products; oil refining; metal fabricating
Industrial production growth rate: NA%
Electricity - production: 7.748 billion kWh (1999)
Electricity - production by source:
fossil fuel: 91.29%
hydro: 8.71%
nuclear: 0%
other: 0% (1999)
Electricity - consumption: 7.86 billion kWh (1999)
Electricity - exports: 0 kWh (1999)
Electricity - imports: 654 million kWh (1999)
Agriculture - products: citrus, grapes, tomatoes, apples, vegetables, potatoes, olives, tobacco; sheep, goats
Exports: $700 million (f.o.b., 2000 est.)
Exports - commodities: foodstuffs and tobacco, textiles, chemicals, precious stones, metal and metal products, electrical equipment and products, jewelry, paper and paper products
Exports - partners: UAE 9%, Saudi Arabia 8%, Syria 6%, US 6%, Kuwait 6%, France 5%, Belgium 5%, Jordan 4% (1999)
Imports: $6.2 billion (f.o.b., 2000 est.)
Imports - commodities: foodstuffs, machinery and transport equipment, consumer goods, chemicals, textiles, metals, fuels, agricultural foods
Imports - partners: Italy 13%, France 11%, Germany 8%, US 7%, Switzerland 6%, Japan, UK, Syria (1999)
Debt - external: $9.6 billion (2000 est.)
Economic aid - recipient: $3.5 billion (pledges 1997-2001)
Currency: Lebanese pound (LBP)
Currency code: LBP
Exchange rates: Lebanese pounds per US dollar - 1,507.5 (January 2001), 1,507.5 (2000), 1,507.8 (1999), 1,516.1 (1998), 1,539.5 (1997), 1,571.4 (1996)
Fiscal year: calendar year

Communications

Telephones - main lines in use: 700,000 (1999)
Telephones - mobile cellular: 580,000 (1999)
Telephone system:
general assessment: telecommunications system severely damaged by civil war; rebuilding well underway
domestic: primarily microwave radio relay and cable
international: satellite earth stations - 2 Intelsat (1 Indian Ocean and 1 Atlantic Ocean) (erratic operations); coaxial cable to Syria; microwave radio relay to Syria but inoperable beyond Syria to Jordan; 3 submarine coaxial cables

Radio broadcast stations: AM 20, FM 22, shortwave 4 (1998)
Radios: 2.85 million (1997)
Television broadcast stations: 15 (plus 5 repeaters) (1995)
Televisions: 1.18 million (1997)
Internet country code: .lb
Internet Service Providers (ISPs): 22 (2000)
Internet users: 227,500 (2000)

Transportation

Railways:
total: 399 km (mostly unusable because of damage in civil war)
standard gauge: 317 km 1.435-m
narrow gauge: 82 km (1999)
Highways:
total: 7,300 km
paved: 6,350 km
unpaved: 950 km (1999 est.)
Waterways: none
Pipelines: crude oil 72 km (none in operation)
Ports and harbors: Antilyas, Batroun, Beirut, Chekka, El Mina, Ez Zahrani, Jbail, Jounie, Naqoura, Sidon, Tripoli, Tyre
Merchant marine:
total: 71 ships (1,000 GRT or over) totaling 379,705 GRT/592,672 DWT
ships by type: bulk 10, cargo 42, chemical tanker 1, combination bulk 1, combination ore/oil 1, container 4, liquefied gas 1, livestock carrier 5, refrigerated cargo 1, roll on/roll off 2, vehicle carrier 3
note: includes some foreign-owned ships registered here as a flag of convenience: Netherlands 1, Syria 1 (2000 est.)
Airports: 8 (2000 est.)
Airports - with paved runways:
total: 5
over 3,047 m: 1
2,438 to 3,047 m: 2
1,524 to 2,437 m: 1
under 914 m: 1 (2000 est.)
Airports - with unpaved runways:
total: 3
914 to 1,523 m: 2
under 914 m: 1 (2000 est.)

Military

Military branches: Lebanese Armed Forces (LAF; includes Army, Navy, and Air Force)
Military manpower - availability:
males age 15-49: 980,412 (2001 est.)
Military manpower - fit for military service:
males age 15-49: 605,332 (2001 est.)
Military expenditures - dollar figure: $343 million (FY99/00)
Military expenditures - percent of GDP: 4.8% (FY99/00)

Transnational Issues

Disputes - international: Syrian troops in northern, central, and eastern Lebanon since October 1976; Lebanese government claims Shab'a Farms area of Israeli-occupied Golan Heights as a part of Lebanon from which Hizballah conducts cross-border attacks
Illicit drugs: inconsequential producer of hashish; a Lebanese/Syrian eradication campaign started in the early 1990s has practically eliminated the opium and cannabis crops

Lesotho

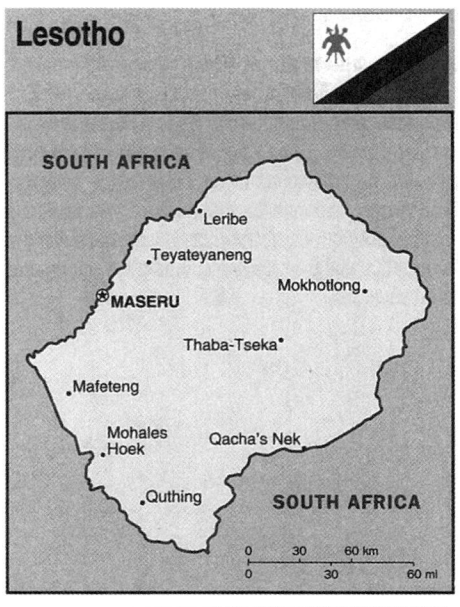

Introduction

Background: Basutoland was renamed the Kingdom of Lesotho upon independence from the UK in 1966. Constitutional government was restored in 1993 after 23 years of military rule.

Geography

Location: Southern Africa, an enclave of South Africa
Geographic coordinates: 29 30 S, 28 30 E
Map references: Africa
Area:
total: 30,355 sq km
land: 30,355 sq km
water: 0 sq km
Area - comparative: slightly smaller than Maryland
Land boundaries:
total: 909 km
border countries: South Africa 909 km
Coastline: 0 km (landlocked)
Maritime claims: none (landlocked)
Climate: temperate; cool to cold, dry winters; hot, wet summers
Terrain: mostly highland with plateaus, hills, and mountains
Elevation extremes:
lowest point: junction of the Orange and Makhaleng Rivers 1,400 m
highest point: Thabana Ntlenyana 3,482 m
Natural resources: water, agricultural and grazing land, some diamonds and other minerals
Land use:
arable land: 11%
permanent crops: 0%
permanent pastures: 66%
forests and woodland: 0%
other: 23% (1993 est.)
Irrigated land: 30 sq km (1993 est.)
Natural hazards: periodic droughts
Environment - current issues: population pressure forcing settlement in marginal areas results in overgrazing, severe soil erosion, and soil exhaustion; desertification; Highlands Water Project controls, stores, and redirects water to South Africa
Environment - international agreements:
party to: Biodiversity, Climate Change, Climate Change-Kyoto Protocol, Desertification, Hazardous Wastes, Marine Dumping, Marine Life Conservation, Ozone Layer Protection, Ship Pollution
signed, but not ratified: Endangered Species, Law of the Sea, Marine Dumping
Geography - note: landlocked; surrounded by South Africa

People

Population: 2,177,062
note: estimates for this country explicitly take into account the effects of excess mortality due to AIDS; this can result in lower life expectancy, higher infant mortality and death rates, lower population and growth rates, and changes in the distribution of population by age and sex than would otherwise be expected (July 2001 est.)
Age structure:
0-14 years: 39.28% (male 430,147; female 424,994)
15-64 years: 56.03% (male 588,440; female 631,404)
65 years and over: 4.69% (male 43,033; female 59,044) (2001 est.)
Population growth rate: 1.49% (2001 est.)
Birth rate: 31.24 births/1,000 population (2001 est.)
Death rate: 15.7 deaths/1,000 population (2001 est.)
Net migration rate: -0.63 migrant(s)/1,000 population (2001 est.)
Sex ratio:
at birth: 1.03 male(s)/female
under 15 years: 1.01 male(s)/female
15-64 years: 0.93 male(s)/female
65 years and over: 0.73 male(s)/female
total population: 0.95 male(s)/female (2001 est.)
Infant mortality rate: 82.77 deaths/1,000 live births (2001 est.)
Life expectancy at birth:
total population: 48.84 years
male: 47.97 years
female: 49.74 years (2001 est.)
Total fertility rate: 4.08 children born/woman (2001 est.)
HIV/AIDS - adult prevalence rate: 23.57% (1999 est.)
HIV/AIDS - people living with HIV/AIDS: 240,000 (1999 est.)
HIV/AIDS - deaths: 16,000 (1999 est.)
Nationality:
noun: Mosotho (singular), Basotho (plural)
adjective: Basotho
Ethnic groups: Sotho 99.7%, Europeans, Asians, and other 0.3%,
Religions: Christian 80%, indigenous beliefs 20%
Languages: Sesotho (southern Sotho), English (official), Zulu, Xhosa
Literacy:
definition: age 15 and over can read and write
total population: 83%
male: 72%
female: 93% (1999 est.)

Government

Country name:
conventional long form: Kingdom of Lesotho
conventional short form: Lesotho
former: Basutoland
Government type: parliamentary constitutional monarchy
Capital: Maseru
Administrative divisions: 10 districts; Berea, Butha-Buthe, Leribe, Mafeteng, Maseru, Mohales Hoek, Mokhotlong, Qacha's Nek, Quthing, Thaba-Tseka
Independence: 4 October 1966 (from UK)
National holiday: Independence Day, 4 October (1966)
Constitution: 2 April 1993
Legal system: based on English common law and Roman-Dutch law; judicial review of legislative acts in High Court and Court of Appeal; has not accepted compulsory ICJ jurisdiction
Suffrage: 18 years of age; universal
Executive branch:
chief of state: King LETSIE III (since 7 February 1996); note - King LETSIE III formerly occupied the throne from November 1990 to February 1995, while his father was in exile
head of government: Prime Minister Pakalitha MOSISILI (since 23 May 1998)
cabinet: Cabinet
elections: none; according to the constitution, the leader of the majority party in the assembly automatically becomes prime minister; the monarch is hereditary, but, under the terms of the constitution which came into effect after the March 1993 election, the monarch is a "living symbol of national unity" with no executive or legislative powers; under traditional law the college of chiefs has the power to determine who is next in the line of succession, who shall serve as regent in the event that the successor is not of mature age, and may even depose the monarch
Legislative branch: bicameral Parliament consists of the Senate (33 members - 22 principal chiefs and 11 other members appointed by the ruling party) and the Assembly (80 seats; members elected by popular vote for five-year terms); note - number of seats in the Assembly rose from 65 to 80 in the May 1998 election; on 28 February 2001, the Senate approved expansion of the Assembly by a further 50 seats in the next election, which may be held as early as January 2002
elections: last held 23 May 1998 (next to be held NA March 2001)
election results: percent of vote by party - LCD 60.7%, BNP 24.5%, other 14.8%; seats by party - LCD 79, BNP 1

Lesotho (continued)

note: results contested; opposition parties claimed the election was fraudulent and staged a coup; Southern African Development Community (SADC) forces intervened in September 1998 and restored order; the Interim Political Authority (IPA) was set up in December 1998 to create a new electoral system and conduct new elections.
Judicial branch: High Court (chief justice appointed by the monarch); Court of Appeal; Magistrate's Court; customary or traditional court
Political parties and leaders: Basotho Congress Party or BCP [Tseliso MAKHAKHE]; Basotho National Party or BNP [Maj. Gen. Justine Metsing LEKHANYA]; Lesotho Congress for Democracy or LCD [Phebe MOTEBANO, chairwoman; Dr. Pakalitha MOSISILI, leader] - the governing party; United Democratic Party or UDP [Charles MOFELI]; Marematlou Freedom Party or MFP and Setlamo Alliance [Vincent MALEBO]; Progressive National Party or PNP [Chief Peete Nkoebe PEETE]; Sefate Democratic Party or SDP [Bofihla NKUEBE]
Political pressure groups and leaders: NA
International organization participation: ACP, AfDB, C, CCC, ECA, FAO, G-77, IBRD, ICAO, ICRM, IDA, IFAD, IFC, IFRCS, ILO, IMF, Intelsat (nonsignatory user), Interpol, IOC, ISO (subscriber), ITU, NAM, OAU, OPCW, SACU, SADC, UN, UNCTAD, UNESCO, UNHCR, UNIDO, UPU, WFTU, WHO, WIPO, WMO, WToO, WTrO
Diplomatic representation in the US:
chief of mission: Ambassador Lebohang Kenneth MOLEKO
chancery: 2511 Massachusetts Avenue NW, Washington, DC 20008
telephone: [1] (202) 797-5533 through 5536
FAX: [1] (202) 234-6815
Diplomatic representation from the US:
chief of mission: Ambassador Katherine H. PETERSON
embassy: 254 Kingsway, Maseru West (Consular Section)
mailing address: P. O. Box 333, Maseru 100, Lesotho
telephone: [266] 312666
FAX: [266] 310116
Flag description: divided diagonally from the lower hoist side corner; the upper half is white, bearing the brown silhouette of a large shield with crossed spear and club; the lower half is a diagonal blue band with a green triangle in the corner

Economy

Economy - overview: Small, landlocked, and mountainous, Lesotho's primary natural resource is water. Its economy is based on subsistence agriculture, livestock, and remittances from miners employed in South Africa. The number of such mineworkers has declined steadily over the past several years. A small manufacturing base depends largely on farm products that support the milling, canning, leather, and jute industries. Agricultural products are exported primarily to South Africa. Proceeds from membership in a common customs union with South Africa form the majority of government revenue. Although drought has decreased agricultural activity over the past few years, completion of a major hydropower facility in January 1998 now permits the sale of water to South Africa, generating royalties for Lesotho. The pace of substantial privatization has increased in recent years. In December 1999, the government embarked on a nine-month IMF staff-monitored program aimed at structural adjustment and stabilization of macroeconomic fundamentals. The government is in the process of applying for a three-year successor program with the IMF under its Poverty Reduction and Growth Facility.
GDP: purchasing power parity - $5.1 billion (2000 est.)
GDP - real growth rate: 2.5% (2000 est.)
GDP - per capita: purchasing power parity - $2,400 (2000 est.)
GDP - composition by sector:
agriculture: 18%
industry: 38%
services: 44% (1999)
Population below poverty line: 49.2% (1999 est.)
Household income or consumption by percentage share:
lowest 10%: 0.9%
highest 10%: 43.4% (1986-87)
Inflation rate (consumer prices): 6% (2000 est.)
Labor force: 700,000 economically active
Labor force - by occupation: 86% of resident population engaged in subsistence agriculture; roughly 35% of the active male wage earners work in South Africa
Unemployment rate: 45% (2000 est.)
Budget:
revenues: $76 million
expenditures: $80 million, including capital expenditures of $15 million (FY99/00 est.)
Industries: food, beverages, textiles, handicrafts; construction; tourism
Industrial production growth rate: 15.5% (1999 est.)
Electricity - production: 0 kWh; note - electricity supplied by South Africa (1999)
Electricity - production by source:
fossil fuel: 0%
hydro: 0%
nuclear: 0%
other: 0% (1999)
Electricity - consumption: 55 million kWh (1999)
Electricity - exports: 0 kWh (1999)
Electricity - imports: 55 million kWh
note: electricity supplied by South Africa (1999)
Agriculture - products: corn, wheat, pulses, sorghum, barley; livestock
Exports: $175 million (f.o.b., 2000 est.)
Exports - commodities: manufactures 75% (clothing, footwear, road vehicles), wool and mohair, food and live animals (1998)
Exports - partners: South African Customs Union 65%, North America 34% (1998)
Imports: $700 million (f.o.b., 2000 est.)
Imports - commodities: food; building materials, vehicles, machinery, medicines, petroleum products (1995)
Imports - partners: South African Customs Union 90%, Asia 7% (1998)
Debt - external: $720 million (2000 est.)
Economic aid - recipient: $123.7 million (1995)
Currency: loti (LSL); South African rand (ZAR)
Currency code: LSL; ZAR
Exchange rates: maloti per US dollar - 7.78307 (January 2001), 6.93983 (2000), 6.10948 (1999), 5.52828 (1998), 4.60796 (1997), 4.29935 (1996); note - the Lesotho loti is at par with the South African rand which is also legal tender; maloti is the plural form of loti
Fiscal year: 1 April - 31 March

Communications

Telephones - main lines in use: 20,000 (1997)
Telephones - mobile cellular: 1,262 (1996)
Telephone system:
general assessment: rudimentary system
domestic: consists of a few landlines, a small microwave radio relay system, and a minor radiotelephone communication system
international: satellite earth station - 1 Intelsat (Atlantic Ocean)
Radio broadcast stations: AM 1, FM 2, shortwave 1 (1998)
Radios: 104,000 (1997)
Television broadcast stations: 1 (2000)
Televisions: 54,000 (1997)
Internet country code: .ls
Internet Service Providers (ISPs): 1 (2000)
Internet users: 1,000 (2000)

Transportation

Railways:
total: 2.6 km; note - owned by, operated by, and included in the statistics of South Africa
narrow gauge: 2.6 km 1.067-m gauge (1995)
Highways:
total: 4,955 km
paved: 887 km
unpaved: 4,068 km (1996)
Waterways: none
Ports and harbors: none
Airports: 29 (2000 est.)
Airports - with paved runways:
total: 4
over 3,047 m: 1
914 to 1,523 m: 1
under 914 m: 2 (2000 est.)
Airports - with unpaved runways:
total: 25
914 to 1,523 m: 4
under 914 m: 21 (2000 est.)

Lesotho (continued)

Military

Military branches: Lesotho Defense Force (LDF; includes Army and Air Wing), Royal Lesotho Mounted Police (RLMP)
Military manpower - availability:
males age 15-49: 515,464 (2001 est.)
Military manpower - fit for military service:
males age 15-49: 277,369 (2001 est.)
Military expenditures - dollar figure: $34 million (1999)
Military expenditures - percent of GDP: NA%
Military - note: The Lesotho Government in 1999 began an open debate on the future structure, size, and role of the armed forces, especially considering the Lesotho Defense Force's (LDF) history of intervening in political affairs.

Transnational Issues

Disputes - international: none

Liberia

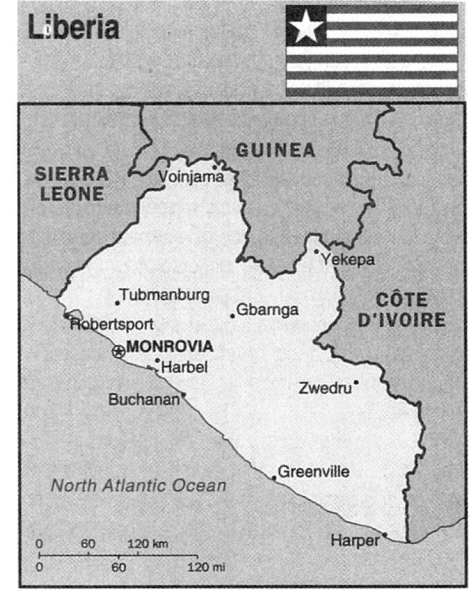

Introduction

Background: Seven years of civil strife were brought to a close in 1996 when free and open presidential and legislative elections were held. President TAYLOR now holds strong executive power with no real political opposition. The years of fighting coupled with the flight of most businesses have disrupted formal economic activity. A still unsettled domestic security situation has slowed the process of rebuilding the social and economic structure of this war-torn country.

Geography

Location: Western Africa, bordering the North Atlantic Ocean, between Cote d'Ivoire and Sierra Leone
Geographic coordinates: 6 30 N, 9 30 W
Map references: Africa
Area:
total: 111,370 sq km
land: 96,320 sq km
water: 15,050 sq km
Area - comparative: slightly larger than Tennessee
Land boundaries:
total: 1,585 km
border countries: Guinea 563 km, Cote d'Ivoire 716 km, Sierra Leone 306 km
Coastline: 579 km
Maritime claims:
territorial sea: 200 NM
Climate: tropical; hot, humid; dry winters with hot days and cool to cold nights; wet, cloudy summers with frequent heavy showers
Terrain: mostly flat to rolling coastal plains rising to rolling plateau and low mountains in northeast
Elevation extremes:
lowest point: Atlantic Ocean 0 m
highest point: Mount Wuteve 1,380 m
Natural resources: iron ore, timber, diamonds, gold, hydropower
Land use:
arable land: 1%
permanent crops: 3%
permanent pastures: 59%
forests and woodland: 18%
other: 19% (1993 est.)
Irrigated land: 20 sq km (1993 est.)
Natural hazards: dust-laden harmattan winds blow from the Sahara (December to March)
Environment - current issues: tropical rain forest subject to deforestation; soil erosion; loss of biodiversity; pollution of coastal waters from oil residue and raw sewage
Environment - international agreements:
party to: Biodiversity, Desertification, Endangered Species, Marine Dumping, Nuclear Test Ban, Ozone Layer Protection, Ship Pollution, Tropical Timber 83, Tropical Timber 94
signed, but not ratified: Climate Change, Environmental Modification, Law of the Sea, Marine Dumping, Marine Life Conservation

People

Population: 3,225,837 (July 2001 est.)
Age structure:
0-14 years: 43.21% (male 698,178; female 695,599)
15-64 years: 53.34% (male 840,103; female 880,403)
65 years and over: 3.45% (male 56,073; female 55,481) (2001 est.)
Population growth rate: 1.92% (2001 est.)
Birth rate: 46.55 births/1,000 population (2001 est.)
Death rate: 16.36 deaths/1,000 population (2001 est.)
Net migration rate: -11 migrant(s)/1,000 population (2001 est.)
note: by the end of 1999, all Liberian refugees, who had fled the domestic strife, were assumed to have returned
Sex ratio:
at birth: 1.03 male(s)/female
under 15 years: 1 male(s)/female
15-64 years: 0.95 male(s)/female
65 years and over: 1.01 male(s)/female
total population: 0.98 male(s)/female (2001 est.)
Infant mortality rate: 132.42 deaths/1,000 live births (2001 est.)
Life expectancy at birth:
total population: 51.41 years
male: 49.96 years
female: 52.91 years (2001 est.)
Total fertility rate: 6.36 children born/woman (2001 est.)
HIV/AIDS - adult prevalence rate: 2.8% (1999 est.)
HIV/AIDS - people living with HIV/AIDS: 39,000 (1999 est.)
HIV/AIDS - deaths: 4,500 (1999 est.)
Nationality:
noun: Liberian(s)
adjective: Liberian
Ethnic groups: indigenous African tribes 95% (including Kpelle, Bassa, Gio, Kru, Grebo, Mano, Krahn, Gola, Gbandi, Loma, Kissi, Vai, and Bella),

Liberia (continued)

Americo-Liberians 2.5% (descendants of immigrants from the US who had been slaves), Congo People 2.5% (descendants of immigrants from the Caribbean who had been slaves)
Religions: indigenous beliefs 40%, Christian 40%, Muslim 20%
Languages: English 20% (official), some 20 ethnic group languages, of which a few can be written and are used in correspondence
Literacy:
definition: age 15 and over can read and write
total population: 38.3%
male: 53.9%
female: 22.4% (1995 est.)
note: these figures are increasing because of the improving school system

Government

Country name:
conventional long form: Republic of Liberia
conventional short form: Liberia
Government type: republic
Capital: Monrovia
Administrative divisions: 13 counties; Bomi, Bong, Grand Bassa, Grand Cape Mount, Grand Gedeh, Grand Kru, Lofa, Margibi, Maryland, Montserrado, Nimba, River Cess, Sinoe
Independence: 26 July 1847
National holiday: Independence Day, 26 July (1847)
Constitution: 6 January 1986
Legal system: dual system of statutory law based on Anglo-American common law for the modern sector and customary law based on unwritten tribal practices for indigenous sector
Suffrage: 18 years of age; universal
Executive branch:
chief of state: President Charles Ghankay TAYLOR (since 2 August 1997); note - the president is both the chief of state and head of government
head of government: President Charles Ghankay TAYLOR (since 2 August 1997); note - the president is both the chief of state and head of government
cabinet: Cabinet appointed by the president and confirmed by the Senate
elections: president elected by popular vote for a six-year term (renewable); election last held 19 July 1997 (next to be held NA July 2003)
election results: Charles Ghankay TAYLOR elected president; percent of vote - Charles Ghankay TAYLOR (NPP) 75.3%, Ellen Johnson SIRLEAF (UP) 9.6%, Alhaji KROMAH (ALCOP) 4%, other 11.1%
Legislative branch: bicameral National Assembly consists of the Senate (26 seats; members elected by popular vote to serve nine-year terms) and the House of Representatives (64 seats; members elected by popular vote to serve six-year terms)
elections: Senate - last held 19 July 1997 (next to be held in NA 2006); House of Representatives - last held 19 July 1997 (next to be held in NA 2003)
election results: Senate - percent of vote by party - NA%; seats by party - NPP 21, UP 3, ALCOP 2; House of Representatives - percent of vote by party - NA%; seats by party - NPP 49, UP 7, ALCOP 3, Alliance of Political Parties 2, UPP 2, LPP 1; note - the Alliance of Political Parties was a coalition of the LAP and the Liberia Unification Party or LUP
Judicial branch: Supreme Court
Political parties and leaders: All Liberia Coalition Party or ALCOP [Lusinee KAMARA]; Liberian Action Party or LAP [Cletus WOTORSON]; Liberian National Union or LINU [Henry MONIBA, chairman]; Liberian People's Party or LPP [Togba-Nah TIPOTEH, chairman]; National Democratic Party of Liberia or NDPL [Isaac DAKINAH]; National Patriotic Party or NPP [Charles Ghankay TAYLOR] - governing party; People's Progressive Party or PPP [Chea CHEAPOO, chairman]; Reformation Alliance Party or RAP [Henry Boimah FAHNBULLEH, chairman]; True Whig Party or TWP [Rudolph SHERMAN, chairman]; United People's Party or UPP [Gabriel Baccus MATTHEWS, chairman]; Unity Party or UP [Charles Clarke]
Political pressure groups and leaders: NA
International organization participation: ACP, AfDB, CCC, ECA, ECOWAS, FAO, G-77, IAEA, IBRD, ICAO, ICFTU, ICRM, IDA, IFAD, IFC, IFRCS, ILO, IMF, IMO, Inmarsat, Intelsat (nonsignatory user), Interpol, IOC, IOM, ITU, NAM, OAU, OPCW, UN, UNCTAD, UNESCO, UNIDO, UPU, WCL, WFTU, WHO, WIPO, WMO
Diplomatic representation in the US:
chief of mission: Ambassador William BULL
chancery: 5201 16th Street NW, Washington, DC 20011
telephone: [1] (202) 723-0437
FAX: [1] (202) 723-0436
consulate(s) general: New York
Diplomatic representation from the US:
chief of mission: Ambassador Bismarck MYRICK
embassy: 111 United Nations Drive, P. O. Box 10-0098, Mamba Point, Monrovia
mailing address: use embassy street address
telephone: [231] 226-370 through 226-380
FAX: [231] 226-148
Flag description: 11 equal horizontal stripes of red (top and bottom) alternating with white; there is a white five-pointed star on a blue square in the upper hoist-side corner; the design was based on the US flag

Economy

Economy - overview: A civil war in 1989-96 destroyed much of Liberia's economy, especially the infrastructure in and around Monrovia. Many businessmen fled the country, taking capital and expertise with them. Some returned during 1997. Many will not return. Richly endowed with water, mineral resources, forests, and a climate favorable to agriculture, Liberia had been a producer and exporter of basic products, while local manufacturing, mainly foreign owned, had been small in scope. The democratically elected government, installed in August 1997, inherited massive international debts and currently relies on revenues from its maritime registry to provide the bulk of its foreign exchange earnings. The restoration of the infrastructure and the raising of incomes in this ravaged economy depend on the implementation of sound macro- and micro-economic policies of the new government, including the encouragement of foreign investment. Recent growth has been from a low base, and continued growth will require major policy successes.
GDP: purchasing power parity - $3.35 billion (2000 est.)
GDP - real growth rate: 15% (2000 est.)
GDP - per capita: purchasing power parity - $1,100 (2000 est.)
GDP - composition by sector:
agriculture: 60%
industry: 10%
services: 30% (2000 est.)
Population below poverty line: 80%
Household income or consumption by percentage share:
lowest 10%: NA%
highest 10%: NA%
Inflation rate (consumer prices): 5% (2000 est.)
Labor force - by occupation: agriculture 70%, industry 8%, services 22% (1999 est.)
Unemployment rate: 70%
Budget:
revenues: $NA
expenditures: $NA, including capital expenditures of $NA
Industries: rubber processing, palm oil processing, diamonds
Industrial production growth rate: NA
Electricity - production: 432 million kWh (1999)
Electricity - production by source:
fossil fuel: 100%
hydro: 0%
nuclear: 0%
other: 0% (1999)
Electricity - consumption: 401.8 million kWh (1999)
Electricity - exports: 0 kWh (1999)
Electricity - imports: 0 kWh (1999)
Agriculture - products: rubber, coffee, cocoa, rice, cassava (tapioca), palm oil, sugarcane, bananas; sheep, goats; timber
Exports: $55 million (f.o.b., 2000 est.)
Exports - commodities: diamonds, iron ore, rubber, timber, coffee, cocoa
Exports - partners: Belgium 53%, Switzerland 9%, US 6%, France 4% (1999)
Imports: $170 million (f.o.b., 2000 est.)
Imports - commodities: fuels, chemicals, machinery, transportation equipment, manufactured goods; rice and other foodstuffs
Imports - partners: South Korea 30%, Italy 24%, Japan 15%, Germany 9% (1999)
Debt - external: $3 billion (1999 est.)
Economic aid - recipient: $200 million pledged (1998)
Currency: Liberian dollar (LRD)
Currency code: LRD

Liberia (continued)

Exchange rates: Liberian dollars per US dollar - 39.8100 (December 2000), 41.0483 (2000), 41.9025 (1999), 41.5075 (1998), 1.0000 (officially fixed rate 1940-97); market exchange rate: Liberian dollars per US dollar - 40 (December 1998), 50 (October 1995)
note: until December 1997, rates were based on a fixed relationship with the US dollar; beginning in January 1998, rates are market determined
Fiscal year: calendar year

Communications

Telephones - main lines in use: 6,000 (1997)
Telephones - mobile cellular: 0 (1995)
Telephone system:
general assessment: telephone and telegraph service via microwave radio relay network; main center is Monrovia
domestic: NA
international: satellite earth station - 1 Intelsat (Atlantic Ocean)
Radio broadcast stations: AM 0, FM 6, shortwave 4 (1999)
Radios: 790,000 (1997)
Television broadcast stations: 2 (plus four low-power repeaters) (2000)
Televisions: 70,000 (1997)
Internet country code: .lr
Internet Service Providers (ISPs): 1 (2000)
Internet users: 300 (2000)

Transportation

Railways:
total: 490 km (328 km single track); note - three rail systems owned and operated by foreign steel and financial interests in conjunction with the Liberian Government; one of these, the Lamco Railroad, closed in 1989 after iron ore production ceased; the other two were shut down by the civil war; large sections of the rail lines have been dismantled; approximately 60 km of railroad track was exported for scrap
standard gauge: 345 km 1.435-m gauge
narrow gauge: 145 km 1.067-m gauge
Highways:
total: 10,600 km
paved: 657 km
unpaved: 9,943 km
note: (there is major deterioration on all highways due to heavy rains and lack of maintenance) (1996 est.)
Waterways: none
Ports and harbors: Buchanan, Greenville, Harper, Monrovia
Merchant marine:
total: 1,478 ships (1,000 GRT or over) totaling 49,456,361 GRT/76,620,648 DWT
ships by type: barge carrier 3, bulk 324, cargo 97, chemical tanker 163, combination bulk 20, combination ore/oil 38, container 245, liquefied gas 97, multi-functional large-load carrier 4, passenger 24, petroleum tanker 310, refrigerated cargo 74, roll on/roll off 19, short-sea passenger 3, specialized tanker 12, vehicle carrier 45

note: includes some foreign-owned ships registered here as a flag of convenience: Argentina 8, Australia 1, Ashmore and Cartier Islands 1, Austria 5, Bermuda 5, Belgium 5, Burma 1, Brazil 8, Canada 1, China 28, Chile 7, Costa Rica 8, Cyprus 27, Denmark 4, Ecuador 1, Germany 117, Greece 83, Hong Kong 54, Croatia 9, Indonesia 2, India 8, Israel 1, Italy 8, Japan 85, South Korea 8, Latvia 15, Monaco 28, Mexico 6, Malaysia 1, Nigeria 1, Netherlands 7, Norway 86, Netherlands Antilles 1, NZ 1, Poland 2, Portugal 2, Philippines 1, Russia 22, Saudi Arabia 20, South Africa 1, Slovenia 1, Singapore 30, Spain 1, Sweden 8, Switzerland 23, UAE 5, Taiwan 10, UK 15, US 85, Uruguay 1, Vietnam 1 (2000 est.)
Airports: 46 (2000 est.)
Airports - with paved runways:
total: 2
over 3,047 m: 1
1,524 to 2,437 m: 1 (2000 est.)
Airports - with unpaved runways:
total: 44
1,524 to 2,437 m: 3
914 to 1,523 m: 5
under 914 m: 36 (2000 est.)

Military

Military branches: Army, Air Force, Navy
Military manpower - availability:
males age 15-49: 715,753 (2001 est.)
Military manpower - fit for military service:
males age 15-49: 385,460 (2001 est.)
Military expenditures - dollar figure: $1 million (FY98)
Military expenditures - percent of GDP: 2% (FY98)

Transnational Issues

Disputes - international: large refugee population from civil war in Sierra Leone
Illicit drugs: increasingly a transshipment point for Southeast and Southwest Asian heroin and South American cocaine for the European and US markets

Libya

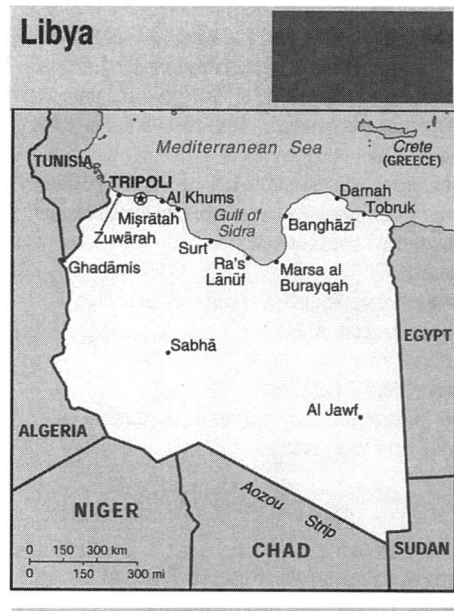

Introduction

Background: Since he took power in a 1969 military coup, Col. Muammar Abu Minyar al-QADHAFI has espoused his own political system - a combination of socialism and Islam - which he calls the Third International Theory. Viewing himself as a revolutionary leader, he used oil funds during the 1970s and 1980s to promote his ideology outside Libya, even supporting subversives and terrorists abroad to hasten the end of Marxism and capitalism. Libyan military adventures failed, e.g., the prolonged foray of Libyan troops into the Aozou Strip in northern Chad was finally repulsed in 1987. Libyan support for terrorism decreased after UN sanctions were imposed in 1992. Those sanctions were suspended in April 1999.

Geography

Location: Northern Africa, bordering the Mediterranean Sea, between Egypt and Tunisia
Geographic coordinates: 25 00 N, 17 00 E
Map references: Africa
Area:
total: 1,759,540 sq km
land: 1,759,540 sq km
water: 0 sq km
Area - comparative: slightly larger than Alaska
Land boundaries:
total: 4,383 km
border countries: Algeria 982 km, Chad 1,055 km, Egypt 1,150 km, Niger 354 km, Sudan 383 km, Tunisia 459 km
Coastline: 1,770 km
Maritime claims:
territorial sea: 12 NM
note: Gulf of Sidra closing line - 32 degrees, 30 minutes north
Climate: Mediterranean along coast; dry, extreme desert interior
Terrain: mostly barren, flat to undulating plains, plateaus, depressions

Libya (continued)

Elevation extremes:
lowest point: Sabkhat Ghuzayyil -47 m
highest point: Bikku Bitti 2,267 m
Natural resources: petroleum, natural gas, gypsum
Land use:
arable land: 1%
permanent crops: 0%
permanent pastures: 8%
forests and woodland: 0%
other: 91% (1993 est.)
Irrigated land: 4,700 sq km (1993 est.)
Natural hazards: hot, dry, dust-laden ghibli is a southern wind lasting one to four days in spring and fall; dust storms, sandstorms
Environment - current issues: desertification; very limited natural fresh water resources; the Great Manmade River Project, the largest water development scheme in the world, is being built to bring water from large aquifers under the Sahara to coastal cities
Environment - international agreements:
party to: Climate Change, Desertification, Marine Dumping, Ozone Layer Protection, Ship Pollution
signed, but not ratified: Biodiversity, Law of the Sea, Nuclear Test Ban

People

Population: 5,240,599
note: includes 662,669 non-nationals, of which an estimated 500,000 or more are Africans living in Libya (July 2001 est.)
Age structure:
0-14 years: 35.41% (male 947,645; female 907,854)
15-64 years: 60.64% (male 1,645,085; female 1,533,066)
65 years and over: 3.95% (male 101,701; female 105,248) (2001 est.)
Population growth rate: 2.42% (2001 est.)
Birth rate: 27.67 births/1,000 population (2001 est.)
Death rate: 3.51 deaths/1,000 population (2001 est.)
Net migration rate: 0 migrant(s)/1,000 population (2001 est.)
Sex ratio:
at birth: 1.05 male(s)/female
under 15 years: 1.04 male(s)/female
15-64 years: 1.07 male(s)/female
65 years and over: 0.97 male(s)/female
total population: 1.06 male(s)/female (2001 est.)
Infant mortality rate: 28.99 deaths/1,000 live births (2001 est.)
Life expectancy at birth:
total population: 75.65 years
male: 73.53 years
female: 77.88 years (2001 est.)
Total fertility rate: 3.64 children born/woman (2001 est.)
HIV/AIDS - adult prevalence rate: 0.05% (1999 est.)
HIV/AIDS - people living with HIV/AIDS: NA
HIV/AIDS - deaths: NA

Nationality:
noun: Libyan(s)
adjective: Libyan
Ethnic groups: Berber and Arab 97%, Greeks, Maltese, Italians, Egyptians, Pakistanis, Turks, Indians, Tunisians
Religions: Sunni Muslim 97%
Languages: Arabic, Italian, English, all are widely understood in the major cities
Literacy:
definition: age 15 and over can read and write
total population: 76.2%
male: 87.9%
female: 63% (1995 est.)

Government

Country name:
conventional long form: Great Socialist People's Libyan Arab Jamahiriya
conventional short form: Libya
local long form: Al Jumahiriyah al Arabiyah al Libiyah ash Shabiyah al Ishtirakiyah al Uzma
local short form: none
Government type: Jamahiriya (a state of the masses) in theory, governed by the populace through local councils; in fact, a military dictatorship
Capital: Tripoli
Administrative divisions: 25 municipalities (baladiyat, singular - baladiyah); Ajdabiya, Al 'Aziziyah, Al Fatih, Al Jabal al Akhdar, Al Jufrah, Al Khums, Al Kufrah, An Nuqat al Khams, Ash Shati', Awbari, Az Zawiyah, Banghazi, Darnah, Ghadamis, Gharyan, Misratah, Murzuq, Sabha, Sawfajjin, Surt, Tarabulus, Tarhunah, Tubruq, Yafran, Zlitan; note - the 25 municipalities may have been replaced by 13 regions
Independence: 24 December 1951 (from Italy)
National holiday: Revolution Day, 1 September (1969)
Constitution: 11 December 1969, amended 2 March 1977
Legal system: based on Italian civil law system and Islamic law; separate religious courts; no constitutional provision for judicial review of legislative acts; has not accepted compulsory ICJ jurisdiction
Suffrage: 18 years of age; universal and compulsory
Executive branch:
chief of state: Revolutionary Leader Col. Muammar Abu Minyar al-QADHAFI (since 1 September 1969); note - holds no official title, but is de facto chief of state
head of government: Secretary of the General People's Committee (Premier) Mubarak al-SHAMEKH (since 2 March 2000)
cabinet: General People's Committee established by the General People's Congress
elections: national elections are indirect through a hierarchy of people's committees; head of government elected by the General People's Congress; election last held 2 March 2000 (next to be held NA)
election results: Mubarak al-SHAMEKH elected premier; percent of General People's Congress vote - NA%
Legislative branch: unicameral General People's Congress (NA seats; members elected indirectly through a hierarchy of people's committees)
Judicial branch: Supreme Court
Political parties and leaders: none
Political pressure groups and leaders: various Arab nationalist movements with almost negligible memberships may be functioning clandestinely, as well as some Islamic elements
International organization participation: ABEDA, AfDB, AFESD, AL, AMF, AMU, CAEU, CCC, ECA, FAO, G-77, IAEA, IBRD, ICAO, ICRM, IDA, IDB, IFAD, IFC, IFRCS, ILO, IMF, IMO, Inmarsat, Intelsat, Interpol, IOC, ISO, ITU, MONUC, NAM, OAPEC, OAU, OIC, OPEC, UN, UNCTAD, UNESCO, UNIDO, UPU, WFTU, WHO, WIPO, WMO, WToO
Diplomatic representation in the US: Libya does not have an embassy in the US
Diplomatic representation from the US: the US suspended all embassy activities in Tripoli on 2 May 1980
Flag description: plain green; green is the traditional color of Islam (the state religion)

Economy

Economy - overview: The socialist-oriented economy depends primarily upon revenues from the oil sector, which contributes practically all export earnings and about one-quarter of GDP. These oil revenues and a small population give Libya one of the highest per capita GDPs in Africa, but little of this income flows down to the lower orders of society. In this statist society, import restrictions and inefficient resource allocations have led to periodic shortages of basic goods and foodstuffs. The nonoil manufacturing and construction sectors, which account for about 20% of GDP, have expanded from processing mostly agricultural products to include the production of petrochemicals, iron, steel, and aluminum. Climatic conditions and poor soils severely limit agricultural output, and Libya imports about 75% of its food requirements. Higher oil prices in 1999 and 2000 led to an increase in export revenues, which improved macroeconomic balances and helped to stimulate the economy. Following the suspension of UN sanctions in 1999, Libya has been trying to increase its attractiveness to foreign investors, and several foreign companies have visited in search of contracts.
GDP: purchasing power parity - $45.4 billion (2000 est.)
GDP - real growth rate: 6.5% (2000 est.)
GDP - per capita: purchasing power parity - $8,900 (2000 est.)
GDP - composition by sector:
agriculture: 7%
industry: 47%
services: 46% (1997 est.)
Population below poverty line: NA%

Libya (continued)

Household income or consumption by percentage share:
lowest 10%: NA%
highest 10%: NA%
Inflation rate (consumer prices): 18.5% (2000 est.)
Labor force: 1.5 million (2000 est.)
Labor force - by occupation: services and government 54%, industry 29%, agriculture 17% (1997 est.)
Unemployment rate: 30% (2000 est.)
Budget:
revenues: $6.85 billion
expenditures: $4.4 billion, including capital expenditures of $NA (2000 est.)
Industries: petroleum, food processing, textiles, handicrafts, cement
Industrial production growth rate: NA%
Electricity - production: 18.9 billion kWh (1999)
Electricity - production by source:
fossil fuel: 100%
hydro: 0%
nuclear: 0%
other: 0% (1999)
Electricity - consumption: 17.577 billion kWh (1999)
Electricity - exports: 0 kWh (1999)
Electricity - imports: 0 kWh (1999)
Agriculture - products: wheat, barley, olives, dates, citrus, vegetables, peanuts, soybeans; cattle
Exports: $13.9 billion (f.o.b., 2000 est.)
Exports - commodities: crude oil, refined petroleum products
Exports - partners: Italy 33%, Germany 24%, Spain 10%, France 5%, Turkey 4%, Tunisia 4% (1999)
Imports: $7.6 billion (f.o.b., 2000 est.)
Imports - commodities: machinery, transport equipment, food, manufactured goods
Imports - partners: Italy 24%, Germany 12%, Tunisia 9%, UK 7%, France 6%, South Korea 5% (1999)
Debt - external: $4.1 billion (2000 est.)
Economic aid - recipient: $8.4 million (1995)
Currency: Libyan dinar (LYD)
Currency code: LYD
Exchange rates: Libyan dinars per US dollar - 0.5101 (January 2001), 0.5081 (2000), 0.4616 (1999), 0.3785 (1998), 0.3891 (1997), 0.3651 (1996)
note: Libya currently has two rates for foreign trade; one for government operations and foreign companies and one for Libyan individuals (0.45 dinars per US dollar in December 1998)
Fiscal year: calendar year

Communications

Telephones - main lines in use: 380,000 (1996)
Telephones - mobile cellular: NA
Telephone system:
general assessment: telecommunications system is being modernized; mobile cellular telephone system became operational in 1996
domestic: microwave radio relay, coaxial cable, cellular, tropospheric scatter, and a domestic satellite system with 14 earth stations
international: satellite earth stations - 4 Intelsat, NA Arabsat, and NA Intersputnik; submarine cables to France and Italy; microwave radio relay to Tunisia and Egypt; tropospheric scatter to Greece; participant in Medarabtel (1999)
Radio broadcast stations: AM 17, FM 4, shortwave 3 (1998)
Radios: 1.35 million (1997)
Television broadcast stations: 12 (plus one low-power repeater) (1998)
Televisions: 730,000 (1997)
Internet country code: .ly
Internet Service Providers (ISPs): 1 (2000)
Internet users: 7,500 (2000)

Transportation

Railways:
note: Libya has had no railroad in operation since 1965, all previous systems having been dismantled; current plans are to construct a 1.435-m standard gauge line from the Tunisian frontier to Tripoli and Misratah, then inland to Sabha, center of a mineral-rich area, but there has been little progress; other plans made jointly with Egypt would establish a rail line from As Sallum, Egypt, to Tobruk with completion originally set for mid-1994; Libya signed contracts with two private companies - Bahne of Egypt and Jez Sistemas Ferroviarios of Spain - in 1998 for the supply of crossings and pointwork (1001)
Highways:
total: 24,484 km
paved: 6,800 km
unpaved: 17,684 km (1996)
Waterways: none
Pipelines: crude oil 4,383 km; petroleum products 443 km (includes liquefied petroleum gas or LPG 256 km); natural gas 1,947 km
Ports and harbors: Al Khums, Banghazi, Darnah, Marsa al Burayqah, Misratah, Ra's Lanuf, Tobruk, Tripoli, Zuwarah
Merchant marine:
total: 28 ships (1,000 GRT or over) totaling 399,725 GRT/654,843 DWT
ships by type: cargo 10, chemical tanker 1, liquefied gas 3, petroleum tanker 6, roll on/roll off 4, short-sea passenger 4 (2000 est.)
Airports: 136 (2000 est.)
Airports - with paved runways:
total: 58
over 3,047 m: 23
2,438 to 3,047 m: 6
1,524 to 2,437 m: 22
914 to 1,523 m: 5
under 914 m: 2 (2000 est.)
Airports - with unpaved runways:
total: 78
over 3,047 m: 4
2,438 to 3,047 m: 2
1,524 to 2,437 m: 14
914 to 1,523 m: 40
under 914 m: 18 (2000 est.)

Military

Military branches: Army, Navy, Air and Air Defense Command
Military manpower - military age: 17 years of age
Military manpower - availability:
males age 15-49: 1,459,400 (2001 est.)
Military manpower - fit for military service:
males age 15-49: 866,012 (2001 est.)
Military manpower - reaching military age annually:
males: 61,694 (2001 est.)
Military expenditures - dollar figure: $1.3 billion (FY99/00)
Military expenditures - percent of GDP: 3.9% (FY99/00)

Transnational Issues

Disputes - international: Libya claims about 19,400 sq km in northern Niger and also a part of southeastern Algeria

Liechtenstein

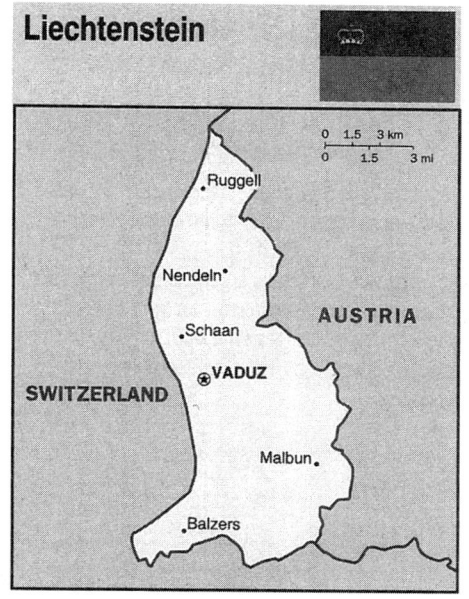

Introduction

Background: The Principality of Liechtenstein was established within the Holy Roman Empire in 1719; it became a sovereign state in 1806. Until the end of World War I, it was closely tied to Austria, but the economic devastation caused by that conflict forced Liechtenstein to conclude a customs and monetary union with Switzerland. Since World War II (in which Liechtenstein remained neutral) the country's low taxes have spurred outstanding economic growth. However, shortcomings in banking regulatory oversight have resulted in concerns about the use of the financial institutions for money laundering.

Geography

Location: Central Europe, between Austria and Switzerland
Geographic coordinates: 47 10 N, 9 32 E
Map references: Europe
Area:
total: 160 sq km
land: 160 sq km
water: 0 sq km
Area - comparative: about 0.9 times the size of Washington, DC
Land boundaries:
total: 76 km
border countries: Austria 35 km, Switzerland 41 km
Coastline: 0 km (landlocked)
Maritime claims: none (landlocked)
Climate: continental; cold, cloudy winters with frequent snow or rain; cool to moderately warm, cloudy, humid summers
Terrain: mostly mountainous (Alps) with Rhine Valley in western third
Elevation extremes:
lowest point: Ruggeller Riet 430 m
highest point: Grauspitz 2,599 m
Natural resources: hydroelectric potential, arable land
Land use:
arable land: 24%
permanent crops: 0%
permanent pastures: 16%
forests and woodland: 35%
other: 25% (1993 est.)
Irrigated land: NA sq km
Natural hazards: NA
Environment - current issues: NA
Environment - international agreements:
party to: Air Pollution, Air Pollution-Nitrogen Oxides, Air Pollution-Sulphur 85, Air Pollution-Sulphur 94, Air Pollution-Volatile Organic Compounds, Biodiversity, Climate Change, Desertification, Endangered Species, Hazardous Wastes, Marine Dumping, Ozone Layer Protection, Ship Pollution, Wetlands
signed, but not ratified: Air Pollution-Persistent Organic Pollutants, Climate Change-Kyoto Protocol, Law of the Sea
Geography - note: along with Uzbekistan, one of only two doubly landlocked countries in the world; variety of microclimatic variations based on elevation

People

Population: 32,528 (July 2001 est.)
Age structure:
0-14 years: 18.41% (male 2,992; female 2,996)
15-64 years: 70.6% (male 11,455; female 11,511)
65 years and over: 10.99% (male 1,439; female 2,135) (2001 est.)
Population growth rate: 0.98% (2001 est.)
Birth rate: 11.53 births/1,000 population (2001 est.)
Death rate: 6.7 deaths/1,000 population (2001 est.)
Net migration rate: 4.98 migrant(s)/1,000 population (2001 est.)
Sex ratio:
at birth: 1.01 male(s)/female
under 15 years: 1 male(s)/female
15-64 years: 1 male(s)/female
65 years and over: 0.67 male(s)/female
total population: 0.95 male(s)/female (2001 est.)
Infant mortality rate: 4.99 deaths/1,000 live births (2001 est.)
Life expectancy at birth:
total population: 78.95 years
male: 75.32 years
female: 82.6 years (2001 est.)
Total fertility rate: 1.5 children born/woman (2001 est.)
HIV/AIDS - adult prevalence rate: NA%
HIV/AIDS - people living with HIV/AIDS: NA
HIV/AIDS - deaths: NA
Nationality:
noun: Liechtensteiner(s)
adjective: Liechtenstein
Ethnic groups: Alemannic 87.5%, Italian, Turkish, and other 12.5%
Religions: Roman Catholic 80%, Protestant 7.4%, unknown 7.7%, other 4.9% (1996)
Languages: German (official), Alemannic dialect
Literacy:
definition: age 10 and over can read and write
total population: 100%
male: 100%
female: 100% (1981 est.)

Government

Country name:
conventional long form: Principality of Liechtenstein
conventional short form: Liechtenstein
local long form: Fuerstentum Liechtenstein
local short form: Liechtenstein
Government type: hereditary constitutional monarchy
Capital: Vaduz
Administrative divisions: 11 communes (gemeinden, singular - gemeinde); Balzers, Eschen, Gamprin, Mauren, Planken, Ruggell, Schaan, Schellenberg, Triesen, Triesenberg, Vaduz
Independence: 23 January 1719 Imperial Principality of Liechtenstein established; 12 July 1806 established independence from the Holy Roman Empire
National holiday: Assumption Day, 15 August
Constitution: 5 October 1921
Legal system: local civil and penal codes; accepts compulsory ICJ jurisdiction, with reservations
Suffrage: 20 years of age; universal
Executive branch:
chief of state: Prince HANS ADAM II (since 13 November 1989, assumed executive powers 26 August 1984); Heir Apparent Prince ALOIS, son of the monarch (born 11 June 1968)
head of government: Head of Government Mario FRICK (since 15 December 1993) and Deputy Head of Government Michael RITTER (since 2 February 1997)
cabinet: Cabinet elected by the Diet; confirmed by the monarch
elections: none; the monarch is hereditary; following legislative elections, the leader of the majority party in the Diet is usually appointed the head of government by the monarch and the leader of the largest minority party in the Diet is usually appointed the deputy head of government by the monarch
Legislative branch: unicameral Diet or Landtag (25 seats; members are elected by direct popular vote under proportional representation to serve four-year terms)
elections: last held on 9-11 February 2001 (next to be held by NA 2005)
election results: percent of vote by party - FBP 49.90%, VU 41.35%, FL 8.71%; seats by party - FBP 13, VU 11, FL 1
Judicial branch: Supreme Court or Oberster Gerichtshof; Superior Court or Obergericht
Political parties and leaders: Fatherland Union or VU [Dr. Oswald KRANZ]; Progressive Citizens' Party or FBP [Dr. Ernst WALCH]; The Free List or FL [Dr. Pepo FRICK, Karin JENNY, Rene HASLER]
Political pressure groups and leaders: NA
International organization participation: CE, EBRD, ECE, EFTA, IAEA, ICRM, IFRCS, Intelsat, Interpol, IOC, ITU, OPCW, OSCE, UN, UNCTAD, UNIDO, UPU, WCL, WHO (observer), WIPO, WTrO

Liechtenstein (continued)

Diplomatic representation in the US: Liechtenstein's Ambassador to the US, Claudia FRITSCHE, is dually accredited to the UN in New York

Diplomatic representation from the US: the US does not have an embassy in Liechtenstein, but the US Ambassador to Switzerland is also accredited to Liechtenstein

Flag description: two equal horizontal bands of blue (top) and red with a gold crown on the hoist side of the blue band

Economy

Economy - overview: Despite its small size and limited natural resources, Liechtenstein has developed into a prosperous, highly industrialized, free-enterprise economy with a vital financial service sector and living standards on a par with the urban areas of its large European neighbors. Low business taxes - the maximum tax rate is 18% - and easy incorporation rules have induced 73,700 holding or so-called letter box companies to establish nominal offices in Liechtenstein, providing 30% of state revenues. The country participates in a customs union with Switzerland and uses the Swiss franc as its national currency. It imports more than 90% of its energy requirements. Liechtenstein has been a member of the European Economic Area (an organization serving as a bridge between European Free Trade Association (EFTA) and EU) since May 1995. The government is working to harmonize its economic policies with those of an integrated Europe.

GDP: purchasing power parity - $730 million (1998 est.)

GDP - real growth rate: NA%

GDP - per capita: purchasing power parity - $23,000 (1998 est.)

GDP - composition by sector:
agriculture: NA%
industry: NA%
services: NA%

Population below poverty line: NA%

Household income or consumption by percentage share:
lowest 10%: NA%
highest 10%: NA%

Inflation rate (consumer prices): 0.5% (1997 est.)

Labor force: 22,891 of which 13,847 are foreigners; 8,231 commute from Austria and Switzerland to work each day

Labor force - by occupation: industry, trade, and building 45%, services 53%, agriculture, fishing, forestry, and horticulture 2% (1997 est.)

Unemployment rate: 1.8% (February 1999)

Budget:
revenues: $424.2 million
expenditures: $414.1 million, including capital expenditures of $NA (1998 est.)

Industries: electronics, metal manufacturing, textiles, ceramics, pharmaceuticals, food products, precision instruments, tourism

Industrial production growth rate: NA%

Electricity - production by source:
fossil fuel: NA%
hydro: NA%
nuclear: NA%
other: NA%

Electricity - consumption: NA kWh
Electricity - exports: NA kWh
Electricity - imports: NA kWh

Agriculture - products: wheat, barley, corn, potatoes; livestock, dairy products

Exports: $2.47 billion (1996)

Exports - commodities: small specialty machinery, dental products, stamps, hardware, pottery

Exports - partners: EU and EFTA countries 60.57% (Switzerland 15.7%) (1995)

Imports: $917.3 million (1996)

Imports - commodities: machinery, metal goods, textiles, foodstuffs, motor vehicles

Imports - partners: EU countries, Switzerland (1996)

Debt - external: $0 (1996)

Economic aid - recipient: none

Currency: Swiss franc (CHF)

Currency code: CHF

Exchange rates: Swiss francs per US dollar - 1.6303 (January 2001), 1.6888 (2000), 1.5022 (1999), 1.4498 (1998), 1.4513 (1997), 1.2360 (1996)

Fiscal year: calendar year

Communications

Telephones - main lines in use: 20,000 (1997)
Telephones - mobile cellular: NA
Telephone system:
general assessment: automatic telephone system
domestic: NA
international: linked to Swiss networks by cable and microwave radio relay

Radio broadcast stations: AM 0, FM 4, shortwave 0 (1998)
Radios: 21,000 (1997)
Television broadcast stations: NA (linked to Swiss networks) (1997)
Televisions: 12,000 (1997)
Internet country code: .li
Internet Service Providers (ISPs): 44 (Liechtenstein and Switzerland) (2000)
Internet users: NA

Transportation

Railways:
total: 18.5 km; note - owned, operated, and included in statistics of Austrian Federal Railways
standard gauge: 18.5 km 1.435-m gauge (electrified)

Highways:
total: 250 km
paved: 250 km
unpaved: 0 km

Waterways: none
Ports and harbors: none
Airports: none

Military

Military - note: defense is the responsibility of Switzerland

Transnational Issues

Disputes - international: Liechtenstein's royal family claims restitution for 1,600 sq km of land in the Czech Republic confiscated in 1918

Illicit drugs: multilateral organizations engaged in issuing international guidelines for financial sector oversight have found gaps in Liechtenstein's financial services controls that make it vulnerable to money laundering

Lithuania

Introduction

Background: Independent between the two World Wars, Lithuania was annexed by the USSR in 1940. On 11 March 1990, Lithuania became the first of the Soviet republics to declare its independence, but this proclamation was not generally recognized until September of 1991 (following the abortive coup in Moscow). The last Russian troops withdrew in 1993. Lithuania subsequently has restructured its economy for eventual integration into Western European institutions.

Geography

Location: Eastern Europe, bordering the Baltic Sea, between Latvia and Russia
Geographic coordinates: 56 00 N, 24 00 E
Map references: Europe
Area:
total: 65,200 sq km
land: 65,200 sq km
water: 0 sq km
Area - comparative: slightly larger than West Virginia
Land boundaries:
total: 1,273 km
border countries: Belarus 502 km, Latvia 453 km, Poland 91 km, Russia (Kaliningrad) 227 km
Coastline: 99 km
Maritime claims:
territorial sea: 12 NM
Climate: transitional, between maritime and continental; wet, moderate winters and summers
Terrain: lowland, many scattered small lakes, fertile soil
Elevation extremes:
lowest point: Baltic Sea 0 m
highest point: Juozapines/Kalnas 292 m
Natural resources: peat, arable land
Land use:
arable land: 39%
permanent crops: 9%
permanent pastures: 6%
forests and woodland: 31%
other: 15% (2001 est.)
Irrigated land: 430 sq km (1993 est.)
Natural hazards: NA
Environment - current issues: contamination of soil and groundwater with petroleum products and chemicals at military bases
Environment - international agreements:
party to: Biodiversity, Climate Change, Hazardous Wastes, Marine Dumping, Ozone Layer Protection, Ship Pollution, Wetlands
signed, but not ratified: Air Pollution-Persistent Organic Pollutants, Climate Change-Kyoto Protocol

People

Population: 3,610,535 (July 2001 est.)
Age structure:
0-14 years: 18.75% (male 345,694; female 331,125)
15-64 years: 67.69% (male 1,181,119; female 1,262,872)
65 years and over: 13.56% (male 165,732; female 323,993) (2001 est.)
Population growth rate: -0.27% (2001 est.)
Birth rate: 10 births/1,000 population (2001 est.)
Death rate: 12.86 deaths/1,000 population (2001 est.)
Net migration rate: 0.15 migrant(s)/1,000 population (2001 est.)
Sex ratio:
at birth: 1.05 male(s)/female
under 15 years: 1.04 male(s)/female
15-64 years: 0.94 male(s)/female
65 years and over: 0.51 male(s)/female
total population: 0.88 male(s)/female (2001 est.)
Infant mortality rate: 14.5 deaths/1,000 live births (2001 est.)
Life expectancy at birth:
total population: 69.25 years
male: 63.3 years
female: 75.5 years (2001 est.)
Total fertility rate: 1.37 children born/woman (2001 est.)
HIV/AIDS - adult prevalence rate: 0.02% (1999 est.)
HIV/AIDS - people living with HIV/AIDS: less than 500 (1999 est.)
HIV/AIDS - deaths: less than 100 (1999 est.)
Nationality:
noun: Lithuanian(s)
adjective: Lithuanian
Ethnic groups: Lithuanian 80.6%, Russian 8.7%, Polish 7%, Byelorussian 1.6%, other 2.1%
Religions: Roman Catholic (primarily), Lutheran, Russian Orthodox, Protestant, Evangelical Christian Baptist, Muslim, Jewish
Languages: Lithuanian (official), Polish, Russian
Literacy:
definition: age 15 and over can read and write
total population: 98%
male: 99%
female: 98% (1989 est.)

Government

Country name:
conventional long form: Republic of Lithuania
conventional short form: Lithuania
local long form: Lietuvos Respublika
local short form: Lietuva
former: Lithuanian Soviet Socialist Republic
Government type: parliamentary democracy
Capital: Vilnius
Administrative divisions: 44 regions (rajonai, singular - rajonas) and 11 municipalities*: Akmenes Rajonas, Alytaus Rajonas, Alytus*, Anyksciu Rajonas, Birstonas*, Birzu Rajonas, Druskininkai*, Ignalinos Rajonas, Jonavos Rajonas, Joniskio Rajonas, Jurbarko Rajonas, Kaisiadoriu Rajonas, Kaunas*, Kauno Rajonas, Kedainiu Rajonas, Kelmes Rajonas, Klaipeda*, Klaipedos Rajonas, Kretingos Rajonas, Kupiskio Rajonas, Lazdiju Rajonas, Marijampole*, Marijampoles Rajonas, Mazeikiu Rajonas, Moletu Rajonas, Neringa* Pakruojo Rajonas, Palanga*, Panevezio Rajonas, Panevezys*, Pasvalio Rajonas, Plunges Rajonas, Prienu Rajonas, Radviliskio Rajonas, Raseiniu Rajonas, Rokiskio Rajonas, Sakiu Rajonas, Salcininku Rajonas, Siauliai*, Siauliu Rajonas, Silales Rajonas, Silutes Rajonas, Sirvintu Rajonas, Skuodo Rajonas, Svencioniu Rajonas, Taurages Rajonas, Telsiu Rajonas, Traku Rajonas, Ukmerges Rajonas, Utenos Rajonas, Varenos Rajonas, Vilkaviskio Rajonas, Vilniaus Rajonas, Vilnius*, Zarasu Rajonas
Independence: 11 March 1990 (independence declared from Soviet Union); 6 September 1991 (Soviet Union recognizes Lithuania's independence)
National holiday: Independence Day, 16 February (1918); note - 16 February 1918 is the date of independence from German, Austrian, Prussian, and Russian occupation, 11 March 1990 is the date of independence from the Soviet Union
Constitution: adopted 25 October 1992
Legal system: based on civil law system; no judicial review of legislative acts
Suffrage: 18 years of age; universal
Executive branch:
chief of state: President Valdas ADAMKUS (since 26 February 1998)
head of government: Premier Algirdas BRAZAUSKAS (since 3 July 2001)
cabinet: Council of Ministers appointed by the president on the nomination of the premier
elections: president elected by popular vote for a five-year term; election last held 21 December 1997 and 4 January 1998 (next to be held NA 2002); premier appointed by the president on the approval of the Parliament
election results: Valdas ADAMKUS elected president; percent of vote - Valdas ADAMKUS 50.4%, Arturas PAULAUSKAS 49.6%
Legislative branch: unicameral Parliament or Seimas (141 seats, 71 members are directly elected by popular vote, 70 are elected by proportional representation; members serve four-year terms)

Lithuania (continued)

elections: last held 8 October 2000 (next to be held NA October 2004)
election results: percent of vote by party - Social Democratic Coalition 31.1%, New Union/Social Liberals 19.6%, Liberal Union 17.2%, TS 8.6%, remaining parties all less than 5%; seats by party - Social Democratic Coalition 52, Liberal Union 34, New Union/Social Liberals 29, TS 9, Farmer's Party 4, Center Union 2, Poles' Electoral Action 2, Modern Christian Democratic Union 1, independents 3, others 5
Judicial branch: Supreme Court; Court of Appeal; judges for both courts appointed by the Parliament
Political parties and leaders: Christian Democratic Party or LKDP [Zigmas ZINKEVICIUS, chairman]; Electoral Action of Lithuanian Poles [Valdemar TOMASZEVSKI, chairman]; Homeland Union/Conservative Party or TS [Vytautas LANDSBERGIS, chairman]; Lithuanian Center Union or LCS [Kestutis GLAVECKAS, chairman]; Lithuanian Farmer's Party or LUP [Ramunas KARBAUSKIS, chairman]; Lithuanian Liberal Union [Rolandas PAKSAS, chairman]; Lithuanian Social Democratic Coalition [Algirdas BRAZAUSKAS, chairman] consists of the Lithuanian Democratic Labor Party or LDDP, the Lithuanian Social Democratic Party or LSPD, and New Democracy; Modern Christian Democratic Union [Vytautas BOGUSIS, chairman]; New Union-Social Liberals [Arturas PAULAUSKAS, chairman]
Political pressure groups and leaders: NA
International organization participation: ACCT (observer), BIS, CBSS, CCC, CE, EAPC, EBRD, ECE, EU (applicant), FAO, IAEA, IBRD, ICAO, ICC, ICFTU, ICRM, IFC, IFRCS, ILO, IMF, IMO, Intelsat (nonsignatory user), Interpol, IOC, IOM, ISO (correspondent), ITU, OPCW, OSCE, PFP, UN, UNCTAD, UNESCO, UNMIK, UPU, WCL, WEU (associate partner), WHO, WIPO, WMO, WTrO (observer)
Diplomatic representation in the US:
chief of mission: Ambassador Vygaudas USACKAS
chancery: 2622 16th Street NW, Washington, DC 20009
telephone: [1] (202) 234-5860
FAX: [1] (202) 328-0466
consulate(s) general: Chicago and New York
Diplomatic representation from the US:
chief of mission: Ambassador John F. TEFFT
embassy: Akmenu 6, 2600 Vilnius
mailing address: American Embassy, Vilnius, PSC 78, Box V, APO AE 09723
telephone: [370] (2) 223-031
FAX: [370] (2) 227-236
Flag description: three equal horizontal bands of yellow (top), green, and red

Economy

Economy - overview: Lithuania, the Baltic state that has conducted the most trade with Russia, has been slowly rebounding from the 1998 Russian financial crisis. High unemployment and weak consumption have held back recovery. GDP growth for 2000 - estimated at 2.9% - fell behind that of Estonia and Latvia, and unemployment is estimated at 10.8%, the country's highest since regaining independence in 1990. For 2001, Lithuanians forecast 3.2% growth, 1.8% inflation, and a fiscal deficit of 3.3%. In early 2001, the Lithuanian Government announced that it will repeg its currency, the litas, to the euro (the litas is currently pegged to the dollar) some time in 2002. Lithuania must ratify 25 agreements along with other legal documents and obligations by 1 May 2001 before gaining World Trade Organization membership. Lithuania was invited to the Helsinki summit in December 1999 and began EU accession talks in early 2000. Privatization of the large, state-owned utilities, particularly in the energy sector, remains a key challenge for 2001.
GDP: purchasing power parity - $26.4 billion (2000 est.)
GDP - real growth rate: 2.9% (2000 est.)
GDP - per capita: purchasing power parity - $7,300 (2000 est.)
GDP - composition by sector:
agriculture: 10%
industry: 33%
services: 57% (1999 est.)
Population below poverty line: NA%
Household income or consumption by percentage share:
lowest 10%: 3.1%
highest 10%: 25.6% (1996)
Inflation rate (consumer prices): 1% (2000 est.)
Labor force: 2 million (2000 est.)
Labor force - by occupation: industry 30%, agriculture 20%, services 50% (1997 est.)
Unemployment rate: 10.8% (2000)
Budget:
revenues: $1.5 billion
expenditures: $1.7 billion, including capital expenditures of $NA (1997 est.)
Industries: metal-cutting machine tools, electric motors, television sets, refrigerators and freezers, petroleum refining, shipbuilding (small ships), furniture making, textiles, food processing, fertilizers, agricultural machinery, optical equipment, electronic components, computers, amber
Industrial production growth rate: 2.3% (2000 est.)
Electricity - production: 13.567 billion kWh (1999)
Electricity - production by source:
fossil fuel: 23.89%
hydro: 3.43%
nuclear: 72.68%
other: 0% (1999)
Electricity - consumption: 9.817 billion kWh (1999)
Electricity - exports: 3.2 billion kWh (1999)
Electricity - imports: 400 million kWh (1999)
Agriculture - products: grain, potatoes, sugar beets, flax, vegetables; beef, milk, eggs; fish
Exports: $3.7 billion (f.o.b., 2000)
Exports - commodities: machinery and equipment 22%, mineral products 15%, chemicals 12%, textiles and clothing, foodstuffs (1999)
Exports - partners: Germany 15.8%, Latvia 12.6%, Russia 6.9%, Belarus 5.8%, Denmark (1999)
Imports: $4.9 billion (f.o.b., 2000)
Imports - commodities: machinery and equipment 18%, mineral products 16%, chemicals 10%, textiles and clothing 10%, transport equipment 7% (1999)
Imports - partners: Russia 20.4%, Germany 16.5%, Denmark 3.8%, Belarus 2.2%, Latvia 2% (1999)
Debt - external: $2.5 billion (2000 est.)
Economic aid - recipient: $228.5 million (1995)
Currency: litas (LTL)
Currency code: LTL
Exchange rates: litai per US dollar - 4.000 (fixed rate since 1 May 1994); note - litai is the plural of litas
Fiscal year: calendar year

Communications

Telephones - main lines in use: 1.048 million (1997)
Telephones - mobile cellular: 297,500 (November 1998)
Telephone system:
general assessment: inadequate, but is being modernized to provide an improved international capability and better residential access
domestic: a national, fiber-optic cable, interurban, trunk system is nearing completion; rural exchanges are being improved and expanded; mobile cellular systems are being installed; access to the Internet is available; still many unsatisfied telephone subscriber applications
international: landline connections to Latvia and Poland; major international connections to Denmark, Sweden, and Norway by submarine cable for further transmission by satellite
Radio broadcast stations: AM 3, FM 112, shortwave 1 (1998)
Radios: 1.9 million (1997)
Television broadcast stations: 20 (plus 30 repeaters) (1995)
Televisions: 1.7 million (1997)
Internet country code: .lt
Internet Service Providers (ISPs): 14 (2000)
Internet users: 225,000 (2000)

Transportation

Railways:
total: 2,002 km
broad gauge: 2,002 km 1.524-m gauge (122 km electrified) (1994)
Highways:
total: 44,000 km
paved: 35,500 km
unpaved: 8,500 km (2000)
Waterways: 600 km (perennially navigable)
Pipelines: crude oil, 105 km; natural gas 760 km (1992)
Ports and harbors: Butinge, Kaunas, Klaipeda
Merchant marine:
total: 50 ships (1,000 GRT or over) totaling 293,168 GRT/327,827 DWT

Lithuania (continued)

ships by type: cargo 26, combination bulk 10, petroleum tanker 2, railcar carrier 1, refrigerated cargo 7, roll on/roll off 1, short-sea passenger 3 (2000 est.)
Airports: 72 (2000 est.)
Airports - with paved runways:
total: 9
over 3,047 m: 2
1,524 to 2,437 m: 4
under 914 m: 3 (2000 est.)
Airports - with unpaved runways:
total: 63
1,524 to 2,437 m: 3
914 to 1,523 m: 5
under 914 m: 55 (2000 est.)

Military

Military branches: Ground Forces, Navy, Air and Air Defense Force, Security Forces (internal and border troops), National Guard (Skat)
Military manpower - military age: 18 years of age
Military manpower - availability:
males age 15-49: 929,389 (2001 est.)
Military manpower - fit for military service:
males age 15-49: 730,363 (2001 est.)
Military manpower - reaching military age annually:
males: 28,506 (2001 est.)
Military expenditures - dollar figure: $181 million (FY99)
Military expenditures - percent of GDP: 1.66% (FY00)

Transnational Issues

Disputes - international: Latvia has not ratified a 1998 maritime boundary agreement with Lithuania (primary concern is oil exploration rights); 1997 border agreement with Russia not yet ratified by Russia
Illicit drugs: transshipment point for opiates and other illicit drugs from Southwest Asia, Latin America, and Western Europe to Western Europe and Scandinavia; limited production of methamphetamine and ecstasy

Luxembourg

Introduction

Background: Founded in 963, Luxembourg became a grand duchy in 1815 and an independent state under the Netherlands. It lost more than half of its territory to Belgium in 1839, but gained a larger measure of autonomy. Full independence was attained in 1867. Overrun by Germany in both World Wars, it ended its neutrality in 1948 when it entered into the Benelux Customs Union and when it joined NATO the following year. In 1957, Luxembourg became one of the six founding countries of the European Economic Community (later the European Union) and in 1999 it joined the euro currency area.

Geography

Location: Western Europe, between France and Germany
Geographic coordinates: 49 45 N, 6 10 E
Map references: Europe
Area:
total: 2,586 sq km
land: 2,586 sq km
water: 0 sq km
Area - comparative: slightly smaller than Rhode Island
Land boundaries:
total: 356 km
border countries: Belgium 148 km, France 73 km, Germany 135 km
Coastline: 0 km (landlocked)
Maritime claims: none (landlocked)
Climate: modified continental with mild winters, cool summers
Terrain: mostly gently rolling uplands with broad, shallow valleys; uplands to slightly mountainous in the north; steep slope down to Moselle flood plain in the southeast
Elevation extremes:
lowest point: Moselle River 133 m
highest point: Buurgplaatz 559 m
Natural resources: iron ore (no longer exploited), arable land
Land use:
arable land: 24%
permanent crops: 1%
permanent pastures: 20%
forests and woodland: 35%
other: 20%
Irrigated land: 10 sq km (including Belgium) (1993 est.)
Natural hazards: NA
Environment - current issues: air and water pollution in urban areas, soil pollution of farmland
Environment - international agreements:
party to: Air Pollution, Air Pollution-Nitrogen Oxides, Air Pollution-Persistent Organic Pollutants, Air Pollution-Sulphur 85, Air Pollution-Sulphur 94, Air Pollution-Volatile Organic Compounds, Biodiversity, Climate Change, Desertification, Endangered Species, Hazardous Wastes, Law of the Sea, Marine Dumping, Nuclear Test Ban, Ozone Layer Protection, Ship Pollution, Tropical Timber 83, Tropical Timber 94, Wetlands
signed, but not ratified: Climate Change-Kyoto Protocol, Environmental Modification
Geography - note: landlocked

People

Population: 442,972 (July 2001 est.)
Age structure:
0-14 years: 18.91% (male 43,051; female 40,711)
15-64 years: 67.03% (male 149,781; female 147,165)
65 years and over: 14.06% (male 24,921; female 37,343) (2001 est.)
Population growth rate: 1.26% (2001 est.)
Birth rate: 12.25 births/1,000 population (2001 est.)
Death rate: 8.88 deaths/1,000 population (2001 est.)
Net migration rate: 9.26 migrant(s)/1,000 population (2001 est.)
Sex ratio:
at birth: 1.07 male(s)/female
under 15 years: 1.06 male(s)/female
15-64 years: 1.02 male(s)/female
65 years and over: 0.67 male(s)/female
total population: 0.97 male(s)/female (2001 est.)
Infant mortality rate: 4.77 deaths/1,000 live births (2001 est.)
Life expectancy at birth:
total population: 77.3 years
male: 74.02 years
female: 80.8 years (2001 est.)
Total fertility rate: 1.7 children born/woman (2001 est.)
HIV/AIDS - adult prevalence rate: 0.16% (1999 est.)
HIV/AIDS - people living with HIV/AIDS: NA
HIV/AIDS - deaths: less than 100 (1999 est.)
Nationality:
noun: Luxembourger(s)
adjective: Luxembourg

Luxembourg (continued)

Ethnic groups: Celtic base (with French and German blend), Portuguese, Italian, Slavs (from Montenegro, Albania, and Kosovo) and European (guest and resident workers)
Religions: the greatest preponderance of the population is Roman Catholic with a very few Protestants, Jews, and Muslims
note: 1979 legislation forbids the collection of religious statistics
Languages: Luxembourgish (national language), German (administrative language), French (administrative language)
Literacy:
definition: age 15 and over can read and write
total population: 100%
male: 100%
female: 100% (2000 est.)

Government

Country name:
conventional long form: Grand Duchy of Luxembourg
conventional short form: Luxembourg
local long form: Grand Duche de Luxembourg
local short form: Luxembourg
Government type: constitutional monarchy
Capital: Luxembourg
Administrative divisions: 3 districts; Diekirch, Grevenmacher, Luxembourg
Independence: 1839 (from the Netherlands)
National holiday: National Day (Birthday of Grand Duchess Charlotte) 23 June
Constitution: 17 October 1868, occasional revisions
Legal system: based on civil law system; accepts compulsory ICJ jurisdiction
Suffrage: 18 years of age; universal and compulsory
Executive branch:
chief of state: Grand Duke HENRI (since 7 October 2000); Heir Apparent Prince GUILLAUME (son of the monarch, born 11 November 1981);
head of government: Prime Minister Jean-Claude JUNCKER (since 1 January 1995) and Vice Prime Minister Lydie POLFER (since 7 August 1999)
cabinet: Council of Ministers recommended by the prime minister and appointed by the monarch
elections: none; the monarch is hereditary; prime minister and vice prime minister appointed by the monarch, following popular election to the Chamber of Deputies; they are responsible to the Chamber of Deputies
note: government coalition - CSV and DP
Legislative branch: unicameral Chamber of Deputies or Chambre des Deputes (60 seats; members are elected by direct popular vote to serve five-year terms)
elections: last held 13 June 1999 (next to be held by NA June 2004)
election results: percent of vote by party - CSV 29.79%, DP 21.58%, LSAP 23.75%, ADR 10.36%, Green Party 9.09%, the Left 3.77%; seats by party - CSV 19, DP 15, LSAP 13, ADR 6, Green Party 5, the Left 2
note: the Council of State or Conseil d'Etat, which has 21 members who are appointed and dismissed by the Grand Duke based on proposals from the government, the Chamber of Deputies, or the Council of State, is an advisory body whose views are considered by the Chamber of Deputies
Judicial branch: judicial courts and tribunals (3 Justices of the Peace, 2 district courts, and 1 Supreme Court of Appeals); administrative courts and tribunals (State Prosecutor's Office, administrative courts and tribunals, and the Constitutional Court); judges for all courts are appointed for life by the monarch
Political parties and leaders: Action Committee for Democracy and Justice or ADR [Robert MEHLEN]; Christian Social People's Party or CSV (known also as Christian Social Party or PCS) [Erna HENNICOT-SCHOEPGES]; Democratic Party or DP [Lydie POLFER]; Green Party [Abbes JACOBY and Felix BRAS]; Luxembourg Socialist Workers' Party or LSAP [Jean ASSELBORN]; Marxist and Reformed Communist Party DEI LENK (the Left) [no formal leadership]; other minor parties
Political pressure groups and leaders: ABBL (bankers' association); ALEBA (financial sector trade union); Centrale Paysanne (federation of agricultural producers); CEP (professional sector chamber); CGFP (trade union representing civil service); Chambre de Commerce (Chamber of Commerce); Chambre des Metiers (Chamber of Artisans); FEDIL (federation of industrialists); LCGP (center-right trade union); OGBL (center-left trade union)
International organization participation: ACCT, Australia Group, Benelux, CCC, CE, EAPC, EBRD, ECE, EIB, EMU, EU, FAO, IAEA, IBRD, ICAO, ICC, ICFTU, ICRM, IDA, IEA, IFAD, IFC, IFRCS, ILO, IMF, IMO, Intelsat, Interpol, IOC, IOM, ISO, ITU, NATO, NEA, NSG, OECD, OPCW, OSCE, PCA, UN, UNCTAD, UNESCO, UNIDO, UPU, WCL, WEU, WHO, WIPO, WMO, WTrO, ZC
Diplomatic representation in the US:
chief of mission: Ambassador Arlette CONZEMIUS
chancery: 2200 Massachusetts Avenue NW, Washington, DC 20008
telephone: [1] (202) 265-4171
FAX: [1] (202) 328-8270
consulate(s) general: New York and San Francisco
Diplomatic representation from the US:
chief of mission: Ambassador James C. HORMEL
embassy: 22 Boulevard Emmanuel-Servais, L-2535 Luxembourg City
mailing address: American Embassy Luxembourg, Unit 1410, APO AE 09126-1410 (official mail); American Embassy Luxembourg, PSC 9, Box 9500, APO AE 09123 (personal mail)
telephone: [352] 46 01 23
FAX: [352] 46 14 01
Flag description: three equal horizontal bands of red (top), white, and light blue; similar to the flag of the Netherlands, which uses a darker blue and is shorter; design was based on the flag of France

Economy

Economy - overview: The stable, high-income economy features solid growth, low inflation, and low unemployment. The industrial sector, initially dominated by steel, has become increasingly diversified to include chemicals, rubber, and other products. Growth in the financial sector has more than compensated for the decline in steel. Services, especially banking, account for a substantial proportion of the economy. Agriculture is based on small family-owned farms. The economy depends on foreign and trans-border workers for 30% of its labor force. Luxembourg has a custom union with Belgium and the Netherlands, and, as a member of the EU, enjoys the advantages of the open European market. It joined with 10 other EU members to launch the euro on 1 January 1999.
GDP: purchasing power parity - $15.9 billion (2000 est.)
GDP - real growth rate: 5.7% (2000 est.)
GDP - per capita: purchasing power parity - $36,400 (2000 est.)
GDP - composition by sector:
agriculture: 1%
industry: 30%
services: 69% (2000 est.)
Population below poverty line: NA%
Household income or consumption by percentage share:
lowest 10%: NA%
highest 10%: NA%
Inflation rate (consumer prices): 7.8% (2000 est.)
Labor force: 248,000 (of whom 70,200 are foreign cross-border workers primarily from France, Belgium, and Germany) (2000)
Labor force - by occupation: services 83.2%, industry 14.3%, agriculture 2.5% (1998 est.)
Unemployment rate: 2.7% (2000 est.)
Budget:
revenues: $5.6 billion
expenditures: $5.6 billion, including capital expenditures of $NA (2000 est.)
Industries: banking, iron and steel, food processing, chemicals, metal products, engineering, tires, glass, aluminum
Industrial production growth rate: 7.8% (2000 est.)
Electricity - production: 648 million kWh (1999)
Electricity - production by source:
fossil fuel: 36.88%
hydro: 53.09%
nuclear: 0%
other: 10.03% (1999)
Electricity - consumption: 6.149 billion kWh (1999)
Electricity - exports: 655 million kWh (1999)
Electricity - imports: 6.201 billion kWh (1999)
Agriculture - products: barley, oats, potatoes, wheat, fruits, wine grapes; livestock products
Exports: $7.6 billion (f.o.b., 2000)
Exports - commodities: machinery and equipment, steel products, chemicals, rubber products, glass

Luxembourg (continued)

Exports - partners: EU 75% (Germany 25%, France 21%, Belgium 13%, UK 8%, Italy 6%, Netherlands 5%), US 4% (1999)
Imports: $10 billion (c.i.f., 2000)
Imports - commodities: minerals, metals, foodstuffs, quality consumer goods
Imports - partners: EU 81% (Belgium 35%, Germany 26%, France 12%, Netherlands 4%), US 9% (1999)
Debt - external: $NA
Economic aid - donor: ODA, $160 million (1999)
Currency: Luxembourg franc (LUF); euro (EUR)
note: on 1 January 1999, the EU introduced the euro as a common currency that is now being used by financial institutions in Luxembourg at a fixed rate of 40.3399 Luxembourg francs per euro and will replace the local currency for all transactions in 2002
Currency code: LUF; EUR
Exchange rates: euros per US dollar - 1.0659 (January 2001), 1.0854 (2000), 0.9386 (1999); Luxembourg francs per US dollar - 34.77 (January 1999), 36.299 (1998), 35.774 (1997), 30.962 (1996); note - the Luxembourg franc is at par with the Belgian franc, which circulates freely in Luxembourg
Fiscal year: calendar year

Communications

Telephones - main lines in use: 314,700 (1999)
Telephones - mobile cellular: 215,741 (2000)
Telephone system:
general assessment: highly developed, completely automated and efficient system, mainly buried cables
domestic: nationwide cellular telephone system; buried cable
international: 3 channels leased on TAT-6 coaxial submarine cable (Europe to North America)
Radio broadcast stations: AM 2, FM 9, shortwave 2 (1999)
Radios: 285,000 (1997)
Television broadcast stations: 5 (1999)
Televisions: 285,000 (1998 est.)
Internet country code: .lu
Internet Service Providers (ISPs): 8 (2000)
Internet users: 86,000 (1999)

Transportation

Railways:
total: 274 km
standard gauge: 274 km 1.435-m gauge (242 km electrified; 178 km double track) (1998)
Highways:
total: 5,166 km
paved: 5,166 km (including 118 km of expressways)
unpaved: 0 km (1999)
Waterways: 37 km (on the Moselle)
Pipelines: petroleum products 48 km
Ports and harbors: Mertert
Merchant marine:
total: 50 ships (1,000 GRT or over) totaling 988,450 GRT/1,313,498 DWT
ships by type: bulk 2, chemical tanker 11, container 2, liquefied gas 18, passenger 4, petroleum tanker 6, roll on/roll off 7
note: includes some foreign-owned ships registered here as a flag of convenience: Belgium 4 (2000 est.)
Airports: 2 (2000 est.)
Airports - with paved runways:
total: 1
over 3,047 m: 1 (2000 est.)
Airports - with unpaved runways:
total: 1
under 914 m: 1 (2000 est.)
Heliports: 1 (2000 est.)

Military

Military branches: Army; note - the government abolished the Gendarmerie
Military manpower - military age: 19 years of age
Military manpower - availability:
males age 15-49: 112,714 (2001 est.)
Military manpower - fit for military service:
males age 15-49: 92,817 (2001 est.)
Military manpower - reaching military age annually:
males: 2,565 (2001 est.)
Military expenditures - dollar figure: $131 million (FY98/99)
Military expenditures - percent of GDP: 1% (FY98/99)

Transnational Issues

Disputes - international: none

Macau
(special administrative region of China)

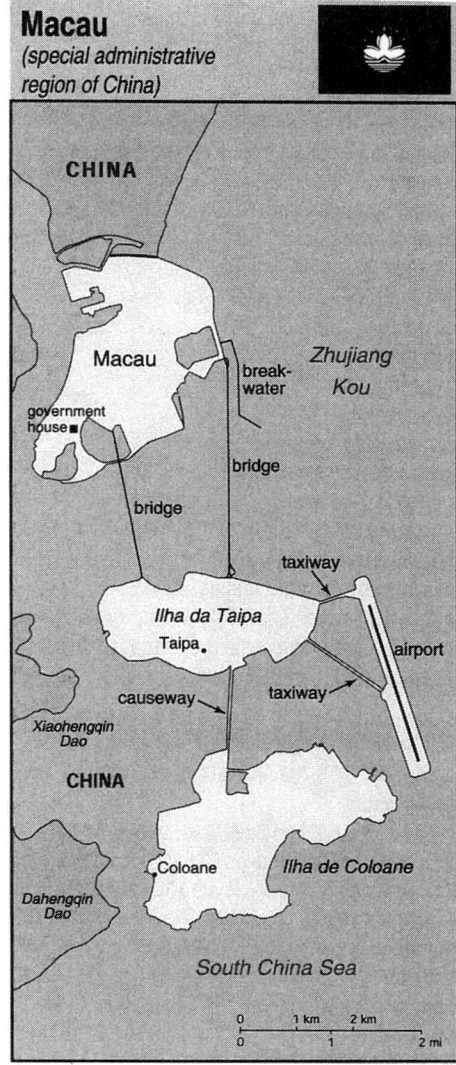

Introduction

Background: Colonized by the Portuguese in the 16th century, Macau was the first European settlement in the Far East. Pursuant to an agreement signed by China and Portugal on 13 April 1987, Macau became the Macau Special Administrative Region (SAR) of China on 20 December 1999. China has promised that, under its "one country, two systems" formula, China's socialist economic system will not be practiced in Macau and that Macau will enjoy a high degree of autonomy in all matters except foreign and defense affairs.

Geography

Location: Eastern Asia, bordering the South China Sea and China
Geographic coordinates: 22 10 N, 113 33 E
Map references: Southeast Asia
Area:
total: 21 sq km
land: 21 sq km
water: 0 sq km
Area - comparative: about 0.1 times the size of Washington, DC

Macau (continued)

Land boundaries:
total: 0.34 km
border countries: China 0.34 km
Coastline: 40 km
Maritime claims: not specified
Climate: subtropical; marine with cool winters, warm summers
Terrain: generally flat
Elevation extremes:
lowest point: South China Sea 0 m
highest point: Coloane Alto 174 m
Natural resources: NEGL
Land use:
arable land: 0%
permanent crops: 2%
permanent pastures: 0%
forests and woodland: 0%
other: 98% (1998 est.)
Irrigated land: NA sq km
Natural hazards: typhoons
Environment - current issues: NA
Geography - note: essentially urban; one causeway and two bridges connect the two islands of Coloane and Taipa to the peninsula on mainland

People

Population: 453,733 (July 2001 est.)
Age structure:
0-14 years: 22.68% (male 53,291; female 49,615)
15-64 years: 70.08% (male 150,538; female 167,431)
65 years and over: 7.24% (male 13,287; female 19,571) (2001 est.)
Population growth rate: 1.79% (2001 est.)
Birth rate: 12.36 births/1,000 population (2001 est.)
Death rate: 3.71 deaths/1,000 population (2001 est.)
Net migration rate: 9.25 migrant(s)/1,000 population (2001 est.)
Sex ratio:
at birth: 1.05 male(s)/female
under 15 years: 1.07 male(s)/female
15-64 years: 0.9 male(s)/female
65 years and over: 0.68 male(s)/female
total population: 0.92 male(s)/female (2001 est.)
Infant mortality rate: 4.47 deaths/1,000 live births (2001 est.)
Life expectancy at birth:
total population: 81.69 years
male: 78.88 years
female: 84.64 years (2001 est.)
Total fertility rate: 1.31 children born/woman (2001 est.)
HIV/AIDS - adult prevalence rate: NA%
HIV/AIDS - people living with HIV/AIDS: NA
HIV/AIDS - deaths: NA
Nationality:
noun: Chinese
adjective: Chinese
Ethnic groups: Chinese 95%, Macanese (mixed Portuguese and Asian ancestry), Portuguese, other
Religions: Buddhist 50%, Roman Catholic 15%, none and other 35% (1997 est.)

Languages: Portuguese, Chinese (Cantonese)
Literacy:
definition: age 15 and over can read and write
total population: 90%
male: 93%
female: 86% (1981 est.)

Government

Country name:
conventional long form: Macau Special Administrative Region
conventional short form: Macau
local long form: Aomen Tebie Xingzhengqu (Chinese); Regiao Administrativa Especial de Macau (Portuguese)
local short form: Aomen (Chinese); Macau (Portuguese)
Dependency status: special administrative region of China
Government type: NA
Administrative divisions: none (special administrative region of China)
Independence: none (special administrative region of China)
National holiday: National Day (Anniversary of the Founding of the People's Republic of China), 1 October (1949); note - 20 December 1999 is celebrated as Macau Special Administrative Region Establishment Day
Constitution: Basic Law, approved in March 1993 by China's National People's Congress, is Macau's "mini-constitution"
Legal system: based on Portuguese civil law system
Suffrage: direct election 18 years of age, universal for permanent residents living in Macau for the past seven years; indirect election limited to organizations registered as "corporate voters" (257 are currently registered) and a 300-member Election Committee drawn from broad regional groupings, municipal organizations, and central government bodies
Executive branch:
chief of state: President of China JIANG Zemin (since 27 March 1993)
head of government: Chief Executive Edmund HO Hau-wah (since 20 December 1999)
cabinet: Executive Council consists of all five government secretaries, three legislators, and two businessmen
elections: NA
Legislative branch: unicameral Legislative Council or LEGCO (23 seats; 8 elected by popular vote, 8 by indirect vote, and 7 appointed by the chief executive; members serve four-year terms)
elections: last held 22 September 1996 (next to be held by 15 October 2001)
election results: percent of vote by party - NA%; seats by party - APPEM 2, UNIPRO 2, CODEM 1, UDM 1, UPD 1, ANMD 1
Judicial branch: The Court of Final Appeal in the Macau Special Administrative Region

Political parties and leaders: the following is a listing of those associations that participated in the last legislative elections: Associacao de Novo Macau Democratico or ANMD [leader NA]; Associacao Promotora para a Economia de Macau or APPEM [leader NA]; Convergencia para o Desenvolvimento or CODEM [leader NA]; Uniao Geral para o Desenvolvimento de Macau or UDM [leader NA]; Uniao para o Desenvolvimento or UPD [leader NA]; Uniao Promotora para o Progresso or UNIPRO [leader NA]
note: there are no formal political parties, but civic associations are used instead
Political pressure groups and leaders: Catholic Church [Domingos LAM, bishop]; Macau Society of Tourism and Entertainment or STDM [Stanley HO, managing director]; Union for Democracy Development [Antonio NG Kuok-cheong, leader]
International organization participation: CCC, ESCAP (associate), IMO (associate), Interpol (subbureau), UNESCO (associate), WMO, WToO (associate), WTrO
Diplomatic representation in the US: none (special administrative region of China)
Diplomatic representation from the US: the US has no offices in Macau, and US interests are monitored by the US Consulate General in Hong Kong
Flag description: light green with a lotus flower above a stylized bridge and water in white, beneath an arc of five gold, five-pointed stars: one large in center of arc and four smaller

Economy

Economy - overview: The economy is based largely on tourism (including gambling) and textile and fireworks manufacturing. Efforts to diversify have spawned other small industries - toys, artificial flowers, and electronics. The tourist sector has accounted for roughly 25% of GDP, and the clothing industry has provided about three-fourths of export earnings; the gambling industry probably represents over 40% of GDP. More than 8 million tourists visited Macau in 2000. Macau depends on China for most of its food, fresh water, and energy imports. Japan and Hong Kong are the main suppliers of raw materials and capital goods. Output dropped 5% in 1998 and 3% in 1999, with a small 2% gain in 2000. Macau reverted to Chinese administration on 20 December 1999. Gang violence, a dark spot in the economy, probably will be reduced in 2000-01 to the advantage of the tourism sector.
GDP: purchasing power parity - $7.82 billion (2000 est.)
GDP - real growth rate: 2% (2000 est.)
GDP - per capita: purchasing power parity - $17,500 (2000 est.)
GDP - composition by sector:
agriculture: 1%
industry: 25%
services: 74% (2000 est.)
Population below poverty line: NA%

Macau (continued)

Household income or consumption by percentage share:
lowest 10%: NA%
highest 10%: NA%
Inflation rate (consumer prices): -1.8% (2000 est.)
Labor force: 283,450 (1999)
Labor force - by occupation: restaurants and hotels 26%, manufacturing 22%, other services 52% (2000 est.)
Unemployment rate: 6.6% (2000)
Budget:
revenues: $1.26 billion
expenditures: $1.22 billion, including capital expenditures of $175 million (1999 est.)
Industries: clothing, textiles, toys, electronics, footwear, tourism, gambling
Industrial production growth rate: NA%
Electricity - production: 1.355 billion kWh (1999)
Electricity - production by source:
fossil fuel: 100%
hydro: 0%
nuclear: 0%
other: 0% (1999)
Electricity - consumption: 1.422 billion kWh (1999)
Electricity - exports: 3 million kWh (1999)
Electricity - imports: 165 million kWh (1999)
Agriculture - products: rice, vegetables
Exports: $2.6 billion (f.o.b., 2000 est.)
Exports - commodities: textiles, clothing, toys, electronics, cement, footwear, machinery
Exports - partners: US 47%, EU 30%, China 9.2%, Hong Kong 6.7% (1999)
Imports: $2.4 billion (c.i.f., 2000 est.)
Imports - commodities: raw materials, foodstuffs, capital goods, fuels, consumer goods
Imports - partners: China 36%, Hong Kong 18%, EU 13%, Taiwan 10%, Japan 7% (1999)
Debt - external: $1.7 billion (1997)
Economic aid - recipient: $NA
Currency: pataca (MOP)
Currency code: MOP
Exchange rates: patacas per US dollar - 8.033 (January 2001), 8.025 (2000), 7.990 (1999), 7.978 (1998), 7.974 (1997), 7.966 (1996); note - linked to the Hong Kong dollar at the rate of 1.03 patacas per Hong Kong dollar
Fiscal year: calendar year

Communications

Telephones - main lines in use: 176,837 (2000)
Telephones - mobile cellular: 120,957 (2000)
Telephone system:
general assessment: fairly modern communication facilities maintained for domestic and international services
domestic: NA
international: HF radiotelephone communication facility; access to international communications carriers provided via Hong Kong and China; satellite earth station - 1 Intelsat (Indian Ocean)
Radio broadcast stations: AM 0, FM 2, shortwave 0 (1998)
Radios: 160,000 (1997)
Television broadcast stations: 0 (receives Hong Kong broadcasts) (1997)
Televisions: 49,000 (1997)
Internet country code: .mo
Internet Service Providers (ISPs): 1 (2000)
Internet users: 40,000 (2000)

Transportation

Railways: 0 km
Highways:
total: 50 km
paved: 50 km
unpaved: 0 km (2001)
Waterways: none
Ports and harbors: Macau
Merchant marine: none (2000 est.)
Airports: 1 (2000 est.)
Airports - with paved runways:
total: 1
over 3,047 m: 1 (2000 est.)

Military

Military branches: Macau garrison of China's People's Liberation Army (PLA) includes about 500 troops
Military manpower - availability:
males age 15-49: 125,737 (2001 est.)
Military manpower - fit for military service:
males age 15-49: 69,191 (2001 est.)
Military - note: responsibility for defense reverted to China on 20 December 1999

Transnational Issues

Disputes - international: none

Macedonia, The Former Yugoslav Republic of

Introduction

Background: International recognition of The Former Yugoslav Republic of Macedonia's (FYROM) independence from Yugoslavia in 1991 was delayed by Greece's objection to the new state's use of what it considered a Hellenic name and symbols. Greece finally lifted its trade blockade in 1995, and the two countries agreed to normalize relations, despite continued disagreement over FYROM's use of "Macedonia." FYROM's large Albanian minority and the de facto independence of neighboring Kosovo continue to be sources of ethnic tension.

Geography

Location: Southeastern Europe, north of Greece
Geographic coordinates: 41 50 N, 22 00 E
Map references: Europe
Area:
total: 25,333 sq km
land: 24,856 sq km
water: 477 sq km
Area - comparative: slightly larger than Vermont
Land boundaries:
total: 748 km
border countries: Albania 151 km, Bulgaria 148 km, Greece 228 km, Yugoslavia 221 km
Coastline: 0 km (landlocked)
Maritime claims: none (landlocked)
Climate: warm, dry summers and autumns and relatively cold winters with heavy snowfall
Terrain: mountainous territory covered with deep basins and valleys; three large lakes, each divided by a frontier line; country bisected by the Vardar River
Elevation extremes:
lowest point: Vardar River 50 m
highest point: Golem Korab (Maja e Korabit) 2,753 m
Natural resources: chromium, lead, zinc, manganese, tungsten, nickel, low-grade iron ore, asbestos, sulfur, timber, arable land

Macedonia, The Former Yugoslav Republic of (continued)

Land use:
arable land: 24%
permanent crops: 2%
permanent pastures: 25%
forests and woodland: 39%
other: 10% (1993 est.)
Irrigated land: 830 sq km (1993 est.)
Natural hazards: high seismic risks
Environment - current issues: air pollution from metallurgical plants
Environment - international agreements:
party to: Air Pollution, Biodiversity, Climate Change, Endangered Species, Hazardous Wastes, Law of the Sea, Marine Dumping, Ozone Layer Protection, Ship Pollution, Wetlands
signed, but not ratified: none of the selected agreements
Geography - note: landlocked; major transportation corridor from Western and Central Europe to Aegean Sea and Southern Europe to Western Europe

People

Population: 2,046,209 (July 2001 est.)
Age structure:
0-14 years: 22.92% (male 243,715; female 225,349)
15-64 years: 66.94% (male 688,484; female 681,225)
65 years and over: 10.14% (male 92,043; female 115,393) (2001 est.)
Population growth rate: 0.43% (2001 est.)
Birth rate: 13.5 births/1,000 population (2001 est.)
Death rate: 7.7 deaths/1,000 population (2001 est.)
Net migration rate: -1.54 migrant(s)/1,000 population (2001 est.)
Sex ratio:
at birth: 1.08 male(s)/female
under 15 years: 1.08 male(s)/female
15-64 years: 1.01 male(s)/female
65 years and over: 0.8 male(s)/female
total population: 1 male(s)/female (2001 est.)
Infant mortality rate: 12.95 deaths/1,000 live births (2001 est.)
Life expectancy at birth:
total population: 74.02 years
male: 71.79 years
female: 76.43 years (2001 est.)
Total fertility rate: 1.79 children born/woman (2001 est.)
HIV/AIDS - adult prevalence rate: less than 0.01% (1999 est.)
HIV/AIDS - people living with HIV/AIDS: less than 100 (1999 est.)
HIV/AIDS - deaths: less than 100 (1999 est.)
Nationality:
noun: Macedonian(s)
adjective: Macedonian
Ethnic groups: Macedonian 66.6%, Albanian 22.7%, Turkish 4%, Roma 2.2%, Serb 2.1%, other 2.4% (1994)
Religions: Macedonian Orthodox 67%, Muslim 30%, other 3%
Languages: Macedonian 70%, Albanian 21%, Turkish 3%, Serbo-Croatian 3%, other 3%
Literacy:
definition: NA
total population: NA%
male: NA%
female: NA%

Government

Country name:
conventional long form: The Former Yugoslav Republic of Macedonia
conventional short form: none
local long form: Republika Makedonija
local short form: Makedonija
abbreviation: FYROM
Government type: emerging democracy
Capital: Skopje
Administrative divisions: 123 municipalities (opstini, singular - opstina); Aracinovo, Bac, Belcista, Berovo, Bistrica, Bitola, Blatec, Bogdanci, Bogomila, Bogovinje, Bosilovo, Brvenica, Cair (Skopje), Capari, Caska, Cegrane, Centar (Skopje), Centar Zupa, Cesinovo, Cucer-Sandevo, Debar, Delcevo, Delogozdi, Demir Hisar, Demir Kapija, Dobrusevo, Dolna Banjica, Dolneni, Dorce Petrov (Skopje), Drugovo, Dzepciste, Gazi Baba (Skopje), Gevgelija, Gostivar, Gradsko, Ilinden, Izvor, Jegunovce, Kamenjane, Karbinci, Karpos (Skopje), Kavadarci, Kicevo, Kisela Voda (Skopje), Klecevce, Kocani, Konce, Kondovo, Konopiste, Kosel, Kratovo, Kriva Palanka, Krivogastani, Krusevo, Kuklis, Kukurecani, Kumanovo, Labunista, Lipkovo, Lozovo, Lukovo, Makedonska Kamenica, Makedonski Brod, Mavrovi Anovi, Meseista, Miravci, Mogila, Murtino, Negotino, Negotino-Poloska, Novaci, Novo Selo, Oblesevo, Ohrid, Orasac, Orizari, Oslomej, Pehcevo, Petrovec, Plasnia, Podares, Prilep, Probistip, Radovis, Rankovce, Resen, Rosoman, Rostusa, Samokov, Saraj, Sipkovica, Sopiste, Sopotnika, Srbinovo, Star Dojran, Staravina, Staro Nagoricane, Stip, Struga, Strumica, Studenicani, Suto Orizari (Skopje), Sveti Nikole, Tearce, Tetovo, Topolcani, Valandovo, Vasilevo, Velesta, Veles, Vevcani, Vinica, Vitoliste, Vranestica, Vrapciste, Vratnica, Vrutok, Zajas, Zelenikovo, Zileno, Zitose, Zletovo, Zrnovci
note: the seven municipalities followed by Skopje in parentheses collectively constitute "greater Skopje"
Independence: 17 September 1991 (from Yugoslavia)
National holiday: Uprising Day, 2 August (1903)
Constitution: adopted 17 November 1991, effective 20 November 1991
note: Democratic Party for Albanians (DPA), which is now a member party of the government, is calling for a rewrite of the constitution to declare ethnic Albanians a constituent national group and allow for greater regional autonomy
Legal system: based on civil law system; judicial review of legislative acts
Suffrage: 18 years of age; universal
Executive branch:
chief of state: President Boris TRAJKOVSKI (since 15 December 1999)
head of government: Prime Minister Ljubco GEORGIEVSKI (since 30 November 1998)
cabinet: Council of Ministers elected by the majority vote of all the deputies in the Assembly; note - current cabinet formed by the government coalition parties VMRO-DPMNE, LDP, and DPA
elections: president elected by popular vote for a five-year term; election last held 14 November 1999 (next to be held NA October 2004); prime minister elected by parliament; election last held NA November 1998 (next to be held NA 2002)
election results: Boris TRAJKOVSKI elected president on second-round ballot; percent of vote - Boris TRAJKOVSKI 52.4%, Tito PETKOVSKI 46.2%
Legislative branch: unicameral Assembly or Sobranje (120 seats - 85 members are elected by popular vote, 35 members come from lists of candidates submitted by parties based on the percentage that parties gain from the overall vote; all serve four-year terms)
elections: last held 18 October and 1 November 1998 (next to be held NA 2002)
election results: percent of vote by party - NA%; seats by party - VMRO-DPMNE 43, SDSM 27, PDP 14, DA 13, DPA 11, VMRO-VMRO 6, LDP 4, SP 1, Roma Party 1
Judicial branch: Constitutional Court; Judicial Court of the Republic; judges for both courts are elected by the Judicial Council
Political parties and leaders: Democratic Alternative or DA [Vasil TUPURKOVSKI, president]; Democratic Party for Albanians or DPA [Arben XHAFERI, president]; Internal Macedonian Revolutionary Organization - Democratic Party for Macedonian National Unity or VMRO-DPMNE [Ljubcho GEORGIEVSKI, president]; Internal Macedonian Revolutionary Organization-True Macedonian Reform Option or VMRO-VMRO [Boris STOJMANOV]; Liberal Democratic Party or LDP [Risto GUSTERVO]; Party for Democratic Prosperity or PDP [Imeri IMERI, president]; Social-Democratic Alliance of Macedonia or SDSM (former Communist Party) [Branko CRVENKOVSKI, president]; Socialist Party of Macedonia or SP [Ljubisav IVANOV, president]; Union of Romanies of Macedonia or SRM [leader NA]
Political pressure groups and leaders: NA
International organization participation: ACCT (associate), BIS, CCC, CE, CEI, EAPC, EBRD, ECE, FAO, IAEA, IBRD, ICAO, ICRM, IDA, IFAD, IFC, IFRCS, ILO, IMF, IMO, Intelsat (nonsignatory user), Interpol, IOC, IOM (observer), ISO, ITU, OPCW, OSCE, PFP, UN, UNCTAD, UNESCO, UNIDO, UPU, WCL, WHO, WIPO, WMO, WToO, WTrO (observer)
Diplomatic representation in the US:
chief of mission: Ambassador Ljubica Z. ACEVSKA
chancery: 3050 K Street, NW, Suite 210, Washington, DC 20007
telephone: [1] (202) 337 3063
FAX: [1] (202) 337-3093
consulate(s) general: New York

Macedonia, The Former Yugoslav Republic of (continued)

Diplomatic representation from the US:
chief of mission: Ambassador Michael M. EINIK
embassy: Bul. Ilinden bb, 91000 Skopje
mailing address: American Embassy Skopje, Department of State, Washington, DC 20521-7120 (pouch)
telephone: [389] (91) 116-180
FAX: [389] (91) 117-103
Flag description: a rising yellow sun with eight rays extending to the edges of the red field

Economy

Economy - overview: At independence in November 1991, Macedonia was the least developed of the Yugoslav republics, producing a mere 5% of the total federal output of goods and services. The collapse of Yugoslavia ended transfer payments from the center and eliminated advantages from inclusion in a de facto free trade area. An absence of infrastructure, UN sanctions on its largest market Yugoslavia, and a Greek economic embargo hindered economic growth until 1996. GDP has subsequently increased each year, rising by 5% in 2000. Successful privatization in 2000 boosted the country's reserves to over $700 million. Also, the leadership demonstrated a continuing commitment to economic reform, free trade, and regional integration. Inflation jumped to 11% in 2000, largely due to higher oil prices.
GDP: purchasing power parity - $9 billion (2000 est.)
GDP - real growth rate: 5% (2000 est.)
GDP - per capita: purchasing power parity - $4,400 (2000 est.)
GDP - composition by sector:
agriculture: 12%
industry: 25%
services: 63% (2000)
Population below poverty line: 25% (2000 est.)
Household income or consumption by percentage share:
lowest 10%: NA%
highest 10%: NA%
Inflation rate (consumer prices): 11% (2000 est.)
Labor force: 1 million (1999 est.)
Labor force - by occupation: agriculture NA%, industry NA%, services NA%
Unemployment rate: 32% (2000)
Budget:
revenues: $1.06 billion
expenditures: $1 billion, including capital expenditures of $107 million (1996 est.)
Industries: coal, metallic chromium, lead, zinc, ferronickel, textiles, wood products, tobacco
Industrial production growth rate: 3% (2000)
Electricity - production: 6.395 billion kWh (1999)
Electricity - production by source:
fossil fuel: 82.25%
hydro: 17.75%
nuclear: 0%
other: 0% (1999)
Electricity - consumption: 5.992 billion kWh (1999)
Electricity - exports: 30 million kWh (1999)
Electricity - imports: 75 million kWh (1999)
Agriculture - products: rice, tobacco, wheat, corn, millet, cotton, sesame, mulberry leaves, citrus, vegetables; beef, pork, poultry, mutton
Exports: $1.4 billion (f.o.b., 2000 est.)
Exports - commodities: food, beverages, tobacco; miscellaneous manufactures, iron and steel
Exports - partners: Germany 22%, Yugoslavia 22%, US 12%, Greece 7%, Italy 6% (2000)
Imports: $2 billion (f.o.b., 2000 est.)
Imports - commodities: machinery and equipment, chemicals, fuels; food products
Imports - partners: Germany 13%, Ukraine 13%, Russia 10%, Yugoslavia 8%, Greece 8% (2000)
Debt - external: $1.4 billion (2000)
Economic aid - recipient: $100 million from the EU (2000)
Currency: Macedonian denar (MKD)
Currency code: MKD
Exchange rates: Macedonian denars per US dollar - 64.757 (January 2001), 65.904 (2000), 56.902 (1999), 54.462 (1998), 50.004 (1997), 39.981 (1996)
Fiscal year: calendar year

Communications

Telephones - main lines in use: 408,000 (1997)
Telephones - mobile cellular: 12,362 (1997)
Telephone system:
general assessment: NA
domestic: NA
international: NA
Radio broadcast stations: AM 29, FM 20, shortwave 0 (1998)
Radios: 410,000 (1997)
Television broadcast stations: 31 (plus 166 repeaters) (1995)
Televisions: 510,000 (1997)
Internet country code: .mk
Internet Service Providers (ISPs): 6 (2000)
Internet users: 30,000 (2000)

Transportation

Railways:
total: 699 km
standard gauge: 699 km 1.435-m gauge (233 km electrified)
note: a 56-km extension of the Kumanovo-Beljakovci line to the Bulgarian border at Gyveshevo is under construction (2001)
Highways:
total: 8,684 km
paved: 5,540 km (including 133 km of expressways)
unpaved: 3,144 km (1997)
Waterways:
note: lake transport only, on the Greek and Albanian borders
Pipelines: 10 km
Ports and harbors: none
Airports: 16 (2000 est.)
Airports - with paved runways:
total: 10
2,438 to 3,047 m: 2
under 914 m: 8 (2000 est.)
Airports - with unpaved runways:
total: 6
914 to 1,523 m: 3
under 914 m: 3 (2000 est.)

Military

Military branches: Army (includes Air and Air Defense Forces), Police Force
Military manpower - military age: 19 years of age
Military manpower - availability:
males age 15-49: 548,183 (2001 est.)
Military manpower - fit for military service:
males age 15-49: 442,053 (2001 est.)
Military manpower - reaching military age annually:
males: 17,905 (2001 est.)
Military expenditures - dollar figure: $76.3 million (FY00/01)
Military expenditures - percent of GDP: 2.17% (FY00/01)

Transnational Issues

Disputes - international: dispute with Greece over its name; February 2001 agreement with Yugoslavia settled alignment of boundary, stipulating implementation within two years
Illicit drugs: increasing transshipment point for Southwest Asian heroin and hashish; minor transit point for South American cocaine destined for Europe

Madagascar

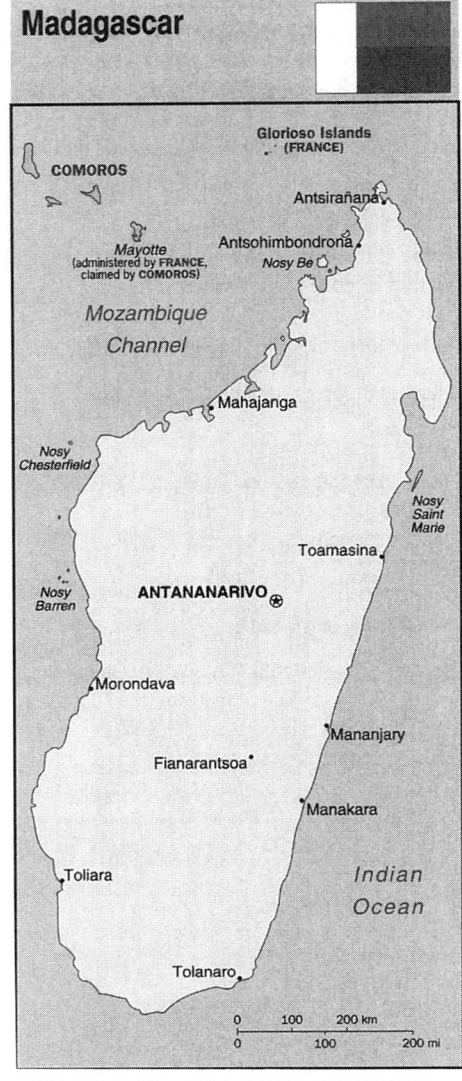

Introduction

Background: Formerly an independent kingdom, Madagascar became a French colony in 1886, but regained its independence in 1960. During 1992-93, free presidential and National Assembly elections were held, ending 17 years of single-party rule. In 1997 in the second presidential race, Didier RATSIRAKA, the leader during the 1970s and 1980s, was returned to the presidency.

Geography

Location: Southern Africa, island in the Indian Ocean, east of Mozambique
Geographic coordinates: 20 00 S, 47 00 E
Map references: Africa
Area:
total: 587,040 sq km
land: 581,540 sq km
water: 5,500 sq km
Area - comparative: slightly less than twice the size of Arizona
Land boundaries: 0 km
Coastline: 4,828 km
Maritime claims:
contiguous zone: 24 NM
continental shelf: 200 NM or 100 NM from the 2,500-m deep isobath
exclusive economic zone: 200 NM
territorial sea: 12 NM
Climate: tropical along coast, temperate inland, arid in south
Terrain: narrow coastal plain, high plateau and mountains in center
Elevation extremes:
lowest point: Indian Ocean 0 m
highest point: Maromokotro 2,876 m
Natural resources: graphite, chromite, coal, bauxite, salt, quartz, tar sands, semiprecious stones, mica, fish, hydropower
Land use:
arable land: 4%
permanent crops: 1%
permanent pastures: 41%
forests and woodland: 40%
other: 14% (1993 est.)
Irrigated land: 10,870 sq km (1993 est.)
Natural hazards: periodic cyclones
Environment - current issues: soil erosion results from deforestation and overgrazing; desertification; surface water contaminated with raw sewage and other organic wastes; several species of flora and fauna unique to the island are endangered
Environment - international agreements:
party to: Biodiversity, Climate Change, Desertification, Endangered Species, Hazardous Wastes, Marine Dumping, Marine Life Conservation, Nuclear Test Ban, Ozone Layer Protection, Ship Pollution, Wetlands
signed, but not ratified: Law of the Sea
Geography - note: world's fourth-largest island; strategic location along Mozambique Channel

People

Population: 15,982,563 (July 2001 est.)
Age structure:
0-14 years: 45.02% (male 3,607,803; female 3,587,532)
15-64 years: 51.77% (male 4,093,720; female 4,180,430)
65 years and over: 3.21% (male 239,839; female 273,239) (2001 est.)
Population growth rate: 3.02% (2001 est.)
Birth rate: 42.66 births/1,000 population (2001 est.)
Death rate: 12.42 deaths/1,000 population (2001 est.)
Net migration rate: 0 migrant(s)/1,000 population (2001 est.)
Sex ratio:
at birth: 1.03 male(s)/female
under 15 years: 1.01 male(s)/female
15-64 years: 0.98 male(s)/female
65 years and over: 0.88 male(s)/female
total population: 0.99 male(s)/female (2001 est.)
Infant mortality rate: 83.58 deaths/1,000 live births (2001 est.)
Life expectancy at birth:
total population: 55.35 years
male: 53.08 years
female: 57.68 years (2001 est.)
Total fertility rate: 5.8 children born/woman (2001 est.)
HIV/AIDS - adult prevalence rate: 0.15% (1999 est.)
HIV/AIDS - people living with HIV/AIDS: 11,000 (1999 est.)
HIV/AIDS - deaths: 870 (1999 est.)
Nationality:
noun: Malagasy (singular and plural)
adjective: Malagasy
Ethnic groups: Malayo-Indonesian (Merina and related Betsileo), Cotiers (mixed African, Malayo-Indonesian, and Arab ancestry - Betsimisaraka, Tsimihety, Antaisaka, Sakalava), French, Indian, Creole, Comoran
Religions: indigenous beliefs 52%, Christian 41%, Muslim 7%
Languages: French (official), Malagasy (official)
Literacy:
definition: age 15 and over can read and write
total population: 80%
male: 88%
female: 73% (1990 est.)

Government

Country name:
conventional long form: Republic of Madagascar
conventional short form: Madagascar
local long form: Republique de Madagascar
local short form: Madagascar
former: Malagasy Republic
Government type: republic
Capital: Antananarivo
Administrative divisions: 6 provinces (faritany); Antananarivo, Antsiranana, Fianarantsoa, Mahajanga, Toamasina, Toliara
Independence: 26 June 1960 (from France)
National holiday: Independence Day, 26 June (1960)
Constitution: 19 August 1992 by national referendum
Legal system: based on French civil law system and traditional Malagasy law; has not accepted compulsory ICJ jurisdiction
Suffrage: 18 years of age; universal
Executive branch:
chief of state: President Didier RATSIRAKA (since 10 February 1997)
head of government: Prime Minister Tantely Rene Gabriot ANDRIANARIVO (since NA 1998)
cabinet: Council of Ministers appointed by the prime minister
elections: president elected by popular vote for a five-year term; election last held 29 December 1996 (next to be held NA November 2001); prime minister appointed by the president from a list of candidates nominated by the National Assembly

Madagascar (continued)

election results: Didier RATSIRAKA elected president; percent of vote - Didier RATSIRAKA (AREMA) 50.7%, Albert ZAFY (AFFA) 49.3%

Legislative branch: unicameral National Assembly or Assemblee Nationale (150 seats; members are directly elected by popular vote to serve four-year terms); note - the legislature is scheduled to become a bicameral Parliament with the establishment of a Senate; two-thirds of the seats of this Senate will be filled by regional assemblies whose members will be elected by popular vote; the remaining one-third of the seats will be appointed by the president; the total number of seats will be determined by the National Assembly; all members will serve four-year terms

elections: National Assembly - last held 17 May 1998 (next to be held NA 2002)

election results: National Assembly - percent of vote by party - NA%; seats by party - AREMA 63, LEADER/Fanilo 16, AVI 14, RPSD 11, AFFA 6, MFM 3, AKFM/Fanavaozana 3, GRAD/Iloafo 1, Fihaonana 1, independents 32

Judicial branch: Supreme Court or Cour Supreme; High Constitutional Court or Haute Cour Constitutionnelle

Political parties and leaders: Action, Truth, Development, and Harmony or AFFA [Professor Albert ZAFY]; Association for the Rebirth of Madagascar or AREMA [leader vacant]; Congress Party for Malagasy Independence or AKFM/Fanavaozana; Economic Liberalism and Democratic Action for National Recovery or LEADER/Fanilo [Herizo RAZAFIMAHALEO]; Fihaonana Rally or Fihaonana [Guy RAZANAMASY]; Group of Reflection and Action for the Development of Madagascar or GRAD/Iloafo; Judged by Your Work or AVI [Norbert RATSIRAHONANA]; Movement for the Progress of Madagascar or MFM [Manandafy RAKOTONIRINA]; Renewal of the Social Democratic Party or RPSD [Evariste MARSON]; Tranobe (Big House) [Ny Hasina ANDRIAMANJATO]

Political pressure groups and leaders: Federalist Movement; National Council of Christian Churches or FFKM

International organization participation: ACCT, ACP, AfDB, CCC, ECA, FAO, G-77, IAEA, IBRD, ICAO, ICC, ICFTU, ICRM, IDA, IFAD, IFC, IFRCS, ILO, IMF, IMO, InOC, Intelsat, Interpol, IOC, IOM (observer), ISO (correspondent), ITU, NAM, OAU, OPCW, UN, UNCTAD, UNESCO, UNHCR, UNIDO, UPU, WCL, WFTU, WHO, WIPO, WMO, WToO, WTrO

Diplomatic representation in the US:
chief of mission: Ambassador Zina ANDRIANARIVELO-RAZAFY
chancery: 2374 Massachusetts Avenue NW, Washington, DC 20008
telephone: [1] (202) 265-5525, 5526
consulate(s) general: New York

Diplomatic representation from the US:
chief of mission: Ambassador Shirley E. BARNES
embassy: 14-16 Rue Rainitovo, Antsahavola, Antananarivo
mailing address: B. P. 620, Antsahavola, Antananarivo
telephone: [261] (20) 22-212-57
FAX: [261] (20) 22-345-39

Flag description: two equal horizontal bands of red (top) and green with a vertical white band of the same width on hoist side

Economy

Economy - overview: Madagascar faces problems of chronic malnutrition, underfunded health and education facilities, a roughly 3% annual population growth rate, and severe loss of forest cover, accompanied by erosion. Agriculture, including fishing and forestry, is the mainstay of the economy, accounting for 30% of GDP and contributing more than 70% to export earnings. Industry features textile manufacturing and the processing of agricultural products. Growth in output in 1992-97 averaged less than the growth rate of the population. Growth has been held back by antigovernment strikes and demonstrations, a decline in world coffee prices, and the erratic commitment of the government to economic reform. The extent of government reforms, outside financial aid, and foreign investment will be key determinants of future growth. For 2001, growth should again be about 5%.

GDP: purchasing power parity - $12.3 billion (2000 est.)

GDP - real growth rate: 4.8% (2000 est.)

GDP - per capita: purchasing power parity - $800 (2000 est.)

GDP - composition by sector:
agriculture: 30%
industry: 14%
services: 56% (1999 est.)

Population below poverty line: 70% (1994 est.)

Household income or consumption by percentage share:
lowest 10%: 1.9%
highest 10%: 36.7% (1993)

Inflation rate (consumer prices): 10% (1999 est.)

Labor force: 7 million (1999)

Unemployment rate: NA%

Budget:
revenues: $553 million
expenditures: $735 million, including capital expenditures of $NA (1998 est.)

Industries: meat processing, soap, breweries, tanneries, sugar, textiles, glassware, cement, automobile assembly plant, paper, petroleum, tourism

Industrial production growth rate: 3% (2000 est.)

Electricity - production: 810 million kWh (1999)

Electricity - production by source:
fossil fuel: 37.04%
hydro: 62.96%
nuclear: 0%
other: 0% (1999)

Electricity - consumption: 753.3 million kWh (1999)

Electricity - exports: 0 kWh (1999)

Electricity - imports: 0 kWh (1999)

Agriculture - products: coffee, vanilla, sugarcane, cloves, cocoa, rice, cassava (tapioca), beans, bananas, peanuts; livestock products

Exports: $538 million (f.o.b., 1998)

Exports - commodities: coffee, vanilla, shellfish, sugar; cotton cloth, chromite, petroleum products

Exports - partners: France 41%, US 19%, Germany 13%, UK 8%, Japan 6% (1999)

Imports: $693 million (f.o.b., 1998)

Imports - commodities: intermediate manufactures, capital goods, petroleum, consumer goods, food

Imports - partners: France 34%, Hong Kong 6%, China 6%, Japan 5%, Singapore 4% (1999)

Debt - external: $4.4 billion (1999)

Economic aid - recipient: $838 million (1997)

Currency: Malagasy franc (MGF)

Currency code: MGF

Exchange rates: Malagasy francs per US dollar - 6,656.3 (November 2000), 6,283.8 (1999), 5,441.4 (1998), 5,090.9 (1997), 4,061.3 (1996)

Fiscal year: calendar year

Communications

Telephones - main lines in use: 43,000 (1997)

Telephones - mobile cellular: 4,000 (1997)

Telephone system:
general assessment: system is above average for the region
domestic: open-wire lines, coaxial cables, microwave radio relay, and tropospheric scatter links
international: submarine cable to Bahrain; satellite earth stations - 1 Intelsat (Indian Ocean) and 1 Intersputnik (Atlantic Ocean region)

Radio broadcast stations: AM 2 (plus 8 repeater stations), FM 7, shortwave 5 (1998)

Radios: 3.05 million (1997)

Television broadcast stations: 1 (plus 36 repeaters) (1997)

Televisions: 325,000 (1997)

Internet country code: .mg

Internet Service Providers (ISPs): 2 (2000)

Internet users: 8,000 (2000)

Transportation

Railways:
total: 883 km
narrow gauge: 883 km 1.000-m gauge (1994)

Highways:
total: 49,837 km
paved: 5,781 km
unpaved: 44,056 km (1996)

Waterways:
note: of local importance only

Ports and harbors: Antsiranana, Antsohimbondrona, Mahajanga, Toamasina, Toliara

Merchant marine:
total: 13 ships (1,000 GRT or over) totaling 24,819 GRT/34,173 DWT
ships by type: cargo 7, chemical tanker 1, liquefied gas 1, petroleum tanker 2, roll on/roll off 2 (2000 est.)

Madagascar (continued)

Airports: 130 (2000 est.)
Airports - with paved runways:
total: 29
over 3,047 m: 1
2,438 to 3,047 m: 2
1,524 to 2,437 m: 5
914 to 1,523 m: 19
under 914 m: 2 (2000 est.)
Airports - with unpaved runways:
total: 101
1,524 to 2,437 m: 2
914 to 1,523 m: 56
under 914 m: 43 (2000 est.)

Military

Military branches: Popular Armed Forces (includes Intervention Forces, Development Forces, Aeronaval Forces - includes Navy and Air Force), Gendarmerie, Presidential Security Regiment
Military manpower - military age: 20 years of age
Military manpower - availability:
males age 15-49: 3,640,554 (2001 est.)
Military manpower - fit for military service:
males age 15-49: 2,159,767 (2001 est.)
Military manpower - reaching military age annually:
males: 153,856 (2001 est.)
Military expenditures - dollar figure: $29 million (FY94)
Military expenditures - percent of GDP: 1% (FY94)

Transnational Issues

Disputes - international: claims Bassas da India, Europa Island, Glorioso Islands, Juan de Nova Island, and Tromelin Island (all administered by France)
Illicit drugs: illicit producer of cannabis (cultivated and wild varieties) used mostly for domestic consumption; transshipment point for heroin

Malawi

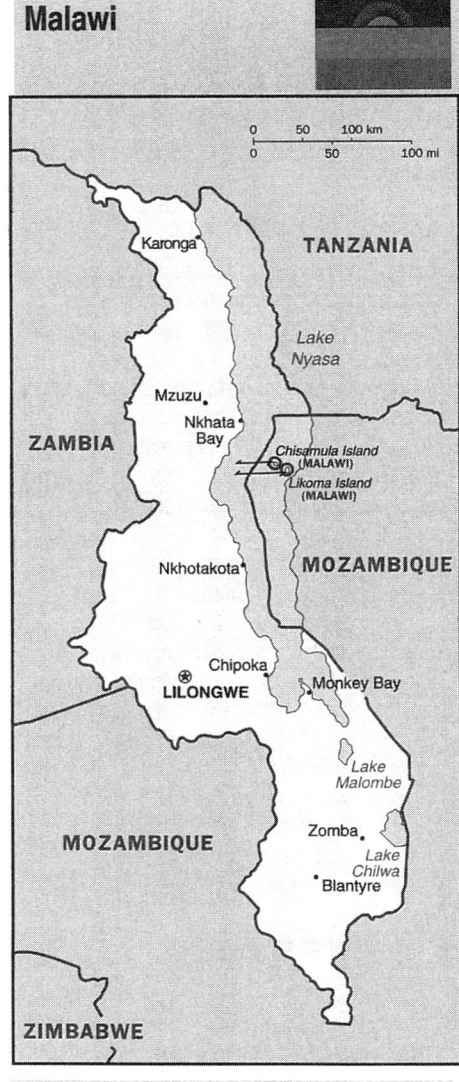

Introduction

Background: Established in 1891, the British protectorate of Nyasaland became the independent nation of Malawi in 1964. After three decades of one-party rule, the country held multiparty elections in 1994 under a provisional constitution, which took full effect the following year. National multiparty elections were held again in 1999.

Geography

Location: Southern Africa, east of Zambia
Geographic coordinates: 13 30 S, 34 00 E
Map references: Africa
Area:
total: 118,480 sq km
land: 94,080 sq km
water: 24,400 sq km
Area - comparative: slightly smaller than Pennsylvania
Land boundaries:
total: 2,881 km
border countries: Mozambique 1,569 km, Tanzania 475 km, Zambia 837 km
Coastline: 0 km (landlocked)
Maritime claims: none (landlocked)
Climate: sub-tropical; rainy season (November to May); dry season (May to November)
Terrain: narrow elongated plateau with rolling plains, rounded hills, some mountains
Elevation extremes:
lowest point: junction of the Shire River and international boundary with Mozambique 37 m
highest point: Sapitwa 3,002 m
Natural resources: limestone, arable land, hydropower, unexploited deposits of uranium, coal, and bauxite
Land use:
arable land: 34%
permanent crops: 0%
permanent pastures: 20%
forests and woodland: 39%
other: 7% (1993 est.)
Irrigated land: 280 sq km (1993 est.)
Natural hazards: NA
Environment - current issues: deforestation; land degradation; water pollution from agricultural runoff, sewage, industrial wastes; siltation of spawning grounds endangers fish populations
Environment - international agreements:
party to: Biodiversity, Climate Change, Desertification, Endangered Species, Environmental Modification, Hazardous Wastes, Marine Dumping, Marine Life Conservation, Nuclear Test Ban, Ozone Layer Protection, Ship Pollution, Wetlands
signed, but not ratified: Law of the Sea
Geography - note: landlocked

People

Population: 10,548,250
note: estimates for this country explicitly take into account the effects of excess mortality due to AIDS; this can result in lower life expectancy, higher infant mortality and death rates, lower population and growth rates, and changes in the distribution of population by age and sex than would otherwise be expected (July 2001 est.)
Age structure:
0-14 years: 44.43% (male 2,348,940; female 2,337,290)
15-64 years: 52.78% (male 2,741,622; female 2,825,966)
65 years and over: 2.79% (male 119,283; female 175,149) (2001 est.)
Population growth rate: 1.5% (2001 est.)
Birth rate: 37.8 births/1,000 population (2001 est.)
Death rate: 22.81 deaths/1,000 population (2001 est.)
Net migration rate: 0 migrant(s)/1,000 population (2001 est.)
Sex ratio:
at birth: 1.03 male(s)/female
under 15 years: 1 male(s)/female
15-64 years: 0.97 male(s)/female
65 years and over: 0.68 male(s)/female
total population: 0.98 male(s)/female (2001 est.)
Infant mortality rate: 121.12 deaths/1,000 live births (2001 est.)

Malawi (continued)

Life expectancy at birth:
total population: 37.08 years
male: 36.61 years
female: 37.55 years (2001 est.)
Total fertility rate: 5.18 children born/woman (2001 est.)
HIV/AIDS - adult prevalence rate: 15.96% (1999 est.)
HIV/AIDS - people living with HIV/AIDS: 800,000 (1999 est.)
HIV/AIDS - deaths: 70,000 (1999 est.)
Nationality:
noun: Malawian(s)
adjective: Malawian
Ethnic groups: Chewa, Nyanja, Tumbuko, Yao, Lomwe, Sena, Tonga, Ngoni, Ngonde, Asian, European
Religions: Protestant 55%, Roman Catholic 20%, Muslim 20%, indigenous beliefs
Languages: English (official), Chichewa (official), other languages important regionally
Literacy:
definition: age 15 and over can read and write
total population: 58%
male: 72.8%
female: 43.4% (1999 est.)

Government

Country name:
conventional long form: Republic of Malawi
conventional short form: Malawi
former: British Central African Protectorate, Nyasaland Protectorate, Nyasaland
Government type: multiparty democracy
Capital: Lilongwe
Administrative divisions: 24 districts; Blantyre, Chikwawa, Chiradzulu, Chitipa, Dedza, Dowa, Karonga, Kasungu, Lilongwe, Machinga (Kasupe), Mangochi, Mchinji, Mulanje, Mwanza, Mzimba, Ntcheu, Nkhata Bay, Nkhotakota, Nsanje, Ntchisi, Rumphi, Salima, Thyolo, Zomba; note - there may be three new districts named Balaka, Likoma, and Phalombe
Independence: 6 July 1964 (from UK)
National holiday: Independence Day, 6 July (1964)
Constitution: 18 May 1994
Legal system: based on English common law and customary law; judicial review of legislative acts in the Supreme Court of Appeal; has not accepted compulsory ICJ jurisdiction
Suffrage: 18 years of age; universal
Executive branch:
chief of state: President Bakili MULUZI (since 21 May 1994); note - the president is both the chief of state and head of government
head of government: President Bakili MULUZI (since 21 May 1994); note - the president is both the chief of state and head of government
cabinet: 36-member Cabinet named by the president
elections: president elected by popular vote for a five-year term; election last held 15 June 1999 (next to be held NA 2004)
election results: Bakili MULUZI reelected president; percent of vote - Bakili MULUZI (UDF) 51.4%, Gwandaguluwe CHAKUAMBA (MCP-AFORD) 44.3%
Legislative branch: unicameral National Assembly (193 seats; members elected by popular vote to serve five-year terms)
elections: last held 15 June 1999 (next to be held NA 2004)
election results: percent of vote by party - UDF 48%, MCP 34%, AFORD 15%, others 3%; seats by party - UDF 94, MCP 66, AFORD 29, others 4
Judicial branch: Supreme Court of Appeal; High Court (chief justice appointed by the president, puisne judges appointed on the advice of the Judicial Service Commission); magistrate's courts
Political parties and leaders: Alliance for Democracy or AFORD [Chakufwa CHIHANA, president]; Malawi Congress Party or MCP [Gwanda CHAKUAMBA, president, John TEMBO, vice president]; Malawi Democratic Party or MDP [Kampelo KALUA, president]; National Independence Party; Social Democratic Party or SDP [Eston KAKHOME, president]; United Democratic Front or UDF [Bakili MULUZI] - governing party
Political pressure groups and leaders: NA
International organization participation: ACP, AfDB, C, CCC, ECA, FAO, G-77, IBRD, ICAO, ICFTU, ICRM, IDA, IFAD, IFC, IFRCS, ILO, IMF, IMO, Intelsat, Interpol, IOC, ISO (correspondent), ITU, NAM, OAU, OPCW, SADC, UN, UNCTAD, UNESCO, UNIDO, UNMIK, UPU, WFTU, WHO, WIPO, WMO, WToO, WTrO
Diplomatic representation in the US:
chief of mission: Ambassador Paul Tony Steven KANDIERO
chancery: 2408 Massachusetts Avenue NW, Washington, DC 20008
telephone: [1] (202) 797-1007
Diplomatic representation from the US:
chief of mission: Ambassador Roger A. MEECE
embassy: Area 40, Plot 24, Kenyatta Road
mailing address: P. O. Box 30016, Lilongwe 3, Malawi
telephone: [265] 773 166
FAX: [265] 770 471
Flag description: three equal horizontal bands of black (top), red, and green with a radiant, rising, red sun centered in the black band
Government - note: the executive exerts considerable influence over the legislature

Economy

Economy - overview: Landlocked Malawi ranks among the world's least developed countries. The economy is predominately agricultural, with about 90% of the population living in rural areas. Agriculture accounts for 37% of GDP and 85% of export revenues. The economy depends on substantial inflows of economic assistance from the IMF, the World Bank, and individual donor nations. In late 2000, Malawi was approved for relief under the Heavily Indebted Poor Countries (HIPC) program. The government faces strong challenges, e.g., to fully develop a market economy, to improve educational facilities, to face up to environmental problems, and to deal with the rapidly growing problem of HIV/AIDS.
GDP: purchasing power parity - $9.4 billion (2000 est.)
GDP - real growth rate: 3% (2000 est.)
GDP - per capita: purchasing power parity - $900 (2000 est.)
GDP - composition by sector:
agriculture: 37%
industry: 29%
services: 34% (1998 est.)
Population below poverty line: 54% (FY90/91 est.)
Household income or consumption by percentage share:
lowest 10%: NA%
highest 10%: NA%
Inflation rate (consumer prices): 29.5% (2000)
Labor force: 3.5 million
Labor force - by occupation: agriculture 86% (1997 est.)
Unemployment rate: NA%
Budget:
revenues: $490 million
expenditures: $523 million, including capital expenditures of $NA (FY99/00 est.)
Industries: tobacco, tea, sugar, sawmill products, cement, consumer goods
Industrial production growth rate: NA%
Electricity - production: 1.025 billion kWh (1999)
Electricity - production by source:
fossil fuel: 2.44%
hydro: 97.56%
nuclear: 0%
other: 0% (1999)
Electricity - consumption: 950 million kWh (1999)
Electricity - exports: 3 million kWh (1999)
Electricity - imports: 0 kWh (1999)
Agriculture - products: tobacco, sugarcane, cotton, tea, corn, potatoes, cassava (tapioca), sorghum, pulses; cattle, goats
Exports: $416 million (f.o.b., 2000)
Exports - commodities: tobacco, tea, sugar, cotton, coffee, peanuts, wood products
Exports - partners: South Africa 16%, Germany 16%, US 15%, Netherlands 7%, Japan (1999)
Imports: $435 million (f.o.b., 2000)
Imports - commodities: food, petroleum products, semimanufactures, consumer goods, transportation equipment
Imports - partners: South Africa 43%, Zimbabwe 14%, UK 5%, Germany 5%, Zambia, Japan, US (1999)
Debt - external: $2.9 billion (2000 est.)
Economic aid - recipient: $427 million (1999)
Currency: Malawian kwacha (MWK)
Currency code: MWK
Exchange rates: Malawian kwachas per US dollar - 80.0946 (December 2000), 59.5438 (2000), 44.0881 (1999), 31.0727 (1998), 16.4442 (1997), 15.3085 (1996)
Fiscal year: 1 July - 30 June

Malawi (continued)

Communications

Telephones - main lines in use: 37,000 (1997)
Telephones - mobile cellular: 7,000 (1997)
Telephone system:
general assessment: NA
domestic: fair system of open-wire lines, microwave radio relay links, and radiotelephone communications stations
international: satellite earth stations - 2 Intelsat (1 Indian Ocean and 1 Atlantic Ocean)
Radio broadcast stations: AM 9, FM 4 (plus 15 repeater stations), shortwave 3 (1998)
Radios: 2.6 million (1997)
Television broadcast stations: 1 (1999)
Televisions: 0 (1999)
Internet country code: .mw
Internet Service Providers (ISPs): 8 (2001)
Internet users: 10,000 (2000)

Transportation

Railways:
total: 789 km
narrow gauge: 789 km 1.067-m gauge
Highways:
total: 16,451 km
paved: 3,126 km
unpaved: 13,325 km (1997)
Waterways: 144 km
note: on Lake Nyasa (Lake Malawi) and Shire Riverall
Ports and harbors: Chipoka, Monkey Bay, Nkhata Bay, Nkhotakota, Chilumba
Airports: 44 (2000 est.)
Airports - with paved runways:
total: 6
over 3,047 m: 1
1,524 to 2,437 m: 1
914 to 1,523 m: 4 (2000 est.)
Airports - with unpaved runways:
total: 38
1,524 to 2,437 m: 1
914 to 1,523 m: 14
under 914 m: 23 (2000 est.)

Military

Military branches: Army (includes Air Wing and Naval Detachment), Police (includes paramilitary Mobile Force Unit)
Military manpower - availability:
males age 15-49: 2,466,708 (2001 est.)
Military manpower - fit for military service:
males age 15-49: 1,265,893 (2001 est.)
Military expenditures - dollar figure: $9.5 million (FY00/01)
Military expenditures - percent of GDP: 0.76% (FY00/01)

Transnational Issues

Disputes - international: dispute with Tanzania over the boundary in Lake Nyasa (Lake Malawi)

Malaysia

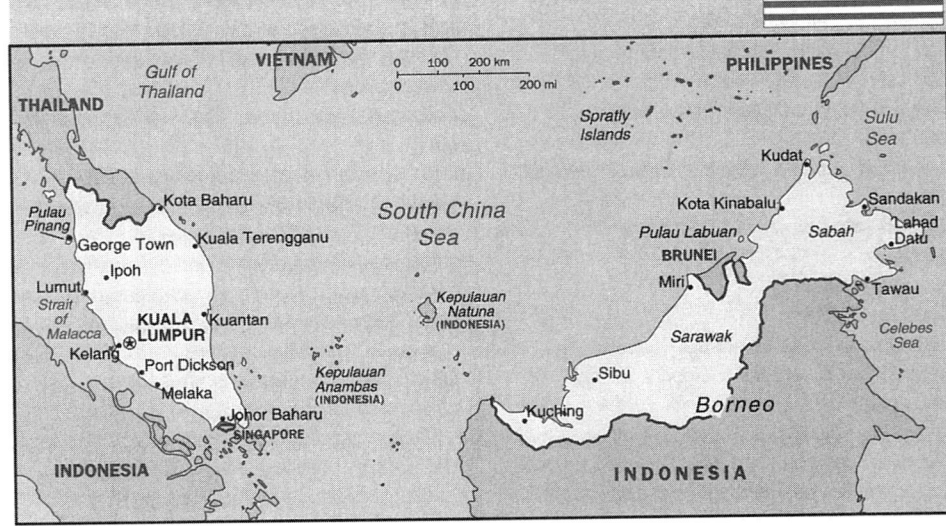

Introduction

Background: Malaysia was created in 1963 through the merging of Malaya (independent in 1957) and the former British Singapore, both of which formed West Malaysia, and Sabah and Sarawak in north Borneo, which composed East Malaysia. The first three years of independence were marred by hostilities with Indonesia. Singapore separated from the union in 1965.

Geography

Location: Southeastern Asia, peninsula and northern one-third of the island of Borneo, bordering Indonesia and the South China Sea, south of Vietnam
Geographic coordinates: 2 30 N, 112 30 E
Map references: Southeast Asia
Area:
total: 329,750 sq km
land: 328,550 sq km
water: 1,200 sq km
Area - comparative: slightly larger than New Mexico
Land boundaries:
total: 2,669 km
border countries: Brunei 381 km, Indonesia 1,782 km, Thailand 506 km
Coastline: 4,675 km (Peninsular Malaysia 2,068 km, East Malaysia 2,607 km)
Maritime claims:
continental shelf: 200-m depth or to the depth of exploitation; specified boundary in the South China Sea
exclusive economic zone: 200 NM
territorial sea: 12 NM
Climate: tropical; annual southwest (April to October) and northeast (October to February) monsoons
Terrain: coastal plains rising to hills and mountains
Elevation extremes:
lowest point: Indian Ocean 0 m
highest point: Gunung Kinabalu 4,100 m
Natural resources: tin, petroleum, timber, copper, iron ore, natural gas, bauxite
Land use:
arable land: 3%
permanent crops: 12%
permanent pastures: 0%
forests and woodland: 68%
other: 17% (1993 est.)
Irrigated land: 2,941 sq km (1998 est.)
Natural hazards: flooding, landslides
Environment - current issues: air pollution from industrial and vehicular emissions; water pollution from raw sewage; deforestation; smoke/haze from Indonesian forest fires
Environment - international agreements:
party to: Biodiversity, Climate Change, Desertification, Endangered Species, Hazardous Wastes, Law of the Sea, Marine Dumping, Marine Life Conservation, Nuclear Test Ban, Ozone Layer Protection, Ship Pollution, Tropical Timber 83, Tropical Timber 94, Wetlands
signed, but not ratified: Climate Change-Kyoto Protocol
Geography - note: strategic location along Strait of Malacca and southern South China Sea

People

Population: 22,229,040 (July 2001 est.)
Age structure:
0-14 years: 34.5% (male 3,943,324; female 3,724,634)
15-64 years: 61.35% (male 6,828,670; female 6,808,623)
65 years and over: 4.15% (male 404,042; female 519,747) (2001 est.)
Population growth rate: 1.96% (2001 est.)
Birth rate: 24.75 births/1,000 population (2001 est.)
Death rate: 5.2 deaths/1,000 population (2001 est.)
Net migration rate: 0 migrant(s)/1,000 population (2001 est.)

Malaysia (continued)

note: does not reflect net flow of an unknown number of illegal immigrants from other countries in the region

Sex ratio:
at birth: 1.07 male(s)/female
under 15 years: 1.06 male(s)/female
15-64 years: 1 male(s)/female
65 years and over: 0.78 male(s)/female
total population: 1.01 male(s)/female (2001 est.)

Infant mortality rate: 20.31 deaths/1,000 live births (2001 est.)

Life expectancy at birth:
total population: 71.11 years
male: 68.48 years
female: 73.92 years (2001 est.)

Total fertility rate: 3.24 children born/woman (2001 est.)

HIV/AIDS - adult prevalence rate: 0.42% (1999 est.)

HIV/AIDS - people living with HIV/AIDS: 49,000 (1999 est.)

HIV/AIDS - deaths: 1,900 (1999 est.)

Nationality:
noun: Malaysian(s)
adjective: Malaysian

Ethnic groups: Malay and other indigenous 58%, Chinese 27%, Indian 8%, others 7% (2000)

Religions: Islam, Buddhism, Daoism, Hinduism, Christianity, Sikhism; note - in addition, Shamanism is practiced in East Malaysia

Languages: Bahasa Melayu (official), English, Chinese dialects (Cantonese, Mandarin, Hokkien, Hakka, Hainan, Foochow), Tamil, Telugu, Malayalam, Panjabi, Thai; note - in addition, in East Malaysia several indigenous languages are spoken, the largest of which are Iban and Kadazan

Literacy:
definition: age 15 and over can read and write
total population: 83.5%
male: 89.1%
female: 78.1% (1995 est.)

Government

Country name:
conventional long form: none
conventional short form: Malaysia
former: Federation of Malaysia

Government type: constitutional monarchy
note: Malaya (what is now Peninsular Malaysia) formed 31 August 1957; Federation of Malaysia (Malaya, Sabah, Sarawak, and Singapore) formed 9 July 1963 (Singapore left the federation on 9 August 1965); nominally headed by the paramount ruler and a bicameral Parliament consisting of a nonelected upper house and an elected lower house; Peninsular Malaysian states - hereditary rulers in all but Melaka, Penang, Sabah, and Sarawak, where governors are appointed by the Malaysian Government; powers of state governments are limited by the federal constitution; under terms of the federation, Sabah and Sarawak retain certain constitutional prerogatives (e.g., the right to maintain their own immigration controls); Sabah - holds 20 seats in House of Representatives, with foreign affairs, defense, internal security, and other powers delegated to federal government; Sarawak - holds 28 seats in House of Representatives, with foreign affairs, defense, internal security, and other powers delegated to federal government

Capital: Kuala Lumpur

Administrative divisions: 13 states (negeri-negeri, singular - negeri) and 2 federal territories* (wilayah-wilayah persekutuan, singular - wilayah persekutuan); Johor, Kedah, Kelantan, Labuan*, Melaka, Negeri Sembilan, Pahang, Perak, Perlis, Pulau Pinang, Sabah, Sarawak, Selangor, Terengganu, Wilayah Persekutuan*
note: the city of Kuala Lumpur is located within the federal territory of Wilayah Persekutuan; the terms therefore are not interchangeable; there may be a new federal territory named Putrajaya

Independence: 31 August 1957 (from UK)

National holiday: Independence Day/Malaysia Day, 31 August (1957)

Constitution: 31 August 1957, amended 16 September 1963

Legal system: based on English common law; judicial review of legislative acts in the Supreme Court at request of supreme head of the federation; has not accepted compulsory ICJ jurisdiction

Suffrage: 21 years of age; universal

Executive branch:
chief of state: Paramount Ruler Sultan TUNKU SALAHUDDIN Abdul Aziz Shah ibni Al-Marhum Sultan Hisammuddin Alam Shah (since 26 April 1999); Deputy Paramount Ruler Sultan MIZAN Zainal Abidin ibni A-Marhum Sultan Mahmud Al-Muktafi Billah Shah
head of government: Prime Minister Dr. MAHATHIR bin Mohamad (since 16 July 1981); Deputy Prime Minister ABDULLAH bin Ahmad Badawi (since 8 January 1999)
cabinet: Cabinet appointed by the prime minister from among the members of Parliament with consent of the paramount ruler
elections: paramount ruler and deputy paramount ruler elected by and from the hereditary rulers of nine of the states for five-year terms; election last held 27 February 1999 (next to be held NA 2004); prime minister designated from among the members of the House of Representatives; following legislative elections, the leader of the party that wins a plurality of seats in the House of Representatives becomes prime minister
election results: Sultan TUNKU SALAHUDDIN Abdul Aziz Shah ibni Al-Marhum Sultan Hisammuddin Alam Shah elected paramount ruler; Sultan MIZAN Zainal Abidin ibni A-Marhum Sultan Mahmud Al-Muktafi Billah Shah elected deputy paramount ruler

Legislative branch: bicameral Parliament or Parlimen consists of nonelected Senate or Dewan Negara (69 seats; 43 appointed by the paramount ruler, 26 appointed by the state legislatures) and the House of Representatives or Dewan Rakyat (193 seats; members elected by popular vote weighted toward the rural Malay population to serve five-year terms)
elections: House of Representatives - last held 29 November 1999 (next must be held by 20 December 2004)
election results: House of Representatives - percent of vote by party - NF 56%, other 44%; seats by party - NF 148, PAS 27, DAP 10, NJP 5, PBS 3

Judicial branch: Federal Court (judges appointed by the paramount ruler on the advice of the prime minister)

Political parties and leaders: Alternative Coalition or Barisan Alternatif-BA (includes the following parties: Party Islam Se-Malaysia or PAS [FADZIL Mohamad Noor], National Justice Party or NJP [WAN AZIZAH Wan Ismail], Democratic Action Party or DAP [LIM Kit Siang], and Malaysian People's Party or PRM [SYED HUSIN]); National Front or NF (ruling coalition dominated by the United Malays National Organization or UMNO [MAHATHIR bin Mohammad], includes the following parties: Malaysian Indian Congress or MIC [S. Samy VELLU], Malaysian Chinese Association or MCA [LING Liong Sik], Gerakan Rakyat Malaysia or Gerakan [LIM Keng Yaik], Parti Pesaka Bumiputra Bersatu or PBB [Patinggi Haji Abdul TAIB Mahmud], Parti Angkatan Keadilan Rakyat Bersatu or Akar [PANDIKAR Amin Mulia], Parti Bangsa Dayak Sarawak or PBDS [Leo MOGGIE], Sarawak United People's Party or SUPP [George CHAN Hong Nam], Liberal Democratic Party or LDP [CHONG Kah Kiat], Sabah Progressive Party or SAPP [YONG Teck Lee], People's Progressive Party or PPP [M. KAYVEAS], Parti Bersatu Rakyat Sabah or PBRS [Joseph KURUP], Sarawak National Party or SNAP [Amar James WONG], Parti Demokratik Sabah or PDS [leader NA], and United Pasok Momogun Kadazan Organization or UPKO (state level only) [Bernard DOMPOK]); Parti Bersatu Sabah or PBS [Joseph PAIRIN Kitingan]; Parti Bersekutu [HARRIS Salleh]; State Reform Party of Sarawak or STAR [PATAU Rubis]

Political pressure groups and leaders: NA

International organization participation: APEC, ARF, AsDB, ASEAN, BIS, C, CCC, CP, ESCAP, FAO, G-15, G-77, IAEA, IBRD, ICAO, ICFTU, ICRM, IDA, IDB, IFAD, IFC, IFRCS, IHO, ILO, IMF, IMO, Inmarsat, Intelsat, Interpol, IOC, ISO, ITU, MINURSO, MONUC, NAM, OIC, OPCW, UN, UNCTAD, UNESCO, UNIDO, UNIKOM, UNMEE, UNMIBH, UNMIK, UNTAET, UPU, WCL, WFTU, WHO, WIPO, WMO, WToO, WTrO

Diplomatic representation in the US:
chief of mission: Ambassador GHAZZALI Sheikh Abdul Khalid
chancery: 2401 Massachusetts Avenue NW, Washington, DC 20008
telephone: [1] (202) 328-2700
FAX: [1] (202) 483-7661
consulate(s) general: Los Angeles and New York

Diplomatic representation from the US:
chief of mission: Ambassador B. Lynn PASCOE
embassy: 376 Jalan Tun Razak, 50400 Kuala Lumpur
mailing address: P. O. Box No. 10035, 50700 Kuala Lumpur; American Embassy Kuala Lumpur, APO AP 96535-8152

Malaysia (continued)

telephone: [60] (3) 2168-5000
FAX: [60] (3) 2168-4961
Flag description: 14 equal horizontal stripes of red (top) alternating with white (bottom); there is a blue rectangle in the upper hoist-side corner bearing a yellow crescent and a yellow fourteen-pointed star; the crescent and the star are traditional symbols of Islam; the design was based on the flag of the US

Economy

Economy - overview: GDP grew at 8.6% in 2000, mainly on the strength of double-digit export growth and continued government fiscal stimulus. As an oil exporter, Malaysia also benefited from higher petroleum prices. Higher export revenues allowed the country to register a current account surplus, but foreign exchange reserves have been declining - from a peak of $34.5 billion in April 2000 to $29.7 billion by December - as foreign investors pulled money out of the country. Despite this development, Kuala Lumpur is unlikely to abandon its currency peg soon. An economic slowdown in key Western markets, especially the United States, and lower world demand for electronics products will slow GDP growth to 3%-6% in 2001, according to private forecasters. Over the longer term, Malaysia's failure to make substantial progress on key reforms of the corporate and financial sectors clouds prospects for sustained growth and the return of critical foreign investment.
GDP: purchasing power parity - $223.7 billion (2000 est.)
GDP - real growth rate: 8.6% (2000 est.)
GDP - per capita: purchasing power parity - $10,300 (2000 est.)
GDP - composition by sector:
agriculture: 14%
industry: 44%
services: 42% (2000)
Population below poverty line: 6.8% (1997 est.)
Household income or consumption by percentage share:
lowest 10%: 1.4%
highest 10%: 20.4% (1997 est.)
Inflation rate (consumer prices): 1.7% (2000)
Labor force: 9.6 million (2000 est.)
Labor force - by occupation: local trade and tourism 28%, manufacturing 27%, agriculture, forestry, and fisheries 16%, services 10%, government 10%, construction 9% (2000 est.)
Unemployment rate: 2.8% (2000 est.)
Budget:
revenues: $16.4 billion
expenditures: $17.8 billion, including capital expenditures of $43 billion (2000 est.)
Industries: Peninsular Malaysia - rubber and oil palm processing and manufacturing, light manufacturing industry, electronics, tin mining and smelting, logging and processing timber; Sabah - logging, petroleum production; Sarawak - agriculture processing, petroleum production and refining, logging
Industrial production growth rate: 12.1% (2000 est.)
Electricity - production: 59.044 billion kWh (1999)
Electricity - production by source:
fossil fuel: 91.61%
hydro: 8.39%
nuclear: 0%
other: 0% (1999)
Electricity - consumption: 54.872 billion kWh (1999)
Electricity - exports: 50 million kWh (1999)
Electricity - imports: 11 million kWh (1999)
Agriculture - products: Peninsular Malaysia - rubber, palm oil, cocoa, rice; Sabah - subsistence crops, rubber, timber, coconuts, rice; Sarawak - rubber, pepper; timber
Exports: $97.9 billion (2000 est.)
Exports - commodities: electronic equipment, petroleum and liquefied natural gas, chemicals, palm oil, wood and wood products, rubber, textiles
Exports - partners: US 21%, Singapore 18%, Japan 13%, Hong Kong 5%, Netherlands 4%, Taiwan 4%, Thailand 3% (2000 est.)
Imports: $82.6 billion (2000 est.)
Imports - commodities: machinery and transport equipment, chemicals, food, fuel and lubricants
Imports - partners: Japan 21%, US 17%, Singapore 14%, Taiwan 6%, South Korea 5%, Thailand 4%, China 4% (2000 est.)
Debt - external: $41.8 billion (2000 est.)
Currency: ringgit (MYR)
Currency code: MYR
Exchange rates: ringgits per US dollar - 3.8000 (January 2001), 3.8000 (2000), 3.8000 (1999), 3.9244 (1998), 2.8133 (1997), 2.5159 (1996)
Fiscal year: calendar year

Communications

Telephones - main lines in use: 4.5 million (1999)
Telephones - mobile cellular: 2.698 million (1999)
Telephone system:
general assessment: modern system; international service excellent
domestic: good intercity service provided on Peninsular Malaysia mainly by microwave radio relay; adequate intercity microwave radio relay network between Sabah and Sarawak via Brunei; domestic satellite system with 2 earth stations
international: submarine cables to India, Hong Kong, and Singapore; satellite earth stations - 2 Intelsat (1 Indian Ocean and 1 Pacific Ocean) (2001)
Radio broadcast stations: AM 56, FM 31 (plus 13 repeater stations), shortwave 5 (1999)
Radios: 10.9 million (1999)
Television broadcast stations: 27 (plus 15 high-power repeaters) (1999)
Televisions: 10.8 million (1999)
Internet country code: .my
Internet Service Providers (ISPs): 7 (2000)
Internet users: 1.5 million (2000)

Transportation

Railways:
total: 1,801 km
narrow gauge: 1,801 km 1.000-m gauge (148 km electrified) (2000)
Highways:
total: 64,672 km
paved: 48,707 km (including 1,192 km of expressways)
unpaved: 15,965 km
note: in addition to these national and main regional roads, Malaysia has thousands of kilometers of local roads that are maintained by local jurisdictions (1999)
Waterways: 7,296 km
note: Peninsular Malaysia 3,209 km, Sabah 1,569 km, Sarawak 2,518 km
Pipelines: crude oil 1,307 km; natural gas 379 km
Ports and harbors: Bintulu, Kota Kinabalu, Kuantan, Kuching, Kudat, Labuan, Lahad Datu, Lumut, Miri, Pasir Gudang, Penang, Port Dickson, Port Kelang, Sandakan, Sibu, Tanjung Berhala, Tanjung Kidurong, Tawau
Merchant marine:
total: 362 ships (1,000 GRT or over) totaling 5,103,657 GRT/7,574,999 DWT
ships by type: bulk 62, cargo 110, chemical tanker 35, container 60, liquefied gas 20, livestock carrier 1, passenger 2, petroleum tanker 58, refrigerated cargo 1, roll on/roll off 6, specialized tanker 1, vehicle carrier 6 (2000 est.)
Airports: 115 (2000 est.)
Airports - with paved runways:
total: 33
over 3,047 m: 5
2,438 to 3,047 m: 4
1,524 to 2,437 m: 11
914 to 1,523 m: 6
under 914 m: 7 (2000 est.)
Airports - with unpaved runways:
total: 82
1,524 to 2,437 m: 1
914 to 1,523 m: 8
under 914 m: 73 (2000 est.)
Heliports: 1 (2000 est.)

Military

Military branches: Malaysian Army, Royal Malaysian Navy, Royal Malaysian Air Force, Royal Malaysian Police Force, Marine Police, Sarawak Border Scouts
Military manpower - military age: 21 years of age
Military manpower - availability:
males age 15-49: 5,800,456 (2001 est.)
Military manpower - fit for military service:
males age 15-49: 3,514,023 (2001 est.)
Military manpower - reaching military age annually:
males: 196,042 (2001 est.)
Military expenditures - dollar figure: $1.69 billion (FY00 est.)

Malaysia (continued)

Military expenditures - percent of GDP: 2.03% (FY00)

Transnational Issues

Disputes - international: involved in a complex dispute over the Spratly Islands with China, Philippines, Taiwan, Vietnam, and possibly Brunei; Philippines have not fully revoked claim to Sabah State; Pulau Batu Putih (Pedra Branca Island) disputed with Singapore; Sipadan and Ligitan Islands in dispute with Indonesia

Illicit drugs: transit point for some illicit drugs; drug trafficking prosecuted vigorously and carries severe penalties

Maldives

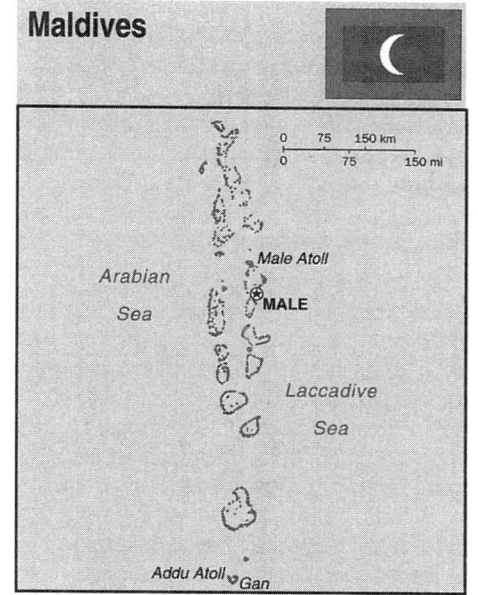

Introduction

Background: The Maldives were long a sultanate, first under Dutch and then under British protection. They became a republic in 1968, three years after independence. Tourism and fishing are being developed on the archipelago.

Geography

Location: Southern Asia, group of atolls in the Indian Ocean, south-southwest of India
Geographic coordinates: 3 15 N, 73 00 E
Map references: Asia
Area:
total: 300 sq km
land: 300 sq km
water: 0 sq km
Area - comparative: about 1.7 times the size of Washington, DC
Land boundaries: 0 km
Coastline: 644 km
Maritime claims: measured from claimed archipelagic baselines
contiguous zone: 24 NM
exclusive economic zone: 200 NM
territorial sea: 12 NM
Climate: tropical; hot, humid; dry, northeast monsoon (November to March); rainy, southwest monsoon (June to August)
Terrain: flat, with white sandy beaches
Elevation extremes:
lowest point: Indian Ocean 0 m
highest point: unnamed location on Wilingili island in the Addu Atoll 2.4 m
Natural resources: fish
Land use:
arable land: 10%
permanent crops: 0%
permanent pastures: 3%
forests and woodland: 3%
other: 84% (1993 est.)
Irrigated land: NA sq km
Natural hazards: low level of islands makes them very sensitive to sea level rise
Environment - current issues: depletion of freshwater aquifers threatens water supplies; global warming and sea level rise; coral reef bleaching
Environment - international agreements:
party to: Biodiversity, Climate Change, Climate Change-Kyoto Protocol, Hazardous Wastes, Law of the Sea, Marine Dumping, Ozone Layer Protection, Ship Pollution
signed, but not ratified: none of the selected agreements
Geography - note: 1,190 coral islands grouped into 26 atolls (200 inhabited islands, plus 80 islands with tourist resorts); archipelago of strategic location astride and along major sea lanes in Indian Ocean

People

Population: 310,764 (July 2001 est.)
Age structure:
0-14 years: 45.63% (male 72,920; female 68,895)
15-64 years: 51.37% (male 81,506; female 78,149)
65 years and over: 3% (male 4,806; female 4,488) (2001 est.)
Population growth rate: 3.01% (2001 est.)
Birth rate: 38.15 births/1,000 population (2001 est.)
Death rate: 8.09 deaths/1,000 population (2001 est.)
Net migration rate: 0 migrant(s)/1,000 population (2001 est.)
Sex ratio:
at birth: 1.05 male(s)/female
under 15 years: 1.06 male(s)/female
15-64 years: 1.04 male(s)/female
65 years and over: 1.07 male(s)/female
total population: 1.05 male(s)/female (2001 est.)
Infant mortality rate: 63.72 deaths/1,000 live births (2001 est.)
Life expectancy at birth:
total population: 62.56 years
male: 61.39 years
female: 63.8 years (2001 est.)
Total fertility rate: 5.5 children born/woman (2001 est.)
HIV/AIDS - adult prevalence rate: 0.05% (1999 est.)
HIV/AIDS - people living with HIV/AIDS: NA
HIV/AIDS - deaths: NA
Nationality:
noun: Maldivian(s)
adjective: Maldivian
Ethnic groups: South Indians, Sinhalese, Arabs
Religions: Sunni Muslim
Languages: Maldivian Dhivehi (dialect of Sinhala, script derived from Arabic), English spoken by most government officials
Literacy:
definition: age 15 and over can read and write
total population: 93.2%
male: 93.3%
female: 93% (1995 est.)

Maldives (continued)

Government

Country name:
conventional long form: Republic of Maldives
conventional short form: Maldives
local long form: Dhivehi Raajjeyge Jumhooriyyaa
local short form: Dhivehi Raajje
Government type: republic
Capital: Male
Administrative divisions: 19 atolls (atholhu, singular and plural) and 1 other first-order administrative division*; Alifu, Baa, Dhaalu, Faafu, Gaafu Alifu, Gaafu Dhaalu, Gnaviyani, Haa Alifu, Haa Dhaalu, Kaafu, Laamu, Lhaviyani, Maale*, Meemu, Noonu, Raa, Seenu, Shaviyani, Thaa, Vaavu
Independence: 26 July 1965 (from UK)
National holiday: Independence Day, 26 July (1965)
Constitution: adopted January 1998
Legal system: based on Islamic law with admixtures of English common law primarily in commercial matters; has not accepted compulsory ICJ jurisdiction
Suffrage: 21 years of age; universal
Executive branch:
chief of state: President Maumoon Abdul GAYOOM (since 11 November 1978); note - the president is both the chief of state and head of government
head of government: President Maumoon Abdul GAYOOM (since 11 November 1978); note - the president is both the chief of state and head of government
cabinet: appointed by the president; note - need not be members of Majlis
elections: president nominated by the Majlis and then that nomination must be ratified by a national referendum (at least a 51% approval margin is required); president elected for a five-year term; election last held 16 October 1998 (next to be held NA October 2003)
election results: President Maumoon Abdul GAYOOM reelected; percent of popular vote - Maumoon Abdul GAYOOM 90.9%
Legislative branch: unicameral People's Council or Majlis (50 seats; 42 elected by popular vote, 8 appointed by the president; members serve five-year terms)
elections: last held 20 November 1999 (next to be held NA November 2004)
election results: percent of vote - NA%; seats - independents 42
Judicial branch: High Court
Political parties and leaders: although political parties are not banned, none exist
Political pressure groups and leaders: none
International organization participation: AsDB, C, CCC, CP, ESCAP, FAO, G-77, IBRD, ICAO, IDA, IDB, IFAD, IFC, IMF, IMO, Intelsat (nonsignatory user), Interpol, IOC, ITU, NAM, OIC, OPCW, SAARC, UN, UNCTAD, UNESCO, UNIDO, UPU, WHO, WMO, WToO, WTrO
Diplomatic representation in the US: Maldives does not have an embassy in the US, but does have a Permanent Mission to the UN in New York
Diplomatic representation from the US: the US does not have an embassy in Maldives; the US Ambassador to Sri Lanka is accredited to Maldives and makes periodic visits there
Flag description: red with a large green rectangle in the center bearing a vertical white crescent; the closed side of the crescent is on the hoist side of the flag

Economy

Economy - overview: Tourism, Maldives largest industry, accounts for 20% of GDP and more than 60% of the Maldives' foreign exchange receipts. Over 90% of government tax revenue comes from import duties and tourism-related taxes. Almost 400,000 tourists visited the islands in 1998. Fishing is a second leading sector. The Maldivian Government began an economic reform program in 1989 initially by lifting import quotas and opening some exports to the private sector. Subsequently, it has liberalized regulations to allow more foreign investment. Agriculture and manufacturing continue to play a minor role in the economy, constrained by the limited availability of cultivable land and the shortage of domestic labor. Most staple foods must be imported. Industry, which consists mainly of garment production, boat building, and handicrafts, accounts for about 18% of GDP. Maldivian authorities worry about the impact of erosion and possible global warming on their low-lying country; 80% of the area is one meter or less above sea level.
GDP: purchasing power parity - $594 million (2000 est.)
GDP - real growth rate: 7.6% (2000 est.)
GDP - per capita: purchasing power parity - $2,000 (2000 est.)
GDP - composition by sector:
agriculture: 20%
industry: 18%
services: 62% (2000 est.)
Population below poverty line: NA%
Household income or consumption by percentage share:
lowest 10%: NA%
highest 10%: NA%
Inflation rate (consumer prices): 3% (2000 est.)
Labor force: 67,000 (1995)
Labor force - by occupation: agriculture 22%, industry 18%, services 60% (1995)
Unemployment rate: NEGL%
Budget:
revenues: $166 million (excluding foreign grants)
expenditures: $192 million, including capital expenditures of $80 million (1999 est.)
Industries: fish processing, tourism, shipping, boat building, coconut processing, garments, woven mats, rope, handicrafts, coral and sand mining
Industrial production growth rate: 4.4% (1996 est.)
Electricity - production: 101 million kWh (1999)
Electricity - production by source:
fossil fuel: 100%
hydro: 0%
nuclear: 0%
other: 0% (1999)
Electricity - consumption: 93.9 million kWh (1999)
Electricity - exports: 0 kWh (1999)
Electricity - imports: 0 kWh (1999)
Agriculture - products: coconuts, corn, sweet potatoes; fish
Exports: $88 million (f.o.b., 2000 est.)
Exports - commodities: fish, clothing
Exports - partners: US, UK, Sri Lanka, Japan
Imports: $372 million (f.o.b., 2000 est.)
Imports - commodities: consumer goods, intermediate and capital goods, petroleum products
Imports - partners: Singapore, India, Sri Lanka, Japan, Canada
Debt - external: $237 million (2000 est.)
Economic aid - recipient: $NA
Currency: rufiyaa (MVR)
Currency code: MVR
Exchange rates: rufiyaa per US dollar - 11.770 (fixed rate since 1995)
Fiscal year: calendar year

Communications

Telephones - main lines in use: 21,000 (1999)
Telephones - mobile cellular: 1,290 (1997)
Telephone system:
general assessment: minimal domestic and international facilities
domestic: interatoll communication through microwave links; all inhabited islands are connected with telephone and fax service
international: satellite earth station - 3 Intelsat (Indian Ocean)
Radio broadcast stations: AM 1, FM 1, shortwave 1 (1998)
Radios: 35,000 (1999)
Television broadcast stations: 1 (1997)
Televisions: 10,000 (1999)
Internet country code: .mv
Internet Service Providers (ISPs): 1 (2000)
Internet users: 2,000 (2000)

Transportation

Railways: 0 km
Highways:
total: NA km
paved: NA km
unpaved: NA km; note - Male has 9.6 km of coral highways within the city (1988 est.)
Waterways: none
Ports and harbors: Gan, Male
Merchant marine:
total: 17 ships (1,000 GRT or over) totaling 58,604 GRT/81,451 DWT
ships by type: cargo 16, short-sea passenger 1 (2000 est.)
Airports: 5 (2000 est.)
Airports - with paved runways:
total: 2
over 3,047 m: 1
2,438 to 3,047 m: 1 (2000 est.)

Maldives (continued)

Airports - with unpaved runways:
total: 3
914 to 1,523 m: 3 (2000 est.)

Military

Military branches: National Security Service
Military manpower - availability:
males age 15-49: 71,856 (2001 est.)
Military manpower - fit for military service:
males age 15-49: 40,006 (2001 est.)
Military expenditures - dollar figure: $NA
Military expenditures - percent of GDP: NA%

Transnational Issues

Disputes - international: none

Mali

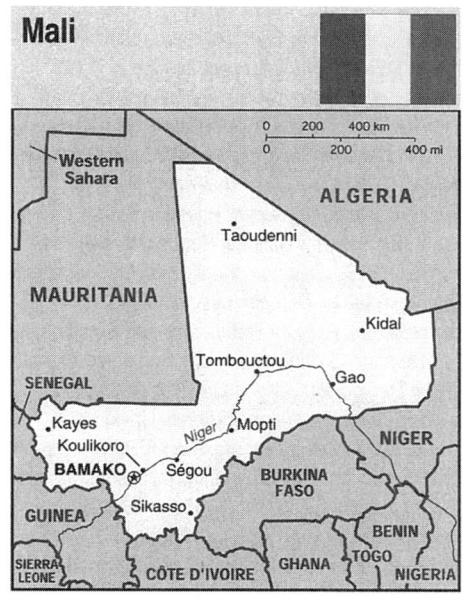

Introduction

Background: The Sudanese Republic and Senegal became independent of France in 1960 as the Mali Federation. When Senegal withdrew after only a few months, the Sudanese Republic was renamed Mali. Rule by dictatorship was brought to a close in 1991 with a transitional government, and in 1992 when Mali's first democratic presidential election was held. Since his reelection in 1997, President KONARE has continued to push through political and economic reforms and to fight corruption. In 1999 he indicated he would not run for a third term.

Geography

Location: Western Africa, southwest of Algeria
Geographic coordinates: 17 00 N, 4 00 W
Map references: Africa
Area:
total: 1.24 million sq km
land: 1.22 million sq km
water: 20,000 sq km
Area - comparative: slightly less than twice the size of Texas
Land boundaries:
total: 7,243 km
border countries: Algeria 1,376 km, Burkina Faso 1,000 km, Guinea 858 km, Cote d'Ivoire 532 km, Mauritania 2,237 km, Niger 821 km, Senegal 419 km
Coastline: 0 km (landlocked)
Maritime claims: none (landlocked)
Climate: subtropical to arid; hot and dry February to June; rainy, humid, and mild June to November; cool and dry November to February
Terrain: mostly flat to rolling northern plains covered by sand; savanna in south, rugged hills in northeast
Elevation extremes:
lowest point: Senegal River 23 m
highest point: Hombori Tondo 1,155 m
Natural resources: gold, phosphates, kaolin, salt, limestone, uranium, hydropower
note: bauxite, iron ore, manganese, tin, and copper deposits are known but not exploited
Land use:
arable land: 2%
permanent crops: 0%
permanent pastures: 25%
forests and woodland: 6%
other: 67% (1993 est.)
Irrigated land: 780 sq km (1993 est.)
Natural hazards: hot, dust-laden harmattan haze common during dry seasons; recurring droughts
Environment - current issues: deforestation; soil erosion; desertification; inadequate supplies of potable water; poaching
Environment - international agreements:
party to: Biodiversity, Climate Change, Desertification, Endangered Species, Hazardous Wastes, Law of the Sea, Marine Dumping, Ozone Layer Protection, Ship Pollution, Wetlands
signed, but not ratified: Climate Change-Kyoto Protocol, Nuclear Test Ban
Geography - note: landlocked

People

Population: 11,008,518 (July 2001 est.)
Age structure:
0-14 years: 47.2% (male 2,612,215; female 2,583,370)
15-64 years: 49.73% (male 2,610,142; female 2,864,127)
65 years and over: 3.07% (male 158,486; female 180,178) (2001 est.)
Population growth rate: 2.97% (2001 est.)
Birth rate: 48.79 births/1,000 population (2001 est.)
Death rate: 18.71 deaths/1,000 population (2001 est.)
Net migration rate: -0.36 migrant(s)/1,000 population (2001 est.)
Sex ratio:
at birth: 1.03 male(s)/female
under 15 years: 1.01 male(s)/female
15-64 years: 0.91 male(s)/female
65 years and over: 0.88 male(s)/female
total population: 0.96 male(s)/female (2001 est.)
Infant mortality rate: 121.44 deaths/1,000 live births (2001 est.)
Life expectancy at birth:
total population: 47.02 years
male: 45.84 years
female: 48.24 years (2001 est.)
Total fertility rate: 6.81 children born/woman (2001 est.)
HIV/AIDS - adult prevalence rate: 2.03% (1999 est.)
HIV/AIDS - people living with HIV/AIDS: 100,000 (1999 est.)
HIV/AIDS - deaths: 9,900 (1999 est.)
Nationality:
noun: Malian(s)
adjective: Malian

Mali (continued)

Ethnic groups: Mande 50% (Bambara, Malinke, Soninke), Peul 17%, Voltaic 12%, Songhai 6%, Tuareg and Moor 10%, other 5%
Religions: Muslim 90%, indigenous beliefs 9%, Christian 1%
Languages: French (official), Bambara 80%, numerous African languages
Literacy:
definition: age 15 and over can read and write
total population: 31%
male: 39.4%
female: 23.1% (1995 est.)

Government

Country name:
conventional long form: Republic of Mali
conventional short form: Mali
local long form: Republique de Mali
local short form: Mali
former: French Sudan and Sudanese Republic
Government type: republic
Capital: Bamako
Administrative divisions: 8 regions (regions, singular - region); Gao, Kayes, Kidal, Koulikoro, Mopti, Segou, Sikasso, Tombouctou
Independence: 22 September 1960 (from France)
National holiday: Independence Day, 22 September (1960)
Constitution: adopted 12 January 1992
Legal system: based on French civil law system and customary law; judicial review of legislative acts in Constitutional Court (which was formally established on 9 March 1994); has not accepted compulsory ICJ jurisdiction
Suffrage: 21 years of age; universal
Executive branch:
chief of state: President Alpha Oumar KONARE (since 8 June 1992)
head of government: Prime Minister Mande SIDIBE (since September 2000)
cabinet: Council of Ministers appointed by the prime minister
elections: president elected by popular vote for a five-year term; election last held 11 May 1997 (next to be held NA May 2002); prime minister appointed by the president
election results: Alpha Oumar KONARE reelected president; percent of vote - Alpha Oumar KONARE 95.9%, Mamadou DIABY 4.1%
Legislative branch: unicameral National Assembly or Assemblee Nationale (147 seats; members are elected by popular vote to serve five-year terms)
elections: last held 20 July and 3 August 1997 (next to be held in two rounds in 2002); note - much of the opposition boycotted the election
election results: percent of vote by party - NA%; seats by party - ADEMA 130, PARENA 8, CDS 4, UDD 3, PDP 2
Judicial branch: Supreme Court or Cour Supreme
Political parties and leaders: Alliance for Democracy or ADEMA [Ibrahim Boubacar KEITA, party chairman]; Block of Alternative for the Renewal of Africa or BARA [Yoro DIAKITE]; Democratic and Social Convention or CDS [Mamadou Bakary SANGARE, chairman]; Movement for the Independence, Renaissance and Integration of Africa or MIRIA [Mohamed Lamine TRAORE, Mouhamedou DICKO]; National Congress for Democratic Initiative or CNID [Mountaga TALL, chairman]; Party for Democracy and Progress or PDP [Me Idrissa TRAORE]; Party for National Renewal or PARENA [Yoro DIAKITE, chairman; Tiebile DRAME, secretary general]; Rally for Democracy and Labor or RDT [Ali GNANGADO]; Rally for Democracy and Progress or RDP [Almamy SYLLA, chairman]; Sudanese Union/ African Democratic Rally or US/RDA [Mamadou Bamou TOURE, secretary general]; Union of Democratic Forces for Progress or UFDP [Youssouf TOURE, secretary general]; Union for Democracy and Development or UDD [Moussa Balla COULIBALY]
Political pressure groups and leaders: Patriotic Movement of the Ghanda Koye or MPGK; United Movement and Fronts of Azawad or MFUA
International organization participation: ACCT, ACP, AfDB, CCC, ECA, ECOWAS, FAO, FZ, G-77, IAEA, IBRD, ICAO, ICFTU, ICRM, IDA, IDB, IFAD, IFC, IFRCS, ILO, IMF, Intelsat, Interpol, IOC, IOM, ISO (subscriber), ITU, MIPONUH, MONUC, NAM, OAU, OIC, OPCW, UN, UN Security Council (temporary), UNAMSIL, UNCTAD, UNESCO, UNIDO, UPU, WADB, WAEMU, WFTU, WHO, WIPO, WMO, WToO, WTrO
Diplomatic representation in the US:
chief of mission: Ambassador Cheick Oumar DIARRAH
chancery: 2130 R Street NW, Washington, DC 20008
telephone: [1] (202) 332-2249, 939-8950
FAX: [1] (202) 332-6603
Diplomatic representation from the US:
chief of mission: Ambassador Michael RANNEBERGER
embassy: Rue Rochester NY and Rue Mohamed V, Bamako
mailing address: B. P. 34, Bamako
telephone: [223] 22 54 70
FAX: [223] 22 37 12
Flag description: three equal vertical bands of green (hoist side), yellow, and red; uses the popular pan-African colors of Ethiopia

Economy

Economy - overview: Mali is among the poorest countries in the world, with 65% of its land area desert or semidesert. Economic activity is largely confined to the riverine area irrigated by the Niger. About 10% of the population is nomadic and some 80% of the labor force is engaged in farming and fishing. Industrial activity is concentrated on processing farm commodities. Mali is heavily dependent on foreign aid and vulnerable to fluctuations in world prices for cotton, its main export. In 1997, the government continued its successful implementation of an IMF-recommended structural adjustment program that is helping the economy grow, diversify, and attract foreign investment. Mali's adherence to economic reform and the 50% devaluation of the African franc in January 1994 have pushed up economic growth to a sturdy 5% average in 1996-2000. Growth should remain around 5% in 2001-02, and inflation should stay less than 2%.
GDP: purchasing power parity - $9.1 billion (2000 est.)
GDP - real growth rate: 4.8% (2000 est.)
GDP - per capita: purchasing power parity - $850 (2000 est.)
GDP - composition by sector:
agriculture: 46%
industry: 21%
services: 33% (1998)
Population below poverty line: NA%
Household income or consumption by percentage share:
lowest 10%: 1.8%
highest 10%: 40.4% (1994)
Inflation rate (consumer prices): 0.8% (2000 est.)
Labor force: NA
Labor force - by occupation: agriculture and fishing 80% (1998 est.)
Unemployment rate: NA%
Budget:
revenues: $730 million
expenditures: $770 million, including capital expenditures of $320 million (1997 est.)
Industries: minor local consumer goods production and food processing; construction; phosphate and gold mining
Industrial production growth rate: NA
Electricity - production: 445 million kWh (1999)
Electricity - production by source:
fossil fuel: 44.94%
hydro: 55.06%
nuclear: 0%
other: 0% (1999)
Electricity - consumption: 413.9 million kWh (1999)
Electricity - exports: 0 kWh (1999)
Electricity - imports: 0 kWh (1999)
Agriculture - products: cotton, millet, rice, corn, vegetables, peanuts; cattle, sheep, goats
Exports: $480 million (f.o.b., 2000 est.)
Exports - commodities: cotton 50%, gold, livestock (1999 est.)
Exports - partners: Italy 18%, Thailand 15%, Germany 7%, Portugal 4% (1999)
Imports: $575 million (f.o.b., 2000 est.)
Imports - commodities: machinery and equipment, construction materials, petroleum, foodstuffs, textiles
Imports - partners: Cote d'Ivoire 19%, France 19%, Senegal 4%, Benelux 3% (1999)
Debt - external: $3 billion (1999)
Economic aid - recipient: $596.4 million (1995)
Currency: Communaute Financiere Africaine franc (XOF); note - responsible authority is the Central Bank of the West African States
Currency code: XOF

Mali (continued)

Exchange rates: Communaute Financiere Africaine francs (XOF) per US dollar - 699.21 (January 2001), 711.98 (2000), 615.70 (1999), 589.95 (1998), 583.67 (1997), 511.55 (1996); note - from 1 January 1999, the XOF is pegged to the euro at a rate of 655.957 XOF per euro
Fiscal year: calendar year

Communications

Telephones - main lines in use: 23,000 (1997)
Telephones - mobile cellular: 2,842 (1997)
Telephone system:
general assessment: domestic system poor but improving; provides only minimal service
domestic: network consists of microwave radio relay, open wire, and radiotelephone communications stations; expansion of microwave radio relay in progress
international: satellite earth stations - 2 Intelsat (1 Atlantic Ocean and 1 Indian Ocean)
Radio broadcast stations: AM 1, FM 14, shortwave 7 (1998)
Radios: 570,000 (1997)
Television broadcast stations: 1 (plus two repeaters) (1997)
Televisions: 45,000 (1997)
Internet country code: .ml
Internet Service Providers (ISPs): 1 (2000)
Internet users: 10,000 (2000)

Transportation

Railways:
total: 729 km (linked to Senegal's rail system through Kayes)
narrow gauge: 729 km 1.000-m gauge
Highways:
total: 15,100 km
paved: 1,827 km
unpaved: 13,273 km (1996)
Waterways: 1,815 km
Ports and harbors: Koulikoro
Airports: 27 (2000 est.)
Airports - with paved runways:
total: 7
2,438 to 3,047 m: 4
1,524 to 2,437 m: 1
914 to 1,523 m: 2 (2000 est.)
Airports - with unpaved runways:
total: 20
1,524 to 2,437 m: 4
914 to 1,523 m: 7
under 914 m: 9 (2000 est.)

Military

Military branches: Army, Air Force, Gendarmerie, Republican Guard, National Guard, National Police (Surete Nationale)
Military manpower - availability:
males age 15-49: 2,284,632 (2001 est.)
Military manpower - fit for military service:
males age 15-49: 1,309,612 (2001 est.)
Military expenditures - dollar figure: $49 million (FY96)
Military expenditures - percent of GDP: 2% (FY96)

Transnational Issues

Disputes - international: none

Malta

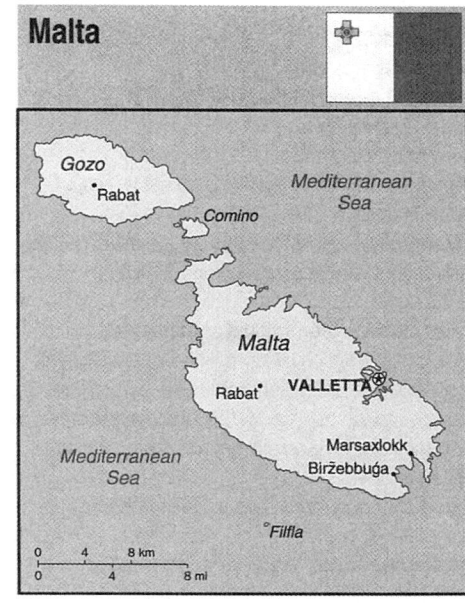

Introduction

Background: Great Britain formally acquired possession of Malta in 1814. The island staunchly supported the UK through both World Wars and remained in the Commonwealth when it became independent in 1964. A decade later Malta became a republic. Over the last 15 years, the island has become a major freight transshipment point, financial center, and tourist destination. It is an official candidate for EU membership.

Geography

Location: Southern Europe, islands in the Mediterranean Sea, south of Sicily (Italy)
Geographic coordinates: 35 50 N, 14 35 E
Map references: Europe
Area:
total: 316 sq km
land: 316 sq km
water: 0 sq km
Area - comparative: slightly less than twice the size of Washington, DC
Land boundaries: 0 km
Coastline: 196.8 km (does not include 56.01 km for the island of Gozo)
Maritime claims:
contiguous zone: 24 NM
continental shelf: 200-m depth or to the depth of exploitation
exclusive fishing zone: 25 NM
territorial sea: 12 NM
Climate: Mediterranean with mild, rainy winters and hot, dry summers
Terrain: mostly low, rocky, flat to dissected plains; many coastal cliffs
Elevation extremes:
lowest point: Mediterranean Sea 0 m
highest point: Ta'Dmejrek 253 m (near Dingli)
Natural resources: limestone, salt, arable land

Malta (continued)

Land use:
arable land: 32%
permanent crops: 3%
permanent pastures: 0%
forests and woodland: 4%
other: 61% (2000 est.)
Irrigated land: 11.45 sq km (2000 est.)
Natural hazards: NA
Environment - current issues: very limited natural fresh water resources; increasing reliance on desalination
Environment - international agreements:
party to: Air Pollution, Biodiversity, Climate Change, Desertification, Endangered Species, Hazardous Wastes, Law of the Sea, Marine Dumping, Nuclear Test Ban, Ozone Layer Protection, Ship Pollution, Wetlands
signed, but not ratified: Climate Change-Kyoto Protocol
Geography - note: the country comprises an archipelago, with only the three largest islands (Malta, Ghawdex or Gozo, and Kemmuna or Comino) being inhabited; numerous bays provide good harbors; Malta and Tunisia are discussing the commercial exploitation of the continental shelf between their countries, particularly for oil exploration

People

Population: 394,583 (July 2001 est.)
Age structure:
0-14 years: 19.98% (male 40,791; female 38,062)
15-64 years: 67.49% (male 133,914; female 132,402)
65 years and over: 12.53% (male 20,643; female 28,771) (2001 est.)
Population growth rate: 0.74% (2001 est.)
Birth rate: 12.75 births/1,000 population (2001 est.)
Death rate: 7.74 deaths/1,000 population (2001 est.)
Net migration rate: 2.37 migrant(s)/1,000 population (2001 est.)
Sex ratio:
at birth: 1.09 male(s)/female
under 15 years: 1.07 male(s)/female
15-64 years: 1.01 male(s)/female
65 years and over: 0.72 male(s)/female
total population: 0.98 male(s)/female (2001 est.)
Infant mortality rate: 5.83 deaths/1,000 live births (2001 est.)
Life expectancy at birth:
total population: 78.1 years
male: 75.64 years
female: 80.79 years (2001 est.)
Total fertility rate: 1.92 children born/woman (2001 est.)
HIV/AIDS - adult prevalence rate: 0.52% (1999 est.)
HIV/AIDS - people living with HIV/AIDS: NA
HIV/AIDS - deaths: less than 100 (1999 est.)
Nationality:
noun: Maltese (singular and plural)
adjective: Maltese

Ethnic groups: Maltese (descendants of ancient Carthaginians and Phoenicians, with strong elements of Italian and other Mediterranean stock)
Religions: Roman Catholic 91%
Languages: Maltese (official), English (official)
Literacy:
definition: age 10 and over can read and write
total population: 88.76%
male: 86.91%
female: 89.55% (1995 census)

Government

Country name:
conventional long form: Republic of Malta
conventional short form: Malta
local long form: Repubblika ta' Malta
local short form: Malta
Government type: republic
Capital: Valletta
Administrative divisions: none (administered directly from Valletta)
Independence: 21 September 1964 (from UK)
National holiday: Independence Day, 21 September (1964)
Constitution: 1964 constitution substantially amended on 13 December 1974
Legal system: based on English common law and Roman civil law; accepts compulsory ICJ jurisdiction, with reservations
Suffrage: 18 years of age; universal
Executive branch:
chief of state: President Guido DE MARCO (since 4 April 1999)
head of government: Prime Minister Eddie FENECH ADAMI (since 6 September 1998); Deputy Prime Minister Lawrence GONZE (since 4 April 1999)
cabinet: Cabinet appointed by the president on the advice of the prime minister
elections: president elected by the House of Representatives for a five-year term; election last held NA April 1999 (next to be held by NA April 2004); following legislative elections, the leader of the majority party or leader of a majority coalition is usually appointed prime minister by the president for a five-year term; the deputy prime minister is appointed by the president on the advice of the prime minister
election results: Guido DE MARCO elected president; percent of House of Representatives vote - 54%
Legislative branch: unicameral House of Representatives (usually 65 seats; note - additional seats are given to the party with the largest popular vote to ensure a legislative majority; members are elected by popular vote on the basis of proportional representation to serve five-year terms)
elections: last held 5 September 1998 (next to be held by September 2003)
election results: percent of vote by party - PN 51.8%, MLP 46.9%, AD 1.2%; seats by party - PN 35, MLP 30
Judicial branch: Constitutional Court; Court of Appeal; judges for both courts are appointed by the president on the advice of the prime minister

Political parties and leaders: Alternativa Demokratika/Alliance for Social Justice or AD [Harry VASSALLO]; Malta Labor Party or MLP [Alfred SANT]; Nationalist Party or PN [Edward FENECH ADAMI]
Political pressure groups and leaders: NA
International organization participation: C, CCC, CE, EBRD, ECE, EU (applicant), FAO, G-77, IAEA, IBRD, ICAO, ICFTU, ICRM, IFAD, IFRCS, ILO, IMF, IMO, Inmarsat, Intelsat, Interpol, IOC, IOM (observer), ISO, ITU, NAM, OPCW, OSCE, PCA, UN, UNCTAD, UNESCO, UNIDO, UPU, WCL, WHO, WIPO, WMO, WToO, WTrO
Diplomatic representation in the US:
chief of mission: Ambassador George SALIBA
chancery: 2017 Connecticut Avenue NW, Washington, DC 20008
telephone: [1] (202) 462-3611, 3612
FAX: [1] (202) 387-5470
consulate(s): New York
Diplomatic representation from the US:
chief of mission: Ambassador George SALIBA
embassy: 3rd Floor, Development House, Saint Anne Street, Floriana, Malta VLT 01
mailing address: P. O. Box 535, Valletta, Malta, CMR 01
telephone: [356] 235960 through 235965
FAX: [356] 243229
Flag description: two equal vertical bands of white (hoist side) and red; in the upper hoist-side corner is a representation of the Saint George Cross, edged in red

Economy

Economy - overview: Major resources are limestone, a favorable geographic location, and a productive labor force. Malta produces only about 20% of its food needs, has limited freshwater supplies, and has no domestic energy sources. The economy is dependent on foreign trade, manufacturing (especially electronics and textiles), and tourism. Malta is privatizing state-controlled firms and liberalizing markets in order to prepare for membership in the European Union. However, the island is divided politically over the question of joining the EU. The sizable budget deficit remains a key concern.
GDP: purchasing power parity - $5.6 billion (2000 est.)
GDP - real growth rate: 3.4% (2000 est.)
GDP - per capita: purchasing power parity - $14,300 (2000 est.)
GDP - composition by sector:
agriculture: 2.8%
industry: 25.5%
services: 71.7% (1999)
Population below poverty line: NA%
Household income or consumption by percentage share:
lowest 10%: NA%
highest 10%: NA%
Inflation rate (consumer prices): 2.5% (2000 est.)
Labor force: 145,901 (1999)

Malta (continued)

Labor force - by occupation: industry 24%, services 71%, agriculture 5% (1999 est.)
Unemployment rate: 4.5% (3rd Quarter 2000)
Budget:
revenues: $1.6 billion
expenditures: $1.73 billion, including capital expenditures of $265.4 million (1999)
Industries: tourism; electronics, ship building and repair, construction; food and beverages, textiles, footwear, clothing, tobacco
Industrial production growth rate: NA%
Electricity - production: 1.65 billion kWh (1999)
Electricity - production by source:
fossil fuel: 100%
hydro: 0%
nuclear: 0%
other: 0% (1999)
Electricity - consumption: 1.534 billion kWh (1999)
Electricity - exports: 0 kWh (1999)
Electricity - imports: 0 kWh (1999)
Agriculture - products: potatoes, cauliflower, grapes, wheat, barley, tomatoes, citrus, cut flowers, green peppers; pork, milk, poultry, eggs
Exports: $2 billion (f.o.b., 1999)
Exports - commodities: machinery and transport equipment, manufactures
Exports - partners: US 21.4%, France 15.2%, Germany 12.6%, UK 9.3%, Italy 4.9% (1999)
Imports: $2.6 billion (f.o.b., 1999)
Imports - commodities: machinery and transport equipment, manufactured and semi-manufactured goods; food, drink, and tobacco
Imports - partners: France 19.1%, Italy 16.7%, UK 10.9%, Germany 10.0%, US 8.5% (1999)
Debt - external: $130 million (1997)
Economic aid - recipient: $NA
Currency: Maltese lira (MTL)
Currency code: MTL
Exchange rates: Maltese liri per US dollar - 0.4370 (January 2001), 0.4376 (2000), 0.3994 (1999), 0.3885 (1998), 0.3857 (1997), 0.3604 (1996)
Fiscal year: 1 April - 31 March

Communications

Telephones - main lines in use: 187,000 (1997)
Telephones - mobile cellular: 17,691 (1997)
Telephone system:
general assessment: automatic system satisfies normal requirements
domestic: submarine cable and microwave radio relay between islands
international: 2 submarine cables; satellite earth station - 1 Intelsat (Atlantic Ocean)
Radio broadcast stations: AM 1, FM 18, shortwave 6 (1999)
Radios: 255,000 (1997)
Television broadcast stations: 6 (2000)
Televisions: 280,000 (1997)
Internet country code: .mt
Internet Service Providers (ISPs): 2 (2000)
Internet users: 40,000 (2000)

Transportation

Railways: 0 km
Highways:
total: 1,742 km
paved: 1,677 km
unpaved: 65 km (1997)
Waterways: none
Ports and harbors: Marsaxlokk, Valletta
Merchant marine:
total: 1,414 ships (1,000 GRT or over) totaling 28,191,090 GRT/46,773,603 DWT
ships by type: bulk 443, cargo 394, chemical tanker 48, combination bulk 12, combination ore/oil 14, container 69, liquefied gas 2, livestock carrier 3, multi-functional large-load carrier 2, passenger 7, passenger/cargo 1, petroleum tanker 296, refrigerated cargo 37, roll on/roll off 50, short-sea passenger 15, specialized tanker 3, vehicle carrier 18
note: includes some foreign-owned ships registered here as a flag of convenience: Argentina 1, Bermuda 1, Belgium 1, Bangladesh 2, Bulgaria 11, China 7, Costa Rica 1, Cuba 2, Cyprus 15, Denmark 1, Estonia 2, Finland 1, Germany 23, Greece 258, Hong Kong 3, Croatia 9, Hungary 1, India 2, Israel 2, Italy 17, South Korea 1, Lebanon 2, Latvia 2, Lithuania 1, Monaco 14, Nigeria 1, Netherlands 10, Norway 31, Poland 8, Romania 3, Russia 39, Singapore 6, Spain 3, Sweden 3, Syria 1, Switzerland 25, UAE 2, Turkey 24, UK 8, Ukraine 9, US 9, Venezuela 1, Vietnam 1 (2000 est.)
Airports: 1 (2000 est.)
Airports - with paved runways:
total: 1
over 3,047 m: 1 (2000 est.)

Military

Military branches: Armed Forces (including land forces, an air squadron, a maritime squadron, and the Revenue Security Corps), Maltese Police Force
Military manpower - availability:
males age 15-49: 98,953 (2001 est.)
Military manpower - fit for military service:
males age 15-49: 78,783 (2001 est.)
Military expenditures - dollar figure: $201 million (FY98)
Military expenditures - percent of GDP: 5.5% (FY98)

Transnational Issues

Disputes - international: none
Illicit drugs: minor transshipment point for hashish from North Africa to Western Europe

Man, Isle of
(British crown dependency)

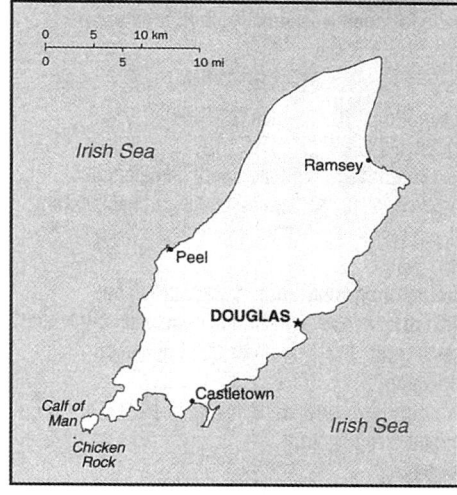

Introduction

Background: Part of the Norwegian Kingdom of the Hebrides until the 13th century when it was ceded to Scotland, the isle came under the British crown in 1765. Current concerns include reviving the almost extinct Manx Celtic language.

Geography

Location: Western Europe, island in the Irish Sea, between Great Britain and Ireland
Geographic coordinates: 54 15 N, 4 30 W
Map references: Europe
Area:
total: 572 sq km
land: 572 sq km
water: 0 sq km
Area - comparative: slightly more than three times the size of Washington, DC
Land boundaries: 0 km
Coastline: 160 km
Maritime claims:
exclusive fishing zone: 12 NM
territorial sea: 12 NM
Climate: cool summers and mild winters; temperate; overcast about one-third of the time
Terrain: hills in north and south bisected by central valley
Elevation extremes:
lowest point: Irish Sea 0 m
highest point: Snaefell 621 m
Natural resources: none
Land use:
arable land: 9%
permanent crops: 0%
permanent pastures: 46%
forests and woodland: 6%
other: 39% (includes 25% mountain and heathland)
Irrigated land: 0 sq km
Natural hazards: NA

Man, Isle of (continued)

Environment - current issues: waste disposal (both household and industrial); transboundary air pollution
Geography - note: one small islet, the Calf of Man, lies to the southwest, and is a bird sanctuary

People

Population: 73,489 (July 2001 est.)
Age structure:
0-14 years: 17.51% (male 6,562; female 6,306)
15-64 years: 65.19% (male 24,061; female 23,845)
65 years and over: 17.3% (male 5,076; female 7,639) (2001 est.)
Population growth rate: 0.52% (2001 est.)
Birth rate: 11.58 births/1,000 population (2001 est.)
Death rate: 11.84 deaths/1,000 population (2001 est.)
Net migration rate: 5.44 migrant(s)/1,000 population (2001 est.)
Sex ratio:
at birth: 1.05 male(s)/female
under 15 years: 1.04 male(s)/female
15-64 years: 1.01 male(s)/female
65 years and over: 0.66 male(s)/female
total population: 0.94 male(s)/female (2001 est.)
Infant mortality rate: 6.42 deaths/1,000 live births (2001 est.)
Life expectancy at birth:
total population: 77.64 years
male: 74.26 years
female: 81.2 years (2001 est.)
Total fertility rate: 1.65 children born/woman (2001 est.)
HIV/AIDS - adult prevalence rate: NA%
HIV/AIDS - people living with HIV/AIDS: NA
HIV/AIDS - deaths: NA
Nationality:
noun: Manxman (men), Manxwoman (women)
adjective: Manx
Ethnic groups: Manx (Norse-Celtic descent), Briton
Religions: Anglican, Roman Catholic, Methodist, Baptist, Presbyterian, Society of Friends
Languages: English, Manx Gaelic
Literacy:
definition: NA
total population: NA%
male: NA%
female: NA%

Government

Country name:
conventional long form: none
conventional short form: Isle of Man
Dependency status: British crown dependency
Government type: parliamentary democracy
Capital: Douglas
Administrative divisions: there are 24 local authorities each with its own elections
Independence: none (British crown dependency)
National holiday: Tynwald Day, 5 July
Constitution: unwritten; note - The Isle of Man Constitution Act, 1961, does not embody the Manx Constitution
Legal system: English common law and Manx statute
Suffrage: 18 years of age; universal
Executive branch:
chief of state: Lord of Mann Queen ELIZABETH II (since 6 February 1952), represented by Lieutenant Governor His Excellency Sir Timothy DAUNT (since 27 October 1995)
head of government: Chief Minister Donald GELLING (since 3 December 1996)
cabinet: Council of Ministers
elections: the monarch is hereditary; lieutenant governor appointed by the monarch for a five-year term; the Chief Minister is elected by the Tynwald; election last held 3 December 1996 (next to be held NA 2001)
election results: Donald GELLING elected chief minister by the Tynwald
Legislative branch: bicameral Tynwald consists of the Legislative Council (a 11-member body composed of the President of Tynwald, the Lord Bishop of Sodor and Man, a nonvoting attorney general, and 8 others named by the House of Keys) and the House of Keys (24 seats; members are elected by popular vote to serve five-year terms)
elections: House of Keys - last held 21 November 1996 (next to be held NA November 2001)
election results: House of Keys - percent of vote by party - NA%; seats by party - independents 24
Judicial branch: High Court of Justice (justices are appointed by the Lord Chancellor of England on the nomination of the lieutenant governor)
Political parties and leaders: there is no party system; members sit as independents
Political pressure groups and leaders: none
International organization participation: none
Diplomatic representation in the US: none (British crown dependency)
Diplomatic representation from the US: none (British crown dependency)
Flag description: red with the Three Legs of Man emblem (Trinacria), in the center; the three legs are joined at the thigh and bent at the knee; in order to have the toes pointing clockwise on both sides of the flag, a two-sided emblem is used

Economy

Economy - overview: Offshore banking, manufacturing, and tourism are key sectors of the economy. The government's policy of offering incentives to high-technology companies and financial institutions to locate on the island has paid off in expanding employment opportunities in high-income industries. As a result, agriculture and fishing, once the mainstays of the economy, have declined in their shares of GDP. Banking and other services now contribute 42% to GDP. Trade is mostly with the UK. The Isle of Man enjoys free access to EU markets.
GDP: purchasing power parity - $1.4 billion (1999 est.)
GDP - real growth rate: 13.5% (1999 est.)
GDP - per capita: purchasing power parity - $18,800 (1999 est.)
GDP - composition by sector:
agriculture: 1%
industry: 9%
services: 90% (1999 est.)
Population below poverty line: NA%
Household income or consumption by percentage share:
lowest 10%: NA%
highest 10%: NA%
Inflation rate (consumer prices): 2.5% (2000 est.)
Labor force: 36,610 (1998)
Labor force - by occupation: agriculture, forestry and fishing 3%, manufacturing 11%, construction 10%, transport and communication 8%, wholesale and retail distribution 11%, professional and scientific services 18%, public administration 6%, banking and finance 18%, tourism 2%, entertainment and catering 3%, miscellaneous services 10%
Unemployment rate: 0.6% (August 2000)
Budget:
revenues: $485 million
expenditures: $463 million, including capital expenditures of $NA (FY00/01 est.)
Industries: financial services, light manufacturing, tourism
Industrial production growth rate: 3.2% (FY96/97)
Agriculture - products: cereals, vegetables; cattle, sheep, pigs, poultry
Exports: $NA
Exports - commodities: tweeds, herring, processed shellfish, beef, lamb
Exports - partners: UK
Imports: $NA
Imports - commodities: timber, fertilizers, fish
Imports - partners: UK
Debt - external: $NA
Economic aid - recipient: $NA
Currency: British pound (GBP); note - there is also a Manx pound
Currency code: GBP
Exchange rates: Manx pounds per US dollar - 0.6764 (January 2001), 0.6596 (2000), 0.6180 (1999), 0.6037 (1998), 0.6106 (1997), 0.6403 (1996); the Manx pound is at par with the British pound
Fiscal year: 1 April - 31 March

Communications

Telephones - main lines in use: 51,000 (1999)
Telephones - mobile cellular: NA
Telephone system:
general assessment: NA
domestic: landline, telefax, mobile cellular telephone system
international: fiber-optic cable, microwave radio relay, satellite earth station, submarine cable

Man, Isle of (continued)

Radio broadcast stations: AM 1, FM 1, shortwave 0 (1998)
Radios: NA
Television broadcast stations: 0 (receives broadcasts from the UK and satellite) (1999)
Televisions: 27,490 (1999)
Internet country code: .im
Internet Service Providers (ISPs): NA
Internet users: NA

Transportation

Railways:
total: 68.5 km (43.5 km electrified)
Highways:
total: 800 km
paved: 800 km
unpaved: 0 km (1999)
Waterways: none
Ports and harbors: Castletown, Douglas, Peel, Ramsey
Merchant marine:
total: 157 ships (1,000 GRT or over) totaling 4,917,402 GRT/8,333,858 DWT
ships by type: bulk 27, cargo 13, chemical tanker 11, combination bulk 3, container 20, liquefied gas 13, petroleum tanker 43, refrigerated cargo 3, roll on/roll off 18, specialized tanker 1, vehicle carrier 5
note: includes some foreign-owned ships registered here as a flag of convenience: Belgium 1, Denmark 1, Germany 1, Netherlands 1, Sweden 1, UK 3 (2000 est.)
Airports: 1 (2000 est.)
Airports - with paved runways:
total: 1
1,524 to 2,437 m: 1 (2000 est.)

Military

Military - note: defense is the responsibility of the UK

Transnational Issues

Disputes - international: none

Marshall Islands

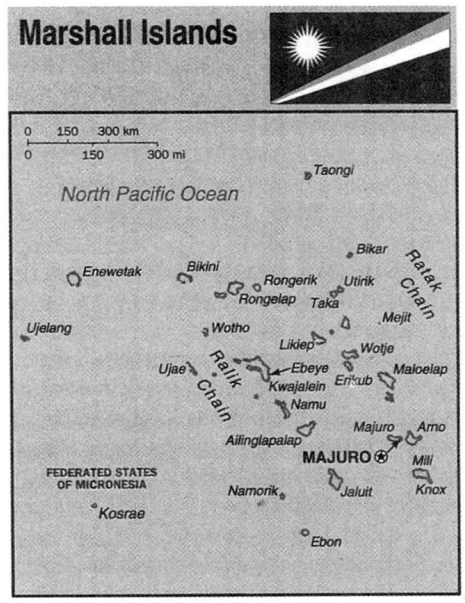

Introduction

Background: After almost four decades under US administration as the easternmost part of the UN Trust Territory of the Pacific Islands, the Marshall Islands attained independence in 1986 under a Compact of Free Association. Compensation claims continue as a result of US nuclear testing on some of the islands between 1947 and 1962.

Geography

Location: Oceania, group of atolls and reefs in the North Pacific Ocean, about one-half of the way from Hawaii to Papua New Guinea
Geographic coordinates: 9 00 N, 168 00 E
Map references: Oceania
Area:
total: 181.3 sq km
land: 181.3 sq km
water: 0 sq km
note: includes the atolls of Bikini, Enewetak, and Kwajalein
Area - comparative: about the size of Washington, DC
Land boundaries: 0 km
Coastline: 370.4 km
Maritime claims:
contiguous zone: 24 NM
exclusive economic zone: 200 NM
territorial sea: 12 NM
Climate: wet season from May to November; hot and humid; islands border typhoon belt
Terrain: low coral limestone and sand islands
Elevation extremes:
lowest point: Pacific Ocean 0 m
highest point: unnamed location on Likiep 10 m
Natural resources: phosphate deposits, marine products, deep seabed minerals
Land use:
arable land: 0%
permanent crops: 60%
permanent pastures: 0%
forests and woodland: 0%
other: 40%
Irrigated land: NA sq km
Natural hazards: occasional typhoons
Environment - current issues: inadequate supplies of potable water
Environment - international agreements:
party to: Biodiversity, Climate Change, Desertification, Law of the Sea, Marine Dumping, Ozone Layer Protection, Ship Pollution
signed, but not ratified: Climate Change-Kyoto Protocol
Geography - note: two archipelagic island chains of 30 atolls and 1,152 islands; Bikini and Enewetak are former US nuclear test sites; Kwajalein, the famous World War II battleground, is now used as a US missile test range

People

Population: 70,822 (July 2001 est.)
Age structure:
0-14 years: 49.29% (male 17,808; female 17,101)
15-64 years: 48.61% (male 17,573; female 16,853)
65 years and over: 2.1% (male 707; female 780) (2001 est.)
Population growth rate: 3.88% (2001 est.)
Birth rate: 45.07 births/1,000 population (2001 est.)
Death rate: 6.23 deaths/1,000 population (2001 est.)
Net migration rate: 0 migrant(s)/1,000 population (2001 est.)
Sex ratio:
at birth: 1.05 male(s)/female
under 15 years: 1.04 male(s)/female
15-64 years: 1.04 male(s)/female
65 years and over: 0.91 male(s)/female
total population: 1.04 male(s)/female (2001 est.)
Infant mortality rate: 39.82 deaths/1,000 live births (2001 est.)
Life expectancy at birth:
total population: 65.84 years
male: 64.04 years
female: 67.73 years (2001 est.)
Total fertility rate: 6.55 children born/woman (2001 est.)
HIV/AIDS - adult prevalence rate: NA%
HIV/AIDS - people living with HIV/AIDS: NA
HIV/AIDS - deaths: NA
Nationality:
noun: Marshallese (singular and plural)
adjective: Marshallese
Ethnic groups: Micronesian
Religions: Christian (mostly Protestant)
Languages: English (universally spoken and is the official language), two major Marshallese dialects from the Malayo-Polynesian family, Japanese
Literacy:
definition: age 15 and over can read and write
total population: 93%
male: 100%
female: 88% (1980 est.)

Marshall Islands (continued)

Government

Country name:
conventional long form: Republic of the Marshall Islands
conventional short form: Marshall Islands
former: Marshall Islands District (Trust Territory of the Pacific Islands)
Government type: constitutional government in free association with the US; the Compact of Free Association entered into force 21 October 1986
Capital: Majuro
Administrative divisions: 33 municipalities; Ailinginae, Ailinglaplap, Ailuk, Arno, Aur, Bikar, Bikini, Bokak, Ebon, Enewetak, Erikub, Jabat, Jaluit, Jemo, Kili, Kwajalein, Lae, Lib, Likiep, Majuro, Maloelap, Mejit, Mili, Namorik, Namu, Rongelap, Rongrik, Toke, Ujae, Ujelang, Utirik, Wotho, Wotje
Independence: 21 October 1986 (from the US-administered UN trusteeship)
National holiday: Constitution Day, 1 May (1979)
Constitution: 1 May 1979
Legal system: based on adapted Trust Territory laws, acts of the legislature, municipal, common, and customary laws
Suffrage: 18 years of age; universal
Executive branch:
chief of state: President Kessai Hesa NOTE (since 3 January 2000); note - the president is both the chief of state and head of government
head of government: President Kessai Hesa NOTE (since 3 January 2000); note - the president is both the chief of state and head of government
cabinet: Cabinet selected by the president from among the members of Parliament
elections: president elected by Parliament from among its own members for a four-year term; election last held 15 November 1999 (next to be held NA November 2003)
election results: Kessai Hesa NOTE elected president; percent of Parliament vote - 100%
Legislative branch: unicameral Parliament or Nitijela (33 seats; members elected by popular vote to serve four-year terms)
elections: last held 15 November 1999 (next to be held NA November 2003)
election results: percent of vote by party - NA%; seats by party - NA
note: the Council of Chiefs is a 12-member body that advises on matters affecting customary law and practice
Judicial branch: Supreme Court; High Court
Political parties and leaders: traditionally there have been no formally organized political parties; what has existed more closely resembles factions or interest groups because they do not have party headquarters, formal platforms, or party structures; the following two "groupings" have competed in legislative balloting in recent years - Kabua Party [Imata KABUA] and United Democratic Party or UDP [Litokwa TOMEING]
Political pressure groups and leaders: NA
International organization participation: ACP, AsDB, ESCAP, FAO, G-77, IAEA, IBRD, ICAO, IDA, IFC, IMF, IMO, Inmarsat, Intelsat (nonsignatory user), Interpol, ITU, OPCW, Sparteca, SPC, SPF, UN, UNCTAD, UNESCO, WHO
Diplomatic representation in the US:
chief of mission: Ambassador Banny DE BRUM
chancery: 2433 Massachusetts Avenue NW, Washington, DC 20008
telephone: [1] (202) 234-5414
FAX: [1] (202) 232-3236
consulate(s) general: Honolulu
Diplomatic representation from the US:
chief of mission: Ambassador Joan M. PLAISTED
embassy: Oceanside, Mejen Weto, Long Island, Majuro
mailing address: P. O. Box 1379, Majuro, Republic of the Marshall Islands 96960-1379
telephone: [692] 247-4011
FAX: [692] 247-4012
Flag description: blue with two stripes radiating from the lower hoist-side corner - orange (top) and white; there is a white star with four large rays and 20 small rays on the hoist side above the two stripes

Economy

Economy - overview: US Government assistance is the mainstay of this tiny island economy. Agricultural production is concentrated on small farms, and the most important commercial crops are coconuts, tomatoes, melons, and breadfruit. Small-scale industry is limited to handicrafts, fish processing, and copra. The tourist industry, now a small source of foreign exchange employing less than 10% of the labor force, remains the best hope for future added income. The islands have few natural resources, and imports far exceed exports. Under the terms of the Compact of Free Association, the US provides roughly $65 million in annual aid. Negotiations were underway in 1999 for an extended agreement. Government downsizing, drought, a drop in construction, and the decline in tourism and foreign investment due to the Asian financial difficulties caused GDP to fall in 1996-98.
GDP: purchasing power parity - $105 million (1998 est.), supplemented by approximately $65 million annual US aid
GDP - real growth rate: -5% (1998 est.)
GDP - per capita: purchasing power parity - $1,670 (1998 est.)
GDP - composition by sector:
agriculture: 15%
industry: 13%
services: 72% (1995)
Population below poverty line: NA%
Household income or consumption by percentage share:
lowest 10%: NA%
highest 10%: NA%
Inflation rate (consumer prices): 5% (1997)
Labor force: NA
Labor force - by occupation: agriculture NA%, industry NA%, services NA%
Unemployment rate: 16% (1991 est.)
Budget:
revenues: $80.1 million
expenditures: $77.4 million, including capital expenditures of $19.5 million (FY95/96 est.)
Industries: copra, fish, tourism, craft items from shell, wood, and pearls, offshore banking (embryonic)
Industrial production growth rate: NA%
Electricity - production by source:
fossil fuel: NA%
hydro: NA%
nuclear: NA%
other: NA%
Agriculture - products: coconuts, tomatoes, melons, cacao, taro, breadfruit, fruits; pigs, chickens
Exports: $28 million (f.o.b., 1997 est.)
Exports - commodities: fish, coconut oil, trochus shells
Exports - partners: US, Japan, Australia
Imports: $58 million (f.o.b., 1997 est.)
Imports - commodities: foodstuffs, machinery and equipment, fuels, beverages and tobacco
Imports - partners: US, Japan, Australia, NZ, Guam, Singapore
Debt - external: $125 million (FY96/97 est.)
Economic aid - recipient: approximately $65 million annually from the US
Currency: US dollar (USD)
Currency code: USD
Exchange rates: the US dollar is used
Fiscal year: 1 October - 30 September

Communications

Telephones - main lines in use: 3,000 (1996)
Telephones - mobile cellular: 365 (1996)
Telephone system:
general assessment: telex services
domestic: Majuro Atoll and Ebeye and Kwajalein islands have regular, seven-digit, direct-dial telephones; other islands interconnected by shortwave radiotelephone (used mostly for government purposes)
international: satellite earth stations - 2 Intelsat (Pacific Ocean); US Government satellite communications system on Kwajalein
Radio broadcast stations: AM 3, FM 4, shortwave 0 (1998)
Radios: NA
Television broadcast stations: 3 (of which two are US military stations) (1997)
Televisions: NA
Internet country code: .mh
Internet Service Providers (ISPs): 1 (2000)
Internet users: 500 (2000)

Transportation

Railways: 0 km
Highways:
total: NA km
paved: NA km
unpaved: NA km

Marshall Islands (continued)

note: paved roads on major islands (Majuro, Kwajalein), otherwise stone-, coral-, or laterite-surfaced roads and tracks
Waterways: none
Ports and harbors: Majuro
Merchant marine:
total: 212 ships (1,000 GRT or over) totaling 9,768,406 GRT/16,242,699 DWT
ships by type: bulk 63, cargo 9, chemical tanker 10, combination ore/oil 2, container 29, liquefied gas 10, multi-functional large-load carrier 1, petroleum tanker 87, vehicle carrier 1
note: includes some foreign-owned ships registered here as a flag of convenience: Cyprus 1, Germany 1, Japan 1, US 6 (2000 est.)
Airports: 16 (2000 est.)
Airports - with paved runways:
total: 4
1,524 to 2,437 m: 3
914 to 1,523 m: 1 (2000 est.)
Airports - with unpaved runways:
total: 12
914 to 1,523 m: 9
under 914 m: 3 (2000 est.)

Military

Military branches: no regular military forces (a coast guard may be established); Police Force
Military expenditures - dollar figure: $NA
Military expenditures - percent of GDP: NA%
Military - note: defense is the responsibility of the US

Transnational Issues

Disputes - international: claims US territory of Wake Island

Martinique
(overseas department of France)

Introduction

Background: Colonized by France in 1635, the island has subsequently remained a French possession except for three brief periods of foreign occupation.

Geography

Location: Caribbean, island in the Caribbean Sea, north of Trinidad and Tobago
Geographic coordinates: 14 40 N, 61 00 W
Map references: Central America and the Caribbean
Area:
total: 1,100 sq km
land: 1,060 sq km
water: 40 sq km
Area - comparative: slightly more than six times the size of Washington, DC
Land boundaries: 0 km
Coastline: 350 km
Maritime claims:
exclusive economic zone: 200 NM
territorial sea: 12 NM
Climate: tropical; moderated by trade winds; rainy season (June to October); vulnerable to devastating cyclones (hurricanes) every eight years on average; average temperature 17.3 degrees C; humid
Terrain: mountainous with indented coastline; dormant volcano
Elevation extremes:
lowest point: Caribbean Sea 0 m
highest point: Montagne Pelee 1,397 m
Natural resources: coastal scenery and beaches, cultivable land
Land use:
arable land: 8%
permanent crops: 8%
permanent pastures: 17%
forests and woodland: 44%
other: 23% (1993 est.)
Irrigated land: 40 sq km (1993 est.)
Natural hazards: hurricanes, flooding, and volcanic activity (an average of one major natural disaster every five years)
Environment - current issues: NA

People

Population: 418,454 (July 2001 est.)
Age structure:
0-14 years: 23.1% (male 49,016; female 47,653)
15-64 years: 66.77% (male 139,106; female 140,291)
65 years and over: 10.13% (male 18,893; female 23,495) (2001 est.)
Population growth rate: 0.93% (2001 est.)
Birth rate: 15.76 births/1,000 population (2001 est.)
Death rate: 6.39 deaths/1,000 population (2001 est.)
Net migration rate: -0.08 migrant(s)/1,000 population (2001 est.)
Sex ratio:
at birth: 1.02 male(s)/female
under 15 years: 1.03 male(s)/female
15-64 years: 0.99 male(s)/female
65 years and over: 0.8 male(s)/female
total population: 0.98 male(s)/female (2001 est.)
Infant mortality rate: 7.8 deaths/1,000 live births (2001 est.)
Life expectancy at birth:
total population: 78.41 years
male: 79.11 years
female: 77.69 years (2001 est.)
Total fertility rate: 1.8 children born/woman (2001 est.)
HIV/AIDS - adult prevalence rate: NA%
HIV/AIDS - people living with HIV/AIDS: NA
HIV/AIDS - deaths: NA
Nationality:
noun: Martiniquais (singular and plural)
adjective: Martiniquais
Ethnic groups: African and African-white-Indian mixture 90%, white 5%, East Indian, Chinese less than 5%
Religions: Roman Catholic 95%, Hindu and pagan African 5%
Languages: French, Creole patois
Literacy:
definition: age 15 and over can read and write
total population: 93%
male: 92%
female: 93% (1982 est.)

Government

Country name:
conventional long form: Department of Martinique
conventional short form: Martinique
local long form: Departement de la Martinique
local short form: Martinique
Dependency status: overseas department of France
Government type: NA
Capital: Fort-de-France

Martinique (continued)

Administrative divisions: none (overseas department of France)
Independence: none (overseas department of France)
National holiday: Bastille Day, 14 July (1789)
Constitution: 28 September 1958 (French Constitution)
Legal system: French legal system
Suffrage: 18 years of age; universal
Executive branch:
chief of state: President Jacques CHIRAC of France (since 17 May 1995); Prefect Jean-Francois CORDET (since NA)
head of government: President of the General Council Claude LISE (since 22 March 1992); President of the Regional Council Alfred MARIE-JEANNE (since NA March 1998)
cabinet: NA
elections: French president elected by popular vote for a seven-year term; prefect appointed by the French president on the advice of the French Ministry of Interior; the presidents of the General and Regional Councils are elected by the members of those councils
Legislative branch: unicameral General Council or Conseil General (45 seats; members are elected by popular vote to serve six-year terms) and a unicameral Regional Assembly or Conseil Regional (41 seats; members are elected by popular vote to serve six-year terms)
elections: General Council - last held NA March 2000 (next to be held NA 2006); Regional Assembly - last held on 15 March 1998 (next to be held by March 2004)
election results: General Council - percent of vote by party - NA%; seats by party - NA; note - the PPM won a plurality; Regional Assembly - percent of vote by party - NA%; seats by party - RPR-UDF 14, MIM 13, PPM 7, left parties 4, PMS 3
note: Martinique elects 2 seats to the French Senate; elections last held NA September 1998 (next to be held September 2001); results - percent of vote by party - NA%; seats by party - PPM 2; Martinique also elects 4 seats to the French National Assembly; elections last held 1 June 1997 (next to be held NA 2002); results - percent of vote by party - NA%; seats by party - RPR 2, PS 1, independent 1
Judicial branch: Court of Appeal or Cour d'Appel
Political parties and leaders: Martinique Independence Movement or MIM [Alfred MARIE-JEANNE]; Martinique Progressive Party or PPM [Camille DARSIERES]; Martinique Socialist Party or PMS [Ernest WAN-AJOUHU]; Rally for the Republic or RPR [Michel CHARLONE]; Union for French Democracy or UDF (replaced by Martinique Forces of Progress) [Jean MAREN]
Political pressure groups and leaders: Association for the Protection of Martinique's Heritage (ecologist) [Garcin MALSA]; Caribbean Revolutionary Alliance or ARC; Central Union for Martinique Workers or CSTM [Marc PULVAR]; Frantz Fanon Circle; League of Workers and Peasants; Proletarian Action Group or GAP; Socialist Revolution Group or GRS [Philippe PIERRE-CHARLES]
International organization participation: FZ, WCL, WFTU
Diplomatic representation in the US: none (overseas department of France)
Diplomatic representation from the US: none (overseas department of France)
Flag description: a light blue background is divided into four quadrants by a white cross; in the center of each rectangle is a white snake; the flag of France is used for official occasions

Economy

Economy - overview: The economy is based on sugarcane, bananas, tourism, and light industry. Agriculture accounts for about 6% of GDP and the small industrial sector for 11%. Sugar production has declined, with most of the sugarcane now used for the production of rum. Banana exports are increasing, going mostly to France. The bulk of meat, vegetable, and grain requirements must be imported, contributing to a chronic trade deficit that requires large annual transfers of aid from France. Tourism has become more important than agricultural exports as a source of foreign exchange. The majority of the work force is employed in the service sector and in administration.
GDP: purchasing power parity - $4.39 billion (1997 est.)
GDP - real growth rate: NA%
GDP - per capita: purchasing power parity - $11,000 (1997 est.)
GDP - composition by sector:
agriculture: 6%
industry: 11%
services: 83% (1997 est.)
Population below poverty line: NA%
Household income or consumption by percentage share:
lowest 10%: NA%
highest 10%: NA%
Inflation rate (consumer prices): 3.9% (1990)
Labor force: 170,000 (1997)
Labor force - by occupation: agriculture 10%, industry 17%, services 73% (1997)
Unemployment rate: 27.2% (1998)
Budget:
revenues: $900 million
expenditures: $2.5 billion, including capital expenditures of $140 million (1996)
Industries: construction, rum, cement, oil refining, sugar, tourism
Industrial production growth rate: NA%
Electricity - production: 1.1 billion kWh (1999)
Electricity - production by source:
fossil fuel: 100%
hydro: 0%
nuclear: 0%
other: 0% (1999)
Electricity - consumption: 1.023 billion kWh (1999)
Electricity - exports: 0 kWh (1999)
Electricity - imports: 0 kWh (1999)
Agriculture - products: pineapples, avocados, bananas, flowers, vegetables, sugarcane
Exports: $250 million (f.o.b., 1997)
Exports - commodities: refined petroleum products, bananas, rum, pineapples
Exports - partners: France 45%, Guadeloupe 28% (1997)
Imports: $2 billion (c.i.f., 1997)
Imports - commodities: petroleum products, crude oil, foodstuffs, construction materials, vehicles, clothing and other consumer goods
Imports - partners: France 62%, Venezuela 6%, Germany 4%, Italy 4%, US 3% (1997)
Debt - external: $180 million (1994)
Economic aid - recipient: $NA; note - substantial annual aid from France
Currency: French franc (FRF); euro (EUR)
Currency code: FRF; EUR
Exchange rates: euros per US dollar - 1.0659 (January 2001), 1.0854 (2000), 0.9386 (1999); French francs per US dollar - 5.8995 (1998), 5.8367 (1997), 5.1155 (1996)
Fiscal year: calendar year

Communications

Telephones - main lines in use: 170,000 (1997)
Telephones - mobile cellular: 15,000 (1997)
Telephone system:
general assessment: domestic facilities are adequate
domestic: NA
international: microwave radio relay to Guadeloupe, Dominica, and Saint Lucia; satellite earth stations - 2 Intelsat (Atlantic Ocean)
Radio broadcast stations: AM 0, FM 14, shortwave 0 (1998)
Radios: 82,000 (1997)
Television broadcast stations: 11 (plus nine repeaters) (1997)
Televisions: 66,000 (1997)
Internet country code: .mq
Internet Service Providers (ISPs): 2 (2000)
Internet users: 5,000 (2000)

Transportation

Railways: 0 km
Highways:
total: 2,724 km (1994)
paved: NA km
unpaved: NA km
Waterways: none
Ports and harbors: Fort-de-France, La Trinite
Merchant marine: none (2000 est.)
Airports: 2 (2000 est.)
Airports - with paved runways:
total: 1
over 3,047 m: 1 (2000 est.)
Airports - with unpaved runways:
total: 1
under 914 m: 1 (2000 est.)

Martinique (continued)

Military

Military branches: French forces (Army, Navy, Air Force), Gendarmerie
Military - note: defense is the responsibility of France

Transnational Issues

Disputes - international: none
Illicit drugs: transshipment point for cocaine and marijuana bound for the US and Europe

Mauritania

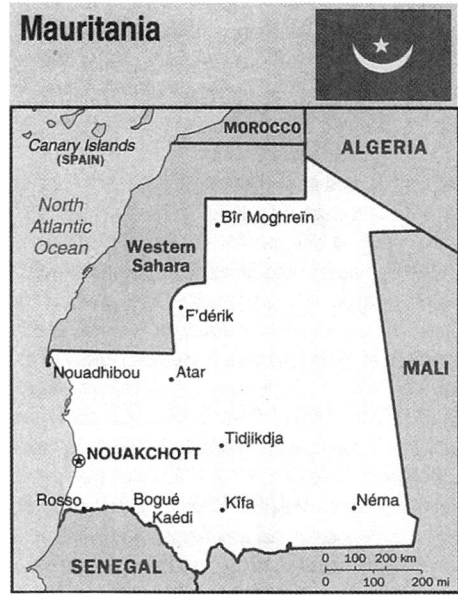

Introduction

Background: Independent from France in 1960, Mauritania annexed the southern third of the former Spanish Sahara (now Western Sahara) in 1976, but relinquished it after three years of raids by the Polisario guerrilla front seeking independence for the territory. Opposition parties were legalized and a new constitution approved in 1991. Two multiparty presidential elections since then were widely seen as being flawed; Mauritania remains, in reality, a one-party state. The country continues to experience ethnic tensions between its black minority population and the dominant Maur (Arab-Berber) populace.

Geography

Location: Northern Africa, bordering the North Atlantic Ocean, between Senegal and Western Sahara
Geographic coordinates: 20 00 N, 12 00 W
Map references: Africa
Area:
total: 1,030,700 sq km
land: 1,030,400 sq km
water: 300 sq km
Area - comparative: slightly larger than three times the size of New Mexico
Land boundaries:
total: 5,074 km
border countries: Algeria 463 km, Mali 2,237 km, Senegal 813 km, Western Sahara 1,561 km
Coastline: 754 km
Maritime claims:
contiguous zone: 24 NM
continental shelf: 200 NM or to the edge of the continental margin
exclusive economic zone: 200 NM
territorial sea: 12 NM
Climate: desert; constantly hot, dry, dusty
Terrain: mostly barren, flat plains of the Sahara; some central hills
Elevation extremes:
lowest point: Sebkha de Ndrhamcha -3 m
highest point: Kediet Ijill 910 m
Natural resources: iron ore, gypsum, fish, copper, phosphate, diamonds, gold
Land use:
arable land: 0%
permanent crops: 0%
permanent pastures: 38%
forests and woodland: 4%
other: 58% (1993 est.)
Irrigated land: 490 sq km (1993 est.)
Natural hazards: hot, dry, dust/sand-laden sirocco wind blows primarily in March and April; periodic droughts
Environment - current issues: overgrazing, deforestation, and soil erosion aggravated by drought are contributing to desertification; very limited natural fresh water resources away from the Senegal which is the only perennial river
Environment - international agreements:
party to: Biodiversity, Climate Change, Desertification, Endangered Species, Hazardous Wastes, Law of the Sea, Marine Dumping, Nuclear Test Ban, Ozone Layer Protection, Ship Pollution, Wetlands
signed, but not ratified: none of the selected agreements
Geography - note: most of the population concentrated in the cities of Nouakchott and Nouadhibou and along the Senegal River in the southern part of the country

People

Population: 2,747,312 (July 2001 est.)
Age structure:
0-14 years: 46.14% (male 634,940; female 632,654)
15-64 years: 51.59% (male 698,433; female 718,883)
65 years and over: 2.27% (male 25,840; female 36,562) (2001 est.)
Population growth rate: 2.93% (2001 est.)
Birth rate: 42.95 births/1,000 population (2001 est.)
Death rate: 13.65 deaths/1,000 population (2001 est.)
Net migration rate: 0 migrant(s)/1,000 population (2001 est.)
Sex ratio:
at birth: 1.03 male(s)/female
under 15 years: 1 male(s)/female
15-64 years: 0.97 male(s)/female
65 years and over: 0.71 male(s)/female
total population: 0.98 male(s)/female (2001 est.)
Infant mortality rate: 76.7 deaths/1,000 live births (2001 est.)
Life expectancy at birth:
total population: 51.14 years
male: 49.06 years
female: 53.29 years (2001 est.)
Total fertility rate: 6.22 children born/woman (2001 est.)
HIV/AIDS - adult prevalence rate: 1.8% (2000 est.)

Mauritania (continued)

HIV/AIDS - people living with HIV/AIDS: 6,600 (1999 est.)
HIV/AIDS - deaths: 610 (1999 est.)
Nationality:
noun: Mauritanian(s)
adjective: Mauritanian
Ethnic groups: mixed Maur/black 40%, Maur 30%, black 30%
Religions: Muslim 100%
Languages: Hasaniya Arabic (official), Pular, Soninke, Wolof (official), French
Literacy:
definition: age 15 and over can read and write
total population: 46.7%
male: 53.4%
female: 40% (1998 est.)

Government

Country name:
conventional long form: Islamic Republic of Mauritania
conventional short form: Mauritania
local long form: Al Jumhuriyah al Islamiyah al Muritaniyah
local short form: Muritaniyah
Government type: republic
Capital: Nouakchott
Administrative divisions: 12 regions (regions, singular - region) and 1 capital district*; Adrar, Assaba, Brakna, Dakhlet Nouadhibou, Gorgol, Guidimaka, Hodh Ech Chargui, Hodh El Gharbi, Inchiri, Nouakchott*, Tagant, Tiris Zemmour, Trarza
Independence: 28 November 1960 (from France)
National holiday: Independence Day, 28 November (1960)
Constitution: 12 July 1991
Legal system: a combination of Shari'a (Islamic law) and French civil law
Suffrage: 18 years of age; universal
Executive branch:
chief of state: President Col. Maaouya Ould Sid Ahmed TAYA (since 12 December 1984)
head of government: Prime Minister Cheik El Avia Ould Mohamed KHOUNA (since 17 November 1998)
cabinet: Council of Ministers
elections: president elected by popular vote for a six-year term; election last held 12 December 1997 (next to be held NA December 2003); prime minister appointed by the president
election results: President Col. Maaouya Ould Sid Ahmed TAYA reelected with 90.9% of the vote
Legislative branch: bicameral legislature consists of the Senate or Majlis al-Shuyukh (56 seats; 17 up for election every two years; members elected by municipal leaders to serve six-year terms) and the National Assembly or Majlis al-Watani (79 seats; members elected by popular vote to serve five-year terms)
elections: Senate - last held 17 April 1998 (next to be held NA 2001); National Assembly - last held 11 and 18 October 1996 (next to be held NA 2001)
election results: Senate - percent of vote by party - NA%; seats by party - NA; National Assembly - percent of vote by party - NA%; seats by party - PRDS 71, AC 1, independents and other 7
Judicial branch: Supreme Court or Cour Supreme; Court of Appeals; lower courts
Political parties and leaders: Action for Change or AC [Messoud Ould BOULKHEIR]; Assembly for Democracy and Unity or RDU [Ahmed Ould SIDI BABA]; Democratic and Social Republican Party or PRDS (ruling party) [President Col. Maaouya Ould Sid Ahmed TAYA]; Mauritanian Party for Renewal and Concorde or PMRC [Molaye El Hassen Ould JIYID]; National Union for Democracy and Development or UNDD [Tidjane KOITA]; Party for Liberty, Equality and Justice or PLEJ [Daouda M'BAGNIGA]; Popular Front or FP [Ch'bih Ould CHEIKH MALAININE]; Popular Progress Alliance or APP [Mohamed El Hafed Ould ISMAEL]; Popular Social and Democratic Union or UPSD [Mohamed Mahmoud Ould MAH]; Progress Force Union or UFP [Mohamed Ould MOLOUD]; Union for Progress and Democracy or UNDD [Naha Mint MOUKNASS]
note: parties legalized by constitution ratified 12 July 1991; however, politics continue to be tribally based
Political pressure groups and leaders: Arab nationalists; Ba'athists; General Confederation of Mauritanian Workers or CGTM [Abdallahi Ould MOHAMED, secretary general]; Independent Confederation of Mauritanian Workers or CLTM [Samory Ould BEYE]; Islamists; Mauritanian Workers Union or UTM [Mohamed Ely Ould BRAHIM, secretary general]
International organization participation: ABEDA, ACCT (associate), ACP, AfDB, AFESD, AL, AMF, AMU, CAEU, CCC, ECA, ECOWAS, FAO, G-77, IBRD, ICAO, ICFTU, ICRM, IDA, IDB, IFAD, IFC, IFRCS, IHO (pending member), ILO, IMF, IMO, Intelsat, Interpol, IOC, ITU, NAM, OAU, OIC, OPCW, UN, UNCTAD, UNESCO, UNIDO, UPU, WCL, WHO, WIPO, WMO, WToO, WTrO
Diplomatic representation in the US:
chief of mission: Ambassador Ahmed Ben Khalifa BEN JIDOU
chancery: 2129 Leroy Place NW, Washington, DC 20008
telephone: [1] (202) 232-5700
FAX: [1] (202) 319-2623
Diplomatic representation from the US:
chief of mission: Ambassador John W. LIMBERT
embassy: Rue Abdallaye, Nouakchott
mailing address: B. P. 222, Nouakchott
telephone: [222] 25-26-60, 25-26-63
FAX: [222] 25-15-92
Flag description: green with a yellow five-pointed star above a yellow, horizontal crescent; the closed side of the crescent is down; the crescent, star, and color green are traditional symbols of Islam

Economy

Economy - overview: A majority of the population still depends on agriculture and livestock for a livelihood, even though most of the nomads and many subsistence farmers were forced into the cities by recurrent droughts in the 1970s and 1980s. Mauritania has extensive deposits of iron ore, which account for half of total exports. The decline in world demand for this ore, however, has led to cutbacks in production. The nation's coastal waters are among the richest fishing areas in the world, but overexploitation by foreigners threatens this key source of revenue. The country's first deepwater port opened near Nouakchott in 1986. In the past, drought and economic mismanagement have resulted in a buildup of foreign debt. In March 1999, the government signed an agreement with a joint World Bank-IMF mission on a $54 million enhanced structural adjustment facility (ESAF). Mauritania withdrew its membership in the Economic Community of West African States (ECOWAS) in 2000. Privatization and debt relief are in full swing, and the rate of economic growth appears to be accelerating, especially in the construction, telecommunication, and information sectors. Diamonds and petroleum are beginning to be explored and exploited.
GDP: purchasing power parity - $5.4 billion (2000 est.)
GDP - real growth rate: 5% (2000 est.)
GDP - per capita: purchasing power parity - $2,000 (2000 est.)
GDP - composition by sector:
agriculture: 25%
industry: 31%
services: 44% (1997)
Population below poverty line: 50% (1996 est.)
Household income or consumption by percentage share:
lowest 10%: 2.3%
highest 10%: 29.9% (1995)
Inflation rate (consumer prices): 4.5% (2000 est.)
Labor force: 750,000 (1999)
Labor force - by occupation: agriculture 47%, services 39%, industry 14%
Unemployment rate: 23% (1995 est.)
Budget:
revenues: $329 million
expenditures: $265 million, including capital expenditures of $75 million (1996 est.)
Industries: fish processing, mining of iron ore and gypsum
Industrial production growth rate: 2.2% (1999)
Electricity - production: 151 million kWh (1999)
Electricity - production by source:
fossil fuel: 82.78%
hydro: 17.22%
nuclear: 0%
other: 0% (1999)
Electricity - consumption: 140.4 million kWh (1999)
Electricity - exports: 0 kWh (1999)

Mauritania (continued)

Electricity - imports: 0 kWh (1999)
Agriculture - products: dates, millet, sorghum, rice, corn, dates; cattle, sheep
Exports: $333 million (f.o.b., 1999)
Exports - commodities: iron ore, fish and fish products, gold
Exports - partners: Japan 18%, France 17%, Italy 16%, Spain 11% (1998)
Imports: $305 million (f.o.b., 1999)
Imports - commodities: machinery and equipment, petroleum products, capital goods, foodstuffs, consumer goods
Imports - partners: France 27%, Benelux 9%, Germany 7%, Spain 7% (1998)
Debt - external: $2.1 billion (1999)
Economic aid - recipient: $300 million (1998)
Currency: ouguiya (MRO)
Currency code: MRO
Exchange rates: ouguiyas per US dollar - 250.870 (December 2000), 238.923 (2000), 209.514 (1999), 188.476 (1998), 151.853 (1997), 137.222 (1996)
Fiscal year: calendar year

Communications

Telephones - main lines in use: 26,000 (2000)
Telephones - mobile cellular: NA
Telephone system:
general assessment: limited system of cable and open-wire lines, minor microwave radio relay links, and radiotelephone communications stations (improvements being made)
domestic: mostly cable and open-wire lines; a recently completed domestic satellite telecommunications system links Nouakchott with regional capitals
international: satellite earth stations - 1 Intelsat (Atlantic Ocean) and 2 Arabsat
Radio broadcast stations: AM 1, FM 2, shortwave 1 (1998)
Radios: 360,000 (1997)
Television broadcast stations: 1 (1997)
Televisions: 87,000 (1998)
Internet country code: .mr
Internet Service Providers (ISPs): 5 (2000)
Internet users: 3,500 (2000)

Transportation

Railways:
total: 750 km (single track); note - owned and operated by government mining company
standard gauge: 750 km 1.435-m gauge (1995)
Highways:
total: 7,660 km
paved: 866 km
unpaved: 6,794 km (1996)
Waterways:
note: ferry traffic on the Senegal River
Ports and harbors: Bogue, Kaedi, Nouadhibou, Nouakchott, Rosso
Merchant marine: none (2000 est.)
Airports: 26 (2000 est.)

Airports - with paved runways:
total: 8
2,438 to 3,047 m: 3
1,524 to 2,437 m: 5 (2000 est.)
Airports - with unpaved runways:
total: 18
2,438 to 3,047 m: 2
1,524 to 2,437 m: 4
914 to 1,523 m: 9
under 914 m: 3 (2000 est.)

Military

Military branches: Army, Navy, Air Force, National Gendarmerie, National Guard, National Police, Presidential Guard
Military manpower - availability:
males age 15-49: 624,375 (2001 est.)
Military manpower - fit for military service:
males age 15-49: 302,699 (2001 est.)
Military expenditures - dollar figure: $41 million (FY97/98)
Military expenditures - percent of GDP: 2.7% (FY97/98)

Transnational Issues

Disputes - international: none

Mauritius

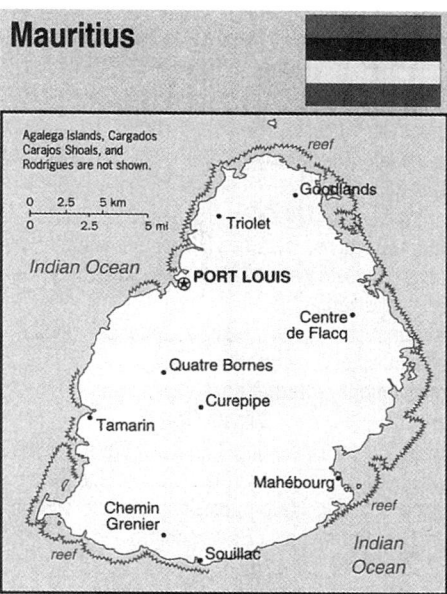

Introduction

Background: Discovered by the Portuguese in 1505, Mauritius was subsequently held by the Dutch, French, and British before independence was attained in 1968. A stable democracy with regular free elections and a positive human rights record, the country has attracted considerable foreign investment and has earned one of Africa's highest per capita incomes. Recent poor weather and declining sugar prices have slowed economic growth leading to some protests over standards of living in the Creole community.

Geography

Location: Southern Africa, island in the Indian Ocean, east of Madagascar
Geographic coordinates: 20 17 S, 57 33 E
Map references: World
Area:
total: 1,860 sq km
land: 1,850 sq km
water: 10 sq km
note: includes Agalega Islands, Cargados Carajos Shoals (Saint Brandon), and Rodrigues
Area - comparative: almost 11 times the size of Washington, DC
Land boundaries: 0 km
Coastline: 177 km
Maritime claims:
continental shelf: 200 NM or to the edge of the continental margin
exclusive economic zone: 200 NM
territorial sea: 12 NM
Climate: tropical, modified by southeast trade winds; warm, dry winter (May to November); hot, wet, humid summer (November to May)
Terrain: small coastal plain rising to discontinuous mountains encircling central plateau
Elevation extremes:
lowest point: Indian Ocean 0 m
highest point: Mont Piton 828 m

Mauritius (continued)

Natural resources: arable land, fish
Land use:
arable land: 49%
permanent crops: 3%
permanent pastures: 3%
forests and woodland: 22%
other: 23% (1993 est.)
Irrigated land: 170 sq km (1993 est.)
Natural hazards: cyclones (November to April); almost completely surrounded by reefs that may pose maritime hazards
Environment - current issues: water pollution, degradation of coral reefs
Environment - international agreements:
party to: Biodiversity, Climate Change, Desertification, Endangered Species, Environmental Modification, Hazardous Wastes, Law of the Sea, Marine Dumping, Marine Life Conservation, Nuclear Test Ban, Ozone Layer Protection, Ship Pollution
signed, but not ratified: none of the selected agreements

People

Population: 1,189,825 (July 2001 est.)
Age structure:
0-14 years: 25.53% (male 153,691; female 150,094)
15-64 years: 68.24% (male 404,940; female 407,056)
65 years and over: 6.23% (male 29,588; female 44,456) (2001 est.)
Population growth rate: 0.88% (2001 est.)
Birth rate: 16.5 births/1,000 population (2001 est.)
Death rate: 6.82 deaths/1,000 population (2001 est.)
Net migration rate: -0.92 migrant(s)/1,000 population (2001 est.)
Sex ratio:
at birth: 1.02 male(s)/female
under 15 years: 1.02 male(s)/female
15-64 years: 0.99 male(s)/female
65 years and over: 0.67 male(s)/female
total population: 0.98 male(s)/female (2001 est.)
Infant mortality rate: 17.19 deaths/1,000 live births (2001 est.)
Life expectancy at birth:
total population: 71.25 years
male: 67.26 years
female: 75.31 years (2001 est.)
Total fertility rate: 2.01 children born/woman (2001 est.)
HIV/AIDS - adult prevalence rate: 0.08% (1999 est.)
HIV/AIDS - people living with HIV/AIDS: NA
HIV/AIDS - deaths: NA
Nationality:
noun: Mauritian(s)
adjective: Mauritian
Ethnic groups: Indo-Mauritian 68%, Creole 27%, Sino-Mauritian 3%, Franco-Mauritian 2%
Religions: Hindu 52%, Christian 28.3% (Roman Catholic 26%, Protestant 2.3%), Muslim 16.6%, other 3.1%
Languages: English (official), Creole, French, Hindi, Urdu, Hakka, Bojpoori
Literacy:
definition: age 15 and over can read and write
total population: 82.9%
male: 87.1%
female: 78.8% (1995 est.)

Government

Country name:
conventional long form: Republic of Mauritius
conventional short form: Mauritius
Government type: parliamentary democracy
Capital: Port Louis
Administrative divisions: 9 districts and 3 dependencies*; Agalega Islands*, Black River, Cargados Carajos Shoals*, Flacq, Grand Port, Moka, Pamplemousses, Plaines Wilhems, Port Louis, Riviere du Rempart, Rodrigues*, Savanne
Independence: 12 March 1968 (from UK)
National holiday: Independence Day, 12 March (1968)
Constitution: 12 March 1968; amended 12 March 1992
Legal system: based on French civil law system with elements of English common law in certain areas
Suffrage: 18 years of age; universal
Executive branch:
chief of state: President Cassam UTEEM (since 1 July 1992) and Vice President Angidi Verriah CHETTIAR (since 28 June 1997)
head of government: Prime Minister Sir Anerood JUGNAUTH (since 17 September 2000) and Deputy Prime Minister Paul BERENGER (since 17 September 2000)
cabinet: Council of Ministers appointed by the president on the recommendation of the prime minister
elections: president and vice president elected by the National Assembly for five-year terms; election last held 28 June 1997 (next to be held NA 2002); prime minister and deputy prime minister appointed by the president and are responsible to the National Assembly
election results: Cassam UTEEM reelected president and Angidi Verriah CHETTIAR elected vice president; percent of vote by the National Assembly - NA%
Legislative branch: unicameral National Assembly (66 seats - 62 elected by popular vote, 4 appointed by the election commission from the losing political parties to give representation to various ethnic minorities; members serve five-year terms)
elections: last held on 11 September 2000 (next to be held by September 2005)
election results: percent of vote by party - MSM/MMM 52.3%, MLP/PSMD 36.9%, OPR 10.8%; seats by party - MSM/MMM 54, MLP/PSMD 6, OPR 2
Judicial branch: Supreme Court
Political parties and leaders: Hizbullah [Cehl Mohamed FAKEEMEEAH]; Mauritian Labor Party or MLP [Navinchandra RAMGOOLAM]; Mauritian Militant Movement or MMM [Paul BERENGER] - in coalition with MSM; Mauritian Militant Renaissance or MMR [Dr. Paramhansa NABABSING]; Mauritian Social Democrat Party or PMSD [Charles Xavier-Luc DUVAL]; Militant Socialist Movement or MSM [Sir Anerood JUGNAUTH] - governing party; Rodrigues Movement or OPR [Joseph (Nicholas) Von MALLY]
Political pressure groups and leaders: various labor unions
International organization participation: ACCT, ACP, AfDB, C, CCC, ECA, FAO, G-77, IAEA, IBRD, ICAO, ICFTU, ICRM, IDA, IFAD, IFC, IFRCS, ILO, IMF, IMO, Inmarsat, InOC, Intelsat, Interpol, IOC, ISO, ITU, NAM, OAU, OPCW, SADC, UN, UN Security Council (temporary), UNCTAD, UNESCO, UNIDO, UPU, WCL, WFTU, WHO, WIPO, WMO, WToO, WTrO
Diplomatic representation in the US:
chief of mission: Ambassador Usha JEETAH
chancery: Suite 441, 4301 Connecticut Avenue NW, Washington, DC 20008
telephone: [1] (202) 244-1491, 1492
FAX: [1] (202) 966-0983
Diplomatic representation from the US:
chief of mission: Ambassador Mark W. ERWIN
embassy: 4th Floor, Rogers House, John Kennedy Street, Port Louis
mailing address: international mail: P. O. Box 544, Port Louis; US mail: American Embassy, Port Louis, Department of State, Washington, DC 20521-2450
telephone: [230] 208-2347, 208-2354, 208-9763 through 9767
FAX: [230] 208-9534
Flag description: four equal horizontal bands of red (top), blue, yellow, and green

Economy

Economy - overview: Since independence in 1968, Mauritius has developed from a low-income, agriculturally based economy to a middle-income diversified economy with growing industrial, financial, and tourist sectors. For most of the period, annual growth has been in the order of 5% to 6%. This remarkable achievement has been reflected in increased life expectancy, lowered infant mortality, and a much-improved infrastructure. Sugarcane is grown on about 90% of the cultivated land area and accounts for 25% of export earnings. The government's development strategy centers on foreign investment. Mauritius has attracted more than 9,000 offshore entities, many aimed at commerce in India and South Africa, and investment in the banking sector alone has reached over $1 billion. Economic performance since 1991 has continued strong with solid growth and low unemployment.
GDP: purchasing power parity - $12.3 billion (2000 est.)
GDP - real growth rate: 7.5% (2000 est.)
GDP - per capita: purchasing power parity - $10,400 (2000 est.)
GDP - composition by sector:
agriculture: 10%
industry: 29%
services: 61% (1996)

Mauritius (continued)

Population below poverty line: 10.6% (1992 est.)
Household income or consumption by percentage share:
lowest 10%: NA%
highest 10%: NA%
Inflation rate (consumer prices): 5.3% (2000 est.)
Labor force: 514,000 (1995)
Labor force - by occupation: construction and industry 36%, services 24%, agriculture and fishing 14%, trade, restaurants, hotels 16%, transportation and communication 7%, finance 3% (1995)
Unemployment rate: 6.4% (1999 est.)
Budget:
revenues: $1.1 billion
expenditures: $1.2 billion, including capital expenditures of $NA (1999 est.)
Industries: food processing (largely sugar milling), textiles, clothing; chemicals, metal products, transport equipment, nonelectrical machinery; tourism
Industrial production growth rate: 8% (2000 est.)
Electricity - production: 1.26 billion kWh (1999)
Electricity - production by source:
fossil fuel: 91.27%
hydro: 8.73%
nuclear: 0%
other: 0% (1999)
Electricity - consumption: 1.172 billion kWh (1999)
Electricity - exports: 0 kWh (1999)
Electricity - imports: 0 kWh (1999)
Agriculture - products: sugarcane, tea, corn, potatoes, bananas, pulses; cattle, goats; fish
Exports: $1.6 billion (f.o.b., 1999)
Exports - commodities: clothing and textiles, sugar, cut flowers, molasses
Exports - partners: UK 32%, France 19%, US 15%, Germany 6%, Italy 4% (1999 est.)
Imports: $2.3 billion (f.o.b., 1999)
Imports - commodities: manufactured goods, capital equipment, foodstuffs, petroleum products, chemicals (1996)
Imports - partners: France 14%, South Africa 11%, India 8%, UK 5% (1999 est.)
Debt - external: $1.9 billion (1998 est.)
Economic aid - recipient: $42 million (1997)
Currency: Mauritian rupee (MUR)
Currency code: MUR
Exchange rates: Mauritian rupees per US dollar - 27.900 (January 2001), 26.250 (2000), 25.186 (1999), 22.993 (1998), 21.057 (1997), 17.948 (1996)
Fiscal year: 1 July - 30 June

Communications

Telephones - main lines in use: 223,000 (1997)
Telephones - mobile cellular: 37,000 (1997)
Telephone system:
general assessment: small system with good service
domestic: primarily microwave radio relay
international: satellite earth station - 1 Intelsat (Indian Ocean); new microwave link to Reunion; HF radiotelephone links to several countries
Radio broadcast stations: AM 5, FM 9, shortwave 2 (1998)
Radios: 420,000 (1997)
Television broadcast stations: 2 (plus 11 repeaters) (1997)
Televisions: 258,000 (1997)
Internet country code: .mu
Internet Service Providers (ISPs): 2 (2000)
Internet users: 55,000 (2000)

Transportation

Railways: 0 km
Highways:
total: 1,910 km
paved: 1,834 km (including 36 km of expressways)
unpaved: 76 km (1998)
Waterways: none
Ports and harbors: Port Louis
Merchant marine:
total: 9 ships (1,000 GRT or over) totaling 61,909 GRT/87,313 DWT
ships by type: cargo 2, combination bulk 2, container 2, liquefied gas 1, refrigerated cargo 2
note: includes a foreign-owned ship registered here as a flag of convenience: India 1 (2000 est.)
Airports: 5 (2000 est.)
Airports - with paved runways:
total: 2
over 3,047 m: 1
914 to 1,523 m: 1 (2000 est.)
Airports - with unpaved runways:
total: 3
914 to 1,523 m: 1
under 914 m: 2 (2000 est.)

Military

Military branches: National Police Force (includes the paramilitary Special Mobile Force or SMF and National Coast Guard)
Military manpower - availability:
males age 15-49: 339,473 (2001 est.)
Military manpower - fit for military service:
males age 15-49: 171,206 (2001 est.)
Military expenditures - dollar figure: $11 million (FY97/98)
Military expenditures - percent of GDP: 0.3% (FY97/98)

Transnational Issues

Disputes - international: claims the Chagos Archipelago (UK-administered British Indian Ocean Territory); claims French-administered Tromelin Island
Illicit drugs: minor consumer and transshipment point for heroin from South Asia; small amounts of cannabis produced and consumed locally

Mayotte
(territorial collectivity of France)

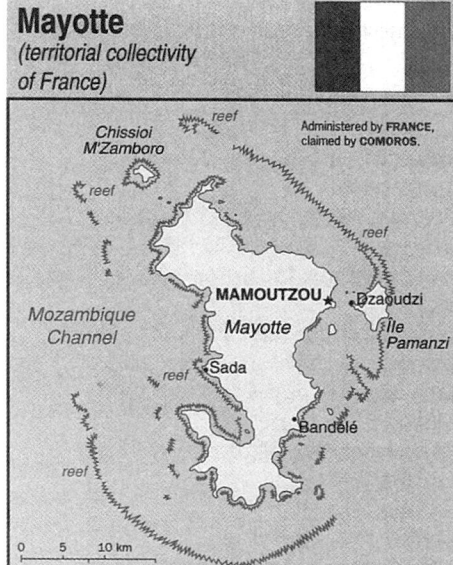

Introduction

Background: Mayotte was ceded to France along with the other Comoros in 1843. It was the only island in the archipelago that voted in 1974 to retain its link with France and forgo independence.

Geography

Location: Southern Africa, island in the Mozambique Channel, about one-half of the way from northern Madagascar to northern Mozambique
Geographic coordinates: 12 50 S, 45 10 E
Map references: Africa
Area:
total: 374 sq km
land: 374 sq km
water: 0 sq km
Area - comparative: slightly more than twice the size of Washington, DC
Land boundaries: 0 km
Coastline: 185.2 km
Maritime claims:
exclusive economic zone: 200 NM
territorial sea: 12 NM
Climate: tropical; marine; hot, humid, rainy season during northeastern monsoon (November to May); dry season is cooler (May to November)
Terrain: generally undulating, with deep ravines and ancient volcanic peaks
Elevation extremes:
lowest point: Indian Ocean 0 m
highest point: Benara 660 m
Natural resources: NEGL
Land use:
arable land: NA%
permanent crops: NA%
permanent pastures: NA%
forests and woodland: NA%
other: NA%
Irrigated land: NA sq km
Natural hazards: cyclones during rainy season

Mayotte (continued)

Environment - current issues: NA
Geography - note: part of Comoro Archipelago; 18 islands

People

Population: 163,366 (July 2001 est.)
Age structure:
0-14 years: 46.59% (male 38,188; female 37,920)
15-64 years: 51.73% (male 46,132; female 38,378)
65 years and over: 1.68% (male 1,361; female 1,387) (2001 est.)
Population growth rate: 4.58% (2001 est.)
Birth rate: 44.39 births/1,000 population (2001 est.)
Death rate: 8.84 deaths/1,000 population (2001 est.)
Net migration rate: 10.28 migrant(s)/1,000 population (2001 est.)
Sex ratio:
at birth: 1.03 male(s)/female
under 15 years: 1.01 male(s)/female
15-64 years: 1.2 male(s)/female
65 years and over: 0.98 male(s)/female
total population: 1.1 male(s)/female (2001 est.)
Infant mortality rate: 69.54 deaths/1,000 live births (2001 est.)
Life expectancy at birth:
total population: 59.83 years
male: 57.77 years
female: 61.96 years (2001 est.)
Total fertility rate: 6.24 children born/woman (2001 est.)
HIV/AIDS - adult prevalence rate: NA%
HIV/AIDS - people living with HIV/AIDS: NA
HIV/AIDS - deaths: NA
Nationality:
noun: Mahorais (singular and plural)
adjective: Mahoran
Ethnic groups: NA
Religions: Muslim 97%, Christian (mostly Roman Catholic)
Languages: Mahorian (a Swahili dialect), French (official language) spoken by 35% of the population
Literacy:
definition: NA
total population: NA%
male: NA%
female: NA%

Government

Country name:
conventional long form: Territorial Collectivity of Mayotte
conventional short form: Mayotte
Dependency status: territorial collectivity of France
Government type: NA
Capital: Mamoutzou
Administrative divisions: none (territorial collectivity of France)
Independence: none (territorial collectivity of France)
National holiday: Bastille Day, 14 July (1789)
Constitution: 28 September 1958 (French Constitution)
Legal system: French law
Suffrage: 18 years of age; universal
Executive branch:
chief of state: President Jacques CHIRAC of France (since 17 May 1995), represented by Prefect Pierre BAYLE (since 15 July 1998)
head of government: President of the General Council Younoussa BAMANA (since NA 1977)
cabinet: NA
elections: French president elected by popular vote for a seven-year term; prefect appointed by the French president on the advice of the French Ministry of the Interior; president of the General Council elected by the members of the General Council for a six-year term
Legislative branch: unicameral General Council or Conseil General (19 seats; members are elected by popular vote to serve three-year terms)
elections: last held 7 October 2000 (next to be held NA 2003)
election results: percent of vote by party - NA%; seats by party - NA
note: Mayotte elects one member of the French Senate; elections last held 24 September 1995 (next to be held 24 September 2001); results - percent of vote by party - NA%; seats by party - MPM 1; Mayotte also elects one member to the French National Assembly; elections last held 25 May and 1 June 1997 (next to be held as a special election on NA May 2002); results - percent of vote by party - UDF/FD 51.7%, RPR 48.3%; seats by party - UDF/FD 1
Judicial branch: Supreme Court or Tribunal Superieur d'Appel
Political parties and leaders: Democratic Front or FD [Youssouf MOUSSA]; Mahoran Popular Movement or MPM [Younoussa BAMANA]; Mahoran Rally for the Republic or RPR [Mansour KAMARDINE]; Movement for Department Status Mayotte or MDM [Henri JEAN-BAPTISTE]; Socialist Party or PS (local branch of French Parti Socialiste) [Ibrahim ABUBACAR]; Union for French Democracy or UDF [Henri JEAN-BAPTISTE]
Political pressure groups and leaders: NA
International organization participation: FZ
Diplomatic representation in the US: none (territorial collectivity of France)
Diplomatic representation from the US: none (territorial collectivity of France)
Flag description: the flag of France is used

Economy

Economy - overview: Economic activity is based primarily on the agricultural sector, including fishing and livestock raising. Mayotte is not self-sufficient and must import a large portion of its food requirements, mainly from France. The economy and future development of the island are heavily dependent on French financial assistance, an important supplement to GDP. Mayotte's remote location is an obstacle to the development of tourism.
GDP: purchasing power parity - $85 million (1998 est.)
GDP - real growth rate: NA%
GDP - per capita: purchasing power parity - $600 (1998 est.)
GDP - composition by sector:
agriculture: NA%
industry: NA%
services: NA%
Population below poverty line: NA%
Household income or consumption by percentage share:
lowest 10%: NA%
highest 10%: NA%
Inflation rate (consumer prices): NA%
Labor force: NA
Unemployment rate: 45% (1997)
Budget:
revenues: $NA
expenditures: $73 million, including capital expenditures of $NA (1991 est.)
Industries: newly created lobster and shrimp industry, construction
Industrial production growth rate: NA%
Electricity - production: NA kWh
Electricity - production by source:
fossil fuel: NA%
hydro: NA%
nuclear: NA%
other: NA%
Electricity - consumption: NA kWh
Agriculture - products: vanilla, ylang-ylang (perfume essence), coffee, copra
Exports: $3.44 million (f.o.b., 1997)
Exports - commodities: ylang-ylang (perfume essence), vanilla, copra, coconuts, coffee, cinnamon
Exports - partners: France 80%, Comoros 15%, Reunion
Imports: $141.3 million (f.o.b., 1997)
Imports - commodities: food, machinery and equipment, transportation equipment, metals, chemicals
Imports - partners: France 66%, Africa 14%, Southeast Asia 11% (1997)
Debt - external: $NA
Economic aid - recipient: $107.7 million (1995); note - extensive French financial assistance
Currency: French franc (FRF); euro (EUR)
Currency code: FRF; EUR
Exchange rates: euros per US dollar - 1.0659 (January 2001), 1.0854 (2000), 0.9386 (1999); French francs per US dollar - 5.8995 (1998), 5.8367 (1997), 5.1155 (1996)
Fiscal year: calendar year

Communications

Telephones - main lines in use: 9,314 (1997)
Telephones - mobile cellular: 0 (2000)
Telephone system:
general assessment: small system administered by French Department of Posts and Telecommunications
domestic: NA

Mayotte (continued)

international: microwave radio relay and HF radiotelephone communications to Comoros and other international connections
Radio broadcast stations: AM 1, FM 4, shortwave 0 (1998)
Radios: NA
Television broadcast stations: 3 (1997)
Televisions: 3,500 (1994)
Internet country code: .yt
Internet Service Providers (ISPs): NA
Internet users: NA

Transportation

Railways: 0 km
Highways:
total: 93 km
paved: 72 km
unpaved: 21 km
Waterways: none
Ports and harbors: Dzaoudzi
Merchant marine: none (2000 est.)
Airports: 1 (2000 est.)
Airports - with paved runways:
total: 1
1,524 to 2,437 m: 1 (2000 est.)

Military

Military - note: defense is the responsibility of France; small contingent of French forces stationed on the island

Transnational Issues

Disputes - international: claimed by Comoros

Mexico

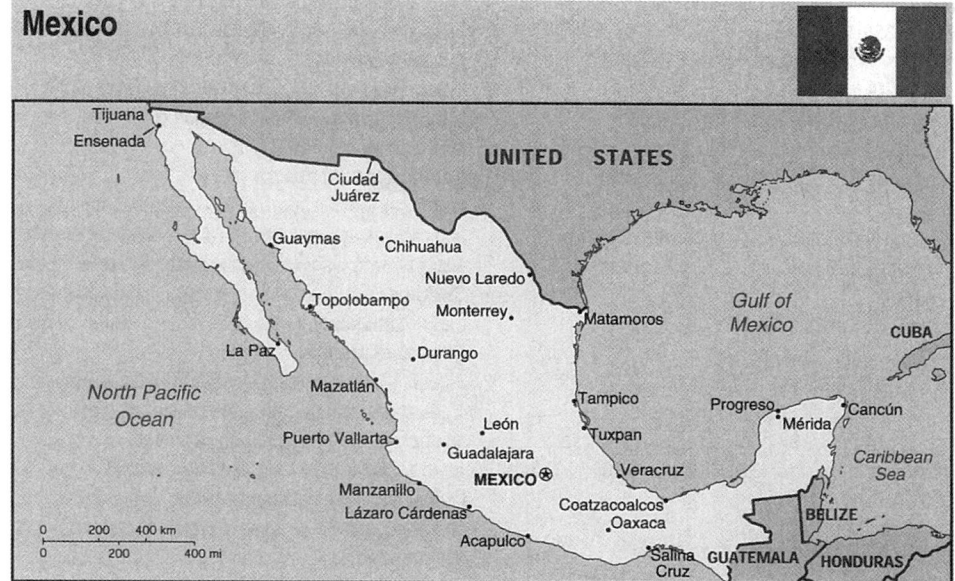

Introduction

Background: The site of advanced Amerindian civilizations, Mexico came under Spanish rule for three centuries before achieving independence early in the 19th century. A devaluation of the peso in late 1994 threw Mexico into economic turmoil, triggering the worst recession in over half a century. The nation continues to make an impressive recovery. Ongoing economic and social concerns include low real wages, underemployment for a large segment of the population, inequitable income distribution, and few advancement opportunities for the largely Amerindian population in the impoverished southern states.

Geography

Location: Middle America, bordering the Caribbean Sea and the Gulf of Mexico, between Belize and the US and bordering the North Pacific Ocean, between Guatemala and the US
Geographic coordinates: 23 00 N, 102 00 W
Map references: North America
Area:
total: 1,972,550 sq km
land: 1,923,040 sq km
water: 49,510 sq km
Area - comparative: slightly less than three times the size of Texas
Land boundaries:
total: 4,538 km
border countries: Belize 250 km, Guatemala 962 km, US 3,326 km
Coastline: 9,330 km
Maritime claims:
contiguous zone: 24 NM
continental shelf: 200 NM or to the edge of the continental margin
exclusive economic zone: 200 NM
territorial sea: 12 NM
Climate: varies from tropical to desert
Terrain: high, rugged mountains; low coastal plains; high plateaus; desert
Elevation extremes:
lowest point: Laguna Salada -10 m
highest point: Volcan Pico de Orizaba 5,700 m
Natural resources: petroleum, silver, copper, gold, lead, zinc, natural gas, timber
Land use:
arable land: 12%
permanent crops: 1%
permanent pastures: 39%
forests and woodland: 26%
other: 22% (1993 est.)
Irrigated land: 61,000 sq km (1993 est.)
Natural hazards: tsunamis along the Pacific coast, volcanoes and destructive earthquakes in the center and south, and hurricanes on the Gulf of Mexico and Caribbean coasts
Environment - current issues: natural fresh water resources scarce and polluted in north, inaccessible and poor quality in center and extreme southeast; raw sewage and industrial effluents polluting rivers in urban areas; deforestation; widespread erosion; desertification; serious air pollution in the national capital and urban centers along US-Mexico border
Environment - international agreements:
party to: Biodiversity, Climate Change, Climate Change-Kyoto Protocol, Desertification, Endangered Species, Hazardous Wastes, Law of the Sea, Marine Dumping, Marine Life Conservation, Nuclear Test Ban, Ozone Layer Protection, Ship Pollution, Wetlands, Whaling
signed, but not ratified: none of the selected agreements
Geography - note: strategic location on southern border of US

People

Population: 101,879,171 (July 2001 est.)
Age structure:
0-14 years: 33.32% (male 17,312,220; female 16,635,438)

Mexico (continued)

15-64 years: 62.28% (male 30,888,015; female 32,558,359)
65 years and over: 4.4% (male 1,997,219; female 2,487,920) (2001 est.)
Population growth rate: 1.5% (2001 est.)
Birth rate: 22.77 births/1,000 population (2001 est.)
Death rate: 5.02 deaths/1,000 population (2001 est.)
Net migration rate: -2.77 migrant(s)/1,000 population (2001 est.)
Sex ratio:
at birth: 1.05 male(s)/female
under 15 years: 1.04 male(s)/female
15-64 years: 0.95 male(s)/female
65 years and over: 0.8 male(s)/female
total population: 0.97 male(s)/female (2001 est.)
Infant mortality rate: 25.36 deaths/1,000 live births (2001 est.)
Life expectancy at birth:
total population: 71.76 years
male: 68.73 years
female: 74.93 years (2001 est.)
Total fertility rate: 2.62 children born/woman (2001 est.)
HIV/AIDS - adult prevalence rate: 0.29% (1999 est.)
HIV/AIDS - people living with HIV/AIDS: 150,000 (1999 est.)
HIV/AIDS - deaths: 4,700 (1999 est.)
Nationality:
noun: Mexican(s)
adjective: Mexican
Ethnic groups: mestizo (Amerindian-Spanish) 60%, Amerindian or predominantly Amerindian 30%, white 9%, other 1%
Religions: nominally Roman Catholic 89%, Protestant 6%, other 5%
Languages: Spanish, various Mayan, Nahuatl, and other regional indigenous languages
Literacy:
definition: age 15 and over can read and write
total population: 89.6%
male: 91.8%
female: 87.4% (1995 est.)

Government

Country name:
conventional long form: United Mexican States
conventional short form: Mexico
local long form: Estados Unidos Mexicanos
local short form: Mexico
Government type: federal republic
Capital: Mexico
Administrative divisions: 31 states (estados, singular - estado) and 1 federal district* (distrito federal); Aguascalientes, Baja California, Baja California Sur, Campeche, Chiapas, Chihuahua, Coahuila de Zaragoza, Colima, Distrito Federal*, Durango, Guanajuato, Guerrero, Hidalgo, Jalisco, Mexico, Michoacan de Ocampo, Morelos, Nayarit, Nuevo Leon, Oaxaca, Puebla, Queretaro de Arteaga, Quintana Roo, San Luis Potosi, Sinaloa, Sonora, Tabasco, Tamaulipas, Tlaxcala, Veracruz-Llave, Yucatan, Zacatecas
Independence: 16 September 1810 (from Spain)
National holiday: Independence Day, 16 September (1810)
Constitution: 5 February 1917
Legal system: mixture of US constitutional theory and civil law system; judicial review of legislative acts; accepts compulsory ICJ jurisdiction, with reservations
Suffrage: 18 years of age; universal and compulsory (but not enforced)
Executive branch:
chief of state: President Vicente FOX Quesada (since 1 December 2000); note - the president is both the chief of state and head of government
head of government: President Vicente FOX Quesada (since 1 December 2000); note - the president is both the chief of state and head of government
cabinet: Cabinet appointed by the president; note - appointment of attorney general requires consent of the Senate
elections: president elected by popular vote for a six-year term; election last held 2 July 2000 (next to be held NA July 2006)
election results: Vicente FOX Quesada elected president; percent of vote - Vicente FOX Quesada (PAN) 42.52%, Francisco LABASTIDA Ochoa (PRI) 36.1%, Cuauhtemoc CARDENAS Solorzano (PRD) 16.64%, other 4.74%
Legislative branch: bicameral National Congress or Congreso de la Union consists of the Senate or Camara de Senadores (128 seats; 96 are elected by popular vote to serve six-year terms, and 32 are allocated on the basis of each party's popular vote) and the Federal Chamber of Deputies or Camara Federal de Diputados (500 seats; 300 members are directly elected by popular vote to serve three-year terms; remaining 200 members are allocated on the basis of each party's popular vote, also for three-year terms)
elections: Senate - last held 2 July 2000 for all of the seats (next to be held NA 2006); Chamber of Deputies - last held 2 July 2000 (next to be held NA 2003)
election results: Senate - percent of vote by party - NA%; seats by party - PRI 59, PAN 45, PRD 17, PVEM 5, PT 1, PCD 1; Chamber of Deputies - percent of vote by party - NA%; seats by party - PRI 211, PAN 208, PRD 50, PVEM 16, PT 7, PCD 3, PSN 3, PAS 2
Judicial branch: Supreme Court of Justice or Corte Suprema de Justicia (judges are appointed by the president with consent of the Senate)
Political parties and leaders: Convergence for Democracy or CD [Dante DELGADO Ranauro]; Institutional Revolutionary Party or PRI [Dulce Maria SAURI Riancho]; Mexican Green Ecological Party or PVEM [Jorge GONZALEZ Torres]; National Action Party or PAN [Luis Felipe BRAVO Mena]; Party of the Democratic Center or PCD [Manuel CAMACHO Solis]; Party of the Democratic Revolution or PRD [Amalia GARCIA Medina]; Party of the Nationalist Society or PSN [Gustavo RIOJAIS Santana]; Social Alliance Party or PAS [Jose Antonio CALDERON Cardoso]; Workers Party or PT [Alberto ANAYA Gutierrez]
Political pressure groups and leaders: Confederation of Employers of the Mexican Republic or COPARMEX; Confederation of Industrial Chambers or CONCAMIN; Confederation of Mexican Workers or CTM; Confederation of National Chambers of Commerce or CONCANACO; Coordinator for Foreign Trade Business Organizations or COECE; Federation of Unions Providing Goods and Services or FESEBES; National Chamber of Transformation Industries or CANACINTRA; National Peasant Confederation or CNC; National Union of Workers or UNT; Regional Confederation of Mexican Workers or CROM; Revolutionary Confederation of Workers and Peasants or CROC; Roman Catholic Church
International organization participation: APEC, BCIE, BIS, Caricom (observer), CCC, CDB, CE (observer), EBRD, ECLAC, FAO, G-3, G-6, G-11, G-15, G-19, G-24, IADB, IAEA, IBRD, ICAO, ICC, ICFTU, ICRM, IDA, IEA (observer), IFAD, IFC, IFRCS, ILO, IMF, IMO, Inmarsat, Intelsat, Interpol, IOC, IOM (observer), ISO, ITU, LAES, LAIA, NAM (observer), NEA, OAS, OECD, OPANAL, OPCW, PCA, RG, UN, UNCTAD, UNESCO, UNIDO, UNITAR, UNU, UPU, WCL, WFTU, WHO, WIPO, WMO, WToO, WTrO
Diplomatic representation in the US:
chief of mission: Ambassador Juan Jose BREMER Martino
chancery: 1911 Pennsylvania Avenue NW, Washington, DC 20006
telephone: [1] (202) 728-1600
FAX: [1] (202) 728-1698
consulate(s) general: Atlanta, Austin, Boston, Chicago, Dallas, Denver, El Paso, Houston, Laredo (Texas), Los Angeles, Miami, New Orleans, New York, Nogales (Arizona), Phoenix, Sacramento, San Antonio, San Diego, San Francisco, San Juan (Puerto Rico)
consulate(s): Albuquerque, Brownsville (Texas), Calexico (California), Corpus Christi, Del Rio (Texas), Detroit, Douglas (Arizona), Eagle Pass (Texas), Fresno (California), McAllen (Texas), Midland (Texas), Orlando, Oxnard (California), Philadelphia, Portland (Oregon), St. Louis, Salt Lake City, San Bernardino, San Jose, Santa Ana (California), Seattle, Tucson
Diplomatic representation from the US:
chief of mission: Ambassador Jeffery DAVIDOW
embassy: Paseo de la Reforma 305, Colonia Cuauhtemoc, 06500 Mexico, Distrito Federal
mailing address: P. O. Box 3087, Laredo, TX 78044-3087
telephone: [52] (5) 209-9100
FAX: [52] (5) 208-3373, 511-9980

Mexico (continued)

consulate(s) general: Ciudad Juarez, Guadalajara, Monterrey, Tijuana
consulate(s): Hermosillo, Matamoros, Merida, Nuevo Laredo, Nogales
Flag description: three equal vertical bands of green (hoist side), white, and red; the coat of arms (an eagle perched on a cactus with a snake in its beak) is centered in the white band

Economy

Economy - overview: Mexico has a free market economy with a mixture of modern and outmoded industry and agriculture, increasingly dominated by the private sector. The number of state-owned enterprises in Mexico has fallen from more than 1,000 in 1982 to fewer than 200 in 2000. The ZEDILLO administration privatized and expanded competition in seaports, railroads, telecommunications, electricity, natural gas distribution, and airports. A strong export sector helped to cushion the economy's decline in 1995 and led the recovery in 1996-2000. Private consumption became the leading driver of growth in 2000, accompanied by increased employment and higher real wages. Mexico still needs to overcome many structural problems as it strives to modernize its economy and raise living standards. Income distribution is very unequal, with the top 20% of income earners accounting for 55% of income. Trade with the US and Canada has tripled since NAFTA was implemented in 1994. Mexico completed free trade agreements with the EU, Israel, El Salvador, Honduras, and Guatemala in 2000, and is pursuing additional trade agreements with countries in Latin America and Asia to lessen its dependence on the US.
GDP: purchasing power parity - $915 billion (2000 est.)
GDP - real growth rate: 7.1% (2000 est.)
GDP - per capita: purchasing power parity - $9,100 (2000 est.)
GDP - composition by sector:
agriculture: 5%
industry: 27%
services: 68% (2000)
Population below poverty line: 27% (1998 est.)
Household income or consumption by percentage share:
lowest 10%: 1.8%
highest 10%: 36.6% (1996)
Inflation rate (consumer prices): 9% (2000 est.)
Labor force: 39.8 million (2000)
Labor force - by occupation: agriculture 20%, industry 24%, services 56% (1998)
Unemployment rate: urban - 2.2% (2000); plus considerable underemployment
Budget:
revenues: $125 billion
expenditures: $130 billion, including capital expenditures of $NA (2000 est.)
Industries: food and beverages, tobacco, chemicals, iron and steel, petroleum, mining, textiles, clothing, motor vehicles, consumer durables, tourism
Industrial production growth rate: 7.5% (2000 est.)
Electricity - production: 182.492 billion kWh (1999)
Electricity - production by source:
fossil fuel: 74.12%
hydro: 17.75%
nuclear: 5.21%
other: 2.92% (1999)
Electricity - consumption: 170.754 billion kWh (1999)
Electricity - exports: 11 million kWh (1999)
Electricity - imports: 1.047 billion kWh (1999)
Agriculture - products: corn, wheat, soybeans, rice, beans, cotton, coffee, fruit, tomatoes; beef, poultry, dairy products; wood products
Exports: $168 billion (f.o.b., 2000), includes in-bond industries (assembly plant operations)
Exports - commodities: manufactured goods, oil and oil products, silver, fruits, vegetables, coffee, cotton
Exports - partners: US 88.6%, Canada 2%, Spain 0.9%, Germany 0.9%, Japan 0.6%, UK 0.6%, Netherlands Antilles 0.5%, Switzerland 0.3% Venezuela 0.3%, Chile 0.3% (2000 est.)
Imports: $176 billion (f.o.b., 2000), includes in-bond industries (assembly plant operations)
Imports - commodities: metal-working machines, steel mill products, agricultural machinery, electrical equipment, car parts for assembly, repair parts for motor vehicles, aircraft, and aircraft parts
Imports - partners: US 73.6%, Japan 3.7%, Germany 3.3%, Canada 2.3%, South Korea 2%, China 1.6%, Taiwan 1.2%, Italy 1%, Brazil 1% (2000 est.)
Debt - external: $162 billion (2000)
Economic aid - recipient: $1.166 billion (1995)
Currency: Mexican peso (MXN)
Currency code: MXN
Exchange rates: Mexican pesos per US dollar - 9.7701 (January 2001), 9.4556 (2000), 9.5604 (1999), 9.1360 (1998), 7.9185 (1997), 7.5994 (1996)
Fiscal year: calendar year

Communications

Telephones - main lines in use: 9.6 million (1998)
Telephones - mobile cellular: 2.02 million (1998)
Telephone system:
general assessment: low telephone density with about 11 main lines per 100 persons; privatized in December 1990; the opening to competition in January 1997 has brightened prospects for development
domestic: adequate telephone service for business and government, but the population is poorly served; domestic satellite system with 120 earth stations; extensive microwave radio relay network; considerable use of fiber-optic cable, coaxial cable, and mobile cellular service
international: satellite earth stations - 32 Intelsat, 2 Solidaridad (giving Mexico improved access to South America, Central America, and much of the US as well as enhancing domestic communications), numerous Inmarsat mobile earth stations; linked to Central American Microwave System of trunk connections; high capacity Columbus-2 fiber-optic submarine cable with access to the US, Virgin Islands, Canary Islands, Morocco, Spain, and Italy (1997)
Radio broadcast stations: AM 865, FM about 500, shortwave 13 (1999)
Radios: 31 million (1997)
Television broadcast stations: 236 (plus repeaters) (1997)
Televisions: 25.6 million (1997)
Internet country code: .mx
Internet Service Providers (ISPs): 51 (2000)
Internet users: 2.5 million (2000)

Transportation

Railways:
total: 31,048 km
standard gauge: 30,958 km 1.435-m gauge (246 km electrified)
narrow gauge: 90 km 0.914-m gauge (1998 est.)
Highways:
total: 323,977 km
paved: 96,221 km (including 6,335 km of expressways)
unpaved: 227,756 km (1997)
Waterways: 2,900 km
note: navigable rivers and coastal canals
Pipelines: crude oil 28,200 km; petroleum products 10,150 km; natural gas 13,254 km; petrochemical 1,400 km
Ports and harbors: Acapulco, Altamira, Coatzacoalcos, Ensenada, Guaymas, La Paz, Lazaro Cardenas, Manzanillo, Mazatlan, Progreso, Salina Cruz, Tampico, Topolobampo, Tuxpan, Veracruz
Merchant marine:
total: 43 ships (1,000 GRT or over) totaling 590,657 GRT/920,456 DWT
ships by type: bulk 2, cargo 1, chemical tanker 4, liquefied gas 3, petroleum tanker 28, roll on/roll off 2, short-sea passenger 3 (2000 est.)
Airports: 1,848 (2000 est.)
Airports - with paved runways:
total: 238
over 3,047 m: 11
2,438 to 3,047 m: 28
1,524 to 2,437 m: 90
914 to 1,523 m: 82
under 914 m: 27 (2000 est.)
Airports - with unpaved runways:
total: 1,610
over 3,047 m: 1
2,438 to 3,047 m: 1
1,524 to 2,437 m: 65
914 to 1,523 m: 470
under 914 m: 1,073 (2000 est.)
Heliports: 2 (2000 est.)

Mexico (continued)

Military

Military branches: National Defense Secretariat (includes Army and Air Force), Navy Secretariat (includes Naval Air and Naval Infantry)
Military manpower - military age: 18 years of age
note: starting in 2000, females will be allowed to volunteer for military service
Military manpower - availability:
males age 15-49: 26,703,300 (2001 est.)
Military manpower - fit for military service:
males age 15-49: 19,394,184 (2001 est.)
Military manpower - reaching military age annually:
males: 1,077,536 (2001 est.)
Military expenditures - dollar figure: $4 billion (FY99)
Military expenditures - percent of GDP: 1% (FY99)

Transnational Issues

Disputes - international: none
Illicit drugs: illicit cultivation of opium poppy (cultivation in 2000 - 1,900 hectares; potential heroin production - 2.4 metric tons) and cannabis cultivation in 2000 - 3,900 hectares; government eradication efforts have been key in keeping illicit crop levels low; major supplier of heroin and marijuana to the US market; continues as the primary transshipment country for US-bound cocaine from South America; two major drug syndicates control majority of drug trafficking throughout the country; primary supplier of methamphetamine to the US market; growing producer and distributor of ecstasy

Micronesia, Federated States of

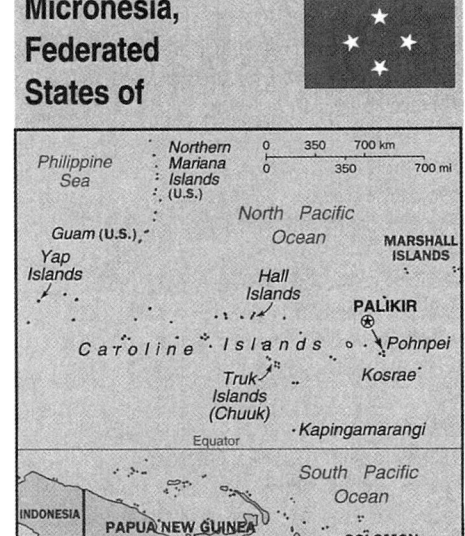

Introduction

Background: In 1979 the Federated States of Micronesia, a UN Trust Territory under US administration, adopted a constitution. In 1986 independence was attained under a Compact of Free Association with the United States. Present concerns include large-scale unemployment, overfishing, and overdependence on US aid.

Geography

Location: Oceania, island group in the North Pacific Ocean, about three-quarters of the way from Hawaii to Indonesia
Geographic coordinates: 6 55 N, 158 15 E
Map references: Oceania
Area:
total: 702 sq km
land: 702 sq km
water: 0 sq km
note: includes Pohnpei (Ponape), Truk (Chuuk) Islands, Yap Islands, and Kosrae
Area - comparative: four times the size of Washington, DC
Land boundaries: 0 km
Coastline: 6,112 km
Maritime claims:
exclusive economic zone: 200 NM
territorial sea: 12 NM
Climate: tropical; heavy year-round rainfall, especially in the eastern islands; located on southern edge of the typhoon belt with occasionally severe damage
Terrain: islands vary geologically from high mountainous islands to low, coral atolls; volcanic outcroppings on Pohnpei, Kosrae, and Truk
Elevation extremes:
lowest point: Pacific Ocean 0 m
highest point: Totolom 791 m
Natural resources: forests, marine products, deep-seabed minerals
Land use:
arable land: NA%
permanent crops: NA%
permanent pastures: NA%
forests and woodland: NA%
other: NA%
Irrigated land: NA sq km
Natural hazards: typhoons (June to December)
Environment - current issues: overfishing
Environment - international agreements:
party to: Biodiversity, Climate Change, Climate Change-Kyoto Protocol, Desertification, Hazardous Wastes, Law of the Sea, Marine Dumping, Ozone Layer Protection, Ship Pollution
signed, but not ratified: none of the selected agreements
Geography - note: four major island groups totaling 607 islands

People

Population: 134,597 (July 2001 est.)
Age structure:
0-14 years: NA%
15-64 years: NA%
65 years and over: NA%
HIV/AIDS - adult prevalence rate: NA%
HIV/AIDS - people living with HIV/AIDS: NA
HIV/AIDS - deaths: NA
Nationality:
noun: Micronesian(s)
adjective: Micronesian; Kosrae(s), Pohnpeian(s), Trukese, Yapese
Ethnic groups: nine ethnic Micronesian and Polynesian groups
Religions: Roman Catholic 50%, Protestant 47%, other and none 3%
Languages: English (official and common language), Trukese, Pohnpeian, Yapese, Kosrean
Literacy:
definition: age 15 and over can read and write
total population: 89%
male: 91%
female: 88% (1980 est.)

Government

Country name:
conventional long form: Federated States of Micronesia
conventional short form: none
former: Ponape, Truk, and Yap Districts (Trust Territory of the Pacific Islands)
abbreviation: FSM
Government type: constitutional government in free association with the US; the Compact of Free Association entered into force 3 November 1986
Capital: Palikir
Administrative divisions: 4 states; Chuuk (Truk), Kosrae, Pohnpei, Yap

Micronesia, Federated States of (continued)

Independence: 3 November 1986 (from the US-administered UN Trusteeship)
National holiday: Constitution Day, 10 May (1979)
Constitution: 10 May 1979
Legal system: based on adapted Trust Territory laws, acts of the legislature, municipal, common, and customary laws
Suffrage: 18 years of age; universal
Executive branch:
chief of state: President Leo A. FALCAM (since 21 July 1999); Vice President Redley KILLION (since 21 July 1999); note - the president is both the chief of state and head of government
head of government: President Leo A. FALCAM (since 21 July 1999); Vice President Redley KILLION (since 21 July 1999); note - the president is both the chief of state and head of government
cabinet: Cabinet
elections: president and vice president elected by Congress from among the four senators-at-large for four-year terms; election last held NA May 1999 (next to be held NA May 2003)
election results: Leo A. FALCAM elected president; percent of Congress vote - NA%; Redley KILLION elected vice president; percent of Congress vote - NA%
Legislative branch: unicameral Congress (14 seats; members elected by popular vote; four - one elected from each of state - to serve four-year terms and 10 - elected from single-member districts delineated by population - to serve two-year terms)
elections: elections for four-year term seats last held 2 March 1999 (next to be held NA March 2003); elections for two-year term seats last held 6 March 2001 (next to be held NA March 2003)
election results: percent of vote - NA%; seats - independents 14
Judicial branch: Supreme Court
Political parties and leaders: no formal parties
International organization participation: ACP, AsDB, ESCAP, G-77, IBRD, ICAO, IDA, IFC, IMF, Intelsat, IOC, ITU, OPCW, Sparteca, SPC, SPF, UN, UNCTAD, UNESCO, WHO, WMO
Diplomatic representation in the US:
chief of mission: Ambassador Jesse Bibiano MAREHALAU
chancery: 1725 N Street NW, Washington, DC 20036
telephone: [1] (202) 223-4383
FAX: [1] (202) 223-4391
consulate(s) general: Honolulu and Tamuning (Guam)
Diplomatic representation from the US:
chief of mission: Ambassador Diane E. WATSON
embassy: address NA, Kolonia
mailing address: P. O. Box 1286, Kolonia, Pohnpei, Federated States of Micronesia 96941
telephone: [691] 320-2187
FAX: [691] 320-2186
Flag description: light blue with four white five-pointed stars centered; the stars are arranged in a diamond pattern

Economy

Economy - overview: Economic activity consists primarily of subsistence farming and fishing. The islands have few mineral deposits worth exploiting, except for high-grade phosphate. The potential for a tourist industry exists, but the remoteness of the location and a lack of adequate facilities hinder development. In 1996, the country experienced a 20% reduction in revenues from the Compact of Free Association - the agreement between the US and Micronesia in which Micronesia receives $1.3 billion in financial and technical assistance over a 15-year period until 2001 - as a result of the second step-down under the agreement. Since these revenues accounted for 57% of consolidated government revenues, reduced Compact funding resulted in a severe depression. While Micronesia's economy appears to have bottomed out in 1999, the country's medium-term economic outlook remains fragile due to likely further reductions in external grants made under the US Compact funding. Geographical isolation and a poorly developed infrastructure remain major impediments to long-term growth.
GDP: purchasing power parity - $263 million (1999 est.)
note: GDP is supplemented by grant aid, averaging perhaps $100 million annually
GDP - real growth rate: 0.3% (1999 est.)
GDP - per capita: purchasing power parity - $2,000 (1999 est.)
GDP - composition by sector:
agriculture: 19%
industry: 4%
services: 77% (1996 est.)
Population below poverty line: NA%
Household income or consumption by percentage share:
lowest 10%: NA%
highest 10%: NA%
Inflation rate (consumer prices): 2.6% (FY98/99)
Labor force: NA
Labor force - by occupation: two-thirds are government employees
Unemployment rate: 16% (1999 est.)
Budget:
revenues: $161 million ($69 million less grants)
expenditures: $160 million, including capital expenditures of $NA (1998 est.)
Industries: tourism, construction, fish processing, craft items from shell, wood, and pearls
Industrial production growth rate: NA%
Electricity - production: NA kWh
Electricity - production by source:
fossil fuel: NA%
hydro: NA%
nuclear: NA%
other: NA%
Electricity - consumption: NA kWh
Agriculture - products: black pepper, tropical fruits and vegetables, coconuts, cassava (tapioca), sweet potatoes; pigs, chickens
Exports: $73 million (f.o.b., 1996 est.)
Exports - commodities: fish, garments, bananas, black pepper
Exports - partners: Japan, US, Guam
Imports: $168 million (c.i.f., 1996 est.)
Imports - commodities: food, manufactured goods, machinery and equipment, beverages
Imports - partners: US, Japan, Australia
Debt - external: $111 million (1997 est.)
Economic aid - recipient: under terms of the Compact of Free Association, the US will provide $1.3 billion in grant aid during the period 1986-2001
Currency: US dollar (USD)
Currency code: USD
Exchange rates: the US dollar is used
Fiscal year: 1 October - 30 September

Communications

Telephones - main lines in use: 8,000 (1997)
Telephones - mobile cellular: NA
Telephone system:
general assessment: adequate system
domestic: islands interconnected by shortwave radiotelephone (used mostly for government purposes)
international: satellite earth stations - 4 Intelsat (Pacific Ocean)
Radio broadcast stations: AM 5, FM 1, shortwave 0 (1998)
Radios: NA
Television broadcast stations: 2 (1997)
Televisions: NA
Internet country code: .fm
Internet Service Providers (ISPs): 1 (2000)
Internet users: 2,000 (2000)

Transportation

Railways: 0 km
Highways:
total: 240 km
paved: 42 km
unpaved: 198 km (1996)
Waterways: none
Ports and harbors: Colonia (Yap), Kolonia (Pohnpei), Lele, Moen
Merchant marine: none (2000 est.)
Airports: 7 (2000 est.)
Airports - with paved runways:
total: 6
1,524 to 2,437 m: 4
914 to 1,523 m: 2 (2000 est.)
Airports - with unpaved runways:
total: 1
914 to 1,523 m: 1 (2000 est.)

Military

Military - note: Federated States of Micronesia (FSM) is a sovereign, self-governing state in free association with the US; FSM is totally dependent on the US for its defense

Transnational Issues

Disputes - international: none

Midway Islands
(territory of the US)

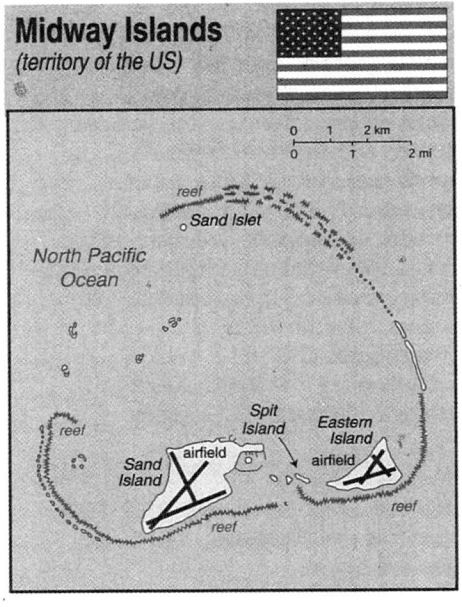

Introduction

Background: The US took formal possession of the islands in 1867. The laying of the trans-Pacific cable, which passed through the islands, brought the first residents in 1903. Between 1935 and 1947, Midway was used as a refueling stop for trans-Pacific flights. The US naval victory over a Japanese fleet off Midway in 1942 was one of the turning points of World War II. The islands continued to serve as a naval station until closed in 1993. Today the islands are a wildlife refuge open to the public.

Geography

Location: Oceania, atoll in the North Pacific Ocean, about one-third of the way from Honolulu to Tokyo
Geographic coordinates: 28 13 N, 177 22 W
Map references: Oceania
Area:
total: 6.2 sq km
land: 6.2 sq km
water: 0 sq km
note: includes Eastern Island, Sand Island, and Spit Island
Area - comparative: about nine times the size of The Mall in Washington, DC
Land boundaries: 0 km
Coastline: 15 km
Maritime claims:
exclusive economic zone: 200 NM
territorial sea: 12 NM
Climate: subtropical, but moderated by prevailing easterly winds
Terrain: low, nearly level
Elevation extremes:
lowest point: Pacific Ocean 0 m
highest point: unnamed location 13 m
Natural resources: wildlife, terrestrial and aquatic
Land use:
arable land: 0%
permanent crops: 0%
permanent pastures: 0%
forests and woodland: 0%
other: 100%
Irrigated land: 0 sq km (1998)
Natural hazards: NA
Environment - current issues: NA
Geography - note: a coral atoll managed as a national wildlife refuge and open to the public for wildlife-related recreation in the form of wildlife observation and photography, sport fishing, snorkeling, and scuba diving

People

Population: no indigenous inhabitants; approximately 150 people make up the staff of US Fish and Wildlife Service and their services cooperator living at the atoll (July 2001 est.)

Government

Country name:
conventional long form: none
conventional short form: Midway Islands
Dependency status: unincorporated territory of the US; formerly administered from Washington, DC, by the US Navy, under Naval Facilities Engineering Command, Pacific Division; this facility has been operationally closed since 10 September 1993; on 31 October 1996, through a presidential executive order, the jurisdiction and control of the atoll was transferred to the Fish and Wildlife Service of the US Department of the Interior as part of the National Wildlife Refuge system
Legal system: the laws of the US, where applicable, apply
Flag description: the flag of the US is used

Economy

Economy - overview: The economy is based on providing support services for the national wildlife refuge activities located on the islands. All food and manufactured goods must be imported.

Transportation

Highways:
total: 32 km
paved: NA km
unpaved: NA km
Waterways: none
Pipelines: 7.8 km
Ports and harbors: Sand Island
Airports: 3 (2000 est.)
Airports - with paved runways:
total: 2
1,524 to 2,437 m: 2 (2000 est.)
Airports - with unpaved runways:
total: 1
914 to 1,523 m: 1 (2000 est.)

Military

Military - note: defense is the responsibility of the US

Transnational Issues

Disputes - international: none

Moldova

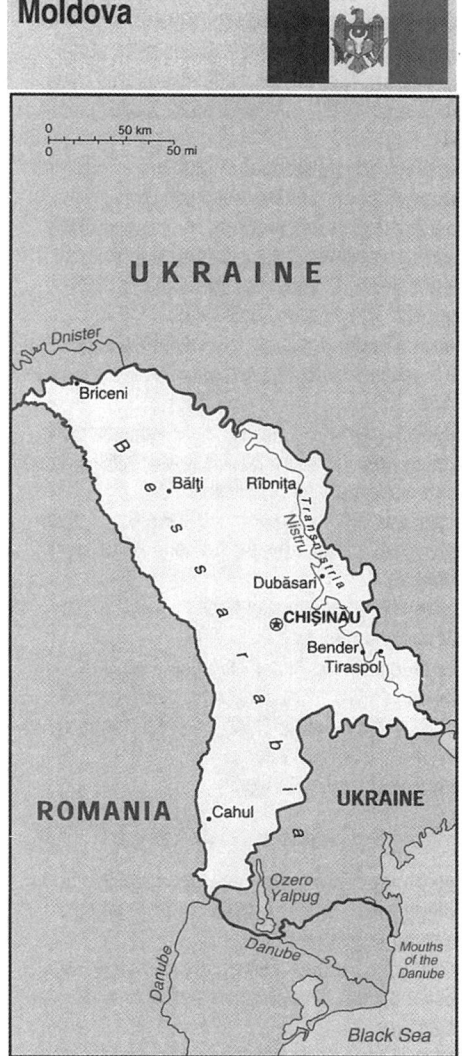

Introduction

Background: Formerly ruled by Romania, Moldova became part of the Soviet Union at the close of World War II. Although independent from the USSR since 1991, Russian forces have remained on Moldovan territory east of the Nistru (Dnister) River supporting the Slavic majority population, mostly Ukrainians and Russians, who have proclaimed a "Transnistria" republic. One of the poorest nations in Europe and plagued by a moribund economy, in 2001 Moldova became the first former Soviet state to elect a communist as its president.

Geography

Location: Eastern Europe, northeast of Romania
Geographic coordinates: 47 00 N, 29 00 E
Map references: Commonwealth of Independent States
Area:
total: 33,843 sq km
land: 33,371 sq km
water: 472 sq km
Area - comparative: slightly larger than Maryland
Land boundaries:
total: 1,389 km
border countries: Romania 450 km, Ukraine 939 km
Coastline: 0 km (landlocked)
Maritime claims: none (landlocked)
Climate: moderate winters, warm summers
Terrain: rolling steppe, gradual slope south to Black Sea
Elevation extremes:
lowest point: Nistru (Dnister) River 2 m
highest point: Dealul Balanesti 430 m
Natural resources: lignite, phosphorites, gypsum, arable land
Land use:
arable land: 53%
permanent crops: 14%
permanent pastures: 13%
forests and woodland: 13%
other: 7% (1993 est.)
Irrigated land: 3,110 sq km (1993 est.)
Natural hazards: landslides (57 cases in 1998)
Environment - current issues: heavy use of agricultural chemicals, including banned pesticides such as DDT, has contaminated soil and groundwater; extensive soil erosion from poor farming methods
Environment - international agreements:
party to: Air Pollution, Biodiversity, Climate Change, Desertification, Hazardous Wastes, Marine Dumping, Ozone Layer Protection, Ship Pollution
signed, but not ratified: Air Pollution-Persistent Organic Pollutants
Geography - note: landlocked

People

Population: 4,431,570 (July 2001 est.)
Age structure:
0-14 years: 22.44% (male 506,303; female 488,311)
15-64 years: 67.62% (male 1,437,492; female 1,559,090)
65 years and over: 9.94% (male 163,473; female 276,901) (2001 est.)
Population growth rate: 0.05% (2001 est.)
Birth rate: 13.35 births/1,000 population (2001 est.)
Death rate: 12.6 deaths/1,000 population (2001 est.)
Net migration rate: -0.3 migrant(s)/1,000 population (2001 est.)
Sex ratio:
at birth: 1.05 male(s)/female
under 15 years: 1.04 male(s)/female
15-64 years: 0.92 male(s)/female
65 years and over: 0.59 male(s)/female
total population: 0.91 male(s)/female (2001 est.)
Infant mortality rate: 42.74 deaths/1,000 live births (2001 est.)
Life expectancy at birth:
total population: 64.6 years
male: 60.15 years
female: 69.26 years (2001 est.)
Total fertility rate: 1.67 children born/woman (2001 est.)
HIV/AIDS - adult prevalence rate: 0.2% (1999 est.)
HIV/AIDS - people living with HIV/AIDS: 4,500 (1999 est.)
HIV/AIDS - deaths: less than 100 (1999 est.)
Nationality:
noun: Moldovan(s)
adjective: Moldovan
Ethnic groups: Moldovan/Romanian 64.5%, Ukrainian 13.8%, Russian 13%, Gagauz 3.5%, Jewish 1.5%, Bulgarian 2%, other 1.7% (1989 est.)
note: internal disputes with ethnic Slavs in the Transnistrian region
Religions: Eastern Orthodox 98.5%, Jewish 1.5%, Baptist (only about 1,000 members) (1991)
Languages: Moldovan (official, virtually the same as the Romanian language), Russian, Gagauz (a Turkish dialect)
Literacy:
definition: age 15 and over can read and write
total population: 96%
male: 99%
female: 94% (1989 est.)

Government

Country name:
conventional long form: Republic of Moldova
conventional short form: Moldova
local long form: Republica Moldova
local short form: none
former: Soviet Socialist Republic of Moldova; Moldavia
Government type: republic
Capital: Chisinau
Administrative divisions: 10 juletule (singular - juletul), 1 municipality*, and 1 autonomous territorial unit**; Balti, Cahul, Chisinau, Chisinau*, Dubasari, Edinet, Gagauzia**, Lapusna, Orhei, Soroca, Tighina, Ungheni
Independence: 27 August 1991 (from Soviet Union)
National holiday: Independence Day, 27 August (1991)
Constitution: new constitution adopted 28 July 1994; replaces old Soviet constitution of 1979
Legal system: based on civil law system; Constitutional Court reviews legality of legislative acts and governmental decisions of resolution; it is unclear if Moldova accepts compulsory ICJ jurisdiction but accepts many UN and Organization for Security and Cooperation in Europe (OSCE) documents
Suffrage: 18 years of age; universal
Executive branch:
chief of state: President Vladimir VORONIN (since 4 April 2001)
head of government: Prime Minister Vasile TARLEV (since 15 April 2001), three Deputy Prime Ministers: Valerian CRISTEA, Andrei CUCU, and Dmitri TODOROGLO (all since 19 April 2001)
cabinet: selected by prime minister, subject to approval of Parliament
elections: president elected by Parliament for a four-year term; election last held 4 April 2001; presidential elections were scheduled for December

Moldova (continued)

2000, but in July 2000, Parliament canceled direct popular elections; Parliament's failure to chose a new president in December 2000 led to early parliamentary elections (moved up a year to February 2001); according to the Moldovan constitution, the president, on consulting with Parliament, will designate a candidate for the office of prime minister; within 15 days from designation, the prime minister-designate will request a vote of confidence from the Parliament regarding his/her work program and entire cabinet; prime minister designated on 15 April 2001, cabinet received vote of confidence on 19 April 2001
election results: Vladimir VORONIN elected president; parliamentary votes - Vladimir VORONIN 71, Dumitru BRAGHIS 15, Valerian CHRISTEA 3; Vasile TARLEV elected Prime Minister; parliamentary votes of confidence - 75 of 101
Legislative branch: unicameral Parliament or Parlamentul (101 seats; parties and electoral blocs, as well as independent candidates, elected by popular vote to serve four-year terms)
elections: last held 25 February 2001 (next to be held NA 2005)
election results: percent of vote by party - PCM 50.1%, Braghis Alliance 13.4%, PPCD 8.2%, other parties 28.3%; seats by party - PCM 71, Braghis Alliance 19, PPCD 11
Judicial branch: Supreme Court; Constitutional Court (the sole authority for constitutional judicature)
Political parties and leaders: Braghis Alliance [Dumitru BRAGHIS]; Popular Christian Democratic Party or PPCD [Iurie ROSCA]; Communist Party or PCM [Vladimir VORONIN, first chairman]
Political pressure groups and leaders: NA
International organization participation: ACCT, BIS, BSEC, CCC, CE, CEI, CIS, EAPC, EBRD, ECE, FAO, IAEA, IBRD, ICAO, ICFTU, IDA, IFAD, IFC, ILO, IMF, Intelsat (nonsignatory user), Interpol, IOC, IOM (observer), ISO (correspondent), ITU, OPCW, OSCE, PFP, UN, UNCTAD, UNESCO, UNIDO, UPU, WHO, WIPO, WMO, WToO, WTrO (observer)
Diplomatic representation in the US:
chief of mission: Ambassador Ceslav CIOBANU
chancery: 2101 S Street NW, Washington, DC 20008
telephone: [1] (202) 667-1130
FAX: [1] (202) 667-1204
Diplomatic representation from the US:
chief of mission: Ambassador Rudolf Vilem PERINA
embassy: Strada Alexei Mateevicie, #103, Chisinau 2009
mailing address: use embassy street address; pouch address - American Embassy Chisinau, Department of State, Washington, DC 20521-7080
telephone: [373] (2) 23-37-72
FAX: [373] (2) 23-30-44
Flag description: same color scheme as Romania - three equal vertical bands of blue (hoist side), yellow, and red; emblem in center of flag is of a Roman eagle of gold outlined in black with a red beak and talons carrying a yellow cross in its beak and a green olive branch in its right talons and a yellow scepter in its left talons; on its breast is a shield divided horizontally red over blue with a stylized ox head, star, rose, and crescent all in black-outlined yellow

Economy

Economy - overview: Moldova enjoys a favorable climate and good farmland but has no major mineral deposits. As a result, the economy depends heavily on agriculture, featuring fruits, vegetables, wine, and tobacco. Moldova must import all of its supplies of oil, coal, and natural gas, largely from Russia. Energy shortages contributed to sharp production declines after the breakup of the Soviet Union in 1991. As part of an ambitious reform effort, Moldova introduced a convertible currency, freed all prices, stopped issuing preferential credits to state enterprises, backed steady land privatization, removed export controls, and freed interest rates. Yet these efforts could not offset the impact of political and economic difficulties, both internal and regional. In 1998, the economic troubles of Russia, by far Moldova's leading trade partner, were a major cause of the 8.6% drop in GDP. In 1999, GDP fell again, by 4.4%, the fifth drop in the past seven years; exports were down, and energy supplies continued to be erratic. GDP declined slightly in 2000, with a serious drought hurting agriculture. Growth should turn positive in 2001.
GDP: purchasing power parity - $11.3 billion (2000 est.)
GDP - real growth rate: -1.5% (2000 est.)
GDP - per capita: purchasing power parity - $2,500 (2000 est.)
GDP - composition by sector:
agriculture: 31%
industry: 35%
services: 34% (1998)
Population below poverty line: 75% (1999 est.)
Household income or consumption by percentage share:
lowest 10%: 2.7%
highest 10%: 25.8% (1992)
Inflation rate (consumer prices): 32% (2000 est.)
Labor force: 1.7 million (1998)
Labor force - by occupation: agriculture 40%, industry 14%, other 46% (1998)
Unemployment rate: 1.9% (includes only officially registered unemployed; large numbers of underemployed workers) (November 2000)
Budget:
revenues: $536 million
expenditures: $594 million, including capital expenditures of $NA (1998 est.)
Industries: food processing, agricultural machinery, foundry equipment, refrigerators and freezers, washing machines, hosiery, sugar, vegetable oil, shoes, textiles
Industrial production growth rate: 3% (2000 est.)
Electricity - production: 4.155 billion kWh (1999)
Electricity - production by source:
fossil fuel: 93.62%
hydro: 6.38%
nuclear: 0%
other: 0% (1999)
Electricity - consumption: 5.78 billion kWh (1999)
Electricity - exports: 0 kWh (1999)
Electricity - imports: 1.916 billion kWh (1999)
Agriculture - products: vegetables, fruits, wine, grain, sugar beets, sunflower seed, tobacco; beef, milk
Exports: $500 million (f.o.b., 2000)
Exports - commodities: foodstuffs 57%, wine, tobacco; textiles and footwear, machinery (1999)
Exports - partners: Russia 41%, Romania 9%, Germany 8%, Ukraine 7%, Italy, Belarus (1999)
Imports: $761 million (f.o.b., 2000)
Imports - commodities: mineral products and fuel 38%, machinery and equipment, chemicals, textiles (1999)
Imports - partners: Russia 21%, Romania 16%, Ukraine 14%, Germany 12%, Italy 6%, Belarus (1999)
Debt - external: $900 million (2000)
Economic aid - recipient: $100.8 million (1995); note - $547 million from the IMF and World Bank (1992-99)
Currency: Moldovan leu (MDL)
Currency code: MDL
Exchange rates: lei per US dollar - 12.3728 (January 2001), 12.4342 (2000), 10.5158 (1999), 5.3707 (1998), 4.6236 (1997), 4.6045 (1996); note - lei is the plural form of leu
Fiscal year: calendar year

Communications

Telephones - main lines in use: 627,000 (1997)
Telephones - mobile cellular: 2,200 (1997)
Telephone system:
general assessment: inadequate, outmoded, poor service outside Chisinau, some effort to modernize is under way
domestic: new subscribers face long wait for service; mobile cellular telephone service being introduced
international: service through Romania and Russia via landline; satellite earth stations - Intelsat, Eutelsat, and Intersputnik
Radio broadcast stations: AM 7, FM 50, shortwave 3 (1998)
Radios: 3.22 million (1997)
Television broadcast stations: 1 (plus 30 repeaters) (1995)
Televisions: 1.26 million (1997)
Internet country code: .md
Internet Service Providers (ISPs): 2 (1999)
Internet users: 15,000 (2000)

Transportation

Railways:
total: 1,328 km
broad gauge: 1,328 km 1.520-m gauge (1992)
Highways:
total: 12,300 km
paved: 10,738 km (these roads are said to be hard-surfaced, and include, in addition to conventionally paved roads, some that are surfaced with gravel or other coarse aggregate, making them trafficable in all weather)

Moldova (continued)

unpaved: 1,562 km (these roads are made of unstabilized earth and are difficult to negotiate in wet weather) (1996)
Waterways: 424 km (1994)
Pipelines: natural gas 310 km (1992)
Ports and harbors: none
Airports: 30 (2000 est.)
Airports - with paved runways:
total: 7
over 3,047 m: 1
2,438 to 3,047 m: 2
1,524 to 2,437 m: 3
under 914 m: 1 (2000 est.)
Airports - with unpaved runways:
total: 23
2,438 to 3,047 m: 4
1,524 to 2,437 m: 1
914 to 1,523 m: 4
under 914 m: 14 (2000 est.)

Military

Military branches: Ground Forces, Air and Air Defense Forces, Republic Security Forces (internal and border troops)
Military manpower - military age: 18 years of age
Military manpower - availability:
males age 15-49: 1,164,018 (2001 est.)
Military manpower - fit for military service:
males age 15-49: 921,210 (2001 est.)
Military manpower - reaching military age annually:
males: 42,268 (2001 est.)
Military expenditures - dollar figure: $6 million (FY99)
Military expenditures - percent of GDP: 1% (FY99)

Transnational Issues

Disputes - international: separatist Transnistria region, comprising the area between the Nistru (Dniester) River and Ukraine, has its own de facto government, dominated by Moldovan Slavs
Illicit drugs: limited cultivation of opium poppy and cannabis, mostly for CIS consumption; transshipment point for illicit drugs from Southwest Asia via Central Asia to Russia, Western Europe, and possibly the US

Monaco

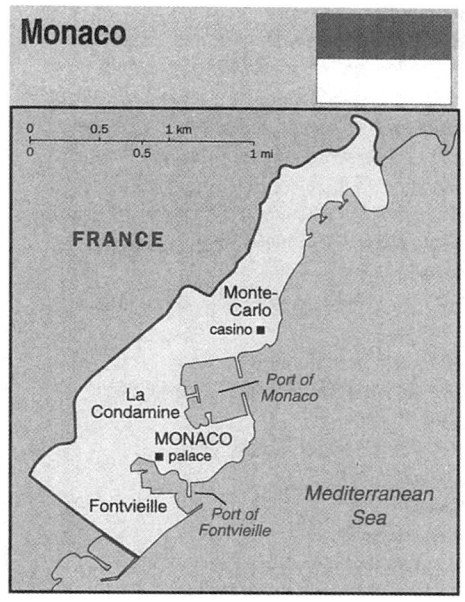

Introduction

Background: Economic development was spurred in the late 19th century with a railroad linkup to France and the opening of a casino. Since then, the principality's mild climate, splendid scenery, and gambling facilities have made Monaco world famous as a tourist and recreation center.

Geography

Location: Western Europe, bordering the Mediterranean Sea on the southern coast of France, near the border with Italy
Geographic coordinates: 43 44 N, 7 24 E
Map references: Europe
Area:
total: 1.95 sq km
land: 1.95 sq km
water: 0 sq km
Area - comparative: about three times the size of The Mall in Washington, DC
Land boundaries:
total: 4.4 km
border countries: France 4.4 km
Coastline: 4.1 km
Maritime claims:
territorial sea: 12 NM
Climate: Mediterranean with mild, wet winters and hot, dry summers
Terrain: hilly, rugged, rocky
Elevation extremes:
lowest point: Mediterranean Sea 0 m
highest point: Mont Agel 140 m
Natural resources: none
Land use:
arable land: 0%
permanent crops: 0%
permanent pastures: 0%
forests and woodland: 0%
other: 100% (urban area)
Irrigated land: NA sq km
Natural hazards: NA
Environment - current issues: NA
Environment - international agreements:
party to: Air Pollution, Biodiversity, Climate Change, Desertification, Endangered Species, Hazardous Wastes, Law of the Sea, Marine Dumping, Ozone Layer Protection, Ship Pollution, Wetlands, Whaling
signed, but not ratified: Climate Change-Kyoto Protocol
Geography - note: second smallest independent state in the world (after Holy See); almost entirely urban

People

Population: 31,842 (July 2001 est.)
Age structure:
0-14 years: 15.32% (male 2,503; female 2,375)
15-64 years: 62.23% (male 9,731; female 10,083)
65 years and over: 22.45% (male 2,921; female 4,229) (2001 est.)
Population growth rate: 0.46% (2001 est.)
Birth rate: 9.74 births/1,000 population (2001 est.)
Death rate: 13 deaths/1,000 population (2001 est.)
Net migration rate: 7.85 migrant(s)/1,000 population (2001 est.)
Sex ratio:
at birth: 1.05 male(s)/female
under 15 years: 1.05 male(s)/female
15-64 years: 0.97 male(s)/female
65 years and over: 0.69 male(s)/female
total population: 0.91 male(s)/female (2001 est.)
Infant mortality rate: 5.83 deaths/1,000 live births (2001 est.)
Life expectancy at birth:
total population: 78.98 years
male: 75.04 years
female: 83.12 years (2001 est.)
Total fertility rate: 1.76 children born/woman (2001 est.)
HIV/AIDS - adult prevalence rate: NA%
HIV/AIDS - people living with HIV/AIDS: NA
HIV/AIDS - deaths: NA
Nationality:
noun: Monegasque(s) or Monacan(s)
adjective: Monegasque or Monacan
Ethnic groups: French 47%, Monegasque 16%, Italian 16%, other 21%
Religions: Roman Catholic 90%
Languages: French (official), English, Italian, Monegasque
Literacy:
definition: NA
total population: 99%
male: NA%
female: NA%

Government

Country name:
conventional long form: Principality of Monaco
conventional short form: Monaco
local long form: Principaute de Monaco
local short form: Monaco
Government type: constitutional monarchy
Capital: Monaco

Monaco (continued)

Administrative divisions: none; there are no first-order administrative divisions as defined by the US Government, but there are four quarters (quartiers, singular - quartier); Fontvieille, La Condamine, Monaco-Ville, Monte-Carlo
Independence: 1419 (beginning of the rule by the House of Grimaldi)
National holiday: National Day (Prince of Monaco Holiday), 19 November
Constitution: 17 December 1962
Legal system: based on French law; has not accepted compulsory ICJ jurisdiction
Suffrage: 21 years of age; universal
Executive branch:
chief of state: Prince RAINIER III (since 9 May 1949); Heir Apparent Prince ALBERT Alexandre Louis Pierre, son of the monarch (born 14 March 1958)
head of government: Minister of State Patrick LECLERQUE (since 5 January 2000)
cabinet: Council of Government is under the authority of the monarch
elections: none; the monarch is hereditary; minister of state appointed by the monarch from a list of three French national candidates presented by the French Government
Legislative branch: unicameral National Council or Conseil National (18 seats; members are elected by popular vote to serve five-year terms)
elections: last held 1 and 8 February 1998 (next to be held NA January 2003)
election results: percent of vote by party - NA%; seats by party - UND 18
Judicial branch: Supreme Court or Tribunal Supreme (judges appointed by the monarch on the basis of nominations by the National Council)
Political parties and leaders: National and Democratic Union or UND [leader NA]; National Union for the Future of Monaco or UNAM [leader NA]; Rally for the Monegasque Family [leader NA]
Political pressure groups and leaders: NA
International organization participation: ACCT, ECE, IAEA, ICAO, ICRM, IFRCS, IHO, IMO, Inmarsat, Intelsat, Interpol, IOC, ITU, OPCW, OSCE, UN, UNCTAD, UNESCO, UPU, WHO, WIPO, WMO, WToO
Diplomatic representation in the US: Monaco does not have an embassy in the US
consulate(s) general: New York
Diplomatic representation from the US: the US does not have an embassy in Monaco; the US Consul General in Marseille (France) is accredited to Monaco
Flag description: two equal horizontal bands of red (top) and white; similar to the flag of Indonesia which is longer and the flag of Poland which is white (top) and red

Economy

Economy - overview: Monaco, situated on the French Mediterranean coast, is a popular resort, attracting tourists to its casino and pleasant climate. The Principality has successfully sought to diversify into services and small, high-value-added, nonpolluting industries. The state has no income tax and low business taxes and thrives as a tax haven both for individuals who have established residence and for foreign companies that have set up businesses and offices. The state retains monopolies in a number of sectors, including tobacco, the telephone network, and the postal service. Living standards are high, roughly comparable to those in prosperous French metropolitan areas. Monaco does not publish national income figures; the estimates below are extremely rough.
GDP: purchasing power parity - $870 million (1999 est.)
GDP - real growth rate: NA%
GDP - per capita: purchasing power parity - $27,000 (1999 est.)
GDP - composition by sector:
agriculture: NA%
industry: NA%
services: NA%
Population below poverty line: NA%
Household income or consumption by percentage share:
lowest 10%: NA%
highest 10%: NA%
Inflation rate (consumer prices): NA%
Labor force: 30,540 (January 1994)
Unemployment rate: 3.1% (1998)
Budget:
revenues: $518 million
expenditures: $531 million, including capital expenditures of $NA (1995)
Industries: tourism, construction, small-scale industrial and consumer products
Industrial production growth rate: NA%
Electricity - consumption: NA kWh
Electricity - imports: NA kWh
note: electricity supplied by France (1999)
Agriculture - products: none
Exports: $NA; full customs integration with France, which collects and rebates Monegasque trade duties; also participates in EU market system through customs union with France
Imports: $NA; full customs integration with France, which collects and rebates Monegasque trade duties; also participates in EU market system through customs union with France
Debt - external: $NA
Economic aid - recipient: $NA
Currency: French franc (FRF); euro (EUR)
Currency code: FRF; EUR
Exchange rates: euros per US dollar - 1.0659 (January 2001), 1.0854 (2000), 0.9386 (1999); French francs per US dollar - 5.8995 (1998), 5.8367 (1997), 5.1155 (1996)
Fiscal year: calendar year

Communications

Telephones - main lines in use: 31,027 (1995)
Telephones - mobile cellular: NA
Telephone system:
general assessment: modern automatic telephone system
domestic: NA
international: no satellite earth stations; connected by cable into the French communications system
Radio broadcast stations: AM 1, FM NA, shortwave 8 (1998)
Radios: 34,000 (1997)
Television broadcast stations: 5 (1998)
Televisions: 25,000 (1997)
Internet country code: .mc
Internet Service Providers (ISPs): 2 (2000)
Internet users: NA

Transportation

Railways:
total: 1.7 km
standard gauge: 1.7 km 1.435-m gauge
Highways:
total: 50 km
paved: 50 km
unpaved: 0 km (2001)
Waterways: none
Ports and harbors: Monaco
Merchant marine: none (2000 est.)
Airports: linked to airport in Nice, France, by helicopter service
Heliports: 1 (shuttle service between the international airport at Nice, France, and Monaco's heliport at Fontvieille)

Military

Military - note: defense is the responsibility of France

Transnational Issues

Disputes - international: none

Mongolia

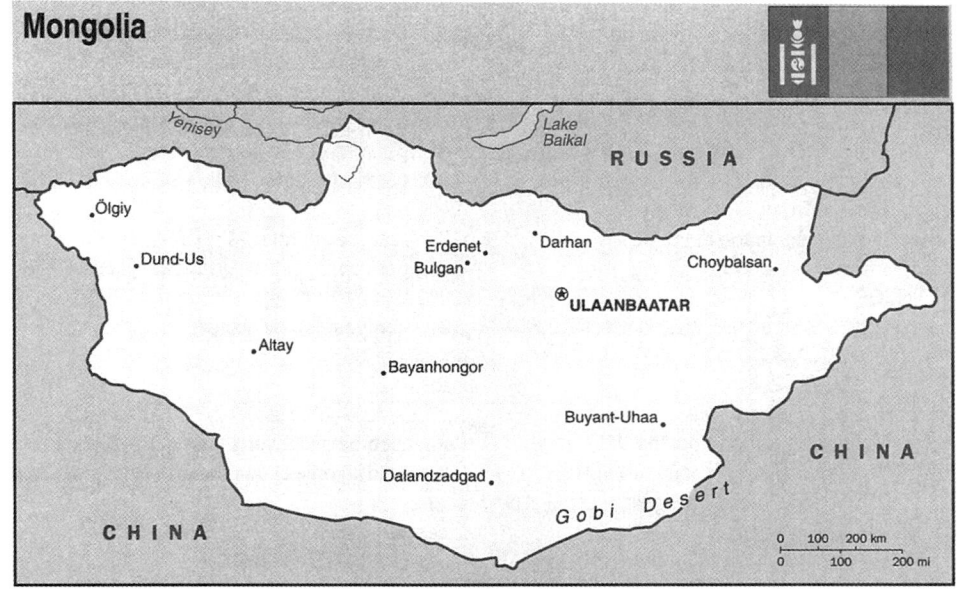

Introduction

Background: Long a province of China, Mongolia won its independence in 1921 with Soviet backing. A communist regime was installed in 1924. During the early 1990s, the ex-communist Mongolian People's Revolutionary Party (MPRP) gradually yielded its monopoly on power. In 1996, the Democratic Union Coalition (DUC) defeated the MPRP in a national election. Over the next four years the Coalition implemented a number of key reforms to modernize the economy and institutionalize democratic reforms. However, the former communists were a strong opposition that stalled additional reforms and made implementation difficult. In 2000, the MPRP won 72 of the 76 seats in Parliament and completely reshuffled the government. While it continues many of the reform policies, the MPRP is focusing on social welfare and public order priorities.

Geography

Location: Northern Asia, between China and Russia
Geographic coordinates: 46 00 N, 105 00 E
Map references: Asia
Area:
total: 1.565 million sq km
land: 1.565 million sq km
water: 0 sq km
Area - comparative: slightly smaller than Alaska
Land boundaries:
total: 8,161.9 km
border countries: China 4,676.9 km, Russia 3,485 km
Coastline: 0 km (landlocked)
Maritime claims: none (landlocked)
Climate: desert; continental (large daily and seasonal temperature ranges)
Terrain: vast semidesert and desert plains, grassy steppe, mountains in west and southwest; Gobi Desert in south-central
Elevation extremes:
lowest point: Hoh Nuur 518 m
highest point: Nayramadlin Orgil (Huyten Orgil) 4,374 m
Natural resources: oil, coal, copper, molybdenum, tungsten, phosphates, tin, nickel, zinc, wolfram, fluorspar, gold, silver, iron, phosphate
Land use:
arable land: 5.7%
permanent crops: 0%
permanent pastures: 81%
forests and woodland: 11.4%
other: 1.9% (2000 est.)
Irrigated land: 800 sq km (1993 est.)
Natural hazards: dust and snow storms, grassland and forest fires, drought and "zud", which is a combination of drought followed by harsh winter conditions
Environment - current issues: limited natural fresh water resources in some areas; policies of the former communist regime promoting rapid urbanization and industrial growth have raised concerns about their negative effects on the environment; the burning of soft coal in power plants and the lack of enforcement of environmental laws have severely polluted the air in Ulaanbaatar; deforestation, overgrazing, the converting of virgin land to agricultural production have increased soil erosion from wind and rain; desertification and mining activities have also had a deleterious effect on the environment
Environment - international agreements:
party to: Biodiversity, Climate Change, Climate Change-Kyoto Protocol, Desertification, Endangered Species, Environmental Modification, Hazardous Wastes, Law of the Sea, Marine Dumping, Ozone Layer Protection, Ship Pollution, Wetlands
signed, but not ratified: none of the selected agreements
Geography - note: landlocked; strategic location between China and Russia

People

Population: 2,654,999 (July 2001 est.)
Age structure:
0-14 years: 32.99% (male 445,252; female 430,758)
15-64 years: 63.13% (male 837,771; female 838,384)
65 years and over: 3.88% (male 44,436; female 58,398) (2001 est.)
Population growth rate: 1.47% (2001 est.)
Birth rate: 21.8 births/1,000 population (2001 est.)
Death rate: 7.1 deaths/1,000 population (2001 est.)
Net migration rate: 0 migrant(s)/1,000 population (2001 est.)
Sex ratio:
at birth: 1.05 male(s)/female
under 15 years: 1.03 male(s)/female
15-64 years: 1 male(s)/female
65 years and over: 0.76 male(s)/female
total population: 1 male(s)/female (2001 est.)
Infant mortality rate: 53.5 deaths/1,000 live births (2001 est.)
Life expectancy at birth:
total population: 64.26 years
male: 62.14 years
female: 66.5 years (2001 est.)
Total fertility rate: 2.39 children born/woman (2001 est.)
HIV/AIDS - adult prevalence rate: less than 0.01% (1999 est.)
HIV/AIDS - people living with HIV/AIDS: less than 100 (1999 est.)
HIV/AIDS - deaths: NA
Nationality:
noun: Mongolian(s)
adjective: Mongolian
Ethnic groups: Mongol (predominantly Khalkha) 85%, Turkic (of which Kazakh is the largest group) 7%, Tungusic 4.6%, other (including Chinese and Russian) 3.4% (1998)
Religions: Tibetan Buddhist Lamaism 96%, Muslim (primarily in the southwest), Shamanism, and Christian 4% (1998)
Languages: Khalkha Mongol 90%, Turkic, Russian (1999)
Literacy:
definition: age 15 and over can read and write
total population: 97%
male: 98%
female: 97.5% (2000)

Government

Country name:
conventional long form: none
conventional short form: Mongolia
local long form: none
local short form: Mongol Uls
former: Outer Mongolia
Government type: parliamentary
Capital: Ulaanbaatar

Mongolia (continued)

Administrative divisions: 18 provinces (aymguud, singular - aymag) and 3 municipalities* (hotuud, singular - hot); Arhangay, Bayanhongor, Bayan-Olgiy, Bulgan, Darhan*, Dornod, Dornogovi, Dundgovi, Dzavhan, Erdenet*, Govi-Altay, Hentiy, Hovd, Hovsgol, Omnogovi, Ovorhangay, Selenge, Suhbaatar, Tov, Ulaanbaatar*, Uvs
note: there may be a new province named Gobi-Sumber; further, there may now be 21 provinces and 1 capital city instead of 18 provinces and 3 municipalities
Independence: 11 July 1921 (from China)
National holiday: Independence Day/Revolution Day, 11 July (1921)
Constitution: 12 February 1992
Legal system: blend of Russian, Chinese, Turkish, and Western systems of law that combines aspects of a parliamentary system with some aspects of a presidential system; constitution ambiguous on judicial review of legislative acts; has not accepted compulsory ICJ jurisdiction
Suffrage: 18 years of age; universal
Executive branch:
chief of state: President Natsagiyn BAGABANDI (since 20 June 1997)
head of government: Prime Minister Nambaryn ENKHBAYAR (since 26 July 2000)
cabinet: Cabinet appointed by the State Great Hural in consultation with the president
elections: president nominated by parties in the State Great Hural and elected by popular vote for a four-year term; election last held 20 May 2001 (next to be held NA May 2005); following legislative elections, the leader of the majority party or majority coalition is usually elected prime minister by the State Great Hural; election last held 2 July 2000 (next to be held NA 2004)
election results: Natsagiyn BAGABANDI reelected president; percent of vote - NA%; Nambaryn ENKHBAYAR elected prime minister by a vote in the State Great Hural of 68 to 3
Legislative branch: unicameral State Great Hural (76 seats; members elected by popular vote to serve four-year terms)
elections: last held 2 July 2000 (next to be held NA July 2004)
election results: percent of vote by party - NA%; seats by party - MPRP 72, other 4
Judicial branch: Supreme Court (serves as appeals court for people's and provincial courts, but rarely overturns verdicts of lower courts; judges are nominated by the General Council of Courts for approval by the president)
Political parties and leaders: Citizens' Will Party or CWP (also called Civil Will Party) [Sanjaasurengyn OYUN]; Democratic Party or DP [D. DORLIGAN]; Mongolian People's Revolutionary Party or MPRP [Nambaryn ENKHBAYAR]; Mongolian Democratic New Socialist Party or MDNSP [B. ERDENEBAT]; Mongolian Republican Party or MRP [B. JARGALSAIHAN]
note: the MPRP is the ruling party

Political pressure groups and leaders: NA
International organization participation: ARF (dialogue partner), AsDB, ASEAN (observer), CCC, EBRD, ESCAP, FAO, G-77, IAEA, IBRD, ICAO, ICFTU, ICRM, IDA, IFAD, IFC, IFRCS, ILO, IMF, IMO, Intelsat, Interpol, IOC, ISO, ITU, NAM, OPCW, UN, UNCTAD, UNESCO, UNIDO, UPU, WHO, WIPO, WMO, WToO, WTrO
Diplomatic representation in the US:
chief of mission: Ambassador Jalbuugiyn CHOINHOR
chancery: 2833 M Street NW, Washington, DC 20007
telephone: [1] (202) 333-7117
FAX: [1] (202) 298-9227
consulate(s) general: New York
Diplomatic representation from the US:
chief of mission: Ambassador John DINGER
embassy: inner north side of the Big Ring, just west of the Selbe Gol, Ulaanbaatar
mailing address: United States Embassy in Mongolia, P. O. Box 1021, Ulaanbaatar 13; PSC 461, Box 300, FPO AP 96521-0002
telephone: [976] (11) 329095
FAX: [976] (11) 320776
Flag description: three equal, vertical bands of red (hoist side), blue, and red; centered on the hoist-side red band in yellow is the national emblem ("soyombo" - a columnar arrangement of abstract and geometric representation for fire, sun, moon, earth, water, and the yin-yang symbol)

Economy

Economy - overview: Economic activity traditionally has been based on agriculture and breeding of livestock. Mongolia also has extensive mineral deposits: copper, coal, molybdenum, tin, tungsten, and gold account for a large part of industrial production. Soviet assistance, at its height one-third of GDP, disappeared almost overnight in 1990-91, at the time of the dismantlement of the USSR. Mongolia was driven into deep recession, which was prolonged by the Mongolian People's Revolutionary Party's (MPRP) reluctance to undertake serious economic reform. The Democratic Coalition (DC) government has embraced free-market economics, easing price controls, liberalizing domestic and international trade, and attempting to restructure the banking system and the energy sector. Major domestic privatization programs were undertaken, as well as the fostering of foreign investment through international tender of the oil distribution company, a leading cashmere company, and banks. Reform was held back by the ex-communist MPRP opposition and by the political instability brought about through four successive governments under the DC. Economic growth picked up in 1997-99 after stalling in 1996 due to a series of natural disasters and declines in world prices of copper and cashmere. In August and September 1999, the economy suffered from a temporary Russian ban on exports of oil and oil products, and Mongolia remains vulnerable in this sector. Mongolia joined the World Trade Organization (WTrO) in 1997.

The international donor community pledged over $300 million per year at the last Consultative Group Meeting, held in Ulaanbaatar in June 1999. The MPRP government, elected in July 2000, is anxious to improve the investment climate; it must also deal with a heavy burden of external debt.
GDP: purchasing power parity - $4.7 billion (2000 est.)
GDP - real growth rate: -1% (2000 est.)
GDP - per capita: purchasing power parity - $1,780 (2000 est.)
GDP - composition by sector:
agriculture: 36%
industry: 22%
services: 42% (2000 est.)
Population below poverty line: 40% (2000 est.)
Household income or consumption by percentage share:
lowest 10%: 2.9%
highest 10%: 24.5% (1995)
Inflation rate (consumer prices): 7.6% (1999)
Labor force: 1.3 million (1999)
Labor force - by occupation: primarily herding/agricultural
Unemployment rate: NA%
Budget:
revenues: $262 million
expenditures: $328 million, including capital expenditures of $NA (2000 est.)
Industries: construction materials, mining (particularly coal and copper); food and beverages, processing of animal products
Industrial production growth rate: 2.4% (2000 est.)
Electricity - production: 2.671 billion kWh (1999)
Electricity - production by source:
fossil fuel: 100%
hydro: 0%
nuclear: 0%
other: 0% (1999)
Electricity - consumption: 2.767 billion kWh (1999)
Electricity - exports: 80 million kWh (1999)
Electricity - imports: 363 million kWh (1999)
Agriculture - products: wheat, barley, potatoes, forage crops; sheep, goats, cattle, camels, horses
Exports: $454.3 million (f.o.b., 1999)
Exports - commodities: copper, livestock, animal products, cashmere, wool, hides, fluorspar, other nonferrous metals
Exports - partners: China 60%, US 20%, Russia 9%, Japan 2% (2000 est.)
Imports: $510.7 million (c.i.f., 1999)
Imports - commodities: machinery and equipment, fuels, food products, industrial consumer goods, chemicals, building materials, sugar, tea
Imports - partners: Russia 33%, China 21%, Japan 12%, South Korea 10%, US 4% (1999)
Debt - external: $760 million (2000 est.)
Economic aid - recipient: $200 million (1998 est.)
Currency: togrog/tugrik (MNT)
Currency code: MNT

Mongolia (continued)

Exchange rates: togrogs/tugriks per US dollar - 1,097.00 (December 2000), 1,076.67 (2000), 1,072.37 (1999), 840.83 (1998), 789.99 (1997), 548.40 (1996)
Fiscal year: calendar year

Communications

Telephones - main lines in use: 104,100 (1999)
Telephones - mobile cellular: 110,000 (2001)
Telephone system:
general assessment: very low density: about 3.5 telephones for each thousand persons
domestic: NA
international: satellite earth station - 1 Intersputnik (Indian Ocean Region)
Radio broadcast stations: AM 7, FM 9, shortwave 4 (2001)
Radios: 155,900 (1999)
Television broadcast stations: 4 (plus 18 provincial repeaters and many low powered repeaters) (1999)
Televisions: 168,800 (1999)
Internet country code: .mn
Internet Service Providers (ISPs): 5 (2001)
Internet users: between 10,000 and 15,000 (2001)

Transportation

Railways: 1,815 km
broad gauge: 1,815 km 1.524-m gauge (2001)
Highways:
total: 3,387 km
paved: 1,563 km
unpaved: 1,824 km
note: there are also 45,862 km of rural roads that consist of rough, unimproved, cross-country tracks (2000)
Waterways: 400 km (1999)
Ports and harbors: none
Airports: 34 (2000 est.)
Airports - with paved runways:
total: 8
2,438 to 3,047 m: 7
under 914 m: 1 (2000 est.)
Airports - with unpaved runways:
total: 26
over 3,047 m: 3
2,438 to 3,047 m: 5
1,524 to 2,437 m: 10
914 to 1,523 m: 3
under 914 m: 5 (2000 est.)

Military

Military branches: Mongolian Armed Forces (includes General Purpose Forces, Air and Air Defense Forces, Civil Defense Troops); note - Border Troops are under Ministry of Justice and Home Affairs in peacetime
Military manpower - military age: 18 years of age
Military manpower - availability:
males age 15-49: 748,779 (2001 est.)
Military manpower - fit for military service:
males age 15-49: 486,491 (2001 est.)
Military manpower - reaching military age annually:
males: 30,230 (2001 est.)
Military expenditures - dollar figure: $25.5 million (FY01)
Military expenditures - percent of GDP: 2.3% (FY01)

Transnational Issues

Disputes - international: none

Montserrat
(overseas territory of the UK)

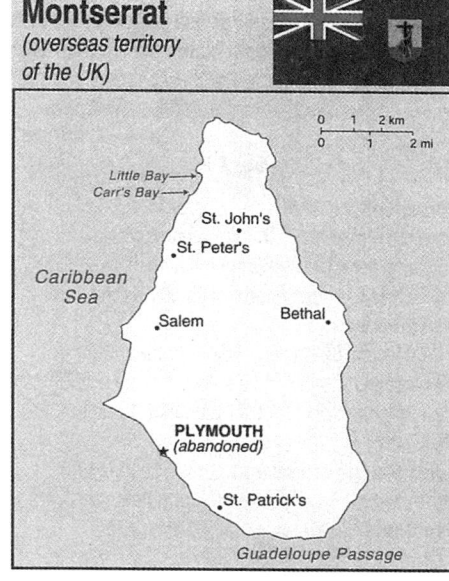

Introduction

Background: Much of this island has been devastated and two-thirds of the population has fled abroad due to the eruption of the Soufriere Hills volcano that began on 18 July 1995.

Geography

Location: Caribbean, island in the Caribbean Sea, southeast of Puerto Rico
Geographic coordinates: 16 45 N, 62 12 W
Map references: Central America and the Caribbean
Area:
total: 100 sq km
land: 100 sq km
water: 0 sq km
Area - comparative: about 0.6 times the size of Washington, DC
Land boundaries: 0 km
Coastline: 40 km
Maritime claims:
exclusive fishing zone: 200 NM
territorial sea: 3 NM
Climate: tropical; little daily or seasonal temperature variation
Terrain: volcanic islands, mostly mountainous, with small coastal lowland
Elevation extremes:
lowest point: Caribbean Sea 0 m
highest point: Chances Peak (in the Soufriere Hills) 914 m
Natural resources: NEGL
Land use:
arable land: 20%
permanent crops: 0%
permanent pastures: 10%
forests and woodland: 40%
other: 30% (1993 est.)
Irrigated land: NA sq km

Montserrat (continued)

Natural hazards: severe hurricanes (June to November); volcanic eruptions (full-scale eruptions of the Soufriere Hills volcano occurred during 1996-97)
Environment - current issues: land erosion occurs on slopes that have been cleared for cultivation

People

Population: 7,574
note: an estimated 8,000 refugees left the island following the resumption of volcanic activity in July 1995; some have returned (July 2001 est.)
Age structure:
0-14 years: 23.83% (male 907; female 898)
15-64 years: 64.66% (male 2,341; female 2,556)
65 years and over: 11.51% (male 464; female 408) (2001 est.)
Population growth rate: 13.39% (2001 est.)
Birth rate: 17.43 births/1,000 population (2001 est.)
Death rate: 7.53 deaths/1,000 population (2001 est.)
Net migration rate: 123.98 migrant(s)/1,000 population (2001 est.)
Sex ratio:
at birth: 1.05 male(s)/female
under 15 years: 1.01 male(s)/female
15-64 years: 0.92 male(s)/female
65 years and over: 1.14 male(s)/female
total population: 0.96 male(s)/female (2001 est.)
Infant mortality rate: 8.19 deaths/1,000 live births (2001 est.)
Life expectancy at birth:
total population: 78.03 years
male: 75.95 years
female: 80.22 years (2001 est.)
Total fertility rate: 1.82 children born/woman (2001 est.)
HIV/AIDS - adult prevalence rate: NA%
HIV/AIDS - people living with HIV/AIDS: NA
HIV/AIDS - deaths: NA
Nationality:
noun: Montserratian(s)
adjective: Montserratian
Ethnic groups: black, white
Religions: Anglican, Methodist, Roman Catholic, Pentecostal, Seventh-Day Adventist, other Christian denominations
Languages: English
Literacy:
definition: age 15 and over has ever attended school
total population: 97%
male: 97%
female: 97% (1970 est.)

Government

Country name:
conventional long form: none
conventional short form: Montserrat
Dependency status: overseas territory of the UK
Government type: NA
Capital: Plymouth (abandoned in 1997 due to volcanic activity; interim government buildings have been built at Brades, in the Carr's Bay/Little Bay vicinity at the northwest end of Montserrat)
Administrative divisions: 3 parishes; Saint Anthony, Saint Georges, Saint Peter's
Independence: none (overseas territory of the UK)
National holiday: Birthday of Queen ELIZABETH II, second Saturday in June (1926)
Constitution: present constitution came into force 19 December 1989
Legal system: English common law and statutory law
Suffrage: 18 years of age; universal
Executive branch:
chief of state: Queen ELIZABETH II (since 6 February 1952), represented by Governor Anthony John ABBOTT (since NA September 1997)
head of government: Chief Minister David BRANDT (since 22 August 1997)
cabinet: Executive Council consists of the governor, the chief minister, three other ministers, the attorney general, and the finance secretary
elections: the monarch is hereditary; governor appointed by the monarch; following legislative elections, the leader of the majority party usually becomes chief minister; note - as a result of the last election, a coalition party was formed between NPP, NDP, and one of the independent candidates
Legislative branch: unicameral Legislative Council (11 seats, 7 popularly elected; members serve five-year terms)
elections: last held 11 November 1996 (next to be held by NA November 2001)
election results: percent of vote by party - NA%; seats by party - PPA 2, MNR 2, NPP 1, independent 2
Judicial branch: Eastern Caribbean Supreme Court (based in Saint Lucia, one judge of the Supreme Court is a resident of the islands and presides over the High Court)
Political parties and leaders: Movement for National Reconstruction or MNR [Percival Austin BRAMBLE]; National Development Party or NDP [leader NA]; National Progressive Party or NPP [Reuben T. MEADE]; People's Progressive Alliance or PPA [John A. OSBORNE]
Political pressure groups and leaders: NA
International organization participation: Caricom, CDB, ECLAC (associate), ICFTU, Interpol (subbureau), OECS, WCL
Diplomatic representation in the US: none (overseas territory of the UK)
Diplomatic representation from the US: none (overseas territory of the UK)
Flag description: blue, with the flag of the UK in the upper hoist-side quadrant and the Montserratian coat of arms centered in the outer half of the flag; the coat of arms features a woman standing beside a yellow harp with her arm around a black cross

Economy

Economy - overview: Severe volcanic activity, which began in July 1995, has put a damper on this small, open economy. A catastrophic eruption in June 1997 closed the airports and seaports, causing further economic and social dislocation. Two-thirds of the 12,000 inhabitants fled the island. Some began to return in 1998, but lack of housing limited the number. The agriculture sector continued to be affected by the lack of suitable land for farming and the destruction of crops. Prospects for the economy depend largely on developments in relation to the volcano and on public sector construction activity. The UK committed to a three year $125 million aid program in 1999 to help reconstruct the economy.
GDP: purchasing power parity - $31 million (1999 est.)
GDP - real growth rate: -1.5% (1999 est.)
GDP - per capita: purchasing power parity - $5,000 (1999 est.)
GDP - composition by sector:
agriculture: 5.4%
industry: 13.6%
services: 81% (1996 est.)
Population below poverty line: NA%
Household income or consumption by percentage share:
lowest 10%: NA%
highest 10%: NA%
Inflation rate (consumer prices): 5% (1998)
Labor force: 4,521 (1992); note - recently lowered by flight of people from volcanic activity
Labor force - by occupation: agriculture NA%, industry NA%, services NA%
Unemployment rate: 20% (1996 est.)
Budget:
revenues: $31.4 million
expenditures: $31.6 million, including capital expenditures of $8.4 million (1997 est.)
Industries: tourism, rum, textiles, electronic appliances
Industrial production growth rate: NA%
Electricity - production: 10 million kWh (1999)
Electricity - production by source:
fossil fuel: 100%
hydro: 0%
nuclear: 0%
other: 0% (1999)
Electricity - consumption: 9.3 million kWh (1999)
Electricity - exports: 0 kWh (1999)
Electricity - imports: 0 kWh (1999)
Agriculture - products: cabbages, carrots, cucumbers, tomatoes, onions, peppers; livestock products
Exports: $1.5 million (1998)
Exports - commodities: electronic components, plastic bags, apparel, hot peppers, live plants, cattle
Exports - partners: US, Antigua and Barbuda (1993)
Imports: $26 million (1998)

Montserrat (continued)

Imports - commodities: machinery and transportation equipment, foodstuffs, manufactured goods, fuels, lubricants, and related materials
Imports - partners: US, UK, Trinidad and Tobago, Japan, Canada (1993)
Debt - external: $8.9 million (1997)
Economic aid - recipient: $9.8 million (1995); note - about $100 million (1996-98) in reconstruction aid from the UK; Country Policy Plan (1999) is a three-year program for spending $122.8 million in British budgetary assistance
Currency: East Caribbean dollar (XCD)
Currency code: XCD
Exchange rates: East Caribbean dollars per US dollar - 2.7000 (fixed rate since 1976)
Fiscal year: 1 April - 31 March

Communications

Telephones - main lines in use: 4,000 (1997)
Telephones - mobile cellular: 70 (1994)
Telephone system:
general assessment: NA
domestic: NA
international: NA
Radio broadcast stations: AM 1, FM 2, shortwave 0 (1998)
Radios: 7,000 (1997)
Television broadcast stations: 1 (1997)
Televisions: 3,000 (1997)
Internet country code: .ms
Internet Service Providers (ISPs): 17 (2000)
Internet users: NA

Transportation

Railways: 0 km
Highways:
total: 269 km
paved: 203 km
unpaved: 66 km (1995)
Waterways: none
Ports and harbors: Plymouth (abandoned), Little Bay (anchorages and ferry landing), Carr's Bay
Merchant marine: none (2000 est.)
Airports: 1 (2000 est.)
Airports - with paved runways:
total: 1
under 914 m: 1 (2000 est.)

Military

Military branches: Police Force
Military - note: defense is the responsibility of the UK

Transnational Issues

Disputes - international: none
Illicit drugs: transshipment point for South American narcotics destined for the US and Europe

Morocco

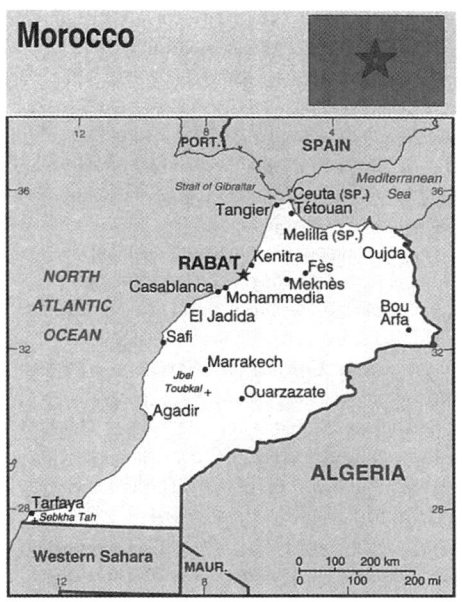

Introduction

Background: Morocco's long struggle for independence from France ended in 1956. The internationalized city of Tangier was turned over to the new country that same year. Morocco virtually annexed Western Sahara during the late 1970s, but final resolution on the status of the territory remains unresolved. Gradual political reforms in the 1990s resulted in the establishment of a bicameral legislature in 1997.

Geography

Location: Northern Africa, bordering the North Atlantic Ocean and the Mediterranean Sea, between Algeria and Western Sahara
Geographic coordinates: 32 00 N, 5 00 W
Map references: Africa
Area:
total: 446,550 sq km
land: 446,300 sq km
water: 250 sq km
Area - comparative: slightly larger than California
Land boundaries:
total: 2,017.9 km
border countries: Algeria 1,559 km, Western Sahara 443 km, Spain (Ceuta) 6.3 km, Spain (Melilla) 9.6 km
Coastline: 1,835 km
Maritime claims:
contiguous zone: 24 NM
continental shelf: 200-m depth or to the depth of exploitation
exclusive economic zone: 200 NM
territorial sea: 12 NM
Climate: Mediterranean, becoming more extreme in the interior
Terrain: northern coast and interior are mountainous with large areas of bordering plateaus, intermontane valleys, and rich coastal plains
Elevation extremes:
lowest point: Sebkha Tah -55 m
highest point: Jbel Toubkal 4,165 m
Natural resources: phosphates, iron ore, manganese, lead, zinc, fish, salt
Land use:
arable land: 21%
permanent crops: 1%
permanent pastures: 47%
forests and woodland: 20%
other: 11% (1993 est.)
Irrigated land: 12,580 sq km (1993 est.)
Natural hazards: northern mountains geologically unstable and subject to earthquakes; periodic droughts
Environment - current issues: land degradation/desertification (soil erosion resulting from farming of marginal areas, overgrazing, destruction of vegetation); water supplies contaminated by raw sewage; siltation of reservoirs; oil pollution of coastal waters
Environment - international agreements:
party to: Biodiversity, Climate Change, Desertification, Endangered Species, Hazardous Wastes, Marine Dumping, Nuclear Test Ban, Ozone Layer Protection, Ship Pollution, Wetlands, Whaling
signed, but not ratified: Environmental Modification, Law of the Sea
Geography - note: strategic location along Strait of Gibraltar

People

Population: 30,645,305 (July 2001 est.)
Age structure:
0-14 years: 34.39% (male 5,368,784; female 5,170,891)
15-64 years: 60.93% (male 9,270,095; female 9,402,561)
65 years and over: 4.68% (male 646,567; female 786,407) (2001 est.)
Population growth rate: 1.71% (2001 est.)
Birth rate: 24.16 births/1,000 population (2001 est.)
Death rate: 5.94 deaths/1,000 population (2001 est.)
Net migration rate: -1.15 migrant(s)/1,000 population (2001 est.)
Sex ratio:
at birth: 1.05 male(s)/female
under 15 years: 1.04 male(s)/female
15-64 years: 0.99 male(s)/female
65 years and over: 0.82 male(s)/female
total population: 1 male(s)/female (2001 est.)
Infant mortality rate: 48.11 deaths/1,000 live births (2001 est.)
Life expectancy at birth:
total population: 69.43 years
male: 67.2 years
female: 71.76 years (2001 est.)
Total fertility rate: 3.05 children born/woman (2001 est.)
HIV/AIDS - adult prevalence rate: 0.03% (1999 est.)
HIV/AIDS - people living with HIV/AIDS: NA

Morocco (continued)

HIV/AIDS - deaths: NA
Nationality:
noun: Moroccan(s)
adjective: Moroccan
Ethnic groups: Arab-Berber 99.1%, other 0.7%, Jewish 0.2%
Religions: Muslim 98.7%, Christian 1.1%, Jewish 0.2%
Languages: Arabic (official), Berber dialects, French often the language of business, government, and diplomacy
Literacy:
definition: age 15 and over can read and write
total population: 43.7%
male: 56.6%
female: 31% (1995 est.)

Government

Country name:
conventional long form: Kingdom of Morocco
conventional short form: Morocco
local long form: Al Mamlakah al Maghribiyah
local short form: Al Maghrib
Government type: constitutional monarchy
Capital: Rabat
Administrative divisions: 37 provinces and 2 wilayas*; Agadir, Al Hoceima, Azilal, Beni Mellal, Ben Slimane, Boulemane, Casablanca*, Chaouen, El Jadida, El Kelaa des Srarhna, Er Rachidia, Essaouira, Fes, Figuig, Guelmim, Ifrane, Kenitra, Khemisset, Khenifra, Khouribga, Laayoune, Larache, Marrakech, Meknes, Nador, Ouarzazate, Oujda, Rabat-Sale*, Safi, Settat, Sidi Kacem, Tanger, Tan-Tan, Taounate, Taroudannt, Tata, Taza, Tetouan, Tiznit
note: three additional provinces of Ad Dakhla (Oued Eddahab), Boujdour, and Es Smara as well as parts of Tan-Tan and Laayoune fall within Moroccan-claimed Western Sahara; decentralization/regionalization law passed by the legislature in March 1997 creating many new provinces/regions; specific details and scope of the reorganization not yet available
Independence: 2 March 1956 (from France)
National holiday: Throne Day (accession of King MOHAMED VI to the throne), 30 July (1999)
Constitution: 10 March 1972, revised 4 September 1992, amended (to create bicameral legislature) September 1996
Legal system: based on Islamic law and French and Spanish civil law system; judicial review of legislative acts in Constitutional Chamber of Supreme Court
Suffrage: 21 years of age; universal
Executive branch:
chief of state: King MOHAMED VI (since 23 July 1999)
head of government: Prime Minister Abderrahmane YOUSSOUFI (since 14 March 1998)
cabinet: Council of Ministers appointed by the monarch
elections: none; the monarch is hereditary; prime minister appointed by the monarch following legislative elections
Legislative branch: bicameral Parliament consists of an upper house or Chamber of Counselors (270 seats; members elected indirectly by local councils, professional organizations, and labor syndicates for nine-year terms; one-third of the members are renewed every three years) and a lower house or Chamber of Representatives (325 seats; members elected by popular vote for five-year terms)
elections: Chamber of Counselors - last held 15 September 2000 (next to be held NA 2002); Chamber of Representatives - last held 14 November 1997 (next to be held NA November 2002)
election results: Chamber of Counselors - percent of vote by party - NA%; seats by party - NA; Chamber of Representatives - percent of vote by party - NA%; seats by party - USFP 57, UC 50, RNI 46, MP 40, MDS 32, IP 32, MNP 19, PND 10, MPCD 9, PPS 9, FFD 9, PSD 5, OADP 4, PA 2, PDI 1
note: CDT, UTM, UGTM, UNMT are all labor unions listed under Political pressure groups and leaders; see explanation in the description of Parliament
Judicial branch: Supreme Court (judges are appointed on the recommendation of the Supreme Council of the Judiciary, presided over by the monarch)
Political parties and leaders: Action Party or PA [Muhammad IDRISS]; Constitutional Union or UC [leader NA]; Democratic Forces Front or FFD [Thami KHIARI]; Democratic Socialist Party or PSD [Issa OUARDIGHI]; Democratic Party for Independence or PDI [Thami EL-OUAZZANI, Said BOUACHRINE]; Istiqlal Party or IP [Abbas El-FASSI]; Labor Party or UT [leader NA]; National Democratic Party or PND [Mohamed Arsalane EL-JADIDI]; National Popular Movement or MNP [Mahjoubi AHERDANE]; National Rally of Independents or RNI [Ahmed OSMAN]; Organization of Democratic and Popular Action or OADP [Mohamed BEN SAID ait Idder]; Party of Progress and Socialism or PPS [Moulay Ismail ALAOUI]; Popular Constitutional and Democratic Movement or MPCD (has become Party of Justice and Development or PJD) [Dr. Abdelkarim KHATIB]; Popular Movement or MP [Mohamed LAENSER]; Social Democratic Movement or MDS [Mahmoud ARCHANE]; Socialist Union of Popular Forces or USFP [Abd ar-Rahman EL-YOUSSOUFI]
Political pressure groups and leaders: Association of Popular Trade Unions or ADP [leader NA]; Democratic Confederation of Labor or CDT [Noubir AMAOUI]; Democratic National Trade Union or USND [leader NA]; Democratic Trade Union or SD [leader NA]; General Union of Moroccan Workers or UGTM [Abderrazzak AFILAL]; Labor Union Commissions or CS [leader NA]; Moroccan National Workers Union or UNMT [leader NA]; Moroccan Union of Workers or UTM [Mahjoub BENSEDIQ]; Party of Shura and Istiqla [Abdelwaheb MAASH]
International organization participation: ABEDA, ACCT (associate), AfDB, AFESD, AL, AMF, AMU, CCC, EBRD, ECA, FAO, G-77, IAEA, IBRD, ICAO, ICC, ICFTU, ICRM, IDA, IDB, IFAD, IFC, IFRCS, IHO, ILO, IMF, IMO, Intelsat, Interpol, IOC, IOM, ISO, ITU, MONUC, NAM, OAS (observer), OIC, OPCW, OSCE (partner), UN, UNCTAD, UNESCO, UNHCR, UNIDO, UPU, WCL, WHO, WIPO, WMO, WToO, WTrO
Diplomatic representation in the US:
chief of mission: Ambassador Abdullah MAAROUFI
chancery: 1601 21st Street NW, Washington, DC 20009
telephone: [1] (202) 462-7979 through 7982
FAX: [1] (202) 265-0161
consulate(s) general: New York
Diplomatic representation from the US:
chief of mission: Ambassador Edward M. GABRIEL
embassy: 2 Avenue de Mohamed El Fassi, Rabat
mailing address: PSC 74, Box 3, APO AE 90718
telephone: [212] (37) 76 22 65
FAX: [212] (37) 76 56 61
consulate(s) general: Casablanca
Flag description: red with a green pentacle (five-pointed, linear star) known as Solomon's seal in the center of the flag; green is the traditional color of Islam

Economy

Economy - overview: Morocco faces the problems typical of developing countries - restraining government spending, reducing constraints on private activity and foreign trade, and achieving sustainable economic growth. Following structural adjustment programs supported by the IMF, World Bank, and the Paris Club, the dirham is now fully convertible for current account transactions, and reforms of the financial sector have been implemented. Drought conditions depressed activity in the key agricultural sector and contributed to a stagnant economy in 1999 and 2000. During that time, however, Morocco reported large foreign exchange inflows from the sale of a mobile telephone license and partial privatization of the state-owned telecommunications company. Favorable rainfalls have led Morocco to predict a growth of 1% for 2001. Formidable long-term challenges include: servicing the external debt; preparing the economy for freer trade with the EU; and improving education and attracting foreign investment to boost living standards and job prospects for Morocco's youthful population.
GDP: purchasing power parity - $105 billion (2000 est.)
GDP - real growth rate: 0.8% (2000 est.)
GDP - per capita: purchasing power parity - $3,500 (2000 est.)
GDP - composition by sector:
agriculture: 15%
industry: 33%
services: 52% (1999 est.)
Population below poverty line: 19% (1999 est.)
Household income or consumption by percentage share:
lowest 10%: 2.6%
highest 10%: 30.9% (1998-99)
Inflation rate (consumer prices): 2% (2000 est.)
Labor force: 11 million (1997 est.)

Morocco (continued)

Labor force - by occupation: agriculture 50%, services 35%, industry 15% (1999 est.)
Unemployment rate: 23% (1999 est.)
Budget:
revenues: $9.6 billion
expenditures: $8.6 billion, including capital expenditures of $2.1 billion (2001 est.)
Industries: phosphate rock mining and processing, food processing, leather goods, textiles, construction, tourism
Industrial production growth rate: 0.5% (1999 est.)
Electricity - production: 13.695 billion kWh (1999)
Electricity - production by source:
fossil fuel: 89.19%
hydro: 10.81%
nuclear: 0%
other: 0% (1999)
Electricity - consumption: 13.441 billion kWh (1999)
Electricity - exports: 0 kWh (1999)
Electricity - imports: 705 million kWh (1999)
Agriculture - products: barley, wheat, citrus, wine, vegetables, olives; livestock
Exports: $7.6 billion (f.o.b., 2000 est.)
Exports - commodities: phosphates and fertilizers, food and beverages, minerals
Exports - partners: France 35%, Spain 9%, UK 8%, Germany 7%, US 5% (1999)
Imports: $12.2 billion (f.o.b., 1999 est.)
Imports - commodities: semiprocessed goods, machinery and equipment, food and beverages, consumer goods, fuel
Imports - partners: France 32%, Spain 12%, Italy 7%, Germany 6%, UK 6% (1999)
Debt - external: $18.4 billion (2000 est.)
Economic aid - recipient: $565.6 million (1995)
Currency: Moroccan dirham (MAD)
Currency code: MAD
Exchange rates: Moroccan dirhams per US dollar - 10.590 (January 2001), 10.626 (2000), 9.804 (1999), 9.604 (1998), 9.527 (1997), 8.716 (1996)
Fiscal year: calendar year

Communications

Telephones - main lines in use: 1.391 million (1998)
Telephones - mobile cellular: 116,645 (1998)
Telephone system:
general assessment: modern system with all important capabilities; however density is low with only 4.6 main lines available for each 100 persons
domestic: good system composed of open-wire lines, cables, and microwave radio relay links; Internet available but expensive; principal switching centers are Casablanca and Rabat; national network nearly 100% digital using fiber-optic links; improved rural service employs microwave radio relay
international: 7 submarine cables; satellite earth stations - 2 Intelsat (Atlantic Ocean) and 1 Arabsat; microwave radio relay to Gibraltar, Spain, and Western Sahara; coaxial cable and microwave radio relay to Algeria; participant in Medarabtel; fiber-optic cable link from Agadir to Algeria and Tunisia (1998)
Radio broadcast stations: AM 27, FM 25, shortwave 6 (1998)
Radios: 6.64 million (1997)
Television broadcast stations: 35 (plus 66 repeaters) (1995)
Televisions: 3.1 million (1997)
Internet country code: .ma
Internet Service Providers (ISPs): 8 (2000)
Internet users: 120,000 (1999)

Transportation

Railways:
total: 1,907 km
standard gauge: 1,907 km 1.435-m gauge (1,003 km electrified; 540 km double track)
Highways:
total: 57,847 km
paved: 30,254 km (including 327 km of expressways)
unpaved: 27,593 km (1998)
Waterways: none
Pipelines: crude oil 362 km; petroleum products 491 km (abandoned); natural gas 241 km
Ports and harbors: Agadir, El Jadida, Casablanca, El Jorf Lasfar, Kenitra, Mohammedia, Nador, Rabat, Safi, Tangier; also Spanish-controlled Ceuta and Melilla
Merchant marine:
total: 41 ships (1,000 GRT or over) totaling 223,052 GRT/272,786 DWT
ships by type: cargo 9, chemical tanker 6, container 5, petroleum tanker 3, refrigerated cargo 9, roll on/roll off 8, short-sea passenger 1 (2000 est.)
Airports: 69 (2000 est.)
Airports - with paved runways:
total: 26
over 3,047 m: 10
2,438 to 3,047 m: 5
1,524 to 2,437 m: 9
914 to 1,523 m: 1
under 914 m: 1 (2000 est.)
Airports - with unpaved runways:
total: 43
2,438 to 3,047 m: 1
1,524 to 2,437 m: 11
914 to 1,523 m: 20
under 914 m: 11 (2000 est.)
Heliports: 1 (2000 est.)

Military

Military branches: Royal Armed Forces (includes Army, Navy, Air Force), Gendarmerie, Auxiliary Forces
Military manpower - military age: 18 years of age
Military manpower - availability:
males age 15-49: 8,182,073 (2001 est.)
Military manpower - fit for military service:
males age 15-49: 5,160,374 (2001 est.)
Military manpower - reaching military age annually:
males: 348,380 (2001 est.)
Military expenditures - dollar figure: $1.4 billion (FY99/00)
Military expenditures - percent of GDP: 4% (FY99/00)

Transnational Issues

Disputes - international: claims and administers Western Sahara, but sovereignty is unresolved and the UN is attempting to hold a referendum on the issue; the UN-administered cease-fire has been in effect since September 1991; Spain controls five places of sovereignty (plazas de soberania) on and off the coast of Morocco - the coastal enclaves of Ceuta and Melilla which Morocco contests, as well as the islands of Penon de Alhucemas, Penon de Velez de la Gomera, and Islas Chafarinas
Illicit drugs: illicit producer of hashish; trafficking on the increase for both domestic and international drug markets; shipments of hashish mostly directed to Western Europe; transit point for cocaine from South America destined for Western Europe

Mozambique

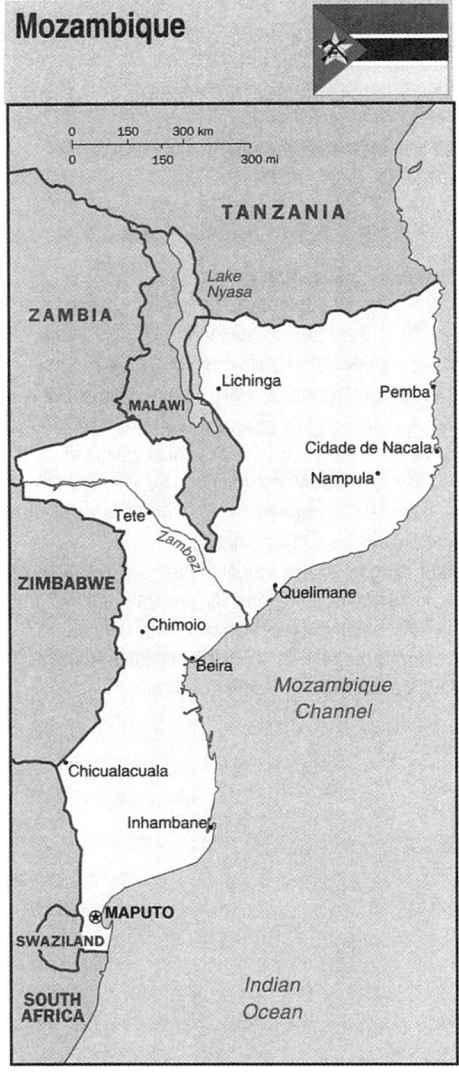

Introduction

Background: Almost five centuries as a Portuguese colony came to a close with independence in 1975. Large-scale emigration by whites, economic dependence on South Africa, a severe drought, and a prolonged civil war hindered the country's development. The ruling party formally abandoned Marxism in 1989, and a new constitution the following year provided for multiparty elections and a free market economy. A UN-negotiated peace agreement with rebel forces ended the fighting in 1992.

Geography

Location: Southern Africa, bordering the Mozambique Channel, between South Africa and Tanzania
Geographic coordinates: 18 15 S, 35 00 E
Map references: Africa
Area:
total: 801,590 sq km
land: 784,090 sq km
water: 17,500 sq km
Area - comparative: slightly less than twice the size of California
Land boundaries:
total: 4,571 km
border countries: Malawi 1,569 km, South Africa 491 km, Swaziland 105 km, Tanzania 756 km, Zambia 419 km, Zimbabwe 1,231 km
Coastline: 2,470 km
Maritime claims:
exclusive economic zone: 200 NM
territorial sea: 12 NM
Climate: tropical to subtropical
Terrain: mostly coastal lowlands, uplands in center, high plateaus in northwest, mountains in west
Elevation extremes:
lowest point: Indian Ocean 0 m
highest point: Monte Binga 2,436 m
Natural resources: coal, titanium, natural gas, hydropower, tantalum, graphite
Land use:
arable land: 4%
permanent crops: 0%
permanent pastures: 56%
forests and woodland: 18%
other: 22% (1993 est.)
Irrigated land: 1,200 sq km (2000 est.)
Natural hazards: severe droughts and floods occur in central and southern provinces; devastating cyclones
Environment - current issues: a long civil war and recurrent drought in the hinterlands have resulted in increased migration of the population to urban and coastal areas with adverse environmental consequences; desertification; pollution of surface and coastal waters
Environment - international agreements:
party to: Biodiversity, Climate Change, Desertification, Endangered Species, Hazardous Wastes, Law of the Sea, Marine Dumping, Ozone Layer Protection, Ship Pollution
signed, but not ratified: none of the selected agreements

People

Population: 19,371,057
note: estimates for this country explicitly take into account the effects of excess mortality due to AIDS; this can result in lower life expectancy, higher infant mortality and death rates, lower population and growth rates, and changes in the distribution of population by age and sex than would otherwise be expected; the 1997 Mozambican census reported a population of 16,099,246 (July 2001 est.)
Age structure:
0-14 years: 42.72% (male 4,124,093; female 4,152,135)
15-64 years: 54.53% (male 5,222,477; female 5,339,615)
65 years and over: 2.75% (male 221,678; female 311,059) (2001 est.)
Population growth rate: 1.3% (2001 est.)
Birth rate: 37.2 births/1,000 population (2001 est.)
Death rate: 24.21 deaths/1,000 population (2001 est.)
Net migration rate: 0 migrant(s)/1,000 population (2001 est.)
Sex ratio:
at birth: 1.03 male(s)/female
under 15 years: 0.99 male(s)/female
15-64 years: 0.98 male(s)/female
65 years and over: 0.71 male(s)/female
total population: 0.98 male(s)/female (2001 est.)
Infant mortality rate: 139.2 deaths/1,000 live births (2001 est.)
Life expectancy at birth:
total population: 36.45 years
male: 37.25 years
female: 35.62 years (2001 est.)
Total fertility rate: 4.82 children born/woman (2001 est.)
HIV/AIDS - adult prevalence rate: 13.22% (1999 est.)
HIV/AIDS - people living with HIV/AIDS: 1.2 million (1999 est.)
HIV/AIDS - deaths: 98,000 (1999 est.)
Nationality:
noun: Mozambican(s)
adjective: Mozambican
Ethnic groups: indigenous tribal groups 99.66% (Shangaan, Chokwe, Manyika, Sena, Makua, and others), Europeans 0.06%, Euro-Africans 0.2%, Indians 0.08%
Religions: indigenous beliefs 50%, Christian 30%, Muslim 20%
Languages: Portuguese (official), indigenous dialects
Literacy:
definition: age 15 and over can read and write
total population: 42.3%
male: 58.4%
female: 27% (1998 est.)

Government

Country name:
conventional long form: Republic of Mozambique
conventional short form: Mozambique
local long form: Republica de Mocambique
local short form: Mocambique
former: Portuguese East Africa
Government type: republic
Capital: Maputo
Administrative divisions: 10 provinces (provincias, singular - provincia); Cabo Delgado, Gaza, Inhambane, Manica, Maputo, Nampula, Niassa, Sofala, Tete, Zambezia
Independence: 25 June 1975 (from Portugal)
National holiday: Independence Day, 25 June (1975)
Constitution: 30 November 1990
Legal system: based on Portuguese civil law system and customary law
Suffrage: 18 years of age; universal
Executive branch:
chief of state: President Joaquim Alberto CHISSANO (since 6 November 1986); note - before being popularly elected, CHISSANO was elected

Mozambique (continued)

president by Frelimo's Central Committee 4 November 1986 (reelected by the Committee 30 July 1989)
head of government: Prime Minister Pascoal MOCUMBI (since NA December 1994)
cabinet: Cabinet
elections: president elected by popular vote for a five-year term; election last held 3-5 December 1999 (next to be held NA 2004); prime minister appointed by the president
election results: Joaquim Alberto CHISSANO reelected president; percent of vote - Joaquim Alberto CHISSANO 52.29%, Afonso DHLAKAMA 47.71%
Legislative branch: unicameral Assembly of the Republic or Assembleia da Republica (250 seats; members are directly elected by popular vote on a secret ballot to serve five-year terms)
elections: last held 3-5 December 1999 (next to be held NA 2004)
election results: percent of vote by party - Frelimo 48.54%, Renamo-UE 38.81%; seats by party - Frelimo 133, Renamo-UE 117
note: Renamo-UE ran as a multiparty coalition; none of the other opposition parties received the 5% required to win parliamentary seats
Judicial branch: Supreme Court (the court of final appeal; some of its professional judges are appointed by the president and some are elected by the Assembly); other courts include an Administrative Court, customs courts, maritime courts, courts marshal, labor courts
note: although the constitution provides for the creation of a separate Constitutional Court, one has never been established; in its absence the Supreme Court reviews constitutional cases
Political parties and leaders: Front for the Liberation of Mozambique (Frente de Liberatacao de Mocambique) or Frelimo [Joaquim Alberto CHISSANO, chairman]; Mozambique National Resistance - Electoral Union (Resistencia Nacional Mocambicana - Uniao Eleitoral) or Renamo-UE [Afonso DHLAKAMA, president]
Political pressure groups and leaders: NA
International organization participation: ACP, AfDB, C, CCC, ECA, FAO, G-77, IBRD, ICAO, ICFTU, ICRM, IDA, IDB, IFAD, IFC, IFRCS, IHO, ILO, IMF, IMO, Inmarsat, Intelsat, Interpol, IOC, IOM (observer), ISO (correspondent), ITU, NAM, OAU, OIC, OPCW, SADC, UN, UNCTAD, UNESCO, UNHCR, UNIDO, UNTAET, UPU, WFTU, WHO, WIPO, WMO, WToO, WTrO
Diplomatic representation in the US:
chief of mission: Ambassador Marcos Geraldo NAMASHULUA
chancery: Suite 570, 1990 M Street NW, Washington, DC 20036
telephone: [1] (202) 293-7146
FAX: [1] (202) 835-0245
Diplomatic representation from the US:
chief of mission: Ambassador Sharon P. WILKINSON
embassy: Avenida Kenneth Kuanda 193, Maputo
mailing address: P. O. Box 783, Maputo
telephone: [258] (1) 492797
FAX: [258] (1) 490114
Flag description: three equal horizontal bands of green (top), black, and yellow with a red isosceles triangle based on the hoist side; the black band is edged in white; centered in the triangle is a yellow five-pointed star bearing a crossed rifle and hoe in black superimposed on an open white book

Economy

Economy - overview: Before the peace accord of October 1992, Mozambique's economy was devastated by a protracted civil war and socialist mismanagement. In 1994, it ranked as one of the poorest countries in the world. Since then, Mozambique has undertaken a series of economic reforms. Almost all aspects of the economy have been liberalized to some extent. More than 900 state enterprises have been privatized. A value-added tax, introduced in 1999, launched the government's comprehensive tax reform program. Pending are much needed commercial code reform and greater private sector involvement in the transportation, telecommunications, and energy sectors. Since 1996, inflation has been low and foreign exchange rates relatively stable. Albeit from a small base, Mozambique's economy grew at an annual 10% rate in 1997-99, one of the highest growth rates in the world. Growth slowed and inflation rose in 2000 due to devastating flooding in the early part of the year. Both indicators should recover in 2001. The country depends on foreign assistance to balance the budget and to pay for a trade imbalance in which imports greatly outnumber exports. The trade situation should improve in the medium term, however, as trade and transportation links to South Africa and the rest of the region have been improved and sizeable foreign investments are beginning to materialize. Among these investments are metal production (aluminum, steel), natural gas, power generation, agriculture, fishing, timber, and transportation services. Mozambique has received a formal cancellation of a large portion of its external debt through an IMF initiative and is scheduled to receive additional relief.
GDP: purchasing power parity - $19.1 billion (2000 est.)
GDP - real growth rate: 3.8% (2000 est.)
GDP - per capita: purchasing power parity - $1,000 (2000 est.)
GDP - composition by sector:
agriculture: 44%
industry: 19%
services: 37% (1999 est.)
Population below poverty line: 70% (2000 est.)
Household income or consumption by percentage share:
lowest 10%: 2.5%
highest 10%: 31.7% (1996-97)
Inflation rate (consumer prices): 11.4% (2000 est.)
Labor force: 7.4 million (1997 est.)
Labor force - by occupation: agriculture 81%, industry 6%, services 13% (1997 est.)
Unemployment rate: 21% (1997 est.)
Budget:
revenues: $466.9 million
expenditures: $1.004 billion, including capital expenditures of $502.5 million (2000 est.)
Industries: food, beverages, chemicals (fertilizer, soap, paints), petroleum products, textiles, cement, glass, asbestos, tobacco
Industrial production growth rate: 7.2% (1999)
Electricity - production: 2.3 billion kWh (1999)
Electricity - production by source:
fossil fuel: 13.04%
hydro: 86.96%
nuclear: 0%
other: 0% (1999)
Electricity - consumption: 307 million kWh (1999)
Electricity - exports: 1.9 billion kWh (1999)
Electricity - imports: 68 million kWh (1999)
Agriculture - products: cotton, cashew nuts, sugarcane, tea, cassava (tapioca), corn, rice, coconuts, sisal, tropical fruits; beef, poultry
Exports: $390 million (f.o.b., 2000 est.)
Exports - commodities: prawns 40%, cashews, cotton, sugar, citrus, timber; bulk electricity (2000)
Exports - partners: EU 27%, South Africa 26%, Zimbabwe 15%, India 12%, US 5%, Japan 4% (1999 est.)
Imports: $1.4 billion (c.i.f., 2000 est.)
Imports - commodities: machinery and equipment, mineral products, chemicals, metals, foodstuffs, textiles (2000)
Imports - partners: South Africa 44%, EU 16%, US 6.5%, Japan 6.5%, Pakistan 3%, India 3% (1999 est.)
Debt - external: $1.4 billion (2000 est.)
Economic aid - recipient: $1.04 billion (1998)
Currency: metical (MZM)
Currency code: MZM
Exchange rates: meticais per US dollar - 17,331.0 (January 2001), 5,199.8 (2000), 12,775.1 (1999), 11,874.6 (1998), 11.543.6 (1997), 11,293.8 (1996)
Fiscal year: calendar year

Communications

Telephones - main lines in use: 65,354 (2000)
Telephones - mobile cellular: 18,500 (2000)
Telephone system:
general assessment: fair system but not available generally (telephone density is only 3.5 telephones for each 1,000 persons)
domestic: the system consists of open-wire lines and trunk connection by microwave radio relay and tropospheric scatter
international: satellite earth stations - 5 Intelsat (2 Atlantic Ocean and 3 Indian Ocean)
Radio broadcast stations: AM 13, FM 16, shortwave 12 (2000)
Radios: 730,000 (1997)
Television broadcast stations: 1 (2000)
Televisions: 67,600 (2000)
Internet country code: .mz

Mozambique (continued)

Internet Service Providers (ISPs): 8 (2000)
Internet users: 6,250
note: 150 corporate accounts and 6,100 individual accounts (2000)

Transportation

Railways:
total: 3,131 km
narrow gauge: 2,988 km 1.067-m gauge; 143 km 0.762-m gauge (1994)
Highways:
total: 30,400 km
paved: 5,685 km
unpaved: 24,715 km (1996)
Waterways: 3,750 km (navigable routes)
Pipelines: crude oil 306 km; petroleum products 289 km
note: not operating
Ports and harbors: Beira, Inhambane, Maputo, Nacala, Pemba, Quelimane
Merchant marine:
total: 3 ships (1,000 GRT or over) totaling 4,125 GRT/ 7,024 DWT
ships by type: cargo 3 (2000 est.)
Airports: 168 (2000 est.)
Airports - with paved runways:
total: 22
over 3,047 m: 1
2,438 to 3,047 m: 3
1,524 to 2,437 m: 10
914 to 1,523 m: 3
under 914 m: 5 (2000 est.)
Airports - with unpaved runways:
total: 146
2,438 to 3,047 m: 1
1,524 to 2,437 m: 16
914 to 1,523 m: 37
under 914 m: 92 (2000 est.)

Military

Military branches: Army, Naval Command, Air and Air Defense Forces, Militia
Military manpower - availability:
males age 15-49: 4,627,052 (2001 est.)
Military manpower - fit for military service:
males age 15-49: 2,670,933 (2001 est.)
Military expenditures - dollar figure: $35.1 million (2000 est.)
Military expenditures - percent of GDP: 1% (2000 est.)

Transnational Issues

Disputes - international: none
Illicit drugs: Southern African transit point for South Asian hashish, South Asian heroin, and South American cocaine probably destined for the European and South African markets; producer of cannabis (for local consumption) and methaqualone (for export to South Africa)

Namibia

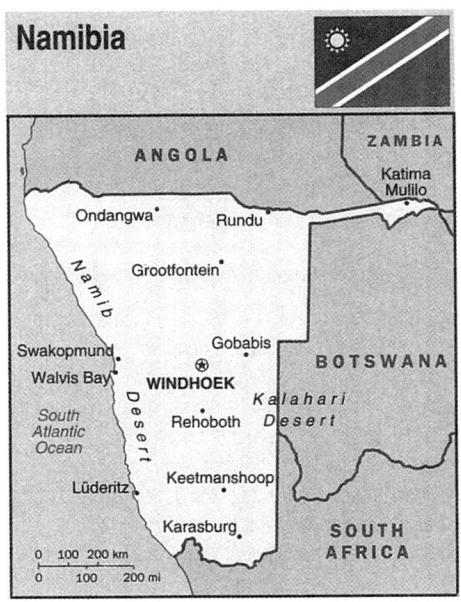

Introduction

Background: South Africa occupied the German colony of Sud-West Afrika during World War I and administered it as a mandate until after World War II when it annexed the territory. In 1966 the Marxist South-West Africa People's Organization (SWAPO) guerrilla group launched a war of independence for the area that was soon named Namibia, but it was not until 1988 that South Africa agreed to end its administration in accordance with a UN peace plan for the entire region. Independence came in 1990.

Geography

Location: Southern Africa, bordering the South Atlantic Ocean, between Angola and South Africa
Geographic coordinates: 22 00 S, 17 00 E
Map references: Africa
Area:
total: 825,418 sq km
land: 825,418 sq km
water: 0 sq km
Area - comparative: slightly more than half the size of Alaska
Land boundaries:
total: 3,824 km
border countries: Angola 1,376 km, Botswana 1,360 km, South Africa 855 km, Zambia 233 km
Coastline: 1,572 km
Maritime claims:
contiguous zone: 24 NM
exclusive economic zone: 200 NM
territorial sea: 12 NM
Climate: desert; hot, dry; rainfall sparse and erratic
Terrain: mostly high plateau; Namib Desert along coast; Kalahari Desert in east
Elevation extremes:
lowest point: Atlantic Ocean 0 m
highest point: Konigstein 2,606 m
Natural resources: diamonds, copper, uranium, gold, lead, tin, lithium, cadmium, zinc, salt, vanadium, natural gas, hydropower, fish

note: suspected deposits of oil, coal, and iron ore
Land use:
arable land: 1%
permanent crops: 0%
permanent pastures: 46%
forests and woodland: 22%
other: 31% (1993 est.)
Irrigated land: 60 sq km (1993 est.)
Natural hazards: prolonged periods of drought
Environment - current issues: very limited natural fresh water resources; desertification
Environment - international agreements:
party to: Antarctic-Marine Living Resources, Biodiversity, Climate Change, Desertification, Endangered Species, Hazardous Wastes, Law of the Sea, Marine Dumping, Ozone Layer Protection, Ship Pollution, Wetlands
signed, but not ratified: none of the selected agreements

People

Population: 1,797,677
note: estimates for this country explicitly take into account the effects of excess mortality due to AIDS; this can result in lower life expectancy, higher infant mortality and death rates, lower population and growth rates, and changes in the distribution of population by age and sex than would otherwise be expected (July 2001 est.)
Age structure:
0-14 years: 42.74% (male 389,028; female 379,229)
15-64 years: 53.54% (male 480,075; female 482,375)
65 years and over: 3.72% (male 29,109; female 37,861) (2001 est.)
Population growth rate: 1.38% (2001 est.)
Birth rate: 34.71 births/1,000 population (2001 est.)
Death rate: 20.9 deaths/1,000 population (2001 est.)
Net migration rate: 0 migrant(s)/1,000 population (2001 est.)
Sex ratio:
at birth: 1.03 male(s)/female
under 15 years: 1.03 male(s)/female
15-64 years: 1 male(s)/female
65 years and over: 0.77 male(s)/female
total population: 1 male(s)/female (2001 est.)
Infant mortality rate: 71.66 deaths/1,000 live births (2001 est.)
Life expectancy at birth:
total population: 40.62 years
male: 42.48 years
female: 38.71 years (2001 est.)
Total fertility rate: 4.83 children born/woman (2001 est.)
HIV/AIDS - adult prevalence rate: 19.54% (1999 est.)
HIV/AIDS - people living with HIV/AIDS: 160,000 (1999 est.)
HIV/AIDS - deaths: 18,000 (1999 est.)
Nationality:
noun: Namibian(s)
adjective: Namibian

Namibia (continued)

Ethnic groups: black 87.5%, white 6%, mixed 6.5%
note: about 50% of the population belong to the Ovambo tribe and 9% to the Kavangos tribe; other ethnic groups are: Herero 7%, Damara 7%, Nama 5%, Caprivian 4%, Bushmen 3%, Baster 2%, Tswana 0.5%
Religions: Christian 80% to 90% (Lutheran 50% at least), indigenous beliefs 10% to 20%
Languages: English 7% (official), Afrikaans common language of most of the population and about 60% of the white population, German 32%, indigenous languages: Oshivambo, Herero, Nama
Literacy:
definition: age 15 and over can read and write
total population: 38%
male: 45%
female: 31% (1960 est.)

Government

Country name:
conventional long form: Republic of Namibia
conventional short form: Namibia
former: German Southwest Africa, South-West Africa
Government type: republic
Capital: Windhoek
Administrative divisions: 13 regions; Caprivi, Erongo, Hardap, Karas, Khomas, Kunene, Ohangwena, Okavango, Omaheke, Omusati, Oshana, Oshikoto, Otjozondjupa
Independence: 21 March 1990 (from South African mandate)
National holiday: Independence Day, 21 March (1990)
Constitution: ratified 9 February 1990; effective 12 March 1990
Legal system: based on Roman-Dutch law and 1990 constitution
Suffrage: 18 years of age; universal
Executive branch:
chief of state: President Sam Shafishuna NUJOMA (since 21 March 1990); note - the president is both the chief of state and head of government
head of government: President Sam Shafishuna NUJOMA (since 21 March 1990); note - the president is both the chief of state and head of government
cabinet: Cabinet appointed by the president from among the members of the National Assembly
elections: president elected by popular vote for a five-year term; election last held 30 November-1 December 1999 (next to be held NA 2004)
election results: Sam Shafishuna NUJOMA elected president; percent of vote - Sam Shafishuna NUJOMA 77%
Legislative branch: bicameral legislature consists of the National Council (26 seats; two members are chosen from each regional council to serve six-year terms) and the National Assembly (72 seats; members are elected by popular vote to serve five-year terms)
elections: National Council - elections for regional councils, to determine members of the National Council, held 30 November-1 December 1998 (next to be held by December 2004); National Assembly - last held 30 November-1 December 1999 (next to be held by December 2004)
election results: National Council - percent of vote by party - NA%; seats by party - SWAPO 21, DTA 4, UDF 1; National Assembly - percent of vote by party - SWAPO 76%, COD 10%, DTA 9%, UDF 3%, MAG 1%, other 1%; seats by party - SWAPO 55, COD 7, DTA 7, UDF 2, MAG 1,
note: the National Council is primarily an advisory body
Judicial branch: Supreme Court (judges appointed by the president on the recommendation of the Judicial Service Commission)
Political parties and leaders: Congress of Democrats or COD [Ben ULENGA]; Democratic Turnhalle Alliance of Namibia or DTA [Katuutire KAURA, president]; Monitor Action Group or MAG [Kosie PRETORIUS]; South West Africa People's Organization or SWAPO [Sam NUJOMA]; United Democratic Front or UDF [Justus GAROEB]
Political pressure groups and leaders: NA
International organization participation: AfDB, C, CCC, ECA, FAO, G-77, IAEA, IBRD, ICAO, ICRM, IFAD, IFC, IFRCS, ILO, IMF, IMO, Intelsat, Interpol, IOC, IOM (observer), ISO (correspondent), ITU, NAM, OAU, OPCW, SACU, SADC, UN, UNCTAD, UNESCO, UNHCR, UNIDO, UNMEE, UNTAET, UPU, WCL, WHO, WIPO, WMO, WToO, WTrO
Diplomatic representation in the US:
chief of mission: Ambassador Leonard Nangolo IIPUMBU
chancery: 1605 New Hampshire Avenue NW, Washington, DC 20009
telephone: [1] (202) 986-0540
FAX: [1] (202) 986-0443
Diplomatic representation from the US:
chief of mission: Ambassador Jeffrey A. BADER
embassy: Ausplan Building, 14 Lossen Street, Private Bag 12029 Ausspannplatz, Windhoek
mailing address: use embassy street address
telephone: [264] (61) 221601
FAX: [264] (61) 229792
Flag description: a large blue triangle with a yellow sunburst fills the upper left section and an equal green triangle (solid) fills the lower right section; the triangles are separated by a red stripe that is contrasted by two narrow white-edge borders

Economy

Economy - overview: The economy is heavily dependent on the extraction and processing of minerals for export. Mining accounts for 20% of GDP. Namibia is the fourth-largest exporter of nonfuel minerals in Africa and the world's fifth-largest producer of uranium. Rich alluvial diamond deposits make Namibia a primary source for gem-quality diamonds. Namibia also produces large quantities of lead, zinc, tin, silver, and tungsten. Half of the population depends on agriculture (largely subsistence agriculture) for its livelihood. Namibia must import some of its food. Although per capita GDP is four times the per capita GDP of Africa's poorer countries, the majority of Namibia's people live in pronounced poverty because of large-scale unemployment, the great inequality of income distribution, and the large amount of wealth going to foreigners. The Namibian economy has close links to South Africa. GDP growth in 2000 was led by gains in the diamond and fish sectors. Agreement has been reached on the privatization of several more enterprises in coming years, which should stimulate long-run foreign investment. Growth in 2001 could be 5.5% provided the world economy remains stable.
GDP: purchasing power parity - $7.6 billion (2000 est.)
GDP - real growth rate: 4% (2000 est.)
GDP - per capita: purchasing power parity - $4,300 (2000 est.)
GDP - composition by sector:
agriculture: 12%
industry: 25%
services: 63% (1999 est.)
Population below poverty line: NA%
Household income or consumption by percentage share:
lowest 10%: NA%
highest 10%: NA%
Inflation rate (consumer prices): 9.1% (2000)
Labor force: 500,000
Labor force - by occupation: agriculture 47%, industry 20%, services 33% (1999 est.)
Unemployment rate: 30% to 40%, including underemployment (1997 est.)
Budget:
revenues: $883 million
expenditures: $950 million, including capital expenditures of $NA (1998)
Industries: meatpacking, fish processing, dairy products; mining (diamond, lead, zinc, tin, silver, tungsten, uranium, copper)
Industrial production growth rate: NA
Electricity - production: 1.198 billion kWh (1999)
Electricity - production by source:
fossil fuel: 2%
hydro: 98%
nuclear: 0%
other: 0% (1999)
Electricity - consumption: 1.948 billion kWh (1999)
Electricity - exports: 56 million kWh (1999)
Electricity - imports: 890 million kWh
note: supplied by South Africa (1999)
Agriculture - products: millet, sorghum, peanuts; livestock; fish
Exports: $1.4 billion (f.o.b., 2000 est.)
Exports - commodities: diamonds, copper, gold, zinc, lead, uranium; cattle, processed fish, karakul skins
Exports - partners: UK 43%, South Africa 26%, Spain 14%, France 8%, Japan (1998 est.)
Imports: $1.6 billion (f.o.b., 2000 est.)
Imports - commodities: foodstuffs; petroleum products and fuel, machinery and equipment, chemicals

Namibia (continued)

Imports - partners: South Africa 81%, US 4%, Germany 2% (1997 est.)
Debt - external: $217 million (2000 est.)
Economic aid - recipient: $127 million (1998)
Currency: Namibian dollar (NAD); South African rand (ZAR)
Currency code: NAD; ZAR
Exchange rates: Namibian dollars per US dollar - 7.78307 (January 2001), 6.93983 (2000), 6.10948 (1999), 5.52828 (1998), 4.60796 (1997), 4.29935 (1996)
Fiscal year: 1 April - 31 March

Communications

Telephones - main lines in use: 100,848 (1997)
Telephones - mobile cellular: NA
Telephone system:
general assessment: good system; about 6 telephones for each 100 persons
domestic: good urban services; fair rural service; microwave radio relay links major towns; connections to other populated places are by open wire; 100% digital
international: fiber-optic cable to South Africa, microwave radio relay link to Botswana, direct links to other neighboring countries; connected to Africa ONE and South African Far East (SAFE) submarine cables through South Africa; satellite earth stations - 4 Intelsat
Radio broadcast stations: AM 2, FM 34, shortwave 5 (1998)
Radios: 232,000 (1997)
Television broadcast stations: 8 (plus about 20 low-power repeaters) (1997)
Televisions: 60,000 (1997)
Internet country code: .na
Internet Service Providers (ISPs): 2 (2000)
Internet users: 9,000 (1999)

Transportation

Railways:
total: 2,382 km
narrow gauge: 2,382 km 1.067-m gauge; single track (1995)
Highways:
total: 63,258 km
paved: 5,250 km
unpaved: 58,008 km (1997 est.)
Waterways: none
Ports and harbors: Luderitz, Walvis Bay
Merchant marine: none (2000 est.)
Airports: 131 (2000 est.)
Airports - with paved runways:
total: 21
over 3,047 m: 2
2,438 to 3,047 m: 2
1,524 to 2,437 m: 13
914 to 1,523 m: 4 (2000 est.)
Airports - with unpaved runways:
total: 110
2,438 to 3,047 m: 2
1,524 to 2,437 m: 21
914 to 1,523 m: 69
under 914 m: 18 (2000 est.)

Military

Military branches: National Defense Force (Army), Police
Military manpower - availability:
males age 15-49: 427,067 (2001 est.)
Military manpower - fit for military service:
males age 15-49: 255,016 (2001 est.)
Military expenditures - dollar figure: $104.4 million (2001)
Military expenditures - percent of GDP: 2.6% (FY97/98)

Transnational Issues

Disputes - international: none

Nauru

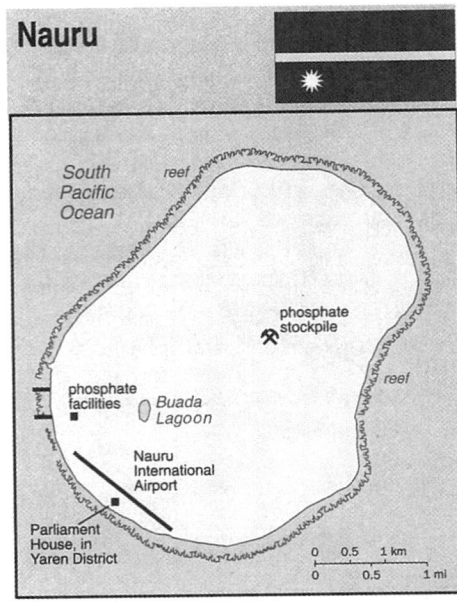

Introduction

Background: Nauru's phosphate deposits began to be mined early in the 20th century by a German-British consortium; the island was occupied by Australian forces in World War I. Upon achieving independence in 1968, Nauru became the smallest independent republic in the world; it joined the UN in 1999.

Geography

Location: Oceania, island in the South Pacific Ocean, south of the Marshall Islands
Geographic coordinates: 0 32 S, 166 55 E
Map references: Oceania
Area:
total: 21 sq km
land: 21 sq km
water: 0 sq km
Area - comparative: about 0.1 times the size of Washington, DC
Land boundaries: 0 km
Coastline: 30 km
Maritime claims:
contiguous zone: 24 NM
exclusive economic zone: 200 NM
territorial sea: 12 NM
Climate: tropical; monsoonal; rainy season (November to February)
Terrain: sandy beach rises to fertile ring around raised coral reefs with phosphate plateau in center
Elevation extremes:
lowest point: Pacific Ocean 0 m
highest point: unnamed location along plateau rim 61 m
Natural resources: phosphates
Land use:
arable land: 0%
permanent crops: 0%
permanent pastures: 0%
forests and woodland: 0%
other: 100% (1993 est.)

Nauru (continued)

Irrigated land: NA sq km
Natural hazards: periodic droughts
Environment - current issues: limited natural fresh water resources, roof storage tanks collect rainwater, but mostly dependent on a single, aging desalination plant; intensive phosphate mining during the past 90 years - mainly by a UK, Australia, and NZ consortium - has left the central 90% of Nauru a wasteland and threatens limited remaining land resources
Environment - international agreements:
party to: Biodiversity, Climate Change, Desertification, Law of the Sea, Marine Dumping, Ship Pollution
signed, but not ratified: none of the selected agreements
Geography - note: Nauru is one of the three great phosphate rock islands in the Pacific Ocean - the others are Banaba (Ocean Island) in Kiribati and Makatea in French Polynesia; only 53 km south of Equator

People

Population: 12,088 (July 2001 est.)
Age structure:
0-14 years: 40.33% (male 2,510; female 2,365)
15-64 years: 57.97% (male 3,475; female 3,533)
65 years and over: 1.7% (male 103; female 102) (2001 est.)
Population growth rate: 2% (2001 est.)
Birth rate: 27.22 births/1,000 population (2001 est.)
Death rate: 7.2 deaths/1,000 population (2001 est.)
Net migration rate: 0 migrant(s)/1,000 population (2001 est.)
Sex ratio:
at birth: 1.05 male(s)/female
under 15 years: 1.06 male(s)/female
15-64 years: 0.98 male(s)/female
65 years and over: 1.01 male(s)/female
total population: 1.01 male(s)/female (2001 est.)
Infant mortality rate: 10.71 deaths/1,000 live births (2001 est.)
Life expectancy at birth:
total population: 61.2 years
male: 57.7 years
female: 64.88 years (2001 est.)
Total fertility rate: 3.61 children born/woman (2001 est.)
HIV/AIDS - adult prevalence rate: NA%
HIV/AIDS - people living with HIV/AIDS: NA
HIV/AIDS - deaths: NA
Nationality:
noun: Nauruan(s)
adjective: Nauruan
Ethnic groups: Nauruan 58%, other Pacific Islander 26%, Chinese 8%, European 8%
Religions: Christian (two-thirds Protestant, one-third Roman Catholic)
Languages: Nauruan (official, a distinct Pacific Island language), English widely understood, spoken, and used for most government and commercial purposes

Literacy:
definition: NA
total population: NA%
male: NA%
female: NA%

Government

Country name:
conventional long form: Republic of Nauru
conventional short form: Nauru
former: Pleasant Island
Government type: republic
Capital: no official capital; government offices in Yaren District
Administrative divisions: 14 districts; Aiwo, Anabar, Anetan, Anibare, Baiti, Boe, Buada, Denigomodu, Ewa, Ijuw, Meneng, Nibok, Uaboe, Yaren
Independence: 31 January 1968 (from the Australia-, NZ-, and UK-administered UN trusteeship)
National holiday: Independence Day, 31 January (1968)
Constitution: 29 January 1968
Legal system: acts of the Nauru Parliament and British common law
Suffrage: 20 years of age; universal and compulsory
Executive branch:
chief of state: President Bernard DOWIYOGO (since 19 April 2000); note - the president is both the chief of state and head of government
head of government: President Bernard DOWIYOGO (since 19 April 2000); note - the president is both the chief of state and head of government
cabinet: Cabinet appointed by the president from among the members of Parliament
elections: president elected by Parliament for a three-year term; election last held 8 April 2000 (next to be held NA 2003)
election results: Bernard DOWIYOGO elected president by a vote in Parliament of nine to eight
note: former President Rene HARRIS was deposed in a no-confidence vote; this is the eighth change of government in Nauru since the fall of the Lagumont HARRIS government in a no-confidence motion in early November 1996; six of the last eight governments have resulted because of parliamentary no-confidence motions
Legislative branch: unicameral Parliament (18 seats; members elected by popular vote to serve three-year terms)
elections: last held 9 April 2000 (next to be held NA April 2003)
election results: percent of vote - NA%; seats - independents 18
Judicial branch: Supreme Court
Political parties and leaders: loose multiparty system; Democratic Party [Kennan ADEANG]; Nauru Party (informal) [Bernard DOWIYOGO]
Political pressure groups and leaders: NA
International organization participation: ACP, AsDB, C, ESCAP, ICAO, Intelsat (nonsignatory user), Interpol, IOC, ITU, OPCW, Sparteca, SPC, SPF, UN, UNESCO, UPU, WHO

Diplomatic representation in the US: Nauru does not have an embassy in the US, but does have a UN office at 800 2nd Avenue, Suite 400 D, New York, New York 10017; telephone: (212) 937-0074
consulate(s): Hagatna (Guam)
Diplomatic representation from the US: the US does not have an embassy in Nauru; the US Ambassador to Fiji is accredited to Nauru
Flag description: blue with a narrow, horizontal, yellow stripe across the center and a large white 12-pointed star below the stripe on the hoist side; the star indicates the country's location in relation to the Equator (the yellow stripe) and the 12 points symbolize the 12 original tribes of Nauru

Economy

Economy - overview: Revenues of this tiny island have come from exports of phosphates, but reserves are expected to be exhausted within five to ten years. Phosphate production has declined since 1989, as demand has fallen in traditional markets and as the marginal cost of extracting the remaining phosphate increases, making it less internationally competitive. While phosphates have given Nauruans one of the highest per capita incomes in the Third World, few other resources exist with most necessities being imported, including fresh water from Australia. The rehabilitation of mined land and the replacement of income from phosphates are serious long-term problems. In anticipation of the exhaustion of Nauru's phosphate deposits, substantial amounts of phosphate income have been invested in trust funds to help cushion the transition and provide for Nauru's economic future. The government has been borrowing heavily from the trusts to finance fiscal deficits. To cut costs the government has called for a freezing of wages, a reduction of over-staffed public service departments, privatization of numerous government agencies, and closure of some overseas consulates. In recent years Nauru has encouraged the registration of offshore banks and corporations. Tens of billions of dollars have been channeled through their accounts. Few comprehensive statistics on the Nauru economy exist, with estimates of Nauru's per capita GDP varying widely.
GDP: purchasing power parity - $59 million (2000 est.)
GDP - real growth rate: NA%
GDP - per capita: purchasing power parity - $5,000 (2000 est.)
GDP - composition by sector:
agriculture: NA%
industry: NA%
services: NA%
Population below poverty line: NA%
Household income or consumption by percentage share:
lowest 10%: NA%
highest 10%: NA%
Inflation rate (consumer prices): -3.6% (1993)
Labor force - by occupation: employed in mining phosphates, public administration, education, and transportation

Nauru (continued)

Unemployment rate: 0%
Budget:
revenues: $23.4 million
expenditures: $64.8 million, including capital expenditures of $NA (FY95/96)
Industries: phosphate mining, financial services, coconut products
Industrial production growth rate: NA%
Electricity - production: 30 million kWh (1999)
Electricity - production by source:
fossil fuel: 100%
hydro: 0%
nuclear: 0%
other: 0% (1999)
Electricity - consumption: 27.9 million kWh (1999)
Electricity - exports: 0 kWh (1999)
Electricity - imports: 0 kWh (1999)
Agriculture - products: coconuts
Exports: $25.3 million (f.o.b., 1991)
Exports - commodities: phosphates
Exports - partners: Australia, NZ
Imports: $21.1 million (c.i.f., 1991)
Imports - commodities: food, fuel, manufactures, building materials, machinery
Imports - partners: Australia, UK, NZ, Japan
Debt - external: $33.3 million
Economic aid - recipient: $2.25 million from Australia (FY96/97 est.)
Currency: Australian dollar (AUD)
Currency code: AUD
Exchange rates: Australian dollars per US dollar - 1.7995 (January 2001), 1.7173 (2000), 1.5497 (1999), 1.5888 (1998), 1.3439 (1997), 1.2773 (1996)
Fiscal year: 1 July - 30 June

Communications

Telephones - main lines in use: 2,000 (1996)
Telephones - mobile cellular: 450 (1994)
Telephone system:
general assessment: adequate local and international radiotelephone communications provided via Australian facilities
domestic: NA
international: satellite earth station - 1 Intelsat (Pacific Ocean)
Radio broadcast stations: AM 1, FM 0, shortwave 0 (1998)
Radios: 7,000 (1997)
Television broadcast stations: 1 (1997)
Televisions: 500 (1997)
Internet country code: .nr
Internet Service Providers (ISPs): 1 (2000)
Internet users: NA

Transportation

Railways:
total: 5 km; note - used to haul phosphates from the center of the island to processing facilities on the southwest coast
Highways:
total: 30 km
paved: 24 km
unpaved: 6 km (1998 est.)
Waterways: none
Ports and harbors: Nauru
Merchant marine: none (2000 est.)
Airports: 1 (2000 est.)
Airports - with paved runways:
total: 1
1,524 to 2,437 m: 1 (2000 est.)

Military

Military branches: no regular armed forces; Directorate of the Nauru Police Force
Military manpower - availability:
males age 15-49: 3,018 (2001 est.)
Military manpower - fit for military service:
males age 15-49: 1,661 (2001 est.)
Military expenditures - dollar figure: $NA
Military expenditures - percent of GDP: NA%
Military - note: Nauru maintains no defense forces; under an informal agreement, defense is the responsibility of Australia

Transnational Issues

Disputes - international: none

Navassa Island
(territory of the US)

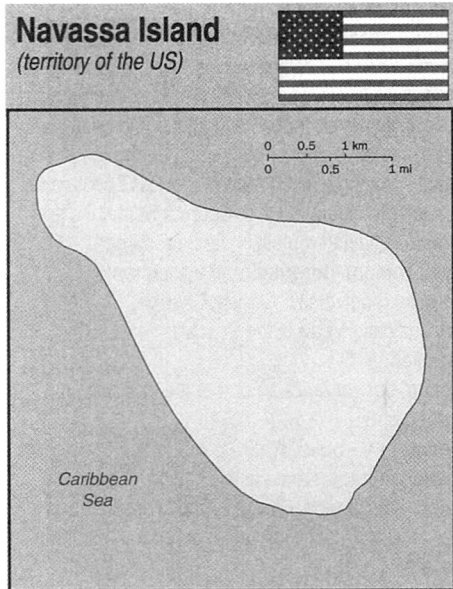

Introduction

Background: This uninhabited island was claimed by the US in 1857 for its guano, and mining took place between 1865 and 1898. The lighthouse, built in 1917, was shut down in 1996 and administration of Navassa Island transferred from the Coast Guard to the Department of the Interior. A 1998 scientific expedition to the island described it as a unique preserve of Caribbean biodiversity; the following year it became a National Wildlife Refuge.

Geography

Location: Caribbean, island in the Caribbean Sea, about one-fourth of the way from Haiti to Jamaica
Geographic coordinates: 18 25 N, 75 02 W
Map references: Central America and the Caribbean
Area:
total: 5.2 sq km
land: 5.2 sq km
water: 0 sq km
Area - comparative: about nine times the size of The Mall in Washington, DC
Land boundaries: 0 km
Coastline: 8 km
Maritime claims:
exclusive economic zone: 200 NM
territorial sea: 12 NM
Climate: marine, tropical
Terrain: raised coral and limestone plateau, flat to undulating; ringed by vertical white cliffs (9 to 15 m high)
Elevation extremes:
lowest point: Caribbean Sea 0 m
highest point: unnamed location on southwest side 77 m
Natural resources: guano
Land use:
arable land: 0%
permanent crops: 0%

Navassa Island (continued)

permanent pastures: 10%
forests and woodland: 0%
other: 90%
Irrigated land: 0 sq km (1998)
Natural hazards: NA
Environment - current issues: NA
Geography - note: strategic location 160 km south of the US Naval Base at Guantanamo Bay, Cuba; mostly exposed rock, but enough grassland to support goat herds; dense stands of fig-like trees, scattered cactus

People

Population: uninhabited
note: transient Haitian fishermen and others camp on the island (July 2001 est.)

Government

Country name:
conventional long form: none
conventional short form: Navassa Island
Dependency status: unincorporated territory of the US; administered from Washington, DC, by the Fish and Wildlife Service, US Department of the Interior; in September 1996, the Coast Guard ceased operations and maintenance of Navassa Island Light, a 46-meter-tall lighthouse located on the southern side of the island; there has also been a private claim advanced against the island
Legal system: the laws of the US, where applicable, apply
Flag description: the flag of the US is used

Economy

Economy - overview: no economic activity

Transportation

Waterways: none
Ports and harbors: none; offshore anchorage only

Military

Military - note: defense is the responsibility of the US

Transnational Issues

Disputes - international: claimed by Haiti

Nepal

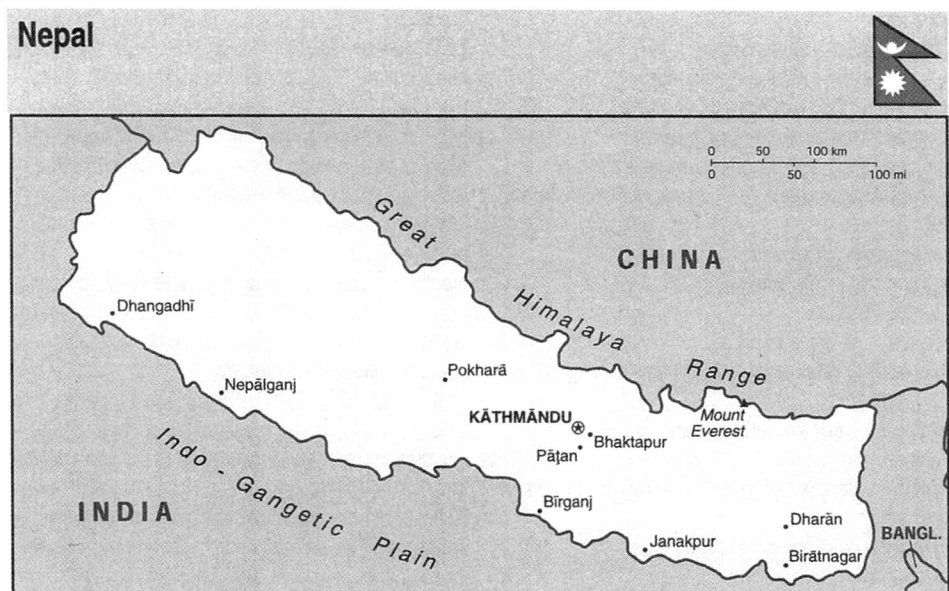

Introduction

Background: In 1951, the Nepalese monarch ended the century-old system of rule by hereditary premiers and instituted a cabinet system of government. Reforms in 1990 established a multiparty democracy within the framework of a constitutional monarchy. The refugee issue of some 100,000 Bhutanese in Nepal remains unresolved; 90% of these displaced persons are housed in seven United Nations Offices of the High Commissioner for Refugees (UNHCR) camps.

Geography

Location: Southern Asia, between China and India
Geographic coordinates: 28 00 N, 84 00 E
Map references: Asia
Area:
total: 140,800 sq km
land: 136,800 sq km
water: 4,000 sq km
Area - comparative: slightly larger than Arkansas
Land boundaries:
total: 2,926 km
border countries: China 1,236 km, India 1,690 km
Coastline: 0 km (landlocked)
Maritime claims: none (landlocked)
Climate: varies from cool summers and severe winters in north to subtropical summers and mild winters in south
Terrain: Terai or flat river plain of the Ganges in south, central hill region, rugged Himalayas in north
Elevation extremes:
lowest point: Kanchan Kalan 70 m
highest point: Mount Everest 8,850 m (1999 est.)
Natural resources: quartz, water, timber, hydropower, scenic beauty, small deposits of lignite, copper, cobalt, iron ore
Land use:
arable land: 17%
permanent crops: 0%
permanent pastures: 15%
forests and woodland: 42%
other: 26% (1993 est.)
Irrigated land: 8,500 sq km (1993 est.)
Natural hazards: severe thunderstorms, flooding, landslides, drought, and famine depending on the timing, intensity, and duration of the summer monsoons
Environment - current issues: deforestation (overuse of wood for fuel and lack of alternatives); contaminated water (with human and animal wastes, agricultural runoff, and industrial effluents); wildlife conservation; vehicular emissions
Environment - international agreements:
party to: Biodiversity, Climate Change, Desertification, Endangered Species, Hazardous Wastes, Law of the Sea, Marine Dumping, Nuclear Test Ban, Ozone Layer Protection, Ship Pollution, Tropical Timber 83, Tropical Timber 94, Wetlands
signed, but not ratified: Marine Dumping, Marine Life Conservation
Geography - note: landlocked; strategic location between China and India; contains eight of world's 10 highest peaks

People

Population: 25,284,463 (July 2001 est.)
Age structure:
0-14 years: 40.35% (male 5,267,234; female 4,933,910)
15-64 years: 56.16% (male 7,264,575; female 6,934,384)
65 years and over: 3.49% (male 437,813; female 446,547) (2001 est.)
Population growth rate: 2.32% (2001 est.)
Birth rate: 33.4 births/1,000 population (2001 est.)
Death rate: 10.22 deaths/1,000 population (2001 est.)
Net migration rate: 0 migrant(s)/1,000 population (2001 est.)

Nepal (continued)

Sex ratio:
at birth: 1.05 male(s)/female
under 15 years: 1.07 male(s)/female
15-64 years: 1.05 male(s)/female
65 years and over: 0.98 male(s)/female
total population: 1.05 male(s)/female (2001 est.)
Infant mortality rate: 74.14 deaths/1,000 live births (2001 est.)
Life expectancy at birth:
total population: 58.22 years
male: 58.65 years
female: 57.77 years (2001 est.)
Total fertility rate: 4.58 children born/woman (2001 est.)
HIV/AIDS - adult prevalence rate: 0.29% (1999 est.)
HIV/AIDS - people living with HIV/AIDS: 34,000 (1999 est.)
HIV/AIDS - deaths: 2,500 (1999 est.)
Nationality:
noun: Nepalese (singular and plural)
adjective: Nepalese
Ethnic groups: Brahman, Chetri, Newar, Gurung, Magar, Tamang, Rai, Limbu, Sherpa, Tharu, and others (1995)
Religions: Hinduism 86.2%, Buddhism 7.8%, Islam 3.8%, other 2.2%
note: only official Hindu state in the world (1995)
Languages: Nepali (official; spoken by 90% of the population), about a dozen other languages and about 30 major dialects; note - many in government and business also speak English (1995)
Literacy:
definition: age 15 and over can read and write
total population: 27.5%
male: 40.9%
female: 14% (1995 est.)
People - note: refugee issue over the presence in Nepal of approximately 98,700 Bhutanese refugees, 90% of whom are in seven United Nations Office of the High Commissioner for Refugees (UNHCR) camps

Government

Country name:
conventional long form: Kingdom of Nepal
conventional short form: Nepal
Government type: parliamentary democracy and constitutional monarchy
Capital: Kathmandu
Administrative divisions: 14 zones (anchal, singular and plural); Bagmati, Bheri, Dhawalagiri, Gandaki, Janakpur, Karnali, Kosi, Lumbini, Mahakali, Mechi, Narayani, Rapti, Sagarmatha, Seti
Independence: 1768 (unified by Prithvi Narayan Shah)
National holiday: Birthday of King GYANENDRA, 7 July (1946)
Constitution: 9 November 1990
Legal system: based on Hindu legal concepts and English common law; has not accepted compulsory ICJ jurisdiction
Suffrage: 18 years of age; universal
Executive branch:
chief of state: King GYANENDRA Bir Bikram Shah (succeeded to the throne 4 June 2001 following the death of his nephew King DIPENDRA Bir Bikram Shah)
head of government: Prime Minister Girija Prasad KOIRALA (since 22 March 2000)
cabinet: Cabinet appointed by the monarch on the recommendation of the prime minister
elections: none; the monarch is hereditary; following legislative elections, the leader of the majority party or leader of a majority coalition is usually appointed prime minister by the monarch
note: King BIRENDRA Bir Bikram Shah Dev died in a bloody shooting at the royal palace on 1 June 2001 that also claimed the lives of most of the royal family; King BIRENDRA's son, Crown Price DIPENDRA, is believed to have been responsible for the shootings before fatally wounding himself; immediately following the shootings and while still clinging to life, DIPENDRA was crowned king; he died three days later and was succeeded by his uncle
Legislative branch: bicameral Parliament consists of the National Council (60 seats; 35 appointed by the House of Representatives, 10 by the king, and 15 elected by an electoral college; one-third of the members elected every two years to serve six-year terms) and the House of Representatives (205 seats; members elected by popular vote to serve five-year terms)
elections: House of Representatives - last held 3 and 17 May 1999 (next to be held NA May 2004)
election results: House of Representatives - percent of vote by party - NC 37.3%, CPN/UML 31.6%, NDP 10.4%, NSP 3.2%, Rastriya Jana Morcha 1.4%, Samyukta Janmorcha Nepal 0.8%, NWPP 0.5%, others 14.8%; seats by party - NC 113, CPN/UML 69, NDP 11, NSP 5, Rastriya Jana Morcha 5, Samyukta Janmorcha Nepal 1, NWPP 1
Judicial branch: Supreme Court or Sarbochha Adalat (chief justice is appointed by the monarch on recommendation of the Constitutional Council; the other judges are appointed by the monarch on the recommendation of the Judicial Council)
Political parties and leaders: Communist Party of Nepal/United Marxist-Leninist or CPN/UML [Madhav Kumar NEPAL, general secretary]; National Democratic Party or NDP (also called Rastriya Prajantra Party or RPP) [Surya Bahadur THAPA, chairman]; Nepal Sadbhavana (Goodwill) Party or NSP [Gajendra Narayan SINGH, president]; Nepal Workers and Peasants Party or NWPP [Narayan Man BIJUKCHHE, party chair]; Nepali Congress or NC [Girija Prasad KOIRALA, party president, Sushil KOIRALA, general secretary]; Rastriya Jana Morcha [Chitra Bahadur K. C., chairman]; Samyukta Janmorcha Nepal [Lila Mani POKHAREL, general secretary]
Political pressure groups and leaders: Maoist guerrilla-based insurgency; numerous small, left-leaning student groups in the capital; several small, radical Nepalese antimonarchist groups
International organization participation: AsDB, CCC, CP, ESCAP, FAO, G-77, IBRD, ICAO, ICFTU, ICRM, IDA, IFAD, IFC, IFRCS, ILO, IMF, IMO, Intelsat, Interpol, IOC, ISO (correspondent), ITU, MONUC, NAM, OPCW, SAARC, UN, UNCTAD, UNESCO, UNFICYP, UNIDO, UNIFIL, UNMEE, UNMIBH, UNMIK, UNMOP, UNMOT, UNTAET, UPU, WFTU, WHO, WIPO, WMO, WToO, WTrO (observer)
Diplomatic representation in the US:
chief of mission: Ambassador Damodar Prasad GAUTAM
chancery: 2131 Leroy Place NW, Washington, DC 20008
telephone: [1] (202) 667-4550
FAX: [1] (202) 667-5534
consulate(s) general: New York
Diplomatic representation from the US:
chief of mission: Ambassador Ralph FRANK
embassy: Pani Pokhari, Kathmandu
mailing address: use embassy street address
telephone: [977] (1) 411179, 410531
FAX: [977] (1) 419963
Flag description: red with a blue border around the unique shape of two overlapping right triangles; the smaller, upper triangle bears a white stylized moon and the larger, lower triangle bears a white 12-pointed sun

Economy

Economy - overview: Nepal is among the poorest and least developed countries in the world with nearly half of its population living below the poverty line. Agriculture is the mainstay of the economy, providing a livelihood for over 80% of the population and accounting for 41% of GDP. Industrial activity mainly involves the processing of agricultural produce including jute, sugarcane, tobacco, and grain. Production of textiles and carpets has expanded recently and accounted for about 80% of foreign exchange earnings in the past three years. Agricultural production is growing by about 5% on average as compared with annual population growth of 2.3%. Since May 1991, the government has been moving forward with economic reforms, particularly those that encourage trade and foreign investment, e.g., by reducing business licenses and registration requirements in order to simplify investment procedures. The government has also been cutting expenditures by reducing subsidies, privatizing state industries, and laying off civil servants. More recently, however, political instability - five different governments over the past few years - has hampered Kathmandu's ability to forge consensus to implement key economic reforms. Nepal has considerable scope for accelerating economic growth by exploiting its potential in hydropower and tourism, areas of recent foreign investment interest. Prospects for foreign trade or investment in other sectors will remain poor, however, because of the small size of the economy, its technological backwardness, its remoteness, its landlocked geographic location, and its susceptibility

Nepal (continued)

to natural disaster. The international community's role of funding more than 60% of Nepal's development budget and more than 28% of total budgetary expenditures will likely continue as a major ingredient of growth.
GDP: purchasing power parity - $33.7 billion (2000 est.)
GDP - real growth rate: 3.7% (2000 est.)
GDP - per capita: purchasing power parity - $1,360 (2000 est.)
GDP - composition by sector:
agriculture: 41%
industry: 22%
services: 37% (2000 est.)
Population below poverty line: 42% (FY95/96 est.)
Household income or consumption by percentage share:
lowest 10%: 3.2%
highest 10%: 29.8% (1995-96)
Inflation rate (consumer prices): 3.3% (FY99/00 est.)
Labor force: 10 million (1996 est.)
note: severe lack of skilled labor
Labor force - by occupation: agriculture 81%, services 16%, industry 3%
Unemployment rate: NA%; substantial underemployment (1999)
Budget:
revenues: $536 million
expenditures: $818 million, including capital expenditures of $NA (FY96/97 est.)
Industries: tourism, carpet, textile; small rice, jute, sugar, and oilseed mills; cigarette; cement and brick production
Industrial production growth rate: NA%
Electricity - production: 1.255 billion kWh (1999)
Electricity - production by source:
fossil fuel: 9.56%
hydro: 90.44%
nuclear: 0%
other: 0% (1999)
Electricity - consumption: 1.309 billion kWh (1999)
Electricity - exports: 68 million kWh (1999)
Electricity - imports: 210 million kWh (1999)
Agriculture - products: rice, corn, wheat, sugarcane, root crops; milk, water buffalo meat
Exports: $485 million (f.o.b., 1998), but does not include unrecorded border trade with India
Exports - commodities: carpets, clothing, leather goods, jute goods, grain
Exports - partners: India 33%, US 26%, Germany 25% (FY97/98)
Imports: $1.2 billion (f.o.b., 1998)
Imports - commodities: gold, machinery and equipment, petroleum products, fertilizer
Imports - partners: India 31%, China/Hong Kong 16%, Singapore 14% (FY97/98)
Debt - external: $2.4 billion (1997)
Economic aid - recipient: $411 million (FY97/98)
Currency: Nepalese rupee (NPR)
Currency code: NPR
Exchange rates: Nepalese rupees per US dollar - 74.129 (January 2001), 71.104 (2000), 68.239 (1999), 65.976 (1998), 58.010 (1997), 56.692 (1996)
Fiscal year: 16 July - 15 July

Communications

Telephones - main lines in use: 236,816 (January 2000)
Telephones - mobile cellular: NA
Telephone system:
general assessment: poor telephone and telegraph service; fair radiotelephone communication service and mobile cellular telephone network
domestic: NA
international: radiotelephone communications; microwave landline to India; satellite earth station - 1 Intelsat (Indian Ocean)
Radio broadcast stations: AM 6, FM 5, shortwave 1 (January 2000)
Radios: 840,000 (1997)
Television broadcast stations: 1 (plus 9 repeaters) (1998)
Televisions: 130,000 (1997)
Internet country code: .np
Internet Service Providers (ISPs): 6 (2000)
Internet users: 35,000 (2000)

Transportation

Railways:
total: 59 km; note - all in Kosi close to Indian border
narrow gauge: 59 km 0.762-m gauge (2000)
Highways:
total: 13,223 km
paved: 4,073 km
unpaved: 9,150 km (April 1999)
Waterways: none
Ports and harbors: none
Airports: 45 (2000 est.)
Airports - with paved runways:
total: 8
over 3,047 m: 1
1,524 to 2,437 m: 1
914 to 1,523 m: 6 (2000 est.)
Airports - with unpaved runways:
total: 37
1,524 to 2,437 m: 1
914 to 1,523 m: 7
under 914 m: 29 (2000 est.)

Military

Military branches: Royal Nepalese Army (includes Royal Nepalese Army Air Service), Nepalese Police Force
Military manpower - military age: 17 years of age
Military manpower - availability:
males age 15-49: 6,295,990 (2001 est.)
Military manpower - fit for military service:
males age 15-49: 3,272,077 (2001 est.)
Military manpower - reaching military age annually:
males: 292,589 (2001 est.)
Military expenditures - dollar figure: $44 million (FY96/97)
Military expenditures - percent of GDP: 0.9% (FY96/97)

Transnational Issues

Disputes - international: approximately 98,700 Bhutanese refugees in Nepal
Illicit drugs: illicit producer of cannabis for the domestic and international drug markets; transit point for opiates from Southeast Asia to the West

Netherlands

Introduction

Background: The Kingdom of the Netherlands was formed in 1815. In 1830 Belgium seceded and formed a separate kingdom. The Netherlands remained neutral in World War I but suffered a brutal invasion and occupation by Germany in World War II. A modern, industrialized nation, the Netherlands is also a large exporter of agricultural products. The country was a founding member of NATO and the EC, and participated in the introduction of the euro in 1999.

Geography

Location: Western Europe, bordering the North Sea, between Belgium and Germany
Geographic coordinates: 52 30 N, 5 45 E
Map references: Europe
Area:
total: 41,526 sq km
land: 33,883 sq km
water: 7,643 sq km
Area - comparative: slightly less than twice the size of New Jersey
Land boundaries:
total: 1,027 km
border countries: Belgium 450 km, Germany 577 km
Coastline: 451 km
Maritime claims:
exclusive fishing zone: 200 NM
territorial sea: 12 NM
Climate: temperate; marine; cool summers and mild winters
Terrain: mostly coastal lowland and reclaimed land (polders); some hills in southeast
Elevation extremes:
lowest point: Prins Alexanderpolder -7 m
highest point: Vaalserberg 321 m
Natural resources: natural gas, petroleum, arable land
Land use:
arable land: 25%
permanent crops: 3%
permanent pastures: 25%
forests and woodland: 8%
other: 39% (1996 est.)
Irrigated land: 6,000 sq km (1996 est.)
Natural hazards: flooding
Environment - current issues: water pollution in the form of heavy metals, organic compounds, and nutrients such as nitrates and phosphates; air pollution from vehicles and refining activities; acid rain
Environment - international agreements:
party to: Air Pollution, Air Pollution-Nitrogen Oxides, Air Pollution-Persistent Organic Pollutants, Air Pollution-Sulphur 85, Air Pollution-Sulphur 94, Air Pollution-Volatile Organic Compounds, Antarctic-Environmental Protocol, Antarctic-Marine Living Resources, Antarctic Treaty, Biodiversity, Climate Change, Desertification, Endangered Species, Environmental Modification, Hazardous Wastes, Law of the Sea, Marine Dumping, Marine Life Conservation, Nuclear Test Ban, Ozone Layer Protection, Ship Pollution, Tropical Timber 83, Tropical Timber 94, Wetlands, Whaling
signed, but not ratified: Biodiversity, Climate Change-Kyoto Protocol
Geography - note: located at mouths of three major European rivers (Rhine, Maas or Meuse, and Schelde)

People

Population: 15,981,472 (July 2001 est.)
Age structure:
0-14 years: 18.38% (male 1,501,925; female 1,436,017)
15-64 years: 67.9% (male 5,518,575; female 5,333,442)
65 years and over: 13.72% (male 899,052; female 1,292,461) (2001 est.)
Population growth rate: 0.55% (2001 est.)
Birth rate: 11.85 births/1,000 population (2001 est.)
Death rate: 8.69 deaths/1,000 population (2001 est.)
Net migration rate: 2.34 migrant(s)/1,000 population (2001 est.)
Sex ratio:
at birth: 1.04 male(s)/female
under 15 years: 1.05 male(s)/female
15-64 years: 1.03 male(s)/female
65 years and over: 0.7 male(s)/female
total population: 0.98 male(s)/female (2001 est.)
Infant mortality rate: 4.37 deaths/1,000 live births (2001 est.)
Life expectancy at birth:
total population: 78.43 years
male: 75.55 years
female: 81.44 years (2001 est.)
Total fertility rate: 1.65 children born/woman (2001 est.)
HIV/AIDS - adult prevalence rate: 0.19% (1999 est.)
HIV/AIDS - people living with HIV/AIDS: 15,000 (1999 est.)
HIV/AIDS - deaths: 100 (1999 est.)
Nationality:
noun: Dutchman(men), Dutchwoman(women)
adjective: Dutch
Ethnic groups: Dutch 91%, Moroccans, Turks, and other 9% (1999 est.)
Religions: Roman Catholic 31%, Protestant 21%, Muslim 4.4%, other 3.6%, unaffiliated 40% (1998)
Languages: Dutch
Literacy:
definition: age 15 and over can read and write
total population: 99% (2000 est.)
male: NA%
female: NA%

Government

Country name:
conventional long form: Kingdom of the Netherlands
conventional short form: Netherlands
local long form: Koninkrijk der Nederlanden
local short form: Nederland
Government type: constitutional monarchy
Capital: Amsterdam; The Hague is the seat of government
Administrative divisions: 12 provinces (provincien, singular - provincie); Drenthe, Flevoland, Friesland, Gelderland, Groningen, Limburg, Noord-Brabant, Noord-Holland, Overijssel, Utrecht, Zeeland, Zuid-Holland
Dependent areas: Aruba, Netherlands Antilles
Independence: 1579 (from Spain)
National holiday: Queen's Day (Birthday of Queen-Mother JULIANA in 1909 and accession to the throne of her oldest daughter BEATRIX in 1980), 30 April
Constitution: adopted 1814; amended many times, last time 17 February 1983
Legal system: civil law system incorporating French penal theory; constitution does not permit judicial review of acts of the States General; accepts compulsory ICJ jurisdiction, with reservations
Suffrage: 18 years of age; universal
Executive branch:
chief of state: Queen BEATRIX (since 30 April 1980); Heir Apparent WILLEM-ALEXANDER (born 27 April 1967), son of the monarch
head of government: Prime Minister Wim KOK (since 22 August 1994) and Vice Prime Ministers Annemarie JORRITSMA (since 3 August 1998) and Els BORST-EILERS (since 3 August 1998)
cabinet: Council of Ministers appointed by the monarch
elections: none; the monarch is hereditary; following Second Chamber elections, the leader of the majority party or leader of a majority coalition is usually appointed prime minister by the monarch; vice prime ministers appointed by the monarch
note: government coalition - PvdA, VVD, and D'66; there is also a Council of State composed of the monarch, heir apparent, and councilors consulted by the executive on legislative and administrative policy
Legislative branch: bicameral States General or Staten Generaal consists of the First Chamber or Eerste Kamer (75 seats; members indirectly elected

Netherlands (continued)

by the country's 12 provincial councils for four-year terms) and the Second Chamber or Tweede Kamer (150 seats; members directly elected by popular vote to serve four-year terms)

elections: First Chamber - last held 25 May 1999 (next to be held NA May 2003); Second Chamber - last held 6 May 1998 (next to be held May 2002)

election results: First Chamber - percent of vote by party - NA%; seats by party - CDA 20, VVD 19, PvdA 15, D'66 4, other 17; Second Chamber - percent of vote by party - PvdA 30.0%, VVD 25.3%, CDA 19.3%, D'66 9.3%, other 16.1%; seats by party - PvdA 45, VVD 38, CDA 29, D'66 14, other 24

Judicial branch: Supreme Court or Hoge Raad (justices are nominated for life by the monarch)

Political parties and leaders: Christian Democratic Appeal or CDA [Jaap de Hoop SCHEFFER]; Democrats '66 or D'66 [Tom DE GRAAF]; Labor Party or PvdA [Wim KOK]; People's Party for Freedom and Democracy (Liberal) or VVD [Hans F. DIJKSTAL]; a host of minor parties

Political pressure groups and leaders: Federation of Netherlands Trade Union Movement (comprising Socialist and Catholic trade unions) and a Protestant trade union; Federation of Catholic and Protestant Employers Associations; Interchurch Peace Council or IKV; large multinational firms; the nondenominational Federation of Netherlands Enterprises

International organization participation: AfDB, AsDB, Australia Group, Benelux, BIS, CCC, CE, CERN, EAPC, EBRD, ECE, ECLAC, EIB, EMU, ESA, ESCAP, EU, FAO, G-10, IADB, IAEA, IBRD, ICAO, ICC, ICFTU, ICRM, IDA, IEA, IFAD, IFC, IFRCS, IHO, ILO, IMF, IMO, Inmarsat, Intelsat, Interpol, IOC, IOM, ISO, ITU, NAM (guest), NATO, NEA, NSG, OAS (observer), OECD, OPCW, OSCE, PCA, UN, UNCTAD, UNESCO, UNFICYP, UNHCR, UNIDO, UNITAR, UNMEE, UNMIBH, UNMIK, UNTSO, UNU, UPU, WCL, WEU, WHO, WIPO, WMO, WToO, WTrO, ZC

Diplomatic representation in the US:
chief of mission: Ambassador Joris M. VOS
chancery: 4200 Linnean Avenue NW, Washington, DC 20008
telephone: [1] (202) 244-5300
FAX: [1] (202) 362-3430
consulate(s) general: Chicago, Houston, Los Angeles, New York
consulate(s): Boston

Diplomatic representation from the US:
chief of mission: Ambassador Cynthia P. SCHNEIDER
embassy: Lange Voorhout 102, 2514 EJ, The Hague
mailing address: PSC 71, Box 1000, APO AE 09715
telephone: [31] (70) 310-9209
FAX: [31] (70) 361-4688
consulate(s) general: Amsterdam

Flag description: three equal horizontal bands of red (top), white, and blue; similar to the flag of Luxembourg, which uses a lighter blue and is longer

Economy

Economy - overview: The Netherlands is a prosperous and open economy depending heavily on foreign trade. The economy is noted for stable industrial relations, moderate inflation, a sizable current account surplus, and an important role as a European transportation hub. Industrial activity is predominantly in food processing, chemicals, petroleum refining, and electrical machinery. A highly mechanized agricultural sector employs no more than 4% of the labor force but provides large surpluses for the food-processing industry and for exports. The Dutch rank third worldwide in value of agricultural exports, behind the US and France. The Dutch economy has expanded by 3% or more in each of the last four years and real GDP growth is likely to be about 3.6% in 2001. The government in 2001 will implement its most comprehensive tax reform since World War II, designed to reduce high income tax levels and redirect the fiscal burden onto consumption. The Dutch were among the first 11 EU countries establishing the euro currency zone on 1 January 1999.

GDP: purchasing power parity - $388.4 billion (2000 est.)

GDP - real growth rate: 4% (2000 est.)

GDP - per capita: purchasing power parity - $24,400 (2000 est.)

GDP - composition by sector:
agriculture: 3.3%
industry: 26.3%
services: 70.4% (2000 est.)

Population below poverty line: NA%

Household income or consumption by percentage share:
lowest 10%: 2.8%
highest 10%: 25.1% (1994)

Inflation rate (consumer prices): 2.6% (2000 est.)

Labor force: 7.2 million (2000)

Labor force - by occupation: services 73%, industry 23%, agriculture 4% (1998 est.)

Unemployment rate: 2.6% (2000 est.)

Budget:
revenues: $134 billion
expenditures: $134 billion, including capital expenditures of $NA (2001 est.)

Industries: agroindustries, metal and engineering products, electrical machinery and equipment, chemicals, petroleum, construction, microelectronics, fishing

Industrial production growth rate: 3.2% (2000)

Electricity - production: 85.294 billion kWh (1999)

Electricity - production by source:
fossil fuel: 90.25%
hydro: 0.11%
nuclear: 4.27%
other: 5.37% (1999)

Electricity - consumption: 97.76 billion kWh (1999)

Electricity - exports: 3.97 billion kWh (1999)

Electricity - imports: 22.407 billion kWh (1999)

Agriculture - products: grains, potatoes, sugar beets, fruits, vegetables; livestock

Exports: $210.3 billion (f.o.b., 2000)

Exports - commodities: machinery and equipment, chemicals, fuels; foodstuffs

Exports - partners: EU 78% (Germany 26%, Belgium-Luxembourg 12%, France 12%, UK 11%, Italy 6%), Central and Eastern Europe, US (2000)

Imports: $201.2 billion (c.i.f., 2000 est.)

Imports - commodities: machinery and transport equipment, chemicals, fuels; foodstuffs, clothing

Imports - partners: EU 56% (Germany 18%, Belgium-Luxembourg 10%, UK 5%, France 6%), US 9%, Central and Eastern Europe (2000)

Debt - external: $0

Economic aid - donor: ODA, $3.5 billion (2000 est.)

Currency: Netherlands guilder (NLG); euro (EUR)
note: on 1 January 1999, the EU introduced the euro as a common currency that is now being used by financial institutions in the Netherlands at a fixed rate of 2.20371 Netherlands guilders per euro and will replace the local currency for all transactions in 2002

Currency code: NLG; EUR

Exchange rates: euros per US dollar - 1.0659 (January 2001), 1.0854 (2000), 0.9386 (1999); Netherlands guilders per US dollar - 1.9837 (1998), 1.9513 (1997), 1.6859 (1996)

Fiscal year: calendar year

Communications

Telephones - main lines in use: 9,132,400 (1999)

Telephones - mobile cellular: 4,081,891 (April 1999)

Telephone system:
general assessment: highly developed and well maintained
domestic: the existing system of multi-conductor cables is gradually being replaced by fiber-optic cables; the density of cellular telephone traffic is rapidly increasing and further modernization of the system is expected in the year 2001, with the introduction of the third generation of the Global System for Mobile Communications (GSM)
international: 5 submarine cables; satellite earth stations - 3 Intelsat (1 Indian Ocean and 2 Atlantic Ocean), 1 Eutelsat, and 1 Inmarsat (Atlantic and Indian Ocean regions) (1996)

Radio broadcast stations: AM 4, FM 58, shortwave 3 (1998)

Radios: 15.3 million (1996)

Television broadcast stations: 21 (plus 26 repeaters) (1995)

Televisions: 8.1 million (1997)

Internet country code: .nl

Internet Service Providers (ISPs): 52 (2000)

Internet users: 6.8 million (2000)

Transportation

Railways:
total: 2,739 km
standard gauge: 2,739 km 1.435-m gauge; (1,991 km electrified) (1998)

Netherlands (continued)

Highways:
total: 125,575 km
paved: 113,018 km (including 2,235 km of expressways)
unpaved: 12,557 km (1998 est.)
Waterways: 5,046 km
note: 47% of total route length is usable by craft of 1,000 metric ton capacity or larger
Pipelines: crude oil 418 km; petroleum products 965 km; natural gas 10,230 km
Ports and harbors: Amsterdam, Delfzijl, Dordrecht, Eemshaven, Groningen, Haarlem, Ijmuiden, Maastricht, Rotterdam, Terneuzen, Utrecht, Vlissingen
Merchant marine:
total: 596 ships (1,000 GRT or over) totaling 4,321,500 GRT/4,877,632 DWT
ships by type: bulk 3, cargo 371, chemical tanker 43, container 59, liquefied gas 21, livestock carrier 1, multi-functional large-load carrier 9, passenger 8, petroleum tanker 26, refrigerated cargo 29, roll on/roll off 18, short-sea passenger 3, specialized tanker 5 (2000 est.)
Airports: 28 (2000 est.)
Airports - with paved runways:
total: 19
over 3,047 m: 2
2,438 to 3,047 m: 7
1,524 to 2,437 m: 6
914 to 1,523 m: 3
under 914 m: 1 (2000 est.)
Airports - with unpaved runways:
total: 9
914 to 1,523 m: 3
under 914 m: 6 (2000 est.)
Heliports: 1 (2000 est.)

Military

Military branches: Royal Netherlands Army, Royal Netherlands Navy (includes Naval Air Service and Marine Corps), Royal Netherlands Air Force, Royal Constabulary
Military manpower - military age: 20 years of age
Military manpower - availability:
males age 15-49: 4,083,349 (2001 est.)
Military manpower - fit for military service:
males age 15-49: 3,555,501 (2001 est.)
Military manpower - reaching military age annually:
males: 96,082 (2001 est.)
Military expenditures - dollar figure: $6.5 billion (FY00/01 est.)
Military expenditures - percent of GDP: 1.5% (FY00/01 est.)

Transnational Issues

Disputes - international: none
Illicit drugs: major European producer of illicit amphetamine and other synthetic drugs; important gateway for cocaine, heroin, and hashish entering Europe; major source of US-bound ecstasy

Netherlands Antilles
(part of the Kingdom of the Netherlands)

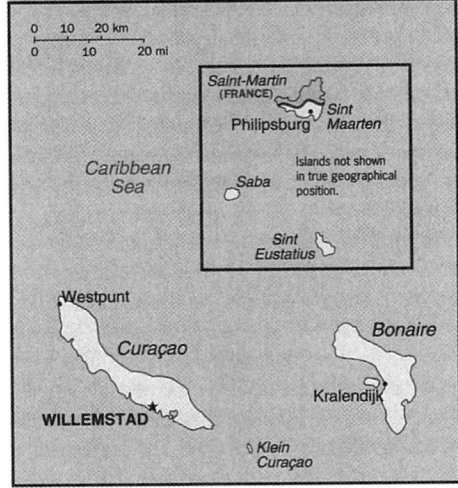

Introduction

Background: Once the center of the Caribbean slave trade, the island of Curacao was hard hit by the abolition of slavery in 1863. Its prosperity (and that of neighboring Aruba) was restored in the early 20th century with the construction of oil refineries to service the newly discovered Venezuelan oil fields. The island of Sint Maarten is shared with France; its northern portion is named Saint Martin and is part of Guadeloupe.

Geography

Location: Caribbean, two island groups in the Caribbean Sea - one includes Curacao and Bonaire north of Venezuela; the other is east of the Virgin Islands
Geographic coordinates: 12 15 N, 68 45 W
Map references: Central America and the Caribbean
Area:
total: 960 sq km
land: 960 sq km
water: 0 sq km
note: includes Bonaire, Curacao, Saba, Sint Eustatius, and Sint Maarten (Dutch part of the island of Saint Martin)
Area - comparative: more than five times the size of Washington, DC
Land boundaries:
total: 10.2 km
border countries: Guadeloupe (Saint Martin) 10.2 km
Coastline: 364 km
Maritime claims:
exclusive fishing zone: 12 NM
territorial sea: 12 NM
Climate: tropical; ameliorated by northeast trade winds
Terrain: generally hilly, volcanic interiors

Elevation extremes:
lowest point: Caribbean Sea 0 m
highest point: Mount Scenery 862 m
Natural resources: phosphates (Curacao only), salt (Bonaire only)
Land use:
arable land: 10%
permanent crops: 0%
permanent pastures: 0%
forests and woodland: 0%
other: 90% (1993 est.)
Irrigated land: NA sq km
Natural hazards: Curacao and Bonaire are south of Caribbean hurricane belt and are rarely threatened; Sint Maarten, Saba, and Sint Eustatius are subject to hurricanes from July to October
Environment - current issues: NA

People

Population: 212,226 (July 2001 est.)
Age structure:
0-14 years: 25.21% (male 27,332; female 26,169)
15-64 years: 66.99% (male 67,562; female 74,599)
65 years and over: 7.8% (male 6,874; female 9,690) (2001 est.)
Population growth rate: 0.97% (2001 est.)
Birth rate: 16.55 births/1,000 population (2001 est.)
Death rate: 6.41 deaths/1,000 population (2001 est.)
Net migration rate: -0.42 migrant(s)/1,000 population (2001 est.)
Sex ratio:
at birth: 1.05 male(s)/female
under 15 years: 1.04 male(s)/female
15-64 years: 0.91 male(s)/female
65 years and over: 0.71 male(s)/female
total population: 0.92 male(s)/female (2001 est.)
Infant mortality rate: 11.4 deaths/1,000 live births (2001 est.)
Life expectancy at birth:
total population: 74.94 years
male: 72.76 years
female: 77.22 years (2001 est.)
Total fertility rate: 2.07 children born/woman (2001 est.)
HIV/AIDS - adult prevalence rate: NA%
HIV/AIDS - people living with HIV/AIDS: NA
HIV/AIDS - deaths: NA
Nationality:
noun: Dutch Antillean(s)
adjective: Dutch Antillean
Ethnic groups: mixed black 85%, Carib Amerindian, white, East Asian
Religions: Roman Catholic, Protestant, Jewish, Seventh-Day Adventist
Languages: Dutch (official), Papiamento (a Spanish-Portuguese-Dutch-English dialect) predominates, English widely spoken, Spanish
Literacy:
definition: age 15 and over can read and write
total population: 98%

Netherlands Antilles (continued)

male: 98%
female: 99% (1981 est.)

Government

Country name:
conventional long form: none
conventional short form: Netherlands Antilles
local long form: none
local short form: Nederlandse Antillen
former: Curacao and Dependencies
Dependency status: part of the Kingdom of the Netherlands; full autonomy in internal affairs granted in 1954; Dutch Government responsible for defense and foreign affairs
Government type: parliamentary
Capital: Willemstad
Administrative divisions: none (part of the Kingdom of the Netherlands)
note: each island has its own government
Independence: none (part of the Kingdom of the Netherlands)
National holiday: Queen's Day (Birthday of Queen-Mother JULIANA in 1909 and accession to the throne of her oldest daughter BEATRIX in 1980), 30 April
Constitution: 29 December 1954, Statute of the Realm of the Netherlands, as amended
Legal system: based on Dutch civil law system, with some English common law influence
Suffrage: 18 years of age; universal
Executive branch:
chief of state: Queen BEATRIX of the Netherlands (since 30 April 1980), represented by Governor General Jaime SALEH (since NA October 1989)
head of government: Prime Minister Miguel POURIER (since 8 November 1999); Deputy Prime Minister Susanne CAMELIA-ROMER (since NA)
note: Miguel POURIER assumed prime ministership following the resignation of Susanne CAMELIA-ROMER
cabinet: Council of Ministers elected by the Staten
elections: the monarch is hereditary; governor general appointed by the monarch for a six-year term; following legislative elections, the leader of the majority party is usually elected prime minister by the Staten; election last held 30 January 1998 (next to be held by NA 2002)
note: government coalition - PDB, DP-St. M, FOL, PLKP, PNP
Legislative branch: unicameral States or Staten (22 seats; members are elected by popular vote to serve four-year terms)
elections: last held 30 January 1998 (next to be held by NA 2002)
election results: percent of vote by party - NA%; seats by party - PAR 4, PNP 3, SPA 1, PDB 2, UPB 1, MAN 2, PLKP 3, WIPM 1, SEA 1, DP-St. M 2, FOL 2; no party won enough seats to form a government
note: the government of Prime Minister Miguel POURIER is a coalition of several parties; current seats by party - PAR 4, PNP 3, FOL 2, MAN 2, UPB 2, DP-St. M 2, PDB 1, SEA 1, WIPM 1, other 4
Judicial branch: Joint High Court of Justice (judges appointed by the monarch)
Political parties and leaders: Antillean Restructuring Party or PAR [Miguel POURIER]; C 93 [Stanley BROWN]; Democratic Party of Bonaire or PDB [Jopi ABRAHAM]; Democratic Party of Curacao or DP [Errol HERNANDEZ]; Democratic Party of Sint Eustatius or DP-St. E [Julian WOODLEY]; Democratic Party of Sint Maarten or DP-St. M [Sarah WESCOTT-WILLIAMS]; Foundation Energetic Management Anti-Narcotics or FAME [Eric LODEWIJKS]; Labor Party People's Crusade or PLKP [Errol COVA]; National People's Party or PNP [Susanne F. C. CAMELIA-ROMER]; New Antilles Movement or MAN [Kenneth GIJSBERTHA]; Patriotic Union of Bonaire or UPB [Ramon BOOI]; Patriotic Movement of Sint Maarten or SPA [Vance JAMES, Jr.]; People's Party or PAPU [Richard Hodi]; Pro Curacao Party or PPK [Winston LOURENS]; Saba Democratic Labor Movement [Steve HASSELL]; Saba Unity Party [Carmen SIMMONDS]; St. Eustatius Alliance or SEA [Kenneth VAN PUTTEN]; Serious Alternative People's Party or Sapp [Julian ROLLOCKS]; Social Action Cause or KAS [Benny DEMEI]; Windward Islands People's Movement or WIPM [Will JOHNSTON]; Workers' Liberation Front or FOL [Anthony GODETT, Rignald LAK, Editha WRIGHT]
note: political parties are indigenous to each island
Political pressure groups and leaders: NA
International organization participation: Caricom (observer), ECLAC (associate), Interpol, IOC, UNESCO (associate), UPU, WCL, WMO, WToO (associate)
Diplomatic representation in the US: none (represented by the Kingdom of the Netherlands)
Diplomatic representation from the US:
chief of mission: Consul General Barbara J. STEPHENSON
consulate(s) general: J. B. Gorsiraweg #1, Willemstad AN, Curacao
mailing address: P. O. Box 158, Willemstad, Curacao
telephone: [599] (9) 4613066
FAX: [599] (9) 4616489
Flag description: white, with a horizontal blue stripe in the center superimposed on a vertical red band, also centered; five white, five-pointed stars are arranged in an oval pattern in the center of the blue band; the five stars represent the five main islands of Bonaire, Curacao, Saba, Sint Eustatius, and Sint Maarten

Economy

Economy - overview: Tourism, petroleum refining, and offshore finance are the mainstays of this small economy, which is closely tied to the outside world. Although GDP has declined slightly in each of the past five years, the islands enjoy a high per capita income and a well-developed infrastructure as compared with other countries in the region. Almost all consumer and capital goods are imported, with Venezuela, the US, and Mexico being the major suppliers. Poor soils and inadequate water supplies hamper the development of agriculture.
GDP: purchasing power parity - $2.4 billion (2000 est.)
GDP - real growth rate: -3.5% (2000 est.)
GDP - per capita: purchasing power parity - $11,400 (2000 est.)
GDP - composition by sector:
agriculture: 1%
industry: 15%
services: 84% (1996 est.)
Population below poverty line: NA%
Household income or consumption by percentage share:
lowest 10%: NA%
highest 10%: NA%
Inflation rate (consumer prices): 6.4% (2000 est.)
Labor force: 89,000
Labor force - by occupation: agriculture 1%, industry 13%, services 86% (1994 est.)
Unemployment rate: 14.9% (1998 est.)
Budget:
revenues: $710.8 million
expenditures: $741.6 million, including capital expenditures of $NA (1997 est.)
Industries: tourism (Curacao, Sint Maarten, and Bonaire), petroleum refining (Curacao), petroleum transshipment facilities (Curacao and Bonaire), light manufacturing (Curacao)
Industrial production growth rate: NA%
Electricity - production: 1.11 billion kWh (1999)
Electricity - production by source:
fossil fuel: 100%
hydro: 0%
nuclear: 0%
other: 0% (1999)
Electricity - consumption: 1.032 billion kWh (1999)
Electricity - exports: 0 kWh (1999)
Electricity - imports: 0 kWh (1999)
Agriculture - products: aloes, sorghum, peanuts, vegetables, tropical fruit
Exports: $276 million (f.o.b., 2000)
Exports - commodities: petroleum products
Exports - partners: US 17.5%, Guatemala 8%, Costa Rica 6.5%, The Bahamas 4.6%, Jamaica 4.1%, Chile 3.4% (1998)
Imports: $1.5 billion (f.o.b., 2000)
Imports - commodities: crude petroleum, food, manufactures
Imports - partners: Venezuela 35.3%, US 21%, Mexico 9.8%, Italy 5.4%, Netherlands 4.8%, Brazil 3.1% (1998)
Debt - external: $1.35 billion (1996)
Economic aid - recipient: IMF provided $61 million in 2000, and the Netherlands continued its support with $40 million
Currency: Netherlands Antillean guilder (ANG)
Currency code: ANG
Exchange rates: Netherlands Antillean guilders per US dollar - 1.790 (fixed rate since 1989)
Fiscal year: calendar year

Netherlands Antilles (continued)

Communications

Telephones - main lines in use: 76,000 (1995)
Telephones - mobile cellular: 13,977 (1996)
Telephone system:
general assessment: generally adequate facilities
domestic: extensive interisland microwave radio relay links
international: submarine cables - 2; satellite earth stations - 2 Intelsat (Atlantic Ocean)
Radio broadcast stations: AM 9, FM 4, shortwave 0 (1998)
Radios: 217,000 (1997)
Television broadcast stations: 3 (there is also a cable service which supplies programs received from various US satellite networks and two Venezuelan channels) (1997)
Televisions: 69,000 (1997)
Internet country code: .an
Internet Service Providers (ISPs): 6
Internet users: 2,000 (2000)

Transportation

Railways: 0 km
Highways:
total: 600 km
paved: 300 km
unpaved: 300 km (1992)
Waterways: none
Ports and harbors: Kralendijk, Philipsburg, Willemstad
Merchant marine:
total: 123 ships (1,000 GRT or over) totaling 1,113,774 GRT/1,397,841 DWT
ships by type: bulk 1, cargo 35, chemical tanker 2, combination ore/oil 3, container 19, liquefied gas 4, multi-functional large-load carrier 19, passenger 1, petroleum tanker 4, refrigerated cargo 28, roll on/roll off 7
note: includes some foreign-owned ships registered here as a flag of convenience: Belgium 8, Germany 1, Italy 1 (2000 est.)
Airports: 5 (2000 est.)
Airports - with paved runways:
total: 5
over 3,047 m: 1
1,524 to 2,437 m: 2
914 to 1,523 m: 1
under 914 m: 1 (2000 est.)

Military

Military branches: Royal Netherlands Navy, Marine Corps, Coast Guard, National Guard, Police Force
Military manpower - military age: 20 years of age
Military manpower - availability:
males age 15-49: 54,284 (2001 est.)
Military manpower - fit for military service:
males age 15-49: 30,405 (2001 est.)
Military manpower - reaching military age annually:
males: 1,610 (2001 est.)

Military - note: defense is the responsibility of the Kingdom of the Netherlands

Transnational Issues

Disputes - international: none
Illicit drugs: money-laundering center; transshipment point for South American drugs bound for the US and Europe

New Caledonia
(overseas territory of France)

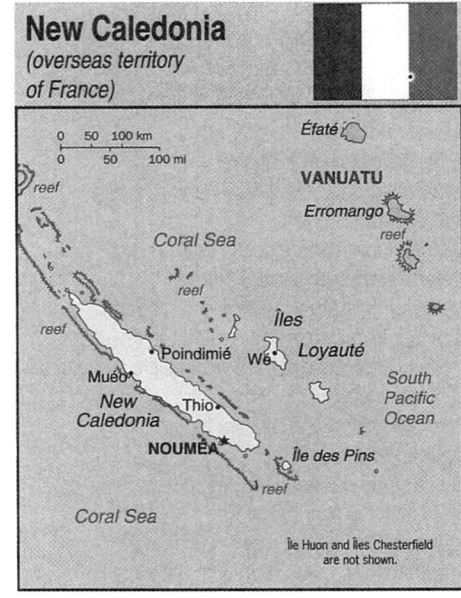

Introduction

Background: Settled by both Britain and France during the first half of the 19th century, the island was made a French possession in 1853. It served as a penal colony for four decades after 1864. Agitation for independence during the 1980s and early 1990s seems to have dissipated.

Geography

Location: Oceania, islands in the South Pacific Ocean, east of Australia
Geographic coordinates: 21 30 S, 165 30 E
Map references: Oceania
Area:
total: 19,060 sq km
land: 18,575 sq km
water: 485 sq km
Area - comparative: slightly smaller than New Jersey
Land boundaries: 0 km
Coastline: 2,254 km
Maritime claims:
exclusive economic zone: 200 NM
territorial sea: 12 NM
Climate: tropical; modified by southeast trade winds; hot, humid
Terrain: coastal plains with interior mountains
Elevation extremes:
lowest point: Pacific Ocean 0 m
highest point: Mont Panie 1,628 m
Natural resources: nickel, chrome, iron, cobalt, manganese, silver, gold, lead, copper
Land use:
arable land: 0%
permanent crops: 0%
permanent pastures: 12%
forests and woodland: 39%
other: 49% (1993 est.)
Irrigated land: 160 sq km (1991)

New Caledonia (continued)

Natural hazards: cyclones, most frequent from November to March
Environment - current issues: erosion caused by mining exploitation and forest fires

People

Population: 204,863 (July 2001 est.)
Age structure:
0-14 years: 30.31% (male 31,674; female 30,416)
15-64 years: 63.95% (male 66,014; female 65,006)
65 years and over: 5.74% (male 5,548; female 6,205) (2001 est.)
Population growth rate: 1.48% (2001 est.)
Birth rate: 20.37 births/1,000 population (2001 est.)
Death rate: 5.62 deaths/1,000 population (2001 est.)
Net migration rate: 0 migrant(s)/1,000 population (2001 est.)
Sex ratio:
at birth: 1.05 male(s)/female
under 15 years: 1.04 male(s)/female
15-64 years: 1.02 male(s)/female
65 years and over: 0.89 male(s)/female
total population: 1.02 male(s)/female (2001 est.)
Infant mortality rate: 8.4 deaths/1,000 live births (2001 est.)
Life expectancy at birth:
total population: 73.02 years
male: 70.08 years
female: 76.11 years (2001 est.)
Total fertility rate: 2.48 children born/woman (2001 est.)
HIV/AIDS - adult prevalence rate: NA%
HIV/AIDS - people living with HIV/AIDS: NA
HIV/AIDS - deaths: NA
Nationality:
noun: New Caledonian(s)
adjective: New Caledonian
Ethnic groups: Melanesian 42.5%, European 37.1%, Wallisian 8.4%, Polynesian 3.8%, Indonesian 3.6%, Vietnamese 1.6%, other 3%
Religions: Roman Catholic 60%, Protestant 30%, other 10%
Languages: French (official), 33 Melanesian-Polynesian dialects
Literacy:
definition: age 15 and over can read and write
total population: 91%
male: 92%
female: 90% (1976 est.)

Government

Country name:
conventional long form: Territory of New Caledonia and Dependencies
conventional short form: New Caledonia
local long form: Territoire des Nouvelle-Caledonie et Dependances
local short form: Nouvelle-Caledonie
Dependency status: overseas territory of France since 1956
Government type: NA
Capital: Noumea
Administrative divisions: none (overseas territory of France); there are no first-order administrative divisions as defined by the US Government, but there are 3 provinces named Iles Loyaute, Nord, and Sud
Independence: none (overseas territory of France); note - a referendum on independence was held in 1998 but did not pass
National holiday: Bastille Day, 14 July (1789)
Constitution: 28 September 1958 (French Constitution)
Legal system: the 1988 Matignon Accords grant substantial autonomy to the islands; formerly under French law
Suffrage: 18 years of age; universal
Executive branch:
chief of state: President of France Jacques CHIRAC (since 17 May 1995), represented by High Commissioner Thierry LATASTE (since 19 July 1999)
head of government: President of the Government Jean LEQUES (since 28 May 1999)
cabinet: Consultative Committee
elections: French president elected by popular vote for a seven-year term; high commissioner appointed by the French president on the advice of the French Ministry of Interior; president of the government elected by the members of the Territorial Congress
Legislative branch: unicameral Territorial Congress or Congres Territorial (54 seats; members are members of the three Provincial Assemblies or Assemblees Provinciales elected by popular vote to serve five-year terms)
elections: last held 9 May 1999 (next to be held NA 2004)
election results: percent of vote by party - NA%; seats by party - RPCR 24, FLNKS 12, UNI 6, FCCI 4, FN 4, Alliance pour la Caledonie 3, LKS 1
note: New Caledonia elects 1 seat to the French Senate; elections last held 27 September 1992 (next to be held NA September 2001); results - percent of vote by party - NA; seats by party - RPR 1; New Caledonia also elects 2 seats to the French National Assembly; elections last held 25 May-1 June 1997 (next to be held NA 2002); resuits - percent of vote by party - NA; seats by party - RPR 2
Judicial branch: Court of Appeal or Cour d'Appel; County Courts; Joint Commerce Tribunal Court; Children's Court
Political parties and leaders: Alliance pour la Caledonie [Didier LEROUX]; Developper Ensemble pour Construire l'Avenir or DEPCA [Robert FROUIN]; Federation des Comites de Coordination des Independantistes or FCCI [Leopold SOREDIE]; Front Uni de Liberation Kanak or FULK [Ernest UNE]; Groupe de l'Alliance Multiraciale or GAM [Dany DALMAYRAE]; Independance et Progres [Alphonse PUJAPUJANE]; Kanak Socialist Front for National Liberation or FLNKS [Rock WAMYTAN] (includes PALIKA, UNI, UC, and UPM); La Caledonie Autrement [Denis MILLIARD]; Loyalty Islands Development Front or FDIL [Cono HAMU]; National Front or FN [Guy GEORGE]; Parti de Liberation Kanak or PALIKA [Charles WASHETINE]; Rally for Caledonia in the Republic or RPCR [Jacques LAFLEUR]; Rally for the Republic or RPR [leader NA]; Renouveau [Thierry VALET]; Socialist Kanak Liberation or LKS [Nidoish NAISSELINE]; Union Caledonienne or UC [Bernard LEPEU]; Union Nationale pour l'Independance or UNI [Paul NEAOUTYINE]; Union Progressiste Melanesienne or UPM [Andre GOPEA]
Political pressure groups and leaders: NA
International organization participation: ESCAP (associate), FZ, ICFTU, SPC, WFTU, WMO
Diplomatic representation in the US: none (overseas territory of France)
Diplomatic representation from the US: none (overseas territory of France)
Flag description: the flag of France is used

Economy

Economy - overview: New Caledonia has more than 20% of the world's known nickel resources. In recent years, the economy has suffered because of depressed international demand for nickel, the principal source of export earnings. Only a negligible amount of the land is suitable for cultivation, and food accounts for about 20% of imports. In addition to nickel, the substantial financial support from France and tourism are keys to the health of the economy. The situation in 1998 was clouded by the spillover of financial problems in East Asia and by lower prices for nickel. Nickel prices jumped in 1999-2000, and large additions were made to capacity. French Government interests in the New Caledonian nickel industry are being transferred to local ownership.
GDP: purchasing power parity - $3 billion (1998 est.)
GDP - real growth rate: 3.5% (1998 est.)
GDP - per capita: purchasing power parity - $15,000 (1998 est.)
GDP - composition by sector:
agriculture: 4%
industry: 30%
services: 66% (1997 est.)
Population below poverty line: NA%
Household income or consumption by percentage share:
lowest 10%: NA%
highest 10%: NA%
Inflation rate (consumer prices): 1.5% (1998 est.)
Labor force: 79,395 (including 15,018 unemployed, 1996)
Labor force - by occupation: agriculture 7%, industry 23%, services 70% (1999 est.)
Unemployment rate: 19% (1996)
Budget:
revenues: $861.3 million
expenditures: $735.3 million, including capital expenditures of $52 million (1996 est.)
Industries: nickel mining and smelting
Industrial production growth rate: -0.6% (1996)
Electricity - production: 1.52 billion kWh (1999)

New Caledonia (continued)

Electricity - production by source:
fossil fuel: 78.95%
hydro: 21.05%
nuclear: 0%
other: 0% (1999)
Electricity - consumption: 1.414 billion kWh (1999)
Electricity - exports: 0 kWh (1999)
Electricity - imports: 0 kWh (1999)
Agriculture - products: vegetables; beef, deer, other livestock products
Exports: $411 million (f.o.b., 1999)
Exports - commodities: ferronickels, nickel ore, fish
Exports - partners: Japan 27%, France 17%, Taiwan 12%, South Korea 9% (1999)
Imports: $843 million (f.o.b., 1999)
Imports - commodities: transport equipment, machinery and electrical equipment, fuels, minerals, wine, sugar, rice
Imports - partners: France 49%, Australia 14%, Singapore 6%, New Zealand 5%, US 5% (1999)
Debt - external: $79 million (1998 est.)
Economic aid - recipient: $880 million annual subsidy from France
Currency: Comptoirs Francais du Pacifique franc (XPF)
Currency code: XPF
Exchange rates: Comptoirs Francais du Pacifique francs (XPF) per US dollar - 127.11 (January 2001), 129.44 (2000), 111.93 (1999), 107.25 (1998), 106.11 (1997), 93.00 (1996); note - linked at the rate of 119.25 XPF to the euro
Fiscal year: calendar year

Communications

Telephones - main lines in use: 47,000 (1997)
Telephones - mobile cellular: 13,040 (1998)
Telephone system:
general assessment: NA
domestic: NA
international: satellite earth station - 1 Intelsat (Pacific Ocean)
Radio broadcast stations: AM 1, FM 5, shortwave 0 (1998)
Radios: 107,000 (1997)
Television broadcast stations: 6 (plus 25 low-power repeaters) (1997)
Televisions: 52,000 (1997)
Internet country code: .nc
Internet Service Providers (ISPs): 1 (2000)
Internet users: 5,000 (2000)

Transportation

Railways: 0 km
Highways:
total: 4,825 km
paved: 2,287 km
unpaved: 2,538 km (1999)
Waterways: none
Ports and harbors: Mueo, Noumea, Thio

Merchant marine:
total: 1 ship (1,000 GRT or over) totaling 1,261 GRT/1,600 DWT
ships by type: cargo 1 (2000 est.)
Airports: 29 (2000 est.)
Airports - with paved runways:
total: 6
over 3,047 m: 1
914 to 1,523 m: 4
under 914 m: 1 (2000 est.)
Airports - with unpaved runways:
total: 23
914 to 1,523 m: 12
under 914 m: 11 (2000 est.)
Heliports: 6 (2000 est.)

Military

Military branches: French Armed Forces (Army, Navy, Air Force, Gendarmerie); Police Force
Military expenditures - dollar figure: $192.3 million (1996)
Military expenditures - percent of GDP: 5.3% (1996)
Military - note: defense is the responsibility of France

Transnational Issues

Disputes - international: Matthew and Hunter Islands east of New Caledonia claimed by France and Vanuatu

New Zealand

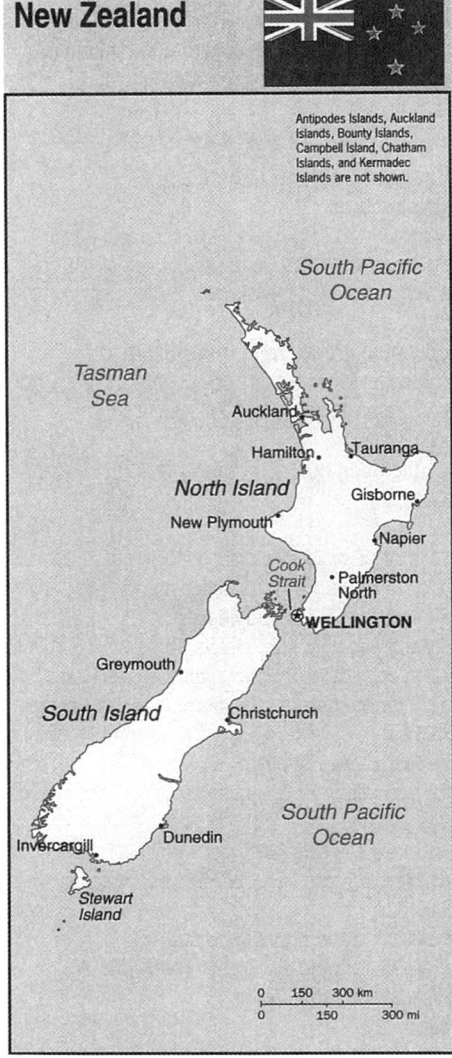

Antipodes Islands, Auckland Islands, Bounty Islands, Campbell Island, Chatham Islands, and Kermadec Islands are not shown.

Introduction

Background: The British colony of New Zealand became an independent dominion in 1907 and supported the UK militarily in both World Wars. New Zealand withdrew from a number of defense alliances during the 1970s and 1980s. In recent years the government has sought to address longstanding native Maori grievances.

Geography

Location: Oceania, islands in the South Pacific Ocean, southeast of Australia
Geographic coordinates: 41 00 S, 174 00 E
Map references: Oceania
Area:
total: 268,680 sq km
land: 268,670 sq km
water: 10 sq km
note: includes Antipodes Islands, Auckland Islands, Bounty Islands, Campbell Island, Chatham Islands, and Kermadec Islands
Area - comparative: about the size of Colorado
Land boundaries: 0 km
Coastline: 15,134 km

New Zealand (continued)

Maritime claims:
continental shelf: 200 NM or to the edge of the continental margin
exclusive economic zone: 200 NM
territorial sea: 12 NM
Climate: temperate with sharp regional contrasts
Terrain: predominately mountainous with some large coastal plains
Elevation extremes:
lowest point: Pacific Ocean 0 m
highest point: Mount Cook 3,764 m
Natural resources: natural gas, iron ore, sand, coal, timber, hydropower, gold, limestone
Land use:
arable land: 9%
permanent crops: 5%
permanent pastures: 50%
forests and woodland: 28%
other: 8% (1993 est.)
Irrigated land: 2,850 sq km (1993 est.)
Natural hazards: earthquakes are common, though usually not severe; volcanic activity
Environment - current issues: deforestation; soil erosion; native flora and fauna hard-hit by species introduced from outside
Environment - international agreements:
party to: Antarctic-Environmental Protocol, Antarctic-Marine Living Resources, Antarctic Treaty, Biodiversity, Climate Change, Desertification, Endangered Species, Environmental Modification, Hazardous Wastes, Law of the Sea, Marine Dumping, Nuclear Test Ban, Ozone Layer Protection, Ship Pollution, Tropical Timber 83, Tropical Timber 94, Wetlands, Whaling
signed, but not ratified: Antarctic Seals, Climate Change-Kyoto Protocol, Marine Life Conservation
Geography - note: about 80% of the population lives in cities; Wellington is the southernmost national capital in the world

People

Population: 3,864,129 (July 2001 est.)
Age structure:
0-14 years: 22.36% (male 442,738; female 421,462)
15-64 years: 66.11% (male 1,281,781; female 1,272,674)
65 years and over: 11.53% (male 193,895; female 251,579) (2001 est.)
Population growth rate: 1.14% (2001 est.)
Birth rate: 14.28 births/1,000 population (2001 est.)
Death rate: 7.56 deaths/1,000 population (2001 est.)
Net migration rate: 4.71 migrant(s)/1,000 population (2001 est.)
Sex ratio:
at birth: 1.04 male(s)/female
under 15 years: 1.05 male(s)/female
15-64 years: 1.01 male(s)/female
65 years and over: 0.77 male(s)/female
total population: 0.99 male(s)/female (2001 est.)
Infant mortality rate: 6.28 deaths/1,000 live births (2001 est.)
Life expectancy at birth:
total population: 77.99 years
male: 75.01 years
female: 81.1 years (2001 est.)
Total fertility rate: 1.8 children born/woman (2001 est.)
HIV/AIDS - adult prevalence rate: 0.06% (1999 est.)
HIV/AIDS - people living with HIV/AIDS: 1,200 (1999 est.)
HIV/AIDS - deaths: less than 100 (1999 est.)
Nationality:
noun: New Zealander(s)
adjective: New Zealand
Ethnic groups: New Zealand European 74.5%, Maori 9.7%, other European 4.6%, Pacific Islander 3.8%, Asian and others 7.4%
Religions: Anglican 24%, Presbyterian 18%, Roman Catholic 15%, Methodist 5%, Baptist 2%, other Protestant 3%, unspecified or none 33% (1986)
Languages: English (official), Maori
Literacy:
definition: age 15 and over can read and write
total population: 99% (1980 est.)
male: NA%
female: NA%

Government

Country name:
conventional long form: none
conventional short form: New Zealand
abbreviation: NZ
Government type: parliamentary democracy
Capital: Wellington
Administrative divisions: 93 counties, 9 districts*, and 3 town districts**; Akaroa, Amuri, Ashburton, Bay of Islands, Bruce, Buller, Chatham Islands, Cheviot, Clifton, Clutha, Cook, Dannevirke, Egmont, Eketahuna, Ellesmere, Eltham, Eyre, Featherston, Franklin, Golden Bay, Great Barrier Island, Grey, Hauraki Plains, Hawera*, Hawke's Bay, Heathcote, Hikurangi**, Hobson, Hokianga, Horowhenua, Hurunui, Hutt, Inangahua, Inglewood, Kaikoura, Kairanga, Kiwitea, Lake, Mackenzie, Malvern, Manaia**, Manawatu, Mangonui, Maniototo, Marlborough, Masterton, Matamata, Mount Herbert, Ohinemuri, Opotiki, Oroua, Otamatea, Otorohanga*, Oxford, Pahiatua, Paparua, Patea, Piako, Pohangina, Raglan, Rangiora*, Rangitikei, Rodney, Rotorua*, Runanga, Saint Kilda, Silverpeaks, Southland, Stewart Island, Stratford, Strathallan, Taranaki, Taumarunui, Taupo, Tauranga, Thames-Coromandel*, Tuapeka, Vincent, Waiapu, Waiheke, Waihemo, Waikato, Waikohu, Waimairi, Waimarino, Waimate, Waimate West, Waimea, Waipa, Waipawa*, Waipukurau*, Wairarapa South, Wairewa, Wairoa, Waitaki, Waitomo*, Waitotara, Wallace, Wanganui, Waverley**, Westland, Whakatane*, Whangarei, Whangaroa, Woodville
note: there may be a new administrative structure of 16 regions (Auckland, Bay of Plenty, Canterbury, Gisborne, Hawke's Bay, Marlborough, Nelson, Northland, Otago, Southland, Taranaki, Tasman, Waikato, Wanganui-Manawatu, Wellington, West Coast) that are subdivided into 57 districts and 16 cities* (Ashburton, Auckland*, Banks Peninsula, Buller, Carterton, Central Hawke's Bay, Central Otago, Christchurch*, Clutha, Dunedin*, Far North, Franklin, Gisborne, Gore, Grey, Hamilton*, Hastings, Hauraki, Horowhenua, Hurunui, Hutt*, Invercargill*, Kaikoura, Kaipara, Kapiti Coast, Kawerau, Mackenzie, Manawatu, Manukau*, Marlborough, Masterton, Matamata Piako, Napier*, Nelson*, New Plymouth, North Shore*, Opotiki, Otorohanga, Palmerston North*, Papakura*, Porirua*, Queenstown Lakes, Rangitikei, Rodney, Rotorua, Ruapehu, Selwyn, Southland, South Taranaki, South Waikato, South Wairarapa, Stratford, Tararua, Tasman, Taupo, Tauranga, Thames Coromandel, Timaru, Upper Hutt*, Waikato, Waimakariri, Waimate, Waipa, Wairoa, Waitakere*, Waitaki, Waitomo, Wanganui, Wellington*, Western Bay of Plenty, Westland, Whakatane, Whangarei)
Dependent areas: Cook Islands, Niue, Tokelau
Independence: 26 September 1907 (from UK)
National holiday: Waitangi Day (Treaty of Waitangi established British sovereignty over New Zealand), 6 February (1840)
Constitution: consists of a series of legal documents, including certain acts of the UK and New Zealand Parliaments and The Constitution Act 1986 which is the principal formal charter
Legal system: based on English law, with special land legislation and land courts for Maoris; accepts compulsory ICJ jurisdiction, with reservations
Suffrage: 18 years of age; universal
Executive branch:
chief of state: Queen ELIZABETH II (since 6 February 1952), represented by Governor General Dame Silvia CARTWRIGHT (since 4 April 2001)
head of government: Prime Minister Helen CLARK (since 10 December 1999) and Deputy Prime Minister Jim ANDERTON (since 10 December 1999)
cabinet: Executive Council appointed by the governor general on the recommendation of the prime minister
elections: none; the monarch is hereditary; governor general appointed by the monarch; following legislative elections, the leader of the majority party or the leader of a majority coalition is usually appointed prime minister by the governor general for a three-year term; deputy prime minister appointed by the governor general
Legislative branch: unicameral House of Representatives - commonly called Parliament (120 seats; members elected by popular vote in single-member constituencies to serve three-year terms)
elections: last held 27 November 1999 (next must be called by November 2002)
election results: percent of vote by party - NA%; seats by party - NZLP 49, NP 39, Alliance 10, ACT New Zealand 9, Green Party 7, NZFP 5, UNZ 1
note: NZLP and Alliance formed the government coalition; the National Party became the opposition party

New Zealand (continued)

Judicial branch: High Court; Court of Appeal
Political parties and leaders: ACT, New Zealand [Richard PREBBLE]; Alliance (a coalition of the New Labor Party, Democratic Party, New Zealand Liberal Party, and Mana Motuhake) [Jim ANDERTON]; Green Party [Jeanette FITZSIMONS and Rod DONALD]; National Party or NP [Jenny SHIPLEY]; New Zealand First Party or NZFP [Winston PETERS]; New Zealand Labor Party or NZLP [Helen CLARK]; United New Zealand or UNZ [Peter DUNNE]
Political pressure groups and leaders: NA
International organization participation: ABEDA, ANZUS (US suspended security obligations to NZ on 11 August 1986), APEC, ARF (dialogue partner), AsDB, ASEAN (dialogue partner), Australia Group, C, CCC, CP, EBRD, ESCAP, FAO, IAEA, IBRD, ICAO, ICFTU, ICRM, IDA, IEA, IFAD, IFC, IFRCS, IHO, ILO, IMF, IMO, Inmarsat, Intelsat, Interpol, IOC, IOM (observer), ISO, ITU, NAM (guest), NSG, OECD, OPCW, PCA, Sparteca, SPC, SPF, UN, UNAMSIL, UNCTAD, UNESCO, UNIDO, UNMIK, UNMOP, UNTAET, UNTSO, UPU, WFTU, WHO, WIPO, WMO, WTrO
Diplomatic representation in the US:
chief of mission: Ambassador James Brendan BOLGER
chancery: 37 Observatory Circle NW, Washington, DC 20008
telephone: [1] (202) 328-4800
FAX: [1] (202) 667-5227
consulate(s) general: Los Angeles, New York
Diplomatic representation from the US:
chief of mission: Ambassador Carol MOSELEY-BRAUN
embassy: 29 Fitzherbert Terrace, Thorndon, Wellington
mailing address: P. O. Box 1190, Wellington; PSC 467, Box 1, FPO AP 96531-1001
telephone: [64] (4) 472-2068
FAX: [64] (4) 478-1701
consulate(s) general: Auckland
Flag description: blue with the flag of the UK in the upper hoist-side quadrant with four red five-pointed stars edged in white centered in the outer half of the flag; the stars represent the Southern Cross constellation

Economy

Economy - overview: Since 1984 the government has accomplished major economic restructuring, moving an agrarian economy dependent on concessionary British market access toward a more industrialized, free market economy that can compete globally. This dynamic growth has boosted real incomes, broadened and deepened the technological capabilities of the industrial sector, and contained inflationary pressures. Inflation remains among the lowest in the industrial world. Per capita GDP has been moving up toward the levels of the big West European economies. New Zealand's heavy dependence on trade leaves its growth prospects vulnerable to economic performance in Asia, Europe, and the US. With the FY00/01 budget pushing up pension and other public outlays, the government's ability to meet fiscal targets will depend on sustained economic growth.
GDP: purchasing power parity - $67.6 billion (2000 est.)
GDP - real growth rate: 3.6% (2000 est.)
GDP - per capita: purchasing power parity - $17,700 (2000 est.)
GDP - composition by sector:
agriculture: 8%
industry: 23%
services: 69% (1999)
Population below poverty line: NA%
Household income or consumption by percentage share:
lowest 10%: 0.3%
highest 10%: 29.8% (1991 est.)
Inflation rate (consumer prices): 2.4% (2000 est.)
Labor force: 1.88 million (2000)
Labor force - by occupation: services 65%, industry 25%, agriculture 10% (1995)
Unemployment rate: 6.3% (2000 est.)
Budget:
revenues: $19.2 billion
expenditures: $19.2 billion, including capital expenditures of $NA (1999 est.)
Industries: food processing, wood and paper products, textiles, machinery, transportation equipment, banking and insurance, tourism, mining
Industrial production growth rate: 6.2% (2000)
Electricity - production: 37.952 billion kWh (1999)
Electricity - production by source:
fossil fuel: 30.49%
hydro: 61.42%
nuclear: 0%
other: 8.09% (1999)
Electricity - consumption: 35.295 billion kWh (1999)
Electricity - exports: 0 kWh (1999)
Electricity - imports: 0 kWh (1999)
Agriculture - products: wheat, barley, potatoes, pulses, fruits, vegetables; wool, beef, dairy products; fish
Exports: $14.6 billion (f.o.b., 2000 est.)
Exports - commodities: dairy products, meat, fish, wool, forestry products, manufactures
Exports - partners: Australia 22%, US 14%, Japan 13%, UK 7% (1999)
Imports: $14.3 billion (f.o.b., 2000 est.)
Imports - commodities: machinery and equipment, vehicles and aircraft, petroleum, consumer goods, plastics
Imports - partners: Australia 24%, US 17%, Japan 12%, UK 4% (1999)
Debt - external: $30.8 billion (2000 est.)
Economic aid - donor: ODA, $123 million (1995)
Currency: New Zealand dollar (NZD)
Currency code: NZD
Exchange rates: New Zealand dollars per US dollar - 2.2502 (January 2001), 2.1863 (2000), 1.8886 (1999), 1.8632 (1998), 1.5083 (1997), 1.4543 (1996)
Fiscal year: 1 July - 30 June

Communications

Telephones - main lines in use: 1.84 million (1997)
Telephones - mobile cellular: 588,000 (1998)
Telephone system:
general assessment: excellent domestic and international systems
domestic: NA
international: submarine cables to Australia and Fiji; satellite earth stations - 2 Intelsat (Pacific Ocean)
Radio broadcast stations: AM 124, FM 290, shortwave 4 (1998)
Radios: 3.75 million (1997)
Television broadcast stations: 41 (plus 52 medium-power repeaters and over 650 low-power repeaters) (1997)
Televisions: 1.926 million (1997)
Internet country code: .nz
Internet Service Providers (ISPs): 36 (2000)
Internet users: 1.34 million (2000)

Transportation

Railways:
total: 3,913 km
narrow gauge: 3,913 km 1.067-m gauge (519 km electrified) (1999)
Highways:
total: 92,200 km
paved: 53,568 km (including at least 144 km of expressways)
unpaved: 38,632 km (1996)
Waterways: 1,609 km
note: of little importance in satisfying total transportation requirements
Pipelines: petroleum products 160 km; natural gas 1,000 km; liquefied petroleum gas or LPG 150 km
Ports and harbors: Auckland, Christchurch, Dunedin, Tauranga, Wellington
Merchant marine:
total: 9 ships (1,000 GRT or over) totaling 72,389 GRT/109,018 DWT
ships by type: bulk 3, cargo 1, container 1, petroleum tanker 2, railcar carrier 1, roll on/roll off 1 (2000 est.)
Airports: 111 (2000 est.)
Airports - with paved runways:
total: 44
over 3,047 m: 2
2,438 to 3,047 m: 1
1,524 to 2,437 m: 10
914 to 1,523 m: 28
under 914 m: 3 (2000 est.)
Airports - with unpaved runways:
total: 67
1,524 to 2,437 m: 1
914 to 1,523 m: 24
under 914 m: 42 (2000 est.)

New Zealand (continued)

Military

Military branches: New Zealand Army, Royal New Zealand Navy, Royal New Zealand Air Force
Military manpower - military age: 20 years of age
Military manpower - availability:
males age 15-49: 1,000,102 (2001 est.)
Military manpower - fit for military service:
males age 15-49: 841,915 (2001 est.)
Military manpower - reaching military age annually:
males: 26,480 (2001 est.)
Military expenditures - dollar figure: $883 million (FY97/98)
Military expenditures - percent of GDP: 1.1% (FY97/98)

Transnational Issues

Disputes - international: territorial claim in Antarctica (Ross Dependency)

Nicaragua

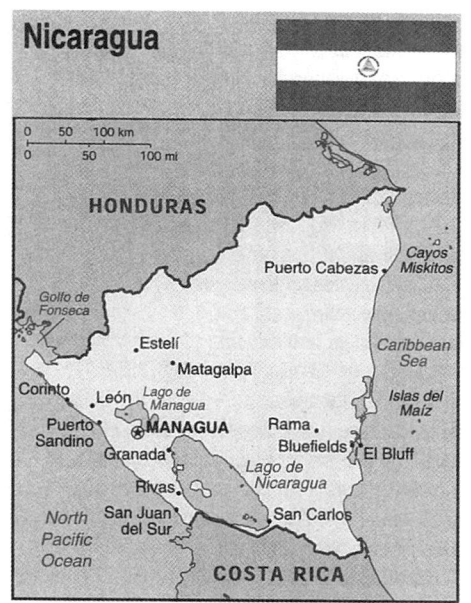

Introduction

Background: Settled as a colony of Spain in the 1520s, Nicaragua gained its independence in 1821. Violent opposition to governmental manipulation and corruption spread to all classes by 1978 and resulted in a short-lived civil war that brought the Marxist Sandinista guerrillas to power in 1979. Nicaraguan aid to leftist rebels in El Salvador caused the US to sponsor anti-Sandinista contra guerrillas through much of the 1980s. Free elections in 1990 and again in 1996 saw the Sandinistas defeated. The country has slowly rebuilt its economy during the 1990s, but was hard hit by Hurricane Mitch in 1998.

Geography

Location: Middle America, bordering both the Caribbean Sea and the North Pacific Ocean, between Costa Rica and Honduras
Geographic coordinates: 13 00 N, 85 00 W
Map references: Central America and the Caribbean
Area:
total: 129,494 sq km
land: 120,254 sq km
water: 9,240 sq km
Area - comparative: slightly smaller than the state of New York
Land boundaries:
total: 1,231 km
border countries: Costa Rica 309 km, Honduras 922 km
Coastline: 910 km
Maritime claims:
continental shelf: natural prolongation
territorial sea: 200 NM
Climate: tropical in lowlands, cooler in highlands
Terrain: extensive Atlantic coastal plains rising to central interior mountains; narrow Pacific coastal plain interrupted by volcanoes
Elevation extremes:
lowest point: Pacific Ocean 0 m
highest point: Mogoton 2,438 m
Natural resources: gold, silver, copper, tungsten, lead, zinc, timber, fish
Land use:
arable land: 9%
permanent crops: 1%
permanent pastures: 46%
forests and woodland: 27%
other: 17% (1993 est.)
Irrigated land: 880 sq km (1993 est.)
Natural hazards: destructive earthquakes, volcanoes, landslides, and occasionally severe hurricanes
Environment - current issues: deforestation; soil erosion; water pollution; Hurricane Mitch damage
Environment - international agreements:
party to: Biodiversity, Climate Change, Climate Change-Kyoto Protocol, Desertification, Endangered Species, Hazardous Wastes, Law of the Sea, Marine Dumping, Nuclear Test Ban, Ozone Layer Protection, Ship Pollution, Wetlands
signed, but not ratified: Environmental Modification

People

Population: 4,918,393 (July 2001 est.)
Age structure:
0-14 years: 38.98% (male 976,087; female 941,141)
15-64 years: 58.08% (male 1,418,555; female 1,438,096)
65 years and over: 2.94% (male 62,963; female 81,551) (2001 est.)
Population growth rate: 2.15% (2001 est.)
Birth rate: 27.64 births/1,000 population (2001 est.)
Death rate: 4.82 deaths/1,000 population (2001 est.)
Net migration rate: -1.33 migrant(s)/1,000 population (2001 est.)
Sex ratio:
at birth: 1.05 male(s)/female
under 15 years: 1.04 male(s)/female
15-64 years: 0.99 male(s)/female
65 years and over: 0.77 male(s)/female
total population: 1 male(s)/female (2001 est.)
Infant mortality rate: 33.66 deaths/1,000 live births (2001 est.)
Life expectancy at birth:
total population: 69.05 years
male: 67.1 years
female: 71.11 years (2001 est.)
Total fertility rate: 3.18 children born/woman (2001 est.)
HIV/AIDS - adult prevalence rate: 0.2% (1999 est.)
HIV/AIDS - people living with HIV/AIDS: 4,900 (1999 est.)
HIV/AIDS - deaths: 360 (1999 est.)
Nationality:
noun: Nicaraguan(s)
adjective: Nicaraguan
Ethnic groups: mestizo (mixed Amerindian and white) 69%, white 17%, black 9%, Amerindian 5%

Nicaragua (continued)

Religions: Roman Catholic 85%, Protestant
Languages: Spanish (official)
note: English and indigenous languages on Atlantic coast
Literacy:
definition: age 15 and over can read and write
total population: 65.7%
male: 64.6%
female: 66.6% (1995 est.)

Government

Country name:
conventional long form: Republic of Nicaragua
conventional short form: Nicaragua
local long form: Republica de Nicaragua
local short form: Nicaragua
Government type: republic
Capital: Managua
Administrative divisions: 15 departments (departamentos, singular - departamento), 2 autonomous regions* (regiones autonomistas, singular - region autonomista); Boaco, Carazo, Chinandega, Chontales, Esteli, Granada, Jinotega, Leon, Madriz, Managua, Masaya, Matagalpa, Nueva Segovia, Rio San Juan, Rivas, Atlantico Norte*, Atlantico Sur*
Independence: 15 September 1821 (from Spain)
National holiday: Independence Day, 15 September (1821)
Constitution: 9 January 1987, with reforms in 1995 and 2000
Legal system: civil law system; Supreme Court may review administrative acts
Suffrage: 16 years of age; universal
Executive branch:
chief of state: President Arnoldo ALEMAN Lacayo (since 10 January 1997); Vice President Leopoldo NAVARRO (since 24 October 2000); note - the president is both chief of state and head of government
head of government: President Arnoldo ALEMAN Lacayo (since 10 January 1997); Vice President Leopoldo NAVARRO (since 24 October 2000); note - the president is both chief of state and head of government
cabinet: Council of Ministers appointed by the president
elections: president and vice president elected on the same ticket by popular vote for a five-year term; election last held 20 October 1996 (next to be held 4 November 2001); note - in July 1995 the term of the office of the president was amended to five years
election results: Arnoldo ALEMAN Lacayo (Liberal Alliance - ruling party - includes PLC, PALI, PLIUN, and PUCA) 51.03%, Daniel ORTEGA Saavedra (FSLN) 37.75%, Guillermo OSORNO (PCCN) 4.10%, Noel VIDAURRE (PCN) 2.26%, Benjamin LANZAS (PRONAL) 0.53%, other (18 other candidates) 4.33%
Legislative branch: unicameral National Assembly or Asamblea Nacional (93 seats; members are elected by proportional representation to serve five-year terms)
elections: last held 20 October 1996 (next to be held 4 November 2001)
election results: percent of vote by party - Liberal Alliance (ruling party - includes PLC, PALI, PLIUN, and PUCA) 46.03%, FSLN 36.55%, PCCN 3.73%, PCN 2.12%, MRS 1.33%; seats by party - Liberal Alliance 42, FSLN 36, PCCN 4, PCN 3, PRONAL 2, MRS 1, PRN 1, PC 1, PLI 1, AU 1, UNO-96 Alliance 1
Judicial branch: Supreme Court or Corte Suprema (16 judges elected for seven-year terms by the National Assembly)
Political parties and leaders: Conservative Party of Nicaragua or PCN [Dr. Fernando AGUERO Rocha]; Independent Liberal Party or PLI [Virgilio GODOY]; Liberal Alliance (ruling alliance including Liberal Constitutional Party or PLC, New Liberal Party or PALI, Independent Liberal Party for National Unity or PLIUN, and Central American Unionist Party or PUCA) [leader NA]; National Conservative Party or PC [Pedro SOLARZANO, Noel VIDAURRE]; National Project or PRONAL [Benjamin LANZAS]; Nicaraguan Party of the Christian Path or PCCN [Guillermo OSORNO, Roberto RODRIGUEZ]; Nicaraguan Resistance Party or PRN [Salvador TALAVERA]; Sandinista National Liberation Front or FSLN [Daniel ORTEGA Saavedra]; Sandinista Renovation Movement or MRS [Sergio RAMIREZ]; Unity Alliance or AU [Alejandro SERRANO]; Union Nacional Opositora 96 or UNO-96 [Alfredo CESAR Aguirre]
Political pressure groups and leaders: National Workers Front or FNT is a Sandinista umbrella group of eight labor unions including Farm Workers Association or ATC; Health Workers Federation or FETASALUD; Heroes and Martyrs Confederation of Professional Associations or CONAPRO; National Association of Educators of Nicaragua or ANDEN; National Union of Employees or UNE; National Union of Farmers and Ranchers or UNAG; Sandinista Workers Central or CST; and Union of Journalists of Nicaragua or UPN; Permanent Congress of Workers or CPT is an umbrella group of four non-Sandinista labor unions: Autonomous Nicaraguan Workers Central or CTN-A; Confederation of Labor Unification or CUS; Independent General Confederation of Labor or CGT-I; and Labor Action and Unity Central or CAUS; Nicaraguan Workers' Central or CTN is an independent labor union; Superior Council of Private Enterprise or COSEP is a confederation of business groups
International organization participation: BCIE, CACM, CCC, ECLAC, FAO, G-77, IADB, IAEA, IBRD, ICAO, ICFTU, ICRM, IDA, IFAD, IFC, IFRCS, ILO, IMF, IMO, Intelsat, Interpol, IOC, IOM, ISO (correspondent), ITU, LAES, LAIA (observer), NAM, OAS, OPANAL, OPCW, PCA, UN, UNCTAD, UNESCO, UNHCR, UNIDO, UPU, WCL, WHO, WIPO, WMO, WToO, WTrO
Diplomatic representation in the US:
chief of mission: Ambassador Alfonso ORTEGA Urbina
chancery: 1627 New Hampshire Avenue NW, Washington, DC 20009
telephone: [1] (202) 939-6570
FAX: [1] (202) 939-6542
consulate(s) general: Houston, Los Angeles, Miami, New Orleans, New York
Diplomatic representation from the US:
chief of mission: Ambassador Oliver P. GARZA
embassy: Apartado Postal 327, Kilometer 4.5 Carretera Sur, Managua
mailing address: APO AA 34021
telephone: [505] (2) 662298, 666010, 666012, 666013, 666015, 666018, 666026, 666027, 666032, 666033
FAX: [505] (2) 669074
Flag description: three equal horizontal bands of blue (top), white, and blue with the national coat of arms centered in the white band; the coat of arms features a triangle encircled by the words REPUBLICA DE NICARAGUA on the top and AMERICA CENTRAL on the bottom; similar to the flag of El Salvador, which features a round emblem encircled by the words REPUBLICA DE EL SALVADOR EN LA AMERICA CENTRAL centered in the white band; also similar to the flag of Honduras, which has five blue stars arranged in an X pattern centered in the white band

Economy

Economy - overview: Nicaragua, one of the hemisphere's poorest countries, faces low per capita income, flagging socio-economic indicators, and huge external debt. While the country has made progress toward macro-economic stabilization over the past few years, a banking crisis and scandal has shaken the economy. Managua will continue to be dependent on international aid and debt relief under the Heavily Indebted Poor Countries (HIPC) initiative. Donors have made aid conditional on improving governability, the openness of government financial operation, poverty alleviation, and human rights. Nicaragua met the conditions for additional debt service relief in December 2000. Growth should remain moderate to high in 2001.
GDP: purchasing power parity - $13.1 billion (2000 est.)
GDP - real growth rate: 5% (2000 est.)
GDP - per capita: purchasing power parity - $2,700 (2000 est.)
GDP - composition by sector:
agriculture: 31.6%
industry: 22.8%
services: 45.6% (1999)
Population below poverty line: 50% (2000 est.)
Household income or consumption by percentage share:
lowest 10%: 1.6%
highest 10%: 39.8% (1993)
Inflation rate (consumer prices): 11% (2000 est.)
Labor force: 1.7 million (1999)
Labor force - by occupation: services 43%, agriculture 42%, industry 15% (1999 est.)
Unemployment rate: 20% plus considerable underemployment (1999 est.)

Nicaragua (continued)

Budget:
revenues: $734 million
expenditures: $836 million, including capital expenditures of $NA (1999 est.)
Industries: food processing, chemicals, machinery and metal products, textiles, clothing, petroleum refining and distribution, beverages, footwear, wood
Industrial production growth rate: 4.4% (2000 est.)
Electricity - production: 2.349 billion kWh (1999)
Electricity - production by source:
fossil fuel: 67.26%
hydro: 17.71%
nuclear: 0%
other: 15.03% (1999)
Electricity - consumption: 2.265 billion kWh (1999)
Electricity - exports: 20 million kWh (1999)
Electricity - imports: 100 million kWh (1999)
Agriculture - products: coffee, bananas, sugarcane, cotton, rice, corn, tobacco, sesame, soya, beans; beef, veal, pork, poultry, dairy products
Exports: $631 million (f.o.b., 2000 est.)
Exports - commodities: coffee, shrimp and lobster, cotton, tobacco, beef, sugar, bananas; gold
Exports - partners: US 37.7%, El Salvador 12.5%, Germany 9.8%, Costa Rica 5.1%, Spain 2.5%, France 2.1% (1999)
Imports: $1.6 billion (f.o.b., 2000 est.)
Imports - commodities: machinery and equipment, raw materials, petroleum products, consumer goods
Imports - partners: US 34.5%, Costa Rica 11.4%, Guatemala 7.3%, Panama 6.9%, Venezuela 5.9%, El Salvador 5.5% (1999)
Debt - external: $6.4 billion (2000 est.)
Economic aid - recipient: NA
Currency: gold cordoba (NIO)
Currency code: NIO
Exchange rates: gold cordobas per US dollar - 12.96 (November 2000), 12.69 (2000 est.), 11.81 (1999), 10.58 (1998), 9.45 (1997), 8.44 (1996)
Fiscal year: calendar year

Communications

Telephones - main lines in use: 140,000 (1996)
Telephones - mobile cellular: 7,911 (1997)
Telephone system:
general assessment: inadequate system being upgraded by foreign investment
domestic: low-capacity microwave radio relay and wire system being expanded; connected to Central American Microwave System
international: satellite earth stations - 1 Intersputnik (Atlantic Ocean region) and 1 Intelsat (Atlantic Ocean)
Radio broadcast stations: AM 63, FM 32, shortwave 1 (1998)
Radios: 1.24 million (1997)
Television broadcast stations: 3 (plus seven low-power repeaters) (1997)
Televisions: 320,000 (1997)
Internet country code: .ni
Internet Service Providers (ISPs): 3 (2000)
Internet users: 20,000 (2000)

Transportation

Highways:
total: 16,382 km
paved: 1,818 km
unpaved: 14,564 km (1998)
Waterways: 2,220 km (including 2 large lakes)
Pipelines: crude oil 56 km
Ports and harbors: Bluefields, Corinto, El Bluff, Puerto Cabezas, Puerto Sandino, Rama, San Juan del Sur
Merchant marine: none (2000 est.)
Airports: 182 (2000 est.)
Airports - with paved runways:
total: 11
2,438 to 3,047 m: 2
1,524 to 2,437 m: 3
914 to 1,523 m: 3
under 914 m: 3 (2000 est.)
Airports - with unpaved runways:
total: 171
1,524 to 2,437 m: 1
914 to 1,523 m: 25
under 914 m: 145 (2000 est.)

Military

Military branches: Army, Navy, Air Force
Military manpower - military age: 18 years of age
Military manpower - availability:
males age 15-49: 1,269,322 (2001 est.)
Military manpower - fit for military service:
males age 15-49: 779,267 (2001 est.)
Military manpower - reaching military age annually:
males: 58,232 (2001 est.)
Military expenditures - dollar figure: $26 million (FY98)
Military expenditures - percent of GDP: 1.2% (FY98)

Transnational Issues

Disputes - international: territorial disputes with Colombia over the Archipelago de San Andres y Providencia and Quita Sueno Bank; with respect to the maritime boundary question in the Golfo de Fonseca, the ICJ referred to the line determined by the 1900 Honduras-Nicaragua Mixed Boundary Commission and advised that some tripartite resolution among El Salvador, Honduras, and Nicaragua likely would be required; maritime boundary dispute with Honduras in the Caribbean Sea is before the ICJ; legal dispute over navigational rights of San Juan River on border with Costa Rica
Illicit drugs: transshipment point for cocaine destined for the US and transshipment point for arms-for-drugs dealing

Niger

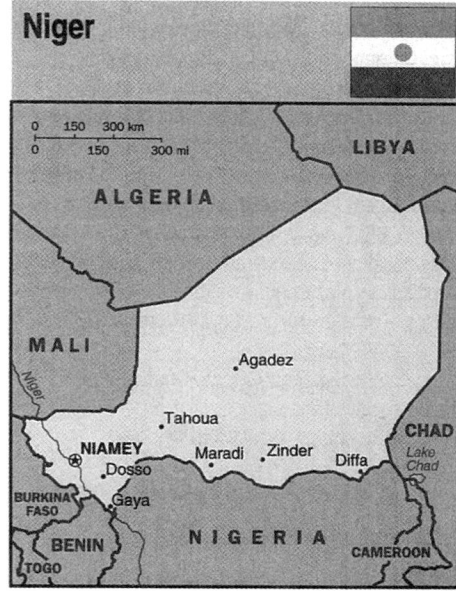

Introduction

Background: Not until 1993, 33 years after independence from France, did Niger hold its first free and open elections. A 1995 peace accord ended a five-year Tuareg insurgency in the north. Coups in 1996 and 1999 were followed by the creation of a National Reconciliation Council that effected a transition to civilian rule in December 1999.

Geography

Location: Western Africa, southeast of Algeria
Geographic coordinates: 16 00 N, 8 00 E
Map references: Africa
Area:
total: 1.267 million sq km
land: 1,266,700 sq km
water: 300 sq km
Area - comparative: slightly less than twice the size of Texas
Land boundaries:
total: 5,697 km
border countries: Algeria 956 km, Benin 266 km, Burkina Faso 628 km, Chad 1,175 km, Libya 354 km, Mali 821 km, Nigeria 1,497 km
Coastline: 0 km (landlocked)
Maritime claims: none (landlocked)
Climate: desert; mostly hot, dry, dusty; tropical in extreme south
Terrain: predominately desert plains and sand dunes; flat to rolling plains in south; hills in north
Elevation extremes:
lowest point: Niger River 200 m
highest point: Mont Greboun 1,944 m
Natural resources: uranium, coal, iron ore, tin, phosphates, gold, petroleum
Land use:
arable land: 3%
permanent crops: 0%
permanent pastures: 7%
forests and woodland: 2%
other: 88% (1993 est.)

Niger (continued)

Irrigated land: 660 sq km (1993 est.)
Natural hazards: recurring droughts
Environment - current issues: overgrazing; soil erosion; deforestation; desertification; wildlife populations (such as elephant, hippopotamus, giraffe, and lion) threatened because of poaching and habitat destruction
Environment - international agreements:
party to: Biodiversity, Climate Change, Desertification, Endangered Species, Environmental Modification, Hazardous Wastes, Marine Dumping, Nuclear Test Ban, Ozone Layer Protection, Ship Pollution, Wetlands
signed, but not ratified: Climate Change-Kyoto Protocol, Law of the Sea
Geography - note: landlocked

People

Population: 10,355,156 (July 2001 est.)
Age structure:
0-14 years: 47.97% (male 2,528,484; female 2,439,051)
15-64 years: 49.75% (male 2,518,400; female 2,633,677)
65 years and over: 2.28% (male 123,589; female 111,955) (2001 est.)
Population growth rate: 2.72% (2001 est.)
Birth rate: 50.68 births/1,000 population (2001 est.)
Death rate: 22.71 deaths/1,000 population (2001 est.)
Net migration rate: -0.73 migrant(s)/1,000 population (2001 est.)
Sex ratio:
at birth: 1.03 male(s)/female
under 15 years: 1.04 male(s)/female
15-64 years: 0.96 male(s)/female
65 years and over: 1.1 male(s)/female
total population: 1 male(s)/female (2001 est.)
Infant mortality rate: 123.57 deaths/1,000 live births (2001 est.)
Life expectancy at birth:
total population: 41.59 years
male: 41.74 years
female: 41.44 years (2001 est.)
Total fertility rate: 7.08 children born/woman (2001 est.)
HIV/AIDS - adult prevalence rate: 1.35% (1999 est.)
HIV/AIDS - people living with HIV/AIDS: 64,000 (1999 est.)
HIV/AIDS - deaths: 6,500 (1999 est.)
Nationality:
noun: Nigerien(s)
adjective: Nigerien
Ethnic groups: Hausa 56%, Djerma 22%, Fula 8.5%, Tuareg 8%, Beri Beri (Kanouri) 4.3%, Arab, Toubou, and Gourmantche 1.2%, about 1,200 French expatriates
Religions: Muslim 80%, remainder indigenous beliefs and Christians
Languages: French (official), Hausa, Djerma

Literacy:
definition: age 15 and over can read and write
total population: 13.6%
male: 20.9%
female: 6.6% (1995 est.)

Government

Country name:
conventional long form: Republic of Niger
conventional short form: Niger
local long form: Republique du Niger
local short form: Niger
Government type: republic
Capital: Niamey
Administrative divisions: 7 departments (departementes, singular - departement), and 1 capital district* (capitale district); Agadez, Diffa, Dosso, Maradi, Niamey*, Tahoua, Tillaberi, Zinder
Independence: 3 August 1958 (from France)
National holiday: Republic Day, 18 December (1958)
Constitution: the constitution of January 1993 was revised by national referendum on 12 May 1996 and again by referendum on 18 July 1999
Legal system: based on French civil law system and customary law; has not accepted compulsory ICJ jurisdiction
Suffrage: 18 years of age; universal
Executive branch:
chief of state: President Mamadou TANDJA (since 22 December 1999); note - the president is both chief of state and head of government
head of government: President Mamadou TANDJA (since 22 December 1999); note - the president is both chief of state and head of government; Prime Minister Hama AMADOU (since 31 December 1999) was appointed by the president and shares some executive responsibilities with the president
note: President Ibrahim BARE was assassinated on 9 April 1999; subsequent elections were held under the nine-month provisional government of Major Daouda Mallam WANKE
cabinet: 23-member cabinet appointed by President TANDJA
elections: president elected by popular vote for a five-year term; last held 24 November 1999 (next to be held NA 2004)
election results: Mamadou TANDJA elected president; percent of vote - Mamadou TANDJA 59.9%, Mahamadou ISSOUFOU 40.1%
Legislative branch: unicameral National Assembly (83 seats, members elected by popular vote for five-year terms)
elections: last held 24 November 1999 (next to be held NA 2004)
election results: percent of vote by party - NA%; seats by party - MNSD-Nassara 38, CDS-Rahama 17, PNDS-Tarayya 16, RDP-Jama'a 8, ANDPS-Zaman Lahiya 4
Judicial branch: State Court or Cour d'Etat; Court of Appeal or Cour d'Appel

Political parties and leaders: Democratic Rally of the People-Jama'a or RDP-Jama'a [Hamid ALGABID]; Democratic and Social Convention-Rahama or CDS-Rahama [Mahamane OUSMANE]; National Movement for a Developing Society-Nassara or MNSD-Nassara [Mamadou TANDJA, chairman]; Nigerien Alliance for Democracy and Social Progress-Zaman Lahiya or ANDPS-Zaman Lahiya [Moumouni Adamou DJERMAKOYE]; Nigerien Party for Democracy and Socialism-Tarayya or PNDS-Tarayya [Mahamadou ISSOUFOU]; Union of Democratic Patriots and Progressives-Chamoua or UPDP-Chamoua [Professor Andre' SALIFOU, chairman]
Political pressure groups and leaders: NA
International organization participation: ACCT, ACP, AfDB, CCC, ECA, ECOWAS, Entente, FAO, FZ, G-77, IAEA, IBRD, ICAO, ICFTU, ICRM, IDA, IDB, IFAD, IFC, IFRCS, ILO, IMF, Intelsat, Interpol, IOC, ITU, MIPONUH, MONUC, NAM, OAU, OIC, OPCW, UN, UNCTAD, UNESCO, UNIDO, UPU, WADB, WAEMU, WCL, WFTU, WHO, WIPO, WMO, WToO, WTrO
Diplomatic representation in the US:
chief of mission: Ambassador Joseph DIATTA
chancery: 2204 R Street NW, Washington, DC 20008
telephone: [1] (202) 483-4224 through 4227
Diplomatic representation from the US:
chief of mission: Ambassador Charles O. CECIL
embassy: Rue Des Ambassades, Niamey
mailing address: B. P. 11201, Niamey
telephone: [227] 72 26 61 through 72 26 64
FAX: [227] 73 31 67
Flag description: three equal horizontal bands of orange (top), white, and green with a small orange disk (representing the sun) centered in the white band; similar to the flag of India, which has a blue spoked wheel centered in the white band

Economy

Economy - overview: Niger is a poor, landlocked Sub-Saharan nation, whose economy centers on subsistence agriculture, animal husbandry, reexport trade, and increasingly less on uranium, because of declining world demand. The 50% devaluation of the West African franc in January 1994 boosted exports of livestock, cowpeas, onions, and the products of Niger's small cotton industry. The government relies on bilateral and multilateral aid - which was suspended following the April 1999 coup d'etat - for operating expenses and public investment. In 2000, the World Bank approved a structural adjustment loan of $35 million to help support fiscal reforms. However, reforms could prove difficult given the government's bleak financial situation.
GDP: purchasing power parity - $10 billion (2000 est.)
GDP - real growth rate: 3.5% (2000 est.)
GDP - per capita: purchasing power parity - $1,000 (2000 est.)

Niger (continued)

GDP - composition by sector:
agriculture: 40%
industry: 18%
services: 42% (1998)
Population below poverty line: 63% (1993 est.)
Household income or consumption by percentage share:
lowest 10%: 0.8%
highest 10%: 35.4% (1995)
Inflation rate (consumer prices): 2.8% (2000 est.)
Labor force: 70,000 receive regular wages or salaries
Labor force - by occupation: agriculture 90%, industry and commerce 6%, government 4%
Unemployment rate: NA%
Budget:
revenues: $377 million, including $146 million from foreign sources
expenditures: $377 million, including capital expenditures of $105 million (1999 est.)
Industries: uranium mining, cement, brick, textiles, food processing, chemicals, slaughterhouses
Industrial production growth rate: NA%
Electricity - production: 200 million kWh (1999)
Electricity - production by source:
fossil fuel: 100%
hydro: 0%
nuclear: 0%
other: 0% (1999)
Electricity - consumption: 401 million kWh (1999)
Electricity - exports: 0 kWh (1999)
Electricity - imports: 215 million kWh (1999)
Agriculture - products: cowpeas, cotton, peanuts, millet, sorghum, cassava (tapioca), rice; cattle, sheep, goats, camels, donkeys, horses, poultry
Exports: $385 million (f.o.b., 1999)
Exports - commodities: uranium ore 65%, livestock products, cowpeas, onions (1998 est.)
Exports - partners: France 45%, Nigeria 27%, UK 11% (1999)
Imports: $317 million (f.o.b., 1999)
Imports - commodities: consumer goods, primary materials, machinery, vehicles and parts, petroleum, cereals
Imports - partners: France 22%, Cote d'Ivoire 15%, Nigeria 8%, US 3% (1999)
Debt - external: $1.3 billion (1999 est.)
Economic aid - recipient: $341 million (1997)
note: the IMF approved a $73 million poverty reduction and growth facility for Niger in 2000 and announced $115 million in debt relief under the Heavily Indebted Poor Countries (HIPC) initiative
Currency: Communaute Financiere Africaine franc (XOF); note - responsible authority is the Central Bank of the West African States
Currency code: XOF
Exchange rates: Communaute Financiere Africaine francs (XOF) per US dollar - 699.21 (January 2001), 711.98 (2000), 615.70 (1999), 589.95 (1998), 583.67 (1997), 511.55 (1996); note - from 1 January 1999, the XOF is pegged to the euro at a rate of 655.957 XOF per euro
Fiscal year: calendar year

Communications

Telephones - main lines in use: 16,000 (1997)
Telephones - mobile cellular: 13,000 (1995)
Telephone system:
general assessment: small system of wire, radio telephone communications, and microwave radio relay links concentrated in the southwestern area of Niger
domestic: wire, radiotelephone communications, and microwave radio relay; domestic satellite system with 3 earth stations and 1 planned
international: satellite earth stations - 2 Intelsat (1 Atlantic Ocean and 1 Indian Ocean)
Radio broadcast stations: AM 5, FM 5, shortwave 4 (1998)
Radios: 680,000 (1997)
Television broadcast stations: 10 (plus seven low-power repeaters) (1997)
Televisions: 125,000 (1997)
Internet country code: .ne
Internet Service Providers (ISPs): 1 (2000)
Internet users: 3,000 (2000)

Transportation

Railways: 0 km
Highways:
total: 10,100 km
paved: 798 km
unpaved: 9,302 km (1996)
Waterways: 300 km
note: the Niger River is navigable from Niamey to Gaya on the Benin frontier from mid-December through March
Ports and harbors: none
Airports: 27 (2000 est.)
Airports - with paved runways:
total: 9
2,438 to 3,047 m: 2
1,524 to 2,437 m: 6
under 914 m: 1 (2000 est.)
Airports - with unpaved runways:
total: 18
1,524 to 2,437 m: 1
914 to 1,523 m: 15
under 914 m: 2 (2000 est.)

Military

Military branches: Army, Air Force, National Gendarmerie, Republican Guard, National Police
Military manpower - military age: 18 years of age
Military manpower - availability:
males age 15-49: 2,202,608 (2001 est.)
Military manpower - fit for military service:
males age 15-49: 1,190,787 (2001 est.)
Military manpower - reaching military age annually:
males: 108,993 (2001 est.)
Military expenditures - dollar figure: $20 million (FY96)
Military expenditures - percent of GDP: 1.1% (FY96)

Transnational Issues

Disputes - international: Libya claims about 19,400 sq km in northern Niger; delimitation of international boundaries in the vicinity of Lake Chad, the lack of which led to border incidents in the past, has been completed and awaits ratification by Cameroon, Chad, Niger, and Nigeria

Nigeria

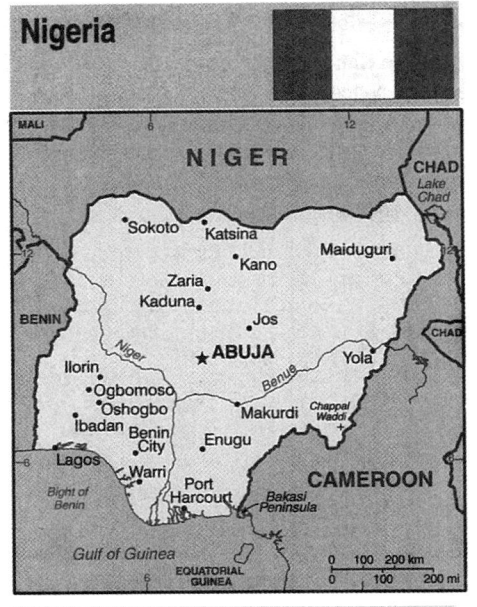

Introduction

Background: Following nearly 16 years of military rule, a new constitution was adopted in 1999 and a peaceful transition to civilian government completed. The new president faces the daunting task of rebuilding a petroleum-based economy, whose revenues have been squandered through corruption and mismanagement, and institutionalizing democracy. In addition, the OBASANJO administration must defuse longstanding ethnic and religious tensions, if it is to build a sound foundation for economic growth and political stability.

Geography

Location: Western Africa, bordering the Gulf of Guinea, between Benin and Cameroon
Geographic coordinates: 10 00 N, 8 00 E
Map references: Africa
Area:
total: 923,768 sq km
land: 910,768 sq km
water: 13,000 sq km
Area - comparative: slightly more than twice the size of California
Land boundaries:
total: 4,047 km
border countries: Benin 773 km, Cameroon 1,690 km, Chad 87 km, Niger 1,497 km
Coastline: 853 km
Maritime claims:
continental shelf: 200-m depth or to the depth of exploitation
exclusive economic zone: 200 NM
territorial sea: 12 NM
Climate: varies; equatorial in south, tropical in center, arid in north
Terrain: southern lowlands merge into central hills and plateaus; mountains in southeast, plains in north
Elevation extremes:
lowest point: Atlantic Ocean 0 m
highest point: Chappal Waddi 2,419 m
Natural resources: natural gas, petroleum, tin, columbite, iron ore, coal, limestone, lead, zinc, arable land
Land use:
arable land: 33%
permanent crops: 3%
permanent pastures: 44%
forests and woodland: 12%
other: 8% (1993 est.)
Irrigated land: 9,570 sq km (1993 est.)
Natural hazards: periodic droughts
Environment - current issues: soil degradation; rapid deforestation; desertification
Environment - international agreements:
party to: Biodiversity, Climate Change, Desertification, Endangered Species, Hazardous Wastes, Law of the Sea, Marine Dumping, Marine Life Conservation, Nuclear Test Ban, Ozone Layer Protection, Ship Pollution
signed, but not ratified: none of the selected agreements

People

Population: 126,635,626
note: estimates for this country explicitly take into account the effects of excess mortality due to AIDS; this can result in lower life expectancy, higher infant mortality and death rates, lower population and growth rates, and changes in the distribution of population by age and sex than would otherwise be expected (July 2001 est.)
Age structure:
0-14 years: 43.71% (male 27,842,225; female 27,514,197)
15-64 years: 53.47% (male 34,456,738; female 33,259,194)
65 years and over: 2.82% (male 1,780,862; female 1,782,410) (2001 est.)
Population growth rate: 2.61% (2001 est.)
Birth rate: 39.69 births/1,000 population (2001 est.)
Death rate: 13.91 deaths/1,000 population (2001 est.)
Net migration rate: 0.28 migrant(s)/1,000 population (2001 est.)
Sex ratio:
at birth: 1.03 male(s)/female
under 15 years: 1.01 male(s)/female
15-64 years: 1.04 male(s)/female
65 years and over: 1 male(s)/female
total population: 1.02 male(s)/female (2001 est.)
Infant mortality rate: 73.34 deaths/1,000 live births (2001 est.)
Life expectancy at birth:
total population: 51.07 years
male: 51.07 years
female: 51.07 years (2001 est.)
Total fertility rate: 5.57 children born/woman (2001 est.)
HIV/AIDS - adult prevalence rate: 5.06% (1999 est.)
HIV/AIDS - people living with HIV/AIDS: 2.7 million (1999 est.)
HIV/AIDS - deaths: 250,000 (1999 est.)
Nationality:
noun: Nigerian(s)
adjective: Nigerian
Ethnic groups: Nigeria, which is Africa's most populous country, is composed of more than 250 ethnic groups; the following are the most populous and politically influential: Hausa and Fulani 29%, Yoruba 21%, Igbo (Ibo) 18%, Ijaw 10%, Kanuri 4%, Ibibio 3.5%, Tiv 2.5%
Religions: Muslim 50%, Christian 40%, indigenous beliefs 10%
Languages: English (official), Hausa, Yoruba, Igbo (Ibo), Fulani
Literacy:
definition: age 15 and over can read and write
total population: 57.1%
male: 67.3%
female: 47.3% (1995 est.)

Government

Country name:
conventional long form: Federal Republic of Nigeria
conventional short form: Nigeria
Government type: republic transitioning from military to civilian rule
Capital: Abuja; note - on 12 December 1991 the capital was officially transferred from Lagos to Abuja; most federal government offices have now made the move to Abuja
Administrative divisions: 36 states and 1 territory*; Abia, Abuja Federal Capital Territory*, Adamawa, Akwa Ibom, Anambra, Bauchi, Bayelsa, Benue, Borno, Cross River, Delta, Ebonyi, Edo, Ekiti, Enugu, Gombe, Imo, Jigawa, Kaduna, Kano, Katsina, Kebbi, Kogi, Kwara, Lagos, Nassarawa, Niger, Ogun, Ondo, Osun, Oyo, Plateau, Rivers, Sokoto, Taraba, Yobe, Zamfara
Independence: 1 October 1960 (from UK)
National holiday: Independence Day, 1 October (1960)
Constitution: NA 1999 new constitution adopted
Legal system: based on English common law, Islamic Shariah law (only in some northern states), and traditional law
Suffrage: 18 years of age; universal
Executive branch:
chief of state: President Olusegun OBASANJO (since 29 May 1999); note - the president is both the chief of state and head of government
head of government: President Olusegun OBASANJO (since 29 May 1999); note - the president is both the chief of state and head of government
cabinet: Federal Executive Council
elections: president is elected by popular vote for no more than two four-year terms; election last held 27 February 1999 (next to be held NA 2003)
election results: Olusegun OBASANJO elected president; percent of vote - Olusegun OBASANJO (PDP) 62.8%, Olu FALAE (APP-AD) 37.2%

Nigeria (continued)

Legislative branch: bicameral National Assembly consists of Senate (109 seats, three from each state and one from the Federal Capital Territory; members elected by popular vote to serve four-year terms) and House of Representatives (360 seats, members elected by popular vote to serve four-year terms)
elections: Senate - last held 20-24 February 1999 (next to be held NA 2003); House of Representatives - last held 20-24 February 1999 (next to be held NA 2003)
election results: Senate - percent of vote by party - PDP 58%, APP 23%, AD 19%; seats by party - PDP 67, APP 23, AD 19; House of Representatives - percent of vote by party - PDP 58%, APP 30%, AD 12%; seats by party - PDP 221, APP 70, AD 69
Judicial branch: Supreme Court (judges appointed by the Provisional Ruling Council); Federal Court of Appeal (judges are appointed by the federal government on the advice of the Advisory Judicial Committee)
Political parties and leaders: All People's Party or APP [Alhaji Yusuf ALI]; Alliance for Democracy or AD [contested between Yusuf MAMMAN and Alhasi Adamu ABDULKADIR]; People's Democratic Party or PDP [Barnabas GEMADE]
Political pressure groups and leaders: NA
International organization participation: ACP, AfDB, C, CCC, ECA, ECOWAS, FAO, G-15, G-19, G-24, G-77, IAEA, IBRD, ICAO, ICC, ICFTU, ICRM, IDA, IFAD, IFC, IFRCS, IHO, ILO, IMF, IMO, Inmarsat, Intelsat, Interpol, IOC, ISO, ITU, MINURSO, MONUC, NAM, OAU, OIC, OPCW, OPEC, PCA, UN, UNCTAD, UNESCO, UNHCR, UNIDO, UNIKOM, UNITAR, UNMEE, UNMIBH, UNMIK, UNMOP, UNMOT, UNTAET, UNU, UPU, WFTU, WHO, WIPO, WMO, WToO, WTrO
Diplomatic representation in the US:
chief of mission: Ambassador Jibril AMINU
chancery: 1333 16th Street NW, Washington, DC 20036
telephone: [1] (202) 986-8400
FAX: [1] (202) 775-1385
consulate(s) general: Atlanta and New York
Diplomatic representation from the US:
chief of mission: Ambassador Howard Franklin JETER
embassy: 8 Mambilla Drive, Abuja
mailing address: P. O. Box 554, Lagos
telephone: [234] (1) 261-0050, -0078
FAX: [234] (1) 261-0257
Flag description: three equal vertical bands of green (hoist side), white, and green

Economy

Economy - overview: The oil-rich Nigerian economy, long hobbled by political instability, corruption, and poor macroeconomic management, is undergoing substantial economic reform under the new civilian administration. Nigeria's former military rulers failed to diversify the economy away from overdependence on the capital-intensive oil sector, which provides 20% of GDP, 95% of foreign exchange earnings, and about 65% of budgetary revenues. The largely subsistence agricultural sector has failed to keep up with rapid population growth, and Nigeria, once a large net exporter of food, now must import food. Following the signing of an IMF stand-by agreement in August 2000, Nigeria received a debt-restructuring deal from the Paris Club and a $1 billion loan from the IMF, both contingent on economic reforms. Increases in foreign investment and oil production combined with high world oil prices should push growth over 4% in 2001-02.
GDP: purchasing power parity - $117 billion (2000 est.)
GDP - real growth rate: 3.5% (2000 est.)
GDP - per capita: purchasing power parity - $950 (2000 est.)
GDP - composition by sector:
agriculture: 40%
industry: 40%
services: 20% (1999 est.)
Population below poverty line: 45% (2000 est.)
Household income or consumption by percentage share:
lowest 10%: 1.6%
highest 10%: 40.8% (1996-97)
Inflation rate (consumer prices): 6.5% (2000 est.)
Labor force: 66 million (1999 est.)
Labor force - by occupation: agriculture 70%, industry 10%, services 20% (1999 est.)
Unemployment rate: 28% (1992 est.)
Budget:
revenues: $3.4 billion
expenditures: $3.6 billion, including capital expenditures of $NA (2000 est.)
Industries: crude oil, coal, tin, columbite, palm oil, peanuts, cotton, rubber, wood, hides and skins, textiles, cement and other construction materials, food products, footwear, chemicals, fertilizer, printing, ceramics, steel
Industrial production growth rate: 1.5% (2000 est.)
Electricity - production: 18.7 billion kWh (1999)
Electricity - production by source:
fossil fuel: 52.94%
hydro: 47.06%
nuclear: 0%
other: 0% (1999)
Electricity - consumption: 17.372 billion kWh (1999)
Electricity - exports: 19 million kWh (1999)
Electricity - imports: 0 kWh (1999)
Agriculture - products: cocoa, peanuts, palm oil, corn, rice, sorghum, millet, cassava (tapioca), yams, rubber; cattle, sheep, goats, pigs; timber; fish
Exports: $22.2 billion (f.o.b., 2000 est.)
Exports - commodities: petroleum and petroleum products 95%, cocoa, rubber
Exports - partners: US 36%, India 9%, Spain 8%, Brazil 6%, France 6%, (1999)
Imports: $10.7 billion (f.o.b., 2000 est.)
Imports - commodities: machinery, chemicals, transport equipment, manufactured goods, food and live animals
Imports - partners: UK 11%, Germany 10%, US 9%, France 8%, China 6% (1999)
Debt - external: $32 billion (2000 est.)
Economic aid - recipient: ODA $250 million (1998)
Currency: naira (NGN)
Currency code: NGN
Exchange rates: nairas per US dollar - 110.005 (January 2001), 101.697 (2000), 92.338 (1999), 21.886 (1998), 21.886 (1997), 21.884 (1996)
Fiscal year: calendar year

Communications

Telephones - main lines in use: 500,000 (2000)
Telephones - mobile cellular: 26,700 (1997)
Telephone system:
general assessment: an inadequate system, further limited by poor maintenance; major expansion is required and a start has been made
domestic: intercity traffic is carried by coaxial cable, microwave radio relay, a domestic communications satellite system with 19 earth stations, and a coastal submarine cable; mobile cellular facilities and the Internet are available
international: satellite earth stations - 3 Intelsat (2 Atlantic Ocean and 1 Indian Ocean); coaxial submarine cable SAFE (South African Far East)
Radio broadcast stations: AM 82, FM 35, shortwave 11 (1998)
Radios: 23.5 million (1997)
Television broadcast stations: 2 government-controlled; note - in addition, in 1993, 14 licenses to operate private television stations were granted (1999)
Televisions: 6.9 million (1997)
Internet country code: .ng
Internet Service Providers (ISPs): 11 (2000)
Internet users: 100,000 (2000)

Transportation

Railways:
total. 3,557 km
narrow gauge. 3,505 km 1.067-m gauge
standard gauge. 52 km 1.435-m gauge
note. years of neglect of both the rolling stock and the right-of-way have seriously reduced the capacity and utility of the system; a project to restore Nigeria's railways is now underway
Highways.
total. 194,394 km
paved. 60,068 km (including 1,194 km of expressways)
unpaved. 134,326 km
note. many of the roads reported as paved may be graveled; because of poor maintenance and years of heavy freight traffic - in part the result of the failure of the railroad system - most of the road system is barely usable (1997)
Waterways. 8,575 km
note. consisting of the Niger and Benue rivers and smaller rivers and creeks
Pipelines. crude oil 2,042 km; petroleum products 3,000 km; natural gas 500 km

Nigeria (continued)

Ports and harbors: Calabar, Lagos, Onne, Port Harcourt, Sapele, Warri
Merchant marine:
total: 41 ships (1,000 GRT or over) totaling 357,372 GRT/636,254 DWT
ships by type: bulk 1, cargo 10, chemical tanker 4, petroleum tanker 24, roll on/roll off 1, specialized tanker 1 (2000 est.)
Airports: 70 (2000 est.)
Airports - with paved runways:
total: 36
over 3,047 m: 7
2,438 to 3,047 m: 10
1,524 to 2,437 m: 10
914 to 1,523 m: 7
under 914 m: 2 (2000 est.)
Airports - with unpaved runways:
total: 34
1,524 to 2,437 m: 2
914 to 1,523 m: 14
under 914 m: 18 (2000 est.)
Heliports: 1 (2000 est.)

Military

Military branches: Army, Navy, Air Force
Military manpower - military age: 18 years of age
Military manpower - availability:
males age 15-49: 29,940,922 (2001 est.)
Military manpower - fit for military service:
males age 15-49: 17,201,367 (2001 est.)
Military manpower - reaching military age annually:
males: 1,375,112 (2001 est.)
Military expenditures - dollar figure: $360 million (FY00)
Military expenditures - percent of GDP: 10% (FY00)

Transnational Issues

Disputes - international: delimitation of international boundaries in the vicinity of Lake Chad, the lack of which led to border incidents in the past, has been completed and awaits ratification by Cameroon, Chad, Niger, and Nigeria; dispute with Cameroon over land and maritime boundaries around the Bakasi Peninsula is currently before the ICJ; tripartite maritime boundary and economic zone dispute with Equatorial Guinea and Cameroon is currently before the ICJ
Illicit drugs: facilitates movement of heroin en route from Southeast and Southwest Asia to Western Europe and North America; increasingly a transit route for cocaine from South America intended for European, East Asian, and North American markets

Niue
(self-governing in free association with New Zealand)

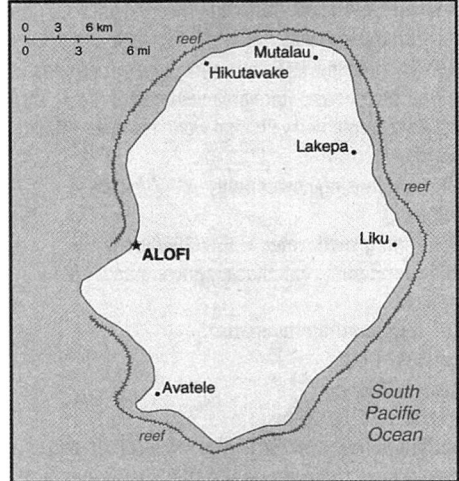

Introduction

Background: Niue's remoteness, as well as cultural and linguistic differences between its Polynesian inhabitants and those of the rest of the Cook Islands, have caused it to be separately administered. The population of the island continues to drop (from a peak of 5,200 in 1966 to 2,100 in 2000) with substantial emigration to New Zealand.

Geography

Location: Oceania, island in the South Pacific Ocean, east of Tonga
Geographic coordinates: 19 02 S, 169 52 W
Map references: Oceania
Area:
total: 260 sq km
land: 260 sq km
water: 0 sq km
Area - comparative: 1.5 times the size of Washington, DC
Land boundaries: 0 km
Coastline: 64 km
Maritime claims:
exclusive economic zone: 200 NM
territorial sea: 12 NM
Climate: tropical; modified by southeast trade winds
Terrain: steep limestone cliffs along coast, central plateau
Elevation extremes:
lowest point: Pacific Ocean 0 m
highest point: unnamed location near Mutalau settlement 68 m
Natural resources: fish, arable land
Land use:
arable land: 19%
permanent crops: 8%
permanent pastures: 4%
forests and woodland: 19%
other: 50% (1993 est.)
Irrigated land: NA sq km
Natural hazards: typhoons
Environment - current issues: increasing attention to conservationist practices to counter loss of soil fertility from traditional slash and burn agriculture
Environment - international agreements:
party to: Biodiversity, Climate Change, Climate Change-Kyoto Protocol, Desertification
signed, but not ratified: Law of the Sea
Geography - note: one of world's largest coral islands

People

Population: 2,124 (July 2001 est.)
Age structure:
0-14 years: NA%
15-64 years: NA%
65 years and over: NA%
Population growth rate: 0.5% (2001 est.)
Birth rate: NA births/1,000 population
Death rate: NA deaths/1,000 population
Net migration rate: NA migrant(s)/1,000 population
Infant mortality rate: NA deaths/1,000 live births
Life expectancy at birth:
total population: NA years
male: NA years
female: NA years
Total fertility rate: NA children born/woman
HIV/AIDS - adult prevalence rate: NA%
HIV/AIDS - people living with HIV/AIDS: NA
HIV/AIDS - deaths: NA
Nationality:
noun: Niuean(s)
adjective: Niuean
Ethnic groups: Polynesian (with some 200 Europeans, Samoans, and Tongans)
Religions: Ekalesia Niue (Niuean Church - a Protestant church closely related to the London Missionary Society) 75%, Latter-Day Saints 10%, other 15% (mostly Roman Catholic, Jehovah's Witnesses, Seventh-Day Adventist)
Languages: Polynesian closely related to Tongan and Samoan, English
Literacy:
definition: NA
total population: 95%
male: NA%
female: NA%

Government

Country name:
conventional long form: none
conventional short form: Niue
former: Savage Island
Dependency status: self-governing in free association with New Zealand; Niue fully responsible for internal affairs; New Zealand retains responsibility for external affairs
Government type: self-governing parliamentary democracy
Capital: Alofi

Niue (continued)

Administrative divisions: none; note - there are no first-order administrative divisions as defined by the US Government, but there are 14 villages each with its own village council whose members are elected and serve three-year terms
Independence: on 19 October 1974, Niue became a self-governing parliamentary government in free association with New Zealand
National holiday: Waitangi Day (Treaty of Waitangi established British sovereignty over New Zealand), 6 February (1840)
Constitution: 19 October 1974 (Niue Constitution Act)
Legal system: English common law
Suffrage: 18 years of age; universal
Executive branch:
chief of state: Queen ELIZABETH II (since 6 February 1952); the UK and New Zealand are represented by New Zealand High Commissioner John BRYAN (since NA May 2000)
head of government: Premier Sani LAKATANI (since 1 April 1999)
cabinet: Cabinet consists of the premier and three ministers
elections: the monarch is hereditary; premier elected by the Legislative Assembly for a three-year term; election last held 19 March 1999 (next to be held NA March 2002)
election results: Sani LAKATANI elected premier; percent of Legislative Assembly vote - NA%
Legislative branch: unicameral Legislative Assembly (20 seats; members elected by popular vote to serve three-year terms; six elected from a common roll and 14 are village representatives)
elections: last held 19 March 1999 (next to be held NA March 2002)
election results: percent of vote by party - NA%; seats by party - NPP 9, independents 11
Judicial branch: Supreme Court of New Zealand; High Court of Niue
Political parties and leaders: Niue People's Action Party or NPP [Sani LAKATANI]
Political pressure groups and leaders: NA
International organization participation: ACP, ESCAP (associate), FAO, Intelsat (nonsignatory user), Sparteca, SPC, SPF, UNESCO, WHO, WMO
Diplomatic representation in the US: none (self-governing territory in free association with New Zealand)
Diplomatic representation from the US: none (self-governing territory in free association with New Zealand)
Flag description: yellow with the flag of the UK in the upper hoist-side quadrant; the flag of the UK bears five yellow five-pointed stars - a large one on a blue disk in the center and a smaller one on each arm of the bold red cross

Economy

Economy - overview: Government expenditures regularly exceed revenues, and the shortfall is made up by critically needed grants from New Zealand that are used to pay wages to public employees. Niue has cut government expenditures by reducing the public service by almost half. The agricultural sector consists mainly of subsistence gardening, although some cash crops are grown for export. Industry consists primarily of small factories to process passion fruit, lime oil, honey, and coconut cream. The sale of postage stamps to foreign collectors is an important source of revenue. The island in recent years has suffered a serious loss of population because of migration of Niueans to New Zealand. Efforts to increase GDP include the promotion of tourism and a financial services industry.
GDP: purchasing power parity - $4.5 million (1997 est.)
GDP - real growth rate: NA%
GDP - per capita: purchasing power parity - $2,800 (1997 est.)
GDP - composition by sector:
agriculture: NA%
industry: NA%
services: NA%
Population below poverty line: NA%
Household income or consumption by percentage share:
lowest 10%: NA%
highest 10%: NA%
Inflation rate (consumer prices): 1% (1995)
Labor force: 450 (1992 est.)
Labor force - by occupation: most work on family plantations; paid work exists only in government service, small industry, and the Niue Development Board
Unemployment rate: NA%
Budget:
revenues: $NA
expenditures: $NA, including capital expenditures of $NA
Industries: tourism, handicrafts, food processing
Industrial production growth rate: NA%
Electricity - production: 3 million kWh (1999)
Electricity - production by source:
fossil fuel: 100%
hydro: 0%
nuclear: 0%
other: 0% (1999)
Electricity - consumption: 2.8 million kWh (1999)
Electricity - exports: 0 kWh (1999)
Electricity - imports: 0 kWh (1999)
Agriculture - products: coconuts, passion fruit, honey, limes, taro, yams, cassava (tapioca), sweet potatoes; pigs, poultry, beef cattle
Exports: $117,500 (f.o.b., 1989)
Exports - commodities: canned coconut cream, copra, honey, passion fruit products, pawpaws, root crops, limes, footballs, stamps, handicrafts
Exports - partners: NZ 89%, Fiji, Cook Islands, Australia
Imports: $4.1 million (c.i.f., 1989)
Imports - commodities: food, live animals, manufactured goods, machinery, fuels, lubricants, chemicals, drugs
Imports - partners: NZ 59%, Fiji 20%, Japan 13%, Samoa, Australia, US
Debt - external: $NA
Economic aid - recipient: $8.3 million (1995)
Currency: New Zealand dollar (NZD)
Currency code: NZD
Exchange rates: New Zealand dollars per US dollar - 2.2502 (January 2001), 2.1863 (2000), 1.8886 (1999), 1.8629 (1998), 1.5082 (1997), 1.4543 (1996)
Fiscal year: 1 April - 31 March

Communications

Telephones - main lines in use: 376 (1991)
Telephones - mobile cellular: 0 (1991)
Telephone system:
general assessment: primitive system
domestic: single-line telephone system connects all villages on island
international: NA
Radio broadcast stations: AM 1, FM 1, shortwave 0 (1998)
Radios: 1,000 (1997)
Television broadcast stations: 1 (1997)
Televisions: NA
Internet country code: .nu
Internet Service Providers (ISPs): 1 (2000)
Internet users: NA

Transportation

Railways: 0 km
Highways:
total: 234 km
paved: 86 km
unpaved: 148 km (106 km of which is access and plantation road) (2001)
Waterways: none
Ports and harbors: none; offshore anchorage only
Merchant marine: none (2000 est.)
Airports: 1 (2000 est.)
Airports - with paved runways:
total: 1
1,524 to 2,437 m: 1 (2000 est.)

Military

Military branches: Police Force
Military - note: defense is the responsibility of New Zealand

Transnational Issues

Disputes - international: none

Norfolk Island
(territory of Australia)

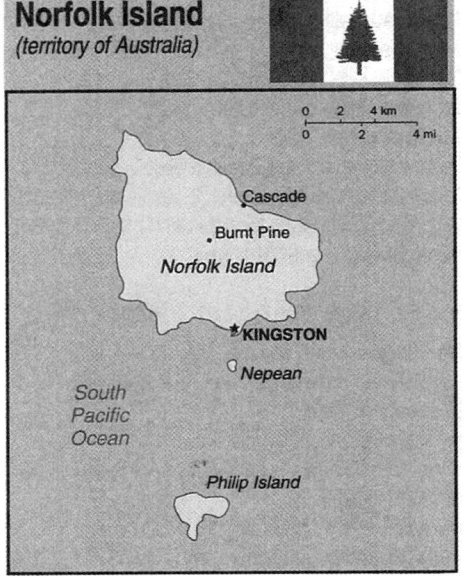

Introduction

Background: Two British attempts at establishing the island as a penal colony (1788-1814 and 1825-55) were ultimately abandoned. In 1856, the island was resettled by Pitcairn Islanders, descendants of the Bounty mutineers and their Tahitian companions.

Geography

Location: Oceania, island in the South Pacific Ocean, east of Australia
Geographic coordinates: 29 02 S, 167 57 E
Map references: Oceania
Area:
total: 34.6 sq km
land: 34.6 sq km
water: 0 sq km
Area - comparative: about 0.2 times the size of Washington, DC
Land boundaries: 0 km
Coastline: 32 km
Maritime claims:
exclusive fishing zone: 200 NM
territorial sea: 3 NM
Climate: subtropical, mild, little seasonal temperature variation
Terrain: volcanic formation with mostly rolling plains
Elevation extremes:
lowest point: Pacific Ocean 0 m
highest point: Mount Bates 319 m
Natural resources: fish
Land use:
arable land: 0%
permanent crops: 0%
permanent pastures: 25%
forests and woodland: 0%
other: 75% (1993 est.)
Irrigated land: NA sq km
Natural hazards: typhoons (especially May to July)
Environment - current issues: NA

People

Population: 1,879 (July 2001 est.)
Age structure:
0-14 years: NA%
15-64 years: NA%
65 years and over: NA%
Population growth rate: -0.71% (2001 est.)
Birth rate: NA births/1,000 population
Death rate: NA deaths/1,000 population
Net migration rate: NA migrant(s)/1,000 population
Infant mortality rate: NA deaths/1,000 live births
Life expectancy at birth:
total population: NA years
male: NA years
female: NA years
Total fertility rate: NA children born/woman
HIV/AIDS - adult prevalence rate: NA%
HIV/AIDS - people living with HIV/AIDS: NA
HIV/AIDS - deaths: NA
Nationality:
noun: Norfolk Islander(s)
adjective: Norfolk Islander(s)
Ethnic groups: descendants of the Bounty mutineers, Australian, New Zealander, Polynesians
Religions: Anglican 39%, Roman Catholic 11.7%, Uniting Church in Australia 16.4%, Seventh-Day Adventist 4.4%, none 9.2%, unknown 16.9%, other 2.4% (1986)
Languages: English (official), Norfolk a mixture of 18th century English and ancient Tahitian

Government

Country name:
conventional long form: Territory of Norfolk Island
conventional short form: Norfolk Island
Dependency status: territory of Australia; Canberra administers Commonwealth responsibilities on Norfolk Island through the Department of Environment, Sport, and Territories
Government type: NA
Capital: Kingston
Administrative divisions: none (territory of Australia)
Independence: none (territory of Australia)
National holiday: Pitcairners Arrival Day, 8 June (1856)
Constitution: Norfolk Island Act of 1979
Legal system: based on the laws of Australia, local ordinances and acts; English common law applies in matters not covered by either Australian or Norfolk Island law
Suffrage: 18 years of age; universal
Executive branch:
chief of state: Queen ELIZABETH II (since 6 February 1952); the UK and Australia are represented by Administrator Anthony J. MESSNER (since 4 August 1997)
head of government: Assembly President and Chief Minister Ronald Coane NOBBS (since 23 February 2000)
cabinet: Executive Council is made up of four of the nine members of the Legislative Assembly; the council devises government policy and acts as an advisor to the Administrator
elections: the monarch is hereditary; administrator appointed by the governor general of Australia; chief minister elected by the Legislative Assembly for a term of not more than three years; election last held 23 February 2000 (next to be held by March 2003)
election results: Ronald Coane NOBBS elected chief minister; percent of Legislative Assembly vote - NA%
Legislative branch: unicameral Legislative Assembly (9 seats; members elected by electors who have nine equal votes each but only four votes can be given to any one candidate; members serve three-year terms)
elections: last held 23 February 2000 (next to be held by March 2003)
election results: percent of vote - NA%; seats - independents 9
Judicial branch: Supreme Court; Court of Petty Sessions
Political parties and leaders: none
Political pressure groups and leaders: none
International organization participation: none
Diplomatic representation in the US: none (territory of Australia)
Diplomatic representation from the US: none (territory of Australia)
Flag description: three vertical bands of green (hoist side), white, and green with a large green Norfolk Island pine tree centered in the slightly wider white band

Economy

Economy - overview: Tourism, the primary economic activity, has steadily increased over the years and has brought a level of prosperity unusual among inhabitants of the Pacific islands. The agricultural sector has become self-sufficient in the production of beef, poultry, and eggs.
GDP: purchasing power parity - $NA
GDP - real growth rate: NA%
GDP - per capita: purchasing power parity - $NA
GDP - composition by sector:
agriculture: NA%
industry: NA%
services: NA%
Population below poverty line: NA%
Household income or consumption by percentage share:
lowest 10%: NA%
highest 10%: NA%
Inflation rate (consumer prices): NA%
Labor force: 1,395 (1991 est.)
Labor force - by occupation: tourism NA%, subsistence agriculture NA%
Unemployment rate: NA%
Budget:
revenues: $4.6 million
expenditures: $4.8 million, including capital expenditures of $NA (FY92/93)
Industries: tourism

Norfolk Island (continued)

Industrial production growth rate: NA%
Electricity - production: NA kWh
Electricity - production by source:
fossil fuel: NA%
hydro: NA%
nuclear: NA%
other: NA%
Electricity - consumption: NA kWh
Agriculture - products: Norfolk Island pine seed, Kentia palm seed, cereals, vegetables, fruit; cattle, poultry
Exports: $1.5 million (f.o.b., FY91/92)
Exports - commodities: postage stamps, seeds of the Norfolk Island pine and Kentia palm, small quantities of avocados
Exports - partners: Australia, other Pacific island countries, NZ, Asia, Europe
Imports: $17.9 million (c.i.f., FY91/92)
Imports - commodities: NA
Imports - partners: Australia, other Pacific island countries, NZ, Asia, Europe
Debt - external: $NA
Economic aid - recipient: $NA
Currency: Australian dollar (AUD)
Currency code: AUD
Exchange rates: Australian dollars per US dollar - 1.7995 (January 2001), 1.7173 (2000), 1.5497 (1999), 1.5888 (1998), 1.3439 (1997), 1.2773 (1996)
Fiscal year: 1 July - 30 June

Communications

Telephones - main lines in use: 1,087 (1983)
Telephones - mobile cellular: 0 (1983)
Telephone system:
general assessment: adequate
domestic: NA
international: radiotelephone service with Sydney (Australia)
Radio broadcast stations: AM 0, FM 3, shortwave 0 (1998)
Radios: 2,500 (1996)
Television broadcast stations: 1 (local programming station plus two repeaters that bring in Australian programs by satellite) (1998)
Televisions: 1,200 (1996)
Internet country code: .nf
Internet Service Providers (ISPs): 2 (2000)
Internet users: NA

Transportation

Railways: 0 km
Highways:
total: 80 km
paved: 53 km
unpaved: 27 km (2001)
Waterways: none
Ports and harbors: none; loading jetties at Kingston and Cascade
Merchant marine: none (2000 est.)
Airports: 1 (2000 est.)
Airports - with paved runways:
total: 1
1,524 to 2,437 m: 1 (2000 est.)

Military

Military - note: defense is the responsibility of Australia

Transnational Issues

Disputes - international: none

Northern Mariana Islands
(commonwealth in political union with the US)

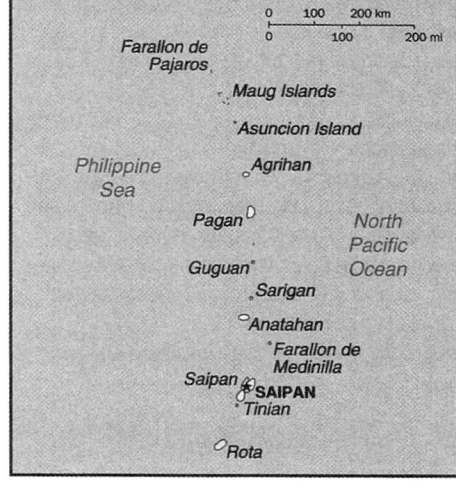

Introduction

Background: Under US administration as part of the UN Trust Territory of the Pacific, the people of the Northern Mariana Islands decided in the 1970s not to seek independence but instead to forge closer links with the US. Negotiations for territorial status began in 1972. A covenant to establish a commonwealth in political union with the US was approved in 1975. A new government and constitution went into effect in 1978.

Geography

Location: Oceania, islands in the North Pacific Ocean, about three-quarters of the way from Hawaii to the Philippines
Geographic coordinates: 15 12 N, 145 45 E
Map references: Oceania
Area:
total: 477 sq km
land: 477 sq km
water: 0 sq km
note: includes 14 islands including Saipan, Rota, and Tinian
Area - comparative: 2.5 times the size of Washington, DC
Land boundaries: 0 km
Coastline: 1,482 km
Maritime claims:
exclusive economic zone: 200 NM
territorial sea: 12 NM
Climate: tropical marine; moderated by northeast trade winds, little seasonal temperature variation; dry season December to June, rainy season July to October
Terrain: southern islands are limestone with level terraces and fringing coral reefs; northern islands are volcanic

Northern Mariana Islands (continued)

Elevation extremes:
lowest point: Pacific Ocean 0 m
highest point: unnamed location on Agrihan 965 m
Natural resources: arable land, fish
Land use:
arable land: 21%
permanent crops: 0%
permanent pastures: 19%
forests and woodland: 0%
other: 60%
Irrigated land: NA sq km
Natural hazards: active volcanoes on Pagan and Agrihan; typhoons (especially August to November)
Environment - current issues: contamination of groundwater on Saipan may contribute to disease; clean-up of landfill; protection of endangered species conflicts with development
Geography - note: strategic location in the North Pacific Ocean

People

Population: 74,612 (July 2001 est.)
Age structure:
0-14 years: 23.55% (male 8,929; female 8,639)
15-64 years: 74.72% (male 26,242; female 29,509)
65 years and over: 1.73% (male 639; female 654) (2001 est.)
Population growth rate: 3.62% (2001 est.)
Birth rate: 20.6 births/1,000 population (2001 est.)
Death rate: 2.4 deaths/1,000 population (2001 est.)
Net migration rate: 18 migrant(s)/1,000 population (2001 est.)
Sex ratio:
at birth: 1.06 male(s)/female
under 15 years: 1.03 male(s)/female
15-64 years: 0.89 male(s)/female
65 years and over: 0.98 male(s)/female
total population: 0.92 male(s)/female (2001 est.)
Infant mortality rate: 5.7 deaths/1,000 live births (2001 est.)
Life expectancy at birth:
total population: 75.74 years
male: 72.65 years
female: 79.02 years (2001 est.)
Total fertility rate: 1.76 children born/woman (2001 est.)
HIV/AIDS - adult prevalence rate: NA%
HIV/AIDS - people living with HIV/AIDS: NA
HIV/AIDS - deaths: NA
Nationality:
noun: NA
adjective: NA
Ethnic groups: Chamorro, Carolinians and other Micronesians, Caucasian, Japanese, Chinese, Korean
Religions: Christian (Roman Catholic majority, although traditional beliefs and taboos may still be found)
Languages: English, Chamorro, Carolinian
note: 86% of population speaks a language other than English at home

Literacy:
definition: age 15 and over can read and write
total population: 97%
male: 97%
female: 96% (1980 est.)

Government

Country name:
conventional long form: Commonwealth of the Northern Mariana Islands
conventional short form: Northern Mariana Islands
former: Mariana Islands District (Trust Territory of the Pacific Islands)
Dependency status: commonwealth in political union with the US; federal funds to the Commonwealth administered by the US Department of the Interior, Office of Insular Affairs
Government type: commonwealth; self-governing with locally elected governor, lieutenant governor, and legislature
Capital: Saipan
Administrative divisions: none (commonwealth in political union with the US); there are no first-order administrative divisions as defined by the US Government, but there are four municipalities at the second order; Northern Islands, Rota, Saipan, Tinian
Independence: none (commonwealth in political union with the US)
National holiday: Commonwealth Day, 8 January (1978)
Constitution: Covenant Agreement effective 4 November 1986 and the Constitution of the Commonwealth of the Northern Mariana Islands effective 1 January 1978
Legal system: based on US system, except for customs, wages, immigration laws, and taxation
Suffrage: 18 years of age; universal; indigenous inhabitants are US citizens but do not vote in US presidential elections
Executive branch:
chief of state: President George W. BUSH of the US (since 20 January 2001); Vice President Richard B. CHENEY (since 20 January 2001)
head of government: Governor Pedro P. TENORIO (since NA January 1998) and Lieutenant Governor Jesus R. SABLAN (since NA January 1998)
cabinet: NA
elections: US president and vice president elected on the same ticket for four-year terms; governor and lieutenant governor elected on the same ticket by popular vote for four-year terms; election last held in NA November 1997 (next to be held NA November 2001)
election results: Pedro P. TENORIO elected governor in a three-way race; percent of vote - Pedro P. TENORIO (Republican Party) 47%
Legislative branch: bicameral Legislature consists of the Senate (9 seats; members are elected by popular vote to serve four-year staggered terms) and the House of Representatives (18 seats; members are elected by popular vote to serve two-year terms)

elections: Senate - last held 9 November 1999 (next to be held NA November 2001); House of Representatives - last held 9 November 1999 (next to be held NA November 2001)
election results: Senate - percent of vote by party - NA%; seats by party - Republican Party 6, Democratic Party 2, Reform Party 1; House of Representatives - percent of vote by party - NA%; seats by party - Republican Party 10, Democratic Party 8
note: the Commonwealth does not have a nonvoting delegate in the US Congress; instead, it has an elected official or "resident representative" located in Washington, DC; seats by party - Republican Party 1 (Juan N. BABAUTA)
Judicial branch: Commonwealth Supreme Court; Superior Court; Federal District Court
Political parties and leaders: Democratic Party [Dr. Carlos S. CAMACHO]; Republican Party [Benigno R. FITIAL]
Political pressure groups and leaders: NA
International organization participation: ESCAP (associate), Interpol (subbureau), SPC
Flag description: blue, with a white, five-pointed star superimposed on the gray silhouette of a latte stone (a traditional foundation stone used in building) in the center, surrounded by a wreath

Economy

Economy - overview: The economy benefits substantially from financial assistance from the US. The rate of funding has declined as locally generated government revenues have grown. The key tourist industry employs about 50% of the work force and accounts for roughly one-fourth of GDP. Japanese tourists predominate. Annual tourist entries have exceeded one-half million in recent years, but financial difficulties in Japan have caused a temporary slowdown. The agricultural sector is made up of cattle ranches and small farms producing coconuts, breadfruit, tomatoes, and melons. Garment production is by far the most important industry with employment of 12,000 mostly Chinese workers and sizable shipments to the US under duty and quota exemptions.
GDP: purchasing power parity - $900 million (2000 est.)
note: GDP numbers reflect US spending
GDP - real growth rate: NA%
GDP - per capita: purchasing power parity - $12,500 (2000 est.)
GDP - composition by sector:
agriculture: NA%
industry: NA%
services: NA%
Population below poverty line: NA%
Household income or consumption by percentage share:
lowest 10%: NA%
highest 10%: NA%
Inflation rate (consumer prices): 1.2% (1997 est.)
Labor force: 6,006 total indigenous labor force; 2,699 unemployed; 28,717 foreign workers (1995)

Northern Mariana Islands (continued)

Labor force - by occupation: NA
Unemployment rate: NA%
Budget:
revenues: $221 million
expenditures: $213 million, including capital expenditures of $17.7 million (1996)
Industries: tourism, construction, garments, handicrafts
Industrial production growth rate: NA%
Electricity - production: NA kWh
Electricity - consumption: NA kWh
Agriculture - products: coconuts, fruits, vegetables; cattle
Exports: $NA
Exports - commodities: garments
Exports - partners: US
Imports: $NA
Imports - commodities: food, construction equipment and materials, petroleum products
Imports - partners: US, Japan
Debt - external: $NA
Economic aid - recipient: extensive funding from US
Currency: US dollar (USD)
Currency code: USD
Exchange rates: the US dollar is used
Fiscal year: 1 October - 30 September

Communications

Telephones - main lines in use: 21,000 (1996)
Telephones - mobile cellular: 1,200 (1995)
Telephone system:
general assessment: NA
domestic: NA
international: satellite earth stations - 2 Intelsat (Pacific Ocean)
Radio broadcast stations: AM 2, FM 3, shortwave 1 (1998)
Radios: NA
Television broadcast stations: 1 (on Saipan and one station planned for Rota; in addition, two cable services on Saipan provide varied programming from satellite networks) (1997)
Televisions: NA
Internet country code: .mp
Internet Service Providers (ISPs): 1 (2000)
Internet users: NA

Transportation

Railways: 0 km
Highways:
total: 362 km
paved: NA km
unpaved: NA km (1991)
Waterways: none
Ports and harbors: Saipan, Tinian
Merchant marine: none (2000 est.)
Airports: 6 (2000 est.)
Airports - with paved runways:
total: 3
2,438 to 3,047 m: 1
1,524 to 2,437 m: 2 (2000 est.)

Airports - with unpaved runways:
total: 3
2,438 to 3,047 m: 1
under 914 m: 2 (2000 est.)
Heliports: 1 (2000 est.)

Military

Military - note: defense is the responsibility of the US

Transnational Issues

Disputes - international: none

Norway

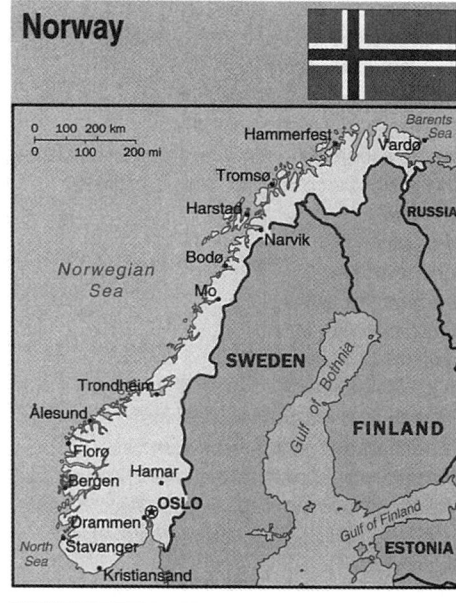

Introduction

Background: Despite its neutrality, Norway was not able to avoid occupation by Germany in World War II. In 1949, neutrality was abandoned and Norway became a member of NATO. Discovery of oil and gas in adjacent waters in the late 1960s boosted Norway's economic fortunes. The current focus is on containing spending on the extensive welfare system and planning for the time when petroleum reserves are depleted. In referenda held in 1972 and 1994, Norway rejected joining the EU.

Geography

Location: Northern Europe, bordering the North Sea and the North Atlantic Ocean, west of Sweden
Geographic coordinates: 62 00 N, 10 00 E
Map references: Europe
Area:
total: 324,220 sq km
land: 307,860 sq km
water: 16,360 sq km
Area - comparative: slightly larger than New Mexico
Land boundaries:
total: 2,515 km
border countries: Finland 729 km, Sweden 1,619 km, Russia 167 km
Coastline: 21,925 km (includes mainland 3,419 km, large islands 2,413 km, long fjords, numerous small islands, and minor indentations 16,093 km)
Maritime claims:
contiguous zone: 10 NM
continental shelf: 200 NM
exclusive economic zone: 200 NM
territorial sea: 4 NM
Climate: temperate along coast, modified by North Atlantic Current; colder interior with increased precipitation and colder summers causing glaciers to grow; rainy year-round on west coast
Terrain: glaciated; mostly high plateaus and rugged mountains broken by fertile valleys; small, scattered

Norway (continued)

plains; coastline deeply indented by fjords; arctic tundra in north

Elevation extremes:
lowest point: Norwegian Sea 0 m
highest point: Galdhopiggen 2,469 m

Natural resources: petroleum, copper, natural gas, pyrites, nickel, iron ore, zinc, lead, fish, timber, hydropower

Land use:
arable land: 3%
permanent crops: 0%
permanent pastures: 0%
forests and woodland: 27%
other: 70% (1993 est.)

Irrigated land: 970 sq km (1993 est.)

Natural hazards: rockslides, avalanches

Environment - current issues: water pollution; acid rain damaging forests and adversely affecting lakes, threatening fish stocks; air pollution from vehicle emissions

Environment - international agreements:
party to: Air Pollution, Air Pollution-Nitrogen Oxides, Air Pollution-Persistent Organic Pollutants, Air Pollution-Sulphur 85, Air Pollution-Sulphur 94, Air Pollution-Volatile Organic Compounds, Antarctic-Environmental Protocol, Antarctic-Marine Living Resources, Antarctic Seals, Antarctic Treaty, Biodiversity, Climate Change, Desertification, Endangered Species, Environmental Modification, Hazardous Wastes, Law of the Sea, Marine Dumping, Nuclear Test Ban, Ozone Layer Protection, Ship Pollution, Tropical Timber 83, Tropical Timber 94, Wetlands, Whaling
signed, but not ratified: Air Pollution-Volatile Organic Compounds, Climate Change-Kyoto Protocol

Geography - note: about two-thirds mountains; some 50,000 islands off its much indented coastline; strategic location adjacent to sea lanes and air routes in North Atlantic; one of most rugged and longest coastlines in world; Norway is the only NATO member having a land boundary with Russia

People

Population: 4,503,440 (July 2001 est.)

Age structure:
0-14 years: 19.99% (male 462,673; female 437,514)
15-64 years: 64.91% (male 1,482,346; female 1,440,832)
65 years and over: 15.1% (male 282,307; female 397,768) (2001 est.)

Population growth rate: 0.49% (2001 est.)

Birth rate: 12.6 births/1,000 population (2001 est.)

Death rate: 9.83 deaths/1,000 population (2001 est.)

Net migration rate: 2.11 migrant(s)/1,000 population (2001 est.)

Sex ratio:
at birth: 1.07 male(s)/female
under 15 years: 1.06 male(s)/female
15-64 years: 1.03 male(s)/female
65 years and over: 0.71 male(s)/female
total population: 0.98 male(s)/female (2001 est.)

Infant mortality rate: 3.94 deaths/1,000 live births (2001 est.)

Life expectancy at birth:
total population: 78.79 years
male: 75.87 years
female: 81.92 years (2001 est.)

Total fertility rate: 1.81 children born/woman (2001 est.)

HIV/AIDS - adult prevalence rate: less than 100 (1999 est.)

HIV/AIDS - people living with HIV/AIDS: 1,600 (1999 est.)

HIV/AIDS - deaths: 8 (1999)

Nationality:
noun: Norwegian(s)
adjective: Norwegian

Ethnic groups: Norwegian (Nordic, Alpine, Baltic), Sami 20,000

Religions: Evangelical Lutheran 86% (state church), other Protestant and Roman Catholic 3%, other 1%, none and unknown 10% (1997)

Languages: Norwegian (official)
note: small Sami- and Finnish-speaking minorities

Literacy:
definition: age 15 and over can read and write
total population: 100%
male: NA%
female: NA%

Government

Country name:
conventional long form: Kingdom of Norway
conventional short form: Norway
local long form: Kongeriket Norge
local short form: Norge

Government type: constitutional monarchy

Capital: Oslo

Administrative divisions: 19 provinces (fylker, singular - fylke); Akershus, Aust-Agder, Buskerud, Finnmark, Hedmark, Hordaland, More og Romsdal, Nordland, Nord-Trondelag, Oppland, Oslo, Ostfold, Rogaland, Sogn og Fjordane, Sor-Trondelag, Telemark, Troms, Vest-Agder, Vestfold

Dependent areas: Bouvet Island, Jan Mayen, Svalbard

Independence: 7 June 1905 Norway declared the union with Sweden dissolved; 26 October 1905 Sweden agreed to the repeal of the union

National holiday: Constitution Day, 17 May (1814); note - 17 May 1814 is the date of independence from Sweden, 7 June 1905 is the date Norway declared the union with Sweden was dissolved

Constitution: 17 May 1814, modified in 1884

Legal system: mixture of customary law, civil law system, and common law traditions; Supreme Court renders advisory opinions to legislature when asked; accepts compulsory ICJ jurisdiction, with reservations

Suffrage: 18 years of age; universal

Executive branch:
chief of state: King HARALD V (since 17 January 1991); Heir Apparent Crown Prince HAAKON MAGNUS, son of the monarch (born 20 July 1973)
head of government: Prime Minister Jens STOLTENBERG (since 17 March 2000)
cabinet: State Council appointed by the monarch with the approval of the Parliament
elections: none; the monarch is hereditary; following parliamentary elections, the leader of the largest party or leader of a coalition is usually appointed prime minister by the monarch with the approval of the Parliament

Legislative branch: modified unicameral Parliament or Storting which, for certain purposes, divides itself into two chambers (165 seats; members are elected by popular vote by proportional representation to serve four-year terms)
elections: last held 15 September 1997 (next to be held 10 September 2001)
election results: percent of vote by party - Labor Party 35%, Center Party 7.9%, Conservative Party 14.3%, Christian People's Party 13.7%, Socialist Left Party 6%, Progress Party 15.3%, Liberal Party 4.4%, other parties 1.6%; seats by party - Labor Party 65, Center Party 11, Conservative Party 23, Christian People's Party 25, Socialist Left Party 9, Progress Party 25, Liberal Party 6, other parties 1
note: for certain purposes, the Parliament divides itself into two chambers and elects one-fourth of its membership to an upper house or Lagting

Judicial branch: Supreme Court or Hoyesterett (justices appointed by the monarch)

Political parties and leaders: Center Party [Odd Roger ENOKSEN]; Christian People's Party [Kiell Magne BONDEVIK]; Conservative Party [Jan PETERSEN]; Labor Party [Jens STOLTENBERG]; Liberal Party [Lars SPONHEIM]; Progress Party [Carl I. HAGEN]; Socialist Left Party [Kristin HALVORSEN]

Political pressure groups and leaders: NA

International organization participation: AfDB, AsDB, Australia Group, BIS, CBSS, CCC, CE, CERN, EAPC, EBRD, ECE, EFTA, ESA, FAO, IADB, IAEA, IBRD, ICAO, ICC, ICFTU, ICRM, IDA, IEA, IFAD, IFC, IFRCS, IHO, ILO, IMF, IMO, Inmarsat, Intelsat, Interpol, IOC, IOM, ISO, ITU, MINURSO, NAM (guest), NATO, NC, NEA, NIB, NSG, OAS (observer), OECD, OPCW, OSCE, PCA, UN, UN Security Council (temporary), UNCTAD, UNESCO, UNHCR, UNIDO, UNMEE, UNMIBH, UNMIK, UNMOP, UNTAET, UNTSO, UPU, WEU (associate), WHO, WIPO, WMO, WTrO, ZC

Diplomatic representation in the US:
chief of mission: Ambassador Tom Erik VRAALSEN
chancery: 2720 34th Street NW, Washington, DC 20008
telephone: [1] (202) 333-6000
FAX: [1] (202) 337-0870
consulate(s) general: Houston, Miami, Minneapolis, New York, and San Francisco

Diplomatic representation from the US:
chief of mission: Ambassador Robin Chandler DUKE
embassy: Drammensveien 18, 0244 Oslo
mailing address: PSC 69, Box 1000, APO AE 09707
telephone: [47] (22) 44 85 50
FAX: [47] (22) 43 07 77

Norway (continued)

Flag description: red with a blue cross outlined in white that extends to the edges of the flag; the vertical part of the cross is shifted to the hoist side in the style of the Dannebrog (Danish flag)

Economy

Economy - overview: The Norwegian economy is a prosperous bastion of welfare capitalism, featuring a combination of free market activity and government intervention. The government controls key areas, such as the vital petroleum sector (through large-scale state enterprises). The country is richly endowed with natural resources - petroleum, hydropower, fish, forests, and minerals - and is highly dependent on its oil production and international oil prices; in 1999, oil and gas accounted for 35% of exports. Only Saudi Arabia exports more oil than Norway. Oslo opted to stay out of the EU during a referendum in November 1994. Growth picked up in 2000 to 2.7%, compared to the meager 0.8% of 1999, but may fall back in 2001. The government moved ahead with privatization in 2000, even proposing the sale of up to one-third of the 100% state-owned oil company Statoil. Despite their high per capita income and generous welfare benefits, Norwegians worry about that time in the next two decades when the oil and gas begin to run out. Accordingly, Norway has been saving its oil-boosted budget surpluses in a Government Petroleum Fund, which is invested abroad and now is valued at more than $43 billion.
GDP: purchasing power parity - $124.1 billion (1999 est.)
GDP - real growth rate: 2.7% (2000 est.)
GDP - per capita: purchasing power parity - $27,700 (2000 est.)
GDP - composition by sector:
agriculture: 2%
industry: 25%
services: 73% (1999)
Population below poverty line: NA%
Household income or consumption by percentage share:
lowest 10%: 4.1%
highest 10%: 21.8% (1995)
Inflation rate (consumer prices): 2.9% (2000 est.)
Labor force: 2.4 million (2000 est.)
Labor force - by occupation: services 74%, industry 22%, agriculture, forestry, and fishing 4% (1995)
Unemployment rate: 3% (2000 est.)
Budget:
revenues: $71.7 billion
expenditures: $57.6 billion, including capital expenditures of $NA (2000 est.)
Industries: petroleum and gas, food processing, shipbuilding, pulp and paper products, metals, chemicals, timber, mining, textiles, fishing
Industrial production growth rate: 3% (2000 est.)
Electricity - production: 121.084 billion kWh (1999)
Electricity - production by source:
fossil fuel: 0.63%
hydro: 99.11%
nuclear: 0%
other: 0.26% (1999)
Electricity - consumption: 110.795 billion kWh (1999)
Electricity - exports: 8.28 billion kWh (1999)
Electricity - imports: 6.467 billion kWh (1999)
Agriculture - products: barley, other grains, potatoes; beef, milk; fish
Exports: $59.2 billion (f.o.b., 2000 est.)
Exports - commodities: petroleum and petroleum products, machinery and equipment, metals, chemicals, ships, fish
Exports - partners: EU 73% (UK 17%, Germany 11%, Netherlands 10%, Sweden 9%), US 5% (1999)
Imports: $35.2 billion (f.o.b., 2000 est.)
Imports - commodities: machinery and equipment, chemicals, metals, foodstuffs
Imports - partners: EU 66% (Sweden 15%, Germany 12%, UK 9%, Denmark 7%), US 10%, Japan (1999)
Debt - external: $0 (Norway is a net external creditor)
Economic aid - donor: ODA, $1.4 billion (1998)
Currency: Norwegian krone (NOK)
Currency code: NOK
Exchange rates: Norwegian kroner per US dollar - 8.7784 (January 2001), 8.8018 (2000), 7.7992 (1999), 7.5451 (1998), 7.0734 (1997), 6.4498 (1996)
Fiscal year: calendar year

Communications

Telephones - main lines in use: 2.735 million (1998)
Telephones - mobile cellular: 2,080,408 (1998)
Telephone system:
general assessment: modern in all respects; one of the most advanced telecommunications networks in Europe
domestic: Norway has a domestic satellite system; moreover the prevalence of rural areas encourages the wide use of cellular mobile systems instead of fixed wire systems
international: 2 buried coaxial cable systems; 4 coaxial submarine cables; satellite earth stations - NA Eutelsat, NA Intelsat (Atlantic Ocean), and 1 Inmarsat (Atlantic and Indian Ocean regions); note - Norway shares the Inmarsat earth station with the other Nordic countries (Denmark, Finland, Iceland, and Sweden) (1999)
Radio broadcast stations: AM 5, FM at least 650, shortwave 1 (1998)
Radios: 4.03 million (1997)
Television broadcast stations: 360 (plus 2,729 repeaters) (1995)
Televisions: 2.03 million (1997)
Internet country code: .no
Internet Service Providers (ISPs): 13 (2000)
Internet users: 2.36 million (October 2000)

Transportation

Railways:
total: 4,012 km
standard gauge: 4,012 km 1.435-m gauge (2,530 km electrified; 96 km double track) (1998)
Highways:
total: 91,180 km
paved: 67,838 km (including 109 km of expressways)
unpaved: 23,342 km (1999)
Waterways: 1,577 km (along west coast)
note: navigable by 2.4 m maximum draft vessels
Pipelines: refined petroleum products 53 km
Ports and harbors: Bergen, Drammen, Floro, Hammerfest, Harstad, Haugesund, Kristiansand, Larvik, Narvik, Oslo, Porsgrunn, Stavanger, Tromso, Trondheim
Merchant marine:
total: 764 ships (1,000 GRT or over) totaling 20,667,370 GRT/32,100,208 DWT
ships by type: bulk 89, cargo 139, chemical tanker 114, combination bulk 9, combination ore/oil 37, container 15, liquefied gas 84, passenger 10, petroleum tanker 151, refrigerated cargo 10, roll on/roll off 45, short-sea passenger 22, specialized tanker 1, vehicle carrier 38
note: includes some foreign-owned ships registered here as a flag of convenience: Germany 1, Japan 1, Mexico 1, Sweden 1 (2000 est.)
Airports: 103 (2000 est.)
Airports - with paved runways:
total: 67
over 3,047 m: 1
2,438 to 3,047 m: 12
1,524 to 2,437 m: 12
914 to 1,523 m: 14
under 914 m: 28 (2000 est.)
Airports - with unpaved runways:
total: 36
914 to 1,523 m: 5
under 914 m: 31 (2000 est.)
Heliports: 1 (2000 est.)

Military

Military branches: Norwegian Army, Royal Norwegian Navy (includes Coast Artillery and Coast Guard), Royal Norwegian Air Force, Home Guard
Military manpower - military age: 20 years of age
Military manpower - availability:
males age 15-49: 1,101,384 (2001 est.)
Military manpower - fit for military service:
males age 15-49: 913,534 (2001 est.)
Military manpower - reaching military age annually:
males: 27,341 (2001 est.)
Military expenditures - dollar figure: $3.113 billion (FY98)
Military expenditures - percent of GDP: 2.1% (FY98)

Transnational Issues

Disputes - international: territorial claim in Antarctica (Queen Maud Land); Svalbard is the focus of a maritime boundary dispute between Norway and Russia

Oman

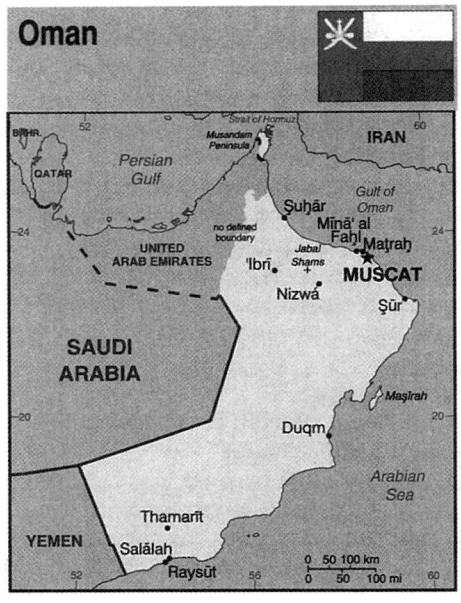

Introduction

Background: In 1970, QABOOS bin Said Al Said ousted his father and has ruled as sultan ever since. His extensive modernization program has opened the country to the outside world and has preserved a long-standing political and military relationship with the UK. Oman's moderate, independent foreign policy has sought to maintain good relations with all Middle Eastern countries.

Geography

Location: Middle East, bordering the Arabian Sea, Gulf of Oman, and Persian Gulf, between Yemen and UAE
Geographic coordinates: 21 00 N, 57 00 E
Map references: Middle East
Area:
total: 212,460 sq km
land: 212,460 sq km
water: 0 sq km
Area - comparative: slightly smaller than Kansas
Land boundaries:
total: 1,374 km
border countries: Saudi Arabia 676 km, UAE 410 km, Yemen 288 km
Coastline: 2,092 km
Maritime claims:
contiguous zone: 24 NM
exclusive economic zone: 200 NM
territorial sea: 12 NM
Climate: dry desert; hot, humid along coast; hot, dry interior; strong southwest summer monsoon (May to September) in far south
Terrain: central desert plain, rugged mountains in north and south
Elevation extremes:
lowest point: Arabian Sea 0 m
highest point: Jabal Shams 2,980 m
Natural resources: petroleum, copper, asbestos, some marble, limestone, chromium, gypsum, natural gas
Land use:
arable land: 0%
permanent crops: 0%
permanent pastures: 5%
forests and woodland: 0%
other: 95% (1993 est.)
Irrigated land: 580 sq km (1993 est.)
Natural hazards: summer winds often raise large sandstorms and dust storms in interior; periodic droughts
Environment - current issues: rising soil salinity; beach pollution from oil spills; very limited natural fresh water resources
Environment - international agreements:
party to: Biodiversity, Climate Change, Desertification, Hazardous Wastes, Law of the Sea, Marine Dumping, Ozone Layer Protection, Ship Pollution, Whaling
signed, but not ratified: none of the selected agreements
Geography - note: strategic location on Musandam Peninsula adjacent to Strait of Hormuz, a vital transit point for world crude oil

People

Population: 2,622,198
note: includes 527,078 non-nationals (July 2001 est.)
Age structure:
0-14 years: 41.51% (male 554,727; female 533,627)
15-64 years: 56.12% (male 894,978; female 576,672)
65 years and over: 2.37% (male 32,863; female 29,331) (2001 est.)
Population growth rate: 3.43% (2001 est.)
Birth rate: 37.96 births/1,000 population (2001 est.)
Death rate: 4.1 deaths/1,000 population (2001 est.)
Net migration rate: 0.48 migrant(s)/1,000 population (2001 est.)
Sex ratio:
at birth: 1.05 male(s)/female
under 15 years: 1.04 male(s)/female
15-64 years: 1.55 male(s)/female
65 years and over: 1.12 male(s)/female
total population: 1.3 male(s)/female (2001 est.)
Infant mortality rate: 22.52 deaths/1,000 live births (2001 est.)
Life expectancy at birth:
total population: 72.04 years
male: 69.9 years
female: 74.29 years (2001 est.)
Total fertility rate: 6.04 children born/woman (2001 est.)
HIV/AIDS - adult prevalence rate: 0.11% (1999 est.)
HIV/AIDS - people living with HIV/AIDS: NA
HIV/AIDS - deaths: NA
Nationality:
noun: Omani(s)
adjective: Omani
Ethnic groups: Arab, Baluchi, South Asian (Indian, Pakistani, Sri Lankan, Bangladeshi), African
Religions: Ibadhi Muslim 75%, Sunni Muslim, Shi'a Muslim, Hindu
Languages: Arabic (official), English, Baluchi, Urdu, Indian dialects
Literacy:
definition: NA
total population: approaching 80%
male: NA%
female: NA%

Government

Country name:
conventional long form: Sultanate of Oman
conventional short form: Oman
local long form: Saltanat Uman
local short form: Uman
former: Muscat and Oman
Government type: monarchy
Capital: Muscat
Administrative divisions: 6 regions (mintaqat, singular - mintaqah) and 2 governorates* (muhafazat, singular - muhafazah) Ad Dakhiliyah, Al Batinah, Al Wusta, Ash Sharqiyah, Az Zahirah, Masqat, Musandam*, Zufar*; note - the US Embassy in Oman reports that Masqat is a governorate, but this has not been confirmed by the US Board of Geographic Names (BGN)
Independence: 1650 (expulsion of the Portuguese)
National holiday: Birthday of Sultan QABOOS, 18 November (1940)
Constitution: none; note - on 6 November 1996, Sultan QABOOS issued a royal decree promulgating a new basic law which, among other things, clarifies the royal succession, provides for a prime minister, bars ministers from holding interests in companies doing business with the government, establishes a bicameral legislature, and guarantees basic civil liberties for Omani citizens
Legal system: based on English common law and Islamic law; ultimate appeal to the monarch; has not accepted compulsory ICJ jurisdiction
Suffrage: in Oman's most recent elections in 2000, limited to approximately 175,000 Omanis chosen by the government to vote in elections for the Majlis ash-Shura
Executive branch:
chief of state: Sultan and Prime Minister QABOOS bin Said Al Said (since 23 July 1970); note - the monarch is both the chief of state and head of government
head of government: Sultan and Prime Minister QABOOS bin Said Al Said (since 23 July 1970); note - the monarch is both the chief of state and head of government
cabinet: Cabinet appointed by the monarch
elections: none; the monarch is hereditary
Legislative branch: bicameral Majlis Oman consists of an upper chamber or Majlis al-Dawla (48 seats; members appointed by the monarch; has advisory powers only) and a lower chamber or Majlis al-Shura (83 seats; members elected by limited suffrage, however, the monarch makes final selections and can negate election results; body has some limited power to propose legislation, but otherwise has only advisory powers)

Oman (continued)

elections: last held NA September 2000 (next to be held NA September 2003)
election results: NA; note - two women were elected for the first time to Majlis al-Shura, about 100,000 people voted
Judicial branch: Supreme Court
note: the nascent civil court system, administered by region, has non-Islamic judges as well as traditional Islamic judges
Political parties and leaders: none
Political pressure groups and leaders: none
International organization participation: ABEDA, AFESD, AL, AMF, CCC, ESCWA, FAO, G-77, GCC, IBRD, ICAO, IDA, IDB, IFAD, IFC, IHO, ILO, IMF, IMO, Inmarsat, Intelsat, Interpol, IOC, ISO (correspondent), ITU, NAM, OIC, OPCW, UN, UNCTAD, UNESCO, UNIDO, UPU, WFTU, WHO, WIPO, WMO, WTrO
Diplomatic representation in the US:
chief of mission: Ambassador Abdallah bin Muhammad bin Aqil al-DHAHAB
chancery: 2535 Belmont Road, NW, Washington, DC 20008
telephone: [1] (202) 387-1980 through 1981, 1988
FAX: [1] (202) 745-4933
Diplomatic representation from the US:
chief of mission: Ambassador John B. CRAIG
embassy: Jameat A'Duwal Al Arabiya Street, Al Khuwair area, Muscat
mailing address: international: P. O. Box 202, Code No. 115, Medinat Al-Sultan Qaboos, Muscat
telephone: [968] 698989
FAX: [968] 699189
Flag description: three horizontal bands of white, red, and green of equal width with a broad, vertical, red band on the hoist side; the national emblem (a khanjar dagger in its sheath superimposed on two crossed swords in scabbards) in white is centered at the top of the vertical band

Economy

Economy - overview: Oman's economic performance improved significantly in 2000 due largely to the upturn in oil prices. The government is moving ahead with privatization of its utilities, the development of a body of commercial law to facilitate foreign investment, and increased budgetary outlays. Oman continues to liberalize its markets and joined the World Trade Organization (WTrO) in November 2000.
GDP: purchasing power parity - $19.6 billion (2000 est.)
GDP - real growth rate: 4.6% (2000 est.)
GDP - per capita: purchasing power parity - $7,700 (2000 est.)
GDP - composition by sector:
agriculture: 3%
industry: 40%
services: 57% (1999 est.)
Population below poverty line: NA%
Household income or consumption by percentage share:
lowest 10%: NA%
highest 10%: NA%
Inflation rate (consumer prices): -0.8% (2000 est.)
Labor force: 850,000 (1997 est.)
Labor force - by occupation: agriculture NA%, industry NA%, services NA%
Unemployment rate: NA%
Budget:
revenues: $4.7 billion
expenditures: $5.9 billion, including capital expenditures of $490 million (1999)
Industries: crude oil production and refining, natural gas production, construction, cement, copper
Industrial production growth rate: 4% (2000 est.)
Electricity - production: 8.63 billion kWh (1999)
Electricity - production by source:
fossil fuel: 100%
hydro: 0%
nuclear: 0%
other: 0% (1999)
Electricity - consumption: 8.026 billion kWh (1999)
Electricity - exports: 0 kWh (1999)
Electricity - imports: 0 kWh (1999)
Agriculture - products: dates, limes, bananas, alfalfa, vegetables; camels, cattle; fish
Exports: $11.1 billion (f.o.b., 2000 est.)
Exports - commodities: petroleum, reexports, fish, metals, textiles
Exports - partners: Japan 27%, China 12%, Thailand 18%, UAE 12%, South Korea 12%, US (1999)
Imports: $4.5 billion (f.o.b., 2000 est.)
Imports - commodities: machinery and transport equipment, manufactured goods, food, livestock, lubricants
Imports - partners: UAE 26% (largely reexports), Japan 16%, UK 9%, Italy 7%, Germany 6%, US (1999)
Debt - external: $4.5 billion (2000 est.)
Economic aid - recipient: $76.4 million (1995)
Currency: Omani rial (OMR)
Currency code: OMR
Exchange rates: Omani rials per US dollar - 0.3845 (fixed rate since 1986)
Fiscal year: calendar year

Communications

Telephones - main lines in use: 201,000 (1997)
Telephones - mobile cellular: 59,822 (1997)
Telephone system:
general assessment: modern system consisting of open wire, microwave, and radiotelephone communication stations; limited coaxial cable
domestic: open wire, microwave, radiotelephone communications, and a domestic satellite system with 8 earth stations
international: satellite earth stations - 2 Intelsat (Indian Ocean) and 1 Arabsat
Radio broadcast stations: AM 3, FM 9, shortwave 2 (1999)
Radios: 1.4 million (1997)
Television broadcast stations: 13 (plus 25 low-power repeaters) (1999)
Televisions: 1.6 million (1997)
Internet country code: .om
Internet Service Providers (ISPs): 1 (2000)
Internet users: 50,000 (2000)

Transportation

Railways: 0 km
Highways:
total: 32,800 km
paved: 9,840 km (including 550 km of expressways)
unpaved: 22,960 km (1996)
Pipelines: crude oil 1,300 km; natural gas 1,030 km
Ports and harbors: Matrah, Mina' al Fahl, Mina' Raysut
Merchant marine:
total: 4 ships (1,000 GRT or over) totaling 18,167 GRT/11,307 DWT
ships by type: cargo 2, passenger 1, passenger/cargo 1 (2000 est.)
Airports: 143 (2000 est.)
Airports - with paved runways:
total: 6
over 3,047 m: 4
2,438 to 3,047 m: 1
914 to 1,523 m: 1 (2000 est.)
Airports - with unpaved runways:
total: 137
over 3,047 m: 2
2,438 to 3,047 m: 6
1,524 to 2,437 m: 56
914 to 1,523 m: 37
under 914 m: 36 (2000 est.)
Heliports: 1 (2000 est.)

Military

Military branches: Army, Navy, Air Force, paramilitary (includes Royal Oman Police)
Military manpower - military age: 14 years of age
Military manpower - availability:
males age 15-49: 771,919 (2001 est.)
Military manpower - fit for military service:
males age 15-49: 429,811 (2001 est.)
Military manpower - reaching military age annually:
males: 26,469 (2001 est.)
Military expenditures - dollar figure: $2.4 billion (FY00)
Military expenditures - percent of GDP: 13% (FY00)

Transnational Issues

Disputes - international: boundary with the UAE has not been bilaterally defined; northern section in the Musandam Peninsula is an administrative boundary

Pacific Ocean

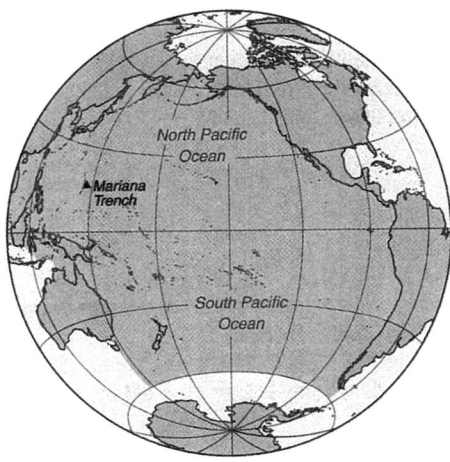

Introduction

Background: The Pacific Ocean is the largest of the world's five oceans (followed by the Atlantic Ocean, Indian Ocean, Southern Ocean, and Arctic Ocean). Strategically important access waterways include the La Perouse, Tsugaru, Tsushima, Taiwan, Singapore, and Torres Straits. The decision by the International Hydrographic Organization in the spring of 2000 to delimit a fifth ocean, the Southern Ocean, removed the portion of the Pacific Ocean south of 60 degrees south.

Geography

Location: body of water between the Southern Ocean, Asia, Australia, and the Western Hemisphere
Geographic coordinates: 0 00 N, 160 00 W
Map references: World
Area:
total: 155.557 million sq km
note: includes Bali Sea, Bering Sea, Bering Strait, Coral Sea, East China Sea, Flores Sea, Gulf of Alaska, Gulf of Tonkin, Java Sea, Philippine Sea, Savu Sea, Sea of Japan, Sea of Okhotsk, South China Sea, Tasman Sea, Timor Sea, and other tributary water bodies
Area - comparative: about 15 times the size of the US; covers about 28% of the global surface; larger than the total land area of the world
Coastline: 135,663 km
Climate: planetary air pressure systems and resultant wind patterns exhibit remarkable uniformity in the south and east; trade winds and westerly winds are well-developed patterns, modified by seasonal fluctuations; tropical cyclones (hurricanes) may form south of Mexico from June to October and affect Mexico and Central America; continental influences cause climatic uniformity to be much less pronounced in the eastern and western regions at the same latitude in the North Pacific Ocean; the western Pacific is monsoonal - a rainy season occurs during the summer months, when moisture-laden winds blow from the ocean over the land, and a dry season during the winter months, when dry winds blow from the Asian landmass back to the ocean; tropical cyclones (typhoons) may strike southeast and east Asia from May to December
Terrain: surface currents in the northern Pacific are dominated by a clockwise, warm-water gyre (broad circular system of currents) and in the southern Pacific by a counterclockwise, cool-water gyre; in the northern Pacific, sea ice forms in the Bering Sea and Sea of Okhotsk in winter; in the southern Pacific, sea ice from Antarctica reaches its northernmost extent in October; the ocean floor in the eastern Pacific is dominated by the East Pacific Rise, while the western Pacific is dissected by deep trenches, including the Mariana Trench, which is the world's deepest
Elevation extremes:
lowest point: Challenger Deep in the Mariana Trench -10,924 m
highest point: sea level 0 m
Natural resources: oil and gas fields, polymetallic nodules, sand and gravel aggregates, placer deposits, fish
Natural hazards: surrounded by a zone of violent volcanic and earthquake activity sometimes referred to as the "Pacific Ring of Fire"; subject to tropical cyclones (typhoons) in southeast and east Asia from May to December (most frequent from July to October); tropical cyclones (hurricanes) may form south of Mexico and strike Central America and Mexico from June to October (most common in August and September); cyclical El Nino/La Nina phenomenon occurs in the equatorial Pacific, influencing weather in the Western Hemisphere and the western Pacific; ships subject to superstructure icing in extreme north from October to May; persistent fog in the northern Pacific can be a maritime hazard from June to December
Environment - current issues: endangered marine species include the dugong, sea lion, sea otter, seals, turtles, and whales; oil pollution in Philippine Sea and South China Sea
Geography - note: the major chokepoints are the Bering Strait, Panama Canal, Luzon Strait, and the Singapore Strait; the Equator divides the Pacific Ocean into the North Pacific Ocean and the South Pacific Ocean; dotted with low coral islands and rugged volcanic islands in the southwestern Pacific Ocean

Economy

Economy - overview: The Pacific Ocean is a major contributor to the world economy and particularly to those nations its waters directly touch. It provides low-cost sea transportation between East and West, extensive fishing grounds, offshore oil and gas fields, minerals, and sand and gravel for the construction industry. In 1996, over 60% of the world's fish catch came from the Pacific Ocean. Exploitation of offshore oil and gas reserves is playing an ever-increasing role in the energy supplies of Australia, NZ, China, US, and Peru. The high cost of recovering offshore oil and gas, combined with the wide swings in world prices for oil since 1985, has slowed but not stopped new drillings.

Transportation

Ports and harbors: Bangkok (Thailand), Hong Kong, Kao-hsiung (Taiwan), Los Angeles (US), Manila (Philippines), Pusan (South Korea), San Francisco (US), Seattle (US), Shanghai (China), Singapore, Sydney (Australia), Vladivostok (Russia), Wellington (NZ), Yokohama (Japan)
Transportation - note: Inside Passage offers protected waters from southeast Alaska to Puget Sound (Washington state)

Transnational Issues

Disputes - international: some maritime disputes (see littoral states)

Pakistan

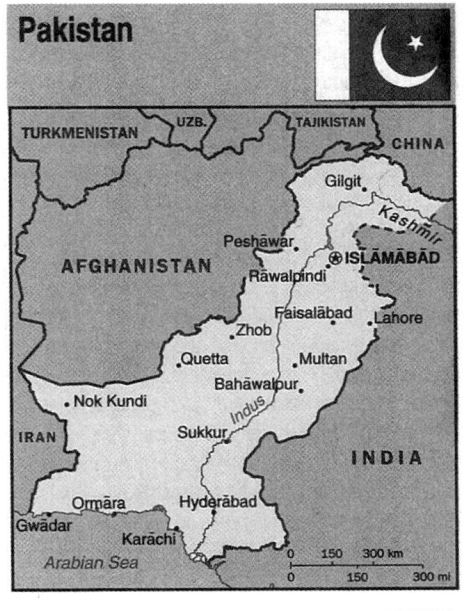

Introduction

Background: The separation in 1947 of British India into the Muslim state of Pakistan (with two sections West and East) and largely Hindu India was never satisfactorily resolved. A third war between these countries in 1971 resulted in East Pakistan seceding and becoming the separate nation of Bangladesh. A dispute over the state of Kashmir is ongoing. In response to Indian nuclear weapons testing, Pakistan conducted its own tests in 1998.

Geography

Location: Southern Asia, bordering the Arabian Sea, between India on the east and Iran and Afghanistan on the west and China in the north
Geographic coordinates: 30 00 N, 70 00 E
Map references: Asia
Area:
total: 803,940 sq km
land: 778,720 sq km
water: 25,220 sq km
Area - comparative: slightly less than twice the size of California
Land boundaries:
total: 6,774 km
border countries: Afghanistan 2,430 km, China 523 km, India 2,912 km, Iran 909 km
Coastline: 1,046 km
Maritime claims:
contiguous zone: 24 NM
continental shelf: 200 NM or to the edge of the continental margin
exclusive economic zone: 200 NM
territorial sea: 12 NM
Climate: mostly hot, dry desert; temperate in northwest; arctic in north
Terrain: flat Indus plain in east; mountains in north and northwest; Balochistan plateau in west
Elevation extremes:
lowest point: Indian Ocean 0 m
highest point: K2 (Mt. Godwin-Austen) 8,611 m
Natural resources: land, extensive natural gas reserves, limited petroleum, poor quality coal, iron ore, copper, salt, limestone
Land use:
arable land: 27%
permanent crops: 1%
permanent pastures: 6%
forests and woodland: 5%
other: 61% (1993 est.)
Irrigated land: 171,100 sq km (1993 est.)
Natural hazards: frequent earthquakes, occasionally severe especially in north and west; flooding along the Indus after heavy rains (July and August)
Environment - current issues: water pollution from raw sewage, industrial wastes, and agricultural runoff; limited natural fresh water resources; a majority of the population does not have access to potable water; deforestation; soil erosion; desertification
Environment - international agreements:
party to: Biodiversity, Climate Change, Desertification, Endangered Species, Environmental Modification, Hazardous Wastes, Law of the Sea, Marine Dumping, Ozone Layer Protection, Ship Pollution, Wetlands
signed, but not ratified: Marine Life Conservation, Nuclear Test Ban
Geography - note: controls Khyber Pass and Bolan Pass, traditional invasion routes between Central Asia and the Indian Subcontinent

People

Population: 144,616,639 (July 2001 est.)
Age structure:
0-14 years: 40.47% (male 30,131,400; female 28,391,891)
15-64 years: 55.42% (male 40,977,543; female 39,164,663)
65 years and over: 4.11% (male 2,918,872; female 3,032,270) (2001 est.)
Population growth rate: 2.11% (2001 est.)
Birth rate: 31.21 births/1,000 population (2001 est.)
Death rate: 9.26 deaths/1,000 population (2001 est.)
Net migration rate: -0.84 migrant(s)/1,000 population (2001 est.)
Sex ratio:
at birth: 1.05 male(s)/female
under 15 years: 1.06 male(s)/female
15-64 years: 1.05 male(s)/female
65 years and over: 0.96 male(s)/female
total population: 1.05 male(s)/female (2001 est.)
Infant mortality rate: 80.5 deaths/1,000 live births (2001 est.)
Life expectancy at birth:
total population: 61.45 years
male: 60.61 years
female: 62.32 years (2001 est.)
Total fertility rate: 4.41 children born/woman (2001 est.)
HIV/AIDS - adult prevalence rate: 0.1% (1999 est.)
HIV/AIDS - people living with HIV/AIDS: 74,000 (1999 est.)
HIV/AIDS - deaths: 6,500 (1999 est.)
Nationality:
noun: Pakistani(s)
adjective: Pakistani
Ethnic groups: Punjabi, Sindhi, Pashtun (Pathan), Baloch, Muhajir (immigrants from India at the time of partition and their descendants)
Religions: Muslim 97% (Sunni 77%, Shi'a 20%), Christian, Hindu, and other 3%
Languages: Punjabi 48%, Sindhi 12%, Siraiki (a Punjabi variant) 10%, Pashtu 8%, Urdu (official) 8%, Balochi 3%, Hindko 2%, Brahui 1%, English (official and lingua franca of Pakistani elite and most government ministries), Burushaski, and other 8%
Literacy:
definition: age 15 and over can read and write
total population: 42.7%
male: 55.3%
female: 29% (1998)

Government

Country name:
conventional long form: Islamic Republic of Pakistan
conventional short form: Pakistan
former: West Pakistan
Government type: federal republic
Capital: Islamabad
Administrative divisions: 4 provinces, 1 territory*, and 1 capital territory**; Balochistan, Federally Administered Tribal Areas*, Islamabad Capital Territory**, North-West Frontier Province, Punjab, Sindh
note: the Pakistani-administered portion of the disputed Jammu and Kashmir region includes Azad Kashmir and the Northern Areas
Independence: 14 August 1947 (from UK)
National holiday: Republic Day, 23 March (1956)
Constitution: 10 April 1973, suspended 5 July 1977, restored with amendments 30 December 1985; suspended 15 October 1999
Legal system: based on English common law with provisions to accommodate Pakistan's status as an Islamic state; accepts compulsory ICJ jurisdiction, with reservations
Suffrage: 21 years of age; universal; separate electorates and reserved parliamentary seats for non-Muslims
Executive branch:
note: following a military takeover on 12 October 1999, Chief of Army Staff and Chairman of the Joint Chiefs of Staff Committee, Gen. Pervez MUSHARRAF suspended Pakistan's constitution and assumed the additional title of Chief Executive; exercising the powers of the head of the government, he appointed an eight-member National Security Council to function as Pakistan's supreme governing body; President Mohammad Rafiq TARAR remains the ceremonial chief of state; on 12 May 2000,

Pakistan (continued)

Pakistan's Supreme Court unanimously validated the October 1999 coup and granted MUSHARRAF executive and legislative authority for three years from the coup date
chief of state: President Mohammad Rafiq TARAR (since 31 December 1997)
head of government: Chief Executive Gen. Pervez MUSHARRAF (since 12 October 1999)
cabinet: Cabinet appointed by the chief executive
elections: president elected by Parliament for a five-year term; election last held 31 December 1997 (next to be held NA 2002); following legislative elections, the leader of the majority party or leader of a majority coalition is usually elected prime minister by the National Assembly; election last held 3 February 1997 (next to be held NA); note - Gen. Pervez MUSHARRAF overthrew the government of Prime Minister Mohammad Nawaz SHARIF in the military takeover of 12 October 1999; in May 2000, the Supreme Court validated the October 1999 coup and set a three-year limit in office for Chief Executive MUSHARRAF
election results: Rafiq TARAR elected president; percent of Parliament and provincial vote - NA%; results are for the last election for prime minister prior to the military takeover of 12 October 1999 - Mohammad Nawaz SHARIF elected prime minister; percent of National Assembly vote - NA%
Legislative branch: note - Gen. Pervez MUSHARRAF dissolved Parliament following the military takeover of 12 October 1999; bicameral Parliament or Majlis-e-Shoora consists of the Senate (87 seats; members indirectly elected by provincial assemblies to serve six-year terms; one-third of the members up for election every two years) and the National Assembly (217 seats - 10 represent non-Muslims; members elected by popular vote to serve five-year terms)
elections: Senate - last held 12 March 1997 (next to be held NA); National Assembly - last held 3 February 1997 (next to be held NA); note - no timetable has yet been given for elections following the military takeover
election results: Senate - percent of vote by party - NA%; seats by party - PML/N 30, PPP 17, ANP 7, MQM/A 6, JWP 5, BNP 4, JUI/F 2, PML/J 2, BNM/M 1, PKMAP 1, TJP 1, independents 6, vacant 5; National Assembly - percent of vote by party - NA%; seats by party - PML/N 137, PPP 18, MQM/A 12, ANP 10, BNP 3, JWP 2, JUI/F 2, PPP/SB 1, NPP 1, independents 21, minorities 10; note - Gen. Pervez MUSHARRAF dismissed Parliament 15 October 1999
Judicial branch: Supreme Court (justices appointed by the president); Federal Islamic or Shari'a Court
Political parties and leaders:
note: Gen. Pervez MUSHARRAF dissolved Parliament following the military takeover of 12 October 1999, however, political parties have been allowed to operate; Awami National Party or ANP [Wali KHAN]; Balochistan National Movement/Hayee Group or BNM/H [Dr. HAYEE Baluch]; Baluch National Party or BNP [Sardar Akhtar MENGAL]; Jamhoori Watan Party or JWP [Akbar Khan BUGTI]; Jamiat-al-Hadith or JAH [Sajid MIR]; Jamiat Ulema-i-Islam, Fazlur Rehman faction or JUI/F [Fazlur REHMAN]; Jamiat Ulema-i-Pakistan, Niazi faction or JUP/NI [Abdul Sattar Khan NIAZI]; Millat Party [Farooq LEGHARI]; Milli Yakjheti Council or MYC is an umbrella organization which includes Jamaat-i-Islami or JI [Qazi Hussain AHMED], Jamiat Ulema-i-Islam, Sami-ul-Haq faction or JUI/S [Sami ul-HAQ], Tehrik-I-Jafria Pakistan or TJP [Allama Sajid NAQVI], and Jamiat Ulema-i-Pakistan, Noorani faction or JUP/NO [Shah Ahmad NOORANI]; Mutahida Qaumi Movement, Altaf faction or MQM/A [Altaf HUSSAIN]; National People's Party or NPP [Ghulam Mustapha JATOI]; Pakhtun Khwa Milli Awami Party or PKMAP [Mahmood Khan ACHAKZAI]; Pakhtun Quami Party or PQP [Mohammed AFZAL Khan]; Pakistan Awami Tehrik or PAT [Tahir ul QADRI]; Pakistan Muslim League, Functional Group or PML/F [Pir PAGARO]; Pakistan Muslim League, Junejo faction or PML/J [Hamid Nasir CHATTHA]; Pakistan Muslim League, Nawaz Sharif faction or PML/N [Nawaz SHARIF]; Pakistan National Party or PNP [Hasil BIZENJO]; Pakistan People's Party or PPP [Benazir BHUTTO]; Pakistan People's Party/Shaheed Bhutto or PPP/SB [Ghinva BHUTTO]; Pakistan Tehrik-e-Insaaf or PTI [Imran KHAN]
note: political alliances in Pakistan can shift frequently
Political pressure groups and leaders: military remains important political force; ulema (clergy), landowners, industrialists, and small merchants also influential
International organization participation: AsDB, C (suspended), CCC, CP, ECO, ESCAP, FAO, G-19, G-24, G-77, IAEA, IBRD, ICAO, ICC, ICFTU, ICRM, IDA, IDB, IFAD, IFC, IFRCS, IHO, ILO, IMF, IMO, Inmarsat, Intelsat, Interpol, IOC, IOM, ISO, ITU, MINURSO, MONUC, NAM, OAS (observer), OIC, OPCW, PCA, SAARC, UN, UNAMSIL, UNCTAD, UNESCO, UNHCR, UNIDO, UNIKOM, UNMIBH, UNMIK, UNMOP, UNOMIG, UNTAET, UPU, WCL, WFTU, WHO, WIPO, WMO, WToO, WTrO
Diplomatic representation in the US:
chief of mission: Ambassador Maleeha LODHI
chancery: 2315 Massachusetts Avenue NW, Washington, DC 20008
telephone: [1] (202) 939-6200
FAX: [1] (202) 387-0484
consulate(s) general: Los Angeles and New York
Diplomatic representation from the US:
chief of mission: Ambassador William B. MILAM
embassy: Diplomatic Enclave, Ramna 5, Islamabad
mailing address: P. O. Box 1048, Unit 62200, APO AE 09812-2200
telephone: [92] (51) 2080-0000
FAX: [92] (51) 2276427
consulate(s) general: Karachi
consulate(s): Lahore, Peshawar
Flag description: green with a vertical white band (symbolizing the role of religious minorities) on the hoist side; a large white crescent and star are centered in the green field; the crescent, star, and color green are traditional symbols of Islam

Economy

Economy - overview: Pakistan is a poor, heavily populated country, suffering from internal political disputes, lack of foreign investment, and a costly confrontation with neighboring India. Pakistan's economic outlook continues to be marred by its weak foreign exchange position, which relies on international creditors for hard currency inflows. The MUSHARRAF government will face an estimated $21 billion in foreign debt coming due in 2000-03, despite having rescheduled nearly $2 billion in debt with Paris Club members. Foreign loans and grants provide approximately 25% of government revenue, but debt service obligations total nearly 50% of government expenditure. Although Pakistan successfully negotiated a $600 million IMF Stand-By Arrangement, future loan installments will be jeopardized if Pakistan misses critical IMF benchmarks on revenue collection and the fiscal deficit. MUSHARRAF has complied largely with IMF recommendations to raise petroleum prices, widen the tax net, privatize public sector assets, and improve the balance of trade. However, Pakistan's economic prospects remain uncertain; too little has changed despite the new administration's intentions. Foreign exchange reserves hover at roughly $1 billion, GDP growth hinges on crop performance, the import bill has been hammered by high oil prices, and both foreign and domestic investors remain wary of committing to projects in Pakistan.
GDP: purchasing power parity - $282 billion (2000 est.)
GDP - real growth rate: 4.8% (2000 est.)
GDP - per capita: purchasing power parity - $2,000 (2000 est.)
GDP - composition by sector:
agriculture: 25.4%
industry: 24.9%
services: 49.7% (1999 est.)
Population below poverty line: 40% (2000 est.)
Household income or consumption by percentage share:
lowest 10%: 4.1%
highest 10%: 27.7% (1996)
Inflation rate (consumer prices): 5.2% (2000 est.)
Labor force: 40 million
note: extensive export of labor, mostly to the Middle East, and use of child labor (2000 est.)
Labor force - by occupation: agriculture 44%, industry 17%, services 39% (1999 est.)
Unemployment rate: 6% (FY99/00 est.)
Budget:
revenues: $8.9 billion
expenditures: $11.6 billion, including capital expenditures of $NA (FY00/01 est.)
Industries: textiles, food processing, beverages, construction materials, clothing, paper products, shrimp
Industrial production growth rate: 3.8% (1999 est.)
Electricity - production: 62.078 billion kWh (1999)

Pakistan (continued)

Electricity - production by source:
fossil fuel: 63.38%
hydro: 36.51%
nuclear: 0.11%
other: 0% (1999)
Electricity - consumption: 57.732 billion kWh (1999)
Electricity - exports: 0 kWh (1999)
Electricity - imports: 0 kWh (1999)
Agriculture - products: cotton, wheat, rice, sugarcane, fruits, vegetables; milk, beef, mutton, eggs
Exports: $8.6 billion (f.o.b., FY99/00)
Exports - commodities: textiles (garments, cotton cloth, and yarn), rice, other agricultural products
Exports - partners: US 24%, Hong Kong 7%, UK 7%, Germany 6%, UAE 6% (FY99/00)
Imports: $9.6 billion (f.o.b., FY99/00)
Imports - commodities: machinery, petroleum, petroleum products, chemicals, transportation equipment, edible oils, grains, pulses, flour
Imports - partners: Saudi Arabia 8%, UAE 8%, US 6%, Japan 6%, Malaysia 4% (FY99/00)
Debt - external: $38 billion (2000 est.)
Economic aid - recipient: $2 billion (FY99/00)
Currency: Pakistani rupee (PKR)
Currency code: PKR
Exchange rates: Pakistani rupees per US dollar - 59.152 (January 2001), 52.814 (2000), 49.118 (1999), 44.943 (1998), 40.918 (1997), 35.909 (1996)
Fiscal year: 1 July - 30 June

Communications

Telephones - main lines in use: 2.861 million (March 1999)
Telephones - mobile cellular: 158,000 (1998)
Telephone system:
general assessment: the domestic system is mediocre, but improving; service is adequate for government and business use, in part because major businesses have established their own private systems; since 1988, the government has promoted investment in the national telecommunications system on a priority basis, significantly increasing network capacity; despite major improvements in trunk and urban systems, telecommunication services are still not readily available to the majority of the rural population
domestic: microwave radio relay, coaxial cable, fiber-optic cable, cellular, and satellite networks
international: satellite earth stations - 3 Intelsat (1 Atlantic Ocean and 2 Indian Ocean); 3 operational international gateway exchanges (1 at Karachi and 2 at Islamabad); microwave radio relay to neighboring countries (1999)
Radio broadcast stations: AM 27, FM 1, shortwave 21 (1998)
Radios: 13.5 million (1997)
Television broadcast stations: 22 (plus seven low-power repeaters) (1997)
Televisions: 3.1 million (1997)
Internet country code: .pk
Internet Service Providers (ISPs): 30 (2000)
Internet users: 1.2 million (2000)

Transportation

Railways:
total: 8,163 km
broad gauge: 7,718 km 1.676-m gauge (293 km electrified; 1,037 km double track)
narrow gauge: 445 km 1.000-m gauge (1996 est.) (2000)
Highways:
total: 247,811 km
paved: 141,252 km (including 339 km of expressways)
unpaved: 106,559 km (1998)
Waterways: none
Pipelines: crude oil 250 km; petroleum products 885 km; natural gas 4,044 km (1987)
Ports and harbors: Karachi, Port Muhammad bin Qasim
Merchant marine:
total: 17 ships (1,000 GRT or over) totaling 240,605 GRT/367,040 DWT
ships by type: cargo 13, container 3, petroleum tanker 1 (2000 est.)
Airports: 117 (2000 est.)
Airports - with paved runways:
total: 82
over 3,047 m: 12
2,438 to 3,047 m: 21
1,524 to 2,437 m: 32
914 to 1,523 m: 14
under 914 m: 3 (2000 est.)
Airports - with unpaved runways:
total: 35
1,524 to 2,437 m: 7
914 to 1,523 m: 11
under 914 m: 17 (2000 est.)
Heliports: 8 (2000 est.)

Military

Military branches: Army, Navy, Air Force, Civil Armed Forces, National Guard
Military manpower - military age: 17 years of age
Military manpower - availability:
males age 15-49: 35,770,928 (2001 est.)
Military manpower - fit for military service:
males age 15-49: 21,897,366 (2001 est.)
Military manpower - reaching military age annually:
males: 1,657,723 (2001 est.)
Military expenditures - dollar figure: $2.435 billion (FY99/00)
Military expenditures - percent of GDP: 3.9% (FY99/00)

Transnational Issues

Disputes - international: status of Kashmir with India; water-sharing problems with India over the Indus River (Wular Barrage)
Illicit drugs: key transit area for Southwest Asian heroin moving to Western markets; narcotics still move from Afghanistan into Balochistan Province

Palau

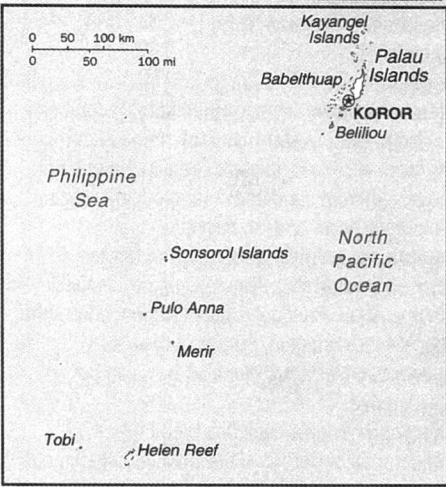

Introduction

Background: After three decades as part of the UN Trust Territory of the Pacific under US administration, this westernmost cluster of the Caroline Islands opted for independent status in 1978 rather than join the Federated States of Micronesia. A Compact of Free Association with the US was approved in 1986, but not ratified until 1993. It entered into force the following year when the islands gained their independence.

Geography

Location: Oceania, group of islands in the North Pacific Ocean, southeast of the Philippines
Geographic coordinates: 7 30 N, 134 30 E
Map references: Oceania
Area:
total: 458 sq km
land: 458 sq km
water: 0 sq km
Area - comparative: slightly more than 2.5 times the size of Washington, DC
Land boundaries: 0 km
Coastline: 1,519 km
Maritime claims:
continental shelf: 200-m depth or to the depth of exploitation
exclusive fishing zone: 12 NM
extended fishing zone: 200 NM
territorial sea: 3 NM
Climate: wet season May to November; hot and humid
Terrain: varying geologically from the high, mountainous main island of Babelthuap to low, coral islands usually fringed by large barrier reefs
Elevation extremes:
lowest point: Pacific Ocean 0 m
highest point: Mount Ngerchelchauus 242 m
Natural resources: forests, minerals (especially gold), marine products, deep-seabed minerals

Palau (continued)

Land use:
arable land: NA%
permanent crops: NA%
permanent pastures: NA%
forests and woodland: NA%
other: NA%
Irrigated land: NA sq km
Natural hazards: typhoons (June to December)
Environment - current issues: inadequate facilities for disposal of solid waste; threats to the marine ecosystem from sand and coral dredging, illegal fishing practices, and overfishing
Environment - international agreements:
party to: Biodiversity, Climate Change, Climate Change-Kyoto Protocol, Desertification, Law of the Sea, Marine Dumping, Ship Pollution
signed, but not ratified: none of the selected agreements
Geography - note: includes World War II battleground of Beliliou (Peleliu) and world-famous rock islands; archipelago of six island groups totaling over 200 islands in the Caroline chain

People

Population: 19,092 (July 2001 est.)
Age structure:
0-14 years: 26.88% (male 2,641; female 2,491)
15-64 years: 68.46% (male 7,128; female 5,943)
65 years and over: 4.66% (male 420; female 469) (2001 est.)
Population growth rate: 1.69% (2001 est.)
Birth rate: 19.64 births/1,000 population (2001 est.)
Death rate: 7.23 deaths/1,000 population (2001 est.)
Net migration rate: 4.45 migrant(s)/1,000 population (2001 est.)
Sex ratio:
at birth: 1.06 male(s)/female
under 15 years: 1.06 male(s)/female
15-64 years: 1.2 male(s)/female
65 years and over: 0.9 male(s)/female
total population: 1.14 male(s)/female (2001 est.)
Infant mortality rate: 16.67 deaths/1,000 live births (2001 est.)
Life expectancy at birth:
total population: 68.89 years
male: 65.77 years
female: 72.19 years (2001 est.)
Total fertility rate: 2.47 children born/woman (2001 est.)
HIV/AIDS - adult prevalence rate: NA%
HIV/AIDS - people living with HIV/AIDS: NA
HIV/AIDS - deaths: NA
Nationality:
noun: Palauan(s)
adjective: Palauan
Ethnic groups: Palauan (Micronesian with Malayan and Melanesian admixtures) 70%, Asian (mainly Filipinos, followed by Chinese, Taiwanese, and Vietnamese) 28%, white 2% (2000 est.)

Religions: Christian (Catholics, Seventh-Day Adventists, Jehovah's Witnesses, the Assembly of God, the Liebenzell Mission, and Latter-Day Saints), Modekngei religion (one-third of the population observes this religion which is indigenous to Palau)
Languages: English and Palauan official in all states except Sonsoral (Sonsorolese and English are official), Tobi (Tobi and English are official), and Angaur (Angaur, Japanese, and English are official)
Literacy:
definition: age 15 and over can read and write
total population: 92%
male: 93%
female: 90% (1980 est.)

Government

Country name:
conventional long form: Republic of Palau
conventional short form: Palau
local long form: Beluu er a Belau
local short form: Belau
former: Palau District (Trust Territory of the Pacific Islands)
Government type: constitutional government in free association with the US; the Compact of Free Association entered into force 1 October 1994
Capital: Koror; note - a new capital is being built about 20 km northeast of Koror
Administrative divisions: 18 states; Aimeliik, Airai, Angaur, Hatobohei, Kayangel, Koror, Melekeok, Ngaraard, Ngarchelong, Ngardmau, Ngatpang, Ngchesar, Ngeremlengui, Ngiwal, Palau Island, Peleliu, Sonsoral, Tobi
Independence: 1 October 1994 (from the US-administered UN Trusteeship)
National holiday: Constitution Day, 9 July (1979)
Constitution: 1 January 1981
Legal system: based on Trust Territory laws, acts of the legislature, municipal, common, and customary laws
Suffrage: 18 years of age; universal
Executive branch:
chief of state: President Tommy Esang REMENGESAU Jr. (since 19 January 2001) and Vice President Sandra PIERANTOZZI (since 19 January 2001); note - the president is both the chief of state and head of government
head of government: President Tommy Esang REMENGESAU Jr. (since 19 January 2001) and Vice President Sandra PIERANTOZZI (since 19 January 2001); note - the president is both the chief of state and head of government
cabinet: Cabinet
elections: president and vice president elected on separate tickets by popular vote for four-year terms; election last held 7 November 2000 (next to be held NA November 2004)
election results: Tommy Esang REMENGESAU Jr. elected president; percent of vote - Tommy Esang REMENGESAU Jr. 53%, Peter SUGIYAMA 46%; Sandra PIERANTOZZI elected vice president; percent of vote - Sandra PIERANTOZZI 52%, Alan SEID 45%

Legislative branch: bicameral Parliament or Olbiil Era Kelulau (OEK) consists of the Senate (16 seats; members elected by popular vote on a population basis to serve four-year terms) and the House of Delegates (16 seats; members elected by popular vote to serve four-year terms)
elections: Senate - last held 7 November 2000 (next to be held NA November 2004); House of Delegates - last held 7 November 2000 (next to be held NA November 2004)
election results: Senate - percent of vote by party - NA%; seats by party - NA; House of Delegates - percent of vote by party - NA%; seats by party - NA
Judicial branch: Supreme Court; National Court; Court of Common Pleas
Political parties and leaders: Palau Nationalist Party [Johnson TORIBIONG]; Ta Belau Party [Kuniwo NAKAMURA]
Political pressure groups and leaders: NA
International organization participation: ACP, ESCAP, FAO, IBRD, ICAO, ICRM, IDA, IFC, IFRCS, IMF, IOC, Sparteca, SPC, SPF, UN, UNCTAD, UNESCO, WHO
Diplomatic representation in the US:
chief of mission: Ambassador Hersey KYOTA
chancery: 1150 18th Street NW, Suite 750, Washington, DC 20036
telephone: [1] (202) 452-6814
FAX: [1] (202) 452-6281
Diplomatic representation from the US:
chief of mission: the Ambassador to the Philippines is accredited to Palau; Charge d'Affaires Allen E. NUGENT
embassy: address NA, Koror
mailing address: P. O. Box 6028, Republic of Palau 96940
telephone: [680] 488-2920, 2990
FAX: [680] 488-2911
Flag description: light blue with a large yellow disk (representing the moon) shifted slightly to the hoist side

Economy

Economy - overview: The economy consists primarily of subsistence agriculture and fishing. The government is the major employer of the work force, relying heavily on financial assistance from the US. The population enjoys a per capita income of twice that of the Philippines and much of Micronesia. Long-run prospects for the tourist sector have been greatly bolstered by the expansion of air travel in the Pacific and the rising prosperity of leading East Asian countries.
GDP: purchasing power parity - $129 million (1998 est.)
note: GDP numbers reflect US spending
GDP - real growth rate: -1.4% (1998 est.)
GDP - per capita: purchasing power parity - $7,100 (1998 est.)
GDP - composition by sector:
agriculture: NA%
industry: NA%
services: NA%

Palau (continued)

Population below poverty line: NA%
Household income or consumption by percentage share:
lowest 10%: NA%
highest 10%: NA%
Inflation rate (consumer prices): NA%
Labor force: 8,300 (1999)
Labor force - by occupation: agriculture NA%, industry NA%, services NA%
Unemployment rate: 2.3% (2000 est.)
Budget:
revenues: $57.7 million
expenditures: $80.8 million, including capital expenditures of $17.1 million (FY98/99 est.)
Industries: tourism, craft items (from shell, wood, pearls), construction, garment making
Industrial production growth rate: NA%
Agriculture - products: coconuts, copra, cassava (tapioca), sweet potatoes
Exports: $14.3 million (f.o.b., 1996)
Exports - commodities: trochus (type of shellfish), tuna, copra, handicrafts
Exports - partners: US, Japan
Imports: $126 million (f.o.b., FY99/00)
Imports - commodities: machinery and equipment, fuels, metals; foodstuffs
Imports - partners: US
Debt - external: $0 (FY99/00)
Economic aid - recipient: $155.8 million (1995); note - the Compact of Free Association with the US, entered into after the end of the UN trusteeship on 1 October 1994, will provide Palau with up to $700 million in US aid over 15 years in return for furnishing military facilities
Currency: US dollar (USD)
Currency code: USD
Exchange rates: the US dollar is used
Fiscal year: 1 October - 30 September

Communications

Telephones - main lines in use: 1,500 (1988)
Telephones - mobile cellular: 0 (1988)
Telephone system:
general assessment: NA
domestic: NA
international: satellite earth station - 1 Intelsat (Pacific Ocean)
Radio broadcast stations: AM 1, FM 0, shortwave 1 (1998)
Radios: 12,000 (1997)
Television broadcast stations: 1 (1997)
Televisions: 11,000 (1997)
Internet country code: .pw
Internet Service Providers (ISPs): NA

Transportation

Railways: 0 km
Highways:
total: 61 km
paved: 36 km
unpaved: 25 km
Waterways: none
Ports and harbors: Koror
Merchant marine: none (2000 est.)
Airports: 3 (2000 est.)
Airports - with paved runways:
total: 1
1,524 to 2,437 m: 1 (2000 est.)
Airports - with unpaved runways:
total: 2
1,524 to 2,437 m: 2 (2000 est.)

Military

Military branches: NA
Military expenditures - dollar figure: $NA
Military expenditures - percent of GDP: NA%
Military - note: defense is the responsibility of the US; under a Compact of Free Association between Palau and the US, the US military is granted access to the islands for 50 years

Transnational Issues

Disputes - international: none

Palmyra Atoll
(territory of the US)

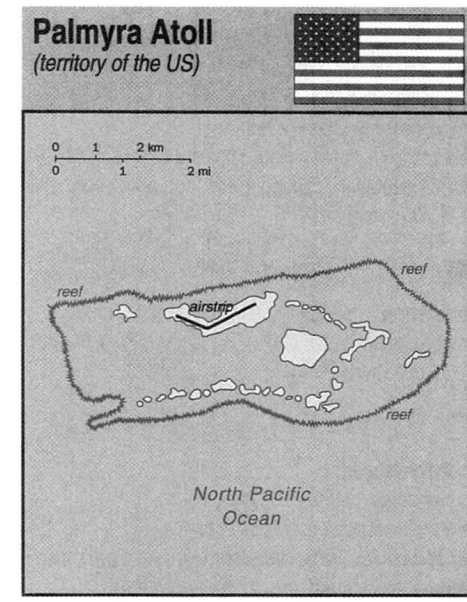

Introduction

Background: The Kingdom of Hawaii claimed the atoll in 1862, and the US included it among the Hawaiian Islands when it annexed the archipelago in 1898. The Hawaii Statehood Act of 1959 did not include Palmyra Atoll, which is now privately owned by the Nature Conservancy. This organization is managing the atoll as a nature preserve. The lagoons and surrounding waters within the 12 nautical mile US territorial seas were transferred to the US Fish and Wildlife service and designated a National Wildlife Refuge in January 2001.

Geography

Location: Oceania, atoll in the North Pacific Ocean, about one-half of the way from Hawaii to American Samoa
Geographic coordinates: 5 52 N, 162 06 W
Map references: Oceania
Area:
total: 11.9 sq km
land: 11.9 sq km
water: 0 sq km
Area - comparative: about 20 times the size of The Mall in Washington, DC
Land boundaries: 0 km
Coastline: 14.5 km
Maritime claims:
exclusive economic zone: 200 NM
territorial sea: 12 NM
Climate: equatorial, hot, and very rainy
Terrain: very low
Elevation extremes:
lowest point: Pacific Ocean 0 m
highest point: unnamed location 2 m
Natural resources: terrestrial and aquatic wildlife
Land use:
arable land: 0%
permanent crops: 0%
permanent pastures: 0%

Palmyra Atoll (continued)

forests and woodland: 100%
other: 0%
Irrigated land: 0 sq km (1993)
Natural hazards: NA
Environment - current issues: NA
Geography - note: about 50 islets covered with dense vegetation, coconut trees, and balsa-like trees up to 30 meters tall

People

Population: no indigenous inhabitants; 4 to 20 Nature Conservancy staff, US Fish and Wildlife staff (July 2001 est.)

Government

Country name:
conventional long form: none
conventional short form: Palmyra Atoll
Dependency status: incorporated territory of the US; privately owned, but administered from Washington, DC, by the Fish and Wildlife Service of the US Department of the Interior
Legal system: the laws of the US, where applicable, apply
Flag description: the flag of the US is used

Economy

Economy - overview: no economic activity

Transportation

Highways: much of the road and many causeways built during World War II are unserviceable and overgrown (2001)
Waterways: none
Ports and harbors: West Lagoon
Airports: 1 (2000 est.)
Airports - with unpaved runways:
total: 1
1,524 to 2,437 m: 1 (2000 est.)

Military

Military - note: defense is the responsibility of the US

Transnational Issues

Disputes - international: none

Panama

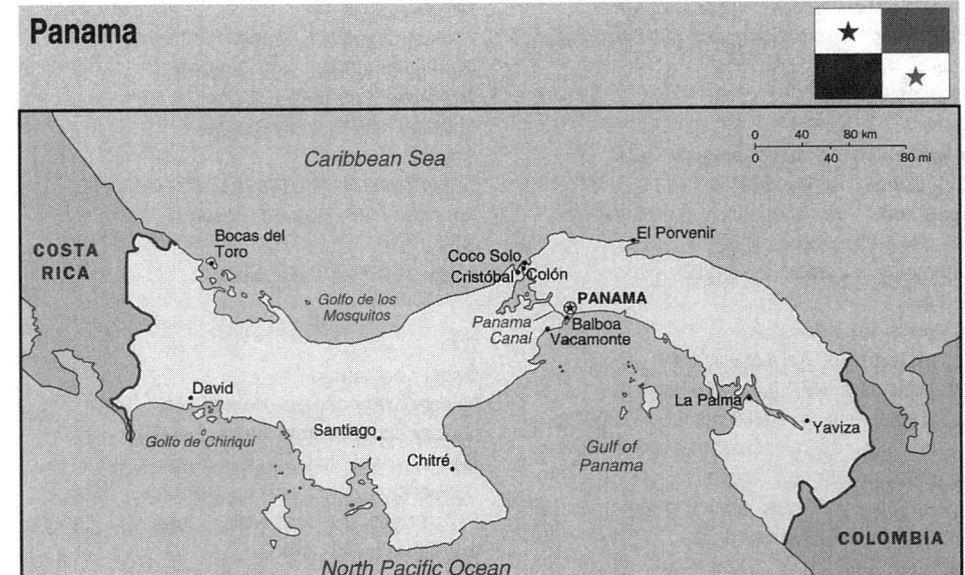

Introduction

Background: With US backing, Panama seceded from Colombia in 1903 and promptly signed a treaty with the US allowing for the construction of a canal and US sovereignty over a strip of land on either side of the structure (the Panama Canal Zone). The Panama Canal was built by the US Army Corps of Engineers between 1904 and 1914. On 7 September 1977, an agreement was signed for the complete transfer of the Canal from the US to Panama by the end of 1999. Certain portions of the Zone and increasing responsibility over the Canal were turned over in the intervening years. With US help, dictator Manuel NORIEGA was deposed in 1989. The entire Panama Canal, the area supporting the Canal, and remaining US military bases were turned over to Panama by or on 31 December 1999.

Geography

Location: Middle America, bordering both the Caribbean Sea and the North Pacific Ocean, between Colombia and Costa Rica
Geographic coordinates: 9 00 N, 80 00 W
Map references: Central America and the Caribbean
Area:
total: 78,200 sq km
land: 75,990 sq km
water: 2,210 sq km
Area - comparative: slightly smaller than South Carolina
Land boundaries:
total: 555 km
border countries: Colombia 225 km, Costa Rica 330 km
Coastline: 2,490 km
Maritime claims:
contiguous zone: 24 NM
exclusive economic zone: 200 NM
territorial sea: 12 NM
Climate: tropical maritime; hot, humid, cloudy; prolonged rainy season (May to January), short dry season (January to May)
Terrain: interior mostly steep, rugged mountains and dissected, upland plains; coastal areas largely plains and rolling hills
Elevation extremes:
lowest point: Pacific Ocean 0 m
highest point: Volcan de Chiriqui 3,475 m
Natural resources: copper, mahogany forests, shrimp, hydropower
Land use:
arable land: 7%
permanent crops: 2%
permanent pastures: 20%
forests and woodland: 44%
other: 27% (1993 est.)
Irrigated land: 320 sq km (1993 est.)
Natural hazards: NA
Environment - current issues: water pollution from agricultural runoff threatens fishery resources; deforestation of tropical rain forest; land degradation and soil erosion threatens siltation of Panama Canal
Environment - international agreements:
party to: Biodiversity, Climate Change, Climate Change-Kyoto Protocol, Desertification, Endangered Species, Hazardous Wastes, Law of the Sea, Marine Dumping, Nuclear Test Ban, Ozone Layer Protection, Ship Pollution, Tropical Timber 83, Tropical Timber 94, Wetlands
signed, but not ratified: Marine Life Conservation
Geography - note: strategic location on eastern end of isthmus forming land bridge connecting North and South America; controls Panama Canal that links North Atlantic Ocean via Caribbean Sea with North Pacific Ocean

People

Population: 2,845,647 (July 2001 est.)
Age structure:
0-14 years: 30.13% (male 436,661; female 420,625)

Panama (continued)

15-64 years: 63.86% (male 920,787; female 896,520)
65 years and over: 6.01% (male 81,682; female 89,372) (2001 est.)
Population growth rate: 1.3% (2001 est.)
Birth rate: 19.06 births/1,000 population (2001 est.)
Death rate: 4.95 deaths/1,000 population (2001 est.)
Net migration rate: -1.1 migrant(s)/1,000 population (2001 est.)
Sex ratio:
at birth: 1.04 male(s)/female
under 15 years: 1.04 male(s)/female
15-64 years: 1.03 male(s)/female
65 years and over: 0.91 male(s)/female
total population: 1.02 male(s)/female (2001 est.)
Infant mortality rate: 20.18 deaths/1,000 live births (2001 est.)
Life expectancy at birth:
total population: 75.68 years
male: 72.94 years
female: 78.53 years (2001 est.)
Total fertility rate: 2.27 children born/woman (2001 est.)
HIV/AIDS - adult prevalence rate: 1.54% (1999 est.)
HIV/AIDS - people living with HIV/AIDS: 24,000 (1999 est.)
HIV/AIDS - deaths: 1,200 (1999 est.)
Nationality:
noun: Panamanian(s)
adjective: Panamanian
Ethnic groups: mestizo (mixed Amerindian and white) 70%, Amerindian and mixed (West Indian) 14%, white 10%, Amerindian 6%
Religions: Roman Catholic 85%, Protestant 15%
Languages: Spanish (official), English 14%
note: many Panamanians bilingual
Literacy:
definition: age 15 and over can read and write
total population: 90.8%
male: 91.4%
female: 90.2% (1995 est.)

Government

Country name:
conventional long form: Republic of Panama
conventional short form: Panama
local long form: Republica de Panama
local short form: Panama
Government type: constitutional democracy
Capital: Panama
Administrative divisions: 9 provinces (provincias, singular - provincia) and one territory* (comarca); Bocas del Toro, Chiriqui, Cocle, Colon, Darien, Herrera, Los Santos, Panama, San Blas*, and Veraguas
Independence: 3 November 1903 (from Colombia; became independent from Spain 28 November 1821)
National holiday: Independence Day, 3 November (1903)
Constitution: 11 October 1972; major reforms adopted 1978, 1983 and 1994

Legal system: based on civil law system; judicial review of legislative acts in the Supreme Court of Justice; accepts compulsory ICJ jurisdiction, with reservations
Suffrage: 18 years of age; universal and compulsory
Executive branch:
chief of state: President Mireya Elisa MOSCOSO Rodriguez (since 1 September 1999); First Vice President Arturo Ulises VALLARINO (since 1 September 1999); Second Vice President Dominador "Kaiser" Baldonero BAZAN Jimenez (since 1 September 1999); note - the president is both the chief of state and head of government
head of government: President Mireya Elisa MOSCOSO Rodriguez (since 1 September 1999); First Vice President Arturo Ulises VALLARINO (since 1 September 1999); Second Vice President Dominador "Kaiser" Baldonero BAZAN Jimenez (since 1 September 1999); note - the president is both the chief of state and head of government
cabinet: Cabinet appointed by the president
elections: president and vice presidents elected on the same ticket by popular vote for five-year terms; election last held 2 May 1999 (next to be held NA May 2004)
election results: Mireya Elisa MOSCOSO Rodriguez elected president; percent of vote - Mireya Elisa MOSCOSO Rodriguez (PA) 44%, Martin TORRIJOS (PRD) 37%
note: government coalition - PA, MOLIRENA, Democratic Change, MORENA, PLN, PS
Legislative branch: unicameral Legislative Assembly or Asamblea Legislativa (71 seats; members are elected by popular vote to serve five-year terms)
elections: last held 2 May 1999 (next to be held NA May 2004)
election results: percent of vote by party - NA%; seats by party - PRD 34, PA 18, PDC 5, PS 4, MOLIRENA 3, PLN 3, Democratic Change 2, PRC 1, MORENA 1
note: legislators from outlying rural districts are chosen on a plurality basis while districts located in more populous towns and cities elect multiple legislators by means of a proportion-based formula
Judicial branch: Supreme Court of Justice or Corte Suprema de Justicia (nine judges appointed for 10-year terms); five superior courts; three courts of appeal
Political parties and leaders: Arnulfista Party or PA [Mireya Elisa MOSCOSO Rodriguez]; Christian Democratic Party or PDC [Ruben AROSEMENA]; Civic Renewal Party or PRC [Serguei DE LA ROSA]; Democratic Change [Ricardo MARTINELLI]; Democratic Revolutionary Party or PRD [Martin TORRIJOS]; National Liberal Party or PLN [Raul ARANGO Gasteazopo]; National Renovation Movement or MORENA [Pedro VALLARINO Cox]; Nationalist Republican Liberal Movement or MOLIRENA [Ramon MORALES]; Solidarity Party or PS [Samuel LEWIS Galindo]
Political pressure groups and leaders: Chamber of Commerce; National Civic Crusade; National Council of Organized Workers or CONATO; National Union of Construction and Similar Workers (SUNTRACS); National Council of Private Enterprise or CONEP; Panamanian Association of Business Executives or APEDE; Panamanian Industrialists Society or SIP; Workers Confederation of the Republic of Panama or CTRP
International organization participation: CCC, ECLAC, FAO, G-77, IADB, IAEA, IBRD, ICAO, ICFTU, ICRM, IDA, IFAD, IFC, IFRCS, ILO, IMF, IMO, Inmarsat, Intelsat, Interpol, IOC, IOM, ISO, ITU, LAES, LAIA (observer), NAM, OAS, OPANAL, OPCW, PCA, RG, UN, UNCTAD, UNESCO, UNIDO, UPU, WCL, WFTU, WHO, WIPO, WMO, WToO, WTrO
Diplomatic representation in the US:
chief of mission: Ambassador Alfredo BOYD
chancery: 2862 McGill Terrace NW, Washington, DC 20008
telephone: [1] (202) 483-1407
consulate(s) general: Atlanta, Houston, Miami, New Orleans, New York, Philadelphia, San Francisco, Tampa
Diplomatic representation from the US:
chief of mission: Ambassador Simon FERRO
embassy: Avenida Balboa and Calle 37, Apartado 6959, Panama City 5
mailing address: American Embassy Panama, Unit 0945, APO AA 34002
telephone: [507] 207-7000
FAX: [507] 227-1964
Flag description: divided into four, equal rectangles; the top quadrants are white (hoist side) with a blue five-pointed star in the center and plain red; the bottom quadrants are plain blue (hoist side) and white with a red five-pointed star in the center

Economy

Economy - overview: Panama's economy is based primarily on a well-developed services sector that accounts for three-fourths of GDP. Services include the Panama Canal, banking, the Colon Free Zone, insurance, container ports, flagship registry, and tourism. A slump in Colon Free Zone and agricultural exports, high oil prices, and the withdrawal of US military forces held back economic growth in 2000. The government plans public works programs, tax reforms, and new regional trade agreements in order to stimulate growth in 2001.
GDP: purchasing power parity - $16.6 billion (2000 est.)
GDP - real growth rate: 2.5% (2000 est.)
GDP - per capita: purchasing power parity - $6,000 (2000 est.)
GDP - composition by sector:
agriculture: 7%
industry: 16.5%
services: 76.5% (1999 est.)
Population below poverty line: 37% (1999 est.)
Household income or consumption by percentage share:
lowest 10%: 1.2%
highest 10%: 35.7% (1997)
Inflation rate (consumer prices): 1.8% (2000 est.)

Panama (continued)

Labor force: 1.1 million (2000 est.)
note: shortage of skilled labor, but an oversupply of unskilled labor
Labor force - by occupation: agriculture 20.8%, industry 18%, services 61.2% (1995 est.)
Unemployment rate: 13% (2000 est.)
Budget:
revenues: $2.8 billion
expenditures: $2.9 billion, including capital expenditures of $471 million (2000 est.)
Industries: construction, petroleum refining, brewing, cement and other construction materials, sugar milling
Industrial production growth rate: 2% (2000 est.)
Electricity - production: 4.413 billion kWh (1999)
Electricity - production by source:
fossil fuel: 27.78%
hydro: 71.65%
nuclear: 0%
other: 0.57% (1999)
Electricity - consumption: 4.049 billion kWh (1999)
Electricity - exports: 95 million kWh (1999)
Electricity - imports: 40 million kWh (1999)
Agriculture - products: bananas, rice, corn, coffee, sugarcane, vegetables; livestock; shrimp
Exports: $5.7 billion (f.o.b., 2000 est.)
Exports - commodities: bananas, shrimp, sugar, coffee, clothing
Exports - partners: US 42%, Germany 11%, Costa Rica 5%, Benelux 4%, Italy 4% (1999)
Imports: $6.9 billion (f.o.b., 2000 est.)
Imports - commodities: capital goods, crude oil, foodstuffs, consumer goods, chemicals
Imports - partners: US 39%, Colon Free Zone 14%, Japan 8%, Ecuador 6%, Mexico 5% (1999)
Debt - external: $7.56 billion (2000 est.)
Economic aid - recipient: $197.1 million (1995)
Currency: balboa (PAB); US dollar (USD)
Currency code: PAB; USD
Exchange rates: balboas per US dollar - 1.000 (fixed rate)
Fiscal year: calendar year

Communications

Telephones - main lines in use: 396,000 (1997)
Telephones - mobile cellular: 17,000 (1997)
Telephone system:
general assessment: domestic and international facilities well developed
domestic: NA
international: 1 coaxial submarine cable; satellite earth stations - 2 Intelsat (Atlantic Ocean); connected to the Central American Microwave System
Radio broadcast stations: AM 101, FM 134, shortwave 0 (1998)
Radios: 815,000 (1997)
Television broadcast stations: 38 (including repeaters) (1998)
Televisions: 510,000 (1997)
Internet country code: .pa
Internet Service Providers (ISPs): 6 (2000)
Internet users: 45,000 (2000)

Transportation

Railways:
total: 355 km
broad gauge: 76 km 1.524-m gauge
narrow gauge: 279 km 0.914-m gauge
Highways:
total: 11,592 km
paved: 4,079 km (including 30 km of expressways)
unpaved: 7,513 km (2000)
Waterways: 882 km
note: 800 km navigable by shallow draft vessels; 82 km Panama Canal
Pipelines: crude oil 130 km (2001)
Ports and harbors: Balboa, Cristobal, Coco Solo, Manzanillo (part of Colon area), Vacamonte
Merchant marine:
total: 4,711 ships (1,000 GRT or over) totaling 111,515,984 GRT/169,655,363 DWT
ships by type: bulk 1,381, cargo 925, chemical tanker 314, combination bulk 71, combination ore/oil 18, container 525, liquefied gas 193, livestock carrier 5, multi-functional large-load carrier 12, passenger 41, passenger/cargo 4, petroleum tanker 544, railcar carrier 2, refrigerated cargo 297, roll on/roll off 106, short-sea passenger 36, specialized tanker 29, vehicle carrier 208
note: includes some foreign-owned ships registered here as a flag of convenience: Argentina 11, Australia 1, Austria 1, Bermuda 21, Belgium 4, The Bahamas 7, Brazil 2, Canada 4, China 154, Chile 4, Cayman Islands 1, Colombia 6, Cuba 7, Cyprus 4, Denmark 12, Egypt 8, Ireland 2, Equatorial Guinea 1, Finland 1, France 4, Germany 17, Greece 248, Hong Kong 158, Honduras 2, Croatia 3, Indonesia 40, India 11, Iran 1, Israel 3, Italy 7, Japan 1,007, Jordan 2, South Korea 223, Latvia 4, Lithuania 1, Liberia 2, Monaco 43, Malta 1, Mexico 5, Malaysia 6, Netherlands 6, Norway 36, Netherlands Antilles 1, Peru 5, Pakistan 1, Portugal 5, Philippines 10, Russia 6, Saudi Arabia 6, Seychelles 2, South Africa 5, Singapore 73, Spain 35, Sweden 4, Syria 11, Switzerland 53, UAE 11, Thailand 15, Taiwan 170, UK 18, US 79, Venezuela 18, Samoa 1 (2000 est.)
Airports: 107 (2000 est.)
Airports - with paved runways:
total: 42
over 3,047 m: 1
2,438 to 3,047 m: 1
1,524 to 2,437 m: 5
914 to 1,523 m: 13
under 914 m: 22 (2000 est.)
Airports - with unpaved runways:
total: 65
914 to 1,523 m: 13
under 914 m: 52 (2000 est.)

Military

Military branches: an amendment to the Constitution abolished the armed forces, but there are security forces (Panamanian Public Forces or PPF includes the Panamanian National Police, National Maritime Service, and National Air Service)
Military manpower - availability:
males age 15-49: 775,966 (2001 est.)
Military manpower - fit for military service:
males age 15-49: 530,916 (2001 est.)
Military expenditures - dollar figure: $128 million (FY99)
Military expenditures - percent of GDP: 1.3% (FY99)
Military - note: on 10 February 1990, the government of then President ENDARA abolished Panama's military and reformed the security apparatus by creating the Panamanian Public Forces; in October 1994, Panama's Legislative Assembly approved a constitutional amendment prohibiting the creation of a standing military force, but allowing the temporary establishment of special police units to counter acts of "external aggression"

Transnational Issues

Disputes - international: none
Illicit drugs: major cocaine transshipment point and major drug money-laundering center; no recent signs of coca cultivation; monitoring of financial transactions is improving; official corruption remains a major problem; Panama was cited by the Financial Action Task Force (FATF) an international organization that includes the US Government, for its lack of cooperation in the fight against international money laundering

Papua New Guinea

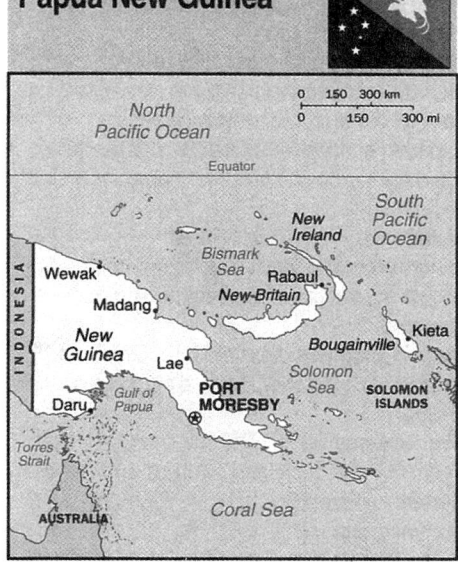

Introduction

Background: The eastern half of the island of New Guinea - second largest in the world - was divided between Germany (north) and the UK (south) in 1885. The latter area was transferred to Australia in 1902, which occupied the northern portion during World War I and continued to administer the combined areas until independence in 1975. A nine-year secessionist revolt on the island of Bougainville ended in 1997, after claiming some 20,000 lives.

Geography

Location: Southeastern Asia, group of islands including the eastern half of the island of New Guinea between the Coral Sea and the South Pacific Ocean, east of Indonesia
Geographic coordinates: 6 00 S, 147 00 E
Map references: Oceania
Area:
total: 462,840 sq km
land: 452,860 sq km
water: 9,980 sq km
Area - comparative: slightly larger than California
Land boundaries:
total: 820 km
border countries: Indonesia 820 km
Coastline: 5,152 km
Maritime claims: measured from claimed archipelagic baselines
continental shelf: 200-m depth or to the depth of exploitation
exclusive fishing zone: 200 NM
territorial sea: 12 NM
Climate: tropical; northwest monsoon (December to March), southeast monsoon (May to October); slight seasonal temperature variation
Terrain: mostly mountains with coastal lowlands and rolling foothills
Elevation extremes:
lowest point: Pacific Ocean 0 m
highest point: Mount Wilhelm 4,509 m
Natural resources: gold, copper, silver, natural gas, timber, oil, fisheries
Land use:
arable land: 0.1%
permanent crops: 1%
permanent pastures: 0%
forests and woodland: 92.9%
other: 6% (1993 est.)
Irrigated land: NA sq km
Natural hazards: active volcanism; situated along the Pacific "Rim of Fire"; the country is subject to frequent and sometimes severe earthquakes; mud slides; tsunamis
Environment - current issues: rain forest subject to deforestation as a result of growing commercial demand for tropical timber; pollution from mining projects; severe drought
Environment - international agreements:
party to: Antarctic Treaty, Biodiversity, Climate Change, Desertification, Endangered Species, Environmental Modification, Hazardous Wastes, Law of the Sea, Marine Dumping, Nuclear Test Ban, Ozone Layer Protection, Ship Pollution, Tropical Timber 83, Tropical Timber 94, Wetlands
signed, but not ratified: Antarctic-Environmental Protocol, Climate Change-Kyoto Protocol
Geography - note: shares island of New Guinea with Indonesia; one of world's largest swamps along southwest coast

People

Population: 5,049,055 (July 2001 est.)
Age structure:
0-14 years: 38.7% (male 993,248; female 960,647)
15-64 years: 57.63% (male 1,507,064; female 1,402,666)
65 years and over: 3.67% (male 87,779; female 97,651) (2001 est.)
Population growth rate: 2.43% (2001 est.)
Birth rate: 32.15 births/1,000 population (2001 est.)
Death rate: 7.88 deaths/1,000 population (2001 est.)
Net migration rate: 0 migrant(s)/1,000 population (2001 est.)
Sex ratio:
at birth: 1.05 male(s)/female
under 15 years: 1.03 male(s)/female
15-64 years: 1.07 male(s)/female
65 years and over: 0.9 male(s)/female
total population: 1.05 male(s)/female (2001 est.)
Infant mortality rate: 58.21 deaths/1,000 live births (2001 est.)
Life expectancy at birth:
total population: 63.46 years
male: 61.39 years
female: 65.64 years (2001 est.)
Total fertility rate: 4.3 children born/woman (2001 est.)
HIV/AIDS - adult prevalence rate: 0.22% (1999 est.)
HIV/AIDS - people living with HIV/AIDS: 5,400 (1999 est.)
HIV/AIDS - deaths: 450 (1999 est.)
Nationality:
noun: Papua New Guinean(s)
adjective: Papua New Guinean
Ethnic groups: Melanesian, Papuan, Negrito, Micronesian, Polynesian
Religions: Roman Catholic 22%, Lutheran 16%, Presbyterian/Methodist/London Missionary Society 8%, Anglican 5%, Evangelical Alliance 4%, Seventh-Day Adventist 1%, other Protestant 10%, indigenous beliefs 34%
Languages: English spoken by 1%-2%, pidgin English widespread, Motu spoken in Papua region
note: 715 indigenous languages
Literacy:
definition: age 15 and over can read and write
total population: 72.2%
male: 81%
female: 62.7% (1995 est.)

Government

Country name:
conventional long form: Independent State of Papua New Guinea
conventional short form: Papua New Guinea
former: Territory of Papua and New Guinea
abbreviation: PNG
Government type: constitutional monarchy with parliamentary democracy
Capital: Port Moresby
Administrative divisions: 20 provinces; Bougainville, Central, Chimbu, Eastern Highlands, East New Britain, East Sepik, Enga, Gulf, Madang, Manus, Milne Bay, Morobe, National Capital, New Ireland, Northern, Sandaun, Southern Highlands, Western, Western Highlands, West New Britain
Independence: 16 September 1975 (from the Australian-administered UN trusteeship)
National holiday: Independence Day, 16 September (1975)
Constitution: 16 September 1975
Legal system: based on English common law
Suffrage: 18 years of age; universal
Executive branch:
chief of state: Queen ELIZABETH II (since 6 February 1952), represented by Governor General Silas ATOPARE (since 13 November 1997)
head of government: Prime Minister Mekere MORAUTA (since NA August 1999); Deputy Prime Minister Michael OGIO (since 3 November 2000)
cabinet: National Executive Council appointed by the governor general on the recommendation of the prime minister
elections: none; the monarch is hereditary; governor general appointed by the National Executive Council; prime minister and deputy prime minister appointed by the governor general for up to five years on the basis of majority support in National Parliament

Papua New Guinea (continued)

Legislative branch: unicameral National Parliament - sometimes referred to as the House of Assembly (109 seats, 89 elected from open electorates and 20 from provincial electorates; members elected by popular vote to serve five-year terms)
elections: last held 14-28 June 1997 (next to be held NA June 2002)
election results: percent of vote by party - PPP 15%, Pangu Pati 14%, NA 14%, PDM 8%, PNC 6%, PAP 5%, UP 3%, NP 1%, PUP 1%, independents 33%; seats by party - PPP 16, Pangu Pati 15, NA 15, PDM 9, PNC 7, PAP 5, UP 3, NP 1, PUP 1, independents 37; note - association with political parties is very fluid

Judicial branch: Supreme Court (the chief justice is appointed by the governor general on the proposal of the National Executive Council after consultation with the minister responsible for justice; other judges are appointed by the Judicial and Legal Services Commission)

Political parties and leaders: National Alliance or NA [Michael SOMARE]; National Party or NP [Michael MEL]; Papua New Guinea United Party or Pangu Pati [Chris HAIVETA]; People's Action Party or PAP [Ted DIRO]; People's Democratic Movement or PDM [Sir Mekere MORAUTA]; People's National Congress or PNC [Simon KAUMI]; People's Progress Party or PPP [Michael NALI]; People's Unity Party or PUP [Alfred KAIABE]; United Party or UP [Rimbiuk PATO]

Political pressure groups and leaders: NA

International organization participation: ACP, APEC, ARF (dialogue partner), AsDB, ASEAN (observer), C, CP, ESCAP, FAO, G-77, IBRD, ICAO, ICFTU, ICRM, IDA, IFAD, IFC, IFRCS, IHO, ILO, IMF, IMO, Intelsat, Interpol, IOC, IOM (observer), ISO (correspondent), ITU, NAM, OPCW, Sparteca, SPC, SPF, UN, UNCTAD, UNESCO, UNIDO, UPU, WFTU, WHO, WIPO, WMO, WTrO

Diplomatic representation in the US:
chief of mission: Ambassador Susan JACOBS
chancery: 1779 Massachusetts Avenue NW, Washington, DC 20036
telephone: [1] (202) 745-3680
FAX: [1] (202) 745-3679

Diplomatic representation from the US:
chief of mission: Ambassador Arma Jane KARAER
embassy: Douglas Street, Port Moresby
mailing address: P. O. Box 1492, Port Moresby
telephone: [675] 321-1455
FAX: [675] 321-3423

Flag description: divided diagonally from upper hoist-side corner; the upper triangle is red with a soaring yellow bird of paradise centered; the lower triangle is black with five, white, five-pointed stars of the Southern Cross constellation centered

Economy

Economy - overview: Papua New Guinea is richly endowed with natural resources, but exploitation has been hampered by the rugged terrain and the high cost of developing infrastructure. Agriculture provides a subsistence livelihood for 85% of the population. Mineral deposits, including oil, copper, and gold, account for 72% of export earnings. The 3.4% average annual growth rate of GDP during 1979-1998 conceals considerable year-to-year variation resulting from external economic shocks, natural disasters, and economic management problems. There has been little growth in the last half of the 1990s, with real GDP in 1999 barely 3% higher than in 1994, not enough to compensate for population growth. A new administration under the leadership of Prime Minister Mekere MORAUTA in July 1999 has promised to restore integrity to state institutions, to stabilize the kina, to restore stability to the national budget, to privatize public enterprises where appropriate, and to ensure ongoing peace on Bougainville. The government has had considerable success in attracting international support, specifically gaining the support of the IMF and the World Bank in securing development assistance loans. Significant challenges remain for MORAUTA, however, including gaining further investor confidence, specifically for the proposed Papua New Guinea-Australia oil pipeline, continuing efforts to privatize government assets, and in maintaining the support from members of Parliament who after 15 July 2001 can dismiss him with a vote of no-confidence.

GDP: purchasing power parity - $12.2 billion (2000 est.)

GDP - real growth rate: 2.9% (2000 est.)

GDP - per capita: purchasing power parity - $2,500 (2000 est.)

GDP - composition by sector:
agriculture: 30%
industry: 35%
services: 35% (1999 est.)

Population below poverty line: 37%

Household income or consumption by percentage share:
lowest 10%: 1.7%
highest 10%: 40.5% (1996)

Inflation rate (consumer prices): 17% (2000 est.)

Labor force: 1.941 million

Labor force - by occupation: agriculture 85%, industry NA%, services NA%

Unemployment rate: NA%

Budget:
revenues: $1.6 billion
expenditures: $1.9 billion, including capital expenditures of $NA (1998 est.)

Industries: copra crushing, palm oil processing, plywood production, wood chip production; mining of gold, silver, and copper; crude oil production; construction, tourism

Industrial production growth rate: NA%

Electricity - production: 1.82 billion kWh (1999)

Electricity - production by source:
fossil fuel: 54.95%
hydro: 45.05%
nuclear: 0%
other: 0% (1999)

Electricity - consumption: 1.693 billion kWh (1999)

Electricity - exports: 0 kWh (1999)

Electricity - imports: 0 kWh (1999)

Agriculture - products: coffee, cocoa, coconuts, palm kernels, tea, rubber, sweet potatoes, fruit, vegetables; poultry, pork

Exports: $2.1 billion (f.o.b., 2000 est.)

Exports - commodities: oil, gold, copper ore, logs, palm oil, coffee, cocoa, crayfish, prawns

Exports - partners: Australia 30%, Japan 12%, Germany 7%, South Korea 4%, Philippines 3%, UK 3% (1999)

Imports: $1 billion (f.o.b., 2000 est.)

Imports - commodities: machinery and transport equipment, manufactured goods, food, fuels, chemicals

Imports - partners: Australia 53%, Singapore 13%, Japan 6%, US 4%, New Zealand 4%, Malaysia 4% (1999)

Debt - external: $2.9 billion (2000 est.)

Economic aid - recipient: $400 million (1999 est.)

Currency: kina (PGK)

Currency code: PGK

Exchange rates: kina per US dollar - 2.81 (October 2000), 2.696 (2000), 2.539 (1999), 2.058 (1998), 1.434 (1997), 1.318 (1996)

Fiscal year: calendar year

Communications

Telephones - main lines in use: 47,000 (1996)

Telephones - mobile cellular: 3,053 (1996)

Telephone system:
general assessment: services are adequate and being improved; facilities provide radiotelephone and telegraph, coastal radio, aeronautical radio, and international radio communication services
domestic: mostly radiotelephone
international: submarine cables to Australia and Guam; satellite earth station - 1 Intelsat (Pacific Ocean); international radio communication service

Radio broadcast stations: AM 8, FM 19, shortwave 28 (1998)

Radios: 410,000 (1997)

Television broadcast stations: 3 (1997)

Televisions: 42,000 (1997)

Internet country code: .pg

Internet Service Providers (ISPs): 3 (2000)

Internet users: 2,000 (2000)

Transportation

Railways: 0 km

Highways:
total: 19,600 km
paved: 686 km
unpaved: 18,914 km (1996 est.)

Waterways: 10,940 km

Ports and harbors: Kieta, Lae, Madang, Port Moresby, Rabaul

Merchant marine:
total: 20 ships (1,000 GRT or over) totaling 35,361 GRT/51,096 DWT
ships by type: bulk 1, cargo 9, chemical tanker 1, combination ore/oil 3, container 1, petroleum tanker 3, roll on/roll off 2 (2000 est.)

Papua New Guinea (continued)

Airports: 492 (2000 est.)
Airports - with paved runways:
total: 20
2,438 to 3,047 m: 2
1,524 to 2,437 m: 13
914 to 1,523 m: 4
under 914 m: 1 (2000 est.)
Airports - with unpaved runways:
total: 472
1,524 to 2,437 m: 13
914 to 1,523 m: 57
under 914 m: 402 (2000 est.)
Heliports: 2 (2000 est.)

Military

Military branches: Papua New Guinea Defense Force (includes Ground, Naval, and Air Forces, and Special Forces Unit)
Military manpower - availability:
males age 15-49: 1,306,159 (2001 est.)
Military manpower - fit for military service:
males age 15-49: 723,012 (2001 est.)
Military expenditures - dollar figure: $42 million (FY98)
Military expenditures - percent of GDP: 1% (FY98)

Transnational Issues

Disputes - international: none

Paracel Islands

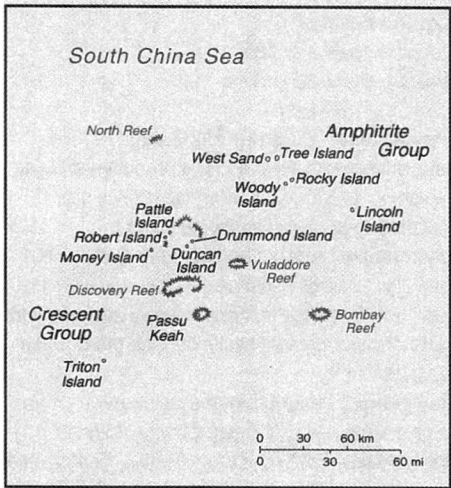

Introduction

Background: This archipelago is surrounded by productive fishing grounds and potentially large oil reserves. In 1932, French Indochina annexed the islands and set up a weather station on Prattle Island; maintenance was continued by its successor Vietnam. China has occupied the Paracel Islands since 1974, when its troops captured a South Vietnamese garrison occupying the western islands. However, the islands are still claimed by Vietnam and Taiwan.

Geography

Location: Southeastern Asia, group of small islands and reefs in the South China Sea, about one-third of the way from central Vietnam to the northern Philippines
Geographic coordinates: 16 30 N, 112 00 E
Map references: Southeast Asia
Area:
total: NA sq km
land: NA sq km
water: 0 sq km
Area - comparative: NA
Land boundaries: 0 km
Coastline: 518 km
Maritime claims: NA
Climate: tropical
Terrain: mostly low and flat
Elevation extremes:
lowest point: South China Sea 0 m
highest point: unnamed location on Rocky Island 14 m
Natural resources: none
Land use:
arable land: 0%
permanent crops: 0%
permanent pastures: 0%
forests and woodland: 0%
other: 100%
Irrigated land: 0 sq km (1993)
Natural hazards: typhoons
Environment - current issues: NA

People

Population: no indigenous inhabitants
note: there are scattered Chinese garrisons (July 2001 est.)

Government

Country name:
conventional long form: none
conventional short form: Paracel Islands

Economy

Economy - overview: China announced plans in 1997 to open the islands for tourism.

Transportation

Waterways: none
Ports and harbors: small Chinese port facilities on Woody Island and Duncan Island being expanded
Airports: 1 (2000 est.)
Airports - with paved runways:
total: 1
1,524 to 2,437 m: 1 (2000 est.)

Military

Military - note: occupied by China

Transnational Issues

Disputes - international: occupied by China, but claimed by Taiwan and Vietnam

Paraguay

Introduction

Background: In the disastrous War of the Triple Alliance (1865-70), Paraguay lost two-thirds of all adult males and much of its territory. It stagnated economically for the next half century. In the Chaco War of 1932-35, large, economically important areas were won from Bolivia. The 35-year military dictatorship of Alfredo STROESSNER was overthrown in 1989, and, despite a marked increase in political infighting in recent years, relatively free and regular presidential elections have been held since then.

Geography

Location: Central South America, northeast of Argentina
Geographic coordinates: 23 00 S, 58 00 W
Map references: South America
Area:
total: 406,750 sq km
land: 397,300 sq km
water: 9,450 sq km
Area - comparative: slightly smaller than California
Land boundaries:
total: 3,920 km
border countries: Argentina 1,880 km, Bolivia 750 km, Brazil 1,290 km
Coastline: 0 km (landlocked)
Maritime claims: none (landlocked)
Climate: subtropical to temperate; substantial rainfall in the eastern portions, becoming semiarid in the far west
Terrain: grassy plains and wooded hills east of Rio Paraguay; Gran Chaco region west of Rio Paraguay mostly low, marshy plain near the river, and dry forest and thorny scrub elsewhere
Elevation extremes:
lowest point: junction of Rio Paraguay and Rio Parana 46 m
highest point: Cerro Pero (Cerro Tres Kandu) 842 m

Natural resources: hydropower, timber, iron ore, manganese, limestone
Land use:
arable land: 6%
permanent crops: 0%
permanent pastures: 55%
forests and woodland: 32%
other: 7% (1993 est.)
Irrigated land: 670 sq km (1993 est.)
Natural hazards: local flooding in southeast (early September to June); poorly drained plains may become boggy (early October to June)
Environment - current issues: deforestation (an estimated 2 million hectares of forest land were lost from 1958-85); water pollution; inadequate means for waste disposal present health risks for many urban residents
Environment - international agreements:
party to: Biodiversity, Climate Change, Climate Change-Kyoto Protocol, Desertification, Endangered Species, Hazardous Wastes, Law of the Sea, Marine Dumping, Ozone Layer Protection, Ship Pollution, Wetlands
signed, but not ratified: Nuclear Test Ban
Geography - note: landlocked; lies between Argentina, Bolivia, and Brazil

People

Population: 5,734,139 (July 2001 est.)
Age structure:
0-14 years: 38.9% (male 1,133,306; female 1,097,360)
15-64 years: 56.39% (male 1,622,743; female 1,610,659)
65 years and over: 4.71% (male 124,321; female 145,750) (2001 est.)
Population growth rate: 2.6% (2001 est.)
Birth rate: 30.88 births/1,000 population (2001 est.)
Death rate: 4.75 deaths/1,000 population (2001 est.)
Net migration rate: -0.09 migrant(s)/1,000 population (2001 est.)
Sex ratio:
at birth: 1.05 male(s)/female
under 15 years: 1.03 male(s)/female
15-64 years: 1.01 male(s)/female
65 years and over: 0.85 male(s)/female
total population: 1.01 male(s)/female (2001 est.)
Infant mortality rate: 29.78 deaths/1,000 live births (2001 est.)
Life expectancy at birth:
total population: 73.92 years
male: 71.44 years
female: 76.52 years (2001 est.)
Total fertility rate: 4.11 children born/woman (2001 est.)
HIV/AIDS - adult prevalence rate: 0.11% (1999 est.)
HIV/AIDS - people living with HIV/AIDS: 3,000 (1999 est.)
HIV/AIDS - deaths: 220 (1999 est.)

Nationality:
noun: Paraguayan(s)
adjective: Paraguayan
Ethnic groups: mestizo (mixed Spanish and Amerindian) 95%
Religions: Roman Catholic 90%, Mennonite, and other Protestant
Languages: Spanish (official), Guarani (official)
Literacy:
definition: age 15 and over can read and write
total population: 92.1%
male: 93.5%
female: 90.6% (1995 est.)

Government

Country name:
conventional long form: Republic of Paraguay
conventional short form: Paraguay
local long form: Republica del Paraguay
local short form: Paraguay
Government type: constitutional republic
Capital: Asuncion
Administrative divisions: 17 departments (departamentos, singular - departamento) and one capital city; Alto Paraguay, Alto Parana, Amambay, Asuncion (city), Boqueron, Caaguazu, Caazapa, Canindeyu, Central, Concepcion, Cordillera, Guaira, Itapua, Misiones, Neembucu, Paraguari, Presidente Hayes, San Pedro
Independence: 14 May 1811 (from Spain)
National holiday: Independence Day, 14 May (1811)
Constitution: promulgated 20 June 1992
Legal system: based on Argentine codes, Roman law, and French codes; judicial review of legislative acts in Supreme Court of Justice
Suffrage: 18 years of age; universal and compulsory up to age 75
Executive branch:
chief of state: President Luis GONZALEZ MACCHI (since 28 March 1999); vice president Julio Cesar FRANCO (since NA August 2000); note - the president is both the chief of state and head of government
head of government: President Luis GONZALEZ MACCHI (since 28 March 1999); vice president Julio Cesar FRANCO (since NA August 2000); note - the president is both the chief of state and head of government
cabinet: Council of Ministers nominated by the president
elections: president and vice president elected on the same ticket by popular vote for five-year terms; election last held 10 May 1998 (next to be held NA May 2003)
election results: Raul CUBAS Grau elected president; percent of vote - 55.3%; resigned 28 March 1999
note: President Luis GONZALEZ MACCHI, formerly president of the Chamber of Senators, constitutionally succeeded President Raul CUBAS Grau, who resigned after being impeached soon after the

Paraguay (continued)

assassination of Vice President Luis Maria ARGANA; the successor to ARGANA was decided in an election held in August 2000
Legislative branch: bicameral Congress or Congreso consists of the Chamber of Senators or Camara de Senadores (45 seats; members are elected by popular vote to serve five-year terms) and the Chamber of Deputies or Camara de Diputados (80 seats; members are elected by popular vote to serve five-year terms)
elections: Chamber of Senators - last held 10 May 1998 (next to be held NA May 2003); Chamber of Deputies - last held 10 May 1998 (next to be held NA May 2003)
election results: Chamber of Senators - percent of vote by party - NA%; seats by party - Colorado Party 25, PLRA 13, PEN 7; Chamber of Deputies - percent of vote by party - NA%; seats by party - Colorado Party 45, PLRA 26, PEN 9
Judicial branch: Supreme Court of Justice or Corte Suprema de Justicia (judges appointed on the proposal of the Counsel of Magistrates or Consejo de la Magistratura)
Political parties and leaders: Authentic Radical Liberal Party or PLRA [Miguel Abdon SAGUIER]; Christian Democratic Party or PDC [Adalina GUITERREZ DE GALEANO]; Febrerista Revolutionary Party or PRF [Carlos Maria LJUBETIC]; National Encounter or PEN [Euclides ACEVEDO]; National Republican Association - Colorado Party [acting president Bader RACHID LICHI]
Political pressure groups and leaders: Ahorristas Estafados or AE; National Workers Central or CNT; Paraguayan Workers Confederation or CPT; Roman Catholic Church; Unitary Workers Central or CUT
International organization participation: CCC, ECLAC, FAO, G-77, IADB, IAEA, IBRD, ICAO, ICFTU, ICRM, IDA, IFAD, IFC, IFRCS, ILO, IMF, IMO, Intelsat, Interpol, IOC, IOM, ISO (correspondent), ITU, LAES, LAIA, Mercosur, NAM (observer), OAS, OPANAL, OPCW, PCA, RG, UN, UNCTAD, UNESCO, UNIDO, UNMEE, UPU, WCL, WHO, WIPO, WMO, WToO, WTrO
Diplomatic representation in the US:
chief of mission: Ambassador Leila RACHID
chancery: 2400 Massachusetts Avenue NW, Washington, DC 20008
telephone: [1] (202) 483-6960 through 6962
FAX: [1] (202) 234-4508
consulate(s) general: Detroit (honorary), Los Angeles, Miami, New Orleans, New York, San Juan (honorary)
Diplomatic representation from the US:
chief of mission: Ambassador David N. GREENLEE
embassy: 1776 Avenida Mariscal Lopez, Casilla Postal 402, Asuncion
mailing address: Unit 4711, APO AA 34036-0001
telephone: [595] (21) 213-715
FAX: [595] (21) 213-728
Flag description: three equal, horizontal bands of red (top), white, and blue with an emblem centered in the white band; unusual flag in that the emblem is different on each side; the obverse (hoist side at the left) bears the national coat of arms (a yellow five-pointed star within a green wreath capped by the words REPUBLICA DEL PARAGUAY, all within two circles); the reverse (hoist side at the right) bears the seal of the treasury (a yellow lion below a red Cap of Liberty and the words Paz y Justicia (Peace and Justice) capped by the words REPUBLICA DEL PARAGUAY, all within two circles)

Economy

Economy - overview: Paraguay has a market economy marked by a large informal sector. The informal sector features both reexport of imported consumer goods to neighboring countries as well as the activities of thousands of microenterprises and urban street vendors. Because of the importance of the informal sector, accurate economic measures are difficult to obtain. A large percentage of the population derives their living from agricultural activity, often on a subsistence basis. The formal economy grew by an average of about 3% annually in 1995-97, but GDP declined slightly in 1998 and 1999. On a per capita basis, real income has stagnated at 1980 levels. Most observers attribute Paraguay's poor economic performance to political uncertainty, corruption, lack of progress on structural reform, substantial internal and external debt, and deficient infrastructure. Growth rebounded slightly in 2000.
GDP: purchasing power parity - $26.2 billion (2000 est.)
GDP - real growth rate: 1% (2000 est.)
GDP - per capita: purchasing power parity - $4,750 (2000 est.)
GDP - composition by sector:
agriculture: 28%
industry: 21%
services: 51% (1999 est.)
Population below poverty line: 36% (2000 est.)
Household income or consumption by percentage share:
lowest 10%: 0.7%
highest 10%: 46.6% (1995)
Inflation rate (consumer prices): 8% (2000 est.)
Labor force: 2 million (2000 est.)
Labor force - by occupation: agriculture 45%
Unemployment rate: 16% (2000 est.)
Budget:
revenues: $1.3 billion
expenditures: $2 billion, including capital expenditures of $700 million (1999 est.)
Industries: sugar, cement, textiles, beverages, wood products
Industrial production growth rate: 0% (2000 est.)
Electricity - production: 51.554 billion kWh (1999)
Electricity - production by source:
fossil fuel: 0.07%
hydro: 99.79%
nuclear: 0%
other: 0.15% (1999)
Electricity - consumption: 1.915 billion kWh (1999)
Electricity - exports: 46.03 billion kWh (1999)
Electricity - imports: 0 kWh (1999)
Agriculture - products: cotton, sugarcane, soybeans, corn, wheat, tobacco, cassava (yucca), fruits, vegetables; beef, pork, eggs, milk; timber
Exports: $3.5 billion (f.o.b., 2000 est.)
Exports - commodities: electricity, soybeans, feed, cotton, meat, edible oils
Exports - partners: Brazil, Argentina, EU
Imports: $3.3 billion (f.o.b., 2000 est.)
Imports - commodities: road vehicles, consumer goods, tobacco, petroleum products, electrical machinery
Imports - partners: Brazil, US, Argentina, Uruguay, EU, Hong Kong
Debt - external: $3 billion (2000 est.)
Economic aid - recipient: $NA
Currency: guarani (PYG)
Currency code: PYG
Exchange rates: guarani per US dollar - 3,570.0 (January 2001), 3,486.4 (2000), 3,119.1 (1999), 2,726.5 (1998), 2,177.9 (1997), 2,056.8 (1996); note - since early 1998, the exchange rate has operated as a managed float; prior to that, the exchange rate was determined freely in the market
Fiscal year: calendar year

Communications

Telephones - main lines in use: 290,475 (2001)
Telephones - mobile cellular: 510,000 (2001)
Telephone system:
general assessment: meager telephone service; principal switching center is Asuncion
domestic: fair microwave radio relay network
international: satellite earth station - 1 Intelsat (Atlantic Ocean)
Radio broadcast stations: AM 46, FM 27, shortwave 6 (three inactive) (1998)
Radios: 925,000 (1997)
Television broadcast stations: 4 (2001)
Televisions: 990,000 (2001)
Internet country code: .py
Internet Service Providers (ISPs): 4 (2000)
Internet users: 20,000 (2000)

Transportation

Railways:
total: 971 km
standard gauge: 441 km 1.435-m gauge
narrow gauge: 60 km 1.000-m gauge
note: there are 470 km of various gauges that are privately owned
Highways:
total: 25,901 km
paved: 3,067 km
unpaved: 22,834 km (2001)
Waterways: 3,100 km
Ports and harbors: Asuncion, Villeta, San Antonio, Encarnacion
Merchant marine:
total: 20 ships (1,000 GRT or over) totaling 31,066 GRT/35,441 DWT

Paraguay (continued)

ships by type: cargo 14, chemical tanker 1, petroleum tanker 3, roll on/roll off 2 (2000 est.)
Airports: 915 (2000 est.)
Airports - with paved runways:
total: 11
over 3,047 m: 3
1,524 to 2,437 m: 4
914 to 1,523 m: 4 (2000 est.)
Airports - with unpaved runways:
total: 904
1,524 to 2,437 m: 29
914 to 1,523 m: 340
under 914 m: 535 (2000 est.)

Military

Military branches: Army, Navy (includes Naval Air and Marines), Air Force
Military manpower - military age: 17 years of age
Military manpower - availability:
males age 15-49: 1,388,436 (2001 est.)
Military manpower - fit for military service:
males age 15-49: 1,001,516 (2001 est.)
Military manpower - reaching military age annually:
males: 58,359 (2001 est.)
Military expenditures - dollar figure: $125 million (FY98)
Military expenditures - percent of GDP: 1.4% (FY98)

Transnational Issues

Illicit drugs: illicit producer of cannabis, most or all of which is consumed in South America; transshipment country for Andean cocaine headed for Southern Cone markets and Europe

Peru

Introduction

Background: After a dozen years of military rule, Peru returned to democratic leadership in 1980. In recent years, bold reform programs and significant progress in curtailing guerrilla activity and drug trafficking have resulted in solid economic growth.

Geography

Location: Western South America, bordering the South Pacific Ocean, between Chile and Ecuador
Geographic coordinates: 10 00 S, 76 00 W
Map references: South America
Area:
total: 1,285,220 sq km
land: 1.28 million sq km
water: 5,220 sq km
Area - comparative: slightly smaller than Alaska
Land boundaries:
total: 5,536 km
border countries: Bolivia 900 km, Brazil 1,560 km, Chile 160 km, Colombia 1,496 km (est.), Ecuador 1,420 km
Coastline: 2,414 km
Maritime claims:
continental shelf: 200 NM
territorial sea: 200 NM
Climate: varies from tropical in east to dry desert in west; temperate to frigid in Andes
Terrain: western coastal plain (costa), high and rugged Andes in center (sierra), eastern lowland jungle of Amazon Basin (selva)
Elevation extremes:
lowest point: Pacific Ocean 0 m
highest point: Nevado Huascaran 6,768 m
Natural resources: copper, silver, gold, petroleum, timber, fish, iron ore, coal, phosphate, potash, hydropower
Land use:
arable land: 3%
permanent crops: 0%
permanent pastures: 21%
forests and woodland: 66%
other: 10% (1993 est.)
Irrigated land: 12,800 sq km (1993 est.)
Natural hazards: earthquakes, tsunamis, flooding, landslides, mild volcanic activity
Environment - current issues: deforestation (some the result of illegal logging); overgrazing of the slopes of the costa and sierra leading to soil erosion; desertification; air pollution in Lima; pollution of rivers and coastal waters from municipal and mining wastes
Environment - international agreements:
party to: Antarctic-Environmental Protocol, Antarctic-Marine Living Resources, Antarctic Treaty, Biodiversity, Climate Change, Desertification, Endangered Species, Hazardous Wastes, Marine Dumping, Nuclear Test Ban, Ozone Layer Protection, Ship Pollution, Tropical Timber 83, Tropical Timber 94, Wetlands, Whaling
signed, but not ratified: Climate Change-Kyoto Protocol
Geography - note: shares control of Lago Titicaca, world's highest navigable lake, with Bolivia

People

Population: 27,483,864 (July 2001 est.)
Age structure:
0-14 years: 34.41% (male 4,803,464; female 4,654,890)
15-64 years: 60.8% (male 8,408,210; female 8,302,943)
65 years and over: 4.79% (male 603,309; female 711,048) (2001 est.)
Population growth rate: 1.7% (2001 est.)
Birth rate: 23.9 births/1,000 population (2001 est.)
Death rate: 5.78 deaths/1,000 population (2001 est.)
Net migration rate: -1.08 migrant(s)/1,000 population (2001 est.)
Sex ratio:
at birth: 1.05 male(s)/female
under 15 years: 1.03 male(s)/female
15-64 years: 1.01 male(s)/female
65 years and over: 0.85 male(s)/female
total population: 1.01 male(s)/female (2001 est.)
Infant mortality rate: 39.39 deaths/1,000 live births (2001 est.)
Life expectancy at birth:
total population: 70.3 years
male: 67.9 years
female: 72.81 years (2001 est.)
Total fertility rate: 2.96 children born/woman (2001 est.)
HIV/AIDS - adult prevalence rate: 0.35% (1999 est.)
HIV/AIDS - people living with HIV/AIDS: 48,000 (1999 est.)
HIV/AIDS - deaths: 4,100 (1999 est.)
Nationality:
noun: Peruvian(s)
adjective: Peruvian

Peru (continued)

Ethnic groups: Amerindian 45%, mestizo (mixed Amerindian and white) 37%, white 15%, black, Japanese, Chinese, and other 3%
Religions: Roman Catholic 90%
Languages: Spanish (official), Quechua (official), Aymara
Literacy:
definition: age 15 and over can read and write
total population: 88.7%
male: 94.5%
female: 83% (1995 est.)

Government

Country name:
conventional long form: Republic of Peru
conventional short form: Peru
local long form: Republica del Peru
local short form: Peru
Government type: constitutional republic
Capital: Lima
Administrative divisions: 24 departments (departamentos, singular - departamento) and 1 constitutional province* (provincia constitucional); Amazonas, Ancash, Apurimac, Arequipa, Ayacucho, Cajamarca, Callao*, Cusco, Huancavelica, Huanuco, Ica, Junin, La Libertad, Lambayeque, Lima, Loreto, Madre de Dios, Moquegua, Pasco, Piura, Puno, San Martin, Tacna, Tumbes, Ucayali
note: the 1979 constitution mandated the creation of regions (regiones, singular - region) to function eventually as autonomous economic and administrative entities; so far, 12 regions have been constituted from 23 of the 24 departments - Amazonas (from Loreto), Andres Avelino Caceres (from Huanuco, Pasco, Junin), Arequipa (from Arequipa), Chavin (from Ancash), Grau (from Tumbes, Piura), Inca (from Cusco, Madre de Dios, Apurimac), La Libertad (from La Libertad), Los Libertadores-Huari (from Ica, Ayacucho, Huancavelica), Mariategui (from Moquegua, Tacna, Puno), Nor Oriental del Maranon (from Lambayeque, Cajamarca, Amazonas), San Martin (from San Martin), Ucayali (from Ucayali); formation of another region has been delayed by the reluctance of the constitutional province of Callao to merge with the department of Lima; because of inadequate funding from the central government and organizational and political difficulties, the regions have yet to assume major responsibilities; the 1993 constitution retains the regions but limits their authority; the 1993 constitution also reaffirms the roles of departmental and municipal governments
Independence: 28 July 1821 (from Spain)
National holiday: Independence Day, 28 July (1821)
Constitution: 31 December 1993
Legal system: based on civil law system; has not accepted compulsory ICJ jurisdiction
Suffrage: 18 years of age; universal
Executive branch:
chief of state: President Valentin PANIAGUA (since 22 November 2000); note - the president is both the chief of state and head of government; additionally two vice presidents are provided for by the Constitution, but those positions have not been filled by the interim government
head of government: President Valentin PANIAGUA (since 22 November 2000); note - the president is both the chief of state and head of government; additionally two vice presidents are provided for by the Constitution, but those positions have not been filled by the interim government
note: Prime Minister Javier PEREZ de Cuellar (since 22 November 2000) does not exercise executive power; this power is in the hands of the president
cabinet: Council of Ministers appointed by the president
elections: president elected by popular vote for a five-year term; election last held 9 April 2000 with runoff on 28 May 2000 (special presidential election was held 8 April 2001 with runoff election 3 June 2001) next to be held NA 2006
election results: President PANIAGUA elected in runoff election; percent of vote - Valentin PANIAGUA 51.22%, Alejandro TOLEDO 17.68%; in special runoff election 3 June 2001, Alejandro TOLEDO was elected president; percent of vote NA%
Legislative branch: unicameral Democratic Constituent Congress or Congresso Constituyente Democratico (120 seats; members are elected by popular vote to serve five-year terms)
elections: last held 9 April 2000 (next to be held 8 April 2001)
note: many congressmen defected to and then from former President FUJIMORI's coalition in 2000
election results: percent of vote by party - Peru 2000 42.16%, Peru Possible 23.34%, FIM 7.56%, Somos Peru 7.2%, APRA 5.5%, others 14.24%; seats by party - Peru 2000 52, Peru Possible 29, FIM 9, others 30
Judicial branch: Supreme Court of Justice or Corte Suprema de Justicia (judges are appointed by the National Council of the Judiciary)
Political parties and leaders: American Popular Revolutionary Alliance or APRA [Alan GARCIA]; Andean Rebirth [Ciro GALVEZ Herreria]; Avancemos [leader NA]; Democratic Cause [Jorge SANTISTEVAN]; Independent Moralizing Front or FIM [Fernando OLIVERA Vega]; National Solidarity or SN [Luis CASTANEDA Lossio]; National Unity [Lourdes FLORES Nano]; Peru 2000 [leader NA]; Peru Posible or PP [Alejandro TOLEDO Maniquez]; Popular Action or AP [leader NA]; Popular Agrarian Front of Peru or Frepap [leader NA]; Popular Solution [Carlos BOLONA Behr]; Project Country [Mario Antonio ARRUNATEGUI]; Somos Peru or SP [Alberto ANDRADE]; Union for Peru or UPP [leader NA]; Vamos Vecinos or VV [Absalon VASQUEZ]
Political pressure groups and leaders: leftist guerrilla groups include Shining Path [Abimael GUZMAN Reynoso (imprisoned), Gabriel MACARIO (top leader at-large)]; Tupac Amaru Revolutionary Movement or MRTA [Victor POLAY (imprisoned), Hugo AVALLENEDA Valdez (top leader at-large)]
International organization participation: ABEDA, APEC, CAN, CCC, ECLAC, FAO, G-11, G-15, G-19, G-24, G-77, IADB, IAEA, IBRD, ICAO, ICC, ICFTU, ICRM, IDA, IFAD, IFC, IFRCS, IHO, ILO, IMF, IMO, Inmarsat, Intelsat, Interpol, IOC, IOM, ISO (correspondent), ITU, LAES, LAIA, MONUC, NAM, OAS, OPANAL, OPCW, PCA, RG, UN, UNCTAD, UNESCO, UNIDO, UNMEE, UNTAET, UPU, WCL, WFTU, WHO, WIPO, WMO, WToO, WTrO
Diplomatic representation in the US:
chief of mission: Ambassador Alfonso RIVERO Monsalve
chancery: 1700 Massachusetts Avenue NW, Washington, DC 20036
telephone: [1] (202) 833-9860 through 9869
FAX: [1] (202) 659-8124
consulate(s) general: Chicago, Houston, Los Angeles, Miami, New York, Paterson (New Jersey), San Francisco
Diplomatic representation from the US:
chief of mission: Ambassador John HAMILTON
embassy: Avenida La Encalada, Cuadra 17s/n, Surco, Lima 33
mailing address: P. O. Box 1995, Lima 1; American Embassy (Lima), APO AA 34031-5000
telephone: [51] (1) 434-3000
FAX: [51] (1) 434-3037
Flag description: three equal, vertical bands of red (hoist side), white, and red with the coat of arms centered in the white band; the coat of arms features a shield bearing a llama, cinchona tree (the source of quinine), and a yellow cornucopia spilling out gold coins, all framed by a green wreath

Economy

Economy - overview: The Peruvian economy has become increasingly market-oriented, with major privatizations completed since 1990 in the mining, electricity, and telecommunications industries. Thanks to strong foreign investment and the cooperation between the FUJIMORI government and the IMF and World Bank, growth was strong in 1994-97 and inflation was brought under control. In 1998, El Nino's impact on agriculture, the financial crisis in Asia, and instability in Brazilian markets undercut growth. And 1999 was another lean year for Peru, with the aftermath of El Nino and the Asian financial crisis working its way through the economy. Political instability resulting from the presidential election and FUJIMORI's subsequent departure from office limited economic growth in 2000.
GDP: purchasing power parity - $123 billion (2000 est.)
GDP - real growth rate: 3.6% (2000 est.)
GDP - per capita: purchasing power parity - $4,550 (2000 est.)
GDP - composition by sector:
agriculture: 15%
industry: 42%
services: 43% (1999)
Population below poverty line: 49% (1994 est.)

Peru (continued)

Household income or consumption by percentage share:
lowest 10%: 1.9%
highest 10%: 34.3% (1994)
Inflation rate (consumer prices): 3.7% (2000 est.)
Labor force: 7.6 million (1996 est.)
Labor force - by occupation: agriculture, mining and quarrying, manufacturing, construction, transport, services
Unemployment rate: 7.7%; extensive underemployment (1997)
Budget:
revenues: $8.5 billion
expenditures: $9.3 billion, including capital expenditures of $2 billion (1996 est.)
Industries: mining of metals, petroleum, fishing, textiles, clothing, food processing, cement, auto assembly, steel, shipbuilding, metal fabrication
Industrial production growth rate: 8.5% (2000 est.)
Electricity - production: 18.886 billion kWh (1999)
Electricity - production by source:
fossil fuel: 23.04%
hydro: 76.43%
nuclear: 0%
other: 0.53% (1999)
Electricity - consumption: 17.565 billion kWh (1999)
Electricity - exports: 0 kWh (1999)
Electricity - imports: 1 million kWh (1999)
Agriculture - products: coffee, cotton, sugarcane, rice, wheat, potatoes, plantains, coca; poultry, beef, dairy products, wool; fish
Exports: $7 billion (f.o.b., 2000 est.)
Exports - commodities: fish and fish products, copper, zinc, gold, crude petroleum and byproducts, lead, coffee, sugar, cotton
Exports - partners: US 29%, EU 25%, Andean Community 6%, Japan 4%, Mercosur 3% (1999)
Imports: $7.4 billion (f.o.b., 2000 est.)
Imports - commodities: machinery, transport equipment, foodstuffs, petroleum, iron and steel, chemicals, pharmaceuticals
Imports - partners: US 32%, EU 21%, Andean Community 6%, Mercosur 8%, Japan 5% (1999)
Debt - external: $31 billion (2000 est.)
Economic aid - recipient: $895.1 million (1995)
Currency: nuevo sol (PEN)
Currency code: PEN
Exchange rates: nuevo sol per US dollar - 3.5230 (January 2001), 3.4900 (2000), 3.383 (1999), 2.930 (1998), 2.664 (1997), 2.453 (1996)
Fiscal year: calendar year

Communications

Telephones - main lines in use: 1.509 million (1998)
Telephones - mobile cellular: 504,995 (1998)
Telephone system:
general assessment: adequate for most requirements
domestic: nationwide microwave radio relay system and a domestic satellite system with 12 earth stations
international: satellite earth stations - 2 Intelsat (Atlantic Ocean); Pan American submarine cable
Radio broadcast stations: AM 472, FM 198, shortwave 189 (1999)
Radios: 6.65 million (1997)
Television broadcast stations: 13 (plus 112 repeaters) (1997)
Televisions: 3.06 million (1997)
Internet country code: .pe
Internet Service Providers (ISPs): 10 (2000)
Internet users: 400,000 (2000)

Transportation

Railways:
total: 1,988 km
standard gauge: 1,608 km 1.435-m gauge
narrow gauge: 380 km 0.914-m gauge
Highways:
total: 72,900 km
paved: 8,700 km
unpaved: 64,200 km (1999 est.)
Waterways: 8,808 km
note: 8,600 km of navigable tributaries of Amazon system and 208 km of Lago Titicaca
Pipelines: crude oil 800 km; natural gas and natural gas liquids 64 km
Ports and harbors: Callao, Chimbote, Ilo, Matarani, Paita, Puerto Maldonado, Salaverry, San Martin, Talara, Iquitos, Pucallpa, Yurimaguas
note: Iquitos, Pucallpa, and Yurimaguas are all on the upper reaches of the Amazon and its tributaries
Merchant marine:
total: 6 ships (1,000 GRT or over) totaling 40,623 GRT/61,769 DWT
ships by type: cargo 5, petroleum tanker 1 (2000 est.)
Airports: 233 (2000 est.)
Airports - with paved runways:
total: 46
over 3,047 m: 6
2,438 to 3,047 m: 18
1,524 to 2,437 m: 13
914 to 1,523 m: 8
under 914 m: 1 (2000 est.)
Airports - with unpaved runways:
total: 187
over 3,047 m: 1
2,438 to 3,047 m: 1
1,524 to 2,437 m: 25
914 to 1,523 m: 65
under 914 m: 95 (2000 est.)

Military

Military branches: Army (Ejercito Peruano), Navy (Marina de Guerra del Peru; includes Naval Air, Marines, and Coast Guard), Air Force (Fuerza Aerea del Peru), National Police (Policia Nacional)
Military manpower - military age: 20 years of age
Military manpower - availability:
males age 15-49: 7,205,675 (2001 est.)
Military manpower - fit for military service:
males age 15-49: 4,847,250 (2001 est.)
Military manpower - reaching military age annually:
males: 276,458 (2001 est.)
Military expenditures - dollar figure: $1 billion (FY00)
Military expenditures - percent of GDP: 1.9% (FY00)

Transnational Issues

Disputes - international: none
Illicit drugs: until 1996 the world's largest coca leaf producer, Peru reduced the area of coca under cultivation by 64% to 34,200 hectares between 1996 and the end of 2000; much of the cocaine base is shipped to neighboring Colombia for processing into cocaine for the international drug market; increasing amounts of finished cocaine, however, are being shipped to Europe or to Brazil and Bolivia for use in the Southern Cone or transshipped to world markets

Philippines

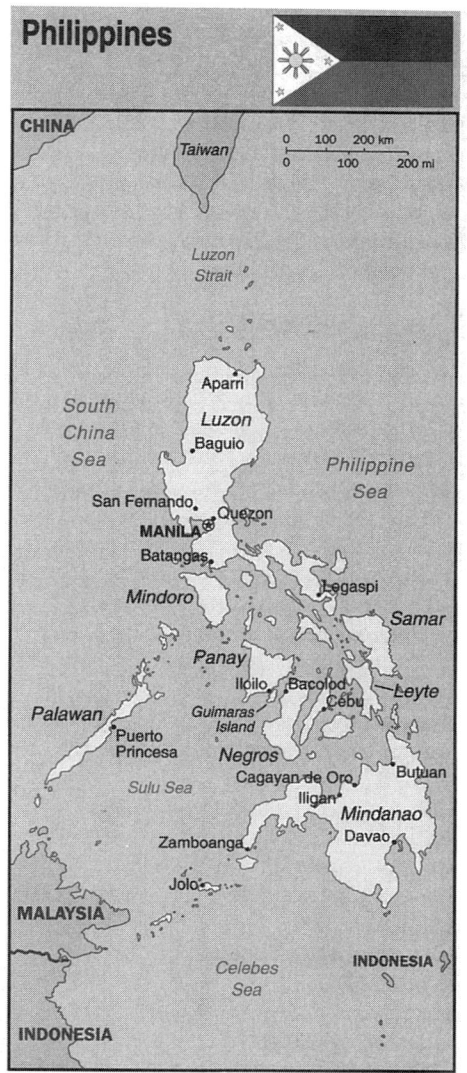

Introduction

Background: The Philippines were ceded by Spain to the US in 1898 following the Spanish-American War. They attained their independence in 1946 after being occupied by the Japanese in World War II. The 21-year rule of Ferdinand MARCOS ended in 1986 when a widespread popular rebellion forced him into exile. In 1992, the US closed down its last military bases on the islands. The Philippines has had two electoral presidential transitions since Marcos' removal by "people power." In January 2001, the Supreme Court declared Joseph ESTRADA unable to rule in view of mass resignations from his government and administered the oath of office to Vice President Gloria MACAPAGAL-ARROYO as his constitutional successor. The government continues to struggle with ongoing Muslim insurgencies in the south.

Geography

Location: Southeastern Asia, archipelago between the Philippine Sea and the South China Sea, east of Vietnam
Geographic coordinates: 13 00 N, 122 00 E
Map references: Southeast Asia
Area:
total: 300,000 sq km
land: 298,170 sq km
water: 1,830 sq km
Area - comparative: slightly larger than Arizona
Land boundaries: 0 km
Coastline: 36,289 km
Maritime claims:
continental shelf: to depth of exploitation
exclusive economic zone: 200 NM
territorial sea: irregular polygon extending up to 100 NM from coastline as defined by 1898 treaty; since late 1970s has also claimed polygonal-shaped area in South China Sea up to 285 NM in breadth
Climate: tropical marine; northeast monsoon (November to April); southwest monsoon (May to October)
Terrain: mostly mountains with narrow to extensive coastal lowlands
Elevation extremes:
lowest point: Philippine Sea 0 m
highest point: Mount Apo 2,954 m
Natural resources: timber, petroleum, nickel, cobalt, silver, gold, salt, copper
Land use:
arable land: 19%
permanent crops: 12%
permanent pastures: 4%
forests and woodland: 46%
other: 19% (1993 est.)
Irrigated land: 15,800 sq km (1993 est.)
Natural hazards: astride typhoon belt, usually affected by 15 and struck by five to six cyclonic storms per year; landslides; active volcanoes; destructive earthquakes; tsunamis
Environment - current issues: uncontrolled deforestation in watershed areas; soil erosion; air and water pollution in Manila; increasing pollution of coastal mangrove swamps which are important fish breeding grounds
Environment - international agreements:
party to: Biodiversity, Climate Change, Desertification, Endangered Species, Hazardous Wastes, Law of the Sea, Marine Dumping, Nuclear Test Ban, Ozone Layer Protection, Ship Pollution, Tropical Timber 83, Tropical Timber 94, Wetlands
signed, but not ratified: Climate Change-Kyoto Protocol

People

Population: 82,841,518 (July 2001 est.)
Age structure:
0-14 years: 36.87% (male 15,547,712; female 14,997,544)
15-64 years: 59.45% (male 24,374,849; female 24,873,595)
65 years and over: 3.68% (male 1,355,046; female 1,692,772) (2001 est.)
Population growth rate: 2.03% (2001 est.)
Birth rate: 27.37 births/1,000 population (2001 est.)
Death rate: 6.04 deaths/1,000 population (2001 est.)
Net migration rate: -1.01 migrant(s)/1,000 population (2001 est.)
Sex ratio:
at birth: 1.05 male(s)/female
under 15 years: 1.04 male(s)/female
15-64 years: 0.98 male(s)/female
65 years and over: 0.8 male(s)/female
total population: 0.99 male(s)/female (2001 est.)
Infant mortality rate: 28.7 deaths/1,000 live births (2001 est.)
Life expectancy at birth:
total population: 67.8 years
male: 64.96 years
female: 70.79 years (2001 est.)
Total fertility rate: 3.42 children born/woman (2001 est.)
HIV/AIDS - adult prevalence rate: 0.07% (1999 est.)
HIV/AIDS - people living with HIV/AIDS: 28,000 (1999 est.)
HIV/AIDS - deaths: 1,200 (1999 est.)
Nationality:
noun: Filipino(s)
adjective: Philippine
Ethnic groups: Christian Malay 91.5%, Muslim Malay 4%, Chinese 1.5%, other 3%
Religions: Roman Catholic 83%, Protestant 9%, Muslim 5%, Buddhist and other 3%
Languages: two official languages - Filipino (based on Tagalog) and English, eight major dialects - Tagalog, Cebuano, Ilocan, Hiligaynon or Ilonggo, Bicol, Waray, Pampango, and Pangasinense
Literacy:
definition: age 15 and over can read and write
total population: 94.6%
male: 95%
female: 94.3% (1995 est.)

Government

Country name:
conventional long form: Republic of the Philippines
conventional short form: Philippines
local long form: Republika ng Pilipinas
local short form: Pilipinas
Government type: republic
Capital: Manila
Administrative divisions: 73 provinces and 61 chartered cities*; Abra, Agusan del Norte, Agusan del Sur, Aklan, Albay, Angeles*, Antique, Aurora, Bacolod*, Bago*, Baguio*, Bais*, Basilan, Basilan City*, Bataan, Batanes, Batangas, Batangas City*, Benguet, Bohol, Bukidnon, Bulacan, Butuan*, Cabanatuan*, Cadiz*, Cagayan, Cagayan de Oro*, Calbayog*, Caloocan*, Camarines Norte, Camarines Sur, Camiguin, Canlaon*, Capiz, Catanduanes, Cavite, Cavite City*, Cebu, Cebu City*, Cotabato*, Dagupan*, Danao*, Dapitan*, Davao City* Davao, Davao del Sur, Davao Oriental, Dipolog*, Dumaguete*, Eastern Samar, General Santos*, Gingoog*, Ifugao, Iligan*, Ilocos Norte, Ilocos Sur, Iloilo, Iloilo City*, Iriga*, Isabela, Kalinga-Apayao, La Carlota*, Laguna, Lanao del Norte, Lanao del Sur,

Philippines (continued)

Laoag*, Lapu-Lapu*, La Union, Legaspi*, Leyte, Lipa*, Lucena*, Maguindanao, Mandaue*, Manila*, Marawi*, Marinduque, Masbate, Mindoro Occidental, Mindoro Oriental, Misamis Occidental, Misamis Oriental, Mountain, Naga*, Negros Occidental, Negros Oriental, North Cotabato, Northern Samar, Nueva Ecija, Nueva Vizcaya, Olongapo*, Ormoc*, Oroquieta*, Ozamis*, Pagadian*, Palawan, Palayan*, Pampanga, Pangasinan, Pasay*, Puerto Princesa*, Quezon, Quezon City*, Quirino, Rizal, Romblon, Roxas*, Samar, San Carlos* (in Negros Occidental), San Carlos* (in Pangasinan), San Jose*, San Pablo*, Silay*, Siquijor, Sorsogon, South Cotabato, Southern Leyte, Sultan Kudarat, Sulu, Surigao*, Surigao del Norte, Surigao del Sur, Tacloban*, Tagaytay*, Tagbilaran*, Tangub*, Tarlac, Tawitawi, Toledo*, Trece Martires*, Zambales, Zamboanga*, Zamboanga del Norte, Zamboanga del Sur

Independence: 4 July 1946 (from US)

National holiday: Independence Day (from Spain), 12 June (1898); note - 12 June 1898 is the date of independence from Spain, 4 July 1946 is the date of independence from the US

Constitution: 2 February 1987, effective 11 February 1987

Legal system: based on Spanish and Anglo-American law; accepts compulsory ICJ jurisdiction, with reservations

Suffrage: 18 years of age; universal

Executive branch:
chief of state: President Gloria MACAPAGAL-ARROYO (since 20 January 2001); note - the president is both the chief of state and head of government
head of government: President Gloria MACAPAGAL-ARROYO (since 20 January 2001); note - the president is both the chief of state and head of government
cabinet: Cabinet appointed by the president with the consent of the Commission of Appointments
elections: president and vice president elected on separate tickets by popular vote for six-year terms; election last held 11 May 1998 (next to be held 16 May 2004)
election results: results of the last presidential election - Joseph Ejercito ESTRADA elected president; percent of vote - approximately 40%; Gloria MACAPAGAL-ARROYO elected vice president; percent of vote - NA%; note - on 20 January 2001, Vice President Gloria MACAPAGAL-ARROYO was sworn in as the constitutional successor to President Joseph ESTRADA after the Supreme Court declared that President ESTRADA was unable to rule in view of the mass resignations from his government; according to the Constitution, only in cases of death, permanent disability, removal from office, or resignation of the president, can the vice president serve for the unexpired term

Legislative branch: bicameral Congress or Kongreso consists of the Senate or Senado (24 seats - one-half elected every three years; members elected by popular vote to serve six-year terms) and the House of Representatives or Kapulungan Ng Mga Kinatawan (204 seats; members elected by popular vote to serve three-year terms; note - additional members may be appointed by the president but the Constitution prohibits the House of Representatives from having more than 250 members)
elections: Senate - last held 11 May 1998 (next to be held 14 May 2001); House of Representatives - elections last held 11 May 1998 (next to be held 14 May 2001)
election results: Senate - percent of vote by party - NA%; seats by party - LAMP 12, Lakas 5, PRP 2, LP 1, other 3; note - the Senate now has only 22 members with one seat vacated when Gloria MACAPAGAL-ARROYO became vice president and another seat vacated upon a senator's death; the two seats can only be filled by election and will remain open until the next regular election in May 2001; House of Representatives - percent of vote by party - NA%; seats by party - LAMP 135, Lakas 37, LP 13, Aksyon Demokratiko 1, other 35

Judicial branch: Supreme Court (justices are appointed for four-year terms by the president on the recommendation of the Judicial and Bar Council)

Political parties and leaders: People Power Coalition or PPC includes: Aksyon Demokratiko or Democratic Action [Raul ROCO], Lakas-NUCD [Gloria MACAPAGAL-ARROYO, titular head, Teofisto GUINGONA, party president], Liberal Party or LP [Florencio ABAD], Probinsiya Muna Development Initiative or Promdi [Lito OSMENA], and Reporma Party [Renato DE VILLA]; Puwersa ng Masa (Force of the Masses) includes: Laban Ng Demokratikong Pilipino (Struggle of Filipino Democrats) or LDP [Eduardo ANGARA], Laban Ng Masang Pilipino or LAMP (Struggle of the Filipino Masses) [Joseph ESTRADA], and People's Reform Party or PRP [Miriam DEFENSOR-SANTIAGO]; Kilusang Bagong Lipunan (New Society Movement) [Imelda MARCOS]; Nacionalista Party [Jose OLIVEROS]; National People's Coalition or NPC [Eduardo COJUANGCO]

Political pressure groups and leaders: NA

International organization participation: APEC, ARF, AsDB, ASEAN, CCC, CP, ESCAP, FAO, G-24, G-77, IAEA, IBRD, ICAO, ICC, ICFTU, ICRM, IDA, IFAD, IFC, IFRCS, IHO, ILO, IMF, IMO, Inmarsat, Intelsat, Interpol, IOC, IOM, ISO, ITU, NAM, OAS (observer), OPCW, UN, UNCTAD, UNESCO, UNHCR, UNIDO, UNMIK, UNTAET, UNU, UPU, WCL, WFTU, WHO, WIPO, WMO, WToO, WTrO

Diplomatic representation in the US:
chief of mission: Ambassador (vacant); Acting Ambassador Ariel ABADILLA
chancery: 1600 Massachusetts Avenue NW, Washington, DC 20036
telephone: [1] (202) 467-9300
FAX: [1] (202) 467-9317
consulate(s) general: Chicago, Honolulu, Los Angeles, New York, San Francisco
consulate(s): San Diego

Diplomatic representation from the US:
chief of mission: Ambassador (vacant); Charge d'Affairs Michael E. MALINOWSKI
embassy: 1201 Roxas Boulevard, Ermita 1000 Manila
mailing address: FPO 96515
telephone: [63] (2) 523-1001
FAX: [63] (2) 522-4361

Flag description: two equal horizontal bands of blue (top) and red with a white equilateral triangle based on the hoist side; in the center of the triangle is a yellow sun with eight primary rays (each containing three individual rays) and in each corner of the triangle is a small yellow five-pointed star

Economy

Economy - overview: In 1998 the Philippine economy - a mixture of agriculture, light industry, and supporting services - deteriorated as a result of spillover from the Asian financial crisis and poor weather conditions. Growth fell to about -0.5% in 1998 from 5% in 1997, but recovered to about 3% in 1999 and 3.6% in 2000. The government has promised to continue its economic reforms to help the Philippines match the pace of development in the newly industrialized countries of East Asia. The strategy includes improving infrastructure, overhauling the tax system to bolster government revenues, moving toward further deregulation and privatization of the economy, and increasing trade integration with the region.

GDP: purchasing power parity - $310 billion (2000 est.)

GDP - real growth rate: 3.6% (2000 est.)

GDP - per capita: purchasing power parity - $3,800 (2000 est.)

GDP - composition by sector:
agriculture: 20%
industry: 32%
services: 48% (1997 est.)

Population below poverty line: 41% (1997 est.)

Household income or consumption by percentage share:
lowest 10%: 1.5%
highest 10%: 39.3% (1998)

Inflation rate (consumer prices): 5% (2000 est.)

Labor force: 48.1 million (2000 est.)

Labor force - by occupation: agriculture 39.8%, government and social services 19.4%, services 17.7%, manufacturing 9.8%, construction 5.8%, other 7.5% (1998 est.)

Unemployment rate: 10% (2000)

Budget:
revenues: $14.5 billion
expenditures: $12.6 billion, including capital expenditures of $NA (1998 est.)

Industries: textiles, pharmaceuticals, chemicals, wood products, food processing, electronics assembly, petroleum refining, fishing

Industrial production growth rate: 4% (2000 est.)

Electricity - production: 40.745 billion kWh (1999)

Electricity - production by source:
fossil fuel: 61.03%
hydro: 18.68%
nuclear: 0%
other: 20.29% (1999)

Philippines (continued)

Electricity - consumption: 37.893 billion kWh (1999)
Electricity - exports: 0 kWh (1999)
Electricity - imports: 0 kWh (1999)
Agriculture - products: rice, coconuts, corn, sugarcane, bananas, pineapples, mangoes; pork, eggs, beef; fish
Exports: $38 billion (f.o.b., 2000 est.)
Exports - commodities: electronic equipment, machinery and transport equipment, garments, coconut products
Exports - partners: US 34%, Japan 14%, Netherlands 8%, Singapore 6%, UK 6%, Hong Kong 4% (1998)
Imports: $35 billion (f.o.b., 2000 est.)
Imports - commodities: raw materials and intermediate goods, capital goods, consumer goods, fuels
Imports - partners: US 22%, Japan 20%, South Korea 8%, Singapore 6%, Taiwan 5%, Hong Kong 4% (1998 est.)
Debt - external: $52 billion (1999)
Economic aid - recipient: ODA, $1.1 billion (1998)
Currency: Philippine peso (PHP)
Currency code: PHP
Exchange rates: Philippine pesos per US dollar - 50.969 (January 2001), 44.192 (2000), 39.089 (1999), 40.893 (1998), 29.471 (1997), 26.216 (1996)
Fiscal year: calendar year

Communications

Telephones - main lines in use: 1.9 million (1997)
Telephones - mobile cellular: 1.959 million (1998)
Telephone system:
general assessment: good international radiotelephone and submarine cable services; domestic and interisland service adequate
domestic: domestic satellite system with 11 earth stations
international: 9 international gateways; satellite earth stations - 3 Intelsat (1 Indian Ocean and 2 Pacific Ocean); submarine cables to Hong Kong, Guam, Singapore, Taiwan, and Japan
Radio broadcast stations: AM 366, FM 290, shortwave 3 (1999)
Radios: 11.5 million (1997)
Television broadcast stations: 31 (1997)
Televisions: 3.7 million (1997)
Internet country code: .ph
Internet Service Providers (ISPs): 33 (2000)
Internet users: 500,000 (2000)

Transportation

Railways:
total: 492 km (an additional 405 km are not in operation)
narrow gauge: 492 km 1.067-m gauge (1996)
Highways:
total: 199,950 km
paved: 39,590 km
unpaved: 160,360 km (1998 est.)
Waterways: 3,219 km
note: limited to vessels with a draft of less than 1.5 m
Pipelines: petroleum products 357 km
Ports and harbors: Batangas, Cagayan de Oro, Cebu, Davao, Guimaras Island, Iligan, Iloilo, Jolo, Legaspi, Manila, Masao, Puerto Princesa, San Fernando, Subic Bay, Zamboanga
Merchant marine:
total: 459 ships (1,000 GRT or over) totaling 5,653,062 GRT/8,512,326 DWT
ships by type: bulk 149, cargo 123, chemical tanker 4, combination bulk 10, container 5, liquefied gas 13, livestock carrier 10, passenger 4, passenger/cargo 12, petroleum tanker 42, refrigerated cargo 21, roll on/roll off 17, short-sea passenger 31, specialized tanker 2, vehicle carrier 16
note: includes some foreign-owned ships registered here as a flag of convenience: Cyprus 1, Denmark 1, Hong Kong 5, Japan 14, Netherlands 1, Singapore 1, UK 1 (2000 est.)
Airports: 288 (2000 est.)
Airports - with paved runways:
total: 76
over 3,047 m: 4
2,438 to 3,047 m: 5
1,524 to 2,437 m: 28
914 to 1,523 m: 28
under 914 m: 11 (2000 est.)
Airports - with unpaved runways:
total: 212
2,438 to 3,047 m: 1
1,524 to 2,437 m: 1
914 to 1,523 m: 81
under 914 m: 129 (2000 est.)
Heliports: 1 (2000 est.)

Military

Military branches: Army, Navy (includes Coast Guard and Marine Corps), Air Force
Military manpower - military age: 20 years of age
Military manpower - availability:
males age 15-49: 21,220,191 (2001 est.)
Military manpower - fit for military service:
males age 15-49: 14,942,363 (2001 est.)
Military manpower - reaching military age annually:
males: 848,181 (2001 est.)
Military expenditures - dollar figure: $995 million (FY98)
Military expenditures - percent of GDP: 1.5% (FY98)

Transnational Issues

Disputes - international: involved in a complex dispute over the Spratly Islands with China, Malaysia, Taiwan, Vietnam, and possibly Brunei; claim to Malaysia's Sabah State has not been fully revoked
Illicit drugs: exports locally produced marijuana and hashish to East Asia, the US, and other Western markets; serves as a transit point for heroin and crystal methamphetamine

Pitcairn Islands
(overseas territory of the UK)

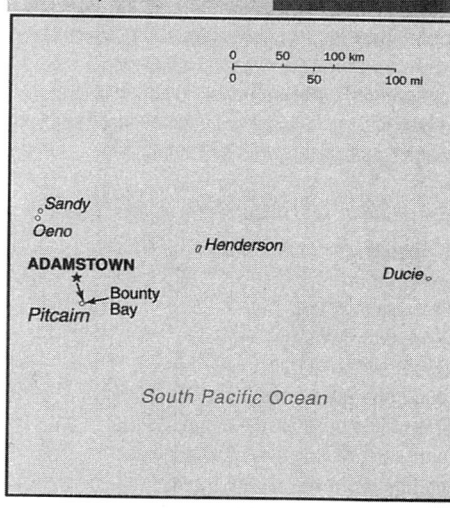

Introduction

Background: Pitcairn Island was discovered in 1767 by the British and settled in 1790 by the Bounty mutineers and their Tahitian companions. Pitcairn was the first Pacific island to become a British colony (in 1838) and today remains the last vestige of that empire in the South Pacific. Outmigration, primarily to New Zealand, has thinned the population from a peak of 233 in 1937 to about 50 today.

Geography

Location: Oceania, islands in the South Pacific Ocean, about one-half of the way from Peru to New Zealand
Geographic coordinates: 25 04 S, 130 06 W
Map references: Oceania
Area:
total: 47 sq km
land: 47 sq km
water: 0 sq km
Area - comparative: about 0.3 times the size of Washington, DC
Land boundaries: 0 km
Coastline: 51 km
Maritime claims:
exclusive economic zone: 200 NM
territorial sea: 3 NM
Climate: tropical, hot, humid; modified by southeast trade winds; rainy season (November to March)
Terrain: rugged volcanic formation; rocky coastline with cliffs
Elevation extremes:
lowest point: Pacific Ocean 0 m
highest point: Pawala Valley Ridge 347 m
Natural resources: miro trees (used for handicrafts), fish
note: manganese, iron, copper, gold, silver, and zinc have been discovered offshore
Land use:
arable land: NA%
permanent crops: NA%

Pitcairn Islands (continued)

permanent pastures: NA%
forests and woodland: NA%
other: NA%
Irrigated land: NA sq km
Natural hazards: typhoons (especially November to March)
Environment - current issues: deforestation (only a small portion of the original forest remains because of burning and clearing for settlement)

People

Population: 47 (July 2001 est.)
Age structure:
0-14 years: NA%
15-64 years: NA%
65 years and over: NA%
Population growth rate: -2.08% (2001 est.)
Birth rate: NA births/1,000 population
Death rate: NA deaths/1,000 population
Net migration rate: NA migrant(s)/1,000 population
Infant mortality rate: NA deaths/1,000 live births
Life expectancy at birth:
total population: NA years
male: NA years
female: NA years
Total fertility rate: NA children born/woman
HIV/AIDS - adult prevalence rate: NA%
HIV/AIDS - people living with HIV/AIDS: NA
HIV/AIDS - deaths: NA
Nationality:
noun: Pitcairn Islander(s)
adjective: Pitcairn Islander
Ethnic groups: descendants of the Bounty mutineers and their Tahitian wives
Religions: Seventh-Day Adventist 100%
Languages: English (official), Pitcairnese (mixture of an 18th century English dialect and a Tahitian dialect)

Government

Country name:
conventional long form: Pitcairn, Henderson, Ducie, and Oeno Islands
conventional short form: Pitcairn Islands
Dependency status: overseas territory of the UK
Government type: NA
Capital: Adamstown
Administrative divisions: none (overseas territory of the UK)
Independence: none (overseas territory of the UK)
National holiday: Birthday of Queen ELIZABETH II, second Saturday in June (1926)
Constitution: 1838; reformed 1904 with additional reforms in 1940; further refined by the Local Government Ordinance of 1964
Legal system: local island by-laws
Suffrage: 18 years of age; universal with three years residency
Executive branch:
chief of state: Queen ELIZABETH II (since 6 February 1952), represented by UK High Commissioner to New Zealand and Governor (nonresident) of the Pitcairn Islands Martin WILLIAMS (since NA May 1998); Commissioner (nonresident) Leon SALT (since NA; is the liaison person between the governor and the Island Council)
head of government: Island Magistrate and Chairman of the Island Council Jay WARREN (since NA)
cabinet: NA
elections: the monarch is hereditary; high commissioner and commissioner appointed by the monarch; island magistrate elected every three years in December by popular vote for a three-year term; last election held NA December 1999 (next to be held NA December 2002)
election results: Lea BROWN elected island magistrate; percent of vote - NA%
Legislative branch: unicameral Island Council (10 seats - 6 elected by popular vote, 1 appointed by the 6 elected members, 2 appointed by the governor, and 1 seat for the Island Secretary; members serve one-year terms)
elections: take place each December; last held NA December 2000 (next to be held NA December 2001)
election results: percent of vote - NA%; seats - all independents
Judicial branch: Island Court (island magistrate presides over the court and is elected every three years)
Political parties and leaders: none
Political pressure groups and leaders: none
International organization participation: SPC
Diplomatic representation in the US: none (overseas territory of the UK)
Diplomatic representation from the US: none (overseas territory of the UK)
Flag description: blue with the flag of the UK in the upper hoist-side quadrant and the Pitcairn Islander coat of arms centered on the outer half of the flag; the coat of arms is yellow, green, and light blue with a shield featuring a yellow anchor

Economy

Economy - overview: The inhabitants of this tiny economy exist on fishing, subsistence farming, handicrafts, and postage stamps. The fertile soil of the valleys produces a wide variety of fruits and vegetables, including citrus, sugarcane, watermelons, bananas, yams, and beans. Bartering is an important part of the economy. The major sources of revenue are the sale of postage stamps to collectors and the sale of handicrafts to passing ships.
GDP: purchasing power parity - $NA
GDP - real growth rate: NA%
GDP - per capita: purchasing power parity - $NA
GDP - composition by sector:
agriculture: NA%
industry: NA%
services: NA%
Population below poverty line: NA%
Household income or consumption by percentage share:
lowest 10%: NA%
highest 10%: NA%
Inflation rate (consumer prices): NA%
Labor force: 12 able-bodied men (1997)
Labor force - by occupation: no business community in the usual sense; some public works; subsistence farming and fishing
Unemployment rate: NA%
Budget:
revenues: $729,884
expenditures: $878,119, including capital expenditures of $NA (FY94/95 est.)
Industries: postage stamps, handicrafts
Industrial production growth rate: NA%
Electricity - production: NA kWh; note - electric power is provided by a small diesel-powered generator
Electricity - consumption: NA kWh
Agriculture - products: wide variety of fruits and vegetables, goats, chickens
Exports: $NA
Exports - commodities: fruits, vegetables, curios, stamps
Exports - partners: NA
Imports: $NA
Imports - commodities: fuel oil, machinery, building materials, flour, sugar, other foodstuffs
Imports - partners: NA
Debt - external: $NA
Economic aid - recipient: $NA
Currency: New Zealand dollar (NZD)
Currency code: NZD
Exchange rates: New Zealand dollars per US dollar - 2.2502 (January 2001), 2.1863 (2000), 1.8886 (1999), 1.8629 (1998), 1.5083 (1997), 1.4543 (1996)
Fiscal year: 1 April - 31 March

Communications

Telephones - main lines in use: 1 (there are 17 telephones on one party line) (1997)
Telephone system:
general assessment: only party line telephone service is available for this small, closely related community
domestic: party line service only
international: radiotelephone
Radio broadcast stations: AM 1, FM 0, shortwave 0 (1998)
Radios: NA
Television broadcast stations: 0 (1997)
Televisions: NA
Internet country code: .pn
Internet Service Providers (ISPs): NA
Internet users: NA

Transportation

Railways: 0 km
Highways:
total: 6.4 km
paved: 0 km
unpaved: 6.4 km
Waterways: none
Ports and harbors: Bounty Bay
Merchant marine: none (2000 est.)
Airports: none

Pitcairn Islands (continued)

Military

Military - note: defense is the responsibility of the UK

Transnational Issues

Disputes - international: none

Poland

Introduction

Background: Poland gained its independence in 1918 only to be overrun by Germany and the Soviet Union in World War II. It became a Soviet satellite country following the war, but one that was comparatively tolerant and progressive. Labor turmoil in 1980 led to the formation of the independent trade union "Solidarity" that over time became a political force and by 1990 had swept parliamentary elections and the presidency. A "shock therapy" program during the early 1990s enabled the country to transform its economy into one of the most robust in Central Europe, boosting hopes for acceptance to the EU. Poland joined the NATO alliance in 1999.

Geography

Location: Central Europe, east of Germany
Geographic coordinates: 52 00 N, 20 00 E
Map references: Europe
Area:
total: 312,685 sq km
land: 304,465 sq km
water: 8,220 sq km
Area - comparative: slightly smaller than New Mexico
Land boundaries:
total: 2,888 km
border countries: Belarus 605 km, Czech Republic 658 km, Germany 456 km, Lithuania 91 km, Russia (Kaliningrad Oblast) 206 km, Slovakia 444 km, Ukraine 428 km
Coastline: 491 km
Maritime claims:
exclusive economic zone: defined by international treaties
territorial sea: 12 NM
Climate: temperate with cold, cloudy, moderately severe winters with frequent precipitation; mild summers with frequent showers and thundershowers
Terrain: mostly flat plain; mountains along southern border
Elevation extremes:
lowest point: Raczki Elblaskie -2 m
highest point: Rysy 2,499 m
Natural resources: coal, sulfur, copper, natural gas, silver, lead, salt, arable land
Land use:
arable land: 47%
permanent crops: 1%
permanent pastures: 13%
forests and woodland: 29%
other: 10% (1993 est.)
Irrigated land: 1,000 sq km (1993 est.)
Natural hazards: NA
Environment - current issues: situation has improved since 1989 due to decline in heavy industry and increased environmental concern by postcommunist governments; air pollution nonetheless remains serious because of sulfur dioxide emissions from coal-fired power plants, and the resulting acid rain has caused forest damage; water pollution from industrial and municipal sources is also a problem, as is disposal of hazardous wastes
Environment - international agreements:
party to: Air Pollution, Antarctic-Environmental Protocol, Antarctic-Marine Living Resources, Antarctic Seals, Antarctic Treaty, Biodiversity, Climate Change, Endangered Species, Environmental Modification, Hazardous Wastes, Law of the Sea, Marine Dumping, Nuclear Test Ban, Ozone Layer Protection, Ship Pollution, Wetlands
signed, but not ratified: Air Pollution-Nitrogen Oxides, Air Pollution-Persistent Organic Pollutants, Air Pollution-Sulphur 94, Climate Change-Kyoto Protocol
Geography - note: historically, an area of conflict because of flat terrain and the lack of natural barriers on the North European Plain

People

Population: 38,633,912 (July 2001 est.)
Age structure:
0-14 years: 18.39% (male 3,640,451; female 3,463,604)
15-64 years: 69.17% (male 13,288,471; female 13,434,753)
65 years and over: 12.44% (male 1,836,816; female 2,969,817) (2001 est.)
Population growth rate: -0.03% (2001 est.)
Birth rate: 10.2 births/1,000 population (2001 est.)
Death rate: 9.98 deaths/1,000 population (2001 est.)
Net migration rate: -0.49 migrant(s)/1,000 population (2001 est.)
Sex ratio:
at birth: 1.06 male(s)/female
under 15 years: 1.05 male(s)/female
15-64 years: 0.99 male(s)/female
65 years and over: 0.62 male(s)/female
total population: 0.94 male(s)/female (2001 est.)
Infant mortality rate: 9.39 deaths/1,000 live births (2001 est.)
Life expectancy at birth:
total population: 73.42 years

Poland (continued)

male: 69.26 years
female: 77.82 years (2001 est.)
Total fertility rate: 1.37 children born/woman (2001 est.)
HIV/AIDS - adult prevalence rate: 0.07% (1999 est.)
HIV/AIDS - people living with HIV/AIDS: NA
HIV/AIDS - deaths: less than 100 (1999 est.)
Nationality:
noun: Pole(s)
adjective: Polish
Ethnic groups: Polish 97.6%, German 1.3%, Ukrainian 0.6%, Byelorussian 0.5% (1990 est.)
Religions: Roman Catholic 95% (about 75% practicing), Eastern Orthodox, Protestant, and other 5%
Languages: Polish
Literacy:
definition: age 15 and over can read and write
total population: 99%
male: 99%
female: 98% (1978 est.)

Government

Country name:
conventional long form: Republic of Poland
conventional short form: Poland
local long form: Rzeczpospolita Polska
local short form: Polska
Government type: republic
Capital: Warsaw
Administrative divisions: 16 provinces (wojewodztwa, singular - wojewodztwo); Dolnoslaskie, Kujawsko-Pomorskie, Lodzkie, Lubelskie, Lubuskie, Malopolskie, Mazowieckie, Opolskie, Podkarpackie, Podlaskie, Pomorskie, Slaskie, Swietokrzyskie, Warminsko-Mazurskie, Wielkopolskie, Zachodniopomorskie
Independence: 11 November 1918 (independent republic proclaimed)
National holiday: Constitution Day, 3 May (1791)
Constitution: 16 October 1997; adopted by the National Assembly 2 April 1997; passed by national referendum 23 May 1997
Legal system: mixture of Continental (Napoleonic) civil law and holdover communist legal theory; changes being gradually introduced as part of broader democratization process; limited judicial review of legislative acts although under the new constitution, the Constitutional Tribunal ruling will become final as of October 1999; court decisions can be appealed to the European Court of Justice in Strasbourg
Suffrage: 18 years of age; universal
Executive branch:
chief of state: President Aleksander KWASNIEWSKI (since 23 December 1995)
head of government: Prime Minister Jerzy BUZEK - Solidarity Electoral Union - (since 31 October 1997), Deputy Prime Ministers Janusz STEINHOFF (since 12 June 2000), Longin KOMOLOWSKI (since 19 October 1999)
cabinet: Council of Ministers responsible to the prime minister and the Sejm; the prime minister proposes, the president appoints, and the Sejm approves the Council of Ministers
elections: president elected by popular vote for a five-year term; election held 8 October 2000 (next to be held NA October 2005); prime minister and deputy prime ministers appointed by the president and confirmed by the Sejm
election results: Aleksander KWASNIEWSKI reelected president; percent of popular vote - Aleksander KWASNIEWSKI 53.9%, Andrzj OLECHOWSKI 17.3%, Marian KRZAKLEWSKI 15.6%, Lech WALESA 1%
Legislative branch: bicameral National Assembly or Zgromadzenie Narodowe consists of the Sejm (460 seats; members are elected under a complex system of proportional representation to serve four-year terms) and the Senate or Senat (100 seats; members are elected by a majority vote on a provincial basis to serve four-year terms)
elections: Sejm elections last held 21 September 1997 (next to be held by NA September 2001); Senate - last held 21 September 1997 (next to be held by NA September 2001)
election results: Sejm - percent of vote by party - AWS 33.8%, SLD 27.1%, UW 13.4%, PSL 7.3%, ROP 5.6%, MNSO 0.4%, other 12.4%; seats by party - AWS 201, SLD 164, UW 60, PSL 27, ROP 6, MNSO 2; Senate - percent of vote by party - NA%; seats by party - AWS 51, SLD 28, UW 8, ROP 5, PSL 3, independents 5; note - seats by party in the Sejm as of February 2001: AWS 175, SLD 161, UW 49, PSL 26, PP 6, KdP 7, ROP-PC 4, independents 31, one seat vacant
note: two seats are assigned to ethnic minority parties
Judicial branch: Supreme Court (judges are appointed by the president on the recommendation of the National Council of the Judiciary for an indefinite period); Constitutional Tribunal (judges are chosen by the Sejm for nine-year terms)
Political parties and leaders: Coalition for Poland or KdP [first name unknown GRABOWSKI]; Confederation for an Independent Poland-Patriotic Camp or KPN-OP (KPN-Fatherland or KPN-O is a small group within the KPN-OP) [Michal JANISZEWSKI]; Democratic Left Alliance or SLD (Social Democracy of Poland) [Leszek MILLER]; Freedom Union or UW [Bronislaw GEREMEK]; German Minority of Lower Silesia or MNSO [Henryk KROLL]; Movement for the Reconstruction of Poland or ROP-PC [Jan OLSZEWSKI]; Polish Accord or PP [Jan LOPUSZANSKI]; Polish Peasant Party or PSL [Jaroslaw KALINOWSKI]; Polish Socialist Party or PPS [Piotr IKONOWICZ]; Solidarity Electoral Action or AWS (includes RS-AWS and Solidarity) [Marian KRZAKLEWSKI]; Social Movement-Solidarity Electoral Action or RS-AWS [Jerzy BUZEK]
Political pressure groups and leaders: All Poland Trade Union Alliance or OPZZ (trade union); Roman Catholic Church; Solidarity (trade union)

International organization participation: ACCT (observer), Australia Group, BIS, BSEC (observer), CBSS, CCC, CE, CEI, CERN, EAPC, EBRD, ECE, EU (applicant), FAO, IAEA, IBRD, ICAO, ICC, ICFTU, ICRM, IDA, IEA (observer), IFC, IFRCS, IHO, ILO, IMF, IMO, Inmarsat, Intelsat, Interpol, IOC, IOM, ISO, ITU, MINURSO, MONUC, NAM (guest), NATO, NSG, OAS (observer), OECD, OPCW, OSCE, PCA, PFP, UN, UNCTAD, UNDOF, UNESCO, UNHCR, UNIDO, UNIFIL, UNIKOM, UNMEE, UNMIBH, UNMIK, UNMOP, UNMOT, UNOMIG, UPU, WCL, WEU (associate), WFTU, WHO, WIPO, WMO, WToO, WTrO, ZC
Diplomatic representation in the US:
chief of mission: Ambassador Przemyslaw GRUDZINSKI
chancery: 2640 16th Street NW, Washington, DC 20009
telephone: [1] (202) 234-3800 through 3802
FAX: [1] (202) 328-6271
consulate(s) general: Chicago, Los Angeles, and New York
Diplomatic representation from the US:
chief of mission: Ambassador Christopher R. HILL
embassy: Aleje Ujazdowskie 29/31 00-054, Warsaw P1
mailing address: American Embassy Warsaw, US Department of State, Washington, DC 20521-5010 (pouch)
telephone: [48] (22) 628-30-41
FAX: [48] (22) 628-82-98
consulate(s) general: Krakow
Flag description: two equal horizontal bands of white (top) and red; similar to the flags of Indonesia and Monaco which are red (top) and white

Economy

Economy - overview: Poland has steadfastly pursued a policy of liberalizing the economy and today stands out as one of the most successful and open transition economies. GDP growth has been strong and steady since 1992 - the best performance in the region. The privatization of small and medium state-owned companies and a liberal law on establishing new firms has allowed for the rapid development of a vibrant private sector. In contrast, Poland's large agricultural sector remains handicapped by structural problems, surplus labor, inefficient small farms, and lack of investment. Restructuring and privatization of "sensitive sectors" (e.g., coal, steel, railroads, and energy) has begun. Structural reforms in health care, education, the pension system, and state administration have resulted in larger than expected fiscal pressures. Further progress in public finance depends mainly on privatization of Poland's remaining state sector. The government's determination to enter the EU as soon as possible affects most aspects of its economic policies. Improving Poland's outsized current account deficit and reining in inflation are priorities. Warsaw leads the region in foreign investment and needs a continued large inflow.

Poland (continued)

GDP: purchasing power parity - $327.5 billion (2000 est.)
GDP - real growth rate: 4.8% (2000 est.)
GDP - per capita: purchasing power parity - $8,500 (2000 est.)
GDP - composition by sector:
agriculture: 3.8%
industry: 36.6%
services: 59.6% (1999)
Population below poverty line: 18.4% (2000 est.)
Household income or consumption by percentage share:
lowest 10%: 3%
highest 10%: 26.3% (1996)
Inflation rate (consumer prices): 10.2% (2000 est.)
Labor force: 17.2 million (1999 est.)
Labor force - by occupation: industry 22.1%, agriculture 27.5%, services 50.4% (1999)
Unemployment rate: 12% (1999)
Budget:
revenues: $49.6 billion
expenditures: $52.3 billion, including capital expenditures of $NA (1999)
Industries: machine building, iron and steel, coal mining, chemicals, shipbuilding, food processing, glass, beverages, textiles
Industrial production growth rate: 4.3% (1999)
Electricity - production: 134.351 billion kWh (1999)
Electricity - production by source:
fossil fuel: 96.43%
hydro: 3.16%
nuclear: 0%
other: 0.41% (1999)
Electricity - consumption: 120.007 billion kWh (1999)
Electricity - exports: 8.43 billion kWh (1999)
Electricity - imports: 3.491 billion kWh (1999)
Agriculture - products: potatoes, fruits, vegetables, wheat; poultry, eggs, pork
Exports: $28.4 billion (f.o.b., 2000)
Exports - commodities: machinery and transport equipment 30.2%, intermediate manufactured goods 25.5%, miscellaneous manufactured goods 20.9%, food and live animals 8.5% (1999)
Exports - partners: Germany 36.1%, Italy 6.5%, Netherlands 5.3%, France 4.8%, UK 4.0%, Czech Republic 3.8% (1999)
Imports: $42.7 billion (f.o.b., 2000)
Imports - commodities: machinery and transport equipment 38.2%, intermediate manufactured goods 20.8%, chemicals 14.3%, miscellaneous manufactured goods 9.5% (1999)
Imports - partners: Germany 25.2%, Italy 9.4%, France 6.8%, Russia 5.8%, UK 4.6%, Netherlands 3.7% (1999)
Debt - external: $57 billion (2000)
Economic aid - recipient: $NA
Currency: zloty (PLN)
Currency code: PLN
Exchange rates: zlotych per US dollar - 4.3126 (December 2000), 4.3461 (2000), 3.9671 (1999), 3.4754 (1998), 3.2793 (1997), 2.6961 (1996)
Fiscal year: calendar year

Communications

Telephones - main lines in use: 8.07 million (1998)
Telephones - mobile cellular: 1.78 million (1998)
Telephone system:
general assessment: underdeveloped and outmoded system; government aimed to have 10 million telephones in service by 2000; the process of partial privatization of the state-owned telephone monopoly has begun; in 1998 there were over 2 million applicants on the waiting list for telephone service
domestic: cable, open wire, and microwave radio relay; 3 cellular networks; local exchanges 56.6% digital
international: satellite earth stations - 2 Intelsat, NA Eutelsat, 2 Inmarsat (Atlantic and Indian Ocean regions), and 1 Intersputnik (Atlantic Ocean region)
Radio broadcast stations: AM 14, FM 777, shortwave 1 (1998)
Radios: 20.2 million (1997)
Television broadcast stations: 179 (plus 256 repeaters) (September 1995)
Televisions: 13.05 million (1997)
Internet country code: .pl
Internet Service Providers (ISPs): 19 (2000)
Internet users: 2.8 million (2000)

Transportation

Railways:
total: 23,420 km
broad gauge: 646 km 1.524-m gauge
standard gauge: 21,639 km 1.435-m gauge (11,626 km electrified; 8,978 km double track)
narrow gauge: 1,135 km various gauges including 1.000-m, 0.785-m, 0.750-m, and 0.600-m (1998)
Highways:
total: 381,046 km
paved: 249,966 km (including 268 km of expressways)
unpaved: 131,080 km (1998)
Waterways: 3,812 km (navigable rivers and canals) (1996)
Pipelines: crude oil and petroleum products 2,280 km; natural gas 17,000 km (1996)
Ports and harbors: Gdansk, Gdynia, Gliwice, Kolobrzeg, Szczecin, Swinoujscie, Ustka, Warsaw, Wroclaw
Merchant marine:
total: 46 ships (1,000 GRT or over) totaling 943,540 GRT/1,532,694 DWT
ships by type: bulk 41, cargo 2, chemical tanker 1, roll on/roll off 1, short-sea passenger 1 (2000 est.)
Airports: 122 (2000 est.)
Airports - with paved runways:
total: 83
over 3,047 m: 3
2,438 to 3,047 m: 29
1,524 to 2,437 m: 42
914 to 1,523 m: 6
under 914 m: 3 (2000 est.)

Airports - with unpaved runways:
total: 39
2,438 to 3,047 m: 1
1,524 to 2,437 m: 4
914 to 1,523 m: 13
under 914 m: 21 (2000 est.)
Heliports: 3 (2000 est.)

Military

Military branches: Army, Navy, Air and Air Defense Force
Military manpower - military age: 19 years of age
Military manpower - availability:
males age 15-49: 10,447,931 (2001 est.)
Military manpower - fit for military service:
males age 15-49: 8,139,245 (2001 est.)
Military manpower - reaching military age annually:
males: 344,781 (2001 est.)
Military expenditures - dollar figure: $3.17 billion (FY00)
Military expenditures - percent of GDP: 1.95% (FY00)

Transnational Issues

Disputes - international: none
Illicit drugs: major illicit producer of amphetamine for the international market; minor transshipment point for Asian and Latin American illicit drugs to Western Europe

Portugal

Introduction

Background: Following its heyday as a world power during the 15th and 16th centuries, Portugal lost much of its wealth and status with the destruction of Lisbon in a 1755 earthquake, occupation during the Napoleonic Wars, and the independence in 1822 of Brazil as a colony. A 1910 revolution deposed the monarchy; for most of the next six decades repressive governments ran the country. In 1974, a left-wing military coup installed broad democratic reforms. The following year Portugal granted independence to all of its African colonies. Portugal entered the EC in 1985.

Geography

Location: Southwestern Europe, bordering the North Atlantic Ocean, west of Spain
Geographic coordinates: 39 30 N, 8 00 W
Map references: Europe
Area:
total: 92,391 sq km
land: 91,951 sq km
water: 440 sq km
note: includes Azores and Madeira Islands
Area - comparative: slightly smaller than Indiana
Land boundaries:
total: 1,214 km
border countries: Spain 1,214 km
Coastline: 1,793 km
Maritime claims:
contiguous zone: 24 NM
continental shelf: 200-m depth or to the depth of exploitation
exclusive economic zone: 200 NM
territorial sea: 12 NM
Climate: maritime temperate; cool and rainy in north, warmer and drier in south
Terrain: mountainous north of the Tagus River, rolling plains in south
Elevation extremes:
lowest point: Atlantic Ocean 0 m
highest point: Ponta do Pico (Pico or Pico Alto) on Ilha do Pico in the Azores 2,351 m
Natural resources: fish, forests (cork), tungsten, iron ore, uranium ore, marble, arable land, hydro power
Land use:
arable land: 26%
permanent crops: 9%
permanent pastures: 9%
forests and woodland: 36%
other: 20% (1993 est.)
Irrigated land: 6,300 sq km (1993 est.)
Natural hazards: Azores subject to severe earthquakes
Environment - current issues: soil erosion; air pollution caused by industrial and vehicle emissions; water pollution, especially in coastal areas
Environment - international agreements:
party to: Air Pollution, Biodiversity, Climate Change, Desertification, Endangered Species, Hazardous Wastes, Law of the Sea, Marine Dumping, Marine Life Conservation, Ozone Layer Protection, Ship Pollution, Tropical Timber 83, Tropical Timber 94, Wetlands
signed, but not ratified: Air Pollution-Persistent Organic Pollutants, Air Pollution-Volatile Organic Compounds, Climate Change-Kyoto Protocol, Environmental Modification, Nuclear Test Ban
Geography - note: Azores and Madeira Islands occupy strategic locations along western sea approaches to Strait of Gibraltar

People

Population: 10,066,253 (July 2001 est.)
Age structure:
0-14 years: 16.96% (male 877,379; female 830,242)
15-64 years: 67.42% (male 3,321,473; female 3,465,481)
65 years and over: 15.62% (male 637,207; female 934,471) (2001 est.)
Population growth rate: 0.18% (2001 est.)
Birth rate: 11.51 births/1,000 population (2001 est.)
Death rate: 10.21 deaths/1,000 population (2001 est.)
Net migration rate: 0.5 migrant(s)/1,000 population (2001 est.)
Sex ratio:
at birth: 1.07 male(s)/female
under 15 years: 1.06 male(s)/female
15-64 years: 0.96 male(s)/female
65 years and over: 0.68 male(s)/female
total population: 0.92 male(s)/female (2001 est.)
Infant mortality rate: 5.94 deaths/1,000 live births (2001 est.)
Life expectancy at birth:
total population: 75.94 years
male: 72.44 years
female: 79.68 years (2001 est.)
Total fertility rate: 1.48 children born/woman (2001 est.)
HIV/AIDS - adult prevalence rate: 0.74% (1999 est.)
HIV/AIDS - people living with HIV/AIDS: 36,000 (1999 est.)
HIV/AIDS - deaths: 280 (1999 est.)
Nationality:
noun: Portuguese (singular and plural)
adjective: Portuguese
Ethnic groups: homogeneous Mediterranean stock; citizens of black African descent who immigrated to mainland during decolonization number less than 100,000
Religions: Roman Catholic 94%, Protestant (1995)
Languages: Portuguese
Literacy:
definition: age 15 and over can read and write
total population: 87.4%
male: NA%
female: NA%

Government

Country name:
conventional long form: Portuguese Republic
conventional short form: Portugal
local long form: Republica Portuguesa
local short form: Portugal
Government type: parliamentary democracy
Capital: Lisbon
Administrative divisions: 18 districts (distritos, singular - distrito) and 2 autonomous regions* (regioes autonomas, singular - regiao autonoma); Aveiro, Acores (Azores)*, Beja, Braga, Braganca, Castelo Branco, Coimbra, Evora, Faro, Guarda, Leiria, Lisboa, Madeira*, Portalegre, Porto, Santarem, Setubal, Viana do Castelo, Vila Real, Viseu
Independence: 1140 (independent republic proclaimed 5 October 1910)
National holiday: Portugal Day, 10 June (1580)
Constitution: 25 April 1976, revised 30 October 1982, 1 June 1989, 5 November 1992, and 3 September 1997
Legal system: civil law system; the Constitutional Tribunal reviews the constitutionality of legislation; accepts compulsory ICJ jurisdiction, with reservations
Suffrage: 18 years of age; universal
Executive branch:
chief of state: President Jorge SAMPAIO (since 9 March 1996)

Portugal (continued)

head of government: Prime Minister Antonio Manuel de Oliviera GUTERRES (since 28 October 1995)
cabinet: Council of Ministers appointed by the president on the recommendation of the prime minister
note: there is also a Council of State that acts as a consultative body to the president
elections: president elected by popular vote for a five-year term; election last held 14 January 2001 (next to be held NA January 2006); following legislative elections, the leader of the majority party or leader of a majority coalition is usually appointed prime minister by the president
election results: Jorge SAMPAIO re-elected president; percent of vote - Jorge SAMPAIO (Socialist) 55.8%, Joaquim FERREIRA Do Amaral (Social Democrat) 34.5%, Antonio ABREU (Communist) 5.1%
Legislative branch: unicameral Assembly of the Republic or Assembleia da Republica (230 seats; members are elected by popular vote to serve four-year terms)
elections: last held 10 October 1999 (next to be held by NA October 2003)
election results: percent of vote by party - NA%; seats by party - PS 115, PSD 81, PCP 15, PP 15, PEV 2, The Left Bloc 2
Judicial branch: Supreme Court or Supremo Tribunal de Justica (judges appointed for life by the Conselho Superior da Magistratura)
Political parties and leaders: The Greens or PEV [leader NA]; Popular Party or PP [Paulo PORTAS]; Portuguese Communist Party/United Democratic Coalition or PCP/CDU [Carlos CARVALHAS]; Portuguese Socialist Party or PS [Antonio GUTERRES]; Social Democratic Party or PSD [leader vacant]; The Left Bloc [no leader]
Political pressure groups and leaders: NA
International organization participation: AfDB, Australia Group, BIS, CCC, CE, CERN, EAPC, EBRD, ECE, ECLAC, EIB, EMU, ESA, EU, FAO, IADB, IAEA, IBRD, ICAO, ICC, ICFTU, ICRM, IDA, IEA, IFAD, IFC, IFRCS, IHO, ILO, IMF, IMO, Inmarsat, Intelsat, Interpol, IOC, IOM, ISO, ITU, LAIA (observer), MINURSO, NAM (guest), NATO, NEA, NSG, OAS (observer), OECD, OPCW, OSCE, PCA, UN, UNCTAD, UNESCO, UNIDO, UNMIBH, UNMIK, UNMOP, UNTAET, UPU, WCL, WEU, WFTU, WHO, WIPO, WMO, WToO, WTrO, ZC
Diplomatic representation in the US:
chief of mission: Ambassador Joao Alberto Bacelar ROCHA PARIS
chancery: 2125 Kalorama Road NW, Washington, DC 20008
telephone: [1] (202) 328-8610
FAX: [1] (202) 462-3726
consulate(s) general: Boston, New York, Newark (New Jersey), and San Francisco
consulate(s): Los Angeles, New Bedford (Massachusetts), Providence (Rhode Island)
Diplomatic representation from the US:
chief of mission: Ambassador Gerald S. MCGOWAN
embassy: Avenida das Forcas Armadas, 1600 Lisbon
mailing address: PSC 83, APO AE 09726
telephone: [351] (21) 727-3300
FAX: [351] (21) 726-9109
consulate(s): Ponta Delgada (Azores)
Flag description: two vertical bands of green (hoist side, two-fifths) and red (three-fifths) with the Portuguese coat of arms centered on the dividing line

Economy

Economy - overview: Portugal is an upcoming capitalist economy with a per capita GDP two-thirds that of the four big West European economies. The country qualified for the European Monetary Union (EMU) in 1998 and joined with 10 other European countries in launching the euro on 1 January 1999. The year 2000 was marked by moderation in growth, inflation, and unemployment. The country continues to run a sizable trade deficit. The government is working to reform the tax system, to modernize capital plant, and to increase the country's competitiveness in the increasingly integrated world markets. Growth is expected to fall off slightly in 2001. Improvement in the education sector is critical to the long-run catch-up process.
GDP: purchasing power parity - $159 billion (2000 est.)
GDP - real growth rate: 2.7% (2000 est.)
GDP - per capita: purchasing power parity - $15,800 (2000 est.)
GDP - composition by sector:
agriculture: 4%
industry: 36%
services: 60% (1999 est.)
Population below poverty line: NA%
Household income or consumption by percentage share:
lowest 10%: 3.1%
highest 10%: 28.4% (1995 est.)
Inflation rate (consumer prices): 2.8% (2000 est.)
Labor force: 5 million (1999)
Labor force - by occupation: services 60%, industry 30%, agriculture 10% (1999 est.)
Unemployment rate: 4.3% (2000 est.)
Budget:
revenues: $48.6 billion
expenditures: $50.7 billion, including capital expenditures of $7.7 billion (2000 est.)
Industries: textiles and footwear; wood pulp, paper, and cork; metalworking; oil refining; chemicals; fish canning; wine; tourism
Industrial production growth rate: 2.9% (1999 est.)
Electricity - production: 41.696 billion kWh (1999)
Electricity - production by source:
fossil fuel: 79.97%
hydro: 17.25%
nuclear: 0%
other: 2.78% (1999)
Electricity - consumption: 37.915 billion kWh (1999)
Electricity - exports: 4.49 billion kWh (1999)
Electricity - imports: 3.628 billion kWh (1999)
Agriculture - products: grain, potatoes, olives, grapes; sheep, cattle, goats, poultry, beef, dairy products
Exports: $26.1 billion (f.o.b., 2000 est.)
Exports - commodities: clothing and footwear, machinery, chemicals, cork and paper products, hides
Exports - partners: EU 83% (Germany 20%, Spain 18%, France 14%, UK 12%, Netherlands 5%, Benelux 5%, Italy), US 5% (1999)
Imports: $41 billion (f.o.b., 2000 est.)
Imports - commodities: machinery and transport equipment, chemicals, petroleum, textiles, agricultural products
Imports - partners: EU 78% (Spain 25%, Germany 15%, France 11%, Italy 8%, UK 7%, Netherlands 5%), US 3%, Japan 3% (1998)
Debt - external: $13.1 billion (1997 est.)
Economic aid - donor: ODA, $271 million (1995)
Currency: Portuguese escudo (PTE); euro (EUR)
note: on 1 January 1999, the EU introduced the euro as a common currency that is now being used by financial institutions in Portugal at a fixed rate of 200.482 Portuguese escudos per euro and will replace the local currency for all transactions in 2002
Currency code: PTE; EUR
Exchange rates: euros per US dollar - 1.0659 (January 2001), 1.0854 (2000), 0.9386 (1999); Portuguese escudos per US dollar - 180.10 (1998), 175.31 (1997), 154.24 (1996)
Fiscal year: calendar year

Communications

Telephones - main lines in use: 5.3 million (end 1998)
Telephones - mobile cellular: 3,074,194 (1999)
Telephone system:
general assessment: undergoing rapid development in recent years, Portugal's telephone system, by the end of 1998, achieved a state-of-the-art network with broadband, high-speed capabilities and a main line telephone density of 53%
domestic: integrated network of coaxial cables, open wire, microwave radio relay, and domestic satellite earth stations
international: 6 submarine cables; satellite earth stations - 3 Intelsat (2 Atlantic Ocean and 1 Indian Ocean), NA Eutelsat; tropospheric scatter to Azores; note - an earth station for Inmarsat (Atlantic Ocean region) is planned
Radio broadcast stations: AM 47, FM 172 (many are repeaters), shortwave 2 (1998)
Radios: 3.02 million (1997)
Television broadcast stations: 62 (plus 166 repeaters)
note: includes Azores and Madeira Islands (1995)
Televisions: 3.31 million (1997)
Internet country code: .pt
Internet Service Providers (ISPs): 16 (2000)
Internet users: 700,000 (2000)

Transportation

Railways:
total: 2,850 km
broad gauge: 2,576 km 1.668-m gauge (623 km electrified; 426 km double track)

Portugal (continued)

narrow gauge: 274 km 1.000-m gauge (1998)
Highways:
total: 68,732 km
paved: 59,110 km (including 797 km of expressways)
unpaved: 9,622 km (1999)
Waterways: 820 km
note: relatively unimportant to national economy, used by shallow-draft craft limited to 300 metric-ton or less cargo capacity
Pipelines: crude oil 22 km; petroleum products 58 km; natural gas 700 km
note: the secondary lines for the natural gas pipeline that will be 300 km long have not yet been built
Ports and harbors: Aveiro, Funchal (Madeira Islands), Horta (Azores), Leixoes, Lisbon, Porto, Ponta Delgada (Azores), Praia da Vitoria (Azores), Setubal, Viana do Castelo
Merchant marine:
total: 158 ships (1,000 GRT or over) totaling 1,053,586 GRT/1,611,238 DWT
ships by type: bulk 14, cargo 84, chemical tanker 16, container 10, liquefied gas 7, multi-functional large-load carrier 1, petroleum tanker 11, refrigerated cargo 1, roll on/roll off 6, short-sea passenger 4, vehicle carrier 4
note: includes some foreign-owned ships registered here as a flag of convenience: Spain 1 (2000 est.)
Airports: 66 (2000 est.)
Airports - with paved runways:
total: 40
over 3,047 m: 5
2,438 to 3,047 m: 9
1,524 to 2,437 m: 4
914 to 1,523 m: 17
under 914 m: 5 (2000 est.)
Airports - with unpaved runways:
total: 26
914 to 1,523 m: 1
under 914 m: 25 (2000 est.)

Military

Military branches: Army, Navy (includes Marines), Air Force, National Republican Guard
Military manpower - military age: 20 years of age
Military manpower - availability:
males age 15-49: 2,530,466 (2001 est.)
Military manpower - fit for military service:
males age 15-49: 2,030,759 (2001 est.)
Military manpower - reaching military age annually:
males: 71,404 (2001 est.)
Military expenditures - dollar figure: $2.458 billion (FY97)
Military expenditures - percent of GDP: 2.6% (FY97)

Transnational Issues

Illicit drugs: important gateway country for Latin American cocaine and Southwest Asian heroin entering the European market; transshipment point for hashish from North Africa to Europe; consumer of Southwest Asian heroin

Puerto Rico
(commonwealth associated with the US)

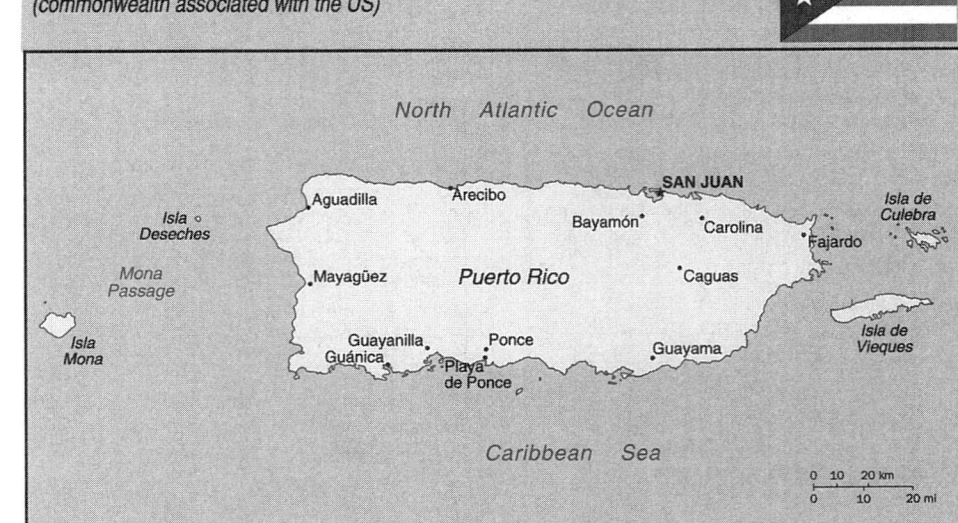

Introduction

Background: Discovered by Columbus in 1493, the island was ceded by Spain to the US in 1898 following the Spanish-American War. A popularly elected governor has served since 1948. In plebiscites held in 1967 and 1993, voters chose to retain commonwealth status.

Geography

Location: Caribbean, island between the Caribbean Sea and the North Atlantic Ocean, east of the Dominican Republic
Geographic coordinates: 18 15 N, 66 30 W
Map references: Central America and the Caribbean
Area:
total: 9,104 sq km
land: 8,959 sq km
water: 145 sq km
Area - comparative: slightly less than three times the size of Rhode Island
Land boundaries: 0 km
Coastline: 501 km
Maritime claims:
exclusive economic zone: 200 NM
territorial sea: 12 NM
Climate: tropical marine, mild; little seasonal temperature variation
Terrain: mostly mountains, with coastal plain belt in north; mountains precipitous to sea on west coast; sandy beaches along most coastal areas
Elevation extremes:
lowest point: Caribbean Sea 0 m
highest point: Cerro de Punta 1,338 m
Natural resources: some copper and nickel; potential for onshore and offshore oil
Land use:
arable land: 4%
permanent crops: 5%
permanent pastures: 26%
forests and woodland: 16%
other: 49% (1993 est.)
Irrigated land: 390 sq km (1993 est.)
Natural hazards: periodic droughts; hurricanes
Environment - current issues: erosion; occasional drought causing water shortages
Geography - note: important location along the Mona Passage - a key shipping lane to the Panama Canal; San Juan is one of the biggest and best natural harbors in the Caribbean; many small rivers and high central mountains ensure land is well watered; south coast relatively dry; fertile coastal plain belt in north

People

Population: 3,937,316 (July 2001 est.)
Age structure:
0-14 years: 23.73% (male 478,441; female 455,800)
15-64 years: 65.72% (male 1,242,245; female 1,345,421)
65 years and over: 10.55% (male 177,083; female 238,326) (2001 est.)
Population growth rate: 0.54% (2001 est.)
Birth rate: 15.26 births/1,000 population (2001 est.)
Death rate: 7.77 deaths/1,000 population (2001 est.)
Net migration rate: -2.13 migrant(s)/1,000 population (2001 est.)
Sex ratio:
at birth: 1.06 male(s)/female
under 15 years: 1.05 male(s)/female
15-64 years: 0.92 male(s)/female
65 years and over: 0.74 male(s)/female
total population: 0.93 male(s)/female (2001 est.)
Infant mortality rate: 9.51 deaths/1,000 live births (2001 est.)
Life expectancy at birth:
total population: 75.76 years
male: 71.28 years
female: 80.48 years (2001 est.)
Total fertility rate: 1.9 children born/woman (2001 est.)

Puerto Rico (continued)

HIV/AIDS - adult prevalence rate: NA%
HIV/AIDS - people living with HIV/AIDS: NA
HIV/AIDS - deaths: NA
Nationality:
noun: Puerto Rican(s) (US citizens)
adjective: Puerto Rican
Ethnic groups: NA
Religions: Roman Catholic 85%, Protestant and other 15%
Languages: Spanish, English
Literacy:
definition: age 15 and over can read and write
total population: 89%
male: 90%
female: 88% (1980 est.)

Government

Country name:
conventional long form: Commonwealth of Puerto Rico
conventional short form: Puerto Rico
Dependency status: commonwealth associated with the US
Government type: commonwealth
Capital: San Juan
Administrative divisions: none (commonwealth associated with the US); there are no first-order administrative divisions as defined by the US Government, but there are 78 municipalities (municipios, singular - municipio) at the second order; Adjuntas, Aguada, Aguadilla, Aguas Buenas, Aibonito, Anasco, Arecibo, Arroyo, Barceloneta, Barranquitas, Bayamon, Cabo Rojo, Caguas, Camuy, Canovanas, Carolina, Catano, Cayey, Ceiba, Ciales, Cidra, Coamo, Comerio, Corozal, Culebra, Dorado, Fajardo, Florida, Guanica, Guayama, Guayanilla, Guaynabo, Gurabo, Hatillo, Hormigueros, Humacao, Isabela, Jayuya, Juana Diaz, Juncos, Lajas, Lares, Las Marias, Las Piedras, Loiza, Luquillo, Manati, Maricao, Maunabo, Mayaguez, Moca, Morovis, Naguabo, Naranjito, Orocovis, Patillas, Penuelas, Ponce, Quebradillas, Rincon, Rio Grande, Sabana Grande, Salinas, San German, San Juan, San Lorenzo, San Sebastian, Santa Isabel, Toa Alta, Toa Baja, Trujillo Alto, Utuado, Vega Alta, Vega Baja, Vieques, Villalba, Yabucoa, Yauco
Independence: none (commonwealth associated with the US)
National holiday: US Independence Day, 4 July (1776)
Constitution: ratified 3 March 1952; approved by US Congress 3 July 1952; effective 25 July 1952
Legal system: based on Spanish civil code
Suffrage: 18 years of age; universal; indigenous inhabitants are US citizens but do not vote in US presidential elections
Executive branch:
chief of state: President George W. BUSH of the US (since 20 January 2001); Vice President Richard B. CHENEY (since 20 January 2001)
head of government: Governor Sila M. CALDERON (since NA January 2001)
cabinet: appointed by the governor with the consent of the legislature
elections: US president and vice president elected on the same ticket for four-year terms; governor elected by popular vote for a four-year term; election last held 7 November 2000 (next to be held NA November 2004)
election results: Sila M. CALDERON (PDP) elected governor; percent of vote - 48.8%
Legislative branch: bicameral Legislative Assembly consists of the Senate (28 seats; members are directly elected by popular vote to serve four-year terms) and the House of Representatives (54 seats; members are directly elected by popular vote to serve four-year terms)
elections: Senate - last held 7 November 2000 (next to be held NA November 2004); House of Representatives - last held 7 November 2000 (next to be held NA November 2004)
election results: Senate - percent of vote by party - NA%; seats by party - PNP 19, PPD 7, PIP 1, other 1; House of Representatives - percent of vote by party - NA%; seats by party - PNP 30, PPD 20, PIP 1, other 3
note: Puerto Rico elects one nonvoting representative to the US House of Representatives; elections last held 7 November 2000 (next to be held NA November 2004); results - percent of vote by party - NA; seats by party - PPD 1 (Anibal ACEVEDO-VILA)
Judicial branch: Supreme Court; Superior Courts; Municipal Courts (justices for all these courts appointed by the governor with the consent of the Senate)
Political parties and leaders: National Democratic Party [Celeste BENITEZ]; National Republican Party of Puerto Rico [Luis FERRE]; New Progressive Party or PNP [Pedro ROSSELLO]; Popular Democratic Party or PPD [Hector Luis ACEVEDO]; Puerto Rican Independence Party or PIP [Ruben BERRIOS Martinez]
Political pressure groups and leaders: Armed Forces for National Liberation or FALN; Armed Forces of Popular Resistance; Boricua Popular Army (also known as the Macheteros); Volunteers of the Puerto Rican Revolution
International organization participation: Caricom (observer), ECLAC (associate), FAO (associate), ICFTU, Interpol (subbureau), IOC, WCL, WFTU, WHO (associate)
Diplomatic representation in the US: none (commonwealth associated with the US)
Diplomatic representation from the US: none (commonwealth associated with the US)
Flag description: five equal horizontal bands of red (top and bottom) alternating with white; a blue isosceles triangle based on the hoist side bears a large, white, five-pointed star in the center; design based on the US flag

Economy

Economy - overview: Puerto Rico has one of the most dynamic economies in the Caribbean region. A diverse industrial sector has surpassed agriculture as the primary locus of economic activity and income. Encouraged by duty-free access to the US and by tax incentives, US firms have invested heavily in Puerto Rico since the 1950s. US minimum wage laws apply. Sugar production has lost out to dairy production and other livestock products as the main source of income in the agricultural sector. Tourism has traditionally been an important source of income, with estimated arrivals of nearly 5 million tourists in 1999. Prospects for 2001 are clouded by a probable slowing down in both the construction and tourist sectors and by increasing inflation, particularly in energy and food prices; estimated growth will be 2%.
GDP: purchasing power parity - $39 billion (2000 est.)
GDP - real growth rate: 2.8% (2000 est.)
GDP - per capita: purchasing power parity - $10,000 (2000 est.)
GDP - composition by sector:
agriculture: 1%
industry: 45%
services: 54% (1999 est.)
Population below poverty line: NA%
Household income or consumption by percentage share:
lowest 10%: NA%
highest 10%: NA%
Inflation rate (consumer prices): 5.7% (2000 est.)
Labor force: 1.3 million (2000)
Labor force - by occupation: agriculture 3%, industry 20%, services 77% (2000 est.)
Unemployment rate: 9.5% (2000)
Budget:
revenues: $6.7 billion
expenditures: $9.6 billion, including capital expenditures of $NA (FY99/00)
Industries: pharmaceuticals, electronics, apparel, food products; tourism
Industrial production growth rate: NA%
Electricity - production: 16.76 billion kWh (1999)
Electricity - production by source:
fossil fuel: 98.45%
hydro: 1.55%
nuclear: 0%
other: 0% (1999)
Electricity - consumption: 15.587 billion kWh (1999)
Electricity - exports: 0 kWh (1999)
Electricity - imports: 0 kWh (1999)
Agriculture - products: sugarcane, coffee, pineapples, plantains, bananas; livestock products, chickens
Exports: $38.5 billion (f.o.b., 2000)
Exports - commodities: pharmaceuticals, electronics, apparel, canned tuna, rum, beverage concentrates, medical equipment

Puerto Rico (continued)

Exports - partners: US 88% (2000)
Imports: $27 billion (c.i.f., 2000)
Imports - commodities: chemicals, machinery and equipment, clothing, food, fish, petroleum products
Imports - partners: US 60% (2000)
Debt - external: $NA
Economic aid - recipient: $NA
Currency: US dollar (USD)
Currency code: USD
Exchange rates: the US dollar is used
Fiscal year: 1 July - 30 June

Communications

Telephones - main lines in use: 1.322 million (1997)
Telephones - mobile cellular: 169,265 (1996)
Telephone system:
general assessment: modern system, integrated with that of the US by high-capacity submarine cable and Intelsat with high-speed data capability
domestic: digital telephone system; cellular telephone service
international: satellite earth station - 1 Intelsat; submarine cable to US
Radio broadcast stations: AM 72, FM 17, shortwave 0 (1998)
Radios: 2.7 million (1997)
Television broadcast stations: 18 (plus three stations of the US Armed Forces Radio and Television Service) (1997)
Televisions: 1.021 million (1997)
Internet country code: .pr
Internet Service Providers (ISPs): 76 (2000)
Internet users: 110,000 (2000)

Transportation

Railways:
total: 96 km
narrow gauge: 96 km 1.000-m gauge, rural, narrow-gauge system for hauling sugarcane; no passenger service
Highways:
total: 14,400 km
paved: 14,400 km
unpaved: 0 km (1996 est.)
Waterways: none
Ports and harbors: Guanica, Guayanilla, Guayama, Playa de Ponce, San Juan
Airports: 28 (2000 est.)
Airports - with paved runways:
total: 19
over 3,047 m: 3
1,524 to 2,437 m: 3
914 to 1,523 m: 7
under 914 m: 6 (2000 est.)
Airports - with unpaved runways:
total: 9
914 to 1,523 m: 2
under 914 m: 7 (2000 est.)

Military

Military branches: paramilitary National Guard, Police Force
Military - note: defense is the responsibility of the US

Transnational Issues

Disputes - international: none

Qatar

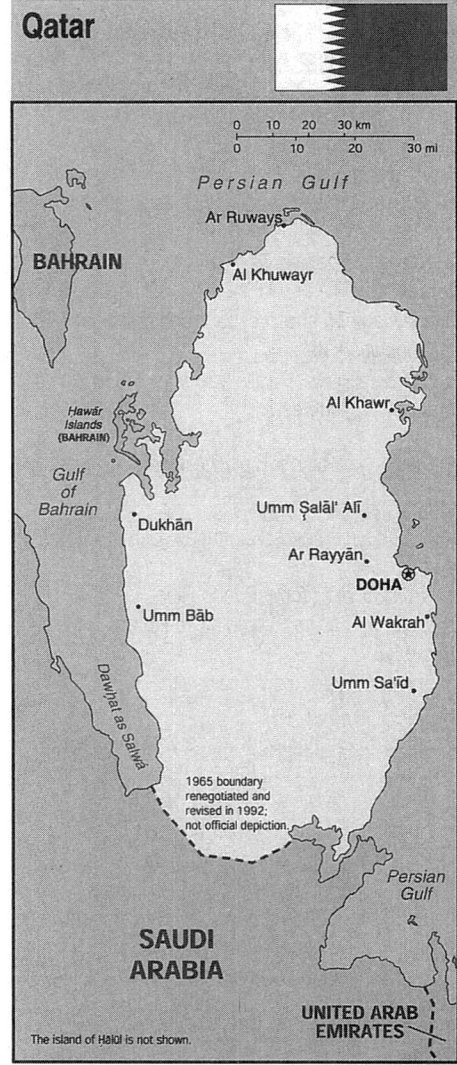

Introduction

Background: Ruled by the Al Thani family since the mid-1800s, Qatar transformed itself from a poor British protectorate noted mainly for pearling into an independent state with significant oil and natural gas revenues. During the late 1980s and early 1990s, the Qatari economy was crippled by a continuous siphoning off of petroleum revenues by the amir who had ruled the country since 1972. He was overthrown by his son, the current Amir HAMAD bin Khalifa Al Thani, in a bloodless coup in 1995. In 2001, Qatar resolved its longstanding border disputes with both Bahrain and Saudi Arabia. Oil and natural gas revenues enable Qatar to have a per capita income not far below the leading industrial countries of Western Europe.

Geography

Location: Middle East, peninsula bordering the Persian Gulf and Saudi Arabia
Geographic coordinates: 25 30 N, 51 15 E
Map references: Middle East

Qatar (continued)

Area:
total: 11,437 sq km
land: 11,437 sq km
water: 0 sq km
Area - comparative: slightly smaller than Connecticut
Land boundaries:
total: 60 km
border countries: Saudi Arabia 60 km
Coastline: 563 km
Maritime claims:
contiguous zone: 24 NM
exclusive economic zone: as determined by bilateral agreements or the median line
territorial sea: 12 NM
Climate: desert; hot, dry; humid and sultry in summer
Terrain: mostly flat and barren desert covered with loose sand and gravel
Elevation extremes:
lowest point: Persian Gulf 0 m
highest point: Qurayn Abu al Bawl 103 m
Natural resources: petroleum, natural gas, fish
Land use:
arable land: 1%
permanent crops: 0%
permanent pastures: 5%
forests and woodland: 0%
other: 94% (1993 est.)
Irrigated land: 80 sq km (1993 est.)
Natural hazards: haze, dust storms, sandstorms common
Environment - current issues: limited natural fresh water resources are increasing dependence on large-scale desalination facilities
Environment - international agreements:
party to: Biodiversity, Climate Change, Desertification, Hazardous Wastes, Marine Dumping, Ozone Layer Protection, Ship Pollution
signed, but not ratified: Law of the Sea
Geography - note: strategic location in central Persian Gulf near major petroleum deposits

People

Population: 769,152 (July 2001 est.)
Age structure:
0-14 years: 25.77% (male 101,155; female 97,086)
15-64 years: 71.75% (male 391,178; female 160,665)
65 years and over: 2.48% (male 13,625; female 5,443) (2001 est.)
Population growth rate: 3.18% (2001 est.)
Birth rate: 15.91 births/1,000 population (2001 est.)
Death rate: 4.26 deaths/1,000 population (2001 est.)
Net migration rate: 20.12 migrant(s)/1,000 population (2001 est.)
Sex ratio:
at birth: 1.05 male(s)/female
under 15 years: 1.04 male(s)/female
15-64 years: 2.43 male(s)/female
65 years and over: 2.5 male(s)/female
total population: 1.92 male(s)/female (2001 est.)
Infant mortality rate: 21.44 deaths/1,000 live births (2001 est.)
Life expectancy at birth:
total population: 72.62 years
male: 70.16 years
female: 75.21 years (2001 est.)
Total fertility rate: 3.17 children born/woman (2001 est.)
HIV/AIDS - adult prevalence rate: 0.09% (1999 est.)
HIV/AIDS - people living with HIV/AIDS: NA
HIV/AIDS - deaths: NA
Nationality:
noun: Qatari(s)
adjective: Qatari
Ethnic groups: Arab 40%, Pakistani 18%, Indian 18%, Iranian 10%, other 14%
Religions: Muslim 95%
Languages: Arabic (official), English commonly used as a second language
Literacy:
definition: age 15 and over can read and write
total population: 79%
male: 79%
female: 80% (1995 est.)

Government

Country name:
conventional long form: State of Qatar
conventional short form: Qatar
local long form: Dawlat Qatar
local short form: Qatar
note: closest approximation of the native pronunciation falls between cutter and gutter, but not like guitar
Government type: traditional monarchy
Capital: Doha
Administrative divisions: 9 municipalities (baladiyat, singular - baladiyah); Ad Dawhah, Al Ghuwayriyah, Al Jumayliyah, Al Khawr, Al Wakrah, Ar Rayyan, Jarayan al Batinah, Madinat ash Shamal, Umm Salal
Independence: 3 September 1971 (from UK)
National holiday: Independence Day, 3 September (1971)
Constitution: provisional constitution enacted 19 April 1972; in July 1999 Amir HAMAD issued a decree forming a committee to draft a permanent constitution
Legal system: discretionary system of law controlled by the amir, although civil codes are being implemented; Islamic law is significant in personal matters
Suffrage: suffrage is limited to municipal elections
Executive branch:
chief of state: Amir HAMAD bin Khalifa Al Thani (since 27 June 1995 when, as crown prince, he ousted his father, Amir KHALIFA bin Hamad Al Thani, in a bloodless coup); Crown Prince JASSIM bin Hamad bin Khalifa Al Thani, third son of the monarch (selected crown prince by the monarch 22 October 1996); note - Amir HAMAD also holds the positions of minister of defense and commander-in-chief of the armed forces
head of government: Prime Minister ABDALLAH bin Khalifa Al Thani, brother of the monarch (since 30 October 1996); Deputy Prime Minister MUHAMMAD bin Khalifa Al Thani, brother of the monarch (since 20 January 1998)
cabinet: Council of Ministers appointed by the monarch
elections: none; the monarch is hereditary
note: in March 1999 Qatar held nationwide elections for a 29-member Central Municipal Council, which has consultative powers aimed at improving the provision of municipal services
Legislative branch: unicameral Advisory Council or Majlis al-Shura (35 seats; members appointed)
note: the constitution calls for elections for part of this consultative body, but no elections have been held since 1970, when there were partial elections to the body; Council members have their terms extended every four years since
Judicial branch: Court of Appeal
Political parties and leaders: none
Political pressure groups and leaders: none
International organization participation: ABEDA, AFESD, AL, AMF, CCC, ESCWA, FAO, G-77, GCC, IAEA, IBRD, ICAO, ICRM, IDB, IFAD, IFRCS, IHO (pending member), ILO, IMF, IMO, Inmarsat, Intelsat, Interpol, IOC, ISO (correspondent), ITU, NAM, OAPEC, OIC, OPCW, OPEC, UN, UNCTAD, UNESCO, UNIDO, UPU, WHO, WIPO, WMO, WTrO
Diplomatic representation in the US:
chief of mission: Ambassador Badr Umar al-DAFA
chancery: 4200 Wisconsin Avenue NW, Washington, DC 20016
telephone: [1] (202) 274-1600
FAX: [1] (202) 237-0061
consulate(s) general: Houston
Diplomatic representation from the US:
chief of mission: Ambassador Elizabeth Davenport MCKUNE
embassy: 22 February Road, Doha
mailing address: P. O. Box 2399, Doha
telephone: [974] 488 4101
FAX: [974] 488 4298
note: workweek is Saturday-Wednesday
Flag description: maroon with a broad white serrated band (nine white points) on the hoist side

Economy

Economy - overview: Oil accounts for more than 30% of GDP, roughly 80% of export earnings, and 66% of government revenues. Proved oil reserves of 3.7 billion barrels should ensure continued output at current levels for 23 years. Oil has given Qatar a per capita GDP comparable to that of the leading West European industrial countries. Qatar's proved reserves of natural gas exceed 7 trillion cubic meters, more than 5% of the world total, third largest in the

Qatar (continued)

world. Production and export of natural gas are becoming increasingly important. Long-term goals feature the development of offshore petroleum and the diversification of the economy. In 2000, Qatar posted its highest ever trade surplus of $6 billion, due mainly to high oil prices and increased natural gas exports.
GDP: purchasing power parity - $15.1 billion (2000 est.)
GDP - real growth rate: 4% (2000 est.)
GDP - per capita: purchasing power parity - $20,300 (2000 est.)
GDP - composition by sector:
agriculture: 1%
industry: 49%
services: 50% (1996 est.)
Population below poverty line: NA%
Household income or consumption by percentage share:
lowest 10%: NA%
highest 10%: NA%
Inflation rate (consumer prices): 2.5% (2000)
Labor force: 233,000 (1993 est.)
Unemployment rate: NA%
Budget:
revenues: $3.9 billion
expenditures: $4 billion, including capital expenditures of $NA (1999 est.)
Industries: crude oil production and refining, fertilizers, petrochemicals, steel reinforcing bars, cement
Industrial production growth rate: NA%
Electricity - production: 9 billion kWh (1999)
Electricity - production by source:
fossil fuel: 100%
hydro: 0%
nuclear: 0%
other: 0% (1999)
Electricity - consumption: 8.37 billion kWh (1999)
Electricity - exports: 0 kWh (1999)
Electricity - imports: 0 kWh (1999)
Agriculture - products: fruits, vegetables; poultry, dairy products, beef; fish
Exports: $9.8 billion (f.o.b., 2000 est.)
Exports - commodities: petroleum products 80%, fertilizers, steel
Exports - partners: Japan 52%, Singapore 9%, South Korea 8%, US, UAE (1998)
Imports: $3.8 billion (f.o.b., 2000 est.)
Imports - commodities: machinery and transport equipment, food, chemicals
Imports - partners: UK 10%, Japan 8%, Germany 6%, US 6%, Italy 6% (1998)
Debt - external: $13.1 billion (2000 est.)
Economic aid - recipient: $NA
Currency: Qatari rial (QAR)
Currency code: QAR
Exchange rates: Qatari rials per US dollar - 3.6400 (fixed rate)
Fiscal year: 1 April - 31 March

Communications

Telephones - main lines in use: 142,000 (1997)
Telephones - mobile cellular: 43,476 (1997)
Telephone system:
general assessment: modern system centered in Doha
domestic: NA
international: tropospheric scatter to Bahrain; microwave radio relay to Saudi Arabia and UAE; submarine cable to Bahrain and UAE; satellite earth stations - 2 Intelsat (1 Atlantic Ocean and 1 Indian Ocean) and 1 Arabsat
Radio broadcast stations: AM 6, FM 5, shortwave 1 (1998)
Radios: 256,000 (1997)
Television broadcast stations: 2 (plus three repeaters) (1997)
Televisions: 230,000 (1997)
Internet country code: .qa
Internet Service Providers (ISPs): 1 (2000)
Internet users: 45,000 (2000)

Transportation

Railways: 0 km
Highways:
total: 1,230 km
paved: 1,107 km
unpaved: 123 km (1996 est.)
Waterways: none
Pipelines: crude oil 235 km; natural gas 400 km
Ports and harbors: Doha, Halul Island, Umm Sa'id (Musay'id)
Merchant marine:
total: 25 ships (1,000 GRT or over) totaling 677,992 GRT/1,049,447 DWT
ships by type: cargo 10, combination ore/oil 2, container 7, petroleum tanker 6 (2000 est.)
Airports: 4 (2000 est.)
Airports - with paved runways:
total: 2
over 3,047 m: 2 (2000 est.)
Airports - with unpaved runways:
total: 2
914 to 1,523 m: 1
under 914 m: 1 (2000 est.)
Heliports: 1 (2000 est.)

Military

Military branches: Army, Navy, Air Force, Public Security
Military manpower - military age: 18 years of age
Military manpower - availability:
males age 15-49: 312,116
note: includes non-nationals (2001 est.)
Military manpower - fit for military service:
males age 15-49: 163,642 (2001 est.)
Military manpower - reaching military age annually:
males: 6,797 (2001 est.)
Military expenditures - dollar figure: $723 million (FY00/01)
Military expenditures - percent of GDP: 10% (FY00/01)

Transnational Issues

Disputes - international: in March of 2001, the International Court of Justice (ICJ) awarded the Hawar Islands to Bahrain and adjusted its maritime boundary with Qatar; a final border resolution was agreed to with Saudi Arabia in March of 2001

Reunion
(overseas department of France)

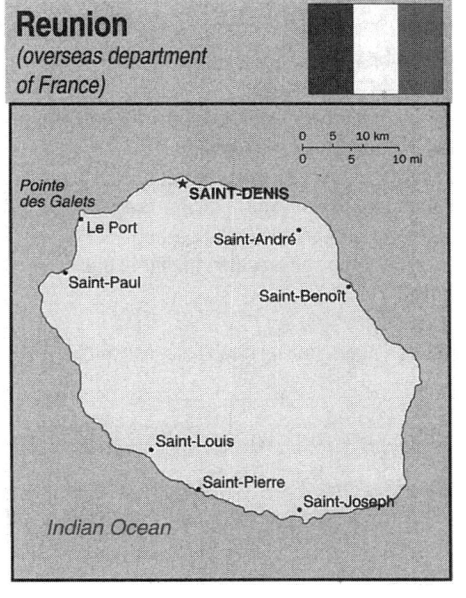

Introduction

Background: The Portuguese discovered the uninhabited island in 1513. From the 17th to the 19th centuries, French immigration supplemented by influxes of Africans, Chinese, Malays, and Malabar Indians gave the island its ethnic mix. The opening of the Suez Canal in 1869 cost the island its importance as a stopover on the East Indies trade route.

Geography

Location: Southern Africa, island in the Indian Ocean, east of Madagascar
Geographic coordinates: 21 06 S, 55 36 E
Map references: World
Area:
total: 2,512 sq km
land: 2,502 sq km
water: 10 sq km
Area - comparative: slightly smaller than Rhode Island
Land boundaries: 0 km
Coastline: 207 km
Maritime claims:
exclusive economic zone: 200 NM
territorial sea: 12 NM
Climate: tropical, but temperature moderates with elevation; cool and dry from May to November, hot and rainy from November to April
Terrain: mostly rugged and mountainous; fertile lowlands along coast
Elevation extremes:
lowest point: Indian Ocean 0 m
highest point: Piton des Neiges 3,069 m
Natural resources: fish, arable land, hydropower
Land use:
arable land: 17%
permanent crops: 2%
permanent pastures: 5%
forests and woodland: 35%
other: 41% (1993 est.)
Irrigated land: 60 sq km (1993 est.)
Natural hazards: periodic, devastating cyclones (December to April); Piton de la Fournaise on the southeastern coast is an active volcano
Environment - current issues: NA

People

Population: 732,570 (July 2001 est.)
Age structure:
0-14 years: 32.07% (male 120,259; female 114,669)
15-64 years: 62.25% (male 224,347; female 231,698)
65 years and over: 5.68% (male 16,892; female 24,705) (2001 est.)
Population growth rate: 1.57% (2001 est.)
Birth rate: 21.26 births/1,000 population (2001 est.)
Death rate: 5.52 deaths/1,000 population (2001 est.)
Net migration rate: 0 migrant(s)/1,000 population (2001 est.)
Sex ratio:
at birth: 1.05 male(s)/female
under 15 years: 1.05 male(s)/female
15-64 years: 0.97 male(s)/female
65 years and over: 0.68 male(s)/female
total population: 0.97 male(s)/female (2001 est.)
Infant mortality rate: 8.49 deaths/1,000 live births (2001 est.)
Life expectancy at birth:
total population: 72.93 years
male: 69.53 years
female: 76.49 years (2001 est.)
Total fertility rate: 2.58 children born/woman (2001 est.)
HIV/AIDS - adult prevalence rate: NA%
HIV/AIDS - people living with HIV/AIDS: NA
HIV/AIDS - deaths: NA
Nationality:
noun: Reunionese (singular and plural)
adjective: Reunionese
Ethnic groups: French, African, Malagasy, Chinese, Pakistani, Indian
Religions: Roman Catholic 86%, Hindu, Muslim, Buddhist (1995)
Languages: French (official), Creole widely used
Literacy:
definition: age 15 and over can read and write
total population: 79%
male: 76%
female: 80% (1982 est.)

Government

Country name:
conventional long form: Department of Reunion
conventional short form: Reunion
local long form: none
local short form: Ile de la Reunion
former: Bourbon Island
Dependency status: overseas department of France
Government type: NA
Capital: Saint-Denis
Administrative divisions: none (overseas department of France); there are no first-order administrative divisions as defined by the US Government, but there are 4 arrondissements, 24 communes, and 47 cantons
Independence: none (overseas department of France)
National holiday: Bastille Day, 14 July (1789)
Constitution: 28 September 1958 (French Constitution)
Legal system: French law
Suffrage: 18 years of age; universal
Executive branch:
chief of state: President Jacques CHIRAC of France (since 17 May 1995), represented by Prefect Robert POMMIES (since NA 1996)
head of government: President of the General Council Jean-Luc POUDROUX (since NA March 1998) and President of the Regional Council Paul VERGES (since NA March 1993)
cabinet: NA
elections: French president elected by popular vote for a seven-year term; prefect appointed by the French president on the advice of the French Ministry of the Interior; the presidents of the General and Regional Councils are elected by the members of those councils
Legislative branch: unicameral General Council (47 seats; members are elected by direct popular vote to serve six-year terms) and a unicameral Regional Council (45 seats; members are elected by direct popular vote to serve six-year terms)
elections: General Council - last held NA March 1994 (next to be held NA 2000); Regional Council - last held 15 March 1998 (next to be held NA 2004)
election results: General Council - percent of vote by party - NA%; seats by party - PCR 12, PS 12, UDF 11, RPR 5, others 7; Regional Council - percent of vote by party - NA%; seats by party - PCR 7, UDF 8, PS 6, RPR 4, various right-wing candidates 15, various left-wing candidates 5
note: Reunion elects three representatives to the French Senate; elections last held 14 April 1996 (next to be held NA 2001); results - percent of vote by party - NA%; seats by party - RPR 1, PCR 2; Reunion also elects five deputies to the French National Assembly; elections last held 25 May and 1 June 1997 (next to be held NA 2002); results - percent of vote by party - NA%; seats by party - PCR 3, PS 1, and RPR-UDF 1
Judicial branch: Court of Appeals or Cour d'Appel
Political parties and leaders: Communist Party of Reunion or PCR [Paul VERGES]; Rally for the Republic or RPR [Andre Maurice PIHOUEE]; Socialist Party or PS [Jean-Claude FRUTEAU]; Union for French Democracy or UDF [Gilbert GERARD]
Political pressure groups and leaders: NA
International organization participation: FZ, InOC, WFTU
Diplomatic representation in the US: none (overseas department of France)

Reunion (continued)

Diplomatic representation from the US: none (overseas department of France)
Flag description: the flag of France is used

Economy

Economy - overview: The economy has traditionally been based on agriculture. Sugarcane has been the primary crop for more than a century, and in some years it accounts for 85% of exports. The government has been pushing the development of a tourist industry to relieve high unemployment, which amounts to more than 40% of the labor force. The gap in Reunion between the well-off and the poor is extraordinary and accounts for the persistent social tensions. The white and Indian communities are substantially better off than other segments of the population, often approaching European standards, whereas minority groups suffer the poverty and unemployment typical of the poorer nations of the African continent. The outbreak of severe rioting in February 1991 illustrates the seriousness of socioeconomic tensions. The economic well-being of Reunion depends heavily on continued financial assistance from France.
GDP: purchasing power parity - $3.4 billion (1998 est.)
GDP - real growth rate: 3.8% (1998 est.)
GDP - per capita: purchasing power parity - $4,800 (1998 est.)
GDP - composition by sector:
agriculture: NA%
industry: NA%
services: NA%
Population below poverty line: NA%
Household income or consumption by percentage share:
lowest 10%: NA%
highest 10%: NA%
Inflation rate (consumer prices): NA%
Labor force: 261,000 (1995)
Labor force - by occupation: agriculture 8%, industry 19%, services 73% (1990)
Unemployment rate: 42.8% (1998)
Budget:
revenues: NA
expenditures: NA
Industries: sugar, rum, cigarettes, handicraft items, flower oil extraction
Industrial production growth rate: NA%
Electricity - production: 1.1 billion kWh (1999)
Electricity - production by source:
fossil fuel: 54.55%
hydro: 45.45%
nuclear: 0%
other: 0% (1999)
Electricity - consumption: 1.023 billion kWh (1999)
Electricity - exports: 0 kWh (1999)
Electricity - imports: 0 kWh (1999)
Agriculture - products: sugarcane, vanilla, tobacco, tropical fruits, vegetables, corn
Exports: $214 million (f.o.b., 1997)
Exports - commodities: sugar 63%, rum and molasses 4%, perfume essences 2%, lobster 3%, (1993)
Exports - partners: France 74%, Japan 6%, Comoros 4% (1994)
Imports: $2.5 billion (c.i.f., 1997)
Imports - commodities: manufactured goods, food, beverages, tobacco, machinery and transportation equipment, raw materials, and petroleum products
Imports - partners: France 64%, Bahrain 3%, Germany 3%, Italy 3% (1994)
Debt - external: $NA
Economic aid - recipient: $NA; note - substantial annual subsidies from France
Currency: French franc (FRF); euro (EUR)
Currency code: FRF; EUR
Exchange rates: euros per US dollar - 1.06594 (January 2001), 1.08540 (2000), 0.9386 (1999); French francs per US dollar - 5.8995 (1998), 5.8367 (1997), 5.1155 (1996)
Fiscal year: calendar year

Communications

Telephones - main lines in use: 236,500 (1997)
Telephones - mobile cellular: 85,000 (1999)
Telephone system:
general assessment: adequate system; principal center is Saint-Denis
domestic: modern open wire and microwave radio relay network
international: radiotelephone communication to Comoros, France, Madagascar; new microwave route to Mauritius; satellite earth station - 1 Intelsat (Indian Ocean)
Radio broadcast stations: AM 2, FM 55, shortwave 0 (1998)
Radios: 173,000 (1997)
Television broadcast stations: 22 (plus 18 low-power repeaters) (1997)
Televisions: 127,000 (1997)
Internet country code: .re
Internet Service Providers (ISPs): 1 (2000)
Internet users: 10,000 (2000)

Transportation

Railways: 0 km
Highways:
total: 2,784 km
paved: 2,187 km
unpaved: 597 km (1987 est.)
Waterways: none
Ports and harbors: Le Port, Pointe des Galets
Merchant marine:
total: 1 ship (1,000 GRT or over) totaling 28,264 GRT/ 44,885 DWT
ships by type: chemical tanker 1 (2000 est.)
Airports: 2 (2000 est.)
Airports - with paved runways:
total: 2
2,438 to 3,047 m: 1
914 to 1,523 m: 1 (2000 est.)

Military

Military branches: French forces (Army, Navy, Air Force, and Gendarmerie)
Military manpower - military age: 18 years of age
Military manpower - availability:
males age 15-49: 190,846 (2001 est.)
Military manpower - fit for military service:
males age 15-49: 97,497 (2001 est.)
Military manpower - reaching military age annually:
males: 6,243 (2001 est.)
Military - note: defense is the responsibility of France

Transnational Issues

Disputes - international: none

Romania

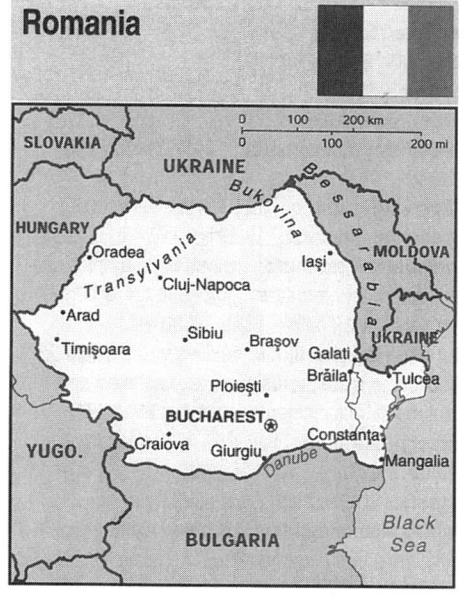

Introduction

Background: Soviet occupation following World War II led to the formation of a communist "peoples republic" in 1947 and the abdication of the king. The decades-long rule of President Nicolae CEAUSESCU became increasingly draconian through the 1980s. He was overthrown and executed in late 1989. Former communists dominated the government until 1996 when they were swept from power. Much economic restructuring remains to be carried out before Romania can achieve its hope of joining the EU.

Geography

Location: Southeastern Europe, bordering the Black Sea, between Bulgaria and Ukraine
Geographic coordinates: 46 00 N, 25 00 E
Map references: Europe
Area:
total: 237,500 sq km
land: 230,340 sq km
water: 7,160 sq km
Area - comparative: slightly smaller than Oregon
Land boundaries:
total: 2,508 km
border countries: Bulgaria 608 km, Hungary 443 km, Moldova 450 km, Yugoslavia 476 km, Ukraine (north) 362 km, Ukraine (east) 169 km
Coastline: 225 km
Maritime claims:
contiguous zone: 24 NM
continental shelf: 200-m depth or to the depth of exploitation
exclusive economic zone: 200 NM
territorial sea: 12 NM
Climate: temperate; cold, cloudy winters with frequent snow and fog; sunny summers with frequent showers and thunderstorms
Terrain: central Transylvanian Basin is separated from the Plain of Moldavia on the east by the Carpathian Mountains and separated from the Walachian Plain on the south by the Transylvanian Alps
Elevation extremes:
lowest point: Black Sea 0 m
highest point: Moldoveanu 2,544 m
Natural resources: petroleum (reserves declining), timber, natural gas, coal, iron ore, salt, arable land, hydropower
Land use:
arable land: 41%
permanent crops: 3%
permanent pastures: 21%
forests and woodland: 29%
other: 6% (1993 est.)
Irrigated land: 31,020 sq km (1993 est.)
Natural hazards: earthquakes most severe in south and southwest; geologic structure and climate promote landslides
Environment - current issues: soil erosion and degradation; water pollution; air pollution in south from industrial effluents; contamination of Danube delta wetlands
Environment - international agreements:
party to: Air Pollution, Antarctic Treaty, Biodiversity, Climate Change, Desertification, Endangered Species, Environmental Modification, Hazardous Wastes, Law of the Sea, Marine Dumping, Nuclear Test Ban, Ozone Layer Protection, Ship Pollution, Wetlands
signed, but not ratified: Air Pollution-Persistent Organic Pollutants, Antarctic-Environmental Protocol, Climate Change-Kyoto Protocol
Geography - note: controls most easily traversable land route between the Balkans, Moldova, and Ukraine

People

Population: 22,364,022 (July 2001 est.)
Age structure:
0-14 years: 17.95% (male 2,054,323; female 1,959,196)
15-64 years: 68.51% (male 7,605,751; female 7,715,434)
65 years and over: 13.54% (male 1,255,880; female 1,773,438) (2001 est.)
Population growth rate: -0.21% (2001 est.)
Birth rate: 10.8 births/1,000 population (2001 est.)
Death rate: 12.28 deaths/1,000 population (2001 est.)
Net migration rate: -0.6 migrant(s)/1,000 population (2001 est.)
Sex ratio:
at birth: 1.06 male(s)/female
under 15 years: 1.05 male(s)/female
15-64 years: 0.99 male(s)/female
65 years and over: 0.71 male(s)/female
total population: 0.95 male(s)/female (2001 est.)
Infant mortality rate: 19.36 deaths/1,000 live births (2001 est.)
Life expectancy at birth:
total population: 70.16 years
male: 66.36 years
female: 74.19 years (2001 est.)
Total fertility rate: 1.35 children born/woman (2001 est.)
HIV/AIDS - adult prevalence rate: 0.02% (1999 est.)
HIV/AIDS - people living with HIV/AIDS: 7,000 (1999 est.)
HIV/AIDS - deaths: 350 (1999 est.)
Nationality:
noun: Romanian(s)
adjective: Romanian
Ethnic groups: Romanian 89.5%, Hungarian 7.1%, Roma 1.8%, German 0.5%, Ukrainian 0.3%, other 0.8% (1992)
Religions: Romanian Orthodox 70%, Roman Catholic 3%, Uniate Catholic 3%, Protestant 6%, unaffiliated 18%
Languages: Romanian, Hungarian, German
Literacy:
definition: age 15 and over can read and write
total population: 97%
male: 98%
female: 95% (1992 est.)

Government

Country name:
conventional long form: none
conventional short form: Romania
local long form: none
local short form: Romania
Government type: republic
Capital: Bucharest
Administrative divisions: 40 counties (judete, singular - judet) and 1 municipality* (municipiu); Alba, Arad, Arges, Bacau, Bihor, Bistrita-Nasaud, Botosani, Braila, Brasov, Bucuresti*, Buzau, Calarasi, Caras-Severin, Cluj, Constanta, Covasna, Dimbovita, Dolj, Galati, Gorj, Giurgiu, Harghita, Hunedoara, Ialomita, Iasi, Maramures, Mehedinti, Mures, Neamt, Olt, Prahova, Salaj, Satu Mare, Sibiu, Suceava, Teleorman, Timis, Tulcea, Vaslui, Vilcea, Vrancea
Independence: 1881 (from Turkey; republic proclaimed 30 December 1947)
National holiday: Unification Day (of Romania and Transylvania), 1 December (1918)
Constitution: 8 December 1991
Legal system: former mixture of civil law system and communist legal theory; is now based on the constitution of France's Fifth Republic
Suffrage: 18 years of age; universal
Executive branch:
chief of state: President Ion ILIESCU (since 20 December 2000)
head of government: Prime Minister Adrian NASTASE (since 29 December 2000)
cabinet: Council of Ministers appointed by the prime minister
elections: president elected by popular vote for a four-year term; election last held 26 November 2000, with runoff between the top two candidates held 10 December 2000 (next to be held NA November/December 2004); prime minister appointed by the president
election results: percent of vote - Ion ILIESCU 66.84%, Corneliu Vadim TUDOR 33.16%

Romania (continued)

Legislative branch: bicameral Parliament or Parlament consists of the Senate or Senat (140 seats; members are elected by direct popular vote on a proportional representation basis to serve four-year terms) and the Chamber of Deputies or Adunarea Deputatilor (345 seats; members are elected by direct popular vote on a proportional representation basis to serve four-year terms)
elections: Senate - last held 26 November 2000 (next to be held in the fall of 2004); Chamber of Deputies - last held 26 November 2000 (next to be held in the fall of 2004)
election results: Senate - percent of vote by party - PDSR 37.1%, PRM 21.0%, PD 7.6%, PNL 7.5%, UDMR 6.9%; seats by party - PDSR 65, PRM 37, PD 13, PNL 13, UDMR 12; Chamber of Deputies - percent of vote by party - PDSR 36.6%, PRM 19.5%, PD 7.0%, PNL, 6.9%, UDMR 6.8%; seats by party - PDSR 155, PRM 84, PD 31, PNL 30, UDMR 27, ethnic minorities 18
Judicial branch: Supreme Court of Justice (judges are appointed by the president on the recommendation of the Superior Council of Magistrates)
Political parties and leaders: Democratic Party or PD [Petre ROMAN]; Democratic Union of Hungarians in Romania or UDMR [Bela MARKO]; National Liberal Party or PNL [Mircea IONESCU-QUINTUS]; Party of Social Democracy in Romania or PDSR [Adrian NASTASE]; Romania Mare Party (Greater Romanian Party) or PRM [Corneliu Vadim TUDOR]; The Democratic Convention or CDR [Ion DIACONESCU]
Political pressure groups and leaders: various human rights and professional associations
International organization participation: ACCT, Australia Group, BIS, BSEC, CCC, CE, CEI, EAPC, EBRD, ECE, EU (applicant), FAO, G-9, G-77, IAEA, IBRD, ICAO, ICFTU, ICRM, IFAD, IFC, IFRCS, ILO, IMF, IMO, Inmarsat, Intelsat, Interpol, IOC, IOM, ISO, ITU, LAIA (observer), MONUC, NAM (guest), NSG, OAS (observer), OPCW, OSCE, PCA, PFP, UN, UNCTAD, UNESCO, UNIDO, UNIKOM, UNMEE, UNMIBH, UNMIK, UPU, WCL, WEU (associate partner), WFTU, WHO, WIPO, WMO, WToO, WTrO, ZC
Diplomatic representation in the US:
chief of mission: Ambassador (vacant)
chancery: 1607 23rd Street NW, Washington, DC 20008
telephone: [1] (202) 332-4846, 4848, 4851
FAX: [1] (202) 232-4748
consulate(s) general: Chicago, Los Angeles, and New York
Diplomatic representation from the US:
chief of mission: Ambassador James C. ROSAPEPE
embassy: Strada Tudor Arghezi 7-9, Bucharest
mailing address: American Embassy Bucharest, Department of State, Washington, DC 20521-5260 (pouch)
telephone: [40] (1) 210 40 42
FAX: [40] (1) 210 03 95
branch office: Cluj-Napoca

Flag description: three equal vertical bands of blue (hoist side), yellow, and red; the national coat of arms that used to be centered in the yellow band has been removed; now similar to the flag of Chad, also resembles the flags of Andorra and Moldova

Economy

Economy - overview: Romania, one of the poorest countries in Central and Eastern Europe, began the transition from communism in 1989 with a largely obsolete industrial base and a pattern of output unsuited to the country's needs. Over the past decade economic restructuring has lagged behind most other countries in the region. Consequently, living standards have continued to fall - real wages are down over 40%. Corruption too has worsened. The EU ranks Romania last among enlargement candidates, and the European Bank for Reconstruction and Development (EBRD) rates Romania's transition progress the region's worst. The country emerged in 2000 from a punishing three-year recession thanks to strong demand in EU export markets. A new government elected in November 2000 promises to promote economic reform. Bucharest hopes to receive financial and technical assistance from international financial institutions and Western governments; negotiations over a new IMF standby agreement are to begin early in 2001. If reform stalls, Romania's ability to borrow from both public and private sources could quickly dry up, leading to another financial crisis.
GDP: purchasing power parity - $132.5 billion (2000 est.)
GDP - real growth rate: 2.2% (2000 est.)
GDP - per capita: purchasing power parity - $5,900 (2000 est.)
GDP - composition by sector:
agriculture: 13.9%
industry: 32.6%
services: 53.5% (2000)
Population below poverty line: 44.5% (2000)
Household income or consumption by percentage share:
lowest 10%: 3.8%
highest 10%: 20.2% (1992)
Inflation rate (consumer prices): 45.7% (2000 est.)
Labor force: 9.9 million (1999 est.)
Labor force - by occupation: agriculture 40%, industry 25%, services 35% (1998)
Unemployment rate: 11.5% (1999)
Budget:
revenues: $11.7 billion
expenditures: $12.4 billion, including capital expenditures of $NA (1999 est.)
Industries: textiles and footwear, light machinery and auto assembly, mining, timber, construction materials, metallurgy, chemicals, food processing, petroleum refining
Industrial production growth rate: 8% (2000)
Electricity - production: 49.036 billion kWh (1999)

Electricity - production by source:
fossil fuel: 53.99%
hydro: 36.18%
nuclear: 9.81%
other: 0.02% (1999)
Electricity - consumption: 44.768 billion kWh (1999)
Electricity - exports: 1.935 billion kWh (1999)
Electricity - imports: 1.1 billion kWh (1999)
Agriculture - products: wheat, corn, sugar beets, sunflower seed, potatoes, grapes; eggs, sheep
Exports: $11.2 billion (f.o.b., 2000 est.)
Exports - commodities: textiles and footwear 26%, metals and metal products 15%, machinery and equipment 11%, minerals and fuels 6% (1999)
Exports - partners: Italy 23%, Germany 18%, France 6%, Turkey 5%, US (1999)
Imports: $11.9 billion (f.o.b., 2000 est.)
Imports - commodities: machinery and equipment 23%, fuels and minerals 12%, chemicals 9%, textile and products 19% (1999)
Imports - partners: Italy 20%, Germany 19%, France 7%, Russia 6% (1999)
Debt - external: $9.3 billion (2000 est.)
Currency: leu (ROL)
Currency code: ROL
Exchange rates: lei per US dollar - 26,243.0 (January 2001), 21,708.7 (2000), 15,332.8 (1999), 8,875.6 (1998), 7,167.9 (1997), 3,084.2 (1996); note - lei is the plural form of leu
Fiscal year: calendar year

Communications

Telephones - main lines in use: 3.777 million (1997)
Telephones - mobile cellular: 645,500 (1999)
Telephone system:
general assessment: poor domestic service, but improving
domestic: 90% of telephone network is automatic; trunk network is mostly microwave radio relay, with some fiber-optic cable; about one-third of exchange capacity is digital; roughly 3,300 villages have no service
international: satellite earth station - 1 Intelsat; new digital, international, direct-dial exchanges operate in Bucharest; note - Romania is an active participant in several international telecommunication network projects (1999)
Radio broadcast stations: AM 40, FM 202, shortwave 3 (1998)
Radios: 7.2 million (1997)
Television broadcast stations: 48 (plus 392 repeaters) (1995)
Televisions: 5.25 million (1997)
Internet country code: .ro
Internet Service Providers (ISPs): 38 (2000)
Internet users: 600,000 (2000)

Romania (continued)

Transportation

Railways:
total: 11,385 km (3,888 km electrified)
standard gauge: 10,898 km
narrow gauge: 487 km (1996)
Highways:
total: 153,359 km
paved: 103,671 km (including 133 km of expressways)
unpaved: 49,688 km (1998 est.)
Waterways: 1,724 km (1984)
Pipelines: crude oil 2,800 km; petroleum products 1,429 km; natural gas 6,400 km (1992)
Ports and harbors: Braila, Constanta, Galati, Mangalia, Sulina, Tulcea
Merchant marine:
total: 95 ships (1,000 GRT or over) totaling 695,227 GRT/931,598 DWT
ships by type: bulk 10, cargo 71, container 1, passenger 1, passenger/cargo 1, petroleum tanker 4, railcar carrier 2, roll on/roll off 4, specialized tanker 1 (2000 est.)
Airports: 62 (2000 est.)
Airports - with paved runways:
total: 25
over 3,047 m: 3
2,438 to 3,047 m: 10
1,524 to 2,437 m: 12 (2000 est.)
Airports - with unpaved runways:
total: 37
1,524 to 2,437 m: 2
914 to 1,523 m: 12
under 914 m: 23 (2000 est.)
Heliports: 1 (2000 est.)

Military

Military branches: Army, Navy, Air and Air Defense Forces, Paramilitary Forces, Civil Defense
Military manpower - military age: 20 years of age
Military manpower - availability:
males age 15-49: 5,899,536 (2001 est.)
Military manpower - fit for military service:
males age 15-49: 4,962,807 (2001 est.)
Military manpower - reaching military age annually:
males: 179,951 (2001 est.)
Military expenditures - dollar figure: $720 million (FY00)
Military expenditures - percent of GDP: 2.2% (FY00)

Transnational Issues

Disputes - international: none
Illicit drugs: important transshipment point for Southwest Asian heroin transiting the Balkan route and small amounts of Latin American cocaine bound for Western Europe

Russia

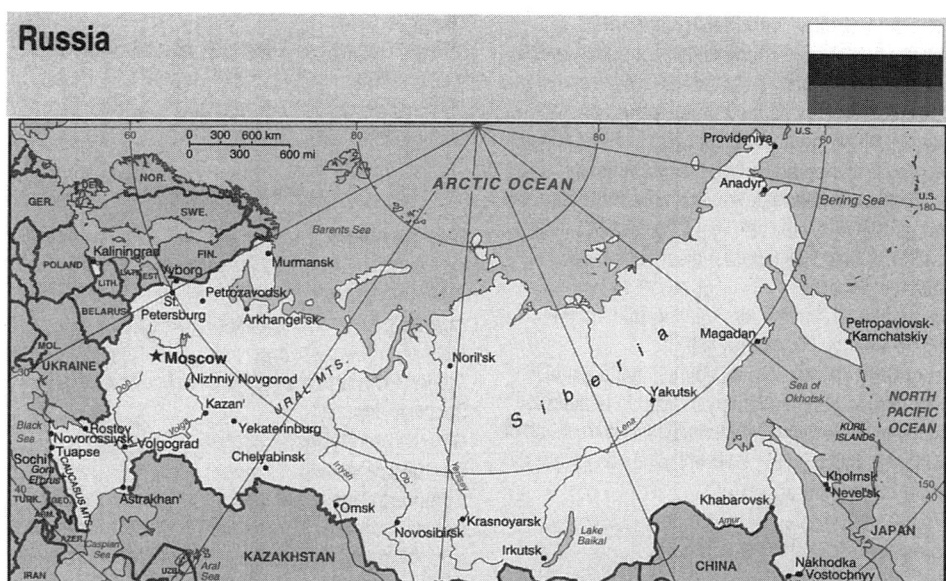

Introduction

Background: The defeat of the Russian Empire in World War I led to the seizure of power by the communists and the formation of the USSR. The brutal rule of Josef STALIN (1924-53) strengthened Russian dominance of the Soviet Union at a cost of tens of millions of lives. The Soviet economy and society stagnated in the following decades until General Secretary Mikhail GORBACHEV (1985-91) introduced glasnost (openness) and perestroika (restructuring) in an attempt to modernize communism, but his initiatives inadvertently released forces that by December 1991 splintered the USSR into 15 independent republics. Since then, Russia has struggled in its efforts to build a democratic political system and market economy to replace the strict social, political, and economic controls of the communist period.

Geography

Location: Northern Asia (that part west of the Urals is sometimes included with Europe), bordering the Arctic Ocean, between Europe and the North Pacific Ocean
Geographic coordinates: 60 00 N, 100 00 E
Map references: Asia
Area:
total: 17,075,200 sq km
land: 16,995,800 sq km
water: 79,400 sq km
Area - comparative: slightly less than 1.8 times the size of the US
Land boundaries:
total: 19,961 km
border countries: Azerbaijan 284 km, Belarus 959 km, China (southeast) 3,605 km, China (south) 40 km, Estonia 294 km, Finland 1,313 km, Georgia 723 km, Kazakhstan 6,846 km, North Korea 19 km, Latvia 217 km, Lithuania (Kaliningrad Oblast) 227 km, Mongolia 3,485 km, Norway 167 km, Poland (Kaliningrad Oblast) 206 km, Ukraine 1,576 km
Coastline: 37,653 km
Maritime claims:
continental shelf: 200-m depth or to the depth of exploitation
exclusive economic zone: 200 NM
territorial sea: 12 NM
Climate: ranges from steppes in the south through humid continental in much of European Russia; subarctic in Siberia to tundra climate in the polar north; winters vary from cool along Black Sea coast to frigid in Siberia; summers vary from warm in the steppes to cool along Arctic coast
Terrain: broad plain with low hills west of Urals; vast coniferous forest and tundra in Siberia; uplands and mountains along southern border regions
Elevation extremes:
lowest point: Caspian Sea -28 m
highest point: Gora El'brus 5,633 m
Natural resources: wide natural resource base including major deposits of oil, natural gas, coal, and many strategic minerals, timber
note: formidable obstacles of climate, terrain, and distance hinder exploitation of natural resources
Land use:
arable land: 8%
permanent crops: 0%
permanent pastures: 4%
forests and woodland: 46%
other: 42% (1993 est.)
Irrigated land: 40,000 sq km (1993 est.)
Natural hazards: permafrost over much of Siberia is a major impediment to development; volcanic activity in the Kuril Islands; volcanoes and earthquakes on the Kamchatka Peninsula
Environment - current issues: air pollution from heavy industry, emissions of coal-fired electric plants, and transportation in major cities; industrial, municipal, and agricultural pollution of inland waterways and sea coasts; deforestation; soil erosion; soil contamination from improper application of agricultural chemicals; scattered areas of sometimes intense radioactive contamination; ground water contamination from toxic waste

Russia (continued)

Environment - international agreements:
party to: Air Pollution, Air Pollution-Nitrogen Oxides, Air Pollution-Sulphur 85, Antarctic-Environmental Protocol, Antarctic-Marine Living Resources, Antarctic Seals, Antarctic Treaty, Biodiversity, Climate Change, Endangered Species, Environmental Modification, Hazardous Wastes, Law of the Sea, Marine Dumping, Nuclear Test Ban, Ozone Layer Protection, Ship Pollution, Tropical Timber 83, Wetlands, Whaling
signed, but not ratified: Air Pollution-Sulphur 94, Climate Change-Kyoto Protocol
Geography - note: largest country in the world in terms of area but unfavorably located in relation to major sea lanes of the world; despite its size, much of the country lacks proper soils and climates (either too cold or too dry) for agriculture

People

Population: 145,470,197 (July 2001 est.)
Age structure:
0-14 years: 17.41% (male 12,915,026; female 12,405,341)
15-64 years: 69.78% (male 49,183,000; female 52,320,962)
65 years and over: 12.81% (male 5,941,944; female 12,703,924) (2001 est.)
Population growth rate: -0.35% (2001 est.)
Birth rate: 9.35 births/1,000 population (2001 est.)
Death rate: 13.85 deaths/1,000 population (2001 est.)
Net migration rate: 0.98 migrant(s)/1,000 population (2001 est.)
Sex ratio:
at birth: 1.05 male(s)/female
under 15 years: 1.04 male(s)/female
15-64 years: 0.94 male(s)/female
65 years and over: 0.47 male(s)/female
total population: 0.88 male(s)/female (2001 est.)
Infant mortality rate: 20.05 deaths/1,000 live births (2001 est.)
Life expectancy at birth:
total population: 67.34 years
male: 62.12 years
female: 72.83 years (2001 est.)
Total fertility rate: 1.27 children born/woman (2001 est.)
HIV/AIDS - adult prevalence rate: 0.18% (1999 est.)
HIV/AIDS - people living with HIV/AIDS: 130,000 (1999 est.)
HIV/AIDS - deaths: 850 (1999 est.)
Nationality:
noun: Russian(s)
adjective: Russian
Ethnic groups: Russian 81.5%, Tatar 3.8%, Ukrainian 3%, Chuvash 1.2%, Bashkir 0.9%, Byelorussian 0.8%, Moldavian 0.7%, other 8.1%
Religions: Russian Orthodox, Muslim, other
Languages: Russian, other

Literacy:
definition: age 15 and over can read and write
total population: 98%
male: 100%
female: 97% (1989 est.)

Government

Country name:
conventional long form: Russian Federation
conventional short form: Russia
local long form: Rossiyskaya Federatsiya
local short form: Rossiya
former: Russian Empire, Russian Soviet Federative Socialist Republic
Government type: federation
Capital: Moscow
Administrative divisions: 49 oblasts (oblastey, singular - oblast), 21 republics* (respublik, singular - respublika), 10 autonomous okrugs**(avtonomnykh okrugov, singular - avtonomnyy okrug), 6 krays*** (krayev, singular - kray), 2 federal cities (singular - gorod)****, and 1 autonomous oblast*****(avtonomnaya oblast'); Adygeya (Maykop)*, Aginskiy Buryatskiy (Aginskoye)**, Altay (Gorno-Altaysk)*, Altayskiy (Barnaul)***, Amurskaya (Blagoveshchensk), Arkhangel'skaya, Astrakhanskaya, Bashkortostan (Ufa)*, Belgorodskaya, Bryanskaya, Buryatiya (Ulan-Ude)*, Chechnya (Groznyy)*, Chelyabinskaya, Chitinskaya, Chukotskiy (Anadyr')**, Chuvashiya (Cheboksary)*, Dagestan (Makhachkala)*, Evenkiyskiy (Tura)**, Ingushetiya (Nazran')*, Irkutskaya, Ivanovskaya, Kabardino-Balkariya (Nal'chik)*, Kaliningradskaya, Kalmykiya (Elista)*, Kaluzhskaya, Kamchatskaya (Petropavlovsk-Kamchatskiy), Karachayevo-Cherkesiya (Cherkessk)*, Kareliya (Petrozavodsk)*, Kemerovskaya, Khabarovskiy***, Khakasiya (Abakan)*, Khanty-Mansiyskiy (Khanty-Mansiysk)**, Kirovskaya, Komi (Syktyvkar)*, Koryakskiy (Palana)**, Kostromskaya, Krasnodarskiy***, Krasnoyarskiy***, Kurganskaya, Kurskaya, Leningradskaya, Lipetskaya, Magadanskaya, Mariy-El (Yoshkar-Ola)*, Mordoviya (Saransk)*, Moskovskaya, Moskva (Moscow)****, Murmanskaya, Nenetskiy (Nar'yan-Mar)**, Nizhegorodskaya, Novgorodskaya, Novosibirskaya, Omskaya, Orenburgskaya, Orlovskaya (Orel), Penzenskaya, Permskaya, Komi-Permyatskiy (Kudymkar)**, Primorskiy (Vladivostok)***, Pskovskaya, Rostovskaya, Ryazanskaya, Sakha (Yakutsk)*, Sakhalinskaya (Yuzhno-Sakhalinsk), Samarskaya, Sankt-Peterburg (Saint Petersburg)****, Saratovskaya, Severnaya Osetiya-Alaniya [North Ossetia] (Vladikavkaz)*, Smolenskaya, Stavropol'skiy***, Sverdlovskaya (Yekaterinburg), Tambovskaya, Tatarstan (Kazan')*, Taymyrskiy (Dudinka)**, Tomskaya, Tul'skaya, Tverskaya, Tyumenskaya, Tyva (Kyzyl)*, Udmurtiya (Izhevsk)*, Ul'yanovskaya, Ust'-Ordynskiy Buryatskiy (Ust'-Ordynskiy)**, Vladimirskaya, Volgogradskaya, Vologodskaya, Voronezhskaya, Yamalo-Nenetskiy (Salekhard)**, Yaroslavskaya, Yevreyskaya*****;

note - when using a place name with an adjectival ending 'skaya' or 'skiy,' the word Oblast' or Avonomnyy Okrug or Kray should be added to the place name
note: the autonomous republics of Chechnya and Ingushetiya were formerly the autonomous republic of Checheno-Ingushetia (the boundary between Chechnya and Ingushetia has yet to be determined); administrative divisions have the same names as their administrative centers (exceptions have the administrative center name following in parentheses)
Independence: 24 August 1991 (from Soviet Union)
National holiday: Russia Day, 12 June (1990)
Constitution: adopted 12 December 1993
Legal system: based on civil law system; judicial review of legislative acts
Suffrage: 18 years of age; universal
Executive branch:
chief of state: President Vladimir Vladimirovich PUTIN (acting president since 31 December 1999, president since 7 May 2000)
head of government: Premier Mikhail Mikhaylovich KASYANOV (since 7 May 2000); First Deputy Premier Aleksey Leonidovich KUDRIN (since 18 May 2000), Deputy Premiers Aleksey Vasilyevich GORDEYEV (since 20 May 2000), Viktor Borisovich KHRISTENKO (since 31 May 1999), Ilya Iosifovich KLEBANOV (since 31 May 1999), Valentina Ivanovna MATVIYENKO (since 22 September 1998)
cabinet: Ministries of the Government or "Government" composed of the premier and his deputies, ministers, and other agency heads; all are appointed by the president
note: there is also a Presidential Administration (PA) that provides staff and policy support to the president, drafts presidential decrees, and coordinates policy among government agencies; a Security Council also reports directly to the president
elections: president elected by popular vote for a four-year term; election last held 26 March 2000 (next to be held NA 2004); note - no vice president; if the president dies in office, cannot exercise his powers because of ill health, is impeached, or resigns, the premier succeeds him; the premier serves as acting president until a new presidential election is held, which must be within three months; premier appointed by the president with the approval of the Duma
election results: Vladimir Vladimirovich PUTIN elected president; percent of vote - PUTIN 52.9%, Gennadiy Aadreyevich ZYUGANOV 29.2%, Grigoriy Alekseyevich YAVLINSKIY 5.8%
Legislative branch: bicameral Federal Assembly or Federalnoye Sobraniye consists of the Federation Council or Sovet Federatsii (178 seats; as of July 2000, members appointed by the top executive and legislative officials in each of the 89 federal administrative units - oblasts, krays, republics, autonomous okrugs and oblasts, and the federal cities of Moscow and Saint Petersburg; members serve four-year terms) and the State Duma or Gosudarstvennaya Duma (450 seats; half elected by proportional representation from party lists winning at

Russia (continued)

least 5% of the vote, and half from single-member constituencies; members are elected by direct popular vote to serve four-year terms)
elections: State Duma - last held 19 December 1999 (next to be held NA December 2003)
election results: State Duma - percent of vote received by parties clearing the 5% threshold entitling them to a proportional share of the 225 party list seats - KPRF 24.29%, Unity 23.32%, OVR 13.33%, Union of Right Forces 8.52%, LDPR 5.98%, Yabloko 5.93%; seats by party - KPRF 113, Unity 72, OVR 67, Union of Rightist Forces 29, LDPR 17, Yabloko 21, other 16, independents 106, repeat election required 8, vacant 1
Judicial branch: Constitutional Court; Supreme Court; Superior Court of Arbitration; judges for all courts are appointed for life by the Federation Council on the recommendation of the president
Political parties and leaders: Agrarian Party [Mikhail Ivanovich LAPSHIN]; Communist Party of the Russian Federation or KPRF [Gennadiy Andreyevich ZYUGANOV]; Fatherland-All Russia or OVR [Yuriy Mikhailovich LUZHKOV]; Liberal Democratic Party of Russia or LDPR [Vladimir Volfovich ZHIRINOVSKIY]; Union of Right Forces [Anatoliy Borisovich CHUBAYS, Yegor Timurovich GAYDAR, Irina Mutsuovna KHAKAMADA, Boris Yefimovich NEMTSOV]; Unity [Sergey Kuzhugetovich SHOYGU]; Yabloko Bloc [Grigoriy Alekseyevich YAVLINSKIY]
note: some 150 political parties, blocs, and movements registered with the Justice Ministry as of the 19 December 1998 deadline to be eligible to participate in the 19 December 1999 Duma elections; of these, 36 political organizations actually qualified to run slates of candidates on the Duma party list ballot, 6 parties cleared the 5% threshold to win a proportional share of the 225 party seats in the Duma, 9 other organizations hold seats in the Duma: Bloc of Nikolayev and Academician Fedorov, Congress of Russian Communities, Movement in Support of the Army, Our Home Is Russia, Party of Pensioners, Power to the People, Russian All-People's Union, Russian Socialist Party, and Spiritual Heritage; primary political blocs include pro-market democrats - (Yabloko Bloc and Union of Right Forces), anti-market and/or ultranationalist (Communist Party of the Russian Federation and Liberal Democratic Party of Russia)
Political pressure groups and leaders: NA
International organization participation: APEC, ASEAN (dialogue partner), BIS, BSEC, CBSS, CCC, CE, CERN (observer), CIS, EAPC, EBRD, ECE, ESCAP, G- 8, IAEA, IBRD, ICAO, ICC, ICFTU, ICRM, IDA, IFC, IFRCS, IHO, ILO, IMF, IMO, Inmarsat, Intelsat, Interpol, IOC, IOM (observer), ISO, ITU, LAIA (observer), MINURSO, MONUC, NAM (guest), NSG, OAS (observer), OPCW, OSCE, PCA, PFP, UN, UN Security Council, UNAMSIL, UNCTAD, UNESCO, UNHCR, UNIDO, UNIKOM, UNITAR, UNMEE, UNMIBH, UNMIK, UNMOP, UNOMIG, UNTAET, UNTSO, UPU, WFTU, WHO, WIPO, WMO, WToO, WTrO (observer), ZC

Diplomatic representation in the US:
chief of mission: Ambassador Yuriy Viktorovich USHAKOV
chancery: 2650 Wisconsin Avenue NW, Washington, DC 20007
telephone: [1] (202) 298-5700, 5701, 5704, 5708
FAX: [1] (202) 298-5735
consulate(s) general: New York, San Francisco, and Seattle
Diplomatic representation from the US:
chief of mission: Ambassador James F. COLLINS
embassy: Novinskiy Bul'var 19/23, 121099 Moscow
mailing address: APO AE 09721
telephone: [7] (095) 728-5000
FAX: [7] (095) 728-5203
consulate(s) general: Saint Petersburg, Vladivostok, Yekaterinburg
Flag description: three equal horizontal bands of white (top), blue, and red

Economy

Economy - overview: A decade after the implosion of the Soviet Union in 1991, Russia is still struggling to establish a modern market economy and achieve strong economic growth. In contrast to its trading partners in Central Europe - which were able to overcome the initial production declines that accompanied the launch of market reforms within three to five years - Russia saw its economy contract for five years, as the executive and legislature dithered over the implementation of many of the basic foundations of a market economy. Russia achieved a slight recovery in 1997, but the government's stubborn budget deficits and the country's poor business climate made it vulnerable when the global financial crisis swept through in 1998. The crisis culminated in the August depreciation of the ruble, a debt default by the government, and a sharp deterioration in living standards for most of the population. The economy rebounded in 1999 and 2000, buoyed by the competitive boost from the weak ruble and a surging trade surplus fueled by rising world oil prices. This recovery, along with a renewed government effort in 2000 to advance lagging structural reforms, have raised business and investor confidence over Russia's prospects in its second decade of transition. Yet serious problems persist. Russia remains heavily dependent on exports of commodities, particularly oil, natural gas, metals, and timber, which account for over 80% of exports, leaving the country vulnerable to swings in world prices. Russia's agricultural sector remains beset by uncertainty over land ownership rights, which has discouraged needed investment and restructuring. Another threat is negative demographic trends, fueled by low birth rates and a deteriorating health situation - including an alarming rise in AIDS cases - that have contributed to a nearly 2% drop in the population since 1992. Russia's industrial base is increasingly dilapidated and must be replaced or modernized if the country is to achieve sustainable economic growth. Other problems include widespread corruption, capital flight, and brain drain.

GDP: purchasing power parity - $1.12 trillion (2000 est.)
GDP - real growth rate: 6.3% (2000 est.)
GDP - per capita: purchasing power parity - $7,700 (2000 est.)
GDP - composition by sector:
agriculture: 7%
industry: 34%
services: 59% (1999 est.)
Population below poverty line: 40% (1999 est.)
Household income or consumption by percentage share:
lowest 10%: 1.7%
highest 10%: 38.7% (1998)
Inflation rate (consumer prices): 20.6% (2000 est.)
Labor force: 66 million (1997)
Labor force - by occupation: agriculture 15%, industry 30%, services 55% (1999 est.)
Unemployment rate: 10.5% (2000 est.), plus considerable underemployment
Budget:
revenues: $40 billion
expenditures: $33.7 billion, including capital expenditures of $NA (2000 est.)
Industries: complete range of mining and extractive industries producing coal, oil, gas, chemicals, and metals; all forms of machine building from rolling mills to high-performance aircraft and space vehicles; shipbuilding; road and rail transportation equipment; communications equipment; agricultural machinery, tractors, and construction equipment; electric power generating and transmitting equipment; medical and scientific instruments; consumer durables, textiles, foodstuffs, handicrafts
Industrial production growth rate: 8.8% (2000 est.)
Electricity - production: 798.065 billion kWh (1999)
Electricity - production by source:
fossil fuel: 66.31%
hydro: 19.79%
nuclear: 13.9%
other: 0% (1999)
Electricity - consumption: 728.2 billion kWh (1999)
Electricity - exports: 20 billion kWh (1999)
Electricity - imports: 6 billion kWh (1999)
Agriculture - products: grain, sugar beets, sunflower seed, vegetables, fruits; beef, milk
Exports: $105.1 billion (2000 est.)
Exports - commodities: petroleum and petroleum products, natural gas, wood and wood products, metals, chemicals, and a wide variety of civilian and military manufactures
Exports - partners: US 8.8%, Germany 8.5%, Ukraine 6.5%, Belarus 5.1%, Italy 5%, Netherlands 4.8% (1999)
Imports: $44.2 billion (2000 est.)
Imports - commodities: machinery and equipment, consumer goods, medicines, meat, grain, sugar, semifinished metal products

Russia (continued)

Imports - partners: Germany 13.8%, Belarus 10.7%, Ukraine 8.3%, US 7.9%, Kazakhstan 4.6%, Italy 3.8% (1999)
Debt - external: $163 billion (2000 est.)
Economic aid - recipient: $8.523 billion (1995)
Currency: Russian ruble (RUR)
Currency code: RUR
Exchange rates: Russian rubles per US dollar - 28.3592 (January 2001), 28.1292 (2000), 24.6199 (1999), 9.7051 (1998), 5,785 (1997), 5,121 (1996)
note: the post-1 January 1998 ruble is equal to 1,000 of the pre-1 January 1998 rubles
Fiscal year: calendar year

Communications

Telephones - main lines in use: 30 million (1998)
Telephones - mobile cellular: 2.5 million (October 2000)
Telephone system:
general assessment: the telephone system has undergone significant changes in the 1990s; there are more than 1,000 companies licensed to offer communication services; access to digital lines has improved, particularly in urban centers; Internet and e-mail services are improving; Russia has made progress toward building the telecommunications infrastructure necessary for a market economy; however, a large demand for main line service remains unsatisfied
domestic: cross-country digital trunk lines run from Saint Petersburg to Khabarovsk, and from Moscow to Novorossiysk; the telephone systems in 60 regional capitals have modern digital infrastructures; cellular services, both analog and digital, are available in many areas; in rural areas, the telephone services are still outdated, inadequate, and low density
international: Russia is connected internationally by three undersea fiber-optic cables; digital switches in several cities provide more than 50,000 lines for international calls; satellite earth stations provide access to Intelsat, Intersputnik, Eutelsat, Inmarsat, and Orbita systems
Radio broadcast stations: AM 420, FM 447, shortwave 56 (1998)
Radios: 61.5 million (1997)
Television broadcast stations: 7,306 (1998)
Televisions: 60.5 million (1997)
Internet country code: .ru
Internet Service Providers (ISPs): 35 (2000)
Internet users: 9.2 million (2000)

Transportation

Railways:
total: 149,000 km
note: 86,000 km are in common carrier service; 63,000 km serve specific industries and are not available for common carrier use; 40,000 km of the railway in common carrier use are electrified
broad gauge: 149,000 km 1.520-m gauge (1998)
Highways:
total: 952,000 km
paved: 752,000 km (including, in addition to about 336,000 km of conventionally paved roads, about 416,000 km of roads, the surfaces of which have been stabilized with gravel or other coarse aggregates, making them trafficable in wet weather)
unpaved: 200,000 km (these roads are made of unstabilized earth and are difficult to negotiate in wet weather) (1998)
Waterways: 95,900 km (total routes in general use)
note: routes with navigation guides serving the Russian River Fleet-95,900 km; routes with night navigational aids-60,400 km; man-made navigable routes-16,900 km (Jan 1994)
Pipelines: crude oil 48,000 km; petroleum products 15,000 km; natural gas 140,000 km (June 1993 est.)
Ports and harbors: Arkhangel'sk, Astrakhan', Kaliningrad, Kazan', Khabarovsk, Kholmsk, Krasnoyarsk, Moscow, Murmansk, Nakhodka, Nevel'sk, Novorossiysk, Petropavlovsk-Kamchatskiy, Saint Petersburg, Rostov, Sochi, Tuapse, Vladivostok, Volgograd, Vostochnyy, Vyborg
Merchant marine:
total: 878 ships (1,000 GRT or over) totaling 4,314,485 GRT/5,344,958 DWT
ships by type: barge carrier 1, bulk 20, cargo 543, chemical tanker 4, combination bulk 21, combination ore/oil 7, container 31, multi-functional large-load carrier 1, passenger 35, passenger/cargo 3, petroleum tanker 164, refrigerated cargo 24, roll on/roll off 17, short-sea passenger 7
note: includes a foreign-owned ship registered here as a flag of convenience: Reunion 1 (2000 est.)
Airports: 2,743 (2000 est.)
Airports - with paved runways:
total: 471
over 3,047 m: 56
2,438 to 3,047 m: 178
1,524 to 2,437 m: 76
914 to 1,523 m: 69
under 914 m: 92 (2000 est.)
Airports - with unpaved runways:
total: 2,272
over 3,047 m: 28
2,438 to 3,047 m: 118
1,524 to 2,437 m: 204
914 to 1,523 m: 324
under 914 m: 1,598 (2000 est.)

Military

Military branches: Ground Forces, Navy, Air Force, Strategic Rocket Forces
Military manpower - military age: 18 years of age
Military manpower - availability:
males age 15-49: 38,866,147 (2001 est.)
Military manpower - fit for military service:
males age 15-49: 30,337,743 (2001 est.)
Military manpower - reaching military age annually:
males: 1,242,778 (2001 est.)
Military expenditures - dollar figure: $NA
Military expenditures - percent of GDP: NA%

Transnational Issues

Disputes - international: dispute over at least two small sections of the boundary with China remains to be settled, despite 1997 boundary agreement; islands of Etorofu, Kunashiri, and Shikotan and the Habomai group occupied by the Soviet Union in 1945, now administered by Russia, claimed by Japan; Caspian Sea boundaries are not yet determined among Azerbaijan, Iran, Kazakhstan, Russia, and Turkmenistan; Estonian and Russian negotiators reached a technical border agreement in December 1996, which has not been signed or ratified by Russia as of February 2001; draft treaty delimiting the boundary with Latvia has not been signed; 1997 border agreement with Lithuania not yet ratified; has made no territorial claim in Antarctica (but has reserved the right to do so) and does not recognize the claims of any other nation; Svalbard is the focus of a maritime boundary dispute between Norway and Russia
Illicit drugs: limited cultivation of illicit cannabis and opium poppy and producer of amphetamine, mostly for domestic consumption; government has active eradication program; increasingly used as transshipment point for Southwest and Southeast Asian opiates and cannabis and Latin American cocaine to Western Europe, possibly to the US, and growing domestic market; major source of heroin precursor chemicals; corruption and organized crime are major concerns; heroin an increasing threat in domestic drug market

Rwanda

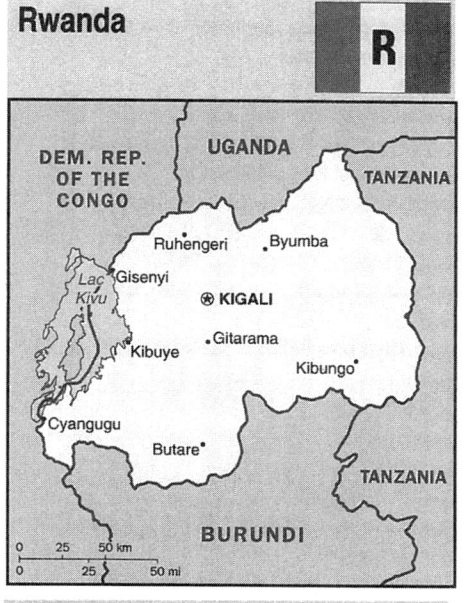

Introduction

Background: In 1959, three years before independence, the majority ethnic group, the Hutus overthrew the ruling Tutsi king. Over the next several years thousands of Tutsis were killed, and some 150,000 driven into exile in neighboring countries. The children of these exiles later formed a rebel group, the Rwandan Patriotic Front (RPF) and began a civil war in 1990. The war, along with several political and economic upheavals, exacerbated ethnic tensions culminating in April 1994 in the genocide of roughly 800,000 Tutsis and moderate Hutus. The Tutsi rebels defeated the Hutu regime and ended the killing in July 1994, but approximately 2 million Hutu refugees - many fearing Tutsi retribution - fled to neighboring Burundi, Tanzania, Uganda, and Zaire, now called the Democratic Republic of the Congo (DROC). Since then most of the refugees have returned to Rwanda. Despite substantial international assistance and political reforms - including Rwanda's first local elections in March 1999 - the country continues to struggle to boost investment and agricultural output and to foster reconciliation. A series of massive population displacements, a nagging Hutu extremist insurgency, and Rwandan involvement in two wars over the past four years in the neighboring DROC continue to hinder Rwanda's efforts.

Geography

Location: Central Africa, east of Democratic Republic of the Congo
Geographic coordinates: 2 00 S, 30 00 E
Map references: Africa
Area:
total: 26,338 sq km
land: 24,948 sq km
water: 1,390 sq km
Area - comparative: slightly smaller than Maryland
Land boundaries:
total: 893 km
border countries: Burundi 290 km, Democratic Republic of the Congo 217 km, Tanzania 217 km, Uganda 169 km
Coastline: 0 km (landlocked)
Maritime claims: none (landlocked)
Climate: temperate; two rainy seasons (February to April, November to January); mild in mountains with frost and snow possible
Terrain: mostly grassy uplands and hills; relief is mountainous with altitude declining from west to east
Elevation extremes:
lowest point: Rusizi River 950 m
highest point: Volcan Karisimbi 4,519 m
Natural resources: gold, cassiterite (tin ore), wolframite (tungsten ore), methane, hydropower, arable land
Land use:
arable land: 35%
permanent crops: 13%
permanent pastures: 18%
forests and woodland: 22%
other: 12% (1993 est.)
Irrigated land: 40 sq km (1993 est.)
Natural hazards: periodic droughts; the volcanic Virunga mountains are in the northwest along the border with Democratic Republic of the Congo
Environment - current issues: deforestation results from uncontrolled cutting of trees for fuel; overgrazing; soil exhaustion; soil erosion; widespread poaching
Environment - international agreements:
party to: Biodiversity, Climate Change, Desertification, Endangered Species, Marine Dumping, Nuclear Test Ban, Ship Pollution
signed, but not ratified: Law of the Sea
Geography - note: landlocked; predominantly rural population

People

Population: 7,312,756
note: estimates for this country explicitly take into account the effects of excess mortality due to AIDS; this can result in lower life expectancy, higher infant mortality and death rates, lower population and growth rates, and changes in the distribution of population by age and sex than would otherwise be expected (July 2001 est.)
Age structure:
0-14 years: 42.4% (male 1,555,878; female 1,544,942)
15-64 years: 54.73% (male 1,989,501; female 2,013,012)
65 years and over: 2.87% (male 83,769; female 125,654) (2001 est.)
Population growth rate: 1.16% (2001 est.)
Birth rate: 33.97 births/1,000 population (2001 est.)
Death rate: 21.13 deaths/1,000 population (2001 est.)
Net migration rate: -1.21 migrant(s)/1,000 population (2001 est.)
Sex ratio:
at birth: 1.03 male(s)/female
under 15 years: 1.01 male(s)/female
15-64 years: 0.99 male(s)/female
65 years and over: 0.67 male(s)/female
total population: 0.99 male(s)/female (2001 est.)
Infant mortality rate: 118.92 deaths/1,000 live births (2001 est.)
Life expectancy at birth:
total population: 38.99 years
male: 38.35 years
female: 39.65 years (2001 est.)
Total fertility rate: 4.89 children born/woman (2001 est.)
HIV/AIDS - adult prevalence rate: 11.21% (1999 est.)
HIV/AIDS - people living with HIV/AIDS: 400,000 (1999 est.)
HIV/AIDS - deaths: 40,000 (1999 est.)
Nationality:
noun: Rwandan(s)
adjective: Rwandan
Ethnic groups: Hutu 84%, Tutsi 15%, Twa (Pygmoid) 1%
Religions: Roman Catholic 52.7%, Protestant 24%, Adventist 10.4%, Muslim 1.9%, indigenous beliefs and other 6.5%, none 4.5% (1996)
Languages: Kinyarwanda (official) universal Bantu vernacular, French (official), English (official), Kiswahili (Swahili) used in commercial centers
Literacy:
definition: age 15 and over can read and write
total population: 48%
male: 52%
female: 45% (1995 est.)

Government

Country name:
conventional long form: Rwandese Republic
conventional short form: Rwanda
local long form: Republika y'u Rwanda
local short form: Rwanda
former: Ruanda
Government type: republic; presidential, multiparty system
Capital: Kigali
Administrative divisions: 12 prefectures (in French - prefectures, singular - prefecture; in Kinyarwanda - plural - NA, singular - prefegitura); Butare, Byumba, Cyangugu, Gikongoro, Gisenyi, Gitarama, Kibungo, Kibuye, Kigali Rurale, Kigali-ville, Umutara, Ruhengeri
Independence: 1 July 1962 (from Belgium-administered UN trusteeship)
National holiday: Independence Day, 1 July (1962)
Constitution: on 5 May 1995, the Transitional National Assembly adopted as Fundamental Law the constitution of 18 June 1991, provisions of the 1993 Arusha peace accord, the July 1994 Declaration by the Rwanda Patriotic Front, and the November 1994 multiparty protocol of understanding

Rwanda (continued)

Legal system: based on German and Belgian civil law systems and customary law; judicial review of legislative acts in the Supreme Court; has not accepted compulsory ICJ jurisdiction

Suffrage: 18 years of age; universal adult

Executive branch:
chief of state: President Maj. Gen. Paul KAGAME (FPR) (since 22 April 2000)
head of government: Prime Minister Bernard MAKUZA (since 8 March 2000)
cabinet: Council of Ministers appointed by the president
elections: normally the president is elected by popular vote for a five-year term; special election for new president by deputies of the National Assembly and governmental ministers held 17 April 2000 (next national election to be held NA 2003); prime minister is appointed by the president
election results: Paul KAGAME (FPR) elected president in a special parliamentary/ministerial ballot receiving 81 of a possible 86 votes

Legislative branch: unicameral Transitional National Assembly or Assemblee Nationale de Transition (a power-sharing body with 70 seats established on 12 December 1994 following a multiparty protocol of understanding; members were named by their parties, number of seats per party predetermined by the Arusha peace accord)
note: four additional seats, two for women and two for youth, added in 2001
elections: the last national legislative elections were held 16 December 1988 for the National Development Council (the legislature prior to the advent of the Transitional National Assembly); no elections have been held for the Transitional National Assembly as the distribution of seats was predetermined by the Arusha peace accord
election results: percent of vote by party - NA%; seats by party - FPR 13, MDR 13, PSD 13, PL 13, PDC 6, RPA 6, PSR 2, PDI 2, UDPR 2; note - the distribution of seats was predetermined, four additional seats (two for women and two for youth) added in 2001

Judicial branch: Supreme Court; communal courts; appeals courts

Political parties and leaders: Centrist Democratic Party or PDC [Jean-Nipomuscene NAYINZIRA]; Democratic Socialist Party or PSD [Charles NTAKIRUTINKA, Vincent BIRUTA, Augusin IYAMUREMYE]; Democratic Popular Union of Rwanda or UDPR [Adrien RANGIRA]; Democratic Republican Movement or MDR [Celestin KABANDA, Emile NTWARABAKIGA, Christian MARARA]; Islamic Democratic Party or PDI [Andre BUMAYA]; Liberal Party or PL [Pie MUGABO, Enock KABERA, Prosper MUGIRANEZA]; Rwanda Patriotic Army or RPA [Maj. Gen. Paul KAGAME, commander]; Rwanda Patriotic Front or FPR [Maj. Gen. Paul KAGAME]; Rwandan Socialist Party or PSR [Medard RUTIJANWA]

Political pressure groups and leaders: IBUKA - association of genocide survivors

International organization participation: ACCT, ACP, AfDB, CCC, CEEAC, CEPGL, ECA, FAO, G-77, IBRD, ICAO, ICFTU, ICRM, IDA, IFAD, IFC, IFRCS, ILO, IMF, Intelsat, Interpol, IOC, IOM (observer), ISO (correspondent), ITU, NAM, OAU, OPCW, UN, UNCTAD, UNESCO, UNIDO, UPU, WCL, WHO, WIPO, WMO, WToO, WTrO

Diplomatic representation in the US:
chief of mission: Ambassador Richard SEZIBERA
chancery: 1714 New Hampshire Ave. NW, Washington, DC 20009
telephone: [1] (202) 232-2882
FAX: [1] (202) 232-4544

Diplomatic representation from the US:
chief of mission: Ambassador George M. STAPLES
embassy: Boulevard de la Revolution, Kigali
mailing address: B. P. 28, Kigali
telephone: [250] 756 01 through 03, 721 26, 771 47
FAX: [250] 721 28

Flag description: three equal vertical bands of red (hoist side), yellow, and green with a large black letter R centered in the yellow band; uses the popular pan-African colors of Ethiopia; similar to the flag of Guinea, which has a plain yellow band

Economy

Economy - overview: Rwanda is a rural country with about 90% of the population engaged in (mainly subsistence) agriculture. It is the most densely populated country in Africa; is landlocked; and has few natural resources and minimal industry. Primary exports are coffee and tea. The 1994 genocide decimated Rwanda's fragile economic base, severely impoverished the population, particularly women, and eroded the country's ability to attract private and external investment. However, Rwanda has made significant progress in stabilizing and rehabilitating its economy. GDP has rebounded, and inflation has been curbed. In June 1998, Rwanda signed an Enhanced Structural Adjustment Facility (ESAF) with the IMF. Rwanda has also embarked upon an ambitious privatization program with the World Bank. Continued growth in 2001 depends on the maintenance of international aid levels and the strengthening of world prices of coffee and tea.

GDP: purchasing power parity - $6.4 billion (2000 est.)

GDP - real growth rate: 5.8% (2000 est.)

GDP - per capita: purchasing power parity - $900 (2000 est.)

GDP - composition by sector:
agriculture: 40%
industry: 20%
services: 40% (2000 est.)

Population below poverty line: 70% (2000 est.)

Household income or consumption by percentage share:
lowest 10%: 4.2%
highest 10%: 24.2% (1983-85)

Inflation rate (consumer prices): 4% (2000)

Labor force: 3.6 million

Labor force - by occupation: agriculture 90%

Unemployment rate: NA%

Budget:
revenues: $198 million
expenditures: $411 million, including capital expenditures of $NA (2000 est.)

Industries: cement, agricultural products, small-scale beverages, soap, furniture, shoes, plastic goods, textiles, cigarettes

Industrial production growth rate: 8.7% (1998 est.)

Electricity - production: 132 million kWh (1999)

Electricity - production by source:
fossil fuel: 3.03%
hydro: 96.97%
nuclear: 0%
other: 0% (1999)

Electricity - consumption: 191.8 million kWh (1999)

Electricity - exports: 1 million kWh (1999)

Electricity - imports: 70 million kWh (1999)

Agriculture - products: coffee, tea, pyrethrum (insecticide made from chrysanthemums), bananas, beans, sorghum, potatoes; livestock

Exports: $68.4 million (f.o.b., 2000 est.)

Exports - commodities: coffee, tea, hides, tin ore

Exports - partners: Germany, Belgium, Pakistan, Italy, Kenya

Imports: $245.9 million (f.o.b., 2000 est.)

Imports - commodities: foodstuffs, machinery and equipment, steel, petroleum products, cement and construction material

Imports - partners: Kenya, Tanzania, US, Benelux, France, India

Debt - external: $1.3 billion (1999)

Economic aid - recipient: $591.5 million (1997); note - in summer 1998, Rwanda presented its policy objectives and development priorities to donor governments resulting in multiyear pledges in the amount of $250 million

Currency: Rwandan franc (RWF)

Currency code: RWF

Exchange rates: Rwandan francs per US dollar - 432.24 (January 2001), 389.70 (2000), 333.94 (1999) 312.31 (1998), 301.53 (1997), 306.82 (1996)

Fiscal year: calendar year

Communications

Telephones - main lines in use: 15,000 (1995)

Telephones - mobile cellular: NA
note: however, Rwanda has mobile cellular service between Kigali and several prefecture capitals (2000)

Telephone system:
general assessment: telephone system primarily serves business and government
domestic: the capital, Kigali, is connected to the centers of the prefectures by microwave radio relay; the remainder of the network depends on wire and HF radiotelephone

Rwanda (continued)

international: international connections employ microwave radio relay to neighboring countries and satellite communications to more distant countries; satellite earth stations - 1 Intelsat (Indian Ocean) in Kigali (includes telex and telefax service)
Radio broadcast stations: AM 0, FM 3, shortwave 1 (1998)
Radios: 601,000 (1997)
Television broadcast stations: 2 (1997)
Televisions: NA; probably less than 1,000 (1997)
Internet country code: .rw
Internet Service Providers (ISPs): 1 (2000)
Internet users: 1,000 (2000)

Transportation

Railways: 0 km
Highways:
total: 12,000 km
paved: 1,000 km
unpaved: 11,000 km (1997 est.)
Waterways:
note: Lac Kivu navigable by shallow-draft barges and native craft
Ports and harbors: Cyangugu, Gisenyi, Kibuye
Airports: 8 (2000 est.)
Airports - with paved runways:
total: 4
over 3,047 m: 1
914 to 1,523 m: 2
under 914 m: 1 (2000 est.)
Airports - with unpaved runways:
total: 4
914 to 1,523 m: 1
under 914 m: 3 (2000 est.)

Military

Military branches: Army, Navy, Air Force
Military manpower - availability:
males age 15-49: 1,815,633 (2001 est.)
Military manpower - fit for military service:
males age 15-49: 924,544 (2001 est.)
Military expenditures - dollar figure: $58 million (FY01)
Military expenditures - percent of GDP: 3.2% (FY01)

Transnational Issues

Disputes - international: Rwandan military forces are supporting the rebel forces in the civil war in the Democratic Republic of the Congo

Saint Helena
(overseas territory of the UK)

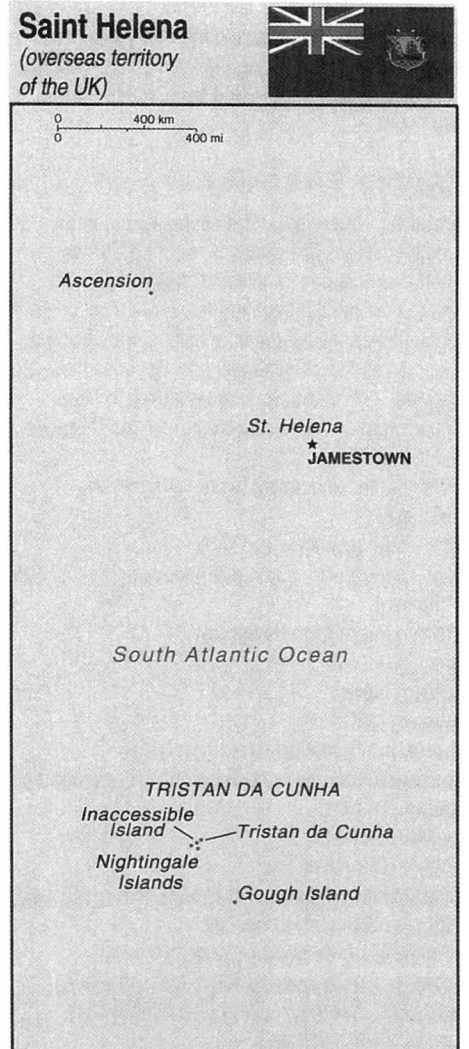

Introduction

Background: Uninhabited when first discovered by the Portuguese in 1502, St. Helena was garrisoned by the British during the 17th century. It acquired fame as the place of Napoleon BONAPARTE's exile, from 1815 until his death in 1821, but its importance as a port of call declined after the opening of the Suez Canal in 1869. Ascension Island is the site of a US Air Force auxiliary airfield; Gough Island has a meteorological station.

Geography

Location: islands in the South Atlantic Ocean, about mid-way between South America and Africa
Geographic coordinates: 15 56 S, 5 42 W
Map references: Africa
Area:
total: 410 sq km
land: 410 sq km
water: 0 sq km
note: includes St. Helena Island, Ascension, and the island group of Tristan da Cunha, which consists of Tristan da Cunha Island, Gough Island, Inaccessible Island, and the three Nightingale Islands
Area - comparative: slightly more than two times the size of Washington, DC
Land boundaries: 0 km
Coastline: 60 km
Maritime claims:
exclusive fishing zone: 200 NM
territorial sea: 12 NM
Climate: Saint Helena - tropical; marine; mild, tempered by trade winds; Tristan da Cunha - temperate; marine, mild, tempered by trade winds (tends to be cooler than Saint Helena)
Terrain: Saint Helena - rugged, volcanic; small scattered plateaus and plains
note: the other islands of the group have a volcanic origin
Elevation extremes:
lowest point: Atlantic Ocean 0 m
highest point: Queen Mary's Peak on Tristan da Cunha 2,060 m
Natural resources: fish
Land use:
arable land: 6%
permanent crops: 0%
permanent pastures: 6%
forests and woodland: 6%
other: 82% (1993 est.)
Irrigated land: NA sq km
Natural hazards: active volcanism on Tristan da Cunha
Environment - current issues: NA
Geography - note: harbors at least 40 species of plants unknown anywhere else in the world; Ascension is a breeding ground for sea turtles and sooty terns

People

Population: 7,266 (July 2001 est.)
Age structure:
0-14 years: 19.08% (male 699; female 687)
15-64 years: 71.72% (male 2,711; female 2,500)
65 years and over: 9.2% (male 286; female 383) (2001 est.)
Population growth rate: 0.72% (2001 est.)
Birth rate: 13.49 births/1,000 population (2001 est.)
Death rate: 6.33 deaths/1,000 population (2001 est.)
Net migration rate: 0 migrant(s)/1,000 population (2001 est.)
Sex ratio:
at birth: 1.04 male(s)/female
under 15 years: 1.02 male(s)/female
15-64 years: 1.08 male(s)/female
65 years and over: 0.75 male(s)/female
total population: 1.04 male(s)/female (2001 est.)
Infant mortality rate: 22.38 deaths/1,000 live births (2001 est.)
Life expectancy at birth:
total population: 77.01 years
male: 74.13 years
female: 80.04 years (2001 est.)
Total fertility rate: 1.53 children born/woman (2001 est.)

Saint Helena (continued)

HIV/AIDS - adult prevalence rate: NA%
HIV/AIDS - people living with HIV/AIDS: NA
HIV/AIDS - deaths: NA
Nationality:
noun: Saint Helenian(s)
adjective: Saint Helenian
Ethnic groups: African descent 50%, white 25%, Chinese 25%
Religions: Anglican (majority), Baptist, Seventh-Day Adventist, Roman Catholic
Languages: English
Literacy:
definition: age 20 and over can read and write
total population: 97%
male: 97%
female: 98% (1987 est.)

Government

Country name:
conventional long form: none
conventional short form: Saint Helena
Dependency status: overseas territory of the UK
Government type: NA
Capital: Jamestown
Administrative divisions: 1 administrative area and 2 dependencies*; Ascension*, Saint Helena, Tristan da Cunha*
Independence: none (overseas territory of the UK)
National holiday: Birthday of Queen ELIZABETH II, second Saturday in June (1926)
Constitution: 1 January 1989
Legal system: NA
Suffrage: NA years of age
Executive branch:
chief of state: Queen ELIZABETH II (since 6 February 1952)
head of government: Governor and Commander in Chief David HOLLAMBY (since NA June 1999)
cabinet: Executive Council consists of the governor, two ex officio officers, and six elected members of the Legislative Council
elections: none; the monarch is hereditary; governor is appointed by the monarch
Legislative branch: unicameral Legislative Council (15 seats, including the speaker, 3 ex officio and 12 elected members; members are elected by popular vote to serve four-year terms)
elections: last held 9 July 1997 (next to be held NA August 2001)
election results: percent of vote - NA%; seats - independents 15
Judicial branch: Supreme Court; Magistrate's Court; Small Debts Court; Juvenile Court
Political parties and leaders: none
Political pressure groups and leaders: none
International organization participation: ICFTU
Diplomatic representation in the US: none (overseas territory of the UK)
Diplomatic representation from the US: none (overseas territory of the UK)
Flag description: blue with the flag of the UK in the upper hoist-side quadrant and the Saint Helenian shield centered on the outer half of the flag; the shield features a rocky coastline and three-masted sailing ship

Economy

Economy - overview: The economy depends largely on financial assistance from the UK, which amounted to about $5 million in 1997 or almost one-half of annual budgetary revenues. The local population earns income from fishing, the raising of livestock, and sales of handicrafts. Because there are few jobs, 25% of the work force has left to seek employment on Ascension Island, on the Falklands, and in the UK.
GDP: purchasing power parity - $18 million (1998 est.)
GDP - real growth rate: NA%
GDP - per capita: purchasing power parity - $2,500 (1998 est.)
GDP - composition by sector:
agriculture: NA%
industry: NA%
services: NA%
Population below poverty line: NA%
Household income or consumption by percentage share:
lowest 10%: NA%
highest 10%: NA%
Inflation rate (consumer prices): 3.2% (1997 est.)
Labor force: 3,500 (1998 est.)
note: 1,200 of whom are working offshore
Labor force - by occupation: agriculture and fishing 6%, industry (mainly construction) 48%, services 46% (1987 est.)
Unemployment rate: 14% (1998 est.)
Budget:
revenues: $11.2 million
expenditures: $11 million, including capital expenditures of $NA (FY92)
Industries: construction, crafts (furniture, lacework, fancy woodwork), fishing
Industrial production growth rate: NA%
Electricity - production: 6 million kWh (1999)
Electricity - production by source:
fossil fuel: 100%
hydro: 0%
nuclear: 0%
other: 0% (1999)
Electricity - consumption: 5.6 million kWh (1999)
Electricity - exports: 0 kWh (1999)
Electricity - imports: 0 kWh (1999)
Agriculture - products: corn, potatoes, vegetables; timber; fish, crawfish (on Tristan da Cunha)
Exports: $704,000 (f.o.b., 1995)
Exports - commodities: fish (frozen, canned, and salt-dried skipjack, tuna), coffee, handicrafts
Exports - partners: South Africa, UK
Imports: $14.434 million (c.i.f., 1995)
Imports - commodities: food, beverages, tobacco, fuel oils, animal feed, building materials, motor vehicles and parts, machinery and parts
Imports - partners: UK, South Africa
Debt - external: $NA
Economic aid - recipient: $12.6 million (1995); note - $5.3 million from UK (1997)
Currency: Saint Helenian pound (SHP)
Currency code: SHP
Exchange rates: Saint Helenian pounds per US dollar - 0.6764 (January 2001), 0.6596 (2000), 0.6180 (1999), 0.6037 (1998), 0.6047 (1997), 0.6403 (1996); note - the Saint Helenian pound is at par with the British pound
Fiscal year: 1 April - 31 March

Communications

Telephones - main lines in use: 2,000 (1997)
Telephones - mobile cellular: 0 (1997)
Telephone system:
general assessment: can communicate with any place in the world
domestic: automatic network
international: HF radiotelephone from Saint Helena to Ascension which is a major coaxial submarine cable relay point between South Africa, Portugal, and UK ; satellite earth stations - 2 Intelsat (Atlantic Ocean)
Radio broadcast stations: AM 1, FM 0, shortwave 0 (1998)
Radios: 3,000 (1997)
Television broadcast stations: 0 (1997)
Televisions: 2,000 (1997)
Internet country code: .sh
Internet Service Providers (ISPs): 1 (2000)
Internet users: NA
Communications - note: Gough Island has a meteorological station

Transportation

Railways: 0 km
Highways:
total: NA km (Saint Helena 118 km, Ascension NA km, Tristan da Cunha NA km)
paved: 180.7 km (Saint Helena 100 km, Ascension 480 km, Tristan da Cunha 2.70 km)
unpaved: NA km (Saint Helena 20 km, Ascension NA km, Tristan da Cunha NA km)
Waterways: none
Ports and harbors: Georgetown (on Ascension), Jamestown
Merchant marine: none (2000 est.)
Airports: 1 (2000 est.)
Airports - with paved runways:
total: 1
over 3,047 m: 1 (2000 est.)

Military

Military - note: defense is the responsibility of the UK

Transnational Issues

Disputes - international: none

Saint Kitts and Nevis

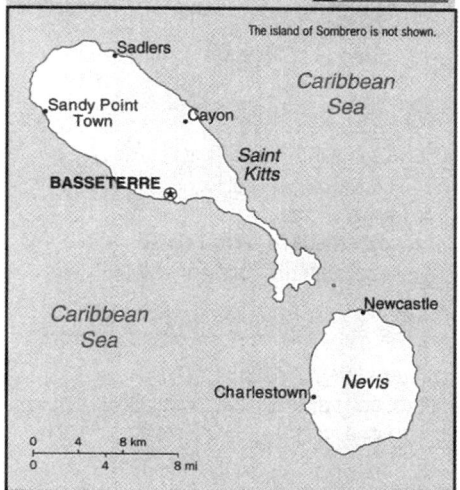

Introduction

Background: First settled by the British in 1623, the islands became an associated state with full internal autonomy in 1967. The island of Anguilla rebelled and was allowed to secede in 1971. Saint Kitts and Nevis achieved independence in 1983. In 1998, a vote in Nevis on a referendum to separate from Saint Kitts fell short of the two-thirds majority needed.

Geography

Location: Caribbean, islands in the Caribbean Sea, about one-third of the way from Puerto Rico to Trinidad and Tobago
Geographic coordinates: 17 20 N, 62 45 W
Map references: Central America and the Caribbean
Area:
total: 261 sq km (Saint Kitts 168 sq km; Nevis 93 sq km)
land: 261 sq km
water: 0 sq km
Area - comparative: 1.5 times the size of Washington, DC
Land boundaries: 0 km
Coastline: 135 km
Maritime claims:
contiguous zone: 24 NM
continental shelf: 200 NM or to the edge of the continental margin
territorial sea: 12 NM
exclusive economic zone: 200 NM
Climate: tropical tempered by constant sea breezes; little seasonal temperature variation; rainy season (May to November)
Terrain: volcanic with mountainous interiors
Elevation extremes:
lowest point: Caribbean Sea 0 m
highest point: Mount Liamuiga 1,156 m
Natural resources: arable land
Land use:
arable land: 22%
permanent crops: 17%
permanent pastures: 3%
forests and woodland: 17%
other: 41% (1993 est.)
Irrigated land: NA sq km
Natural hazards: hurricanes (July to October)
Environment - current issues: NA
Environment - international agreements:
party to: Biodiversity, Climate Change, Desertification, Endangered Species, Hazardous Wastes, Law of the Sea, Marine Dumping, Ozone Layer Protection, Ship Pollution, Whaling
signed, but not ratified: none of the selected agreements

People

Population: 38,756 (July 2001 est.)
Age structure:
0-14 years: 29.84% (male 5,909; female 5,654)
15-64 years: 61.37% (male 11,870; female 11,915)
65 years and over: 8.79% (male 1,406; female 2,002) (2001 est.)
Population growth rate: -0.11% (2001 est.)
Birth rate: 18.78 births/1,000 population (2001 est.)
Death rate: 9.21 deaths/1,000 population (2001 est.)
Net migration rate: -10.68 migrant(s)/1,000 population (2001 est.)
Sex ratio:
at birth: 1.06 male(s)/female
under 15 years: 1.05 male(s)/female
15-64 years: 1 male(s)/female
65 years and over: 0.7 male(s)/female
total population: 0.98 male(s)/female (2001 est.)
Infant mortality rate: 16.28 deaths/1,000 live births (2001 est.)
Life expectancy at birth:
total population: 71.01 years
male: 68.22 years
female: 73.97 years (2001 est.)
Total fertility rate: 2.41 children born/woman (2001 est.)
HIV/AIDS - adult prevalence rate: NA%
HIV/AIDS - people living with HIV/AIDS: NA
HIV/AIDS - deaths: NA
Nationality:
noun: Kittitian(s), Nevisian(s)
adjective: Kittitian, Nevisian
Ethnic groups: predominantly black some British, Portuguese, and Lebanese
Religions: Anglican, other Protestant, Roman Catholic
Languages: English
Literacy:
definition: age 15 and over has ever attended school
total population: 97%
male: 97%
female: 98% (1980 est.)

Government

Country name:
conventional long form: Federation of Saint Kitts and Nevis
conventional short form: Saint Kitts and Nevis
former: Federation of Saint Christopher and Nevis
Government type: constitutional monarchy with Westminster-style parliament
Capital: Basseterre
Administrative divisions: 14 parishes; Christ Church Nichola Town, Saint Anne Sandy Point, Saint George Basseterre, Saint George Gingerland, Saint James Windward, Saint John Capisterre, Saint John Figtree, Saint Mary Cayon, Saint Paul Capisterre, Saint Paul Charlestown, Saint Peter Basseterre, Saint Thomas Lowland, Saint Thomas Middle Island, Trinity Palmetto Point
Independence: 19 September 1983 (from UK)
National holiday: Independence Day, 19 September (1983)
Constitution: 19 September 1983
Legal system: based on English common law
Suffrage: 18 years of age; universal
Executive branch:
chief of state: Queen ELIZABETH II (since 6 February 1952), represented by Governor General Perlette LOUISY (since September 1997)
head of government: Prime Minister Dr. Denzil DOUGLAS (since 6 July 1995) and Deputy Prime Minister Sam CONDOR (since 6 July 1995)
cabinet: Cabinet appointed by the governor general in consultation with the prime minister
elections: none; the monarch is hereditary; the governor general is appointed by the monarch; following legislative elections, the leader of the majority party or leader of a majority coalition is usually appointed prime minister by the governor general; deputy prime minister appointed by the governor general
Legislative branch: unicameral National Assembly (14 seats, 3 appointed and 11 popularly elected from single-member constituencies; members serve five-year terms)
elections: last held 6 March 2000 (next to be held by July 2005)
election results: percent of vote by party - NA%; seats by party - SKNLP 8, CCM 2, NRP 1
Judicial branch: Eastern Caribbean Supreme Court (based on Saint Lucia; one judge of the Supreme Court resides in Saint Kitts and Nevis)
Political parties and leaders: Concerned Citizens Movement or CCM [Vance AMORY]; Nevis Reformation Party or NRP [Joseph PARRY]; People's Action Movement or PAM [Lindsey GRANT]; Saint Kitts and Nevis Labor Party or SKNLP [Dr. Denzil DOUGLAS]
Political pressure groups and leaders: NA
International organization participation: ACP, C, Caricom, CDB, ECLAC, FAO, G-77, IBRD, ICFTU, ICRM, IDA, IFAD, IFC, IFRCS, ILO, IMF, Interpol, IOC, OAS, OECS, OPANAL, OPCW, UN, UNCTAD, UNESCO, UNIDO, UPU, WCL, WHO, WIPO, WTrO

Saint Kitts and Nevis (continued)

Diplomatic representation in the US:
chief of mission: Ambassador Dr. Osbert W. LIBURD
chancery: 3216 New Mexico Avenue NW, Washington, DC 20016
telephone: [1] (202) 686-2636
FAX: [1] (202) 686-5740
Diplomatic representation from the US: the US does not have an embassy in Saint Kitts and Nevis; the US Ambassador in Barbados is accredited to Saint Kitts and Nevis
Flag description: divided diagonally from the lower hoist side by a broad black band bearing two white, five-pointed stars; the black band is edged in yellow; the upper triangle is green, the lower triangle is red

Economy

Economy - overview: The economy has traditionally depended on the growing and processing of sugarcane; decreasing world prices have hurt the industry in recent years. Tourism, export-oriented manufacturing, and offshore banking activity have assumed larger roles. Most food is imported. The government has undertaken a program designed to revitalize the faltering sugar sector. It is also working to improve revenue collection in order to better fund social programs. In 1997 some leaders in Nevis were urging separation from Saint Kitts on the basis that Nevis was paying far more in taxes than it was receiving in government services, but the vote on cessation failed in August 1998. In late September 1998, Hurricane Georges caused approximately $445 million in damages and limited GDP growth for the year.
GDP: purchasing power parity - $274 million (2000 est.)
GDP - real growth rate: 5% (2000 est.)
GDP - per capita: purchasing power parity - $7,000 (2000 est.)
GDP - composition by sector:
agriculture: 5.5%
industry: 22.5%
services: 72% (1996)
Population below poverty line: NA%
Household income or consumption by percentage share:
lowest 10%: NA%
highest 10%: NA%
Inflation rate (consumer prices): 2.5% (2000 est.)
Labor force: 18,172 (June 1995)
Labor force - by occupation: NA
Unemployment rate: 4.5% (1997)
Budget:
revenues: $64.1 million
expenditures: $73.3 million, including capital expenditures of $10.4 million (1997 est.)
Industries: sugar processing, tourism, cotton, salt, copra, clothing, footwear, beverages
Industrial production growth rate: NA%
Electricity - production: 90 million kWh (1999)
Electricity - production by source:
fossil fuel: 100%
hydro: 0%
nuclear: 0%
other: 0% (1999)
Electricity - consumption: 83.7 million kWh (1999)
Electricity - exports: 0 kWh (1999)
Electricity - imports: 0 kWh (1999)
Agriculture - products: sugarcane, rice, yams, vegetables, bananas; fish
Exports: $53.2 million (2000 est.)
Exports - commodities: machinery, food, electronics, beverages, tobacco
Exports - partners: US 68.5%, UK 22.3%, Caricom countries 5.5% (1995 est.)
Imports: $151.5 million (2000 est.)
Imports - commodities: machinery, manufactures, food, fuels
Imports - partners: US 42.4%, Caricom countries 17.2%, UK 11.3% (1995 est.)
Debt - external: $115.1 million (1998)
Economic aid - recipient: $5.5 million (1995)
Currency: East Caribbean dollar (XCD)
Currency code: XCD
Exchange rates: East Caribbean dollars per US dollar - 2.7000 (fixed rate since 1976)
Fiscal year: calendar year

Communications

Telephones - main lines in use: 17,000 (1997)
Telephones - mobile cellular: 205 (1997)
Telephone system:
general assessment: good interisland and international connections
domestic: interisland links to Antigua and Barbuda and Saint Martin (Guadeloupe and Netherlands Antilles) are handled by VHF/UHF/SHF radiotelephone
international: international calls are carried by radiotelephone to Antigua and Barbuda and switched there to submarine cable or to Intelsat; or carried to Saint Martin (Guadeloupe and Netherlands Antilles) by radiotelephone and switched to Intelsat
Radio broadcast stations: AM 3, FM 1, shortwave 0 (1998)
Radios: 28,000 (1997)
Television broadcast stations: 1 (plus three repeaters) (1997)
Televisions: 10,000 (1997)
Internet country code: .kn
Internet Service Providers (ISPs): 16 (2000)
Internet users: 2,000 (2000)

Transportation

Railways:
total: 58 km
narrow gauge: 58 km 0.762-m gauge on Saint Kitts to serve sugarcane plantations (1995)
Highways:
total: 320 km
paved: 136 km
unpaved: 184 km (1996 est.)
Waterways: none
Ports and harbors: Basseterre, Charlestown
Merchant marine: none (2000 est.)
Airports: 2 (2000 est.)
Airports - with paved runways:
total: 2
1,524 to 2,437 m: 1
914 to 1,523 m: 1 (2000 est.)

Military

Military branches: Royal Saint Kitts and Nevis Police Force, Coast Guard, Royal Saint Kitts and Nevis Defense Force
Military expenditures - dollar figure: $NA
Military expenditures - percent of GDP: NA%

Transnational Issues

Disputes - international: none
Illicit drugs: transshipment point for South American drugs destined for the US and Europe

Saint Lucia

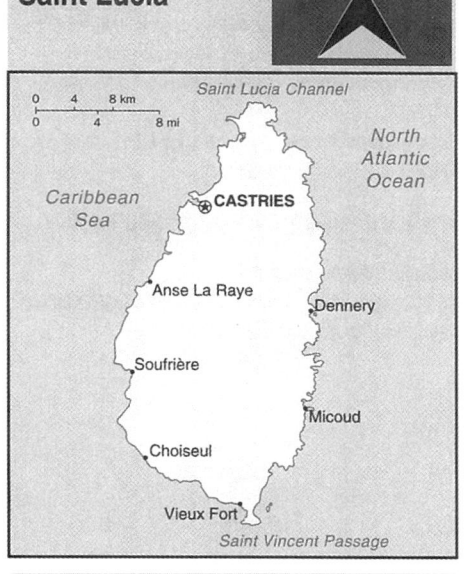

Introduction

Background: The island, with its fine natural harbor at Castries, was contested between England and France throughout the 17th and early 18th centuries (changing possession 14 times); it was finally ceded to the UK in 1814. Self-government was granted in 1967 and independence in 1979.

Geography

Location: Caribbean, island between the Caribbean Sea and North Atlantic Ocean, north of Trinidad and Tobago
Geographic coordinates: 13 53 N, 60 68 W
Map references: Central America and the Caribbean
Area:
total: 620 sq km
land: 610 sq km
water: 10 sq km
Area - comparative: 3.5 times the size of Washington, DC
Land boundaries: 0 km
Coastline: 158 km
Maritime claims:
contiguous zone: 24 NM
continental shelf: 200 NM or to the edge of the continental margin
exclusive economic zone: 200 NM
territorial sea: 12 NM
Climate: tropical, moderated by northeast trade winds; dry season from January to April, rainy season from May to August
Terrain: volcanic and mountainous with some broad, fertile valleys
Elevation extremes:
lowest point: Caribbean Sea 0 m
highest point: Mount Gimie 950 m
Natural resources: forests, sandy beaches, minerals (pumice), mineral springs, geothermal potential
Land use:
arable land: 8%
permanent crops: 21%
permanent pastures: 5%
forests and woodland: 13%
other: 53% (1993 est.)
Irrigated land: 10 sq km (1993 est.)
Natural hazards: hurricanes and volcanic activity
Environment - current issues: deforestation; soil erosion, particularly in the northern region
Environment - international agreements:
party to: Biodiversity, Climate Change, Desertification, Endangered Species, Environmental Modification, Hazardous Wastes, Law of the Sea, Marine Dumping, Ozone Layer Protection, Ship Pollution, Whaling
signed, but not ratified: Climate Change-Kyoto Protocol

People

Population: 158,178 (July 2001 est.)
Age structure:
0-14 years: 32.13% (male 25,951; female 24,874)
15-64 years: 62.59% (male 48,568; female 50,430)
65 years and over: 5.28% (male 3,120; female 5,235) (2001 est.)
Population growth rate: 1.23% (2001 est.)
Birth rate: 21.8 births/1,000 population (2001 est.)
Death rate: 5.36 deaths/1,000 population (2001 est.)
Net migration rate: -4.15 migrant(s)/1,000 population (2001 est.)
Sex ratio:
at birth: 1.07 male(s)/female
under 15 years: 1.04 male(s)/female
15-64 years: 0.96 male(s)/female
65 years and over: 0.6 male(s)/female
total population: 0.96 male(s)/female (2001 est.)
Infant mortality rate: 15.22 deaths/1,000 live births (2001 est.)
Life expectancy at birth:
total population: 72.57 years
male: 69 years
female: 76.39 years (2001 est.)
Total fertility rate: 2.38 children born/woman (2001 est.)
HIV/AIDS - adult prevalence rate: NA%
HIV/AIDS - people living with HIV/AIDS: NA
HIV/AIDS - deaths: NA
Nationality:
noun: Saint Lucian(s)
adjective: Saint Lucian
Ethnic groups: black 90%, mixed 6%, East Indian 3%, white 1%
Religions: Roman Catholic 90%, Protestant 7%, Anglican 3%
Languages: English (official), French patois
Literacy:
definition: age 15 and over has ever attended school
total population: 67%
male: 65%
female: 69% (1980 est.)

Government

Country name:
conventional long form: none
conventional short form: Saint Lucia
Government type: Westminster-style parliamentary democracy
Capital: Castries
Administrative divisions: 11 quarters; Anse-la-Raye, Castries, Choiseul, Dauphin, Dennery, Gros Islet, Laborie, Micoud, Praslin, Soufriere, Vieux Fort
Independence: 22 February 1979 (from UK)
National holiday: Independence Day, 22 February (1979)
Constitution: 22 February 1979
Legal system: based on English common law
Suffrage: 18 years of age; universal
Executive branch:
chief of state: Queen ELIZABETH II (since 6 February 1952), represented by Governor General Dr. Perlette LOUISY (since September 1997)
head of government: Prime Minister Kenneth ANTHONY (since 24 May 1997) and Deputy Prime Minister Mario MICHEL (since 24 May 1997)
cabinet: Cabinet appointed by the governor general on the advice of the prime minister
elections: none; the monarch is hereditary; the governor general is appointed by the monarch; following legislative elections, the leader of the majority party or leader of a majority coalition is usually appointed prime minister by the governor general
Legislative branch: bicameral Parliament consists of the Senate (11 seats; six members appointed on the advice of the prime minister, three on the advice of the leader of the opposition, and two after consultation with religious, economic, and social groups) and the House of Assembly (17 seats; members are elected by popular vote from single-member constituencies to serve five-year terms)
elections: House of Assembly - last held 23 May 1997 (next to be held NA 2002)
election results: House of Assembly - percent of vote by party - NA%; seats by party - SLP 16, UWP 1
Judicial branch: Eastern Caribbean Supreme Court (jurisdiction extends to Anguilla, Antigua and Barbuda, the British Virgin Islands, Dominica, Grenada, Montserrat, Saint Kitts and Nevis, Saint Lucia, and Saint Vincent and the Grenadines)
Political parties and leaders: National Freedom Party or NFP [Martinus FRANCOIS]; Saint Lucia Labor Party or SLP [Kenneth ANTHONY]; United Workers Party or UWP [Dr. Morella JOSEPH]
Political pressure groups and leaders: NA
International organization participation: ACCT (associate), ACP, C, Caricom, CDB, ECLAC, FAO, G-77, IBRD, ICAO, ICFTU, ICRM, IDA, IFAD, IFC, IFRCS, ILO, IMF, IMO, Intelsat (nonsignatory user), Interpol, IOC, ISO (subscriber), ITU, NAM, OAS, OECS, OPANAL, OPCW, UN, UNCTAD, UNESCO, UNIDO, UPU, WCL, WFTU, WHO, WIPO, WMO, WTrO

Saint Lucia (continued)

Diplomatic representation in the US:
chief of mission: Ambassador Sonia Merlyn JOHNNY
chancery: 3216 New Mexico Avenue NW, Washington, DC 20016
telephone: [1] (202) 364-6792 through 6795
FAX: [1] (202) 364-6728
consulate(s) general: Miami and New York
Diplomatic representation from the US: the US does not have an embassy in Saint Lucia; the US Ambassador in Barbados is accredited to Saint Lucia
Flag description: blue, with a gold isosceles triangle below a black arrowhead; the upper edges of the arrowhead have a white border

Economy

Economy - overview: The recent changes in the EU import preference regime and the increased competition from Latin American bananas have made economic diversification increasingly important in Saint Lucia. Improvement in the construction sector and growth of the tourism industry helped expand GDP in 1998-99. The agriculture sector registered its fifth year of decline in 1997 primarily because of a severe decline in banana production. The manufacturing sector is the most diverse in the Eastern Caribbean, and the government is beginning to develop regulations for the small offshore financial sector.
GDP: purchasing power parity - $700 million (2000 est.)
GDP - real growth rate: 0.5% (2000 est.)
GDP - per capita: purchasing power parity - $4,500 (2000 est.)
GDP - composition by sector:
agriculture: 10.7%
industry: 32.3%
services: 57% (1996 est.)
Population below poverty line: NA%
Household income or consumption by percentage share:
lowest 10%: NA%
highest 10%: NA%
Inflation rate (consumer prices): 2.5% (2000 est.)
Labor force: 43,800
Labor force - by occupation: agriculture 43.4%, services 38.9%, industry and commerce 17.7% (1983 est.)
Unemployment rate: 15% (1996 est.)
Budget:
revenues: $141.2 million
expenditures: $146.7 million, including capital expenditures of $25.1 million (FY97/98 est.)
Industries: clothing, assembly of electronic components, beverages, corrugated cardboard boxes, tourism, lime processing, coconut processing
Industrial production growth rate: -8.9% (1997 est.)
Electricity - production: 110 million kWh (1999)
Electricity - production by source:
fossil fuel: 100%
hydro: 0%
nuclear: 0%
other: 0% (1999)

Electricity - consumption: 102.3 million kWh (1999)
Electricity - exports: 0 kWh (1999)
Electricity - imports: 0 kWh (1999)
Agriculture - products: bananas, coconuts, vegetables, citrus, root crops, cocoa
Exports: $68.3 million (2000 est.)
Exports - commodities: bananas 41%, clothing, cocoa, vegetables, fruits, coconut oil
Exports - partners: UK 50%, US 24%, Caricom countries 16% (1995)
Imports: $319.4 million (2000 est.)
Imports - commodities: food 23%, manufactured goods 21%, machinery and transportation equipment 19%, chemicals, fuels
Imports - partners: US 36%, Caricom countries 22%, UK 11%, Japan 5%, Canada 4% (1995)
Debt - external: $131.6 million (1998)
Economic aid - recipient: $51.8 million (1995)
Currency: East Caribbean dollar (XCD)
Currency code: XCD
Exchange rates: East Caribbean dollars per US dollar - 2.7000 (fixed rate since 1976)
Fiscal year: 1 April - 31 March

Communications

Telephones - main lines in use: 37,000 (1997)
Telephones - mobile cellular: 1,600 (1997)
Telephone system:
general assessment: adequate system
domestic: system is automatically switched
international: direct microwave radio relay link with Martinique and Saint Vincent and the Grenadines; tropospheric scatter to Barbados; international calls beyond these countries are carried by Intelsat from Martinique
Radio broadcast stations: AM 2, FM 7 (plus 3 repeaters), shortwave 0 (1998)
Radios: 111,000 (1997)
Television broadcast stations: 3 (of which two are commercial stations and one is a community antenna television or CATV channel) (1997)
Televisions: 32,000 (1997)
Internet country code: .lc
Internet Service Providers (ISPs): 15 (2000)
Internet users: 5,000 (2000)

Transportation

Railways: 0 km
Highways:
total: 1,210 km
paved: 63 km
unpaved: 1,147 km (1996 est.)
Waterways: none
Ports and harbors: Castries, Vieux Fort
Merchant marine: none (2000 est.)
Airports: 2 (2000 est.)
Airports - with paved runways:
total: 2
2,438 to 3,047 m: 1
1,524 to 2,437 m: 1 (2000 est.)

Military

Military branches: Royal Saint Lucia Police Force (includes Special Service Unit), Coast Guard
Military expenditures - dollar figure: $5 million (FY91/92)
Military expenditures - percent of GDP: 2% (FY91/92)

Transnational Issues

Disputes - international: none
Illicit drugs: transit point for South American drugs destined for the US and Europe

Saint Pierre and Miquelon
(territorial collectivity of France)

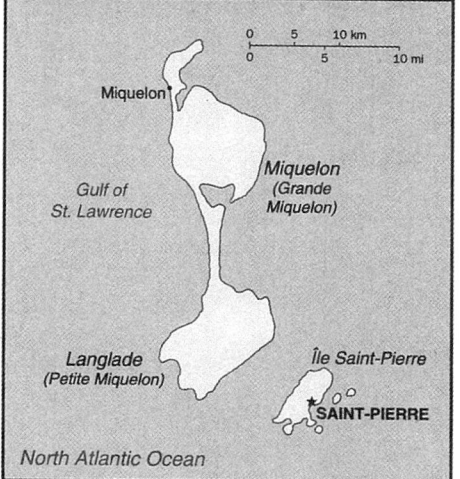

Introduction

Background: First settled by the French in the early 17th century, the islands represent the sole remaining vestige of France's once vast North American possessions.

Geography

Location: Northern North America, islands in the North Atlantic Ocean, south of Newfoundland (Canada)
Geographic coordinates: 46 50 N, 56 20 W
Map references: North America
Area:
total: 242 sq km
land: 242 sq km
water: 0 sq km
note: includes eight small islands in the Saint Pierre and the Miquelon groups
Area - comparative: 1.5 times the size of Washington, DC
Land boundaries: 0 km
Coastline: 120 km
Maritime claims:
exclusive economic zone: 200 NM
territorial sea: 12 NM
Climate: cold and wet, with much mist and fog; spring and autumn are windy
Terrain: mostly barren rock
Elevation extremes:
lowest point: Atlantic Ocean 0 m
highest point: Morne de la Grande Montagne 240 m
Natural resources: fish, deepwater ports
Land use:
arable land: 13%
permanent crops: 0%
permanent pastures: 0%
forests and woodland: 4%
other: 83% (1993 est.)
Irrigated land: NA sq km
Natural hazards: persistent fog throughout the year can be a maritime hazard
Environment - current issues: NA
Geography - note: vegetation scanty

People

Population: 6,928 (July 2001 est.)
Age structure:
0-14 years: 25.85% (male 917; female 874)
15-64 years: 64.22% (male 2,273; female 2,176)
65 years and over: 9.93% (male 291; female 397) (2001 est.)
Population growth rate: 0.43% (2001 est.)
Birth rate: 15.88 births/1,000 population (2001 est.)
Death rate: 6.64 deaths/1,000 population (2001 est.)
Net migration rate: -4.91 migrant(s)/1,000 population (2001 est.)
Sex ratio:
at birth: 1.06 male(s)/female
under 15 years: 1.05 male(s)/female
15-64 years: 1.04 male(s)/female
65 years and over: 0.73 male(s)/female
total population: 1.01 male(s)/female (2001 est.)
Infant mortality rate: 8.39 deaths/1,000 live births (2001 est.)
Life expectancy at birth:
total population: 77.77 years
male: 75.51 years
female: 80.13 years (2001 est.)
Total fertility rate: 2.12 children born/woman (2001 est.)
HIV/AIDS - adult prevalence rate: NA%
HIV/AIDS - people living with HIV/AIDS: NA
HIV/AIDS - deaths: NA
Nationality:
noun: Frenchman(men), Frenchwoman(women)
adjective: French
Ethnic groups: Basques and Bretons (French fishermen)
Religions: Roman Catholic 99%
Languages: French
Literacy:
definition: age 15 and over can read and write
total population: 99%
male: 99%
female: 99% (1982 est.)

Government

Country name:
conventional long form: Territorial Collectivity of Saint Pierre and Miquelon
conventional short form: Saint Pierre and Miquelon
local long form: Departement de Saint-Pierre et Miquelon
local short form: Saint-Pierre et Miquelon
Dependency status: self-governing territorial collectivity of France
Government type: NA
Capital: Saint-Pierre
Administrative divisions: none (territorial collectivity of France); note - there are no first-order administrative divisions approved by the US Government, but there are two communes - Saint Pierre, Miquelon
Independence: none (territorial collectivity of France; has been under French control since 1763)
National holiday: Bastille Day, 14 July (1789)
Constitution: 28 September 1958 (French Constitution)
Legal system: French law with special adaptations for local conditions, such as housing and taxation
Suffrage: 18 years of age; universal
Executive branch:
chief of state: President Jacques CHIRAC of France (since 17 May 1995), represented by Prefect Remi THUAU (since NA)
head of government: President of the General Council Bernard LE SOAVEC (since NA 1996)
cabinet: NA
elections: French president elected by popular vote for a seven-year term; election last held 7 May 1995 (next to be held NA May 2002); prefect appointed by the French president on the advice of the French Ministry of Interior; president of the General Council is elected by the members of the council
Legislative branch: unicameral General Council or Conseil General (19 seats - 15 from Saint Pierre and 4 from Miquelon; members are elected by popular vote to serve six-year terms)
elections: elections last held NA April 2000 (next to be held NA April 2006)
election results: percent of vote by party - NA%; seats by party - NA
note: Saint Pierre and Miquelon elect 1 seat to the French Senate; elections last held NA September 1995 (next to be held NA September 2004); results - percent of vote by party - NA; seats by party - RPR 1; Saint Pierre and Miquelon also elects 1 seat to the French National Assembly; elections last held 25 May-1 June 1997 (next to be held NA 2002); results - percent of vote by party - NA; seats by party - UDF 1
Judicial branch: Superior Tribunal of Appeals or Tribunal Superieur d'Appel
Political parties and leaders: Rassemblement pour la Republique or RPR [leader NA]; Socialist Party or PS [leader NA]; Union pour la Democratie Francaise or UDF [leader NA]
Political pressure groups and leaders: NA
International organization participation: FZ, WFTU
Diplomatic representation in the US: none (territorial collectivity of France)
Diplomatic representation from the US: none (territorial collectivity of France)
Flag description: a yellow sailing ship facing the hoist side rides on a dark blue background with a black wave line under the ship; on the hoist side, a vertical band is divided into three parts: the top part is red with a green diagonal cross extending to the

Saint Pierre and Miquelon (continued)

corners overlaid by a white cross dividing the square into four sections; the middle part has a white background with an ermine pattern; the third part has a red background with two stylized yellow lions outlined in black, one on top of the other; the flag of France is used for official occasions

Economy

Economy - overview: The inhabitants have traditionally earned their livelihood by fishing and by servicing fishing fleets operating off the coast of Newfoundland. The economy has been declining, however, because of disputes with Canada over fishing quotas and a steady decline in the number of ships stopping at Saint Pierre. In 1992, an arbitration panel awarded the islands an exclusive economic zone of 12,348 sq km to settle a longstanding territorial dispute with Canada, although it represents only 25% of what France had sought. The islands are heavily subsidized by France to the great betterment of living standards. The government hopes an expansion of tourism will boost economic prospects.
GDP: purchasing power parity - $74 million (1996 est.); supplemented by annual payments from France of about $60 million
GDP - real growth rate: NA%
GDP - per capita: purchasing power parity - $11,000 (1996 est.)
GDP - composition by sector:
agriculture: NA%
industry: NA%
services: NA%
Population below poverty line: NA%
Household income or consumption by percentage share:
lowest 10%: NA%
highest 10%: NA%
Inflation rate (consumer prices): 2.1% (1991-96 average)
Labor force: 3,000 (1997)
Labor force - by occupation: fishing 18%, industry (mainly fish-processing) 41%, services 41% (1996 est.)
Unemployment rate: 9.8% (1997)
Budget:
revenues: $70 million
expenditures: $60 million, including capital expenditures of $24 million (1996 est.)
Industries: fish processing and supply base for fishing fleets; tourism
Industrial production growth rate: NA%
Electricity - production: 40 million kWh (1999)
Electricity - production by source:
fossil fuel: 100%
hydro: 0%
nuclear: 0%
other: 0% (1999)
Electricity - consumption: 37.2 million kWh (1999)
Electricity - exports: 0 kWh (1999)
Electricity - imports: 0 kWh (1999)
Agriculture - products: vegetables; poultry, cattle, sheep, pigs; fish
Exports: $12 million (f.o.b., 1999)
Exports - commodities: fish and fish products, soybeans, animal feed, mollusks and crustaceans, fox and mink pelts
Exports - partners: US 43%, Egypt 14%, Japan 11%, Colombia 8% (1999)
Imports: $55 million (f.o.b., 1999)
Imports - commodities: meat, clothing, fuel, electrical equipment, machinery, building materials
Imports - partners: France 44%, Canada 40% (1999)
Debt - external: $NA
Economic aid - recipient: approximately $65 million in annual grants from France
Currency: French franc (FRF); euro (EUR)
Currency code: FRF; EUR
Exchange rates: euros per US dollar - 1.06594 (January 2001), 1.08540 (2000), 0.93863 (1999); French francs per US dollar - 5.8995 (1998), 5.8367 (1997), 5.1155 (1996)
Fiscal year: calendar year

Communications

Telephones - main lines in use: 4,000 (1997)
Telephones - mobile cellular: 0 (1994)
Telephone system:
general assessment: adequate
domestic: NA
international: radiotelephone communication with most countries in the world; 1 earth station in French domestic satellite system
Radio broadcast stations: AM 1, FM 4, shortwave 0 (1998)
Radios: 4,000 (1997)
Television broadcast stations: 0 (there are, however, two repeaters which rebroadcast programs from France, Canada, and the US) (1997)
Televisions: 4,000 (1997)
Internet country code: .pm
Internet Service Providers (ISPs): 1 (2000)
Internet users: NA

Transportation

Railways: 0 km
Highways:
total: 114 km
paved: 69 km
unpaved: 45 km (1994 est.)
Waterways: none
Ports and harbors: Saint Pierre
Merchant marine: none (2000 est.)
Airports: 2 (2000 est.)
Airports - with paved runways:
total: 2
1,524 to 2,437 m: 1
914 to 1,523 m: 1 (2000 est.)

Military

Military - note: defense is the responsibility of France

Transnational Issues

Disputes - international: none

Saint Vincent and the Grenadines

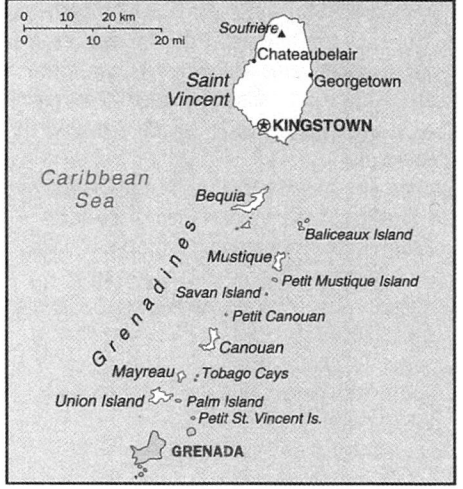

Introduction

Background: Disputed between France and Great Britain in the 18th century, Saint Vincent was ceded to the latter in 1783. Autonomy was granted in 1969, and independence in 1979.

Geography

Location: Caribbean, islands in the Caribbean Sea, north of Trinidad and Tobago
Geographic coordinates: 13 15 N, 61 12 W
Map references: Central America and the Caribbean
Area:
total: 389 sq km (Saint Vincent 344 sq km)
land: 389 sq km
water: 0 sq km
Area - comparative: twice the size of Washington, DC
Land boundaries: 0 km
Coastline: 84 km
Maritime claims:
contiguous zone: 24 NM
continental shelf: 200 NM
exclusive economic zone: 200 NM
territorial sea: 12 NM
Climate: tropical; little seasonal temperature variation; rainy season (May to November)
Terrain: volcanic, mountainous
Elevation extremes:
lowest point: Caribbean Sea 0 m
highest point: Soufriere 1,234 m
Natural resources: hydropower, cropland
Land use:
arable land: 10%
permanent crops: 18%
permanent pastures: 5%
forests and woodland: 36%
other: 31% (1993 est.)
Irrigated land: 10 sq km (1993 est.)
Natural hazards: hurricanes; Soufriere volcano on the island of Saint Vincent is a constant threat
Environment - current issues: pollution of coastal waters and shorelines from discharges by pleasure yachts and other effluents; in some areas, pollution is severe enough to make swimming prohibitive
Environment - international agreements:
party to: Biodiversity, Climate Change, Desertification, Endangered Species, Environmental Modification, Hazardous Wastes, Law of the Sea, Marine Dumping, Ozone Layer Protection, Ship Pollution, Whaling
signed, but not ratified: Climate Change-Kyoto Protocol
Geography - note: the administration of the islands of the Grenadines group is divided between Saint Vincent and the Grenadines and Grenada

People

Population: 115,942 (July 2001 est.)
Age structure:
0-14 years: 29.61% (male 17,466; female 16,865)
15-64 years: 64.04% (male 38,074; female 36,179)
65 years and over: 6.35% (male 3,162; female 4,196) (2001 est.)
Population growth rate: 0.4% (2001 est.)
Birth rate: 17.91 births/1,000 population (2001 est.)
Death rate: 6.16 deaths/1,000 population (2001 est.)
Net migration rate: -7.72 migrant(s)/1,000 population (2001 est.)
Sex ratio:
at birth: 1.03 male(s)/female
under 15 years: 1.04 male(s)/female
15-64 years: 1.05 male(s)/female
65 years and over: 0.75 male(s)/female
total population: 1.03 male(s)/female (2001 est.)
Infant mortality rate: 16.61 deaths/1,000 live births (2001 est.)
Life expectancy at birth:
total population: 72.56 years
male: 70.83 years
female: 74.34 years (2001 est.)
Total fertility rate: 2.06 children born/woman (2001 est.)
HIV/AIDS - adult prevalence rate: NA%
HIV/AIDS - people living with HIV/AIDS: NA
HIV/AIDS - deaths: NA
Nationality:
noun: Saint Vincentian(s) or Vincentian(s)
adjective: Saint Vincentian or Vincentian
Ethnic groups: black 66%, mixed 19%, East Indian 6%, Carib Amerindian 2%
Religions: Anglican 47%, Methodist 28%, Roman Catholic 13%, Seventh-Day Adventist, Hindu, other Protestant
Languages: English, French patois
Literacy:
definition: age 15 and over has ever attended school
total population: 96%
male: 96%
female: 96% (1970 est.)

Government

Country name:
conventional long form: none
conventional short form: Saint Vincent and the Grenadines
Government type: parliamentary democracy; independent sovereign state within the Commonwealth
Capital: Kingstown
Administrative divisions: 6 parishes; Charlotte, Grenadines, Saint Andrew, Saint David, Saint George, Saint Patrick
Independence: 27 October 1979 (from UK)
National holiday: Independence Day, 27 October (1979)
Constitution: 27 October 1979
Legal system: based on English common law
Suffrage: 18 years of age; universal
Executive branch:
chief of state: Queen ELIZABETH II (since 6 February 1952), represented by Governor General David JACK (since 29 September 1989)
head of government: Prime Minister Ralph GONSALVES (since 29 March 2001)
cabinet: Cabinet appointed by the governor general on the advice of the prime minister
elections: none; the monarch is hereditary; the governor general is appointed by the monarch; following legislative elections, the leader of the majority party is usually appointed prime minister by the governor general; deputy prime minister appointed by the governor general on the advice of the prime minister
Legislative branch: unicameral House of Assembly (21 seats, 15 elected representatives and 6 appointed senators; representatives are elected by popular vote from single-member constituencies to serve five-year terms)
elections: last held 28 March 2001 (next to be held by NA March 2006)
election results: percent of vote by party - NA%; seats by party - ULP 12, NDP 3
Judicial branch: Eastern Caribbean Supreme Court (based on Saint Lucia; one judge of the Supreme Court resides in Saint Vincent and the Grenadines)
Political parties and leaders: National Reform Party or NRP [Joel MIGUEL]; New Democratic Party or NDP [Arnhim EUSTACE]; People's Progressive Movement or PPM [Ken BOYEA]; Progressive Labor Party or PLP [leader NA]; United People's Movement or UPM [Adrian SAUNDERS]; Unity Labor Party or ULP [Ralph GONSALVES] (formed by the coalition of Saint Vincent Labor Party or SVLP and the Movement for National Unity or MNU)
Political pressure groups and leaders: NA
International organization participation: ACP, C, Caricom, CDB, ECLAC, FAO, G-77, IBRD, ICAO, ICFTU, ICRM, IDA, IFAD, IFRCS, ILO, IMF, IMO, Intelsat (nonsignatory user), Interpol, IOC, ITU, OAS, OECS, OPANAL, OPCW, UN, UNCTAD, UNESCO, UNIDO, UPU, WCL, WFTU, WHO, WIPO, WTrO

Saint Vincent and the Grenadines (continued)

Diplomatic representation in the US:
chief of mission: Ambassador Ellsworth JOHN
chancery: 3216 New Mexico Avenue NW, Washington, DC 20016
telephone: [1] (202) 364-6730
FAX: [1] (202) 364-6736

Diplomatic representation from the US: the US does not have an embassy in Saint Vincent and the Grenadines; the US Ambassador in Barbados is accredited to Saint Vincent and the Grenadines

Flag description: three vertical bands of blue (hoist side), gold (double width), and green; the gold band bears three green diamonds arranged in a V pattern

Economy

Economy - overview: Agriculture, dominated by banana production, is the most important sector of this lower-middle-income economy. The services sector, based mostly on a growing tourist industry, is also important. The government has been relatively unsuccessful at introducing new industries, and a high unemployment rate persists. The continuing dependence on a single crop represents the biggest obstacle to the islands' development; tropical storms wiped out substantial portions of crops in both 1994 and 1995. The tourism sector has considerable potential for development over the next decade. Recent growth has been stimulated by strong activity in the construction sector and an improvement in tourism. There is a small manufacturing sector and a small offshore financial sector whose particularly restrictive secrecy laws have caused some international concern.

GDP: purchasing power parity - $322 million (2000 est.)

GDP - real growth rate: 2% (2000 est.)

GDP - per capita: purchasing power parity - $2,800 (2000 est.)

GDP - composition by sector:
agriculture: 10.6%
industry: 17.5%
services: 71.9% (1996 est.)

Population below poverty line: NA%

Household income or consumption by percentage share:
lowest 10%: NA%
highest 10%: NA%

Inflation rate (consumer prices): 2% (1999 est.)

Labor force: 67,000 (1984 est.)

Labor force - by occupation: agriculture 26%, industry 17%, services 57% (1980 est.)

Unemployment rate: 22% (1997 est.)

Budget:
revenues: $85.7 million
expenditures: $98.6 million, including capital expenditures of $25.7 million (1997 est.)

Industries: food processing, cement, furniture, clothing, starch

Industrial production growth rate: -0.9% (1997 est.)

Electricity - production: 82 million kWh (1999)

Electricity - production by source:
fossil fuel: 73.17%
hydro: 26.83%
nuclear: 0%
other: 0% (1999)

Electricity - consumption: 76.3 million kWh (1999)

Electricity - exports: 0 kWh (1999)

Electricity - imports: 0 kWh (1999)

Agriculture - products: bananas, coconuts, sweet potatoes, spices; small numbers of cattle, sheep, pigs, goats; fish

Exports: $53.7 million (2000 est.)

Exports - commodities: bananas 39%, eddoes and dasheen (taro), arrowroot starch, tennis racquets

Exports - partners: Caricom countries 49%, UK 16%, US 10% (1995)

Imports: $185.6 million (2000 est.)

Imports - commodities: foodstuffs, machinery and equipment, chemicals and fertilizers, minerals and fuels

Imports - partners: US 36%, Caricom countries 28%, UK 13% (1995)

Debt - external: $99.3 million (1998)

Economic aid - recipient: $47.5 million (1995); note - EU $34.5 million (1998)

Currency: East Caribbean dollar (XCD)

Currency code: XCD

Exchange rates: East Caribbean dollars per US dollar - 2.7000 (fixed rate since 1976)

Fiscal year: calendar year

Communications

Telephones - main lines in use: 20,500 (1998)

Telephones - mobile cellular: NA

Telephone system:
general assessment: adequate system
domestic: islandwide, fully automatic telephone system; VHF/UHF radiotelephone from Saint Vincent to the other islands of the Grenadines
international: VHF/UHF radiotelephone from Saint Vincent to Barbados; new SHF radiotelephone to Grenada and to Saint Lucia; access to Intelsat earth station in Martinique through Saint Lucia

Radio broadcast stations: AM 1, FM 3, shortwave 0 (1998)

Radios: 77,000 (1997)

Television broadcast stations: 1 (plus three repeaters) (1997)

Televisions: 18,000 (1997)

Internet country code: .vc

Internet Service Providers (ISPs): 15 (2000)

Internet users: 2,000 (2000)

Transportation

Railways: 0 km

Highways:
total: 1,040 km
paved: 320 km
unpaved: 720 km (1996 est.)

Waterways: none

Ports and harbors: Kingstown

Merchant marine:
total: 800 ships (1,000 GRT or over) totaling 6,705,336 GRT/10,134,002 DWT
ships by type: barge carrier 1, bulk 131, cargo 395, chemical tanker 29, combination bulk 12, combination ore/oil 1, container 46, liquefied gas 7, livestock carrier 3, multi-functional large-load carrier 4, passenger 2, petroleum tanker 56, refrigerated cargo 42, roll on/roll off 49, short-sea passenger 11, specialized tanker 10, vehicle carrier 1
note: includes some foreign-owned ships registered here as a flag of convenience: China 4, Ireland 1, France 1, Greece 3, Hong Kong 1, Croatia 10, India 1, Japan 2, Monaco 1, Netherlands 1, Norway 2, Netherlands Antilles 1, Pakistan 1, Russia 1, Slovenia 5, UAE 1 (2000 est.)

Airports: 6 (2000 est.)

Airports - with paved runways:
total: 5
914 to 1,523 m: 3
under 914 m: 2 (2000 est.)

Airports - with unpaved runways:
total: 1
under 914 m: 1 (2000 est.)

Military

Military branches: Royal Saint Vincent and the Grenadines Police Force (includes Special Service Unit), Coast Guard

Military expenditures - dollar figure: $NA

Military expenditures - percent of GDP: NA%

Transnational Issues

Disputes - international: none

Illicit drugs: transshipment point for South American drugs destined for the US and Europe

Samoa

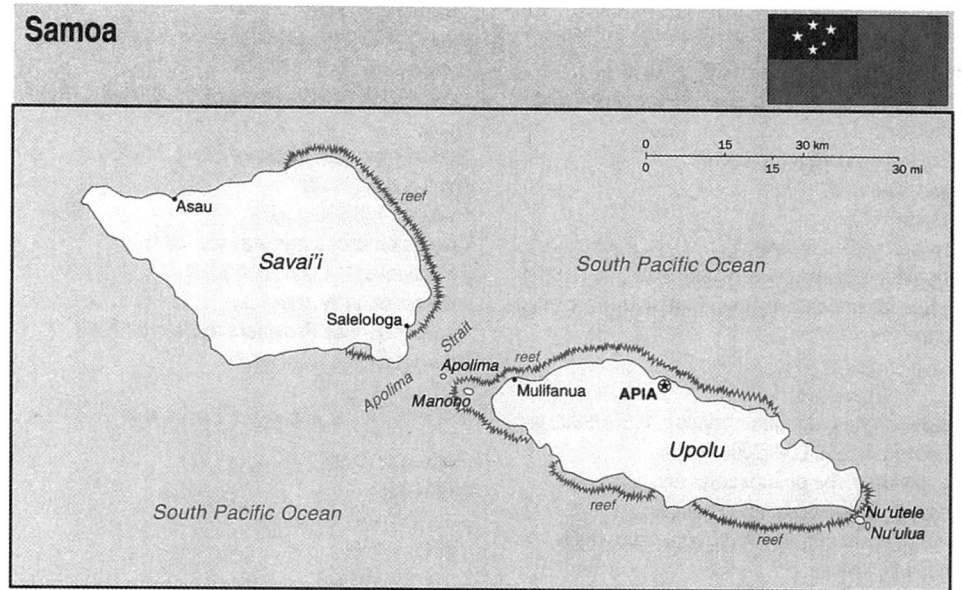

Introduction

Background: New Zealand occupied the German protectorate of Western Samoa at the outbreak of World War I in 1914. It continued to administer the islands as a mandate and then as a trust territory until 1962, when the islands became the first Polynesian nation to reestablish independence in the 20th century. The country dropped the "Western" from its name in 1997.

Geography

Location: Oceania, group of islands in the South Pacific Ocean, about one-half of the way from Hawaii to New Zealand
Geographic coordinates: 13 35 S, 172 20 W
Map references: Oceania
Area:
total: 2,860 sq km
land: 2,850 sq km
water: 10 sq km
Area - comparative: slightly smaller than Rhode Island
Land boundaries: 0 km
Coastline: 403 km
Maritime claims:
exclusive economic zone: 200 NM
territorial sea: 12 NM
Climate: tropical; rainy season (October to March), dry season (May to October)
Terrain: narrow coastal plain with volcanic, rocky, rugged mountains in interior
Elevation extremes:
lowest point: Pacific Ocean 0 m
highest point: Mauga Silisili 1,857 m
Natural resources: hardwood forests, fish, hydropower
Land use:
arable land: 19%
permanent crops: 24%
permanent pastures: 0%
forests and woodland: 47%
other: 10%
Irrigated land: NA sq km
Natural hazards: occasional typhoons; active volcanism
Environment - current issues: soil erosion
Environment - international agreements:
party to: Biodiversity, Climate Change, Climate Change-Kyoto Protocol, Desertification, Law of the Sea, Marine Dumping, Nuclear Test Ban, Ozone Layer Protection, Ship Pollution
signed, but not ratified: none of the selected agreements

People

Population: 179,058 (July 2001 est.)
Age structure:
0-14 years: 31.88% (male 29,009; female 28,069)
15-64 years: 62.44% (male 70,491; female 41,304)
65 years and over: 5.68% (male 4,739; female 5,446) (2001 est.)
Population growth rate: -0.23% (2001 est.)
Birth rate: 15.59 births/1,000 population (2001 est.)
Death rate: 6.29 deaths/1,000 population (2001 est.)
Net migration rate: -11.62 migrant(s)/1,000 population (2001 est.)
Sex ratio:
at birth: 1.05 male(s)/female
under 15 years: 1.03 male(s)/female
15-64 years: 1.71 male(s)/female
65 years and over: 0.87 male(s)/female
total population: 1.39 male(s)/female (2001 est.)
Infant mortality rate: 31.75 deaths/1,000 live births (2001 est.)
Life expectancy at birth:
total population: 69.5 years
male: 66.77 years
female: 72.37 years (2001 est.)
Total fertility rate: 3.4 children born/woman (2001 est.)
HIV/AIDS - adult prevalence rate: NA%
HIV/AIDS - people living with HIV/AIDS: NA
HIV/AIDS - deaths: NA
Nationality:
noun: Samoan(s)
adjective: Samoan
Ethnic groups: Samoan 92.6%, Euronesians 7% (persons of European and Polynesian blood), Europeans 0.4%
Religions: Christian 99.7% (about one-half of population associated with the London Missionary Society; includes Congregational, Roman Catholic, Methodist, Latter-Day Saints, Seventh-Day Adventist)
Languages: Samoan (Polynesian), English
Literacy:
definition: age 15 and over can read and write
total population: 97%
male: 97%
female: 97% (1971 est.)

Government

Country name:
conventional long form: Independent State of Samoa
conventional short form: Samoa
former: Western Samoa
Government type: constitutional monarchy under native chief
Capital: Apia
Administrative divisions: 11 districts; A'ana, Aiga-i-le-Tai, Atua, Fa'asaleleaga, Gaga'emauga, Gagaifomauga, Palauli, Satupa'itea, Tuamasaga, Va'a-o-Fonoti, Vaisigano
Independence: 1 January 1962 (from New Zealand-administered UN trusteeship)
National holiday: Independence Day Celebration, 1 June (1962); note - 1 January 1962 is the date of independence from the New Zealand-administered UN trusteeship, 1 June 1962 is the date that independence is celebrated
Constitution: 1 January 1962
Legal system: based on English common law and local customs; judicial review of legislative acts with respect to fundamental rights of the citizen; has not accepted compulsory ICJ jurisdiction
Suffrage: 21 years of age; universal
Executive branch:
chief of state: Chief Susuga MALIETOA Tanumafili II (cochief of state from 1 January 1962 until becoming sole chief of state 5 April 1963)
head of government: Prime Minister TUILA'EPA Sailele Malielegaoi (since 24 November 1998); note - TUILA'EPA served as deputy prime minister since 1992; he assumed the prime ministership in November 1998 when former Prime Minister TOFILAU Eti Alesana resigned in poor health; the post of deputy prime minister is currently vacant
cabinet: Cabinet consists of 12 members, appointed by the chief of state with the prime minister's advice
elections: upon the death of Chief Susuga MALIETOA Tanumafili II, a new chief of state will be elected by the Legislative Assembly to serve a five-year term; prime minister appointed by the chief of state with the approval of the Legislative Assembly

Samoa (continued)

Legislative branch: unicameral Legislative Assembly or Fono (49 seats - 47 elected by Samoans, 2 elected by non-Samoans; only chiefs (matai) may stand for election to the Fono; members serve five-year terms)
elections: last held 4 March 2001 (next to be held by March 2006)
election results: percent of vote by party - NA%; seats by party - HRPP 23, SNDP 13, independents 13
Judicial branch: Supreme Court; Court of Appeal
Political parties and leaders: Human Rights Protection Party or HRPP [TUILA'EPA Sailele Malielegaoi, chairman]; Samoa All People's Party or SAPP [Matatumua NAIMOAGA]; Samoan National Development Party or SNDP [TAPUA Tamasese Efi, chairman] (opposition); Samoa National Party [FETU Tiatia, party secretary]; Samoan Progressive Conservative Party [LEOTA Ituau Ale]
Political pressure groups and leaders: NA
International organization participation: ACP, AsDB, C, ESCAP, FAO, G-77, IBRD, ICAO, ICFTU, ICRM, IDA, IFAD, IFC, IFRCS, IMF, IMO, Intelsat (nonsignatory user), IOC, ITU, OPCW, Sparteca, SPC, SPF, UN, UNCTAD, UNESCO, UPU, WHO, WIPO, WMO, WTrO (observer)
Diplomatic representation in the US:
chief of mission: Ambassador Tuiloma Neroni SLADE
chancery: 800 Second Avenue, Suite 400D, New York, NY 10017
telephone: [1] (212) 599-6196, 6197
FAX: [1] (212) 599-0797
Diplomatic representation from the US:
chief of mission: Ambassador Carol MOSELEY BRAUN (Ambassador to New Zealand and Samoa, resides in Wellington, New Zealand)
embassy: 5th floor, Beach Road, Apia
mailing address: P. O. Box 3430, Apia
telephone: [685] 21631
FAX: [685] 22030
Flag description: red with a blue rectangle in the upper hoist-side quadrant bearing five white five-pointed stars representing the Southern Cross constellation

Economy

Economy - overview: The economy of Samoa has traditionally been dependent on development aid, family remittances from overseas, and agricultural exports. The country is vulnerable to devastating storms. Agriculture employs two-thirds of the labor force, and furnishes 90% of exports, featuring coconut cream, coconut oil, and copra. The manufacturing sector mainly processes agricultural products. Tourism is an expanding sector, accounting for 15% of GDP; about 85,000 tourists visited the islands in 2000. The Samoan Government has called for deregulation of the financial sector, encouragement of investment, and continued fiscal discipline. Observers point to the flexibility of the labor market as a basic strength for future economic advances. Foreign reserves are in a relatively healthy state, the external debt is stable, and inflation is low.

GDP: purchasing power parity - $571 million (2000 est.)
GDP - real growth rate: 6.8% (2000 est.)
GDP - per capita: purchasing power parity - $3,200 (2000 est.)
GDP - composition by sector:
agriculture: 15%
industry: 24%
services: 61% (2000 est.)
Population below poverty line: NA%
Household income or consumption by percentage share:
lowest 10%: NA%
highest 10%: NA%
Inflation rate (consumer prices): 0.8% (2000 est.)
Labor force: 90,000 (2000 est.)
Labor force - by occupation: agriculture 65%, services 30%, industry 5% (1995 est.)
Unemployment rate: NA%; note - substantial underemployment
Budget:
revenues: $74.8 million
expenditures: $81.4 million, including capital expenditures of $NA (1999 est.)
Industries: food processing, building materials, auto parts
Industrial production growth rate: 10% (2000 est.)
Electricity - production: 100 million kWh (1999)
Electricity - production by source:
fossil fuel: 60%
hydro: 40%
nuclear: 0%
other: 0% (1999)
Electricity - consumption: 93 million kWh (1999)
Electricity - exports: 0 kWh (1999)
Electricity - imports: 0 kWh (1999)
Agriculture - products: coconuts, bananas, taro, yams
Exports: $17 million (f.o.b., 2000)
Exports - commodities: coconut oil and cream, copra, fish, beer
Exports - partners: American Samoa 59%, US 18%, Germany 9%, New Zealand 8% (2000 est.)
Imports: $90 million (f.o.b., 2000)
Imports - commodities: machinery and equipment, industrial supplies, foodstuffs
Imports - partners: New Zealand 37%, Australia 24%, Fiji 14%, US 14% (2000 est.)
Debt - external: $180 million (1998 est.)
Economic aid - recipient: $42.9 million (1995)
Currency: tala (WST)
Currency code: WST
Exchange rates: tala per US dollar - 3.3400 (January 2001), 3.2712 (2000), 3.0120 (1999), 2.9429 (1998), 2.5562 (1997), 2.4618 (1996)
Fiscal year: calendar year

Communications

Telephones - main lines in use: 8,000 (1997)
Telephones - mobile cellular: 1,545 (February 1998)
Telephone system:
general assessment: adequate
domestic: NA
international: satellite earth station - 1 Intelsat (Pacific Ocean)
Radio broadcast stations: AM 1, FM 3, shortwave 0 (1998)
Radios: 178,000 (1997)
Television broadcast stations: 6 (1997)
Televisions: 11,000 (1997)
Internet country code: .ws
Internet Service Providers (ISPs): 2 (2000)
Internet users: 500 (2000)

Transportation

Railways: 0 km
Highways:
total: 790 km
paved: 332 km
unpaved: 458 km (1996 est.)
Waterways: none
Ports and harbors: Apia, Asau, Mulifanua, Salelologa
Airports: 3 (2000 est.)
Airports - with paved runways:
total: 1
2,438 to 3,047 m: 1 (2000 est.)
Airports - with unpaved runways:
total: 2
under 914 m: 2 (2000 est.)

Military

Military branches: no regular armed services; Samoa Police Force
Military expenditures - dollar figure: $NA
Military expenditures - percent of GDP: NA%
Military - note: Samoa has no formal defense structure or regular armed forces; informal defense ties exist with NZ, which is required to consider any Samoan request for assistance under the 1962 Treaty of Friendship

Transnational Issues

Disputes - international: none

San Marino

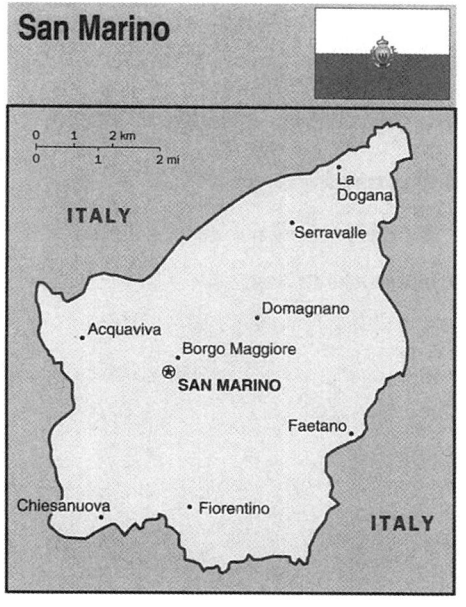

Introduction

Background: The third smallest state in Europe (after The Holy See and Monaco) also claims to be the world's oldest republic. According to tradition, it was founded by a Christian stonemason named Marinus in 301 A.D. San Marino's foreign policy is aligned with that of Italy. Social and political trends in the republic also track closely with those of its larger neighbor.

Geography

Location: Southern Europe, an enclave in central Italy
Geographic coordinates: 43 46 N, 12 25 E
Map references: Europe
Area:
total: 61.2 sq km
land: 61.2 sq km
water: 0 sq km
Area - comparative: about 0.3 times the size of Washington, DC
Land boundaries:
total: 39 km
border countries: Italy 39 km
Coastline: 0 km (landlocked)
Maritime claims: none (landlocked)
Climate: Mediterranean; mild to cool winters; warm, sunny summers
Terrain: rugged mountains
Elevation extremes:
lowest point: Torrente Ausa 55 m
highest point: Monte Titano 755 m
Natural resources: building stone
Land use:
arable land: 17%
permanent crops: 0%
permanent pastures: 0%
forests and woodland: 0%
other: 83% (1993 est.)
Irrigated land: NA sq km
Natural hazards: NA
Environment - current issues: NA
Environment - international agreements:
party to: Biodiversity, Climate Change, Desertification, Marine Dumping, Nuclear Test Ban, Ship Pollution
signed, but not ratified: Air Pollution
Geography - note: landlocked; smallest independent state in Europe after the Holy See and Monaco; dominated by the Apennines

People

Population: 27,336 (July 2001 est.)
Age structure:
0-14 years: 15.88% (male 2,241; female 2,100)
15-64 years: 67.94% (male 9,048; female 9,525)
65 years and over: 16.18% (male 1,902; female 2,520) (2001 est.)
Population growth rate: 1.45% (2001 est.)
Birth rate: 10.76 births/1,000 population (2001 est.)
Death rate: 7.68 deaths/1,000 population (2001 est.)
Net migration rate: 11.45 migrant(s)/1,000 population (2001 est.)
Sex ratio:
at birth: 1.09 male(s)/female
under 15 years: 1.07 male(s)/female
15-64 years: 0.95 male(s)/female
65 years and over: 0.75 male(s)/female
total population: 0.93 male(s)/female (2001 est.)
Infant mortality rate: 6.21 deaths/1,000 live births (2001 est.)
Life expectancy at birth:
total population: 81.23 years
male: 77.68 years
female: 85.1 years (2001 est.)
Total fertility rate: 1.3 children born/woman (2001 est.)
HIV/AIDS - adult prevalence rate: NA%
HIV/AIDS - people living with HIV/AIDS: NA
HIV/AIDS - deaths: NA
Nationality:
noun: Sammarinese (singular and plural)
adjective: Sammarinese
Ethnic groups: Sammarinese, Italian
Religions: Roman Catholic
Languages: Italian
Literacy:
definition: age 10 and over can read and write
total population: 96%
male: 97%
female: 95% (1976 est.)

Government

Country name:
conventional long form: Republic of San Marino
conventional short form: San Marino
local long form: Repubblica di San Marino
local short form: San Marino
Government type: independent republic
Capital: San Marino
Administrative divisions: 9 municipalities (castelli, singular - castello); Acquaviva, Borgo Maggiore, Chiesanuova, Domagnano, Faetano, Fiorentino, Monte Giardino, San Marino, Serravalle
Independence: 3 September 301
National holiday: Founding of the Republic, 3 September (301)
Constitution: 8 October 1600; electoral law of 1926 serves some of the functions of a constitution
Legal system: based on civil law system with Italian law influences; has not accepted compulsory ICJ jurisdiction
Suffrage: 18 years of age; universal
Executive branch:
chief of state: cochiefs of state Captain Regent Luigi LONFERNINI and Captain Regent Fabio BERARDI (for the period 1 April 2001-30 September 2001)
head of government: Secretary of State for Foreign and Political Affairs Gabriele GATTI (since NA July 1986)
cabinet: Congress of State elected by the Great and General Council for a five-year term
elections: cochiefs of state (captain regents) elected by the Great and General Council for a six-month term; election last held NA March 2001 (next to be held NA September 2001); secretary of state for foreign and political affairs elected by the Great and General Council for a five-year term; election last held NA June 1998 (next to be held NA June 2003)
election results: Luigi LONFERNINI and Fabio BERARDI elected captain regents; percent of legislative vote - NA; Gabriele GATTI reelected secretary of state for foreign and political affairs; percent of legislative vote - NA
note: the popularly elected parliament (Grand and General Council) selects two of its members to serve as the Captains Regent (cochiefs of state) for a six-month period; they preside over meetings of the Grand and General Council and its cabinet (Congress of State) which has ten other members, all selected by the Grand and General Council; assisting the captains regent are three secretaries of state - Foreign Affairs, Internal Affairs, and Finance - and several additional secretaries; the secretary of state for Foreign Affairs has assumed many of the prerogatives of a prime minister
Legislative branch: unicameral Grand and General Council or Consiglio Grande e Generale (60 seats; members are elected by direct popular vote to serve five-year terms)
elections: last held 31 May 1998 (next likely to be held by NA June 2001)
election results: percent of vote by party - PDCS 40.8%, PSS 23.3%, PPDS 18.6%, APDS 9.8%, RC 3.3%, SR 4.2%; seats by party - PDCS 25, PSS 14, PPDS 11, APDS 6, RC 2, SR 2
Judicial branch: Council of Twelve or Consiglio dei XII
Political parties and leaders: Communist Refoundation or RC [Ivan FOSHI]; Ideas in Movement or IM [Alessandro ROSSI]; San Marino Christian Democratic Party or PDCS [Pier Marino

San Marino (continued)

MENICUCCI]; San Marino Popular Alliance of Democrats or APDS [Mario VENTURINI]; San Marino Progressive Democratic Party or PPDS [Claudio FELICI]; San Marino Socialist Party or PSS [Augusto CASALI]; Socialists for Reform or SR [Renzo GIARDI]
Political pressure groups and leaders: NA
International organization participation: CE, ECE, FAO, IBRD, ICAO, ICFTU, ICRM, IFRCS, ILO, IMF, IOC, IOM (observer), ITU, OPCW, OSCE, UN, UNCTAD, UNESCO, UPU, WHO, WIPO, WToO
Diplomatic representation in the US: San Marino does not have an embassy in the US
honorary consulate(s) general: Washington, DC, and New York
honorary consulate(s): Detroit
Diplomatic representation from the US: the US does not have an embassy in San Marino; the US Consul General in Florence (Italy) is accredited to San Marino
Flag description: two equal horizontal bands of white (top) and light blue with the national coat of arms superimposed in the center; the coat of arms has a shield (featuring three towers on three peaks) flanked by a wreath, below a crown and above a scroll bearing the word LIBERTAS (Liberty)

Economy

Economy - overview: The tourist sector contributes over 50% of GDP. In 1999 more than 3 million tourists visited San Marino. The key industries are banking, wearing apparel, electronics, and ceramics. Main agricultural products are wine and cheeses. The per capita level of output and standard of living are comparable to those of the most prosperous regions of Italy, which supplies much of its food.
GDP: purchasing power parity - $860 million (2000 est.)
GDP - real growth rate: 8% (2000 est.)
GDP - per capita: purchasing power parity - $32,000 (2000 est.)
GDP - composition by sector:
agriculture: NA%
industry: NA%
services: NA%
Population below poverty line: NA%
Household income or consumption by percentage share:
lowest 10%: NA%
highest 10%: NA%
Inflation rate (consumer prices): 2.2% (2000)
Labor force: 18,500 (1999)
Labor force - by occupation: services 60%, industry 38%, agriculture 2% (1998 est.)
Unemployment rate: 3% (1999)
Budget:
revenues: $400 million
expenditures: $400 million, including capital expenditures of $NA (2000 est.)
Industries: tourism, banking, textiles, electronics, ceramics, cement, wine
Industrial production growth rate: 6% (1997 est.)
Electricity - production: NA kWh
Electricity - production by source:
fossil fuel: NA%
hydro: NA%
nuclear: NA%
other: NA%
Electricity - consumption: NA kWh
Electricity - exports: 0 kWh
note: electric power supplied by Italy (1999)
Electricity - imports: NA kWh
note: electricity supplied by Italy
Agriculture - products: wheat, grapes, corn, olives; cattle, pigs, horses, beef, cheese, hides
Exports: trade data are included with the statistics for Italy
Exports - commodities: building stone, lime, wood, chestnuts, wheat, wine, baked goods, hides, ceramics
Imports: trade data are included with the statistics for Italy
Imports - commodities: wide variety of consumer manufactures, food
Debt - external: $NA
Economic aid - recipient: $NA
Currency: Italian lira (ITL); euro (EUR)
Currency code: ITL; EUR
Exchange rates: euros per US dollar - 1.06594 (January 2001), 1.08540 (2000), 0.93863 (1999); Italian lire per US dollar - 1,736.2 (1998), 1,703.1 (1997), 1,542.9 (1996)
Fiscal year: calendar year

Communications

Telephones - main lines in use: 18,000 (1998)
Telephones - mobile cellular: 3,010 (1998)
Telephone system:
general assessment: adequate connections
domestic: automatic telephone system completely integrated into Italian system
international: connected to Italian international network
Radio broadcast stations: AM 0, FM 3, shortwave 0 (1998)
Radios: 16,000 (1997)
Television broadcast stations: 1 (San Marino residents also receive broadcasts from Italy) (1997)
Televisions: 9,000 (1997)
Internet country code: .sm
Internet Service Providers (ISPs): 2 (2000)
Internet users: NA

Transportation

Railways: 0 km; note - there is a 1.5 km cable railway connecting the city of San Marino to Borgo Maggiore
Highways:
total: 220 km
paved: NA km
unpaved: NA km
Waterways: none
Ports and harbors: none
Airports: none

Military

Military branches: Voluntary Military Force, Police Force
Military expenditures - dollar figure: $700,000 (FY00)
Military expenditures - percent of GDP: NA%

Transnational Issues

Disputes - international: none

Sao Tome and Principe

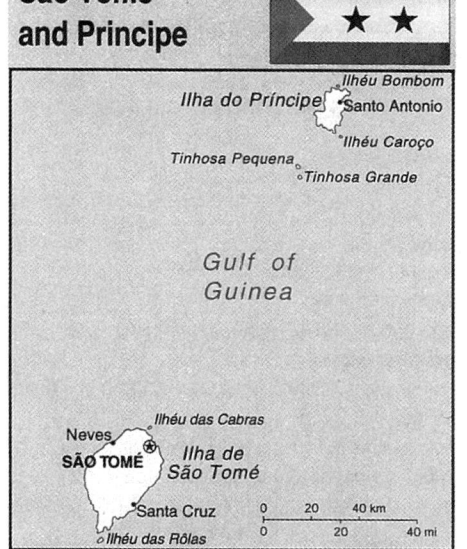

Introduction

Background: Discovered and claimed by Portugal in the late 15th century, the islands' sugar-based economy gave way to coffee and cocoa in the 19th century - all grown with plantation slave labor, a form of which lingered into the 20th century. Although independence was achieved in 1975, democratic reforms were not instituted until the late 1980s. The first free elections were held in 1991.

Geography

Location: Western Africa, islands in the Gulf of Guinea, straddling the Equator, west of Gabon
Geographic coordinates: 1 00 N, 7 00 E
Map references: Africa
Area:
total: 1,001 sq km
land: 1,001 sq km
water: 0 sq km
Area - comparative: more than five times the size of Washington, DC
Land boundaries: 0 km
Coastline: 209 km
Maritime claims: measured from claimed archipelagic baselines
exclusive economic zone: 200 NM
territorial sea: 12 NM
Climate: tropical; hot, humid; one rainy season (October to May)
Terrain: volcanic, mountainous
Elevation extremes:
lowest point: Atlantic Ocean 0 m
highest point: Pico de Sao Tome 2,024 m
Natural resources: fish, hydropower
Land use:
arable land: 2%
permanent crops: 36%
permanent pastures: 1%
forests and woodland: 0%
other: 61% (1993 est.)
Irrigated land: 100 sq km (1993 est.)
Natural hazards: NA
Environment - current issues: deforestation; soil erosion and exhaustion
Environment - international agreements:
party to: Biodiversity, Climate Change, Desertification, Environmental Modification, Law of the Sea, Marine Dumping, Ship Pollution
signed, but not ratified: none of the selected agreements

People

Population: 165,034 (July 2001 est.)
Age structure:
0-14 years: 47.7% (male 39,857; female 38,859)
15-64 years: 48.28% (male 38,430; female 41,246)
65 years and over: 4.02% (male 3,034; female 3,608) (2001 est.)
Population growth rate: 3.18% (2001 est.)
Birth rate: 42.74 births/1,000 population (2001 est.)
Death rate: 7.54 deaths/1,000 population (2001 est.)
Net migration rate: -3.38 migrant(s)/1,000 population (2001 est.)
Sex ratio:
at birth: 1.03 male(s)/female
under 15 years: 1.03 male(s)/female
15-64 years: 0.93 male(s)/female
65 years and over: 0.84 male(s)/female
total population: 0.97 male(s)/female (2001 est.)
Infant mortality rate: 48.96 deaths/1,000 live births (2001 est.)
Life expectancy at birth:
total population: 65.59 years
male: 64.15 years
female: 67.07 years (2001 est.)
Total fertility rate: 6.02 children born/woman (2001 est.)
HIV/AIDS - adult prevalence rate: NA%
HIV/AIDS - people living with HIV/AIDS: NA
HIV/AIDS - deaths: NA
Nationality:
noun: Sao Tomean(s)
adjective: Sao Tomean
Ethnic groups: mestico, angolares (descendants of Angolan slaves), forros (descendants of freed slaves), servicais (contract laborers from Angola, Mozambique, and Cape Verde), tongas (children of servicais born on the islands), Europeans (primarily Portuguese)
Religions: Christian 80% (Roman Catholic, Evangelical Protestant, Seventh-Day Adventist)
Languages: Portuguese (official)
Literacy:
definition: age 15 and over can read and write
total population: 73%
male: 85%
female: 62% (1991 est.)

Government

Country name:
conventional long form: Democratic Republic of Sao Tome and Principe
conventional short form: Sao Tome and Principe
local long form: Republica Democratica de Sao Tome e Principe
local short form: Sao Tome e Principe
Government type: republic
Capital: Sao Tome
Administrative divisions: 2 provinces; Principe, Sao Tome
note: Principe has had self-government since 29 April 1995
Independence: 12 July 1975 (from Portugal)
National holiday: Independence Day, 12 July (1975)
Constitution: approved March 1990; effective 10 September 1990
Legal system: based on Portuguese legal system and customary law; has not accepted compulsory ICJ jurisdiction
Suffrage: 18 years of age; universal
Executive branch:
chief of state: President Miguel TROVOADA (since 4 April 1991)
head of government: Prime Minister Guilherma Posser da COSTA (since 30 December 1998)
cabinet: Council of Ministers appointed by the president on the proposal of the prime minister
elections: president elected by popular vote for a five-year term; election last held 30 June and 21 July 1996 (next to be held NA July 2001); prime minister chosen by the National Assembly and approved by the president
election results: Miguel TROVOADA reelected president in Sao Tome's second multiparty presidential election; percent of vote - Miguel TROVOADA 52.74%, Manuel Pinto da COSTA 47.26%
Legislative branch: unicameral National Assembly or Assembleia Nacional (55 seats; members are elected by direct popular vote to serve five-year terms)
elections: last held 8 November 1998 (next to be held NA November 2003)
election results: percent of vote by party - MLSTP-PSD 56%, PCD 14.5%, ADI 29%; seats by party - MLSTP-PSD 31, ADI 16, PCD 8
Judicial branch: Supreme Court (judges are appointed by the National Assembly)
Political parties and leaders: Independent Democratic Action or ADI [Carlos NEVES]; Movement for the Liberation of Sao Tome and Principe-Social Democratic Party or MLSTP-PSD [Manuel Pinto Da COSTA]; Party for Democratic Convergence or PCD [Aldo BANDEIRA]; Democratic Renovation Party [Armindo GRACA]; other small parties
Political pressure groups and leaders: NA
International organization participation: ACCT, ACP, AfDB, CEEAC, ECA, FAO, G-77, IBRD, ICAO, ICRM, IDA, IFAD, IFRCS, ILO, IMF, IMO, Intelsat

Sao Tome and Principe (continued)

(nonsignatory user), Interpol, IOC, IOM (observer), ITU, NAM, OAU, UN, UNCTAD, UNESCO, UNIDO, UPU, WCL, WHO, WIPO, WMO, WToO, WTrO (observer)
Diplomatic representation in the US: Sao Tome and Principe does not have an embassy in the US, but does have a Permanent Mission to the UN, headed by First Secretary Domingos Augusto FERREIRA, located at 122 East 42nd Street, Suite 1604, New York, NY 10168, telephone [1] (212) 317-0533
Diplomatic representation from the US: the US does not have an embassy in Sao Tome and Principe; the Ambassador to Gabon is accredited to Sao Tome and Principe on a nonresident basis and makes periodic visits to the islands
Flag description: three horizontal bands of green (top), yellow (double width), and green with two black five-pointed stars placed side by side in the center of the yellow band and a red isosceles triangle based on the hoist side; uses the popular pan-African colors of Ethiopia

Economy

Economy - overview: This small poor island economy has become increasingly dependent on cocoa since independence 25 years ago. However, cocoa production has substantially declined because of drought and mismanagement. The resulting shortage of cocoa for export has created a persistent balance-of-payments problem. Sao Tome has to import all fuels, most manufactured goods, consumer goods, and a significant amount of food. Over the years, it has been unable to service its external debt and has had to depend on concessional aid and debt rescheduling. Sao Tome benefited from $200 million in debt relief in December 2000 under the Highly Indebted Poor Countries (HIPC) program. Considerable potential exists for development of a tourist industry, and the government has taken steps to expand facilities in recent years. The government also has attempted to reduce price controls and subsidies, but economic growth has remained sluggish. Sao Tome is also optimistic that significant petroleum discoveries are forthcoming in its territorial waters in the oil-rich waters of the Gulf of Guinea. Corruption scandals continue to weaken the economy. At the same time, progress in the economic reform program has attracted international financial institutions' support, and GDP growth will likely rise to at least 4% in 2001-02.
GDP: purchasing power parity - $178 million (2000 est.)
GDP - real growth rate: 3% (2000 est.)
GDP - per capita: purchasing power parity - $1,100 (2000 est.)
GDP - composition by sector:
agriculture: 23%
industry: 19%
services: 58% (1997 est.)
Population below poverty line: NA%
Household income or consumption by percentage share:
lowest 10%: NA%
highest 10%: NA%
Inflation rate (consumer prices): 5% (2000 est.)
Labor force: NA
Labor force - by occupation: population mainly engaged in subsistence agriculture and fishing
note: shortages of skilled workers
Unemployment rate: NA%
Budget:
revenues: $58 million
expenditures: $114 million, including capital expenditures of $54 million (1993 est.)
Industries: light construction, textiles, soap, beer; fish processing; timber
Industrial production growth rate: NA%
Electricity - production: 17 million kWh (1999)
Electricity - production by source:
fossil fuel: 41.18%
hydro: 58.82%
nuclear: 0%
other: 0% (1999)
Electricity - consumption: 15.8 million kWh (1999)
Electricity - exports: 0 kWh (1999)
Electricity - imports: 0 kWh (1999)
Agriculture - products: cocoa, coconuts, palm kernels, copra, cinnamon, pepper, coffee, bananas, papayas, beans; poultry; fish
Exports: $3.2 million (f.o.b., 2000 est.)
Exports - commodities: cocoa 90%, copra, coffee, palm oil
Exports - partners: Netherlands 18%, Germany 9%, Portugal 9% (1998)
Imports: $40 million (f.o.b., 2000 est.)
Imports - commodities: machinery and electrical equipment, food products, petroleum products
Imports - partners: Portugal 42%, US 20%, South Africa 6% (1998)
Debt - external: $268 million (2000)
Economic aid - recipient: $200 million in December 2000 under the HIPC program
Currency: dobra (STD)
Currency code: STD
Exchange rates: dobras per US dollar - 2390.04 (December 2000), 7,119.0 (1999), 6,883.2 (1998), 4,552.5 (1997), 2,203.2 (1996)
Fiscal year: calendar year

Communications

Telephones - main lines in use: 3,000 (1997)
Telephones - mobile cellular: 6,942 (1997)
Telephone system:
general assessment: adequate facilities
domestic: minimal system
international: satellite earth station - 1 Intelsat (Atlantic Ocean)
Radio broadcast stations: AM 2, FM 4, shortwave 0 (1998)
Radios: 38,000 (1997)
Television broadcast stations: 2 (1997)
Televisions: 23,000 (1997)
Internet country code: .st
Internet Service Providers (ISPs): 2 (2000)
Internet users: 500 (2000)

Transportation

Railways: 0 km
Highways:
total: 320 km
paved: 218 km
unpaved: 102 km (1996 est.)
Waterways: none
Ports and harbors: Santo Antonio, Sao Tome
Merchant marine:
total: 39 ships (1,000 GRT or over) totaling 130,843 GRT/149,048 DWT
ships by type: bulk 3, cargo 21, chemical tanker 1, container 3, liquefied gas 1, livestock carrier 1, petroleum tanker 1, refrigerated cargo 2, roll on/roll off 5, specialized tanker 1 (2000 est.)
Airports: 2 (2000 est.)
Airports - with paved runways:
total: 2
1,524 to 2,437 m: 1
914 to 1,523 m: 1 (2000 est.)

Military

Military branches: Army, Navy, Security Police
Military manpower - availability:
males age 15-49: 34,205 (2001 est.)
Military manpower - fit for military service:
males age 15-49: 18,043 (2001 est.)
Military expenditures - dollar figure: $1 million (FY94)
Military expenditures - percent of GDP: 1.5% (FY94)

Transnational Issues

Disputes - international: none

Saudi Arabia

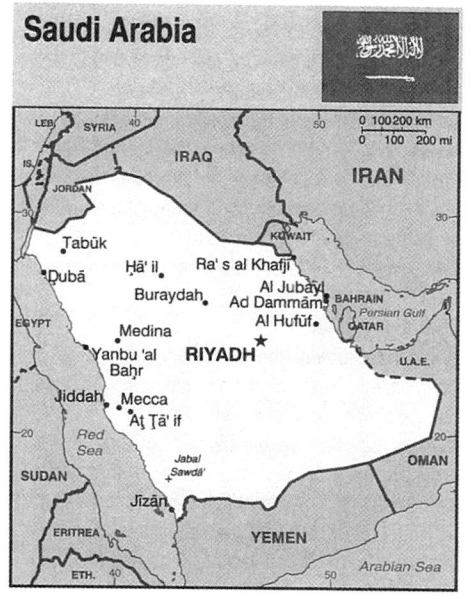

Introduction

Background: In 1902 Abdul al-Aziz Ibn SAUD captured Riyadh and set out on a 30-year campaign to unify the Arabian peninsula. In the 1930s, the discovery of oil transformed the country. Following Iraq's invasion of Kuwait in 1990, Saudi Arabia accepted the Kuwaiti royal family and 400,000 refugees while allowing Western and Arab troops to deploy on its soil for the liberation of Kuwait the following year. A burgeoning population, aquifer depletion, and an economy largely dependent on petroleum output and prices are all major governmental concerns.

Geography

Location: Middle East, bordering the Persian Gulf and the Red Sea, north of Yemen
Geographic coordinates: 25 00 N, 45 00 E
Map references: Middle East
Area:
total: 1,960,582 sq km
land: 1,960,582 sq km
water: 0 sq km
Area - comparative: slightly more than one-fifth the size of the US
Land boundaries:
total: 4,415 km
border countries: Iraq 814 km, Jordan 728 km, Kuwait 222 km, Oman 676 km, Qatar 60 km, UAE 457 km, Yemen 1,458 km
Coastline: 2,640 km
Maritime claims:
contiguous zone: 18 NM
continental shelf: not specified
territorial sea: 12 NM
Climate: harsh, dry desert with great extremes of temperature
Terrain: mostly uninhabited, sandy desert
Elevation extremes:
lowest point: Persian Gulf 0 m
highest point: Jabal Sawda' 3,133 m
Natural resources: petroleum, natural gas, iron ore, gold, copper
Land use:
arable land: 2%
permanent crops: 0%
permanent pastures: 56%
forests and woodland: 1%
other: 41% (1993 est.)
Irrigated land: 4,350 sq km (1993 est.)
Natural hazards: frequent sand and dust storms
Environment - current issues: desertification; depletion of underground water resources; the lack of perennial rivers or permanent water bodies has prompted the development of extensive seawater desalination facilities; coastal pollution from oil spills
Environment - international agreements:
party to: Climate Change, Desertification, Endangered Species, Hazardous Wastes, Law of the Sea, Marine Dumping, Ozone Layer Protection, Ship Pollution
signed, but not ratified: none of the selected agreements
Geography - note: extensive coastlines on Persian Gulf and Red Sea provide great leverage on shipping (especially crude oil) through Persian Gulf and Suez Canal

People

Population: 22,757,092
note: includes 5,360,526 non-nationals (July 2001 est.)
Age structure:
0-14 years: 42.52% (male 4,932,465; female 4,743,908)
15-64 years: 54.8% (male 7,290,840; female 5,179,393)
65 years and over: 2.68% (male 334,981; female 275,505) (2001 est.)
Population growth rate: 3.27% (2001 est.)
Birth rate: 37.34 births/1,000 population (2001 est.)
Death rate: 5.94 deaths/1,000 population (2001 est.)
Net migration rate: 1.32 migrant(s)/1,000 population (2001 est.)
Sex ratio:
at birth: 1.05 male(s)/female
under 15 years: 1.04 male(s)/female
15-64 years: 1.41 male(s)/female
65 years and over: 1.22 male(s)/female
total population: 1.23 male(s)/female (2001 est.)
Infant mortality rate: 51.25 deaths/1,000 live births (2001 est.)
Life expectancy at birth:
total population: 68.09 years
male: 66.4 years
female: 69.85 years (2001 est.)
Total fertility rate: 6.25 children born/woman (2001 est.)
HIV/AIDS - adult prevalence rate: 0.01% (1999 est.)
HIV/AIDS - people living with HIV/AIDS: NA
HIV/AIDS - deaths: NA
Nationality:
noun: Saudi(s)
adjective: Saudi or Saudi Arabian
Ethnic groups: Arab 90%, Afro-Asian 10%
Religions: Muslim 100%
Languages: Arabic
Literacy:
definition: age 15 and over can read and write
total population: 62.8%
male: 71.5%
female: 50.2% (1995 est.)

Government

Country name:
conventional long form: Kingdom of Saudi Arabia
conventional short form: Saudi Arabia
local long form: Al Mamlakah al Arabiyah as Suudiyah
local short form: Al Arabiyah as Suudiyah
Government type: monarchy
Capital: Riyadh
Administrative divisions: 13 provinces (mintaqat, singular - mintaqah); Al Bahah, Al Hudud ash Shamaliyah, Al Jawf, Al Madinah, Al Qasim, Ar Riyad, Ash Sharqiyah (Eastern Province), 'Asir, Ha'il, Jizan, Makkah, Najran, Tabuk
Independence: 23 September 1932 (Unification of the Kingdom)
National holiday: Unification of the Kingdom, 23 September (1932)
Constitution: governed according to Shari'a (Islamic law); the Basic Law that articulates the government's rights and responsibilities was introduced in 1993
Legal system: based on Islamic law, several secular codes have been introduced; commercial disputes handled by special committees; has not accepted compulsory ICJ jurisdiction
Suffrage: none
Executive branch:
chief of state: King and Prime Minister FAHD bin Abd al-Aziz Al Saud (since 13 June 1982); Crown Prince and First Deputy Prime Minister ABDALLAH bin Abd al-Aziz Al Saud (half-brother to the monarch, heir to the throne since 13 June 1982, regent from 1 January to 22 February 1996); note - the monarch is both the chief of state and head of government
head of government: King and Prime Minister FAHD bin Abd al-Aziz Al Saud (since 13 June 1982); Crown Prince and First Deputy Prime Minister ABDALLAH bin Abd al-Aziz Al Saud (half-brother to the monarch, heir to the throne since 13 June 1982, regent from 1 January to 22 February 1996); note - the monarch is both the chief of state and head of government
cabinet: Council of Ministers is appointed by the monarch and includes many royal family members
elections: none; the monarch is hereditary
Legislative branch: a consultative council (90 members and a chairman appointed by the monarch for four-year terms)
Judicial branch: Supreme Council of Justice

Saudi Arabia (continued)

Political parties and leaders: none allowed
Political pressure groups and leaders: none
International organization participation: ABEDA, AfDB, AFESD, AL, AMF, BIS, CCC, ESCWA, FAO, G-19, G-77, GCC, IAEA, IBRD, ICAO, ICC, ICRM, IDA, IDB, IFAD, IFC, IFRCS, ILO, IMF, IMO, Inmarsat, Intelsat, Interpol, IOC, ISO, ITU, NAM, OAPEC, OAS (observer), OIC, OPCW, OPEC, UN, UNCTAD, UNESCO, UNIDO, UPU, WFTU, WHO, WIPO, WMO, WTrO (observer)
Diplomatic representation in the US:
chief of mission: Ambassador BANDAR bin Sultan bin Abd al-Aziz Al Saud
chancery: 601 New Hampshire Avenue NW, Washington, DC 20037
telephone: [1] (202) 342-3800
consulate(s) general: Houston, Los Angeles, and New York
Diplomatic representation from the US:
chief of mission: Ambassador Wyche FOWLER, Jr.
embassy: Collector Road M, Diplomatic Quarter, Riyadh
mailing address: American Embassy Riyadh, Unit 61307, APO AE 09803-1307; International Mail: P. O. Box 94309, Riyadh 11693
telephone: [966] (1) 488-3800
FAX: [966] (1) 488-7360
consulate(s) general: Dhahran, Jiddah (Jeddah)
Flag description: green with large white Arabic script (that may be translated as There is no God but God; Muhammad is the Messenger of God) above a white horizontal saber (the tip points to the hoist side); green is the traditional color of Islam

Economy

Economy - overview: This is an oil-based economy with strong government controls over major economic activities. Saudi Arabia has the largest reserves of petroleum in the world (26% of the proved reserves), ranks as the largest exporter of petroleum, and plays a leading role in OPEC. The petroleum sector accounts for roughly 75% of budget revenues, 40% of GDP, and 90% of export earnings. About 35% of GDP comes from the private sector. Roughly 5 million foreign workers play an important role in the Saudi economy, for example, in the oil and service sectors. Saudi Arabia was a key player in the successful efforts of OPEC and other oil producing countries to raise the price of oil in 1999-2000 to its highest level since the Gulf war by reducing production. Riyadh expects to have a moderate budget deficit in 2001, in part because of increased spending for education and other social programs. The government in 1999 announced plans to begin privatizing the electricity companies, which follows the ongoing privatization of the telecommunications company. The government is expected to continue calling for private sector growth to lessen the kingdom's dependence on oil and increase employment opportunities for the swelling Saudi population. Shortages of water and rapid population growth will constrain government efforts to increase self-sufficiency in agricultural products.

GDP: purchasing power parity - $232 billion (2000 est.)
GDP - real growth rate: 4% (2000 est.)
GDP - per capita: purchasing power parity - $10,500 (2000 est.)
GDP - composition by sector:
agriculture: 6%
industry: 47%
services: 47% (1998 est.)
Population below poverty line: NA%
Household income or consumption by percentage share:
lowest 10%: NA%
highest 10%: NA%
Inflation rate (consumer prices): 0.5% (2000)
Labor force: 7 million
note: 35% of the population in the 15-64 age group is non-national (July 1998 est.)
Labor force - by occupation: agriculture 12%, industry 25%, services 63% (1999 est.)
Unemployment rate: NA%
Budget:
revenues: $66 billion
expenditures: $66 billion, including capital expenditures of $NA (2000 est.)
Industries: crude oil production, petroleum refining, basic petrochemicals, cement, construction, fertilizer, plastics
Industrial production growth rate: 1% (1997 est.)
Electricity - production: 120 billion kWh (1999)
Electricity - production by source:
fossil fuel: 100%
hydro: 0%
nuclear: 0%
other: 0% (1999)
Electricity - consumption: 111.6 billion kWh (1999)
Electricity - exports: 0 kWh (1999)
Electricity - imports: 0 kWh (1999)
Agriculture - products: wheat, barley, tomatoes, melons, dates, citrus; mutton, chickens, eggs, milk
Exports: $81.2 billion (f.o.b., 2000)
Exports - commodities: petroleum and petroleum products 90%
Exports - partners: Japan 18%, US 18%, France 4%, South Korea, Singapore, India (1999)
Imports: $30.1 billion (f.o.b., 2000)
Imports - commodities: machinery and equipment, foodstuffs, chemicals, motor vehicles, textiles
Imports - partners: US 25%, Japan 10%, Germany 7%, Italy 5%, France, UK (1999)
Debt - external: $26.3 billion (2000 est.)
Economic aid - donor: pledged $100 million in 1993 to fund reconstruction of Lebanon; since 1993, Saudi Arabia has committed $208 million for assistance to the Palestinians
Currency: Saudi riyal (SAR)
Currency code: SAR
Exchange rates: Saudi riyals per US dollar - 3.7450 (fixed rate since June 1986)
Fiscal year: calendar year

Communications

Telephones - main lines in use: 3.1 million (1998)
Telephones - mobile cellular: 1 million
note: in 1998, the government contracted for the installation of 575,000 additional Group Speciale Mobile (GSM) cellular telephone lines over 15 months to raise the total number of subscribers to more than one million; Riyadh planned to further expand the GSM system in 1999 by adding an additional one million lines (1998)
Telephone system:
general assessment: modern system
domestic: extensive microwave radio relay, coaxial cable, and fiber-optic cable systems
international: microwave radio relay to Bahrain, Jordan, Kuwait, Qatar, UAE, Yemen, and Sudan; coaxial cable to Kuwait and Jordan; submarine cable to Djibouti, Egypt and Bahrain; satellite earth stations - 5 Intelsat (3 Atlantic Ocean and 2 Indian Ocean), 1 Arabsat, and 1 Inmarsat (Indian Ocean region)
Radio broadcast stations: AM 43, FM 31, shortwave 2 (1998)
Radios: 6.25 million (1997)
Television broadcast stations: 117 (1997)
Televisions: 5.1 million (1997)
Internet country code: .sa
Internet Service Providers (ISPs): 42 (2001)
Internet users: 400,000 (2001)

Transportation

Railways:
total: 1,390 km
standard gauge: 1,390 km 1.435-m gauge (448 km double track) (1992)
Highways:
total: 146,524 km
paved: 44,104 km
unpaved: 102,420 km (1997 est.)
Waterways: none
Pipelines: crude oil 6,400 km; petroleum products 150 km; natural gas 2,200 km (includes natural gas liquids 1,600 km)
Ports and harbors: Ad Dammam, Al Jubayl, Duba, Jiddah, Jizan, Rabigh, Ra's al Khafji, Mishab, Ras Tanura, Yanbu' al Bahr, Madinat Yanbu' al Sinaiyah
Merchant marine:
total: 71 ships (1,000 GRT or over) totaling 1,154,619 GRT/1,533,732 DWT
ships by type: cargo 11, chemical tanker 8, container 5, liquefied gas 1, livestock carrier 3, passenger 1, petroleum tanker 18, refrigerated cargo 3, roll on/roll off 13, short-sea passenger 8 (2000 est.)
Airports: 206 (2000 est.)
Airports - with paved runways:
total: 70
over 3,047 m: 31
2,438 to 3,047 m: 11
1,524 to 2,437 m: 23
914 to 1,523 m: 3
under 914 m: 2 (2000 est.)

Saudi Arabia (continued)

Airports - with unpaved runways:
total: 136
2,438 to 3,047 m: 5
1,524 to 2,437 m: 77
914 to 1,523 m: 39
under 914 m: 15 (2000 est.)
Heliports: 5 (2000 est.)

Military

Military branches: Land Force (Army), Navy, Air Force, Air Defense Force, National Guard, Ministry of Interior Forces (paramilitary)
Military manpower - military age: 17 years of age
Military manpower - availability:
males age 15-49: 5,894,691 (2001 est.)
Military manpower - fit for military service:
males age 15-49: 3,291,185 (2001 est.)
Military manpower - reaching military age annually:
males: 233,402 (2001 est.)
Military expenditures - dollar figure: $18.3 billion (FY00)
Military expenditures - percent of GDP: 13% (FY00)

Transnational Issues

Disputes - international: a final border resolution was agreed to with Qatar in March of 2001; location and status of boundary with UAE is not final, de facto boundary reflects a 1974 agreement; a June 2000 treaty delimited the boundary with Yemen, but final demarcation requires adjustments based on tribal considerations
Illicit drugs: death penalty for traffickers; increasing consumption of heroin and cocaine

Senegal

Introduction

Background: Independent from France in 1960, Senegal joined with The Gambia to form the nominal confederation of Senegambia in 1982. However, the envisaged integration of the two countries was never carried out, and the union was dissolved in 1989. Despite peace talks, a southern separatist group sporadically has clashed with government forces since 1982. Senegal has a long history of participating in international peacekeeping.

Geography

Location: Western Africa, bordering the North Atlantic Ocean, between Guinea-Bissau and Mauritania
Geographic coordinates: 14 00 N, 14 00 W
Map references: Africa
Area:
total: 196,190 sq km
land: 192,000 sq km
water: 4,190 sq km
Area - comparative: slightly smaller than South Dakota
Land boundaries:
total: 2,640 km
border countries: The Gambia 740 km, Guinea 330 km, Guinea-Bissau 338 km, Mali 419 km, Mauritania 813 km
Coastline: 531 km
Maritime claims:
contiguous zone: 24 NM
continental shelf: 200 NM or to the edge of the continental margin
exclusive economic zone: 200 NM
territorial sea: 12 NM
Climate: tropical; hot, humid; rainy season (May to November) has strong southeast winds; dry season (December to April) dominated by hot, dry, harmattan wind
Terrain: generally low, rolling, plains rising to foothills in southeast
Elevation extremes:
lowest point: Atlantic Ocean 0 m
highest point: unnamed feature near Nepen Diakha 581 m
Natural resources: fish, phosphates, iron ore
Land use:
arable land: 12%
permanent crops: 0%
permanent pastures: 16%
forests and woodland: 54%
other: 18% (1993 est.)
Irrigated land: 710 sq km (1993 est.)
Natural hazards: lowlands seasonally flooded; periodic droughts
Environment - current issues: wildlife populations threatened by poaching; deforestation; overgrazing; soil erosion; desertification; overfishing
Environment - international agreements:
party to: Biodiversity, Climate Change, Desertification, Endangered Species, Hazardous Wastes, Law of the Sea, Marine Dumping, Marine Life Conservation, Nuclear Test Ban, Ozone Layer Protection, Ship Pollution, Wetlands, Whaling
signed, but not ratified: Marine Dumping
Geography - note: The Gambia is almost an enclave of Senegal

People

Population: 10,284,929 (July 2001 est.)
Age structure:
0-14 years: 44.07% (male 2,279,996; female 2,252,255)
15-64 years: 52.88% (male 2,603,829; female 2,834,328)
65 years and over: 3.05% (male 155,877; female 158,644) (2001 est.)
Population growth rate: 2.93% (2001 est.)
Birth rate: 37.46 births/1,000 population (2001 est.)
Death rate: 8.35 deaths/1,000 population (2001 est.)
Net migration rate: 0.21 migrant(s)/1,000 population (2001 est.)
Sex ratio:
at birth: 1.03 male(s)/female
under 15 years: 1.01 male(s)/female
15-64 years: 0.92 male(s)/female
65 years and over: 0.98 male(s)/female
total population: 0.96 male(s)/female (2001 est.)
Infant mortality rate: 56.75 deaths/1,000 live births (2001 est.)
Life expectancy at birth:
total population: 62.56 years
male: 60.94 years
female: 64.22 years (2001 est.)
Total fertility rate: 5.12 children born/woman (2001 est.)
HIV/AIDS - adult prevalence rate: 1.77% (1999 est.)
HIV/AIDS - people living with HIV/AIDS: 79,000 (1999 est.)
HIV/AIDS - deaths: 7,800 (1999 est.)

Senegal (continued)

Nationality:
noun: Senegalese (singular and plural)
adjective: Senegalese
Ethnic groups: Wolof 43.3%, Pular 23.8%, Serer 14.7%, Jola 3.7%, Mandinka 3%, Soninke 1.1%, European and Lebanese 1%, other 9.4%
Religions: Muslim 92%, indigenous beliefs 6%, Christian 2% (mostly Roman Catholic)
Languages: French (official), Wolof, Pulaar, Jola, Mandinka
Literacy:
definition: age 15 and over can read and write
total population: 33.1%
male: 43%
female: 23.2% (1995 est.)

Government

Country name:
conventional long form: Republic of Senegal
conventional short form: Senegal
local long form: Republique du Senegal
local short form: Senegal
Government type: republic under multiparty democratic rule
Capital: Dakar
Administrative divisions: 10 regions (regions, singular - region); Dakar, Diourbel, Fatick, Kaolack, Kolda, Louga, Saint-Louis, Tambacounda, Thies, Ziguinchor
Independence: 4 April 1960 (from France); complete independence was achieved upon dissolution of federation with Mali on 20 August 1960
National holiday: Independence Day, 4 April (1960)
Constitution: 3 March 1963, revised 1991
Legal system: based on French civil law system; judicial review of legislative acts in Constitutional Court; the Council of State audits the government's accounting office; has not accepted compulsory ICJ jurisdiction
Suffrage: 18 years of age; universal
Executive branch:
chief of state: President Abdoulaye WADE (since 1 April 2000)
head of government: Prime Minister Madior BOYE (since 3 March 2001)
cabinet: Council of Ministers appointed by the prime minister in consultation with the president
elections: president elected by popular vote for a seven-year term; election last held 27 February and 19 March 2000 (next to be held 27 February 2007); prime minister appointed by the president
election results: Abdoulaye WADE elected president; percent of vote in the second round of voting - Abdoulaye WADE (PDS) 58.49%, Abdou DIOUF (PS) 41.51%
Legislative branch: unicameral National Assembly or Assemblee Nationale (120 seats; members are elected by direct popular vote to serve five-year terms)
note: the former National Assembly, dissolved in the spring of 2001, had 140 seats
elections: last held 29 April 2001 (next to be held NA 2006)
election results: percent of vote by party - NA%; seats by party - SOPI Coalition 89, AFP 11, PS 10, other 10
Judicial branch: Constitutional Court; Council of State; Court of Final Appeals or Cour de Cassation; Court of Appeals; note-the judicial system was reformed in 1992
Political parties and leaders: African Party for Democracy and Socialism or And Jef (also known as PADS/AJ) [Landing SAVANE, secretary general]; African Party of Independence [Majhemout DIOP]; Alliance of Forces of Progress or AFP [Moustapha NIASSE]; Democratic and Patriotic Convention or CDP (also known as Garab-Gi) [Dr. Iba Der THIAM]; Democratic League-Labor Party Movement or LD-MPT [Dr. Abdoulaye BATHILY]; Front for Socialism and Democracy or FSD [Cheikh Abdoulaye DIEYE]; Gainde Centrist Bloc or BGC [Jean-Paul DIAS]; Independence and Labor Party or PIT [Amath DANSOKHO]; National Democratic Rally or RND [Madier DIOUF]; Senegalese Democratic Party or PDS [Abdoulaye WADE]; Senegalese Democratic Party-Renewal or PDS-R [Serigne Lamine DIOP, secretary general]; Senegalese Democratic Union-Renewal or UDS-R [Mamadou Puritain FALL]; Socialist Party or PS [President Abdou DIOUF]; SOPI Coalition (a 40-party coalition led by the PDS) [Abdoulaye WADE]; Union for Democratic Renewal or URD [Djibo Leyti KA]; other small parties
Political pressure groups and leaders: labor; Muslim brotherhoods; students; teachers
International organization participation: ACCT, ACP, AfDB, CCC, ECA, ECOWAS, FAO, FZ, G-15, G-77, IAEA, IBRD, ICAO, ICC, ICFTU, ICRM, IDA, IDB, IFAD, IFC, IFRCS, ILO, IMF, IMO, Inmarsat, Intelsat, Interpol, IOC, IOM, ITU, MINURSO, MIPONUH, MONUC, NAM, OAU, OIC, OPCW, PCA, UN, UNCTAD, UNESCO, UNIDO, UNIKOM, UNMIBH, UNMIK, UNTAET, UPU, WADB, WAEMU, WCL, WFTU, WHO, WIPO, WMO, WToO, WTrO
Diplomatic representation in the US:
chief of mission: Ambassador Mamadou Mansour SECK
chancery: 2112 Wyoming Avenue NW, Washington, DC 20008
telephone: [1] (202) 234-0540
Diplomatic representation from the US:
chief of mission: Ambassador Harriet L. ELAM-THOMAS
embassy: Avenue Jean XXIII at the corner of Rue Kleber, Dakar
mailing address: B. P. 49, Dakar
telephone: [221] 823-4296, 823-7384
FAX: [221] 822-2991
Flag description: three equal vertical bands of green (hoist side), yellow, and red with a small green five-pointed star centered in the yellow band; uses the popular pan-African colors of Ethiopia

Economy

Economy - overview: In January 1994, Senegal undertook a bold and ambitious economic reform program with the support of the international donor community. This reform began with a 50% devaluation of Senegal's currency, the CFA franc, which is linked at a fixed rate to the French franc. Government price controls and subsidies have been steadily dismantled. After seeing its economy contract by 2.1% in 1993, Senegal made an important turnaround, thanks to the reform program, with real growth in GDP averaging 5% annually in 1995-99. Annual inflation has been pushed down to 2%, and the fiscal deficit has been cut to less than 1.5% of GDP. Investment rose steadily from 13.8% of GDP in 1993 to 16.5% in 1997. As a member of the West African Economic and Monetary Union (UEMOA), Senegal is working toward greater regional integration with a unified external tariff. Senegal also realized full Internet connectivity in 1996, creating a miniboom in information technology-based services. Private activity now accounts for 82% of GDP. On the negative side, Senegal faces deep-seated urban problems of chronic unemployment, juvenile delinquency, and drug addiction. Real GDP growth is expected to rise above 6%, while inflation is likely to hold at 2% in 2001-02.
GDP: purchasing power parity - $16 billion (2000 est.)
GDP - real growth rate: 5.7% (2000 est.)
GDP - per capita: purchasing power parity - $1,600 (2000 est.)
GDP - composition by sector:
agriculture: 19%
industry: 20%
services: 61% (1997 est.)
Population below poverty line: NA%
Household income or consumption by percentage share:
lowest 10%: 1.4%
highest 10%: 42.8% (1991)
Inflation rate (consumer prices): 1.5% (2000 est.)
Labor force: NA
Labor force - by occupation: agriculture 60%
Unemployment rate: NA%; urban youth 40%
Budget:
revenues: $885 million
expenditures: $885 million, including capital expenditures of $125 million (1996 est.)
Industries: agricultural and fish processing, phosphate mining, fertilizer production, petroleum refining, construction materials
Industrial production growth rate: 7% (1998 est.)
Electricity - production: 1.27 billion kWh (1999)
Electricity - production by source:
fossil fuel: 100%
hydro: 0%
nuclear: 0%
other: 0% (1999)
Electricity - consumption: 1.181 billion kWh (1999)

Senegal (continued)

Electricity - exports: 0 kWh (1999)
Electricity - imports: 0 kWh (1999)
Agriculture - products: peanuts, millet, corn, sorghum, rice, cotton, tomatoes, green vegetables; cattle, poultry, pigs; fish
Exports: $959 million (f.o.b., 2000)
Exports - commodities: fish, ground nuts (peanuts), petroleum products, phosphates, cotton
Exports - partners: France 17%, India 17%, Italy 12%, Spain 6%, Mali 6%, Cote d'Ivoire 4% (1999)
Imports: $1.3 billion (f.o.b., 2000)
Imports - commodities: foods and beverages, consumer goods, capital goods, petroleum products
Imports - partners: France 30%, Nigeria 7%, Italy 6%, Thailand 5%, Germany 4%, US 4% (1999)
Debt - external: $4.1 billion (1998 est.)
Economic aid - recipient: $647.5 million (1995)
Currency: Communaute Financiere Africaine franc (XOF); note - responsible authority is the Central Bank of the West African States
Currency code: XOF
Exchange rates: Communaute Financiere Africaine francs (XOF) per US dollar - 699.21 (January 2001), 711.98 (2000), 615.70 (1999), 589.95 (1998), 583.67 (1997), 511.55 (1966); note - from 1 January 1999, the XOF is pegged to the euro at a rate of 655.957 XOF per euro
Fiscal year: calendar year

Communications

Telephones - main lines in use: 116,000 (1997)
Telephones - mobile cellular: 1,149 (1996)
Telephone system:
general assessment: good system
domestic: above-average urban system; microwave radio relay, coaxial cable and fiber-optic cable in trunk system
international: 4 submarine cables; satellite earth station - 1 Intelsat (Atlantic Ocean)
Radio broadcast stations: AM 10, FM 14, shortwave 0 (1998)
Radios: 1.24 million (1997)
Television broadcast stations: 1 (1997)
Televisions: 361,000 (1997)
Internet country code: .sn
Internet Service Providers (ISPs): 1 (2000)
Internet users: 30,000 (2000)

Transportation

Railways:
total: 906 km
narrow gauge: 906 km 1.000-meter gauge (70 km double track)
Highways:
total: 14,576 km
paved: 4,271 km
unpaved: 10,305 km (1996 est.)
Waterways: 897 km
note: 785 km on the Senegal river, and 112 km on the Saloum river

Ports and harbors: Dakar, Kaolack, Matam, Podor, Richard Toll, Saint-Louis, Ziguinchor
Airports: 20 (2000 est.)
Airports - with paved runways:
total: 10
over 3,047 m: 1
1,524 to 2,437 m: 7
914 to 1,523 m: 2 (2000 est.)
Airports - with unpaved runways:
total: 10
1,524 to 2,437 m: 5
914 to 1,523 m: 4
under 914 m: 1 (2000 est.)

Military

Military branches: Army, Navy, Air Force, National Gendarmerie, National Police (Surete Nationale)
Military manpower - military age: 18 years of age
Military manpower - availability:
males age 15-49: 2,311,063 (2001 est.)
Military manpower - fit for military service:
males age 15-49: 1,207,360 (2001 est.)
Military manpower - reaching military age annually:
males: 114,189 (2001 est.)
Military expenditures - dollar figure: $68 million (FY97)
Military expenditures - percent of GDP: 1.4% (FY97)

Transnational Issues

Disputes - international: none
Illicit drugs: transshipment point for Southwest and Southeast Asian heroin moving to Europe and North America; illicit cultivator of cannabis

Seychelles

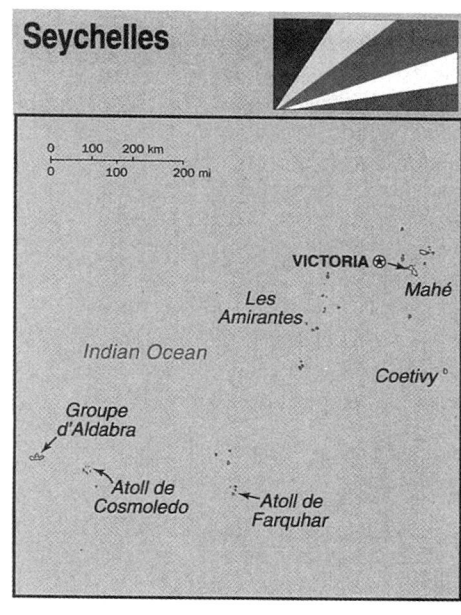

Introduction

Background: A lengthy struggle between France and Great Britain for the islands ended in 1814, when they were ceded to the latter. Independence came in 1976. Socialist rule was brought to a close with a new constitution and free elections in 1993.

Geography

Location: Eastern Africa, group of islands in the Indian Ocean, northeast of Madagascar
Geographic coordinates: 4 35 S, 55 40 E
Map references: Africa
Area:
total: 455 sq km
land: 455 sq km
water: 0 sq km
Area - comparative: 2.5 times the size of Washington, DC
Land boundaries: 0 km
Coastline: 491 km
Maritime claims:
contiguous zone: 24 NM
continental shelf: 200 NM or to the edge of the continental margin
exclusive economic zone: 200 NM
territorial sea: 12 NM
Climate: tropical marine; humid; cooler season during southeast monsoon (late May to September); warmer season during northwest monsoon (March to May)
Terrain: Mahe Group is granitic, narrow coastal strip, rocky, hilly; others are coral, flat, elevated reefs
Elevation extremes:
lowest point: Indian Ocean 0 m
highest point: Morne Seychellois 905 m
Natural resources: fish, copra, cinnamon trees
Land use:
arable land: 2%
permanent crops: 13%

Seychelles (continued)

permanent pastures: 0%
forests and woodland: 11%
other: 74% (1993 est.)
Irrigated land: NA sq km
Natural hazards: lies outside the cyclone belt, so severe storms are rare; short droughts possible
Environment - current issues: water supply depends on catchments to collect rainwater
Environment - international agreements:
party to: Biodiversity, Climate Change, Desertification, Endangered Species, Hazardous Wastes, Law of the Sea, Marine Dumping, Nuclear Test Ban, Ozone Layer Protection, Ship Pollution
signed, but not ratified: Climate Change-Kyoto Protocol
Geography - note: 40 granitic and about 50 coralline islands

People

Population: 79,715 (July 2001 est.)
Age structure:
0-14 years: 28.27% (male 11,367; female 11,167)
15-64 years: 65.47% (male 25,453; female 26,737)
65 years and over: 6.26% (male 1,673; female 3,318) (2001 est.)
Population growth rate: 0.49% (2001 est.)
Birth rate: 17.66 births/1,000 population (2001 est.)
Death rate: 6.65 deaths/1,000 population (2001 est.)
Net migration rate: -6.15 migrant(s)/1,000 population (2001 est.)
Sex ratio:
at birth: 1.03 male(s)/female
under 15 years: 1.02 male(s)/female
15-64 years: 0.95 male(s)/female
65 years and over: 0.5 male(s)/female
total population: 0.93 male(s)/female (2001 est.)
Infant mortality rate: 17.3 deaths/1,000 live births (2001 est.)
Life expectancy at birth:
total population: 70.69 years
male: 65.17 years
female: 76.37 years (2001 est.)
Total fertility rate: 1.83 children born/woman (2001 est.)
HIV/AIDS - adult prevalence rate: NA%
HIV/AIDS - people living with HIV/AIDS: NA
HIV/AIDS - deaths: NA
Nationality:
noun: Seychellois (singular and plural)
adjective: Seychelles
Ethnic groups: Seychellois (mixture of Asians, Africans, Europeans)
Religions: Roman Catholic 90%, Anglican 8%, other 2%
Languages: English (official), French (official), Creole
Literacy:
definition: age 15 and over can read and write
total population: 58%
male: 56%
female: 60% (1971 est.)

Government

Country name:
conventional long form: Republic of Seychelles
conventional short form: Seychelles
Government type: republic
Capital: Victoria
Administrative divisions: 23 administrative districts; Anse aux Pins, Anse Boileau, Anse Etoile, Anse Louis, Anse Royale, Baie Lazare, Baie Sainte Anne, Beau Vallon, Bel Air, Bel Ombre, Cascade, Glacis, Grand' Anse (on Mahe), Grand' Anse (on Praslin), La Digue, La Riviere Anglaise, Mont Buxton, Mont Fleuri, Plaisance, Pointe La Rue, Port Glaud, Saint Louis, Takamaka
Independence: 29 June 1976 (from UK)
National holiday: Constitution Day, 18 June (1993)
Constitution: 18 June 1993
Legal system: based on English common law, French civil law, and customary law
Suffrage: 17 years of age; universal
Executive branch:
chief of state: President France Albert RENE (since 5 June 1977); note - the president is both the chief of state and head of government
head of government: President France Albert RENE (since 5 June 1977); note - the president is both the chief of state and head of government
cabinet: Council of Ministers appointed by the president
elections: president elected by popular vote for a five-year term; election last held 20-22 March 1998 (next to be held by NA 2003)
election results: France Albert RENE reelected president; percent of vote - France Albert RENE (SPPF) 66.7%, Wavel RAMKALAWAN (UO) 19.5%, Sir James MANCHAM (DP) 13.8%
Legislative branch: unicameral National Assembly or Assemblee Nationale (34 seats - 25 elected by popular vote, 9 allocated on a proportional basis to parties winning at least ten percent of the vote; members serve five-year terms)
elections: last held 20-22 March 1998 (next to be held by NA 2003)
election results: percent of vote by party - SPPF 61.7%, UO 26.1%, DP 12.1%; seats by party - SPPF 30, UO 3, DP 1
note: the 9 awarded seats are apportioned according to the share of each party in the total vote
Judicial branch: Court of Appeal; Supreme Court; judges for both courts are appointed by the president
Political parties and leaders: Democratic Party or DP [James MANCHAM]; Seychelles National Party or SNP (formerly the United Opposition or UO) [Wavel RAMKALAWAN]; Seychelles People's Progressive Front or SPPF [France Albert RENE] - the governing party
Political pressure groups and leaders: Roman Catholic Church; trade unions
International organization participation: ACCT, ACP, AfDB, C, CCC, ECA, FAO, G-77, IBRD, ICAO, ICFTU, ICRM, IFAD, IFC, IFRCS, ILO, IMF, IMO, InOC, Intelsat (nonsignatory user), Interpol, IOC, ITU, NAM, OAU, OPCW, SADC, UN, UNCTAD, UNESCO, UNIDO, UPU, WHO, WIPO, WMO, WToO, WTrO (observer)
Diplomatic representation in the US:
chief of mission: Ambassador Claude Sylvestre MOREL
chancery: 800 Second Avenue, Suite 400C, New York, NY 10017
telephone: [1] (212) 972-1785
FAX: [1] (212) 972-1786
Diplomatic representation from the US: the US does not have an embassy in Seychelles; the ambassador to Mauritius is accredited to Seychelles
Flag description: five oblique bands of blue (hoist side), yellow, red, white, and green (bottom) radiating from the bottom of the hoist side

Economy

Economy - overview: Since independence in 1976, per capita output in this Indian Ocean archipelago has expanded to roughly seven times the old near-subsistence level. Growth has been led by the tourist sector, which employs about 30% of the labor force and provides more than 70% of hard currency earnings, and by tuna fishing. In recent years the government has encouraged foreign investment in order to upgrade hotels and other services. At the same time, the government has moved to reduce the dependence on tourism by promoting the development of farming, fishing, and small-scale manufacturing. The vulnerability of the tourist sector was illustrated by the sharp drop in 1991-92 due largely to the Gulf war. Although the industry has rebounded, the government recognizes the continuing need for upgrading the sector in the face of stiff international competition. Other issues facing the government are the curbing of the budget deficit and further privatization of public enterprises. Growth slowed in 1998-2000, due to sluggish tourist and tuna sectors. Tight controls on exchange rates and the scarcity of foreign exchange have hindered short-term economic prospects. The black market value of the Seychelles ruppee is half the official exchange rate; without a devaluation of the currency the tourist sector should remain sluggish as vacationers seek cheaper destinations such as Comoros, Mauritius, and Madagascar.
GDP: purchasing power parity - $610 million (2000 est.)
GDP - real growth rate: 1.5% (2000 est.)
GDP - per capita: purchasing power parity - $7,700 (2000 est.)
GDP - composition by sector:
agriculture: 3.1%
industry: 26.3%
services: 70.6% (1999)
Population below poverty line: NA%
Household income or consumption by percentage share:
lowest 10%: NA%
highest 10%: NA%

Seychelles (continued)

Inflation rate (consumer prices): 6% (1999 est.)
Labor force: 30,900 (1996)
Labor force - by occupation: industry 19%, services 71%, agriculture 10% (1989)
Unemployment rate: NA%
Budget:
revenues: $249 million
expenditures: $262 million, including capital expenditures of $NA (1998 est.)
Industries: fishing; tourism; processing of coconuts and vanilla, coir (coconut fiber) rope, boat building, printing, furniture; beverages
Industrial production growth rate: NA%
Electricity - production: 160 million kWh (1999)
Electricity - production by source:
fossil fuel: 100%
hydro: 0%
nuclear: 0%
other: 0% (1999)
Electricity - consumption: 148.8 million kWh (1999)
Electricity - exports: 0 kWh (1999)
Electricity - imports: 0 kWh (1999)
Agriculture - products: coconuts, cinnamon, vanilla, sweet potatoes, cassava (tapioca), bananas; broiler chickens; tuna fish
Exports: $111 million (f.o.b., 1999)
Exports - commodities: fish, cinnamon bark, copra, petroleum products (reexports)
Exports - partners: France, UK, Netherlands, Italy, China, Germany, Japan
Imports: $440 million (c.i.f., 1999)
Imports - commodities: machinery and equipment, foodstuffs, petroleum products, chemicals
Imports - partners: South Africa, UK, China, Singapore, France, Italy
Debt - external: $240 million (1999 est.)
Economic aid - recipient: $16.4 million (1995)
Currency: Seychelles rupee (SCR)
Currency code: SCR
Exchange rates: Seychelles rupees per US dollar - 6.0397 (November 2000), 5.6009 (2000), 5,3426 (1999), 5.2622 (1998), 5.0263 (1997), 4.9700 (1996)
Fiscal year: calendar year

Communications

Telephones - main lines in use: 19,635 (1997)
Telephones - mobile cellular: 16,316 (1999)
Telephone system:
general assessment: effective system
domestic: radiotelephone communications between islands in the archipelago
international: direct radiotelephone communications with adjacent island countries and African coastal countries; satellite earth station - 1 Intelsat (Indian Ocean)
Radio broadcast stations: AM 1, FM 2, shortwave 2 (1998)
Radios: 42,000 (1997)
Television broadcast stations: 2 (plus 9 repeaters) (1997)
Televisions: 11,000 (1997)
Internet country code: .sc
Internet Service Providers (ISPs): 1 (2000)
Internet users: 5,000 (2000)

Transportation

Railways: 0 km
Highways:
total: 280 km
paved: 176 km
unpaved: 104 km (1996 est.)
Waterways: none
Ports and harbors: Victoria
Merchant marine:
total: 1 ship (1,000 GRT or over) totaling 5,353 GRT/ 7,638 DWT
ships by type: cargo 1 (2000 est.)
Airports: 14 (2000 est.)
Airports - with paved runways:
total: 6
2,438 to 3,047 m: 1
914 to 1,523 m: 3
under 914 m: 2 (2000 est.)
Airports - with unpaved runways:
total: 8
914 to 1,523 m: 4
under 914 m: 4 (2000 est.)

Military

Military branches: Army, Coast Guard, air wing, National Guard, Presidential Protection Unit, Police Force
Military manpower - availability:
males age 15-49: 22,951 (2001 est.)
Military manpower - fit for military service:
males age 15-49: 11,452 (2001 est.)
Military expenditures - dollar figure: $13 million (FY93)
Military expenditures - percent of GDP: 2.8% (FY93)

Transnational Issues

Disputes - international: claims the Chagos Archipelago (UK-administered British Indian Ocean Territory)

Sierra Leone

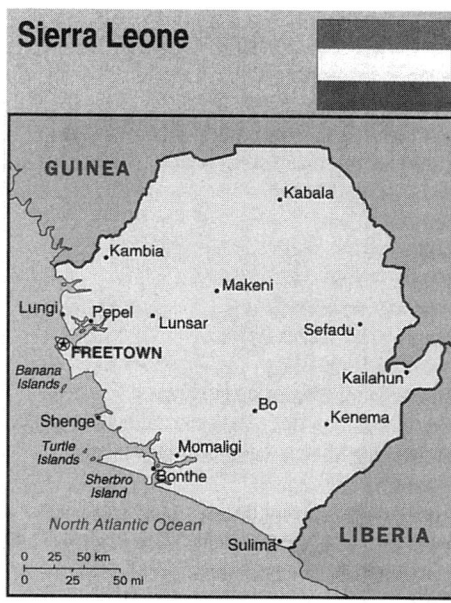

Introduction

Background: Since 1991, civil war between the government and the Revolutionary United Front (RUF) has resulted in tens of thousands of deaths and the displacement of more than 2 million people (well over one-third of the population) many of whom are now refugees in neighboring countries. A peace agreement, signed in July 1999, collapsed in May 2000 after the RUF took over 500 UN peacekeepers hostage. The RUF stepped up attacks on Guinea in December 2000, despite a cease-fire that it signed with the Freetown government one month earlier. As of late 2000, up to 13,000 UN peacekeepers were protecting the capital and key towns in the south. A UK force of 750 was helping to reinforce security and train the Sierra Leone army.

Geography

Location: Western Africa, bordering the North Atlantic Ocean, between Guinea and Liberia
Geographic coordinates: 8 30 N, 11 30 W
Map references: Africa
Area:
total: 71,740 sq km
land: 71,620 sq km
water: 120 sq km
Area - comparative: slightly smaller than South Carolina
Land boundaries:
total: 958 km
border countries: Guinea 652 km, Liberia 306 km
Coastline: 402 km
Maritime claims:
territorial sea: 200 NM
continental shelf: 200-m depth or to the depth of exploitation
Climate: tropical; hot, humid; summer rainy season (May to December); winter dry season (December to April)

Sierra Leone (continued)

Terrain: coastal belt of mangrove swamps, wooded hill country, upland plateau, mountains in east
Elevation extremes:
lowest point: Atlantic Ocean 0 m
highest point: Loma Mansa (Bintimani) 1,948 m
Natural resources: diamonds, titanium ore, bauxite, iron ore, gold, chromite
Land use:
arable land: 7%
permanent crops: 1%
permanent pastures: 31%
forests and woodland: 28%
other: 33% (1993 est.)
Irrigated land: 290 sq km (1993 est.)
Natural hazards: dry, sand-laden harmattan winds blow from the Sahara (December to February); sandstorms, dust storms
Environment - current issues: rapid population growth pressuring the environment; overharvesting of timber, expansion of cattle grazing, and slash-and-burn agriculture have resulted in deforestation and soil exhaustion; civil war depleting natural resources; overfishing
Environment - international agreements:
party to: Biodiversity, Climate Change, Desertification, Endangered Species, Environmental Modification, Law of the Sea, Marine Dumping, Marine Life Conservation, Nuclear Test Ban, Ship Pollution, Wetlands
signed, but not ratified: none of the selected agreements

People

Population: 5,426,618 (July 2001 est.)
Age structure:
0-14 years: 44.73% (male 1,190,207; female 1,237,326)
15-64 years: 52.12% (male 1,351,455; female 1,477,155)
65 years and over: 3.15% (male 84,364; female 86,111) (2001 est.)
Population growth rate: 3.61% (2001 est.)
Birth rate: 45.11 births/1,000 population (2001 est.)
Death rate: 19.19 deaths/1,000 population (2001 est.)
Net migration rate: 10.23 migrant(s)/1,000 population (2001 est.)
note: by the end of 1999 refugees from Sierra Leone are assumed to be returning
Sex ratio:
at birth: 1.03 male(s)/female
under 15 years: 0.96 male(s)/female
15-64 years: 0.91 male(s)/female
65 years and over: 0.98 male(s)/female
total population: 0.94 male(s)/female (2001 est.)
Infant mortality rate: 146.52 deaths/1,000 live births (2001 est.)
Life expectancy at birth:
total population: 45.6 years
male: 42.69 years
female: 48.61 years (2001 est.)
Total fertility rate: 6.01 children born/woman (2001 est.)
HIV/AIDS - adult prevalence rate: 2.99% (1999 est.)
HIV/AIDS - people living with HIV/AIDS: 68,000 (1999 est.)
HIV/AIDS - deaths: 8,200 (1999 est.)
Nationality:
noun: Sierra Leonean(s)
adjective: Sierra Leonean
Ethnic groups: 20 native African tribes 90% (Temne 30%, Mende 30%, other 30%), Creole 10% (descendants of freed Jamaican slaves who were settled in the Freetown area in the late-18th century), refugees from Liberia's recent civil war, small numbers of Europeans, Lebanese, Pakistanis, and Indians
Religions: Muslim 60%, indigenous beliefs 30%, Christian 10%
Languages: English (official, regular use limited to literate minority), Mende (principal vernacular in the south), Temne (principal vernacular in the north), Krio (English-based Creole, spoken by the descendants of freed Jamaican slaves who were settled in the Freetown area, a lingua franca and a first language for 10% of the population but understood by 95%)
Literacy:
definition: age 15 and over can read and write English, Mende, Temne, or Arabic
total population: 31.4%
male: 45.4%
female: 18.2% (1995 est.)

Government

Country name:
conventional long form: Republic of Sierra Leone
conventional short form: Sierra Leone
Government type: constitutional democracy
Capital: Freetown
Administrative divisions: 3 provinces and 1 area*; Eastern, Northern, Southern, Western*
Independence: 27 April 1961 (from UK)
National holiday: Independence Day, 27 April (1961)
Constitution: 1 October 1991; subsequently amended several times
Legal system: based on English law and customary laws indigenous to local tribes; has not accepted compulsory ICJ jurisdiction
Suffrage: 18 years of age; universal
Executive branch:
chief of state: President Ahmad Tejan KABBAH (since 29 March 1996, reinstated 10 March 1998); note - the president is both the chief of state and head of government
head of government: President Ahmad Tejan KABBAH (since 29 March 1996, reinstated 10 March 1998); note - the president is both the chief of state and head of government
cabinet: Ministers of State appointed by the president with the approval of the House of Representatives; the cabinet is responsible to the president
elections: president elected by popular vote for a five-year term; election held 26-27 February and 15 March 1996 (next to be held NA September 2001); note - president's tenure of office is limited to two five-year terms
election results: Ahmad Tejan KABBAH elected president; percent of vote - Ahmad Tejan KABBAH (SLPP) 59.5%, John KAREFA-SMART (UNPP) 40.5%
Legislative branch: unicameral House of Representatives (80 seats - 68 elected by popular vote, 12 filled by paramount chiefs elected in separate elections; members serve five-year terms)
elections: last held 26-27 February 1996 (next to be held NA 2001)
election results: percent of vote by party - SLPP 36.1%, UNPP 21.6%, PDP 15.3%, APC 5.7%, NUP 5.3%, DCP 4.8%, other 11.2%; seats by party - SLPP 27, UNPP 17, PDP 12, APC 5, NUP 4, DCP 3; note - first elections since the former House of Representatives was shut down by the military coup of 29 April 1992
Judicial branch: Supreme Court; Appeals Court; High Court
Political parties and leaders: All People's Congress or APC [Edward Mohammed TURAY, chairman]; Democratic Centre Party or DCP [Adu Aiah KOROMA]; National Democratic Alliance or NDA [Amadu M. B. JALLOH]; National Republican Party or NRP [Sahr Stephen MAMBU]; National Unity Party or NUP [Dr. John KARIMU, chairman]; People's Democratic Party or PDP [Thaimu BANGURA, chairman]; People's Progressive Party or PPP [Abass Chernok BUNDU, chairman]; Revolutionary United Front Party or RUFP [Foday SANKOH, chairman]; Sierra Leone People's Party or SLPP [President Ahmad Tejan KABBAH, chairman]; United National People's Party or UNPP [John KARIFA-SMART in exile, Raymond KAMARA, acting leader]
Political pressure groups and leaders: Trade Unions and Student Unions
International organization participation: ACP, AfDB, C, CCC, ECA, ECOWAS, FAO, G-77, IAEA, IBRD, ICAO, ICFTU, ICRM, IDA, IDB, IFAD, IFC, IFRCS, ILO, IMF, IMO, Intelsat (nonsignatory user), Interpol, IOC, ITU, NAM, OAU, OIC, OPCW, UN, UNCTAD, UNESCO, UNIDO, UPU, WCL, WFTU, WHO, WIPO, WMO, WToO, WTrO
Diplomatic representation in the US:
chief of mission: Ambassador John Ernest LEIGH
chancery: 1701 19th Street NW, Washington, DC 20009
telephone: [1] (202) 939-9261 through 9263
FAX: [1] (202) 483-1793
Diplomatic representation from the US:
chief of mission: Ambassador Joseph H. MELROSE, Jr.
embassy: Corner of Walpole and Siaka Stevens Streets, Freetown
mailing address: use embassy street address
telephone: [232] (22) 226481 through 226485
FAX: [232] (22) 225471

Sierra Leone (continued)

Flag description: three equal horizontal bands of light green (top), white, and light blue

Economy

Economy - overview: Sierra Leone is an extremely poor African nation with tremendous inequality in income distribution. It does have substantial mineral, agricultural, and fishery resources. However, the economic and social infrastructure is not well developed, and serious social disorders continue to hamper economic development. About two-thirds of the working-age population engages in subsistence agriculture. Manufacturing consists mainly of the processing of raw materials and of light manufacturing for the domestic market. Bauxite and rutile mines have been shut down by civil strife. The major source of hard currency is found in the mining of diamonds, the large majority of which are smuggled out of the country. The resurgence of internal warfare in 1999 brought another substantial drop in GDP, with GNP recovering part of the way in 2000. The fate of the economy depends upon the maintenance of domestic peace and the continued receipt of substantial aid from abroad.
GDP: purchasing power parity - $2.7 billion (2000 est.)
GDP - real growth rate: 4.2% (2000 est.)
GDP - per capita: purchasing power parity - $510 (2000 est.)
GDP - composition by sector:
agriculture: 43%
industry: 26%
services: 31% (1999)
Population below poverty line: 68% (1989 est.)
Household income or consumption by percentage share:
lowest 10%: 0.5%
highest 10%: 43.6% (1989)
Inflation rate (consumer prices): 15% (2000 est.)
Labor force: 1.369 million (1981 est.)
note: only about 65,000 wage earners (1985)
Labor force - by occupation: agriculture NA%, industry NA%, services NA%
Unemployment rate: NA%
Budget:
revenues: $96 million
expenditures: $351 million, including capital expenditures of $NA (2000 est.)
Industries: mining (diamonds); small-scale manufacturing (beverages, textiles, cigarettes, footwear); petroleum refining
Industrial production growth rate: NA%
Electricity - production: 240 million kWh (1999)
Electricity - production by source:
fossil fuel: 100%
hydro: 0%
nuclear: 0%
other: 0% (1999)
Electricity - consumption: 223.2 million kWh (1999)
Electricity - exports: 0 kWh (1999)
Electricity - imports: 0 kWh (1999)
Agriculture - products: rice, coffee, cocoa, palm kernels, palm oil, peanuts; poultry, cattle, sheep, pigs; fish
Exports: $65 million (f.o.b., 2000 est.)
Exports - commodities: diamonds, rutile, cocoa, coffee, fish
Exports - partners: Belgium 38%, US 6%, Italy 4%, UK 4% (1999)
Imports: $145 million (f.o.b., 2000 est.)
Imports - commodities: foodstuffs, machinery and equipment, fuels and lubricants, chemicals
Imports - partners: UK 34%, US 8%, Italy 7%, Nigeria 5% (1999)
Debt - external: $1.28 billion (1999)
Economic aid - recipient: $203.7 million (1995)
Currency: leone (SLL)
Currency code: SLL
Exchange rates: leones per US dollar - 1,653.39 (January 2001), 2,092.13 (2000), 1,804.20 (1999), 1,563.62 (1998), 981.48 (1997), 920.73 (1996)
Fiscal year: calendar year

Communications

Telephones - main lines in use: 17,000 (1997)
Telephones - mobile cellular: 650 (1999)
Telephone system:
general assessment: marginal telephone and telegraph service
domestic: national microwave radio relay trunk system, made unserviceable by military activities, is now operating from Freetown to Bo and Kenema (April 2001)
international: satellite earth station - 1 Intelsat (Atlantic Ocean)
Radio broadcast stations: AM 1, FM 9, shortwave 1 (1999)
Radios: 1.12 million (1997)
Television broadcast stations: 2 (1999)
Televisions: 53,000 (1997)
Internet country code: .sl
Internet Service Providers (ISPs): 1 (2000)
Internet users: 2,000 (2000)

Transportation

Railways:
total: 84 km used on a limited basis because the mine at Marampa is closed
narrow gauge: 84 km 1.067-m gauge
Highways:
total: 11,300 km
paved: 904 km
unpaved: 10,396 km (1999 est.)
Waterways: 800 km (of which 600 km navigable year round)
Ports and harbors: Bonthe, Freetown, Pepel
Merchant marine:
total: 1 ship (1,000 GRT or over) totaling 2,057 GRT/ 3,498 DWT
ships by type: cargo 1 (2000 est.)
Airports: 11 (2000 est.)
Airports - with paved runways:
total: 1
over 3,047 m: 1 (2000 est.)
Airports - with unpaved runways:
total: 10
914 to 1,523 m: 7
under 914 m: 3 (2000 est.)
Heliports: 1 (2000 est.)

Military

Military branches: Army
Military manpower - availability:
males age 15-49: 1,161,790 (2001 est.)
Military manpower - fit for military service:
males age 15-49: 563,631 (2001 est.)
Military expenditures - dollar figure: $46 million (FY96/97)
Military expenditures - percent of GDP: 2% (FY96/97)

Transnational Issues

Disputes - international: civil war has engendered massive refugee movements into neighboring Guinea and Liberia

Singapore

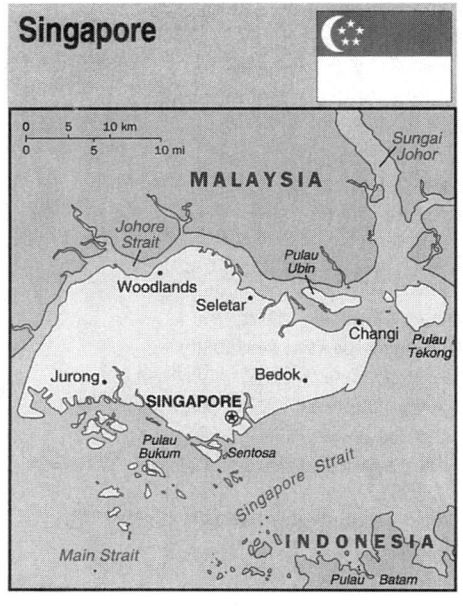

Introduction

Background: Founded as a British trading colony in 1819, Singapore joined Malaysia in 1963, but withdrew two years later and became independent. It subsequently became one of the world's most prosperous countries, with strong international trading links (its port is one of the world's busiest) and with per capita GDP above that of the leading nations of Western Europe.

Geography

Location: Southeastern Asia, islands between Malaysia and Indonesia
Geographic coordinates: 1 22 N, 103 48 E
Map references: Southeast Asia
Area:
total: 647.5 sq km
land: 637.5 sq km
water: 10 sq km
Area - comparative: slightly more than 3.5 times the size of Washington, DC
Land boundaries: 0 km
Coastline: 193 km
Maritime claims:
exclusive fishing zone: within and beyond territorial sea, as defined in treaties and practice
territorial sea: 3 NM
Climate: tropical; hot, humid, rainy; two distinct monsoon seasons - Northeastern monsoon from December to March and Southwestern monsoon from June to September; inter-monsoon - frequent afternoon and early evening thunderstorms
Terrain: lowland; gently undulating central plateau contains water catchment area and nature preserve
Elevation extremes:
lowest point: Singapore Strait 0 m
highest point: Bukit Timah 166 m
Natural resources: fish, deepwater ports
Land use:
arable land: 2%
permanent crops: 6%
permanent pastures: 0%
forests and woodland: 5%
other: 87% (1993 est.)
Irrigated land: NA sq km
Natural hazards: NA
Environment - current issues: industrial pollution; limited natural fresh water resources; limited land availability presents waste disposal problems; seasonal smoke/haze resulting from forest fires in Indonesia
Environment - international agreements:
party to: Biodiversity, Climate Change, Desertification, Endangered Species, Hazardous Wastes, Law of the Sea, Marine Dumping, Nuclear Test Ban, Ozone Layer Protection, Ship Pollution
signed, but not ratified: none of the selected agreements
Geography - note: focal point for Southeast Asian sea routes

People

Population: 4,300,419 (July 2001 est.)
Age structure:
0-14 years: 17.89% (male 397,124; female 372,058)
15-64 years: 75.16% (male 1,575,381; female 1,656,838)
65 years and over: 6.95% (male 130,815; female 168,203) (2001 est.)
Population growth rate: 3.5% (2001 est.)
Birth rate: 12.8 births/1,000 population (2001 est.)
Death rate: 4.24 deaths/1,000 population (2001 est.)
Net migration rate: 26.45 migrant(s)/1,000 population (2001 est.)
Sex ratio:
at birth: 1.08 male(s)/female
under 15 years: 1.07 male(s)/female
15-64 years: 0.95 male(s)/female
65 years and over: 0.78 male(s)/female
total population: 0.96 male(s)/female (2001 est.)
Infant mortality rate: 3.62 deaths/1,000 live births (2001 est.)
Life expectancy at birth:
total population: 80.17 years
male: 77.22 years
female: 83.35 years (2001 est.)
Total fertility rate: 1.22 children born/woman (2001 est.)
HIV/AIDS - adult prevalence rate: 0.19% (1999 est.)
HIV/AIDS - people living with HIV/AIDS: 4,000 (1999 est.)
HIV/AIDS - deaths: 210 (1999 est.)
Nationality:
noun: Singaporean(s)
adjective: Singapore
Ethnic groups: Chinese 76.7%, Malay 14%, Indian 7.9%, other 1.4%
Religions: Buddhist (Chinese), Muslim (Malays), Christian, Hindu, Sikh, Taoist, Confucianist
Languages: Chinese (official), Malay (official and national), Tamil (official), English (official)
Literacy:
definition: age 15 and over can read and write
total population: 93.5%
male: 97%
female: 89.8% (1999)

Government

Country name:
conventional long form: Republic of Singapore
conventional short form: Singapore
Government type: parliamentary republic
Capital: Singapore
Administrative divisions: none
Independence: 9 August 1965 (from Malaysia)
National holiday: Independence Day, 9 August (1965)
Constitution: 3 June 1959, amended 1965 (based on preindependence State of Singapore Constitution)
Legal system: based on English common law; has not accepted compulsory ICJ jurisdiction
Suffrage: 21 years of age; universal and compulsory
Executive branch:
chief of state: President Sellapan Rama (S. R.) NATHAN (since 1 September 1999)
head of government: Prime Minister GOH Chok Tong (since 28 November 1990) and Deputy Prime Ministers LEE Hsien Loong (since 28 November 1990) and Tony TAN Keng Yam (since 1 August 1995)
cabinet: Cabinet appointed by the president, responsible to Parliament
elections: president elected by popular vote for a six-year term; election last held 28 August 1999 (next to be held NA August 2005); following legislative elections, the leader of the majority party or the leader of a majority coalition is usually appointed prime minister by the president; deputy prime ministers appointed by the president
election results: Sellapan Rama (S. R.) NATHAN elected president unopposed
Legislative branch: unicameral Parliament (83 seats; members elected by popular vote to serve five-year terms)
elections: last held 2 January 1997 (next to be held by 26 August 2002)
election results: percent of vote by party - PAP 65% (in contested constituencies), other 35%; seats by party - PAP 81, WP 1, SPP 1; note - subsequent to the election, there was a change in the distribution of seats, the new distribution is as follows: PAP 80, WP 1, SPP 1, vacant 1
Judicial branch: Supreme Court (chief justice is appointed by the president with the advice of the prime minister, other judges are appointed by the president with the advice of the chief justice); Court of Appeals

Singapore (continued)

Political parties and leaders: People's Action Party or PAP [GOH Chok Tong, secretary general] - the governing party; Singapore Democratic Party or SDP [CHEE Soon Juan]; Singapore People's Party or SPP [CHIAM See Tong]; Workers' Party or WP [J. B. JEYARETNAM]
Political pressure groups and leaders: NA
International organization participation: APEC, ARF, AsDB, ASEAN, Australia Group (observer), BIS, C, CCC, CP, ESCAP, G-77, IAEA, IBRD, ICAO, ICC, ICFTU, ICRM, IFC, IFRCS, IHO, ILO, IMF, IMO, Inmarsat, Intelsat, Interpol, IOC, ISO, ITU, NAM, OPCW, PCA, UN, UN Security Council (temporary), UNCTAD, UNIKOM, UNMEE, UNTAET, UPU, WHO, WIPO, WMO, WTrO
Diplomatic representation in the US:
chief of mission: Ambassador CHAN Heng Chee
chancery: 3501 International Place NW, Washington, DC 20008
telephone: [1] (202) 537-3100
FAX: [1] (202) 537-0876
consulate(s) general: Los Angeles, San Francisco
consulate(s): New York
Diplomatic representation from the US:
chief of mission: Ambassador (vacant)
embassy: 27 Napier Road, Singapore 258508
mailing address: PSC Box 470, FPO AP 96534-0001
telephone: [65] 476-9100
FAX: [65] 476-9340
Flag description: two equal horizontal bands of red (top) and white; near the hoist side of the red band, there is a vertical, white crescent (closed portion is toward the hoist side) partially enclosing five white five-pointed stars arranged in a circle

Economy

Economy - overview: Singapore is blessed with a highly developed and successful free-market economy, a remarkably open and corruption-free business environment, stable prices, and the fifth highest per capita GDP in the world. Exports, particularly in electronics and chemicals, and services are the main drivers of the economy. Mainly because of robust exports, especially electronic goods, the economy grew 10.1% in 2000. Forecasters, however, are projecting only 4%-6% growth in 2001 largely because of weaker global demand, especially in the US. The government promotes high levels of savings and investment through a mandatory savings scheme and spends heavily in education and technology. It also owns government-linked companies (GLCs) - particularly in manufacturing - that operate as commercial entities. As Singapore looks to a future increasingly marked by globalization, the country is positioning itself as the region's financial and high-tech hub.
GDP: purchasing power parity - $109.8 billion (2000 est.)
GDP - real growth rate: 10.1% (2000 est.)
GDP - per capita: purchasing power parity - $26,500 (2000 est.)
GDP - composition by sector:
agriculture: NEGL%
industry: 30%
services: 70%
Population below poverty line: NA%
Household income or consumption by percentage share:
lowest 10%: NA%
highest 10%: NA%
Inflation rate (consumer prices): 1.4% (2000)
Labor force: 2.1 million (2000)
Labor force - by occupation: financial, business, and other services 35%, manufacturing 21%, construction 13%, transportation and communication 9%
Unemployment rate: 3% (2000 est.)
Budget:
revenues: $18.1 billion
expenditures: $17.1 billion, including capital expenditures of $9.5 billion (FY99/00 est.)
Industries: electronics, chemicals, financial services, oil drilling equipment, petroleum refining, rubber processing and rubber products, processed food and beverages, ship repair, entrepot trade, biotechnology
Industrial production growth rate: 14% (2000 est.)
Electricity - production: 27.381 billion kWh (1999)
Electricity - production by source:
fossil fuel: 100%
hydro: 0%
nuclear: 0%
other: 0% (1999)
Electricity - consumption: 25.464 billion kWh (1999)
Electricity - exports: 0 kWh (1999)
Electricity - imports: 0 kWh (1999)
Agriculture - products: rubber, copra, fruit, orchids, vegetables; poultry, eggs, fish, ornamental fish
Exports: $137 billion (f.o.b., 2000)
Exports - commodities: machinery and equipment (including electronics), chemicals, mineral fuels
Exports - partners: US 19%, Malaysia 17%, Hong Kong 8%, Japan 7%, Taiwan 5%, Thailand 4%, UK 4%, Netherlands 3.8%, China 3%, South Korea 3%, Germany 3% (1999)
Imports: $127 billion (f.o.b., 2000)
Imports - commodities: machinery and equipment, mineral fuels, chemicals, foodstuffs
Imports - partners: US 17%, Japan 17%, Malaysia 16%, Thailand 5%, China 5%, Taiwan 4%, Germany 3%, Saudi Arabia 3% (1999)
Debt - external: $9.7 billion (2000)
Economic aid - recipient: $NA
Currency: Singapore dollar (SGD)
Currency code: SGD
Exchange rates: Singapore dollars per US dollar - 1.7365 (January 2001), 1.7240 (2000), 1.6950 (1999), 1.6736 (1998), 1.4848 (1997), 1.4100 (1996)
Fiscal year: 1 April - 31 March

Communications

Telephones - main lines in use: 1.928 million (November 2000)
Telephones - mobile cellular: 2.333 million (November 2000)
Telephone system:
general assessment: major consideration given to serving business interests; excellent international service
domestic: excellent domestic facilities
international: submarine cables to Malaysia (Sabah and Peninsular Malaysia), Indonesia, and the Philippines; satellite earth stations - 2 Intelsat (1 Indian Ocean and 1 Pacific Ocean), and 1 Inmarsat (Pacific Ocean region)
Radio broadcast stations: AM 0, FM 16, shortwave 2 (1998)
Radios: 2.6 million (2000)
Television broadcast stations: 6 (2000)
Televisions: 1.33 million (1997)
Internet country code: .sg
Internet Service Providers (ISPs): 9 (2000)
Internet users: 1.74 million (2000)

Transportation

Railways:
total: 38.6 km
narrow gauge: 38.6 km 1.000-m gauge
note: there is a 83 km mass transit system with 48 stations
Highways:
total: 3,150 km
paved: 3,066 km (including 150 km of expressways)
unpaved: 84 km (2000)
Waterways: none
Ports and harbors: Singapore
Merchant marine:
total: 879 ships (1,000 GRT or over) totaling 20,849,168 GRT/33,215,317 DWT
ships by type: bulk 134, cargo 111, chemical tanker 63, combination bulk 10, combination ore/oil 6, container 167, liquefied gas 28, livestock carrier 2, multi-functional large-load carrier 4, passenger 1, petroleum tanker 295, refrigerated cargo 7, roll on/roll off 7, short-sea passenger 1, specialized tanker 10, vehicle carrier 33
note: includes some foreign-owned ships registered here as a flag of convenience: Australia 1, Bermuda 12, Belgium 6, China 9, Denmark 29, Germany 8, Greece 1, Hong Kong 20, Indonesia 9, Japan 32, South Korea 3, Netherlands 2, Norway 9, Russia 1, Sweden 22, Thailand 22, Taiwan 17, UK 3, US 10 (2000 est.)
Airports: 9 (2000 est.)
Airports - with paved runways:
total: 9
over 3,047 m: 2
2,438 to 3,047 m: 1
1,524 to 2,437 m: 4
914 to 1,523 m: 1
under 914 m: 1 (2000 est.)
Heliports: 1 (2000 est.)

Singapore (continued)

Military

Military branches: Army, Navy, Air Force, People's Defense Force, Police Force
Military manpower - availability:
males age 15-49: 1,316,815 (2001 est.)
Military manpower - fit for military service:
males age 15-49: 959,636 (2001 est.)
Military expenditures - dollar figure: $5 billion (FY00/01 est.)
Military expenditures - percent of GDP: 4.5% (FY00/01 est.)

Transnational Issues

Disputes - international: Pedra Branca Island (Pulau Batu Putih) disputed with Malaysia
Illicit drugs: as a transportation and financial services hub, Singapore is vulnerable, despite strict laws and enforcement, to use as a transit point for Golden Triangle heroin and as a venue for money laundering

Slovakia

Introduction

Background: In 1918 the Slovaks joined the closely related Czechs to form Czechoslovakia. Following the chaos of World War II, Czechoslovakia became a communist nation within Soviet-ruled Eastern Europe. Soviet influence collapsed in 1989 and Czechoslovakia once more became free. The Slovaks and the Czechs agreed to separate peacefully on 1 January 1993. Historic, political, and geographic factors have caused Slovakia to experience more difficulty in developing a modern market economy than some of its Central European neighbors.

Geography

Location: Central Europe, south of Poland
Geographic coordinates: 48 40 N, 19 30 E
Map references: Europe
Area:
total: 48,845 sq km
land: 48,800 sq km
water: 45 sq km
Area - comparative: about twice the size of New Hampshire
Land boundaries:
total: 1,355 km
border countries: Austria 91 km, Czech Republic 215 km, Hungary 515 km, Poland 444 km, Ukraine 90 km
Coastline: 0 km (landlocked)
Maritime claims: none (landlocked)
Climate: temperate; cool summers; cold, cloudy, humid winters
Terrain: rugged mountains in the central and northern part and lowlands in the south
Elevation extremes:
lowest point: Bodrok River 94 m
highest point: Gerlachovsky Stit 2,655 m
Natural resources: brown coal and lignite; small amounts of iron ore, copper and manganese ore; salt; arable land
Land use:
arable land: 31%
permanent crops: 3%
permanent pastures: 17%
forests and woodland: 41%
other: 8% (1993 est.)
Irrigated land: 800 sq km (1993 est.)
Natural hazards: NA
Environment - current issues: air pollution from metallurgical plants presents human health risks; acid rain damaging forests
Environment - international agreements:
party to: Air Pollution, Air Pollution-Nitrogen Oxides, Air Pollution-Sulphur 85, Air Pollution-Sulphur 94, Air Pollution-Volatile Organic Compounds, Antarctic Treaty, Biodiversity, Climate Change, Endangered Species, Environmental Modification, Hazardous Wastes, Law of the Sea, Marine Dumping, Nuclear Test Ban, Ozone Layer Protection, Ship Pollution, Wetlands
signed, but not ratified: Air Pollution-Persistent Organic Pollutants, Antarctic-Environmental Protocol, Climate Change-Kyoto Protocol
Geography - note: landlocked

People

Population: 5,414,937 (July 2001 est.)
Age structure:
0-14 years: 18.86% (male 522,563; female 498,832)
15-64 years: 69.6% (male 1,872,496; female 1,896,249)
65 years and over: 11.54% (male 236,996; female 387,801) (2001 est.)
Population growth rate: 0.13% (2001 est.)
Birth rate: 10.05 births/1,000 population (2001 est.)
Death rate: 9.25 deaths/1,000 population (2001 est.)
Net migration rate: 0.53 migrant(s)/1,000 population (2001 est.)

Slovakia (continued)

Sex ratio:
at birth: 1.05 male(s)/female
under 15 years: 1.05 male(s)/female
15-64 years: 0.99 male(s)/female
65 years and over: 0.61 male(s)/female
total population: 0.95 male(s)/female (2001 est.)
Infant mortality rate: 8.97 deaths/1,000 live births (2001 est.)
Life expectancy at birth:
total population: 73.97 years
male: 69.95 years
female: 78.2 years (2001 est.)
Total fertility rate: 1.25 children born/woman (2001 est.)
HIV/AIDS - adult prevalence rate: less than 0.01% (1999 est.)
HIV/AIDS - people living with HIV/AIDS: 400 (1999 est.)
HIV/AIDS - deaths: less than 100 (1999 est.)
Nationality:
noun: Slovak(s)
adjective: Slovak
Ethnic groups: Slovak 85.7%, Hungarian 10.6%, Roma 1.6% (the 1992 census figures underreport the Gypsy/Romany community, which is about 500,000), Czech, Moravian, Silesian 1.1%, Ruthenian and Ukrainian 0.6%, German 0.1%, Polish 0.1%, other 0.2% (1996)
Religions: Roman Catholic 60.3%, atheist 9.7%, Protestant 8.4%, Orthodox 4.1%, other 17.5%
Languages: Slovak (official), Hungarian
Literacy:
definition: NA
total population: NA%
male: NA%
female: NA%

Government

Country name:
conventional long form: Slovak Republic
conventional short form: Slovakia
local long form: Slovenska Republika
local short form: Slovensko
Government type: parliamentary democracy
Capital: Bratislava
Administrative divisions: 8 regions (kraje, singular - kraj); Banskobystricky, Bratislavsky, Kosicky, Nitriansky, Presovsky, Trenciansky, Trnavsky, Zilinsky
Independence: 1 January 1993 (Czechoslovakia split into the Czech Republic and Slovakia)
National holiday: Constitution Day, 1 September (1992)
Constitution: ratified 1 September 1992, fully effective 1 January 1993; changed in September 1998 to allow direct election of the president; amended February 2001 to allow Slovakia to apply for NATO and EU membership
Legal system: civil law system based on Austro-Hungarian codes; has not accepted compulsory ICJ jurisdiction; legal code modified to comply with the obligations of Organization on Security and Cooperation in Europe (OSCE) and to expunge Marxist-Leninist legal theory
Suffrage: 18 years of age; universal
Executive branch:
chief of state: President Rudolf SCHUSTER (since 15 June 1999)
head of government: Prime Minister Mikulas DZURINDA (since 30 October 1998)
cabinet: Cabinet appointed by the president on the recommendation of the prime minister
elections: president elected by direct popular vote for a five-year term; election last held 29 May 1999 (next to be held NA May/June 2004); following National Council elections, the leader of the majority party or the leader of a majority coalition is usually appointed prime minister by the president
election results: Rudolf SCHUSTER elected president in the first direct, popular election; percent of vote - Rudolf SCHUSTER 57%
note: government coalition - SDK, SDL, SMK, SOP, KDH
Legislative branch: unicameral National Council of the Slovak Republic or Narodna Rada Slovenskej Republiky (150 seats; members are elected on the basis of proportional representation to serve four-year terms)
elections: last held 25-26 September 1998 (next to be held NA September 2002)
election results: percent of vote by party - HZDS 27%, SDK 26.3%, SDL 14.7%, SMK 9.1%, SNS 9.1%, SOP 8%; seats by party - governing coalition 93 (SDK 42, SDL 23, SMK 15, SOP 13), opposition 57 (HZDS 43, SNS 14)
Judicial branch: Supreme Court (judges are elected by the National Council); Constitutional Court (judges appointed by president from group of nominees approved by the National Council)
Political parties and leaders: Christian Democratic Movement or KDH [Pavol HRUSOVSKY]; Liberal Democratic Union or LDU [Jan BUDAJ]; Movement for a Democratic Slovakia or HZDS [Vladimir MECIAR]; Party of Civic Understanding or SOP [Pavol HAMZIK]; Party of the Democratic Left or SDL [Jozef MIGAS]; Party of the Hungarian Coalition or SMK [Bela BUGAR]; Slovak Democratic and Christian Union or SDKU [Mikulas DZURINDA]; note - this is DZURINDA's new party for 2002 elections; he remains chairman of a rump and splintering SDK; Slovak Democratic Coalition or SDK (loose parliamentary club grouping representing members of the smaller SSDS, SZS, and those committed to run under SDKU in 2002) [Mikulas DZURINDA]; Slovak National Party or SNS [Anna MALIKOVA]
Political pressure groups and leaders: Association of Employers of Slovakia; Association of Towns and Villages or ZMOS; Confederation of Trade Unions or KOZ; Metal Workers Unions or KOVO and METALURG
International organization participation: Australia Group, BIS, BSEC (observer), CCC, CE, CEI, CERN, EAPC, EBRD, ECE, EU (applicant), FAO, IAEA, IBRD, ICAO, ICC, ICFTU, ICRM, IDA, IFC, IFRCS, ILO, IMF, IMO, Inmarsat, Intelsat (nonsignatory user), Interpol, IOC, IOM, ISO, ITU, NAM (guest), NSG, OECD, OPCW, OSCE, PCA, PFP, UN, UNCTAD, UNDOF, UNESCO, UNIDO, UNMEE, UNTSO, UPU, WCL, WEU (associate partner), WFTU, WHO, WIPO, WMO, WToO, WTrO, ZC
Diplomatic representation in the US:
chief of mission: Ambassador Martin BUTORA
chancery: Suite 250, 2201 Wisconsin Avenue NW, Washington, DC 20007; note - new chancery opening in June 2001 at International Court NW, Washington, DC
telephone: [1] (202) 965-5161
FAX: [1] (202) 965-5166
Diplomatic representation from the US:
chief of mission: Ambassador Carl SPIELVOGEL
embassy: Hviezdoslavovo Namestie 4, 81102 Bratislava
mailing address: use embassy street address
telephone: [421] (7) 5443-3338
FAX: [421] (7) 5443-0096
Flag description: three equal horizontal bands of white (top), blue, and red superimposed with the Slovak cross in a shield centered on the hoist side; the cross is white centered on a background of red and blue

Economy

Economy - overview: Slovakia continues the difficult transition from a centrally planned economy to a modern market economy. The economic slowdown in 1999 stemmed from large budget and current account deficits, fast-growing external debt, and persistent corruption. Even though GDP growth reached only 2.2% in 2000, the year was marked by positive developments such as foreign direct investment of $1.5 billion, strong export performance, restructuring and privatization in the banking sector, entry into the OECD, and initial efforts to stem corruption. Strong challenges face the government in 2001, especially the maintenance of fiscal balance, the further privatization of the economy, and the reduction of unemployment.
GDP: purchasing power parity - $55.3 billion (2000 est.)
GDP - real growth rate: 2.2% (2000 est.)
GDP - per capita: purchasing power parity - $10,200 (2000 est.)
GDP - composition by sector:
agriculture: 4.5%
industry: 29.3%
services: 66.2% (1999 est.)
Population below poverty line: NA%
Household income or consumption by percentage share:
lowest 10%: 5.1%
highest 10%: 18.2% (1992)
Inflation rate (consumer prices): 12.2% (2000 est.)
Labor force: 3 million (1999)

Slovakia (continued)

Labor force - by occupation: industry 29.3%, agriculture 8.9%, construction 8%, transport and communication 8.2%, services 45.6% (1994)
Unemployment rate: 17% (2000 est.)
Budget:
revenues: $5.2 billion
expenditures: $5.6 billion, including capital expenditures of $NA (1999)
Industries: metal and metal products; food and beverages; electricity, gas, coke, oil, nuclear fuel; chemicals and manmade fibers; machinery; paper and printing; earthenware and ceramics; transport vehicles; textiles; electrical and optical apparatus; rubber products
Industrial production growth rate: 9.3% (2000 est.)
Electricity - production: 22.582 billion kWh (1999)
Electricity - production by source:
fossil fuel: 37.56%
hydro: 18.27%
nuclear: 44.17%
other: 0% (1999)
Electricity - consumption: 21.471 billion kWh (1999)
Electricity - exports: 930 million kWh (1999)
Electricity - imports: 1.4 billion kWh (1999)
Agriculture - products: grains, potatoes, sugar beets, hops, fruit; pigs, cattle, poultry; forest products
Exports: $12 billion (f.o.b., 2000 est.)
Exports - commodities: machinery and transport equipment 39.4%, intermediate manufactured goods 27.5%, miscellaneous manufactured goods 13%, chemicals 8% (1999)
Exports - partners: EU 59.7% (Germany 27.8%, Austria 8%, Italy 8.9%), Czech Republic 18.1% (1999)
Imports: $12.8 billion (f.o.b., 2000 est.)
Imports - commodities: machinery and transport equipment 37.7%, intermediate manufactured goods 18%, fuels 13%, chemicals 11%, miscellaneous manufactured goods 9.5% (1999)
Imports - partners: EU 51.4% (Germany 26%, Italy 7.1%), Czech Republic 16.6%, Russia 11.9% (1999)
Debt - external: $10.3 billion (2000 est.)
Economic aid - recipient: $421.9 million (1995)
Currency: Slovak koruna (SKK)
Currency code: SKK
Exchange rates: koruny per US dollar - 48.09 (March 2001), 46.395 (2000), 41.363 (1999), 35.233 (1998), 33.616 (1997), 30.654 (1996)
Fiscal year: calendar year

Communications

Telephones - main lines in use: 1,934,558 (1998)
Telephones - mobile cellular: 736,662 (April 1999)
Telephone system:
general assessment: a modernization and privatization program is increasing accessibility to telephone service, reducing the waiting time for new subscribers, and generally improving service quality
domestic: predominantly an analog system that is now receiving digital equipment and is being enlarged with fiber-optic cable, especially in the larger cities; mobile cellular capability has been added
international: three international exchanges (one in Bratislava and two in Banska Bystrica) are available; Slovakia is participating in several international telecommunications projects that will increase the availability of external services
Radio broadcast stations: AM 15, FM 78, shortwave 2 (1998)
Radios: 3.12 million (1997)
Television broadcast stations: 38 (plus 864 repeaters) (1995)
Televisions: 2.62 million (1997)
Internet country code: .sk
Internet Service Providers (ISPs): 6 (2000)
Internet users: 700,000 (2000)

Transportation

Railways:
total: 3,660 km
broad gauge: 102 km 1.520-m gauge
standard gauge: 3,507 km 1.435-m gauge (1,505 km electrified; 1,011 km double track)
narrow gauge: 51 km (46 km 1,000-m gauge; 5 km 0.750-m gauge) (1998)
Highways:
total: 17,710 km
paved: 17,533 km (including 288 km of expressways)
unpaved: 177 km (1998 est.)
Waterways: 172 km (all on the Danube)
Pipelines: petroleum products NA km; natural gas 2,700 km
Ports and harbors: Bratislava, Komarno
Merchant marine:
total: 3 ships (1,000 GRT or over) totaling 15,041 GRT/19,517 DWT
ships by type: cargo 3 (2000 est.)
Airports: 35 (2000 est.)
Airports - with paved runways:
total: 18
over 3,047 m: 1
2,438 to 3,047 m: 3
1,524 to 2,437 m: 3
914 to 1,523 m: 3
under 914 m: 8 (2000 est.)
Airports - with unpaved runways:
total: 17
2,438 to 3,047 m: 1
914 to 1,523 m: 9
under 914 m: 7 (2000 est.)

Military

Military branches: Ground Forces, Air and Air Defense Forces, Territorial Defense Forces, Civil Defense Force
Military manpower - military age: 18 years of age
Military manpower - availability:
males age 15-49: 1,487,093 (2001 est.)
Military manpower - fit for military service:
males age 15-49: 1,136,811 (2001 est.)
Military manpower - reaching military age annually:
males: 45,502 (2001 est.)
Military expenditures - dollar figure: $380 million (FY00)
Military expenditures - percent of GDP: 1.71% (FY00)

Transnational Issues

Disputes - international: Gabcikovo/Nagymaros Dam dispute with Hungary is before the ICJ
Illicit drugs: transshipment point for Southwest Asian heroin bound for Western Europe

Slovenia

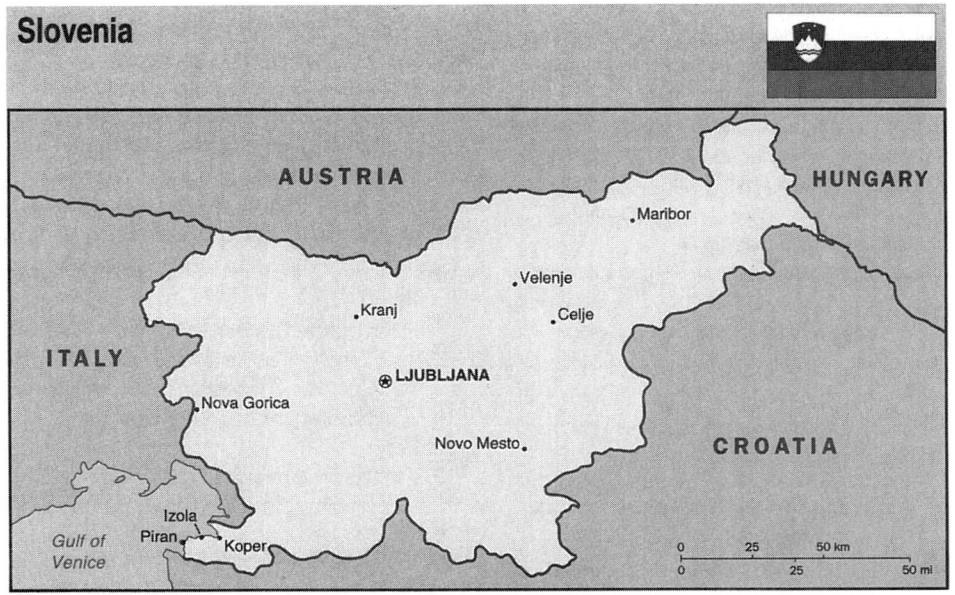

Introduction

Background: In 1918 the Slovenes joined the Serbs and Croats in forming a new nation, renamed Yugoslavia in 1929. After World War II, Slovenia became a republic of the renewed Yugoslavia, which though communist, distanced itself from Moscow's rule. Dissatisfied with the exercise of power of the majority Serbs, the Slovenes succeeded in establishing their independence in 1991. Historical ties to Western Europe, a strong economy, and a stable democracy make Slovenia a leading candidate for future membership in the EU and NATO.

Geography

Location: Southeastern Europe, eastern Alps bordering the Adriatic Sea, between Austria and Croatia
Geographic coordinates: 46 00 N, 15 00 E
Map references: Europe
Area:
total: 20,253 sq km
land: 20,253 sq km
water: 0 sq km
Area - comparative: slightly smaller than New Jersey
Land boundaries:
total: 1,165 km
border countries: Austria 330 km, Croatia 501 km, Italy 232 km, Hungary 102 km
Coastline: 46.6 km
Maritime claims: NA
Climate: Mediterranean climate on the coast, continental climate with mild to hot summers and cold winters in the plateaus and valleys to the east
Terrain: a short coastal strip on the Adriatic, an alpine mountain region adjacent to Italy and Austria, mixed mountain and valleys with numerous rivers to the east
Elevation extremes:
lowest point: Adriatic Sea 0 m
highest point: Triglav 2,864 m
Natural resources: lignite coal, lead, zinc, mercury, uranium, silver, hydropower
Land use:
arable land: 12%
permanent crops: 3%
permanent pastures: 24%
forests and woodland: 54%
other: 7% (1996 est.)
Irrigated land: 20 sq km (1993 est.)
Natural hazards: flooding and earthquakes
Environment - current issues: Sava River polluted with domestic and industrial waste; pollution of coastal waters with heavy metals and toxic chemicals; forest damage near Koper from air pollution (originating at metallurgical and chemical plants) and resulting acid rain
Environment - international agreements:
party to: Air Pollution, Air Pollution-Sulphur 94, Biodiversity, Climate Change, Endangered Species, Hazardous Wastes, Law of the Sea, Marine Dumping, Nuclear Test Ban, Ozone Layer Protection, Ship Pollution, Wetlands
signed, but not ratified: Air Pollution-Persistent Organic Pollutants, Climate Change-Kyoto Protocol

People

Population: 1,930,132 (July 2001 est.)
Age structure:
0-14 years: 16.09% (male 159,428; female 151,134)
15-64 years: 69.61% (male 681,333; female 662,170)
65 years and over: 14.3% (male 101,354; female 174,713) (2001 est.)
Population growth rate: 0.14% (2001 est.)
Birth rate: 9.32 births/1,000 population (2001 est.)
Death rate: 9.98 deaths/1,000 population (2001 est.)
Net migration rate: 2.11 migrant(s)/1,000 population (2001 est.)
Sex ratio:
at birth: 1.06 male(s)/female
under 15 years: 1.05 male(s)/female
15-64 years: 1.03 male(s)/female
65 years and over: 0.58 male(s)/female
total population: 0.95 male(s)/female (2001 est.)
Infant mortality rate: 4.51 deaths/1,000 live births (2001 est.)
Life expectancy at birth:
total population: 75.08 years
male: 71.2 years
female: 79.17 years (2001 est.)
Total fertility rate: 1.28 children born/woman (2001 est.)
HIV/AIDS - adult prevalence rate: 0.02% (1999 est.)
HIV/AIDS - people living with HIV/AIDS: 200 (1999 est.)
HIV/AIDS - deaths: less than 100 (1999 est.)
Nationality:
noun: Slovene(s)
adjective: Slovenian
Ethnic groups: Slovene 88%, Croat 3%, Serb 2%, Bosniak 1%, Yugoslav 0.6%, Hungarian 0.4%, other 5% (1991)
Religions: Roman Catholic 68.8%, Uniate Catholic 2%, Lutheran 1%, Muslim 1%, atheist 4.3%, other 22.9%
Languages: Slovenian 91%, Serbo-Croatian 6%, other 3%
Literacy:
definition: NA
total population: 99%
male: NA%
female: NA%

Government

Country name:
conventional long form: Republic of Slovenia
conventional short form: Slovenia
local long form: Republika Slovenija
local short form: Slovenija
Government type: parliamentary democratic republic
Capital: Ljubljana
Administrative divisions: 136 municipalities (obcine, singular - obcina) and 11 urban municipalities* (mestne obcine , singular - mestna obcina) Ajdovscina, Beltinci, Bled, Bohinj, Borovnica, Bovec, Brda, Brezice, Brezovica, Cankova-Tisina, Celje*, Cerklje na Gorenjskem, Cerknica, Cerkno, Crensovci, Crna na Koroskem, Crnomelj, Destrnik-Trnovska Vas, Divaca, Dobrepolje, Dobrova-Horjul-Polhov Gradec, Dol pri Ljubljani, Domzale, Dornava, Dravograd, Duplek, Gorenja Vas-Poljane, Gorisnica, Gornja Radgona, Gornji Grad, Gornji Petrovci, Grosuplje, Hodos Salovci, Hrastnik, Hrpelje-Kozina, Idrija, Ig, Ilirska Bistrica, Ivancna Gorica, Izola, Jesenice, Jursinci, Kamnik, Kanal, Kidricevo, Kobarid, Kobilje, Kocevje, Komen, Koper*, Kozje, Kranj*, Kranjska Gora, Krsko, Kungota, Kuzma, Lasko, Lenart, Lendava, Litija, Ljubljana*, Ljubno, Ljutomer, Logatec, Loska Dolina, Loski Potok, Luce, Lukovica, Majsperk, Maribor*, Medvode, Menges, Metlika, Mezica,

Slovenia (continued)

Miren-Kostanjevica, Mislinja, Moravce, Moravske Toplice, Mozirje, Murska Sobota*, Muta, Naklo, Nazarje, Nova Gorica*, Novo Mesto*, Odranci, Ormoz, Osilnica, Pesnica, Piran, Pivka, Podcetrtek, Podvelka-Ribnica, Postojna, Preddvor, Ptuj*, Puconci, Race-Fram, Radece, Radenci, Radlje ob Dravi, Radovljica, Ravne-Prevalje, Ribnica, Rogasevci, Rogaska Slatina, Rogatec, Ruse, Semic, Sencur, Sentilj, Sentjernej, Sentjur pri Celju, Sevnica, Sezana, Skocjan, Skofja Loka, Skofljica, Slovenj Gradec*, Slovenska Bistrica, Slovenske Konjice, Smarje pri Jelsah, Smartno ob Paki, Sostanj, Starse, Store, Sveti Jurij, Tolmin, Trbovlje, Trebnje, Trzic, Turnisce, Velenje*, Velike Lasce, Videm, Vipava, Vitanje, Vodice, Vojnik, Vrhnika, Vuzenica, Zagorje ob Savi, Zalec, Zavrc, Zelezniki, Ziri, Zrece
note: there may be 45 more municipalities
Independence: 25 June 1991 (from Yugoslavia)
National holiday: Independence Day/Statehood Day, 25 June (1991)
Constitution: adopted 23 December 1991, effective 23 December 1991
Legal system: based on civil law system
Suffrage: 18 years of age; universal (16 years of age, if employed)
Executive branch:
chief of state: President Milan KUCAN (since 22 April 1990)
head of government: Prime Minister Janez DRNOVSEK (since 15 October 2000);
cabinet: Council of Ministers nominated by the prime minister and elected by the National Assembly
elections: president elected by popular vote for a five-year term; election last held 24 November 1997 (next to be held NA 2002); following National Assembly elections, the leader of the majority party or the leader of a majority coalition is usually nominated to become prime minister by the president and elected by the National Assembly; election last held 15 October 2000 (next to be held NA October 2004)
election results: Milan KUCAN elected president; percent of vote - Milan KUCAN 56.3%, Janez PODOBNIK 18%; Janez DRNOVSEK elected prime minister; percent of National Assembly vote - NA
Legislative branch: unicameral National Assembly or Drzavni Zbor (90 seats, 40 are directly elected and 50 are selected on a proportional basis; note - the numbers of directly elected and proportionally elected seats varies with each election; members are elected by popular vote to serve four-year terms)
elections: National Assembly - last held 15 October 2000 (next to be held NA October 2004)
election results: percent of vote by party - LDS 36%, SDS 16%, ZLSD 12%, SLS/SKD 10%, NSI 9%, SMS 4%, SNS 4%, DeSUS 5%, other 4%; seats by party - LDS 34, SDS 14, ZLDS 11, SLS/SKD 9, NSI 8, SMS 4, SNS 4, DeSUS 4, other 2
note: the National Council or Drzavni Svet is an advisory body with limited legislative powers; it may propose laws and ask to review any National Assembly decisions; in the election of NA November 1997, 40 members were elected to represent local, professional, and socioeconomic interests (next election to be held in the fall of 2002)
Judicial branch: Supreme Court (judges are elected by the National Assembly on the recommendation of the Judicial Council); Constitutional Court (judges elected for nine-year terms by the National Assembly and nominated by the president)
Political parties and leaders: Democratic Party of Retired (Persons) of Slovenia or DeSUS [Janko KUSAR]; Liberal Democratic or LDS [Janez DRNOVSEK, chairman]; New Slovenia or NSI [Andrej BAJUK, chairman]; Slovene National Party or SNS [Zmago JELINCIC, chairman]; Slovene People's Party or SLS (Slovenian People's Party or SLS and Slovenian Christian Democrats or SKD merged in April 2000) [Franc ZAGOZEN, chairman]; Slovene Youth Party or SMS [leader NA]; Social Democratic Party of Slovenia or SDS [Janez JANSA, chairman]; United List of Social Democrats (former Communists and allies) or ZLSD [Borut PAHOR, chairman]
Political pressure groups and leaders: NA
International organization participation: ABEDA, ACCT (observer), BIS, CCC, CE, CEI, EAPC, EBRD, ECE, EU (applicant), FAO, IADB, IAEA, IBRD, ICAO, ICRM, IDA, IFC, IFRCS, ILO, IMF, IMO, Intelsat (nonsignatory user), Interpol, IOC, IOM, ISO, ITU, NAM (guest), NSG, OPCW, OSCE, PFP, UN, UNCTAD, UNESCO, UNFICYP, UNIDO, UNTAET, UNTSO, UPU, WEU (associate partner), WHO, WIPO, WMO, WToO, WTrO
Diplomatic representation in the US:
chief of mission: Ambassador Davorin KRACUN
chancery: 1525 New Hampshire Avenue NW, Washington, DC 20036
telephone: [1] (202) 667-5363
FAX: [1] (202) 667-4563
consulate(s) general: New York
consulate(s): Cleveland
Diplomatic representation from the US:
chief of mission: Ambassador Nancy ELY-RAPHEL
embassy: Presernova 31, SI-1000 Ljubljana
mailing address: P. O. Box 254, Presernova 31, 1000 Ljubljana; American Embassy Ljubljana, Department of State, Washington, DC 20521-7140
telephone: [386] (01) 200-5500
FAX: [386] (01) 200-5555
Flag description: three equal horizontal bands of white (top), blue, and red, with the Slovenian seal (a shield with the image of Triglav, Slovenia's highest peak, in white against a blue background at the center; beneath it are two wavy blue lines depicting seas and rivers, and above it are three six-pointed stars arranged in an inverted triangle which are taken from the coat of arms of the Counts of Celje, the great Slovene dynastic house of the late 14th and early 15th centuries); the seal is located in the upper hoist side of the flag centered in the white and blue bands

Economy

Economy - overview: Although Slovenia enjoys one of the highest GDPs per capita among the transition economies of Central Europe, it needs to speed up the privatization process and the dismantling of restrictions on foreign investment. About 45% of the economy remains in state hands, and the level of foreign direct investment inflows as a percent of GDP is the lowest in the region. Analysts are predicting between 4.0% and 4.2% growth for 2001. Export growth is expected to slow in 2001 and 2002 as EU markets soften. Inflation rose from 6.1% to 8.9% in 2000 and remains a matter of concern.
GDP: purchasing power parity - $22.9 billion (2000 est.)
GDP - real growth rate: 4.5% (2000 est.)
GDP - per capita: purchasing power parity - $12,000 (2000 est.)
GDP - composition by sector:
agriculture: 4%
industry: 35%
services: 61% (1999 est.)
Population below poverty line: NA%
Household income or consumption by percentage share:
lowest 10%: 3.2%
highest 10%: 20.7% (1995)
Inflation rate (consumer prices): 8.9% (2000 est.)
Labor force: 857,400
Labor force - by occupation: agriculture NA%, industry NA%, services NA%
Unemployment rate: 7.1% (1997 est.)
Budget:
revenues: $8.11 billion
expenditures: $8.32 billion, including capital expenditures of $NA (1997 est.)
Industries: ferrous metallurgy and rolling mill products, aluminum reduction and rolled products, lead and zinc smelting, electronics (including military electronics), trucks, electric power equipment, wood products, textiles, chemicals, machine tools
Industrial production growth rate: 6.2% (2000)
Electricity - production: 12.451 billion kWh (1999)
Electricity - production by source:
fossil fuel: 34.44%
hydro: 29.58%
nuclear: 35.98%
other: 0% (1999)
Electricity - consumption: 10.024 billion kWh (1999)
Electricity - exports: 2.2 billion kWh (1999)
Electricity - imports: 645 million kWh (1999)
Agriculture - products: potatoes, hops, wheat, sugar beets, corn, grapes; cattle, sheep, poultry
Exports: $8.9 billion (f.o.b., 2000)
Exports - commodities: manufactured goods, machinery and transport equipment, chemicals, food
Exports - partners: Germany 31%, Italy 14%, Croatia 8%, Austria 7%, France 6% (1999)
Imports: $9.9 billion (f.o.b., 2000)

Slovenia (continued)

Imports - commodities: machinery and transport equipment, manufactured goods, chemicals, fuels and lubricants, food
Imports - partners: Germany 21%, Italy 17%, France 11%, Austria 8%, Croatia 4%, Hungary, Russia (1999)
Debt - external: $6.2 billion (2000)
Economic aid - recipient: ODA, $5 million (1993)
Currency: tolar (SIT)
Currency code: SIT
Exchange rates: tolars per US dollar - 225.93 (January 2001), 222.66 (2000), 181.77 (1999), 166.13 (1998), 159.69 (1997), 135.36 (1996)
Fiscal year: calendar year

Communications

Telephones - main lines in use: 722,000 (1997)
Telephones - mobile cellular: 1 million (2000)
Telephone system:
general assessment: NA
domestic: 100% digital (2000)
international: NA
Radio broadcast stations: AM 17, FM 160, shortwave 0 (1998)
Radios: 805,000 (1997)
Television broadcast stations: 48 (2001)
Televisions: 710,000 (1997)
Internet country code: .si
Internet Service Providers (ISPs): 11 (2000)
Internet users: 460,000 (1999)

Transportation

Railways:
total: 1,201 km
standard gauge: 1,201 km 1.435-m gauge (489 km electrified) (1999)
Highways:
total: 19,586 km
paved: 17,745 km (including 249 km of expressways)
unpaved: 1,841 km (1998 est.)
Waterways: NA
Pipelines: crude oil 290 km; natural gas 305 km
Ports and harbors: Izola, Koper, Piran
Airports: 14 (2000 est.)
Airports - with paved runways:
total: 6
over 3,047 m: 1
2,438 to 3,047 m: 1
1,524 to 2,437 m: 1
914 to 1,523 m: 2
under 914 m: 1 (2000 est.)
Airports - with unpaved runways:
total: 8
1,524 to 2,437 m: 2
914 to 1,523 m: 2
under 914 m: 4 (2000 est.)

Military

Military branches: Slovenian Army (includes Air and Naval Forces)
Military manpower - military age: 19 years of age
Military manpower - availability:
males age 15-49: 523,336 (2001 est.)
Military manpower - fit for military service:
males age 15-49: 416,237 (2001 est.)
Military manpower - reaching military age annually:
males: 14,513 (2001 est.)
Military expenditures - dollar figure: $370 million (FY00)
Military expenditures - percent of GDP: 1.7% (FY00)

Transnational Issues

Disputes - international: progress with Croatia on discussions of adjustments to land boundary, but problems remain in defining maritime boundary in Gulf of Piran; Austria has minor dispute with Slovenia over nuclear power plants and post-World War II treatment of German-speaking minorities
Illicit drugs: minor transit point for cocaine and Southwest Asian heroin bound for Western Europe, and for precursor chemicals

Solomon Islands

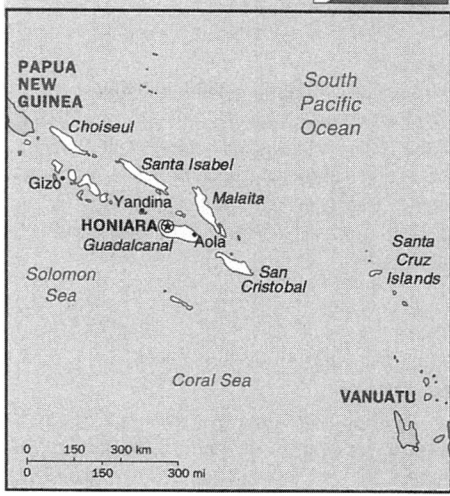

Introduction

Background: The UK established a protectorate over the Solomon Islands in the 1890s. Some of the bitterest fighting of World War II occurred on these islands. Self-government was achieved in 1976 and independence two years later. Current issues include government deficits, deforestation, and malaria control.

Geography

Location: Oceania, group of islands in the South Pacific Ocean, east of Papua New Guinea
Geographic coordinates: 8 00 S, 159 00 E
Map references: Oceania
Area:
total: 28,450 sq km
land: 27,540 sq km
water: 910 sq km
Area - comparative: slightly smaller than Maryland
Land boundaries: 0 km
Coastline: 5,313 km
Maritime claims: measured from claimed archipelagic baselines
continental shelf: 200 NM
exclusive economic zone: 200 NM
territorial sea: 12 NM
Climate: tropical monsoon; few extremes of temperature and weather
Terrain: mostly rugged mountains with some low coral atolls
Elevation extremes:
lowest point: Pacific Ocean 0 m
highest point: Mount Makarakomburu 2,447 m
Natural resources: fish, forests, gold, bauxite, phosphates, lead, zinc, nickel
Land use:
arable land: 1%
permanent crops: 1%
permanent pastures: 1%
forests and woodland: 88%
other: 9% (1993 est.)
Irrigated land: NA sq km

Solomon Islands (continued)

Natural hazards: typhoons, but they are rarely destructive; geologically active region with frequent earth tremors; volcanic activity
Environment - current issues: deforestation; soil erosion; much of the surrounding coral reefs are dead or dying
Environment - international agreements:
party to: Biodiversity, Climate Change, Desertification, Environmental Modification, Law of the Sea, Marine Dumping, Marine Life Conservation, Ozone Layer Protection, Ship Pollution, Whaling
signed, but not ratified: Climate Change-Kyoto Protocol

People

Population: 480,442 (July 2001 est.)
Age structure.
0-14 years. 43.79% (male 107,229; female 103,162)
15-64 years. 53.15% (male 129,315; female 126,021)
65 years and over. 3.06% (male 7,190; female 7,525) (2001 est.)
Population growth rate. 2.98% (2001 est.)
Birth rate. 34.05 births/1,000 population (2001 est.)
Death rate. 4.27 deaths/1,000 population (2001 est.)
Net migration rate. 0 migrant(s)/1,000 population (2001 est.)
Sex ratio.
at birth. 1.05 male(s)/female
under 15 years. 1.04 male(s)/female
15-64 years. 1.03 male(s)/female
65 years and over. 0.96 male(s)/female
total population. 1.03 male(s)/female (2001 est.)
Infant mortality rate. 24.47 deaths/1,000 live births (2001 est.)
Life expectancy at birth.
total population. 71.55 years
male. 69.12 years
female. 74.1 years (2001 est.)
Total fertility rate. 4.65 children born/woman (2001 est.)
HIV/AIDS - adult prevalence rate. NA%
HIV/AIDS - people living with HIV/AIDS. NA
HIV/AIDS - deaths. NA
Nationality.
noun. Solomon Islander(s)
adjective. Solomon Islander
Ethnic groups. Melanesian 93%, Polynesian 4%, Micronesian 1.5%, European 0.8%, Chinese 0.3%, other 0.4%
Religions. Anglican 34%, Roman Catholic 19%, Baptist 17%, United (Methodist/Presbyterian) 11%, Seventh-Day Adventist 10%, other Protestant 5%, indigenous beliefs 4%
Languages. Melanesian pidgin in much of the country is lingua franca, English spoken by 1%-2% of population
note. 120 indigenous languages
Literacy.
definition. NA
total population. NA%
male. NA%
female. NA%

Government

Country name:
conventional long form: none
conventional short form: Solomon Islands
former: British Solomon Islands
Government type: parliamentary democracy
Capital: Honiara
Administrative divisions: 7 provinces and 1 town*; Central, Guadalcanal, Honiara*, Isabel, Makira, Malaita, Temotu, Western; note - there may be two new provinces of Choiseul (Lauru) and Rennell/Bellona and the administrative unit of Honiara may have been abolished
Independence: 7 July 1978 (from UK)
National holiday: Independence Day, 7 July (1978)
Constitution: 7 July 1978
Legal system: English common law
Suffrage: 21 years of age; universal
Executive branch:
chief of state: Queen ELIZABETH II (since 6 February 1952), represented by Governor General Father John LAPLI (since NA 1999)
head of government: Prime Minister Mannaseh Damukana SOGAVARE (since 1 July 2000); Assistant Prime Minister Nathaniel WAENA (since 1 July 2000); Deputy Prime Minister Allan KEMAKEZA (since 1 July 2000); note - Prime Minister Bartholomew ULUFA'ALU was forced to resign his position in June 2000 following the armed takeover of the capital by elements supporting the opposition parties; Mannaseh Damukana SOGAVARE, who had been opposition leader, was then elected prime minister at a sitting of National Parliament on 30 June 2000
cabinet: Cabinet appointed by the governor general on the advice of the prime minister from among the members of Parliament
elections: none; the monarch is hereditary; governor general appointed by the monarch on the advice of Parliament for up to five years; following legislative elections, the leader of the majority party or the leader of a majority coalition is usually elected prime minister by Parliament; deputy prime minister appointed by the governor general on the advice of the prime minister from among the members of Parliament
Legislative branch: unicameral National Parliament (50 seats; members elected from single member constituencies by popular vote to serve four-year terms)
elections: last held 6 August 1997 (next to be held by August 2001)
election results: percent of vote by party - NA%; seats by party - GNUR 21, PAP 7, NAPSI 5, SILP 4, UP 4, independents 6, other 3
Judicial branch: Court of Appeal
Political parties and leaders: there are two main coalitions - Coalition for National Unity, Reconciliation, and Peace or CNURP and Alliance for Change; the CNURP took power on 30 June 2000, it comprises members of the Liberal Party, People's Alliance Party, and the United Party, as well as a number of independents; the Alliance for Change, represents the former government and now is the opposition; in general, Solomon Islands politics is characterized by fluid coalitions; Group for National Unity and Reconciliation or GNUR [leader NA]; Liberal Party [Bartholomew ULUFA'ALU]; National Action Party of Solomon Islands or NAPSI [Francis SAEMALA]; People's Alliance Party or PAP [George LEPPING]; People's Progressive Party [Mannaseh Damukana SOGAVARE]; Solomon Islands Labor Party or SILP [Joses TUHANUKU]; United Party or UP [leader NA]
Political pressure groups and leaders: NA
International organization participation: ACP, AsDB, C, ESCAP, FAO, G-77, IBRD, ICAO, ICRM, IDA, IFAD, IFC, IFRCS, ILO, IMF, IMO, Intelsat (nonsignatory user), IOC, ITU, Sparteca, SPC, SPF, UN, UNCTAD, UNESCO, UPU, WFTU, WHO, WMO, WTrO
Diplomatic representation in the US:
chief of mission: Ambassador (vacant); Charge d'Affaires ad interim Jeremiah MANELE
chancery: 800 Second Avenue, Suite 400L, New York, NY 10017
telephone: [1] (212) 599-6192, 6193
FAX: [1] (212) 661-8925
Diplomatic representation from the US: the US does not have an embassy in Solomon Islands (embassy closed July 1993); the ambassador to Papua New Guinea is accredited to the Solomon Islands
Flag description: divided diagonally by a thin yellow stripe from the lower hoist-side corner; the upper triangle (hoist side) is blue with five white five-pointed stars arranged in an X pattern; the lower triangle is green

Economy

Economy - overview: The bulk of the population depends on agriculture, fishing, and forestry for at least part of their livelihood. Most manufactured goods and petroleum products must be imported. The islands are rich in undeveloped mineral resources such as lead, zinc, nickel, and gold. However, severe ethnic violence, the closing of key business enterprises, and an empty government treasury have led to a continuing economic downslide. Deliveries of crucial fuel supplies (including those for electrical generation) by tankers have become sporadic due to the government's inability to pay and attacks against ships. Telecommunications are threatened by the lack of technical and maintenance staff many of whom have left the country.
GDP: purchasing power parity - $900 million (2000 est.)
GDP - real growth rate: 1% (2000 est.)
GDP - per capita: purchasing power parity - $2,000 (2000 est.)
GDP - composition by sector:
agriculture: 50%
industry: 3.5%
services: 46.5% (1995)

Solomon Islands (continued)

Population below poverty line: NA%
Household income or consumption by percentage share:
lowest 10%: NA%
highest 10%: NA%
Inflation rate (consumer prices): 10% (1999 est.)
Labor force: 26,842
Labor force - by occupation: agriculture NA%, industry NA%, services NA%
Unemployment rate: NA%
Budget:
revenues: $147 million
expenditures: $168 million, including capital expenditures of $NA (1997 est.)
Industries: fish (tuna), mining, timber
Industrial production growth rate: NA%
Electricity - production: 30 million kWh (1999)
Electricity - production by source:
fossil fuel: 100%
hydro: 0%
nuclear: 0%
other: 0% (1999)
Electricity - consumption: 27.9 million kWh (1999)
Electricity - exports: 0 kWh (1999)
Electricity - imports: 0 kWh (1999)
Agriculture - products: cocoa, beans, coconuts, palm kernels, rice, potatoes, vegetables, fruit; cattle, pigs; timber; fish
Exports: $165 million (f.o.b., 1999 est.)
Exports - commodities: timber, fish, palm oil, cocoa, copra
Exports - partners: Japan 35.5%, other Asian countries 47.3% (1999)
Imports: $152 million (f.o.b., 1999 est.)
Imports - commodities: plant and equipment, manufactured goods, food and live animals, fuels, chemicals
Imports - partners: Australia 38.5%, Singapore 15%, Japan 10.6%, NZ 6.2% (1999)
Debt - external: $152.4 million (1998)
Economic aid - recipient: $47 million (1999 est.), mainly from Japan, Australia, China, and NZ
Currency: Solomon Islands dollar (SBD)
Currency code: SBD
Exchange rates: Solomon Islands dollars per US dollar - 5.0968 (November 2000), 5.0864 (2000), 4.8381 (1999), 4.8156 (1998), 3.7169 (1997), 3.5664 (1996)
Fiscal year: calendar year

Communications

Telephones - main lines in use: 8,000 (1997)
Telephones - mobile cellular: 658 (1997)
Telephone system:
general assessment: NA
domestic: NA
international: satellite earth station - 1 Intelsat (Pacific Ocean)
Radio broadcast stations: AM 3, FM 0, shortwave 0 (1998)
Radios: 57,000 (1997)
Television broadcast stations: 0 (1997)
Televisions: 3,000 (1997)
Internet country code: .sb
Internet Service Providers (ISPs): 1 (2000)
Internet users: 3,000 (2000)

Transportation

Railways: 0 km
Highways:
total: 1,360 km
paved: 34 km
unpaved: 1,326 km (includes about 800 km of private plantation roads) (1996 est.)
Waterways: none
Ports and harbors: Aola Bay, Honiara, Lofung, Noro, Viru Harbor, Yandina
Merchant marine: none (2000 est.)
Airports: 31 (2000 est.)
Airports - with paved runways:
total: 2
1,524 to 2,437 m: 1
914 to 1,523 m: 1 (2000 est.)
Airports - with unpaved runways:
total: 29
1,524 to 2,437 m: 1
914 to 1,523 m: 10
under 914 m: 18 (2000 est.)

Military

Military branches: no regular military forces; Solomon Islands National Reconnaissance and Surveillance Force; Royal Solomon Islands Police (RSIP)
Military expenditures - dollar figure: $NA
Military expenditures - percent of GDP: NA%

Transnational Issues

Disputes - international: none

Somalia

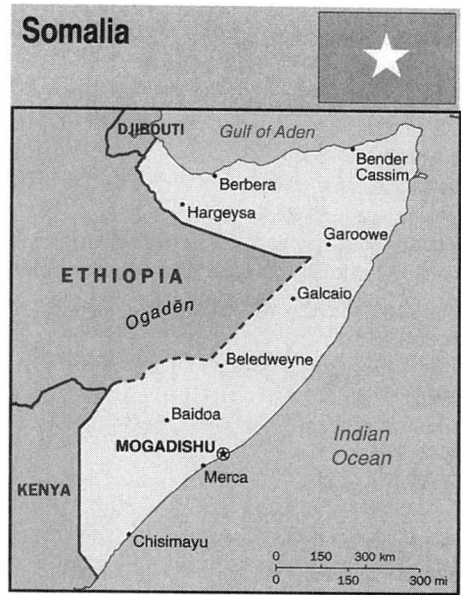

Introduction

Background: A SIAD BARRE regime was ousted in January 1991; turmoil, factional fighting, and anarchy followed for nine years. In May of 1991, northern clans declared an independent Republic of Somaliland which now includes the administrative regions of Awdal, Woqooyi Galbeed, Togdheer, Sanaag, and Sool. Although not recognized by any government, this entity has maintained a stable existence, aided by the overwhelming dominance of the ruling clan and economic infrastructure left behind by British, Russian, and American military assistance programs. The regions of Bari and Nugaal comprise a neighboring self-declared Republic of Puntland, which has also made strides towards reconstructing legitimate, representative government. Beginning in 1993, a two-year UN humanitarian effort (primarily in the south) was able to alleviate famine conditions, but when the UN withdrew in 1995, having suffered significant casualties, order still had not been restored. A Transitional National Government (TNG) was created in October 2000 in Arta, Djibouti which was attended by a broad representation of Somali clans. The TNG has a three-year mandate to create a permanent national Somali government. The TNG does not recognize Somaliland or Puntland as independent republics but so far has been unable to reunite them with the unstable regions in the south; numerous warlords and factions are still fighting for control of Mogadishu and the other southern regions.

Geography

Location: Eastern Africa, bordering the Gulf of Aden and the Indian Ocean, east of Ethiopia
Geographic coordinates: 10 00 N, 49 00 E
Map references: Africa
Area:
total: 637,657 sq km
land: 627,337 sq km
water: 10,320 sq km

Somalia (continued)

Area - comparative: slightly smaller than Texas
Land boundaries:
total: 2,366 km
border countries: Djibouti 58 km, Ethiopia 1,626 km, Kenya 682 km
Coastline: 3,025 km
Maritime claims:
territorial sea: 200 NM
Climate: principally desert; December to February - northeast monsoon, moderate temperatures in north and very hot in south; May to October - southwest monsoon, torrid in the north and hot in the south, irregular rainfall, hot and humid periods (tangambili) between monsoons
Terrain: mostly flat to undulating plateau rising to hills in north
Elevation extremes:
lowest point: Indian Ocean 0 m
highest point: Shimbiris 2,416 m
Natural resources: uranium and largely unexploited reserves of iron ore, tin, gypsum, bauxite, copper, salt
Land use:
arable land: 2%
permanent crops: 0%
permanent pastures: 69%
forests and woodland: 26%
other: 3% (1993 est.)
Irrigated land: 1,800 sq km (1993 est.)
Natural hazards: recurring droughts; frequent dust storms over eastern plains in summer; floods during rainy season
Environment - current issues: famine; use of contaminated water contributes to human health problems; deforestation; overgrazing; soil erosion; desertification
Environment - international agreements:
party to: Endangered Species, Law of the Sea, Marine Dumping, Ship Pollution
signed, but not ratified: Marine Dumping, Nuclear Test Ban
Geography - note: strategic location on Horn of Africa along southern approaches to Bab el Mandeb and route through Red Sea and Suez Canal

People

Population: 7,488,773
note: this estimate was derived from an official census taken in 1975 by the Somali Government; population counting in Somalia is complicated by the large number of nomads and by refugee movements in response to famine and clan warfare (July 2001 est.)
Age structure:
0-14 years: 44.54% (male 1,670,320; female 1,665,329)
15-64 years: 52.69% (male 1,993,750; female 1,952,437)
65 years and over: 2.77% (male 91,511; female 115,426) (2001 est.)
Population growth rate: 3.48% (2001 est.)
Birth rate: 47.23 births/1,000 population (2001 est.)
Death rate: 18.35 deaths/1,000 population (2001 est.)
Net migration rate: 5.96 migrant(s)/1,000 population (2001 est.)
Sex ratio:
at birth: 1.03 male(s)/female
under 15 years: 1 male(s)/female
15-64 years: 1.02 male(s)/female
65 years and over: 0.79 male(s)/female
total population: 1.01 male(s)/female (2001 est.)
Infant mortality rate: 123.97 deaths/1,000 live births (2001 est.)
Life expectancy at birth:
total population: 46.6 years
male: 44.99 years
female: 48.25 years (2001 est.)
Total fertility rate: 7.11 children born/woman (2001 est.)
HIV/AIDS - adult prevalence rate: NA%
HIV/AIDS - people living with HIV/AIDS: NA
HIV/AIDS - deaths: NA
Nationality:
noun: Somali(s)
adjective: Somali
Ethnic groups: Somali 85%, Bantu, Arabs 30,000
Religions: Sunni Muslim
Languages: Somali (official), Arabic, Italian, English
Literacy:
definition: age 15 and over can read and write
total population: 24%
male: 36%
female: 14% (1990 est.)

Government

Country name:
conventional long form: none
conventional short form: Somalia
former: Somali Republic, Somali Democratic Republic
Government type: parliamentary
Capital: Mogadishu
Administrative divisions: 18 regions (plural - NA, singular - gobolka); Awdal, Bakool, Banaadir, Bari, Bay, Galguduud, Gedo, Hiiraan, Jubbada Dhexe, Jubbada Hoose, Mudug, Nugaal, Sanaag, Shabeellaha Dhexe, Shabeellaha Hoose, Sool, Togdheer, Woqooyi Galbeed
Independence: 1 July 1960 (from a merger of British Somaliland, which became independent from the UK on 26 June 1960, and Italian Somaliland, which became independent from the Italian-administered UN trusteeship on 1 July 1960, to form the Somali Republic)
National holiday: Foundation of the Somali Republic, 1 July (1960)
Constitution: 25 August 1979, presidential approval 23 September 1979
note: the Transitional National Government formed in October 2000 has a mandate to create a new constitution and hold elections within three years
Legal system: NA
Suffrage: 18 years of age; universal
Executive branch:
chief of state: ABDIKASSIM Salad Hassan (since 26 August 2000); note - Interim President ABDIKASSIM was chosen for a three-year term by a 245-member National Assembly serving as a transitional government; the present political situation is still unstable, particularly in the south, with interclan fighting and random banditry
head of government: ALI Khalifa Galaydh, appointed by the president 8 October 2000
cabinet: appointed by the prime minister and sworn in on 20 October 2000
election results: ABDIKASSIM Salad Hassan was elected president of an interim government at the Djibouti-sponsored Arta Peace Conference on 26 August 2000 by a broad representation of Somali clans that comprised a transitional National Assembly.
Legislative branch: unicameral People's Assembly or Golaha Shacbiga
note: fledgling parliament; a transitional 245-member National Assembly began to meet on 13 August 2000 in the town of Arta, Djibouti and is now based in Mogadishu
Judicial branch: following the breakdown of national government, most regions have reverted to Islamic (Shari'a) law with a provision for appeal of all sentences
Political parties and leaders: none
Political pressure groups and leaders: numerous clan and subclan factions are currently vying for power
International organization participation: ACP, AfDB, AFESD, AL, AMF, CAEU, ECA, FAO, G-77, IBRD, ICAO, ICRM, IDA, IDB, IFAD, IFC, IFRCS, ILO, IMF, IMO, Intelsat, Interpol, IOC, IOM (observer), ITU, NAM, OAU, OIC, UN, UNCTAD, UNESCO, UNHCR, UNIDO, UPU, WFTU, WHO, WIPO, WMO, WTrO (observer)
Diplomatic representation in the US: Somalia does not have an embassy in the US (ceased operations on 8 May 1991)
Diplomatic representation from the US: the US does not have an embassy in Somalia; US interests are represented by the US Embassy in Nairobi at Moi Avenue and Haile Selassie Avenue; mail address: P. O. Box 30137, Unit 64100, Nairobi; APO AE 09831; telephone: [254] (2) 334141; FAX [254] (2) 340838
Flag description: light blue with a large white five-pointed star in the center; design based on the flag of the UN (Italian Somaliland was a UN trust territory)
Government - note: An interim Transitional National Government - with a president, prime minister, and 245-member National Assembly - was formed in October 2000. However, other governing bodies continue to exist and control various cities and regions of the country, including Somaliland, Puntland, and traditional clan and faction strongholds.

Economy

Economy - overview: One of the world's poorest and least developed countries, Somalia has few resources. Moreover, much of the economy has been devastated by the civil war. Agriculture is the most important sector, with livestock accounting for about 40% of GDP and about 65% of export earnings. Nomads and semi-nomads, who are dependent upon livestock for their livelihood, make up a large portion of

Somalia (continued)

the population. Livestock and bananas are the principal exports; sugar, sorghum, corn, fish, and qat are products for the domestic market. The small industrial sector, based on the processing of agricultural products, accounts for 10% of GDP; most facilities have been shut down because of the civil strife. Moreover, ongoing civil disturbances in Mogadishu and outlying areas have interfered with any substantial economic advance and with international aid arrangements. Due to the civil strife, economic data is susceptible to an exceptionally wide margin of error.

GDP: purchasing power parity - $4.3 billion (2000 est.)
GDP - real growth rate: NA%
GDP - per capita: purchasing power parity - $600 (2000 est.)
GDP - composition by sector:
agriculture: 60%
industry: 10% (largely shut down in 2000)
services: 30% (2000 est.)
Population below poverty line: NA%
Household income or consumption by percentage share:
lowest 10%: NA%
highest 10%: NA%
Inflation rate (consumer prices): over 100% (businesses print their own money) (2000 est.)
Labor force: 3.7 million (very few are skilled laborers) (1993 est.)
Labor force - by occupation: agriculture (mostly pastoral nomadism) 71%, industry and services 29%
Unemployment rate: NA%
Budget:
revenues: $NA
expenditures: $NA, including capital expenditures of $NA
Industries: a few small industries, including sugar refining, textiles, petroleum refining (mostly shut down), wireless communication
Industrial production growth rate: NA%
Electricity - production: 260 million kWh (1999)
Electricity - production by source:
fossil fuel: 100%
hydro: 0%
nuclear: 0%
other: 0% (1999)
Electricity - consumption: 241.8 million kWh (1999)
Electricity - exports: 0 kWh (1999)
Electricity - imports: 0 kWh (1999)
Agriculture - products: cattle, sheep, goats; bananas, sorghum, corn, sugarcane, mangoes, sesame seeds, beans; fish
Exports: $186 million (f.o.b., 1999 est.)
Exports - commodities: livestock, bananas, hides, fish (1999)
Exports - partners: Saudi Arabia 53%, Yemen 19%, UAE 14%, Italy 5%, Pakistan 2% (1999)
Imports: $314 million (f.o.b., 1999 est.)
Imports - commodities: manufactures, petroleum products, foodstuffs, construction materials (1995)
Imports - partners: Djibouti 24%, Kenya 14%, Brazil 13%, Saudi Arabia 10%, India 9% (1999)
Debt - external: $2.6 billion (1999 est.)
Economic aid - recipient: $191.5 million (1995)
Currency: Somali shilling (SOS)
Currency code: SOS
Exchange rates: Somali shillings per US dollar - 11,000 (November 2000), 2,620 (January 1999), 7,500 (November 1997 est.), 7,000 (January 1996 est.), 5,000 (1 January 1995), 2,616 (1 July 1993)
note: the Republic of Somaliland, a self-declared independent country not recognized by any foreign government, issues its own currency, the Somaliland shilling
Fiscal year: NA

Communications

Telephones - main lines in use: NA
Telephones - mobile cellular: NA
Telephone system:
general assessment: the public telecommunications system was completely destroyed or dismantled by the civil war factions; all relief organizations depend on their own private systems
domestic: recently, local cellular telephone systems have been established in Mogadishu and in several other population centers
international: international connections are available from Mogadishu by satellite
Radio broadcast stations: AM 0, FM 0, shortwave 4 (1988)
Radios: 470,000 (1997)
Television broadcast stations: 1 (1997)
Televisions: 135,000 (1997)
Internet country code: .so
Internet Service Providers (ISPs): 1 (2000)
Internet users: 200 (2000)

Transportation

Railways: 0 km
Highways:
total: 22,100 km
paved: 2,608 km
unpaved: 19,492 km (1996 est.)
Waterways: none
Pipelines: crude oil 15 km
Ports and harbors: Bender Cassim (Boosaaso), Berbera, Chisimayu (Kismaayo), Merca, Mogadishu
Merchant marine: none (2000 est.)
Airports: 62 (2000 est.)
Airports - with paved runways:
total: 5
over 3,047 m: 4
1,524 to 2,437 m: 1 (2000 est.)
Airports - with unpaved runways:
total: 57
2,438 to 3,047 m: 4
1,524 to 2,437 m: 13
914 to 1,523 m: 29
under 914 m: 11 (2000 est.)

Military

Military branches: A Somali National Army is being reformed under the interim government; numerous factions and clans maintain independent militias, and the Somaliland and Puntland regional governments maintain their own security and police forces
Military manpower - availability:
males age 15-49: 1,825,302 (2001 est.)
Military manpower - fit for military service:
males age 15-49: 1,011,400 (2001 est.)
Military expenditures - dollar figure: $NA
Military expenditures - percent of GDP: NA%

Transnational Issues

Disputes - international: most of the southern half of the boundary with Ethiopia is a Provisional Administrative Line; territorial dispute with Ethiopia over the Ogaden

South Africa

Introduction

Background: After the British seized the Cape of Good Hope area in 1806, many of the Dutch settlers (the Boers) trekked north to found their own republics. The discovery of diamonds (1867) and gold (1886) spurred wealth and immigration and intensified the subjugation of the native inhabitants. The Boers resisted British encroachments, but were defeated in the Boer War (1899-1902). The resulting Union of South Africa operated under a policy of apartheid - the separate development of the races. The 1990s brought an end to apartheid politically and ushered in black majority rule.

Geography

Location: Southern Africa, at the southern tip of the continent of Africa
Geographic coordinates: 29 00 S, 24 00 E
Map references: Africa
Area:
total: 1,219,912 sq km
land: 1,219,912 sq km
water: 0 sq km
note: includes Prince Edward Islands (Marion Island and Prince Edward Island)
Area - comparative: slightly less than twice the size of Texas
Land boundaries:
total: 4,750 km
border countries: Botswana 1,840 km, Lesotho 909 km, Mozambique 491 km, Namibia 855 km, Swaziland 430 km, Zimbabwe 225 km
Coastline: 2,798 km
Maritime claims:
contiguous zone: 24 NM
continental shelf: 200-m depth or to the depth of exploitation
exclusive economic zone: 200 NM
territorial sea: 12 NM
Climate: mostly semiarid; subtropical along east coast; sunny days, cool nights
Terrain: vast interior plateau rimmed by rugged hills and narrow coastal plain
Elevation extremes:
lowest point: Atlantic Ocean 0 m
highest point: Njesuthi 3,408 m
Natural resources: gold, chromium, antimony, coal, iron ore, manganese, nickel, phosphates, tin, uranium, gem diamonds, platinum, copper, vanadium, salt, natural gas
Land use:
arable land: 10%
permanent crops: 1%
permanent pastures: 67%
forests and woodland: 7%
other: 15% (1993 est.)
Irrigated land: 12,700 sq km (1993 est.)
Natural hazards: prolonged droughts
Environment - current issues: lack of important arterial rivers or lakes requires extensive water conservation and control measures; growth in water usage threatens to outpace supply; pollution of rivers from agricultural runoff and urban discharge; air pollution resulting in acid rain; soil erosion; desertification
Environment - international agreements:
party to: Antarctic-Environmental Protocol, Antarctic-Marine Living Resources, Antarctic Seals, Antarctic Treaty, Biodiversity, Climate Change, Desertification, Endangered Species, Hazardous Wastes, Law of the Sea, Marine Dumping, Marine Life Conservation, Nuclear Test Ban, Ozone Layer Protection, Ship Pollution, Wetlands, Whaling
signed, but not ratified: none of the selected agreements
Geography - note: South Africa completely surrounds Lesotho and almost completely surrounds Swaziland

People

Population: 43,586,097
note: South Africa took a census October 1996 which showed a population of 40,583,611 (after an official adjustment for a 6.8% underenumeration based on a postenumeration survey); estimates for this country explicitly take into account the effects of excess mortality due to AIDS; this can result in lower life expectancy, higher infant mortality and death rates, lower population and growth rates, and changes in the distribution of population by age and sex than would otherwise be expected (July 2001 est.)
Age structure:
0-14 years: 32.01% (male 7,023,639; female 6,928,559)
15-64 years: 63.11% (male 13,264,654; female 14,244,484)
65 years and over: 4.88% (male 798,914; female 1,325,847) (2001 est.)
Population growth rate: 0.26% (2001 est.)
Birth rate: 21.12 births/1,000 population (2001 est.)
Death rate: 16.77 deaths/1,000 population (2001 est.)
Net migration rate: -1.73 migrant(s)/1,000 population (2001 est.)
Sex ratio:
at birth: 1.02 male(s)/female
under 15 years: 1.01 male(s)/female
15-64 years: 0.93 male(s)/female
65 years and over: 0.6 male(s)/female
total population: 0.94 male(s)/female (2001 est.)
Infant mortality rate: 60.33 deaths/1,000 live births (2001 est.)
Life expectancy at birth:
total population: 48.09 years
male: 47.64 years
female: 48.56 years (2001 est.)
Total fertility rate: 2.43 children born/woman (2001 est.)
HIV/AIDS - adult prevalence rate: 19.94% (1999 est.)
HIV/AIDS - people living with HIV/AIDS: 4.2 million (1999 est.)
HIV/AIDS - deaths: 250,000 (1999 est.)
Nationality:
noun: South African(s)
adjective: South African
Ethnic groups: black 75.2%, white 13.6%, Colored 8.6%, Indian 2.6%
Religions: Christian 68% (includes most whites and Coloreds, about 60% of blacks and about 40% of Indians), Muslim 2%, Hindu 1.5% (60% of Indians), indigenous beliefs and animist 28.5%
Languages: 11 official languages, including Afrikaans, English, Ndebele, Pedi, Sotho, Swazi, Tsonga, Tswana, Venda, Xhosa, Zulu
Literacy:
definition: age 15 and over can read and write
total population: 81.8%
male: 81.9%
female: 81.7% (1995 est.)

Government

Country name:
conventional long form: Republic of South Africa
conventional short form: South Africa
former: Union of South Africa
abbreviation: RSA
Government type: republic
Capital: Pretoria; note - Cape Town is the legislative center and Bloemfontein the judicial center
Administrative divisions: 9 provinces; Eastern Cape, Free State, Gauteng, KwaZulu-Natal, Mpumalanga, North-West, Northern Cape, Northern Province, Western Cape
Independence: 31 May 1910 (from UK)
National holiday: Freedom Day, 27 April (1994)
Constitution: 10 December 1996; this new constitution was certified by the Constitutional Court on 4 December 1996, was signed by then President MANDELA on 10 December 1996, and entered into effect on 3 February 1997; it is being implemented in phases
Legal system: based on Roman-Dutch law and English common law; accepts compulsory ICJ jurisdiction, with reservations
Suffrage: 18 years of age; universal

South Africa (continued)

Executive branch:
chief of state: President Thabo MBEKI (since 16 June 1999); Executive Deputy President Jacob ZUMA (since 17 June 1999); note - the president is both the chief of state and head of government
head of government: President Thabo MBEKI (since 16 June 1999); Executive Deputy President Jacob ZUMA (since 17 June 1999); note - the president is both the chief of state and head of government
cabinet: Cabinet appointed by the president
elections: president elected by the National Assembly for a five-year term; election last held 2 June 1999 (next scheduled for sometime between May and July 2004)
election results: Thabo MBEKI elected president; percent of National Assembly vote - 100% (by acclamation)
note: ANC-IFP governing coalition
Legislative branch: bicameral parliament consisting of the National Assembly (400 seats; members are elected by popular vote under a system of proportional representation to serve five-year terms) and the National Council of Provinces (90 seats, 10 members elected by each of the nine provincial legislatures for five-year terms; has special powers to protect regional interests, including the safeguarding of cultural and linguistic traditions among ethnic minorities); note - following the implementation of the new constitution on 3 February 1997 the former Senate was disbanded and replaced by the National Council of Provinces with essentially no change in membership and party affiliations, although the new institution's responsibilities have been changed somewhat by the new constitution
elections: National Assembly and National Council of Provinces - last held 2 June 1999 (next to be held NA 2004)
election results: National Assembly - percent of vote by party - ANC 66.4%, DP 9.6%, IFP 8.6%, NP 6.9%, UDM 3.4%, ACDP 1.4%, FF 0.8%, other 2.9%; seats by party - ANC 266, DP 38, IFP 34, NP 28, UDM 14, ACDP 6, FF 3, other 11; National Council of Provinces - percent of vote by party - NA%; seats by party - ANC 61, NP 17, FF 4, IFP 5, DP 3
Judicial branch: Constitutional Court; Supreme Court of Appeals; High Courts; Magistrate Courts
Political parties and leaders: African Christian Democratic Party or ACDP [Kenneth MESHOE, president]; African National Congress or ANC [Thabo MBEKI, president]; Democratic Alliance (formed from the merger of the Democratic Party or DP and the New National Party or NP) [Anthony LEON, leader]; Freedom Front or FF [Constand VILJOEN, president]; Inkatha Freedom Party or IFP [Mangosuthu BUTHELEZI, president]; Pan-Africanist Congress or PAC [Stanley MOGOBA, president]; United Democratic Movement or UDM [Bantu HOLOMISA]
Political pressure groups and leaders: Congress of South African Trade Unions or COSATU [Zwelinzima VAVI, general secretary]; South African Communist Party or SACP [Blade NZIMANDE, general secretary]; South African National Civics Organization or SANCO [Mlungisi HLONGWANE, national president]; note - COSATU and SACP are in a formal alliance with the ANC
International organization participation: ACP, AfDB, BIS, C, CCC, ECA, FAO, G-77, IAEA, IBRD, ICAO, ICC, ICFTU, ICRM, IDA, IFAD, IFC, IFRCS, IHO, ILO, IMF, IMO, Inmarsat, Intelsat, Interpol, IOC, IOM, ISO, ITU, MONUC, NAM, NSG, OAU, OPCW, PCA, SACU, SADC, UN, UNCTAD, UNESCO, UNHCR, UNIDO, UNITAR, UNMEE, UPU, WCL, WFTU, WHO, WIPO, WMO, WToO, WTrO, ZC
Diplomatic representation in the US:
chief of mission: Ambassador Makate Sheila SISULU
chancery: 3051 Massachusetts Avenue NW, Washington, DC 20008
telephone: [1] (202) 232-4400
FAX: [1] (202) 265-1607
consulate(s) general: Chicago, Los Angeles, and New York
Diplomatic representation from the US:
chief of mission: Ambassador Delano E. LEWIS, Sr.
embassy: 877 Pretorius Street, Pretoria
mailing address: P. O. Box 9536, Pretoria 0001
telephone: [27] (12) 342-1048
FAX: [27] (12) 342-2244
consulate(s) general: Cape Town, Durban, Johannesburg
Flag description: two equal width horizontal bands of red (top) and blue separated by a central green band which splits into a horizontal Y, the arms of which end at the corners of the hoist side; the Y embraces a black isosceles triangle from which the arms are separated by narrow yellow bands; the red and blue bands are separated from the green band and its arms by narrow white stripes
note: prior to 26 April 1994, the flag was actually four flags in one - three miniature flags reproduced in the center of the white band of the former flag of the Netherlands, which had three equal horizontal bands of orange (top), white, and blue; the miniature flags were a vertically hanging flag of the old Orange Free State with a horizontal flag of the UK adjoining on the hoist side and a horizontal flag of the old Transvaal Republic adjoining on the other side

Economy

Economy - overview: South Africa is a middle-income, developing country with an abundant supply of resources, well-developed financial, legal, communications, energy, and transport sectors, a stock exchange that ranks among the 10 largest in the world, and a modern infrastructure supporting an efficient distribution of goods to major urban centers throughout the region. However, growth has not been strong enough to cut into the 30% unemployment, and daunting economic problems remain from the apartheid era, especially the problems of poverty and lack of economic empowerment among the disadvantaged groups. Other problems are crime, corruption, and HIV/AIDS. At the start of 2000, President MBEKI vowed to promote economic growth and foreign investment, and to reduce poverty by relaxing restrictive labor laws, stepping up the pace of privatization, and cutting unneeded governmental spending.
GDP: purchasing power parity - $369 billion (2000 est.)
GDP - real growth rate: 3% (2000 est.)
GDP - per capita: purchasing power parity - $8,500 (2000 est.)
GDP - composition by sector:
agriculture: 5%
industry: 30%
services: 65% (1999 est.)
Population below poverty line: 50% (2000 est.)
Household income or consumption by percentage share:
lowest 10%: 1.1%
highest 10%: 45.9% (1994)
Inflation rate (consumer prices): 5.3% (2000 est.)
Labor force: 17 million economically active (2000)
Labor force - by occupation: agriculture 30%, industry 25%, services 45% (1999 est.)
Unemployment rate: 30% (2000 est.)
Budget:
revenues: $31.1 billion
expenditures: $34.4 billion, including capital expenditures of $NA billion (FY01/02)
Industries: mining (world's largest producer of platinum, gold, chromium), automobile assembly, metalworking, machinery, textile, iron and steel, chemicals, fertilizer, foodstuffs
Industrial production growth rate: 2.4% (2000 est.)
Electricity - production: 186.903 billion kWh (1999)
Electricity - production by source:
fossil fuel: 92.74%
hydro: 0.39%
nuclear: 6.87%
other: 0% (1999)
Electricity - consumption: 172.393 billion kWh (1999)
Electricity - exports: 3.884 billion kWh (1999)
Electricity - imports: 2.457 billion kWh (1999)
Agriculture - products: corn, wheat, sugarcane, fruits, vegetables; beef, poultry, mutton, wool, dairy products
Exports: $30.8 billion (f.o.b., 2000 est.)
Exports - commodities: gold, diamonds, other metals and minerals, machinery and equipment
Exports - partners: UK, Italy, Japan, US, Germany
Imports: $27.6 billion (f.o.b., 2000 est.)
Imports - commodities: machinery, foodstuffs and equipment, chemicals, petroleum products, scientific instruments
Imports - partners: Germany, US, UK, Japan
Debt - external: $25.6 billion (2000 est.)
Economic aid - recipient: $676.3 million
Currency: rand (ZAR)
Currency code: ZAR
Exchange rates: rand per US dollar - 7.60 (March 2001), 6.93983 (2000), 6.10948 (1999), 5.52828 (1998), 4.60796 (1997), 4.29935 (1996)
Fiscal year: 1 April - 31 March

South Africa (continued)

Communications

Telephones - main lines in use: 5.075 million (1999)
Telephones - mobile cellular: over 2,000,000 (1999)
Telephone system:
general assessment: the system is the best developed and most modern in Africa
domestic: consists of carrier-equipped open-wire lines, coaxial cables, microwave radio relay links, fiber-optic cable, radiotelephone communication stations, and wireless local loops; key centers are Bloemfontein, Cape Town, Durban, Johannesburg, Port Elizabeth, and Pretoria
international: 2 submarine cables; satellite earth stations - 3 Intelsat (1 Indian Ocean and 2 Atlantic Ocean)
Radio broadcast stations: AM 14, FM 347 (plus 243 repeaters), shortwave 1 (1998)
Radios: 13.75 million (1997)
Television broadcast stations: 556 (plus 144 network repeaters) (1997)
Televisions: 5.2 million (1997)
Internet country code: .za
Internet Service Providers (ISPs): 44 (2000)
Internet users: 1.82 million (2000)

Transportation

Railways:
total: 21,431 km
narrow gauge: 20,995 km 1.067-m gauge (9,087 km electrified); 436 km 0.610-m gauge (1995)
Highways:
total: 534,131 km
paved: 63,027 km (including 2,032 km of expressways)
unpaved: 471,104 km (1998 est.)
Waterways: NA
Pipelines: crude oil 931 km; petroleum products 1,748 km; natural gas 322 km
Ports and harbors: Cape Town, Durban, East London, Mosselbaai, Port Elizabeth, Richards Bay, Saldanha
Merchant marine:
total: 8 ships (1,000 GRT or over) totaling 271,650 GRT/268,604 DWT
ships by type: container 6, petroleum tanker 2 (2000 est.)
Airports: 741 (2000 est.)
Airports - with paved runways:
total: 142
over 3,047 m: 9
2,438 to 3,047 m: 5
1,524 to 2,437 m: 47
914 to 1,523 m: 71
under 914 m: 10 (2000 est.)
Airports - with unpaved runways:
total: 599
1,524 to 2,437 m: 33
914 to 1,523 m: 304
under 914 m: 262 (2000 est.)

Military

Military branches: South African National Defense Force or SANDF (includes Army, Navy, Air Force, and Medical Services), South African Police Service or SAPS
Military manpower - military age: 18 years of age
Military manpower - availability:
males age 15-49: 11,469,812 (2001 est.)
Military manpower - fit for military service:
males age 15-49: 6,977,328 (2001 est.)
Military manpower - reaching military age annually:
males: 466,399 (2001 est.)
Military expenditures - dollar figure: $2 billion (FY00/01)
Military expenditures - percent of GDP: 1.5% (FY99/00)
Military - note: the National Defense Force continues to integrate former military, black homelands forces, and ex-opposition forces

Transnational Issues

Disputes - international: Swaziland has asked South Africa to open negotiations on reincorporating some nearby South African territories that are populated by ethnic Swazis or that were long ago part of the Swazi Kingdom
Illicit drugs: transshipment center for heroin, hashish, marijuana, and possibly cocaine; cocaine consumption on the rise; world's largest market for illicit methaqualone, usually imported illegally from India through various east African countries; illicit cultivation of marijuana

South Georgia and the South Sandwich Islands
(overseas territory of the UK, also claimed by Argentina)

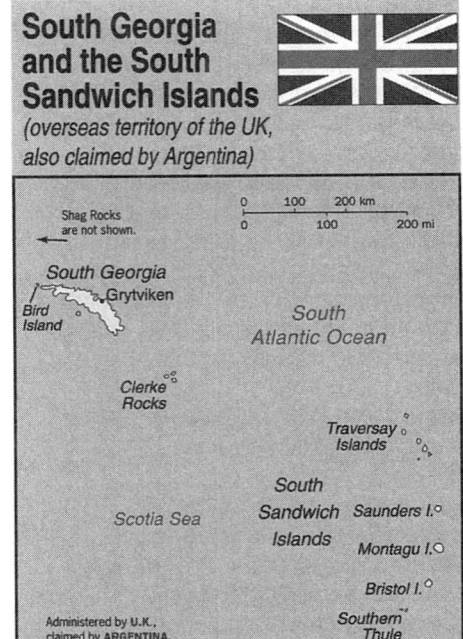

Introduction

Background: The islands lie approximately 1,000 km east of the Falkland Islands. Grytviken, on South Georgia, was a 19th and early 20th century whaling station. The famed explorer Ernest SHACKLETON stopped there in 1914 en route to his ill-fated attempt to cross Antarctica on foot. He returned some 20 months later with a few companions in a small boat and arranged a successful rescue for the rest of his crew, stranded off the Antarctic Peninsula. He died in 1922 on a subsequent expedition and is buried in Grytviken. Today, the station houses a small military garrison. The islands have large bird and seal populations and, recognizing the importance of preserving the marine stocks in adjacent waters, the UK, in 1993, extended the exclusive fishing zone from 12 miles to 200 miles around each island.

Geography

Location: Southern South America, islands in the South Atlantic Ocean, east of the tip of South America
Geographic coordinates: 54 30 S, 37 00 W
Map references: Antarctic Region
Area:
total: 3,903 sq km
land: 3,903 sq km
water: 0 sq km
note: includes Shag Rocks, Black Rock, Clerke Rocks, South Georgia Island, Bird Island, and the South Sandwich Islands, which consist of some nine islands
Area - comparative: slightly larger than Rhode Island
Land boundaries: 0 km
Coastline: NA km
Maritime claims:
exclusive fishing zone: 200 NM
territorial sea: 12 NM

South Georgia and the South Sandwich Islands (continued)

Climate: variable, with mostly westerly winds throughout the year interspersed with periods of calm; nearly all precipitation falls as snow
Terrain: most of the islands, rising steeply from the sea, are rugged and mountainous; South Georgia is largely barren and has steep, glacier-covered mountains; the South Sandwich Islands are of volcanic origin with some active volcanoes
Elevation extremes:
lowest point: Atlantic Ocean 0 m
highest point: Mount Paget (South Georgia) 2,934 m
Natural resources: fish
Land use:
arable land: 0%
permanent crops: 0%
permanent pastures: 0%
forests and woodland: 0%
other: 100% (largely covered by permanent ice and snow with some sparse vegetation consisting of grass, moss, and lichen)
Irrigated land: 0 sq km (1993)
Natural hazards: the South Sandwich Islands have prevailing weather conditions that generally make them difficult to approach by ship; they are also subject to active volcanism
Environment - current issues: NA
Geography - note: the north coast of South Georgia has several large bays, which provide good anchorage; reindeer, introduced early in this century, live on South Georgia

People

Population: no indigenous inhabitants
note: the small military garrison on South Georgia withdrew in March 2001, to be replaced by a permanent group of scientists of the British Antarctic Survey which also has a biological station on Bird Island; the South Sandwich Islands are uninhabited (July 2001 est.)

Government

Country name:
conventional long form: South Georgia and the South Sandwich Islands
conventional short form: none
Dependency status: overseas territory of the UK, also claimed by Argentina; administered from the Falkland Islands by UK civil commissioner Donald A. LAMONT, representing Queen ELIZABETH II; Grytviken, formerly a whaling station on South Georgia, is the garrison town
National holiday: Liberation Day, 14 June (1982)
Constitution: adopted 3 October 1985
Legal system: the laws of the UK, where applicable, apply
Diplomatic representation in the US: none (overseas territory of the UK, also claimed by Argentina)
Diplomatic representation from the US: none (overseas territory of the UK, also claimed by Argentina)
Flag description: the flag of the UK is used

Economy

Economy - overview: Some fishing takes place in adjacent waters. There is a potential source of income from harvesting fin fish and krill. The islands receive income from postage stamps produced in the UK.
Budget:
revenues: $291,777
expenditures: $451,000, including capital expenditures of $NA (1988 est.)
Electricity - production by source:
fossil fuel: NA%
hydro: NA%
nuclear: NA%
other: NA%
Electricity - consumption: NA kWh

Communications

Telephone system:
general assessment: NA
domestic: NA
international: coastal radiotelephone station at Grytviken
Radio broadcast stations: none
Television broadcast stations: 0 (1997)
Internet country code: .gs

Transportation

Waterways: none
Ports and harbors: Grytviken
Airports: none

Military

Military - note: defense is the responsibility of the UK

Transnational Issues

Disputes - international: claimed by Argentina

Southern Ocean

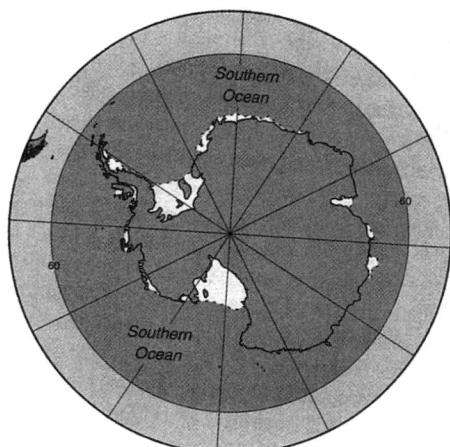

Introduction

Background: A decision by the International Hydrographic Organization in the spring of 2000 delimited a fifth world ocean - the Southern Ocean - from the southern portions of the Atlantic Ocean, Indian Ocean, and Pacific Ocean. The Southern Ocean extends from the coast of Antarctica north to 60 degrees south latitude which coincides with the Antarctic Treaty Limit. The Southern Ocean is now the fourth largest of the world's five oceans (after the Pacific Ocean, Atlantic Ocean, and Indian Ocean, but larger than the Arctic Ocean).

Geography

Location: body of water between 60 degrees south latitude and Antarctica
Geographic coordinates. 65 00 S, 0 00 E (nominally), but the Southern Ocean has the unique distinction of being a large circumpolar body of water totally encircling the continent of Antarctica; this ring of water lies between 60 degrees south latitude and the coast of Antarctica, and encompasses 360 degrees of longitude
Map references. Antarctic Region
Area.
total. 20.327 million sq km
note. includes Amundsen Sea, Bellingshausen Sea, part of the Drake Passage, Ross Sea, a small part of the Scotia Sea, Weddell Sea, and other tributary water bodies
Area - comparative. slightly more than twice the size of the US
Coastline. 17,968 km
Climate. sea temperatures vary from about 10 degrees Celsius to -2 degrees Celsius; cyclonic storms travel eastward around the continent and frequently are intense because of the temperature contrast between ice and open ocean; the ocean area from about latitude 40 south to the Antarctic Circle has the strongest average winds found anywhere on Earth; in winter the ocean freezes outward to

Southern Ocean (continued)

65 degrees south latitude in the Pacific sector and 55 degrees south latitude in the Atlantic sector, lowering surface temperatures well below 0 degrees Celsius; at some coastal points intense persistent drainage winds from the interior keep the shoreline ice-free throughout the winter
Terrain: the Southern Ocean is deep, 4,000 to 5,000 meters over most of its extent with only limited areas of shallow water; the Antarctic continental shelf is generally narrow and unusually deep - its edge lying at depths of 400 to 800 meters (the global mean is 133 meters); the Antarctic icepack grows from an average minimum of 2.6 million square kilometers in March to about 18.8 million square kilometers in September, better than a sixfold increase in area; the Antarctic Circumpolar Current (21,000 km in length) moves perpetually eastward; it is the world's largest ocean current, transporting 130 million cubic meters of water per second - 100 times the flow of all the world's rivers
Elevation extremes:
lowest point: -7,235 m at the southern end of the South Sandwich Trench
highest point: sea level 0 m
Natural resources: probable large and possible giant oil and gas fields on the continental margin, manganese nodules, possible placer deposits, sand and gravel, fresh water as icebergs, squid, whales, and seals - none exploited; krill, fishes
Natural hazards: huge icebergs with drafts up to several hundred meters; smaller bergs and iceberg fragments; sea ice (generally 0.5 to 1 meter thick) with sometimes dynamic short-term variations and with large annual and interannual variations; deep continental shelf floored by glacial deposits varying widely over short distances; high winds and large waves much of the year; ship icing, especially May-October; most of region is remote from sources of search and rescue
Environment - current issues: increased solar ultraviolet radiation resulting from the Antarctic ozone hole in recent years, reducing marine primary productivity (phytoplankton) by as much as 15% and damaging the DNA of some fish; illegal, unreported, and unregulated fishing in recent years, especially the landing of an estimated five to six times more Patagonian toothfish than the regulated fishery, which is likely to affect the sustainability of the stock; large amount of incidental mortality of seabirds resulting from long-line fishing for toothfish
note: the now-protected fur seal population is making a strong comeback after severe overexploitation in the 18th and 19th centuries
Environment - international agreements: the Southern Ocean is subject to all international agreements regarding the world's oceans; in addition, it is subject to these agreements specific to the Antarctic region: International Whaling Commission (prohibits commercial whaling south of 40 degrees south [south of 60 degrees south between 50 degrees and 130 degrees west]); Convention on the Conservation of Antarctic Seals (limits sealing); Convention on the Conservation of Antarctic Marine Living Resources (regulates fishing)

note: many nations (including the US) prohibit mineral resource exploration and exploitation south of the fluctuating Polar Front (Antarctic Convergence) which is in the middle of the Antarctic Circumpolar Current and serves as the dividing line between the very cold polar surface waters to the south and the warmer waters to the north
Geography - note: the major chokepoint is the Drake Passage between South America and Antarctica; the Polar Front (Antarctic Convergence) is the best natural definition of the northern extent of the Southern Ocean; it is a distinct region at the middle of the Antarctic Circumpolar Current that separates the very cold polar surface waters to the south from the warmer waters to the north; the Front and the Current extend entirely around Antarctica, reaching south of 60 degrees south near New Zealand and near 48 degrees south in the far South Atlantic coinciding with the path of the maximum westerly winds

Economy

Economy - overview: Fisheries in 1998-99 (1 July to 30 June) landed 119,898 metric tons, of which 85% was krill and 14% Patagonian toothfish. International agreements were adopted in late 1999 to reduce illegal, unreported, and unregulated fishing, which in the 1998-99 season landed five to six times more Patagonian toothfish than the regulated fishery. In the 1999-2000 antarctic summer 13,193 tourists, most of them seaborne, visited the Southern Ocean and Antarctica, compared to 10,013 the previous year. Nearly 16,000 tourists are expected during the 2000-01 season.

Transportation

Ports and harbors: McMurdo, Palmer, and offshore anchorages in Antarctica
note: few ports or harbors exist on the southern side of the Southern Ocean; ice conditions limit use of most of them to short periods in midsummer; even then some cannot be entered without icebreaker escort; most antarctic ports are operated by government research stations and, except in an emergency, are not open to commercial or private vessels; vessels in any port south of 60 degrees south are subject to inspection by Antarctic Treaty observers
Transportation - note: Drake Passage offers alternative to transit through the Panama Canal

Transnational Issues

Disputes - international: Antarctic Treaty defers claims (see Antarctic Treaty Summary in the Antarctica entry); sections (some overlapping) claimed by Argentina, Australia, Chile, France, New Zealand, Norway, and UK; the US and most other nations do not recognize the maritime claims of other nations and have made no claims themselves (the US and Russia have reserved the right to do so); no formal claims have been made in the sector between 90 degrees west and 150 degrees west

Spain

Introduction

Background: Spain's powerful world empire of the 16th and 17th centuries ultimately yielded command of the seas to England. Subsequent failure to embrace the mercantile and industrial revolutions caused the country to fall behind Britain, France, and Germany in economic and political power. Spain remained neutral in World Wars I and II, but suffered through a devastating Civil War (1936-39). In the second half of the 20th century, it has played a catch-up role in the western international community. Continuing concerns are large-scale unemployment and the Basque separatist movement.

Geography

Location: Southwestern Europe, bordering the Bay of Biscay, Mediterranean Sea, North Atlantic Ocean, and Pyrenees Mountains, southwest of France
Geographic coordinates: 40 00 N, 4 00 W
Map references: Europe
Area:
total: 504,782 sq km
land: 499,542 sq km
water: 5,240 sq km
note: includes Balearic Islands, Canary Islands, and five places of sovereignty (plazas de soberania) on and off the coast of Morocco - Ceuta, Melilla, Islas Chafarinas, Penon de Alhucemas, and Penon de Velez de la Gomera
Area - comparative: slightly more than twice the size of Oregon
Land boundaries:
total: 1,917.8 km
border countries: Andorra 63.7 km, France 623 km, Gibraltar 1.2 km, Portugal 1,214 km, Morocco (Ceuta) 6.3 km, Morocco (Melilla) 9.6 km
Coastline: 4,964 km
Maritime claims:
contiguous zone: 24 NM

Spain (continued)

exclusive economic zone: 200 NM (applies only to the Atlantic Ocean)
territorial sea: 12 NM
Climate: temperate; clear, hot summers in interior, more moderate and cloudy along coast; cloudy, cold winters in interior, partly cloudy and cool along coast
Terrain: large, flat to dissected plateau surrounded by rugged hills; Pyrenees in north
Elevation extremes:
lowest point: Atlantic Ocean 0 m
highest point: Pico de Teide (Tenerife) on Canary Islands 3,718 m
Natural resources: coal, lignite, iron ore, uranium, mercury, pyrites, fluorspar, gypsum, zinc, lead, tungsten, copper, kaolin, potash, hydropower, arable land
Land use:
arable land: 30%
permanent crops: 9%
permanent pastures: 21%
forests and woodland: 32%
other: 8% (1993 est.)
Irrigated land: 34,530 sq km (1993 est.)
Natural hazards: periodic droughts
Environment - current issues: pollution of the Mediterranean Sea from raw sewage and effluents from the offshore production of oil and gas; water quality and quantity nationwide; air pollution; deforestation; desertification
Environment - international agreements:
party to: Air Pollution, Air Pollution-Nitrogen Oxides, Air Pollution-Sulphur 94, Air Pollution-Volatile Organic Compounds, Antarctic-Environmental Protocol, Antarctic-Marine Living Resources, Antarctic Treaty, Biodiversity, Climate Change, Endangered Species, Environmental Modification, Hazardous Wastes, Law of the Sea, Marine Dumping, Marine Life Conservation, Nuclear Test Ban, Ozone Layer Protection, Ship Pollution, Tropical Timber 83, Tropical Timber 94, Wetlands, Whaling
signed, but not ratified: Air Pollution-Persistent Organic Pollutants, Climate Change-Kyoto Protocol, Desertification
Geography - note: strategic location along approaches to Strait of Gibraltar

People

Population: 40,037,995 (July 2001 est.)
Age structure:
0-14 years: 14.62% (male 3,015,851; female 2,835,763)
15-64 years: 68.2% (male 13,701,065; female 13,605,314)
65 years and over: 17.18% (male 2,881,334; female 3,998,668) (2001 est.)
Population growth rate: 0.1% (2001 est.)
Birth rate: 9.26 births/1,000 population (2001 est.)
Death rate: 9.13 deaths/1,000 population (2001 est.)
Net migration rate: 0.87 migrant(s)/1,000 population (2001 est.)
Sex ratio:
at birth: 1.07 male(s)/female
under 15 years: 1.06 male(s)/female
15-64 years: 1.01 male(s)/female
65 years and over: 0.72 male(s)/female
total population: 0.96 male(s)/female (2001 est.)
Infant mortality rate: 4.92 deaths/1,000 live births (2001 est.)
Life expectancy at birth:
total population: 78.93 years
male: 75.47 years
female: 82.62 years (2001 est.)
Total fertility rate: 1.15 children born/woman (2001 est.)
HIV/AIDS - adult prevalence rate: 0.58% (1999 est.)
HIV/AIDS - people living with HIV/AIDS: 120,000 (1999 est.)
HIV/AIDS - deaths: 2,000 (1999 est.)
Nationality:
noun: Spaniard(s)
adjective: Spanish
Ethnic groups: composite of Mediterranean and Nordic types
Religions: Roman Catholic 99%, other 1%
Languages: Castilian Spanish (official) 74%, Catalan 17%, Galician 7%, Basque 2%
Literacy:
definition: age 15 and over can read and write
total population: 97%
male: NA%
female: NA%

Government

Country name:
conventional long form: Kingdom of Spain
conventional short form: Spain
local short form: Espana
Government type: parliamentary monarchy
Capital: Madrid
Administrative divisions: 17 autonomous communities (comunidades autonomas, singular - comunidad autonoma); Andalucia, Aragon, Asturias, Baleares (Balearic Islands), Canarias (Canary Islands), Cantabria, Castilla-La Mancha, Castilla y Leon, Cataluna, Communidad Valencian, Extremadura, Galicia, La Rioja, Madrid, Murcia, Navarra, Pais Vasco (Basque Country)
note: there are five places of sovereignty on and off the coast of Morocco: Ceuta and Melilla are administered as autonomous communities; Islas Chafarinas, Penon de Alhucemas, and Penon de Velez de la Gomera are under direct Spanish administration
Independence: 1492 (expulsion of the Moors and unification)
National holiday: Hispanic Day, 12 October
Constitution: 6 December 1978, effective 29 December 1978
Legal system: civil law system, with regional applications; has not accepted compulsory ICJ jurisdiction
Suffrage: 18 years of age; universal
Executive branch:
chief of state: King JUAN CARLOS I (since 22 November 1975); Heir Apparent Prince FELIPE, son of the monarch, born 30 January 1968
head of government: President of the Government Jose Maria AZNAR Lopez (since 5 May 1996); First Vice President Juan Jose LUCAS (since 28 February 2000) and Second Vice President (and Minister of Economy) Rodrigo RATO Figaredo (since 5 May 1996)
cabinet: Council of Ministers designated by the president
note: there is also a Council of State that is the supreme consultative organ of the government
elections: the monarch is hereditary; president proposed by the monarch and elected by the National Assembly following legislative elections; election last held 12 March 2000 (next to be held NA March 2004); vice presidents appointed by the monarch on proposal of the president
election results: Jose Maria AZNAR Lopez (PP) elected president; percent of National Assembly vote - 44%
Legislative branch: bicameral; General Courts or National Assembly or Las Cortes Generales consists of the Senate or Senado (259 seats - 208 members directly elected by popular vote and the other 51 appointed by the regional legislatures to serve four-year terms) and the Congress of Deputies or Congreso de los Diputados (350 seats; members are elected by popular vote on block lists by proportional representation to serve four-year terms)
elections: Senate - last held 12 March 2000 (next to be held NA March 2004); Congress of Deputies - last held 12 March 2000 (next to be held NA March 2004)
election results: Senate - percent of vote by party - NA%; seats by party - PP 127, PSOE 61, CiU 8, PNV 6, CC 5, PIL 1; Congress of Deputies - percent of vote by party - PP 44.5%, PSOE 34%, CiU 4.2%, IU 5.4%, PNV 1.5%, CC 1%, BNG 1.3%; seats by party - PP 183, PSOE 125, CiU 15, IU 8, PNV 7, CC 4, BNG 3, other 5
Judicial branch: Supreme Court or Tribunal Supremo
Political parties and leaders: Basque Nationalist Party or PNV [Xabier ARZALLUS Antia]; Canarian Coalition or CC (a coalition of five parties) [Paulino RIVERO]; Convergence and Union or CiU [Jordi PUJOL i Soley, secretary general] (a coalition of the Democratic Convergence of Catalonia or CDC [Jordi PUJOL i Soley] and the Democratic Union of Catalonia or UDC [Josep Antoni DURAN y LLEIDA]); Galician Nationalist Bloc or BNG [Xose Manuel BEIRAS]; Party of Independents from Lanzarote or PIL [Dimas MARTIN Martin]; Popular Party or PP [Jose Maria AZNAR Lopez]; Spanish Socialist Workers Party or PSOE [Jose Luis Rodriguez ZAPATERO]; United Left or IU (a coalition of parties including the PCE and other small parties) [Gaspar LLAMAZARES]

Spain (continued)

Political pressure groups and leaders: business and landowning interests; Catholic Church; Euskal Herritarok or EH [Herri BATASUNA]; free labor unions (authorized in April 1977); on the extreme left, the Basque Fatherland and Liberty or ETA and the First of October Antifascist Resistance Group or GRAPO use terrorism to oppose the government; Opus Dei; Socialist General Union of Workers or UGT and the smaller independent Workers Syndical Union or USO; university students; Workers Confederation or CC.OO

International organization participation: AfDB, AsDB, Australia Group, BIS, CCC, CE, CERN, EAPC, EBRD, ECE, ECLAC, EIB, EMU, ESA, EU, FAO, IADB, IAEA, IBRD, ICAO, ICC, ICFTU, ICRM, IDA, IEA, IFAD, IFC, IFRCS, IHO, ILO, IMF, IMO, Inmarsat, Intelsat, Interpol, IOC, IOM (observer), ISO, ITU, LAIA (observer), NATO, NEA, NSG, OAS (observer), OECD, OPCW, OSCE, PCA, UN, UNCTAD, UNESCO, UNHCR, UNIDO, UNMEE, UNMIBH, UNMIK, UNTAET, UNU, UPU, WCL, WEU, WHO, WIPO, WMO, WToO, WTrO, ZC

Diplomatic representation in the US:
chief of mission: Ambassador Francisco Javier RUPEREZ
chancery: 2375 Pennsylvania Avenue NW, Washington, DC 20037
telephone: [1] (202) 452-0100, 728-2340
FAX: [1] (202) 833-5670
consulate(s) general: Boston, Chicago, Houston, Los Angeles, Miami, New Orleans, New York, San Francisco, and San Juan (Puerto Rico)

Diplomatic representation from the US:
chief of mission: Ambassador Edward L. ROMERO
embassy: Serrano 75, 28006 Madrid
mailing address: APO AE 09642
telephone: [34] (91) 587-2200
FAX: [34] (91) 587-2303
consulate(s) general: Barcelona

Flag description: three horizontal bands of red (top), yellow (double width), and red with the national coat of arms on the hoist side of the yellow band; the coat of arms includes the royal seal framed by the Pillars of Hercules, which are the two promontories (Gibraltar and Ceuta) on either side of the eastern end of the Strait of Gibraltar

Economy

Economy - overview: Spain's mixed capitalist economy supports a GDP that on a per capita basis is 80% that of the four leading West European economies. Its center-right government successfully worked to gain admission to the first group of countries launching the European single currency on 1 January 1999. The AZNAR administration has continued to advocate liberalization, privatization, and deregulation of the economy and has introduced some tax reforms to that end. Unemployment has been steadily falling under the AZNAR administration but remains the highest in the EU at 14%. The government intends to make further progress in changing labor laws and reforming pension schemes, which are key to the sustainability of both Spain's internal economic advances and its competitiveness in a single currency area. Adjusting to the monetary and other economic policies of an integrated Europe - and further reducing unemployment - will pose challenges to Spain in the next few years.

GDP: purchasing power parity - $720.8 billion (2000 est.)

GDP - real growth rate: 4% (2000 est.)

GDP - per capita: purchasing power parity - $18,000 (2000 est.)

GDP - composition by sector:
agriculture: 4%
industry: 31%
services: 65% (1999)

Population below poverty line: NA%

Household income or consumption by percentage share:
lowest 10%: 2.8%
highest 10%: 25.2% (1990)

Inflation rate (consumer prices): 3.4% (2000 est.)

Labor force: 17 million (2000)

Labor force - by occupation: services 64%, manufacturing, mining, and construction 28%, agriculture 8% (1997 est.)

Unemployment rate: 14% (2000 est.)

Budget:
revenues: $105 billion
expenditures: $109 billion, including capital expenditures of $12.8 billion (2000 est.)

Industries: textiles and apparel (including footwear), food and beverages, metals and metal manufactures, chemicals, shipbuilding, automobiles, machine tools, tourism

Industrial production growth rate: 4.5% (2000 est.)

Electricity - production: 197.694 billion kWh (1999)

Electricity - production by source:
fossil fuel: 57.71%
hydro: 12.1%
nuclear: 28.28%
other: 1.91% (1999)

Electricity - consumption: 189.57 billion kWh (1999)

Electricity - exports: 6.23 billion kWh (1999)

Electricity - imports: 11.945 billion kWh (1999)

Agriculture - products: grain, vegetables, olives, wine grapes, sugar beets, citrus; beef, pork, poultry, dairy products; fish

Exports: $120.5 billion (f.o.b., 2000 est.)

Exports - commodities: machinery, motor vehicles; foodstuffs, other consumer goods

Exports - partners: EU 71% (France 20%, Germany 12%, Italy 9%, Portugal 9%, UK 8%), Latin America 6%, US 5% (2000)

Imports: $153.9 billion (f.o.b., 2000 est.)

Imports - commodities: machinery and equipment, fuels, chemicals, semifinished goods; foodstuffs, consumer goods (1997)

Imports - partners: EU 68% (France 18%, Germany 16%, Italy 9%, UK 7%, Benelux 8%), US 8%, OPEC 5%, Latin America 4%, Japan 3% (1999)

Debt - external: $90 billion (1993 est.)

Economic aid - donor: ODA, $1.3 billion (1995)

Currency: Spanish peseta (ESP); euro (EUR)
note: on 1 January 1999, the EU introduced the euro as a common currency that is now being used by financial institutions in Spain at a fixed rate of 166.386 Spanish pesetas per euro and will replace the local currency for all transactions in 2002

Currency code: ESP; EUR

Exchange rates: euros per US dollar - 1.0659 (January 2001), 1.0854 (2000), 0.9386 (1999); pesetas per US dollar - 149.40 (1998), 146.41 (1997), 126.66 (1996)

Fiscal year: calendar year

Communications

Telephones - main lines in use: 17.336 million (1999)

Telephones - mobile cellular: 8.394 million (1999)

Telephone system:
general assessment: generally adequate, modern facilities; teledensity is 44 main lines for each 100 persons
domestic: NA
international: 22 coaxial submarine cables; satellite earth stations - 2 Intelsat (1 Atlantic Ocean and 1 Indian Ocean), NA Eutelsat; tropospheric scatter to adjacent countries

Radio broadcast stations: AM 208, FM 715, shortwave 1 (1998)

Radios: 13.1 million (1997)

Television broadcast stations: 224 (plus 2,105 repeaters)
note: these figures include 11 television broadcast stations and 88 repeaters in the Canary Islands (1995)

Televisions: 16.2 million (1997)

Internet country code: .es

Internet Service Providers (ISPs): 56 (2000)

Internet users: 4.6 million (2000)

Transportation

Railways:
total: 13,950 km
broad gauge: 12,781 km 1.668-m gauge (6,358 km electrified; 2,295 km double track)
standard gauge: 525 km 1.435-m gauge (525 km electrified)
narrow gauge: 644 km 1.000-m gauge (438 km electrified) (1998)

Highways:
total: 346,858 km
paved: 343,389 km (including 9,063 km of expressways)
unpaved: 3,469 km (1997 est.)

Waterways: 1,045 km (of minor economic importance)

Pipelines: crude oil 265 km; petroleum products 1,794 km; natural gas 1,666 km

Ports and harbors: Aviles, Barcelona, Bilbao, Cadiz, Cartagena, Castellon de la Plana, Ceuta, Huelva, La Coruna, Las Palmas (Canary Islands),

Spain (continued)

Malaga, Melilla, Pasajes, Gijon, Santa Cruz de Tenerife (Canary Islands), Santander, Tarragona, Valencia, Vigo

Merchant marine:
total: 135 ships (1,000 GRT or over) totaling 1,208,730 GRT/1,773,378 DWT
ships by type: bulk 10, cargo 26, chemical tanker 10, container 9, liquefied gas 2, livestock carrier 1, passenger 1, petroleum tanker 24, refrigerated cargo 5, roll on/roll off 35, short-sea passenger 8, specialized tanker 1, vehicle carrier 3 (2000 est.)

Airports: 110 (2000 est.)

Airports - with paved runways:
total: 75
over 3,047 m: 15
2,438 to 3,047 m: 10
1,524 to 2,437 m: 18
914 to 1,523 m: 19
under 914 m: 13 (2000 est.)

Airports - with unpaved runways:
total: 35
1,524 to 2,437 m: 1
914 to 1,523 m: 9
under 914 m: 25 (2000 est.)

Heliports: 2 (2000 est.)

Military

Military branches: Army, Navy, Air Force, Marines, Civil Guard, National Police, Coastal Civil Guard
Military manpower - military age: 20 years of age
Military manpower - availability:
males age 15-49: 10,551,945 (2001 est.)
Military manpower - fit for military service:
males age 15-49: 8,448,150 (2001 est.)
Military manpower - reaching military age annually:
males: 281,043 (2001 est.)
Military expenditures - dollar figure: $6 billion (FY97)
Military expenditures - percent of GDP: 1.1% (FY97)

Transnational Issues

Disputes - international: Gibraltar issue with UK; Spain controls five places of sovereignty (plazas de soberania) on and off the coast of Morocco - the coastal enclaves of Ceuta and Melilla, which Morocco contests, as well as the islands of Penon de Alhucemas, Penon de Velez de la Gomera, and Islas Chafarinas

Illicit drugs: key European gateway country for Latin American cocaine and North African hashish entering the European market; transshipment point for and consumer of Southwest Asian heroin

Spratly Islands

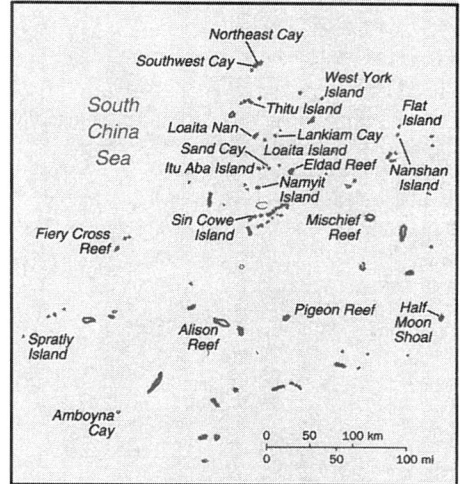

Introduction

Background: Rich fishing grounds and the potential for gas and oil deposits have caused this archipelago to be claimed in its entirety by China, Taiwan, and Vietnam, while portions are claimed by Malaysia and the Philippines. All five parties have occupied certain islands or reefs, and occasional clashes have occurred between Chinese and Vietnamese naval forces

Geography

Location: Southeastern Asia, group of reefs and islands in the South China Sea, about two-thirds of the way from southern Vietnam to the southern Philippines
Geographic coordinates: 8 38 N, 111 55 E
Map references: Southeast Asia
Area:
total: less than 5 sq km
land: less than 5 sq km
water: 0 sq km
note: includes 100 or so islets, coral reefs, and sea mounts scattered over an area of nearly 410,000 sq km of the central South China Sea
Area - comparative: NA
Land boundaries: 0 km
Coastline: 926 km
Maritime claims: NA
Climate: tropical
Terrain: flat
Elevation extremes:
lowest point: South China Sea 0 m
highest point: unnamed location on Southwest Cay 4 m
Natural resources: fish, guano, undetermined oil and natural gas potential
Land use:
arable land: 0%
permanent crops: 0%
permanent pastures: 0%
forests and woodland: 0%
other: 100%
Irrigated land: 0 sq km (1993)
Natural hazards: typhoons; serious maritime hazard because of numerous reefs and shoals
Environment - current issues: NA
Geography - note: strategically located near several primary shipping lanes in the central South China Sea; includes numerous small islands, atolls, shoals, and coral reefs

People

Population: no indigenous inhabitants
note: there are scattered garrisons occupied by personnel of several claimant states (July 2001 est.)

Government

Country name:
conventional long form: none
conventional short form: Spratly Islands

Economy

Economy - overview: Economic activity is limited to commercial fishing. The proximity to nearby oil- and gas-producing sedimentary basins suggests the potential for oil and gas deposits, but the region is largely unexplored, and there are no reliable estimates of potential reserves; commercial exploitation has yet to be developed.

Transportation

Waterways: none
Ports and harbors: none; offshore anchorage only
Airports: 4 (2000 est.)
Airports - with paved runways:
total: 1
914 to 1,523 m: 1 (2000 est.)
Airports - with unpaved runways:
total: 3
914 to 1,523 m: 1
under 914 m: 2 (2000 est.)

Military

Military - note: Spratly Islands consist of more than 100 small islands or reefs, of which about 45 are claimed and occupied by China, Malaysia, the Philippines, Taiwan, and Vietnam

Transnational Issues

Disputes - international: all of the Spratly Islands are claimed by China, Taiwan, and Vietnam; parts of them are claimed by Malaysia and the Philippines; in 1984, Brunei established an exclusive fishing zone that encompasses Louisa Reef in the southern Spratly Islands, but has not publicly claimed the island; in 2000, China joined ASEAN discussions towards creating a South China Sea "code of conduct" - a non-legally binding confidence building measure

Sri Lanka

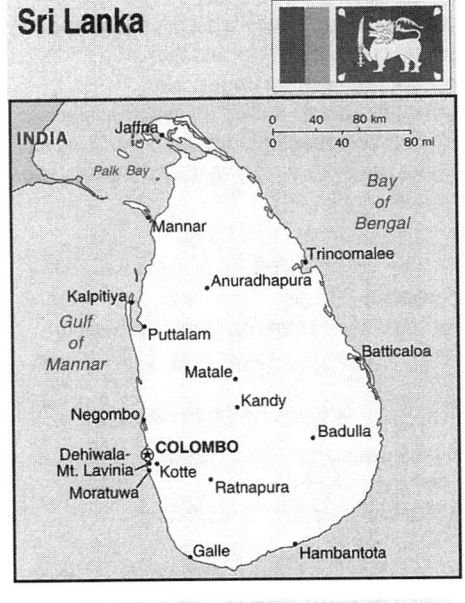

Introduction

Background: Occupied by the Portuguese in the 16th century and the Dutch in the 17th century, the island was ceded to the British in 1802. As Ceylon it became independent in 1948; its name was changed in 1972. Tensions between the Sinhalese majority and Tamil separatists erupted in violence in the mid-1980s. Tens of thousands have died in an ethnic war that continues to fester.

Geography

Location: Southern Asia, island in the Indian Ocean, south of India
Geographic coordinates: 7 00 N, 81 00 E
Map references: Asia
Area:
total: 65,610 sq km
land: 64,740 sq km
water: 870 sq km
Area - comparative: slightly larger than West Virginia
Land boundaries: 0 km
Coastline: 1,340 km
Maritime claims:
contiguous zone: 24 NM
continental shelf: 200 NM or to the edge of the continental margin
exclusive economic zone: 200 NM
territorial sea: 12 NM
Climate: tropical monsoon; northeast monsoon (December to March); southwest monsoon (June to October)
Terrain: mostly low, flat to rolling plain; mountains in south-central interior
Elevation extremes:
lowest point: Indian Ocean 0 m
highest point: Pidurutalagala 2,524 m
Natural resources: limestone, graphite, mineral sands, gems, phosphates, clay, hydropower
Land use:
arable land: 14%
permanent crops: 15%
permanent pastures: 7%
forests and woodland: 32%
other: 32% (1993 est.)
Irrigated land: 5,500 sq km (1993 est.)
Natural hazards: occasional cyclones and tornadoes
Environment - current issues: deforestation; soil erosion; wildlife populations threatened by poaching and urbanization; coastal degradation from mining activities and increased pollution; freshwater resources being polluted by industrial wastes and sewage runoff; waste disposal; air pollution in Colombo
Environment - international agreements:
party to: Biodiversity, Climate Change, Desertification, Endangered Species, Environmental Modification, Hazardous Wastes, Law of the Sea, Marine Dumping, Nuclear Test Ban, Ozone Layer Protection, Ship Pollution, Wetlands
signed, but not ratified: Marine Life Conservation
Geography - note: strategic location near major Indian Ocean sea lanes

People

Population: 19,408,635 (July 2001 est.)
note: since the outbreak of hostilities between the government and armed Tamil separatists in the mid-1980s, several hundred thousand Tamil civilians have fled the island; as of mid-1999, approximately 66,000 were housed in 133 refugee camps in south India, another 40,000 lived outside the Indian camps, and more than 200,000 Tamils have sought refuge in the West
Age structure:
0-14 years: 25.99% (male 2,578,618; female 2,464,928)
15-64 years: 67.39% (male 6,369,881; female 6,708,852)
65 years and over: 6.62% (male 615,253; female 671,103) (2001 est.)
Population growth rate: 0.87% (2001 est.)
Birth rate: 16.58 births/1,000 population (2001 est.)
Death rate: 6.43 deaths/1,000 population (2001 est.)
Net migration rate: -1.43 migrant(s)/1,000 population (2001 est.)
Sex ratio:
at birth: 1.05 male(s)/female
under 15 years: 1.05 male(s)/female
15-64 years: 0.95 male(s)/female
65 years and over: 0.92 male(s)/female
total population: 0.97 male(s)/female (2001 est.)
Infant mortality rate: 16.08 deaths/1,000 live births (2001 est.)
Life expectancy at birth:
total population: 72.09 years
male: 69.58 years
female: 74.73 years (2001 est.)
Total fertility rate: 1.95 children born/woman (2001 est.)
HIV/AIDS - adult prevalence rate: 0.07% (1999 est.)
HIV/AIDS - people living with HIV/AIDS: 7,500 (1999 est.)
HIV/AIDS - deaths: 490 (1999 est.)
Nationality:
noun: Sri Lankan(s)
adjective: Sri Lankan
Ethnic groups: Sinhalese 74%, Tamil 18%, Moor 7%, Burgher, Malay, and Vedda 1%
Religions: Buddhist 70%, Hindu 15%, Christian 8%, Muslim 7% (1999)
Languages: Sinhala (official and national language) 74%, Tamil (national language) 18%, other 8%
note: English is commonly used in government and is spoken competently by about 10% of the population
Literacy:
definition: age 15 and over can read and write
total population: 90.2%
male: 93.4%
female: 87.2% (1995 est.)

Government

Country name:
conventional long form: Democratic Socialist Republic of Sri Lanka
conventional short form: Sri Lanka
former: Serendib, Ceylon
Government type: republic
Capital: Colombo; note - Sri Jayewardenepura Kotte is the legislative capital
Administrative divisions: 8 provinces; Central, North Central, North Eastern, North Western, Sabaragamuwa, Southern, Uva, Western; note - North Eastern province may have been divided in two - Northern and Eastern
Independence: 4 February 1948 (from UK)
National holiday: Independence Day, 4 February (1948)
Constitution: adopted 16 August 1978
Legal system: a highly complex mixture of English common law, Roman-Dutch, Muslim, Sinhalese, and customary law; has not accepted compulsory ICJ jurisdiction
Suffrage: 18 years of age; universal
Executive branch:
chief of state: President Chandrika Bandaranaike KUMARATUNGA (since 12 November 1994); note - Ratnasiri WICKRAMANAYAKE (since 10 August 2000) is the prime minister; in Sri Lanka the president is considered to be both the chief of state and the head of the government, this is in contrast to the more common practice of dividing the roles between the president and the prime minister when both offices exist
head of government: President Chandrika Bandaranaike KUMARATUNGA (since 12 November 1994); note - Ratnasiri WICKRAMANAYAKE (since 10 August 2000) is the prime minister; in Sri Lanka the president is considered to be both the chief of state and the head of the government, this is in contrast to

Sri Lanka (continued)

the more common practice of dividing the roles between the president and the prime minister when both offices exist
cabinet: Cabinet appointed by the president in consultation with the prime minister
elections: president elected by popular vote for a six-year term; election last held 21 December 1999 (next to be held NA December 2005)
election results: Chandrika Bandaranaike KUMARATUNGA reelected president; percent of vote - Chandrika Bandaranaike KUMARATUNGA (PA) 51%, Ranil WICKREMASINGHE (UNP) 42%, other 7%
Legislative branch: unicameral Parliament (225 seats; members elected by popular vote on the basis of a modified proportional representation system by district to serve six-year terms)
elections: last held 10 October 2000 (next to be held NA October 2006)
election results: percent of vote by party - PA 45.11%, UNP 40.22%, JVP 6%, NUA 2.29%, SU 1.48%, TULF 1.23%, other 3.67%; seats by party - PA 107, UNP 89, JVP 10, TULF 5, EPDP 4, NUA 4, TELO 3, ACTC 1, SU 1, independent 1
Judicial branch: Supreme Court; Court of Appeals; judges for both courts are appointed by the president
Political parties and leaders: All Ceylon Tamil Congress or ACTC [Nalliah GURUPAUAN]; Ceylon Workers Congress or CLDC [Arumugam THONDAMAN]; Communist Party [Raja COLLURE]; Democratic United National (Lalith) Front or DUNLF [Srimani ATHULATHMUDALI]; Eelam People's Democratic Party or EPDP [Douglas DEVANANDA]; Eelam People's Revolutionary Liberation Front or EPRLF [Suresh PREMACHANDRA]; Janatha Vimukthi Peramuna or JVP [Tilvan SILVA]; National Unity Alliance or NUA [leader NA]; People's Alliance or PA [Chandrika Bandaranaike KUMARATUNGA]; People's Liberation Organization of Tamil Eelam or PLOTE [D. SIDDATHAN]; Sihala Urumaya or SU [leader NA]; Sri Lanka Freedom Party or SLFP [Chandrika Bandaranaike KUMARATUNGA]; Sri Lanka Muslim Congress or SLMC [Rauff HAKEEM and Ferial ASHRAFF]; Sri Lanka Progressive Front or SLPF [leader NA]; Tamil Eelam Liberation Organization or TELO [SUBRAMANIUM]; Tamil United Liberation Front or TULF [R. SAMPATHAN]; United National Party or UNP [Ranil WICKREMASINGHE]; Upcountry People's Front or UPF [P. CHANDRASEKARAN]; several ethnic Tamil and Muslim parties, represented in either parliament or provincial councils
Political pressure groups and leaders: Buddhist clergy; labor unions; Liberation Tigers of Tamil Eelam or LTTE (insurgent group fighting for a separate state); radical chauvinist Sinhalese groups such as the National Movement Against Terrorism; Sinhalese Buddhist lay groups
International organization participation: AsDB, C, CCC, CP, ESCAP, FAO, G-24, G-77, IAEA, IBRD, ICAO, ICC, ICFTU, ICRM, IDA, IFAD, IFC, IFRCS, IHO, ILO, IMF, IMO, Inmarsat, Intelsat, Interpol, IOC, IOM, ISO, ITU, NAM, OAS (observer), OPCW, PCA, SAARC, UN, UNCTAD, UNESCO, UNIDO, UNTAET, UNU, UPU, WCL, WFTU, WHO, WIPO, WMO, WToO, WTrO
Diplomatic representation in the US:
chief of mission: Ambassador Warnasena RASAPUTRAM
chancery: 2148 Wyoming Avenue NW, Washington, DC 20008
telephone: [1] (202) 483-4025 (through 4028)
FAX: [1] (202) 232-7181
consulate(s) general: Los Angeles
consulate(s): New York
Diplomatic representation from the US:
chief of mission: Ambassador E. Ashley WILLS
embassy: 210 Galle Road, Colombo 3
mailing address: P. O. Box 106, Colombo
telephone: [94] (1) 448007
FAX: [94] (1) 437345
Flag description: yellow with two panels; the smaller hoist-side panel has two equal vertical bands of green (hoist side) and orange; the other panel is a large dark red rectangle with a yellow lion holding a sword, and there is a yellow bo leaf in each corner; the yellow field appears as a border that goes around the entire flag and extends between the two panels

Economy

Economy - overview: In 1977, Colombo abandoned statist economic policies and its import substitution trade policy for market-oriented policies and export-oriented trade. Sri Lanka's most dynamic sectors now are food processing, textiles and apparel, food and beverages, telecommunications, and insurance and banking. By 1996 plantation crops made up only 20% of exports (compared with 93% in 1970), while textiles and garments accounted for 63%. GDP grew at an annual average rate of 5.5% throughout the 1990s until a drought and a deteriorating security situation lowered growth to 3.8% in 1996. The economy rebounded in 1997-98 with growth of 6.4% and 4.7% - but slowed to 4.3% in 1999. Growth increased to 5.6% in 2000, with growth in tourism and exports leading the way. But a resurgence of civil war between the Sinhalese and the minority Tamils and a possible slowdown in tourism dampen prospects for 2001. For the next round of reforms, the central bank of Sri Lanka recommends that Colombo expand market mechanisms in nonplantation agriculture, dismantle the government's monopoly on wheat imports, and promote more competition in the financial sector.
GDP: purchasing power parity - $62.7 billion (2000 est.)
GDP - real growth rate: 5.6% (2000 est.)
GDP - per capita: purchasing power parity - $3,250 (2000 est.)
GDP - composition by sector:
agriculture: 21%
industry: 19%
services: 60% (1998)
Population below poverty line: 22% (1997 est.)
Household income or consumption by percentage share:
lowest 10%: 1.8%
highest 10%: 39.7% (1995-96 est.)
Inflation rate (consumer prices): 8.5% (2000 est.)
Labor force: 6.6 million (1998)
Labor force - by occupation: services 45%, agriculture 38%, industry 17% (1998 est.)
Unemployment rate: 8.8% (1999 est.)
Budget:
revenues: $3 billion
expenditures: $3 billion, including capital expenditures of $NA (2000 est.)
Industries: processing of rubber, tea, coconuts, and other agricultural commodities; clothing, cement, petroleum refining, textiles, tobacco
Industrial production growth rate: 4% (1999)
Electricity - production: 6.026 billion kWh (1999)
Electricity - production by source:
fossil fuel: 29.9%
hydro: 70.1%
nuclear: 0%
other: 0% (1999)
Electricity - consumption: 5.604 billion kWh (1999)
Electricity - exports: 0 kWh (1999)
Electricity - imports: 0 kWh (1999)
Agriculture - products: rice, sugarcane, grains, pulses, oilseed, spices, tea, rubber, coconuts; milk, eggs, hides, beef
Exports: $5.2 billion (f.o.b., 2000)
Exports - commodities: textiles and apparel, tea, diamonds, coconut products, petroleum products
Exports - partners: US 39%, UK 13%, Middle East 8%, Germany 5%, Japan 4% (1999)
Imports: $6.1 billion (f.o.b., 2000)
Imports - commodities: machinery and equipment, textiles, petroleum, foodstuffs
Imports - partners: Japan 10%, India 9%, Hong Kong 8%, Singapore 8%, South Korea 6% (1999)
Debt - external: $9.9 billion (2000)
Economic aid - recipient: $577 million (1998)
Currency: Sri Lankan rupee (LKR)
Currency code: LKR
Exchange rates: Sri Lankan rupees per US dollar - 83.506 (January 2001), 77.005 (2000), 70.635 (1999), 64.450 (1998), 58.995 (1997), 55.271 (1996)
Fiscal year: calendar year

Communications

Telephones - main lines in use: 494,509 (1998)
Telephones - mobile cellular: 228,604 (1999)
Telephone system:
general assessment: very inadequate domestic service, particularly in rural areas; some hope for improvement with privatization of national telephone company and encouragement to private investment; good international service (1999)
domestic: national trunk network consists mostly of digital microwave radio relay; fiber-optic links now in use in Colombo area and two fixed wireless local loops have been installed; competition is strong in mobile cellular systems; telephone density remains low at 2.6 main lines per 100 persons (1999)

Sri Lanka (continued)

international: submarine cables to Indonesia and Djibouti; satellite earth stations - 2 Intelsat (Indian Ocean) (1999)
Radio broadcast stations: AM 26, FM 45, shortwave 1 (1998)
Radios: 3.85 million (1997)
Television broadcast stations: 21 (1997)
Televisions: 1.53 million (1997)
Internet country code: .lk
Internet Service Providers (ISPs): 5 (2000)
Internet users: 65,000 (2000)

Transportation

Railways:
total: 1,463 km
broad gauge: 1,404 km 1.676-m gauge
narrow gauge: 59 km 0.762-m gauge (1996)
Highways:
total: 11,285 km
paved: 10,721 km
unpaved: 564 km (1998 est.)
Waterways: 430 km (navigable by shallow-draft craft)
Pipelines: crude oil and petroleum products 62 km (1987)
Ports and harbors: Colombo, Galle, Jaffna, Trincomalee
Merchant marine:
total: 20 ships (1,000 GRT or over) totaling 149,902 GRT/247,852 DWT
ships by type: bulk 1, cargo 16, container 1, petroleum tanker 1, refrigerated cargo 1 (2000 est.)
Airports: 14 (2000 est.)
Airports - with paved runways:
total: 12
over 3,047 m: 1
1,524 to 2,437 m: 5
914 to 1,523 m: 6 (2000 est.)
Airports - with unpaved runways:
total: 2
1,524 to 2,437 m: 1
under 914 m: 1 (2000 est.)

Military

Military branches: Army, Navy, Air Force, Police Force
Military manpower - military age: 18 years of age
Military manpower - availability:
males age 15-49: 5,304,323 (2001 est.)
Military manpower - fit for military service:
males age 15-49: 4,119,511 (2001 est.)
Military manpower - reaching military age annually:
males: 193,522 (2001 est.)
Military expenditures - dollar figure: $719 million (FY98)
Military expenditures - percent of GDP: 4.2% (FY98)

Transnational Issues

Disputes - international: none

Sudan

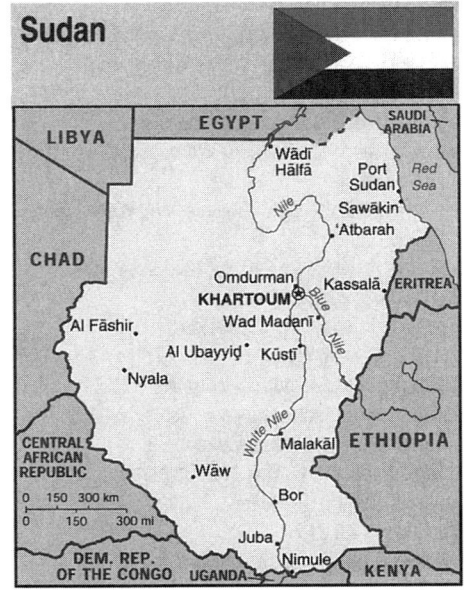

Introduction

Background: Military dictatorships promulgating an Islamic government have mostly run the country since independence from the UK in 1956. Over the past two decades, a civil war pitting black Christians and animists in the south against the Arab-Muslims of the north has cost at least 1.5 million lives in war- and famine-related deaths, as well as the displacement of millions of others.

Geography

Location: Northern Africa, bordering the Red Sea, between Egypt and Eritrea
Geographic coordinates: 15 00 N, 30 00 E
Map references: Africa
Area:
total: 2,505,810 sq km
land: 2.376 million sq km
water: 129,810 sq km
Area - comparative: slightly more than one-quarter the size of the US
Land boundaries:
total: 7,687 km
border countries: Central African Republic 1,165 km, Chad 1,360 km, Democratic Republic of the Congo 628 km, Egypt 1,273 km, Eritrea 605 km, Ethiopia 1,606 km, Kenya 232 km, Libya 383 km, Uganda 435 km
Coastline: 853 km
Maritime claims:
contiguous zone: 18 NM
continental shelf: 200-m depth or to the depth of exploitation
territorial sea: 12 NM
Climate: tropical in south; arid desert in north; rainy season (April to October)
Terrain: generally flat, featureless plain; mountains in east and west
Elevation extremes:
lowest point: Red Sea 0 m
highest point: Kinyeti 3,187 m

Natural resources: petroleum; small reserves of iron ore, copper, chromium ore, zinc, tungsten, mica, silver, gold, hydropower
Land use:
arable land: 5%
permanent crops: 0%
permanent pastures: 46%
forests and woodland: 19%
other: 30% (1993 est.)
Irrigated land: 19,460 sq km (1993 est.)
Natural hazards: dust storms
Environment - current issues: inadequate supplies of potable water; wildlife populations threatened by excessive hunting; soil erosion; desertification
Environment - international agreements:
party to: Biodiversity, Climate Change, Desertification, Endangered Species, Law of the Sea, Marine Dumping, Nuclear Test Ban, Ozone Layer Protection, Ship Pollution
signed, but not ratified: none of the selected agreements
Geography - note: largest country in Africa; dominated by the Nile and its tributaries

People

Population: 36,080,373 (July 2001 est.)
Age structure:
0-14 years: 44.62% (male 8,227,011; female 7,870,783)
15-64 years: 53.29% (male 9,619,218; female 9,608,469)
65 years and over: 2.09% (male 425,898; female 328,994) (2001 est.)
Population growth rate: 2.79% (2001 est.)
Birth rate: 37.89 births/1,000 population (2001 est.)
Death rate: 10.04 deaths/1,000 population (2001 est.)
Net migration rate: 0.04 migrant(s)/1,000 population (2001 est.)
Sex ratio:
at birth: 1.05 male(s)/female
under 15 years: 1.05 male(s)/female
15-64 years: 1 male(s)/female
65 years and over: 1.29 male(s)/female
total population: 1.03 male(s)/female (2001 est.)
Infant mortality rate: 68.67 deaths/1,000 live births (2001 est.)
Life expectancy at birth:
total population: 56.94 years
male: 55.85 years
female: 58.08 years (2001 est.)
Total fertility rate: 5.35 children born/woman (2001 est.)
HIV/AIDS - adult prevalence rate: 0.99% (1999 est.)
HIV/AIDS - people living with HIV/AIDS: NA
HIV/AIDS - deaths: NA
Nationality:
noun: Sudanese (singular and plural)
adjective: Sudanese

Sudan (continued)

Ethnic groups: black 52%, Arab 39%, Beja 6%, foreigners 2%, other 1%
Religions: Sunni Muslim 70% (in north), indigenous beliefs 25%, Christian 5% (mostly in south and Khartoum)
Languages: Arabic (official), Nubian, Ta Bedawie, diverse dialects of Nilotic, Nilo-Hamitic, Sudanic languages, English
note: program of "Arabization" in process
Literacy:
definition: age 15 and over can read and write
total population: 46.1%
male: 57.7%
female: 34.6% (1995 est.)

Government

Country name:
conventional long form: Republic of the Sudan
conventional short form: Sudan
local long form: Jumhuriyat as-Sudan
local short form: As-Sudan
former: Anglo-Egyptian Sudan
Government type: transitional - ruling military junta took power in 1989; government is dominated by members of Sudan's National Islamic Front (NIF), a fundamentalist political organization, which uses the National Congress Party (NCP) as its legal front
Capital: Khartoum
Administrative divisions: 26 states (wilayat, singular - wilayah); A'ali an Nil, Al Bahr al Ahmar, Al Buhayrat, Al Jazirah, Al Khartum, Al Qadarif, Al Wahdah, An Nil al Abyad, An Nil al Azraq, Ash Shamaliyah, Bahr al Jabal, Gharb al Istiwa'iyah, Gharb Bahr al Ghazal, Gharb Darfur, Gharb Kurdufan, Janub Darfur, Janub Kurdufan, Junqali, Kassala, Nahr an Nil, Shamal Bahr al Ghazal, Shamal Darfur, Shamal Kurdufan, Sharq al Istiwa'iyah, Sinnar, Warab
Independence: 1 January 1956 (from Egypt and UK)
National holiday: Independence Day, 1 January (1956)
Constitution: 12 April 1973, suspended following coup of 6 April 1985; interim constitution of 10 October 1985 suspended following coup of 30 June 1989; new constitution implemented on 30 June 1998 partially suspended 12 December 1999 by President BASHIR
Legal system: based on English common law and Islamic law; as of 20 January 1991, the now defunct Revolutionary Command Council imposed Islamic law in the northern states; Islamic law applies to all residents of the northern states regardless of their religion; some separate religious courts; accepts compulsory ICJ jurisdiction, with reservations
Suffrage: 17 years of age; universal, but noncompulsory
Executive branch:
chief of state: President Lt. Gen. Umar Hasan Ahmad al-BASHIR (since 16 October 1993); First Vice President Ali Uthman Muhammad TAHA (since 17 February 1998), Second Vice President Moses MACHAR (since 12 February 2001); note - the president is both the chief of state and head of government
head of government: President Lt. Gen. Umar Hasan Ahmad al-BASHIR (since 16 October 1993); First Vice President Ali Uthman Muhammad TAHA (since 17 February 1998), Second Vice President Moses MACHAR (since 12 February 2001); note - the president is both the chief of state and head of government
cabinet: Council of Ministers appointed by the president; note - the National Congress Party (front for the National Islamic Front or NIF) dominates BASHIR's cabinet
elections: president elected by popular vote for a five-year term; election last held 13-23 December 2000 (next to be held NA 2005)
election results: Umar Hasan Ahmad al-BASHIR reelected president; percent of vote - Umar Hasan Ahmad al-BASHIR 86.5%, Ja'afar Muhammed NUMAYRI 9.6%, three other candidates received less than a combined 4% of the vote
note: BASHIR assumed supreme executive power in 1989 and retained it through several transitional governments in the early and mid-90s before being popularly elected for the first time in March 1996
Legislative branch: unicameral National Assembly (400 seats; 275 elected by popular vote, 125 elected by a supra assembly of interest groups known as the National Congress)
elections: last held 13-23 December 2000 (next to be held NA)
election results: NA; few parties participated in the 2000 elections
note: on 12 December 1999, BASHIR dismissed the National Assembly during an internal power struggle between the president and speaker of the National Assembly Hasan al-TURABI
Judicial branch: Supreme Court; Special Revolutionary Courts
Political parties and leaders: the government allows political "associations" under a 1998 law revised in 2000; to obtain government approval parties must accept the constitution and refrain from advocating or using violence against the regime; approved parties include the National Congress Party or NCP [Ibrahim Ahmed UMAR], Popular National Congress [Hassan al-TURABI], and a handful of minor pro-government parties
Political pressure groups and leaders: National Congress Party [Ibrahim Ahmed UMAR] (front for the National Islamic Front or NIF); Popular National Congress [Hassan al-TURABI]; Umma [Sadiq al-MAHDI]; Democratic Unionist Party [Muhammed Uthman AL-MIRGHANI]; National Democratic Alliance [Muhammed Uthman AL-MIRGHANI, chairman]; Sudan People's Liberation Army [Dr. John GARANG]
International organization participation: ABEDA, ACP, AfDB, AFESD, AL, AMF, CAEU, CCC, ECA, FAO, G-77, IAEA, IBRD, ICAO, ICRM, IDA, IDB, IFAD, IFC, IFRCS, IGAD, ILO, IMF, IMO, Intelsat, Interpol, IOC, IOM, ISO (correspondent), ITU, NAM, OAU, OIC, OPCW, PCA, UN, UNCTAD, UNESCO, UNHCR, UNIDO, UNU, UPU, WFTU, WHO, WIPO, WMO, WToO, WTrO (observer)
Diplomatic representation in the US:
chief of mission: Ambassador Mahdi Ibrahim MAHAMMAD (recalled to Khartoum in August 1998)
chancery: 2210 Massachusetts Avenue NW, Washington, DC 20008
telephone: [1] (202) 338-8565
FAX: [1] (202) 667-2406
Diplomatic representation from the US: US officials at the US Embassy in Khartoum were moved for security reasons in February 1996 and have been relocated to the US Embassies in Nairobi, Kenya, and Cairo, Egypt, from where they make periodic visits to Khartoum; the US Embassy in Khartoum is located on Sharia Abdul Latif Avenue; mailing address - P. O. Box 699, Khartoum; APO AE 09829; telephone - [249] (11) 774611 or 774700; FAX - [249] (11) 774137; the US Embassy in Nairobi, Kenya is located in the Interim Office Building on Mombasa Road, Nairobi; mailing address - P. O. Box 30137, Box 21A, Unit 64100, APO AE 09831; telephone - [254] (2) 751613; FAX - [254] (2) 743204; the US Embassy in Cairo, Egypt is located at (North Gate) 8, Kamel El-Din Salah Street, Garden City, Cairo; mailing address - Unit 64900, APO AE 09839-4900; telephone - [20] (2) 3557371; FAX - [20] (2) 3573200
Flag description: three equal horizontal bands of red (top), white, and black with a green isosceles triangle based on the hoist side

Economy

Economy - overview: Sudan is buffeted by civil war, chronic instability, adverse weather, weak world agricultural prices, a drop in remittances from abroad, and counterproductive economic policies. The private sector's main areas of activity are agriculture (which employs 80% of the work force), trading, and light industry which is mostly processing of agricultural goods. Most of the 1990s were characterized by sluggish economic growth as the IMF suspended lending, declared Sudan a non-cooperative state, and threatened to expel Sudan from the IMF. Starting in 1997, Sudan began implementing IMF macroeconomic reforms which have successfully stabilized inflation at 10% or less. Sudan continues to have limited international credit resources as over 75% of Sudan's debt of $24.9 billion is in arrears and Khartoum's continued prosecution of the civil war works to isolate Sudan. In 1999, Sudan began exporting oil and in 1999-2000 had recorded its first trade surpluses. Current oil production stands at 185,000 barrels per day, of which about 70% is exported and the rest refined for domestic consumption. Despite its many infrastructure problems, Sudan's increased oil production, the return of regular rainfall, and recent investments in irrigation schemes should allow the country to achieve economic growth of 6% in 2001.

Sudan (continued)

GDP: purchasing power parity - $35.7 billion (2000 est.)
GDP - real growth rate: 7% (2000 est.)
GDP - per capita: purchasing power parity - $1,000 (2000 est.)
GDP - composition by sector:
agriculture: 39%
industry: 17%
services: 44% (1998 est.)
Population below poverty line: NA%
Household income or consumption by percentage share:
lowest 10%: NA%
highest 10%: NA%
Inflation rate (consumer prices): 10% (2000 est.)
Labor force: 11 million (1996 est.)
Labor force - by occupation: agriculture 80%, industry and commerce 10%, government 6%, unemployed 4% (1996 est.)
Unemployment rate: 4% (1996 est.)
Budget:
revenues: $1.2 billion
expenditures: $1.3 billion, including capital expenditures of $NA (2000 est.)
Industries: cotton ginning, textiles, cement, edible oils, sugar, soap distilling, shoes, petroleum refining, pharmaceuticals, armaments
Industrial production growth rate: 5% (1996 est.)
Electricity - production: 1.76 billion kWh (1999)
Electricity - production by source:
fossil fuel: 42.05%
hydro: 57.95%
nuclear: 0%
other: 0% (1999)
Electricity - consumption: 1.637 billion kWh (1999)
Electricity - exports: 0 kWh (1999)
Electricity - imports: 0 kWh (1999)
Agriculture - products: cotton, groundnuts (peanuts), sorghum, millet, wheat, gum arabic, sugarcane, cassara, mangos, papaya, bananas, sweet potatoes, sesame; sheep, livestock
Exports: $1.7 billion (f.o.b., 2000 est.)
Exports - commodities: oil and petroleum products, cotton, sesame, livestock, groundnuts, gum arabic, sugar
Exports - partners: Saudi Arabia 16%, Italy 10%, Germany 5%, France 3%, Thailand 3% (1999)
Imports: $1.2 billion (f.o.b., 2000 est.)
Imports - commodities: foodstuffs, manufactured goods, machinery and transport equipment, medicines and chemicals, textiles
Imports - partners: China 14.7%, Libya 14.7%, Saudi Arabia 8.9%, UK 8.7%, France 6.7% (1999)
Debt - external: $24.9 billion (2000 est.)
Economic aid - recipient: $187 million (1997)
Currency: Sudanese dinar (SDD)
Currency code: SDD
Exchange rates: Sudanese dinars per US dollar - 257.44 (January 2001), 257.12 (2000), 252.55 (1999), 200.80 (1998), 157.57 (1997), 125.08 (1996)
Fiscal year: calendar year

Communications

Telephones - main lines in use: 400,000 (2000)
Telephones - mobile cellular: 20,000 (2000)
Telephone system:
general assessment: large, well-equipped system by regional standards and being upgraded; cellular communications started in 1996 and have expanded substantially
domestic: consists of microwave radio relay, cable, radiotelephone communications, tropospheric scatter, and a domestic satellite system with 14 earth stations
international: satellite earth stations - 1 Intelsat (Atlantic Ocean) and 1 Arabsat (2000)
Radio broadcast stations: AM 12, FM 1, shortwave 1 (1998)
Radios: 7.55 million (1997)
Television broadcast stations: 3 (1997)
Televisions: 2.38 million (1997)
Internet country code: .sd
Internet Service Providers (ISPs): 1 (2000)
Internet users: 10,000 (2000)

Transportation

Railways:
total: 5,311 km
narrow gauge: 4,595 km 1.067-m gauge; 716 km 1.6096-m gauge plantation line
note: the main line linking Khartoum to Port Sudan carries over two-thirds of Sudan's rail traffic
Highways:
total: 11,900 km
paved: 4,320 km
unpaved: 7,580 km (1996 est.)
Waterways: 5,310 km
Pipelines: refined products 815 km
Ports and harbors: Juba, Khartoum, Kusti, Malakal, Nimule, Port Sudan, Sawakin
Merchant marine:
total: 4 ships (1,000 GRT or over) totaling 38,093 GRT/49,727 DWT
ships by type: cargo 2, roll on/roll off 2 (2000 est.)
Airports: 61 (2000 est.)
Airports - with paved runways:
total: 12
over 3,047 m: 1
2,438 to 3,047 m: 8
1,524 to 2,437 m: 3 (2000 est.)
Airports - with unpaved runways:
total: 49
1,524 to 2,437 m: 15
914 to 1,523 m: 25
under 914 m: 9 (2000 est.)
Heliports: 1 (2000 est.)

Military

Military branches: Army, Navy, Air Force, Popular Defense Force Militia
Military manpower - military age: 18 years of age
Military manpower - availability:
males age 15-49: 8,436,732 (2001 est.)
Military manpower - fit for military service:
males age 15-49: 5,194,862 (2001 est.)
Military manpower - reaching military age annually:
males: 398,294 (2001 est.)
Military expenditures - dollar figure: $550 million (FY98)
Military expenditures - percent of GDP: NA%

Transnational Issues

Disputes - international: administrative boundary with Kenya does not coincide with international boundary; Egypt asserts its claim to the "Hala'ib Triangle," a barren area of 20,580 sq km under partial Sudanese administration that is defined by an administrative boundary which supersedes the treaty boundary of 1899

Suriname

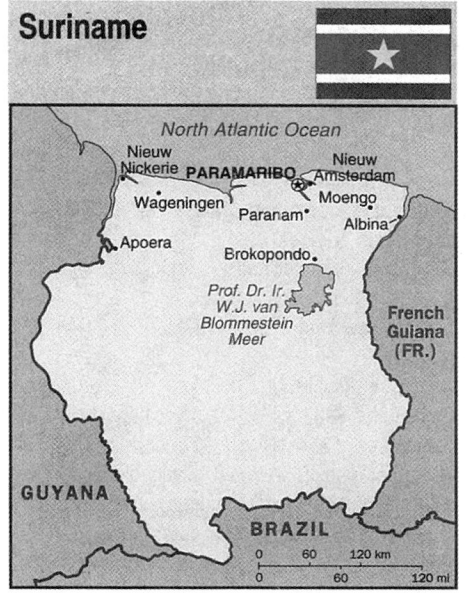

Introduction

Background: Independence from the Netherlands was granted in 1975. Five years later the civilian government was replaced by a military regime that soon declared a socialist republic. It continued to rule through a succession of nominally civilian administrations until 1987, when international pressure finally brought about a democratic election. In 1989, the military overthrew the civilian government, but a democratically elected government returned to power in 1991.

Geography

Location: Northern South America, bordering the North Atlantic Ocean, between French Guiana and Guyana
Geographic coordinates: 4 00 N, 56 00 W
Map references: South America
Area:
total: 163,270 sq km
land: 161,470 sq km
water: 1,800 sq km
Area - comparative: slightly larger than Georgia
Land boundaries:
total: 1,707 km
border countries: Brazil 597 km, French Guiana 510 km, Guyana 600 km
Coastline: 386 km
Maritime claims:
exclusive economic zone: 200 NM
territorial sea: 12 NM
Climate: tropical; moderated by trade winds
Terrain: mostly rolling hills; narrow coastal plain with swamps
Elevation extremes:
lowest point: unnamed location in the coastal plain -2 m
highest point: Juliana Top 1,230 m
Natural resources: timber, hydropower, fish, kaolin, shrimp, bauxite, gold, and small amounts of nickel, copper, platinum, iron ore
Land use:
arable land: 0%
permanent crops: 0%
permanent pastures: 0%
forests and woodland: 96%
other: 4% (1993 est.)
note: there are 94,927 hectares of arable land, 7,195 hectares of permanent crops, and 15,000 hectares of permanent pastures
Irrigated land: 600 sq km (1993 est.)
Natural hazards: NA
Environment - current issues: deforestation as timber is cut for export; pollution of inland waterways by small-scale mining activities
Environment - international agreements:
party to: Biodiversity, Climate Change, Desertification, Endangered Species, Law of the Sea, Marine Dumping, Nuclear Test Ban, Ozone Layer Protection, Ship Pollution, Tropical Timber 94, Wetlands
signed, but not ratified: none of the selected agreements
Geography - note: mostly tropical rain forest; great diversity of flora and fauna that, for the most part, is increasingly threatened by new development; relatively small population, most of which lives along the coast

People

Population: 433,998 (July 2001 est.)
Age structure:
0-14 years: 31.62% (male 70,314; female 66,924)
15-64 years: 62.71% (male 138,969; female 133,193)
65 years and over: 5.67% (male 11,194; female 13,404) (2001 est.)
Population growth rate: 0.6% (2001 est.)
Birth rate: 20.53 births/1,000 population (2001 est.)
Death rate: 5.68 deaths/1,000 population (2001 est.)
Net migration rate: -8.87 migrant(s)/1,000 population (2001 est.)
Sex ratio:
at birth: 1.05 male(s)/female
under 15 years: 1.05 male(s)/female
15-64 years: 1.04 male(s)/female
65 years and over: 0.84 male(s)/female
total population: 1.03 male(s)/female (2001 est.)
Infant mortality rate: 24.27 deaths/1,000 live births (2001 est.)
Life expectancy at birth:
total population: 71.63 years
male: 68.97 years
female: 74.42 years (2001 est.)
Total fertility rate: 2.47 children born/woman (2001 est.)
HIV/AIDS - adult prevalence rate: 1.26% (1999 est.)
HIV/AIDS - people living with HIV/AIDS: 3,000 (1999 est.)
HIV/AIDS - deaths: 210 (1999 est.)
Nationality:
noun: Surinamer(s)
adjective: Surinamese
Ethnic groups: Hindustani (also known locally as "East Indians"; their ancestors emigrated from northern India in the latter part of the 19th century) 37%, Creole (mixed white and black) 31%, Javanese 15%, "Maroons" (their African ancestors were brought to the country in the 17th and 18th centuries as slaves and escaped to the interior) 10%, Amerindian 2%, Chinese 2%, white 1%, other 2%
Religions: Hindu 27.4%, Muslim 19.6%, Roman Catholic 22.8%, Protestant 25.2% (predominantly Moravian), indigenous beliefs 5%
Languages: Dutch (official), English (widely spoken), Sranang Tongo (Surinamese, sometimes called Taki-Taki, is native language of Creoles and much of the younger population and is lingua franca among others), Hindustani (a dialect of Hindi), Javanese
Literacy:
definition: age 15 and over can read and write
total population: 93%
male: 95%
female: 91% (1995 est.)

Government

Country name:
conventional long form: Republic of Suriname
conventional short form: Suriname
local long form: Republiek Suriname
local short form: Suriname
former: Netherlands Guiana, Dutch Guiana
Government type: constitutional democracy
Capital: Paramaribo
Administrative divisions: 10 districts (distrikten, singular - distrikt); Brokopondo, Commewijne, Coronie, Marowijne, Nickerie, Para, Paramaribo, Saramacca, Sipaliwini, Wanica
Independence: 25 November 1975 (from Netherlands)
National holiday: Independence Day, 25 November (1975)
Constitution: ratified 30 September 1987
Legal system: based on Dutch legal system incorporating French penal theory
Suffrage: 18 years of age; universal
Executive branch:
chief of state: President Runaldo Ronald VENETIAAN (since 12 August 2000); Vice President Jules Rattankoemar AJODHIA (since 12 August 2000); note - the president is both the chief of state and head of government
head of government: President Runaldo Ronald VENETIAAN (since 12 August 2000); Vice President Jules Rattankoemar AJODHIA (since 12 August 2000); note - the president is both the chief of state and head of government
cabinet: Cabinet of Ministers appointed by the president from among the members of the National Assembly
elections: president and vice president elected by the National Assembly or, if no presidential or vice presidential candidate receives a constitutional majority vote in the National Assembly after two votes,

Suriname (continued)

by the larger People's Assembly (869 representatives from the national, local, and regional councils), for five-year terms; election last held 6 May 2000 (next to be held NA May 2005)
note: widespread demonstrations during the summer of 1999 led to the calling of elections a year early
election results: Runaldo Ronald VENETIAAN elected president; percent of legislative vote - 72.5; National Assembly elected the president - Runaldo Ronald VENETIAAN (New Front) 37 votes, Rashied DOEKHIE (NDP) 10 votes
Legislative branch: unicameral National Assembly or Nationale Assemblee (51 seats; members are elected by popular vote to serve five-year terms)
elections: last held 5 May 2000 (next to be held NA May 2005)
election results: percent of vote by party - NA%; seats by party - NF 33, MC 10, DNP 2000 3, DA '91 2, PVF 2, PALU 1
note: widespread demonstrations during the summer of 1999 led to the calling of elections a year early
Judicial branch: Court of Justice (justices are nominated for life)
Political parties and leaders: Democratic Alternative '91 or DA '91 (a coalition of the Alternative Forum or AF and Party for Brotherhood and Unity in Politics or BEP, formed in January 1991) [S. RAMKHELAWAN]; Democratic National Platform 2000 or DNP 2000 (coalition of two parties, Democratic Party and Democrats of the 21st Century) [Jules WIJDENBOSCH]; Independent Progressive Democratic Alternative or OPDA [Joginder RAMKHILAWAN]; Millennium Combination or MC (a coalition of three parties, Democratic Alternative, Party for National Unity and Solidarity, and National Democratic Party) [leader NA]; National Democratic Party or NDP [Desire BOUTERSE]; Naya Kadam or NK [leader NA]; Party for Renewal and Democracy or BVD [Tjan GOBARDHAN]; Party of National Unity and Solidarity or KTPI [Willy SOEMITA]; Pertjaja Luhur [Paul SOMOHARDJO]; Progressive Workers' and Farm Laborers' Union or PALU [Ir Iwan KROLIS]; The New Front or NF (a coalition of four parties Suriname National Party or NPS, Progressive Reform Party or VHP, Suriname Labor Party or SPA, and Pertjaja Luhur) [Ronald R. VENETIAAN]; The Progressive Development Alliance (a combination of three parties, Renewed Progressive Party or HPP, Party of the Federation of Land Workers or PVF, and Suriname Progressive People's Party or PSV) [Harry KISOENSINGH]
Political pressure groups and leaders: General Liberation and Development Party or ABOP [Ronnie BRUNSWIJK]; Mandela Bushnegro Liberation Movement [Leendert ADAMS]; Tucayana Amazonica [Alex JUBITANA, Thomas SABAJO]; Union for Liberation and Democracy [Kofi AFONGPONG]
International organization participation: ACP, Caricom, ECLAC, FAO, G-77, IADB, IBRD, ICAO, ICFTU, ICRM, IDB, IFAD, IHO, ILO, IMF, IMO, Intelsat (nonsignatory user), Interpol, IOC, ITU, LAES, NAM, OAS, OIC, OPANAL, OPCW, PCA, UN, UNCTAD, UNESCO, UNIDO, UPU, WCL, WHO, WIPO, WMO, WTrO
Diplomatic representation in the US:
chief of mission: Ambassador (vacant)
chancery: Suite 460, 4301 Connecticut Avenue NW, Washington, DC 20008
telephone: [1] (202) 244-7488
FAX: [1] (202) 244-5878
consulate(s) general: Miami
Diplomatic representation from the US:
chief of mission: Ambassador Daniel A. JOHNSON
embassy: Dr. Sophie Redmondstraat 129, Paramaribo
mailing address: Department of State, 3390 Paramaribo Place, Washington, DC, 20521-3390
telephone: [597] 472900
FAX: [597] 420800
Flag description: five horizontal bands of green (top, double width), white, red (quadruple width), white, and green (double width); there is a large, yellow, five-pointed star centered in the red band

Economy

Economy - overview: The economy is dominated by the bauxite industry, which accounts for more than 15% of GDP and 70% of export earnings. After assuming power in the fall of 1996, the WIJDENBOSCH government ended the structural adjustment program of the previous government, claiming it was unfair to the poorer elements of society. Tax revenues fell as old taxes lapsed and the government failed to implement new tax alternatives. By the end of 1997, the allocation of new Dutch development funds was frozen as Surinamese Government relations with the Netherlands deteriorated. Economic growth slowed in 1998, with decline in the mining, construction, and utility sectors. Rampant government expenditures, poor tax collection, a bloated civil service, and reduced foreign aid in 1999 contributed to the fiscal deficit, estimated at 11% of GDP. The government sought to cover this deficit through monetary expansion, which led to a dramatic increase in inflation and exchange rate depreciation. Suriname's economic prospects for the medium term will depend on renewed commitment to responsible monetary and fiscal policies and to the introduction of structural reforms to liberalize markets and promote competition. The new government of Ronald VENETIAAN has begun an austerity program, raised taxes, and attempted to control spending. the exchange rate has responded by stabilizing. The Dutch Government has restarted the aid flow, which will allow Suriname to access international development financing.
GDP: purchasing power parity - $1.48 billion (1999 est.)
GDP - real growth rate: -1% (1999 est.)
GDP - per capita: purchasing power parity - $3,400 (1999 est.)
GDP - composition by sector:
agriculture: 13%
industry: 22%
services: 65% (1998 est.)
Population below poverty line: NA%
Household income or consumption by percentage share:
lowest 10%: NA%
highest 10%: NA%
Inflation rate (consumer prices): 78% (2000 est.)
Labor force: 100,000
Labor force - by occupation: agriculture NA%, industry NA%, services NA%
Unemployment rate: 20% (1997)
Budget:
revenues: $393 million
expenditures: $403 million, including capital expenditures of $34 million (1997 est.)
Industries: bauxite and gold mining, alumina production, lumbering, food processing, fishing
Industrial production growth rate: 6.5% (1994 est.)
Electricity - production: 1.937 billion kWh (1999)
Electricity - production by source:
fossil fuel: 25.92%
hydro: 74.08%
nuclear: 0%
other: 0% (1999)
Electricity - consumption: 1.801 billion kWh (1999)
Electricity - exports: 0 kWh (1999)
Electricity - imports: 0 kWh (1999)
Agriculture - products: paddy rice, bananas, palm kernels, coconuts, plantains, peanuts; beef, chickens; forest products; shrimp
Exports: $443 million (f.o.b., 1999)
Exports - commodities: alumina, crude oil, lumber, shrimp and fish, rice, bananas
Exports - partners: US 23%, Norway 19%, Netherlands 11%, France, Japan, UK (1999)
Imports: $525 million (f.o.b., 1999)
Imports - commodities: capital equipment, petroleum, foodstuffs, cotton, consumer goods
Imports - partners: US 35%, Netherlands 15%, Trinidad and Tobago 12%, Japan, UK, Brazil (1999)
Debt - external: $512 million (2000 est.)
Economic aid - recipient: Netherlands provided $37 million for project and program assistance, European Development Fund $4 million, Belgium $2 million (1998)
Currency: Surinamese guilder (SRG)
Currency code: SRG
Exchange rates: Surinamese guilders per US dollar - 2,178.50 (December 2000), 987.50 (December 1999), 401.00 (December 1998), 401.00 (December 1997), 401.26 (December 1996)
note: beginning in July 1994, the central bank midpoint exchange rate was unified and became market determined; during 1998, the exchange rate splintered into four distinct rates; in January 1999 the government floated the guilder, but subsequently fixed it when the black-market rate plunged; the government currently allows trading within a band of SRG 500 around the official rate
Fiscal year: calendar year

Suriname (continued)

Communications

Telephones - main lines in use: 64,000 (1997)
Telephones - mobile cellular: 4,090 (1997)
Telephone system:
general assessment: international facilities are good
domestic: microwave radio relay network
international: satellite earth stations - 2 Intelsat (Atlantic Ocean)
Radio broadcast stations: AM 4, FM 13, shortwave 1 (1998)
Radios: 300,000 (1997)
Television broadcast stations: 3 (plus seven repeaters) (2000)
Televisions: 63,000 (1997)
Internet country code: .sr
Internet Service Providers (ISPs): 2 (2000)
Internet users: 10,000 (2000)

Transportation

Railways:
total: 166 km (single track)
standard gauge: 80 km 1.435-m gauge
narrow gauge: 86 km 1.000-m gauge
note: Suriname railroads are not in operation (2000)
Highways:
total: 4,530 km
paved: 1,178 km
unpaved: 3,352 km (1996 est.)
Waterways: 1,200 km
note: most important means of transport; oceangoing vessels with drafts ranging up to 7 m can navigate many of the principal waterways
Ports and harbors: Albina, Moengo, New Nickerie, Paramaribo, Paranam, Wageningen
Merchant marine:
total: 3 ships (1,000 GRT or over) totaling 3,432 GRT/4,525 DWT
ships by type: cargo 1, container 1, petroleum tanker 1 (2000 est.)
Airports: 46 (2000 est.)
Airports - with paved runways:
total: 5
over 3,047 m: 1
914 to 1,523 m: 1
under 914 m: 3 (2000 est.)
Airports - with unpaved runways:
total: 41
1,524 to 2,437 m: 1
914 to 1,523 m: 5
under 914 m: 35 (2000 est.)

Military

Military branches: National Army (includes small Navy and Air Force elements), Civil Police
Military manpower - availability:
males age 15-49: 121,656 (2001 est.)
Military manpower - fit for military service:
males age 15-49: 71,344 (2001 est.)
Military expenditures - dollar figure: $8.5 million (FY97 est.)
Military expenditures - percent of GDP: 1.6% (FY97 est.)

Transnational Issues

Disputes - international: area disputed by French Guiana between Riviere Litani and Riviere Marouini (both headwaters of the Lawa); area disputed by Guyana between New (Upper Courantyne) and Courantyne/Koetari [Kutari] rivers (all headwaters of the Courantyne)
Illicit drugs: transshipment point for South American drugs destined for Europe and Brazil; transshipment point for arms-for-drugs dealing

Svalbard
(territory of Norway)

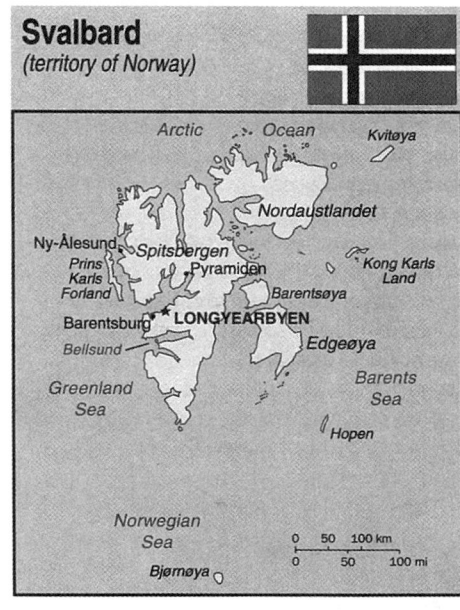

Introduction

Background: First discovered by the Norwegians in the 12th century, the islands served as an international whaling base during the 17th and 18th centuries. Norway's sovereignty was recognized in 1920; five years later it officially took over the territory.

Geography

Location: Northern Europe, islands between the Arctic Ocean, Barents Sea, Greenland Sea, and Norwegian Sea, north of Norway
Geographic coordinates: 78 00 N, 20 00 E
Map references: Arctic Region
Area:
total: 62,049 sq km
land: 62,049 sq km
water: 0 sq km
note: includes Spitsbergen and Bjornoya (Bear Island)
Area - comparative: slightly smaller than West Virginia
Land boundaries: 0 km
Coastline: 3,587 km
Maritime claims:
exclusive fishing zone: 200 NM unilaterally claimed by Norway but not recognized by Russia
territorial sea: 4 NM
Climate: arctic, tempered by warm North Atlantic Current; cool summers, cold winters; North Atlantic Current flows along west and north coasts of Spitsbergen, keeping water open and navigable most of the year
Terrain: wild, rugged mountains; much of high land ice covered; west coast clear of ice about one-half of the year; fjords along west and north coasts
Elevation extremes:
lowest point: Arctic Ocean 0 m
highest point: Newtontoppen 1,717 m
Natural resources: coal, copper, iron ore, phosphate, zinc, wildlife, fish

Svalbard (continued)

Land use:
arable land: 0%
permanent crops: 0%
permanent pastures: 0%
forests and woodland: 0%
other: 100% (no trees, and the only bushes are crowberry and cloudberry)
Irrigated land: NA sq km
Natural hazards: ice floes often block up the entrance to Bellsund (a transit point for coal export) on the west coast and occasionally make parts of the northeastern coast inaccessible to maritime traffic
Environment - current issues: NA
Geography - note: northernmost part of the Kingdom of Norway; consists of nine main islands; glaciers and snowfields cover 60% of the total area

People

Population: 2,332 (July 2001 est.)
Age structure:
0-14 years: NA%
15-64 years: NA%
65 years and over: NA%
Population growth rate: -3.55% (2001 est.)
Birth rate: NA births/1,000 population
Death rate: NA deaths/1,000 population
Net migration rate: NA migrant(s)/1,000 population
Infant mortality rate: NA deaths/1,000 live births
Life expectancy at birth:
total population: NA years
male: NA years
female: NA years
Total fertility rate: NA children born/woman
HIV/AIDS - adult prevalence rate: 0% (2001)
HIV/AIDS - people living with HIV/AIDS: 0 (2001)
HIV/AIDS - deaths: 0 (2001)
Ethnic groups: Norwegian 55.4%, Russian and Ukrainian 44.3%, other 0.3% (1998)
Languages: Russian, Norwegian

Government

Country name:
conventional long form: none
conventional short form: Svalbard (sometimes referred to as Spitzbergen)
Dependency status: territory of Norway; administered by the Ministry of Industry, Oslo, through a governor (sysselmann) residing in Longyearbyen, Spitsbergen; by treaty (9 February 1920) sovereignty was given to Norway
Government type: NA
Capital: Longyearbyen
Independence: none (territory of Norway)
National holiday: NA
Legal system: NA
Executive branch:
chief of state: King HARALD V of Norway (since 17 January 1991)
head of government: Governor Morten RUUD (since NA November 1998) and Assistant Governor Odd Redar HUMLEGAARD (since NA)
elections: none; the monarch is hereditary; governor and assistant governor responsible to the Polar Department of the Ministry of Justice
International organization participation: none
Flag description: the flag of Norway is used

Economy

Economy - overview: Coal mining is the major economic activity on Svalbard. The treaty of 9 February 1920 gives the 41 signatories equal rights to exploit mineral deposits, subject to Norwegian regulation. Although US, UK, Dutch, and Swedish coal companies have mined in the past, the only companies still mining are Norwegian and Russian. The settlements on Svalbard are essentially company towns. The Norwegian state-owned coal company employs nearly 60% of the Norwegian population on the island, runs many of the local services, and provides most of the local infrastructure. There is also some trapping of seal, polar bear, fox, and walrus.
GDP: purchasing power parity - $NA
GDP - real growth rate: NA%
GDP - per capita: purchasing power parity - $NA
Population below poverty line: NA%
Household income or consumption by percentage share:
lowest 10%: NA%
highest 10%: NA%
Inflation rate (consumer prices): NA%
Labor force: NA
Budget:
revenues: $11.5 million
expenditures: $11.5 million, including capital expenditures of $NA (1998 est.)
Industrial production growth rate: NA%
Electricity - production: NA kWh
Electricity - production by source:
fossil fuel: NA%
hydro: NA%
nuclear: NA%
other: NA%
Electricity - consumption: NA kWh
Exports: $NA
Imports: $NA
Economic aid - recipient: $8.2 million from Norway (1998)
Currency: Norwegian krone (NOK)
Currency code: NOK
Exchange rates: Norwegian kroner per US dollar - 8.7784 (January 2001), 8.8018 (2000), 7.7992 (1999), 7.5451 (1998), 7.0734 (1997), 6.4498 (1996)

Communications

Telephones - main lines in use: NA
Telephones - mobile cellular: NA
Telephone system:
general assessment: probably adequate
domestic: local telephone service
international: satellite earth station - 1 of unknown type (for communication with Norwegian mainland only)
Radio broadcast stations: AM 1, FM 1 (plus 2 repeaters), shortwave 0 (1998)
Radios: NA
Television broadcast stations: NA
Televisions: NA
Internet country code: .sj
Internet Service Providers (ISPs): 13 (Svalbard and Jan Mayen) (2000)
Internet users: NA

Transportation

Railways: 0 km
Highways:
total: NA km
paved: NA km
unpaved: NA km
Waterways: none
Ports and harbors: Barentsburg, Longyearbyen, Ny-Alesund, Pyramiden
Merchant marine: none (2000 est.)
Airports: 4 (2000 est.)
Airports - with paved runways:
total: 1
1,524 to 2,437 m: 1 (2000 est.)
Airports - with unpaved runways:
total: 3
under 914 m: 3 (2000 est.)

Military

Military - note: demilitarized by treaty (9 February 1920)

Transnational Issues

Disputes - international: focus of a maritime boundary dispute between Norway and Russia

Swaziland

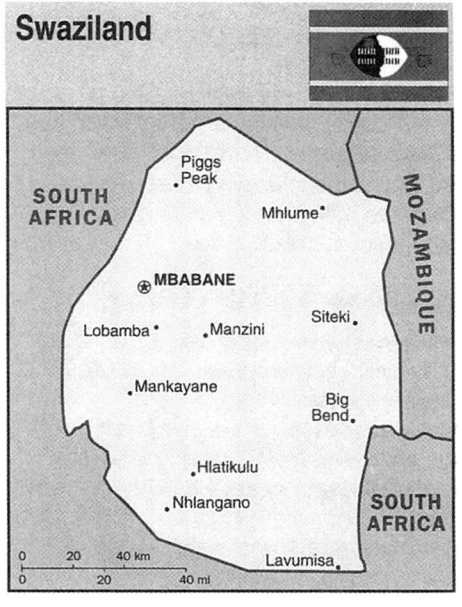

Introduction

Background: Autonomy for the Swazis of southern Africa was guaranteed by the British in the late 19th century; independence was granted 1968. Student and labor unrest during the 1990s have pressured the monarchy (one of the oldest on the continent) to grudgingly allow political reform and greater democracy.

Geography

Location: Southern Africa, between Mozambique and South Africa
Geographic coordinates: 26 30 S, 31 30 E
Map references: Africa
Area:
total: 17,363 sq km
land: 17,203 sq km
water: 160 sq km
Area - comparative: slightly smaller than New Jersey
Land boundaries:
total: 535 km
border countries: Mozambique 105 km, South Africa 430 km
Coastline: 0 km (landlocked)
Maritime claims: none (landlocked)
Climate: varies from tropical to near temperate
Terrain: mostly mountains and hills; some moderately sloping plains
Elevation extremes:
lowest point: Great Usutu River 21 m
highest point: Emlembe 1,862 m
Natural resources: asbestos, coal, clay, cassiterite, hydropower, forests, small gold and diamond deposits, quarry stone, and talc
Land use:
arable land: 11%
permanent crops: 0%
permanent pastures: 62%
forests and woodland: 7%
other: 20% (1993 est.)
Irrigated land: 670 sq km (1993 est.)
Natural hazards: NA
Environment - current issues: limited supplies of potable water; wildlife populations being depleted because of excessive hunting; overgrazing; soil degradation; soil erosion
Environment - international agreements:
party to: Biodiversity, Climate Change, Endangered Species, Marine Dumping, Nuclear Test Ban, Ozone Layer Protection, Ship Pollution
signed, but not ratified: Desertification, Law of the Sea
Geography - note: landlocked; almost completely surrounded by South Africa

People

Population: 1,104,343
note: estimates for this country explicitly take into account the effects of excess mortality due to AIDS; this can result in lower life expectancy, higher infant mortality and death rates, lower population and growth rates, and changes in the distribution of population by age and sex than would otherwise be expected (July 2001 est.)
Age structure:
0-14 years: 45.53% (male 250,327; female 252,479)
15-64 years: 51.88% (male 276,186; female 296,728)
65 years and over: 2.59% (male 11,687; female 16,936) (2001 est.)
Population growth rate: 1.83% (2001 est.)
Birth rate: 40.12 births/1,000 population (2001 est.)
Death rate: 21.84 deaths/1,000 population (2001 est.)
Net migration rate: 0 migrant(s)/1,000 population (2001 est.)
Sex ratio:
at birth: 1.03 male(s)/female
under 15 years: 0.99 male(s)/female
15-64 years: 0.93 male(s)/female
65 years and over: 0.69 male(s)/female
total population: 0.95 male(s)/female (2001 est.)
Infant mortality rate: 109.19 deaths/1,000 live births (2001 est.)
Life expectancy at birth:
total population: 38.62 years
male: 37.86 years
female: 39.4 years (2001 est.)
Total fertility rate: 5.82 children born/woman (2001 est.)
HIV/AIDS - adult prevalence rate: 25.25% (1999 est.)
HIV/AIDS - people living with HIV/AIDS: 130,000 (1999 est.)
HIV/AIDS - deaths: 7,100 (1999 est.)
Nationality:
noun: Swazi(s)
adjective: Swazi
Ethnic groups: African 97%, European 3%
Religions: Protestant 55%, Muslim 10%, Roman Catholic 5%, indigenous beliefs 30%
Languages: English (official, government business conducted in English), siSwati (official)
Literacy:
definition: age 15 and over can read and write
total population: 76.7%
male: 78%
female: 75.6% (1995 est.)

Government

Country name:
conventional long form: Kingdom of Swaziland
conventional short form: Swaziland
Government type: monarchy; independent member of Commonwealth
Capital: Mbabane; note - Lobamba is the royal and legislative capital
Administrative divisions: 4 districts; Hhohho, Lubombo, Manzini, Shiselweni
Independence: 6 September 1968 (from UK)
National holiday: Independence Day, 6 September (1968)
Constitution: none; constitution of 6 September 1968 was suspended 12 April 1973; a new constitution was promulgated 13 October 1978, but was not formally presented to the people; since then a few more outlines for a constitution have been compiled under the Constitutional Review Commission (CRC), but so far none have been accepted
Legal system: based on South African Roman-Dutch law in statutory courts and Swazi traditional law and custom in traditional courts; has not accepted compulsory ICJ jurisdiction
Suffrage: 18 years of age
Executive branch:
chief of state: King MSWATI III (since 25 April 1986)
head of government: Prime Minister Sibusiso Barnabas DLAMINI (since 9 August 1996)
cabinet: Cabinet recommended by the prime minister and confirmed by the monarch
elections: none; the monarch is hereditary; prime minister appointed by the monarch
Legislative branch: bicameral Parliament or Libandla, an advisory body, consists of the Senate (30 seats - 10 appointed by the House of Assembly and 20 appointed by the monarch; members serve five-year terms) and the House of Assembly (65 seats - 10 appointed by the monarch and 55 elected by popular vote; members serve five-year terms)
elections: House of Assembly - last held 16 and 24 October 1998 (next to be held NA 2003)
election results: House of Assembly - balloting is done on a nonparty basis; candidates for election are nominated by the local council of each constituency and for each constituency the three candidates with the most votes in the first round of voting are narrowed to a single winner by a second round
Judicial branch: High Court; Court of Appeal; judges for both courts are appointed by the monarch

Swaziland (continued)

Political parties and leaders: Imbokodvo National Movement or INM [leader NA]; Ngwane National Libertatory Congress or NNLC [Obed DLAMINI, president]; People's United Democratic Movement or PUDEMO [Mario MASUKU, president]; Swaziland National Front or SWANAFRO [Elmond SHONGWE, president]; Swaziland Progressive Party or SPP [J. J. NQUKU, president]; Swaziland United Front or SUF [Matsapa SHONGWE, leader]
note: political parties are banned by the constitution promulgated on 13 October 1978; illegal parties are prohibited from holding large public gatherings; the organizations listed are political associations
Political pressure groups and leaders: NA
International organization participation: ACP, AfDB, C, CCC, ECA, FAO, G-77, IBRD, ICAO, ICFTU, ICRM, IDA, IFAD, IFC, IFRCS, ILO, IMF, Intelsat, Interpol, IOC, ITU, NAM, OAU, OPCW, SACU, SADC, UN, UNCTAD, UNESCO, UNIDO, UPU, WHO, WIPO, WMO, WToO, WTrO
Diplomatic representation in the US:
chief of mission: Ambassador Mary Madzandza KANYA
chancery: 3400 International Drive NW, Washington, DC 20008
telephone: [1] (202) 362-6683
FAX: [1] (202) 244-8059
Diplomatic representation from the US:
chief of mission: Ambassador Gregory L. JOHNSON
embassy: Central Bank Building, Warner Street, Mbabane
mailing address: P. O. Box 199, Mbabane
telephone: [268] 404-6441 through 404-6445
FAX: [268] 404-5959
Flag description: three horizontal bands of blue (top), red (triple width), and blue; the red band is edged in yellow; centered in the red band is a large black and white shield covering two spears and a staff decorated with feather tassels, all placed horizontally

Economy

Economy - overview: In this small landlocked economy, subsistence agriculture occupies more than 60% of the population. Manufacturing features a number of agroprocessing factories. Mining has declined in importance in recent years: diamond mines have shut down because of the depletion of easily accessible reserves; high-grade iron ore deposits were depleted by 1978; and health concerns have cut world demand for asbestos. Exports of soft drink concentrate, sugar, and wood pulp are the main earners of hard currency. Surrounded by South Africa, except for a short border with Mozambique, Swaziland is heavily dependent on South Africa from which it receives four-fifths of its imports and to which it sends two-thirds of its exports. Remittances from the Southern African Customs Union and Swazi workers in South African mines substantially supplement domestically earned income. The government is trying to improve the atmosphere for foreign investment. Overgrazing, soil depletion, drought, and sometimes floods persist as problems for the future. Prospects for 2001 are strengthened by government millennium projects for a new convention center, additional hotels, an amusement park, a new airport, and stepped-up roadbuilding and factory construction plans.
GDP: purchasing power parity - $4.4 billion (2000 est.)
GDP - real growth rate: 2.4% (2000 est.)
GDP - per capita: purchasing power parity - $4,000 (2000 est.)
GDP - composition by sector:
agriculture: 10%
industry: 46%
services: 44% (1998 est.)
Population below poverty line: NA%
Household income or consumption by percentage share:
lowest 10%: NA%
highest 10%: NA%
Inflation rate (consumer prices): 6.4% (2000 est.)
Labor force: NA
Labor force - by occupation: private sector 70%, public sector 30%
Unemployment rate: 22% (1995 est.)
Budget:
revenues: $400 million
expenditures: $450 million, including capital expenditures of $115 million (FY96/97)
Industries: mining (coal and asbestos), wood pulp, sugar, soft drink concentrates
Industrial production growth rate: 3.7% (FY95/96)
Electricity - production: 375 million kWh (1999)
Electricity - production by source:
fossil fuel: 53.33%
hydro: 46.67%
nuclear: 0%
other: 0% (1999)
Electricity - consumption: 198 million kWh (1999)
Electricity - exports: 852 million kWh (1999)
Electricity - imports: 701 million kWh
note: supplied by South Africa (1999)
Agriculture - products: sugarcane, cotton, corn, tobacco, rice, citrus, pineapples, sorghum, peanuts; cattle, goats, sheep
Exports: $881 million (f.o.b., 2000)
Exports - commodities: soft drink concentrates, sugar, wood pulp, cotton yarn, refrigerators, citrus and canned fruit
Exports - partners: South Africa 65%, EU 12%, Mozambique 11%, US 5% (1998)
Imports: $928 million (f.o.b., 2000)
Imports - commodities: motor vehicles, machinery, transport equipment, foodstuffs, petroleum products, chemicals
Imports - partners: South Africa 84%, EU 5%, Japan 2%, Singapore 2% (1998)
Debt - external: $281 million (2000 est.)
Economic aid - recipient: $55 million (1995)
Currency: lilangeni (SZL)
Currency code: SZL
Exchange rates: emalangeni per US dollar - 7.7803 (January 2001), 6.9056 (2000), 6.1087 (1999), 5.4807 (1998), 4.6032 (1997), 4.2706 (1996); note - the Swazi lilangeni is at par with the South African rand; emalangeni is the plural form of lilangeni
Fiscal year: 1 April - 31 March

Communications

Telephones - main lines in use: 33,500 (2000)
Telephones - mobile cellular: 30,000 (2000)
Telephone system:
general assessment: not a modern system
domestic: system consists of carrier-equipped, open-wire lines and low-capacity, microwave radio relay
international: satellite earth station - 1 Intelsat (Atlantic Ocean)
Radio broadcast stations: AM 7, FM 6 (2000)
Radios: 155,000 (1997)
Television broadcast stations: 10 (2000)
Televisions: 21,000 (1997)
Internet country code: .sz
Internet Service Providers (ISPs): 3 (2000)
Internet users: 4,000 (2000)

Transportation

Railways:
total: 297 km; note - includes 71 km which are not in use
narrow gauge: 297 km 1.067-m gauge
Highways:
total: 2,896 km (1997 est.)
paved: NA km
unpaved: NA km
Waterways: none
Ports and harbors: none
Airports: 18 (2000 est.)
Airports - with paved runways:
total: 1
2,438 to 3,047 m: 1 (2000 est.)
Airports - with unpaved runways:
total: 17
914 to 1,523 m: 7
under 914 m: 10 (2000 est.)

Military

Military branches: Umbutfo Swaziland Defense Force (Army), Royal Swaziland Police Force
Military manpower - availability:
males age 15-49: 248,084 (2001 est.)
Military manpower - fit for military service:
males age 15-49: 143,618 (2001 est.)
Military expenditures - dollar figure: $19.198 million (FY00/01)
Military expenditures - percent of GDP: 4.75% (FY00/01)

Swaziland (continued)

Transnational Issues

Disputes - international: Swaziland has asked South Africa to open negotiations on reincorporating some nearby South African territories that are populated by ethnic Swazis or that were long ago part of the Swazi Kingdom

Sweden

Introduction

Background: A military power during the 17th century, Sweden has not participated in any war in almost two centuries. An armed neutrality was preserved in both World Wars. Sweden's long-successful economic formula of a capitalist system interlarded with substantial welfare elements has recently been undermined by high unemployment, rising maintenance costs, and a declining position in world markets. Indecision over the country's role in the political and economic integration of Europe caused Sweden not to join the EU until 1995, and to forgo the introduction of the euro in 1999.

Geography

Location: Northern Europe, bordering the Baltic Sea, Gulf of Bothnia, Kattegat, and Skagerrak, between Finland and Norway
Geographic coordinates: 62 00 N, 15 00 E
Map references: Europe
Area:
total: 449,964 sq km
land: 410,934 sq km
water: 39,030 sq km
Area - comparative: slightly larger than California
Land boundaries:
total: 2,205 km
border countries: Finland 586 km, Norway 1,619 km
Coastline: 3,218 km
Maritime claims:
continental shelf: 200-m depth or to the depth of exploitation
exclusive economic zone: agreed boundaries or midlines
territorial sea: 12 NM (adjustments made to return a portion of straits to high seas)
Climate: temperate in south with cold, cloudy winters and cool, partly cloudy summers; subarctic in north
Terrain: mostly flat or gently rolling lowlands; mountains in west
Elevation extremes:
lowest point: Baltic Sea 0 m
highest point: Kebnekaise 2,111 m
Natural resources: zinc, iron ore, lead, copper, silver, timber, uranium, hydropower
Land use:
arable land: 7%
permanent crops: 0%
permanent pastures: 1%
forests and woodland: 68%
other: 24% (1993 est.)
Irrigated land: 1,150 sq km (1993 est.)
Natural hazards: ice floes in the surrounding waters, especially in the Gulf of Bothnia, can interfere with maritime traffic
Environment - current issues: acid rain damaging soils and lakes; pollution of the North Sea and the Baltic Sea
Environment - international agreements:
party to: Air Pollution, Air Pollution-Nitrogen Oxides, Air Pollution-Persistent Organic Pollutants, Air Pollution-Sulphur 85, Air Pollution-Sulphur 94, Air Pollution-Volatile Organic Compounds, Antarctic-Environmental Protocol, Antarctic-Marine Living Resources, Antarctic Treaty, Biodiversity, Climate Change, Desertification, Endangered Species, Environmental Modification, Hazardous Wastes, Law of the Sea, Marine Dumping, Nuclear Test Ban, Ozone Layer Protection, Ship Pollution, Tropical Timber 83, Tropical Timber 94, Wetlands, Whaling
signed, but not ratified: Climate Change-Kyoto Protocol
Geography - note: strategic location along Danish Straits linking Baltic and North Seas

People

Population: 8,875,053 (July 2001 est.)
Age structure:
0-14 years: 18.19% (male 828,308; female 786,353)
15-64 years: 64.53% (male 2,911,949; female 2,814,730)
65 years and over: 17.28% (male 649,296; female 884,417) (2001 est.)
Population growth rate: 0.02% (2001 est.)

Sweden (continued)

Birth rate: 9.91 births/1,000 population (2001 est.)
Death rate: 10.61 deaths/1,000 population (2001 est.)
Net migration rate: 0.91 migrant(s)/1,000 population (2001 est.)
Sex ratio:
at birth: 1.06 male(s)/female
under 15 years: 1.05 male(s)/female
15-64 years: 1.03 male(s)/female
65 years and over: 0.73 male(s)/female
total population: 0.98 male(s)/female (2001 est.)
Infant mortality rate: 3.47 deaths/1,000 live births (2001 est.)
Life expectancy at birth:
total population: 79.71 years
male: 77.07 years
female: 82.5 years (2001 est.)
Total fertility rate: 1.53 children born/woman (2001 est.)
HIV/AIDS - adult prevalence rate: 0.08% (1999 est.)
HIV/AIDS - people living with HIV/AIDS: 3,000 (1999 est.)
HIV/AIDS - deaths: less than 100 (1999 est.)
Nationality:
noun: Swede(s)
adjective: Swedish
Ethnic groups: indigenous population: Swedes and Finnish and Sami minorities; foreign-born or first-generation immigrants: Finns, Yugoslavs, Danes, Norwegians, Greeks, Turks
Religions: Lutheran 87%, Roman Catholic, Orthodox, Baptist, Muslim, Jewish, Buddhist
Languages: Swedish
note: small Lapp- and Finnish-speaking minorities
Literacy:
definition: age 15 and over can read and write
total population: 99% (1979 est.)
male: NA%
female: NA%

Government

Country name:
conventional long form: Kingdom of Sweden
conventional short form: Sweden
local long form: Konungariket Sverige
local short form: Sverige
Government type: constitutional monarchy
Capital: Stockholm
Administrative divisions: 21 counties (lan, singular and plural); Blekinge, Dalarnas, Gavleborgs, Gotlands, Hallands, Jamtlands, Jonkopings, Kalmar, Kronobergs, Norrbottens, Orebro, Ostergotlands, Skane, Sodermanlands, Stockholms, Uppsala, Varmlands, Vasterbottens, Vasternorrlands, Vastmanlands, Vastra Gotalands
Independence: 6 June 1523 (Gustav VASA elected king)
National holiday: Flag Day, 6 June
Constitution: 1 January 1975
Legal system: civil law system influenced by customary law; accepts compulsory ICJ jurisdiction, with reservations
Suffrage: 18 years of age; universal
Executive branch:
chief of state: King CARL XVI GUSTAF (since 19 September 1973); Heir Apparent Princess VICTORIA Ingrid Alice Desiree, daughter of the monarch (born 14 July 1977)
head of government: Prime Minister Goran PERSSON (since 21 March 1996)
cabinet: Cabinet appointed by the prime minister
elections: the monarch is hereditary; prime minister elected by the Parliament; election last held NA September 1998 (next to be held NA 2002)
election results: Goran PERSSON reelected prime minister with 131 out of 349 votes
Legislative branch: unicameral Parliament or Riksdag (349 seats; members are elected by popular vote on a proportional representation basis to serve four-year terms)
elections: last held 20 September 1998 (next to be held NA September 2002)
election results: percent of vote by party - Social Democrats 36.5%, Moderates 22.7%, Left Party 12%, Christian Democrats 11.8%, Center Party 5.1%, Liberal Party 4.7%, Greens 4.5%; seats by party - Social Democrats 131, Moderates 82, Left Party 43, Christian Democrats 42, Center Party 18, Liberal Party 17, Greens 16
Judicial branch: Supreme Court or Hogsta Domstolen (judges are appointed by the prime minister and the cabinet)
Political parties and leaders: Center Party [Lennart DALEUS]; Christian Democratic Party [Alf SVENSSON]; Communist Workers' Party [Rolf HAGEL]; Green Party [no formal leader but party spokesperson is Briger SCHLAUG]; Left Party or VP (formerly Communist) [Gudrun SCHYMAN]; Liberal People's Party [Lars LEIJONBORG]; Moderate Party (conservative) [Bo LUNDGREN]; New Democracy Party [Vivianne FRANZEN]; Social Democratic Party [Goran PERSSON]
Political pressure groups and leaders: NA
International organization participation: AfDB, AsDB, Australia Group, BIS, CBSS, CCC, CE, CERN, EAPC, EBRD, ECE, EIB, ESA, EU, FAO, G- 6, G- 9, G-10, IADB, IAEA, IBRD, ICAO, ICC, ICFTU, ICRM, IDA, IEA, IFAD, IFC, IFRCS, IHO, ILO, IMF, IMO, Inmarsat, Intelsat, Interpol, IOC, IOM, ISO, ITU, MINURSO, NAM (guest), NC, NEA, NIB, NSG, OAS (observer), OECD, OPCW, OSCE, PCA, PFP, UN, UNCTAD, UNESCO, UNHCR, UNIDO, UNIKOM, UNITAR, UNMEE, UNMIBH, UNMIK, UNMOGIP, UNMOP, UNOMIG, UNTAET, UNTSO, UPU, WEU (observer), WFTU, WHO, WIPO, WMO, WTrO, ZC
Diplomatic representation in the US:
chief of mission: Ambassador Jan ELIASSON
chancery: 1501 M Street NW, Washington, DC 20005-1702
telephone: [1] (202) 467-2600
FAX: [1] (202) 467-2699
consulate(s) general: Los Angeles and New York
Diplomatic representation from the US:
chief of mission: Ambassador Lyndon Lowell OLSON, Jr.
embassy: Dag Hammarskjolds VAG 31, SE-11589 Stockholm
mailing address: American Embassy Stockholm, Department of State, Washington, DC 20521-5750 (pouch)
telephone: [46] (8) 783 53 00
FAX: [46] (8) 661 19 64
Flag description: blue with a yellow cross that extends to the edges of the flag; the vertical part of the cross is shifted to the hoist side in the style of the Dannebrog (Danish flag)

Economy

Economy - overview: Aided by peace and neutrality for the whole twentieth century, Sweden has achieved an enviable standard of living under a mixed system of high-tech capitalism and extensive welfare benefits. It has a modern distribution system, excellent internal and external communications, and a skilled labor force. Timber, hydropower, and iron ore constitute the resource base of an economy heavily oriented toward foreign trade. Privately owned firms account for about 90% of industrial output, of which the engineering sector accounts for 50% of output and exports. Agriculture accounts for only 2% of GDP and 2% of the jobs. In recent years, however, this extraordinarily favorable picture has been somewhat clouded by budgetary difficulties, high unemployment, and a gradual loss of competitiveness in international markets. Sweden has harmonized its economic policies with those of the EU, which it joined at the start of 1995. GDP growth is forecast for 4% in 2001.
GDP: purchasing power parity - $197 billion (2000 est.)
GDP - real growth rate: 4.3% (2000 est.)
GDP - per capita: purchasing power parity - $22,200 (2000 est.)
GDP - composition by sector:
agriculture: 2.2%
industry: 27.9%
services: 69.9% (1999)
Population below poverty line: NA%
Household income or consumption by percentage share:
lowest 10%: 3.7%
highest 10%: 20.1% (1992)
Inflation rate (consumer prices): 1.2% (2000 est.)
Labor force: 4.4 million (2000 est.)
Labor force - by occupation: agriculture 2%, industry 24%, services 74% (2000 est.)
Unemployment rate: 6% (2000 est.)
Budget:
revenues: $133 billion
expenditures: $125.2 billion, including capital expenditures of $NA (2000 est.)

Sweden (continued)

Industries: iron and steel, precision equipment (bearings, radio and telephone parts, armaments), wood pulp and paper products, processed foods, motor vehicles
Industrial production growth rate: 7% (2000 est.)
Electricity - production: 146.633 billion kWh (1999)
Electricity - production by source:
fossil fuel: 5.53%
hydro: 47.24%
nuclear: 45.42%
other: 1.81% (1999)
Electricity - consumption: 128.819 billion kWh (1999)
Electricity - exports: 15.9 billion kWh (1999)
Electricity - imports: 8.35 billion kWh (1999)
Agriculture - products: grains, sugar beets, potatoes; meat, milk
Exports: $95.5 billion (f.o.b., 2000)
Exports - commodities: machinery 35%, motor vehicles, paper products, pulp and wood, iron and steel products, chemicals
Exports - partners: EU 55% (Germany 11%, UK 10%, Denmark 6%, Finland 5%, France 5%), US 9%, Norway 8% (1999)
Imports: $80 billion (f.o.b., 2000)
Imports - commodities: machinery, petroleum and petroleum products, chemicals, motor vehicles, iron and steel; foodstuffs, clothing
Imports - partners: EU 67% (Germany 18%, UK 10%, Denmark 7%, France 6%), Norway 8%, US 6% (1999)
Debt - external: $66.5 billion (1994)
Economic aid - donor: ODA, $1.7 billion (1997)
Currency: Swedish krona (SEK)
Currency code: SEK
Exchange rates: Swedish kronor per US dollar - 9.4669 (January 2001), 9.1622 (2000), 8.2624 (1999), 7.9499 (1998), 7.6349 (1997), 6.7060 (1996)
Fiscal year: calendar year

Communications

Telephones - main lines in use: 6.017 million (December 1998)
Telephones - mobile cellular: 3.835 million (October 1998)
Telephone system:
general assessment: excellent domestic and international facilities; automatic system
domestic: coaxial and multiconductor cables carry most of the voice traffic; parallel microwave radio relay systems carry some additional telephone channels
international: 5 submarine coaxial cables; satellite earth stations - 1 Intelsat (Atlantic Ocean), 1 Eutelsat, and 1 Inmarsat (Atlantic and Indian Ocean regions); note - Sweden shares the Inmarsat earth station with the other Nordic countries (Denmark, Finland, Iceland, and Norway)
Radio broadcast stations: AM 1, FM 265, shortwave 1 (1998)
Radios: 8.25 million (1997)
Television broadcast stations: 169 (plus 1,299 repeaters) (1995)
Televisions: 4.6 million (1997)
Internet country code: .se
Internet Service Providers (ISPs): 29 (2000)
Internet users: 4.5 million (2000)

Transportation

Railways:
total: 12,821 km (includes 3,594 km of privately owned railways)
standard gauge: 12,821 km 1.435-m gauge (7,918 km electrified and 1,152 km double track) (1998)
Highways:
total: 210,907 km
paved: 163,453 km (including 1,439 km of expressways)
unpaved: 47,454 km (1998 est.)
Waterways: 2,052 km
note: navigable for small steamers and barges
Pipelines: natural gas 84 km
Ports and harbors: Gavle, Goteborg, Halmstad, Helsingborg, Hudiksvall, Kalmar, Karlshamn, Malmo, Solvesborg, Stockholm, Sundsvall
Merchant marine:
total: 167 ships (1,000 GRT or over) totaling 2,205,370 GRT/1,663,091 DWT
ships by type: bulk 5, cargo 28, chemical tanker 31, combination ore/oil 4, liquefied gas 1, passenger 1, petroleum tanker 29, railcar carrier 1, roll on/roll off 40, short-sea passenger 4, specialized tanker 6, vehicle carrier 17 (2000 est.)
Airports: 255 (2000 est.)
Airports - with paved runways:
total: 147
over 3,047 m: 3
2,438 to 3,047 m: 11
1,524 to 2,437 m: 80
914 to 1,523 m: 28
under 914 m: 25 (2000 est.)
Airports - with unpaved runways:
total: 108
914 to 1,523 m: 5
under 914 m: 103 (2000 est.)
Heliports: 1 (2000 est.)

Military

Military branches: Swedish Army, Royal Swedish Navy, Swedish Air Force
Military manpower - military age: 19 years of age
Military manpower - availability:
males age 15-49: 2,062,566 (2001 est.)
Military manpower - fit for military service:
males age 15-49: 1,803,995 (2001 est.)
Military manpower - reaching military age annually:
males: 51,506 (2001 est.)
Military expenditures - dollar figure: $5 billion (FY98)
Military expenditures - percent of GDP: 2.1% (FY98)

Transnational Issues

Disputes - international: none

Switzerland

Introduction

Background: Switzerland's independence and neutrality have long been honored by the major European powers and Switzerland was not involved in either of the two World Wars. The political and economic integration of Europe over the past half century, as well as Switzerland's role in many UN and international organizations, may be rendering obsolete the country's concern for neutrality.

Geography

Location: Central Europe, east of France, north of Italy
Geographic coordinates: 47 00 N, 8 00 E
Map references: Europe
Area:
total: 41,290 sq km
land: 39,770 sq km
water: 1,520 sq km
Area - comparative: slightly less than twice the size of New Jersey
Land boundaries:
total: 1,852 km
border countries: Austria 164 km, France 573 km, Italy 740 km, Liechtenstein 41 km, Germany 334 km
Coastline: 0 km (landlocked)
Maritime claims: none (landlocked)
Climate: temperate, but varies with altitude; cold, cloudy, rainy/snowy winters; cool to warm, cloudy, humid summers with occasional showers
Terrain: mostly mountains (Alps in south, Jura in northwest) with a central plateau of rolling hills, plains, and large lakes
Elevation extremes:
lowest point: Lake Maggiore 195 m
highest point: Dufourspitze 4,634 m
Natural resources: hydropower potential, timber, salt
Land use:
arable land: 10%
permanent crops: 2%
permanent pastures: 28%
forests and woodland: 32%
other: 28% (1993 est.)
Irrigated land: 250 sq km (1993 est.)
Natural hazards: avalanches, landslides, flash floods
Environment - current issues: air pollution from vehicle emissions and open-air burning; acid rain; water pollution from increased use of agricultural fertilizers; loss of biodiversity
Environment - international agreements:
party to: Air Pollution, Air Pollution-Nitrogen Oxides, Air Pollution-Persistent Organic Pollutants, Air Pollution-Sulphur 85, Air Pollution-Sulphur 94, Air Pollution-Volatile Organic Compounds, Antarctic Treaty, Biodiversity, Climate Change, Desertification, Endangered Species, Environmental Modification, Hazardous Wastes, Marine Dumping, Marine Life Conservation, Nuclear Test Ban, Ozone Layer Protection, Ship Pollution, Tropical Timber 83, Tropical Timber 94, Wetlands, Whaling
signed, but not ratified: Antarctic-Environmental Protocol, Climate Change-Kyoto Protocol, Law of the Sea
Geography - note: landlocked; crossroads of northern and southern Europe; along with southeastern France and northern Italy, contains the highest elevations in Europe

People

Population: 7,283,274 (July 2001 est.)
Age structure:
0-14 years: 16.97% (male 634,030; female 601,929)
15-64 years: 67.73% (male 2,505,450; female 2,427,408)
65 years and over: 15.3% (male 453,366; female 661,091) (2001 est.)
Population growth rate: 0.27% (2001 est.)
Birth rate: 10.12 births/1,000 population (2001 est.)
Death rate: 8.77 deaths/1,000 population (2001 est.)
Net migration rate: 1.37 migrant(s)/1,000 population (2001 est.)
Sex ratio:
at birth: 1.05 male(s)/female
under 15 years: 1.05 male(s)/female
15-64 years: 1.03 male(s)/female
65 years and over: 0.69 male(s)/female
total population: 0.97 male(s)/female (2001 est.)
Infant mortality rate: 4.48 deaths/1,000 live births (2001 est.)
Life expectancy at birth:
total population: 79.73 years
male: 76.85 years
female: 82.76 years (2001 est.)
Total fertility rate: 1.47 children born/woman (2001 est.)
HIV/AIDS - adult prevalence rate: 0.46% (1999 est.)
HIV/AIDS - people living with HIV/AIDS: 17,000 (1999 est.)
HIV/AIDS - deaths: 150 (1999 est.)
Nationality:
noun: Swiss (singular and plural)
adjective: Swiss
Ethnic groups: German 65%, French 18%, Italian 10%, Romansch 1%, other 6%
Religions: Roman Catholic 46.1%, Protestant 40%, other 5%, none 8.9% (1990)
Languages: German (official) 63.7%, French (official) 19.2%, Italian (official) 7.6%, Romansch 0.6%, other 8.9%
Literacy:
definition: age 15 and over can read and write
total population: 99% (1980 est.)
male: NA%
female: NA%

Government

Country name:
conventional long form: Swiss Confederation
conventional short form: Switzerland
local long form: Schweizerische Eidgenossenschaft (German), Confederation Suisse (French), Confederazione Svizzera (Italian)
local short form: Schweiz (German), Suisse (French), Svizzera (Italian)
Government type: federal republic
Capital: Bern
Administrative divisions: 26 cantons (cantons, singular - canton in French; cantoni, singular - cantone in Italian; kantone, singular - kanton in German); Aargau, Ausser-Rhoden, Basel-Landschaft, Basel-Stadt, Bern, Fribourg, Geneve, Glarus, Graubunden, Inner-Rhoden, Jura, Luzern, Neuchatel, Nidwalden, Obwalden, Sankt Gallen, Schaffhausen, Schwyz, Solothurn, Thurgau, Ticino, Uri, Valais, Vaud, Zug, Zurich
Independence: 1 August 1291 (Founding of the Swiss Confederation)
National holiday: Founding of the Swiss Confederation, 1 August (1291)
Constitution: 29 May 1874
Legal system: civil law system influenced by customary law; judicial review of legislative acts,

Switzerland (continued)

except with respect to federal decrees of general obligatory character; accepts compulsory ICJ jurisdiction, with reservations
Suffrage: 18 years of age; universal
Executive branch:
chief of state: President Moritz LEUENBERGER (since 1 January 2001); Vice President Kaspar VILLIGER (since 1 January 2001); note - the president is both the chief of state and head of government
head of government: President Moritz LEUENBERGER (since 1 January 2001); Vice President Kaspar VILLIGER (since 1 January 2001); note - the president is both the chief of state and head of government
cabinet: Federal Council or Bundesrat (in German), Conseil Federal (in French), Consiglio Federale (in Italian) elected by the Federal Assembly from among its own members for a four-year term
elections: president and vice president elected by the Federal Assembly from among the members of the Federal Council for one-year terms that run concurrently; election last held 6 December 2000 (next to be held NA December 2001)
election results: Moritz LEUENBERGER elected president; percent of Federal Assembly vote - 76%; Kaspar VILLIGER elected vice president; percent of legislative vote - 72%
Legislative branch: bicameral Federal Assembly or Bundesversammlung (in German), Assemblee Federale (in French), Assemblea Federale (in Italian) consists of the Council of States or Standerat (in German), Conseil des Etats (in French), Consiglio degli Stati (in Italian) (46 seats - members serve four-year terms) and the National Council or Nationalrat (in German), Conseil National (in French), Consiglio Nazionale (in Italian) (200 seats - members are elected by popular vote on a basis of proportional representation to serve four-year terms)
elections: Council of States - last held in 1999 (each canton determines when the next election will be held); National Council - last held 24 October 1999 (next to be held NA October 2003)
election results: Council of States - percent of vote by party - NA%; seats by party - FDP 18, CVP 15, SVP 7, SPS 6; National Council - percent of vote by party - SPS 22.5%, SVP 22.6%, FDP 19.9%, CVP 15.8%, other small parties all under 5%; seats by party - SPS 51, SVP 44, FDP 43, CVP 35, Greens 9, other small parties 18
Judicial branch: Federal Supreme Court (judges elected for six-year terms by the Federal Assembly)
Political parties and leaders: Christian Democratic People's Party (Christichdemokratische Volkspartei der Schweiz or CVP, Parti Democrate-Chretien Suisse or PDC, Partito Democratico-Cristiano Popolare Svizzero or PDC, Partida Cristiandemocratica dalla Svizra or PCD) [Adalbert DURRER, president]; Green Party (Grune Partei der Schweiz or Grune, Parti Ecologiste Suisse or Les Verts, Partito Ecologista Svizzero or I Verdi, Partida Ecologica Svizra or La Verda) [Ruedi BAUMANN, president]; Radical Free Democratic Party (Freisinnig-Demokratische Partei der Schweiz or FDP, Parti Radical-Democratique Suisse or PRD, Partitio Liberal-Radicale Svizzero or PLR) [Franz STEINEGGER, president]; Social Democratic Party (Sozialdemokratische Partei der Schweiz or SPS, Parti Socialist Suisse or PSS, Partito Socialista Svizzero or PSS, Partida Socialdemocratica de la Svizra or PSS) [Christiane BRUNNER, president]; Swiss People's Party (Schweizerische Volkspartei or SVP, Union Democratique du Centre or UDC, Unione Democratica de Centro or UDC, Uniun Democratica dal Center or UDC) [Ueli MAURER, president]; and other minor parties
Political pressure groups and leaders: NA
International organization participation: ACCT, AfDB, AsDB, Australia Group, BIS, CCC, CE, CERN, EAPC, EBRD, ECE, EFTA, ESA, FAO, G-10, IADB, IAEA, IBRD, ICAO, ICC, ICFTU, ICRM, IDA, IEA, IFAD, IFC, IFRCS, ILO, IMF, IMO, Inmarsat, Intelsat, Interpol, IOC, IOM, ISO, ITU, LAIA (observer), MONUC, NAM (guest), NEA, NSG, OAS (observer), OECD, OPCW, OSCE, PCA, PFP, UN (observer), UNCTAD, UNESCO, UNHCR, UNIDO, UNITAR, UNMEE, UNMIBH, UNMIK, UNMOP, UNOMIG, UNTSO, UNU, UPU, WCL, WHO, WIPO, WMO, WToO, WTrO, ZC
Diplomatic representation in the US:
chief of mission: Ambassador Alfred DEFAGO
chancery: 2900 Cathedral Avenue NW, Washington, DC 20008
telephone: [1] (202) 745-7900
FAX: [1] (202) 387-2564
consulate(s) general: Atlanta, Chicago, Houston, Los Angeles, New York, and San Francisco
consulate(s): Boston
Diplomatic representation from the US:
chief of mission: Ambassador J. Richard FREDERICKS
embassy: Jubilaeumstrasse 93, 3001 Bern
mailing address: use embassy street address
telephone: [41] (31) 357 70 11
FAX: [41] (31) 357 73 44
Flag description: red square with a bold, equilateral white cross in the center that does not extend to the edges of the flag

Economy

Economy - overview: Switzerland, a prosperous and stable modern market economy with a per capita GDP 20% above that of the big western European economies, experienced solid growth of 3% in 2000, but growth is expected to fall back to about 2% in 2001. The Swiss in recent years have brought their economic practices largely into conformity with the EU's to enhance their international competitiveness. Although the Swiss are not pursuing full EU membership in the near term, in 1999 Bern and Brussels signed agreements to further liberalize trade ties, and the agreements should come into force in 2001. Switzerland is still considered a safe haven for investors, because it has maintained a degree of bank secrecy and has kept up the franc's long-term external value.
GDP: purchasing power parity - $207 billion (2000 est.)
GDP - real growth rate: 3% (2000 est.)
GDP - per capita: purchasing power parity - $28,600 (2000 est.)
GDP - composition by sector:
agriculture: 2.8%
industry: 31.1%
services: 66.1% (1995)
Population below poverty line: NA%
Household income or consumption by percentage share:
lowest 10%: 2.8%
highest 10%: 25.2% (1992)
Inflation rate (consumer prices): 1.5% (2000 est.)
Labor force: 3.9 million (964,000 foreign workers, mostly Italian) (1998 est.)
Labor force - by occupation: services 69.1%, industry 26.3%, agriculture 4.6% (1998 est.)
Unemployment rate: 1.9% (2000 est.)
Budget:
revenues: $32.66 billion
expenditures: $34.89 billion, including capital expenditures of $2.3 billion (1998 est.)
Industries: machinery, chemicals, watches, textiles, precision instruments
Industrial production growth rate: 8.6% (2000 est.)
Electricity - production: 66.768 billion kWh (1999)
Electricity - production by source:
fossil fuel: 3.44%
hydro: 59.16%
nuclear: 35.43%
other: 1.97% (1999)
Electricity - consumption: 51.862 billion kWh (1999)
Electricity - exports: 31.955 billion kWh (1999)
Electricity - imports: 21.723 billion kWh (1999)
Agriculture - products: grains, fruits, vegetables; meat, eggs
Exports: $91.3 billion (f.o.b., 2000)
Exports - commodities: machinery, chemicals, metals, watches, agricultural products
Exports - partners: EU 65.8% (Germany 22.6%, France 9.2%, Italy 8.0%, UK 5.5%, Austria 3.2%), US 12.4%, Japan 4.0% (1999)
Imports: $91.6 billion (f.o.b., 2000)
Imports - commodities: machinery, chemicals, vehicles, metals; agricultural products, textiles
Imports - partners: EU 77.7% (Germany 31.0%, France 12.0%, Italy 9.7%, Netherlands 5.1%, UK 5.7%), US 7.1%, Japan 2.9% (1999)
Debt - external: $NA
Economic aid - donor: ODA, $1.1 billion (1995)
Currency: Swiss franc (CHF)
Currency code: CHF
Exchange rates: Swiss francs per US dollar - 1.6303 (January 2001), 1.6888 (2000), 1.5022 (1999), 1.4498 (1998), 1.4513 (1997), 1.2360 (1996)
Fiscal year: calendar year

Switzerland (continued)

Communications

Telephones - main lines in use: 4.82 million (1998)
Telephones - mobile cellular: 1.967 million (1999)
Telephone system:
general assessment: excellent domestic and international services
domestic: extensive cable and microwave radio relay networks
international: satellite earth stations - 2 Intelsat (Atlantic Ocean and Indian Ocean)
Radio broadcast stations: AM 4, FM 113 (plus many low power stations), shortwave 2 (1998)
Radios: 7.1 million (1997)
Television broadcast stations: 115 (plus 1,919 repeaters) (1995)
Televisions: 3.31 million (1997)
Internet country code: .ch
Internet Service Providers (ISPs): 44 (Switzerland and Liechtenstein) (2000)
Internet users: 2.4 million (2000)

Transportation

Railways:
total: 4,492 km (1,564 km double track)
standard gauge: 3,317 km 1.435-m gauge (3,288 km electrified)
narrow gauge: 1,165 km 1.000-m gauge (1,165 km electrified); 10 km 0.800-m gauge (1998)
Highways:
total: 71,059 km (including 1,638 km of expressways) (1998 est.)
paved: NA km
unpaved: NA km
Waterways: 65 km
note: The Rhine carries heavy traffic on the Basel-Rheinfelden and Schaffhausen-Bodensee stretches; there are also 12 navigable lakes
Pipelines: crude oil 314 km; natural gas 1,506 km
Ports and harbors: Basel
Merchant marine:
total: 24 ships (1,000 GRT or over) totaling 435,966 GRT/780,458 DWT
ships by type: bulk 12, cargo 6, chemical tanker 5, petroleum tanker 1
note: includes some foreign-owned ships registered here as a flag of convenience: UK 1 (2000 est.)
Airports: 67 (2000 est.)
Airports - with paved runways:
total: 42
over 3,047 m: 3
2,438 to 3,047 m: 4
1,524 to 2,437 m: 13
914 to 1,523 m: 7
under 914 m: 15 (2000 est.)
Airports - with unpaved runways:
total: 25
under 914 m: 25 (2000 est.)

Military

Military branches: Army, Air Force, Frontier Guards, Fortification Guards
Military manpower - military age: 20 years of age
Military manpower - availability:
males age 15-49: 1,849,034 (2001 est.)
Military manpower - fit for military service:
males age 15-49: 1,570,918 (2001 est.)
Military manpower - reaching military age annually:
males: 42,597 (2001 est.)
Military expenditures - dollar figure: $3.1 billion (FY98)
Military expenditures - percent of GDP: 1.2% (FY98)

Transnational Issues

Disputes - international: none
Illicit drugs: because of more stringent government regulations, used significantly less as a money-laundering center; transit country for and consumer of South American cocaine and Southwest Asian heroin

Syria

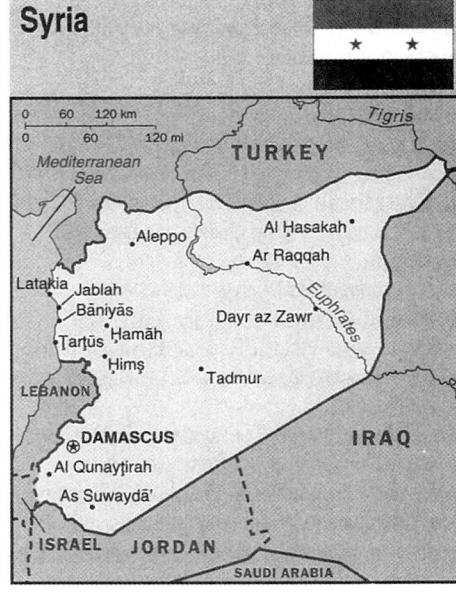

Introduction

Background: Following the breakup of the Ottoman Empire during World War I, Syria was administered by the French until independence in 1946. In the 1967 Arab-Israeli War, Syria lost the Golan Heights to Israel. Since 1976, Syrian troops have been stationed in Lebanon, ostensibly in a peacekeeping capacity. In recent years, Syria and Israel have held occasional peace talks over the return of the Golan Heights.

Geography

Location: Middle East, bordering the Mediterranean Sea, between Lebanon and Turkey
Geographic coordinates: 35 00 N, 38 00 E
Map references: Middle East
Area:
total: 185,180 sq km
land: 184,050 sq km
water: 1,130 sq km
note: includes 1,295 sq km of Israeli-occupied territory
Area - comparative: slightly larger than North Dakota
Land boundaries:
total: 2,253 km
border countries: Iraq 605 km, Israel 76 km, Jordan 375 km, Lebanon 375 km, Turkey 822 km
Coastline: 193 km
Maritime claims:
contiguous zone: 41 NM
territorial sea: 35 NM
Climate: mostly desert; hot, dry, sunny summers (June to August) and mild, rainy winters (December to February) along coast; cold weather with snow or sleet periodically hitting Damascus
Terrain: primarily semiarid and desert plateau; narrow coastal plain; mountains in west
Elevation extremes:
lowest point: unnamed location near Lake Tiberias -200 m
highest point: Mount Hermon 2,814 m

Syria (continued)

Natural resources: petroleum, phosphates, chrome and manganese ores, asphalt, iron ore, rock salt, marble, gypsum, hydropower
Land use:
arable land: 28%
permanent crops: 4%
permanent pastures: 43%
forests and woodland: 3%
other: 22% (1993 est.)
Irrigated land: 9,060 sq km (1993 est.)
Natural hazards: dust storms, sandstorms
Environment - current issues: deforestation; overgrazing; soil erosion; desertification; water pollution from dumping of raw sewage and wastes from petroleum refining; inadequate supplies of potable water
Environment - international agreements:
party to: Biodiversity, Climate Change, Desertification, Hazardous Wastes, Marine Dumping, Nuclear Test Ban, Ozone Layer Protection, Ship Pollution, Wetlands
signed, but not ratified: Environmental Modification
Geography - note: there are 42 Israeli settlements and civilian land use sites in the Israeli-occupied Golan Heights (August 1999 est.)

People

Population: 16,728,808
note: in addition, there are about 38,200 people living in the Israeli-occupied Golan Heights - 18,200 Arabs (16,500 Druze and 1,700 Alawites) and about 20,000 Israeli settlers (July 2001 est.)
Age structure:
0-14 years: 39.92% (male 3,440,060; female 3,238,576)
15-64 years: 56.87% (male 4,868,816; female 4,644,870)
65 years and over: 3.21% (male 261,036; female 275,450) (2001 est.)
Population growth rate: 2.54% (2001 est.)
Birth rate: 30.64 births/1,000 population (2001 est.)
Death rate: 5.21 deaths/1,000 population (2001 est.)
Net migration rate: 0 migrant(s)/1,000 population (2001 est.)
Sex ratio:
at birth: 1.06 male(s)/female
under 15 years: 1.06 male(s)/female
15-64 years: 1.05 male(s)/female
65 years and over: 0.95 male(s)/female
total population: 1.05 male(s)/female (2001 est.)
Infant mortality rate: 33.8 deaths/1,000 live births (2001 est.)
Life expectancy at birth:
total population: 68.77 years
male: 67.63 years
female: 69.98 years (2001 est.)
Total fertility rate: 3.95 children born/woman (2001 est.)
HIV/AIDS - adult prevalence rate: 0.01% (1999 est.)
HIV/AIDS - people living with HIV/AIDS: NA
HIV/AIDS - deaths: NA
Nationality:
noun: Syrian(s)
adjective: Syrian
Ethnic groups: Arab 90.3%, Kurds, Armenians, and other 9.7%
Religions: Sunni Muslim 74%, Alawite, Druze, and other Muslim sects 16%, Christian (various sects) 10%, Jewish (tiny communities in Damascus, Al Qamishli, and Aleppo)
Languages: Arabic (official); Kurdish, Armenian, Aramaic, Circassian widely understood; French, English somewhat understood
Literacy:
definition: age 15 and over can read and write
total population: 70.8%
male: 85.7%
female: 55.8% (1997 est.)

Government

Country name:
conventional long form: Syrian Arab Republic
conventional short form: Syria
local long form: Al Jumhuriyah al Arabiyah as Suriyah
local short form: Suriyah
former: United Arab Republic (with Egypt)
Government type: republic under military regime since March 1963
Capital: Damascus
Administrative divisions: 14 provinces (muhafazat, singular - muhafazah); Al Hasakah, Al Ladhiqiyah, Al Qunaytirah, Ar Raqqah, As Suwayda', Dar'a, Dayr az Zawr, Dimashq, Halab, Hamah, Hims, Idlib, Rif Dimashq, Tartus
Independence: 17 April 1946 (from League of Nations mandate under French administration)
National holiday: Independence Day, 17 April (1946)
Constitution: 13 March 1973
Legal system: based on Islamic law and civil law system; special religious courts; has not accepted compulsory ICJ jurisdiction
Suffrage: 18 years of age; universal
Executive branch:
chief of state: President Bashar al-ASAD (since 17 July 2000); Vice Presidents Abd al-Halim ibn Said KHADDAM (since 11 March 1984) and Muhammad Zuhayr MASHARIQA (since 11 March 1984)
head of government: Prime Minister Muhammad Mustafa MIRU (since 13 March 2000), Deputy Prime Ministers Lt. Gen. Mustafa TALAS (since 11 March 1984), Khalid RA'D (since 13 March 2000), Muhammad NAJI 'UTRI (since 13 March 2000)
cabinet: Council of Ministers appointed by the president
elections: president elected by popular vote for a seven-year term; referendum/election last held 10 July 2000 - after the death of President Hafez al-ASAD, father of Bashar al-ASAD - (next to be held NA 2007); vice presidents appointed by the president; prime minister and deputy prime ministers appointed by the president
election results: Bashar al-ASAD elected president; percent of vote - Bashar al-ASAD 97.29%
note: Hafiz al-ASAD died 10 June 2000; 20 June 2000 the Ba'th Party nominated Bashar al-ASAD for president and presented his name to the People's Council 25 June 2000
Legislative branch: unicameral People's Council or Majlis al-shaab (250 seats; members elected by popular vote to serve four-year terms)
elections: last held 30 November-1 December 1998 (next to be held NA 2002)
election results: percent of vote by party - NPF 67%, non-NPF 33%; seats by party - NPF 167, independents 83; note - the constitution guarantees that the Ba'th Party (part of the NPF alliance) receive one-half of the seats
Judicial branch: Supreme Constitutional Court (justices are appointed for four-year terms by the president); High Judicial Council; Court of Cassation; State Security Courts
Political parties and leaders: National Progressive Front or NPF (includes the Ba'th Party, ASU, Arab Socialist Party, Socialist Unionist Democratic Party, ASP, SCP) [President Bashar al-ASAD]; Arab Socialist Renaissance (Ba'th) Party (governing party) [Bashar al-ASAD, secretary general of the party, and chairman of the National Progressive Front after the death of Hafiz al-ASAD on 10 June 2000]; Arab Socialist Unionist Movement or ASU [Sami SOUFAN]; Arab Socialist Party [Abd al-Ghani KANNUT]; Socialist Unionist Democratic Party [Ahmad al-ASAD]; Syrian Arab Socialist Party or ASP [Safwan KOUDSI]; Syrian Communist Party or SCP [Yusuf FAYSAL]
Political pressure groups and leaders: conservative religious leaders; Muslim Brotherhood (operates in exile in Jordan and Yemen); non-Ba'th parties have little effective political influence
International organization participation: ABEDA, AFESD, AL, AMF, CAEU, CCC, ESCWA, FAO, G-24, G-77, IAEA, IBRD, ICAO, ICC, ICRM, IDA, IDB, IFAD, IFC, IFRCS, IHO, ILO, IMF, IMO, Intelsat, Interpol, IOC, ISO, ITU, NAM, OAPEC, OIC, UN, UNCTAD, UNESCO, UNIDO, UNRWA, UPU, WFTU, WHO, WMO, WToO
Diplomatic representation in the US:
chief of mission: Ambassador Rustum al-ZU'BI
chancery: 2215 Wyoming Avenue NW, Washington, DC 20008
telephone: [1] (202) 232-6313
FAX: [1] (202) 234-9548
Diplomatic representation from the US:
chief of mission: Ambassador Ryan C. CROCKER
embassy: Abou Roumaneh, Al-Mansur Street, No. 2, Damascus
mailing address: P. O. Box 29, Damascus
telephone: [963] (11) 333-2814
FAX: [963] (11) 224-7938
Flag description: three equal horizontal bands of red (top), white, and black, with two small green five-pointed stars in a horizontal line centered in the white band; similar to the flag of Yemen, which has a

Syria (continued)

plain white band, and of Iraq, which has three green stars (plus an Arabic inscription) in a horizontal line centered in the white band; also similar to the flag of Egypt, which has a heraldic eagle centered in the white band

Economy

Economy - overview: Syria's predominantly statist economy is on a shaky footing because of Damascus's failure to implement extensive economic reform. The dominant agricultural sector remains underdeveloped, with roughly 80% of agricultural land still dependent on rain-fed sources. Although Syria has sufficient water supplies in the aggregate at normal levels of precipitation, the great distance between major water supplies and population centers poses serious distribution problems. The water problem is exacerbated by rapid population growth, industrial expansion, and increased water pollution. Private investment is critical to the modernization of the agricultural, energy, and export sectors. Oil production is leveling off, and the efforts of the nonoil sector to penetrate international markets have fallen short. Syria's inadequate infrastructure, outmoded technological base, and weak educational system make it vulnerable to future shocks and hamper competition with neighbors such as Jordan and Israel. The government recognizes the need to open the economy to additional domestic and foreign investment.
GDP: purchasing power parity - $50.9 billion (2000 est.)
GDP - real growth rate: 3.5% (2000 est.)
GDP - per capita: purchasing power parity - $3,100 (2000 est.)
GDP - composition by sector:
agriculture: 29%
industry: 22%
services: 49% (1997)
Population below poverty line: 15%-25%
Household income or consumption by percentage share:
lowest 10%: NA%
highest 10%: NA%
Inflation rate (consumer prices): 1.5% (2000 est.)
Labor force: 4.7 million (1998 est.)
Labor force - by occupation: agriculture 40%, industry 20%, services 40% (1996 est.)
Unemployment rate: 20% (2000 est.)
Budget:
revenues: $2.25 billion
expenditures: $5.4 billion, including capital expenditures of $NA (2000 est.)
Industries: petroleum, textiles, food processing, beverages, tobacco, phosphate rock mining
Industrial production growth rate: NA%
Electricity - production: 17.94 billion kWh (1999)
Electricity - production by source:
fossil fuel: 57.64%
hydro: 42.36%
nuclear: 0%
other: 0% (1999)
Electricity - consumption: 16.684 billion kWh (1999)
Electricity - exports: 0 kWh (1999)
Electricity - imports: 0 kWh (1999)
Agriculture - products: wheat, barley, cotton, lentils, chickpeas, olives, sugar beets; beef, mutton, eggs, poultry, milk
Exports: $4.8 billion (f.o.b., 2000 est.)
Exports - commodities: petroleum 65%, textiles 10%, manufactured goods 10%, fruits and vegetables 7%, raw cotton 5%, live sheep 2%, phosphates 1% (1998 est.)
Exports - partners: Germany 21%, Italy 12%, France 10%, Saudi Arabia 9%, Turkey 8% (1999 est.)
Imports: $3.5 billion (f.o.b., 2000 est.)
Imports - commodities: machinery and equipment 23%, foodstuffs/animals 20%, metal and metal products 15%, textiles 10%, chemicals 10% (1998 est.)
Imports - partners: France 11%, Italy 8%, Germany 7%, Turkey 5%, China 4% (1999 est.)
Debt - external: $22 billion (2000 est.)
Economic aid - recipient: $199 million (1997 est.)
Currency: Syrian pound (SYP)
Currency code: SYP
Exchange rates: Syrian pounds per US dollar - 46 (2000), 46 (1998), 41.9 (January 1997)
Fiscal year: calendar year

Communications

Telephones - main lines in use: 1.313 million (1997)
Telephones - mobile cellular: NA
Telephone system:
general assessment: fair system currently undergoing significant improvement and digital upgrades, including fiber-optic technology
domestic: coaxial cable and microwave radio relay network
international: satellite earth stations - 1 Intelsat (Indian Ocean) and 1 Intersputnik (Atlantic Ocean region); 1 submarine cable; coaxial cable and microwave radio relay to Iraq, Jordan, Lebanon, and Turkey; participant in Medarabtel
Radio broadcast stations: AM 14, FM 2, shortwave 1 (1998)
Radios: 4.15 million (1997)
Television broadcast stations: 44 (plus 17 repeaters) (1995)
Televisions: 1.05 million (1997)
Internet country code: .sy
Internet Service Providers (ISPs): 1 (2000)
Internet users: 20,000 (2000)

Transportation

Railways:
total: 2,750 km
standard gauge: 2,423 km 1.435-m gauge
narrow gauge: 327 km 1.050-m gauge
note: rail link between Syria and Iraq replaced in 2000 (2000)
Highways:
total: 36,377 km
paved: 26,299 km (including 877 km of expressways)
unpaved: 10,078 km (1999 est.)
Waterways: 870 km (minimal economic importance)
Pipelines: crude oil 1,304 km; petroleum products 515 km
Ports and harbors: Baniyas, Jablah, Latakia, Tartus
Merchant marine:
total: 133 ships (1,000 GRT or over) totaling 425,392 GRT/612,097 DWT
ships by type: bulk 11, cargo 117, livestock carrier 4, roll on/roll off 1 (2000 est.)
Airports: 100 (2000 est.)
Airports - with paved runways:
total: 24
over 3,047 m: 5
2,438 to 3,047 m: 16
914 to 1,523 m: 1
under 914 m: 2 (2000 est.)
Airports - with unpaved runways:
total: 76
1,524 to 2,437 m: 2
914 to 1,523 m: 11
under 914 m: 63 (2000 est.)
Heliports: 2 (2000 est.)

Military

Military branches: Syrian Arab Army, Syrian Arab Navy, Syrian Arab Air Force, Syrian Arab Air Defense Forces, Police and Security Force
Military manpower - military age: 19 years of age
Military manpower - availability:
males age 15-49: 4,384,528 (2001 est.)
Military manpower - fit for military service:
males age 15-49: 2,448,630 (2001 est.)
Military manpower - reaching military age annually:
males: 200,859 (2001 est.)
Military expenditures - dollar figure: $921 million (FY00 est.); note - based on official budget data that may understate actual spending
Military expenditures - percent of GDP: 5.9% (FY98)

Transnational Issues

Disputes - international: Golan Heights is Israeli occupied; dispute with upstream riparian Turkey over Turkish water development plans for the Tigris and Euphrates rivers; Syrian troops in northern, central, and eastern Lebanon since October 1976
Illicit drugs: a transit point for opiates and hashish bound for regional and Western markets

Taiwan

Entry follows Zimbabwe

Tajikistan

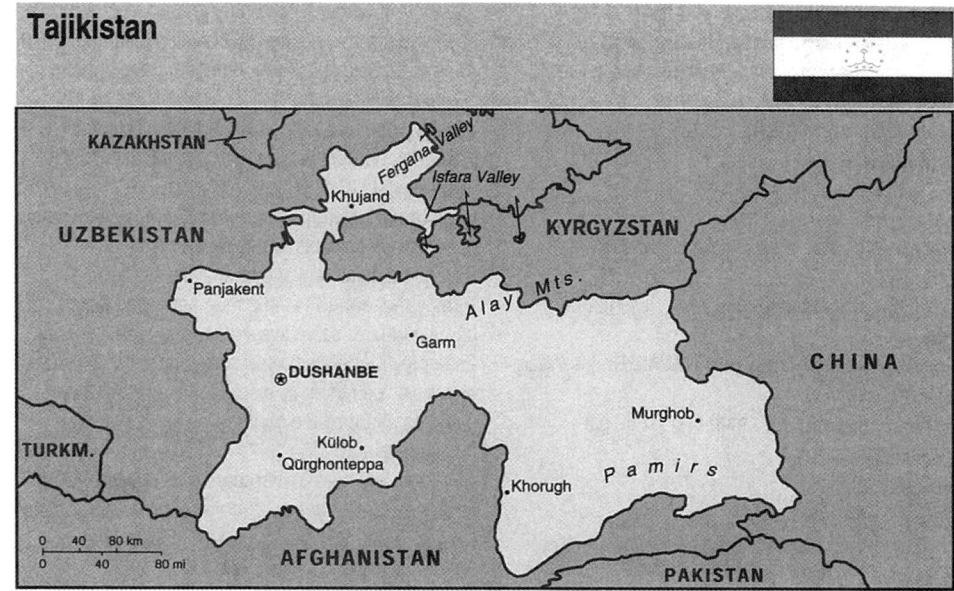

Introduction

Background: Tajikistan has experienced three changes in government and a five-year civil war since it gained independence in 1991 from the USSR. A peace agreement among rival factions was signed in 1997, and implementation reportedly completed by late 1999. Part of the agreement required the legalization of opposition political parties prior to the 1999 elections, which occurred, but such parties have made little progress in successful participation in government. Random criminal and political violence in the country remains a complication impairing Tajikistan's ability to engage internationally.

Geography

Location: Central Asia, west of China
Geographic coordinates: 39 00 N, 71 00 E
Map references: Commonwealth of Independent States
Area:
total: 143,100 sq km
land: 142,700 sq km
water: 400 sq km
Area - comparative: slightly smaller than Wisconsin
Land boundaries:
total: 3,651 km
border countries: Afghanistan 1,206 km, China 414 km, Kyrgyzstan 870 km, Uzbekistan 1,161 km
Coastline: 0 km (landlocked)
Maritime claims: none (landlocked)
Climate: midlatitude continental, hot summers, mild winters; semiarid to polar in Pamir Mountains
Terrain: Pamir and Alay mountains dominate landscape; western Fergana Valley in north, Kofarnihon and Vakhsh Valleys in southwest
Elevation extremes:
lowest point: Syrdariya 300 m
highest point: Pik Imeni Ismail Samani 7,495 m
Natural resources: hydropower, some petroleum, uranium, mercury, brown coal, lead, zinc, antimony, tungsten, silver, gold

Land use:
arable land: 6%
permanent crops: 0%
permanent pastures: 25%
forests and woodland: 4%
other: 65% (1993 est.)
Irrigated land: 6,390 sq km (1993 est.)
Natural hazards: NA
Environment - current issues: inadequate sanitation facilities; increasing levels of soil salinity; industrial pollution; excessive pesticides; part of the basin of the shrinking Aral Sea suffers from severe overutilization of available water for irrigation and associated pollution
Environment - international agreements:
party to: Biodiversity, Climate Change, Desertification, Environmental Modification, Marine Dumping, Ozone Layer Protection, Ship Pollution
signed, but not ratified: none of the selected agreements
Geography - note: landlocked

People

Population: 6,578,681 (July 2001 est.)
Age structure:
0-14 years: 41.18% (male 1,367,194; female 1,341,967)
15-64 years: 54.22% (male 1,773,605; female 1,793,345)
65 years and over: 4.6% (male 131,009; female 171,561) (2001 est.)
Population growth rate: 2.12% (2001 est.)
Birth rate: 33.23 births/1,000 population (2001 est.)
Death rate: 8.57 deaths/1,000 population (2001 est.)
Net migration rate: -3.49 migrant(s)/1,000 population (2001 est.)
Sex ratio:
at birth: 1.05 male(s)/female
under 15 years: 1.02 male(s)/female
15-64 years: 0.99 male(s)/female

Tajikistan (continued)

65 years and over: 0.76 male(s)/female
total population: 0.99 male(s)/female (2001 est.)
Infant mortality rate: 116.09 deaths/1,000 live births (2001 est.)
Life expectancy at birth:
total population: 64.18 years
male: 61.09 years
female: 67.42 years (2001 est.)
Total fertility rate: 4.29 children born/woman (2001 est.)
HIV/AIDS - adult prevalence rate: less than 0.01% (1999 est.)
HIV/AIDS - people living with HIV/AIDS: less than 100 (1999 est.)
HIV/AIDS - deaths: less than 100 (1999 est.)
Nationality:
noun: Tajikistani(s)
adjective: Tajikistani
Ethnic groups: Tajik 64.9%, Uzbek 25%, Russian 3.5% (declining because of emigration), other 6.6%
Religions: Sunni Muslim 80%, Shi'a Muslim 5%
Languages: Tajik (official), Russian widely used in government and business
Literacy:
definition: age 15 and over can read and write
total population: 98%
male: 99%
female: 97% (1989 est.)

Government

Country name:
conventional long form: Republic of Tajikistan
conventional short form: Tajikistan
local long form: Jumhurii Tojikiston
local short form: none
former: Tajik Soviet Socialist Republic
Government type: republic
Capital: Dushanbe
Administrative divisions: 2 oblasts (viloyatho, singular - viloyat) and one autonomous oblast* (viloyati mukhtori); Viloyati Mukhtori Kuhistoni Badakhshon* (Khorugh - formerly Khorog), Viloyati Khatlon (Qurghonteppa - formerly Kurgan-Tyube), Viloyati Leninobod (Khujand - formerly Leninabad)
note: the administrative center name follows in parentheses
Independence: 9 September 1991 (from Soviet Union)
National holiday: Independence Day, 9 September (1991)
Constitution: 6 November 1994
Legal system: based on civil law system; no judicial review of legislative acts
Suffrage: 18 years of age; universal
Executive branch:
chief of state: President Emomali RAHMONOV (since 6 November 1994; head of state and Supreme Assembly chairman since 19 November 1992)
head of government: Prime Minister Oqil OQILOV (since 20 January 1999)
cabinet: Council of Ministers appointed by the president, approved by the Supreme Assembly
elections: president elected by popular vote for a seven-year term; election last held 6 November 1999 (next to be held NA 2006); prime minister appointed by the president
election results: Emomali RAHMONOV elected president; percent of vote - Emomali RAHMONOV 97%, Davlat USMON 2%
Legislative branch: bicameral Supreme Assembly or Majlisi Oli consists of the Assembly of Representatives (lower chamber) or Majlisi Namoyandagon (63 seats; members are elected by popular vote to serve five-year terms) and National Assembly (upper chamber) or Majlisi Milliy (33 seats; members are indirectly elected, 25 selected by local deputies, 8 appointed by the president; all to serve five-year terms)
elections: last held 27 February and 12 March 2000 for the Assembly of Representatives (next to be held NA 2005) and 23 March 2000 for the National Assembly (next to be held NA 2005)
election results: Assembly of Representatives - percent of vote by party - PDPT 65%, Communist Party 20%, Islamic Rebirth Party 7.5%, other 7.5%; seats by party - NA; National Assembly - percent of vote by party - NA%; seats by party - NA
Judicial branch: Supreme Court (judges are appointed by the president)
Political parties and leaders: Congress of People's Unity of Tajikistan [Saiffidin TURAYEV]; Democratic Party or TDP [Mahmadruzi ISKANDAROV, chairman]; Islamic Rebirth Party [Muhammadsharif HIMMAT-ZODA, chairman]; Lali Badakhshan Movement [Atobek AMIRBEKOV]; National Movement Party [Hakim MUHHABATOV]; Party of Justice and Development [Rahmatullo ZOIROV]; People's Democratic Party of Tajikistan or PDPT [Emomali RAHMONOV]; Rastokhez (Rebirth) Movement [Tohiri ABDUJABBOR]; Socialist Party [Sherali KENJAEV]; Tajik Communist Party or CPT [Shodi SHABDOLOV]; Adolatho "Justice" Party [Abdurahmon KARIMOV, chairman]
Political pressure groups and leaders: NA
International organization participation: AsDB, CCC, CIS, EAPC, EBRD, ECE, ECO, ESCAP, FAO, IBRD, ICAO, ICRM, IDA, IDB, IFAD, IFC, IFRCS, ILO, IMF, Intelsat, IOC, IOM, ITU, OIC, OPCW, OSCE, UN, UNCTAD, UNESCO, UNIDO, UPU, WFTU, WHO, WIPO, WMO, WTrO (observer)
Diplomatic representation in the US: Tajikistan does not have an embassy in the US, but does have a permanent mission to the UN: address - 136 East 67th Street, New York, NY 10021, telephone - [1] (212) 472-7645, FAX - [1] (212) 628-0252; permanent representative to the UN is Rashid ALIMOV
Diplomatic representation from the US:
chief of mission: Ambassador Robert P. J. FINN
embassy: temporarily collocated with the US Embassy in Almaty (Kazakhstan)
mailing address: use embassy street address
telephone: NA
FAX: NA
Flag description: three horizontal stripes of red (top), a wider stripe of white, and green; a gold crown surmounted by seven gold, five-pointed stars is located in the center of the white stripe

Economy

Economy - overview: Tajikistan has the lowest per capita GDP among the 15 former Soviet republics. Cotton is the most important crop. Mineral resources, varied but limited in amount, include silver, gold, uranium, and tungsten. Industry consists only of a large aluminum plant, hydropower facilities, and small obsolete factories mostly in light industry and food processing. The Tajikistani economy has been gravely weakened by six years of civil conflict and by the loss of subsidies from Moscow and of markets for its products. Most of its people live in abject poverty. Tajikistan depends on aid from Russia and Uzbekistan and on international humanitarian assistance for much of its basic subsistence needs. The future of Tajikistan's economy and the potential for attracting foreign investment depend upon stability and continued progress in the peace process.
GDP: purchasing power parity - $7.3 billion (2000 est.)
GDP - real growth rate: 5.1% (2000 est.)
GDP - per capita: purchasing power parity - $1,140 (2000 est.)
GDP - composition by sector:
agriculture: 19.8%
industry: 18.1%
services: 62.1% (1998)
Population below poverty line: 80% (2000 est.)
Household income or consumption by percentage share:
lowest 10%: NA%
highest 10%: NA%
Inflation rate (consumer prices): 33% (2000 est.)
Labor force: 1.9 million (1996)
Labor force - by occupation: agriculture 50%, industry 20%, services 30% (1997 est.)
Unemployment rate: 5.7% includes only officially registered unemployed; also large numbers of underemployed workers and unregistered unemployed people (December 1998)
Budget:
revenues: $146 million
expenditures: $196 million, including capital expenditures of $NA (2000 est.)
Industries: aluminum, zinc, lead, chemicals and fertilizers, cement, vegetable oil, metal-cutting machine tools, refrigerators and freezers
Industrial production growth rate: 10% (2000 est.)
Electricity - production: 15.623 billion kWh (1999)
Electricity - production by source:
fossil fuel: 1.9%
hydro: 98.1%
nuclear: 0%
other: 0% (1999)
Electricity - consumption: 14.729 billion kWh (1999)

Tajikistan (continued)

Electricity - exports: 3.9 billion kWh (1999)
Electricity - imports: 4.1 billion kWh (1999)
Agriculture - products: cotton, grain, fruits, grapes, vegetables; cattle, sheep, goats
Exports: $761 million (f.o.b., 2000 est.)
Exports - commodities: aluminum, electricity, cotton, fruits, vegetable oil, textiles
Exports - partners: Liechtenstein 26%, Uzbekistan 20%, Russia 8% (1998)
Imports: $782 million (f.o.b., 2000 est.)
Imports - commodities: electricity, petroleum products, aluminum oxide, machinery and equipment, foodstuffs
Imports - partners: Europe 32.3%, Uzbekistan 29%, Russia 13.6% (1998)
Debt - external: $1.3 billion (1999 est.)
Economic aid - recipient: $64.7 million (1995)
Currency: somoni
Currency code: SM
Exchange rates: Tajikistani somoni per US dollar - 2.2 (January 2001), 1550 (January 2000), 998 (January 1999), 350 (January 1997), 284 (January 1996)
note: the new unit of exchange was introduced on 30 October 2000, with one somoni equal to 1,000 of the old Tajikistani rubles
Fiscal year: calendar year

Communications

Telephones - main lines in use: 363,000 (1997)
Telephones - mobile cellular: 2,500 (1997)
Telephone system:
general assessment: poorly developed and not well maintained; many towns are not reached by the national network
domestic: cable and microwave radio relay
international: linked by cable and microwave radio relay to other CIS republics and by leased connections to the Moscow international gateway switch; Dushanbe linked by Intelsat to international gateway switch in Ankara (Turkey); satellite earth stations - 1 Orbita and 2 Intelsat
Radio broadcast stations: AM 9, FM 6, shortwave 5 (1998)
Radios: 1.291 million (1991)
Television broadcast stations: 0 (there are, however, repeaters that relay programs from Russia, Iran, and Turkey) (1997)
Televisions: 860,000 (1991)
Internet country code: .tj
Internet Service Providers (ISPs): NA
Internet users: 2,000 (2000)

Transportation

Railways:
total: 480 km in common carrier service; does not include industrial lines (1990)
Highways:
total: 13,700 km
paved: 11,330 km (these roads are said to be hard-surfaced, and include, in addition to conventionally paved roads, some that are surfaced with gravel or other coarse aggregate, making them trafficable in all weather)
unpaved: 2,370 km (these roads are made of unstabilized earth and are difficult to negotiate in wet weather) (1996)
Waterways: none
Pipelines: natural gas 400 km (1992)
Ports and harbors: none
Airports: 53 (2000 est.)
Airports - with paved runways:
total: 2
1,524 to 2,437 m: 1
under 914 m: 1 (2000 est.)
Airports - with unpaved runways:
total: 51
over 3,047 m: 1
1,524 to 2,437 m: 2
914 to 1,523 m: 12
under 914 m: 36 (2000 est.)

Military

Military branches: Army, Air Force, Air Defense Forces, Presidential National Guard, Security Forces (internal and border troops)
Military manpower - military age: 18 years of age
Military manpower - availability:
males age 15-49: 1,586,700 (2001 est.)
Military manpower - fit for military service:
males age 15-49: 1,300,252 (2001 est.)
Military manpower - reaching military age annually:
males: 72,056 (2001 est.)
Military expenditures - dollar figure: $17 million (FY97)
Military expenditures - percent of GDP: 1.8% (FY97)

Transnational Issues

Disputes - international: portions of Tajikistan's northern and western border with Uzbekistan and its eastern border with China have not been officially demarcated; territorial dispute with Kyrgyzstan on northern boundary in Isfara Valley area
Illicit drugs: major transshipment zone for heroin and opiates from Afghanistan going to Russia and Western Europe; limited illicit cultivation of cannabis, mostly for domestic consumption

Tanzania

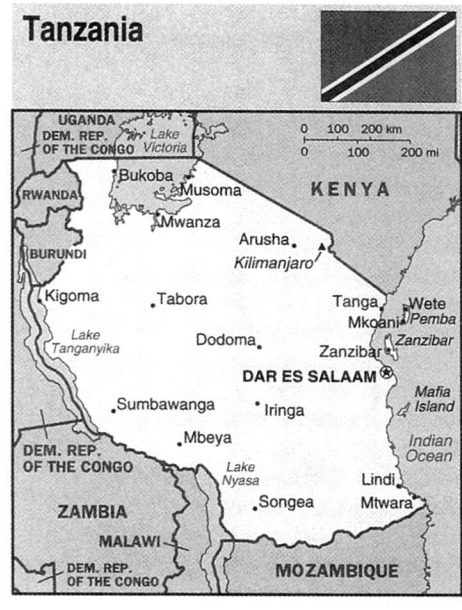

Introduction

Background: Shortly after independence, Tanganyika and Zanzibar merged to form the nation of Tanzania in 1964. One-party rule came to an end in 1995 with the first democratic elections held in the country since the 1970s. Zanzibar's semi-autonomous status and popular opposition have led to two contentious elections since 1995, which the ruling party won despite international observers' claims of voting irregularities.

Geography

Location: Eastern Africa, bordering the Indian Ocean, between Kenya and Mozambique
Geographic coordinates: 6 00 S, 35 00 E
Map references: Africa
Area:
total: 945,087 sq km
land: 886,037 sq km
water: 59,050 sq km
note: includes the islands of Mafia, Pemba, and Zanzibar
Area - comparative: slightly larger than twice the size of California
Land boundaries:
total: 3,402 km
border countries: Burundi 451 km, Kenya 769 km, Malawi 475 km, Mozambique 756 km, Rwanda 217 km, Uganda 396 km, Zambia 338 km
Coastline: 1,424 km
Maritime claims:
exclusive economic zone: 200 NM
territorial sea: 12 NM
Climate: varies from tropical along coast to temperate in highlands
Terrain: plains along coast; central plateau; highlands in north, south
Elevation extremes:
lowest point: Indian Ocean 0 m
highest point: Kilimanjaro 5,895 m

Tanzania (continued)

Natural resources: hydropower, tin, phosphates, iron ore, coal, diamonds, gemstones, gold, natural gas, nickel
Land use:
arable land: 3%
permanent crops: 1%
permanent pastures: 40%
forests and woodland: 38%
other: 18% (1993 est.)
Irrigated land: 1,500 sq km (1993 est.)
Natural hazards: flooding on the central plateau during the rainy season; drought
Environment - current issues: soil degradation; deforestation; desertification; destruction of coral reefs threatens marine habitats; recent droughts affected marginal agriculture
Environment - international agreements:
party to: Biodiversity, Climate Change, Desertification, Endangered Species, Hazardous Wastes, Law of the Sea, Marine Dumping, Ozone Layer Protection, Ship Pollution
signed, but not ratified: Nuclear Test Ban
Geography - note: Kilimanjaro is highest point in Africa

People

Population: 36,232,074
note: estimates for this country explicitly take into account the effects of excess mortality due to AIDS; this can result in lower life expectancy, higher infant mortality and death rates, lower population and growth rates, and changes in the distribution of population by age and sex than would otherwise be expected (July 2001 est.)
Age structure:
0-14 years: 44.76% (male 8,152,438; female 8,063,520)
15-64 years: 52.35% (male 9,387,737; female 9,581,518)
65 years and over: 2.89% (male 473,498; female 573,363) (2001 est.)
Population growth rate: 2.61% (2001 est.)
Birth rate: 39.65 births/1,000 population (2001 est.)
Death rate: 12.95 deaths/1,000 population (2001 est.)
Net migration rate: -0.64 migrant(s)/1,000 population (2001 est.)
Sex ratio:
at birth: 1.03 male(s)/female
under 15 years: 1.01 male(s)/female
15-64 years: 0.98 male(s)/female
65 years and over: 0.83 male(s)/female
total population: 0.99 male(s)/female (2001 est.)
Infant mortality rate: 79.41 deaths/1,000 live births (2001 est.)
Life expectancy at birth:
total population: 51.98 years
male: 51.04 years
female: 52.95 years (2001 est.)
Total fertility rate: 5.42 children born/woman (2001 est.)

HIV/AIDS - adult prevalence rate: 8.09% (1999 est.)
HIV/AIDS - people living with HIV/AIDS: 1.3 million (1999 est.)
HIV/AIDS - deaths: 140,000 (1999 est.)
Nationality:
noun: Tanzanian(s)
adjective: Tanzanian
Ethnic groups: mainland - native African 99% (of which 95% are Bantu consisting of more than 130 tribes), other 1% (consisting of Asian, European, and Arab); Zanzibar - Arab, native African, mixed Arab and native African
Religions: mainland - Christian 45%, Muslim 35%, indigenous beliefs 20%; Zanzibar - more than 99% Muslim
Languages: Kiswahili or Swahili (official), Kiunguju (name for Swahili in Zanzibar), English (official, primary language of commerce, administration, and higher education), Arabic (widely spoken in Zanzibar), many local languages
note: Kiswahili (Swahili) is the mother tongue of the Bantu people living in Zanzibar and nearby coastal Tanzania; although Kiswahili is Bantu in structure and origin, its vocabulary draws on a variety of sources, including Arabic and English, and it has become the lingua franca of central and eastern Africa; the first language of most people is one of the local languages
Literacy:
definition: age 15 and over can read and write Kiswahili (Swahili), English, or Arabic
total population: 67.8%
male: 79.4%
female: 56.8% (1995 est.)

Government

Country name:
conventional long form: United Republic of Tanzania
conventional short form: Tanzania
former: United Republic of Tanganyika and Zanzibar
Government type: republic
Capital: Dar es Salaam; note - legislative offices have been transferred to Dodoma, which is planned as the new national capital; the National Assembly now meets there on regular basis
Administrative divisions: 25 regions; Arusha, Dar es Salaam, Dodoma, Iringa, Kagera, Kigoma, Kilimanjaro, Lindi, Mara, Mbeya, Morogoro, Mtwara, Mwanza, Pemba North, Pemba South, Pwani, Rukwa, Ruvuma, Shinyanga, Singida, Tabora, Tanga, Zanzibar Central/South, Zanzibar North, Zanzibar Urban/West
Independence: 26 April 1964; Tanganyika became independent 9 December 1961 (from UK-administered UN trusteeship); Zanzibar became independent 19 December 1963 (from UK); Tanganyika united with Zanzibar 26 April 1964 to form the United Republic of Tanganyika and Zanzibar; renamed United Republic of Tanzania 29 October 1964

National holiday: Union Day (Tanganyika and Zanzibar), 26 April (1964)
Constitution: 25 April 1977; major revisions October 1984
Legal system: based on English common law; judicial review of legislative acts limited to matters of interpretation; has not accepted compulsory ICJ jurisdiction
Suffrage: 18 years of age; universal
Executive branch:
chief of state: President Benjamin William MKAPA (since 23 November 1995); Vice President Omar Ali JUMA (since 23 November 1995); note - the president is both chief of state and head of government
head of government: President Benjamin William MKAPA (since 23 November 1995); Vice President Omar Ali JUMA (since 23 November 1995); note - the president is both chief of state and head of government
note: Zanzibar elects a president who is head of government for matters internal to Zanzibar; Amani Abeid KARUME was elected to that office on 29 October 2000
cabinet: Cabinet ministers, including the prime minister, are appointed by the president from among the members of the National Assembly
elections: president and vice president elected on the same ballot by popular vote for five-year terms; election last held 29 October 2000 (next to be held NA October 2005); prime minister appointed by the president
election results: Benjamin William MKAPA reelected president; percent of vote - Benjamin William MKAPA 71.7%, Ibrahim Haruna LIPUMBA 16.3%, Augustine Lyatonga MREME 7.8%, John Momose CHEYO 4.2%
Legislative branch: unicameral National Assembly or Bunge (274 seats - 232 elected by popular vote, 37 allocated to women nominated by the president, five to members of the Zanzibar House of Representatives; members serve five-year terms); note - in addition to enacting laws that apply to the entire United Republic of Tanzania, the Assembly enacts laws that apply only to the mainland; Zanzibar has its own House of Representatives to make laws especially for Zanzibar (the Zanzibar House of Representatives has 50 seats, directly elected by universal suffrage to serve five-year terms)
elections: last held 29 October 2000 (next to be held NA October 2005)
election results: National Assembly: percent of vote by party - NA%; seats by party - CCM 244, CUF 16, CHADEMA 4, TLP 3, UDP 2, Zanzibar representatives 5; Zanzibar House of Representatives: percent of vote by party - NA%; seats by party - CCM 34, CUF 16
Judicial branch: Permanent Commission of Enquiry (official ombudsman); Court of Appeal (consists of a chief justice and four judges); High Court (consists of a Jaji Kiongozi and 29 judges appointed by the president; holds regular sessions in all regions); District Courts; Primary Courts (limited jurisdiction and appeals can be made to the higher courts)

Tanzania (continued)

Political parties and leaders: Chama Cha Demokrasia na Maendeleo or CHADEMA [Bob MAKANI, chairman]; Chama Cha Mapinduzi or CCM (Revolutionary Party) [Benjamin William MKAPA, chairman]; Civic United Front or CUF [Seif Sharif HAMAD, secretary-general]; Democratic Party (unregistered) [Reverend Christopher MTIKLA, leader]; National Convention for Construction and Reform or NCCR [Kassim MAGUTU, secretary-general]; Tanzania Labor Party or TLP [Augustine Lyatonga MREMA, chairman]; Union for Multiparty Democracy or UMD [leader NA]; United Democratic Party or UDP [John CHEYO, leader]
Political pressure groups and leaders: NA
International organization participation: ACP, AfDB, C, CCC, EADB, ECA, FAO, G- 6, G-77, IAEA, IBRD, ICAO, ICC, ICFTU, ICRM, IDA, IFAD, IFC, IFRCS, ILO, IMF, IMO, Inmarsat, Intelsat, Interpol, IOC, IOM, ISO, ITU, MONUC, NAM, OAU, OPCW, SADC, UN, UNCTAD, UNESCO, UNHCR, UNIDO, UNMEE, UPU, WFTU, WHO, WIPO, WMO, WToO, WTrO
Diplomatic representation in the US:
chief of mission: Ambassador Mustafa Salim NYANG'ANYI
chancery: 2139 R Street NW, Washington, DC 20008
telephone: [1] (202) 939-6125
FAX: [1] (202) 797-7408
Diplomatic representation from the US:
chief of mission: Charge d'Affaires Wanda NESBITT
embassy: 140 Msese Road, Kinondoni District, Dar es Salaam
mailing address: P. O. Box 9123, Dar es Salaam
telephone: [255] (22) 666010 through 666015
FAX: [255] (22) 666701
Flag description: divided diagonally by a yellow-edged black band from the lower hoist-side corner; the upper triangle (hoist side) is green and the lower triangle is blue

Economy

Economy - overview: Tanzania is one of the poorest countries in the world. The economy is heavily dependent on agriculture, which accounts for half of GDP, provides 85% of exports, and employs 80% of the work force. Topography and climatic conditions, however, limit cultivated crops to only 4% of the land area. Industry is mainly limited to processing agricultural products and light consumer goods. The World Bank, the International Monetary Fund, and bilateral donors have provided funds to rehabilitate Tanzania's deteriorated economic infrastructure. Growth in 1991-2000 featured a pick up in industrial production and a substantial increase in output of minerals, led by gold. Natural gas exploration in the Rufiji Delta looks promising and production could start by 2002. Recent banking reforms have helped increase private sector growth and investment. Continued donor support and solid macroeconomic policies should allow Tanzania to achieve real GDP growth of 6% in 2001 and in 2002.
GDP: purchasing power parity - $25.1 billion (2000 est.)
GDP - real growth rate: 5.2% (2000 est.)
GDP - per capita: purchasing power parity - $710 (2000 est.)
GDP - composition by sector:
agriculture: 49%
industry: 17%
services: 34% (1998 est.)
Population below poverty line: 51.1% (1991 est.)
Household income or consumption by percentage share:
lowest 10%: 2.9%
highest 10%: 30.2% (1993)
Inflation rate (consumer prices): 6% (2000 est.)
Labor force: 13.495 million
Labor force - by occupation: agriculture 80%, industry and commerce 20% (2000 est.)
Unemployment rate: NA%
Budget:
revenues: $1.21 billion
expenditures: $1.36 billion, including capital expenditures of $NA (1999 est.)
Industries: primarily agricultural processing (sugar, beer, cigarettes, sisal twine), diamond and gold mining, oil refining, shoes, cement, textiles, wood products, fertilizer, salt
Industrial production growth rate: 8.4% (1999 est.)
Electricity - production: 2.248 billion kWh (1999)
Electricity - production by source:
fossil fuel: 22.24%
hydro: 77.76%
nuclear: 0%
other: 0% (1999)
Electricity - consumption: 2.134 billion kWh (1999)
Electricity - exports: 0 kWh (1999)
Electricity - imports: 43 million kWh (1999)
Agriculture - products: coffee, sisal, tea, cotton, pyrethrum (insecticide made from chrysanthemums), cashew nuts, tobacco, cloves (Zanzibar), corn, wheat, cassava (tapioca), bananas, fruits, vegetables; cattle, sheep, goats
Exports: $937 million (f.o.b., 2000 est.)
Exports - commodities: coffee, manufactured goods, cotton, cashew nuts, minerals, tobacco, sisal (1996)
Exports - partners: India 20%, UK 10%, Germany 8%, Japan 8%, Netherlands 8%, Belgium 4% (1998)
Imports: $1.57 billion (f.o.b., 2000 est.)
Imports - commodities: consumer goods, machinery and transportation equipment, industrial raw materials, crude oil
Imports - partners: South Africa 8%, Japan 8%, UK 8%, Kenya 7%, India 6%, US 5% (1998)
Debt - external: $6.8 billion (2000 est.)
Economic aid - recipient: $963 million (1997)
Currency: Tanzanian shilling (TZS)
Currency code: TZS
Exchange rates: Tanzanian shillings per US dollar - 803.34 (December 2000), 800.41 (2000), 744.76 (1999), 664.67 (1998), 612.12 (1997), 579.98 (1996)
Fiscal year: 1 July - 30 June

Communications

Telephones - main lines in use: 127,000 (1998)
Telephones - mobile cellular: 30,000 (1999)
Telephone system:
general assessment: fair system operating below capacity and being modernized for better service; VSAT (very small aperture terminal) system under construction
domestic: trunk service provided by open wire, microwave radio relay, tropospheric scatter, and fiber-optic cable; some links being made digital
international: satellite earth stations - 2 Intelsat (1 Indian Ocean and 1 Atlantic Ocean)
Radio broadcast stations: AM 12, FM 11, shortwave 2 (1998)
Radios: 8.8 million (1997)
Television broadcast stations: 3 (1999)
Televisions: 103,000 (1997)
Internet country code: .tz
Internet Service Providers (ISPs): 6 (2000)
Internet users: 25,000 (2000)

Transportation

Railways:
total: 3,569 km (1995)
narrow gauge: 2,600 km 1.000-m gauge; 969 km 1.067-m gauge
note: the Tanzania-Zambia Railway Authority (TAZARA), which operates 1,860 km of 1.067-m narrow gauge track between Dar es Salaam and Kapiri Mposhi in Zambia (of which 969 km are in Tanzania and 891 km are in Zambia) is not a part of Tanzania Railways Corporation; because of the difference in gauge, this system does not connect to Tanzania Railways
Highways:
total: 88,200 km
paved: 3,704 km
unpaved: 84,496 km (1996 est.)
Waterways:
note: Lake Tanganyika, Lake Victoria, and Lake Nyasa are principal avenues of commerce between Tanzania and its neighbors on those lakes
Pipelines: crude oil 982 km
Ports and harbors: Bukoba, Dar es Salaam, Kigoma, Kilwa Masoko, Lindi, Mtwara, Mwanza, Pangani, Tanga, Wete, Zanzibar
Merchant marine:
total: 8 ships (1,000 GRT or over) totaling 21,987 GRT/27,121 DWT
ships by type: cargo 2, passenger/cargo 2, petroleum tanker 2, roll on/roll off 1, short-sea passenger 1 (2000 est.)
Airports: 126 (2000 est.)
Airports - with paved runways:
total: 11
over 3,047 m: 2
2,438 to 3,047 m: 2
1,524 to 2,437 m: 5
914 to 1,523 m: 1
under 914 m: 1 (2000 est.)

Tanzania (continued)

Airports - with unpaved runways:
total: 115
1,524 to 2,437 m: 17
914 to 1,523 m: 63
under 914 m: 35 (2000 est.)

Military

Military branches: Tanzanian People's Defense Force or TPDF (includes Army, Navy, and Air Force), paramilitary Police Field Force Unit, Militia
Military manpower - availability:
males age 15-49: 8,365,337 (2001 est.)
Military manpower - fit for military service:
males age 15-49: 4,841,095 (2001 est.)
Military expenditures - dollar figure: $21 million (FY98/99)
Military expenditures - percent of GDP: 0.2% (FY98/99)

Transnational Issues

Disputes - international: dispute with Malawi over the boundary in Lake Nyasa (Lake Malawi); a resurvey of the latitudinal boundary with Uganda in 2000 revealed a 300-meter discrepancy that both sides are currently adjudicating
Illicit drugs: growing role in transshipment of Southwest and Southeast Asian heroin and South American cocaine destined for South African, European, and US markets and of South Asian methaqualone bound for Southern Africa

Thailand

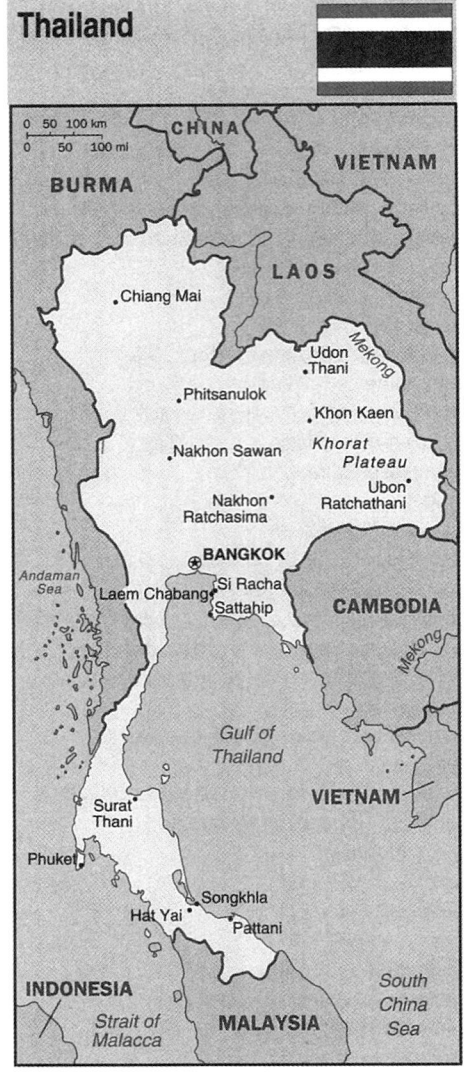

Introduction

Background: A unified Thai kingdom was established in the mid-14th century; it was known as Siam until 1939. Thailand is the only southeast Asian country never to have been taken over by a European power. A bloodless revolution in 1932 led to a constitutional monarchy. In alliance with Japan during World War II, Thailand became a US ally following the conflict.

Geography

Location: Southeastern Asia, bordering the Andaman Sea and the Gulf of Thailand, southeast of Burma
Geographic coordinates: 15 00 N, 100 00 E
Map references: Southeast Asia
Area:
total: 514,000 sq km
land: 511,770 sq km
water: 2,230 sq km
Area - comparative: slightly more than twice the size of Wyoming
Land boundaries:
total: 4,863 km
border countries: Burma 1,800 km, Cambodia 803 km, Laos 1,754 km, Malaysia 506 km
Coastline: 3,219 km
Maritime claims:
continental shelf: 200-m depth or to the depth of exploitation
exclusive economic zone: 200 NM
territorial sea: 12 NM
Climate: tropical; rainy, warm, cloudy southwest monsoon (mid-May to September); dry, cool northeast monsoon (November to mid-March); southern isthmus always hot and humid
Terrain: central plain; Khorat Plateau in the east; mountains elsewhere
Elevation extremes:
lowest point: Gulf of Thailand 0 m
highest point: Doi Inthanon 2,576 m
Natural resources: tin, rubber, natural gas, tungsten, tantalum, timber, lead, fish, gypsum, lignite, fluorite, arable land
Land use:
arable land: 34%
permanent crops: 6%
permanent pastures: 2%
forests and woodland: 26%
other: 32% (1993 est.)
Irrigated land: 44,000 sq km (1993 est.)
Natural hazards: land subsidence in Bangkok area resulting from the depletion of the water table; droughts
Environment - current issues: air pollution from vehicle emissions; water pollution from organic and factory wastes; deforestation; soil erosion; wildlife populations threatened by illegal hunting
Environment - international agreements:
party to: Climate Change, Endangered Species, Hazardous Wastes, Marine Dumping, Marine Life Conservation, Nuclear Test Ban, Ozone Layer Protection, Ship Pollution, Tropical Timber 83, Tropical Timber 94, Wetlands
signed, but not ratified: Biodiversity, Climate Change-Kyoto Protocol, Law of the Sea
Geography - note: controls only land route from Asia to Malaysia and Singapore

People

Population: 61,797,751
note: estimates for this country explicitly take into account the effects of excess mortality due to AIDS; this can result in lower life expectancy, higher infant mortality and death rates, lower population and growth rates, and changes in the distribution of population by age and sex than would otherwise be expected (July 2001 est.)
Age structure:
0-14 years: 23.43% (male 7,380,273; female 7,099,506)
15-64 years: 69.95% (male 21,304,051; female 21,921,383)
65 years and over: 6.62% (male 1,796,325; female 2,296,213) (2001 est.)
Population growth rate: 0.91% (2001 est.)

Thailand (continued)

Birth rate: 16.63 births/1,000 population (2001 est.)
Death rate: 7.54 deaths/1,000 population (2001 est.)
Net migration rate: 0 migrant(s)/1,000 population (2001 est.)
Sex ratio:
at birth: 1.05 male(s)/female
under 15 years: 1.04 male(s)/female
15-64 years: 0.97 male(s)/female
65 years and over: 0.78 male(s)/female
total population: 0.97 male(s)/female (2001 est.)
Infant mortality rate: 30.49 deaths/1,000 live births (2001 est.)
Life expectancy at birth:
total population: 68.86 years
male: 65.64 years
female: 72.24 years (2001 est.)
Total fertility rate: 1.87 children born/woman (2001 est.)
HIV/AIDS - adult prevalence rate: 2.15% (1999 est.)
HIV/AIDS - people living with HIV/AIDS: 755,000 (1999 est.)
HIV/AIDS - deaths: 66,000 (1999 est.)
Nationality:
noun: Thai (singular and plural)
adjective: Thai
Ethnic groups: Thai 75%, Chinese 14%, other 11%
Religions: Buddhism 95%, Muslim 3.8%, Christianity 0.5%, Hinduism 0.1%, other 0.6% (1991)
Languages: Thai, English (secondary language of the elite), ethnic and regional dialects
Literacy:
definition: age 15 and over can read and write
total population: 93.8%
male: 96%
female: 91.6% (1995 est.)

Government

Country name:
conventional long form: Kingdom of Thailand
conventional short form: Thailand
former: Siam
Government type: constitutional monarchy
Capital: Bangkok
Administrative divisions: 76 provinces (changwat, singular and plural); Amnat Charoen, Ang Thong, Buriram, Chachoengsao, Chai Nat, Chaiyaphum, Chanthaburi, Chiang Mai, Chiang Rai, Chon Buri, Chumphon, Kalasin, Kamphaeng Phet, Kanchanaburi, Khon Kaen, Krabi, Krung Thep Mahanakhon (Bangkok), Lampang, Lamphun, Loei, Lop Buri, Mae Hong Son, Maha Sarakham, Mukdahan, Nakhon Nayok, Nakhon Pathom, Nakhon Phanom, Nakhon Ratchasima, Nakhon Sawan, Nakhon Si Thammarat, Nan, Narathiwat, Nong Bua Lamphu, Nong Khai, Nonthaburi, Pathum Thani, Pattani, Phangnga, Phatthalung, Phayao, Phetchabun, Phetchaburi, Phichit, Phitsanulok, Phra Nakhon Si Ayutthaya, Phrae, Phuket, Prachin Buri, Prachuap Khiri Khan, Ranong, Ratchaburi, Rayong, Roi Et, Sa Kaeo, Sakon Nakhon, Samut Prakan, Samut Sakhon, Samut Songkhram, Sara Buri, Satun, Sing Buri, Sisaket, Songkhla, Sukhothai, Suphan Buri, Surat Thani, Surin, Tak, Trang, Trat, Ubon Ratchathani, Udon Thani, Uthai Thani, Uttaradit, Yala, Yasothon
Independence: 1238 (traditional founding date; never colonized)
National holiday: Birthday of King PHUMIPHON, 5 December (1927)
Constitution: new constitution signed by King PHUMIPHON on 11 October 1997
Legal system: based on civil law system, with influences of common law; has not accepted compulsory ICJ jurisdiction
Suffrage: 18 years of age; universal and compulsory
Executive branch:
chief of state: King PHUMIPHON Adunyadet (since 9 June 1946)
head of government: Prime Minister THAKSIN Chinnawat (since NA January 2001)
cabinet: Council of Ministers
note: there is also a Privy Council
elections: none; the monarch is hereditary; prime minister designated from among the members of the House of Representatives; following a national election for the House of Representatives, the leader of the party that can organize a majority coalition usually becomes prime minister
Legislative branch: bicameral National Assembly or Rathasapha consists of the Senate or Wuthisapha (200 seats; members elected by popular vote to serve four-year terms) and the House of Representatives or Sapha Phuthaen Ratsadon (500 seats; members elected by popular vote to serve four-year terms)
elections: Senate - last held 4 March, 29 April, 4 June, 9 July, and 22 July 2000 (next to be held NA March 2004); House of Representatives - last held 6 January 2001 (next to be held NA January 2005)
election results: Senate - percent of vote by party - NA%; seats by party - NA; House of Representatives - percent of vote by party - NA%; seats by party - TRT 248, DP 128, TNP 41, NAP 36, NDP 29, other 18
Judicial branch: Supreme Court or Sandika (judges appointed by the monarch)
Political parties and leaders: Democratic Party or DP (Prachathipat Party) [CHUAN Likphai]; Liberal Democratic Party or LDP (Seri Tham) [PHINIT Charusombat]; Mass Party or MP [CHALERM Yoobamrung, SOPHON Petchsavang]; National Development Party or NDP (Chat Phattana) [KORN Dabbaransi]; New Aspiration Party or NAP (Khwamwang Mai) [Gen. CHAWALIT Yongchaiyut]; Phalang Dharma Party or PDP (Phalang Tham) [CHAIWAT Sinsuwong]; Social Action Party or SAP (Kitsangkhom Party) [leader vacant]; Solidarity Party or SP (Ekkaphap Party) [CHAIYOT Sasomsap]; Thai Citizen's Party or TCP (Prachakon Thai) [SAMAK Sunthonwet]; Thai Nation Party or TNP (Chat Thai Party) [BANHAN Sinlapa-acha]; Thai Rak Thai Party or TRT [THAKSIN Chinnawat]
Political pressure groups and leaders: NA
International organization participation: APEC, ARF, AsDB, ASEAN, BIS, CCC, CP, ESCAP, FAO, G-77, IAEA, IBRD, ICAO, ICC, ICFTU, ICRM, IDA, IFAD, IFC, IFRCS, IHO, ILO, IMF, IMO, Inmarsat, Intelsat, Interpol, IOC, IOM, ISO, ITU, NAM, OAS (observer), OIC (observer), OPCW, OSCE (partner), PCA, UN, UNCTAD, UNESCO, UNHCR, UNIDO, UNIKOM, UNITAR, UNMIBH, UNTAET, UNU, UPU, WCL, WFTU, WHO, WIPO, WMO, WToO, WTrO
Diplomatic representation in the US:
chief of mission: Ambassador TEJ Bunnag
chancery: 1024 Wisconsin Avenue NW, Washington, DC 20007
telephone: [1] (202) 944-3600
FAX: [1] (202) 944-3611
consulate(s) general: Chicago, Los Angeles, and New York
Diplomatic representation from the US:
chief of mission: Ambassador Richard E. HECKLINGER
embassy: 120/22 Wireless Road, Bangkok
mailing address: APO AP 96546
telephone: [66] (2) 205-4000
FAX: [66] (2) 254-1171
consulate(s) general: Chiang Mai
Flag description: five horizontal bands of red (top), white, blue (double width), white, and red

Economy

Economy - overview: After enjoying the world's highest growth rate from 1985 to 1995 - averaging almost 9% annually - increased speculative pressure on Thailand's currency in 1997 led to a crisis that uncovered financial sector weaknesses and forced the government to float the baht. Long pegged at 25 to the dollar, the baht reached its lowest point of 56 to the dollar in January 1998 and the economy contracted by 10.2% that same year. Thailand entered a recovery stage in 1999, expanding 4.2% and grew about the same amount in 2000, largely due to strong exports - which increased about 20% in 2000. An ailing financial sector and the slow pace of corporate debt restructuring, combined with a softening of global demand, is likely to slow growth in 2001.
GDP: purchasing power parity - $413 billion (2000 est.)
GDP - real growth rate: 4.2% (2000 est.)
GDP - per capita: purchasing power parity - $6,700 (2000 est.)
GDP - composition by sector:
agriculture: 13%
industry: 40%
services: 47% (1999)
Population below poverty line: 12.5% (1998 est.)
Household income or consumption by percentage share:
lowest 10%: 2.5%
highest 10%: 37.1% (1992)
Inflation rate (consumer prices): 2.1% (2000 est.)
Labor force: 32.6 million (1997 est.)

Thailand (continued)

Labor force - by occupation: agriculture 54%, industry 15%, services 31% (1996 est.)
Unemployment rate: 3.7% (2000 est.)
Budget:
revenues: $19 billion
expenditures: $21 billion, including capital expenditures of $NA (2000 est.)
Industries: tourism; textiles and garments, agricultural processing, beverages, tobacco, cement, light manufacturing, such as jewelry; electric appliances and components, computers and parts, integrated circuits, furniture, plastics; world's second-largest tungsten producer and third-largest tin producer
Industrial production growth rate: 3% (2000 est.)
Electricity - production: 89.431 billion kWh (1999)
Electricity - production by source:
fossil fuel: 91.17%
hydro: 3.81%
nuclear: 0%
other: 5.02% (1999)
Electricity - consumption: 83.991 billion kWh (1999)
Electricity - exports: 200 million kWh (1999)
Electricity - imports: 1.02 billion kWh (1999)
Agriculture - products: rice, cassava (tapioca), rubber, corn, sugarcane, coconuts, soybeans
Exports: $68.2 billion (f.o.b., 2000 est.)
Exports - commodities: computers and parts, textiles, integrated circuits, rice
Exports - partners: US 22%, Japan 14%, Singapore 9%, Hong Kong 5%, Netherlands 4%, Malaysia 4%, UK 4% (1999)
Imports: $61.8 billion (f.o.b., 2000 est.)
Imports - commodities: capital goods, intermediate goods and raw materials, consumer goods, fuels
Imports - partners: Japan 26%, US 14%, Singapore 6%, China 5%, Malaysia 5%, Taiwan 5% (1999)
Debt - external: $90 billion (2000 est.)
Economic aid - recipient: $131.5 million (1998 est.)
Currency: baht (THB)
Currency code: THB
Exchange rates: baht per US dollar - 43.078 (January 2001), 40.112 (2000), 37.814 (1999), 41.359 (1998), 31.364 (1997), 25.343 (1996)
Fiscal year: 1 October - 30 September

Communications

Telephones - main lines in use: 5.4 million (1998)
Telephones - mobile cellular: 2.3 million (1998)
Telephone system:
general assessment: service to general public adequate, but investment in technological upgrades reduced by recession; bulk of service to government activities provided by multichannel cable and microwave radio relay network
domestic: microwave radio relay and multichannel cable; domestic satellite system being developed
international: satellite earth stations - 2 Intelsat (1 Indian Ocean and 1 Pacific Ocean)

Radio broadcast stations: AM 204, FM 334, shortwave 6 (1999)
Radios: 13.96 million (1997)
Television broadcast stations: 5 (all in Bangkok; plus 131 repeaters) (1997)
Televisions: 15.19 million (1997)
Internet country code: .th
Internet Service Providers (ISPs): 15 (2000)
Internet users: 1 million (2000)

Transportation

Railways:
total: 3,940 km
narrow gauge: 3,940 km 1.000-m gauge (99 km double track)
Highways:
total: 64,600 km
paved: 62,985 km
unpaved: 1,615 km (1996 est.)
Waterways: 4,000 km
note: 3,701 km are navigable throughout the year by boats with drafts up to 0.9 meters; numerous minor waterways serve shallow-draft native craft
Pipelines: petroleum products 67 km; natural gas 350 km
Ports and harbors: Bangkok, Laem Chabang, Pattani, Phuket, Sattahip, Si Racha, Songkhla
Merchant marine:
total: 294 ships (1,000 GRT or over) totaling 1,845,972 GRT/2,923,914 DWT
ships by type: bulk 36, cargo 133, chemical tanker 3, combination bulk 1, container 14, liquefied gas 20, multi-functional large-load carrier 3, passenger 1, petroleum tanker 61, refrigerated cargo 13, roll on/roll off 2, short-sea passenger 2, specialized tanker 5 (2000 est.)
Airports: 110 (2000 est.)
Airports - with paved runways:
total: 59
over 3,047 m: 6
2,438 to 3,047 m: 11
1,524 to 2,437 m: 21
914 to 1,523 m: 17
under 914 m: 4 (2000 est.)
Airports - with unpaved runways:
total: 51
1,524 to 2,437 m: 1
914 to 1,523 m: 16
under 914 m: 34 (2000 est.)
Heliports: 2 (2000 est.)

Military

Military branches: Royal Thai Army, Royal Thai Navy (includes Royal Thai Marine Corps), Royal Thai Air Force, Paramilitary Forces
Military manpower - military age: 18 years of age
Military manpower - availability:
males age 15-49: 17,717,268 (2001 est.)
Military manpower - fit for military service:
males age 15-49: 10,646,818 (2001 est.)
Military manpower - reaching military age annually:
males: 567,659 (2001 est.)
Military expenditures - dollar figure: $1.775 billion (FY00)
Military expenditures - percent of GDP: 1.4% (FY00)

Transnational Issues

Disputes - international: parts of the border with Laos are indefinite; parts of border with Cambodia are indefinite; sporadic border hostilities with Burma over border alignment and ethnic Shan rebels operating in cross-border region
Illicit drugs: a minor producer of opium, heroin, and marijuana; illicit transit point for heroin en route to the international drug market from Burma and Laos; eradication efforts have reduced the area of cannabis cultivation and shifted some production to neighboring countries; opium poppy cultivation has been reduced by eradication efforts; also a drug money-laundering center; minor role in amphetamine production for regional consumption; increasing indigenous abuse of methamphetamine

Togo

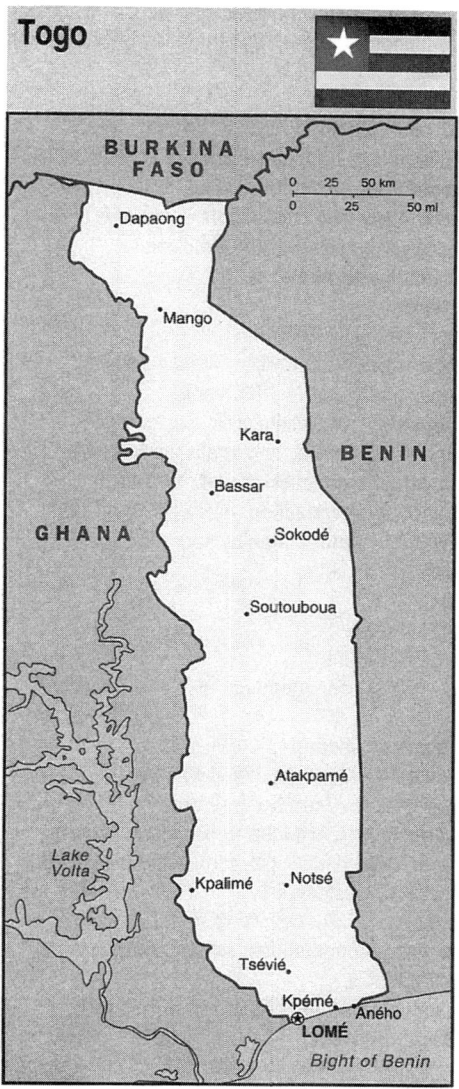

Introduction

Background: French Togoland became Togo in 1960. General Gnassingbe EYADEMA, installed as military ruler in 1967, is Africa's longest-serving head of state. Despite the facade of multiparty elections that resulted in EYADEMA's victory in 1993, the government continues to be dominated by the military. In addition, Togo has come under fire from international organizations for human rights abuses and is plagued by political unrest. Most bilateral and multilateral aid to Togo remains frozen.

Geography

Location: Western Africa, bordering the Bight of Benin, between Benin and Ghana
Geographic coordinates: 8 00 N, 1 10 E
Map references: Africa
Area:
total: 56,785 sq km
land: 54,385 sq km
water: 2,400 sq km
Area - comparative: slightly smaller than West Virginia
Land boundaries:
total: 1,647 km
border countries: Benin 644 km, Burkina Faso 126 km, Ghana 877 km
Coastline: 56 km
Maritime claims:
exclusive economic zone: 200 NM
territorial sea: 30 NM
Climate: tropical; hot, humid in south; semiarid in north
Terrain: gently rolling savanna in north; central hills; southern plateau; low coastal plain with extensive lagoons and marshes
Elevation extremes:
lowest point: Atlantic Ocean 0 m
highest point: Mont Agou 986 m
Natural resources: phosphates, limestone, marble, arable land
Land use:
arable land: 38%
permanent crops: 7%
permanent pastures: 4%
forests and woodland: 17%
other: 34% (1993 est.)
Irrigated land: 70 sq km (1993 est.)
Natural hazards: hot, dry harmattan wind can reduce visibility in north during winter; periodic droughts
Environment - current issues: deforestation attributable to slash-and-burn agriculture and the use of wood for fuel; water pollution presents health hazards and hinders the fishing industry; air pollution increasing in urban areas
Environment - international agreements:
party to: Biodiversity, Climate Change, Desertification, Endangered Species, Law of the Sea, Marine Dumping, Nuclear Test Ban, Ozone Layer Protection, Ship Pollution, Tropical Timber 83, Tropical Timber 94, Wetlands
signed, but not ratified: none of the selected agreements

People

Population: 5,153,088
note: estimates for this country explicitly take into account the effects of excess mortality due to AIDS; this can result in lower life expectancy, higher infant mortality and death rates, lower population and growth rates, and changes in the distribution of population by age and sex than would otherwise be expected (July 2001 est.)
Age structure:
0-14 years: 45.63% (male 1,179,650; female 1,171,748)
15-64 years: 51.92% (male 1,302,197; female 1,373,247)
65 years and over: 2.45% (male 54,651; female 71,595) (2001 est.)
Population growth rate: 2.6% (2001 est.)
Birth rate: 37.04 births/1,000 population (2001 est.)
Death rate: 11.24 deaths/1,000 population (2001 est.)
Net migration rate: 0.15 migrant(s)/1,000 population (2001 est.)
Sex ratio:
at birth: 1.03 male(s)/female
under 15 years: 1.01 male(s)/female
15-64 years: 0.95 male(s)/female
65 years and over: 0.76 male(s)/female
total population: 0.97 male(s)/female (2001 est.)
Infant mortality rate: 70.43 deaths/1,000 live births (2001 est.)
Life expectancy at birth:
total population: 54.35 years
male: 52.38 years
female: 56.38 years (2001 est.)
Total fertility rate: 5.32 children born/woman (2001 est.)
HIV/AIDS - adult prevalence rate: 5.98% (1999 est.)
HIV/AIDS - people living with HIV/AIDS: 130,000 (1999 est.)
HIV/AIDS - deaths: 14,000 (1999 est.)
Nationality:
noun: Togolese (singular and plural)
adjective: Togolese
Ethnic groups: native African (37 tribes; largest and most important are Ewe, Mina, and Kabre) 99%, European and Syrian-Lebanese less than 1%
Religions: indigenous beliefs 59%, Christian 29%, Muslim 12%
Languages: French (official and the language of commerce), Ewe and Mina (the two major African languages in the south), Kabye (sometimes spelled Kabiye) and Dagomba (the two major African languages in the north)
Literacy:
definition: age 15 and over can read and write
total population: 51.7%
male: 67%
female: 37% (1995 est.)

Government

Country name:
conventional long form: Togolese Republic
conventional short form: Togo
local long form: Republique Togolaise
local short form: none
former: French Togoland
Government type: republic under transition to multiparty democratic rule
Capital: Lome
Administrative divisions: 5 regions (regions, singular - region); De La Kara, Des Plateaux, Des Savanes, Du Centre, Maritime
Independence: 27 April 1960 (from French-administered UN trusteeship)
National holiday: Independence Day, 27 April (1960)
Constitution: multiparty draft constitution approved by High Council of the Republic 1 July 1992; adopted by public referendum 27 September 1992
Legal system: French-based court system
Suffrage: NA years of age; universal adult

Togo (continued)

Executive branch:
chief of state: President Gen. Gnassingbe EYADEMA (since 14 April 1967)
head of government: Prime Minister Agbeyome KODJO (since 29 August 2000)
cabinet: Council of Ministers appointed by the president and the prime minister
elections: president elected by popular vote for a five-year term; election last held 21 June 1998 (next to be held NA 2003); prime minister appointed by the president
election results: Gnassingbe EYADEMA reelected president; percent of vote - Gnassingbe EYADEMA 52.13%, Gilchrist OLYMPIO 34.12%, other 13.75%
Legislative branch: unicameral National Assembly (81 seats; members are elected by popular vote to serve five-year terms)
elections: last held 21 March 1999 (next due to be held NA October 2001)
election results: percent of vote by party - NA%; seats by party - RPT 79, independents 2
note: Togo's main opposition parties boycotted the election because of EYADEMA's alleged manipulation of 1998 presidential polling; in March of 1999, opposition parties entered into negotiations with the president over the establishment of an independent electoral commission and a new round of legislative elections, now scheduled for October 2001
Judicial branch: Court of Appeal or Cour d'Appel; Supreme Court or Cour Supreme
Political parties and leaders: Action Committee for Renewal or CAR [Yawovi AGBOYIBO]; Coordination des Forces Nouvelles or CFN [Joseph KOFFIGOH]; Democratic Convention of African Peoples or CDPA [Leopold GNININVI]; Party for Democracy and Renewal or PDR [Zarifou AYEVA]; Patriotic Pan-African Convergence or CPP [Edem KODJO]; Rally of the Togolese People or RPT [President Gen. Gnassingbe EYADEMA]; Union of Forces for Change or UFC [Gilchrist OLYMPIO (in exile), Jeane-Pierre FABRE, general secretary in Togo]; Union of Independent Liberals or ULI [Jacques AMOUZO]
note: Rally of the Togolese People or RPT, led by President EYADEMA, was the only party until the formation of multiple parties was legalized 12 April 1991
Political pressure groups and leaders: NA
International organization participation: ACCT, ACP, AfDB, CCC, ECA, ECOWAS, Entente, FAO, FZ, G-77, IBRD, ICAO, ICC, ICFTU, ICRM, IDA, IDB, IFAD, IFC, IFRCS, ILO, IMF, IMO, Intelsat, Interpol, IOC, ITU, MIPONUH, NAM, OAU, OIC, OPCW, UN, UNCTAD, UNESCO, UNIDO, UPU, WADB, WAEMU, WCL, WFTU, WHO, WIPO, WMO, WToO, WTrO
Diplomatic representation in the US:
chief of mission: Ambassador Akoussoulelov BODJONA
chancery: 2208 Massachusetts Avenue NW, Washington, DC 20008
telephone: [1] (202) 234-4212
FAX: [1] (202) 232-3190

Diplomatic representation from the US:
chief of mission: Ambassador Karl HOFMANN
embassy: Angle Rue Kouenou and Rue 15 Beniglato, Lome
mailing address: B. P. 852, Lome
telephone: [228] 21 29 91 through 21 29 94
FAX: [228] 21 79 52
Flag description: five equal horizontal bands of green (top and bottom) alternating with yellow; there is a white five-pointed star on a red square in the upper hoist-side corner; uses the popular pan-African colors of Ethiopia

Economy

Economy - overview: This small sub-Saharan economy is heavily dependent on both commercial and subsistence agriculture, which provides employment for 65% of the labor force. Some basic foodstuffs must still be imported. Together, cocoa, coffee, and cotton generate some 40% of export earnings, with cotton being the most significant cash crop despite falling prices on the world market. In the industrial sector, phosphate mining is by far the most important activity. Togo is the world's fourth largest producer, and geological advantages keep production costs low. The recently privatized mining operation, Office Togolais des Phosphates (OTP), is slowly recovering from a steep fall in prices in the early 1990's, but continues to face the challenge of tough foreign competition, exacerbated by weakening demand. Togo serves as a regional commercial and trade center. It continues to expand its duty-free export-processing zone (EPZ), launched in 1989, which has attracted enterprises from France, Italy, Scandinavia, the US, India, and China and created jobs for Togolese nationals. The government's decade-long effort, supported by the World Bank and the IMF, to implement economic reform measures, encourage foreign investment, and bring revenues in line with expenditures has stalled. Progress depends on following through on privatization, increased openness in government financial operations, progress towards legislative elections, and possible downsizing of the military, on which the regime has depended to stay in place. Lack of foreign aid, deterioration of the financial sector, energy shortages, and depressed commodity prices continue to constrain economic growth; however, Togo did realize a 3% gain in GDP in 1999. The takeover of the national power company by a Franco-Canadian consortium in 2000 should ease the energy crisis and if successful legislative elections pave the way for increased aid, growth should rise to 5% a year in 2001-02.
GDP: purchasing power parity - $7.3 billion (2000 est.)
GDP - real growth rate: 3.4% (2000 est.)
GDP - per capita: purchasing power parity - $1,500 (2000 est.)
GDP - composition by sector:
agriculture: 42%
industry: 21%
services: 37% (1997)

Population below poverty line: 32% (1989 est.)
Household income or consumption by percentage share:
lowest 10%: NA%
highest 10%: NA%
Inflation rate (consumer prices): 2.5% (2000 est.)
Labor force: 1.74 million (1996)
Labor force - by occupation: agriculture 65%, industry 5%, services 30% (1998 est.)
Unemployment rate: NA%
Budget:
revenues: $232 million
expenditures: $252 million, including capital expenditures of $NA (1997 est.)
Industries: phosphate mining, agricultural processing, cement; handicrafts, textiles, beverages
Industrial production growth rate: NA%
Electricity - production: 92 million kWh (1999)
Electricity - production by source:
fossil fuel: 97.83%
hydro: 2.17%
nuclear: 0%
other: 0% (1999)
Electricity - consumption: 511.6 million kWh (1999)
Electricity - exports: 0 kWh (1999)
Electricity - imports: 426 million kWh
note: electricity supplied by Ghana (1999)
Agriculture - products: coffee, cocoa, cotton, yams, cassava (tapioca), corn, beans, rice, millet, sorghum; livestock; fish
Exports: $336 million (f.o.b., 2000)
Exports - commodities: cotton, phosphates, coffee, cocoa
Exports - partners: Nigeria, Brazil, Canada, Philippines (1999)
Imports: $452 million (f.o.b., 2000)
Imports - commodities: machinery and equipment, foodstuffs, petroleum products
Imports - partners: Ghana, China, France, Cote d'Ivoire (1999)
Debt - external: $1.5 billion (1999)
Economic aid - recipient: $201.1 million (1995)
Currency: Communaute Financiere Africaine franc (XOF); note - responsible authority is the Central Bank of the West African States
Currency code: XOF
Exchange rates: Communaute Financiere Africaine francs (XOF) per US dollar - 699.21 (January 2001), 711.98 (2000), 615.70 (1999), 589.95 (1998), 583.67 (1997), 511.55 (1996); note - from 1 January 1999, the XOF is pegged to the euro at a rate of 655.957 XOF per euro
Fiscal year: calendar year

Communications

Telephones - main lines in use: 25,000 (1997)
Telephones - mobile cellular: 2,995 (1997)
Telephone system:
general assessment: fair system based on a network of microwave radio relay routes supplemented by open-wire lines and a mobile cellular system

Togo (continued)

domestic: microwave radio relay and open-wire lines for conventional system; cellular system has capacity of 10,000 telephones
international: satellite earth stations - 1 Intelsat (Atlantic Ocean) and 1 Symphonie
Radio broadcast stations: AM 2, FM 9, shortwave 4 (1998)
Radios: 940,000 (1997)
Television broadcast stations: 3 (plus two repeaters) (1997)
Televisions: 73,000 (1997)
Internet country code: .tg
Internet Service Providers (ISPs): 3 (2000)
Internet users: 10,000 (2000)

Transportation

Railways:
total: 525 km (1995)
narrow gauge: 525 km 1.000-m gauge
Highways:
total: 7,520 km
paved: 2,376 km
unpaved: 5,144 km (1996 est.)
Waterways: 50 km (Mono river)
Ports and harbors: Kpeme, Lome
Merchant marine:
total: 1 ship (1,000 GRT or over) totaling 2,603 GRT/ 2,800 DWT
ships by type: specialized tanker 1 (2000 est.)
Airports: 9 (2000 est.)
Airports - with paved runways:
total: 2
2,438 to 3,047 m: 2 (2000 est.)
Airports - with unpaved runways:
total: 7
914 to 1,523 m: 5
under 914 m: 2 (2000 est.)

Military

Military branches: Army, Navy, Air Force, Gendarmerie
Military manpower - availability:
males age 15-49: 1,175,528 (2001 est.)
Military manpower - fit for military service:
males age 15-49: 616,622 (2001 est.)
Military expenditures - dollar figure: $27 million (FY96)
Military expenditures - percent of GDP: 2% (FY96)

Transnational Issues

Disputes - international: none
Illicit drugs: transit hub for Nigerian heroin and cocaine traffickers

Tokelau
(territory of New Zealand)

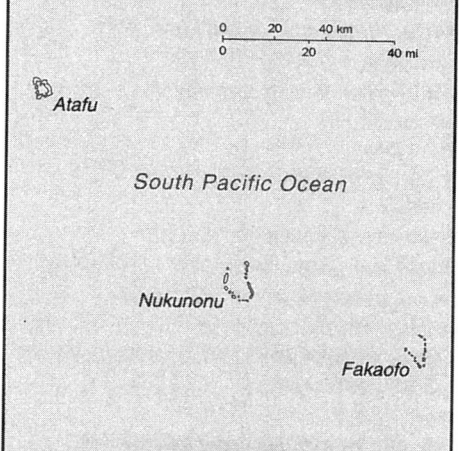

Introduction

Background: Originally settled by Polynesian emigrants from surrounding island groups, the Tokelau Islands were made a British protectorate in 1889. They were transferred to New Zealand administration in 1925. According to a UN report, these low-lying islands will disappear in the 21st century, if global warming continues to raise sea levels.

Geography

Location: Oceania, group of three islands in the South Pacific Ocean, about one-half of the way from Hawaii to New Zealand
Geographic coordinates: 9 00 S, 172 00 W
Map references: Oceania
Area:
total: 10 sq km
land: 10 sq km
water: 0 sq km
Area - comparative: about 17 times the size of The Mall in Washington, DC
Land boundaries: 0 km
Coastline: 101 km
Maritime claims:
exclusive economic zone: 200 NM
territorial sea: 12 NM
Climate: tropical; moderated by trade winds (April to November)
Terrain: low-lying coral atolls enclosing large lagoons
Elevation extremes:
lowest point: Pacific Ocean 0 m
highest point: unnamed location 5 m
Natural resources: NEGL
Land use:
arable land: 0% (soil is thin and infertile)
permanent crops: 0%
permanent pastures: 0%
forests and woodland: 0%
other: 100% (1993 est.)
Irrigated land: NA sq km
Natural hazards: lies in Pacific typhoon belt
Environment - current issues: very limited natural resources and overcrowding are contributing to emigration to New Zealand

People

Population: 1,445 (July 2001 est.)
Age structure:
0-14 years: NA%
15-64 years: NA%
65 years and over: NA%
Population growth rate: -0.92% (2001 est.)
Birth rate: NA births/1,000 population
Death rate: NA deaths/1,000 population
Net migration rate: NA migrant(s)/1,000 population
Infant mortality rate: NA deaths/1,000 live births
Life expectancy at birth:
total population: NA years
male: NA years
female: NA years
Total fertility rate: NA children born/woman
HIV/AIDS - adult prevalence rate: NA%
HIV/AIDS - people living with HIV/AIDS: NA
HIV/AIDS - deaths: NA
Nationality:
noun: Tokelauan(s)
adjective: Tokelauan
Ethnic groups: Polynesian
Religions: Congregational Christian Church 70%, Roman Catholic 28%, other 2%
note: on Atafu, all Congregational Christian Church of Samoa; on Nukunonu, all Roman Catholic; on Fakaofo, both denominations, with the Congregational Christian Church predominant
Languages: Tokelauan (a Polynesian language), English

Government

Country name:
conventional long form: none
conventional short form: Tokelau
Dependency status: territory of New Zealand; note - Tokelauans are drafting a constitution, developing institutions and patterns of self-government as Tokelau moves toward free association with Wellington
Government type: NA
Capital: none; each atoll has its own administrative center
Administrative divisions: none (territory of New Zealand)
Independence: none (territory of New Zealand)
National holiday: Waitangi Day (Treaty of Waitangi established British sovereignty over New Zealand), 6 February (1840)
Constitution: administered under the Tokelau Islands Act of 1948, as amended in 1970
Legal system: British and local statutes
Suffrage: 21 years of age; universal

Tokelau (continued)

Executive branch:
chief of state: Queen ELIZABETH II (since 6 February 1952); the UK and New Zealand are represented by Administrator Lindsay WATT (since NA March 1993)
head of government: Aliki Faipule FALIMATEAO (since NA 1997)
cabinet: the Council of Faipule, consisting of three elected leaders, one from each atoll; functions as a cabinet
elections: none; the monarch is hereditary; administrator appointed by the Minister of Foreign Affairs and Trade in New Zealand; the head of government is chosen from the Council of Faipule and serves a one-year term
Legislative branch: unicameral General Fono (45 seats - 15 from each of the three atolls; members chosen by each atoll's Council of Elders or Taupulega to serve three-year terms); note - the Tokelau Amendment Act of 1996 confers legislative power on the General Fono
Judicial branch: Supreme Court in New Zealand exercises civil and criminal jurisdiction in Tokelau
Political parties and leaders: none
Political pressure groups and leaders: none
International organization participation: SPC, WHO (associate)
Diplomatic representation in the US: none (territory of New Zealand)
Diplomatic representation from the US: none (territory of New Zealand)
Flag description: the flag of New Zealand is used

Economy

Economy - overview: Tokelau's small size (three villages), isolation, and lack of resources greatly restrain economic development and confine agriculture to the subsistence level. The people must rely on aid from New Zealand to maintain public services, annual aid being substantially greater than GDP. The principal sources of revenue come from sales of copra, postage stamps, souvenir coins, and handicrafts. Money is also remitted to families from relatives in New Zealand.
GDP: purchasing power parity - $1.5 million (1993 est.)
GDP - real growth rate: NA%
GDP - per capita: purchasing power parity - $1,000 (1993 est.)
GDP - composition by sector:
agriculture: NA%
industry: NA%
services: NA%
Population below poverty line: NA%
Household income or consumption by percentage share:
lowest 10%: NA%
highest 10%: NA%
Inflation rate (consumer prices): NA%
Labor force: NA
Unemployment rate: NA%
Budget:
revenues: $430,830
expenditures: $2.8 million, including capital expenditures of $37,300 (1987 est.)
Industries: small-scale enterprises for copra production, woodworking, plaited craft goods; stamps, coins; fishing
Industrial production growth rate: NA%
Electricity - production: NA kWh
Electricity - production by source:
fossil fuel: NA%
hydro: NA%
nuclear: NA%
other: NA%
Electricity - consumption: NA kWh
Agriculture - products: coconuts, copra, breadfruit, papayas, bananas; pigs, poultry, goats
Exports: $98,000 (f.o.b., 1983)
Exports - commodities: stamps, copra, handicrafts
Exports - partners: NZ
Imports: $323,400 (c.i.f., 1983)
Imports - commodities: foodstuffs, building materials, fuel
Imports - partners: NZ
Debt - external: $0
Economic aid - recipient: $3.8 million (1995)
Currency: New Zealand dollar (NZD)
Currency code: NZD
Exchange rates: New Zealand dollars per US dollar - 2.2502 (January 2001), 2.1863 (2000), 1.8886 (1999), 1.8632 (1998), 1.5083 (1997), 1.4543 (1996)
Fiscal year: 1 April - 31 March

Communications

Telephones - main lines in use: NA
Telephones - mobile cellular: 0 (2001)
Telephone system:
general assessment: adequate
domestic: radiotelephone service between islands
international: radiotelephone service to Samoa; government-regulated telephone service (TeleTok), with 3 satellite earth stations, established in 1997
Radio broadcast stations: AM NA, FM NA, shortwave NA
note: each atoll has a radio broadcast station of unknown type that broadcasts shipping and weather reports (1998)
Radios: 1,000 (1997)
Television broadcast stations: NA
Televisions: NA
Internet country code: .tk
Internet Service Providers (ISPs): 1 (2000)
Internet users: NA

Transportation

Railways: 0 km
Highways:
total: NA km
paved: NA km
unpaved: NA km
Waterways: none
Ports and harbors: none; offshore anchorage only
Merchant marine: none (2000 est.)
Airports: none; lagoon landings by amphibious aircraft from Samoa

Military

Military - note: defense is the responsibility of New Zealand

Transnational Issues

Disputes - international: none

Tonga

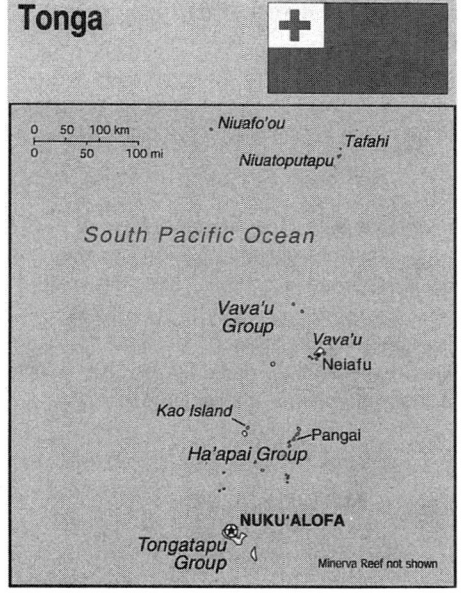

Introduction

Background: The archipelago of "The Friendly Islands" was united into a Polynesian kingdom in 1845. It became a constitutional monarchy in 1875 and a British protectorate in 1900. Tonga acquired its independence in 1970 and became a member of the Commonwealth of Nations. It remains the only monarchy in the Pacific.

Geography

Location: Oceania, archipelago in the South Pacific Ocean, about two-thirds of the way from Hawaii to New Zealand
Geographic coordinates: 20 00 S, 175 00 W
Map references: Oceania
Area:
total: 748 sq km
land: 718 sq km
water: 30 sq km
Area - comparative: four times the size of Washington, DC
Land boundaries: 0 km
Coastline: 419 km
Maritime claims:
continental shelf: 200-m depth or to the depth of exploitation
exclusive economic zone: 200 NM
territorial sea: 12 NM
Climate: tropical; modified by trade winds; warm season (December to May), cool season (May to December)
Terrain: most islands have limestone base formed from uplifted coral formation; others have limestone overlying volcanic base
Elevation extremes:
lowest point: Pacific Ocean 0 m
highest point: unnamed location on Kao Island 1,033 m
Natural resources: fish, fertile soil
Land use:
arable land: 24%
permanent crops: 43%
permanent pastures: 6%
forests and woodland: 11%
other: 16% (1993 est.)
Irrigated land: NA sq km
Natural hazards: cyclones (October to April); earthquakes and volcanic activity on Fonuafo'ou
Environment - current issues: deforestation results as more and more land is being cleared for agriculture and settlement; some damage to coral reefs from starfish and indiscriminate coral and shell collectors; overhunting threatens native sea turtle populations
Environment - international agreements:
party to: Biodiversity, Climate Change, Desertification, Law of the Sea, Marine Life Conservation, Nuclear Test Ban, Ozone Layer Protection, Ship Pollution
signed, but not ratified: none of the selected agreements
Geography - note: archipelago of 170 islands (36 inhabited)

People

Population: 104,227 (July 2001 est.)
Age structure:
0-14 years: 40.93% (male 21,739; female 20,916)
15-64 years: 54.99% (male 28,231; female 29,082)
65 years and over: 4.08% (male 1,912; female 2,347) (2001 est.)
Population growth rate: 1.79% (2001 est.)
Birth rate: 23.59 births/1,000 population (2001 est.)
Death rate: 5.74 deaths/1,000 population (2001 est.)
Net migration rate: 0 migrant(s)/1,000 population (2001 est.)
Sex ratio:
at birth: 1.05 male(s)/female
under 15 years: 1.04 male(s)/female
15-64 years: 0.97 male(s)/female
65 years and over: 0.81 male(s)/female
total population: 0.99 male(s)/female (2001 est.)
Infant mortality rate: 14.08 deaths/1,000 live births (2001 est.)
Life expectancy at birth:
total population: 68.25 years
male: 65.83 years
female: 70.78 years (2001 est.)
Total fertility rate: 3 children born/woman (2001 est.)
HIV/AIDS - adult prevalence rate: NA%
HIV/AIDS - people living with HIV/AIDS: NA
HIV/AIDS - deaths: NA
Nationality:
noun: Tongan(s)
adjective: Tongan
Ethnic groups: Polynesian, Europeans about 300
Religions: Christian (Free Wesleyan Church claims over 30,000 adherents)
Languages: Tongan, English
Literacy:
definition: can read and write Tongan and/or English
total population: 98.5%
male: 98.4%
female: 98.7% (1996 est.)

Government

Country name:
conventional long form: Kingdom of Tonga
conventional short form: Tonga
former: Friendly Islands
Government type: hereditary constitutional monarchy
Capital: Nuku'alofa
Administrative divisions: 3 island groups; Ha'apai, Tongatapu, Vava'u
Independence: 4 June 1970 (from UK protectorate)
National holiday: Independence Day, 4 June (1970)
Constitution: 4 November 1875, revised 1 January 1967
Legal system: based on English law
Suffrage: 21 years of age; universal
Executive branch:
chief of state: King Taufa'ahau TUPOU IV (since 16 December 1965)
head of government: Prime Minister Prince Lavaka ata ULUKALALA (since NA February 2000) and Deputy Prime Minister Tevita TOPOU (since NA January 2001)
cabinet: Cabinet appointed by the monarch
note: there is also a Privy Council that consists of the monarch and the Cabinet
elections: none; the monarch is hereditary; prime minister and deputy prime minister appointed for life by the monarch
Legislative branch: unicameral Legislative Assembly or Fale Alea (30 seats - 12 reserved for cabinet ministers sitting ex officio, nine for nobles selected by the country's 33 nobles, and nine elected by popular vote; members serve three-year terms)
elections: last held NA March 1999 (next to be held NA 2002)
election results: percent of vote - pro-democratic 40%; seats - pro-democratic 5, traditionalist 4
Judicial branch: Supreme Court (judges are appointed by the monarch); Court of Appeal (consists of the Privy Council with the addition of the chief justice of the Supreme Court)
Political parties and leaders: Human Rights and Democracy Movement [Huliki WATAB, chairman, Viliami FUKOFUKA, president, 'Akilisi POHIVA, vice president]
Political pressure groups and leaders: Pro-Democracy and Human Rights Movement [leader NA]
International organization participation: ACP, AsDB, C, ESCAP, FAO, G-77, IBRD, ICAO, ICFTU, ICRM, IDA, IFAD, IFC, IFRCS, IHO, IMF, IMO, Intelsat (nonsignatory user), Interpol, IOC, ITU, Sparteca, SPC, SPF, UN, UNCTAD, UNESCO, UNIDO, UPU, WHO, WIPO, WMO, WTrO (observer)

Tonga (continued)

Diplomatic representation in the US: Tonga does not have an embassy in the US; Ambassador Fetu'utolo TUPOU, resides in London; address: Embassy of the Kingdom of Tonga, c/o Tonga High Commission, 36 Molyneux Street, London W1H 6AB, telephone [44] (171) 724-5828, FAX [44] (171) 723-9074
consulate(s) general: San Francisco
Diplomatic representation from the US: the US does not have an embassy in Tonga; the ambassador to Fiji is accredited to Tonga
Flag description: red with a bold red cross on a white rectangle in the upper hoist-side corner

Economy

Economy - overview: Tonga has a small, open economy with a narrow export base in agricultural goods, which contributes 30% to GDP. Squash, coconuts, bananas, and vanilla beans are the main crops, and agricultural exports make up two-thirds of total exports. The country must import a high proportion of its food, mainly from New Zealand. The industrial sector accounts for only 10% of GDP. Tourism is the primary source of hard currency earnings. The country remains dependent on sizable external aid and remittances from Tongan communities overseas to offset its trade deficit. The government is emphasizing the development of the private sector, especially the encouragement of investment, and is committing increased funds for health and education. Tonga has a reasonable basic infrastructure and well-developed social services.
GDP: purchasing power parity - $225 million (2000 est.)
GDP - real growth rate: 5% (2000 est.)
GDP - per capita: purchasing power parity - $2,200 (2000 est.)
GDP - composition by sector:
agriculture: 30%
industry: 10%
services: 60% (1997)
Population below poverty line: NA%
Household income or consumption by percentage share:
lowest 10%: NA%
highest 10%: NA%
Inflation rate (consumer prices): 7% (2000 est.)
Labor force: 34,000 (FY96/97)
Labor force - by occupation: agriculture 65% (1997 est.)
Unemployment rate: 13.3% (FY96/97)
Budget:
revenues: $49 million
expenditures: $120 million, including capital expenditures of $75 million (FY96/97 est.)
Industries: tourism, fishing
Industrial production growth rate: 8.6% (FY98/99)
Electricity - production: 35 million kWh (1999)
Electricity - production by source:
fossil fuel: 100%
hydro: 0%
nuclear: 0%
other: 0% (1999)
Electricity - consumption: 32.6 million kWh (1999)
Electricity - exports: 0 kWh (1999)
Electricity - imports: 0 kWh (1999)
Agriculture - products: squash, coconuts, copra, bananas, vanilla beans, cocoa, coffee, ginger, black pepper; fish
Exports: $8 million (f.o.b., 1998)
Exports - commodities: squash, fish, vanilla beans
Exports - partners: Japan 53%, US 18%, NZ 6%, Australia 6% (1997 est.)
Imports: $69 million (f.o.b., 1998)
Imports - commodities: foodstuffs, machinery and transport equipment, fuels, chemicals
Imports - partners: NZ 30%, Australia 19%, US 11%, UK 11%, Japan 3% (1997 est.)
Debt - external: $62 million (1998)
Economic aid - recipient: $38.8 million (1995)
Currency: pa'anga (TOP)
Currency code: TOP
Exchange rates: pa'anga per US dollar - 1.9885 (January 2001), 1.7585 (2000), 1.5991 (1999), 1.4920 (1998), 1.2635 (1997), 1.2323 (1996)
Fiscal year: 1 July - 30 June

Communications

Telephones - main lines in use: 8,000 (1996)
Telephones - mobile cellular: 302 (1996)
Telephone system:
general assessment: NA
domestic: NA
international: satellite earth station - 1 Intelsat (Pacific Ocean)
Radio broadcast stations: AM 1, FM 2, shortwave 1 (2001)
Radios: 61,000 (1997)
Television broadcast stations: 1 (2001)
Televisions: 2,000 (1997)
Internet country code: .to
Internet Service Providers (ISPs): 2 (2000)
Internet users: 1,000 (2000)

Transportation

Railways: 0 km
Highways:
total: 680 km
paved: 184 km
unpaved: 496 km (1996 est.)
Waterways: none
Ports and harbors: Neiafu, Nuku'alofa, Pangai
Merchant marine:
total: 8 ships (1,000 GRT or over) totaling 20,626 GRT/29,468 DWT
ships by type: bulk 1, cargo 2, liquefied gas 3, petroleum tanker 1, roll on/roll off 1 (2000 est.)
Airports: 6 (2000 est.)
Airports - with paved runways:
total: 1
2,438 to 3,047 m: 1 (2000 est.)
Airports - with unpaved runways:
total: 5
1,524 to 2,437 m: 1
914 to 1,523 m: 2
under 914 m: 2 (2000 est.)

Military

Military branches: Tonga Defense Services (includes Royal Tongan Marines, Tongan Royal Guards, Maritime Force, Police); note - a new Air Wing which will be subordinate to the Defense Ministry is being developed
Military expenditures - dollar figure: $NA
Military expenditures - percent of GDP: NA%

Transnational Issues

Disputes - international: none

Trinidad and Tobago

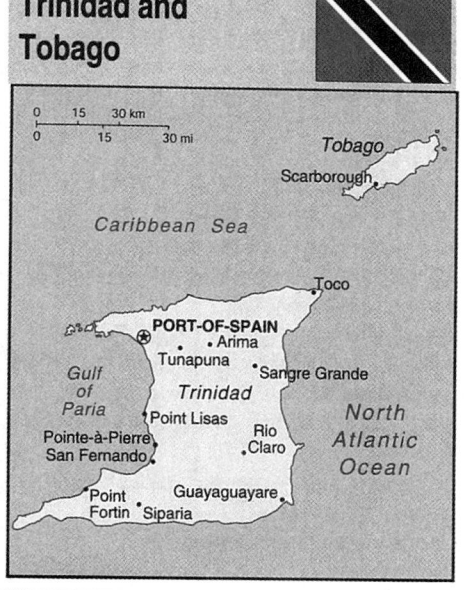

Introduction

Background: The islands came under British control in the 19th century; independence was granted in 1962. The country is one of the most prosperous in the Caribbean thanks largely to petroleum and natural gas production and processing. Tourism, mostly in Tobago, is targeted for expansion and is growing.

Geography

Location: Caribbean, islands between the Caribbean Sea and the North Atlantic Ocean, northeast of Venezuela
Geographic coordinates: 11 00 N, 61 00 W
Map references: Central America and the Caribbean
Area:
total: 5,128 sq km
land: 5,128 sq km
water: 0 sq km
Area - comparative: slightly smaller than Delaware
Land boundaries: 0 km
Coastline: 362 km
Maritime claims:
contiguous zone: 24 NM
continental shelf: 200 NM or to the outer edge of the continental margin
exclusive economic zone: 200 NM
territorial sea: 12 NM
Climate: tropical; rainy season (June to December)
Terrain: mostly plains with some hills and low mountains
Elevation extremes:
lowest point: Caribbean Sea 0 m
highest point: El Cerro del Aripo 940 m
Natural resources: petroleum, natural gas, asphalt
Land use:
arable land: 15%
permanent crops: 9%
permanent pastures: 2%
forests and woodland: 46%
other: 28% (1993 est.)
Irrigated land: 220 sq km (1993 est.)
Natural hazards: outside usual path of hurricanes and other tropical storms
Environment - current issues: water pollution from agricultural chemicals, industrial wastes, and raw sewage; oil pollution of beaches; deforestation; soil erosion
Environment - international agreements:
party to: Biodiversity, Climate Change, Climate Change-Kyoto Protocol, Desertification, Endangered Species, Hazardous Wastes, Law of the Sea, Marine Dumping, Marine Life Conservation, Nuclear Test Ban, Ozone Layer Protection, Ship Pollution, Tropical Timber 83, Tropical Timber 94, Wetlands
signed, but not ratified: none of the selected agreements

People

Population: 1,169,682 (July 2001 est.)
Age structure:
0-14 years: 24.1% (male 143,730; female 138,160)
15-64 years: 69.2% (male 415,898; female 393,551)
65 years and over: 6.7% (male 34,785; female 43,558) (2001 est.)
Population growth rate: -0.51% (2001 est.)
Birth rate: 13.73 births/1,000 population (2001 est.)
Death rate: 8.82 deaths/1,000 population (2001 est.)
Net migration rate: -9.97 migrant(s)/1,000 population (2001 est.)
Sex ratio:
at birth: 1.05 male(s)/female
under 15 years: 1.04 male(s)/female
15-64 years: 1.06 male(s)/female
65 years and over: 0.8 male(s)/female
total population: 1.03 male(s)/female (2001 est.)
Infant mortality rate: 24.98 deaths/1,000 live births (2001 est.)
Life expectancy at birth:
total population: 68.27 years
male: 65.74 years
female: 70.92 years (2001 est.)
Total fertility rate: 1.81 children born/woman (2001 est.)
HIV/AIDS - adult prevalence rate: 1.05% (1999 est.)
HIV/AIDS - people living with HIV/AIDS: 7,800 (1999 est.)
HIV/AIDS - deaths: 530 (1999 est.)
Nationality:
noun: Trinidadian(s), Tobagonian(s)
adjective: Trinidadian, Tobagonian
Ethnic groups: black 39.5%, East Indian (a local term - primarily immigrants from northern India) 40.3%, mixed 18.4%, white 0.6%, Chinese and other 1.2%
Religions: Roman Catholic 29.4%, Hindu 23.8%, Anglican 10.9%, Muslim 5.8%, Presbyterian 3.4%, other 26.7%
Languages: English (official), Hindi, French, Spanish, Chinese
Literacy:
definition: age 15 and over can read and write
total population: 97.9%
male: 98.8%
female: 97% (1995 est.)

Government

Country name:
conventional long form: Republic of Trinidad and Tobago
conventional short form: Trinidad and Tobago
Government type: parliamentary democracy
Capital: Port-of-Spain
Administrative divisions: 8 counties, 3 municipalities*, and 1 ward**; Arima*, Caroni, Mayaro, Nariva, Port-of-Spain*, Saint Andrew, Saint David, Saint George, Saint Patrick, San Fernando*, Tobago**, Victoria
Independence: 31 August 1962 (from UK)
National holiday: Independence Day, 31 August (1962)
Constitution: 1 August 1976
Legal system: based on English common law; judicial review of legislative acts in the Supreme Court; has not accepted compulsory ICJ jurisdiction
Suffrage: 18 years of age; universal
Executive branch:
chief of state: President Arthur Napoleon Raymond ROBINSON (since 19 March 1997)
head of government: Prime Minister Basdeo PANDAY (since 9 November 1995)
cabinet: Cabinet appointed from among the members of Parliament
elections: president elected by an electoral college, which consists of the members of the Senate and House of Representatives, for a five-year term; election last held 11 December 2000 (next to be held by NA 2005); prime minister appointed from among the members of Parliament; following legislative elections, the leader of the majority party in the House of Representatives is usually appointed prime minister
election results: Arthur Napoleon Raymond ROBINSON elected president; percent of electoral college vote - 69%
Legislative branch: bicameral Parliament consists of the Senate (31 seats; members appointed by the president for a maximum term of five years) and the House of Representatives (36 seats; members are elected by popular vote to serve five-year terms)
elections: House of Representatives - last held 11 December 2000 (next to be held by December 2005)
election results: House of Representatives - percent of vote - UNC 58.1%, PNM 40.8%, NAR 1.1%; seats by party - UNC 19, PNM 16, NAR 1
note: Tobago has a unicameral House of Assembly, with 15 members serving four-year terms
Judicial branch: Supreme Court of Judicature (comprised of the High Court of Justice and the Court of Appeals; the chief justice is appointed by the president on the advice of the prime minister and the leader of the opposition; other justices are appointed

Trinidad and Tobago (continued)

by the president on the advice of the Judicial and Legal Service Commission); High Court of Justice; Court of Appeals; The Majistracy (hears minor civil cases and summary criminal cases)
Political parties and leaders: National Alliance for Reconstruction or NAR [Hochay CHARLES]; People's Empowerment Party or PEP [leader NA]; People's National Movement or PNM [Patrick MANNING]; United National Congress or UNC [Basdeo PANDAY]
Political pressure groups and leaders: Jamaat Al Musilmeen [Abu BAKR]
International organization participation: ACP, C, Caricom, CCC, CDB, ECLAC, FAO, G-24, G-77, IADB, IBRD, ICAO, ICFTU, ICRM, IDA, IFAD, IFC, IFRCS, IHO, ILO, IMF, IMO, Intelsat, Interpol, IOC, ISO, ITU, LAES, NAM, OAS, OPANAL, OPCW, UN, UNCTAD, UNESCO, UNIDO, UNU, UPU, WCL, WFTU, WHO, WIPO, WMO, WTrO
Diplomatic representation in the US:
chief of mission: Ambassador (vacant)
chancery: 1708 Massachusetts Avenue NW, Washington, DC 20036
telephone: [1] (202) 467-6490
FAX: [1] (202) 785-3130
consulate(s) general: Miami and New York
Diplomatic representation from the US:
chief of mission: Ambassador Edward E. SHUMAKER, III (until April, 2001)
embassy: 15 Queen's Park West, Port-of-Spain
mailing address: P. O. Box 752, Port-of-Spain
telephone: [1] (868) 622-6371 through 6376, 6176
FAX: [1] (868) 628-5462
Flag description: red with a white-edged black diagonal band from the upper hoist side

Economy

Economy - overview: Trinidad and Tobago has earned a reputation as an excellent investment site for international businesses. Successful economic reforms were implemented in 1995, and foreign investment and trade are flourishing. Persistently high unemployment remains one of the chief challenges of the government. The petrochemical sector has spurred growth in other related sectors, reinforcing the government's commitment to economic diversification. Tourism is growing, especially in the pleasure boat sector. New investment and construction also will continue to drive the economy.
GDP: purchasing power parity - $11.2 billion (2000 est.)
GDP - real growth rate: 5% (2000 est.)
GDP - per capita: purchasing power parity - $9,500 (2000 est.)
GDP - composition by sector:
agriculture: 2%
industry: 44%
services: 54% (1998 est.)
Population below poverty line: 21% (1992 est.)
Household income or consumption by percentage share:
lowest 10%: NA%
highest 10%: NA%
Inflation rate (consumer prices): 3.2% (2000 est.)
Labor force: 558,700 (1998)
Labor force - by occupation: construction and utilities 12.4%, manufacturing, mining, and quarrying 14%, agriculture 9.5%, services 64.1% (1997 est.)
Unemployment rate: 12.8% (2000)
Budget:
revenues: $1.54 billion
expenditures: $1.6 billion, including capital expenditures of $117.3 million (1998)
Industries: petroleum, chemicals, tourism, food processing, cement, beverage, cotton textiles
Industrial production growth rate: 3.8% (2000)
Electricity - production: 4.9 billion kWh (1999)
Electricity - production by source:
fossil fuel: 99.59%
hydro: 0%
nuclear: 0%
other: 0.41% (1999)
Electricity - consumption: 4.557 billion kWh (1999)
Electricity - exports: 0 kWh (1999)
Electricity - imports: 0 kWh (1999)
Agriculture - products: cocoa, sugarcane, rice, citrus, coffee, vegetables; poultry
Exports: $3.2 billion (f.o.b., 2000)
Exports - commodities: petroleum and petroleum products, chemicals, steel products, fertilizer, sugar, cocoa, coffee, citrus, flowers
Exports - partners: US 39.3%, Caricom countries 26.1%, Latin America 9.5%, EU 5.7% (1999)
Imports: $3 billion (f.o.b., 2000 est.)
Imports - commodities: machinery, transportation equipment, manufactured goods, food, live animals
Imports - partners: US 39.8%, Venezuela 11.9%, EU 11%, Caricom 4.8% (1999)
Debt - external: $2.8 billion (2000 est.)
Economic aid - recipient: $121.4 million (1995)
Currency: Trinidad and Tobago dollar (TTD)
Currency code: TTD
Exchange rates: Trinidad and Tobago dollars per US dollar - 6.2688 (January 2001), 6.2998 (2000), 6.2989 (1999), 6.2983 (1998), 6.2517 (1997), 6.0051 (1996)
Fiscal year: 1 October - 30 September

Communications

Telephones - main lines in use: 243,000 (1997)
Telephones - mobile cellular: 17,411 (1997)
Telephone system:
general assessment: excellent international service; good local service
domestic: NA
international: satellite earth station - 1 Intelsat (Atlantic Ocean); tropospheric scatter to Barbados and Guyana
Radio broadcast stations: AM 2, FM 12, shortwave 0 (1998)
Radios: 680,000 (1997)
Television broadcast stations: 4 (1997)
Televisions: 425,000 (1997)
Internet country code: .tt
Internet Service Providers (ISPs): 17 (2000)
Internet users: 30,000 (2000)

Transportation

Railways: minimal agricultural railroad system near San Fernando; railway service was discontinued in 1968
Highways:
total: 8,320 km
paved: 4,252 km
unpaved: 4,068 km (1996 est.)
Waterways: none
Pipelines: crude oil 1,032 km; petroleum products 19 km; natural gas 904 km
Ports and harbors: Pointe-a-Pierre, Point Fortin, Point Lisas, Port-of-Spain, Scarborough, Tembladora
Merchant marine:
total: 2 ships (1,000 GRT or over) totaling 2,439 GRT/4,040 DWT
ships by type: cargo 1, petroleum tanker 1 (2000 est.)
Airports: 6 (2000 est.)
Airports - with paved runways:
total: 3
over 3,047 m: 1
2,438 to 3,047 m: 1
1,524 to 2,437 m: 1 (2000 est.)
Airports - with unpaved runways:
total: 3
914 to 1,523 m: 1
under 914 m: 2 (2000 est.)

Military

Military branches: Trinidad and Tobago Defense Force (includes Ground Forces, Coast Guard, and Air Wing), Trinidad and Tobago Police Service
Military manpower - availability:
males age 15-49: 346,043 (2001 est.)
Military manpower - fit for military service:
males age 15-49: 247,297 (2001 est.)
Military expenditures - dollar figure: $83 million (FY94)
Military expenditures - percent of GDP: NA%

Transnational Issues

Disputes - international: none
Illicit drugs: transshipment point for South American drugs destined for the US and Europe; producer of cannabis

Tromelin Island
(possession of France)

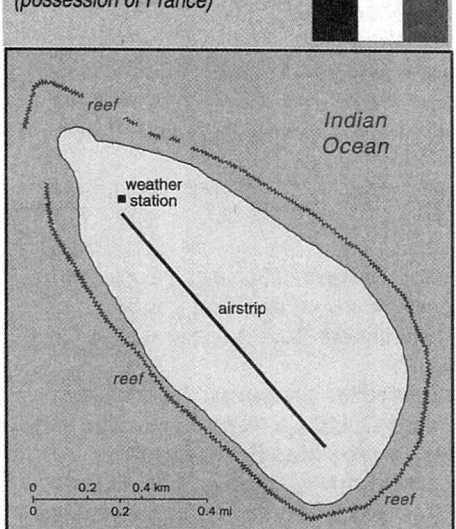

Introduction

Background: First explored by the French in 1776, the island came under the jurisdiction of Reunion in 1814. At present, it serves as a sea turtle sanctuary and is the site of an important meteorological station.

Geography

Location: Southern Africa, island in the Indian Ocean, east of Madagascar
Geographic coordinates. 15 52 S, 54 25 E
Map references. Africa
Area.
total. 1 sq km
land. 1 sq km
water. 0 sq km
Area - comparative. about 1.7 times the size of The Mall in Washington, DC
Land boundaries. 0 km
Coastline. 3.7 km
Maritime claims.
continental shelf. 200-m depth or to the depth of exploitation
exclusive economic zone. 200 NM
territorial sea. 12 NM
Climate. tropical
Terrain. low, flat, and sandy
Elevation extremes.
lowest point. Indian Ocean 0 m
highest point. unnamed location 7 m
Natural resources. fish
Land use.
arable land. 0%
permanent crops. 0%
permanent pastures. 0%
forests and woodland. 0%
other. 100% (scattered bushes)
Irrigated land. 0 sq km (1993)
Natural hazards. NA
Environment - current issues. NA
Geography - note. climatologically important location for forecasting cyclones; wildlife sanctuary

People

Population: uninhabited (July 2001 est.)

Government

Country name:
conventional long form: none
conventional short form: Tromelin Island
local long form: none
local short form: Ile Tromelin
Dependency status: possession of France; administered by a high commissioner of the Republic, resident in Reunion
Legal system: the laws of France, where applicable, apply
Flag description: the flag of France is used

Economy

Economy - overview: no economic activity

Communications

Communications - note: important meteorological station

Transportation

Waterways: none
Ports and harbors: none; offshore anchorage only
Airports: 1 (2000 est.)
Airports - with unpaved runways:
total: 1
under 914 m: 1 (2000 est.)

Military

Military - note: defense is the responsibility of France

Transnational Issues

Disputes - international: claimed by Madagascar and Mauritius

Tunisia

Introduction

Background: Following independence from France in 1956, President Habib BOURGIUBA established a strict one-party state. He dominated the country for 31 years, repressing Islamic fundamentalism and establishing rights for women unmatched by any other Arab nation. In recent years, Tunisia has taken a moderate, non-aligned stance in its foreign relations. Domestically, it has sought to diffuse rising pressure for a more open political society.

Geography

Location: Northern Africa, bordering the Mediterranean Sea, between Algeria and Libya
Geographic coordinates: 34 00 N, 9 00 E
Map references: Africa
Area:
total: 163,610 sq km
land: 155,360 sq km
water: 8,250 sq km
Area - comparative: slightly larger than Georgia
Land boundaries:
total: 1,424 km
border countries: Algeria 965 km, Libya 459 km

Tunisia (continued)

Coastline: 1,148 km
Maritime claims:
contiguous zone: 24 NM
territorial sea: 12 NM
Climate: temperate in north with mild, rainy winters and hot, dry summers; desert in south
Terrain: mountains in north; hot, dry central plain; semiarid south merges into the Sahara
Elevation extremes:
lowest point: Shatt al Gharsah -17 m
highest point: Jebel ech Chambi 1,544 m
Natural resources: petroleum, phosphates, iron ore, lead, zinc, salt
Land use:
arable land: 19%
permanent crops: 13%
permanent pastures: 20%
forests and woodland: 4%
other: 44% (1993 est.)
Irrigated land: 3,850 sq km (1993 est.)
Natural hazards: NA
Environment - current issues: toxic and hazardous waste disposal is ineffective and presents human health risks; water pollution from raw sewage; limited natural fresh water resources; deforestation; overgrazing; soil erosion; desertification
Environment - international agreements:
party to: Biodiversity, Climate Change, Desertification, Endangered Species, Environmental Modification, Hazardous Wastes, Law of the Sea, Marine Dumping, Nuclear Test Ban, Ozone Layer Protection, Ship Pollution, Wetlands
signed, but not ratified: Marine Life Conservation
Geography - note: strategic location in central Mediterranean; Malta and Tunisia are discussing the commercial exploitation of the continental shelf between their countries, particularly for oil exploration

People

Population: 9,705,102 (July 2001 est.)
Age structure:
0-14 years: 28.74% (male 1,440,636; female 1,348,133)
15-64 years: 65.12% (male 3,157,988; female 3,161,596)
65 years and over: 6.14% (male 296,930; female 299,819) (2001 est.)
Population growth rate: 1.15% (2001 est.)
Birth rate: 17.11 births/1,000 population (2001 est.)
Death rate: 4.99 deaths/1,000 population (2001 est.)
Net migration rate: -0.67 migrant(s)/1,000 population (2001 est.)
Sex ratio:
at birth: 1.08 male(s)/female
under 15 years: 1.07 male(s)/female
15-64 years: 1 male(s)/female
65 years and over: 0.99 male(s)/female
total population: 1.02 male(s)/female (2001 est.)
Infant mortality rate: 29.04 deaths/1,000 live births (2001 est.)

Life expectancy at birth:
total population: 73.92 years
male: 72.35 years
female: 75.62 years (2001 est.)
Total fertility rate: 1.99 children born/woman (2001 est.)
HIV/AIDS - adult prevalence rate: 0.04% (1999 est.)
HIV/AIDS - people living with HIV/AIDS: NA
HIV/AIDS - deaths: NA
Nationality:
noun: Tunisian(s)
adjective: Tunisian
Ethnic groups: Arab 98%, European 1%, Jewish and other 1%
Religions: Muslim 98%, Christian 1%, Jewish and other 1%
Languages: Arabic (official and one of the languages of commerce), French (commerce)
Literacy:
definition: age 15 and over can read and write
total population: 66.7%
male: 78.6%
female: 54.6% (1995 est.)

Government

Country name:
conventional long form: Republic of Tunisia
conventional short form: Tunisia
local long form: Al Jumhuriyah at Tunisiyah
local short form: Tunis
Government type: republic
Capital: Tunis
Administrative divisions: 23 governorates; Ariana (Aryanah), Beja (Bajah), Ben Arous (Bin 'Arus), Bizerte (Banzart), El Kef (Al Kaf), Gabes (Qabis), Gafsa (Qafsah), Jendouba (Jundubah), Kairouan (Al Qayrawan), Kasserine (Al Qasrayn), Kebili (Qibili), Mahdia (Al Mahdiyah), Medenine (Madanin), Monastir (Al Munastir), Nabeul (Nabul), Sfax (Safaqis), Sidi Bou Zid (Sidi Bu Zayd), Siliana (Silyanah), Sousse (Susah), Tataouine (Tatawin), Tozeur (Tawzar), Tunis, Zaghouan (Zaghwan)
Independence: 20 March 1956 (from France)
National holiday: Independence Day, 20 March (1956)
Constitution: 1 June 1959; amended 12 July 1988
Legal system: based on French civil law system and Islamic law; some judicial review of legislative acts in the Supreme Court in joint session
Suffrage: 20 years of age; universal
Executive branch:
chief of state: President Zine El Abidine BEN ALI (since 7 November 1987)
head of government: Prime Minister Mohamed GHANNOUCHI (since 17 November 1999)
cabinet: Council of Ministers appointed by the president
elections: president elected by popular vote for a five-year term; election last held 24 October 1999 (next to be held NA 2004); prime minister appointed by the president

election results: President Zine El Abidine BEN ALI reelected for a third term without opposition; percent of vote - Zine El Abidine BEN ALI nearly 100%
Legislative branch: unicameral Chamber of Deputies or Majlis al-Nuwaab (182 seats; members elected by popular vote to serve five-year terms)
elections: last held 24 October 1999 (next to be held NA 2004)
election results: percent of vote by party - RCD 92%; seats by party - RCD 148, MDS 13, UDU 7, PUP 7, Al-Tajdid 5, PSL 2; note - reforms enabled opposition parties to win up to 20% of seats; the opposition increased number of seats from 19 to 34
Judicial branch: Court of Cassation or Cour de Cassation
Political parties and leaders: Al-Tajdid Movement [Adel CHAOUCH]; Constitutional Democratic Rally Party (Rassemblement Constitutionnel Democratique) or RCD [President Zine El Abidine BEN ALI (official ruling party)]; Liberal Social Party or PSL [Mounir BEJI]; Movement of Democratic Socialists or MDS [Khamis CHAMMARI]; Popular Unity Party or PUP [Mohamed Belhaj AMOR]; Unionist Democratic Union or UDU [Abderrahmane TLILI]
Political pressure groups and leaders: the Islamic fundamentalist party, Al Nahda (Renaissance), is outlawed
International organization participation: ABEDA, ACCT, AfDB, AFESD, AL, AMF, AMU, BSEC (observer), CCC, ECA, FAO, G-77, IAEA, IBRD, ICAO, ICC, ICFTU, ICRM, IDA, IDB, IFAD, IFC, IFRCS, IHO, ILO, IMF, IMO, Inmarsat, Intelsat, Interpol, IOC, IOM, ISO, ITU, MIPONUH, MONUC, NAM, OAS (observer), OAU, OIC, OPCW, OSCE (partner), UN, UN Security Council (temporary), UNCTAD, UNESCO, UNHCR, UNIDO, UNMEE, UNMIBH, UNMIK, UPU, WFTU, WHO, WIPO, WMO, WToO, WTrO
Diplomatic representation in the US:
chief of mission: Ambassador Hatem ATALLAH
chancery: 1515 Massachusetts Avenue NW, Washington, DC 20005
telephone: [1] (202) 862-1850
Diplomatic representation from the US:
chief of mission: Ambassador Rust DEMMING
embassy: 144 Avenue de la Liberte, 1002 Tunis-Belvedere
mailing address: use embassy street address
telephone: [216] (1) 782-566
FAX: [216] (1) 789-719
Flag description: red with a white disk in the center bearing a red crescent nearly encircling a red five-pointed star; the crescent and star are traditional symbols of Islam

Economy

Economy - overview: Tunisia has a diverse economy, with important agricultural, mining, energy, tourism, and manufacturing sectors. Governmental control of economic affairs while still heavy has gradually lessened over the past decade with

Tunisia (continued)

increasing privatization, simplification of the tax structure, and a prudent approach to debt. Real growth averaged 5.5% in the past four years, and inflation is slowing. Growth in tourism and increased trade have been key elements in this steady growth. Tunisia's association agreement with the European Union entered into force on 1 March 1998, the first such accord between the EU and Mediterranean countries to be activated. Under the agreement Tunisia will gradually remove barriers to trade with the EU over the next decade. Broader privatization, further liberalization of the investment code to increase foreign investment, and improvements in government efficiency are among the challenges for the future.

GDP: purchasing power parity - $62.8 billion (2000 est.)
GDP - real growth rate: 5% (2000 est.)
GDP - per capita: purchasing power parity - $6,500 (2000 est.)
GDP - composition by sector:
agriculture: 14%
industry: 32%
services: 54% (1999 est.)
Population below poverty line: 6% (2000 est.)
Household income or consumption by percentage share:
lowest 10%: 2.3%
highest 10%: 30.7% (1990)
Inflation rate (consumer prices): 3% (2000 est.)
Labor force: 2.65 million (2000 est.)
note: shortage of skilled labor
Labor force - by occupation: services 55%, industry 23%, agriculture 22% (1995 est.)
Unemployment rate: 15.6% (2000 est.)
Budget:
revenues: $7.5 billion
expenditures: $8.1 billion, including capital expenditures to $1.6 billion (2000 est.)
Industries: petroleum, mining (particularly phosphate and iron ore), tourism, textiles, footwear, food, beverages
Industrial production growth rate: 4.1% (2000 est.)
Electricity - production: 9.173 billion kWh (1999)
Electricity - production by source:
fossil fuel: 99.2%
hydro: 0.8%
nuclear: 0%
other: 0% (1999)
Electricity - consumption: 8.677 billion kWh (1999)
Electricity - exports: 19 million kWh (1999)
Electricity - imports: 165 million kWh (1999)
Agriculture - products: olives, olive oil, grain, dairy products, tomatoes, citrus fruit, beef, sugar beets, dates, almonds
Exports: $6.1 billion (f.o.b., 2000 est.)
Exports - commodities: textiles, mechanical goods, phosphates and chemicals, agricultural products, hydrocarbons
Exports - partners: Germany 28%, France 22%, Italy 17%, Belgium 5%, Libya 4% (1999)

Imports: $8.4 billion (f.o.b., 2000 est.)
Imports - commodities: machinery and equipment, hydrocarbons, chemicals, food
Imports - partners: France 23%, Germany 23%, Italy 15%, Belgium 3% (1999)
Debt - external: $13 billion (2000 est.)
Economic aid - recipient: $933.2 million (1995); note - ODA, $90 million (1998 est.)
Currency: Tunisian dinar (TND)
Currency code: TND
Exchange rates: Tunisian dinars per US dollar - 1.3753 (January 2001), 1.4667 (November 2000), 1.1862 (1999), 1.1387 (1998), 1.1059 (1997), 0.9734 (1996)
Fiscal year: calendar year

Communications

Telephones - main lines in use: 654,000 (1997)
Telephones - mobile cellular: 50,000 (1998)
Telephone system:
general assessment: above the African average and continuing to be upgraded; key centers are Sfax, Sousse, Bizerte, and Tunis; Internet access available
domestic: trunk facilities consist of open-wire lines, coaxial cable, and microwave radio relay
international: 5 submarine cables; satellite earth stations - 1 Intelsat (Atlantic Ocean) and 1 Arabsat; coaxial cable and microwave radio relay to Algeria and Libya; participant in Medarabtel; two international gateway digital switches
Radio broadcast stations: AM 7, FM 20, shortwave 2 (1998)
Radios: 2.06 million (1997)
Television broadcast stations: 26 (plus 76 repeaters) (1995)
Televisions: 920,000 (1997)
Internet country code: .tn
Internet Service Providers (ISPs): 1 (2000)
Internet users: 110,000 (2000)

Transportation

Railways:
total: 2,168 km
standard gauge: 471 km 1.435-m gauge
narrow gauge: 1,687 km 1.000-m gauge
dual gauge: 10 km 1.000-m and 1.435-m gauges (three rails)
Highways:
total: 23,100 km
paved: 18,226 km
unpaved: 4,874 km (1996 est.)
Waterways: none
Pipelines: crude oil 797 km; petroleum products 86 km; natural gas 742 km
Ports and harbors: Bizerte, Gabes, La Goulette, Sfax, Sousse, Tunis, Zarzis
Merchant marine:
total: 15 ships (1,000 GRT or over) totaling 149,554 GRT/156,861 DWT
ships by type: bulk 2, cargo 4, chemical tanker 3, liquefied gas 1, petroleum tanker 1, short-sea passenger 3, specialized tanker 1 (2000 est.)

Airports: 32 (2000 est.)
Airports - with paved runways:
total: 15
over 3,047 m: 3
2,438 to 3,047 m: 6
1,524 to 2,437 m: 3
914 to 1,523 m: 3 (2000 est.)
Airports - with unpaved runways:
total: 17
1,524 to 2,437 m: 2
914 to 1,523 m: 8
under 914 m: 7 (2000 est.)

Military

Military branches: Army, Navy, Air Force, paramilitary forces, National Guard
Military manpower - military age: 20 years of age
Military manpower - availability:
males age 15-49: 2,739,566 (2001 est.)
Military manpower - fit for military service:
males age 15-49: 1,561,484 (2001 est.)
Military manpower - reaching military age annually:
males: 105,146 (2001 est.)
Military expenditures - dollar figure: $356 million (FY99)
Military expenditures - percent of GDP: 1.5% (FY99)

Transnational Issues

Disputes - international: none

Turkey

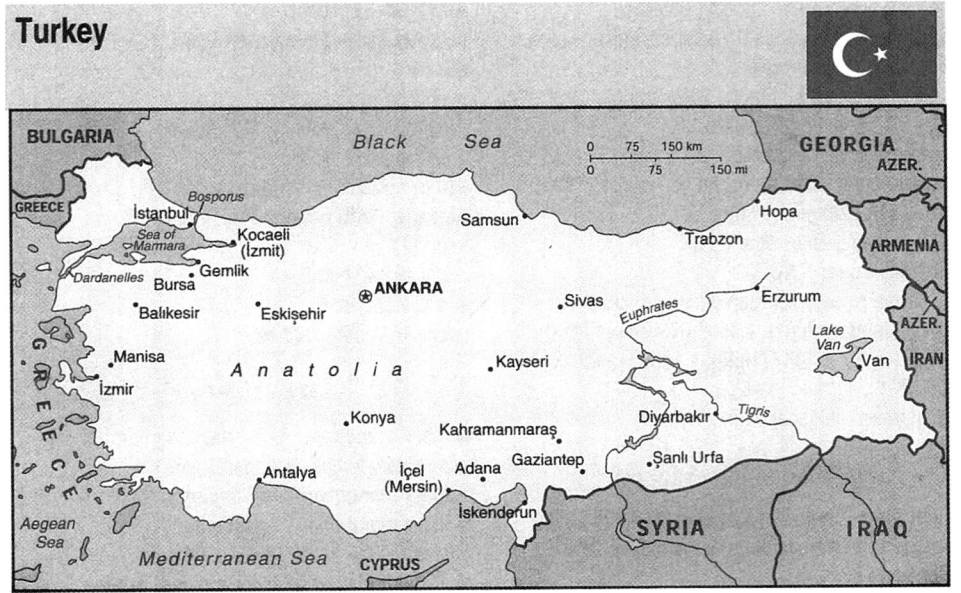

Introduction

Background: Turkey was created in 1923 from the Turkish remnants of the Ottoman Empire. Soon thereafter the country instituted secular laws to replace traditional religious fiats. In 1945 Turkey joined the UN and in 1952 it became a member of NATO. Turkey occupied the northern portion of Cyprus in 1974 to prevent a Greek takeover of the island; relations between the two countries remain strained. Periodic military offensives against Kurdish separatists have dislocated part of the population in southeast Turkey and have drawn international condemnation.

Geography

Location: southeastern Europe and southwestern Asia (that portion of Turkey west of the Bosporus is geographically part of Europe), bordering the Black Sea, between Bulgaria and Georgia, and bordering the Aegean Sea and the Mediterranean Sea, between Greece and Syria
Geographic coordinates: 39 00 N, 35 00 E
Map references: Middle East
Area:
total: 780,580 sq km
land: 770,760 sq km
water: 9,820 sq km
Area - comparative: slightly larger than Texas
Land boundaries:
total: 2,627 km
border countries: Armenia 268 km, Azerbaijan 9 km, Bulgaria 240 km, Georgia 252 km, Greece 206 km, Iran 499 km, Iraq 331 km, Syria 822 km
Coastline: 7,200 km
Maritime claims:
exclusive economic zone: in Black Sea only: to the maritime boundary agreed upon with the former USSR
territorial sea: 6 NM in the Aegean Sea; 12 NM in Black Sea and in Mediterranean Sea
Climate: temperate; hot, dry summers with mild, wet winters; harsher in interior
Terrain: mostly mountains; narrow coastal plain; high central plateau (Anatolia)
Elevation extremes:
lowest point: Mediterranean Sea 0 m
highest point: Mount Ararat 5,166 m
Natural resources: antimony, coal, chromium, mercury, copper, borate, sulfur, iron ore, arable land, hydropower
Land use:
arable land: 32%
permanent crops: 4%
permanent pastures: 16%
forests and woodland: 26%
other: 22% (1993 est.)
Irrigated land: 36,740 sq km (1993 est.)
Natural hazards: very severe earthquakes, especially in northern Turkey, along an arc extending from the Sea of Marmara to Lake Van
Environment - current issues: water pollution from dumping of chemicals and detergents; air pollution, particularly in urban areas; deforestation; concern for oil spills from increasing Bosporus ship traffic
Environment - international agreements:
party to: Air Pollution, Antarctic Treaty, Biodiversity, Desertification, Endangered Species, Hazardous Wastes, Marine Dumping, Nuclear Test Ban, Ozone Layer Protection, Ship Pollution, Wetlands
signed, but not ratified: Antarctic-Environmental Protocol, Environmental Modification
Geography - note: strategic location controlling the Turkish Straits (Bosporus, Sea of Marmara, Dardanelles) that link Black and Aegean Seas

People

Population: 66,493,970 (July 2001 est.)
Age structure:
0-14 years: 28.42% (male 9,620,291; female 9,276,347)
15-64 years: 65.45% (male 22,116,599; female 21,401,165)
65 years and over: 6.13% (male 1,878,571; female 2,200,997) (2001 est.)
Population growth rate: 1.24% (2001 est.)
Birth rate: 18.31 births/1,000 population (2001 est.)
Death rate: 5.95 deaths/1,000 population (2001 est.)
Net migration rate: 0 migrant(s)/1,000 population (2001 est.)
Sex ratio:
at birth: 1.05 male(s)/female
under 15 years: 1.04 male(s)/female
15-64 years: 1.03 male(s)/female
65 years and over: 0.85 male(s)/female
total population: 1.02 male(s)/female (2001 est.)
Infant mortality rate: 47.34 deaths/1,000 live births (2001 est.)
Life expectancy at birth:
total population: 71.24 years
male: 68.89 years
female: 73.71 years (2001 est.)
Total fertility rate: 2.12 children born/woman (2001 est.)
HIV/AIDS - adult prevalence rate: 0.01% (1999 est.)
HIV/AIDS - people living with HIV/AIDS: NA
HIV/AIDS - deaths: NA
Nationality:
noun: Turk(s)
adjective: Turkish
Ethnic groups: Turkish 80%, Kurdish 20%
Religions: Muslim 99.8% (mostly Sunni), other 0.2% (Christian and Jews)
Languages: Turkish (official), Kurdish, Arabic, Armenian, Greek
Literacy:
definition: age 15 and over can read and write
total population: 85%
male: 94%
female: 77% (2000)

Government

Country name:
conventional long form: Republic of Turkey
conventional short form: Turkey
local long form: Turkiye Cumhuriyeti
local short form: Turkiye
Government type: republican parliamentary democracy
Capital: Ankara
Administrative divisions: 80 provinces (iller, singular - il); Adana, Adiyaman, Afyon, Agri, Aksaray, Amasya, Ankara, Antalya, Ardahan, Artvin, Aydin, Balikesir, Bartin, Batman, Bayburt, Bilecik, Bingol, Bitlis, Bolu, Burdur, Bursa, Canakkale, Cankiri, Corum, Denizli, Diyarbakir, Edirne, Elazig, Erzincan, Erzurum, Eskisehir, Gaziantep, Giresun, Gumushane, Hakkari, Hatay, Icel, Igdir, Isparta, Istanbul, Izmir, Kahramanmaras, Karabuk, Karaman, Kars, Kastamonu, Kayseri, Kilis, Kirikkale, Kirklareli,

Turkey (continued)

Kirsehir, Kocaeli, Konya, Kutahya, Malatya, Manisa, Mardin, Mugla, Mus, Nevsehir, Nigde, Ordu, Osmaniye, Rize, Sakarya, Samsun, Sanliurfa, Siirt, Sinop, Sirnak, Sivas, Tekirdag, Tokat, Trabzon, Tunceli, Usak, Van, Yalova, Yozgat, Zonguldak; note - there may be another province called Duzce

Independence: 29 October 1923 (successor state to the Ottoman Empire)

National holiday: Independence Day, 29 October (1923)

Constitution: 7 November 1982

Legal system: derived from various European continental legal systems; accepts compulsory ICJ jurisdiction, with reservations

Suffrage: 18 years of age; universal

Executive branch:
chief of state: President Ahmed Necdet SEZER (since 16 May 2000)
head of government: Prime Minister Bulent ECEVIT (since 11 January 1999)
cabinet: Council of Ministers appointed by the president on the nomination of the prime minister
note: there is also a National Security Council that serves as an advisory body to the president and the cabinet
elections: president elected by the National Assembly for a seven-year term; election last held 5 May 2000 (next scheduled to be held NA May 2007); prime minister and deputy prime minister appointed by the president
election results: Ahmed Necdet SEZER elected president on the third ballot; percent of National Assembly vote - 60%
note: president must have a two-thirds majority of the National Assembly on the first two ballots and a simple majority on the third ballot

Legislative branch: unicameral Grand National Assembly of Turkey or Turkiye Buyuk Millet Meclisi (550 seats; members are elected by popular vote to serve five-year terms)
elections: last held 18 April 1999 (next to be held NA 2004)
election results: percent of vote by party - NA%; seats by party - DSP 136, MHP 130, FP 110, DYP 86, ANAP 88; note - as of 7 March 2000 seating was DSP 136, MHP 127, FP 103, DYP 85, ANAP 88 independents 6, vacancies 5

Judicial branch: Constitutional Court (judges are appointed by the president); Court of Appeals (judges are elected by the Supreme Council of Judges and Prosecutors)

Political parties and leaders: Democratic Left Party or DSP [Bulent ECEVIT]; Motherland Party or ANAP [Mesut YILMAZ]; Nationalist Action Party or MHP [Devlet BAHCELI]; True Path Party or DYP [Tansu CILLER]; Virtue Party or FP [Recai KUTAN]
note: Welfare Party or RP [Necmettin ERBAKAN] was officially outlawed on 22 February 1998

Political pressure groups and leaders: Confederation of Revolutionary Workers Unions or DISK [Ridvan BUDAK]; Independent Industrialists and Businessmen's Association or MUSIAD [Erol YARAR]; Moral Rights Workers Union or Hak-Is [Salim USLU]; Turkish Industrialists' and Businessmen's Association or TUSIAD [Muharrem KAYHAN]; Turkish Confederation of Employers' Unions or TISK [Refik BAYDUR]; Turkish Confederation of Labor or Turk-Is [Bayram MERAL]; Turkish Union of Chambers of Commerce and Commodity Exchanges or TOBB [Fuat MIRAS]

International organization participation: AsDB, Australia Group, BIS, BSEC, CCC, CE, CERN (observer), EAPC, EBRD, ECE, ECO, ESCAP, EU (applicant), FAO, IAEA, IBRD, ICAO, ICC, ICFTU, ICRM, IDA, IDB, IEA, IFAD, IFC, IFRCS, IHO, ILO, IMF, IMO, Inmarsat, Intelsat, Interpol, IOC, IOM (observer), ISO, ITU, NATO, NEA, NSG, OAS (observer), OECD, OIC, OPCW, OSCE, PCA, UN, UNCTAD, UNESCO, UNHCR, UNIDO, UNIKOM, UNMIBH, UNMIK, UNOMIG, UNRWA, UNTAET, UPU, WEU (associate), WFTU, WHO, WIPO, WMO, WToO, WTrO

Diplomatic representation in the US:
chief of mission: Ambassador Baki ILKIN
chancery: 2525 Massachusetts Avenue NW, Washington, DC 20008
telephone: [1] (202) 612-6700
FAX: [1] (202) 612-6744
consulate(s) general: Chicago, Houston, Los Angeles, and New York

Diplomatic representation from the US:
chief of mission: Ambassador Robert PEARSON
embassy: Ataturk Bulvarii 110, Ankara
mailing address: PSC 93, Box 5000, APO AE 09823
telephone: [90] (312) 468-6110
FAX: [90] (312) 467-0019
consulate(s) general: Istanbul (closed as of December 2000 for security review)
consulate(s): Adana (closed as of December 2000 for security review)

Flag description: red with a vertical white crescent (the closed portion is toward the hoist side) and white five-pointed star centered just outside the crescent opening

Economy

Economy - overview: Turkey's dynamic economy is a complex mix of modern industry and commerce along with traditional agriculture that still accounts for nearly 40% of employment. It has a strong and rapidly growing private sector, yet the state still plays a major role in basic industry, banking, transport, and communication. The most important industry - and largest exporter - is textiles and clothing, which is almost entirely in private hands. In recent years the economic situation has been marked by erratic economic growth and serious imbalances. Real GNP growth has exceeded 6% in most years, but this strong expansion was interrupted by sharp declines in output in 1994 and 1999. Meanwhile the public sector fiscal deficit has regularly exceeded 10% of GDP - due in large part to the huge burden of interest payments, which now account for more than 40% of central government spending - while inflation has remained in the high double digit range. Perhaps because of these problems, foreign direct investment in Turkey remains low - less than $1 billion annually. Prospects for the future are improving, however, because the ECEVIT government since June 1999 has been implementing an IMF-backed reform program, including a tighter budget, social security reform, banking reorganization, and accelerated privatization. As a result, the fiscal situation is greatly improved and inflation has dropped below 40% - the lowest rate since 1987. The country experienced a financial crisis in late 2000, including sharp drops in the stock market and foreign exchange reserves, but is recovering rapidly, thanks to additional IMF support and the government's commitment to a specific timetable of economic reforms.

GDP: purchasing power parity - $444 billion (2000 est.)

GDP - real growth rate: 6% (2000 est.)

GDP - per capita: purchasing power parity - $6,800 (2000 est.)

GDP - composition by sector:
agriculture: 15%
industry: 29%
services: 56% (1999)

Population below poverty line: NA%

Household income or consumption by percentage share:
lowest 10%: 2.3%
highest 10%: 32.3% (1994)

Inflation rate (consumer prices): 39% (2000 est.)

Labor force: 23 million (2000 est.)
note: about 1.2 million Turks work abroad (1999)

Labor force - by occupation: agriculture 38%, services 38%, industry 24% (2000)

Unemployment rate: 5.6% (plus underemployment of 5.6%) (2000 est.)

Budget:
revenues: $54.5 billion
expenditures: $75.2 billion, including capital expenditures of $3.3 billion (2000)

Industries: textiles, food processing, autos, mining (coal, chromite, copper, boron), steel, petroleum, construction, lumber, paper

Industrial production growth rate: 6.2% (2000 est.)

Electricity - production: 125.3 billion kWh (2000 est.)

Electricity - production by source:
fossil fuel: 71%
hydro: 29%
nuclear: 0%
other: 0% (2000 est.)

Electricity - consumption: 119.5 billion kWh (2000 est.)

Electricity - exports: 350 million kWh (2000 est.)

Electricity - imports: 3.35 billion kWh (2000 est.)

Agriculture - products: tobacco, cotton, grain, olives, sugar beets, pulse, citrus; livestock

Exports: $26.9 billion (f.o.b., 2000 est.)

Turkey (continued)

Exports - commodities: apparel 25.6%, foodstuffs 15.4%, textiles 12.3%, metal manufactures 8.6%, transport equipment 8.1% (1998)
Exports - partners: Germany 18.7%, US 11.4%, UK 7.4%, Italy 6.3%, France 6.0% (2000 est.)
Imports: $55.7 billion (c.i.f., 2000 est.)
Imports - commodities: machinery 28.3%, chemicals 15.2%, semi-finished goods 14.5%, fuels 11%, transport equipment 9.5% (1999)
Imports - partners: Germany 13.1%, Italy 7.9%, US 7.2%, Russia 7.0%, France 6.6%, UK 5.0% (2000 est.)
Debt - external: $109 billion (2000 est.)
Economic aid - recipient: ODA, $195 million (1993)
Currency: Turkish lira (TRL)
Currency code: TRL
Exchange rates: Turkish liras per US dollar - 677,621 (December 2000), 625,219 (2000), 418,783 (1999), 260,724 (1998), 151,865 (1997), 81,405 (1996)
Fiscal year: calendar year

Communications

Telephones - main lines in use: 19.5 million (1999)
Telephones - mobile cellular: 12.1 million (1999)
Telephone system:
general assessment: undergoing rapid modernization and expansion, especially cellular telephones
domestic: additional digital exchanges are permitting a rapid increase in subscribers; the construction of a network of technologically advanced intercity trunk lines, using both fiber-optic cable and digital microwave radio relay is facilitating communication between urban centers; remote areas are reached by a domestic satellite system; the number of subscribers to mobile cellular telephone service is growing rapidly
international: international service is provided by three submarine fiber-optic cables in the Mediterranean and Black Seas, linking Turkey with Italy, Greece, Israel, Bulgaria, Romania, and Russia, by 12 Intelsat earth stations, and by 328 mobile satellite terminals in the Inmarsat and Eutelsat systems
Radio broadcast stations: AM 16, FM 72, shortwave 6 (1998)
Radios: 11.3 million (1997)
Television broadcast stations: 635 (plus 2,934 repeaters) (1995)
Televisions: 20.9 million (1997)
Internet country code: .tr
Internet Service Providers (ISPs): 22 (2000)
Internet users: 2 million (2000)

Transportation

Railways:
total: 8,607 km
standard gauge: 8,607 km 1.435-m gauge (1,524 km electrified) (1999)
Highways:
total: 382,397 km
paved: 95,599 km (including 1,726 km of expressways)
unpaved: 286,798 km (1999 est.)
Waterways: 1,200 km (approximately)
Pipelines: crude oil 1,738 km; petroleum products 2,321 km; natural gas 708 km
Ports and harbors: Gemlik, Hopa, Iskenderun, Istanbul, Izmir, Kocaeli (Izmit), Icel (Mersin), Samsun, Trabzon
Merchant marine:
total: 548 ships (1,000 GRT or over) totaling 5,617,302 GRT/9,088,451 DWT
ships by type: bulk 140, cargo 242, chemical tanker 41, combination bulk 5, combination ore/oil 6, container 21, liquefied gas 6, passenger/cargo 1, petroleum tanker 43, refrigerated cargo 3, roll on/roll off 25, short-sea passenger 10, specialized tanker 5 (2000 est.)
Airports: 121 (2000 est.)
Airports - with paved runways:
total: 86
over 3,047 m: 16
2,438 to 3,047 m: 29
1,524 to 2,437 m: 19
914 to 1,523 m: 16
under 914 m: 6 (2000 est.)
Airports - with unpaved runways:
total: 35
1,524 to 2,437 m: 1
914 to 1,523 m: 8
under 914 m: 26 (2000 est.)
Heliports: 2 (2000 est.)

Military

Military branches: Land Force, Navy (includes Naval Air and Naval Infantry), Air Force, Coast Guard, Gendarmerie
Military manpower - military age: 20 years of age
Military manpower - availability:
males age 15-49: 18,882,272 (2001 est.)
Military manpower - fit for military service:
males age 15-49: 11,432,438 (2001 est.)
Military manpower - reaching military age annually:
males: 674,805 (2001 est.)
Military expenditures - dollar figure: $10.6 billion (FY99)
Military expenditures - percent of GDP: 5.6% (FY99)

Transnational Issues

Disputes - international: complex maritime, air, and territorial disputes with Greece in Aegean Sea; Cyprus question with Greece; dispute with downstream riparian states (Syria and Iraq) over water development plans for the Tigris and Euphrates rivers; traditional demands regarding former Armenian lands in Turkey have subsided
Illicit drugs: key transit route for Southwest Asian heroin to Western Europe and - to a far lesser extent the US - via air, land, and sea routes; major Turkish, Iranian, and other international trafficking organizations operate out of Istanbul; laboratories to convert imported morphine base into heroin are in remote regions of Turkey as well as near Istanbul; government maintains strict controls over areas of legal opium poppy cultivation and output of poppy straw concentrate

Turkmenistan

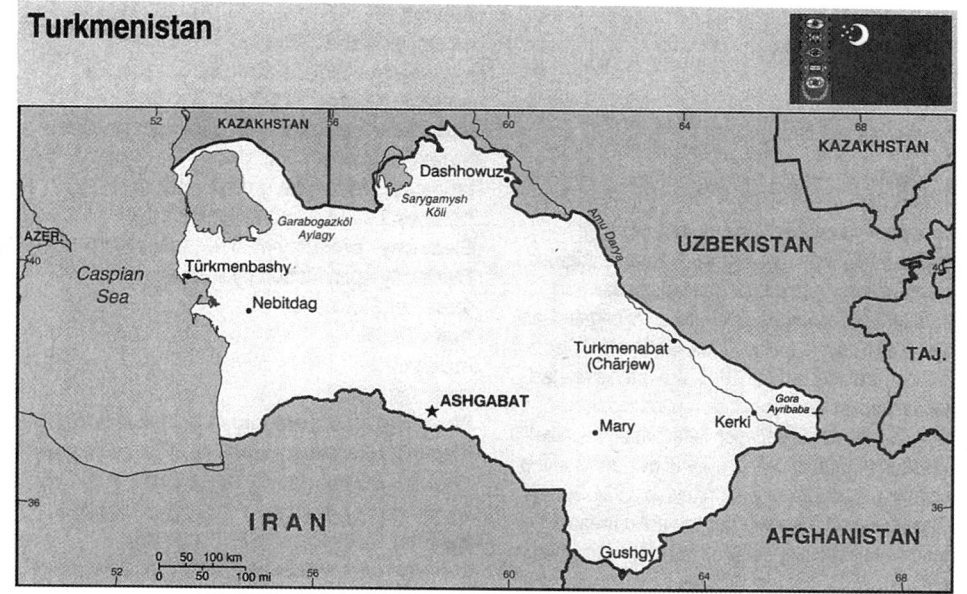

Introduction

Background: Annexed by Russia between 1865 and 1885, Turkmenistan became a Soviet republic in 1925. It achieved its independence upon the dissolution of the USSR in 1991. President NIYAZOV retains absolute control over the country and opposition is not tolerated. Extensive hydrocarbon/natural gas reserves could prove a boon to this underdeveloped country if extraction and delivery projects can be worked out.

Geography

Location: Central Asia, bordering the Caspian Sea, between Iran and Kazakhstan
Geographic coordinates: 40 00 N, 60 00 E
Map references: Commonwealth of Independent States
Area:
total: 488,100 sq km
land: 488,100 sq km
water: 0 sq km
Area - comparative: slightly larger than California
Land boundaries:
total: 3,736 km
border countries: Afghanistan 744 km, Iran 992 km, Kazakhstan 379 km, Uzbekistan 1,621 km
Coastline: 0 km; note - Turkmenistan borders the Caspian Sea (1,768 km)
Maritime claims: none (landlocked)
Climate: subtropical desert
Terrain: flat-to-rolling sandy desert with dunes rising to mountains in the south; low mountains along border with Iran; borders Caspian Sea in west
Elevation extremes:
lowest point: Vpadina Akchanaya -81.00 m; note - Sarygamysh Koli is a lake in northern Turkmenistan with a water level that fluctuates above and below the elevation of Vpadina Akchanaya (the lake has dropped as low as -110 m)
highest point: Gora Ayribaba 3,139 m
Natural resources: petroleum, natural gas, coal, sulfur, salt
Land use:
arable land: 3%
permanent crops: 0%
permanent pastures: 63%
forests and woodland: 8%
other: 26% (1993 est.)
Irrigated land: 13,000 sq km (1993 est.)
Natural hazards: NA
Environment - current issues: contamination of soil and groundwater with agricultural chemicals, pesticides; salination, water-logging of soil due to poor irrigation methods; Caspian Sea pollution; diversion of a large share of the flow of the Amu Darya into irrigation contributes to that river's inability to replenish the Aral Sea; desertification
Environment - international agreements:
party to: Biodiversity, Climate Change, Climate Change-Kyoto Protocol, Desertification, Hazardous Wastes, Marine Dumping, Ozone Layer Protection, Ship Pollution
signed, but not ratified: none of the selected agreements
Geography - note: landlocked

People

Population: 4,603,244 (July 2001 est.)
Age structure:
0-14 years: 37.88% (male 891,758; female 852,104)
15-64 years: 58.09% (male 1,313,303; female 1,360,690)
65 years and over: 4.03% (male 70,800; female 114,589) (2001 est.)
Population growth rate: 1.85% (2001 est.)
Birth rate: 28.55 births/1,000 population (2001 est.)
Death rate: 8.98 deaths/1,000 population (2001 est.)
Net migration rate: -1.04 migrant(s)/1,000 population (2001 est.)
Sex ratio:
at birth: 1.05 male(s)/female
under 15 years: 1.05 male(s)/female
15-64 years: 0.97 male(s)/female
65 years and over: 0.62 male(s)/female
total population: 0.98 male(s)/female (2001 est.)
Infant mortality rate: 73.25 deaths/1,000 live births (2001 est.)
Life expectancy at birth:
total population: 61 years
male: 57.43 years
female: 64.76 years (2001 est.)
Total fertility rate: 3.58 children born/woman (2001 est.)
HIV/AIDS - adult prevalence rate: 0.01% (1999 est.)
HIV/AIDS - people living with HIV/AIDS: less than 100 (1999 est.)
HIV/AIDS - deaths: less than 100 (1999 est.)
Nationality:
noun: Turkmen(s)
adjective: Turkmen
Ethnic groups: Turkmen 77%, Uzbek 9.2%, Russian 6.7%, Kazakh 2%, other 5.1% (1995)
Religions: Muslim 89%, Eastern Orthodox 9%, unknown 2%
Languages: Turkmen 72%, Russian 12%, Uzbek 9%, other 7%
Literacy:
definition: age 15 and over can read and write
total population: 98%
male: 99%
female: 97% (1989 est.)

Government

Country name:
conventional long form: none
conventional short form: Turkmenistan
local long form: none
local short form: Turkmenistan
former: Turkmen Soviet Socialist Republic
Government type: republic
Capital: Ashgabat
Administrative divisions: 5 welayatlar (singular - welayat): Ahal Welayaty (Ashgabat), Balkan Welayaty (Nebitdag), Dashhowuz Welayaty (formerly Tashauz), Lebap Welayaty (Charjew), Mary Welayaty
note: administrative divisions have the same names as their administrative centers (exceptions have the administrative center name following in parentheses)
Independence: 27 October 1991 (from the Soviet Union)
National holiday: Independence Day, 27 October (1991)
Constitution: adopted 18 May 1992
Legal system: based on civil law system
Suffrage: 18 years of age; universal
Executive branch:
chief of state: President and Chairman of the Cabinet of Ministers Saparmurat NIYAZOV (since 27 October 1990, when the first direct presidential election occurred); note - the president is both the chief of state and head of government

Turkmenistan (continued)

head of government: President and Chairman of the Cabinet of Ministers Saparmurat NIYAZOV (since 27 October 1990, when the first direct presidential election occurred); note - the president is both the chief of state and head of government
cabinet: Council of Ministers appointed by the president
note: NIYAZOV's term in office was extended indefinitely on 28 December 1999 by the Assembly (Majlis) during a session of the People's Council (Halk Maslahaty)
elections: president elected by popular vote for a five-year term; election last held 21 June 1992 (next scheduled to be held NA); note - President NIYAZOV was unanimously approved as president for life by the Assembly on 28 December 1999; deputy chairmen of the cabinet of ministers are appointed by the president
election results: Saparmurat NIYAZOV elected president without opposition; percent of vote - Saparmurat NIYAZOV 99.5%
Legislative branch: under the 1992 constitution, there are two parliamentary bodies, a unicameral People's Council or Halk Maslahaty (more than 100 seats, some of which are elected by popular vote and some of which are appointed; meets infrequently) and a unicameral Assembly or Majlis (50 seats; members are elected by popular vote to serve five-year terms)
elections: People's Council - NA; Assembly - last held 12 December 1999 (next to be held NA 2004)
election results: Assembly - percent of vote by party - NA%; seats by party - NA; note - all 50 elected officials preapproved by President NIYAZOV; most are from the DPT
Judicial branch: Supreme Court (judges are appointed by the president)
Political parties and leaders: Democratic Party of Turkmenistan or DPT [Saparmurat NIYAZOV]
note: formal opposition parties are outlawed; unofficial, small opposition movements exist underground or in foreign countries
Political pressure groups and leaders: NA
International organization participation: AsDB, CCC, CIS, EAPC, EBRD, ECE, ECO, ESCAP, FAO, IBRD, ICAO, ICRM, IDB, IFC, IFRCS, ILO, IMF, IMO, Intelsat (nonsignatory user), IOC, IOM (observer), ISO (correspondent), ITU, NAM, OIC, OPCW, OSCE, PFP, UN, UNCTAD, UNESCO, UNIDO, UPU, WFTU, WHO, WIPO, WMO, WToO, WTrO (observer)
Diplomatic representation in the US:
chief of mission: Ambassador Mered ORAZOV
chancery: 2207 Massachusetts Avenue NW, Washington, DC 20008
telephone: [1] (202) 588-1500
FAX: [1] (202) 588-0697
Diplomatic representation from the US:
chief of mission: Ambassador Steven R. MANN
embassy: 9 Pushkin Street, Ashgabat, Turkmenistan 774000
mailing address: use embassy street address
telephone: [9] (9312) 35-00-45
FAX: [9] (9312) 51-13-05
Flag description: green field with a vertical red stripe near the hoist side, containing five carpet guls (designs used in producing rugs) stacked above two crossed olive branches similar to the olive branches on the UN flag; a white crescent moon and five white stars appear in the upper corner of the field just to the fly side of the red stripe

Economy

Economy - overview: Turkmenistan is largely desert country with intensive agriculture in irrigated oases and huge gas (fifth largest reserves in the world) and oil resources. One-half of its irrigated land is planted in cotton, making it the world's tenth largest producer. Until the end of 1993, Turkmenistan had experienced less economic disruption than other former Soviet states because its economy received a boost from higher prices for oil and gas and a sharp increase in hard currency earnings. In 1994, Russia's refusal to export Turkmen gas to hard currency markets and mounting debts of its major customers in the former USSR for gas deliveries contributed to a sharp fall in industrial production and caused the budget to shift from a surplus to a slight deficit. With an authoritarian ex-communist regime in power and a tribally based social structure, Turkmenistan has taken a cautious approach to economic reform, hoping to use gas and cotton sales to sustain its inefficient economy. Privatization goals remain limited. In 1998-2000, Turkmenistan suffered from the continued lack of adequate export routes for natural gas and from obligations on extensive short-term external debt. At the same time, however, total exports rose sharply because of higher international oil and gas prices. Prospects in the near future are discouraging because of widespread internal poverty and the burden of foreign debt. IMF assistance would seem to be necessary, yet the government is not as yet ready to accept IMF requirements. Turkmenistan's 1999 deal to ship 20 billion cubic meters (bcm) of natural gas through Russia's Gazprom pipeline helped alleviate the 2000 fiscal shortfall. Inadequate fiscal restraint and the tenuous nature of Turkmenistan's 2001 gas deals, combined with a lack of economic reform, will limit progress in the near term.
GDP: purchasing power parity - $19.6 billion (2000 est.)
GDP - real growth rate: 16% (2000 est.)
GDP - per capita: purchasing power parity - $4,300 (2000 est.)
GDP - composition by sector:
agriculture: 25%
industry: 43%
services: 32% (1999 est.)
Population below poverty line: 58% (1999 est.)
Household income or consumption by percentage share:
lowest 10%: 2.6%
highest 10%: 31.7% (1998)
Inflation rate (consumer prices): 14% (2000 est.)
Labor force: 2.34 million (1996)
Labor force - by occupation: agriculture 44%, industry 19%, services 37% (1996)
Unemployment rate: NA%
Budget:
revenues: $588.6 million
expenditures: $658.2 million, including capital expenditures of $NA (1999 est.)
Industries: natural gas, oil, petroleum products, textiles, food processing
Industrial production growth rate: 18% (2000 est.)
Electricity - production: 8.371 billion kWh (1999)
Electricity - production by source:
fossil fuel: 99.94%
hydro: 0.06%
nuclear: 0%
other: 0% (1999)
Electricity - consumption: 4.785 billion kWh (1999)
Electricity - exports: 4.1 billion kWh (1999)
Electricity - imports: 1.1 billion kWh (1999)
Agriculture - products: cotton, grain; livestock
Exports: $2.4 billion (f.o.b., 2000 est.)
Exports - commodities: gas 33%, oil 30%, cotton fiber 18%, textiles 8% (1999)
Exports - partners: Ukraine, Iran, Turkey, Russia, Kazakhstan, Tajikistan, Azerbaijan
Imports: $1.65 billion (c.i.f., 2000 est.)
Imports - commodities: machinery and equipment 60%, foodstuffs 15% (1999)
Imports - partners: Ukraine, Turkey, Russia, Germany, US, Kazakhstan, Uzbekistan
Debt - external: $2.5 billion (2000 est.)
Economic aid - recipient: $27.2 million (1995)
Currency: Turkmen manat (TMM)
Currency code: TMM
Exchange rates: Turkmen manats per US dollar - 5,200 (January 2001), 5,200 (January 2000), 5,350 (January 1999), 4,070 (January 1997), 2,400 (January 1996)
Fiscal year: calendar year

Communications

Telephones - main lines in use: 363,000 (1997)
Telephones - mobile cellular: 4,300 (1998)
Telephone system:
general assessment: poorly developed
domestic: NA
international: linked by cable and microwave radio relay to other CIS republics and to other countries by leased connections to the Moscow international gateway switch; a new telephone link from Ashgabat to Iran has been established; a new exchange in Ashgabat switches international traffic through Turkey via Intelsat; satellite earth stations - 1 Orbita and 1 Intelsat
Radio broadcast stations: AM 16, FM 8, shortwave 2 (1998)
Radios: 1.225 million (1997)
Television broadcast stations: 3 (much programming relayed from Russia and Turkey) (1997)
Televisions: 820,000 (1997)
Internet country code: .tm
Internet Service Providers (ISPs): NA
Internet users: 2,000 (2000)

Turkmenistan (continued)

Transportation

Railways:
total: 2,187 km
broad gauge: 2,187 km 1.520-m gauge (1996 est.)
Highways:
total: 24,000 km
paved: 19,488 km (these roads are said to be hard-surfaced, and include, in addition to conventionally paved roads, some that are surfaced with gravel or other coarse aggregate, making them trafficable in all weather)
unpaved: 4,512 km (these roads are made of unstabilized earth and are difficult to negotiate in wet weather) (1996)
Waterways: the Amu Darya is an important inland waterway for Turkmenistan
Pipelines: crude oil 250 km; natural gas 4,400 km
Ports and harbors: Turkmenbashi
Merchant marine:
total: 1 ship (1,000 GRT or over) totaling 6,459 GRT/ 8,865 DWT
ships by type: container 1 (2000 est.)
Airports: 76 (2000 est.)
Airports - with paved runways:
total: 13
2,438 to 3,047 m: 9
1,524 to 2,437 m: 4 (2000 est.)
Airports - with unpaved runways:
total: 63
2,438 to 3,047 m: 7
1,524 to 2,437 m: 5
914 to 1,523 m: 10
under 914 m: 41 (2000 est.)

Military

Military branches: Ministry of Defense (Army, Air and Air Defense, Navy, Border Troops, and Internal Troops), National Guard
Military manpower - military age: 18 years of age
Military manpower - availability:
males age 15-49: 1,173,500 (2001 est.)
Military manpower - fit for military service:
males age 15-49: 952,218 (2001 est.)
Military manpower - reaching military age annually:
males: 48,292 (2001 est.)
Military expenditures - dollar figure: $90 million (FY99)
Military expenditures - percent of GDP: 3.4% (FY99)

Transnational Issues

Disputes - international: Caspian Sea boundaries are not yet determined among Azerbaijan, Iran, Kazakhstan, Russia, and Turkmenistan
Illicit drugs: limited illicit cultivator of opium poppy, mostly for domestic consumption; limited government eradication program; increasingly used as transshipment point for illicit drugs from Southwest Asia to Russia and Western Europe; also a transshipment point for acetic anhydride destined for Afghanistan

Turks and Caicos Islands
(overseas territory of the UK)

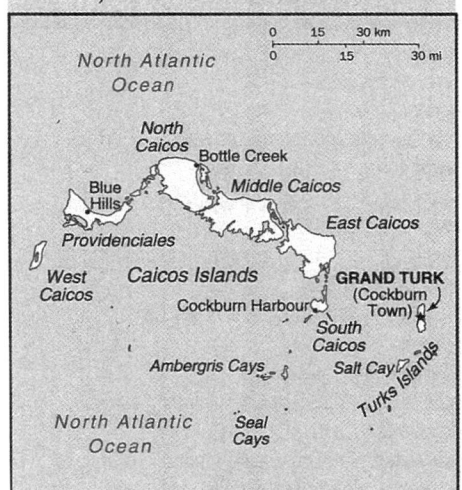

Introduction

Background: The islands were part of the UK's Jamaican colony until 1962, when they assumed the status of a separate crown colony upon Jamaica's independence. The governor of The Bahamas oversaw affairs from 1965 to 1973. With Bahamian independence, the islands received a separate governor in 1973. Although independence was agreed upon for 1982, the policy was reversed and the islands are presently a British overseas territory.

Geography

Location: Caribbean, two island groups in the North Atlantic Ocean, southeast of The Bahamas
Geographic coordinates: 21 45 N, 71 35 W
Map references: Central America and the Caribbean
Area:
total: 430 sq km
land: 430 sq km
water: 0 sq km
Area - comparative: 2.5 times the size of Washington, DC
Land boundaries: 0 km
Coastline: 389 km
Maritime claims:
exclusive fishing zone: 200 NM
territorial sea: 12 NM
Climate: tropical; marine; moderated by trade winds; sunny and relatively dry
Terrain: low, flat limestone; extensive marshes and mangrove swamps
Elevation extremes:
lowest point: Caribbean Sea 0 m
highest point: Blue Hills 49 m
Natural resources: spiny lobster, conch
Land use:
arable land: 2%
permanent crops: 0%
permanent pastures: 0%
forests and woodland: 0%
other: 98% (1993 est.)
Irrigated land: NA sq km
Natural hazards: frequent hurricanes
Environment - current issues: limited natural fresh water resources, private cisterns collect rainwater
Geography - note: 30 islands (eight inhabited)

People

Population: 18,122 (July 2001 est.)
Age structure:
0-14 years: 32.58% (male 2,996; female 2,908)
15-64 years: 63.51% (male 6,050; female 5,459)
65 years and over: 3.91% (male 316; female 393) (2001 est.)
Population growth rate: 3.41% (2001 est.)
Birth rate: 24.89 births/1,000 population (2001 est.)
Death rate: 4.47 deaths/1,000 population (2001 est.)
Net migration rate: 13.69 migrant(s)/1,000 population (2001 est.)
Sex ratio:
at birth: 1.05 male(s)/female
under 15 years: 1.03 male(s)/female
15-64 years: 1.11 male(s)/female
65 years and over: 0.8 male(s)/female
total population: 1.07 male(s)/female (2001 est.)
Infant mortality rate: 18.06 deaths/1,000 live births (2001 est.)
Life expectancy at birth:
total population: 73.52 years
male: 71.37 years
female: 75.77 years (2001 est.)
Total fertility rate: 3.22 children born/woman (2001 est.)
HIV/AIDS - adult prevalence rate: NA%
HIV/AIDS - people living with HIV/AIDS: NA
HIV/AIDS - deaths: NA
Nationality:
noun: none
adjective: none
Ethnic groups: black
Religions: Baptist 41.2%, Methodist 18.9%, Anglican 18.3%, Seventh-Day Adventist 1.7%, other 19.9% (1980)
Languages: English (official)
Literacy:
definition: age 15 and over has ever attended school
total population: 98%
male: 99%
female: 98% (1970 est.)

Government

Country name:
conventional long form: none
conventional short form: Turks and Caicos Islands
Dependency status: overseas territory of the UK
Government type: NA
Capital: Cockburn Town (on Grand Turk)
Administrative divisions: none (overseas territory of the UK)

Turks and Caicos Islands (continued)

Independence: none (overseas territory of the UK)
National holiday: Constitution Day, 30 August (1976)
Constitution: introduced 30 August 1976; suspended in 1986; restored and revised 5 March 1988
Legal system: based on laws of England and Wales, with a small number adopted from Jamaica and The Bahamas
Suffrage: 18 years of age; universal
Executive branch:
chief of state: Queen ELIZABETH II (since 6 February 1953), represented by Governor Mervyn JONES (since 27 January 2000)
head of government: Chief Minister Derek H. TAYLOR (since 31 January 1995)
cabinet: Executive Council consists of three ex officio members and five appointed by the governor from among the members of the Legislative Council
elections: none; the monarch is hereditary; governor appointed by the monarch; chief minister appointed by the governor
Legislative branch: unicameral Legislative Council (19 seats, of which 13 are popularly elected; members serve four-year terms)
elections: last held 4 March 1999 (next to be held by NA 2003)
election results: percent of vote by party - PDM 52.2%, PNP 40.9%, independent 6.9%; seats by party - PDM 9, PNP 4
Judicial branch: Supreme Court
Political parties and leaders: People's Democratic Movement or PDM [Derek H. TAYLOR]; Progressive National Party or PNP [Washington MISICK]; United Democratic Party or UDP [Wendal SWANN]
Political pressure groups and leaders: NA
International organization participation: Caricom (associate), CDB, Interpol (subbureau)
Diplomatic representation in the US: none (overseas territory of the UK)
Diplomatic representation from the US: none (overseas territory of the UK)
Flag description: blue, with the flag of the UK in the upper hoist-side quadrant and the colonial shield centered on the outer half of the flag; the shield is yellow and contains a conch shell, lobster, and cactus

Economy

Economy - overview: The Turks and Caicos economy is based on tourism, fishing, and offshore financial services. Most capital goods and food for domestic consumption are imported. The US was the leading source of tourists in 1996, accounting for more than half of the 87,000 visitors; tourist arrivals had risen to 93,000 by 1998. Major sources of government revenue include fees from offshore financial activities and customs receipts.
GDP: purchasing power parity - $128 million (1999 est.)
GDP - real growth rate: 8.7% (1999 est.)
GDP - per capita: purchasing power parity - $7,300 (1999 est.)
GDP - composition by sector:
agriculture: NA%
industry: NA%
services: NA%
Population below poverty line: NA%
Household income or consumption by percentage share:
lowest 10%: NA%
highest 10%: NA%
Inflation rate (consumer prices): 4% (1995)
Labor force: 4,848 (1990 est.)
Labor force - by occupation: about 33% in government and 20% in agriculture and fishing; significant numbers in tourism, financial, and other services (1997 est.)
Unemployment rate: 10% (1997 est.)
Budget:
revenues: $47 million
expenditures: $33.6 million, including capital expenditures of $NA (1997-1998 est.)
Industries: tourism, offshore financial services
Industrial production growth rate: NA%
Electricity - production: 5 million kWh (1999)
Electricity - production by source:
fossil fuel: 100%
hydro: 0%
nuclear: 0%
other: 0% (1999)
Electricity - consumption: 4.6 million kWh (1999)
Electricity - exports: 0 kWh (1999)
Electricity - imports: 0 kWh (1999)
Agriculture - products: corn, beans, cassava (tapioca), citrus fruits; fish
Exports: $4.7 million (1993)
Exports - commodities: lobster, dried and fresh conch, conch shells
Exports - partners: US, UK
Imports: $46.6 million (1993)
Imports - commodities: food and beverages, tobacco, clothing, manufactures, construction materials
Imports - partners: US, UK
Debt - external: $NA
Economic aid - recipient: $4.1 million (1997)
Currency: US dollar (USD)
Currency code: USD
Exchange rates: the US dollar is used
Fiscal year: calendar year

Communications

Telephones - main lines in use: 3,000 (1994)
Telephones - mobile cellular: 0 (1994)
Telephone system:
general assessment: fair cable and radiotelephone services
domestic: NA
international: 2 submarine cables; satellite earth station - 1 Intelsat (Atlantic Ocean)
Radio broadcast stations: AM 3 (one inactive), FM 6, shortwave 0 (1998)
Radios: 8,000 (1997)
Television broadcast stations: 0 (broadcasts from The Bahamas are received; cable television is established) (1997)
Televisions: NA
Internet country code: .tc
Internet Service Providers (ISPs): 14 (2000)
Internet users: NA

Transportation

Railways: 0 km
Highways:
total: 121 km
paved: 24 km
unpaved: 97 km
Waterways: none
Ports and harbors: Grand Turk, Providenciales
Merchant marine: none (2000 est.)
Airports: 8 (2000 est.)
Airports - with paved runways:
total: 4
1,524 to 2,437 m: 3
914 to 1,523 m: 1 (2000 est.)
Airports - with unpaved runways:
total: 4
914 to 1,523 m: 2
under 914 m: 2 (2000 est.)

Military

Military - note: defense is the responsibility of the UK

Transnational Issues

Disputes - international: none
Illicit drugs: transshipment point for South American narcotics destined for the US and Europe

Tuvalu

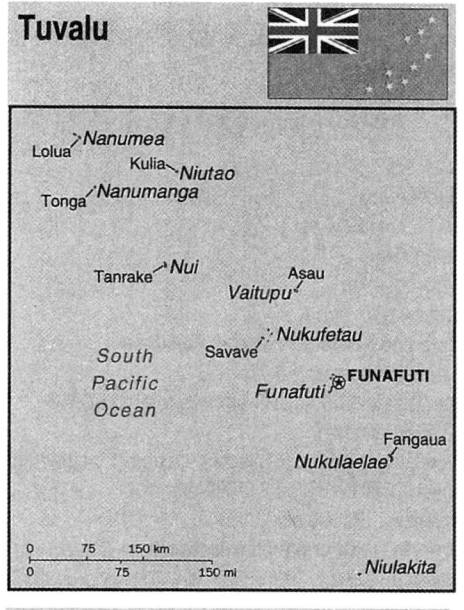

Introduction

Background: In 1974, ethnic differences within the British colony of the Gilbert and Ellice Islands caused the Polynesians of the Ellice Islands to vote for separation from the Micronesians of the Gilbert Islands. The following year, the Ellice Islands became the separate British colony of Tuvalu. Independence was granted in 1978. In 2000, Tuvalu negotiated a contract leasing its Internet domain name ".tv" for $50 million in royalties over the next dozen years.

Geography

Location: Oceania, island group consisting of nine coral atolls in the South Pacific Ocean, about one-half of the way from Hawaii to Australia
Geographic coordinates: 8 00 S, 178 00 E
Map references: Oceania
Area:
total: 26 sq km
land: 26 sq km
water: 0 sq km
Area - comparative: 0.1 times the size of Washington, DC
Land boundaries: 0 km
Coastline: 24 km
Maritime claims:
contiguous zone: 24 NM
exclusive economic zone: 200 NM
territorial sea: 12 NM
Climate: tropical; moderated by easterly trade winds (March to November); westerly gales and heavy rain (November to March)
Terrain: very low-lying and narrow coral atolls
Elevation extremes:
lowest point: Pacific Ocean 0 m
highest point: unnamed location 5 m
Natural resources: fish
Land use:
arable land: 0%
permanent crops: 0%
permanent pastures: 0%
forests and woodland: 0%
other: 100% (1993 est.)
Irrigated land: NA sq km
Natural hazards: severe tropical storms are usually rare, but, in 1997, there were three cyclones; low level of islands make them very sensitive to changes in sea level
Environment - current issues: since there are no streams or rivers and groundwater is not potable, most water needs must be met by catchment systems with storage facilities (the Japanese Government has built one desalination plant and plans to build one other); beachhead erosion because of the use of sand for building materials; excessive clearance of forest undergrowth for use as fuel; damage to coral reefs from the spread of the Crown of Thorns starfish; Tuvalu is very concerned about global increases in greenhouse gas emissions and their effect on rising sea levels, which threaten the country's underground water table
Environment - international agreements:
party to: Climate Change, Climate Change-Kyoto Protocol, Desertification, Marine Dumping, Ozone Layer Protection, Ship Pollution
signed, but not ratified: Biodiversity, Law of the Sea

People

Population: 10,991 (July 2001 est.)
Age structure:
0-14 years: 33.28% (male 1,862; female 1,796)
15-64 years: 61.6% (male 3,241; female 3,529)
65 years and over: 5.12% (male 236; female 327) (2001 est.)
Population growth rate: 1.4% (2001 est.)
Birth rate: 21.56 births/1,000 population (2001 est.)
Death rate: 7.55 deaths/1,000 population (2001 est.)
Net migration rate: 0 migrant(s)/1,000 population (2001 est.)
Sex ratio:
at birth: 1.04 male(s)/female
under 15 years: 1.04 male(s)/female
15-64 years: 0.92 male(s)/female
65 years and over: 0.72 male(s)/female
total population: 0.94 male(s)/female (2001 est.)
Infant mortality rate: 22.65 deaths/1,000 live births (2001 est.)
Life expectancy at birth:
total population: 66.65 years
male: 64.52 years
female: 68.88 years (2001 est.)
Total fertility rate: 3.09 children born/woman (2001 est.)
HIV/AIDS - adult prevalence rate: NA%
HIV/AIDS - people living with HIV/AIDS: NA
HIV/AIDS - deaths: NA
Nationality:
noun: Tuvaluan(s)
adjective: Tuvaluan
Ethnic groups: Polynesian 96%
Religions: Church of Tuvalu (Congregationalist) 97%, Seventh-Day Adventist 1.4%, Baha'i 1%, other 0.6%
Languages: Tuvaluan, English
Literacy:
definition: NA
total population: NA%
male: NA%
female: NA%

Government

Country name:
conventional long form: none
conventional short form: Tuvalu
former: Ellice Islands
Government type: constitutional monarchy with a parliamentary democracy; began debating republic status in 1992
Capital: Funafuti
Administrative divisions: none
Independence: 1 October 1978 (from UK)
National holiday: Independence Day, 1 October (1978)
Constitution: 1 October 1978
Legal system: NA
Suffrage: 18 years of age; universal
Executive branch:
chief of state: Queen ELIZABETH II (since 6 February 1952), represented by Governor General Sir Tomasi PUAPUA (since 26 June 1998)
head of government: Acting Prime Minister Lagitupu (of Nanumea) TUILIMU (since 8 December 2000); note - TUILIMU took over after Prime Minister Ionatana IONATANA died suddenly of a heart attack on 8 December 2000
cabinet: Cabinet appointed by the governor general on the recommendation of the prime minister
elections: the monarch is hereditary; governor general appointed by the monarch on the recommendation of the prime minister; prime minister and deputy prime minister elected by and from the members of Parliament; election last held 27 April 1999 (next to be held NA 2002)
election results: results of the last election for prime minister - Ionatana IONATANA elected prime minister; percent of Parliament vote - NA%; Lagitupu (of Nanumea) TUILIMU elected deputy prime minister; percent of Parliament vote - NA%; note - Deputy Prime Minister Lagitupu (of Nanumea) TUILIMU became acting prime minister following the death of Prime Minister Ionatana IONATANA on 8 December 2000
Legislative branch: unicameral Parliament or Fale I Fono, also called House of Assembly (12 seats; members elected by popular vote to serve four-year terms)
elections: last held 26-27 March 1998 (next to be held by NA 2002)
election results: percent of vote - NA%; seats - independents 12

Tuvalu (continued)

Judicial branch: High Court (a chief justice visits twice a year to preside over its sessions; its rulings can be appealed to the Court of Appeal in Fiji); eight Island Courts (with limited jurisdiction)
Political parties and leaders: there are no political parties but members of Parliament usually align themselves in informal groupings
Political pressure groups and leaders: none
International organization participation: ACP, AsDB, C, ESCAP, IFRCS (associate), Intelsat (nonsignatory user), ITU, Sparteca, SPC, SPF, UN, UNCTAD, UNESCO, UPU, WHO, WTrO (applicant)
Diplomatic representation in the US: Tuvalu does not have an embassy in the US
Diplomatic representation from the US: the US does not have an embassy in Tuvalu; the US ambassador to Fiji is accredited to Tuvalu
Flag description: light blue with the flag of the UK in the upper hoist-side quadrant; the outer half of the flag represents a map of the country with nine yellow five-pointed stars symbolizing the nine islands

Economy

Economy - overview: Tuvalu consists of a densely populated, scattered group of nine coral atolls with poor soil. The country has no known mineral resources and few exports. Subsistence farming and fishing are the primary economic activities. Government revenues largely come from the sale of stamps and coins and worker remittances. About 1,000 Tuvaluans work in Nauru in the phosphate mining industry. Nauru has begun repatriating Tuvaluans, however, as phosphate resources decline. Substantial income is received annually from an international trust fund established in 1987 by Australia, NZ, and the UK and supported also by Japan and South Korea. Thanks to wise investments and conservative withdrawals, this Fund has grown from an initial $17 million to over $35 million in 1999. The US government is also a major revenue source for Tuvalu, with 1999 payments from a 1988 treaty on fisheries at about $9 million, a total which is expected to rise annually. In an effort to reduce its dependence on foreign aid, the government is pursuing public sector reforms, including privatization of some government functions and personnel cuts of up to 7%. In 1998, Tuvalu began deriving revenue from use of its area code for "900" lines and in 2000, from the sale of its ".tv" Internet domain name. Royalties from these new technology sources could raise GDP three or more times over the next decade. In 1999, with merchandise exports falling and finance reaching less than 5% of imports, continued reliance was placed on fishing and telecommunications license fees, remittances from overseas workers, official transfers, and investment income from overseas assets to cover the trade deficit.
GDP: purchasing power parity - $11.6 million (1999 est.)
GDP - real growth rate: 3% (1999 est.)
GDP - per capita: purchasing power parity - $1,100 (1999 est.)
GDP - composition by sector:
agriculture: NA%
industry: NA%
services: NA%
Population below poverty line: NA%
Household income or consumption by percentage share:
lowest 10%: NA%
highest 10%: NA%
Inflation rate (consumer prices): 7% (1999 est.)
Labor force: NA
Labor force - by occupation: people make a living mainly through exploitation of the sea, reefs, and atolls and from wages sent home by those working abroad (mostly workers in the phosphate industry and sailors)
Unemployment rate: NA%
Budget:
revenues: $6.2 million
expenditures: $6.1 million, including capital expenditures of $NA (1998 est.)
Industries: fishing, tourism, copra
Industrial production growth rate: NA%
Electricity - production by source:
fossil fuel: NA%
hydro: NA%
nuclear: NA%
other: NA%
Agriculture - products: coconuts; fish
Exports: $165,000 (f.o.b., 1989)
Exports - commodities: copra
Exports - partners: Fiji, Australia, NZ
Imports: $4.4 million (c.i.f., 1989)
Imports - commodities: food, animals, mineral fuels, machinery, manufactured goods
Imports - partners: Fiji, Australia, NZ
Debt - external: $NA
Economic aid - recipient: $13 million (1999 est.); note - major donors are Japan and Australia
Currency: Australian dollar (AUD); note - there is also a Tuvaluan dollar
Currency code: AUD
Exchange rates: Tuvaluan dollars or Australian dollars per US dollar - 1.7995 (January 2001), 1.7173 (2000), 1.5497 (1999), 1.5888 (1998), 1.3439 (1997), 1.2773 (1996)
Fiscal year: calendar year

Communications

Telephones - main lines in use: 1,000 (1997)
Telephones - mobile cellular: 0 (1994)
Telephone system:
general assessment: serves particular needs for internal communications
domestic: radiotelephone communications between islands
international: NA
Radio broadcast stations: AM 1, FM 0, shortwave 0 (1998)
Radios: 4,000 (1997)
Television broadcast stations: 0 (1997)
Televisions: 800
Internet country code: .tv
Internet Service Providers (ISPs): 1 (2000)
Internet users: NA

Transportation

Railways: 0 km
Highways:
total: 8 km (1996 est.)
paved: 0 km
unpaved: 8 km
Waterways: none
Ports and harbors: Funafuti, Nukufetau
Merchant marine:
total: 9 ships (1,000 GRT or over) totaling 52,135 GRT/68,300 DWT
ships by type: cargo 5, passenger/cargo 1, petroleum tanker 1, roll on/roll off 2 (2000 est.)
Airports: 1 (2000 est.)
Airports - with unpaved runways:
total: 1
1,524 to 2,437 m: 1 (2000 est.)

Military

Military branches: no regular military forces; Police Force includes Maritime Surveillance Unit for search and rescue missions and surveillance operations
Military expenditures - dollar figure: $NA
Military expenditures - percent of GDP: NA%

Transnational Issues

Disputes - international: none

Uganda

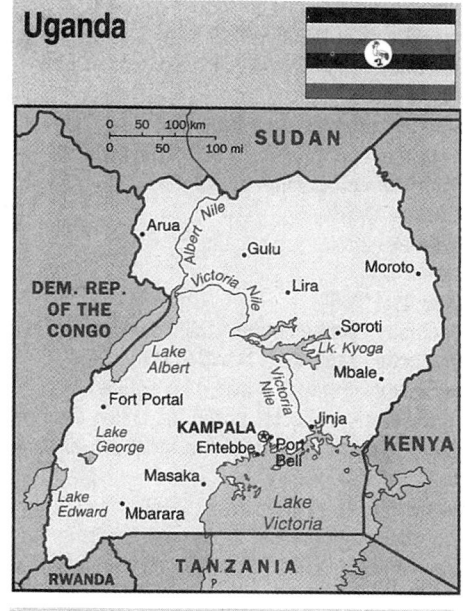

Introduction

Background: Uganda achieved independence from the UK in 1962. The dictatorial regime of Idi AMIN (1971-79) was responsible for the deaths of some 300,000 opponents; guerrilla war and human rights abuses under Milton OBOTE (1980-85) claimed another 100,000 lives. During the 1990s the government promulgated non-party presidential and legislative elections.

Geography

Location: Eastern Africa, west of Kenya
Geographic coordinates: 1 00 N, 32 00 E
Map references: Africa
Area:
total: 236,040 sq km
land: 199,710 sq km
water: 36,330 sq km
Area - comparative: slightly smaller than Oregon
Land boundaries:
total: 2,698 km
border countries: Democratic Republic of the Congo 765 km, Kenya 933 km, Rwanda 169 km, Sudan 435 km, Tanzania 396 km
Coastline: 0 km (landlocked)
Maritime claims: none (landlocked)
Climate: tropical; generally rainy with two dry seasons (December to February, June to August); semiarid in northeast
Terrain: mostly plateau with rim of mountains
Elevation extremes:
lowest point: Lake Albert 621 m
highest point: Margherita Peak on Mount Stanley 5,110 m
Natural resources: copper, cobalt, hydropower, limestone, salt, arable land
Land use:
arable land: 25%
permanent crops: 9%
permanent pastures: 9%
forests and woodland: 28%
other: 29% (1993 est.)
Irrigated land: 90 sq km (1993 est.)
Natural hazards: NA
Environment - current issues: draining of wetlands for agricultural use; deforestation; overgrazing; soil erosion; water hyacinth infestation in Lake Victoria; poaching is widespread
Environment - international agreements:
party to: Biodiversity, Climate Change, Desertification, Endangered Species, Hazardous Wastes, Law of the Sea, Marine Dumping, Marine Life Conservation, Nuclear Test Ban, Ozone Layer Protection, Ship Pollution, Wetlands
signed, but not ratified: Environmental Modification
Geography - note: landlocked

People

Population: 23,985,712
note: estimates for this country explicitly take into account the effects of excess mortality due to AIDS; this can result in lower life expectancy, higher infant mortality and death rates, lower population and growth rates, and changes in the distribution of population by age and sex than would otherwise be expected (July 2001 est.)
Age structure:
0-14 years: 51.08% (male 6,150,038; female 6,100,880)
15-64 years: 46.78% (male 5,613,499; female 5,607,526)
65 years and over: 2.14% (male 244,216; female 269,553) (2001 est.)
Population growth rate: 2.93% (2001 est.)
Birth rate: 47.52 births/1,000 population (2001 est.)
Death rate: 17.97 deaths/1,000 population (2001 est.)
Net migration rate: -0.29 migrant(s)/1,000 population (2001 est.)
note: according to the UNHCR, by the end of 1999, Uganda was host to 218,000 refugees from a number of neighboring countries, including: Sudan 200,600, Rwanda 8,000, and Democratic Republic of the Congo 8,000
Sex ratio:
at birth: 1.03 male(s)/female
under 15 years: 1.01 male(s)/female
15-64 years: 1 male(s)/female
65 years and over: 0.91 male(s)/female
total population: 1 male(s)/female (2001 est.)
Infant mortality rate: 91.3 deaths/1,000 live births (2001 est.)
Life expectancy at birth:
total population: 43.37 years
male: 42.59 years
female: 44.17 years (2001 est.)
Total fertility rate: 6.88 children born/woman (2001 est.)
HIV/AIDS - adult prevalence rate: 8.3% (1999 est.)
HIV/AIDS - people living with HIV/AIDS: 820,000 (1999 est.)
HIV/AIDS - deaths: 110,000 (1999 est.)
Nationality:
noun: Ugandan(s)
adjective: Ugandan
Ethnic groups: Baganda 17%, Karamojong 12%, Basogo 8%, Iteso 8%, Langi 6%, Rwanda 6%, Bagisu 5%, Acholi 4%, Lugbara 4%, Bunyoro 3%, Batoro 3%, non-African (European, Asian, Arab) 1%, other 23%
Religions: Roman Catholic 33%, Protestant 33%, Muslim 16%, indigenous beliefs 18%
Languages: English (official national language, taught in grade schools, used in courts of law and by most newspapers and some radio broadcasts), Ganda or Luganda (most widely used of the Niger-Congo languages, preferred for native language publications in the capital and may be taught in school), other Niger-Congo languages, Nilo-Saharan languages, Swahili, Arabic
Literacy:
definition: age 15 and over can read and write
total population: 61.8%
male: 73.7%
female: 50.2% (1995 est.)

Government

Country name:
conventional long form: Republic of Uganda
conventional short form: Uganda
Government type: republic
Capital: Kampala
Administrative divisions: 45 districts; Adjumani, Apac, Arua, Bugiri, Bundibugyo, Bushenyi, Busia, Gulu, Hoima, Iganga, Jinja, Kabale, Kabarole, Kalangala, Kampala, Kamuli, Kapchorwa, Kasese, Katakwi, Kibale, Kiboga, Kisoro, Kitgum, Kotido, Kumi, Lira, Luwero, Masaka, Masindi, Mbale, Mbarara, Moroto, Moyo, Mpigi, Mubende, Mukono, Nakasongola, Nebbi, Ntungamo, Pallisa, Rakai, Rukungiri, Sembabule, Soroti, Tororo
Independence: 9 October 1962 (from UK)
National holiday: Independence Day, 9 October (1962)
Constitution: 8 October 1995; adopted by the interim, 284-member Constituent Assembly, charged with debating the draft constitution that had been proposed in May 1993; the Constituent Assembly was dissolved upon the promulgation of the constitution in October 1995
Legal system: in 1995, the government restored the legal system to one based on English common law and customary law; accepts compulsory ICJ jurisdiction, with reservations
Suffrage: 18 years of age; universal
Executive branch:
chief of state: President Lt. Gen. Yoweri Kaguta MUSEVENI (since seizing power 29 January 1986); note - the president is both chief of state and head of government
head of government: President Lt. Gen. Yoweri Kaguta MUSEVENI (since seizing power 29 January 1986); Prime Minister Apollo NSIBAMBI (since 5 April 1999); note - the president is both chief of state and head of government; the prime minister assists the president in the supervision of the cabinet

Uganda (continued)

cabinet: Cabinet appointed by the president from among elected legislators

elections: president reelected by popular vote for a five-year term; election last held 12 March 2001 (next to be held NA 2006); note - first popular election for president since independence in 1962 was held in 1996; prime minister appointed by the president

election results: Lt. Gen. Yoweri Kaguta MUSEVENI elected president; percent of vote - Lt. Gen. Yoweri Kaguta MUSEVENI 69.3%, Kizza BESIGYE 27.8%

Legislative branch: unicameral National Assembly (276 members - 214 directly elected by popular vote, 62 nominated by legally established special interest groups and approved by the president - women 39, army 10, disabled 5, youth 5, labor 3; members serve five-year terms)

elections: last held 27 June 1996 (next to be held May or June 2001);

election results: percent of vote by party - NA%; seats by party - NA; note - election campaigning by party was not permitted

Judicial branch: Court of Appeal (judges are appointed by the president and approved by the legislature); High Court (judges are appointed by the president)

Political parties and leaders: only one political organization, the National Resistance Movement or NRM [President MUSEVENI, chairman] is allowed to operate unfettered; note - the president maintains that the NRM is not a political party, but a movement which claims the loyalty of all Ugandans

note: the new constitution requires the suspension of political parties while the Movement system is in governanace; of the political parties that exist but are prohibited from sponsoring candidates, the most important are the Ugandan People's Congress or UPC [Milton OBOTE]; Democratic Party or DP [Paul SSEMOGERERE]; Conservative Party or CP [Joshua S. MAYANJA-NKANGI]; Justice Forum [Muhammad Kibirige MAYANJA]; and National Democrats Forum [Chapaa KARUHANGA]

Political pressure groups and leaders: NA

International organization participation: ACP, AfDB, C, CCC, EADB, ECA, FAO, G-77, IAEA, IBRD, ICAO, ICFTU, ICRM, IDA, IDB, IFAD, IFC, IFRCS, IGAD, ILO, IMF, Intelsat, Interpol, IOC, IOM, ISO (correspondent), ITU, NAM, OAU, OIC, OPCW, PCA, UN, UNCTAD, UNESCO, UNHCR, UNIDO, UPU, WFTU, WHO, WIPO, WMO, WToO, WTrO

Diplomatic representation in the US:

chief of mission: Ambassador Edith Grace SSEMPALA

chancery: 5911 16th Street NW, Washington, DC 20011

telephone: [1] (202) 726-7100 through 7102, 0416

FAX: [1] (202) 726-1727

Diplomatic representation from the US:

chief of mission: Ambassador Martin G. BRENNAN

embassy: Parliament Avenue, Kampala

mailing address: P. O. Box 7007, Kampala

telephone: [256] (41) 259792, 259793, 259795

FAX: [256] (41) 259794

Flag description: six equal horizontal bands of black (top), yellow, red, black, yellow, and red; a white disk is superimposed at the center and depicts a red-crested crane (the national symbol) facing the hoist side

Economy

Economy - overview: Uganda has substantial natural resources, including fertile soils, regular rainfall, and sizable mineral deposits of copper and cobalt. Agriculture is the most important sector of the economy, employing over 80% of the work force. Coffee is the major export crop and accounts for the bulk of export revenues. Since 1986, the government - with the support of foreign countries and international agencies - has acted to rehabilitate and stabilize the economy by undertaking currency reform, raising producer prices on export crops, increasing prices of petroleum products, and improving civil service wages. The policy changes are especially aimed at dampening inflation and boosting production and export earnings. In 1990-2000, the economy turned in a solid performance based on continued investment in the rehabilitation of infrastructure, improved incentives for production and exports, reduced inflation, gradually improved domestic security, and the return of exiled Indian-Ugandan entrepreneurs. Ongoing Ugandan involvement in the war in the Democratic Republic of the Congo, corruption within the government, and slippage in the government's determination to press reforms raise doubts about the continuation of strong growth. In 2000, Uganda qualified for enhanced HIPC debt relief worth $1.3 billion and Paris Club debt relief worth $145 million. These amounts combined with the original Highly Indebted Poor Countries HIPC debt relief add up to about $2 billion. Growth for 2001 should be somewhat lower than in 2000, because of a decline in the price of coffee, Uganda's principal export.

GDP: purchasing power parity - $26.2 billion (2000 est.)

GDP - real growth rate: 6% (2000 est.)

GDP - per capita: purchasing power parity - $1,100 (2000 est.)

GDP - composition by sector:

agriculture: 43%

industry: 17%

services: 40% (1998 est.)

Population below poverty line: 55% (1993 est.)

Household income or consumption by percentage share:

lowest 10%: 3%

highest 10%: 33.4% (1992)

Inflation rate (consumer prices): 6.5% (2000)

Labor force: 8.361 million (1993 est.)

Labor force - by occupation: agriculture 82%, industry 5%, services 13% (1999 est.)

Unemployment rate: NA%

Budget:

revenues: $959 million

expenditures: $1.04 billion, including capital expenditures of $NA (FY98/99 est.)

Industries: sugar, brewing, tobacco, cotton textiles, cement

Industrial production growth rate: 7% (1999)

Electricity - production: 1.326 billion kWh (1999)

Electricity - production by source:

fossil fuel: 0.98%

hydro: 99.02%

nuclear: 0%

other: 0% (1999)

Electricity - consumption: 1.06 billion kWh (1999)

Electricity - exports: 174 million kWh (1999)

Electricity - imports: 1 million kWh (1999)

Agriculture - products: coffee, tea, cotton, tobacco, cassava (tapioca), potatoes, corn, millet, pulses; beef, goat meat, milk, poultry

Exports: $500.1 million (f.o.b., 1999)

Exports - commodities: coffee, fish and fish products, tea; electrical products, iron and steel

Exports - partners: Spain, Germany, Belgium, Netherlands, Hungary, Kenya (1999)

Imports: $1.1 billion (f.o.b., 1999)

Imports - commodities: vehicles, petroleum, medical supplies; cereals

Imports - partners: Kenya 27.5%, US 21.2%, France 19.3, UK 5%, India 4% (1999)

Debt - external: $3.6 billion (2000 est.)

Economic aid - recipient: $1.4 billion (2000)

Currency: Ugandan shilling (UGX)

Currency code: UGX

Exchange rates: Ugandan shillings per US dollar - 1,700 (February 2001), 1,830.4 (January 2001), 1,644.5 (2000), 1,454.8 (1999), 1,240.2 (1998), 1,083.0 (1997), 1,046.1 (1996)

Fiscal year: 1 July - 30 June

Communications

Telephones - main lines in use: 50,074; however, 80,868 main lines were installed (1998)

Telephones - mobile cellular: 9,000 (1998)

Telephone system:

general assessment: seriously inadequate; two cellular systems have been introduced, but a sharp increase in the number of main lines is essential; e-mail and Internet services are available

domestic: intercity traffic by wire, microwave radio relay, and radiotelephone communication stations, fixed and mobile cellular systems for short range traffic

international: satellite earth stations - 1 Intelsat (Atlantic Ocean) and 1 Inmarsat; analog links to Kenya and Tanzania

Radio broadcast stations: AM 19, FM 4, shortwave 5 (1998)

Radios: 2.6 million (1997)

Television broadcast stations: 8 (plus one low-power repeater) (1999)

Televisions: 315,000 (1997)

Internet country code: .ug

Internet Service Providers (ISPs): 2 (2000)

Internet users: 25,000 (2000)

Uganda (continued)

Transportation

Railways:
total: 1,241 km
narrow gauge: 1,241 km 1.000-m gauge
note: a program to rehabilitate the railroad is underway (1995)
Highways:
total: 27,000 km
paved: 1,800 km
unpaved: 25,200 km (of which about 4,800 km are all-weather roads) (1990 est.)
Waterways: Lake Victoria, Lake Albert, Lake Kyoga, Lake George, Lake Edward, Victoria Nile, Albert Nile
Ports and harbors: Entebbe, Jinja, Port Bell
Merchant marine:
total: 3 ships (1,000 GRT or over) totaling 5,091 GRT/ 8,229 DWT
ships by type: roll on/roll off
note: these ships are in cargo and passenger service on Uganda's inland waterways (2000 est.)
Airports: 28 (2000 est.)
Airports - with paved runways:
total: 4
over 3,047 m: 3
1,524 to 2,437 m: 1 (2000 est.)
Airports - with unpaved runways:
total: 24
2,438 to 3,047 m: 1
1,524 to 2,437 m: 6
914 to 1,523 m: 9
under 914 m: 8 (2000 est.)
Heliports: 1 (2000 est.)

Military

Military branches: Army, Air Wing, Marine Unit
Military manpower - availability:
males age 15-49: 5,118,755 (2001 est.)
Military manpower - fit for military service:
males age 15-49: 2,778,457 (2001 est.)
Military expenditures - dollar figure: $95 million (FY98/99)
Military expenditures - percent of GDP: 1.9% (FY98/99)

Transnational Issues

Disputes - international: the Ugandan military is deployed to the Democratic Republic of Congo in support of rebel forces in that country's civil war; a resurvey of the latitudinal boundary with Tanzania in 2000 revealed a 300-meter discrepancy that both sides are currently adjudicating

Ukraine

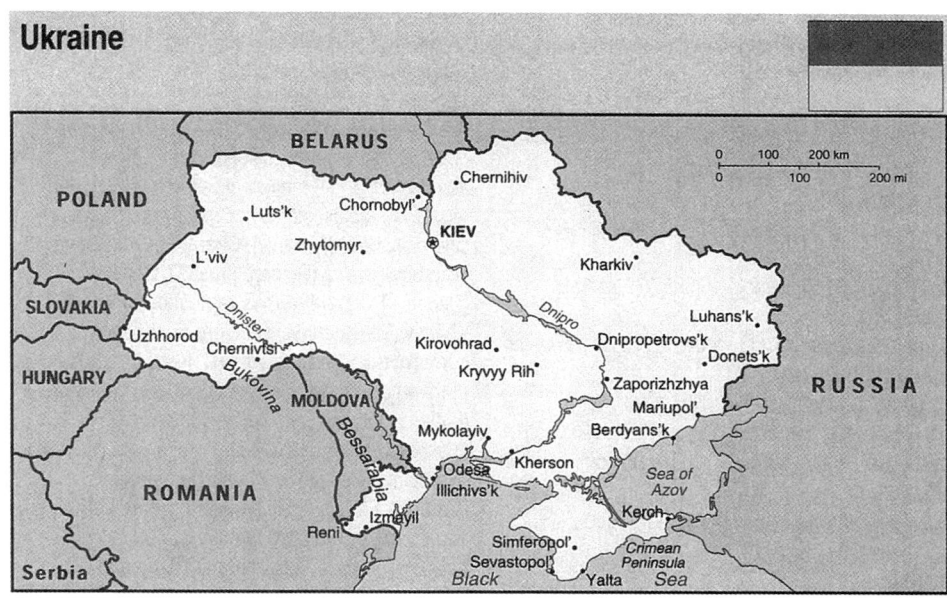

Introduction

Background: Richly endowed in natural resources, Ukraine has been fought over and subjugated for centuries; its 20th-century struggle for liberty is not yet complete. A short-lived independence from Russia (1917-1920) was followed by brutal Soviet rule that engineered two artificial famines (1921-22 and 1932-33) in which over 8 million died, and World War II, in which German and Soviet armies were responsible for some 7 million more deaths. Although independence was attained in 1991 with the dissolution of the USSR, true freedom remains elusive as many of the former Soviet elite remain entrenched, stalling efforts at economic reform, privatization, and civic liberties.

Geography

Location: Eastern Europe, bordering the Black Sea, between Poland and Russia
Geographic coordinates: 49 00 N, 32 00 E
Map references: Commonwealth of Independent States
Area:
total: 603,700 sq km
land: 603,700 sq km
water: 0 sq km
Area - comparative: slightly smaller than Texas
Land boundaries:
total: 4,558 km
border countries: Belarus 891 km, Hungary 103 km, Moldova 939 km, Poland 428 km, Romania (south) 169 km, Romania (west) 362 km, Russia 1,576 km, Slovakia 90 km
Coastline: 2,782 km
Maritime claims:
continental shelf: 200-m or to the depth of exploitation
exclusive economic zone: 200 NM
territorial sea: 12 NM
Climate: temperate continental; Mediterranean only on the southern Crimean coast; precipitation disproportionately distributed, highest in west and north, lesser in east and southeast; winters vary from cool along the Black Sea to cold farther inland; summers are warm across the greater part of the country, hot in the south
Terrain: most of Ukraine consists of fertile plains (steppes) and plateaus, mountains being found only in the west (the Carpathians), and in the Crimean Peninsula in the extreme south
Elevation extremes:
lowest point: Black Sea 0 m
highest point: Hora Hoverla 2,061 m
Natural resources: iron ore, coal, manganese, natural gas, oil, salt, sulfur, graphite, titanium, magnesium, kaolin, nickel, mercury, timber, arable land
Land use:
arable land: 58%
permanent crops: 2%
permanent pastures: 13%
forests and woodland: 18%
other: 9% (1993 est.)
Irrigated land: 26,050 sq km (1993 est.)
Natural hazards: NA
Environment - current issues: inadequate supplies of potable water; air and water pollution; deforestation; radiation contamination in the northeast from 1986 accident at Chornobyl' Nuclear Power Plant
Environment - international agreements:
party to: Air Pollution, Air Pollution-Nitrogen Oxides, Air Pollution-Sulphur 85, Antarctic-Marine Living Resources, Antarctic Treaty, Biodiversity, Climate Change, Endangered Species, Environmental Modification, Hazardous Wastes, Law of the Sea, Marine Dumping, Ozone Layer Protection, Ship Pollution, Wetlands
signed, but not ratified: Air Pollution-Persistent Organic Pollutants, Air Pollution-Sulphur 94, Air Pollution-Volatile Organic Compounds, Antarctic-Environmental Protocol, Climate Change-Kyoto Protocol

Ukraine (continued)

Geography - note: strategic position at the crossroads between Europe and Asia; second-largest country in Europe

People

Population: 48,760,474 (July 2001 est.)
Age structure:
0-14 years: 17.3% (male 4,310,158; female 4,127,677)
15-64 years: 68.57% (male 15,965,079; female 17,468,035)
65 years and over: 14.13% (male 2,275,004; female 4,614,521) (2001 est.)
Population growth rate: -0.78% (2001 est.)
Birth rate: 9.31 births/1,000 population (2001 est.)
Death rate: 16.43 deaths/1,000 population (2001 est.)
Net migration rate: -0.63 migrant(s)/1,000 population (2001 est.)
Sex ratio:
at birth: 1.05 male(s)/female
under 15 years: 1.04 male(s)/female
15-64 years: 0.91 male(s)/female
65 years and over: 0.49 male(s)/female
total population: 0.86 male(s)/female (2001 est.)
Infant mortality rate: 21.4 deaths/1,000 live births (2001 est.)
Life expectancy at birth:
total population: 66.15 years
male: 60.62 years
female: 71.96 years (2001 est.)
Total fertility rate: 1.29 children born/woman (2001 est.)
HIV/AIDS - adult prevalence rate: 0.96% (1999 est.)
HIV/AIDS - people living with HIV/AIDS: 240,000 (1999 est.)
HIV/AIDS - deaths: 4,000 (1999 est.)
Nationality:
noun: Ukrainian(s)
adjective: Ukrainian
Ethnic groups: Ukrainian 73%, Russian 22%, Jewish 1%, other 4%
Religions: Ukrainian Orthodox - Moscow Patriarchate, Ukrainian Orthodox - Kiev Patriarchate, Ukrainian Autocephalous Orthodox, Ukrainian Catholic (Uniate), Protestant, Jewish
Languages: Ukrainian, Russian, Romanian, Polish, Hungarian
Literacy:
definition: age 15 and over can read and write
total population: 98%
male: 100%
female: 97% (1989 est.)

Government

Country name:
conventional long form: none
conventional short form: Ukraine
local long form: none
local short form: Ukrayina
former: Ukrainian National Republic, Ukrainian State, Ukrainian Soviet Socialist Republic
Government type: republic
Capital: Kiev (Kyyiv)
Administrative divisions: 24 oblasti (singular - oblast'), 1 autonomous republic* (avtomnaya respublika), and 2 municipalities (mista, singular - misto) with oblast status**; Cherkas'ka (Cherkasy), Chernihivs'ka (Chernihiv), Chernivets'ka (Chernivtsi), Dnipropetrovs'ka (Dnipropetrovs'k), Donets'ka (Donets'k), Ivano-Frankivs'ka (Ivano-Frankivs'k), Kharkivs'ka (Kharkiv), Khersons'ka (Kherson), Khmel'nyts'ka (Khmel'nyts'kyy), Kirovohrads'ka (Kirovohrad), Kyyiv**, Kyyivs'ka (Kiev), Luhans'ka (Luhans'k), L'vivs'ka (L'viv), Mykolayivs'ka (Mykolayiv), Odes'ka (Odesa), Poltavs'ka (Poltava), Avtonomna Respublika Krym* (Simferopol'), Rivnens'ka (Rivne), Sevastopol'**, Sums'ka (Sumy), Ternopil's'ka (Ternopil'), Vinnyts'ka (Vinnytsya), Volyns'ka (Luts'k), Zakarpats'ka (Uzhhorod), Zaporiz'ka (Zaporizhzhya), Zhytomyrs'ka (Zhytomyr); note - when using a place name with an adjectival ending 's'ka' or 'z'ka,' the word Oblast' should be added to the place name
note: oblasts have the administrative center name following in parentheses
Independence: 24 August 1991 (from Soviet Union)
National holiday: Independence Day, 24 August (1991)
Constitution: adopted 28 June 1996
Legal system: based on civil law system; judicial review of legislative acts
Suffrage: 18 years of age; universal
Executive branch:
chief of state: President Leonid D. KUCHMA (since 19 July 1994)
head of government: Prime Minister Anatoliy KINAKH (since 29 May 2001), First Deputy Prime Minister Oleh DUBYNA (since 29 May 2001)
cabinet: Cabinet of Ministers appointed by the president and approved by the Supreme Council
note: there is also a National Security and Defense Council or NSDC originally created in 1992 as the National Security Council, but significantly revamped and strengthened under President KUCHMA; the NSDC staff is tasked with developing national security policy on domestic and international matters and advising the president; a Presidential Administration that helps draft presidential edicts and provides policy support to the president; and a Council of Regions that serves as an advisory body created by President KUCHMA in September 1994 that includes chairmen of the Kyyiv (Kiev) and Sevastopol' municipalities and chairmen of the oblasti
elections: president elected by popular vote for a five-year term; election last held 31 October and 14 November 1999 (next to be held NA 2004); prime minister and deputy prime ministers appointed by the president and approved by the Supreme Council
election results: Leonid D. KUCHMA elected president; percent of vote - Leonid KUCHMA 57.7%, Petro SYMONENKO 38.8%
Legislative branch: unicameral Supreme Council or Verkhovna Rada (450 seats; under Ukraine's new election law, half of the Supreme Council's seats are allocated on a proportional basis to those parties that gain 4% or more of the national electoral vote; the other 225 members are elected by popular vote in single-mandate constituencies; all serve four-year terms)
elections: last held 29 March 1998 (next to be held NA 2002)
election results: percent of vote by party (for parties clearing 4% hurdle on 29 March 1998) - Communist Party 24.7%, Rukh (combined) 9.4%, SPU/SelPU 8.6%, PZU 5.3%, People's Democratic Party 5.0%, Hromada Party 4.7%, Progressive Socialist Party 4.0%, United Social Democratic Party 4.0%; seats by party (as of 25 February 2000) - Communist Party 115, PRVU 36, Fatherland Party 35, United Social Democratic Party 34, People's Democratic Party 27, Trudova Ukrayina Party 27, Rukh K 27, left-center 23, PZU 18, Rukh U 17, SelPU 15, Hromada Party 14, Reforms-Congress 12, independents 14, unaffiliated 31, vacant 5
Judicial branch: Supreme Court; Constitutional Court
Political parties and leaders: Communist Party of Ukraine [Petro SYMONENKO]; Fatherland (Motherland) All Ukrainian Party [Yuliya TYMOSHENKO, chairperson]; Green Party of Ukraine or PZU [Vitaliy KONONOV, chairman]; Hromada [Pavlo LAZARENKO]; Party of Regional Revival of Ukraine or PRVU [Volodymyr RYBAK]; Peasant Party of Ukraine or SelPU [Serhiy DOVHAN]; People's Democratic Party [Valeriy PUSTOVOYTENKO, chairman]; People's Movement of Ukraine or Rukh U [Hennadiy UDOVENKO, chairman]; Progressive Socialist Party [Nataliya VITRENKO]; Reforms and Order Party/Reforms-Congress [Viktor PYNZENYK]; Socialist Party of Ukraine or SPU [Oleksandr MOROZ, chairman]; Solidarity [leader NA]; Trudova Ukrayina/Working Ukraine [Igor SHAROV, chairman]; Ukrainian Popular Movement or Rukh K [Yuriy KOSTENKO, chairman]; United Social Democratic Party of Ukraine [Viktor MEDVEDCHUK]
note: and numerous smaller parties
Political pressure groups and leaders: NA
International organization participation: BSEC, CCC, CE, CEI, CIS, EAPC, EBRD, ECE, IAEA, IBRD, ICAO, ICRM, IFC, IFRCS, IHO, ILO, IMF, IMO, Inmarsat, Intelsat (nonsignatory user), Interpol, IOC, IOM (observer), ISO, ITU, MONUC, NAM (observer), NSG, OAS (observer), OPCW, OSCE, PCA, PFP, UN, UN Security Council (temporary), UNAMSIL, UNCTAD, UNESCO, UNIDO, UNIFIL, UNMEE, UNMIBH, UNMIK, UNMOP, UNMOT, UNTAET, UPU, WCL, WFTU, WHO, WIPO, WMO, WToO, WTrO (observer), ZC
Diplomatic representation in the US:
chief of mission: Ambassador Konstantin Ivanovych HRYSHCHENKO
chancery: 3350 M Street NW, Washington, DC 20007

Ukraine (continued)

telephone: [1] (202) 333-0606
FAX: [1] (202) 333-0817
consulate(s) general: Chicago and New York
Diplomatic representation from the US:
chief of mission: Ambassador Carlos PASCUAL
embassy: 10 Yuria Kotsubynskoho, 254053 Kiev 53
mailing address: use embassy street address
telephone: [380] (44) 490-4000
FAX: [380] (44) 244-7350
Flag description: two equal horizontal bands of azure (top) and golden yellow represent grainfields under a blue sky

Economy

Economy - overview: After Russia, the Ukrainian republic was far and away the most important economic component of the former Soviet Union, producing about four times the output of the next-ranking republic. Its fertile black soil generated more than one-fourth of Soviet agricultural output, and its farms provided substantial quantities of meat, milk, grain, and vegetables to other republics. Likewise, its diversified heavy industry supplied the unique equipment (for example, large diameter pipes) and raw materials to industrial and mining sites (vertical drilling apparatus) in other regions of the former USSR. Ukraine depends on imports of energy, especially natural gas, to meet some 85% of its annual energy requirements. Shortly after independence in late 1991, the Ukrainian Government liberalized most prices and erected a legal framework for privatization, but widespread resistance to reform within the government and the legislature soon stalled reform efforts and led to some backtracking. Output in 1992-99 fell to less than 40% the 1991 level. Loose monetary policies pushed inflation to hyperinflationary levels in late 1993. Ukraine's dependence on Russia for energy supplies and the lack of significant structural reform have made the Ukrainian economy vulnerable to external shocks. Now in his second term, President KUCHMA has pledged to reduce the number of government agencies and streamline the regulation process, create a legal environment to encourage entrepreneurs and protect ownership rights, and enact a comprehensive tax overhaul. Reforms in the more politically sensitive areas of structural reform and land privatization are still lagging. Outside institutions - particularly the IMF - have encouraged Ukraine to quicken the pace and scope of reforms and have threatened to withdraw financial support. GDP in 2000 showed strong export-based growth of 6% - the first growth since independence - and industrial production grew 12.9%. As the capacity for further export-based economic expansion diminishes, GDP growth in 2001 is likely to decline to around 3%.
GDP: purchasing power parity - $189.4 billion (2000 est.)
GDP - real growth rate: 6% (2000 est.)
GDP - per capita: purchasing power parity - $3,850 (2000 est.)
GDP - composition by sector:
agriculture: 12%
industry: 26%
services: 62% (1998 est.)
Population below poverty line: 50% (1999 est.)
Household income or consumption by percentage share:
lowest 10%: 3.9%
highest 10%: 26.4% (1996)
Inflation rate (consumer prices): 25.8% (2000 est.)
Labor force: 22.8 million (yearend 1997)
Labor force - by occupation: industry 32%, agriculture 24%, services 44% (1996)
Unemployment rate: 4.3% officially registered; large number of unregistered or underemployed workers (December 1999)
Budget:
revenues: $8.3 billion
expenditures: $8.8 billion, including capital expenditures of $NA (1999 est.)
Industries: coal, electric power, ferrous and nonferrous metals, machinery and transport equipment, chemicals, food processing (especially sugar)
Industrial production growth rate: 12.9% (2000 est.)
Electricity - production: 157.823 billion kWh (1999)
Electricity - production by source:
fossil fuel: 47.67%
hydro: 9.65%
nuclear: 42.67%
other: 0.01% (1999)
Electricity - consumption: 146.675 billion kWh (1999)
Electricity - exports: 2.3 billion kWh (1999)
Electricity - imports: 2.2 billion kWh (1999)
Agriculture - products: grain, sugar beets, sunflower seeds, vegetables; beef, milk
Exports: $14.6 billion (2000 est.)
Exports - commodities: ferrous and nonferrous metals, fuel and petroleum products, machinery and transport equipment, food products
Exports - partners: Russia 24%, Europe 30%, US 5% (2000 est.)
Imports: $15 billion (2000 est.)
Imports - commodities: energy, machinery and parts, transportation equipment, chemicals
Imports - partners: Russia 42%, Europe 29%, US 3% (2000 est.)
Debt - external: $10.3 billion (2000)
Economic aid - recipient: $637.7 million (1995); IMF Extended Funds Facility $2.2 billion (1998)
Currency: hryvnia (UAH)
Currency code: UAH
Exchange rates: hryvnia per US dollar - 5.4331 (January 2001), 5.4402 (2000), 4.1304 (1999), 2.4495 (1998), 1.8617 (1997), 1.8295 (1996)
Fiscal year: calendar year

Communications

Telephones - main lines in use: 9.45 million (April 1999)
Telephones - mobile cellular: 236,000 (1998)
Telephone system:
general assessment: Ukraine's telecommunication development plan, running through 2005, emphasizes improving domestic trunk lines, international connections, and the mobile cellular system
domestic: at independence in December 1991, Ukraine inherited a telephone system that was antiquated, inefficient, and in disrepair; more than 3.5 million applications for telephones could not be satisfied; telephone density is now rising slowly and the domestic trunk system is being improved; the mobile cellular telephone system is expanding at a high rate
international: two new domestic trunk lines are a part of the fiber-optic Trans-Asia-Europe (TAE) system and three Ukrainian links have been installed in the fiber-optic Trans-European Lines (TEL) project which connects 18 countries; additional international service is provided by the Italy-Turkey-Ukraine-Russia (ITUR) fiber-optic submarine cable and by earth stations in the Intelsat, Inmarsat, and Intersputnik satellite systems
Radio broadcast stations: AM 134, FM 289, shortwave 4 (1998)
Radios: 45.05 million (1997)
Television broadcast stations: at least 33 (plus 21 repeaters that relay broadcasts from Russia) (1997)
Televisions: 18.05 million (1997)
Internet country code: .ua
Internet Service Providers (ISPs): 32 (2000)
Internet users: 200,000 (2000)

Transportation

Railways:
total: 23,350 km
broad gauge: 23,350 km 1.524-m gauge (8,600 km electrified)
Highways:
total: 176,310 km
paved: 170,139 km (including 1,770 km of expressways); note - (these roads are said to be hard-surfaced, and include, in addition to conventionally paved roads, some that are surfaced with gravel or other coarse aggregate, making them trafficable in all weather)
unpaved: 6,171 km (these roads are made of unstabilized earth and are difficult to negotiate in wet weather) (1998 est.)
Waterways: 4,499 km
note: (1,672 km are on the Pryp'yat' and Dnistr) (1990)
Pipelines: crude oil 4,000 km (1995); petroleum products 4,500 km (1995); natural gas 34,400 km (1998)
Ports and harbors: Berdyans'k, Illichivs'k, Izmayil, Kerch, Kherson, Kiev (Kyyiv), Mariupol', Mykolayiv, Odesa, Reni, Sevastopol'

Ukraine (continued)

Merchant marine:
total: 156 ships (1,000 GRT or over) totaling 757,582 GRT/841,755 DWT
ships by type: bulk 8, cargo 110, container 3, liquefied gas 2, passenger 11, passenger/cargo 2, petroleum tanker 14, railcar carrier 2, roll on/roll off 2, short-sea passenger 2 (2000 est.)
Airports: 718 (2000 est.)
Airports - with paved runways:
total: 114
over 3,047 m: 14
2,438 to 3,047 m: 50
1,524 to 2,437 m: 21
914 to 1,523 m: 3
under 914 m: 26 (2000 est.)
Airports - with unpaved runways:
total: 604
over 3,047 m: 13
2,438 to 3,047 m: 37
1,524 to 2,437 m: 52
914 to 1,523 m: 45
under 914 m: 457 (2000 est.)

Military

Military branches: Army, Navy, Air Force, Air Defense Force, Internal Troops, Border Troops
Military manpower - military age: 18 years of age
Military manpower - availability:
males age 15-49: 12,285,623 (2001 est.)
Military manpower - fit for military service:
males age 15-49: 9,630,184 (2001 est.)
Military manpower - reaching military age annually:
males: 390,823 (2001 est.)
Military expenditures - dollar figure: $500 million (FY99)
Military expenditures - percent of GDP: 1.4% (FY99)

Transnational Issues

Disputes - international: has made no territorial claim in Antarctica (but has reserved the right to do so) and does not recognize the claims of any other nation
Illicit drugs: limited cultivation of cannabis and opium poppy, mostly for CIS consumption; some synthetic drug production for export to West; limited government eradication program; used as transshipment point for opiates and other illicit drugs from Africa, Latin America, and Turkey, and to Europe and Russia; drug-related money laundering a minor, but growing, problem

United Arab Emirates

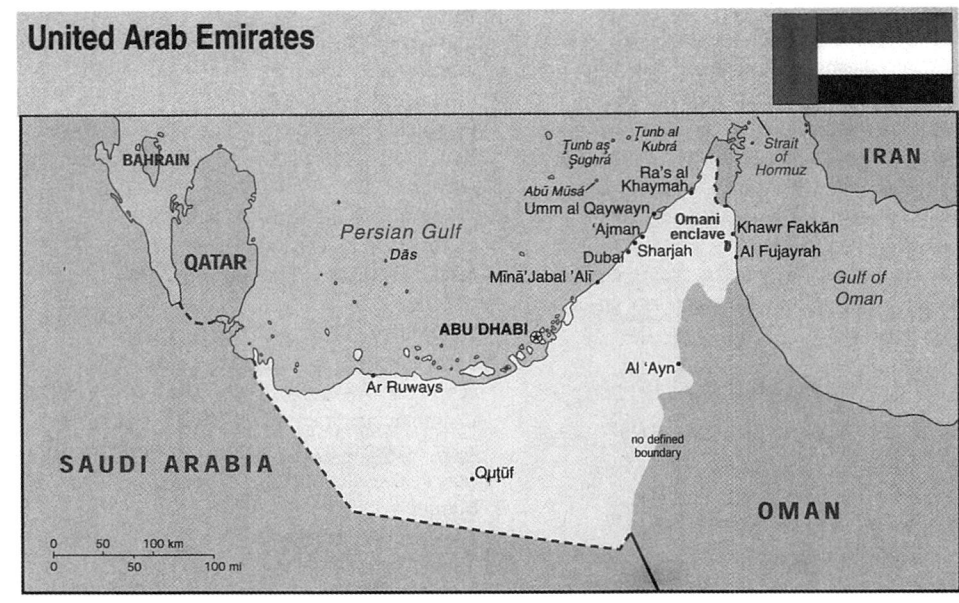

Introduction

Background: The Trucial States of the Persian Gulf coast granted the UK control of their defense and foreign affairs in 19th century treaties. In 1971, six of these states - Abu Zaby, 'Ajman, Al Fujayrah, Ash Shariqah, Dubayy, and Umm al Qaywayn - merged to form the UAE. They were joined in 1972 by Ra's al Khaymah. The UAE's per capita GDP is not far below those of the leading West European nations. Its generosity with oil revenues and its moderate foreign policy stance have allowed it to play a vital role in the affairs of the region.

Geography

Location: Middle East, bordering the Gulf of Oman and the Persian Gulf, between Oman and Saudi Arabia
Geographic coordinates: 24 00 N, 54 00 E
Map references: Middle East
Area:
total: 82,880 sq km
land: 82,880 sq km
water: 0 sq km
Area - comparative: slightly smaller than Maine
Land boundaries:
total: 867 km
border countries: Oman 410 km, Saudi Arabia 457 km
Coastline: 1,318 km
Maritime claims:
contiguous zone: 24 NM
continental shelf: 200 NM or to the edge of the continental margin
exclusive economic zone: 200 NM
territorial sea: 12 NM
Climate: desert; cooler in eastern mountains
Terrain: flat, barren coastal plain merging into rolling sand dunes of vast desert wasteland; mountains in east
Elevation extremes:
lowest point: Persian Gulf 0 m
highest point: Jabal Yibir 1,527 m
Natural resources: petroleum, natural gas
Land use:
arable land: 0%
permanent crops: 0%
permanent pastures: 2%
forests and woodland: 0%
other: 98% (1993 est.)
Irrigated land: 50 sq km (1993 est.)
Natural hazards: frequent sand and dust storms
Environment - current issues: lack of natural freshwater resources being overcome by desalination plants; desertification; beach pollution from oil spills
Environment - international agreements:
party to: Biodiversity, Climate Change, Desertification, Endangered Species, Hazardous Wastes, Marine Dumping, Ozone Layer Protection, Ship Pollution
signed, but not ratified: Law of the Sea
Geography - note: strategic location along southern approaches to Strait of Hormuz, a vital transit point for world crude oil

People

Population: 2,407,460
note: includes 1,576,472 non-nationals (July 2001 est.)
Age structure:
0-14 years: 28.86% (male 354,298; female 340,498)
15-64 years: 68.74% (male 1,047,839; female 607,020)
65 years and over: 2.4% (male 40,626; female 17,179) (2001 est.)
Population growth rate: 1.59% (2001 est.)
Birth rate: 18.11 births/1,000 population (2001 est.)
Death rate: 3.79 deaths/1,000 population (2001 est.)
Net migration rate: 1.61 migrant(s)/1,000 population (2001 est.)

United Arab Emirates (continued)

Sex ratio:
at birth: 1.05 male(s)/female
under 15 years: 1.04 male(s)/female
15-64 years: 1.73 male(s)/female
65 years and over: 2.36 male(s)/female
total population: 1.5 male(s)/female (2001 est.)
Infant mortality rate: 16.68 deaths/1,000 live births (2001 est.)
Life expectancy at birth:
total population: 74.29 years
male: 71.84 years
female: 76.86 years (2001 est.)
Total fertility rate: 3.23 children born/woman (2001 est.)
HIV/AIDS - adult prevalence rate: 0.18% (1999 est.)
HIV/AIDS - people living with HIV/AIDS: NA
HIV/AIDS - deaths: NA
Nationality:
noun: Emirati(s)
adjective: Emirati
Ethnic groups: Emirati 19%, other Arab and Iranian 23%, South Asian 50%, other expatriates (includes Westerners and East Asians) 8% (1982)
note: less than 20% are UAE citizens (1982)
Religions: Muslim 96% (Shi'a 16%), Christian, Hindu, and other 4%
Languages: Arabic (official), Persian, English, Hindi, Urdu
Literacy:
definition: age 15 and over can read and write
total population: 79.2%
male: 78.9%
female: 79.8% (1995 est.)

Government

Country name:
conventional long form: United Arab Emirates
conventional short form: none
local long form: Al Imarat al Arabiyah al Muttahidah
local short form: none
former: Trucial Oman, Trucial States
abbreviation: UAE
Government type: federation with specified powers delegated to the UAE federal government and other powers reserved to member emirates
Capital: Abu Dhabi
Administrative divisions: 7 emirates (imarat, singular - imarah); Abu Zaby (Abu Dhabi), 'Ajman, Al Fujayrah, Ash Shariqah (Sharjah), Dubayy (Dubai), Ra's al Khaymah, Umm al Qaywayn
Independence: 2 December 1971 (from UK)
National holiday: Independence Day, 2 December (1971)
Constitution: 2 December 1971 (made permanent in 1996)
Legal system: federal court system introduced in 1971; all emirates except Dubayy (Dubai) and Ra's al Khaymah have joined the federal system; all emirates have secular and Islamic law for civil, criminal, and high courts
Suffrage: none
Executive branch:
chief of state: President ZAYID bin Sultan Al Nuhayyan (since 2 December 1971), ruler of Abu Zaby (Abu Dhabi) (since 6 August 1966) and Vice President MAKTUM bin Rashid al-Maktum (since 8 October 1990), ruler of Dubayy (Dubai)
head of government: Prime Minister MAKTUM bin Rashid al-Maktum (since 8 October 1990), ruler of Dubayy (Dubai); Deputy Prime Minister SULTAN bin Zayid Al Nuhayyan (since 20 November 1990)
cabinet: Council of Ministers appointed by the president
note: there is also a Federal Supreme Council (FSC) which is composed of the seven emirate rulers; the council is the highest constitutional authority in the UAE; establishes general policies and sanctions federal legislation, Abu Zaby (Abu Dhabi) and Dubayy (Dubai) rulers have effective veto power; meets four times a year
elections: president and vice president elected by the FSC (a group of seven electors) for five-year terms; election last held NA October 1996 (next to be held NA October 2001); prime minister and deputy prime minister appointed by the president
election results: ZAYID bin Sultan Al Nuhayyan reelected president; percent of FSC vote - NA, but believed to be unanimous; MAKTUM bin Rashid al-Maktum elected vice president; percent of FSC vote - NA%, but believed to be unanimous
Legislative branch: unicameral Federal National Council or Majlis al-Ittihad al-Watani (40 seats; members appointed by the rulers of the constituent states to serve two-year terms)
elections: none
note: reviews legislation, but cannot change or veto
Judicial branch: Union Supreme Court (judges are appointed by the president)
Political parties and leaders: none
Political pressure groups and leaders: NA
International organization participation: ABEDA, AFESD, AL, AMF, CAEU, CCC, ESCWA, FAO, G-77, GCC, IAEA, IBRD, ICAO, ICRM, IDA, IDB, IFAD, IFC, IFRCS, IHO, ILO, IMF, IMO, Inmarsat, Intelsat, Interpol, IOC, ISO, ITU, NAM, OAPEC, OIC, OPCW, OPEC, UN, UNCTAD, UNESCO, UNIDO, UPU, WHO, WIPO, WMO, WTrO
Diplomatic representation in the US:
chief of mission: Ambassador Asri Said Ahmad al-DHAHIRI
chancery: Suite 700, 1255 22nd Street NW, Washington, DC 20037
telephone: [1] (202) 955-7999
Diplomatic representation from the US:
chief of mission: Ambassador Theodore H. KATTOUF
embassy: Al-Sudan Street, Abu Dhabi
mailing address: P. O. Box 4009, Abu Dhabi; American Embassy Abu Dhabi, Department of State, Washington, DC 20521-6010 (pouch); note - work week is Saturday through Wednesday
telephone: [971] (2) 4436691
FAX: [971] (2) 4435441
consulate(s) general: Dubai
Flag description: three equal horizontal bands of green (top), white, and black with a thicker vertical red band on the hoist side

Economy

Economy - overview: The UAE has an open economy with a high per capita income and a sizable annual trade surplus. Its wealth is based on oil and gas output (about 33% of GDP), and the fortunes of the economy fluctuate with the prices of those commodities. Since 1973, the UAE has undergone a profound transformation from an impoverished region of small desert principalities to a modern state with a high standard of living. At present levels of production, oil and gas reserves should last for more than 100 years. Despite higher oil revenues in 1999-2000, the government has not drawn back from the economic reforms implemented during the 1998 oil price depression. The government has increased spending on job creation and infrastructure expansion and is opening up its utilities to greater private-sector involvement.
GDP: purchasing power parity - $54 billion (2000 est.)
GDP - real growth rate: 4% (2000 est.)
GDP - per capita: purchasing power parity - $22,800 (2000 est.)
GDP - composition by sector:
agriculture: 3%
industry: 52%
services: 45% (1996 est.)
Population below poverty line: NA%
Household income or consumption by percentage share:
lowest 10%: NA%
highest 10%: NA%
Inflation rate (consumer prices): 4.5% (2000 est.)
Labor force: 1.4 million (1998 est.)
note: 75% of the population in the 15-64 age group is non-national (July 1998 est.)
Labor force - by occupation: services 60%, industry 32%, agriculture 8% (1996 est.)
Unemployment rate: NA%
Budget:
revenues: $6.5 billion
expenditures: $7.3 billion, including capital expenditures of $NA (2000 est.)
Industries: petroleum, fishing, petrochemicals, construction materials, some boat building, handicrafts, pearling
Industrial production growth rate: 4% (2000)
Electricity - production: 36.7 billion kWh (1999)
Electricity - production by source:
fossil fuel: 100%
hydro: 0%
nuclear: 0%
other: 0% (1999)

United Arab Emirates (continued)

Electricity - consumption: 34.131 billion kWh (1999)
Electricity - exports: 0 kWh (1999)
Electricity - imports: 0 kWh (1999)
Agriculture - products: dates, vegetables, watermelons; poultry, eggs, dairy products; fish
Exports: $46 billion (f.o.b., 2000 est.)
Exports - commodities: crude oil 45%, natural gas, reexports, dried fish, dates
Exports - partners: Japan 30%, India 7%, Singapore 6%, South Korea 4%, Oman, Iran (1999)
Imports: $34 billion (f.o.b., 2000 est.)
Imports - commodities: machinery and transport equipment, chemicals, food
Imports - partners: Japan 9%, US 8%, UK 8%, Italy 6%, Germany, South Korea (1999)
Debt - external: $12.6 billion (2000 est.)
Economic aid - recipient: $NA
Currency: Emirati dirham (AED)
Currency code: AED
Exchange rates: Emirati dirhams per US dollar - central bank mid-point rate: 3.6725 (since 1998); 3.6711 (1997), 3.6710 (1995-96)
Fiscal year: calendar year

Communications

Telephones - main lines in use: 915,223 (1998)
Telephones - mobile cellular: 1 million (1999)
Telephone system:
general assessment: modern system consisting of microwave radio relay and coaxial cable; key centers are Abu Dhabi and Dubai
domestic: microwave radio relay and coaxial cable
international: satellite earth stations - 3 Intelsat (1 Atlantic Ocean and 2 Indian Ocean) and 1 Arabsat; submarine cables to Qatar, Bahrain, India, and Pakistan; tropospheric scatter to Bahrain; microwave radio relay to Saudi Arabia
Radio broadcast stations: AM 13, FM 7, shortwave 2 (1998)
Radios: 820,000 (1997)
Television broadcast stations: 15 (1997)
Televisions: 310,000 (1997)
Internet country code: .ae
Internet Service Providers (ISPs): 1 (2000)
Internet users: 400,000 (2000)

Transportation

Railways: 0 km
Highways:
total: 1,088 km
paved: 1,088 km
unpaved: 0 km (1998 est.)
Waterways: none
Pipelines: crude oil 830 km; natural gas, including natural gas liquids, 870 km
Ports and harbors: 'Ajman, Al Fujayrah, Das Island, Khawr Fakkan, Mina' Jabal 'Ali, Mina' Khalid, Mina' Rashid, Mina' Saqr, Mina' Zayid, Umm al Qaywayn

Merchant marine:
total: 70 ships (1,000 GRT or over) totaling 1,094,256 GRT/1,421,333 DWT
ships by type: cargo 16, chemical tanker 3, container 17, liquefied gas 1, livestock carrier 1, passenger 1, petroleum tanker 24, roll on/roll off 6, specialized tanker 1 (2000 est.)
Airports: 40 (2000 est.)
Airports - with paved runways:
total: 22
over 3,047 m: 8
2,438 to 3,047 m: 3
1,524 to 2,437 m: 4
914 to 1,523 m: 3
under 914 m: 4 (2000 est.)
Airports - with unpaved runways:
total: 18
over 3,047 m: 1
2,438 to 3,047 m: 1
1,524 to 2,437 m: 4
914 to 1,523 m: 9
under 914 m: 3 (2000 est.)
Heliports: 2 (2000 est.)

Military

Military branches: Army, Navy, Air Force, Air Defense, paramilitary (includes Federal Police Force)
Military manpower - military age: 18 years of age
Military manpower - availability:
males age 15-49: 778,842
note: includes non-nationals (2001 est.)
Military manpower - fit for military service:
males age 15-49: 420,484 (2001 est.)
Military manpower - reaching military age annually:
males: 25,482 (2001 est.)
Military expenditures - dollar figure: $1.6 billion (FY00)
Military expenditures - percent of GDP: 3.1% (FY00)

Transnational Issues

Disputes - international: location and status of boundary with Saudi Arabia is not final, de facto boundary reflects 1974 agreement; boundary with Oman has not been bilaterally defined; northern section in the Musandam Peninsula is an administrative boundary; claims two islands in the Persian Gulf occupied by Iran: Lesser Tunb (called Tunb as Sughra in Arabic by UAE and Jazireh-ye Tonb-e Kuchek in Persian by Iran) and Greater Tunb (called Tunb al Kubra in Arabic by UAE and Jazireh-ye Tonb-e Bozorg in Persian by Iran); claims island in the Persian Gulf jointly administered with Iran (called Abu Musa in Arabic by UAE and Jazireh-ye Abu Musa in Persian by Iran) - over which Iran has taken steps to exert unilateral control since 1992, including access restrictions and a military build-up on the island; the UAE has garnered significant diplomatic support in the region in protesting these Iranian actions

Illicit drugs: growing role as heroin transshipment and money-laundering center due to its proximity to southwest Asian producing countries and the bustling free trade zone in Dubai

United Kingdom

Introduction

Background: Great Britain, the dominant industrial and maritime power of the 19th century, played a leading role in developing parliamentary democracy and in advancing literature and science. At its zenith, the British Empire stretched over one-fourth of the earth's surface. The first half of the 20th century saw the UK's strength seriously depleted in two World Wars. The second half witnessed the dismantling of the Empire and the UK rebuilding itself into a modern and prosperous European nation. As one of five permanent members of the UN Security Council, a founding member of NATO, and of the Commonwealth, the UK pursues a global approach to foreign policy; it currently is weighing the degree of its integration with continental Europe. A member of the EU, it chose to remain outside of the European Monetary Union for the time being. Constitutional reform is also a significant issue in the UK. Regional assemblies with varying degrees of power opened in Scotland, Wales, and Northern Ireland in 1999.

Geography

Location: Western Europe, islands including the northern one-sixth of the island of Ireland between the North Atlantic Ocean and the North Sea, northwest of France
Geographic coordinates: 54 00 N, 2 00 W
Map references: Europe
Area:
total: 244,820 sq km
land: 241,590 sq km
water: 3,230 sq km
note: includes Rockall and Shetland Islands
Area - comparative: slightly smaller than Oregon
Land boundaries:
total: 360 km
border countries: Ireland 360 km
Coastline: 12,429 km
Maritime claims:
continental shelf: as defined in continental shelf orders or in accordance with agreed upon boundaries
exclusive fishing zone: 200 NM
territorial sea: 12 NM
Climate: temperate; moderated by prevailing southwest winds over the North Atlantic Current; more than one-half of the days are overcast
Terrain: mostly rugged hills and low mountains; level to rolling plains in east and southeast
Elevation extremes:
lowest point: Fenland -4 m
highest point: Ben Nevis 1,343 m
Natural resources: coal, petroleum, natural gas, tin, limestone, iron ore, salt, clay, chalk, gypsum, lead, silica, arable land
Land use:
arable land: 25%
permanent crops: 0%
permanent pastures: 46%
forests and woodland: 10%
other: 19% (1993 est.)
Irrigated land: 1,080 sq km (1993 est.)
Natural hazards: NA
Environment - current issues: continues to reduce greenhouse gas emissions (has meet Kyoto Protocol target of a 12.5% reduction from 1990 levels and hopes to reduce even more); small particulate emissions, largely from vehicular traffic, remain a problem; solid waste continues to rise and recycling is very limited
Environment - international agreements:
party to: Air Pollution, Air Pollution-Nitrogen Oxides, Air Pollution-Sulphur 94, Air Pollution-Volatile Organic Compounds, Antarctic-Environmental Protocol, Antarctic-Marine Living Resources, Antarctic Seals, Antarctic Treaty, Biodiversity, Climate Change, Desertification, Endangered Species, Environmental Modification, Hazardous Wastes, Law of the Sea, Marine Dumping, Marine Life Conservation, Nuclear Test Ban, Ozone Layer Protection, Ship Pollution, Tropical Timber 83, Tropical Timber 94, Wetlands, Whaling
signed, but not ratified: Air Pollution-Persistent Organic Pollutants, Climate Change-Kyoto Protocol
Geography - note: lies near vital North Atlantic sea lanes; only 35 km from France and now linked by tunnel under the English Channel; because of heavily indented coastline, no location is more than 125 km from tidal waters

People

Population: 59,647,790 (July 2001 est.)
Age structure:
0-14 years: 18.89% (male 5,778,415; female 5,486,114)
15-64 years: 65.41% (male 19,712,932; female 19,304,771)
65 years and over: 15.7% (male 3,895,921; female 5,469,637) (2001 est.)
Population growth rate: 0.23% (2001 est.)
Birth rate: 11.54 births/1,000 population (2001 est.)
Death rate: 10.35 deaths/1,000 population (2001 est.)
Net migration rate: 1.07 migrant(s)/1,000 population (2001 est.)
Sex ratio:
at birth: 1.05 male(s)/female
under 15 years: 1.05 male(s)/female
15-64 years: 1.02 male(s)/female
65 years and over: 0.71 male(s)/female
total population: 0.97 male(s)/female (2001 est.)
Infant mortality rate: 5.54 deaths/1,000 live births (2001 est.)
Life expectancy at birth:
total population: 77.82 years
male: 75.13 years
female: 80.66 years (2001 est.)
Total fertility rate: 1.73 children born/woman (2001 est.)
HIV/AIDS - adult prevalence rate: 0.11% (1999 est.)
HIV/AIDS - people living with HIV/AIDS: 31,000 (1999 est.)
HIV/AIDS - deaths: 450 (1999 est.)
Nationality:
noun: Briton(s), British (collective plural)
adjective: British
Ethnic groups: English 81.5%, Scottish 9.6%, Irish 2.4%, Welsh 1.9%, Ulster 1.8%, West Indian, Indian, Pakistani, and other 2.8%
Religions: Anglican 27 million, Roman Catholic 9 million, Muslim 1 million, Presbyterian 800,000, Methodist 760,000, Sikh 400,000, Hindu 350,000, Jewish 300,000 (1991 est.)
Languages: English, Welsh (about 26% of the population of Wales), Scottish form of Gaelic (about 60,000 in Scotland)
Literacy:
definition: age 15 and over has completed five or more years of schooling
total population: 99% (1978 est.)
male: NA%
female: NA%

United Kingdom (continued)

Government

Country name:
conventional long form: United Kingdom of Great Britain and Northern Ireland
conventional short form: United Kingdom
abbreviation: UK
Government type: constitutional monarchy
Capital: London
Administrative divisions:
England: 47 boroughs, 36 counties*, 29 London boroughs**, 12 cities and boroughs***, 10 districts****, 12 cities*****, 3 royal boroughs******; Barking and Dagenham**, Barnet**, Barnsley, Bath and North East Somerset****, Bedfordshire*, Bexley**, Birmingham***, Blackburn with Darwen, Blackpool, Bolton, Bournemouth, Bracknell Forest, Bradford***, Brent**, Brighton and Hove, City of Bristol*****, Bromley**, Buckinghamshire*, Bury, Calderdale, Cambridgeshire*, Camden**, Cheshire*, Cornwall*, Coventry***, Croydon**, Cumbria*, Darlington, Derby*****, Derbyshire*, Devon*, Doncaster, Dorset*, Dudley, Durham*, Ealing**, East Riding of Yorkshire****, East Sussex*, Enfield**, Essex*, Gateshead, Gloucestershire*, Greenwich**, Hackney**, Halton, Hammersmith and Fulham**, Hampshire*, Haringey**, Harrow**, Hartlepool, Havering**, Herefordshire*, Hertfordshire*, Hillingdon**, Hounslow**, Isle of Wight*, Islington**, Kensington and Chelsea******, Kent*, City of Kingston upon Hull*****, Kingston upon Thames******, Kirklees, Knowsley, Lambeth**, Lancashire*, Leeds***, Leicester*****, Leicestershire*, Lewisham**, Lincolnshire*, Liverpool***, City of London*****, Luton, Manchester***, Medway, Merton**, Middlesbrough, Milton Keynes, Newcastle upon Tyne***, Newham**, Norfolk*, Northamptonshire*, North East Lincolnshire****, North Lincolnshire****, North Somerset****, North Tyneside, Northumberland*, North Yorkshire*, Nottingham*****, Nottinghamshire*, Oldham, Oxfordshire*, Peterborough*****, Plymouth*****, Poole, Portsmouth*****, Reading, Redbridge**, Redcar and Cleveland, Richmond upon Thames**, Rochdale, Rotherham, Rutland****, Salford***, Shropshire*, Sandwell, Sefton, Sheffield***, Slough, Solihull, Somerset*, Southampton*****, Southend-on-Sea, South Gloucestershire****, South Tyneside, Southwark**, Staffordshire*, St. Helens, Stockport, Stockton-on-Tees, Stoke-on-Trent*****, Suffolk*, Sunderland***, Surrey*, Sutton**, Swindon, Tameside, Telford and Wrekin****, Thurrock, Torbay, Tower Hamlets**, Trafford, Wakefield***, Walsall, Waltham Forest**, Wandsworth**, Warrington, Warwickshire*, West Berkshire****, Westminster***, West Sussex*, Wigan, Wiltshire*, Windsor and Maidenhead******, Wirral, Wokingham****, Wolverhampton, Worcestershire*, York*****
Northern Ireland: 24 districts, 2 cities*; Antrim, Ards, Armagh, Ballymena, Ballymoney, Banbridge, Belfast*, Carrickfergus, Castlereagh, Coleraine, Cookstown, Craigavon, Down, Dungannon, Fermanagh, Larne, Limavady, Lisburn, Derry*, Magherafelt, Moyle, Newry and Mourne, Newtownabbey, North Down, Omagh, Strabane;
Scotland: 32 council areas; Aberdeen City, Aberdeenshire, Angus, Argyll and Bute, The Scottish Borders, Clackmannanshire, Dumfries and Galloway, Dundee City, East Ayrshire, East Dunbartonshire, East Lothian, East Renfrewshire, City of Edinburgh, Falkirk, Fife, Glasgow City, Highland, Inverclyde, Midlothian, Moray, North Ayrshire, North Lanarkshire, Orkney Islands, Perth and Kinross, Renfrewshire, Shetland Islands, South Ayrshire, South Lanarkshire, Stirling, West Dunbartonshire, Eilean Siar (Western Isles), West Lothian
Wales: 11 county boroughs, 9 counties*, 2 cities and counties**; Isle of Anglesey*, Blaenau Gwent, Bridgend, Caerphilly, Cardiff**, Ceredigion*, Carmarthenshire*, Conwy, Denbighshire*, Flintshire*, Gwynedd, Merthyr Tydfil, Monmouthshire*, Neath Port Talbot, Newport, Pembrokeshire*, Powys*, Rhondda Cynon Taff, Swansea**, Torfaen, The Vale of Glamorgan*, Wrexham
Dependent areas: Anguilla, Bermuda, British Indian Ocean Territory, British Virgin Islands, Cayman Islands, Falkland Islands, Gibraltar, Guernsey, Jersey, Isle of Man, Montserrat, Pitcairn Islands, Saint Helena, South Georgia and the South Sandwich Islands, Turks and Caicos Islands
Independence: England has existed as a unified entity since the 10th century; the union between England and Wales was enacted under the Statute of Rhuddlan in 1284; in the Act of Union of 1707, England and Scotland agreed to permanent union as Great Britain; the legislative union of Great Britain and Ireland was implemented in 1801, with the adoption of the name the United Kingdom of Great Britain and Ireland; the Anglo-Irish treaty of 1921 formalized a partition of Ireland; six northern Irish counties remained part of the United Kingdom as Northern Ireland and the current name of the country, the United Kingdom of Great Britain and Northern Ireland, was adopted in 1927
National holiday: Birthday of Queen ELIZABETH II, celebrated on the second Saturday in June (1926)
Constitution: unwritten; partly statutes, partly common law and practice
Legal system: common law tradition with early Roman and modern continental influences; no judicial review of Acts of Parliament; accepts compulsory ICJ jurisdiction, with reservations; British courts and legislation are increasingly subject to review by European Union courts
Suffrage: 18 years of age; universal
Executive branch:
chief of state: Queen ELIZABETH II (since 6 February 1952); Heir Apparent Prince CHARLES (son of the queen, born 14 November 1948)
head of government: Prime Minister Anthony C. L. (Tony) BLAIR (since 2 May 1997)
cabinet: Cabinet of Ministers appointed by the prime minister
elections: none; the monarch is hereditary; the prime minister is the leader of the majority party in the House of Commons (assuming there is no majority party, a prime minister would have a majority coalition or at least a coalition that was not rejected by the majority)
Legislative branch: bicameral Parliament comprised of House of Lords (consists of approximately 500 life peers, 92 hereditary peers and 26 clergy) and House of Commons (659 seats; members are elected by popular vote to serve five-year terms unless the House is dissolved earlier)
elections: House of Lords - no elections (some proposals for further reform include elections); House of Commons - last held 7 June 2001 (next to be held by NA May 2006)
election results: House of Commons - percent of vote by party - NA%; seats by party - Labor 412, Conservative and Unionist 166, Liberal Democrat 52, other 29
note: in 1998 elections were held for a Northern Ireland Parliament (because of unresolved disputes among existing parties, the transfer of power from London to Northern Ireland came only at the end of 1999 and was rescinded in February 2000); in 1999 there were elections for a new Scottish Parliament and a new Welsh Assembly
Judicial branch: House of Lords (highest court of appeal; several Lords of Appeal in Ordinary are appointed by the monarch for life); Supreme Courts of England, Wales, and Northern Ireland (comprising the Courts of Appeal, the High Courts of Justice, and the Crown Courts); Scotland's Court of Session and Court of the Justiciary
Political parties and leaders: Conservative and Unionist Party [William HAGUE]; Democratic Unionist Party (Northern Ireland) [Rev. Ian PAISLEY]; Labor Party [Anthony (Tony) Blair]; Liberal Democrats [Charles KENNEDY]; Party of Wales (Plaid Cymru) [Ieuan Wyn JONES]; Scottish National Party or SNP [John SWINNEY]; Sinn Fein (Northern Ireland) [Gerry ADAMS]; Social Democratic and Labor Party or SDLP (Northern Ireland) [John HUME]; Ulster Unionist Party (Northern Ireland) [David TRIMBLE]
Political pressure groups and leaders: Campaign for Nuclear Disarmament; Confederation of British Industry; National Farmers' Union; Trades Union Congress
International organization participation: AfDB, AsDB, Australia Group, BIS, C, CCC, CDB (non-regional), CE, CERN, EAPC, EBRD, ECA (associate), ECE, ECLAC, EIB, ESA, ESCAP, EU, FAO, G- 5, G- 7, G-10, IADB, IAEA, IBRD, ICAO, ICC, ICFTU, ICRM, IDA, IEA, IFAD, IFC, IFRCS, IHO, ILO, IMF, IMO, Inmarsat, Intelsat, Interpol, IOC, IOM (observer), ISO, ITU, MONUC, NAM (guest), NATO, NEA, NSG, OAS (observer), OECD, OPCW, OSCE, PCA, SPC, UN, UN Security Council, UNAMSIL, UNCTAD, UNESCO, UNFICYP, UNHCR, UNIDO, UNIKOM, UNMIBH, UNMIK, UNOMIG, UNRWA, UNTAET, UNU, UPU, WCL, WEU, WHO, WIPO, WMO, WTrO, ZC

United Kingdom *(continued)*

Diplomatic representation in the US:
chief of mission: Ambassador Sir Christopher J. R. MEYER
chancery: 3100 Massachusetts Avenue NW, Washington, DC 20008
telephone: [1] (202) 588-6500
FAX: [1] (202) 588-7870
consulate(s) general: Atlanta, Boston, Chicago, Cleveland, Houston, Los Angeles, New York, and San Francisco
consulate(s): Dallas, Denver, Miami, Orlando (reports to Atlanta), San Juan, and Seattle

Diplomatic representation from the US:
chief of mission: Ambassador Philip LADER
embassy: 24/31 Grosvenor Square, London, W1A1AE
mailing address: PSC 801, Box 40, FPO AE 09498-4040
telephone: [44] (0) 207499-9000 (switchboard)
FAX: [44] (171) 409-1637
consulate(s) general: Belfast, Edinburgh

Flag description: blue with the red cross of Saint George (patron saint of England) edged in white superimposed on the diagonal red cross of Saint Patrick (patron saint of Ireland) and which is superimposed on the diagonal white cross of Saint Andrew (patron saint of Scotland); known as the Union Flag or Union Jack; the design and colors (especially the Blue Ensign) have been the basis for a number of other flags including other Commonwealth countries and their constituent states or provinces, as well as British overseas territories

Economy

Economy - overview: The UK, a leading trading power and financial center, deploys an essentially capitalistic economy, one of the quartet of trillion dollar economies of Western Europe. Over the past two decades the government has greatly reduced public ownership and contained the growth of social welfare programs. Agriculture is intensive, highly mechanized, and efficient by European standards, producing about 60% of food needs with only 1% of the labor force. The UK has large coal, natural gas, and oil reserves; primary energy production accounts for 10% of GDP, one of the highest shares of any industrial nation. Services, particularly banking, insurance, and business services, account by far for the largest proportion of GDP while industry continues to decline in importance. The economy has grown steadily, at just above or below 3%, for the last several years. The BLAIR government has put off the question of participation in the euro system until after the next election, in June of 2001; Chancellor of the Exchequer BROWN has identified some key economic tests to determine whether the UK should join the common currency system, but it will largely be a political decision. A serious short-term problem is foot-and-mouth disease, which by early 2001 had broken out in nearly 600 farms and slaughterhouses and had resulted in the killing of 400,000 animals.

GDP: purchasing power parity - $1.36 trillion (2000 est.)
GDP - real growth rate: 3% (2000 est.)
GDP - per capita: purchasing power parity - $22,800 (2000 est.)
GDP - composition by sector:
agriculture: 1.7%
industry: 24.9%
services: 73.4% (1999)
Population below poverty line: 17%
Household income or consumption by percentage share:
lowest 10%: 2.6%
highest 10%: 27.3% (1991)
Inflation rate (consumer prices): 2.4% (2000 est.)
Labor force: 29.2 million (1999)
Labor force - by occupation: agriculture 1%, industry 19%, services 80% (1996 est.)
Unemployment rate: 5.5% (2000 est.)
Budget:
revenues: $555.2 billion
expenditures: $510.8 billion, including capital expenditures of $37.7 billion (FY00)
Industries: machine tools, electric power equipment, automation equipment, railroad equipment, shipbuilding, aircraft, motor vehicles and parts, electronics and communications equipment, metals, chemicals, coal, petroleum, paper and paper products, food processing, textiles, clothing, and other consumer goods
Industrial production growth rate: 2% (2000)
Electricity - production: 342.771 billion kWh (1999)
Electricity - production by source:
fossil fuel: 69.38%
hydro: 1.55%
nuclear: 26.68%
other: 2.39% (1999)
Electricity - consumption: 333.012 billion kWh (1999)
Electricity - exports: 265 million kWh (1999)
Electricity - imports: 14.5 billion kWh (1999)
Agriculture - products: cereals, oilseed, potatoes, vegetables; cattle, sheep, poultry; fish
Exports: $282 billion (f.o.b., 2000)
Exports - commodities: manufactured goods, fuels, chemicals; food, beverages, tobacco
Exports - partners: EU 58% (Germany 12%, France 10%, Netherlands 8%), US 15% (1999)
Imports: $324 billion (f.o.b., 2000)
Imports - commodities: manufactured goods, machinery, fuels; foodstuffs
Imports - partners: EU 53% (Germany 14%, France 9%, Netherlands 7%), US 13%, Japan 5% (1999)
Debt - external: $NA
Economic aid - donor: ODA, $3.4 billion (1997)
Currency: British pound (GBP)
Currency code: GBP
Exchange rates: British pounds per US dollar - 0.6764 (January 2001), 0.6596 (2000), 0.6180 (1999), 0.6037 (1998), 0.6106 (1997), 0.6403 (1996)
Fiscal year: 1 April - 31 March

Communications

Telephones - main lines in use: 34.878 million (1997)
Telephones - mobile cellular: 13 million (yearend 1998)
Telephone system:
general assessment: technologically advanced domestic and international system
domestic: equal mix of buried cables, microwave radio relay, and fiber-optic systems
international: 40 coaxial submarine cables; satellite earth stations - 10 Intelsat (7 Atlantic Ocean and 3 Indian Ocean), 1 Inmarsat (Atlantic Ocean region), and 1 Eutelsat; at least 8 large international switching centers
Radio broadcast stations: AM 219, FM 431, shortwave 3 (1998)
Radios: 84.5 million (1997)
Television broadcast stations: 228 (plus 3,523 repeaters) (1995)
Televisions: 30.5 million (1997)
Internet country code: .uk, .gb
Internet Service Providers (ISPs): 245 (2000)
Internet users: 19.47 million (2000)

Transportation

Railways:
total: 16,878 km
broad gauge: 342 km 1.600-m gauge (190 km double track); note - all 1.600-m gauge track, of which 342 km is in common carrier use, and is in Northern Ireland
standard gauge: 16,536 km 1.435-m gauge (4,928 km electrified; 12,591 km double or multiple track) (1996)
Highways:
total: 371,603 km
paved: 371,603 km (including 3,303 km of expressways)
unpaved: 0 km (1998 est.)
Waterways: 3,200 km
Pipelines: crude oil (almost all insignificant) 933 km; petroleum products 2,993 km; natural gas 12,800 km
Ports and harbors: Aberdeen, Belfast, Bristol, Cardiff, Dover, Falmouth, Felixstowe, Glasgow, Grangemouth, Hull, Leith, Liverpool, London, Manchester, Peterhead, Plymouth, Portsmouth, Scapa Flow, Southampton, Sullom Voe, Tees, Tyne
Merchant marine:
total: 200 ships (1,000 GRT or over) totaling 3,934,776 GRT/3,760,240 DWT
ships by type: bulk 4, cargo 31, chemical tanker 11, combination ore/oil 1, container 47, liquefied gas 3, passenger 14, passenger/cargo 1, petroleum tanker 52, refrigerated cargo 4, roll on/roll off 19, short-sea passenger 10, specialized tanker 1, vehicle carrier 2
note: includes some foreign-owned ships registered here as a flag of convenience: Denmark 1 (2000 est.)
Airports: 489 (2000 est.)
Airports - with paved runways:
total: 349
over 3,047 m: 10
2,438 to 3,047 m: 33

United Kingdom (continued)

1,524 to 2,437 m: 162
914 to 1,523 m: 89
under 914 m: 55 (2000 est.)
Airports - with unpaved runways:
total: 140
1,524 to 2,437 m: 1
914 to 1,523 m: 23
under 914 m: 116 (2000 est.)
Heliports: 11 (2000 est.)

Military

Military branches: Army, Royal Navy (includes Royal Marines), Royal Air Force
Military manpower - availability:
males age 15-49: 14,599,199 (2001 est.)
Military manpower - fit for military service:
males age 15-49: 12,139,930 (2001 est.)
Military expenditures - dollar figure: $36.884 billion (FY97)
Military expenditures - percent of GDP: 2.7% (FY97)

Transnational Issues

Disputes - international: Northern Ireland issue with Ireland (historic peace agreement signed 10 April 1998); Gibraltar issue with Spain; Argentina claims Falkland Islands (Islas Malvinas); Argentina claims South Georgia and the South Sandwich Islands; Mauritius and the Seychelles claim Chagos Archipelago (UK-administered British Indian Ocean Territory); Rockall continental shelf dispute involving Denmark and Iceland; territorial claim in Antarctica (British Antarctic Territory) overlaps Argentine claim and partially overlaps Chilean claim; disputes with Iceland, Denmark, and Ireland over the Faroe Islands continental shelf boundary outside 200 NM
Illicit drugs: gateway country for Latin American cocaine entering the European market; major consumer of synthetic drugs, producer of limited amounts of synthetic drugs and synthetic precursor chemicals; major consumer of Southwest Asian heroin; money-laundering center

United States

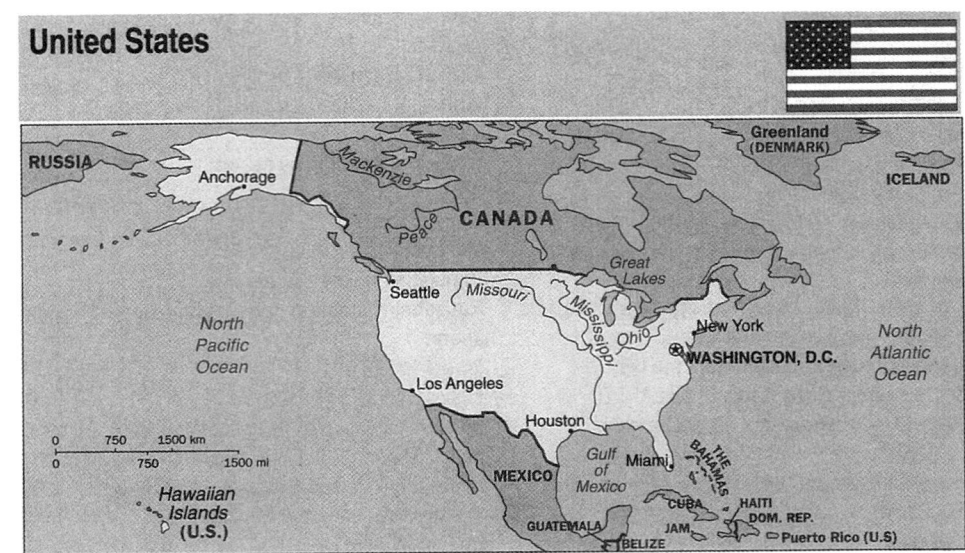

Introduction

Background: The United States became the world's first modern democracy after its break with Great Britain (1776) and the adoption of a constitution (1789). During the 19th century, many new states were added to the original 13 as the nation expanded across the North American continent and acquired a number of overseas possessions. The two most traumatic experiences in the nation's history were the Civil War (1861-65) and the Great Depression of the 1930s. Buoyed by victories in World Wars I and II and the end of the Cold War in 1991, the US remains the world's most powerful nation-state. The economy is marked by steady growth, low unemployment and inflation, and rapid advances in technology.

Geography

Location: North America, bordering both the North Atlantic Ocean and the North Pacific Ocean, between Canada and Mexico
Geographic coordinates: 38 00 N, 97 00 W
Map references: North America
Area:
total: 9,629,091 sq km
land: 9,158,960 sq km
water: 470,131 sq km
note: includes only the 50 states and District of Columbia
Area - comparative: about one-half the size of Russia; about three-tenths the size of Africa; about one-half the size of South America (or slightly larger than Brazil); slightly larger than China; about two and one-half times the size of Western Europe
Land boundaries:
total: 12,248 km
border countries: Canada 8,893 km (including 2,477 km with Alaska), Cuba 29 km (US Naval Base at Guantanamo Bay), Mexico 3,326 km
note: Guantanamo Naval Base is leased by the US and thus remains part of Cuba
Coastline: 19,924 km
Maritime claims:
contiguous zone: 24 NM
continental shelf: not specified
exclusive economic zone: 200 NM
territorial sea: 12 NM
Climate: mostly temperate, but tropical in Hawaii and Florida, arctic in Alaska, semiarid in the great plains west of the Mississippi River, and arid in the Great Basin of the southwest; low winter temperatures in the northwest are ameliorated occasionally in January and February by warm chinook winds from the eastern slopes of the Rocky Mountains
Terrain: vast central plain, mountains in west, hills and low mountains in east; rugged mountains and broad river valleys in Alaska; rugged, volcanic topography in Hawaii
Elevation extremes:
lowest point: Death Valley -86 m
highest point: Mount McKinley 6,194 m
Natural resources: coal, copper, lead, molybdenum, phosphates, uranium, bauxite, gold, iron, mercury, nickel, potash, silver, tungsten, zinc, petroleum, natural gas, timber
Land use:
arable land: 19%
permanent crops: 0%
permanent pastures: 25%
forests and woodland: 30%
other: 26% (1993 est.)
Irrigated land: 207,000 sq km (1993 est.)
Natural hazards: tsunamis, volcanoes, and earthquake activity around Pacific Basin; hurricanes along the Atlantic and Gulf of Mexico coasts; tornadoes in the midwest and southeast; mud slides in California; forest fires in the west; flooding; permafrost in northern Alaska, a major impediment to development
Environment - current issues: air pollution resulting in acid rain in both the US and Canada; the US is the largest single emitter of carbon dioxide from the burning of fossil fuels; water pollution from runoff

United States (continued)

of pesticides and fertilizers; very limited natural fresh water resources in much of the western part of the country require careful management; desertification
Environment - international agreements:
party to: Air Pollution, Air Pollution-Nitrogen Oxides, Antarctic-Environmental Protocol, Antarctic-Marine Living Resources, Antarctic Seals, Antarctic Treaty, Climate Change, Desertification, Endangered Species, Environmental Modification, Marine Dumping, Marine Life Conservation, Nuclear Test Ban, Ozone Layer Protection, Ship Pollution, Tropical Timber 83, Tropical Timber 94, Wetlands, Whaling
signed, but not ratified: Air Pollution-Persistent Organic Pollutants, Air Pollution-Volatile Organic Compounds, Biodiversity, Climate Change-Kyoto Protocol, Hazardous Wastes
Geography - note: world's third-largest country (after Russia and Canada)

People

Population: 278,058,881 (July 2001 est.)
Age structure:
0-14 years: 21.12% (male 30,034,674; female 28,681,253)
15-64 years: 66.27% (male 91,371,753; female 92,907,199)
65 years and over: 12.61% (male 14,608,948; female 20,455,054) (2001 est.)
Population growth rate: 0.9% (2001 est.)
Birth rate: 14.2 births/1,000 population (2001 est.)
Death rate: 8.7 deaths/1,000 population (2001 est.)
Net migration rate: 3.5 migrant(s)/1,000 population (2001 est.)
Sex ratio:
at birth: 1.05 male(s)/female
under 15 years: 1.05 male(s)/female
15-64 years: 0.98 male(s)/female
65 years and over: 0.71 male(s)/female
total population: 0.96 male(s)/female (2001 est.)
Infant mortality rate: 6.76 deaths/1,000 live births (2001 est.)
Life expectancy at birth:
total population: 77.26 years
male: 74.37 years
female: 80.05 years (2001 est.)
Total fertility rate: 2.06 children born/woman (2001 est.)
HIV/AIDS - adult prevalence rate: 0.61% (1999 est.)
HIV/AIDS - people living with HIV/AIDS: 850,000 (1999 est.)
HIV/AIDS - deaths: 20,000 (1999 est.)
Nationality:
noun: American(s)
adjective: American
Ethnic groups: white 83.5%, black 12.4%, Asian 3.3%, Amerindian 0.8% (1992)
note: a separate listing for Hispanic is not included because the US Census Bureau considers Hispanic to mean a person of Latin American descent (especially of Cuban, Mexican, or Puerto Rican origin) living in the US who may be of any race or ethnic group (white, black, Asian, etc.)
Religions: Protestant 56%, Roman Catholic 28%, Jewish 2%, other 4%, none 10% (1989)
Languages: English, Spanish (spoken by a sizable minority)
Literacy:
definition: age 15 and over can read and write
total population: 97%
male: 97%
female: 97% (1979 est.)

Government

Country name:
conventional long form: United States of America
conventional short form: United States
abbreviation: US or USA
Government type: federal republic; strong democratic tradition
Capital: Washington, DC
Administrative divisions: 50 states and 1 district*; Alabama, Alaska, Arizona, Arkansas, California, Colorado, Connecticut, Delaware, District of Columbia*, Florida, Georgia, Hawaii, Idaho, Illinois, Indiana, Iowa, Kansas, Kentucky, Louisiana, Maine, Maryland, Massachusetts, Michigan, Minnesota, Mississippi, Missouri, Montana, Nebraska, Nevada, New Hampshire, New Jersey, New Mexico, New York, North Carolina, North Dakota, Ohio, Oklahoma, Oregon, Pennsylvania, Rhode Island, South Carolina, South Dakota, Tennessee, Texas, Utah, Vermont, Virginia, Washington, West Virginia, Wisconsin, Wyoming
Dependent areas: American Samoa, Baker Island, Guam, Howland Island, Jarvis Island, Johnston Atoll, Kingman Reef, Midway Islands, Navassa Island, Northern Mariana Islands, Palmyra Atoll, Puerto Rico, Virgin Islands, Wake Island
note: from 18 July 1947 until 1 October 1994, the US administered the Trust Territory of the Pacific Islands, but recently entered into a new political relationship with all four political units: the Northern Mariana Islands is a commonwealth in political union with the US (effective 3 November 1986); Palau concluded a Compact of Free Association with the US (effective 1 October 1994); the Federated States of Micronesia signed a Compact of Free Association with the US (effective 3 November 1986); the Republic of the Marshall Islands signed a Compact of Free Association with the US (effective 21 October 1986)
Independence: 4 July 1776 (from Great Britain)
National holiday: Independence Day, 4 July (1776)
Constitution: 17 September 1787, effective 4 March 1789
Legal system: based on English common law; judicial review of legislative acts; accepts compulsory ICJ jurisdiction, with reservations
Suffrage: 18 years of age; universal
Executive branch:
chief of state: President George W. BUSH (since 20 January 2001) and Vice President Richard B. CHENEY (since 20 January 2001); note - the president is both the chief of state and head of government
head of government: President George W. BUSH (since 20 January 2001) and Vice President Richard B. CHENEY (since 20 January 2001); note - the president is both the chief of state and head of government
cabinet: Cabinet appointed by the president with Senate approval
elections: president and vice president elected on the same ticket by a college of representatives who are elected directly from each state; president and vice president serve four-year terms; election last held 7 November 2000 (next to be held NA November 2004)
election results: George W. BUSH elected president; percent of popular vote - George W. BUSH (Republican Party) 48%, Albert A. GORE, Jr. (Democratic Party) 48%, Ralph NADER (Green Party) 3%, other 1%
Legislative branch: bicameral Congress consists of Senate (100 seats, one-third are renewed every two years; two members are elected from each state by popular vote to serve six-year terms) and House of Representatives (435 seats; members are directly elected by popular vote to serve two-year terms)
elections: Senate - last held 7 November 2000 (next to be held 4 November 2002); House of Representatives - last held 7 November 2000 (next to be held 4 November 2002)
election results: Senate - percent of vote by party - NA%; seats by party - Republican Party 50, Democratic Party 50; House of Representatives - percent of vote by party - NA%; seats by party - Republican Party 221, Democratic Party 211, independent 2, vacant 1
Judicial branch: Supreme Court (its nine justices are appointed for life by the president with confirmation by the Senate); United States Courts of Appeal; United States District Courts; State and County Courts
Political parties and leaders: Democratic Party [Terence McAULIFFE, national committee chairman]; Republican Party [James S. GILMORE III, national committee chairman]; several other groups or parties of minor political significance
Political pressure groups and leaders: NA
International organization participation: APEC, ARF (dialogue partner), AsDB, ASEAN (dialogue partner), Australia Group, BIS, CCC, CE (observer), CERN (observer), CP, EAPC, EBRD, ECE, ECLAC, ESCAP, FAO, G-5, G-7, G-10, IADB, IAEA, IBRD, ICAO, ICC, ICFTU, ICRM, IDA, IEA, IFAD, IFC, IFRCS, IHO, ILO, IMF, IMO, Inmarsat, Intelsat, Interpol, IOC, IOM, ISO, ITU, MINURSO, MIPONUH, NAM (guest), NATO, NEA, NSG, OAS, OECD, OPCW, OSCE, PCA, SPC, UN, UN Security Council, UNCTAD, UNHCR, UNIKOM, UNITAR, UNMEE, UNMIBH, UNMIK, UNOMIG, UNRWA, UNTAET, UNTSO, UNU, UPU, WCL, WHO, WIPO, WMO, WTrO, ZC
Flag description: thirteen equal horizontal stripes of red (top and bottom) alternating with white; there is a blue rectangle in the upper hoist-side corner bearing

United States (continued)

50 small, white, five-pointed stars arranged in nine offset horizontal rows of six stars (top and bottom) alternating with rows of five stars; the 50 stars represent the 50 states, the 13 stripes represent the 13 original colonies; known as Old Glory; the design and colors have been the basis for a number of other flags, including Chile, Liberia, Malaysia, and Puerto Rico

Economy

Economy - overview: The US has the largest and most technologically powerful economy in the world, with a per capita GDP of $36,200. In this market-oriented economy, private individuals and business firms make most of the decisions, and government buys needed goods and services predominantly in the private marketplace. US business firms enjoy considerably greater flexibility than their counterparts in Western Europe and Japan in decisions to expand capital plant, lay off surplus workers, and develop new products. At the same time, they face higher barriers to entry in their rivals' home markets than the barriers to entry of foreign firms in US markets. US firms are at or near the forefront in technological advances, especially in computers and in medical, aerospace, and military equipment, although their advantage has narrowed since the end of World War II. The onrush of technology largely explains the gradual development of a "two-tier labor market" in which those at the bottom lack the education and the professional/technical skills of those at the top and, more and more, fail to get comparable pay raises, health insurance coverage, and other benefits. Since 1975, practically all the gains in household income have gone to the top 20% of households. The years 1994-2000 witnessed solid increases in real output, low inflation rates, and a drop in unemployment to below 5%. Long-term problems include inadequate investment in economic infrastructure, rapidly rising medical costs of an aging population, sizable trade deficits, and stagnation of family income in the lower economic groups. Growth weakened in the fourth quarter of 2000; growth for the year 2001 almost certainly will be substantially lower than the strong 5% of 2000. The outlook for 2001 is further clouded by the continued economic problems of Japan, Russia, Indonesia, Brazil, and many other countries.
GDP: purchasing power parity - $9.963 trillion (2000 est.)
GDP - real growth rate: 5% (2000 est.)
GDP - per capita: purchasing power parity - $36,200 (2000 est.)
GDP - composition by sector:
agriculture: 2%
industry: 18%
services: 80% (1999)
Population below poverty line: 12.7% (1999 est.)
Household income or consumption by percentage share:
lowest 10%: 1.8%
highest 10%: 30.5% (1997)
Inflation rate (consumer prices): 3.4% (2000)
Labor force: 140.9 million (includes unemployed) (2000)
Labor force - by occupation: managerial and professional 30.2%, technical, sales and administrative support 29.2%, services 13.5%, manufacturing, mining, transportation, and crafts 24.6%, farming, forestry, and fishing 2.5% (2000)
note: figures exclude the unemployed
Unemployment rate: 4% (2000)
Budget:
revenues: $1.828 trillion
expenditures: $1.703 trillion, including capital expenditures of $NA (1999)
Industries: leading industrial power in the world, highly diversified and technologically advanced; petroleum, steel, motor vehicles, aerospace, telecommunications, chemicals, electronics, food processing, consumer goods, lumber, mining
Industrial production growth rate: 5.6% (2000 est.)
Electricity - production: 3.678 trillion kWh (1999)
Electricity - production by source:
fossil fuel: 69.64%
hydro: 8.31%
nuclear: 19.8%
other: 2.25% (1999)
Electricity - consumption: 3.45 trillion kWh (1999)
Electricity - exports: 14 billion kWh (1999)
Electricity - imports: 43 billion kWh (1999)
Agriculture - products: wheat, other grains, corn, fruits, vegetables, cotton; beef, pork, poultry, dairy products; forest products; fish
Exports: $776 billion (f.o.b., 2000 est.)
Exports - commodities: capital goods, automobiles, industrial supplies and raw materials, consumer goods, agricultural products
Exports - partners: Canada 23%, Mexico 14%, Japan 8%, UK 5%, Germany 4%, France, Netherlands (2000)
Imports: $1.223 trillion (f.o.b., 2000 est.)
Imports - commodities: crude oil and refined petroleum products, machinery, automobiles, consumer goods, industrial raw materials, food and beverages
Imports - partners: Canada 19%, Japan 11%, Mexico 11%, China 8%, Germany 5%, UK, Taiwan (2000)
Debt - external: $862 billion (1995 est.)
Economic aid - donor: ODA, $6.9 billion (1997)
Currency: US dollar (USD)
Currency code: USD
Exchange rates: British pounds per US dollar - 0.6764 (January 2001), 0.6596 (2000), 0.6180 (1999), 0.6037 (1998), 0.6106 (1997), 0.6403 (1996); Canadian dollars per US dollar - 1.5032 (January 2001), 1.4851 (2000), 1.4857 (1999), 1.4835 (1998), 1.3846 (1997), 1.3635 (1996); French francs per US dollar - 5.65 (January 1999), 5.8995 (1998), 5.8367 (1997), 5.1155 (1996), 4.9915 (1995), 5.5520 (1994); Italian lire per US dollar - 1,668.7 (January 1999), 1,763.2 (1998), 1,703.1 (1997), 1,542.9 (1996), 1,628.9 (1995), 1,612.4 (1994); Japanese yen per US dollar - 117.10 (January 2001), 107.77 (2000), 113.91 (1999), 130.91 (1998), 120.99 (1997), 108.78 (1996); German deutsche marks per US dollar - 1.69 (January 1999), 1.9692 (1998), 1.7341 (1997), 1.5048 (1996), 1.4331 (1995), 1.6228 (1994); euros per US dollar - 1.06594 (January 2001), 1.08540 (2000), 0.93863 (1999)
note: financial institutions in France, Italy, and Germany and eight other European countries started using the euro on 1 January 1999 with the euro replacing the local currency in consenting countries for all transactions in 2002
Fiscal year: 1 October - 30 September

Communications

Telephones - main lines in use: 194 million (1997)
Telephones - mobile cellular: 69.209 million (1998)
Telephone system:
general assessment: a very large, technologically advanced, multipurpose communications system
domestic: a large system of fiber-optic cable, microwave radio relay, coaxial cable, and domestic satellites carries every form of telephone traffic; a rapidly growing cellular system carries mobile telephone traffic throughout the country
international: 24 ocean cable systems in use; satellite earth stations - 61 Intelsat (45 Atlantic Ocean and 16 Pacific Ocean), 5 Intersputnik (Atlantic Ocean region), and 4 Inmarsat (Pacific and Atlantic Ocean regions) (2000)
Radio broadcast stations: AM 4,762, FM 5,542, shortwave 18 (1998)
Radios: 575 million (1997)
Television broadcast stations: more than 1,500 (including nearly 1,000 stations affiliated with the five major networks - NBC, ABC, CBS, FOX, and PBS; in addition, there are about 9,000 cable TV systems) (1997)
Televisions: 219 million (1997)
Internet country code: .us
Internet Service Providers (ISPs): 7,800 (2000 est.)
Internet users: 148 million (2000)

Transportation

Railways:
total: 240,000 km mainline routes (nongovernment owned)
standard gauge: 240,000 km 1.435-m gauge (1989)
Highways:
total: 6,348,227 km
paved: 3,732,757 km (including 88,727 km of expressways)
unpaved: 2,615,470 km (1997 est.)
Waterways: 41,009 km
note: navigable inland channels, exclusive of the Great Lakes
Pipelines: petroleum products 276,000 km; natural gas 331,000 km (1991)

United States (continued)

Ports and harbors: Anchorage, Baltimore, Boston, Charleston, Chicago, Duluth, Hampton Roads, Honolulu, Houston, Jacksonville, Los Angeles, New Orleans, New York, Philadelphia, Port Canaveral, Portland (Oregon), Prudhoe Bay, San Francisco, Savannah, Seattle, Tampa, Toledo

Merchant marine:
total: 376 ships (1,000 GRT or over) totaling 10,814,622 GRT/14,416,517 DWT
ships by type: barge carrier 9, bulk 68, cargo 29, chemical tanker 13, combination bulk 3, container 80, liquefied gas 1, multi-functional large-load carrier 3, passenger 9, passenger/cargo 1, petroleum tanker 98, roll on/roll off 49, short-sea passenger 3, specialized tanker 1, vehicle carrier 9 (2000 est.)

Airports: 14,720 (2000 est.)

Airports - with paved runways:
total: 5,174
over 3,047 m: 182
2,438 to 3,047 m: 220
1,524 to 2,437 m: 1,331
914 to 1,523 m: 2,440
under 914 m: 1,001 (2000 est.)

Airports - with unpaved runways:
total: 9,546
over 3,047 m: 3
2,438 to 3,047 m: 6
1,524 to 2,437 m: 164
914 to 1,523 m: 1,675
under 914 m: 7,698 (2000 est.)

Heliports: 131 (2000 est.)

Military

Military branches: Department of the Army, Department of the Navy (includes Marine Corps), Department of the Air Force
note: the Coast Guard is normally subordinate to the Department of Transportation, but in wartime reports to the Department of the Navy

Military manpower - military age: 18 years of age

Military manpower - availability:
males age 15-49: 70,819,436 (2001 est.)

Military manpower - fit for military service: NA (2001 est.)

Military manpower - reaching military age annually:
males: 2,039,414 (2001 est.)

Military expenditures - dollar figure: $276.7 billion (FY99 est.)

Military expenditures - percent of GDP: 3.2% (FY99 est.)

Transnational Issues

Disputes - international: maritime boundary disputes with Canada (Dixon Entrance, Beaufort Sea, Strait of Juan de Fuca, Machias Seal Island); US Naval Base at Guantanamo Bay is leased from Cuba and only mutual agreement or US abandonment of the area can terminate the lease; Haiti claims Navassa Island; US has made no territorial claim in Antarctica (but has reserved the right to do so) and does not recognize the claims of any other nation; Marshall Islands claims Wake Island

Illicit drugs: consumer of cocaine shipped from Colombia through Mexico and the Caribbean; consumer of heroin, marijuana, and increasingly methamphetamine from Mexico; consumer of high-quality Southeast Asian heroin; illicit producer of cannabis, marijuana, depressants, stimulants, hallucinogens, and methamphetamine; money-laundering center

Uruguay

Introduction

Background: A violent Marxist urban guerrilla movement, the Tupamaros, launched in the late 1960s, led Uruguay's president to agree to military control of his administration in 1973. By the end of the year the rebels had been crushed, but the military continued to expand its hold throughout the government. Civilian rule was not restored until 1985. Uruguay's political and labor conditions are among the freest on the continent.

Geography

Location: Southern South America, bordering the South Atlantic Ocean, between Argentina and Brazil

Geographic coordinates: 33 00 S, 56 00 W

Map references: South America

Area:
total: 176,220 sq km
land: 173,620 sq km
water: 2,600 sq km

Area - comparative: slightly smaller than the state of Washington

Land boundaries:
total: 1,564 km
border countries: Argentina 579 km, Brazil 985 km

Coastline: 660 km

Maritime claims:
contiguous zone: 24 NM
continental shelf: 200-m depth or to the depth of exploitation
exclusive economic zone: 200 NM
territorial sea: 12 NM

Climate: warm temperate; freezing temperatures almost unknown

Terrain: mostly rolling plains and low hills; fertile coastal lowland

Elevation extremes:
lowest point: Atlantic Ocean 0 m
highest point: Cerro Catedral 514 m

Uruguay (continued)

Natural resources: arable land, hydropower, minor minerals, fisheries
Land use:
arable land: 7%
permanent crops: 0%
permanent pastures: 77%
forests and woodland: 6%
other: 10% (1997 est.)
Irrigated land: 7,700 sq km (1997 est.)
Natural hazards: seasonally high winds (the pampero is a chilly and occasional violent wind which blows north from the Argentine pampas), droughts, floods; because of the absence of mountains, which act as weather barriers, all locations are particularly vulnerable to rapid changes in weather fronts
Environment - current issues: water pollution from meat packing/tannery industry; inadequate solid/hazardous waste disposal
Environment - international agreements:
party to: Antarctic-Environmental Protocol, Antarctic-Marine Living Resources, Antarctic Treaty, Biodiversity, Climate Change, Climate Change-Kyoto Protocol, Desertification, Endangered Species, Environmental Modification, Hazardous Wastes, Law of the Sea, Marine Dumping, Marine Life Conservation, Ozone Layer Protection, Ship Pollution, Tropical Timber 94, Wetlands
signed, but not ratified: Marine Dumping, Nuclear Test Ban

People

Population: 3,360,105 (July 2001 est.)
Age structure:
0-14 years: 24.39% (male 419,932; female 399,605)
15-64 years: 62.61% (male 1,038,785; female 1,064,891)
65 years and over: 13% (male 180,130; female 256,762) (2001 est.)
Population growth rate: 0.78% (2001 est.)
Birth rate: 17.36 births/1,000 population (2001 est.)
Death rate: 9.03 deaths/1,000 population (2001 est.)
Net migration rate: -0.51 migrant(s)/1,000 population (2001 est.)
Sex ratio:
at birth: 1.06 male(s)/female
under 15 years: 1.05 male(s)/female
15-64 years: 0.98 male(s)/female
65 years and over: 0.7 male(s)/female
total population: 0.95 male(s)/female (2001 est.)
Infant mortality rate: 14.7 deaths/1,000 live births (2001 est.)
Life expectancy at birth:
total population: 75.44 years
male: 72.11 years
female: 78.96 years (2001 est.)
Total fertility rate: 2.36 children born/woman (2001 est.)
HIV/AIDS - adult prevalence rate: 0.33% (1999 est.)
HIV/AIDS - people living with HIV/AIDS: 6,000 (1999 est.)
HIV/AIDS - deaths: 150 (1999 est.)
Nationality:
noun: Uruguayan(s)
adjective: Uruguayan
Ethnic groups: white 88%, mestizo 8%, black 4%, Amerindian, practically nonexistent
Religions: Roman Catholic 66% (less than one-half of the adult population attends church regularly), Protestant 2%, Jewish 1%, nonprofessing or other 31%
Languages: Spanish, Portunol, or Brazilero (Portuguese-Spanish mix on the Brazilian frontier)
Literacy:
definition: age 15 and over can read and write
total population: 97.3%
male: 96.9%
female: 97.7% (1995 est.)

Government

Country name:
conventional long form: Oriental Republic of Uruguay
conventional short form: Uruguay
local long form: Republica Oriental del Uruguay
local short form: Uruguay
former: Banda Oriental, Cisplatine Province
Government type: constitutional republic
Capital: Montevideo
Administrative divisions: 19 departments (departamentos, singular - departamento); Artigas, Canelones, Cerro Largo, Colonia, Durazno, Flores, Florida, Lavalleja, Maldonado, Montevideo, Paysandu, Rio Negro, Rivera, Rocha, Salto, San Jose, Soriano, Tacuarembo, Treinta y Tres
Independence: 25 August 1825 (from Brazil)
National holiday: Independence Day, 25 August (1825)
Constitution: 27 November 1966, effective February 1967, suspended 27 June 1973, new constitution rejected by referendum 30 November 1980; two constitutional reforms approved by plebiscite 26 November 1989 and 7 January 1997
Legal system: based on Spanish civil law system; accepts compulsory ICJ jurisdiction
Suffrage: 18 years of age; universal and compulsory
Executive branch:
chief of state: President Jorge BATLLE (since 1 March 2000) and Vice President Luis HIERRO (since 1 March 2000); note - the president is both the chief of state and head of government
head of government: President Jorge BATLLE (since 1 March 2000) and Vice President Luis HIERRO (since 1 March 2000); note - the president is both the chief of state and head of government
cabinet: Council of Ministers appointed by the president with parliamentary approval
elections: president and vice president elected on the same ticket by popular vote for five-year terms; election last held 31 October 1999 with run-off election on 28 November 1999 (next to be held NA 2004)
election results: Jorge BATLLE elected president; percent of vote - Jorge BATLLE 52% in a runoff against Tabare VAZQUEZ 44%
Legislative branch: bicameral General Assembly or Asamblea General consists of Chamber of Senators or Camara de Senadores (30 seats; members are elected by popular vote to serve five-year terms) and Chamber of Representatives or Camara de Representantes (99 seats; members are elected by popular vote to serve five-year terms)
elections: Chamber of Senators - last held 31 October 1999 (next to be held NA 2004); Chamber of Representatives - last held 31 October 1999 (next to be held NA 2004)
election results: Chamber of Senators - percent of vote by party - NA%; seats by party - Encuentro Progresista 12, Colorado Party 10, Blanco 7, New Sector/Space Coalition 1; Chamber of Representatives - percent of vote by party - NA%; seats by party - Encuentro Progresista 40, Colorado Party 33, Blanco 22, New Sector/Space Coalition 4
Judicial branch: Supreme Court (judges are nominated by the president and elected for 10-year terms by the General Assembly)
Political parties and leaders: Colorado Party [Jorge BATLLE]; National Party or Blanco [Alberto VOLONTE]; New Sector/Space Coalition or Nuevo Espacio [Rafael MICHELINI]; Progressive Encounter in the Broad Front or Encuentro Progresista [Tabare VAZQUEZ]
Political pressure groups and leaders: NA
International organization participation: CCC, ECLAC, FAO, G-11, G-77, IADB, IAEA, IBRD, ICAO, ICC, ICRM, IFAD, IFC, IFRCS, IHO, ILO, IMF, IMO, Intelsat, Interpol, IOC, IOM, ISO, ITU, LAES, LAIA, Mercosur, MINURSO, MONUC, NAM (observer), OAS, OPANAL, OPCW, PCA, RG, UN, UNCTAD, UNESCO, UNIDO, UNIKOM, UNMEE, UNMOGIP, UNMOT, UNOMIG, UNTAET, UPU, WCL, WFTU, WHO, WIPO, WMO, WToO, WTrO
Diplomatic representation in the US:
chief of mission: Ambassador Hugo FERNANDEZ Faingold
chancery: 2715 M Street, NW, Washington, DC 20007
telephone: [1] (202) 331-1313 through 1316
FAX: [1] (202) 331-8142
consulate(s) general: Chicago, Los Angeles, Miami, and New York
Diplomatic representation from the US:
chief of mission: Ambassador Christopher C. ASHBY
embassy: Lauro Muller 1776, Montevideo 11100
mailing address: APO AA 34035
telephone: [598] (2) 408-777, 203-6061
FAX: [598] (2) 48 86 11
Flag description: nine equal horizontal stripes of white (top and bottom) alternating with blue; there is a white square in the upper hoist-side corner with a yellow sun bearing a human face known as the Sun of May and 16 rays alternately triangular and wavy

Uruguay (continued)

Economy

Economy - overview: Uruguay's economy is characterized by an export-oriented agricultural sector, a well-educated workforce, relatively even income distribution, and high levels of social spending. After averaging growth of 5% annually in 1996-98, in 1999-2000 the economy suffered from lower demand in Argentina and Brazil, which together account for about half of Uruguay's exports. Despite the severity of the trade shocks, Uruguay's financial indicators remained more stable than those of its neighbors, a reflection of its solid reputation among investors and its investment-grade sovereign bond rating - one of only two in Latin America. Challenges for the government of President Jorge BATLLE include expanding Uruguay's trade ties beyond its MERCOSUR trade partners and reducing the costs of public services. GDP fell by 1.1% in 2000 and will grow by perhaps 1.5% in 2001.
GDP: purchasing power parity - $31 billion (2000 est.)
GDP - real growth rate: -1.1% (2000 est.)
GDP - per capita: purchasing power parity - $9,300 (2000 est.)
GDP - composition by sector:
agriculture: 10%
industry: 28%
services: 62% (1999)
Population below poverty line: NA%
Household income or consumption by percentage share:
lowest 10%: NA%
highest 10%: NA%
Inflation rate (consumer prices): 4.8% (2000 est.)
Labor force: 1.5 million (1999 est.)
Labor force - by occupation: agriculture NA%, industry NA%, services NA%
Unemployment rate: 14% (2000 est.)
Budget:
revenues: $4 billion
expenditures: $4.6 billion, including capital expenditures of $500 million (2000 est.)
Industries: food processing, electrical machinery, transportation equipment, petroleum products, textiles, chemicals, beverages
Industrial production growth rate: -2.1% (2000 est.)
Electricity - production: 5.704 billion kWh (1999)
Electricity - production by source:
fossil fuel: 3.86%
hydro: 95.44%
nuclear: 0%
other: 0.7% (1999)
Electricity - consumption: 5.89 billion kWh (1999)
Electricity - exports: 215 million kWh (1999)
Electricity - imports: 800 million kWh (1999)
Agriculture - products: wheat, rice, barley, corn, sorghum; livestock; fish
Exports: $2.6 billion (f.o.b., 2000 est.)
Exports - commodities: meat, rice, leather products, vehicles, dairy products, wool, electricity
Exports - partners: MERCOSUR partners 45%, EU 20%, US 7% (1999 est.)
Imports: $3.4 billion (f.o.b., 2000 est.)
Imports - commodities: road vehicles, electrical machinery, metal manufactures, heavy industrial machinery, crude petroleum
Imports - partners: MERCOSUR partners 43%, EU 20%, US 11% (1999 est.)
Debt - external: $8 billion (2000 est.)
Economic aid - recipient: $NA
Currency: Uruguayan peso (UYU)
Currency code: UYU
Exchange rates: Uruguayan pesos per US dollar - 12.5610 (January 2001), 12.0996 (2000), 11.3393 (1999), 10.4719 (1998), 9.4418 (1997), 7.9718 (1996)
Fiscal year: calendar year

Communications

Telephones - main lines in use: 850,000 (2000)
Telephones - mobile cellular: 300,000 (2000)
Telephone system:
general assessment: some modern facilities
domestic: most modern facilities concentrated in Montevideo; new nationwide microwave radio relay network
international: satellite earth stations - 2 Intelsat (Atlantic Ocean)
Radio broadcast stations: AM 94, FM 115, shortwave 14 (seven are inactive) (1998)
Radios: 1.97 million (1997)
Television broadcast stations: 26 (plus ten low-power repeaters for the Montevideo station) (1997)
Televisions: 782,000 (1997)
Internet country code: .uy
Internet Service Providers (ISPs): 7 (2000)
Internet users: 300,000 (2000)

Transportation

Railways:
total: 2,073 km
standard gauge: 2,073 km 1.435-m gauge (2000)
Highways:
total: 8,983 km
paved: 8,085 km
unpaved: 898 km (1999 est.)
Waterways: 1,600 km (used by coastal and shallow-draft river craft)
Ports and harbors: Fray Bentos, Montevideo, Nueva Palmira, Paysandu, Punta del Este, Colonia, Piriapolis
Merchant marine:
total: 2 ships (1,000 GRT or over) totaling 7,752 GRT/ 5,228 DWT
ships by type: petroleum tanker 1, roll on/roll off 1 (2000 est.)
Airports: 64 (2000 est.)
Airports - with paved runways:
total: 15
2,438 to 3,047 m: 1
1,524 to 2,437 m: 5
914 to 1,523 m: 8
under 914 m: 1 (2000 est.)
Airports - with unpaved runways:
total: 49
1,524 to 2,437 m: 2
914 to 1,523 m: 16
under 914 m: 31 (2000 est.)

Military

Military branches: Army, Navy (includes Naval Air Arm, Coast Guard, Marines), Air Force, Police (Coracero Guard, Grenadier Guard)
Military manpower - availability:
males age 15-49: 817,535 (2001 est.)
Military manpower - fit for military service:
males age 15-49: 661,777 (2001 est.)
Military expenditures - dollar figure: $172 million (FY98)
Military expenditures - percent of GDP: 0.9% (FY98)

Transnational Issues

Disputes - international: none

Uzbekistan

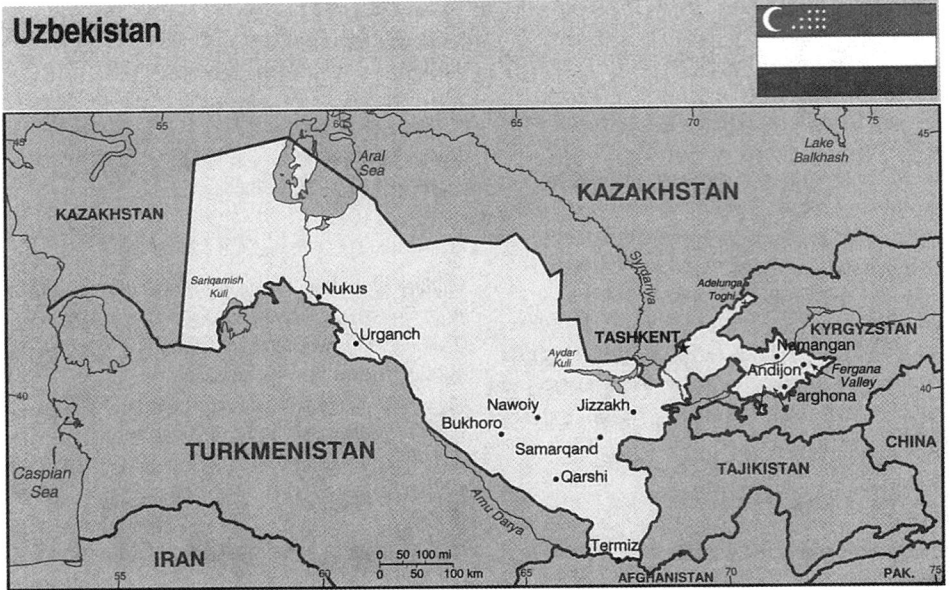

Introduction

Background: Russia conquered Uzbekistan in the late 19th century. Stiff resistance to the Red Army after World War I was eventually suppressed and a socialist republic set up in 1925. During the Soviet era, intensive production of "white gold" (cotton) and grain led to overuse of agrochemicals and the depletion of water supplies, which have left the land poisoned and the Aral Sea and certain rivers half dry. Independent since 1991, the country seeks to gradually lessen its dependence on agriculture while developing its mineral and petroleum reserves. Current concerns include insurgency by Islamic militants based in Tajikistan and Afghanistan, a non-convertible currency, and the curtailment of human rights and democratization.

Geography

Location: Central Asia, north of Afghanistan
Geographic coordinates: 41 00 N, 64 00 E
Map references: Commonwealth of Independent States
Area:
total: 447,400 sq km
land: 425,400 sq km
water: 22,000 sq km
Area - comparative: slightly larger than California
Land boundaries:
total: 6,221 km
border countries: Afghanistan 137 km, Kazakhstan 2,203 km, Kyrgyzstan 1,099 km, Tajikistan 1,161 km, Turkmenistan 1,621 km
Coastline: 0 km; note - Uzbekistan includes the southern portion of the Aral Sea with a 420 km shoreline
Maritime claims: none (doubly landlocked)
Climate: mostly midlatitude desert, long, hot summers, mild winters; semiarid grassland in east
Terrain: mostly flat-to-rolling sandy desert with dunes; broad, flat intensely irrigated river valleys along course of Amu Darya, Sirdaryo (Syr Darya), and Zarafshon; Fergana Valley in east surrounded by mountainous Tajikistan and Kyrgyzstan; shrinking Aral Sea in west
Elevation extremes:
lowest point: Sariqarnish Kuli -12 m
highest point: Adelunga Toghi 4,301 m
Natural resources: natural gas, petroleum, coal, gold, uranium, silver, copper, lead and zinc, tungsten, molybdenum
Land use:
arable land: 9%
permanent crops: 1%
permanent pastures: 46%
forests and woodland: 3%
other: 41% (1993 est.)
Irrigated land: 40,000 sq km (1993 est.)
Natural hazards: NA
Environment - current issues: drying up of the Aral Sea is resulting in growing concentrations of chemical pesticides and natural salts; these substances are then blown from the increasingly exposed lake bed and contribute to desertification; water pollution from industrial wastes and the heavy use of fertilizers and pesticides is the cause of many human health disorders; increasing soil salination; soil contamination from agricultural chemicals, including DDT
Environment - international agreements:
party to: Biodiversity, Climate Change, Climate Change-Kyoto Protocol, Desertification, Endangered Species, Environmental Modification, Hazardous Wastes, Marine Dumping, Ozone Layer Protection, Ship Pollution
signed, but not ratified: none of the selected agreements
Geography - note: along with Liechtenstein, one of the only two doubly landlocked countries in the world

People

Population: 25,155,064 (July 2001 est.)
Age structure:
0-14 years: 36.32% (male 4,646,341; female 4,489,265)
15-64 years: 59.06% (male 7,351,908; female 7,504,626)
65 years and over: 4.62% (male 466,029; female 696,895) (2001 est.)
Population growth rate: 1.6% (2001 est.)
Birth rate: 26.1 births/1,000 population (2001 est.)
Death rate: 8 deaths/1,000 population (2001 est.)
Net migration rate: -2.06 migrant(s)/1,000 population (2001 est.)
Sex ratio:
at birth: 1.05 male(s)/female
under 15 years: 1.03 male(s)/female
15-64 years: 0.98 male(s)/female
65 years and over: 0.67 male(s)/female
total population: 0.98 male(s)/female (2001 est.)
Infant mortality rate: 71.92 deaths/1,000 live births (2001 est.)
Life expectancy at birth:
total population: 63.81 years
male: 60.24 years
female: 67.56 years (2001 est.)
Total fertility rate: 3.06 children born/woman (2001 est.)
HIV/AIDS - adult prevalence rate: less than 0.01% (1999 est.)
HIV/AIDS - people living with HIV/AIDS: less than 100 (1999 est.)
HIV/AIDS - deaths: less than 100 (1999 est.)
Nationality:
noun: Uzbekistani(s)
adjective: Uzbekistani
Ethnic groups: Uzbek 80%, Russian 5.5%, Tajik 5%, Kazakh 3%, Karakalpak 2.5%, Tatar 1.5%, other 2.5% (1996 est.)
Religions: Muslim 88% (mostly Sunnis), Eastern Orthodox 9%, other 3%
Languages: Uzbek 74.3%, Russian 14.2%, Tajik 4.4%, other 7.1%
Literacy:
definition: age 15 and over can read and write
total population: 99%
male: 99%
female: 99% (yearend 1996)

Government

Country name:
conventional long form: Republic of Uzbekistan
conventional short form: Uzbekistan
local long form: Uzbekiston Respublikasi
local short form: none
former: Uzbek Soviet Socialist Republic
Government type: republic; effectively authoritarian presidential rule, with little power outside the executive branch
Capital: Tashkent (Toshkent)

Uzbekistan (continued)

Administrative divisions: 12 wiloyatlar (singular - wiloyat), 1 autonomous republic* (respublikasi), and 1 city** (shahri); Andijon Wiloyati, Bukhoro Wiloyati, Farghona Wiloyati, Jizzakh Wiloyati, Khorazm Wiloyati (Urganch), Namangan Wiloyati, Nawoiy Wiloyati, Qashqadaryo Wiloyati (Qarshi), Qoraqalpoghiston* (Nukus), Samarqand Wiloyati, Sirdaryo Wiloyati (Guliston), Surkhondaryo Wiloyati (Termiz), Toshkent Shahri**, Toshkent Wiloyati
note: administrative divisions have the same names as their administrative centers (exceptions have the administrative center name following in parentheses)
Independence: 1 September 1991 (from Soviet Union)
National holiday: Independence Day, 1 September (1991)
Constitution: new constitution adopted 8 December 1992
Legal system: evolution of Soviet civil law; still lacks independent judicial system
Suffrage: 18 years of age; universal
Executive branch:
chief of state: President Islom KARIMOV (since 24 March 1990, when he was elected president by the then Supreme Soviet)
head of government: Prime Minister Otkir SULTONOV (since 21 December 1995)
cabinet: Cabinet of Ministers appointed by the president with approval of the Supreme Assembly
elections: president elected by popular vote for a five-year term; election last held 9 January 2000 (next to be held NA January 2005); note - extension of President KARIMOV's original term for an additional five years overwhelmingly approved - 99.6% of total vote in favor - by national referendum held 27 March 1995; prime minister and deputy ministers appointed by the president
election results: Islom KARIMOV reelected president; percent of vote - Islom KARIMOV 91.9%, Abdulkhafiz DZHALALOV 4.2%
Legislative branch: unicameral Supreme Assembly or Oliy Majlis (250 seats; members elected by popular vote to serve five-year terms)
elections: last held 5 December and 19 December 1999 (next to be held NA December 2004)
election results: percent of vote by party - NA%; seats by party - NDP 48, Self-Sacrificers Party 34, Fatherland Progress Party 20, Adolat Social Democratic Party 11, MTP 10, citizens' groups 16, local government 110, vacant 1
note: not all seats in the last Supreme Assembly election were contested; all parties in the Supreme Assembly support President KARIMOV
Judicial branch: Supreme Court (judges are nominated by the president and confirmed by the Supreme Assembly)
Political parties and leaders: Adolat (Justice) Social Democratic Party [Anwar JURABAYEV, first secretary]; Democratic National Rebirth Party (Milly Tiklanish) or MTP [Aziz KAYUMOV, chairman]; Fatherland Progress Party [Anwar Z. YOLDASHEV]; People's Democratic Party or NDP (formerly Communist Party) [Abdulkhafiz JALOLOV, first secretary]; Self-Sacrificers Party or Fidokorlar National Democratic Party [Ahtam TURSUNOV, first secretary]
Political pressure groups and leaders: Birlik (Unity) Movement [Abdurakhim PULAT, chairman]; Erk (Freedom) Democratic Party [Muhammad SOLIH, chairman] was banned 9 December 1992; Human Rights Society of Uzbekistan [Abdumanob PULAT, chairman]; Independent Human Rights Society of Uzbekistan [Mikhail ARDZINOV, chairman]
International organization participation: AsDB, CCC, CIS, EAPC, EBRD, ECE, ECO, ESCAP, IAEA, IBRD, ICAO, ICRM, IDA, IFC, IFRCS, ILO, IMF, Intelsat, Interpol, IOC, ISO, ITU, NAM, OIC, OPCW, OSCE, PFP, UN, UNCTAD, UNESCO, UNIDO, UPU, WFTU, WHO, WIPO, WMO, WToO, WTrO (observer)
Diplomatic representation in the US:
chief of mission: Ambassador Shavkat HAMRAKULOV
chancery: 1746 Massachusetts Avenue NW, Washington, DC 20036
telephone: [1] (202) 887-5300
FAX: [1] (202) 293-6804
consulate(s) general: New York
Diplomatic representation from the US:
chief of mission: Ambassador John Edward HERBST
embassy: 82 Chilanzarskaya, Tashkent 700115
mailing address: use embassy street address; US Embassy Tashkent, Department of State, Washington, DC 20521-7110
telephone: [998] (71) 120-5444
FAX: [998] (71) 120-6335
Flag description: three equal horizontal bands of blue (top), white, and green separated by red fimbriations with a white crescent moon and 12 white stars in the upper hoist-side quadrant

Economy

Economy - overview: Uzbekistan is a dry, landlocked country of which 10% consists of intensely cultivated, irrigated river valleys. More than 60% of its population lives in densely populated rural communities. Uzbekistan is now the world's third largest cotton exporter, a large producer of gold and oil, and a regionally significant producer of chemicals and machinery. Following independence in December 1991, the government sought to prop up its Soviet-style command economy with subsidies and tight controls on production and prices. Faced with high rates of inflation, however, the government began to reform in mid-1994, by introducing tighter monetary policies, expanding privatization, slightly reducing the role of the state in the economy, and improving the environment for foreign investors. The state continues to be a dominating influence in the economy and has so far failed to bring about much-needed structural changes. The IMF suspended Uzbekistan's $185 million standby arrangement in late 1996 because of governmental steps that made impossible fulfillment of Fund conditions. Uzbekistan has responded to the negative external conditions generated by the Asian and Russian financial crises by tightening export and currency controls within its already largely closed economy. Economic policies that have repelled foreign investment are a major factor in the economy's stagnation. A growing debt burden, persistent inflation, and a poor business climate led to stagnant growth in 2000, with little improvement predicted for 2001.
GDP: purchasing power parity - $60 billion (2000 est.)
GDP - real growth rate: 2.1% (2000 est.)
GDP - per capita: purchasing power parity - $2,400 (2000 est.)
GDP - composition by sector:
agriculture: 28%
industry: 21%
services: 51% (1999 est.)
Population below poverty line: NA%
Household income or consumption by percentage share:
lowest 10%: 3.1%
highest 10%: 25.2% (1993)
Inflation rate (consumer prices): 40% (2000 est.)
Labor force: 11.9 million (1998 est.)
Labor force - by occupation: agriculture 44%, industry 20%, services 36% (1995)
Unemployment rate: 10% plus another 20% underemployed (1999 est.)
Budget:
revenues: $4 billion
expenditures: $4.1 billion, including capital expenditures of $NA (1999 est.)
Industries: textiles, food processing, machine building, metallurgy, natural gas, chemicals
Industrial production growth rate: 6.4% (2000 est.)
Electricity - production: 42.876 billion kWh (1999)
Electricity - production by source:
fossil fuel: 86.4%
hydro: 13.6%
nuclear: 0%
other: 0% (1999)
Electricity - consumption: 43.455 billion kWh (1999)
Electricity - exports: 3.92 billion kWh (1999)
Electricity - imports: 7.5 billion kWh (1999)
Agriculture - products: cotton, vegetables, fruits, grain; livestock
Exports: $2.9 billion (f.o.b., 2000 est.)
Exports - commodities: cotton, gold, natural gas, mineral fertilizers, ferrous metals, textiles, food products, automobiles
Exports - partners: Russia 13%, Switzerland 10%, UK 10%, Belgium 3%, Kazakhstan 4%, Tajikistan 4% (1999)
Imports: $2.6 billion (f.o.b., 2000 est.)
Imports - commodities: machinery and equipment, chemicals, metals; foodstuffs
Imports - partners: Russia 14%, South Korea 14%, Germany 11%, US 8%, Turkey 4%, Kazakhstan 4% (1999)

Uzbekistan (continued)

Debt - external: $3.3 billion (1999 est.)
Economic aid - recipient: $276.6 million (1995)
Currency: Uzbekistani sum (UZS)
Currency code: UZS
Exchange rates: Uzbekistani sums per US dollar - 325.0 (January 2001), 141.4 (January 2000), 111.9 (February 1999), 110.95 (December 1998), 75.8 (September 1997), 41.1 (1996)
Fiscal year: calendar year

Communications

Telephones - main lines in use: 1.98 million (1999)
Telephones - mobile cellular: 26,000 (1998)
Telephone system:
general assessment: antiquated and inadequate; in serious need of modernization
domestic: the domestic telephone system is being expanded and technologically improved, particularly in Tashkent and Samarqand, under contracts with prominent companies in industrialized countries; moreover, by 1998, six cellular networks had been placed in operation - four of the GSM type (Global System for Mobile Communication), one D-AMPS type (Digital Advanced Mobile Phone System), and one AMPS type (Advanced Mobile Phone System)
international: linked by landline or microwave radio relay with CIS member states and to other countries by leased connection via the Moscow international gateway switch; after the completion of the Uzbek link to the Trans-Asia-Europe (TAE) fiber-optic cable, Uzbekistan will be independent of Russian facilities for international communications; Inmarsat also provides an international connection, albeit an expensive one; satellite earth stations - NA (1998)
Radio broadcast stations: AM 20, FM 7, shortwave 10 (1998)
Radios: 10.8 million (1997)
Television broadcast stations: 4 (plus two repeaters that relay Russian, Kazakh, Kyrgyz, and Tadzhik programs) (1997)
Televisions: 6.4 million (1997)
Internet country code: .uz
Internet Service Providers (ISPs): 42 (2000)
Internet users: 7,500 (2000)

Transportation

Railways:
total: 3,380 km in common carrier service; does not include industrial lines
broad gauge: 3,380 km 1.520-m gauge (300 km electrified) (1993)
Highways:
total: 81,600 km
paved: 71,237 km ((these roads are said to be hard-surfaced, and include, in addition to conventionally paved roads, some that are surfaced with gravel or other coarse aggregate, making them trafficable in all weather)
unpaved: 10,363 km (these roads are made of unstabilized earth and are difficult to negotiate in wet weather) (1996)

Waterways: 1,100 km (1990)
Pipelines: crude oil 250 km; petroleum products 40 km; natural gas 810 km (1992)
Ports and harbors: Termiz (Amu Darya river)
Airports: 267 (2000 est.)
Airports - with paved runways:
total: 10
over 3,047 m: 3
2,438 to 3,047 m: 5
under 914 m: 2 (2000 est.)
Airports - with unpaved runways:
total: 257
over 3,047 m: 3
2,438 to 3,047 m: 8
1,524 to 2,437 m: 11
914 to 1,523 m: 13
under 914 m: 222

Military

Military branches: Army, Air and Air Defense Forces, Security Forces (internal and border troops), National Guard
Military manpower - military age: 18 years of age
Military manpower - availability:
males age 15-49: 6,550,587 (2001 est.)
Military manpower - fit for military service:
males age 15-49: 5,318,418 (2001 est.)
Military manpower - reaching military age annually:
males: 274,602 (2001 est.)
Military expenditures - dollar figure: $200 million (FY97)
Military expenditures - percent of GDP: 2% (FY97)

Transnational Issues

Disputes - international: occasional target of Islamic insurgents based in Tajikistan and Afghanistan
Illicit drugs: limited illicit cultivation of cannabis and very small amounts of opium poppy, mostly for domestic consumption, almost entirely eradicated by an effective government eradication program; increasingly used as transshipment point for illicit drugs from Afghanistan to Russia and Western Europe and for acetic anhydride destined for Afghanistan

Vanuatu

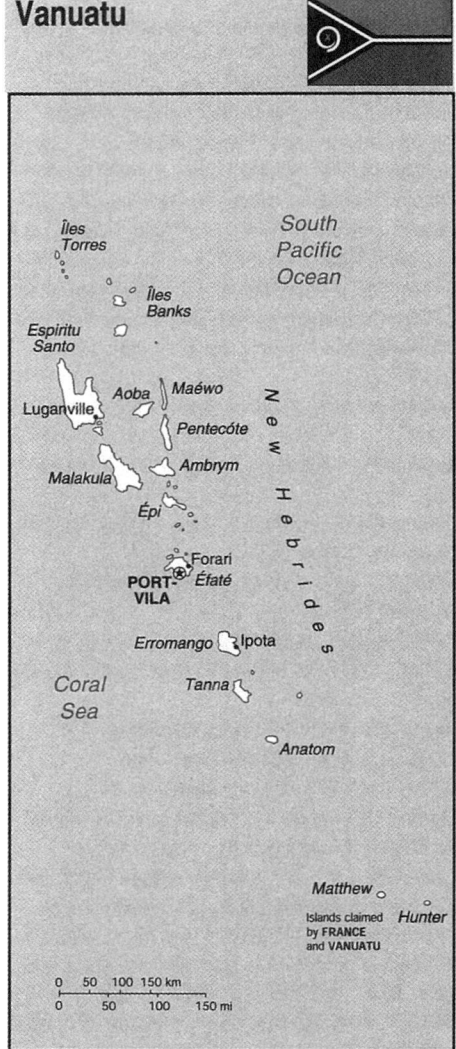

Introduction

Background: The British and French who settled the New Hebrides in the 19th century, agreed in 1906 to an Anglo-French Condominium, which administered the islands until independence in 1980.

Geography

Location: Oceania, group of islands in the South Pacific Ocean, about three-quarters of the way from Hawaii to Australia
Geographic coordinates: 16 00 S, 167 00 E
Map references: Oceania
Area:
total: 12,200 sq km
land: 12,200 sq km
water: 0 sq km
note: includes more than 80 islands
Area - comparative: slightly larger than Connecticut
Land boundaries: 0 km
Coastline: 2,528 km
Maritime claims: measured from claimed archipelagic baselines
contiguous zone: 24 NM

Vanuatu (continued)

continental shelf: 200 NM or to the edge of the continental margin
exclusive economic zone: 200 NM
territorial sea: 12 NM
Climate: tropical; moderated by southeast trade winds
Terrain: mostly mountains of volcanic origin; narrow coastal plains
Elevation extremes:
lowest point: Pacific Ocean 0 m
highest point: Tabwemasana 1,877 m
Natural resources: manganese, hardwood forests, fish
Land use:
arable land: 2%
permanent crops: 10%
permanent pastures: 2%
forests and woodland: 75%
other: 11% (1993 est.)
Irrigated land: NA sq km
Natural hazards: tropical cyclones or typhoons (January to April); volcanism causes minor earthquakes
Environment - current issues: a majority of the population does not have access to a potable and reliable supply of water; deforestation
Environment - international agreements:
party to: Biodiversity, Climate Change, Desertification, Endangered Species, Law of the Sea, Marine Dumping, Ozone Layer Protection, Ship Pollution, Tropical Timber 94
signed, but not ratified: none of the selected agreements

People

Population: 192,910 (July 2001 est.)
Age structure:
0-14 years: 36.35% (male 35,822; female 34,299)
15-64 years: 60.43% (male 59,764; female 56,808)
65 years and over: 3.22% (male 3,348; female 2,869) (2001 est.)
Population growth rate: 1.7% (2001 est.)
Birth rate: 25.4 births/1,000 population (2001 est.)
Death rate: 8.38 deaths/1,000 population (2001 est.)
Net migration rate: 0 migrant(s)/1,000 population (2001 est.)
Sex ratio:
at birth: 1.05 male(s)/female
under 15 years: 1.04 male(s)/female
15-64 years: 1.05 male(s)/female
65 years and over: 1.17 male(s)/female
total population: 1.05 male(s)/female (2001 est.)
Infant mortality rate: 61.05 deaths/1,000 live births (2001 est.)
Life expectancy at birth:
total population: 60.95 years
male: 59.58 years
female: 62.39 years (2001 est.)
Total fertility rate: 3.19 children born/woman (2001 est.)

HIV/AIDS - adult prevalence rate: NA%
HIV/AIDS - people living with HIV/AIDS: NA
HIV/AIDS - deaths: NA
Nationality:
noun: Ni-Vanuatu (singular and plural)
adjective: Ni-Vanuatu
Ethnic groups: indigenous Melanesian 94%, French 4%, Vietnamese, Chinese, Pacific Islanders
Religions: Presbyterian 36.7%, Anglican 15%, Roman Catholic 15%, indigenous beliefs 7.6%, Seventh-Day Adventist 6.2%, Church of Christ 3.8%, other 15.7%
Languages: English (official), French (official), pidgin (known as Bislama or Bichelama)
Literacy:
definition: age 15 and over can read and write
total population: 53%
male: 57%
female: 48% (1979 est.)

Government

Country name:
conventional long form: Republic of Vanuatu
conventional short form: Vanuatu
former: New Hebrides
Government type: republic
Capital: Port-Vila
Administrative divisions: 6 provinces; Malampa, Penama, Sanma, Shefa, Tafea, Torba
Independence: 30 July 1980 (from France and UK)
National holiday: Independence Day, 30 July (1980)
Constitution: 30 July 1980
Legal system: unified system being created from former dual French and British systems
Suffrage: 18 years of age; universal
Executive branch:
chief of state: President Father John BANI (since 25 March 1999)
head of government: Prime Minister Edward NATAPEI (since 16 April 2001); Deputy Prime Minister Serge VOHOR (since 16 April 2001)
cabinet: Council of Ministers appointed by the prime minister, responsible to Parliament
elections: president elected for a four-year term by an electoral college consisting of Parliament and the presidents of the regional councils for a five-year term; election for president last held 25 March 1999 (next to be held NA 2003); following legislative elections, the leader of the majority party or majority coalition is usually elected prime minister by Parliament from among its members; election for prime minister last held 16 April 2001 (next to be held NA 2002)
election results: Father John BANI elected president; percent of electoral college vote - NA%; Edward NATAPEI elected prime minister by Parliament with a total of 27 out of 52 votes
note: the government of Prime Minister Barak SOPE was ousted in a no confidence vote on 14 April 2001 and Edward NATAPEI was elected the new prime minister by Parliament

Legislative branch: unicameral Parliament (52 seats; members elected by popular vote to serve four-year terms)
elections: last held 6 March 1998 (next to be held NA 2002)
election results: percent of vote by party - NA%; seats by party - VP 18, UMP 12, NUP 11, other and independent 11; note - political party associations are fluid; there have been four changes of government since the November 1995 elections
note: the National Council of Chiefs advises on matters of custom and land
Judicial branch: Supreme Court (chief justice is appointed by the president after consultation with the prime minister and the leader of the opposition, three other justices are appointed by the president on the advice of the Judicial Service Commission)
Political parties and leaders: Melanesian Progressive Party or MPP [Barak SOPE]; National United Party or NUP [Willie TITONGOA]; Union of Moderate Parties or UMP [Serge VOHOR]; Vanuaaku Party (Our Land Party) or VP [Edward NATAPEI]; Vanuatu Republican Party [Maxime Carlot KORMAN]
Political pressure groups and leaders: NA
International organization participation: ACCT, ACP, AsDB, C, ESCAP, FAO, G-77, IBRD, ICAO, ICFTU, ICRM, IDA, IFC, IFRCS, IMF, IMO, Intelsat (nonsignatory user), IOC, ITU, NAM, Sparteca, SPC, SPF, UN, UNCTAD, UNESCO, UNIDO, UNMIBH, UNTAET, UPU, WFTU, WHO, WMO, WTrO (observer)
Diplomatic representation in the US: Vanuatu does not have an embassy in the US, it does, however, have a Permanent Mission to the UN
Diplomatic representation from the US: the US does not have an embassy in Vanuatu; the ambassador to Papua New Guinea is accredited to Vanuatu
Flag description: two equal horizontal bands of red (top) and green with a black isosceles triangle (based on the hoist side) all separated by a black-edged yellow stripe in the shape of a horizontal Y (the two points of the Y face the hoist side and enclose the triangle); centered in the triangle is a boar's tusk encircling two crossed namele leaves, all in yellow

Economy

Economy - overview: The economy is based primarily on subsistence or small-scale agriculture which provides a living for 65% of the population. Fishing, offshore financial services, and tourism, with about 50,000 visitors in 1997, are other mainstays of the economy. Mineral deposits are negligible; the country has no known petroleum deposits. A small light industry sector caters to the local market. Tax revenues come mainly from import duties. Economic development is hindered by dependence on relatively few commodity exports, vulnerability to natural disasters, and long distances from main markets and between constituent islands. The most recent natural disaster, a severe earthquake in November 1999 followed by a tsunami, caused extensive damage to the northern island of Pentecote and left thousands

Vanuatu (continued)

homeless. GDP growth has risen less than 3% on average in the 1990s. In response to foreign concerns, the government is moving to tighten regulation of its offshore financial center.
GDP: purchasing power parity - $245 million (1999 est.)
GDP - real growth rate: -2.5% (1999 est.)
GDP - per capita: purchasing power parity - $1,300 (1999 est.)
GDP - composition by sector:
agriculture: 20%
industry: 9%
services: 71% (1999 est.)
Population below poverty line: NA%
Household income or consumption by percentage share:
lowest 10%: NA%
highest 10%: NA%
Inflation rate (consumer prices): 2.5% (1999 est.)
Labor force: NA
Labor force - by occupation: agriculture 65%, services 32%, industry 3% (1995 est.)
Unemployment rate: NA%
Budget:
revenues: $94.4 million
expenditures: $99.8 million, including capital expenditures of $30.4 million (1996 est.)
Industries: food and fish freezing, wood processing, meat canning
Industrial production growth rate: 1% (1997 est.)
Electricity - production: 35 million kWh (1999)
Electricity - production by source:
fossil fuel: 100%
hydro: 0%
nuclear: 0%
other: 0% (1999)
Electricity - consumption: 32.6 million kWh (1999)
Electricity - exports: 0 kWh (1999)
Electricity - imports: 0 kWh (1999)
Agriculture - products: copra, coconuts, cocoa, coffee, taro, yams, coconuts, fruits, vegetables; fish, beef
Exports: $25.3 million (f.o.b., 1999)
Exports - commodities: copra, kava, beef, cocoa, timber, coffee
Exports - partners: Japan 32%, Germany 14%, Spain 8%, New Caledonia 7%, Australia 2% (1997 est.)
Imports: $77.2 million (f.o.b., 1999)
Imports - commodities: machinery and equipment, foodstuffs, fuels
Imports - partners: Japan 52%, Australia 20%, New Caledonia, Singapore, New Zealand, France, Fiji (1997 est.)
Debt - external: $48 million (1997 est.)
Economic aid - recipient: $45.8 million (1995)
Currency: vatu (VUV)
Currency code: VUV
Exchange rates: vatu per US dollar - 143.95 (December 2000), 137.82 (2000), 129.08 (1999), 127.52 (1998), 115.87 (1997), 111.72 (1996)
Fiscal year: calendar year

Communications

Telephones - main lines in use: 4,000 (1996)
Telephones - mobile cellular: 154 (1996)
Telephone system:
general assessment: NA
domestic: NA
international: satellite earth station - 1 Intelsat (Pacific Ocean)
Radio broadcast stations: AM 2, FM 2, shortwave 1 (1998)
Radios: 62,000 (1997)
Television broadcast stations: 1 (1997)
Televisions: 2,000 (1997)
Internet country code: .vu
Internet Service Providers (ISPs): 1 (2000)
Internet users: 3,000 (2000)

Transportation

Railways: 0 km
Highways:
total: 1,070 km
paved: 256 km
unpaved: 814 km (1996 est.)
Waterways: none
Ports and harbors: Forari, Port-Vila, Santo (Espiritu Santo)
Merchant marine:
total: 54 ships (1,000 GRT or over) totaling 1,067,384 GRT/1,330,543 DWT
ships by type: bulk 23, cargo 7, chemical tanker 3, combination bulk 2, container 1, liquefied gas 3, petroleum tanker 2, refrigerated cargo 7, vehicle carrier 6
note: includes some foreign-owned ships registered here as a flag of convenience: Australia 2, Canada 1, China 1, France 1, Greece 1, Hong Kong 1, Japan 22, Netherlands 1, Norway 1, Switzerland 1, US 4 (2000 est.)
Airports: 32 (2000 est.)
Airports - with paved runways:
total: 2
2,438 to 3,047 m: 1
914 to 1,523 m: 1 (2000 est.)
Airports - with unpaved runways:
total: 30
1,524 to 2,437 m: 2
914 to 1,523 m: 11
under 914 m: 17 (2000 est.)

Military

Military branches: no regular military forces; Vanuatu Police Force (VPF; includes the paramilitary Vanuatu Mobile Force or VMF)
Military expenditures - dollar figure: $NA
Military expenditures - percent of GDP: NA%

Transnational Issues

Disputes - international: claims Matthew and Hunter Islands east of New Caledonia

Venezuela

Introduction

Background: Venezuela was one of the three countries that emerged from the collapse of Gran Colombia in 1830 (the others being Colombia and Ecuador). For most of the first half of the 20th century, Venezuela was ruled by generally benevolent military strongmen, who promoted the oil industry and allowed for some social reforms. Democratically elected governments have held sway since 1959. Current concerns include: drug-related conflicts along the Colombian border, increasing internal drug consumption, overdependence on the petroleum industry with its price fluctuations, and irresponsible mining operations that are endangering the rain forest and indigenous peoples.

Geography

Location: Northern South America, bordering the Caribbean Sea and the North Atlantic Ocean, between Colombia and Guyana
Geographic coordinates: 8 00 N, 66 00 W
Map references: South America, Central America and the Caribbean
Area:
total: 912,050 sq km
land: 882,050 sq km
water: 30,000 sq km
Area - comparative: slightly more than twice the size of California
Land boundaries:
total: 4,993 km
border countries: Brazil 2,200 km, Colombia 2,050 km, Guyana 743 km
Coastline: 2,800 km
Maritime claims:
contiguous zone: 15 NM
continental shelf: 200-m depth or to the depth of exploitation
exclusive economic zone: 200 NM
territorial sea: 12 NM

Venezuela (continued)

Climate: tropical; hot, humid; more moderate in highlands
Terrain: Andes Mountains and Maracaibo Lowlands in northwest; central plains (llanos); Guiana Highlands in southeast
Elevation extremes:
lowest point: Caribbean Sea 0 m
highest point: Pico Bolivar (La Columna) 5,007 m
Natural resources: petroleum, natural gas, iron ore, gold, bauxite, other minerals, hydropower, diamonds
Land use:
arable land: 4%
permanent crops: 1%
permanent pastures: 20%
forests and woodland: 34%
other: 41% (1993 est.)
Irrigated land: 1,900 sq km (1993 est.)
Natural hazards: subject to floods, rockslides, mudslides; periodic droughts
Environment - current issues: sewage pollution of Lago de Valencia; oil and urban pollution of Lago de Maracaibo; deforestation; soil degradation; urban and industrial pollution, especially along the Caribbean coast; threat to the rainforest ecosystem from irresponsible mining operations
Environment - international agreements:
party to: Antarctic Treaty, Biodiversity, Climate Change, Desertification, Endangered Species, Hazardous Wastes, Marine Dumping, Marine Life Conservation, Nuclear Test Ban, Ozone Layer Protection, Ship Pollution, Tropical Timber 83, Tropical Timber 94, Wetlands
signed, but not ratified: Marine Dumping
Geography - note: on major sea and air routes linking North and South America

People

Population: 23,916,810 (July 2001 est.)
Age structure:
0-14 years: 32.11% (male 3,962,517; female 3,716,880)
15-64 years: 63.17% (male 7,581,589; female 7,526,467)
65 years and over: 4.72% (male 515,687; female 613,670) (2001 est.)
Population growth rate: 1.56% (2001 est.)
Birth rate: 20.65 births/1,000 population (2001 est.)
Death rate: 4.92 deaths/1,000 population (2001 est.)
Net migration rate: -0.15 migrant(s)/1,000 population (2001 est.)
Sex ratio:
at birth: 1.08 male(s)/female
under 15 years: 1.07 male(s)/female
15-64 years: 1.01 male(s)/female
65 years and over: 0.84 male(s)/female
total population: 1.02 male(s)/female (2001 est.)
Infant mortality rate: 25.37 deaths/1,000 live births (2001 est.)
Life expectancy at birth:
total population: 73.31 years
male: 70.29 years
female: 76.56 years (2001 est.)
Total fertility rate: 2.46 children born/woman (2001 est.)
HIV/AIDS - adult prevalence rate: 0.49% (1999 est.)
HIV/AIDS - people living with HIV/AIDS: 62,000 (1999 est.)
HIV/AIDS - deaths: 2,000 (1999 est.)
Nationality:
noun: Venezuelan(s)
adjective: Venezuelan
Ethnic groups: Spanish, Italian, Portuguese, Arab, German, African, indigenous people
Religions: nominally Roman Catholic 96%, Protestant 2%, other 2%
Languages: Spanish (official), numerous indigenous dialects
Literacy:
definition: age 15 and over can read and write
total population: 91.1%
male: 91.8%
female: 90.3% (1995 est.)

Government

Country name:
conventional long form: Bolivarian Republic of Venezuela
conventional short form: Venezuela
local long form: Republica Bolivariana de Venezuela
local short form: Venezuela
Government type: federal republic
Capital: Caracas
Administrative divisions: 23 states (estados, singular - estado),1 federal district* (distrito federal), and 1 federal dependency** (dependencia federal); Amazonas, Anzoategui, Apure, Aragua, Barinas, Bolivar, Carabobo, Cojedes, Delta Amacuro, Dependencias Federales**, Distrito Federal*, Falcon, Guarico, Lara, Merida, Miranda, Monagas, Nueva Esparta, Portuguesa, Sucre, Tachira, Trujillo, Vargas, Yaracuy, Zulia
note: the federal dependency consists of 11 federally controlled island groups with a total of 72 individual islands
Independence: 5 July 1811 (from Spain)
National holiday: Independence Day, 5 July (1811)
Constitution: 30 December 1999
Legal system: based on organic laws as of July 1999; open, adversarial court system; has not accepted compulsory ICJ jurisdiction
Suffrage: 18 years of age; universal
Executive branch:
chief of state: President Hugo CHAVEZ Frias (since 3 February 1999); Vice President Adina BASTIDAS Castillo; note - the president is both the chief of state and head of government
head of government: President Hugo CHAVEZ Frias (since 3 February 1999); Vice President Adina BASTIDAS Castillo; note - the president is both the chief of state and head of government
cabinet: Council of Ministers appointed by the president
elections: president elected by popular vote for a six-year term; election last held 30 July 2000 (next to be held NA 2006)
election results: Hugo CHAVEZ Frias elected president; percent of vote - 60%
note: government coalition - Patriotic Pole or Polo Patriotico consists of MVR, MAS, and PPT
Legislative branch: unicameral National Assembly or Asamblea Nacional; 165 seats; members elected by popular vote to serve five-year terms; three seats reserved for the indigenous peoples of Venezuela
elections: last held 30 July 2000 (next to be held NA 2005)
election results: Pro-government: percent of vote by party - NA%; seats by party - MVR 92, MAS 6, indigenous 3, other parties 7; Opposition: percent of vote by party - NA%; seats by party - AD 33, COPEI 6, Justice First 5, other parties 13
Judicial branch: Supreme Tribunal of Justice or Tribuna Suprema de Justicia (magistrates are elected by the National Assembly for a single 12-year term)
Political parties and leaders: Brave Peoples Alliance or ABP [leader NA]; Democratic Action or AD [Henry RAMOS Allup]; Fifth Republic Movement or MVR [leader Luis MIQUILENA]; Homeland for All or PPT [Pablo MEDINA]; Justice First [leader NA]; Movement Toward Socialism or MAS [Felipe MUJICA]; National Convergence or Convergencia [Dr. Rafael CALDERA Rodriguez]; Radical Cause or La Causa R [Andres VELASQUEZ]; Social Christian Party or COPEI [Jose CURIEL]; Venezuela Project or PV [Henrique SALAS Ronier]
Political pressure groups and leaders: FEDECAMARAS, a conservative business group; VECINOS groups; Venezuelan Confederation of Workers or CTV (labor organization dominated by the Democratic Action)
International organization participation: CAN, Caricom (observer), CCC, CDB, ECLAC, FAO, G- 3, G-11, G-15, G-19, G-24, G-77, IADB, IAEA, IBRD, ICAO, ICC, ICFTU, ICRM, IFAD, IFC, IFRCS, IHO, ILO, IMF, IMO, Intelsat, Interpol, IOC, IOM, ISO, ITU, LAES, LAIA, NAM, OAS, OPANAL, OPCW, OPEC, PCA, RG, UN, UNCTAD, UNESCO, UNHCR, UNIDO, UNIKOM, UNU, UPU, WCL, WFTU, WHO, WIPO, WMO, WToO, WTrO
Diplomatic representation in the US:
chief of mission: Ambassador Alfredo TORO Hardy
chancery: 1099 30th Street NW, Washington, DC 20007
telephone: [1] (202) 342-2214
FAX: [1] (202) 342-6820
consulate(s) general: Boston, Chicago, Houston, Miami, New Orleans, New York, San Francisco, and San Juan (Puerto Rico)
Diplomatic representation from the US:
chief of mission: Ambassador Donna J. HRINAK
embassy: Calle F con Calle Suapure, Urbanizacion Colinas de Valle Arriba, Caracas 1080
mailing address: P. O. Box 62291, Caracas 1060-A; APO AA 34037

Venezuela (continued)

telephone: [58] (2) 975-6411
FAX: [58] (2) 975-6710
Flag description: three equal horizontal bands of yellow (top), blue, and red with the coat of arms on the hoist side of the yellow band and an arc of seven white five-pointed stars centered in the blue band

Economy

Economy - overview: The petroleum sector dominates the economy, accounting for roughly a third of GDP, around 80% of export earnings, and more than half of government operating revenues. Venezuelan officials estimate that GDP grew by 3.2% in 2000. A strong rebound in international oil prices fueled the recovery from the steep recession in 1999. Nevertheless, a weak nonoil sector and capital flight undercut the recovery. The bolivar is widely believed to be overvalued by as much as 50%. The government is still rebuilding after massive flooding and landslides in December 1999 caused an estimated $15 billion to $20 billion in damage.
GDP: purchasing power parity - $146.2 billion (2000 est.)
GDP - real growth rate: 3.2% (2000 est.)
GDP - per capita: purchasing power parity - $6,200 (2000 est.)
GDP - composition by sector:
agriculture: 5%
industry: 24%
services: 71% (1999 est.)
Population below poverty line: 67% (1997 est.)
Household income or consumption by percentage share:
lowest 10%: 1.5%
highest 10%: 35.6% (1995)
Inflation rate (consumer prices): 13% (2000)
Labor force: 9.9 million (1999)
Labor force - by occupation: services 64%, industry 23%, agriculture 13% (1997 est.)
Unemployment rate: 14% (2000 est.)
Budget:
revenues: $26.4 billion
expenditures: $27 billion, including capital expenditures of $NA (2000 est.)
Industries: petroleum, iron ore mining, construction materials, food processing, textiles, steel, aluminum, motor vehicle assembly
Industrial production growth rate: NA
Electricity - production: 81.215 billion kWh (1999)
Electricity - production by source:
fossil fuel: 32.16%
hydro: 67.84%
nuclear: 0%
other: 0% (1999)
Electricity - consumption: 75.53 billion kWh (1999)
Electricity - exports: 0 kWh (1999)
Electricity - imports: 0 kWh (1999)
Agriculture - products: corn, sorghum, sugarcane, rice, bananas, vegetables, coffee; beef, pork, milk, eggs; fish
Exports: $32.8 billion (f.o.b., 2000)
Exports - commodities: petroleum, bauxite and aluminum, steel, chemicals, agricultural products, basic manufactures
Exports - partners: US and Puerto Rico 57%, Colombia, Brazil, Japan, Germany, Netherlands, Italy (1999)
Imports: $14.7 billion (f.o.b., 2000)
Imports - commodities: raw materials, machinery and equipment, transport equipment, construction materials
Imports - partners: US 53%, Japan, Colombia, Italy, Germany, France, Brazil, Canada (1999)
Debt - external: $34 billion (2000)
Economic aid - recipient: $35 million with more assistance likely as a result of flooding (1999)
Currency: bolivar (VEB)
Currency code: VEB
Exchange rates: bolivares per US dollar - 699.700 (January 2001), 679.960 (2000), 605.717 (1999), 547.556 (1998), 488.635 (1997), 417.333 (1996)
Fiscal year: calendar year

Communications

Telephones - main lines in use: 2,600,000.00; however, 3,500,000 were installed (1998)
Telephones - mobile cellular: 2 million (1998)
Telephone system:
general assessment: modern and expanding
domestic: domestic satellite system with 3 earth stations; recent substantial improvement in telephone service in rural areas; substantial increase in digitalization of exchanges and trunk lines; installation of a national interurban fiber-optic network capable of digital multimedia services
international: 3 submarine coaxial cables; satellite earth stations - 1 Intelsat (Atlantic Ocean) and 1 PanAmSat; participating with Colombia, Ecuador, Peru, and Bolivia in the construction of an international fiber-optic network
Radio broadcast stations: AM 201, FM NA (20 in Caracas), shortwave 11 (1998)
Radios: 10.75 million (1997)
Television broadcast stations: 66 (plus 45 repeaters) (1997)
Televisions: 4.1 million (1997)
Internet country code: .ve
Internet Service Providers (ISPs): 16 (2000)
Internet users: 400,000 (2000)

Transportation

Railways:
total: 584 km (248 km privately owned)
standard gauge: 584 km 1.435-m gauge
Highways:
total: 96,155 km
paved: 32,308 km
unpaved: 63,847 km (1997 est.)
Waterways: 7,100 km
note: Rio Orinoco and Lago de Maracaibo accept oceangoing vessels
Pipelines: crude oil 6,370 km; petroleum products 480 km; natural gas 4,010 km
Ports and harbors: Amuay, Bajo Grande, El Tablazo, La Guaira, La Salina, Maracaibo, Matanzas, Palua, Puerto Cabello, Puerto la Cruz, Puerto Ordaz, Puerto Sucre, Punta Cardon
Merchant marine:
total: 36 ships (1,000 GRT or over) totaling 490,160 GRT/897,694 DWT
ships by type: bulk 7, cargo 10, liquefied gas 2, passenger/cargo 1, petroleum tanker 7, roll on/roll off 8, short-sea passenger 1 (2000 est.)
Airports: 371 (2000 est.)
Airports - with paved runways:
total: 124
over 3,047 m: 4
2,438 to 3,047 m: 12
1,524 to 2,437 m: 32
914 to 1,523 m: 59
under 914 m: 17 (2000 est.)
Airports - with unpaved runways:
total: 247
1,524 to 2,437 m: 10
914 to 1,523 m: 97
under 914 m: 140 (2000 est.)
Heliports: 1 (2000 est.)

Military

Military branches: National Armed Forces (Fuerzas Armadas Nacionales or FAN) includes Ground Forces or Army (Fuerzas Terrestres or Ejercito), Naval Forces (Fuerzas Navales or Armada), Air Force (Fuerzas Aereas or Aviacion), Armed Forces of Cooperation or National Guard (Fuerzas Armadas de Cooperacion or Guardia Nacional)
Military manpower - military age: 18 years of age
Military manpower - availability:
males age 15-49: 6,524,809 (2001 est.)
Military manpower - fit for military service:
males age 15-49: 4,701,062 (2001 est.)
Military manpower - reaching military age annually:
males: 246,185 (2001 est.)
Military expenditures - dollar figure: $934 million (FY99)
Military expenditures - percent of GDP: 0.9% (FY99)

Transnational Issues

Disputes - international: claims all of Guyana west of the Essequibo (river); maritime boundary dispute with Colombia in the Gulf of Venezuela
Illicit drugs: illicit producer of opium for the international drug trade on a small scale; however, large quantities of cocaine, heroin, and marijuana transit the country from Colombia bound for US and Europe; important money-laundering center; active eradication program primarily targeting opium; increasing signs of drug-related activities by Colombian insurgents on border

Vietnam

Introduction

Background: France occupied all of Vietnam by 1884. Independence was declared after World War II, but the French continued to rule until 1954 when they were defeated by communist forces under Ho Chi MINH, who took control of the north. US economic and military aid to South Vietnam grew through the 1960s in an attempt to bolster the government, but US armed forces were withdrawn following a cease-fire agreement in 1973. Two years later North Vietnamese forces overran the south. Economic reconstruction of the reunited country has proven difficult as aging Communist Party leaders have only grudgingly initiated reforms necessary for a free market.

Geography

Location: Southeastern Asia, bordering the Gulf of Thailand, Gulf of Tonkin, and South China Sea, alongside China, Laos, and Cambodia
Geographic coordinates: 16 00 N, 106 00 E
Map references: Southeast Asia
Area:
total: 329,560 sq km
land: 325,360 sq km
water: 4,200 sq km
Area - comparative: slightly larger than New Mexico
Land boundaries:
total: 4,639 km
border countries: Cambodia 1,228 km, China 1,281 km, Laos 2,130 km
Coastline: 3,444 km (excludes islands)
Maritime claims:
contiguous zone: 24 NM
continental shelf: 200 NM or to the edge of the continental margin
exclusive economic zone: 200 NM
territorial sea: 12 NM
Climate: tropical in south; monsoonal in north with hot, rainy season (mid-May to mid-September) and warm, dry season (mid-October to mid-March)
Terrain: low, flat delta in south and north; central highlands; hilly, mountainous in far north and northwest
Elevation extremes:
lowest point: South China Sea 0 m
highest point: Ngoc Linh 3,143 m
Natural resources: phosphates, coal, manganese, bauxite, chromate, offshore oil and gas deposits, forests, hydropower
Land use:
arable land: 17%
permanent crops: 4%
permanent pastures: 1%
forests and woodland: 30%
other: 48% (1993 est.)
Irrigated land: 18,600 sq km (1993 est.)
Natural hazards: occasional typhoons (May to January) with extensive flooding
Environment - current issues: logging and slash-and-burn agricultural practices contribute to deforestation and soil degradation; water pollution and overfishing threaten marine life populations; groundwater contamination limits potable water supply; growing urban industrialization and population migration are rapidly degrading environment in Hanoi and Ho Chi Minh City
Environment - international agreements:
party to: Biodiversity, Climate Change, Desertification, Endangered Species, Environmental Modification, Hazardous Wastes, Law of the Sea, Marine Dumping, Ozone Layer Protection, Ship Pollution, Wetlands
signed, but not ratified: Climate Change-Kyoto Protocol, Nuclear Test Ban

People

Population: 79,939,014 (July 2001 est.)
Age structure:
0-14 years: 32.13% (male 13,266,585; female 12,415,384)
15-64 years: 62.44% (male 24,357,343; female 25,556,187)
65 years and over: 5.43% (male 1,722,094; female 2,621,421) (2001 est.)
Population growth rate: 1.45% (2001 est.)
Birth rate: 21.23 births/1,000 population (2001 est.)
Death rate: 6.22 deaths/1,000 population (2001 est.)
Net migration rate: -0.49 migrant(s)/1,000 population (2001 est.)
Sex ratio:
at birth: 1.07 male(s)/female
under 15 years: 1.07 male(s)/female
15-64 years: 0.95 male(s)/female
65 years and over: 0.66 male(s)/female
total population: 0.97 male(s)/female (2001 est.)
Infant mortality rate: 30.24 deaths/1,000 live births (2001 est.)
Life expectancy at birth:
total population: 69.56 years
male: 67.12 years
female: 72.19 years (2001 est.)
Total fertility rate: 2.49 children born/woman (2001 est.)
HIV/AIDS - adult prevalence rate: 0.24% (1999 est.)
HIV/AIDS - people living with HIV/AIDS: 100,000 (1999 est.)
HIV/AIDS - deaths: 2,500 (1999 est.)
Nationality:
noun: Vietnamese (singular and plural)
adjective: Vietnamese
Ethnic groups: Vietnamese 85%-90%, Chinese, Hmong, Thai, Khmer, Cham, mountain groups
Religions: Buddhist, Hoa Hao, Cao Dai, Christian (predominantly Roman Catholic, some Protestant), indigenous beliefs, Muslim
Languages: Vietnamese (official), English (increasingly favored as a second language), some French, Chinese, and Khmer; mountain area languages (Mon-Khmer and Malayo-Polynesian)
Literacy:
definition: age 15 and over can read and write
total population: 93.7%
male: 96.5%
female: 91.2% (1995 est.)

Government

Country name:
conventional long form: Socialist Republic of Vietnam
conventional short form: Vietnam
local long form: Cong Hoa Xa Hoi Chu Nghia Viet Nam
local short form: Viet Nam
abbreviation: SRV
Government type: Communist state
Capital: Hanoi
Administrative divisions: 58 provinces (tinh, singular and plural), 3 municipalities* (thu do, singular and plural); An Giang, Bac Giang, Bac Kan, Bac Lieu, Bac Ninh, Ba Ria-Vung Tau, Ben Tre, Binh Dinh, Binh Duong, Binh Phuoc, Binh Thuan, Ca Mau, Can Tho, Cao Bang, Dac Lak, Da Nang, Dong Nai, Dong Thap, Gia Lai, Ha Giang, Hai Duong, Hai Phong*, Ha Nam, Ha Noi*, Ha Tay, Ha Tinh, Hoa Binh, Ho Chi Minh*, Hung Yen, Khanh Hoa, Kien Giang, Kon Tum, Lai Chau, Lam Dong, Lang Son, Lao Cai, Long An, Nam Dinh, Nghe An, Ninh Binh, Ninh Thuan, Phu Tho, Phu

Vietnam (continued)

Yen, Quang Binh, Quang Nam, Quang Ngai, Quang Ninh, Quang Tri, Soc Trang, Son La, Tay Ninh, Thai Binh, Thai Nguyen, Thanh Hoa, Thua Thien-Hue, Tien Giang, Tra Vinh, Tuyen Quang, Vinh Long, Vinh Phuc, Yen Bai

Independence: 2 September 1945 (from France)
National holiday: Independence Day, 2 September (1945)
Constitution: 15 April 1992
Legal system: based on communist legal theory and French civil law system
Suffrage: 18 years of age; universal
Executive branch:
chief of state: President Tran Duc LUONG (since 24 September 1997) and Vice President Nguyen Thi BINH (since NA October 1992)
head of government: Prime Minister Phan Van KHAI (since 25 September 1997); First Deputy Prime Minister Nguyen Tan DUNG (since 29 September 1997); Deputy Prime Ministers Nguyen Cong TAN (since 29 September 1997), Nguyen Manh CAM (since 29 September 1997), and Pham Gia KHIEM (since 29 September 1997)
cabinet: Cabinet appointed by the president on the proposal of the prime minister and ratification of the National Assembly
elections: president elected by the National Assembly from among its members for a five-year term; election last held 25 September 1997 (next to be held when National Assembly meets following legislative elections in NA 2002); prime minister appointed by the president from among the members of the National Assembly; deputy prime ministers appointed by the prime minister
election results: Tran Duc LUONG elected president; percent of National Assembly vote - NA%
Legislative branch: unicameral National Assembly or Quoc-Hoi (450 seats; members elected by popular vote to serve five-year terms)
elections: last held 20 July 1997 (next to be held NA 2002)
election results: percent of vote by party - CPV 92%, other 8% (the 8% are not CPV members but are approved by the CPV to stand for election); seats by party - CPV or CPV-approved 450
Judicial branch: Supreme People's Court (chief justice is elected for a five-year term by the National Assembly on the recommendation of the president)
Political parties and leaders: only party - Communist Party of Vietnam or CPV [Le Kha PHIEU, general secretary]
Political pressure groups and leaders: none
International organization participation: ACCT, APEC, ARF, AsDB, ASEAN, CCC, ESCAP, FAO, G-77, IAEA, IBRD, ICAO, ICRM, IDA, IFAD, IFC, IFRCS, ILO, IMF, IMO, Inmarsat, Intelsat, Interpol, IOC, IOM (observer), ISO, ITU, NAM, OPCW, UN, UNCTAD, UNESCO, UNIDO, UPU, WFTU, WHO, WIPO, WMO, WToO, WTrO (observer)
Diplomatic representation in the US:
chief of mission: Ambassador-designate Nguyen Tam CHIEN
chancery: 1233 20th Street NW, Washington, DC 20036, Suite 400
telephone: [1] (202) 861-0737
FAX: [1] (202) 861-0917
consulate(s) general: San Francisco
Diplomatic representation from the US:
chief of mission: Ambassador Douglas B. "Pete" PETERSON
embassy: 7 Lang Ha Road, Ba Dinh District, Hanoi
mailing address: PSC 461, Box 400, FPO AP 96521-0002
telephone: [84] (4) 8431500
FAX: [84] (4) 8351510
consulate(s) general: Ho Chi Minh City
Flag description: red with a large yellow five-pointed star in the center

Economy

Economy - overview: Vietnam is a poor, densely populated country that has had to recover from the ravages of war, the loss of financial support from the old Soviet Bloc, and the rigidities of a centrally planned economy. Substantial progress was achieved from 1986 to 1996 in moving forward from an extremely low starting point - growth averaged around 9% per year from 1993 to 1997. The 1997 Asian financial crisis highlighted the problems existing in the Vietnamese economy but, rather than prompting reform, reaffirmed the government's belief that shifting to a market oriented economy leads to disaster. GDP growth of 8.5% in 1997 fell to 6% in 1998 and 5% in 1999. Growth continued at the moderately strong level of 5.5%, a level that should be matched in 2001. These numbers mask some major difficulties in economic performance. Many domestic industries, including coal, cement, steel, and paper, have reported large stockpiles of inventory and tough competition from more efficient foreign producers; this problem apparently eased in 2000. Foreign direct investment fell dramatically, from $8.3 billion in 1996 to about $1.6 billion in 1999. Meanwhile, Vietnamese authorities have moved slowly in implementing the structural reforms needed to revitalize the economy and produce more competitive, export-driven industries.
GDP: purchasing power parity - $154.4 billion (2000 est.)
GDP - real growth rate: 5.5% (2000 est.)
GDP - per capita: purchasing power parity - $1,950 (2000 est.)
GDP - composition by sector:
agriculture: 25%
industry: 35%
services: 40% (1999 est.)
Population below poverty line: 37% (1998 est.)
Household income or consumption by percentage share:
lowest 10%: 3.5%
highest 10%: 29% (1993)
Inflation rate (consumer prices): -0.6% (2000 est.)
Labor force: 38.2 million (1998 est.)
Labor force - by occupation: agriculture 67%, industry and services 33% (1997 est.)
Unemployment rate: 25% (1995 est.)
Budget:
revenues: $5.3 billion
expenditures: $5.6 billion, including capital expenditures of $1.8 billion (1999 est.)
Industries: food processing, garments, shoes, machine building, mining, cement, chemical fertilizer, glass, tires, oil, coal, steel, paper
Industrial production growth rate: 10.7% (2000 est.)
Electricity - production: 22.985 billion kWh (1999)
Electricity - production by source:
fossil fuel: 47.71%
hydro: 52.29%
nuclear: 0%
other: 0% (1999)
Electricity - consumption: 21.376 billion kWh (1999)
Electricity - exports: 0 kWh (1999)
Electricity - imports: 0 kWh (1999)
Agriculture - products: paddy rice, corn, potatoes, rubber, soybeans, coffee, tea, bananas, sugar; poultry, pigs; fish
Exports: $14.3 billion (f.o.b., 2000 est.)
Exports - commodities: crude oil, marine products, rice, coffee, rubber, tea, garments, shoes
Exports - partners: China, Japan, Germany, Australia, US, France, Singapore, UK, Taiwan
Imports: $15.2 billion (f.o.b., 2000 est.)
Imports - commodities: machinery and equipment, petroleum products, fertilizer, steel products, raw cotton, grain, cement, motorcycles
Imports - partners: Japan, Singapore, South Korea, Taiwan, China, Thailand, Hong Kong, Malaysia, Indonesia, France, US, Sweden
Debt - external: $13.2 billion (2000)
Economic aid - recipient: $2.1 billion in credits and grants pledged by international donors for 2000
Currency: dong (VND)
Currency code: VND
Exchange rates: dong per US dollar - 14,530 (January 2001), 14,020 (January 2000), 13,900 (December 1998), 11,100 (December 1996), 11,193 (1995 average), 11,000 (October 1994)
Fiscal year: calendar year

Communications

Telephones - main lines in use: 2.6 million (2000)
Telephones - mobile cellular: 730,155 (2000)
Telephone system:
general assessment: Vietnam is putting considerable effort into modernization and expansion of its telecommunication system, but its performance continues to lag behind that of its more modern neighbors
domestic: all provincial exchanges are digitalized and connected to Hanoi, Da Nang, and Ho Chi Minh City by fiber-optic cable or microwave radio relay networks; since 1991, main lines in use have been substantially increased and the use of mobile telephones is growing rapidly

Vietnam (continued)

international: satellite earth stations - 2 Intersputnik (Indian Ocean region)
Radio broadcast stations: AM 65, FM 7, shortwave 29 (1999)
Radios: 8.2 million (1997)
Television broadcast stations: at least 7 (plus 13 repeaters) (1998)
Televisions: 3.57 million (1997)
Internet country code: .vn
Internet Service Providers (ISPs): 5 (2000)
Internet users: 121,000 (2000)

Transportation

Railways:
total: 2,652 km
standard gauge: 166 km 1.435-m gauge
narrow gauge: 2,249 km 1.000-m gauge
dual gauge: 237 km NA-m gauges (three rails) (1998)
Highways:
total: 93,300 km
paved: 23,418 km
unpaved: 69,882 km (1996 est.)
Waterways: 17,702 km
note: more than 5,149 km are navigable at all times by vessels up to 1.8 m draft
Pipelines: petroleum products 150 km
Ports and harbors: Cam Ranh, Da Nang, Haiphong, Ho Chi Minh City, Ha Long, Quy Nhon, Nha Trang, Vinh, Vung Tau
Merchant marine:
total: 143 ships (1,000 GRT or over) totaling 705,388 GRT/1,071,902 DWT
ships by type: bulk 8, cargo 108, chemical tanker 1, combination bulk 1, container 2, liquefied gas 2, petroleum tanker 18, refrigerated cargo 3 (2000 est.)
Airports: 34 (2000 est.)
Airports - with paved runways:
total: 17
over 3,047 m: 8
2,438 to 3,047 m: 3
1,524 to 2,437 m: 4
under 914 m: 2 (2000 est.)
Airports - with unpaved runways:
total: 17
over 3,047 m: 1
1,524 to 2,437 m: 1
914 to 1,523 m: 7
under 914 m: 8 (2000 est.)

Military

Military branches: People's Army of Vietnam (PAVN) (includes Ground Forces, Navy, and Air Force), Coast Guard
Military manpower - military age: 17 years of age
Military manpower - availability:
males age 15-49: 21,704,588 (2001 est.)
Military manpower - fit for military service:
males age 15-49: 13,673,438 (2001 est.)
Military manpower - reaching military age annually:
males: 961,124 (2001 est.)
Military expenditures - dollar figure: $650 million (FY98)
Military expenditures - percent of GDP: 2.5% (FY98)

Transnational Issues

Disputes - international: maritime boundary with Cambodia not defined; involved in a complex dispute over the Spratly Islands with China, Malaysia, Philippines, Taiwan, and possibly Brunei; maritime boundary agreement with China in the Gulf of Tonkin awaits ratification; Paracel Islands occupied by China but claimed by Vietnam and Taiwan; portions of boundary with Cambodia are in dispute; agreement on land border with China was signed in December 1999, but details of alignment have not yet been made public
Illicit drugs: minor producer of opium poppy with 2,100 hectares cultivated in 1999, capable of producing 11 metric tons of opium; probable minor transit point for Southeast Asian heroin; opium/heroin/methamphetamine addiction problems

Virgin Islands
(territory of the US)

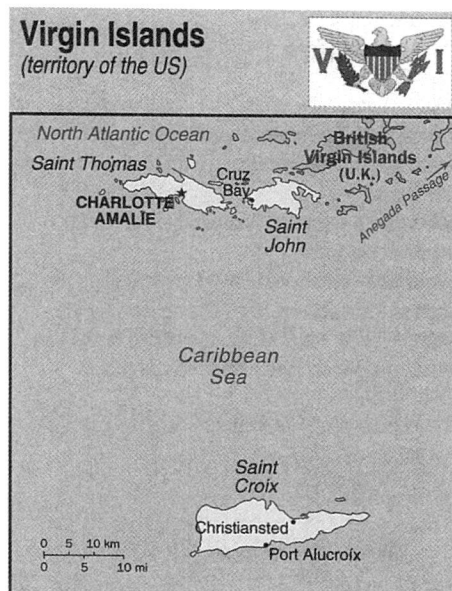

Introduction

Background: During the 17th century, the archipelago was divided into two territorial units, one English and the other Danish. Sugarcane, produced by slave labor, drove the islands' economy during the 18th and early 19th centuries. In 1917, the US purchased the Danish portion, which had been in economic decline since the abolition of slavery in 1848.

Geography

Location: Caribbean, islands between the Caribbean Sea and the North Atlantic Ocean, east of Puerto Rico
Geographic coordinates: 18 20 N, 64 50 W
Map references: Central America and the Caribbean
Area:
total: 352 sq km
land: 349 sq km
water: 3 sq km
Area - comparative: twice the size of Washington, DC
Land boundaries: 0 km
Coastline: 188 km
Maritime claims:
exclusive economic zone: 200 NM
territorial sea: 12 NM
Climate: subtropical, tempered by easterly trade winds, relatively low humidity, little seasonal temperature variation; rainy season May to November
Terrain: mostly hilly to rugged and mountainous with little level land
Elevation extremes:
lowest point: Caribbean Sea 0 m
highest point: Crown Mountain 474 m
Natural resources: sun, sand, sea, surf
Land use:
arable land: 15%
permanent crops: 6%

Virgin Islands (continued)

permanent pastures: 26%
forests and woodland: 6%
other: 47% (1993 est.)
Irrigated land: NA sq km
Natural hazards: several hurricanes in recent years; frequent and severe droughts and floods; occasional earthquakes
Environment - current issues: lack of natural freshwater resources
Geography - note: important location along the Anegada Passage - a key shipping lane for the Panama Canal; Saint Thomas has one of the best natural, deepwater harbors in the Caribbean

People

Population: 122,211 (July 2001 est.)
Age structure:
0-14 years: 27.27% (male 17,121; female 16,204)
15-64 years: 63.92% (male 35,391; female 42,727)
65 years and over: 8.81% (male 4,638; female 6,130) (2001 est.)
Population growth rate: 1.06% (2001 est.)
Birth rate: 15.9 births/1,000 population (2001 est.)
Death rate: 5.47 deaths/1,000 population (2001 est.)
Net migration rate: 0.12 migrant(s)/1,000 population (2001 est.)
Sex ratio:
at birth: 1.06 male(s)/female
under 15 years: 1.06 male(s)/female
15-64 years: 0.83 male(s)/female
65 years and over: 0.76 male(s)/female
total population: 0.88 male(s)/female (2001 est.)
Infant mortality rate: 9.43 deaths/1,000 live births (2001 est.)
Life expectancy at birth:
total population: 78.27 years
male: 74.38 years
female: 82.39 years (2001 est.)
Total fertility rate: 2.25 children born/woman (2001 est.)
HIV/AIDS - adult prevalence rate: NA%
HIV/AIDS - people living with HIV/AIDS: NA
HIV/AIDS - deaths: NA
Nationality:
noun: Virgin Islander(s)
adjective: Virgin Islander
Ethnic groups: black 80%, white 15%, other 5%
note: West Indian (45% born in the Virgin Islands and 29% born elsewhere in the West Indies) 74%, US mainland 13%, Puerto Rican 5%, other 8%
Religions: Baptist 42%, Roman Catholic 34%, Episcopalian 17%, other 7%
Languages: English (official), Spanish, Creole
Literacy:
definition: NA
total population: NA%
male: NA%
female: NA%

Government

Country name:
conventional long form: United States Virgin Islands
conventional short form: Virgin Islands
former: Danish West Indies
Dependency status: organized, unincorporated territory of the US with policy relations between the Virgin Islands and the US under the jurisdiction of the Office of Insular Affairs, US Department of the Interior
Government type: NA
Capital: Charlotte Amalie
Administrative divisions: none (territory of the US); there are no first-order administrative divisions as defined by the US Government, but there are three islands at the second order; Saint Croix, Saint John, Saint Thomas
National holiday: Transfer Day (from Denmark to the US), 27 March (1917)
Constitution: Revised Organic Act of 22 July 1954
Legal system: based on US laws
Suffrage: 18 years of age; universal; note - indigenous inhabitants are US citizens but do not vote in US presidential elections
Executive branch:
chief of state: President George W. BUSH of the US (since 20 January 2001); Vice President Richard B. CHENEY (Since 20 January 2001)
head of government: Governor Dr. Charles Wesley TURNBULL (since 5 January 1999) and Lieutenant Governor Gererd LUZ James II (since 5 January 1999)
cabinet: NA
elections: US president and vice president elected on the same ticket for four-year terms; governor and lieutenant governor elected on the same ticket by popular vote for four-year terms; election last held 3 November 1998 (next to be held NA November 2002)
election results: Dr. Charles Wesley TURNBULL elected governor; percent of vote - Dr. Charles W. TURNBULL (Democrat) 58.9%, former Governor Roy L. SCHNEIDER (ICM) 41.1%
Legislative branch: unicameral Senate (15 seats; members are elected by popular vote to serve two-year terms)
elections: last held 7 November 2000 (next to be held NA November 2002)
election results: percent of vote by party - NA%; seats by party - Democratic Party 6, ICM 2, independents 7
note: the Virgin Islands elects one non-voting representative to the US House of Representatives; election last held 7 November 2000 (next to be held NA November 2002); results - Donna M. CHRISTIAN-CHRISTENSON (Democrat) elected
Judicial branch: US District Court of the Virgin Islands (under Third Circuit jurisdiction); Territorial Court (judges appointed by the governor for 10-year terms)
Political parties and leaders: Democratic Party [Arturo WATLINGTON]; Independent Citizens' Movement or ICM [Usie RICHON]; Republican Party [Gary SCROUVE]
Political pressure groups and leaders: NA
International organization participation: ECLAC (associate), Interpol (subbureau), IOC
Diplomatic representation in the US: none (territory of the US)
Diplomatic representation from the US: none (territory of the US)
Flag description: white, with a modified US coat of arms in the center between the large blue initials V and I; the coat of arms shows a yellow eagle holding an olive branch in one talon and three arrows in the other with a superimposed shield of vertical red and white stripes below a blue panel

Economy

Economy - overview: Tourism is the primary economic activity, accounting for more than 70% of GDP and 70% of employment. The islands normally host 2 million visitors a year. The manufacturing sector consists of petroleum refining, textiles, electronics, pharmaceuticals, and watch assembly. The agricultural sector is small, with most food being imported. International business and financial services are a small but growing component of the economy. One of the world's largest petroleum refineries is at Saint Croix. The islands are subject to substantial damage from storms. The government is working to improve fiscal discipline, support construction projects in the private sector, expand tourist facilities, and protect the environment.
GDP: purchasing power parity - $1.8 billion (2000 est.)
GDP - real growth rate: NA%
GDP - per capita: purchasing power parity - $15,000 (2000 est.)
GDP - composition by sector:
agriculture: NA%
industry: NA%
services: NA%
Population below poverty line: NA%
Household income or consumption by percentage share:
lowest 10%: NA%
highest 10%: NA%
Inflation rate (consumer prices): NA%
Labor force: 47,443 (1990 est.)
Labor force - by occupation: agriculture 1%, industry 20%, services 79% (1990 est.)
Unemployment rate: 4.9% (March 1999)
Budget:
revenues: $364.4 million
expenditures: $364.4 million, including capital expenditures of $NA (1990 est.)
Industries: tourism, petroleum refining, watch assembly, rum distilling, construction, pharmaceuticals, textiles, electronics
Industrial production growth rate: NA%
Electricity - production: 1.02 billion kWh (1999)
Electricity - production by source:
fossil fuel: 100%
hydro: 0%
nuclear: 0%
other: 0% (1999)

Virgin Islands (continued)

Electricity - consumption: 948.6 million kWh (1999)
Electricity - exports: 0 kWh (1999)
Electricity - imports: 0 kWh (1999)
Agriculture - products: fruit, vegetables, sorghum; Senepol cattle
Exports: $NA
Exports - commodities: refined petroleum products
Exports - partners: US, Puerto Rico
Imports: $NA
Imports - commodities: crude oil, foodstuffs, consumer goods, building materials
Imports - partners: US, Puerto Rico
Debt - external: $NA
Economic aid - recipient: $NA
Currency: US dollar (USD)
Currency code: USD
Exchange rates: the US dollar is used
Fiscal year: 1 October - 30 September

Communications

Telephones - main lines in use: 62,000 (1997)
Telephones - mobile cellular: 2,000 (1992)
Telephone system:
general assessment: NA
domestic: modern, uses fiber-optic cable and microwave radio relay
international: submarine cable and satellite communications; satellite earth stations - NA
Radio broadcast stations: AM 5, FM 11, shortwave 0 (1998)
Radios: 107,000 (1997)
Television broadcast stations: 2 (1997)
Televisions: 68,000 (1997)
Internet country code: .vi
Internet Service Providers (ISPs): 50 (2000)
Internet users: 12,000 (2000)

Transportation

Railways: 0 km
Highways:
total: 856 km
paved: NA km
unpaved: NA km
Waterways: none
Ports and harbors: Charlotte Amalie, Christiansted, Cruz Bay, Port Alucroix
Merchant marine: none (2000 est.)
Airports: 2
note: international airports on Saint Thomas and Saint Croix (2000 est.)
Airports - with paved runways:
total: 2
1,524 to 2,437 m: 2 (2000 est.)

Military

Military - note: defense is the responsibility of the US

Transnational Issues

Disputes - international: none

Wake Island
(territory of the US)

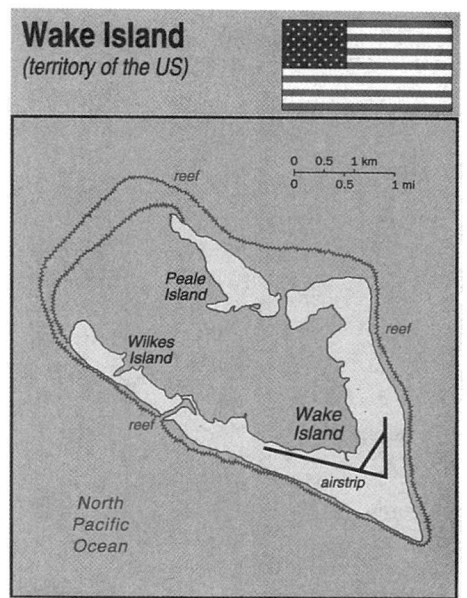

Introduction

Background: The US annexed Wake Island in 1899 for a cable station. An important air and naval base was constructed in 1940-41. In December 1941 the island was captured by the Japanese and held until the end of World War II. In subsequent years, Wake was developed as a stopover and refueling site for military and commercial aircraft transiting the Pacific. Since 1974, the island's airstrip has been used by the US military and some commercial cargo planes, as well as for emergency landings. There are over 700 landings a year on the island.

Geography

Location: Oceania, atoll in the North Pacific Ocean, about two-thirds of the way from Hawaii to the Northern Mariana Islands
Geographic coordinates: 19 17 N, 166 36 E
Map references: Oceania
Area:
total: 6.5 sq km
land: 6.5 sq km
water: 0 sq km
Area - comparative: about 11 times the size of The Mall in Washington, DC
Land boundaries: 0 km
Coastline: 19.3 km
Maritime claims:
exclusive economic zone: 200 NM
territorial sea: 12 NM
Climate: tropical
Terrain: atoll of three coral islands built up on an underwater volcano; central lagoon is former crater, islands are part of the rim
Elevation extremes:
lowest point: Pacific Ocean 0 m
highest point: unnamed location 6 m
Natural resources: none
Land use:
arable land: 0%
permanent crops: 0%
permanent pastures: 0%
forests and woodland: 0%
other: 100%
Irrigated land: 0 sq km (1998)
Natural hazards: occasional typhoons
Environment - current issues: NA
Geography - note: strategic location in the North Pacific Ocean; emergency landing location for transpacific flights

People

Population: no indigenous inhabitants
note: US military personnel have left the island, but civilian personnel remain; as of December 2000, one US Army civilian and 123 civilian contractor personnel were present (January 2001 est.)
HIV/AIDS - people living with HIV/AIDS: NA

Government

Country name:
conventional long form: none
conventional short form: Wake Island
Dependency status: unincorporated territory of the US; administered from Washington, DC, by the Department of the Interior; activities on the island are managed by the US Army under a US Air Force permit
Legal system: the laws of the US, where applicable, apply
Flag description: the flag of the US is used

Economy

Economy - overview: Economic activity is limited to providing services to contractors located on the island. All food and manufactured goods must be imported.
Electricity - production: NA kWh

Communications

Telephone system:
general assessment: satellite communications; 1 DSN circuit off the Overseas Telephone System (OTS)
domestic: NA
international: NA
Radio broadcast stations: AM 0, FM NA, shortwave NA
note: Armed Forces Radio/Television Service (AFRTS) radio service provided by satellite (1998)
Television broadcast stations: 0 (1997)

Transportation

Waterways: none
Ports and harbors: none; two offshore anchorages for large ships
Airports: 1 (2000 est.)
Airports - with paved runways:
total: 1
2,438 to 3,047 m: 1 (2000 est.)

Wake Island (continued)

Transportation - note: formerly an important commercial aviation base, now used by US military, some commercial cargo planes, and for emergency landings

Military

Military - note: defense is the responsibility of the US

Transnational Issues

Disputes - international: claimed by Marshall Islands

Wallis and Futuna
(overseas territory of France)

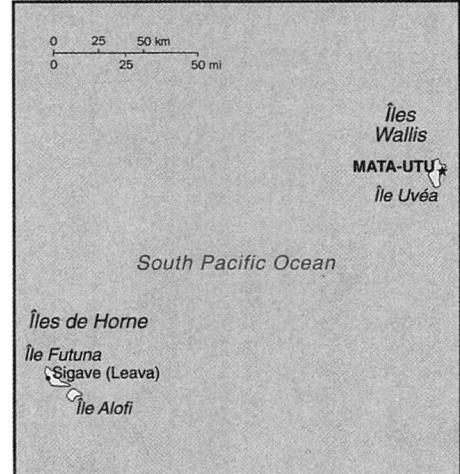

Introduction

Background: Although discovered by the Dutch and the British in the 17th and 18th centuries, it was the French who declared a protectorate over the islands in 1842. In 1959, the inhabitants of the islands voted to become a French overseas territory.

Geography

Location: Oceania, islands in the South Pacific Ocean, about two-thirds of the way from Hawaii to New Zealand
Geographic coordinates: 13 18 S, 176 12 W
Map references: Oceania
Area:
total: 274 sq km
land: 274 sq km
water: 0 sq km
note: includes Ile Uvea (Wallis Island), Ile Futuna (Futuna Island), Ile Alofi, and 20 islets
Area - comparative: 1.5 times the size of Washington, DC
Land boundaries: 0 km
Coastline: 129 km
Maritime claims:
exclusive economic zone: 200 NM
territorial sea: 12 NM
Climate: tropical; hot, rainy season (November to April); cool, dry season (May to October); rains 2,500-3,000 mm per year (80% humidity); average temperature 26.6 degrees C
Terrain: volcanic origin; low hills
Elevation extremes:
lowest point: Pacific Ocean 0 m
highest point: Mont Singavi 765 m
Natural resources: NEGL
Land use:
arable land: 5%
permanent crops: 20%
permanent pastures: 0%
forests and woodland: 0%
other: 75% (1993 est.)
Irrigated land: NA sq km
Natural hazards: NA
Environment - current issues: deforestation (only small portions of the original forests remain) largely as a result of the continued use of wood as the main fuel source; as a consequence of cutting down the forests, the mountainous terrain of Futuna is particularly prone to erosion; there are no permanent settlements on Alofi because of the lack of natural fresh water resources
Geography - note: both island groups have fringing reefs

People

Population: 15,435 (July 2001 est.)
Age structure:
0-14 years: NA%
15-64 years: NA%
65 years and over: NA%
Population growth rate: NA%
Birth rate: NA births/1,000 population
Death rate: NA deaths/1,000 population
Net migration rate: NA migrant(s)/1,000 population
Infant mortality rate: NA deaths/1,000 live births
Life expectancy at birth:
total population: NA years
male: NA years
female: NA years
Total fertility rate: NA children born/woman
HIV/AIDS - adult prevalence rate: NA%
HIV/AIDS - people living with HIV/AIDS: NA
HIV/AIDS - deaths: NA
Nationality:
noun: Wallisian(s), Futunan(s), or Wallis and Futuna Islanders
adjective: Wallisian, Futunan, or Wallis and Futuna Islander
Ethnic groups: Polynesian
Religions: Roman Catholic 100%
Languages: French, Wallisian (indigenous Polynesian language)
Literacy:
definition: age 15 and over can read and write
total population: 50%
male: 50%
female: 50% (1969 est.)

Government

Country name:
conventional long form: Territory of the Wallis and Futuna Islands
conventional short form: Wallis and Futuna
local long form: Territoire des Iles Wallis et Futuna
local short form: Wallis et Futuna
Dependency status: overseas territory of France
Government type: NA
Capital: Mata-Utu (on Ile Uvea)
Administrative divisions: none (overseas territory of France); there are no first-order administrative divisions as defined by the US Government, but there are three kingdoms named Alo, Sigave, Wallis

Wallis and Futuna (continued)

Independence: none (overseas territory of France)
National holiday: Bastille Day, 14 July (1789)
Constitution: 28 September 1958 (French Constitution)
Legal system: French legal system
Suffrage: 18 years of age; universal
Executive branch:
chief of state: President Jacques CHIRAC of France (since 17 May 1995), represented by High Administrator Christian DORS (since NA)
head of government: President of the Territorial Assembly Soane UHILA (since NA)
cabinet: Council of the Territory consists of three kings and three members appointed by the high administrator on the advice of the Territorial Assembly
note: there are three traditional kings with limited powers
elections: French president elected by popular vote for a seven-year term; high administrator appointed by the French president on the advice of the French Ministry of the Interior; the presidents of the Territorial Government and the Territorial Assembly are elected by the members of the assembly
Legislative branch: unicameral Territorial Assembly or Assemblee Territoriale (20 seats; members are elected by popular vote to serve five-year terms)
elections: last held 16 March 1997 (next to be held NA March 2002)
election results: percent of vote by party - NA%; seats by party - RPR 14, other 6
note: Wallis and Futuna elects one senator to the French Senate and one deputy to the French National Assembly; French Senate - elections last held 27 September 1998 (next to be held by NA September 2007); results - percent of vote by party - NA; seats - RPR 1; French National Assembly - elections last held 25 May-1 June 1997 (next to be held by NA March 2002); results - percent of vote by party - NA; seats - RPR 1
Judicial branch: none; justice generally administered under French law by the high administrator, but the three traditional kings administer customary law and there is a magistrate in Mata-Utu
Political parties and leaders: Lua Kae Tahi (Giscardians) [leader NA]; Mouvement des Radicaux de Gauche or MRG [leader NA]; Rally for the Republic or RPR [Clovis LOGOLOGOFOLAU]; Taumu'a Lelei [Soane Muni UHILA]; Union Populaire Locale or UPL [Falakiko GATA]; Union Pour la Democratie Francaise or UDF [leader NA]
Political pressure groups and leaders: NA
International organization participation: FZ, SPC
Diplomatic representation in the US: none (overseas territory of France)
Diplomatic representation from the US: none (overseas territory of France)
Flag description: a large white modified Maltese cross centered on a red background; the flag of France outlined in white on two sides is in the upper hoist quadrant; the flag of France is used for official occasions

Economy

Economy - overview: The economy is limited to traditional subsistence agriculture, with about 80% of the labor force earning its livelihood from agriculture (coconuts and vegetables), livestock (mostly pigs), and fishing. About 4% of the population is employed in government. Revenues come from French Government subsidies, licensing of fishing rights to Japan and South Korea, import taxes, and remittances from expatriate workers in New Caledonia.
GDP: purchasing power parity - $30 million (1997 est.)
GDP - real growth rate: NA%
GDP - per capita: purchasing power parity - $2,000 (1997 est.)
GDP - composition by sector:
agriculture: NA%
industry: NA%
services: NA%
Population below poverty line: NA%
Household income or consumption by percentage share:
lowest 10%: NA%
highest 10%: NA%
Inflation rate (consumer prices): NA%
Labor force: NA
Labor force - by occupation: agriculture, livestock, and fishing 80%, government 4% (est.)
Unemployment rate: NA%
Budget:
revenues: $20 million
expenditures: $17 million, including capital expenditures of $NA (1998 est.)
Industries: copra, handicrafts, fishing, lumber
Industrial production growth rate: NA%
Electricity - production: NA kWh
Electricity - production by source:
fossil fuel: NA%
hydro: NA%
nuclear: NA%
other: NA%
Electricity - consumption: NA kWh
Agriculture - products: breadfruit, yams, taro, bananas; pigs, goats
Exports: $250,000 (f.o.b., 1999)
Exports - commodities: copra, chemicals, construction materials
Exports - partners: Italy 40%, Croatia 15%, US 14%, Denmark 13%
Imports: $300 million (f.o.b., 1999)
Imports - commodities: chemicals, machinery, passenger ships, consumer goods
Imports - partners: France 97%, Australia 2%, New Zealand 1%
Debt - external: $NA
Economic aid - recipient: assistance from France
Currency: Comptoirs Francais du Pacifique franc (XPF)
Currency code: XPF
Exchange rates: Comptoirs Francais du Pacifique francs (XPF) per US dollar - 1127.11 (January 2001), 129.43 (2000), 111.93 (1999), 107.25 (1998), 106.11 (1997), 93.00 (1996); note - linked at the rate of 119.25 XPF to the euro
Fiscal year: calendar year

Communications

Telephones - main lines in use: 1,125 (1994)
Telephones - mobile cellular: 0 (1994)
Telephone system:
general assessment: NA
domestic: NA
international: NA
Radio broadcast stations: AM 1, FM 0, shortwave 0 (2000)
Radios: NA
Television broadcast stations: 2 (2000)
Televisions: NA
Internet country code: .wf
Internet Service Providers (ISPs): 1 (2000)
Internet users: NA

Transportation

Railways: 0 km
Highways:
total: 120 km (Ile Uvea 100 km, Ile Futuna 20 km)
paved: 16 km (all on Ile Uvea)
unpaved: 104 km (Ile Uvea 84 km, Ile Futuna 20 km)
Waterways: none
Ports and harbors: Leava, Mata-Utu
Merchant marine:
total: 4 ships (1,000 GRT or over) totaling 48,853 GRT/43,128 DWT
ships by type: passenger 3, petroleum tanker 1
note: includes some foreign-owned ships registered here as a flag of convenience: France 1 (2000 est.)
Airports: 2 (2000 est.)
Airports - with paved runways:
total: 1
1,524 to 2,437 m: 1 (2000 est.)
Airports - with unpaved runways:
total: 1
914 to 1,523 m: 1 (2000 est.)

Military

Military - note: defense is the responsibility of France

Transnational Issues

Disputes - international: none

West Bank

West Bank is Israeli occupied with current status subject to the Israeli-Palestinian Interim Agreement - permanent status to be determined through further negotiation.

Introduction

Background: The Israel-PLO Declaration of Principles on Interim Self-Government Arrangements (the DOP), signed in Washington on 13 September 1993, provided for a transitional period not exceeding five years of Palestinian interim self-government in the Gaza Strip and the West Bank. Under the DOP, Israel agreed to transfer certain powers and responsibilities to the Palestinian Authority, which includes the Palestinian Legislative Council elected in January 1996, as part of interim self-governing arrangements in the West Bank and Gaza Strip. A transfer of powers and responsibilities for the Gaza Strip and Jericho took place pursuant to the Israel-PLO 4 May 1994 Cairo Agreement on the Gaza Strip and the Jericho Area and in additional areas of the West Bank pursuant to the Israel-PLO 28 September 1995 Interim Agreement, the Israel-PLO 15 January 1997 Protocol Concerning Redeployment in Hebron, the Israel-PLO 23 October 1998 Wye River Memorandum, and the 4 September 1999 Sharm el-Sheikh Agreement. The DOP provides that Israel will retain responsibility during the transitional period for external security and for internal security and public order of settlements and Israeli citizens. Permanent status is to be determined through direct negotiations, which resumed in September 1999 after a three-year hiatus. An intifadah broke out in September 2000; the resulting widespread violence in the West Bank and Gaza Strip, Israel's military response, and instability in the Palestinian Authority are undermining progress toward a permanent settlement.

Geography

Location: Middle East, west of Jordan
Geographic coordinates: 32 00 N, 35 15 E
Map references: Middle East
Area:
total: 5,860 sq km
land: 5,640 sq km
water: 220 sq km
note: includes West Bank, Latrun Salient, and the northwest quarter of the Dead Sea, but excludes Mt. Scopus; East Jerusalem and Jerusalem No Man's Land are also included only as a means of depicting the entire area occupied by Israel in 1967
Area - comparative: slightly smaller than Delaware
Land boundaries:
total: 404 km
border countries: Israel 307 km, Jordan 97 km
Coastline: 0 km (landlocked)
Maritime claims: none (landlocked)
Climate: temperate, temperature and precipitation vary with altitude, warm to hot summers, cool to mild winters
Terrain: mostly rugged dissected upland, some vegetation in west, but barren in east
Elevation extremes:
lowest point: Dead Sea -408 m
highest point: Tall Asur 1,022 m
Natural resources: arable land
Land use:
arable land: 27%
permanent crops: 0%
permanent pastures: 32%
forests and woodland: 1%
other: 40%
Irrigated land: NA sq km
Natural hazards: droughts
Environment - current issues: adequacy of fresh water supply; sewage treatment
Geography - note: landlocked; highlands are main recharge area for Israel's coastal aquifers; there are 231 Israeli settlements and civilian land use sites in the West Bank and 29 in East Jerusalem (August 1999 est.)

People

Population: 2,090,713 (July 2001 est.)
note: in addition, there are some 176,000 Israeli settlers in the West Bank and about 173,000 in East Jerusalem (August 1999 est.)
Age structure:
0-14 years: 44.61% (male 478,232; female 454,439)
15-64 years: 51.8% (male 552,661; female 530,230)
65 years and over: 3.59% (male 32,629; female 42,522) (2001 est.)
Population growth rate: 3.48% (2001 est.)
Birth rate: 35.83 births/1,000 population (2001 est.)
Death rate: 4.37 deaths/1,000 population (2001 est.)
Net migration rate: 3.29 migrant(s)/1,000 population (2001 est.)
Sex ratio:
at birth: 1.06 male(s)/female
under 15 years: 1.05 male(s)/female
15-64 years: 1.04 male(s)/female
65 years and over: 0.77 male(s)/female
total population: 1.04 male(s)/female (2001 est.)
Infant mortality rate: 21.78 deaths/1,000 live births (2001 est.)
Life expectancy at birth:
total population: 72.28 years
male: 70.58 years
female: 74.07 years (2001 est.)
Total fertility rate: 4.9 children born/woman (2001 est.)
HIV/AIDS - adult prevalence rate: NA%
HIV/AIDS - people living with HIV/AIDS: NA
HIV/AIDS - deaths: NA
Nationality:
noun: NA
adjective: NA
Ethnic groups: Palestinian Arab and other 83%, Jewish 17%
Religions: Muslim 75% (predominantly Sunni), Jewish 17%, Christian and other 8%
Languages: Arabic, Hebrew (spoken by Israeli settlers and many Palestinians), English (widely understood)
Literacy:
definition: NA
total population: NA%
male: NA%
female: NA%

Government

Country name:
conventional long form: none
conventional short form: West Bank

Economy

Economy - overview: Economic output in the West Bank is governed by the Paris Economic Protocol of April 1994 between Israel and the Palestinian Authority. Real per capita GDP for the West Bank and Gaza Strip (WBGS) declined by 36.1% between 1992 and 1996 owing to the combined effect of falling aggregate incomes and rapid population growth. The downturn in economic activity was largely the result of Israeli closure policies - the imposition of border closures in response to security incidents in Israel - which disrupted established labor and commodity market relationships between Israel and the WBGS. The most serious social effect of this downturn was

West Bank (continued)

rising unemployment; unemployment in the WBGS during the 1980s was generally under 5%; by 1995 it had risen to over 20%. Since 1997 Israel's use of comprehensive closures has decreased and, in 1998, Israel implemented new policies to reduce the impact of closures and other security procedures on the movement of Palestinian goods and labor. These changes fueled an almost three-year long economic recovery in the West Bank and Gaza Strip; real GDP grew by 5% in 1998 and 6% in 1999. Recovery was upended in the last quarter of 2000 with the outbreak of Palestinian violence, which triggered tight Israeli closures of Palestinian self-rule areas and a severe disruption of trade and labor movements.

GDP: purchasing power parity - $3.1 billion (2000 est.)
GDP - real growth rate: -7.5% (2000 est.)
GDP - per capita: purchasing power parity - $1,500 (2000 est.)
GDP - composition by sector:
agriculture: 9%
industry: 28%
services: 63%
note: includes Gaza Strip (1999 est.)
Population below poverty line: NA%
Household income or consumption by percentage share:
lowest 10%: NA%
highest 10%: NA%
Inflation rate (consumer prices): 3% (includes Gaza Strip) (2000 est.)
Labor force: NA
Labor force - by occupation: services 66%, industry 21%, agriculture 13% (1996)
Unemployment rate: 40% (includes Gaza Strip) (yearend 2000)
Budget:
revenues: $1.6 billion
expenditures: $1.73 billion, including capital expenditures of $NA
note: includes Gaza Strip (1999 est.)
Industries: generally small family businesses that produce cement, textiles, soap, olive-wood carvings, and mother-of-pearl souvenirs; the Israelis have established some small-scale, modern industries in the settlements and industrial centers
Industrial production growth rate: NA%
Electricity - production: NA kWh; note - most electricity imported from Israel; East Jerusalem Electric Company buys and distributes electricity to Palestinians in East Jerusalem and its concession in the West Bank; the Israel Electric Company directly supplies electricity to most Jewish residents and military facilities; at the same time, some Palestinian municipalities, such as Nablus and Janin, generate their own electricity from small power plants
Electricity - production by source:
fossil fuel: NA%
hydro: NA%
nuclear: NA%
other: NA%
Electricity - consumption: NA kWh
Electricity - imports: NA kWh
Agriculture - products: olives, citrus, vegetables; beef, dairy products
Exports: $682 million (includes Gaza Strip) (f.o.b., 1998 est.)
Exports - commodities: olives, fruit, vegetables, limestone
Exports - partners: Israel, Jordan, Gaza Strip
Imports: $2.5 billion (includes Gaza Strip) (c.i.f., 1998 est.)
Imports - commodities: food, consumer goods, construction materials
Imports - partners: Israel, Jordan, Gaza Strip
Debt - external: $108 million (includes Gaza Strip) (1997 est.)
Economic aid - recipient: $121 million disbursed (includes Gaza Strip) (2000)
Currency: new Israeli shekel (ILS); Jordanian dinar (JOD)
Currency code: ILS; JOD
Exchange rates: new Israeli shekels per US dollar - 4.0810 (December 2000), 4.0773 (2000), 4.1397 (1999), 3.8001 (1998), 3.4494 (1997), 3.1917 (1996); Jordanian dinars per US dollar - fixed rate of 0.7090 (from 1996)
Fiscal year: calendar year (since 1 January 1992)

Communications

Telephones - main lines in use: 95,729 (total for West Bank and Gaza Strip) (1997)
Telephones - mobile cellular: NA
Telephone system:
general assessment: NA
domestic: NA
international: NA
note: Israeli company BEZEK and the Palestinian company PALTEL are responsible for communication services in the West Bank
Radio broadcast stations: AM 1, FM 0, shortwave 0
note: the Palestinian Broadcasting Corporation broadcasts from an AM station in Ramallah on 675 kHz; numerous local, private stations are reported to be in operation (2000)
Radios: NA; note - most Palestinian households have radios (1999)
Television broadcast stations: NA
Televisions: NA; note - many Palestinian households have televisions (1999)
Internet Service Providers (ISPs): 8 (1999)
Internet users: 23,520 (includes Gaza Strip) (1999)

Transportation

Railways: 0 km
Highways:
total: 4,500 km
paved: 2,700 km
unpaved: 1,800 km (1997 est.)
note: Israelis have developed many highways to service Jewish settlements
Waterways: none
Ports and harbors: none
Airports: 3 (2000 est.)
Airports - with paved runways:
total: 3
2,438 to 3,047 m: 1
1,524 to 2,437 m: 1
under 914 m: 1 (2000 est.)

Military

Military branches: NA
Military expenditures - dollar figure: $NA
Military expenditures - percent of GDP: NA%

Transnational Issues

Disputes - international: West Bank and Gaza Strip are Israeli-occupied with current status subject to the Israeli-Palestinian Interim Agreement - permanent status to be determined through further negotiation

Western Sahara

Introduction

Background: Morocco virtually annexed the northern two-thirds of Western Sahara (formerly Spanish Sahara) in 1976, and the rest of the territory in 1979, following Mauritania's withdrawal. A guerrilla war with the Polisario Front contesting Rabat's sovereignty ended in a 1991 cease-fire; a referendum on final status has been repeatedly postponed and is not expected to occur until at least 2002.

Geography

Location: Northern Africa, bordering the North Atlantic Ocean, between Mauritania and Morocco
Geographic coordinates: 24 30 N, 13 00 W
Map references: Africa
Area:
total: 266,000 sq km
land: 266,000 sq km
water: 0 sq km
Area - comparative: about the size of Colorado
Land boundaries:
total: 2,046 km
border countries: Algeria 42 km, Mauritania 1,561 km, Morocco 443 km
Coastline: 1,110 km
Maritime claims: contingent upon resolution of sovereignty issue
Climate: hot, dry desert; rain is rare; cold offshore air currents produce fog and heavy dew
Terrain: mostly low, flat desert with large areas of rocky or sandy surfaces rising to small mountains in south and northeast
Elevation extremes:
lowest point: Sebjet Tah -55 m
highest point: unnamed location 463 m
Natural resources: phosphates, iron ore
Land use:
arable land: 0%
permanent crops: 0%
permanent pastures: 19%
forests and woodland: 0%
other: 81%
Irrigated land: NA sq km
Natural hazards: hot, dry, dust/sand-laden sirocco wind can occur during winter and spring; widespread harmattan haze exists 60% of time, often severely restricting visibility
Environment - current issues: sparse water and lack of arable land
Environment - international agreements:
party to: none of the selected agreements
signed, but not ratified: none of the selected agreements

People

Population: 250,559 (July 2001 est.)
Age structure:
0-14 years: NA%
15-64 years: NA%
65 years and over: NA%
HIV/AIDS - adult prevalence rate: NA%
HIV/AIDS - people living with HIV/AIDS: NA
HIV/AIDS - deaths: NA
Nationality:
noun: Sahrawi(s), Sahraoui(s)
adjective: Sahrawian, Sahraouian
Ethnic groups: Arab, Berber
Religions: Muslim
Languages: Hassaniya Arabic, Moroccan Arabic
Literacy:
definition: NA
total population: NA%
male: NA%
female: NA%

Government

Country name:
conventional long form: none
conventional short form: Western Sahara
former: Spanish Sahara
Government type: legal status of territory and question of sovereignty unresolved; territory contested by Morocco and Polisario Front (Popular Front for the Liberation of the Saguia el Hamra and Rio de Oro), which in February 1976 formally proclaimed a government-in-exile of the Sahrawi Arab Democratic Republic (SADR); territory partitioned between Morocco and Mauritania in April 1976, with Morocco acquiring northern two-thirds; Mauritania, under pressure from Polisario guerrillas, abandoned all claims to its portion in August 1979; Morocco moved to occupy that sector shortly thereafter and has since asserted administrative control; the Polisario's government-in-exile was seated as an OAU member in 1984; guerrilla activities continued sporadically, until a UN-monitored cease-fire was implemented 6 September 1991
Capital: none
Administrative divisions: none (under de facto control of Morocco)
Suffrage: none; a UN-sponsored voter identification campaign has yet to be completed
Executive branch: none
Political pressure groups and leaders: none
International organization participation: none
Diplomatic representation in the US: none
Diplomatic representation from the US: none

Economy

Economy - overview: Western Sahara, a territory poor in natural resources and lacking sufficient rainfall, depends on pastoral nomadism, fishing, and phosphate mining as the principal sources of income for the population. Most of the food for the urban population must be imported. All trade and other economic activities are controlled by the Moroccan Government. Incomes and standards of living are substantially below the Moroccan level.
GDP: purchasing power parity - $NA
GDP - real growth rate: NA%
GDP - per capita: purchasing power parity - $NA
GDP - composition by sector:
agriculture: NA%
industry: NA%
services: 40%-45% (1996 est.)
Population below poverty line: NA%
Household income or consumption by percentage share:
lowest 10%: NA%
highest 10%: NA%
Inflation rate (consumer prices): NA%
Labor force: 12,000
Labor force - by occupation: animal husbandry and subsistence farming 50%
Unemployment rate: NA%
Budget:
revenues: $NA
expenditures: $NA, including capital expenditures of $NA
Industries: phosphate mining, handicrafts
Industrial production growth rate: NA%
Electricity - production: 90 million kWh (1999)
Electricity - production by source:
fossil fuel: 100%
hydro: 0%
nuclear: 0%
other: 0% (1999)
Electricity - consumption: 83.7 million kWh (1999)
Electricity - exports: 0 kWh (1999)
Electricity - imports: 0 kWh (1999)
Agriculture - products: fruits and vegetables (grown in the few oases); camels, sheep, goats (kept by nomads)
Exports: $NA
Exports - commodities: phosphates 62%
Exports - partners: Morocco claims and administers Western Sahara, so trade partners are included in overall Moroccan accounts
Imports: $NA
Imports - commodities: fuel for fishing fleet, foodstuffs
Imports - partners: Morocco claims and administers Western Sahara, so trade partners are included in overall Moroccan accounts

Western Sahara (continued)

Debt - external: $NA
Economic aid - recipient: $NA
Currency: Moroccan dirham (MAD)
Currency code: MAD
Exchange rates: Moroccan dirhams per US dollar - 10.590 (January 2001), 10.626 (2000), 9.804 (1999), 9.604 (1998), 9.527 (1997), 8.716 (1996)
Fiscal year: calendar year

Communications

Telephones - main lines in use: about 2,000 (1999 est.)
Telephones - mobile cellular: 0 (1999)
Telephone system:
general assessment: sparse and limited system
domestic: NA
international: tied into Morocco's system by microwave radio relay, tropospheric scatter, and satellite; satellite earth stations - 2 Intelsat (Atlantic Ocean) linked to Rabat, Morocco
Radio broadcast stations: AM 2, FM 0, shortwave 0 (1998)
Radios: 56,000 (1997)
Television broadcast stations: NA
Televisions: 6,000 (1997)
Internet country code: .eh
Internet Service Providers (ISPs): 1 (2000)
Internet users: NA

Transportation

Railways: 0 km
Highways:
total: 6,200 km
paved: 1,350 km
unpaved: 4,850 km (1991 est.)
Waterways: none
Ports and harbors: Ad Dakhla, Cabo Bojador, Laayoune (El Aaiun)
Airports: 11 (2000 est.)
Airports - with paved runways:
total: 3
2,438 to 3,047 m: 3 (2000 est.)
Airports - with unpaved runways:
total: 8
1,524 to 2,437 m: 1
914 to 1,523 m: 4
under 914 m: 3 (2000 est.)
Heliports: 1 (2000 est.)

Military

Military branches: NA
Military expenditures - dollar figure: $NA
Military expenditures - percent of GDP: NA%

Transnational Issues

Disputes - international: claimed and administered by Morocco, but sovereignty is unresolved and the UN is attempting to hold a referendum on the issue; the UN-administered cease-fire has been in effect since September 1991

World

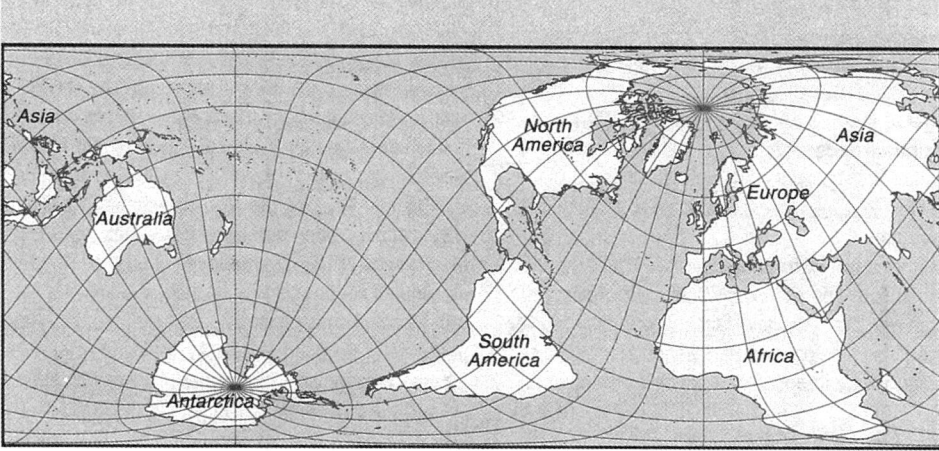

Introduction

Background: Globally, the 20th century was marked by: (a) two devastating world wars; (b) the Great Depression of the 1930s; (c) the end of vast colonial empires; (d) rapid advances in science and technology, from the first airplane flight at Kitty Hawk, North Carolina (US) to the landing on the moon; (e) the Cold War between the Western alliance and the Warsaw Pact nations; (f) a sharp rise in living standards in North America, Europe, and Japan; (g) increased concerns about the environment, including loss of forests, shortages of energy and water, the drop in biological diversity, and air pollution; (h) the onset of the AIDS epidemic; and (i) the ultimate emergence of the US as the only world superpower. The planet's population continues to explode: from 1 billion in 1820, to 2 billion in 1930, 3 billion in 1960, 4 billion in 1974, 5 billion in 1988, and 6 billion in 2000. For the 21st century, the continued exponential growth in science and technology raises both hopes (e.g., advances in medicine) and fears (e.g., development of even more lethal weapons of war).

Geography

Map references: World, Time Zones
Area:
total: 510.072 million sq km
land: 148.94 million sq km
water: 361.132 million sq km
note: 70.8% of the world's surface is water, 29.2% is land
Area - comparative: land area about 16 times the size of the US
Land boundaries: the land boundaries in the world total 251,480.24 km (not counting shared boundaries twice)
Coastline: 356,000 km
Maritime claims:
contiguous zone: 24 NM claimed by most, but can vary
continental shelf: 200-m depth claimed by most or to depth of exploitation; others claim 200 NM or to the edge of the continental margin
exclusive fishing zone: 200 NM claimed by most, but can vary
exclusive economic zone: 200 NM claimed by most, but can vary
territorial sea: 12 NM claimed by most, but can vary
note: boundary situations with neighboring states prevent many countries from extending their fishing or economic zones to a full 200 NM; 43 nations and other areas that are landlocked include Afghanistan, Andorra, Armenia, Austria, Azerbaijan, Belarus, Bhutan, Bolivia, Botswana, Burkina Faso, Burundi, Central African Republic, Chad, Czech Republic, Ethiopia, Holy See (Vatican City), Hungary, Kazakhstan, Kyrgyzstan, Laos, Lesotho, Liechtenstein, Luxembourg, Malawi, Mali, Moldova, Mongolia, Nepal, Niger, Paraguay, Rwanda, San Marino, Slovakia, Swaziland, Switzerland, Tajikistan, The Former Yugoslav Republic of Macedonia, Turkmenistan, Uganda, Uzbekistan, West Bank, Zambia, Zimbabwe
Climate: two large areas of polar climates separated by two rather narrow temperate zones from a wide equatorial band of tropical to subtropical climates
Terrain: the greatest ocean depth is the Mariana Trench at 10,924 m in the Pacific Ocean
Elevation extremes:
lowest point: Bentley Subglacial Trench -2,540 m
highest point: Mount Everest 8,850 m (1999 est.)
Natural resources: the rapid using up of nonrenewable mineral resources, the depletion of forest areas and wetlands, the extinction of animal and plant species, and the deterioration in air and water quality (especially in Eastern Europe, the former USSR, and China) pose serious long-term problems that governments and peoples are only beginning to address

World (continued)

Land use:
arable land: 10%
permanent crops: 1%
permanent pastures: 26%
forests and woodland: 32%
other: 31% (1993 est.)
Irrigated land: 2,481,250 sq km (1993 est.)
Natural hazards: large areas subject to severe weather (tropical cyclones), natural disasters (earthquakes, landslides, tsunamis, volcanic eruptions)
Environment - current issues: large areas subject to overpopulation, industrial disasters, pollution (air, water, acid rain, toxic substances), loss of vegetation (overgrazing, deforestation, desertification), loss of wildlife, soil degradation, soil depletion, erosion

People

Population: 6,157,400,560 (July 2001 est.)
Age structure:
0-14 years: 29.6% (male 933,647,850; female 886,681,514)
15-64 years: 63.4% (male 1,975,418,386; female 1,931,021,694)
65 years and over: 7% (male 188,760,223; female 241,449,691) (2001 est.)
Population growth rate: 1.25% (2001 est.)
Birth rate: 21.37 births/1,000 population (2001 est.)
Death rate: 8.93 deaths/1,000 population (2001 est.)
Sex ratio:
at birth: 1.05 male(s)/female
under 15 years: 1.05 male(s)/female
15-64 years: 1.02 male(s)/female
65 years and over: 0.78 male(s)/female
total population: 1.05 male(s)/female (2001 est.)
Infant mortality rate: 52.61 deaths/1,000 live births (2001 est.)
Life expectancy at birth:
total population: 63.79 years
male: 62.15 years
female: 65.51 years (2001 est.)
Total fertility rate: 2.73 children born/woman (2001 est.)
HIV/AIDS - adult prevalence rate: NA%
HIV/AIDS - people living with HIV/AIDS: NA
HIV/AIDS - deaths: NA

Government

Administrative divisions: 267 nations, dependent areas, other, and miscellaneous entries
Legal system: all members of the UN plus Switzerland are parties to the statute that established the International Court of Justice (ICJ) or World Court

Economy

Economy - overview: Growth in global output (gross world product, GWP) rose to 4.8% in 2000 from 3.5% in 1999, despite continued low growth in Japan, severe financial difficulties in other East Asian countries, and widespread dislocations in several transition economies. The US economy continued its remarkable sustained prosperity, growing at 5% in 2000, although growth slowed in fourth quarter 2000; the US accounted for 23% of GWP. The EU economies grew at 3.3% and produced 20% of GWP. China, the second largest economy in the world, continued its strong growth and accounted for 10% of GWP. Japan grew at only 1.3% in 2000; its share in GWP is 7%. As usual, the 15 successor nations of the USSR and the other old Warsaw Pact nations experienced widely different rates of growth. The developing nations also varied in their growth results, with many countries facing population increases that eat up gains in output. Externally, the nation-state, as a bedrock economic-political institution, is steadily losing control over international flows of people, goods, funds, and technology. Internally, the central government often finds its control over resources slipping as separatist regional movements - typically based on ethnicity - gain momentum, e.g., in many of the successor states of the former Soviet Union, in the former Yugoslavia, in India, and in Canada. In Western Europe, governments face the difficult political problem of channeling resources away from welfare programs in order to increase investment and strengthen incentives to seek employment. The addition of 80 million people each year to an already overcrowded globe is exacerbating the problems of pollution, desertification, underemployment, epidemics, and famine. Because of their own internal problems and priorities, the industrialized countries devote insufficient resources to deal effectively with the poorer areas of the world, which, at least from the economic point of view, are becoming further marginalized. Continued financial difficulties in East Asia, Russia, and many African nations, as well as the slowdown in US economic growth, cast a shadow over short-term global economic prospects; GWP probably will grow at 3-4% in 2001. The introduction of the euro as the common currency of much of Western Europe in January 1999, while paving the way for an integrated economic powerhouse, poses serious economic risks because of varying levels of income and cultural and political differences among the participating nations. (For specific economic developments in each country of the world in 2000, see the individual country entries.)
GDP: GWP (gross world product) - purchasing power parity - $43.6 trillion (2000 est.)
GDP - real growth rate: 4.8% (2000 est.)
GDP - per capita: purchasing power parity - $7,200 (2000 est.)
GDP - composition by sector:
agriculture: 4%
industry: 32%
services: 64% (1999 est.)
Household income or consumption by percentage share:
lowest 10%: NA%
highest 10%: NA%
Inflation rate (consumer prices): all countries 25%; developed countries 1% to 3% typically; developing countries 5% to 60% typically (2000 est.)
note: national inflation rates vary widely in individual cases, from stable prices in Japan to hyperinflation in a number of Third World countries
Labor force: NA
Labor force - by occupation: agricultue NA%, industry NA%, services NA%
Unemployment rate: 30% combined unemployment and underemployment in many non-industrialized countries; developed countries typically 4%-12% unemployment (2000 est.)
Industries: dominated by the onrush of technology, especially in computers, robotics, telecommunications, and medicines and medical equipment; most of these advances take place in OECD nations; only a small portion of non-OECD countries have succeeded in rapidly adjusting to these technological forces; the accelerated development of new industrial (and agricultural) technology is complicating already grim environmental problems
Industrial production growth rate: 6% (2000 est.)
Electricity - production by source:
fossil fuel: NA%
hydro: NA%
nuclear: NA%
other: NA%
Exports: $6 trillion (f.o.b., 2000 est.)
Exports - commodities: the whole range of industrial and agricultural goods and services
Exports - partners: in value, about 75% of exports from the developed countries
Imports: $6 trillion (f.o.b., 2000 est.)
Imports - commodities: the whole range of industrial and agricultural goods and services
Imports - partners: in value, about 75% of imports by the developed countries
Debt - external: $2 trillion for less developed countries (2000 est.)
Economic aid - recipient: traditional worldwide foreign aid $50 billion (1997 est.)

Communications

Telephones - main lines in use: NA
Telephones - mobile cellular: NA
Telephone system:
general assessment: NA
domestic: NA
international: NA
Radio broadcast stations: AM NA, FM NA, shortwave NA
Radios: NA
Television broadcast stations: NA
Televisions: NA
Internet Service Providers (ISPs): 10,350 (2000 est.)
Internet users: 407.1 million (2000 est.)

World (continued)

Transportation

Railways:
total: 1,201,337 km includes about 190,000 to 195,000 km of electrified routes of which 147,760 km are in Europe, 24,509 km in the Far East, 11,050 km in Africa, 4,223 km in South America, and 4,160 km in North America; note - fastest speed in daily service is 300 km/hr attained by France's Societe Nationale des Chemins-de-Fer Francais (SNCF) Le Train a Grande Vitesse (TGV) - Atlantique line
broad gauge: 251,153 km
standard gauge: 710,754 km
narrow gauge: 239,430 km
Highways:
total: NA km
paved: NA km
unpaved: NA km
Ports and harbors: Chiba, Houston, Kawasaki, Kobe, Marseille, Mina' al Ahmadi (Kuwait), New Orleans, New York, Rotterdam, Yokohama

Military

Military expenditures - dollar figure: aggregate real expenditure on arms worldwide in 1999 remained at approximately the 1998 level, about three-quarters of a trillion dollars (1999 est.)
Military expenditures - percent of GDP: roughly 2% of gross world product (1999 est.)

Yemen

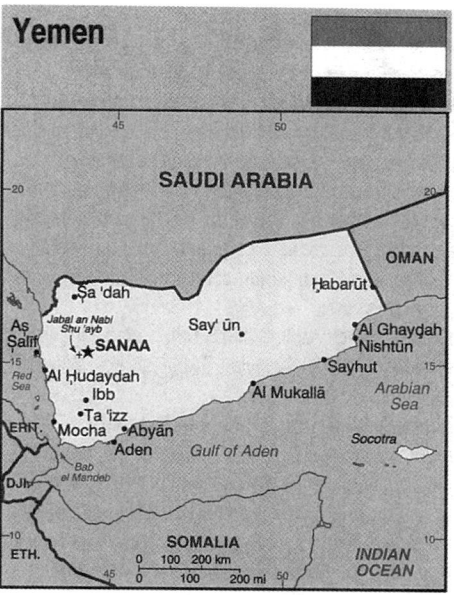

Introduction

Background: North Yemen became independent of the Ottoman Empire in 1918. The British, who had set up a protectorate area around the southern port of Aden in the 19th century, withdrew in 1967 from what became South Yemen. Three years later, the southern government adopted a Marxist orientation. The massive exodus of hundreds of thousands of Yemenis from the south to the north contributed to two decades of hostility between the states. The two countries were formally unified as the Republic of Yemen in 1990. A southern secessionist movement in 1994 was quickly subdued. In 2000, Saudi Arabia and Yemen agreed to a delimitation of their border.

Geography

Location: Middle East, bordering the Arabian Sea, Gulf of Aden, and Red Sea, between Oman and Saudi Arabia
Geographic coordinates: 15 00 N, 48 00 E
Map references: Middle East
Area:
total: 527,970 sq km
land: 527,970 sq km
water: 0 sq km
note: includes Perim, Socotra, the former Yemen Arab Republic (YAR or North Yemen), and the former People's Democratic Republic of Yemen (PDRY or South Yemen)
Area - comparative: slightly larger than twice the size of Wyoming
Land boundaries:
total: 1,746 km
border countries: Oman 288 km, Saudi Arabia 1,458 km
Coastline: 1,906 km
Maritime claims:
contiguous zone: 24 NM
continental shelf: 200 NM or to the edge of the continental margin
exclusive economic zone: 200 NM
territorial sea: 12 NM
Climate: mostly desert; hot and humid along west coast; temperate in western mountains affected by seasonal monsoon; extraordinarily hot, dry, harsh desert in east
Terrain: narrow coastal plain backed by flat-topped hills and rugged mountains; dissected upland desert plains in center slope into the desert interior of the Arabian Peninsula
Elevation extremes:
lowest point: Arabian Sea 0 m
highest point: Jabal an Nabi Shu'ayb 3,760 m
Natural resources: petroleum, fish, rock salt, marble, small deposits of coal, gold, lead, nickel, and copper, fertile soil in west
Land use:
arable land: 3%
permanent crops: 13%
permanent pastures: 33.5%
forests and woodland: 4%
other: 46.5% (1999)
Irrigated land: 5,674 sq km (1999)
Natural hazards: sandstorms and dust storms in summer
Environment - current issues: very limited natural fresh water resources; inadequate supplies of potable water; overgrazing; soil erosion; desertification
Environment - international agreements:
party to: Biodiversity, Climate Change, Desertification, Endangered Species, Environmental Modification, Hazardous Wastes, Law of the Sea, Marine Dumping, Ozone Layer Protection, Ship Pollution
signed, but not ratified: Nuclear Test Ban
Geography - note: strategic location on Bab el Mandeb, the strait linking the Red Sea and the Gulf of Aden, one of world's most active shipping lanes

People

Population: 18,078,035 (July 2001 est.)
Age structure:
0-14 years: 47.21% (male 4,340,436; female 4,195,076)
15-64 years: 49.79% (male 4,598,301; female 4,402,402)
65 years and over: 3% (male 274,202; female 267,618) (2001 est.)
Population growth rate: 3.38% (2001 est.)
Birth rate: 43.36 births/1,000 population (2001 est.)
Death rate: 9.58 deaths/1,000 population (2001 est.)
Net migration rate: 0 migrant(s)/1,000 population (2001 est.)
Sex ratio:
at birth: 1.05 male(s)/female
under 15 years: 1.03 male(s)/female
15-64 years: 1.04 male(s)/female
65 years and over: 1.02 male(s)/female
total population: 1.04 male(s)/female (2001 est.)
Infant mortality rate: 68.53 deaths/1,000 live births (2001 est.)

Yemen (continued)

Life expectancy at birth:
total population: 60.21 years
male: 58.45 years
female: 62.05 years (2001 est.)
Total fertility rate: 6.97 children born/woman (2001 est.)
HIV/AIDS - adult prevalence rate: 0.01% (1999 est.)
HIV/AIDS - people living with HIV/AIDS: NA
HIV/AIDS - deaths: NA
Nationality:
noun: Yemeni(s)
adjective: Yemeni
Ethnic groups: predominantly Arab; but also Afro-Arab, South Asians, Europeans
Religions: Muslim including Shaf'i (Sunni) and Zaydi (Shi'a), small numbers of Jewish, Christian, and Hindu
Languages: Arabic
Literacy:
definition: age 15 and over can read and write
total population: 38%
male: 53%
female: 26% (1990 est.)

Government

Country name:
conventional long form: Republic of Yemen
conventional short form: Yemen
local long form: Al Jumhuriyah al Yamaniyah
local short form: Al Yaman
Government type: republic
Capital: Sanaa
Administrative divisions: 17 governorates (muhafazat, singular - muhafazah); Abyan, 'Adan, Al Bayda', Al Hudaydah, Al Jawf, Al Mahrah, Al Mahwit, 'Ataq, Dhamar, Hadhramawt, Hajjah, Ibb, Lahij, Ma'rib, Sa'dah, San'a', Ta'izz
note: there may be three more governorates: Al Daleh, Shabwah, and the capital city of Sana'a
Independence: 22 May 1990, Republic of Yemen was established with the merger of the Yemen Arab Republic [Yemen (Sanaa) or North Yemen] and the Marxist-dominated People's Democratic Republic of Yemen [Yemen (Aden) or South Yemen]; previously North Yemen had become independent on NA November 1918 (from the Ottoman Empire) and South Yemen had become independent on 30 November 1967 (from the UK)
National holiday: Unification Day, 22 May (1990)
Constitution: 16 May 1991; amended 29 September 1994 and February 2001
Legal system: based on Islamic law, Turkish law, English common law, and local tribal customary law; has not accepted compulsory ICJ jurisdiction
Suffrage: 18 years of age; universal
Executive branch:
chief of state: President Field Marshall Ali Abdallah SALIH (since 22 May 1990, the former president of North Yemen, assumed office upon the merger of North and South Yemen); Vice President Maj. Gen. Abd al-Rab Mansur al-HADI (since 3 October 1994)
head of government: Prime Minister Abd al-Qadir BA JAMAL (since 4 April 2001)
cabinet: Council of Ministers appointed by the president on the advice of the prime minister
elections: president elected by direct, popular vote for a five-year term (a new constitution amendment extends the term by two years to a seven-year term); election last held 23 September 1999 (next to be held NA 2006); vice president appointed by the president; prime minister and deputy prime ministers appointed by the president
election results: Ali Abdallah SALIH elected president; percent of vote: Ali Abdallah SALIH 96.3%, Najeeb Qahtan AL-SHAABI 3.7%
Legislative branch: a new constitutional amendment ratified on 20 February 2001 created a bicameral legislature consisting of a Shura Council (111 seats; members appointed by the president) and a House of Representatives (301 seats; members elected by popular vote to serve six-year terms)
elections: last held 27 April 1997 (next to be held 27 April 2003)
election results: percent of vote by party - NA%; seats by party - GPC 189, Islah 52, Nasserite Unionist Party 3, National Arab Socialist Baath Party 2, independents 54, election pending 1; latest seats by party: GPC 223, Islah 64, Nasserite Unionist Party 3, National Arab Socialist Baath Party 2, YSP 2, independents 7
Judicial branch: Supreme Court
Political parties and leaders: there are over 12 political parties active in Yemen, some of the more prominent are: General People's Congress or GPC [President Ali Abdallah SALIH]; Islamic Reform Grouping or Islah [Shaykh Abdallah bin Husayn al-AHMAR]; National Arab Socialist Baath Party [Dr. Qassim SALAAM]; Nasserite Unionist Party [Abdel Malik al-MAKHLAFI]; Yemeni Socialist Party or YSP [Ali Salih MUQBIL]
note: President SALIH's General People's Congress or GPC won a landslide victory in the April 1997 legislative election and no longer governs in coalition with Shaykh Abdallah bin Husayn al-AHMAR's Islamic Reform Grouping or Islah - the two parties had been in coalition since the end of the civil war in 1994; the YSP, a loyal opposition party, boycotted the April 1997 legislative election, but announced that it would participate in Yemen's first local elections to be held in February 2001; these local elections aim to decentralize political power and are a key element of the government's political reform program
Political pressure groups and leaders: NA
International organization participation: ACC, AFESD, AL, AMF, CAEU, CCC, ESCWA, FAO, G-77, IAEA, IBRD, ICAO, ICRM, IDA, IDB, IFAD, IFC, IFRCS, ILO, IMF, IMO, Intelsat, Interpol, IOC, IOM, ITU, NAM, OAS (observer), OIC, OPCW, UN, UNCTAD, UNESCO, UNIDO, UPU, WFTU, WHO, WIPO, WMO, WToO, WTrO (observer)
Diplomatic representation in the US:
chief of mission: Ambassador Abd al-Wahhab Abdallah al-HAJRI
chancery: Suite 705, 2600 Virginia Avenue NW, Washington, DC 20037
telephone: [1] (202) 965-4760
FAX: [1] (202) 337-2017
Diplomatic representation from the US:
chief of mission: Ambassador Barbara K. BODINE
embassy: Dhahar Himyar Zone, Sheraton Hotel District, Sanaa
mailing address: P. O. Box 22347, Sanaa
telephone: [967] (1) 303-161
FAX: [967] (1) 303-182
Flag description: three equal horizontal bands of red (top), white, and black; similar to the flag of Syria which has two green stars and of Iraq which has three green stars (plus an Arabic inscription) in a horizontal line centered in the white band; also similar to the flag of Egypt which has a heraldic eagle centered in the white band

Economy

Economy - overview: Yemen, one of the poorest countries in the Arab world, reported strong growth in the mid-1990s with the onset of oil production, but was harmed by low oil prices in 1998. Yemen has embarked on an IMF-supported structural adjustment program designed to modernize and streamline the economy, which has led to foreign debt relief and restructuring. Aided by higher oil prices in 1999-2000, Yemen worked to maintain tight control over spending and implement additional components of the IMF program. A high population growth rate of nearly 3.4% and internal political dissension complicate the government's task.
GDP: purchasing power parity - $14.4 billion (2000 est.)
GDP - real growth rate: 6% (2000 est.)
GDP - per capita: purchasing power parity - $820 (2000 est.)
GDP - composition by sector:
agriculture: 20%
industry: 42%
services: 38% (1998)
Population below poverty line: 19% (1992 est.)
Household income or consumption by percentage share:
lowest 10%: 2.3%
highest 10%: 30.8% (1992)
Inflation rate (consumer prices): 10% (2000 est.)
Labor force: NA
Labor force - by occupation: most people are employed in agriculture and herding; services, construction, industry, and commerce account for less than one-fourth of the labor force
Unemployment rate: 30% (1995 est.)
Budget:
revenues: $3 billion
expenditures: $3.1 billion, including capital expenditures of $NA (2001 est.)
Industries: crude oil production and petroleum refining; small-scale production of cotton textiles and leather goods; food processing; handicrafts; small aluminum products factory; cement

Yemen (continued)

Industrial production growth rate: NA%
Electricity - production: 2.4 billion kWh (1999)
Electricity - production by source:
fossil fuel: 100%
hydro: 0%
nuclear: 0%
other: 0% (1999)
Electricity - consumption: 2.232 billion kWh (1999)
Electricity - exports: 0 kWh (1999)
Electricity - imports: 0 kWh (1999)
Agriculture - products: grain, fruits, vegetables, pulses, qat (mildly narcotic shrub), coffee, cotton; dairy products, livestock (sheep, goats, cattle, camels), poultry; fish
Exports: $4.2 billion (f.o.b., 2000 est.)
Exports - commodities: crude oil, coffee, dried and salted fish
Exports - partners: Thailand 34%, China 26%, South Korea 14%, Japan 3% (1999)
Imports: $2.7 billion (f.o.b., 2000 est.)
Imports - commodities: food and live animals, machinery and equipment
Imports - partners: Saudi Arabia 10%, UAE 8%, US 7%, France 7%, Italy 6% (1999)
Debt - external: $4.4 billion (2000)
Economic aid - recipient: $176.1 million (1995)
Currency: Yemeni rial (YER)
Currency code: YER
Exchange rates: Yemeni rials per US dollar - 164.590 (October 2000), 160.683 (2000), 155.718 (1999), 135.882 (1998), 129.281 (1997), 94.157 (1996)
Fiscal year: calendar year

Communications

Telephones - main lines in use: 291,359 (1999)
Telephones - mobile cellular: 32,042 (2000)
Telephone system:
general assessment: since unification in 1990, efforts have been made to create a national telecommunications network
domestic: the national network consists of microwave radio relay, cable, tropospheric scatter, and GSM cellular mobile telephone systems
international: satellite earth stations - 3 Intelsat (2 Indian Ocean and 1 Atlantic Ocean), 1 Intersputnik (Atlantic Ocean region), and 2 Arabsat; microwave radio relay to Saudi Arabia and Djibouti
Radio broadcast stations: AM 6, FM 1, shortwave 2 (1998)
Radios: 1.05 million (1997)
Television broadcast stations: 7 (plus several low-power repeaters) (1997)
Televisions: 470,000 (1997)
Internet country code: .ye
Internet Service Providers (ISPs): 1 (2000)
Internet users: 12,000 (2000)

Transportation

Railways: 0 km
Highways:
total: 69,263 km
paved: 9,963 km
unpaved: 59,300 km (1999)
Waterways: none
Pipelines: crude oil 644 km; petroleum products 32 km
Ports and harbors: Aden, Al Hudaydah, Al Mukalla, As Salif, Mocha, Nishtun
Merchant marine:
total: 4 ships (1,000 GRT or over) totaling 15,075 GRT/23,562 DWT
ships by type: cargo 1, petroleum tanker 3 (2000 est.)
Airports: 50 (2000 est.)
Airports - with paved runways:
total: 13
over 3,047 m: 2
2,438 to 3,047 m: 8
1,524 to 2,437 m: 1
914 to 1,523 m: 1
under 914 m: 1 (2000 est.)
Airports - with unpaved runways:
total: 37
over 3,047 m: 2
2,438 to 3,047 m: 9
1,524 to 2,437 m: 8
914 to 1,523 m: 13
under 914 m: 5 (2000 est.)

Military

Military branches: Army, Navy, Coast Guard, Air Force, Air Defense Forces, Presidential Guards, paramilitary (includes Police)
Military manpower - military age: 14 years of age
Military manpower - availability:
males age 15-49: 4,103,093 (2001 est.)
Military manpower - fit for military service:
males age 15-49: 2,303,257 (2001 est.)
Military manpower - reaching military age annually:
males: 238,690 (2001 est.)
Military expenditures - dollar figure: $414 million (FY99)
Military expenditures - percent of GDP: 7.6% (FY99)

Transnational Issues

Disputes - international: a June 2000 treaty delimited the boundary with Saudi Arabia, but final demarcation requires adjustments based on tribal considerations

Yugoslavia

Introduction

Background: The Kingdom of Serbs, Croats, and Slovenes was formed in 1918; its name was changed to Yugoslavia in 1929. Occupation by Nazi Germany in 1941 was resisted by various partisan bands that fought themselves as well as the invaders. The group headed by Marshal TITO took full control upon German expulsion in 1945. Although communist in name, his new government successfully steered its own path between the Warsaw Pact nations and the West for the next four and a half decades. In the early 1990s, post-TITO Yugoslavia began to unravel along ethnic lines: Slovenia, Croatia, and The Former Yugoslav Republic of Macedonia all declared their independence in 1991; Bosnia and Herzegovina in 1992. The remaining republics of Serbia and Montenegro declared a new "Federal Republic of Yugoslavia" in 1992 and, under President Slobodan MILOSEVIC, Serbia led various military intervention efforts to unite Serbs in neighboring republics into a "Greater Serbia." All of these efforts were ultimately unsuccessful. In 1999, massive expulsions by Serbs of ethnic Albanians living in the autonomous republic of Kosovo provoked an international response, including the NATO bombing of Serbia and the stationing of NATO and Russian peacekeepers in Kosovo. Blatant attempts to manipulate presidential balloting in October of 2000 were followed by massive nationwide demonstrations and strikes that saw the election winner, Vojislav KOSTUNICA, replace MILOSEVIC.

Geography

Location: Southeastern Europe, bordering the Adriatic Sea, between Albania and Bosnia and Herzegovina
Geographic coordinates: 44 00 N, 21 00 E
Map references: Europe
Area:
total: 102,350 sq km

Yugoslavia (continued)

land: 102,136 sq km
water: 214 sq km
Area - comparative: slightly smaller than Kentucky
Land boundaries:
total: 2,246 km
border countries: Albania 287 km, Bosnia and Herzegovina 527 km, Bulgaria 318 km, Croatia (north) 241 km, Croatia (south) 25 km, Hungary 151 km, The Former Yugoslav Republic of Macedonia 221 km, Romania 476 km
Coastline: 199 km
Maritime claims: NA
Climate: in the north, continental climate (cold winters and hot, humid summers with well distributed rainfall); central portion, continental and Mediterranean climate; to the south, Adriatic climate along the coast, hot, dry summers and autumns and relatively cold winters with heavy snowfall inland
Terrain: extremely varied; to the north, rich fertile plains; to the east, limestone ranges and basins; to the southeast, ancient mountains and hills; to the southwest, extremely high shoreline with no islands off the coast
Elevation extremes:
lowest point: Adriatic Sea 0 m
highest point: Daravica 2,656 m
Natural resources: oil, gas, coal, antimony, copper, lead, zinc, nickel, gold, pyrite, chrome, hydropower, arable land
Land use:
arable land: 40%
permanent crops: 0%
permanent pastures: 20.7%
forests and woodland: 17.3%
other: 22% (1998 est.)
Irrigated land: NA sq km
Natural hazards: destructive earthquakes
Environment - current issues: pollution of coastal waters from sewage outlets, especially in tourist-related areas such as Kotor; air pollution around Belgrade and other industrial cities; water pollution from industrial wastes dumped into the Sava which flows into the Danube
Environment - international agreements:
party to: Air Pollution, Climate Change, Hazardous Wastes, Marine Dumping, Marine Life Conservation, Nuclear Test Ban, Ozone Layer Protection, Ship Pollution
signed, but not ratified: Biodiversity
Geography - note: controls one of the major land routes from Western Europe to Turkey and the Near East; strategic location along the Adriatic coast

People

Population: 10,677,290
note: all data dealing with population is subject to considerable error because of the dislocations caused by military action and ethnic cleansing (July 2001 est.)
Age structure:
0-14 years: 19.8% (male 1,095,905; female 1,024,123)
15-64 years: 65.3% (male 3,415,728; female 3,553,343)
65 years and over: 14.9% (male 681,559; female 906,632) (2001 est.)
Population growth rate: -0.27% (2001 est.)
Birth rate: 12.61 births/1,000 population (2001 est.)
Death rate: 10.54 deaths/1,000 population (2001 est.)
Net migration rate: -4.71 migrant(s)/1,000 population (2001 est.)
Sex ratio:
at birth: 1.08 male(s)/female
under 15 years: 1.08 male(s)/female
15-64 years: 0.96 male(s)/female
65 years and over: 0.75 male(s)/female
total population: 0.95 male(s)/female (2001 est.)
Infant mortality rate: 17.42 deaths/1,000 live births (2001 est.)
Life expectancy at birth:
total population: 73.5 years
male: 70.57 years
female: 76.67 years (2001 est.)
Total fertility rate: 1.75 children born/woman (2001 est.)
HIV/AIDS - adult prevalence rate: NA%
HIV/AIDS - people living with HIV/AIDS: NA
HIV/AIDS - deaths: NA
Nationality:
noun: Serb(s); Montenegrin(s)
adjective: Serbian; Montenegrin
Ethnic groups: Serb 62.6%, Albanian 16.5%, Montenegrin 5%, Hungarian 3.3%, other 12.6% (1991)
Religions: Orthodox 65%, Muslim 19%, Roman Catholic 4%, Protestant 1%, other 11%
Languages: Serbian 95%, Albanian 5%
Literacy:
definition: age 15 and over can read and write
total population: 93%
male: 97.2%
female: 88.9% (1991)

Government

Country name:
conventional long form: Federal Republic of Yugoslavia
conventional short form: Yugoslavia
local long form: Savezna Republika Jugoslavija
local short form: Jugoslavija
Government type: republic
Capital: Belgrade
Administrative divisions: 2 republics (republike, singular - republika); and 2 nominally autonomous provinces* (autonomn pokrajine, singular - autonomna pokrajina); Kosovo*, Montenegro, Serbia, Vojvodina*
Independence: 27 April 1992 (Federal Republic of Yugoslavia or FRY formed as self-proclaimed successor to the Socialist Federal Republic of Yugoslavia or SFRY)
National holiday: Republic Day, 29 November
Constitution: 27 April 1992
Legal system: based on civil law system
Suffrage: 16 years of age, if employed; 18 years of age, universal
Executive branch:
chief of state: President Vojislav KOSTUNICA (since 7 October 2000)
head of government: Prime Minister Zoran ZIZIC (since 25 January 2001); Deputy Prime Minister Miroljub LABUS (since 25 January 2001)
cabinet: Federal Executive Council
elections: president elected by direct popular vote for up to two, four-year terms; election last held 24 September 2000 (next to be held NA 2004); prime minister appointed by the president
election results: Vojislav KOSTUNICA elected president; percent of vote - Vojislav KOSTUNICA 55%, Slobodan MILOSEVIC 35%
Legislative branch: bicameral Federal Assembly or Savezna Skupstina consists of the Chamber of Republics or Vece Republika (40 seats - 20 Serbian, 20 Montenegrin; members distributed on the basis of party representation in the republican assemblies to serve four-year terms; note - the Assembly passed a new constitutional amendment calling for direct elections for the deputies to the upper chamber) and the Chamber of Citizens or Vece Gradjana (138 seats - 108 Serbian with half elected by constituency majorities and half by proportional representation, 30 Montenegrin with six elected by constituency and 24 proportionally; members serve four-year terms)
elections: Chamber of Republics - last held 24 September 2000 (next to be held NA 2004); Chamber of Citizens - last held 24 September 2000 (next to be held NA 2004)
election results: Chamber of Republics - percent of vote by party - NA%; seats by party - SNP 19, DOS 10, SPS/JUL 7, SRS 2, SPO 1, SNS 1; note - seats are filled on a proportional basis to reflect the composition of the legislatures of the republics of Montenegro and Serbia; since 1998 Serbia has effectively barred Montenegro from its constitutional right to delegate deputies to the Chamber of Republics; Chamber of Citizens - percent of vote by party - NA%; seats by party - DOS 55, SPS/JUL 46, SNP 28, SRS 4, SNS 2, other 3
Judicial branch: Federal Court or Savezni Sud; Constitutional Court; judges for both courts are elected by the Federal Assembly for nine-year terms
Political parties and leaders: Alliance of Vojvodina Hungarians or SVM [Jozsef KASZA]; Civic Alliance of Serbia or GSS [Vesna PESIC]; Coalition Sandzak [Rasim JAJIC]; Coalition Sumadija [Branislav KOVACEVIC]; Democratic Alternative of DA [Nebojsa COVIC]; Democratic Center or DC [Dragoljub MICUNOVIC]; Democratic Christian Party of Serbia of DHSS [Vladan BATIC]; Democratic League of Kosovo or LDK [Dr. Ibrahim RUGOVA, president]; Democratic Opposition of Serbia or DOS [leader NA]; Democratic Party or DS [Zoran DJINDJIC]; Democratic Party of Serbia or DSS [Vojislav KOSTUNICA]; Democratic Party of Socialists of Montenegro or DPS [Milo

Yugoslavia (continued)

DJUKANOVIC]; Movement for a Democratic Serbia or PDS [Momcilo PERISIC]; New Democracy or ND [Dusan MIHAJLOVIC]; New Serbia [Velimir ILIC and Milan St. PROTIC]; People's Party of Montenegro or NS [Dragan SOC]; Serb People's Party or SNS [leader NA]; Serbian Radical Party or SRS [Vojislav SESELJ]; Serbian Renewal Movement or SPO [Vuk DRASKOVIC, president]; Serbian Socialist Party or SPS (former Communist Party) [Slobodan MILOSEVIC]; Social Democracy or SD [Vuk OBRADOVIC]; Social Democratic Union or SDU [Zarko KORAC]; Socialist People's Party of Montenegro or SNP [Momir BULATOVIC]; Yugoslav United Left or JUL [Ljubisa RISTIC]

Political pressure groups and leaders: Alliance for the Future of Kosovo or AAK [leader RAMUSH]; Group of 17 Independent Economists or G-17 [leader NA]; National Movement for the Liberation of Kosovo or LKCK [Sabit GASHI]; Otpor Student Resistance Movement [leader NA]; Political Council for Presevo, Meveda and Bujanovac or PCPMB [leader NA]; The People's Movement for Kosovo or LPK [leader NA]

International organization participation: BIS, CE (guest), FAO (applicant), G-9, G-15, G-24, G-77, IAEA, ICAO, ICC, ICFTU, ICRM, IFAD, IFRCS, IHO, ILO, IMF, IMO, Inmarsat, Intelsat, IOC, IOM (observer), ISO, ITU, NAM, OPCW, OSCE, UN, UNCTAD, UNESCO, UNIDO, UPU, WHO, WIPO, WMO, WTrO (observer)

Diplomatic representation in the US:
chief of mission: Ambassador Milan PROTIC
chancery: 2410 California St. NW, Washington, DC 20008
note: Yugoslavia restored its diplomatic mission in the US in November 2000 after temporarily ceasing its operations at the beginning of the March 1999 NATO bombing campaign

Diplomatic representation from the US:
chief of mission: Ambassador (vacant); Charge d'Affaires William MONTGOMERY
embassy: Kneza Milosa 30, 11000 Belgrade
note: the US reestablished relations with Yugoslavia 17 November 2000; the embassy is not scheduled to open for business until extensive renovations have been completed

Economy

Economy - overview: The swift collapse of the Yugoslav federation in 1991 was followed by highly destructive warfare, the destabilization of republic boundaries, and the breakup of important interrepublic trade flows. Output in Yugoslavia dropped by half in 1992-93. Like the other former Yugoslav republics, it had depended on its sister republics for large amounts of energy and manufactures. Wide differences in climate, mineral resources, and levels of technology among the republics accentuated this interdependence, as did the communist practice of concentrating much industrial output in a small number of giant plants. The breakup of many of the trade links, the sharp drop in output as industrial plants lost suppliers and markets, and the destruction of physical assets in the fighting all have contributed to the economic difficulties of the republics. Hyperinflation ended with the establishment of a new currency unit in June 1993; prices were relatively stable from 1995 through 1997, but inflationary pressures resurged in 1998. Reliable statistics continue to be hard to come by, and the GDP estimate is extremely rough. The economic boom anticipated by the government after the suspension of UN sanctions in December 1995 has failed to materialize. Government mismanagement of the economy is largely to blame, but the damage to Yugoslavia's infrastructure and industry by the NATO bombing during the war in Kosovo have added to problems. All sanctions now have been lifted. Yugoslavia is in the first stage of economic reform. Severe electricity shortages are chronic, the result of lack of investment by former regimes, depleted hydropower reservoirs due to extended drought, and lack of funds. GDP growth in 2000 was perhaps 15%, which made up for a large part of the 20% decline of 1999.

GDP: purchasing power parity - $24.2 billion (2000 est.)

GDP - real growth rate: 15% (2000 est.)

GDP - per capita: purchasing power parity - $2,300 (2000 est.)

GDP - composition by sector:
agriculture: 20%
industry: 50%
services: 30% (1998 est.)

Population below poverty line: NA%

Household income or consumption by percentage share:
lowest 10%: NA%
highest 10%: NA%

Inflation rate (consumer prices): 42% (1999 est.)

Labor force: 1.6 million (1999 est.)

Labor force - by occupation: agriculture NA%, industry NA%, services NA%

Unemployment rate: 30% (2000 est.)

Budget:
revenues: $NA
expenditures: $NA, including capital expenditures of $NA

Industries: machine building (aircraft, trucks, and automobiles; tanks and weapons; electrical equipment; agricultural machinery); metallurgy (steel, aluminum, copper, lead, zinc, chromium, antimony, bismuth, cadmium); mining (coal, bauxite, nonferrous ore, iron ore, limestone); consumer goods (textiles, footwear, foodstuffs, appliances); electronics, petroleum products, chemicals, and pharmaceuticals

Industrial production growth rate: -22% (1999 est.)

Electricity - production: 34.455 billion kWh (1999)

Electricity - production by source:
fossil fuel: 70%
hydro: 30%
nuclear: 0%
other: 0% (1999)

Electricity - consumption: 33.006 billion kWh (1999)

Electricity - exports: 960 million kWh (1999)

Electricity - imports: 1.923 billion kWh (1999)

Agriculture - products: cereals, fruits, vegetables, tobacco, olives; cattle, sheep, goats

Exports: $1.5 billion (1999)

Exports - commodities: manufactured goods, food and live animals, raw materials

Exports - partners: Bosnia and Herzegovina, Italy, The Former Yugoslav Republic of Macedonia, Germany (1998)

Imports: $3.3 billion (1999)

Imports - commodities: machinery and transport equipment, fuels and lubricants, manufactured goods, chemicals, food and live animals, raw materials

Imports - partners: Germany, Italy, Russia, The Former Yugoslav Republic of Macedonia (1998)

Debt - external: $14.1 billion (1999 est.)

Economic aid - recipient: $NA

Currency: new Yugoslav dinar (YUM); note - in Montenegro the German deutsche mark is legal tender (1999)

Currency code: YUM

Exchange rates: new Yugoslav dinars per US dollar - official rate: 10.0 (December 1998), 5.85 (December 1997), 5.02 (September 1996), 1.5 (early 1995); black market rate: 14.5 (December 1998), 8.9 (December 1997), 2 to 3 (early 1995)

Fiscal year: calendar year

Communications

Telephones - main lines in use: 2.017 million (1995)

Telephones - mobile cellular: 87,000 (1997)

Telephone system:
general assessment: NA
domestic: NA
international: satellite earth station - 1 Intelsat (Atlantic Ocean)

Radio broadcast stations: AM 113, FM 194, shortwave 2 (1998)

Radios: 3.15 million (1997)

Television broadcast stations: more than 771 (including 86 strong stations and 685 low-power stations, plus 20 repeaters in the principal networks; also numerous local or private stations in Serbia and Vojvodina) (1997)

Televisions: 2.75 million (1997)

Internet Service Providers (ISPs): 9 (2000)

Internet users: 80,000 (2000)

Transportation

Railways:
total: 4,095 km
standard gauge: 4,095 km 1.435-m gauge (1,377 km partially electrified since 1992)
note: during to the 1999 Kosovo conflict, the Serbian rail system suffered significant damage due to bridge destruction; many rail bridges have been rebuilt, but the bridge over the Danube at Novi Sad was still down in early 2000; however, a by-pass is available; Montenegrin rail lines remain intact

Yugoslavia (continued)

Highways:
total: 48,603 km
paved: 28,822 km (including 560 km of expressways)
unpaved: 19,781 km (1998 est.)
note: because of the 1999 Kosovo conflict, many road bridges were destroyed; since the end of the conflict in June 1999, there has been an intensive program to either rebuild bridges or build by-pass routes
Waterways: 587 km
note: The Danube River, which connects Europe with the Black Sea, runs through Serbia; since early 2000, a pontoon bridge, replacing a destroyed conventional bridge, has obstructed river traffic at Novi Sad; the obstruction can be bypassed by a canal system but inadequate lock size limits the size of vessels which may pass (2001)
Pipelines: crude oil 415 km; petroleum products 130 km; natural gas 2,110 km
Ports and harbors: Bar, Belgrade, Kotor, Novi Sad, Pancevo, Tivat, Zelenika
Merchant marine:
total: 1 ship (1,000 GRT or over) totaling 2,437 GRT/ 400 DWT
ships by type: short-sea passenger 1 (2000 est.)
Airports: 47 (2000 est.)
Airports - with paved runways:
total: 19
over 3,047 m: 2
2,438 to 3,047 m: 5
1,524 to 2,437 m: 5
914 to 1,523 m: 3
under 914 m: 4 (2000 est.)
Airports - with unpaved runways:
total: 28
1,524 to 2,437 m: 2
914 to 1,523 m: 12
under 914 m: 14 (2000 est.)
Heliports: 2 (2000 est.)

Military

Military branches: Army (including ground forces with border troops, naval forces, air and air defense forces)
Military manpower - military age: 19 years of age
Military manpower - availability:
males ages 15-49: 2,600,362 (2001 est.)
Military manpower - fit for military service:
males age 15-49: 2,088,595 (2001 est.)
Military manpower - reaching military age annually:
males: 82,542 (2001 est.)
Military expenditures - dollar figure: $760 million (FY00)
Military expenditures - percent of GDP: NA%

Transnational Issues

Disputes - international: Albanian majority in Kosovo seeks independence from Yugoslavia; Croatia and Yugoslavia are negotiating the status of the strategically important Prevlaka Peninsula, which is currently under a UN military observer mission (UNMOP); the February 2001 agreement with the Former Yugoslav Republic of Macedonia settled alignment of boundary, stipulating implementation within two years
Illicit drugs: transshipment point for Southwest Asian heroin moving to Western Europe on the Balkan route

Zambia

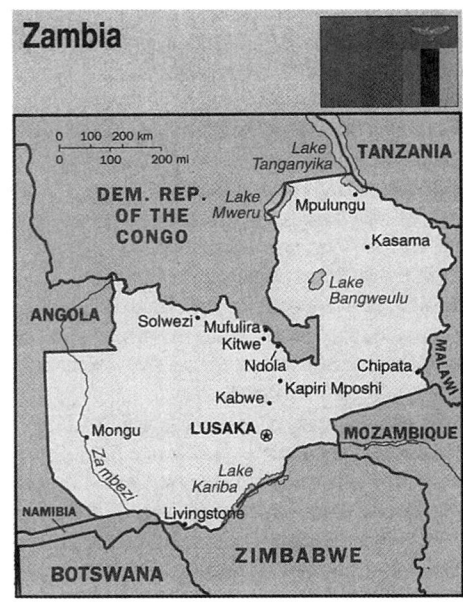

Introduction

Background: The territory of Northern Rhodesia was administered by the South Africa Company from 1891 until takeover by the UK in 1923. During the 1920s and 1930s, advances in mining spurred development and immigration. The name was changed to Zambia upon independence in 1964. In the 1980s and 1990s, declining copper prices and a prolonged drought hurt the economy. Elections in 1991 brought an end to one-party rule, but the subsequent vote in 1996 saw blatant harassment of opposition parties.

Geography

Location: Southern Africa, east of Angola
Geographic coordinates: 15 00 S, 30 00 E
Map references: Africa
Area:
total: 752,614 sq km
land: 740,724 sq km
water: 11,890 sq km
Area - comparative: slightly larger than Texas
Land boundaries:
total: 5,664 km
border countries: Angola 1,110 km, Democratic Republic of the Congo 1,930 km, Malawi 837 km, Mozambique 419 km, Namibia 233 km, Tanzania 338 km, Zimbabwe 797 km
Coastline: 0 km (landlocked)
Maritime claims: none (landlocked)
Climate: tropical; modified by altitude; rainy season (October to April)
Terrain: mostly high plateau with some hills and mountains
Elevation extremes:
lowest point: Zambezi river 329 m
highest point: unnamed location in Mafinga Hills 2,301 m
Natural resources: copper, cobalt, zinc, lead, coal, emeralds, gold, silver, uranium, hydropower

Zambia (continued)

Land use:
arable land: 7%
permanent crops: 0%
permanent pastures: 40%
forests and woodland: 39%
other: 14% (1993 est.)
Irrigated land: 460 sq km (1993 est.)
Natural hazards: tropical storms (November to April)
Environment - current issues: air pollution and resulting acid rain in the mineral extraction and refining region; chemical runoff into watersheds; poaching seriously threatens rhinoceros, elephant, antelope, and large cat populations; deforestation; soil erosion; desertification; lack of adequate water treatment presents human health risks
Environment - international agreements:
party to: Biodiversity, Climate Change, Desertification, Endangered Species, Hazardous Wastes, Law of the Sea, Marine Dumping, Nuclear Test Ban, Ozone Layer Protection, Ship Pollution, Wetlands
signed, but not ratified: Climate Change-Kyoto Protocol
Geography - note: landlocked

People

Population: 9,770,199
note: estimates for this country explicitly take into account the effects of excess mortality due to AIDS; this can result in lower life expectancy, higher infant mortality and death rates, lower population and growth rates, and changes in the distribution of population by age and sex than would otherwise be expected (July 2001 est.)
Age structure:
0-14 years: 47.36% (male 2,324,128; female 2,303,349)
15-64 years: 50.14% (male 2,433,250; female 2,465,747)
65 years and over: 2.5% (male 105,694; female 138,031) (2001 est.)
Population growth rate: 1.93% (2001 est.)
Birth rate: 41.46 births/1,000 population (2001 est.)
Death rate: 21.97 deaths/1,000 population (2001 est.)
Net migration rate: -0.16 migrant(s)/1,000 population (2001 est.)
Sex ratio:
at birth: 1.03 male(s)/female
under 15 years: 1.01 male(s)/female
15-64 years: 0.99 male(s)/female
65 years and over: 0.77 male(s)/female
total population: 0.99 male(s)/female (2001 est.)
Infant mortality rate: 90.89 deaths/1,000 live births (2001 est.)
Life expectancy at birth:
total population: 37.29 years
male: 37.06 years
female: 37.53 years (2001 est.)
Total fertility rate: 5.53 children born/woman (2001 est.)
HIV/AIDS - adult prevalence rate: 19.95% (1999 est.)
HIV/AIDS - people living with HIV/AIDS: 870,000 (1999 est.)
HIV/AIDS - deaths: 99,000 (1999 est.)
Nationality:
noun: Zambian(s)
adjective: Zambian
Ethnic groups: African 98.7%, European 1.1%, other 0.2%
Religions: Christian 50%-75%, Muslim and Hindu 24%-49%, indigenous beliefs 1%
Languages: English (official), major vernaculars - Bemba, Kaonda, Lozi, Lunda, Luvale, Nyanja, Tonga, and about 70 other indigenous languages
Literacy:
definition: age 15 and over can read and write English
total population: 78.2%
male: 85.6%
female: 71.3% (1995 est.)

Government

Country name:
conventional long form: Republic of Zambia
conventional short form: Zambia
former: Northern Rhodesia
Government type: republic
Capital: Lusaka
Administrative divisions: 9 provinces; Central, Copperbelt, Eastern, Luapula, Lusaka, Northern, North-Western, Southern, Western
Independence: 24 October 1964 (from UK)
National holiday: Independence Day, 24 October (1964)
Constitution: 2 August 1991
Legal system: based on English common law and customary law; judicial review of legislative acts in an ad hoc constitutional council; has not accepted compulsory ICJ jurisdiction
Suffrage: 18 years of age; universal
Executive branch:
chief of state: President Frederick CHILUBA (since 2 November 1991); Vice President Enoch KAVINDELE (since 4 May 2001); note - the president is both the chief of state and head of government
head of government: President Frederick CHILUBA (since 2 November 1991); Vice President Enoch KAVINDELE (since 4 May 2001); note - the president is both the chief of state and head of government
cabinet: Cabinet appointed by the president from among the members of the National Assembly
elections: president elected by popular vote for a five-year term; election last held 18 November 1996 (next to be held NA October 2001); vice president appointed by the president
election results: Frederick CHILUBA reelected president; percent of vote - Frederick CHILUBA 72.5%, Dean MUNGO'MBA 12.6%, Humphrey MULEMBA 7%, Akashambatwa LEWANIKA 4.7%, Chama CHAKOMBOKA 3.2%
Legislative branch: unicameral National Assembly (150 seats; members are elected by popular vote to serve five-year terms)
elections: last held 18 November 1996 (next to be held NA December 2001)
election results: percent of vote by party - NA%; seats by party - MMD 131, NP 5, Zadeco 2, AZ 2, independents 10
Judicial branch: Supreme Court (the final court of appeal; justices are appointed by the president); High Court (has unlimited jurisdiction to hear civil and criminal cases)
Political parties and leaders: Agenda for Zambia or AZ [Akashambatwa LEWANIKA]; Labor Party or LP [Chibiza MFUNI]; Liberal Progressive Front or LPF [Roger CHONGWE, president]; Movement for Democratic Process or MDP [Chama CHAKOMBOKA]; Movement for Multiparty Democracy or MMD [Frederick CHILUBA]; National Party or NP [Daniel LISULO]; Republican Party or RP [Ben MWILA]; Social Democratic Party or SDP [Gwendoline Konie]; United National Independence Party or UNIP [Tilyenji KAUNDA]; United Party for National Development or UPND [Anderson MAZOKA]; Zambia Democratic Congress or Zadeco [Eden JERRY, acting head]
Political pressure groups and leaders: NA
International organization participation: ACP, AfDB, C, CCC, ECA, FAO, G-19, G-77, IAEA, IBRD, ICAO, ICFTU, ICRM, IDA, IFAD, IFC, IFRCS, ILO, IMF, Intelsat, Interpol, IOC, IOM, ITU, MONUC, NAM, OAU, OPCW, PCA, SADC, UN, UNAMSIL, UNCTAD, UNESCO, UNIDO, UNMEE, UNMIK, UNTAET, UPU, WHO, WIPO, WMO, WToO, WTrO
Diplomatic representation in the US:
chief of mission: Ambassador Atan SHANSONGA
chancery: 2419 Massachusetts Avenue NW, Washington, DC 20008
telephone: [1] (202) 265-9717 through 9719
FAX: [1] (202) 332-0826
Diplomatic representation from the US:
chief of mission: Ambassador David B. DUNN
embassy: corner of Independence and United Nations Avenues
mailing address: P. O. Box 31617, Lusaka
telephone: [260] (1) 250-955
FAX: [260] (1) 252-225
Flag description: green with a panel of three vertical bands of red (hoist side), black, and orange below a soaring orange eagle, on the outer edge of the flag

Economy

Economy - overview: Despite progress in privatization and budgetary reform, Zambia's economy has a long way to go. Privatization of government-owned copper mines relieved the government from covering mammoth losses generated by the industry and greatly improved the chances for copper mining to return to profitability and spur economic growth. In late 2000, Zambia was determined to be eligible for debt relief under the Heavily Indebted Poor Countries (HIPC) initiative. Inflation and unemployment rates remain high, but the GDP growth rate should rise in 2001.
GDP: purchasing power parity - $8.5 billion (2000 est.)

Zambia (continued)

GDP - real growth rate: 4% (2000 est.)
GDP - per capita: purchasing power parity - $880 (2000 est.)
GDP - composition by sector:
agriculture: 18%
industry: 27%
services: 55% (1999 est.)
Population below poverty line: 86% (1993 est.)
Household income or consumption by percentage share:
lowest 10%: 1.6%
highest 10%: 39.2% (1995)
Inflation rate (consumer prices): 27.3% (2000 est.)
Labor force: 3.4 million
Labor force - by occupation: agriculture 85%, industry 6%, services 9%
Unemployment rate: 50% (2000 est.)
Budget:
revenues: $900 million
expenditures: $1 billion, including capital expenditures of NA million (1999 est.)
Industries: copper mining and processing, construction, foodstuffs, beverages, chemicals, textiles, fertilizer
Industrial production growth rate: 6.1% (2000 est.)
Electricity - production: 7.642 billion kWh (1999)
Electricity - production by source:
fossil fuel: 0.55%
hydro: 99.45%
nuclear: 0%
other: 0% (1999)
Electricity - consumption: 5.926 billion kWh (1999)
Electricity - exports: 1.6 billion kWh (1999)
Electricity - imports: 419 million kWh (1999)
Agriculture - products: corn, sorghum, rice, peanuts, sunflower seed, vegetables, flowers, tobacco, cotton, sugarcane, cassava (tapioca); cattle, goats, pigs, poultry, milk, eggs, hides; coffee
Exports: $928 million (f.o.b., 2000 est.)
Exports - commodities: copper, cobalt, electricity, tobacco
Exports - partners: Japan, Saudi Arabia, India, Thailand, South Africa, US, Malaysia (1997)
Imports: $1.05 billion (f.o.b., 2000 est.)
Imports - commodities: machinery, transportation equipment, fuels, petroleum products, electricity, fertilizer; foodstuffs, clothing
Imports - partners: South Africa 48%, Saudi Arabia, UK, Zimbabwe (1997)
Debt - external: $6.5 billion (2000)
Economic aid - recipient: $1.99 billion (1995)
Currency: Zambian kwacha (ZMK)
Currency code: ZMK
Exchange rates: Zambian kwacha per US dollar - 4,024.53 (January 2001), 3,110.84 (2000), 2,388.02 (1999), 1,862.07 (1998), 1,314.50 (1997), 1,207.90 (1996)
Fiscal year: calendar year

Communications

Telephones - main lines in use: 77,935 (in addition there are about 40,000 fixed telephones in wireless local loop connections) (1997)
Telephones - mobile cellular: 6,000 (1998)
Telephone system:
general assessment: facilities are among the best in Sub-Saharan Africa
domestic: high-capacity microwave radio relay connects most larger towns and cities; several cellular telephone services in operation; Internet service is widely available; very small aperture terminal (VSAT) networks are operated by private firms
international: satellite earth stations - 2 Intelsat (1 Indian Ocean and 1 Atlantic Ocean)
Radio broadcast stations: AM 19, FM 5, shortwave 4 (1998)
Radios: 1.03 million (1997)
Television broadcast stations: 9 (1997)
Televisions: 277,000 (1997)
Internet country code: .zm
Internet Service Providers (ISPs): 3 (2000)
Internet users: 15,000 (2000)

Transportation

Railways:
total: 2,164 km (1995)
narrow gauge: 2,164 km 1.067-m gauge (13 km double track)
note: the total includes 891 km of the Tanzania-Zambia Railway Authority (TAZARA), which operates 1,860 km of 1.067-m narrow gauge track between Dar es Salaam and Kapiri Mposhi where it connects to the Zambia Railways system; TAZARA is not a part of the Zambia Railways system; Zambia Railways assets are scheduled for concessioning in 2001
Highways:
total: 66,781 km
paved: NA km
unpaved: NA km (1997 est.)
Waterways: 2,250 km
note: includes Lake Tanganyika and the Zambezi and Luapula rivers
Pipelines: crude oil 1,724 km
Ports and harbors: Mpulungu
Airports: 112 (2000 est.)
Airports - with paved runways:
total: 13
over 3,047 m: 1
2,438 to 3,047 m: 3
1,524 to 2,437 m: 5
914 to 1,523 m: 3
under 914 m: 1 (2000 est.)
Airports - with unpaved runways:
total: 99
2,438 to 3,047 m: 1
1,524 to 2,437 m: 2
914 to 1,523 m: 65
under 914 m: 31 (2000 est.)

Military

Military branches: Army, Air Force, National Service, police
Military manpower - availability:
males age 15-49: 2,246,640 (2001 est.)
Military manpower - fit for military service:
males age 15-49: 1,193,047 (2001 est.)
Military expenditures - dollar figure: $76 million (FY97)
Military expenditures - percent of GDP: 1.8% (FY97)

Transnational Issues

Illicit drugs: transshipment point for moderate amounts of methaqualone, small amounts of heroin, and cocaine bound for Southern Africa and possibly Europe; regional money-laundering center

Zimbabwe

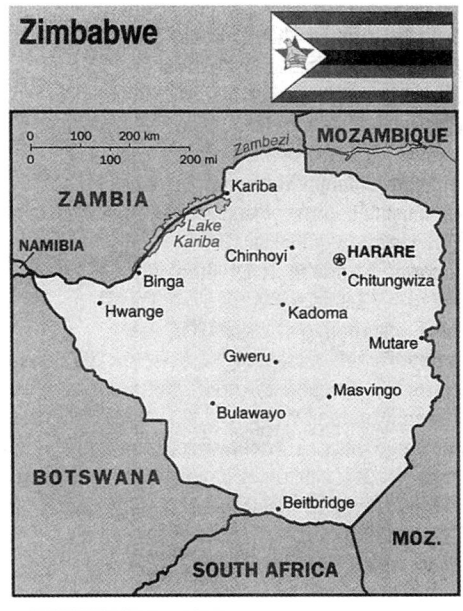

Introduction

Background: The UK annexed Southern Rhodesia from the South Africa Company in 1923. A 1961 constitution was formulated to keep whites in power. In 1965 the government unilaterally declared its independence, but the UK did not recognize the act and demanded voting rights for the black African majority in the country (then called Rhodesia). UN sanctions and a guerrilla uprising finally led to free elections in 1979 and independence (as Zimbabwe) in 1980. Robert MUGABE, the nation's first prime minister, has been the country's only ruler (as president since 1987) and has dominated the country's political system since independence.

Geography

Location: Southern Africa, between South Africa and Zambia
Geographic coordinates: 20 00 S, 30 00 E
Map references: Africa
Area:
total: 390,580 sq km
land: 386,670 sq km
water: 3,910 sq km
Area - comparative: slightly larger than Montana
Land boundaries:
total: 3,066 km
border countries: Botswana 813 km, Mozambique 1,231 km, South Africa 225 km, Zambia 797 km
Coastline: 0 km (landlocked)
Maritime claims: none (landlocked)
Climate: tropical; moderated by altitude; rainy season (November to March)
Terrain: mostly high plateau with higher central plateau (high veld); mountains in east
Elevation extremes:
lowest point: junction of the Runde and Save rivers 162 m
highest point: Inyangani 2,592 m
Natural resources: coal, chromium ore, asbestos, gold, nickel, copper, iron ore, vanadium, lithium, tin, platinum group metals
Land use:
arable land: 7%
permanent crops: 0%
permanent pastures: 13%
forests and woodland: 23%
other: 57% (1993 est.)
Irrigated land: 1,930 sq km (1993 est.)
Natural hazards: recurring droughts; floods and severe storms are rare
Environment - current issues: deforestation; soil erosion; land degradation; air and water pollution; the black rhinoceros herd - once the largest concentration of the species in the world - has been significantly reduced by poaching
Environment - international agreements:
party to: Biodiversity, Climate Change, Desertification, Endangered Species, Law of the Sea, Marine Dumping, Ozone Layer Protection, Ship Pollution
signed, but not ratified: none of the selected agreements
Geography - note: landlocked

People

Population: 11,365,366
note: estimates for this country explicitly take into account the effects of excess mortality due to AIDS; this can result in lower life expectancy, higher infant mortality and death rates, lower population and growth rates, and changes in the distribution of population by age and sex than would otherwise be expected (July 2001 est.)
Age structure:
0-14 years: 38.68% (male 2,223,332; female 2,172,479)
15-64 years: 57.69% (male 3,319,982; female 3,236,286)
65 years and over: 3.63% (male 208,785; female 204,502) (2001 est.)
Population growth rate: 0.15% (2001 est.)
Birth rate: 24.68 births/1,000 population (2001 est.)
Death rate: 23.22 deaths/1,000 population (2001 est.)
Net migration rate: 0 migrant(s)/1,000 population (2001 est.)
note: there is a small but steady flow of Zimbabweans into South Africa in search of better paid employment
Sex ratio:
at birth: 1.03 male(s)/female
under 15 years: 1.02 male(s)/female
15-64 years: 1.03 male(s)/female
65 years and over: 1.02 male(s)/female
total population: 1.02 male(s)/female (2001 est.)
Infant mortality rate: 62.61 deaths/1,000 live births (2001 est.)
Life expectancy at birth:
total population: 37.13 years
male: 38.51 years
female: 35.7 years (2001 est.)
Total fertility rate: 3.28 children born/woman (2001 est.)
HIV/AIDS - adult prevalence rate: 25.06% (1999 est.)
HIV/AIDS - people living with HIV/AIDS: 1.5 million (1999 est.)
HIV/AIDS - deaths: 160,000 (1999 est.)
Nationality:
noun: Zimbabwean(s)
adjective: Zimbabwean
Ethnic groups: African 98% (Shona 71%, Ndebele 16%, other 11%), mixed and Asian 1%, white less than 1%
Religions: syncretic (part Christian, part indigenous beliefs) 50%, Christian 25%, indigenous beliefs 24%, Muslim and other 1%
Languages: English (official), Shona, Sindebele (the language of the Ndebele, sometimes called Ndebele), numerous but minor tribal dialects
Literacy:
definition: age 15 and over can read and write English
total population: 85%
male: 90%
female: 80% (1995 est.)

Government

Country name:
conventional long form: Republic of Zimbabwe
conventional short form: Zimbabwe
former: Southern Rhodesia, Rhodesia
Government type: parliamentary democracy
Capital: Harare
Administrative divisions: 8 provinces and 2 cities* with provincial status; Bulawayo*, Harare*, Manicaland, Mashonaland Central, Mashonaland East, Mashonaland West, Masvingo, Matabeleland North, Matabeleland South, Midlands
Independence: 18 April 1980 (from UK)
National holiday: Independence Day, 18 April (1980)
Constitution: 21 December 1979
Legal system: mixture of Roman-Dutch and English common law
Suffrage: 18 years of age; universal
Executive branch:
chief of state: Executive President Robert Gabriel MUGABE (since 31 December 1987); Co-Vice Presidents Simon Vengai MUZENDA (since 31 December 1987) and Joseph MSIKA (since 23 December 1999); note - the president is both the chief of state and head of government
head of government: Executive President Robert Gabriel MUGABE (since 31 December 1987); Co-Vice Presidents Simon Vengai MUZENDA (since 31 December 1987) and Joseph MSIKA (since 23 December 1999); note - the president is both the chief of state and head of government
cabinet: Cabinet appointed by the president; responsible to the House of Assembly

Zimbabwe (continued)

elections: presidential candidates nominated with a nomination paper signed by at least 10 registered voters (at least one from each province) and elected by popular vote; election last held 16-17 March 1996 (next to be held NA March 2002); co-vice presidents appointed by the president

election results: Robert Gabriel MUGABE reelected president; percent of electoral college vote - Robert Gabriel MUGABE 92.7%, Abel MUZOREWA 4.8%; Ndabaningi SITHOLE 2.4%

Legislative branch: unicameral parliament, called House of Assembly (150 seats - 120 elected by popular vote for six-year terms, 12 nominated by the president, 10 occupied by traditional chiefs chosen by their peers, and 8 occupied by provincial governors)

elections: last held 24-25 June 2000 (next to be held NA 2006)

election results: percent of vote by party - ZANU-PF 47.2%, MDC 45.6%, ZANU-Ndonga 0.7%, United Parties 0.7%; seats by party - ZANU-PF 63, MDC 56, ZANU-Ndonga 1

Judicial branch: Supreme Court; High Court

Political parties and leaders: Movement for Democratic Change or MDC [Morgan TSVANGIRAI]; Popular Democratic Front or PDF [Austin CHAKAODZA]; United Parties [Abel MUZOREWA]; Zimbabwe African National Union-Ndonga or ZANU-Ndonga [Ndabaningi SITHOLE]; Zimbabwe African National Union-Patriotic Front or ZANU-PF [Robert MUGABE]; Zimbabwe Unity Movement or ZUM [Edgar TEKERE]

Political pressure groups and leaders: National Constitutional Assembly or NCA

International organization participation: ACP, AfDB, C, CCC, ECA, FAO, G-15, G-77, IAEA, IBRD, ICAO, ICFTU, ICRM, IDA, IFAD, IFC, IFRCS, ILO, IMF, Intelsat, Interpol, IOC, IOM (observer), ISO, ITU, NAM, OAU, OPCW, PCA, SADC, UN, UNCTAD, UNESCO, UNIDO, UNMIK, UNTAET, UPU, WCL, WFTU, WHO, WIPO, WMO, WToO, WTrO

Diplomatic representation in the US:
chief of mission: Ambassador Simbi Veke MUBAKO
chancery: 1608 New Hampshire Avenue NW, Washington, DC 20009
telephone: [1] (202) 332-7100
FAX: [1] (202) 483-9326

Diplomatic representation from the US:
chief of mission: Ambassador (vacant); Charge d'Affaires Earl M. IRVING
embassy: 172 Herbert Chitepo Avenue, Harare
mailing address: P. O. Box 3340, Harare
telephone: [263] (4) 250-593
FAX: [263] (4) 796487

Flag description: seven equal horizontal bands of green, yellow, red, black, red, yellow, and green with a white isosceles triangle edged in black with its base on the hoist side; a yellow Zimbabwe bird is superimposed on a red five-pointed star in the center of the triangle

Economy

Economy - overview: The government of Zimbabwe faces a wide variety of difficult economic problems as it struggles to consolidate earlier moves to develop a market-oriented economy. Its involvement in the war in the Democratic Republic of the Congo, for example, has already drained hundreds of millions of dollars from the economy. Badly needed support from the IMF suffers delays in part because of the country's failure to meet budgetary goals. Inflation rose from an annual rate of 32% in 1998 to 59% in 1999 and 60% in 2000. The economy is being steadily weakened by excessive government deficits and AIDS; Zimbabwe has the highest rate of infection in the world. Per capita GDP, which is twice the average of the poorer sub-Saharan nations, will increase little if any in the near-term, and Zimbabwe will suffer continued frustrations in developing its agricultural and mineral resources.

GDP: purchasing power parity - $28.2 billion (2000 est.)

GDP - real growth rate: -6.1% (2000 est.)

GDP - per capita: purchasing power parity - $2,500 (2000 est.)

GDP - composition by sector:
agriculture: 28%
industry: 32%
services: 40% (1997 est.)

Population below poverty line: 60% (1999 est.)

Household income or consumption by percentage share:
lowest 10%: 1.8%
highest 10%: 46.9% (1990)

Inflation rate (consumer prices): 60% (2000 est.)

Labor force: 5.5 million (2000 est.)

Labor force - by occupation: agriculture 66%, services 24%, industry 10% (1996 est.)

Unemployment rate: 50% (2000 est.)

Budget:
revenues: $2.5 billion
expenditures: $2.9 billion, including capital expenditures of $279 million (FY96/97 est.)

Industries: mining (coal, gold, copper, nickel, tin, clay, numerous metallic and nonmetallic ores), steel, wood products, cement, chemicals, fertilizer, clothing and footwear, foodstuffs, beverages

Industrial production growth rate: NA%

Electricity - production: 5.78 billion kWh (1999)

Electricity - production by source:
fossil fuel: 69.98%
hydro: 30.02%
nuclear: 0%
other: 0% (1999)

Electricity - consumption: 6.939 billion kWh (1999)

Electricity - exports: 0 kWh (1999)

Electricity - imports: 1.564 billion kWh (1999)

Agriculture - products: corn, cotton, tobacco, wheat, coffee, sugarcane, peanuts; cattle, sheep, goats, pigs

Exports: $1.8 billion (f.o.b., 2000 est.)

Exports - commodities: tobacco 29%, gold 7%, ferroalloys 7%, cotton 5% (1999 est.)

Exports - partners: South Africa 10%, UK 9%, Malawi 8%, Botswana 8%, Japan 7%, (1999 est.)

Imports: $1.3 billion (f.o.b., 2000 est.)

Imports - commodities: machinery and transport equipment 35%, other manufactures 18%, chemicals 17%, fuels 14% (1999 est.)

Imports - partners: South Africa 46%, UK 6%, China 4%, Germany 4%, US 3% (1999 est.)

Debt - external: $4.1 billion (2000 est.)

Economic aid - recipient: $200 million (2000 est.)

Currency: Zimbabwean dollar (ZWD)

Currency code: ZWD

Exchange rates: Zimbabwean dollars per US dollar - 54.9451 (January 2001), 43.2900 (2000), 38.3142 (1999), 21.4133 (1998), 11.8906 (1997), 9.9206 (1996)

Fiscal year: 1 July - 30 June

Communications

Telephones - main lines in use: 212,000 (in addition there are about 20,000 fixed telephones in wireless local loop connections) (1997)

Telephones - mobile cellular: 70,000 (1999)

Telephone system:
general assessment: system was once one of the best in Africa, but now suffers from poor maintenance; more than 100,000 outstanding requests for connection despite an equally large number of installed but unused main lines
domestic: consists of microwave radio relay links, open-wire lines, radiotelephone communication stations, fixed wireless local loop installations, and a substantial mobile cellular network; Internet connection is available in Harare and planned for all major towns and for some of the smaller ones
international: satellite earth stations - 2 Intelsat; two international digital gateway exchanges (in Harare and Gweru)

Radio broadcast stations: AM 7, FM 20 (plus 17 repeater stations), shortwave 1 (1998)

Radios: 1.14 million (1997)

Television broadcast stations: 16 (1997)

Televisions: 370,000 (1997)

Internet country code: .zw

Internet Service Providers (ISPs): 6 (2000)

Internet users: 30,000 (1999)

Transportation

Railways:
total: 2,759 km (1995)
narrow gauge: 2,759 km 1.067-m gauge (313 km electrified; 42 km double track) (1995 est.)

Highways:
total: 18,338 km
paved: 8,692 km
unpaved: 9,646 km (1996 est.)

Zimbabwe (continued)

Waterways: the Mazoe and Zambezi rivers are used for transporting chrome ore from Harare to Mozambique
Pipelines: petroleum products 212 km
Ports and harbors: Binga, Kariba
Airports: 455 (2000 est.)
Airports - with paved runways:
total: 18
over 3,047 m: 3
2,438 to 3,047 m: 2
1,524 to 2,437 m: 4
914 to 1,523 m: 9 (2000 est.)
Airports - with unpaved runways:
total: 437
1,524 to 2,437 m: 4
914 to 1,523 m: 209
under 914 m: 224 (2000 est.)

Military

Military branches: Zimbabwe National Army, Air Force of Zimbabwe, Zimbabwe Republic Police (includes Police Support Unit, Paramilitary Police)
Military manpower - availability:
males age 15-49: 2,996,631 (2001 est.)
Military manpower - fit for military service:
males age 15-49: 1,860,167 (2001 est.)
Military expenditures - dollar figure: $127 million (FY99/00)
Military expenditures - percent of GDP: 3.1% (FY99/00)

Transnational Issues

Illicit drugs: significant transit point for African cannabis and South Asian heroin, mandrax, and methamphetamines destined for the South African and European markets

Taiwan

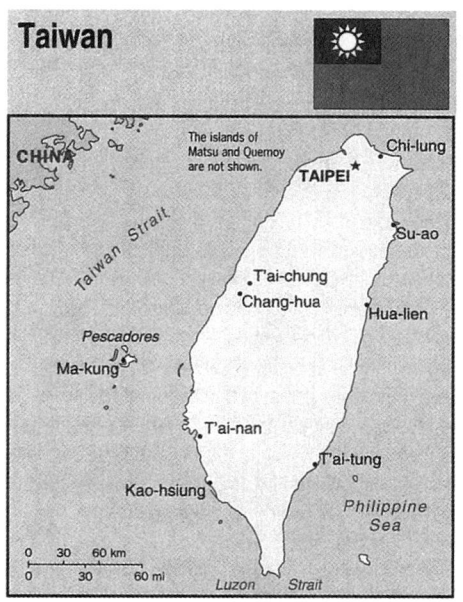

Introduction

Background: In 1895, military defeat forced China to cede Taiwan to Japan, however it reverted to Chinese control after World War II. Following the communist victory on the mainland in 1949, 2 million Nationalists fled to Taiwan and established a government using the 1947 constitution drawn up for all of China. Over the next five decades, the ruling authorities gradually democratized and incorporated the native population within its governing structure. Throughout this period, the island has prospered to become one of East Asia's economic "Tigers." The dominant political issue continues to be the relationship between Taiwan and China and the question of eventual reunification.

Geography

Location: Eastern Asia, islands bordering the East China Sea, Philippine Sea, South China Sea, and Taiwan Strait, north of the Philippines, off the southeastern coast of China
Geographic coordinates: 23 30 N, 121 00 E
Map references: Southeast Asia
Area:
total: 35,980 sq km
land: 32,260 sq km
water: 3,720 sq km
note: includes the Pescadores, Matsu, and Quemoy
Area - comparative: slightly smaller than Maryland and Delaware combined
Land boundaries: 0 km
Coastline: 1,566.3 km
Maritime claims:
exclusive economic zone: 200 NM
territorial sea: 12 NM
Climate: tropical; marine; rainy season during southwest monsoon (June to August); cloudiness is persistent and extensive all year
Terrain: eastern two-thirds mostly rugged mountains; flat to gently rolling plains in west
Elevation extremes:
lowest point: South China Sea 0 m
highest point: Yu Shan 3,997 m
Natural resources: small deposits of coal, natural gas, limestone, marble, and asbestos
Land use:
arable land: 24%
permanent crops: 1%
permanent pastures: 5%
forests and woodland: 55%
other: 15%
Irrigated land: NA sq km
Natural hazards: earthquakes and typhoons
Environment - current issues: air pollution; water pollution from industrial emissions, raw sewage; contamination of drinking water supplies; trade in endangered species; low-level radioactive waste disposal
Environment - international agreements:
party to: none of the selected agreements
signed, but not ratified: none of the selected agreements

People

Population: 22,370,461 (July 2001 est.)
Age structure:
0-14 years: 21.22% (male 2,470,270; female 2,276,108)
15-64 years: 69.97% (male 7,944,451; female 7,707,250)
65 years and over: 8.81% (male 1,034,230; female 938,152) (2001 est.)
Population growth rate: 0.8% (2001 est.)
Birth rate: 14.31 births/1,000 population (2001 est.)
Death rate: 6 deaths/1,000 population (2001 est.)
Net migration rate: -0.34 migrant(s)/1,000 population (2001 est.)
Sex ratio:
at birth: 1.09 male(s)/female
under 15 years: 1.09 male(s)/female
15-64 years: 1.03 male(s)/female
65 years and over: 1.1 male(s)/female
total population: 1.05 male(s)/female (2001 est.)
Infant mortality rate: 6.93 deaths/1,000 live births (2001 est.)
Life expectancy at birth:
total population: 76.54 years
male: 73.81 years
female: 79.51 years (2001 est.)
Total fertility rate: 1.76 children born/woman (2001 est.)
HIV/AIDS - people living with HIV/AIDS: NA
HIV/AIDS - deaths: NA
Nationality:
noun: Chinese (singular and plural)
adjective: Chinese
Ethnic groups: Taiwanese (including Hakka) 84%, mainland Chinese 14%, aborigine 2%
Religions: mixture of Buddhist, Confucian, and Taoist 93%, Christian 4.5%, other 2.5%
Languages: Mandarin Chinese (official), Taiwanese (Min), Hakka dialects

Taiwan (continued)

Literacy:
definition: age 15 and over can read and write
total population: 86% (1980 est.); note - literacy for the total population has reportedly increased to 94% (1998 est.)
male: 93% (1980 est.)
female: 79% (1980 est.)

Government

Country name:
conventional long form: none
conventional short form: Taiwan
local long form: none
local short form: T'ai-wan
former: Formosa
Government type: multiparty democratic regime headed by popularly elected president
Capital: Taipei
Administrative divisions: since in the past the authorities claimed to be the government of all China, the central administrative divisions include the provinces of Fu-chien (some 20 offshore islands of Fujian Province including Quemoy and Matsu) and Taiwan (the island of Taiwan and the Pescadores islands); note - the more commonly referenced administrative divisions are those of Taiwan Province - 16 counties (hsien, singular and plural), 5 municipalities* (shih, singular and plural), and 2 special municipalities** (chuan-shih, singular and plural); Chang-hua, Chia-i, Chia-i*, Chi-lung*, Hsin-chu, Hsin-chu*, Hua-lien, I-lan, Kao-hsiung, Kao-hsiung**, Miao-li, Nan-t'ou, P'eng-hu, P'ing-tung, T'ai-chung, T'ai-chung*, T'ai-nan, T'ai-nan*, T'ai-pei, T'ai-pei**, T'ai-tung, T'ao-yuan, and Yun-lin; the provincial capital is at Chung-hsing-hsin-ts'un
note: Taiwan uses the Wade-Giles system for romanization
National holiday: Republic Day (Anniversary of the Chinese Revolution), 10 October (1911)
Constitution: 1 January 1947, amended in 1992, 1994, 1997, and 1999
Legal system: based on civil law system; accepts compulsory ICJ jurisdiction, with reservations
Suffrage: 20 years of age; universal
Executive branch:
chief of state: President CHEN Shui-bien (20 May 2000) and Vice President Annette LU (since 20 May 2000)
head of government: Premier (President of the Executive Yuan) CHANG Chun-hsiung (since NA October 2000) and Vice Premier (Vice President of the Executive Yuan) LAI In-jaw (since NA October 2000)
cabinet: Executive Yuan appointed by the president
elections: president and vice president elected on the same ticket by popular vote for four-year terms; election last held 18 March 2000 (next to be held NA March 2004); premier appointed by the president; vice premiers appointed by the president on the recommendation of the premier
election results: CHEN Shui-bien elected president; percent of vote - CHEN Shui-bien (DPP) 39.3%, James SOONG (independent) 36.84%, LIEN Chan (KMT) 23.1%, HSU Hsin-liang (independent) 0.63%, LEE Ao (CNP) 0.13%
Legislative branch: unicameral Legislative Yuan (225 seats - 168 elected by popular vote, 41 elected on the basis of the proportion of nationwide votes received by participating political parties, eight elected from overseas Chinese constituencies on the basis of the proportion of nationwide votes received by participating political parties, eight elected by popular vote among the aboriginal populations; members serve three-year terms) and unicameral National Assembly (300 seats, note - total number of seats has been reduced from 334 to 300 since the last election; members are elected by proportional representation based on the election of the Legislative Yuan and serve four-year terms)
elections: Legislative Yuan - last held 5 December 1998 (next to be held NA December 2001); National Assembly - last held 23 March 1996 (next to be held NA June 2002)
election results: Legislative Yuan - percent of vote by party - KMT 46%, DPP 29%, CNP 7%, independents 10%, other parties 8%; seats by party - KMT 123, DPP 70, CNP 11, independents 15, other parties 6; subsequent to the election there have been some changes in the distribution of seats in the Legislative Yuan due to new party formation and party defections, the new distribution is as follows - KMT 114, DPP 66, PFP 17, NP 9, other/independent 19; National Assembly - percent of vote by party - KMT 55%, DPP 30%, CNP 14%, other 1%; seats by party - KMT 183, DPP 99, CNP 46, other 6
Judicial branch: Judicial Yuan (justices appointed by the president with the consent of the National Assembly; note - beginning in 2003, justices will be appointed by the president with the consent of the Legislative Yuan)
Political parties and leaders: Chinese New Party or CNP [HAU Lang-bin]; Democratic Progressive Party or DPP [Frank HSIEH, chairman]; Kuomintang or KMT (Nationalist Party) [LIEN Chan, chairman]; New Party or NP [LI Ching-hwa]; People First Party or PFP [James SOONG, chairman]; other minor parties
Political pressure groups and leaders: Taiwan independence movement, various business and environmental groups
note: debate on Taiwan independence has become acceptable within the mainstream of domestic politics on Taiwan; political liberalization and the increased representation of opposition parties in Taiwan's legislature have opened public debate on the island's national identity; a broad popular consensus has developed that Taiwan currently enjoys de facto independence and - whatever the ultimate outcome regarding reunification or independence - that Taiwan's people must have the deciding voice; advocates of Taiwan independence oppose the stand that the island will eventually reunify with mainland China; goals of the Taiwan independence movement include establishing a sovereign nation on Taiwan and entering the UN; other organizations supporting Taiwan independence include the World United Formosans for Independence and the Organization for Taiwan Nation Building
International organization participation: APEC, AsDB, BCIE, ICC, ICFTU, IFRCS, IOC, WCL, WTrO (observer)
Diplomatic representation in the US: none; unofficial commercial and cultural relations with the people of the US are maintained through a private instrumentality, the Taipei Economic and Cultural Representative Office (TECRO) in the US with headquarters in Taipei and field offices in Washington and 12 other US cities
Diplomatic representation from the US: none; unofficial commercial and cultural relations with the people on Taiwan are maintained through a private corporation, the American Institute in Taiwan (AIT), which has its headquarters in Rosslyn, Virginia (telephone: [1] (703) 525-8474 and FAX: [1] (703) 841-1385) and offices in Taipei at #7 Lane 134, Hsin Yi Road, Section 3, telephone [886] (2) 2709-2000, FAX [886] (2) 2702-7675, and in Kao-hsiung at #2 Chung Cheng 3rd Road, 5th Floor, telephone [886] (7) 224-0154 through 0157, FAX [886] (7) 223-8237, and the American Trade Center at Room 3208 International Trade Building, Taipei World Trade Center, 333 Keelung Road Section 1, Taipei 10548, telephone [886] (2) 2720-1550, FAX [886] (2) 2757-7162
Flag description: red with a dark blue rectangle in the upper hoist-side corner bearing a white sun with 12 triangular rays

Economy

Economy - overview: Taiwan has a dynamic capitalist economy with gradually decreasing guidance of investment and foreign trade by government authorities. In keeping with this trend, some large government-owned banks and industrial firms are being privatized. Real growth in GDP has averaged about 8% during the past three decades. Exports have grown even faster and have provided the primary impetus for industrialization. Inflation and unemployment are low; the trade surplus is substantial; and foreign reserves are the world's fourth largest. Agriculture contributes 3% to GDP, down from 35% in 1952. Traditional labor-intensive industries are steadily being moved offshore and replaced with more capital- and technology-intensive industries. Taiwan has become a major investor in China, Thailand, Indonesia, the Philippines, Malaysia, and Vietnam. The tightening of labor markets has led to an influx of foreign workers, both legal and illegal. Because of its conservative financial approach and its entrepreneurial strengths, Taiwan suffered little compared with many of its neighbors from the Asian financial crisis in 1998-99. Growth in 2001 will depend largely on conditions in Taiwan's export markets and may be about 5%.

Taiwan (continued)

GDP: purchasing power parity - $386 billion (2000 est.)
GDP - real growth rate: 6.3% (2000 est.)
GDP - per capita: purchasing power parity - $17,400 (2000 est.)
GDP - composition by sector:
agriculture: 3%
industry: 33%
services: 64% (1999 est.)
Population below poverty line: 1% (1999 est.)
Household income or consumption by percentage share:
lowest 10%: NA%
highest 10%: NA%
Inflation rate (consumer prices): 1.3% (2000 est.)
Labor force: 9.8 million (2000 est.)
Labor force - by occupation: services 55%, industry 37%, agriculture 8% (1999 est.)
Unemployment rate: 3% (2000 est.)
Budget:
revenues: $42.74 billion
expenditures: $48.8 billion, including capital expenditures of $NA (2001 est.)
Industries: electronics, petroleum refining, chemicals, textiles, iron and steel, machinery, cement, food processing
Industrial production growth rate: 8% (2000 est.)
Electricity - production: 139.676 billion kWh (1999)
Electricity - production by source:
fossil fuel: 67.26%
hydro: 6.32%
nuclear: 26.42%
other: 0% (1999)
Electricity - consumption: 129.899 billion kWh (1999)
Electricity - exports: 0 kWh (1999)
Electricity - imports: 0 kWh (1999)
Agriculture - products: rice, corn, vegetables, fruit, tea; pigs, poultry, beef, milk; fish
Exports: $148.38 billion (f.o.b., 2000)
Exports - commodities: machinery and electrical equipment 51%, metals, textiles, plastics, chemicals
Exports - partners: US 23.5%, Hong Kong 21.1%, Europe 16%, ASEAN 12.2%, Japan 11.2% (2000)
Imports: $140.01 billion (c.i.f., 2000)
Imports - commodities: machinery and electrical equipment 51%, minerals, precision instruments
Imports - partners: Japan 27.5%, US 17.9%, Europe 13.6% (2000)
Debt - external: $40 billion (2000)
Currency: new Taiwan dollar (TWD)
Currency code: TWD
Exchange rates: new Taiwan dollars per US dollar - 33.082 (yearend 2000), 31.395 (yearend 1999), 32.216 (1998), 32.052 (1997), 27.5 (1996)
Fiscal year: 1 July - 30 June (up to FY98/99); 1 July 1999 - 31 December 2000 for FY00; calendar year (after FY00)

Communications

Telephones - main lines in use: 12.49 million (September 2000)
Telephones - mobile cellular: 16 million (September 2000)
Telephone system:
general assessment: provides telecommunications service for every business and private need
domestic: thoroughly modern; completely digitalized
international: satellite earth stations - 2 Intelsat (1 Pacific Ocean and 1 Indian Ocean); submarine cables to Japan (Okinawa), Philippines, Guam, Singapore, Hong Kong, Indonesia, Australia, Middle East, and Western Europe (1999)
Radio broadcast stations: AM 218, FM 333, shortwave 50 (1999)
Radios: 16 million (1994)
Television broadcast stations: 29 (plus two repeaters) (1997)
Televisions: 8.8 million (1998)
Internet country code: .tw
Internet Service Providers (ISPs): 8 (2000)
Internet users: 6.4 million (2000)

Transportation

Railways:
total: 4,600 km (519 km electrified)
narrow gauge: 4,600 km 1.067-m
note: only 1,108 km of route length (including the electrified part) is used in common carrier service by the Taiwan Railway Administration; the remaining 3,492 km is dedicated to industrial use (1999)
Highways:
total: 34,901 km
paved: 31,271 km (including 538 km of expressways)
unpaved: 3,630 km (1998 est.)
Waterways: NA
Pipelines: petroleum products 3,400 km; natural gas 1,800 km (1999)
Ports and harbors: Chi-lung (Keelung), Hua-lien, Kao-hsiung, Su-ao, T'ai-chung
Merchant marine:
total: 167 ships (1,000 GRT or over) totaling 4,768,145 GRT/7,508,941 DWT
ships by type: bulk 45, cargo 29, combination bulk 1, container 65, petroleum tanker 17, refrigerated cargo 8, roll on/roll off 2 (2000 est.)
Airports: 39 (2000 est.)
Airports - with paved runways:
total: 35
over 3,047 m: 8
2,438 to 3,047 m: 9
1,524 to 2,437 m: 8
914 to 1,523 m: 7
under 914 m: 3 (2000 est.)
Airports - with unpaved runways:
total: 4
1,524 to 2,437 m: 1
under 914 m: 3 (2000 est.)
Heliports: 3 (2000 est.)

Military

Military branches: Army, Navy (includes Marines), Air Force, Coastal Patrol and Defense Command, Armed Forces Reserve Command, Combined Service Forces
Military manpower - military age: 19 years of age
Military manpower - availability:
males age 15-49: 6,575,689 (2001 est.)
Military manpower - fit for military service:
males age 15-49: 5,025,856 (2001 est.)
Military manpower - reaching military age annually:
males: 198,766 (2001 est.)
Military expenditures - dollar figure: $8.042 billion (FY98/99)
Military expenditures - percent of GDP: 2.8% (FY98/99)

Transnational Issues

Disputes - international: involved in complex dispute over the Spratly Islands with China, Malaysia, Philippines, Vietnam, and possibly Brunei; Paracel Islands occupied by China, but claimed by Vietnam and Taiwan; claims Japanese-administered Senkaku-shoto (Senkaku Islands/Diaoyu Tai), as does China
Illicit drugs: transit point for heroin and methamphetamine; major problem with domestic consumption of methamphetamine and heroin

Appendix A:

Abbreviations

A	ABEDA	Arab Bank for Economic Development in Africa
	ACC	Arab Cooperation Council
	ACCT	Agency for the French-Speaking Community
	ACP Group	African, Caribbean, and Pacific Group of States
	AfDB	African Development Bank
	AFESD	Arab Fund for Economic and Social Development
	Air Pollution	Convention on Long-Range Transboundary Air Pollution
	Air Pollution-Nitrogen Oxides	Protocol to the 1979 Convention on Long-Range Transboundary Air Pollution Concerning the Control of Emissions of Nitrogen Oxides or Control of Emissions of Nitrogen Oxides or Their Transboundary Fluxes
	Air Pollution-Persistent Organic Pollutants	Protocol to the 1979 Convention on Long-Range Transboundary Air Pollution on Persistent Organic Pollutants
	Air Pollution-Sulphur 85	Protocol to the 1979 Convention on Long-Range Transboundary Air Pollution on the Reduction of Sulphur Emissions or Their Transboundary Fluxes by at Least 30%
	Air Pollution-Sulphur 94	Protocol to the 1979 Convention on Long-Range Transboundary Air Pollution on Further Reduction of Sulphur Emissions
	Air Pollution-Volatile Organic Compounds	Protocol to the 1979 Convention on Long-Range Transboundary Air Pollution Concerning the Control of Emissions of Volatile Organic Compounds or Their Transboundary Fluxes
	AL	Arab League
	AMF	Arab Monetary Fund
	AMU	Arab Maghreb Union
	Antarctic-Environmental Protocol	Protocol on Environmental Protection to the Antarctic Treaty
	ANZUS	Australia-New Zealand-United States Security Treaty
	APEC	Asia-Pacific Economic Cooperation
	Arabsat	Arab Satellite Communications Organization
	ARF	ASEAN Regional Forum
	AsDB	Asian Development Bank
	ASEAN	Association of Southeast Asian Nations
	Autodin	Automatic Digital Network
B	Benelux	Benelux Economic Union
	Biodiversity	Convention on Biological Diversity
	BIS	Bank for International Settlements
	BSEC	Black Sea Economic Cooperation Zone
C	C	Commonwealth
	CACM	Central American Common Market
	CAEU	Council of Arab Economic Unity
	CAN	Andean Community of Nations
	Caricom	Caribbean Community and Common Market
	CB	citizen's band mobile radio communications
	CBSS	Council of the Baltic Sea States

Appendix A: Abbreviations *(continued)*

	CCC	Customs Cooperation Council
	CDB	Caribbean Development Bank
	CE	Council of Europe
	CEI	Central European Initiative
	CEMA	Council for Mutual Economic Assistance; also known as CMEA or Comecon
	CEMAC	Monetary and Economic Community of Central Africa
	CEPGL	Economic Community of the Great Lakes Countries
	CERN	European Organization for Nuclear Research
	c.i.f.	cost, insurance, and freight
	CIS	Commonwealth of Independent States
	CITES	see Endangered Species
	Climate Change	United Nations Framework Convention on Climate Change
	Climate Change-Kyoto Protocol	Kyoto Protocol to the United Nations Framework Convention on Climate Change
	COCOM	Coordinating Committee on Export Controls
	Comsat	Communications Satellite Corporation
	CP	Colombo Plan
	CY	calendar year
D	DC	developed country
	Desertification	United Nations Convention to Combat Desertification in Those Countries Experiencing Serious Drought and/or Desertification, Particularly in Africa
	DSN	Defense Switched Network
	DWT	deadweight ton
E	EADB	East African Development Bank
	EAPC	Euro-Atlantic Partnership Council
	EBRD	European Bank for Reconstruction and Development
	EC	European Community
	ECA	Economic Commission for Africa
	ECE	Economic Commission for Europe
	ECLAC	Economic Commission for Latin America and the Caribbean
	ECO	Economic Cooperation Organization
	ECOSOC	Economic and Social Council
	ECOWAS	Economic Community of West African States
	ECS	European Coal and Steel Community
	EEC	European Economic Community
	EFTA	European Free Trade Association
	EIB	European Investment Bank
	EMU	European Monetary Union
	Endangered Species	Convention on the International Trade in Endangered Species of Wild Flora and Fauna (CITES)
	Entente	Council of the Entente
	Environmental Modification	Convention on the Prohibition of Military or Any Other Hostile Use of Environmental Modification Techniques
	ESA	European Space Agency

Appendix A: Abbreviations *(continued)*

	ESCAP	Economic and Social Commission for Asia and the Pacific
	ESCWA	Economic and Social Commission for Western Asia
	est.	estimate
	EU	European Union
	Euratom	European Atomic Energy Community
	Eutelsat	European Telecommunications Satellite Organization
	Ex-Im	Export-Import Bank of the United States
F	FAO	Food and Agriculture Organization
	FAX	facsimile
	f.o.b.	free on board
	FLS	Front Line States
	FRG	Federal Republic of Germany (West Germany); used for information dated before 3 October 1990 or CY91
	FSU	former Soviet Union
	FY	fiscal year
	FYROM	The Former Yugoslav Republic of Macedonia
	FZ	Franc Zone
G	G-2	Group of 2
	G-3	Group of 3
	G-5	Group of 5
	G-6	Group of 6
	G-7	Group of 7
	G-8	Group of 8
	G-9	Group of 9
	G-10	Group of 10
	G-11	Group of 11
	G-15	Group of 15
	G-19	Group of 19
	G-24	Group of 24
	G-30	Group of 30
	G-33	Group of 33
	G-77	Group of 77
	GATT	General Agreement on Tariffs and Trade; now WTrO
	GCC	Gulf Cooperation Council
	GDP	gross domestic product
	GDR	German Democratic Republic (East Germany); used for information dated before 3 October 1990 or CY91
	GNP	gross national product
	GRT	gross register ton
	GWP	gross world product
H	Habitat	United Nations Center for Human Settlements
	Hazardous Wastes	Basel Convention on the Control of Transboundary Movements of Hazardous Wastes and Their Disposal
	HF	high-frequency

Appendix A: Abbreviations *(continued)*

I	IADB	Inter-American Development Bank
	IAEA	International Atomic Energy Agency
	IBEC	International Bank for Economic Cooperation
	IBRD	International Bank for Reconstruction and Development (World Bank)
	ICAO	International Civil Aviation Organization
	ICC	International Chamber of Commerce
	ICJ	International Court of Justice (World Court)
	ICRC	International Committee of the Red Cross
	ICRM	International Red Cross and Red Crescent Movement
	ICTR	International Criminal Tribunal for Rwanda
	ICTY	International Criminal Tribunal for the former Yugoslavia
	IDA	International Development Association
	IDB	Islamic Development Bank
	IEA	International Energy Agency
	IFAD	International Fund for Agricultural Development
	IFC	International Finance Corporation
	IFCTU	International Federation of Christian Trade Unions
	IFRCS	International Federation of Red Cross and Red Crescent Societies
	IGAD	Inter-Governmental Authority on Development
	IGADD	Inter-Governmental Authority on Drought and Development
	IHO	International Hydrographic Organization
	IIB	International Investment Bank
	ILO	International Labor Organization
	IMF	International Monetary Fund
	IMO	International Maritime Organization
	Inmarsat	International Mobile Satellite Organization
	InOC	Indian Ocean Commission
	INSTRAW	International Research and Training Institute for the Advancement of Women
	Intelsat	International Telecommunications Satellite Organization
	Interpol	International Criminal Police Organization
	Intersputnik	International Organization of Space Communications
	IOC	International Olympic Committee
	IOM	International Organization for Migration
	ISO	International Organization for Standardization
	ITU	International Telecommunication Union
K	kHz	kilohertz
	km	kilometer
	kW	kilowatt
	kWh	kilowatt-hour
L	LAES	Latin American Economic System
	LAIA	Latin American Integration Association
	Law of the Sea	United Nations Convention on the Law of the Sea (LOS)
	LDC	less developed country

Appendix A: Abbreviations *(continued)*

	LLDC	least developed country
	London Convention	see Marine Dumping
	LOS	see Law of the Sea
M	m	meter
	Marecs	Maritime European Communications Satellite
	Marine Dumping	Convention on the Prevention of Marine Pollution by Dumping Wastes and Other Matter
	Marine Life Conservation	Convention on Fishing and Conservation of Living Resources of the High Seas
	MARPOL	see Ship Pollution
	Medarabtel	Middle East Telecommunications Project of the International Telecommunications Union
	Mercosur	Southern Cone Common Market
	MHz	megahertz
	MINURSO	United Nations Mission for the Referendum in Western Sahara
	MONUC	United Nations Organization Mission in the Democratic Republic of the Congo
N	NA	not available
	NAM	Nonaligned Movement
	NATO	North Atlantic Treaty Organization
	NC	Nordic Council
	NEA	Nuclear Energy Agency
	NEGL	negligible
	NIB	Nordic Investment Bank
	NIC	newly industrializing country
	NIE	newly industrializing economy
	NIS	new independent states
	NM	nautical mile
	NMT	Nordic Mobile Telephone
	NSG	Nuclear Suppliers Group
	Nuclear Test Ban	Treaty Banning Nuclear Weapons Tests in the Atmosphere, in Outer Space, and Under Water
	NZ	New Zealand
O	OAPEC	Organization of Arab Petroleum Exporting Countries
	OAS	Organization of American States
	OAU	Organization of African Unity
	ODA	official development assistance
	OECD	Organization for Economic Cooperation and Development
	OECS	Organization of Eastern Caribbean States
	OIC	Organization of the Islamic Conference
	OOF	other official flows
	OPCW	Organization for the Prohibition of Chemical Weapons
	OPEC	Organization of Petroleum Exporting Countries
	OSCE	Organization for Security and Cooperation in Europe
	Ozone Layer Protection	Montreal Protocol on Substances That Deplete the Ozone Layer

Appendix A: Abbreviations *(continued)*

P	PCA	Permanent Court of Arbitration
	PDRY	People's Democratic Republic of Yemen [Yemen (Aden) or South Yemen]; used for information dated before 22 May 1990 or CY91
	PFP	Partnership for Peace
R	Ramsar	see Wetlands
	RG	Rio Group
S	SAARC	South Asian Association for Regional Cooperation
	SACU	Southern African Customs Union
	SADC	Southern African Development Community
	SFRY	Socialist Federal Republic of Yugoslavia
	SHF	super-high-frequency
	Ship Pollution	Protocol of 1978 Relating to the International Convention for the Prevention of Pollution From Ships, 1973 (MARPOL)
	Sparteca	South Pacific Regional Trade and Economic Cooperation Agreement
	SPC	South Pacific Commission
	SPF	South Pacific Forum
	sq km	square kilometer
	sq mi	square mile
T	TAT	Trans-Atlantic Telephone
	Tropical Timber 83	International Tropical Timber Agreement, 1983
	Tropical Timber 94	International Tropical Timber Agreement, 1994
U	UAE	United Arab Emirates
	UHF	ultra-high-frequency
	UK	United Kingdom
	UN	United Nations
	UNAMIR	United Nations Assistance Mission for Rwanda
	UNAMSIL	United Nations Mission in Sierra Leone
	UNAVEM III	United Nations Angola Verification Mission III
	UNCRO	United Nations Confidence Restoration Operation in Croatia
	UNCTAD	United Nations Conference on Trade and Development
	UNDCP	United Nations Drug Control Program
	UNDOF	United Nations Disengagement Observer Force
	UNDP	United Nations Development Program
	UNEP	United Nations Environment Program
	UNESCO	United Nations Educational, Scientific, and Cultural Organization
	UNFICYP	United Nations Peace-keeping Force in Cyprus
	UNHCR	United Nations High Commissioner for Refugees
	UNHCRHR	United Nations High Commissioner for Human Rights
	UNICEF	United Nations Children's Fund
	UNICRI	United Nations Interregional Crime and Justice Research Institute
	UNIDIR	United Nations Disarmament Research
	UNIDO	United Nations Industrial Development Organization
	UNIFIL	United Nations Interim Force in Lebanon
	UNIKOM	United Nations Iraq-Kuwait Observation Mission

Appendix A: Abbreviations *(continued)*

	UNITAR	United Nations Institute for Training and Research
	UNMEE	United Nations Mission in Ethiopia and Eritrea
	UNMIBH	United Nations Mission in Bosnia and Herzegovina
	UNMIK	United Nations Interim Administration Mission in Kosovo
	UNMOGIP	United Nations Military Observer Group in India and Pakistan
	UNMOP	United Nations Mission of Observers in Prevlaka
	UNMOT	United Nations Mission of Observers in Tajikistan
	UNMOVIC	United Nations Monitoring and Verification Commission
	UNOMIG	United Nations Observer Mission in Georgia
	UNOMSIL	United Nations Mission of Observers in Sierra Leone
	UNRISD	United Nations Research Institute for Social Development
	UNRWA	United Nations Relief and Works Agency for Palestine Refugees in the Near East
	UNSMIH	United Nations Support Mission in Haiti
	UNTAET	United Nations Transitional Administration in East Timor
	UNTSO	United Nations Truce Supervision Organization
	UNU	United Nations University
	UPU	Universal Postal Union
	US	United States
	USSR	Union of Soviet Socialist Republics (Soviet Union); used for information dated before 25 December 1991
	USSR/EE	Union of Soviet Socialist Republics/Eastern Europe
V	VHF	very-high-frequency
	VSAT	very small aperture terminal
W	WADB	West African Development Bank
	WAEMU	West African Economic and Monetary Union
	WCL	World Confederation of Labor
	Wetlands	Convention on Wetlands of International Importance Especially As Waterfowl Habitat
	WEU	Western European Union
	WFC	World Food Council
	WFP	World Food Program
	WFTU	World Federation of Trade Unions
	Whaling	International Convention for the Regulation of Whaling
	WHO	World Health Organization
	WIPO	World Intellectual Property Organization
	WMO	World Meteorological Organization
	WP	Warsaw Pact
	WTO	see WToO for World Tourism Organization or WTrO for World Trade Organization
	WToO	World Tourism Organization
	WTrO	World Trade Organization
Y	YAR	Yemen Arab Republic [Yemen (Sanaa) or North Yemen]; used for information dated before 22 May 1990 or CY91
Z	ZC	Zangger Committee

Appendix B:

International Organizations and Groups

advanced developing countries	another term for those less developed countries (LDCs) with particularly rapid industrial development; see newly industrializing economies (NIEs)
advanced economies	a term used by the International Monetary FUND (IMF) for the top group in its hierarchy of advanced economies, countries in transition, and developing countries; it includes the following 28 advanced economies: Australia, Austria, Belgium, Canada, Denmark, Finland, France, Germany, Greece, Hong Kong, Iceland, Ireland, Israel, Italy, Japan, South Korea, Luxembourg, Netherlands, NZ, Norway, Portugal, Singapore, Spain, Sweden, Switzerland, Taiwan, UK, US; *note*—this group would presumably also cover the following seven smaller countries of Andorra, Bermuda, Faroe Islands, Holy See, Liechtenstein, Monaco, and San Marino which are included in the more comprehensive group of "developed countries"
African, Caribbean, and Pacific Group of States (ACP Group) *established*—6 June 1975 *aim*—to manage their preferential economic and aid relationship with the EU	*members*—(77) Angola, Antigua and Barbuda, The Bahamas, Barbados, Belize, Benin, Botswana, Burkina Faso, Burundi, Cameroon, Cape Verde, Central African Republic, Chad, Comoros, Democratic Republic of the Congo, Republic of the Congo, Cook Islands, Cote d'Ivoire, Djibouti, Dominica, Dominican Republic, Equatorial Guinea, Eritrea, Ethiopia, Fiji, Gabon, The Gambia, Ghana, Grenada, Guinea, Guinea-Bissau, Guyana, Haiti, Jamaica, Kenya, Kiribati, Lesotho, Liberia, Madagascar, Malawi, Mali, Marshall Islands, Mauritania, Mauritius, Federated States of Micronesia, Mozambique, Namibia, Nauru, Niger, Nigeria, Niue, Palau, Papua New Guinea, Rwanda, Saint Kitts and Nevis, Saint Lucia, Saint Vincent and the Grenadines, Samoa, Sao Tome and Principe, Senegal, Seychelles, Sierra Leone, Solomon Islands, Somalia, South Africa, Sudan, Suriname, Swaziland, Tanzania, Togo, Tonga, Trinidad and Tobago, Tuvalu, Uganda, Vanuatu, Zambia, Zimbabwe
African Development Bank (AfDB) *note*—also known as Banque Africaine de Developpement (BAD) *established*—4 August 1963 *aim*—to promote economic and social development	*regional members*—(53) Algeria, Angola, Benin, Botswana, Burkina Faso, Burundi, Cameroon, Cape Verde, Central African Republic, Chad, Comoros, Democratic Republic of the Congo, Republic of the Congo, Cote d'Ivoire, Djibouti, Egypt, Equatorial Guinea, Eritrea, Ethiopia, Gabon, The Gambia, Ghana, Guinea, Guinea-Bissau, Kenya, Lesotho, Liberia, Libya, Madagascar, Malawi, Mali, Mauritania, Mauritius, Morocco, Mozambique, Namibia, Niger, Nigeria, Rwanda, Sao Tome and Principe, Senegal, Seychelles, Sierra Leone, Somalia, South Africa, Sudan, Swaziland, Tanzania, Togo, Tunisia, Uganda, Zambia, Zimbabwe *nonregional members*—(24) Argentina, Austria, Belgium, Brazil, Canada, China, Denmark, Finland, France, Germany, India, Italy, Japan, South Korea, Kuwait, Netherlands, Norway, Portugal, Saudi Arabia, Spain, Sweden, Switzerland, UK, US
Agency for the French-Speaking Community (ACCT) *note*—formerly Agency for Cultural and Technical Cooperation *established*—20 March 1970; name changed 1996 *aim*—to promote cultural and technical cooperation among French-speaking countries	*members*—(41) Belgium, Benin, Bulgaria, Burkina Faso, Burundi, Cambodia, Cameroon, Canada, Cape Verde, Central African Republic, Chad, Comoros, Democratic Republic of the Congo, Republic of the Congo, Cote d'Ivoire, Djibouti, Dominica, Equatorial Guinea, France, Gabon, Guinea, Haiti, Laos, Lebanon, Luxembourg, Madagascar, Mali, Mauritius, Moldova, Monaco, Niger, Romania, Rwanda, Sao Tome and Principe, Senegal, Seychelles, Switzerland, Togo, Tunisia, Vanuatu, Vietnam *associate members*—(7) Albania, Egypt, Guinea-Bissau, The Former Yugoslav Republic of Macedonia, Mauritania, Morocco, Saint Lucia *observers*—(4) Czech Republic, Lithuania, Poland, Slovenia *participating governments*—(2) New Brunswick (Canada), Quebec (Canada)
Agency for the Prohibition of Nuclear Weapons in Latin America and the Caribbean (OPANAL) *note*—acronym from Organismo para la Proscripcion de las Armas Nucleares en la America Latina y el Caribe (OPANAL) *established*—14 February 1967 under the Treaty of Tlatelolco *effective*—25 April 1969 on the 11th ratification of the treaty *aim*—to encourage the peaceful uses of atomic energy and prohibit nuclear weapons	*members*—(32) Antigua and Barbuda, Argentina, The Bahamas, Barbados, Belize, Bolivia, Brazil, Chile, Colombia, Costa Rica, Dominica, Dominican Republic, Ecuador, El Salvador, Grenada, Guatemala, Guyana, Haiti, Honduras, Jamaica, Mexico, Nicaragua, Panama, Paraguay, Peru, Saint Kitts and Nevis, Saint Lucia, Saint Vincent and the Grenadines, Suriname, Trinidad and Tobago, Uruguay, Venezuela; *note*—Cuba signed the treaty but did not ratify it

Appendix B: International Organizations and Groups (continued)

Andean Community of Nations (CAN)

note—formerly known as the Andean Group (AG), the Andean Parliament, and most recently as the Andean Common Market (Ancom)
established—26 May 1969; present name adopted 1 October 1992
effective—16 October 1969
aim—to promote harmonious development through economic integration

members—(5) Bolivia, Colombia, Ecuador, Peru, Venezuela

Arab Bank for Economic Development in Africa (ABEDA)

note—also known as Banque Arabe de Developpement Economique en Afrique (BADEA)
established—18 February 1974
effective—16 September 1974
aim—to promote economic development

members—(17 plus the Palestine Liberation Organization) Algeria, Bahrain, Egypt, Iraq, Jordan, Kuwait, Lebanon, Libya, Mauritania, Morocco, Oman, Qatar, Saudi Arabia, Sudan, Syria, Tunisia, UAE, Palestine Liberation Organization; note—these are all the members of the Arab League excluding Comoros, Djibouti, Somalia, Yemen

Arab Cooperation Council (ACC)

established—16 February 1989
aim—to promote economic cooperation and integration, possibly leading to an Arab Common Market

members—(4) Egypt, Iraq, Jordan, Yemen

Arab Fund for Economic and Social Development (AFESD)

established—16 May 1968
aim—to promote economic and social development

members—(20 plus the Palestine Liberation Organization) Algeria, Bahrain, Djibouti, Egypt, Iraq (suspended 1993), Jordan, Kuwait, Lebanon, Libya, Mauritania, Morocco, Oman, Qatar, Saudi Arabia, Somalia (suspended 1993), Sudan, Syria, Tunisia, UAE, Yemen, Palestine Liberation Organization

Arab League (AL)

note—also known as League of Arab States (LAS)
established—22 March 1945
aim—to promote economic, social, political, and military cooperation

members—(21 plus the Palestine Liberation Organization) Algeria, Bahrain, Comoros, Djibouti, Egypt, Iraq, Jordan, Kuwait, Lebanon, Libya, Mauritania, Morocco, Oman, Qatar, Saudi Arabia, Somalia, Sudan, Syria, Tunisia, UAE, Yemen, Palestine Liberation Organization

Arab Maghreb Union (AMU)

established—17 February 1989
aim—to promote cooperation and integration among the Arab states of northern Africa

members—(5) Algeria, Libya, Mauritania, Morocco, Tunisia

Arab Monetary Fund (AMF)

established—27 April 1976
effective—2 February 1977
aim—to promote Arab cooperation, development, and integration in monetary and economic affairs

members—(20 plus the Palestine Liberation Organization) Algeria, Bahrain, Djibouti, Egypt, Iraq, Jordan, Kuwait, Lebanon, Libya, Mauritania, Morocco, Oman, Qatar, Saudi Arabia, Somalia, Sudan, Syria, Tunisia, UAE, Yemen, Palestine Liberation Organization

Asia-Pacific Economic Cooperation (APEC)

established—7 November 1989
aim—to promote trade and investment in the Pacific basin

members—(21) Australia, Brunei, Canada, Chile, China, Hong Kong, Indonesia, Japan, South Korea, Malaysia, Mexico, NZ, Papua New Guinea, Peru, Philippines, Russia, Singapore, Taiwan, Thailand, US, Vietnam
observers—(3) Association of Southeast Asian Nations, Pacific Economic Cooperation Conference, South Pacific Forum

Appendix B: International Organizations and Groups *(continued)*

Asian Development Bank (AsDB) *established*—19 December 1966 *aim*—to promote regional economic cooperation	*regional members*—(43) Afghanistan, Australia, Azerbaijan, Bangladesh, Bhutan, Burma, Cambodia, China, Cook Islands, Fiji, Hong Kong, India, Indonesia, Japan, Kazakhstan, Kiribati, South Korea, Kyrgyzstan, Laos, Malaysia, Maldives, Marshall Islands, Federated States of Micronesia, Mongolia, Nauru, Nepal, NZ, Pakistan, Papua New Guinea, Philippines, Samoa, Singapore, Solomon Islands, Sri Lanka, Taiwan, Tajikistan, Thailand, Tonga, Turkmenistan, Tuvalu, Uzbekistan, Vanuatu, Vietnam *nonregional members*—(16) Austria, Belgium, Canada, Denmark, Finland, France, Germany, Italy, Netherlands, Norway, Spain, Sweden, Switzerland, Turkey, UK, US
Association of Southeast Asian Nations (ASEAN) *established*—8 August 1967 *aim*—to encourage regional economic, social, and cultural cooperation among the non-Communist countries of Southeast Asia	*members*—(10) Brunei, Burma, Cambodia, Indonesia, Laos, Malaysia, Philippines, Singapore, Thailand, Vietnam *observers*—(1) Papua New Guinea *dialogue partners*—(11) Australia, Canada, China, EU, India, Japan, South Korea, NZ, Russia, US, UNDP
ASEAN Regional Forum (ARF) *established*—NA 1994 *aim*—to foster constructive dialogue and consultation on political and security issues of common interest and concern	*members*—(10) Brunei, Burma, Cambodia, Indonesia, Laos, Malaysia, Philippines, Singapore, Thailand, Vietnam *dialogue partners*—(13) Australia, Canada, China, EU, India, Japan, North Korea, South Korea, Mongolia, NZ, Papua New Guinea, Russia, US
Australia Group *established*—NA 1984 *aim*—to consult on and coordinate export controls related to chemical and biological weapons	*members*—(33) Argentina, Australia, Austria, Belgium, Canada, Cyprus, Czech Republic, Denmark, European Commission, Finland, France, Germany, Greece, Hungary, Iceland, Ireland, Italy, Japan, South Korea, Luxembourg, Netherlands, NZ, Norway, Poland, Portugal, Romania, Slovakia, Spain, Sweden, Switzerland, Turkey, UK, US *observers*—(1) Singapore
Australia-New Zealand-United States Security Treaty (ANZUS) *established*—1 September 1951 *effective*—29 April 1952 *aim*—to implement a trilateral mutual security agreement, although the US suspended security obligations to NZ on 11 August 1986; Australia and the US continue to hold annual meetings	*members*—(3) Australia, NZ, US
Bank for International Settlements (BIS) *established*—20 January 1930 *effective*—17 March 1930 *aim*—to promote cooperation among central banks in international financial settlements	*members*—(49) Argentina, Australia, Austria, Belgium, Bosnia and Herzegovina, Brazil, Bulgaria, Canada, China, Croatia, Czech Republic, Denmark, Estonia, Finland, France, Germany, Greece, Hong Kong, Hungary, Iceland, India, Ireland, Italy, Japan, South Korea, Latvia, Lithuania, The Former Yugoslav Republic of Macedonia, Malaysia, Mexico, Netherlands, Norway, Poland, Portugal, Romania, Russia, Saudi Arabia, Singapore, Slovakia, Slovenia, South Africa, Spain, Sweden, Switzerland, Thailand, Turkey, UK, US, Yugoslavia
Benelux Economic Union (Benelux) *note*—acronym from Belgium, Netherlands, and Luxembourg *established*—3 February 1958 *effective*—1 November 1960 *aim*—to develop closer economic cooperation and integration	*members*—(3) Belgium, Luxembourg, Netherlands
Big Seven *note*—membership is the same as the Group of 7 *established*—NA 1975 *aim*—to discuss and coordinate major economic policies	*members*—(7) Big Six (Canada, France, Germany, Italy, Japan, UK) plus the US

Appendix B: International Organizations and Groups *(continued)*

Big Six *note*—not to be confused with the Group of 6 *established*—NA 1967 *aim*—to foster economic cooperation	*members*—(6) Canada, France, Germany, Italy, Japan, UK
Black Sea Economic Cooperation Zone (BSEC) *established*—25 June 1992 *aim*—to enhance regional stability through economic cooperation	*members*—(11) Albania, Armenia, Azerbaijan, Bulgaria, Georgia, Greece, Moldova, Romania, Russia, Turkey, Ukraine *observers*—(7) Austria, Egypt, Israel, Italy, Poland, Slovakia, Tunisia
Caribbean Community and Common Market (Caricom) *established*—4 July 1973 *effective*—1 August 1973 *aim*—to promote economic integration and development, especially among the less developed countries	*members*—(14) Antigua and Barbuda, The Bahamas, Barbados, Belize, Dominica, Grenada, Guyana, Jamaica, Montserrat, Saint Kitts and Nevis, Saint Lucia, Saint Vincent and the Grenadines, Suriname, Trinidad and Tobago *associate members*—(3) Anguilla, British Virgin Islands, Turks and Caicos Islands *observers*—(10) Aruba, Bermuda, Cayman Islands, Colombia, Dominican Republic, Haiti, Mexico, Netherlands Antilles, Puerto Rico, Venezuela; *note*—when Haiti has deposited an appropriate instrument of accession with the Secretary General, it will become a full member of the Community
Caribbean Development Bank (CDB) *established*—18 October 1969 *effective*—26 January 1970 *aim*—to promote economic development and cooperation	*regional members*—(20) Anguilla, Antigua and Barbuda, The Bahamas, Barbados, Belize, British Virgin Islands, Cayman Islands, Colombia, Dominica, Grenada, Guyana, Jamaica, Mexico, Montserrat, Saint Kitts and Nevis, Saint Lucia, Saint Vincent and the Grenadines, Trinidad and Tobago, Turks and Caicos Islands, Venezuela *nonregional members*—(5) Canada, China, Germany, Italy, UK
Central African Customs and Economic Union (UDEAC)	see Monetary and Economic Community of Central Africa (CEMAC)
Central African States Development Bank (BDEAC) *note*—acronym from Banque de Developpement des Etats de l'Afrique Centrale *established*—3 December 1975 *aim*—to provide loans for economic development	*members*—(9) Cameroon, Central African Republic, Chad, Republic of the Congo, Equatorial Guinea, France, Gabon, Germany, Kuwait
Central American Bank for Economic Integration (BCIE) *note*—acronym from Banco Centroamericano de Integracion Economico *established*—13 December 1960 signature of Articles of Agreement; 31 May 1961 began operations *aim*—to promote economic integration and development	*members*—(5) Costa Rica, El Salvador, Guatemala, Honduras, Nicaragua *nonregional members*—(4) Argentina, Colombia, Mexico, Taiwan
Central American Common Market (CACM) *established*—13 December 1960, collapsed in 1969, reinstated in 1991 *aim*—to promote establishment of a Central American Common Market	*members*—(5) Costa Rica, El Salvador, Guatemala, Honduras, Nicaragua; *note*—Panama, although not a member, pursues full regional cooperation

Appendix B: International Organizations and Groups *(continued)*

Central European Initiative (CEI) *note*—evolved from the Quadrilateral Initiative and the Hexagonal Initiative *established*—11 November 1989 as the Quadrilateral Initiative, 27 July 1991 became the Hexagonal Initiative, NA July 1992 present name adopted *aim*—to form an economic and political cooperation group for the region between the Adriatic and the Baltic Seas	*members*—(17) Albania, Austria, Belarus, Bosnia and Herzegovina, Bulgaria, Croatia, Czech Republic, Hungary, Italy, The Former Yugoslav Republic of Macedonia, Moldova, Poland, Romania, Slovakia, Slovenia, Ukraine, Yugoslavia
centrally planned economies	a term applied mainly to the traditionally communist states that looked to the former USSR for leadership; most are now evolving toward more democratic and market-oriented systems; also known formerly as the Second World or as the communist countries; through the 1980s, this group included Albania, Bulgaria, Cambodia, China, Cuba, Czechoslovakia, GDR, Hungary, North Korea, Laos, Mongolia, Poland, Romania, USSR, Vietnam, Yugoslavia
Colombo Plan (CP) *established*—NA May 1950 proposal was adopted; 1 July 1951 commenced full operations *aim*—to promote economic and social development in Asia and the Pacific	*members*—(24) Afghanistan, Australia, Bangladesh, Bhutan, Burma, Cambodia, Fiji, India, Indonesia, Iran, Japan, South Korea, Laos, Malaysia, Maldives, Nepal, NZ, Pakistan, Papua New Guinea, Philippines, Singapore, Sri Lanka, Thailand, US
Commonwealth (C) *note*—also known as Commonwealth of Nations *established*—31 December 1931 *aim*—to foster multinational cooperation and assistance, as a voluntary association that evolved from the British Empire	*members*—(54) Antigua and Barbuda, Australia, The Bahamas, Bangladesh, Barbados, Belize, Botswana, Brunei, Cameroon, Canada, Cyprus, Dominica, Fiji, The Gambia, Ghana, Grenada, Guyana, India, Jamaica, Kenya, Kiribati, Lesotho, Malawi, Malaysia, Maldives, Malta, Mauritius, Mozambique, Namibia, Nauru, NZ, Nigeria, Pakistan (suspended), Papua New Guinea, Saint Kitts and Nevis, Saint Lucia, Saint Vincent and the Grenadines, Samoa, Seychelles, Sierra Leone, Singapore, Solomon Islands, South Africa, Sri Lanka, Swaziland, Tanzania, Tonga, Trinidad and Tobago, Tuvalu, Uganda, UK, Vanuatu, Zambia, Zimbabwe
Commonwealth of Independent States (CIS) *established*—8 December 1991 *effective*—21 December 1991 *aim*—to coordinate intercommonwealth relations and to provide a mechanism for the orderly dissolution of the USSR	*members*—(12) Armenia, Azerbaijan, Belarus, Georgia, Kazakhstan, Kyrgyzstan, Moldova, Russia, Tajikistan, Turkmenistan, Ukraine, Uzbekistan
communist countries	traditionally the Marxist-Leninist states with authoritarian governments and command economies based on the Soviet model; most of the original and the successor states are no longer communist; see centrally planned economies
Coordinating Committee on Export Controls (COCOM)	established in 1949 to control the export of strategic products and technical data from member countries to proscribed destinations; members were Australia, Belgium, Canada, Denmark, France, Germany, Greece, Italy, Japan, Luxembourg, Netherlands, Norway, Portugal, Spain, Turkey, UK, US; abolished 31 March 1994; COCOM members established a new organization, the Wassenaar Arrangement, with expanded membership on 12 July 1996 which focuses on nonproliferation export controls as opposed to East-West control of advanced technology
Council for Mutual Economic Assistance (CEMA) *note*—also known as CMEA or Comecon	established 25 January 1949 to promote the development of socialist economies and abolished 1 January 1991; members included Afghanistan (observer), Albania (had not participated since 1961 break with USSR), Angola (observer), Bulgaria, Cuba, Czechoslovakia, Ethiopia (observer), GDR, Hungary, Laos (observer), Mongolia, Mozambique (observer), Nicaragua (observer), Poland, Romania, USSR, Vietnam, Yemen (observer), Yugoslavia (associate)
Council of Arab Economic Unity (CAEU) *established*—3 June 1957 *effective*—30 May 1964 *aim*—to promote economic integration among Arab nations	*members*—(11 plus the Palestine Liberation Organization) Egypt, Iraq, Jordan, Kuwait, Libya, Mauritania, Somalia, Sudan, Syria, UAE, Yemen, Palestine Liberation Organization

Appendix B: International Organizations and Groups *(continued)*

Council of Europe (CE)

established—5 May 1949
effective—3 August 1949
aim—to promote increased unity and quality of life in Europe

members—(43) Albania, Andorra, Armenia, Austria, Azerbaijan, Belgium, Bulgaria, Croatia, Cyprus, Czech Republic, Denmark, Estonia, Finland, France, Georgia, Germany, Greece, Hungary, Iceland, Ireland, Italy, Latvia, Liechtenstein, Lithuania, Luxembourg, The Former Yugoslav Republic of Macedonia, Malta, Moldova, Netherlands, Norway, Poland, Portugal, Romania, Russia, San Marino, Slovakia, Slovenia, Spain, Sweden, Switzerland, Turkey, Ukraine, UK
guests—(2) Bosnia and Herzegovina, Yugoslavia
observers—(5) Canada, Israel, Japan, Mexico, US

Council of the Baltic Sea States (CBSS)

established—6 March 1992
aim—to promote cooperation among the Baltic Sea states in the areas of aid to new democratic institutions, economic development, humanitarian aid, energy and the environment, cultural programs and education, and transportation and communication

members—(12) Denmark, Estonia, EU, Finland, Germany, Iceland, Latvia, Lithuania, Norway, Poland, Russia, Sweden

Council of the Entente (Entente)

established—29 May 1959
aim—to promote economic, social, and political coordination

members—(5) Benin, Burkina Faso, Cote d'Ivoire, Niger, Togo

countries in transition

a term used by the International Monetary FUND (IMF) for the middle group in its hierarchy of advanced economies, countries in transition, and developing countries; recently published IMF statistics include the following 28 countries in transition: Albania, Armenia, Azerbaijan, Belarus, Bosnia and Herzegovina, Bulgaria, Croatia, Czech Republic, Estonia, Georgia, Hungary, Kazakhstan, Kyrgyzstan, Latvia, Lithuania, The Former Yugoslav Republic of Macedonia, Moldova, Mongolia, Poland, Romania, Russia, Slovakia, Slovenia, Tajikistan, Turkmenistan, Ukraine, Uzbekistan, Yugoslavia; *note*—this group is identical to the group traditionally referred to as the "former USSR/Eastern Europe" except for the addition of Mongolia

Customs Cooperation Council (CCC)

note—also known as World Customs Organization (WCO)
established—15 December 1950
aim—to promote international cooperation in customs matters

members—(153) Albania, Algeria, Andorra, Angola, Argentina, Armenia, Australia, Austria, Azerbaijan, The Bahamas, Bangladesh, Barbados, Belarus, Belgium, Benin, Bermuda, Bolivia, Botswana, Brazil, Brunei, Bulgaria, Burkina Faso, Burma, Burundi, Cameroon, Canada, Cape Verde, Central African Republic, Chile, China, Colombia, Comoros, Democratic Republic of the Congo, Republic of the Congo, Cote d'Ivoire, Croatia, Cuba, Cyprus, Czech Republic, Denmark, Ecuador, Egypt, Eritrea, Estonia, Ethiopia, Fiji, Finland, France, Gabon, The Gambia, Georgia, Germany, Ghana, Greece, Guatemala, Guinea, Guyana, Haiti, Hong Kong, Hungary, Iceland, India, Indonesia, Iran, Iraq, Ireland, Israel, Italy, Jamaica, Japan, Jordan, Kazakhstan, Kenya, South Korea, Kuwait, Kyrgyzstan, Latvia, Lebanon, Lesotho, Liberia, Libya, Lithuania, Luxembourg, Macau, The Former Yugoslav Republic of Macedonia, Madagascar, Malawi, Malaysia, Maldives, Mali, Malta, Mauritania, Mauritius, Mexico, Moldova, Mongolia, Morocco, Mozambique, Namibia, Nepal, Netherlands, NZ, Nicaragua, Niger, Nigeria, Norway, Oman, Pakistan, Panama, Paraguay, Peru, Philippines, Poland, Portugal, Qatar, Romania, Russia, Rwanda, Saudi Arabia, Senegal, Seychelles, Sierra Leone, Singapore, Slovakia, Slovenia, South Africa, Spain, Sri Lanka, Sudan, Swaziland, Sweden, Switzerland, Syria, Tajikistan, Tanzania, Thailand, Togo, Trinidad and Tobago, Tunisia, Turkey, Turkmenistan, Uganda, Ukraine, UAE, UK, US, Uruguay, Uzbekistan, Venezuela, Vietnam, Yemen, Zambia, Zimbabwe

developed countries (DCs)

the top group in the hierarchy of developed countries (DCs), former USSR/Eastern Europe (former USSR/EE), and less developed countries (LDCs); includes the market-oriented economies of the mainly democratic nations in the Organization for Economic Cooperation and Development (OECD), Bermuda, Israel, South Africa, and the European ministates; also known as the First World, high-income countries, the North, industrial countries; generally have a per capita GDP in excess of $10,000 although four OECD countries and South Africa have figures well under $10,000 and two of the excluded OPEC countries have figures of more than $10,000; the 35 DCs are: Andorra, Australia, Austria, Belgium, Bermuda, Canada, Denmark, Faroe Islands, Finland, France, Germany, Greece, Holy See, Iceland, Ireland, Israel, Italy, Japan, Liechtenstein, Luxembourg, Malta, Mexico, Monaco, Netherlands, NZ, Norway, Portugal, San Marino, South Africa, Spain, Sweden, Switzerland, Turkey, UK, US; *note*—similar to the new International Monetary Fund (IMF) term "advanced economies" which adds Hong Kong, South Korea, Singapore, and Taiwan but drops Malta, Mexico, South Africa, and Turkey

Appendix B: International Organizations and Groups *(continued)*

developing countries	a term used by the International Monetary Fund (IMF) for the bottom group in its hierarchy of advanced economies, countries in transition, and developing countries; recently published IMF statistics include the following 126 developing countries: Afghanistan, Algeria, Angola, Antigua and Barbuda, Argentina, Aruba, The Bahamas, Bahrain, Bangladesh, Barbados, Belize, Benin, Bhutan, Bolivia, Botswana, Brazil, Burkina Faso, Burma, Burundi, Cambodia, Cameroon, Cape Verde, Central African Republic, Chad, Chile, China, Colombia, Comoros, Democratic Republic of the Congo, Republic of the Congo, Costa Rica, Cote d'Ivoire, Cyprus, Djibouti, Dominica, Dominican Republic, Ecuador, Egypt, El Salvador, Equatorial Guinea, Ethiopia, Fiji, Gabon, The Gambia, Ghana, Grenada, Guatemala, Guinea, Guinea-Bissau, Guyana, Haiti, Honduras, India, Indonesia, Iran, Iraq, Jamaica, Jordan, Kenya, Kiribati, Kuwait, Laos, Lebanon, Lesotho, Liberia, Libya, Madagascar, Malawi, Malaysia, Maldives, Mali, Malta, Marshall Islands, Mauritania, Mauritius, Mexico, Federated States of Micronesia, Morocco, Mozambique, Namibia, Nepal, Netherlands Antilles, Nicaragua, Niger, Nigeria, Oman, Pakistan, Panama, Papua New Guinea, Paraguay, Peru, Philippines, Qatar, Rwanda, Saint Kitts and Nevis, Saint Lucia, Saint Vincent and the Grenadines, Samoa, Sao Tome and Principe, Saudi Arabia, Senegal, Seychelles, Sierra Leone, Solomon Islands, Somalia, South Africa, Sri Lanka, Sudan, Suriname, Swaziland, Syria, Tanzania, Thailand, Togo, Trinidad and Tobago, Tunisia, Turkey, UAE, Uganda, Uruguay, Vanuatu, Venezuela, Vietnam, Yemen, Zambia, Zimbabwe; *note*—this category would presumably also cover the following 46 other countries that are traditionally included in the more comprehensive group of "less developed countries": American Samoa, Anguilla, British Virgin Islands, Brunei, Cayman Islands, Christmas Island, Cocos Islands, Cook Islands, Cuba, Eritrea, Falkland Islands, French Guiana, French Polynesia, Gaza Strip, Gibraltar, Greenland, Grenada, Guadeloupe, Guam, Guernsey, Jersey, North Korea, Macau, Isle of Man, Martinique, Mayotte, Montserrat, Nauru, New Caledonia, Niue, Norfolk Island, Northern Mariana Islands, Palau, Pitcairn Islands, Puerto Rico, Reunion, Saint Helena, Saint Pierre and Miquelon, Tokelau, Tonga, Turks and Caicos Islands, Tuvalu, Virgin Islands, Wallis and Futuna, West Bank, Western Sahara
East African Development Bank (EADB) *established*—6 June 1967 *effective*—1 December 1967 *aim*—to promote economic development	*members*—(3) Kenya, Tanzania, Uganda
Economic and Social Council (ECOSOC) *established*—26 June 1945 *effective*—24 October 1945 *aim*—to coordinate the economic and social work of the UN; includes five regional commissions (Economic Commission for Africa, Economic Commission for Europe, Economic Commission for Latin America and the Caribbean, Economic and Social Commission for Asia and the Pacific, Economic and Social Commission for Western Asia) and 9 functional commissions (Commission for Social Development, Commission on Human Rights, Commission on Narcotic Drugs, Commission on the Status of Women, Commission on Population and Development, Statistical Commission, Commission on Science and Technology for Development, Commission on Sustainable Development, and Commission on Crime Prevention and Criminal Justice)	*members*—(54) selected on a rotating basis from all regions
Economic Community of the Great Lakes Countries (CEPGL) *note*—acronym from Communaute Economique des Pays des Grands Lacs *established*—20 September 1976 *aim*—to promote regional economic cooperation and integration	*members*—(3) Burundi, Democratic Republic of the Congo, Rwanda

Appendix B: International Organizations and Groups *(continued)*

Economic Community of West African States (ECOWAS) *established*—28 May 1975 *aim*—to promote regional economic cooperation	*members*—(16) Benin, Burkina Faso, Cape Verde, Cote d'Ivoire, The Gambia, Ghana, Guinea, Guinea-Bissau, Liberia, Mali, Mauritania, Niger, Nigeria, Senegal, Sierra Leone, Togo
Economic Cooperation Organization (ECO) *established*—27-29 January 1985 *aim*—to promote regional cooperation in trade, transportation, communications, tourism, cultural affairs, and economic development	*members*—(10) Afghanistan, Azerbaijan, Iran, Kazakhstan, Kyrgyzstan, Pakistan, Tajikistan, Turkey, Turkmenistan, Uzbekistan *associate member*—(1) "Turkish Republic of Northern Cyprus"
Euro-Atlantic Partnership Council (EAPC) *note*—began as the North Atlantic Cooperation Council (NACC); an extension of NATO *established*—8 November 1991 *effective*—20 December 1991 *aim*—to discuss cooperation on mutual political and security issues	*members*—(46) Albania, Armenia, Austria, Azerbaijan, Belarus, Belgium, Bulgaria, Canada, Croatia, Czech Republic, Denmark, Estonia, Finland, France, Georgia, Germany, Greece, Hungary, Iceland, Ireland, Italy, Kazakhstan, Kyrgyzstan, Latvia, Lithuania, Luxembourg, The Former Yugoslav Republic of Macedonia, Moldova, Netherlands, Norway, Poland, Portugal, Romania, Russia, Slovakia, Slovenia, Spain, Sweden, Switzerland, Tajikistan, Turkey, Turkmenistan, Ukraine, UK, US, Uzbekistan
European Bank for Reconstruction and Development (EBRD) *established*—8-9 January 1990 (proposals made); 15 April 1991 (bank inaugurated) *aim*—to facilitate the transition of seven centrally planned economies in Europe (Bulgaria, former Czechoslovakia, Hungary, Poland, Romania, former USSR, and former Yugoslavia) to market economies by committing 60% of its loans to privatization	*members*—(61) Albania, Armenia, Australia, Austria, Azerbaijan, Belarus, Belgium, Bosnia and Herzegovina, Bulgaria, Canada, Croatia, Cyprus, Czech Republic, Denmark, Egypt, EU, European Investment Bank (EIB), Estonia, Finland, France, Georgia, Germany, Greece, Hungary, Iceland, Ireland, Israel, Italy, Japan, Kazakhstan, South Korea, Kyrgyzstan, Latvia, Liechtenstein, Lithuania, Luxembourg, The Former Yugoslav Republic of Macedonia, Malta, Mexico, Moldova, Mongolia, Morocco, Netherlands, NZ, Norway, Poland, Portugal, Romania, Russia, Slovakia, Slovenia, Spain, Sweden, Switzerland, Tajikistan, Turkey, Turkmenistan, Ukraine, UK, US, Uzbekistan; *note*—includes all 25 members of the OECD; also includes the EU as a single entity
European Community (or European Communities, EC)	was established 8 April 1965 to integrate the European Atomic Energy Community (Euratom), the European Coal and Steel Community (ESC), the European Economic Community (EEC or Common Market), and to establish a completely integrated common market and an eventual federation of Europe; merged into the European Union (EU) on 7 February 1992; member states at the time of merger were Belgium, Denmark, France, Germany, Greece, Ireland, Italy, Luxembourg, Netherlands, Portugal, Spain, UK
European Free Trade Association (EFTA) *established*—4 January 1960 *effective*—3 May 1960 *aim*—to promote expansion of free trade	*members*—(4) Iceland, Liechtenstein, Norway, Switzerland
European Investment Bank (EIB) *established*—25 March 1957 *effective*—1 January 1958 *aim*—to promote economic development of the EU and its predecessors, the EEC and the EC	*members*—(15) Austria, Belgium, Denmark, Finland, France, Germany, Greece, Ireland, Italy, Luxembourg, Netherlands, Portugal, Spain, Sweden, UK

Appendix B: International Organizations and Groups *(continued)*

European Monetary Union (EMU) *note*—an integral part of the European Union; also known as the European Economic and Monetary Union *proposed*—1-2 December 1969 at summit conference of heads of government *signed*—7 February 1992 (Maastricht Treaty) *aim*—to promote a single market by creating a single currency, the euro; time table—2 May 1998: European exchange rates fixed for 1 January 1999; 1 January 1999: all banks and stock exchanges begin using euros; 1 January 2002: the euro goes into circulation; 1 July 2002 local currencies no longer accepted	*members*—(12) Austria, Belgium, Finland, France, Germany, Greece, Ireland, Italy, Luxembourg, Netherlands, Portugal, Spain; *note*—Denmark, Sweden, and UK decided not to join
European Organization for Nuclear Research (CERN) *note*—acronym retained from the predecessor organization Conseil Europeenne pour la Recherche Nucleaire *established*—1 July 1953 *effective*—29 September 1954 *aim*—to foster nuclear research for peaceful purposes only	*members*—(20) Austria, Belgium, Bulgaria, Czech Republic, Denmark, Finland, France, Germany, Greece, Hungary, Italy, Netherlands, Norway, Poland, Portugal, Slovakia, Spain, Sweden, Switzerland, UK *observers*—(7) European Commission, Israel, Japan, Russia, Turkey, United Nations Educational, Scientific, and Cultural Organization (UNESCO), US
European Space Agency (ESA) *established*—31 May 1975 *aim*—to promote peaceful cooperation in space research and technology	*members*—(15) Austria, Belgium, Denmark, Finland, France, Germany, Ireland, Italy, Netherlands, Norway, Portugal, Spain, Sweden, Switzerland, UK *cooperating state*—(1) Canada
European Union (EU) *note*—evolved from the European Community (EC) *established*—7 February 1992 *effective*—1 November 1993 *aim*—to coordinate policy among the 15 members in three fields: economics, building on the European Economic Community's (EEC) efforts to establish a common market and eventually a common currency to be called the 'euro', which superseded the EU's accounting unit, the ECU; defense, within the concept of a Common Foreign and Security Policy (CFSP); and justice and home affairs, including immigration, drugs, terrorism, and improved living and working conditions	*members*—(15) Austria, Belgium, Denmark, Finland, France, Germany, Greece, Ireland, Italy, Luxembourg, Netherlands, Portugal, Spain, Sweden, UK *membership applicants*—(13) Bulgaria, Cyprus, Czech Republic, Estonia, Hungary, Latvia, Lithuania, Malta, Poland, Romania, Slovakia, Slovenia, Turkey
First World	another term for countries with advanced, industrialized economies; this term is fading from use; see developed countries (DCs)

Appendix B: International Organizations and Groups *(continued)*

Food and Agriculture Organization (FAO) *established*—16 October 1945 *aim*—to raise living standards and increase availability of agricultural products, as a UN specialized agency	*members*—(180) Afghanistan, Albania, Algeria, Angola, Antigua and Barbuda, Argentina, Armenia, Australia, Austria, Azerbaijan, The Bahamas, Bahrain, Bangladesh, Barbados, Belgium, Belize, Benin, Bhutan, Bolivia, Bosnia and Herzegovina, Botswana, Brazil, Bulgaria, Burkina Faso, Burma, Burundi, Cambodia, Cameroon, Canada, Cape Verde, Central African Republic, Chad, Chile, China, Colombia, Comoros, Democratic Republic of the Congo, Republic of the Congo, Cook Islands, Costa Rica, Cote d'Ivoire, Croatia, Cuba, Cyprus, Czech Republic, Denmark, Djibouti, Dominica, Dominican Republic, Ecuador, Egypt, El Salvador, Equatorial Guinea, Eritrea, Estonia, Ethiopia, EU, Fiji, Finland, France, Gabon, The Gambia, Georgia, Germany, Ghana, Greece, Grenada, Guatemala, Guinea, Guinea-Bissau, Guyana, Haiti, Honduras, Hungary, Iceland, India, Indonesia, Iran, Iraq, Ireland, Israel, Italy, Jamaica, Japan, Jordan, Kazakhstan, Kenya, Kiribati, North Korea, South Korea, Kuwait, Kyrgyzstan, Laos, Latvia, Lebanon, Lesotho, Liberia, Libya, Lithuania, Luxembourg, The Former Yugoslav Republic of Macedonia, Madagascar, Malawi, Malaysia, Maldives, Mali, Malta, Marshall Islands, Mauritania, Mauritius, Mexico, Moldova, Mongolia, Morocco, Mozambique, Namibia, Nepal, Netherlands, NZ, Nicaragua, Niger, Nigeria, Niue, Norway, Oman, Pakistan, Palau, Panama, Papua New Guinea, Paraguay, Peru, Philippines, Poland, Portugal, Qatar, Romania, Rwanda, Saint Kitts and Nevis, Saint Lucia, Saint Vincent and the Grenadines, Samoa, San Marino, Sao Tome and Principe, Saudi Arabia, Senegal, Seychelles, Sierra Leone, Slovakia, Slovenia, Solomon Islands, Somalia, South Africa, Spain, Sri Lanka, Sudan, Suriname, Swaziland, Sweden, Switzerland, Syria, Tajikistan, Tanzania, Thailand, Togo, Tonga, Trinidad and Tobago, Tunisia, Turkey, Turkmenistan, Uganda, UAE, UK, US, Uruguay, Vanuatu, Venezuela, Vietnam, Yemen, Zambia, Zimbabwe *applicant member*—(1) Yugoslavia
former Soviet Union (FSU)	former term often used to identify as a group the successor nations to the Soviet Union or USSR; this group of 15 countries consists of Armenia, Azerbaijan, Belarus, Estonia, Georgia, Kazakhstan, Kyrgyzstan, Latvia, Lithuania, Moldova, Russia, Tajikistan, Turkmenistan, Ukraine, Uzbekistan
former USSR/Eastern Europe (former USSR/EE)	the middle group in the hierarchy of developed countries (DCs), former USSR/Eastern Europe (former USSR/EE), and less developed countries (LDCs); these countries are in political and economic transition and may well be grouped differently in the near future; this group of 27 countries consists of Albania, Armenia, Azerbaijan, Belarus, Bosnia and Herzegovina, Bulgaria, Croatia, Czech Republic, Estonia, Georgia, Hungary, Kazakhstan, Kyrgyzstan, Latvia, Lithuania, The Former Yugoslav Republic of Macedonia, Moldova, Poland, Romania, Russia, Slovakia, Slovenia, Tajikistan, Turkmenistan, Ukraine, Uzbekistan, Yugoslavia; this group is identical to the IMF group "countries in transition" except for the IMF's inclusion of Mongolia
Four Dragons	the four small Asian less developed countries (LDCs) that have experienced unusually rapid economic growth; also known as the Four Tigers; this group consists of Hong Kong, South Korea, Singapore, Taiwan; these countries are included in the IMF's "advanced economies" group
Franc Zone (FZ) *note*—also known as Conference des Ministres des Finances des Pays de la Zone Franc *established*—NA 1964 *aim*—to form a monetary union among countries whose currencies are linked to the French franc	*members*—(16) Benin, Burkina Faso, Cameroon, Central African Republic, Chad, Comoros, Republic of the Congo, Cote d'Ivoire, Equatorial Guinea, France, Gabon, Guinea-Bissau, Mali, Niger, Senegal, Togo; *note*—France includes metropolitan France, the four overseas departments of France (French Guiana, Guadeloupe, Martinique, Reunion), the two territorial collectivities of France (Mayotte, Saint Pierre and Miquelon), and the three overseas territories of France (French Polynesia, New Caledonia, Wallis and Futuna)
Front Line States (FLS)	established to achieve black majority rule in South Africa; has since gone out of existence; members included Angola, Botswana, Mozambique, Namibia, Tanzania, Zambia, Zimbabwe
General Agreement on Tariffs and Trade (GATT)	see the World Trade Organization (WTrO)
Group of 2 (G-2)	informal term that came into use about 1986; to facilitate bilateral economic cooperation between the two most powerful economic giants Japan, US
Group of 3 (G-3) *established*—NA September 1990 *aim*—mechanism for policy coordination	*members*—(3) Colombia, Mexico, Venezuela
Group of 5 (G-5) *established*—22 September 1985 *aim*—to coordinate the economic policies of five major noncommunist economic powers	*members*—(5) France, Germany, Japan, UK, US

Appendix B: International Organizations and Groups *(continued)*

Group of 6 (G-6)

note—also known as Groupe des Six Sur le Desarmement; not to be confused with the Big Six
established—22 May 1984
aim—to achieve nuclear disarmament

members—(6) Argentina, Greece, India, Mexico, Sweden, Tanzania

Group of 7 (G-7)

note—membership is the same as the Big Seven
established—22 September 1985
aim—to facilitate economic cooperation among the seven major noncommunist economic powers

members—(7) Group of 5 (France, Germany, Japan, UK, US) plus Canada and Italy

Group of 8 (G-8)

established—NA October 1975
aim—to facilitate economic cooperation among the developed countries (DCs) that participated in the Conference on International Economic Cooperation (CIEC), held in several sessions between NA December 1975 and 3 June 1977

members—(9) Canada, EU (as one member), France, Germany, Italy, Japan, Russia, UK, US

Group of 9 (G-9)

established—NA
aim—to discuss matters of mutual interest on an informal basis

members—(9) Austria, Belgium, Bulgaria, Denmark, Finland, Hungary, Romania, Sweden, Yugoslavia

Group of 10 (G-10)

note—also known as the Paris Club; includes the wealthiest members of the IMF who provide most of the money to be loaned and act as the informal steering committee; name persists in spite of the addition of Switzerland on NA April 1984
established—NA October 1962
aim—to coordinate credit policy

members—(11) Belgium, Canada, France, Germany, Italy, Japan, Netherlands, Sweden, Switzerland, UK, US
nonstate participants—(4) BIS, EU, IMF, OECD

Group of 11 (G-11)

note—also known as the Cartagena Group
established—21-22 June 1984, in Cartagena, Colombia
aim—to provide a forum for largest debtor nations in Latin America

members—(11) Argentina, Bolivia, Brazil, Chile, Colombia, Dominican Republic, Ecuador, Mexico, Peru, Uruguay, Venezuela

Group of 15 (G-15)

note—byproduct of the Nonaligned Movement
established—NA September 1989
aim—to promote economic cooperation among developing nations; to act as the main political organ for the Nonaligned Movement

members—(15) Algeria, Argentina, Brazil, Egypt, India, Indonesia, Jamaica, Malaysia, Mexico, Nigeria, Peru, Senegal, Venezuela, Yugoslavia, Zimbabwe

Group of 24 (G-24)

established—1 August 1989
aim—to promote the interests of developing countries in Africa, Asia, and Latin America within the IMF

members—(24) Algeria, Argentina, Brazil, Colombia, Democratic Republic of the Congo, Cote d'Ivoire, Egypt, Ethiopia, Gabon, Ghana, Guatemala, India, Iran, Lebanon, Mexico, Nigeria, Pakistan, Peru, Philippines, Sri Lanka, Syria, Trinidad and Tobago, Venezuela, Yugoslavia

Appendix B: International Organizations and Groups *(continued)*

Group of 77 (G-77) *established*—15 June 1964 was set up; NA October 1967 first ministerial meeting *aim*—to promote economic cooperation among developing countries; name persists in spite of increased membership	*members*—(131 plus the Palestine Liberation Organization) Afghanistan, Algeria, Angola, Antigua and Barbuda, Argentina, The Bahamas, Bahrain, Bangladesh, Barbados, Belize, Benin, Bhutan, Bolivia, Bosnia and Herzegovina, Botswana, Brazil, Brunei, Burkina Faso, Burma, Burundi, Cambodia, Cameroon, Cape Verde, Central African Republic, Chad, Chile, China, Colombia, Comoros, Democratic Republic of the Congo, Republic of the Congo, Costa Rica, Cote d'Ivoire, Cuba, Cyprus, Djibouti, Dominica, Dominican Republic, Ecuador, Egypt, El Salvador, Equatorial Guinea, Ethiopia, Fiji, Gabon, The Gambia, Ghana, Grenada, Guatemala, Guinea, Guinea-Bissau, Guyana, Haiti, Honduras, India, Indonesia, Iran, Iraq, Jamaica, Jordan, Kenya, North Korea, South Korea, Kuwait, Laos, Lebanon, Lesotho, Liberia, Libya, Madagascar, Malawi, Malaysia, Maldives, Mali, Malta, Marshall Islands, Mauritania, Mauritius, Federated States of Micronesia, Mongolia, Morocco, Mozambique, Namibia, Nepal, Nicaragua, Niger, Nigeria, Oman, Pakistan, Panama, Papua New Guinea, Paraguay, Peru, Philippines, Qatar, Romania, Rwanda, Saint Kitts and Nevis, Saint Lucia, Saint Vincent and the Grenadines, Samoa, Sao Tome and Principe, Saudi Arabia, Senegal, Seychelles, Sierra Leone, Singapore, Solomon Islands, Somalia, South Africa, Sri Lanka, Sudan, Suriname, Swaziland, Syria, Tanzania, Thailand, Togo, Tonga, Trinidad and Tobago, Tunisia, Uganda, UAE, Uruguay, Vanuatu, Venezuela, Vietnam, Yemen, Yugoslavia, Zambia, Zimbabwe, Palestine Liberation Organization
Gulf Cooperation Council (GCC) *note*—also known as the Cooperation Council for the Arab States of the Gulf *established*—25 May 1981 *aim*—to promote regional cooperation in economic, social, political, and military affairs	*members*—(6) Bahrain, Kuwait, Oman, Qatar, Saudi Arabia, UAE
high-income countries	another term for the industrialized countries with high per capita GDPs; see developed countries (DCs)
Indian Ocean Commission (InOC) *established*—21 December 1982 *aim*—to organize and promote regional cooperation in all sectors, especially economic	*members*—(5) Comoros, France (for Reunion), Madagascar, Mauritius, Seychelles
industrial countries	another term for the developed countries; see developed countries (DCs)
Inter-American Development Bank (IADB) *note*—also known as Banco Interamericano de Desarrollo (BID) *established*—8 April 1959 *effective*—30 December 1959 *aim*—to promote economic and social development in Latin America	*members*—(46) Argentina, Austria, The Bahamas, Barbados, Belgium, Belize, Bolivia, Brazil, Canada, Chile, Colombia, Costa Rica, Croatia, Denmark, Dominican Republic, Ecuador, El Salvador, Finland, France, Germany, Guatemala, Guyana, Haiti, Honduras, Israel, Italy, Jamaica, Japan, Mexico, Netherlands, Nicaragua, Norway, Panama, Paraguay, Peru, Portugal, Slovenia, Spain, Suriname, Sweden, Switzerland, Trinidad and Tobago, UK, US, Uruguay, Venezuela
Inter-Governmental Authority on Development (IGAD) *note*—formerly known as Inter-Governmental Authority on Drought and Development (IGADD) *established*—15-16 January 1986 as the Inter-Governmental Authority on Drought and Development *revitalized*—21 March 1996 as the Inter-Governmental Authority on Development *aim*—to promote a social, economic, and scientific community among its members	*members*—(6) Djibouti, Eritrea, Ethiopia, Kenya, Sudan, Uganda

Appendix B: International Organizations and Groups (continued)

International Atomic Energy Agency (IAEA)

established—26 October 1956
effective—29 July 1957
aim—to promote peaceful uses of atomic energy

members—(130) Afghanistan, Albania, Algeria, Angola, Argentina, Armenia, Australia, Austria, Bangladesh, Belarus, Belgium, Benin, Bolivia, Bosnia and Herzegovina, Brazil, Bulgaria, Burkina Faso, Burma, Cambodia, Cameroon, Canada, Chile, China, Colombia, Democratic Republic of the Congo, Costa Rica, Cote d'Ivoire, Croatia, Cuba, Cyprus, Czech Republic, Denmark, Dominican Republic, Ecuador, Egypt, El Salvador, Estonia, Ethiopia, Finland, France, Gabon, Georgia, Germany, Ghana, Greece, Guatemala, Haiti, Holy See, Hungary, Iceland, India, Indonesia, Iran, Iraq, Ireland, Israel, Italy, Jamaica, Japan, Jordan, Kazakhstan, Kenya, South Korea, Kuwait, Latvia, Lebanon, Liberia, Libya, Liechtenstein, Lithuania, Luxembourg, The Former Yugoslav Republic of Macedonia, Madagascar, Malaysia, Mali, Malta, Marshall Islands, Mauritius, Mexico, Moldova, Monaco, Mongolia, Morocco, Namibia, Netherlands, NZ, Nicaragua, Niger, Nigeria, Norway, Pakistan, Panama, Paraguay, Peru, Philippines, Poland, Portugal, Qatar, Romania, Russia, Saudi Arabia, Senegal, Sierra Leone, Singapore, Slovakia, Slovenia, South Africa, Spain, Sri Lanka, Sudan, Sweden, Switzerland, Syria, Tanzania, Thailand, Tunisia, Turkey, Uganda, Ukraine, UAE, UK, US, Uruguay, Uzbekistan, Venezuela, Vietnam, Yemen, Yugoslavia, Zambia, Zimbabwe

International Bank for Reconstruction and Development (IBRD)

note—also known as the World Bank
established—22 July 1944
effective—27 December 1945
aim—to provide economic development loans; a UN specialized agency

members—(182) Afghanistan, Albania, Algeria, Angola, Antigua and Barbuda, Argentina, Armenia, Australia, Austria, Azerbaijan, The Bahamas, Bahrain, Bangladesh, Barbados, Belarus, Belgium, Belize, Benin, Bhutan, Bolivia, Bosnia and Herzegovina, Botswana, Brazil, Brunei, Bulgaria, Burkina Faso, Burma, Burundi, Cambodia, Cameroon, Canada, Cape Verde, Central African Republic, Chad, Chile, China, Colombia, Comoros, Democratic Republic of the Congo, Republic of the Congo, Costa Rica, Cote d'Ivoire, Croatia, Cyprus, Czech Republic, Denmark, Djibouti, Dominica, Dominican Republic, Ecuador, Egypt, El Salvador, Equatorial Guinea, Eritrea, Estonia, Ethiopia, Fiji, Finland, France, Gabon, The Gambia, Georgia, Germany, Ghana, Greece, Grenada, Guatemala, Guinea, Guinea-Bissau, Guyana, Haiti, Honduras, Hungary, Iceland, India, Indonesia, Iran, Iraq, Ireland, Israel, Italy, Jamaica, Japan, Jordan, Kazakhstan, Kenya, Kiribati, South Korea, Kuwait, Kyrgyzstan, Laos, Latvia, Lebanon, Lesotho, Liberia, Libya, Lithuania, Luxembourg, The Former Yugoslav Republic of Macedonia, Madagascar, Malawi, Malaysia, Maldives, Mali, Malta, Marshall Islands, Mauritania, Mauritius, Mexico, Federated States of Micronesia, Moldova, Mongolia, Morocco, Mozambique, Namibia, Nepal, Netherlands, NZ, Nicaragua, Niger, Nigeria, Norway, Oman, Pakistan, Palau, Panama, Papua New Guinea, Paraguay, Peru, Philippines, Poland, Portugal, Qatar, Romania, Russia, Rwanda, Saint Kitts and Nevis, Saint Lucia, Saint Vincent and the Grenadines, Samoa, San Marino, Sao Tome and Principe, Saudi Arabia, Senegal, Seychelles, Sierra Leone, Singapore, Slovakia, Slovenia, Solomon Islands, Somalia, South Africa, Spain, Sri Lanka, Sudan, Suriname, Swaziland, Sweden, Switzerland, Syria, Tajikistan, Tanzania, Thailand, Togo, Tonga, Trinidad and Tobago, Tunisia, Turkey, Turkmenistan, Uganda, Ukraine, UAE, UK, US, Uruguay, Uzbekistan, Vanuatu, Venezuela, Vietnam, Yemen, Zambia, Zimbabwe

International Chamber of Commerce (ICC)

established—NA 1919
aim—to promote free trade and private enterprise and to represent business interests at national and international levels

members—(78 national councils) Algeria, Argentina, Australia, Austria, Bahrain, Bangladesh, Belgium, Brazil, Burkina Faso, Cameroon, Canada, Caribbean, Chile, China, Colombia, Cote d'Ivoire, Cuba, Cyprus, Czech Republic, Denmark, Ecuador, Egypt, Finland, France, Germany, Ghana, Greece, Greenland, Hong Kong, Hungary, Iceland, India, Indonesia, Iran, Ireland, Israel, Italy, Japan, Jordan, South Korea, Kuwait, Lebanon, Lithuania, Luxembourg, Madagascar, Mexico, Morocco, Netherlands, NZ, Nigeria, Norway, Pakistan, Peru, Philippines, Poland, Portugal, Russia, Saudi Arabia, Senegal, Singapore, Slovakia, South Africa, Spain, Sri Lanka, Sweden, Switzerland, Syria, Taiwan, Tanzania, Thailand, Togo, Tunisia, Turkey, UK, US, Uruguay, Venezuela, Yugoslavia

International Civil Aviation Organization (ICAO)

established—7 December 1944
effective—4 April 1947
aim—to promote international cooperation in civil aviation; a UN specialized agency

members—(187) Afghanistan, Albania, Algeria, Andorra, Angola, Antigua and Barbuda, Argentina, Armenia, Australia, Austria, Azerbaijan, The Bahamas, Bahrain, Bangladesh, Barbados, Belarus, Belgium, Belize, Benin, Bhutan, Bolivia, Bosnia and Herzegovina, Botswana, Brazil, Brunei, Bulgaria, Burkina Faso, Burma, Burundi, Cambodia, Cameroon, Canada, Cape Verde, Central African Republic, Chad, Chile, China, Colombia, Comoros, Democratic Republic of the Congo, Republic of the Congo, Cook Islands, Costa Rica, Cote d'Ivoire, Croatia, Cuba, Cyprus, Czech Republic, Denmark, Djibouti, Dominican Republic, Ecuador, Egypt, El Salvador, Equatorial Guinea, Eritrea, Estonia, Ethiopia, Fiji, Finland, France, Gabon, The Gambia, Georgia, Germany, Ghana, Greece, Grenada, Guatemala, Guinea, Guinea-Bissau, Guyana, Haiti, Honduras, Hungary, Iceland, India, Indonesia, Iran, Iraq, Ireland, Israel, Italy, Jamaica, Japan, Jordan, Kazakhstan, Kenya, Kiribati, North Korea, South Korea, Kuwait, Kyrgyzstan, Laos, Latvia, Lebanon, Lesotho, Liberia, Libya, Lithuania, Luxembourg, The Former Yugoslav Republic of Macedonia, Madagascar, Malawi, Malaysia, Maldives, Mali, Malta, Marshall Islands, Mauritania, Mauritius, Mexico, Federated States of Micronesia, Moldova, Monaco, Mongolia, Morocco, Mozambique, Namibia, Nauru, Nepal, Netherlands, NZ, Nicaragua, Niger, Nigeria, Norway, Oman, Palau, Pakistan, Panama, Papua New Guinea, Paraguay, Peru, Philippines, Poland, Portugal, Qatar, Romania, Russia, Rwanda, Saint Lucia, Saint Vincent and the Grenadines, Samoa, San Marino, Sao Tome and Principe, Saudi Arabia, Senegal, Seychelles, Sierra Leone, Singapore, Slovakia, Slovenia, Solomon Islands, Somalia, South Africa, Spain, Sri Lanka, Sudan, Suriname, Swaziland, Sweden, Switzerland, Syria, Tajikistan, Tanzania, Thailand, Togo, Tonga, Trinidad and Tobago, Tunisia, Turkey, Turkmenistan, Uganda, Ukraine, UAE, UK, US, Uruguay, Uzbekistan, Vanuatu, Venezuela, Vietnam, Yemen, Yugoslavia, Zambia, Zimbabwe

Appendix B: International Organizations and Groups *(continued)*

International Committee of the Red Cross (ICRC) *established*—17 February 1863 *aim*—to provide humanitarian aid in wartime	*members*—(25 individuals) all Swiss nationals
International Confederation of Free Trade Unions (ICFTU) *established*—NA December 1949 *aim*—to promote the trade union movement	*members*—(221 affiliated organizations in the following 148 countries) Algeria, Angola, Antigua and Barbuda, Argentina, Australia, Austria, Azerbaijan, The Bahamas, Bangladesh, Barbados, Basque Country, Belgium, Belize, Benin, Bermuda, Botswana, Brazil, Bulgaria, Burkina Faso, Cameroon, Canada, Cape Verde, Central African Republic, Chad, Chile, China, Colombia, Democratic Republic of the Congo, Republic of the Congo, Cook Islands, Costa Rica, Cote d'Ivoire, Croatia, Curacao, Cyprus, Czech Republic, Denmark, Djibouti, Dominica, Dominican Republic, Ecuador, El Salvador, Eritrea, Estonia, Falkland Islands, Fiji, Finland, France, French Polynesia, Gabon, The Gambia, Georgia, Germany, Ghana, Greece, Grenada, Guatemala, Guinea, Guinea-Bissau, Guyana, Holy See, Honduras, Hong Kong, Hungary, Iceland, India, Indonesia, Ireland, Israel, Italy, Jamaica, Japan, Jordan, Kenya, Kiribati, South Korea, Latvia, Lebanon, Liberia, Lithuania, Luxembourg, Madagascar, Malawi, Malaysia, Mali, Malta, Mauritania, Mauritius, Mexico, Moldova, Mongolia, Montserrat, Morocco, Mozambique, Nepal, Netherlands, New Caledonia, NZ, Nicaragua, Niger, Nigeria, Norway, Pakistan, Panama, Papua New Guinea, Paraguay, Peru, Philippines, Poland, Portugal, Puerto Rico, Romania, Russia, Rwanda, Saint Helena, Saint Kitts and Nevis, Saint Lucia, Saint Vincent and the Grenadines, Samoa, San Marino, Senegal, Seychelles, Sierra Leone, Singapore, Slovakia, South Africa, Spain, Sri Lanka, Suriname, Swaziland, Sweden, Switzerland, Taiwan, Tanzania, Thailand, Togo, Tonga, Trinidad and Tobago, Tunisia, Turkey, Uganda, UK, US, Vanuatu, Venezuela, Yugoslavia, Zambia, Zimbabwe
International Court of Justice (ICJ) *note*—also known as the World Court *established*—3 February 1946 superseded Permanent Court of International Justice *aim*—primary judicial organ of the UN	*members*—(15 judges) elected by the UN General Assembly and Security Council to represent all principal legal systems
International Criminal Police Organization (Interpol) *established*—NA September 1923 set up as the International Criminal Police Commission; 13 June 1956 constitution modified and present name adopted *aim*—to promote international cooperation among police authorities in fighting crime	*members*—(178) Albania, Algeria, Andorra, Angola, Antigua and Barbuda, Argentina, Armenia, Aruba, Australia, Austria, Azerbaijan, The Bahamas, Bahrain, Bangladesh, Barbados, Belarus, Belgium, Belize, Benin, Bolivia, Bosnia and Herzegovina, Botswana, Brazil, Brunei, Bulgaria, Burkina Faso, Burma, Burundi, Cambodia, Cameroon, Canada, Cape Verde, Central African Republic, Chad, Chile, China, Colombia, Comoros, Democratic Republic of the Congo, Republic of the Congo, Costa Rica, Cote d'Ivoire, Croatia, Cuba, Cyprus, Czech Republic, Denmark, Djibouti, Dominica, Dominican Republic, Ecuador, Egypt, El Salvador, Equatorial Guinea, Eritrea, Estonia, Ethiopia, Fiji, Finland, France, Gabon, The Gambia, Georgia, Germany, Ghana, Greece, Grenada, Guatemala, Guinea, Guinea-Bissau, Guyana, Haiti, Honduras, Hungary, Iceland, India, Indonesia, Iran, Iraq, Ireland, Israel, Italy, Jamaica, Japan, Jordan, Kazakhstan, Kenya, South Korea, Kuwait, Kyrgyzstan, Laos, Latvia, Lebanon, Lesotho, Liberia, Libya, Liechtenstein, Lithuania, Luxembourg, The Former Yugoslav Republic of Macedonia, Madagascar, Malawi, Malaysia, Maldives, Mali, Malta, Marshall Islands, Mauritania, Mauritius, Mexico, Moldova, Monaco, Mongolia, Morocco, Mozambique, Namibia, Nauru, Nepal, Netherlands, Netherlands Antilles, NZ, Nicaragua, Niger, Nigeria, Norway, Oman, Pakistan, Panama, Papua New Guinea, Paraguay, Peru, Philippines, Poland, Portugal, Qatar, Romania, Russia, Rwanda, Saint Kitts and Nevis, Saint Lucia, Saint Vincent and the Grenadines, Sao Tome and Principe, Saudi Arabia, Senegal, Seychelles, Sierra Leone, Singapore, Slovakia, Slovenia, Somalia, South Africa, Spain, Sri Lanka, Sudan, Suriname, Swaziland, Sweden, Switzerland, Syria, Tanzania, Thailand, Togo, Tonga, Trinidad and Tobago, Tunisia, Turkey, Uganda, Ukraine, UAE, UK, US, Uruguay, Uzbekistan, Venezuela, Vietnam, Yemen, Zambia, Zimbabwe *subbureaus*—(14) American Samoa, Anguilla, Bermuda, British Virgin Islands, Cayman Islands, Gibraltar, Guam, Hong Kong, Macau, Montserrat, Northern Mariana Islands, Puerto Rico, Turks and Caicos Islands, Virgin Islands

Appendix B: International Organizations and Groups *(continued)*

International Development Association (IDA)

established—26 January 1960
effective—24 September 1960
aim—UN specialized agency and IBRD affiliate that provides economic loans for low-income countries

members—(161)
Part I—(27 developed countries) Australia, Austria, Belgium, Canada, Denmark, EU, Finland, France, Germany, Iceland, Ireland, Italy, Japan, Kuwait, Luxembourg, Netherlands, NZ, Norway, Portugal, Russia, South Africa, Spain, Sweden, Switzerland, UAE, UK, US
Part II—(134 less developed countries) Afghanistan, Albania, Algeria, Angola, Argentina, Armenia, Azerbaijan, Bangladesh, Belize, Benin, Bhutan, Bolivia, Bosnia and Herzegovina, Botswana, Brazil, Burkina Faso, Burma, Burundi, Cambodia, Cameroon, Cape Verde, Central African Republic, Chad, Chile, China, Colombia, Comoros, Democratic Republic of the Congo, Republic of the Congo, Costa Rica, Cote d'Ivoire, Croatia, Cyprus, Czech Republic, Djibouti, Dominica, Dominican Republic, Ecuador, Egypt, El Salvador, Equatorial Guinea, Eritrea, Ethiopia, Fiji, Gabon, The Gambia, Georgia, Ghana, Greece, Grenada, Guatemala, Guinea, Guinea-Bissau, Guyana, Haiti, Honduras, Hungary, India, Indonesia, Iran, Iraq, Israel, Jordan, Kazakhstan, Kenya, Kiribati, South Korea, Kyrgyzstan, Laos, Latvia, Lebanon, Lesotho, Liberia, Libya, The Former Yugoslav Republic of Macedonia, Madagascar, Malawi, Malaysia, Maldives, Mali, Marshall Islands, Mauritania, Mauritius, Mexico, Federated States of Micronesia, Moldova, Mongolia, Morocco, Mozambique, Nepal, Nicaragua, Niger, Nigeria, Oman, Pakistan, Palau, Panama, Papua New Guinea, Paraguay, Peru, Philippines, Poland, Rwanda, Saint Kitts and Nevis, Saint Lucia, Saint Vincent and the Grenadines, Samoa, Sao Tome and Principe, Saudi Arabia, Senegal, Sierra Leone, Slovakia, Slovenia, Solomon Islands, Somalia, Sri Lanka, Sudan, Swaziland, Syria, Tajikistan, Tanzania, Thailand, Togo, Tonga, Trinidad and Tobago, Tunisia, Turkey, Uganda, Uzbekistan, Vanuatu, Vietnam, Yemen, Zambia, Zimbabwe

International Energy Agency (IEA)

established—15 November 1974
aim—to promote cooperation on energy matters, especially emergency oil sharing and relations between oil consumers and oil producers; established by the OECD

members—(25) Australia, Austria, Belgium, Canada, Czech Republic, Denmark, Finland, France, Germany, Greece, Hungary, Ireland, Italy, Japan, Luxembourg, Netherlands, NZ, Norway, Portugal, Spain, Sweden, Switzerland, Turkey, UK, US
observers—(15) Commission of the European Communities, Iceland, South Korea, Mexico, Poland

International Federation of Red Cross and Red Crescent Societies (IFRCS)

note—formerly known as League of Red Cross and Red Crescent Societies (LORCS)
established—5 May 1919
aim—to organize, coordinate, and direct international relief actions; to promote humanitarian activities; to represent and encourage the development of National Societies; to bring help to victims of armed conflicts, refugees, and displaced people; to reduce the vulnerability of people through development programs

members—(176) Afghanistan, Albania, Algeria, Andorra, Angola, Antigua and Barbuda, Argentina, Armenia, Australia, Austria, Azerbaijan, The Bahamas, Bahrain, Bangladesh, Barbados, Belarus, Belgium, Belize, Benin, Bolivia, Botswana, Brazil, Brunei, Bulgaria, Burkina Faso, Burma, Burundi, Cambodia, Cameroon, Canada, Cape Verde, Central African Republic, Chad, Chile, China, Colombia, Democratic Republic of the Congo, Republic of the Congo, Costa Rica, Cote d'Ivoire, Croatia, Cuba, Czech Republic, Denmark, Djibouti, Dominica, Dominican Republic, Ecuador, Egypt, El Salvador, Equatorial Guinea, Estonia, Ethiopia, Fiji, Finland, France, The Gambia, Georgia, Germany, Ghana, Greece, Grenada, Guatemala, Guinea, Guinea-Bissau, Guyana, Haiti, Honduras, Hungary, Iceland, India, Indonesia, Iran, Iraq, Ireland, Italy, Jamaica, Japan, Jordan, Kenya, Kiribati, North Korea, South Korea, Kuwait, Kyrgyzstan, Laos, Latvia, Lebanon, Lesotho, Liberia, Libya, Liechtenstein, Lithuania, Luxembourg, The Former Yugoslav Republic of Macedonia, Madagascar, Malawi, Malaysia, Mali, Malta, Mauritania, Mauritius, Mexico, Monaco, Mongolia, Morocco, Mozambique, Namibia, Nepal, Netherlands, NZ, Nicaragua, Niger, Nigeria, Norway, Pakistan, Palau, Panama, Papua New Guinea, Paraguay, Peru, Philippines, Poland, Portugal, Qatar, Romania, Russia, Rwanda, Saint Kitts and Nevis, Saint Lucia, Saint Vincent and the Grenadines, Samoa, San Marino, Sao Tome and Principe, Saudi Arabia, Senegal, Seychelles, Sierra Leone, Singapore, Slovakia, Slovenia, Solomon Islands, Somalia, South Africa, Spain, Sri Lanka, Sudan, Suriname, Swaziland, Sweden, Switzerland, Syria, Taiwan, Tajikistan, Tanzania, Thailand, Togo, Tonga, Trinidad and Tobago, Tunisia, Turkey, Turkmenistan, Uganda, Ukraine, UAE, UK, US, Uruguay, Uzbekistan, Vanuatu, Venezuela, Vietnam, Yemen, Yugoslavia, Zambia, Zimbabwe
associate members—(4) Comoros, Cyprus, Gabon, Tuvalu

Appendix B: International Organizations and Groups *(continued)*

International Finance Corporation (IFC) *established*—25 May 1955 *effective*—24 July 1956 *aim*—to support private enterprise in international economic development; a UN specialized agency and IBRD affiliate	*members*—(174) Afghanistan, Albania, Algeria, Angola, Antigua and Barbuda, Argentina, Armenia, Australia, Austria, Azerbaijan, The Bahamas, Bahrain, Bangladesh, Barbados, Belarus, Belgium, Belize, Benin, Bolivia, Bosnia and Herzegovina, Botswana, Brazil, Bulgaria, Burkina Faso, Burma, Burundi, Cambodia, Cameroon, Canada, Cape Verde, Central African Republic, Chad, Chile, China, Colombia, Comoros, Democratic Republic of the Congo, Republic of the Congo, Costa Rica, Cote d'Ivoire, Croatia, Cyprus, Czech Republic, Denmark, Djibouti, Dominica, Dominican Republic, Ecuador, Egypt, El Salvador, Equatorial Guinea, Eritrea, Estonia, Ethiopia, Fiji, Finland, France, Gabon, The Gambia, Georgia, Germany, Ghana, Greece, Grenada, Guatemala, Guinea, Guinea-Bissau, Guyana, Haiti, Honduras, Hungary, Iceland, India, Indonesia, Iran, Iraq, Ireland, Israel, Italy, Jamaica, Japan, Jordan, Kazakhstan, Kenya, Kiribati, South Korea, Kuwait, Kyrgyzstan, Laos, Latvia, Lebanon, Lesotho, Liberia, Libya, Lithuania, Luxembourg, The Former Yugoslav Republic of Macedonia, Madagascar, Malawi, Malaysia, Maldives, Mali, Marshall Islands, Mauritania, Mauritius, Mexico, Federated States of Micronesia, Moldova, Mongolia, Morocco, Mozambique, Namibia, Nepal, Netherlands, NZ, Nicaragua, Niger, Nigeria, Norway, Oman, Pakistan, Palau, Panama, Papua New Guinea, Paraguay, Peru, Philippines, Poland, Portugal, Romania, Russia, Rwanda, Saint Kitts and Nevis, Saint Lucia, Samoa, Saudi Arabia, Senegal, Seychelles, Sierra Leone, Singapore, Slovakia, Slovenia, Solomon Islands, Somalia, South Africa, Spain, Sri Lanka, Sudan, Swaziland, Sweden, Switzerland, Syria, Tajikistan, Tanzania, Thailand, Togo, Tonga, Trinidad and Tobago, Tunisia, Turkey, Turkmenistan, Uganda, Ukraine, UAE, UK, US, Uruguay, Uzbekistan, Vanuatu, Venezuela, Vietnam, Yemen, Zambia, Zimbabwe
International Fund for Agricultural Development (IFAD) *established*—NA November 1974 *aim*—to promote agricultural development; a UN specialized agency	*members*—(161) *Category I*—(22 industrialized aid contributors) Australia, Austria, Belgium, Canada, Denmark, Finland, France, Germany, Greece, Ireland, Italy, Japan, Luxembourg, Netherlands, NZ, Norway, Portugal, Spain, Sweden, Switzerland, UK, US *Category II*—(12 petroleum-exporting aid contributors) Algeria, Gabon, Indonesia, Iran, Iraq, Kuwait, Libya, Nigeria, Qatar, Saudi Arabia, UAE, Venezuela *Category III*—(127 aid recipients) Afghanistan, Albania, Angola, Antigua and Barbuda, Argentina, Armenia, Azerbaijan, Bangladesh, Barbados, Belize, Benin, Bhutan, Bolivia, Bosnia and Herzegovina, Botswana, Brazil, Burkina Faso, Burma, Burundi, Cambodia, Cameroon, Cape Verde, Central African Republic, Chad, Chile, China, Colombia, Comoros, Democratic Republic of the Congo, Republic of the Congo, Cook Islands, Costa Rica, Cote d'Ivoire, Croatia, Cuba, Cyprus, Djibouti, Dominica, Dominican Republic, Ecuador, Egypt, El Salvador, Equatorial Guinea, Eritrea, Ethiopia, Fiji, The Gambia, Georgia, Ghana, Grenada, Guatemala, Guinea, Guinea-Bissau, Guyana, Haiti, Honduras, India, Israel, Jamaica, Jordan, Kazakhstan, Kenya, North Korea, South Korea, Kyrgyzstan, Laos, Lebanon, Lesotho, Liberia, The Former Yugoslav Republic of Macedonia, Madagascar, Malawi, Malaysia, Maldives, Mali, Malta, Mauritania, Mauritius, Mexico, Moldova, Mongolia, Morocco, Mozambique, Namibia, Nepal, Nicaragua, Niger, Oman, Pakistan, Panama, Papua New Guinea, Paraguay, Peru, Philippines, Romania, Rwanda, Saint Kitts and Nevis, Saint Lucia, Saint Vincent and the Grenadines, Samoa, Sao Tome and Principe, Senegal, Seychelles, Sierra Leone, Solomon Islands, Somalia, South Africa, Sri Lanka, Sudan, Suriname, Swaziland, Syria, Tajikistan, Tanzania, Thailand, Togo, Tonga, Trinidad and Tobago, Tunisia, Turkey, Uganda, Uruguay, Vietnam, Yemen, Yugoslavia, Zambia, Zimbabwe
International Hydrographic Organization (IHO) *note*—name changed from International Hydrographic Bureau on 22 September 1970 *established*—NA June 1919 *effective*—NA June 1921 *aim*—to train hydrographic surveyors and nautical cartographers to achieve standardization in nautical charts and electronic chart displays; to provide advice on nautical cartography and hydrography; to develop the sciences in the field of hydrography and techniques used for descriptive oceanography	*members*—(68) Algeria, Argentina, Australia, Bahrain, Belgium, Brazil, Canada, Chile, China, Colombia, Democratic Republic of the Congo, Croatia, Cuba, Cyprus, Denmark, Dominican Republic, Ecuador, Egypt, Estonia, Fiji, Finland, France, Germany, Greece, Guatemala, Iceland, India, Indonesia, Iran, Italy, Japan, North Korea, South Korea, Malaysia, Monaco, Morocco, Mozambique, Netherlands, NZ, Nigeria, Norway, Oman, Pakistan, Papua New Guinea, Peru, Philippines, Poland, Portugal, Russia, Singapore, South Africa, Spain, Sri Lanka, Suriname, Sweden, Syria, Thailand, Tonga, Trinidad and Tobago, Tunisia, Turkey, Ukraine, UAE, UK, US, Uruguay, Venezuela, Yugoslavia *membership pending*—(5) Bangladesh, Bulgaria, Jamaica, Mauritania, Qatar

Appendix B: International Organizations and Groups *(continued)*

International Labor Organization (ILO) *established*—28 June 1919 set up as part of Treaty of Versailles; 11 April 1919 became operative; 14 December 1946 affiliated with the UN *aim*—to deal with world labor issues; a UN specialized agency	*members*—(175) Afghanistan, Albania, Algeria, Angola, Antigua and Barbuda, Argentina, Armenia, Australia, Austria, Azerbaijan, The Bahamas, Bahrain, Bangladesh, Barbados, Belarus, Belgium, Belize, Benin, Bolivia, Bosnia and Herzegovina, Botswana, Brazil, Bulgaria, Burkina Faso, Burma, Burundi, Cambodia, Cameroon, Canada, Cape Verde, Central African Republic, Chad, Chile, China, Colombia, Comoros, Democratic Republic of the Congo, Republic of the Congo, Costa Rica, Cote d'Ivoire, Croatia, Cuba, Cyprus, Czech Republic, Denmark, Djibouti, Dominica, Dominican Republic, Ecuador, Egypt, El Salvador, Equatorial Guinea, Eritrea, Estonia, Ethiopia, Fiji, Finland, France, Gabon, The Gambia, Georgia, Germany, Ghana, Greece, Grenada, Guatemala, Guinea, Guinea-Bissau, Guyana, Haiti, Honduras, Hungary, Iceland, India, Indonesia, Iran, Iraq, Ireland, Israel, Italy, Jamaica, Japan, Jordan, Kazakhstan, Kenya, Kiribati, South Korea, Kuwait, Kyrgyzstan, Laos, Latvia, Lebanon, Lesotho, Liberia, Libya, Lithuania, Luxembourg, The Former Yugoslav Republic of Macedonia, Madagascar, Malawi, Malaysia, Mali, Malta, Mauritania, Mauritius, Mexico, Moldova, Mongolia, Morocco, Mozambique, Namibia, Nepal, Netherlands, NZ, Nicaragua, Niger, Nigeria, Norway, Oman, Pakistan, Panama, Papua New Guinea, Paraguay, Peru, Philippines, Poland, Portugal, Qatar, Romania, Russia, Rwanda, Saint Kitts and Nevis, Saint Lucia, Saint Vincent and the Grenadines, San Marino, Sao Tome and Principe, Saudi Arabia, Senegal, Seychelles, Sierra Leone, Singapore, Slovakia, Slovenia, Solomon Islands, Somalia, South Africa, Spain, Sri Lanka, Sudan, Suriname, Swaziland, Sweden, Switzerland, Syria, Tajikistan, Tanzania, Thailand, Togo, Trinidad and Tobago, Tunisia, Turkey, Turkmenistan, Uganda, Ukraine, UAE, UK, US, Uruguay, Uzbekistan, Venezuela, Vietnam, Yemen, Yugoslavia, Zambia, Zimbabwe
International Maritime Organization (IMO) *note*—name changed from Intergovernmental Maritime Consultative Organization (IMCO) on 22 May 1982 *established*—6 March 1948 set up as the Inter-Governmental Maritime Consultative Organization *effective*—17 March 1958 *aim*—to deal with international maritime affairs; a UN specialized agency	*members*—(158) Albania, Algeria, Angola, Antigua and Barbuda, Argentina, Australia, Austria, Azerbaijan, The Bahamas, Bahrain, Bangladesh, Barbados, Belgium, Belize, Benin, Bolivia, Bosnia and Herzegovina, Brazil, Brunei, Bulgaria, Burma, Cambodia, Cameroon, Canada, Cape Verde, Chile, China, Colombia, Democratic Republic of the Congo, Republic of the Congo, Costa Rica, Cote d'Ivoire, Croatia, Cuba, Cyprus, Czech Republic, Denmark, Djibouti, Dominica, Dominican Republic, Ecuador, Egypt, El Salvador, Equatorial Guinea, Eritrea, Estonia, Ethiopia, Fiji, Finland, France, Gabon, The Gambia, Georgia, Germany, Ghana, Greece, Grenada, Guatemala, Guinea, Guinea-Bissau, Guyana, Haiti, Honduras, Hungary, Iceland, India, Indonesia, Iran, Iraq, Ireland, Israel, Italy, Jamaica, Japan, Jordan, Kazakhstan, Kenya, North Korea, South Korea, Kuwait, Latvia, Lebanon, Liberia, Libya, Lithuania, Luxembourg, The Former Yugoslav Republic of Macedonia, Madagascar, Malawi, Malaysia, Maldives, Malta, Marshall Islands, Mauritania, Mauritius, Mexico, Monaco, Mongolia, Morocco, Mozambique, Namibia, Nepal, Netherlands, NZ, Nicaragua, Nigeria, Norway, Oman, Pakistan, Panama, Papua New Guinea, Paraguay, Peru, Philippines, Poland, Portugal, Qatar, Romania, Russia, Saint Lucia, Saint Vincent and the Grenadines, Samoa, Sao Tome and Principe, Saudi Arabia, Senegal, Seychelles, Sierra Leone, Singapore, Slovakia, Slovenia, Solomon Islands, Somalia, South Africa, Spain, Sri Lanka, Sudan, Suriname, Sweden, Switzerland, Syria, Tanzania, Thailand, Togo, Tonga, Trinidad and Tobago, Tunisia, Turkey, Turkmenistan, Ukraine, UAE, UK, US, Uruguay, Vanuatu, Venezuela, Vietnam, Yemen, Yugoslavia *associate members*—(2) Hong Kong, Macau
International Mobile Satellite Organization (Inmarsat) *note*—formerly International Maritime Satellite Organization *established*—3 September 1976 *effective*—16 July 1979 *aim*—to provide worldwide communications for commercial, distress, and safety applications, at sea, in the air, and on land	*members*—(86) Algeria, Argentina, Australia, The Bahamas, Bahrain, Bangladesh, Belarus, Belgium, Bosnia and Herzegovina, Brazil, Brunei, Bulgaria, Cameroon, Canada, Chile, China, Colombia, Costa Rica, Croatia, Cuba, Cyprus, Czech Republic, Denmark, Egypt, Finland, France, Gabon, Georgia, Germany, Ghana, Greece, Hungary, Iceland, India, Indonesia, Iran, Iraq, Israel, Italy, Japan, Kenya, South Korea, Kuwait, Latvia, Lebanon, Liberia, Malaysia, Malta, Marshall Islands, Mauritius, Mexico, Monaco, Mozambique, Netherlands, NZ, Nigeria, Norway, Oman, Pakistan, Panama, Peru, Philippines, Poland, Portugal, Qatar, Romania, Russia, Saudi Arabia, Senegal, Singapore, Slovakia, South Africa, Spain, Sri Lanka, Sweden, Switzerland, Tanzania, Thailand, Tunisia, Turkey, Ukraine, UAE, UK, US, Vietnam, Yugoslavia

Appendix B: International Organizations and Groups *(continued)*

International Monetary Fund (IMF) *established*—22 July 1944 *effective*—27 December 1945 *aim*—to promote world monetary stability and economic development; a UN specialized agency	*members*—(183) Afghanistan, Albania, Algeria, Angola, Antigua and Barbuda, Argentina, Armenia, Australia, Austria, Azerbaijan, The Bahamas, Bahrain, Bangladesh, Barbados, Belarus, Belgium, Belize, Benin, Bhutan, Bolivia, Bosnia and Herzegovina, Botswana, Brazil, Brunei, Bulgaria, Burkina Faso, Burma, Burundi, Cambodia, Cameroon, Canada, Cape Verde, Central African Republic, Chad, Chile, China, Colombia, Comoros, Democratic Republic of the Congo, Republic of the Congo, Costa Rica, Cote d'Ivoire, Croatia, Cyprus, Czech Republic, Denmark, Djibouti, Dominica, Dominican Republic, Ecuador, Egypt, El Salvador, Equatorial Guinea, Eritrea, Estonia, Ethiopia, Fiji, Finland, France, Gabon, The Gambia, Georgia, Germany, Ghana, Greece, Grenada, Guatemala, Guinea, Guinea-Bissau, Guyana, Haiti, Honduras, Hungary, Iceland, India, Indonesia, Iran, Iraq, Ireland, Israel, Italy, Jamaica, Japan, Jordan, Kazakhstan, Kenya, Kiribati, South Korea, Kuwait, Kyrgyzstan, Laos, Latvia, Lebanon, Lesotho, Liberia, Libya, Lithuania, Luxembourg, The Former Yugoslav Republic of Macedonia, Madagascar, Malawi, Malaysia, Maldives, Mali, Malta, Marshall Islands, Mauritania, Mauritius, Mexico, Federated States of Micronesia, Moldova, Mongolia, Morocco, Mozambique, Namibia, Nepal, Netherlands, NZ, Nicaragua, Niger, Nigeria, Norway, Oman, Pakistan, Palau, Panama, Papua New Guinea, Paraguay, Peru, Philippines, Poland, Portugal, Qatar, Romania, Russia, Rwanda, Saint Kitts and Nevis, Saint Lucia, Saint Vincent and the Grenadines, Samoa, San Marino, Sao Tome and Principe, Saudi Arabia, Senegal, Seychelles, Sierra Leone, Singapore, Slovakia, Slovenia, Solomon Islands, Somalia, South Africa, Spain, Sri Lanka, Sudan, Suriname, Swaziland, Sweden, Switzerland, Syria, Tajikistan, Tanzania, Thailand, Togo, Tonga, Trinidad and Tobago, Tunisia, Turkey, Turkmenistan, Uganda, Ukraine, UAE, UK, US, Uruguay, Uzbekistan, Vanuatu, Venezuela, Vietnam, Yemen, Yugoslavia, Zambia, Zimbabwe
International Olympic Committee (IOC) *established*—23 June 1894 *aim*—to promote the Olympic ideals and administer the Olympic games: 2002 Winter Olympics in Salt Lake City, United States; 2004 Summer Olympics in Athens, Greece; 2006 Winter Olympics in Turin, Italy	*National Olympic Committees*—(199 and the Palestine Liberation Organization) Afghanistan, Albania, Algeria, American Samoa, Andorra, Angola, Antigua and Barbuda, Argentina, Armenia, Aruba, Australia, Austria, Azerbaijan, The Bahamas, Bahrain, Bangladesh, Barbados, Belarus, Belgium, Belize, Benin, Bermuda, Bhutan, Bolivia, Bosnia and Herzegovina, Botswana, Brazil, British Virgin Islands, Brunei, Bulgaria, Burkina Faso, Burma, Burundi, Cambodia, Cameroon, Canada, Cape Verde, Cayman Islands, Central African Republic, Chad, Chile, China, Colombia, Comoros, Democratic Republic of the Congo, Republic of the Congo, Cook Islands, Costa Rica, Cote d'Ivoire, Croatia, Cuba, Cyprus, Czech Republic, Denmark, Djibouti, Dominica, Dominican Republic, Ecuador, Egypt, El Salvador, Equatorial Guinea, Eritrea, Estonia, Ethiopia, Fiji, Finland, France, Gabon, The Gambia, Georgia, Germany, Ghana, Greece, Grenada, Guam, Guatemala, Guinea, Guinea-Bissau, Guyana, Haiti, Honduras, Hong Kong, Hungary, Iceland, India, Indonesia, Iran, Iraq, Ireland, Israel, Italy, Jamaica, Japan, Jordan, Kazakhstan, Kenya, North Korea, South Korea, Kuwait, Kyrgyzstan, Laos, Latvia, Lebanon, Lesotho, Liberia, Libya, Liechtenstein, Lithuania, Luxembourg, The Former Yugoslav Republic of Macedonia, Madagascar, Malawi, Malaysia, Maldives, Mali, Malta, Mauritania, Mauritius, Mexico, Federated States of Micronesia, Moldova, Monaco, Mongolia, Morocco, Mozambique, Namibia, Nauru, Nepal, Netherlands, Netherlands Antilles, NZ, Nicaragua, Niger, Nigeria, Norway, Oman, Pakistan, Palau, Panama, Papua New Guinea, Paraguay, Peru, Philippines, Poland, Portugal, Puerto Rico, Qatar, Romania, Russia, Rwanda, Saint Kitts and Nevis, Saint Lucia, Saint Vincent and the Grenadines, Samoa, San Marino, Sao Tome and Principe, Saudi Arabia, Senegal, Seychelles, Sierra Leone, Singapore, Slovakia, Slovenia, Solomon Islands, Somalia, South Africa, Spain, Sri Lanka, Sudan, Suriname, Swaziland, Sweden, Switzerland, Syria, Taiwan, Tajikistan, Tanzania, Thailand, Togo, Tonga, Trinidad and Tobago, Tunisia, Turkey, Turkmenistan, Uganda, Ukraine, UAE, UK, US, Uruguay, Uzbekistan, Vanuatu, Venezuela, Vietnam, Virgin Islands, Yemen, Yugoslavia, Zambia, Zimbabwe, Palestine Liberation Organization
International Organization for Migration (IOM) *note*—established as Provisional Intergovernmental Committee for the Movement of Migrants from Europe; renamed Intergovernmental Committee for European Migration (ICEM) on 15 November 1952; renamed Intergovernmental Committee for Migration (ICM) in November 1980; current name adopted 14 November 1989 *established*—5 December 1951 *aim*—to facilitate orderly international emigration and immigration	*members*—(79) Albania, Algeria, Angola, Argentina, Armenia, Australia, Austria, Bangladesh, Belgium, Belize, Benin, Bolivia, Bulgaria, Burkina Faso, Canada, Chile, Colombia, Costa Rica, Cote d'Ivoire Croatia, Cyprus, Czech Republic, Denmark, Dominican Republic, Ecuador, Egypt, El Salvador, Finland, France, Germany, Greece, Guatemala, Guinea, Guinea-Bissau, Haiti, Honduras, Hungary, Israel, Italy, Japan, Jordan, Kenya, South Korea, Kyrgyzstan, Latvia, Liberia, Lithuania, Luxembourg, Mali, Morocco, Netherlands, Nicaragua, Norway, Pakistan, Panama, Paraguay, Peru, Philippines, Poland, Portugal, Romania, Senegal, Slovakia, Slovenia, South Africa, Sri Lanka, Sudan, Sweden, Switzerland, Tajikistan, Tanzania, Thailand, Tunisia, Uganda, US, Uruguay, Venezuela, Yemen, Zambia *observers*—(43) Afghanistan, Belarus, Bhutan, Bosnia and Herzegovina, Brazil, Cambodia, Cape Verde, Democratic Republic of the Congo, Republic of the Congo, Cuba, Estonia, Ethiopia, Georgia, Ghana, Holy See, India, Indonesia, Iran, Ireland, Jamaica, Kazakhstan, The Former Yugoslav Republic of Macedonia, Madagascar, Malta, Mexico, Moldova, Mozambique, Namibia, NZ, Papua New Guinea, Russia, Rwanda, San Marino, Sao Tome and Principe, Somalia, Spain, Turkey, Turkmenistan, Ukraine, UK, Vietnam, Yugoslavia, Zimbabwe

Appendix B: International Organizations and Groups *(continued)*

International Organization for Standardization (ISO)

established—NA February 1947
aim—to promote the development of international standards with a view to facilitating international exchange of goods and services and to developing cooperation in the sphere of intellectual, scientific, technological and economic activity

members—(91 national standards organizations) Algeria, Argentina, Armenia, Australia, Austria, Bangladesh, Barbados, Belarus, Belgium, Bosnia and Herzegovina, Botswana, Brazil, Bulgaria, Canada, Chile, China, Colombia, Costa Rica, Croatia, Cuba, Cyprus, Czech Republic, Denmark, Ecuador, Egypt, Ethiopia, Finland, France, Germany, Ghana, Greece, Hungary, Iceland, India, Indonesia, Iran, Ireland, Israel, Italy, Jamaica, Japan, Kazakhstan, Kenya, North Korea, South Korea, Kuwait, Libya, Luxembourg, The Former Yugoslav Republic of Macedonia, Malaysia, Malta, Mauritius, Mexico, Mongolia, Morocco, Netherlands, NZ, Nigeria, Norway, Pakistan, Panama, Philippines, Poland, Portugal, Romania, Russia, Saudi Arabia, Singapore, Slovakia, Slovenia, South Africa, Spain, Sri Lanka, Sweden, Switzerland, Syria, Tanzania, Thailand, Trinidad and Tobago, Tunisia, Turkey, Ukraine, UAE, UK, US, Uruguay, Uzbekistan, Venezuela, Vietnam, Yugoslavia, Zimbabwe
correspondent members—(34) Albania, Azerbaijan, Bahrain, Bolivia, Brunei, Cameroon, Democratic Republic of the Congo, Cote d'Ivoire, El Salvador, Estonia, Guatemala, Honduras, Hong Kong, Jordan, Kyrgyzstan, Latvia, Lebanon, Lithuania, Madagascar, Malawi, Moldova, Mozambique, Namibia, Nepal, Nicaragua, Oman, Papua New Guinea, Paraguay, Peru, Qatar, Rwanda, Sudan, Turkmenistan, Uganda
subscriber members—(11) Benin, Burkina Faso, Cambodia, Comoros, Dominican Republic, Fiji, Grenada, Guyana, Lesotho, Mali, Saint Lucia

International Red Cross and Red Crescent Movement (ICRM)

established—NA 1928
aim—to promote worldwide humanitarian aid through the International Committee of the Red Cross (ICRC) in wartime, and International Federation of Red Cross and Red Crescent Societies (IFRCS; formerly League of Red Cross and Red Crescent Societies or LORCS) in peacetime

National Societies—(176 countries); *note*—same as membership for International Federation of Red Cross and Red Crescent Societies (IFRCS)

International Telecommunication Union (ITU)

established—17 May 1865 set up as the International Telegraph Union; 9 December 1932 adopted present name
effective—1 January 1934; affiliated with the UN—15 November 1947
aim—to deal with world telecommunications issues; a UN specialized agency

members—(189) Afghanistan, Albania, Algeria, Andorra, Angola, Antigua and Barbuda, Argentina, Armenia, Australia, Austria, Azerbaijan, The Bahamas, Bahrain, Bangladesh, Barbados, Belarus, Belgium, Belize, Benin, Bhutan, Bolivia, Bosnia and Herzegovina, Botswana, Brazil, Brunei, Bulgaria, Burkina Faso, Burma, Burundi, Cambodia, Cameroon, Canada, Cape Verde, Central African Republic, Chad, Chile, China, Colombia, Comoros, Democratic Republic of the Congo, Republic of the Congo, Costa Rica, Cote d'Ivoire, Croatia, Cuba, Cyprus, Czech Republic, Denmark, Djibouti, Dominica, Dominican Republic, Ecuador, Egypt, El Salvador, Equatorial Guinea, Eritrea, Estonia, Ethiopia, Fiji, Finland, France, Gabon, The Gambia, Georgia, Germany, Ghana, Greece, Grenada, Guatemala, Guinea, Guinea-Bissau, Guyana, Haiti, Holy See, Honduras, Hungary, Iceland, India, Indonesia, Iran, Iraq, Ireland, Israel, Italy, Jamaica, Japan, Jordan, Kazakhstan, Kenya, Kiribati, North Korea, South Korea, Kuwait, Kyrgyzstan, Laos, Latvia, Lebanon, Lesotho, Liberia, Libya, Liechtenstein, Lithuania, Luxembourg, The Former Yugoslav Republic of Macedonia, Madagascar, Malawi, Malaysia, Maldives, Mali, Malta, Marshall Islands, Mauritania, Mauritius, Mexico, Federated States of Micronesia, Moldova, Monaco, Mongolia, Morocco, Mozambique, Namibia, Nauru, Nepal, Netherlands, NZ, Nicaragua, Niger, Nigeria, Norway, Oman, Pakistan, Panama, Papua New Guinea, Paraguay, Peru, Philippines, Poland, Portugal, Qatar, Romania, Russia, Rwanda, Saint Lucia, Saint Vincent and the Grenadines, Samoa, San Marino, Sao Tome and Principe, Saudi Arabia, Senegal, Seychelles, Sierra Leone, Singapore, Slovakia, Slovenia, Solomon Islands, Somalia, South Africa, Spain, Sri Lanka, Sudan, Suriname, Swaziland, Sweden, Switzerland, Syria, Tajikistan, Tanzania, Thailand, Togo, Tonga, Trinidad and Tobago, Tunisia, Turkey, Turkmenistan, Tuvalu, Uganda, Ukraine, UAE, UK, US, Uruguay, Uzbekistan, Vanuatu, Venezuela, Vietnam, Yemen, Yugoslavia, Zambia, Zimbabwe

Appendix B: International Organizations and Groups *(continued)*

International Telecommunications Satellite Organization (Intelsat) *established*—20 August 1964 set up as the Telecommunications Satellite Consortium; 12 February 1973 adopted present name *aim*—to develop and operate a global commercial telecommunications satellite system	*members*—(143) Afghanistan, Algeria, Angola, Argentina, Armenia, Australia, Austria, Azerbaijan, The Bahamas, Bahrain, Bangladesh, Barbados, Belgium, Benin, Bhutan, Bolivia, Bosnia and Herzegovina, Botswana, Brazil, Brunei, Bulgaria, Burkina Faso, Cameroon, Canada, Cape Verde, Central African Republic, Chad, Chile, China, Colombia, Comoros, Democratic Republic of the Congo, Republic of the Congo, Costa Rica, Cote d'Ivoire, Croatia, Cyprus, Czech Republic, Denmark, Dominican Republic, Ecuador, Egypt, El Salvador, Equatorial Guinea, Ethiopia, Fiji, Finland, France, Gabon, Germany, Ghana, Greece, Guatemala, Guinea, Haiti, Holy See, Honduras, Hungary, Iceland, India, Indonesia, Iran, Iraq, Ireland, Israel, Italy, Jamaica, Japan, Jordan, Kazakhstan, Kenya, South Korea, Kuwait, Kyrgyzstan, Lebanon, Libya, Liechtenstein, Luxembourg, Madagascar, Malawi, Malaysia, Mali, Malta, Mauritania, Mauritius, Mexico, Federated States of Micronesia, Monaco, Mongolia, Morocco, Mozambique, Namibia, Nepal, Netherlands, NZ, Nicaragua, Niger, Nigeria, Norway, Oman, Pakistan, Panama, Papua New Guinea, Paraguay, Peru, Philippines, Poland, Portugal, Qatar, Romania, Russia, Rwanda, Saudi Arabia, Senegal, Singapore, Somalia, South Africa, Spain, Sri Lanka, Sudan, Swaziland, Sweden, Switzerland, Syria, Tajikistan, Tanzania, Thailand, Togo, Trinidad and Tobago, Tunisia, Turkey, Uganda, UAE, UK, US, Uruguay, Uzbekistan, Venezuela, Vietnam, Yemen, Yugoslavia, Zambia, Zimbabwe *nonsignatory users*—(42) Albania, Antigua and Barbuda, Belarus, Belize, Burma, Burundi, Cambodia, Cook Islands, Cuba, Djibouti, Eritrea, The Gambia, Guinea-Bissau, Guyana, Kiribati, North Korea, Laos, Latvia, Lesotho, Liberia, Lithuania, The Former Yugoslav Republic of Macedonia, Maldives, Marshall Islands, Moldova, Nauru, Niue, Saint Lucia, Saint Vincent and the Grenadines, Samoa, Sao Tome and Principe, Seychelles, Sierra Leone, Slovakia, Slovenia, Solomon Islands, Suriname, Tonga, Turkmenistan, Tuvalu, Ukraine, Vanuatu
Islamic Development Bank (IDB) *established*—15 December 1973 by declaration of intent *effective*—12 August 1974 *aim*—to promote Islamic economic aid and social development	*members*—(52 plus the Palestine Liberation Organization) Afghanistan, Albania, Algeria, Azerbaijan, Bahrain, Bangladesh, Benin, Brunei, Burkina Faso, Cameroon, Chad, Comoros, Djibouti, Egypt, Gabon, The Gambia, Guinea, Guinea-Bissau, Indonesia, Iran, Iraq, Jordan, Kazakhstan, Kuwait, Kyrgyzstan, Lebanon, Libya, Malaysia, Maldives, Mali, Mauritania, Morocco, Mozambique, Niger, Oman, Pakistan, Qatar, Saudi Arabia, Senegal, Sierra Leone, Somalia, Sudan, Suriname, Syria, Tajikistan, Togo, Tunisia, Turkey, Turkmenistan, Uganda, UAE, Yemen, Palestine Liberation Organization
Latin American Economic System (LAES) *note*—also known as Sistema Economico Latinoamericana (SELA) *established*—17 October 1975 *aim*—to promote economic and social development through regional cooperation	*members*—(28) Argentina, The Bahamas, Barbados, Belize, Bolivia, Brazil, Chile, Colombia, Costa Rica, Cuba, Dominican Republic, Ecuador, El Salvador, Grenada, Guatemala, Guyana, Haiti, Honduras, Jamaica, Mexico, Nicaragua, Panama, Paraguay, Peru, Suriname, Trinidad and Tobago, Uruguay, Venezuela *observers*—(21) Andean Promotion Corporation, China, Costa Rica, Dominican Republic, El Salvador, EEC, Guatemala, Honduras, IADB, Inter-American Institute for Agricultural Cooperation, Italy, Nicaragua, OAS, Panama, Portugal, Romania, Russia, Spain, Switzerland, UN Development Program, UN Economic Commission for Latin America and the Caribbean
Latin American Integration Association (LAIA) *note*—also known as Asociacion Latinoamericana de Integracion (ALADI) *established*—12 August 1980 *effective*—18 March 1981 *aim*—to promote freer regional trade	*members*—(12) Argentina, Bolivia, Brazil, Chile, Colombia, Cuba, Ecuador, Mexico, Paraguay, Peru, Uruguay, Venezuela *observers*—(22) China, Commission of the European Communities, Corporacion Andina de Fomento, Costa Rica, Dominican Republic, El Salvador, Guatemala, Honduras, Inter-American Development Bank, Inter-American Institute for Cooperation on Agriculture, Italy, Latin America Economic System, Nicaragua, Organization of American States, Panama, Portugal, Romania, Russia, Spain, Switzerland, United Nations Development Program, United Nations Economic Commission for Latin America and the Caribbean
least developed countries (LLDCs)	that subgroup of the less developed countries (LDCs) initially identified by the UN General Assembly in 1971 as having no significant economic growth, per capita GDPs normally less than $1,000, and low literacy rates; also known as the undeveloped countries; the 42 LLDCs are: Afghanistan, Bangladesh, Benin, Bhutan, Botswana, Burkina Faso, Burma, Burundi, Cape Verde, Central African Republic, Chad, Comoros, Djibouti, Equatorial Guinea, Eritrea, Ethiopia, The Gambia, Guinea, Guinea-Bissau, Haiti, Kiribati, Laos, Lesotho, Malawi, Maldives, Mali, Mauritania, Mozambique, Nepal, Niger, Rwanda, Samoa, Sao Tome and Principe, Sierra Leone, Somalia, Sudan, Tanzania, Togo, Tuvalu, Uganda, Vanuatu, Yemen

Appendix B: International Organizations and Groups (continued)

less developed countries (LDCs)	the bottom group in the hierarchy of developed countries (DCs), former USSR/Eastern Europe (former USSR/EE), and less developed countries (LDCs); mainly countries and dependent areas with low levels of output, living standards, and technology; per capita GDPs are generally below $5,000 and often less than $1,500; however, the group also includes a number of countries with high per capita incomes, areas of advanced technology, and rapid rates of growth; includes the advanced developing countries, developing countries, Four Dragons (Four Tigers), least developed countries (LLDCs), low-income countries, middle-income countries, newly industrializing economies (NIEs), the South, Third World, underdeveloped countries, undeveloped countries; the 172 LDCs are: Afghanistan, Algeria, American Samoa, Angola, Anguilla, Antigua and Barbuda, Argentina, Aruba, The Bahamas, Bahrain, Bangladesh, Barbados, Belize, Benin, Bhutan, Bolivia, Botswana, Brazil, British Virgin Islands, Brunei, Burkina Faso, Burma, Burundi, Cambodia, Cameroon, Cape Verde, Cayman Islands, Central African Republic, Chad, Chile, China, Christmas Island, Cocos Islands, Colombia, Comoros, Democratic Republic of the Congo, Republic of the Congo, Cook Islands, Costa Rica, Cote d'Ivoire, Cuba, Cyprus, Djibouti, Dominica, Dominican Republic, Ecuador, Egypt, El Salvador, Equatorial Guinea, Eritrea, Ethiopia, Falkland Islands, Fiji, French Guiana, French Polynesia, Gabon, The Gambia, Gaza Strip, Ghana, Gibraltar, Greenland, Grenada, Guadeloupe, Guam, Guatemala, Guernsey, Guinea, Guinea-Bissau, Guyana, Haiti, Honduras, Hong Kong, India, Indonesia, Iran, Iraq, Jamaica, Jersey, Jordan, Kenya, Kiribati, North Korea, South Korea, Kuwait, Laos, Lebanon, Lesotho, Liberia, Libya, Macau, Madagascar, Malawi, Malaysia, Maldives, Mali, Isle of Man, Marshall Islands, Martinique, Mauritania, Mauritius, Mayotte, Federated States of Micronesia, Mongolia, Montserrat, Morocco, Mozambique, Namibia, Nauru, Nepal, Netherlands Antilles, New Caledonia, Nicaragua, Niger, Nigeria, Niue, Norfolk Island, Northern Mariana Islands, Oman, Palau, Pakistan, Panama, Papua New Guinea, Paraguay, Peru, Philippines, Pitcairn Islands, Puerto Rico, Qatar, Reunion, Rwanda, Saint Helena, Saint Kitts and Nevis, Saint Lucia, Saint Pierre and Miquelon, Saint Vincent and the Grenadines, Samoa, Sao Tome and Principe, Saudi Arabia, Senegal, Seychelles, Sierra Leone, Singapore, Solomon Islands, Somalia, Sri Lanka, Sudan, Suriname, Swaziland, Syria, Taiwan, Tanzania, Thailand, Togo, Tokelau, Tonga, Trinidad and Tobago, Tunisia, Turks and Caicos Islands, Tuvalu, UAE, Uganda, Uruguay, Vanuatu, Venezuela, Vietnam, Virgin Islands, Wallis and Futuna, West Bank, Western Sahara, Yemen, Zambia, Zimbabwe; *note*—similar to the new International Monetary Fund (IMF) term "developing countries" which adds Malta, Mexico, South Africa, and Turkey but omits in its recently published statistics American Samoa, Anguilla, British Virgin Islands, Brunei, Cayman Islands, Christmas Island, Cocos Islands, Cook Islands, Cuba, Eritrea, Falkland Islands, French Guiana, French Polynesia, Gaza Strip, Gibraltar, Greenland, Grenada, Guadeloupe, Guam, Guernsey, Jersey, North Korea, Macau, Isle of Man, Martinique, Mayotte, Montserrat, Nauru, New Caledonia, Niue, Norfolk Island, Northern Mariana Islands, Palau, Pitcairn Islands, Puerto Rico, Reunion, Saint Helena, Saint Pierre and Miquelon, Tokelau, Tonga, Turks and Caicos Islands, Tuvalu, Virgin Islands, Wallis and Futuna, West Bank, Western Sahara
low-income countries	another term for those less developed countries with below-average per capita GDPs; see less developed countries (LDCs)
middle-income countries	another term for those less developed countries with above-average per capita GDPs; see less developed countries (LDCs)
Monetary and Economic Community of Central Africa (CEMAC) *note*—was formerly the Central African Customs and Economic Union (UDEAC) *established*—8 December 1964 *effective*—1 January 1966 *aim*—to promote the establishment of a Central African Common Market	*members*—(6) Cameroon, Central African Republic, Chad, Republic of the Congo, Equatorial Guinea, Gabon
Near Abroad	Russian term for the 14 non-Russian successor states of the USSR, in which 25 million ethnic Russians live and in which Moscow has expressed a strong national security interest; the 14 countries are Armenia, Azerbaijan, Belarus, Estonia, Georgia, Kazakhstan, Kyrgyzstan, Latvia, Lithuania, Moldova, Tajikistan, Turkmenistan, Ukraine, Uzbekistan
new independent states (NIS)	a term referring to all those countries of the FSU except the Baltic countries (Estonia, Latvia, Lithuania)
newly industrializing countries (NICs)	former term for the newly industrializing economies; see newly industrializing economies (NIEs)
newly industrializing economies (NIEs)	that subgroup of the less developed countries (LDCs) that has experienced particularly rapid industrialization of their economies; formerly known as the newly industrializing countries (NICs); also known as advanced developing countries; usually includes the Four Dragons (Hong Kong, South Korea, Singapore, Taiwan), and Brazil

Appendix B: International Organizations and Groups *(continued)*

Nonaligned Movement (NAM) *established*—1-6 September 1961 *aim*—to establish political and military cooperation apart from the traditional East or West blocs	*members*—(113 plus the Palestine Liberation Organization) Afghanistan, Algeria, Angola, The Bahamas, Bahrain, Bangladesh, Barbados, Belarus, Belize, Benin, Bhutan, Bolivia, Botswana, Brunei, Burkina Faso, Burma, Burundi, Cambodia, Cameroon, Cape Verde, Central African Republic, Chad, Chile, Colombia, Comoros, Democratic Republic of the Congo, Republic of the Congo, Cote d'Ivoire, Cuba, Cyprus, Djibouti, Ecuador, Egypt, Equatorial Guinea, Eritrea, Ethiopia, Gabon, The Gambia, Ghana, Grenada, Guatemala, Guinea, Guinea-Bissau, Guyana, Honduras, India, Indonesia, Iran, Iraq, Jamaica, Jordan, Kenya, North Korea, Kuwait, Laos, Lebanon, Lesotho, Liberia, Libya, Madagascar, Malawi, Malaysia, Maldives, Mali, Malta, Mauritania, Mauritius, Mongolia, Morocco, Mozambique, Namibia, Nepal, Nicaragua, Niger, Nigeria, Oman, Pakistan, Panama, Papua New Guinea, Peru, Philippines, Qatar, Rwanda, Saint Lucia, Sao Tome and Principe, Saudi Arabia, Senegal, Seychelles, Sierra Leone, Singapore, Somalia, South Africa, Sri Lanka, Sudan, Suriname, Swaziland, Syria, Tanzania, Thailand, Togo, Trinidad and Tobago, Tunisia, Turkmenistan, Uganda, UAE, Uzbekistan, Vanuatu, Venezuela, Vietnam, Yemen, Yugoslavia, Zambia, Zimbabwe, Palestine Liberation Organization *observers*—(16) Antigua and Barbuda, Armenia, Azerbaijan, Brazil, China, Costa Rica, Croatia, Dominica, Dominican Republic, El Salvador, Kazakhstan, Kyrgyzstan, Mexico, Paraguay, Ukraine, Uruguay *guests*—(28) Australia, Austria, Bosnia and Herzegovina, Bulgaria, Canada, Finland, France, Germany, Greece, Holy See, Hungary, Ireland, Italy, Japan, South Korea, Netherlands, NZ, Norway, Poland, Portugal, Romania, Russia, Slovakia, Slovenia, Sweden, Switzerland, UK, US
Nordic Council (NC) *established*—16 March 1952 *effective*—12 February 1953 *aim*—to promote regional economic, cultural, and environmental cooperation	*members*—(5) Denmark (including Faroe Islands and Greenland), Finland, Iceland, Norway, Sweden *observers*—(3) the Sami (Lapp) local parliaments of Finland, Norway, and Sweden
Nordic Investment Bank (NIB) *established*—4 December 1975 *effective*—1 June 1976 *aim*—to promote economic cooperation and development	*members*—(5) Denmark (including Faroe Islands and Greenland), Finland, Iceland, Norway, Sweden
North	a popular term for the rich industrialized countries generally located in the northern portion of the Northern Hemisphere; the counterpart of the South; see developed countries (DCs)
North Atlantic Treaty Organization (NATO) *established*—4 April 1949 *aim*—to promote mutual defense and cooperation	*members*—(19) Belgium, Canada, Czech Republic, Denmark, France, Germany, Greece, Hungary, Iceland, Italy, Luxembourg, Netherlands, Norway, Poland, Portugal, Spain, Turkey, UK, US
Nuclear Energy Agency (NEA) *note*—also known as OECD Nuclear Energy Agency *established*—1 February 1958 *aim*—to promote the peaceful uses of nuclear energy; associated with OECD	*members*—(27) Australia, Austria, Belgium, Canada, Czech Republic, Denmark, Finland, France, Germany, Greece, Hungary, Iceland, Ireland, Italy, Japan, South Korea, Luxembourg, Mexico, Netherlands, Norway, Portugal, Spain, Sweden, Switzerland, Turkey, UK, US
Nuclear Suppliers Group (NSG) *note*—also known as the London Suppliers Group or the London Group *established*—NA 1974 *effective*—NA 1975 *aim*—to establish guidelines for exports of nuclear materials, processing equipment for uranium enrichment, and technical information to countries of proliferation concern and regions of conflict and instability	*members*—(39) Argentina, Australia, Austria, Belarus, Belgium, Brazil, Bulgaria, Canada, Cyprus, Czech Republic, Denmark, Finland, France, Germany, Greece, Hungary, Ireland, Italy, Japan, South Korea, Latvia, Luxembourg, Netherlands, NZ, Norway, Poland, Portugal, Romania, Russia, Slovakia, Slovenia, South Africa, Spain, Sweden, Switzerland, Turkey, Ukraine, UK, US *observers*—(1) European Commission

Appendix B: International Organizations and Groups *(continued)*

Organization for Economic Cooperation and Development (OECD) *established*—14 December 1960 *effective*—30 September 1961 *aim*—to promote economic cooperation and development	*members*—(30) Australia, Austria, Belgium, Canada, Czech Republic, Denmark, Finland, France, Germany, Greece, Hungary, Iceland, Ireland, Italy, Japan, South Korea, Luxembourg, Mexico, Netherlands, NZ, Norway, Poland, Portugal, Slovakia, Spain, Sweden, Switzerland, Turkey, UK, US *special member*—(1) EU
Organization for Security and Cooperation in Europe (OSCE) *note*—formerly the Conference on Security and Cooperation in Europe (CSCE) established 3 July 1975 *established*—1 January 1995 *aim*—to foster the implementation of human rights, fundamental freedoms, democracy, and the rule of law; to act as an instrument of early warning, conflict prevention, and crisis management; and to serve as a framework for conventional arms control and confidence building measures	*members*—(55) Albania, Andorra, Armenia, Austria, Azerbaijan, Belarus, Belgium, Bosnia and Herzegovina, Bulgaria, Canada, Croatia, Cyprus, Czech Republic, Denmark, Estonia, Finland, France, Georgia, Germany, Greece, Holy See, Hungary, Iceland, Ireland, Italy, Kazakhstan, Kyrgyzstan, Latvia, Liechtenstein, Lithuania, Luxembourg, The Former Yugoslav Republic of Macedonia, Malta, Moldova, Monaco, Netherlands, Norway, Poland, Portugal, Romania, Russia, San Marino, Slovakia, Slovenia, Spain, Sweden, Switzerland, Tajikistan, Turkey, Turkmenistan, Ukraine, UK, US, Uzbekistan, Yugoslavia *partners for cooperation*—(9) Algeria, Egypt, Israel, Japan, Jordan, South Korea, Morocco, Thailand, Tunisia
Organization for the Prohibition of Chemical Weapons (OPCW) *established*—29 April 1997 *aim*—to enforce the Convention on the Prohibition of the Development, Production, Stockpiling and Use of Chemical Weapons and on Their Destruction; to provide a forum for consultation and cooperation among the signatories of the Convention	*members*—(174) Afghanistan, Albania, Algeria, Argentina, Armenia, Australia, Austria, Azerbaijan, The Bahamas, Bahrain, Bangladesh, Belarus, Belgium, Benin, Bhutan, Bolivia, Bosnia and Herzegovina, Botswana, Brazil, Brunei, Bulgaria, Burkina Faso, Burma, Burundi, Cambodia, Cameroon, Canada, Cape Verde, Central African Republic, Chad, Chile, China, Colombia, Comoros, Democratic Republic of the Congo, Republic of the Congo, Cook Islands, Costa Rica, Cote d'Ivoire, Croatia, Cuba, Cyprus, Czech Republic, Denmark, Djibouti, Dominica, Dominican Republic, Ecuador, El Salvador, Eritrea, Equatorial Guinea, Estonia, Ethiopia, Fiji, Finland, France, Gabon, The Gambia, Georgia, Germany, Ghana, Greece, Grenada, Guatemala, Guinea, Guinea-Bissau, Guyana, Haiti, Holy See, Honduras, Hungary, Iceland, India, Indonesia, Iran, Ireland, Israel, Italy, Jamaica, Japan, Jordan, Kazakhstan, Kenya, Kiribati, South Korea, Kuwait, Kyrgyzstan, Laos, Latvia, Lesotho, Liberia, Liechtenstein, Lithuania, Luxembourg, The Former Yugoslav Republic of Macedonia, Madagascar, Malawi, Malaysia, Maldives, Mali, Malta, Marshall Islands, Mauritania, Mauritius, Mexico, Federated States of Micronesia, Moldova, Monaco, Mongolia, Morocco, Mozambique, Namibia, Nauru, Nepal, Netherlands, NZ, Nicaragua, Niger, Nigeria, Norway, Oman, Pakistan, Panama, Papua New Guinea, Paraguay, Peru, Philippines, Poland, Portugal, Qatar, Romania, Russia, Rwanda, Saint Kitts and Nevis, Saint Lucia, Saint Vincent and the Grenadines, Samoa, San Marino, Saudi Arabia, Senegal, Seychelles, Sierra Leone, Singapore, Slovakia, Slovenia, South Africa, Spain, Sri Lanka, Sudan, Suriname, Swaziland, Sweden, Switzerland, Tajikistan, Tanzania, Thailand, Togo, Trinidad and Tobago, Tunisia, Turkey, Turkmenistan, Uganda, Ukraine, UAE, UK, US, Uruguay, Uzbekistan, Venezuela, Vietnam, Yemen, Yugoslavia, Zambia, Zimbabwe
Organization of African Unity (OAU) *established*—25 May 1963 *aim*—to promote unity and cooperation among African states	*members*—(53) Algeria, Angola, Benin, Botswana, Burkina Faso, Burundi, Cameroon, Cape Verde, Central African Republic, Chad, Comoros, Democratic Republic of the Congo, Republic of the Congo, Cote d'Ivoire, Djibouti, Egypt, Equatorial Guinea, Eritrea, Ethiopia, Gabon, The Gambia, Ghana, Guinea, Guinea-Bissau, Kenya, Lesotho, Liberia, Libya, Madagascar, Malawi, Mali, Mauritania, Mauritius, Mozambique, Namibia, Niger, Nigeria, Rwanda, Sahrawi Arab Democratic Republic, Sao Tome and Principe, Senegal, Seychelles, Sierra Leone, Somalia, South Africa, Sudan, Swaziland, Tanzania, Togo, Tunisia, Uganda, Zambia, Zimbabwe
Organization of American States (OAS) *established*—14 April 1890 as the International Union of American Republics; 30 April 1948 adopted present charter *effective*—13 December 1951 *aim*—to promote regional peace and security as well as economic and social development	*members*—(35) Antigua and Barbuda, Argentina, The Bahamas, Barbados, Belize, Bolivia, Brazil, Canada, Chile, Colombia, Costa Rica, Cuba (excluded from formal participation since 1962), Dominica, Dominican Republic, Ecuador, El Salvador, Grenada, Guatemala, Guyana, Haiti, Honduras, Jamaica, Mexico, Nicaragua, Panama, Paraguay, Peru, Saint Kitts and Nevis, Saint Lucia, Saint Vincent and the Grenadines, Suriname, Trinidad and Tobago, US, Uruguay, Venezuela *observers*—(50) Algeria, Angola, Austria, Azerbaijan, Belgium, Bosnia and Herzegovina, Bulgaria, Croatia, Cyprus, Czech Republic, Denmark, Egypt, Equatorial Guinea, EU, Finland, France, Germany, Ghana, Greece, Holy See, Hungary, India, Ireland, Israel, Italy, Japan, Kazakhstan, South Korea, Latvia, Lebanon, Morocco, Netherlands, Norway, Pakistan, Philippines, Poland, Portugal, Romania, Russia, Saudi Arabia, Spain, Sri Lanka, Sweden, Switzerland, Thailand, Tunisia, Turkey, Ukraine, UK, Yemen

Appendix B: International Organizations and Groups (continued)

Organization of Arab Petroleum Exporting Countries (OAPEC) *established*—9 January 1968 *aim*—to promote cooperation in the petroleum industry	*members*—(10) Algeria, Bahrain, Egypt, Iraq, Kuwait, Libya, Qatar, Saudi Arabia, Syria, UAE
Organization of Eastern Caribbean States (OECS) *established*—18 June 1981 *effective*—4 July 1981 *aim*—to promote political, economic, and defense cooperation	*members*—(7) Antigua and Barbuda, Dominica, Grenada, Montserrat, Saint Kitts and Nevis, Saint Lucia, Saint Vincent and the Grenadines *associate members*—(2) Anguilla, British Virgin Islands
Organization of Petroleum Exporting Countries (OPEC) *established*—14 September 1960 *aim*—to coordinate petroleum policies	*members*—(11) Algeria, Indonesia, Iran, Iraq, Kuwait, Libya, Nigeria, Qatar, Saudi Arabia, UAE, Venezuela
Organization of the Islamic Conference (OIC) *established*—22-25 September 1969 *aim*—to promote Islamic solidarity in economic, social, cultural, and political affairs	*members*—(55 plus the Palestine Liberation Organization) Afghanistan, Albania, Algeria, Azerbaijan, Bahrain, Bangladesh, Benin, Brunei, Burkina Faso, Cameroon, Chad, Comoros, Djibouti, Egypt, Gabon, The Gambia, Guinea, Guinea-Bissau, Guyana, Indonesia, Iran, Iraq, Jordan, Kazakhstan, Kuwait, Kyrgyzstan, Lebanon, Libya, Malaysia, Maldives, Mali, Mauritania, Morocco, Mozambique, Niger, Nigeria, Oman, Pakistan, Qatar, Saudi Arabia, Senegal, Sierra Leone, Somalia, Sudan, Suriname, Syria, Tajikistan, Togo, Tunisia, Turkey, Turkmenistan, Uganda, UAE, Uzbekistan, Yemen, Palestine Liberation Organization *observers*—(12) Bosnia and Herzegovina, Central African Republic, Cote d'Ivoire, ECO, LAS, NAM, Moro National Liberation Front of the Philippines, OAU, Thailand, Turkish Muslim Community of Kirbris, "Turkish Republic of Northern Cyprus", UN
Pacific Community *note*—formerly known as the South Pacific Commission (SPC) *established*—6 February 1947 *effective*—29 July 1948 *aim*—to promote regional cooperation in economic and social matters	*members*—(27) American Samoa, Australia, Cook Islands, Fiji, France, French Polynesia, Guam, Kiribati, Marshall Islands, Federated States of Micronesia, Nauru, New Caledonia, NZ, Niue, Northern Mariana Islands, Palau, Papua New Guinea, Pitcairn Islands, Samoa, Solomon Islands, Tokelau, Tonga, Tuvalu, UK, US, Vanuatu, Wallis and Futuna
Partnership for Peace (PFP) *established*—10-11 January 1994 *aim*—to expand and intensify political and military cooperation throughout Europe, increase stability, diminish threats to peace, and build relationships by promoting the spirit of practical cooperation and commitment to democratic principles that underpin NATO; program under the auspices of NATO	*members*—(29) Albania, Armenia, Austria, Azerbaijan, Belarus, Bulgaria, Croatia, Czech Republic, Estonia, Finland, Georgia, Hungary, Ireland, Kazakhstan, Kyrgyzstan, Latvia, Lithuania, The Former Yugoslav Republic of Macedonia, Moldova, Poland, Romania, Russia, Slovakia, Slovenia, Sweden, Switzerland, Turkmenistan, Ukraine, Uzbekistan
Permanent Court of Arbitration (PCA) *established*—29 July 1899 *aim*—to facilitate the settlement of international disputes	*members*—(78) Argentina, Australia, Austria, Belarus, Belgium, Bolivia, Brazil, Bulgaria, Canada, Chile, China, Colombia, Democratic Republic of the Congo, Croatia, Cuba, Cyprus, Czech Republic, Denmark, Dominican Republic, Ecuador, Egypt, El Salvador, Finland, France, Germany, Greece, Guatemala, Guyana, Haiti, Honduras, Hungary, India, Iran, Iraq, Israel, Italy, Japan, Jordan, South Korea, Laos, Lebanon, Luxembourg, Malta, Mexico, Netherlands, NZ, Nicaragua, Nigeria, Norway, Pakistan, Panama, Paraguay, Peru, Poland, Portugal, Romania, Russia, Senegal, Singapore, Slovakia, South Africa, Spain, Sri Lanka, Sudan, Suriname, Sweden, Switzerland, Thailand, Turkey, Uganda, Ukraine, UK, US, Uruguay, Venezuela, Zambia, Zimbabwe

Appendix B: International Organizations and Groups *(continued)*

Rio Group (RG) *note*—formerly known as Grupo de los Ocho, established in December 1986; composed of the Contadora Group and the Lima Group *established*—NA 1988 *aim*—to consult on regional Latin American issues	*members*—(12) Argentina, Bolivia, Brazil, Chile, Colombia, Ecuador, Mexico, Panama, Paraguay, Peru, Uruguay, Venezuela
Second World	another term for the traditionally Marxist-Leninist states of the USSR and Eastern Europe, with authoritarian governments and command economies based on the Soviet model; the term is fading from use; see centrally planned economies
socialist countries	in general, countries in which the government owns and plans the use of the major factors of production; *note*—the term is sometimes used incorrectly as a synonym for communist countries
South	a popular term for the poorer, less industrialized countries generally located south of the developed countries; the counterpart of the North; see less developed countries (LDCs)
South Asian Association for Regional Cooperation (SAARC) *established*—8 December 1985 *aim*—to promote economic, social, and cultural cooperation	*members*—(7) Bangladesh, Bhutan, India, Maldives, Nepal, Pakistan, Sri Lanka
South Pacific Forum (SPF) *established*—5 August 1971 *aim*—to promote regional cooperation in political matters	*members*—(16) Australia, Cook Islands, Fiji, Kiribati, Marshall Islands, Federated States of Micronesia, Nauru, NZ, Niue, Palau, Papua New Guinea, Samoa, Solomon Islands, Tonga, Tuvalu, Vanuatu
South Pacific Regional Trade and Economic Cooperation Agreement (Sparteca) *established*—NA 1981 *aim*—to redress unequal trade relationships of Australia and New Zealand with small island economies in the Pacific region	*members*—(16) Australia, Cook Islands, Fiji, Kiribati, Marshall Islands, Federated States of Micronesia, Nauru, NZ, Niue, Palau, Papua New Guinea, Samoa, Solomon Islands, Tonga, Tuvalu, Vanuatu
Southern African Customs Union (SACU) *established*—11 December 1969 *aim*—to promote free trade and cooperation in customs matters	*members*—(5) Botswana, Lesotho, Namibia, South Africa, Swaziland
Southern African Development Community (SADC) *note*—evolved from the Southern African Development Coordination Conference (SADCC) *established*—17 August 1992 *aim*—to promote regional economic development and integration	*members*—(14) Angola, Botswana, Democratic Republic of the Congo, Lesotho, Malawi, Mauritius, Mozambique, Namibia, Seychelles, South Africa, Swaziland, Tanzania, Zambia, Zimbabwe

Appendix B: International Organizations and Groups *(continued)*

Southern Cone Common Market (Mercosur) or Southern Common Market

note—also known as Mercado Comun del Cono Sur (Mercosur)
established—26 March 1991
aim—to increase regional economic cooperation

members—(4) Argentina, Brazil, Paraguay, Uruguay
associate member—(2) Bolivia, Chile

Third World

another term for the less developed countries; the term is obsolescent; see less developed countries (LDCs)

underdeveloped countries

refers to those less developed countries with the potential for above-average economic growth; see less developed countries (LDCs)

undeveloped countries

refers to those extremely poor less developed countries (LDCs) with little prospect for economic growth; see least developed countries (LLDCs)

United Nations (UN)

established—26 June 1945
effective—24 October 1945
aim—to maintain international peace and security and to promote cooperation involving economic, social, cultural, and humanitarian problems

constituent organizations—the UN is composed of six principal organs and numerous subordinate agencies and bodies as follows:
1) Secretariat
2) General Assembly: International Research and Training Institute for the Advancement of Women (INSTRAW), United Nations Center for Human Settlements (Habitat), United Nations Children's Fund (UNICEF), United Nations Conference on Trade and Development (UNCTAD), United Nations Development Program (UNDP), United Nations Drug Control Program (UNDCP), United Nations Environment Program (UNEP), United Nations High Commissioner for Human Rights (UNHCHR), United Nations High Commissioner for Refugees (UNHCR), United Nations Institute for Disarmament Research (UNIDIR), United Nations Institute for Training and Research (UNITAR), United Nations Interregional Crime and Justice Research Institute (UNICRI), United Nations Population Fund (UNFPA), United Nations Relief and Works Agency for Palestine Refugees in the Near East (UNRWA), United Nations Research Institute for Social Development (UNRISD), and United Nations University (UNU), World Food Program (WFP)
3) Security Council: International Criminal Tribunal for the Former Yugoslavia (ICTY), International Criminal Tribunal for Rwanda (ICTR), United Nations Compensation Commission, United Nations Disengagement Observer Force (UNDOF), United Nations Interim Administration Mission in Kosovo (UNMIK), United Nations Interim Force in Lebanon (UNIFIL), United Nations Iraq/Kuwait Boundary Demarcation Commission, United Nations Iraq-Kuwait Observation Mission (UNIKOM), United Nations Military Observer Group in India and Pakistan (UNMOGIP), United Nations Mission for the Referendum in Western Sahara (MINURSO), United Nations Mission in Bosnia and Herzegovina (UNMIBH), United Nations Mission in Ethiopia and Eritrea (UNMEE), United Nations Mission in Sierra Leone (UNAMSIL), United Nations Mission of Observers in Prevlaka (UNMOP), United Nations Monitoring and Verification Commission (UNMOVIC), United Nations Observer Mission in Georgia (UNOMIG), United Nations Organization Mission in the Democratic Republic of the Congo (MONUC), United Nations Peace-Keeping Force in Cyprus (UNFICYP), United Nations Transitional Administration in East Timor (UNTAET), and United Nations Truce Supervision Organization (UNTSO)
4) Economic and Social Council (ECOSOC): Commission for Social Development, Commission on Crime Prevention and Criminal Justice, Commission on Human Rights, Commission on Narcotics Drugs, Commission on Population and Development, Commission on Science and Technology for Development, Commission on Sustainable Development, Commission on the Status of Women, Economic and Social Commission for Asia and the Pacific (ESCAP), Economic and Social Commission for Western Asia (ESCWA), Economic Commission for Africa (ECA), Economic Commission for Europe (ECE), Economic Commission for Latin America and the Caribbean (ECLAC), Food and Agriculture Organization of the United Nations (FAO), International Atomic Energy Agency (IAEA), International Bank for Reconstruction and Development (IBRD), International Civil Aviation Organization (ICAO), International Development Association (IDA), International Finance Corporation (IFC), International Fund for Agricultural Development (IFAD), International Labor Organization (ILO), International Maritime Organization (IMO), International Monetary Fund (IMF), International Telecommunication Union (ITU), Statistical Commission, United Nations Educational, Scientific, and Cultural Organization (UNESCO), United Nations Industrial Development Organization (UNIDO), Universal Postal Union (UPU), World Health Organization (WHO), World Intellectual Property Organization (WIPO), World Meteorological Organization (WMO), World Tourism Organization (WToO), and World Trade Organization (WTrO)
5) Trusteeship Council (inactive; no trusteeships at this time)
6) International Court of Justice (ICJ)

Appendix B: International Organizations and Groups *(continued)*

United Nations (UN) *(continued)*	*UN members*—(189) Afghanistan, Albania, Algeria, Andorra, Angola, Antigua and Barbuda, Argentina, Armenia, Australia, Austria, Azerbaijan, The Bahamas, Bahrain, Bangladesh, Barbados, Belarus, Belgium, Belize, Benin, Bhutan, Bolivia, Bosnia and Herzegovina, Botswana, Brazil, Brunei, Bulgaria, Burkina Faso, Burma, Burundi, Cambodia, Cameroon, Canada, Cape Verde, Central African Republic, Chad, Chile, China, Colombia, Comoros, Democratic Republic of the Congo, Republic of the Congo, Costa Rica, Cote d'Ivoire, Croatia, Cuba, Cyprus, Czech Republic, Denmark, Djibouti, Dominica, Dominican Republic, Ecuador, Egypt, El Salvador, Equatorial Guinea, Eritrea, Estonia, Ethiopia, Fiji, Finland, France, Gabon, The Gambia, Georgia, Germany, Ghana, Greece, Grenada, Guatemala, Guinea, Guinea-Bissau, Guyana, Haiti, Honduras, Hungary, Iceland, India, Indonesia, Iran, Iraq, Ireland, Israel, Italy, Jamaica, Japan, Jordan, Kazakhstan, Kenya, Kiribati, North Korea, South Korea, Kuwait, Kyrgyzstan, Laos, Latvia, Lebanon, Lesotho, Liberia, Libya, Liechtenstein, Lithuania, Luxembourg, The Former Yugoslav Republic of Macedonia, Madagascar, Malawi, Malaysia, Maldives, Mali, Malta, Marshall Islands, Mauritania, Mauritius, Mexico, Federated States of Micronesia, Moldova, Monaco, Mongolia, Morocco, Mozambique, Namibia, Nauru, Nepal, Netherlands, NZ, Nicaragua, Niger, Nigeria, Norway, Oman, Pakistan, Palau, Panama, Papua New Guinea, Paraguay, Peru, Philippines, Poland, Portugal, Qatar, Romania, Russia, Rwanda, Saint Kitts and Nevis, Saint Lucia, Saint Vincent and the Grenadines, Samoa, San Marino, Sao Tome and Principe, Saudi Arabia, Senegal, Seychelles, Sierra Leone, Singapore, Slovakia, Slovenia, Solomon Islands, Somalia, South Africa, Spain, Sri Lanka, Sudan, Suriname, Swaziland, Sweden, Syria, Tajikistan, Tanzania, Thailand, Togo, Tonga, Trinidad and Tobago, Tunisia, Turkey, Turkmenistan, Tuvalu, Uganda, Ukraine, UAE, UK, US, Uruguay, Uzbekistan, Vanuatu, Venezuela, Vietnam, Yemen, Yugoslavia, Zambia, Zimbabwe; *note*—all UN members are represented in the General Assembly *observers*—(2 plus the Palestine Liberation Organization) Holy See, Switzerland, Palestine Liberation Organization
United Nations Children's Fund (UNICEF) *note*—acronym retained from the predecessor organization, UN International Children's Emergency Fund *established*—11 December 1946 *aim*—to help establish child health and welfare services	*members*—(36) selected on a rotating basis from all regions
United Nations Civilian Police Mission in Haiti (MIPONUH)	established 28 November 1997; to support the professionalization of the Haitian National Police; established by UN Security Council; members were Argentina, Benin, Canada, France, India, Mali, Niger, Senegal, Togo, Tunisia, US; mission ended March 2000
United Nations Conference on Trade and Development (UNCTAD) *established*—30 December 1964 *aim*—to promote international trade	*members*—(191) all UN members plus Holy See, Switzerland
United Nations Development Program (UNDP) *established*—22 November 1965 *aim*—to provide technical assistance to stimulate economic and social development	*members (executive board)*—(36) selected on a rotating basis from all regions
United Nations Disengagement Observer Force (UNDOF) *established*—31 May 1974 *aim*—to observe the 1973 Arab-Israeli cease-fire; established by the UN Security Council	*members*—(5) Austria, Canada, Japan, Poland, Slovakia

Appendix B: International Organizations and Groups *(continued)*

United Nations Educational, Scientific, and Cultural Organization (UNESCO) *established*—16 November 1945 *effective*—4 November 1946 *aim*—to promote cooperation in education, science, and culture	*members*—(188) Afghanistan, Albania, Algeria, Andorra, Angola, Antigua and Barbuda, Argentina, Armenia, Australia, Austria, Azerbaijan, The Bahamas, Bahrain, Bangladesh, Barbados, Belarus, Belgium, Belize, Benin, Bhutan, Bolivia, Bosnia and Herzegovina, Botswana, Brazil, Bulgaria, Burkina Faso, Burma, Burundi, Cambodia, Cameroon, Canada, Cape Verde, Central African Republic, Chad, Chile, China, Colombia, Comoros, Democratic Republic of the Congo, Republic of the Congo, Cook Islands, Costa Rica, Cote d'Ivoire, Croatia, Cuba, Cyprus, Czech Republic, Denmark, Djibouti, Dominica, Dominican Republic, Ecuador, Egypt, El Salvador, Equatorial Guinea, Eritrea, Estonia, Ethiopia, Fiji, Finland, France, Gabon, The Gambia, Georgia, Germany, Ghana, Greece, Grenada, Guatemala, Guinea, Guinea-Bissau, Guyana, Haiti, Honduras, Hungary, Iceland, India, Indonesia, Iran, Iraq, Ireland, Israel, Italy, Jamaica, Japan, Jordan, Kazakhstan, Kenya, Kiribati, North Korea, South Korea, Kuwait, Kyrgyzstan, Laos, Latvia, Lebanon, Lesotho, Liberia, Libya, Lithuania, Luxembourg, The Former Yugoslav Republic of Macedonia, Madagascar, Malawi, Malaysia, Maldives, Mali, Malta, Marshall Islands, Mauritania, Mauritius, Mexico, Federated States of Micronesia, Moldova, Monaco, Mongolia, Morocco, Mozambique, Namibia, Nauru, Nepal, Netherlands, NZ, Nicaragua, Niger, Nigeria, Niue, Norway, Oman, Pakistan, Palau, Panama, Papua New Guinea, Paraguay, Peru, Philippines, Poland, Portugal, Qatar, Romania, Russia, Rwanda, Saint Kitts and Nevis, Saint Lucia, Saint Vincent and the Grenadines, Samoa, San Marino, Sao Tome and Principe, Saudi Arabia, Senegal, Seychelles, Sierra Leone, Slovakia, Slovenia, Solomon Islands, Somalia, South Africa, Spain, Sri Lanka, Sudan, Suriname, Swaziland, Sweden, Switzerland, Syria, Tajikistan, Tanzania, Thailand, Togo, Tonga, Trinidad and Tobago, Tunisia, Turkey, Turkmenistan, Tuvalu, Uganda, Ukraine, UAE, UK, Uruguay, Uzbekistan, Vanuatu, Venezuela, Vietnam, Yemen, Yugoslavia, Zambia, Zimbabwe *associate members*—(5) Aruba, British Virgin Islands, Cayman Islands, Macau, Netherlands Antilles
United Nations Environment Program (UNEP) *established*—15 December 1972 *aim*—to promote international cooperation on all environmental matters	*members*—(58) selected on a rotating basis from all regions
United Nations General Assembly *established*—26 June 1945 *effective*—24 October 1945 *aim*—to function as the primary deliberative organ of the UN	*members*—(189) all UN members are represented in the General Assembly
United Nations High Commissioner for Refugees (UNHCR) *established*—3 December 1949 *effective*—1 January 1951 *aim*—to ensure the humanitarian treatment of refugees and find permanent solutions to refugee problems	*members (executive committee)*—(57) Algeria, Argentina, Australia, Austria, Bangladesh, Belgium, Brazil, Canada, Chile, China, Colombia, Democratic Republic of the Congo, Cote d'Ivoire, Denmark, Ethiopia, Finland, France, Germany, Greece, Holy See, Hungary, Iceland, India, Iran, Ireland, Israel, Italy, Japan, South Korea, Lebanon, Lesotho, Madagascar, Morocco, Mozambique, Namibia, Netherlands, Nicaragua, Nigeria, Norway, Pakistan, Philippines, Poland, Russia, Somalia, South Africa, Spain, Sudan, Sweden, Switzerland, Tanzania, Thailand, Tunisia, Turkey, Uganda, UK, US, Venezuela
United Nations Industrial Development Organization (UNIDO) *established*—17 November 1966 *effective*—1 January 1967 *aim*—UN specialized agency that promotes industrial development especially among the members	*members*—(169) Afghanistan, Albania, Algeria, Angola, Argentina, Armenia, Austria, Azerbaijan, The Bahamas, Bahrain, Bangladesh, Barbados, Belarus, Belgium, Belize, Benin, Bhutan, Bolivia, Bosnia and Herzegovina, Botswana, Brazil, Bulgaria, Burkina Faso, Burma, Burundi, Cambodia, Cameroon, Cape Verde, Central African Republic, Chad, Chile, China, Colombia, Comoros, Democratic Republic of the Congo, Republic of the Congo, Costa Rica, Cote d'Ivoire, Croatia, Cuba, Cyprus, Czech Republic, Denmark, Djibouti, Dominica, Dominican Republic, Ecuador, Egypt, El Salvador, Equatorial Guinea, Eritrea, Ethiopia, Fiji, Finland, France, Gabon, The Gambia, Georgia, Germany, Ghana, Greece, Grenada, Guatemala, Guinea, Guinea-Bissau, Guyana, Haiti, Honduras, Hungary, India, Indonesia, Iran, Iraq, Ireland, Israel, Italy, Jamaica, Japan, Jordan, Kazakhstan, Kenya, North Korea, South Korea, Kuwait, Kyrgyzstan, Laos, Lebanon, Lesotho, Liberia, Libya, Lithuania, Luxembourg, The Former Yugoslav Republic of Macedonia, Madagascar, Malawi, Malaysia, Maldives, Mali, Malta, Mauritania, Mauritius, Mexico, Moldova, Mongolia, Morocco, Mozambique, Namibia, Nepal, Netherlands, NZ, Nicaragua, Niger, Nigeria, Norway, Oman, Pakistan, Panama, Papua New Guinea, Paraguay, Peru, Philippines, Poland, Portugal, Qatar, Romania, Russia, Rwanda, Saint Kitts and Nevis, Saint Lucia, Saint Vincent and the Grenadines, Sao Tome and Principe, Saudi Arabia, Senegal, Seychelles, Sierra Leone, Slovakia, Slovenia, Somalia, South Africa, Spain, Sri Lanka, Sudan, Suriname, Swaziland, Sweden, Switzerland, Syria, Tajikistan, Tanzania, Thailand, Togo, Tonga, Trinidad and Tobago, Tunisia, Turkey, Turkmenistan, Uganda, Ukraine, UAE, UK, Uruguay, Uzbekistan, Vanuatu, Venezuela, Vietnam, Yemen, Yugoslavia, Zambia, Zimbabwe

Appendix B: International Organizations and Groups *(continued)*

United Nations Institute for Training and Research (UNITAR) *established*—11 December 1963 adoption of the resolution establishing the Institute *effective*—24 March 1965 *aim*—to help the UN become more effective through training and research	*members (Board of Trustees)*—(20) Austria, Brazil, Cameroon, Chile, China, Egypt, France, Ghana, Ireland, Japan, Kuwait, Mexico, Netherlands, Nigeria, Russia, South Africa, Sweden, Switzerland, Thailand, US; *note*—the UN Secretary General can appoint up to 30 members
United Nations Interim Administration Mission in Kosovo (UNMIK) *established*—10 June 1999 *aim*—to promote the establishment of substantial autonomy and self-government in Kosovo; to perform basic civilian administrative functions; to support the reconstruction of key infrastructure and humanitarian and disaster relief	*members*—(49) Argentina, Austria, Bangladesh, Belgium, Bolivia, Bulgaria, Canada, Czech Republic, Denmark, Egypt, Estonia, Fiji, Finland, France, Germany, Ghana, Hungary, Iceland, India, Ireland, Italy, Jordan, Kenya, Kyrgyzstan, Lithuania, Malawi, Malaysia, Nepal, Netherlands, NZ, Nigeria, Norway, Pakistan, Philippines, Poland, Portugal, Romania, Russia, Senegal, Spain, Sweden, Switzerland, Tunisia, Turkey, Ukraine UK, US, Zambia, Zimbabwe
United Nations Interim Force in Lebanon (UNIFIL) *established*—19 March 1978 *aim*—to confirm the withdrawal of Israeli forces, and assist in reestablishing Lebanese authority in southern Lebanon; established by the UN Security Council	*members*—(10) Fiji, Finland, France, Ghana, India, Ireland, Italy, Nepal, Poland, Ukraine
United Nations Iraq-Kuwait Observation Mission (UNIKOM) *established*—9 April 1991 *aim*—to observe and monitor the demilitarized zone established between Iraq and Kuwait; established by the UN Security Council	*members*—(33) Argentina, Austria, Bangladesh, Canada, China, Denmark, Fiji, Finland, France, Germany, Ghana, Greece, Hungary, India, Indonesia, Ireland, Italy, Kenya, Malaysia, Nigeria, Pakistan, Poland, Romania, Russia, Senegal, Singapore, Sweden, Thailand, Turkey, UK, US, Uruguay, Venezuela
United Nations Military Observer Group in India and Pakistan (UNMOGIP) *established*—24 January 1949 *aim*—to observe the 1949 India-Pakistan cease-fire; established by the UN Security Council	*members*—(9) Belgium, Chile, Denmark, Finland, Hungary, Italy, South Korea, Sweden, Uruguay
United Nations Mission for the Referendum in Western Sahara (MINURSO) *established*—29 April 1991 *aim*—to supervise the cease-fire and conduct a referendum in Western Sahara; established by the UN Security Council	*members*—(30) Argentina, Austria, Bangladesh, Belgium, China, Egypt, El Salvador, France, Ghana, Greece, Guinea, Honduras, Hungary, India, Ireland, Italy, Jordan, Kenya, South Korea, Malaysia, Nigeria, Norway, Pakistan, Poland, Portugal, Russia, Senegal, Sweden, US, Uruguay
United Nations Mission in Bosnia and Herzegovina (UNMIBH) *established*—21 December 1995 *aim*—to establish an International Police Task Force (IPTF) to implement the Dayton Peace Agreement in Bosnia and Herzegovina	*members*—(45) Argentina, Austria, Bangladesh, Bulgaria, Canada, Chile, Czech Republic, Denmark, Egypt, Estonia, Fiji, Finland, France, Germany, Ghana, Greece, Hungary, Iceland, India, Indonesia, Ireland, Italy, Jordan, Kenya, Malaysia, Nepal, Netherlands, Nigeria, Norway, Pakistan, Poland, Portugal, Romania, Russia, Senegal, Spain, Sweden, Switzerland, Thailand, Tunisia, Turkey, Ukraine, UK, US, Vanuatu

Appendix B: International Organizations and Groups *(continued)*

United Nations Mission in Sierra Leone (UNAMSIL)

established—22 October 1999
aim—to cooperate with the Government of Sierra Leone and the other parties to the Peace Agreement in the implementation of the agreement; to monitor the military and security situation in Sierra Leone; to monitor the disarmament and demobilization of combatants and members of the Civil Defense Forces (CFD); to assist in monitoring respect for international humanitarian law

members—(30) Bangladesh, Bolivia, Canada, Croatia, Czech Republic, Denmark, Egypt, France, The Gambia, Ghana, Guinea, Indonesia, Jordan, Kenya, Kyrgyzstan, Malaysia, Mali, Nepal, NZ, Nigeria, Norway, Pakistan, Russia, Slovakia, Sweden, Thailand, Ukraine, UK, Uruguay, Zambia

United Nations Mission of Observers in Prevlaka (UNMOP)

established—1 February 1996
aim—to monitor the demilitarization of the Prevlaka peninsula in southern Croatia

members—(25) Argentina, Bangladesh, Belgium, Brazil, Canada, Czech Republic, Denmark, Egypt, Finland, Ghana, Indonesia, Ireland, Jordan, Kenya, Nepal, NZ, Nigeria, Norway, Pakistan, Poland, Portugal, Russia, Sweden, Switzerland, Ukraine

United Nations Mission of Observers in Tajikistan (UNMOT)

established 16 December 1994; to monitor and investigate violations of the cease-fire of 17 September 1994 between Tajikistan and the Tajik opposition and to assist in the political negotiation process; established by the UN Security Council; members were Austria, Bangladesh, Bulgaria, Czech Republic, Denmark, Ghana, Indonesia, Jordan, Nepal, Nigeria, Poland, Ukraine, Uruguay; mission ended May 2000

United Nations Monitoring and Verification Commission (UNMOVIC)

note—formerly known as United Nations Special Commission for the Elimination of Iraq's Weapons of Mass Destruction (UNSCOM)
established—NA December 1999
aim—to identify, account for, and eliminate Iraq's weapons of mass destruction and the capacity to produce them

members—(22) Australia, Austria, Belgium, Canada, China, Czech Republic, Finland, France, Germany, Indonesia, Italy, Japan, Netherlands, Nigeria, Norway, Poland, Russia, Sri Lanka, Sweden, UK, US, Venezuela

United Nations Observer Mission in Georgia (UNOMIG)

established—24 August 1993
aim—to verify compliance with the cease-fire agreement, to monitor weapons exclusion zone, and to supervise CIS peacekeeping force for Abkhazia; established by the UN Security Council

members—(22) Albania, Austria, Bangladesh, Czech Republic, Denmark, Egypt, France, Germany, Greece, Hungary, Indonesia, Jordan, South Korea, Pakistan, Poland, Russia, Sweden, Switzerland, Turkey, UK, US, Uruguay

United Nations Organization Mission in the Democratic Republic of the Congo (MONUC)

established—30 November 1999
aim—to establish contacts with the signatories to the cease-fire agreement and to plan for the observation of the cease-fire and disengagement of forces

members—(36) Algeria, Bangladesh, Belgium, Benin, Bolivia, Burkina Faso, Canada, Czech Republic, Denmark, Egypt, France, Ghana, India, Jordan, Kenya, Libya, Malaysia, Mali, Morocco, Nepal, Niger, Nigeria, Pakistan, Peru, Poland, Romania, Russia, Senegal, South Africa, Switzerland, Tunisia, Ukraine, UK, Tanzania, Uruguay, Zambia

Appendix B: International Organizations and Groups *(continued)*

United Nations Peace-keeping Force in Cyprus (UNFICYP) *established*—4 March 1964 *aim*—to serve as a peacekeeping force between Greek Cypriots and Turkish Cypriots in Cyprus; established by the UN Security Council	*members*—(10) Argentina, Austria, Canada, Finland, Hungary, Ireland, Nepal, Netherlands, Slovenia, UK
United Nations Population Fund (UNFPA) *note*—acronym retained from predecessor organization UN Fund for Population Activities *established*—NA July 1967 *aim*—to assist both developed and developing countries to deal with their population problems	*members (executive board)*—(36) selected on a rotating basis from all regions
United Nations Preventive Deployment Force (UNPREDEP)	established 31 March 1995; to monitor border activity in the Former Yugoslav Republic of Macedonia; members were Argentina, Bangladesh, Belgium, Brazil, Canada, Czech Republic, Denmark, Egypt, Finland, Ghana, Indonesia, Ireland, Jordan, Kenya, Nepal, NZ, Nigeria, Norway, Pakistan, Poland, Portugal, Russia, Sweden, Switzerland, Turkey, Ukraine, US; mandate ended 25 March 1999
United Nations Relief and Works Agency for Palestine Refugees in the Near East (UNRWA) *established*—8 December 1949 *aim*—to provide assistance to Palestinian refugees	*members (advisory commission)*—(10) Belgium, Egypt, France, Japan, Jordan, Lebanon, Syria, Turkey, UK, US
United Nations Research Institute for Social Development (UNRISD) *established*—NA 1963 *aim*—to conduct research into the problems of economic development during different phases of economic growth	*members*—no country members, but a Board of Directors consisting of a chairman appointed by the UN secretary general and 11 individual members
United Nations Secretariat *established*—26 June 1945 *effective*—24 October 1945 *aim*—to serve as the primary administrative organ of the UN; a Secretary General is appointed for a five-year term by the General Assembly on the recommendation of the Security Council	*members*—the UN Secretary General and staff
United Nations Security Council *established*—26 June 1945 *effective*—24 October 1945 *aim*—to maintain international peace and security	*permanent members*—(5) China, France, Russia, UK, US *nonpermanent members*—(10) elected for two-year terms by the UN General Assembly; Bangladesh (2000-01), Colombia (2001-02), Ireland (2001-02), Jamaica (2000-01), Mali (2000-01), Mauritius (2001-02), Norway (2001-02), Singapore (2001-02), Tunisia (2000-01), Ukraine (2000-01)
United Nations Transitional Administration in East Timor (UNTAET) *established*—25 October 1999 *aim*—to provide security throughout the territory of East Timor; to establish an effective administration; to ensure the coordination and delivery of humanitarian assistance; to support capacity-building for self-government	*members*—(47) Australia, Austria, Bangladesh, Benin, Bolivia, Bosnia and Herzegovina, Brazil, Canada, Cape Verde, Chile, China, Denmark, Egypt, Fiji, France, Ghana, Ireland, Jordan, Kenya, South Korea, Malaysia, Mozambique, Namibia, Nepal, NZ, Nigeria, Norway, Pakistan, Peru, Philippines, Portugal, Russia, Senegal, Singapore, Slovenia, Spain, Sri Lanka, Sweden, Thailand, Turkey, Ukraine, UK, US, Uruguay, Vanuatu, Zambia, Zimbabwe

Appendix B: International Organizations and Groups *(continued)*

United Nations Truce Supervision Organization (UNTSO) *established*—NA June 1948 *aim*—to supervise the 1948 Arab-Israeli cease-fire; currently supports timely deployment of reinforcements to other peacekeeping operations in the region as needed; initially established by the UN Security Council	*members*—(22) Argentina, Australia, Austria, Belgium, Canada, Chile, China, Denmark, Estonia, Finland, France, Ireland, Italy, Netherlands, NZ, Norway, Russia, Slovakia, Slovenia, Sweden, Switzerland, US
United Nations Trusteeship Council	established on 26 June 1945, effective on 24 October 1945, to supervise the administration of the 11 UN trust territories; members were China, France, Russia, UK, US; it formally suspended operations 1 November 1995 after the Trust Territory of the Pacific Islands (Palau) became the Republic of Palau, a constitutional government in free association with the US; the Trusteeship Council was not dissolved
United Nations University (UNU) *established*—3 December 1973 *aim*—to conduct research in development, welfare, and human survival and to train scholars	*members*—(24 members of UNU Council and the Rector are appointed by the Secretary General of the United Nations and the Director General of UNESCO)
Universal Postal Union (UPU) *established*—9 October 1874, affiliated with the UN 15 November 1947 *effective*—1 July 1948 *aim*—to promote international postal cooperation; a UN specialized agency	*members*—(189) Afghanistan, Albania, Algeria, Angola, Antigua and Barbuda, Argentina, Armenia, Australia, Austria, Azerbaijan, The Bahamas, Bahrain, Bangladesh, Barbados, Belarus, Belgium, Belize, Benin, Bhutan, Bolivia, Bosnia and Herzegovina, Botswana, Brazil, Brunei, Bulgaria, Burkina Faso, Burma, Burundi, Cambodia, Cameroon, Canada, Cape Verde, Central African Republic, Chad, Chile, China, Colombia, Comoros, Democratic Republic of the Congo, Republic of the Congo, Costa Rica, Cote d'Ivoire, Croatia, Cuba, Cyprus, Czech Republic, Denmark, Djibouti, Dominica, Dominican Republic, Ecuador, Egypt, El Salvador, Equatorial Guinea, Eritrea, Estonia, Ethiopia, Fiji, Finland, France, Gabon, The Gambia, Georgia, Germany, Ghana, Greece, Grenada, Guatemala, Guinea, Guinea-Bissau, Guyana, Haiti, Holy See, Honduras, Hungary, Iceland, India, Indonesia, Iran, Iraq, Ireland, Israel, Italy, Jamaica, Japan, Jordan, Kazakhstan, Kenya, Kiribati, North Korea, South Korea, Kuwait, Kyrgyzstan, Laos, Latvia, Lebanon, Lesotho, Liberia, Libya, Liechtenstein, Lithuania, Luxembourg, The Former Yugoslav Republic of Macedonia, Madagascar, Malawi, Malaysia, Maldives, Mali, Malta, Mauritania, Mauritius, Mexico, Moldova, Monaco, Mongolia, Morocco, Mozambique, Namibia, Nauru, Nepal, Netherlands, Netherlands Antilles, NZ, Nicaragua, Niger, Nigeria, Norway, Oman, Overseas Territories of the UK, Pakistan, Panama, Papua New Guinea, Paraguay, Peru, Philippines, Poland, Portugal, Qatar, Romania, Russia, Rwanda, Saint Kitts and Nevis, Saint Lucia, Saint Vincent and the Grenadines, Samoa, San Marino, Sao Tome and Principe, Saudi Arabia, Senegal, Seychelles, Sierra Leone, Singapore, Slovakia, Slovenia, Solomon Islands, Somalia, South Africa, Spain, Sri Lanka, Sudan, Suriname, Swaziland, Sweden, Switzerland, Syria, Tajikistan, Tanzania, Thailand, Togo, Tonga, Trinidad and Tobago, Tunisia, Turkey, Turkmenistan, Tuvalu, Uganda, Ukraine, UAE, UK, US, Uruguay, Uzbekistan, Vanuatu, Venezuela, Vietnam, Yemen, Yugoslavia, Zambia, Zimbabwe
Warsaw Pact (WP)	established 14 May 1955 to promote mutual defense; members met 1 July 1991 to dissolve the alliance; member states at the time of dissolution were Bulgaria, Czechoslovakia, Hungary, Poland, Romania, and the USSR; earlier members included GDR and Albania
West African Development Bank (WADB) *note*—also known as Banque Ouest-Africaine de Developpement (BOAD); is a financial institution of WAEMU *established*—14 November 1973 *aim*—to promote regional economic development and integration	*regional members*—(8) Benin, Burkina Faso, Cote d'Ivoire, Guinea-Bissau, Mali, Niger, Senegal, Togo *international/nonregional members*—(5) African Development Bank, Belgium, European Investment Bank, France, Germany

Appendix B: International Organizations and Groups *(continued)*

West African Economic and Monetary Union (WAEMU) *note*—also known as Union Economique et Monetaire Ouest Africaine (UEMOA) *established*—1 August 1994 *aim*—to increase competitiveness of members' economic markets; to create a common market	*members*—(8) Benin, Burkina Faso, Cote d'Ivoire, Guinea-Bissau, Mali, Niger, Senegal, Togo
Western European Union (WEU) *established*—23 October 1954 *effective*—6 May 1955 *aim*—to provide mutual defense and to move toward political unification	*members*—(10) Belgium, France, Germany, Greece, Italy, Luxembourg, Netherlands, Portugal, Spain, UK *associate members*—(6) Czech Republic, Hungary, Iceland, Norway, Poland, Turkey *associate partners*—(7) Bulgaria, Estonia, Latvia, Lithuania, Romania, Slovakia, Slovenia *observers*—(5) Austria, Denmark, Finland, Ireland, Sweden
World Bank Group	includes International Bank for Reconstruction and Development (IBRD), International Development Association (IDA), and International Finance Corporation (IFC)
World Confederation of Labor (WCL) *established*—19 June 1920 as the International Federation of Christian Trade Unions (IFCTU), renamed 4 October 1968 *aim*—to promote the trade union movement	*members*—(101 national organizations) Antigua and Barbuda, Argentina, Aruba, Austria, Bangladesh, Belgium, Belize, Benin, Bolivia, Bonaire Island, Brazil, Bulgaria, Burkina Faso, Cameroon, Canada, Central African Republic, Chad, Chile, Colombia, Democratic Republic of the Congo, Republic of the Congo, Costa Rica, Cote d'Ivoire, Cuba, Cyprus, Czech Republic, Dominica, Dominican Republic, Ecuador, El Salvador, France, French Guiana, Gabon, The Gambia, Ghana, Guadeloupe, Guatemala, Guinea, Guyana, Haiti, Honduras, Hong Kong, Hungary, India, Indonesia, Iran, Italy, Japan, Kazakhstan, South Korea, Liberia, Liechtenstein, Lithuania, Luxembourg, The Former Yugoslav Republic of Macedonia, Madagascar, Malaysia, Malta, Martinique, Mauritania, Mauritius, Mexico, Montserrat, Morocco, Namibia, Netherlands, Netherlands Antilles, Nicaragua, Niger, Pakistan, Panama, Paraguay, Peru, Philippines, Poland, Portugal, Puerto Rico, Romania, Rwanda, Saint Lucia, Saint Vincent and the Grenadines, Sao Tome and Principe, Senegal, Sierra Leone, Singapore, Slovakia, South Africa, Spain, Sri Lanka, Switzerland, Taiwan, Thailand, Togo, Trinidad and Tobago, Ukraine, US, Uruguay, Venezuela, Vietnam, Windward Islands, Zambia, Zimbabwe
World Federation of Trade Unions (WFTU) *established*—3 October 1945 *aim*—to promote the trade union movement	*members*—(125 and the Palestine Liberation Organization) Afghanistan, Albania, Angola, Antigua and Barbuda, Argentina, Armenia, Australia, Austria, Azerbaijan, Bahrain, Bangladesh, Barbados, Belarus, Benin, Bolivia, Botswana, Brazil, Bulgaria, Burkina Faso, Cambodia, Cameroon, Canada, Chile, Colombia, Democratic Republic of the Congo, Republic of the Congo, Costa Rica, Cote d'Ivoire, Cuba, Cyprus, Czech Republic, Djibouti, Dominican Republic, Ecuador, Egypt, El Salvador, Eritrea, Ethiopia, Fiji, Finland, France, French Guiana, The Gambia, Ghana, Greece, Guadeloupe, Guatemala, Guinea, Guinea-Bissau, Guyana, Haiti, Honduras, Hungary, India, Indonesia, Iran, Iraq, Jamaica, Japan, Jordan, Kazakhstan, North Korea, Kuwait, Kyrgyzstan, Laos, Lebanon, Lesotho, Liberia, Libya, Madagascar, Malawi, Malaysia, Mali, Martinique, Mauritius, Mexico, Mozambique, Nepal, New Caledonia, NZ, Niger, Nigeria, Oman, Pakistan, Panama, Papua New Guinea, Peru, Philippines, Poland, Portugal, Puerto Rico, Reunion, Romania, Russia, Saint Lucia, Saint Pierre and Miquelon, Saint Vincent and the Grenadines, Saudi Arabia, Senegal, Sierra Leone, Slovakia, Solomon Islands, Somalia, South Africa, Sri Lanka, Sudan, Sweden, Syria, Tajikistan, Tanzania, Thailand, Togo, Trinidad and Tobago, Tunisia, Turkey, Turkmenistan, Uganda, Ukraine, Uruguay, Uzbekistan, Vanuatu, Venezuela, Vietnam, Yemen, Zimbabwe, Palestine Liberation Organization
World Food Program (WFP) *established*—24 November 1961 *aim*—to provide food aid in support of economic development or disaster relief; an ECOSOC organization	*members*—(36) selected on a rotating basis from all regions

Appendix B: International Organizations and Groups *(continued)*

World Health Organization (WHO) *established*—22 July 1946 *effective*—7 April 1948 *aim*—to deal with health matters worldwide; a UN specialized agency	*members*—(191) Afghanistan, Albania, Algeria, Andorra, Angola, Antigua and Barbuda, Argentina, Armenia, Australia, Austria, Azerbaijan, The Bahamas, Bahrain, Bangladesh, Barbados, Belarus, Belgium, Belize, Benin, Bhutan, Bolivia, Bosnia and Herzegovina, Botswana, Brazil, Brunei, Bulgaria, Burkina Faso, Burma, Burundi, Cambodia, Cameroon, Canada, Cape Verde, Central African Republic, Chad, Chile, China, Colombia, Comoros, Democratic Republic of the Congo, Republic of the Congo, Cook Islands, Costa Rica, Cote d'Ivoire, Croatia, Cuba, Cyprus, Czech Republic, Denmark, Djibouti, Dominica, Dominican Republic, Ecuador, Egypt, El Salvador, Equatorial Guinea, Eritrea, Estonia, Ethiopia, Fiji, Finland, France, Gabon, The Gambia, Georgia, Germany, Ghana, Greece, Grenada, Guatemala, Guinea, Guinea-Bissau, Guyana, Haiti, Honduras, Hungary, Iceland, India, Indonesia, Iran, Iraq, Ireland, Israel, Italy, Jamaica, Japan, Jordan, Kazakhstan, Kenya, Kiribati, North Korea, South Korea, Kuwait, Kyrgyzstan, Laos, Latvia, Lebanon, Lesotho, Liberia, Libya, Lithuania, Luxembourg, The Former Yugoslav Republic of Macedonia, Madagascar, Malawi, Malaysia, Maldives, Mali, Malta, Marshall Islands, Mauritania, Mauritius, Mexico, Federated States of Micronesia, Moldova, Monaco, Mongolia, Morocco, Mozambique, Namibia, Nauru, Nepal, Netherlands, NZ, Nicaragua, Niue, Niger, Nigeria, Norway, Oman, Pakistan, Palau, Panama, Papua New Guinea, Paraguay, Peru, Philippines, Poland, Portugal, Qatar, Romania, Russia, Rwanda, Saint Kitts and Nevis, Saint Lucia, Saint Vincent and the Grenadines, Samoa, San Marino, Sao Tome and Principe, Saudi Arabia, Senegal, Seychelles, Sierra Leone, Singapore, Slovakia, Slovenia, Solomon Islands, Somalia, South Africa, Spain, Sri Lanka, Sudan, Suriname, Swaziland, Sweden, Switzerland, Syria, Tajikistan, Tanzania, Thailand, Togo, Tonga, Trinidad and Tobago, Tunisia, Turkey, Turkmenistan, Tuvalu, Uganda, Ukraine, UAE, UK, US, Uruguay, Uzbekistan, Vanuatu, Venezuela, Vietnam, Yemen, Yugoslavia, Zambia, Zimbabwe *associate members*—(2) Puerto Rico, Tokelau *observers*—(2) Holy See, Liechtenstein
World Intellectual Property Organization (WIPO) *established*—14 July 1967 *effective*—26 April 1970 *aim*—to furnish protection for literary, artistic, and scientific works; a UN specialized agency	*members*—(177) Albania, Algeria, Andorra, Angola, Antigua and Barbuda, Argentina, Armenia, Australia, Austria, Azerbaijan, The Bahamas, Bahrain, Bangladesh, Barbados, Belarus, Belgium, Belize, Benin, Bhutan, Bolivia, Bosnia and Herzegovina, Botswana, Brazil, Brunei, Bulgaria, Burkina Faso, Burma, Burundi, Cambodia, Cameroon, Canada, Cape Verde, Central African Republic, Chad, Chile, China, Colombia, Democratic Republic of the Congo, Republic of the Congo, Costa Rica, Cote d'Ivoire, Croatia, Cuba, Cyprus, Czech Republic, Denmark, Dominica, Dominican Republic, Ecuador, Egypt, El Salvador, Equatorial Guinea, Eritrea, Estonia, Ethiopia, Fiji, Finland, France, Gabon, The Gambia, Georgia, Germany, Ghana, Greece, Grenada, Guatemala, Guinea, Guinea-Bissau, Guyana, Haiti, Holy See, Honduras, Hungary, Iceland, India, Indonesia, Iraq, Ireland, Israel, Italy, Jamaica, Japan, Jordan, Kazakhstan, Kenya, North Korea, South Korea, Kuwait, Kyrgyzstan, Laos, Latvia, Lebanon, Lesotho, Liberia, Libya, Liechtenstein, Lithuania, Luxembourg, The Former Yugoslav Republic of Macedonia, Madagascar, Malawi, Malaysia, Mali, Malta, Mauritania, Mauritius, Mexico, Moldova, Monaco, Mongolia, Morocco, Mozambique, Namibia, Nepal, Netherlands, NZ, Nicaragua, Niger, Nigeria, Norway, Oman, Pakistan, Panama, Papua New Guinea, Paraguay, Peru, Philippines, Poland, Portugal, Qatar, Romania, Russia, Rwanda, Saint Kitts and Nevis, Saint Lucia, Saint Vincent and the Grenadines, Samoa, San Marino, Sao Tome and Principe, Saudi Arabia, Senegal, Seychelles, Sierra Leone, Singapore, Slovakia, Slovenia, Somalia, South Africa, Spain, Sri Lanka, Sudan, Suriname, Swaziland, Sweden, Switzerland, Tajikistan, Tanzania, Thailand, Togo, Tonga, Trinidad and Tobago, Tunisia, Turkey, Turkmenistan, Uganda, Ukraine, UAE, UK, US, Uruguay, Uzbekistan, Venezuela, Vietnam, Yemen, Yugoslavia, Zambia, Zimbabwe
World Meteorological Organization (WMO) *established*—11 October 1947 *effective*—4 April 1951 *aim*—to sponsor meteorological cooperation; a UN specialized agency	*members*—(185) Afghanistan, Albania, Algeria, Angola, Antigua and Barbuda, Argentina, Armenia, Australia, Austria, Azerbaijan, The Bahamas, Bahrain, Bangladesh, Barbados, Belarus, Belgium, Belize, Benin, Bolivia, Bosnia and Herzegovina, Botswana, Brazil, British Caribbean Territories, Brunei, Bulgaria, Burkina Faso, Burma, Burundi, Cambodia, Cameroon, Canada, Cape Verde, Central African Republic, Chad, Chile, China, Colombia, Comoros, Democratic Republic of the Congo, Republic of the Congo, Cook Islands, Costa Rica, Cote d'Ivoire, Croatia, Cuba, Cyprus, Czech Republic, Denmark, Djibouti, Dominica, Dominican Republic, Ecuador, Egypt, El Salvador, Eritrea, Estonia, Ethiopia, Fiji, Finland, France, French Polynesia, Gabon, The Gambia, Georgia, Germany, Ghana, Greece, Guatemala, Guinea, Guinea-Bissau, Guyana, Haiti, Honduras, Hong Kong, Hungary, Iceland, India, Indonesia, Iran, Iraq, Ireland, Israel, Italy, Jamaica, Japan, Jordan, Kazakhstan, Kenya, North Korea, South Korea, Kuwait, Kyrgyzstan, Laos, Latvia, Lebanon, Lesotho, Liberia, Libya, Lithuania, Luxembourg, Macau, The Former Yugoslav Republic of Macedonia, Madagascar, Malawi, Malaysia, Maldives, Mali, Malta, Mauritania, Mauritius, Mexico, Federated States of Micronesia, Moldova, Monaco, Mongolia, Morocco, Mozambique, Namibia, Nepal, Netherlands, Netherlands Antilles, New Caledonia, NZ, Nicaragua, Niger, Nigeria, Niue, Norway, Oman, Pakistan, Panama, Papua New Guinea, Paraguay, Peru, Philippines, Poland, Portugal, Qatar, Romania, Russia, Rwanda, Saint Lucia, Samoa, Sao Tome and Principe, Saudi Arabia, Senegal, Seychelles, Sierra Leone, Singapore, Slovakia, Slovenia, Solomon Islands, Somalia, South Africa, Spain, Sri Lanka, Sudan, Suriname, Swaziland, Sweden, Switzerland, Syria, Tajikistan, Tanzania, Thailand, Togo, Tonga, Trinidad and Tobago, Tunisia, Turkey, Turkmenistan, Uganda, Ukraine, UAE, UK, US, Uruguay, Uzbekistan, Vanuatu, Venezuela, Vietnam, Yemen, Yugoslavia, Zambia, Zimbabwe

Appendix B: International Organizations and Groups *(continued)*

World Tourism Organization (WToO) *established*—2 January 1975 *aim*—to promote tourism as a means of contributing to economic development, international understanding, and peace	*members*—(135) Afghanistan, Albania, Algeria, Andorra, Angola, Argentina, Armenia, Austria, Bangladesh, Benin, Bolivia, Bosnia and Herzegovina, Botswana, Brazil, Bulgaria, Burkina Faso, Burma, Burundi, Cambodia, Cameroon, Canada, Central African Republic, Chad, Chile, China, Colombia, Democratic Republic of the Congo, Republic of the Congo, Costa Rica, Cote d'Ivoire, Croatia, Cuba, Cyprus, Czech Republic, Djibouti, Dominican Republic, Ecuador, Egypt, El Salvador, Equatorial Guinea, Eritrea, Ethiopia, Fiji, Finland, France, Gabon, The Gambia, Georgia, Germany, Ghana, Greece, Guatemala, Guinea, Guinea-Bissau, Haiti, Hungary, India, Indonesia, Iran, Iraq, Israel, Italy, Jamaica, Japan, Jordan, Kazakhstan, Kenya, North Korea, South Korea, Kuwait, Kyrgyzstan, Laos, Lebanon, Lesotho, Libya, The Former Yugoslav Republic of Macedonia, Madagascar, Malawi, Malaysia, Maldives, Mali, Malta, Mauritania, Mauritius, Mexico, Moldova, Monaco, Mongolia, Morocco, Mozambique, Namibia, Nepal, Netherlands, Nicaragua, Niger, Nigeria, Pakistan, Panama, Paraguay, Peru, Philippines, Poland, Portugal, Romania, Russia, Rwanda, San Marino, Sao Tome and Principe, Senegal, Seychelles, Sierra Leone, Slovakia, Slovenia, South Africa, Spain, Sri Lanka, Sudan, Swaziland, Switzerland, Syria, Tanzania, Thailand, Togo, Tunisia, Turkey, Turkmenistan, Uganda, Ukraine, Uruguay, Uzbekistan, Venezuela, Vietnam, Yemen, Zambia, Zimbabwe *associate members*—(6) Aruba, Flanders, Hong Kong, Macau, Madeira Islands, Netherlands Antilles *observers*—(2) Holy See, Palestine Liberation Organization
World Trade Organization (WTrO) *note*—succeeded General Agreement on Tariff and Trade (GATT) *established*—15 April 1994 *effective*—1 January 1995 *aim*—to provide a means to resolve trade conflicts between members and to carry on negotiations with the goal of further lowering and/or eliminating tariffs and other trade barriers	*members*—(140) Albania, Angola, Antigua and Barbuda, Argentina, Australia, Austria, Bahrain, Bangladesh, Barbados, Belgium, Belize, Benin, Bolivia, Botswana, Brazil, Brunei, Bulgaria, Burkina Faso, Burma, Burundi, Cameroon, Canada, Central African Republic, Chad, Chile, Colombia, Democratic Republic of the Congo, Republic of the Congo, Costa Rica, Cote d'Ivoire, Croatia, Cuba, Cyprus, Czech Republic, Denmark, Djibouti, Dominica, Dominican Republic, Ecuador, Egypt, El Salvador, Estonia, EU, Fiji, Finland, France, Gabon, The Gambia, Georgia, Germany, Ghana, Greece, Grenada, Guatemala, Guinea, Guinea-Bissau, Guyana, Haiti, Honduras, Hong Kong, Hungary, Iceland, India, Indonesia, Ireland, Israel, Italy, Jamaica, Japan, Jordan, Kenya, South Korea, Kuwait, Kyrgyzstan, Latvia, Lesotho, Liechtenstein, Luxembourg, Macau, Madagascar, Malawi, Malaysia, Maldives, Mali, Malta, Mauritania, Mauritius, Mexico, Mongolia, Morocco, Mozambique, Namibia, Netherlands, NZ, Nicaragua, Niger, Nigeria, Norway, Oman, Pakistan, Panama, Papua New Guinea, Paraguay, Peru, Philippines, Poland, Portugal, Qatar, Romania, Rwanda, Saint Kitts and Nevis, Saint Lucia, Saint Vincent and the Grenadines, Senegal, Sierra Leone, Singapore, Slovakia, Slovenia, Solomon Islands, South Africa, Spain, Sri Lanka, Suriname, Swaziland, Sweden, Switzerland, Tanzania, Thailand, Togo, Trinidad and Tobago, Tunisia, Turkey, Uganda, UAE, UK, US, Uruguay, Venezuela, Zambia, Zimbabwe *observers*—(34) Algeria, Andorra, Armenia, Azerbaijan, The Bahamas, Belarus, Bhutan, Bosnia and Herzegovina, Cambodia, Cape Verde, China, Ethiopia, The Former Yugoslav Republic of Macedonia, Holy See, Kazakhstan, Laos, Lebanon, Lithuania, Moldova, Nepal, Russia, Samoa, Sao Tome and Principe, Saudi Arabia, Seychelles, Sudan, Taiwan, Tonga, Ukraine, Uzbekistan, Vanuatu, Vietnam, Yemen, Yugoslavia; *note*—must start accession negotiations within five years of becoming observers
Zangger Committee (ZC) *established*—early 1970s *aim*—to establish guidelines for the export control provisions of the Nonproliferation of Nuclear Weapons Treaty (NPT)	*members*—(33) Argentina, Australia, Austria, Belgium, Bulgaria, Canada, China, Czech Republic, Denmark, Finland, France, Germany, Greece, Hungary, Ireland, Italy, Japan, South Korea, Luxembourg, Netherlands, Norway, Poland, Portugal, Romania, Russia, Slovakia, South Africa, Spain, Sweden, Switzerland, Ukraine, UK, US

Appendix C:

Selected International Environmental Agreements

Air Pollution	see Convention on Long-Range Transboundary Air Pollution
Air Pollution-Nitrogen Oxides	see Protocol to the 1979 Convention on Long-Range Transboundary Air Pollution Concerning the Control of Emissions of Nitrogen Oxides or Their Transboundary Fluxes
Air Pollution-Persistent Organic Pollutants	see Protocol to the 1979 Convention on Long-Range Transboundary Air Pollution on Persistent Organic Pollutants
Air Pollution-Sulphur 85	see Protocol to the 1979 Convention on Long-Range Transboundary Air Pollution on the Reduction of Sulphur Emissions or Their Transboundary Fluxes by at least 30%
Air Pollution-Sulphur 94	see Protocol to the 1979 Convention on Long-Range Transboundary Air Pollution on Further Reduction of Sulphur Emissions
Air Pollution-Volatile Organic Compounds	see Protocol to the 1979 Convention on Long-Range Transboundary Air Pollution Concerning the Control of Emissions of Volatile Organic Compounds or Their Transboundary Fluxes
Antarctic-Environmental Protocol	see Protocol on Environmental Protection to the Antarctic Treaty
Antarctic Treaty *opened for signature*—1 December 1959 *entered into force*—23 June 1961 *objective*—to ensure that Antarctica is used for peaceful purposes only (such as international cooperation in scientific research); to defer the question of territorial claims asserted by some nations and not recognized by others; to provide an international forum for management of the region; applies to land and ice shelves south of 60 degrees South latitude	*parties*—(44) Argentina, Australia, Austria, Belgium, Brazil, Bulgaria, Canada, Chile, China, Colombia, Cuba, Czech Republic, Denmark, Ecuador, Finland, France, Germany, Greece, Guatemala, Hungary, India, Italy, Japan, North Korea, South Korea, Netherlands, NZ, Norway, Papua New Guinea, Peru, Poland, Romania, Russia, Slovakia, South Africa, Spain, Sweden, Switzerland, Turkey, Ukraine, UK, US, Uruguay, Venezuela
Basel Convention on the Control of Transboundary Movements of Hazardous Wastes and Their Disposal *note*—abbreviated as Hazardous Wastes *opened for signature*—22 March 1989 *entered into force*—5 May 1992 *objective*—to reduce transboundary movements of wastes subject to the Convention to a minimum consistent with the environmentally sound and efficient management of such wastes; to minimize the amount and toxicity of wastes generated and ensure their environmentally sound management as closely as possible to the source of generation; and to assist LDCs in environmentally sound management of the hazardous and other wastes they generate	*parties*—(143) Albania, Algeria, Andorra, Antigua and Barbuda, Argentina, Armenia, Australia, Austria, The Bahamas, Bahrain, Bangladesh, Barbados, Belarus, Belgium, Belize, Benin, Bolivia, Botswana, Brazil, Bulgaria, Burkina Faso, Burundi, Cameroon, Canada, Cape Verde, Chile, China, Colombia, Comoros, Democratic Republic of the Congo, Costa Rica, Cote d'Ivoire, Croatia, Cuba, Cyprus, Czech Republic, Denmark, Dominica, Dominican Republic, Ecuador, Egypt, El Salvador, Estonia, Ethiopia, EU, Finland, France, The Gambia, Georgia, Germany, Greece, Guatemala, Guinea, Honduras, Hungary, Iceland, India, Indonesia, Iran, Ireland, Israel, Italy, Japan, Jordan, Kenya, Kiribati, South Korea, Kuwait, Kyrgyzstan, Latvia, Lebanon, Lesotho, Liechtenstein, Lithuania, Luxembourg, The Former Yugoslav Republic of Macedonia, Madagascar, Malawi, Malaysia, Maldives, Mali, Malta, Mauritania, Mauritius, Mexico, Federated States of Micronesia, Moldova, Monaco, Mongolia, Morocco, Mozambique, Namibia, Nepal, Netherlands, NZ, Nicaragua, Niger, Nigeria, Norway, Oman, Pakistan, Panama, Papua New Guinea, Paraguay, Peru, Philippines, Poland, Portugal, Qatar, Romania, Russia, Saint Kitts and Nevis, Saint Lucia, Saint Vincent and the Grenadines, Saudi Arabia, Senegal, Seychelles, Singapore, Slovakia, Slovenia, South Africa, Spain, Sri Lanka, Sweden, Switzerland, Syria, Tanzania, Thailand, Trinidad and Tobago, Tunisia, Turkey, Turkmenistan, Uganda, Ukraine, UAE, UK, Uruguay, Uzbekistan, Venezuela, Vietnam, Yemen, Yugoslavia, Zambia *countries that have signed, but not yet ratified*—(3) Afghanistan, Haiti, US
Biodiversity	see Convention on Biological Diversity
Convention for the Conservation of Antarctic Seals *note*—abbreviated as Antarctic Seals *opened for signature*—NA *entered into force*—NA *objective*—NA	*parties*—(16) Argentina, Australia, Belgium, Brazil, Canada, Chile, France, Germany, Italy, Japan, Norway, Poland, Russia, South Africa, UK, US *countries that have signed, but not yet ratified*—(1) NZ

Appendix C: Selected International Environmental Agreements *(continued)*

Convention on Biological Diversity *note*—abbreviated as Biodiversity *opened for signature*—5 June 1992 *entered into force*—29 December 1993 *objective*—to develop national strategies for the conservation and sustainable use of biological diversity	*parties*—(180) Albania, Algeria, Angola, Antigua and Barbuda, Argentina, Armenia, Australia, Austria, Azerbaijan, The Bahamas, Bahrain, Bangladesh, Barbados, Belarus, Belgium, Belize, Benin, Bhutan, Bolivia, Botswana, Brazil, Bulgaria, Burkina Faso, Burma, Burundi, Cambodia, Cameroon, Canada, Cape Verde, Central African Republic, Chad, Chile, China, Colombia, Comoros, Democratic Republic of the Congo, Republic of the Congo, Cook Islands, Costa Rica, Cote d'Ivoire, Croatia, Cuba, Cyprus, Czech Republic, Denmark, Djibouti, Dominica, Dominican Republic, Ecuador, Egypt, El Salvador, Equatorial Guinea, Eritrea, Estonia, Ethiopia, EU, Fiji, Finland, France, Gabon, The Gambia, Georgia, Germany, Ghana, Greece, Grenada, Guatemala, Guinea, Guinea-Bissau, Guyana, Haiti, Honduras, Hungary, Iceland, India, Indonesia, Iran, Ireland, Israel, Italy, Jamaica, Japan, Jordan, Kazakhstan, Kenya, Kiribati, North Korea, South Korea, Kyrgyzstan, Laos, Latvia, Lebanon, Lesotho, Liberia, Liechtenstein, Lithuania, Luxembourg, The Former Yugoslav Republic of Macedonia, Madagascar, Malawi, Malaysia, Maldives, Mali, Malta, Marshall Islands, Mauritania, Mauritius, Mexico, Federated States of Micronesia, Moldova, Monaco, Mongolia, Morocco, Mozambique, Namibia, Nauru, Nepal, Netherlands, NZ, Nicaragua, Niger, Nigeria, Niue, Norway, Oman, Pakistan, Palau, Panama, Papua New Guinea, Paraguay, Peru, Philippines, Poland, Portugal, Qatar, Romania, Russia, Rwanda, Saint Kitts and Nevis, Saint Lucia, Saint Vincent and the Grenadines, Samoa, San Marino, Sao Tome and Principe, Senegal, Seychelles, Sierra Leone, Singapore, Slovakia, Slovenia, Solomon Islands, South Africa, Spain, Sri Lanka, Sudan, Suriname, Swaziland, Sweden, Switzerland, Syria, Tajikistan, Tanzania, Togo, Tonga, Trinidad and Tobago, Tunisia, Turkey, Turkmenistan, Uganda, Ukraine, UAE, UK, Uruguay, Uzbekistan, Vanuatu, Venezuela, Vietnam, Yemen, Zambia, Zimbabwe *countries that have signed, but not yet ratified*—(7) Afghanistan, Kuwait, Libya, Thailand, Tuvalu, US, Yugoslavia
Climate Change	see United Nations Framework Convention on Climate Change
Climate Change-Kyoto Protocol	see Kyoto Protocol to the United Nations Framework Convention on Climate Change
Convention on Fishing and Conservation of Living Resources of the High Seas *note*—abbreviated as Marine Life Conservation *opened for signature*—29 April 1958 *entered into force*—20 March 1966 *objective*—to solve through international cooperation the problems involved in the conservation of living resources of the high seas, considering that because of the development of modern technology some of these resources are in danger of being overexploited	*parties*—(38) Australia, Belgium, Bosnia and Herzegovina, Burkina Faso, Cambodia, Colombia, Denmark, Dominican Republic, Fiji, Finland, France, Haiti, Jamaica, Kenya, Lesotho, Madagascar, Malawi, Malaysia, Mauritius, Mexico, Netherlands, Nigeria, Portugal, Senegal, Sierra Leone, Solomon Islands, South Africa, Spain, Switzerland, Thailand, Tonga, Trinidad and Tobago, Uganda, UK, US, Uruguay, Venezuela, Yugoslavia *countries that have signed, but not yet ratified*—(21) Afghanistan, Argentina, Bolivia, Canada, China, Costa Rica, Cuba, Ghana, Iceland, Indonesia, Iran, Ireland, Israel, Lebanon, Liberia, Nepal, NZ, Pakistan, Panama, Sri Lanka, Tunisia
Convention on Long-Range Transboundary Air Pollution *note*—abbreviated as Air Pollution *opened for signature*—13 November 1979 *entered into force*—16 March 1983 *objective*—to protect the human environment against air pollution and to gradually reduce and prevent air pollution, including long-range transboundary air pollution	*parties*—(48) Armenia, Austria, Belarus, Belgium, Bosnia and Herzegovina, Bulgaria, Canada, Croatia, Cyprus, Czech Republic, Denmark, Estonia, EU, Finland, France, Georgia, Germany, Greece, Hungary, Iceland, Ireland, Italy, Kazakhstan, Kyrgyzstan, Latvia, Liechtenstein, Lithuania, Luxembourg, The Former Yugoslav Republic of Macedonia, Malta, Moldova, Monaco, Netherlands, Norway, Poland, Portugal, Romania, Russia, Slovakia, Slovenia, Spain, Sweden, Switzerland, Turkey, Ukraine, UK, US, Yugoslavia *countries that have signed, but not yet ratified*—(2) Holy See, San Marino
Convention on the Conservation of Antarctic Marine Living Resources *note*—abbreviated as Antarctic-Marine Living Resources *opened for signature*—NA *entered into force*—NA *objective*—NA	*parties*—(30) Argentina, Australia, Belgium, Brazil, Bulgaria, Canada, Chile, EU, Finland, France, Germany, Greece, India, Italy, Japan, South Korea, Namibia, Netherlands, NZ, Norway, Peru, Poland, Russia, South Africa, Spain, Sweden, Ukraine, UK, US, Uruguay

Appendix C: Selected International Environmental Agreements *(continued)*

Convention on the International Trade in Endangered Species of Wild Flora and Fauna (CITES) *note*—abbreviated as Endangered Species *opened for signature*—3 March 1973 *entered into force*—1 July 1975 *objective*—to protect certain endangered species from overexploitation by means of a system of import/export permits	*parties*—(152) Afghanistan, Algeria, Antigua and Barbuda, Argentina, Australia, Austria, Azerbaijan, The Bahamas, Bangladesh, Barbados, Belarus, Belgium, Belize, Benin, Bolivia, Botswana, Brazil, Brunei, Bulgaria, Burkina Faso, Burma, Burundi, Cambodia, Cameroon, Canada, Central African Republic, Chad, Chile, China, Colombia, Comoros, Democratic Republic of the Congo, Republic of the Congo, Costa Rica, Cote d'Ivoire, Croatia, Cuba, Cyprus, Czech Republic, Denmark, Djibouti, Dominica, Dominican Republic, Ecuador, Egypt, El Salvador, Equatorial Guinea, Eritrea, Estonia, Ethiopia, Fiji, Finland, France, Gabon, The Gambia, Georgia, Germany, Ghana, Greece, Grenada, Guatemala, Guinea, Guinea-Bissau, Guyana, Honduras, Hungary, Iceland, India, Indonesia, Iran, Israel, Italy, Jamaica, Japan, Jordan, Kazakhstan, Kenya, South Korea, Latvia, Liberia, Liechtenstein, Luxembourg, The Former Yugoslav Republic of Macedonia, Madagascar, Malawi, Malaysia, Mali, Malta, Mauritania, Mauritius, Mexico, Monaco, Mongolia, Morocco, Mozambique, Namibia, Nepal, Netherlands, NZ, Nicaragua, Niger, Nigeria, Norway, Pakistan, Panama, Papua New Guinea, Paraguay, Peru, Philippines, Poland, Portugal, Romania, Russia, Rwanda, Saint Kitts and Nevis, Saint Lucia, Saint Vincent and the Grenadines, Saudi Arabia, Senegal, Seychelles, Sierra Leone, Singapore, Slovakia, Slovenia, Somalia, South Africa, Spain, Sri Lanka, Sudan, Suriname, Swaziland, Sweden, Switzerland, Tanzania, Thailand, Togo, Trinidad and Tobago, Tunisia, Turkey, Uganda, Ukraine, UAE, UK, US, Uruguay, Uzbekistan, Vanuatu, Venezuela, Vietnam, Yemen, Zambia, Zimbabwe *countries that have signed, but not yet ratified*—(3) Ireland, Kuwait, Lesotho
Convention on the Prevention of Marine Pollution by Dumping Wastes and Other Matter (London Convention) *note*—abbreviated as Marine Dumping *opened for signature*—29 December 1972 *entered into force*—30 August 1975 *objective*—to control pollution of the sea by dumping and to encourage regional agreements supplementary to the Convention	*parties*—(78) Afghanistan, Antigua and Barbuda, Argentina, Australia, Azerbaijan, Barbados, Belarus, Belgium, Brazil, Canada, Cape Verde, Chile, China, Democratic Republic of the Congo, Costa Rica, Cote d'Ivoire, Croatia, Cuba, Cyprus, Denmark, Dominican Republic, Egypt, Finland, France, Gabon, Germany, Greece, Guatemala, Haiti, Honduras, Hong Kong (associate member), Hungary, Iceland, Iran, Ireland, Italy, Jamaica, Japan, Jordan, Kenya, Kiribati, South Korea, Libya, Luxembourg, Malta, Mexico, Monaco, Morocco, Nauru, Netherlands, NZ, Nigeria, Norway, Oman, Pakistan, Panama, Papua New Guinea, Philippines, Poland, Portugal, Russia, Saint Lucia, Seychelles, Slovenia, Solomon Islands, South Africa, Spain, Suriname, Sweden, Switzerland, Tonga, Tunisia, Ukraine, UAE, UK, US, Vanuatu, Yugoslavia
Convention on the Prohibition of Military or Any Other Hostile Use of Environmental Modification Techniques *note*—abbreviated as Environmental Modification *opened for signature*—10 December 1976 *entered into force*—5 October 1978 *objective*—to prohibit the military or other hostile use of environmental modification techniques in order to further world peace and trust among nations	*parties*—(68) Afghanistan, Algeria, Antigua and Barbuda, Argentina, Australia, Austria, Bangladesh, Belarus, Belgium, Benin, Brazil, Bulgaria, Canada, Cape Verde, Chile, Costa Rica, Cuba, Cyprus, Czech Republic, Denmark, Dominica, Egypt, Finland, Germany, Ghana, Greece, Guatemala, Hungary, Iceland, India, Ireland, Italy, Japan, North Korea, South Korea, Kuwait, Laos, Malawi, Mauritius, Mongolia, Netherlands, NZ, Niger, Norway, Pakistan, Papua New Guinea, Poland, Romania, Russia, Saint Lucia, Saint Vincent and the Grenadines, Sao Tome and Principe, Sierra Leone, Slovakia, Solomon Islands, Spain, Sri Lanka, Sweden, Switzerland, Tajikistan, Tunisia, Ukraine, UK, US, Uruguay, Uzbekistan, Vietnam, Yemen *countries that have signed, but not yet ratified*—(15) Bolivia, Democratic Republic of the Congo, Ethiopia, Holy See, Iran, Iraq, Lebanon, Liberia, Luxembourg, Morocco, Nicaragua, Portugal, Syria, Turkey, Uganda
Convention on Wetlands of International Importance Especially as Waterfowl Habitat (Ramsar) *note*—abbreviated as Wetlands *opened for signature*—2 February 1971 *entered into force*—21 December 1975 *objective*—to stem the progressive encroachment on and loss of wetlands now and in the future, recognizing the fundamental ecological functions of wetlands and their economic, cultural, scientific, and recreational value	*parties*—(123) Albania, Algeria, Argentina, Armenia, Australia, Austria, The Bahamas, Bahrain, Bangladesh, Belarus, Belgium, Belize, Benin, Bolivia, Botswana, Brazil, Bulgaria, Burkina Faso, Cambodia, Canada, Chad, Chile, China, Colombia, Comoros, Democratic Republic of the Congo, Republic of the Congo, Costa Rica, Cote d'Ivoire, Croatia, Czech Republic, Denmark, Ecuador, Egypt, El Salvador, Estonia, Finland, France, Gabon, The Gambia, Georgia, Germany, Ghana, Greece, Guatemala, Guinea, Guinea-Bissau, Honduras, Hungary, Iceland, India, Indonesia, Iran, Ireland, Israel, Italy, Jamaica, Japan, Jordan, Kenya, South Korea, Latvia, Lebanon, Libya, Liechtenstein, Lithuania, Luxembourg, The Former Yugoslav Republic of Macedonia, Madagascar, Malawi, Malaysia, Mali, Malta, Mauritania, Mexico, Moldova, Monaco, Mongolia, Morocco, Namibia, Nepal, Netherlands, NZ, Nicaragua, Niger, Nigeria, Norway, Pakistan, Panama, Papua New Guinea, Paraguay, Peru, Philippines, Poland, Portugal, Romania, Russia, Senegal, Sierra Leone, Slovakia, Slovenia, South Africa, Spain, Sri Lanka, Suriname, Sweden, Switzerland, Syria, Tanzania, Thailand, Togo, Trinidad and Tobago, Tunisia, Turkey, Uganda, Ukraine, UK, US, Uruguay, Venezuela, Vietnam, Yugoslavia, Zambia
Desertification	see United Nations Convention to Combat Desertification in those Countries Experiencing Serious Drought and/or Desertification, Particularly in Africa
Endangered Species	see Convention on the International Trade in Endangered Species of Wild Flora and Fauna (CITES)
Environmental Modification	see Convention on the Prohibition of Military or Any Other Hostile Use of Environmental Modification Techniques

Appendix C: Selected International Environmental Agreements *(continued)*

Hazardous Wastes	see Basel Convention on the Control of Transboundary Movements of Hazardous Wastes and Their Disposal
International Convention for the Regulation of Whaling *note*—abbreviated as Whaling *opened for signature*—2 December 1946 *entered into force*—10 November 1948 *objective*—to protect all species of whales from overhunting; to establish a system of international regulation for the whale fisheries to ensure proper conservation and development of whale stocks; and to safeguard for future generations the great natural resources represented by whale stocks	*parties*—(41) Antigua and Barbuda, Argentina, Australia, Austria, Brazil, Chile, China, Costa Rica, Denmark, Dominica, Finland, France, Germany, Grenada, Guinea, India, Ireland, Italy, Japan, Kenya, South Korea, Mexico, Monaco, Morocco, Netherlands, NZ, Norway, Oman, Peru, Russia, Saint Kitts and Nevis, Saint Lucia, Saint Vincent and the Grenadines, Senegal, Solomon Islands, South Africa, Spain, Sweden, Switzerland, UK, US
International Tropical Timber Agreement, 1983 *note*—abbreviated as Tropical Timber 83 *opened for signature*—18 November 1983 *entered into force*—1 April 1985; this agreement expired when the International Tropical Timber Agreement, 1994, went into force *objective*—to provide an effective framework for cooperation between tropical timber producers and consumers and to encourage the development of national policies aimed at sustainable utilization and conservation of tropical forests and their genetic resources	*parties*—(54) Australia, Austria, Belgium, Bolivia, Brazil, Burma, Cameroon, Canada, China, Colombia, Democratic Republic of the Congo, Republic of the Congo, Cote d'Ivoire, Denmark, Ecuador, Egypt, EU, Fiji, Finland, France, Gabon, Germany, Ghana, Greece, Guyana, Honduras, India, Indonesia, Ireland, Italy, Japan, South Korea, Liberia, Luxembourg, Malaysia, Nepal, Netherlands, NZ, Norway, Panama, Papua New Guinea, Peru, Philippines, Portugal, Russia, Spain, Sweden, Switzerland, Thailand, Togo, Trinidad and Tobago, UK, US, Venezuela
International Tropical Timber Agreement, 1994 *note*—abbreviated as Tropical Timber 94 *opened for signature*—26 January 1994 *entered into force*—1 January 1997 *objective*—to ensure that by the year 2000 exports of tropical timber originate from sustainably managed sources; to establish a fund to assist tropical timber producers in obtaining the resources necessary to reach this objective	*parties*—(58) Australia, Austria, Belgium, Bolivia, Brazil, Burma, Cambodia, Cameroon, Canada, Central African Republic, China, Colombia, Democratic Republic of the Congo, Republic of the Congo, Cote d'Ivoire, Denmark, Ecuador, Egypt, EU, Fiji, Finland, France, Gabon, Germany, Ghana, Greece, Guyana, Honduras, India, Indonesia, Ireland, Italy, Japan, South Korea, Liberia, Luxembourg, Malaysia, Nepal, Netherlands, NZ, Norway, Panama, Papua New Guinea, Peru, Philippines, Portugal, Spain, Suriname, Sweden, Switzerland, Thailand, Togo, Trinidad and Tobago, UK, US, Uruguay, Vanuatu, Venezuela *countries that have signed, but not yet ratified*—(1) Ireland
Kyoto Protocol to the United Nations Framework Convention on Climate Change *note*—abbreviated as Climate Change-Kyoto Protocol *opened for signature*—16 March 1998, but not yet in force *objective*—to further reduce greenhouse gas emissions by enhancing the national programs of developed countries aimed at this goal and by establishing percentage reduction targets for the developed countries	*parties*—(32) Antigua and Barbuda, Azerbaijan, The Bahamas, Barbados, Bolivia, Cyprus, Ecuador, El Salvador, Equatorial Guinea, Fiji, Georgia, Guatemala, Guinea, Honduras, Jamaica, Kiribati, Lesotho, Maldives, Mexico, Federated States of Micronesia, Mongolia, Nicaragua, Niue, Palau, Panama, Paraguay, Samoa, Trinidad and Tobago, Turkmenistan, Tuvalu, Uruguay, Uzbekistan *countries that have signed, but not yet ratified*—(64) Argentina, Australia, Austria, Belgium, Brazil, Bulgaria, Canada, Chile, China, Cook Islands, Costa Rica, Croatia, Cuba, Czech Republic, Denmark, Egypt, Estonia, EU, Finland, France, Germany, Greece, Indonesia, Ireland, Israel, Italy, Japan, Kazakhstan, South Korea, Latvia, Liechtenstein, Lithuania, Luxembourg, Malaysia, Mali, Malta, Marshall Islands, Monaco, Netherlands, NZ, Niger, Norway, Papua New Guinea, Peru, Philippines, Poland, Portugal, Romania, Russia, Saint Lucia, Saint Vincent and the Grenadines, Seychelles, Slovakia, Slovenia, Solomon Islands, Spain, Sweden, Switzerland, Thailand, Ukraine, UK, US, Vietnam, Zambia
Law of the Sea	see United Nations Convention on the Law of the Sea (LOS)
Marine Dumping	see Convention on the Prevention of Marine Pollution by Dumping Wastes and Other Matter (London Convention)
Marine Life Conservation	see Convention on Fishing and Conservation of Living Resources of the High Seas

Appendix C: Selected International Environmental Agreements *(continued)*

Montreal Protocol on Substances That Deplete the Ozone Layer *note*—abbreviated as Ozone Layer Protection *opened for signature*—16 September 1987 *entered into force*—1 January 1989 *objective*—to protect the ozone layer by controlling emissions of substances that deplete it	*parties*—(175) Albania, Algeria, Angola, Antigua and Barbuda, Argentina, Armenia, Australia, Austria, Azerbaijan, The Bahamas, Bahrain, Bangladesh, Barbados, Belarus, Belgium, Belize, Benin, Bolivia, Bosnia and Herzegovina, Botswana, Brazil, Brunei, Bulgaria, Burkina Faso, Burma, Burundi, Cameroon, Canada, Central African Republic, Chad, Chile, China, Colombia, Comoros, Democratic Republic of the Congo, Republic of the Congo, Costa Rica, Cote d'Ivoire, Croatia, Cuba, Cyprus, Czech Republic, Denmark, Djibouti, Dominica, Dominican Republic, Ecuador, Egypt, El Salvador, Estonia, Ethiopia, EU, Fiji, Finland, France, Gabon, The Gambia, Georgia, Germany, Ghana, Greece, Grenada, Guatemala, Guinea, Guyana, Haiti, Honduras, Hungary, Iceland, India, Indonesia, Iran, Ireland, Israel, Italy, Jamaica, Japan, Jordan, Kazakhstan, Kenya, Kiribati, North Korea, South Korea, Kuwait, Kyrgyzstan, Laos, Latvia, Lebanon, Lesotho, Liberia, Libya, Liechtenstein, Lithuania, Luxembourg, The Former Yugoslav Republic of Macedonia, Madagascar, Malawi, Malaysia, Maldives, Mali, Malta, Marshall Islands, Mauritania, Mauritius, Mexico, Federated States of Micronesia, Moldova, Monaco, Mongolia, Morocco, Mozambique, Namibia, Nepal, Netherlands, NZ, Nicaragua, Niger, Nigeria, Norway, Oman, Pakistan, Panama, Papua New Guinea, Paraguay, Peru, Philippines, Poland, Portugal, Qatar, Romania, Russia, Saint Kitts and Nevis, Saint Lucia, Saint Vincent and the Grenadines, Samoa, Saudi Arabia, Senegal, Seychelles, Singapore, Slovakia, Slovenia, Solomon Islands, South Africa, Spain, Sri Lanka, Sudan, Suriname, Swaziland, Sweden, Switzerland, Syria, Tajikistan, Tanzania, Thailand, Togo, Tonga, Trinidad and Tobago, Tunisia, Turkey, Turkmenistan, Tuvalu, Uganda, Ukraine, UAE, UK, US, Uruguay, Uzbekistan, Vanuatu, Venezuela, Vietnam, Yemen, Yugoslavia, Zambia, Zimbabwe
Nuclear Test Ban	see Treaty Banning Nuclear Weapons Tests in the Atmosphere, in Outer Space, and Under Water
Ozone Layer Protection	see Montreal Protocol on Substances That Deplete the Ozone Layer
Protocol of 1978 Relating to the International Convention for the Prevention of Pollution From Ships, 1973 (MARPOL) *note*—abbreviated as Ship Pollution *opened for signature*—17 February 1978 *entered into force*—2 October 1983 *objective*—to preserve the marine environment through the complete elimination of pollution by oil and other harmful substances and the minimization of accidental discharge of such substances	*parties*—(115) Algeria, Antigua and Barbuda, Argentina, Australia, Austria, The Bahamas, Barbados, Belarus, Belgium, Belize, Benin, Bolivia, Brazil, Brunei, Bulgaria, Burma, Cambodia, Canada, Chile, China, Colombia, Comoros, Cote d'Ivoire, Croatia, Cuba, Cyprus, Czech Republic, Denmark, Djibouti, Dominica, Dominican Republic, Ecuador, Egypt, Equatorial Guinea, Estonia, Finland, France, Gabon, The Gambia, Georgia, Germany, Ghana, Greece, Guatemala, Guyana, Hong Kong (associate member), Hungary, Iceland, India, Indonesia, Ireland, Israel, Italy, Jamaica, Japan, Kazakhstan, Kenya, North Korea, South Korea, Latvia, Lebanon, Liberia, Lithuania, Luxembourg, Malaysia, Malta, Marshall Islands, Mauritania, Mauritius, Mexico, Monaco, Morocco, Netherlands, NZ, Nicaragua, Norway, Oman, Pakistan, Panama, Papua New Guinea, Peru, Poland, Portugal, Romania, Russia, Saint Kitts and Nevis, Saint Lucia, Saint Vincent and the Grenadines, Sao Tome and Principe, Senegal, Seychelles, Singapore, Slovakia, Slovenia, South Africa, Spain, Sri Lanka, Suriname, Sweden, Switzerland, Syria, Togo, Tonga, Trinidad and Tobago, Tunisia, Turkey, Tuvalu, Ukraine, UK, US, Uruguay, Vanuatu, Venezuela, Vietnam, Yugoslavia
Protocol on Environmental Protection to the Antarctic Treaty *note*—abbreviated as Antarctic-Environmental Protocol *opened for signature*—4 October 1991 *entered into force*—14 January 1998 *objective*—to provide for comprehensive protection of the Antarctic environment and dependent and associated ecosystems; applies to the area covered by the Antarctic Treaty	*parties*—(27) Argentina, Australia, Belgium, Brazil, Bulgaria, Chile, China, Ecuador, Finland, France, Germany, India, Italy, Japan, South Korea, Netherlands, NZ, Norway, Peru, Poland, Russia, South Africa, Spain, Sweden, UK, US, Uruguay *countries that have signed, but not yet ratified*—(16) Austria, Canada, Colombia, Cuba, Czech Republic, Denmark, Greece, Guatemala, Hungary, North Korea, Papua New Guinea, Romania, Slovakia, Switzerland, Turkey, Ukraine
Protocol to the 1979 Convention on Long-Range Transboundary Air Pollution Concerning the Control of Emissions of Nitrogen Oxides or Their Transboundary Fluxes *note*—abbreviated as Air Pollution-Nitrogen Oxides *opened for signature*—31 October 1988 *entered into force*—14 February 1991 *objective*—to provide for the control or reduction of nitrogen oxides and their transboundary fluxes	*parties*—(28) Austria, Belarus, Belgium, Bulgaria, Canada, Czech Republic, Denmark, Estonia, EU, Finland, France, Germany, Greece, Hungary, Ireland, Italy, Liechtenstein, Luxembourg, Netherlands, Norway, Russia, Slovakia, Spain, Sweden, Switzerland, Ukraine, UK, US *countries that have signed, but not yet ratified*—(1) Poland

Appendix C: Selected International Environmental Agreements *(continued)*

Protocol to the 1979 Convention on Long-Range Transboundary Air Pollution Concerning the Control of Emissions of Volatile Organic Compounds or Their Transboundary Fluxes *note*—abbreviated as Air Pollution-Volatile Organic Compounds *opened for signature*—18 November 1991 *entered into force*—29 September 1997 *objective*—to provide for the control and reduction of emissions of volatile organic compounds in order to reduce their transboundary fluxes so as to protect human health and the environment from adverse effects	*parties*—(20) Austria, Belgium, Bulgaria, Czech Republic, Denmark, Estonia, Finland, France, Germany, Hungary, Italy, Liechtenstein, Luxembourg, Netherlands, Norway, Slovakia, Spain, Sweden, Switzerland, UK *countries that have signed, but not yet ratified*—(7) Canada, EU, Greece, Norway, Portugal, Ukraine, US
Protocol to the 1979 Convention on Long-Range Transboundary Air Pollution on Further Reduction of Sulphur Emissions *note*—abbreviated as Air Pollution-Sulphur 94 *opened for signature*—14 June 1994 *entered into force*—5 August 1998 *objective*—to provide for a further reduction in sulfur emissions or transboundary fluxes	*parties*—(23) Austria, Belgium, Canada, Croatia, Czech Republic, Denmark, EU, Finland, France, Germany, Greece, Ireland, Italy, Liechtenstein, Luxembourg, Netherlands, Norway, Slovakia, Slovenia, Spain, Sweden, Switzerland, UK *countries that have signed, but not yet ratified*—(5) Bulgaria, Hungary, Poland, Russia, Ukraine
Protocol to the 1979 Convention on Long-Range Transboundary Air Pollution on Persistent Organic Pollutants *note*—abbreviated as Air Pollution-Persistent Organic Pollutants *opened for signature*—24 June 1998, but not yet in force *objective*—to provide for the control and reduction of emissions of persistent organic pollutants in order to reduce their transboundary fluxes so as to protect human health and the environment from adverse effects	*parties*—(6) Canada, Luxembourg, Netherlands, Norway, Sweden, Switzerland *countries that have signed, but not yet ratified*—(30) Armenia, Austria, Belgium, Bulgaria, Croatia, Cyprus, Czech Republic, Denmark, EU, Finland, France, Germany, Greece, Hungary, Iceland, Ireland, Italy, Latvia, Liechtenstein, Lithuania, Moldova, Poland, Portugal, Romania, Slovakia, Slovenia, Spain, Ukraine, UK, US
Protocol to the 1979 Convention on Long-Range Transboundary Air Pollution on the Reduction of Sulphur Emissions or Their Transboundary Fluxes by at Least 30% *note*—abbreviated as Air Pollution-Sulphur 85 *opened for signature*—8 July 1985 *entered into force*—2 September 1987 *objective*—to provide for a 30% reduction in sulfur emissions or transboundary fluxes by 1993	*parties*—(22) Austria, Belarus, Belgium, Bulgaria, Canada, Czech Republic, Denmark, Estonia, Finland, France, Germany, Hungary, Italy, Liechtenstein, Luxembourg, Netherlands, Norway, Russia, Slovakia, Sweden, Switzerland, Ukraine
Ship Pollution	see Protocol of 1978 Relating to the International Convention for the Prevention of Pollution From Ships, 1973 (MARPOL)

Appendix C: Selected International Environmental Agreements *(continued)*

Treaty Banning Nuclear Weapon Tests in the Atmosphere, in Outer Space, and Under Water *note*—abbreviated as Nuclear Test Ban *opened for signature*—5 August 1963 *entered into force*—10 October 1963 *objective*—to obtain an agreement on general and complete disarmament under strict international control in accordance with the objectives of the United Nations; to put an end to the armaments race and eliminate incentives for the production and testing of all kinds of weapons, including nuclear weapons	*parties*—(113) Afghanistan, Antigua and Barbuda, Argentina, Armenia, Australia, Austria, The Bahamas, Bangladesh, Belgium, Benin, Bhutan, Bolivia, Bosnia and Herzegovina, Botswana, Brazil, Bulgaria, Burma, Canada, Central African Republic, Chad, China, Colombia, Democratic Republic of the Congo, Costa Rica, Cote d'Ivoire, Croatia, Cyprus, Czech Republic, Denmark, Dominican Republic, Ecuador, Egypt, El Salvador, Fiji, Finland, Gabon, The Gambia, Germany, Ghana, Greece, Guatemala, Honduras, Hungary, Iceland, India, Indonesia, Iran, Iraq, Ireland, Israel, Italy, Jamaica, Japan, Jordan, Kenya, South Korea, Kuwait, Laos, Lebanon, Liberia, Luxembourg, Madagascar, Malawi, Malaysia, Malta, Mauritania, Mauritius, Mexico, Morocco, Nepal, Netherlands, NZ, Nicaragua, Niger, Nigeria, Norway, Panama, Papua New Guinea, Peru, Philippines, Poland, Romania, Russia, Rwanda, Samoa, San Marino, Senegal, Seychelles, Sierra Leone, Singapore, Slovakia, Slovenia, South Africa, Spain, Sri Lanka, Sudan, Suriname, Swaziland, Sweden, Switzerland, Syria, Thailand, Togo, Tonga, Trinidad and Tobago, Tunisia, Turkey, Uganda, UK, US, Venezuela, Yugoslavia, Zambia *countries that have signed, but not yet ratified*—(17) Algeria, Burkina Faso, Burundi, Cameroon, Chile, Ethiopia, Haiti, Libya, Mali, Pakistan, Paraguay, Portugal, Somalia, Tanzania, Uruguay, Vietnam, Yemen
Tropical Timber 83	see International Tropical Timber Agreement, 1983
Tropical Timber 94	see International Tropical Timber Agreement, 1994
United Nations Convention on the Law of the Sea (LOS) *note*—abbreviated as Law of the Sea *opened for signature*—10 December 1982 *entered into force*—16 November 1994 *objective*—to set up a comprehensive new legal regime for the sea and oceans; to include rules concerning environmental standards as well as enforcement provisions dealing with pollution of the marine environment	*parties*—(135) Algeria, Angola, Antigua and Barbuda, Argentina, Australia, Austria, The Bahamas, Bahrain, Barbados, Belgium, Belize, Benin, Bolivia, Bosnia and Herzegovina, Botswana, Brazil, Brunei, Bulgaria, Burma, Cameroon, Cape Verde, Chile, China, Comoros, Democratic Republic of the Congo, Cook Islands, Costa Rica, Cote d'Ivoire, Croatia, Cuba, Cyprus, Czech Republic, Djibouti, Dominica, Egypt, Equatorial Guinea, EU, Fiji, Finland, France, Gabon, The Gambia, Georgia, Germany, Ghana, Greece, Grenada, Guatemala, Guinea, Guinea-Bissau, Guyana, Haiti, Honduras, Iceland, India, Indonesia, Iraq, Ireland, Italy, Jamaica, Japan, Jordan, Kenya, South Korea, Kuwait, Laos, Lebanon, Luxembourg, The Former Yugoslav Republic of Macedonia, Malaysia, Maldives, Mali, Malta, Marshall Islands, Mauritania, Mauritius, Mexico, Federated States of Micronesia, Monaco, Mongolia, Mozambique, Namibia, Nauru, Nepal, Netherlands, NZ, Nicaragua, Nigeria, Norway, Oman, Pakistan, Palau, Panama, Papua New Guinea, Paraguay, Philippines, Poland, Portugal, Romania, Russia, Saint Kitts and Nevis, Saint Lucia, Saint Vincent and the Grenadines, Samoa, Sao Tome and Principe, Saudi Arabia, Senegal, Seychelles, Sierra Leone, Singapore, Slovakia, Slovenia, Solomon Islands, Somalia, South Africa, Spain, Sri Lanka, Sudan, Suriname, Sweden, Tanzania, Togo, Tonga, Trinidad and Tobago, Tunisia, Uganda, Ukraine, UK, Uruguay, Vanuatu, Vietnam, Yemen, Yugoslavia, Zambia, Zimbabwe *countries that have signed, but not yet ratified*—(35) Afghanistan, Bangladesh, Belarus, Bhutan, Burkina Faso, Burundi, Cambodia, Canada, Central African Republic, Chad, Colombia, Republic of the Congo, Denmark, Dominican Republic, El Salvador, Ethiopia, Hungary, Iran, North Korea, Lesotho, Liberia, Libya, Liechtenstein, Madagascar, Malawi, Morocco, Niger, Niue, Qatar, Rwanda, Swaziland, Switzerland, Thailand, Tuvalu, UAE
United Nations Convention to Combat Desertification in Those Countries Experiencing Serious Drought and/or Desertification, Particularly in Africa *note*—abbreviated as Desertification *opened for signature*—14 October 1994 *entered into force*—26 December 1996 *objective*—to combat desertification and mitigate the effects of drought through national action programs that incorporate long-term strategies supported by international cooperation and partnership arrangements	*parties*—(172) Afghanistan, Albania, Algeria, Angola, Antigua and Barbuda, Argentina, Armenia, Australia, Austria, Azerbaijan, The Bahamas, Bahrain, Bangladesh, Barbados, Belgium, Belize, Benin, Bolivia, Botswana, Brazil, Burkina Faso, Burma, Burundi, Cambodia, Cameroon, Canada, Cape Verde, Central African Republic, Chad, Chile, China, Colombia, Comoros, Democratic Republic of the Congo, Republic of the Congo, Cook Islands, Costa Rica, Cote d'Ivoire, Croatia, Cuba, Cyprus, Czech Republic, Denmark, Djibouti, Dominica, Dominican Republic, Ecuador, Egypt, El Salvador, Equatorial Guinea, Eritrea, Ethiopia, EU, Fiji, Finland, France, Gabon, The Gambia, Georgia, Germany, Ghana, Greece, Grenada, Guatemala, Guinea, Guinea-Bissau, Guyana, Haiti, Honduras, Hungary, Iceland, India, Indonesia, Iran, Ireland, Israel, Italy, Jamaica, Japan, Jordan, Kazakhstan, Kenya, Kiribati, South Korea, Kuwait, Kyrgyzstan, Laos, Lebanon, Lesotho, Liberia, Libya, Liechtenstein, Luxembourg, Madagascar, Malawi, Malaysia, Mali, Malta, Marshall Islands, Mauritania, Mauritius, Mexico, Federated States of Micronesia, Moldova, Monaco, Mongolia, Morocco, Mozambique, Namibia, Nauru, Nepal, Netherlands, NZ, Nicaragua, Niger, Nigeria, Niue, Norway, Oman, Pakistan, Palau, Panama, Papua New Guinea, Paraguay, Peru, Philippines, Portugal, Qatar, Romania, Rwanda, Saint Kitts and Nevis, Saint Lucia, Saint Vincent and the Grenadines, Samoa, San Marino, Sao Tome and Principe, Saudi Arabia, Senegal, Seychelles, Sierra Leone, Singapore, Solomon Islands, South Africa, Spain, Sri Lanka, Sudan, Suriname, Swaziland, Sweden, Switzerland, Syria, Tajikistan, Tanzania, Togo, Tonga, Trinidad and Tobago, Tunisia, Turkey, Turkmenistan, Tuvalu, Uganda, UAE, UK, US, Uruguay, Uzbekistan, Vanuatu, Venezuela, Vietnam, Yemen, Zambia, Zimbabwe

Appendix C: Selected International Environmental Agreements *(continued)*

United Nations Framework Convention on Climate Change *note*—abbreviated as Climate Change *opened for signature*—9 May 1992 *entered into force*—21 March 1994 *objective*—to achieve stabilization of greenhouse gas concentrations in the atmosphere at a low enough level to prevent dangerous anthropogenic interference with the climate system	*parties*—(186) Albania, Algeria, Angola, Antigua and Barbuda, Argentina, Armenia, Australia, Austria, Azerbaijan, The Bahamas, Bahrain, Bangladesh, Barbados, Belarus, Belgium, Belize, Benin, Bhutan, Bolivia, Bosnia and Herzegovina, Botswana, Brazil, Bulgaria, Burkina Faso, Burma, Burundi, Cambodia, Cameroon, Canada, Cape Verde, Central African Republic, Chad, Chile, China, Colombia, Comoros, Democratic Republic of the Congo, Republic of the Congo, Cook Islands, Costa Rica, Cote d'Ivoire, Croatia, Cuba, Cyprus, Czech Republic, Denmark, Djibouti, Dominica, Dominican Republic, Ecuador, Egypt, El Salvador, Equatorial Guinea, Eritrea, Estonia, Ethiopia, EU, Fiji, Finland, France, Gabon, The Gambia, Georgia, Germany, Ghana, Greece, Grenada, Guatemala, Guinea, Guinea-Bissau, Guyana, Haiti, Honduras, Hungary, Iceland, India, Indonesia, Iran, Ireland, Israel, Italy, Jamaica, Japan, Jordan, Kazakhstan, Kenya, Kiribati, North Korea, South Korea, Kuwait, Kyrgyzstan, Laos, Latvia, Lebanon, Lesotho, Libya, Liechtenstein, Lithuania, Luxembourg, The Former Yugoslav Republic of Macedonia, Madagascar, Malawi, Malaysia, Maldives, Mali, Malta, Marshall Islands, Mauritania, Mauritius, Mexico, Federated States of Micronesia, Moldova, Monaco, Mongolia, Morocco, Mozambique, Namibia, Nauru, Nepal, Netherlands, NZ, Nicaragua, Niger, Nigeria, Niue, Norway, Oman, Pakistan, Palau, Panama, Papua New Guinea, Paraguay, Peru, Philippines, Poland, Portugal, Qatar, Romania, Russia, Rwanda, Saint Kitts and Nevis, Saint Lucia, Saint Vincent and the Grenadines, Samoa, San Marino, Sao Tome and Principe, Saudi Arabia, Senegal, Seychelles, Sierra Leone, Singapore, Slovakia, Slovenia, Solomon Islands, South Africa, Spain, Sri Lanka, Sudan, Suriname, Swaziland, Sweden, Switzerland, Syria, Tajikistan, Tanzania, Thailand, Togo, Tonga, Trinidad and Tobago, Tunisia, Turkmenistan, Tuvalu, Uganda, Ukraine, UAE, UK, US, Uruguay, Uzbekistan, Vanuatu, Venezuela, Vietnam, Yemen, Yugoslavia, Zambia, Zimbabwe *countries that have signed, but not yet ratified*—(2) Afghanistan, Liberia
Wetlands	see Convention on Wetlands of International Importance Especially As Waterfowl Habitat (Ramsar)
Whaling	see International Convention for the Regulation of Whaling

Appendix D:

Cross-Reference List of Country Data Codes

FIPS 10-4:	Countries, Dependencies, Areas of Special Sovereignty, and Their Principal Administrative Divisions (FIPS PUB 10-4) is maintained by the Office of the Geographer and Global Issues (Department of State) and published by the National Institute of Standards and Technology (Department of Commerce). FIPS 10-4 codes are intended for general use throughout the US Government, especially in activities associated with the mission of the Department of State and national defense programs.
ISO 3166:	Codes for the Representation of Names of Countries (ISO 3166) is prepared by the International Organization for Standardization. ISO 3166 includes two- and three-character alphabetic codes and three-digit numeric codes that may be needed for activities involving exchange of data with international organizations that have adopted that standard. Except for the numeric codes, ISO 3166 codes have been adopted in the US as FIPS 104-1: American National Standard Codes for the Representation of Names of Countries, Dependencies, and Areas of Special Sovereignty for Information Interchange.
Internet:	The Internet country code is the two-letter digraph maintained by the International Organization for Standardization (ISO) in *the ISO 3166 Alpha-2 list* and used by the Internet Assigned Numbers Authority (IANA) to establish country-coded top-level domains (ccTLDs).

Entity	FIPS 10-4	ISO 3166			Internet	Comment
Afghanistan	AF	C	AFG	004	.af	
Albania	AL	AL	ALB	008	.al	
Algeria	AG	DZ	DZA	012	.dz	
American Samoa	AQ	AS	ASM	016	.as	
Andorra	AN	AD	AND	020	.ad	
Angola	AO	AO	AGO	024	.ao	
Anguilla	AV	AI	AIA	660	.ai	
Antarctica	AY	AQ	ATA	010	.aq	ISO defines as the territory south of 60 degrees south latitude
Antigua and Barbuda	AC	AG	ATG	028	.ag	
Argentina	AR	AR	ARG	032	.ar	
Armenia	AM	AM	ARM	051	.am	
Aruba	AA	AW	ABW	533	.aw	
Ashmore and Cartier Islands	AT	—	—	—	—	ISO includes with Australia
Australia	AS	AU	AUS	036	.au	ISO includes Ashmore and Cartier Islands, Coral Sea Islands
Austria	AU	AT	AUT	040	.at	
Azerbaijan	AJ	AZ	AZE	031	.az	
Bahamas, The	BF	BS	BHS	044	.bs	
Bahrain	BA	BH	BHR	048	.bh	
Baker Island	FQ	—	—	—	—	ISO includes with the US Minor Outlying Islands
Bangladesh	BG	BD	BGD	050	.bd	
Barbados	BB	BB	BRB	052	.bb	
Bassas da India	BS	—	—	—	—	ISO includes with the Miscellaneous (French) Indian Ocean Islands
Belarus	BO	BY	BLR	112	.by	
Belgium	BE	BE	BEL	056	.be	
Belize	BH	BZ	BLZ	084	.bz	

Appendix D: Cross-Reference List of Country Data Codes (continued)

Entity	FIPS 10-4	ISO 3166			Internet	Comment
Benin	BN	BJ	BEN	204	.bj	
Bermuda	BD	BM	BMU	060	.bm	
Bhutan	BT	BT	BTN	064	.bt	
Bolivia	BL	BO	BOL	068	.bo	
Bosnia and Herzegovina	BK	BA	BIH	070	.ba	
Botswana	BC	BW	BWA	072	.bw	
Bouvet Island	BV	BV	BVT	074	.bv	
Brazil	BR	BR	BRA	076	.br	
British Indian Ocean Territory	IO	IO	IOT	086	.io	
British Virgin Islands	VI	VG	VGB	092	.vg	
Brunei	BX	BN	BRN	096	.bn	
Bulgaria	BU	BG	BGR	100	.bg	
Burkina Faso	UV	BF	BFA	854	.bf	
Burma	BM	MM	MMR	104	.mm	ISO uses the name Myanmar
Burundi	BY	BI	BDI	108	.bi	
Cambodia	CB	KH	KHM	116	.kh	
Cameroon	CM	CM	CMR	120	.cm	
Canada	CA	CA	CAN	124	.ca	
Cape Verde	CV	CV	CPV	132	.cv	
Cayman Islands	CJ	KY	CYM	136	.ky	
Central African Republic	CT	CF	CAF	140	.cf	
Chad	CD	TD	TCD	148	.td	
Chile	CI	CL	CHL	152	.cl	
China	CH	CN	CHN	156	.cn	see also Taiwan
Christmas Island	KT	CX	CXR	162	.cx	
Clipperton Island	IP	—	—	—	—	ISO includes with French Polynesia
Cocos (Keeling) Islands	CK	CC	CCK	166	.cc	
Colombia	CO	CO	COL	170	.co	
Comoros	CN	KM	COM	174	.km	
Congo, Democratic Republic of the	CG	ZR	ZAR	180	.cd	formerly Zaire
Congo, Republic of the	CF	CG	COG	178	.cg	
Cook Islands	CW	CK	COK	184	.ck	
Coral Sea Islands	CR	—	—	—	—	ISO includes with Australia
Costa Rica	CS	CR	CRI	188	.cr	
Cote d'Ivoire	IV	CI	CIV	384	.ci	
Croatia	HR	HR	HRV	191	.hr	
Cuba	CU	CU	CUB	192	.cu	
Cyprus	CY	CY	CYP	196	.cy	
Czech Republic	EZ	CZ	CZE	203	.cz	
Denmark	DA	DK	DNK	208	.dk	
Djibouti	DJ	DJ	DJI	262	.dj	

Appendix D: Cross-Reference List of Country Data Codes *(continued)*

Entity	FIPS 10-4	ISO 3166			Internet	Comment
Dominica	DO	DM	DMA	212	.dm	
Dominican Republic	DR	DO	DOM	214	.do	
East Timor	—	TP	TMP	626	.tp	FIPS includes with Indonesia
Ecuador	EC	EC	ECU	218	.ec	
Egypt	EG	EG	EGY	818	.eg	
El Salvador	ES	SV	SLV	222	.sv	
Equatorial Guinea	EK	GQ	GNQ	226	.gq	
Eritrea	ER	ER	ERI	232	.er	
Estonia	EN	EE	EST	233	.ee	
Ethiopia	ET	ET	ETH	231	.et	
Europa Island	EU	—	—	—	—	ISO includes with the Miscellaneous (French) Indian Ocean Islands
Falkland Islands (Islas Malvinas)	FA	FK	FLK	238	.fk	
Faroe Islands	FO	FO	FRO	234	.fo	
Fiji	FJ	FJ	FJI	242	.fj	
Finland	FI	FI	FIN	246	.fi	
France	FR	FR	FRA	250	.fr	
France, Metropolitan	—	FX	FXX	249	.fx	ISO limits to the European part of France, excluding French Guiana, French Polynesia, French Southern and Antarctic Lands, Guadeloupe, Martinique, Mayotte, New Caledonia, Reunion, Saint Pierre and Miquelon, Wallis and Futuna
French Guiana	FG	GF	GUF	254	.gf	
French Polynesia	FP	PF	PYF	258	.pf	ISO includes Clipperton Island
French Southern and Antarctic Lands	FS	TF	ATF	260	.tf	FIPS 10-4 does not include the French-claimed portion of Antarctica (Terre Adelie)
Gabon	GB	GA	GAB	266	.ga	
Gambia, The	GA	GM	GMB	270	.gm	
Gaza Strip	GZ	—	—	—	—	
Georgia	GG	GE	GEO	268	.ge	
Germany	GM	DE	DEU	276	.de	
Ghana	GH	GH	GHA	288	.gh	
Gibraltar	GI	GI	GIB	292	.gi	
Glorioso Islands	GO	—	—	—	—	ISO includes with the Miscellaneous (French) Indian Ocean Islands
Greece	GR	GR	GRC	300	.gr	
Greenland	GL	GL	GRL	304	.gl	
Grenada	GJ	GD	GRD	308	.gd	
Guadeloupe	GP	GP	GLP	312	.gp	
Guam	GQ	GU	GUM	316	.gu	
Guatemala	GT	GT	GTM	320	.gt	
Guernsey	GK	—	—	—	.gg	ISO includes with the United Kingdom

Appendix D: Cross-Reference List of Country Data Codes *(continued)*

Entity	FIPS 10-4	ISO 3166			Internet	Comment
Guinea	GV	GN	GIN	324	.gn	
Guinea-Bissau	PU	GW	GNB	624	.gw	
Guyana	GY	GY	GUY	328	.gy	
Haiti	HA	HT	HTI	332	.ht	
Heard Island and McDonald Islands	HM	HM	HMD	334	.hm	
Holy See (Vatican City)	VT	VA	VAT	336	.va	
Honduras	HO	HN	HND	340	.hn	
Hong Kong	HK	HK	HKG	344	.hk	
Howland Island	HQ	—	—	—	—	ISO includes with the US Minor Outlying Islands
Hungary	HU	HU	HUN	348	.hu	
Iceland	IC	IS	ISL	352	.is	
India	IN	IN	IND	356	.in	
Indonesia	ID	ID	IDN	360	.id	
Iran	IR	IR	IRN	364	.ir	
Iraq	IZ	IQ	IRQ	368	.iq	
Ireland	EI	IE	IRL	372	.ie	
Israel	IS	IL	ISR	376	.il	
Italy	IT	IT	ITA	380	.it	
Jamaica	JM	JM	JAM	388	.jm	
Jan Mayen	JN	—	—	—	—	ISO includes with Svalbard
Japan	JA	JP	JPN	392	.jp	
Jarvis Island	DQ	—	—	—	—	ISO includes with the US Minor Outlying Islands
Jersey	JE	—	—	—	.je	ISO includes with the United Kingdom
Johnston Atoll	JQ	—	—	—	—	ISO includes with the US Minor Outlying Islands
Jordan	JO	JO	JOR	400	.jo	
Juan de Nova Island	JU	—	—	—	—	ISO includes with the Miscellaneous (French) Indian Ocean Islands
Kazakhstan	KZ	KZ	KAZ	398	.kz	
Kenya	KE	KE	KEN	404	.ke	
Kingman Reef	KQ	—	—	—	—	ISO includes with the US Minor Outlying Islands
Kiribati	KR	KI	KIR	296	.ki	
Korea, North	KN	KP	PRK	408	.kp	
Korea, South	KS	KR	KOR	410	.kr	
Kuwait	KU	KW	KWT	414	.kw	
Kyrgyzstan	KG	KG	KGZ	417	.kg	
Laos	LA	LA	LAO	418	.la	
Latvia	LG	LV	LVA	428	.lv	
Lebanon	LE	LB	LBN	422	.lb	
Lesotho	LT	LS	LSO	426	.ls	

Appendix D: Cross-Reference List of Country Data Codes *(continued)*

Entity	FIPS 10-4	ISO 3166			Internet	Comment
Liberia	LI	LR	LBR	430	.lr	
Libya	LY	LY	LBY	434	.ly	
Liechtenstein	LS	LI	LIE	438	.li	
Lithuania	LH	LT	LTU	440	.lt	
Luxembourg	LU	LU	LUX	442	.lu	
Macau	MC	MO	MAC	446	.mo	
Macedonia, The Republic of	MK	MK	MKD	807	.mk	
Madagascar	MA	MG	MDG	450	.mg	
Malawi	MI	MW	MWI	454	.mw	
Malaysia	MY	MY	MYS	458	.my	
Maldives	MV	MV	MDV	462	.mv	
Mali	ML	ML	MLI	466	.ml	
Malta	MT	MT	MLT	470	.mt	
Man, Isle of	IM	—	—	—	.im	ISO includes with the United Kingdom
Marshall Islands	RM	MH	MHL	584	.mh	
Martinique	MB	MQ	MTQ	474	.mq	
Mauritania	MR	MR	MRT	478	.mr	
Mauritius	MP	MU	MUS	480	.mu	
Mayotte	MF	YT	MYT	175	.yt	
Mexico	MX	MX	MEX	484	.mx	
Micronesia, Federated States of	FM	FM	FSM	583	.fm	
Midway Islands	MQ	—	—	—	—	ISO includes with the US Minor Outlying Islands
Miscellaneous (French) Indian Ocean Islands	—	—	—	—	—	ISO includes Bassas da India, Europa Island, Glorioso Islands, Juan de Nova Island, Tromelin Island
Moldova	MD	MD	MDA	498	.md	
Monaco	MN	MC	MCO	492	.mc	
Mongolia	MG	MN	MNG	496	.mn	
Montserrat	MH	MS	MSR	500	.ms	
Morocco	MO	MA	MAR	504	.ma	
Mozambique	MZ	MZ	MOZ	508	.mz	
Myanmar	—	—	—	—	—	see Burma
Namibia	WA	NA	NAM	516	.na	
Nauru	NR	NR	NRU	520	.nr	
Navassa Island	BQ	—	—	—	—	
Nepal	NP	NP	NPL	524	.np	
Netherlands	NL	NL	NLD	528	.nl	
Netherlands Antilles	NT	AN	ANT	530	.an	
New Caledonia	NC	NC	NCL	540	.nc	
New Zealand	NZ	NZ	NZL	554	.nz	
Nicaragua	NU	NI	NIC	558	.ni	

Appendix D: Cross-Reference List of Country Data Codes *(continued)*

Entity	FIPS 10-4	ISO 3166			Internet	Comment
Niger	NG	NE	NER	562	.ne	
Nigeria	NI	NG	NGA	566	.ng	
Niue	NE	NU	NIU	570	.nu	
Norfolk Island	NF	NF	NFK	574	.nf	
Northern Mariana Islands	CQ	MP	MNP	580	.mp	
Norway	NO	NO	NOR	578	.no	
Oman	MU	OM	OMN	512	.om	
Pakistan	PK	PK	PAK	586	.pk	
Palau	PS	PW	PLW	585	.pw	
Palmyra Atoll	LQ	—	—	—	—	ISO includes with the US Minor Outlying Islands
Panama	PM	PA	PAN	591	.pa	
Papua New Guinea	PP	PG	PNG	598	.pg	
Paracel Islands	PF	—	—	—	—	
Paraguay	PA	PY	PRY	600	.py	
Peru	PE	PE	PER	604	.pe	
Philippines	RP	PH	PHL	608	.ph	
Pitcairn Islands	PC	PN	PCN	612	.pn	
Poland	PL	PL	POL	616	.pl	
Portugal	PO	PT	PRT	620	.pt	
Puerto Rico	RQ	PR	PRI	630	.pr	
Qatar	QA	QA	QAT	634	.qa	
Reunion	RE	RE	REU	638	.re	
Romania	RO	RO	ROM	642	.ro	
Russia	RS	RU	RUS	643	.ru	
Rwanda	RW	RW	RWA	646	.rw	
Saint Helena	SH	SH	SHN	654	.sh	
Saint Kitts and Nevis	SC	KN	KNA	659	.kn	
Saint Lucia	ST	LC	LCA	662	.lc	
Saint Pierre and Miquelon	SB	PM	SPM	666	.pm	
Saint Vincent and the Grenadines	VC	VC	VCT	670	.vc	
Samoa	WS	WS	WSM	882	.ws	
San Marino	SM	SM	SMR	674	.sm	
Sao Tome and Principe	TP	ST	STP	678	.st	
Saudi Arabia	SA	SA	SAU	682	.sa	
Senegal	SG	SN	SEN	686	.sn	
Seychelles	SE	SC	SYC	690	.sc	
Sierra Leone	SL	SL	SLE	694	.sl	
Singapore	SN	SG	SGP	702	.sg	
Slovakia	LO	SK	SVK	703	.sk	
Slovenia	SI	SI	SVN	705	.si	
Solomon Islands	BP	SB	SLB	090	.sb	

Appendix D: Cross-Reference List of Country Data Codes (continued)

Entity	FIPS 10-4	ISO 3166			Internet	Comment
Somalia	SO	SO	SOM	706	.so	
South Africa	SF	ZA	ZAF	710	.za	
South Georgia and the Islands	SX	GS	SGS	239	.gs	
Spain	SP	ES	ESP	724	.es	
Spratly Islands	PG	—	—	—	—	
Sri Lanka	CE	LK	LKA	144	.lk	
Sudan	SU	SD	SDN	736	.sd	
Suriname	NS	SR	SUR	740	.sr	
Svalbard	SV	SJ	SJM	744	.sj	ISO includes Jan Mayen
Swaziland	WZ	SZ	SWZ	748	.sz	
Sweden	SW	SE	SWE	752	.se	
Switzerland	SZ	CH	CHE	756	.ch	
Syria	SY	SY	SYR	760	.sy	
Taiwan	TW	TW	TWN	158	.tw	
Tajikistan	TI	TJ	TJK	762	.tj	
Tanzania	TZ	TZ	TZA	834	.tz	
Thailand	TH	TH	THA	764	.th	
Togo	TO	TG	TGO	768	.tg	
Tokelau	TL	TK	TKL	772	.tk	
Tonga	TN	TO	TON	776	.to	
Trinidad and Tobago	TD	TT	TTO	780	.tt	
Tromelin Island	TE	—	—	—	—	ISO includes with the Miscellaneous Islands
Tunisia	TS	TN	TUN	788	.tn	
Turkey	TU	TR	TUR	792	.tr	
Turkmenistan	TX	TM	TKM	795	.tm	
Turks and Caicos Islands	TK	TC	TCA	796	.tc	
Tuvalu	TV	TV	TUV	798	.tv	
Uganda	UG	UG	UGA	800	.ug	
Ukraine	UP	UA	UKR	804	.ua	
United Arab Emirates	TC	AE	ARE	784	.ae	
United Kingdom	UK	GB	GBR	826	.uk	ISO includes Guernsey, Isle of Man, Jersey
United States	US	US	USA	840	.us	
United States Minor Outlying Islands	—	UM	UMI	581	.um	ISO includes Baker Island, Howland Island, Jarvis Island, Johnston Atoll, Kingman Reef, Midway Islands, Palmyra Atoll, Wake Island
Uruguay	UY	UY	URY	858	.uy	
Uzbekistan	UZ	UZ	UZB	860	.uz	
Vanuatu	NH	VU	VUT	548	.vu	
Venezuela	VE	VE	VEN	862	.ve	
Vietnam	VM	VN	VNM	704	.vn	

Appendix D: Cross-Reference List of Country Data Codes *(continued)*

Entity	FIPS 10-4	ISO 3166			Internet	Comment
Virgin Islands	VQ	VI	VIR	850	.vi	
Virgin Islands (UK)	—	—	—	—	.vg	see British Virgin Islands
Virgin Islands (US)	—	—	—	—	.vi	see Virgin Islands
Wake Island	WQ	—	—	—	—	ISO includes with the US Minor Outlying Islands
Wallis and Futuna	WF	WF	WLF	876	.wf	
West Bank	WE	—	—	—	—	
Western Sahara	WI	EH	ESH	732	.eh	
Western Samoa	—	—	—	—	.ws	see Samoa
World	—	—	—	—	—	the *Factbook* uses the W data code from DIAM 65-18 *Geopolitical* Data Elements and *Related Features*, Data Standard No. 3, December 1994, published by the Defense Intelligence Agency
Yemen	YM	YE	YEM	887	.ye	
Yugoslavia	—	YU	YUG	891	.yu	
Zaire	—	—	—	—	—	see Democratic Republic of the Congo
Zambia	ZA	ZM	ZWB	894	.zm	
Zimbabwe	ZI	ZW	ZWE	716	.zw	

Appendix E:

Cross-Reference List of Hydrographic Data Codes

IHO 23-4th:	*Limits of Oceans and Seas*, Special Publication 23, Draft 4th Edition 1986, published by the International Hydrographic Bureau of the International Hydrographic Organization
IHO 23-3rd:	*Limits of Oceans and Seas*, Special Publication 23, 3rd Edition 1953, published by the International Hydrographic Organization
ACIC M 49-1:	*Chart of Limits of Seas and Oceans*, revised January 1958, published by the Aeronautical Chart and Information Center (ACIC), United States Air Force; note - ACIC is now part of the National Imagery and Mapping Agency (NIMA)
DIAM 65-18:	*Geopolitical Data Elements and Related Features*, Data Standard No. 4, Defense Intelligence Agency Manual 65-18, December 1994, published by the Defense Intelligence Agency
	The US Government has not yet adopted a standard for hydrographic codes similar to the Federal Information Processing Standards (FIPS) 10-4 country codes. The names and limits of the following oceans and seas are not always directly comparable because of differences in the customers, needs, and requirements of the individual organizations. Even the number of principal water bodies varies from organization to organization. *Factbook* users, for example, find the Atlantic Ocean and Pacific Ocean entries useful, but none of the following standards include those oceans in their entirety. Nor is there any provision for combining codes or overcodes to aggregate water bodies. The recently delimited Southern Ocean is not included.

Principal Oceans and Seas of the World With Hydrographic Codes by Institution

	IHO 23-4th	IHO 23-3rd*	ACIC M 49-1	DIAM 65-18
Arctic Ocean	9	17	A	5A
Atlantic Ocean	—	—	—	—
North Atlantic Ocean	1	23	B	1A
South Atlantic Ocean	4	32	C	2A
Baltic Sea	2	1	B26	7B
Indian Ocean	5	45	F	6A
Mediterranean Sea	3.1	28	B11	—
Eastern Mediterranean	3.1.2	28 B	—	8E
Western Mediterranean	3.1.1	28 A	—	8W
Pacific Ocean	—	—	—	—
North Pacific Ocean	7	57	D	3A
South Pacific Ocean	8	61	E	4A
South China and Eastern Archipelagic Seas	6	49, 48	D18 plus others	3U plus others

* The letters after the numbers are subdivisions, not footnotes.

Appendix F:

Cross-Reference List of Geographic Names

This appendix cross-references a wide variety of geographic names to the appropriate *Factbook* 'country' entry. Additional information is included in parentheses.

	Name	Entry in *The World Factbook*	Latitude (deg min)	Longitude (deg min)
A	Abidjan (capital)	Cote d'Ivoire	5 19 N	4 02 W
	Abkhazia (region)	Georgia	43 00 N	41 00 E
	Abu Dhabi (capital)	United Arab Emirates	24 28 N	54 22 E
	Abu Musa (island)	Iran	25 52 N	55 03 E
	Abuja (capital)	Nigeria	9 12 N	7 11 E
	Abyssinia (former name for Ethiopia)	Ethiopia	8 00 N	38 00 E
	Acapulco (city)	Mexico	16 51 N	99 55 W
	Accra (capital)	Ghana	5 33 N	0 13 W
	Adamstown (capital)	Pitcairn Islands	25 04 S	130 05 W
	Addis Ababa (capital)	Ethiopia	9 02 N	38 42 E
	Adelie Land (Terre Adelie) (claimed by France)	Antarctica	66 30 S	139 00 E
	Aden (city)	Yemen	12 46 N	45 01 E
	Aden, Gulf of	Indian Ocean	12 30 N	48 00 E
	Admiralty Island	United States (Alaska)	57 44 N	134 20 W
	Admiralty Islands	Papua New Guinea	2 10 S	147 00 E
	Adriatic Sea	Atlantic Ocean	42 30 N	16 00 E
	Adygey (region)	Russia	44 30 N	40 10 E
	Aegean Islands	Greece	38 00 N	25 00 E
	Aegean Sea	Atlantic Ocean	38 30 N	25 00 E
	Afars and Issas, French Territory of the (FTAI) (former name for Djibouti)	Djibouti	11 30 N	43 00 E
	Afghanestan (local name for Afghanistan)	Afghanistan	33 00 N	65 00 E
	Agalega Islands	Mauritius	10 25 S	56 40 E
	Agana (city; former name for Hagatna)	Guam	13 28 N	144 45 E
	Ajaccio (city)	France (Corsica)	41 55 N	8 44 E
	Ajaria (region)	Georgia	41 45 N	42 10 E
	Akmola (city; former name for Astana)	Kazakhstan	51 10 N	71 30 E
	Aksai Chin (region)	China (de facto), India (claimed)	35 00 N	79 00 E
	Al Arabiyah as Suudiyah (local name for Saudi Arabia)	Saudi Arabia	25 00 N	45 00 E
	Al Bahrayn (local name for Bahrain)	Bahrain	26 00 N	50 33 E
	Al Imarat al Arabiyah al Muttahidah (local name for the United Arab Emirates)	United Arab Emirates	24 00 N	54 00 E
	Al Iraq (local name for Iraq)	Iraq	33 00 N	44 00 E
	Al Jaza'ir (local name for Algeria)	Algeria	28 00 N	3 00 E
	Al Kuwayt (local name for Kuwait)	Kuwait	29 30 N	45 45 E
	Al Maghrib (local name for Morocco)	Morocco	32 00 N	5 00 W
	Al Urdun (local name for Jordan)	Jordan	31 00 N	36 00 E
	Al Yaman (local name for Yemen)	Yemen	15 00 N	48 00 E
	Aland Islands	Finland	60 15 N	20 00 E
	Alaska (state)	United States	65 00 N	153 00 W
	Alaska, Gulf of	Pacific Ocean	58 00 N	145 00 W
	Alboran Sea	Atlantic Ocean	36 00 N	2 30 W

Appendix F: Cross-Reference List of Geographic Names *(continued)*

Name	Entry in *The World Factbook*	Latitude (deg min)	Longitude (deg min)
Aldabra Islands (Groupe d'Aldabra)	Seychelles	9 25 S	46 22 E
Alderney (island)	Guernsey	49 43 N	2 12 W
Aleutian Islands	United States (Alaska)	52 00 N	176 00 W
Alexander Archipelago (island group)	United States (Alaska)	57 00 N	134 00 W
Alexander Island	Antarctica	71 00 S	70 00 W
Alexandretta (region; former name for Iskenderun)	Turkey	36 34 N	36 08 E
Alexandria (city)	Egypt	31 12 N	29 54 E
Algiers (capital)	Algeria	36 47 N	2 03 E
Alhucemas, Penon de (island group)	Spain	35 13 N	3 53 W
Alma-Ata (city; former name for Almaty)	Kazakhstan	43 15 N	76 57 E
Almaty (former capital)	Kazakhstan	43 15 N	76 57 E
Alofi (capital)	Niue	19 01 S	169 55 E
Alphonse Island	Seychelles	7 01 S	52 45 E
Alsace (region)	France	48 30 N	7 20 E
Amami Strait	Pacific Ocean	28 40 N	129 30 E
Amindivi Islands (former name for Laccadive Islands)	India	11 30 N	72 30 E
Amirante Isles (Les Amirantes) (island group)	Seychelles	6 00 S	53 10 E
Amman (capital)	Jordan	31 57 N	35 56 E
Amsterdam (capital)	Netherlands	52 23 N	4 54 E
Amsterdam Island (Ile Amsterdam)	French Southern and Antarctic Lands	37 52 S	77 32 E
Amundsen Sea	Southern Ocean	72 30 S	112 00 W
Amur River	China, Russia	52 56 N	141 10 E
Amurskiy Liman (strait)	Pacific Ocean	53 00 N	141 30 E
Anadyrskiy Zaliv (gulf)	Pacific Ocean	64 00 N	177 00 E
Anatolia (region)	Turkey	39 00 N	35 00 E
Andaman Islands	India	12 00 N	92 45 E
Andaman Sea	Indian Ocean	10 00 N	95 00 E
Andorra la Vella (capital)	Andorra	42 30 N	1 30 E
Andros (island)	Greece	37 45 N	24 42 E
Andros Island	The Bahamas	24 26 N	77 57 W
Anegada Passage	Atlantic Ocean	18 30 N	63 40 W
Angkor Wat (ruins)	Cambodia	13 26 N	103 50 E
Anglo-Egyptian Sudan (former name for Sudan)	Sudan	15 00 N	30 00 E
Anjouan (island)	Comoros	12 15 S	44 25 E
Ankara (capital)	Turkey	39 56 N	32 52 E
Annobon (island)	Equatorial Guinea	1 25 S	5 36 E
Antananarivo (capital)	Madagascar	18 52 S	47 30 E
Antigua (island)	Antigua and Barbuda	14 34 N	90 44 W
Antipodes Islands	New Zealand	49 41 S	178 43 E
Antwerp (city)	Belgium	51 13 N	4 25 E
Aomen (local Chinese short-form name for Macau)	Macau	22 10 N	113 33 E
Aozou Strip (region)	Chad	22 00 N	18 00 E
Apia (capital)	Samoa	13 50 S	171 44 N
Aqaba, Gulf of	Indian Ocean	29 00 N	34 30 E
Arab, Shatt al (river)	Iran, Iraq	29 57 N	48 34 E
Arabian Sea	Indian Ocean	15 00 N	65 00 E
Arafura Sea	Pacific Ocean	9 00 S	133 00 E

Appendix F: Cross-Reference List of Geographic Names *(continued)*

Name	Entry in *The World Factbook*	Latitude (deg min)	Longitude (deg min)
Aral Sea	Kazakhstan, Uzbekistan	45 00 N	60 00 E
Argun River	China, Russia	53 20 N	121 28 E
Aru Sea	Pacific Ocean	6 15 S	135 00 E
Ascension Island	Saint Helena	7 57 S	14 22 W
Ashgabat (capital)	Turkmenistan	37 57 N	58 23 E
Ashkhabad (see Ashgabat)	Turkmenistan	37 57 N	58 23 E
Asmara (capital)	Eritrea	15 20 N	38 53 E
Asmera (see Asmara)	Eritrea	15 20 N	38 53 E
As-Sudan (local name for Sudan)	Sudan	15 00 N	30 00 E
Assumption Island	Seychelles	9 46 S	46 34 E
Astana (Akmola) (capital)	Kazakhstan	51 10 N	71 30 E
Asuncion (capital)	Paraguay	25 16 S	57 40 W
Asuncion Island	Northern Mariana Islands	19 40 N	145 24 E
Atacama (desert)	Chile	23 00 S	70 10 W
Atacama (region)	Chile	24 30 S	69 15 W
Athens (capital)	Greece	37 59 N	23 44 E
Attu Island	United States	52 55 N	172 57 E
Auckland Islands	New Zealand	51 00 S	166 30 E
Australes, Iles (Iles Tubuai) (island group)	French Polynesia	23 20 S	151 00 W
Avarua (capital)	Cook Islands	21 12 S	159 46 W
Axel Heiberg Island	Canada	79 30 N	90 00 W
Azad Kashmir (region)	Pakistan	34 30 N	74 00 E
Azarbaycan (local name for Azerbaijan)	Azerbaijan	40 30 N	47 30 E
Azerbaidzhan (local name for Azerbaijan)	Azerbaijan	40 30 N	47 30 E
Azores (islands)	Portugal	38 30 N	28 00 W
Azov, Sea of	Atlantic Ocean	49 00 N	36 00 E
B Bab el Mandeb (strait)	Indian Ocean	12 40 N	43 20 E
Babuyan Channel	Pacific Ocean	18 44 N	121 40 E
Babuyan Islands	Philippines	19 10 N	121 40 E
Baffin Bay	Arctic Ocean	73 00 N	66 00 W
Baffin Island	Canada	68 00 N	70 00 W
Baghdad (capital)	Iraq	33 21 N	44 25 E
Baki (see Baku)	Azerbaijan	40 23 N	49 51 E
Baku (capital)	Azerbaijan	40 23 N	49 51 E
Baky (see Baku)	Azerbaijan	40 23 N	49 51 E
Balabac Strait	Pacific Ocean	7 35 N	117 00 E
Balearic Islands	Spain	39 30 N	3 00 E
Balearic Sea (Iberian Sea)	Atlantic Ocean	40 30 N	2 00 E
Bali (island)	Indonesia	8 20 S	115 00 E
Bali Sea	Indian Ocean	7 45 S	115 30 E
Balintang Channel	Pacific Ocean	19 49 N	121 40 E
Balintang Islands	Philippines	19 55 N	122 10 E
Balkan Peninsula	Albania, Bosnia and Herzegovina, Bulgaria, Croatia, Greece, The Former Yugoslav Republic of Macedonia, Romania, Slovenia, Turkey (European part), Yugoslavia	42 00 N	23 00 E
Balleny Islands	Antarctica	67 00 S	163 00 E
Balochistan (region)	Pakistan	28 00 N	63 00 E
Baltic Sea	Atlantic Ocean	57 00 N	19 00 E

Appendix F: Cross-Reference List of Geographic Names *(continued)*

Name	Entry in *The World Factbook*	Latitude (deg min)	Longitude (deg min)
Bamako (capital)	Mali	12 39 N	8 00 W
Banaba (Ocean Island)	Kiribati	0 52 S	169 35 E
Banat (region)	Hungary, Romania, Yugoslavia	45 30 N	21 00 E
Banda Sea	Pacific Ocean	5 00 S	128 00 E
Bandar Seri Begawan (capital)	Brunei	4 52 S	114 55 E
Bangka (island)	Indonesia	2 30 S	106 00 E
Bangkok (capital)	Thailand	13 45 N	100 31 E
Bangui (capital)	Central African Republic	4 22 N	18 35 E
Banjul (capital)	The Gambia	13 28 N	16 39 W
Banks Island	Australia	10 12 S	142 16 E
Banks Island	Canada	75 15 N	121 30 W
Banks Islands (Iles Banks)	Vanuatu	14 00 S	167 30 E
Barbuda (island)	Antigua and Barbuda	17 38 N	61 48 W
Barents Sea	Arctic Ocean	74 00 N	36 00 E
Barranquilla (city)	Colombia	10 59 N	74 48 W
Bashi Channel	Pacific Ocean	22 00 N	121 00 E
Basilan Strait	Pacific Ocean	6 49 N	122 05 E
Basque Provinces	Spain	43 00 N	2 30 W
Bass Strait	Pacific Ocean	39 20 S	145 30 E
Basse-Terre (capital)	Guadeloupe	16 00 N	61 44 W
Basseterre (capital)	Saint Kitts and Nevis	17 18 N	62 43 W
Bastia (city)	France (Corsica)	42 42 N	9 27 E
Basutoland (former name for Lesotho)	Lesotho	29 30 S	28 30 E
Batan Islands	Philippines	20 30 N	121 50 E
Bavaria (Bayern) (region)	Germany	48 30 N	11 30 E
Beagle Channel	Atlantic Ocean	54 53 S	68 10 W
Bear Island (see Bjornoya)	Svalbard	74 26 N	19 05 E
Beaufort Sea	Arctic Ocean	73 00 N	140 00 W
Bechuanaland (former name for Botswana)	Botswana	22 00 S	24 00 E
Beijing (capital)	China	39 56 N	116 24 E
Beirut (capital)	Lebanon	33 53 N	35 30 E
Bekaa Valley	Lebanon	34 00 N	36 05 E
Belau (Palau Islands)	Palau	7 30 N	134 30 E
Belep Islands (Iles Belep)	New Caledonia	19 45 S	163 40 E
Belgian Congo (former name for Democratic Republic of the Congo)	Democratic Republic of the Congo	0 00 N	25 00 E
Belgie (local name for Belgium)	Belgium	50 50 N	4 00 E
Belgique (local name for Belgium)	Belgium	50 50 N	4 00 E
Belgrade (capital)	Yugoslavia	44 50 N	20 30 E
Belize City (capital)	Belize	17 30 N	88 12 W
Belle Isle, Strait of	Atlantic Ocean	51 35 N	56 30 W
Bellingshausen Sea	Southern Ocean	71 00 S	85 00 W
Belmopan (capital)	Belize	17 15 N	88 46 W
Belorussia (former name for Belarus)	Belarus	53 00 N	28 00 E
Benadir (region; former name of Italian Somaliland)	Somalia	4 00 N	46 00 E
Bengal, Bay of	Indian Ocean	15 00 N	90 00 E
Berau, Gulf of	Pacific Ocean	2 30 S	132 30 E
Bering Island	Russia	55 00 N	166 30 E
Bering Sea	Pacific Ocean	60 00 N	175 00 W

Appendix F: Cross-Reference List of Geographic Names *(continued)*

Name	Entry in *The World Factbook*	Latitude (deg min)	Longitude (deg min)
Bering Strait	Pacific Ocean	65 30 N	169 00 W
Berkner Island	Antarctica	79 30 S	49 30 W
Berlin (capital)	Germany	52 31 N	13 24 E
Berlin, East (former name for eastern sector of Berlin)	Germany	52 30 N	13 33 E
Berlin, West (former name for western sector of Berlin)	Germany	52 30 N	12 20 E
Bern (capital)	Switzerland	46 57 N	7 26 E
Bessarabia (region)	Moldova, Romania, Ukraine	47 00 N	28 30 E
Bharat (local name for India)	India	20 00 N	77 00 E
Bhopal (city)	India	23 16 N	77 24 E
Biafra (region)	Nigeria	5 30 N	7 30 E
Big Diomede Island	Russia	65 46 N	169 06 W
Bijagos, Arquipelago dos (island group)	Guinea-Bissau	11 25 N	16 20 W
Bikini Atoll	Marshall Islands	11 35 N	165 23 E
Bilbao (city)	Spain	43 15 N	2 58 W
Bioko (island)	Equatorial Guinea	3 30 N	8 42 E
Biscay, Bay of	Atlantic Ocean	44 00 N	4 00 W
Bishkek (capital)	Kyrgyzstan	42 54 N	74 36 E
Bishop Rock	United Kingdom	49 52 N	6 27 W
Bismarck Archipelago (island group)	Papua New Guinea	5 00 S	150 00 E
Bismarck Sea	Pacific Ocean	4 00 S	148 00 E
Bissau (capital)	Guinea-Bissau	11 51 N	15 35 W
Bjornoya (Bear Island)	Svalbard	74 26 N	19 05 E
Black Forest (region)	Germany	48 00 N	8 15 E
Black Rock (island)	South Georgia and the South Sandwich Islands	53 39 S	41 48 W
Black Sea	Atlantic Ocean	43 00 N	35 00 E
Bloemfontein (city, judicial center)	South Africa	29 12 S	26 07 E
Bo Hai (gulf)	Pacific Ocean	38 00 N	120 00 E
Boa Vista (island)	Cape Verde	16 05 N	22 50 W
Bogota (capital)	Colombia	4 36 N	74 05 W
Bohemia (region)	Czech Republic	50 00 N	14 30 E
Bombay (see Mumbai)	India	18 58 N	72 50 E
Bonaire (island)	Netherlands Antilles	12 10 N	68 15 W
Bonifacio, Strait of	Atlantic Ocean	41 01 N	14 00 E
Bonin Islands	Japan	27 00 N	140 10 E
Bonn (capital)	Germany	50 44 N	7 05 E
Bophuthatswana (enclave region)	South Africa	26 30 S	25 30 E
Bora-Bora (island)	French Polynesia	16 30 S	151 45 W
Bordeaux (city)	France	44 50 N	0 34 W
Borneo (island)	Brunei, Indonesia, Malaysia	0 30 N	114 00 E
Bornholm (island)	Denmark	55 10 N	15 00 E
Bosna i Hercegovina (local name for Bosnia and Herzegovina)	Bosnia and Herzegovina	44 00 N	18 00 E
Bosnia (political region)	Bosnia and Herzegovina	44 00 N	18 00 E
Bosporus (strait)	Atlantic Ocean	41 00 N	29 00 E
Bothnia, Gulf of	Atlantic Ocean	63 00 N	20 00 E
Bougainville (island)	Papua New Guinea	6 00 S	155 00 E
Bougainville Strait	Pacific Ocean	6 40 S	156 10 E
Bounty Islands	New Zealand	47 43 S	174 00 E

Appendix F: Cross-Reference List of Geographic Names *(continued)*

Name	Entry in *The World Factbook*	Latitude (deg min)	Longitude (deg min)
Bourbon Island (former name of Reunion)	Reunion	21 06 S	55 36 E
Brasilia (capital)	Brazil	15 47 S	47 55 W
Bratislava (capital)	Slovakia	48 09 N	17 07 E
Brazzaville (capital)	Republic of the Congo	4 16 S	15 17 E
Bridgetown (capital)	Barbados	13 06 N	59 37 W
Brisbane (city)	Australia	27 28 S	153 02 E
Bristol Bay	Pacific Ocean	57 00 N	160 00 W
Bristol Channel	Atlantic Ocean	51 18 N	3 30 W
Britain (see Great Britain)	United Kingdom	54 00 N	2 00 W
British Bechuanaland (region; former name for northwest South Africa)	South Africa	27 30 S	23 30 E
British Central African Protectorate (former name of Nyasaland)	Malawi	13 30 S	34 00 E
British East Africa (former name for British possessions in eastern Africa)	Kenya, Tanzania, Uganda	1 00 N	38 00 E
British Guiana (former name for Guyana)	Guyana	5 00 N	59 00 W
British Honduras (former name for Belize)	Belize	17 15 N	88 45 W
British Solomon Islands (former name for Solomon Islands)	Solomon Islands	8 00 S	159 00 E
British Somaliland (former name for northern Somalia)	Somalia	10 00 N	49 00 E
Brussels (capital)	Belgium	50 50 N	4 20 E
Bubiyan (island)	Kuwait	29 47 N	48 10 E
Bucharest (capital)	Romania	44 26 N	26 06 E
Budapest (capital)	Hungary	47 30 N	19 05 E
Buenos Aires (capital)	Argentina	34 36 S	58 27 W
Bujumbura (capital)	Burundi	3 23 S	29 22 E
Bukovina (region)	Romania, Ukraine	48 00 N	26 00 E
Byelarus (local name for Belarus)	Belarus	53 00 N	28 00 E
Byelorussia (former name for Belarus)	Belarus	53 00 N	28 00 E
C Cabinda (province)	Angola	5 33 S	12 12 E
Cabo Verde (local name for Cape Verde)	Cape Verde	16 00 N	24 00 W
Cabot Strait	Atlantic Ocean	47 20 N	59 30 W
Caicos Islands	Turks and Caicos Islands	21 56 N	71 58 W
Cairo (capital)	Egypt	30 03 N	31 15 E
California, Gulf of	Pacific Ocean	28 00 N	112 00 W
Cameroun (local name for Cameroon)	Cameroon	6 00 N	12 00 E
Campbell Island	New Zealand	52 33 S	169 09 E
Campeche, Bay of	Atlantic Ocean	20 00 N	94 00 W
Canal Zone (former name for US possessions in Panama)	Panama	9 00 N	79 45 W
Canarias Sea	Atlantic Ocean	28 00 N	16 00 W
Canary Islands	Spain	28 00 N	15 30 W
Canberra (capital)	Australia	35 17 S	149 08 E
Cancun (city)	Mexico	21 10 N	86 50 W
Canton (Guangzhou) (city)	China	23 06 N	113 16 E
Canton Island (Kanton Island)	Kiribati	2 49 S	171 40 W
Cape Juby (region; former name for Southern Morocco)	Morocco	27 53 N	12 58 W
Cape of Good Hope (cape; also alternate name for Cape Province of South Africa)	South Africa	34 15 S	18 25 E

Appendix F: Cross-Reference List of Geographic Names (continued)

Name	Entry in The World Factbook	Latitude (deg min)	Longitude (deg min)
Cape Province (region; former name for Northern, Western, and Eastern Cape Provinces of South Africa)	South Africa	31 30 S	22 30 E
Cape Town (legislative capital)	South Africa	33 57 S	18 28 W
Caracas (capital)	Venezuela	10 30 N	66 56 W
Cargados Carajos Shoals	Mauritius	16 25 S	59 38 E
Caribbean Sea	Atlantic Ocean	15 00 N	73 00 W
Caroline Islands	Federated States of Micronesia, Palau	7 30 N	148 00 E
Carpatho-Ukraine (region; former name for Zakarpats'ka oblast')	Ukraine	48 22 N	23 32 E
Carpentaria, Gulf of	Pacific Ocean	14 00 S	139 00 E
Castries (capital)	Saint Lucia	14 01 N	61 00 W
Catalonia (region)	Spain	42 00 N	2 00 E
Cato Island	Australia	23 15 S	155 32 E
Caucasus (region)	Russia	42 00 N	45 00 E
Cayenne (capital)	French Guiana	4 56 N	52 20 W
Celebes (island)	Indonesia	2 00 S	121 00 E
Celebes Sea	Pacific Ocean	3 00 N	122 00 E
Celtic Sea	Atlantic Ocean	51 00 N	6 30 W
Central African Empire (former name for Central African Republic)	Central African Republic	7 00 N	21 00 E
Ceram (Seram) Sea	Pacific Ocean	2 30 S	129 30 E
Ceska Republika (local name for Czech Republic)	Czech Republic	49 45 N	15 30 E
Ceskoslovensko (former local name for Czechoslovakia)	Czech Republic, Slovakia	49 00 N	17 30 E
Ceuta (city)	Spain	35 53 N	5 19 W
Ceylon (former name for Sri Lanka)	Sri Lanka	7 00 N	81 00 E
Chafarinas, Islas (island)	Spain	35 12 N	2 26 W
Chagos Archipelago (Oil Islands)	British Indian Ocean Territory	6 00 S	71 30 E
Challenger Deep (Mariana Trench)	Pacific Ocean	11 22 N	142 36 E
Channel Islands	Guernsey, Jersey	49 20 N	2 20 W
Charlotte Amalie (capital)	Virgin Islands	18 21 N	64 56 W
Chatham Islands	New Zealand	44 00 S	176 30 W
Chechnya (Chechnia) (region)	Russia	43 15 N	45 40 E
Cheju Strait	Pacific Ocean	34 00 N	126 30 E
Cheju-do (island)	Korea, South	33 20 N	126 30 E
Chennai (Madras) (city)	India	13 04 N	80 16 E
Chesterfield Islands (Iles Chesterfield)	New Caledonia	19 52 S	158 15 E
Chihli, Gulf of (see Bo Hai)	Pacific Ocean	38 30 N	120 00 E
Chiloe (island)	Chile	42 50 S	74 00 W
China, People's Republic of	China	35 00 N	105 00 E
China, Republic of	Taiwan	23 30 N	105 00 E
Chisinau (capital)	Moldova	47 00 N	28 50 E
Choiseul (island)	Solomon Islands	7 05 S	121 00 E
Choson (local name for North Korea)	North Korea	40 00 N	127 00 E
Christmas Island (Indian Ocean)	Australia	10 25 S	105 39 E
Christmas Island (Kiritimati) (Pacific Ocean)	Kiribati	1 52 N	157 20 W
Chukchi Sea	Arctic Ocean	69 00 N	171 00 W
Chuuk Islands (Truk Islands)	Federated States of Micronesia	7 25 N	151 47 W

Appendix F: Cross-Reference List of Geographic Names *(continued)*

Name	Entry in *The World Factbook*	Latitude (deg min)	Longitude (deg min)
Cilicia (region)	Turkey	36 50 N	34 30 E
Ciskei (enclave)	South Africa	33 00 S	27 00 E
Citta del Vaticano (local name for Vatican City)	Holy See	41 54 N	12 27 E
Cochin China (region)	Vietnam	11 00 N	107 00 E
Coco, Isla del (island)	Costa Rica	5 32 N	87 04 W
Cocos Islands	Cocos (Keeling) Islands	12 30 S	96 50 E
Colombo (capital)	Sri Lanka	6 56 N	79 51 E
Colon, Archipielago de (Galapagos Islands)	Ecuador	0 00 N	90 30 W
Commander Islands (Komandorskiye Ostrova)	Russia	55 00 N	167 00 E
Comores (local name for Comoros)	Comoros	12 10 S	44 15 E
Con Son (islands)	Vietnam	8 43 N	106 36 E
Conakry (capital)	Guinea	9 31 N	13 43 W
Confederatio Helvetica (local name for Switzerland)	Switzerland	47 00 N	8 00 E
Congo (Brazzaville) (former name for Republic of the Congo)	Republic of the Congo	1 00 S	15 00 E
Congo (Leopoldville) (former name for the Democratic Republic of the Congo)	Democratic Republic of the Congo	0 00 N	25 00 E
Constantinople (city; former name for Istanbul)	Turkey	41 01 N	28 58 E
Cook Strait	Pacific Ocean	41 15 S	174 30 E
Copenhagen (capital)	Denmark	55 40 N	12 35 E
Coral Sea	Pacific Ocean	15 00 S	150 00 E
Corfu (island)	Greece	39 40 N	19 45 E
Corinth (region)	Greece	37 56 N	22 56 E
Corisco (island)	Equatorial Guinea	0 55 N	9 19 E
Corn Islands (Islas del Maiz)	Nicaragua	12 15 N	83 00 W
Corocoro Island	Guyana, Venezuela	3 38 N	66 50 W
Corsica (Corse) (island)	France	42 00 N	9 00 E
Cosmoledo Group (Atoll de Cosmoledo) (island group)	Seychelles	9 43 S	47 35 E
Cotonou (seat of government)	Benin	6 21 N	2 26 E
Cotopaxi (volcano)	Ecuador	0 39 S	78 26 W
Courantyne River	Guyana, Suriname	5 57 N	57 06 W
Cozumel (island)	Mexico	20 30 N	86 55 W
Crete (island)	Greece	35 15 N	24 45 E
Crimea (region)	Ukraine	45 00 N	34 00 E
Crimean Peninsula	Ukraine	45 00 N	34 00 E
Crooked Island Passage	Atlantic Ocean	22 55 N	74 35 W
Crozet Islands (Iles Crozet)	French Southern and Antarctic Lands	46 30 S	51 00 E
Cyclades (island group)	Greece	37 00 N	25 10 E
Cyrenaica (region)	Libya	31 00 N	22 00 E
Czechoslovakia (former name for the entity that subsequently split into the Czech Republic and Slovakia)	Czech Republic, Slovakia	49 00 N	18 00 E
D Dagestan (region)	Russia	43 00 N	47 00 E
Dahomey (former name for Benin)	Benin	9 30 N	2 15 E
Daito Islands	Japan	43 00 N	17 00 E
Dakar (capital)	Senegal	14 40 N	17 26 W
Dalmatia (region)	Croatia	43 00 N	17 00 E
Daman (Damao) (city)	India	20 10 N	73 00 E
Damascus (capital)	Syria	33 30 N	36 18 E
Danger Islands (see Pukapuka Atoll)	Cook Islands	10 53 S	165 49 W

Appendix F: Cross-Reference List of Geographic Names *(continued)*

Name	Entry in *The World Factbook*	Latitude (deg min)	Longitude (deg min)
Danish Straits	Atlantic Ocean	58 00 N	11 00 E
Danish West Indies (former name for the Virgin Islands)	Virgin Islands	18 20 N	64 50 W
Danmark (local name)	Denmark	56 00 N	10 00 E
Danzig (city; former name for Gdansk)	Poland	54 23 N	18 40 E
Dao Bach Long Vi (island)	Vietnam	20 08 N	107 44 E
Dar es Salaam (capital)	Tanzania	6 48 S	39 17 E
Dardanelles (strait)	Atlantic Ocean	40 15 N	26 25 E
Davis Strait	Atlantic Ocean	67 00 N	57 00 W
Dead Sea	Israel, Jordan, West Bank	32 30 N	35 30 E
Deception Island	Antarctica	62 56 S	60 34 W
Denmark Strait	Atlantic Ocean	67 00 N	24 00 W
D'Entrecasteaux Islands	Papua New Guinea	9 30 S	150 40 E
Desolation Islands (Isles Kerguelen)	French Southern and Antarctic Lands	49 30 S	69 30 E
Deutschland (local name for Germany)	Germany	51 00 N	9 00 E
Devils Island (Ile du Diable)	French Guiana	5 17 N	52 35 W
Devon Island	Canada	76 00 N	87 00 W
Dhaka (capital)	Bangladesh	23 43 N	90 25 E
Dhivehi Raajje (local name for Maldives)	Maldives	3 15 N	73 00 E
Dhofar (region)	Oman	17 00 N	54 10 E
Diego Garcia (island)	British Indian Ocean Territory	7 20 S	72 25 E
Diego Ramirez (islands)	Chile	56 30 S	68 43 W
Dilmun (former name for Bahrain)	Bahrain	7 00 N	81 00 E
Diomede Islands	Russia (Big Diomede), United States (Little Diomede)	65 47 N	169 00 W
Diu (region)	India	20 42 N	70 59 E
Djibouti (capital)	Djibouti	11 30 N	43 15 E
Dnieper (river)	Belarus, Russia, Ukraine (Dnyapro, Dnepr, Dnipro)	46 30 N	32 18 E
Dniester (river)	Moldova, Ukraine (Nistru, Dnister)	46 18 N	30 17 E
Dobruja (region)	Bulgaria, Romania	43 30 N	28 00 E
Dodecanese (island group)	Greece	36 00 N	27 05 E
Dodoma (city)	Tanzania	6 11 S	35 45 E
Doha (capital)	Qatar	25 17 N	51 32 E
Donets Basin	Russia, Ukraine	48 15 N	38 30 E
Douala (city)	Cameroon	4 03 N	9 42 E
Douglas (capital)	Man, Isle of	54 09 N	4 28 W
Dover, Strait of	Atlantic Ocean	51 00 N	1 30 E
Drake Passage	Atlantic Ocean, Southern Ocean	60 00 S	60 00 W
Druk Yul (local name for Bhutan)	Bhutan	27 30 N	90 30 E
Dubai (city)	United Arab Emirates	25 18 N	55 18 E
Dubayy (see Dubai)	United Arab Emirates	25 18 N	55 18 E
Dublin (capital)	Ireland	53 20 N	6 15 W
Dushanbe (capital)	Tajikistan	38 35 N	68 48 E
Dutch Antilles (former name for the Netherlands Antilles)	Netherlands Antilles	52 05 N	4 18 E
Dutch East Indies (former name for Indonesia)	Indonesia	5 00 S	120 00 E
Dutch Guiana (former name for Suriname)	Suriname	4 00 N	56 00 W
Dutch West Indies (former name for the Netherlands Antilles)	Netherlands Antilles	52 05 N	4 18 E
Dzungarian Gate (valley)	China, Kazakhstan	45 25 N	82 25 E

Appendix F: Cross-Reference List of Geographic Names *(continued)*

	Name	Entry in *The World Factbook*	Latitude (deg min)	Longitude (deg min)
E	East China Sea	Pacific Ocean	30 00 N	126 00 E
	East Frisian Islands	Germany	53 44 N	7 25 E
	East Germany (German Democratic Republic) (former name for eastern portion of Germany)	Germany	52 00 N	13 00 E
	East Korea Strait (Eastern Channel or Tsushima Strait)	Pacific Ocean	34 00 N	129 00 E
	East Pakistan (former name for Bangladesh)	Bangladesh	24 00 N	90 00 E
	East Siberian Sea	Arctic Ocean	74 00 N	166 00 E
	East Timor (Portuguese Timor)	Indonesia	9 00 S	126 00 E
	Easter Island (Isla de Pascua)	Chile	27 07 S	109 22 W
	Eastern Channel (East Korea Strait or Tsushima Strait)	Pacific Ocean	34 00 N	129 00 E
	Eastern Samoa (former name for American Samoa)	American Samoa	14 20 S	170 00 W
	Eesti (local name for Estonia)	Estonia	59 00 N	26 00 E
	Eire (local name for Ireland)	Ireland	53 00 N	8 00 W
	Elba (island)	Italy	42 46 N	10 17 E
	Elemi Triangle (region)	Ethiopia (claimed), Kenya (de facto), Sudan (claimed)	5 00 N	35 30 E
	Ellada (local name for Greece)	Greece	39 00 N	22 00 E
	Ellas (local name for Greece)	Greece	39 00 N	22 00 E
	Ellef Ringnes Island	Canada	78 00 N	103 00 W
	Ellesmere Island	Canada	81 00 N	80 00 W
	Ellice Islands	Tuvalu	8 00 S	178 00 E
	Ellsworth Land (region)	Antarctica	75 00 S	92 00 W
	Elobey, Islas de (island group)	Equatorial Guinea	0 59 N	9 33 E
	Enderbury Island	Kiribati	3 08 S	171 05 W
	Enewetak Atoll (Eniwetok Atoll)	Marshall Islands	11 30 N	162 15 E
	England (region)	United Kingdom	52 30 N	1 30 W
	English Channel	Atlantic Ocean	50 20 N	1 00 W
	Eniwetok Atoll (see Enewetak Atoll)	Marshall Islands	11 30 N	162 15 E
	Eolie, Isole (island group)	Italy	38 30 N	15 00 E
	Epirus, Northern (region)	Albania, Greece	40 00 N	20 30 E
	Ertra (local name for Eritrea)	Eritrea	15 00 N	39 00 E
	Espana	Spain	40 00 N	4 00 W
	Essequibo (region) (claimed by Venezuela)	Guyana	6 59 N	58 23 W
	Etorofu (Iturup) (island)	Russia (de facto)	44 55 N	147 40 E
F	Farquhar Group (Atoll de Farquhar) (island group)	Seychelles	10 10 S	51 10 E
	Fergana Valley	Kyrgyzstan, Tajikistan, Uzbekistan	41 00 N	72 00 E
	Fernando de Noronha (island group)	Brazil	3 51 S	32 25 W
	Fernando Po (island) (see Bioko)	Equatorial Guinea	3 30 N	8 42 E
	Filipinas (local name for the Philippines)	Philippines	13 00 N	122 00 E
	Finland, Gulf of	Atlantic Ocean	60 00 N	27 00 E
	Flores (island)	Indonesia	8 45 S	121 00 E
	Flores Sea	Pacific Ocean	7 40 S	119 45 E
	Florida, Straits of	Atlantic Ocean	25 00 N	79 45 W
	Former Soviet Union (FSU)	Armenia, Azerbaijan, Belarus, Estonia, Georgia, Kazakhstan, Kyrgyzstan, Latvia, Lithuania, Moldova, Russia, Tajikistan, Turkmenistan, Ukraine, Uzbekistan		
	Formosa (island)	Taiwan	23 30 N	121 00 E
	Formosa Strait (see Taiwan Strait)	Pacific Ocean	24 00 N	119 00 E

Appendix F: Cross-Reference List of Geographic Names (continued)

Name	Entry in *The World Factbook*	Latitude (deg min)	Longitude (deg min)
Foroyar (local name for Faroe Islands)	Faroe Islands	62 00 N	7 00 W
Fort-de-France (capital)	Martinique	14 36 N	61 05 W
Franz Josef Land (island group)	Russia	81 00 N	55 00 E
Freetown (capital)	Sierra Leone	8 30 N	13 15 W
French Cameroon (former name for Cameroon)	Cameroon	6 00 N	12 00 E
French Guinea (former name for Guinea)	Guinea	11 00 N	10 00 W
French Indochina (former name for French possessions in southeast Asia)	Cambodia, Laos, Vietnam	15 00 N	107 00 E
French Morocco (former name for Morocco)	Morocco	32 00 N	5 00 W
French Somaliland (former name for Djibouti)	Djibouti	11 30 N	43 00 W
French Sudan (former name for Mali)	Mali	17 00 N	4 00 W
French Territory of the Afars and Issas (FTAI) (former name for Djibouti)	Djibouti	11 30 N	43 00 E
French Togoland (former name for Togo)	Togo	8 00 N	1 10 E
French West Indies (former name for French possessions in the West Indies)	Guadeloupe, Martinique	16 30 N	62 00 W
Friendly Islands	Tonga	20 00 S	175 00 W
Frisian Islands	Denmark, Germany, Netherlands	53 35 N	6 40 E
Frunze (city; former name for Bishkek)	Kyrgyzstan	42 54 N	74 36 E
Funafuti (capital)	Tuvalu	8 30 S	179 12 E
Fundy, Bay of	Atlantic Ocean	45 00 N	66 00 W
Futuna Islands (Hoorn Islands/Iles de Horne)	Wallis and Futuna	14 19 S	178 05 W
Fyn (island)	Denmark	55 20 N	10 25 E
Gaborone (capital)	Botswana	24 45 S	25 55 E
Galapagos Islands (Archipielago de Colon)	Ecuador	0 00 N	90 30 W
Galicia (region)	Poland, Ukraine	49 30 N	23 00 E
Galicia (region)	Spain	42 45 N	8 10 E
Galilee (region)	Israel	32 54 N	35 20 E
Galleons Passage	Atlantic Ocean	11 00 N	60 55 W
Gambier Islands (Iles Gambier)	French Polynesia	23 09 S	134 58 W
Gaspar Strait	Pacific Ocean	3 00 S	107 00 E
Gdansk (Danzig) (city)	Poland	54 23 N	18 40 E
Geneva (city)	Switzerland	46 12 N	6 10 E
Genoa (city)	Italy	44 25 N	8 57 E
George Town (capital)	Cayman Islands	19 20 N	81 23 W
George Town (city)	Malaysia	5 26 N	100 16 E
George Town (city)	The Bahamas	23 30 N	75 46 W
Georgetown (capital)	Guyana	6 48 N	58 10 W
Georgetown (city)	The Gambia	13 30 N	14 47 W
German Democratic Republic (East Germany) (former name for eastern portion of Germany)	Germany	52 00 N	13 00 E
German Southwest Africa (former name for Namibia)	Namibia	22 00 S	17 00 E
Germany, Federal Republic of	Germany	51 00 N	9 00 E
Gibraltar (city, peninsula)	Gibraltar	36 11 N	5 22 W
Gibraltar, Strait of	Atlantic Ocean	35 57 N	5 36 W
Gidi Pass	Egypt	30 13 N	33 09 E
Gilbert Islands	Kiribati	1 25 N	173 00 E
Goa (state)	India	14 20 N	74 00 E

Appendix F: Cross-Reference List of Geographic Names *(continued)*

Name	Entry in *The World Factbook*	Latitude (deg min)	Longitude (deg min)
Gobi (desert)	China, Mongolia	42 30 N	107 00 E
Godthab (Nuuk) (capital)	Greenland	64 11 N	51 44 W
Golan Heights (region)	Syria	33 00 N	35 45 E
Gold Coast (former name for Ghana)	Ghana	8 00 N	2 00 W
Golfo San Jorge (gulf)	Atlantic Ocean	46 00 S	66 00 W
Golfo San Matias (gulf)	Atlantic Ocean	41 30 S	64 00 W
Good Hope, Cape of	South Africa	34 24 S	18 30 E
Goteborg (city)	Sweden	57 43 N	11 58 E
Gotland (island)	Sweden	57 30 N	18 33 E
Gough Island	Saint Helena	40 10 S	9 45 W
Graham Land (region)	Antarctica	65 00 S	64 00 W
Gran Chaco (region)	Argentina, Paraguay	24 00 S	60 00 W
Grand Bahama (island)	The Bahamas	26 40 N	78 35 W
Grand Banks (fishing ground)	Atlantic Ocean	47 06 N	55 48 W
Grand Cayman (island)	Cayman Islands	19 20 N	81 20 W
Grand Turk (Cockburn Town) (capital)	Turks and Caicos Islands	21 28 N	71 08 W
Great Australian Bight	Indian Ocean	35 00 S	130 00 E
Great Belt (Store Baelt) (strait)	Atlantic Ocean	55 30 N	11 00 E
Great Bitter Lake	Egypt	30 20 N	32 23 E
Great Britain (island)	United Kingdom	54 00 N	2 00 W
Great Channel	Indian Ocean	6 25 N	94 20 E
Great Inagua (island)	The Bahamas	21 00 N	73 20 W
Great Rift Valley	Ethiopia, Kenya	0 30 N	36 00 E
Greater Sunda Islands	Brunei, Indonesia, Malaysia	2 00 S	110 00 E
Green Islands	Papua New Guinea	4 30 S	154 10 E
Greenland Sea	Arctic Ocean	79 00 N	5 00 W
Grenadines, Northern (island group)	Saint Vincent and the Grenadines	13 15 N	61 12 W
Grenadines, Southern (island group)	Grenada	12 07 N	61 40 W
Grytviken (South Georgia) (town)	South Georgia and the South Sandwich Islands	54 15 S	36 45 W
Guadalcanal (island)	Solomon Islands	9 32 S	160 12 E
Guadalupe, Isla de (island)	Mexico	29 11 N	118 17 W
Guantanamo Bay (US Naval Base)	Cuba	20 00 N	75 08 W
Guatemala (capital)	Guatemala	14 38 N	90 31 W
Guinea Ecuatorial (local name for Equatorial Guinea)	Equatorial Guinea	2 00 N	10 00 E
Guinea, Gulf of	Atlantic Ocean	3 00 N	2 30 E
Guine-Bissau (local name for Guinea-Bissau)	Guinea-Bissau	12 00 N	15 00 E
Guinee (local name for Guinea)	Guinea	11 00 N	10 00 E
Guyane Francaise (local name for French Guiana)	French Guiana	4 00 N	53 00 W

H

Name	Entry in *The World Factbook*	Latitude (deg min)	Longitude (deg min)
Ha'apai Group (island group)	Tonga	19 42 S	174 29 W
Habomai Islands	Russia (de facto)	43 30 N	146 10 E
Hadhramaut (region)	Yemen	15 00 N	50 00 E
Hagatna (Agana) (capital)	Guam	13 28 N	144 45 E
Hague, The (seat of government)	Netherlands	52 05 N	4 18 E
Haifa (city)	Israel	32 50 N	35 00 E
Hainan Dao (island)	China	19 00 N	109 30 E
Haiphong (city)	Vietnam	20 52 N	106 41 E
Halaib Triangle (region)	Egypt (claimed), Sudan (de facto)	22 30 N	35 00 E
Halmahera (island)	Indonesia	1 00 N	128 00 E

Appendix F: Cross-Reference List of Geographic Names *(continued)*

Name	Entry in *The World Factbook*	Latitude (deg min)	Longitude (deg min)
Halmahera Sea	Pacific Ocean	0 30 S	129 00 E
Hamilton (capital)	Bermuda	32 17 N	64 46 W
Han-guk (local name for South Korea)	South Korea	37 00 N	127 30 E
Hanoi (capital)	Vietnam	21 02 N	105 51 E
Harare (capital)	Zimbabwe	17 50 S	31 03 E
Harvey Islands (former name for Cook Islands)	Cook Islands	21 14 S	159 46 W
Hatay (province)	Turkey	36 30 N	36 15 E
Havana (capital)	Cuba	23 08 N	82 22 W
Hawaii (island)	United States	19 45 N	155 45 W
Hawaiian Islands	United States	21 00 N	157 45 W
Hawar (island)	Bahrain	25 40 N	50 47 E
Hayastan (local name for Armenia)	Armenia	40 00 N	45 00 E
Heard Island	Heard Island and McDonald Islands	53 06 S	73 30 E
Hejaz (region)	Saudi Arabia	24 30 N	38 30 E
Helsinki (capital)	Finland	60 10 N	24 58 E
Herzegovina (political region)	Bosnia and Herzegovina	44 00 N	18 00 E
Hiiumaa (island)	Estonia	58 50 N	22 30 E
Hispaniola (island)	Dominican Republic, Haiti	18 45 N	71 00 W
Ho Chi Minh City (Saigon)	Vietnam	10 45 N	106 40 E
Hokkaido (island)	Japan	44 00 N	143 00 E
Holland (region)	Netherlands	52 30 N	5 45 E
Hong Kong (special administrative region)	Hong Kong	22 15 N	114 10 E
Honiara (capital)	Solomon Islands	9 26 S	159 57 E
Honshu (island)	Japan	36 00 N	138 00 E
Hormuz, Strait of	Indian Ocean	26 34 N	56 15 E
Horn of Africa (region)	Djibouti, Eritrea, Ethiopia, Somalia	8 00 N	48 00 E
Horn, Cape (Cabo de Hornos)	Chile	55 59 S	67 16 W
Horne, Iles de (island group)	Wallis and Futuna	14 19 S	178 05 W
Hrvatska (local name for Croatia)	Croatia	45 10 N	15 30 E
Hudson Bay	Arctic Ocean	60 00 N	86 00 W
Hudson Strait	Arctic Ocean	62 00 N	71 00 W
Hunter Island	New Caledonia, Vanuatu	22 24 S	172 06 E
Iberian Peninsula	Portugal, Spain	40 00 N	5 00 W
Iceland Sea	Arctic Ocean	68 00 N	20 00 W
Ifni (region; former name of part of Spanish West Africa)	Morocco	29 22 N	10 09 W
Inaccessible Island	Saint Helena	37 17 S	12 40 W
Indochina (region)	Cambodia, Laos, Vietnam	15 00 N	107 00 E
Ingushetia (region)	Russia	43 15 N	45 00 E
Inhambane (region)	Mozambique	22 30 S	34 30 E
Inini (former name for French Guiana)	French Guiana	4 00 N	53 00 W
Inland Sea	Japan	34 20 N	133 30 E
Inner Hebrides (islands)	United Kingdom	56 30 N	6 20 W
Inner Mongolia (Nei Mongol) (region)	China	42 00 N	113 00 E
Ionian Islands	Greece	38 30 N	20 30 E
Ionian Sea	Atlantic Ocean	38 30 N	18 00 E
Irian Jaya (province)	Indonesia	5 00 S	138 00 E
Irish Sea	Atlantic Ocean	53 30 N	5 20 W
Iron Gate (river gorge)	Romania, Yugoslavia	44 41 N	22 31 E

Appendix F: Cross-Reference List of Geographic Names *(continued)*

	Name	Entry in *The World Factbook*	Latitude (deg min)	Longitude (deg min)
	Iskenderun (Alexandretta) (region)	Turkey	36 34 N	36 08 E
	Islamabad (capital)	Pakistan	33 42 N	73 10 E
	Island (local name for Iceland)	Iceland	65 00 N	18 00 W
	Islas Malvinas (island group)	Falkland Islands (Islas Malvinas)	51 45 S	59 00 W
	Istanbul (city)	Turkey	41 01 N	28 58 E
	Istrian Peninsula	Croatia, Slovenia	45 00 N	14 00 E
	Italia (local name for Italy)	Italy	42 50 N	12 50 E
	Italian East Africa (former name for Italian possessions in eastern Africa)	Eritrea, Ethiopia, Somalia	8 00 N	38 00 E
	Italian Somaliland (former name for southern Somalia)	Somalia	10 00 N	49 00 E
	Ittihad al-Imarat al-Arabiyah (local name for the United Arab Emirates)	United Arab Emirates	24 00 N	54 00 E
	Iturup (see Etorofu) (island)	Russia (de facto)	44 55 N	147 40 E
	Ityop'iya (local name for Ethiopia)	Ethiopia	8 00 N	38 00 E
	Ivory Coast (former name for Cote d'Ivoire)	Cote d'Ivoire	8 00 N	5 00 W
	Iwo Jima (island)	Japan	24 47 N	141 20 E
	Izmir (region)	Turkey	38 25 N	27 10 E
J	Jakarta (capital)	Indonesia	6 10 S	106 48 E
	James Bay	Arctic Ocean	54 00 N	80 00 W
	Jamestown (capital)	Saint Helena	15 56 S	5 44 W
	Jammu (city)	India	32 42 N	74 52 E
	Jammu and Kashmir (region)	India, Pakistan	34 00 N	76 00 E
	Japan, Sea of	Pacific Ocean	40 00 N	135 00 E
	Jars, Plain of	Laos	19 27 N	103 10 E
	Java (island)	Indonesia	7 30 S	110 00 E
	Java Sea	Pacific Ocean	5 00 S	110 00 E
	Jerusalem (capital, proclaimed)	Israel, West Bank	31 47 N	35 14 E
	Jiddah (Jeddah) (city)	Saudi Arabia	21 30 N	39 12 E
	Johannesburg (city)	South Africa	26 15 S	28 00 E
	Joseph Bonaparte Gulf	Pacific Ocean	14 00 S	128 45 E
	Juan de Fuca, Strait of	Pacific Ocean	48 18 N	124 00 W
	Juan Fernandez, Islas de (island group)	Chile	33 00 S	80 00 W
	Jubal, Strait of	Indian Ocean	27 40 N	33 55 E
	Judaea (region)	Israel, West Bank	31 35 N	35 00 E
	Jugoslavia, Jugoslavija (local names for Yugoslavia)	Yugoslavia	43 00 N	21 00 E
	Jutland (region)	Denmark	56 00 N	9 15 E
	Juventud, Isla de la (Isle of Youth)	Cuba	21 40 N	82 50 W
K	Kabardino-Balkaria (region)	Russia	43 30 N	43 30 E
	Kabul (capital)	Afghanistan	34 31 N	69 12 E
	Kaduna (city)	Nigeria	10 33 N	7 27 E
	Kailas Range	China, India	30 00 N	82 00 E
	Kalaallit Nunaat (local name for Greenland)	Greenland	72 00 N	40 00 W
	Kalahari (desert)	Botswana, Namibia	24 30 S	21 00 E
	Kalimantan (region)	Indonesia	0 00 N	115 00 E
	Kaliningrad (region; formerly part of East Prussia)	Russia	54 30 N	21 00 E
	Kamaran (island)	Yemen	15 21 N	42 34 E
	Kamchatka Peninsula (Poluostrov Kamchatka)	Russia	56 00 N	160 00 E
	Kampala (capital)	Uganda	0 19 N	32 25 E

Appendix F: Cross-Reference List of Geographic Names *(continued)*

Name	Entry in *The World Factbook*	Latitude (deg min)	Longitude (deg min)
Kampuchea (former name for Cambodia)	Cambodia	13 00 N	105 00 E
Kane Basin (portion of channel)	Arctic Ocean	79 30 N	68 00 W
Kanton Island	Kiribati	2 49 S	171 40 W
Kara Sea	Arctic Ocean	76 00 N	80 00 E
Karachevo-Cherkessia (region)	Russia	43 40 N	41 50 E
Karafuto (island; former name for southern Sakhalin Island)	Russia	50 00 N	143 00 E
Karakoram Pass	China, India	35 30 N	77 50 E
Karelia (region)	Finland, Russia	63 15 N	30 48 E
Karelian Isthmus	Russia	60 25 N	30 00 E
Karimata Strait	Pacific Ocean	2 05 S	108 40 E
Kashmir (region)	India, Pakistan	34 00 N	76 00 E
Katanga (region)	Democratic Republic of the Congo	10 00 S	26 00 E
Kathmandu (capital)	Nepal	27 43 N	85 19 E
Kattegat (strait)	Atlantic Ocean	57 00 N	11 00 E
Kauai Channel	Pacific Ocean	21 45 N	158 50 W
Kazakstan (former name for Kazakhstan)	Kazakhstan	48 00 N	68 00 E
Keeling Islands	Cocos (Keeling) Islands	12 30 S	96 50 E
Kerguelen, Iles (island group)	French Southern and Antarctic Lands	49 30 S	69 30 E
Kermadec Islands	New Zealand	29 50 S	178 15 W
Kerulen River	China, Mongolia	48 48 N	117 00 E
Khabarovsk (city)	Russia	48 27 N	135 06 E
Khanka, Lake	China, Russia	45 00 N	132 24 E
Khartoum (capital)	Sudan	15 36 N	32 32 E
Khios (island)	Greece	38 22 N	26 04 E
Khmer Republic (former name for Cambodia)	Cambodia	13 00 N	105 00 E
Khuriya Muriya Islands (Kuria Muria Islands)	Oman	17 30 N	56 00 E
Khyber Pass	Afghanistan, Pakistan	34 05 N	71 10 E
Kibris (Turkish local name for Cyprus)	Cyprus	35 00 N	33 00 E
Kiel Canal (Nord-Ostsee Kanal)	Atlantic Ocean	53 53 N	9 08 E
Kiev (capital)	Ukraine	50 26 N	30 31 E
Kigali (capital)	Rwanda	1 57 S	30 04 E
Kingston (capital)	Jamaica	18 00 N	76 48 W
Kingston (capital)	Norfolk Island	29 03 S	167 58 E
Kingstown (capital)	Saint Vincent and the Grenadines	13 09 N	61 14 W
Kinshasa (capital)	Democratic Republic of the Congo	4 18 S	15 18 E
Kipros (Greek local name for Cyprus)	Cyprus	35 00 N	33 00 E
Kirghiziya (former name for Kyrgyzstan)	Kyrgyzstan	41 00 N	75 00 E
Kirgizia (former name for Kyrgyzstan)	Kyrgyzstan	41 00 N	75 00 E
Kirguizstan (local name for Kyrgyzstan)	Kyrgyzstan	41 00 N	75 00 E
Kiritimati (Christmas Island)	Kiribati	1 52 N	157 20 W
Kishinev (see Chisinau)	Moldova	47 00 N	28 50 E
Kithira Strait	Atlantic Ocean	36 00 N	23 00 E
Kobe (city)	Japan	34 41 N	135 10 E
Kodiak Island	United States	57 49 N	152 23 W
Kola Peninsula (Kol'skiy Poluostrov)	Russia	67 20 N	37 00 E
Kolonia (town; former capital) (see Palikir)	Federated States of Micronesia	6 58 N	158 13 E
Korea Bay	Pacific Ocean	39 00 N	124 00 E
Korea Strait	Pacific Ocean	34 00 N	129 00 E

Appendix F: Cross-Reference List of Geographic Names *(continued)*

Name	Entry in *The World Factbook*	Latitude (deg min)	Longitude (deg min)
Korea, Democratic People's Republic of	North Korea	40 00 N	127 00 E
Korea, Republic of	South Korea	37 00 N	127 30 E
Koror (capital)	Palau	7 20 N	134 29 E
Kosovo (region)	Yugoslavia	42 30 N	21 00 E
Kosrae (island)	Federated States of Micronesia	5 20 N	163 00 E
Kowloon (city)	Hong Kong	22 18 N	114 10 E
Kra, Isthmus of	Burma, Thailand	10 20 N	99 00 E
Krakatoa (volcano)	Indonesia	6 07 S	105 24 E
Kuala Lumpur (capital)	Malaysia	3 10 N	101 42 E
Kunashiri (Kunashir) (island)	Russia (de facto)	44 20 N	146 00 E
Kunlun Mountains	China	36 00 N	84 00 E
Kuril Islands	Russia (de facto)	46 10 N	152 00 E
Kuwait (capital)	Kuwait	29 20 N	47 59 E
Kuznetsk Basin	Russia	54 00 N	86 00 E
Kwajalein Atoll	Marshall Islands	9 05 N	167 20 E
Kyushu (island)	Japan	33 00 N	131 00 E
Kyyiv (see Kiev)	Ukraine	50 26 N	30 31 E
L La Paz (capital)	Bolivia	16 30 S	68 09 W
La Perouse Strait	Pacific Ocean	45 45 N	142 00 E
Labrador (peninsula, region)	Canada	54 00 N	62 00 W
Labrador Sea	Atlantic Ocean	60 00 N	55 00 W
Laccadive Islands	India	10 00 N	73 00 E
Laccadive Sea	Indian Ocean	7 00 N	76 00 E
Lagos (capital)	Nigeria	6 27 N	3 24 E
Lake Erie	Atlantic Ocean	42 30 N	81 00 W
Lake Huron	Atlantic Ocean	45 00 N	83 00 W
Lake Michigan	Atlantic Ocean	43 30 N	87 30 W
Lake Ontario	Atlantic Ocean	43 30 N	78 00 W
Lake Superior	Atlantic Ocean	48 00 N	88 00 W
Lakshadweep (Laccadive Islands)	India	10 00 N	73 00 E
Lantau Island	Hong Kong	22 15 N	113 55 E
Lao (local name for Laos)	Laos	18 00 N	105 00 E
Laptev Sea	Arctic Ocean	76 00 N	126 00 E
Las Palmas (city)	Spain (Canary Islands)	28 06 N	15 24 W
Latakia (region)	Syria	36 00 N	35 50 E
Latvija (local name for Latvia)	Latvia	57 00 N	25 00 E
Lau Group (island group)	Fiji	18 20 S	178 30 E
Lefkosa (see Nicosia)	Cyprus	35 10 N	33 22 E
Lemnos (island)	Greece	39 54 N	25 21 E
Leningrad (see Saint Petersburg)	Russia	59 55 N	30 15 E
Lesser Sunda Islands	Indonesia	9 00 S	120 00 E
Lesvos (island)	Greece	39 15 N	26 15 E
Leyte (island)	Philippines	10 50 N	124 50 E
Liancourt Rocks (claimed by Japan)	South Korea	37 15 N	131 50 E
Liaodong Wan (gulf)	Pacific Ocean	40 30 N	121 20 E
Liban (local name for Lebanon)	Lebanon	33 50 N	36 50 E
Libreville (capital)	Gabon	0 23 N	9 27 E
Lietuva (local name for Lithuania)	Lithuania	56 00 N	24 00 E

Appendix F: Cross-Reference List of Geographic Names *(continued)*

Name	Entry in *The World Factbook*	Latitude (deg min)	Longitude (deg min)
Ligurian Sea	Atlantic Ocean	43 30 N	9 00 E
Lilongwe (capital)	Malawi	13 59 S	33 44 E
Lima (capital)	Peru	12 03 S	77 03 W
Lincoln Sea	Arctic Ocean	83 00 N	56 00 W
Line Islands	Jarvis Island, Kingman Reef, Kiribati, Palmyra Atoll	0 05 N	157 00 W
Lion, Gulf of	Atlantic Ocean	43 20 N	4 00 E
Lisbon (capital)	Portugal	38 43 N	9 08 W
Little Belt (Lille Baelt) (strait)	Atlantic Ocean	55 05 N	9 55 E
Ljubljana (capital)	Slovenia	46 03 N	14 31 E
Llanos (region)	Venezuela	8 00 N	68 00 W
Lobamba (city)	Swaziland	26 27 S	31 12 E
Lombok (island)	Indonesia	8 28 S	116 40 E
Lombok Strait	Indian Ocean	8 30 S	115 50 E
Lome (capital)	Togo	6 08 N	1 13 E
London (capital)	United Kingdom	51 30 N	0 10 W
Longyearbyen (town)	Svalbard	78 13 N	15 33 E
Lord Howe Island	Australia	31 30 S	159 00 E
Lorraine (region)	France	48 42 N	6 11 E
Louisiade Archipelago	Papua New Guinea	11 00 S	153 00 E
Lourenco Marques (city) (former name for Maputo)	Mozambique	25 56 S	32 34 E
Loyalty Islands (Iles Loyaute)	New Caledonia	21 00 S	167 00 E
Luanda (capital)	Angola	8 48 S	13 14 E
Lubnan (local name for Lebanon)	Lebanon	33 50 N	36 50 E
Lubumbashi (city)	Democratic Republic of the Congo	11 40 S	27 28 E
Lusaka (capital)	Zambia	15 25 S	28 17 E
Luxembourg (capital)	Luxembourg	49 45 N	6 10 E
Luzon (island)	Philippines	16 00 N	121 00 E
Luzon Strait	Pacific Ocean	20 30 N	121 00 E
Lyakhov Islands	Russia	73 45 N	138 00 E

M

Name	Entry in *The World Factbook*	Latitude (deg min)	Longitude (deg min)
Macao	Macau	22 10 N	113 33 E
Macedonia	The Former Yugoslav Republic of Macedonia	41 50 N	22 00 E
Macquarie Island	Australia	30 07 S	147 24 E
Madagasikara (local name for Madagascar)	Madagascar	20 00 S	47 00 E
Maddalena, Isola	Italy	41 13 N	09 24 E
Madeira Islands	Portugal	32 40 N	16 45 W
Madras (see Chennai) (city)	India	13 04 N	80 16 E
Madrid (capital)	Spain	40 24 N	3 41 W
Magellan, Strait of	Atlantic Ocean	54 00 S	71 00 W
Maghreb (region)	Algeria, Libya, Mauritania, Morocco, Tunisia	30 00 N	5 00 E
Magreb (local name for Morocco)	Morocco	32 00 N	5 00 W
Magyarorszag (local name for Hungary)	Hungary	47 00 N	20 00 E
Mahe Island	Seychelles	4 41 S	55 30 E
Maiz, Islas del (Corn Islands)	Nicaragua	12 15 N	83 00 W
Majorca Island (Isla de Mallorca)	Spain	39 30 N	3 00 E
Majuro (capital)	Marshall Islands	7 05 N	171 08 E
Makassar Strait	Pacific Ocean	2 00 S	117 30 E
Makedonija (local name for Macedonia)	The Former Yugoslav Republic of Macedonia	41 50 N	22 00 E

Appendix F: Cross-Reference List of Geographic Names (continued)

Name	Entry in *The World Factbook*	Latitude (deg min)	Longitude (deg min)
Malabo (capital)	Equatorial Guinea	3 45 N	8 47 E
Malacca, Strait of	Indian Ocean	2 30 N	101 20 E
Malagasy Republic	Madagascar	20 00 S	47 00 E
Malay Archipelago	Brunei, Indonesia, Malaysia, Papua New Guinea, Philippines	2 30 N	120 00 E
Malay Peninsula	Malaysia, Thailand	7 10 N	100 35 E
Male (capital)	Maldives	4 10 N	73 31 E
Mallorca (Majorca) (island)	Spain	39 30 N	3 00 E
Malmady (region)	Belgium	50 26 N	6 02 E
Malpelo, Isla de (island)	Colombia	4 00 N	90 30 W
Malta Channel	Atlantic Ocean	56 44 N	26 53 E
Malvinas, Islas (island group)	Falkland Islands (Islas Malvinas)	51 45 S	59 00 W
Mamoutzou (capital)	Mayotte	12 47 S	45 14 E
Managua (capital)	Nicaragua	12 09 N	86 17 W
Manama (capital)	Bahrain	26 13 N	50 35 E
Manchukuo (former state)	China	44 00 N	124 00 E
Manchuria (region)	China	44 00 N	124 00 E
Manila (capital)	Philippines	14 35 N	121 00 E
Manipa Strait	Pacific Ocean	3 20 S	127 23 E
Mannar, Gulf of	Indian Ocean	8 30 N	79 00 E
Manua Islands	American Samoa	14 13 S	169 35 W
Maputo (capital)	Mozambique	25 58 S	32 35 E
Marcus Island (Minami-tori-shima)	Japan	24 16 N	154 00 E
Margarita, Isla (island)	Venezuela	10 00 N	64 00 W
Mariana Islands	Guam, Northern Mariana Islands	16 00 N	145 30 E
Marie Byrd Land (region)	Antarctica	77 00 S	130 00 E
Marion Island	South Africa	46 51 S	37 52 E
Marmara, Sea of	Atlantic Ocean	40 40 N	28 15 E
Marquesas Islands (Iles Marquises)	French Polynesia	9 00 S	139 30 W
Martin Vaz, Ilhas (island group)	Brazil	20 30 S	28 51 W
Mas a Tierra (Robinson Crusoe Island)	Chile	33 38 S	78 52 W
Mascarene Islands	Mauritius, Reunion	21 00 S	57 00 E
Maseru (capital)	Lesotho	29 28 S	27 30 E
Mata-Utu (capital)	Wallis and Futuna	13 57 S	171 56 W
Matsu (island)	Taiwan	26 13 N	119 56 E
Matthew Island	New Caledonia, Vanuatu	22 20 S	171 20 E
Mauritanie (local name for Mauritania)	Mauritania	20 00 N	12 00 W
Mazatlan (city)	Mexico	23 13 N	106 25 W
Mbabane (capital)	Swaziland	26 18 S	31 06 E
McDonald Islands	Heard Island and McDonald Islands	53 06 S	73 30 E
Mecca (city)	Saudi Arabia	21 27 N	39 49 E
Mediterranean Sea	Atlantic Ocean	36 00 N	15 00 E
Melilla (exclave)	Spain	35 19 N	2 58 W
Memel (region)	Lithuania	55 43 N	21 30 E
Mesopotamia (region)	Iraq	33 00 N	44 00 E
Messina, Strait of	Atlantic Ocean	38 15 N	15 35 E
Mexico (capital)	Mexico	19 24 N	99 09 W
Mexico, Gulf of	Atlantic Ocean	25 00 N	90 00 W

Appendix F: Cross-Reference List of Geographic Names (continued)

Name	Entry in *The World Factbook*	Latitude (deg min)	Longitude (deg min)
Middle Congo (former name for Republic of the Congo)	Republic of the Congo	1 00 S	15 00 E
Milwaukee Deep (Puerto Rico Trench)	Atlantic Ocean	19 55 N	65 27 W
Minami-tori-shima (Marcus Island)	Japan	24 16 N	154 00 E
Mindanao (island)	Philippines	8 00 N	125 00 E
Mindanao Sea	Pacific Ocean	9 15 N	124 30 E
Mindoro (island)	Philippines	12 50 N	121 05 E
Mindoro Strait	Pacific Ocean	12 20 N	120 40 E
Mingrelia (region)	Georgia	42 30 N	41 52 E
Minicoy Island	India	8 17 N	73 02 E
Minorca Island (Isla de Menorca)	Spain	40 00 N	4 00 E
Minsk (capital)	Belarus	53 54 N	27 34 E
Misr (local name for Egypt)	Egypt	27 00 N	30 00 E
Mitla Pass	Egypt	30 02 N	32 54 E
Mocambique (local name for Mozambique)	Mozambique	18 15 S	35 00 E
Mogadishu (capital)	Somalia	2 04 N	45 22 E
Moldavia (region)	Moldova, Romania	47 00 N	29 00 E
Molucca Sea	Pacific Ocean	2 00 N	127 00 E
Moluccas (Spice Islands)	Indonesia	2 00 S	28 00 E
Mombasa (city)	Kenya	4 03 S	39 40 E
Mona Passage	Atlantic Ocean	18 30 N	67 45 W
Monaco (capital)	Monaco	43 44 N	7 25 E
Mongol Uls (local name for Mongolia)	Mongolia	46 00 N	105 00 E
Monrovia (capital)	Liberia	6 18 N	10 47 W
Montenegro (political region)	Yugoslavia	42 30 N	19 00 E
Monterrey (city)	Mexico	25 40 N	100 19 W
Montevideo (capital)	Uruguay	34 53 S	56 11 W
Montreal (city)	Canada	45 31 N	73 34 W
Moravia (region)	Czech Republic	49 30 N	17 00 E
Moravian Gate (pass)	Czech Republic	49 35 N	17 50 E
Moroni (capital)	Comoros	11 41 S	43 16 E
Mortlock Islands (Nomoi Islands)	Federated States of Micronesia	5 30 N	153 40 E
Moscow (capital)	Russia	55 45 N	37 35 E
Mount Pinatubo (volcano)	Philippines	15 08 N	120 21 E
Mozambique Channel	Indian Ocean	19 00 S	41 00 E
Muritaniyah (local name for Mauritania)	Mauritania	20 00 N	12 00 W
Musandam Peninsula	Oman, United Arab Emirates	26 18 N	56 24 E
Muscat (capital)	Oman	23 37 N	58 35 E
Muscat and Oman (former name for Oman)	Oman	21 00 N	57 00 E
Myanma, Myanmar	Burma	22 00 N	98 00 E
Nagorno-Karabakh (region)	Azerbaijan	40 00 N	46 40 E
Nairobi (capital)	Kenya	1 17 S	36 49 E
Namib (desert)	Namibia	24 00 S	15 00 E
Nampo-shoto (island group)	Japan	30 00 N	140 00 E
Nassau (capital)	The Bahamas	25 05 N	77 21 W
Natal (region)	South Africa	29 00 S	30 25 E
Natuna Besar Islands	Indonesia	3 30 N	102 30 E
Natuna Sea	Pacific Ocean	3 30 N	108 00 E

N

Appendix F: Cross-Reference List of Geographic Names *(continued)*

Name	Entry in *The World Factbook*	Latitude (deg min)	Longitude (deg min)
Naxcivan (region)	Azerbaijan	39 20 N	45 20 E
Naxos (island)	Greece	37 05 N	25 30 E
N'Djamena (capital)	Chad	12 07 N	15 03 E
Nederland (local name for the Netherlands)	Netherlands	52 30 N	5 45 E
Nederlandse Antillen (local name for the Netherlands Antilles)	Netherlands Antilles	12 15 N	68 45 W
Negev (region)	Israel	30 30 N	34 55 E
Negros (island)	Philippines	10 00 N	123 00 E
Nejd (region)	Saudi Arabia	24 05 N	45 15 E
Netherlands East Indies (former name for Indonesia)	Indonesia	5 00 S	120 00 E
Netherlands Guiana (former name for Suriname)	Suriname	4 00 N	56 00 W
Nevis (island)	Saint Kitts and Nevis	17 09 N	62 35 W
New Britain (island)	Papua New Guinea	6 00 S	150 00 E
New Delhi (capital)	India	28 36 N	77 12 E
New Guinea (island)	Indonesia, Papua New Guinea	5 00 S	140 00 E
New Hebrides (island group)	Vanuatu	16 00 S	167 00 E
New Ireland (island)	Papua New Guinea	3 20 N	152 00 E
New Siberian Islands	Russia	75 00 N	142 00 E
New Territories (mainland region)	Hong Kong	22 24 N	114 10 E
Newfoundland (island, with mainland area, and a province)	Canada	52 00 N	56 00 W
Niamey (capital)	Niger	13 31 N	2 07 E
Nicobar Islands	India	8 00 N	93 30 E
Nicosia (capital)	Cyprus	35 10 N	33 22 E
Nightingale Island	Saint Helena	37 25 S	12 30 W
Nihon (local name for Japan)	Japan	36 00 N	138 00 E
Nippon (local name for Japan)	Japan	36 00 N	138 00 E
Nomoi Islands (Mortlock Islands)	Federated States of Micronesia	5 30 N	153 40 E
Norge (local name for Norway)	Norway	62 00 N	10 00 E
Norman Isles (Channel Islands)	Guernsey, Jersey	49 20 N	2 20 W
North Atlantic Ocean	Atlantic Ocean	30 00 N	45 00 W
North Channel	Atlantic Ocean	55 10 N	5 40 W
North Frisian Islands	Denmark, Germany	54 50 N	8 12 E
North Greenland Sea	Arctic Ocean	78 00 N	5 00 W
North Island	New Zealand	39 00 S	176 00 E
North Korea	North Korea	40 00 N	127 00 E
North Ossetia (region)	Russia	43 00 N	44 10 E
North Pacific Ocean	Pacific Ocean	30 00 N	165 00 W
North Sea	Atlantic Ocean	56 00 N	4 00 E
North Vietnam (former name for northern portion of Vietnam)	Vietnam	23 00 N	106 00 E
North Yemen (Yemen Arab Republic)	Yemen	15 00 N	44 00 E
Northeast Providence Channel	Atlantic Ocean	25 40 N	77 09 W
Northern Cyprus (region)	Cyprus	35 15 N	33 44 E
Northern Epirus (region)	Albania, Greece	40 00 N	20 30 E
Northern Grenadines (political region)	Saint Vincent and the Grenadines	12 45 N	61 15 W
Northern Ireland	United Kingdom	54 40 N	6 45 W
Northern Rhodesia (former name for Zambia)	Zambia	15 00 S	30 00 E
Northwest Passages	Arctic Ocean	74 40 N	100 00 W

Appendix F: Cross-Reference List of Geographic Names *(continued)*

Name	Entry in *The World Factbook*	Latitude (deg min)	Longitude (deg min)
Northwest Territories (region)	Canada	64 05 N	117 10 W
Norwegian Sea	Atlantic Ocean	66 00 N	6 00 E
Nouakchott (capital)	Mauritania	18 06 N	15 57 W
Noumea (capital)	New Caledonia	22 16 S	166 27 E
Nouvelle-Caledonie (local name for New Caledonia)	New Caledonia	21 30 S	165 30 E
Nouvelles Hebrides (former name for Vanuatu)	Vanuatu	16 00 S	167 00 E
Novaya Zemlya (islands)	Russia	74 00 N	57 00 E
Nubia (region)	Egypt, Sudan	20 30 N	33 00 E
Nuku'alofa (capital)	Tonga	21 08 S	175 12 W
Nunavut (region)	Canada	72 00 N	90 00 W
Nuuk (Godthab) (capital)	Greenland	64 11 N	51 44 W
Nyasaland (former name for Malawi)	Malawi	13 30 S	34 00 E
Nyassa (region)	Mozambique	13 30 S	37 00 E
O Oahu (island)	United States (Hawaii)	21 30 N	158 00 W
Ocean Island (Banaba)	Kiribati	0 52 S	169 35 E
Ocean Island (Kure Island)	United States	28 25 N	178 20 W
Oesterreich (local name for Austria)	Austria	47 20 N	13 20 E
Ogaden (region)	Ethiopia, Somalia	7 00 N	46 00 E
Oil Islands (Chagos Archipelago)	British Indian Ocean Territory	6 00 S	71 30 E
Okhotsk, Sea of	Pacific Ocean	53 00 N	150 00 E
Okinawa (island group)	Japan	26 30 N	128 00 E
Oland (island)	Sweden	56 45 N	16 40 E
Oman, Gulf of	Indian Ocean	24 30 N	58 30 E
Ombai Strait	Pacific Ocean	8 30 S	125 00 E
Oran (city)	Algeria	35 43 N	0 43 W
Orange River Colony (region; former name of Free State Province of South Africa)	South Africa	28 20 S	26 40 E
Oranjestad (capital)	Aruba	12 33 N	70 06 W
Oresund (The Sound) (strait)	Atlantic Ocean	55 50 N	12 40 E
Orkney Islands	United Kingdom	59 00 N	3 00 W
Oslo (capital)	Norway	59 55 N	10 45 E
Osumi Strait (Van Diemen Strait)	Pacific Ocean	31 00 N	131 00 E
Otranto, Strait of	Atlantic Ocean	40 00 N	19 00 E
Ottawa (capital)	Canada	45 20 N	73 58 W
Ouagadougou (capital)	Burkina Faso	12 22 N	1 31 W
Outer Hebrides (islands)	United Kingdom	57 45 N	7 00 W
Outer Mongolia (region)	Mongolia	46 00 N	105 00 E
P Pacific Islands, Trust Territory of the	Marshall Islands, Federated States of Micronesia, Northern Mariana Islands, Palau	10 00 N	155 00 E
Pagan (island)	Northern Mariana Islands	18 08 N	145 47 E
Pago Pago (capital)	American Samoa	14 16 S	170 42 W
Palawan (island)	Philippines	9 30 N	118 30 E
Palermo (city)	Italy	38 07 N	13 21 E
Palestine (region)	Israel, West Bank	32 00 N	35 15 E
Palikir (capital)	Federated States of Micronesia	6 55 N	158 08 E
Palk Strait	Indian Ocean	10 00 N	79 45 E
Pamirs (mountains)	China, Tajikistan	38 00 N	73 00 E
Pampas (region)	Argentina	35 00 N	63 00 W

Appendix F: Cross-Reference List of Geographic Names *(continued)*

Name	Entry in *The World Factbook*	Latitude (deg min)	Longitude (deg min)
Panama (capital)	Panama	8 58 N	79 32 W
Panama Canal	Panama	9 00 N	79 45 W
Panama, Gulf of	Pacific Ocean	8 00 N	79 30 W
Panay (island)	Philippines	11 15 N	122 30 E
Pantelleria, Isola di (island)	Italy	36 47 N	12 00 E
Papeete (capital)	French Polynesia	17 32 S	149 34 W
Paramaribo (capital)	Suriname	5 50 N	55 10 W
Parece Vela (island)	Japan	20 20 N	136 00 E
Paris (capital)	France	48 52 N	2 20 E
Pascua, Isla de (Easter Island)	Chile	27 07 S	109 22 W
Pashtunistan (region)	Afghanistan, Pakistan	32 00 N	69 00 E
Passion, Ile de la (island)	Clipperton Island	10 17 N	109 13 W
Patagonia (region)	Argentina	48 00 S	61 00 W
Peking (see Beijing)	China	39 56 N	116 24 E
Pelagian Islands (Isole Pelagie)	Italy	35 40 N	12 40 E
Peleliu (Beliliou) (island)	Palau	7 01 N	134 15 E
Peloponnese (peninsula)	Greece	37 30 N	22 25 E
Pemba Island	Tanzania	7 31 S	39 25 E
Penang Island	Malaysia	5 23 N	100 15 E
Pentland Firth (channel)	Atlantic Ocean	58 44 N	3 13 W
Perim (island)	Yemen	12 39 N	43 25 E
Perouse Strait, La	Pacific Ocean	44 45 N	142 00 E
Persia (former name for Iran)	Iran	32 00 N	53 00 E
Persian Gulf	Indian Ocean	27 00 N	51 00 E
Pescadores (islands)	Taiwan	23 30 N	119 30 E
Peter I Island	Antarctica	68 48 S	90 35 W
Philip Island	Norfolk Island	29 08 S	167 57 E
Philippine Sea	Pacific Ocean	20 00 N	134 00 E
Phnom Penh (capital)	Cambodia	11 33 N	104 55 E
Phoenix Islands	Kiribati	3 30 S	172 00 W
Pilipinas (local name for the Philippines)	Philippines	13 00 N	122 00 E
Pinatubo, Mount (volcano)	Philippines	15 08 N	120 21 E
Pines, Isle of (former name for Isla de la Juventud) (island)	Cuba	21 40 N	82 50 W
Pleasant Island	Nauru	0 32 S	166 55 E
Plymouth (capital)	Montserrat	16 44 N	62 14 W
Polska (local name)	Poland	52 00 N	20 00 E
Polynesie Francaise (local name for French Polynesia)	French Polynesia	15 00 S	140 00 W
Pomerania (region)	Germany, Poland	53 40 N	15 35 E
Ponape (Pohnpei) (island)	Federated States of Micronesia	6 55 N	158 15 E
Port Louis (capital)	Mauritius	20 10 S	57 30 E
Port Moresby (capital)	Papua New Guinea	9 30 S	147 10 E
Port-au-Prince (capital)	Haiti	18 32 N	72 20 W
Port-of-Spain (capital)	Trinidad and Tobago	10 39 N	61 31 W
Porto-Novo (capital)	Benin	6 29 N	2 37 E
Portuguese East Africa (former name for Mozambique)	Mozambique	18 15 S	35 00 E
Portuguese Guinea (former name for Guinea-Bissau)	Guinea-Bissau	12 00 N	15 00 W
Portuguese Timor (former name for East Timor)	Indonesia	9 00 S	126 00 E
Port-Vila (capital)	Vanuatu	17 44 S	168 19 E

Appendix F: Cross-Reference List of Geographic Names *(continued)*

Name	Entry in *The World Factbook*	Latitude (deg min)	Longitude (deg min)
Poznan (city)	Poland	52 25 N	16 55 E
Prague (capital)	Czech Republic	40 55 N	21 00 E
Praia (capital)	Cape Verde	14 55 N	23 31 W
Prathet Thai (local name for Thailand)	Thailand	15 00 N	100 00 E
Pretoria (capital)	South Africa	25 45 S	28 10 E
Prevlaka peninsula	Croatia	42 24 N	18 31 E
Pribilof Islands	United States	57 00 N	170 00 W
Prince Edward Island	Canada	46 20 N	63 20 W
Prince Edward Islands	South Africa	46 35 S	38 00 E
Prince Patrick Island	Canada	76 30 N	119 00 W
Principe (island)	Sao Tome and Principe	1 38 N	7 25 E
Prussia (region)	Germany, Poland, Russia	53 00 N	14 00 E
Pukapuka Atoll	Cook Islands	10 53 S	165 49 W
Punjab (region)	India, Pakistan	30 50 N	73 30 E
Puntland (region)	Somalia	8 21 N	49 08 E
P'yongyang (capital)	North Korea	39 01 N	125 45 E
Q Qazaqstan (local name for Kazakhstan)	Kazakhstan	48 00 N	68 00 E
Qita Ghazzah (local name Gaza Strip)	Gaza Strip	31 25 N	34 20 E
Quebec (province)	Canada	52 00 N	72 00 W
Queen Charlotte Islands	Canada	53 00 N	132 00 W
Queen Elizabeth Islands	Canada	78 00 N	95 00 W
Queen Maud Land (claimed by Norway)	Antarctica	73 30 S	12 00 E
Quemoy (island)	Taiwan	24 27 N	118 23 E
Quito (capital)	Ecuador	0 13 S	78 30 W
R Rabat (capital)	Morocco	34 02 N	6 51 W
Ralik Chain (island group)	Marshall Islands	8 00 N	167 00 E
Rangoon (Yangon) (capital)	Burma	16 47 N	96 10 E
Rapa Nui (Easter Island)	Chile	27 07 S	109 22 W
Ratak Chain (island group)	Marshall Islands	9 00 N	171 00 E
Red Sea	Indian Ocean	20 00 N	38 00 E
Redonda (island)	Antigua and Barbuda	16 55 N	62 19 W
Republica Dominicana (local name for Dominican Republic)	Dominican Republic	19 00 N	70 40 W
Republique Centrafricain (local name for Central African Republic)	Central African Republic	7 00 N	21 00 E
Republique Francaise (local name for France)	France	46 00 N	2 00 E
Republique Gabonaise (local name for Gabon)	Gabon	1 00 S	11 45 E
Republique Rwandaise (local name for Rwanda)	Rwanda	2 00 S	30 00 E
Republique Togolaise (local name for Togo)	Togo	8 00 N	1 10 E
Revillagigedo Island	United States (Alaska)	55 35 N	131 06 W
Revillagigedo Islands	Mexico	19 00 N	112 45 W
Reykjavik (capital)	Iceland	19 00 N	111 30 W
Rhodes (island)	Greece	36 10 N	28 00 E
Rhodesia (region)	Zimbabwe	20 00 S	30 00 E
Rhodesia, Northern (former name for Zambia)	Zambia	15 00 S	30 00 E
Rhodesia, Southern (former name for Zimbabwe)	Zimbabwe	20 00 S	30 00 E
Riga (capital)	Latvia	56 57 N	24 06 E
Riga, Gulf of	Atlantic Ocean	57 30 N	23 30 E
Rio de la Plata (gulf)	Atlantic Ocean	35 00 S	59 00 W

Appendix F: Cross-Reference List of Geographic Names (continued)

	Name	Entry in The World Factbook	Latitude (deg min)	Longitude (deg min)
	Rio de Oro (region)	Western Sahara	23 45 N	15 45 W
	Rio Muni (mainland region)	Equatorial Guinea	1 30 N	10 00 E
	Riyadh (capital)	Saudi Arabia	24 38 N	46 43 E
	Road Town (capital)	British Virgin Islands	18 27 N	64 37 W
	Robinson Crusoe Island (Mas a Tierra)	Chile	33 38 S	78 52 W
	Rocas, Atol das (island)	Brazil	3 51 S	33 49 W
	Rockall (island)	United Kingdom	57 35 N	13 48 W
	Rodrigues (island)	Mauritius	19 42 S	63 25 E
	Rome (capital)	Italy	41 54 N	12 29 E
	Roncador Cay (island)	Colombia	13 32 N	80 03 W
	Roosevelt Island	Antarctica	79 30 S	162 00 W
	Roseau (capital)	Dominica	15 18 N	61 24 W
	Ross Dependency (claimed by New Zealand)	Antarctica	80 00 S	180 00 E
	Ross Island	Antarctica	81 30 S	175 00 W
	Ross Sea	Antarctica, Southern Ocean	76 00 S	175 00 W
	Rossiya (local name for Russia)	Russia	60 00 N	100 00 E
	Rota (island)	Northern Mariana Islands	14 10 N	145 12 E
	Rotuma (island)	Fiji	12 30 S	177 30 E
	Ruanda (former name for Rwanda)	Rwanda	2 00 S	30 00 E
	Rub al Khali (desert)	Saudi Arabia	19 30 N	49 00 E
	Rumelia (region)	Albania, Bulgaria, The Former Yugoslav Republic of Macedonia	42 00 N	22 30 E
	Ruthenia (region; former name for Carpatho-Ukraine)	Ukraine	48 22 N	23 32 E
	Ryukyu Islands	Japan	26 30 N	128 00 E
S	Saar (region)	Germany	49 25 N	7 00 E
	Saaremaa (island)	Estonia	58 25 N	22 30 E
	Saba (island)	Netherlands Antilles	17 38 N	63 10 W
	Sabah (state)	Malaysia	5 20 N	117 10 E
	Sable Island	Canada	43 55 N	59 50 W
	Safety Islands (Iles du Salut)	French Guiana	5 20 N	52 37 W
	Sahara Occidental (former name for Western Sahara)	Western Sahara	24 30 N	13 00 W
	Sahel (region)	Burkina Faso, Chad, The Gambia, Guinea-Bissau, Mali, Mauritania, Niger, Senegal	15 00 N	8 00 W
	Saigon (city; former name for Ho Chi Minh City)	Vietnam	10 45 N	106 40 E
	Saint Barthelemy (Saint Bart's) (island)	Guadeloupe	17 55 N	62 52 W
	Saint Brandon (Cargados Carajos Shoals)	Mauritius	16 25 S	59 38 E
	Saint Christopher (island)	Saint Kitts and Nevis	17 20 N	62 45 W
	Saint Christopher and Nevis	Saint Kitts and Nevis	17 20 N	62 45 W
	Saint Eustatius (island)	Netherlands Antilles	17 30 N	63 00 W
	Saint George's (capital)	Grenada	12 03 N	61 45 W
	Saint George's Channel	Atlantic Ocean	52 00 N	6 00 W
	Saint Helens, Mount (volcano)	United States	46 15 N	122 12 W
	Saint Helier (capital)	Jersey	49 12 N	2 37 W
	Saint John (city)	Canada (New Brunswick)	45 16 N	66 04 W
	Saint John's (capital)	Antigua and Barbuda	17 06 N	61 51 W
	Saint Lawrence Island	United States	49 30 N	67 00 W
	Saint Lawrence Seaway	Atlantic Ocean	49 15 N	67 00 W
	Saint Lawrence, Gulf of	Atlantic Ocean	48 00 N	62 00 W

Appendix F: Cross-Reference List of Geographic Names *(continued)*

Name	Entry in *The World Factbook*	Latitude (deg min)	Longitude (deg min)
Saint Paul Island	Canada	47 12 N	60 09 W
Saint Paul Island	United States	57 11 N	170 16 W
Saint Paul Island (Ile Saint-Paul)	French Southern and Antarctic Lands	38 43 S	77 29 E
Saint Peter and Saint Paul Rocks (Penedos de Sao Pedro e Sao Paulo)	Brazil	0 23 N	29 23 W
Saint Peter Port (capital)	Guernsey	49 27 N	2 32 W
Saint Petersburg (city; former capital)	Russia	59 55 N	30 15 E
Saint Thomas (island)	Virgin Islands	18 21 N	64 55 W
Saint Vincent Passage	Atlantic Ocean	13 30 N	61 00 W
Saint-Denis (capital)	Reunion	20 52 S	55 28 E
Saint-Martin (Sint Maarten) (island)	Guadeloupe	18 04 N	63 04 W
Saint-Pierre (capital)	Saint Pierre and Miquelon	46 46 N	56 11 W
Saipan (island)	Northern Mariana Islands	15 12 N	145 45 E
Sak'art'velo (local name for Georgia)	Georgia	42 00 N	43 30 E
Sakhalin Island (Ostrov Sakhalin)	Russia	51 00 N	143 00 E
Sakishima Islands	Japan	24 30 N	124 00 E
Sala y Gomez, Isla (island)	Chile	26 28 S	105 00 W
Salisbury (city; former name for Harare)	Zimbabwe	17 50 S	105 00 W
Salzburg (city)	Austria	47 48 N	13 02 E
Samar (island)	Philippines	12 00 N	125 00 E
Samaria (region)	West Bank	32 15 N	35 10 E
Samoa Islands	American Samoa, Samoa	14 00 S	171 00 W
Samos (island)	Greece	37 48 N	26 44 E
San Ambrosio, Isla (island)	Chile	26 21 S	79 52 W
San Andres y Providencia, Archipielago (island group)	Colombia	13 00 N	81 30 W
San Bernardino Strait	Pacific Ocean	12 32 N	124 10 E
San Felix, Isla (island)	Chile	26 17 S	80 05 W
San Jose (capital)	Costa Rica	9 56 N	84 05 W
San Juan (capital)	Puerto Rico	18 28 N	66 07 W
San Marino (capital)	San Marino	43 56 N	12 25 E
San Salvador (capital)	El Salvador	13 42 N	89 12 W
Sanaa (capital)	Yemen	15 21 N	44 12 E
Sandzak (region)	Yugoslavia	43 05 N	19 45 E
Santa Cruz (city)	Bolivia	17 48 S	63 10 W
Santa Cruz Islands	Solomon Islands	11 00 S	166 15 E
Santa Sede (local name for the Holy See)	Holy See	41 54 N	12 27 E
Santiago (capital)	Chile	33 27 S	70 40 W
Santo Antao (island)	Cape Verde	17 05 N	25 10 W
Santo Domingo (capital)	Dominican Republic	18 28 N	69 54 W
Sao Pedro e Sao Paulo, Penedos de (rocks)	Brazil	0 23 N	29 23 W
Sao Tiago (island)	Cape Verde	15 05 N	23 40 W
Sao Tome (island)	Sao Tome and Principe	0 12 N	6 39 E
Sapudi Strait	Pacific Ocean	7 05 S	114 10 E
Sarajevo (capital)	Bosnia and Herzegovina	43 52 N	18 25 E
Sarawak (state)	Malaysia	2 30 N	113 30 E
Sardinia (island)	Italy	40 00 N	9 00 E
Sargasso Sea (region)	Atlantic Ocean	30 00 N	55 00 W
Sark (island)	Guernsey	49 26 N	2 21 W

Appendix F: Cross-Reference List of Geographic Names (continued)

Name	Entry in *The World Factbook*	Latitude (deg min)	Longitude (deg min)
Savage Island (former name for Niue)	Niue	19 02 S	169 52 W
Savu Sea	Pacific Ocean	9 30 S	122 00 E
Saxony (region)	Germany	51 00 N	13 00 E
Schleswig-Holstein (region)	Germany	54 31 N	9 33 E
Schweiz (local German name for Switzerland)	Switzerland	47 00 N	8 00 E
Scopus, Mount	Israel, West Bank	31 48 N	35 14 E
Scotia Sea	Atlantic Ocean, Southern Ocean	56 00 S	40 00 W
Scotland (region)	United Kingdom	57 00 N	4 00 W
Scott Island	Antarctica	67 24 S	179 55 W
Senegambia (region; former name of confederation of Senegal and The Gambia)	The Gambia, Senegal	13 50 N	15 25 W
Senyavin Islands	Federated States of Micronesia	6 55 N	158 00 E
Seoul (capital)	South Korea	37 34 N	127 00 E
Serbia and Montenegro	Yugoslavia	43 00 N	21 00 E
Serendib (former name for Sri Lanka)	Sri Lanka	7 00 N	81 00 E
Serrana Bank (shoal)	Colombia	14 25 N	80 16 W
Serranilla Bank (shoal)	Colombia	15 51 N	79 46 W
Settlement, The (capital)	Christmas Island	18 44 N	64 19 W
Severnaya Zemlya (Northland) (island group)	Russia	79 30 N	98 00 E
Shaba (region)	Democratic Republic of the Congo	8 00 S	27 00 E
Shag Island	Heard Island and McDonald Islands	53 00 S	72 30 E
Shag Rocks	South Georgia and the South Sandwich Islands	53 33 S	42 02 W
Shetland Islands	United Kingdom	60 30 N	1 30 W
Shikoku (island)	Japan	33 45 N	133 30 E
Shikotan (island)	Russia (de facto)	43 47 N	146 45 E
Shqiperia (local name for Albania)	Albania	41 00 N	20 00 E
Siam (former name for Thailand)	Thailand	15 00 N	100 00 E
Siberia (region)	Russia	60 00 N	100 00 E
Sibutu Passage	Pacific Ocean	4 50 N	119 35 E
Sicily (island)	Italy	37 30 N	14 00 E
Sicily, Strait of	Atlantic Ocean	37 20 N	11 20 E
Sidra, Gulf of	Atlantic Ocean	31 30 N	18 00 E
Sikkim (state)	India	27 50 N	88 30 E
Silesia (region)	Czech Republic, Germany, Poland	51 00 N	17 00 E
Sinai Peninsula	Egypt	29 30 N	34 00 E
Singapore (capital)	Singapore	1 17 N	103 51 E
Singapore Strait	Pacific Ocean	1 15 N	104 00 E
Sinkiang (Xinjiang) (city)	China	42 00 N	86 00 E
Sint Eustatius (island)	Netherlands Antilles	17 29 N	62 58 W
Sint Maarten (Saint-Martin) (island)	Netherlands Antilles	18 04 N	63 04 W
Sjaelland (island)	Denmark	55 30 N	12 00 E
Skagerrak (strait)	Atlantic Ocean	57 45 N	9 00 E
Skopje (capital)	The Former Yugoslav Republic of Macedonia	41 59 N	21 26 E
Slavonia (region)	Croatia	45 27 N	18 00 E
Slovenija (local name for Slovenia)	Slovenia	46 00 N	15 00 E
Slovensko (local name for Slovakia)	Slovakia	48 40 N	19 30 E
Smyrna (region; former name for Izmir)	Turkey	38 25 N	27 10 E
Society Islands (Iles de la Societe)	French Polynesia	17 00 S	150 00 W

Appendix F: Cross-Reference List of Geographic Names (continued)

Name	Entry in The World Factbook	Latitude (deg min)	Longitude (deg min)
Socotra (island)	Yemen	12 30 N	54 00 E
Sofia (capital)	Bulgaria	42 41 N	23 19 E
Solomon Islands, northern	Papua New Guinea	6 00 S	155 00 E
Solomon Islands, southern	Solomon Islands	8 00 S	159 00 E
Solomon Sea	Pacific Ocean	8 00 S	153 00 E
Somaliland (region)	Somalia	9 30 N	46 00 E
Somers Islands (former name for Bermuda)	Bermuda	32 20 N	64 45 W
Songkhla (city)	Thailand	7 12 N	100 36 E
Sound, The (Oresund) (strait)	Atlantic Ocean	55 50 N	12 40 E
South Atlantic Ocean	Atlantic Ocean	30 00 S	15 00 W
South China Sea	Pacific Ocean	10 00 N	113 00 E
South Georgia (island)	South Georgia and the South Sandwich Islands	54 15 S	36 45 W
South Island	New Zealand	43 00 S	171 00 E
South Korea	South Korea	37 00 N	127 30 E
South Orkney Islands	Antarctica	61 00 S	45 00 W
South Ossetia (region)	Georgia	42 20 N	44 00 E
South Pacific Ocean	Pacific Ocean	30 00 S	130 00 W
South Sandwich Islands	South Georgia and the South Sandwich Islands	57 45 S	26 30 W
South Shetland Islands	Antarctica	62 00 S	59 00 W
South Tyrol (region)	Italy	46 30 N	10 30 E
South Vietnam (former name for the southern portion of Vietnam)	Vietnam	12 00 N	108 00 E
South Yemen (People's Democratic Republic of Yemen)	Yemen	14 00 N	48 00 E
Southern Grenadines (island group)	Grenada	12 20 N	61 30 W
Southern Rhodesia (former name for Zimbabwe)	Zimbabwe	20 00 S	30 00 E
South-West Africa (former name for Namibia)	Namibia	22 00 S	17 00 E
Soviet Union (former name of a large Eurasian empire, roughly coequal with the former Russian Empire)	Armenia, Azerbaijan, Belarus, Estonia, Georgia, Kazakhstan, Kyrgyzstan, Latvia, Lithuania, Moldova, Russia, Tajikistan, Turkmenistan, Ukraine, Uzbekistan		
Spanish Guinea (former name for Equatorial Guinea)	Equatorial Guinea	2 00 N	10 00 E
Spanish Morocco (former name for northern Morocco)	Morocco	32 00 N	7 00 W
Spanish North Africa (exclaves)	Spain (Ceuta, Islas Chafarinas, Melilla, Penon de Alhucemas, Penon de Velez de la Gomera)	35 15 N	4 00 W
Spanish Sahara (former name)	Western Sahara	24 30 N	13 00 W
Spanish West Africa (former name for Ifni and Spanish Sahara)	Morocco, Western Sahara	25 00 N	13 00 W
Spice Islands (Moluccas)	Indonesia	2 00 S	28 00 E
Spitsbergen (island)	Svalbard	78 00 N	20 00 E
Srbija-Crna Gora (local name for Serbia and Montenegro)	Yugoslavia	44 00 N	21 00 E
St. John's (city)	Canada (Newfoundland)	47 34 N	52 43 W
Stanley (capital)	Falkland Islands (Islas Malvinas)	51 42 S	57 41 W
Stockholm (capital)	Sweden	59 20 N	18 03 E
Stuttgart (city)	Germany	48 46 N	9 11 E
Sucre (city)	Bolivia	19 02 S	65 17 W
Suez Canal	Egypt	29 55 N	32 33 E
Suez, Gulf of	Indian Ocean	28 10 N	33 27 E
Suisse (local French name for Switzerland)	Switzerland	47 00 N	8 00 E
Sulawesi (Celebes) (island)	Indonesia	2 00 S	121 00 E
Sulawesi Sea	Pacific Ocean	3 00 N	122 00 E

Appendix F: Cross-Reference List of Geographic Names *(continued)*

	Name	Entry in *The World Factbook*	Latitude (deg min)	Longitude (deg min)
	Sulu Archipelago (island group)	Philippines	6 00 N	121 00 E
	Sulu Sea	Pacific Ocean	8 00 N	120 00 E
	Sumatra (island)	Indonesia	0 00 N	102 00 E
	Sumba (island)	Indonesia	10 00 S	120 00 E
	Sumba Strait	Pacific Ocean	9 10 S	120 00 E
	Sumbawa (island)	Indonesia	8 30 S	118 00 E
	Sunda Islands (Soenda Isles)	Indonesia, Malaysia	2 00 S	110 00 E
	Sunda Strait	Indian Ocean	6 00 S	105 45 E
	Suomi (local name for Finland)	Finland	64 00 N	26 00 E
	Surigao Strait	Pacific Ocean	10 15 N	125 23 E
	Surinam (former name for Suriname)	Suriname	4 00 N	56 00 W
	Suriyah (local name for Syria)	Syria	35 00 N	38 00 E
	Surtsey (volcanic island)	Iceland	63 17 N	20 40 W
	Suva (capital)	Fiji	18 08 S	178 25 E
	Sverdlovsk (Yekaterinburg) (city)	Russia	56 50 N	60 39 E
	Sverige (local name for Sweden)	Sweden	62 00 N	15 00 E
	Svizzera (local Italian name for Switzerland)	Switzerland	47 00 N	8 00 E
	Swains Island	American Samoa	11 03 S	171 15 W
	Swan Islands	Honduras	17 25 S	83 56 W
T	Tadzhikistan (former name for Tadjikistan)	Tadjikistan	39 00 N	71 00 E
	Tahiti (island)	French Polynesia	17 37 S	149 27 W
	Taipei (capital)	Taiwan	25 03 N	121 30 E
	Taiwan Strait	Pacific Ocean	24 00 N	119 00 E
	Tallinn (capital)	Estonia	59 25 N	24 45 E
	Tanganyika (former name for the mainland portion of Tanzania)	Tanzania	6 00 S	35 00 E
	Tangier (city)	Morocco	35 48 N	5 45 W
	Tannu-Tuva (region)	Russia	51 25 N	94 45 E
	Tarawa (island)	Kiribati	1 25 N	173 00 E
	Tartary, Gulf of	Pacific Ocean	50 00 N	141 00 E
	Tashkent (capital)	Uzbekistan	41 20 N	69 18 E
	Tasman Sea	Pacific Ocean	4 30 S	168 00 E
	Tasmania (island)	Australia	43 00 S	147 00 E
	Tatar Strait	Pacific Ocean	50 00 N	141 00 E
	Taymyr Peninsula (Poluostrov Taymyr)	Russia	76 00 N	104 00 E
	T'bilisi (capital)	Georgia	41 43 N	44 49 E
	Tchad (local name for Chad)	Chad	15 00 N	19 00 E
	Tegucigalpa (capital)	Honduras	14 06 N	87 13 W
	Tehran (capital)	Iran	35 40 N	51 26 E
	Tel Aviv (capital, de facto)	Israel	32 05 N	34 48 E
	Teluk Bone (gulf)	Pacific Ocean	4 00 S	120 45 E
	Teluk Tomini (gulf)	Pacific Ocean	0 30 S	121 00 E
	Terre Adelie (Adelie Land) (claimed by France)	Antarctica	66 30 S	139 00 E
	Terres Australes et Antarctiques Francaises (local name for the French Southern and Antarctic Lands)	French Southern and Antarctic Lands	43 00 S	67 00 E
	Thailand, Gulf of	Pacific Ocean	10 00 N	101 00 E
	Thimphu (capital)	Bhutan	27 28 N	89 39 E
	Thuringia (region)	Germany	51 00 N	11 00 E

Appendix F: Cross-Reference List of Geographic Names *(continued)*

Name	Entry in *The World Factbook*	Latitude (deg min)	Longitude (deg min)
Thurston Island	Antarctica	72 20 S	99 00 W
Tiberias, Lake	Israel	32 48 N	35 35 E
Tibet (Xizang) (province)	China	32 00 N	90 00 E
Tibilisi (see T'bilisi)	Georgia	41 43 N	44 49 E
Tien Shan (mountains)	China, Kyrgyzstan	42 00 N	80 00 E
Tierra del Fuego (island, island group)	Argentina, Chile	54 00 S	69 00 W
Timor (island)	Indonesia	9 00 S	125 00 E
Timor Leste (former name for East Timor)	East Timor	9 00 N	126 00 E
Timor Sea	Pacific Ocean	11 00 S	128 00 E
Tinian (island)	Northern Mariana Islands	15 00 N	145 38 E
Tiran, Strait of	Indian Ocean	28 00 N	34 27 E
Tirana (capital)	Albania	41 20 N	19 50 E
Tirane (see Tirana)	Albania	41 20 N	19 50 E
Tirol (region)	Austria, Italy	47 00 N	11 00 E
Tobago (island)	Trinidad and Tobago	11 15 N	60 40 W
Tokyo (capital)	Japan	35 42 N	139 46 E
Tonkin, Gulf of	Pacific Ocean	20 00 N	108 00 E
Torres Strait	Pacific Ocean	10 25 S	142 10 E
Torshavn (capital)	Faroe Islands	62 01 N	6 46 W
Toshkent (see Tashkent)	Uzbekistan	41 20 N	69 18 E
Transcarpathia (region; alternate name for Carpatho-Ukraine)	Ukraine	48 22 N	23 32 E
Transjordan (former name for Jordan)	Jordan	31 00 N	36 00 E
Transkei (enclave)	South Africa	32 15 S	28 15 E
Transvaal (region; former name for northeastern South Africa)	South Africa	25 10 S	29 25 E
Transylvania (region)	Romania	46 30 N	24 00 E
Trindade, Ilha de (island)	Brazil	20 31 S	29 20 W
Trinidad (island)	Trinidad and Tobago	10 22 N	61 15 W
Tripoli (capital)	Libya	32 54 N	13 11 E
Tripoli (city)	Lebanon	34 26 N	35 51 E
Tripolitania (region)	Libya	31 00 N	14 00 E
Tristan da Cunha Group (island group)	Saint Helena	37 04 S	12 19 W
Trobriand Islands	Papua New Guinea	8 38 S	151 04 E
Trucial Coast (former name for the United Arab Emirates)	United Arab Emirates	24 00 N	54 00 E
Trucial Oman (former name for the United Arab Emirates)	United Arab Emirates	24 00 N	54 00 E
Trucial States (former name for the United Arab Emirates)	United Arab Emirates	24 00 N	54 00 E
Truk Islands (former name for the Chuuk Islands)	Federated States of Micronesia	7 25 N	151 47 E
Tsugaru Strait	Pacific Ocean	41 35 N	141 00 E
Tuamotu Islands (Iles Tuamotu)	French Polynesia	19 00 S	142 00 W
Tubuai Islands (Iles Tubuai)	French Polynesia	23 00 S	150 00 W
Tunb al Kubra (island)	Iran	26 14 N	55 19 E
Tunb as Sughra (island)	Iran	26 14 N	55 09 E
Tunis (capital)	Tunisia	36 48 N	10 11 E
Turin (city)	Italy	45 04 N	7 40 E
Turkish Straits	Atlantic Ocean	40 40 N	28 00 E
Turkiye (local name for Turkey)	Turkey	39 00 N	35 00 E
Turkmenia (former name for Turkmenistan)	Turkmenistan	40 00 N	60 00 E

Appendix F: Cross-Reference List of Geographic Names (continued)

	Name	Entry in *The World Factbook*	Latitude (deg min)	Longitude (deg min)
	Turkmeniya (former name for Turkmenistan)	Turkmenistan	40 00 N	60 00 E
	Turks Island Passage	Atlantic Ocean	21 40 N	71 00 W
	Tuscany (region)	Italy	43 25 N	11 00 E
	Tutuila (island)	American Samoa	14 18 S	170 42 W
	Tyrol, South (region)	Italy	46 30 N	10 30 E
	Tyrrhenian Sea	Atlantic Ocean	40 00 N	12 00 E
U	Ubangi-Shari (former name for the Central African Republic	Central African Republic	6 38 N	20 33 E
	Ukrayina (local name for Ukraine)	Ukraine	49 00 N	32 00 E
	Ulaanbaatar (capital)	Mongolia	47 55 N	106 53 E
	Ullung-do (island)	South Korea	37 29 N	130 52 E
	Ulster (region)	Ireland, United Kingdom	54 35 N	7 00 W
	Uman (local name for Oman)	Oman	21 00 N	57 00 E
	Unimak Pass (strait)	Pacific Ocean	54 20 N	164 50 W
	Union of Soviet Socialist Republics (USSR) (former name of a large Eurasian empire, roughly coequal with the former Russian Empire)	Armenia, Azerbaijan, Belarus, Estonia, Georgia, Kazakhstan, Kyrgyzstan, Latvia, Lithuania, Moldova, Russia, Tajikistan, Turkmenistan, Ukraine, Uzbekistan		
	United Arab Republic (UAR) (former name for a federation between Egypt and Syria)	Egypt, Syria		
	Upper Volta (former name for Burkina Faso)	Burkina Faso	13 00 N	2 00 W
	Ural Mountains	Kazakhstan, Russia	60 00 N	60 00 E
	Urdunn (local name for Jordan)	Jordan	31 00 N	36 00 E
	Urundi (former name for Burundi)	Burundi	3 30 S	30 00 E
	Ussuri River	China, Russia	48 28 N	135 02 E
V	Vaduz (capital)	Liechtenstein	47 09 N	9 31 E
	Vakhan (Wakhan Corridor)	Afghanistan	37 00 N	73 00 E
	Valletta (capital)	Malta	35 54 N	14 31 E
	Valley, The (capital)	Anguilla	18 13 N	63 04 W
	Van Diemen Strait (Osumi Strait)	Pacific Ocean	31 00 N	131 00 E
	Vancouver Island	Canada	49 45 N	126 00 W
	Vatican City (capital)	Holy See	41 54 N	12 27 E
	Velez de la Gomera, Penon de (island)	Spain	35 11 N	4 18 W
	Venda (enclave)	South Africa	23 00 S	31 00 E
	Verde Island Passage	Pacific Ocean	13 34 N	120 51 E
	Victoria (capital)	Seychelles	4 38 S	55 27 E
	Victoria (city; former name of seaport city in Hong Kong colony)	Hong Kong	22 17 N	114 09 E
	Victoria (island)	Canada	71 00 N	110 00 W
	Victoria Land (region)	Antarctica	72 00 S	155 00 E
	Vienna (capital)	Austria	48 12 N	16 22 E
	Vientiane (capital)	Laos	17 58 N	102 36 E
	Vilnius (capital)	Lithuania	54 41 N	25 19 E
	Viti Levu (island)	Fiji	18 00 S	178 00 E
	Vladivostok (city)	Russia	43 10 N	131 56 E
	Vojvodina (region)	Yugoslavia	45 35 N	20 00 E
	Volcano Islands	Japan	25 00 N	141 00 E
	Vostok Island	Kiribati	10 06 S	152 23 W
	Vrangelya, Ostrov (Wrangel Island)	Russia	71 14 N	179 36 W

Appendix F: Cross-Reference List of Geographic Names *(continued)*

	Name	Entry in *The World Factbook*	Latitude (deg min)	Longitude (deg min)
W	Wake Atoll	Wake Island	19 17 N	166 36 E
	Wakhan Corridor (see Vakhan)	Afghanistan	37 00 N	73 00 E
	Walachia (region)	Romania	44 45 N	26 05 E
	Wales (region)	United Kingdom	52 30 N	3 30 W
	Wallis Islands	Wallis and Futuna	13 17 S	176 10 W
	Walvis Bay (former exclave) (city)	Namibia	22 59 S	14 31 E
	Warsaw (capital)	Poland	52 15 N	21 00 E
	Washington, DC (capital)	United States	38 53 N	77 02 W
	Weddell Sea	Southern Ocean	72 00 S	45 00 W
	Wellington (capital)	New Zealand	41 28 S	174 51 E
	West Frisian Islands	Netherlands	53 26 N	5 30 E
	West Germany (Federal Republic of Germany) (former name for western portion of Germany)	Germany	53 22 N	5 20 E
	West Island (capital)	Cocos (Keeling) Islands	12 10 S	96 55 E
	West Korea Strait (Western Channel)	Pacific Ocean	34 40 N	129 00 E
	West Pakistan (former name for western portion of Pakistan)	Pakistan	30 00 N	70 00 E
	West Siberian Plain	Russia	60 00 N	75 00 E
	Western Channel (West Korea Strait)	Pacific Ocean	34 40 N	129 00 E
	Western Samoa (former name for Samoa)	Samoa	13 35 S	172 20 W
	Wetar Strait	Pacific Ocean	8 20 S	126 30 E
	White Sea	Arctic Ocean	65 30 N	38 00 E
	Wilkes Land (region)	Antarctica	71 00 S	120 00 E
	Willemstad (capital)	Netherlands Antilles	12 06 N	68 56 W
	Windhoek (capital)	Namibia	22 34 S	17 06 E
	Windward Passage	Atlantic Ocean	20 00 N	73 50 W
	Wrangel Island (Ostrov Vrangelya)	Russia	71 14 N	179 36 W
X	Xianggang (local name for Hong Kong)	Hong Kong	22 15 N	114 10 E
Y	Y'israel (local name for Israel)	Israel	31 30 N	34 45 E
	Yaitopya (local name for Ethiopia)	Ethiopia	8 00 N	38 00 E
	Yalu River	China, North Korea	39 55 N	124 20 E
	Yamoussoukro (capital)	Cote d'Ivoire	6 49 N	5 17 W
	Yangon (see Rangoon)	Burma	16 47 N	96 10 E
	Yaounde (capital)	Cameroon	3 52 N	11 31 E
	Yap Islands	Federated States of Micronesia	9 30 N	138 00 E
	Yaren (governmental center)	Nauru	0 32 S	166 55 E
	Yekaterinburg (city; former name for Sverdlovsk)	Russia	56 50 N	60 39 E
	Yellow Sea	Pacific Ocean	36 00 N	123 00 E
	Yemen (Aden) (People's Democratic Republic of Yemen) (former name for southern portion of Yemen)	Yemen	14 00 N	46 00 E
	Yemen (Sanaa) (Yemen Arab Republic) (former name for northern portion of Yemen)	Yemen	15 00 N	44 00 E
	Yemen Arab Republic (former name for northern portion of Yemen)	Yemen	15 00 N	44 00 E
	Yemen, North (Yemen Arab Republic) (former name for northern portion of Yemen)	Yemen	15 00 N	44 00 E
	Yemen, People's Democratic Republic of (former name for southern portion of Yemen)	Yemen	14 00 N	46 00 E
	Yemen, South (People's Democratic Republic of Yemen) (former name for southern portion of Yemen)	Yemen	14 00 N	46 00 E

Appendix F: Cross-Reference List of Geographic Names *(continued)*

	Name	Entry in *The World Factbook*	Latitude (deg min)	Longitude (deg min)
	Yerevan (capital)	Armenia	40 11 N	44 30 E
	Youth, Isle of (Isla de la Juventud)	Cuba	21 40 N	82 50 W
	Yucatan Channel	Atlantic Ocean	21 45 N	85 45 W
	Yucatan Peninsula	Mexico	19 30 N	89 00 W
	Yugoslavia, Socialist Federal Republic	Bosnia and Herzegovina, Croatia, The Former Yugoslav Republic of Macedonia, Serbia and Montenegro (now Yugoslavia), Slovenia	43 00 N	19 00 E
Z	Zagreb (capital)	Croatia	45 48 N	15 58 E
	Zaire (former name for the Democratic Republic of the Congo)	Democratic Republic of the Congo	15 00 S	30 00 E
	Zakhalinskiy Zaliv (bay)	Pacific Ocean	54 00 N	142 00 E
	Zaliv Shelikhova (bay)	Pacific Ocean	60 00 N	157 30 E
	Zambezia (region)	Mozambique	16 00 S	37 00 E
	Zanzibar (island)	Tanzania	6 10 S	39 11 E
	Zhong Guo (local name for China)	China	35 00 N	105 00 E
	Zhonghua (local name for China)	China	35 00 N	105 00 E
	Zion, Mount (locale in Jerusalem)	Israel, West Bank	31 46 N	35 14 E
	Zurich (city)	Switzerland	47 23 N	8 32 E